HOW DO YOU FIND "A PHILIPPINE TREE" OF 5 LETTERS?

It's as easy as falling off a log: just look under **TREE**, and below to **(PHILIPPINES —)**. Are you looking for a synonym for **PROJECTION**? You'll find 63 . . . with an additional 27 subcategories! Whether your questions are geographical, etymological, mythological, biblical, literary, dramatic, or operatic, the answers are here, in a single handy volume guaranteed to expand your word-power and provide endless hours of entertainment.

Student, scholar, wordsmith, crossword-puzzler . . . we've got the name, the fame, and the game for you! Where else would you find an entry to compare to . . .

TALKER YENTA CAMPER POTGUN
  CAUSEUR SPIELER
  (IDLE —) WHIFFLER
  (NOISY —) BLELLUM
  (PROFESSIONAL —) JAWSMITH
  (SENSELESS —) RATTLE

The
New York Times
CONCISE
CROSSWORD PUZZLE DICTIONARY

**Also published by
Warner Books**

THE NEW YORK TIMES CROSSWORD PUZZLE DICTIONARY
by Tom Pulliam and Clare Grundman

THE SYNONYM FINDER
by J.I. Rodale

The New York Times

CONCISE

CROSSWORD PUZZLE DICTIONARY

by Tom Pulliam, Clare Grundman,
and Gorton Carruth

A HUDSON GROUP BOOK

WARNER BOOKS

A Time Warner Company

WARNER BOOKS EDITION

Concise edition copyright © 1987 by Warner Books, Inc.
Copyright © 1974, 1977, 1984 by Thomas Pulliam and Clare Grundman
All rights reserved.

Published by arrangement with Times Books,
a division of Random House, Inc., 201 East 50th Street,
New York, N.Y. 10022.

Produced in association with Morningside Editorial Associates, Inc.

Designed by Martin Connell

Warner Books, Inc.
1271 Avenue of the Americas
New York, N.Y. 10020

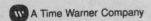 A Time Warner Company

Printed in the United States of America

First Mass Market Paperback Printing: August, 1987

15 14 13 12 11

PREFACE

When we created the original *New York Times Crossword Puzzle Dictionary* in 1974, it was our aim to produce the most comprehensive and useful book of its kind for the crossword puzzle fan. Called "the biggest and the best available" it contained over 500,000 words and was received enthusiastically by an encouragingly large number of readers. Ten years later, in a second edition under our editorship, the book was enlarged by more than 100,000 new words, bringing the total to over 600,000 words, and the book in all its editions has been used by hundreds of thousands of readers.

At the same time we had been hearing from crossword puzzle fans that they would like to find a similar book, embodying as many features as possible of the large *New York Times Crossword Puzzle Dictionary*, but in a more portable form—a handy, pocket-sized reference that could be thrown into a weekend bag, carried on a plane trip, or used to help in solving the daily newspaper puzzle while riding to work by bus or train. *The New York Times Concise Crossword Puzzle Dictionary* has been created to fill that need.

Obviously, it was not possible to include all of the words and features of the larger book. Nor would an arbitrary elimination of all long or seldom-seen words have served the purpose. Instead, as longtime compilers and solvers of crossword puzzles ourselves, we have selected word by word the entries most likely to be useful. The result is this book of over 700 pages containing more than 350,000 words—long enough to answer most needs, yet compact enough to be portable.

You will find this the easiest to use of all crossword puzzle dictionaries. After each entry word are grouped its synonyms arranged by their number of letters and then alphabetized so that you can quickly find the very word that fills the spaces in the puzzle. Many entry words are followed by subentries, placed in parentheses, which serve to qualify or narrow the search for the word you want. Do you require a "Philippine tree" of five letters? By quick reference to **TREE** and, below it, to **(PHILIPPINES —)**, you soon find many possibilities from which to select the best.

Among the popular features found also in the larger

volume are the geographical boxes. Covering all the countries of the world and the U.S. states, they are found alphabetically listed among the main entries but separated by a double line from adjoining entries. You no longer need to be stumped when seeking "river" or "province" of Spain!

Other user-friendly devices include key prefixes and suffixes; mythological and biblical relationships; and characters from major operas and novels. For example, by referring to the entry **APEX** you will find the prefix APIC and the suffix ACE; the entry **HERCULES** reveals that IPHICLES was his brother; and under **FAUST** you find that GRETCHEN is one of the characters in the Gounod opera.

Finally, another feature, which seems obvious for a crossword puzzle dictionary but is not found in most of them, is that all words are printed in easy-to-read capital letters. Furthermore, for this *Concise* edition, special care has been taken to select an especially legible typeface.

We wish to express our thanks to all of you who have used and recommended the original *New York Times Crossword Puzzle Dictionary*. We believe that you will find this shorter, concise dictionary an equally effective companion on your word-seeking safaris. Use it with pleasure and satisfaction.

Tom Pulliam
Clare Grundman
Gorton Carruth

1987

A

A AY ARY PER EACH ALPHA
AARDVARK ANTEATER EDENTATE
AARDWOLF HYAENID
AARON (BROTHER OF —) MOSES
(BURIAL PLACE OF —) HOR
(FATHER OF —) AMRAM
(MOTHER OF —) JOCHEBED
(SISTER OF —) MIRIAM
(SON OF —) ABIHU NADAB ELEAZAR
ITHAMAR
(WIFE OF —) ELISHEBA
AB HATI
ABACA HEMP FIBER LUPIS LINAGA
MANILA
ABACK SHORT
ABACUS SOROBAN SHWANPAN
ABAFT AFT BACK BAFT ABAFF ASTERN
BEHIND REARWARD
ABALONE EAR PAUA AWABI NACRE
ORMER UHLLO ASSEIR
ABANDON EGO CAST DROP FLEE JUNK
QUIT SINK ABAND ALLAY CHUCK DITCH
EXPEL LEAVE PLANT REMIT SCRAP
WAIVE YIELD ABJURE BANISH BETRAY
DESERT DISUSE DIVEST EXPOSE FOREGO
FORHOO FORLET MAROON RECANT
REFUSE REJECT RELENT RESIGN SLOUGH
VACATE DEPLORE DISCARD FORFEIT
FORSAKE SCUTTLE ABDICATE
FORSWEAR JETTISON RASHNESS
RELINQUISH
ABANDONED BAD LEFT LORN LOST
VACANT CORRUPT FORLORN PROJECT
DEPRAVED DERELICT DESERTED
DESOLATE FLAGRANT FORSAKEN
ABANDONMENT BURIAL APOSTASY
ABATEMENT
ABASE SINK VAIL AVALE AVILE BLAME
DEMIT LOWER SHAME ABJECT DEBASE
DEFAME DEJECT DEMEAN DEPOSE
GROVEL HUMBLE LESSEN MEEKEN
REDUCE DEGRADE DEPRESS MORTIFY
DIMINISH DISGRACE DISHONOR
ABASED ABAISSE
ABASH AWE COW DASH AVALE SHAME
HUMBLE CONFUSE MORTIFY BEWILDER
BROWBEAT CONFOUND
ABASHED BLANK CHEAP SHAMED
ASHAMED FOOLISH SHEEPISH
ABATE EBB END LOW CALM CURB FAIK
FALL MEND OMIT SLOW SOFT VAIL VOID
WANE ALLAY ALLOW ANNUL APPAL
BREAK CHECK LOWER QUASH RELAX
REMIT SLAKE ASLAKE DEDUCT LESSEN
PACIFY REBATE REDUCE RELENT
ABOLISH ASSUAGE NULLIFY QUALIFY
SLACKEN SUBSIDE DECREASE DIMINISH
MITIGATE MODERATE PALLIATE
ABATEMENT DELF FALL ALLAY DELFT

LETUP GUSSET MIOSIS DECREASE
DISCOUNT
(— OF DISEASE) LYSIS
ABAXIAL DORSAL
ABBA FATHER
ABBE MONK CLERIC CURATE PRIEST
ABBESS AMMA VICARESS
ABBEY ABADIA ABBAYE PRIORY
CONVENT NUNNERY CLOISTER
ABBOT ABBAS COARB
ABBREVIATE CUT CLIP DOCK PRUNE
DIGEST ABRIDGE BOBTAIL CURTAIL
SHORTEN CONDENSE CONTRACT
TRUNCATE
ABBREVIATED SHORT CRYPTIC
ABBREVIATION LAPSE SIGLUM SYMBOL
ABC ALPHABET
ABDERITE FOOL SCOFFER SIMPLETON
ABDICATE CEDE QUIT DEMIT EXPEL
LEAVE REMIT DEPOSE DISOWN FOREGO
RESIGN RETIRE VACATE ABANDON
DISCLAIM RENOUNCE
ABDICATION DRIFT
ABDOMEN BOUK WOMB ALVUS APRON
BELLY MELON MIRAC PLEON THARM
PAUNCH VENTER STOMACH
ABDOMINAL BELLY HEMAL COELIAC
VENTRAL VISCERAL
ABDUCT LURE TAKE STEAL ABDUCE
KIDNAP RAVISH SPIRIT CAPTURE
ABDUCTION APAGOGE
ABDUCTION FROM THE SERAGLIO
(CHARACTER IN —) OSMIN PASHA
BLONDE BELMONTE PEDRILLO
CONSTANZE
(COMPOSER OF —) MOZART
ABEAM ABREAST
ABECEDARIAN TYRO NOVICE LEARNER
BEGINNER
ABED SICK RESTING RETIRED SLEEPING
ABEL (BROTHER OF —) CAIN SETH
(FATHER OF —) ADAM
(MOTHER OF —) EVE
(PARENT OF —) ADAM
ABE LINCOLN IN ILLINOIS
(AUTHOR OF —) SHERWOOD
(CHARACTER IN —) ABE ANN GALE
MARY SETH TODD GREEN SPEED
GRAHAM JIMMIE MENTOR NINIAN
BOWLING DOUGLAS EDWARDS HERNDON
RUTLEDGE
ABELMOSK MUSK MALLOW
ABERDEEN ANGUS BLACK DODDY
DODDIE
ABERRANT WILD CLAMMY DEVIANT
ABNORMAL STRAYING VARIABLE
ABERRATION SLIP WARP ERROR FAULT
LAPSE MANIA DELIRIUM DELUSION
INSANITY

ABET AID EGG BACK HELP BOOST COACH ASSIST FOMENT INCITE SECOND SUCCOR UPHOLD COMFORT CONNIVE ESPOUSE FORWARD FURTHER SUPPORT SUSTAIN ADVOCATE BEFRIEND

ABETTOR FAUTOR ADVOCATE PROMOTER

ABHOR UG IRK HATE SHUN DETEST LOATHE DESPISE DISLIKE EXECRATE ABOMINATE

ABHORRENCE HATE ODIUM HATRED HORROR DISGUST DISLIKE AVERSION LOATHING

ABHORRENT ODIOUS UGSOME HATEFUL INFAMOUS REPUGNANT

ABIDE BE WIN WON BEAR BIDE KEEP LAST LEND LENG LIVE REST STAY WAIT ABEAR AWAIT DELAY EXIST HABIT PAUSE STAND SWELL TARRY ENDURE HARBOR LINGER REMAIN RESIDE SUBMIT INHABIT SOJOURN SUBSIST SUSTAIN CONTINUE TOLERATE

ABIDING FAST STABLE LASTING

ABIGAIL MAID
(HUSBAND OF —) DAVID NABAL JETHER
(SON OF —) AMASA DANIEL CHILEAB

ABIHAIL (DAUGHTER OF —) ESTHER
(FATHER OF —) HURI ELIAB
(HUSBAND OF —) ABISHUR REHOBOAM
(SON OF —) ZURIEL

ABILITY CAN MAY CLAY EASE FORM HAND CLASS FLAIR FORCE MIGHT POWER SKILL STUFF VERVE ENERGY ENGINE STROKE TALENT CALIBER CUNNING FACULTY POTENCY APTITUDE CAPACITY STRENGTH
(BATTING —) STICKWORK
(CREATIVE —) IMAGINATION
(INVENTIVE —) CONTRIVANCE
(MENTAL —) INGENY BRAINPOWER

ABIMELECH (BROTHER OF —) JOTHAM
(FATHER OF —) GIDEON ABIATHA

ABJECT LOW BASE MEAN POOR SUNK VILE PRONE SORRY CRAVEN MENIAL PALTRY SORDID SUPINE FAWNING FORLORN IGNOBLE SERVILE SLAVISH BEGGARLY CRINGING DEGRADED DOWNCAST LISTLESS WRETCHED

ABJURE DENY SPURN ESCHEW RECALL RECANT REJECT RESIGN REVOKE ABANDON DISAVOW DISCLAIM FORSWEAR RENOUNCE

ABLAUT APOPHONY

ABLAZE AFIRE BURNING GLOWING RADIANT GLEAMING INFLAMED

ABLE APT BIG CAN FIT ADEPT SMART CLEVER EXPERT FACILE FITTED POTENT STRONG CAPABLE DOUGHTY DEXTROUS POSSIBLE POWERFUL SKILLFUL SUITABLE TALENTED VIGOROUS

ABLUTION BATH LOTION BAPTISM BATHING WASHING

ABNEGATE DENY ABJURE FOREGO REFUSE REJECT DISAVOW DISCLAIM FORSWEAR RENOUNCE

ABNER (BROTHER OF —) KISH
(FATHER OF —) NER
(SLAYER OF —) JOAB
(SON OF —) JAASIEL
(WIFE OF —) RIZPAH

ABNORMAL QUEER UTTER ERRATIC UNUSUAL VICIOUS ABERRANT ATYPICAL FREAKISH TERATOID ANOMALOUS MONSTROUS

ABNORMALITY ATAXY ATAXIA LETHAL ANOMALY DEMENTIA

ABOARD ON ONTO ACROSS ATHWART

ABODE COT DAR HUT INN WON BODE CELL FLAT HALL HOME NEST OMEN REST SEAT TENT WOON BEING BOWER DELAY HAUNT HOUSE MANOR PITCH RESET SIEGE SUITE ABIDAL BIDING ESTATE ADDRESS COTTAGE HABITAT LODGING MANSION SITTING CUNABULA DOMICILE DWELLING TENEMENT
(— OF DEAD) DAR AARU HELL ARALU HADES ORCUS SHEOL HEAVEN SHADES XIBALBA
(— OF DELIGHT) ELYSIUM
(— OF EVIL POWERS) ABYSS
(— OF GIANTS) UTGARD
(— OF GODS) MERU ASGARD OLYMPUS
(— OF LOST SOULS) ABADDON
(— OF SOULS) LIMBO
(ANIMAL —) ZOO MENAGERIE
(CELESTIAL —) HEAVEN
(FILTHY —) STY STYE
(MISERABLE —) DOGHOLE
(SHELTERED —) SHADE

ABOLISH END BLOT KILL ABATE ANNUL ERASE FORDO QUASH CANCEL EFFACE FOREDO RECALL REPEAL REVOKE VACATE DESTROY NULLIFY RESCIND REVERSE ABROGATE

ABOLITION EXTINCTION

ABOMINABLE VILE RUSTY CURSED ODIOUS ROTTEN BEASTLY HATEFUL HEINOUS

ABOMINATE HATE ABHOR DETEST LOATHE EXECRATE

ABOMINATION EVIL CRIME CURSE HORROR PLAGUE DISGUST AVERSION

ABORIGINAL ABO YAO FIRST NATAL BINGHI NATIVE SAVAGE NATURAL PRIMARY ORIGINAL
(— WOMAN) GIN

ABORIGINE KHA TODA ALFUR BAIGA BLACK BOONG DASYU MAORI MYALL ALFURO ARUNTA BINGHI INDIAN KIPPER KODAGA NATIVE SAVAGE ADIBASI CHINHWAN WARRAGAL

ABORT SLIP

ABORTION FAILURE CASTLING FETICIDE MISBIRTH

ABORTIVE IDLE VAIN BLIND FUTILE BOOTLESS

ABOUND SNY FLOW TEEM COVER FLEET SWARM REDOUND OVERFLOW

ABOUNDING RIFE FLUSH COPIOUS REPLETE TEEMING ABUNDANT AFFLUENT PROLIFIC

ABOUT BY IN OF ON RE SAY AWAY NEAR

SOME UMBE UPON ANENT ASTIR CIRCA
ABROAD ACTIVE ALMOST AROUND
CIRCUM TOWARD CIRCITER

ABOVE ON UP OER SUP ATOP OVER PAST
UPON ALOFT SUPRA BEFORE BEYOND
HIGHER OVERHEAD SUPERIOR

ABRADE RUB BARK FILE FRET GALL RASP
SAND WEAR CHAFE ERASE GRATE GRIND
SCORE SCUFF SCOTCH SCRAPE IRRITATE

ABRAHAM (BIRTHPLACE OF —) UR
(BROTHER OF —) HARAN NAHOR
(CONCUBINE OF —) HAGAR
(FATHER OF —) TERAH
(GRANDFATHER OF —) NAHOR
(GRANDSON OF —) ESAU
(NEPHEW OF —) LOT
(SON OF —) ISAAC MEDAN SHUAH
MIDIAN ZIMRAN ISHMAEL JOKSHAN
(WIFE OF —) SARAH KETURAH

ABRASION BURN GALL OUCH SCAR
SORE GRAZE BRUISE BLASTING

ABRASIVE SAND EMERY PUMICE
QUARTZ SILICA ALUNDUM ERODENT
ABRADANT CORUNDUM PUMICITE
SCRUBBER

ABREAST EVEN AFRONT BESIDE
HANGING

ABRI SHED COVER DUGOUT SHELTER

ABRIDGE CUT DOCK ELIDE LIMIT RAZEE
REDUCE SHRINK CURTAIL DEPRIVE
REWRITE SHORTEN ABSTRACT BREVIATE
COMPRESS CONDENSE CONTRACT
DIMINISH RETRENCH SIMPLIFY
ABBREVIATE

ABRIDGEMENT BRIEF DIGEST PRECIS
RESUME SKETCH COMPEND EPITOME
PANDECT SUMMARY SUMMULA
ABSTRACT BREVIARY SYNOPSIS

ABROAD OFF ASEA AWAY ABOUT ASTIR
FORTH ABREED AFIELD ASTRAY WIDELY
DISTANT OVERSEA

ABROGATE ANNUL QUASH REMIT
CANCEL REPEAL REVOKE VACATE
ABOLISH NULLIFY RESCIND DISSOLVE

ABRUPT BOLD CURT DEAD FAST RUDE
BLUFF BLUNT BRIEF HASTY ICTIC PLUMP
QUICK ROUGH SHARP SHEER SHORT
STEEP STUNT SURLY TERSE TOTAL
CRUSTY SUDDEN ANGULAR BRUSQUE
PRERUPT VIOLENT HEADLONG VERTICAL
PRECIPITATE

ABRUPTLY BANG SHARP SHORT
STEEPLY SUDDENLY

ABSALOM (FATHER OF —) DAVID
(MOTHER OF —) MAACHAH
(SISTER OF —) TAMAR
(SLAYER OF —) JOAB

ABSALOM, ABSALOM
(AUTHOR OF —) FAULKNER
(CHARACTER IN —) BON ROSA ELLEN
HENRY JUDITH SHREVE SUTPEN THOMAS
CHARLES COMPSON GOODHUE QUENTIN
MCCANNON COLDFIELD

ABSAROKA CROW

ABSCESS BOIL SORE ULCER FESTER
LESION QUINSY VOMICA EXITURE
GUMBOIL PARULIS APOSTEME SQUINACY

ABSCISSA X COSINE

ABSCISSION APOCOPE

ABSCOND GO FLY RUN BOLT FLEE HIDE
QUIT ELOPE SCRAM DECAMP DEPART
DESERT ESCAPE

ABSENCE CUT LACK VOID WANT BLANK
LEAVE DEFECT REMOVE VACUUM
DEFAULT FAILURE VACANCY FURLOUGH
(— FROM DUTY) LIBERTY
(— FROM ONE'S COUNTRY) EXILE
(— OF AN ORGAN) AGENESIA
AGENESIS
(— OF FAMILIARITY) DISTANCE
(— OF FEELING) APATHY
(— OF FEVER) APYREXY APYREXIA
(— OF FORM) ENTROPY
(— OF GOVERNMENT) ANARCHY
(— OF INHIBITIONS) ANIMALITY
(— OF LIGHT) BLACK DARKNESS
(— OF MARRIAGE) AGAMY
(— OF PAIN) ANODYNIA
(— OF TASTE) AGEUSIA
(— OF TRUMPS) CHICANE
(— OF TRUTH) FALSEHOOD

ABSENT CUT OFF OUT AWAY AWOL
GONE LOST DESERT MUSING LACKING
MISSING WANTING ABSORBED
DREAMING

ABSENTMINDED MUSED MUSING
DISTRAIT DREAMING ABSTRACTED

ABSENTMINDEDNESS STARGAZING

ABSINTHE AJENJO GENIPI

ABSOLUTE GOD ONE DEAD DOWN FINE
FREE MERE PURE RANK REAL SELF TRUE
VERY BLANK CLEAR FIXED PLUMB SHEER
STARK TOTAL UTTER WHOLE ENTIRE
PROPER SEVERE SIMPLE SQUARE
BRAHMAN CERTAIN PERFECT PLENARY
COMPLETE
(NOT —) NISI FINITE CONDITIONAL

ABSOLUTELY YEA YES AMEN BONE
COLD DEAD FAIR JUST PLAT SLAP PLAIN
PLUMB STARK BARELY FLATLY SIMPLY
WHOLLY SHEERLY ENTIRELY

ABSOLUTION EXCUSE PARDON SHRIFT

ABSOLVE FREE QUIT CLEAR LOOSE
REMIT ACQUIT EXCUSE EXEMPT FINISH
PARDON SHRIVE UNBIND CLEANSE
FORGIVE JUSTIFY RELEASE DISPENSE
LIBERATE OVERLOOK

ABSORB EAT FIX SOP SUP BLOT SOAK
SUCK TAKE AMUSE DRINK MERGE RIVET
UNITE DEVOUR ENGAGE ENGULF
ENWRAP IMBIBE INGEST OCCUPY
SPONGE STIFLE COMBINE CONSUME
ENGROSS IMMERSE INVOLVE OCCLUDE
SWALLOW

ABSORBED DEEP GONE LOST RAPT
SUNK FIXED ABSENT BURIED ENRAPT
INTENT PLUNGED RIVETED WRAPPED
IMMERSED ABSTRACTED

ABSORBENT BASE DOPE SPONGY
ANTACID SORBENT

ABSTAIN DENY FAST KEEP STAY AVOID
CEASE SPARE SPURN WAIVE DESIST
DISUSE ESCHEW FOREGO REFUSE

REJECT FORBEAR REFRAIN RESTRAIN
TEETOTAL WITHHOLD

ABSTAINER TOTE RECHABITE

ABSTENTION CELIBACY CHASTITY

ABSTERGE WIPE BATHE CLEAN PURGE
RINSE

ABSTINENCE ENCRATY

ABSTINENT SOBER ABSTEMIOUS

ABSTRACT CULL DEED DRAW NOTE
PART PURE TAKE BRIEF IDEAL STEAL
ABSORB DEDUCT DETACH DIGEST
DIVERT DOCKET PRECIS REMOVE
ABRIDGE COMPEND EXCERPT ISOLATE
PURLOIN SECRETE SUMMARY VIDIMUS
DISCRETE SEPARATE SYLLABUS
SYNOPSIS WITHDRAW
(NOT —) CONCRETE

ABSTRACTION STUDY ENTITY ABSENCE
REVERIE ABSTRACT QUODDITY

ABSTRUSE DARK DEEP HIGH HIDDEN
MYSTIC REMOTE SECRET SUBTLE
OBSCURE ABSTRACT ESOTERIC
PROFOUND METAPHYSICAL

ABSURD RICH WILD DOTTY DROLL FALSE
INANE INEPT SILLY SCREWY STUPID
ASININE FATUOUS FOOLISH LAPUTAN
FABULOUS COCKAMAMY RIDICULOUS

ABSURDITY BETISE FATUITY FOOLERY
FOPPERY NONSENSE

ABUNDANCE COPY FLOW MORT SONS
CHEAP DEPTH FLUSH FOUTH POWER
RIVER ROUTH ROWTH SCADS STORE
BOUNTY FOISON GALORE LAVISH
OODLES PLENTY RICHES TALENT LIBERTY
WEALTH FLUENCY SATIETY FULLNESS
OPULENCE RIMPTION PLENITUDE

ABUNDANT FAT LUSH MUCH RANK RICH
RIFE AMPLE FLUSH HEFTY LARGE OPIME
GALORE HEARTY APLENTY COPIOUS
FERTILE FULSOME LIBERAL OPULENT
PROFUSE REPLETE TEEMING UBERANT
AFFLUENT FRUITFUL GENEROUS
NUMEROUS PLENTIFUL

ABUSE MAR MOB TAX DRUB FLAY GAFF
HARM HURT MAUL RAIL RUIN SLAM
TEEN VAIN BASTE BLAST CRIME CURSE
FAULT GRIEF SCOLD SLANG SPOIL
BERATE DEFILE INJURE INSULT MALIGN
MISUSE PUNISH RAVISH REVILE VILIFY
AFFRONT DECEIVE FALSIFY OBLOQUY
OUTRAGE PERVERT PROFANE SLANDER
TRADUCE UPBRAID VIOLATE DISHONOR
MALTREAT MISTREAT REPROACH

ABUSIVE FOUL DIRTY SHREWD CORRUPT
CHEATING INSOLENT LIBELOUS

ABUT BUTT JOIN REST TOUCH ADJOIN
BORDER

ABUTMENT CRIB PIER ALETTE BUTTRESS

ABUTTING FLUSH ADJACENT

ABYSMAL DEEP DREARY PROFOUND
UNENDING WRETCHED

ABYSS PIT POT DEEP GULF HELL VOID
ABYSM CHAOS CHASM DEPTH GORGE
BOTTOM DOWNFALL

ACACIA GUM JAM KOA WOLD BABUL
MULGA MYALL SIRIS THORN TIMBE
VEREK ARABIC BABLAH BINDER GIDGEE

HASHAB LEGUME LOCUST MIMOSA
SALLEE WATTLE YARRAN

ACADEMIC IVY RIGID FORMAL CLASSIC
DONNISH ERUDITE LEARNED POMPIER
PEDANTIC

ACADEMY LYCEE CRUSCA LYCEUM
SCHOOL ACADEME COLLEGE SOCIETY
YESHIVA SEMINARY
(RIDING —) MANEGE

ACADIAN CAJUN

ACALEPH MEDUSA

ACANTHA FIN SPINE THORN PRICKLE

ACAPU WALNUT CHAPERNO

ACARID MITE NYMPH

ACAUDAL BOBBED ANUROUS TAILLESS

ACCEDE LET AGREE ALLOW ENTER
GRANT YIELD ASSENT COMPLY CONCUR
CONCEDE CONFORM CONSENT

ACCELERATE GUN REV RUN HYPO JAZZ
RACE URGE DRIVE FAVOR FORCE HURRY
SPEED HASTEN ADVANCE FORWARD
FURTHER QUICKEN DISPATCH EXPEDITE
INCREASE THROTTLE

ACCELERATION PICKUP SPEEDUP

ACCELERATOR GAS GUN SPEEDER
BETATRON BEVATRON THROTTLE
(LINEAR —) LINAC

ACCENT BLAS BURR MARK TONE ACUTE
GRAVE ICTUS PITCH PULSE SOUND
THROB VERGE LENGTH RHYTHM STRESS
EMPHASIS
(DORIC —) PLATEASM
(IRISH —) BROGUE
(MUSICAL —) BEAT
(WITHOUT AN —) ATONIC

ACCENTED FZ SFZ TONIC STRONG
MARCATO

ACCEPT BUY EAT BEAR FANG HAVE
HOLD JUMP TAKE ADMIT ADOPT AGREE
ALLOW HONOR INFER MARRY ASSENT
ASSUME POCKET APPROVE BELIEVE
CONCEDE EMBRACE ESPOUSE RECEIVE
(— BETS) BOOK
(— EAGERLY) LEAP
(— INHERITANCE) ADIATE
(— READILY) SWALLOW
(— WITHOUT QUESTION) ABIDE

ACCEPTABLE LIEF VALID WELCOME
GRACIOUS PASSABLE PLEASANT

ACCEPTANCE PASS ADITIO CREDENCE
CURRENCY

ACCEPTED GOING VULGAR POPULAR
APPROVED CREDITED ORTHODOX
STANDARD
(NOT —) OUT
(WIDELY —) INVETERATE

ACCESS WAY ADIT DOOR GATE PATH
ROAD ENTRY GOING ROUTE AVENUE
COMING PORTAL STREET ADVANCE
APPROACH ENTRANCE

ACCESSIBILITY EXPOSURE

ACCESSIBLE NEAR OPEN HANDY
PATENT AFFABLE PRESENT FAMILIAR
SOCIABLE

ACCESSORY HAT AIDE ALLY TOOL
EXTRA SCARF HELPER ABETTOR

ADAPTER ADAPTOR ADJUNCT ANCILLA FIXTURE ADDITIVE ORNAMENT

ACCIACCATURA MORDENT

ACCIDENT HAP CASE LUCK EVENT CHANCE HAZARD INJURY MISHAP FORTUNE QUALITY CALAMITY CASUALTY DISASTER FORTUITY INCIDENT
(— IN CAR RACING) SHUNT
(AUTOMOBILE —) FATAL

ACCIDENTAL ODD CASUAL CHANCE RANDOM EXTERNAL

ACCLAIM CRY CLAP FAME HAIL LAUD ROOT CHEER CLAIM ECLAT EXTOL SHOUT PRAISE APPLAUD HOSANNA OVATION PLAUDIT APPLAUSE

ACCLIMATIZE ADAPT HARDEN SEASON

ACCLIVITY BANK BROW HILL RISE GRADE PITCH SLANT SLOPE TALUS ASCENT HEIGHT INCLINE

ACCOLADE EMMY KISS RITE SIGN AWARD HONOR KUDOS MEDAL OSCAR TOKEN GARLAND

ACCOMMODATE AID BOW FIT GIVE HELP HOLD LEND SORT SUIT ADAPT BOARD DEFER FAVOR HOUSE LODGE SERVE YIELD ADJUST COMPLY OBLIGE SETTLE CONFORM GARRISON

ACCOMMODATION LOAN BERTH CLASS BERTHAGE GIFFGAFF

ACCOMPANIED FRAUGHT

ACCOMPANIMENT BURDEN ESCORT OOMPAH ADJUNCT DESCANT SUPPORT OBLIGATO

ACCOMPANY SEE FARE JOIN LEAD TEND BRING PILOT ASSIST ATTEND CONCUR CONVEY CONVOY ESCORT FOLLOW SECOND SQUIRE COEXIST CONDUCT CONSORT CHAPERON

ACCOMPANYING FELLOW ADJUNCT

ACCOMPLICE PAL AIDE ALLY CHUM BUDDY CRONY SHILL TILER COHORT FELLOW HELPER ABETTOR FEODARY PARTNER

ACCOMPLISH DO GO END WIN FILL WORK ENACT EQUIP FETCH FORTH SWING AFFORD ATTAIN EFFECT FINISH MANAGE ACHIEVE COMPASS EXECUTE FULFILL OPERATE PERFECT PERFORM REALIZE SUCCEED COMPLETE CONTRIVE ENGINEER

ACCOMPLISHED APT ABLE ARCH DONE ADEPT ENDED GREAT EXPERT TALENTED

ACCOMPLISHMENT ART END DEED FEAT CRAFT SKILL EFFECT TALENT QUALITY FRUITION LEARNING

ACCORD GIVE JIBE JUMP SUIT UNIT AGREE ALLOW AWARD BEFIT GRANT LEVEL STAND TALLY UNITY ACCEDE ADJUST ASSENT BESTOW COMPLY CONCUR SETTLE UNISON COMPORT COMPOSE CONCEDE CONCERT CONCORD CONSENT CONSORT HARMONY RAPPORT RESPOND SYMPATHY

ACCORDING (— TO) AD BY AUX SEC PURSUANT

ACCORDINGLY SO THEN THUS HENCE IGITUR

ACCORDION LANTUM FLAUTINO

ACCOST HAIL MASH MEET ASSAY BOARD GREET SPEAK ACCESS BROACH HALLOO SALUTE ADDRESS SOLICIT APPROACH

ACCOUNT TAB BILL BOOK DEEM DRAW ITEM NICK NOTE RATE SAKE TALE TELL TEXT WORD AUDIT BLAME CHALK COUNT JUDGE SCORE STATE STORY VALUE WORTH DETAIL ESTEEM LEGEND NOTICE PROFIT REASON RECKON RECORD REGARD RELATE RENDER REPORT REPUTE TREATY COMPUTE EXPLAIN JOURNAL NARRATE PROCESS RECITAL CONSIDER ESTIMATE TREATISE
(— FOR) SAVE EXPLAIN
(ACCURATE —) GRIFF
(CREDIT —) TICK
(LONG —) ILIAD MEGILLAH

ACCOUNTABILITY DETAIL LIABILITY

ACCOUNTABLE LIABLE AMENABLE

ACCOUNTANT CLERK SIRCAR AUDITOR PESHKAR PUTWARI KULKARNI

ACCOUNTING TASK REASON COSTING

ACCOUTER ARM RIG GIRD ARRAY DRESS EQUIP ATTIRE CLOTHE OUTFIT FURNISH PROVIDE

ACCOUTERMENTS GEAR DRESS ATTIRE

ACCREDIT ALLOT VOUCH CREDIT DEPUTE APPOINT APPROVE ASCRIBE BELIEVE CERTIFY CONFIRM ENDORSE LICENSE SANCTION

ACCRETION GAIN GROWTH DEPOSIT EXUDATE ADDITION INCREASE

ACCRUE ADD WIN EARN GAIN GROW PILE ARISE ENSUE INCUR ISSUE MATURE RESULT ACQUIRE COLLECT REDOUND INCREASE

ACCUMULATE DRAW GROW HEAP MASS PILE SAVE AMASS HOARD STACK STORE TOTAL ACCRUE GARNER GATHER MUSTER SCRAPE COLLECT HARVEST INCREASE

ACCUMULATION DRIP DUMP FUND GAIN HEAP MASS PILE LODGE STACK STORE DEBRIS GARNER BACKLOG CUMULUS DEPOSIT DOSSIER MORAINE DIVIDEND INTEREST
(— OF FLUID) EDEMA ASCITES
(— OF FORCE) CHARGE
(— OF TRIFLES) FLOTSAM
(— ON CONCRETE) LAITANCE

ACCURACY NICETY FIDELITY JUSTNESS PRECISION
(— OF ADJUSTMENT) TRAM

ACCURATE JUST LEAL NICE TRUE CLOSE EXACT FLUSH RIGHT NARROW PROPER SEVERE STRICT CAREFUL CORRECT PRECISE FAITHFUL PUNCTUAL RIGOROUS TRUTHFUL

ACCUSATION BEEF WITE BLAME CAUSE CRIME POINT APPEAL ATTACK CHARGE DELATION

ACCUSATORY WRAYFUL

ACCUSE TAX CALL FILE SLUR TASK WITE WRAY ARGUE BLAME TAINT TOUCH WHITE APPEAL ATTACH ATTACK BECALL

CHARGE DEFAME DELATE INDICT ARRAIGN CENSURE IMPEACH TRADUCE CHASTISE COMPLAIN

ACCUSTOM USE HAFT WONT ADAPT BREAK DRILL HABIT HAUNT INURE TRAIN ADDICT ADJUST INDUCE SEASON TOUGHEN ACQUAINT

ACCUSTOMED TAME USED WONT USUAL INURED CHRONIC CURRENT

ACE JOT ONE PIP ATOM CARD HERO MARK TOPS UNIT ADEPT FLYER POINT EXPERT AVIATOR
(— OF CLUBS) BASTA BASTO
(— OF SPADES) SPADILLE
(— OF TRUMPS) TIB HONOR PUNTO
(THREE —S) GLEEK

ACERB ACID HARD SOUR TART ACRID HARSH SHARP BITTER SEVERE

ACERBITY ACRIMONY ASPERITY SEVERITY TARTNESS

ACETIC SOUR SHARP ZOONIC

ACETYLENE TOLAN ALKYNE ETHYNE

ACHE NAG NIP HURT LONG PAIN PANG PINE RACK SMART THROB YEARN DESIRE MISERY STITCH STOUND TWINGE TWITCH ANGUISH SORENESS

ACHENE CYPSELA UTRICLE

ACHIEVE DO END GET WIN EARN GAIN HAVE MAKE FETCH FORCE NOTCH REACH SCORE AFFORD ARRIVE ATTAIN EFFECT FINISH OBTAIN COMPASS EXPLOIT FULFILL PERFORM PROCURE PRODUCE REALIZE SUCCEED TRIUMPH COMPLETE CONCLUDE CONTRIVE ACCOMPLISH

ACHIEVEMENT ACT JOB DEED FEAT WORK ACTION CAREER RESULT EXPLOIT PROWESS

ACHILLES PELIDES
(COMPANION OF —) PATROCLUS
(FATHER OF —) PELEUS
(FRIEND OF —) PATROCLUS
(HORSE OF —) XANTHUS
(MOTHER OF —) THETIS
(SLAYER OF —) PARIS

ACHROMATIC GRAY GREY NEUTRAL

ACID DRY DIAL DOPA KEEN PABA SOUR TART ACERB ACRID ALGIN AMINO CERIN EAGER HARSH LYSIN MALIC OLEUM RHEIN SHARP ULMIC ABRINE BITING BITTER GLYCIN LYSINE NIACIN PROLIN SERINE VALINE ACETOSE CERASIN FILICIN GLYCINE PROLINE STEARIN VINEGAR

ACIDITY ACOR VERDURE ACERBITY SOURNESS VERJUICE

ACIS (FATHER OF —) FAUNUS
(LOVER OF —) GALATEA
(MOTHER OF —) SYMAETHIS
(SLAYER OF —) POLYPHEMUS

ACKNOWLEDGE NOD OWN AVER AVOW SIGN ADMIT ADOPT ALLOW GRANT THANK YIELD ACCEDE ACCEPT ANSWER ASSENT AVOUCH FATHER REWARD CONCEDE CONFESS DECLARE OBSERVE PROFESS DISCLOSE RECOGNIZE

ACKNOWLEDGEMENT GRANT THANK

AVOWAL CREDIT SHRIFT APOLOGY RECOGNITION
(— OF MISTAKE) JEOFAIL
(— OF SIN) PECCAVI

ACME IT ACE CAP TOP APEX CULM HIGH PEAK CREST PITCH POINT STATE APOGEE CLIMAX CRISIS HEIGHT HEYDAY SUMMIT ZENITH SUBLIME PINNACLE

ACNE WHELK ROSACEA

ACOLYTE BOY HELPER NOVICE SERVER LEARNER PATENER THURIFER

ACOMIA BALDNESS

ACONITE BIKH NAPELLUS

ACORN NUT GLAND OVEST BALANUS BELLOTA
(PL.) MAST CAMATA PANNAGE CAMATINA

ACOUSTICS SONICS PHONICS

ACQUAINT KNOW TELL TEACH VERSE ADVISE INFORM NOTIFY SCHOOL APPRISE

ACQUAINTANCE HABIT COUSIN FRIEND GOSSIP PICKUP AFFINITY FAMILIAR INTIMATE
(PRACTICAL —) PRACTICE
(PL.) KITH SOCIETY

ACQUAINTED ACQUENT VERSANT

ACQUIESCE BOW ABIDE AGREE YIELD ACCEDE ACCEPT ASSENT COMPLY CONCUR SUBMIT CONCEDE CONFIRM CONFORM CONSENT

ACQUIRE ADD BAG BUY GET WIN EARN FORM GAIN GRAB HAVE MAKE REAP ADOPT AMASS ANNEX BEGET GLEAN LEARN REACH SEIZE STEAL ATTAIN DERIVE EFFECT GARNER OBTAIN SECURE SNATCH COLLECT DEVELOP PROCURE RECEIVE CONTRACT

ACQUISITION WIN GAIN LUCRE GETTING
(DISHONEST —) GRAFT

ACQUIT PAY FREE QUIT CLEAR QUIET BEHAVE BESTOW EXCUSE PARDON ABSOLVE COMPORT CONDUCT RELEASE REQUITE LIBERATE OVERLOOK

ACQUITTAL EXCUSE ABSOLUTION

ACRE LAND FIELD STANG ARPENT COLLOP FARMHOLD
(QUARTER —) ROOD
(120 —S) HIDE
(2-3RDS —) COVER

ACRID HOT ACID KEEN SOUR HARSH ROUGH SHARP SURLY BITING BITTER CAUSTIC PUNGENT REEKING UNSAVORY VIRULENT

ACRIMONIOUS MAD ACID KEEN ACRID ANGRY GRUFF HARSH IRATE SHARP SURLY BITTER CAUSTIC STINGING VIRULENT

ACRIMONY VIRUS ACERBITY ASPERITY PUNGENCY SOURNESS ANIMOSITY

ACROBAT ZANY KINKER GYMNAST TOPPLER TUMBLER BALANCER AERIALIST

ACROPOLIS FORT HILL CITADEL

ACROSS OVER SPAN YOND CROSS ABOARD THWART ATHWART OPPOSITE TRAVERSE

ACROSTIC ABC AGLA DORA GAME POEM PHRASE PUZZLE

ACT BE DO GO APE LET BILL COME DEAL DEED DORA FACT FEAT JEST MAKE MOVE PART PASS PLAY SKIT TURN WORK DRAMA EDICT EMOTE EXERT FEIGN GRACE KARMA MODEL SCENE SHIFT STUNT ACTION BEHAVE BESTIR DECREE MANAGE COMPORT EXECUTE EXPLOIT PERFORM PORTRAY PRETEND STATUTE FUNCTION PRETENSE SIMULATE
(— AFFECTEDLY) MIMP
(— AWKWARDLY) HOCKER
(— BEFORE) ANTICIPATE
(— BLUNDERINGLY) BULL
(— DECEITFULLY) DOUBLE
(— DISHONESTLY) FUDGE
(— IN THEATER) GAFF
(— INDECISIVELY) DITHER
(— OF APPROVAL) EUGE
(— OF KINDNESS) CARESS BENEFIT
(— OF LABOR) DILIGENCE
(— OF PRAYER) DEVOTION
(— OF STUPIDITY) BETISE
(— OF TRICKERY) COG
(— OUT) ENACT DRAMATIZE
(— PLAYFULLY) DALLY BANTER
(— SPORTIVELY) DAFF
(— SUDDENLY) FLASH
(— TIMIDLY) NESH
(— TOGETHER) AGREE COACT CONCUR CONCORD
(— UPON) TOUCH AFFECT HANDLE
(— VIGOROUSLY) TWIG
(COMICAL —) JIG
(CONVENTIONAL —) AMENITY
(CORRUPT —) DEPRAVITY
(CRIMINAL —) INFAMY
(DARING —) ESCAPADE
(DECEPTIVE —) FEINT
(ECCENTRIC —) CANTRIP
(FOOLISH —) DIDO IDIOTISM
(FORBIDDEN —) CRIME
(FORMAL —) CEREMONY
(HASTY —) FLING
(HOSTILE —) BLOW
(INJURIOUS —) SPOIL
(LAUDATORY —) COUP
(LITURGICAL —) LAVABO
(LIVELY —) JIG
(MERITORIOUS —) MITZVAH
(OFFENSIVE —) AFFRONT
(OFFICIAL —S) ACTA
(PLAYFUL —) RAILLERY
(RUDE —) INCIVILITY
(THOUGHTLESS —) FOLLY
(UNMANNERLY —) SOLECISM
(UNUSUAL —) STUNT
(VARIETY —) SKETCH

ACTION ACT AIR DAP JOB PAS CASE DEED FACT FRAY GEST PLOY SHOW STEP SUIT WORK DOING EDICT FIGHT FLING ISSUE THING VENUE AFFAIR AGENCY BATTLE COMBAT PRAXIS CONDUCT FACTION GESTURE PROCESS ACTIVITY BEHAVIOR BUSINESS CONFLICT FUNCTION PRACTICE
(ABSURD —S) BOSH
(ANTAGONISTIC —) ATOMISM
(BLAMEWORTHY —) WITE
(CAPRICIOUS —) FREAK
(COOPERATIVE —) SYNERGISM
(COURT —) LAW SUIT ASSIZE LAWSUIT QUERELA
(CRUEL —) RUTH
(CUSTOMARY —) COURSE
(EXTEMPORE —) SCHEDIASM
(FRIVOLOUS —) DALLIANCE
(HOSTILE —) OPPOSITION
(IMPULSIVE —) STAMPEDE
(INDIRECT —) WINDLASS
(INITIAL —) LEADOFF INDUCTION
(LEGAL —) DEBT SUIT ACCOUNT DETINET DETINUE PROCEEDING
(MEAN —S) DOGGERY
(MILITARY —) SWEEP OPERATION
(ODD —S) JIMJAMS
(PLAYFUL —) FUN FROLIC
(RASH —) HASTE
(REPEATED —) DRUM DOUBLE
(SUDDEN —) FLISK
(SYMBOLIC —) CHARADE
(TACTLESS —) GAUCHERIE
(VIOLENT —) AFFRAY
(WHIMSICAL —S) HUMORS
(WILY —) WRINKLE

ACTIVATE SPARK ELICIT

ACTIVATOR GOAD

ACTIVE UP BUSY GAIN PERT RASH SPRY TRIG YEPE ABOUT AGILE ALERT ALIVE ASTIR BRISK FRESH LIGHT LUSTY NIPPY PEART QUICK READY SMART SNELL SPICY SPRIG STOUT SWANK VIVID BOUNCY CLEVER DIRECT FIERCE HEARTY LIVELY LIVING MOVING NIMBLE PROMPT SPEEDY SPRUCE DASHING DYNAMIC HOPPING HUMMING KINETIC STHENIC ANIMATED ATHLETIC DILIGENT SPIRITED VIGOROUS

ACTIVITY ACT ADO GOG VIR FIZZ LIFE PLAY PUSH STIR BLAST CAPER EVENT HEART RALLY TRADE VIGOR ACTION AGENCY BUSTLE ENERGY HUSTLE AGILITY CALLING BUSINESS EXERCISE FUNCTION

ACTOR HAM DOER HERO LEAD MIME STAR AGENT BUFFO COMIC DROLL EXTRA HEAVY MIMIC SUPER ARTIST BUSKER DISEUR MUMMER PLAYER PUPPET STAGER TOMMER ARTISTE DISEUSE HISTRIO TROUPER COMEDIAN HISTRION JUVENILE THESPIAN
(INDIFFERENT —) JAY
(INEPT —) HAM
(INFERIOR —) SHINE

ACTRESS DIVA STAR INGENUE STARLET FARCEUSE PREMIERE THESPIAN

ACTUAL GOOD HARD REAL TRUE VERY BODILY FACTUAL GENUINE CONCRETE DEFINITE EXISTING MATERIAL POSITIVE TANGIBLE

ACTUALITY ACT FACT BEING VERITY REALITY

ACTUALLY BUT DONE TRULY FAIRLY ITSELF REALLY

ACTUATE ACT EGG RUN DRAW MOVE URGE ENACT IMPEL ROUSE START AROUSE COMPEL EXCITE INCITE INDUCE AGITATE ANIMATE ENLIVEN INSPIRE SHARPEN MOTIVATE PERSUADE

ACUITY FINENESS

ACUMEN WIT INSIGHT CAPACITY KEENNESS SAGACITY

ACUTE ACID FINE HIGH KEEN TART HEAVY QUICK SHARP SMART ASTUTE SHREWD SHRILL SUBTLE TREBLE URGENT CRUCIAL INTENSE POINTED VIOLENT CRITICAL INCISIVE POIGNANT (MOST —) DIRE (NOT —) SLOW GRAVE CHRONIC

ACUTENESS DEPTH SENSE ACUITY ACUMEN SAGACITY SUBTLETY

ADAD RAMMAN

ADAGE SAW DICT REDE TEXT WORD AXIOM MAXIM MOTTO HOMILY SAYING TRUISM BROMIDE PRECEPT PROVERB APHORISM APOTHEGM

ADAM ADE EDIE ADKIN (GRANDSON OF —) ENOS ENOCH (SON OF —) ABEL CAIN SETH (TEACHER OF —) RAISEL (WIFE OF —) EVE LILITH

ADAMANT FIRM GRIM HARD SOLID STONY ADAMAS DIAMOND UNMOVED OBDURATE STUBBORN

ADAMANTINE FIRM BORON STONE VAJRA

ADAM BEDE (AUTHOR OF —) ELIOT (CHARACTER IN —) ADAM SETH DINAH HETTY ARTHUR BARTLE IRVINE MARTIN MASSEY MORRIS POYSER SORREL DONNITHORNE

ADAM'S APPLE GUZZLE

ADAM'S NEEDLE YUCCA

ADAPT FIT PLY PUT EDIT MOLD SORT SUIT AGREE HUMOR INURE SHAPE TALLY ADJUST CHANGE COMPLY DERIVE DOCTOR TEMPER CONFORM FASHION PREPARE QUALIFY CONTRIVE

ADAPTABLE LABILE ELASTIC PLASTIC PLIABLE

ADAPTED FIT FOR FITTED SUITED CONGENIAL

ADD EKE SAY TOT CAST FOOT GAIN JOIN LEND PLUS AFFIX ANNEX TOTAL UNITE ACCRUE ADJECT APPEND ATTACH CONFER FIGURE RECKON SUPPLY ACCRETE COMBINE COMPILE COMPUTE ENLARGE INCREASE (— ALCOHOL) SPIKE (— FUEL) BEET (— TO) ADORN ENRICH AUGMENT (— UP) SUM TOT COUNT TOTAL AMOUNT

ADDED AND EKE PLUS ADJUNCT

ADDER KRAIT VIPER ELAPID HAGWORM HYPNALE

ADDICT FAN BUFF DOPE HYPE USER COKEY COKIE FIEND HOPPY HOUND SLAVE DEVOTE JUNKIE DELIVER DEVOTEE HABITUE HOPHEAD SNIFTER ACCUSTOM

ADDICTED GIVEN PRONE HOOKED BIBULOUS

ADDICTION HABIT MONKEY BIBACITY

ADDITION AND EKE ELL TAB TOO ALSO ELSE GAIN PLUS AFFIX RIDER ACCESS ACCRUE AUGEND ENCORE PREFIX ADJUNCT CODICIL JOINING PENDANT UNITING ADDENDUM INCREASE

ADDITIONAL NEW ELSE MORE ADDED EXTRA FRESH OTHER ANOTHER BESIDES FURTHER ACCESSORY

ADDLE MIRE AMAZE FILTH RIPEN SPOIL CURDLE MUDDLE AGITATE CONFUSE BEFUDDLE BEWILDER

ADDLED ASEA EMPTY PUTRID MUDDLED UNSOUND

ADDRESS AIM SUE WOO CALL HAIL HOME PRAY TACT TALK TURN ABODE APPLY BOARD COURT DRESS GREET POISE SKILL SPEAK TREAT ACCOST APPEAL CHARGE DIRECT EULOGY MANNER PARLEY SALUTE SERMON SPEECH CONDUCT CONSIGN ENTRUST LECTURE ORATION DEDICATE DELIVERY HARANGUE PETITION

ADEPT ACE APT ABLE HANDY ADROIT ARTIST CRAFTY EXPERT MASTER VERSED ANCIENT ARTISTE CAPABLE DEXTROUS SKILLFUL PROFICIENT

ADEQUATE DUE FIT ABLE FAIR FULL GOOD MEET WELL AMPLE EQUAL DECENT ENOUGH PROPER SUITABLE SATISFACTORY

ADHERE HEW HUG GLUE HOLD JOIN KEEP LINK ABIDE AFFIX APPLY CLING STICK UNITE ATTACH CEMENT CLEAVE COHERE ACCRETE PERSIST

ADHERENT IST ITE AIDE ALLY ADEPT FACTOR VOTARY BELIEVER DISCIPLE FAITHFUL FOLLOWER PARTISAN RETAINER SERVITOR

ADHESIVE GUM WAX BOND GLUE SIZE TAPE DABBY PASTE TACKY BINDER CEMENT CLINGY GLUTEN MASTIC STICKY MUCILAGE TENACIOUS

ADIPOSE FAT HARD SUET FATTY OBESE PURSY SQUAT TALLOW

ADIT DOOR ENTRY STULM ACCESS TUNNEL PASSAGE APPROACH ENTRANCE

ADJACENT NEAR NIGH CLOSE FLUSH HANDY BESIDE NEARBY MEETING VICINAL ABUTTING TOUCHING CONTIGUOUS

ADJOIN ADD ABUT BUTT JOIN LINE TACK TOUCH UNITE ACCOST APPEND ATTACH BORDER CONTACT NEIGHBOR

ADJOINING VICINAL

ADJOURN END MOVE RISE STAY ARISE CLOSE DEFER DELAY RECESS SUSPEND DISSOLVE POSTPONE

ADJUDGE TRY DEEM FIND GIVE HOLD RATE ALLOT AWARD GRANT JUDGE

ORDER ADDEEM DECIDE DECREE ORDAIN
REGARD CONDEMN SENTENCE
(— GUILTY) DAMN
(— NOT GUILTY) ABSOLVE
ADJUDICATE ACT TRY HEAR PASS RULE
JUDGE DECIDE RECKON REGARD SETTLE
ADJUDGE CONSIDER SENTENCE
ADJUNCT AID HELP PART ANNEX
PHRASE ANCILLA EPITHET FITTING
APPENDIX ORNAMENT
ADJURE ASK BEG BID BIND PRAY CRAVE
PLEAD SWEAR APPEAL CHARGE OBTEST
BESEECH COMMAND CONJURE CONTEST
ENTREAT REQUEST
ADJUST FIT FIX SET CAST EASE FORM
GEAR LINE PARE RATE SIZE SORT SUIT
TRIM TRUE ADAPT ALIGN ALINE COAPT
EQUAL FRAME PATCH RIGHT SHAPE
ATTUNE HAMMER ORIENT SETTLE
SQUARE TEMPER ARRANGE BALANCE
COMPOSE CONCERT CONFORM CORRECT
JUSTIFY PREPARE RECTIFY
ADJUSTMENT FIT GEAR MISE TRIM
FITNESS CHANCERY
ADJUTANT AIDE ALLY ARGALA HELPER
HURGILA MARABOU
ADJUVANT AIDE HELPER ADJUNCT
HELPFUL
ADMAN HUCKSTER
ADMETUS (FATHER OF —) PHERES
(WIFE OF —) ALCESTIS
ADMINISTER DO RUN DEAL DEEM DOSE
GIVE MOVE RULE APPLY SERVE TREAT
DIRECT GOVERN MANAGE SETTLE
SUPPLY TENDER CONDUCT CONTROL
EXECUTE FURNISH HUSBAND DISPENSE
(— FORCIBLY) HAND
(— SACRAMENT) BISHOP HOUSEL
ADMINISTRATION HELM RULE SWAY
POLICY TAHSIL CONDUCT DIOCESE
ECONOMY RECTORY REGIMEN CARRIAGE
DISPOSAL MINISTRY
(— OF OATH) JURATION
(REVENUE —) HACIENDA
ADMINISTRATOR CAID HELM
MANAGER TRUSTEE DIRECTOR
EXECUTOR MINISTER
(INCA —) CURACA
(MORMON —) APOSTLE
ADMIRABLE FINE GOOD HIGH GRAND
GREAT PROUD DIVINE AMIABLE CAPITAL
ELEGANT RIPPING
ADMIRAL FLAG CAPITAN FLAGMAN
NAVARCH
ADMIRATION FUROR GLORY ESTEEM
LIKING WONDER CONCEIT WORSHIP
ADMIRE DIG LIKE LOVE ADORE EXTOL
HONOR PRIZE VALUE ESTEEM MARVEL
REGARD REVERE WONDER ADULATE
APPROVE DELIGHT IDOLIZE RESPECT
VENERATE
ADMIRER FAN BEAU LOVER SWAIN
AMATEUR DEVOTEE FOLLOWER
IDOLATER
(PL.) FOLLOWING
ADMISSION FEE ADIT CALL ENTRY
ACCESS CHARGE ENTREE TICKET

CONSENT INGRESS ENTRANCE
RECEPTION CONCESSION
ADMIT LET OWN AVER AVOW BEAR TAKE
AGREE ALLOW ENTER GRANT ACCEDE
ACCEPT ASSENT ENROLL INDUCT PERMIT
SUFFER CONCEDE CONFESS INCLUDE
PROFESS RECEIVE SUFFICE INITIATE
(— AS MEMBER) INDUCT
(— AS VALID) SUSTAIN
ADMITTANCE ACCESS ENTRANCE
ADMITTING THOUGH
ADMIXTURE DASH ALLOY BLEND SHADE
SPICE TINGE DOLLOP FLAVOR LEAVEN
STREAK MIXTURE SOUPCON COMPOUND
INFUSION
ADMONISH WARN CHIDE SCOLD ADVISE
ENJOIN EXHORT NOTIFY REBUKE REMIND
SCHOOL CAUTION COUNSEL MONITOR
REPROVE
ADMONITION ADVICE CAVEAT HOMILY
CAUTION LECTURE REPROOF WARNING
REMINDER
ADO DEED FUSS ROUT STIR WORK HURRY
TOUSE BOTHER BUSTLE EFFORT FLURRY
HUBBUB POTHER RUCKUS BLATHER
SPUTTER TROUBLE TURMOIL
ADOBE MUD CLAY SILT TAPIA MUDCAP
ADOLESCENCE TEENS YOUTH NONAGE
PUBERTY MINORITY
ADOLESCENT LAD TEEN YOUNG YOUTH
TEENER IMMATURE TEENAGER
ADONIS ADON
(FATHER OF —) CINYRAS
(MOTHER OF —) MYRRH MYRRHA
ADOPT TAKE STEAL ACCEPT ASSUME
ATTACH BORROW CHOOSE FATHER
FOLLOW FOSTER MOTHER ACQUIRE
EMBRACE ESPOUSE RECEIVE WELCOME
ADVOCATE ARROGATE
ADORABLE LOVELY LOVABLE CHARMING
ADORATION HOMAGE WORSHIP
DEVOTION
ADORE DOTE LAUD LOVE EXALT EXTOL
HONOR ADMIRE ESTEEM PRAISE REVERE
GLORIFY IDOLIZE WORSHIP VENERATE
ADORN DUB FIG SET BEAD DECK FOIL
GAUD GILD LACE OUCH POSH STUD
SWAG TRIM ARRAY BEDUB BEGEM
CROWN DIGHT DRAPE DRESS FRONT
GRACE HIGHT INLAY JEWEL PRICK PRIMP
PRINK ROUGE SPRIG TRICK ATTIRE
BECOME BEDECK BETRIM BLAZON
BROOCH CLOTHE COLLAR DAMASK
DIADEM EMBOSS ENAMEL ENRICH
ENROBE FIGURE INSTAL INVEST PURFLE
TASSEL APPAREL BEDIGHT BEDIZEN
COMMEND EMPEARL FEATHER FURNISH
GARNISH GLORIFY SPANGLE VARNISH
BEAUTIFY DECORATE EMBLAZON
ORNAMENT
ADORNED CLAD BESEEN DAEDAL
ORNATE CLOTHED COLORED FIGURED
ADORNMENT DRESS PRIDE BEAUTY
DECORE TINSEL DECKING PRANKING
ADRIFT ASEA LOST AWAFT LIGAN LOOSE
AFLOAT DERELICT FLOATING UNMOORED
ADROIT DEFT EASY FEAT GOOD NEAT

SLIM ADEPT HANDY READY SMART TRICK ARTFUL CLEVER EXPERT HABILE NIMBLE CUNNING DEXTROUS HANDSOME SKILLFUL

ADROITNESS ART EASE TACT KNACK SKILL ADDRESS FACILITY

ADULATE FAWN LAUD GLOSS GLOZE PRAISE FLATTER

ADULATION GLOSE GLOZE PRAISE FLATTERY

ADULT MAN FULL MANLY MATURE GROWNUP

ADULTERATE CUT MIX DASH LOAD ALLOY TAINT DEBASE DEFILE DILUTE EXTEND WEAKEN CORRUPT FALSIFY VITIATE DENATURE

ADULTERATED CUT SHAM IMPURE CORRUPT SPURIOUS

ADUMBRATE IMAGE SHADE VAGUE OBSCURE SUGGEST INTIMATE

ADUMBRATION SHADE SHADOW PHANTASM

ADVANCE COME GO AID PAY SOP WAY BULL CITE COME DASH GAIN HELP INCH LAUD LEND LIFT LOAN MARK MOVE NEAR NOSE PASS PUSH RISE SHOW STEP AVANT BOOST BRING CREEP ENTER EXALT EXTOL FAVOR FORGE MARCH OFFER PLACE SERVE SPEED THROW ASSIGN ASSIST BETTER EXTEND GROWTH HASTEN INROAD PREFER PREPAY STRIDE STRIKE THRIVE TRAVEL BENEFIT DEVELOP ELEVATE ENHANCE FORWARD FURTHER HEADWAY IMPROVE PROCEED PROMOTE PROPOSE PROSPER SUCCEED HEIGHTEN INCREASE PROGRESS

ADVANCED FAR DEEP GONE HIGH LATE AHEAD FORWARD LIBERAL VANWARD FOREMOST
(— IN YEARS) SENIOR ELDERLY
(MOST —) EXTREME FARTHEST FOREMOST HEADMOST

ADVANTAGE USE VAN BEST BOOT DROP EDGE GAIN GOOD JUMP MEND ODDS PULL SAKE AVAIL BULGE FAVOR LAUGH POINT SPEED START STEAD USAGE BEHALF BETTER EFFECT PROFIT ACCOUNT BENEFIT CAPITAL EXPLOIT PURPOSE UTILITY HANDICAP INTEREST LEVERAGE
(ACCIDENTAL —) FLUKE
(UNDUE —) ABUSE

ADVANTAGEOUS GOOD WELL GOLDEN PLUMMY SPEEDY USEFUL

ADVENT COMING INCOME ARRIVAL APPROACH PAROUSIA

ADVENTITIOUS CASUAL FOREIGN STRANGE ACQUIRED EPISODIC ACCESSORY

ADVENTURE LARK RISK EVENT GESTE PERIL QUEST CHANCE DANGER HAZARD EMPRISE FORTUNE ESCAPADE JEOPARDY

ADVENTURER ROUTIER ARGONAUT PICAROON

ADVENTUROUS BOLD RASH DARING ERRANT AUNTROUS RECKLESS

ADVERSARY FOE ENEMY RIVAL SATAN FOEMAN OPPONENT

ADVERSE FOE ILL EVIL CROSS LOATH AVERSE COUNTER FROWARD HOSTILE OPPOSED CONTRARY INIMICAL OPPOSING OPPOSITE

ADVERSITY ILL WOE DECAY NIGHT MISERY SORROW ILLNESS TROUBLE CALAMITY DISTRESS MISFORTUNE

ADVERTISE CRY BARK BILL CALL PLUG PUFF STAR WARN BLURB INFORM NOTIFY PARADE DECLARE DISPLAY OBSERVE PLACARD PUBLISH ANNOUNCE PROCLAIM

ADVERTISEMENT AD BILL SIGN BLURB CHANT PITCH PROMO CACHET NOTICE POSTER TEASER AFFICHE PLACARD STUFFER CIRCULAR HANDBILL

ADVERTISING BUSH BILLING PUFFERY
(EXTRAVAGANT —) HYPE

ADVICE LORE NEWS REDE STEER NOTICE CAUTION COUNSEL OPINION TIDINGS GUIDANCE MONITION

ADVISABLE BOOK PROPER PRUDENT

ADVISE SAY REDE TELL WARN WISE COACH GUIDE ADJURE CONFER DEVISE EXHORT INFORM PONDER REVEAL COUNSEL ACQUAINT ADMONISH RECOMMEND

ADVISER AIDE TOUT COACH COMES TUTOR DOCTOR EGERIA LAWYER NESTOR MONITOR STARETS TEACHER ATTORNEY DIRECTOR PREACHER

ADVISORY URGING PRUDENT

ADVOCATE PRO ABET BACK PUSH URGE VOGT ADOPT FAVOR PLEAD ASSERT BACKER DEFEND LAWYER PATRON SYNDIC ABETTOR APOSTLE DECLAIM ENDORSE ESPOUSE EXPOUND PATRIOT PLEADER PROMOTE SUPPORT ATTORNEY CHAMPION PARTISAN PREACHER PROPONENT

AEGIR HLER GYMIR

AEGIS EGIS SHIELD AUSPICE DEFENCE

AENEAS (COMPANION OF —) ACHATES
(FATHER OF —) ANCHISES
(GREAT-GRANDSON OF —) BRUT
(MOTHER OF —) VENUS APHRODITE
(SON OF —) IULUS ASCANIUS
(WIFE OF —) CREUSA LAVINIA

AENEID (AUTHOR OF —) VIRGIL
(CHARACTER IN —) ANNA DIDO JUNO
VENUS AENEAS PALLAS TURNUS
EVANDER LATINUS LAVINIA ANCHISES
ASCANIUS

AEOLUS (BROTHER OF —) DORUS
XUTHUS
(DAUGHTER OF —) ARNE CANACE
ALCYONE HALCYONE
(FATHER OF —) HELLEN HIPPOTES
(MOTHER OF —) ORSEIS
(SON OF —) ATHAMAS CRETHEUS
SISYPHUS SALMONEUS

AEON AGE EON ERA AEVUM CYCLE KALPA

AERATE AERIFY CHARGE INFLATE

AERIAL AERY AERY AIRY AERIE LOFTY DIPOLE UNREAL ANTENNA ETHEREAL

AEROBE BACTERIUM
AEROEMBOLISM BENDS
AEROFOIL SLAT ROTOR
AERONAUT PILOT SKYMAN
AEROPLANE (SEE AIRPLANE)
AERUGO RUST PATINA
AESTHETIC ARTISTIC ESTHETIC
   TASTEFUL
AFAR OFF AWAY REMOTE DANAKIL
   DANKALI DISTANT
AFARA LIMBA
AFFABLE FAIR OPEN BLAND CIVIL FRANK
   SUAVE BENIGN FACILE GENIAL SOCIAL
   URBANE AMIABLE CORDIAL GENERAL
   LIKABLE CHARMING FAMILIAR FRIENDLY
   GRACIOUS PLEASANT SOCIABLE
   TOWARDLY
AFFAIR DO JOB CASE GEAR PLOY BRAWL
   CAUSE EVENT FIGHT LEVEE PARTY
   THING ACTION BATTLE MATTER
   BLOWOUT CONCERN FUNERAL
   HOEDOWN JOURNEY LIAISON PALAVER
   SHEBANG BUSINESS ENDEAVOR
   INTRIGUE OCCASION PROCEEDING
   (CONFUSED —) SCHEMOZZLE
   (CRITICAL —) KANKEDORT
   (LOVE —) LOVE AMOUR INTRIGUE
   (SOCIAL —) FORMAL JUNKET SUPPER
   (STATE —S) ESTATE
AFFECT AIL HIT BEAR MELT MOVE POSE
   SHAM STIR SWAY ALLOT ALTER ANNOY
   ASSAY COLOR DRIVE FANCY FEIGN
   HAUNT IMPEL MINCE SHOCK TOUCH
   ASPIRE ASSIGN ASSUME CHANGE
   SOFTEN STRIKE THRILL ATTINGE
   BEWITCH CONCERN IMPRESS PRETEND
   PROFESS INTEREST SIMULATE
   (— BY HANDLING) TOUCH
   (— FAVORABLY) LIKE
   (— INJURIOUSLY) INTERESS
   (— STRONGLY) HIT HOLD SURPRISE
   (— WITH EXCITEMENT) BLOW
AFFECTATION AIR AIRS POSE SHAM
   FRILL GRACE MINCE CHICHI CONCEIT
   DISPLAY FOPPERY PIETISM PRETENSE
AFFECTED MOY AIRY CAMP FEAT APISH
   POSEY CHICHI FALLAL FEISTY FORMAL
   PRETTY QUAINT FEIGNED MINIKIN
   STILTED TAFFETA INVOLVED PRECIEUX
   PRECIOUS
AFFECTION LOVE ALOHA AMOUR BOTCH
   FLAME HEART DOTAGE ESTEEM MALADY
   REGARD AILMENT CHARITY EMOTION
   FEELING PASSION SYMPTOM DEARNESS
   DEVOTION FONDNESS KINDNESS
   TENDENCY
AFFECTIONATE DEAR FOND WARM
   ARDENT DOTING LOVING TENDER
   AMOROUS CORDIAL DEVOTED EARNEST
   ZEALOUS ATTACHED PARENTAL
   SISTERLY
AFFIANCED INTENDED
AFFIDAVIT DAVY OATH AFFIANT
AFFILIATE ALLY UNIT ADOPT MERGE
   UNITE ATTACH BRANCH RELATE
   CHAPTER
AFFINITY KIN FAMILY LIKING AVIDITY

   KINDRED KINSHIP RAPPORT ALLIANCE
   RELATION SYMPATHY COGNATION
AFFIRM PUT AVER AVOW TAKE POSIT
   STATE SWEAR VOUCH ADHERE ALLEGE
   ASSERT ATTEST AVOUCH DEPOSE
   RATIFY SUBMIT THREAP VERIFY
   CONFIRM DECLARE PROFESS PROTEST
   TESTIFY MAINTAIN
AFFIRMATION SAY VOW YES AMEN
   OATH WORD DIXIT PONENT THESIS
   AVERMENT
AFFIRMATIVE AY AYE NOD YAH YEA YEP
   YES AMEN YEAH PONENT DOGMATIC
   POSITIVE
AFFIX ADD FIX PIN SET CASE CLIP FAST
   JOIN NAIL SEAL SIGN ANNEX STAMP
   UNITE ANCHOR APPEND ATTACH FASTEN
   STAPLE CONNECT PLASTER SUBJOIN
AFFLATUS FURY FUROR FRENZY VISION
   IMPULSE
AFFLICT AIL RUE TRY VEX FIRE HOLD
   HURT PAIN PINE RACK BESET CURSE
   GRILL GRIPE HARRY PINCH PRESS SEIZE
   SMITE VISIT WOUND WRING BURDEN
   GRIEVE HARASS HUMBLE INFEST
   MOLEST PESTER STRAIN STRESS STRIKE
   CHASTEN INFLICT OPPRESS SCOURGE
   TORMENT TROUBLE DISTRESS LACERATE
   STRAITEN
AFFLICTED SAD SORRY AILING WOEFUL
   GRIEVED HAUNTED SMITTEN IMPAIRED
   STRICKEN TROUBLED
AFFLICTION WOE EVIL LOSS PAIN SORE
   CROSS GRIEF PRESS SMART BUFFET
   DURESS MISERY PATHOS PLAGUE
   SORROW STRESS AILMENT DISEASE
   ILLNESS PASSION PURSUIT SCOURGE
   TORTURE TROUBLE CALAMITY DISTRESS
   HARDSHIP SEVERITY SICKNESS
   VEXATION
AFFLUENCE EASE PLENTY RICHES
   WEALTH FORTUNE OPULENCE
AFFLUENT FAT RICH FLUSH RIVER
   BRANCH COPIOUS FLOWING HALCYON
   OPULENT WEALTHY ABUNDANT
AFFORD GO BEAR GIVE LEND GRANT
   INCUR OFFER STAND YIELD SUPPLY
   ACHIEVE FURNISH PRODUCE PROVIDE
AFFRONT CUT DEFY SLAP ABUSE PEEVE
   HARASS INJURE INSULT NETTLE OFFEND
   SLIGHT ASSAULT OFFENSE OUTRAGE
   PROVOKE IRRITATE CONTUMELY
AFGHAN RUG COVER DURANI HAZARA
   PATHAN BLANKET PAKHTUN ACHAKZAI
   COVERLET

AFGHANISTAN

CAPITAL: KABUL
COIN: PUL ABBASI AMANIA AFGHANI
LAKE: HELMAND
LANGUAGE: DARI PASHTO PUSHTU
   BALOCHI BALUCHI
MEASURE: JERIB KAROH
MOUNTAIN: KOH SAFEO CHAGAI PAMIRS
   SULAIMAN

NATIVE: SISTANI
PARLIAMENT: SHURA
PROVINCE: GHOR FARAH HERAT KABUL KUNAR KUNUZ LOGAR MAZAR ZABUL GHAZNI KAPISA PARWAN WARDAK
RIVER: LORA OXUS CABUL FARAH HARUT INDUS KABUL KHASH KUNAR KOKCHA KUNDUZ HELMAND MURGHAB AMUDARYA
SEA: DARYA
TOWN: RUI JURM NANI WAMA ASMAR BALKH DOSHI HERAT KABUL KUNAR MARUF MATUN MUKUR PAHRA TULAK URGAN CHAMAN GHAZNI KUNDUZ NAUZAD PANJAO RUSTAK SANGAN SAROBI TUKZAR WASHIR BAGHLAN BAMIYAN DILARAM KANDAHAR
TRIBE: SAFI TURK ULUS KAFIR TAJIK UZBEK BALOCH BALUCH HAZARA KIRGIZ PATHAN
WEIGHT: PAU PAW SER SIR KARWAR KHURDS

AFICIONADO FAN AMATEUR DEVOTEE FOLLOWER
AFIELD ABROAD ASTRAY
AFIRE EAGER ABLAZE AFLAME ARDENT BURNING FLAMING
AFLOAT ASEA ASWIM AWAFT AWASH ADRIFT BUOYED NATANT FLOODED
AFOOT ABOUT ASTIR ABROAD WALKING
AFOREMENTIONED SAID SUCH
AFORESAID SAME DITTO NAMED PRIOR PREVIOUS
AFORETIME ERE FORMER FORMERLY
AFRAID PAVID TIMID AGHAST CRAVEN SCARED ALARMED ANXIOUS CHICKEN FEARFUL COWARDLY GHASTFUL TIMOROUS
AFRESH ANEW ANON OVER AGAIN NEWLY DENOVO ENCORE REPEATED
AFRIKAANS TAAL DUTCH
AFRO NATURAL
AFT BACK REAR ABAFT AFTER ASTERN BEHIND
AFTER A AB BY TO AFT EFT FOR SIN ANON NEXT PAST POST SYNE ABAFT APRES INFRA LATER SINCE ASTERN BEHIND BEYOND
AFTERBIRTH HEAM SECUNDINE SOOTERKIN
AFTERBODY TONNEAU
AFTERMATH FOG LOSS ISSUE ROWEN TRAIL ARRISH EDDISH EDGREW EFFECT PROFIT RESULT SEQUEL UPSHOT STUBBLE BACKWASH
AFTERNOON AFTER TARDE UNDERN EVENING TEATIME
AFTERTASTE TWANG FAREWELL
AFTERTHOUGHT FOOTNOTE
AFTERWARD EFT POST SITH THEN APRES LATER EFTSOON EFTSOONS
AGAIN OR BIS EFT YET ANEW ANON BACK MORE OVER NEWLY AFRESH DENOVO ENCORE ITERUM FRESHLY FURTHER MOREOVER

AGAINST BY IN UP CON NON ANTI INTO WITH ANENT UNTIL AVERSE CONTRA VERSUS FERNENT FORNENT OPPOSED
AGALLOCH AGGUR ALOES GAROO TAMBAC LINALOE CALAMBAC
AGAMEMNON (BROTHER OF —) MENELAUS
 (DAUGHTER OF —) ELECTRA IPHIGENIA
 (FATHER OF —) PLISTHENES
 (GRANDFATHER OF —) ATREUS
 (SON OF —) ORESTES
 (WIFE OF —) CLYTEMNESTRA
AGAPE LOVE OPEN FEAST GAPING YAWNING
AGAR MOSS GELOSE KANTEN
AGARIC BLEWITS BLUSHER FLYBANE LEPIOTA
AGASP EAGER GASPING
AGATE TAW ONYX RUBY SARD MARBLE PEBBLE QUARTZ
AGAVE ALOE LILY AMOLE DATIL SISAL LILIUM MAGUEY MESCAL PULQUE ZAPUPE CANTALA KERATTO TEQUILA SOAPWEED
AGE DAY ELD EON ERA AEON EDGE OLAM TIME CYCLE EPOCH RIPEN WORLD YEARS MATURE MELLOW PERIOD SIECLE WITHER CENTURY DEVELOP OLDNESS SENESCE DURATION ETERNITY LIFETIME MAJORITY MATURITY
 (— OF MOON) EPACT
 (— OF 100 YEARS) CENTENARY
 (ADVANCED —) DOTAGE
 (BEING UNDER 13 YEARS OF —) PRETEEN
 (EARLY MIDDLE —) SUMMER
 (GREAT —) ANTIQUITY GRANDEVITY
 (OLD —) CRUTCH SENIUM VETUSTRY SENILITY
AGED OLD RIPE ANILE HOARY OLDEN PASSE FEEBLE INFIRM MATURE SENILE WINTRY YEARED ANCIENT ELDERLY OGYGIAN WINTERED
AGELESS ETERNAL TIMELESS
AGENCY DINT HAND CHECK FORCE LEVER MEANS ORGAN PROXY ACTION BUREAU MEDIUM OFFICE ARBITER BENEFIT FACULTY ACTIVITY MINISTRY
AGENDUM SLATE DOCKET RECORD RITUAL PROGRAM
AGENT SPY AMIN DOER GENE ACTOR BUYER CAUSE ENVOY MEANS ORGAN PROXY ASSIGN BROKER BURSAR COMMIS DEALER DEPUTY ENGINE FACTOR FITTER MEDIUM MINION MUKTAR SELLER SYNDIC VAKEEL WALLAH BAILIFF CHANNEL FACIENT FEDERAL OFFICER PESHKAR PROCTOR SCALPER ATTORNEY AUMILDAR CATALYST EMISSARY EXECUTOR MINISTER MOOKHTAR OPERATOR PROMOTER QUAESTOR SENESCHAL MAINSPRING
 (— OF CROMWELL) AGITATOR
 (ANTIKNOCK —) ADDITIVE ALKYLATE
 (CLEANSING —) SOAP
 (DESTRUCTIVE —) DEVOURER

(EMPLOYMENT —) PADRONE
(ENFORCEMENT —) LAW
(ESPIONAGE —) COURIER
(FISCAL —) STEWARD
(HEALING —) BALSAM
(MEDICINAL —) DRASTIC
(NARCOTIC —) NARC NARK GAZER
(OXIDIZING —) NINHYDRIN
(PRESS —) FLACK
(SUBVERSIVE —) STOOGE
(SWEETENING —) DULCIN
(UNDERCOVER —) SPOOK
(VOLATILE —) SPIRIT
(WETTING —) SPREADER

AGGLOMERATE HEAP LUMP MASS PILE
SLAG GATHER CLUSTER COLLECT

AGGLOMERATION HORDE FAVELLA
CONGERIE

AGGRANDIZE LIFT BOOST EXALT RAISE
ADVANCE AUGMENT DIGNIFY ELEVATE
ENLARGE MAGNIFY PROMOTE INCREASE

AGGRAVATE IRK NAG VEX TWIT ANGER
ANNOY TAUNT TEASE BURDEN PESTER
WORSEN BEDEVIL MAGNIFY PROVOKE
AGGRIEVE HEIGHTEN INCREASE IRRITATE

AGGRAVATED ACUTE

AGGREEABLE ACCEPTABLE

AGGREGATE ADD ALL SET SUM BULK
COMB FLOC GOUT LATH MASS BLOCK
BUNCH CLASS CLONE COVER CROWD
FIELD GROSS SHOOT TOTAL UNITE
WHOLE AMOUNT DOMAIN VOLUME
COLLECT ENSEMBLE MANIFOLD
MULTEITY TOTALITY

AGGREGATION HERD NEST CLUMP
FLOCK GORGE GROUP SWARM COLONY
FAMILY NATION SYSTEM CLUSTER
CONGERIE

AGGRESSION WAR RAID ATTACK
INJURY ASSAULT OFFENSE INVASION

AGGRESSIVE BUTCH PUSHY PUSHING
AGONISTIC

AGGRESSIVENESS CRUST DEFIANCE
BELLICOSITY

AGGRIEVE HARM HURT PAIN HARRY
WRONG INJURE AFFLICT OPPRESS
TROUBLE DISTRESS

AGGRIEVED SORE OFFENDED

AGILE DEFT FAST SPRY WIRY ADEPT
ALERT BRISK CATTY ELFIN FLEET LITHE
NIFTY NIPPY QUICK WITHY ACTIVE
ADROIT LIMBER LISSOM LIVELY NIMBLE
SUPPLE SPRINGY ATHLETIC

AGILITY LEVITY SLEIGHT ACTIVITY
SALIENCE

AGITATE FAN IRK JAR VEX FRET FUSS
MOVE PLOT RILE ROCK STIR TEEM
ALARM BROIL CHURN DRIVE HARRY
IMPEL QUAKE ROUSE SHAKE AROUSE
DEVISE EXCITE FOMENT HARASS INCITE
JOSTLE JUMBLE RATTLE RUFFLE SEETHE
ACTUATE DISCUSS DISTURB PERTURB
TORMENT TROUBLE ACTIVATE
CONVULSE DISQUIET DISTRACT

AGITATED WILD HECTIC STORMY
YEASTY UNQUIET FEVERISH FLURRIED
SEETHING

AGITATION JAR JOG BOIL FEAR FLAP
FRET FURY GUST HEAT ITCH JERK JOLT
SNIT ALARM HURRY QUAKE SHAKE
STORM TWEAK YEAST BREEZE BUSTLE
DITHER ENERGY FLURRY FRENZY MOTION
QUIVER RIPPLE SHAKES TREMOR
TUMULT WELTER EMOTION FERMENT
FLUSTER FLUTTER MADNESS RAMPAGE
TEMPEST TURMOIL DISQUIET PAROXYSM
UPHEAVAL COMMOTION

AGNATE AKIN ALLIED COGNATE KINDRED

AGNOMEN NAME ALIAS EPITHET
SURNAME COGNOMEN NICKNAME

AGNOSTIC ATHEIST DOUBTER SKEPTIC
NESCIENT

AGO BY BACK ERST GONE PAST SYNE
YORE ABACK AGONE SINCE

AGOG AVID KEEN ASTIR EAGER LIVELY
EXCITED VIGILANT

AGONIZE BEAR RACK STRAIN WRITHE

AGONY ACHE PAIN PANG DOLOR GRIEF
GRIPE PANIC THROE TRIAL ACHING
ANGUISH ANXIETY EMOTION TORMENT
TORTURE TRAVAIL DISTRESS PAROXYSM

AGOUTI CAPA CAVY PACA

AGRARIAN RURAL PASTORAL PRAEDIAL

AGREE FIT GEE HIT PAN YES GIBE JIBE
MEET SORT SUIT ADMIT ALLOW ATONE
BLEND CHECK CLICK CLOSE GRANT
HITCH LEVEL MATCH STAND TALLY
UNITE YIELD ACCEDE ACCEPT ACCORD
ADHERE ASSENT ASSORT COMPLY
CONCUR COTTON ENGAGE SETTLE
SQUARE SUBMIT ARRANGE BARGAIN
CONCEDE CONFORM CONSENT PROMISE
COINCIDE CONTRACT COVENANT
(— MUTUALLY) STIPULATE
(— TO) ACCEPT
(— TO JOIN) ADHERE
(— WITH) SIT LIKE SIDE TAIL ANSWER

AGREEABLE AMEN EASY FAIR FINE
GOOD KIND LIEF NICE SOFT DULCE JOLIE
JOLLY LITHE LUSTY READY SAPID SUAVE
SWEET COMELY DAINTY DULCET KINDLY
LIKELY MELLOW SAVORY SMOOTH
SUITED ADAPTED AMIABLE WELCOME
WILLING WINSOME AMENABLE
CHARMING DELICATE GRATEFUL
LIKESOME LOVESOME OBLIGING
PLACABLE PLEASANT PLEASING
PURSUANT SOCIABLE SUITABLE
THANKFUL CONGENIAL PALATABLE

AGREEING CONNATE CONTENT
ACCORDING

AGREEMENT GO FIT NOD AXIS BOND
DEAL FINE PACT COVIN LEASE MATCH
TERMS TOUCH TRUTH TRYST UNITY
ACCORD ACTION ASSENT CARTEL
COMITY DICKER LEAGUE PACTUM
PLEDGE TREATY UNISON ANALOGY
BARGAIN CLOSING CLOSURE COMPACT
CONCERT CONSENT CONSORT ENTENTE
HARMONY ONENESS PACTION RAPPORT
CONTRACT DIAPASON SANCTION
SYMPATHY

AGRICULTURAL ARABLE GEOPONIC
GEOPONICAL

AGRICULTURE FARMING GAINAGE TILLAGE AGRONOMY
AGRICULTURIST THO FARMER GROWER SANTAL PLANTER RANCHER
AGRIMONY CLIVE BONESET BORWORT HEMPWEED
AGROUND ASHORE BEACHED STRANDED
AGUE CHILL FEVER MALARIA QUARTAN SHAKING SHIVERS
AGUEWEED BONESET
AHAB (FATHER OF —) OMRI
  (NEIGHBOR OF —) NABOTH
  (WIFE OF —) JEZEBEL
AHAZIAH (FATHER OF —) AHAB JEHORAM
  (MOTHER OF —) JEZEBEL ATHALIAH
AHEAD ON UP ALEE FORE AFORE ALONG BEFORE ONWARD ALREADY ENDWAYS ENDWISE FORWARD LEADING ADVANCED ANTERIOR
  (— OF TIME) FAST
  (STRAIGHT —) FORERIGHT
AHOY AVAST
AHUEHUETE CEDAR SABINO CYPRESS
AH WILDERNESS (AUTHOR OF —) ONEILL
  (CHARACTER IN —) BELLE DAVID MILLER MURIEL RICHARD MCCOMBER
AID KEY ABET BACK HAND HELP PONY ALLAY BOOST COACH FAVOR GRANT SERVE SPEED TREAT ASSIST CRUTCH FRIEND PROFIT RELIEF REMEDY RESCUE SECOND SUCCOR SUPPLY UPHOLD ADVANCE ANCILLA BACKING BENEFIT COMFORT ENDORSE FORWARD FURTHER RELIEVE SERVICE SUBSIDY SUPPORT
  (— A VESSEL) HOVEL
  (— SECRETLY) SUBAID
  (COMPLEXION —) FUCUS
AIDA (CHARACTER IN —) AIDA AMNERIS RADAMES AMONASRO
  (COMPOSER OF —) VERDI
AIDE BEAGLE DEPUTY SECOND OFFICER ORDERLY ADJUTANT
AIGRETTE EGRET HERON PLUME SPRAY
AIL FAIL PAIN PINE AFFECT BOTHER FALTER SUFFER AFFLICT DECLINE TROUBLE COMPLAIN DISTRESS
AILANTHUS SUMAC SUMACH
AILING SICK CRAZY SOBER SICKLY UNWELL
AILMENT AIL ILL PIP COUGH MALADY DISEASE ILLNESS DISORDER SICKNESS WEAKNESS
  (SUDDEN —) WAFF
AIM END LAY TRY BEAD BEAM BEND BENT BUTT GOAL HEAD HOLD LEAD MARK PLAN SAKE SEEK VIEW DRIVE ESSAY GUESS LEVEL POINT PRICK SCOPE SIGHT TRAIN ASPIRE DESIGN DIRECT ESTEEM INTEND INTENT OBJECT SCHEME STRIVE ADDRESS ATTEMPT MEANING PRETEND PURPOSE RESPECT ENDEAVOR ESTIMATE PRETENSE STEERING
  (— A KICK) FLING
  (— AT) EYE AFFECT

  (— FURTIVELY) STEAL
  (— INDIRECTLY) GLANCE
AIMLESS IDLE BLIND CHANCE RANDOM DRIFTING
AIMLESSNESS FLANERIE
AIR AER PEW SKY ARIA AURA BROW FEEL LILT LOFT MIEN PORT POSE SONG TELL TUNE VENT WIND ETHER FRILL OZONE UTTER VOICE AERATE ALLURE ASPECT BROACH MANNER MELODY REGARD REGION STRAIN VANITY BEARING DISPLAY EXHIBIT EXPRESS ATTITUDE BEHAVIOR CARRIAGE PRESENCE
  (— EXHALED) BLAST
  (— IN MOTION) BREATH
  (BOASTFUL —) PARADO
  (CONFIDENT —) BRAVURA
  (COOL —) FRESCO
  (COQUETTISH —) MINAUDERIE
  (FETID —) REEK
  (FOUL —) DIRT
  (HAUGHTY —S) ALTITUDES
  (MUSICAL —) ARIA SOLO TUNE BRAWL MELODY ARIETTA BRAVURA CANZONE MUSETTE CAVATINE
  (POMPOUS —) SWELL
  (PUT ON —S) PROSS
  (STALE —) STEAM
  (STIFLING —) SMORE
  (THE —) GATE
  (WARM —) OAM
  (PL.) LUGS FRONT
AIRCRAFT KITE BLIMP CRAFT FLYER PLANE GLIDER AEROBUS AIRSHIP BALLOON AERODYNE AEROSTAT AIRLINER AIRPLANE AUTOGIRO GYRODYNE
  (UNIDENTIFIED —) UFO BOGY BOGEY BOGIE
AIRCRAFTSMAN ERK
AIRCREWMAN KICKER AIREDALE
AIRFOIL FIN FLAP SLAT BLADE SURFACE AEROFOIL ELEVATOR
AIRILY JAUNTILY
AIRLESS STUFFY STIFLING
AIRLINE FEEDER SKYWAY NONSKED
AIRMAN ACE FLIER FLYER BIRDMAN WARBIRD AERONAUT
AIRPLANE BUS CUB JET MIG SST GYRO KITE SHIP ZERO AVION CAMEL CRATE FLIER FLYER GOTHA JENNY LINER PLANE SCOUT BOMBER COPTER FOKKER GLIDER JENNIE PUSHER AVIETTE BIPLANE CLIPPER FIGHTER FLYAWAY SPOTTER AEROSTAT ALBATROS KAMIKAZE SEAPLANE SKYCOACH SKYCRAFT TRIPLANE TURBOJET WARPLANE AEROPLANE MONOPLANE
  (PART OF —) FIN POD TAB FLAP WING BLADE CABIN PYLON RADAR ENGINE RUDDER AILERON COCKPIT COWLING SPOILER ELEVATOR REVERSER STABILIZER SUPPRESSOR
  (REMOTE-CONTROLLED —) DRONE
AIRPORT DROME AIRPARK JETPORT SCUTTLE AIRDROME AIRFIELD

AIRTIGHT SEALED AIRPROOF HERMETIC
AIRY GAY COOL RARE THIN EMPTY HUFFY
LIGHT MERRY WINDY AERIAL BLITHE
BREEZY FLUFFY JAUNTY JOCUND LIVELY
HAUGHTY JOCULAR SFOGATO AFFECTED
ANIMATED DEBONAIR DELICATE
ETHEREAL FLIPPANT GRACEFUL TRIFLING
VOLATILE
AISLE WAY LANE NAVE WALK ALLEE
ALLEY FEEDWAY GANGWAY PASSAGE
CORRIDOR
AJAR OPEN DISCORDANT
AJAX AIAS
(FATHER OF —) OILEUS TELAMON
(MOTHER OF —) ERIBOEA PERIBOEA
AKIMBO ANGLED
AKIN SIB LIKE NEAR NIGH ALIKE CLOSE
AGNATE ALLIED COUSIN COGNATE
GERMANE RELATED SIMILAR
(— ON MALE SIDE) AGNATIC
ALA AXIL DRUM WING AXILLA RECESS
NOSEWING

ALABAMA

CAPITAL: MONTGOMERY
COUNTY: LEE BIBB CLAY DALE PIKE
COOSA HENRY LAMAR MACON PERRY
BLOUNT BUTLER COFFEE DALLAS
ELMORE ETOWAH GENEVA GREENE
MARION MONROE MORGAN SHELBY
SUMTER WILCOX CHILTON
LAKE: MARTIN
MOUNTAIN: CHEAHA LOOKOUT RACCOON
NATIVE: LIZARD
RIVER: PEA COOSA CAHABA MOBILE
SIPSEY TENSAW CONECUH PERDIDO
SEPULGA WARRIOR TOMBIGBEE
STATE BIRD: YELLOWHAMMER
STATE FISH: TARPON
STATE FLOWER: CAMELLIA
STATE TREE: PINE LONGLEAF
TOWN: OPP PIPER SELMA ATHENS
CORONA HEFLIN JASPER LANETT LINDEN
MARION MOBILE SAMSON BREWTON
FLORALA GADSDEN ANNISTON

ALABASTER GYPSUM TECALI ONYCHITE
ALACRITY HASTE SPEED CELERITY
RAPIDITY
ALAMEDA MALL WALK
ALAR PTERIC WINGED AXILLARY
WINGLIKE
ALARM COW DIN BELL FEAR ALERT
CLOCK DAUNT NOISE PANIC ROUSE
SCARE SIREN START STILL UPSET
ALARUM APPALL AROUSE ATTACK
BUZZER DISMAY EXCITE FRIGHT OUTCRY
SIGNAL TERROR TOCSIN DISTURB
STARTLE TERRIFY WARNING AFFRIGHT
DISQUIET FRIGHTEN SURPRISE
ALARMING SCARY FEARFUL
ALAS AY ACH HEU OCH VAE WOE EHEU
HECH ALACK HELAS

ALASKA

CAPITAL: JUNEAU
ISLAND: ADAK ATKA ATTU UMNAK
KODIAK UNIMAK AFOGNAK DIOMEDE
NUNIVAK
ISLAND GROUP: RAT ALEUTIAN PRIBILOF
ANDREANOF
LAKE: NAKNEK ILIAMNA
MOUNTAIN: BONA VETA SPURR KATMAI
PAVLOF FORAKER MCKINLEY
MOUNTAIN RANGE: CRAZY BROOKS
KAIYUH CHUGACH KILBUCK WRANGELL
NATIVE: ALEUT AHTENA ESKIMO INGALIK
KOYUKON TLINGIT
PENINSULA: KENAI SEWARD
RIVER: CHENA KOBUK YUKON COPPER
NOATAK TANANA KOYUKUK SUSITNA
CHULITNA COLVILLE
STATE BIRD: PTARMIGAN
STATE FLOWER: FORGETMENOT
STATE TREE: SPRUCE
TOWN: EEK NOME RUBY KENAI SITKA
BARROW JUNEAU KODIAK NENANA
SKAGWAY ANCHORAGE FAIRBANKS
KETCHIKAN
VOLCANO: KUKAK SPURR GRIGGS KATMAI
MAGEIK MARTIN PAVLOF DOUGLAS
ILIAMNA REDOUBT TORBERT TRIDENT
WRANGELL

ALB AUBE CAMISIA CHRISOM VESTMENT
ALBACORE TUNA TUNNY LONGFIN
MACKEREL SCOMBRID

ALBANIA

ANCIENT PEOPLE: ILLYRIAN
CAPITAL: TIRANA
COIN: LEK FRANC GUINTAR
KING: ZOG
LAKE: ULZE OHRID PRESPA SCUTARI
OHRIDSKO
MOUNTAIN: KORAB SHALA PINDUS
KORITNIK
REGION: EPIRUS
RIVER: MAT DRIN OSUM SEMAN BOJANA
ERZENI SEMENI VIJOSE SHKUMBI
TOWN: LIN FIER KLOS LESH BERAT CROIA
DUKAT KORCE KRUJE PECIN BOGEN
QUKES RUBIC SPASH VLONE VLORE
AVLONA BERATI BITSAN DARDHE
DURRES KORRCE PERMET PRESHE
TIRANA VALONA ALESSIO DURAZZO
KORITZA SCUTARI SHKODER
TRIBE: GEG CHAM GHEG TOSK

ALBANIAN GEG GHEG ARNAUT SKIPETAR
ALBATROSS GONY GOONY NELLY
QUAKER SEABIRD ALCATRAS BLUEBIRD
STINKPOT
ALBEIT THOUGH HOWBEIT
ALBERTA (CAPITAL OF —) EDMONTON

(LAKE OF —) BANFF JASPER WATERTON
(RIVER OF —) BOW OLDMAN WAPITI ATHABASCA
(TOWN OF —) CALGARY REDDEER
ALBINO LEUCAETHIOP
ALBUM BOOK RECORD VOLUME REGISTER
ALBUMEN WHITE
ALBUMIN ALBUMEN PHASELIN SYNTONIN
ALBURNUM SAP BLEA SPLINT SAPWOOD
ALCAEUS (DAUGHTER OF —) ANAXO
(FATHER OF —) PERSEUS ANDROGEUS
(MOTHER OF —) ANDROMEDA
(SON OF —) AMPHITRYON
ALCESTIS (AUTHOR OF —) EURIPIDES
(CHARACTER IN —) APOLLO ADMETUS ALCESTIS HERCULES THANATOS
(FATHER OF —) PELIAS
(HUSBAND OF —) ADMETUS
ALCHEMIST ADEPT ARTIST CHEMIC CHEMIST HERMETIC
(AUTHOR OF —) JONSON
(CHARACTER IN —) DOL ABEL FACE SURLY COMMON DAPPER MAMMON PLIANT SUBTLE ANANIAS DRUGGER EPICURE KASTRIL LOVEWIT WHOLESOME TRIBULATION
ALCHEMY ART MAGIC CHYMIA SPAGYRIC
(GOD OF —) HERMES
ALCIBIADES (FATHER OF —) CLINIAS
(MOTHER OF —) DINOMACHE
ALCIMEDES (BROTHER OF —) ARGUS MEDEUS PHERES MERMERUS TISANDER THESSALUS
(FATHER OF —) JASON
(MOTHER OF —) MEDEA
ALCMENE (FATHER OF —) ELECTRYON
(HUSBAND OF —) AMPHITRYON
(SON OF —) HERCULES IPHICLES
ALCOVE BAY NOOK BOWER NICHE ORIEL STALL CARREL RECESS CUBICLE DINETTE RETREAT
ALDER ARN OLER ALNUS ELDER SAGEROSE
ALDERMAN BAILIE SENIOR HEADMAN
ALE NOG BASS BEER BOCK BREW FLIP MILD CLINK DARBY LAGER NAPPY STOUT PORTER BITTERS
(— BREWED WITH BRACKISH WATER) TIPPER
(— MIXED WITH SWEETENER) BRAGGET
(INFERIOR —) SWANKY
(NEW —) SWATS
(SOUR —) ALEGAR
(SPICED —) SWIG
(STRONG —) MUM HUFF BURTON STINGO HUFFCAP
(WEAK —) TWOPENNY
ALEE AHEAD LEEWARD
ALEHOUSE PUB TAVERN BARROOM MUGHOUSE POTHOUSE
ALERT APT GAY HEP HIP FOXY KEEN LIVE PERT TRIG WAKE WARN WARY ACUTE AGILE ALARM ALIVE AWAKE AWARE BRISK EAGER ERECT MERRY NIPPY PEART QUICK READY SHARP SIREN SLICK SWIFT ACTIVE ALARUM BRIGHT DAPPER LIVELY NIMBLE PROMPT SLIPPY TOCSIN CAREFUL KNOWING WAKEFUL PREPARED VIGILANT WATCHFUL
ALERTNESS SNAP APTNESS APTITUDE
(MENTAL —) WIT
ALEWIFE BANG ALLICE BUCKIE HERRING POMPANO WALLEYE GRAYBACK GREYBACK SAWBELLY SKIPJACK
ALEXANDER ALEX PARIS ELLICK ISKANDER
(BIRTHPLACE OF —) PELLA
(FATHER OF —) SIMON
(HORSE OF —) BUCEPHALUS
ALFALFA HAY MEDIC FODDER LEGUME LUCERNE
ALGA NORI FUCUS SLOKE DESMID DIATOM FUNORI NOSTOC

ALGERIA

CAPITAL: ALGIERS
CAVALRYMAN: SPAHI SPAHEE
DEPARTMENT: ORAN ALGER ALGIERS CONSTANTINE
HILL: TELL
HOLY MAN: MARABOUT
MEASURE: PIK REBIS TARRI TERMIN
MONASTERY: RIBAT
MOUNTAIN: AISSA ATLAS AURES DAHRA TAHAT CHELIA AHAGGAR MOUYDIR DJURJURA
NATIVE: BERBER KABYLE
RIVER: SHELIF CHELIFF MEDJERDA
RULER: BEY DEY
SHIP: XEBEC
TERRITORY: AINSEFRA GHARDALA TOUGGOURT
TOWN: BONE ORAN AFLOU ARZEW BATNA BLIDA MEDEA SAIDA SETIF TENES ABADLA ANNABA AUMALE BARIKA BECHAR BEJAIA BENOUD BISKRA BOUGIE DELLYS DJANET DJELFA DZIOUA FRENDA GUELMA SKIKDA BOGHARI MASCARA MILIANA NEGRINE NEMOURS OUARGLA TEBESSA TLEMCEN
WEIGHT: ROTL

ALGID COLD COOL CHILLY CLAMMY
ALIAS OTHER AYLESS ASSUMED EPITHET
ALIBI PLEA EXCUSE APOLOGY PRETEXT
ALIDADE INDEX DIOPTER
ALIEN EXOTIC REMOTE ADVERSE DENIZEN FOREIGN INVADER OUTLAND STRANGE STRANGER
ALIENATE PART AVERT CONVEY DEVEST FORFEIT SUBVERT AMORTIZE ESTRANGE SEPARATE TRANSFER
ALIENIST PSYCHOPATH PSYCHIATRIST
ALIGHT DROP LAND REST STOP LIGHT PERCH ROOST ARRIVE SETTLE DESCEND

ALIGN TRAM TRUE ALINE ARRAY DRESS RANGE ADJUST ARRANGE MARSHAL

ALIKE AKIN BOTH LIKE SAME EQUAL SQUARE SIMILAR UNIFORM

ALIMENT PAP FOOD FUEL BROMA MANNA VIANDS PABULUM RATIONS

ALIMONY ALIMENT

ALIVE BUSY KEEN SPRY VIVE AGILE ALERT ASTIR AWARE BEING BRISK FRESH GREEN QUICK VITAL EXTANT LIVING ANIMATE EXISTENT

ALKALI LYE REH BASE SALT SODA CAUSTIC

ALKALOID BASE ERGOT BRUCIN ESERIN ACONINE CAFFEIN COCAINE CODEINE NEOPINE QUININE

ALL ANY SUM EACH FULL TOTE EVERY GROSS OMNES QUITE TOTAL WHOLE ENTIRE SOLELY PLENARY ENTIRELY EVERYONE TOTALITY

ALLAY AID LAY CALM COOL EASE HELP HUSH STAY ABATE CHECK DELAY QUELL QUIET SALVE SLAKE STILL LESSEN PACIFY QUENCH REDUCE SOFTEN SOLACE SOOTHE STANCH SUBDUE TEMPER APPEASE ASSUAGE COMFORT COMPOSE LIGHTEN MOLLIFY RELIEVE REPRESS STAUNCH MITIGATE PALLIATE

ALLEGE SAY AVER AVOW CITE URGE CLAIM INFER PLEAD QUOTE STATE SWEAR TRUMP VOUCH ADDUCE AFFIRM ASSERT CHARGE DEPOSE ESSOIN RECITE ADVANCE ASCRIBE DECLARE PRESENT PROFESS PROPOSE MAINTAIN

ALLEGED SUPPOSED SURMISED

ALLEGIANCE FOY TIE DUTY FAITH HONOR FEALTY HOMAGE LOYALTY SERVICE TRIBUTE DEVOTION FIDELITY

ALLEGORY MYTH TALE FABLE STORY EMBLEM PARABLE APOLOGUE METAPHOR

ALLERGY ATOPY IDIOBLAPSIS

ALLEVIATE AID BALM CALM CURE EASE HELP ABATE ALLAY QUIET LENIFY LESSEN PACIFY SOFTEN SOLACE SOOTHE SUCCOR TEMPER ASSUAGE COMPOSE CONSOLE CORRECT LENIATE LIGHTEN MOLLIFY RELEASE RELIEVE DIMINISH MITIGATE MODERATE PALLIATE

ALLEY MIG ROW WAY LANE MALL MEWS PASS PATH VENT WALK WIND AISLE ALLEE BLIND BYWAY ENTRY PEEWEE PASSAGE
(BLIND —) LOKE STOP CLOSE POCKET IMPASSE

ALL FOR LOVE (AUTHOR OF —) DRYDEN
(CHARACTER IN —) ANTONY OCTAVIA OCTAVIUS CLEOPATRA DOLABELLA VENTIDIUS

ALLIANCE AXIS PACT UNION ACCORD FUSION LEAGUE TREATY COMPACT ENTENTE SOCIETY AFFINITY COVENANT FEDERACY

ALLIED SIB AKIN AGNATE COUSIN JOINED LINKED UNITED COGNATE CONNATE FEDERAL GERMANE KINDRED RELATED SIMILAR RELATIVE

ALLIGATOR GATOR NIGER CAIMAN CAYMAN JACARE LAGARTO TRAVOIS LORICATE
(MALE —) BULL

ALLNESS OMNEITY OMNITUDE

ALLOCATE DEAL DOLE METE RATE ALLOT AWARD SHARE ASSIGN

ALLOT FIX SET BILL CAST DEAL DOLE GIVE MARK METE PART RATE SORT ALLOW AWARD GRANT SHARE ACCORD AFFECT ASSIGN BESTOW DEPUTE DESIGN DIRECT INTEND ORDAIN ACCOUNT APPOINT DESTINE PRORATE SPECIFY ALLOCATE

ALLOTMENT CUT LOT DOLE SHARE RATION LOTTERY PORTION DIVISION PITTANCE

ALLOW LET BEAR GIVE HAVE LEND LOAN ADMIT DEFER GRANT LEAVE STAND YIELD ACCEPT ACCORD ASSIGN BESTOW ENABLE ENDURE PERMIT SUFFER APPROVE CONCEDE CONFESS LICENSE SANCTION TOLERATE

ALLOWANCE FEE AGIO BOTE DOLE EASE EDGE GIFT HIRE ODDS RATE GRANT LEAVE RATIO SHARE STINT BOUNTY MARGIN RATING SALARY ALIMENT ALIMONY LEAKAGE PENSION PORTION PREBEND STIPEND
(— FOR EXPENSES) DIET
(— FOR MAINTENANCE) ALIMENT
(— FOR THICKNESS) BOXING
(— FOR WASTE) TRET
(— FOR WEIGHT) BUG TARE DRAFT DRAUGHT
(— OF ARROWS) SHEAF
(— OF FOOD) DIET BOUCHE DIETARY
(— OF TIME OR DISTANCE) LAW
(CLOTHING —) INLAY
(CORRECTIVE —) SALT
(EXTRA —) BUCKSHEE
(NEGATIVE —) INTERFERENCE

ALLOWING THOUGH

ALLOY MIX ASEM BIDRI BRASS DURAL INVAR MONEL TERNE ALBATA ALNICO ALUMEL BILLON BRONZE CERMET NIELLO PEWTER SOLDER TOMBAC AMALGAM BABBITT

ALL QUIET ON WESTERN FRONT (AUTHOR OF —) REMARQUE
(CHARACTER IN —) PAUL KROPP ALBERT BAUMER MULLER TJADENS KEMMERICH STANILAUS KATCYINSKY

ALLSPICE BUBBY PIMENTO

ALL'S WELL THAT ENDS WELL (AUTHOR OF —) SHAKESPEARE
(CHARACTER IN —) DIANA LAFEU HELENA BERTRAM LAVACHE MARIANA PAROLLES VIOLENTA

ALLUDE HINT IMPLY POINT REFER GLANCE RELATE CONNOTE MENTION SUGGEST INDICATE INTIMATE

ALLURE IT AIR COY WIN WOO BAIT DRAW LEAD LURE MOVE SWAY WILE ANGLE BRIBE CHARM COURT DECOY

SNARE TEMPT ENTICE ENTRAP INDUCE
INVITE SEDUCE ATTRACT BEGUILE
ENSNARE BLANDISH INVEIGLE PERSUADE
ALLUREMENT BAIT CORD LURE GLAMOR
ALLURING GREEN TAKING SIRENIC
SUGARED CATCHING CHARMING
ENTICING FETCHING TEMPTING
ALLUSION HINT TWIT TOUCH GLANCE
INKLING MENTION INNUENDO
ALLY PAL AIDE JOIN UNION UNITE FRIEND
HELPER CONNECT PARTNER ADHERENT
ALMANAC ORDO PADDY CALENDAR
ALMIGHTY GOD GREAT CREATOR
EXTREME JEHOVAH INFINITE POWERFUL
PUISSANT OMNIPOTENT
ALMOST JUST LIKE MOST MUCH NEAR
NIGH ABOUT CLOSE MOSTLY NEARLY
PRACTICALLY
ALMS DOLE GIFT BOUNTY MAUNDY
RELIEF ALMOIGN CHARITY HANDOUT
DONATION GRATUITY
ALOE PITA AGAVE
ALOFT UP HIGH ABOVE UPWARD
SKYWARD OVERHEAD
ALONE ALL ONE BARE LORN ONLY SOLE
SOLO ALOOF APART SOLUS SIMPLY
SINGLE SOLELY UNIQUE FORLORN
DESOLATE DETACHED ISOLATED
SEPARATE SOLITARY
ALONG ON UP VIA AWAY WITH AHEAD
BESIDE ONWARD FORWARD
ALONGSIDE AT BY ASIDE CLOSE
ABOARD BESIDE ABREAST
ALOOF DRY ICY SHY COLD COOL ABACK
ALONE APART PROUD FROSTY REMOTE
SILENT DISTANT REMOVED RESERVED
ALPHABET ABC KUFIC LATIN ONMUN
BISAYA BRAHMI GLAGOL HANGUL
HANKUL KAITHI NAGARI ROMAJI
SARADA TAGALA VISAYA ALJAMIA
FUTHARK KALEKAH LETTERS PESHITO
(ARABIC —) BA FA HA RA TA YA ZA
AYN DAD DAL JIM KAF KHA LAM MIM
NUN QAF SAD SIN THA WAW ZAY ALIF
DHAL SHIN GHAYN
(GREEK —) MU NU PI XI CHI ETA PHI
PSI RHO TAU BETA IOTA ZETA ALPHA
DELTA GAMMA KAPPA OMEGA SIGMA
THETA LAMBDA EPSILON OMICRON
UPSILON
(HEBREW —) HE PE MEM NUN SIN TAW
WAW AYIN BETH HETH KAPH QOPH
RESH SHIN TETH YODH ALEPH GIMEL
SADHE ZAYIN DALETH LAMEDH SAMEKH
ALREADY EEN NOW DONE EVEN SINCE
BEFORE
ALSO SO AND EKE TOO YET ERST MORE
PLUS ALONG DITTO BESIDES FURTHER
LIKEWISE MOREOVER
ALTAR ARA BEMA BOMOS TABLE SHRINE
CHANCEL ESCHARA
ALTER COOK DRAW EDIT GELD MOVE
TURN VARY VEER ADAPT AMEND BREAK
ELIDE EMEND FORGE RESET SHAPE SHIFT
ADJUST CENSOR CHANGE DEFORM
IMMUTE MODIFY MUTATE NEUTER

REVISE CONVERT CORRECT CORRUPT
DISTORT FASHION QUALIFY
(— APPEARANCE) WRY
(— BOUNDARIES) DEACON
(— BRANDS) DUFF
(— DIRECTION) BREAK
(— STANCE) CLOSE
ALTERCATION SPAT TIFF TILT BRAWL
BROIL CROSS FIGHT BARNEY BICKER
FRACAS JANGLE STRIFE CONTEST
DISPUTE QUARREL WRANGLE SQUABBLE
ALTERNATE ELSE VARY OTHER RECUR
SHIFT CHANGE ROTATE SECOND
SEESAW EXCHANGE INTERMIT
ALTERNATIVE OR FORK HORN CHOICE
EITHER OPTION ELECTION
ALTERNATOR MAGNETO
ALTHAEA MALLOW
(FATHER OF —) THESTIUS
(HUSBAND OF —) OENEUS
(SON OF —) MELEAGER
ALTHOUGH EEN EVEN THAT WHEN
WHILE ALBEIT THOUGH DESPITE
WHEREAS
ALTITUDE APEX PEAK PITCH HEIGHT
STATURE
ALTOGETHER NUDE QUITE SHEER
FREELY WHOLLY TOTALLY UTTERLY
ENTIRELY
ALUM MIGITE STYPTIC
ALUMNUS GRAD GRADUATE
ALWAYS AY AYE EEN EER EVER STILL
SEMPRE FOREVER EVERMORE
AMA CUP AMULA CRUET VESSEL CHALICE
AMADAVAT WAXBILL TIGERBIRD
AMADOU PUNK TINDER
AMAH NURSE SERVANT
AMAIN GREATLY FORCIBLY
AMALGAM ALLOY MAGNESIA
ARQUERITE
AMALGAMATE MIX FUSE JOIN ALLOY
BLEND MARRY MERGE UNITE MINGLE
COMBINE
AMALGAMATION MERGER ADDITION
AMANUENSIS PENMAN SCRIBE TYPIST
RECORDER
AMARYLLIS LILY AGAVE CRINUM
SNOWFLAKE
AMASS HEAP HILL MASS PILE SAVE
GROSS HOARD STACK STORE GATHER
COLLECT COMPILE CONGEST ASSEMBLE
ACCUMULATE
AMATEUR HAM TYRO NOVICE VOTARY
DABBLER DEVOTEE FANCIER BEGINNER
AMATEURISH BUSH TYRONIC
AMATORY EROTIC LOVING TENDER
AMOROUS GALLANT
AMAZE AWE STUN ALARM WONDER
ASTOUND CONFUSE IMPRESS PERPLEX
STAGGER STUPEFY ASTONISH BEWILDER
CONFOUND DUMFOUND FRIGHTEN
SURPRISE
AMAZEMENT FRENZY WONDER
MADNESS SURPRISE CONSTERNATION
AMAZON VIRAGO
AMBASSADOR AGENT ENVOY VAKIL

DEPUTY LEGATE NUNCIO DIPLOMAT
MINISTER

AMBER GRIS RESIN FUSTIC SUCCIN
YELLOW BURMITE ELECTRUM

AMBERGRIS AMBER AMBRACAN

AMBIENCE MILIEU AMBIANCE

AMBIGUITY AMBAGE PARADOX

AMBIGUOUS DARK VAGUE DOUBLE
FORKED CRYPTIC DUBIOUS DOUBTFUL
SPURIOUS
(NOT —) EXPRESS

AMBIT LIMIT SCOPE SPACE BOUNDS
EXTENT SPHERE CIRCUIT COMPASS
BOUNDARY PRECINCT

AMBITION GOAL HOPE WISH DESIRE
PURPOSE PRETENSION

AMBITIOUS AVID BOLD HIGH KEEN
EAGER EMULOUS ASPIRANT ASPIRING

AMBIVALENT EQUIVOCAL

AMBLE GAIT MOOCH MEANDER SAUNTER

AMBO DESK PULPIT

AMBROSIA AMRITA KINGWEED

AMBULATE GAD HIKE MOVE WALK

AMBUSCADE WAYLAY BUSHMENT

AMBUSH NAB LURE LURK TRAP WAIT
AWAIT BLIND CATCH COVER SNARE
WATCH WAYLAY

AMELIA (AUTHOR OF —) FIELDING
(CHARACTER IN —) BOOTH JAMES
TRENT AMELIA HARRIS ATKINSON
HARRISON MATTHEWS ELIZABETH

AMELIORATE EASE HELP MEND AMEND
EMEND BETTER REFORM IMPROVE
PROMOTE

AMEN YEA TRULY ASSENT SOBEIT VERILY
APPROVAL SANCTION

AMENABLE OPEN LIABLE PLIANT
SUBJECT OBEDIENT MALLEABLE

AMEND HEAL MEND ALTER ATONE
EMEND BETTER CHANGE DOCTOR
REFORM REMEDY REPAIR REPEAL REVISE
CONVERT CORRECT IMPROVE RECTIFY
RESTORE

AMENDMENT RIDER REFORM SLEEPER

AMENDS APOLOGY REDRESS

AMENITY COMITY SUAVITY CIVILITY
COURTESY MILDNESS

AMENT CHAT IDIOT IULUS MORON
CATKIN CATTAIL GOSLING IMBECILE

AMERCE FINE MULCT PUNISH SCONCE
CONDEMN FORFEIT

AMERICAN YANK GRINGO YANKEE
YANQUI WESTERN
(— OF EUROPEAN STOCK) WASP
(AUTHOR OF —) JAMES
(CHARACTER IN —) BREAD CINTRE
CLAIRE NEWMAN NIOCHE TRISTRAM
VALENTIN BELLEGARDE CHRISTOPHER

AMERICAN TRAGEDY
(AUTHOR OF —) DREISER
(CHARACTER IN —) ALDEN CLYDE
SAMUEL SONDRA ROBERTA FINCHLEY
GRIFFITHS

AMIABLE GOOD KIND WARM SWEET
CLEVER GENIAL GENTLE LOVING
MELLOW SMOOTH TENDER AFFABLE
LOVABLE WINSOME CHARMING

ENGAGING FRIENDLY OBLIGING
PLEASING

AMICABLE KIND FRIENDLY NEIGHBORLY

AMICE CAPE COWL HOOD EPHOD
ALMUCE TIPPET VESTMENT

AMID IN AMONG AMIDST DURING
AMONGST BETWEEN

AMISS ILL AWRY AGLEY ASKEW WRONG
AGRIEF ASTRAY FAULTY IMPROPER

AMITY PEACE ACCORD CONCORD
HARMONY

AMMONIA HARTSHORN

AMMONITE POLYPOD BACULITE
CACULOID CERATITE SALIGRAM

AMMUNITION AMMO ARMS SHOT
BOMBS FODDER POWDER SHELLS
BULLETS GRENADES MATERIAL
MATERIEL ORDNANCE

AMNESIA LAPSE FORGETFULNESS

AMNESTY PARDON OBLIVION

AMOEBA AMEBA AMEBULA PROTEUS
RHIZOPOD

AMOK MAD AMUCK CRAZY CRAZED
VIOLENT FRENZIED

AMONG IN MID AMID INTO WITH MIDST
AMIDST WITHIN BETWEEN

AMOR EROS LOVE CUPID AMOROSO

AMORAL NEUTRAL NONMORAL

AMOROUS FOND WARM JOLLY MUSHY
NUTTY ARDENT COQUET EROTIC LOVELY
LOVING SPOONY TENDER WANTON
AMATORY AMIABLE FERVENT GALLANT
JEALOUS

AMORPHOUS VAGUE DEFORMED
FORMLESS RESINOUS

AMOUNT GOB LOT SUM TOT ANTE BODY
DOSE KIND LEVY MESS UNIT CHUNK
COUNT GROSS PRICE STACK STORE
STUFF TOTAL WHOLE DEGREE DOSAGE
EFFECT EXTENT FIGURE MATTER
NUMBER SUPPLY QUANTUM SIGNIFY
SLATHER QUANTITY
(— BORNE BY BEAST) SEAM
(— CARRIED AT ONE TIME) GANG
(— DUE) BILL SCORE
(— HELD) CAPACITY
(— OF BASS) BOOMINESS
(— OF CONCRETE) LIFT
(— OF DYE) STRIKE
(— OF FLOW) STRENGTH
(— OF FREIGHT) CARLOAD
(— OF GAS) BREATH
(— OF HERRINGS) CRANNAGE
(— OF LEAKAGE) SLIP
(— OF LIQUOR) SLUG
(— OF MEDICINE) DOSAGE
(— OF MONEY) BEAN BOND CASH
SCOT
(— OF OIL) ALLOWABLE
(— OF PAYMENT) FOOTAGE
(— OF POWDER) INCREMENT
(— OF SOIL) INTHROW
(— OF WATER) CATCHMENT
(— OF WORK) ASSIGNMENT
(— OWED) LIABILITY OBLIGATION
(— PAID) COST
(— TURNED BY SPADE) GRAFT

(APPRECIABLE —) BEANS
(COMPLETE —) FULL
(CONSIDERABLE —) MIGHT HANTLE HATFUL
(EXACT —) NICK
(EXTRA —) BONUS
(GREAT —) MICKLE INFINITY MOUNTAIN
(GROSS —) SLUMP
(INADEQUATE —) DEFICIENCY
(INDEFINITE —) BAIT SNAG SOME
(INFINITESIMAL —) IOTA
(INSIGNIFICANT —) SCRAT PEANUTS
(LARGE —) GOB LOB JUNT LUMP MINT RAFT SNAG SWAG SIEGE SLASH SPATE BOODLE BONANZA MUCHNESS
(LAVISH —) SLATHER
(LEAST POSSIBLE —) GRAIN AMBSACE
(LIMITED —) SPRINKLING
(MINUTE —) HAIR FLEABITE
(RENT —) GALE
(SIZABLE —) CHUNK SMART
(SLIGHT —) SNACK TINGE
(SMALL —) ACE BIT DAB TAD DITE DRAM DRIB FLOW HINT HOOT INCH LICK MITE SNAP SONG SPOT SPECK SPURT TRACE SMIDGE CAPSULE GLIMMER SMIDGEN
(SMALLEST —) JOT STIVER
(TENFOLD —) DECUPLE
(USUAL —) GRIST
(WHOLE —) ALL SUBSTANCE
(YEARLY —) ANNUITY
AMOUR DRURY INTRIGUE PARAMOUR
AMPERSAND AND ALSO PLUS
AMPHIBIA BATRACHIA
AMPHIBIAN EFT FROG NEWT RANA TOAD SIREN SNAKE AXOLOTL CAUDATE PROTEUS TADPOLE SALAMANDER
AMPHIBOLE EDENITE ORALITE URALITE ASBESTOS CROSSITE TREMOLITE SMARAGDITE
AMPHICTYON (FATHER OF —) DEUCALION
(MOTHER OF —) PYRRHA
AMPHITHEATER BOWL OVAL ARENA CAVEA CIRCUS CIRQUE STADIUM THEATER
AMPHITRITE (FATHER OF —) NEREUS OCEANUS
(HUSBAND OF —) NEPTUNE POSEIDON
(MOTHER OF —) TETHYS
(SON OF —) TRITON
AMPHITRYON (AUTHOR OF —) PLAUTUS
(CHARACTER IN —) SOSIA ALCMENA JUPITER MERCURY AMPHITRYON
(DOG OF —) LAELAPS
(FATHER OF —) ALCAEUS
(MOTHER OF —) HIPPONOME
(WIFE OF —) ALCMENE
AMPHORA JUG URN VASE PELIKE
AMPLE BIG FAIR FULL GOOD MUCH RICH WIDE BROAD GREAT LARGE PLUMP ROOMY ROUND ENOUGH HEARTY PLENTY PROLIX COPIOUS LIBERAL OPULENT WEALTHY ABUNDANT ADEQUATE GENEROUS HANDSOME SPACIOUS PLENTIFUL
AMPLIFIER BOOSTER REPEATER
AMPLIFY PAD SWELL WIDEN DILATE EXPAND EXTEND STRESS AUGMENT ENLARGE STRETCH HEIGHTEN INCREASE LENGTHEN MULTIPLY
AMPLITUDE BULK LATITUDE OPULENCE
AMPLY LARGE
AMPUTATE CUT LOP PRUNE SEVER CURTAIL
AMPUTATION APOCOPE ABLATION
AMULET GEM JUJU MOJO PLUM CHARM IMAGE TOKEN FETISH GRIGRI MASCOT SAPHIE TABLET ABRAXAS PERIAPT CHURINGA TALISMAN PHYLACTERY
AMUSE GAME ENJOY SPORT ABSORB DELUDE DIVERT ENGAGE FROLIC PLEASE SOLACE TICKLE BEGUILE DISPORT GRATIFY BEWILDER DISTRACT RECREATE
AMUSEMENT FAD FUN JEU GAME JEST PLAY MIRTH SPORT MUSERY PASTIME LAUGHTER PLEASURE
AMUSING RICH COMIC DROLL FUNNY MERRY WITTY COMICAL FOOLISH KILLING RISIBLE FARCICAL HUMOROUS PLEASANT SPORTFUL
AMYLASE PTYALIN DIASTASE
AN ONE ARTICLE
ANA EVENTS OMNIANA SAYINGS
ANABAPTIST DIPPER ABECEDARIAN
ANACHRONISM SOLECISM
ANACONDA BOA ABOLLA SUCURI CAMOUDIE
ANADEM CROWN DIADEM FILLET WREATH CHAPLET CORONET GARLAND
ANAGOGICAL MYSTICAL
ANAGRAM REBUS PUZZLE METAGRAM LOGOGRIPH
ANAL PODICAL
ANALGESIC ANODYNE CODEINE ANTIPYRIN PHENALGIN
ANALOGOUS LIKE SIMILAR
ANALOGY PARALLEL
(CLOSE —) PARITY
ANALYSIS TEST INDEX STUDY ANATOMY AUTOPSY SOLUTION
(BLOWPIPE —) PYROLOGY
(CHARACTER —) PSYCHOGRAPH
(ECONOMIC —) DYNAMICS
(LOGICAL —) SYLLOGISM
ANALYTIC SUBTLE REGULAR
ANALYTICAL CLINICAL DIVISIVE
ANALYZE RUN SIFT ASSAY BREAK PARSE SENSE STUDY WEIGH ASSESS DIVIDE REDUCE DISSECT EXAMINE ITEMIZE RESOLVE TITRATE UNPIECE APPRAISE CONSTRUE DIAGNOSE SEPARATE
ANANIAS LIAR SIDRACH
(FATHER OF —) NEDEBAEUS
(WIFE OF —) SAPPHIRA
ANARCHIST RED PROVO REBEL NIHILIST REDSHIRT
ANARCHY RIOT CHAOS REVOLT LICENSE MISRULE DISORDER
ANATHEMA WOE OATH CURSE CENSURE

ANATHEMATIZE BAN CURSE ACCURSE
EXECRATE
ANATOMY TOPOLOGY
(— OF HORSE) HIPPOTOMY
(MICROSCOPIC —) HISTOLOGY
(VEGETABLE —) PHYTOTOMY
ANCESTOR ADAM EBER HETH ROOT SIRE
DORUS ELDER STOCK APETUS ATAVUS
AUTHOR EPONYM FATHER PARENT
STIPES ANCIENT EPAPHUS IAPETUS
DARDANUS FOREBEAR FOREGOER
MILESIUS MYRMIDON SECURE
PREDECESSOR PRIMOGENITOR
ANCESTRAL AVAL AVITIC LINEAL
FAMILIAL
ANCESTRY KIN RACE SEED ATHEL
FAMILY ORIGIN PEOPLE SOURCE STRAIN
DESCENT KINDRED LINEAGE BREEDING
PEDIGREE
ANCHOR FIX BIND DRAG HOOK MOOR
REST SPUD STOP AFFIX BERTH BOWER
KEDGE RIVET SHEET STOCK ATTACH
DROGUE FASTEN KEDGER SECURE
CONNECT DEADMAN GRAPNEL
MUDHOOK SUPPORT COCKBILL
(PART OF —) ARM EYE KEY PEE PIN
BALL BILL HEAD HOOP PALM RING
CROWN FLUKE STOCK TREND THROAT
ANCHORAGE DOCK STAY HARBOR
REFUGE RIDING MOORAGE BERTHAGE
ROOTHOLD
ANCHORITE MONK HERMIT ASCETIC
EREMITE RECLUSE STYLITE
ANCHOVY SPRAT HERRING SARDINE
ANCIENT ELD OLD AGED AULD HOAR
IAGO YORE EARLY ELDER HOARY OLDEN
BYGONE ENSIGN FORMER NOETIC PISTOL
PRIMAL ANTIQUE ARCHAIC ARCHEAN
CLASSIC OGYGIAN HISTORIC NOACHIAN
OBSOLETE PRIMEVAL PRISTINE
ANCILLA HELPER ADJUNCT SERVANT
ANCON ELBOW CORBEL CONSOLE
AND ET SO TOO ALSO PLUS BESIDES
FURTHER MOREOVER
(— SO FORTH) ETC USW
ANDIRON DOG CHENET COBIRON
FIREDOG HESSIAN
ANDORRA (LANGUAGE OF —)
CATALAN
(NATIVE OF —) ANDOSIAN
(RIVER OF —) VALIRA
ANDREA CHENIER
(CHARACTER IN —) ANDREA COIGNY
GERARD CHENIER MADELEINE
(COMPOSER OF —) GIORDANO
ANDROCLES AND THE LION
(AUTHOR OF —) SHAW
(CHARACTER IN —) LAVINIA MEGAERA
ANDROCLES FERROVIUS
ANDROID ROBOT AUTOMATON
ANDROMACHE (AUTHOR OF —)
EURIPIDES
(CHARACTER IN —) PELEUS THETIS
ORESTES PYRRHUS HERMIONE
MENELAUS MOLOSSUS ANDROMACHE
NEOPTOLEMUS
(FATHER OF —) EETION

(HUSBAND OF —) HECTOR HELENUS
NEOPTOLEMUS
(SON OF —) PIELUS ASTYANAX
MOLOSSUS PERGAMUS
ANDROMEDA (FATHER OF —)
CEPHEUS
(MOTHER OF —) CASSIOPEA
(RESCUER OF —) PERSEUS
ANECDOTAL LITERARY
ANECDOTE GAG TOY JOKE TALE YARN
EVENT STORY SKETCH HAGGADA
EXEMPLUM
ANEMIC LOW PALE WEAK MEALY
WATERY LIFELESS
(PREF.) CHLOR(O)
ANEMONE LILY CRASS POLYP OPELET
BOWBELLS SNOWDROP
ANENT ON RE ABOUT ANENST BESIDE
TOWARD AGAINST OPPOSITE
ANESTHESIA BLOCK CORYL SPINAL
ANESTHETIC GAS ETHER ACOINE
EVIPAN OPIATE COCAINE DULLING
METOPRYL PARAFORM PROCAINE
SEDATIVE PHENOCAIN
ANESTHETIZE FREEZE ETHERIZE
ANEW OVER AGAIN NEWLY AFRESH
ITERUM
ANGEL MAH DEVA EBUS ARIEL DULIA
NAKIR YAKSA ABDIEL ARIOCH BACKER
BELIAL CHERUB NEKKAR SERAPH SPIRIT
THRONE UZZIEL YAKSHA ISRAFEL
RAPHAEL SPONSOR WATCHER ZADKIEL
ZOPHIEL APOLLYON GUARDIAN ITHURIEL
SUPERNAL
(— OF DEATH) AZRAEL SAMMAEL
(DESTROYING —) ABADDON
(FALLEN —S) HELL
(GUARDIAN —) YAKSA YAKSHA YAKSHI
(RECORDING —) SIJIL SIJILL
(PL.) HOST FRAVASHI SERAPHIM
ANGELFISH MONK ANGEL QUOTT RHINA
SQUAT MONACH CICHLID FLATFISH
MONKFISH
ANGELIC SAINTLY BEATIFIC CHERUBIC
HEAVENLY SERAPHIC
ANGER IRE IRK MAD VEX BATE BILE
BURN CRAB FELL FUME FURY GALL GRIM
HUFF MOOD RAGE RILE ROIL TIFF ANNOY
GRIPE IRISH PIQUE SPUNK WRATH
BOTHER CHOLER DANDER ENRAGE
EXCITE GRIEVE MONKEY NETTLE OFFEND
RANCOR SPLEEN TEMPER WARMTH
BURNING DUDGEON EMOTION INCENSE
INFLAME PASSION PROVOKE STOMACH
ACRIMONY DISTRESS IRRITATE
VEXATION
ANGERED SORE AGRAMED PELTISH
INCENSED
ANGLE BOB DIP ELL OUT TEE CANT COIN
COOK DRAW FISH FORK KNEE LEAD
NOOK PEAK SITE WICK ANCON AXIAL
BEVEL BIGHT COIGN DRAFT DRIFT
ELBOW FLEAM GROIN GUISE INGLE
PHASE POINT QUOIN SLANT SLOPE
ASPECT CANTON CORNEL CORNER
DIRECT OCTANT SCHEME SQUARE
TORNUS AZIMUTH BASTION DRAUGHT

GIMMICK KNUCKLE PERIGON RAVELIN
SALIENT DIHEDRAL FISHHOOK INTRIGUE
SHOULDER OBLIQUITY
(— OF BEVEL) FLEAM FLEEM
(— OF BOWSPRIT) STEEVE STEEVING
(— OF CLUB HEAD) LIE
(— OF EYELIDS) CANTHUS
(— OF HAT BRIM) BREAK
(— OF HIPBONE) HOOK
(— OF LEAF) AXIL
(— OF RAFTER) HEEL
(— OF TIMBER KNEE) BREECH
(DRIFT —) LEEWAY
(OBTUSE —) HEEL BULLNOSE
(ROCK —) DIEDRE
(ROOF —) HIP FASTIGIUM
(ROUND —) PERIGON
(SALIENT —) ARIS ARRIS PIEND
ANGLED CANTED NOOKED ANGULATE
ANGLER MONK FRIAR THIEF RODSTER
SPINNER ALLMOUTH FROGFISH
MONKFISH PISCATOR TOADFISH
WALTONIAN
ANGLEWORM ESS WORM FISHWORM
ANGLICAN EPISCOPAL
ANGLO CAUCASIAN

ANGOLA

CAPITAL: LUANDA
COIN: MACUTA
DISTRICT: CABINDA
KINGDOM: BAKONGO
LANGUAGE: BANTU KIMBUNDU
MOUNTAIN: LOVITI
PLATEAU: PLANALTO
PORT: LOBITO LUANDA
RIVER: CONGO CUITO KASAI CUANDO
   CUANZA CUNENE KUNENE KWANDO
   KWANZA CUBANGO
TOWN: LOBITO LUANDA LUBANGO
   BENGUELA MOSSAMEDES NOVALISBOA
TRIBE: BANTU KIKONGO
WATERFALL: RUACANA

ANGORA CAT GOAT RABBIT
ANGRY MAD EVIL GRIM HIGH ROSY SORE
WARM WAXY WILD CROOK CROSS
GRAME HUFFY IRATE MOODY VEXED
WROTH CHAFED FUMING FUMOUS
HEATED IREFUL LOADED FRETFUL
FURIOUS HOPPING IRACUND PAINFUL
SPLEENY UPTIGHT CHOLERIC INFLAMED
RIGOROUS SPITFIRE TEMPERED
VEHEMENT PASSIONATE
ANGUISH WOE ACHE HARM HURT PAIN
PANG RACK AGONY ANGST DOLOR GRIEF
THROE MISERY REGRET SORROW
REMORSE TORMENT TORTURE TRAVAIL
DISTRESS
ANGULAR BONY EDGY LEAN SLIM THIN
GAUNT SHARP ABRUPT POINTED
SCRAWNY CORNERED
ANHYDROUS DRY DESICCATED
ANIMADVERSION BLAME CENSURE

REPROOF WARNING MONITION
REPROACH
ANIMAL
(ALSO SEE UNDER SPECIFIC
HEADINGS) DEER BEAST BIPED BLACK
BRUTE GRADE GROSS LUSTY STRAY
BRUTAL CARNAL DAPPLE DESPOT
FLESHY KICKER MAMMAL RODENT
SORREL SPONGE SYLVAN BEASTIE
BREEDER CARRION CRITTER SENSUAL
BURROWER CREATURE ORGANISM
PREDATOR
(— FOR MARKET) STOCKER
(— INHABITED BY SPIRIT) GUACA
HUACA
(— LIVING IN CAVES) TROGLOBITE
(— OF LITTLE VALUE) SCALAWAG
SKALAWAG
(— RESEMBLING MAN) HOMINOID
(— WITH BLACK COAT AND
MARKINGS) PARSON
(— WITH DOCKED TAIL) CURTAL
(—S AS RENT) CAIN
(BEEF —) BONER GRASSER
(BOVINE —) BOSS BRUTE
(BROKEN-DOWN —) CROCK
(COLD-BLOODED —) ECTOTHERM
(DECOY —) COACH
(DOMESTIC —) DOER SCRUB BESTIAL
FOLLOWER SCRUBBER
(DRAFT —) AVER AIVER
(EMACIATED —) FRAME SKELETON
(FABULOUS —) KYLIN BUNYIP DRAGON
ACEPHAL GRIFFIN GRIFFON GRYPHON
UNICORN SEMITAUR TRAGELAPH
(FEMALE —) HEN SHE LADY JENNY
SHEDER
(FOOTLESS —) APOD APODE
(FOSSIL —) ZOOLITE
(GRASSHOPPER-EATING —)
WHANGAM
(GRAY —) GRIZZLE
(GRAZING —) HERBAGER
(GREEDY —) GORB
(HYPOTHETICAL —) PROAVIS
(LOWER —) BEAST CREATURE
(MALE —) HE TOM BUCK BULL JACK
STAG JOHNNY BACHELOR
(MATURE —) SENIOR
(MEAT —) CHOPPER
(MYTHICAL —) HODAG KYLIN
MOONACK
(PACK —) HUNIA SUMPTER
(PET —) CADE
(PURSUED —S) GAME
(SADDLE —) LOPER
(SCRAWNY —) SCRAG
(SHORN —) SHEAR
(SKINNY —) SCRAE
(SLUGGISH —) DRUMBLE
(SOLID-HOOFED —) SOLIPED
(SPOTTED —) CALICO
(STOCKY —) BLOCK
(THICKSET —) NUGGET
(TOTEM —) EPONYM
(UNBRANDED —) SLICK
(UNCASTRATED —) ENTIRE

(UNWEANED —) SUCKER
(WANDERING —) STRAY ESTRAY
(WARM-BLOODED —) ENDOTHERM HAEMATHERM
(WATER —) AQUATIC AQUATILE
(WEAK —) DRAG DOWNER
(WILD —) SAVAGE WILDLING
(WORTHLESS —) CARRION
(YOUNG —) HOG BIRD HOGG JOEY SHOT TOTO STORE JUNIOR PULLUS FATLING LITTLIN KINDLING LITTLING SUCKLING YOUNGLET
(2-HORNED —) BICORN BICORNE
(PL.) ZOA FAUNA NECTON NEKTON

ANIMATE ACT PEP FIRE MOVE PERK STIR URGE ALIVE BRISK CHEER DRIVE FLUSH IMBUE IMPEL LIGHT LIVEN QUICK ROUSE VITAL AROUSE BRIGHT EXCITE INCITE INDUCE KINDLE LIVING SPIRIT VIVIFY ACTUATE ENLIVEN INSPIRE QUICKEN ACTIVATE ENERGIZE INSPIRIT VITALIZE

ANIMATED UP GAY GLAD VIVE ALIVE BRISK QUICK VITAL VIVID ACTIVE ARDENT BLITHE BOUNCY BRISKY LIVELY LIVING SPARKY SPUNKY BUOYANT JOCULAR BOUNCING SPIRITED VIGOROUS

ANIMATION BRIO VERVE

ANIME COPAL ELEMI RESIN ROSIN ANIMATO

ANIMISM NATURISM

ANIMOSITY HATE PIQUE SPITE ANIMUS ENMITY HATRED MALICE RANCOR DISLIKE ACRIMONY

ANIMUS MIND WILL EFFORT ENMITY SPIRIT TEMPER ATTITUDE

ANISE ANET DILL CUMEN FENNEL

ANKH TAU

ANKLE HOCK TALUS WRIST TARSUS

ANKLEBONE TALUS ASTRAGAL

ANKLET SHOE SOCK BANGLE FETTER SHACKLE

ANNA KARENINA (AUTHOR OF —) TOLSTOY
(CHARACTER IN —) ANNA KITTY LEVIN ALEXEI STEPAN KARENIN VRONSKY OBLONSKY KONSTANTINE SHTCHERBATSKY

ANNALS FASTI NIHONGI REGISTER

ANNEAL BAKE FUSE HEAT SMELT TEMPER INFLAME TOUGHEN

ANNELID NAID WORM LUGWORM SERPULA ANNULATE SANDWORM

ANNEX ADD ELL JOIN AFFIX SEIZE UNITE APPEND ATTACH FASTEN ACQUIRE CONNECT FIXTURE POSTFIX SUBJOIN ADDITION

ANNIHILATE END OUT KILL RAZE RUIN SLAY ANNUL ERASE WRECK DELETE DEVOUR QUENCH REDUCE ABOLISH DESTROY EXPUNGE DECIMATE PULVERIZE

ANNIHILATION FANA NEGATION

ANNIVERSARY FETE MASS FEAST ANNUAL JUBILEE YEARDAY BIRTHDAY FESTIVAL
(100TH —) CENTENNIAL

(1000TH —) MILLENIUM
(150TH —) SESQUICENTENNIAL
(200TH —) BIMILLENARY BIMILLENNIUM
(25TH —) SEMIJUBILEE
(50TH —) SEMICENTENNIAL

ANNOTATE EDIT NOTE GLOSS NOTIFY POSTIL REMARK COMMENT EXPLAIN FOOTNOTE

ANNOTATION APOSTIL COMMENT SCHOLION SCHOLIUM

ANNOTATOR NOTIST SCHOLIAST

ANNOUNCE BID CRY BODE CALL SCRY SHOW SING TELL BRUIT CLAIM KNELL STATE VOICE ASSERT BLAZON BROACH DENOTE HERALD INFORM PREACH REPORT REVEAL SIGNAL DECLARE DIVULGE PUBLISH SIGNIFY DENOUNCE PROCLAIM RENOUNCE SENTENCE

ANNOUNCEMENT BID CRY HAT BILL CALL LEAD ALARM BANNS BLURB EDICT ALARUM DECREE DICTUM NOTICE GAZETTE BULLETIN CIRCULAR DECISION RESCRIPT PROCLAMATION

ANNOUNCER NEBO PAGE CRIER EMCEE CALLER HERALD NUNCIO SPIELER NUNCIATE

ANNOY BUG EAT EGG GET GIG IRE IRK NAG TRY VEX BAIT BORE BURN FRET FUSS GALL GRIG HARM HAZE HUFF PAIN RILE ROIL CHAFE DEVIL GRATE HARRY PEEVE PIQUE SPITE TEASE THORN UPSET WEARY WORRY BADGER BOTHER ENRAGE HARASS HECKLE HECTOR INFEST INJURE MADDEN MOLEST NEEDLE NETTLE OFFEND PESTER POTTER RATTLE RUFFLE TICKLE BEDEVIL DISTURB TROUBLE ACERBATE DISTRESS IRRITATE PERSECUTE

ANNOYANCE FASH PEST WEED CROSS GRIEF SPITE THORN INSECT DISGUST FASHERY TROUBLE UMBRAGE NUISANCE PINPRICK

ANNOYED SORE INSULTED

ANNOYING PESKY HATEFUL IRKSOME NOISOME PAINFUL FRETSOME NIGGLING SPITEFUL TIRESOME

ANNUAL BOOK PLANT FLOWER YEARLY ANNUARY ETESIAN GIFTBOOK PERIODIC YEARBOOK

ANNUITY CENSO CONSOL INCOME PENSION TONTINE

ANNUL NULL TOLL UNDO VOID AVOID BLANK ELIDE ERASE QUASH REMIT CANCEL NEGATE RECALL REPEAL REVERT REVOKE VACATE ABOLISH CASHIER DESTROY NULLIFY RESCIND RETRACT REVERSE VACUATE ABROGATE ARROGATE DEROGATE DISSOLVE

ANNULAR BANDED CYCLIC RINGED ANNULATE CIRCULAR

ANNULET RING RIDGE FILLET ANNULUS MOLDING

ANNULUS RING COLLAR

ANOA BUFFALO SAPIUTAN

ANODYNE BALM OPIATE REMEDY SOOTHER NARCOTIC SEDATIVE

ANOINT FAT OIL RUB BALM CERE NARD

ANELE CREAM CROWN SALVE SMEAR CHRISM GREASE SPREAD

ANOMALOUS ODD STRANGE UNUSUAL ABNORMAL ATYPICAL PECULIAR

ANON ANEW ONCE SOON AGAIN LATER AFRESH THENCE SHORTLY

ANONYMOUS UNKNOWN NAMELESS UNSIGNED

ANOTHER NEW THAT ALIAS FRESH SECOND

ANSWER DO IT SAY SIT ECHO PLEA SUIT ATONE AVAIL COVER REACT REPLY LETTER REJOIN RESULT RETORT RETURN RIPOST COUNTER DEFENSE FULFILL RESPOND SATISFY ANTIPHON COMEBACK REBUTTAL REPARTEE RESPONSE SOLUTION

ANSWERABLE EQUAL LIABLE FITTING ADEQUATE AMENABLE

ANT GYNE MIRE EMMET KELEP NURSE SLAVE AMAZON DRIVER ERGATE NASUTE WORKER PISMIRE PISSANT SOLDIER TERMITE FORMICID

ANTA PIER PEDESTAL PILASTER

ANTAGONISM WAR ANIMUS ENMITY QUARREL AVERSION CONFLICT

ANTAGONIST FOE ENEMY PARTY RIVAL FOEMAN BATTLER WARRIOR OPPONENT OPPOSITE

ANTAGONISTIC ADVERSE COUNTER HOSTILE CONTRARY INIMICAL OPPONENT OPPOSITE

ANTE PAY STAKE

ANTEATER TAPIR NUMBAT ECHIDNA TAMANDU AARDVARK AARDWOLF DASYURID EDENTATE PANGOLIN TAMANDUA TAMANOIR

ANTECEDENT FORE CAUSE PRIOR FORMER REASON PREMISE PREVIOUS PRECEDING

ANTEDATE PRECEDE PREDATE PREEXIST

ANTELOPE GNU SAT KOB BUCK DODA GUIB IBEX KOBA KUDU ORYX PUKU SUNI TOPI ADDAX BEIRA BOHOR BONGO BUBAL ELAND GORAL GUIBA NAGOR NYALA ORIBI SABLE SAIGA SASIN SEROW TAKIN BUBALE CHOUKA DIKDIK DUIKER DZEREN GOORAL IMPALA KOODOO NILGAI PYGARG RHEBOK BLAUBOK BLESBOK CHAMOIS GAZELLE GEMSBOK GERENUK RHEEBOK SASSABY BOSCHBOK REEDBUCK PRONGHORN (YOUNG —) KID LAMB

ANTENNA DISH HORN LOOP PALP AERIAL DIPOLE FEELER TACTOR WHISKER MONOPOLE PARABOLA RADIATOR

ANTERIOR FRONT PRIOR BEFORE FORMER VENTRAL PREVIOUS

ANTEROOM HALL FOYER LOBBY ENTRANCE

ANTHEM HYMN SONG AGNUS MOTET PSALM INTROIT (JAPANESE —) KIMIGAYO

ANTHER TIP AGLET CHIVE THECA

ANTHOLOGY ANA POSY ALBUM SYLVA CORPUS READER GARLAND SYNTAGMA

ANTHRACITE CULM

ANTHRAX SANG CHARBON BLACKLEG

ANTHROPOLOGIST TOTEMIST CULTURALIST

ANTHROPOPHAGITE CANNIBAL

ANTIBIOTIC BIOTIC ABIOTIC HUMULON TYLOSIN CIRCULIN CITRININ CLAVACIN CLAVATIN COLISTIN FRADICIN HUMULONE NEOMYCIN NYSTATIN SUBTILIN POLYMYCIN PUROMYCIN OLIGOMYCIN PENICILLIN RIFAMPICIN

ANTIC TOY DIDO FOOL WILD CAPER CLOWN COMIC DROLL MERRY PRANK STUNT GAMBOL BUFFOON CAPRICE GAMBADO

ANTICIPATE BEAT HOPE JUMP WISH AUGUR AWAIT DREAD PSYCH SENSE STALL EXPECT FORESEE OBVIATE PORTEND PREPARE PREVENT PROPOSE SUPPOSE ANTEDATE FORECAST

ANTICIPATION AUGURY OPINION THOUGHT PROSPECT PROLEPSIS PRESCIENCE PREMONITION

ANTICLIMAX BATHOS

ANTIDOTE BEZOAR EMETIC REMEDY THERIAC DELETERY

ANTIGONE (AUTHOR OF —) SOPHOCLES (BROTHER OF —) POLYNICES (CHARACTER IN —) CREON HAEMON ISMENE ANTIGONE TIRESIAS (FATHER OF —) OEDIPUS (MOTHER OF —) JOCASTA

ANTIPATHY HATE ODIUM ENMITY NAUSEA RANCOR ALLERGY DISGUST DISLIKE AVERSION DISTASTE LOATHING

ANTIPHUS (BROTHER OF —) MESTHLES (FATHER OF —) PRIAM TALAEMENES (HALF-BROTHER OF —) ISUS (MOTHER OF —) HECUBA

ANTIPODAL ANTARCTIC

ANTIPYRETIC SALOL MALARIN THALLIN THALLINE

ANTIQUARY ARCHAIST ANTIQUARIAN

ANTIQUATED OLD AGED FUSTY MOSSY PASSE FOSSIL VOIDED ANCIENT ARCHAIC NOACHIAN OBSOLETE OUTDATED OUTMODED TIMEWORN

ANTIQUE RELIC VIRTU NOETIC ANCIENT ARCHAIC NOACHIC NOACHIAN OUTMODED

ANTIQUITY ELD OLD PAST YORE OLDNESS

ANTISEPTIC EGOL KAVA AMIDO AMINE EUSOL AMADOL IODINE PHENOL ALCOHOL ASEPTIC STERILE CREOSOTE METAPHEN TEREBENE MERBROMIN

ANTISOCIAL HOSTILE ANARCHIST

ANTITHETICAL OPPOSITE

ANTITOXIN SERUM BIOLOGIC

ANTLER DAG HORN KNOB ROYAL SHOOT SPIKE BOSSET DEERHORN SURROYAL

ANTONY AND CLEOPATRA (AUTHOR OF —) SHAKESPEARE (CHARACTER IN —) EROS IRAS MENAS PHILO ALEXAS ANTONY GALLUS SCARUS SEXTUS SILIUS TAURUS AGRIPPA

LEPIDUS MARDIAN OCTAVIA THYREUS
VARRIUS CANIDIUS CHARMIAN
DERCETAS DIOMEDES DOMITIUS
MECAENAS OCTAVIUS SELEUCUS
CLEOPATRA DEMETRIUS DOLABELLA
VENTIDIUS EUPHRONIUS MENECRATES
PROCULEIUS

ANTONYM OPPOSITE

ANUS ASS ARSE BUNG VENT SIEGE
TEWEL

ANVIL BLOCK INCUS STAKE TEEST
STETHY STITHY BICKERN BEAKIRON

ANXIETY CARE CARK FEAR FRAY PAIN
ALARM DOUBT DREAD PANIC WORRY
ANGUISH CAUTION CHAGRIN CONCERN
SCRUPLE TENSION THOUGHT TROUBLE
DISQUIET SUSPENSE SOLICITUDE

ANXIOUS AGOG BUSY FOND EAGER
UPSET AFRAID UNEASY CAREFUL
UNQUIET DESIROUS RESTLESS
THOUGHTY WATCHFUL CONCERNED

ANY A AN AY ALL ARY EVER SOME WHAT

ANYBODY ANY ONE ANYONE SOMEONE

ANYTHING THAT AUGHT OUGHT

APACE FAST QUICK QUICKLY RAPIDLY
SPEEDILY

APACHE YUMA PADUCA CIBECUE
VAQUERO QUERECHO MESCALERO

APART BY OFF AWAY ELSE ALONE ALOOF
ASIDE SOLUS SPLIT LONELY SUNDRY
ASUNDER ENISLED REMOVED SEVERED
SEPARATE PIECEMEAL

APARTMENT PAD WON DIGS FLAT HALL
ROOM ABODE BOWER OECUS ORIEL
ROOMS SALON SOLAR SUITE ANDRON
CLOSET DECKER DINGLE DUPLEX
GROTTO LYCEUM SALOON SINGLE
SOLLAR SPENCE STANZA BUTTERY
CHAMBER COCKPIT GALLERY MANSION
PRIVACY BUILDING EPHEBEUM
SHOWROOM SOLARIUM TENEMENT
THALAMUS MAISONETTE
(— FOR IDOL) TING
(— IN CASTLE) BOWER
(— IN CHURCH) SACRISTY
(— OF WARSHIP) COCKPIT
(BACHELOR —) GARCONNIERE
(OUTER —) BUT
(PRIVATE —) MAHAL PARADISE
(RENTED —) LET
(PL.) GYNAECEUM

APATHETIC CALM COLD COOL DEAD
DOWF DULL BLASE DOWFF INERT STOIC
GLASSY SUPINE TORPID ADENOID
PASSIVE UNMOVED LISTLESS SLUGGISH
LETHARGIC PERFUNCTORY

APATHY SLOTH ACEDIA CAFARD PHLEGM
TORPOR LANGUOR DOLDRUMS
DULLNESS LETHARGY OMISSION
STOICISM STOLIDITY

APATITE IJOLITE MOROXITE
PHOSPHORINE

APAYAO ISNEG

APE KRA LAR PAN BOOR COPY DUPE FOOL
MAHA MIME MOCK SHAM BEROK CLOWN
MAGOT MIMIC ORANG PONGO PYGMY
APELET BABOON GELADA GIBBON
LANGUR MARTEN MARTIN MONKEY
OURANG PARROT PONGID SIMIAN SIMIID
BUFFOON COPYCAT EMULATE GORILLA
IMITATE PORTRAY PRIMATE SATYRUS
SIAMANG DURUKULI IMITATOR
MANTEGAR SIMULATE ORANGUTAN
(— STUDY) PITHECOLOGY
(PREF.) PITHEC(O)
(SUFF.) PITHECUS

APEAK VERTICAL

APEIRON MATTER

APER BOAR MIME SNOB CLOWN MOCKER
BUFFOON COPYCAT

APERCU DIGEST GLANCE PRECIS SKETCH
INSIGHT OUTLINE

APERIENT LAX OPENER CASCARA

APERIODIC DEADBEAT

APERITIF WHET CINZANO DUBONNET

APERTURE F EYE GAP OPE VUE BOLE
BORE HOLE LEAK PASS PORE RIMA SLIT
SLOT VENT BREAK CHASM CLEFT CRACK
LIGHT MOUTH PUPIL STOMA CUTOUT
HIATUS KEYWAY LOUVER WINDOW
FISSURE KEYHOLE OPENING ORIFICE
OSTIOLE PINHOLE PUNCTUM SWALLOW
TROMPIL APERTION FENESTRA
LOOPHOLE OVERTURE SPIRACLE

APEX EPI PIN TIP TOP ACME AUGE CONE
CUSP NOON PEAK RUFF CREST HIGHT
PITCH POINT SPIRE APOGEE CLIMAX
CRISIS CUPULA GENION HEIGHT SUMMIT
TITTLE VERTEX ZENITH CACUMEN
EVEREST PAPILLA PUNCTUM PINNACLE
(— OF HELMET) CREST
(PREF.) APIC(O)
(SUFF.) ACE

APHAREUS (BROTHER OF —)
LEUCIPPUS
(FATHER OF —) PERIERES
(MOTHER OF —) GORGOPHONE
(SON OF —) IDAS LYNCEUS
(WIFE OF —) ARENE

APHASIA ALALIA ALEXIA JARGON
APHEMIA ASYMBOLIA

APHID APHIS LOUSE APTERA BLIGHT
COLLIER DIMERAN MIGRANS PUCERON
BLACKFLY GREENFLY GYNOPARA
HOMOPTER

APHIDAS (DAUGHTER OF —) ANTIA
(FATHER OF —) ARCAS
(MOTHER OF —) ERATO MEGANIRA
CHRYSOPELIA
(SON OF —) ALEUS

APHORISM SAW ADAGE AXIOM GNOME
MAXIM MOTTO SUTRA SUTTA DICTUM
SAYING WISDOM EPIGRAM PRECEPT
PROVERB APOTHEGM PISHOGUE

APHORISTIC GNOMIC

APHRODISIAC DEWTRY DAMIANA
VENEREAL VENEREOUS

APHRODITE VENUS CYPRIS URANIA
ANTHEIA MYLITTA CYTHEREA PANDEMOS
(FATHER OF —) ZEUS JUPITER
(HUSBAND OF —) VULCAN
(MOTHER OF —) DIONE
(SON OF —) EROS CUPID AENEAS

APIARIST SKEPPIST

APIARY HIVE SKEP BEEYARD BEEHOUSE
APICULTURE BEEKEEPING
APIECE UP ALL PER EACH SERIATIM
APIKORES BECORESH
APIO ARRACACH ARRACACHA
APIOS SOIA SOJA GLYCINE
APIS HAPI
　(FATHER OF —) APOLLO PHORONEUS
　(MOTHER OF —) LAODICE
APISH SILLY FOPPISH AFFECTED
APITONG BAGAC HAPITON KERUING
APIUM UMBEL
APLITE HAPLITE
APLOMB TACT NERVE POISE SURETY
　COOLNESS
APOCALYPSE SHOWING REVELATION
APOCHRYPHA PSEUDEPIGRAPHA
APOCRISIARY RESPONSAL
APOCRYPHAL SHAM FALSE UNREAL
　DOUBTFUL FABULOUS FICTIOUS
APODAL FOOTLESS
APOGEE ACME APEX AUGE PEAK CLIMAX
　ZENITH
APOGON AMIA CARDINAL
APOLLO SUN PAEAN DELIUS AGYIEUS
　APOLLON LYKEIOS PATROUS PHOEBUS
　PYTHIUS CYNTHIUS PYTHAEUS
　(FATHER OF —) ZEUS JUPITER
　(MOTHER OF —) LETO LATONA
　(SISTER OF —) DIANA ARTEMIS
APOLLYON DEVIL SATAN ABADDON
APOLOGETIC SORRY
APOLOGUE MYTH FABLE STORY
　APOLOGY PARABLE ALLEGORY
APOLOGY PLEA ALIBI AMENDS EXCUSE
　PARDON REGRET PRETEXT SCRUPLE
　APOLOGIA
APOPHYGE SCAPE ESCAPE
APOPLEXY ESCA SHOCK STROKE
　POPLESIE
APOSTASY FALL LAPSE
APOSTATE RAT LAPSED CONVERT
　HERETIC PERVERT SECEDER DESERTER
　DISLOYAL RECREANT RENEGADE
　TURNCOAT
APOSTLE ESCAPE TEACHER DISCIPLE
　FOLLOWER PREACHER
　(BIBLICAL —) JOHN JUDE LEVI PAUL
　DENIS JAMES JUDAS PETER SIMON
　ANDREW PHILIP THOMAS DIDYMUS
　MATTHEW BARNABAS MATTHIAS
APOSTLE BIRD CATBIRD
APOSTROPHE TUISM TURNWAY
　TURNTALE
APOTHECARY CHEMIC SPICER CHEMICK
　DRUGGIST
APOTHECIUM CUP PELTA TRICA SHIELD
　ARDELLA LIRELLA PATELLA
APOTHEGM SAW DICT ADAGE AXIOM
　GNOME MAXIM SUTRA DICTUM SAYING
　SUTTAH PROVERB APHORISM SENTENCE
APOTHEOSIS DEIFICATION
　CONSECRATION
APOTHEOSIZE DEIFY EXALT ELEVATE
　GLORIFY CANONIZE
APPAIM (FATHER OF —) NADAB
APPALL STUN APPAL DAUNT SHOCK

DISMAY REDUCE REVOLT WEAKEN
ASTOUND DEPRESS DISGUST DISMISS
HORRIFY TERRIFY AFFRIGHT ASTONISH
ENFEEBLE FRIGHTEN OVERCOME
APPALLING AWFUL AWESOME FEARFUL
　TERRIBLE TERRIFIC
APPANAGE GRANT ADJUNCT APANAGE
APPARATUS AID BOX GUN LOG SET
ADON DRAG ETNA FAKE GEAR GRIP HECK
HELM LAMP LIFT STOW TIRE TOOL
BURET GANCH HOIST HORSE LEECH
RELAY SCUBA SHEAR SIREN SONAR
STILL STOVE SWING BUDDLE BUFFER
COILER COOKER DEVICE DINGUS ENGINE
FEEDER FILTER FOGGER GADGET GEYSER
GRAITH LADDER LIFTER MILKER ORRERY
OUTFIT REFLUX SEESAW SHEARS
SMOKER SMUDGE TACKLE TIPPLE
TREMIE TROMPE AERATOR ALEMBIC
APPAREL AUTOMAT BAGGAGE BALANCE
BASCULE BURETTE DERRICK ECHELON
FURNACE GASOGEN GRILLER HOISTER
INHALER ISOTRON MACHINE MEGAFOG
PINCERS PRESSER SOXHLET SPRAYER
STIRRER TELEPIX TREMOLO TRIMMER
UTENSIL AGITATOR AQUALUNG
BLOWDOWN CALUTRON CONVEYER
CONVEYOR CRYOSTAT DIALYZER
DIAPHOTE DIGESTER DRENCHER
DUMBBELL EOLIPILE EQUIPAGE
ERGOSTAT GASIFIER GAZOGENE
INJECTOR ISOSCOPE JACQUARD
OSMOGENE OZONIZER PULMOTOR
PURIFIER RECORDER REDUCTOR
REHEATER SCRUBBER SOFTENER
STRIPPER ABSORPTIOMETER
　(— IN STOMACH OF LOBSTER) LADY
　(SEGMENTAL —) BRAINSTEM
　(SUFF.) STAT(IC) STAT(ICS)
APPAREL DECK FARE GARB GEAR ROBE
SECT TIRE WEAR WEDE ADORN ARRAY
BESEE CLOTH DRESS EQUIP HABIT TUNIC
ATTIRE CLOTHE GRAITH OUTFIT PARURE
ROBING CLOBBER COSTUME FURNISH
GARMENT HARNESS PREPARE RAIMENT
VESTURE CLOTHING FOOTWEAR
HEADWEAR WARDROBE
　(HEAD —) MILLINERY
　(MILITARY —) WARENTMENT
　(RICH —) ARRAY
APPARENT OPEN BREEM BREME CLEAR
OVERT PLAIN FORMAL PARENT PATENT
PHANIC CERTAIN EVIDENT GLARING
OBVIOUS SEEMING SHALLOW VISIBLE
DISTINCT ILLUSORY MANIFEST
PALPABLE PROBABLE SEMBLANT
SEMBLABLE OSTENSIBLE
APPARENTLY (PREF.) QUASI
APPARITION HUE HANT SHOW DREAM
FANCY FETCH GHOST HAUNT IMAGE
LARVA PHASM SHADE SHAPE SPOOK
ASPECT DOUBLE IDOLUM SOWLTH
SPIRIT SPRITE STOUND SWARTH TAISCH
THURSE THYON WRAITH DISPLAY
EIDOLON FANTASY FEATURE PHANTOM
SPECTER SPECTRE EPIPHANY ILLUSION

PHANTASM PRESENCE REVENANT
SPECTRUM SEMBLANCE

APPARITOR BEADLE PARURE PARITOR
SUMMONER

APPEAL ASK BEG BID CRY CALL CASE
PLEA SEEK SUIT APPLY CHARM CLEPE
REFER SPEAK ACCUSE ADJURE AVOUCH
INVOKE PRAYER SUMMON ADDRESS
CONJURE ENTREAT IMPLORE REQUEST
SOLICIT APPROACH ENTREATY PETITION
ADJURATION
(— TO) APPLY AVOUCH INVOKE
ARRAIGN
(SEX —) IT OOMPH

APPEALING CUTE NICE CATCHY CLEVER
CUNNING SUGARED PLEASANT
(STRIKINGLY —) ZINGY

APPEAR BID CAR EYE GET COME DAWN
FARE LOOK LOOM MAKE MEET PEER
REAR RISE SEEM WALK ARISE ENTER
ISSUE KITHE KYTHE OCCUR SOUND
THINK ARRIVE BESEEM EMERGE INFORM
REGARD SPRING BLOSSOM COMPEAR
DEVELOP OUTCROP RESEMBLE
(— AND DISAPPEAR) COOK
(— BRIEFLY) GLINT
(— DIRECTLY BEFORE) AFFRONT
(— SUDDENLY) BURST
(— UNEXPECTEDLY) BLOOM IRRUPT
(PREF.) PHANER(O) PHANTA PHANTO

APPEARANCE AIR CUT HUE CAST FARE
FORM GARB IDEA LATE LEEN LOOK MIEN
SHOW VIEW BLUSH COLOR EIDOS FAVOR
FRONT GUISE HABIT PHASE PHASM
SHAPE SIGHT SOUND SPICE ASPECT
EFFECT FACIES FAVOUR MANNER
OBJECT OSTENT REGARD VISAGE
ARRIVAL DISPLAY FARRAND FASHION
FEATURE GLIMPSE OUTSIDE RESPECT
SHOWING SPECIES ARTEFACT ARTIFACT
EPIPHANY ILLUSION LIKENESS PRESENCE
PRETENSE SEMBLANCE
(— OF LIGHT ON HAIR) HAG
(CLOUDED —) HAZE CHILL
(CONSPICUOUS —) FIGURE
(DISTINCTIVE —) AURA
(FIRST —) DAWN DEBUT SPRING
(IMPOVERISHED —) BEGGARY
(MERE —) INTENTIONAL
(MOCK —) SIMULACRUM
(MOTTLED —) ROE DAPPLE
(MOTTLED SKY —) BLINK
(OUTWARD —) FACE SEEM FACADE
APPAREL BALLOON SEEMING SURFACE
(PERSONAL —) PRESENCE
(SUPERNATURAL —) APPARITION
(SURFACE —) TOUR BLOOM
(UNGAINLY —) ANGULARITY
(VAGUE —) BLUR

APPEASE LAY PAY CALM EASE HUSH
SATE ALLAY ATONE QUIET SLAKE STILL
DEFRAY MODIFY PACIFY PLEASE SOFTEN
SOOTHE ASSUAGE CONTENT DULCIFY
GRATIFY MOLLIFY PLACATE SATISFY
STICKLE SUFFICE SWEETEN MITIGATE
PROPITIATE

APPELLATION NAME TERM STYLE TITLE

EPITHET SURNAME COGNOMEN
NICKNAME

APPEND ADD PIN TAG CLIP HANG JOIN
TACK AFFIX ANNEX ADJOIN ATTACH
FASTEN AUGMENT SUBJOIN

APPENDAGE ARM AWN FIN LEG TAB
TAG ARIL BARB FLAP HOOK HORN LIMB
LOBE SPUR TAIL AFFIX BEARD RIDER
SCALE WHISK PALPUS PAPPUS STYLET
SUFFIX ADJUNCT ANTENNA AURICLE
CODICIL EARLOBE FIXTURE PENDANT
ADDITION ADHERENT ASCIDIUM
BRACHIUM FILAMENT PENDICLE

APPENDIX EKE ANNEX LABEL VERMIX
AURICLE CODICIL PENDANT ADDENDUM
EPILOGUE

APPETITE MAW YEN LUST URGE WILL
ZEST BELLY BLOOD GORGE GREED
GUSTO TASTE DESIRE FAMINE GENIUS
HUNGER LIKING RELISH BULIMIA
CRAVING EDACITY LONGING PASSION
STOMACH WANTING CUPIDITY
FONDNESS TENDENCY
(— LOSS) ANOREXIA
(ANIMAL —) BLOOD
(CANINE —) PHAGEDENA
(EXCESSIVE —) LIMOSIS GULOSITY
POLYPHAGIA
(PERVERTED —) MALACIA

APPETIZER WHET SAUCE CANAPE
RELISH SAVORY APERITIF COCKTAIL

APPETIZING NICE GUSTY SAVORY
GUSTFUL GUSTABLE PALATABLE

APPLAUD HUM CLAP LAUD RISE ROOT
CHEER EXTOL HUZZA PRAISE ACCLAIM
APPROVE ENDORSE HOSANNA PLAUDIT

APPLAUSE CLAP HAND BRAVO CHEER
ECLAT HUZZA SALVO HURRAH PRAISE
ACCLAIM OVATION CLAPPING

APPLE PIP CRAB POME PIPPIN PUFFIN
RENNET RUSSET BALDWIN CODLING
COSTARD POMEROY RUDDOCK WINESAP
CORTLAND GREENING JONATHAN
MCINTOSH NONESUCH PARADISE
POMANDER
(— OF PERU) JIMSON JIMPSON
SHOOFLY
(BITTER —) COLOCYNTH
(CRAB —) CRAB SCRAB WHARRE
POWITCH
(EMU —) COLANE
(GOLDEN —) BEL BAEL
(PEELED —) DUMPLING
(SHRIVELED —) CRUMPLING
(SLICED DRIED —S) SCHNITZ
(SMALL —) CODLIN CODLING
(SMALL —S) GRIGGLES
(THORN —) MAD METEL

APPLIANCE GEAR IRON TOOL CLAMP
DEVICE ENGINE FABRIC GADGET JUICER
MACHINE UTENSIL

APPLICABLE APT FIT MEET PROPER
USEFUL FITTING PLIABLE APPOSITE
RELATIVE RELEVANT SUITABLE
(UNIVERSALLY —) CATHOLIC
(WIDELY —) BROAD

APPLICANT PROSPECT

APPLICATION USE FORM BLANK TOPIC APPEAL EFFORT ADDRESS REQUEST EPITHEME PETITION SEDULITY
(— OF KNOWLEDGE) PRACTICE
(— TO WRONG PURPOSE) ABUSE
(MEDICINAL —) PLASTER DRESSING FRONTING LENITIVE
(MENTAL —) INTENTION

APPLY ASK LAY PLY PUT RUB SET USE BEAR BEND CLAP DAUB GIVE MOVE SEEK TOIL TURN WORK ADAPT LABOR LIKEN REFER SMEAR APPEAL BESTOW COMPLY DEVOTE DIRECT EMPLOY EXTEND RESORT COMPARE CONFORM IMPRESS OVERLAY PERTAIN REQUEST SOLICIT UTILIZE DEDICATE DISPENSE MINISTER PETITION
(— BRAKE) BUR
(— COSMETICS) DO POP
(— GREASE) ARM
(— HOT CLOTHS) FOMENT
(— IMPROPERLY) ABUSE
(— ONESELF) ATTEND INTEND MUCKLE ADDRESS
(— PIGMENT) DRAG

APPOINT ARM FIX SET CALL DECK GIVE MAKE NAME ALLOT ARRAY AWARD DIGHT ELECT ENACT EQUIP PLACE POINT SLATE ASSIGN CREATE DECREE DEPUTE DETAIL DEVISE DIRECT ENTAIL ORDAIN OUTFIT SETTLE ARRAIGN CONFIRM DISPOSE FURNISH RESOLVE TAILZIE DELEGATE DEPUTIZE NOMINATE

APPOINTMENT DATE BERTH ORDER TRYST BILLET OFFICE COMMAND STATION CREATION DELEGACY POSITION

APPORTION LOT DEAL DOLE MARK METE PART RATE ALLOT AWARD GRANT SHARE WEIGH ASSESS ASSIGN DIVIDE PARCEL RATION ARRANGE BALANCE QUARTER ALLOCATE

APPRAISE METE RATE ASSAY GAUGE JUDGE PRICE PRIZE VALUE ASSESS ESTEEM EVALUE PONDER PRAISE SURVEY ADJUDGE ANALYZE COMMEND ESTIMATE EVALUATE

APPRECIABLE ANY SENSIBLE PERCEPTIBLE

APPRECIATE DIG FEEL LOVE PRIZE SAVOR TASTE VALUE ADMIRE ESTEEM APPROVE CHERISH REALIZE INCREASE TREASURE

APPRECIATION EYE GUSTO SENSE CONCEIT PERCEPTION

APPREHEND COP GET NAB SEE FEAR HEAR KNOW NOTE SCAN TAKE VIEW CATCH DREAD GRASP SEIZE ARREST BEHOLD DETAIN INTEND INTUIT CAPTURE REALIZE RECEIVE SUPPOSE CONCEIVE DISCOVER OVERTAKE PERCEIVE

APPREHENSION FEAR PAIN PANG ALARM DOUBT DREAD FANCY WORRY ARREST DISMAY NOESIS ANXIETY CAPTURE CONCERN DISTRUST COGNITION

APPREHENSIVE APT JUMPY FEARED MORBID ANXIOUS FEARFUL JEALOUS NERVOUS DOUBTFUL

APPRENTICE CUB TYRO CADET DEVIL HELPER NOVICE LEARNER TRAINEE BEGINNER SERVITOR

APPRISE WARN TEACH ADVISE INFORM NOTIFY REVEAL ACQUAINT DISCLOSE INSTRUCT

APPROACH TRY ADIT COME COST DRAW NEAR ROAD BOARD CLOSE COAST ESSAY VERGE ACCEDE ACCESS ACCOST ADVENT APPEAL BROACH COMING IMPEND ADVANCE CONTACT PREFACE SUCCEED CONVERGE
(— FROM WINDWARD) BEAR
(— GAME) DRAW
(— HOSTILELY) SWAY
(— NEAR) TOUCH
(— OF NIGHT) FALL
(— TENDENCY) ADIENCE
(INVITING —) PASS

APPROBATION TEST FAVOR PROOF TRIAL ASSENT PRAISE REGARD REPUTE PLAUDIT APPLAUSE APPROVAL SANCTION

APPROPRIATE ADD APT DUE FIT PAT AKIN CRIB GOOD GRAB GRIP HELP JUST MEET SUIT TAKE ANNEX RIGHT STEAL USURP ASSUME BORROW DECENT DEVOTE DIGEST GATHER KINDLY PILFER PIRATE PROPER TIMELY WORTHY APROPOS FITTING GERMANE IMPOUND PREEMPT PURLOIN RELATED ARROGATE BECOMING DESERVED EMBEZZLE HANDSOME RELEVANT RIGHTFUL SUITABLE

APPROVAL AMEN ECLAT ASSENT ESTEEM CONSENT PLAUDIT SUPPORT APPLAUSE BLESSING SANCTION SUFFRAGE

APPROVE DO OK BUY DIG TRY AMEN LIKE OKAY PASS TEST VOTE ALLOW BLESS CLEAR FAVOR PROVE VALUE ACCEPT ADMIRE CONCUR RATIFY APPLAUD CERTIFY COMMEND CONFIRM CONSENT ENDORSE SUPPORT ACCREDIT SANCTION

APPROXIMATE NEAR ABOUT CIRCA CLOSE ROUGH GENERAL ESTIMATE

APPROXIMATELY SAY MUCH NIGH SOME ABOUT CIRCA ALMOST AROUND NEARLY ROUGHLY

APPURTENANCE GEAR ADJUNCT APPANAGE

APRON BIB CAP BASE RAMP TIER COVER CANVAS DICKEY RUNWAY SHIELD TARMAC PINAFORE

APROPOS APT FIT PAT MEET TIMELY RELEVANT SUITABLE

APSE BEMA NICHE CONCHA EXEDRA RECESS

APT FIT PAT ABLE DEFT FAIN FEAT KEEN WONT ADEPT ALERT HAPPY PRONE QUICK READY CLEVER DOCILE LIABLE LIKELY PRETTY SUITED CAPABLE FITTING WILLING DISPOSED INCLINED SKILLFUL SUITABLE

APTERYX KIWI
APTITUDE ART BENT GIFT CRAFT FLAIR HABIT KNACK SKILL VERVE GENIUS TALENT ABILITY FACULTY FITNESS CAPACITY
AQUEDUCT DUCT CANAL CHANNEL CONDUIT
ARAB WAIF GAMIN NOMAD SAUDI TATAR SEMITE URCHIN BEDOUIN SARACEN
ARABESQUE ORNATE

ARABIA

COIN: LARI CARAT DINAR KABIK RIYAL
DESERT: NYD ANKAF DEHNA NAFUD NEFUD
GARMENT: ABA HAIK CABAAN BURNOUS
HOLY CITY: MECCA MEDINA
HOLY LAND: HEJAZ
ISLAND: SOCOTRA
JUDGE: CADI
KINGDOM: NEJD
MEASURE: DEN SAA FERK KIST ACHIR BARID CABDA CAFIZ COVID CUDDY MAKUK QASAB TEMAN WOIBE ZUDDA ARTABA
MOUNTAIN: NEBO HOREB SINAI
PORT: ADEN
RULER: AMIR EMIR AMEER EMEER
STATE: ASIR OMAN YEMEN KUWAIT
TOWN: ABHA ADEN BEDA BERA HAIL RIAD SANA TAIF DUBAI HAUTA HOFUF JIDDA MECCA MOCHA QATIF TAIZZ YENBO ANAIZA MANAMA MATRAH MEDINA RIYADH SALALA SHAQRA BURAIDA HODEIDA MUKALLA ONEIZAH SHARJAH
TRIBE: AUS ASIR IRAD TEMA KEDAR DIENDEL SHUKRIA
WEIGHT: ROTL BAHAR CHEKI KELLA MAUND NASCH NEVAT OCQUE OUKIA RATEL TOMAN VAKIA BOKARD DIRHEM

ARABLE FERTILE PLOWABLE TILLABLE
ARACHNID CRAB MITE TICK ACARID SPIDER SCORPION
ARBALEST BALISTER CROSSBOW
ARBITER JUDGE CRITIC UMPIRE ADVISER DAYSMAN REFEREE
ARBITRARY SEVERE THETIC WILLFUL ABSOLUTE DESPOTIC MASTERLY
ARBITRATE DECIDE MEDIATE
ARBITRATOR REF JUDGE UMPIRE ARBITER REFEREE MEDIATOR
ARBOR BAR AXLE BEAM BOWER SHAFT STAFF STALK TRAIL GARDEN RAMADA BERCEAU MANDREL ORCHARD PERGOLA
ARC BOW ARCH BEND HALO CURVE ORBIT SPARK FOGBOW COMPASS RAINBOW
(— OF HORIZON) AZIMUTH AMPLITUDE
(ELECTRIC —) SPARK
ARCADE LOGGIA STREET GALLERY PORTICO CLOISTER
ARCANE RUNIC HIDDEN SECRET MYSTERIOUS
ARCH ARC BOW COY SLY BEND COVE
DOME HOOP OGEE PERT SPAN CHIEF CURVE GREAT OGIVE PRIME SAUCY SWEEP VAULT BRIDGE CAMBER CLEVER FORNIX IMPISH MANTEL SPRING WICKET ZYGOMA CONCAVE CUNNING GATEWAY ROGUISH TESTUDO WAGGISH
(PART OF —) PIER CHORD IMPOST PILLAR ABUTMENT EXTRADOS INTRADOS KEYSTONE SKEWBACK SPANDREL SPRINGER VOUSSOIR
ARCHAEOLOGIST POTHUNTER PREHISTORIAN
ARCHAIC OLD ANCIENT ANTIQUE HISTORIC OBSOLETE
ARCHANGEL SATAN URIEL GABRIEL MICHAEL RAPHAEL HIERARCH
ARCHBISHOP HATTO PRELATE PRIMATE ORDINARY
ARCHER BOW CLIM CUPID BOWMAN SHOOTER PANDARUS
ARCHERY TOXOLOGY
ARCHETYPE IDEA MODEL FIGURE SAMPLE ESSENCE EXAMPLE PARAGON PATTERN EXEMPLAR ORIGINAL PROTOTYPE
ARCHING CAMBER
ARCHITECT MAKER ARTIST ARTISAN BUILDER CREATOR PLANNER DESIGNER SURVEYOR
ARCHITECTURAL TECTONIC
ARCHITRAVE EPISTYLE PLATBAND
ARCHLUTE THEORBO
ARC LAMP MONOPHOTE
ARCTIC ICY COLD COOL GELID POLAR BOREAL CHILLY FRIGID GALOSH NORTHERN OVERSHOE
ARDENT HOT AVID FOND KEEN LIVE WARM EAGER FIERY SHARP ABLAZE FERVID FIERCE STRONG TORRID AMOROUS BURNING CORDIAL DEVOTED EARNEST FEELING FERVENT FLAMING GLOWING INTENSE SHINING ZEALOUS DESIROUS FEVERISH FLAGRANT ROMANTIC SANGUINE SCALDING VEHEMENT
ARDOR DASH EDGE ELAN FIRE GLOW HEAT LOVE ZEST FLAME GUSTO HEART VERVE WRATH DESIRE FERVOR METTLE SPIRIT SPLEEN WARMTH PASSION DEVOTION FEROCITY VIOLENCE VIVACITY
ARDUOUS HARD LOFTY STEEP STIFF SEVERE TRYING ONEROUS EXACTING TIRESOME TOILSOME
AREA BELT PALE SIZE ZONE BASIN COURT FIELD PLACE RANGE REALM SCENE SCOPE SPACE TRACT AREOLA EXTENT GROUND LOCALE REGION SECTOR SPHERE SPREAD ACREAGE CIRCUIT COMPASS CONTENT COUNTRY ENVIRON EXPANSE KINGDOM PURLIEU SURFACE CAPACITY DISTRICT ENCEINTE PLOTTAGE PROVINCE
(— AT INTERSECTION) CIRCUS
(— BETWEEN FILLETS) CANALIS
(— IN BACTERIAL CULTURE) PLAQUE
(— IN CARTOON) BALLOON
(— IN HOSTILE TERRITORY) AIRHEAD

(— OF ACTIVITY) METIER
(— OF EXPERIENCE) BOOK
(— OF FLAG) CANTON
(— OF OLDER LAND) KIPUKA
(— OF OPEN WATER AMID ICE) POLYNYA
(— OF RIDGES) BILO
(— OF TIMBERLAND) CHENA
(— ON MOON) MARE WANE TERRA
(— UNIT) TAN YOKE LABOR VIRGATE PLETHRON PLOWGANG PLOWGATE
(BLANK —) BITE HOLE
(COMBAT —) GLACIS
(CONTINENTAL —) MOARIA
(CULTURAL —) HORIZON
(CURLING —) PARISH
(DARK — OF MOON) MARE MARIA
(DENUDED —) BURN
(DIKED —) SLUSHPIT
(ELONGATED —) BELT
(ENCLOSED —) FOLD SEPT
(EXTRAMURAL —) BANLIEUE
(FENCED —) CAGE COMPOUND
(FERTILE —) HAMMOCK
(FLOORING —) SQUARE
(FORTIFIED —) BASTION ENCEINTE
(GATHERING —) MANDAPA
(HUNTING —) SURROUND
(INFESTED —) FLYBELT
(LOW-LYING —) GLADE SWALE COULEE COULIE GUTTER
(LUMINOUS —) AUREOLA AUREOLE
(MINE —) SQUEEZE
(NUCLEAR —) HEARTH ECUMENE
(OPEN —) COURT LAUND CAMPUS SQUARE HAGGARD
(OVERGROWN —) COGONAL
(PASTURE —) SOUM
(PAVED —) CAUSEY
(PLOWED —) BREAK
(RESIDENTIAL —) BANLIEU BANLIEUE
(SHOPPING —) MALL
(SLUM —) STEW
(SMALL —) AREOLA
(SMOKING —) BULLPEN
(STERN —) AFTERPART
(SUBURBAN —) ADDITION FAUBOURG
(SUNKEN —) SAG
(SWAMPY —) SLASH
(TEST —) MILACRE
(TIDAL —) CLAMFLAT
(TRANSITION —) ECOTONE
(TREELESS —) SLICK
(TUMID —) CERE
(UNCLEARED —) BUSH
(UPLAND —) COTEAU
(VOLCANIC —) SOLFATARA
(WASTE —) FOREST
(WOODED —) HAG BOSK BOSQUE
ARENA AREA LIST OVAL RING RINK COURT FIELD SCENE SCOPE SPACE STAGE CIRCUS CIRQUE REGION SPHERE COCKPIT STADIUM TERRAIN THEATER BULLRING
ARENACEOUS SANDY GRITTY
AREOLA PIT AREA RING SPOT SPACE

ARES MARS ENYALIUS GRADIVUS QUIRINUS
(FATHER OF —) ZEUS JUPITER
(MOTHER OF —) ENYO HERA JUNO
(SON OF —) REMUS CYCNUS ROMULUS
ARGENT LUNA MOON PEARL WHITE BLANCH SILVER CRYSTAL SHINING SILVERY

ARGENTINA

CAPITAL: BUENOSAIRES
COIN: PESO CENTAVO
DANCE: TANGO CUANDO GAUCHO
INDIAN: LULE GUARANI
LAKE: VIEDMA CARDIEL FAGNANO MUSTERS
MEASURE: SINO VARA LEGUA CUADRA FANEGA LASTRE MANZANA
MOUNTAIN: TORO ANDES CHATO LAUDO MAIPU POTRO CONICO PISSIS RINCON FAMATINA MURALLON OLIVARES TRONADOR ZAPALERI ACONCAGUA INCAHUASI
PLAIN: PAMPA PAMPAS
PORT: ROSARIO
PROVINCE: CHACO JUJUY SALTA CHUBUT CORDOBA FORMOSA LARIOJA MENDOZA NEUQUEN TUCUMAN MISIONES
REGION: CHACO PATAGONIA
RIVER: SALI ATUEL CHICO COYLE DULCE LIMAY NEGRO PLATA TEUCO BLANCO CHUBUT CUARTO FLORES GRANDE PARANA QUINTO SALADO
TOWN: AZUL GOYA ORAN PUAN BAHIA JUNIN LANUS LUJAN METAN SALTA PARANA RAWSON RUFINO VIEDMA ZARATE BOLIVAR CORDOBA DOLORES FORMOSA LABANDA MENDOZA NEUQUEN POSADAS RAFAELA ROSARIO TUCUMAN USHUAIA
VOLCANO: LANIN MAIPU DOMUYO PETEROA TUPUNGATO
WATERFALL: IGUAZU
WEIGHT: LAST GRANO LIBRA QUINTAL TONELADA

ARGOSY SHIP FLEET GALLEON
ARGOT CANT FLASH LINGO SLANG JARGON PATOIS DIALECT
ARGUE JAW CHOP FUSS MOOT MOVE SPAR CAVIL PLEAD PROVE TREAT ACCUSE DEBATE HASSLE REASON CONTEND CONTEST COUNTER DISCUSS DISPUTE WRANGLE MAINTAIN
ARGUMENT ROW AGON BEEF CASE FUSS PLEA TEXT CLASH LEMMA PROOF THEME TOPIC COMBAT DEBATE HASSLE MATTER TUSSLE APAGOGE DEFENSE DILEMMA DISPUTE POLEMIC RHUBARB SOPHISM SORITES SUMMARY CLINCHER
ARGUMENTATIVE ERISTIC FORENSIC
ARGUS (FATHER OF —) ZEUS JUPITER PHRIXUS

(MOTHER OF —) ARGIA NIOBE
CHALCIOPE
(SLAYER OF —) HERMES MERCURY
ARIA AIR SOLO SONG TUNE MELODY
SORTIE ARIETTA SORTITA
ARIADNE (FATHER OF —) MINOS
(HUSBAND OF —) THESEUS
(MOTHER OF —) PASIPHAE
ARID DRY BALD BARE DULL LEAN BARREN
DESERT JEJUNE MEAGER PARCHED
STERILE THIRSTY WITHERED
ARIDITY DROUGHT SICCITY
ARIL POD COATING
ARISE WAX COME FLOW FORM GROW
LIFT REAR RISE SOAR STEM AWAKE
BEGIN BUILD ISSUE MOUNT RAISE
STAND START SURGE TOWER WAKEN
ACCRUE AMOUNT APPEAR ASCEND
ATTAIN DERIVE HAPPEN SPRING
DEVELOP EMANATE PROCEED
ARISTOCRACY CLASS ELITE GENTRY
ARISTOI SAMURAI NOBILITY OPTIMACY
ARISTOCRAT LORD NOBLE JUNKER
GRANDEE PARVENU PATRICIAN
ARISTOCRATIC HIGH TONY NOBLE
QUALITY CAVALIER BELGRAVIAN
ARISTOTELIAN PERIPATETIC
ARITHMETIC SUM ALGORISM

ARIZONA

CAPITAL: PHOENIX
COUNTY: GILA PIMA YUMA PINAL APACHE
MOHAVE NAVAJO COCHISE YAVAPAI
INDIAN: HOPI PIMA YUMA NAVAHO
NAVAJO PAPAGO HUALAPAI
MOUNTAIN: BANGS GROOM LEMMON
TURRET
MOUNTAIN RANGE: GILA KOFA MOHAWK
GALIURO HUALPAI
RIVER: GILA SALT ZUNI VERDE PUERCO
COLORADO
STATE BIRD: CACTUSWREN
STATE FLOWER: SAGUARO
STATE NICKNAME: OCOTILLO
STATE TREE: PALOVERDE
TOWN: AJO ELOY MESA NACO YUMA
GLOBE LEUPP TEMPE BISBEE JEROME
MCNARY SALOME TOLTEC TUCSON
KINGMAN NOGALES PHOENIX PRESCOTT
FLAGSTAFF TOMBSTONE

ARK BIN BOX BOAT SHIP BARGE CHEST
HUTCH BASKET COFFER REFUGE
SHELTER

ARKANSAS

CAPITAL: LITTLEROCK
COUNTY: LEE CLAY DREW PIKE POLK POPE
YELL BOONE CROSS DESHA IZARD
LOGAN SHARP STONE BAXTER CHICOT
LONOKE SEARCY

INDIAN: CADDO OSAGE QUAPAW
CHOCTAW CHEROKEE
LAKE: CONWAY NIMROD GREESON
NORFORK OUACHITA
MOUNTAIN RANGE: OZARK OUACHITA
NATIVE: TOOTHPICK
NICKNAME: WONDER
RIVER: RED WHITE SALINE BUFFALO
CURRENT OUACHITA
STATE BIRD: MOCKINGBIRD
STATE FLOWER: APPLE BLOSSOM
STATE TREE: SHORTLEAFPINE
TOWN: COY CUY KEO OLA ROE ULM ALMA
BONO CASA DELL DIAZ MORO ENOLA
PERLA RISON RONDO WYNNE ALICIA
JASPER PIGGOTT

ARM FIN OAR BOOM LIMB WING BLADE
BOUGH CRANE EQUIP FIORD FIRTH
FORCE INLET MIGHT POWER RIFLE
BRANCH CRUTCH MEMBER OUTFIT
PINION RADIAL SLEEVE WEAPON FLIPPER
FORTIFY FURNISH PREPARE PROTECT
PROVIDE SUPPORT FORELIMB SOUPBONE
(— HOLDING FLINT) HAMMER
(— OF BARNACLE) CIRRUS CIRRHUS
(— OF CHAIR) ELBOW
(— OF CRANE) JIB GIBBET RAMHEAD
(— OF GIN) START
(— OF PROPELLER) BLADE
(— OF RECORD PLAYER) PICKUP
(— OF SEA) COVE FLOW MEER MERE
BRACE CANAL FIRTH FRITH GRAIN
FRETUM ESTUARY EURIPUS
(— OF SPINNING MULE) SICKLE
(— OF WINDMILL) VANE WHIP
(— WITH GAFF) HEEL
(INDEX —) DIOPTER
(IRON —) CRANE
(LEVER —) SWEEP
(PITCHING —) SOUPBONE
ARMADA NAVY FLEET FLOTILLA
ARMADILLO APAR PEBA POYOU TATOU
BOLITA MATACO MULITA PELUDO
KABASSOU PANGOLIN
ARMATURE ARMING KEEPER LIFTER
ARMBAND BRASSARD
ARMCHAIR BERGERE FAUTEUIL
ARMED FLUTE HEELED DAGGERED
WEAPONED

ARMENIA

ANCIENT NAME: MINNI
CAPITAL: ERIVAN
KING: ASHOT GAGIK TRDAT ZAREH DIKRAN
ARTAKIAS ARTASHES TIGRANES
ZARIADES
KINGDOM: URARTU VANNIC CILICIA
SOPHENE ARDSRUNI
LAKE: VAN SEVAN URMIA
MOUNTAIN: ARA ALAGEZ ARARAT
TAURUS ALADAGH ARAGATS
NATIVE: ARMEN GOMER
RIVER: KUR ARAS KURA ARAKS CYRUS

HALYS ZANGA ARAXES RAZDAN TIGRIS
EUPHRATES
TOWN: VAN SIVAS BITLIS EREVAN ERIVAN
ERZURUM TRABZON YEREVAN

ARMHOLE SCYE OXTER ARMSIZE
ARMISTICE LULL PEACE TRUCE
ARMOR
(AND SPECIFIC PIECES THEREOF)
BACK EGIS JAMB MAIL TACE BRACE
CULET GUIGE PLATE SCALE STEEL TASSE
ARMLET BEAVER CUISSE GORGET
GREAVE RONDEL SHIELD TASSET TUILLE
AILETTE CORSLET CUIRASS DEFENSE
EPAULET HAUBERK PALETTE ROUNDEL
VENTAIL BRASSARD PAULDRON
VAMBRACE
(— ON TREE) TROPHY
(— PLATE) TUILLE
(ELBOW —) CUBITIERE
(FOOT —) SABBATON SOLLERET
(HEAD —) CASQUE HELMET PALLET
SCONCE
(HORSE —) BARB BARD CRINET
CHAMFRON CRINIERE
(LEATHER —) CORIUM
(LEG —) BOOT JAMB CUISH CUISSE
GREAVE TUILLE JAMBEAU CHAUSSES
(NECK —) COLLAR GORGET
(PADDED —) GAMBESON
(SUIT OF —) CAST STAND
ARMOR-BEARER SQUIRE ARMIGER
CUSTREL
ARMORY ARSENAL
ARMPIT ALA OXTER AXILLA
ARMS AND THE MAN
(AUTHOR OF —) SHAW
(CHARACTER IN —) LOUKA RAINA
NICOLA PETKOFF SERGIUS CATHERINE
BLUNTSCHLI
ARMY HOST IMPI MAIN ARRAY CROWD
FORCE HORDE POWER RANKS COHORT
LEGION NUMBER THRONG TROOPS
MILITIA MILITARY
AROMA NOSE ODOR NIDOR SAVOR
SCENT SMELL SNUFF SPICE FLAVOR
BOUQUET PERFUME REDOLENCE
(— OF WINE) BLOOM
AROMATIC BALMY SPICY SWEET
ODOROUS PIQUANT PUNGENT FRAGRANT
REDOLENT
AROUND NEAR ABOUT CIRCA CIRCUM
ENVIRON
AROUSE CALL CITE HEAT MOVE REAR
SPUR STIR WAKE WHET ALARM ALERT
AWAKE EVOKE PIQUE RAISE RALLY
ROUSE ROUST SHAKE STEER WAKEN
ABRAID AWAKEN ELICIT EXCITE FOMENT
INCITE INDUCE KINDLE REVIVE SUMMON
ACTUATE AGITATE INCENSE INFLAME
INSPIRE PROVOKE
ARPEGGIO SWEEP ROULADE FLOURISH
ARRAIGN TRY CITE ARGUE ACCUSE
CHARGE IMPUTE INDICT SUMMON
IMPEACH
ARRANGE DO FIX LAY SET CAST FILE

FORM PLAN PLAT SIZE SORT TIER WORK
ADAPT AGREE ALIGN ALINE ARRAY
CURRY DRAPE DRESS FRAME GRADE
ORDER PITCH RANGE SCORE SHAPE
SHIFT SPACE STALL TRICK ADJUST
CODIFY DESIGN DEVISE FETTLE SETTLE
APPOINT CATALOG COLLATE COMPOSE
CONCERT DISPOSE MARSHAL PREPARE
CLASSIFY ORGANIZE REGULATE
TABULATE
(— FASTIDIOUSLY) PREEN
(— HAIR) SET TED COIF TRUSS
(— HARMONIOUSLY) GRADATE
(— IN FLOCKS) HIRSEL
(— IN FOLDS) DRAPE
(— IN LAYERS) DESS TIER
(— IN ROW) RACE
(— STRAW) HAULM
(— SYSTEMATICALLY) DIGEST
(— WITH BEST AT TOP) DEACON
ARRANGEMENT FIX LAY DEAL PLAT
RANK ARRAY DRAPE ORDER SETUP
DESIGN LAYOUT SCHEME SETOUT
SYSTEM POSTURE ATTITUDE DISPOSAL
GROUPING SEQUENCE
ARRANT BAD THIEF OUTLAW ROBBER
VAGRANT OUTRIGHT RASCALLY
ARRAS DRAPERY TAPESTRY
ARRAY FIG ARMY DECK DOLL GALA GARB
HOST POMP RANK ROBE VEST ADORN
ALIGN ALINE DRESS EQUIP HABIT ORDER
ATTIRE BEDECK CLOTHE DEVISE FETTLE
FINERY SETOUT APPAREL ARRANGE
COMPANY DISPLAY DISPOSE MARSHAL
ARREST COP FIX LAG NAB NIP VAG BALK
CURB FALL GLOM GRAB HALT HOLD JAIL
KEEP NAIL NICK PULL REST STAY STOP
ARRET CATCH CHECK DELAY PINCH
SEIZE STILL ATTACH BRIDLE COLLAR
DETAIN ENGAGE FINGER HINDER RETARD
THWART CAPTURE CUSTODY SUSPEND
IMPRISON OBSTRUCT RESTRAIN
ARRESTING BOLD SEIZING MAGNETIC
PLEASING STRIKING
ARRIVAL COMER VENUE ADVENT
COMING REACHING
ARRIVE GO COME FALL FLOW GAIN LAND
LIGHT OCCUR REACH WORTH ACCEDE
APPEAR ATTAIN HAPPEN OBTAIN
(— AT) GET HIT FIND GAIN HENT MAKE
BRING EDUCE FETCH GUESS SEIZE
ATTAIN DERIVE ESTIMATE
ARROGANCE PRIDE SWANK HUBRIS
BOBANCE CONCEIT DISDAIN EGOTISM
HAUTEUR BOLDNESS
ARROGANT BOLD COXY HIGH COCKY
GREAT HUFFY LOFTY PROUD SURLY
CHESTY FIERCE LORDLY UPPISH UPPITY
WANTON FORWARD FROSTED HAUGHTY
HAUTAIN HUFFISH POMPOUS STATELY
AFFECTED ASSUMING CAVALIER
IMPUDENT SUPERIOR
ARROGATE GRAB TAKE CLAIM SEIZE
USURP ASSUME
ARROW PIN ROD BOLT DART REED SHOT
BLUNT FLANE ROVER SHAFT FLIGHT

DOGBOLT MISSILE POINTER PROJECT
QUARREL SAGITTA
(FIRE —) MALLEOLUS
(PART OF —) TIP BUTT HEAD NOCK
PILE POINT SHAFT FEATHER FLETCHING
(POISONED —) DERRID SUMPIT
ARROWHEAD BUNT FORK HEAD PILE
FLUKE POINT
ARROWROOT PIA ARUM MUSA SAGU
ARARU CANNA TACCA TIKOR ARARAO
ARROWSMITH (AUTHOR OF —) LEWIS
(CHARACTER IN —) MAX ALMUS
JOYCE LEORA SILVA TERRY LANYON
MARTIN GUSTAVE WICKETT GOTTLIEB
SONDELIUS ARROWSMITH PICKERBAUGH
ARROYO DRAW BROOK CREEK GULCH
GULLY HONDO ZANJA RAVINE STREAM
CHANNEL
ARSENAL ARMORY SUPPLY MAGAZINE
ARSON FIRE CRIME FELONY BURNING
ART WILE CRAFT KNACK MAGIC SKILL
TRADE CALLING CUNNING DESCANT
FACULTY FINESSE MYSTERY SCIENCE
APTITUDE ARTIFICE BUSINESS LEARNING
PRACTICE
(— OF APPLYING TESTS) DOCIMASY
(— OF BLAZONING) ARMORY
(— OF CALCULATING) ALGORISM
ALGORITHM
(— OF FLOWER ARRANGEMENT)
IKEBANA
(— OF HORSEMANSHIP) MANEGE
(— OF PREPARING COLORS)
GUMPTION
(— OF SPEECH) RHETORIC
(— OF TYING KNOTS IN PATTERN)
MACRAME
(DIABOLIC —) DEVILRY DEVILTRY
(DRAMATIC —) STAGE
(JUNK —) NEODADA
(LEG —) CHEESECAKE
(MAGIC —) WITHCRAFT
(MYSTERIOUS —) CABALA KABALA
CABBALA KABBALA QABBALA
CABBALAH KABBALAH QABBALAH
(OCCULT —) THEURGY
ARTEMIS UPIS DELIA DIANA PHOEBE
CYNTHIA AMARYSIA
ARTERY WAY PATH ROAD AORTA PULSE
ROUTE COURSE RADIAL STREET VESSEL
CAROTID CONDUIT HIGHWAY SCIATIC
CERVICAL CORONARY
ARTFUL APT SLY FOXY WILY AGILE
PAWKY SUAVE ADROIT CLEVER CRAFTY
FACILE PRETTY QUAINT SCHEMY
SHREWD SMOOTH TRICKY CROOKED
CUNNING KNOWING POLITIC SUBTILE
VULPINE DEXTROUS SCHEMING
STEALTHY
ARTFULNESS CUNNING ARTIFICE
SUBTLETY
ARTHRITIS GOUT CARPITIS
ARTICLE A AN YE LOT ONE THE BOOK
ITEM TERM BRIEF ESSAY PAPER PIECE
PLANK POINT STORY THEME THING
CLAUSE DETAIL NOTICE OBJECT REPORT

FEATURE BROCHURE DOCTRINE
PARTICLE TREATISE
(— OF CLOTHING) DUD DIDO APRON
CLOUT DICKY FANCY THING CASUAL
DICKEY GARMENT COINTISE CREATION
(— OF FOOD) CATE KNACK
(— OF FURNITURE) STICK
(— OF LITTLE WORTH) DIDO
(— OF SILK) SQUEEZE
(— OF TRADE) PADNAG
(— OF UNUSUAL SIZE) IMPERIAL
(—S OF FAITH) CREDENDA
(—S OF MERCHANDISE) CHAFFER
(CAST-IRON —S) KENTLEDGE
(CHEAP —) CAMELOT
(DECORATIVE —) LACQUER
(FANCY —) CONCEIT
(FIVE —S) HAND
(GENUINE —) GOODS
(INFERIOR —S) SHODDY
(MISCELLANEOUS —S) SUNDRIES
(NONDESCRIPT —) DOODAD WHATNOT
(SECONDHAND —) JUNK
(SHOWY —) FRIPPERY
(VALUABLE —S) SWAG
(WORTHLESS —) TRANGAM
ARTICULATE JOIN CLEAR JOINT SPEAK
UNITE UTTER VOCAL ACCENT FLUENT
VERBAL EXPRESS JOINTED PHONATE
DISTINCT
ARTIFACT CELT DISC DISK BATON
HUACA BRONZE EOLITH GORGET RONDEL
SKEWER ABRADER SCRAPER
ARTIFICE ART GIN JET GAUD HOAX JOUK
PLAN PLOT RUSE TURN WILE BLIND
CHEAT CRAFT CROOK DODGE FEINT
FRAUD GUILE SHIFT SKILL STALL TRICK
DECEIT DEVICE CHICANE CUNNING
DODGERY EVASION FINESSE SHUFFLE
SLEIGHT COZENAGE DISGUISE INTRIGUE
MANEUVER PRETENSE TRICKERY
ARTIFICER WRIGHT ARTIFEX WORKMAN
DAEDALUS MECHANIC
ARTIFICIAL CUTE SHAM BOGUS DUMMY
FAKED FALSE ARTFUL ERSATZ FORGED
UNREAL ASSUMED BASTARD FEIGNED
PLASTIC AFFECTED POSTICHE SPURIOUS
ARTILLERY (OR PIECE THEREOF) ARMS
GUNS DRAKE SAKER CANNON MINION
HEAVIES LANTACA CANNONRY
ORDNANCE
ARTILLERYMAN GUNNER LASCAR
REDLEG ENGINEER
ARTISAN SMITH ARTIST COOPER
ARTIFEX WORKMAN MECHANIC
ARTIST (ALSO SEE PAINTER) DAB POET
ACTOR ADEPT BRUSH DANCER ETCHER
EXPERT MASTER SINGER WIZARD
ARTISAN ARTISTE ARTSMAN OPERANT
PAINTER SCHEMER ANIMATOR COLORIST
IDEALIST MAGICIAN MUSICIAN
SCULPTOR SKETCHER STIPPLER
PRIMITIVE
ARTISTIC DAEDAL EXPERT ESTHETIC
ARTLESS NAIF OPEN FRANK NAIVE PLAIN
SEELY CANDID RUSTIC SIMPLE GIRLISH
NATURAL INNOCENT

ARTY CHICHI
ARUM ARAD TARO AROID TUCKAHOE
AS SO FOR HOW QUA ALSO LIKE SOME
THAT THUS TILL WHEN EQUAL SINCE
WHILE BECAUSE EQUALLY SIMILAR
(— FAR AS) TO INTO
(— IT WERE) FAIRLY
(— LONG AS) SOBEIT
(— TO) QUOAD
(— WELL) EVEN
(— WELL AS) FORBY FORBYE
(— YET) HITHERTO
ASBESTOS XYLITE AMIANTH WOODROCK
ASCEND UP RISE SOAR UPGO ARISE
CLIMB MOUNT SCALE STAIR TOWER
ASPIRE CLIMAX UPRISE CLAMBER
ESCALATE PROGRESS
ASCENDANCY SWAY POWER CONTROL
MASTERY SUCCESS DOMINION PRESTIGE
ASCENT HILL RAMP RISE UPGO CLIMB
GLORY GRADE MOUNT RAISE SCEND
SLOPE STEEP STEPS UPWAY STAIRS
UPHILL UPRISE INCLINE UPGRADE
UPSWING EMINENCE GRADIENT
ASCERTAIN GET SEE SET TRY FEEL FIND
TELL COUNT GLEAN LEARN ATTAIN
FIGURE ANALYSE ANALYZE APPRISE
APPRIZE COMPUTE MEASURE UNEARTH
DISCOVER
ASCETIC NUN MONK SOFI SUFI YATI
YOGI DANDY FAKIR FRIAR SADHU SOFEE
STOIC YOGIN CHASTE ESSENE HERMIT
SADDHU SEVERE SOOFEE STRICT
ADAMITE AUSTERE BHIKSHU DEVOTEE
EREMITE RECLUSE SRAMANA STYLITE
TAPASVI AVADHUTA MARABOUT
NAZARITE SANNYASI
(PL.) THERAPEUTAE
ASCIDIAN POLYP CUNGEBOI CUNGEVOI
TETHYDAN TUNICATE
ASCIDIUM PITCHER VASCULUM
ASCOCARP ASCOMA
ASCOGONIUM ARCHICARP
ASCOMA CUPULE
ASCRIBABLE DUE
ASCRIBE LAY ARET EVEN GIVE APPLY
BLAME COUNT GUESS IMPLY INFER
PLACE REFER TITLE ACCUSE ALLEGE
ARETTE ASSIGN ATTACH CHARGE CREDIT
IMPUTE PREFER RECKON RELATE
ASCRIVE ENTITLE ACCREDIT ARROGATE
DEDICATE INSCRIBE INTITULE
ASCRIPTION LAUD CREDIT ADDITION
ASCUS BAG SAC THECA ASCELLUS
ASEA LOST ADDLED ADRIFT PUZZLED
SAILING CONFUSED
ASEMIA ASYMBOLIA
ASENATH (FATHER OF —) POTIPHERAH
(HUSBAND OF —) JOSEPH
(SON OF —) EPHRAIM MANASSEH
ASEXUAL AGAMIC AGAMOUS
(PREF.) AGAM(O)
ASH AS ALS ASE ASS FIG RON COKE
SORB ARTAR ASHEN EMBER FRAIN
ROWAN CINDER CORPSE DOTTEL DOTTLE
WICKEN CLINKER RESIDUE DOGBERRY
FRAXINUS HOOPWOOD WINETREE

(SILKY —) CEDAR
(PL.) ASE AXAN KELP SOIL ASHEN VAREC
WASTE BREEZE CINDERS PULVERIN
ASHAMED MEAN NACE NAIS ABASHED
HANGDOG HONTOUS SHAMEFACED
ASHBEL (FATHER OF —) BENJAMIN
ASH-BLOND CENDRE
ASH-COLORED CINEREAL CINEREOUS
ASHEN WAN GRAY GREY PALE WAXEN
WHITE PALLID GHASTLY BLANCHED
CINEREAL
ASHER (FATHER OF —) JACOB
(MOTHER OF —) ZILPAH
ASHES (— OF CREMATED BODY)
CREMAINS
(PREF.) CINE SPODO TEPHRA TEPHRO
ASHKENAZ (FATHER OF —) GOMER
ASHKOKO CONY DAMAN HYRAX
ASHLAR ASELAR RANGEWORK
ASHORE ACOST ALAND AGROUND
BEACHED STRANDED
ASHTAVAKRA (FATHER OF —)
KAHODA
ASHTRAY SPITKID SPITKIT
ASHUR FEROHER
(FATHER OF —) HEZRON
(MOTHER OF —) ABIAH
(WIFE OF —) HELAH
ASHVATH (FATHER OF —) JAPHLET
ASHWEED GOUTWEED
ASIA (FATHER OF —) OCEANUS
(HUSBAND OF —) IAPETUS
(MOTHER OF —) TETHYS
(SON OF —) ATLAS EPIMETHEUS
PROMETHEUS PROMETHUS
ASIDE BY BYE OFF AGEE AWAY GONE
NEAR PAST AGLEY ALOOF APART ASKEW
FORBY ASLANT ASTRAY BESIDE BEYOND
BYHAND FORBYE FORTHBY LATERAL
PRIVATE WHISPER OVERHAND RESERVED
SECRETLY SEPARATE SIDEWISE
OVERBOARD
ASININE DULL CRASS DENSE INEPT SILLY
ABSURD ASSISH OBTUSE SIMPLE STUPID
DOLTISH FATUOUS FOOLISH IDIOTIC
ASIUS (FATHER OF —) DYMAS
HYRTACUS
(SISTER OF —) HECUBA
(SLAYER OF —) AJAX IDOMENUS
ASK BEG SPY SUE FAND PRAY QUIZ
CLAIM CRAVE EXACT FRAYN PLEAD
QUERY SPEAK SPEER SPEIR SPELL SPERE
ADJURE DEMAND DESIRE EXAMIN
EXPECT FRAIST FRAYNE INVITE BESEECH
BESPEAK CONSULT ENTREAT IMPLORE
INQUIRE REQUEST REQUIRE SOLICIT
PETITION QUESTION
(— ALMS) CANT THIG
(— FOR) BEG BID CRY DUN LAIT SEEK
BESPEAK INQUIRE REQUEST
(— PAYMENT) CHARGE
ASKANCE AWRY ASKEW ASKILE
CROOKED SIDEWAYS
ASKEW CAM CAM AGEE ALOP AWRY AZEW
AGLEE AGLEY AMISS ATILT CRAZY GLEED
TIPSY ASKANT ASLANT ATWIST FLOOEY

SKEWED SKIVIE ASQUINT CROOKED
OBLIQUE BIASWISE COCKEYED SIDELING
ASKING ROGATION
ASLANT ASIDE SLOPE
(PREF.) PLAGI(O)
ASLEEP DEAD FAST IDLE LATENT
NUMBED DORMANT NAPPING
ASOCIAL EGREGIOUS
ASOKA (FATHER OF —) BINDUSARA
ASOPUS (DAUGHTER OF —) ORNIA
THEBE AEGINA ASOPIS CLEONE PIRENE
SINOPE CHALCIS CORCYRA SALAMIS
TANAGRA THESPEIA
(SON OF —) ISMENUS PELASGUS
(WIFE OF —) METOPE
ASP ESP ASPIC ASPIDE URAEUS
ASPAR (FATHER OF —) ARDABURIUS
ASPARAGUS LILY GRASS SPRUE
ASPERGE SPARAGE SPERAGE
(— GARNISH) PRINCESS
ASPATHA (FATHER OF —) HAMAN
ASPECT AIR HUE WAY AURA BROW FACE
HAND KIND LEER LOOK MIEN SIDE VIEW
VULT ANGLE COLOR DECIL FACET GUISE
IMAGE NORMA PHASE SIGHT STAGE
TRINE VIZOR DECILE FACIES
FIGURE GLANCE MANNER PHASIS
REGARD VISAGE APPAREL BEARING
ESSENCE FEATURE MALEFIC OUTLOOK
RESPECT RETRAIT SEXTILE SHOWING
SPECIES CARRIAGE CONSPECT
FOREHEAD OUTSIGHT PROSPECT
QUINTILE CHARACTER SEMBLANCE
(— OF CURVE) INSIDE
(— OF EMOTION) AFFECT
(— OF MOON) CRESCENT
(— OF MUSICAL NUANCES) AGOGICS
(BALEFUL —) DISASTER
(CULTURAL —) EMANATION
(DETERMINING —) HEART
(EXTERNAL —) PHYSIOGNOMY
(FACIAL —) EXPRESSION
(LANGUAGE —) DURATIVE
(PRIMARY —) HIGHWAY
(QUARTILE —) SQUARE
(SECONDARY —) BYWAY
ASPEN APS ASP ALAMO NITHER POPLAR
POPPLE QUAKER QUAKING TREMBLE
ASPER AKCHA AKCHEH OTHMANY
ASPERGILLUM HYSSOP SPRINKLE
STRINKLE
ASPERITY IRE RIGOR ACERBITY
ACRIMONY TARTNESS ANIMOSITY
ASPERSE SKIT SLUR SPOT ABUSE DECRY
LIBEL SPRAY DEFAME DEFILE MALIGN
REVILE SHOWER VILIFY APPEACH
BLACKEN DETRACT LAMPOON SLANDER
TARNISH TRADUCE BESMIRCH FORSPEAK
SPRINKLE
ASPERSION SLUR BAPTISM CALUMNY
INNUENDO
ASPHALT BREA PITCH SLIME FILLER
MANJAK BITUMEN CUTBACK MANJACK
BYERLITE UINTAITE
ASPHALTUM CONGO
ASPHODEL KNAVERY AFFODILL
ASPHYXIA APNEA APNOEA ACROTISM

ASPIC JELLY GELATIN GELATINE
LAVENDER
ASPIRATE ROUGH SPIRITUS
ASPIRATION GOAL IDEAL DESIRE RECOIL
SIGHTS AMBITION PRETENSION
ASPIRE AIM STY HOPE LONG MINT RISE
SEEK SOAR WISH ETTLE MOUNT TOWER
YEARN ASCEND ATTAIN DESIRE PRETEND
ASPIRING ASPIRANT
ASRIEL (FATHER OF —) GILEAD
ASS DOLT FOOL JADE KHUR MOKE BURRO
CHUMP CUDDY DICKY DUNCE EQUID
GUDDA HINNY CUDDIE DAPPLE DICKEY
DONKEY ONAGER ASINEGO ASSHEAD
JACKASS LONGEAR MALTESE SOLIPED
IMBECILE
(FEMALE —) JENNY JENNET
(MALE —S) JACKSTOCK
(WILD —) KIANG KULAN KYANG KIYANG
KOULAN ONAGER HEMIPPE CHIGETAI
GHORKHAR HEMIONUS
(PL.) JACKSTOCK
(PREF.) ONISCI ONO
ASSAI MANICOLE
ASSAIL WOO BEAT FRAY HOOT JUMP
PELT SAIL ASSAY BESET PRESS SHOCK
STONE WHACK WHANG ACCUSE ATTACK
BATTER BICKER BULLET HURTLE IMPUGN
INFEST INSULT INVADE MALIGN MOLEST
OFFEND OPPUGN RATTLE SAILYE SCATHE
STRIKE ASSAULT ATTEMPT BELABOR
BESEIGE BOMBARD CATCALL ENFORCE
ASSEMBLE BLUDGEON TOMAHAWK
ASSAILANT ONSETTER
ASSAM (MOUNTAIN OF —) JAPVO
(STATE OF —) KHASI MANIPUR
(TOWN OF —) IMPHAL SADIYA
GAUHATI SHILLONG
(TRIBE OF —) AO AKA AOR AHOM GARO
NAGA
ASSARACUS (BROTHER OF —) ILUS
GANYMEDE
(FATHER OF —) TROS
(MOTHER OF —) CALLIRRHOE
(SISTER OF —) CLEOPATRA
(SON OF —) CAPYS
ASSART SART THWAITE
ASSASSIN THAG THUG BRAVE BRAVO
FEDAI FIDAI CUTTLE FIDAWI KILLER
SLAYER RUFFIAN STABBER TORPEDO
HACKSTER MURDERER SICARIUS
ASSASSINATE KILL SLAY MURDER
REMOVE
ASSASSINATION THUGGEE
ASSAULT MUG BEAT BLOW COSH FRAY
RAID SLUG ABUSE ALARM ASSAY BRUNT
HARRY ONSET POISE POUND SHOCK
SMITE STORM STOUR VENUE AFFRAY
ALARUM ASSAIL ATTACK BREACH
BUFFET CHARGE ENGINE EXTENT
HOLDUP INSULT INVADE NAPALM
ONFALL STOUND STOUSH THRUST
YOKING ATTEMPT BOMBARD DESCENT
LAMBAST PURSUIT RUNNING VIOLATE
INVASION OUTBURST
ASSAY RUN SAY TRY TEST ESSAY PROOF

PROVE TOUCH TRIAL ASSAIL ATTACK
EFFORT ANALYZE ATTEMPT EXAMINE
TASTING ANALYSIS APPRAISE ENDEAVOR
ESTIMATE HARDSHIP

ASSAYER POTDAR TESTER

ASSAYING DOCIMASY

ASSEMBLAGE ARMY BODY CAMP CLOT
COMA CREW HERD HOST MASS PACK
RUCK BUNCH COURT CROWD DRIFT
DROVE FLOCK GROUP LEVEE POSSE
QUIRE SALON SWARM CONVOY THRONG
CLUSTER COMPANY COMPLEX SOCIETY
ASSEMBLY CONGRESS PARLIAMENT
(— OF FOSSILS) COLONY
(— OF INTEGERS) IDEAL
(CONFUSED —) FARRAGO

ASSEMBLE FIT LAY BULK CALL HERD
HOST KNOT MASS MEET AMASS FLOCK
PIECE RALLY TROOP UNITE COUPLE
GATHER HUDDLE MUSTER COLLECT
COMPILE CONVENE CONVOKE
CONGREGATE

ASSEMBLY SUM BEVY DIET DUMA FEIS
RAAD AGORA BOGEY BOULE COURT
COVEN CURIA FORUM GROUP JUNTA
LEVEE PARTY PRESS SYNOD TROOP
AENACH ASSIZE GEMOTE MAJLIS
PARADE POWWOW SENATE CHAMBER
CHAPTER COLLEGE COMITIA COMPANY
CONSORT CONVENT COUNCIL FOLKMOT
HUSTING LANDTAG MEETING SESSION
SOCIETY AUDIENCE CONCLAVE
CONGRESS TRIBUNAL
(— OF BLESSED) HEAVEN
(— OF ELDERS) KGOTLA
(— OF WITCHES) COVEN SABBATH
(AFTERNOON —) LEVEE
(BOY SCOUT —) JAMBOREE
(CLOSED —) CONCLAVE

ASSENT AYE BOW NOD YEA YES AMEN
SEAL ADMIT AGREE GRANT YIELD
ACCEDE ACCEPT ACCORD COMPLY
CONCUR SUBMIT APPROVE CONCEDE
CONFESS CONFORM CONSENT
SANCTION SUFFRAGE

ASSERT BRAG SHOW VOICE AFFIRM
ALLEGE ASSURE AVOUCH DEFEND
DEPONE DEPOSE UPHOLD ADVANCE
CONFIRM CONTEND DECLARE PROTEST
SUPPORT ADVOCATE CHAMPION
MAINTAIN

ASSERTION VOW FACT CLAIM VOUCH
AVERMENT
(— OF MASCULINITY) MACHISMO
(BOASTFUL —) JACTATION
(DUBIOUS —) PLINYISM

ASSERTIVE BRASH DOGMATIC POSITIVE

ASSESS TAX CESS DOOM LEVY SCOT
TOLL AGIST PRICE STENT VALUE CHARGE
SAMPLE MEASURE APPRAISE ESTIMATE

ASSESSMENT FEE TAX CESS DUTY LEVY
SCOT TOLL PRICE RATAL TITHE WORTH
IMPOST PURVEY SURTAX TARIFF
TAXATION

ASSESSOR JUDGE RATER CESSOR
AUDITOR STENTOR TAXATOR

ASSETS GOODS MEANS MONEY STOCK

CREDIT WEALTH CAPITAL EFFECTS
ACCOUNTS PROPERTY RESOURCE

ASSEVERATE SAY VOW AVER AVOW
STATE SWEAR AFFIRM ALLEGE ASSERT
ASSURE DECLARE PROTEST

ASSEVERATION VOW OATH

ASSIDUOUS BUSY ACTIVE DEVOTED
STUDIED DILIGENT SEDULOUS STUDIOUS

ASSIGN FIX PUT SET CAST CEDE DEAL
DOLE GIVE METE RATE ALLOT ALLOW
APPLY AWARD ENDOW REFER SHIFT
ADDUCE ALLEGE ATTACH CHARGE
CONVEY DESIGN DIRECT ENTAIL ORDAIN
APPOINT ASCRIBE CONSIGN DISPOSE
ENTITLE SPECIFY ALLOCATE DELEGATE
TRANSFER

ASSIGNATION DATE MEET TRYST
MEETING

ASSIGNMENT DUTY TASK CHORE GRIND
STINT LESSON HOMEWORK PLACEMENT

ASSIMILATE MIX FUSE ADAPT ALTER
BLEND LEARN MERGE ABSORB DIGEST
CONCOCT

ASSIST AID ABET BACK HELP JOIN AVAIL
BOOST COACH FAVOR NURSE SERVE
SPEED ESCORT PROMPT SECOND SQUIRE
SUCCOR BENEFIT COMFORT FURTHER
RELIEVE SUPPORT SUSTAIN

ASSOCIATE MIX PAL AIDE ALLY BAND
CHUM HERD JOIN LINK MATE PEER YOKE
BLEND BUDDY CRONY MATCH TROOP
ATTACH ATTEND COHORT COUSIN
FASTEN FELLOW FRIEND HELPER
HOBNOB MEMBER MINGLE RELATE
ADJUNCT BRACKET COMMUNE
COMPANY COMPEER COMRADE
CONNECT CONSORT PARTNER CONFRERE
FAMILIAR FEDERATE FOLLOWER
INTIMATE

ASSOCIATION BODY BUND CLUB HUNT
TONG ARTEL BOARD GUILD HANSA
UNION CARTEL COMITY GRANGE LEAGUE
LEGION LYCEUM SCHOLA VEREIN
CIRCUIT COMPANY CONSORT CONTACT
CONVENT COUNCIL SOCIETY SOROSIS
AFFINITY ALLIANCE ASSEMBLY
INTIMACY SODALITY ORGANIZATION
(— OF FOSSILS) FAUNULE
(ANTAGONISTIC —) ANTIBIOSIS
(BOOK-SELLERS' —) CONGER
(CLOSE —) HARNESS INTIMACY
(EMPLOYERS' —) GREMIO
(FARMERS' —) GRANGE
(IN —) ALONG
(LABOR —) ARTEL UNION
(RELIGIOUS —) SAMAJ
(SECRET —) CABAL
(STUDENTS' —) CORPS
(SYMBIOTIC —) ACAROPHILY

ASSORT BOLT CULL SUIT WINNOW
(— COINS) SHROFF

ASSORTMENT BAG LOT SET OLIO
BATCH BUNCH GROUP SUITE RAGBAG
MIXTURE
(— OF TYPE) BILL FONT

ASSUAGE CALM EASE ABATE ALLAY
DELAY SALVE SLAKE STILL LENIFY

LESSEN MODIFY PACIFY QUENCH
REDUCE SOFTEN SOLACE SOOTHE
TEMPER APPEASE COMFORT MOLLIFY
QUALIFY RELIEVE SATISFY DIMINISH
MITIGATE MODERATE

ASSUME DON PUT BEAR DARE GIVE
MASK SHAM TAKE ADOPT ANNEX CLOAK
FEIGN GUESS INFER USURP ACCEPT
AFFECT CLOTHE FIGURE BELIEVE
PREMISE PRESUME PRETEND RECEIVE
SUPPOSE SURMISE SIMULATE
PERSONATE

ASSUMED ALIAS FALSE GIVEN FEIGNED
AFFECTED BORROWED

ASSUMING LOFTY UPPITY AFFECTED
ARROGANT SUPERIOR

ASSUMPTION THESIS FICTION SURMISE
PRETENSE PRESUMPTION

ASSURANCE FACE GALL BRASS CHEEK
FAITH NERVE TRUST APLOMB BELIEF
CREDIT COURAGE PROMISE WARRANT
AUDACITY BOLDNESS COOLNESS
SECURITY

ASSURE AVER TELL CINCH VOUCH
ASSERT AVOUCH ENSURE INSURE
PLEDGE SECURE CERTIFY CONFIRM
DECLARE HEARTEN PROMISE PROTEST
WARRANT CONVINCE PERSUADE

ASSURED BOLD CALM COLD FIRM PERT
SURE FACILE SECURE CERTAIN POSITIVE

ASSUREDLY AMEN SOON INDEED
SICCAR SURELY VERILY HARDILY

ASTER ARNICA COCASH AMELLUS
BEEWEED BONESET CYTASTER
MONASTER STARWORT STOKESIA

ASTERISK MARK STAR ASTERISM
WINDMILL

ASTERN AFT BAFT HIND REAR ABAFT
APOOP BEHIND BACKWARD

ASTEROID EROS HEBE IRIS JUNO CERES
DIONE FLORA IRENE METIS VESTA
ASTREA EGERIA EUROPA HYGEIA PALLAS
PLANET PSYCHE THALIA THEMIS THETIS
ELECTRA EUNOMIA FORTUNA LUTETIA
CALLIOPE MASSALIA PLANTOID
STARFISH STARLIKE VICTORIA

ASTHMA PHTHISIC

ASTHMATIC PURSY WHEEZY PANTING
PUFFING

ASTIR UP AGOG ABOUT AFOOT ALERT
GOING ACTIVE AROUND MOVING
ROUSED EXCITED STIRRING VIGILANT

ASTONISH AWE DAZE AMAZE KNOCK
SHOCK MARVEL ASTOUND IMPRESS
STARTLE BEWILDER CONFOUND
SURPRISE

ASTONISHING AMAZING FABULOUS
MARVELOUS

ASTONISHMENT DISMAY MARVEL
WONDER SURPRISE

ASTOUND BEAT STUN ABASH AMAZE
SHOCK APPALL STAGGER STUPEFY
TERRIFY ASTONISH CONFOUND
SURPRISE

ASTOUNDING STUNNING

ASTRAEA (FATHER OF —) ZEUS
JUPITER

(MOTHER OF —) THEMIS
(SISTER OF —) PUDICITIA

ASTRAL REMOTE STARRY STELLAR
SIDEREAL STARLIKE

ASTRAY AWRY LOST AGLEY AMISS
ASIDE WRONG ABROAD AFIELD ERRANT
ERRING FAULTY DEVIOUS FORLORN
SINNING MISTAKEN

ASTRIDE ATOP ABOARD SPANNING

ASTRINGENT ACID ALUM SOUR TART
ACERB HARSH ROUGH STERN MASTIC
PONTIC SEVERE TANNIN AUSTERE
BINDING CATECHU PUCKERY RHATANY
STYPTIC

ASTROLOGY STARCRAFT

ASTRONOMICAL FAR HUGE GREAT
URANIC DISTANT IMMENSE COLOSSAL
INFINITE

ASTUTE SLY FOXY KEEN WILY ACUTE
CANNY QUICK SHARP SMART CLEVER
CRAFTY NASUTE SHREWD CUNNING
KNOWING SKILLED

ASUNDER APART SPLIT ATWAIN SUNDRY
DIVIDED DIVORCED

ASYLUM ARK HOME JAIL COVER GRITH
HAVEN BEDLAM HARBOR REFUGE
ALSATIA COLLEGE HOSPICE RETREAT
SHELTER BUGHOUSE MADHOUSE
NUTHOUSE

ASYMMETRIC PEDIAL

AS YOU LIKE IT (AUTHOR OF —)
SHAKESPEARE
(CHARACTER IN —) ADAM CELIA
CORIN PHEBE AMIENS AUDREY DENNIS
JAQUES LEBEAU OLIVER CHARLES
MARTEXT ORLANDO SILVIUS WILLIAM
ROSALIND FREDERICK TOUCHSTONE

AT BY IN TO TIL TILL UNTO THERE HEREAT
(— ALL) ANY EER EVER HALF OUGHT
SOEVER HOWEVER

ATALANTA (CHARACTER IN —)
MERCURY ATALANTA MELEAGER
(COMPOSER OF —) HANDEL
(FATHER OF —) IASUS
(HUSBAND OF —) MELANION
HIPPOMENES
(MOTHER OF —) CLYMENE

ATAMAN CHIEF JUDGE HETMAN
HEADMAN

ATAVISM REVERSION

ATELIER SHOP STUDIO BOTTEGA
WORKSHOP

ATES SWEETSOP

ATHALIAH (FATHER OF —) AHAB
(HUSBAND OF —) JEHORAM
(MOTHER OF —) JEZEBEL

ATHEIST ZENDIK DOUBTER INFIDEL
NASTIKA AGNOSTIC

ATHENA ALEA AUGE NIKE ALERA AREIA
ERGANE HIPPIA HYGEIA ITONIA PALLAS
POLIAS AIANTIS MINERVA APATURIA

ATHENIAN ATTIC CHORAGUS

ATHLETE PRO BLUE JOCK STAR BOXER
COLOR CRACK CUTEY CUTIE TURNER
ACROBAT AMATEUR GYMNAST TUMBLER
GAMESTER WRESTLER PENTATHLETE

ATHLETIC AGILE BURLY LUSTY VITAL

BRAWNY GYMNIC ROBUST SINEWY
STRONG MUSCULAR POWERFUL
VIGOROUS

ATHLETICS GAMES SPORT EXERCISE

ATHWART CROSS ABOARD ACROSS
ASLANT OBLIQUE SIDEWISE TRAVERSE

ATLAS BOOK LIST MAPS TOME TITAN
TELAMON MAINSTAY
(DAUGHTERS OF —) ATLANTIDES
(FATHER OF —) IAPETUS
(MOTHER OF —) CLYMENE
(WIFE OF —) PLEIONE

ATMOSPHERE AIR SKY AURA FEEL LIFT
MOOD TONE AROMA CLIME DECOR
ETHER PLACE SMELL NIMBUS SPHERE
WELKIN FEELING AMBIENCE
(— OF DISCOURAGEMENT) CHILL
(CHARACTERISTIC —) VIBE
(NOXIOUS —) MIASMA
(SECTION OF —) SOLENOID
(SENSED —) KARMA
(STALE —) FROUST FROWST
(STUFFY —) FUG
(SUFFOCATING —) STIFLE

ATMOSPHERIC AERIAL

ATMOSPHERICS STATIC SPHERICS

ATOM ACE BIT ION JOT IOTA MITE MOTE
WHIT ATOMY HENAD MONAD SHADE
SPECK TINGE HEPTAD TETRAD BODIKIN
ISOTOPE NUCLIDE RADICAL MOLECULE
PARTICLE CORPUSCLE SCINTILLA

ATOMIC TINY MINUTE NUCLEAR

ATOMIZE PULVERIZE

ATOMIZER SPRAY SCENTER SPRAYER
AIRBRUSH ODORATOR PERFUMER

ATONE AGREE AMEND ACCORD ANSWER
RANSOM REDEEM REPENT APPEASE
EXPIATE RESTORE SATISFY

ATONEMENT MEND RANSOM MICHTAM
PENANCE SATISFACTION

ATREUS (BROTHER OF —) THYESTES
(FATHER OF —) PELOPS
(HALF-BROTHER OF —) THYESTES
(MOTHER OF —) HIPPODAMIA
(SON OF —) MENELAUS
(WIFE OF —) AEROPE

ATRIP AWEIGH

ATRIUM HALL COURT CAVITY AURICLE
CHAMBER PASSAGE

ATROCIOUS BAD DARK RANK VILE
AWFUL BLACK CRUEL GROSS BRUTAL
ODIOUS SAVAGE WICKED HEINOUS
UNGODLY VIOLENT FLAGRANT GRIEVOUS
HORRIBLE TERRIBLE MONSTROUS

ATROPHY RUST STUNT TABES MACIES
SHRINK STARVE WITHER WASTING
STULTIFY

ATTACH ADD FIX PUT SET SEW TAG TIE
BIND BOLT GLUE HANG JOIN LINK SPAN
TAKE WELD ADOPT AFFIX ANNEX CLING
HINGE HITCH LATCH PASTE SCREW
STICK UNITE ADHERE ADJOIN APPEND
ARREST CEMENT DEVOTE ENGAGE
ENTAIL FASTEN ASCRIBE CONNECT
ESPOUSE SUBJOIN

ATTACHED FAST FOND ADNATE DOTING
ADJUNCT SESSILE

ATTACHMENT ARM GAG BAIL DRUM
FLAY HEAD LOVE SHIM SHOE AMOUR
CHUCK CRUSH FENCE GUARD AFFAIR
BINDER BUMPER DOODAD DREDGE
FETISH HEMMER LAPPET MARKER
PICKUP SHIELD SIDING ADAPTOR
CREASER DROPPER FITTING HOLDING
JOINTER SPANNER DEVOTION FASTNESS
FIXATION FONDNESS

ATTACK FIT HIT HOP MUG SIC BAIT
BOMB BOUT CLAW COSH DINT FRAY
GANG HOOK JUMP PANG RAID RISE
RUSH TURN WADE ABUSE ALARM BESET
BLAST BLITZ BOARD BRUNT CHECK
DRIVE FIGHT FLUSH FORAY FORCE
HARRY ICTUS ONSET SALLY SMITE
SPASM SPELL STORM ACCUSE ACTION
AFFRAY ASSAIL BATTLE BICKER CHARGE
CRISIS INDICT INFEST INSULT INVADE
OFFEND ONRUSH POUNCE RUFFLE
SHOWER SORTIE STRIKE STROKE TACKLE
TAKING THRUST AGGRESS ASPERSE
ASSAULT BARRAGE BELABOR BESEIGE
BOMBARD CENSURE CRUSADE OFFENSE
POTSHOT SEIZURE PAROXYSM SKIRMISH
SURPRISE OFFENSIVE
(— IN COCKFIGHT) SHUFFLE
(— OF ILLNESS) GO DWALM ACCESS
(— OF SICKNESS) WHIP SEIZURE
(— TO ROB) THUG
(— WITH SHOUTS) HUE
(— WITH WORDS) STOUSH
(— ZEALOUSLY) CRUSADE
(BOMBING —) PRANG
(CHESS —) FORK
(CRITICAL —) SLATING
(FENCING —) GLIDE
(LIGHT —) TOUCH
(NIGHT —) CAMISADO
(SLIGHT —) WAFF
(SUDDEN —) ICTUS RAPTUS SURPRISE
(SUICIDAL —) KAMIKAZE
(SURPRISE —) ALARM ALARUM
(VERBAL —) FIRE BLUDGEON

ATTACKER AGGRESSOR OFFENDANT

ATTAIN GO GET HIT WIN COME EARN
GAIN RISE ARISE CATCH COVER FETCH
PROVE REACH TOUCH ACCEDE AMOUNT
ARRIVE ASPIRE EFFECT OBTAIN SECURE
ACHIEVE ACQUIRE PROCURE SUCCEED
OVERTAKE

ATTAR OIL OTTO ESSENCE PERFUME

ATTEMPT GO PUT SAY SHY TRY BOUT
DARE DASH HACK JUMP MIND SEEK
SHOT SLAP STAB WAGE WORK ASSAY
BEGIN ESSAY ETTLE FLING FRAME OFFER
ONSET PRESS PROOF PROVE START
TEMPT TRIAL WHACK EFFORT STRIVE
PRETEND PROFFER VENTURE CONATION
ENDEAVOR EXERTION

ATTEND GO SEE HEAR HEED LIST MIND
OYES OYEZ STAY TEND WAIT APPLY
AUDIT AWAIT GUARD NURSE SERVE
TREAT VISIT WATCH ASSIST ESCORT
FOLLOW HARKEN LISTEN SECOND
SHADOW SQUIRE CONDUCT CONSORT

ESQUIRE HEARKEN PERPEND ACCOMPANY
(— A LADY) WAIT
(— FUNERAL) FOLLOW
(— REGULARLY) KEEP
(— TO) MIND TREAT FETTLE INTEND
(— UPON) TENT CHASE CHAPERON

ATTENDANCE GATE NUMBER REGARD PRESENCE

ATTENDANT BOY LAD JACK MAID PAGE PEON ZANY CADDY COMES GROOM GUIDE USHER VALET CADDIE EMILIA ESCORT FRIEND GILLIE JAEGER MINION PORTER SQUIRE VARLET WAITER YEOMAN FOOTBOY LINKMAN ORDERLY PAGEBOY SERVANT FOLLOWER HANDMAID HENCHMAN HOUSEMAN MINISTER MYRMIDON
(— OF CYBELE) CORYBANT
(CROSSING —) GATEMAN
(KNIGHT'S —) SWAIN CUSTREL ESQUIRE
(PALACE —) BOSTANGI
(PROCTOR'S —) BULLDOG
(YOUNG —) BOY LAD JACK PAGE KNIGHT
(PL.) MEINY STAFF CORTEGE RETINUE

ATTENTION EAR CARE HEED HIST MARK MIND NOTE COURT GUARD STUDY DETAIL FAVORS NOTICE REGARD ACCOUNT ACHTUNG ADDRESS HEARING RESPECT THOUGHT AUDIENCE
(— TO PETTY ITEMS) MICROLOGY
(AMOROUS —) GALLANTRY
(FIXED —) DHARANA
(FLATTERING —) HOMAGE
(PLEASING —) INCENSE
(SPECIAL —) ACCENT

ATTENTIVE WARY ALERT AWAKE CIVIL CLOSE SHARP INTENT POLITE CAREFUL GALLANT HEEDFUL LISTFUL MINDFUL PRESENT DILIGENT OBEDIENT STUDIOUS THOUGHTY VIGILANT WATCHFUL
(— TO) IMMINENT

ATTENUATE SAP DRAW FINE THIN WATER DILUTE LESSEN RAREFY REDUCE WEAKEN SLENDER DECREASE DIMINISH EMACIATE ENFEEBLE TAPERING

ATTENUATED GAUNT AERIAL DILUTED SPINDLY FINESPUN SMORZATO

ATTENUATION LOSS

ATTEST CHOP SEAL SIGN PROVE STATE SWEAR VOUCH ADJURE AFFIRM INVOKE RECORD CERTIFY CONFESS CONFIRM CONSIGN TESTIFY WARRANT WITNESS EVIDENCE INDICATE MANIFEST

ATTESTATION VOUCH DOCKET RECORD

ATTESTED SWORN CERTIFIED

ATTIC LOFT CELER SOLAR GARRET TALLET GRENIER COCKLOFT

ATTILA (BROTHER OF —) BLEDA
(CHARACTER IN —) LEO EZIO ATTILA FORESTO ODABELLA
(COMPOSER OF —) VERDI
(FATHER OF —) MUNDZUK
(WIFE OF —) HILDA ILDICO

ATTIRE (ALSO SEE DRESS) BUSK SUIT TIRE ADORN ARRAY DRESS HABIT ENROBE PLIGHT TOILET ADDRESS APPAREL DUBBING PANOPLY ACCOUTER EQUIPAGE FEATHERS
(EPISCOPAL —) PONTIFICAL
(FORMAL —) BALLDRESS
(SHINING —) SHEEN

ATTITUDE AIR CUE SET BIAS MIEN MOOD POSE SIDE ANGLE FRAME HEART PHASE SHAPE SHELL SIGHT SLANT STAND ACTION ANIMUS ASPECT MANNER SPIRIT STANCE BEARING FEELING GESTURE POSTURE STATION STOMACH BEHAVIOR CROTCHET HABITUDE POSITION
(— OF HUNTING DOG) POINT
(PREVAILING —) STREAM

ATTORNEY DOER AGENT AVOUE PROXY DEPUTY FACTOR LAWYER LEGIST MUKTAR SYNDIC VAKEEL PROCTOR ADVOCATE PROSECUTOR

ATTRACT BAIT CALL DRAW LURE PULL WIND BRING CATCH CHARM COURT FETCH TEMPT ALLURE ATTACH ENGAGE ENLIST ENTICE GATHER INVITE SEDUCE STRIKE BEWITCH PROCURE INTEREST MAGNETIZE
(— FISH) CHUM

ATTRACTION BAIT CALL CARD DRAW PULL CHARM DRAFT FAVOR SPELL APPEAL DESIRE MAGNET COITION DRAUGHT GRAVITY ADHESION AFFINITY COHESION CONTRACT PENCHANT SIDESHOW WITCHERY

ATTRACTIVE BRAW CHIC CUTE FAIR FOXY GOOD NICE BONNY DISHY FATAL JOLLY NIFTY SWEET COMELY FLASHY FRUITY LOVELY PRETTY SAVORY SNAZZY TAKING TRICKY AMIABLE CIRCEAN CUNNING EYEABLE EYESOME GRADELY LIKABLE WINNING WINSOME ALLURING CHARMING ENGAGING ENTICING FEATURED FETCHING GRACEFUL GRACIOUS HANDSOME INVITING SPECIOUS TEMPTING VENEREAN PERSONABLE
(— TO OPPOSITE SEX) EPIGAMIC
(FALSELY —) MERETRICIOUS
(NOT —) FOUL INCURIOUS
(STRIKINGLY —) ZINGY

ATTRACTIVENESS CHARM GRACE LOOKS BEAUTY GLAMOR AMENITY GLITTER AFFINITY

ATTRIBUTABLE DUE

ATTRIBUTE OWE PUT GIVE MARK SIGN TYPE ALLOT BADGE BLAME CHARM PLACE POWER REFER ALLEGE ALLUDE ARRECT ASSERT ASSIGN BESTOW CHARGE CREDIT IMPUTE PREFER REPUTE SYMBOL ADJUNCT APANAGE ASCRIBE COUNTER ESSENCE PERTAIN QUALITY ACCREDIT APPANAGE ARROGATE GRANDITY INTITULE PROPERTY PROPRIUM STRENGTH
(— WRONGFULLY) FOIST
(—S OF ROCKS) GEOLOGY
(PL.) SARIRA SHARIRA

ATTRIBUTION ACCENT THEORY ANIMISM ETIOLOGY

ATTRITION WEAR GRIEF REGRET SORROW ANGUISH ABRASION BLASTING FRICTION

ATTUNE KEY TUNE ADAPT AGREE ACCORD ADJUST TEMPER PREPARE

ATUA AKUA DEMON SPIRIT

ATYPICAL BIZARRE ABERRANT GROTESQUE

AUBADE ALBA

AUBERGE INN ALBERGO

AUBERGINE EGGPLANT

AUBURN ABRAM BLOND CACHA CUTCH BLONDE CACHOU CATECHU GOREVAN TULIPWOOD

AU COURANT CONTEMPORARY

AUCTION CANT ROUP SALE VEND COKER TRADE BARTER BRIDGE HAMMER OUTCRY TROVER VENDUE OUTROOP UNCTION DISPOSAL KNOCKOUT

AUCTIONEER CRIER CRYER OUTCRIER

AUDACIOUS BOLD BRASH BRAVE HARDY SAUCY AUDACE BRAZEN CHEEKY DARING FORWARD ARROGANT FEARLESS IMPUDENT INSOLENT INTREPID SPIRITED BAREFACED
(NOT —) CIVIL

AUDACITY CHEEK NERVE COURAGE BOLDNESS TEMERITY PRESUMPTION

AUDIBLE RIFE ALOUD CLEAR HEARD AUTOMATIC

AUDIENCE EAR PIT FANS AUDIT COURT FLOOR HOUSE PUBLIC GALLERY HEARING ASSEMBLY AUDITORY TRIBUNAL

AUDIT SCAN CHECK PROBE RECKON VERIFY ACCOUNT EXAMINE INQUIRE INSPECT ESTIMATE

AUDITION HEARING

AUDITOR CENSOR HEARER APPOSER PITTITE DISCIPLE LISTENER

AUDITORIUM HALL ROOM CAVEA FRONT ODEUM THEATER AUDITORY

AUDITORY ORAL OTIC AURAL AUDILE ACOUSTIC AUDITIVE

AUGER BIT POD BORE BORER GRILL GIMLET WIMBLE PIERCER TEREBRA

AUGHT CIPHER NAUGHT WORTHY NOTHING VALIANT ANYTHING

AUGMENT ADD EKE FEED GROW HELP URGE BOOST EXALT SWELL APPEND DILATE EXPAND EXTEND AMPLIFY BALLOON ENHANCE ENLARGE IMPROVE INFLAME MAGNIFY COMPOUND HEIGHTEN INCREASE MULTIPLY

AUGMENTED SHARP EXTREME

AUGUR BODE OMEN SEER AUSPEX DIVINE BETOKEN FORESEE PORTEND PREDICT PRESAGE PROMISE PROPHET SIGNIFY FOREBODE FORESHOW FORETELL FOREWARN INDICATE PROPHESY

AUGURY OMEN SIGN SOOTH TOKEN RITUAL AUSPICE HANDSEL PRESAGE

AUGUST AWFUL GRAND NOBLE KINGLY SERENE SOLEMN EXALTED STATELY IMPOSING MAJESTIC

AUK FALK LOOM ARRIE DIVER MURRE NODDY SCOUT MARROT PUFFIN DOVEKIE PENGUIN PYGOPOD WILLOCK GAREFOWL ROCKBIRD RAZORBILL

AUNT TIA BAWD AUNTY NAUNT TANTA TANTE AUNTIE GOSSIP

AURA AIR HALO ODOR PUFF AROMA SAVOR SMELL BREEZE ESSENCE FEELING (CHARACTERISTIC —) VIBE (SENSED —) KARMA

AURAL OTIC

AUREATE GOLDEN ORNATE ROCOCO YELLOW

AUREOLE HALO CROWN GLORY LIGHT AREOLA CORONA GLORIA NIMBUS VESICA

AUROCHS TUR UROX URUS BISON WISENT BONASUS

AURORA EOS DAWN DRAPERY MORNING

AURORA BOREALIS DANCERS STREAMERS

AUSPICE CARE OMEN SIGN AUGURY PORTENT GUIDANCE
(PL.) EGIS AEGIS

AUSPICIOUS FAIR GOOD WHITE BRIGHT CHANCY DEXTER FAVORING PROPITIOUS PROSPEROUS

AUSTERE BARE COLD HARD SOUR BLEAK GRAVE GRUFF HARSH RIGID ROUGH SHARP STERN STIFF BITTER CHASTE FORMAL RUGGED SEVERE SIMPLE SOMBER STRICT SULLEN ASCETIC CRABBED EARNEST SERIOUS GRANITIC RIGOROUS PURITANICAL

AUSTERITY RIGOR CATOISM RIGORISM SIMPLICITY

AUSTRALIA

ABORIGINE: MYALL
CAPE: HOWE
CAPITAL: CANBERRA
COIN: DUMP POUND SHILLING
DESERT: GIBSON TANAMI SIMPSON
HARBOR: DARWIN BRISBANE FREMANTLE MELBOURNE NEWCASTLE
LAKE: EYRE COWAN FROME BARLEE BULLOO LEFROY AMADEUS BLANCHE EVERARD GREGORY TORRENS GAIRDNER
LANGUAGE: YABBER
MEASURE: SAUM
MOUNTAIN: OLGA BRUCE LEGGE CRADLE GARNET GAWLER MAGNET STUART BONGONG GREGORY WILHELM KOSCIUSKO
MOUNTAIN RANGE: DARLING FLINDERS
NATIVE: ABO MARA BINGE AUSSIE DIGGER BILLIJIM WARRAGAL
PENINSULA: EYRE
RIVER: DALY SWAN BULLO COMET FINKE ISAAC PAROO ROPER SNOWY YARRA BARCOO BARWON CULGOA DAWSON DEGREY DARLING FITZROY LACHLAN STAATEN WARREGO BURDEKIN FLINDERS GEORGINA VICTORIA
SEA: CORAL TIMOR TASMAN ARAFURA

SOLDIER: DIGGER SWADDY BILLIJIM
STATE: TASMANIA VICTORIA
   QUEENSLAND
STRAIT: TORRES
TOWN: AYR YASS DUBBO PERTH WAGGA
   ALBURY AUBURN CAIRNS CASINO
   COBURG DARWIN HOBART MACKAY
   SYDNEY BENDIGO GEELONG KOGARAH
   MILDURA MITCHAM ADELAIDE BRISBANE
   ESSENDON RANDWICK RINGWOOD
   MELBOURNE TOOWOOMBA

AUSTRALIAN ANZAC AUSSIE DIGGER
   AUSTRAL KANGAROO WARRAGAL

AUSTRIA

ANCIENT PEOPLE: HUNS AVARS
   RAETIANS SLOVENES BAVARIANS
CAPITAL: WIEN VIENNA
COIN: DUCAT KRONE FLORIN HELLER
   ZEHNER GROSCHEN SCHILLING
LAKE: ALMSEE FERTOTO MONDSEE
   BODENSEE TRAUNSEE CONSTANCE
   NEUSIEDLER
MEASURE: FASS FUSS JOCH MASS MUTH
   YOKE HALBE LINIE MEILE METZE PFIFF
   PUNKT ACHTEL BECHER SEIDEL DLAFTER
   VIERTEL DREILING
MOUNTAIN: STUBAI EISENERZ RHATIKON
   KITZBUHEL
NATIVE: STYRIAN TYROLEAN
PASS: LOIBL ARLBERG BRENNER PLOCKEN
PROVINCE: TIROL TYROL STYRIA VIENNA
   SALZBURG CARINTHIA VORARLBERG
RIVER: INN MUR DRAU ENNS KAMP LECH
   MURZ RAAB DONAU MARCH SALZA
   THAYA TRAUN DANUBE SALZACH
TOWN: ENNS GRAZ LECH LINZ RIED WELS
   WIEN GMUND LIENZ STEYR TRAUN
   LEOBEN VIENNA BREGENZ MODLING
   SPITTAL VILLACH DORNBIRN SALZBURG
   INNSBRUCK
WATERFALL: KRIMML GASTEIN GOLLING
WEIGHT: MARC SAUM UNZE DENAT
   KARCH PFUND STEIN CENTNER PFENNIG
   VIERLING

AUTHENTIC PURE REAL SURE TRUE
   EXACT PUCCA RIGHT VALID ACTUAL
   DINKUM PROPER CORRECT GENUINE
   SINCERE CREDIBLE OFFICIAL ORIGINAL
   RELIABLE
AUTHENTICATE SEAL PROVE VOUCH
   ATTEST SIGNET VERIFY APPROVE
   CONFIRM LEGALIZE
AUTHOR DOER JUDE SIRE JUDAS MAKER
   RULER AUCTOR FACTOR FORGER PARENT
   PENMAN SCRIBE SOURCE WRITER
   ANCIENT CLASSIC CREATOR ELOHIST
   FOUNDER ANCESTOR BEGETTER
   COMPILER COMPOSER IDEALIST
   IMMORTAL INVENTOR JEHOVIST
   ORIGINAL PAYYETAN PRODUCER
   (BAD —) BLOTTER

AUTHORITATIVE GRAVE CLASSIC
   OFFICIAL ORACULAR POSITIVE
   TEXTUARY MAGISTERIAL
AUTHORITY LAW ROD SEE BALL RULE
   SWAY BOARD FAITH POWER RIGHT
   STAMP SWING TITLE ARTIST AUTHOR
   CREDIT EMPERY EXPERT FASCES PUNDIT
   REGENT REGIME WEIGHT COMMAND
   CONTROL DYNASTY FACULTY LEADING
   LICENSE SCEPTER WARRANT DISPOSAL
   DOMINION DOMINIUM HEGEMONY
   LORDSHIP PRESTIGE SANCTION
   STRENGTH
   (— OF SWITZERLAND) BUNDESRAT
   (ARBITRARY —) ABOVE
   (MORAL —) MANA
   (ONE HIGHEST IN —) SUPREMO
   (ROYAL —) SCEPTRE SOVRANTY
   (SPIRITUAL —) KEYS KHILAFAT
   (SUPREME —) SAY SIRCAR
   (TEACHING —) MAGISTERIUM
   (UNLIMITED —) AUTOCRACY
   (PL.) ISNAD SIRCAR
AUTHORIZATION FIAT BERAT
   PASSPORT SANCTION WARRANTY
   PERMISSION
AUTHORIZE LET VEST ALLOW CLEAR
   CLOTHE PERMIT RATIFY APPROVE
   EMPOWER ENDORSE ENTITLE INDORSE
   JUSTIFY LICENSE WARRANT ACCREDIT
   DELEGATE LEGALIZE SANCTION
AUTHORIZED LEGAL OFFICIAL
AUTO (ALSO SEE AUTOMOBILE) CRATE
   CHUMMY LIZZIE
AUTOBIOGRAPHY VITA MEMOIR
AUTOCRACY MONARCHY
AUTOCRAT CHAM CZAR TSAR TZAR
   MOGUL CAESAR DESPOT AUTARCH
   MONARCH DICTATOR MONOCRAT
AUTOCRATIC ABSOLUTE
AUTOGRAPH NAME SIGN MANUAL
   INSCRIBE
AUTOMATIC REFLEX MACHINE
   MECHANICAL
AUTOMATON GOLEM ROBOT AUTOMA
   ANDROID MACHINE
AUTOMOBILE BUG BUS CAR SIX AUTO
   FOUR HEAP JEEP PONY TRAP BUGGY
   COACH COUPE CRATE EIGHT PONEY
   RACER SEDAN BUCKET CHUMMY
   CUSTOM JALOPY JUNKER SALOON
   WHEELS AUTOCAR COMPACT FLIVVER
   HACKNEY HARDTOP MACHINE MINICAR
   PHAETON STEAMER TORPEDO VOITURE
   CARRYALL DRAGSTER ELECTRIC
   ROADSTER SQUADROL SUBURBAN
   VICTORIA HATCHBACK NOTCHBACK
   (CONVERTIBLE —) DROPHEAD
   (DEMONSTRATOR —) DEMO
   (MIDGET —) DOODLEBUG
   (NOISY —) BANGER
   (SMALL —) MINI
AUTONOMOUS FREE SEPARATE
AUTONOMY SOVEREIGNTY
   SEPARATENESS
AUTOPSY NECROPSY

AUTUMN FALL KHARIF FALLTIME
MATURITY

AUXILIARY SUB AIDE ALLY AIDING
BRANCH HELPER ABETTOR ADJUNCT
HELPING PARTNER ADJUTANT
ANCILLARY PERIPHERAL
(PL.) FOEDERATI

AVAIL DO AID USE BOOT HELP SERVE
SKILL STEAD VALUE MOMENT PROFIT
BENEFIT PREVAIL SERVICE SUCCEED
SUFFICE UTILIZE
(— ONESELF) EMBRACE IMPROVE
SUBSERVE

AVAILABLE FIT FREE OPEN FLUSH
HANDY LOOSE READY PATENT USABLE
PRESENT VISIBLE

AVALANCHE SLIDE LAWINE VOLLENGE

AVARICE GREED MAMMON MISERY
AVIDITY CUPIDITY RAPACITY

AVARICIOUS CLOSE GREEDY HAVING
HUNGRY SORDID STINGY GRIPING
ITCHING MISERLY COVETOUS GRASPING

AVATAR BALARAMA EPIPHANY

AVENGE REPAY RIGHT VISIT WRACK
WREAK PUNISH REQUITE REVENGE
SATISFY CHASTISE

AVENGER KANAIMA NEMESIS WREAKER

AVENUE RUE WAY GATE MALL PIKE
ROAD ALLEE ALLEY DRIVE ENTRY
ACCESS ARCADE ARTERY RIDING STREET
AVENIDA OPENING PASSAGE

AVER SAY CLAIM PROVE STATE SWEAR
AFFIRM ALLEGE ASSERT ASSURE
AVOUCH DEPOSE VERIFY DECLARE
JUSTIFY PROFESS PROTEST

AVERAGE PAR SUM DUTY FAIR MEAN
NORM RULE SOSO RATIO USUAL VALUE
CHARGE MEDIAL MEDIAN MEDIUM
MIDDLE NORMAL TARIFF ESTIMATE
MEDIOCRE MIDDLING MODERATE
ORDINARY STANDARD

AVERSE LOTH BALKY LOATH AFRAID
ADVERSE AGAINST OPPOSED BACKWARD
INIMICAL OPPOSITE PERVERSE
RELUCTANT

AVERSION HATE ODIUM ENMITY HATRED
HORROR PHOBIA REGRET DISDAIN
DISGUST DISLIKE MISLIKE DISTASTE

AVERT WRY BEND FEND MOVE SHUN
TURN WARD AVOID DETER DODGE
EVADE PARRY SHEER TWIST DEFRAY
DIVERT RETARD SHIELD DEFLECT
EXPIATE PREVENT ALIENATE

AVIARY CAGE HOUSE VOLARY ORNITHON

AVIATOR ACE FLIER FLYER PILOT
AIRMAN ICARUS BIRDMAN LUFBERY
SOLOIST

AVID AGOG KEEN WARM EAGER ARDENT
GREEDY HUNGRY JEJUNE ANXIOUS
ATHIRST CRAVING LONGING THIRSTY
DESIROUS GRASPING

AVIDITY AVARICE CUPIDITY

AVIFAUNA BIRDS ORNIS BIRDLIFE

AVOCET TILTER YELPER SCOOPER

AVOID FLY SHY BALK FLEE MISS PASS
QUIT SAVE SHUN VOID ABHOR AVERT
BURKE DITCH DODGE ELUDE EVADE

FEIGN HEDGE PARRY SHIFT SHIRK SKIRT
SLACK SPARE START ABJURE BYPASS
DETOUR ESCAPE ESCHEW REFUTE
REMOVE VACATE ABSTAIN DECLINE
FORBEAR FORSAKE REFRAIN
(— A PUNCH) SLIP
(— COMMITMENT) FUDGE
(— EXPENSE) HELP MISS SKIVE
(— OVERWORKING) FAVOR
(— RESPONSIBILITY) BLUDGE
(— SUPERHIGHWAY) SHUNPIKE

AVOIDANCE DODGE OUTLET EVASION
ESCHEWAL
(— OF RISK) CAUTION

AVOUCH AVER ASSERT

AVOW OWN BIND ADMIT STATE AFFIRM
ASSERT AVOUCH DEPONE DEPOSE
DEVOTE CONFESS DECLARE JUSTIFY
PROFESS MAINTAIN

AVOWAL OATH WORD PROTEST

AVOWED FRANK SWORN STATED
DECLARED

AWAIT BIDE HEED KEEP PEND STAY TEND
WAIT ABIDE TARRY WATCH ATTEND
EXPECT IMPEND REMAIN WAYLAY

AWAKE STIR WAKE ALERT ALIVE AWARE
ROUSE ACTIVE AROUSE AWAKEN EXCITE
CAREFUL HEEDFUL STARTLE VIGILANT

AWAKEN STIR AROUSE BESTIR EXCITE
KINDLE

AWAKENING REVIVAL WAKEFUL

AWARD GIVE KUDO ALLOT GRANT
MEDAL PRICE PRIZE ACCORD ADDEEM
ASSIGN BESTOW BOUNTY CONFER
DECIDE ADJUDGE APPOINT CONSIGN
CUSTODY KEEPING ACCOLADE
SENTENCE
(MOVIE —) OSCAR
(RADIO OR TELEVISION —) CLIO
(RECORDING —) GRAMMIE
(THEATER —) OBIE
(THEATRICAL —) TONY
(WRITING —) HUGO
(PL.) DESERTS

AWARE HEP SURE WARY WISE ALERT
ALIVE AWAKE KNOWING MINDFUL
APPRISED INFORMED SENSIBLE
SENTIENT VIGILANT WATCHFUL

AWARENESS EAR FEEL SENSE FEELING
INSIGHT COGNITION SENSATION
PERCEPTION

AWAY BY TO FRO OFF OUT VIA WAY
AFAR GONE PAST SCAT YOND ALONG
APART ASIDE FORTH HENCE ABROAD
ABSENT BEGONE ONWARD THENCE
DISTANT
(— FROM) DOWN WITH ALONE ALOOF
APART BESIDE
(— FROM HOME) AFIELD OUTLAND
(— FROM PORT) AFLOAT
(FARTHER —) BEYOND

AWE COW FEAR AMAZE DAUNT DREAD
SCARE FRIGHT HORROR REGARD TERROR
WONDER BUFFALO RESPECT ASTONISH
BEWILDER OVERCOME

AWE-INSPIRING GODFUL SOLEMN

AWESOME RELIGIO FEARSOME OLYMPIAN
AWESOME EERY FELL HOLY AWFUL EERIE WEIRD SOLEMN DREADED GHOSTLY
AWFUL DIRE FINE UGLY DREAD GHAST AUGUST HORRID AWESOME FEARFUL HIDEOUS SATANIC DREADFUL SHOCKING TERRIBLE
AWFULLY AWFUL FIERCE
AWKWARD UNCO FALSE FUDGY GAWKY INAPT INEPT SPLAY STIFF CLUMSY GAUCHE RUSTIC STICKY THUMBY UNEASY WOODEN ADVERSE BOORISH CUBBISH FROWARD HALTING LOUTISH LUMPISH STILTED UNCANNY UNCOUTH UNHANDY UNREADY BUNGLING CLOWNISH FECKLESS LUBBERLY PERVERSE UNGAINLY UNTOWARD UNWIELDY MALADROIT
(NOT —) FACILE
AWL BROD BROG NAIL PROD BROACH DRIVER ELSHIN FIBULA GIMLET SCRIBER
AWN EAR BARB BEAK PILE ARISTA BRISTLE
(— OF BARLEY) HORN
(— OF OATS) JAG JAGG
(PL.) BEARD
AWNED BARBATE
AWNING TILT BLIND SHADE VELUM CANOPY TIENDA SUNBLIND SUNSHADE VELARIUM
AWRY CAM WRY AGEE BIAS SKEW AGLEY AMISS ASKEW SNAFU WONKY WRONG ACROSS ASKANCE ASQUINT ATHWART CROOKED OBLIQUE PERVERSE
AX ADZ AXE ADZE BIFACE POLEAX BROADAX CHOPPER CLEAVER HATCHET PULASKI TWIBILL FRANCISC PALSTAVE SUNDERER TOMAHAWK
(DOUBLE —) LABRYS
(HEADSMAN'S —) MANNAIA
(MASON'S —) CAVEL
(PART OF —) EAR EYE BUTT FACE HAFT HEAD POLL BLADE HELVE HANDLE
(WOODEN —) MACANA
AXIAL VENTRAL
AXIL ALA
AXILLA AXIS ARMPIT SHOULDER
AXIOM SAW ADAGE MAXIM MOTTO BYWORD DICTUM SAYING TRUISM PRECEPT PROVERB APHORISM APOTHEGM POSTULATE
AXIOMATIC PRIMITIVE
AXIS NUT AXLE STEM ARBOR HINGE STALK CAUDEX CENTER CHITRA RACHIS SPINDLE SYMPODE TENDRIL AXLETREE
AXLE BAR COD PIN AXIS ARBOR BOGIE SHAFT SLEEVE MANDREL SPINDLE SUCCULA
AXOLOTL SIREDON
AXON PROCESS
AYE AY PRO YEA YES EVER ALWAYS ASSENT FOREVER
AZALEA ERICA MINERVA CARDINAL
AZIMUTH ZN ARC BEARING
AZTEC MEXICAN TENOCHCA
AZURE BICE BLUE JOVE COBALT JOVIAL JUPITER CERULEAN SAPPHIRE

B

B BEE BAKER BRAVO
(— FLAT) ZA BEMOL
BAA MAA BLEAT
BABBITT PHILISTINE
(AUTHOR OF —) LEWIS
(CHARACTER IN —) TED MYRA PAUL
TANIS ZILLA GEORGE VERONA BABBITT
JUDIQUE REISLING
BABBLE CHAT GASH KNAP PURL CLACK
PRATE CACKLE DITHER GABBLE GAGGLE
GOSSIP JANGLE MURMUR PALTER PIFFLE
RABBLE TUMULT BLABBER BLATHER
BLUSTER CHATTER CLATTER PRATTLE
SMATTER TWADDLE
BABEL DIN MEDLEY TUMULT CHARIVARI
CONFUSION
BABOON APE DRILL ADONIS BAVIAN
CHACMA GIRRIT BABUINA MANDRILL
HAMADRYAD
BABUSHKA SCARF KERCHIEF
BABY BABE CHAP DOLL JOEY TOTO
WEAN BAIRN CHILD HUMOR SPOIL
CODDLE FONDLE INFANT MOPPET
PAMPER PUPPET SQUALL BAMBINO
INDULGE PAPOOSE PREEMIE
BABY CARRIAGE PRAM BUGGY WAGON
GOCART STROLLER PERAMBULATOR
BABYISH TIDDY PULING SIMPLE PUERILE
CHILDISH
BABYLONIA CHALDEA
BACCHANAL DEVOTEE REVELER
CAROUSER
BACCHANTE FROW MAENAD
BACCHUS LIBER LYAEUS BROMIUS
DIONYSUS
(AUNT OF —) INO
(FATHER OF —) ZEUS JUPITER
(MOTHER OF —) SEMELE
BACHELOR BACH GARCON WANTER
BENEDICT CELIBATE
BACILLUS GERM VIRUS MICROBE
BACK AID FRO ABET HIND NAPE REAR
TAIL AGAIN BROAD CHINE NOTUM SPINE
SPLAT STERN VOUCH ASSIST DORSUM
RETRAL SECOND SOOTHE UPHOLD
VERIFY ENDORSE FINANCE POSTERN
SPONSOR SUPPORT SUSTAIN FULLBACK
HALFBACK MAINTAIN
(— A ROWBOAT) STERN
(— OF ANIMAL) RIG TERGUM
(— OF ARCHERY TARGET) BOSS
(— OF BOOK) DORSE SPINE
(— OF BULL) ROOF
(— OF HAND) OPISTHENAR
(— OF HEAD) NODDLE NIDDICK
OCCIPUT
(— OF INSECT) NOTUM
(— OF NECK) NAPE NUQUE SCRUFF

(— OF PAGE) FV
(— OUT) BEG JIB DUCK FLUNK
CRAWFISH
(— TO BACK) ADDORSED
(— UP) ABET VERIFY
BACKACHE NOTALGIA
BACKBITING CATTY DETRACTION
BACKBONE BACK GRIT GUTS CHINE
NERVE PLUCK RIDGE SPINE METTLE
SPIRIT GRISTLE STAMINA VERTEBRA
(— OF FISH) GRATE
BACKCOUNTRY BUSH STICKS BOONIES
BACKLAND BACKVELD BOONDOCKS
BACKFIELD SECONDARY
BACKFIRE BOOMERANG
BACKGAMMON IRISH LURCH TABLE
FAYLES GAMMON TABLES TICKTACK
VERQUERE
(— MAN) BLOT TABLEMAN
BACKGROUND REAR GROUND OFFING
LINEAGE SETTING BACKDROP DISTANCE
EXTERIOR OFFSCAPE TRAINING
EDUCATION
(— OF FLOWERS) BOCAGE
(MUSICAL —) SUPPORT
BACKHANDED AWKWARD
BACKING AID EGIS AEGIS BACKUP
BEHIND LINING MUSLIN SUPPORT
FINANCING
BACKLOG RESERVE SURPLUS
BACKSLIDE FALL LAPSE DESERT REVERT
RELAPSE
BACKSPIN DRAG UNDERCUT UNDERSPIN
BACKSTITCH PURL
BACKSTOP BUTT
BACK TALK LIP SASS
BACKWARD FRO LAX YON DARK DULL
LOTH INAPT LOATH AVERSE AVERSE
BYGONE POSTIC RETRAD RETRAL STUPID
ARRIERE BASHFUL LAGGARD LAGGING
REVERSE UPSTAGE DILATORY IGNORANT
PERVERSE REARWARD RINKYDINK
TAILFIRST
BACKWATER EBB COVE BAYOU SHEAVE
SLOUGH RETRACT RETREAT BACKWASH
BILLABONG
BACKWOODSMAN HICK WOODSY
BUCKSKIN HILLBILLY
BACON PIG BARD MEAT PORK PRIZE
SPECK FLITCH GAMMON RUSTIC
SAWNEY GAMBONE SOWBELLY
BACTERIUM ROD COLI GERM AEROBE
COCCUS CYTODE ANTHRAX CHOLERA
MICROBE PROTEUS SARCINA VIBRION
BACILLUS LISTERIA PATHOGEN
BOTULINUS CYTOPHAGA HEMOPHILE
INFECTANT INFECTION SPIRILLUM
BAD DUD ILL SAD EVIL HARD LEWD POOR
PUNK SICK SOUR VILE LOUSY NASTY

SORRY WEARY WORST WRONG ARRANT
FAULTY ROTTEN SEVERE SHREWD
SINFUL UNKIND WICKED BALEFUL
BANEFUL CHRONIC CORRUPT FEARFUL
HARMFUL HEINOUS HURTFUL IMMORAL
INUTILE NAUGHTY SPOILED TAINTED
UNLUCKY UNSOUND VICIOUS ANNOYING
CRIMINAL DEPRAVED DOGGEREL
FIENDISH FLAGRANT INFERIOR SINISTER
UNSUITED
(OUTRAGEOUSLY —) GRIEVOUS
(OUTSTANDINGLY —) ARRANT
PIACULAR
(RATHER —) INDIFFERENT
(VERY —) ALMIGHTY EXECRABLE
BADGE PIN BLUE MARK SIGN STAR
COLOR CREST CROSS FAVOR HONOR
ORDER PATCH TOKEN WINGS BUTTON
EMBLEM ENSIGN FASCES GARTER GIGLIO
PLAQUE SHIELD SYMBOL CHEVRON
EPAULET FEATHER BRASSARD INSIGNIA
SCAPULAR VERNICLE EPAULETTE
(JAPANESE —) MON KIRIMON
(RUSSIAN —) ZNAK
BADGER NAG GRAY GREY GRIS ANNOY
BRACE BROCK BRUSH HURON RATEL
TEASE WORRY BAUSON BOTHER HAGGLE
HARASS HECKLE MELINE PESTER TELEDU
WOMBAT GRISARD TORMENT
(AUSTRALIAN —) WOMBAT
(COMPANY OF —S) CETE
(LIKE A —) MELINE
BADINAGE FOOL CHAFF BANTER
RAILLERY TRIFLING
BADMINTON POONA
BADNESS MALICE PRAVITY UNVALUE
EVILNESS
BAD-TEMPERED FOUL ANGRY STINGY
CRABBED GROUCHY
BAFFLE FOX GET BALK BEAT FOIL LICK
MATE POSE STOP UNDO CHEAT CHECK
ELUDE EVADE STICK STUMP BOGGLE
DEFEAT DELUDE OUTWIT PUZZLE RESIST
THWART BUFFALO CONFUSE DECEIVE
QUIBBLE BEWILDER CONFOUND
BAG BUCK KIT MAT NET PAD POD POT SAC
CELL DRAG GRIP LOBE MAIL POCK POKE
SACK TOOT TRAP WOMB BELLY BOUGE
BULSE CATCH DILLY HUSSY POUCH
PURSE SCRIP SEIZE SNARE STEAL
BLOUSE CAVITY ENTRAP MATAPI
POCKET POUNCE SACHET SEABAG
VALISE WALLET ALFORJA BALLOON
BEANBAG BLISTER BUCKRAM CANTINA
CAPCASE CAPTURE CUSHION GAMEBAG
GOMUKHI HANDBAG HOLDALL RETICLE
SANDBAG SATCHEL TRAVOIS CARRYALL
ENVELOPE FOLLICLE KNAPSACK
MONEYBAG OVERSLIP POCHETTE
RETICULE RUCKSACK SUITCASE
WINESKIN WEEKENDER
(— BULGING) SWAG
(— FOR LETTERS) MAIL POUCH
KAREETA MAILBAG POSTBAG
(— FOR TOOLS) WALLET
(— OF ANISEED) DRAG
(— WITH POCKETS) TIDE TIDY

(AUSTRALIAN —) SWAG DILLI SHIRT
SHAMMY
(GAS —) CELL
(GRAB —) FISHPOND
(HAWSE —) JACKASS
(LEATHER —) JAG ASKOS BUDGE
MUSSUK
(NET —) SNOOD GARLAND
(SEWING —) HUSSY
(SLEEPING —) FUMBA FLEABAG
SLEEPER
BAGATELLE TRUNK VERSE CANNON
TRIFLE NOTHING
BAGEL ROLL BIALY
BAGGAGE ARMS GEAR MINX SWAG
CUTTY STUFF TRASH WENCH HARLOT
REFUSE TRASHY TRUNKS CLOTHES
DUNNAGE EFFECTS PLUNDER RUBBISH
SUMPTER VALISES
BAGGY LOOSE POCKY PURSY FLABBY
PUFFED SACCATE
BAGNIO BAIN BATH PRISON BROTHEL
HOTHOUSE
BAGPIPE MUSE PIPE PIVA DRONE TITTY
BIGNOU MUSETTE PIFFERO SAMBUKE
DULCIMER ZAMPOGNA CORNEMUSE
SYMPHONIA
(PART OF —) BAG CORD PIPE DRONE
MOUNT STOCK TASSEL CHANTER
WINDBAG BLOWPIPE
BAGUETTE CHAPLET
BAIL BOW DIP HOOP LADE LAVE RING
RYND YOKE LADLE SCOOP THROW
BUCKET HANDLE PLEDGE SECURE
SURETY VADIUM CAUTION CUSTODY
DELIVER RELEASE REPLEVY SECURITY
GUARANTEE
(— OUT) ABANDON
BAILIFF FOUD GRAB HIND AGENT REEVE
SAFFO SCULT STAFF BEADLE DEPUTY
FACTOR GRIEVE PORTER SCHOUT
VARLET BUMTRAP GRIPPER PROVOST
PUTTOCK SHERIFF STEWARD HUISSIER
OVERSEER TIPSTAFF CATCHPOLL
CONSTABLE
BAILIWICK AREA FIELD DOMAIN OFFICE
PROVINCE
BAIT BOB BOG COG DAP LUG BITE CAST CHUM
FEED HALT HANK LURE PLUG TAIL
DECOY HOUND SHACK SLATE
SQUID STALE TEMPT TRAIN WORRY
ALLURE ATTACK BADGER ENTICE
HARASS HECKLE HECTOR PROVOKE
TORMENT
(— FOR BIRDS) SHRAP
(— FOR COD) CAPELIN
(GREASY —) ROGUE
(GROUND —) BERLEY
(MAGGOT —) GENTLE
(SCENTED —) DRAG
BAKE DRY BURN COCT COOK FIRE BATCH
BROIL GRILL PARCH ROAST ANNEAL
HARDEN BISCUIT PISTATE SCALLOP
CLAMBAKE ESCALLOP
(— EGGS) SHIRR
(— THOROUGHLY) SOAK

BAKER OVEN FIRER BAXTER BURNER
FURNACE ROASTER
BALANCE BEAM EVEN REST SWAY TRIM
COVER POISE SCALE WEIGH ADJUST
CANCEL EQUATE KELVIN KILTER OFFSET
SANITY SQUARE LIBRATE OVERRUN
RESIDUE EQUALITY EQUALIZE EQUATION
SERENITY PROPORTION
BALANCED EVEN EQUAL LEVEL APOISE
KITTLE WEIGHED COMPLETE QUADRATE
TOGETHER
BALCONY ORIEL PORCH STOOP CIRCLE
GAZEBO PIAZZA PODIUM SOLLAR
BALAGAN GALLERY MIRADOR PERGOLA
TERRACE BRATTICE CANTORIA
VERANDAH MEZZANINE
BALD RAW BARE BASE BOLD CRUDE
NAKED PLAIN CALLOW PALTRY PEELED
PILLED SIMPLE EPILOSE LITERAL
POLLARD GLABROUS HAIRLESS
TONSURED
BALDERDASH ROT GUFF PUNK TRASH
TRIPE DRIVEL JARGON FLUBDUB
NONSENSE RIGMAROLE
BALDNESS ACOMIA CALVITY ALOPECIA
ATRICHIA OPHIASIS CALVITIES
BALDRIC BELT LACE GIRDLE ZODIAC
BALTEUS SUPPORT NECKLACE
BALE NO NOT WOE EVIL FIRE HARM PYRE
BLOCK CRATE DEATH BALLOT BUNDLE
SEROON SORROW PACKAGE SARPLER
BALEARIC ISLANDS (ISLAND OF —)
IBIZA CABRERA MAJORCA MINORCA
CONEJERA
(MEASURE OF —) PALMO MISURA
QUARTA QUARTIN BARCELLA
(TOWN OF —) IBIZA MAHON PALMA
(WEIGHT OF —) CARGO CORTA
QUARTANO
BALEEN WHALEBONE
BALEFUL BAD EVIL DEADLY MALIGN
SULLEN MALEFIC NOXIOUS RUINOUS
SINISTER WRETCHED MALEFICENT
BALI (CAPITAL OF —) DENPASAR
(DANCE OF —) ARDJA BARIS KRISS
BARONG KETJAK MONKEY DJANGER
(MOUNTAIN OF —) AGOENG
(MUSICAL INSTRUMENT OF —)
GAMELAN
(RICE FIELD OF —) SAWAII
(STRAIT OF —) LOMBOK
(TOWN OF —) SINGARADJA
BALK GAG HEN JIB SHY BEAM BILK BUCK
FOIL LICK MISS OMIT PROP SHUN SKIP
SLIP STAY STOP AVOID BLOCK CHECK
CLAMP DEMUR HUNCH MOUND REBEL
RIDGE STAKE STICK WAVER BAFFLE
DEFEAT FALTER HINDER IMPEDE OUTWIT
REFUSE STRAIN THWART BLUNDER
BALL BAL BAL FLY HOP NOB ORB PEA
TOY BEAD BOWL CLEW CLUE KNOB
KNOP KNUR PICK PILL POME PROM TRAP
DANCE EDGER FAULT FLOAT GLOBE
GLOME HURLY ORBIT PEARL PUPPY
SHAPE SNACK SPORT TRUCK BULLET
BUTTON HOOKER HURLEY MOONIE
MUDDLE PEELEE PELLET PELOTA

POMMEL POMPON RONDEL RUNDLE
SPHERE SQUASH BALLOON CONFUSE
FLOATER GLOBULE INCURVE INSHOOT
KNAPPAN LEATHER MANDREL PELOTON
RIDOTTO SLITTER ASSEMBLY BASEBALL
BISCAYEN FANDANGO FOOTBALL
GROUNDER HANDBALL QUENELLE
SOFTBALL SPHEROID TRAPBALL
(— AS SHIP'S SIGNAL) SHAPE
(— FOR MUSKET) GOLI SLUG
(— OF CLAY) KNICKER
(— OF RICE OR MEAT) PINDA
(— OF THREAD) COP CLEW CLUE GOME
BOTTOM COPPIN WHARROW
(— OF THUMB) THENAR CUSHION
(— OF WASTE IRON) COBBLE
(— USED IN SHINTY) PEG
(—S OF MEDICI FAMILY) PALLE
(BILLIARD —) SPOT IVORY SNOOKER
(BOWLED —) TICE CURVE SKYER
BAILER BUMPER FIZZER GOOGLY KICKER
POODLE SEAMER YORKER CREEPER
SNORTER SPINNER BREAKBACK
CROSSOVER INSWINGER
(BOWLING —) DODO JACK
(CORK —) PLUMBER
(CRICKET —) SNICK SHOOTER
(DECORATIVE —) DRAGEE
(FIVES —) SNACK
(GOLF —) PUTTY
(HARD —) SNUG
(HOCKEY —) NUN NUR ORR
(INK —) PUMPET
(MEAT —S) CECILS
(SKITTLE —) CHEESE
(TENNIS —) PALM
(WOODEN —) KNUR
BALLAD JIG LAY LILT POEM SONG CAROL
DERRY FANCY BALLET CARVAL SONNET
CANZONE CORRIDO GWERZIOU
SINGSONG
BALLAST BED CRIB LOAD TRIM POISE
STONE BOTTOM BURDEN GRAVEL
WEIGHT BALANCE SANDBAG
BALLET BALLAD MASQUE BOURREE
PANTOMIME
(— MOVEMENT) VOLE TEMPS APLOMB
OUVERT POINTE RELEVE RETIRE
ALLONGE ARRONDI ASSEMBLE ATTITUDE
ARABESQUE
BALLOON BAG BALL BLIMP EXPAND
GASBAG AIRSHIP DISTEND DRACHEN
INFLATE SAUSAGE SKYHOOK AEROSTAT
ENVELOPE DIRIGIBLE
(TRIAL —) KITE
BALLOT BALE POLL VOTE PROXY VOICE
BILLET CHOICE POLICY TICKET
SUFFRAGE
BALLROOM SALOON
BALLYHOO BALLY HOOPLA
BALM OIL DAUB SALVE ANOINT BALSAM
EMBALM LOTION RELIEF SOLACE
SOOTHE ANODYNE COMFORT PERFUME
UNGUENT OINTMENT
(— OF GILEAD) CANADA OPOBALSAM
BALMY MILD SOFT BLAND MOONY
SUNNY SWEET GENTLE SERENE HEALING

LENIENT AROMATIC BALSAMIC DRESSING FRAGRANT SOOTHING
BALONEY BUNK HOOEY BUSHWAH
BALSAM RIGA TOLU UMIRI COPALM GURJUN STORAX COPAIBA AMPALAYA BDELLIUM
BALSAM FIR SAPIN BAUMIER
BALTIC (— GULF) RIGA DANZIG BOTHNIA FINLAND
(— ISLAND) AERO DAGO FARO OSEL ALAND ALSEN OESEL OLAND GOTLAND HIIUMAA BORNHOLM
(— PORT) KIEL RIGA MEMEL REVAL DANZIG GDANSK TALINN LEIPAJA
(— RIVER) ODER ODRA DVINA VIADUA
(— TOWN) MEMEL DANZIG GDANSK LEIPAJA
BALUSTER SPOKE BANISTER COLUMELLA
BALUSTRADE PARAPET RAILING BALCONET BANISTER
BAMBOO DHA CANE REED BATAK GLUMAL GUADUA TONKIN BATAKAN WHANGEE
(— SACRED) NANDIN
(— WOVEN) SAWALI
BAMBOOZLE DUPE HAVE CHEAT COZEN GRILL CAJOLE HUMBUG BUFFALO DECEIVE DEFRAUD MYSTIFY PERPLEX
BAN BAR TABU VETO BLOCK CURSE EDICT ORDER TABOO BANISH CENSOR ENJOIN FORBID HINDER INVOKE NOTICE OUTLAW CONDEMN EXCLUDE ANATHEMA DENOUNCE EXECRATE PROHIBIT
(— ON NEWS) BLACKOUT
BANAL FLAT CORNY INANE SILLY STALE TRITE VAPID JEJUNE INSIPID MUNDANE TRIVIAL
BANANA MUSA SABA ENSETE FINGER SAGING LACATAN PLATANO SUNBEAM PLANTAIN
BAND BAR GAD HUB TIE BEAD BELT BEND BOND CORD CREW CUFF FESS GANG GIRT HOOD HOOP KNOT LACE RING SASH SHOE TAPE WISP ZONE AMPYX BRAID CHOIR CLAMP COVEY COVIN CRAPE CROWN FLOCK FRAME GIRTH GORGE GUARD LABEL NOISE PANEL PRIDE QUIRE SABOT SNOOD STRAP STRIP STROP TRACK TRIBE UNITE WITHE ARMLET BINDER BORDER BUNDLE CLAVUS COHORT COLLAR COLLET COPULA CRAVAT DECKLE FASCIA FETTER FILLET FRIEZE FRINGE FUNNEL GAMMON GARTER GASKET GIRDLE LEGLET RADULA REGULA SCREED STRAKE STRIPE SWATHE TETHER BINDING BLANKET CIRCLET COMPANY FERRULE FRONTAL GARLAND HATBAND NECKTIE ORPHREY PALLIUM PIGTAIL SHACKLE SWADDLE VINCULUM
(— ACROSS SUNSPOT) BRIDGE
(— AROUND MAST) PARREL
(— FOR HEAD) VITTA
(— IN BRAIN) LIGULA FRENULUM FUNICULUS

(— IN ROCKS) FAHLBAND
(— OF CLAY) COTTLE
(— OF COLOR) SOCK SLASH STRIA LACING FASCIOLE
(— OF CRAPE) WEED SCARF
(— OF INDIANS) SHIVWITS
(— OF PILLAGERS) SKINNERS
(— OF PIPERS) POVERTY
(— OF PURPLE) CLAVUS
(— OF STRAW) GAD SIMMON
(— OF TISSUE) TISSUE
(— OF 13 WITCHES) COVEN
(— ON SHIELD) ENDORSE
(— TO COMPRESS CHEEKS) CAPISTRUM
(ARMED —) JATHA POSSE
(ARMOR —) TONLET
(CIRCULAR —) HOOP RING ANNULE WREATH
(DANCE —) CHORO COMBO
(DECORATIVE —) PATTE LEGLET CORNICE ARCHIVOLT
(DIVIDING —) CLOISON
(EUCHARISTIC —) MANIPLE
(FOREHEAD —) INFULA
(IRON —) FRET GATE TRUSS FUNNEL STRAKE
(LACE —) SCALLOP
(MUSICIANS —) CONCERT
(RADIO —) CHANNEL
(RESONANCE —) FORMANT
(STREET —) MARIACHI
(TRIBAL —) AIMAK
BANDAGE BAND BELT BIND TAPE BRACE DRESS GALEA LINEN SLING SWATH TRUSS BINDER COLLAR FASCIA FILLET LIGATE ROLLER SWATHE ROLLING SWADDLE TRUSSER CINCTURE LIGAMENT LIGATURE
(— FOR NOSE) ACCIPITER
(EYE —) MUFFLER
(FINGER —) HOVEL
(JAW —) FUNDA
(PL.) SWADDLING
BANDIT CACA TORY BRAVO THIEF BANISH HAIDUK OUTLAW ROBBER BANDIDO BRIGAND LADRONE TULISAN MARAUDER MIQUELET PICAROON
(PL.) MANZAS
BANDLEADER MASTER MAESTRO CHORAGUS CONDUCTOR
BANDSTAND KIOSK
BANDY VIE BAND SWAP TRADE RACKET STRIVE CHAFFER CONTEND DISCUSS CARRIAGE EXCHANGE
(— WORDS) REVIE GIFFGAFF
BANE WOE BONE EVIL HARM KILL PEST RUIN CURSE DEATH VENOM INJURY MURDER POISON SLAYER NEMESIS SCOURGE MISCHIEF NUISANCE
BANEFUL BAD ILL EVIL VILE HARMFUL HURTFUL NOXIOUS RUINOUS VENOMOUS SINISTRAL PERNICIOUS
BANG RAP BAFF BEAT BLOW BOOT DRUB SLAM SWAP BLAFF CLASH CRACK DRIVE EXCEL FORCE IMPEL POUND SLAKE SLUMP SOUND THUMP WHACK WHUMP

CUDGEL ENERGY STRIKE THRASH
THWACK
BANGLADESH (CAPITAL OF —) DACCA
(MONEY OF —) TAKA
(NATIVE OF —) BENGALI
(RIVER OF —) GANGES
(TOWN IN —) KHULNA CHITTAGONG
CHITTAGONG
BANGLE ORNAMENT
BANISH BAN EJECT EXILE EXPEL WAIVE
DEPORT DISPEL OUTLAW ABANDON
CONDEMN DISMISS DIVORCE EXCLUDE
DISPLACE RELEGATE
BANISHED FUGITIVE
BANISTER RAILING BALUSTER
BANJO BOX BANJORINE
BANK BAR COP RIM ROW BRAE BUTT
CAJA DIKE DUNE DYKE EDGE HILL MASS
PILE RAKE RAMP RIPA RIVE SAND SCAR
SEAT SIDE TIER WEIR BANCO BENCH
BLUFF BRINK COAST DITCH EARTH
FENCE LEVEE MARGE MOUND MOUNT
RIDGE SHELF SHOAL SHORE SLOPE
STACK STAGE TRUST BANQUE CAISSE
CAUSEY CRADGE DEGREE DEPEND
MARGIN RIVAGE STRAND DEPOSIT
LOMBARD SHALLOW
(— A FIRE) REST
(— FOR DRYING BRICKS) HACK
(— OF CANAL) BERM BERME HEELPATH
(— OF EARTH) COP DAM DITCH
(— OF RIVER) RIPA WHARF STRAND
(— OF SAND OR MUD) BAR SCALP
(— OF SNOW) WREATH SNOWDRIFT
(— OF TURF) SUNK
(OVERHANGING —) BREW HOVER
(RUSSIAN —) CRAPETTE
(STEEP —) HEUCH HEUGH WOUGH
BARRANCA BARRANCO
BANKER BOOK FACTOR LOMBARD
MARWARI SPONSOR TAILLEUR
FINANCIER
BANKNOTE CRISP FLIMSY SCREEN
(FORGED —) STUMER
BANKRUPT BUST BREAK BROKE SMASH
BROKEN BUSTED DYVOUR DEPLETE
BANKRUPTCY SMASH FAILURE
SMASHUP
BANNER FANE FLAG JACK COLOR
ENSIGN FANNON PENNON LABARUM
PENNANT SALIENT BANDEROL
FOREMOST GONFALON STANDARD
STREAMER VEXILLUM BEAUSEANT
ORIFLAMME
(— ON TRUMPET) TABARD
(FUNERAL —) BANNEROL GUMPHION
(PL.) ENSIGNRY
BANQUET FETE MEAL FEAST DINNER
JUNKET REGALE REPAST SPREAD
CONVIVE CAROUSAL FESTIVAL
SYMPOSIUM
BANSHEE BOW SIDHE
BANTAM COCK GRIG BANTY DANDY
SAUCY CHICKEN SEBRIGHT COMBATIVE
BANTER KID RAG CHIP FOOL JEST JOKE
JOSH MOCK QUIZ RAIL RAZZ CHAFF
JOLLY RALLY ROAST TAUNT TRICK

DELUDE DERIDE HAGGLE SATIRE
BADINAGE CHAFFING RAILLERY RIDICULE
BANTU ILA BULU GOGO GUHA HEHE
YAKA ZULU DUALA KAMBA KIOKO
KONDE KONGO LAMBA SHONA SWAZI
BANYAI BASUTO DAMARA HERERO
KAFFIR THONGA YAKALA CABINDA
MASHONA SWAHILI WACHAGA
(— LANGUAGE) ILA RONGA NYANJA
THONGA NYAMWEZI
BAOBAB MOWANA IMBONDO TEBELDI
CALABASH ADANSONIA
BAPTISM CLEANSING IMMERSION
PALINGENY PERFUSION
BAPTIST DIPPER DOPPER DIDAPPER
TRASKITE
BAPTIZE DIP NAME HEAVE PLUNGE
PURIFY ASPERSE CLEANSE IMMERSE
CHRISTEN SPRINKLE
BAR BAN DAM FID FOX LAW RIB ROD
AXLE BALK BAND BANK BEAM BOLT
BOOM CORE DRAG FLAT GATE HIDE JOKE
LOCK OUST POLE RACK RAIL REEF SAVE
SHUT SKID SLAB SLAT SLIP SNIB STOP
TREE YARD ARBOR BENCH BLOCK BRACE
CATCH CLASP CLOSE COURT CRAMP
DETER EASER EMBAR ESTOP FENCE
HEDGE LEVER PERCH PILOT SHAFT
SHAPE SPELL SPOON SPRAG STAFF
STANG STAVE STRAP STRIP STRUT
TRACE BATTEN BILLET BISTRO BODEGA
BROOCH BUMPER CRUTCH EXCEPT
FASTEN FORBID GRILLE HINDER LADDER
PEELER RADIAL RETURN SALOON STRIPE
TANGLE TILLER TOGGLE BARRIER
BOLSTER CONFINE COUNTER EXCLUDE
PREVENT SPINDLE TOPRAIL TRUNDLE
ASTRAGAL
(— FOR TAPPING FURNACE) LANCET
(— IN FABRIC) BARRE
(— IN RIVER) CHAR SANDBAR
(— IN SEA) SWASH
(— OF CULTIVATOR) ARCH
(— OF DOOR) SLOT STANG
(— OF ELECTRIC SWITCH) BLADE
(— OF GATE) SPAR LEDGE
(— OF HARROW) BULL
(— OF LOOM) EASER SWORD BATTEN
BACKSTAY
(— OF RAYS) SHOOT
(— OF STEEL) BLOOM BILLET STIRRUP
(— OF WAGON) SHETH
(— ON SIDE OF BOWSPRIT) WHISKER
(— ON WINDMILL) UPLONG
(— SUPPORTING MILLSTONE)
MOLINE
(— WITH SHACKLES) BILBOES
(— WITH SPIKES) HERISSON
(CAST IRON —) SOW
(CONNECTING —) ZYGON
(HERALDIC —) FESS HUMET LABEL
(JOINTED —) CHILL
(MINING —) MOIL
(NOTCHED —) RISP SKEY
(PAIR OF —S) GEMEL GEMMEL
(REFRESHMENT —) BUFFET CANTEEN
(SOAP FRAME —) SESS

(STIRRING —) CRUTCH
(TAMPING —) STEMMER
(TYPEWRITER —) BAIL BALE SPACER
SHUTTLE
(WEAVING —) TEMPLE
(WHEEL —) AXLE SPOKE
BARB AWN BUR JAG BARR FILE HAIR
HERL HOOK BEARD POINT RIDGE SPEAR
BARBULE BRISTLE FILAMENT
(— OF ARROW) HOOK WING BEARD
WITTER
(— OF FEATHER) HERL RAMUS
PINNULA FILAMENT
(— OF HARPOON) FLUKE
BARBADOS (CAPITAL OF —)
BRIDGETOWN
(MOUNTAIN OF —) HILLABY
(NATIVE OF —) BIM
BARBARIAN HUN BOOR GOTH RUDE
WILD ALIEN BRUTE SAVAGE VANDAL
RUFFIAN
BARBARIC GROSS ATROCIOUS
BARBARITY FERITY CRUELTY FELLNESS
FEROCITY RUDENESS SAVAGERY
BRUTALITY
BARBAROUS FELL RUDE WILD CRUEL
BRUTAL FIERCE GOTHIC BESTIAL
FOREIGN HUNNISH INHUMAN SLAVISH
UNCIVIL IGNORANT CUTTHROAT
FEROCIOUS PRIMITIVE
BARBER NAI FIGARO POLLER SHAVER
TONSOR SCRAPER TONSURE
BARBER OF SEVILLE
(CHARACTER IN —) BERTHA FIGARO
ROSINA BARTOLO LINDORO ALMAVIVA
(COMPOSER OF —) ROSSINI
BARBITAL VERONAL
BARBITURATE DOWNER SECONAL
BARCHESTER TOWERS
(AUTHOR OF —) TROLLOPE
(CHARACTER IN —) BOLD SLOPE
ARABIN BERTIE NERONI ELEANOR
GRANTLY HARDING OBADIAH PROUDIE
SEPTIMUS STANHOPE CHARLOTTE
ETHELBERT QUIVERFUL
BARD MUSE POET SCOP DRUID RUNER
SKALD OSSIAN SINGER MINSTREL
TALIESEN
BARE DRY BALD LEAN MERE NUDE POOR
THIN ALONE BLEAK CRUDE EMPTY
NAKED PLAIN SCANT STARK WASTE
BARREN CALLOW DENUDE DIVEST
EXPOSE MEAGER PALTRY REVEAL
SIMPLE DIVULGE EXPOSED UNCOVER
DESOLATE DISCLOSE STRIPPED
DESTITUTE
BARELY JUST ONLY FANIT HARDLY
MERELY POORLY SIMPLY SCANTILY
SCARCELY SLIGHTLY
BARGAIN BUY WOD COPE DEAL MART
PACT PICK SALE SELL TROG CHEAP
FIGHT PRICE STEAL BARTER DICKER
HAGGLE NIFFER PALTER CHAFFER
CHEAPEN COMPACT CONTEND CONTEST
CONTRACT COVENANT PURCHASE
(— HARD) PRIG
(— IN MINING) STURT

BARGE ARK BOX HOY TOW TUB BARK
PRAM RAFT SCOW TROW BARCA CASCO
FOIST LUNGE LURCH VIXEN BARQUE
BUGERO DREDGE GALLEY REBUKE
TENDER THRUST DROGHER GONDOLA
LIGHTER TOWBOAT
(COAL —) KEEL
(TOWED —) BUTTY
BARK BAG BAY RUB TAN YAP YIP COAT
COTO DITA HOWL HUSK OPEN PEEL PELT
PILL RIND SKIN TAPA YELP YIPE BARCA
BARGE COUGH SHELL SHOUT STRIP
ABRADE BOWWOW CASSIA CORTEX
GIRDLE
(AROMATIC —) CANELLA CULILAWAN
(EXTERIOR OF —) ROSS
(INNER —) BAST
(LAYER OF —) HAT
BARKER DOORMAN SPIELER
BARLEY BENT SPRAT LICORN HORDEUM
WHITECORN
(AWN OF —) HORN
(GROUND —) TSAMBA
(HULLED —) PTISAN
(REFUSE —) SHAG FLINTS
BARN BYRE AMBAR LATHE STALL
GRANGE STABLE SKIPPER COWHOUSE
(COW —) SAUR SHIPPON
(PART OF —) BAY HIP DOOR EAVE
APRON GABLE RIDGE VERGE AWNING
CUPOLA DORMER PENTHOUSE
VENTILATOR WEATHERVANE
BARNSTORM TOUR
BARNYARD PIGHTLE BACKSIDE
FARMYARD
BAROMETER GLASS ANEROID
OROMETER STATOSCOPE
BARON THANE DAIMIO BARONET
FREEMAN FREIHERR
BARONY HAN DOMAIN
BAROQUE GOTHIC ORNATE ROCOCO
GROTESQUE IRREGULAR
BARRACKS HOOCH
BARRACUDA KAKU SPET BARRY PELON
SNAKE SNOEK BECUNA PICUDA SCOOTS
SENNET VICUDA KATONKEL SCOOTERS
BARRAGE VOLLEY BARRIER DRUMFIRE
UMBRELLA CANNONADE FUSILLADE
BARREL KEG TUN VAT BUTT CASK DRUM
WOOD BOWIE QUILL SHELL STAND
UNION FESSEL GIRNEL HOGGET RUMBLE
RUNLET TIERCE CISTERN PACKAGE
RATTLER RUNDLET TUMBLER CYLINDER
HOGSHEAD KILDERKIN
(— OF FEATHER) CALAMUS
(— OF REVOLVER) CHAMBER
(CAPSTAN —) SPOOL
(HERRING —) CADE CRAN
(PART OF —) HEAD HOOP CHIME STAVE
BOTTOM
(SMALL —) KEG KIT CADE KNAG
RUNLET BARRICO RUNDLET
(TAR —) CLAVIE
BARREN DRY ARID BARE DEAD DOUR
DULL LEAN NUDE POOR SALT ADDLE
BLEAK BLUNT DUSTY EMPTY GAUNT
GHAST NAKED STARK STERN WASTE

BARREN DESERT EFFETE FALLOW HUNGRY JEJUNE MEAGER STUPID SAPLESS STERILE DESOLATE IMPOTENT TREELESS
(NOT —) FACILE FECUND
(PL.) LANDES

BARREN GROUND (AUTHOR OF —) GLASGOW
(CHARACTER IN —) JASON RUFUS GENEVA JOSIAH NATHAN OAKLEY PEDLAR DORINDA ELLGOOD GREYLOCK

BARRICADE BAR STOP BLOCK CLOSE FENCE ABATIS PRISON BARRIER DEFENSE FORTIFY OBSTRUCT RAMFORCE REVETMENT ROADBLOCK

BARRIER ALP BAR DAM BALK BOMA CRIB DIKE DOOR DYKE FOSS GATE PALE STOP WALL BOUND CHAIN FENCE FOSSE GRILL HEDGE LIMIT STILE CORDON GLACIS GRILLE HURDLE SCREEN BARRAGE CURTAIN PARAPET RAILING RAMPART BOUNDARY FORTRESS FRONTIER STOCKADE
(— ACROSS RIVER) STILL KIDDLE
(PROTECTIVE —) REDOUBT
(TRAFFIC —) SEPARATOR

BARRING BUT SAVE CLOSED

BARRISTER BARMAN LAWYER COUNSEL TEMPLAR ADVOCATE ATTORNEY SERJEANT

BARROOM PUB CAFE HOUSE SALOON CANTINA DOGGERY GROCERY TAPROOM DRAMSHOP DRINKERY GROGGERY GROGSHOP

BARROW HOG BANK BIER DUNE HILL TUMP GRAVE GURRY HURLY MOUND SEDAN TRUCK GALGAL KURGAN NAVETA HILLOCK TROLLEY TUMULUS MOUNTAIN PUSHCART

BARTENDER MIXER BARMAN BARMAID SKINKER TAPSTER

BARTER CHAP COPE HAWK SWAP TROG VEND CORSE TRADE TRUCK DICKER NIFFER SCORSE BARGAIN CHAFFER TRAFFIC TRUCKLE COMMERCE EXCHANGE

BARTERED BRIDE
(CHARACTER IN —) JASEK JENIK KECAL MICHA TOBIAS MARENKA ESMERALDA
(COMPOSER OF —) SMETANA

BASALT MARBLE NAVITE DIABASE GHIZITE KULAITE AUGANITE BANDAITE BASANITE DOLERITE ANAMESITE ARAPAHITE MELAPHYRE SUDBURITE VARIOLITE
(DECOMPOSED —) WACKE

BASE BED DEN LOW EVIL FOOT FOUL LEWD MEAN POOR RELY REST ROOT SACK STEM STEP VILE BASIS BLOCK CHEAP DIRTY FIRST MUDDY PETTY SNIDE SOCLE STAND STOOL WORSE ABJECT BOTTOM COARSE COMMON GROUND GRUBBY HUMBLE MENIAL PALTRY RASCAL SHABBY SORDID VULGAR BASTARD CAITIFF CURRISH DEBASED HANGDOG IGNOBLE OUTPOST PEASANT SERVILE SLAVISH SUPPORT CHURLISH DEGRADED INFAMOUS INFERIOR PEDESTAL PEDIMENT RASCALLY SCULLION SHAMEFUL STANDARD UNWORTHY WRETCHED
(— IN QUALITY) LEADEN
(— OF CANNON) SOUL
(— OF OPERATIONS) BOOK HOME
(— OF OVULE) CHALAZA
(— OF PETAL) CLAW
(— OF PLANT) CAUDEX
(— OF POLLINIUM) DISC DISK
(— OF ROCK) MAGMA
(— OF TUBER) HEEL
(HIDDEN —) LAIR
(HOME —) DEN
(LEAF —) FOVEA
(LOGARITHM —) E RADIX
(SECOND —) KEYSTONE

BASEBALL PILL APPLE DUSTER FLOATER INSHOOT LEATHER BEANBALL HARDBALL HORSEHIDE STICKBALL

BASEBOARD GRIN SKIRT PLINTH MOPBOARD SKIRTING

BASELESS IDLE UNFOUNDED

BASEMENT CELLAR TAHKHANA

BASHFUL COY SHY TIMID MODEST PUDENT ASHAMED DAUNTED BACKWARD BLUSHING PUDIBUND RETIRING SHEEPISH SKITTISH

BASHFULNESS PUDOR SHYNESS

BASIC BASE BASAL VITAL BOTTOM BEDROCK CENTRAL CLASSIC PRIMARY CARDINAL ULTIMATE ELEMENTAL ESSENTIAL

BASIN PAN BOWL COVE DISH DOCK EWER FLOW FONT GULF LAKE SINK TANK LAVER STOUP CHAFER HOLLOW LAVABO MARINA VALLEY VESSEL PISCINA BIRDBATH CESSPOOL LAVATORY VANITORY WASHBOWL
(DESERT —) PLAYA
(GEOLOGICAL —) BOLSON
(MOUNTAIN —) HOYA PUNA
(ROCK —) KEEVE KIEVE

BASIS BASE FOOT FORM FUND ROOT SILL RADIX STOCK BOTTOM GROUND BEDROCK FOOTING PREMISE SUPPORT GRAVAMEN AUTHORITY CRITERION FUNDAMENT SUBSTANCE

BASK SUN LAZE WARM BATHE ENJOY REVEL REJOICE

BASKET ARK COB FAN HOT KIT LUG PAD PED PEG POT RIP TOP CAUL COOP CORF CRIB GOAL KISH SKEP TILL TOUR TRUG CHEST CRATE CREEL DEVIL DILLY GRATE MAUND NATTE SCULL SWILL WILLY BEACON COFFIN CRADLE DOSSER FANNER FASCET GABION HAMPER HOPPET JICARA JUNKET KIBSEY MURLIN PETARA POTTLE SERPET TAPPET WINDLE CANASTA CORBEIL CRESSET FLASKET HANAPER MURLAIN PANNIER SCUTTLE SKEOUGH SKIPPET CANISTER
(— FOR CRUMBS) VOIDER
(— FOR EELS) BUCK COURGE
(— FOR FIGS) TAP CABAS FRAIL TAPNET

(— FOR FRUIT) CALA MOLLY CALATHOS
(FISH —) CRAN HASK

BAS-RELIEF PLAQUETTE

BASS LOW CHUB DEEP DRUM FOOT BASSO DRONE HURON ROCHE BURDEN CHERNA GROUND REDEYE SINGER STRIPE BARFISH BOURDON BROWNIE GROWLER JEWFISH STRIPER BACHELOR BIGMOUTH BLUEFISH CABRILLA CONTINUO ROCKFISH SPOTTAIL STREAKER TALLYWAG

BASSOON CURTAL FAGOTT BOMBARD

BAST LIBER RAMIE PHLOEM NOSEBURN

BASTARD BASE FALSE COWSON HYBRID IMPURE GETLING LOWBRED MONGREL BANTLING BASEBORN MISBEGET NAMELESS SPURIOUS

BASTE SEW CANE DRUB LARD TACK SAUCE CUDGEL PUNISH STITCH THRASH

BASTION JETTY BULWARK LUNETTE MOINEAU
(PART OF —) FACE RAMP ANGLE FLANK GORGE CURTAIN BANQUETTE

BAT CAT HIT WAD BEAT CLUB GAIT JACK LUMP MASS SWAT TRAP WINK BANDY BATON BRICK CHUCK FUNGO HARPY SPREE STICK ALIPED BEETLE CUDGEL DRIVER KALONG PADDLE POMMEL RACKET STRIKE STROKE WILLOW NOCTULE VAMPIRE BLUDGEON SEROTINE BARBASTEL REREMOUSE CHEIROPTER

BATCH LOT BREW CAST CROP MASS MESS SORT BUNCH GROUP FORMULA MIXTURE QUANTITY
(— OF EGGS) SETTING
(— OF GRAIN) GRIST

BATFISH ANGLER DIABLO MALTHE DEVILFISH

BATH DIP TUB BAIN TOSH LAVER STEEP BAGNIO DOUCHE MIKVAH PICKLE PLUNGE SHOWER SPONGE BALNEUM LAVACRE ABLUTION
(FOOT —) PEDILUVIUM
(HOT —) STEW SCALD
(MUD —) ILLUTATION
(PHOTOGRAPHIC —) FIXER
(SITZ —) BIDET SEMICUPE INSESSION
(STEAM —) SAUNA

BATHE TUB BASK LAVE STEW WASH CLEAN DOUSE EMBAY SOUSE STEEP FOMENT SHOWER SPLASH IMMERSE PERVADE SUFFUSE PERMEATE

BATHHOUSE STEW SAUNA BAGNIO CABANA BALNEARY

BATHROBE PEIGNOIR

BATHROOM BIFFY BALNEARY

BATHSHEBA (FATHER OF —) ELIAM AMMIEL
(HUSBAND OF —) DAVID URIAH
(SON OF —) NATHAN SHIMEA SHOBAB SOLOMON

BATON ROD BURN WAND STAFF STICK BASTON CUDGEL BOURDON SCEPTER BAGUETTE TRUNCHEON

BATSMAN BAT BATTER HITTER SLOGGER SLUGGER STRIKER

BATTEN END LAY RIB SLEY CLEAT LEDGE ENRICH FATTEN THRIVE FERTILIZE

BATTER RAM BEAT DENT MAIM MAUL DINGE PASTE POUND SMASH BRUISE BUFFET HAMMER HITTER PUMMEL TUMBLE BATSMAN BOMBARD CRIPPLE DESTROY SHATTER SLUGGER STRIKER DEMOLISH

BATTERCAKE WAFFLE CRUMPET

BATTERY PILE SINK TIRE TROOP EXCITER SINKBOX
(GUN —) SWINGER

BATTLE WAR CAMP DUEL FEUD FRAY MEET TILT TOIL BRUSH FIELD FIGHT JOUST ACTION AFFAIR AFFRAY COMBAT STRIVE CONTEND CONTEST WARFARE CONFLICT SKIRMISH STRUGGLE ENCOUNTER

BATTLE-AX POLEAX SPARTH TWIBIL BROADAX HALBERD FAUCHARD FRANCISC

BATTLE CRY CRY BANZAI ENSIGN GERONIMO BEAUSEANT

BATTLEFIELD ARENA TAHUA CHAMPAIGN

BATTLEMENT KERNEL MERION PINION BARMKIN CORNELLE MURDRESS

BATTY BATS BUGGY CRAZY SILLY FOOLISH

BAUBLE BOW TOY BEAD GAUD BUTTON GEWGAW TRIFLE TRINKET GIMCRACK PLAYTHING

BAWDY LEWD DIRTY SCARLET

BAWL CRY HOWL ROAR YAWP SHOUT BELLOW BOOHOO OUTCRY

BAY ARM DAM RIA VOE BANK BARK COVE GULF HOLE HOPE LOCH ROAN WICK YAWP BAHIA BASIN BAYOU BERRY BIGHT CREEK FIORD HAVEN HORSE INLET LOUGH MOUTH ORIEL QUEST SINUS SPEAK HARBOR LAUREL RECESS TONGUE WINDOW ENCLOSE ESTUARY MALABAR SILANGA ULULATE CHESTNUT
(— OF BARN) GOAF SKEELING
(— OF LIBRARY) CLASSIS

BAYBERRY AUSU PIMIENTA WAXBERRY

BAYOU SLUE BROOK CREEK INLET RIVER SLOUGH STREAM RIVULET BACKWATER

BAY WINDOW ORIEL MIRADOR

BAZAAR FAIR FETE SALE AGORA BURSE CHOWK MARKET ALCAZAR CANTEEN BOOKFAIR EMPORIUM

BE ARE LIVE ABIDE EXIST OCCUR REMAIN BREATHE CONSIST SUBSIST CONTINUE

BEACH BANK MOOR RIPA SAND SLIP COAST PLAYA SHORE SHILLA STRAND SEASIDE LAKESHORE
(PROJECTING —) CUSP
(SANDY —) MACHAIR

BEACON MARK PIKE SIGN FANAL GUIDE PHAROS SIGNAL CRESSET SEAMARK WARNING BALEFIRE

BEAD NIB POT DROP FOAM GAUD FILET GRAIN KNURL PEARL QUIRK SIGHT ARANGO BAGUET BAUBLE BUBBLE CORNET FILLET PELLET POPPET RONDEL

WAMPUM DEWDROP GLOBULE MOLDING TRINKET CABOCHON

BEADLE CRIER MACER POKER USHER BEDRAL BUMBLE HARMAN HERALD BAILIFF SUMMONER

BEAK NEB NIB BILL NOSE PIKE PROW LORUM SNOUT TUTEL NOZZLE ROSTRUM MANDIBLE CAPITULUM
(— OF SHELL) UMBO
(— OF SHIP) SPERON

BEAKED NASUTE

BEAKER CUP HORN TASS BIKER BOCAL BOUSE GLASS BARECA

BEAM BAR RAY TIE BALK BEAK BOOM EMIT GLOW SILL SKID SPAR STUD ARBOR CABER FLASH GLEAM JOIST LIGHT SHAPE SHINE SHOOT SMILE SPEAR STOCK CAMBER FLITCH GIRDER GLANCE HEADER MANTEL NEEDLE RAFTER SUMMER TIMBER TREVIS BALANCE CATHEAD CHANNEL CHEVRON PINRAIL RADIATE SLEEPER SUPPORT TRANSOM TRIMMER AXLETREE ROOFTREE
(— OF LIGHT) CHINK GLEED SHAFT PENCIL SIGNAL STREAM SUNBEAM
(HIGH —) BRIGHTS
(LARGE —) BALK LACE SUMMER
(LOW —) DIM
(WEAVER'S —) TRAM TAVIL

BEAMING GAY ROSY BRIGHT LUCENT RADIANT SHINING

BEAN BON NIB FAVA GRAM HEAD LIMA POLE SNAP BRAIN CARAT PULSE SKULL CACOON CASTER FELLOW KIDNEY LENTIL NOGGIN RUNNER THRASH CALABAR

BEAR CUB CAST GEST GIVE HAVE HOLD LIFT TEEM TOTE URSA WEAR ABIDE ALLOW BEGET BREED BRING BROOK BROWN BRUIN CARRY DRIVE ISSUE KOALA POLAR PRESS SPARE STAND STICK THOLE THROW WEIGH WIELD YIELD AFFORD BEHAVE BRUANG CONVEY ENDURE IMPORT KINDLE KODIAK PIERCE RENDER SUFFER THRUST UPHOLD WOMBAT ARCTOID COMFORT CONDUCT GRIZZLY PRODUCE STOMACH SUPPORT SUSTAIN UNDERGO SILVERTIP
(— EXPENSES) DEFRAY
(— FLOWERS) FLOURISH
(— FRUIT) FRUCTIFY
(— INVESTIGATION) WASH
(— ON) CONCERN
(— OUT) PROPORT
(— PATIENTLY) DIGEST
(— UP) CAPE ENDURE SUSTAIN
(— WITH CREDIT) BROOK
(— WITNESS) TEEM SPEAK ATTEST DEPOSE
(— YOUNG) FIND CALVE CHILD
(MALE —) BOAR

BEARD AWN BARB DEFY FACE FUZZ NECK NOSE PEAK TUFT ARISTA BEAVER GOATEE TASSEL BARBULE VANDYKE IMPERIAL WHISKERS BILLYGOAT
(— OF GRAIN) AIL AWN
(SMALL —) BARBET

BEARDED AWNIE HAIRY BARBED BARBATE HIRSUTE POGONIATE WHISKERED

BEARDLESS NOT IMBERBE POLLARD

BEARER HAMAL MACER BEADLE HOLDER PACKER PORTER CARRIER PINCERN CHAPRASI PORTATOR MESSENGER SUPPORTER
(— OF GREAT BURDEN) ATLAS
(ARMOR —) ESQUIRE
(BURDEN —) HAMAL
(CROZIER —) CROCIARY
(CUP —) SAKI COPPER
(PALANQUIN —) BOY SIRDAR MUSAHAR
(SHIELD —) SQUIRE ESCUDERO
(STANDARD —) ANCIENT
(STRETCHER —) BRANCARDIER
(SWORD —) PORTGLAIVE

BEARING AIR BALL DUCT MIEN ORLE PORT RUBY BIRTH FRONT GESTE HABIT JEWEL POISE SETUP TENUE TREND ALLURE ASPECT BILLET CHARGE COURSE GIGLIO MANNER ORIENT SADDLE THRUST ADDRESS AZIMUTH CONDUCT FASHION GESTURE MEANING POSTURE PURPORT SUPPORT ATTITUDE BEHAVIOR CARRIAGE DELIVERY DEMEANOR PEDESTAL PRESENCE PRESSURE RELATION STANDARD TENDENCY REFERENCE
(— FRUIT) FRUCTED
(— OUTWARD) EFFERENT
(ARROGANT —) HUFF
(HERALDIC —) GAD DELF ENTE GORE MARK ORLE PALL WEEL CROWN DELFT FUSIL LAVER PHEON BILLET DEVICE ENSIGN GOUTTE CHAPLET CLARION DEMIVOL PLASQUE QUARTER ORDINARY QUENTISE TRESSURE
(PERSONAL —) GARB

BEARLIKE URSINE

BEARSKIN BUSBY

BEAST BETE HOOF BRUTE VACHE ANIMAL MONSTER VENISON BEHEMOTH BLIGHTER
(— OF BURDEN) JUMENT SUMPTER
(CASTRATED —) SPADO
(DEAD —) MORKIN
(FABULOUS —) YALE THRIS BAGWYN TRICORN DINGMAUL EPIMACUS OPINICUS GYASCUTUS
(STURDY —) NUGGET
(WILD —) FERINE OUTLAW UNBEAST
(WILD —S) ZIIM
(3-HORNED —) TRICORN

BEASTLY GROSS ANIMAL BRUTAL WICKED BESTIAL BRUTISH INHUMAN SWINISH OFFENSIVE

BEAT BAT BUM COB FAN LAM PLY PUG PUN TAN TAP TIE WAX BAFF BAIT BANG BASH BATE BELT BEST BLOW BOLT BRAY BUFF CANE CAST CLAP CLUB COMB CRAB DINT DRUB DUMP FELL FLAP FLOG FRAP GROW HAZE JOWL KILL LACE LAMP LASH LICK LUMP LUSH MAUL

MELL MILL PALE PANT PELT ROUT SLAM
SLAT SLOG SOCK STUB SWAP TACK TICK
TRIM TUCK WARP WELT WHIP WHOP
WIPE BANDY BASTE BATON BIRCH
CHURN CLINK CREAM CURRY DOUSE
DRESS DRIVE FIGHT FILCH FLAIL FLANK
FORGE ICTUS INLAY KNOCK LABOR
POUND PULSE PUNCH ROUGH SCOUR
SKELP STAMP STRAP SWACK SWING
THROB THUMP TREAD TRUMP UPEND
WHACK WORST ACCENT BAMBOO
BATTER BOUNCE BUFFET COTTON
CUDGEL DEFEAT FETTLE HAMMER
LARRUP LATHER OUTRUN PUMMEL
REBUKE RHYTHM SQUASH STOUND
STRIKE STRIPE STROKE SWINGE SWITCH
THRASH THREAP THRESH TICKLE
WAGGLE WALLOP ASSAULT BELABOR
BLISTER CADENCE CANVASS CONQUER
CONTUSE EXHAUST FATIGUE KNUCKLE
LAMBAST PULSATE SHELLAC SURPASS
TROUNCE VIBRATE MALLEATE PALPITATE
(— ABOUT) BUSK BANGLE
(— AGAINST) BLAD
(— BACK) REBUFF
(— BARLEY) PAIL WARM
(— CLOTHES) BATTLE
(— DOWN) LAY FELL FULL ABATE
FLASH
(— EGGS) CAST
(— FIBERS) BRUSH
(— IT) LAM
(— OF DRUM) RUFF RAPPEL RATTAN
(— OF HEART) DUNT STROKE
(— ON BUTTOCKS) COB
(— SEVERELY) DRUB LUMP SOAK
BASTE SOUSE LATHER
(— WINGS) BATE FLAP
(— WITH HAMMER) DOLLY
(— WITH WHIP) SJAMBOK
(MUSICAL —) BOUNCE BATTUTA
(WEAK —) ARSIS
BEATEN BEAT PARTY TRITE TRADED
BEATIFIC DEIFIC ELYSIAN
BEATIFY SAINT HALLOW HEAVEN
ENCHANT GLORIFY SANCTIFY
BEATING COB LICK DOUSE PULSE STICK
HAZING HIDING TATTOO BASHING
BATTERY BELTING DUSTING LICKING
SKELPIN WELTING WHALING BIRCHING
DRESSING DRUBBING WHIPPING
STRAPPADO
BEATITUDE JOY BLISS BENISON
MACARISM HAPPINESS
BEAU BOY CHAP BLADE DANDY FLAME
LOVER SPARK SWELL ADONIS ESCORT
FELLOW GARCON STEADY SUITOR
ADMIRER COURTER COXCOMB GALLANT
BEAUTIFUL FAIR FINE GLAD GOOD BELLE
BONNY LUSTY SHEEN BLITHE BONNIE
COMELY DECORE FREELY LOVELY POETIC
PRETTY VENUST ANGELIC ELEGANT
CHARMING DELICATE ESTHETIC
FAIRSOME GORGEOUS GRACEFUL
HANDSOME LUCULENT SPECIOUS
MAGNIFICENT
BEAUTIFY GILD ADORN GRACE HIGHT

PREEN PRIMP PRUNE BEAUTY BEDECK
ENAMEL ADONIZE ENHANCE GARNISH
GLORIFY DECORATE EMBELLISH
PULCHRIFY
BEAUTY FACE FAIR FORM GLEE BELLE
CHARM FAVOR GLORY GRACE PRIDE
FINERY LOOKER LOVELY POLISH
DECORUM FEATURE SPLENDOR
(— OF FORM) SYMMETRY
(— OF STYLE) ELEGANCE
BEAVER BOOMER CASTOR RODENT
PRALINE MUSHROOM SEWELLEL
STARLING
BECAUSE AS SO FOR THAT BEING CAUSE
SINCE THEN FORWHY THROUGH
INASMUCH
BECCAFICO FIGEATER FIGPECKER
BECHE-DE-MER PIDGIN TREPANG
BECKON BOW NOD WAG BECK WAFT
WAVE CURTSY SUMMON BIDDING
COMMAND GESTURE
BECLOUD HIDE MASK BEDIM DARKEN
MUDDLE MYSTIFY OBSCURE
BECOME GO FIT GET SET SIT WAX COME
FALL GROW PASS SUIT TAKE WEAR
ADORN BEFIT GRACE PROVE WORTH
BEFALL BESEEM BETIDE CHANGE
BEHOOVE FLATTER PROCEED
BECOMING FIT FEAT GOOD FITTY RIGHT
COMELY DUEFUL GAINLY PROPER
DECOROUS HANDSOME SUITABLE
WISELIKE
BED COT HAY KIP PAD PAN BAND BASE
BODY BUNK DOWN FLOP FORM PLOT
SACK VEIN WADI BERTH COUCH FLOCK
GRATE GROVE LAYER ROOST BORDER
BOTTOM CRADLE GIRDLE HOTBED LITTER
MATRIX OSIERY PALLET STRATA
CHANNEL FLEABAG HAMMOCK LODGING
QUARTER REPOSAL SETTING STRATUM
SUBSOIL TRUCKLE TRUNDLE BASSINET
(— DOWN) DOSS
(— IN WAGON) KATEL
(— OF ANIMAL) LAIR KENNEL
(— OF CLAY) CLOD
(— OF COAL) BRAT DELF SEAM
(— OF EMBERS) GRIESHOCH
(— OF FIRE CLAY) THILL
(— OF FURNACE) HEARTH
(— OF GUN-CARRIAGE) FLASK
(— OF HAND PRESS) COFFIN
(— OF OYSTERS) PLANT
(— OF REFUSE) NITRIARY
(— OF ROCK) CAP PLUM
(— OF ROSES) ROSARY
(— OF SEDIMENT) WARP
(— OF SHELLFISH) BANK
(— OF STONES) SHINGLE
(— OF STREAM) DRAW WASH NULLA
BILLABONG STREAMWAY
(CREEK —) COULEE COULIE
(DRIED LAKE —) CHOTT SEBKA
(FEATHER —) TIE TYE
(FOLDING —) SLAWBANK
(LOW —) LOWBOY
(OYSTER —) STEW LAYER SCALP
CLAIRE LAYING OYSTERAGE

(RUBBLE —) CALLOW
(SEED —) SEMINARY
(WATER-BEARING —) AQUAFER
AQUIFER
(WOODEN —) RUSTBANK
BEDAUB CLAG CLAT DAUB MOIL SOIL
SLAKE SMEAR PARGET SLUBBER
SLAISTER
BEDBUG CIMEX CHINCH COREID VERMIN
CIMICID PUNAISE CONENOSE
BEDCHAMBER RUELLE BEDROOM
CUBICLE
BEDCLOTHES COVER BEDDING
BEDCOVER COMFORTER PALAMPORE
BEDDING BEDROLL DOMESTICS
BEDECK GEM BEDO LARD TRAP ADORN
ARRAY DIGHT GRACE PRINK ORNAMENT
EMBELLISH
BEDEVIL ABUSE ANNOY BESET WORRY
HARASS MUDDLE PESTER BEWITCH
CONFUSE TORMENT
BEDIZEN DAUB ADORN ARRAY BEDAUB
BEDLAM RIOT NOISE RUDAS ASYLUM
TUMULT UPROAR MADNESS MADHOUSE
BETHLEHEM
BEDOUIN ARAB MOOR NOMAD BADAWI
BEDRAGGLED FORLORN SHOPWORN
BEDRIDDEN ILL AILING BEDFAST
BEDROLL BINDLE
BEDROOM FLAT BERTH CABIN DORMER
BOUDOIR CHAMBER WARDROBE
BEE DOR FLY APIS BEVY KING RING KARBI
MASON NOMIA NURSE PARTY DINGAR
DRONER FROLIC NOTION WORKER
MELISSA RAISING SERPENT STINGER
TRIGONA ANDRENID ANGELITO
HONEYBEE QUILTING SHUCKING
BEECH BUCK BIRCH MYRTLE FLINDOSA
BEEF BULLY GRIPE JERKY CASSON
CUTTER CHARQUI COMPLAIN PASTRAMI
(— FOR SLAUGHTER) MART
(BOILED —) BOUILLI
(BROILED —) CHURRASCO
(CORN —) BULLY
(CUT OF —) SEY LOIN RUMP SIDE
BARON CHINE CHUCK FLANK ROAST
ROUND SHANK STEAK ALOYAU CUTLET
SADDLE BRISKET KNUCKLE QUARTER
SIRLOIN EDGEBONE SHOULDER
AITCHBONE NINEHOLES RATTLERAN
(GROUND —) HAMBURGER
(INFERIOR —) COMPOUND
(JERKED —) TASAJO BILTONG CHARQUI
(LEAN —) LIRE
(SALTED —) JUNK VIFDA
BEEFY HEAVY HEFTY SOLID BRAWNY
FLESHY
BEEHIVE GUM BUTT HIVE SKEP SWARM
APIARY HOPPET ALVEARY SWARMER
BEEHOUSE
BEELZEBUB DEVIL
BEER ALE MUM BIER BOCK BREW FARO
GAIL GROG GYLE HOPS MALT MILD SCUD
SUDS CHICA KVASS LAGER POMBE
QUASS STOUT WEISS CHICHA PORTER
SPRUCE WALLOP ZYTHUM CERVEZA
PANGASI PHARAOH PILSNER TANKARD

(BAD —) TACK TAPLASH
(HOT — AND GIN) PURL
(INFERIOR —) BELCH SWANKY
(SMALL —) TIFF GROUT
(SOUR —) BEEREGAR
(STRONG —) HUFF NAPPY DOUBLE
STINGO
(THIN —) PRITCH SWIPES
(TIBETAN —) CHANG
(WARM — AND OATMEAL) STORRY
(WEAK —) BEVERAGE
BEET CHARD MANGEL MANGOLD
STECHLING
(SUGAR —) BOLTER
BEETLE BAT BOB JUT RAM BEAT BUZZ
FOWL MAUL MELL STAG TURK AMARA
ATLAS BORER BULGE CAROB CHUCK
CLOCK DRIVE HISPA LYCID SAGRA TIGER
CHAFER CLERID COCUYO ELATER
MALLET MELOID PESTLE PRUNER
SCARAB WEEVIL BRUCHID CLOCKER
FIREFLY GIRDLER HORNBUG LADYBUG
PROJECT SKIPPER SNAPPER SOLDIER
TICKLER CURCULIO GLOWWORM
HARDBACK LADYBIRD OVERHANG
SKIPJACK LONGICORN
BEFALL HAP COME TIDE TIME OCCUR
BECOME BETIDE HAPPEN
BEFITTING FIT DECENT PROPER WORTHY
SEEMING BECOMING DECOROUS
BEFOG CLOUD CONFUSE MYSTIFY
BEFORE TO ERE ANTE FORE SAID TILL
YORE AHEAD AVANT FIRST FRONT PRIOR
UNTIL FORMER RATHER SOONER
ALREADY EARLIER
BEFRIEND AID ABET HELP FAVOR ASSIST
FOSTER FRIEND SUCCOR SUPPORT
SUSTAIN
BEFUDDLE ADDLE BESOT MUDDLE
BECLOUD CONFUSE FLUSTER MYSTIFY
STUPEFY
BEG ASK BID CRY SUE WOO COAX MOVE
MUMP PRAY SEEK CADGE CRAVE MOOCH
PLEAD TEASE YEARN ADJURE BESEECH
ENTREAT IMPLORE REQUEST SOLICIT
PETITION OBSECRATE PANHANDLE
BEGET GET BEAR HAVE SIRE BREED YIELD
CREATE FATHER CONCEIVE ENGENDER
GENERATE PROCREATE
BEGGAR PROG RUIN ASKER LAZAR
ROGUE TRAMP CADGER CANTER
MUMPER PARIAH PAUPER WRETCH
ALMSMAN MENDICANT SCHNORRER
BEGGARS' OPERA (AUTHOR OF —)
GAY
(CHARACTER IN —) LUCY POLLY
LOCKIT PEACHUM MACHEATH
BEGIN FALL HEAD JUMP LEAD OPEN RISE
ARISE ENTER FRONT START COMMENCE
INITIATE
BEGINNER BOOT PUNK TYRO NOVICE
ROOKIE AMATEUR ENTRANT RECRUIT
STUDENT TRAINEE FRESHMAN
NEOPHYTE NEWCOMER
BEGINNING EGG DAWN GERM HEAD RISE
ROOT SEED ALPHA BIRTH DEBUT ENTRY
FIRST FRONT ONSET START AURORA

INCOME ORIGIN OUTSET SOURCE SPRING GENESIS INFANCY INITIAL NASCENT OPENING SUNRISE ENTRANCE

BEGRUDGE ENVY GRUDGE MALIGN JALOUSE

BEGUILE FOX COAX GULL LURE VAMP WILE AMUSE CHARM CHEAT COZEN ELUDE EVADE TEMPT TRICK DELUDE DIVERT ENTRAP DECEIVE ENSNARE FLATTER MISLEAD

BEHALF PART SAKE SIDE FAVOR SCORE STEAD PROFIT BENEFIT SUPPORT INTEREST

BEHAVE DO ACT BEAR FARE KEEP MAKE PLAY WALK WORK CARRY REACT TREAT ACQUIT DEMEAN DEPORT HANDLE COMPORT CONDUCT FUNCTION REGULATE

BEHAVIOR AIR MIEN RULE FRONT GUISE HABIT USAGE ACTION COURSE MANNER BEARING COMPORT CONDUCT DECORUM FASHION ATTITUDE BREEDING CARRIAGE FUNCTION
(ARROGANT —) SIDE SWAGGER
(COURTEOUS —) COMITY COURTESY
(DECENT —) CIVILITY
(FOOLISH —) SIMPLES SOTTISE
(GOAL-DIRECTED —) HORME
(IMPROPER —) MISCONDUCT
(LIVELY —) TITTUP
(LOUTISH —) BUFFOONERY
(RIOTOUS —) RAMPAGE
(SILLY —) SPOONISM
(STUDIED —) ART
(UNDERHANDED —) SKULLDUGGERY

BEHIND AFT PAST RUMP ABAFT AFTER LATER PASSE TARDY ASTERN BACKWARD

BEHOLD LO EYE SEE SPY ECCE ESPY GAZE HOLD LOOK SCAN STOP VIEW SIGHT VOILA WATCH ASPECT DESCRY REGARD DISCERN OBSERVE WITNESS

BEHOLDEN OWING BOUNDEN OBLIGED INDEBTED

BEHOOVE FIT NEED SUIT BEFIT OUGHT BELONG REQUIRE

BEIGE TAN ECRU GREGE DORADO SUNBURN

BEING ENS ESSE SELF HUMAN SHAPE ANIMAL ENTITY EXTANT LIVING MORTAL PERSON SYSTEM PRESENT REALITY CREATURE EXISTENT PRESENCE
(ANIMATE —) LIFE JAGAT
(CELESTIAL —) ANGEL CHERUB SERAPH WATCHER DIVINITY
(DIMINUTIVE —) ELF GNOME
(DIVINE —) DEV DEVA DEMIGOD
(EVIL —) DEVIL GHOUL
(FABULOUS —) TENGU TORNIT
(HUMAN —) BODY BUCK JACK SOUL BLADE HUMAN SLIME ANIMAL ADAMITE CREATURE RATIONAL CHRISTIAN
(IDEAL —) IMMORTAL
(IMAGINARY —) SYLPH TERMAGANT
(INNERMOST —) HEART
(INTRINSIC —) ESSENCE
(LEGENDARY —) GIANT

(MATERIAL —) HYLIC
(PERFECT —) GOD
(PHYSICAL —) FLESH
(SUPERNATURAL —) DEV MAN AKUA ATUA DEVA JANN ZEMI ADARO BALAM DAEVA DEMON FAIRY TROLL WIGHT DAEMON GARUDA GODKIN SPIRIT GODLING FOLLETTO HAMINGJA
(SUPREME —) DEITY MONAD NYAMBE NZAMBI CREATOR
(TRUE —) OUSIA

BELABOR PLY BEAT DRUB LASH WORK ASSAIL BOUNCE CUDGEL HAMMER HAMPER THRASH THWACK

BELCH BURP ERUCT ERUCTATE

BELDAM HAG FURY CRONE ALECTO ERINYS VIRAGO BELDAME JEZEBEL TISIPHONE

BELEAGUER BELAY BESET ASSAULT BESEIGE BLOCKADE SURROUND

BELFRY SHED TOWER BELLHOUSE

BELGIUM

CAPITAL: BRUSSELS BRUXELLES
MEASURE: VAT AUNE LAST PIED CARAT PERCHE BOISSEAU
MOUNTAIN: BOTRANGE
NAME: BELGIE BELGIQUE
PLATEAU: ARDENNES HOHEVENN
PORT: OSTEND ANTWERP
PROVINCE: LIEGE NAMUR ANTWERP BRABANT HAINAUT LIMBURG FLANDERS
RIVER: LYS DYLE MAAS MARK YSER BOUCQ DEMER LESSE MEUSE NETHE RUPEL SENNE DENDER ESCAUT MANJEL OURTHE SAMBRE SEMOIS VESDRE WARCHE AMBLEVE SCHELDT
TOWN: AS AAT ANS ATH HAL HUY MOL SPA AATH AMAY ASSE BOOM BREE DOEL GAND GEEL GENK GENT HOEI LIER LOOZ MONS VISE WAHA ZELE AALST ALOST ARLON CINEY EEKLO ESSEN EUPEN EVERE GENCK GHENT HEIST IEPER JETTE JUMET LIEGE NAMUR RONSE TIELT UCCLE VORST WEZET YNOIR YPRES AARLEN ANVERS BERGEN BILZEN BRUGES DEURNE ELSENE IZEGEM LEUVEN LIERRE MERXEM OPWIJK OSTEND ANTWERP ARDOOIE BERCHEM DOORWIK HERSTAL HOBOKEN IXELLES LOUVAIN MECHLIN ROULERS SERAING TONGRES TOURNAI BRUSSELS COURTRAI KORTRIJK MECHELEN MOUSCRON TONGEREN TURNHOUT VERVIERS WATERLOO
WEIGHT: LAST CARAT LIVRE POUND CHARGE CHARIOT ESTERLIN

BELIE BELONG DEFAME FALSIFY SLANDER TRADUCE DISGUISE MISREPRESENT

BELIEF ISM MIND SECT TROW VIEW VOTE WEEN CAUSE CREDO CREED DOGMA FAITH TENET TROTH TRUST CREDIT GROUND FEELING HOLDING OPINION CREDENCE DOCTRINE RELIANCE

(— IN DEVILS) DIABOLISM
(— IN GHOSTS) EIDOLISM
(CONVENTIONAL —) PIETY
(FALSE —) DELUSION
(GROUNDLESS —) CANARD
(SHALLOW —) BALLOON
(UNFOUNDED —) FICTON
BELIEVABLE PLAUSIBLE
BELIEVE BUY DEEM FEEL HOLD TAKE
TROW WEEN CREED FAITH FANCY GUESS
JUDGE THINK TRUST ACCEPT CREDIT
ESTEEM EXPECT DARESAY SUPPOSE
ACCREDIT CONSIDER
(— ERRONEOUSLY) FEIGN
(— NAIVELY) SWALLOW
(— UNCRITICALLY) EAT
BELIEVER IST ADHERENT
BELITTLE DECRY DWARF SNEER BEMEAN
SLIGHT DETRACT MINIMIZE DENIGRATE
DISCREDIT DISPARAGE
BELL HUB TOM CALL FAIR GONG RING
ROAR CHIME KNELL TENOR BASKET
BELLOW BUBBLE TAPPER TOLLER
TREBLE TRIPLE VESPER ANGELUS
BLOSSOM CAMPANA COROLLA COWBELL
JANGLER JINGLER LOWBELL SKELLAT
TAMBOUR TINKLER DINGDONG
DOORBELL HANDBELL HAWKBELL
(ALARM —) TOCSIN
(CLOSED —) CROTAL
(EVENING —) CURFEW
(FUNERAL —) TELLER
(HAND —) CLAG
(LARGE —) SIGNUM
(LOWEST —) BOURDON
(PART OF —) BOW LIP HEAD CROWN
MOUTH WAIST CLAPPER SHOULDER
(PASSING —) KNELL
(SACRING —) SQUILLA
(SLEIGH —) GRELOT CROTALUM
BELLADONNA DWALE BANEWORT
NIGHTSHADE
BELLE SPARK TOAST
(SPANISH —) MAJA
BELLICOSE MAD IRATE HOSTILE
WARLIKE MILITANT
BELLIGERENT BRISTLY HOSTILE
WARLIKE CHOLERIC FIGHTING JINGOIST
COMBATIVE IRASCIBLE LITIGIOUS
WRANGLING PUGNACIOUS
BELLOW CRY LOW MOO YAP BAWL BELL
ROAR YAWP BLORE CROON SHOUT
CLAMOR BLUSTER
BELLOWS LUNGS FEEDER SANDER
WINKER SYLPHON WINDBAG EXPELLER
(SMALL —) PLUFF
(STORAGE —) RESERVOIR
BELLWETHER MASTER
BELLY BAG COD GUT MAW POD FILL KYTE
WAME WOMB BOSOM BULGE FRONT
GORGE TRIPE HUNGER PAUNCH VENTER
ABDOMEN BALLOON STOMACH APPETITE
BELONG BE GO FIT LIE BEAR FALL RELY
APPLY BELIE INHERE RELATE PERTAIN
SUBSCRIBE
BELONGINGS DUDS FARE GEAR GOODS
TRAPS ASSETS DUFFEL ESTATE

BAGGAGE EFFECTS CHATTELS PROPERTY
FURNITURE
BELOVED DEAR IDOL CHERI SWEET
ADORED CHERIE DARLING PRECIOUS
BELOW DOWN AFTER INFRA NEATH
SOTTO UNDER BENEATH
BELT AREA BAND BEAT GIRD RING SASH
SLUG ZONE GIRTH STRAP STRIP SWATH
TRACT WAIST BODICE CESTUS CINGLE
GIRDLE REGION STRIPE SWATHE CIRCUIT
CINCTURE ENCIRCLE
(— OF FOG) BLANKET
(ASTROLOGICAL —) CLIMATE
(CONVEYOR —) HAUL
(ENDLESS —) APRON CREEPER
(GREEK —) ZOSTER
(MACHINE —) SWIFTER
(MINERAL —) RANGE
BELVEDERE GAZEBO LOOKOUT
BENCH PEW BANC BANK DAIS SEAT
CHAIR JUDGE STOOL SEDILE SETTEE
SETTLE TRESTLE
(— FOR DAIRY TUBS) TRAM
(— FOR KNEADING DOUGH) BREAK
(OUTDOOR —) EXEDRA
(PLAYER'S —) WOOD
(ROWER'S —) BANK THOFT ZYGON
THWART
(SHOEMAKER'S —) FORME
(WORKMAN'S —) SIEGE
BEND BOW PLY SAG WRY ARCH DOME
FLEX FOLD HOOK KINK TURN ANGLE
BATON BIGHT BREAK CRIMP CROOK
CURVE DROOP HUNCH INBOW KNEEL
PLICA SLANT STOOP TWIST BOUGHT
BUCKLE CROUCH
BENDER JAG BUST DRUNK SPREE
WHOPPER
BENEATH BELOW LOWER UNDER
BENEDICTION AMEN PRAYER BENISON
BERAKAH BLESSING
BENEFACTOR ANGEL DONOR FRIEND
HELPER PATRON SAVIOR PROMOTER
BENEFICE FEE FEU FIEF CURACY
CANONRY PRELACY RECTORY SINECURE
VICARAGE
BENEFICENCE BOON GIFT GRACE
BOUNTY CHARITY GOODNESS KINDNESS
BENEFICENT KINDLY AMIABLE
GRACIOUS
BENEFICIAL GOOD USEFUL HEALTHY
HELPFUL SALUTARY BENIGNANT
DESIRABLE ENJOYABLE HEALTHFUL
LUCRATIVE REWARDING WHOLESOME
PROFITABLE
BENEFICIARY HEIR USER DONEE
LEGATEE FEUDATORY
BENEFIT AID USE BOON GAIN GIFT GOOD
HELP SAKE AVAIL BOOST FRUIT STEAD
ASSIST BEHALF FRINGE PROFIT USANCE
IMPROVE SERVICE INTEREST
BENEVOLENCE BOUNTY GOODNESS
GOODWILL HUMANITY
BENEVOLENT GOOD BENIGN KINDLY
LOVING AMIABLE LIBERAL GENEROUS
ALTRUISTIC
BEN HUR (AUTHOR OF —) WALLACE

(CHARACTER IN —) HUR IRAS JUDAH ESTHER TIRZAH MESSALA BALTHASAR SIMONIDES

BENIGN GOOD KIND MILD BLAND SWEET GENIAL GENTLE AFFABLE GRACIOUS SALUTARY FAVORABLE WHOLESOME

BENIGNANT KIND BLAND GENIAL LIBERAL GRACIOUS MERCIFUL

BENJAMIN (FATHER OF —) HARIM JACOB BILHAN
(MOTHER OF —) RACHEL
(SON OF —) ARD EHI BELA GERA ROSH ASHBEL BECHER HUPPIM MUPPIM NAAMAN

BENT AIM BIAS CAST CURB TURN BOUND BOWED COUDE FLAIR HUMOR KNACK PRONE TASTE TREND AKIMBO BIASED CURVED DOGLEG HOOKED LIKING SWAYED ARCUATE CROOKED EMBOWED IMPETUS INTENSE LEANING LEVELED PRONATE STOOPED APTITUDE PENCHANT TENDENCY

BENUMB DAZE NUMB STUN CHILL DEADEN STOUND STIFFEN STUPEFY TORPEFY

BEOWULF (AUTHOR OF —) UNKNOWN
(CHARACTER IN —) WIGLAF BEOWULF GRENDEL HIGELAC UNFERTH AESCHERE HONDSCIO HROTHGAR

BEQUEATH GIVE WILL ENDOW LEAVE BESTOW DEVISE LEGATE COMMEND TRANSMIT

BEQUEST GIFT WILL LEGACY BEQUEATH HERITAGE ENDOWMENT BENEFACTION

BERATE JAW NAG LASH RAIL ABUSE CHIDE SCOLD SCORE REVILE CENSURE REPROVE UPBRAID CHASTISE

BERCEUSE CRADLESONG WIEGENLIED

BEREAVE WIDOW DIVEST SADDEN DEPRIVE DESPOIL

BERG FLOE BARROW ICEBERG

BERRY DEW HAW CRAN POHA RASP BLACK CUBEB GRAPE CURRANT ALLSPICE COWBERRY DEWBERRY HAWEBAKE PERSIMMON POKEBERRY SASKATOON PEPPERCORN SHEEPBERRY POMEGRANATE

BERTH BED JOB BUNK DOCK SLIP CABIN PLACE UPPER BILLET LODGING MOORING

BESEECH ASK BEG BID CRY SUE WOO PRAY CRAVE PLEAD PRESS ADJURE APPEAL ENTREAT IMPLORE SOLICIT OBSECRATE

BESIDE BY ALONG ANENT ASIDE FORBY ABREAST AGAINST FORNENT ADJACENT

BESIDES TO AND BUT TOO YET ALSO ELSE MORE OVER THEN WITH ABOVE AGAIN SUPRA BEYOND EXCEPT WITHAL LIKEWISE MOREOVER

BESIEGE BELAY BESET SIEGE STORM ATTACK OBSESS PESTER PLAGUE COMPASS SOLICIT SURROUND BELEAGUER

BESMIRCH TAR DASH SLUR SOIL SMEAR SULLY SLURRY SMIRCH ASPERSE BLACKEN DISCOLOR

BESPATTER BLOT DASH SOIL SPOT PLASH STAIN SULLY ASPERSE SCATTER

BEST ACE BEAT GOOD MOST PICK TOPS ELITE EXCEL WORST CHOICE DEFEAT FINEST FLOWER OUTWIT TIPTOP UTMOST CONQUER LARGEST OPTIMUM GREATEST TOPNOTCH

BESTIAL LOW VILE WILD BRUTE FERAL BRUTAL FILTHY BEASTLY BRUTISH INHUMAN SENSUAL DEPRAVED

BESTIR STIR AWAKE SHIFT AROUSE HUSTLE

BESTOW ADD PUT CAST GIVE SEND ALLOT ALLOW APPLY AWARD GRANT LODGE PLACE SPEND ACCORD CONFER DEVOTE DONATE EMPLOY ENTAIL IMPART IMPOSE COMMEND DISPOSE ENLARGE INDULGE PARTAKE PRESENT BEQUEATH

BET BAS BOX LAY PUT SET VIE ANTE BACK BRAG CHIP HOLD JACK NOIR PAIR PLAY PUNT RISK WAGE HEDGE ROUGE STAKE WAGER GAMBLE HAZARD MANQUE
(— AGAINST) MILK COPPER
(— AT LONG ODDS) SKINNER
(— BOLDLY) BLUFF
(— CHIP) CHECK
(FARO —) SLEEPER
(HEDGING —) SAVER
(POKER —) BLIND

BETOKEN MARK NOTE SHOW SIGN AUGUR ASSERT DENOTE EVINCE BESPEAK EXPRESS PORTEND PRESAGE SIGNIFY FOREBODE FORESHOW INDICATE

BETRAY BLAB BLOW SELL SING TELL UNDO WRAY CROSS FALSE PEACH SPILL ACCUSE DELUDE DESERT REVEAL SNITCH SQUEAL BEGUILE DECEIVE FALSIFY MISLEAD DISCLOSE
(— CONFIDENCES) SPILL

BETRAYER RAT JUDAS SKUNK SEDUCER TRAITOR DERELICT RECREANT SQUEALER

BETROTH TOKEN TROTH ENGAGE ENSURE PLEDGE PLIGHT ESPOUSE PROMISE AFFIANCE CONTRACT

BETROTHED VOWED ASSURED ENGAGED HANDFAST INTENDED

BETTER AID TOP MEND AMEND EMEND EXCEL SAFER WISER BIGGER EXCEED REFORM ADVANCE CHOICER CORRECT GREATER IMPROVE PROMOTE RECTIFY RELIEVE SUPPORT SURPASS EMINENCE INCREASE SUPERIOR
(— A SCORE) BREAK
(— THAN ORDINARY) EXTRA

BETWEEN AMID AMONG ENTRE TWEEN TWEESH AVERAGE BETWIXT

BEVEL CANT EDGE ANGLE BEZEL MITER SLANT SLOPE SNAPE CHAMFER INCLINE OBLIQUE

BEVERAGE ADE ALE CUP NOG POP RUM SAP TEA BEER BREW CHIA GROG MATE MEAD MILK NIPA SODA WINE CIDER COCOA DRAFT DRINK JULEP LAGER NEGUS PUNCH SMASH TWIST WATER

COFFEE EGGNOG LIQUID LIQUOR NECTAR
PORTER CORDIAL LIMEADE POTABLE
COCKTAIL LEMONADE POTATION
SANGAREE CHOCOLATE GINGERADE
ORANGEADE
(— FROM COW'S MILK) KEFIR
(— FROM PEPPERS) KAVA
(— FROM SAP) TUBA
(— OF BUTTERMILK AND WATER)
BLAND
(— OF CHAMPAGNE) POPE
(— OF HONEY AND WATER)
METHEGLIN
(— OF HOT MILK) POSSET
(— OF PORT WINE) BISHOP
(— OF VINEGAR AND WATER) POSCA
(ALCOHOLIC —) DEW SAKE SAKI
SHRUB ARRACK FIREWATER STIMULANT
(COLA —) DOPE
(EFFERVESCENT —) FIZZ
(FERMENTED —) BASI KAVA KUMISS
(FRUIT —) BEVERAGE
(INSIPID —) WASH
(MEXICAN —) TEPACHE
(POLYNESIAN —) AVA KAVA
(WEAK —) LAP
BEVY HERD PACK COVEY DROVE FLOCK
GROUP SWARM FLIGHT SCHOOL
COMPANY
BEWAIL CRY RUE KEEN MOAN SIGH WAIL
WEEP MOURN BEMOAN GRIEVE LAMENT
DEPLORE COMPLAIN
BEWARE CAVE HEED SHUN WARD AVOID
ESCHEW WARNING
BEWILDER FOG FOX BEAT DAZE FOIL
STUN ABASH ADDLE AMAZE DIZZY
BAFFLE BEMUSE BOTHER DAZZLE
MUDDLE PUZZLE BUFFALO CONFUSE
MYSTIFY NONPLUS PERPLEX STAGGER
STUPEFY ASTONISH CONFOUND
DISTRACT ENTANGLE SURPRISE
BEWILDERED ASEA LOST AGAPE DAZED
MAZED WILSOME CONFUSED HELPLESS
PERPLEXED
BEWILDERMENT AWE FOG DAZE
AMAZEMENT CONFUSION PERPLEXITY
BEWITCH HEX CHARM SPELL ENAMOR
ENTICE GLAMOR HOODOO ATTRACT
BEDEVIL DELIGHT ENCHANT
BEYOND BY OVER YOND ABOVE ASIDE
ULTRA YONDER BENEATH BESIDES
FURTHER WITHOUT OVERMORE
SUPERIOR HEREAFTER
BEZEL RIM TOP EDGE OUCH SEAL CROWN
FACET FLANGE MARQUISE
BHUTAN (ASSEMBLY OF —) TSONGDU
(CAPITAL OF —) THIMPHU
(CURRENCY OF —) PAISA RUPEE
(LANGUAGE OF —) DZONGKHA
(RIVER OF —) MACHU MANAS AMOCHU
BIAS PLY BENT SWAY WARP COLOR
FAVOR POISE SLANT SLOPE BIGOTRY
INCLINE OBLIQUE DIAGONAL TENDENCY
PREJUDICE
BIASED ANGLED COLORED PARTIAL
BIB BRAT POUT APRON FEEDER TUCKER
(CHILD'S —) BISHOP

(LEATHER —) DICK
BIBLE BOOK VULGATE SCRIPTURE
(BOOK OF —) EX CHR COL COR DAN
EPH GAL GEN HAB HAG HEB HOS JER
JOB KIN LAM LEV MAL MIC NAH NEH
NUM PET REV ROM SAM TIM ACTS AMOS
CANT DEUT EZEK EZRA JOEL JOHN JUDE
JUDG LUKE MARK MATT OBAD PHIL
PROV RUTH SONG ZECH ZEPH HOSEA
JAMES JONAH KINGS MICAH NAHUM
PETER THESS TITUS DANIEL ECCLES
ESTHER EXODUS HAGGAI ISAIAH
JOSHUA JUDGES PHILEM PSALMS
ROMANS SAMUEL EZEKIEL GENESIS
HEBREWS MALACHI MATTHEW
NUMBERS OBADIAH TIMOTHY JEREMIAH
NEHEMIAH PHILEMON PROVERBS
CANTICLES EPHESIANS GALATIANS
LEVITICUS ZECHARIAH ZEPHANIAH
CHRONICLES COLOSSIANS REVELATION
CORINTHIANS DEUTERONOMY
PHILIPPIANS ECCLESIASTES
LAMENTATIONS THESSALONIANS
BICKER WAR SPAR TIFF ARGUE BRAWL
CAVIL FIGHT ASSAIL ATTACK BATTLE
CONTEND DISPUTE QUARREL QUIBBLE
WRANGLE SQUABBLE
BICYCLE BIKE CYCLE WHEEL JIGGER
SAFETY TANDEM TRIPLET ROADSTER
(PART OF —) ARM LUG RIM CLIP FORK
POST RACK RING SEAT STAY STEM TIRE
CHAIN GUARD PEDAL SHIFT SPOKE
FENDER HANGER SADDLE DOWNTUBE
SPROCKET CHAINWHEEL DERAILLEUR
BID GO BEG CALL TELL WISH OFFER
ORDER ADJURE CHARGE DIRECT ENJOIN
INVITE REVEAL SUMMON TENDER
COMMAND DECLARE ENTREAT PROFFER
ANNOUNCE PROCLAIM PROPOSAL
(— ADIEU) TEACH
(— AT AUCTION) CRY
BIDE STAY WAIT ABIDE AWAIT TARRY
ENDURE REMAIN SUFFER SOJOURN
CONTINUE TOLERATE
BIER PYRE FRAME HORSE COFFIN HEARSE
LITTER SUPPORT
BIG FAT BOLD HUGE MUCH VAST BULKY
CHIEF GRAND GREAT GROSS HUSKY
LARGE MIGHTY EMINENT LEADING
MASSIVE POMPOUS VIOLENT BOASTFUL
BOUNCING ENORMOUS GENEROUS
GIGANTIC IMPOSING PLUMPING
PREGNANT
BIGFOOT SASQUATCH
BIGHORN AOUDAD ARGALI CIMARRON
BIGHT BAY BEND BITE COIL GULF LOOP
ANGLE CURVE INLET NOOSE POCKET
BIGNESS BULK
BIGOT CAFARD ZEALOT FANATIC
MUMPSIMUS
BIGOTED BIASED NARROW HIDEBOUND
ILLIBERAL SECTARIAN
BIGOTRY INTOLERANCE
BILE GALL VENOM CHOLER ATRABILE
MELANCHOLY
BILK DO GYP BALK HOAX CHEAT COZEN

TRICK DELUDE FLEECE DECEIVE
DEFRAUD SWINDLE
BILL ACT DUN NEB NIB TAB BEAK CHIT
NOTE PECK CHECK ENTRY LIBEL SCORE
CARESS CHARGE DOCKET INDICT PECKER
PICKAX POSTER STRIKE INVOICE
MATTOCK PLACARD PROGRAM STATUTE
BILLHOOK DOCUMENT PETITION
(— OF ANCHOR) PEE PEAK
(— OF COMPLAINT) QUERELA
(— OF CREDIT) ANGEL
(— OF DIVORCE) GET
(— OF EXCHANGE) SOLA HUNDI
DEVISE
(— OF FARE) MENU CARTE
(— OF PARCELS) FACTURE
(DOLLAR —) BUCK SPOT SINGLE
FROGSKIN
(REVOLUTIONARY —) ASSIGNAT
(10-DOLLAR —) TEN TENNER SAWBUCK
(100-DOLLAR —) CENTURY
(2-DOLLAR —) DEUCE
(5-DOLLAR —) FIN VEE FIVE FIVER
BILLET BAR HUT LOG NOTE PASS POST
BERTH HOUSE LODGE STICK STRAP
COUPON ENROLL HARBOR LETTER
NOTICE TICKET EPISTLE MISSIVE
DOCUMENT FIREWOOD QUARTERS
(— SOLDIERS) CESS
BILLFOLD WALLET NOTECASE
BILLINGSGATE ABUSE SLAPDASH
BILLION MILLIARD
BILLOW SEA BLOW WAVE BULGE FLOAT
SURGE SWELL RIPPLE ROLLER WALLOW
BREAKER UNDULATE
BILLY CLUB GOAT MACE BATON CUDGEL
BLUDGEON BLACKJACK TRUNCHEON
BILLY BUDD (CHARACTER IN —)
BUDD VERE BILLY CLAGGART
(COMPOSER OF —) BRITTEN
BIN ARK BOX CART CRIB FRAME HUTCH
STALL STORE WAGON BASKET BUNKER
HAMPER MANGER POCKET TROUGH
(— FOR CEMENT) SILO
(— FOR FISH) KENCH
(— FOR GRAIN) ARK
BIND JAM TIE FAST GIRD GYVE HOLD
HOOP KNIT KNOT LASH NAIL TAPE
BRACE CHAIN CINCH GIRTH STICK STRAP
TRUSS ATTACH BUNDLE COMMIT
ENGAGE FETTER FREEZE GARTER GIRDLE
LIGATE OBLIGE SWATHE TETHER
BANDAGE CONFINE ENCHAIN GRAPPLE
SHACKLE SWADDLE OBLIGATE RESTRAIN
(— A FALCON) MAIL
(— BY LEASE) THIRL
(— BY PLEDGE) GAGE SWEAR
(— IN BUNDLE) KID BAVIN
(— INTO SHEAVES) GAVEL THRAVE
(— ONESELF) ADHERE
(— TO SECRECY) TILE
(— TOGETHER) LIME FAGOT SEIZE
CEMENT ASTRINGE RELIGATE COLLIGATE
(— UP) KILT BAVIN TRUSS
(— WINGS) PINION
BINDER BAND BEAM BOND CORD ROPE

BALER COVER FRAME LEVER FILLET
FOLDER GIRDER HEADER BOOKMAKER
BINDING TAG BAND CORD ROPE TAPE
COVER VALID EDGING RIBBON BOUNDEN
WEBBING FAITHFUL STRINGENT
OBLIGATORY
(— FAST) IRON
(— OF BOOK) BOCK FACE
(— OF GOLD) BISSET
(— ON DRESS) FENT
BINGE BAT BLOW BUST SOAK TEAR TOOT
BEANO PARTY SOUSE SPREE CAROUSAL
BINGO KENO BEANO LOTTO BRANDY
SCREENO TOMBOLA
BINOCULARS GLASS
BIOGRAPHY BIO LIFE VITA MEMOIR
ACCOUNT HISTORY RECOUNT
BIOLOGIST NATURALIST
BIOTITE MICA ANOMITE MEROXENE
RUBELLAN
BIRCH CANE FLOG WHIP ALDER ALNUS
CANOE HICKORY
BIRD JAY NUN PIE CHAT COOT CROW
DOVE FOWL JACK KNOT RUFF WING
BAKER BRANT CHUCK CLEAR COVEY
EGRET FLIER FLYER GOOSE HOBBY
JUNCO PEWEE PEWIT RAVEN SWIFT
TWITE BULBUL DIPPER DRIVER DRONGO
DUCKER DUNLIN FALCON FINGER
GROUSE GUINEA HOOPOE HOOTER
NESTER OSCINE PHOEBE SHRIKE SILVAN
SITTER SYLVAN TURNIX VERDIN YAWPER
ANTBIRD BABBLER BLUEJAY BUNTING
CATBIRD CHIRPER COTINGA COURLAN
FEATHER FLAPPER FLICKER FLOPPER
GRACKLE HORNERO IRRISOR JACKDAW
KINGLET MOULTER PEACOCK PERCHER
QUILLER REDWING SCRAPER SKINNER
SKYLARK SUNBIRD TINAMOU TOMFOOL
WAXWING ACCENTOR AIRPLANE
AMADAVAT ANNOTINE BLACKCAP
BLACKNEB BLUEBIRD BOBOLINK
BOBWHITE CAGELING CARINATE
COCKBIRD FIREBIRD FIRETAIL GROSBEAK
GRUIFORM IBISBILL JUVENILE KILLDEER
KINGBIRD LOBEFOOT LONGSPUR
OXPECKER PALMIPED PHEASANT
PLUMIPED POORWILL PREACHER
SONGBIRD SURFBIRD SWAMPHEN
THRASHER THROSTLE TITMOUSE
TREMBLER WHINCHAT WOODCHAT
WOODCOCK YEARBIRD CROSSBILL
ROADRUNNER MOCKINGBIRD
(— OF BRILLIANT PLUMAGE) TODY
JALAP BARBET ORIOLE TROGON
JACAMAR KIROMBO MINIVET TANAGER
(— OF INDIA) BAYA KALA SHAMA
(— OF OMEN) WAYBIRD
(— OF PREY) OWL HAWK KITE EAGLE
GLEDE STOOP EAGLET ELANET BUZZARD
GOSHAWK STOOPER VULTURE
ACCIPITER
(AFRICAN —) TAHA QUELEA TOURACO
UMBRETTE NAPECREST
(AUSTRALIAN —) EMU ROA LORY
ARARA LEIPOA BOOBOOK BUSTARD

FIGBIRD WAYBUNG BELLBIRD LORIKEET
LYREBIRD MANUCODE
(BIG-BEAKED —) BECARD HORNBILL
(CRESTED —) KAGU COPPY HOATZIN
TOPKNOT
(CROCODILE —) TROCHIL
(DECOY —) CALL STOOL
(DIVING —) AUK LOON GREBE DARTER
DOPPER DUCKER GRAYLING PLUNGEON
(EUROPEAN —) ANI DAW MEW QUA
CIRL DARR KITE MALL MORO QUIS ROOK
STAG WHIM YITE AMSEL BOONK GLEDE
MAVIS MERLE OUZEL SACER SAKER
SERIN TARIN TEREK TERIN WHAUP
AVOCET CUCKOO CUSHAT GAYLAG
GODWIT MARTEN MERLIN MISSEL
REDCAP WHEWER WINDLE WINNEL
WRANNY BITTERN BUSTARD HAYBIRD
KESTREL MOTACIL ORTOLAN SAKERET
STARNEL WHISKEY WINNARD WITWALL
BARGOOSE CHEPSTER DOTTEREL
GARGANEY REDSTART WHEATEAR
WHEYBIRD WHIMBREL WRANNOCK
YOLDRING
(EXTINCT —) MOA DODO JIBI KIWI
MAMO RUKH OFFBIRD
(FABULOUS —) FUM ROC FUNG
HALCYON OOFBIRD WHISTLER
(FEMALE —) HEN JENNY
(FICTITIOUS —) JAYHAWK PHOENIX
(FISH-CATCHING —) OSPREY CRABIER
(FLEDGLING —) SQUAB
(FLIGHTLESS —) EMU GOR MOA DODO
EYAS GORB GULL KAGU KIWI CALLOW
GORLIN APTERYX GORLING NESTLER
OSTRICH PENGUIN BUBBLING NESTLING
(FRIGATE —) IOA IWA
(FRUIT-EATING —) COLY
(GALLOWS —) HEMPY
(GAME —) QUAIL SNIPE COLIMA
GROUSE INCOME FLAPPER INCOMER
(GREEN —) SIRGANG
(HAWAIIAN —) IO OO AVA IOA IWA
OOA IIWI JIBI KOAE MAMO MOHO OMAO
OOAA KAMAO PALILA
(HORN-HEADED —) KAMICHI
(INJURED —) CRIPPLE
(LARGEST —) LAMMERGEIER
(LIMICOLINE —) PRATINCOLE
(MADAGASCAR —) KIROMBO
(MECHANICAL —) ORTHOPTER
(MYTHICAL —) FUM ROC GANZA
SIMURGH
(NEW ZEALAND —) KEA MOA OII ROA
HUIA KAKA KIWI KOKO KUKU KULU PEHO
RURU TITI WEKA POAKA KAKAPO
KOKAKO KUKUPA APTERYX KORIMAKO
MOREPORK NOTORNIS
(PASSERINE —) QUIT FINCH SPARROW
STARNEL SWALLOW SYLVIID DREPANID
FALCONET FERNBIRD GRALLINA
JACKBIRD OVENBIRD
(RAPACIOUS —) SKUA JAEGER
(RASORIAL —) SCRATCHER
(RUNNING —) COURSER
(SAMOAN —) IAO
(SEA —) AUK ERNE GONY GULL PINK

SMEW TERN EIDER SOLAN FULMAR
GANNET HAGDON OSPREY PETREL
PUFFIN PELICAN SEAFOWL MURRELET
MALLEMUCK
(SHORE —) REE RAIL SORA SNIPE STILT
WADER AVOCET CURLEW PLOVER
WILLET WRYBILL SHEATHBILL
(SHORT-TAILED —) BREVE
(SINGING —) LARK WREN PIPIT ROBIN
VEERY VIREO CANARY LINNET MOCKER
ORIOLE OSCINE SINGER THRUSH
WARBLER FAUVETTE REDSTART
NIGHTINGALE
(SMALL —) TIT TODY WREN PEGGY
PIPIT TYDIE VIREO DICKEY LINNET SISKIN
TOMTIT CREEPER SPARROW TITLARK
COCORICO GNATSNAP PERCOLIN
STARLING WHEATEAR
(SOUTH AMERICAN —) GUAN MINA
MITU MYNA RARA TOCA BAKER CHAJA
JOPIM TURCO BARBET BECARD CHUNGA
TOUCAN CARIAMA OILBIRD BELLBIRD
BOATBILL CARACARA GUACHARO
HOACTZIN PUFFBIRD SCREAMER
TAPACOLO TERUTERO
(STYLIZED —) DISTELFINK
(TROPICAL —) ANI GUAN KOAE TODY
BOSUN JALAP BARBET BECARD MOTMOT
TROGON JACAMAR MANAKIN WIGTAIL
LONGTAIL SALTATOR
(WADING —) HERN IBIS RAIL SORA
CRANE HERON SNIPE STILT STORK
ARGALA AVOCET GODWIT JACANA
LIMPKIN BOATBILL FLAMINGO SHOEBILL
SHOEBIRD SANDERLING
(YOUNG —) EYA GULL PIPER CHEEPER
FLAPPER NESTLER BIRDIKIN NESTLING
BIRTH BEAR FALL BLOOD ORIGIN
BEARING BORNING DESCENT GENESIS
LINEAGE DELIVERY GENITURE NASCENCY
NATALITY NATIVITY
BIRTHMARK MOLE NEVUS SPILOMA
BISCUIT BUN ROLL RUSK SNAP BREAD
SCONE WAFER COOKIE MUFFIN SIMNEL
CRACKER PRETZEL HARDTACK
ZWIEBACK
BISECT FORK CROSS HALVE SPLIT
CLEAVE DIVIDE MIDDLE SEPARATE
BISHOP ABBA LAWN PAPA POPE COARB
EPARCH EXARCH PRIEST PRIMUS
PONTIFF PRELATE PRIMATE DIOCESAN
ORDINARY PONTIFEX PATRIARCH
BISON BOVINE WISENT AUROCHS
BONASUS BUFFALO
BISTRO BAR CAFE TAVERN WINESHOP
ESTAMINET NIGHTCLUB
BIT ACE FID JOT NIP ORT PIP TAD WEE
ATOM BITE CHIP DOIT DRIB IOTA ITEM
MITE MOTE PART SNIP SPOT WHIT
AUGER BLADE CRUMB DRILL PIECE
POINT SCRAP SHRED SMACK SNACK
SPECK TASTE MORSEL SIPPET SMIDGE
TITTLE TRIFLE GLIMMER MORCEAU
PORTION SMIDGEN FRACTION FRAGMENT
(— OF KEY) WEB
(— OF METAL) FLITTER
(— OF TOAST) SNIPPET

(CUTTING —) CHASER
(DRILL —) CROWN
(FANCIFUL —) FLAM
(FIPPENY —) SIXPENCE
(HORSE'S —) KEVEL SNODE CANNON
PELHAM SCATCH SNAFFLE BASTONET
(LEAST —) FIG JOT RAP HANG LICK
GHOST GROAT RIZZOM STITCH
(LITTLE —) PICK TOUCH BITTOCK
REMNANT SOUPCON
(ONE — PER SECOND) BAUD
(ONE BILLION —S) GIGABIT
(ONE-QUARTER —) GILL
(SEQUENCE OF —S) BYTE
(SMALL —) BLEB GLIM SPUNK
(SMALL —S) SMATTER
BITE BIT CUT EAT JAW NIP BAIT CHEW
FOOD GNAW HOLD MEAL SNAP TAKE
CHAMP CHEAT GNASH PINCH SEIZE
SMART SNACK STING CRUNCH MORSEL
NIBBLE CORRODE MORSURE PARTAKE
SLANDER
BITING HOT ACID HOAR KEEN ACRID
NIPPY QUICK SHARP SNELL BITTER
RODENT SEVERE SHREWD CAUSTIC
CUTTING MORDANT NIPPING PUNGENT
INCISIVE PIERCING POIGNANT SCALDING
SCATHING STINGING ACIDULOUS
MORDACIOUS
BITTER ACID KEEN RUDE SALT SORE
SOUR TART ACERB ACRID ASPER BLEAK
HARSH IRATE SHARP BITING PICRIC
SEVERE SEARE CAUSTIC CRABBED
CUTTING FERVENT GALLING PAINFUL
PUNGENT SATIRIC POIGNANT SARDONIC
STINGING
BITTERNESS RUE ACOR BILE GALL
ENMITY MALICE RANCOR ACERBITY
ACRIDITY ACRIMONY ASPERITY
FERVENCY SEVERITY
BITTER VETCH ERS
BITUMEN TAR CONGO PITCH MALTHA
ASPHALT
BIVALENT DIATOMIC
BIVALVE CLAM SPAT PINNA COCKLE
MUSSEL OYSTER MOLLUSK PANDORA
SCALLOP TOHEROA
BIVOUAC CAMP ETAPE WATCH ENCAMP
SHELTER
BIZARRE ODD ANTIC OUTRE QUEER
QUAINT BAROQUE CURIOUS FANCIFUL
ECCENTRIC FANTASTIC GROTESQUE
OUTLANDISH
BLAB CHAT BLATE CHEEP CLACK BABBLE
BETRAY GOSSIP REVEAL SQUEAL TATTLE
CHATTER CLATTER
BLACK DHU JET DARK EBON FOUL INKY
NOIR SOOT DUSKY MURKY NEGRO NOIRE
RAVEN SABLE SOOTY TARRY THICK
ATROUS BRUNET DISMAL GLOOMY
PITCHY SULLEN MELANIC SWARTHY
(— AND BLUE) LIVID
(— OUT) CONK
(BONE —) SPODIUM
(BROWNISH —) LAVA
(GREENISH —) CORBEAU
(IVORY —) ABAISER

(VIOLET —) CROW
BLACK ARROW (AUTHOR OF —)
STEVENSON
(CHARACTER IN —) DICK ELLIS OATES
DANIEL JOANNA OLIVER SEDLEY
LAWLESS RICHARD SHELTON BRACKLEY
DUCKWORTH
BLACKBALL PILL BALLOT EXCLUDE
OSTRACIZE
BLACKBERRY AGAWAM LAWTON
BRAMBLE DEWBERRY MULBERRY
ROSACEAN
BLACKBIRD ANI DAW PIE CROW MERL
COLLY OUZEL RAVEN COWBIRD GRACKLE
JACKDAW REDWING
BLACK BUCK SASIN
BLACKEN INK TAR CHAR CORK SMUT
SOIL SOOT CLOUD SMOKY SULLY
BEFOUL DARKEN DEFAME MALIGN
SMIRCH SMUTCH VILIFY ASPERSE
SLANDER TRADUCE BESMIRCH
BLACKFISH TAUTOG DOGFISH GRAMPUS
POTHEAD HARDHEAD
BLACKFOOT KAINAH PIEGAN SIKSIKA
SIHASAPA
BLACKGUARD GAMIN ROTTER LADRONE
SKELLUM VAGRANT BLAGGARD
CRIMINAL LARRIKIN VAGABOND
SCOUNDREL
BLACK GUM TUPELO HORNPIPE
STINKWOOD
BLACKHEAD COMEDO
BLACKJACK OAK SAP SAP CLUB COSH DUCK
FLAG JACK BILLY JERKIN BLUDGEON
BLACKMAIL BRIBE COERCE EXTORT
RANSOM
BLACKSMITH LOHAR SHOER SMITH
VULCAN FARRIER STRIKER IRONSMITH
BLACKSNAKE WHIP QUIRT RACER
ELAPID RUNNER COLUBRID
BLACKTHORN HAW SLOE GRIBBLE
SLOEBUSH
BLACK WIDOW POKOMOO
BLADDER SAC VES VESICA AMPULLA
BLISTER UROCYST UTRICLE VESICLE
BLADE FIN OAR SAW WEB BOWL EDGE
FLAG HEAD LEAF WEAK BLOOD BRAND
DANDY FLUKE GUIDE KNIFE LANCE
SHEAR SPARK SWORD BLUNGE BUCKET
BUSTER CUTTER DOCTOR FOIBLE
HEDDLE RIPPER SCYTHE SICKLE TOLEDO
BAYONET CHIPPER GALLANT SCALPEL
SCAPULA SCRAPER
(— OF FAN) VANE
(— OF GRASS) PILE CHIRE SPEAR SPIRE
STRAP TRANEEN
(— OF KNIFE) TANG GRAIN
(— OF LEAF) LIMB LAMINA
(— OF MORION) COMB
(— OF OAR) PALM PEEL PELL WASH
(— OF SCISSORS) BILL
(— OF YOUNG GRAIN) SORAGE
(CULTIVATOR —) SWEEP DUCKFOOT
(SKATE —) RUNNER
BLAME CALL CHOP HURT LACK ONUS
TWIT CHIDE FAULT GUILT ODIUM PINCH
TOUCH ACCUSE BUMBLE BURDEN

CHARGE DIRDUM PLIGHT REBUKE REVILE ASCRIBE CENSURE CONDEMN CULPATE OBLOQUY REPROOF REPROVE SLANDER UPBRAID REPROACH

BLAMELESS PURE ENTIRE PERFECT INNOCENT SACKLESS SPOTLESS RIGHTEOUS

BLAMEWORTHY GUILTY CRIMINAL CULPABLE REPROBATE

BLANCH FADE PALE CHALK SCALD APPALL BLEACH BLENCH WHITEN ETIOLATE

BLAND COLD KIND MILD OILY OPEN SOFT SLEEK SUAVE BENIGN BREEZY GENIAL GENTLE SMOOTH URBANE AFFABLE AMIABLE LENIENT GRACIOUS UNCTUOUS

BLANDISH COAX CHARM ALLURE BLANCH CAJOLE FONDLE SMOOTH FLATTER WHEEDLE

BLANK BARE FLAN FORM SHOT VOID ANNUL BLIND CHASM CLEAN EMPTY FALSE SPACE WASTE WHITE COUPON VACANT UNMIXED VACUOUS UNFILLED

BLANKET RUG WRAP COTTA COVER LAYER MANTA QUILT SHEET THROW AFGHAN GLOBAL MANTLE PALLET PONCHO SERAPE STIFLE STROUD SMOTHER COVERLET MACKINAW
(— A VESSEL) WRONG
(— OF SKINS) KAROSS
(— WITH BOMBS) SATURATE
(BUSHMAN'S —) BLUEY
(QUILTED —) BROT
(SADDLE —) CORONA

BLANKNESS VACUITY NEGATION

BLARE PEAL BLAST NOISE BLAZON SCREAM FANFARE TANTARA TRUMPET

BLARNEY CON TAFFY BUTTER CAJOLE SAWDER FLATTER WHEEDLE

BLASPHEME ABUSE CURSE DEFAME REVILE PROFANE

BLASPHEMOUS BAD RIBALD IMPIOUS PROFANE

BLASPHEMY CALUMNY CURSING IMPIETY ANATHEMA SWEARING

BLAST NIP BANG BLOW FRAP GALE RUIN RUST SHOT WIND BLAME SPLIT STUNT TRUMP ATTACK BLIGHT FORBID REBUFF VOLLEY WITHER BLUSTER DESPOIL EXPLODE SHATTER SHRIVEL DYNAMITE OUTBURST PROCLAIM
(— OF WIND) GUST RISE PERRY PIRRIE VENTOSITY
(— ON HORN) TOOT PRYSE
(— WITH COLD) SNEAP
(FURIOUS —) SNIFTER
(RAINY —) BLATTER

BLATANT GLIB LOUD BRASH GROSS NOISY SILLY VOCAL COARSE GARISH TONANT VULGAR BRAWLING STRIDENT

BLATHER STIR BLEAT BABBLE WAFFLE BLITHER PRATTLE NONSENSE

BLAUBOK ETAAC BLUEBOK

BLAZE BURN FIRE GLOW LUNT MARK SHOT SPOT FLAME FLARE FLASH GLARE GLEAM GLORY INGLE SHINE STEAM

TORCH BLAZON BONFIRE PIONEER SPLENDOR

BLAZING AFIRE FIERY LIGHT FLAMING FLARING

BLAZON DECK SHOW ADORN BLARE BLAZE BOAST DEPICT SHIELD DECLARE DISPLAY EXHIBIT PUBLISH

BLEACH SUN WASH CHALK POACH BLANCH BLENCH PURIFY WHITEN DECOLOR LIGHTEN BLONDINE ETIOLATE PEROXIDE

BLEACHERS SCAFFOLD

BLEAK DIM RAW COLD DOUR GRAY PALE OURIE STARK BITTER BLEACH DISMAL DREARY FRIGID PALLID CUTTING DESOLATE CHEERLESS

BLEAK HOUSE (AUTHOR OF —) DICKENS
(CHARACTER IN —) JO ADA JOHN ALLAN CLARE FLITE GUPPY KROOK BUCKET ESTHER RAWDON DEDLOCK JELLYBY RICHARD WILLIAM CARSTONE CHADBAND JARNDYCE SKIMPOLE LEICESTER SUMMERSON WOODCOURT TULKINGHORN

BLEAT BAA BLAT BLATE BLATHER BLUSTER WHICKER

BLEED FLUX MILK WEEP BLOOD LEECH MULCT SWEAT SWINDLE

BLEMISH MAR BLOT BLUR DENT FLAW GALL LACK MAIM MARK MOIL MOLE RIFT SCAR SLUR SPOT VICE WANT BLAME BOTCH CLOUD CRACK FAULT FLECK SPECK STAIN TAINT TOUCH BLOTCH BREACH DEFAME DEFECT IMPAIR INJURE MACULA SMIRCH STIGMA DEFAULT FISSURE SUNSPOT
(— IN CLOTH) AMPER SULLY
(— IN PAPER) FISHEYE
(PRINTING —) MACKLE

BLENCH FOIL SHUN AVOID ELUDE EVADE QUAIL SHAKE SHIRK TRICK BAFFLE BLANCH BLEACH FLINCH RECOIL SHRINK DECEIVE

BLEND MIX RUN BLOT FUSE JOIN MELT ADMIX CREAM GRADE MERGE PUREE SHADE SMEAR SPOIL STAIN TINGE UNITE COMMIX MINGLE COMBINE CONFUSE CORRUPT GRADATE MIXTURE POLLUTE COALESCE TINCTURE
(— OF NOISES) CHARM
(— OF SHERRY) SOLERA
(— OF WINES) CUVEE

BLENDE JACK SPHALERITE

BLENDED FONDU FUSED MIXED MERGED MINGLED CONFLATE CONFLUENT

BLESS KEEP SAIN WAVE ADORE CROSS EXTOL FAVOR GUARD THANK VISIT HALLOW PRAISE APPROVE BEATIFY GLORIFY PROTECT PRESERVE SANCTIFY

BLESSED HOLY BLEST HAPPY SEELY DIVINE JOYFUL SACRED BHAGAVAT BLISSFUL BLOOMING HALLOWED HEAVENLY CELESTIAL

BLESSING BOON GIFT SAIN BLISS GRACE PRAISE BENISON WORSHIP FELICITY BEATITUDE

BLIGHT NIP FIRE RUIN RUST SMUT BLAST
FROST SNEAP MILDEW WITHER DESTROY
BLIND BET POT ANTE BOMA DARK DEAD
DULL HIDE HOOD SEEL BLANK CLOAK
SHADE STAKE STALL WAGER AMBUSH
DARKEN DAZZLE SCREEN SECRET
AIMLESS BANDAGE ECLIPSE EYELESS
OBSCURE PRETEXT SHUTTER ABORTIVE
ARTIFICE BLINDING HOODWINK
IGNORANT JALOUSIE UMBRELLA
VENETIAN
(— IN ONE EYE) PEED GLEED
(HALF —) STARBLIND
BLINDFOLD MOP DARK BLINK BLUFF
SCARF MUFFLE BANDAGE BLINDER
OBSCURE ENCLOSER
BLINDNESS BISSON CECITY MYOPSY
ANOPSIA MEROPIA ABLEPSIA DARKNESS
IGNORANCE
(— TO TRUTH) AVIDYA
(COLOR —) ACHROBIA
(DAY —) HEMERALOPIA
(NIGHT —) NYCTALOPIA
(PARTIAL —) MEROPIA HEMIOPSIA
(RED-GREEN —) DALTONISM
(SNOW —) CHIONABLEPSIA
(TEMPORARY —) MOONBLINK
BLINK BAT PINK SHUN WINK CHEAT
FLASH GLEAM SHINE TRICK GLANCE
IGNORE CONDONE GLIMMER GLIMPSE
NEGLECT NICTATE SPARKLE TWINKLE
BLINKER EYE BLINK BLUFF LIGHT SIGNAL
WINKER BLINDER FLASHER GOGGLES
BLIP PIP ECHO
BLISS JOY EDEN GLORY ANANDA HEAVEN
DELIGHT ECSTASY NIRVANA RAPTURE
FELICITY GLADNESS PARADISE
PLEASURE
BLISSFUL HOLY SEELY BLITHE BLESSED
ELYSIAN UTOPIAN BEATIFIED GLORIFIED
BLISTER BLEB BLOW BOIL BURN BLAIN
BULGE BULLA TOPIC VESIC APHTHA
BUBBLE CUPOLA SCORCH TETTER
SCALDER SKELLER VESICLE VESICATE
BLISTERED BULLATE
BLITHE GAY GLAD BONNY BUXOM HAPPY
JOLLY MERRY JOVIAL JOYOUS LIVELY
GAYSOME JOCULAR WINSOME
CHEERFUL GLADSOME SPRIGHTLY
BLIZZARD BLOW GALE WIND BURAN
PURGA RETORT SNIFTER SQUELCHER
BLOAT BLOW FLOAT SWELL EXPAND
TUMEFY DISTEND FERMENT INFLATE
BLOATED FOZY CURED FOGGY HOVEN
PUFFY TUMID SODDEN TURGID
POMPOUS REPLETE
BLOB WEN BEAD BLEB BOIL CLOT DAUB
DROP GOUT LUMP MARK MASS BUBBLE
DOLLOP PIMPLE BLEMISH BLISTER
BLOSSOM GLOBULE PUSTULE SPLOTCH
BLOC RING BLOK CABAL PARTY UNION
CLIQUE BENELUX FACTION
BLOCK COB COG DIE DOG FID HOB HUB
JAM KEY NOG ROW TOP BALK BASE
BEAR BILK BUCK CAKE CLOG CUBE
DRUM FOIL FOUL FROG HEAD JAMB
MASS STAY STOP TRIG BRICK CHECK

CLAMP CLEAT CLOSE COVER DETER
DOLLY DUMMY FLOAT NUDGE PARRY
PATCH SHAPE SLUMP SPIKE SPOKE
STOCK STUFF STUMP DOMINO HINDER
IMPEDE KIBOSH MONKEY MUFFLE
OPPOSE QUERRE SCOTCH SNATCH
SQUARE STREET STYMIE TAPLET
THWART WAYLAY BOLLOCK BOLSTER
CONDEMN DEADEYE INHIBIT PREVENT
RAMHEAD TROLLEY BLOCKADE
KEYSTONE MONOLITH OBSTACLE
OBSTRUCT STOPPAGE BRIQUETTE
(— A WHEEL) SCOTE
(— AT SPAR END) STEEVE
(— FOR SKIDDING LOGS) BICYCLE
(— FOR SLAVE SALES) CATASTA
(— IN SPEAKING) STAMMER
(— OF BUILDINGS) INSULA
(— OF COAL) JUD
(— OF EARTH'S CRUST) HORST
(— OF GRANITE) SET
(— OF ICE) SERAC
(— OF LAND) FORTY
(— OF SEATS) CUNEUS
(— OF TIMBER) BOLT JUGGLE
(— SUPPORTING MAST) STEP
(— THE WAY) SCOAT
(— UP) BAR DAM CLOY QUIRT
CONDEMN OPPILATE FORECLOSE
(— WITH HOLE IN IT) WAPP EUPHROE
(— WITH PROJECTING CORE) SETTLE
(—S OF STONE) DIMENSION
(ARCHITECTURAL —) DRUM STONE
DENTIL IMPOST MUTULE PLINTH
DOSSERET
(CHOPPING —) HACKLOG
(CLAY —) DRAWBAR
(FAULT —) MASSIF
(FELTED —) DAMPER
(FOOTBALL —) CRACKBACK
(FULCRUM —) GLUT
(FUSE —) CUTOUT
(HOSPITAL —) PAVILION
(IRON —) USE VOL BITT ANVIL CHAIR
(LOGGING —) LEAD JUMBO
(NAUTICAL —) CHOCK HEART STOCK
SADDLE DEADEYE FAIRLEAD
(ORNAMENTAL —) BOSS MODILLION
(PAVING —) SET CUBE STONE
WHEELER
(PLASTER —) BATTER
(POLISHING —) BUFF FLOAT RABOT
(PRINTING —) CUT QUAD RISER
QUADRAT
(PULLEY —) CRAWL
(SANDSTONE —) SARSEN
(SQUARED —) MITCHEL
(STUMBLING —) HURTING
(TACKLE —) CALO TONGUE
(VAULTING —) BUCK HORSE
BLOCKADE DAM BLOCK SIEGE BESIEGE
EMBARGO OBSTRUCT BARRICADE
BELEAGUER
BLOCKAGE LOGJAM
BLOCKHEAD ASS LUG OAF CLOT COOT
DOLT FOOL MOME BOOBY CHUMP
CUDDY IDIOT NINNY DIMWIT NITWIT

JACKASS LACKWIT TOMFOOL BONEHEAD CLODPATE DUMMKOPF

BLOCKHOUSE SPUR PUNTAL GARRISON

BLOKE MAN CHAP COVE TOFF BLOAK JOKER FELLOW

BLOND FAIR LIGHT BLONDE FLAXEN GOLDEN YELLOW

BLOOD KIN SAP GORE LIFE MOOD RACE SANG BLADE CRUOR FLESH FLUID SERUM CLARET GALLANT KINSHIP KINSMAN LINEAGE RELATION

BLOODHOUND LYAM LIMER BANDOG SLEUTH

BLOODSHED DEATH CARNAGE VIOLENCE SLAUGHTER

BLOODSHOT RED INFLAMED

BLOODSTAINED GORY

BLOODSUCKER LEECH SPONGER VAMPIRE

BLOODTHIRSTY BLOODY CARNAL SANGUINE TIGERISH FEROCIOUS MURDEROUS SANGUINARY

BLOODY GORY RUDE CRUEL RUDDY PLUCKY CRIMSON BLEEDING DEATHFUL HEMATOSE FEROCIOUS MERCILESS MURDEROUS SANGUINARY

BLOOM BLOW HAZE KNOT BLUSH BLOSSOM FLOURISH
(— OF WILLOW) GULL
(— ON INSECT) POLLEN
(— ON SHELL) CUTICLE
(— ON TREE) GOSLING
(METAL —S) HEAT
(POWDERY —) PRUINA

BLOSSOM BUD BELL BLOW BLOOM FLOWER BURGEON PROSPER FLOURISH

BLOT MAR BLOB BLUR DAUB SOIL SPOT BLACK SMEAR SPECK STAIN SULLY BLOTCH CANCEL DAMAGE EFFACE IMPAIR SHADOW SMIRCH SMUDGE STIGMA BLEMISH ECLIPSE EXPUNGE OBSCURE TARNISH DISGRACE REPROACH

BLOUSE MIDDY SHIRT SMOCK TUNIC CAMISA GUIMPE JUMPER CASAQUE VAREUSE CAMISOLE CASAQUIN JIRKINET

BLOW BOB COB COP CUT DAB FAN HIT JAB JAR PAT PEG POP RAP TAP TIP BAFF BANG BASH BEAT BELT BIFF BLAW BRAG BULL BUMP BUTT CHAP CHOP CONK CUFF DASH DENT DINT DRUB FLAP GALE GUST HACK HURT JOLT LEAD LEFT LICK PANT PLUG PUFF SCUD SLAM SLAP SLUG SOCK SWAT THUD WELT WHOP WIND BINGE BOAST BURST CLOUT CLUNK FLICK IMPEL KNOCK PANDY PASTE PLUMP PLUNK PUNCH RIGHT SHOCK SLASH SMACK SMASH SMITE SPANK STORM THUMP WHACK BUFFET DEPART LARRUP REBUKE STROKE THWACK WALLOP BLOSSOM BLUSTER CRUSHER INFLATE CALAMITY DISASTER KNOCKOUT
(— ABRASIVES) BLAST
(— CEMENT) KIBOSH
(— GUSTILY) FLAW TUCK WINNOW
(— IN PUFFS) FAFF
(— NOSE) SNITE

(— OFF STEAM) SNIFT
(— ON CHEEK) ALAPA
(— SOFTLY) BREATHE
(— UP) BOMB BLAST DYNAMITE SUFFLATE
(— VIOLENTLY) STORM
(— WITH FOOT) BOOT KICK SPURN
(FENCING —) MONTANT
(GENTLE —) CHUCK
(GLANCING —) SCUFF
(MOCK —) FEINT

BLOWGUN SUMPIT SARBACANE PEASHOOTER

BLOWSY DOWDY FROWZY

BLUBBER CRY FAT SOB WAIL WEEP SPECK WHINE SLOBBER WHIMPER

BLUDGEON BAT HIT SAP CLUB COSH MACE BILLY STICK BLACKJACK TRUNCHEON

BLUE (ALSO SEE COLOR) SAD SKY AQUA BICE GLUM TEAL WOAD AZURE BERYL LIVID COBALT GLOOMY INDIGO LUPINE CELESTE CYANINE GENTIAN LOBELIA PEACOCK CERULEAN DEJECTED LITERARY MIDNIGHT SAPPHIRE WEDGWOOD

BLUE GUM FEVERGUM EUCALYPTUS

BLUEPRINT MAP PLAN PLOT DRAFT TRACE SKETCH DIAGRAM PROJECT CYANOTYPE

BLUFF BANK BRAG CURT FOOL RUDE BLUNT BRAVE BURLY CLIFF FRANK GRUFF SHORT SURLY WINDY ABRUPT CRUSTY BRUSQUE DECEIVE UNCIVIL CHURLISH HOODWINK

BLUNDER ERR BALK BONE BOOB BULL FLUB ROIL SKEW SLIP TRIP BONER BOTCH BREAK ERROR FAULT FLUFF GAFFE LAPSE MISDO BOGGLE BOOBOO BUMBLE BUNGLE FUMBLE HOWLER MUDDLE BLOOMER BLOOPER CONFUSE DERANGE FAILURE MISTAKE STUMBLE

BLUNDERING AWKWARD BUMBLING

BLUNT BALD CURT DULL FLAT SNUB ABATE BLUFF BRUSK INERT PLAIN CANDID CLUMSY DEADEN OBTUND OBTUSE STUBBY STUPID BRUSQUE

BLUR DIM FOG BLOT FADE MIST SLUR SOIL BLEAR CLOUD SMEAR STAIN SULLY SMUDGE STIGMA BLEMISH CONFUSE OBSCURE

BLURB AD BOLT PUFF RAVE BRIEF NOTICE

BLURRED FAINT FUZZY MUZZY VAGUE WOOZY BLEARY BLURRY CLOUDY SMEARY SMUDGY WOOLLY CLOUDED EDGELESS

BLURT BOLT PLUMP BLUNDER EXCLAIM

BLUSH GLOW COLOR FLUSH GLEAM ROUGE TINGE MANTLE REDDEN CRIMSON SCARLET LIKENESS

BLUSTER BEEF BLOW HUFF RAGE RAIL RANT BLAST BOAST BULLY NOISE STORM BABBLE BELLOW HECTOR TUMULT BRAVADO FLUSTER ROISTER SWAGGER THREATEN RODOMONTADE

BLUSTERING LOUD BLUFF BRASH BULLY ARROGANT BULLYING

BOA BOMA ABOMA JIBOA SCARF THROW PYTHON ANACONDA

BOAR HOG SUID SWINE BARROW HOGGET TUSKER SOUNDER

BOARD EAT TOE DECK DIET FARE JOIN KEEP LATH SIGN SLAT TRAY CLEAR COURT FOUND HOUSE LODGE MEALS PANEL PLANK STAGE STALL TABLE COMMON PALLET SIDING TUCKER CABINET CHAMBER COUNCIL ENPLANE ENTRAIN PALETTE PLANCHE TRANSOM ASSEMBLY TRIBUNAL
(— FOR FALCON'S MEAT) HACK
(— OF BRIDGE) CHESS
(— OF LOOM) CARD
(— OF MILL WHEEL) AWE
(— ON CALF'S NOSE) BLAB
(— OVER) BERTH
(— WITH GROOVE) COULISSE
(— WITH HANDLE) CLAPPER
(— WITH NUMBER) SLATE
(— WITH PINS) RIDDLE
(— WITH TEETH) HACKLE RUFFER
(CHESS —) TABLER
(DRAWING —) COQUILLE
(EXHIBITION —) FRAME
(GAME —) HALMA
(HEART-SHAPED —) PLANCHET
(MORTAR —) HAWK
(PULP-PRESSING —) COUCH
(TANNING —) BEAM
(WARPING —) BARTREE

BOARDING LIVERY

BOARDINGHOUSE FONDA HOUSE PENSION

BOARDWALK MARINA DUCKBOARD

BOAST GAB BEEF BLOW BRAG CROW POMP PUFF RAVE WIND YELP BLAST BRAVE EXTOL EXULT GLORY PRATE QUACK VAPOR VAUNT BOUNCE CLAMOR FLAUNT INSULT MENACE BLUSTER DISPLAY GLORIFY SWAGGER FLOURISH THREATEN

BOASTER BLOW CROWER GASCON PRATER SHAKER BLOWOFF BRAGGER BRAVADO BLOWHARD BRAGGART FANFARON GLORIOSO JINGOIST RODOMONT

BOASTFUL BIG HIGH COCKY BOBADIL FANFARON GLORIOUS GASCONADE THRASONIC

BOAT BUM CAT COT DOW TUB ACON BAIT BARK BRIG CHOP COCK DHOW DINK DUMP RAFT SHIP SKAG TACK YAWL BANCA BARCA BATEL BULLY CANOE CRAFT FERRY FOIST FORTY JOLLY KETCH LAKER LINER OOLAK PIECE PILOT RACER SKIFF WHIFF XEBEC BAIDAK BANGKA BATEAU BILALO BOTTOM CAIQUE CAYUCO COCKLE CUTTER DREDGE DRIVER DUGOUT FLATTY GALLEY GARVEY GLIDER JIGGER KEELER NAGGAR PEAPOD PICARD PINKIE PULWAR SCAPHE SCHUYT SETTEE SKERRY TANKER TIMBER TOGGER TROUGH VESSEL
WHERRY AIRBOAT ANGEYOK BALLOON BUMBOAT CAISSON CARRIER CORACLE CRUISER CURRACH DRIFTER FLYBOAT FOYBOAT FRIGATE GAIASSA GEORDIE HOVELER HUFFLER KELLECK NACELLE PEARLER PIRAGUA SCOOTER SHIKARA SKIPPET SPONGER SPYBOAT STEAMER TUMBREL VEDETTE BALANGAY BILLYBOY BOOMBOAT BUMBARGE CANALLER CHELINGA COCKBOAT DAHABEAH DUCKBOAT FIREBOAT FLAGBOAT KEELBOAT LIFEBOAT MONOXYLE OYSTERER PALANDER SAILBOAT SCHOONER SURFBOAT TRANSFER OUTRIGGER
(— OF MALTA) DGHAISA
(— WITH SAILS AND OARS) LYMPHIAD
(ABANDONED —) DERELICT
(CHINESE —) JUNK SAMPAN
(CLUMSY —) HOOKER DROGHER
(COLLEGE —) TORPID
(DISPATCH —) AVISO PACKET
(ESKIMO —) KAMIK UMIAK
(FERRY —) BAC CUTT
(FISHING —) COG BOVO BUSS DONI CANOA COBLE DHONI NOBBY PYKAR SMACK VINTA BALDIE BAWLEY BORLEY DOGGER DROVER FISHER KUPHAR NICKEY SANDAL SCAFFY SEINER SEXERN TOSHER VOLYER CARAVEL CRABBER DRAGGER FOLLYER POOKAUN SHARPIE SKAFFIE TRAWLER DRAGBOAT GAROOKUH SHRIMPER
(FLAT-BOTTOM —) ARK BAC BUN DORY FLAT PLAT PRAM PUNT SCOW BARGE COBLE DOREY FLOAT MOSES PRAAM SHOUT BATEAU BUGEYE GAYYOU PUTELI GONDOLA LIGHTER FLATBOAT GUNDELOW JOHNBOAT
(FLY —) BUSS FLUTE FLIGHT
(GANGES —) PUTELI
(HIGHLAND —) BIRLINN
(INCENSE —) NEF SHIP NAVICULA
(MALAY —) COROCORE GALLIVAT
(MORTAR —) PALANDER
(OPEN —) WHIFF LERRET SHALLOP
(PATROL —) SPITKID
(RACING —) SIX FOUR EIGHT SCULL SHELL SINGLE TORPID SCULLER
(SHIP'S —) GIG MOSES DINGHY LAUNCH TENDER PINNACE
(SKIN —) BIDAR ANGEYOK BIDARKA BULLBOAT
(SMALL —) CARTOPPER
(WICKER —) KUFA GOOFA CORACLE
(3-OAR —) RANDAN
(6-OAR —) SEXERN
(8-OAR —) SHIP

BOATMAN DANDY PHAON BARGER CHARON YAWLER HOBBLER HOVELER HUFFLER COBLEMAN VOYAGEUR WATERMAN GONDOLIER

BOATSWAIN BOSN BOSUN SERANG TINDAL

BOB BOW CUT DAB DIP JOG POP RAP TAP BALL BLOW BUFF CLIP CLOD COIN CORK

GRUB JEER JERK JEST KNOB BUNCH
CHEAT DANCE FILCH FLOAT SHAKE
TAUNT BUFFET CURTSY POMMEL STRIKE
WEIGHT CLUSTER HAIRCUT PAGEBOY
PENDANT PLUMMET REFRAIN SHILLING

BOBBIN PIN CORD REEL BRAID SPOOL
BROCHE RATCHET SPINDLE

BOBBLE ERROR

BOBOLINK SUCKER BUNTING MAYBIRD
ORTOLAN REEDBIRD RICEBIRD

BOBSLED BOB DRAY BOBLET RIPPER
TRAVERSE

BOBWHITE COLIN QUAIL PARTRIDGE

BODE OMEN SIGN AUGUR HERALD
MESSAGE PORTEND PRESAGE FOREBODE
FORECAST FORESHOW FORETELL
INDICATE

BODICE CHOLI GILET WAIST BASQUE
BOLERO CORSET CORSAGE

BODILY SOLID SOMAL ACTUAL CARNAL
FLESHLY SOMATIC CORPORAL ENTIRELY
EXTERNAL MATERIAL PERSONAL
PHYSICAL CORPOREAL

BODKIN AWL PIN POINT BROACH
DAGGER NEEDLE HAIRPIN PONIARD
STILETTO

BODY BAND BOOK BUCK BULK CREW
FORM HEAD MASS MOLD NAVE RIND
SOMA FLESH FRAME HABIT STIFF TORSO
TRUNK CORPSE EXTENT PERSON
ANATOMY CADAVER CARCASS COMPANY
QUANTUM TEXTURE MAJORITY
PERSONNEL
(— OF ARROW) SHAFT STELE
(— OF BELIEVERS) FAITH
(— OF CANONS) CHAPTER
(— OF CARDINALS) CONCLAVE
(— OF CHILDREN) INFANTRY
(— OF CHRISTIANS) KOINONIA
COMMUNION
(— OF DOCTRINES) DOGMA
(— OF ECHINODERM) DISC DISK
(— OF EVIDENCE) CASE CORPUS
(— OF FIBERS) FORNIX
(— OF HELMET) BELL
(— OF LAW) CODE HALAKA SHARIA
PANDECT HALACHAH
(— OF MUSCLE) BELLY
(— OF OFFICERS) BUREAU
(— OF ORE) BUNCH MANTO
(— OF PIGMENT) EYESPOT IMPASTO
(— OF POETRY) EPOS
(— OF PRINCIPLES) ORGANON
(— OF ROCK) DIKE HORSE STOCK
BIOHERM MUDFLOW INTRUSION
(— OF SINGERS) CHORUS
(— OF STUDENTS) CLASS
(— OF TEN) DECURY
(— OF TENANTS) GAVEL HOMAGE
(— OF THIEVES) SCHOOL
(— OF TRADITIONS) HADITH
(— OF TROOPS) FORCE TAXIS AMBUSH
BATTLE CONREY SCREEN SQUARE
BRIGADE LASHKAR SUPPORT BATTALIA
GARRISON
(— OF TYPE) SHANK
(— OF VASSALS) BAN MANRED

(— OF WARRIORS) IMPI
(— OF WATER) BAY RIP SEA BAHR
FORD HEAD LAKE LAVE POND POOL
WAVE ABYSS BAYOU DRINK FLOOD
OCEAN SHARD SWASH LAGOON NYANZA
STREAM FLOWAGE SWALLOW
(— OF WELLBORN MEN) COMITATUS
(— OF WRITINGS) SMRITI
(— OF 12 MEN) DOUZAINE
(— POLITIC) ESTATE
(CART —) SIRPEA
(CELESTIAL —) SUN BALL COMET
PLANET SPHERE ELEMENT ASTEROID
PLANETOID SATELLITE
(COMPACT —) GLOBE
(CONDUCTING —) GROUND
(CORPORATE —) SOCIETY
(DEAD —) LICH MORT CADAVER
CARCASS CARRION SUBJECT
(ECCLESIASTICAL —) CLASSIS
(ELASTIC —) CUSHION
(EXTENDED) LENGTH
(FAT —) EPIPLOON
(GOVERNING —) KAHAL SYNOD
DURBAR SENATE DECARCHY DIRECTORY
(HAT —) HOOD
(HYALINE —) DRUSE
(IMMUNE —) DESMON
(JUDICIAL —) FORUM
(LEGISLATIVE —) CHAMBER ASSEMBLY
CONGRESS LAGTHING PARLIAMENT
(MAIN — OF ARMY) BATTLE
(MATHEMATICAL —) FILAMENT
(MORMON —) BISHOPRIC
(MORTAL —) KHET
(PRESBYTERIAN —) SESSION
JUDICATORY
(RELIGIOUS —) SECT CONVENT
(REPRODUCTIVE —) EGG GEMMA
SPORE GEMMULA
(SONOROUS —) PHONIC
(SPIRITUAL —) SAHU
(SWELLING —) BOSS
(WAGON —) BED BUCK PUNT

BODYGUARD THANE ESCORT RETINUE

BOER TAKHAAR AFRIKANER

BOG FEN HAG CARR CESS FLOW MIRE
MOOR MOSS OOZE QUAG SINK SLUE
SPEW WASH MARSH SLADE SWAMP
MORASS MUSKEG POLDER SLOUGH
QUAGMIRE

BOGEY BUG COW HAG DEVIL GNOME
BOOGER GOBLIN BUGABOO BUGBEAR
SPECTER

BOGGLE BALK FOIL STOP ALARM DEMUR
SCARE START BAFFLE PERPLEX
STUMBLE FRIGHTEN HESITATE

BOGGY WET DEEP MIRY SOFT FENNY
FOGGY MOSSY MARSHY QUAGGY
SLOBBY SWAMPY SQUASHY

BOGUS FAKE SHAM FALSE PHONY
SPURIOUS

BOHEME, LA (CHARACTER IN —) MIMI
COLLINE MUSETTA RODOLFO MARCELLO
SCHAUNARD
(COMPOSER OF —) PUCCINI

BOHEMIAN ARTY PICARO ARTISTIC

BOIL FRY PET BILE BUCK BUMP COOK QUAT RAGE SORE STYE TEEM BLAIN STEAM BETRAY BUBBLE DECOCT PIMPLE RISING SEETHE SIMMER INFLAME CARBUNCLE

BOILER REEF STILL COPPER KETTLE RETORT ALEMBIC CALDRON FURNACE (SALT —) WELLER

BOILING FERVID FERVENT SCALDING SEETHING ELIXATION

BOISTEROUS HIGH LOUD RUDE WILD BURLY NOISY RANDY ROUGH WINDY COARSE RUGGED STORMY STRONG UNRULY FURIOUS ROARING VIOLENT BIGMOUTH LARRIKIN STRIDENT VEHEMENT

BOLD BIG HARD KEEN PERT RASH RUDE TALL BRASH BRAVE HARDY JOLLY LARGE MANLY NERVY PAWKY PEART SAUCY STEEP STOUT ABRUPT BRASSY BRAZEN DARING FIERCE HEROIC PLUCKY PRETTY STRONG ASSURED DASHING DEFIANT FORWARD HAUGHTY VALIANT ARROGANT FAMILIAR FEARLESS IMMODEST IMPUDENT INTREPID MALAPERT POWERFUL RESOLUTE TEMEROUS

BOLDNESS BROW DARE FACE GALL CHEEK NERVE PLUCK VIGOR DARING BRAVERY COURAGE FREEDOM AUDACITY TEMERITY

BOLE STEM TRUNK TIMBER

BOLIVIA

CAPITAL: LAPAZ SUCRE
COIN: TOMIN CENTAVO
DEPARTMENT: LAPAZ ORURO PANDO ELBENI POTOSI TARIJA
INDIAN: URO INCA ITEN MOXO URAN ARAWAK AYMARA CHARCA CHICHA IXIAMA TACANA PUQUINA QUECHUA SIRIONE TUMUPASA
LAKE: POOPO COIPASA ROGAGUA AULLAGAS TITICACA
MEASURE: LEAGUE CELEMIN
MOUNTAIN: JARA CUSCO CUZCO PUPUYA SAJAMA SORATA ILLAMPU ANCOHUMA ILLIMANI
MOUNTAINS: ANDES SUNSAS
PLATEAU: ALTIPLANO
RIVER: BENI YATA ABUNA APERE BOOPI LAUCA ORTON BAURES GRANDE ICHILO ITENEZ MADIDI MAMORE MIZQUE TARIJA YACUMA GUAPORE ITONAMA MACHUPO BENECITO INAMBARI
TOWN: IVO ICLA ITAU MOJO POJO SAYA YACO YATA YURA CLIZA LAPAZ LLICA ORURO QUIME SUCRE UNCIA UYUNI ZONGO GUAQUI POTOSI TARIJA
VOLCANO: OLLAGUE
WEIGHT: LIBRA MARCO

BOLL POD BULB KNOB ONION BUBBLE CAPSULE
BOLLARD BITT KEVEL DOLPHIN DEADHEAD

(—S AND BITTS) APOSTLES

BOLL WEEVIL PICUDO

BOLO MACHETE SUNDANG

BOLSHEVISM COMMUNISM SOVIETISM

BOLSTER AID PAD JACK PILLOW CUSHION HEADING STIFFEN SUPPORT

BOLT BAR KEY PIN ROD RUN BEAT DART DUMP FLEE GULP LOCK PAWL SHUT SLOT ARROW CLOSE ELOPE FLASH GORGE LATCH RIVET SHAFT STOCK DECAMP DESERT FASTEN FLIGHT PINTLE SAFETY SECURE STREAK TOGGLE DOGBOLT MISSILE QUARREL FASTENER STAMPEDE
(— FOOD) SKOFF
(DOOR —) DRAWBOLT
(FIERY —) RESHEPH
(LIGHTNING —) SHAFT
(THUNDER —) FULMEN

BOMB DUD EGG BOOM PRANG SHELL SQUIB ASHCAN SALUTE AEROSOL BOMBARD GRENADE FIREBALL

BOMBARD BOMB CRUMP SHELL ATTACK BATTER BOTTLE STRAFE

BOMBARDMENT BLITZ SIEGE ATTACK RAFALE STRAFE BATTERY SHELLING

BOMBASTIC PUFFY TUMID VOCAL WINDY FLUENT HEROIC MOUTHY TURGID BLOATED FLOWERY FUSTIAN OROTUND POMPOUS RANTING STILTED SWOLLEN INFLATED SWELLING

BONA FIDE LEVEL GENUINE AUTHENTIC

BONBON CANDY CREAM GOODY DAINTY CARAMEL

BOND TIE VOW BAIL BAND GLUE GYVE HOLD KNOT LINK NOTE YOKE CHAIN NEXUS BINDER CEMENT COPULA COUPLE ESCROW FETTER LEAGUE PLEDGE SOLDER LIAISON LIBERTY LINKAGE MANACLE SHACKLE STATUTE ADHESIVE CONTRACT COVENANT LIGAMENT LIGATION LIGATURE MORTGAGE SECURITY VINCULUM

BONDAGE YOKE THRALL HELOTRY SERFDOM SLAVERY BONDSHIP THIRLING CAPTIVITY SERVITUDE

BONDMAN CARL ESNE PEON SERF CHURL HELOT SLAVE STOOGE SURETY THRALL VASSAL CHATTEL PEASANT SERVANT VILLEIN BONDSMAN

BONE OS HIP RIB ULNA BLADE FEMUR HYOID ILIUM INCUS JUGAL TALUS TIBIA CANNON COCCYX CONCHA COPULA CUBOID EPURAL FIBULA NUCHAL RADIAL SPLINT ZYGOMA
(ANKLE —) TALUS
(HIP —) HUGGIN
(PUBIC —) PECTEN
(SHIN —) CNEMIS
(THIGH —) FEMUR

BONER BUBU FLUB ERROR BRODIE BLOOPER BLUNDER MISTAKE

BONESET COMFREY AGUEWEED EUPATORY HEMPWEEK

BONFIRE BLAZE TAWNIE BALEFIRE

BONNET CAP HAT COWL HOOD POKE COVER TOQUE CAPOTE MOBCAP

CHAPEAU CORONET LEGHORN
BALMORAL
BONNY GAY FINE MERRY PLUMP BLITHE
BONNIE PRETTY STRONG HEALTHY
HANDSOME BEAUTIFUL
BONUS TIP GIFT MEED AWARD BRIBE
PILON PRIZE SPIFF REWARD CUMSHAW
DOUCEUR PREMIUM SUBSIDY DIVIDEND
TANTIEME LAGNIAPPE
BON VIVANT SPORT EPICURE
BONY HARD LANK THIN LANKY STIFF
TOUGH OSTEAL SKINNY ANGULAR
OSSEOUS SCRAGGY SKELETAL
BOOB ASS OAF FOOL GOON DUNCE
BOODLE LOOT SWAG GRAFT PLUNDER
BOOJUM SNARK
BOOK MO LOG CHAP FORM OPUS TEXT
TOME ALBUM BIBLE CANON CANTO
CODEX DIARY ENTER FOLIO GUIDE LIBER
QUIRE BODONI DOCKET LEDGER MANUAL
MISSAL RECORD TICKET VOLUME
BLOTTER CATALOG GRAMMAR JOURNAL
LAWBOOK LEXICON OMNIBUS SPELLER
WRITING BANKBOOK BROCHURE
CALCULUS CASEBOOK CASHBOOK
CHAPBOOK COOKBOOK COPYBOOK
DOCUMENT GIFTBOOK HANDBOOK
HARDBACK JESTBOOK JUVENILE
LIBRETTO PASTORAL POSTBOOK
REGISTER SONGBOOK STUDBOOK
TWENTYMO PAPERBACK
(— BACK) DORSE
(— FOR HARVARD GRADUATE)
DETUR
(— OF CHARTS) WAGONER PORTOLAN
(— OF HERALDRY) ARMORY ARMORIAL
(— OF MAPS) ATLAS
(— OF PSALMS) PSALTER TEHILLIM
(— OF RULES) HOYLE
(— OF SERVICES) PIE
(— OF SOLUTIONS) KEY
(— OF THE MASS) ORDO
(—S KEPT IN PRINT) BACKLIST
(CHINESE —) CHING
(ELEMENTARY —) PRIMER
(FOLDED —) ORIHON
(JOKE —) JOE JESTBOOK
(MEMORANDUM —) AGENDA JOTTER
TICKLER
(MINIATURE —) BIBELOT
(RECORD —) LIBER TICKLER
(RELIGIOUS —) KITAB KORAN GOSPEL
HORARY PROSAR GRADUAL KYRIALE
BREVIARY MEGILLAH ORDINARY
SYNAXARY
(UNBOUND —) CAHIER
BOOM JIB BEAM POLE ROAR SPAR
RESOUND BOWSPRIT FLOURISH
(CRANE —) ARM GIB JIB
BOON BENE GIFT GOOD FAVOR GRANT
BOUNTY BENEFIT BLESSING INTIMATE
BENEFACTION
BOOR CAD OAF BORE HICK KERN LOUT
PILL SLOB CHURL CLOWN LUBBER
LUMMOX RUSTIC BUMPKIN PEASANT
VILLAIN BOEOTIAN
BOORISH ILL RUDE GAWKY ROUGH

SURLY CLUMSY RUSTIC SULLEN VULGAR
AWKWARD LOUTISH UNCOUTH VILLAIN
BOEOTIAN
BOORISHNESS VILLAINY GROBIANISM
BOOST AID LEG ABET BACK HELP LIFT
PLUG PUSH COACH EXALT HOIST RAISE
ASSIST ADVANCE COMMEND ELEVATE
ENDORSE PROMOTE INCREASE
BOOT PAC GAIN HALF HELP KICK PUNT
SHOE AVAIL EJECT SPOIL BUSKIN
CRAKOW FUMBLE GAITER GALOSH
MUKLUK SHEATH HESSIAN BALMORAL
BOOTH BOX COOP LOGE SHED SHOP
CABIN CRAME HOUSE KIOSK LODGE
STALL STAND SUKKAH
BOOTY GAIN LOOT PELF PREY SACK
SWAG GRAFT PRIZE FLEECE SPOILS
PILLAGE PLUNDER
BORDER HEM RIM TAB ABUT BRIM CURB
DADO EAVE EDGE LINE MARK ORLE RAND
SIDE TRIM WELT BOUND BRINK COAST
DRAFT FLANK FRAME LIMIT MARCH
MARGE SHORE SKIRT VERGE ADJOIN
EDGING FRINGE MARGIN SELVAGE
VALANCE BOUNDARY FRONTIER
NEIGHBOR OUTSKIRT SURROUND
(— OF EXTERNAL EAR) HELIX
(— OF LACE) PICOT
(— OF ROCK) SALBAND
(— OF SAIL) DOUBLING
(— OF SHIELD) BORDURE
(— OF STREAM) ROND
(— ON) ABUT ACCOST AFFRONT
NEIGHBOR
(FLOWERED —) FLOROON
(ORNAMENTAL —) PURL WAGE FRAME
FRINGE MATTING DENTELLE TRESSURE
(RIBBON —) FRILAL
BORE BIT CUT IRK TAP DRAG HOLE PALL
PILL REAM SINK TIDE ANNOY DRILL
EAGRE GOUGE PRICK PUNCH WEARY
GIMLET PIERCE THRUST TUNNEL
CALIBER DIAMETER
(— OF CANNON) SOUL CHASE
BORED BLASE WEARY ENNUYEE TEDIOUS
SATIATED
BOREDOM YAWN ENNUI ACEDIA TEDIUM
BORING DIM DRY FLAT SLOW STODGY
STUPID TIRING LUMPISH TEDIOUS
PIERCING TIRESOME
BORIS GODUNOV
(CHARACTER IN —) BORIS PIMEN
DMITRY GRIGORY MISSAIL RANGONI
SHUISKY VARLAAM
(COMPOSER OF —) MUSSORGSKY
BORN NEE INNATE NASCENT NATURAL
ORIGINAL
BORNE RODE CARRIED ENDURED

BORNEO

BAY: ADANG KUMAI SAMPIT
CAPE: ARU DATU LOJAR PUTING SAMBAR
SELATAN
MOUNTAIN: RAJA SARAN NIJAAN
TEBANG

MOUNTAINS: IRAN MULLER SCHWANER
NATIVE: DYAK
RIVER: ARUT IWAN BAHAU BERAU KAJAN
   PADAS PAWAN BARITO KAPUAS SEBUKU
   KAHAJAN MAHAKAM MENDAWI
   PEMBUANG
TOWN: KUMAI SAMBAS SAMPIT MALINAU
   PAGATAN SANGGAU SINTANG TARAKAN
   KETAPANG
WEIGHT: PARA CHAPAH

BOROUGH BURG CITY PORT TOWN WICK
   BURGH CASTLE COUNTY CITADEL
   FORTESS VILLAGE TOWNSHIP
BORROW COPY HIRE LOAN TAKE ADOPT
   STEAL PLEDGE
BOSH ROT JOKE TALK TOSH FUDGE
   TRASH BUSHWA HUMBUG TRIVIA
BOSOM BUST CLOSE HEART SINUS
   BREAST DESIRE DICKEY RECESS
   EMBRACE INTIMATE
BOSS HUB NOB ORB BEAD KNOB KNOP
   KNOT NAIL NAVE STUD BULLY BWANA
   CHIEF ORDER OWNER BROOCH BUTTON
   DIRECT HONCHO MANAGE MASTER
   CAPTAIN FOREMAN HEADMAN MANAGER
   DIRECTOR DOMINEER OMPHALOS
   OVERSEER
   (— OF LOGGING CAMP) BULLY
   (— OF SHIELD) UMBO
   (MINE —) SHIFTER
   (POLITICAL —) CACIQUE CAUDILLO
   (STRAW —) BULL LEADER
BOSSY PUSHY
BOTCH MAR BOIL FLUB MEND MESS
   MULL FLUFF FUDGE SPOIL BOLLIX
   BUNGLE JUMBLE BLUNDER BUTCHER
BOTH ALL TWO EQUALLY
BOTHER ADO AIL BUG IRK NAG VEX FAZE
   FUSS JADE WORK ANNOY KNOCK TEASE
   WORRY BADGER BUSTLE CUMBER
   DITHER FLURRY HARASS MEDDLE
   MOLEST PESTER PLAGUE POTHER
   PUTTER PUZZLE TAMPER CONFUSE
   DISTURB PERPLEX TROUBLE BEWILDER
   DISTRESS IRRITATE NUISANCE

BOTSWANA

CAPITAL: GABERONES
COIN: RAND
DESERT: KALAHARI
LAKE: DOW NGAMI
LANGUAGE: BANTU CLICK KHOISAN
   SETSWANA
MOUNTAIN: TSODILO
NATIVE: BANTU TSWANA BUSHMAN
RIVER: NATA OKWA CHOBE NOSOB
   CUANDO MOLOPO SHASHI CUBANGO
   LIMPOPO OKAVANGO
TOWN: KANYE ORAPA TSANE SEROWE
   LOBOTSI MOCHUDI PALAPYE THAMAGA
   GABERONES

BOTTLE JUG BOSS SKIN VIAL AMPUL
   ASKOS BOCAL CRUET CRUSE FIFTH
   FLASK GOURD PHIAL SPLIT CARAFE
   FIASCO FLACON FLAGON MAGNUM
   NURSER SIPHON VESSEL DECANTER
   DEMIJOHN REHOBOAM
   (— IN WICKER) CARBOY DEMIJOHN
   (EGYPTIAN —) DORUCK
   (EMPTY —) MARINE
   (HOT-WATER —) PIG
   (LARGE —) KIT JEROBOAM
   (LEATHER —) BOOT JACK DUBBA
   BUDGET MATARA BOMBARD BORACHIO
   WHINNOCK WINESKIN
   (OVERSIZED —) BALTHAZAR
   (PART OF —) LIP CORK KICK NECK
   PUNT MOUTH MUZZLE CAPSULE
   SHOULDER
   (PILGRIM'S —) AMPULLA
   (SMALL —) VIAL AMPUL PHIAL SPLIT
   FLACON AMPOULE TICKLER CRUISKEN
   CRUISKEEN
   (18 —S OF WINE) RIDDLE
   (40 —S) KEMPLE
BOTTOM ASS BED ARSE BASE FLAT
   FOOT FUND LEES REAR ROOT BASIS
   DREGS FLOOR NADIR FUNDUS GROUND
   GUTTER BEDROCK SUPPORT SURFACE
   BUTTOCKS SEDIMENT
BOUGH ARM LEG LIMB TWIG SHOOT
   SPRIG BRANCH RAMAGE OFFSHOOT
BOULDER KNOB ROCK STONE GRAYBACK
   MEGALITH
BOULEVARD DRIVE PRADO AVENUE
   STREET ALAMEDA HIGHWAY TERRACE
BOUNCE DAP HOP BANG BLOW BUMP
   FIRE JUMP LEAP SACK BOUND CAROM
   EJECT KNOCK VERVE SPIRIT SPRING
   STRIKE DISMISS REBOUND SWAGGER
   RICOCHET
BOUND END HOP SKIP DART JUMP LEAP
   MERE RISE SCUD SKIP AMBIT BOURN
   FIXED LIMIT START VAULT VERGE
   BORDER BOUNCE CAVORT CURVET
   DEFINE GAMBOL HURDLE LIABLE OBLIGE
   PRANCE SPRING CERTAIN CHAINED
   CONFINE CONTAIN GAMBADO SALTATE
   SECURED TRUSSED CONFINED DESTINED
   ENCLOSED FRONTIER PINIONED
   SHACKLED
BOUNDARY END RIM EDGE LINE MARK
   MERE META METE PALE TERM WALL
   BOURN CLOSE FENCE FRAME FRONT
   HEDGE LIMIT MARCH SHORE VERGE
   BORDER BARRIER COMPASS OUTLINE
   FRONTIER PRECINCT TERMINUS
   PERIMETER PERIPHERY
BOUNDER ROUE
BOUNDLESS VAST UNTOLD ENDLESS
   ETERNAL INFINITE UNLIMITED
BOUNTEOUS BOON CROWNED LIBERAL
   PLENTEOUS
BOUNTIFUL GOOD LUSH RICH AMPLE
   LAVISH LIBERAL PROFUSE ABUNDANT
   GENEROUS
BOUNTY BOON GIFT MEED AWARD
   BONUS GRANT WORTH REWARD VIRTUE

LARGESS PREMIUM PRESENT PROWESS
SUBSIDY GOODNESS GRATUITY
KINDNESS
BOUQUET AURA ODOR POSY AROMA
BLOOM CIGAR SHEAF SPRAY SHOWER
CORSAGE NOSEGAY
BOUT GO JOB FALL TURN CRASH ESSAY
FIGHT MATCH ROUND TRIAL ATTACK
COURSE FRACAS ASSAULT ATTEMPT
CONTEST CONFLICT
(DRINKING —) BAT BEND BUST SPREE
RANDAN SCREED SPLORE CAROUSE
WASSAIL
BOW ARC LEG NOD TIE YEW ARCH BAIL
BEND DUCK FOLD KNEE LATH MOVE
PROW STEM TURN CROOK CURVE DEFER
HONOR KNEEL STICK STOOP YIELD
ARCHER ASSENT BUCKLE CRINGE
CROUCH CURTSY FIDDLE RIBBON
SALAAM SALUTE SCRAPE SUBMIT
SWERVE DEPRESS INCLINE INFLECT
RAINBOW ARBALEST CRESCENT
OBEISANCE
(— DOWN) ALOUT HUMBLE
(— LOW) BINGE
(— OF PLOW) DRAIL
(— OF VESSEL) HEAD PROW STEM
ENTRANCE
(— ON SCRAPER) BAIL
(— SLIGHTLY) ADDRESS
(PART OF —) DIP TIP BACK FACE GRIP
LIMB LOOP NOCK BELLY BRIDGE HANDLE
RECURVE SERVING BOWSTRING
BOWER NOOK ABODE ARBOR BERCEAU
CHAMBER PERGOLA RETREAT SHELTER
TRELLIS
BOWL CUP PAN TRAY ARENA BASIN
JORUM KITTY LAVER PHIAL PITCH
BEAKER CRATER KETTLE MORTAR PIGGIN
TROUGH TUREEN VESSEL BRIMMER
SCYPHUS SKYPHOS STADIUM TRUNDLE
AQUARIUM FISHBOWL LAVATORY
MONTEITH PORRINGER
(— ILLEGALLY) JERK
(— OF PIPE) CHILLUM STUMMEL
(— ON PEDESTAL) TAZZA SALVER
(— OUT) YORK
(— THAT TOUCHED JACK) TOUCHER
(— WITH TWO HANDLES) CAP DEPAS
(DRINKING —) TUN TASS
(MARBLE CUTTER'S —) SEBILLA
(OBLONG —) PITCHI
(PUNCH —) SNEAKER
(SHALLOW —) CAP COUPE WHISKIN
(SMALL —) JACK
(SOUP —) ECUELLE
(SUGAR —) SUGAR SUCRIER
(TOILET —) HOPPER
(WOODEN —) CAP BOWIE COGIE KITTY
ROGAN BASSIE BICKER
BOWLEGGED BANDY VALGUS
BOWLER HAT POT DERBY KEGLER
PINMAN SPINNER TRUNDLER
BOWLING BOWLS KEGLING TENPINS
BOWMAN ARCHER
BOX BED BIN GIG KIT PYX TYE ARCA

BOOT CAGE CASE CIST CRIB CUFF CYST
LOGE MILL PACK SEAT SLAP SLUG SPAR
STOW TILL TRAY CADDY CHEST CLOUT
CRATE FIGHT HUTCH PUNCH STALL
TRUNK ASCHAM BUFFET BUNKER
CARTON CASKET COFFER COFFIN
DRAWER GRILLE HAMPER HATBOX
HAYBOX HOPPER ICEBOX SHRINE STRIKE
VANITY ARCANUM BANDBOX BATTERY
CABINET CARRIER CASHBOX CASQUET
CONFINE DICEBOX DREDGER ENCLOSE
FREEZER HANAPER PACKAGE PILLBOX
SANDBOX SHELTER JUNCTION
MATCHBOX POMANDER SHOWCASE
(— FOR CARRYING COAL) DAN
(— FOR CUTLERY) CANTEEN
(— FOR FIRE) CHAUFFER
(— FOR FISH) CAR NID
(— FOR MONEY OFFERING) ARCA
LADLE
(— FOR SALT) DRAB
(— FOR SEAL) SKIPPET
(— FOR SEED) LEAP
(— FOR TOBACCO) BUTT DOSS CADDY
SARATOGA
(— IN TIMEPIECE) BARREL
(— IN WHEEL HUB) FUR
(— OF BIRCHBARK) MOCUCK
(— OF CYLINDER) BUSH
(— OF ORGAN) BOOT SWELL
(— TO SHELTER BELL) SCONCE
(BERRY —) HALLOCK
(BREAD —) BARGE
(CANDLE —) BARK
(CIRCULAR —) THIMBLE
(COLLECTION —) BROD
(COMPASS —) KETTLE BINNACLE
(FANCY —) ETUI
(FLOATING —) CAISSON
(FOUNDRY —) FRAME
(IRON —) HANGER
(JUGGLER'S —) TRANKA
(MONEY —) CASH SAFE PIRLIE
(PIVOTING —) TOUR
(PRINTING —) TURTLE
(REFRIGERATOR —) COOLER
(SHALLOW —) FLAT BACKET HARBOR
(SNUFF —) MILL MULL
(TEA —) CADDY
(TIN —) TRUMMEL VASCULUM
BOXER PUG CHAMP BANTAM MILLER
TANKER WELTER BRUISER CRUISER
FIGHTER SLUGGER SPARRER BUFFETER
PUGILIST SOUTHPAW
BOY BO BUB GUY HIM LAD TAD BOYO
CHAP NINO PAGE PUER BUDDY GAMIN
GROOM KNAVE SWAIN VALET YOUTH
GAFFER GARCON MASTER NIPPER
RASCAL SHAVER URCHIN GOSSOON
SERVANT MUCHACHO SPALPEEN
(— DRESSED AS WOMAN) MALINCHE
(— OF FREE BIRTH) CAMILLUS
(ALTAR —) ACOLYTE THURIFER
(AWKWARD —) CUB CALF GRUMMET
(BOLD —) SPALPEEN
(CHIMNEY SWEEPER'S —) CHUMMY

(CHOIR —) CHILD
(CLEANING —) BUSBOY
(COLLIER'S —) HODDER
(EFFEMINATE —) SISSY MOLLYCODDLE
(ERRAND —) GALOPIN
(FIRST-YEAR —) GYTE
(HEAD —) SENIOR CAPTAIN
(ILL-MANNERED —) CUB
(MISCHIEVOUS —) NICKUM
(NON-JEWISH —) SHEGETZ
(PERT —) CRACK
(ROGUISH —) CRACK GAMIN URCHIN
(SAUCY —) NACKET
(SERVING —) KNAVE PEDEE CHOKRA
  MOUSSE FOOTBOY GOSSOON
(SILLY —) CALF
(SPRIGHTLY —) CRACK
(TOWN —) CAD
(YOUNG —) LAD SONNY YOUTH NIPPER
BOYCOTT SHUN AVOID DEBAR
  BLACKBALL
BOYFRIEND BEAU STEADY
BRACE LEG TIE TWO BIND CASE GIRD
  JACK KNEE LACE PAIR PROP STAY STUD
  CLAMP CRANK GIRTH POISE RIDER
  SHORE STOCK STRUT ANKLET BINDER
  CLENCH COLLAR COUPLE CRUTCH
  FASTEN SPLINT STRING BRACKET
  REFRESH SPANNER STIFFEN SUPPORT
  BITSTOCK BUTTRESS
BRACELET BAND RING CHAIN ARMLET
  BANGLE GRIVNA ARMILLA CIRCLET
  MANACLE POIGNET RACETTE HANDCUFF
  WRISTLET
  (— USED AS MONEY) MANILLA
  (SHELL —) SANKHA
BRACER TONIC SHORER STIFFENER
  STIMULANT
BRACING CRISP QUICK TONIC DUNNAGE
BRACKEN FERN BRAKE
BRACKET COCK FORK GATE ANCON
  BRACE CLASS CRANE CRANK CROOK
  LEVEL STRUT TRUSS BRIDGE CORBEL
  COUPLE SCONCE CONSOLE DERRICK
  GATELEG SPONSON CATEGORY
  CROTCHET SPECKLED STRADDLE
  MODILLION CANTILEVER
BRACKISH SALTY SALINE SALTISH
  NAUSEOUS
BRACT HUSK LEAF GLUME LEMMA PALEA
  SCALE SPADIX SPATHE PHYLLARY
BRAD PIN NAIL PRIG RIVET SPRIG
BRAG GAB BLAH BLOW CROW DEFY FACE
  HUFF PUFF WIND BLUFF BOAST PREEN
  STRUT VAUNT ROISTER SWAGGER
  FLOURISH
BRAGGART PUFF BLOWER CROWER
  GASCON HECTOR BLOWOFF BOASTER
  BOBADIL BLOWHARD CACAFUGO
  PAROLLES RODOMONT
BRAID CUE GIMP LACE PLAT TAIL FANCY
  LACET MILAN ORRIS PLAIT QUEUE TRESS
  TWINE WEAVE BOBBIN CORDON EDGING
  GALLON LACING RIBBON ENTWINE
  ORNAMENT RICKRACK SOUTACHE
  TRIMMING

BRAIN BEAN HARN MIND PATE WITS
  SKULL NODDLE CEREBRUM
BRAINLESS SILLY STUPID FOOLISH
  WITLESS
BRAKE CLOG CURB DRAG FERN LOCK
  SKID SLOW STAY TRAP BLOCK CHECK
  COPSE DELAY DETER SNARE BRIDLE
  HINDER RETARD STAYER BRACKEN
  DEADMAN STOPPER THICKET RETARDER
BRAMBLE BRIER RHAMN THORN JAGGER
  STICKER
BRANCH ARM LEG RAY RUN BROG FORK
  LIMB PART SNAG SPUR STEM STUD
  TWIG YARD AXITE BOUGH BRIAR BRIER
  CREEK PRONG RAMUS SHOOT SPRAY
  SPRIG STICK VIMEN WITHE DIVIDE
  GROWTH LEADER MEMBER PHYLUM
  RAMIFY RUNNER STOLON STREAM
  DIVERGE FURCATE LATERAL RAMULUS
  TENDRIL OFFSHOOT SPRANGLE
  (— OF ANTLER) SPELLER ADVANCER
  (— OF COLONY) STIPE
  (— OF FAMILY) SEPT
  (— OF FEATHER) BARB
  (— OF HORN) RIAL ANTLER
  (— OF LEARNING) ART STUDY
  FACULTY KNOWLEDGE
  (— OF MATHEMATICS) ALGEBRA
  CALCULUS
  (DEAD —) FLAG
  (EVERGREEN —S) GREENS
  (MINE —) LEADER
  (PALM —) LULAB
  (RAILWAY —) LYE
  (SMALL —) RICE
  (YOUNGER —) CADET
BRANCHED FORKED RAMOSE CLADOSE
BRANCHIA GILL
BRAND BURN CHOP KIND MARK NOTE
  SEAR SORT LABEL STAIN STAMP SWORD
  TORCH MARQUE STIGMA
BRANDISH WAG WAVE SHAKE SWING
  WIELD FLAUNT QUAVER RUFFLE
  FLUTTER SWAGGER FLOURISH
BRANDY FINE JACK MARC BINGO MOBBY
  PEACH RAKIA COGNAC GRAPPA KIRSCH
  AQUAVIT ARMAGNAC CALVADOS
  SLIVOVITZ
BRASH GAY BOLD RASH HASTY NERVY
  SAUCY FORWARD IMPUDENT TACTLESS
  BALDFACED
BRASS ALLOY MONEY NERVE BRAZEN
  BRONZE ORMOLU
BRASSARD ARMBAND
BRASSIERE BANDEAU
BRASSY LOUD RUDE BRAZEN COARSE
  SHRILL IMPUDENT STRIDENT
  OVERBLOWN
BRAT GET IMP APRON BAIRN CHILD
  INFANT TERROR URCHIN BANTLING
BRAVADO POMP BRAVE PRIDE HECTOR
  BLUSTER BOMBAST BRAVERY SWAGGER
  VAUNTERY GASCONISM
BRAVE BOLD BRAW DARE DEFY FACE
  FINE GAME GOOD BOAST BRAVO BULLY
  HARDY JOLLY MANLY STIFF STOUT

VAUNT BREAST DARING HEROIC MANFUL
PLUCKY SANNUP STURDY DOUGHTY
GALLANT SOLDIER SWAGGER VALIANT
VENTURE WARRIOR CAVALIER FEARLESS
INTREPID LIONLIKE STALWART SUPERIOR
VALOROUS VIRTUOUS

BRAVE NEW WORLD
(AUTHOR OF —) HUXLEY
(CHARACTER IN —) JOHN MARX
MOND CROWNE LENINA WATSON
BERNARD MUSTAPHA HELMHOLTZ

BRAVERY GRIT VALOR SPIRIT VIRTUE
BRAVADO BRAVURA COURAGE HEROISM
MANHOOD PROWESS BOLDNESS
CHIVALRY

BRAVO OLE RAH BULLY BANDIT
APPLAUSE

BRAWL DIN ROW BEEF FRAY RIOT BROIL
CHIDE CLASH FIGHT MELEE REVEL
SCOLD SCRAP AFFRAY BICKER FRACAS
RUFFLE RUMPUS SHINDY STRIFE
TUMULT UPROAR BRANGLE DISCORD
DISPUTE QUARREL SCUFFLE WRANGLE
COMPLAIN SQUABBLE

BRAWLING NOISY BLATANT

BRAWN BEEF PORK FLESH SINEW
MUSCLE MANPOWER STRENGTH

BRAWNY BEEFY FLESHY ROBUST
SINEWY SQUARE STRONG STURDY
CALLOUS MUSCULAR POWERFUL
STALWART

BRAY CRY MIX RUB BEAT CRUSH GRIND
POUND STAMP BRUISE HEEHAW OUTCRY
PESTLE THRASH WHINNY

BRAZEN BOLD CALM HARD PERT BRASS
HARDY HARSH SASSY BRASSY BLATANT
CALLOUS FORWARD IMMODEST
IMPUDENT INSOLENT

BRAZIER HEARTH BRASERO HIBACHI
SCALDINO

BRAZIL

BAY: MARAJO IGRANDE SEPETIBA
GUANABARA
CAPE: FRIO BLANCO BUZIOS GURUPY
ORANGE SAOTOME
CAPITAL: BRASILIA
COIN: JOE REIS CONTO DOBRA HALFJOE
MILREIS CRUZEIRO
ESTUARY: PARA
FALLS: IGUACU IGUASSU
INDIAN: ANTA ACROA ARARA ARAUA
BRAVO CARIB GUANA ARAWAK CARAJA
CARAYAN JAVAHAI TARIANA BOTOCUDO
CHAMBIOA
ISLAND: MARACA MARAJO BANANAL
CARDOSO CAVIANA MEXIANA COMPRIDA
LAKE: AIMA FEIA MIRIM
MEASURE: PE MOIO PIPA SACK VARA
BRACA FANGA LEGOA MILHA PALMO
PASSO TONEL CANADA COVADO CUARTA
LEAGUE QUARTO TAREFA ALQUIER
GARRAFA ALQUEIRE
MOUNTAINS: MAR GERAL ORGAN PIAUI

ACARAI GURUPI ORGAOS PARIMA
AMAMBAI CARAJAS GRADAUS
RONCADOR TOMBADOR
NATIVE: CABOCLO CURIBOCA MAMELUCO
PAULISTA
PORT: RIO PARA BAHIA BELEM NATAL
SANTOS PELOTAS SALVADOR
RIVER: APA ICA DOCE GEIO IVAI JARI
PARA PARU SONO TEFE ABUNA ANAUA
APORE CAPIM CLARO CORUA ICANA IRIRI
ITAPI JURUA JUTAI MANSO NEGRO
PARDO PIAUI PRETO TIETE TURVO
URUBU VERDE XINGU AJUANA AMAZON
ARINOS BALSAS BRANCO CANUMA
CONTAS CUIABA DEMINI GRAJAU
GRANDE GURUPI IBICUI IGUACU JAPURA
JAVARI MEARIM MORTES MUCURI
PARANA PURPUS RONURO SANGUE
TACUTU TIBAGI UATUMA UAUPES
VELHAS CORUMBA IGUASSU MADEIRA
PARAIBA SUCURIU TAPAJOS TAQUARI
TEODORO URUGUAI ARAGUAIA PADAUIRI
PARACATU PARAGUAI PARNAIBA
SOLIMOES TARAUACA
STATE: ACRE PARA AMAPA BAHIA CEARA
GOIAS GOYAZ PIAUI PARANA PIAUHY
ALAGOAS GUAPORE PARAIBA RORAIMA
SERGIPE AMAZONAS MARANHAO
PARAHIBA PARAHYBA RONDONIA
SAOPAULO
TOWN: ACU EXU ICO IPU ITU JAU LUZ RIO
UBA BAGE FARO IBIA IJUI ITAI LAPA LINS
PARA PIUI TUPA UNAI BAHIA BAIAO
BAURU BELEM CEARA NATAL NEVES
CAMPOS CUIABA ILHEUS MACEIO
MANAOS MANAUS OLINDA RECIFE
SANTOS ARACAJU CARUARU CITORIA
GOIANIA ITABUNA JUNDIAI NITEROI
PELOTAS TAUBATE UBERABA ANAPOLIS
BRASILIA CAMPINAS CURITIBA
LONDRINA SALVADOR SOROCABA
TERESINA
WATERFALL: GLASS IGUAZU
WEIGHT: BAG ONCA LIBRA ARROBA
OITAVA ARRATEL QUILATE QUINTAL
TONELADA

BRAZIL NUT JUVIA CASTANA
BREACH GAP FLAW RENT RIFT BURST
CHASM CLEFT CRACK PAUSE SPLIT
WOUND BRUISE HERNIA HIATUS SCHISM
ASSAULT BLEMISH DISPUTE FISSURE
OPENING QUARREL RUPTURE BREAKING
CREVASSE FRACTION FRACTURE
INTERVAL OUTBREAK TRESPASS
(— IN DIKE) GOOL
(— OF CONTINUITY) SALTUS
(— OF DUTY) BARRATRY
(— OF FAITH) TREASON
(— OF GRAMMAR) SOLECISM
(— OF MORALITY) SCAPE VAGARY
(— OF PEACE) AFFRAY FRACTION
(— OF UNITY) SOHISM
BREAD BUN PAN LOAF PAIN PONE ROLL
RUSK BATCH CHAPON HALLAH MATZOS
PANNAM SIMNEL BANNOCK POPOVER

STOLLEN CORNCAKE HARDTACK
SOFTTACK TORTILLA ZWIEBACK
PUMPERNICKEL
(— AND MILK) POBS PANADA POBBIES
(BATCH OF —) CAST
(BUTTERED —) CAPER
(DRY —) TOKE
(EUCHARISTIC —) BODY HOST AZYME
(FANCY —) BRAID
(MAIZE —) PIKI
(OATMEAL —) ANACK JANNOCK
(POTATO —) FADGE
(QUICK —) SCONE
(S. AFRICAN —) DIKA
(SLICE OF —) TARTINE TRENCHER
(SMALL LOAF OF —) COB
(SMALL PIECE OF —) SIPPET MEALOCK
(SOPPED —) MISER BREWIS BROWIS
(SWEET —) BUN BROWNIE STOLLEN
(TOASTED —) SIPPET
(UNLEAVENED —) AZYME BANNOCK
CHAPATTI
(WHEAT —) CHEAT HOVIS COCKET
MANCHET
BREADFRUIT MASI RIMAS CAMANSI
CASTANA ANTIPOLO
BREADTH BEAM
BREAK GO CUT JAR LOP TEN BUST CHIP
DRAG FALL FLAW KNAP PART RUIN SLIP
SNAP STEP STOP TEAR TURN UNDO
WASH WORK ALTER BURST CHECK
CHINK CLEFT COMMA CRACK DAUNT
FRACT LAPSE PAUSE SEVER SMASH
SOLVE WOUND CHANGE CLEAVE
CRANNY HIATUS IMPAIR LACUNA PIERCE
SPRING CAESURA CRACKLE CREVICE
DESTROY DISABLE FISSURE INTERIM
OPENING RESPITE RUPTURE BREATHER
CREVASSE DIERESIS FRACTURE
FRAGMENT INTERVAL SEPARATE
(— APART) SUNDER DISRUPT SHATTER
(— AWAY) BOLT ESCAPE
(— BOULDERS) BULLDOZE
(— DOWN) CONK FAIL GIVE CRAZE
CROCK PLASH TRAIK BRUISE TUMBLE
ANALYZE FOUNDER REFRACT COLLAPSE
INFRINGE
(— FORTH) BOIL ERUPT EVENT FLASH
EXPLODE
(— FROM ICE MASS) CALVE
(— GLASS) SHREND DRAGADE
(— IN) ENTER
(— IN PIECES) CHAP DICE KNAP CRASH
CRAZE SMASH SMOKE SHIVER CRUMBLE
FRITTER SMATTER DEMOLISH DIFFRACT
DISJOINT SPLINTER STRAMASH
(— IN WAVES) JABBLE
(— IN YARN) SMASH
(— INTO) BROACH IRRUPT
(— INTO FOAM) COMB
(— INWARD) STAVE
(— LANCE) TAINT
(— OF CONTINUITY) SALTUS
(— OFF) NUB DROP SNAP CEASE LEAVE
ABRUPT DIREMPT PRETERMIT
(— OFF END) SNUB
(— OPEN) BUST CHOP FORCE

(— ORE) COB SPALL SPAWL
(— OUT) ERUPT START ASSURD STRIKE
(— RANKS) DISMISS
(— SHARPLY) KNACK
(— SILENCE) QUETCH
(— SKIN) GALL
(— SLATE) SCULP
(— STONE) CAVIL KEVEL
(— THE BACK) CHINE
(— THROUGH) BEAT FORCE BREACH
(— THROUGH SHELL) PIP
(— UP) BUCK FALL MELT FLOUR SEVER
SPALE SPLIT STASH INCIDE DEGRADE
DIFFUSE DISBAND DISSECT DISTURB
REFRACT SCARIFY SCATTER DISJOINT
DISPERSE DISSOLVE DISUNIFY
FRAGMENT
(— UP EARTH) HACK FALLOW
(— UP SIEGE) LEVY
(— WATER) FIN
(— WINDOWS) NICK
BREAKDOWN BURNOUT DEBACLE
COLLAPSE DILUTION
BREAKER SURF WAVE BILLOW COMBER
ROLLER CRACKER
(— OF WORD) WARLOCK
(CIRCUIT —) CUTOUT
(ROCK —) ALLIGATOR
BREAKFAST BRUNCH DEJEUNER
BREAKING BREACH BREAKUP FRACTION
FRACTURE SOLUTION
BREAKWATER COB DAM DIKE MOLE
PIER PILE QUAY JETTY
BREAM TAI CARP SCUP SHAD SARGUS
OLDWIFE SUNFISH FLATFISH
BREAST DUG BUMP FACE BOOBY BOSOM
BRAVE BUBBY CHEST HEART THORAX
BRISKET
BREASTBONE STERNUM XIPHOID
BREASTPLATE EGIS URIM AEGIS
GORGET LORICA SHIELD THORAX
CUIRASS PECTORAL
BREASTWORK FORT REDAN PARAPET
RAMPART BARBETTE
BREATH AIR GASP HUFF LIFE PANT PUFF
SIGH WAFT WIND BLAST PAUSE SCENT
SMELL VAPOR WHIFF BREEZE FLATUS
PNEUMA HALITUS INSTANT RESPITE
SUSPIRE SPIRACLE
(— OF WIND) SPIRIT
(BAD —) OZOSTOMIA
(DIVINE —) NEPHESH
(LIFE —) PRANA SPIRIT
(STINKING —) FUMOSITY
BREATHE LIVE PANT PUFF SIGH VENT
EXIST EXUDE SPEAK SPIRE UTTER
ASPIRE EXHALE INHALE WHEEZE RESPIRE
(— HEAVILY) FOB PECH SOUGH
THROTTLE
(— LABORIOUSLY) GASP
(— NOISILY) SOUGH SNOTTER
(— UPON) FAN
BREATHER PAUSE
BREATHING ALIVE GASPING AFFLATUS
SPIRATION
BREECH BORE BUTT BLOCK BUTTOCKS
DERRIERE

BREECHES HOSE CHAPS JEANS LEVIS
SLOPS TREWS BREEKS TIGHTS
JODHPURS KNICKERS TROUSERS
PANTALOON
BREED GET ILK BEAR KIND RACE REAR
SORT BEGET BROOD CASTE CAUSE
CLASS HATCH ISSUE RAISE STOCK
TRAIN CREATE STRAIN EDUCATE
NOURISH PRODUCE PROGENY SPECIES
VARIETY GENERATE INSTRUCT
(DWARF —) TOY
BREEDING ORIGIN DESCENT NURTURE
BEHAVIOR CIVILITY TRAINING
BREEZE AIR AURA BLOW GALE GUST STIR
WIND BLAST WALTZ ZEPHYR FRESHEN
WHISPER
(COOL —) DOCTOR
(GENTLE —) AIR AURA ZEPHYR
(LAND —) TERRAL
(STIFF —) STOUR TIFTER
BREEZY AIRY BRISK FRESH WINDY
BRETON ARMORICAN
BREVIARY ORDO DIGEST EPITOME
SUMMARY ABSTRACT
BREVITY SYNTOMY LACONISM
BRIEFNESS SHORTNESS TERSENESS
BREW ALE MIX BEER BOIL MAKE PLOT
HATCH STOUT DEVISE FOMENT SEETHE
CONCOCT PREPARE CONTRIVE
BREWERY BRASSERIE
BRIBE BUY FEE FIX OIL ROB SOP TIP BAIT
GIFT PALM BONUS GRAFT STEAL SUGAR
TEMPT EXTORT GREASE PAYOLA
SUBORN CORRUPT SWEETEN GRATUITY
BRIC-A-BRAC CURIO VIRTU BIBELOT
TRUMPERY
BRICK BAT MARL PAVE TILE BLOCK
QUARL SLOPE SPLIT STONE CUTTER
HEADER PAVIOR CLINKER
(— WALL) NECK
(CRACKED —) CHUFF SHUFF
(FINAL HALF —) JACK
(IMPERFECT —) SHIPPER BURNOVER
(PILE OF —S) HACK CLAMP
(SECOND QUALITY —S) BRINDLES
(SECOND-RATE —) GRIZZLE
(SOFT —) CUTTER RUBBER PICKING
(SQUARE —) QUADREL
(SUN-DRIED —) BAT ADOBE
(WOODEN —) DOOK
BRIDAL NUPTIAL
BRIDE KALLAH SPOUSE SHULAMITE
BRIDE OF LAMMERMOOR
(AUTHOR OF —) SCOTT
(CHARACTER IN —) LUCY CALEB
EDGAR FRANK ASHTON HAYSTON
WILLIAM RAVENSWOOD BALDERSTONE
BRIDESHEAD REVISITED
(AUTHOR OF —) WAUGH
(CHARACTER IN —) BOY REX CARA
KURT BERYL CELIA JULIA RYDER BRIDEY
ANTHONY BLANCHE CHARLES MOTTRAM
CORDELIA MUSPRATT SAMGRASS
MARCHMAIN MULCASTER SEBASTIAN
BRIDESHEAD
BRIDGE WAY LINK PONS PONT REST
SPAN CROSS SIRAT RUNWAY AUCTION
BASCULE BIFROST CONNECT PASSAGE
PONTOON TRESTLE VIADUCT CONTRACT
TRAVERSE DUPLICATE
(— OF MUSICAL INSTRUMENT)
MAGAS CHEVALET CHEVILLE
(— TO PARADISE) ALSIRAT
(ARCADED —) RIALTO
(CONTRACT —) CHICAGO GHOULIE
PLAFOND
(FLUE —) ALTAR
(GATEWAY —) GOUT
(HOSE —) JUMPER
(IMPEDANCE —) DIPLEXER
(NATURAL —) ARCH
(PLANK —) LIGGER
(ROPE SUSPENSION —) JOOLA
(RUDE —) CLAPPER
BRIDGE OF SAN LUIS REY
(AUTHOR OF —) WILDER
(CHARACTER IN —) PIO JAIME PILAR
MANUEL PEPITA ESTEBAN JUNIPER
PERICHOLE MONTEMAYOR
BRIDLE BIT CURB REIN RULE BRAKE
BRANK CHECK GUIDE GOVERN HALTER
SUBDUE CONTROL REPRESS SNAFFLE
RESTRAIN SUPPRESS
BRIEF FEW CURT WRIT BLURB BREVE
PITHY QUICK SHORT TERSE ABRUPT
COMMON CURTAL LITTLE SNIPPY
SUDDEN CAPSULE COMPACT CONCISE
LACONIC OUTLINE SUMMARY FLEETING
FLITTING SUCCINCT SYLLABUS
BRIEF CASE FOLIO TASHIE
BRIEFLY BRIEF ENFIN SHORTLY
BRIG RIG JAIL PRISON GEORDIE
BRIGADE TERZO CAMPOO
BRIGAND THIEF BANDIT PIRATE ROBBER
CATERAN LADRONE ROUTIER PICAROON
BRIGHT APT GAY FINE GLAD HIGH LIVE
ROSY ACUTE AGLOW ALERT BRAVE
CLEAR CRISP FRESH JOLLY LIGHT LUCID
NITID QUICK RIANT SHARP SHEER SHINY
SMART SUNNY TINNY VIVID WHITE
WITTY CHEERY CLEVER FLASHY FLORID
GARISH LIMPID LIVELY LUCENT ORIENT
SERENE SHRILL SILVER FULGENT
LAMBENT RADIANT RINGING SHINING
ANIMATED CHEERFUL FLASHING
GLEAMING LIGHTFUL LUMINOUS
LUSTROUS SPLENDID STARLIKE
SUNSHINY
BRIGHTEN GILD BLOOM CHEER CLEAR
FLAME LIGHT LIVEN SHINE POLISH
ANIMATE BURNISH ENLIVEN FURBISH
LIGHTEN REFRESH SMARTEN ILLUMINE
BRIGHTLY GAY CLEAR LIGHT SHEEN
BRIGHT FRESHLY
BRIGHTNESS SUN BLAZE BLOOM ECLAT
FLAME GLARE GLEAM GLINT GLORY
GLOSS LIGHT NITOR SHEEN SHINE
ACUMEN BRIGHT CANDOR FULGOR
LUSTER CLARITY GLITTER NITENCY
SPARKLE RADIANCE SPLENDOR
BRILLIANCE
BRILLIANCE FAME BLARE BLAZE ECLAT
FLAME GLARE GLORY SHINE VALUE

KEENNESS RADIANCE SPLENDOR
VIVACITY REFULGENCE

BRILLIANCY FIRE BLARE ECLAT GLORY
CLARITY GLITTER RADIANCE SPLENDOR

BRILLIANT GAY GOOD KEEN SAGE WISE
QUICK VIVID BRIGHT CLEVER GIFTED
LIVELY BRAVURA EMINENT FLAMING
GLARING LAMBENT LOZENGE PRISMAL
RADIANT SHINING BLINDING DAZZLING
GLORIOUS INSPIRED LUCULENT
LUMINOUS SPLENDID
(TRANSIENTLY —) METEORIC

BRIM LIP RIM EDGE BLUFF BRINK MARGE
VERGE BORDER MARGIN
(— OF HAT) FLAP LEAF POKE BRINK
TARFE SLOUCH

BRIMMING BIG FULL ABRIM

BRIMSTONE SULFUR VIRAGO SPITFIRE

BRINE SEA MAIN SALT BRACK LEACH
OCEAN TEARS PICKLE MARINADE

BRING LAY WIN BEAR BUCK CALL FIRK
LEAD STOP TAKE CARRY DRIVE ENDUE
FETCH INCUR ARRIVE CONVEY DEDUCE
CONDUCE CONDUCT EXHIBIT PROCURE
PRODUCE
(— ABOUT) DO SEE BREW MAKE STAY
TEEM CAUSE DIGHT FRAME INFER
MOYEN SHAPE SWING CREATE EFFECT
INVOKE SECURE SPIRIT COMPASS
CONDUCE INSPIRE OPERATE PROCURE
PRODUCE CATALYZE OCCASION
TRANSACT PERPETRATE
(— BACK) REFER EFFECT RECALL
REDUCE REDUCT RELATE RETURN REVIVE
REVOKE PRODUCE RESTORE OCCASION
RETRIEVE TRANSACT
(— BEFORE) HAUL
(— CHARGE) APPEACH
(— DOWN) LAY DROP FALL FELL STOP
ABATE COUCH EMBASE SOFTEN DECLINE
DESCEND DISMOUNT OVERTHROW
(— FORTH) CAST FOAL GIVE MAKE
TEEM EDUCE HATCH ISSUE SPAWN
THROW PROFER DELIVER TRADUCE
ENGENDER PROCREATE
(— FORTH YOUNG) EAN KID YEAN
(— FORWARD) CITE LEAD INFER
ADDUCE ALLEGE ADJOUST ADVANCE
PROPOSE
(— IN) EARN INFER USHER IMPORT
INDUCE INVECT REPORT RETURN
ADHIBIT
(— INTO BATTLE) COMMIT
(— INTO COURT) SIST
(— INTO DISGRACE) FOUL
(— LOW) AVALE DEGRADE SUPPLANT
(— ON) INFER INDUCE
(— ONESELF) GET
(— OUT) DRAW ACCENT ELICIT
DISINTER HEIGHTEN
(— OVER) CONVERT
(— SHIP INTO POSITION) EASE
(— TO A HALT) STICK
(— TO AN END) DO END FIT DOCK
DRAW REDD CEASE FORDO DECIDE
EXPIRE FINISH FOREDO FULFIL DISJOIN

INCLUDE COMPLETE CONCLUDE
DISSOLVE SURCEASE
(— TO BAY) CORNER
(— TO BEAR) EXERT
(— TO HEEL) FACE
(— TO LIFE) EVOKE ANIMATE
(— TO LIGHT) GRUB REAP DREDGE
ELICIT EXPOSE REVEAL UNEARTH
DISCLOSE DISCOVER
(— TO NAUGHT) DASH FOIL UNDO
NEGATE CONFUTE DESTROY
(— TO PERFECTION) RIPEN
(— TO STOP) CURB HALT ARREST
(— TO THE GROUND) GRASS
(— TOGETHER) JOIN AMASS RAISE
UNITE ADDUCT CONFER CORRAL ENGAGE
ENLINK GATHER SUMMON COLLATE
COLLECT COMPILE COMPORT ASSEMBLE
CONFLATE ENSEMBLE
(— UP) REAR BREED NURSE RAISE
TRAIN NURSLE NUZZLE UPREAR
EDUCATE NOURISH

BRINK END EVE LIP RIM BANK BRIM EDGE
FOSS MARGE SHORE VERGE BORDER
MARGIN PRECIPICE

BRINY SALTY SALINE BRACKISH
MURIATED

BRIOCHE ROLL STICH SAVARIN

BRISK GAY BUSY CANT FAST KEEN PERT
RACY RASH SPRY TRIG VIVE AGILE ALERT
ALIVE CRISP FRESH FRISK NIPPY PEART
PEPPY PERKY QUICK ZIPPY ACTIVE
BREEZY DAPPER LIVELY NIMBLE SNAPPY
VIVACE ALLEGRO CHIPPER HUMMING
ROUSING ANIMATED SPANKING SPIRITED

BRISKNESS ALACRITY VIRITOOT

BRISTLE AWN JAG RIB BARB HAIR SETA
TELA BRUSH STRUT CHAETA PALPUS
RUFFLE SETULA STRIGA STYLET
STUBBLE WHISKER ACICULUM
FRENULUM SPICULUM VIBRISSA

BRISTLY SETOSE STUBBY SCRUBBY

BRITISH ENGLISH BRITANNIC WHITEHALL

BRITON CELT SCOT BRYTHON

BRITTANY ARMORICA
(NATIVE OF —) BRETON

BRITTLE DRY WEAK CRISP FRAIL SHORT
CRISPY FEEBLE FICKLE SLIGHT BRICKLE
FRAGILE FRIABLE DELICATE

BROACH AIR AWL CUT PIN TAP OPEN
SHED SPIT SPUR STAB VENT BEGIN
DRIFT PRICK VOICE DRIVER FIBULA
LAUNCH PIERCE REAMER ENLARGE
EXPRESS PUBLISH WIDENER

BROAD DEEP FREE VAST WIDE AMPLE
BEAMY GROSS LARGE ROOMY STOUT
THICK COARSE GLOBAL GENERAL
LIBERAL OBVIOUS SPACIOUS TOLERANT

BROADCAST AIR SOW SEED SEND
CARRY RADIO STREW AIRING SPREAD
DECLARE DIFFUSE PUBLISH SCATTER
ANNOUNCE TELEVISE TRANSMIT

BROADEN WIDEN DILATE EXPAND
EXTEND SPREAD ENNOBLE

BROADSWORD BILL KRIS GLAIVE
HANGER SPATHA CUTLASS FERRARA
CLAYMORE MONTANTO SCIMITAR

BROBDINGNAGIAN HUGE
BROCHURE TRACT BOOKLET PAMPHLET
  TREATISE
BROIL ROW BURN CHAR FEUD FRAY GRID
  HEAT TOIL BRAWL GRILL MELEE SCRAP
  BRAISE TUMULT CONTEST DISPUTE
  QUARREL BARBECUE CONFLICT
BROILER GRILL SEARER CHICKEN
  POUSSIN
BROKE LOW BUST STONY BANKRUPT
BROKEN DOWN RENT TORN BLOWN
  BURST KAPUT TAMED RUINED SHAKEN
  CRACKED CRUSHED FRACTED REDUCED
  SUBDUED WHIPPED BANKRUPT
  CONTRITE RUPTURED TATTERED
  WEAKENED
BROKER AGENT BANYAN CORSER
  DEALER FACTOR JOBBER CHANGER
  PEDDLER REALTOR HUCKSTER
  MERCHANT
BROKERAGE AGIOTAGE
BRONZE AES TAN BROWN STATUE
  GUNMETAL
  (ANTIQUE —) CACAO
  (GILDED —) VERMEIL
  (MEDAL —) CALABASH
BROOCH BAR PIN BOSS OUCH CAMEO
  CLASP SLIDE FIBULA
BROOD FRY NYE SET MOPE NEST NIDE
  TEAM COVEY FLOCK GLOOM GROUP
  HATCH HOVER ISSUE SEDGE STOCK
  WORRY YOUNG CLUTCH FAMILY LITTER
  PONDER PROGENY COGITATE INCUBATE
  MEDITATE
BROOK RUN BEAR BURN GILL LAKE RILL
  RUSH ABIDE BAYOU BOURN CREEK
  ARROYO BRANCH ENDURE GUTTER
  RUNLET RUNNEL STREAM SUFFER
  STOMACH TOLERATE
  (RIPPLING —) PURL
  (SALT —) LICK
BROOM MOP SWAB WISP BESOM BRUSH
  SCRUB SWEEP WHISK
BROTH BREE SOUP STOCK LIQUOR
  POTTAGE BOUILLON CONSOMME
BROTHEL CRIB HOUSE BAGNIO
  BORDELLO CATHOUSE SERAGLIO
BROTHER FRA KIN PAL SIB BRER MATE
  MONK PEER BUDDY FRERE FRIAR
  FELLOW FRATER GERMAN COMRADE
  SIBLING
  (HUSBAND'S —) LEVIR
  (LAY —) SCOLOG
  (WIFE'S —) AFFINE
  (YOUNGER —) CADET
BROTHERHOOD GUILD LODGE ORDER
  FRIARY SODALITY
  (— OF FREEMASONS) CRAFT
  (LITERARY —) FELIBRIGE
BROTHER-IN-LAW MAUGH
BROTHERS KARAMAZOV
  (AUTHOR OF —) DOSTOEVSKI
  (CHARACTER IN —) IVAN ALEXEY
  DMITRI FYODOR ALYOSHA KATRINA
  ZOSSIMA GRUSHENKA SMERDYAKOV
BROW TOP EDGE MIEN BRINK CREST
  EAVES FRONT RIDGE SLOPE FOREHEAD

BROWBEAT BOSS ABASH BULLY
  BOUNCE HECTOR DEPRESS DUMBCOW
  OUTFACE SWAGGER
BROWN (ALSO SEE COLOR) DUN TAN
  ARAB COOK SEAR ACORN BRUNO DUSKY
  HAZEL PABLO SEDGE SEPIA TAWNY
  TOAST UMBER APACHE BEAVER BRUNET
  MANILA RUSSET SENNET TANNED
  FUSCOUS OXBLOOD POMPEII PRAIRIE
  REDWOOD TANBARK TOBACCO VESUVIN
  BRUNETTE
BROWNIE NIS NISSE COOKY DOBBY NISSE
  GOBLIN URUISG
BROWSE CROP FEED GRAZE FORAGE
  NIBBLE PASTURE
BRUISE JAM BASH BRAY DENT HURT
  MAIM MAUL SORE STUN CRUSH POUND
  PUNCH BATTER BREACH INTUSE
  MANGLE SHINER CONTUND CROWNER
  (— FLAX) BRAKE
BRUNET DARK BLACK BROWN GYPSY
  MORENA SWARTHY MORENITA
BRUNT JAR BLOW JOLT CLASH FORCE
  ONSET SHOCK EFFORT IMPACT STRAIN
  STRESS ASSAULT OUTBURST VIOLENCE
BRUSH DIP TIP CARD COMB DUST FLAT
  SKIM SWAB BROOM CLEAN COPSE FIGHT
  FITCH GRAZE LINER SABLE SCRUB SCUFF
  SWEEP SWOOP WHISK BADGER BATTLE
  DAUBER DUSTER PENCIL SPONGE
  STROKE TEASEL CLEANSE FOXTAIL
  GRAINER GROOMER STIPPLE STRIPER
  THICKET SCRUBBER SKIRMISH STIPPLER
  (— ASIDE) SCUFF
  (— IN DANCING) SCUFFLE
  (— OF TWIGS) COW
  (— TO CLEAN SHIP BOTTOM) HOG
  (BLUNT —) BLENDER
  (ELECTRIC —) DOCTOR
  (FLESH —) SCRAPER STRIGIL
BRUSHWOOD RUSH BRAKE BRUSH
  COPSE SCRUB COPPET RAMMEL COPPICE
  THICKET
BRUSQUE CURT RUDE BLUFF BLUNT
  GRUFF HASTY ROUGH SHORT ABRUPT
  VIOLENT CAVALIER IMPOLITE
BRUTAL CRUEL FERAL GROSS CARNAL
  COARSE SAVAGE BEASTLY BESTIAL
  BRUTISH INHUMAN INSOLENT RUTHLESS
BRUTE BETE BEAST GROSS YAHOO
  ANIMAL SAVAGE BESTIAL RUFFIAN
BRUTISH FELL CRUEL BRUTAL CARNAL
  FIERCE SAVAGE STUPID BESTIAL
  INHUMAN SENSUAL GADARENE
BUBBLE AIR BEAD BELL BLEB BLOB BOIL
  FOAM GLOB EMPTY BURBLE DELUDE
  SEETHE BLISTER GLOBULE DELUSIVE
  (— IN GLASS) BOIL REAM SEED
  BLISTER
  (PL.) SUDS
BUCCANEER PIRATE RIFLER ROBBER
  VIKING CORSAIR MARINER SPOILER
  MAROONER PICAROON
BUCK FOB RAM BUTT DEER DUDE MALE
  REAR STAG BLOOD DANDY PITCH SASIN
  DOLLAR OPPOSE RESIST STRIVE
  SAWBUCK

(— IN 1ST YEAR) FAWN
(— IN 2ND YEAR) PRICKET
(— IN 3RD YEAR) SORREL
(— IN 4TH YEAR) SORE
(— STEADILY) SUNFISH
(— UP) BRACE
BUCKET TUB BAIL GRAB PAIL SKIP SCOOP STOUP BAILER DIPPER HOPPET VESSEL SNAPPER CANNIKIN
BUCKLE BOW BEND CURL KINK OUCH TACK WARP CLASP MARRY STRAP FIBULA FASTENER
BUCKLER PELTA SCUTE TARGE SHIELD ROTELLA ROUNDEL RONDACHE
BUCOLIC IDYL LOCAL NAIVE RURAL FARMER RUSTIC SIMPLE AGRESTIC PASTORAL
BUD EYE GEM IMP PIP BULB BURR CION GERM GROW KNOT CLOVE SCION SHOOT BUTTON FLOWER SPROUT BLOSSOM PLUMULE TENDRON
BUDDENBROOKS (AUTHOR OF —) MANN
(CHARACTER IN —) TOM JEAN TONI ERICA GERDA HANNO JOHANN THOMAS ANTONIE GRUNLICH CHRISTIAN PERMANEDER
BUDDHA FO FOH BUTSU JATAKA GAUTAMA SRAMANA DAIBUTSU
(FATHER OF —) SUDDHODANA
(SON OF —) KAHULA
BUDDHISM DAIJO FOISM KEGON CHANISM LAMAISM HINAYANA
BUDDY BUD PAL MATE COBBER DIGGER BROTHER COMRADE COMPADRE TENTMATE
BUDGE MOVE STIR MOVEMENT
BUFF ASH TAN SHINE BUFFET POLISH
BUFFALO OX ANOA ARNA BISON HAMPER CARABAO CARIBOU GAZELLE OVERAWE ZAMOUSE BEWILDER SAPIUTAN SELADANG
BUFFER PAD FROG BUMPER FENDER CUSHION
BUFFET BOX BEAT BLOW CUFF SLAP TOSS KNOCK SCUFF SMITE BATTER FILLIP SERVER STRIKE THRASH CREDENZA
BUFFOON WAG WIT APER FOOL JAPE MIME ZANY ACTOR ANTIC CLOWN COMIC DROLL JESTER MUMMER STOOGE FARCEUR JUGGLER PIERROT TOMFOOL HUMORIST MERRYMAN PANTALOON SCARAMOUCH PUNCHINELLO
BUFFOONERY JAPERY ZANYISM CLOWNERY TOMFOOLERY
BUG (ALSO SEE INSECT) DOR FLAW GERM MITE BOGEY ROACH BEDBUG BEETLE CHINCH ELATER INSECT TINGID CIMICID STRIDER CONENOSE HEMIPTER
BUGABOO FEAR OGRE ALARM BOGEY BODACH GOBLIN BUGBEAR SPECTER
BUGBEAR COW OGRE BOGIE BUGABOO FEARBABE SCAREBUG
BUGGY CART SHAY TRAP NUTTY CALESA CABOOSE CALESIN FOOLISH DEMENTED INFESTED ROADSTER STANHOPE

BUGLE HORN CLARION TRUMPET
(PART OF —) CUP RIM BELL BITE EDGE
BUILD SET FORM MAKE REAR EDIFY ERECT FOUND FRAME RAISE SHAPE COMPILE FASHION ASSEMBLE PHYSIQUE
(— FIRE) CHUNK
(— HASTILY) CLAP
(— NEST) AERIE NIDIFY
(— UP) AGGRADE
(BODY —) HABITUS
BUILDING GIN CASA FLAT JAIL PILE SHED SHOP ABBEY HOTEL HOUSE IGLOO STORE STUDY ARMORY CHAPEL GARAGE LYCEUM PALACE SCHOOL BREWERY COLLEGE EDIFICE FACTORY FOUNDRY MANSION PALAZZO STATION SYNAGOG ATHENEUM BASILICA CHANCERY DWELLING EPHEBEUM FIRETRAP HOTHOUSE ICEHOUSE MAGAZINE SERAPEUM TENEMENT VELODROME OBSERVATORY PLANETARIUM
(— FOR AIRCRAFT) DOCK
(— OF STONE) KAABA CASHEL TRUDDO TRULLO
(— ON POSTS) PATAKA
(— WITH TRIANGULAR FRONT) AFRAME
(BUDDHIST —) TOPE
(CIRCULAR —) THOLOS ROTUNDA
(CRUDE —) SHANTY
(DILAPIDATED —) ROOKERY FIRETRAP
(EXHIBITION —) MUSEUM
(FARM —) BARN STABLE HACIENDA
(FORTIFIED —) CASTLE
(GLOOMY —) MAUSOLEUM
(GRAIN —) GARNER
(JAI ALAI —) FRONTON
(MOVABLE —) TURRET
(ORNAMENTAL —) ALCOVE
(PUBLIC —) CASINO THEATER COLISEUM
(QUARANTINE —) LAZARET
(SACRED —) CHURCH MOSQUE TEMPLE SACRARY PANTHEON SARAPEUM
(SLIGHT —) SHED
(SMALL —) HUT COOP HOCK EDICULE
(SPORTS —) CAGE
(STATELY —) DOME
(STORAGE —) BARN HORREUM
(SUBSIDIARY —) ANNEX
(TALL —) SKYSCRAPER
(TRADE —) HALL
(UNCOMFORTABLE —) ARK
BULB BUD CORM KNOB LAMP SEED CHIVE CLOVE GLOBE ONION SWELL TUBER CROCUS GARLIC SCILLA PHOTOFLASH

BULGARIA

ASSEMBLY: SOBRANJE
CAPE: EMINE SABLA KURATAN
CAPITAL: SOFIA
COIN: LEV LEW STOTINKA
COMMUNE: SLIVEN SLIVNO SISTOVA
GULF: BURGAS
MEASURE: OKA OKE KRINE LEKHE

MOUNTAIN: BOTEV SAPKA MUSALA VIKHREN

MOUNTAINS: PIRIN BALKAN RHODOPE

PEOPLE: SLAV TATAR BULGAR SLAVIC

RIVER: LOM VIT ARDA OSMA ISKER MESTA DANUBE MARICA OGOSTA STRUMA YANTRA MARITSA STRYAMA TUNDZHA

TOWN: RILA RUSE AYTOS BUTAN BYCLU ELENA ISKRA STARA VARNA BLEVEN BURGAS DULOVO LEVSKY PLEVNA SHUMEN SHUMLA SLIVEN SLIVNO WIDDIN YAMBOL ZAGORA GABROVO KARLOVO PLOVDIV SISTOVA TIRNOVO RUSTCHUK

WEIGHT: OKA OKE TOVAR

BULGE BAG JUT SAG BUMP HUMP KNOB LUMP BLOAT POUCH SWELL BEETLE BILLOW EXTEND PUCKER BLISTER PROJECT PROTRUDE SWELLING PROJECTION

BULGING FULL BOWED GOUTY PUDGY TUMID CONVEX TOROSE GIBBOUS SWOLLEN BOUFFANT

BULK BODY HEAP HEFT HULK HULL LUMP MASS PILE SIZE CARGO GROSS MIGHT POWER CORPSE EXTENT VOLUME BIGNESS MAJORITY QUANTITY

BULKHEAD CHECK BATTERY PARTITION

BULKY BIG MAIN BURLY GROSS LARGE LUSTY PUDGY STOUT CLUMSY STODGY HULKING LUMPING MASSIVE WEIGHTY CUMBROUS UNWIELDY

BULL COP APIS BEEF BILL MALE SEAL SLIP TORO ZEBU BONER BOVID BRUTE EDICT ERROR BOVINE BUSHWA LETTER TAURUS BULLOCK IRISHISM

BULLDOZE COW RAM BULLY FORCE SCOOP COERCE BROWBEAT BULLYRAG

BULLET BALL LEAD PILL SHOT SLUG DUMDUM PELLET TRACER MISSILE MUSHROOM WADCUTTER

(**PL.**) BALL LEAD STUFF

BULLETIN ITEM MEMO NOTICE POSTER REPORT SERIAL PROGRAM NEWSBILL

BULLFIGHT CORRIDA NOVILLADA

BULLFIGHTER TORERO MATADOR PICADOR CAPEADOR TOREADOR NOVILLERO

BULL'S-EYE EYE BULL DUMP GOLD BLANK OXEYE WHITE TARGET ROUNDEL

BULLY COW BOSS FACE FINE GOOD HAZE MATE BRAVE BRAVO GREAT JOLLY CUTTER HARASS HECTOR JOVIAL TYRANT BLUSTER BOUNCER DARLING DASHING GALLANT ROISTER RUFFIAN SWAGGER BANGSTER BROWBEAT BULLDOZE DOMINEER

BULRUSH REED RISP RUSH TULE SEDGE GLUMAL CATTAIL PAPYRUS

BULWARK FORT WALL FENCE JETTY MOUND WARDER BASTION DEFENSE PARAPET RAMPART

BUM BEG HOBO IDLER MOOCH STIFF TRAMP GUZZLE SPONGE LAYABOUT VAGABOND BINDLESTIFF

BUMP HIP HIT BANG BLOW BOOM JOLT JOWL KNOB LUMP WHOP BARGE BULGE CLASH CLOUT KNOCK THUMP BOUNCE IMPACT JOUNCE NODULE STRIKE COLLIDE CONFLICT SWELLING

(— IN SKI RUN) MOGUL

(— ON WHALE'S HEAD) HOVEL

BUMPKIN JAY YAP BOOR CLOD GAWK HICK LOUT RUBE TYKE CHURL CLOWN YAHOO YOKEL FARMER LUMMOX RUSTIC BUCOLIC CAUBOGE

BUN PUG CHOU BRICK COOKIE

BUNCH SET BALE CLEW CLUB KNOB KNOT PACK TUFT WISP CLUMP FAGOT FLOCK CLUTCH GAGGLE HUDDLE

(— OF BANANAS) HAND STEM

(— OF FLAX) HEAD STRICK

(— OF FLOWERS) BOWPOT BOUQUET BOUGHPOT

(— OF FRUIT) HOG STRAP

(— OF GRAIN) RIP

(— OF GRAPES) RAISIN

(— OF GRASS) WHISK

(— OF HAIR) COB

(— OF HERBS) BOUQUET

(— OF IVY) BUSH

(— OF TOBACCO LEAVES) HAND BREAK

(— OF TWIGS) COW KOW

(— UP) SHRUG

(SMALL —) WISP

BUNDLE LOT PAD TOD WAD BALE BOLT GARB HANK HAUL HEAD KNOT LOCK PACK ROLL SWAG BLUEY BUNCH FAGOT GROUP SHEAF SKEIN TRACE TRUSS BATTEN BINDLE FARDEL FASCES GATHER PACKET PARCEL PACKAGE

(— OF BOARDS) BOLT

(— OF CELLULOSE) MICROFIBRIL

(— OF FASCINES) ROULEAU

(— OF FIBRILS) AXONEME

(— OF FILAMENTS) BYSSUS

(— OF FLAX) BEET HEAD

(— OF HAIR) LEECH

(— OF HAY, STRAW, ETC.) WAP WASE WISP GAVEL SHEAF BATTEN BOLTIN BOTTLE TIPPLE WINDLING

(— OF HEATH) KID

(— OF HIDES) KIP

(— OF NERVE FIBERS) TRACT COLUMN

(— OF PAPERS) SPUR DUFTER

(— OF RODS) FASCES

(— OF SACKS) BADGER

(— OF SACRED TWIGS) BARSOM

(— OF THONGS) KNOUT

(— OF TOBACCO) CARROT

(— OF TWIGS) BIRCH BROOM FAGGOT

(— OF WOOD) PIMP BAVIN FAGOT

(— OF YARN) HAUL SLIP

(— OF 60 SKINS) TURN

(BUSHMAN'S —) DRUM BLUEY

BUNG CORK DOOK PLUG SPILE STOPPER

BUNGLE ERR FLUB GOOF MESS MUCK MUFF BOTCH FAULT FLUFF FUDGE MISDO SPOIL BOLLIX BUMBLE FOOZLE FUMBLE MANGLE MUDDLE BLUNDER

BUNGLING CLUMSY AWKWARD

BUNK BED BLAH SACK BERTH HOKUM
HOOEY LODGE SLEEP BALONEY
TWADDLE BUNCOMBE MALARKEY
NONSENSE

BUNTING FLAG FINCH TOWHEE
COWBIRD ETAMINE OATFOWL ORTOLAN
BOBOLINK RICEBIRD RINGBIRD

BUOY WAFT ELATE FLOAT BEACON
MARKER SUSTAIN LEVITATE

BUOYANT GAY CORKY HAPPY LIGHT
BLITHE BOUNCY FLOATY LIVELY ELASTIC
HOPEFUL JOCULAR LILTING SPRINGY
ANIMATED CHEERFUL SANGUINE
SPIRITED VOLATILE

BURDEN TAX VEX CARE DRAG DUTY
LADE LOAD ONUS TASK CARGO CRUSH
DRONE LABOR CHARGE CUMBER ENTAIL
HAMPER IMPOSE WEIGHT BALLAST
FREIGHT HAGRIDE ONERATE OPPRESS
REFRAIN REPRISE SUMPTER TROUBLE
ENCUMBER HANDICAP PRESSURE
MILLSTONE RESPONSIBILITY

BURDENSOME HEAVY IRKSOME
ONEROUS WEIGHTY CUMBROUS
GRIEVOUS GRINDING LOADSOME

BUREAU DESK CHEST AGENCY OFFICE
CENTRAL DRESSER

BUREAUCRAT MANDARIN

BURGLAR YEGG CRACK THIEF GOPHER
ROBBER RAFFLES YEGGMAN PETERMAN
PICKLOCK

BURGLARY BREAK CRACK THEFT
LARCENY ROBBERY STEALAGE

BURIAL PLACE AHU TOMB GRAVE
BURIAL GIGUNU LAYSTOW PYRAMID
CATACOMB CEMETERY GOLGOTHA
LAYSTALL

BURLAP GUNNY CROCUS BAGGING
HESSIAN SACKING WRAPPING

BURLESQUE APE ODD COPY JEST MIME
SKIT DROLL FARCE REVUE COMEDY
OVERDO PARODY BUFFOON JOCULAR
MIMICRY MOCKERY OVERACT DOGGEREL
RIDICULE TRAVESTY

BURLY BIG FAT BLUFF BULKY GROSS
HEAVY HUSKY LARGE LUSTY NOBLE
OBESE STOUT THICK STATELY IMPOSING

BURMA

BAY: BENGAL HUNTER HEANZAY
CAPITAL: RANGOON
DIVISION: PEGU MAGWE ARAKAN
KARENNI SAGAING MANDALAY
IRRAWADDY TENASSERIM
GULF: MARTABAN
MEASURE: LY DHA GON LAN MAU NGU
SAO TAO TAT BYEE DAIN PHAN SEIT
TAUN TENG THAT SALAY SHITA THUOC
LAMANY PALGAT TRUONG CHAIVAI
OKTHABAH
MONEY: KYAT
MOUNTAIN: POPA NATTAUNG SARAMATI
VICTORIA
MOUNTAINS: CHIN NAGA DAWNA
KACHIN KARENNI PEGUYOMA

NATIVE: AO VU WA LAI LAO MON PYU TAI
CHIN KADU KUKI LOLO MIAO NAGA
SEMA SGAU SGAW SHAN THAI KAREN
KHMER LHOTA BIRMAN BURMAN KACHIN
RENGMA PALAUNG ARAKANESE
PLATEAU: SHAN
PORT: AKYAB BASSEIN HENZADA
MOULMEIN
RIVER: HKA NMAI PEGU MEKONG SALWIN
SHWELI KALADAN MALIKHA MYITNGE
SALWEEN SITTANG CHINDWIN
INDAWGYI IRRAWADDY
SEA: ANDAMAN
TOWN: YE AVA PEGU AKYAB BHAMO
KARBE KATHA MINBU PAPUN PROME
TAVOY HSENWI HSIPAW LASHIO
MAYMYO MONYWA SHWEBO BASSEIN
HENZADA PAKOKKU RANGOON
MANDALAY MOULMEIN
WEIGHT: TA CAN MAT MOO PAI VIS BINH
DONG KYAT RUAY VISS BAHAR BEHAR
CANDY TICAL TICUL ABUCCO PEIKTHA

BURN CHAR FIRE GLOW RAZE SEAR SERE
BLAZE BROIL CENSE FLAME FLARE
PARCH ROAST SCALD SINGE WATER
IGNIFY SCORCH SIZZLE STREAM
COMBUST CONSUME CREMATE INCENSE
RIVULET SMOLDER AMBUSTION

BURNER KORO BAKER PILOT BUNSEN
CENSER BATSWING CALCINER GASLIGHT
THURIBLE WELSBACH

BURNING HOT FIRE LIVE AFIRE ANGRY
CALID EAGER FIERY QUICK ABLAZE
ARDENT FERVID TORRID CAUSTIC
FERVENT FLAMING GLARING GLOWING
INTENSE MORDANT SHINING FLAGRANT

BURRO ASS DONKEY

BURROW BED DEN DIG BURY HEAP HOLE
MINE MOLE ROOT COUCH MOUND
FURROW TUNNEL GALLERY PASSAGE
SHELTER EXCAVATE WORMHOLE

BURSAR PURSER CASHIER

BURST POP BLOW BUST DASH GUSH
GUST REND SCAT BLAST BREAK CRACK
ERUPT FLASH SALVO SPASM SPLIT
START STAVE BROKEN DAMAGE INJURY
EXPLODE IMPLODE RUPTURE SHATTER
OUTBREAK
(— ASUNDER) OUTRIVE
(— FORTH) ERUPT SALLY EXPIRE
BALLOON
(— IN) IRRUPT IMPLODE
(— INTO FRAGMENTS) FLITTER
(— INTO LAUGHTER) BUFF
(— OF ACTIVITY) BRASH SPURT
SPRINT SPLURGE
(— OF ARTILLERY) GRAZE RAFALE
(— OF CHEERS) SALVO
(— OF ENERGY) BANG
(— OF FIRING) COUGH
(— OF HARMONIOUS SOUND)
DIAPASON
(— OF LIGHT) FLASH GLORY
(— OF SPEED) KICK FLUTTER
(— OF TEARS) BLURT

(— OF TEMPER) FUFF BOUTADE
(— OF WIND) FLAW
(— OPEN) DEHISCE UPBRAST
(— OUT) BUFF PRORUMP
(— THE HEART) RIVE

BURUNDI

CAPITAL: BUJUMBURA
COIN: FRANC
LAKE: RUGWERO TSHOHOHA
NATIVE: TWA HUTU BANTU PYGMY TUTSI
WATUSI
RIVER: KAGERA RUVUBU RUZIZI
AKANYARU MALAGARAZI
TOWN: NGOZI BURURI KITEGA MUYINGA
BUJUMBURA

BURY URN HIDE RAKE TURF VEIL CLOAK
COVER EARTH GRAVE INTER INURN
PLANT VAULT ENTOMB INHUME SHROUD
CONCEAL ENGROSS IMMERSE REPRESS
SECRETE SUBMERGE
BUS CAMION JITNEY JEEPNEY MINIBUS
BUSBOY OMNIBUS PICCOLO
BUSH TOD CLUMP GROVE SHRUB
BRANCH MAQUIS BOSCAGE OUTBACK
THICKET
BUSHEL LOT EPHAH BUCKET MODIUS
(1-HALF —) TOVET
(1-HALF TO 3-4THS —) CABOT
(1-4TH —) PECK
(1.6 —) FANEGA
(3 TO 5 —S) SACK
(3-4THS —) SKIPPLE
(4 —S) COMB COOMB
(41.28 —) WEY
(8 —S) SEAM
BUSHING BUSH COAK DRILL LINER
BOUCHE COLLET LINING SLEEVE
BOUCHON FERRULE GROMMET PADDING
(HALF —) STEP
BUSINESS ADO ART BIZ JOB CARE FEAT
FIRM FUSS GAME LINE TASK WORK
CRAFT ERGON TRADE TRUCK AFFAIR
CUSTOM EMPLOY ERRAND MATTER
METIER OFFICE RACKET ACCOUNT
CALLING CONCERN TRADING TRAFFIC
ACTIVITY COMMERCE INDUSTRY
INTEREST VOCATION OCCUPATION
BUSINESSMAN TYCOON POACHER
BOURGEOIS CONVERTER
BUSKIN BOOT SHOE CALIGA BOTTINE
COTHURN BRODEKIN
BUST BUMP FAIL RUIN TAME BOSOM
BREAK BURST CHEST FLUNK SPREE
BRONZE DEMOTE REDUCE STATUE
DEGRADE DISMISS FAILURE
BUSTLE ADO FRAY FUSS JUMP STIR
WHIR FRISK HASTE WHIRL BUMBLE
ENERGY FLURRY HUSTLE POTHER
RACKET RUFFLE TATTER THRONG
TUMULT UNREST UPROAR CLATTER
CLUTTER SCUFFLE ACTIVITY SPLUTTER
STRUGGLE
BUSY FAST FELL APPLY BRISK QUICK
ACTIVE EIDENT EMPLOY INTENT LIVELY
OCCUPY THRONG UNIDLE ENGAGED
HOPPING HUMMING OPEROSE WORKING
DILIGENT EMPLOYED EXERCISE
OCCUPIED SEDULOUS TIRELESS
UNTIRING PRAGMATIC
BUSYBODY SNOOP EARWIG MARPLOT
MEDDLER SNOOPER FACTOTUM
QUIDNUNC
BUT LO SED YEA YET MERE ONLY SAVE
ARRAH STILL ALWAYS EXCEPT UNLESS
BESIDES HOWBEIT HOWEVER
BUTCHER KILL SLAY BUTCH SPOIL
BUNGLE MURDER BOTCHER BRAINER
FLESHER MEATMAN PORKMAN
SLAUGHTER
BUTLER YEOMAN BOTELER SERVANT
STEWARD CELLARER MAJORDOMO
BUTT JUT MOT PIT PUT RAM TOY TUP
BUCK BUNT CART CASK FOOL GOAD
GOAL GOAT HORN JOLT PIPE POLL PUSH
STUB TOPE HINGE JOINT MOUND SCOPE
STOCK STUMP BREECH TARGET THRUST
BEEHIVE BUTTOCK PARAPET PROJECT
RIDICULE
(— FOR RIDICULE) GAME SPORT STALE
COCKSHY
(— OF CIGAR) DOCK SNIPE
(— OF HORSEHIDE) SHELL
(— OF JOKE) JEST SCOGGIN
JESTWORD
(CIGARETTE —) BUMPER
(HALF —) BEND
BUTTE HILL PICACHO
BUTTER SHEA CLART COCUM BEURRE
CAJOLE SPREAD BLARNEY FLATTER
(ARTIFICIAL —) BOSH OLEO BOSCH
MARGARINE
(PRUNE —) LEKVAR
BUTTERCUP CYME ANEMONE CROWTOE
GOLDCUP KINGCUP CROWFOOT
FROGWORT PASQUEFLOWER
BUTTERFISH GUNNEL POMPANO
WHITING PALOMETA SKIPJACK
BUTTERFLY IO BLUE ARGUS ELFIN
GHOST NYMPH QUEEN SATYR SWIFT
WHITE ZEBRA ADONIS ALPINE APOLLO
CALIGO COPPER DANAID HOPPER IDALIA
JUGATE MORPHO PIERID PROGNE
PSYCHE SULFUR THECLA URSULA VIOLET
YELLOW ADMIRAL BUCKEYE DIURNAL
DOLPHIN EMPEROR MONARCH SKIPPER
TROILUS TUSSOCK VANESSA VICEROY
ARTHEMIS CECROPIA CRESCENT
GRAYLING HESPERID ITHOMIID
BUTTERMILK WHIG JOCOQUE
SOURDOOK
(— AND WATER) BLAND
BUTTOCKS BUM CAN HAM ARSE BUNS
BUTT DOCK PRAT SEAT TAIL CROUP
FANNY SLATS STERN BEHIND BOTTOM
BREECH HEINIE CRUPPER KEISTER
BACKSIDE DERRIERE POSTERIOR
BUTTON BUD ZIP BOSS CHIN DOME
HOOK KNOB SPUR TUFT BADGE CATCH
GLIDE OLIVE PEARL BAUBLE BOUTON
BUCKLE GLIDER SHINER TOGGLE TROCHE

DEWDROP HORNTIP KNICKER NETSUKE
REGULUS DOORBELL FASTENER
OLIVETTE

BUTTRESS NOSE PIER PILE PROP STAY
BRACE ALLETTE OUTSHOT SUPPORT
ABUTMENT

BUXOM AMPLE JOLLY PLUMP PRONE
BLITHE FLORID BOUNCING OBLIGING
YIELDING JUNOESQUE

BUY GAIN HAVE SHOP TAKE BRIBE TRADE
MARKET RANSOM REDEEM SECURE
ACQUIRE CHAFFER PURCHASE

BUYER CHAP AGENT CATER BEGGER
EMPTOR PATRON VENDEE CHAPMAN
SHOPPER CUSTOMER PROSPECT
(— OF CLOTH) REDUBBER

BUZZ HUM BURR CALL DASH HISS RING
WHIR PHONE WHISPER

BUZZARD HAWK PERN BUTEO GLEDE
HARPY CURLEW PREYER PUTTOCK
VULTURE BROMVOEL

BUZZER BEE BELL ALARM HOWLER
SIGNAL WHIZZER

BY AT OF TO AGO PAR PER ABUT ANON
INTO NEAR PAST TILL APART ASIDE
CLOSE BESIDE TOWARD THROUGH
(— AND BY) BELIVE BIMEBY

(— FAR) EASILY
(— HEART) PERQUEIR
(— HOOK OR CROOK) HABNAB
(— MEANS OF) PER MOYENANT
(— NO MEANS) NA
(— REASON OF THIS) HEREAT
(— STEALTH) STOWLINS
(— SURPRISE) ABACK
(— THE DAY) PD
(— THE ORDER OF) O
(— THE WAY) APROPOS
(— THIS TIME) ALREADY
(— WAY OF) VIA
(GONE —) AGO PAST
(NEAR —) GIN

BYGONE PAST YORE OLDEN FORMER
ANCIENT ELAPSED DEPARTED PRETERIT

BYPASS JUMP SHUN AVOID EVADE
SHUNT CUTOFF DETOUR CIRCUIT
OUTFLANK

BYPATH LANE BYWAY UNDERWALK

BY-PRODUCT SCRAP SHORTS
EFFLUVIUM MIDDLINGS OUTGROWTH

BYWAY LANE PATH ALLEY BYPATH
BYWALK OUTWAY SIDEWAY

BYWORD ADAGE AXIOM MOTTO PHRASE
SAYING PROVERB NICKNAME

C

C CEE COCA CHARLIE HUNDRED

CAB FLY TAXI ARABA CABIN GHARRI
CRAWLER HACKNEY TAXICAB COUPELET
(HINDU —) JUDKA
(LOW-HUNG —) HERDIC
(2-PONY —) KOSONG
(4-WHEELED —) BOUNDER DROSHKY
GROWLER

CABAL PLOT RING JUNTA PARTY CLIQUE
SCHEME SECRET COUNCIL FACTION
INTRIGUE CAMARILLA

CABALISTIC MYSTIC

CABARET CAFE TAVERN

CABBAGE CHOU KALE CROUT SAVOY
STEAL PECHAY PILFER OXHEART
PAKCHOI PURLOIN COLEWORT KOHLRABI

CABDRIVER HACK CABBY CABMAN
COCHER MUSHER HACKMAN

CABIN BOX CAB COT DEN HUT CELL CRIB
SHED TILT BOOTH CHOZA COACH CUDDY
HOVEL LODGE SHACK BOHAWN CABANA
CASITA REFUGE SALOON SHANTY
SHELTY COTTAGE HUDDOCK MUDSILL
(— ON SHIP'S DECK) TEXAS
ROUNDHOUSE
(DOUBLE —) SADDLEBAG
(RUSSIAN LOG —) IZBA

CABINET BOX BUHL CASE FILE SINK
AMBRY BAHUT BOARD CABIN CHEST
BAFFLE BUREAU CLOSET ICEBOX
ALMIRAH BOUDOIR COMMODE CONSOLE
COUNCIL ETAGERE FREEZER JUKEBOX
WHATNOT CELLARET CUPBOARD
MINISTRY SHOWCASE VARGUENO
MONOCLEID
(FILING —) MORGUE

CABLE GUY TOW CORD FAST LINK ROPE
STAY WIRE GANGER STRAND TETHER
COAXIAL CATENARY HIGHLINE
TELEGRAM UMBILICAL
(— WITH EYE AT EACH END) STRAP
(CHAIN —) BOOM
(DERRICK —) BACKSTAY
(SPLICED —) SHOT
(SUSPENDED —) ROPEWAY

CABOOSE CAB CAR VAN BUGGY
CRUMMY GALLEY PALACE BOUNCER
COOKROOM DOGHOUSE

CACAO BROMA COCOA ARRIBA COCKER
CRIOLLO FORASTERO

CACHE BURY HIDE DEPOT STASH STORE
SCREEN CONCEAL DEPOSIT TREASURE

CACHET SEAL STAMP WAFER ESSENCE
KONSEAL

CACKLE CONK CLACK LAUGH BABBLE
GABBLE GAGGLE GIGGLE GOSSIP TITTER
CHATTER SNICKER TWADDLE LAUGHTER

CACOPHONOUS HARSH RAUCOUS
JANGLING STRIDENT

CACTUS NOPAL BAVOSO CARDON
CEREUS CHAUTE CHINOA CHOLLA
COCHAL MESCAL PEYOTE BISNAGA
SAGUARO PITAHAYA

CAD CUR BOOR HEEL CHURL MUCKER
RASCAL ROTTER BOUNDER DASTARD
BLIGHTER

CADAVER BODY STIFF CORPSE CARCASS

CADAVEROUS PALE GAUNT LIVID
PALLID GHASTLY HAGGARD

CADENCE BEAT FALL IAMB LILT PACE
TONE METER SWING THROB DACTYL
IAMBUS JINGLE RHYTHM BACCHIC
ANAPAEST MOVEMENT

CADET SON DODO GOAT PLEBE YOUTH
JUNIOR

CADGE BEG BUM HAWK MOOCH SPONGE
SCROUNGE

CADGER BUM PACKMAN SPONGER
HUCKSTER SCAMBLER

CADMUS (DAUGHTER OF —) INO
AGAVE SEMELE AUTONOE
(FATHER OF —) AGENOR
(MOTHER OF —) TELEPHASSA
(SISTER OF —) EUROPA
(SON OF —) POLYDORUS
(WIFE OF —) HARMONIA

CADRE CORE FRAME

CADUCEUS WAND STAFF SCEPTER
KERYKEION

CAESURA REST STOP BREAK PAUSE
INTERVAL DIAERESIS

CAFE BARROOM CABARET ESTAMINET

CAGE BOX CAR MEW PEN COOP CORF
CRIB GOAL GRATE HUTCH AVIARY
BASKET PRISON CHANTRY CONFINE
ENCLOSE SHELTER TUMBREL CARRIAGE
ELEVATOR IMPRISON RETAINER
(— FOR HAWKS) MEW
(— FOR HENS) CAVIE
(— OF MINE SHAFT) GIG
(— OF TRAM) CABIN
(BIRD —) AVIARY PINJRA VOLARY
BIRDCAGE
(FIRE —) CRESSET
(LOBSTER —) CORF CREEL

CAGED PENT CAPTIVE

CAIN (BROTHER OF —) ABEL SETH
(FATHER OF —) ADAM
(MOTHER OF —) EVE
(SON OF —) ENOCH

CAIRN MOUND GALGAL CATSTONE
STONEMAN

CAISSON BOX PONT CAMEL CHEST
WAGON COFFER PONTON SAUCER
CAMAILE CHAMBER PONTOON

CAITIFF BASE MEAN VILE COWARD
WICKED CAPTIVE COWARDLY PRISONER
WRETCHED

CAJOLE COG CON JIG COAX FLAM
CARNY CHEAT CURRY DECOY FRAIK

INGLE JOLLY TEASE DELUDE DIDDLE
ENTICE FRAISE HUMBUG BEGUILE
FLATTER PALAVER TWEEDLE WHEEDLE
BLANDISH

CAJOLERY FRAIK TAFFY BUTTER FRAISE
WHILLY BLARNEY DAUBERY FLATTERY

CAKE BAR BUN NUT WIG BAKE BALL
LUMP MASS MOLE PUFF TART ARVAL
BATTY BLOCK BOXTY COOKY CRUST
CUPID FADGE SCONE TORTE WAFER
WEDGE CIMBAL COOKIE ECLAIR GATEAU
HALLAH HARDEN KICHEL KUCHEN
NACKET PARKIN PASTRY POPLIN TABLET
BANBURY BRIOCHE BROWNIE CARAWAY
CRUMPET CUPCAKE HOECAKE MANCHET
NUTCAKE OATCAKE PANCAKE PLASTER
KUGELHOF MADELINE MARZIPAN
SEEDCAKE SOLIDIFY
(— OF CLAY) PLATTEN
(— OF COCONUT PULP) POONAC
(— OF MEAL) DODGER
(— OF RUBBER) BISCUIT
(ALMOND —) RATAFIA
(CREOLE RICE —) CALA
(FANCY —) SUNKET
(FLAT —) PLATE BUNUELO GALETTE
PLACENT CHRIMSEL
(FOURTH PART OF —) FARL
(FRIED —) WONDER CRULLER
DOUGHNUT
(GINGER —) BOLIVAR
(GRIDDLE —) LATKE FLIPPER FRITTER
FLAPJACK
(HOLIDAY —) SIMNEL
(HONEY —) LEKACH
(LAMB AND WHEAT —) KIBBE
(LEAVENED —) BAP
(NEW YEAR'S —) HAGMENA HOGMANAY
(OATEN —) BANNOCK
(OIL —) GRIT POONAC
(PLUM —) SIMNEL
(POTATO —) FADGE
(PRESS —) CACHAZA
(RUM —) BABA
(SEED —) WIG SEEDCAKE
(TEA —) LUNN SCONE PIKELET
(THIN —) WAFER JUMBLE BANNOCK
TORTILLA
(UNLEAVENED —) CHAPATI CHAPATTI
(YEAST —) KOJI
(PL.) AMSATH COLYBA

CAKES AND ALE (AUTHOR OF —)
MAUGHAM
(CHARACTER IN —) AMY KEAR KEMP
ALROY ROSIE EDWARD GEORGE
ASHENDEN TRAFFORD DRIFFIELD

CALABASH GOURD CURUBA JICARA

CALABOOSE JUG BRIG JAIL STIR POKEY
PRISON CABOOSE BASTILLE HOOSEGOW

CALAMITOUS BAD SAD DIRE EVIL
BLACK FATAL BITTER DISMAL TRAGIC
WOEFUL ADVERSE BALEFUL DIREFUL
HAPLESS RUINOUS UNHAPPY UNLUCKY
GRIEVOUS TRAGICAL WRETCHED

CALAMITY ILL WOE BLOW DOOM EVIL
RUIN RUTH SLAP HYDRA STORM WRACK
MISERY ONCOME PLAGUE SORROW
EXTREME SCOURGE ACCIDENT DISASTER
DISTRESS FATALITY JUDGMENT
MISCHIEF

CALCIFY CRETIFY

CALCINING BURNING

CALCIUM LIME

CALCIUM CARBONATE WHITING
DRIPSTONE

CALCULATE AIM SUM CALK CAST PLAN
RATE TELL COUNT FRAME THINK CIPHER
DESIGN EXPECT FIGURE NUMBER
RECKON ACCOUNT AVERAGE COMPUTE
PREPARE CONSIDER ESTIMATE FORECAST
(— BY ASTROLOGY) ERECT

CALCULATING COLD WISE BRITTLE
CAUTIOUS

CALCULATION CARE SHARE ACCOUNT
CALCULUS FORECAST PRUDENCE
(PL.) FIGURES

CALCULATOR TABLE ABACUS ABACIST
SOROBAN COMPUTER ISOGRAPH

CALCULUS STONE UROLITH ANALYSIS

CALDRON POT RED VAT LEAD BOILER
KETTLE TRIPOD VESSEL CALDERA

CALEB (DAUGHTER OF —) ACHSAH
(FATHER OF —) HEZRON JEPHUNNEH
(SON OF —) HUR

CALENDAR ORDO DIARY FASTI ALMANAC
CALENDS JOURNAL REGISTER SCHEDULE
(— OF MARTYRS) MENOLOGY

CALENDER TABBY SCHREINER

CALF BOY LEG DOLT VEAL VEAU BOSSY
DOGIE PODDY RANNY SOOKY YOUTH
WEANER BULCHIN FATLING SLEEPER
(LIKE A —) VITULINE
(PREMATURE —) SLINK
(UNBRANDED —) LONGEAR SLEEPER
(YEARLING —) BUD DAIRT
(YOUNG —) DEACON
(PL.) CAURE

CALIBER BORE RANK DEGREE TALENT
ABILITY BREADTH COMPASS QUALITY
CAPACITY DIAMETER MAGNITUDE
(HIGH —) STATURE

CALICO BLAY PINTO SALLO CHINTZ
SALLOO CROYDON SPOTTED DUNGAREE
GOLDFISH

CALIFORNIA

CAPITAL: SACRAMENTO

COLLEGE: MILLS POMONA WHITTIER

COUNTY: INYO KERN MONO NAPA YOLO
YUBA MARIN MODOC COLUSA LASSEN
MERCED PLACER PLUMAS SHASTA
SOLANO SONOMA SUTTER TEHAMA
TULARE ALAMEDA VENTURA SISKIYOU
CALAVERAS

DESERT: MOJAVE COLORADO

INDIAN: HUPA POMO YANA YUKI KAROK
MAIDU MIWOK WAPPO WIYOT YUROK
PATWIN SHASTA TOLOWA YOKUTS
CHUMASH LUISENO SALINAN SERRANO
DIEGUENO

LAKE: MONO SODA EAGLE OWENS TAHOE
SALTON TULARE ALMANOR BERRYESSA

MOUNTAIN: MUIR LASSEN SHASTA WHITNEY
PARK: LASSEN SEQUOIA YOSEMITE
RIVER: EEL MAD PIT KERN OWENS PUTAH STONY FEATHER KLAMATH RUBICON TRINITY SACRAMENTO
STATE BIRD: QUAIL
STATE FLOWER: POPPY
STATE NICKNAME: GOLDEN
STATE TREE: REDWOOD
TOWN: LODI AZUSA CHICO CHINO INDIO BLYTHE CARMEL COVINA EUREKA FRESNO LOMPOC MERCED OXNARD POMONA SONOMA TULARE ALAMEDA BURBANK GARDENA NEEDLES SALINAS VALLEJO VISALIA ALTADENA BERKELEY PASADENA REDLANDS CUCAMONGA
UNIVERSITY: USC UCLA CALTECH STANFORD

CALIPH ABU ALI BEKR IMAM OMAR OTHMAN ABBASID UMAYYAD
CALK JAG NAP PAY COPY CORK FILL STOP CAULK CLOSE HORSE ROUGH CAREEN CALTROP CHINTZE OCCLUDE SILENCE
CALKING OAKUM
CALL HO BAN BID CRY CUP DUB HOY SAY SEE CITE COOP HAIL JERK NAME NOTE PAGE STOP TERM TOOT YELL BEDUB CLAIM CLEPE HALLO HIGHT HOLLA PHONE ROUSE SHOUT SPEAK STYLE UTTER VISIT VOUCH WAKEN YODEL ACCUSE APPEAL AROUSE BECALL CHANGE DEMAND HALLOA HALLOO INVITE INVOKE MUSTER SUMMON ADDRESS APPOINT BEHIGHT BETITLE COMMAND CONVENE CONVOKE DECLARE ENTITLE IMPEACH INQUIRE WHISTLE ANNOUNCE ASSEMBLE NOMINATE PROCLAIM
(— A BET) STAY
(— ALOUD) COUNT
(— BACK) RECALL REVOKE
(— COARSELY) ROUP
(— DOWN) BRAWL DEVOCATE IMPRECATE
(— FOR) CRY TAKE CLAIM EXACT DEMAND DESIRE COLLECT SOLICIT
(— FOR HELP) SOS
(— FOR HOGS) SOOK SOOEY
(— FOR PARLEY) CHAMADE
(— FORTH) STIR EVOKE ELICIT INDUCE INVOKE ATTRACT PROVOKE SUGGEST
(— HOUNDS) LIFT
(— IN MARBLES) DUBS
(— IN WHIST) ABUNDANCE
(— INTO QUESTION) IMPUGN OPPUGN
(— LOUDLY) CRY HAIL ACCLAIM
(— MAN BY MAN) ARRAY
(— ON TELEPHONE) BUZZ
(— TO ARMS) ALARM ALARUM RAPPEL
(— TO BELLBOY) FRONT
(— TO CAT) CHEET
(— TO COURT) ARRAIGN
(— TO COWS) PROO SOOK COBOSS SOOKIE
(— TO FOOD) SOSS

(— TO HORSE) HIE HUP WAY PROO
(— TO MIND) CITE MING RECORD BETHINK RECOLLECT
(— TO PRAYER) ADAN AZAN
(— TO READINESS) ALERT
(— TO SPARROW) PHIP PHIPPE
(— TO WITNESS) APPEAL
(BIRD'S —) WEET
(BOATSWAIN'S —) WINDING
(BRIDGE —) DOUBLE
(BUGLE —) POST HALLALI STABLES
(CLOSE —) TOUCH
(DUCK —) SQUAWKER
(FRIENDLY —) CEILIDH
(HUNTING —) MOT RECHATE RECHEAT
(MORNING —) MATIN
(NAUTICAL —) AHOY
(SHEPHERD'S —) OVEY
CALLING ART JOB WAY HAIL RANK TRADE CAREER METIER NAMING OUTCRY MISSION PURSUIT STATION SUMMONS WARNING BUSINESS FUNCTION SHOUTING VOCATION
CALLIOPE (FATHER OF —) ZEUS JUPITER
(MOTHER OF —) MNEMOSYNE
(SON OF —) ORPHEUS
CALLOUS HARD HORNY TOUGH OBTUSE TORPID OBDURATE
CALLOW BALD BARE CRUDE GREEN SQUAB JEJUNE IMMATURE YOUTHFUL
CALM LEE COOL EASY EVEN FAIR FLAT HUSH LULL MILD REST SOFT STAY ABATE ALLAY CHARM LEVEL PEACE QUELL QUIET SLEEK SOBER STILL STOIC APLOMB DEFUSE DOCILE GENTLE IRENIC PACIFY PLACID SEDATE SERENE SETTLE SILENT SMOOTH SOOTHE STEADY APPEASE ASSUAGE COMPOSE GLACIAL HALCYON MOLLIFY PACIFIC PATIENT PLACATE RESTFUL UNMOVED COMPOSED DECOROUS MODERATE PEACEFUL RESTRAIN SERENITY TRANQUIL
CALMNESS LULL POISE PHLEGM REPOSE ATARAXY COOLNESS SERENITY SOBRIETY STILLNESS
CALOMEL TURPETH
CALUMNY SLUR DEPRAVE OBLOQUY ASPERSION
CALVARY GOLGOTHA
CALVINIST GENEVAN GOMARIAN
CALYX CUP POP HULL HUSK LEAF CULOT SEPAL SHUCK
CAM COG AWRY LOBE ASKEW SNAIL LIFTER TAPPET CROOKED TRIPPET

CAMBODIA

CAPE: SAMIT
CAPITAL: PNOMPENH PHNOMPENH
COIN: RIEL PUTTAN PIASTER
GULF: SIAM
LAKE: TONLESAP
MOUNTAIN: PAN AURAL
MOUNTAINS: DANGREK CARDAMOM ELEPHANT

NATIVE: CHAM KHMER
RIVER: SAN SEN BASSAC MEKONG PORONG SREPOK SEKHONG TONLESAP
TOWN: REAM TAKEO KAMPOT KRATIE PURSAT KOHNIEH KRACHEH ROVIENG SAMRONG PNOMPENH SISOPHON
WEIGHT: MACE TAEL

CAMBRIC BATISTE PERCALE
CAMEL OONT DELOUL FENDER HAGEEN MEHARI CAISSON TYLOPOD BACTRIAN DROMEDARY
CAMELLIA JAPONICA
CAMELOPARD GIRAFFE
CAMEO GEM CARVING PHALERA RELIEVO ANAGLYPH
CAMERA KODAK MINICAM PANORAM ENLARGER MINIATURE VERASCOPE (PART OF —) LUG BODY DOOR KNOB LENS LOCK CRANK DRIVE FOCUS LATCH SCALE STRAP TIMER BUTTON SENSOR SOCKET WINDOW ADVANCE BELLOWS LANYARD RELEASE SHUTTER PHOTOCELL TRANSDUCER VIEWFINDER
CAMILLE (AUTHOR OF —) DUMAS (CHARACTER IN —) DUVAL ARMAND NANINE CAMILLE GAUTIER PRUDENCE VARVILLE
CAMOMILE OXEYE MORGAN MAYWEED
CAMOUFLAGE FAKE HIDE DAZZLE MUFFLE SCREEN CONCEAL DISGUISE
CAMP TENT DOUAR ETAPE HORDE SIEGE CASTLE LAAGER BIVOUAC HUTMENT LASHKAR LODGING MAHALLA PALANKA ZAREEBA QUARTERS
CAMPAIGN BLITZ DRIVE PLAIN WHOOP CANVASS CRUSADE JOURNEY SERVICE SOLICIT WARFARE
CAMPANILE TOWER BELFRY CLOCHER STEEPLE CARILLON
CAMPHOR ASARONE BORNEOL MENTHOL
CAMPUS GATE QUAD YARD FIELD
CAN CUP JUG MAY POT TIN FIRE JAIL BILLY CADDY ESHIN OILER SHALL BOTTLE CANIKIN DISMISS GROWLER PIPETTE BILLYCAN CONSERVE PRESERVE (— FOR LIQUOR) JACK (— ON WHEELS) DANDY (BULGED —) SWELL FLIPPER (DEFECTIVE —) SPRINGER (LEAKY —) LEAKER (MILK —) CHURN (TIN —) DESTROYER (TRASH —) DUSTBIN
CANAANITE ARKITE HIVITE AMORITE JEBUSITE

CANADA
(ALSO SEE SPECIFIC PROVINCES)
BAY: JAMES HUDSON UNGAVA GEORGIAN
CAPITAL: OTTAWA
ISLAND: READ BANKS BYLOT COATS DEVON SABLE BAFFIN MANSEL VICTORIA ANTICOSTI VANCOUVER

ISLANDS: PARRY BELCHER BATHURST MAGDALEN
LAKE: BEAR CREE GARRY RAINY SLAVE LOUISE SIMCOE ABITIBI DUBAWNT NIPIGON KOOTENAY OKANAGAN NIPISSING
MOUNTAIN: LOGAN ROYAL ROBSON TREMBLANT
MOUNTAIN RANGE: SKEENA CARIBOO PEMBINA STELIAS COLUMBIA LAURENTIAN
NATIVE: CANUCK
PARK: YOHO BANFF ACADIA JASPER
PENINSULA: GASPE BOOTHIA MELVILLE
PROVINCE: BC NB NS MAN ONT PEI QUE ALTA SASK QUEBEC ALBERTA ONTARIO MANITOBA NOVASCOTIA NEWBRUNSWICK NEWFOUNDLAND SASKATCHEWAN
RIVER: HAY RED BACK PEEL PEACE SLAVE YUKON FRASER NELSON OTTAWA SKEENA THELON KOKOSAK PEMBINA PETAWAWA SAGUENAY MACKENZIE RICHELIEU
STRAIT: CABOT DEASE HECATE HUDSON GEORGIA
SYMBOL: MAPLELEAF
TERRITORY: YUKON
TOWN: HULL BANFF LAVAL GUELPH OSHAWA REGINA SARNIA CALGARY HALIFAX MONCTON NANAIMO SUDBURY TORONTO WELLAND WINDSOR KINGSTON MONTREAL VICTORIA WINNIPEG SASKATOON VANCOUVER
UNIVERSITY: MCGILL DALHOUSIE
WATERFALL: DELLA PANTHER TAKAKKAW

CANADA GOOSE HONKER BUSTARD OUTARDE
CANADIAN CANUCK
CANAILLE MOB FLOUR RABBLE DOGGERY RIFFRAFF
CANAL CUT CANO DUCT LODE PIPE TUBE BAYOU DITCH DRAIN FOSSA ESTERO GROOVE KENNEL STRAIT TRENCH CHANNEL CONDUIT FOREBAY RACEWAY SHIPWAY TOWPATH AQUEDUCT MILLRACE PROSODUS VOLKMANN (ALIMENTARY —) GUT ENTERON INTESTINE (ANATOMICAL —) SCALA MEATUS (CARINAL —) LACUNA
CANARD DUCK HOAX RUMOR GRAPEVINE
CANARY DICKY FRILL SERIN LIZARD ROLLER CAYENNE CHOPPER JONQUIL SQUEALER

CANARY ISLANDS
CAPITAL: SANTACRUZ
ISLAND: ROCA CLARA FERRO LOBOS PALMA ROCCA GOMERA HIERRO INFERNO GRACIOSA TENERIFE LANZAROTE
MEASURE: FANEGADA

MOUNTAIN: TEYDE LACRUZ ELCUMBRE TENERIFE
PROVINCE: LASPALMAS
TOWN: LAGUNA ARRECIFE VALVERDE
VOLCANO: TENEGUIA

CANCEL BLOT DASH DELE OMIT UNDO WIPE ABORT ANNUL BELAY CROSS ERASE QUASH REMIT SCRUB DELETE EFFACE KILLER REMOVE REVOKE ABOLISH DESTROY EXPUNGE NULLIFY RESCIND RETRACT SCRATCH ABROGATE OVERRIDE OBLITERATE
CANDID FAIR JUST OPEN PURE BLUNT CLEAR FRANK NAIVE PLAIN HONEST ARTLESS SINCERE INNOCENT STRAIGHT PLAINSPOKEN
CANDIDA (AUTHOR OF —) SHAW (CHARACTER IN —) MORELL CANDIDA MARCHBANKS
CANDIDATE NOMINEE ASPIRANT PROSPECT
CANDIDE (AUTHOR OF —) VOLTAIRE (CHARACTER IN —) CACAMBO CANDIDE PANGLOSS PAQUETTE CUNEGONDE
CANDLE DIP WAX GLIM SPERM TAPER TOLLY TORCH BOUGIE CIERGE TALLOW PRICKET
CANDLEHOLDER SPIDER
CANDLESTICK BUGIA DYKER JESSE STICK CRUSIE LAMPAD SCONCE PRICKET FLAMBEAU TORCHERE
CANDOR PURITY FAIRNESS KINDNESS INTEGRITY SIMPLICITY
CANDY DROP KISS ROCK CREAM CRISP DULCE FUDGE GLACE GUNDY LOLLY SQUIB SWEET TAFFY BONBON COMFIT HUMBUG NOUGAT PATTIE BRITTLE CARAMEL GUMDROP LOLLIPOP PEPPERMINT
CANE ROD BEAT FLOG PIPE REED STEM TUBE WAND WHIP BIRCH LANCE STAFF STICK SWISH WADDY BAMBOO KEBBIE PUNISH RATTAN CALAMUS MALACCA SCOURGE WHANGEE
(BLACK —) JAPAN
(END OF —) FRAZE
CANFIELD KLONDIKE
CANNON GUN BASE SHOT TUBE CAROM CRACK MOYEN PIECE SACRE SACRI SAKER THIEF BARKER BICORN CURTAL FALCON JINGAL LICORN MORTAR BASTARD BOMBARD BULLDOG LOMBARD MOYENNE ROBINET SERPENT UNICORN CULVERIN HOWITZER OERLIKON
(— OF BELL) EAR
(CARRIAGE OF —) NADRIER
(DUMMY —) QUAKER
(PART OF —) BASE BORE FACE KNOB NECK OGEE RING VENT CHASE FILET SWELL BREECH BUTTON FILLET MUZZLE CHAMBER DOLPHIN GUNLOCK RIMBASE ASTRAGAL CASCABEL TRUNNION REINFORCE
CANNULA TROCAR

CANNY SLY WARY WILY WISE COONY LUCKY PAWKY CLEVER FRUGAL SHREWD CAREFUL CUNNING KNOWING PRUDENT SKILLFUL
CANOE AMA LISI PAHI PROA ARAWA BANCA BIRCH BUNGO KAYAK KOLEK PRAHU UMIAK VINTA BAIDAR BAROTO CORIAL CUNNER DUGOUT PUNGEY ALMADIA BIDARKA BUCKEYE CANADER CORACLE PIRAGUA PIROGUE BALANGAY FALTBOAT FOLDBOAT
CANON LAW CODE HYMN LAUD LIST ROTA RULE AXIOM ROUND TENET ACTION DECREE GNOMON BROCARD LIBRARY PRECEPT STATUTE
CANONICAL ACCEPTED ORTHODOX (NOT —) APOCHRYPHAL
CANOPY SKY CEIL COPE DAIS HOOD TILT CHUPA CROWN SHADE AWNING BUBBLE CELURE HUPPAH PELMET TESTER MARQUEE SHELTER BASILICA PAVILION SHAMIANA TABENACLE
(— ABOVE THRONE) STATE
(— FOR LIVESTOCK) HOVEL
(— OF ALTAR) DAIS CIBORIUM
(— OF HEAVEN) VAULT
(— OVER BROODER) HOVER
(BED —) TESTER SPARVER
(HEARSE —) MAJESTY
CANT TIP HEEL LEAN LIST SING TILT TURN ARGOT BEVEL CHANT DRIFT LINGO MERRY NICHE PITCH SLANG SLANT SLOPE WHINE CAREEN INTONE JARGON LIVELY PATOIS PATTER DIALECT INCLINE WHEEDLE CHEERFUL
CANTANKEROUS ILL CURSED CUSSED ORNERY KICKISH PIGGISH CANKERED CONTRARY PERVERSE
CANTATA MOTET SERENATA VILLANCICO
CANTEEN BAR FLASK BAZAAR CANTINA
CANTER JOG RUN GAIT LOPE PACE RACK AUBIN ROGUE BEGGAR WHINER TRIPPLE SNUFFLER VAGABOND
CANTERBURY TALES
(AUTHOR OF —) CHAUCER
(CHARACTER IN —) NUN COOK DYER HOST MONK WIFE CLERK FRIAR REEVE DOCTOR KNIGHT MILLER PARSON PRIEST SQUIRE WEAVER YEOMAN CHAUCER PLOWMAN SHIPMAN FRANKLIN MANCIPLE MERCHANT PARDONER PRIORESS SERGEANT SUMMONER CARPENTER HABERDASHER
CANTICLE ODE HYMN LAUD SONG CANTO ANTHEM HIRMOS BRAVURA MAGNIFICAT
CANTO AIR BOOK DUAN RUNE SONG VERSE MELODY PASSUS CANTICLE
CANTON ANGLE UNION CORNER VOLOST PORTION QUARTER SECTION DISTRICT DIVISION
(HALF —) ESQUIRE
CANTOR HAZAN SINGER CHANTER CHAZZAN SOLOIST PSALMIST
CANVAS FLY DUCK PATA SAIL TARP TENT CLOTH SCRIM TOILE BALINE

BURLAP MUSLIN PICTURE POLDAVY
SACKING SCUTAGE PAINTING SAILCLOTH
(— FOR CONVEYING GRAIN) APRON
(OLD CONDEMNED —) RUMBOWLINE
(RUBBERIZED —) TOSH
(STUFFED —) BOLSTER
(TARRED —) COAT

CANVASBACK CAN DIVER CHEVAL
DUCKER POCHARD BULLNECK

CANVASS BEAT CASE DRUM HAWK POLL
SIFT RANDY STUDY DEBATE PEDDLE
SEARCH AGITATE DISCUSS EXAMINE
SOLICIT TROUNCE CAMPAIGN CONSIDER

CANYON CAJON CHASM COULE GORGE
GULCH ARROYO CANADA RAVINE

CAP FEZ HAT LID PAD POT TAJ TAM TIP
TOP ACME COIF CORK COWL DINK DOME
DOWD ETON GAGE HURE JOAN KEEP
KEPI MATE BERET BUSBY CHIEF COVER
CROWN EXCEL FANON GALEA HOUVE
KULAH MUTCH OUTDO PHANO SEIZE
SHAKO TOPEE BARRAD BARRET BEANIE
BIGGIN BIRRUS BONNET CALPAC CLIMAX
COCKUP CORNET GALERA HELMET
JINNAH MOBCAP PILEUS PINNER PRIMER
PUZZLE SUMMIT TABARD TURBAN
ALOPEKE BIRETTA CALOTTE CAMAURO
CAPITAL CEREVIS CHAPEAU CHECHIA
CLOSURE COMMODE FERRULE FLATCAP
FORAGER HEADCAP OVERLIE OVERTOP
PERPLEX PETASOS PILLBOX PILLION
SOWBACK SURPASS THIMBLE TURNCAP
ACROSOME BALMORAL BEARSKIN
BYCOCKET CAPELINE CHAPERON
COONSKIN PHRYGIUM SKEWBACK
SKULLCAP TARBOOSH
(— FOR PILEDRIVER) PUNCH
(— OF FLAGSTAFF) TRUCK
(— OF FOAM) HOOD
(— OF PIER) CUSHION
(— OF PYXIDIUM) LID
(— OF WATCH) DOME CROWN
(— ON MAST) TRUCK
(ACADEMIC —) MORTARBOARD
(BISHOP'S —) HURA HURE
(CANADIAN —) TUQUE
(CHIMNEY —) GRANNY
(HORSEMAN'S —) MONTERO
(ICE —) BRAE CALOTTE
(JESTER'S —) COXCOMB FOOLSCAP
(MILITARY —) KEPI BUSBY SHAKO
(MOUNTAIN —) SCALP
(PERCUSSION —) AMORCE CAPSULE
(PERUVIAN —) CHULLO
(POPE'S —) CAMAURO
(ROOT —) CALYPTRA
(TRIANGULAR —) KALPAK
(WOMAN'S —) TOY CAUL DOWD JOAN
KELL MUTCH COMMODE VOLUPER
BIGGONET
(WOOLEN —) BOINA TOQUE TUQUE

CAPABILITY POWER ABILITY FACULTY
POTENCY CAPACITY

CAPABLE APT CAN FIT ABLE GOOD
ADEPT EXPERT SKILLED POWERFUL

CAPACIOUS FULL WIDE AMPLE BROAD
LARGE ROOMY GOODLY SPACIOUS

CAPACITOR CONDENSER

CAPACITY GIFT SIZE TURN FLAIR FORCE
KNACK POWER SKILL SPACE AGENCY
BURDEN ENERGY EXTENT GENIUS
SPREAD TALENT VOLUME ABILITY
CALIBER CONTENT FACULTY FITNESS
QUALITY APTITUDE INSTINCT STRENGTH
INFLUENCE

CAPARISON DECK TRAP HOUSE
COVERING TRAPPING

CAPE RAS GAPE HEAD HOOK LOOK NECK
NESS SKAW WRIT AMICE CAPPA CLOAK
FICHU ORALE SAGUM STARE STOLE
TALMA BERTHA BYRRUS CABAAN
DOLMAN MANTLE SONTAG TABARD
TIPPET CHLAMYS TANJONG VANDYKE
HEADLAND MANTILLA MOZZETTA
PELERINE SEALSKIN RAINPROOF
(— OF SKINS) KAROSS
(— OF STRAW) MINO
(BULLFIGHTER'S —) CAPA
(CLERGICAL —) ALMUCE
(DRESSING —) TOILET
(FEATHER —) AHUULA
(HOODED —) HUKE DOMINO
(LACE OR SILK —) VISITE
(LOW —) TANG
(PAPAL —) FANO FANON FANUM ORALE
PHANO
(RAIN —) CAPOTE

CAPER HOP JET DIDO HOIT JUMP LEAP
ROMP SKIP SKIT ANTIC BRANK DANCE
FLING FLISK FRISK PRANK CAVORT
CURVET FROLIC GAMBOL PRANCE
SPRING TITTUP VAGARY COURANT
GAMBADO CAPRIOLE

CAPITAL CAP CASH CITY FUND GOOD
MAIN RARE SEAT BASIC CHIEF FATAL
GREAT MAJOR MONEY STOCK VITAL
DEADLY HEADLY IMPOST LETTER
MORTAL PRIMAL UNCIAL WEALTH
CENTRAL LEADING RADICAL SERIOUS
WEIGHTY CHAPITER CHAPTREL
DOSSERET
(— OF HEAVEN) AMARAVATI
(— OF HELL) PANDEMONIUM
(DIVISION OF —) ABACUS
(GAMBLER'S —) STAKE
(INADEQUATE —) SHOESTRING

CAPITOL STATEHOUSE

CAPRICE FAD TOY KINK MOOD WHIM
ANTIC CRANK FANCY FREAK HUMOR
QUIRK MAGGOT NOTION SPLEEN TEMPER
VAGARY WHIMSY CONCEIT CROCHET
IMPULSE TANTRUM WHIMSEY

CAPRICIOUS DIZZY DODDY FLUKY
MOODY CHANCY FICKLE FITFUL KITTLE
PLATTY WANTON COMICAL ERRATIC
FLIGHTY MAGGOTY MOONISH PEEVISH
VAGRANT WAYWARD FANCIFUL
FREAKISH HUMOROUS PERVERSE
SKITTISH UNSTEADY VARIABLE
VOLATILE CROTCHETY FANTASTIC
VAGARIOUS

CAPSIZE COUP KEEL PURL UPSET
WRONG WHEMMLE OVERTURN

CAPSTAN CRAB DRUM DANDY HOIST
LEVER CYLINDER WINDLASS
CAPSULE POD URN CASE CYST
PILL SEED PEARL SHELL THECA WAFER
AMPULE CACHET SHEATH OTOCYST
SEEDBOX SILIQUE PERICARP PYXIDIUM
CAPTAIN BOH CID BAAS HEAD BARAK
CHIEF LEADER MASTER SOTNIK
FOREMAN HEADMAN MANAGER
PATROON SKIPPER FLUELLEN GOVERNOR
SUBAHDAR
(— OF ARAB VESSEL) NACODAR
(— OF CAVALRY) RESSALDAR
RITMASTER
(— OF CRICKET TEAM) SKIPPER
(— OF CURLING TEAM) SKIP
(— OF PRIVATEER) CAPER
(— OF SHIP) WAFTER
(STRICT —) SUNDOWNER
CAPTAINS COURAGEOUS
(AUTHOR OF —) KIPLING
(CHARACTER IN —) DAN JACK DISKO
TROOP CHEYNE HARVEY MANUEL
SALTERS
CAPTION TITLE LEADER LEGEND
HEADING SUBHEAD CITATION HEADLINE
SUBTITLE
CAPTIOUS TESTY CRAFTY SEVERE
CARPING CYNICAL FRETFUL PEEVISH
TETTISH CATCHING CONTRARY CRITICAL
CAPTIVATE WIN TAKE CATCH CHARM
ALLURE ENAMOR PLEASE RAVISH
SUBDUE ATTRACT BEWITCH CAPTIVE
CAPTURE ENCHANT ENTHRALL
OVERTAKE SURPRISE
CAPTIVATING TAKING KILLING
WINNING WINSOME CATCHING
CAPTIVE SLAVE DANIEL ENAMOR THRALL
BRISEIS CAITIFF PRISONER
CAPTIVITY IRON CHAINS DURESS
BONDAGE SERFDOM SLAVERY
CAPTOR TAKER VICTOR CATCHER
CAPTURE BAG COP FIX GET NAB NET
WIN FALL FANG GRAB HOOK LAND PREY
SNIB TAKE TRAP TREE CARRY CATCH
FORCE PINCH PRIZE PURSE RAVEN SEIZE
SWOOP ARREST CORRAL
ENTRAP GOBBLE OBTAIN TAKING
SEIZURE
(— BACKGAMMON PIECE) HIT
(— BIRDS) TOODLE
(— GAME) SATCHEL
(— OF ALL PRIZES) SWEEP
(— TROUT) TICKLE
CAPUCHIN MONKEY CAY SAI CEPID
SAJOU WEEPER SAPAJOU RINGTAIL
CAPYBARA CAVY CARPINCHO
CAR BOX BUS PIG AUTO BUNK DOLL
DRAG DUMP GRIP JEEP RATH TRAM
ZULU BOGEY COACH CRATE DINER
DUMMY GURRY HUTCH JIMMY RATHA
SEDAN STOCK TRAIN TRUCK WRONG
BASKET BOXCAR BUFFET CHIPPY
DINGHY DUPLEX HOPPER JIGGER JINGLE
SALOON SETOFF SMOKER TOURER
AWKWARD CHARIOT COMBINE FLATCAR
FREEZER GIRAFFE GONDOLA HANDCAR

SIDECAR TELPHER TRAILER TROLLEY
VEHICLE VETTURA AMPHICAR DRAGSTER
HORSECAR OUTSIDER QUADRIGA
ROADSTER SINISTER
(— FOR TRAIN CREW) CABOOSE
(— ON RAIL) TROLLEY
(BAGGAGE —) BLIND
(CABLE —) GONDOLA
(COAL —) HUTCH JIMMY WAGON
WAGGON
(ELECTRIC —) TELPHER
(ELEVATOR —) CAB CAGE
(EMPTY —) EMPTY IDLER
(JAUNTING —) SIDECAR
(LOG —) BUNK
(LOW-WHEELED —) HUTCH TRUCKLE
(MINE —) SKIP LARRY BARNEY GIRAFFE
GUNBOAT
(MONORAIL —) GYROCAR
(OBSERVATION —) BUGGY
(OLD —) JUNKER
(POLICE —) CRUISER
(SMALL —) MINICAB
(TROLLEY —) SHORT
(USED —) DOG
CARAPACE CRUST SHELL LORICA
SHIELD CALAPASH
CARAVAN VAN TREK TRIP FLEET TRAIN
CAFILA COFFLE CONVOY SAFARI TRAVEL
JOURNEY CONDUCTA
CARAVANSARY INN KHAN SERAI
ZAYAT HOSTEL IMARET CHOULTRY
CARBINE STEN MUSKET DRAGOON
ESCOPET
CARBOHYDRATE SUGAR AMYLAN
GELOSE INULIN STARCH FUCOSAN
GLUCIDE CELLULIN DEXTRINE DEXTROSE
GLYCOGEN GRAMININ PENTOSAN
TRITICIN CELLULOSE PARAMYLUM
POLYSACCHARIDE
CARBON COAL COKE COPY SOOT
DIAMOND CHARCOAL GRAPHITE
CARBORUNDUM EMERY ABRASIVE
SILUNDUM
CARBUNCLE RUBY PYROPE ANTHRAX
CHARBOCLE
CARCASS BEEF BODY BOUK CASE CULL
BLOCK MUMMY CORPSE CARRION
(— OF WHALE) KRENG
CARD ACE PAM CLUB COMB FACE FIVE
FOUR JACK KING MENU PLAN BALOP
BLANK CARTE CHART CHECK DEUCE
DUMMY EIGHT ENTRY FICHE GREEN
HEART HONOR JOKER QUEEN STIFF
TAROT TEASE FILLER KICKER KNIGHT
PIGEON READER SECOND TICKET
DIAMOND PROGRAM STOPPER TAROCCO
SCHEDULE STRIPPER
(— IN OMBRE) MANILLE
(— LAST IN BAY) HOCK HOCKELTY
(— WOOL) TUM ROVE
(ACE OF CLUBS —) BASTA MATADOR
PUPPYFOOT
(ACE OF SPADES —) MATADOR
SPADILLE
(ACE OF TRUMPS —) TIB
(AVIATOR'S —) CARNET

(CLUB —) OAK
(COMPASS —) FLY ROSE
(CRIBBAGE —S) CRIB
(DEAD —) SLEEPER
(DIAMOND —) PICK CARREAU
(DISCARDED —S) CRIB
(DRAWING —) BLOWOFF
(FARO —) SODA
(FOUR —) CATER QUATRE
(FOURTH —) CASE
(HIGHEST UNPLAYED —) COMMAND
(JOKER —) BRAGGER MISTIGRIS
(KING, QUEEN OR KNAVE —) COST
FACE
(KNAVE —) PAM TOM JACK BOWER
EQUES MAKER NODDY COQUIN KNIGHT
PICARO VARLET WENZEL CUSTREL
PEASANT VILLAIN VARLETTO
(LAYOUT OF —S) TABLEAU
(LOW —) GUARD
(MARKED —) STAMP
(POSTAL —) COVER
(PULLING —S) TIRE
(QUEEN AND KNAVE —S) INTRIGO
INTRIGUE
(RUN OF —S) SEQUENCE
(SPADE —) PICK DIGGER
(STOCK —) TALON
(THIRD HIGHEST TRUMP —) BASTA
(THREE —) TREY THREE
(WILD —) FREAK
(3 ACE —S) CORONA
(3 FACE —S) GLEEK
(3 —S IN SEQUENCE) TIERCE
FOURCHETTE
(3 —S OF KIND) TRIO TRICON PAIRIAL
TRIPLET
(4 OF TRUMPS —) TIDDY
(5 FACE —S) BLAZE
(7, 8 AND 9 —S) VOIDS
CARDIGAN CORGI WAMUS JACKET
SWEATER
CARDINAL MAIN BASIC CHIEF VITAL
ALEPHA CLERIC PRINCE RADICAL
CARDINAL BIRD CARNAL REDBIRD
REDLEGS GROSBEAK REDSHANK
CARE DOW HOW CARK CURE DUTY FASH
FRET HEED KEEP MIND PASS RECK SOIN
TEND TENT WISH YEME COUNT GRIEF
GUARD NURSE PAINS TRUST WORRY
BURDEN CHARGE CUMBER DESIRE
GRIEVE REGARD ANXIETY AUSPICE
CAUTION CHERISH CONCERN CULTURE
CUSTODY KEEPING RESPECT RUNNING
SCRUPLE THOUGHT TUITION BUSINESS
PRECAUTION SOLICITUDE
(— FOR) KNOW MIND RECK TEND WARD
FORCE NURSE SAVOR FATHER MATTER
REGARD CHERISH PROCURE
(— FOR ONESELF) BACH
(— OF HOUSEHOLD) HUSBANDRY
(— OF LIVESTOCK) CHORE
(JUDICIOUS —) LEISURE
(WATCHFUL —) TENDANCE OVERSIGHT
CAREEN GIP CANT HEEL KEEL LIST TILT
VEER LURCH SLOPE SWIFT INCLINE
CAREER RUN WAY LIFE ROAD RUSH

TRADE CHARGE COURSE GALLOP
CALLING CARIERE PURSUIT
CAREFREE EASY FRANK HAPPY BREEZY
DEGAGE HOLIDAY DEBONAIR
CAREFUL BUSY WARY CANNY CHARY
CLOSE EXACT HOOLY TENTY CHOICE
DAINTY EIDENT EYEFUL FRUGAL
NARROW TENDER ANXIOUS CURIOUS
GUARDED HEEDFUL PRUDENT THRIFTY
ACCURATE CAUTIOUS CRITICAL
DILIGENT DISCREET GINGERLY TROUBLED
VIGILANT WATCHFUL OBSERVANT
METICULOUS SOLICITOUS PUNCTILIOUS
CARELESS LAX COOL EASY RASH MESSY
SLACK CASUAL RAKISH REMISS SLOPPY
UNTIDY UNWARY CURSORY LANGUID
HEEDLESS LISTLESS MINDLESS
RECKLESS SLIPSHOD SLOVENLY
NEGLECTFUL SLATTERNLY
CARESS HUG PAT PET BILL CLAP DAUT
KISS NECK NURSE CODDLE COSSET
CUDDLE FONDLE PAMPER STROKE
CHERISH EMBRACE FLATTER BLANDISH
CANOODLE LALLYGAG
CARETAKER KEEPER WARDER JANITOR
CARGO BULK LOAD BURDEN LADING
FREIGHT PORTAGE SHIPLOAD SHIPMENT
CARIBOU STAG RANGIFER REINDEER
CARICATURE APE COPY MOCK SKIT
FARCE LIBEL MIMIC SQUIB OVERDO
PARODY SATIRE CARTOON TRAVESTY
BURLESQUE
CARMEN (CHARACTER IN —) JOSE
CARMEN ZUNIGA MICAELA ESCAMILLO
(COMPOSER OF —) BIZET
CARMINE RED LAKE CRIMSON SCARLET
CARNAGE MURDER POGROM BUTCHERY
MASSACRE BLOODSHED SLAUGHTER
CARNAL CROW LEWD GROSS ANIMAL
BODILY SEXUAL BESTIAL BRUTISH
EARTHLY FLESHLY SECULAR SENSUAL
WORLDLY PANDEMIC PHYSICAL
CARNATION JACK PINK FLAKE BIZARRE
PICOTEE DAYBREAK DIANTHUS
GRENADINE MALMAISON
CARNELIAN SARD COPPER
CARNIVAL FETE SHOW CARNY CANVAS
APOKREA REVELRY FASCHING FESTIVAL
CARNIVORE CAT DOG FOX BEAR COON
LION LYNX MINK PUMA SEAL WOLF
CIVET GENET HYENA OTTER PANDA
PEKAN RATEL SABLE STOAT TIGER
BADGER COUGAR ERMINE FELINE FERRET
FISHER FOUSSA JACKAL JAGUAR
MARTEN OCELOT POSSUM SERVAL
WEASEL DASYURE GLUTTON LEOPARD
MEERKAT POLECAT RACCOON TIGRESS
AARDWOLF MONGOOSE OPOSSUM
CAROL LAY NOEL SING SONG DITTY
YODEL WARBLE WASSAIL MADRIGAL
AGUINALDO
CAROM BOUNCE CANNON GLANCE
STRIKE REBOUND BILLIARD CARAMBOLE
CAROUSAL BAT LARK ORGY RIOT ROMP
TOOT BINGE FEAST RANDY REVEL ROUSE
SPRAY SPREE FROLIC SHINDY REVELRY
WASSAIL DRINKING FESTIVAL JAMBOREE

CAROUSE HELL RANT TEAR TOOT BINGE
BIRLE BOUSE DRINK QUAFF RANDY
REVEL ROUSE SPREE TOAST COURANT
JOLLIFY WASSAIL

CARP KOI NAG BITE DRUM SING SNAG
TALK YERK CAVIL PINCH PRATE SCOLD
SPEAK CENSOR NIBBLE RECITE TWITCH
CENSURE CHATTER QUIBBLE COMPLAIN
GOLDFISH
(CRUCIAN —) GIBEL
(LAKE —) DRUM LAKER
(PREF.) CYPRIN(O)

CARPENTER ANT LOHAR FITTER FRAMER
HOUSER JOINER PINNER WRIGHT
BUILDER HOWSOUR WOODMAN
INDENTER TECTONIC TIMBERER
PITWRIGHT SHIPWRIGHT
(SHIP'S —) CHIPS

CARPET MAT RUG AGRA KALI KUBA
HERAT SARUK SCOLD SUMAK TAPET
TAPIS TEKKE USHAK AFGHAN FLOSSA
FRIEZE KASHAN KIDDER KIRMAN LAVEHR
NAMMAD RUNNER SAROUK SAXONY
SELJUK SMYRNA TABRIZ VELVET
WILTON DHURRIE GIORDES HAMADAN
INGRAIN ISPAHAN SHEMAKA TEHERAN
AKHISSAR AMRITSAR BRUSSELS
COVERING FOOTPACE KARABAGH
MOQUETTE TAPESTRY TURCOMAN
VENETIAN AXMINSTER SITRINGEE
(HOLY —) KISWA
(PILELESS —) KILIM GELEEM

CARRIAGE AIR CAB CAR FLY GIG RIG SET
ARBA BIGA CART CHAR DRAG DUKE
EKKA GAIT HACK MIEN SHAY TEAM TRAP
WYNN ARABA BANDY BRAKE BRETT
BUGGY CHAIR COACH COUPE FRONT
JUTKA MIDGE NODDY PANEL POISE
SADOO SETUP SULKY TENUE TONGA
TRUCK WAGON BURDEN CALASH CHAISE
CISIUM CONVOY DENNET FIACRE
GOCART HANSOM HERDIC KOSONG
LANDAU MANNER SPIDER SURREY
TANDEM TELEGA TROIKA BEARING
BERLINE BOUNDER BRITSKA CALECHE
CALESIN CARAVAN CARIOLE CAROCHE
CHARIOT CONDUCT CROYDON DOGCART
DOSADOS DROSHKY HACKNEY MINIBUS
PHAETON POSCHAY SHANDRY SKYHOOK
TALLYHO TARTANA TILBURY TRANSIT
TROLLEY UNICORN VECTURE VETTURA
VOITURE VOLANTE WAFTAGE BAROUCHE
BEHAVIOR BROUGHAM CARRYALL
CLARENCE CURRICLE DEARBORN
DEMEANOR DORMEUSE PRESENCE
ROCKAWAY SOCIABLE STANHOPE
TARANTAS TOURNURE VICTORIA
(— OF HANDPRESS) COFFIN
(— OF HORSE) AIR
(AMMUNITION —) CAISSON
(CEREMONIAL —) RATH
(ELEVATED —) LIFT
(GUN —) CHASSIS
(INDIAN —) RUT EKKA BANDY GHARRY
(JAVANESE —) SADO
(LIVERY —) REMISE
(LOG —) DRAG

(PUBLIC —) FLY OMNIBUS
CARRIER HOD BASE JEEP SHIP TRAM
BUGGY HAMAL KAHAR MACER PLANE
SABOT TAMEN BARKIS BEARER COOLIE
HODMAN JAGGER PACKER PORTER
RUNNER DRAYMAN DROGHER FLATTOP
CARGADOR CARRYALL PORTATOR
RAILROAD TEAMSTER
(COAL —) FLATIRON
(COLOR —) LURRIER
(ENDLESS —) TAILER
(FIRE —) PORTFIRE
(MAIL —) COURIER POSTMAN
(WATER —) BHISTI BHEESTY
CARRION OFFAL CORPSE REFUSE ROTTEN
CARCASS CORRUPT DOGMEAT CROWBAIT
CARRY HUG LUG BEAR CART DRAY HAVE
HUMP PACK PORT TAKE TOTE TUMP
BRING BROOK FERRY GUIDE POISE
BEHAVE CONVEY CONVOY DEPORT
EXTEND COMPORT CONTAIN PORTAGE
SUPPORT SUSTAIN TRANSFER TRANSMIT
(— AWAY) FIRK DRAIN REAVE SWEEP
TRUSS ABLATE ASPORT
(— EFFIGY) GUY
(— FORWARD) EXTEND
(— IN OXCART) KURVEY
(— LIQUOR) BOOTLEG
(— OFF) RAP HENT LIFE SACK FETCH
HEAVE RIFLE SCOUR SWOOP ABDUCT
BRAZEN KIDNAP SPIRIT
(— ON) DO RUN WAR HAVE LEAD LEVY
WAGE APPLY DRIVE ENSUE FIGHT TRAIN
CREATE DEMEAN FOLLOW MANAGE
OCCUPY CONDUCT EXERCISE MAINTAIN
TRANSACT
(— ONESELF) HOLD
(— ONWARD) CONTINUE
(— OUT) DO ACT END GIVE LAST HONOR
AFFORD EFFECT ACHIEVE EXECUTE
FULFILL PERFORM SATISFY PERPETRATE
(— UPWARD) RAP ESCALATE
(SUFF.) GER(ENCE) GER(ENT) GER(OUS)
PHER PHORA PHORE(SIS) PHORIA
PHOROUS PHORUS
CART CAR POT RUT BUTT CHAR COUP
DRAY HAUL LOAD PUTT RUTH TOTE
WAIN ARABA BOGEY DANDY DILLY
DOLLY SULKY TONGA TRUCK WAGON
BARROW CADDIE CHAISE CISIUM
DUMPER GHARRY JINKER KURUMA
LIMBER CARRETA CHARIOT DOGCART
GUJERAT MORFREY SHANDRY TROLLEY
TRUNDLE TUMBLER TUMBREL
DUMPCART HANDCART PUSHCART
(— WITH TANK) TUMBLER
(BULLOCK —) BANDY HACKERY
(COSTER'S —) TROLL
(COVERED —) JINGLE CARIOLE
(FARMER'S —) PUTT GAMBO
(FREIGHT —) CARRETON
(LOG —) TUG BUNK
(LUMBER —) GILL BUMMER
(MILKMAN'S —) PRAM
(OX —) RECKLA
(PARCELS —) FLY
(TIMBER —) CUTS

(TIP —) COOP COUP COUPE
(UNDERSLUNG —) FLOAT
(2-PONY —) KOSONG
(2-WHEELED —) BANDY BUGGY SULKY
CARRETA TUMBREL
(3-WHEELED —) PORTER
CARTEL PACT POOL PAPER TRUST
CORNER CONTRACT SYNDICATE
CARTILAGE COPULA TISSUE CRICOID
EPIURAL GRISTLE RADIALE STERNUM
TARSALE THYROID CHONDRUS EPIPUBIS
HYPOHYAL SESAMOID TURBINAL
(— UNDER DOG'S TONGUE) LYTTA
CARTON BOX CASE SHELL
CARTRIDGE BAG CASE HULL BLANK
SHELL SHORT BULLET MAGNUM PATRON
CAPSULE TORPEDO HANDLOAD
SHOTSHELL
(PART OF —) RIM CASE HEAD NOSE
SLUG CRIMP BULLET JACKET PRIMER
(TAPE —) CASSETTE
CARVE CUT BREAK MINCE SHEAR SPLAY
INCISE SCULPT ENCHASE ENGRAVE
DISJOINT
CARVING CAMEO GLYPH IVORY SCRIVE
GLYPTIC MASKOID NICKING APLUSTRE
INTAGLIO TRIPTYCH PETROGLYPH
(CIRCULAR —) TONDO
CASCADE FALL LINN FORCE SPOUT
CATARACT
CASE BOX POD POT PYX BUNK CASK
DEED DESK DOCK FILE PACK PAIR ROLL
SUIT TICK BRACE BRIEF BULLA BURSE
CADDY CASUS CAUSE COVER CRATE
EVENT FOLIO FOREL HUSSY PRESS SHELL
STATE THECA TRIAL ACTION AFFAIR
APPEAL BINDER BOXING CARTON
CASING CELLAR CHANCE CHRISM
COFFIN COUPLE LOCKET LORICA MATTER
PETARD POPPET QUIVER RIDDLE SHEATH
SHRINE STATOR SURVEY VALISE VANITY
CABINET CAMISIA CAPSULE COUNTER
ENCLOSE ENVELOP EXAMPLE GEARBOX
HOLDALL HOUSING HUMIDOR INCLOSE
LAWSUIT PACKAGE SATCHEL ACCIDENT
ARGUMENT CARRYALL ENVELOPE
EQUIPAGE INSTANCE KNAPSACK
PACKSACK SHOWCASE PORTFOLIO
(— CONTAINING ELEVATOR BELT)
LEG
(— ENCLOSING CLOCK DIAL) HOOD
(— FOR BOTTLES) CELLARET
(— FOR CARDS) SHOE
(— FOR COMPASS) BINNACLE
(— FOR EXPLOSIVES) TRUNK
(— FOR JEWELS) TYE
(— FOR MAINSPRING) BARILLET
(— FOR MOLD) COPE CHAPE
(— FOR MUMMY) SLEDGE
(— FOR PISTOL) HOLSTER
(— FOR PULLEY) BLOCK
(— FOR RIFLE) BOOT
(— FOR SEWING ITEMS) HUSSY
(— FOR TOOLS) TROUSSE
(— FOR TWEEZERS) BUBBLEBOW
(— FOR WRITING MATERIALS)
STANDISH

(— IN WATCH) DOME BARREL
(— OF FLOUR BOLTER) HUTCH
(— OF VENETIAN BLIND) HEADBOX
(— WITH COMPARTMENTS) RIDDLE
(BONY —) CARAPACE
(CARTRIDGE —) DOP CARTOUCHE
(COSMETIC —) COMPACT
(COURT —) LAWSUIT
(EGG —) OVISAC OOTHECA
(FIREWORKS —) LANCE
(GRAMMATICAL —) DATIVE ESSIVE
LATIVE ELATIVE FACTIVE ABLATIVE
EQUATIVE ERGATIVE GENITIVE ILLATIVE
LOCATIVE VOCATIVE ACCUSATIVE
(HOPELESS —) GONER
(LARVA —) INDUSIUM
(LUGGAGE —) IMPERIAL
(ORNAMENTAL —) ETUI
(PAPER —) COFFIN
(PILLOW —) SLIP
(WICKER —) HASK BARROW HANAPER
(WING —) SHARD
(WRITING —) KALAMDAN
CASHIER BREAK DEALER POTDAR
PURSER CHECKER DISMISS
CASING BODY CASE HULL SHOE SKIN
TIRE DERMA EPHOD LINER STOCK TRUNK
BOXING COFFIN COLLET JACKET LINING
SHEATH COWLING HOUSING THIMBLE
COVERING
CASK KEG TUB TUN VAT BUTT COWL
DRUM KNAG PIPE RAPE SLIP TREE WOOD
BULGE FOIST BARECA BARREL CASQUE
DOLIUM FIRKIN OCTAVE TIERCE BARRICO
SACKBUT HOGSHEAD PUNCHEON
QUARDEEL KILDERKIN
CASKET BOX TYE CASE CASK CIST TOMB
CHEST ACERRA CHASSE COFFER COFFIN
CADENAS CASSETTE
CASSANDRA (BROTHER OF —)
HELENUS
(FATHER OF —) PRIAM
(HUSBAND OF —) AGAMEMNON
(MOTHER OF —) HECUBA
(SLAYER OF —) CLYTEMNESTRA
CASSOCK GOWN SLOP VEST APRON
GIPPO PELISSE SOUTANE ZIMARRA
CASSOWARY EMU MOORUP RATITE
CAST PUT SET DART HURL MOLD PICK
SHED SLAT SLIP SPEW TINT TOSS WHOP
BLOCK BRAID CHUCK DRIVE EJECT FLIRT
HEAVE PITCH SHADE SHAPE SLING
STAMP THROW TINGE INJECT STRIND
THRILL AGARWAL CASHIER DEPOSIT
MOULAGE
(— A SPELL) TAKE HOODOO BESPELL
BEWITCH FORSPEAK
(— ASIDE) DICE FLING
(— ASPERSIONS) SLUR SKLENT
APPEACH
(— AWAY) DUMP SHOVE DEJECT
REJECT
(— DICE) WHIRL
(— DISCREDIT) GLANCE
(— DOWN) DASH DUMP HURL SINK
ABASE AMATE AMORT AWARP STREW
ABATTU ABJECT DECAST DEJECT

DEMISS THRING ECLIPSE RUINATE DEJECTED
(— FORTH) SPEW WARP BELCH BRAID LAUNCH
(— GLOOM) DUSK CLOUD DARKEN DEPRESS
(— IN A MOLD) STRIKE
(— LOTS) CAVEL
(— METAL) YET
(— OF DICE) COUP DEUCE
(— OF HERRINGS) WARP
(— OF LANGUAGE) IDIOM
(— OF NET) SHOT SHOOT
(— OFF) DAFF JILT MOLT SHED DITCH LOSSE SHAKE SLIRT SLUFF WAIVE CASTEN DEVEST REFUSE REJECT SLOUGH ABDICATE RENOUNCE
(— ON GROUND) TERRE
(— OUT) EGEST EJECT EXPEL BANISH ABANDON EXTRUDE OSTRACIZE
(— SHADOW) ADUMBRATE
(— UP) SUM LEVY UPBRAID
(FRESHLY —) GREEN
CASTAWAY WAIF WEFT TRAMP CRUSOE REJECT OUTCAST DERELICT STRANDED
CASTIGATE LASH SCARE SCORE BERATE PUNISH STRAFE SUBDUE CENSURE CHASTEN CORRECT REPROVE CHASTISE KEELHAUL LAMBASTE
CASTLE BURY FORT KEEP ROCK ABODE COURT MORRO PIECE CASBAH BASTILE BOROUGH CHATEAU CITADEL SCHLOSS UDOLPHO BASTILLE CASTELET CASTILLO FASTNESS FORTRESS
(— IN CHESS) JUEZ ROOK TOUR JUDGE TOWER
(PART OF —) KEEP MOAT WARD MOUNT TOWER WHARF BAILEY BRIDGE DONJON TURRET BASTION BULWARK DUNGEON OUTWORK RAMPART BARBICAN CASEMATE GATEHOUSE BATTLEMENT DRAWBRIDGE PORTCULLIS
(SMALL —) PEEL TOWER CASTLET CHATELET
CASTLE OF OTRANTO
(AUTHOR OF —) WALPOLE
(CHARACTER IN —) CONRAD JEROME MANFRED MATILDA ISABELLA THEODORE
CASTRATE CUT FIX GIB GELD SPAY ALTER DESEX CHANGE EUNUCH NEUTER
CASUAL GLIB BLITHE CHANCE FOLKSY RANDOM CURSORY LEISURE NATURAL OFFHAND RUNNING GLANCING INFORMAL
CASUALTY LOSS DEATH CHANCE HAZARD INJURY MISHAP ACCIDENT DISASTER
CAT TAB EYRA FLOG LION LYNX PARD PUMA PUSS CHAUS CIVET FELID KITTY MEWER MOGGY OUNCE PUSSY SMOKE TABBY TIGER TILER ZIBET ANGORA COUGAR FELINE JAGUAR KITTEN MALKIN MARGAY MIAUER MOUSER OCELOT SERVAL BURMESE CARACAL CHEETAH KUICHUA LEOPARD LINSANG PANTHER PERSIAN SIAMESE TIGRESS WILDCAT WRAWLER BAUDRONS

(— GROUP) CLOWDER
(FEMALE —) QUEEN WHEENCAT
(MALE —) GIB TOM TOMCAT
(TAILLESS —) RUMPY
CATACLYSM FLOOD DELUGE DEBACLE DISASTER UPHEAVAL
CATACOMB TOMB CRYPT VAULT CEMETERY HYPOGEUM
(PL.) ARENARIAE
CATALEPSY TRANCE SEIZURE CATATONY
CATALOG BILL BOOK LIST ROLL ROTA BRIEF INDEX RECORD ROSTER ARRANGE NOTITIA BULLETIN CALENDAR CLASSIFY REGISTER SCHEDULE SYLLABUS INVENTORY
CATAMARAN RAFT TROW BALSA FLOAT GUNBOAT JANGADA MONITOR AUNTSARY
CATAMOUNT LYNX PUMA COUGAR
CATAPULT BIBLE SLING SWEEP THROW HURTLE LAUNCH ONAGER ALACRAN BRICOLE PEDRERO TORMENT TRABUCH WARWOLF BALLISTA CROSSBOW DONDAINE LAUNCHER MANGONEL MARTINET SCORPION SPRINGAL STONEBOW
CATARACT FALL LINN FALLS FLOOD DELUGE CASCADE NIAGARA OVERFALL VICTORIA
CATASTROPHE ACCIDENT CALAMITY DISASTER CATACLYSM
CATCH BAG COB COG COP GET GIN NAB NET NIP DRAW GLOM SNAP HAUL HAWK HOLD HOOK LAND MAKE MEET MESS NAIL NICK PAWL SAVE SEAR SNAG SNAP SNIB STOP TAKE TRAP TREE VANG CLASP CREEL FETCH GLOVE GRASP HITCH KNACK LASSO LATCH SEIZE SNARE TRICK TROLL ARREST ATTAIN BUTTON CLUTCH CORNER CORRAL DETECT DETENT ENGAGE ENMESH ENTRAP LOCKET NOBBLE NOODLE SNATCH TAKING TURNEL ATTRACT CAPTURE ENSNARE GIMMICK GRAPNEL RELEASE SPRINGE TRIGGER CONTRACT ENTANGLE OVERTAKE SURPRISE
(— AT PROPER TIME) NICK
(— ATTENTION) FLAG
(— BIRDS) BATFOWL BIRDLIME
(— EELS) SNIGGLE
(— FIRE) SPUNK IGNITE KINDLE
(— FISH) JAB JIG GILL HANG GILLNET
(— FISH WITH HANDS) GUDDLE GRABBLE HANDFAST
(— IN VOICE) FETCH
(— OF DOOR) LATCH SNECK SNICK
(— OF FISH) FARE HAUL SHOT TACK TRIP SHACK
(— ONE'S BREATH) GASP CHINK
(— SIGHT OF) SPY ESPY SPOT DESCRY
(CRICKET —) DOLLY
(RATCHET —) CLICK
(SAFETY —) CLEVIS
CATCHING CATCHY TAKING ALLURING ARRESTING
CATCHWORD CUE TAG MOTTO BYWORD PHRASE SLOGAN

CATECHISM QUIZ GUIDE MANUAL CARRITCH QUESTIONS

CATEGORICAL DIRECT ABSOLUTE EXPLICIT KNOCKDOWN

CATEGORY WAY RANK CLASS FIELD GENRE GENUS ORDER STYLE FAMILY LEAGUE NUMBER SERIES SPECIES DIVISION

CATER CUT HUMOR SERVE TREAT PANDER PURVEY SUPPLY PROVIDE

CATERPILLAR MUGA AWETO ERUCA CANKER LOOPER PALMER PORINA RISPER TAILOR WOUBIT CUTWORM TRACTOR WEBWORM HANGWORM HORNWORM SILKWORM SKINWORM WORTWORM PALMERWORM

CATERWAUL CRY HOWL WAIL MIAUL WRAWL

CATFISH CUSK ELOD POUT RAAD BAGRE DORAD RAASH DOCMAC GOONCH GOUJON HASSAR MADTOM MUDCAT BARBUDO COBBLER FIDDLER SILURID WALLAGO BULLHEAD BULLPOUT FLATHEAD

CATHEDRAL DOM SEE DUOMO SOBOR MARTYRY MEMORIA MINSTER BASILICA (PART OF —) ARCH ROOF CROSS GABLE IMAGE LABEL SPIRE TOWER BELFRY FINIAL LINTEL LOUVER PORTAL WINDOW CROCKET GALLERY LOZENGE MOLDING MULLION TRACERY TREFOIL PINNACLE TYMPANUM DRIPSTONE THROATING TRIFORIUM CINQUEFOIL CLERESTORY QUATREFOIL

CATHOLIC BROAD GENERAL LIBERAL TOLERANT

CATKIN TAG GULL AGLET AMENT PUSSY CACHRYS CATTAIL GOSLING

CATTAIL DOD FLAG MUSK RUSH TULE AMENT BAYON BLECK RAUPO REREE WONGA CATKIN BULRUSH

CATTLE FEE GIR DHAN GAUR KINE NEAT NOWT OXEN ZEBU DEVON STOCK ANKOLI DURHAM GALYAK ONGOLE ROTHER SINDHI SUSSEX BESTIAL NELLORE REDPOLL COMPOUND OUTSIGHT TUBICORN

CAUCASIAN WHITE EUROPEAN JAPHETIC PALEFACE

CAUL WEB KELL VEIL GALEA KERCHER MEMBRANE

CAULIFLOWER BROCCOLI SNOWBALL CHOUFLEUR

CAUSE DO AIM GAR ISM KEY LET WAY CASE CHAT FATE HOTI LEAD MAKE MOVE ROOT SAKE SPUR SUIT AGENT BASIS BREED CAUSA FRAME PARTY SKILL SLAKE WREAK YIELD CREATE EFFECT ELICIT GOSSIP GROUND INDUCE INVOKE MALADY MANNER MATTER MOTIVE OBJECT ORIGIN PARENT REASON RESORT SOURCE SPEECH SPRING CHESOUN CONCERN PRODUCE PROVOKE QUARREL SUBJECT BUSINESS ENGENDER GENERATE MOVEMENT WHEREFORE MAINSPRING
— A SORE) RANKLE

(— DAMAGE) DAMNIFY
(— FOR COMPLAINT) COMEBACK
(— OF RUIN) BANE
(— OF TERROR) AFFRIGHT
(— OF TROUBLE) TRACHLE
(— PAIN) URN
(— TO ARCH) ROACH
(— TO CONTRACT) PUCKER
(— TO CROUCH) COUCH
(— TO DESERT) DEFECT
(— TO END) ACHIEVE
(— TO MOVE RAPIDLY) GIG
(— TO PROJECT) JET
(— TO RESULT) ISSUE
(— TO STICK) MIRE
(— TO SWELL) BINGE EMBOSS
(— TO THICKEN) CURD
(FINAL —) END

CAUSTIC LYE ACID TART ACRID QUICK SALTY SHARP SNELL ACIDIC BITING BITTER SEVERE BURNING CUTTING ERODENT MORDANT NIPPING PUNGENT PYROTIC SATIRIC ALKALINE DIERETIC SCATHING SNAPPISH STINGING ACIDULOUS SARCASTIC MORDACIOUS

CAUTERIZE BURN CHAR FIRE SEAR BRAND SINGE

CAUTION CARE FEAR HEED WARN GUARD ADVICE CAUTEL CAVEAT EXHORT ANXIETY COUNSEL PRECEPT PROVISO WARNING ADMONISH FORECAST FOREWARN MONITION PRUDENCE WARINESS

CAUTIOUS SHY SAFE WARY ALERT CANNY CHARY TENDER TIPTOE CAREFUL CURIOUS FEARFUL GUARDED PRUDENT DISCREET VIGILANT

CAVALCADE RIDE MARCH TRAIN PARADE SAFARI COMPANY JOURNEY PAGEANT

CAVALIER GAY CURT EASY FINE BRAVE FRANK RIDER ESCORT KNIGHT BRUSQUE GALLANT HAUGHTY OFFHAND ROYALIST

CAVALLERIA RUSTICANA (CHARACTER IN —) LOLA ALFIO TURIDDU SANTUZZA (COMPOSER OF —) MASCAGNI

CAVALRYMAN SOWAR SPAHI HUSSAR LANCER REITER COURIER DRAGOON SABREUR TROOPER HORSEMAN

CAVE DEN COVE HOLE LAIR MINE SINK CACHE CAVEA CRYPT DELVE SLADE SPEOS STORE UPSET CAVERN CAVITY CELLAR DUGOUT GROTTO HOLLOW PANTRY PLUNGE SHROUD SPELUNK COLLAPSE OVERTURN

CAVEAT BEWARE NOTICE CAUTION WARNING

CAVE-DWELLER HORITE TROGLODYTE

CAVERN DEN CAVE COVE GROT HOLE LAIR WEEM CROFT VAULT ANTRUM CAVITY GROTTO HOLLOW SPELUNK

CAVIL CARP HAGGLE QUARREL QUIBBLE

CAVITY CUP PIT SAC AXIL CAVE CELL DALK DENT DUCT HOLE MINE VEIN VOID WELL WOMB ABYSS BOSOM BURSA CRYPT DRUSE FOSSA GOUGE MOUTH

SCOOP SINUS ANTRUM AREOLE ATRIUM
AXILLA BORING CAECUM CAMERA
CAVERN COELIA COTYLE CRATER
GROTTO HOLLOW POCKET RECESS
SOCKET VACUUM VOMICA ABDOMEN
CHAMBER CISTERN DIOCOEL LOCULUS
MORTISE VACUITY VACUOLE VESICLE
EPICOELE FOLLICLE
(— IN BONE) LACUNA
(— IN CASTING) CORE
(— IN HEAD OF WHALE) CASE
(— IN HILLSIDE) ABRI
(— IN LAVA) AMYGDULE
(— IN MINE) BAG
(— IN ROCK) KETTLE
(— MADE BY SEALS) IGLOO
(— OF SEA-SHELL) FLUE
(ALTAR —) TOMB
(BODY —) GUT BELLY CLOACA THORAX
ABDOMEN STOMACH PSEUDOCOEL
PERICARDIUM
(CHEST —) THORAX
(CRYSTAL-LINED —) VUGG DRUSE
GEODE
(GUN —) BORE
(NASAL —) CAVUM
(SUBTERRANEAN —) SLUGGA
CAVORT PLAY BOUND CAPER CURVET
GAMBOL PRANCE
CAVY PONY AGOUTI APEREA CAPYBARA
CAYUSE PONY BRONCO MUSTANG
CEASE BOW CUT DIE END BALK DROP
HALT HOLD LIFT QUIT REST SHUT STAY
STOP STOW AVAST CLOSE DOWSE
LEAVE PAUSE PETER STINT WAIVE
DESIST EXPIRE FINISH FORGET ABSTAIN
REFRAIN SUSPEND INTERMIT SURCEASE
CEASELESS EVER ENDLESS ETERNAL
IMMORTAL UNENDING
CEDAR SUGI TOON SAVIN AROLLA
DEODAR SABINA TUMION CYPRESS
JUNIPER WAXWING CALANTAS
PAHAUTEA
CEDE GIVE AWARD GRANT LEAVE WAIVE
YIELD ASSIGN RESIGN SUBMIT CONCEDE
RENOUNCE
CEILING TOP DOME LOFT CUPOLA
SCREEN CURTAIN PLAFOND TESTUDO
COVERING OVERHEAD
CELEBRATE FETE KEEP SING CHANT
DITTY EXTOL HONOR REVEL BESING
PRAISE ELEGIZE GLORIFY OBSERVE
EULOGIZE PROCLAIM
CELEBRATED KEPT FAMED NOTED
FAMOUS EMINENT FEASTED RENOMME
STORIED FABULOUS GLORIOUS NOTIFIED
OBSERVED RENOWNED
CELEBRATION FETE GALA RITE FESTA
REVEL CUSTOM DOMENT EASTER FIESTA
RENOWN SIMHAH BLOWOUT HAGMENA
HOLIDAY JUBILEE PASCHAL SHINDIG
BIRTHDAY HOGMANAY OCCASION
POTLATCH SHIVAREE FESTIVITY
CELEBRITY FAME LION NAME STAR
CELEB ECLAT RENOWN REPUTE
CELERITY HASTE HURRY SPEED

DISPATCH RAPIDITY VELOCITY
SWIFTNESS
CELESTIAL HOLY DIVINE URANIC
ANGELIC CHINESE EMPYREAL ETHEREAL
HEAVENLY OLYMPIAN
CELIBACY CHASTITY VIRGINITY
CELIBATE CHASTE SINGLE BACHELOR
SPINSTER
CELL BOX EGG BOOT CAGE CYTE GERM
HOLE JAIL ASCUS CABIN CLINK CRYPT
GLAND OOTID TMEMA TORIL VAULT
ZOOID ANAXON CEPTOR COCCUS
CYTODE GAMETE GONIUM INAXON
NEURON PRISON ZYGOTE AGAMETE
AMEBULA CHAMBER CUBICLE DUNGEON
HAPLOID MYOCYTE NEURONE OOBLAST
UTRICLE VESICLE
CELLAR CAVE VAULT BODEGA FAVISSA
BASEMENT HYPOGEUM
CELT GAEL GAUL MANX IRISH WELSH
BRETON BRITON EOLITH BRYTHON
CORNISH
CELTIC ERSE GAEL SCOTCH
CEMENT FIX TIE GLUE HEAL JOIN KNIT
LIME SLIP GROUT PASTE PUTTY STICK
UNITE BINDER COHERE FASTEN FILLER
MASTIC MORTAR SOLDER ASPHALT
ADHESIVE SOLIDIFY
CEMETERY HOWF LITTEN CHARNEL
BONEYARD CATACOMB GOLGOTHA
URNFIELD NECROPOLIS
CENOTAPH TOMB
CENSER INCENSER THURIBLE
CASSOLETTE
CENSOR CRITIC SCREEN SYNDIC
LAUNDER RESTRICT SUPPRESS
CENSORIOUS SEVERE BLAMING
CARPING BLAMEFUL CAPTIOUS CRITICAL
CULPABLE SLASHING
CENSURE BAN HIT NIP RAP TAX CARP
DRUB FLAY HELL LASH SLAP TASK
BLAME CHIDE CURSE DECRY FAULT
JUDGE PINCH SCOLD SLATE TAUNT
ACCUSE ATTACK BERATE CHARGE
REBUFF REBUKE STRAFE TIRADE BLISTER
CHASTEN CONDEMN DECRIAL IMPEACH
IMPROVE INVEIGH REPROOF REPROVE
SCARIFY TRADUCE TROUNCE UPBRAID
BACKBITE CHASTISE REPROACH
SATIRIZE SENTENCE STRICTURE
ADMONITION
CENSUS LIST POLL COUNT LUSTRUM
CENT RED DUIT SANT BROWNIE CENTAVO
STUIVER
(ODD —S) BREAKAGE
(12 1-2 —S) LEVY
CENTAUR CHIRON NESSUS HORSEMAN
BUCENTAUR SAGITTARY
CENTER EYE MID AXIS CORE NAVE SEAT
SNAP FOCUS HEART MIDST PIVOT SPINE
MIDDLE STAPLE ESSENCE NUCLEUS
OMPHALOS SNAPBACK
(— FOR SPINDLE) GIG
(— FOR TARGET) EYE PIN PINHOLE
(— OF ACTIVITY) HUB HIVE
(— OF ARCH) COOM

(— OF ATTRACTION) FOCUS STAGE
CYNOSURE POLESTAR
(— OF BASKET) SLATHER
(— OF CITY) DOWNTOWN
(— OF CULTURE) ATHENS
(— OF DIAMOND) WELL
(— OF ESCUTCHEON) NOMBRIL
(— OF FIGURE) CENTROID
(— OF FISHING NET) BUNT
(— OF FLOWER) EYE
(— OF HURRICANE) EYE
(— OF POPULATION) CITY
(— OF POWER) SEE SIEGE
(— OF STAGE) LIMELIGHT
(— OF STRENGTH) GANGLION
(BASKETBALL —) PIVOTMAN
(COMMERCIAL —) MACHI EMPORIUM
(INTIMATE —) BOSOM
(LATHE —) PIKE
(NERVOUS —) BRAIN NIDUS
(NEURAL —) APPESTAT
(TRADING —) BEACH EXCHANGE
CENTIGRADE CELSIUS
CENTIME RAPPEN
CENTRAL MID AXIAL BASIC CHIEF FOCAL
PRIME MEDIAN MIDDLE CAPITAL
LEADING NUCLEAR PIVOTAL PRIMARY
CARDINAL DOMINANT

CENTRAL AFRICAN REPUBLIC

CAPITAL: BANGUI
COIN: FRANC
NATIVE: BAYA SARA BANDA BWAKA
SANGO YAKOMA BANZIRI MANDJIA
RIVER: BOMU NANA CHARI KOTTO MBARI
MPOKO OUAKA OUHAM CHINKO LOBAYE
SANGHA UBANGI
TOWN: OBO IPPY BIRAO BOUAR KEMBE
NDELE NGOTO PAOUA RAFAI ZEMIO
BABOUA BAKALA BANGUI BOZOUM
BAMBARI GRIMARI ZEMONGO BERBERATI
BOSSANGOA

CENTRIFUGE CYCLONE SEPARATOR
CENTURY AGE TON SECLE SIECLE
(14TH —) TRECENTO
CENTURY PLANT ALOE PITA AGAVE
MAGUEY CANTALA TEQUILA MONOCARP
CEPHALOPOD SQUID CUTTLE INKFISH
OCTOPUS SPIRULA DIBRANCH SCAPHITE
CEREAL RYE BEAN BRAN CORN MUSH
OATS RICE SAMP TEFF ARZUN GRAIN
MAIZE SPELT WHEAT BARLEY BINDER
FARINA HOMINY PABLUM OATMEAL
SOYBEAN PORRIDGE
CEREBRATION THOUGHT
CEREMENT SHROUD
CEREMONIAL FORM RITE STIFF FORMAL
RITUAL SOLEMN PRECISE STUDIED
TRIUMPH
CEREMONY BRIS FETE FORM GAUD
HAKO ORGY POMP RITE SEAL SHOW
SIGN SING DANCE BERITH BRIDAL
BURIAL EXEQUY HOMAGE KERIAH
MALKAH MAUNDY NIPTER OFFICE

PARADE POWWOW REVIEW RITUAL
SALUTE BAPTISM DISPLAY MELAVEH
OVATION PAGEANT PANAGIA TAHARAH
ACCOLADE APOLUSIS ASPERGES
COEMPTIO CRIOBOLY ENCAENIA
EXERCISE FUNCTION MARRIAGE
OCCASION INAUGURAL INDUCTION
OBSERVANCE
(GRADUATION —) CAPPING
(HAZING —) CREELING
(MARRIAGE —) ESPOUSAL
(TEA —) CHANOYU
CERES DEMETER
(DAUGHTER OF —) PROSERPINE
PHERREPHATTA
(FATHER OF —) SATURN
(MOTHER OF —) VESTA
CERTAIN COLD COOL DEAD FAST FIRM
FREE REAL SURE TRUE BOUND CLEAR
EXACT FIXED PLAIN ACTUAL SECURE
STATED ASSURED PERFECT PRECISE
SETTLED ABSOLUTE CONSTANT OFFICIAL
PALPABLE POSITIVE RELIABLE RESOLVED
UNERRING CONFIDENT
CERTAINLY AY AYE AMEN SURE TRULY
INDEED SURELY VERILY EVERMORE
FORSOOTH SECURELY NATURALLY
CERTAINTY YEA PIPE CINCH SURETY
SURENESS CONSTANCY
CERTIFICATE BOND CHECK DEMIT
JURAT SCRIP TITLE ATTEST CEDULA
COUPON INDENT PATENT TICKET VERIFY
CERTIFY DIPLOMA VOUCHER WARRANT
WAYBILL JUDGMENT NAVICERT
REGISTER REGISTRY SECURITY
(CUSTOMHOUSE —) COCKET
(MARRIAGE —) LINES
(MINER'S —) LICENCE LICENSE
(PILOT'S —) BRANCH
(SERVANT'S —) CHIT
CERTIFICATION PASS STAMP
APPROVAL HECHSHER CLEARANCE
DISCHARGE
CERTIFIED SWORN
CERTIFY AVOW SWEAR AFFIRM ASSURE
ATTEST DEPOSE EVINCE VERIFY
APPROVE ENDORSE LICENSE TESTIFY
ACCREDIT
CESSATION END HALT HUSH LULL REST
STAY STOP BREAK CEASE CLOSE LETUP
PAUSE SLACK TRUCE CUTOFF DEMISE
DISUSE PERIOD RECESS CLOSURE
RESPITE ABEYANCE BLACKOUT
INTERVAL SHUTDOWN STOPPAGE
SURCEASE SUSPENSE
(— OF HOSTILITIES) TRUCE INDUCIAE
ARMISTICE
(— OF LIFE) DEATH
(— OF RESPIRATION) APNEA
(— OF WORK) HARTAL
CETACEAN ORC CETE ORCA SUSU
WHALE BELUGA COWFISH DOLPHIN
GRAMPUS NARWHAL PORPOISE
CEYLON (SEE SRI LANKA) SERENDIP
TAPROBANE TAPROBANE

CHAD

CAPITAL: NDJAMENA
COIN: FRANC FRANCCFA
LAKE: CHAD
NATIVE: ARAB SARA KREDA MASSA
TOUBOU KAMADJA MOUNDAN
PLATEAU: ENNEDI
RIVER: CHARI SHARI LOGONE BAHRAOUK
TOWN: ATI BOL LAI MAO FADA FAYA
MONGO ABECHE BOKORO BONGOR
LARGEAU MOUNDOU FORTLAMY
MOUSSORO

CHAFE IRK RUB VEX FRET FUME GALL
HEAT JOSH RAGE WARM WEAR ANGER
ANNOY GRIND SCOLD WORRY ABRADE
BANTER EXCITE HARASS NETTLE RANKLE
INCENSE INFLAME IRRITATE
CHAFF HAY ROT BRAN CHIP GRIT GUFF
JOSH QUIZ RAZZ DROSS GLUME HULLS
HUSKS JOLLY RALLY STRAW TEASE
TRASH BANTER REFUSE TAILING
RAILLERY RIDICULE
CHAFFINCH PINK CHINK SPINK TWINK
ROBERD SCOBBY SHILFA SKELLY
ROBINET SNABBIE WETBIRD
CHAGRIN ENVY SPITE VEXATION
CHAGRINED SICK ASHAMED
CHAIN FOB GUY NET ROW SET TOW TUG
BIND BOND CURB FAST GYVE JOIN LINE
LINK SEAL TEAM CABLE GROUP LEASH
SHEET SLING TRACE TRAIN CATENA
COLLAR CORDON FASTEN FETTER
HANGER HOBBLE JIGGER LINKER SECURE
SERIES STRING TETHER TOGGLE
BOBSTAY CHIGNON CONNECT LASHING
MANACLE NETWORK PENDANT SHACKLE
BRACELET NECKLACE RESTRAIN
STROBILA
(— FOR ANCHOR) CATFALL PAINTER
(— FOR BINDING) JACKER TACKLER
(— FOR WRAPPING MAST)
WOOLDING
(— OF AUTHORITIES) ISNAD
(— OF DUNES) SEIF
(— OF MOUNTAINS) RANGE
(— OF ROCKS) REEF
(— ON CONVICT'S LEG) SLANG
(— TO BIND CATTLE) SEAL
(DECORATIVE —) FESTOON
(ENDLESS —) CREEPER
(MAGIC —) GLEIPNIR
(SHORT —) SHANK
(SUSPENDED —) CATENARY
(WATCH —) FOB ALBERT
CHAIR KEEP SEAT HORSE SEDAN STOOL
ESTATE OFFICE PULPIT ROCKER SADDLE
SITTER TONJON CACOLET COMMODE
FANBACK GONDOLA SITTING VOYEUSE
WINDSOR ARMCHAIR CARRIAGE
CATHEDRA FAUTEUIL
(— OF STATE) THRONE
(— SLUNG FROM POLE) KAGO
TALABON

(— WITH CANOPY) STATE
(BISHOP'S —) CATHEDRA FALDSTOOL
(EASY —) COGSWELL
(GREEK —) KLISMOS
(MINING —) DOG
(PART OF —) ARM EAR LEG BACK POST
RUNG SEAT SLAT CREST STILE STUMP
ROCKER ARMREST SPINDLE BACKRAIL
HEADPIECE
(PORTABLE —) SEDAN
(SEDAN —) NORIMONO
(SPRING —) PERCH
(THRONE —) SHINZA
CHAIRMAN HEAD CHAIR EMCEE
SPEAKER CONVENER DIRECTOR
MODERATOR
CHAISE GIG SHAY CALESIN CARRIAGE
CURRICLE SHANDRYDAN
CHAISE LONGUE DAYBED DUCHESSE
CHALCEDONY ONYX OPAL SARD AGATE
CHERT PRASE CATEYE JASPER QUARTZ
ENHYROS OPALINE SARDINE SARDIUS
CORNELIAN
CHALICE AMA CUP BOWL CALIX GRAIL
REGAL GOBLET KRASIS
CHALK CORK PALE TALC TICK CRETA
FLOUR SCORE BLANCH BLEACH CRAYON
RUBBLE WHITEN ACCOUNT WHITING
(GREEN —) PRASINE
(HARD —) HURLOCK
(RED —) RUBRIC
(SURVEYOR'S —) KEEL
CHALLENGE VIE CALL DARE DEFY FACE
GAGE ASSAY BLAME BRAVE CLAIM
QUERY STUMP ACCUSE APPEAL BANTER
CARTEL CHARGE DEMAND FORBID
IMPUGN INVITE ARRAIGN CENSURE
IMPEACH PROVOKE REPROVE SOLICIT
SUMMONS CHAMPION DEFIANCE
GAUNTLET QUESTION
CHAMBER ODA AGER CELL CIST DOME
FLAT FOLD HALL IWAN KIVA ROOM SALE
TOMB BOWER CAVUM COURT GOMER
HOUSE STOVE STOVE ATRIUM CAMARA
CAMERA COFFER HEADER HOLLOW
MIHRAB SENATE SOLLAR SPRING
STANZA BEDROOM CAISSON CHANNEL
CUBICLE FAVISSA GALLERY DIFFUSER
SMOKEBOX
(— FOR MOLTEN GLASS) FONT
(— IN FURNACE) SHAFT DOGHOUSE
(— OF EAR) SACCULE UTRICLE
(— POT) JORDAN JEROBOAM
(AIR —) SPONSON
(AUDIENCE —) DURBAR
(BOMBPROOF —) CASEMATE
(CLIMATE CONTROL —) BIOTRON
(FIRE —) ARCH STOVE COCKLE FIREBOX
(FORTIFICATION —) BUNKER
(OPEN —) LANTERN
(ORGAN —) SWELL
(PISTON —) BARREL
(PRIVATE —) CLOSET CONCLAVE
(PUEBLO —) KIVA ESTUFA
(SLEEPING —) BEDROOM WARDROBE
(SMALL —) LOCULUS
(SUPPLY —) MAGAZINE

(UNDERGROUND —) CAVE CRYPT CAVERN SERDAB HYPOGEE
(WATERTIGHT —) CAISSON
CHAMFER BEVEL CHIME CHINE FLUTE CIPHER FURROW GROOVE
CHAMOIS IZARD AOUDAD
CHAMP BITE CHAW MASH CHOMP GNASH TRAMPLE
CHAMPAGNE BUBBLY SIMKIN BELLEEK SILLERY
CHAMPION ACE AID FAN ABET BACK BOSS DEFY HERO KEMP DEFEND KNIGHT PATRON SQUIRE VICTOR ESPOUSE PALADIN PROTECT ADVOCATE DEFENDER
CHANCE DIE HAP LOT CAST DRAW FATE LUCK ODDS RISK SHOT TIDE BREAK STAKE CASUAL GAMBLE HAPPEN MISHAP RANDOM AIMLESS FORTUNE STUMBLE VANTAGE VENTURE ACCIDENT FORTUITY OPPORTUNITY
(ADVERSE —) HAZARD
(EVEN —) TOSSUP
(SLIGHT —) PRAYER
CHANCEL BEMA CHOIR ADYTUM
CHANDELIER CORONA LUSTER PHAROS PENDANT GASELIER
CHANGE CHOP FLOP MOLT MOVE ODDS PEAL TURN VARY VEER WARP WEND ADAPT ALTER AMEND BREAK COINS EMEND SHIFT ADJUST BECOME DIFFER IMMUTE MODIFY MUTATE REVAMP REVISE SWITCH COMMUTE CONVERT CUTOVER DEVIATE DENATURE INNOVATE MUTATION REVISION TRANSFER VARIANCE
(— APPEARANCE) DISGUISE
(— COLOR) TURN
(— COURSE) GYBE JIBE
(— DIRECTION) CUT CANT CHOP HAUL KNEE VEER ANGLE BREAK SHIFT
(— FOR BETTER) HELP
(— FOR WORSE) BEDEVIL
(— FORM) DEVELOP
(— GAIT) BREAK
(— GRADUALLY) PASS GRADUATE
(— IN COURSE) SHEER
(— IN DIRECTION) JOG KNEE STEP
(— IN ELEVATION) FORK
(— IN LAKE LEVEL) SEICHE
(— IN SIZE) ASTOGENY
(— INTO VAPOR) FLASH
(— MONEY) WISSEL
(— OF FORM) SET
(— OF GEAR) KICKDOWN
(— OF MIND) CAPRICE
(— OF MOOD) VARY
(— OF PITCH) MOTION INFLECT
(— OF SEA LEVEL) EUSTACY
(— OF SOUND) BREAKING
(— OF WORD) ANAGRAM
(— ONE'S HEART) REPENT
(— PACE) BREAK
(— POSITION) STIR FLEET HOTCH
(— QUICKLY) FLY
(— RESIDENCE) FLIT
(— SHAPE) DRAW CREEP DEFORM
(ABNORMAL —) LESION

(ABRUPT —) DOGLEG SALTATION
(GEAR —) KICKDOWN
(GRADUAL —) DRIFT
(PRESSURE —) ALLOBAR
(SHORT —) FLUFF
(SMALL —) GROCERY
(UNEXPECTED —) SWITCH
CHANGEABLE GIDDY LIGHT WINDY CHOPPY FICKLE FITFUL LABILE MOBILE MOTLEY SHIFTY ERRATIC MUTABLE PROTEAN UNSTAID VARIANT VARIOUS MOVEABLE SKITTISH TICKLISH UNSTABLE VARIABLE VOLATILE CHAMELEON VERSATILE
CHANNEL CUT GAT RUT CANO CAVA DIKE DUCT FLUE KILL LANE PIPE RACE SLEW VALE VEIN WADI BAYOU CANAL CARRY DITCH DRAIN FLUME GLYPH GUIDE RIVER SINUS SLIDE STRIA SWASH AIRWAY ALVEUS ARROYO ARTERY BRANCH COURSE CUTOFF ESTERO FURROW GROOVE GULLET GUTTER HOLLOW KEYWAY LAGOON MEDIUM RABBET RESACA RIVOSE RUNWAY SLOUGH SLUICE STRAIT STRAND STREAM THROAT TROUGH CONDUCT CONDUIT CULVERT PASSAGE RACEWAY RIVULET SILANGA TIDEWAY AQUEDUCT GUIDEWAY
(— FOR MOLTEN METAL) SOW GATE RUNNER
(— IN CLOTH) FLUTE
(— IN ICE FIELD) LEAD
(— IN MOLD) SPRAY
(— OF AQUEDUCT) SPECUS
(— ON A DECK) CHIMB CHIME
(— ON WHALE) SCARF
(ARTIFICIAL —) GAT GOUT
(DRAINAGE —) GAW
(ENGLISH —) SLEEVE
(INCLINED —) SHOOT
(INFORMATION —) PIPELINE
(IRRIGATION —) AUWAI DROVE
(LYMPH —) CISTERNA
(SECONDARY —) BINNACLE
(SLOPING —) CHUTE
CHANT CANT SING SONG TONE CAROL PSALM ANTHEM CANTUS INTONE LITANY WARBLE CHORTLE INTROIT PROSODE REQUIEM WORSHIP ALLELUIA ANTIPHON CANTICLE SINGSONG PLAINSONG
CHAOS PIE GULF MESS VOID ABYSS BABEL CHASM JUMBLE TOPHET ANARCHY MIXTURE DISORDER SHAMBLES TOHUBOHU
CHAOTIC MUDDLED CONFUSED FORMLESS TUMULTUARY
CHAP BOY BUY DOG LAD MAN RAP WAG BEAN BEAT BIRD BLOW CHOP COVE DICK DUCK HIND JOHN MASH MATE NABS SNAP BILLY BLOKE BUCKO BUYER CLEFT CRACK FRUIT KNOCK LOVER RUMMY SCOUT SPLIT SPORT SWIPE TRADE YOUTH BARTER BREACH CODGER FELLOW GAFFER KIPPER SHAVER STRIKE STROKE BROTHER FISSURE ROUGHEN BLIGHTER

(— HANDS) RACK SPRAY
(— IN SKIN) KIN KIBE
(FINE —) BULLY
(OLD —) BO GEEZER
(PLUCKY —) COCK
(QUEER —) GALOOT
(S.AFRICAN —) KEREL
(YOUNG —) GAFFER
CHAPARRAL MONTE CHAMISAL
BUCKTHORN
CHAPEL CAGE CRYPT PORCH SALEM
BETHEL BEULAH CHURCH HAIKAL
SHRINE CHANTRY ORATORY SACRARY
BETHESDA DIACONIA FERETORY
PARABEMA SACELLUM
(UNDERGROUND —) SHROUDS
CHAPERON ATTEND DUENNA ESCORT
MATRON GRIFFIN PROTECT GUARDIAN
CHAPLAIN PADRE LEVITE ALMONER
ALTARIST ORDINARY
CHAPTER BODY CELL PACE POST COURT
LODGE BRANCH CABILDO CAPITAL
CORRECT COUNCIL MEETING SECTION
ASSEMBLY
(— OF BOOK) CAPITAL
(— OF KORAN) SURA
(— OF SOCIETY) CAMP CIRCLE
CHAR BURN SEAR BROIL SINGE TROUT
SCORCH BLACKEN TORGOCH REDBELLY
SAIBLING SALMONID SANDBANK
(PL.) SALVELINI
CHARACTER AURA BENT CLEF DASH
FLAT FORM KIND MAKE MARK MOLD
NOTE PART ROLE RUNE SIGN SORT TONE
TYPE BRAND COLOR ETHOS FIBER HABIT
HEART HUMOR INDEX SAVOR STAMP
TENOR TOKEN TRAIT WRITE CARACT
CIPHER COCKUP DAGGER DIRECT
EMBLEM FIGURE GENIUS HANGER
LETTER MANNER METTLE NATURE
REPUTE SIGLUM SPIRIT STRIPE SYMBOL
CALIBER ESSENCE QUALITY CAPACITY
IDENTITY LIGATURE
(— OF SOIL) LAIR
(ASSUMED —) ROLE FIGURE
INCOGNITO
(BAD —) DROLE BUDMASH
(BASIC —) BOTTOM
(CHIEF —) AGONIST
(CHINESE —) SHOU RADICAL
(COMMON —) COMMUNITY
(FIRM —) BACKBONE
(GIVE — TO) TONE
(GREEK —) SAMPI
(JAPANESE —S) HIBUNCI
(MENDELIAN —) ALLEL ALLELE
(PHYSICAL —) ARMENOID
(PRIME —) ESSENCE
(SHIFTLESS —) BEAT
(STOCK —) BESSY MACCUS
(TESTED —) ASSAY
(TRIED —) TOUCH
(VULGAR —S) ONMUN
CHARACTERISTIC CAST MARK MIEN
AROMA GRACE POINT TOKEN TRAIT
ACCENT NATURE AMENITY FEATURE
QUALITY SPECIES TYPICAL PECULIAR

PROPERTY SYMBOLIC PARAMETER
PROPRIETY PECULIARITY
CHARACTERIZE MARK STYLE DEFINE
DEPICT ENTITLE PORTRAY DESCRIBE
INDICATE INSCRIBE
CHARCOAL COAL CARBO CHARK FUSAIN
SPODIUM SCRIBBET
CHARGE FEE LAP LAY RAP TAX BEEF BILL
BUCK CALL CARE CARK CAST COST
CURE DUES DUTY FILL GIBE KEEP LADE
LIEN LOAD NICK NOTE ONUS RATE REST
RUSH SHOT SIZE SOAK SPAR TASK TOLL
WARD BLAME CAUSE CHALK COUNT
CRIME DEBIT EXTRA ONSET ORDER PRICE
REFER SCORE ACCUSE ADJURE ALLEGE
APPEAL ASSESS ATTACK BURDEN
CAREER CENSUS COURSE CREDIT
DAMAGE DEFAME DEMAND ENJOIN
EXCESS IMPOSE IMPUTE OFFICE SURTAX
TARIFF TOWAGE WEIGHT ANNULET
ARRAIGN ASCRIBE ASSAULT BOATAGE
CARTAGE CENSURE CHEVRON COMMAND
CONCERN CONJURE CORKAGE CORNAGE
CUSTODY DOCKAGE DRAYAGE EXPENSE
HAULAGE IMPEACH KEEPING
(— AGAINST) TILT
(— BATTERY) SOAK BOOST
(— EXCESSIVELY) FLEECE
(— FALSELY) SURMISE
(— OF FIREARM) LOAD AMORCE
(— OF MENTAL ENERGY) CATHEXIS
(— OF METAL) HEAT
(— OF ORE) POST
(— TO BE PAID) LAW
(— UPON PROPERTY) LIEN
(— WITH CRIME) ACCUSE DELATE
INDICT ARTICLE ATTAINT IMPEACH
(— WITH GAS) AERATE
(AGGREGATE —S) BOOK
(CANNON —) GRAPE
(COVER —) COUVERT
(DEPTH —) CAN
(EXPLOSIVE —) CAP BLAST SNAKE
SQUIB TULIP BOOSTER BURSTER IGNITER
(FALSE —) CALUMNY
(HERALDIC —) DELF DROP GYRON
LABEL BEZANT BILLET DRAGON GURGES
BEARING ESQUIRE
(MAILING —) FRANKAGE
(POWDER —) GRAIN
(SHAPED —) BEEHIVE
(SPIRITUAL —) CURE
(TEMPORARY —) CARE
(WINE —) CORKAGE
CHARGER DISH HORSE MOUNT STEED
ACCUSER COURSER PLATTER TROOPER
CHARIOT CAR BIGA CART CHAR RATH
WAIN BUGGY CHAIR ESSED RATHA
TRIGA WAGON CHARET QUADRIGA
CHARITY ALMS DOLE GIFT LOVE PITY
RUTH MERCY BASKET BOUNTY CARITAS
HANDOUT LARGESS LENIENCE
CHARIVARI BABEL SHALLAL SERENADE
SHIVAREE
CHARLATAN FAKE CHEAT FAKER FRAUD
QUACK IMPOSTER MOUNTEBANK
QUACKSALVER

CHARM OBI CALM JINX JUJU LUCK MOJO SNOW ZOGO ALLAY CATCH FAVOR GRACE MAGIC OBEAH OOMPH SPELL WANGA ALLURE AMULET BEAUTY CARACT ENAMOR ENGAGE ENTICE FETISH GLAMOR GRIGRI MANTRA MELODY PLEASE SAPHIE SCARAB SOOTHE SUBDUE VOODOO ABRAXAS ATTRACT BEGUILE BEWITCH CONJURE DELIGHT ENCHANT FLATTER PHILTER SINGING SORCERY ENTHRALL TALISMAN CAPTIVATE MAGNETIZE

CHARMING SWEET GOLDEN AMIABLE DARLING EYESOME TEMPEAN WINNING WINSOME ADORABLE DELICATE GRACEFUL LOVESOME

CHARON (FATHER OF —) EREBUS **(MOTHER OF —)** NOX

CHART MAP CARD PLAN PLAT PLOT ROSE CARTE GRAPH RECORD SCHEME DIAGRAM OUTLINE PROJECT MERCATOR

CHARTER LET BOND DEED HIRE RENT CARTE FUERO GRANT LEASE CHARTA PERMIT CONTRACT

CHARTERHOUSE OF PARMA (AUTHOR OF —) STENDHAL **(CHARACTER IN —)** GINA CONTI DONGO MOSCA CLELIA FAUSTA GILETTI FABRIZIO FERRANTE MARIETTA PIETRANERA

CHASE HUNT SHAG SHOO SICK CHIVY HARRY HOUND SCORE EMBOSS FOLLOW FRIEZE GROOVE HARASS PURSUE QUARRY ENGRAVE HUNTING PURSUIT

CHASM GAP PIT GULF RIFT YAWN ABYSS CANON CHAOS CLEFT GORGE BREACH CANYON HIATUS FISSURE VACANCY APERTURE CREVASSE

CHASTE PURE CLEAN DECENT HONEST MODEST PROPER SEVERE VESTAL VIRGIN PUDICAL REFINED CELIBATE INNOCENT VIRGINLY VIRTUOUS CONTINENT

CHASTEN RATE ABASE SMITE SOBER HUMBLE PUNISH REBUKE REFINE SUBDUE TEMPER AFFLICT CENSURE CORRECT CHASTISE MODERATE RESTRAIN

CHASTISE BEAT FLOG LASH SLAP TRIM WHIP AMEND BLAME SCOLD SPANK STRAP TAUNT ACCUSE BERATE CHARGE PUNISH PURIFY REBUKE THRASH CHASTEN CORRECT REPROVE SCOURGE CASTIGATE

CHASTITY HONOR PURITY VIRTUE HONESTY MODESTY CELIBACY GOODNESS PUDICITY INNOCENCE

CHAT GAS JAW RAP CHIN COZE TALK YARN DALLY PITCH PRATE SPEAK VISIT BABBLE CONFAB GABBLE GIBBER GOSSIP HOBNOB JABBER NATTER CHATTER CONVERSE

CHATEAU HOUSE TOWER CASTLE MANSION SCHLOSS CHATELET FORTRESS

CHATTER GAB JAW YAP BLAB CHAT CHIN GASH TALK TEAR CLACK CLASH PRATE BABBLE CACKLE GABBLE GIBBER GOSSIP JABBER JARGON PALTER YAMMER YATTER BLABBER BRABBLE CHAFFER CLATTER GABNASH PALAVER PRATING PRATTLE TWITTER LOLLYGAG

CHAUVINISM JINGOISM

CHEAP LOW BASE POOR VILE CLOSE GAUDY GROSS KITCH LIGHT MUCKY NASTY SNIDE TATTY TIGHT TINNY ABJECT BRUMMY CHEESY COMMON CRUMMY SHODDY SORDID STINGY TAWDRY TRASHY BARGAIN CHINTZY TINHORN INFERIOR TWOPENNY BRUMMAGEM PINCHBECK

CHEAT DO COG CON FOB GYP NIP BEAT BILK BITE BURN CLIP CRIB DUPE FAKE FLAM GULL HAVE HOAX JILT JOUK KNAP LIAR MUMP NICK POOP REAM ROOK SELL SHAM SKIN SWAP TRIM BLANK BUNKO COZEN CROOK CULLY DODGE FAKER FRAUD FUDGE GOUGE GUILE KNAVE MULCT PINCH ROGUE SCAMP SCREW SHARP SHORT STICK STIFF STING TOUCH TRICK BLANCH CHISEL DADDLE DECEIT DELUDE DIDDLE EUCHRE FIDDLE FLEECE GREASE HUMBUG HUSTLE ILLUDE NIGGLE OUTWIT RENEGE RIPOFF ABUSION BEGUILE CHICANE DECEIVE DEFRAUD FINAGLE FINESSE MISLEAD PLUNDER QUIBBLE SHARPER SLICKER SWINDLE ARTIFICE CHISELER HOODWINK IMPOSTOR INTRIGUE PICAROON SWINDLER BAMBOOZLE

CHECK BIT DAM LID NAB NIP SET TAB BAIL BALK BEAT BILK BILL CHIT CURB DAMP FACE FOIL KITE PAWL REIN SNIP SNUB STAY STEM STOP STUB TAKE TEST TICK TRIG TURN TWIT ABORT ALLAY ANNUL BLOCK BRAKE CATCH CHIDE CHOKE CROOK DAUNT DELAY DETER DRAFT EMBAR GAUGE LIMIT PAUSE QUELL REPEL STALL STILL STUNT TALLY TAUNT TOKEN WAVER ARREST ATTACK BAFFLE BOTTLE BRIDLE CHEQUE COUPON DAMPEN DEFEAT DETAIN DETENT DURESS HINDER IMPEDE OPPOSE OUTWIT QUENCH REBATE REBUFF REBUKE RETURN SCOTCH STANCH STAYER STIFLE STYMIE TICKET VERIFY COMMAND CONTAIN CONTROL COUNTER CURTAIN DRAUGHT INHIBIT MONITOR REFRAIN REPRESS REPROOF REPROVE REPULSE REVERSE SETBACK SNAFFLE STOPPER TRAMMEL BULKHEAD ENCUMBER HOLDBACK OBSTRUCT PULLBACK RESTRAIN WITHHOLD **(— GRADUALLY)** CUSHION **(— GROWTH)** BLAST STINT STUNT **(— IN GLASS)** SPLIT **(— IN TIMBER)** STARSHAKE **(— MOTION)** SPRAG **(— OF HORSE)** SACCADE **(FORGED —)** STIFF STUMER **(RESTAURANT —)** LAWING **(WORTHLESS —)** DUD STUMER

CHECKER DAM DICE FRET KING PIECE WHITE DAMPER DRAUGHT

CHECKERED PIED VAIR DICED PLAID CHECKY MOTLEY
CHECKERS DRAFTS CHEQUERS DRAUGHTS
CHEEK CHAP CHOP GALL GENA JAMB JOWL LEER SASS BUCCA CRUST NERVE SAUCE AUDACITY TEMERITY
(— OF SPUR) SHANK
(— OF VISE) CHAP
CHEEKBONE MALAR ZYGOMA
CHEEKY BOLD
CHEER OLE RAH FARE FOOD MIND ROOT VIVA YELL BRAVO BRISK ELATE FEAST HEART HUZZA JOLLY MIRTH SHOUT SPORT TIGER WHOOP CANTLE CHERRY GAIETY HOORAY HURRAH HUZZAH SOLACE ACCLAIM ANIMATE APPLAUD CHERISH COMFORT CONSOLE GLADDEN HEARTEN JOLLITY LIGHTEN REFRESH REJOICE SUPPORT UPRAISE APPLAUSE BRIGHTEN HILARITY INSPIRIT RECREATE VIVACITY
(BURST OF —S) SALVO
(GOOD —) WELFARE
(JAPANESE —) BANZAI
(SORRY —) PENANCE
CHEERFUL GAY GLAD GOOD HIGH ROSY BONNY DOUCE HAPPY JOLLY LIGHT MERRY PEART READY SAPPY SUNNY BLITHE BRIGHT CHEERY CHIRPY GENIAL HEARTY JOCUND LIVELY BUOYANT CHIPPER CHIRRUP JOCULAR SMILING WINSOME CHIRRUPY EUPEPTIC FRIENDLY GLADSOME HOMELIKE SANGUINE SUNBEAMY SUNSHINE
CHEERFULNESS JOY GLEE CHEER GAIETY LEVITY SPIRIT JOLLITY BUOYANCY FESTIVAL GLADNESS HILARITY
CHEERLESS SAD BLAE COLD DIRE DRAB GLUM GRAY BLEAK DREAR WASTE DISMAL DREARY GLOOMY WINTRY DOLEFUL FORLORN JOYLESS SUNLESS DEJECTED DESOLATE
CHEESE OKA BLUE BRIE EDAM FETA HAND JACK TRIP APPLE BRICK COLBY CREAM DAISY DERBY GOUDA GRANA KENNO MAHON SWISS WHEEL ASIAGO BRYNZA BURGOS CASSAN DUNLOP MYSOST ROMANO RONCAL SAANEN SBRINZ TILSIT ZAMORA ZIEGER ANGELOT CHEDDAR CHEVRET COTTAGE FONTINA FROMAGE GJEDOST GRUYERE KEBBUCK LASELVA PRIMOST RICOTTA SAPSAGO SERRANO STILTON TETILLA TRUCKLE CHESHIRE EMMENTAL LONGHORN MUENSTER PARMESAN PECORINO RACLETTE SANSIMON TRONCHON LEICESTER PROVOLONE ROQUEFORT WILTSHIRE MOZZARELLA NEUFCHATEL SERVILLETA
CHEETAH CAT OUNCE YOUSE GUEPARD
CHEF COOK COMMIS SAUCIER CUISINIER
CHELA HAND MANUS NIPPER PINCER
CHEMICAL
(ALSO SEE SPECIFIC HEADINGS) ACID

BASE SALT ALKALI BLEACH ADDITIVE ALGICIDE CATALYST
CHEMISE SARK SHIFT SHIRT SIMAR SMOCK CAMISA SHIMMY LINGERIE
CHEMIST ANALYST ASSAYER CHEMICK BENCHMAN COLORIST DRUGGIST
CHERISH AID HUG PET DOTE HAVE HOPE LIKE LOVE SAVE ADORE BOSOM CHEER CLING ENJOY NURSE PRIZE VALUE CARESS ESTEEM FONDLE FOSTER HARBOR MOTHER NESTLE NUZZLE PAMPER REVERE COMFORT EMBOSOM EMBRACE INDULGE NOURISH NURTURE PROTECT SUPPORT SUSTAIN ENSHRINE PRESERVE TREASURE
CHERISHED PET DEAR BOSOM DANDILY AFFECTED PRECIOUS
CHEROOT MANILA TRICHI TRICHY
CHERRY BING DUKE FUJI GEAN MOREL CORNEL MAZARD BURBANK CAPULIN LAMBERT MAHALEB MARASCA MAYDUKE OXHEART PITANGA WINDSOR DURACINE NAPOLEON BIGARREAU MARASCHINO
CHERRY ORCHARD (AUTHOR OF —) CHEKHOV
(CHARACTER IN —) ANYA GAYEV VARYA YASHA DUNYASHA LOPAKHIN RANEVSKY TROFIMOV CHARLOTTE
CHESS SHOGI CHECKER SKITTLES
CHESSMAN PIN KING PIECE CHECKER CHEQUER
(— SET) MEINY MEINIE
(ANY — BUT PAWN) OFFICER
(BISHOP —) ALFIN ARCHER
(CASTLE —) JUEZ ROOK TOUR JUDGE LEDGE TOWER
(KNIGHT —) HORSE CHEVALIER
(PAWN —) PON POUNE
(QUEEN —) FERS FIERS PHEARSE
CHEST ARK BOX KIT PYX ARCA BUST CAJA CASH CYST FUND KIST SAFE AMBRY BAHUT BUIST CADDY FRONT HOARD HUTCH TRUNK ALMOIN BASKET BREAST BUNKER BUREAU CAISSE CAJETA CASKET COFFER COFFIN HAMPER LOCKER LOWBOY SHRINE THORAX WANGAN BRAZIER BRISKET CAISSON CASSONE COMMODE DRAWERS DRESSER ENCLOSE HIGHBOY TOOLBOX CISTVAEN CUPBOARD TREASURY
(— FOR CUTLERY) CANTEEN
(— FOR FISH) CAUF
(— OF ORES) CAXON
(MEDICINE) INRO
CHESTNUT JOKE BROWN HORSE CASTOR MARRON SATIVA CRENATA DENTATA
(HORSE —) CONKER
(POLYNESIAN —) RATA
(WATER —) LING
CHEVALIER CADET NOBLE KNIGHT GALLANT CAVALIER HORSEMAN
CHEVRON BEAM MARK WOUND RAFTER STRIPE ZIGZAG
CHEW CUD EAT GUM BITE CHAM CHAW GNAW NOSH QUID CHAMP CHONK GRIND

MUNCH RUMEN CRUNCH MUMBLE
MEDITATE RUMINATE
CHEWINK FINCH JOREE TOWHEE
GRASSET
CHIC PERT POSH TRIG TRIM KIPPY NATTY
NIFTY SMART CHICHI DAPPER GIGOLO
MODISH ELEGANT STYLISH
CHICANERY DIRT RUSE WILE FEINT
TRICK ARTIFICE INTRIGUE TRICKERY
DECEPTION PETTIFOGGERY
CHICHI TONY
CHICK BIRD GIRL PEEP TICK CHILD NATTY
POULET SCREEN SEQUIN SPROUT
CHICKEN CHUCKIE
CHICKADEE TOMTIT BLACKCAP
TITMOUSE
CHICKEN HEN COCK FOWL BIDDY CAPON
CHICK CHOOK CHUCK FRYER LAYER
POULT SILKY TIMID AFRAID PULLET
SULTAN SUSSEX BROILER POUSSIN
ROASTER ROOSTER ARAUCANA
COCKEREL
CHICKEN POX SOREHEAD VARICELLA
CHIDE FUSS RAIL RATE BLAME CHECK
SCOLD BERATE REBUFF REBUKE THREAT
CENSURE REPROVE UPBRAID WRANGLE
ADMONISH LAMBASTE REPROACH
CHIEF (ALSO SEE CHIEFTAIN) AGA BOH
CID DUX TOP AGHA ARCH BOSS CAID
COCK DEAN DUCE DUKE HEAD HIGH
INCA JARL KHAN KING MAIN MOST ONLY
RAJA ALDER ALPHA ELDER FIRST GREAT
MAJOR PRIMA PRIME RULER THANE
TITAN VITAL CABEZA DEPUTY KEHAYA
LEADER MASTER NAIQUE PRIMAL
RECTOR SHEIKH SHERIF STAPLE TOPMAN
CAPITAL CAPTAIN CENTRAL EMINENT
FOREMAN GENERAL HEADMAN LEADING
PADRONE PRELATE PREMIER PRIMARY
STELLAR SUPREME TRIBUNE CAPITANO
CARDINAL DECURION DIRECTOR
DOMINANT ESPECIAL FOREMOST
GOVERNOR HIERARCH PREMIERE
SAGAMORE STAROSTA PENDRAGON
(— IN INDIA) PRABHU SIRDAR
(— OF ADVOCATES) BATONNIER
(— OF RELIGIOUS ORDER) GENERAL
(— OF TITHING) BORSHOLDING
. (— OF 10 MEN) DEAN
(CHINOOK —) TYEE
(CLAN —) TOISECH
(INDIAN —) SUNCK SACHEM SUNCKE
CACIQUE MOCUDDUM SAGAMORE
(MOHAMMEDAN —) DATO DATTO
SAYID SAYYID
(SCHOOL —) DUX
(SCOTTISH —) MAORMOR
(TIBETAN —) POMBO
(TURKISH —) AGA AGHA
CHIEFLY MAINLY LARGELY
CHIEFTAIN BEG CHAM EMIR HEAD JARL
KHAN ASTUR CHIEF EMEER LEADER
SIRDAR CAUDILLO HIAWATHA
CHILD BOY BUD ELF GET IMP KID LAD
SON TAD TOT BABA BABE BABY BIRD
BRAT CHIT CION GIRL PAGE PUSS TINY
TOTO TROT TYKE BAIRN BIRTH CHICK

ELFIN GAMIN ISSUE SCION TRICK WHELP
CHERUB ENFANT FILIUS FOSTER INFANT
MOPPET NIPPER TODDLE URCHIN
BAMBINO GANGREL GYTLING KINCHIN
KITLING LAMBKIN PAPOOSE PRETEEN
PROGENY SUBTEEN TODDLER YOUNKER
BANTLING DAUGHTER JUVENILE
NURSLING WEANLING
(— OF THE WORLD) WELTKIND
(— UNDER 7 YEARS) INFANS
(BAD-MANNERED —) GOOP
(BAPTISMAL —) CHRISOM
(CHUBBY —) CHUNK
(ELF'S —) AUF OAF CHANGELING
(FAVORITE —) BENJAMIN
(FOSTER —) DAULT NORRY NURRY
FOSTER REARLING
(ILLEGITIMATE —) MISHAP BASTARD
(INNOCENT —) CHRISOM
(LAST-BORN —) DILLING
(LOVED —) JOY
(MERRY —) SUNBEAM
(MISCHIEVOUS —) IMP LIMB TIKE
DICKENS
(NAKED —) SCUDDY
(NEWBORN —) NEONATE STRANGER
(PAUPER —) MINDER
(PLAYFUL —) ELF WANTON
(PLUMP —) FOB FUB
(PRECOCIOUS —) PRODIGY
(PURE —) DOVE
(ROWDY —) HOODLUM
(SMALL —) TAD TOT MITE SPUD KIDDY
TIDDY TOTUM KIDLET PEEWEE TACKER
BAIRNIE
(SPOILED —) CADE COSSET WANTON
COCKNEY
(STUNTED —) URF
(TROUBLESOME —) PICKLE STICHEL
(UNMANNERLY —) SMATCHET
(YOUNG —) BABY JOEY INFANT SQUIRT
GANGREL NESTLER TODDLER BANTLING
INNOCENT LITTLING SUCKLING
(YOUNGEST —) WRIG DILLING
CHILDBIRTH LABOR INLYING TRAVAIL
OXYTOCIA
CHILDISH WEAK DANSY NAIVE PETTY
SILLY YOUNG PULING SIMPLE ASININE
BABYISH CHILDLY FOOLISH KIDDISH
PEEVISH PUERILE UNMANLY IMMATURE
CHILDLESS ORBATE

CHILE

BAY: COOK EYRE NENA TARN LOMAS
OTWAY SARCO DARWIN INUTIL MORENO
STOKES TONGOY DYNELEY INGLESA
SKYRING DESOLATE
CAPE: DYER HORN CHOROS HORNOS
QUILAN TABLAS DESEADO BASCUNAN
CARRANZA
CAPITAL: SANTIAGO
COIN: PESO LIBRA CONDOR ESCUDO
DESERT: ATACAMA
GULF: ANCUD GUAFO PENAS ARAUCO
INDIAN: ONA AUCA INCA ONAN ARAUCA

CHANGO YAHGAN FUEGIAN MAPUCHE
MOLUCHE PAMPEAN PATAGON RANQUEL
ALIKULUF PICUNCHE TSONECAN

ISLAND: LUZ PRAT BYRON GUAFO HOSTE
MOCHA NUEVA NUNEZ VIDAL CHILOE
DAWSON EASTER LENNOX PIAZZI
PICTON QUILAN RIESCO STOSCH TALCAN
ANGAMOS CAMPANA HANOVER REFUGIO
TRANQUI CLARENCE HUAMBLIN
NALCAYEC NAVARINO TRAIGUEN

ISTHMUS: OFQUI

LAKE: TORO RANCO YELCHO PUYEHUE
RUPANCO

MOUNTAIN: MACA TORO CHATO MAIPO
PAINE POTRO PULAR TORRE YOGAN
APIWAN BURNEY CONICO JERVIS
POQUIS RINCON CHALTEL COPIAPO
FITZROY PALPANA VELLUDA COCHRANE
TRONADOR YANTELES

MOUNTAINS: ANDES DARWIN ALMEIDA
DOMEYKO

PENINSULA: HARDY LACUY TAITAO
TUMBES

PORT: LOTA TOME ARICA COQUIMBO

PROVINCE: AISEN ARICA AYSEN MAULE
NUBLE TALCA ARAUCO BIOBIO CAUTIN
CHILOE CURICO OSORNO ATACAMA
LINARES MALLECO COQUIMBO OHIGGINS
SANTIAGO TARAPACA VALDIVIA

RIVER: LOA LAJA YALI ALHUE AZAPA
BRAVO BUENO ELQUI ITATA LAUCA
LLUTA MAIPO MAULE PUELO RAHUE
RAPEL VITOR BIOBIO CAMINA CHOAPA
CHOROS CISNES COLINA HUASCO
LIMARI MORADO PALENA POSCUA
TOLTEN COPIAPO VALDIVIA

TOWN: BOCO CUYA LEBU LOTA OCOA
TOCO TOME ARICA TALCA ARAUCO
CURICO GATICO OSORNO SERENA
TEMUCO VICUNA YUMBEL YUNGAY
CALDERA CHILLAN COPIAPO COQUIMBO
RANCAGUA SANTIAGO VALDIVIA

VOLCANO: LANIN MAIPO ANTUCO
LASCAR LLAIMA OSORNO OYAHUE
TACORA LAUTARO PETEROA SOCOMAP
VILLARICA GUALLATIRI

CHILL ICE RAW AGUE COLD COOL ALGOR
GELID RIGOR SHAKE FRAPPE FREEZE
FRIGID FROSTY SHIVER FRISSON

CHILLING ICY COLD BLEAK EERIE NIPPY
CHILLY WINTRY GLACIAL NIPPING
SHIVERY

CHILLY RAW COLD COOL LASH ALGID
BLEAK NIPPY AGUISH AIRISH ARCTIC
FROSTY FROZEN

CHIME DIN BELL PEAL RING TING TINK
AGREE ACCORD CLOCHE CYMBAL JINGLE
MELODY CONCORD HARMONY SINGSONG

CHIMERA FANCY MIRAGE MOSAIC
POMATO ILLUSION

CHIMERICAL VAIN WILD INSANE
UTOPIAN DELUSIVE FANCIFUL ROMANTIC
IMAGINARY

CHIMNEY BAG LUM TUN FLUE PIPE TUBE
VENT STACK TEWEL FUNNEL LOUVER

TUNNEL FISSURE OPENING ORIFICE
FUMIDUCT SMOKESTACK

CHIMPANZEE APE CHIMP JACKO JOCKO
PYGMY NCHEGA

CHIN JAW CHAT TSIN MENTUM CHOLLER
(— **POINT**) MENTON POGONION
(**DOUBLE —**) BUCCULA CHOLLER

CHINA WARE JAPAN LENOX SPODE
CATHAY PARIAN SEVRES CERAMIC
DRESDEN LIMOGES MEISSEN POTTERY
CINCHONA CROCKERY EGGSHELL
EGGSHELL

CHINA

ABORIGINE: YAO MANS MIAO MANTZU
YAOMIN MIAOTSE

BAY: LAICHOW HANGCHOW

CAPITAL: PEKING TAIPEI PEIPING

COIN: PU CASH CENT MACE TAEL TIAO
YUAN CHIAO SYCEE DOLLAR

DESERT: GOBI ORDOS SHAMO ALASHAN
TAKLAMAKAN

DYNASTY: WU HAN SHU SUI WEI YIN
CHIN CHOU HSIA HSIN MING SUNG TANG
YUAN CHING SHANG

GULF: POHAI CHIHLI TONKIN PECHILI
LIAOTUNG

ISLAND: AMOY FLAT MACAO MATSU
NAMKI CHUSAN HAINAN PRATAS
QUEMOY TAIWAN YUHWAN FORMOSA
HUNGTOW TUNGSHA CHOUCHAN
KULANGSU STAUNTON

LAKE: TAI CHAO KAOYU OLING TELLI
BAMTSO BORNOR EBINOR ERHHAI
KHANKA LOPNOR NAMTSO POYANG
CHALING HUNGTSE KARANOR KOKONOR
HULUNNOR MONTCALM TAROKTSO
TELLINOR TIENCHIH TSINGHAI TUNGTING

MOUNTAIN: OMI OMEI SUNG KAILAS
POBEDA EVEREST MUZTABH SUNGSHAN

MOUNTAINS: ALTAY KUNLUN ALASHAN
KUENLUN MEILING MINSHAN NANLING
NANSHAN TANGLHA BOGDOULA
HIMALAYA TAPASHAN TAYULING
TIENSHAN WUYLISHAN

NATIVE: PAT

PORT: AMOY WUHU AIGUN SHASI
ANTUNG CANTON CHEFOO DAIREN
ICHANG NINGPO PAKHOI SWATOW
SZEMAO WUCHOW YOCHOW FOOCHOW
HUNCHUN MENGTSZ NANKING SAMSHUI
SANTUAO SOOCHOW WENCHOW
CHANGSHA HANGCHOW KIUKIANG
KONGMOON LUNGCHOW SHANGHAI
TENGYUEH TIENTSIN TSINGTAO
WANHSIEN

PROVINCE: HONAN HOPEI HUNAN HUPEI
HUPEN JEHOL KANSU KIRIN TIBET
ANHWEI FUKIEN SHANSI SHENSI
TAIWAN YUNNAN KIANGSI KWANGSI
NGANHUI CHEKIANG KWEICHOW
LIAONING MONGOLIA SHANTUNG
SZECHWAN TSINGHAI MANCHURIA

RESERVOIR: SUNGARI

RIVER: SI HAN ILI MIN NEN PEI WEI AMUR

HUAI LOHO TUNG YALU YUAN YUEN
ARGUN FENHO MACHU PEIHO TARIM
TUMEN WEIHO CHUMAR DRECHU
DZACHU KHOTAN KUMARA LIAOHO
MANASS MEKONG OCHINA URUNGU
YELLOW HOANGHO HWANGHO KERULEN
KIALING SALWEEN SIKIANG SUNGARI
TSANGPO WUKIANG YANGTZE YARKAND
YUKIANG CHERCHEN HANKIANG
HUNGSHUI MINKIANG
SEA: ECHINA SCHINA YELLOW
STRAIT: HAINAN TAIWAN FORMOSA
TOWN: BAI NOH AHPA AMOY ANSI ANTA
AQSU FUYU GUMA HAMI HUMA IPIN
KIAN KISI LINI LOHO LUTA MOHO MOYU
MULI NIYA NOHO NURA OMIN OWPU
RIMA SAKA SIAN TALI TAYU WUHU
WUSU WUTU YAAN CHIAI FUSIN HOFEI
ICHUN JEHOL KIRIN KOKLU LHASA
MACAO PENKI SHASI TAIAN TALAI TUTZE
TUYUN TZEPO WUHAN WUSIH YENKI
YULIN YUMEN ANSHAN ANTUNG
CANTON CHENDU DAIREN FUCHAU
FUSHUN HANKOW HANTAN HARBIN
HOIHOW KALGAN LOYANG LUSHUN
MUKDEN NINGPO PAOTOW PEKING
PENGPU SUCHOW SWATOW TAINAN
TAIPEI TALIEN TSINAN YUNNAN
CHUNGTU FATSHAN FOOCHOW
HANYANG HUHEHOT KAIFENG KUNMING
KWEISUI LANCHOW NANKING PAOTING
PEIPING SOOCHOW TAIYUAN TIANJIN
TZEKUNG URUMCHI WUCHANG YENPING
CHANGSHA CHAOCHOW CHENGTEH
CHINCHOW HANGCHOW KIAOCHOW
KWEIYANG NANCHANG QARAQASH
SHANGHAI SHENYANG SIANGTAN
TANGSHAN TENGCHOW TIENTSIN
TSINGTAO TUNGCHOW CHUNGKING

CHINCHILLA ABROCOME VIZCACHA
CHINK GAP CASH RENT RIFT SCAR CLEFT
CRACK CRANNY RICTUS CREVICE
FISSURE APERTURE
CHIP BIT CUT DIB HEW NIG CLIP HACK
KNAP NICK SNIP SNUB FLAKE PIECE
SCRAP SKELF SLICE SPALE SPALL
WASTE CHISEL GALLET MARKER
SHAVING COSSETTE FRAGMENT
SPLINTER WHITLING
(— OF WOOD) SPOON
(— OUT) DESEAM
(BUFFALO —S) BODEWASH
(CORN —S) FRITOS
(POTATO —) CRISP
(SUPPLY OF —S) STACK
CHIPMUNK CHIPPY GOPHER HACKEE
GRINNIE SQUIRREL
CHIPPER GAY SPRY CHIRP PERKY LIVELY
CHIRRUP TWITTER CHEERFUL
CHIROPODIST PEDICURE CORNCUTTER
CHIRP PIP PEEK PEEP PIPE PULE TWIT
CHEEP CHIRK CHIRM CHIRT TWEET
TWINK CHIPPER CHIRRUP CHITTER
TWITTER WHEETLE WHITTER
CHISEL BUR CUT GAD CHIP ETCH FORM

MOIL PARE SEAT SETT TANG BURIN
CARVE CHEAT GOUGE HARDY SCOOP
SLICK STIFF BROACH FORMER QUARRY
REAMER CHIPPER ENGRAVE GRUBBER
SCOOPER
(BLACKSMITH'S —) HARDIE
(FLINT —) TRANCHET
(ICE —) SPUD
(JEWELER'S —) SCAUPER SCORPER
(PREHISTORIC —) CELT
(STONEMASON'S —) TOOL DROVE
POMMEL TOOLER SPLITTER
(TOOTHED —) GRADINE
(TRIANGULAR —) BUR
(WHEELWRIGHT'S —) BRUZZ
CHISELER CHEAT CROOK COYOTE
GOUGER
CHIT DAB TAB BILL NOTE DRAFT LETTER
VOUCHER
CHITCHAT GAB GASH GUFF TALK
BANTER GOSSIP BAVARDAGE
CHIVALROUS BRAVE CIVIL NOBLE
PREUX GENTLE POLITE GALLANT
GENTEEL VALIANT WARLIKE KNIGHTLY
CHLORIS (BROTHER OF —) AMYCLAS
(FATHER OF —) AMPHION
(HUSBAND OF —) NELEUS ZEPHYRUS
(MOTHER OF —) NIOBE
(SON OF —) NESTOR
CHOCK COG PAD BLOCK BRACE CHUCK
CLEAT SPOKE SPRAG WEDGE SCOTCH
(PL.) STOWWOOD
CHOCOLATE BUD CANDY COCOA
NORFOLK JACOLATT
CHOICE BET ODD TRY BEST FINE FORE
GOOD MIND PICK RARE WALE WILL
CREAM ELITE PRIME VOICE CHOSEN
DAINTY DESIRE FLOWER OPTION PICKED
PLUMMY SELECT DILEMMA ELEGANT
DELICATE ELECTION UNCOMMON
VOLITION PREFERENCE
CHOIR CHAPEL CHORUS CHORALE
CONCERT KAPELLE PSALMODY
CHOIR LEADER CANTOR CHORAGUS
CHORISTER PRECENTOR
CHOKE DAM GAG GOB CLOG DAMP PLUG
STOP CHECK CHOCK CLOSE SCRAG
ACCLOY HINDER IMPEDE STIFLE
CONGEST REPRESS SILENCE SMOLDER
SMOTHER OBSTRUCT STRANGLE
SUPPRESS THROTTLE
CHOLER IRE BILE FURY RAGE ANGER
WRATH SPLEEN TEMPER DISTEMPER
CHOLERIC MAD ANGRY CROSS FIERY
HUFFY TESTY FUMISH IREFUL TOUCHY
BILIOUS ENRAGED IRACUND PEEVISH
PEPPERY WASPISH WRATHFUL
IMPATIENT
CHOOSE OPT TRY CULL LIKE LIST LOVE
LUST PICK TAKE VOTE WALE ADOPT
ELECT ANOINT DECIDE PLEASE PREFER
SELECT EMBRACE ESPOUSE EXTRACT
SEPARATE
CHOOSY PICKY CHOICY FINICAL
CHOP AX AXE CUT HAG HEW JAW LOP
CHAP CHIP DICE GASH HACK HASH RIVE
SLIT CARVE CLEFT CRACK KNOCK NOTCH

SLASH STAMP TRADE TRUCK WHANG
BARTER CHANGE CLEAVE INCISE
EXCHANGE
(— OFF) SNIG
(— SMALL) DEVIL MINCE
(— UP) HACKLE
(— WITH DULL AX) BUTTE
(DOG'S —) FLEW
(PORK —) GRISKIN
CHOPPY BUMPY LUMPY ROUGH SHORT
CHORD DYAD ROLL TONE NERVE TRIAD
TRINE ACCORD STRING TENDON TETRAD
CADENCE CONCORD HARMONY
ARPEGGIO DIAMETER SFORZANDO
CHORE JOB JOT CHAR DUTY TASK
KNACK STINT ERRAND BUSINESS
CHORUS SONG CHOIR DRONE ACCORD
ASSENT BURDEN UNISON CHORALE
REFRAIN RESPONSE
(— IN PLAY) GREX
CHOSEN ELECT ELITE SORTED ELECTED
FANCIED AFFECTED SELECTED
CHRIST KING LORD TRUE JUDGE RANSOM
VERITY MESSIAH SAVIOUR DRIGHTEN
PARAMOUR
(INFANT —) BAMBINO
CHRISTEN NAME KIRSEN BAPTIZE
CHRISTMAS NOEL YULE HOLIDAY
NATIVITY YULETIDE MIDWINTER
CHROMOSOME DYAD IDANT HOMOLOG
ALLOSOME AUTOSOME IDIOSOME
MONOSOME KARYOMERE LEPTONEMA
PLANOSOME
CHRONIC FIXED SEVERE INTENSE
CONSTANT STUBBORN
CHRONICLE BRUT ANNAL DIARY ENACT
RECORD ACCOUNT HISTORY RECITAL
CORNICLE REGISTER
(PL.) ANNALS ARCHIVE PARALIPOMENON
CHRONOLOGICAL TEMPORAL
CHRONOMETER DIAL HACK CLOCK
TIMER WATCH
CHRYSALIS KELL PUPA AURELIA
CHRYSANTHEMUM MUM KIKU OXEYE
SPOON BRUTUS POMPON KIKUMON
KIRIMON AZALEAMUM PYRETHRUM
MARGUERITE
CHUBBY FAT FUBSY PLUMP PUDGY
CHUFFY ROTUND ROLYPOLY
CHUCK HEN LOG PIG CHUG GRUB HURL
JERK LUMP TOSS CHOCK CLUCK PITCH
THROW BOUNCE COLLET DISCARD
CHUCKLE CLUCK EXULT LAUGH GIGGLE
KECKLE SMUDGE TITTER CHORTLE
CHUM CAD PAL BAIT MATE PARD TOLL
BUDDY CRONY AIKANE COBBER COPAIN
FRIEND PARDNER ROOMMATE
(— AROUND) HOBNOB
CHUMMY GREAT MATEY PALLY
FAMILIAR
CHUMP ASS DOLT HEAD BLOCK PUMPKIN
SCHLEMIEL
CHUNK DAB FID GOB PAT WAD SLUG
CHOCK CHUCK PIECE WHANG GOBBET
DORNICK
CHUNKY LUMPY PLUMP SQUAT STOUT
THICK TRUSS BLOCKY CHUBBY STOCKY

CHURCH SEE DOME FANE HIGH KIRK
TERA ABBEY AUTEM FAITH FLOCK KOVIL
SAMAJ TITLE BETHEL CHAPEL CHARGE
HIERON TEMPLE EDIFICE FANACLE
IGLESIA LATERAN MEMORIA MINSTER
ORATORY RECTORY BASILICA EBENEZER
ECCLESIA
CHURCHMAN KIRKMAN
(HIGH —) PUSEYITE PRELATIST
(LOW —) SIM LOWBOY SIMEONITE
CHURL CAD BOOR CARL HIND LOUT SERF
KNAVE BODACH LUBBER RUSTIC VASSAL
YEOMAN BONDMAN FREEMAN HUSBAND
PEASANT VILLEIN CURMUDGEON
CHURLISH MEAN BLUFF GRUFF ROUGH
RUNTY SURLY URSAL CRABBY RUSTIC
SORDID SULLEN VULGAR BOORISH
CARLISH CRABBED INCIVIL PEEVISH
CHURN BOIL KIRN MOIL STIR SHAKE
BUBBLE SEETHE AGITATE
CHUTE RUSH SLIP TUBE FLUME HURRY
RAPID SLIDE HOPPER TROUGH DECLINE
DESCENT DOWNFALL
CICERONE GUIDE PILOT MENTOR
ORATOR COURIER SIGHTSMAN
CID HERO CAMPEADOR
(AUTHOR OF —) CORNEILLE
(CHARACTER IN —) GOMES DIEGUE
SANCHE CHIMENE FERNAND URRAQUE
RODRIGUE
CIDER PERRY PERKIN SWANKY SYDDIR
POMMAGE SCRUMPY BEVERAGE
COCCAGEE
(HARD —) APPLEJACK
(INFERIOR —) SWANKY
CIGAR PURO TOBY WEED BREVA CLARO
SEGAR SHUCK SMOKE CONCHA CORONA
HAVANA MADURO MANILA STOGIE
TWOFER CHEROOT CULEBRA LONDRES
REGALIA TRABUCO COLORADO
LOCOFOCO PANATELA PERFECTO
PICKWICK PURITANO
CIGARETTE CIG FAG BUTT PILL SKAG
CUBEB JOINT SHUCK SMOKE GASPER
REEFER CIGARITO
(— BUTT) ROACH
(MARIHUANA —) JOINT STICK
CINCH BELT GIRD GRIP PIPE SNAP GIRTH
GRAVY BREEZE FASTEN PIANOLA
SINECURE
CINDER ASH TAP COAL GRAY SCAR SLAG
CHARK DROSS EMBER SCORIA CLINKER
RESIDUE
(REFUSE —) BREEZE
(VOLCANIC —) LAPILLUS
(PL.) GLEEDS
CINNAMON CANEL SPICE CASSIA
SANELA STACTE CANELLA BARBASCO
(WILD —) BAYBERRY
CIPHER KEY NIL CODE NULL ZERO AUGHT
OUGHT DECODE DEVICE FIGURE LETTER
NAUGHT NOUGHT NUMBER SYMBOL
NULLITY MONOGRAM
CIRCE SIREN TEMPTER
(BROTHER OF —) AEETES
(FATHER OF —) SOL
(LOVER OF —) ULYSSES ODYSSEUS

(MOTHER OF —) PERSE
(SON OF —) TELEGONUS
CIRCLE DOT LAP ORB CULT DISK GYRE
HALO HOOP IRIS LOOP MARU RING RINK
ROLL TOUR TURN ZONE BLACK CAROL
CLASS CROWN CYCLE GROUP MONDE
ORBIT PEARL REALM RHOMB ROUND
ROWEL SWIRL TWIRL BEZANT CIRCUS
CIRQUE CLIQUE COLLET COLURE
CORDON CORONA DIADEM GIRDLE
RONDEL ROTATE SPIRAL CIRCLET
CIRCUIT COMPANY COMPASS CORONET
COTERIE ENCLOSE HORIZON REVOLVE
SURROUND
(— AROUND ORGAN) ANNULET
(— IN BULL'S-EYE) CARTON
(— OF FRIED DOUGH) POPADUM
(— OF HELL) MALEBOLGE
(— OF MONOLITHS) CROMLECH
(— TRACED BY HORSE) VOLT
(ASTRONOMICAL —) EQUANT
EPICYCLE
(DANCE —) GALLEY
(FAIRY —) RINGLET
(GREAT —) EQUATOR ECLIPTIC
MERIDIAN
(IMAGINARY —) CYCLE DEFERENT
(INNER —) BOSOM
(MYSTIC —) MANDALA
(PARHELIC —) FROSTBOW
(QUARTER —) ARC
(STONE —) CAROL HURLER GORSEDD
CROMLECH
(TRAVERSE —) RACER
(TWO —S) CACHET
CIRCLET BAND HALO HOOP RING CROWN
RIGOL VERGE BANGLE CIRQUE CORONA
WREATH CIRCUIT CORONET VALLARY
BRACELET HEADBAND
CIRCUIT LAP AREA BOUT EYRE ITER LOOP
TOUR WEND ZONE AMBIT CHAIN CYCLE
ORBIT ROUND ROUTE VIRON AMBAGE
CIRCLE DETOUR DOUBLE SPHERE
UMGANG ZODIAC ADAPTER ADDRESS
COMARCA COMPASS COUNTER DIOCESE
DISTRICT
CIRCUITOUS MAZY CURVED CROOKED
DEVIOUS OBLIQUE SINUOUS TWISTED
VAGRANT WINDING FLEXUOUS INDIRECT
RAMBLING TORTUOUS AMBAGIOUS
DECEITFUL DEVIATING WANDERING
ROUNDABOUT
CIRCULAR BILL FLIER ORBAL ORBED
ROUND DODGER FOLDER RINGED
ANNULAR COMPASS CYCLOID DISCOID
HANDOUT RUNDLED ENCYCLIC
GLOBULAR INFINITE NUMMULAR
PAMPHLET DOPESHEET ORBICULAR
CIRCULATE GO AIR MIX MOVE PASS
RISE TURN WALK WIND BANDY TROLL
CANARD PURVEY ROTATE SCURRY
SPHERE SPREAD WANDER CANVASS
CONVECT DIFFUSE PUBLISH CONVOLVE
CIRCULATION ISSUE COURSE
COVERAGE CURRENCY
CIRCUMFERENCE ARC AUGE AMBIT
APSIS GIRTH VERGE BORDER BOUNDS

CIRCLE LIMITS COMPASS BOUNDARY
SURROUND
(— OF SHELL) LIMBUS
CIRCUMLOCUTION AMBAGE CIRCUIT
WINDING VERBIAGE
CIRCUMSCRIBE BOUND FENCE LIMIT
DEFINE CAPTURE CONFINE ENCLOSE
ENVIRON ENCIRCLE RESTRAIN RESTRICT
SURROUND CONSCRIBE
CIRCUMSPECT SHY WARY WISE ALERT
CHARY CAREFUL GUARDED PRUDENT
CAUTIOUS DISCREET VIGILANT
WATCHFUL
CIRCUMSPECTION RESPECT PRUDENCE
WARINESS
CIRCUMSTANCE CASE FACT ITEM
NOTE EVENT PHASE POINT START STATE
THING AFFAIR DETAIL FACTOR PICKLE
CALLING ELEMENT EPISODE INCIDENT
INSTANCE POSITION OCCURRENCE
PARTICULAR
(CRITICAL —S) EXTREMES
(EXECRABLE —) ATROCITY
(LUDICROUS —) JEST
(PL.) CIRCS STATE TERMS ESTATE
FORTUNE
CIRCUMSTANTIAL EXACT FORMAL
MINUTE PRECISE DETAILED ITEMIZED
PARTICULAR
CIRCUMVENT BALK BEAT DISH DUPE
FOIL CHEAT CHECK COZEN EVADE
OUTGO TRICK BAFFLE DELUDE ENTRAP
NOBBLE OUTWIT THWART CAPTURE
DECEIVE DEFRAUD ENSNARE PREVENT
OUTFLANK SURROUND UNDERFONG
CIRCUS RING SHOW ARENA CANVAS
CIRCLE CIRQUE CARNIVAL
(— LOT) TOBER
(— RING) TAN
CISTERCIAN TRAPPIST
CISTERN BAC SAC TUB URN VAT BACK
SUMP TANK URNA WELL LAVER CAVITY
CAISSON CHULTUN CUVETTE STEEPER
FEEDHEAD
CITADEL ARX FORT HALL ALAMO BYRSA
TOWER CASTLE BOROUGH CHESTER
KREMLIN ALHAMBRA FASTNESS
FORTRESS TOOTHILL ACROPOLIS
CITATION CITAL NOTICE MENTION
SUMMONS EPIGRAPH MONITION
AUTHORITY EVOCATION
CITE CALL NAME SIST TELL ALLAY EVOKE
QUOTE REFER ACCUSE ADDUCE ALLEGE
AROUSE AVOUCH EXCITE INVOKE
NOTIFY RECITE REPEAT SUMMON
ADVANCE ARRAIGN BESPEAK EXCERPT
EXTRACT IMPEACH MENTION INDICATE
INSTANCE REHEARSE
CITIZEN CIT ALLY VOTER NATIVE
BURGESS BURGHER CITOYEN CLERUCH
DENIZEN ELECTOR FLATCAP FREEMAN
OPPIDAN SUBJECT TOWNMAN CIVILIAN
COMMONER CONSCIVE DOMESTIC
NATIONAL OCCUPANT RESIDENT
(— OF SECOND CLASS) KNIGHT
HIPPEUS
(—S OF MEDINA) ANSAR

(FOREIGN-BORN —) ALIEN
CITRON LIME CEDRA LEMON CEDRAT
ETHROG YELLOW BERGAMOT
CITY FU WON BURG DORP TOWN URBS
ZION BURGH PIECE PLACE POLIS STEAD
VILLE CENTER CIUDAD STAPLE CHESTER
FREEDOM
(CAPITAL —) SEAT
(CHIEF —) CAPITAL CABECERA
MEGAPOLIS
(RICH —) MAGAZINE
(TREASURE —) RAAMSES
(WICKED —) BABYLON
CIVET CAT CIT GENET RASSE ZIBET
BONDAR FOUSSA MUSANG PAGUMA
CIVETTA FOSSANE LINSANG NANDINE
POLECAT ZINSANG FANALOKA
MONGOOSE TANGALUNG
CIVIC LAY CIVIL SUAVE URBAN POLITE
URBANE CIVICAL SECULAR
CIVIL FAIR HEND SUAVE POLITE URBANE
AFFABLE AMIABLE COURTLY ELEGANT
GALLANT POLITIC REFINED SECULAR
DISCREET GRACIOUS OBLIGING
POLISHED WELLBRED
CIVILIAN CIT CIVVY MOHAIR CITIZEN
TEACHER CIVILIST GOWNSMAN
CIVILITY BONTE COURT COMITY NOTICE
AMENITY COURTESY URBANITY
GENTILITY
CIVILIZATION KULTUR POLICE CULTURE
ECUMENE CIVILITY
CIVILIZE TAME TEACH TRAIN POLISH
REFINE EDUCATE HUMANIZE URBANIZE
CLAD DREST ROBED BESEEN CLEDDE
DECKED ADORNED ARRAYED ATTIRED
CLOTHED COVERED DRESSED SHEATHED
(— IN PURPLE) PORPORATE
(SCANTILY —) SINGLY
CLAIM ASK DUE AVER AVOW CALL CASE
DIBS LIEN PLEA DRAFT PLEAD RIGHT
TITLE ASSERT DEMAND DESIRE ELICIT
EQUITY INTEND RECKON PRETEND
PRETEXT PROFESS SOLICIT ARROGATE
MAINTAIN PRETENSE CHALLENGE
(— IN BUSINESS) CAPITAL
(— TO BE BELIEVED) AUTHORITY
(FALSE —) JACTATION
(FORESTER'S —) PUTURE
(INDIAN LEGAL —) HAK HAKH
(MINING —) SHICER
CLAIRVOYANCE INSIGHT LUCIDITY
SAGACITY TELOPSIS PRECOGNITION
CLAIRVOYANT FEY SEER OMENER
PROPHET SEERESS
CLAM MYA DAUB HUSH GAPER GLAUM
PAHUA RAZOR SHELL SOLEN STICK
ADHERE GWEDUC QUAHOG COQUINA
MOLLUSK STEAMER BULLNOSE
(PART OF —) BEAK FOOT SHELL VALVE
MANTLE SIPHON UMBONE ORIFICE
CLAMBER CLIMB SCALE SPRAWL
RAMMACK SCRABBLE SCRAMBLE
CLAMMY DAMP DANK SOFT WACK
MOIST SAMMY STICKY WAUGHY
FLACCID SQUIDGY
CLAMOR CRY DIN HUE BARK ROAR ROUP

ROUT SONG UTAS WAIL BLARE BOAST
BRUIT CHIRM NOISE OUTAS SHOUT
BELLOW BOWWOW HUBBUB OUTCRY
RACKET TUMULT UPROAR YATTER
(— AGAINST) DECRY
CLAMOROUS LOUD NOISY VOCAL
BLATANT DINSOME BRAWLING
OBSTREPEROUS
CLAMP DOG HOG LUG NIP PIN SET BAIL
BEND BOLT GRIP JACK NAIL VISE YOKE
BLOCK BRACE CLASP CRAMP HORSE
CLINCH FASTEN FASTENER HOLDFAST
(— FOR BASS DRUM) SPUR
(— FOR CORK) AGRAFE
(— FOR FLASK) GLAND
(— ON TUBE) PINCHCOCK
(STORAGE —) GRAVE
CLAN ATI HAN KIN SET SIB CULT GENS
HAPU NAME RACE SECT SEPT SIOL UNIT
AIMAK AYLLU CLASS GENOS GROUP
HORDE PARTY TRIBE CLIQUE FAMILY
KINDRED PHRATRY SOCIETY DIVISION
(— SUBDIVISION) OBE
CLANDESTINE SLY FOXY PRIVY QUIET
SNEAK COVERT HIDDEN SECRET
BOOTLEG FURTIVE ILLICIT BACKDOOR
STEALTHY
CLANG DIN DING PEAL RING CLANK
CLASH NOISE JANGLE TIMBRE
CLANGOR DIN CLAM ROAR CLANG
HUBBUB UPROAR
CLAP BANG FLAP PEAL SLAP SPAT CHEER
CRACK SMITE STRIKE STROKE APPLAUD
PLAUDIT HANDCLAP
(— OF THUNDER) DINT
(— ON) CRACK
CLAPTRAP HOKUM TRASH TRIPE
BLAGUE BUNKUM EYEWASH FUSTIAN
BUNCOMBE NONSENSE TRICKERY
CLARET TERSE PONTAC LAFITTE
BORDEAUX BADMINTON
CLARIFY FINE CLEAN CLEAR PURGE
SNUFF PURIFY REFINE RENDER SERENE
SETTLE CLEANSE EXPLAIN GLORIFY
DEPURATE ELIQUATE SIMPLIFY
CLARINET BONE REED AULOS CLARY
PUNGI CLARONE LAUNEDDAS
(PART OF —) KEY PAD BELL CORK REED
CLAMP COVER BARREL LIGATURE
MOUTHPIECE FINGERPLATE
CLARISSA HARLOWE
(AUTHOR OF —) RICHARDSON
(CHARACTER IN —) HOWE JOHN
JAMES MORDEN ROBERT SOLMES
BELFORD HARLOWE WILLIAM ARABELLA
CLARISSA LOVELACE SINCLAIR
CLARITY GLORY SPLENDOR STRENGTH
CLEARNESS SIMPLICITY
CLASH JAR BANG BOLT BUMP DASH
FRAY SLAM BRAWL BRUNT CHECK
CRASH CROSS FIGHT KNOCK SHOCK
DIFFER HURTLE IMPACT JOSTLE STRIFE
STRIKE THRUST THWART COLLIDE
DISCORD ARGUMENT CONFLICT
CLASP HUG PIN CLIP FOLD GRAB GRIP
HASP HOLD HOOK HOOP KEEP OUCH
STAY BRACE CATCH CLING GRASP SEIZE

SLIDE AGRAFE BROOCH BUCKLE CLENCH
CLUTCH ENFOLD ENWRAP FASTEN
FIBULA EMBRACE ENTWINE BARRETTE
CORSELET FASTENER SURROUND

CLASS ILK FORM KIND RACE RANK RATE
SECT SORT SUIT TYPE YEAR BREED
CASTE GENRE GENUS GRADE GROUP
ORDER RANGE TRIBE CIRCLE CLINIC
FAMILY LEAGUE MISTER NATION
PHYLUM RATING STRAIN STRIPE
CATALOG FACTION LECTURE REGIMEN
SEMINAR SPECIES VARIETY CATEGORY
DESCRIBE DIVISION GENOTYPE
(— OF BARDS) THULIR
(— OF GOODS) BRAND
(— OF OUTCASTS) ETA
(— OF SHASTRAS) SRUTI SHRUTI
(— OF TEASELS) KINGS
(ARISTOCRATIC —) ARISTOI
(CHOICEST —) ROBUR
(DEPRESSED —) PANCHAMA
(FIRST —) GAY
(HEREDITARY —) CASTE
(JAPANESE —) HEIMIN KWAZOKU
(LABORING —) PARAIYAN
PROLETARIAT
(LEARNED —) VATES CLERISY
(LOWER —) BELOW GENTE
(LOWEST —) LAG SCUM
(PEASANT —) JACQUERIE
(SLAVEHOLDING —) CHIVALRY
(SOCIAL —) ESTATE SHIZOKU

CLASSIC VINTAGE AUGUSTAN

CLASSICAL PURE ATTIC GREEK LATIN
ROMAN ACADEMIC HELLENIC

CLASSIFICATION FILE RANK RATE SORT
GENRE GENUS GRADE ORDER TAXIS
RATING SYSTEM ANALYSIS CATEGORY
DIVISION TAXONOMY BREAKDOWN

CLASSIFIED SECRET

CLASSIFY CODE LIST RANK RATE SIZE
SORT SUIT TYPE DRAFT GRADE GROUP
LABEL RANGE ASSORT CODIFY DIGEST
DIVIDE ARRANGE BRACKET BRIGADE
CATALOG DISPOSE MARSHAL REGISTER
PIGEONHOLE

CLATTER DIN JAR CLACK NOISE RUMOR
BABBLE GABBLE GOSSIP RATTLE TATTLE
CHATTER CLUTTER PRATTLE

CLAUSE ITEM PART CLOSE PLANK RIDER
SALVO TROPE MEMBER PHRASE
ADJUNCT ARTICLE PASSAGE PROVISO
SLEEPER APODOSIS PARTICLE PETITION
SENTENCE
(— IN CREED) FILIOQUE
(— IN WRIT) TESTE
(— OF WILL) DEVISE
(ADDITIONAL —) RIDER
(SUBORDINATE —) PROTASIS

CLAVICHORD CLAVIER MANICORD
UNICHORD CLARIGOLD MONOCHORD

CLAVICLE FURCULE COLLARBONE

CLAW DIG CRAB FANG HAND HOOK NAIL
PULL TEAR CHELA COURT GRASP SEIZE
TALON CLUTCH NIPPER POUNCE SCRAPE
SINGLE UNGUIS UNGULA SCRATCH
WHEEDLE SCRABBLE

CLAY BAT PUG WAD BODY BOLE GLEY
LOAM LUTE MARL MIRE ARGIL BRICK
CLOAM EARTH LOESS OCHRE PASTE
RABAT BINDER CLEDGE KAOLIN PUDDLE
SAGGER DAUBING CAMSTONE CIMOLITE
FIRECLAY LATERITE LIFELESS
(— FOR MELTING POTS) TASCO
(— IN GLASS) TEAR
(— IRON) BULL
(— USED MEDICALLY) FANGO
(HARD —) BEND
(HARDENED —) METAL
(INDURATED —) BASS CLUNCH
(PIECE OF FIRED —) TILE
(PIPE —) CAMSTONE
(POTTER'S —) SLIP ARGIL PETUNTSE
(SURPLUS —) SPARE
(TOUGH —) LECK
(3-ARMED, HARD-FIRED —) STILT

CLEAN DO MOP NET DUST FAIR NEAT
PURE REDD RIPE SIDE SMUG SWAB TRIM
WASH WIPE CLEAR CURRY EMPTY FEIGH
SCOUR SCRUB SMART SWEEP TERSE
CHASTE CLEVER KOSHER PURIFY
APINOID BANDBOX CHAMOIS CLEANSE
CLEARLY FURBISH PERFECT SWINGLE
ABSTERGE BACKWASH BRIGHTLY
DEXTROUS ENTIRELY RENOVATE
SCAVENGE SPOTLESS UNSOILED
(— A FUR) DRUM
(— A QUILL) DUTCH
(— BOAT) CAREEN
(— BY SCRAPING) GRAVE
(— BY SMOKE) SMEEK
(— CANNON) SCALE
(— FIREARM) WORM
(— FLAX) SWINGLE
(— IN ACID) BLANCH
(— OUT) USH SPEAR
(— SHIP'S BOTTOM) HOG BREAM
GRAVE
(— UP) DISPATCH
(RITUALLY —) KOSHER

CLEANER SOAP BORAX PURER RAMROD
FLUEMAN SPOTTER CLEANSER

CLEANLY PURE CLEAN ADROIT ARTFUL
CHASTE FAIRLY CORRECT ELEGANT
INNOCENT SKILLFUL

CLEANSE CARD COMB HEAL PICK SOAP
WASH BROOM BRUSH CLEAN CLEAR
DIGHT DRESS FEIGH FLAME FLUSH
PURGE RINSE SCOUR SCRUB SNUFF
PICKLE PURIFY REFINE SPONGE BAPTIZE
CLARIFY DETERGE EXPIATE LAUNDER
ABSTERGE DEPURATE RENOVATE
SCAVENGE SPRINKLE

CLEANSER LYE SOAP CLEANER PURIFIER
DETERGENT DETERSIVE

CLEANSING BATH FLUSH ABLUENT
CLYSMIC WASHING ABLUTION CLEANING
LAVATION DETERGENT MENDATORY
ABSTERGENT
(CEREMONIAL —) LAVABO PURGATION

CLEAR HOT JAM NET RID WAY CAST
EASY FAIR FINE FLAT FREE GAIN GRUB
JUMP NEAT OPEN OVER PURE QUIT REDD
RIFE SHUT SLAM VOID ACUTE ATRIP

AZURE BREAK BREME BRENT BROAD
CHUCK CLEAN CRISP DRIVE LIGHT LUCID
NAKED PLAIN PRINT PRUNE SCOUR
SHARP SMOLT SUNNY SWEEP VIVID
ACQUIT AERIAL ASSOIL BRIGHT CANDID
CLEVER EXCUSE EXEMPT LIMPID LIQUID
LUCENT PATENT PURIFY SERENE SETTLE
SHRILL SMOOTH UNSTOP ABSOLVE
CAPITAL CLARIFY CLARION CRYSTAL
DELIVER DILUCID EVIDENT EXPLAIN
EXPRESS GLARING GRAPHIC LIGHTEN
OBVIOUS RELEASE SILVERY THROUGH
APPARENT BRIGHTEN BULLDOZE
DEFINITE DISTINCT EXPLICIT LUCULENT
LUMINOUS MANIFEST PELLUCID
REVELANT
(— AWAY) FAY FEY FEIGH BANISH
DISPEL DISCUSS
(— FROM) ALOOF
(— LAND) CURE BRUSH SLASH DEADEN
(— OF GROUND) ATRIP AWEIGH
(— OF MUD) SLUTCH
(— OF SCUM) SKIM
(— OF TUFTS) HOB
(— OUT) BLOW HOOK SWAMP SKIDDOO
HIGHTAIL DISCHARGE
(— PATH) FRAY HACK BUSHWACK
(— THROAT) HOICK HOUGH
(— UP) SOLVE ASSOIL RESOLVE
DISSOLVE UNSHADOW
(NOT —) DULL DUSKY FOGGY
INEVIDENT
CLEARANCE ROOM BACKLASH
ALLOWANCE
(— FOR SHIP) PRATIQUE
CLEAR-CUT LUCID SHARP DIRECT
CONCISE DECIDED CHISELED DEFINITE
DISTINCT INCISIVE TRENCHANT
CLEARHEADED LUCID
CLEARING SART FIELD FRITH GLADE
SHADE TRACT ALCOVE ASSART RIDING
RIDDING SLASHING
CLEAR-MINDEDNESS LUCIDITY
CLEAT BITT STUD BLOCK CHOCK KEVEL
LEDGE RANGE WEDGE BATTEN BOLLARD
SUPPORT
CLEAVAGE RIFT CLEFT FISSION FISSURE
DIVISION SCISSION
CLEAVE CUT RIP CHOP HANG HOLD JOIN
LINK PART RELY REND RIFT RIVE SLIT
TEAR BREAK CARVE CHINE CLEFT CLING
CRACK SEVER SHEAR STICK ADHERE
BISECT COHERE DIVIDE FURROW PIERCE
SUNDER FISSURE SEPARATE
CLEF KEY CLIVE CHIAVETTA
CLEFT CUT GAP JAG CHAP CHOP FLAW
GASH RAG NOTCH REFT RIMA RIVE SLIT
BREAK CHASM CHINK CRACK CRENA
GULCH KLOOF RILLE RIVEN SINUS SPLIT
BREACH CLOVEN CRANNY CROTCH
DIVIDE PARTED RECESS RICTUS CREVICE
DIVIDED FISSURE OPENING APERTURE
CREVASSE FRACTURE INCISION
(— BETWEEN HILLS) SLACK RAVINE
(— IN HOOF) SEAM
(— IN THE POSTERIORS) NOCK
(— OF BUTTOCKS) CREASE

CLEMENCY PITY GRACE MERCY LENITY
QUARTER KINDNESS LENIENCY
MILDNESS
CLEMENT MILD SOFT WARM GENTLE
LENIENT MERCIFUL
CLEMENZA DI TITO
(CHARACTER IN —) TITUS ANNIUS
SEXTUS SERVILIA VITELLIA
(COMPOSER OF —) MOZART
CLENCH FIST GRIP GRIT HOLD NAIL
BRACE CLASP CLOSE GRASP CLINCH
CLUTCH DOUBLE
CLEOPATRA (BROTHER OF —) ILUS
ZETES CALAIS GANYMEDE ASSARACUS
(FATHER OF —) IDAS TROS BOREAS
PTOLEMY
(HUSBAND OF —) PHILIP PHINEUS
PTOLEMY MELEAGER
(MOTHER OF —) MARPESSA ORITHYIA
CALLIRRHOE
CLERGY CLOTH CRAPE CHURCH CLERISY
MINISTRY
(BODY OF —) PULPIT
CLERGYMAN ABBA ABBE DEAN PAPA
CANON CLERK FROCK PADRE PILOT
PRIOR RABBI VICAR BISHOP CLERIC
CURATE DEACON DIVINE DOMINE
PAROCH PARSON PASTOR PRIEST
RECTOR SUPPLY CASSOCK PRELATE
CARDINAL CHAPLAIN CLERICAL
DIOCESAN EMERITUS LECTURER
MINISTER ORDINARY PREACHER
REVEREND SQUARSON PRESBYTER
PREBENDARY REVIVALIST
CLERIC ABBE CLERK FROCK DEACON
GALLAH LEVITE PRIEST ACOLYTE
GOLIARD ANAGNOST
CLERICAL BLACK CLERIC CLERKISH
PARSONIC PARSONLY
CLERK BABU AGENT AWARD FILER WRITE
BILLER CLERIC LAYMAN MAPPER
MASTER MUNSHI PANDIT PENMAN
PRIEST PUNDIT SCRIBE SIRCAR TELLER
WRITER YEOMAN ACOLYTE ACTUARY
BOOKMAN COMPOSE GOMASTA
SCHOLAR SHOPMAN CURSITOR
EMPLOYEE MUTSUDDY RECORDER
SALESMAN
CLEVER APT SLY ABLE CUTE DEFT FEAT
FINE FOXY GOOD HEND KEEN NEAT SLIM
SPRY AGILE ALERT CANNY CLEAR FENDY
HANDY HEADY LITHE QUICK SHARP
SLICK SMART WITTY ACTIVE ADROIT
ARTFUL ASTUTE BRIGHT CRAFTY EXPERT
HABILE NEATLY NIMBLE PRETTY
SHREWD SPIFFY SUBTLE AMIABLE
CUNNING GNOSTIC DEXTROUS
HANDSOME OBLIGING SKILLFUL
TALENTED
CLEVERNESS CAN CHIC NOUS TACT
KNACK SKILL ESPRIT INDUSTRY
DEXTERITY
CLICHE COMMONPLACE
CLICK DOT PAWL SLAP TICK AGREE
CATCH SNECK SNICK DETENT PALLET
RATCHET
(HEEL —S) BELLS

(TELEGRAPH —) DASH

CLIENT CEILE PATRON PATIENT CUSTOMER HENCHMAN RETAINER

CLIENTELE PUBLIC CLIENTRY

CLIFF NIP CRAG HILL KLIP ROCK SCAR BLUFF HEUGH SCARP SHORE SLOPE STEEP HEIGHT KRANTZ HILLSIDE PALISADE TRAVERSE
(BROKEN —) CRAG
(ICE —) ICEBLINK
(LINE OF —S) PALISADE

CLIMATE SKY SUN MOOD CLIME HEAVEN REGION TEMPER ATTITUDE
(SCIENCE OF —) PHENOLOGY

CLIMAX CAP TOP ACME APEX HEAD PEAK SHUT CREST CROWN MOUNT SCALE TIGHT APOGEE ASCEND FINISH HEIGHT PAYOFF SUMMIT ZENITH EVEREST CAPSTONE CULMINATION

CLIMB GAD STY RAMP RISE SHIN SOAR CREEP GRIMP MOUNT SCALE SWARM TWINE ASCEND ASCENT BREAST SHINNY SWARVE SWERVE CLAMBER SCRAMBLE TRAVERSE

CLINCH FIX GET HUG TOE BIND GRIP LOCK NAIL SEAL CLAMP CLING GRASP RIVET SEIZE CLENCH CLUTCH FASTEN SECURE CONFIRM EMBRACE GRAPPLE SCUFFLE COMPLETE CONCLUDE HOLDFAST

CLING HUG BANK HANG HOLD RELY CLASP HITCH STICK TRUST ADHERE CLEAVE CLINCH COHERE DEPEND FASTEN SHRINK WITHER CHERISH EMBRACE SHRIVEL CONTRACT

CLINK JUG RAP BEAT BLOW BRIG CASH CLAP COIN JAIL RING CHINK LATCH MONEY JINGLE LOCKUP PRISON STRIKE TINKLE INSTANT JINGLING

CLIP BAT CUT LOP MOW NIG BEAK CHIP CROP DOCK PACE PARE SNIP TRIM BRUSH CLASP MINCE PRUNE SHAVE SHEAR SNICK FASTEN HINDER HOLDER LACING CURTAIL SCISSOR SHORTEN DIMINISH RETAINER
(— A COIN) SHORTEN
(— OF LEAD) TINGLE
(— WOOL) CRUTCH
(CARTRIDGE —) CHARGER
(HAIR —) BARRETTE
(SPRING —) JACK

CLIQUE MOB SET BLOC CLAN CLUB GANG KNOT RING CABAL CROWD GROUP JUNTO CIRCLE COTERIE FACTION CONCLAVE SODALITY CAMARILLA

CLOAK ABA BRAT CAPA CAPE COPE IZAR PALL ROBE VEIL WRAP AMICE BURKA CHOGA COVER GREGO GUISE JELAB MANTA MANTO SAGUM TALAR TALMA ABOLLA CAMAIL CAPOTE CHAMMA PONCHO SCREEN SERAPE SHIELD SHROUD TABARD CASSOCK CHLAMYS CONCEAL MANTEAU PALLIUM PELISSE PELLARD SHELTER SURCOAT ZIMARRA ALBORNOZ BURNOOSE CAPUCHIN DISGUISE MANTILLA

(— OF FEATHERS) MAMO AHUULA
(— WITH CROSSES) ANALABOS
(CORONATION —) SACCOS
(HOODED —) HUKE CAPOT BAUTTA BIRRUS BAVAROY CARDINAL DJELLABA
(INQUISITION —) SANBENITO
(RUSSIAN —) SARAFAN
(SOLDIER'S —) SAGUM MANTEEL
(WATERPROOF —) GOSSAMER

CLOCK BELL CALL DIAL GONG TIME KNOCK METER QUIRK STYLE VERGE WATCH BEETLE CROUCH GHURRY ORLAGE TICKER STRIKER HOROLOGE
(— IN FORM OF SHIP) NEF
(— ON STOCKING) QUIRK GUSHET GUSSET
(— WITH PENDULUM) PENDULE
(PART OF —) BOB ROD BASE DIAL DOOR FACE FOOT HAND HOOD RING ROPE CHAIN CREST PLATE TRUCK FINIAL PLINTH WEIGHT CHAPTER NUMERAL PENDULUM SPANDREL
(WATER —) GHURRY SOLARIUM CLEPSYDRA

CLOD SOD CLOT DOLT LOUT LUMP SLOB TURF CLOUT CLOWN DIVOT EARTH GLEBE GROSS KNOLL YOKEL CLATCH GROUND STUPID BUMPKIN

CLODHOPPER BOOR CLOD SHOE RUSTIC HOBNAIL PLOWMAN

CLOG JAM LOG CLOY CURB DRAG GAUM LOAD LUMP SKID STOP BLOCK CHECK CHOKE DANCE SABOT ADHERE BURDEN CHOPIN DAGGLE FETTER FREEZE HAMPER HOBBLE IMPEDE PATINE SANDAL SECQUE CONGEST SHACKLE TRAMMEL COALESCE OBSTRUCT RESTRAIN

CLOISTER HALL STOA ABBEY AISLE ARCADE FRIARY IMMURE PIAZZA PRIORY CONVENT NUNNERY MONASTERY

CLOISTER AND THE HEARTH
(AUTHOR OF —) READE
(CHARACTER IN —) KATE DENYS ELIAS GILES MARIE PETER BRANDT GERARD MARTIN PIETRO ELIASON MARGARET GHYSBRECHT

CLOSE BY IN CAP END HOT AKIN CHOP CLAP FAST FIRM GRIP HARD HIDE MEET NEAR NIGH QUIT SEAL SHUT SLAM SNUG STOP BLOCK BREAK CEASE CHEAP CHIEF DENSE FENCE FINIS GARTH GROSS ISSUE MUGGY SNECK SOLID STICK STIVY THICK TIGHT BUCKLE BUTTON CLAUSE CLENCH CLUTCH EFFECT FINALE FINISH NARROW NEARBY PERIOD SECRET SETTLE SILENT STINGY STITCH STRAIT STRICT STUFFY THRONG ADJOURN BOROUGH CLOSING COMPACT CONDEMN MISERLY RAMPIRE SHUTTER SIMILAR STOPPER ACCURATE ADJACENT BLOCKADE COMPRESS CONCLUDE FAMILIAR FINALIZE HAIRLINE IMMINENT INTIMATE OBTURATE STIFLING PROXIMATE
(— EYES OF HAWK) SEEL
(— THE MOUTH) STOPPLE
(— TO BATSMAN) SILLY

(— TO QUARRY) HOT
(— TO THE HEART) DEAR
(— TO THE WIND) SHARP
(— WITH A CLICK) SNECK
(PARTIALLY —) HOOD
CLOSED DARK DOWN SHUT UNOPEN
BLOCKED COVERED
CLOSEFISTED MEAN NEAR TIGHT
SNIPPY STINGY MISERLY HANDFAST
CLOSEMOUTHED SECRET SILENT
TACITURN
(NOT —) LEAKY
CLOSET ARK EWRY ROOM SAFE ZETA
AMBRY CUBBY CUDDY PRESS LOCKER
PANTRY CABINET CABINET CONCEAL
PRIVATE CONCLAVE CUPBOARD
GARDEVIN WARDROBE
CLOSING FLY SLAM SNAP CLINCH
CLOSURE CLOTURE CLAUDENT
PHASEOUT BUTTONING
(— DOWN OF OPERATIONS)
PHASEOUT
CLOSURE END GAG BOLT SEAL BOUND
LIMIT ATRESIA FERRULE TENSION
CLAUSURE FINALITY KANGAROO
CLOT GEL CLAG CLAT GOUT LUMP MASS
CLUMP GRUME LOPPER EMBOLUS
THICKEN COAGULUM CONCRETE
SOLIDIFY THROMBUS
CLOTH COAT DRAB ECRU FELT PALL
SEAM WARE BEIGE FOULE GOODS LODEN
LUNGI MOORY PRINT STUPE TAMMY
TIBET TOILE TWEED TWILL ALPACA
BENGAL BYSSUS CANAMO CANVAS
CHADOR CLERGY COVERT DRAPET
DUSTER FABRIC LIVERY LOWELL MELLAY
MULETA NAPKIN RENGUE SARONG
TILLOT WITNEY ACETATE BAGGING
BOULTEL COATING GARMENT JACONET
ORLEANS PANUELO RAIMENT SACKING
TEXTILE WORSTED CHRISMAL CRAMOISY
FROCKING HOMESPUN LAMBSKIN
MATERIAL PHULKARI
(— FOR BELT) SHROUD
(— FOR WIPING TABLE) FILE
(— FOR WRAPPING FABRICS) TILLOT
(— FOR WRAPPING THE DEAD)
CEREMENT
(— HANGING FROM WAISTBAND)
LANGOOTY
(— OF GOLD) CICLATON CHECKLATON
(— OF SINGLE WIDTH) STRAITS
(— REMAINING AFTER CUTTING)
CABBAGE
(— WORN LIKE KILT) LAVALAVA
(— OF GOLD) SONERI
(ALTAR —) TOWEL PENDLE PALLIUM
VESPERAL CATASARKA
(ARABIAN —) HAIK CABAN CABAAN
(BAPTISMAL —) CHRISOM
(BARK —) TAPA
(BED —) COVER SPREAD
(BLACK —) KISWA
(BLUE —) PERSE
(COARSE —) KELT DOZEN DUROY
RUDGE BURREL CANGAN DOWLAS
DOZENS FORFAR FRIEZE HODDEN

KERSEY KHARVA KHARWA STAMIN
STROUD TAPALO WADMAL CAMBAYE
COTONIA DRUGGET FORFARS RAPLOCH
RUGGING SARPLER SOUTAGE FLUSHING
RADEVORE SARCILIS
(COMMUNION —) FANON SINDON
ANIMETTA CORPORAL PURIFICATOR
(COTTON —) BAFT JEAN TOBE ADATI
BLUET CAFFA CRASH DURRY JEANS
KHADI KHAKI SURAT BEAVER CALICO
CANGAN DOWLAS DURRIE GANZIE
HUMHUM KALMUK NANKIN PENANG
CAMBAYE FUSTIAN GALATEA GINGHAM
JACONET KHADDAR LASTING NANKEEN
REGATTA BOGOTANA CRETONNE
DOMESTIC MUSLINET
(CRIMSON —) CRAMASIE CRAMOISY
(DECORATIVE —) SCARF
(EMBROIDERED —) SAMPLER
BAUDEKIN
(FINE —) SINDON
(GLASS —) DORON
(GOAT-WOOL —) ABA SLING
(GREEN —) KENDAL
(GUNNY —) TAT
(HAIR —) ABA CILICE
(HEMP —) PINAYUSA
(HOMESPUN —) KELT KHADI PATTU
PUTTOO HEADING KHADDAR
(INFERIOR —) MOCKADO
(LAP —) GREMIAL
(LINEN —) BRIN LINE GULIX DOWLAS
FORFAR BRABANT LOCKRAM SILESIA
BLANCARD CORPORAL DRILLING
GAMBROON GHENTING LINCLOTH
(LONG —) LUNGI WHITE
(PACK —) MANTA
(PACKING —) SOUTAGE
(PURLOINED —) CABBAGE
(SADDLE —) PANEL NUMNAH
SHABRACK
(SILK —) CAFFA BENGAL PATOLA
LUSTRING
(SOAKED —) BUCK
(SOFT —) RUGINE
(STAGE —) BACKDROP
(STARCHED —) GUIMPE
(STRIPED —) RAY
(STRONG —) CANVAS DURANCE
BARRACAN
(TWILLED —) JANE JEAN BARATHEA
GAMBROON
(UNDYED —) HODDEN
(WASHING —) CHAMOIS
(WAX —) MUMJUMA
(WET —) DAB
(WOOL —) SAY DRAB PUKE BEIGE
BUREL DOZEN DUROY LAINE STARA
TAMMY BURNET DOZENS DUFFEL
HODDEN KENDAL KERSEY MEDLEY
MELTON MUSTER SATARA SAXONY
STAMIN TAMINY TARTAN BASTARD
BLANKET DUNSTER FLANNEL RAPLOCH
ROPLOCH RUGGING BEARSKIN
BOMBAZET BUCKSKIN FLORENCE
SARCILIS VENETIAN PETERSHAM
BOMBAZETTE

(WORSTED —) RASH SHAG BOTANY BOMBAZET

CLOTHE DON RIG TOG BUSK COAT DECK GARB GIRD GOWN ROBE VEST ADORN ARRAY DRESS ENDUE FROCK HABIT ATTIRE BEWRAP SHROUD SWATHE APPAREL VESTURE ACCOUTER

CLOTHES CASE DUDS GARB GEAR SUIT TACK TOGS WEAR DUCKS HABIT ATTIRE SHROUD APPAREL BAGGAGE COSTUME RAIMENT REGALIA THREADS TOGGERY VESTURE WEARING CLOTHING FEATHERS GARMENTS INDUMENT
(CASTOFF —) FRIPPERY
(DAINTY —) PRETTIES
(DRESS —) WAMPUM
(FINE —) BRAWS
(HANDSOME —) BRAVERY
(MOURNING —) DOLE
(SHOWY —) LUGS
(SOAKED —) BUCK

CLOTHING (ALSO SEE CLOTHES) BACK COAT GARB GEAR WEAR ARRAY CLOTH DRESS HABIT STUFF ATTIRE ROBING APPAREL CLOTHES DRAPERY RAIMENT VESTURE INDUMENT KNITWEAR MENSWEAR VESTMENT
(BLACK —) SABLE
(COARSE —) BUREL
(INFORMAL —) PLAYWEAR
(LOWER —) LAP
(MUSLIM —) IHRAM
(NAUTICAL —) SLOPS
(SHEER —) FLIMSIES
(SHOWY —) SHEEN FINERY
(WOMEN'S —) FRILLIES
(WORK —) FATIGUES

CLOUD BLUR DAMP DARK DUST HAZE HIDE MIST PUFF REEK SMUR BEDIM BEFOG DRIFT GLOOM MUDDY SHADE STAIN SULLY SWARM TAINT VAPOR CIRRUS DARKEN DEFAME MUDDLE NEBULA NIMBUS SCREEN SHADOW STIGMA BLACKEN CONFUSE CUMULUS ECLIPSE OBSCURE STRATUS TARNISH NUBILATE OVERCAST
(— OF DUST OR VAPOR) STEW SMOTHER
(— OF MIST) SOP
(— OVER MOUNTAIN) HELM
(FLYING —) RACK
(HIGH —) CIRRUS
(HORIZONTAL —) STRATUS
(MASS OF HIGH —S) RACK
(MASSY —) CUMULUS
(NUCLEAR —) FIREBALL
(RAIN —) NIMBUS

CLOUDY DIM DARK DULL HAZY BLEAR FILMY FOGGY MISTY MUDDY MURKY SHADY GLOOMY LOWERY OPAQUE SMURRY VEILED BLURRED CLOUDED NEBULAR OBSCURE CONFUSED NUBILOUS OVERCAST VAPOROUS

CLOUT BAT BOX DAB HIT BEAT BLOW BUMP CLUB CUFF NAIL SLAP SLUG SWAT SMITE WHACK STRIKE THRASH BOSTHOON

CLOVEN CLEFT SPLIT DIVIDED BISULCATE

CLOVER HAGI HUBAM MEDIC NARDU ALSIKE BERSIM LADINO LUXURY ALFALFA COMFORT LUCERNE MELILOT TREFOIL COWGRASS HAREFOOT NAPOLEON PUSSYCAT SHAMROCK SUCKLING YELLOWTOP

CLOWN OAF APER BOOR FOOL GAUM GOFF JOEY LOUT MIME ZANY ANTIC BUFFO CHURL COMIC FESTE IDIOT MIMER PATCH PUNCH WAMBA ZANNI BODACH HOBBIL JESTER LUBBER RUSTIC STOOGE AUGUSTE BODDAGH BUFFOON BUMPKIN CHARLEY COSTARD MUDHEAD PEASANT PIERROT PLAYBOY SCOFFER TOMFOOL COVIELLO KOYEMSHI MERRYMAN WHITEFACE PUNCHINELLO

CLOWNISH RAW RUDE ZANY GAWKY ROUGH CLUMSY COARSE RUSTIC AWKWARD BOORISH KERNISH LOBBISH LOUTISH UNCIVIL BOEOTIAN UNGAINLY

CLOY GLUT PALL SATE GORGE SATIATE SATISFY SURFEIT SATURATE

CLOYING GOOEY SWEET VANILLA CLOYSOME LUSCIOUS SACCHARINE

CLUB BAT HIT HUI SET BEAT CANE JOIN MACE MAUL TEAM BANDY BATON BUNCH CLOUT LODGE ORDER STAFF YOKEL ZONTA CIRCLE CLIQUE CUDGEL HURLEY KEBBIE LIBBET MACANA NULLAH STRIKE TAIAHA VEREIN WEAPON BOURDON CAMBUCA COUNCIL ATHENEUM BLUDGEON SODALITY SORORITY SPONTOON KNOBKERRY
(— IN PLAYING CARDS) OAK
(— OF ANTENNA) CLAVUS
(BASEBALL —) FARM
(GOLF —) IRON WOOD BAFFY CLEEK MASHY SPOON STICK BRASSY BULGER DRIVER JIGGER LOFTER MASHIE PUTTER BLASTER MIDIRON NIBLICK PITCHER
(MAORI —) MERE MERAI
(POLICEMAN'S —) SAP BILLY SPONTOON NIGHTSTICK
(POLITICAL —) ROTA FASCIO HETAERY
(SPIKED —) ALLIDE
(WAR —) WADDY
(WOMEN'S —) SOROSIS SORORITY

CLUE KEY TIP BALL CLEW HINT IDEA LEAD GUIDE TWINE BOTTOM CLAVIS THREAD INNUENDO

CLUMP TOD BUSH CLOT HEAP KNOT LUMP MASS MOSS TOPE TUFT TUMP BUNCH CLAMP GROUP GROVE PATCH PLUMP STUMP WUDGE DOLLOP BOSCAGE CLUSTER THICKET

CLUMSY NUMB RUDE BLUNT BULKY GAWKY HULKY INAPT INEPT SPLAY STIFF STOGY GAUCHE LUBBER NOGGEN THUMBY WOODEN AWKWARD BOORISH LOUTISH LUMPISH UNHANDY UNREADY BUNGLING CLOWNISH FOOTLESS TACTLESS UNGAINLY UNWIELDY

CLUSTER BOB BUSH CLOT CONE CYME KNOT LUMP TUFT BUNCH CLUMP GROUP SHEAF CENTER COLONY GATHER REGIME

ENVIRON FOLIAGE FASCICLE NUCLEATE
SURROUND
(— AS BEES) BALL KNIT
(— OF BANANAS) HAND
(— OF BRANCHES) SPRAY
(— OF CRYSTALS) DRUSE
(— OF FEATHERS) MUFF
(— OF FIBERS) NEP
(— OF FLOWERS) CYME TRUSS
CORYMB ANTHEMY PANICLE
(— OF HAIRS) MYSTAX
(— OF METAL BALLS) GRAPE
(— OF PILES) DOLPHIN
(— OF PLANTS) BED
(— OF RAYS) AIGRETTE
(— OF SPORES) SORUS
(— OF STARS) PRAESEPE
(— OF TINES) TROCHE
(— OF WOOL) NEP
(CONFUSED —) SPLATTER
(GERM CELL —) MORULA
CLUTCH HUG NAB CLIP FIST GRAB GRIP
NEST BROOD CATCH CLASP GRASP
GRIPE HATCH SEIZE TALON CLENCH
CLINCH FASTEN RETAIN SNATCH
CONTROL
CLUTTER MESS STUFF BUSTLE CUMBER
LITTER CLATTER DISORDER CONFUSION
CLYTEMNESTRA (BROTHER OF —)
CASTOR POLLUX POLYDEUCES
(DAUGHTER OF —) ELECTRA LAODICE
IPHIGENIA IPHINASSA CHRYSOTHEMIS
(FATHER OF —) TYNDAREUS
(HUSBAND OF —) TANTALUS
AGAMEMNON
(LOVER OF —) AEGISTHUS
(MOTHER OF —) LEDA
(SISTER OF —) HELENA
(SON OF —) ORESTES
COACH BUS CAR FLY HACK ARABA
BOGEY CABIN FLIER STAGE TEACH TRAIN
TUTOR ADVISE DIRECT SALOON ADVISER
CONCORD GONDOLA PREPARE RATTLER
TALLYHO CARRIAGE DORMEUSE
(FAST —) FLIER
(HACKNEY —) FIACRE JARVEY
(HEAVY —) DRAG
(SLOW —) SLOWPOKE
(3-WHEELED —) TRICYCLE
COACHMAN JEHU WHIP PILOT COACHY
DRIVER COACHEE COACHER YAMSHIK
YEMSCHIK
COAGULATE GEL SET CAKE CLOT CURD
CURDLE LOBBER LOPPER POSSET
CLABBER CONGEAL THICKEN CONCRETE
SOLIDIFY
COAL RIB BASS DUFF FUEL BLOCK CHARK
EMBER GLEED STOKE BRAZIL BURGEE
CANNEL CARBON CINDER BACKING
BOGHEAD BRIGHTS BYERITE COBBLES
LIGNITE VITRAIN AMPELITE
(— IN PLACE) SOLID
(— PILLAR) STOOK
(— SLAB) SKIP
(BAD —) SMUT
(BED OF —) SEAM
(DIRTY —) RASH

(FINE —) DUFF SCREENINGS
(IMPURE —) SWAD
(LARGE BLOCK OF —) JUD
(LIVE OR GLOWING —) GLEED
(REFUSE —) BREEZE
(SIZE OF —) EGG NUT PEA LUMP RICE
SLACK STOVE BARLEY BROKEN
CHESTNUT WALLSEND BUCKWHEAT
(SLATY —) BASS BONE
(SMALL LUMP OF —) NUBBLING
COALESCE MIX CLOG FUSE JOIN BLEND
MERGE UNITE COHERE MINGLE COMBINE
COALITION FRONT TRUST UNION
FUSION LEAGUE MERGER ENTENTE
ALLIANCE
COAL OIL KEROSENE
COARSE FAT LOW RAW BASE DANK
FOUL HARD LEWD LOUD RANK RUDE
SOUR VILE BAWDY BRASH BROAD
CRASS CRUDE DIRTY GREAT GROSS
HARSH HEAVY LARGE LOOSE PLAIN
RANDY ROUGH STOUR THICK BLOWSY
BRAZEN BRUTAL CALLOW COMMON
EARTHY IMPURE RIBALD RUGGED RUSTIC
VULGAR BLATANT GOATISH LOUTISH
LOWBRED OBSCENE PROFANE RAUCOUS
BARBARIC CLOWNISH HOMESPUN
IMMODEST INDECENT PLEBEIAN
STUBBORN UNCHASTE
COAST BANK LAND RIPA BEACH SHORE
SLIDE BORDER RIVAGE STRAND BOBSLED
SEASIDE SEABOARD SEASHORE
COAT FUR SAC BARK BUFF DAUB FOIL
FOLD HIDE HUSK MIDI RIND SACK SEAL
ZINC BENNY CLOTH COVER CRUST
FROCK GLAZE HABIT JEMMY LAYER
PAINT PLATE SAQUE SHELL ALPACA
DUSTER ENAMEL GROUND INVEST
JACKET JOSEPH KIRTLE MANTLE MELOTE
PARGET PELAGE RABBIT REEFER SILVER
STUCCO TABARD VENEER BOBTAIL
CASSOCK COATING COURTBY CRISPIN
CUTAWAY GARMENT INCRUST KARAKUL
LACQUER OVERLAY PALETOT PELISSE
PLASTER SHELLAC SPENCER SURTOUT
SWAGGER TOPCOAT VESTURE BENJAMIN
MACKINAW MEMBRANE OVERCOAT
SEALSKIN TEGUMENT TRENCHER
OUTERCOAT
(— FOOD) DREDGE
(— LENS) BLOOM
(— OF ARMS) CREST BLAZON
BEARINGS
(— OF BIRD SKINS) TEMIAK
(— OF BLOOD VESSEL) MEDIA
(— OF CARIBOU SKINS) KOOLETAH
(— OF DEFENSE) JACK
(— OF EYE) CHOROID
(— OF EYEBALL) SCLERA
(— OF GRAVEL) BLOTTER
(— OF INDIA) ACHKAN
(— OF MAIL) FROCK BYRNIE SECRET
HAUBERK CATAPHRACT
(— OF ORGAN) INTIMA
(— OF OVULE) PRIMINE
(— OF PLASTER) SET ARRICCIO
BROWNING INTONACO

(— OF SEED) ARIL BRAN EPISPERM
(— OF WOOL) FLEECE
(— WITH ALLOY) TERNE
(— WITH PITCH) PAY
(— WORN UNDER ARMOR)
GAMBESON
(DEER'S WINTER —) BLUE
(FIRST — OF TIN) LIST
(FUR —) ANORAK
(HAIR —) MELOTE
(HOODED —) GREGO CAPOTE
(LONG —) MAXI KAPOTE DJIBBAH
MAXICOAT NEWMARKET
(LOOSE —) CASSOCK PALETOT
INVERNESS
(MILITARY —) TUNIC BLOUSE
BUFFCOAT
(OLD —) MUMMOCK
(RIDING —) JOSEPH
(SACKCLOTH —) SANBENITO
(SEALSKIN —) NETCHA
(SHEEPSKIN —) ZAMARRA
(SHORT —) PEA JUMP MIDI SACK
TERNE JERKIN REEFER PEACOAT
(THREE-QUARTER LENGTH —)
ACHKAN
(WATERPROOF —) BURSATI SLICKER
(WOMAN'S —) CARACO DOLMAN
(WOOLLY —) LANUGO
COATI NASUA TEJON NARICA PISOTE
ARCTOID
COATING (ALSO SEE COAT) FUR GUM
ARIL DOPE FILM HAIR HOAR SKIN BLOOM
GLACE GLAZE ICING SCALE CRUSTA
FINISH JACKET PATINA VENEER BACKING
GILDING LACQUER OVERLAY PLATING
TINNING EMULSION PERIDIUM
PLASTERING
(— OF BACTERIA) SLIME
(— OF GLASS) MOILES FOLIATION
(— OF GLUE) ENAMEL
(— OF ICE) GLAZE
(— OF SEED) TESTA
(— OF TONGUE) ATTER
(CORROSION —) RUST
(POWDERY —) DOWN
(PRUINOUS —) FARINA
(WALL —) GROUT
COAX BEG CANT DUPE FAWN LURE URGE
WILE JOLLY TEASE BANTER CAJOLE
ENTICE SEDUCE BEGUILE FLATTER
IMPLORE WHEEDLE BLANDISH INVEIGLE
PERSUADE
COBBLER PIE SNOB SHEEP SOLER
COZIER BOTCHER CATFISH CRISPIN
POMPANO SADDLER CHUCKLER
SCORPION SNOBSCAT
COBWEB NET TRAP SNARE WEVET
GOSSAMER
COCAINE COKE SNOW
(— MIXED WITH HEROIN) SPEEDBALL
COCK TAP COIL FOWL KORA PILE RICK
GALLO SHOCK STACK STRUT VALVE
FAUCET HAMMER LEADER ROOSTER
(— GUNLOCK) NAB
(— OF HAY) HIPPLE
(— OF THE WALK) KINGFISH

(— WITHOUT COURAGE) CRAVEN
(— WITHOUT SPURS) MUCKNA
(FIGHTING —) FUGIE HEELER
TURNPOKE
(TURKEY —) STAG
(WATER —) KORA
(WEATHER —) FANE VANE
COCKADE KNOT BADGE COCKARD
ROSETTE TRICOLOR
COCKATOO ARA ARARA COCKY GALAH
MACAW PARROT CALANGAY
COCKPIT PIT RING RINK WELL ARENA
CABIN FIELD GALLERA
COCKROACH BUG DRUM ROACH BEETLE
BLATTID DRUMMER KNOCKER
COCKTAIL SOUR ZOOM BRONX CRUSTA
GIBSON MAITAI COBBLER MARTINI
NEGRONI SAZERAC SIDECAR STINGER
SWIZZLE APERITIF DAIQUIRI MARGARITA
COCKY PERT CRANK PERKY JAUNTY
ARROGANT
COCOON POD CLUE KELL SHED SHELL
DOUPION FOLLICLE
COD COR POD CUSK HUSK ROCK DORSE
GADID POUCH SCROD TORSK BURBOT
MULVEL POCKET TOMCOD BACALAO
CODLING MILWELL MORRHUA CABELIAU
DOLEFISH KABBELOW KLIPFISH
ROCKLING
CODDLE PET BABY CADE HUMOR NURSE
SPOIL CARESS COSSET COTTON FONDLE
PAMPER
CODE LAW CANON CODEX DOGMA
CIPHER DIGEST SECRET SIGNAL PRECEPT
(— OF CHIVALRY) BUSHIDO
(— OF LAWS) ADA ADAT PANDECT
SHERIAT DOOMBOOK
(— OF RULES) VINAYA
(— OF WHAT IS FITTING) DECORUM
PROTOCOL
(COMPUTER —) ASCII
(PUNCHCARD —) HOLLERITH
COERCE COW CURB MAKE BULLY CHECK
DRIVE FORCE ORDER COMPEL HIJACK
ENFORCE REPRESS SANDBAG BULLDOZE
RESTRAIN RESTRICT
COFFEE JOE CAFE JAVA MILD MOCHA
BOGOTA BRAZIL JAMOKE SANTOS
TRIAGE ARABICA BOURBON MELANGE
SUMATRA ESPRESSO MAZAGRAN
MEDELLIN TRILLADO
COFFER ARK BOX DAM PYX CHEST
HUTCH TRUNK CASKET CAISSON
CASHBOX CIBORIUM
COFFIN BIER CASE CIST KIST MOLD PALL
CASING CASKET HEARSE THROUGH
(LEADEN —) COPE
COG CAM NOG COCK GEAR CATCH CHOCK
TENON TOOTH WEDGE DECEIVE
WHEEDLE
COGENT GOOD PITHY VALID POTENT
STRONG TELLING FORCIBLE POWERFUL
PREGNANT
COGITATE MULL MUSE PLAN THINK
PONDER CONNATE MEDIATE REFLECT
CONSIDER
COGNATE KIN AKIN ALIKE ALLIED

COGENER KINDRED RELATED SIMILAR RELATIVE

COGNIZANT WISE AWAKE AWARE KNOWING SENSIBLE

COHERE FIT BOND GLUE SUIT AGREE CLING SEIZE STICK UNITE ADHERE CEMENT CLEAVE CONNECT COINCIDE

COHERENCE UNION CONSENT CONTEXT COHESION STRENGTH

COIL CLEW CURL FAKE FURL HANK LINK LOOP ROLL TUFT WIND HELIX ROUND TWINE TWIRL TWIST WHORL WRING DIMMER ENROLL SPIRAL TOROID WINDUP WREATH ENTRAIL INVOLVE RINGLET WREATHE CONVOLVE ENCIRCLE INDUCTOR OVERCOIL

COIN AS BU PU AVO BAN BIT BOO COB DAM DIE DUB ECU FIL JOE KIP LAT LEK LEU LEV LEY ORI PUL SEN SOL TRA WEN WON ZUZ ABAS ANNA ATTE BAHT BATZ BESA CASH CENT CHIP CHON DEMY DIME DOIT DONG DOTT DUMP DURO FELS FILS GILL GROS GROT HARP HOON HWAN JACK JANE KRAN KYAT LEVY LION MAIL MAKE MERK MILL MINT MITE MULE OBAN ONZA OORD PARA PAUL PESA PESO PICE POND POUL QUAN RAND RIAL ROCK RYAL SCAD SENT SINK SIZE SLUG TAEL TARA TARE TARI TARO TIAO TREY TYPE UNIT ACKEY AGNEL AGORA AKCHA ALBUS ALTIN ALTUN AMANI ANGEL ANGLE ASPER BAIOC BAIZA BATTE BEKAR BELGA BETSO BEZZO BISTI BLANC BLANK BODLE BROAD BROWN CHINK CLINK COIGN CONTO COROA CROSS CROWN CUNYE DARIC DINAR DISME DOBLA DUCAT EAGLE EYRIR FANAM FANON FODDA FRANC GAZET GRANO GROAT GROSZ HALER HECTE JACOB JULIO JUSTO KOBAN KRONA KRONE KROON LIARD LIBRA LITRA LIVRE LOUIS MEDAL MEDIN MEDIO MILAN MOHUR MOPUS NOBLE NOMOS OBANG ORKEY ORKYN PAISA PAOLO PARDO PENNY PERAU PESSA PIECE PLACK PLATE POALI POALO PROOF PRUTA QUART QUINE RAPPE REBIA RIDER RIYAL ROYAL RUBLE RUPIA SAIGA SAPEK SCEAT SCUDO SEMIS SHAHI SICCA SMASH SOLDO STAMP STYCA SUCRE TALER TANGA TANKA TEMPO THRIP TICAL TRIME UNCIA UNITE WHITE ABASSI ABBASI AFGHAN AHMADI ARGENT ASSARY AUREUS AZTECA BALBOA BAUBEE BAWBEE BEAVER BEZANT BIANCO BLANCO BOGACH BRONZE CARLIN CENTAS CHAISE COBANG CONDOR COPPER CORONA CUARTO CUNZIE DECIME DENARY DENIER DERHAM DINDER DIOBOL DIRHAM DIXAIN DIZAIN DOBLON DODKIN DOLLAR DOPPIA DOUBLE ESCUDO FLEUR FLORIN FOLLIS FORINT GEORGE GIULIO GOURDE GRIVNA GROSSO GUINEA GULDEN HARPER HELLER ICHIBU ITZEBU JUSLIK KLIPPE KOPECK KORONA KORUNA LAUREL LEPTON MACUTA MAHBUB MAIDEN MANCUS MEDINO MISKAL NICKEL NORKYN OCHAVO OCTAVE ONGARO PADUAN PAGODA PARDAO PATACA PATART PHILIP PRUTAH QUEZAL ROSARY SALUNG SALUTE SATANG SEQUIN SESKIN SHEKEL SHIELD SIGLOS SINKER SIXAIN SOMALO SOVRAN STATER STELLA STIVER TALENT TARGET TESTAO TESTER TESTON THALER THOMAN TOSTON TRIENS TUMAIN TUNGAH TURNER TURNEY TURTLE UNGARO VINTEM XERIFF YUZLIK ZECHIN ZEHNER ZEQUIN

COINCIDE FIT GEE JIBE AGREE TALLY CONCUR

COLD FLU ICY NIP COOL DEAD DULL HARD HOAR AGUED ALGID BLEAK CHILL CRISP FISHY FRORE GELID GLACE RHEUM STONY ARCTIC BITTER BOREAL CHILLY CLAMMY FRIGID FRIGOR FROSTY WINTRY CATARRH CHILLED DISTANT FROSTED GLACIAL SHIVERY UNHEATED

COLD-BLOODED BRUTAL LEEPIT

COLLABORATE AID ASSIST COOPERATE

COLLAPSE CAVE FALL FLOP FOLD GIVE SINK CRASH SLUMP WRECK BUCKLE SHRINK TUMBLE CAPSIZE CROPPER CRUMBLE CRUMPLE DEBACLE DEFLATE FAILURE FLUMMOX FOUNDER SMASHUP CONTRACT DOWNFALL TAILSPIN PROSTRATION

COLLAR NAB BAND BOSS ETON FALL FANO GILL GRAB POKE RING RUFF CHAIN FANON FICHU RUCHE SEIZE STOCK TRASH WHISK BERTHA CHOKER COLLET DICKEY GORGET RABATO SLEEVE TORQUE TUCKER TURNUP BOBECHE CAPTURE CHIGNON CIRCLET PANUELO SHACKLE VANDYKE CARCANET CINCTURE NECKBAND NECKLACE
(— FOR HORSE) BARGHAM BRECHAM
(HIGH —) GILLS JAMPOT
(HORSE —) BRECHAM
(LACE —) SCALLOP
(MAGISTRATE'S —) GOLILLA
(ROMAN —) RABAT
(WHEEL-SHAPED —) RUFF
(WOODEN —) CANG CANGUE

COLLARBONE CLAVICLE

COLLATERAL SIDE MARGIN OBLIQUE INDIRECT PARALLEL SECURITY

COLLATION TEA MEAL LUNCH REPAST READING DEJEUNER

COLLEAGUE AIDE ALLY DEPUTY SOCIUS ADJUNCT COMPEER CONSORT PARTNER CONFRERE

COLLECT TAX CARD CULL DRAW HEAP LEVY LIFT PICK PILE POOL SAVE AMASS CROWD GLEAN GROUP HOARD RAISE STORE SWEEP ACCRUE CONFER GARNER GATHER MUSTER PRAYER ARCHIVE CLUSTER COMPILE CONGEST ENGROSS IMPOUND SYNAPTE ASSEMBLE SCRAMBLE SCROUNGE

COLLECTED CALM COOL SOBER SERENE PRESENT COMPOSED

COLLECTION ANA BAG KIT SET BAND

BEVY CLAN CROP FILE HEAP KNOT LEVY
OLIO ALBUM ANNEX BATCH BUNCH
FLOCK GROUP HOARD KITTY SHEAF
STORE SUITE BUNDLE FARDEL MISHNA
PARCEL RAGBAG ACCOUNT CLUSTER
CONGERY EXHIBIT FISTFUL GALLERY
ASSEMBLY CABOODLE GLOSSARY
(— AT FOX HUNT) CAP
(— OF ANIMALS) ZOO HEAD
(— OF BOOKCASES) STACK
(— OF BOOKS) SET BIBLE CANON
LIBRARY
(— OF CONIFERS) PINETUM
(— OF DATA) GROUND
(— OF FORMULAS) CODEX
(— OF FOUR) TETRAD
(— OF HUTS) BUSTEE
(— OF LAWS) CODE
(— OF MAPS) ATLAS
(— OF OBJECTS) AFFAIR
(— OF OPINIONS) SYMPOSIUM
(— OF PERSONS) BOODLE
(— OF PLANTS) SERTULE
(— OF POEMS) DIVAN DIWAN SYLVA
ANTHOLOGY
(— OF PUS) ABSCESS HYPOPYON
(— OF REVENUES) TAHSIL TEHSIL
(— OF ROCKS) SUITE
(— OF RULES) SUTRA SUTTA
(— OF SAMPLES) SWATCH
(— OF SAYINGS) ANA
(— OF SPECIMENS) CABINET
(— OF STAFFS) SYSTEM
(— OF STORIES) LEGEND
(— OF TIPS) TRONC
(— OF TOOLS) LAYOUT
(— OF TREES) SERINGAL
(— OF UNWANTED ANIMALS)
LARDER
(— OF WRITINGS) CORPUS
(— OF 24 SHEETS) QUIRE
(CONFUSED —) CLUTTER
(MISCELLANEOUS —) OLIO FARDEL
SMYTRIE
(VAST —) CLOUD
COLLEGE TOL HALL LYCEE CAMPUS
COLAGE SCHOOL SIWASH ACADEMY
SEMINARY
COLLIDE HIT RAM BUMP DASH FRAY
HURT BARGE CLASH CRASH KNOCK
SHOCK SMITE WRECK CANNON HURTLE
STRIKE THRUST
COLLIE KELPIE BEARDIE
COLLISION HIT FOUL CLASH CRASH
PRANG SHOCK IMPACT PILEUP SMASHUP
CONFLICT
COLLOQUY CHAT TALK PARLEY
DIALOGUE
COLLUSION DECEIT CAHOOTS SECRECY
PRACTICE

COLOMBIA

CAPE: VELA AGUJA MARZO AUGUSTA
CAPITAL: BOGOTA

COIN: PESO REAL CONDOR PESETA
CENTAVO
GULF: URABA CUPICA DARIEN TIBUGA
TORTUGAS
INDIAN: BORO CUNA HOKA MACU MUZO
PAEZ CARIB CATIO CHOCO COFAN COGUI
CUBEO GUANE PIJAO SEONA ARAWAK
BETOYA CALIMA INGANO SALIVA
TAHAMI TUCANO TUNEBO YAHUNA
ACHAGUA ANDAQUI CHIBCHA CHIMILA
GUAHIBO GUAJIRO PANCHES PUINAVE
PUITOTO QUECHUA TAIRONA GUARAUNO
MOTILONE
ISLAND: BARU NAIPO FUERTE GORGONA
CUSACHON
MEASURE: VARA AZUMBRE CELEMIN
MOUNTAIN: CHITA HUILA PURACE
TOLIMA
MOUNTAINS: ABIBE ANDES BAUDO
COCUY AYAPEL PERIJA TUNAHI
CHAMUSA ORIENGAL
POINT: CRUCES LACRUZ SOLANO
CARIBANA GALLINAS
PORT: LORICA CARTAGENA
PROVINCE: META CAUCA CHOCO HUILA
VALLE ARAUCA BOYACA CALDAS
NARINO TOLIMA VAUPES BOLIVAR
CAQUETA GUAJIRE VICHADA AMAZONAS
PUTUMAYO
RIVER: UVA BITA META MUCO SINU TOMO
UPIA YARI BAUDO CAUCA CESAR ISANA
MESAI NECHI PATIA PAUTO SUCIO
AMAZON ARAUCA ARIARI ATRATO
CAGUAN VAUPES YAPURA CAQUETA
GUAINIA INIRIDA TRUANDO VICHADA
APAPORIS CASANARE GUAVIARE
PUTUMAYO MAGDALENA
TOWN: TEN ANZA BUGA CALI MITU MUZO
PAEZ SIPI TADO TOLU YARI BELLO CHINU
GUAPI NEIVA PASTO TUNJA BOGOTA
CUCUTA IBAGUE QUIBDO SANGIL
CARTAGO LETICIA PALMIRA PEREIRA
POPAYAN GIRARDOT MEDELLIN
MONTERIA CARTAGENA

COLONIST BOOR COLON FATHER
CUTHEAN PIONEER PLANTER SETTLER
EMIGRANT
(— IN SICILY) SIKELIOT
(AUSTRALIAN —) STERLING
COLONNADE ROW STOA PORCH PARVIS
PIAZZA XYSTUS EUSTYLE GALLERY
PARVISE PERGOLA PORTICO TERRACE
CHOULTRY DIASTYLE PERISTYLE
COLONY STATE SWARM APOIKIA
CENOBIUM PLANTATION
(— OF BEES) HIVE SKEP SWARM
COLOR (ALSO SEE SPECIFIC COLOR)
DIP DYE HUE CAST FAKE SUIT TINT TONE
BLUSH GLAZE GLOSS GRAIN PAINT
SHADE STAIN TAINT TASTE TINCT TINGE
TOUCH BANNER BLEACH BOTTOM
CHROMA ENSIGN RADDLE REDDEN
STREAK TEMPER DISTORT PENNANT
PIGMENT STANDARD TINCTURE

(— IMPARTED TO HERRINGS)
GILDING
(— OF BIRD) SMUT
(— OF EYES OF FOWLS) DAW
(— OF HUMAN FLESH) CARNATION
(— OF REFLECTED LIGHT) OVERTONE
(BLUE —) FOG JAY SKY AQUA BICE CIEL
CYAN DUSK NAVY SAXE WOAD AZURE
BERYL CADET CAPRI COPEN DELFT
DIANA DRAKE GRAPE PEARL ROYAL
SLATE SMALT SMOKE VANDA CENDRE
GROTTO INDIGO LUPINE MARINE
MIGNON ORIENT SEVRES VENICE
CELESTE GOBELIN HORIZON LOBELIA
LOGWOOD MATELOT PEACOCK PETUNIA
ABSINTHE BRITTANY CERULEAN
DUCKLING ELECTRIC HYACINTH
LARKSPUR MASCOTTE MAZARINE
MIDNIGHT MOONBEAM SAPPHIRE
TWILIGHT WEDGWOOD
(BROWN —) BAY ELK FOX OAK TAN
ARAB BARK BRAN CLAY CORK CUBA
DEER DRAB DUST ECRU FAWN GOAT
HOPI LAMA LION MESA MUSK SEAL SIAM
TEAK ALOMA AZTEC BEIGE BISON BLOND
BLUSH BRICK BROWN BUNNY CACAO
CAMEL CANNA CLOVE COCOA CONGO
EAGLE FRIAR FUDGE GYPSY HAZEL
HENNA KHAKI MALAY MECCA MUMMY
OTTER PABLO QUAIL SEPIA SIENA SNUFF
SUDAN SUEDE SUMAC TABAC TOAST
TOPAZ AFGHAN ALMOND APACHE
ARGALI AUBURN BAMBOO BEAVER
BISQUE BISTER BLONDE COCHIN COFFEE
CONDOR COOKIE DORADO FALLOW
GINGER GROUSE HAVANA ISABEL
MAROON MERIDA NUTMEG PAWNEE
PLOVER PUEBLO RABBIT RUSSET
SAHARA SANTOS SORREL STUCCO
SUNTAN THRUSH CATTAIL CIGARET
COCONUT COTRINE CRACKER DOGWOOD
DURANGO FILBERT GAZELLE GOREVAN
HARVEST LEATHER MALABAR MIRADOR
MOROCCO MUSCADE MUSTANG
OAKWOOD PERIQUE PRALINE SUNBURN
SUNDOWN TALLYHO TANBARK TOBACCO
TUSCANY BISMARCK CINNAMON
CORDOVAN ETRUSCAN HAZELNUT
ISABELLA KOLINSKY MANDALAY
MOCCASIN MOLESKIN SAUTERNE
SHAGBARK TAMARACK TEAKWOOD
WOODBARK
(DEAD-LEAF —) FILEMOT
(DEEP —) DARK
(FAST —) GRAIN
(GREEN —) BOA FIR IVY ALOE BICE
FERN JADE LEEK MOSS NILE SAGE FAIRY
HOLLY KELLY OLIVE CANNON EMPIRE
HUNTER JASPER LAUREL LIZARD
MEADOW MYRTLE SPRUCE VERDET
CITRINE CORBEAU CRESSON CYPRESS
EMERALD JADEITE JUNIPER NEPTUNE
OLIVINE PERIDOT SEAFOAM VERDURE
BAYBERRY CHASSEUR EMERAUDE
PISTACHE POPINJAY SHAMROCK
TARRAGON VIRIDIAN
(GRIZZLED —) AGOUTI

(OTHER —S) OR ASH BAT DOE DUN JET
TEA CORN CROW DAWN DOVE GRAY
GREY GULL LAVA LEAD MOLE NUDE
PLUM PORT ROAN RUST SAND SOOT
WOOD AMBER BEACH BLACK CAMEO
CREAM EBONY FLESH GRAPE GREGE
MAUVE MOUSE PANSY PHLOX PRUNE
SABLE SPICE THYME AURORA AUTUMN
COLLIE DAHLIA DAMSON FIESTA FUSTIC
GAMBIA MALLOW MODENA NAVAHO
NAVAJO NIMBUS NUTRIA ORCHID
OXFORD OYSTER PEANUT PEBBLE
PIGEON QUAKER RAISIN RESEDA SILVER
TUSCAN VIOLET WALNUT ANNATTO
ARBUTUS BEGONIA BERMUDA BLOSSOM
BRINDLE CARAMEL CORBEAU COWSLIP
CRACKER CRUISER NATURAL PELICAN
PUMPKIN REGATTA ROSEBUD SANDUST
SPARROW SUNBEAM THISTLE VERVAIN
WHEATEN ALUMINUM AMARANTH
AMETHYST BLONDINE CHARCOAL
CLEMATIS CYCLAMEN EGGPLANT
FELDGRAU FLAMINGO GRAPHITE
GUNMETAL IMPERIAL JACINTHE
LAVENDER MULBERRY PALMETTO
ROSEWOOD SAUTERNE SQUIRREL
SUNBURST CARNELIAN
(RED —) DAWN FLEA GOYA LAKE MIST
PUCE RUBY WINE AGATE BRASS BRICK
CANNA CEDAR CORAL FLAME GULES
LILAC MELON NYMPH PEACH PEONY
POPPY ROSET SIENA SPARK TOTEM
ACAJOU ARCHIL AUTUMN AZALEA
BRAZIL CANYON CARROT CATSUP
CERISE CHERRY CHERUB CLARET FRAISE
GAIETY GARNET JOCKEY KERMES
MADDER MALAGA MIKADO MURREY
NECTAR SALMON SHRIMP SIERRA
SULTAN TITIAN TOMATO ANEMONE
BEGONIA BISCUIT BOKHARA CARMINE
CATAWBA CRIMSON CURRANT FIREFLY
FUCHSIA HEATHER KETCHUP LOBSTER
MAGENTA MASCARA OXBLOOD PAPRIKA
POMPEII PONCEAU REDWOOD RUBELLE
SARAVAN SCARLET SINOPLE STAMMEL
SULTANA VERMEIL ALKERMES
AMARANTH BISMARCK BORDEAUX
BURGUNDY CAMELLIA CARDINAL
CHEROKEE CHESTNUT DIANTHUS
DUBONNET EVENGLOW GERANIUM
GRENADIN MAHOGANY MANDARIN
(TONE —) TIMBRE
(YELLOW —) HAY RAT WAX BEAR BUFF
CLAY CORN ECRU FLAX GOLD LARK
MOTH WOLD ACIER ALOMA AZTEC BEIGE
CRASH CREAM GRAIN HONEY IVORY
LEMON MAIZE SHELL STRAW TAUPE
ACACIA ALMOND BANANA CANARY
CATHAY CHROME CITRON CITRUS
CROCUS DORADO FELLOW MASTIC
MIMOSA OXGALL SULFUR SUNRAY
SUNSET ANTIQUE APRICOT BISCUIT
CAVALRY CHAMOIS GAMBOGE JASMINE
JONQUIL LEGHORN PRAIRIE RHUBARB
SAFFRON SUNGLOW ANTELOPE
CALABASH CAPUCINE DAFFODIL

EGGSHELL GOLDMIST MARIGOLD
PRIMROSE SNOWSHOE

COLORADO

CAPITAL: DENVER
COLLEGE: REGIS
COUNTY: BACA MESA YUMA OTERO
OURAY ROUTT GILPIN CHAFFEE
MOUNTAIN: OSO LONGS PIKES ELBERT
MOUNTAIN RANGE: ROCKY
PARK: ESTES
RIVER: YAMPA DOLORES APISHAPA
ARIKAREE GUNNISON PURGATOIRE
STATE FLOWER: COLUMBINE
STATE NICKNAME: CENTENNIAL
STATE TREE: SPRUCE
TOWN: ASPEN DELTA LAMAR GOLDEN
PUEBLO SALIDA ALAMOSA BOULDER
DURANGO GREELEY GUNNISON
LOVELAND TRINIDAD

COLORED FAW HUED BIASED STAINED
(— IN RED) RUBRIC
(— LIKE PIPE BOWL) TROUSERED
(BRILLIANTLY —) SUPERB FLAMING
PSYCHEDELIC
(HIGHLY —) CHROMATIC PRISMATIC
(PARTI —) PIED PIEBALD
(UNIFORMLY —) HARD
COLORFUL GAY BRAVE JUICY VIVID
GORGEOUS
COLORLESS WAN DRAB DULL PALE
ASHEN BLANK PLAIN MOUSEY PALLID
HUELESS NEUTRAL ACHROMIC
ACHROUS ETIOLATE LIFELESS
COLOSSAL BIG HUGE VAST GREAT
JUMBO LARGE IMMENSE TITANIC
ENORMOUS GIGANTIC MONSTROUS
COLOSSUS GIANT TITAN STATUE
MONOLITH
COLT FOAL STAG FILLY POTRO HOGGET
POLEYN EQUULEUS
COLUMN LAT ROW FILE GOAL LINE POLE
POST PROP STUB SHAFT STELE STELA
TORSO TRUNK GNOMON PILLAR STAPLE
SUPPORT CYLINDER PILASTER
(— IN EAR) MODIOLUS
(— OF FIGURES) SUM
(— OF FILAMENTS) SYNEMA
(— OF MOLTEN ROCK) PLUME
(BUDDHIST —) LAT
(FIGURE USED AS —) ATLAS TELAMON
(PART OF —) BASE DADO NECK OVOLO
SHAFT TORUS ABACUS PLINTH REGLET
SCOTIA CAPITAL ECHINUS FLUTING
ASTRAGAL CINCTURE COLARENO
PEDESTAL
(ROCK —) HOODOO
(ROULETTE —) DERNIER
(SPINAL —) HORN SPINE BACKBONE
(STRUCTURAL —) LALLY
(TWISTED —) TORSO
COMA TUFT BUNCH SLEEP SOPOR
STUPOR TORPOR TRANCE
COMATOSE OUT DROWSY LETHARGIC

COMB CARD GILL RACK RAKE REED SEEK
BREAK BRUSH CREST CTENE CURRY
TEASE HACKLE SMOOTH
COMBAT WAR BLOW BOUT COPE DUEL
FRAY MEET TILT CLASH FIGHT JOUST
REPEL STOUR ACTION AFFRAY BATTLE
OPPOSE RESIST STRIFE CONTEND
CONTEST COUNTER DISPUTE SCUFFLE
ARGUMENT CONFLICT STRUGGLE
COMBATIVE BANTAM MILITANT
AGONISTIC BELLICOSE PUGNACIOUS
AGONISTICAL
COMBINATION KEY BLOC CLUB GANG
PACT POOL RING CABAL COMBO GROUP
JUNTO PARTY TRUST UNION CARTEL
CLIQUE FUSION LEAGUE MEDLEY
MERGER AMALGAM COTERIE FACTION
HARMONY JOINING MIXTURE ADDITION
ALLIANCE ENSEMBLE MONOPOLY
(— OF CARDS) SET BUILD FLUSH
SPREAD STRAIGHT
(— OF CIRCUMSTANCES) ACTION
(— OF COLORS) HARLEQUIN
(— OF FACES) FORM
(— OF FIRMS) TRUST
(— OF INTAGLIO FORMS) GRYLLI
(— OF NUMBERS) GIG SADDLE
(— OF TONES) CHORD
COMBINE ADD MIX WED BIND BLOC
CLUB JOIN POOL BLEND GROUP JOINT
MARRY MERGE TOTAL UNITE ABSORB
LEAGUE MEDDLE MERGER MINGLE
SPLICE AMALGAM COMPACT CONJOIN
COALESCE CONDENSE CONTRACT
CUMULATE FEDERATE
COMBUSTION FIRE HEAT FLAME THERM
TUMULT BURNING BACKFIRE
COME BE GET LAY DRAW FALL GROW
PASS ARISE FETCH ISSUE OCCUR REACH
ACCRUE APPEAR ARRIVE BEFALL
EMERGE HAPPEN SPRING ADVANCE
DEVELOP EMANATE PROCEED APPROACH
PRACTICE
(— ABOUT) ARISE CHANCE
(— AFTER) SUE FOLLOW
(— APART) FRAY SHED BREAK STAVE
(— BACK) REVERSE
(— BEFORE) FORERUN PREVENE
ANTECEDE ANTEDATE
(— DOWN) AVALE SWOOP ALIGHT
DESCEND SUCCEED DISMOUNT
(— FORTH) EMIT BREAK ISSUE ACCEDE
FORTHGO FURNACE
(— FORWARD) ACCEDE
(— IN CONTACT) ATTINGE
(— IN SECOND) PLACE
(— IN THIRD) SHOW
(— INTO BLOOM) BURST BLOSSOM
(— INTO COLLISION) MEET CLASH
COLLIDE
(— INTO EXISTENCE) FORM BEGIN
ACCRUE HAPPEN SPRING
(— INTO POSSESSION) ACQUIRE
INHERIT
(— OF AGE) MAJORIZE
(— OFF) HARL PEEL

(— OUT) ISSUE APPEAR EMERGE
EMANATE
(— SUDDENLY) CLAP
(— THROUGH) DELIVER
(— TO) TOUCH ADVENE STRIKE
RECOVER REVERSE
(— TO BELIEVE IN) ADOPT
(— TO CONCLUSION) DECIDE
(— TO DIE) DO DIE SET DROP EXPIRE
FINISH SURCEASE
(— TO GRIEF) FOUNDER
(— TO HAND) OFFER
(— TO LIGHT) SPUNK DEVELOP
(— TO MIND) OCCUR STRIKE
(— TO NOTHING) ABORT
(— TO PASS) SORT BREAK LIGHT
BEFALL BETIDE HAPPEN
(— TO PERFECTION) RIPEN
(— TO TERMS) AGREE TRYST ACCORD
BARGAIN COMPOSE COMPOUND
ACCOMMODATE
(— TOGETHER) ADD HERD JOIN MEET
AMASS CONCUR COUPLE GATHER
COLLECT COMBINE CONVENE ASSEMBLE
(— UNDER) SUBVENE
(— UPON) FIND CROSS INVENT STRIKE
OVERTAKE
COMEDIAN WAG WIT CARD ANTIC
CLOWN COMIC GAGMAN JESTER
BUFFOON FUNSTER FUNMAKER
FUNNYMAN
COMEDY SOCK FARCE LAZZO REVUE
SITCOM TEMACHA TRAVESTY
BACCHIDES SLAPSTICK
COMEDY OF ERRORS
(AUTHOR OF —) SHAKESPEARE
(CHARACTER IN —) LUCE PINCH
AEGEON ANGELO DROMIO ADRIANA
AEMILIA EPHESUS LUCIANA SOLINUS
BALTHAZAR ANTIPHOLUS
COMELINESS GRACE DECORUM
FEATURE VENUSTY PULCHRITUDE
COMELY FAIR GOOD HEND PERT TALL
TIDY BONNY BUXOM DECENT GOODLY
LIKELY LOVELY PRETTY PROPER SEEMLY
VENUST SIGHTLY BECOMING DECOROUS
GRACEFUL HANDSOME PLEASING
SUITABLE
COMET STAR METEOR XIPHIAS
COMFORT AID EASE REST STAY CHEER
LIGHT SOOTH RELIEF REPOSE SOLACE
SOOTHE SUCCOR ASSUAGE CHERISH
CONSOLE GLADDEN REFRESH RELIEVE
SUPPORT SUSTAIN INSPIRIT REASSURE
COMFORTABLE COZY EASY SNUG TRIG
COMFY COUTH CUSHY RELAXED
RESTFUL CHEERFUL DELICATE EUPHORIC
HOMELIKE GEMUTLICH
COMFORTER PUFF COVER EIDER
NAHUM QUILT SCARF TIPPET CHEERER
PACIFIER
COMFREY DAISY BONESET BACKWORT
KNITBACK BRUISEWORT
COMIC DROLL FUNNY STRIP BUFFONE
THALIAN COMEDIAN FARCICAL
COMICAL LOW BASE BUFFO DROLL
FUNNY MERRY WITTY BOUFFE AMUSING

JOCULAR HUMOROUS TICKLISH
SPLITTING
COMING DUE ANON NEXT ADVENT
FUTURE ARRIVAL FORWARD BECOMING
DESERVED
COMMAND BID BECK CALL FIAT RULE
SWAY WILL WORD EDICT EXACT FORCE
HIGHT ORDER POWER UKASE ADJURE
BEHEST CHARGE COMPEL DEMAND
DIRECT ENJOIN GOVERN MASTER
ORDAIN SUMMON APPOINT BIDDING
CONTROL DICTATE MANDATE REQUIRE
BIDDANCE DOMINEER MANDAMUS
COMMANDER CID DUX DUKE EMIR
HEAD CHIEF LEADER MASTER ALCALDE
CAPTAIN DECARCH EMPEROR GENERAL
MARSHAL OFFICER HIPPARCH MYRIARCH
PHYLARCH RISALDAR SERASKER
TETRARCH PROCONSUL
COMMANDMENT LAW RULE ORDER
COMMAND MITZVAH PRECEPT
BODEWORD
COMMEMORATE FETE KEEP FEAST
REMEMBER MEMORIALIZE
COMMEMORATION AWARD MEDAL
PLAQUE JUBILEE MEMORIA EBENEZER
MEMORIAL REMEMBRANCE
COMMENCE OPEN ARISE BEGIN FOUND
START INCEPT LAUNCH SPRING INITIATE
COMMEND PAT LAUD BOOST
EXTOL GRACE BESTOW COMMIT PRAISE
APPLAUD APPROVE BESPEAK ENTRUST
INTRUST BEQUEATH
COMMENDABLE GOOD WORTHY
LOVABLE LAUDABLE
COMMENSURATE EVEN EQUAL
ENOUGH ADEQUATE RELEVANT
COMMENT BARB GIBE TALK ASIDE
NOTATE REMARK CAPTION DISCUSS
EXPLAIN EXPOUND
COMMERCE TRADE BARTER CHANGE
TRAFFIC BUSINESS EXCHANGE
MERCATURE
COMMISSION SEND TASK BOARD
PRESS TRUST BREVET CHARGE DEMAND
DEPUTE ERRAND LEGACY ORDAIN
PERMIT CONSIGN EMPOWER MANDATE
WARRANT DELEGATE
COMMIT DO TAKE ALLOT LEAVE REFER
ASSIGN ENGAGE PERMIT REMAND
COMMEND CONFIDE CONSIGN DELIVER
DEPOSIT ENTRUST INTRUSE INTRUST
BEQUEATH DEDICATE DELEGATE
IMPRISON RELEGATE
COMMITTEE BODY JURY BOARD GROUP
JUNTA BUREAU SOVIET COUNCIL
PRESIDIUM
COMMODITY ITEM WARE GOODS STUFF
STAPLE ARTICLE SHIPMENT
COMMON LAY LOW BASE MEAN RIFE
VILE BANAL CHEAP GREEN GROSS JOINT
OFTEN STALE TACKY TRITE USUAL
COARSE MUTUAL ORNERY PUBLIC
SIMPLE VULGAR AVERAGE CURRENT
DEMOTIC GENERAL GENERIC IGNOBLE
NATURAL POPULAR PROFANE RAFFISH
REGULAR TRIVIAL UNNOBLE FAMILIAR

FREQUENT HABITUAL MEDIOCRE
ORDINARY PLEBEIAN TRIFLING
RECIPROCAL
COMMONPLACE DULL WORN BANAL
DAILY PLAIN PROSY STALE TRITE USUAL
COMMON GARDEN HOMELY TRUISM
VULGAR HUMDRUM INSIPID PROSAIC
TEDIOUS TRIVIAL BANALITY BROMIDIC
EVERYDAY ORDINARY PEDESTRIAN
COMMOTION DO ADO DIN FLAP FRAY
FUSS HELL RIOT STIR FLARE FUROR
HURRY STORM WHIRL BUSTLE FLURRY
FRACAS FURORE HOOPLA POTHER
RUFFLE SQUALL TUMULT UNREST
BLUSTER CLATTER TEMPEST TURMOIL
DISORDER ERUPTION UPHEAVAL
UPRISING
COMMUNICATE SAY GIVE SHOW SIGN
TELL BREAK CONVEY IMPART INFECT
INFORM SIGNAL REVEAL ADDRESS
DECLARE DICTATE DIVULGE CONVERSE
DESCRIBE INTIMATE
COMMUNICATION CALL NOTE WORD
CABLE LETTER SPEECH ADDRESS
MESSAGE LANGUAGE TELEGRAM
MEMORANDUM
(— SERVICE) TELEX
COMMUNIST RED COMMIE SOVIET
COMRADE
COMMUNITY BODY BURG CITY CLAN
STATE THORP COLONY FAMILY HAMLET
NATION PUBLIC COMMUNE KINGDOM
SOCIETY VILLAGE DISTRICT PROVINCE
TOWNSHIP
(— OF ANCHORITES) LAURA
(— OF INTERESTS) KINSHIP
(— OF KNIGHTS TEMPLARS)
PRECEPTORY
(— OF NATURE) RACE
(— OF ORGANISMS) GAMODEME
(— OF TURKS) KIZILBASH
(COOPERATIVE —) PHALANSTERY
(ECOLOGICAL —) PROCLIMAX
(JEWISH —) JEWRY KOLEL ALJAMA
SHTETL JUDAISM SYNAGOG KEHILLAH
(MAORI —) KAIK
(PERUVIAN —) AYLLU COMUNIDAD
(PLANT —) HEATH FOREST ALTERNE
ENCLAVE
(RELIGIOUS —) CENOBY SANGHA
CONVENT CENOBIUM
(RUSSIAN —) MIR
(UTOPIAN —) PANTISOCRACY
(VILLAGE —) IKHWAN
COMPACT BOND FAST FIRM HARD KNIT
PACK PACT SNUG TRIM BRIEF CLOSE
COVIN DENSE GROSS PITHY SOLID TERSE
THICK TIGHT HARDEN LEAGUE SPISSY
STOCKY VANITY CONCISE CONCORD
SERRIED TABLOID ALLIANCE CONDENSE
CONTRACT COVENANT HEAVYSET
SUCCINCT
COMPANION PAL CHUM MATE PEER
BUDDY COMES CRONY MATCH MATEY
COBBER ESCORT FELLOW FRIEND
SHADOW SPOUSE STEADY ACHATES
COMPANY COMPEER COMRADE

CONSORT PARTNER SOCIATE SOCIETY
COMPADRE FAMILIAR HELPMATE
SYNODITE
COMPANIONSHIP FERE SHIP HAUNT
COMPANY SOCIETY AFFINITY
COMPANY MOB SET BAND BEVY BODY
CREW FIRM GANG HERD HOST MANY
SORT TEAM COVEN COVEY CROWD
FLOCK GROUP GUEST HORDE PARTY
SQUAD SUITE TROOP CIRCLE CLIQUE
COHORT DECURY LOCHUS OUTFIT
THRONG TROUPE BATTERY COLLEGE
CONSORT MANIPLE SOCIETY VISITOR
ASSEMBLY PRESENCE
(— OF BADGERS) CETE
(— OF BIRDS) BANK
(— OF BOOKSELLERS) CONGER
(— OF DANCERS) COMPARSA
(— OF HERDSMEN) BOOLY
(— OF HORSEMEN) TROOP
(— OF MARTENS) RICHESSE
(— OF SINGERS) CHOIR CHORUS
(— OF THE FAITHFUL) FOLD
(— OF TRAVELERS) CAFILA
CAVALCADE
(— OF WOMEN) GAGGLE
(— OF WORSHIPPERS) THIASUS
(FINANCIAL —) FACTOR
(FIRE —) SQUAD
(MILITARY —) WATCH DECURY VENLIT
PELOTON VEXILLUM
COMPARABLE LIKE SAME SIMILAR
COMPARE VIE LIKE APPLY EQUAL LIKEN
MATCH TALLY PARIFY RELATE BALANCE
BRACKET COLLATE EXAMINE CONTRAST
ESTIMATE PARALLEL RESEMBLE SIMILIZE
COMPARISON SIMILE ANALOGY
BALANCE DISIMILE LIKENESS METAPHOR
PARALLEL
COMPARTMENT BIN BOX CAB POD
CELL DECK FLUE PANE PART SLOT WELL
ABODE CABIN HATCH HUTCH PANEL
STALL ALCOVE BUNKER GARAGE HOPPER
REGION SMOKER ALVEOLE CABINET
CAPSULE CELLULE CHAMBER HOUSING
LOCULUS SECTION ALVEOLUS DIVISION
PIGEONHOLE
(— FOR COAL) BUNKER
(— FOR TREATING ORE) KITCHEN
(— IN BARN) BAY
(— IN STOVE) BROILER
(— OF COACH) IMPERIAL
(— OF ROOF) SEVERY
(— OF WINDOW) LIGHT
(— ON GAMEBOARD) STORE
(— ON ROULETTE WHEEL) EAGLE
(— ON TRAIN) COUCHETTE
(CARGO —) HOLD
(DETACHABLE —) POD
(GAS-TIGHT —) BALLONET
(GUNNER'S —) BLISTER
(REFRIGERATOR —) CHILLER
(SLEEPING —) CUBICLE
(STAGECOACH —) COUPE
(STORAGE —) BOOT
COMPASS BOW AREA ROSE SIZE TOUR
AMBIT FIELD GAMUT RANGE REACH

COMPASS SCOPE SWEEP TENOR BOUNDS CIRCLE DEGREE EXTENT SPHERE SPREAD VOLUME AZIMUTH CALIBER CIRCUIT CONFINE EMBRACE ENCLOSE HORIZON PELORUS PURVIEW BOUNDARY SURROUND
(— IN SHIP'S CABIN) TELLTALE
(— NEEDLE END) LILY
(— OF MELODY) AMBITUS
(— OF TONES) DIAPASON
(— OF VOICE) GAMUT SCALE
(— POINT) RHUMB
(BELL-MAKING —) CROOK
(PART OF —) PIN CARD DOME HOOD PIVOT HOUSING BINNACLE

COMPASSION RUE PITY GRACE HEART MERCY PIETY SORRY LENITY REMORSE CLEMENCY HUMANITY KINDNESS SYMPATHY

COMPASSIONATE MEEK RUTH SOFT HUMAN GENTLE TENDER CLEMENT PITEOUS GRACIOUS MERCIFUL

COMPATIBLE AKIN CIVIL ARTISTIC SUITABLE

COMPEL MAKE MOVE URGE BRING CAUSE DRIVE EXACT FORCE PRESS SHOVE COERCE ENJOIN EXTORT INCITE OBLIGE ACTUATE COMMAND DRAGOON ENFORCE REQUIRE NECESSITATE

COMPENDIUM LIST BRIEF APERCU DIGEST PRECIS SKETCH SURVEY CATALOG EPITOME LEXICON OUTLINE PANDECT SUMMARY ABSTRACT BREVIARY SYLLABUS SYNOPSIS

COMPENSATE PAY JIBE AGREE ATONE COVER REPAY OFFSET RECOUP REDEEM REWARD SQUARE REDRESS REPRISE REQUITE RESTORE SATISFY DISPENSE EQUALIZE

COMPENSATION BOT FEE PAY HIRE TOLL BONUS WAGES AMENDS OFFSET REWARD SALARY DAMAGES PAYMENT REDRESS STIPEND EARNINGS INTEREST PITTANCE REQUITAL

COMPETE PIT VIE COPE KEMP CLASH MATCH RIVAL STRIVE CONTEND CONTEST EMULATE

COMPETENCE SKILL ABILITY FACULTY CAPACITY

COMPETENT UP APT FIT ABLE GOOD MEET SANE ADEPT SMART TIGHT WORTHY CAPABLE ENDOWED SKILLED ADEQUATE SUITABLE QUALIFIED

COMPETITION DRAW GAME HEAT JUMP MATCH PRIZE TRIAL CONTEST PARAGON RIVALRY CONCOURS CONFLICT

COMPETITOR FOE ENEMY MATCH RIVAL PLAYER AGONIST ENTRANT GAMESTER OPPONENT

COMPILATION ANA BOOK CODE DIGEST DIRECTORY

COMPILE ADD EDIT AMASS GATHER SELECT ARRANGE COLLECT COMPOSE PREPARE

COMPLACENT CALM SMUG PLACID FATUOUS PRIGGISH

COMPLAIN AIL BEEF CARP FRET FUSS KEEN KICK MOAN WAIL YELP BITCH BLEAT BRAWL CROAK GRIPE GROWL GRUMP GRUNT WHINE BEWAIL CHARGE GRIEVE GROUSE HOLLER MURMUR REPINE SQUAWK YAMMER DEPLORE GRUMBLE INVEIGH PROTEST BELLYACHE

COMPLAINT RAP BEEF FUSS HOWL MOAN WAIL BITCH GRIPE GROWL WHINE GROUCH GROUSE GRUDGE HOLLER LAMENT MALADY SQUAWK AILMENT DISEASE GRUMBLE ILLNESS PROTEST QUARREL DISORDER JEREMIAD

COMPLEMENT CREW GANG FORCE TALLY AMOUNT ADJUNCT OBVERSE PENDANT

COMPLETE DO ALL CAP END DEAD FILL FINE FULL PURE RANK VERY CLEAN CROWN EVERY LARGE PLAIN PLUMB POINT PUKKA QUITE RIPEN SOLID SOUND STARK TOTAL UTTER WHOLE EFFECT ENTIRE FINISH GLOBAL INTACT PROPER SINGLE STRICT ACHIEVE CONFIRM EXECUTE FULFILL PERFECT PLENARY REALIZE REPLETE ABSOLUTE CONCLUDE FINALIZE INTEGRAL OUTRIGHT PROFOUND THOROUGH ACCOMPLISH

COMPLETELY ALL FLAT GOOD SLAM SLAP SPAN CLEAN FULLY PLUMB QUITE SHEER SMACK SPANG STARK STOCK UTTER BODILY ENTIRE PURELY WHOLLY DIRECTLY ENTIRELY OUTRIGHT

COMPLEX HARD MAZY MIXED KNOTTY SYSTEM CULTURE NETWORK SINUOUS TANGLED TWISTED ABSTRUSE COMPOUND EQUATION INVOLVED MANIFOLD SYNDROME

COMPLEXION HUE CAST LEER LOOK TINT COLOR HUMOR STATE TENOR TINGE ASPECT TEMPER COLORING
(BAD —) DYSCHROA

COMPLIANCE ASSENT CESSION CONSENT HARMONY OBSEQUY ABIDANCE CIVILITY FACILITY FORMALITY

COMPLIANT EASY MEEK SOFT BUXOM FACILE PLIANT SUPPLE DUCTILE DUTIFUL WILLING OBEDIENT TOWARDLY YIELDING

COMPLICATE PUZZLE TANGLE EMBROIL INVOLVE PERPLEX BEWILDER INTRIGUE INTRICATE

COMPLICATED HARD KNOTTY PROLIX COMPLEX GORDIAN SNARLED TANGLED INVOLVED PLEXIFORM

COMPLICATION KNOT NODE PLOT NODUS SNARL TANGLE INTRIGUE

COMPLIMENT GIFT LAUD EXTOL EULOGY PRAISE SALUTE ADULATE APPLAUD BOUQUET COMMEND FLATTER TRIBUTE ENCOMIUM GRATUITY GREETING

COMPLY CEDE OBEY ABIDE ADAPT AGREE YIELD ACCEDE ACCORD ASSENT SUBMIT CONFORM EMBRACE OBSERVE

COMPONENT KEY FORM ITEM PART UNIT GIVEN FACTOR MEMBER ELEMENT INTEGRAL

COMPORT ACT BEAR KEEP SUIT AGREE

CARRY ACCORD ACQUIT BEHAVE
DEMEAN ENDURE SQUARE CONDUCT
COMPORTMENT DEALING BEHAVIOR
DEMEANOR
COMPOSE PEN SET CALM FORM MAKE
ALLAY CLERK COUCH DRAFT FRAME
ORDER SPELL WRITE ADJUST CREATE
DESIGN INDITE REDACT SETTLE SOOTHE
STEADY ARRANGE COMPILE CONCOCT
DICTATE DISPOSE FASHION PRODUCE
TYPESET COMPRISE REGULATE
COMPOSED SET CALM COOL QUIET
SOBER WROTE DEMURE DIGEST PLACID
SEDATE SERENE WRITTEN DECOROUS
TRANQUIL
COMPOSER BARD POET ODIST AUTHOR
LYRIST PENMAN WRITER CONTEUR
ELEGIST MAESTRO COLORIST ELEGIAST
IDYLLIST MELODIST MONODIST
MUSICIAN PHANTAST TUNESMITH
COMPOSITION ANA OPUS WORK CENTO
DITTY DRAMA FUGUE GETUP PIECE
POESY THEME EULOGY HAIKAI LESSON
MAGGOT MONODY THESIS ARTICLE
COMPOST EPISTLE MIXTURE PICTURE
WRITING ACROSTIC CAUSERIE
COMPOUND DIALOGUE EXERCISE
(— FOR BILLIARD BALLS) COMPO
(— TO BE ACTED) PLAY DRAMA
(— TO FILL LEATHER) STUFF
(AMOROUS —) EROTIC
(ARTISTIC —) COLLAGE
(BAGPIPE —) PORT
(CHORAL —) MOTET CANTATA
ORATORIO
(HUMOROUS —) BURLA
(IMPERFECT —) SOOTERKIN
(INSTRUMENTAL —) AIR GATO FANCY
RONDO GROUND SKETCH SONATA
TIENTO BOURREE CANZONE BERCEUSE
CONCERTO FANTASIA RHAPSODY
SYMPHONY PASSACAGLIA
(LITERARY —) BOOK CENTO DEBAT
ESSAY PIECE COMEDY SATIRE SKETCH
THESIS TREATISE
(MUSICAL —) DUET GLEE IDYL OPUS
SOLO SONG TRIO BURLA CANON DANCE
ELEGY ETUDE FUGUE IDYLL MOTET
NONET SCORE STUDY ADAGIO ARIOSO
AZIONE ENTREE SEPTET SEXTET
BALLADE BOURREE BOUTADE BRAVURA
QUARTET SCHERZO TOCCATA CAVATINA
CHACONNE CLAUSULA CONCERTO
SERENADE SINFONIA SYMPHONY
ANTIPHONY OFFERTORY PROCESSIONAL
(NARRATIVE —) BALLAD
(PLASTIC —) CEMENT
(POETIC —) GLOSS KAVYA
(RELIGIOUS —) MOTET ANTHEM
HYMNIC CANTATA ORATORIO
(VEDIC —) GAYATRI
(VOCAL —) ARIA SOLO SONG CANON
ANTHEM ELEVATIO CONDUCTUS
COMPOSURE MIEN POISE QUIET UNION
REPOSE TEMPER BALANCE POSTURE
CALMNESS SERENITY
COMPOTATION SYMPOSIUM

COMPOUND MIX BASE FILL JOIN ALLOY
AMIDE AMINE BLEND ESTER UNION
ACETAL ADJUST ALKIDE COMMIX IODIDE
JUMBLE KETONE MEDLEY PHENOL
TEMPER URACIL ALCOHOL AMALGAM
AMMONIA COMBINE COMPLEX COMPOSE
COMPOST PREPARE STEROID
COMPREHEND GET SEE KNOW TAKE
COVER GRASP IMPLY LATCH REACH
SAVVY SEIZE SENSE ATTAIN DIGEST
EMBODY FATHOM FOLLOW COMPASS
CONTAIN DISCERN EMBRACE ENCLOSE
IMAGINE INCLUDE REALIZE RECEIVE
SWALLOW CONCEIVE PERCEIVE
COMPREHENSION HOLD GRASP SAVVY
SENSE ESPRIT FATHOM NOESIS UPTAKE
INSIGHT KNOWING
COMPREHENSIVE BIG FULL WIDE
BROAD GRAND LARGE GLOBAL SCOPIC
CONCISE GENERAL GENERIC CATHOLIC
ENCYCLIC SPACIOUS
COMPRESS NIP TIE BALE BIND WRAP
CRAMP CROWD CRUSH PINCH PRESS
SMASH BUNDLE DIGEST GATHER SHRINK
STRAIN ABRIDGE BOLSTER COMPACT
CURTAIL EMBRACE FLATTEN PLEDGET
SQUEEZE SQUINCH ASTRINGE
CONDENSE CONTRACT LAMINATE
PEMMICAN RESTRAIN SUPPRESS
COMPRESSED STRICT CROWDED
SUCCINCT ANGUSTATE COARCTATE
COMPRISE HOLD COVER ATTACH
EMBODY EMPLOY MUSTER COMPOSE
CONTAIN EMBRACE ENCLOSE INCLUDE
INVOLVE CONCEIVE PERCEIVE
COMPUTE ADD SUM CAST RATE COUNT
TALLY VALUE ASSESS CIPHER FIGURE
NUMBER RECKON ACCOUNT BALANCE
ESTIMATE CALCULATE
COMPUTER ADDER ENIAC MANIAC
MAINFRAME PROCESSOR
COMRADE PAL ALLY CHUM MATE PEER
BILLY BUDDY BUTTY CRONY COPAIN
COUSIN DIGGER FRATER FRIEND HEARTY
BROTHER COMPEER CONVIVE CONFRERE
TOVARICH
COMRADESHIP CAMARADERIE
CON ANTI KNOW LOOK PORE READ SCAN
CHEAT GUIDE LEARN STEER STUDY
DIRECT PERUSE REGARD VERSUS
AGAINST DECEIVE EXAMINE INSPECT
OPPOSED SWINDLE
CONCEAL BURY HIDE KEEP MASK VEIL
VEST WRAP BLIND BOSOM CACHE
CLOAK COUCH COVER FEIGN SHADE
BURROW CLOSET DOCTOR HUDDLE
POCKET SCREEN SHADOW SHIELD
SHROUD STIFLE ENVELOP SECRETE
SMOTHER BESCREEN DISGUISE
ENSCONCE
CONCEALED SNUG BLIND PRIVY COVERT
HIDDEN LATENT OCCULT PERDUE
SECRET VEILED COVERED WRAPPED
ABSTRUSE RECONDITE
CONCEDE OWN CEDE GIVE ADMIT AGREE
ALLOW GRANT WAIVE YIELD ACCORD
ASSENT CONFESS ACKNOWLEDGE

CONCEIT EGO IDEA CRANK FANCY KNACK PRIDE QUIRK DEVICE NOTION VAGARY VANITY BIGHEAD CAPRICE EGOTISM

CONCEITED BRAG VAIN COCKY HUFFY PROUD SAUCY BIGGETY ARROGANT SNOBBISH

CONCEIVABLE EARTHLY POSSIBLE

CONCEIVE FORM HOLD MAKE PLAN BEGIN DREAM FANCY FRAME GUESS THINK DESIGN DEVISE IDEATE INTEND PONDER GESTATE IMAGINE REALIZE SUPPOSE SUSPECT CONTRIVE ENVISAGE

CONCENTRATE AIM FIX MASS PILE BUNCH FOCUS UNIFY CENTER FIXATE GATHER SINGLE COMPACT CONGEST DISTILL ENGROSS ESSENCE EXTRACT THICKEN ASSEMBLE CONDENSE FOCALIZE

CONCEPT IDEA FANCY IMAGE CONCEIT OPINION THOUGHT PERCEPTION

CONCEPTION IDEA VIEW FANCY FETUS IMAGE BELIEF DESIGN EMBRYO ENTITY NOTION CONCEIT PURPOSE

CONCERN BEAR CARE FEAR FIRM PART SAKE APPLY CAUSE GRIEF HEART TOUCH WORRY AFFAIR AFFECT CHARGE DIRECT EMPLOY IMPORT MATTER REGARD ANXIETY COMPANY DISTURB INVOLVE PERTAIN RESPECT TROUBLE BUSINESS INTEREST

CONCERNING OF ON RE FOR TILL ABOUT ANENT APROPOS

CONCERT POP UNITE ACCORD ARRANGE BENEFIT CONCORD HARMONY RECITAL

CONCESSION BOON FAVOR GRANT LEASE ALLOWANCE PRIVILEGE

CONCILIATE CALM EASE ATONE HONEY ADJUST PACIFY SOFTEN APPEASE CONCILE MOLLIFY PLACATE SATISFY PROPITIATE

CONCISE CURT NEAT TRIG BRIEF CRISP PITHY SHORT TERSE COMPACT LACONIC POINTED PRECISE SUMMARY TABLOID SUCCINCT

CONCLUDE END AMEN REST CLOSE ESTOP INFER JUDGE LIMIT DECIDE DEDUCE EXPIRE FIGURE FINISH GATHER REASON RECKON SETTLE ACHIEVE ARRANGE RESOLVE SUPPOSE COMPLETE ESTIMATE

CONCLUSION END AMEN CODA LAST CLOSE FINIS ISSUE POINT ENDING FINALE FINISH RESULT THIRTY UPSHOT CURTAIN OUTCOME VERDICT DECISION EPILOGUE

CONCLUSIVE LAST FINAL CERTAIN EXTREME TELLING DECISIVE DEFINITE ULTIMATE

CONCOCT MIX BREW COOK FAKE PLAN PLOT FRAME HATCH THINK DEVISE INVENT REFINE SCHEME COMPOSE PREPARE COMPOUND

CONCORD AGREE AMITY PEACE TERMS UNION UNITY UNISON COMPACT CONCERT HARMONY ONENESS COMMUNITY

CONCRETE FIRM HARD REAL GROUT SOLID ACTUAL CEMENT GUNITE CONGEAL COALESCE POSITIVE TANGIBLE

CONCRETION CLOT KNOT PEARL STONE BEZOAR DOGGER NODULE LITHITE OTOLITH CALCULUS

CONCUR JIBE JOIN AGREE CHECK CHIME UNITE ACCEDE ACCORD ASSENT APPROVE CONSENT COINCIDE CONSPIRE CONVERGE

CONDEMN BAN CAST DAMN DEEM DOOM HISS BLAME DECRY JUDGE AMERCE BANISH DETEST CENSURE CONVICT DENOUNCE REPROACH SENTENCE PROSCRIBE

CONDENSATION STORY DIGEST CAPSULE BOILDOWN

CONDENSE CUT BRIEF DECOCT DIGEST HARDEN LESSEN NARROW REDUCE SHRINK ABRIDGE CAPSULE COMBINE COMPACT DISTILL SHORTEN SQUEEZE THICKEN COMPRESS CONTRACT DIMINISH SOLIDIFY

CONDENSED CURT BRIEF CAPSULE COMPACT CONCISE SUMMARY TABLOID ABSORBED

CONDESCEND DEIGN FAVOR GRANT STOOP ASSENT OBLIGE SUBMIT CONCEDE DESCEND

CONDIMENT SOY HERB MACE SAGE SALT CAPER CURRY SAUCE SPICE THYME CATSUP CLOVES GARLIC PEPPER RELISH CHUTNEY KETCHUP MUSTARD OREGANO PAPRIKA VINEGAR ALLSPICE DRESSING TURMERIC

CONDITION IF WAY CASE FORM MODE RANK TERM TRIM ANGLE CAUSE CLASS COLOR PLACE POINT SHAPE STAGE STATE AGENCY DEGREE ESTATE FETTLE MORALE PLIGHT STATUS FEATHER FOOTING PREMISE PREPARE PROVISO STATION OCCASION POSITION STANDING REQUIREMENT

(— OF ANXIETY) CARK

(CHANCE —) ACCIDENT

(DEBASED —) CACHEXY CACHEXIA

(DEPRESSED —) DOWNBEAT

(DETERMINING —) GROUND

(DIRTY —) CLAT

(DISEASED —) DIEBACK

(DISGRACEFUL —) IGNOMINY

(DRUNKEN —) BUN

(FLOURISHING —) HEALTH

(GENERAL —) VOGUE

(HABITUAL —) TENOR

(MEAN —) DUST

(MISERABLE —) SQUALOR

(MORBID —) HOLDOVER

(NECESSARY —) MEAN

(NEUROTIC —) LATAH

(ORDERLY —) DECENCY

(PAINFUL —) CRICK

(PERMANENT —) HEXIS

(PROPER —) KILTER

(PROTECTIVE —) CALLUS

(SCURFY —) BUCKSKIN

(STATIONARY —) JIB

(SUBLIME —) HEAVEN
(SURROUNDING —) AIR
(TRUE —) SIZE
(UNEQUAL —) ODDS
(UNPROSPEROUS —) ILLTH
(UNWHOLESOME —) MALADY
(WEATHER —S) ELEMENTS
CONDITIONAL EVENTUAL PROVISORY
QUALIFIED
CONDONE BLINK REMIT ACQUIT EXCUSE
FORGET IGNORE PARDON ABSOLVE
FORGIVE OVERLOOK
CONDOR TIFFIN BUZZARD VULTURE
CONDUCT ACT RUN USE BEAR DEED
FARE FORM KEEP LEAD MIEN QUIT SHOW
TAKE WAGE CARRY CHAIR DRESS GESTE
GUIDE HABIT TRAIN USAGE USHER
ACTION ATTEND BEHAVE CONVEY
CONVOY COURSE DEPORT DIRECT
ESCORT GOVERN MANNER SQUIRE
BEARING CHANNEL COMPORT CONDUIT
CONTROL EXECUTE OPERATE BEHAVIOR
CARRIAGE COURTESY DEMEANOR
GUIDANCE REGULATE SHEPHERD
TRANSACT
(APPROPRIATE —) DHARMA
(BRASH —) FACE
(CONVENTIONAL —) PRAXIS
(DISORDERLY —) RANDAN
(DORMANT —) LATENCY
(ETHICAL —) HONOR
(PROPER —) CRICKET
(RECKLESS —) DEVILRY
(RIGHT —) TE TAO
(RIOTOUS —) RANDAN
(SAFE —) KOWL COWLE
(SEDITIOUS —) MISPRISION
(SHOWY —) BRAVADO
(SLOPPY —) SWASH
(VAINGLORIOUS —) HEROICS
(WANTON —) RUFF
(WEAK —) FOLLY
CONDUCTOR LEAD MAIN BRUSH BRIDGE
BUSMAN CARMAN ESCORT FEEDER
LEADER CAPTAIN CATHODE MAESTRO
MANAGER AQUEDUCT BATONIST
CICERONE CONVEYOR DIRECTOR
(— OF FESTIVAL) SKUDLER
(ELECTRIC —) FILAMENT
(LIGHTNING —) ROD
(OMNIBUS —) CAD
(WOMAN —) CLIPPIE
CONDUIT DUCT GOUT MAIN PIPE SINK
TUBE WIRE CABLE CANAL SEWER
HEADER SLUICE TROUGH CARRIER
CHANNEL CHIMNEY CULVERT EXHAUST
LATERAL PASSAGE AQUEDUCT
WASTEWAY
CONE CAP MOXA PINA SCREW SPIRE
BOBBIN CONIOLE FRUSTUM PYRAMID
THIMBLE PASTILLE PINECONE STROBILE
STROBILUS
(— OF CLOTH) VANE
(— OF FIR) YOW YOWIE STROBIL
STROBILE STROBILUS
(— OF GUNPOWDER) PEEOY
(— OF HOP PLANT) BUR

(— OF SILVER AMALGAM) PINA
(— ON LOG END) CAP
(— ON SHOE) CLEAT
(— STRUCTURE) NURAGHE
(HALF —) FORME NAPPE
(ICE CREAM —) ICE CORNET
(INVERTED —) HOPPER
(PAPER —) SPILL COFFIN
(ROPE-MAKING —) TOP
(TOP CUT FROM —) UNGULA
(VOLCANIC —) PUY MONTICULE
CONFECTION CHOW CANDY DULCE
SWEET BONBON COMFIT DAINTY
DRAGEE HALVAH JUNKET NOUGAT
TABLET CARAMEL FONDANT POMFRET
PRALINE SUCCADE CONSERVE DELICACY
MARZIPAN QUIDDANY MARSHMALLOW
CONFEDERACY BUND COVIN JUNTA
UNION LEAGUE ALLIANCE COVENANT
CONFEDERATE AID PAL REB ALLY
REBEL UNITE LEAGUE ABETTOR PARTNER
CONFEDERATION BODY BUND ZUPA
GUEUX UNION LEAGUE COMPACT
HASINAI SOCIETY ALLIANCE COVENANT
CONFER DUB GIVE MEET TALK AWARD
ENDOW GRANT SPEND TREAT BESTOW
DONATE HUDDLE IMPART INVEST
PARLEY POWWOW COMMUNE CONSULT
COUNSEL DISCUSS PRESENT COLLOGUE
CONFERENCE DIET TALK SYNOD TRUST
CAUCUS CONFAB HUDDLE INDABA
KORERO PARLEY PARVIS POWWOW
SUMMIT CIRCUIT COUNCIL MEETING
PALAVER PARLING SEMINAR COLLOQUY
CONCLAVE CONGRESS PRACTICE
PARLIAMENT
CONFESS OWN AVOW SING ADMIT
GRANT REVEAL CONCEDE DIVULGE
PROFESS DISCLOSE ACKNOWLEDGE
CONFESSION CREDO CREED GRANT
AVOWAL SHRIFT PECCAVI COGNOVIT
(MUTUAL —) SHARING
CONFIDE RELY TELL TRUST COMMIT
DEPEND CONSIGN ENTRUST
CONFIDENCE FACE HOPE CHEEK FAITH
TRUST APLOMB BELIEF CREDIT METTLE
MORALE SURETY COUNSEL COURAGE
BOLDNESS CREDENCE RELIANCE
SECURITY SURENESS
CONFIDENT BOLD SMUG SURE COCKY
HARDY SECURE ASSURED CERTAIN
HOPEFUL RELIANT CONSTANT FEARLESS
IMPUDENT POSITIVE SANGUINE
TRUSTFUL
CONFIDENTIAL BOSOM PRIVY CLOSET
COVERT HUSHED INWARD SECRET
PRIVATE ESOTERIC FAMILIAR INTIMATE
CONFINE BAR BOX DAM HEM MEW PEN
PIN STY TIE BIND CAGE COOP CRIB FOLD
HASP JAIL KEEP LACE LOCK SEAL SHUT
STOP STOW CABIN CHAIN CRAMP
CROWD DELAY FENCE HOUSE LIMIT
PINCH STINT THIRL BORDER BOTTLE
COARCT CORRAL EMBANK FETTER
FORBAR HURDLE IMMURE IMPALE
INTERN PINION POCKET PRISON TETHER
ASTRICT CHAMBER COMPASS CONTAIN

IMPOUND INCLUDE MANACLE RECLOSE
SECLUDE SHACKLE TRAMMEL CLOISTER
CONCLUDE IMPRISON RESTRAIN
STRAITEN
CONFINED ILL FAST PENT BOUND CAGED
CLOSE BEDRID SEALED CAPTIVE
CRAMPED LIMITED
CONFINEMENT MEW BOND JAIL WARD
DURANCE SOLITARY
CONFIRM FIX SET SEAL PROVE VOUCH
AFFIRM ASSURE ATTEST AVOUCH
CLINCH FASTEN HARDEN RATIFY
SECOND SETTLE VERIFY APPROVE
ENDORSE FORTIFY JUSTIFY SUPPORT
SUSTAIN ACCREDIT ENTRENCH
SANCTION VALIDATE CORROBORATE
CONFISCATE GRAB SEIZE USURP
CONDEMN ESCHEAT
CONFLAGRATION FIRE BLAZE FEVER
BURNING INFERNO
CONFLICT JAR WAR AGON BOUT DUEL
FRAY MEET RIFT AGONY BROIL BRUSH
CLASH FIGHT GRIPS ACTION BATTLE
COMBAT MUTINY OPPOSE SCRAPE
STRIFE CONTEND CONTEST DISCORD
SCUFFLE WARFARE DISAGREE MILITATE
SKIRMISH STRUGGLE COLLISION
CONFORM GO FIT HEW BEND LEAN
OBEY SUIT ABIDE ADAPT AGREE APPLY
SHAPE YIELD ACCEDE ADJUST ASSENT
COMPLY SETTLE SQUARE SUBMIT
COMPOSE CONFIRM
CONFORMITY FIT ACCORD DHARMA
EQUITY HARMONY JUSTICE KEEPING
ACCURACY AFFINITY JUSTNESS
LIKENESS SYMMETRY CONGRUITY
FORMALITY ACCORDANCE CONSERTION
CONFOUND MIX DASH MAZE ROUT
STAM STUN WHIP ABASH ADDLE AMAZE
APPAL BLAST SPOIL STUMP BAFFLE
DISMAY MINGLE MUDDLE RATTLE
ASTOUND CONFUSE CONFUTE CORRUPT
DESTROY FLUMMOX MISTAKE NONPLUS
PERPLEX PETRIFY STUMBLE STUPEFY
ASTONISH BABELIZE BEWILDER
DISTRACT DUMFOUND SURPRISE
CONFRONT DARE DEFY FACE MEET
BEARD BRAVE FRONT STAND ACCOST
ASSAIL BREAST OPPOSE RESIST
ENVISAGE THREATEN
CONFUSE FOX MIX DASH MAZE MUSS
ROIL ROUT ABASH ADDLE AMAZE BEFOG
BLEND CLOUD MUDDY SNARL STEER
TWIST UPSET BAFFLE BEDAZE BEMUSE
BOTHER DUDDER FLURRY FUDDLE
JUMBLE MUDDLE PUZZLE RAFFLE
RATTLE TWITCH BECLOUD BEDEVIL
BLUNDER BUMBAZE DERANGE DIFFUSE
EMBROIL FLUSTER MISTAKE MYSTIFY
NONPLUS PERPLEX PERTURB SCATTER
SHUFFLE STUPEFY UNRAVEL BEFUDDLE
BEWILDER CONFOUND DISORDER
DISTRACT DUMFOUND ENTANGLE
OBFUSCATE
CONFUSED ASEA LOST DIZZY FOGGY
FUZZY MISTY MUDDY MUZZY VAGUE
BLOTTO CLOUDY BEMUSED BLURRED

CHAOTIC CLOUDED DIFFUSE MIFFLED
OBSCURE RATTLED STUPENT COCKEYED
DERANGED INVOLVED
CONFUSION PI DIN FLAP FUSS MESS
MOIL RIOT BABEL CHAOS HAVOC SNAFU
SNARL ATAXIA BABBLE BEDLAM
BUMBLE HUBBUB JABBLE JUMBLE
MUDDLE POTHER RABBLE RUFFLE
RUMPUS THRONG TOPHET TUMULT
UPROAR WELTER ANARCHY BLUNDER
BLUSTER CLUTTER COBWEBS RUMMAGE
TURMOIL DISARRAY DISORDER
SHAMBLES STRAMASH
CONGEAL GEL ICE SET CANDY CURDLE
FREEZE HARDEN STIFFEN THICKEN
SOLIDIFY
CONGENIAL BOON HAPPY AMIABLE
CONNATE KINDRED
CONGESTION JAM HEAP CROWDING
STOPPAGE
CONGLOMERATE HEAP MASS PILE
ROCK STACK BANKET PSEPHITE
NAGELFLUH

CONGO

CAPITAL: BRAZZAVILLE
COIN: FRANC FRANCCFA
LAKE: MWERU TUMBA UPEMBA LEOPOLD
NATIVE: SUSA VILI MANTU PYGMY
BATEKE MBOCHI WABUMA BAKONGO
BANGALA
PLATEAU: BATEKE
RIVER: UELE CONGO KWILU LULUA NGOKO
NIARI SANGA WAMBA KWENGE LOANGE
SANGHA UBANGI KOUILOU LUBILASH
TOWN: EWO EPENA HOLLE JACOB OKOYO
SEMBE MAKOUA OUESSO ZANAGA
DOLISIE ENYELLE LOUBOMO SOUANKE
DJAMBALA BRAZZAVILLE
TRIBUTARY: LOMAMI UBANGI ARUWIMA
LUALABA LUAPULA ITIMBIRI

CONGRATULATE HUG JOY LAUD GREET
SALUTE FLATTER MACARIZE
CONGREGATE HERD MASS MEET PACK
TEEM GROUP SWARM TROOP GATHER
MUSTER COLLECT CONVENE ASSEMBLE
CONGREGATION BODY FOLD HERD
HOST MASS FLOCK SWARM CHURCH
PARISH COMPANY MEETING ORATORY
SYNAXIS ASSEMBLY BRETHREN
CONGRESS DAIL DIET SYNOD UYEZD
OBLAST POWWOW COUNCIL GORSEDD
MEETING ASSEMBLY CONCLAVE
CONIFER FIR YEW PINE CEDAR LARCH
SPRUCE SOFTWOOD EVERGREEN
CONJECTURE AIM CAST PLOT SHOT
VIEW AUGUR FANCY GUESS OPINE
THINK BELIEF DIVINE THEORY IMAGINE
OPINION PRESUME SUPPOSE SURMISE
SUSPECT
CONJUNCTION AS ET IF OR AND BUT
NOR TIE THAN JOINT SINCE SYNOD
UNION UNITY THOUGH JOINDER
CONJURE PRAY WISH CHARM ENJOIN

INVOKE SUMMON BESEECH COMBINE ENTREAT CONSPIRE CONTRIVE EXORCIZE

CONJURER MAGE PELLAR POWWOW SHAMAN WIZARD WARLOCK ANGEKKOK JONGLEUR MAGICIAN SORCERER

CONNECT COG TIE ALLY BIND BOND GEAR GLUE JOIN KNIT KNOT LINK AFFIX CHAIN MARRY UNITE ATTACH BRIDGE CEMENT COHERE COUPLE FASTEN RELATE SPLICE COMBINE ENCHAIN INVOLVE

CONNECTICUT

CAPITAL: HARTFORD
COLLEGE: TRINITY
COUNTY: TOLLAND WINDHAM
INDIAN: PEQUOT MOHEGAN NIANTIC
STATE BIRD: ROBIN
STATE FLOWER: LAUREL
STATE NICKNAME: NUTMEG
STATE TREE: OAK
TOWN: AVON BETHEL CANAAN COSCOB DARIEN MYSTIC SHARON STORRS WILTON DANBURY MERIDEN NIANTIC NORWALK NORWICH TOLLAND WINDSOR NEWHAVEN SIMSBURY WESTPORT GREENWICH RIDGEFIELD
UNIVERSITY: YALE WESLEYAN

CONNECTION TAP TIE BOND LINK HITCH NEXUS UNION BUCKLE CLEVIS GROUND SUTURE SWIVEL BEARING BOLSTER CONTACT FERRULE HOLDING KINSHIP LIAISON RAPPORT AFFINITY ALLIANCE COMMERCE INTIMACY JUNCTION LIGATION
(ELECTRICAL —) GROUND
(FORKED —) BRANCH
(MECHANICAL —S) LEADOUT

CONNIVE ABET PLOT WINK BLINK CABAL ASSENT FOMENT INCITE COLLUDE

CONNOISSEUR JUDGE CRITIC EXPERT EPICURE GOURMET COGNOSCENTE

CONNUBIAL MARITAL CONJUGAL DOMESTIC

CONQUER WIN BEAT BEST DOWN GAIN LICK ROUT TAME WHIP CRUSH DAUNT DEFEAT HUMBLE MASTER REDUCE SUBDUE PREVAIL SUBJECT SURPASS TRIUMPH OVERCOME SURMOUNT VANQUISH

CONQUEROR HERO MASTER VICTOR WINNER TRIUMPHER

CONQUEST MASTERY SCALING TRIUMPH VICTORY WINNING

CONSCIENCE WORD HEART SENSE SCRUPLE THOUGHT

CONSCIENTIOUS FAIR JUST EXACT RIGID EIDENT HONEST STRICT DUTIFUL UPRIGHT FAITHFUL

CONSCIOUS KEEN ALIVE AWAKE AWARE FEELING KNOWING WITTING RATIONAL SENSIBLE SENTIENT

CONSCIOUSNESS EGO HEART SENSE

SPIRIT FEELING THOUGHT AWARENESS PERCEPTION

CONSCRIPT LEVY DRAFT ENROL ENLIST MUSTER DRAFTEE DRAUGHT RECRUIT

CONSCRIPTION LEVY

CONSECRATE VOW FAIN HOLY BLESS DEIFY ANOINT DEVOTE HALLOW ORDAIN DEDICATE SANCTIFY

CONSECRATED BLEST OBLATE SACRED VOTARY VOTIVE BLESSED HALLOWED HIERATIC

CONSENT HEAR AGREE ALLOW GRANT YIELD ACCEDE ACCORD AFFORD ASSENT BETEEM COMPLY CONCUR PERMIT APPROVE

CONSEQUENCE END EVENT FRUIT ISSUE EFFECT IMPORT MOMENT REPUTE RESULT SEQUEL WEIGHT CONCERN OUTCOME PRODUCE PURPOSE SEQUELA SEQUENT BACKLASH OCCASION OUTGROWTH RAMIFICATION

CONSEQUENTLY SO ERGO THEN THUS HENCE LATER PURSUANT PRESENTLY

CONSERVATIVE SAFE TORY FUSTY QUIET STAID FABIAN HUNKER STABLE BOURBON DIEHARD HARDHAT MODERATE UNIONIST

CONSERVE CAN JAM SAVE GUARD JELLY DEFEND SECURE SHIELD UPHOLD HUSBAND PROTECT SUSTAIN MAINTAIN

CONSIDER AIM SEE CALL CAST DEEM HEED HOLD MULL MUSE RATE SEEM TAKE TALE VIEW ALLOW COUNT ENTER JUDGE POISE SPELL STUDY THINK WEIGH ADVISE BEHOLD DEVISE ESTEEM EXPEND FIGURE IMPUTE PONDER REASON RECKON REGARD REWARD SURVEY BELIEVE CANVASS CONSULT EXAMINE INSPECT REFLECT RESPECT SUPPOSE COGITATE ESTIMATE MEDITATE RUMINATE

CONSIDERABLE FAIR GOOD TIDY BONNY CANNY GREAT LARGE SMART GOODLY PRETTY GOODISH HEALTHY INTENSE NOTABLE SEVERAL POWERFUL

CONSIDERATE KIND MILD NICE GENTLE TENDER CAREFUL HEEDFUL PRUDENT SERIOUS TACTFUL DELICATE GRACIOUS ATTENTIVE

CONSIDERATION SAKE COUNT PRICE TOPIC ASPECT DEBATE ESTEEM MOMENT MOTIVE NOTICE REASON REFLEX REGARD SURVEY ACCOUNT INSIGHT PREMIUM RESPECT THOUGHT ALTRUISM COURTESY DELICACY EMINENCE EMPHASIS GRATUITY PROSPECT SANCTION

CONSIGN DOOM GIVE MAIL SEND SHIP ALLOT AWARD CHECK REMIT YIELD COMMIT DEVOTE REMAND ADDRESS DELIVER DEPOSIT ENTRUST BEQUEATH DELEGATE RELEGATE TRANSFER

CONSIGNMENT INVOICE FOREDOOM SHIPMENT
(— OF TEA) BREAK

CONSIST LIE HOLD RELY REST DWELL

EXIST STAND CONTAIN EMBRACE
COMPRISE

CONSISTENCY BODY UNION DEGREE
CONCORD HARMONY KEEPING EVENNESS
FIRMNESS SOLIDITY SYMMETRY

CONSISTENT EVEN FIRM STEADY
DURABLE LOGICAL REGULAR UNIFORM
COHERENT ENDURING SUITABLE
COMPATIBLE

CONSOLATION SOP RELIEF SOLACE
COMFORT

CONSOLE CALM ALLAY CHEER ORGAN
TABLE SOLACE SOOTHE CABINET
COMFORT RELIEVE SUPPORT SUSTAIN

CONSOLIDATE KNIT MASS POOL WELD
BLEND MERGE UNIFY UNITE HARDEN
MINGLE COMBINE COMPACT COALESCE
COMPRESS CONDENSE ORGANIZE
SOLIDIFY

CONSONANT STOP DENTAL FORTIS
LABIAL LETTER SONANT MUTABLE
PALATAL PLOSIVE SPIRANT ALVEOLAR
ASPIRATE BILABIAL EJECTIVE GEMINATE
HARMONIC SUITABLE

CONSPICUOUS BIG BOLD RANK CLEAR
FAMED PLAIN FAMOUS MARKED PATENT
SIGNAL BLATANT EMINENT GLARING
NOTABLE OBVIOUS POINTED SALIENT
APPARENT EMPHATIC FLAGRANT
MANIFEST STRIKING PROMINENT
NOTICEABLE OUTSTANDING

CONSPIRACY COUP PLAN PLOT CABAL
SCHEME COMPACT INTRIGUE

CONSPIRE ABET PLOT SCHEME COLLUDE
CONNIVE CONTRIVE

CONSTABLE COP BULL BEADLE BEAGLE
KEEPER WARDEN BAILIFF OFFICER
TIPSTAFF

CONSTANT SET EVEN FIRM JUST TRUE
FIXED LOYAL SOLID STILL TRIED STABLE
STEADY CERTAIN CHRONIC DURABLE
FOREVER LASTING REGULAR STAUNCH
UNIFORM ENDURING FAITHFUL POSITIVE
RESOLUTE STANDING PERENNIAL

CONSTELLATION ARA CUP FLY FOX
LEO APUS ARGO COLT CROW CRUX
DOVE GOAT GRUS HARE HARP LION
LYNX LYRA MAST PAVO PLOW SIGN
SWAN TAUR URSA VELA WAIN WOLF
ALTAR ARIES CAMEL CETUS CLOCK
CRANE DRACO EAGLE GROUP HYDRA
INDUS LEPUS LIBRA LUPUS MALUS
MENSA MUSCA NORMA ORION PYXIS
RAVEN TABLE VIRGO WAGON WHALE
ANTLIA AQUILA AURIGA BOOTES
CAELUM CANCER CARINA CORVUS
CRATER CYGNUS DIPPER DORADO
FORNAX GEMINI HYDRUS INDIAN LIZARD
OBELUS OCTANS OKNARI PICTOR PISCES
PISCIS PLOUGH PUPPIS SCALES SCUTUM
TAURUS TIGRIS TOUCAN TUCANA
VOLANS ALGEBAR CEPHEUS CLUSTER
COLUMBA COMPASS DOLPHIN FURNACE
GIRAFFE LACERTA MONARCH OETAEUS
PATTERN PEACOCK PEGASUS PERSEUS
PHOENIX RHOMBUS SAGITTA SCORPIO
SERPENS SERPENT SEXTANS SEXTANT

XIPHIAS AQUARIUS ASTERISM
CHAMPION CIRCINUS CYNOSURE
EQUULEUS ERIDANUS HERCULES
HERDSMAN KASHYAPA QUADRANS
REINDEER RETICULE SCORPION
SCORPIUS SCULPTOR TRIANGLE

CONSTERNATION FEAR ALARM PANIC
DISMAY FRIGHT HORROR TERROR
TREPIDITY

CONSTITUENT ATOM ITEM PART PIECE
VOTER DETAIL FACTOR MATTER MEMBER
ELECTOR ELEMENT FEATURE INTEGRAL

CONSTITUTE BE FIX FORM MAKE ENACT
ERECT FORGE FOUND SHAPE SPELL
CREATE APPOINT COMPOSE FASHION
COMPOUND COMPRISE

CONSTITUTION LAW CODE BEING
CANON HUMOR SETUP STATE ESTATE
HEALTH NATURE TEMPER CHARTER
PHYSIQUE

CONSTRAIN PUT TIE BIND CURB DOOM
FAIN HOLD LEAD URGE CHAIN CHECK
CLASP CRAMP DETER DRIVE FORCE
IMPEL LIMIT PRESS COERCE COMPEL
EVINCE OBLIGE SECURE CONFINE
ENFORCE MANACLE REPRESS OBLIGATE

CONSTRICT TIE BIND CURB GRIP CHOKE
CRAMP LIMIT STRAP HAMPER SHRINK
STRAIN SQUEEZE TIGHTEN COMPRESS
CONDENSE CONTRACT

CONSTRUCT FORM MAKE REAR BUILD
ERECT FRAME MODEL BURROW DEDUCE
DESIGN DEVISE ARRANGE COMPILE
COMPOSE FASHION ENGINEER

CONSTRUCTION BOOM ALTAR FRAME
FABRIC MONSTER SYNESIS APPROACH
BUILDING DWELLING ERECTION

CONSTRUCTIVE PONENT FACTIVE
HELPFUL VIRTUAL CREATIVE IMPLICIT
INFERRED

CONSTRUE INFER INTEND RENDER
ANALYZE DISSECT EXPLAIN EXPOUND
RESOLVE

CONSULT LOOK SEEK TALK ADVISE
CONFER COUNSEL RESOLVE

CONSULTANT EXPERT ADVISER
COUNSEL

CONSUME EAT SUP USE BOLT BURN
CHEW FANG FARE FEED GULP KILL RUST
TAKE WEAR DALLY DRINK RAVEN SPEND
TOOTH WASTE ABSORB DEVOUR
ENGAGE EXPEND FINISH IMBIBE INHALE
VANISH CORRODE DESTROY DWINDLE
ENGROSS EXHAUST SWALLOW
CONTRIVE SQUANDER

CONSUMMATE END FINE FULL RIPE
CLOSE IDEAL SHEER ARRANT EFFECT
FINISH RATIFY ACHIEVE CROWNED
FULFILL PERFECT PERFORM ABSOLUTE
COMPLETE THOROUGH

CONSUMPTION USE DECAY WASTE
EXPENSE WASTING PHTHISIS SPENDING

CONTACT ABUT JOIN KISS MEET CROSS
TOUCH UNION ARRIVE IMPACT MEETING
JUNCTION TANGENCY TOUCHING
(— OF TELEGRAPH KEY) ANVIL
(ELECTRICAL —) HUB POINT

(EVIL —) CONTAGION
(FLEETING —) BRUSH
(FORCIBLE —) IMPACT
(3-POINT —) OSCNODE
CONTAGIOUS TAKING NOXIOUS SMITTLE CATCHING EPIDEMIC
CONTAIN HAVE HOLD KEEP STOW TAKE CARRY CLOSE COVER HOUSE EMBODY ENFOLD HARBOR RETAIN COMPILE EMBRACE ENCLOSE INCLUDE INVOLVE RECEIVE SUSTAIN COMPRISE RESTRAIN
CONTAINER BAG BOX CAN CUP JAR JUG KEG PAN POD POT TIN TUB URN VAT BAIL BOMB CAGE CASE CASK CRIB DRUM EWER FILE FLAT JACK SACK SALT SILO SINK SKIP TANK TUBE VASE ALBUM BASIN BILLY CADDY CHEST CRATE CRUET DEWAR EMPTY FLASK GLASS GOURD POUCH SCOOP SCRAY STAND STOOP STOUP BARREL BASKET BOTTLE BUCKET BUSHEL CARBOY CARTON CASTER CASTOR COOLER CRADLE DUSTER HAMPER HATBOX HOLDER INKPOT MAILER PICNIC RABBIT RIDDLE SHAKER WITJAR AEROSOL AMPULLA BANDBOX BLADDER CAPSULE COASTER COSTREL CRISPER FEEDBOX HANAPER HOLDALL INKWELL PACKAGE SEEDLIP SHIPPER STEEPER CANISTER DECANTER DEMIJOHN ENVELOPE HOGSHEAD HONEYPOT INHOLDER KNAPSACK PUNCHEON SLIPCASE RELIQUARY POCKETBOOK
(— FOR BEER) GROWLER
(— FOR BOBBINS) BUFFALO
(— FOR COINS) BANK
(— FOR EXPLOSIVE CHARGE) CAP
(— FOR FISH) BASS
(— FOR GOLD DUST) SHAMMY
(— FOR HOLY OIL) STOCK
(— FOR PLANTS) BAND
(— MADE OF HOLLOW LOG) GUM
(COFFEE —) INSET
(DESSERT —) COUPE
(DRINK —) DOP
(EARTHENWARE —) STEAN
(FIRECLAY —) SETTER
(RAILROAD —S) BUNKER
(SHELVED —) CABIN
(SHIPPING —) KIT
(SNUFF —) WEASAND
(TOBACCO —) SARATOGA
(VENTILATED —) CHIP
(5-GALLON —) JERICAN JERRICAN
CONTAMINATE FOUL HARM SLUR SOIL STAIN SULLY TAINT BEFOUL DEBASE DEFILE INFECT INJURE POISON CORRUPT DEBAUCH POLLUTE TARNISH VITIATE DISHONOR
CONTAMINATED DIRTY DEGRADED INFECTED
CONTEMPLATE FACE DEIGN MUSE PLAN SCAN VIEW DEIGN STUDY THINK WEIGH BEHOLD DESIGN PONDER REGARD SURVEY PROPOSE REFLECT CONSIDER ENVISAGE ENVISION MEDITATE

CONTEMPLATION MUSE STUDY MUSING PRAYER REGARD INSIGHT
CONTEMPORARY EQUAL COEVAL FELLOW CURRENT PRESENT EXISTENT SIMULTANEOUS
CONTEMPT SCORN SHAME SNEER SLIGHT DISDAIN MOCKERY DEFIANCE DERISION DESPISAL DISGRACE OPPROBRIUM
CONTEMPTIBLE LOW BASE MEAN POOR VILE CHEAP DIRTY DUSTY LOUSY MANGY MUCKY PETTY SORRY ABJECT CRUDDY GRUBBY MEASLY PALTRY SCABBY SCUMMY SCURVY SHABBY SORDID YELLOW PITIFUL SCORNED SLAVISH SQUALID BEGGARLY INFAMOUS INFERIOR PICAYUNE PITIABLE SNEAKING UNWORTHY WRETCHED
CONTEMPTUOUS SNOOTY HAUGHTY ARROGANT FLOUTING INSOLENT SCOFFING SCORNFUL
CONTEND TUG VIE WAR COPE DEAL PLEA RACE WAGE ARGUE BANDY BRAWL CHIDE CLAIM FIGHT ASSERT BATTLE BICKER BUCKLE BUFFET BUSTLE COMBAT DEBATE DIFFER JOSTLE OPPOSE REASON STRIVE COMPETE CONTEST COUNTER DISPUTE QUARREL SCUFFLE WRESTLE CONFLICT CONTRAST MILITATE SQUABBLE STRUGGLE
CONTENT CALM GLAD HAPPY AMOUNT CUBAGE PLEASE APPEASE GRATIFY SATIATE SATISFY SUFFICE WILLING BLISSFUL CAPACITY
CONTENTED COZY VAIN QUIET SATED PLEASED CHEERFUL
CONTENTION WAR FEUD PLEA RIOT TIFF BROIL BICKER COMBAT DEBATE STRIFE CONTEST DISCORD DISPUTE OPINION QUARREL RIVALRY WRANGLE ARGUMENT CONFLICT SQUABBLE STRUGGLE VARIANCE
CONTENTIOUS CROSS PEEVISH PERVERSE BELLICOSE
CONTENTMENT EASE BLISS HEAVEN PLEASURE SATISFACTION
CONTEST GO BEE RUN SUE TRY VIE AGON BOUT COPE DUEL FEUD FRAY GAME PULL RACE TIFF TILT AGONY ARGUE BROIL CLASH DERBY EVENT FIGHT MATCH SPORT TRIAL ACTION BATTLE COMBAT DEBATE DEFEND OPPOSE RESIST SEESAW STRIFE STRIVE TUSSLE CLASSIC COMPETE CONTEND DISPUTE GRAPPLE PROTEST SHUTOUT TOURNEY WARFARE ARGUMENT CONFLICT DOGFIGHT HANDICAP LITIGATE SKIRMISH SLUGFEST STRUGGLE
(— IN WORDS) SPAR
(— NARROWLY WON) SQUEAKER
(ATHLETIC —) BIATHLON
(AUTOMOBILE — ON FROZEN LAKE) ICEKHANA
(CLOSE —) DICE
(DRAWN —) TIE DRAW STALEMATE
(MOCK —) SCIAMACHY

(RACING —) DRAG
(REAPING —) KEMP
CONTESTANT VIER RIVAL PLAYER
AGONIST ENTRANT FINALIST

CONTIGUOUS NEXT NIGH NEARBY
TANGENT ABUTTING ADJACENT
TOUCHING

CONTINGENCY CASE EVENT CHANCE
CONTACT VENTURE ACCIDENT FORTUITY
INCIDENT PROSPECT

CONTINUAL STILL HOURLY ABIDING
ENDLESS ETERNAL LASTING REGULAR
UNDYING UNIFORM CONSTANT
ENDURING UNBROKEN

CONTINUALLY AY AYE EVER STILL
ALWAYS HOURLY STEADY ENDLESS
ETERNAL FOREVER

CONTINUATION SEQUEL DURATION
PROLONGATION

CONTINUE BE DO BIDE HOLD KEEP LAST
LIVE STAY ABIDE CARRY EXIST STICK
ENDURE EXTEND REMAIN RESUME
PERSIST PROCEED PROLONG SURVIVE
SUSTAIN

CONTINUOUS EVEN ENTIRE STEADY
CHRONIC ENDLESS RUNNING UNBROKEN
PERENNIAL PERPETUAL

CONTORT WRY BEND COIL CURL TURN
WARP GNARL SCREW TWIST WREST
CRINGE DEFORM WRITHE DISTORT
PERVERT WREATHE

CONTOUR FORM LINE CURVE GRAPH
SHAPE SWEEP FIGURE OUTLINE PROFILE

CONTRABAND HOT ILLEGAL ILLICIT
SMUGGLED UNLAWFUL

CONTRACT BOND DRAW FORM KNIT
PACT CATCH CLOSE CRAMP INCUR
LEASE LIMIT PINCH CRINGE ENGAGE
GATHER INDENT LESSEN NARROW
PLEDGE POLICY PUCKER REDUCE SHRINK
SUBLET TREATY ABRIDGE CHARTER
COMPACT CURTAIL DEFLATE MANDATE
SHORTEN SHRIVEL WRINKLE ASSIENTO
CONDENSE COVENANT RESTRICT

CONTRACTION TIC TIS AINT CANT ISNT
MAAM WONT CRAMP HADNT HASNT
NISUS SPASM CRASIS GATHER MUSTNT
SHRINK ELISION EPITOME WOULDNT
APNEUSIS TRACTION ABRIDGMENT
ABRIDGMENT

CONTRADICT DENY BELIE CROSS REBUT
IMPUGN NEGATE OPPOSE RECANT
REFUTE COUNTER GAINSAY REVERSE
DISPROVE

CONTRARY BALKY CROSS KICKY
AVERSE ORNERY COUNTER CRABBED
FROWARD HOSTILE INVERSE OPPOSED
PEEVISH RESTIVE REVERSE WAYWARD
CAPTIOUS INIMICAL OPPOSITE PERVERSE
PETULANT

CONTRAST CLASH STRIFE COMPARE
CONTEND DISCORD OPPOSITE

CONTRIBUTE AID ANTE FORK GIVE HELP
MAKE CAUSE SERVE ASSIST BESTOW
CONFER DONATE RENDER SUPPLY
TENDER FURNISH FURTHER PROVIDE

CONTRIBUTION BIT SUM TAX ALMS

BOON GIFT SHARE LARGESS PAYMENT
PRESENT DONATION EXACTION
OFFERING

CONTRITE SORRY HUMBLE RUEFUL
PENITENT SORROWFUL

CONTRITION SORROW PENANCE
PENITENCE

CONTRIVANCE (ALSO SEE DEVICE)
FLY GIN JIG DROP GEAR HARP JACK KITE
LURE PAGE PLAN PLOT RASP REED TOOL
ALARM BRAKE CARRY CHECK DOLLY
DRAFT FLOAT FRAME GUIDE HICKY
KNACK MIXER QUIPU SHIFT SNARE
STOCK ANCHOR DAMPER DECEIT DESIGN
DEVICE DOCTOR DOLLIE ENGINE FABRIC
FANGLE GABION GADGET GIMBAL
HANGER HARROW HEATER HICKEY
HOLDER JIGGER JINKER MARKER
MORTAR MUZZLE POLICY RATTLE
SCHEME SLUICE SPIDER TEASEL WEIGHT
WHEEZE WINDAS WRENCH BOLSTER
CLEANER CLEARER CONCERN COUPLER
CUNNING DINGBAT DRAUGHT FICTION
FISHWAY HUMIDOR KNOCKER MACHINE
PAGEANT PROJECT REDUCER ROASTER
SCRAPER SHEBANG SPANNER STOPPER
TOASTER TRIPPER VOLVELL ADAPTION
ARTIFICE CROTCHET DUTCHMAN
EUPYRION FAKEMENT FORECAST
GOVERNOR INDUSTRY MOLITION
OXIDATOR REGISTER RESOURCE
SCISSORS SQUEEZER SUBTLETY
WITCRAFT

CONTRIVE GET LAY BREW DRAW FIND
MAKE PLAN PLOT WORK FRAME HATCH
SHAPE STAGE WEAVE DESIGN DEVISE
FIGURE INVENT MANAGE SCHEME
WANGLE ACHIEVE CONCOCT CONTEND
FASHION IMAGINE PROCURE CONSPIRE
INTRIGUE

CONTROL BIT LAW RUN CONN CURB
GRIP HAND HAVE HOLD REDE REIN RULE
STAY SWAY CHARM CHECK DAUNT
GRASP GUIDE LEASH ORDER POWER
STEER SWING TREAT WIELD BRIDLE
CHARGE CLUTCH COERCE CORNER
DIRECT GOVERN HANDLE MANAGE
TEMPER COMMAND CONDUCT CONTAIN
CUSTODY FORBEAR MASTERY QUALIFY
DOMINATE DOMINIUM IMPERIUM
MODERATE REGULATE POSSESSION
(— A BULL) MANDAR
(— OF RESOURCES) HUSBANDRY
(— OVER WIFE) MANUS
(ABSOLUTE —) BECK
(FIRE —) BLANKET
(GOVERNMENT —) DIRIGISM
SQUADRISM
(MANUAL —) JOYSTICK

CONTROVERSY SPAT SUIT FUROR
BATTLE COMBAT DEBATE FURORE
HASSLE STRIFE TUSSLE DISPUTE
QUARREL WRANGLE ARGUMENT
TRAVERSE CONTENTION

CONUNDRUM PUN WHIM GUESS
ENIGMA PUZZLE RIDDLE CONCEIT
CROTCHET

CONVENE SIT CALL HOLD MEET UNITE GATHER MUSTER SUMMON CONVOKE ASSEMBLE CONVERGE

CONVENIENCE GAIN BEHOOF LEISURE

CONVENIENT FIT GAIN NIGH HANDY READY CLEVER PROPER SUITED USEFUL COMMODE HELPFUL BECOMING SUITABLE OPPORTUNE COMMODIOUS

CONVENT ABBEY CENOBY FRIARY PRIORY CLOISTER LAMASERY

CONVENTION DIET FORM RULE SYNOD TABOO USAGE CAUCUS CUSTOM TREATY DECORUM MEETING ASSEMBLY CONCLAVE CONGRESS PRACTICE PRECEDENT

CONVENTIONAL RIGHT TRITE USUAL DECENT FORMAL MODISH PROPER CORRECT REGULAR ACCEPTED ORTHODOX CUSTOMARY

CONVERGE JOIN MEET FOCUS CONCUR APPROACH FOCALIZE

CONVERSANT ADEPT EXPERT VERSED SKILLED FAMILIAR

CONVERSATION RAP SAY CHAT CHIN TALE TALK PROSE CONFAB GOSSIP PARLEY POWWOW SPEECH YABBER PALAVER CHITCHAT COLLOQUY DIALOGUE HARANGUE PARLANCE

CONVERSE CHAT CHIN TALK SPEAK CONFER PARLEY REASON COMMUNE DISCUSS EXCHANGE

CONVERT TURN ALTER AMEND APPLY CHANGE DECODE DIRECT NOVICE COMMUTE RESOLVE RESTORE REVERSE DISCIPLE NEOPHYTE PERSUADE PROSELYTE
(— COTTON) LAP
(— INTO CASH) NEGOTIATE
(— INTO LEATHER) TAN TAW
(— INTO LIQUID) BREW
(— INTO PELLETS) PRILL
(— INTO SOAP) SAPONIFY
(— INTO STEEL) ACIERATE
(— INTO STONE) LAPIDIFY
(— SOAP) CLOSE
(— TO CARBON) CHAR

CONVEX BOWED ARCHED CAMBER CURVED BULGING EMBOWED GIBBOUS ROUNDED

CONVEY BEAR CART CEDE HAVE LEAD MEAN PASS SEND SIGN TAKE TOTE WILL BRING CARRY DRIVE FETCH GUIDE ASSIGN DEVISE IMPART YMMOTE AUCTION CHANNEL CHARTER CONDUCT DELIVER DISPOSE ALIENATE BEQUEATH DESCRIBE TRANSFER TRANSMIT
(— AN ESTATE) DEMISE
(— BY ALLUSION) IMPLY
(— FORCIBLY) HUSTLE
(— LEGALLY) DEED GRANT LEASE DEMISE ELOIGN DISPONE
(— NEARER) BRING
(— SECRETLY) CRIM

CONVEYANCE BUS CAR AUTO CART DEED SLED TAXI TRAM GRANT SEDAN STAGE TRAIN WAGON DEMISE CHARTER RATTLER TRAILER TRANSIT TROLLEY VEHICLE CARRIAGE TRANSFER

CONVICT LAG CAST EXILE FELON LIFER TAINT TERMER TRUSTY ATTAINT CAPTIVE CONDEMN CULPRIT IMPEACH REPROVE CRIMINAL JAILBIRD PRISONER SENTENCE

CONVICTION CREDO CREED DOGMA FAITH SENSE TENET BELIEF CONCERN OPINION SENTENCE

CONVINCE ASSURE RESOLVE SATISFY CONCLUDE

CONVINCING SOUND VALID COGENT POTENT EVIDENT TELLING FORCIBLE POWERFUL

CONVIVIAL GAY BOON FESTAL GENIAL JOVIAL SOCIAL FESTIVE HOLIDAY JOCULAR REVELING

CONVOKE CALL HOLD GATHER SUMMON CONVENE ASSEMBLE

CONVOLUTION COIL CURL FOLD TURN WRAP GYRUS SWIRL TWINE TWIRL TWIST WHORL

CONVOY LEAD CARRY GUARD GUIDE PILOT WATCH ATTEND ESCORT CONDUCT SAFEGUARD

CONVULSION FIT SHRUG SPASM THROE ATTACK TUMULT UPROAR PAROXYSM COMMOTION

COOK DO FIX FRY BAKE BOIL CHEF MAKE STEW BROIL GRILL POACH ROAST SCALD SHIRR STEAM BRAISE CODDLE SAUTEE SEETHE SIMMER BROILER GRIDDLE PREPARE

COOKIE CAKE ROCK SNAP KIPFEL BISCUIT BROWNIE OATCAKE PLACENT CRESCENT SEEDCAKE

COOL AIR FAN ICE CALM COLD ALGID ALLAY CHILL FRESH GELID NERVY SOBER STAID WHOLE CHILLY PLACID QUENCH SEDATE SERENE TEMPER UNMOVED COMPOSED MITIGATE MODERATE TRANQUIL NERVELESS NONCHALANT UNFLAPPABLE

COOLNESS FROST NERVE SWALE APLOMB PHLEGM SERENITY

COOP COT MEW PEN CAGE COTE JAIL HUTCH CORRAL CONFINE

COOPERATE TEND AGREE UNITE CONCUR COMBINE CONDUCE CONNIVE CONSPIRE

COORDINATION BOND SKILL HARMONY LIAISON

COP BAG NAB ROB BULL HEAD JOHN LIFT TRAP CATCH FILCH SNARE STEAL SWIPE PEELER CAPTURE

COPE VIE WAR FACE MEET DRESS EQUAL FIGHT MATCH RIVAL WIELD COMBAT OPPOSE STRIVE CONTEND CONTEST GRAPPLE STRUGGLE

COPIOUS FREE FULL GOOD LUSH RANK RICH AMPLE LARGE FLUENT LAVISH DIFFUSE FLOWING FULSOME LENGTHY PROFUSE REPLETE TEEMING UBEROUS ABUNDANT AFFLUENT FRUITFUL GENEROUS NUMEROUS PLENTIFUL

COPPER AES CENT BOBBY PENNY CUPRUM PEELER CARNELIAN

COPY APE CAST ECHO EDIT MIME MOCK DITTO DUMMY IMAGE MIMIC MODEL PRINT TRACE DOUBLE ECTYPE EFFIGY FOLLOW RECORD SHADOW EDITION EMULATE IMITATE PATTERN REPLICA REPRINT RUBBING TRACING LIKENESS RESEMBLE SPECIMEN MICROCOPY MINIATURE PHOTOSTAT

COQUET TOY VAMP DALLY FLIRT TRIFLE BLINKER CELIMENE

CORAL RED PINK AKORI BLOOD POLYP ALCYON PALULE PORITE FUNGIAN OCULINA ACROPORE ASTRAEAN CORALLUM FAVOSITE POLYPITE STAGHORN TUBIPORE ZOOPHYTE MADREPORE MILLEPORE

CORD RIB BAND BOND LACE LASH LINE ROPE WELT BRAID GUARD LEASH NERVE TWINE BINDER BRIDLE CATGUT GIRDLE LASHER SENNET STRING TENDON TOGGLE FUNICLE LANYARD MACRAME SEAMING SEIZING TIEBACK CHENILLE SHOELACE
(— AROUND BOWSTRING) SERVING
(— FOR PIPING) BOBBIN
(— OF CANDLENUT BARK) AEA
(CROCHETING —) CORDE
(ELECTRIC —) FLEX
(EMBROIDERY —) ARRASENE
(FRINGED —) LLAUTU
(HAMMOCK —S) CLEW
(HAWK'S —) CREANCE
(MASON'S —) SKIRREH
(ORNAMENTED —) AGLET AIGLET
(PARACHUTE —) SHROUD
(SACRED —) KUSTI
(SPINAL —) EON AEON NUKE
(TWISTED —) TORSADE
(PREF.) CHORD(O)

CORDIAL REAL WARM CREAM ARDENT CASSIS CLOVES DEVOUT ELIXIR GENIAL HEARTY PASTIS LIQUEUR PERSICO RATAFIA ROSOLIO SINCERE ZEALOUS ANISETTE FRIENDLY GRACIOUS PERSICOT VIGOROUS BENEDICTINE

CORE AME HUB NUT GIST KNOT NAVE PITH FOCUS HEART SPOOL BARREL CENTER KERNEL MATRIX MIDDLE STAPLE ESSENCE NUCLEUS
(— OF COAL) STOCK
(— OF COLUMN) BELL HEART
(— OF CRICKET BALL) QUILT
(— OF LOG) PITH
(— OF MOLD) NOWEL
(EARTH'S HYPOTHETICAL —) NIFE

CORIOLANUS (AUTHOR OF —) SHAKESPEARE
(CHARACTER IN —) CAIUS TITUS BRUTUS JUNIUS TULLUS LARTIUS MARCIUS VALERIA AUFIDIUS COMINIUS MENENIUS SICINIUS VIRGILIA VOLUMNIA

CORK BUNG PLUG FLOAT SUBER BOBBER SOBERIN STOPPER STOPPLE

CORN DENT SALT SAMP GRAIN MAIZE SPIKE CALLUS CLAVUS HELOMA KERNEL NUBBIN
(CRUSHED —) STAMP
(DECORATED EAR OF —) TIPONI
(EAR OF —) ICKER
(GUINEA —) DURRA
(INDIAN —) MAIZE INDIAN NOCAKE
(PARCHED —) ROKEE NOCAKE PINOLE YOKAGE GRADDAN ROKEAGE YOKEAGE
(STRING OF —) TRACE
(UNRIPE EAR OF —) TUCKET

CORNER GET BEND CANT JAMB NOOK TRAP TREE ANGLE BIGHT CATCH COIGN ELBOW INGLE NICHE QUOIN CANTON COLLAR CRANNY RECESS MONOPOLY
(— IN A DRIFT) ARRAGE
(— OF EYE) CANTHUS
(— OF GUNSTOCK) TOE
(— OF MOLDBOARD) SHIN
(— OF SAIL) CLEW CLUE TACK GOOSEWING
(CHIMNEY —) LUG
(LOWER —) CLEW CLUE
(RE-ENTRANT —) DIEDRE
(ROUNDED —) FILET FILLET
(SECRET —) CREEK
(TIGHT —) BOX

CORNICE CAP BAND DRIP EAVE ANCON CROWN ANTEFIX MOLDING SURBASE ASTRAGAL

CORN MEAL MASA SAMP ATOLE HOECAKE

CORNUCOPIA HORN CORNU COFFIN

CORNY BANAL STALE TRITE MICKEY BUCKEYE

COROLLA CUP BELL CUPULE LIGULE PERIANTH

COROLLARY DOGMA PORISM RESULT TRUISM ADJUNCT THEOREM

CORONA BURR CIGAR CROWN GLORY AURORA FILLET ROSARY WREATH AUREOLE CIRCLET CORONET GARLAND LARMIER SCYPHUS

CORONET BAND BURR CROWN TIARA ANADEM CIRCLE DIADEM WREATH CHAPLET GARLAND

CORPORATE UNITED COMBINED

CORPORATION BODY CITY FIRM POUCH TRUST SCHOLA BOROUGH COLLEGE COMMUNE FREEDOM GUILDRY SOCIETY SPONSOR

CORPOREAL REAL HYLIC SOMAL ACTUAL BODILY CARNAL FLESHLY SOMATIC MATERIAL PHYSICAL TANGIBLE

CORPSE BIER BODY CLAY DUST LICH MORT GHOST MUMMY RELIC STIFF TRUCK ZOMBI CORPUS CADAVER CARCASS CARRION

CORPULENT FAT BULKY BURLY FATTY GROSS HUSKY OBESE PLUMP STOUT TUBBY FLESHY GREASY PORTLY ROTUND ADIPOSE WEIGHTY

CORPUSCLE CELL GLOBULE HEMATID HEMOCYTE

CORRAL PEN STY COOP ATAJO POUND TAMBO CONFINE ENCLOSE SURROUND
(ELEPHANT —) KRAAL KEDDAH

CORRECT DUE FIT FIX EDIT JAKE JUST LEAL MARK MEND NICE OKAY SMUG TRUE AMEND CHECK CLEAN EMEND EXACT ORDER RIGHT SOUND ADJUST BETTER CHANGE PROPER PUNISH REBUKE REFORM REMEDY REPAIR REVAMP REVISE SEEMLY STRICT CHASTEN IMPROVE PERFECT PRECISE RECTIFY REDRESS REGULAR REPROVE SINCERE ACCURATE CHASTISE DEFINITE EQUALIZE REGULATE STRAIGHT TRUTHFUL CASTIGATE **(APPROXIMATELY —)** BALLPARK **(GRAMMATICALLY —)** CONGRUE **(MATHEMATICALLY —)** PURE

CORRECTION REFORM CENSURE FLEXURE IMPRINT REDRESS SCOURGE FUGACITY **(— IN COMPUTER PROGRAM)** PATCH

CORRELATIVE OR NOR THEN EQUAL STILL EITHER MUTUAL NEITHER ANALOGUE CONJOINT REDDITIVE

CORRESPOND FIT GEE JIBE SUIT AGREE MATCH TALLY WRITE ACCORD ANSWER CONCUR SQUARE COMPORT RESPOND COINCIDE PARALLEL QUADRATE

CORRESPONDENCE MAIL TALLY ANALOGY CONSENT HARMONY KEEPING LETTERS TRAFFIC SYMMETRY SIMILARITY SIMILITUDE PARALLELISM RESEMBLANCE

CORRESPONDENT NEWSMAN QUADRATE RELEVANT STRINGER SUITABLE

CORRESPONDING LIKE SIMILAR PARALLEL ACCORDANT CONGRUENT

CORRIDOR HALL AISLE ORIEL VISTA ARCADE COULOIR GALLERY PASSAGE COULISSE HALLCIST TRESANCE

CORROBORATE PROVE SECOND APPROVE COMFORT CONFIRM SUPPORT SUSTAIN

CORRODE EAT BITE BURN ETCH FRET GNAW RUST DECAY ERODE WASTE IMPAIR CONSUME

CORROSIVE ACID ACRID ARDENT BITING EATING CAUSTIC EROSIVE FRETFUL MORDANT

CORRUGATED PLAITED WRINKLY FURROWED WRINKLED

CORRUGATION BAT FOLD GILL REED RUGA CREASE PUCKER CRINKLE WRINKLE

CORRUPT BAD ILL LOW ROT EVIL RANK SICK SOIL VILE ADDLE BRIBE FALSE SPOIL STAIN SULLY TAINT VENAL VENOM AUGEAN DEBASE DEFILE FESTER IMPURE INFECT PALTER POISON PUTRID RAVISH ROTTEN SEPTIC ABUSIVE ATTAINT BEGRIME CROOKED DEBAUCH DEGRADE DEPRAVE ENVENOM FALSIFY IMMORAL PECCANT PERVERT POLLUTE PUTREFY SUBVERT VIOLATE VITIATE CONFOUND DEPRAVED PERVERSE POLLUTED PRACTICE SINISTER PERVERTED ADULTERATE CONTAMINATE

CORRUPTION DIRT SOIL VICE DECAY SPOIL TAINT JOBBERY PRAVITY SQUALOR ADULTERY BARRATRY INFECTION MALVERSATION PUTREFACTION

CORSAGE WAIST BODICE BOUQUET CANEZOU

CORSAIR BUG CAPER PIRATE ROBBER PICAROON ROCKFISH

CORSET BELT BUSK STAY STAYS GIRDLE SUPPORT

CORSICA (CAPITAL OF —) AJACCIO **(HARBOR OF —)** BASTIA **(MOUNTAIN OF —)** CINTO ROTONDO **(RIVER OF —)** GOLO TARAVO GRAVONE **(TOWN OF —)** CALVI CORTE ALERIA BASTIA AJACCIO SARTENE **(VEGETATION OF —)** MAQUIS

CORTEGE POMP SUITE TRAIN PARADE RETINUE

CORTEX BARK PEEL RIND MANTLE PALLIUM PERIBLEM PERIDIUM

CORUNDUM RUBY SAND EMERY ADAMAS ALUMINA ABRASIVE AMETHYST SAPPHIRE BARKLYITE

CORUSCATE BLAZE FLASH GLEAM SHINE GLANCE GLISTEN GLITTER RADIATE SPARKLE BRANDISH

COSI FAN TUTTE (CHARACTER IN —) ALFONSO DESPINA FERRANDO DORABELLA GUGLIELMO FIORDILIGI **(COMPOSER OF —)** MOZART

COSMETIC KOHL WASH CREAM FUCUS HENNA LINER PAINT ROUGE BLANCH CERUSE CRAYON ENAMEL POMADE POWDER BLUSHER MASCARA STIBIUM AMANDINE LIPSTICK STIBNITE

COSMIC VAST MUNDANE ORDERLY CATHOLIC INFINITE

COSMOPOLITAN URBAN ECUMENIC PANDEMIC AMPHIGEAN

COSMOS EARTH GLOBE ORDER REALM WORLD FLOWER HEAVEN HARMONY UNIVERSE

COSSACK TURK TATAR ATAMAN HETMAN TARTAR ZAPOROGUE

COST LOSS PAIN SOAK PRICE SPEND STAND VALUE CHARGE DAMAGE OUTLAY SCATHE EXPENSE

COSTA RICA

CAPE: ELENA VELAS BLANCO
CAPITAL: SANJOSE
GULF: DULCE NICOYA PAPAGAYO
INDIAN: BORUCA GUAYMI
ISLAND: COCO
LAKE: ARENAL
MEASURE: VARA CAFIZ CAHIZ FANEGA TERCIA CAJUELA CANTARO MANZANA
MOUNTAIN: BLANCO CHIRRIPO
PENINSULA: OSA NICOYA
POINT: QUEPOS CAHUITA GALONOS LLERENA
PORT: LIMON PUNTARENAS
RIVER: POAS IRAZU MATINA SIXAOLA TENORIA TARCOLES

TOWN: CANAS LIMON VESTA BORUCA NICOYA BAGACES CARTAGO GOLFITO HEREDIA LIBERIA NEGRITA ALAJUELA COLORADO GUAPILES
VOLCANO: POAS IRAZU
WEIGHT: BAG CAJA LIBRA

COSTLY DEAR FINE HIGH RICH DAINTY LAVISH SILVER GORGEOUS PLATINUM PRECIOUS PRODIGAL SPLENDID PRICELESS

COSTUME RIG GARB ROBE SARI SUIT BURKA DRESS GETUP HABIT SHAPE TRUSS ATTIRE DOMINO FORMAL SETOUT TOILET APPAREL BLOOMER CLOTHES POLLERA RAIMENT SCARLET UNIFORM CHARSHAF CLOTHING ENSEMBLE TOILETTE VENETIAN
(ACADEMIC —) GUISE

COT BED HUT MAT COTE FOLD ABODE CABIN COUCH COVER HOUSE STALL CRADLE GURNEY PALLET SHEATH CHARPOY COTTAGE SHELTER BEDSTEAD STRETCHER

COTERIE SET RING CABAL JUNTO MONDE CIRCLE CLIQUE GALAXY SETOUT CENACLE CIRCUIT COLLEGE PLATOON SOCIETY

COTTAGE BOX COT HUT BACH BARI COSH CRIB SHED WALK BOTHY BOWER CABIN HOUSE HOVEL LODGE SHACK BOHAWN CABANA CHALET SHELTER BUNGALOW SHIELING THALTHAN

COTTAGE CHEESE SKYR SMEARCASE SMIERCASE

COTTER KEY MAT PIN BOWPIN FASTEN TOGGLE PEASANT VILLEIN COTTAGER LINCHPIN

COTTON SAK BEAT DRAB FLOG MALO PIMA AGREE BOLLY DERRY MATTA SAKEL SURAT BOMBACE BROACH CODDLE COMBER FABRIC MAARAD MALLOW NANKIN PEELER STAPLE ALGODON BENDERS CANTOON DHURRIE GINNING SILESIA
(— SQUARE) TZUT
(BOLL OF —) SNAP
(NAPPED —) LAMBSKIN
(PAINTED —) INDIENNE
(PIECE OF —) SPONGE
(PRINTED —) SARONG
(RAW —) BAYAL
(SILK —) FLOSS
(STRIPED —) BENGAL
(TREE —) MACO
(TWILLED —) JEAN SALLO SALLOO
(WAD OF —) TAMPON
(WASTE —) GRABBOTS

COUCH BED COT LAY LIE HIDE LAIR LURK SOFA DIVAN INLAY LODGE SNEAK SNOOP BURROW CLOTHE DAYBED LITTER PALLET PLINTH SETTEE CONCEAL HAMMOCK OTTOMAN RECLINE TRANSOM

COUGAR CAT PUMA PAINTER PANTHER CARCAJOU

COUGH BAFF BARK HACK CHINK CROUP TISICK TUSSIS

COUNCIL BODY DAEL DIET DUMA FONO RAAD YUAN BOARD BUNGA CABAL DIVAN DOUMA JUNTA JUNTO SABHA SOBOR SYNOD LUKIKO MAJLIS POWWOW SENATE SOVIET TARYBA CABILDO CABINET CHAMBER CONSULT GERUSIA HUSTING MEETING ASSEMBLY CONCLAVE CONGRESS FOLKMOOT HEEMRAAD MINISTRY RIGSRAAD CAMARILLA PARLIAMENT

COUNCILLOR INDUNA VIZIER FAIPULE SENATOR WISEMAN DECURION

COUNSEL LORE REDE RUNE PUSS WARN CHIDE GUIDE ADVICE ADVISE LEADER ABOGADO CAUTION COUNCIL LECTURE ADMONISH ADVOCATE PRUDENCE
(JUNIOR LEGAL —) DEVIL
(KING'S —) SILK
(SACRED —) TORAH

COUNSELOR SAGE LAWYER MENTOR NESTOR ADVISER ECHEVIN GONZALO PROCTOR STARETS ADVOCATE ATTORNEY REDESMAN

COUNT ADD SUM TOT BANK CAST EARL GRAF NAME RELY RIME SIZE TALE TELL TOTE COMES COMPT COMTE GRAVE JUDGE SCORE TALLY WEIGH CENSUS CONSUL DEPEND ESTEEM FIGURE IMPUTE NUMBER RECKON TOTTLE ACCOUNT ASCRIBE COMPUTE GANELON NUMERATE CALCULATE PALSGRAVE
(— IN BILLIARDS) DOUBLE
(— OF A FIBER) GRIST
(— OF SHEEP OR CATTLE) BREAK
(— ON) LITE RELY

COUNTENANCE AID MUG OWN ABET BROW FACE LEER MIEN PUSS SHOW FAVOR FRONT GRACE ASPECT ENDURE UPHOLD VISAGE APPROVE BEARING CONDUCT ENDORSE FEATURE SUPPORT DEMEANOR SANCTION

COUNTER BAR DIB LOT BANK BUCK CENT CHIP DESK DUMP EDDY FISH JACK KIST PAWN STOP CAROM CHECK FORCE HATCH JETON MERIL PIECE SHELF STALL STAND TABLE TOTER BUFFET COMBAT GEIGER ISLAND JETTON MARKER OPPOSE SQUAIL ADVERSE BUTTOCK CONTEND CURRENT FANTAIL SHAMBLE CONTRARY MAHOGANY OPPOSITE TELLTALE

COUNTERACT CHECK CANCEL OPPOSE RESIST THWART BALANCE CORRECT DESTROY NULLIFY ANTIDOTE NEGATIVE

COUNTERBALANCE COVER WEIGH CANCEL SETOFF BALANCE

COUNTERFEIT BASE COIN COPY DAUB DUFF FAKE IDOL MOCK SHAM BELIE BOGUS DUMMY FALSE FEIGN FLASH FORGE FUDGE GAMMY MIMIC PHONY QUEER ASSUME ERSATZ FORGED PSEUDO TINSEL BASTARD DUFFING FALSIFY FASHION FEIGNED FORGERY IMITATE PHANTASM POSTICHE SIMULATE SPURIOUS SUPPOSED

COUNTERFEITER COINER JACKMAN
JARKMAN SCRATCHER
COUNTERPANE PANE LIGGER
BEDSPREAD
COUNTERPART COPY LIKE MATE SPIT
TWIN FETCH IMAGE MATCH COUSIN
DOUBLE SHADOW BALANCE COUNTER
OBVERSE SIMILAR PARALLEL SIMILITUDE
COUNTERPOINT FOIL DESCANT
CONTRAST FABURDEN
COUNTERSIGN BACK MARK SEAL SIGN
SIGNAL CONFIRM ENDORSE PASSWORD
SANCTION
COUNTLESS INFINITE NUMBERLESS
COUNT OF MONTE CRISTO
(AUTHOR OF —) DUMAS
(CHARACTER IN —) FARIA ALBERT
DANTES EDMOND HAIDEE MONDEGO
MORRELL DANGLARS MERCEDES
FERDINAND VALENTINE VILLEFORT
CADEROUSSE MAXIMILIAN
COUNTRY SOD HICK HOME KITH LAND
PAIS SOIL CLIME EARTH FRITH MARCH
PLAGE REALM STATE TRACT WEALD
GROUND KINTRA KINTRY NATION PEOPLE
REGION STICKS UPLAND DISTRICT
DOMINION PRINCIPALITY
(— OF ORIGIN) HOMELAND
(— ON SEA) SEABOARD
(CABIN —) LOBBY
(FRONTIER —) BORDER
(HOME —) BLIGHTY
(IMAGINARY —) EREWHON LILLIPUT
RURITANIA
(LIMESTONE —) KARST
(MARITIME —) MAREMMA
(MYTHICAL —) UTOPIA LEONNOYS
SVITHIOD SWITHIOD TEUTONIA
(OPEN —) BLED VELD FIELD VELDT
WEALD CAMPAIGN
(PETTY —) TOPARCHY
(ROUGH —) BOONDOCK BUNDOCKS
(RURAL —) OUTBACK
COUNTRYMAN HOB BOOR HIND KERN
TIKE CHURL CLOWN HODGE SWAIN
YOKEL GAFFER JIBARO GRANGER
HAYSEED LANDMAN PAISANO PEASANT
PLOWMAN LANDSMAN
COUNTY AMT LAN SEAT FYLKE SHIRE
DOMAIN PARISH BOROUGH COMITAT
NORFOLK DISTRICT
COUP BLOW DEAL PLAN PLAY FAULT
SCOOP UPSET ATTACK BARTER PUTSCH
STRIKE STROKE CAPSIZE TRAFFIC
COUPLE DUO TIE TWO BOND CASE DYAD
JOIN LINK MATE PAIR SPAN TEAM TWIN
YOKE BRACE LEASH MARRY TWAIN
UNITE GEMINI SPLINE SWINGE BRACKET
CONNECT DOUBLET SHACKLE TWOSOME
(— OF HAWKS) CAST
COURAGE FIRE GRIT GUTS MIND MOOD
PROW SAND SOUL BIELD HEART HONOR
MOXIE NERVE PLUCK SPUNK VALOR
DARING METTLE PECKER SPIRIT VIRTUE
BRAVERY CORAGIO HEROISM MANHOOD
PROWESS STOMACH VENTURE

AUDACITY BOLDNESS FIRMNESS
TENACITY
COURAGEOUS BOLD GAME GOOD
BRAVE GUTSY HARDY LUSTY MANLY
STOUT DARING HEROIC MANFUL PLUCKY
SPUNKY GALLANT SPARTAN STAUNCH
VALIANT FEARLESS INTREPID VALOROUS
COURIER NEWS POST GUIDE SCOUT
KAVASS ESTAFET POSTBOY POSTMAN
PATTAMAR
COURSE FLY LAP RUN WAY BEAT BENT
FLOW GAGE GAME GANG GATE HEAT
HUNT LANE LINE LODE MESS MODE PACE
PATH RACE RACK RILL RINK ROAD ROTA
CLASS CURRY CURVE CYCLE DRAFT
DRIFT DRIVE EMBER GAUGE GREAT
LAPSE LAYER LEDGE MARCH MOYEN
ORBIT PLATE POINT ROUTE SENSE SITHE
SPACE STEPS SWELT SWING TENOR
TRACK TRACT TRADE TRAIL TREND
WEENT ARTERY CAREER COPING CURSUS
DROMOS FURROW GALLOP GIRDER
GUTTER HONORS MANNER METHOD
MOTION RESACA SCHOOL SERIES
SPHERE STREAM STREET SYSTEM
TRIPOS ZODIAC AZIMUTH BEELINE
CHANNEL CIRCUIT CONDUCT DIAULOS
DRAUGHT HIGHWAY LECTURE PASSADE
PASSAGE PATHWAY PROCESS ROUTINE
RUNNING SEMINAR SERVICE STRETCH
SUBJECT SUCCESS TIDEWAY TRAJECT
TRUNDLE CURRENCY CURRICLE
DIADROME DISTANCE ELECTIVE
PROGRESS RECOURSE SEQUENCE
STEERAGE TENDENCY MOTORDROME
(— OF A ROPE) LEAD
(— OF ACTION) LARK TACK TROD VEIN
DANCE CUSTOM ROUTINE DEMARCHE
(— OF BOAT) LEG
(— OF BRICK) BED ROWLOCK SCINTLE
CREASING
(— OF FEEDING) DIET
(— OF KNITTING) BOUT
(— OF LUCK) FORTUNE
(— OF MASONRY) BAHUT STILT
COPING HEADING SKEWBACK
(— OF NATURE) TAO
(— OF PROCEDURE) RULE
(— OF ROADBED) SUBCRUST
(— OF STONES) BED PLINTH
(— OF STUDY) DEBATE COLLEGE
LECTURE SEMINAR ELECTIVE
(— OF TREATMENT) CURE
(— OF WALL) CORNICE
(— WITH GREYHOUNDS) GREW
(BELL-RINGING —) HUNT
(CIRCULAR —) SWEEP CHUKKER
COMPASS
(CURVING —) PIPE
(CUSTOMARY —) GUISE
(DOWNWARD —) DIP DECLINE
TOBOGGAN
(DUE —) TRAIN
(EASY —) PIPE
(EXACT —) BEAM
(FIRST —) ANTEPAST
(LAST —) VOID

(MIDDLE —) MIDS TEMPER
(NATURAL —) RITA
(OBLIQUE —) SKEW
(OVERHANGING —) JET
(PREDETERMINED —) DESTINY
(ROUNDABOUT —) DETOUR WINDLASS
(SETTLED —) BIAS GROOVE
(SKIING —) SCHUSS

COURT BAR SEE SUE WOO FUSS GATE
LEET QUAD ROTA SEAT SEEK SUIT WALE
WARD WYND YARD ARENA BENCH
BUREO CURIA CURRY DAIRI DIVAN
FAVOR FORUM FUERO GARTH JUDGE
PATIO SHIRE SPACE SPARK SPOON
SWEET TEMPT THING THINK YAMEN
ADALAT ALLURE ATRIUM BAILEY
COUNTY DARGAH DURBAR DURGAH
GEMOTE HOMAGE INVITE PALACE
PARVIS PURSUE SPLINT SUITOR TOLSEY
ADAWLUT ADDRESS ASSIZES ATTRACT
BARMOTE DUOVIRI FOREIGN HUSTING
JUSTICE PARVISE RETINUE SOLICIT
TEMENOS AUDIENCE CHANCERY
LAWCOURT SESSIONS TRIBUNAL
(— FAVOR) FAWN
(— OF A HUNDRED) MALL MALLUM
MALLUS
(— OF CIRCUIT JUDGES) EYRE
(— OF FORTRESS) PEEL
(— OF MIKADO) DAIRI
(— ORDER) VACATUR
(ECCLESIASTICAL —) ROTA CURIA
SYNOD COLLOQUY AUDIENCIA
(EXERCISE —) EPHEBEUM
(FORTIFIED —) BAWN
(GERMAN —) FEHM VEHM
(INNER —) PATIO
(MUSLIM —) DIVAN
(REFORMED —) CLASIS
(SMALL —) WYND CORTILE
(SUPREME —) SUDDER
(TURKISH —) GATE

COURTEOUS FAIR HEND CIVIL SUAVE
GENTLE POLITE SMOOTH URBANE
AFFABLE CORDIAL GALLANT GENTEEL
REFINED DEBONAIR GRACIOUS OBLIGING

COURTESAN MADAM THAIS WHORE
GEISHA MADAME AMOROSA DELILAH
PUCELLE DEVADASI
(PL.) DEMIMONDE

COURTESY COMITY BREEDING
ELEGANCE GRATUITY URBANITY

COURTYARD AREA WYND CLOSE CURIA
PATIO TRANCE BALLIUM CORTILE
TETRAGON CURTILAGE

COUSIN COZ KIN AKIN HERO ALLIED
NEPHEW

COVE BAY DEN CHAP HOLE NOOK PASS
SUMP BASIN BAYOU BIGHT CREEK INLET
FELLOW HOLLOW RECESS MOLDING

COVENANT BIND BOND PACT ACCORD
BERITH ENGAGE LEAGUE PLEDGE TREATY
BARGAIN COMPACT CONCORD PROMISE
ALLIANCE CONTRACT DOCUMENT
HANDFAST

COVER DO CAP COT HAP LAP LAY LID
NAP TOP TUP WRY BIND CEIL CLAD
COAT COOM CURE DAUB DECK FACE
FADE FALL FURL GARB GATE HEAD HEAL
HEEL HIDE HILL HOOD LATH LEAD LEAP
LINE MASK PAVE ROOF SILE SPAN TELD
TICK TIDE TILT VEIL WRAP APRON BATHE
BOARD CLOAK CLOUT COPSE CROWN
DRAPE DRESS FENCE FLESH FLOOD
GUISE HATCH KIVER MOUNT RECTO
SCARF SERVE SHADE STREW STUDY
THEAK THEEK TREAD TREAD VERSO
WELME WHALM AWNING BATTER
BINDER BLAZON CANOPY CHALON
CLOTHE DOUBLE EARLAP ENAMEL
ENCASE ENFOLD ENTIRE ENVEIL FOLDER
HACKLE IMMASK INVEST JACKET KIRTLE
MANTLE OVERGO POTLID RUNNER
SCONCE SCREEN SHADOW SHEATH
SHIELD SLEEVE SPREAD SPRING SWATHE
TOILET TOPPER WHAUVE APPAREL
ASPHALT BANDAGE BESTREW BLANKET
CAPSULE CONCEAL CONTECT COUVERT
ELYTRON EMBRACE ENCRUST FASCINE
HEADCAP HOUSING INCRUST KNEECAP
MANHEAD OBSCURE OMNIBUS OVERLAY
PRETEXT SHEATHE SHELTER SHUTTER
TAMPION THIMBLE BEDCOVER COMPRISE
COVERCLE DEBRUISE ENCLOTHE
ENSCONCE HOODWINK IMMANTLE
OVERHAIL OVERSILE OVERWEND
PALLIATE PRETENCE PRETENSE
SLIPOVER SURPOSE
(— A FIRE) BANK DAMP
(— AROUND FLOWER) CYMBA
(— BRICKS) SCOVE
(— BY EXCUSES) ALIBI PALLIATE
(— FOR ALEMBIC) HEAD
(— FOR CHALICE) PALL
(— FOR DIAPER) SOAKER
(— FOR ENGINE) COWLING
(— FOR FOOD) BELL
(— FOR GUN) TAMPION
(— FOR MILITARY CAPE) HAVELOCK
(— FOR PISTON) FOLLOWER
(— FOR POWDER PAN) HAMMER
(— FOR WIRES) BOOTLEG
(— GROUND) HEAT
(— HEARTH) FETTLE
(— OF BALL) CARCASS
(— OF BOILER) VOMIT
(— OF COFFIN) COOM
(— OF HAWSEHOLE) BUCKLER
(— OF MINE CAGE) BONNET
(— OF RIFLE MAGAZINE) GATE
(— OF SPORANGIUM) EPIGONE
(— OF VEGETATION) GROWTH
(— OPPRESSIVELY) SMOTHER
(— OVER) RAKE WELME WHELM
BECLOUD OVERDECK OVERWHELM
(— PLANTS) BAG
(— PROTECTIVELY) SHROUD SHEATHE
(— ROAD) BLIND
(— SOIL WITH CLAY) GAULT
(— UP) HAP BELY FOLD BELIE SALVE
SLEEK HUDDLE
(— WITH ASHES) SOIL
(— WITH BACON) BARD
(— WITH CLAY) CLOAM

(— WITH COWL) MOB
(— WITH CRUMBS) BREAD
(— WITH DOTS) CRIBBLE
(— WITH DROPS) DAG
(— WITH EARTH) BURY HEAL INTER
(— WITH FILM) SKIM
(— WITH FLESH) INCARN
(— WITH FOAM) EMBOSS
(— WITH GOLD) GILD
(— WITH MEAL) MELVIE
(— WITH MUD) BEMUD BELUTE
(— WITH OAKUM) FOTHER
(— WITH PITCH) PAY
(— WITH PLASTER) PARGET
(— WITH SHEATH) GLOVE
(— WITH SOLDER) SPLASH
(— WITH STONE) ASHLAR
(— WITH STRAW) THATCH
(— WITH TIN) BLANCH
(— WITH TOPSOIL) KELLY
(— WITH WATER) DOUSE FLOOD
WHELM OVERFLOW
(— WITH WAX) CERE
(— WITH WEAVING) GRAFT
(— WITH WINGS) BROOD
(BED —S) HEALING
(BEEHIVE —) QUILT
(BOOK —) CASE SIDE
(GLASS —) STRIKE
(PACK —) MANTA
(POSTAL —) ENTIRE
(POT —) BRED
(SADDLE —) PILCH HOUSING
(SLIDING —) BRIDGE
(TABLE —) BAIZE DUCHESSE
(WING — OF BEETLE) SHARD
COVERING (ALSO SEE COVER) BOX
COT FUR HAP KEX LAG ARIL BARB BARK
BOOT CASE CAUL COAT CUFF DECK FILM
HAME HEAD HOOD HULL HUSK KELL
MASK OVER PALL PUFF ROBE ROOF SLIP
SPAT TARP TILE TILT TRAP VEIL APRON
ARMOR BRAID BURSE CRUST DRESS
GLOBE GLOVE HATCH QUILT SCALE
SHELL SKIRT STALL SWARD TESTA
TUNIC TWEEL WREIL ARMING ATTIRE
AWNING BANCAL BANKER CANOPY
CANVAS COVERT DRAPET EMBRYO
ENAMEL FACING FENDER GAITER
GANOIN HACKLE HATCAP HELMET
JACKET MUZZLE PELAGE SADDLE
SCREEN SHEATH SHROUD SINDON
TEGMEN VERNIX BLANKET BUFFONT
CAMISIA CAPPING CAPSULE CEILING
COATING COWLING EARFLAP ENVELOP
EXCIPLE GRATING HAPPING HEALING
HEELCAP HOUSING MUFFLER OVERLAY
PURPORT SARPLER SHADING SHELTER
SHOEING SLIPPER TECTURE TEGMENT
VESTURE WRAPPER ARMGUARD
BLAZONRY BOARDING CASEMENT
CLEADING CLOTHING COMPRESS
COVERLET EGGSHELL EPISPORE
INDUMENT INDUSIUM MANTELET
MANTLING OVERCAST PAVILION
PERICARP SETATION UMBRELLA
TECTORIAL PILLOWCASE

(— FOR ANTENNA) RADOME
(— FOR BENCH) BANKER
(— FOR BOXERS' HANDS) CESTUS
(— FOR EGG) COSY
(— FOR FOREHEAD) BONGRACE
(— FOR NECK) TUCKER PARTLET
(— FOR ROOF APEX) EPI
(— FOR SHOULDERS) STOLE
(— FOR SKI) SKIN
(— FOR STIRRUP) HOOD
(— OF BED) TIKE
(— OF BELL ROPE) GRIP
(— OF BIRD) INDUMENT
(— OF BOW HANDLE) ARMING
(— OF CASH SHORTAGE) LAPPING
(— OF FEATHERS) DOWN
(— OF GILLS) OPERCULUM
(— OF NUTMEG) MACE
(— OF ROOT) CALYPTRA
(— OF ROPE) SERVICE
(— OF VEGETATION) FLEECE
(— WITH IRON) ACIERAGE
(—S FOR NIPPLES) PASTIES
(CAST —S) EXUVIAE
(CHIMNEY —) COWL
(CLOTH —) TOILET
(COARSE —) CADDOW TILLET
(DEFENSIVE —) ARMOR KICKER
(EAR —) EARLAP EARFLAP EARMUFF
OREILET
(EYE —S) GOGGLES
(FLOOR —) RUG TILE CRASH CARPET
LINOLEUM OILCLOTH
(FOUL —) SCUM
(HEAD —) CAP HAT WIG HAIR HIVE
HOOD CURCH BONNET HELMET BIRETTA
CHAPEAU CHAPERON HAVELOCK
HEADRAIL TROTCOZY
(LEG —) BOOT HOSE STOCK GAITER
LEGGIN PEDULE KNEELET LEGGING
STOCKING
(LIGHT —) GRIMING
(LINEN —) BARB
(OUTER —) BARK HIDE HULL HUSK
CRUST TESTA JACKET CARAPACE
(PLANT —) PERIDERM
(PROTECTIVE —) APRON ARMOR SHELL
COCOON
(SADDLE —) MOCHILA
(SEED —) PERIGONE
(SLIGHT —) CYMAR
(STAGE —) HEAVENS
(STERILE —) DRAPE
(STICKY DAMP —) GLET
COVERLET PANE QUILT THROW AFGHAN
CHALON COLCHA LIGGER SPREAD
BLANKET
COVERT DEN LAIR EARTH NICHE PRIVY
ASYLUM HARBOR HIDDEN LATENT
MASKED MYSTIC REFUGE SECRET
COVERED PRIVATE SHELTER THICKET
COVET ACHE ENVY WANT WISH CRAVE
YEARN DESIRE HANKER
COVETOUS AVID EAGER GREEDY STINGY
ENVIOUS MISERLY DESIROUS GRASPING
COVETOUSNESS GREED MISERY
AVARICE CUPIDITY

COVEY BEVY FALL BROOD FLOCK HATCH COVERT COMPANY

COW AWE BEEF BOSS FAZE MULL NOTT ROAN RUNT VACA ABASH BOSSY BROCK BULLY DAUNT QUAIL SCARE BOVINE CRUMMY HEIFER MILKER MULLEY ROTHER SUBDUE BULLOCK CRITTER CRUMMIE DEPRESS MILCHER SQUELCH TERRIFY ALDERNEY BROWBEAT DISPIRIT FRIGHTEN THREATEN
(— ABOUT 3 FEET HIGH) GYNEE
(— BEFORE CALVING) SPRINGER
(BAD-TEMPERED —) RAGER
(BARREN —) DRAPE BARRENER
(DRY —) KEY SEW
(HORNLESS —) NOT MOIL NOTT DODDY MULEY DODDIE HUMLIE MAILIE HUMBLIE POLLARD MOULLEEN
(WHITE-FACED —) HAWKEY HAWKIE
(YOUNG —) QUEY STIRK HEIFER

COWARD LACHE PIKER CRAVEN FUNKER PIGEON CAITIFF CHICKEN DASTARD QUITTER POLTROON RECREANT TURNTAIL

COWARDICE DASTARDY LASHNESS POLTROONERY

COWARDLY SHY FAINT TIMID AFRAID CRAVEN TURPID YELLOW CAITIFF CHICKEN GUTLESS FACELESS POLTROON RECREANT SNEAKING

COWBOY RIDER ROPER WADDY CHARRO GAUCHO HERDER JINETE COWHAND COWHERD COWPOKE HERDBOY LLANERO PUNCHER VAQUERO BUCKAROO JACKAROO OUTRIDER RANCHERO WRANGLER

COWER HUG FAWN HOVER QUAIL SHRUG SQUAT STOOP TOADY WINCE CRINGE CROUCH SHRINK

COWL CAP LID SOE HOOD MONK MITER BONNET SCUTTLE CAPUCHIN

COWSLIP PAIGLE PRIMULA SHOOTER AURICULA CYCLAMEN MARIGOLD PRIMROSE

COXCOMB FOP BUCK DUDE PRIG DANDY PRINCOX POPINJAY

COY SHY ARCH NICE ALOOF CHARY QUIET STILL DEMURE MODEST PROPER BASHFUL DISTANT RESERVED KITTENISH

COYPU DEGU NUTRIA

COZEN COG CON BILK GULL POOP CHEAT TRICK CHISEL GREASE BEGUILE DECEIVE DEFRAUD SWINDLE HOODWINK

COZY RUG BIEN EASY SAFE SNUG CUSHY HOMEY SECURE TOASTY FAMILIAR HOMELIKE SOCIABLE

CRAB GIN UCA BOCO JUEY MAJA ZOEA ANGER ARROW AYUYU BLUEY MAIAN MAJID RACER SANDY THIEF WINCH BUSTER CANCER GROUSE HARPER HERMIT KABURI NIPPER PARTAN PEELER PUNGAR SCRAWL SPRITE BUCKLER BURSTER CABOUCA CANCRID FIDDLER GRUMBLE INACHID OCYPODE PANFISH POLYPOD SHEDDER SOLDIER SPECTER SURIQUE ARACHNID DORIPPID GRAPSOID HORSEMAN IRRITATE LIMULOID LITHODID OCHIDORE OXYSTOME PAGURIAN PORTUNID RANINIAN TRAVELER WINDLASS BRACHYURA

CRABBED SOUR UGLY CRANK CROSS SURLY TESTY BITTER CROOSE CRUSTY MOROSE SULLEN TRYING BOORISH CANKERY CRAMPED CROOKED GNARLED KNOTTED PEEVISH CHURLISH CONTRARY LIVERISH PETULANT VINEGARY

CRABGRASS DRAWK FONIO PANIC DARNEL PANICLE CRABWEED ELEUSINE

CRACK GAG POP BANG BLOW CHIP CHOP CLAP FLAW JEST JIBE JOKE LEAK LICK QUIP REND RIFT RIME RIVE SCAR SLAT SNAP BREAK CHARK CHICK CHINE CHINK CLACK CLEFT CRAKE CRAZE FLAKE FLASH KNICK SCORE SHAKE SLASH SOLVE SPANG SPLIT CLEAVE CRANNY SPIDER SPRING BLEMISH CREVICE FISSURE FRACTURE HAIRLINE
(— A WHIP) YERK FLANK
(— IN FLESH) KIN CHAP KIBE
(— IN FLOOR) STRAKE
(— IN INGOT) SPILL
(— IN MAST) SPRING
(— IN ROCK) GRIKE JOINT
(— IN SEA ICE) RIFTER
(— IN STEEL) CHECK SPILL
(— OPEN) SEAM
(— PETROLEUM) BURN
(— WHILE FIRING) DUNT

CRACKER BAKE LIAR WAFER BONBON POPPER BISCUIT BOASTER BREAKER BURSTER COSAQUE REDNECK SALTINE SNAPPER
(BOILED —S) CUSH
(BROKEN —S) DUNDERFUNK

CRACKLE SNAP BREAK CRACK CRISP CRINKLE SPUTTER CREPITATE

CRACKPOT ERRATIC LUNATIC CRANKISH

CRACKSMAN YEGG BURGLAR PETEMAN

CRADLE COT CRIB REST ROCK WOMB CRATE FRAME CRECHE MATRIX ROCKER SADDLE TROUGH BERCEAU SHELTER BASSINET CUNABULA
(— FOR SHIP) BED SLEE
(— FOR VATS) STILLING STILLION
(— IN ARCHERY) PURSE
(CERAMICS —) CHUM

CRAFT ART BARK BOAT SAIL GUILE SKILL TRADE BARQUE BATEAU DECEIT METIER TALENT VESSEL ABILITY CUNNING PANURGY SLEIGHT APTITUDE ARTIFICE VOCATION

CRAFTY SLY ARCH DEEP FINE FOXY SLIM WILY WISE ADEPT PAWKY SLAPE SLEEK ADROIT ARTFUL ASTUTE CALLID SHREWD SUBTLE TRICKY CUNNING POLITIC SLEIGHT VAFROUS VERSUTE VULPINE CAPTIOUS DEXTROUS JESUITIC

CRAG TOR KNEE NECK ROCK SCAR SPUR ARETE BRACK CLIFF HEUGH

CRAGGY ROUGH ABRUPT KNOTTY CRAGGED KNAGGED

CRAM BAG MUG RAM WAD FILL GLUT

LADE PACK STOW TRIG TUCK URGE
CROWD CRUSH DRIVE FORCE GORGE
LEARN PRESS STUDY STUFF TEACH
STEEVE STODGE

CRAMMED PANG STODGY CHOCKFUL
JAMPACKED

CRAMP CRIB KINK PAIN TUCK CRICK
CRIMP CROWD DOWEL PINCH STUNT
AGRAFE DOGTIE HAMPER HINDER
PESTER CONFINE COMPRESS CONTRACT
RESTRAIN RESTRICT

CRAMPED POKY BOUNDED CRIMPED
SQUEEZY

CRANBERRY ERICAD BOGWORT
PEMBINA ACROSARC BILBERRY
BOGBERRY COWBERRY FENBERRY
FOXBERRY CROWBERRY
(— BUSH) PIMBINA

CRANE HOOK SWAY CYRUS DAVIT
HERON HOIST JENNY RAISE SARUS
TITAN WADER BROLGA JIGGER KULANG
SAHRAS COOLUNG CRAWLER DERRICK
GOLIATH KAIKARA WHOOPER ADJUTANT
GRUIFORM TRAVELER

CRANK NUT WIT BENT SICK WHIM WIND
BRACE LOOSE ROGUE SHAKY THROW
WINCH AILING EVENER GROUCH HANDLE
INFIRM AWKWARD BRACKET FANATIC
LUSTILY

CRANKY UGLY CRAZY CRONK CROSS
LUSTY SHAKY TESTY AILING FIFISH
INFIRM SICKLY CROOKED GROUCHY
PERVERSE TORTUOUS

CRANNY HOLE NOOK CHINK CLEFT
CRACK CORNER CRANNEL CREVICE
FISSURE

CRAPE BAND CURL FRIZ CREPE CRIMP
DRAPE GAUZE SHROUD MOURNING

CRASH BASH FAIL FALL RACK BLAST
BURST CLOTH CRUSH FRUSH PRANG
SHOCK SMASH SOUND FIASCO FRAGOR
HURTLE FAILURE SHATTER STENTER
COLLAPSE ICEQUAKE SPLINTER
STRAMASH
(— OF THUNDER) CLAP

CRASS RAW DULL LOUD RUDE CRUDE
DENSE GROSS ROUGH THICK COARSE
OBTUSE STUPID

CRATE BOX CAR CASE CRIB FLAT SERON
BASKET CRADLE ENCASE HAMPER
HURDLE CARRIER PACKAGE VEHICLE

CRATER CUP PIT CONE HOLE DINOS
FOVEA NICHE CELEBE HOLLOW CALDERA
(LUNAR —) LINNE
(VOLCANIC —) MAAR

CRAVAT TIE ASCOT SCARF STOCK
CHOKER NECKTIE SOUBISE

CRAVE ASK BEG ITCH LONG NEED PRAY
SEEK WISH COVET YEARN DESIRE
HANKER HUNGER LINGER THIRST
BESEECH ENTREAT IMPLORE REQUEST
REQUIRE SOLICIT

CRAVEN AFRAID COWARD SCARED
DASTARD COWARDLY DEFEATED
OVERCOME POLTROON RECREANT
SNEAKING

CRAVING AVID ITCH WANT LETCH
DESIRE HUNGER THIRST LONGING
APPETITE TICKLING
(— FOR LIQUOR) DRY
(— FOR UNNATURAL FOOD) PICA
(ABNORMAL —) BULIMIA

CRAW MAW CRAG CROP STOMACH

CRAWL LAG DRAG FAWN INCH LOOP
SWIM CREEP SLIDE SNAKE TRAIL CRINGE
GROVEL CLAMBER SLITHER TRUDGEN

CRAYFISH DAD CRAB YABBY CAMARON
CRAWDAD LOBSTER CAMBARUS
CRABFISH CRAWFISH

CRAYON PLAN CHALK CONTE PASTEL
PENCIL SKETCH

CRAZE BUG FAD MODE RAGE BREAK
CRACK FUROR MANIA VOGUE WEAKEN
DERANGE DESTROY ASUNDER DISTRACT

CRAZED MAD AMOK LOCO WILD ZANY
BALMY BATTY DAFFY DOTTY GIDDY
MANIC NUTTY POTTY WACKY COOCOO
DOTTLE INSANE LOONEY BERSERK
FANATIC LUNATIC DEMENTED DERANGED
POSSESSED

CRAZY (ALSO SEE CRAZED) APE OFF
BATS BUGS GYTE LOCO NUTS WILD
ZANY BATTY BEANY BUGGY DAFFY DIPPY
DOILT DOTTY FLAKY GOOFY KOOKY
LOONY POTTY CRANKY CUCKOO DOTTLE
FLAKEY FRUITY INSANE SCREWY
BANANAS BONKERS CRACKED LUNATIC
PEEVISH BUGHOUSE COCKEYED
CRACKERS DERANGED MESHUGGA

CREAK CRY GIG RASP CHIRK CRANK
CROAK GRIND GROAN FRATCH SCREAK
SQUEAK COMPLAIN

CREAM DIP BEAT BEST CREME ELITE
FROTH SAUCE BONBON CHOICE
EMULSION OINTMENT

CREASE GAW CLAM FOLD LINE RUGA
SEAM BLOCK CRESS CRIMP PLAIT PLEAT
PRESS SCORE FURROW SUTURE WREATH
CRUMPLE WRINKLE

CREATE COIN FORM MAKE PLAN BUILD
CAUSE ERECT FORGE RAISE SHAPE
WRITE AUTHOR DESIGN INVENT
COMPOSE FASHION IMAGINE PRODUCE
GENERATE CONSTRUCT

CREATIVE FERTILE POIETIC GERMINAL
ORIGINATIVE

CREATOR MAKER AUTHOR FATHER
FORMER VARUNA WORKER KHEPERA
TAGALOA DESIGNER INVENTOR
OPERATOR PRODUCER TANGALOA

CREATURE MAN BEAST BEING DABBA
SLAVE WIGHT ANIMAL FELLOW MINION
PERSON WRETCH CRITTER GANGREL
MINIKIN MINIMUS
(— OF LITTLE VALUE) SHOT
(CANNIBALISTIC —) WINDIGO
(DISORDERLY —) ROIT
(DWARF —) FAIRY GNOME
(ELFLIKE —) PERI
(EVIL —) HELLICAT
(FABLED —) LUNG SIREN MERMAN
WIVERN ALBORAK MERMAID

(LITTLE —) MITING
(MANGY —) RONYON
(MANLIKE —) HOMINID HOMONID HOMINIAN
(MECHANICAL —) GOLEM
(MISERABLE —) SNAKE
(NONSENSE —) SNARK
(SILLY —) GOOSE
(SMALL —) ATOM GRIG BEASTIE
(SPRY —) WHIPPET
(STUNTED —) WIRL URLING WIRLING
(SUPERNATURAL —) DRAGON
(TINY —) ELF ATOMY
(UNDERDEVELOPED —) SLINK
(UNDERSIZED —) DURGAN
(USELESS —) HUSHION
(VICIOUS —) DEVIL
(WORTHLESS —) SCULPIN SNIPJACK
(WRETCHED —) ARMINE
(3 —S OF A KIND) LEASH
CREDIBLE LIKELY CREDENT FAITHFUL PROBABLE TROWABLE PLAUSIBLE
CREDIT LOAN TICK FAITH HONOR MERIT CHARGE ESTEEM IMPUTE ASCRIBE BELIEVE CREANCE CREDENCE
CREDULOUS SIMPLE SPOONY BOOBYISH CREDIBLE GULLIBLE
CREED ISM CULT SECT CREDO DOGMA FAITH TENET BELIEF DOCTRINE SYMBOLUM
CREEK BAY GUT RIA RIO RUN VLY BURN KILL RILL SLUE VLEI WASH WICK BAYOU BIGHT BOGUE BROOK CRICK INLET ARROYO BRANCH ESTERO SLOUGH STREAM ESTUARY RIVULET
(AUSTRALIAN —) COWAL
(TIDE —) SLAKE
CREEP FAWN INCH CRAWL GLIDE PROWL SKULK SLINK STEAL TRAIL CRINGE GROVEL
CREOLE PATOIS CRIOLLO DIALECT HAITIAN MESTIZO
CREON (DAUGHTER OF —) GLAUCE
(FATHER OF —) MENOECEUS
(SISTER OF —) JOCASTA HIPPONOME
CRESCENT HORN LUNE MOON CURVE LUNAR LUNULE SICKLE LUNETTE MENISCUS
CREST TIP TOP ACME APEX EDGE HOOD PEAK RUFF SEAL TUFT CROWN PLUME RIDGE FINIAL HEIGHT HELMET SUMMIT BEARING FEATHER TOPKNOT PINNACLE
(— OF BREAKER) SEEGE
(— OF HELMET) COMB CIMIER
(— OF HILL) KNAP
(— OF MINERAL VEIN) APEX
(— OF MOUNTAIN RANGE) ARETE SAWBACK
(— OF PEACOCK) CHAPLET
(— OF RIDGE) EDGE
(— OF SNOW) CORNICE
(— ON BIRD) CROWN ECKLE COPPLE
(IMPERIAL —) KIKUMON
(WAVE —) FEATHER WHITECAP
CRESTFALLEN COWED DEJECTED

CRETE

BAY: SUDA KANCA KISAMO MESARA
CAPE: BUZA LIANO SALOME SIDERO SPATHA STAVROS LITHINON SIDHEROS
CAPITAL: CANEA
GULF: KHANIA MERABELLO
MOUNTAIN: IDA DIKTE JUKTAS LASITHI THEODORE
TOWN: HAG LATO CANEA KHORA SITIA ZAKRO ANOYIA CANDIA KHANIA KISAMO RETIMO KISAMOS KASTELLI HERAKLION

CRETIN IDIOT
CREVASSE CHASM SPLIT MOULIN SCHRUND CLEAVAGE BERGSCHRUND
CREVICE BORE NOOK PEEP SEAM VEIN BREAK CHINK CLEFT CRACK CRANNY STRAKE FISSURE OPENING CREVASSE
(VOLCANIC —) SOLFATARA
CREW LOT MEN MOB SET BAND GANG HERD TEAM COVIN EIGHT HANDS PARTY SQUAD STAFF THRONG COMPANY RETINUE
CRIB BED BIN BOX CAB COT HUT KEY PONY RACK SKIN TROT CHEAT CRATE FRAME HOVEL STALL STEAL BUNKER CRECHE MANGER PIGSTY PILFER CABBAGE PURLOIN BASSINET
CRICKET GRIG MOLE SNOB CHANGA SADDLE GRYLLID TWIDDLER ORTHOPTERAN
CRICKET ON THE HEARTH
(AUTHOR OF —) DICKENS
(CHARACTER IN —) DOT MAY JOHN CALEB BERTHA EDWARD PLUMMER FIELDING TACKLETON PERRYBINGLE
CRIME SIN EVIL ABUSE ARSON CAPER LIBEL WRONG FELONY INCEST MURDER PIACLE FORGERY MISDEED OFFENSE INIQUITY SABOTAGE VILLAINY MALEFACTION MISDEMEANOR
CRIME AND PUNISHMENT
(AUTHOR OF —) DOSTOEVSKI
(CHARACTER IN —) SONIA DOUNIA LUZHIN PORFIRY PETROVICH RAZUMIHIN MARMELADOV RASKOLNIKOV SVIDRIGAILOV
CRIMINAL BAD YEGG CROOK FELON TOUGH APACHE BASHER DACOIT GUILTY GUNMAN INMATE KILLER NOCENT SLAYER WICKED CONVICT CULPRIT HEINOUS HOODLUM ILLEGAL MOBSTER NOXIOUS CULPABLE GANGSTER JAILBIRD
(HABITUAL —) RECIDIVIST
(PETTY —) ROUNDER
(VIOLENT —) DESPERADO
CRIMSON LAC RED PINK GRAIN BLOODY JOCKEY MAROON MODENA CARMINE SCARLET CRAMOISY CREMOSIN
CRINGE BOW BEND DUCK FAWN BINGE COWER CRAWL CREEP QUAIL SNEAK STOOP WINCE YIELD BUCKLE CROUCH

GROVEL SHRINK SUBMIT ADULATE TRUCKLE

CRINGING ABJECT HANGDOG SERVILE SPANIEL

CRINKLE BEND CURL KINK TURN WIND CREPE CRISP PUCKER RIPPLE RUMPLE RUSTLE CRACKLE CRANKLE FRIZZLE WRINKLE

CRIPPLE MAR GIMP HARM HURT LAME MAIM HOBBLE IMPAIR INJURE SCOTCH WEAKEN DISABLE HANDICAP LAMESTER MUTILATE PARALYZE

CRIPPLED GIMPY COUPLED DISABLED

CRISIS FIT CRUX FLAP HEAD PASS TURN BRUNT PANIC PERIL PINCH POINT STATE STORM TRIAL STRAIT DECISION JUNCTURE

CRISP NEW COLD CURL BRISK CLEAR CURLY FRESH FRIZZ NIPPY PITHY SHARP STIFF TERSE BITING BRIGHT CRISPY LIVELY SNAPPY BRACING BRITTLE CONCISE CRUNCHY FRIABLE INCISIVE

CRITERION LAW NORM RULE TEST TYPE AXIOM CANON CHECK GAUGE MODEL PROOF INDICIA MEASURE PLUMMET STANDARD SHIBBOLETH

CRITIC MOME BOOER JUDGE MOMUS CARPER CENSOR EXPERT PUNDIT ZOILUS DEBUNKER OVERSEER REVIEWER ARISTARCH

CRITICAL EDGY HIGH NICE ACERB ACUTE CHILLY NASUTE SEVERE URGENT ADVERSE CARPING EXIGENT NERVOUS PARLOUS CAPTIOUS CARDINAL DECISIVE EXACTING JUDICIAL PRESSING SLASHING TICKLISH CLIMACTERIC

CRITICISM RAP FIRE FLAK GAFF SLAM BLAME KNOCK ATTACK REVIEW CENSURE COMMENT PANNING QUIBBLE SLASHER SLATING ZOILISM BLUDGEON CRITIQUE DIATRIBE JUDGMENT STRICTURE
(PETTY —) NITPICKING

CRITICIZE HIT PAN RAP RIP CARP CRAB FLAY FLOG SKIN SLAM SLUR TIDE YELP BLAME BLAST CAVIL DECRY GRIPE JUDGE KNOCK ROAST SCORE SLASH SLATE BERATE CRITIC REBUKE REVIEW CENSURE COMMENT CONDEMN EXAMINE SCARIFY BADMOUTH CRITIQUE DENOUNCE TOMAHAWK

CROAK CAW GASP KILL ROUP QUARK GRUMBLE COMPLAIN FOREBODE

CROCHET HOOK KNIT BRAID PLAIT WEAVE CROTCHET

CROCK JAR PIG POT STEAN CHATTY CRITCH GOOLAH PANMUG SMUDGE CRAGGAN TERRINE POTSHERD

CROCKERY CHINA CLOAM DISHES PIGGERY POTWARE CLAYWARE

CROCODILE GOA CROC GATOR MAGAR CAYMAN GAVIAL JACARE DIAPSID SAURIAN LORICATE

CROMLECH QUOIT CIRCLE DOLMEN CROMMEL GORSEDD

CRONE HAG AUNT TROT WITCH BELDAM RIBIBE

CRONY PAL CHUM BILLY GOSSY NETOP GIMMER GOSSIP

CROOK BEND HOOK TURN WARP CHEAT CRANK CURVE HUNCH NIBBY PEDUM STAFF THIEF INDENT CAMBUCA CROSIER POTHOOK SLICKER CHISELER SWINDLER

CROOKED CAM WRY AGEE AWRY BENT AGLEY ASKEW BANDY CRANK FALSE KINKY SNIDE WRONG AKIMBO ARTFUL ASLANT CAMMED CRAFTY CRANKY CURVED DOGLEG HURLED WEEWOW ZIGZAG ASKANCE ASQUINT CORRUPT OBLIQUE TURNING TWISTED WINDING TORTUOUS

CROON HUM LOW BOOM LULL SING WAIL CHIRM CRONY WHINE LAMENT MURMUR TEEDLE COMPLAIN

CROP BOB CUT MAW TOP CLIP CRAW REAP TRAP TRIM WHIP GRAZE SHAVE SHEAR SHIFT SWATH TILTH BROWSE SILAGE CURTAIL CUTTING HARVEST TILLAGE GLEANING
(— CANDLEWICK) SNUFF
(— OF A HAWK) GORGE
(— OF FRUIT) HANG
(— OF GRASS) LEA LEY SWATH
(— OF OYSTERS) SET
(— OF POTATOES) GARDEN
(GREEN —S) SOILAGE
(INDIAN —) RABI KHARIF
(LARGE —) HIT
(RIDING —) ROP
(SECOND-GROWTH —) ROWEN AFTERMATH

CROQUET ROQUE BOMBARD

CROQUETTE CECIL OYSTER KROMESKI

CROSS GO CAM CUT MIX TAU ANKH CRUX FORD PASS ROOD SIGN SOUR SPAN TREE WOOD ANGRY CHUFF SURLY TESTY THRAW TRAVE TRIAL YAPPY BISECT CHUFFY CRABBY CRANKY CROUCH DENIAL GIBBET GROUTY GRUMPY HIPPED OUTWIT PATCHY SIGNUM SNAGGY SNASTY SNUFFY SULLEN THWART TOUCHY WICKED WOOLLY ATHWART CALVARY CRABBED CROSIER FRETFUL FROWARD OBLIQUE PASSAGE PEEVISH PETTISH POTENCE SALTIRE CAMSHACH CROISADE CROTCHED CRUCIFIX DEMISANG FRAMPOLD FRATCHED FRUMPISH PECTORAL PETULANT SNAPPISH SWASTIKA TRAVERSE VEXILLUM
(— BETWEEN GRAPEFRUIT AND TANGERINE) UGLI
(— BY PLANE) HOP
(— ONESELF) SAIN
(— OVER) SPAN TRAJECT
(DOUBLE —) BUSINESS
(MALTESE —) FIREBALL

CROSSBAR RUNG CROWN JUGUM DRIVER TRANSOM
(— IN GATE) SWORD
(— IN SHAFT) STEMPLE
(— OF BALANCE) BEAM
(— OF DOOR) SLOAT
(— OF WINDOW) LOCKET

CROSSBEAM BAR BUNK SPUR TRAVE GIRDER BOLSTER DORMANT TRANSOM TRAVERSE

CROSSBOW BRAKE LATCH TILLER ARBALEST BALISTER BALLISTA STONEBOW
(PART OF —) NUT IRON LOCK GUARD SIGHT STOCK WEDGE GROOVE STIRRUP TRIGGER BOWSTRING

CROSSBREED HUSKY METIS SANGA HYBRID

CROSSED ACROSS SQUINT WOOFED CRUCIAL THWARTING

CROSSING PASS LACED MIXTURE PASSAGE TRAJECT CRUCIATE OPPOSING OVERPASS TRAVERSE CROSSOVER

CROSSROAD LEET VENT WENT CAREFOX CARFOUR COMPITUM

CROTCH FORK POLE POST CLEFT NOTCH STAKE CRUTCH CROTCHET

CROTCHET FAD TOY HOOK KINK WHIM CRANK FANCY FREAK FIZGIG MAGGOT VAGARY CORCHAT CRANKUM

CROUCH BEND DROP FAWN COWER HOVER SQUAT STOOP CRINGE HUDDLE HUNKER SCRUNCH SQUATTER

CROW CAW CRY DAW BRAG DOWP ROOK AYLET BOAST CRAKE EXULT HOODY KELLY RAVEN VAUNT CHOUGH CORBIE CORVUS HOODIE KOKAKO GORCROW JACKDAW SWAGGER ABSAROKA BALDHEAD BLACKNEB GAVELOCK GRAYBACK GREYBACK

CROWBAR PRY SET BETTY JIMMY LEVER SWAPE FORCER GAVELOCK

CROWD HUG JAM MOB CRAM HEAP HERD HOST JOSS MONG PACK PILE PUSH RAFT ROUT RUCK SORT STOW SWAD BUNCH CLOUD COHUE COVEY CRAMP CRUSH CRWTH DROVE FLOCK GROUP HORDE POSSE PRESS ROTTA SERRY SWARM VOLGE WEDGE BOODLE CHORUS CLIQUE HUDDLE IMPACT JOSTLE OUTFIT RABBLE THREAD THRONG THRIMP THRONG THRUST TYMPAN VOLLEY BOUROCK CHROTTA CLUSTER COMPANY CONGEST IMPRESS SCROUGE SQUEEZE THICKEN CABOODLE SANDWICH CONCOURSE GATHERING MULTITUDE CLAMJAMFRY

CROWDED CLOSE DENSE STIFF THICK FILLED THRONG BUNCHED COMPACT SERRIED STUFFED TEEMING NUMEROUS POPULOUS

CROWN CAP TAJ TIP TOP COIN GULL HELM PEAK POLL ADORN BASIL BEZEL CREST CROWN MURAL POLOS REGAL ROUND ROYAL TIARA ANADEM CIRCLE CLIMAX CORONA DIADEM FILLET INVEST LAUREL POTONG REWARD SUMMIT TIMBER TROPHY UPWARD VALLAR VERTEX WREATH AUREOLE CHAPLET CORNICE CORONAL CORONET GARLAND INSTALL PSCHENT STEPHEN TONSURE CORONATE ENTHRONE PINNACLE SURMOUNT
(— OF CHICORY) ENDIVE

(— OF EGYPT) ATEF PSCHENT
(— OF HEAD) NOLL PATE SKULL CANTLE POMMEL FORETOP
(— OF HILL) KNAP
(— OF LAUREL) BAY
(— OF ROCK) KRANTZ
(HALF —) GEORGE ALDERMAN
(PIECE OF —) BULL
(PLANT —) STOOL

CROW'S NEST LOOKOUT

CRUCIAL KEY ACUTE PIVOT SEVERE TRYING PIVOTAL SUPREME TELLING CRITICAL DECISIVE

CRUCIBLE POT DISH ETNA TEST HEARTH MONKEY RETORT FURNACE CROSSLET

CRUCIFIX PAX ROOD CROSS

CRUCIFY VEX HANG KILL HARRY MORTIFY TORMENT TORTURE CRUCIATE

CRUDE ILL RAW BALD BARE RUDE BRUTE CRASS GREEN GROSS HAIRY HARSH ROUGH TACKY CALLOW COARSE DOUGHY SAVAGE UNRIPE VULGAR ARTLESS GLARING SQUALID UNCOUTH AGRESTIC IGNORANT IMMATURE IMPOLITE PRIMITIVE

CRUEL ILL FELL GRIM HARD BLACK BREME BRUTE FELON HARSH STERN WROTH BITTER BLOODY BRUTAL DREARY FIERCE SAVAGE SEVERE UNJUST UNKIND UNMILD WANTON WICKED BESTIAL INHUMAN NERONIC BARBARIC DIABOLIC FELONOUS FIENDISH INHUMANE PITILESS RUTHLESS SADISTIC TYRANNIC TRUCULENT

CRUELTY RIGOR DURESS SADISM DEVILRY FELLNESS SEVERITY

CRUET AMA JAR JUG VIAL CRUSE BOTTLE CASTER GUTTUS AMPULLA BURETTE URCEOLE

CRUISE SAIL TRIP JUNKET STOOGE

CRUISER SHIP VALUER VESSEL WARSHIP ESTIMATOR

CRUMB BIT ORT PIECE MORSEL CRUMBLE REMNANT FRAGMENT
(PL.) PANADA PANURE MOOLINGS

CRUMBLE ROT MULL MUSH BREAK CRUSH DECAY RAVEL SPOIL BUCKLE MOLDER MYRTLE PERISH SLOUGH CORRADE CRIMBLE COLLAPSE

CRUMPLE FOLD MUSS CRUSH SCREW BUCKLE CREASE FURROW RUMPLE SCRUNCH WRINKLE COLLAPSE CONTRACT

CRUNCH BITE CHEW CHOMP CRASH CRUSH GNASH GRIND PRESS GRANCH GROWSE CRAUNCH SCRANCH SCRUNCH

CRUSADE WAR JIHAD CROISEE CAMPAIGN CROCIATE

CRUSADER PILGRIM TEMPLAR EQUITIST REFORMER

CRUSH HUG JAM BEND CHEW CRAM DASH MASH MILL MULL STUB BREAK BRIZZ CHAMP CHECK CRASH CRAZE CROWD FORCE GRIND PRESS QUASH QUELL SMASH SQUAB STAMP TREAD BRUISE BURDEN CRUNCH SCOTCH SQUASH SUBDUE THRONG CONQUER

CONTUSE CRACKLE CRUMPLE DEPRESS DESTROY OPPRESS OVERRUN REPRESS SCRUNCH SHATTER SQUEEZE SQUELCH TRAMPLE COMPRESS OVERCOME SQUABASH SUPPRESS OVERWHELM

CRUSHING FIERCE BRUISING SMASHING SQUABASH

CRUST FUR PIP CAKE HULL RIND SCAB SHELL SKULL COFFIN GRATIN HARDEN RONDLE SCRUFF CALICHE COATING CARAPACE PELLICLE SCUTULUM
(— OF DIKE) SALBAND
(— ON WINE) ARGOL
(PIE —) HUFF COFFIN

CRUSTACEAN BUG APUS CRAB FLEA SCUD ZOEA ALIMA CARID KRILL LOUSE PRAWN SLATER CYPRID ENDITE ISOPOD SHRIMP SLATER SQUILL ARTEMIA COPEPOD CRAYLET DAPHNID DECAPOD GRIBBLE HAYSEED LOBSTER SQUAGGA SQUILLA AMPHIPOD BARNACLE CIRRIPED CRAYFISH GAMMARID LERNAEAN MONOCULE OSTRACOD PAGURIAN SQUILLID BRACHYURA PHYLLOPOD SCHIZOPOD SHELLFISH

CRUSTY CURT BLUFF BLUNT TESTY MOROSE SULLEN CRABBED PEEVISH PETTISH STARCHY SNAPPISH

CRUTCH FORK STILT CROTCH POTENT SADDLE SPRAG

CRUX NUB GIST HALF PITH CROSS POINT PUZZLE RIDDLE PROBLEM

CRY HO CRI FAD HOA HUE OLE PIP SOB YIP BUMP CALL COWL CROW GLAM GOWL HAIL HAWK NOTE OYEZ PULE RAGE RAME RANE REEM RERD ROOP SIKE TOOT WAIL WEEP YELL YELP CLEPE CRAKE CRUNK GREET GROAN QUEAK RUMOR SHOUT SOUND TROAT UTTER VOGUE WHEWL WHINE WHULE WRAWL BELLOW BOOHOO CHIVVY CLAMOR DEMAND LAMENT OUTCRY SCREAM SHRIEK SLOGAN SNIVEL SQUALL SQUAWL SQUEAL TONGUE WIMICK YAMMER FASHION SCREECH PROCLAIM
(— ALOUD) BLART GREDE
(— AT SIGHT OF WHALE) FALL
(— DOWN) DOWNCRY BERATTLE
(— FOR TRUCE) BARLEY
(— HOARSELY) CROUP
(— LIKE ELEPHANT) BARR TRUMPET
(— LIKE PIG) WRINE
(— OF A BAT) CHIP
(— OF ABORIGINES) COOEE
(— OF BACCHANALS) EVOE
(— OF BIRD) CAW COO PEW BOOM CAWK CLANG BIRDCALL
(— OF BITTERN) BILL
(— OF CAT) MEW MEWL MIAOU MIAOW MIAUL MIAUW CALLING
(— OF CONTEMPT) BOO
(— OF DEER) BELL
(— OF ENTHUSIASM) BANZAI
(— OF GOOSE) HONK YANG
(— OF GUINEA HEN) POTRACK
(— OF HOUND) MUTE MUSIC
(— OF JACKAL) PHEAL

(— OF MOURNING) KEEN TANGI
(— OF NEWBORN CHILD) VAGITUS
(— OF RAVEN) QUALM
(— OF SHEEP) BAA BLAT BLEAT
(— OF SNIPE) SCAPE
(— OF SORROW) ULLAGONE
(— OF SURRENDER) KAMERAD
(— OF WATCHMAN) WATCH
(— OUT) BAY BAWL BRAY GALE GAPE HOOT HOWL JERK SCRY BLORE CHIRM CLAIM ESCRY SHOUT HALLOO HOLLER SCREAM SHRIEK THREAP THROPE BREATHE EXCLAIM RECLAIM DISCLAIM PROCLAIM
(— TO CLEAR PASSAGE) HALL
(— TO COMBATANTS) BAILE
(BATTLE —) CRY ENSIGN MONTJOY GERONIMO
(DRINKING —) RIVO
(HOARSE —) CROAK
(HUNTING —) TIVY CHEVY STABOY YOICKS TALLYHO TANTARA TANTIVY PILILLOO
(PROLONGED —) RANE
(RALLYING —) SLOGAN
(RAUCOUS —) CATCALL
(SHRILL) SKIRL SQUEAK SQUEAL SCREECH YALLOCK
(WAR —) DIN ALALA HAVOC BANZAI SLOGAN
(WORDLESS —) KEEN ULULU

CRYING PIPING URGING CLAMANT HEINOUS VAGIENT PRESSING RECREANT

CRYPT PIT CRAFT CROFT VAULT CAVERN GROTTO RECESS SHROUD CHAMBER FOLLICLE

CRYPTIC DARK VAGUE HIDDEN SECRET OBSCURE ELLIPTIC MYSTICAL SIBYLLIC

CRYSTAL ICE DIAL DOME HARD SEED CLEAR GLASS GRAIN LUCID NICOL GLASSY LIMPID MIRROR NEEDLE PEBBLE QUARTZ ACICULA DIAMOND DIPLOID LUNETTE ORTHITE ULEXITE YAJEINE ZOISITE FIVELING FOURLING PELLUCID TRICHITE TRILLING PERIMORPH
(— FOREIGN TO ROCK) XENOCYST
(— OF GREAT STRENGTH) WHISKER
(FINE —) BERYL
(ICE —S IN WATER) FRAZIL
(NEEDLE-SHAPED —S) RAPHIDES
(ROCK —) BRISTOL CITRINE
(TWIN —) TWIN MACLE TWINDLE TWOLING FOURLING

CRYSTALLINE PURE CRYSTAL PELLUCID

CRYSTALLIZE FIX FIRM JELL CANDY SUGAR NEEDLE CONGEAL SOLIDIFY

CUB FRY PEN BEAR CHIT TOTO WHELP LIONET NOVICE CODLING REPORTER
(— SCOUT) WEBELOS

CUBA

BAY: NIPE PIGS
CAPE: CRUZ MAISI LUCRECIA
CAPITAL: HAVANA
COIN: PESO CENTAVO CUARENTA

DANCE: CONGA RUMBA DANZON RHUMBA
   GUARACHA PACHANGA
FALLS: TOA AGABAMA CABURNI
GULF: MEXICO ANAMARIA BATABANO
INDIAN: CARIB TAINO ARAWAK
ISLAND: PINES
ISLANDS: SABANA CAMAGUEY
MEASURE: VARA BOCOY TAREA CORDEL
   FANEGA
MOUNTAIN: TURQUINO
MOUNTAINS: CRISTAL MAESTRA
   ORGANOS TRINIDAD
PROVINCE: HAVANA ORIENTE CAMAGUEY
   MATANZAS
RIVER: ZAZA CAUTO
SWAMP: ZAPATA
TOWN: COLON MANES ALAMAR BAYAMO
   GUINES HAVANA BARACOA HOLGUIN
   PALMIRA ARTEMISA CAMAGUEY
   GUAYABAL MATANZAS SANTIAGO
WEIGHT: LIBRA TERCIO

CUBE CUT DIE KNOB BLOCK EIGHT SOLID
   TIMBO TESSERA BARBASCO QUADRATE
   TESSELLA
CUBICLE BAY CELL ROOM BOOTH CABIN
   NICHE STALL ALCOVE CARREL
CUCKOLD TUP HORN BECCO VULCAN
   WITTOL ACTAEON HORNIFY RAMHEAD
CUCKOO ANI FOOL GOWK KOEL CLOCK
   CRAZY SILLY DIDRIC HUNTER BOOBOOK
   CHATAKA DIEDRIC SIRKEER CHOWCHOW
   PICARIAN RAINBIRD RAINFOWL
CUCUMBER CUKE PEPO GOURD CONGER
   PEPINO GHERKIN PICKLER CUCURBIT
   PEPONIDA PEPONIUM
   (BITTER —) COLOCYNTH
   (SHRIVELED —) CRUMPLING
   (WILD —) SICYOS CREEPER
CUDBEAR CORK PERSIO PERSIS
   CUDWEED
CUDGEL BAT BEAT CANE CLUB DRUB
   KENT MACE RACK RUNG TREE BASTE
   BATON BILLY DRIVE KEBBY KEVEL LINCH
   LINGE SHRUB STAFF STAVE STICK
   THUMP TOWEL ALPEEN BALLOW
   BASTON BILLET GIBBET KEBBIE LIBBET
   THRASH WASTER BELABOR BOURDON
   DRUBBER SWADDLE SWINGLE TROUNCE
   BLUDGEON SHILLALA THWACKER
CUE NOD TAG TIP HINT WINK BRAID PLAIT
   QUEUE TWIST PROMPT SIGNAL PIGTAIL
   (BILLIARD —) MACE MAST STICK
   (MUSICAL —) PRESA
   (SHUFFLEBOARD —) SHOVEL
CUFF BOX BLOW SLAM SLAP SLUG SWAT
   CLOUT FIGHT SCUFF SMITE SOUSE
   BUFFET FENDER MITTEN STRIKE
   COLPHEG SCUFFLE GAUNTLET
CUISINE FOOD MENU TABLE COOKERY
   KITCHEN
CUL-DE-SAC POCKET STRAIT IMPASSE
CULL OPT CAST PICK SIFT SORT ELECT
   GLEAN PLUCK ASSORT CHOOSE GATHER
   REMOVE SELECT SEPARATE
CULMINATION END ACME APEX NOON

BLOOM CREST CROWN POINT APOGEE
   CLIMAX CULMEN HEIGHT PERIOD
   SUMMIT VERTEX ZENITH BLOWOFF
CULPABLE FAULTY GUILTY SINFUL
   IMMORAL BLAMABLE CRIMINAL
CULPRIT FELON CONVICT CRIMINAL
   OFFENDER
CULT CLAN DADA SECT CREED KUKSU
   CHURCH CULTUS DOMNEI MANISM
   NUDISM RITUAL SCHOOL SHINTO
   AMIDISM DADAISM ICONISM MYALISM
   MYSTERY WORSHIP DEVILISM
   HUMANISM SATANISM
   (SUFF.) ISM
CULTIVATE HOE CROP DISC DISK FARM
   GROW PLOW REAR TEND TILL WORK
   DRESS EARTH LABOR NURSE RAISE
   STUDY TRAIN AFFECT FOSTER FURROW
   HARROW MANAGE MANURE PLOUGH
   RATOON SARCLE SCHOOL ACQUIRE
   CHERISH CONTOUR CULTURE EDUCATE
   EMBRACE EXPLOIT HUSBAND IMPROVE
   NOURISH PREPARE SCRATCH CIVILIZE
CULTIVATED TAME CIVIL GROWN
   POLITE POLITIC REFINED CULTURED
   ARTIFICIAL
   (ARTIFICIALLY —) HOTHOUSE
CULTIVATION CROP TILTH FINISH
   GROWTH CULTURE TILLAGE REFINEMENT
   (— IN MANNERS) FINISH
   (MENTAL —) HUMANITY
CULTURE ART AGAR KULLI SLANT TAJIN
   TASTE TILTH JHUKAR POLISH STREAK
   ANANINO AZILIAN IRANISM JHANGAR
   KAYENTA SOCIETY STARTER TILLAGE
   HUMANISM LEARNING
CULTURED CIVIL POLITE LETTERED
CULVERT FOX GOUT DRAIN CONDUIT
   PINNOCK PONCEAU OVERPASS
CUMBERSOME HEAVY CLUMSY
   AWKWARD ONEROUS WEIGHTY
   UNWIELDY
CUMMERBUND BAND BELT SASH
CUNNING ART SLY WIT ARCH CUTE FINE
   FOXY KEEN SLIM WILY WISE CANNY
   CRAFT FAVEL GUILE SHARP SMART
   ADROIT ARTFUL ASTUTE CLEVER CRAFTY
   DAEDAL DECEIT ENGINE FOXERY PRETTY
   QUAINT SHREWD SUBTLE SUPPLE
   TRICKY WISDOM FINESSE KNOWING
   PARLOUS POLITIC PRACTIC SLEIGHT
   VULPINE DEXTROUS SKILLFUL STEALTHY
CUP AMA BOX POT CELL LOTA SHOE
   BOUSE CALIX CHARK COGUE COPPE
   CRUSE DEPAS GLASS KITTY PHIAL SCALE
   STEIN STOOP STOUP THECA BUCKET
   CHOANA COTYLA CRATER CUPULA
   EGGCUP EYECUP FESSEL FINJAN GOBLET
   JICARA KOTYLE MAZARD NOGGIN
   OXHORN POTION RUMKIN TASSIE
   VESSEL BRIMMER CHEERER QUONIAM
   SCYPHUS SHERBET STIRRUP THIMBLE
   GRADUATE PANNIKIN
   (— FOR HOLDING DIAMOND) DOP
   DOPP
   (— FOR PERFUMES) CONCH
   (— FOR YEAST) SKEP

(— IN SAUCER OF ALCOHOL) ETNA
(— OF FLOWER) BELL
(— OF TEA) DISH SPEED OYSTER
(— ON BULLET) GASCHECK
(— WITH COVER) HANAP
(ASSAYING —) CUPEL
(DRINKING —) CAN MUG NUT TIG TUN
TYG HORN TASS TOSS GODET BEAKER
GOBLET HOLMOS QUAICH RUMMER
CHALICE GODDARD TRINKET
(FAIRY —) COOLWORT
(FILLED —) BUMPER
(IRISH —) MADDER METHER
(IRON —) CULOT MUSHROOM
(LARGE —) FACER BLACKJACK
(LEATHER —) WELL GISPIN
(LONG-HANDLED —) CYATH DIPPER
CYATHUS KYATHOS
(MAPLE —) MAZER
(NAUTICAL —) THIEF
(ORNAMENTAL —) TAZZA
(PAPER —) DIXIE
(PASTRY —) DARIOLE
(PRIZE —) PEWTER
(SACRED —) GRAIL
(SHALLOW —) CYLIX TAZZA TASTER
CAPSULE
(SMALL —) DOP NOG TOT DOPP TASS
DOBBIN NOGGIN TASSIE
(SQUARE —) MADDER METHER
(STIRRUP —) BONAILIE
(WOODEN —) COG COGUE CAPPER
CAPPIE METHER QUAICH
CUPBEARER HEBE SAKI CUPPER
GANYMEDE
CUPBOARD CASE SAFE AMBRY CHEST
CUDDY HUTCH PRESS BUFFET CLOSET
LARDER LOCKER PANTRY ARMOIRE
CABINET DRESSER CREDENZA
(ARCHERY —) ASCHAM
CUPID DAN AMOR EROS LOVE PUTTO
CHERUB AMORINO AMOURET AMORETTO
CUPIDITY LUST GREED DESIRE AVARICE
AVIDITY LONGING APPETITE RAPACITY
CUPOLA DOME KILN VAULT BELFRY
TURRET FURNACE LANTERN LOOKOUT
CIMBORIO COCKLOFT
(ROUND —) THOLUS
CUR DOG YAP MUTT TYKE FEIST BRAKJE
MESSAN BOBTAIL MONGREL
CURATOR KEEPER STEWARD GUARDIAN
OVERSEER
CURB BIT FOIL KERB REIN SKID SNUB
BRAKE CHECK CRIMP GUARD LIMIT
ARREST BRIDLE COLLAR GOVERN
HAMPER STIFLE SUBDUE THWART
CONTROL INHIBIT REFRAIN REPRESS
SHACKLE MODERATE RESTRAIN
RESTRICT WITHHOLD
CURE DIP DRY DUN FIX CARE CORN HEAL
HELP JERK MEND SALT SAVE AMEND
BOTEN SMEEK SMOKE CHARGE KIPPER
PRIEST REMEDY SEASON SUCCOR
TEMPER RECOVER RESTORE THERAPY
ANTIDOTE PRESERVE
CURE-ALL BALM AVENS ELIXIR REMEDY
PANACEA THERIAC

CURIOSITY CURIO ODDITY INTEREST
CURIOUS ODD NOSY RARE QUEER
PRYING QUAINT SNOOPY CUNNING
STRANGE UNUSUAL FREAKISH
MEDDLING PECULIAR SINGULAR
CURL BOB BEND COIL FURL KINK LOCK
PURL ROLL WAVE WIND CRIMP CRISP
FRILL FRIZZ SPIRE TRESS TWIST BUCKLE
CURDLE FROWSE MULLET RIPPLE SPIRAL
WRITHE CRINKLE EARLOCK FLEXURE
FRIZZLE FROUNCE RINGLET TENDRIL
LOVELOCK SQUIGGLE
(— HAIR) CROOK
(— OF SMOKE) WREATH
(— OF WIG) SNAKE
(— ON FOREHEAD) CRUCHE CROUCHE
(— UP) CRUMP HUNCH SNIRL HUDDLE
SHRINK SNUGGLE
(METAL —) CHIP
(SMALL —) CROCK
CURLED FUZZY KINKY CIRRATE FRIZZLY
WREATHY CRISPATE CRUMPLED
CURLY WAVY CRISP CRULL OUNDY
CRIMPY RIPPLED CRINKLED
CURMUDGEON CRAB CHURL HUNKS
MISER GLEYDE GROUCH NIGGARD
CURRANT PASA BERRY CASSIS RAISIN
RIZZAR RIZZLE CORINTH
CURRENCY CASH COIN BILLS MONEY
SCRIP SERIES SPECIE PASSAGE
CURRENT NOW WAY EDDY FLOW FLUX
FORD RACE RIFE TIDE VEIN WAFT ALIVE
DRIFT GOING RAPID SWIFT TENOR TREND
USUAL ABROAD COEVAL COMMON
COURSE FLUENT LATEST LIVING MOTION
MOVING RECENT SLUICE STREAM
TONGUE VOLANT COUNTER DRAUGHT
FLOWING FRESHET GENERAL INSTANT
PASSANT PRESENT RUNNING STICKLE
THERMAL TORRENT BACKWASH
FREQUENT MILLRACE TIDERACE
UNDERTOW
(— IN SPEECH) WAIF
(AIR —) DRAFT SHEET SPLIT BREEZE
DOWNCAST DOWNFLOW
(ELECTRIC —) STRAY
(HOT —) BACK
(JAPAN —) KUROSHIO
(PREVAILING —) MAINSTREAM
(RAPID —) SWIFT TONGUE
(PREF.) RHEO
CURRY COMB DRUB KARI CLEAN DRESS
GROOM BRUISE CAJOLE TARKEEAN
(— FAVOR) HUG NUT QUILL COTTON
CUITTLE SMOODGE
CURSE BAN POX DAMN CUSS DAMN OATH
BLAST SHREW SPELL SWEAR DETEST
MAKUTU MALIGN MALISON ANATHEMA
EXECRATE MALEDICTION
CURSORY FAST BRIEF HASTY QUICK
SHORT FITFUL ROVING SPEEDY PASSANT
PASSING SHALLOW CARELESS
RAMBLING
CURT RUDE BLUFF BLUNT BRIEF NIPPY
SHORT TERSE ABRUPT SNIPPY BRUSQUE
CONCISE CRYPTIC LACONIC CAVALIER
SNAPPISH SNIPPETY SUCCINCT

CURTAIL CUT LOP CLIP CROP DOCK PARE
STOP ABATE ELIDE SLASH STUNT
LESSEN REDUCE ABRIDGE BOBTAIL
SHORTEN DIMINISH MINORATE

CURTAIN END BOOM DROP IRIS MASK
VEIL WALL BLIND DRAPE SCENE SHADE
SHEET VELUM COSTER HANGER PURDAH
SCREEN SHROUD CEILING CONCEAL
CORTINE DRAPERY HANGING VITRAGE
ASBESTOS PORTIERE TRAVERSE
(CHURCH —) CLOTH RIDDEL ENDOTHYS
(THEATER —) IRON SCRIM TEASER
TRAVELER TORMENTER

CURVE ARC BOW CUP ESS SAG ARCH
BEND BOUT COME CURB FADE HOOK
LINE OGEE TURN VEER WIND AMBIT
BIGHT BREAK CONIC CROOK CRUMP
CUBIC HELIX NONIC OGIVE PEDAL POLAR
QUIRK SLICE SWEEP SWIRL TARVE
TREND TWIST WITCH BOUGHT CAMBER
CIRCLE DEFLEX JORDAN LITUUS SOLVUS
SPIRAL SPRING TOROID WIMPLE
ADIABAT BRACKET CAUSTIC CIRCUIT
CISSOID COMPASS CONCAVE CONTOUR
COSEISM CURVITY CYCLOID ELLIPSE
ENVELOP FESTOON FLEXURE INCURVE
INFLECT LIMACON PHUGOID PROFILE
QUARTIC SCALLOP SINUATE SOLIDUS
CARDIOID CATENARY CONCHOID
DYGOGRAM ELASTICA EXTRADOS
FADEAWAY INVOLUTE LIGATURE
LIQUIDUS OPHIURID PARABOLA
SINUSOID TONOGRAM TRACTRIX
TROCHOID CATACAUSTIC
(— DESCRIBED BY GRAPH) GRAM
(— IN HANDRAIL) KNEE
(— IN PLANKING) HANG
(— IN SAIL) ROACH
(— OF ARCH) INTRADOS
(— OF BALL) DROP
(— OF BIT) LIBERTY
(— OF COLUMN) APOPHYGE
(— OF FINGERNAIL) GRYPOSIS
(— OF HORSE'S NECK) CREST
(— OF PLANK) SNY
(— OF SHIP'S BOW) FLAIR FLARE
(— OF TIMBER) CUP
(— SATISFYING EQUATION) BRANCH
(CRICKET —) SWERVE
(DOUBLE —) CYMA
(PLANE —) ROSE STROPHOID
(PLANE CUBIC —) WITCH
(VERTICAL —) RAMP

CURVED BENT ROUND WOUND CONVEX
GYRATE HAMATE TURNED ARCUATE
CONCAVE CROOKED EMBOWED FALCATE
SIGMOID AQUILINE

CUSHION BAG COD MAT PAD PUFF SEAT
GADDI TRUSH BUFFER INSOLE PILLOW
SACHET BOLSTER BRIOCHE HASSOCK
KNEELER MUFFLER PILLION
(LACE-MAKERS —) BOTT
(PIN —) PRINCOD
(SEAT —) BANKER
(TAILOR'S —) HAM
(PREF.) PULVILLI PULVINI

CUSP APEX CONE HORN PEAK ANGLE
POINT STYLE TOOTH CORNER SPINODE
ENTOCONE HYPOCONE METACONE
PARACONE

CUSPIDOR GABOON CRACHOIR
SPITTOON

CUSTARD FLAN CREME FLAWN DOUCET
CHARLET PARFAIT FLUMMERY
ZABAGLIONE

CUSTODIAN GUARD KEEPER SEXTON
WARDEN WARDER CURATOR JANITOR
CERBERUS CLAVIGER GUARDIAN
CONCIERGE

CUSTODY BAIL CARE HOLD KEEP WARD
TRUST ARREST CHARGE CONTROL
DURANCE KEEPING SECURITY

CUSTOM FAD TAX USE DUTY FORM
GARB MODE RITE ROTE RULE TOLL
WONT GUISE HABIT HAUNT STYLE
TRADE USAGE VOGUE DHARMA IMPOST
MANNER PRAXIS USANCE COSTUME
FASHION FORMULA TRIBUTE PRACTICE
(BINDING —) LAW
(BUSINESS —) TRADE GOODWILL
(CHILDBIRTH —) COUVADE
(CHURCH —) COMITY
(CORRUPT —) ABUSE
(FESTIVAL —) HOCKING
(OUTMODED —) ARCHAISM
(PRIMITIVE —) COUVADE
(RURAL —) HEAVING
(SECRET —) SANDE
(TEMPORARY —) FAD VOGUE

CUSTOMARY RIFE USED NOMIC USUAL
COMMON VULGAR WONTED CLASSIC
GENERAL REGULAR EVERYDAY FAMILIAR
HABITUAL ORTHODOX

CUSTOMER CHAP COVE BUYER CLIENT
PATRON ACCOUNT PATIENT SHOPPER
PROSPECT

CUT AX ADZ AXE DAG DAP DIE HAG HEW
KIT NIP RIT SAW SNY TAP ADZE BITE
BOLO BOLT BUZZ CHOP DADO FACE FILE
GASH GIRD HASH HEWN JERK KNAP
LIMB MAKE MODE MUSH NICK OCHE
RACE RASH RAZE SIDE SKIN SLOT SMIT
SNEE SNEG SNIB SNUB STOW SUMP
SWAP SWOP TAME TRIM VIDE BLOCK
BREAK CANAL CANCH CHIVE CLEFT
COPSE COUPE CRIMP DRESS FLICK FRITH
GOUGE GRAVE GRIDE GROOP HOWEL
KITTE KNIFE LANCE LATHE NOTCH PLATE
SABER SCALP SCORE SHAPE SHARE
SHIVE SHRED SLICE SPLIT STAMP SWEEP
SWIPE SWISH TOUCH TWITE VOGUE
WHITE ABLATE AJOURE BARBER BISECT
CAMBER CHISEL CLEAVE CORNER
CUTTED DIVIDE FIGURE FLETCH FLITCH
FRENCH IGNORE INCIDE INCISE INDENT
LESSEN MANGLE RASURE REDUCE
RIPPLE SCORCH SCOTCH SCRIBE SCYTHE
SLIGHT SLIVER STRAIT STREAK SULLET
SWINGE TAILYE THWITE TRENCH
AFFRONT CONVERT CURTAIL CUTTING
DIACOPE DISCIDE DISSECT DRAWCUT
ENGRAVE FASHION FRITTER HATCHET
SCALPEL SCISSOR SCUTTLE SECTILE
TAILZEE WHITTLE DISSEVER FRACTION

INCISION INCISURE INTAGLIO LACERATE
MALAHACK RETRENCH THWITTLE
(— A THREAD) CHASE
(— AN OPENING) BREACH
(— AT ANGLE) CANT BEVEL
(— AT RANDOM) SLASH
(— AWAY) COPE SLIT UNDO ABATE
CONCISE
(— BACK) HEAD SPUR
(— BARK) CHIP
(— BEAM) KERF
(— CARS) LIFT
(— CHEESE) HARP
(— CLAY) SLING
(— CORNERS) SKIRT CHAMFER
(— CRUST) CHIP
(— DEEPLY) DIG SHANK
(— DIAGONALLY) CATER SLANT
(— DOWN) MOW FELL STAG STUB
RAZEE SCANT SCARP ABRIDGE SHORTEN
RETRENCH
(— FANCY FIGURE) DASH
(— FISH) SOLAY STEAK
(— FOR FODDER) CHAFF
(— GEAR TEETH) RATCH
(— GLASS) SPLIT
(— GRAIN) BAG FAG CRADLE SWINGE
(— HAIR) DOD
(— IN) INSECT INCISED
(— IN A TREE) FACE
(— IN BARREL STAVE) HOWEL
(— IN EXCAVATIONS) GULLET
(— IN RELIEF) ENCHASE
(— IN SOFT ROCK) CAVATE
(— IN SQUARES) CHECK
(— INTO LARGE SLICES) WHANG
(— INTO SLIPS) ZEST
(— INTO STRIPS) JERK FLETCH FLITCH
JULIENNE
(— INTO TREE) BOX
(— JAGGEDLY) HACK SNAG
(— LEDGES) BENCH
(— LOGS) LUMBER
(— OF FISH) JOWL
(— OF GEM) STAR
(— OF GRAIN) MELL
(— OF MEAT) ARM SEY CROP HOCK
SHIN SIDE CHUCK SHANK STEAK
BRISKET FORESEY ICEBONE SIRLOIN
EDGEBONE FORERIBS
(— OF RIFLING) GROOVE
(— OFF) BOB LOP CLIP CROP DOCK KILL
PARE SHUT SLIT STAG BELEE CROSS
ELIDE PRUNE SCIND SEVER SHAVE
SHEAR SKIVE SLIPE SPIKE COUPED
DECIDE EXEMPT FORCUT RESECT SHIELD
STIFLE SWATCH ABJOINT ABSCIND
ABSCISE ABSCISS CURTAIL EXSCIND
ISOLATE PRECIDE RESCIND AMPUTATE
CLEIDOIC DESECATE RESECATE
RETRENCH TRUNCATE
(— OFF BY BITS) DRIB
(— OFF END) BUTT
(— OFF WOOL) DOD
(— OPEN) SPLAY
(— OUT) DESS DINK CLICK BROACH
EXCIDE EXCISE EXSECT

(— PATH) FRAY
(— SALMON) CHINE
(— SHEEP) TOMAHAWK
(— SHORT) BOB COW HOG LOP BANG
CROP DOCK JIMP SNIB BOBBED CURTAL
HOGGED BOBTAIL CHAPPED CONCISE
SCANTLE PRESCIND
(— TENDONS) ENERVATE
(— THE THROAT) JUGULATE
(— THE WAVES) SNORE
(— THINLY) CURL
(— TO PIECES) CHOP DICE MINCE
BRITTLE FRITTER
(— TO SIZE) TAIL
(— TURF) VELL
(— UNDER) KIRVE
(— UNEVENLY) CHATTER
(— UP) TUSK CARVE CHINE JOINT
PRANK SPOIL TRAIN GOBBET COLLOPED
(— UP SWAN) LIFT
(— WHALE BLUBBER) LEAN FLENSE
(— WITH BACKWARD SLOPE) COOT
(— WITH DIE) DINK BLANK
(— WITH SHEARS) SHIRL
(— WITH SICKLE) BAG REAP
(COLD —S) ASSIETTE
(CREW —) BUTCH FLATTOP
(DEEP NARROW —) JAD
(FENCING —) STRAMAZON
(LARGE —, OF FOOD) DODGE
(NOT —) UNCORVEN
(SHORT —) ATAJO
(SLIGHT —) SNICK SCOTCH
(THIN —) TARGET
CUTE COY KEEN DINKY DUCKY SHARP
CLEVER PRETTY SHREWD CUNNING
DARLING
CUTLASS SWORD CURTAL DUSACK
HANGER TESACK CURTAXE MACHETE
SHABBLE CAMPILAN
CUTTHROAT THUG BRAVO CUTTER
RUFFIAN SWORDER
CUTTING RAW ACID CURT KEEN KERF
TART TWIG ACUTE BLEAK CRISP EDGED
SCION SCRAP SHARP SMART BITING
BITTER BORING JAGGED PIPING SECANT
SEVERE BURNING CAUSTIC MORDANT
PAINFUL PIQUANT SATIRIC SECTION
SLICING CLEARING INCISIVE PIERCING
POIGNANT SCATHING SNAPPISH
TRENCHANT
(— FOR DIRT-CAR TRACK) GULLET
(— FOR WATER) TAJO
(— FROM PLANT) SLIP SHROUD
SARMENT PROPAGULE TRUNCHEON
(— OF DEER) SAY
(— OF TREES) HAG
(— OFF) AVULSION
(— SHORT) ABORTIVE
(DRILL —S) MUD
(OBLIQUE —) BARBING
(SECOND —) ROWEN
(WASTE —) SELVAGE
CUTTLEFISH SEPIA SQUID DECAPOD
INKFISH OCTOPUS
CYBELE RHEA KYBELE AGDISTIS
(DAUGHTER OF —) JUNO

(FATHER OF —) URANUS
(HUSBAND OF —) SATURN
(MOTHER OF —) GAEA
(SON OF —) JUPITER NEPTUNE
CYCLADES (ISLAND OF —) IOS KEOS
DELOS MELOS NAXOS PAROS SYROS
TENOS ANDROS AMORGOS KYTHNOS
SANTORIN SERIPHOS
CYCLE AGE EON ERA AEON BIKE EPOCH
KALPA PEDAL ROUND WHEEL BAKTUN
CIRCLE COURSE PERIOD BICYCLE
CIRCUIT TRICYCLE
(— OF WORK) ROTA JOURNEY
(—S CAUSED BY KARMA) SAMSARA
SANSARA
(BUSINESS —) JUGLAR KITCHIN
(LUNAR —) SAROS
(ONE — PER SECOND) HERTZ
(SECONDARY —) EPICYCLE
CYCLONE GALE GUST WIND BLAST
STORM BAGUIO TORNADO TWISTER
TYPHOON
CYCLOPEAN HUGE VAST STRONG
MASSIVE COLOSSAL GIGANTIC
CYCLOPS ARGES BRONTES COPEPOD
STEROPES
CYLINDER CAN TIN BOMB BURR CAGE
CANE DRUM ROLL SLUG WELL BLOCK
CORER DRAIN FIBER SCREW SHELL
SPOOL STELA BARREL BOBBIN BUTTON
COLUMN COPPER DECKER DOFFER
DUSTER FILTER GABION PISTON PLATEN
ROLLER SCREEN TIPITI TUMBLE SLEEVER
SLUDGER SUCCULA FOLLOWER
GRADUATE NEURAXIS
(— AROUND MOLD) COTTLE
(— FOR DANCE RHYTHM) CLAVE
(— OF STEAM WHISTLE) BELL
(— OF TISSUE) CORTEX
(— OF YARN) CAKE
(— ON LOOM) BEAM
(— WITH PERFORATIONS) FLUSHER
(—S PULLED THROUGH DUCT)
MANDREL
(ARMORED —) BARBETTE
(GLASS —) MUFF
(HOLLOW —) PIPE TUBE
(MARKING —) LEAD
(NAPPING —) GIG
(RELAY —) BATON
(REVOLVING —) BEATER ROLLER
(TOOTHED —) SPROCKET
(WATERMARK —) DANDY
CYLINDRICAL ROUND TERETE TOROSE
CENTRIC TUBULAR TERETIAL
(PREF.) TERETI
CYMBAL ZEL CHIME TARGET CROTALUM
KYMBALON
(PL.) TAL BECKEN PIATTI
CYMBELINE (AUTHOR OF —)
SHAKESPEARE
(CHARACTER IN —) CAIUS HELEN
CLOTEN IMOGEN LUCIUS MORGAN
IACHIMO PISANIO BELARIUS LEONATUS

PHILARIO ARVIRAGUS CORNELIUS
CYMBELINE GUIDERIUS POSTHUMUS
(SON OF —) ARVIRAGUS GUIDERIUS
CYNIC SATYR TIMON DOUBTER
APEMANTUS
CYNICAL SULLEN CURRISH DOGGISH
CAPTIOUS SARDONIC SNARLING
JAQUESIAN MISOGYNIC PESSIMISTIC
MISANTHROPIC
CYNOSURE SHOW LODESTAR
CYPRESS CULL SABINO SIPERS FIREBALL
AHUEHUETE BELVEDERE

CYPRUS

CAPE: GATA GRECO ANDREAS ARNAUTI
ZEVGARI
CAPITAL: NICOSIA
COIN: PARA
MEASURE: OKA OKE PIK CASS DONUM
KOUZA GOMARI KARTOS MEDIMNO
MOUNTAIN: TROODOS
RIVER: PEDIAS PEDIEOS
TOWN: POLIS CITIUM PAPHOS KYRENIA
LARNACA MORPHOU NICOSIA LIMASSOL
FAMAGUSTA
WEIGHT: OKA OKE MOOSA KANTAR

CYRANO DE BERGERAC

(AUTHOR OF —) ROSTAND
(CHARACTER IN —) CYRANO ROXANE
VALVERT DEGUICHE CHRISTIAN
CYST BAG SAC WEN POUCH RANULA
DERMOID HYDATID HYGROMA SACCULE
VESICLE ATHEROMA DACRYOPS
MUCOCELE STEATOMA
CZAR CSAR IVAN TSAR TZAR PETER
NICHOLAS

CZECHOSLOVAKIA

CAPITAL: PRAHA PRAGUE
COIN: DUCAT HALER HELLER KORUNA
DANCE: POLKA REDOWA FURIANT
MEASURE: LAN SAH MIRA KOREC LATRO
STOPA MERICE STRYCH
MOUNTAIN: ORE TATRA SUDETEN
PROVINCE: BOHEMIA MORAVIA SLOVAKIA
REGION: BOHEMIA MORAVIA SLOVAKIA
RIVER: UH MZE VAG VAH DYJE EGER ELBE
GRAU HRON IPEL ISAR ISER LABE NISA
ODER OHRE OLSE OPPA WAAG BECVA
DUNAJ MARCH NITRA SLANA TISZA
DANUBE HORNAD MOLDAU MORAVA
ONDAVA SAZAVA TORYSA VLTAVA
LABOREC LUZNICE BEROUNKA
TOWN: AS ASCH BRNO CHEB EGER MOST
BRUNN OPAVA PLZEN TABOR TUZLA
AUSSIG BILINA KLADUS PILSEN PRESOV
VSETIN ZVOLEN BUDWEIS JIHLAVA
OSTRAVA TEPLITZ

D

D DEE DOG DELTA

DAB DOB PAT BLOW DAUB LICK LUMP SPOT CLOUT SMEAR BLOTCH SPLOTCH FLATFISH FLOUNDER MARYSOLE SANDLING

DABBLE DAB MESS DALLY MEDDLE MUDDLE POTTER TAMPER TRIFLE MOISTEN SMATTER SPATTER

DAD BEAT BLOW PAPA FATHER

DAEDALUS (ANCESTOR OF —) ERECHTHEUS
(NEPHEW OF —) TALUS
(SON OF —) ICARUS

DAFFODIL GLEN LILY DAFFY DILLY JONQUIL ASPHODEL BELLWORT CROWBELL

DAFT WILD BALMY BATTY CRAZY DAFFY GIDDY LOONY POTTY SILLY INSANE FOOLISH IDIOTIC IMBECILE

DAGGER SAX DIRK KRIS SNEE SPUD STAB TANG KATAR POINT PRICK SKEAN STEEL ANLACE BODKIN COUTEL DIESIS HANGER KIRPAN PANADE PINKER POPPER SKHIAN STYLET BALARAO BAYONET COUTEAU DUDGEON KHANJAR OBELISK PONIARD SLASHER STABBER BASELARD PUNCHEON PUNTILLA STILETTO

DAHLIA JICAMA POMPON

DAHOMEY (CAPITAL OF —) PORTONOVO
(PEOPLE OF —) FON FONG BARIBA
(RIVER OF —) NIGER OUEME
(TOWN IN —) KANDI NIKKI ABOMEY OUIDAH COTONOU

DAILY DIARY DIURNAL

DAINTY CATE FINE NICE RARE FRILL NAISH BONBON CHOICE COSTLY MIGNON PICKED REGALO SCARCE SPICED CURIOUS ELEGANT FINICAL FINICKY TAFFETA DELICACY DELICATE ETHEREAL

DAIRY TAMBO LACTARY VACCARY CREAMERY DEYHOUSE

DAIS SEAT BENCH LEWAN STAGE TABLE CANOPY LISSOM PODIUM PULPIT SETTLE ESTRADE TERRACE CHABUTRA HUSTINGS PLATFORM

DAISY BULL GOLD DANDY GOWAN OXEYE BENNET MORGAN SHASTA BONESET COMFREY BACKWORT BONEWORT KNITBACK MOONPENNY BRUISEWORT MARGUERITE

DALE HAW DELL DENE GLEN VALE DINGLE TROUGH VALLEY

DALLY TOY CHAT DAFF FOOL IDLE JAUK PLAY SWAN WAIT DELAY FLIRT SPORT TARRY COQUET DABBLE DAWDLE LINGER LOITER PINGLE TRIFLE WANTON DRINGLE SLIDDER

DAM BAR BAY PEN REE BUND HEAD POND SPUR STAY STEM STOP SUDD WEIR BLOCK CAULD CHECK CHOKE GARTH MOUND POUND STANK ANICUT CAUSEY HINDER MOTHER ANNICUT BARRAGE BARRIER BURROCK MILLDAM RAMPIRE TAPPOON ABOIDEAU BLOCKADE OBSTACLE OBSTRUCT RESTRAIN

DAMAGE MAR BLOT BURN COST HARM HURT JEEL LOSS RUIN SKIN TEEN BLITZ BURST CLOUD CRACK HAVOC PRANG SPOIL WOUND WRONG BATTER CHARGE DANGER DEFACE DEFECT HINDER IMPAIR INJURE INJURY INSULT LESION SCATHE SORROW AFFLICT DAMNIFY DEGRADE DISTURB EXPENSE FOUNDER OFFENSE SCRATCH SCUTTLE SHATTER ACCIDENT BUSINESS DISSERVE FRACTURE FRETTING MISCHIEF SABOTAGE

DAMAGED HURT CRAZY LESED BROKEN CRACKED INJURED

DAMASK LINEN DARNEX DORNICK VALANCE DAMASSIN

DAME DINT LADY WOMAN MATRON

DAMN DEE DEM DOG RAT BLOW BURN DANG DARN DASH DING DRAT DUMB DURN BLAME BLANK BLAST BLESS CURSE WHOOP BEDAMN BUGGER DEVOTE CONDEMN CONSARN DOGGONE GOLDARN CONFOUND

DAMNABLE RUDDY DAMNED ODIOUS ACCURSED INFERNAL

DAMNED DEE LOST BALLY BLAMED BLOODY DARNED DASHED DURNED GORMED TARNAL BLASTED BLESSED CONSARN DOGGONE ETERNAL GOLDARN ACCURSED BLANKETY BLINKING DASHEDLY INFERNAL

DAMP FOG RAW WET DANK DEWY DULL MIST SOFT BLUNT DABBY HUMID JUICY MALMY MOCHY MOIST MUGGY MUNGY MUSTY RAFTY RAINY RAWKY SAPPY SEEPY SOBBY SOGGY WAUGH WEAKY BLIGHT CLAMMY DAMPEN DEADEN MUFFLE QUENCH RHEUMY STUPOR BEDEWED DAMPISH DEPRESS MOISTEN SQUIDGY DEJECTED DISPIRIT HUMIDIFY HUMIDITY MOISTURE
(— OF EVENING) SERENE

DAMPEN DEG DAMP MOIL CHILL CRAMP FREEZE SPONGE MOISTURE

DAMSEL GIRL WENCH MAIDEN MOPPET DAMOSEL DAMOZEL PUCELLE DONZELLA PRINCESS

DANCE BOB HOP MAI SON BALL DRAG DUET DUMP FISH FOOT FRUG HEEL HOOF HORA JAZZ JIVE JUBA JUKE KOLO LEAP LOPE LOUP MASK MILL MOVE PROM SAIL SHAG SKIT STEP BAILE BAMBA BONGO

CANON CAPER CAROL CONGA DANZA
ENTRY FLING FLISK FRIKE FRISK GOPAK
LASYA LIMBO LINDY MAMBO PAVAN
RINKA SALLY SAMBA STOMP SWING
TANGO TRACE TREAD TWIST VOLTA
ALTHEA BALLET BALTER BOOGIE
BOSTON CANCAN CORDAX DANZON
DIDDLE DREHER FADING FORMAL FROLIC
GERMAN HORMOS MASQUE MINUET
MOBBLE MONKEY NRITTA PASSAY
RACKET SHIMMY TODDLE TRESCA
TUMBLE VELETA ANTHEMA BEGUINE
CALINDA COURANT CZARDAS DANSANT
FADDING FARRUCA FOOTING FOXTROT
MEASURE MORISCO PATTERN SALTATE
SARDANA SHUFFLE TEMPETE TRESCHE
TRIPPLE VOLTIZE ZIGANKA AURRESCU
BAMBOULA BUNNYHUG CACHUCHA
CAKEWALK CHACONNE COMPARSA
COONJINE COTILLON ENTRACTE
ESTAMPIE FANDANGO FANTASIA
FLAMENCO GALLIARD GALOPADE
GUARACHA HABANERA HEYDEGUY
HORNPIPE KOLATTAM MATELOTE
MERENGUE SALTATION SHAKEDOWN
CARMAGNOLE SCHOTTISCHE
(— CLUMSILY) BALTER
(— DRAMA) NO NOH
(— FACE TO FACE) SET
(— IN CIRCLE) JIGGER
(— NIMBLY) CANARY
(— RESEMBLING THE POLKA) BERLIN
(ACROBATIC —) ADAGIO
(AFRICAN —) SHOUT
(ARGENTINE —) CUANDO
(AUSTRIAN —) LANDLER
(BALINESE —) KEBYAR LEGONG
(BALLROOM —) SON CONGO COTILLON
(BOHEMIAN —) REDOWA FURIANT
(CARNIVAL —) COOCH FOLIA
(CEREMONIAL —) AREITO CANTICO
DUTUBURI
(COQUETTISH —) PURPOSE
(COUNTRY —) HAY RANT CONFESS
LANDLER MUSETTE ANGLAISE
SARABAND
(COURTSHIP —) CUECA BATUQUE
LEZGINKA
(DANISH —) SEXTUR
(FIESTA —S) AKRIEROS
(FLAMENCO —) ALEGRIAS
(FRENCH —) BAL BOREE BRAWL GAVOT
BRANLE BOURREE BOUTADE GAVOTTE
LAVOLTA
(GAY —) RANT GALLIARD
(GESTURE —) SIVA
(GREEK —) KORDAX ROMAIKA SIKINNIS
(GYPSY —) FARRUCA
(HAITIAN —) JUBA
(HOBBYHORSE —) CALUSAR
(HOLIDAY —) PATTERN
(HUNGARIAN —) KOS
(IMPROMPTU —) BOUTADE
(INDIAN —) IRUSKA KATHAK KANTIKOY
(IRISH —) FADING PLANXTY
(ITALIAN —) FORLANA BERGAMASK
SALTARELLO

(JAPANESE —) BUGAKU KAGURA
(JAVANESE —) SERIMPI
(LIVELY —) JIG REEL GALOP GIGUE
POLKA RUMBA BOLERO CANARY SPRING
BOURREE CORANTO HOEDOWN
GALLIARD GALOPADE HORNPIPE
(MAORI —) HAKA
(MARTIAL —) PYRRHIC
(MEXICAN —) JARABE HUAPANGO
SANDUNGA
(MOURNFUL —) DUMP
(NORWEGIAN —) HALLING
(OLD ENGLISH —) CEBELL MORRIS
ARGEERS ANGLAISE
(OLD-FASHIONED —) LOURE
PASSACAGLIA
(PEASANT —) JOTA DANZON BALITAO
(PERUVIAN —) CUECA KASWA CACHUA
(POLISH —) POLACCA KUJAWIAK
POLONAISE VARSOVIENNE
(POLYNESIAN —) HULA
(PORTUGUESE —) FADO
(ROMAN —) TRIPUDIUM
(ROUND —) RAY BRAUL CAROL WALTZ
CAROLE MAXIXE
(RUSSIAN —) ZIGANKA
(RUSTIC —) HAY HEY HAYMAKER
(SPANISH —) JOTA POLO JALEO
BOLERO JARABE CHACONNE FLAMENCO
GUARACHA MALAGUENA ZAPATEADO
SEGUIDILLA
(SPEAR —) BARIS
(SQUARE —) SQUARE ARGEERS
HOEDOWN LANCERS QUADRILLE
(STATELY —) PAVANE EMMELEIA
SARABAND POLONAISE
(SWORD —) BACUBERT MATACHIN
(VENEZUELAN —) JOROPO
(WEDDING —) CANACUAS
(WEST INDIAN —) LIMBO
DANCER PONY HOOFER HOPPER MAENAD
APSARAS CLOGGER DANSEUR PASCOLA
PRANCER SAILOUR STEPPER BALADINE
BAYADERE DANSEUSE DEVADASI
FIGURANT MORRICER
(BALLET —) ETOILE SOLISTE CORYPHEE
(EGYPTIAN —S) GHAWAZEE
(JAVANESE —) SERIMPI
(JAVANESE —S) BEDOYO
(MASKED —S) GAHE
(SQUARE —S) FLOOR
(SWORD —) MATACHIN
(ZUNI —) SHALAKO
DANDELION CANKER DINDLE HAWKBIT
BLOWBALL
(RUSSIAN —) KOKSAGYZ
DANDER ANGER DUTCH TEMPER
HACKLES PASSION
DANDLE DANCE DIDDLE DOODLE FADDLE
FONDLE PAMPER
DANDRUFF SCURF DANDER FURFUR
PORRIGO
DANDY FOP JAY ADON BEAU BUCK DUDE
FINE JAKE MAJO PRIG TOFF TRIG YAWL
BLOOD JEMMY SWELL ADONIS MIZZEN
BUCKEEN CAPSTAN COXCOMB ELEGANT

FOPPISH JESSAMY MACARONI MUSCADIN SAILBOAT

DANGER FEAR RISK DOUBT PERIL WATHE HAZARD PLIGHT PITFALL VENTURE DISTRESS JEOPARDY

DANGEROUS BAD HOT ILL RUM DEAR FOUL GRAVE NASTY RISKY FICKLE KITTLE SCATHY SHREWD UNSURE AWKWARD FEARFUL PARLOUS UNCANNY DOUBTFUL INSECURE PERILOUS UNCHANCY BREAKNECK WANCHANCY PRECARIOUS PESTIFEROUS

DANGLE BOB LOP HANG LOLL DROOP SWING DANDLE SHOGGLE SUSPEND SWINGLE TROLLOP

DANIEL (FATHER OF —) DAVID (MOTHER OF —) ABIGAIL

DANK WET DAMP HUMID MADID MOIST CLAMMY COARSE DANKISH DRIZZLE WETNESS MOISTURE

DANSEUSE DANCER BALLERINA

DAPPER NEAT TRIM NATTY SPRUCE FINICAL FOPPISH SPARKISH

DAPPLED BLOCKY DOTTED POMELY FLECKED MOTTLED SPOTTED FRECKLED

DARE DAST FACE RISK BRAVE STUMP ASSUME BANTER DACKER ATTEMPT BRAVADE FASHION PRESUME VENTURE

DAREDEVIL MADCAP HARDYDARDY

DARING BOLD DERF PERT RASH WILD BRAVE HARDY MANLY HEROIC COURAGE BOLDNESS DEVILISH FEARLESS STALWART

DARK DIM DUN MUM SAD WAN BASE BLAE DEEP DUSK EBON HARD MALE MURK BLACK BLIND CLOUD DINGY DUSKY FAINT MURKY ROOKY SHADY SOOTY SWART UMBER UNLIT VAGUE CLOSED CLOUDY CYPRUS DIMPSY DISMAL DRUMLY GLOOMY OPAQUE SOMBER SWARTH WICKED APHOTIC MELANIC OBSCURE RAYLESS STYGIAN SUNLESS SWARTHY UNCLEAR ABSTRUSE GLOOMING IGNORANT LOWERING SINISTER CIMMERIAN CALIGINOUS

DARKEN DIM BLUR DULL BEDIM BLIND CLOUD GLOOM SHADE SULLY SWART DEEPEN SHADOW BECLOUD BLACKEN ECLIPSE OBSCURE SLUBBER TARNISH OVERCAST OBFUSCATE

DARKNESS DUSK MURK BLACK GLOOM NIGHT SHADE TAMAS SHADOW DIMNESS PRIVACY SECRECY TENEBRA GLOAMING INIQUITY MIDNIGHT TENEBRES TWILIGHT NIGRITUDE

DARKNESS AT NOON (AUTHOR OF —) KOESTLER (CHARACTER IN —) ARLOVA BOGRAV IVANOV GLETKIN HARELIP KIEFFER MICHAEL NICHOLAS RUBASHOV

DARLING JO JOE PET CHOU CONY DEAR LIFE LOVE NOBS PEAT AROON BULLY CHERI DEARY DUCKS SWEET CHERIE MINION MOPPET OCHREE POPPET ACUSHLA BUNTING CUSHLAM PIGSNEY PINKENY QUERIDA STOREEN DUMPLING

FAVORITE LIEBCHEN MACUSHLA PRECIOUS MAVOURNEEN

DARN DOG BLOW MEND PATCH RENTER REPAIR DOGGONE

DARNED BLAME BLAMED DEUCED DURNED BLESSED

DART JET POP BOLT BUZZ CANE CHOP FLIT JOUK LEAP LICK PILE PLAN PLAY ROUT ARROW BOUND FLAME FLING FLIRT GLEAM GLINT LANCE SCAMP SCOOT SHAFT SHOOT SKITE SKIVE SPEAR SPEED SPRIT START ANCHOR BULTEN ELANCE GLANCE LANCET LAUNCH SPRING SQUIRT STRIKE SUMPIT THRUST JAVELIN MISSILE VERUTUM GAVELOCK SPICULUM BANDERILLA

DASH DAD PEP ZIP BANG BOLT CAST DING DIVE ELAN GIFT HINT HURL LASH LINE PELT RACE RASH RUIN RULE RUSH SHOW SLAM TICK VEIN ABASH ARDOR BLANK BREAK CHAFE CLASH CRASH CRUSH DRIVE ECLAT FLASH FLING FRUSH KNOCK PLASH PLOUT SKITE SLASH SMASH SPEED SPEND SPICE SPURN START STYLE SWASH SWELL TASTE THROW TOUCH TRICK DASHEE DOLLOP ENERGY HURTLE HYPHEN JABBLE RELISH SHIVER SPIRIT SPLASH SPRINT STRAIN STROKE THRUST ABANDON BRAVURA COLLIDE DEPRESS DISPLAY IMPINGE PANACHE SHATTER SPATTER SPLOTCH TANTIVY VIRETOT CONFOUND SPLINTER

(— ABOUT WILDLY) GAD REEL

(— AGAINST) BEAT

(— DOWN) QUELL STRAM STRAMASH

(— IN PIECES) CRASH

(— OF LIQUID) JAW

(— OF SPIRITS) LACE LACING

(— OUT) QUELL

(— TOGETHER) COLLIDE

(— UP) FLURR

(— WITH WATER) JAW BLASH SLASH

DASHING BOLD BULLY DOGGY SHOWY SMART SPICY SWASH SPANKY SWANKY VELOCE STYLISH SWAGGER SPANKING SPIRITED

DASTARD CAD SOT DAFF SNEAK COWARD CRAVEN DULLARD HILDING WITHING POLTROON

DASTARDLY FOUL VILLAIN COWARDLY POLTROON SNEAKING

DATA DOPE FILE FACTS INPUT MATERIAL

DATE DAY ERA DRAG FARD FUSS DATUM SAIDI FRIEND HALAWI JUJUBE RECKON GALLANT ASHARASI DEADLINE

DATED GIVEN PASSE OUTMODED

DATUM FACT ITEM GIVEN DONNEE

DAUB DAB DOB MUD BALM BLOB BLOT CLAG CLAM CLAT CLAY COAT GAUM MOIL SOIL CLART COVER DITCH FLICK PAINT SLAKE SMEAR BEDAUB CLATCH GREASE SMUDGE SPLASH BESMEAR DRIBBLE PLASTER SLUBBER SPLATCH SPLOTCH SLAISTER

DAUGHTER ANAC BINT DAME GIRL

CHILD FILLE FILLY KIBEI REGAN ALUMNA
CADETTE DOCHTER GONERIL CORDELIA
DAUGHTER OF THE REGIMENT
(CHARACTER IN —) MARIE TONZIO
SULPICE COUNTESS
(COMPOSER OF —) DONIZETTI
DAUNT AWE COW DARE FAZE PALL STUN
TAME ABASH CHECK DETER QUAIL
DISMAY SUBDUE CONQUER CONTROL
OVERAWE REPRESS STUPEFY TERRIFY
DISPIRIT OVERCOME
DAUNTLESS BOLD GOOD BRAVE
AWELESS SPARTAN FEARLESS INTREPID
DAVENPORT DESK SOFA COUCH DIVAN
DAVID TAFFY DAWKIN
(COMPANION OF —) JONATHAN
(DAUGHTER OF —) TAMAR
(FATHER OF —) JESSE
(SON OF —) AMNON ABSALOM
(WIFE OF —) ABIGAIL AHINOAM
DAVID COPPERFIELD
(AUTHOR OF —) DICKENS
(CHARACTER IN —) HAM DICK DORA
HEEP JANE MICK ROSA AGNES BETSY
CLARA DAVID EMILY JAMES MEALY
TOMMY URIAH BARKIS DARTLE GRINBY
STRONG WALKER CREAKLE SPENLOW
WILKINS MICAWBER PEGGOTTY
TRADDLES TROTWOOD MURDSTONE
WICKFIELD STEERFORTH
DAVIT CRANE
DAWDLE LAG IDLE JAUK LOAF MUCK
MULL POKE TOIT DALLY DELAY DRILL
KNOCK DADDLE DIDDLE LINGER LOITER
MUCKER PICKLE PIDDLE POTTER PUTTER
TRIFLE FINNICK QUIDDLE SAUNTER
LALLYGAG SHAMMOCK SLUMMOCK
DAWN MORN LIGHT PRIME SHINE SUNUP
AURORA MORROW ORIENT SPRING
UPRISE DAWNING MORNING SUNRISE
COCKCROW DAYBREAK
DAY DEI ERA SUN YOM DATE DIEM TIME
EPOCH LIGHT FRIDAY MONDAY PERIOD
SUNDAY JOURNEY TUESDAY LIFETIME
SATURDAY THURSDAY WEDNESDAY
(— AND NIGHT) KALPA
(— BEFORE) EVE
(— OF JUDGMENT) INQUEST
DOOMSDAY
(— OF ORIGIN) BIRTHDAY
(— OF REST) SABBATH
(— OF ROMAN MONTH) IDES NONES
CALENDS KALENDS
(DOG —S) CANICULE
(FAST —) ASHURA FASTEN
(FIRST — OF AUGUST) LAMMAS
(FIRST — OF MAY) BELTANE
(HOLY —) FEAST HOLIDAY
(HOT —) BROILER ROASTER SCORCHER
(LAST — OF FESTIVAL) APODOSIS
(MARKET —) NUNDINE TIANGUE
(WEEK —) FERIA
(WORK —) WARDAY
(5 NAMELESS —S) UAYEB
(60TH — OF) GHURRY
(8TH — AFTER FEAST) UTAS
(PREF.) HEMER(O)

DAYBREAK DAWN MORN SUNUP
DAWNING DAYLIGHT
DAYDREAM MUSE DREAM DWALM
FANCY VISION FANTASY REVERIE
PHANTASY
DAZE FOG DAMP DARE MAZE ROCK STUN
DAUNT DIZZY SWOON ASTONY BEMUSE
BENUMB DAZZLE DEAFEN MUDDLE
TRANCE CONFUSE PETRIFY STUPEFY
TORPIFY ASTONISH BEWILDER
DUMFOUND PARALYZE
DAZED MAD ASEA DAMP ASSOT DIZZY
MUZZY SILLY TOTTY WOOZY CUCKOO
GROGGY ROTTEN BEMUSED SPOILED
WITLESS ASTONIED BESOTTED DITHERED
DONNERED WITHERED
DAZZLE DAZE BLIND DROWN GLAIK
SHINE FULGOR ECLIPSE BEWILDER
OUTSHINE SURPRISE
DAZZLED BLINDED
DAZZLING FLARE FLASH GLAIK FLASHY
GARISH FLARING FULGENT GLARING
RADIANT DIZZYING GORGEOUS
DEACON CLERIC DOCTOR LAYMAN
LEVITE MASTER PHILIP MINISTER
DEAD LOW AWAY COLD DULL FLAT GONE
MORT NUMB POKY SURE TAME AMORT
BLIND INERT POKEY QUIET SLAIN STARK
VAPID ASLEEP BYGONE FALLEN LAPSED
PARTED REFUSE DEFUNCT EXACTLY
EXPIRED EXTINCT INSIPID SAINTED
STERILE TEDIOUS ABSOLUTE COMPLETE
DECEASED DEPARTED INACTIVE LIFELESS
OBSOLETE SCUPPERED
DEADEN DAMP DULL DUMB KILL MULL
MUTE NUMB SEAR STUN BLUNT SLAKE
BENUMB DAMPEN MUFFLE OBTUND
OPIATE RETARD STIFLE WEAKEN
MORTIFY PETRIFY REPRESS SLUMBER
SMOTHER ASTONISH ENFEEBLE
DEAD END PLACE
(AUTHOR OF —) KINGSLEY
(CHARACTER IN —) KAY JACK DRINA
TOMMY GIMPTY HILTON MARTIN
BABYFACE
DEADLOCK TIE LOGJAM IMPASSE
STANDOFF STOPPAGE
DEADLY WAN DIRE FELL MORT FATAL
FERAL LETHAL MORTAL CAPITAL
DEATHLY FATEFUL RUINOUS MORTIFIC
VENOMOUS VIRULENT PESTILENT
THANATOID PERNICIOUS
DEAF SURD DUNCH DUNNY SORDA
SORDO
DEAL JOB LEND PART SALE TALE WHIZ
ALLOT BOARD BROKE FETCH PLANK
SERVE SEVER SHAKE SHARE SHIFT
TRADE TREAT WIELD YIELD BATTEN
BESTOW DIVIDE HANDLE MEDDLE
NUMBER PARCEL BARGAIN DELIVER
INFLICT PORTION SCATTER DISPENSE
SEPARATE
DEALER CHAP AGENT COPER BADGER
BANKER BROKER CADGER JOBBER
MONGER SELLER TRADER BUTCHER
CHAPMAN CHANDLER MERCHANT
OPERATOR TAILLEUR

(— IN CATTLE) COUPER DROVER
(— IN CHEMICALS) SALTER
DRYSALTER
(— IN DRY GOODS) DRAPER
(— IN GRAIN) SWALER
(— IN OLD CLOTHES) FRIPPER
(— IN PAINTS) COLORMAN
(— IN TEXTILES) MERCER
(CARDS —) FARMER
(COAL —) COLLIER
(SLAVE —) MANGO
(STOCK —) STAG JOBBER OUTSIDER
DEAN DOYEN SENIOR VERGER PREFECT
PROVOST
DEAR HON PET CARA CHER CHOU CONY
FAIR FOND GOOD HIGH LAMB LOVE
NOBS ANGEL BOSOM DEARY HONEY
LOVED SWEET COSTLY POPPET SCARCE
TENDER WORTHY BELOVED DARLING
SPECIAL TOOTSIE ESTEEMED GLORIOUS
PRECIOUS VALUABLE
DEARTH LACK WANT FAMINE PAUCITY
POVERTY SCARCITY
(SUFF.) PENIA
DEATH END BALE BANE DOOM EXIT FATE
MORT OBIT REST DECAY GRAVE GRUEL
LETHE NIGHT SLEEP DEMISE DEPART
ENDING EXITUS EXPIRY MURDER REAPER
CURTAIN DECEASE FUNERAL PARTING
PASSAGE QUIETUS SILENCE BIOLYSIS
CASUALTY CURTAINS FATALITY
NECROSIS THANATOS MORTALITY
NOTHINGNESS
DEATHLESS ETERNAL UNDYING
IMMORTAL
DEATHLY FATAL DEADLY MORTAL
GHASTLY STYGIAN DEATHFUL MORTALLY
DEATH OF A SALESMAN
(AUTHOR OF —) MILLER
(CHARACTER IN —) BIFF HAPPY LINDA
LOMAN WILLY
DEBACLE ROUT STAMPEDE COLLAPSE
DEBASE SINK ALLOY DIRTY LOWER
STOOP DEFILE DEMEAN DILUTE IMPAIR
REDUCE REVILE VILIFY CORRUPT
DEBAUCH DECLINE DEGRADE DEPRAVE
PERVERT PROFANE TRADUCE VITIATE
PROSTITUTE
DEBASED BASE VILE BASTARD CORRUPT
SQUALID CANKERED DEGRADED
DEROGATE
DEBATE MOOT ARGUE FIGHT PLEAD
STUDY ARGUFY COMBAT HASSLE
REASON CONTEND CONTEST DISCUSS
DISPUTE PALAVER QUARREL WRANGLE
ARGUMENT COLLOQUY MILITATE
QUESTION
DEBAUCH FILE TAINT DEBASE DEFILE
MISUSE SEDUCE VILIFY CORRUPT
DEPRAVE MISLEAD POLLUTE VIOLATE
DISHONOR SQUANDER
DEBAUCHEE RIP RAKE ROUE HOLOUR
LECHER RAKEHELL
DEBAUCHERY RIOT RAKERY DEBAUCH
PRIAPISM
DEBILITATED WEAK SEEDY FEEBLE
INFIRM SAPPED ASTHENIC

DEBIT DEBT LOSS CHARGE
DEBONAIR AIRY JAUNTY POLITE
CAVALIER GRACEFUL GRACIOUS
DEBRIS GUCK SLAG DECAY TRASH
WASTE RAFFLE REFUSE RUBBLE
ELUVIUM RUBBISH
DEBT DUE DEBIT FAULT ARREARS
JUDGMENT TRESPASS
DEBTOR OWER PEON SKIP DYVOUR
DEBITOR YIELDER
DEBUT OPENING ENTRANCE
DEBUTANTE BUD DEB INGENUE
ROSEBUD
DECADENT EFFETE DECAYED HOTHOUSE
OVERRIPE
DECANTER CARAFE URCEOLE GARDEVIN
INGESTER
DECAPITATE BEHEAD DECOLLATE
DECAY ROT BLET FADE RUIN SEED WANE
WEAR CROCK DEATH SPOIL WASTE
BLIGHT CANKER CARIES FADING MOLDER
SICKEN WITHER CRUMBLE DECLINE
FAILURE MORTIFY PUTREFY DECREASE
(— IN WOOD) CONK DOZE
(— OF FRUIT) BLETTING
DECEASE DIE FAIL OBIT PASS DEATH
DEMISE PASSAGE
DECEASED DEAD LATE PARTED DEFUNCT
EXTINCT DEPARTED
DECEIT FLUM GAFF GULL RUSE SHAM
TRAP WILE ABUSE CRAFT DOLUS FRAUD
GUILE CAUTEL FELONY CUNNING
FAITERY FICTION ARTIFICE COZENAGE
INTRIGUE SPOOFERY SUBTLETY
TRICKERY TRUMPERY WILINESS
DECEITFUL JIVE BLIND BRAID FALSE
GAUDY JANUS LOOPY PUNIC SNAKY
ARTFUL COVERT CRAFTY DOUBLE FICKLE
HOLLOW ROTTEN TRICKY CUNNING
EVASIVE FICTIVE SIRENIC WINDING
GUILEFUL ILLUSIVE INDIRECT TORTUOUS
MENDACIOUS
DECEIVE BOB BOG CON FOB GAB GUM
KID LIE BILK BRAG BUNK CRAP DUPE
FAKE FLAM FOOL GAFF GULL HAVE
HOAX HYPE JILT JOUK MUCK SELL SHAM
SILE SNOW TURN ABUSE AMUSE BLEAR
BLINK BLUFF CATCH CHEAT COZEN
CROSS CULLY DODGE FEINT GLEEK
GLOZE HOCUS LURCH PATCH SHUCK
SPOOF TRICK TRUMP TRYST BAFFLE
BARRAT BEFLUM BEFOOL BETRAY
BLANCH BUBBLE CAJOLE DELUDE
DIVERT EUCHRE GAMMON HUMBUG
ILLUDE JUGGLE MISUSE NIGGLE SUCKER
WIMPLE BEGUILE DEFRAUD MISLEAD
OVERSEE TRAITOR BEJUGGLE FLIMFLAM
HOODWINK OUTREACH
DECENCY GRACE DECORUM HONESTY
MODESTY CHASTITY
DECENT FAIR CHASTE COMELY HONEST
MODEST PRETTY PROPER SEEMLY
FITTING GRADELY JANNOCK SHAPELY
SIGHTLY DECOROUS GRAITHLY WISELIKE
DECEPTION BAM COG DOR GAG LIE
DOLE FLAM FLUM GAFF GULL HOAX
HYPE MAZE RIDE RUSE SELL SHAM WILE

ABUSE BLIND BLUFF CHEAT COVIN
CRAFT CURVE DOLUS DORRE FAVEL
FRAUD GLAIK GLEEK GUILE MAGIC
SHUCK SNARE SPOOF TRICK BARRAT
CAUTEL DECEIT DUPERY HUMBUG
JUGGLE ABUSION BLAFLUM CHICANE
CUNNING EVASION FALLACY FALSERY
FICTION GULLAGE GULLERY KNAVERY
PRETEXT SLYNESS ARTIFICE DISGUISE
FALSEDAD FLIMFLAM ILLUSION
INTRIGUE PHANTASM PRESTIGE
SUBTLETY TRICKERY TRUMPERY
WILINESS
DECEPTIVE FLAM FALSE ARTFUL
BUBBLE SIRENIC TRICKSY DELUSIVE
DELUSORY FLIMFLAM ILLUSORY
IMPOSING SHAMMISH UNSICKER
DECIDE FIX CAST DEEM HOLD RULE TELL
WILL AWARD JUDGE PATCH PITCH
DECERN DECREE FIGURE REWARD
SETTLE ADJUDGE RESOLVE CONCLUDE
SENTENCE
(— UPON) SET ELECT CHOOSE TERMINE
DECISION ACT END CALL DOOM FIAT
GRIT ARRET AWARD CANON FAITH ISSUE
PARTY PLUCK POINT ACTION CHOICE
CRISIS DECREE RULING VERDICT
JUDGMENT PLACITUM SENTENCE
SUFFRAGE
DECISIVE FATAL FINAL CRISIC PAYOFF
VIRILE CRUCIAL DECIDED CRITICAL
CRUSHING DECRETAL POSITIVE
DECK FIG TOG BANK BUSK BUSS DAUB
DINK FLAT HEAP PINK POOP PROW TRIG
ADORN ARRAY COVER DIZEN DRESS
EQUIP FLOOR HATCH PRANK PRINK
STORE AWNING BEDECK BETRIM BLAZON
CLOTHE ENRICH FETTLE FOCSLE LAUREL
APPAREL BEDIGHT BEDIZEN FEATHER
FLOUNCE GEMMATE BEAUTIFY
DECORATE EMBLAZON PLATFORM
(— OF CARDS) BOOK
(— OUT) BARB TIFF DIZEN SPICK
BEDECK DAIKER FANGLE FINIFY BEDIGHT
(HIGH —) POOP
(LOWEST —) ORLOP
DECKHAND BOATMAN TRIMMER
BARGEMAN ROUSTABOUT
DECLAIM GALE RANT RAVE ROLL MOUTH
ORATE SPEAK SPOUT BLEEZE RECITE
ELOCUTE INVEIGH DENOUNCE DISCLAIM
HARANGUE PERORATE
DECLAMATION FROTHING HARANGUE
RHETORIC SPOUTING PHILIPPIC
DECLARATION BILL CALL DICK TALE
WORD COUNT LIBEL PAROL AVOWAL
ORACLE PAROLE SAYING EXPRESS
PROMISE RESOLVE MANIFEST PLATFORM
DECLARE BID KEN LAY SAY VOW AVER
AVOW DENY MAKE READ SHOW SWAN
TROW VOTE BRUIT POSIT SNORE SOUND
SPEAK STATE TRUTH VOUCH AFFIRM
ALLEGE ASSERT ASSURE AUTHOR
AVOUCH BLAZON DEPONE DESCRY
EXPONE HERALD INDICT NOTIFY PATEFY
RELATE SPRING UPGIVE ACCLAIM
BEHIGHT DISCUSS EXPRESS OUTTELL

PROFESS PROTEST PUBLISH SIGNIFY
TESTIFY ANNOUNCE DENOUNCE
DESCRIBE INDICATE INTIMATE MAINTAIN
MANIFEST NUNCIATE PROCLAIM
RENOUNCE PREDICATE
(— A SAINT) CANONIZE
(— ARBITRARILY) GAVEL
(— INVALID) ANNUL
(— PUBLICLY) CRY
(— UNTRUE) DENY
(— WAR) DEFY
(SOLEMNLY —) AFFY SWEAR
DECLINE BEG DIP EBB SAG SET BALK
BEND BUST DENY DIVE DOWN DROP
FADE FAIL FALL FLAG FLOP HELD SINK
SLIP TURN VAIL WANE WELK BAULK
CHUTE DECAY DROLL DROOP DWINE
FAINT HEALD HIELD LAPSE LOWER QUAIL
REPEL SLACK SLOPE SLUMP SPURN
STOOP STRAY TABES WAIVE DEBASE
DEVALL FALTER REFUSE REJECT RENEGE
SICKEN WEAKEN ATROPHY DESCEND
DESCENT DETRECT DEVIATE DISAVOW
DWINDLE ECLIPSE FAILURE FALLOFF
FORBEAR INFLECT LETDOWN SINKAGE
DECREASE DOWNBEAT DOWNTURN
FOREBEAR LANGUISH TOBOGGAN
WITHDRAW REPUDIATE
DECOMPOSE ROT FOUL FRIT DECAY
ATTACK DIGEST DEGRADE DISSOLVE
DECOMPOSED PUTRID
DECORATE DO BIND BUSK CHIP CITE
DECK EDGE FRET GAUD PINK RAIL RULE
TIFF TIRE TRIM ADORN DRESS FLOCK
FRILL GRAIN INLAY PANEL TRAIL TRICK
BEDECK BUTTON DAMASK EMBOSS
FLOWER FRESCO PARGET POUNCE
PURFLE SPONGE SUBORN CORONET
ENCHASE FESTOON FURNISH GARNISH
FLOURISH ORNAMENT OVERWORK
TITIVATE
DECORATED GIDDY LACED AJOURE
FLAMBE ORNATE ADORNED DAMASSE
FROGGED INCISED WROUGHT COCKADED
DISTINCT FLORETED
DECORATION KEY BUHL FALL FUSS
IKAT DECOR DODAD HONOR MEDAL
PRIDE BOULLE DESIGN DOODAD FINERY
FLORET FRIEZE GOTHIC NIELLO PLAQUE
SETOFF TINSEL ARTWORK BARBOLA
DECKING EPERGNE FLUTING GARNISH
TRACERY BAYADERE DIAMANTE
ESCALLOP FLOURISH FRETWORK
INTARSIA ORNAMENT
(— IN GUEST CHAMBER) XENIUM
(— OF LEAVES) VIGNETTE
(— OF MONKEYS) SINGERIE
(— TECHNIQUE) PLANGI
(BOOK-COVER —) DENTELLE
(CUTOUT —) APPLIQUE
(ENAMEL —) WUTSAI
(FESTIVE —) GALA
(INESSENTIAL —) SPINACH
(MURAL —) TOPIA
(MUSICAL —) GRACE
(PORCELAIN —) KAKIEMON
(POTTERY —) BRODERIE

(RICH —) PARAMENT
(SCANDINAVIAN —) ROSEMALING
DECOROUS CALM GOOD NICE PRIM
DOUCE GRAVE QUIET SOBER STAID
CHASTE DECENT DEMURE MODEST
POLITE PROPER SEDATE SEEMLY SERENE
STEADY FITTING ORDERLY REGULAR
SETTLED BECOMING COMPOSED
MANNERLY
DECOY BAIT LURE DRILL SHILL STALL
STOOL TEMPT ALLURE CALLER CAPPER
ENTICE ENTRAP SEDUCE TOLLER
INVEIGLE
(— FOR GAMBLERS) CAPPER
(— FOR SWINDLERS) BARNARD
BERNARD
(AUCTIONEER'S —) BONNET BUTTON
DECREASE EBB BATE DROP FALL LOSS
SINK WANE ABATE DECAY LAPSE TAPER
WASTE CHANGE IMPAIR LESSEN
NARROW REDUCE SHRINK ATROPHY
CUTDOWN DECLINE DWINDLE SHORTEN
SLACKEN SUBSIDE ABLATION DECIMATE
DIMINISH DOWNTURN MODERATE
RETRENCH
DECREE ACT DIT LAW SET DOOM FIAT
RULE WILL ARRET CANON EDICT ENACT
HATTI IRADE JUDGE ORDER POINT SHAPE
TENET UKASE WRITE ARREST ASSIZE
DICTUM FIRMAN ORDAIN PLACIT RECESS
ADJUDGE APPOINT COMMAND CONSULT
DICTATE DIVORCE MANDATE STATUTE
DECISION JUDGMENT ROGATION
SANCTION SENTENCE ORDINANCE
DECREPIT LAME WEAK BEDRID CREAKY
FEEBLE INFIRM SENILE FAILING INVALID
DEDICATE VOW VOTE DEVOTE DIRECT
HALLOW OBLATE ASCRIBE CHRISTEN
INSCRIBE
DEDICATED HOLY OBLATE SACRED
VOTIVE
DEDUCE DRAW LEAD TAKE BRING DRIVE
FETCH GUESS INFER TRACE DEDUCT
DERIVE ELICIT EVOLVE GATHER COLLECT
EXTRACT CONCLUDE
DEDUCT BATE DOCK TAKE ABATE ALLOW
SHAVE REBATE REMOVE CURTAIL
TRADUCE DISCOUNT SUBTRACT
DEDUCTION AGIO SALT CREDIT REBATE
IMPRESS OFFTAKE DISCOUNT ILLATION
ABATEMENT COROLLARY
DEED ACT BILL BOOK CASE FACT FEAT
FIAT GEST TURN WORK CHART DOING
ISSUE SANAD THING TITLE ACTION
CONVEY ESCROW POTTAH REMISE
SASINE CHARTER EXPLOIT FACTION
PARERGON PRACTICE TRANSFER
PERFORMANCE
(BRUTAL —) ATROCITY
(CHARITABLE —S) ALMS
(EVIL —) MALEFACTION
(GOOD —) BENEFIT MITZVAH
(HEBREW —) STARR
(PART OF —) HABENDUM
(VALIANT —) VALIANCE
(WICKED —) ILL
DEEM LET SAY SEE GIVE HOPE TELL

JUDGE OPINE THINK ESTEEM EXPECT
ORDAIN RECKON REGARD ADJUDGE
BELIEVE SURMISE ANNOUNCE CONSIDER
PROCLAIM
DEEP LOW SAD SEA BASS BOLD ABYSS
BROAD GRAVE GREAT GRUFF HEAVY
OCEAN SOUND STIFF HOLLOW INTENT
STRONG SULLEN ABYSMAL INTENSE
SERIOUS ABSORBED ABSTRUSE
COMPLETE POWERFUL PROFOUND
THOROUGH RECONDITE
DEEPEN CLOUD DARKEN DREDGE
ENHANCE THICKEN HEIGHTEN
DEER ELK RED ROE AXIS BUCK HART HIND
MILU MUSK OLEN PARA PUDU RUSA
SHOU SIKA STAG BROCK MARAL MOOSE
SABIR SPADE CERVID CHITAL CHITRA
FALLOW GUEMAL HANGUL HEARST
PARRAH RASCAL SAMBAR THAMIN
VENADA BROCKET CARIBOU CERVINE
GUAZUTI KASTURA MUNTJAC PLANDOK
VENISON CARJACOU
(— IN 3RD YEAR) SPAY SOREL
SPAYARD
(— UNDER 1 YEAR) KID
(CASTRATED —) HAVIER
(FEMALE —) DOE ROE HIND
(FEMALE — IN 2ND YEAR) TEG
HEARST
(MALE — IN 2ND YEAR) PRICKET
(MALE — IN 4TH YEAR) SORE
STAGGARD
(MALE — OVER 5 YEARS) HART STAG
(RED —) OLEN SPAY MARAL BROCKET
(RUSINE —) AXIS
(YOUNG —) KID FAWN SPITTER
(2-YEAR OLD —) KNOBBER
(PREF.) CERVI
DEERSLAYER (AUTHOR OF —) COOPER
(CHARACTER IN —) HARRY HETTY
NATTY UNCAS BUMPPO HUTTER JUDITH
THOMAS CHINGACHGOOK
DEFACE MAR FOUL RUIN SCAR ERASE
SHAME SPOIL CANCEL DAMAGE DEFAME
DEFORM EFFACE INJURE DESTROY
DETRACT DISTORT SLANDER DISGRACE
DISHONOR MUTILATE
DEFAMATION LIBEL SCANDAL SLANDER
ASPERSION
DEFAME FOUL ABASE BELIE CLOUD
LIBEL NOISE SMEAR ACCUSE CHARGE
DEFACE DEFOUL INJURE MALIGN REVILE
VILIFY ASPERSE BLACKEN BLEMISH
DEBAUCH DETRACT SLANDER TRADUCE
DISHONOR VILIPEND
DEFAULT FAIL FLAW LOSS MORA ERROR
FAULT BLEMISH FAILURE MISTAKE
NEGLECT OFFENSE OMISSION
DEFEAT WIN BEAT BEST CAST DOWN
DRUB FOIL HAVE KILL LACE LICK LOSS
ROUT RUIN SINK SKIN STOP TRAP TRIM
UNDO WHIP BREAK CHECK FLING FLOOR
OUTDO PASTE SKUNK SMITE SWAMP
THROW WASTE WHACK WORST WRACK
BAFFLE CUMBER EUCHRE LARRUP
MASTER MURDER OUTGUN REBUFF
THWACK THWART CLOBBER CONQUER

DEPRIVE DESTROY LICKING REVERSE SETBACK SHELLAC SUBVERT TROUNCE OUTFIGHT OVERCOME VANQUISH WATERLOO OVERPOWER OVERTHROW

DEFECT BUG FLAW LACK MOTE VICE WANT BOTCH CLOUD ERROR FAULT MINUS DAMAGE INJURY LACUNA MALADY PLIGHT BLEMISH DEMERIT FAILING DRAWBACK WEAKNESS SHORTCOMING
(— IN ARTICULATION) PSELLISM
(— IN CRYSTAL) HOLE
(— IN ENAMEL) SCAB SAGGING SCUMMING
(— IN FABRIC) GOUT SCOB BARRE BRACK SMASH
(— IN GLASS) KNOT TEAR STONE WREATH THREADS
(— IN IRON) SEAM
(— IN METAL) SNAKE BLOWHOLE
(— IN PRINTING PLATE) HICKEY
(— IN STEEL) LAP
(— IN TIMBER) LAG SHAN COLLAPSE
(— IN YARN) SINGLING CORKSCREW
(— OF CHARACTER) HOLE SHADE HAMARTIA
(LINT —) SPOT
(SPEECH —) BALBUTIES CLUTTERING
(TELEVISION —) FLOPOVER

DEFECTIVE BAD ILL EVIL FOXY LAME POOR SICK BLIND FALSE FAULTY FLAWED MEAGER RAGGED HALTING VICIOUS

DEFEND HOLD KEEP SAVE WARD WARN COVER GUARD SHEND WATCH FORBID SCREEN SECURE SHIELD UPHOLD BULWARK ESPOUSE EXPOUND JUSTIFY PROPUGN PROTECT SHELTER SUPPORT ADVOCATE CHAMPION CONSERVE MAINTAIN PRESERVE PROHIBIT SAFEGUARD

DEFENSE EGIS FORT PALE ROCK WALL WARD WEAR AEGIS ALIBI FENCE GRITH GUARD TOWER ABATIS ANSWER BEHALF COVERT FRAISE SCONCE BARRIER BASTION BULWARK OUTWORK PARADOS RAMPART SHELTER ADVOCACY FRONTIER SECURITY

DEFENSELESS BARE COLD NAKED SILLY UNARMED HELPLESS

DEFER BOW WAIT DELAY HONOR REMIT STAVE TARRY WAIVE YIELD ESTEEM HUMBLE RETARD REVERE SUBMIT ADJOURN SUSPEND CONSIDER POSTPONE SUSPENSE

DEFIANT BOLD BRAVE STOUT DARING STOCKY INSOLENT STUBBORN OBSTREPEROUS

DEFICIENCY LACK WANT ERROR FAULT MINUS DEARTH DEFECT ABSENCE BLEMISH DEFICIT FAILING FAILURE POVERTY DELETION SCARCITY SHORTAGE
(PREF.) ISCH
(SUFF.) PENIA

DEFICIENT BAD LEAN BLUNT MINUS SCANT BARREN FEEBLE MEAGER SCARCE SKIMPY INDIGENT

DEFILE FOIL FOUL GATE LIME MOIL MUCK SLIP SLOT SMUT SOIL ABUSE CLEFT DIRTY GORGE NOTCH SMEAR STAIN SULLY TAINT BEWRAY DEBASE GULLET RAVISH CORRUPT DEBAUCH DEPRAVE PASSAGE POLLUTE PROFANE SMATTER TARNISH VIOLATE DISHONOR

DEFINE END FIX SET MERE TERM BOUND LIMIT DECIDE CLARIFY DELIMIT EXPLAIN EXPOUND DESCRIBE DISCOVER

DEFINITE SET FIRM HARD SURE CLEAR FINAL FIXED SHARP FINITE FORMED STRAIT CERTAIN EXPRESS LIMITED POINTED PRECISE DISTINCT EMPHATIC EXPLICIT LIMITING POSITIVE PUNCTUAL SPECIFIC

DEFINITIVE LAST FINAL GRAND ORISTIC DEFINITE

DEFLECT WRY BEND COCK SWAY WARP PARRY WREST WRING BAFFLE DETOUR DIVERT SWERVE DEVIATE DIVERGE REFLECT REFRACT

DEFLECTION DROOP SWEEP WINDAGE
(— ON METER) KICK

DEFORM MAR WARP GNARL DEFACE BLEMISH CONTORT DISTORT DIFFORME DISGUISE DISHONOR MISSHAPE

DEFORMED GAMMY WRONG PAULIE CROOKED HIDEOUS MISBORN FORMLESS UNMACKLY

DEFORMITY GALL VICE BLEMISH HARELIP CLUBFOOT FLATFOOT

DEFRAUD ROB BEAT BILK FAKE GULL NICK ROOK TRIM WIPE CHEAT COZEN GOUGE LURCH MULCT SLICK STICK TRICK WRONG BOODLE CHOUSE DECEIVE SKELDER SWINDLE

DEFRAY PAY BEAR AVERT COVER ABSORB EXPEND PREPAY APPEASE REQUITE SATISFY DISBURSE

DEFT FEAT GAIN NEAT TALL TRIM AGILE HANDY NATTY QUICK SLICK ADROIT EXPERT HEPPEN NIMBLE SPRACK SPRUCE DELIVER DEXTROUS SKILLFUL

DEFUNCT DEAD EXTINCT DECEASED DEPARTED FINISHED

DEFY BRAG DARE FACE MOCK BEARD BRAVE STUMP TEMPT FORBID AFFRONT BRAVADE DESPISE DISDAIN OUTDARE OUTFACE CHAMPION DEFIANCE OUTSCOUT RENOUNCE CHALLENGE

DEGENERATE ROT SINK EFFETE DEGRADE DEPRAVE DESCEND DEROGATE

DEGRADE BUST SINK ABASE BREAK DECRY LOWER SHAME SHEND STOOP STRIP UNMAN DEBASE DEMEAN DEMOTE DEPOSE HUMBLE LESSEN REDUCE VILIFY CORRUPT DECLINE DEPRESS DIMINISH DISGRACE DISHONOR DISMOUNT DISPLUME SUPPLANT

DEGRADED BASE BROKE SEAMY ABJECT DEMISS FALLEN SORDID DEBASED OUTCAST

DEGRADING BASE VILE MENIAL SHAMEFUL

DEGREE PEG PIP BANK CAST DEAL FORM
HEAT PEEP POLL RANK RATE RUNG STEP
TERM TIER CLASS HONOR LEVEL ORDER
PITCH PLACE POINT PRICK SHADE STAGE
STAIR EXTENT GRIECE LENGTH MEDIUM
SOEVER DESCENT DIGNITY MEASURE
ACCURACY QUANTITY STANDING
STRENGTH
(— OF CLOSENESS) FIT
(— OF COMBINING POWER) VALENCE
(— OF CONTRAST) GAMMA
(— OF DEVIATION) LEEWAY
(— OF ELEVATION) ASCENT
(— OF ENGAGEMENT) DEPTH
(— OF FLAWLESSNESS) CLARITY
(— OF FORCE) KICK
(— OF HEIGHT) GRADE
(— OF IMPORTANCE) CALIBER
(— OF INFESTATION) BURDEN
(— OF INTOXICATION) EDGE
(— OF KNOWLEDGE) SCIENTER
(— OF LIGHTNESS) VALUE
(— OF MIXTURE) ALLOY
(— OF OPACITY) DENSITY
(— OF PLENTIFULNESS) ABUNDANCE
(— OF PRESTIGE) PLACE
(— OF SLOPE) PITCH SPLAY
(— OF STREAMLINING) FAIRNESS
(— OF THE SOUL) RUACH
(— OF WATER HARDNESS) GRAIN
(— OF WHITENESS) BLEACH
(EXCESSIVE —) EXTREME
(GREATEST —) UTMOST OPTIMUM
(HIGHEST —) PINK SUMMIT SUPREME
SUBLIMITY
(INDEFINITE —) SEEM
(MINUTE —) DROP SHADE
(MUSICAL —) SPACE SUBTONIC
(RABBINICAL —) SEMIKAH
(SMALL —) ACE TAD HAIR INCH IOTA
SHADOW GLIMMER
(SOME —) BIT
(UTMOST —) SUM ACME HEIGHT
EXTREME EXTREMITY
(10 —S OF LONGITUDE) FACE
(15 —S) HOUR
DEIGN STOOP VOUCHSAFE
DEITY (ALSO SEE GOD AND GODDESS)
EA EL KA RA RE SU ABU BEL GAD GOD
RAN SHU SOL AKAL AMEN AMON BAAL
CAGN DEVA FAUN FURY GWYN MIND
MORS RANA SIVA SOBK ALALA ALALU
AMIDA AMITA AMMON DAGAN DAGON
HAOMA HOBAL HORUS HUBAL INUUS
JANUS MIDER MITRA MONAD SATYR
SEBEK SHIVA SIRIS SURYA ZOMBI
ASHIMA ATHTAR BATALA BUNENE
CAISSA FATHER FAUNUS IASION
MARDUK MOLOCH NIBHAZ OANNES
ORISHA ORMAZD ORMUZD RIMMON
SOMNUS SUCHOS SYLVAN VARUNA
ZOMBIE ALASTOR FORSETE FORSETI
GODDESS GODHEAD GODLING GODSHIP
HERSHEF IAPETUS KHEPERA MANITOU
NINURTA NISROCH PHORCUS PHORKYS
RESHEPH SETEBOS SILENUS TAGALOA
TARANIS VIRBIUS BAALPEOR BEELPEOR

BELFAGOR DEVARAJA DIVINITY
ELAGABAL GOVERNOR HACHIMAN
MELKARTH MERODACH PICUMNUS
PILUMNUS SEILENOS SILVANUS
TANGALOA TUTELARY ZEPHYRUS
ZOOMORPH
(AVENGING —) ALASTOR
(HEATHEN —) IDOL
(INFERIOR —) GODKIN GODLING
DEMIURGE PETTYGOD
(SHINTO —) KAMI
(SUPREME —) HANSA
(TUTELARY —) NUMEN GENIUS
DEJECTED BAD LOW SAD DAMP DOWN
GLUM POOR SUNK ABASED ABATTU
DROOPY GLOOMY PINING SOMBER
ALAMORT DUMPISH HANGDOG HANGING
HUMBLED LUMPISH UNHAPPY
DOWNCAST DOWNWARD REPINING
WOBEGONE WRETCHED MELANCHOLY
DEJECTION DAMP GLOOM SLOTH
DISMAY DISMALS HUMDRUM SADNESS
MELANCHOLY

DELAWARE

CAPITAL: DOVER
COUNTY: KENT SUSSEX NEWCASTLE
INDIAN: LENAPE
STATE BIRD: BLUEHEN
STATE FLOWER: PEACH
STATE NICKNAME: FIRST BLUEHEN
DIAMOND
STATE TREE: HOLLY
TOWN: LEWES NEWARK SMYRNA
ELSMERE CLAYMONT WILMINGTON

DELAY LAG LET BODE HOLD LING LITE
MORA SIST SLOW SLUG STAY STOP
WAIT ABIDE ABODE ALLAY BLINE CHECK
DALLY DEFER DEMUR DETER DRIFT
DWELL FRIST PAUSE SLOTH STALL STICK
STINT TARRY TRACT ARREST ATTEND
BELATE DAWDLE DETAIN DILATE DRETCH
ESSOIN HINDER HOLDUP IMPEDE LINGER
LOITER QUENCH RETARD TEMPER
WEAKEN ADJOURN ASSUAGE CONFINE
FORSLOW PROLONG RESPECT RESPITE
SLACKEN SOJOURN DEMURRAL
DILATION FORESLOW HANGFIRE
HESITATE MORATION OBSTRUCT
POSTPONE PROTRACT REPRIEVE
STOPPAGE OBSTRUCTION
(— IN COUNTDOWN) HOLD
(— TRIAL) TRAVERSE
(LEGAL —) DILATOR INDUCIAE
(UNDUE —) LACHES
DELECTABLE TASTY DESIROUS
PLEASING BEAUTIFUL EXQUISITE
DELEGATE NAME SEND ASSIGN COMMIT
DELATE DEPUTE DEPUTY LEGATE
NUNCIO APPOINT CONSIGN EMPOWER
ENTRUST EMISSARY RELEGATE
TRANSFER
DELETE DELE EDIT OMIT BLACK ERASE

PURGE SLASH CANCEL CENSOR DELATE
REMOVE STRIKE DESTROY EXPUNGE
DELETERIOUS BAD HARMFUL HURTFUL
NOXIOUS DAMAGING PERNICIOUS
DELIBERATE COOL PORE SLOW STUDY
THINK ADVISE CONFER DEBATE PONDER
REGARD ADVISED BALANCE BETHINK
CONSULT COUNSEL REFLECT STUDIED
WILLING WITTING CONSIDER DESIGNED
MEASURED MEDITATE STUDIOUS
DELIBERATION ADVICE COUNCIL
COUNSEL LEISURE THOUGHT VISEMENT
DELICACY BIT ROE CATE EASE TACT
FRILL KNACK TASTE CAVIAR DAINTY
JUNKET LUXURY NICETY FINESSE
RAREBIT TRINKET AIRINESS KICKSHAW
LEGERETE NICENESS PLEASURE
SUBTLETY
DELICATE SLY AIRY FINE LACY NESH
NICE SOFT TEAR ZART ELFIN FAIRY FRAIL
LIGHT SILKY CHOICE DAINTY FLIMSY
GENTLE KITTLE MINION PASTEL PETITE
QUEASY SILKEN SLIGHT SUBTLE TENDER
ELEGANT EPICENE FINICAL FRAGILE
MINIKIN REFINED SUBTILE SUMMERY
TAFFETA TENUOUS TIFFANY WILLOWY
CHARMING ETHEREAL FEATHERY
GOSSAMER GRACEFUL HOTHOUSE
LUSCIOUS MIGNIARD PLEASANT
TICKLISH
DELICATESSEN GASTRONOME
CHARCUTERIE
DELICIOUS DAINTY FRIAND DELICATE
SCRUMPTIOUS
DELIGHT JOY GLEE GUST LITE LOVE
SEND TAKE BLESS BLISS CHARM EXULT
FEAST GRACE GUSTO MIRTH REVEL
SAVOR SMACK ADMIRE ARRIDE DELICE
DIVERT LIKING PLEASE RAVISH REGALE
RELISH TICKLE DISPORT ECSTASY
ENCHANT GLADDEN GRATIFY JOYANCE
JOYANCY LECHERY RAPTURE REJOICE
DELICATE ENTRANCE GLADNESS
PLEASURE SAVORING
(— IN) LOVE SAVOR
(PL.) DELICIAE
DELIGHTED GLAD
DELIGHTFUL NICE GREAT JAMMY JOLLY
MERRY SOOTH DREAMY SAVORY
ELYSIAN LEESOME ADORABLE
CHARMING DELICATE GLORIOUS
GORGEOUS HEAVENLY LUSCIOUS
SCRUMPTIOUS
DELINEATE MAP DRAW OFF ETCH LIMN LINE
CHALK CHART FENCE PAINT TOUCH
TRACE DELINE DEPICT DESIGN DEVISE
SKETCH SURVEY EXPRESS OUTLINE
PORTRAY
DELIRIOUS FEY MAD OFF LIGHT MANIC
INSANE RAVING FLIGHTY FRANTIC
LUNATIC MADDING DERANGED FRENETIC
FRENZIED
DELIRIUM FURY MAZE MANIA FRENZY
LUNACY RAVING MADNESS INSANITY
DELIVER DO HIT LAY LET RID BAIL BORN
DEAL FREE GIVE LEND SAVE SELL SEND
TAKE BRING COUGH LIVER SERVE SPEAK

UTTER BETRAY COMMIT CONVEY
EXEMPT PREACH RANSOM REDEEM
RENDER RESCUE RESIGN SUCCOR
COMMEND CONSIGN DECLAIM DICTATE
OUTTAKE PRESENT RECOVER RELEASE
RELIEVE DISPATCH LIBERATE
DELIVERY FLY BAIL FLIER ISSUE RESCUE
ADDRESS AIRDROP BAILMENT SHIPMENT
(— IN SPEAKING) DICTION
(— OF BALL) BOWL
(— WAGON) FLY
(MAIL —) TAPPALL TAPPAUL
DELL HOW DALE GLEN VALE SLADE
DINGLE RAVINE VALLEY
DELUDE BOB JIG BILK DUPE FOOL HOAX
MOCK AMUSE CHEAT COZEN ELUDE
EVADE SPOOF TRICK BAFFLE BANTER
BEFOOL CAJOLE DIDDLE BEGUILE
DECEIVE ENCHANT MISLEAD OVERSEE
HOODWINK INVEIGLE
DELUGE SEA FLOW FLOOD SWAMP
CATARACT INUNDATE OVERFLOW
SATURATE SUBMERGE
DELUSION MAZE DWALE FRAUD TRICK
MIRAGE VISION CHIMERA FALLACY
PHANTOM ILLUSION PHANTASM
DELUXE PALACE ELEGANT ELABORATE
SUMPTUOUS
DELVE DIG DIP CAVE DINT MINE DITCH
PLUMB BRUISE BURROW EXHUME
FATHOM INDENT IMPRESS EXCAVATE
INSCRIBE
DEMAGOGUE CLEON LEADER ORATOR
ROUSER JACOBIN SPEAKER TRIBUNE
JAWSMITH OCHLOCRAT
DEMAND ASK CRY TAX USE CALL NEED
CLAIM CRAVE DRAFT EXACT GAVEL
ORDER QUERY BEHEST CHARGE
DESIRE ELICIT EXPECT SNATCH SUMMON
ARRAIGN COMMAND CONSIST INQUIRE
MANDATE REQUEST REQUIRE SOLICIT
INSTANCE QUESTION
DEMANDING HEFTY EXIGENT
(— ATTENTION) ACUTE
DEMEANOR AIR GARB MIEN PORT
FRONT HABIT ACTION BEARING
CONDUCT FASHION CARRIAGE
PORTANCE
DEMENTED MAD NUTS BUGGY CRAZY
LOONY NUTTY INSANE SKEWED
FATUOUS
DEMERIT MARK FAULT DESERT BROWNIE
(PL.) GIG
DEMETRIUS (BELOVED OF —) CELIA
HERMIA
(MOTHER OF —) TAMORA
DEMIGOD AITU HERO KAMI YIMA ADAPA
SATYR GARUDA PAGODA TRITON
GODLING
(PL.) NEPHILIM
DEMIGODDESS URD NORN HEROINE
DEMISE WILL DEATH CONVEY DECEASE
BEQUEATH
DEMOCRACY POPULACY COMMONALTY
DEMOCRAT DEMO DANITE HUNKER
SNAPPER DEMOCRAW LOCOFOCO
POPOCRAT

DEMOLISH RASE RAZE RUIN BREAK LEVEL WASTE WRECK BATTER DESTROY SHATTER SUBVERT DOWNCAST STRAMASH PULVERIZE

DEMON ALP DEV NAT OKI AITU ATUA BADB BALI BHUT DEVA DOOK OGRE OKEE PUCK RAHU SURT WADE ASURA DEVIL DHOUL FIEND GENIE GHOST JUMBY OTKON SATAN SATYR SURTR TAIPO WITCH ABIGOR ARIOCH BILWIS DAEMON DAIMON DAITYA JUMBIE MAMMON PILWIZ PISACA THURSE VRITRA YAKSHA YAKSHI ASMADAI ASMODAY DEMONIO HARPIER PISACHA VILLAIN WARLOCK ALICHINO ASHMODAI ASMODEUS BAALPEOR BEELPEOR CURUPIRA EUDAEMON OBIDICUT SUCCUBUS WATERMAN
(— OF WOODS) LESIY
(ARABIC —) AFREET
(EVIL —) SHEDU
(FEMALE —) HAG LAMIA PISACHI SUCCUBUS
(NATURE —) GENIUS
(PETTY —) IMP
(WATER —) NICKER

DEMONIAC DEMONIC LUNATIC SATANIC DEVILISH DIABOLIC FIENDISH INFERNAL

DEMONSTRATE GIVE SHOW CLEAR PROVE SPEAK CONVICT DISPLAY PORTRAY CONVINCE MANIFEST

DEMONSTRATION SHOW SIGN TIME PROOF OVATION APODIXIS BALLYHOO MANIFEST
(— OF POWER) MANIFESTATION
(OSTENTATIOUS —) SPLURGE

DEMORALIZE WEAKEN CONFUSE CORRUPT DEPRAVE PERVERT

DEMORALIZING INFECTIOUS SHATTERING

DEMOTE BUMP BUST REDUCE UNRANK DEGRADE DISRATE

DEMURE COY MIM SHY PRIM GRAVE STAID MODEST SEDATE COMPOSED DECOROUS

DEN MEW CAVE COVE DELL DIVE GLEN HELL HOLE LAIR NEST ROOM SHED SINK CABIN CAVEA COUCH HAUNT LODGE SLADE STUDY BURROW CAVERN COVERT GROTTO HOLLOW KENNEL RAVINE RETREAT HIDEAWAY SNUGGERY WORKROOM
(— OF BEAR) WASH
(— OF INIQUITY) DOMDANIEL
(DRINKING —) BOTHAN
(FOUL —) SPITAL
(GAMBLING —) DEADFALL

DENIZEN CITIZEN RESIDENT
(— BY BIRTH) NATIVE
(— OF HELL) HELLION

DENMARK

CAPITAL: COPENHAGEN
COIN: ORA ORE KRONE
COUNTY: AMT FYN RIBE SORO VEJLE AARHUS MARIBO ODENSE TONDER VIBORG AALBORG RANDERS AABENRAA BORNHOLM
INLET: ISE LIM FJORD VEJLE NISSUM ODENSE HORSENS LOGSTOR MARIAGER
ISLAND: OE ALS FYN MON AARO AERO FANO FOHR MORS ROMO BAAGO FAROE LAESO SAMSO SANDO AMAGER SEJERO SUDERO FALSTER SEELAND ZEALAND
MEASURE: ELL FOD MIL POT ALEN FAVN RODE ALBUM KANDE LINJE PAEGL TOMME ACHTEL PAEGEL SKEPPE LANDMIL OLTONDE SKIEPPE VIERTEL FJERDING
PARLIAMENT: RIGSRAAD FOLKETING LANDSTING
RIVER: ASA HOLM OMME STOR GUDEN SKIVE SUSAA VARDE GELSAA STORAA VORGOD GUDENAA LILLEAA LONBORG
TOWN: ARS HOV HALS KOGE NIBE SORO VRAA FARUM HOBRO SKIVE AARHUS DRAGOR KORSOR NYBORG ODENSE SKAGEN STRUER VIBORG AALBORG HERNING HORSENS KOLDING RANDERS ALSINORE BALLERUP GENTOFTE GLOSTRUP ROSKILDE HELSINGOR COPENHAGEN
TRIBE: DANES JUTES ANGLES CIMBRI TEUTONS
WEIGHT: ES LOD ORT VOG LAST MARK PUND UNZE CARAT KVINT POUND QUINT TONDE CENTNER LISPUND QUINTIN LISPOUND SKIPPUND

DENOMINATION CULT NAME SECT CLASS FAITH TITLE VALUE CHURCH SCHOOL SOCIETY CATEGORY

DENOTE GIVE MARK MEAN NAME NOTE SHOW SOUND IMPORT NOTIFY BETOKEN CONNOTE EXPRESS SIGNIFY DESCRIBE INDICATE

DENOUNCE BAN DAMN WRAY ASCRY BASTE BLAST DECRY TAUNT ACCUSE DELATE DESCRY SCATHE ARRAIGN CONDEMN DECLAIM DECLARE UPBRAID EXECRATE THREATEN OBJURGATE

DENSE FAST FIRM CLOSE CRASS GROSS HEAVY MASSY MURKY SILLY SOLID SPISS STIFF THICK TIGHT OBTUSE OPAQUE STUPID COMPACT CROWDED INTENSE SERRIED

DENT BASH BURT DINT DOKE DUNT FAZE NICK CLOUR DELVE DINGE NOTCH STOVE TOOTH BATTER DUNTLE HALLOW INDENT BLEMISH DEPRESS

DENUDE BARE SCALP SHAVE STRIP DIVEST DENUDATE

DENUNCIATION BAN THREAT THUNDER ANATHEMA DIATRIBE

DENY NAY BELIE REPEL ABJURE DISOWN FORBID IMPUGN NEGATE REFUTE REJECT RENEGE CONFUTE DEPRIVE DISAVOW DISPUTE FORSAKE GAINSAY PROTEST SUBLATE WITHSAY ABNEGATE DISALLOW DISCLAIM FORSWEAR RENOUNCE WITHHOLD

DEPART GO DIE WAG BLOW EXIT FLIT HOOK MOVE PACK PART PASS PIKE QUIT SHED STEP VADE VARY VOID WALK WEND WITE AVOID BREAK FOUND LEAVE MOSEY SEVER SHAKE SHIFT START TRUSS AVAUNT BEGONE DECAMP DECEDE DEMISE DESIST DIVIDE PERISH RECEDE REMOVE RETIRE SUNDER SWERVE WANDER ABSCOND DEVIATE FORSAKE RETREAT SKIDDOO VAMOOSE FAREWELL WITHDRAW

DEPARTED DEAD BYGONE DEFUNCT DECEASED DECEDENT

DEPARTMENT PART OKRUG REALM AGENCY BRANCH BUREAU OKROOG SPHERE PORTION AGITPROP CHANCERY DIVISION PROVINCE

DEPARTURE EXIT BREAK DEATH GOING LEAVE OUTGO EGRESS EXODUS HEGIRA DECEASE PARTING RETREAT FAREWELL OFFGOING

DEPEND BANK HANG LEAN PEND RELY REST RIDE STAY TURN BUILD COUNT FOUND HINGE TRUST LIPPEN CONFIDE

DEPENDABILITY SECURITY

DEPENDABLE GOOD SURE TRIG SOLID SOUND THERE SECURE STANCH STEADY CERTAIN RELIABLE SUREFIRE

DEPENDENT CHILD CLIENT MINION SPONGE VASSAL FEODARY RELIANT SERVILE SPONGER SUBJECT BEHOLDEN CLINGING ENCLITIC FOLLOWER RETAINER
(— ON) ILLATIVE
(NOT —) ABSOLUTE

DEPICT HUE DRAW ETCH LIMN ENTER IMAGE PAINT SPEAK WRITE BLAZON DISPLAY EXPRESS PICTURE PORTRAY DESCRIBE EMBLAZON

DEPLETE DRAIN EMPTY PUNISH REDUCE UNLOAD EXHAUST BANKRUPT DIMINISH

DEPLORABLE SAD WOEFUL DOLOROUS GRIEVOUS WAILSOME WRETCHED

DEPLORE RUE MOAN SIGH WAIL MOURN BEMOAN BEWAIL GRIEVE LAMENT REGRET COMPLAIN

DEPORTMENT AIR GEST MIEN HABIT ACTION MANNER ADDRESS BEARING COMPORT CONDUCT GESTURE BREEDING CARRIAGE DEMEANOR MAINTAIN PORTANCE

DEPOSE AVER ABASE SWEAR AFFIRM ASSERT BANISH DEPONE DIVEST REDUCE REMOVE DEGRADE DEPOSIT DESTOOL TESTIFY DETHRONE DISCROWN DISPLACE

DEPOSIT FUR LAY PUT SET ADHI BANK CAKE CRUD DROP DUMP FUND HIDE HOCK PAWN BLOOM CHEST COUCH COVER DEPOT LODGE PLACE SCURF STORE TOSCA BESTOW DEPONE DEPOSE ENTOMB ESCROW GARNER IMPOSE INHUME PLEDGE REPOSE SALINE SCORIA SCROLL SETTLE SINTER TOPHUS ASHFALL CONSIGN HORIZON DILUVIUM SANDBANK PRECIPITATION
(— BALLOT) CAST

(— DRIFT-SAND) SUD
(— EGGS) BLOW SPAWN
(— FOR COPYRIGHT) ENTER
(— IN CHAMPAGNE) GRIFFE
(— IN EARTH) INTER INHUME
(— IN GUN BORE) FOULING
(— IN WINE CASK) CRUST TARTAR
(— OF DEBRIS) BRECCIA
(— OF LOAM) LOESS
(— OF ORE) BLOOM FLAT
(— OF PEBBLES AND SAND) BEACH CASCALHO
(— OF SALT WATER) SOAK
(— ON LEATHER) BLOOM
(— ON LEAVES) HONEYDEW
(— STOLEN ARTICLES) FENCE
(— USED AS FERTILIZER) FALUN
(ALLUVIAL —) APRON DELTA
(ARCHAEOLOGICAL —) LENS
(BANK —S) CASH
(BLACK —) STUPP
(CORNEA —) ARCUS
(EARTHY —) GUHR MARL
(GEOLOGIC —) BLANKET HORIZON
(GLACIAL —) TILL DRIFT ESKER SHEET PLACER MORAINE
(GRAVEL —) LEAD
(KIDNEY —) GRAVEL
(MASS OF SEDIMENTARY —S) GOBI
(MINERAL —) FLAT LODE CARBONA
(MUDDY —) SLUDGE SLUMGULLION
(POWDERY —) BERGMEHL
(SEDIMENTARY —) SILT VARVE
(SHELLY —) CRAG
(SHOAL-WATER —) CULM
(SKELETAL —) CORAL
(STOMACH —) SABURRA
(TARRY —) GUM
(WELDING —) TACK
(PREF.) THESO

DEPOSITORY BANK DROP SAFE AMBRY ATTIC VAULT

DEPOT BANK BASE GARE STATION MAGAZINE TERMINAL TERMINUS

DEPRAVED BAD EVIL UGLY VILE ROTTEN SHREWD WICKED BESTIAL CORRUPT IMMORAL PRAVOUS VICIOUS MISCREANT

DEPRECATE PRAY INVOKE BESEECH

DEPRECIATE FALL LACK SLUR ABASE DECRY SLUMP DEBASE LESSEN REDUCE SHRINK CHEAPEN DEBAUCH DEGRADE DEPRAVE DEPRESS DETRACT DISABLE SLANDER BELITTLE DEROGATE DISCOUNT DISVALUE MINIMIZE PEJORATE VILIPEND

DEPRECIATION AGIO DECRIAL DISCOUNT

DEPRESS BOW COW HIP LOW BATE BEAR BORE DAMP DASH DENT FALL FLAT SINK SUMP ABASE BREAK CHILL COUCH CRUSH FAINT LOWER SLUMP VAPOR WEIGH APPALL DAMPEN DISMAY HUMBLE LESSEN SADDEN SETTLE SICKEN SLOUCH WEAKEN DECLINE DEGRADE DESTROY FLATTEN OPPRESS

REPRESS BROWBEAT DIMINISH DISPIRIT ENFEEBLE

DEPRESSED LOW SAD BLUE DAMP DULL FLAT SICK SUNK COWED WROTH BROODY GLOOMY LONELY SOMBER TRISTE DEJECTED DOWNCAST

DEPRESSING SAD BLUE COLD BLEAK CHILL DREAR DUSKY MUZZY OURIE DISMAL DREARY GLOOMY SOMBER TRISTE OPPRESSIVE

DEPRESSION DIP GAT PAN PIT BUST CROP DAMP DOKE DOWN FALL FOSS GASH GLEN HOLL HOWE SLOT WELL ATRIO BASIN BLUES CANON COWAL CRYPT DINGE FOSSA FOSSE FOVEA GLOOM GROIN NADIR NAVEL ORBIT SCOOP SELLA SINUS SLUMP BLIGHT BUCKLE CAFARD CANYON CAVITY CRATER CUPULE DISMAY FURROW GROOVE GULLEY GUTTER INDENT RAVINE SAUCER SLOUGH SPLEEN VALLEY WALLOW ALVEOLA BLOWOUT BOGHOLE CHAGRIN CLAYPAN CONCAVE COUNTER FOVEOLA SADNESS SALTPAN SINKAGE SINKING VARIOLE BOTHRIUM DOLDRUMS FOLLICLE SINKHOLE SOAKAWAY EPHIPPIUM MELANCHOLY OPPRESSION
(— BEHIND COW'S SHOULDERS) CROP
(— BETWEEN BREASTS) CLEAVAGE
(— BETWEEN HILLS) SWIRE
(— IN BOARD) SKIP
(— IN BOTTLE BOTTOM) KICK
(— IN DECK) COCKPIT
(— IN DOG'S FACE) STOP
(— IN FRUITS) EYE
(— IN GROUND) DALK DELK SOAK SWAG WELL SWALE CHARCO
(— IN MILLSTONE) BOSOM
(— IN NILE VALLEY) KORE
(— IN RANGE) PASS
(— IN RIDGE) COL
(— IN SNOW) SITZMARK
(— IN VELD) COMITJE KOMMETJE
(— OF EAR) SCAPHA
(— OF SPIRITS) JAWFALL
(ARTICULAR —) GLENE
(OBLONG —) CIRCUS
(SMALL —) DENT DIMPLE LACUNA FOLLICLE

DEPRIVE BAR ROB BATE DENY DOCK ABATE DEBAR EMPTY SPOIL STRIP WRONG AMERCE DEFEAT DENUDE DEPOSE DISMAY DIVEST FAMISH HINDER REMOVE ABRIDGE BEGUILE BEREAVE CASHIER CURTAIL DECEIVE DESPOIL DESTROY DISABLE EXHAUST FOREBAR BANKRUPT DENATURE DESOLATE EVACUATE

DEPTH BURY DEEP DROP MOHO ABYSS FATHOM ALTITUDE DEEPNESS PENETRATION

DEPUTY AIDE VICE AGENT ENVOY NABOB PROXY VICAR ANGELO COMMIS CURATE EXARCH FACTOR KEHAYA LEGATE MINION ADJOINT BAILIFF ESCALUS SUBDEAN DELEGATE ORDINARY PYLAGORE TENIENTE VICARIAN

DERANGED OUT GYTE CRAZY CRAZED SKIVIE FRANTIC FURIOUS BUGHOUSE DEMENTED DETRAQUE INFORMAL

DERBY POT CADY KATY RACE BOXER CADDY DICER KELLY SHIRE BOWLER

DERELICT STREET FAILURE BETRAYER CASTAWAY

DERIDE BOO GECK GIBE HOOT JAPE JEER LOUT MOCK TWIT DRAPE FLEER FLOUT KNACK LAUGH RALLY SCOFF SCORN SCOUT TAUNT EXPOSE ILLUDE RIDICULE

DERISION GECK JEER MOCK HOKER SCORN SPORT MOWING ASTEISM MOCKERY CONTEMPT IRRISION RIDICULE

DERISIVE JEERY SNIDE MOWING SATANIC DERISORY IRRISORY SARDONIC SCOFFING

DERIVATION ORIGIN DESCENT PEDIGREE PARENTAGE

DERIVE GET DRAW STEM TAKE BRING CARRY DRIVE FETCH INFER TRACE BORROW CONVEY DEDUCE ELICIT EVOLVE GATHER OBTAIN SPRING DESCEND EXTRACT PROCEED RECEIVE TRADUCE

DEROGATORY BAD

DERRICK JIB RIG LIFT SPAR CRANE DAVIT HOIST STEEVE TACKLE ERECTOR GALLOWS JINNYWINK

DESCEND DIP SYE DIVE DROP DUCK FALL SHED SINK SKIN AVALE LIGHT LOWER SQUAT STOOP SWOOP ALIGHT DERIVE DEVALL SETTLE DECLINE DELAPSE DEVOLVE SUBSIDE SUCCEED DISMOUNT PREPONDERATE

DESCENDANT SON CION HEIR SEED SLIP CHILD SCION BRANCH LINEAL DESCENT DAUGHTER EPIGONUS
(— OF IMMIGRANTS) BRAVA
(— OF JEW) CHUETA
(— OF MOHAMMED) EMIR
(— OF NOAH) AD
(—S OF MOHAMMED) ASHRAF
(INSIGNIFICANT —) TAG
(PL.) SEED STRAIN PROGENY OFFSPRING POSTERITY
(SUFF.) ITE

DESCENDING FALL CADENT DOWNWARD
(— FROM COMMON ANCESTOR) AKIN

DESCENT JET KIN SET DOWN DROP FALL KIND VAIL BIRTH BLOOD CANCH CHUTE ISSUE PITCH SCARP SLOPE STOCK CLEUCH ESCARP RAPPEL STRAIN ASSAULT DECLINE DISSENT EXTRACT FALLOUT INCLINE KINDRED LINEAGE PROGENY ANCESTRY BREEDING DOWNFALL DOWNHILL GLISSADE PEDIGREE PARENTAGE
(— IN MOUNTAINEERING) ABSEIL
(— OF AIRPLANE) LETDOWN APPROACH
(— OF BIRD) STOOP
(— OF DEITY) AVATAR

(— OF LIQUID) DRIBBLE
(— OF MASS) SLIDE
(— OF RIVER) LEAP
(FAMILIAR —) HAVAGE
(OVERWHELMING —) AVALANCHE
(PARACHUTE —) JUMP BAILOUT
(PLUNGING —) SPIN
DESCRIBE GIVE TELL BLAZE PAINT POINT
WRITE DEFINE DENOTE DEPICT DEVISE
RELATE REPORT SKETCH DECLARE
DISPLAY EXPLAIN EXPRESS NARRATE
OUTLINE PICTURE PORTRAY PRESENT
RECOUNT INSCRIBE REHEARSE
DESCRIPTION IMAGE BLAZON SKETCH
SURVEY ACCOUNT DICTION DISPLAY
PICTURE LANDSKIP RELATION TREATISE
DESDEMONA (FATHER OF —)
BRABANTIO
(HUSBAND OF —) OTHELLO
DESECRATE ABUSE DEFILE POLLUTE
PROFANE VIOLATE
DESECRATION PROFANATION
DESERT DUE RAT RUN ARID BOLT FAIL
FLEE MEED SAND TURN GUILT LEAVE
LURCH MERIT PLANT START WAIVE
WASTE BARREN BETRAY DEFECT
EXPOSE LONELY RENEGE REWARD
SHRINK THIRST ABANDON ABSCOND
CHICKEN FORSAKE DESOLATE
RENOUNCE SOLITARY SOLITUDE
WASTABLE
(PREF.) EREM(O)
DESERTED DEAD LONE LONELY FORLORN
DESOLATE FORSAKEN SOLITARY
DESERTER RAT BOLTER BUGOUT
APOSTATE BUSHWACK FUGITIVE
RECREANT RENEGADE RUNAGATE
TURNTAIL
DESERTION BUGOUT RATTERY
APOSTASY
DESERVE EARN MEED RATE MERIT
BENEFIT PROMERIT
DESERVED JUST COMING WORTHY
CONDIGN
DESERVING WORTHY CONDIGN
WORTHFUL ADMIRABLE MERITORIOUS
DESIGN AIM END MAP CAST DRAW GOAL
IDEA MARK MEAN PLAN PLAT PLOT TREE
WORK ALLOT CHECK DECAL DECOR
DRAFT FANCY MODEL MOTIF QUILT
SHAPE STAMP STUDY STYLE BOWPOT
CACHET CORNER CREATE DEVICE DEVISE
DOODAD DOODLE EMBLEM FIGURE
FLORAL FLOWER INCUSE INTEND INTENT
INVENT LAYOUT MODULE OBJECT
OBTENT SCHEME SKETCH SYSTEM
ALLOVER CARVING CHASING COMPOSE
CONCERT COUNSEL DESTINE DIAGRAM
ETCHING FANTASY FASHION OUTLINE
PATTERN PRETEND PROJECT PROPOSE
PURPORT PURPOSE REVERSE SCALLOP
SLEIGHT THOUGHT APPLIQUE CONTRIVE
ENGINEER FILIGREE FLOCKING FORECAST
GRAFFITO INTAGLIO PHANTASY
PLATFORM REMARQUE SINGERIE
STRIPING
(— AS TITLE PAGE) VIGNETTE

(— ON BOOK) TOOL
(— ON CARPET) MEDALLION
(— ON COIN) BEADING
(— ON FABRIC) BATIK
(ARTFUL —) MACHINATION
(BOOK —) FILET FILLET
(CUP-SHAPED —) HUSK
(EMBLEMATIC —) IMPRESS
(ESSENTIAL —) BONES
(FASHION —) FORD
(OUTLINE —) KEYSTONE
(PERFORATED —) POUNCE
(STRIPED —) STRIA
(TESSELLATED —) MOSAIC
(TEXTILE —) STRIPE HAIRLINE
DESIGNATE SET HAIL MARK MEAN
NAME SHOW ELECT LABEL SPEAK STYLE
TITLE ANOINT ASSIGN DENOTE DESIGN
FINGER INTEND SETTLE APPOINT
EARMARK ENTITLE EXPRESS SPECIFY
SURNAME ALLOCATE DESCRIBE IDENTIFY
INDICATE NOMINATE PRESCRIBE
DESIGNATION NAME TYPE LABEL STYLE
TITLE CAPTION HOMONYM ADDITION
DESIGNER STYLER FANCIER PLANNER
PLOTTER SCHEMER STYLIST COLORIST
ENGINEER MEDALIST MOSAICIST
DESIGNING ARTFUL CUNNING JESUITIC
PLANNING PLOTTING SCHEMING
DESIRABLE FAIR GOOD KEEN WORTH
PLUMMY AMIABLE GRADELY HEALTHY
WELCOME ELIGIBLE PLEASING
SALUTARY
DESIRE YEN ACHE CARE ENVY EROS FAIN
HAVE HOPE LIST LUST MIND NEED PANT
URGE WANT WILL WISH WIST ARDOR
COVET CRAVE FANCY GREED MANIA
NISUS QUEST TASTE YEARN AFFECT
DEMAND HANKER HUNGER PREFER
AVARICE AVIDITY CRAVING EROTISM
LONGING PASSION STOMACH AMBITION
APPETITE COVETISE NECESSITY
(— FOR LIFE) TANHA
(— WITH EAGERNESS) ASPIRE
(ARDENT —) THIRST
(IRRITATING —) ITCH
(SEXUAL —) HOTS PRIDE
(STRONG —) CUPIDITY SLAVERING
(UNCONTROLLABLE —) CACOETHES
DESIRE UNDER THE ELMS
(AUTHOR OF —) ONEILL
(CHARACTER IN —) EBEN ABBIE
CABOT PUTNAM EPHRAIM
DESIROUS AVID FAIN FOND LIEF VAIN
EAGER LUSTY ARDENT ANXIOUS THIRSTY
WILLFUL WILLING WISHING COVETOUS
SPIRITED
DESIST HALT QUIT REST STOP WHOA
CEASE LEAVE SPARE ABANDON FORBEAR
FORFEIT RESPITE SUBSIST SURCEASE
DESK PEW AMBO TABLE BUREAU PULPIT
CONSOLE LECTERN PLUTEUS STANDISH
VARGUENO
DESOLATE SAD BARE LORN RUIN SACK
SOLE WILD ALONE BLEAK DREAR GAUNT
STARK UNKET WASTE BARREN DESERT
DISMAL DREARY GLOOMY LONELY

RAVAGE DESTROY FORLORN LACKING
WIDOWED DEPRIVED DESERTED
FORSAKEN SOLITARY WASTEFUL
WOBEGONE

DESOLATION WOE RUIN GLOOM GRIEF
HAVOC WASTE RAVAGE SADNESS

DESPAIR GLOOM UNHOPE WANHOPE

DESPERADO BRAVO BADMAN BANDIT
RUFFIAN CRIMINAL

DESPERATE MAD DIRE RASH EXTREME
FORLORN FRANTIC HEADLONG HOPELESS
PERILOUS RECKLESS

DESPICABLE BUM BASE MEAN VILE
CHEAP DIRTY ABJECT PALTRY SHABBY
SORDID CAITIFF IGNOBLE PITIFUL
PITIABLE UNWORTHY WRETCHED

DESPISE DEFY HATE SCORN SPURN
DETEST LOATHE VILIFY CONTEMN
DISDAIN

DESPONDENT SAD BLUE GLOOMY
FORLORN DEJECTED DOWNCAST
HOPELESS

DESPOT CZAR TSAR TZAR ANARCH
SATRAP TYRANT AUTARCH MONARCH
AUTOCRAT

DESPOTISM TYRANNY AUTARCHY
SULTANISM

DESSERT ICE PIE CAKE BOMBE DOLCE
FRUIT GLACE JELLY AFTERS ECLAIR
JUNKET MOUSSE PASTRY SWEETS
TRIFLE BAKLAVA PARFAIT PUDDING
SHERBET SPUMONE STRUDEL DUMPLING
FLUMMERY FRUMENTY NAPOLEON
PANDOWDY SILLABUB

DESTINATION END GOAL PORT BOURN
BILLET

DESTINE DOOM FATE ALLOT SLATE
DEPUTE DESIGN DEVOTE INTEND ORDAIN
APPOINT PURPOSE SENTENCE

DESTINY LOT DOLE DOOM FATE KARMA
MOIRA STARS KISMET DESTINE FORTUNE

DESTITUTE BARE POOR SANS VOID
CLEAN EMPTY NAKED NEEDY WASTE
BEREFT DEVOID VACANT WASTED
FORLORN LACKING WANTING BANKRUPT
BEGGARED DEFEATED DEPRIVED
DESOLATE FORSAKEN HELPLESS
INDIGENT INNOCENT VIDUATED
PENNILESS

DESTROY BAG EAT END GUT MOW RID
ZAP BLOW CHEW FRAP FULL KILL NULL
RASE RAZE RUIN RUSH SINK SLAY UNDO
VOID BREAK CRACK DECAY ERASE
ERODE QUELL SHOOT SMASH SMITE
SPEED SPEND SPILL SPLIT SPOIL TOTAL
WRACK WRECK BLIGHT CANCEL CUMBER
DEFACE DEFEAT DELETE DEVOUR EFFACE
MURDER QUENCH RANKLE RAVAGE
STARVE STIFLE UPROOT ABOLISH
CONSUME CORRODE DEPRIVE EXPUNGE
FLATTEN MORTIFY NULLIFY OVERRUN
PEREMPT SHATTER SMOTHER SUBVERT
CONFOUND DECIMATE DEMOLISH
DESOLATE DESTRUCT DISSOLVE
FRACTURE FRAGMENT IMMOLATE
OVERTURN SABOTAGE OBLITERATE

DESTROYER CAN HUN DEATH TINCAN

UNDOER VANDAL VICTOR WARSHIP
APOLLYON DEVOURER SABOTEUR

DESTRUCTION BAR END BANE DOGS
DOOM FIRE LOSS RACK RUIN CRUSH
DEATH DECAY GRAVE HAVOC SMASH
STRIP WASTE WRACK DEFEAT DISMAY
ENDING EXPIRY CARNAGE EROSION
UNDOING COLLAPSE DELETION
DISPOSAL DOWNFALL SHAMBLES
RUINATION
(— OF BONES) CARIES
(— OF ENVIRONMENT) ECOCIDE
(— OF SHIP'S PAPERS) SPOLIATION
(CELL —) LYSIS
(GRADUAL —) CORROSION
(MALICIOUS —) SABOTAGE
(UTTER —) PERDITION

DESTRUCTIVE FELL FATAL DEADLY
MORTAL BALEFUL BANEFUL DEATHLY
FATEFUL HARMFUL HURTFUL NOISOME
NOXIOUS RUINOUS PESTILENT

DETACH CUT LOOSE SEVER LOOSEN
UNBIND UNGLUE DISJOIN ISOLATE
UNHINGE UNRIVET SEPARATE UNFASTEN
WITHDRAW

DETACHED CUT COLD FREE ALONE
ALOOF DEADPAN INSULAR ABSTRACT
CLINICAL ISOLATED OUTLYING
SEPARATE UNBIASED

DETAIL CREW ITEM POINT ASSIGN
NICETY RELATE ACCOUNT APPOINT
ARTICLE ITEMIZE MINUTIA NARRATE
SPECIFY INSTANCE

DETAIN HOLD KEEP STAY STOP CHECK
DELAY TARRY ARREST COLLAR HINDER
RETARD IMPRISON RESTRAIN WITHHOLD

DETECT SEE SPY ESPY FIND NOSE SPOT
CATCH SCENT SENSE SMOKE TRACE
DESCRY DIVINE EXPOSE REVEAL
DEVELOP DISCERN UNCOVER DECIPHER
DISCOVER OVERTAKE

DETECTIVE EYE TEC BULL DICK SNOOP
BEAGLE MOUSER SHADOW SHAMUS
SLEUTH TAILER TRACER GUMSHOE
SNOOPER TRAILER HAWKSHAW
SHERLOCK OPERATIVE PINKERTON

DETER BAR BLOCK CHECK DELAY HINDER
RETARD PREVENT DISSUADE PRECLUDE
RESTRAIN

DETERIORATE GO FAIL SOUR WEAR
DECAY ERODE SPILL IMPAIR SICKEN
WORSEN DECLINE PERVERT

DETERMINATION WILL CAUSE ADVICE
BEARING PURPOSE RESOLVE ANALYSIS
BACKBONE DECISION FIRMNESS
FORECAST JUDGMENT SENTENCE

DETERMINE FIT FIX GET TEST ASSAY
JUDGE ADJUST ASSESS ASSIGN CHOOSE
DECERN DECIDE DECREE DEFINE DETECT
DEVISE FIGURE SETTLE ACCOUNT
ADJUDGE ANALYZE ARRANGE COMPUTE
RESOLVE CONCLUDE DISCOVER
PINPOINT

DETERMINED SET BENT FIRM GRIM
BOUND STOUT DOGGED GRITTY INTENT
MULISH STURDY DECIDED SETTLED

DECISIVE FOREGONE PERVERSE
RESOLUTE RESOLVED STUBBORN

DETEST DAMN HATE ABHOR CURSE
LOATHE CONDEMN DESPISE DISLIKE
DENOUNCE EXECRATE ABOMINATE

DETESTABLE FOUL HORRID ODIOUS
BLASTED HATEFUL HELLISH HIDEOUS
ACCURSED DAMNABLE HATEABLE
INFERNAL ABHORRENT ABOMINABLE

DETHRONE DEPOSE DIVEST UNCROWN

DETONATE FIRE BELCH BLAST SHOOT
EXPLODE DETONIZE

DETOUR BYPASS CIRCUIT DIVERSION
ROUNDABOUT

DETRACT TAKE DEDUCT DEFAME DIVERT
VILIFY ASPERSE TRADUCE BELITTLE
DEROGATE DIMINISH MINIMIZE
SUBTRACT

DETRIMENT COST HARM HURT LOSS
SORE WOUND DAMAGE INJURY BEATING
EXPENSE MISCHIEF

DETRIMENTAL ADVERSE HARMFUL
HURTFUL DAMAGING INVIDIOUS
PERNICIOUS PREJUDICIAL

DEUCALION (FATHER OF —)
PROMETHEUS
(MOTHER OF —) CLYMENE
(SON OF —) HELLEN ORESTHEUS
AMPHICTYON
(WIFE OF —) PYRRHA

DEVASTATE HARRY WASTE RAVAGE
ATOMIZE DESTROY PILLAGE PLUNDER
SCOURGE DEMOLISH

DEVASTATING DEADLY LETHAL SAVAGE
CRUSHING FEROCIOUS MURDEROUS

DEVASTATION RUIN SACK HAVOC
WASTE WRACK RAVAGE SACKAGE

DEVELOP BUD RUN BOOM COOK FORM
GROW STEM ARISE BREED BUILD ERECT
RIPEN SHOOT APPEAR BRANCH EVOLVE
EXPAND FLOWER MATURE REVEAL
UNFOLD UNFURL BURGEON EDUCATE
ENLARGE EXPOUND FULFILL UNCOVER
DISCLOSE DISCOVER ENGENDER
GENERATE INCUBATE MANIFEST

DEVELOPMENT DRIFT EVENT HATCH
ESTATE GROWTH DESCENT GENESIS
PROCESS STATURE BREEDING INCREASE
PEDIGREE UPSPRING
(— OF SEX) DIOECISM
(FULL —) BLOW MATURITY
(HIGHEST —) BLOOM
(NORMAL —) APHANISIA
(SUBSEQUENT —) SEQUEL
(THEMATIC —) CONTINUITY
(UNEXPECTED —) ACCIDENT
(PREF.) PLASTO

DEVIATE ERR WRY YAW LEAN MISS
VARY VEER BREAK DRIFT LAPSE SHEER
SPORT STRAY CHANGE DEPART DETOUR
DIVERT RECEDE SWERVE WANDER
DECLINE DEFLECT DIGRESS DIVERGE
INCLINE REFLECT
(— FROM VERTICAL) HADE

DEVIATION BOW YAW JUMP SKEW
TURN DRIFT LAPSE QUIRK SHEER TWIST
CHANGE DETOUR SPREAD ANOMALY

LICENSE LATITUDE SOLECISM VARIANCE
ABERRATION

DEVICE (ALSO SEE INSTRUMENT) ARM
ART DIE DOG DOP EYE FAN FLY FOB GAG
GIN GUN HOG JIG KEY MOP MOT PEN
SET TIP TUP WAY WIT ARCH BELL BOND
BOOM BUFF COIN COMB COUP DARE
DOPP DRAG DRIP FAKE FIRE FLAG FORK
FROG FUSE FUZE GAGE GATE GOBO
GRAB GRIP GYRO HASP HAUL HEAD
HECK HORN IRIS IRON JACK KEEP KITE
LAMP LENS LOCK MOVE MULE MUTE
NAIL PACE PAGE PAWK PLOW POKE
PUMP REEL SEAL SHOE SHUT SIGN SLAY
SLEY SLUR SNAP SPUD STOP STUD
SUMP TOOL TRAP TRIP VICE WEIR WHIM
WHIP WIND WING WOLF ALARM APRON
BADGE BALUN BITCH BLOCK BREAK
BRUSH CHECK CLAMP CODER COVIN
CRAMP CROSS DODGE DRIER DRIFT
DRYER DUMMY FADER FANCY FLAIL
FLARE FLASH FLIRT FLOAT GAUGE
GLAND GORGE GRIPE GUARD GUIDE
GUILE HICKY HINGE HOKUM IMAGE
KAZOO KEYER LADLE LASER LATCH
LEVEL MATCH OTTER PARER PLATE
PUNKA SCREW SHADE SHANK SHIFT
SIEVE SIGHT SIGIL SIREN SIZER SKATE
SLAVE SLICK SLIDE SLING SONDE SPOOL
SPOUT SQUIB STAMP STILL STOOL
STOVE SWEEP SWELL TABLE TABUT
TAMER THIEF TIMER TORCH TRUER
TUNER UNION VERGE AGRAFE AIRWAY
ALARUM ALINER ANCHOR ARREST
BAILER BASTER BEACON BEATER BECKET
BEDDER BEEPER BINDER BLOWER
BOBBIN BOOMER BRIDLE BROOCH
BUCKLE BUFFER BULLEN BUMPER
BUNGEE BUNTER BURNER BUTTON
CHARGE CIPHER DESIGN DIMMER DOFFER
DOTTER DRIVER DROGUE DUMPER
EMBLEM ENGINE EVENER FABRIC FALLER
FEEDER FENDER FILLER FILTER FINDAL
FINDER FORMER GADGET GLAZER
GOFFER GOGGLE GRADER GRATER
GRISLY GUIDER HANGER HEATER HICKEY
HOLDER HOOTER INVENT JIGGER
JOGGER KEEPER KICKER LAYBOY LETOFF
LIFTER LOOPER MARKER MIRROR
MODULE MORTAR MOTHER NAVAID
NIPPLE NONIUS NOTION PACKER PEELER
PICKUP PLAYER PLOUGH PORTER POTEYE
PULLER PUNKAH REROLL RINGER
ROCKET ROLLER ROOTER ROTULA
ROUTER SACKER SADDLE SAFETY
SANDER SCALER SCHEME SCREEN
SEALER SEEKER SENSOR SETTER SHAKER
SHIELD SIFTER SIGNAL SINKER SIPPER
SLEIGH SLICER SLIDER SLIMER SLOPER
SLUICE SOCKET SOLION SORTER SPACER
SPRING STONER STYLUS SUCKER
SWITCH TACTIC TAGGER TAPPER TELLER
TEMPLE TESTER TILLER TRACER TUCKER
TUNNEL TURNER WARMER WASHER
WEANER WEEDER WHEEZE WINDER
WINNOW WORKER

DEVIL IMP MAHU NICK PUCK WOLF
ANNOY BOBBY BOGEY CLOOT DEMON
DEUCE EBLIS FIEND HARRY SATAN
SCRAT SHEDU TAIPO TEASE AMAMON
BELIAL DAEMON DIABLO HORNIE NICKIE
PESTER AMAIMON ANHANGA CLOOTIE
DICKENS GREMLIN LUCIFER MAHOUND
SHAITAN TORMENT WARLOCK WINDIGO
APOLLYON BAALPEOR BEELPEOR
BELFAGOR CAGNAZZO CURUPIRA
MEPHISTO MISCHIEF

DEVILFISH RAY MANTA

DEVIOUS DEEP ERRING ROVING SHIFTY
SUBTLE TRICKY OBLIQUE VAGRANT
WINDING INDIRECT RAMBLING
SCHEMING TORTUOUS

DEVISE AIM CAST COOK FIND GIVE PLAN
PLOT WARP WILL FANCY FRAME LEAVE
SHAPE WEAVE ADVISE CONVEY DECOCT
DESIGN DEVICE DIVIDE DIVINE INVENT
APPOINT ARRANGE COMMENT COMPASS
CONCERT CONCOCT CONSULT IMAGINE
PREPARE PROJECT BEQUEATH CONTRIVE

DEVOID FREE VAIN EMPTY BARREN
VACANT WANTING DESOLATE

DEVOTE VOW ALLY AVOW DOOM GIVE
LEND APPLY ADDICT ATTACH BESTOW
DEPUTE DESIGN DEVOVE EMPLOY
INTEND ADDRESS APPOINT CONSIGN
DEDICATE VENERATE

DEVOTED HIGH TRUE LIEGE LOYAL PIOUS
ARDENT DEVOUT DOOMED ENTIRE
FERVID LOVING OBLATE VOTARY VOTIVE
ADORING ARDUOUS JEALOUS SERIOUS
ZEALOUS ADDICTED ATTACHED
CONSTANT FAITHFUL

DEVOTION ZEAL ARDOR PIETY NOVENA
ANGELUS CULTISM LOYALTY PIETISM
FIDELITY IDOLATRY JEALOUSY RELIGION
NATIONALISM

DEVOUR EAT JAW GULP GORGE RAVEN
WASTE ENGULF CONSUME ENGORGE
SWALLOW

DEVOUT GOOD HOLY WARM GODLY
PIOUS HEARTY INWARD SOLEMN
CORDIAL DEVOTED GODLIKE PITEOUS
SAINTLY SINCERE REVERENT PIETISTIC
PRAYERFUL RELIGIOUS

DEWY DAMP RORY MOIST RORAL GENTLE

DEXTERITY ART CHIC CRAFT KNACK
SKILL STROIL ABILITY ADDRESS AGILITY
APTNESS CUNNING FINESSE SLEIGHT
APTITUDE DEFTNESS FACILITY
(— IN ARMS) CHIVALRY

DEXTEROUS APT FLY DEFT NEAT ADEPT
CANNY CLEAN FEATY HANDY HAPPY
QUICK READY SMART TIGHT ADROIT
ARTFUL CLEVER DRAFTY CUNNING
SKILLFUL

DIABOLICAL CRUEL WICKED DEMONIC
HELLISH INHUMAN SATANIC VIOLENT
DEMONIAC DEVILISH DIABOLIC FIENDISH
INFERNAL

DIADEM TAJ CROWN TIARA ANADEM
CIRCLE EMBLEM FILLET CIRCUIT
CORONET HEADBAND

DIAGNOSE ANALYZE IDENTIFY

DIAGONAL BIAS SLANT SLASH SOLIDUS
VIRGULE

DIAGRAM MAP PLAN PLOT TREE CARTE
CHART EPURE GRAPH DESIGN FIGURE
SCHEMA SCHEME SYMBOL ISOGRAM

DIAL NOB FACE KNOB DIACLE JIGGER
AZIMUTH CRYSTAL DECLINER HOROLOGE
INCLINER

DIALECT (ALSO SEE LANGUAGE) HO KA
WU GEG GIZ KHA LAI SAC TWI AMOY
CANI CANT DRAA EFIK EGBA EPIC GEEZ
GHEG GONA GUEG IOWA ITZA KORA
MANX NAMA NORN OGAM PALI SAUK
SHOR SOGA TALK TCHI TOSK TUBA
ALTAI ARGOT ASURI ATTIC CONOY
DORIC FANTI GHEEZ GHESE HAKKA
IDIOM IONIC IOWAY IRAQI KANSA KAREL
KOINE LADIN LINGO MAZUR MOPAN
MUKRI NGOKO OGHAM PARSI PUNIC
SABIR SAXON SCOTS SLANG TIGRE
TSCHI VALVE VOGUL ZMUDZ AEOLIC
AGNEAN ASANTE ATSINA AWADHI
BADAGA BRETON BROGUE CANTON
CREOLE DEBATE DUNGAN FAEROE
FANTEE FURLAN GASCON GULLAH
GUTNIC HARARI HARAYA IBANAG ISINAI
ITAVES JARGON KABYLE KANSAS
KHAMIR KORANA KVITSH LADAKI
LADINO LAHULI LALLAN LEDDEN LIBYAN
PARSEE PATOIS PATTER PICARD SANTEE
SCOTCH SHARRA SKAGIT SPEECH
SUDANI SWATOW SYRIAC SZEKEL
TAVAST TONGUE TUSCAN YANKEE
ZENAGA

DIALOGUE ION CRITO PATTER PHAEDO
TIMAEUS COLLOQUY DUOLOGUE
EPILOGUE EXCHANGE COLLOCUTION

DIAMETER BORE GAUGE WIDTH MODULE
(— OF BULLET) CALIBER
(— OF PELVIS) CONJUGATA
(— OF PUPIL) APERTURE
(— OF WIRE) GAUGE

DIAMOND GEM ICE BORT PICK ROCK
ROSE BAHIA DORJE FANCY FIELD JEWEL
MELEE POINT RHOMB SANCY SPARK
TABLE VAJRA ADAMAS CARBON JAEGER
ORLOFF PENCIL REGENT RONDEL SHINER
TABLET ADAMANT BRIOLET CARREAU
FISHEYE INFIELD LOZENGE PREMIER
RHOMBUS SPARKLE CORUNDUM
KOHINOOR RONDELLE SPARKLER
BRIOLETTE
(— CUT TOO THIN) FISHEYE
(— MOLDER) DOP
(— USED FOR ENGRAVING) SHARP
(BLACK —) CARBONADO
(FLAT —) LASQUE
(GLAZIER'S —) QUARREL
(IMITATION —) SCHLENTER
(INFERIOR GRADE OF —) FLAT
(PERFECT —) PARAGON
(PURE WHITE —) RIVER
(ROUGH —) BRAIT
(SINGLE —) SOLITAIRE
(TRANSPARENT —) CRYSTAL
(YELLOW —) CANARY

DIANA LUCINA TRIVIA ARTEMIS

(BROTHER OF —) APOLLO
(FATHER OF —) JUPITER
(MOTHER OF —) LATONA
DIAPHANOUS CLEAR SHEER FRAGILE
VAPOROUS
DIAPHRAGM IRIS SLIT APRON SKIRT
WAFER PLATEN MIDRIFF SKIRTING
TRAVERSE TYMPANUM
DIARY LOG RECORD DAYBOOK DIURNAL
JOURNAL REGISTER EPHEMERIS
DIATRIBE SATIRE SCREED HARANGUE
INVECTIVE
DICE CHOP CUBE BONES CRAPS FLATS
LOWMEN REJECT CHECKER IVORIES
(— GAME) SET RAPHE MUMCHANCE
(— HAVING FOUR SPOTS) QUATRE
(FALSE —) GOAD TATS GOURD
GRAVIERS SQUARIER STOPDICE
(HIGHEST THROW AT —) APHRODITE
(LOADED —) TOPS DOCTOR
(LOWEST THROW AT —) AMBSACE
(PAIRED NUMBERS AT —) DUPLET
DOUBLETS
(2, 3, OR 12 ON 1ST —) MISSOUT
DICHOTOMY DUALITY
DICKER SWAP BARTER HAGGLE BARGAIN
CHAFFER EXCHANGE
DICTATE SAW SAY DITE TELL UTTER
WRITE DECREE DICTUM ENJOIN IMPOSE
INDITE ORDAIN COMMAND DELIVER
REQUIRE WARRANT DICTAMEN
PRESCRIBE
DICTATOR CHAM CZAR DUCE TSAR
CAESAR PENDRAGON
DICTATORIAL BOSSY LORDLY CZARIST
POMPOUS TSARIST ARROGANT
DOGMATIC POSITIVE ARBITRARY
MAGISTERIAL
DICTION STYLE IMAGERY LANGUAGE
PARLANCE VERBIAGE
DICTIONARY GRADUS ALVEARY
CALEPIN LEXICON GLOSSARY
WORDBOOK THESAURUS
DIE GO BED END HOB HUB PIP ROT SIX
TAT BOSS COIN CONK CUBE DADO DEAD
DICE DROP EXIT FADE FALL MARK MOLD
PART PASS PIKE PILE SEAL TINE WANE
CROAK FORCE FUDGE IVORY PRINT
PUNCH QUAIL SHAPE SNUFF SPILL
STAMP STOCK CHANCE DEMISE DEPART
EXPIRE FINISH FORMER MATRIX MULLAR
PATRIX PERISH ROLLER STARVE STRIKE
TRANCE VANISH WITHER DECEASE
SUCCUMB TESSERA INTAGLIO LANGUISH
MISCARRY PUNCHEON TRESPASS
(— AWAY) FAIL SWOON
(— BEFORE) PREDECEASE
(— BY HANGING) SWING
(— DOWN) FLIT SINK ABATE
(— FOR DRAWING WIRE) WHIRTLE
(— FOR MAKING DRAINPIPE) DOD
(— FOR MOLDING BRICK) KICK
(— FROM HUNGER) AFFAMISH
(— OF COLD) STARVE
(— OF PEDESTAL) SOLIDUM
(— WITH 4 SPOTS) QUATRE

(— WITH 6 SPOTS) CISE SICE SISE
SIZE
(COINING —) SICCA
(FRAUDULENT —) FULHAM
(HOLLOW —) GOURD
(IMPROPER —) FLAT
(LOADED —) TAT DOCTOR FULHAM
HIGHMAN LANGRET
(LOWER —) BED
(REVOLVING —) DREIDEL
DIET FARE FAST FOOD BOARD HOFTAG
REDUCE SEIMAS VIANDS LANDTAG
REGIMEN RIKSDAG CONGRESS KREISTAG
VOLKSTAG
DIFFER VARY DISCORD DISSENT DIVERGE
DISAGREE
DIFFERENCE CHASM CLASH BREACH
CHANGE ANOMALY BRISURE DISCORD
DISPUTE VARIETY DISTANCE DIVISION
IMPARITY VARIANCE
(— IN ELEVATION) HEAD
(— IN EXCHANGE) AGIO
(— IN LATITUDE) SOUTHING
(— IN LONGITUDE) EASTING
(— IN PITCH) COMMA INTERVAL
(— IN PRESSURE) DRAFT
(— IN WIDTH) BILGE
(— OF OPINION) DISSENT ARGUMENT
(— OF VESSEL'S DRAFT) DRAG
(ANGULAR —) EXPLEMENT
(GRADED —) GRADIENT
(MINUTE —) SHADE
(PRICE —) BASIS
(SMALL —) HAIRLINE
DIFFERENT OTHER DIVERS SUNDRY
UNLIKE ANOTHER DISTANT DIVERSE
SEVERAL STRANGE UNUSUAL VARIANT
VARIOUS CONTRARY MANIFOLD
SEPARATE OTHERWISE
DIFFICULT ILL HARD WICK CRAMP
CRANK GREAT HEAVY SPINY STEEP STIFF
AUGEAN CRABBY CRANKY KNOTTY
SEVERE STICKY STRAIT STRONG TICKLE
UNEASY UPHILL WICKED ARDUOUS
AWKWARD COMPLEX CRABBED DIFFUSE
LABORED OBSCURE PAINFUL PERPLEX
SERIOUS ABSTRACT CUMBROUS
FIENDISH PUZZLING SCABROUS
STUBBORN TICKLISH
(— TO BEAR) BITTER
(— TO COMPREHEND) STRANGE
(— TO FOLLOW) DIRTY
(— TO GRASP) FUGITIVE
(— TO HANDLE) SPINOUS
(— TO MANAGE) SURLY STURDY
(— TO OBTAIN) CLOSE
(— TO PLEASE) CURIOUS
(— TO RAISE) DORTY
(— TO SATISFY) CHOOSY CHOOSEY
(— TO UNDERSTAND) DEEP HIGH
SUBTLE CRABBED ABSTRACT ABSTRUSE
ESOTERIC
(PREF.) DYS MOGI
DIFFICULTY ADO BOX ILL JAM RUB
BUMP CLOG COIL HEAT JAMB KNOT
LOCK NODE PAIN SNAG SORE CHECK
DOUBT GRIEF NODUS PRESS RIGOR

STAND BOGGLE BUNKER PLIGHT PLUNGE RUBBER SCRAPE STRAIT BARRIER DICKENS PITFALL PROBLEM SQUEEZE ASPERITY DISTRESS HARDNESS HARDSHIP OBSTACLE SEVERITY STRUGGLE

DIFFIDENT SHY BLATE CHARY MODEST BACKWARD RESERVED RETIRING SHEEPISH

DIG HOE NIP CLAW DIKE GIRD GORE GRUB MINE MOOT PICK POKE PROD ROOT SINK SLAM SMUG SPIT SPUD SUMP DELVE DITCH DWELL GRAFT GRAVE LODGE POACH PROBE SNOUT SPADE START STOCK BURROW DREDGE EXHUME HOLLOW PLUNGE SHOVEL THRUST TUNNEL COSTEAN UNEARTH EXCAVATE
(— OUT) SCOOP STUMP EXHUME
(— OUT CREVICES) FOSSICK
(— PEAT) SHEUGH
(— POTATOES) LIFT
(— TRENCHES) GRIP COSTEAN
(— UP) CAST GRUB STUB SPADE STOCK EXHUME UPGRAVE DISINTER
(— WITH NAILS) SCRAPE
(— WITH SNOUT) GROUT
(— WITH STICK) CROW

DIGEST CODE ENDUE INDUE RIPEN CODIFY DECOCT DOCKET MATURE SEETHE CONCOCT EPITOME PANDECT SUMMARY CONDENSE SYLLABUS

DIGESTION PEPSIS EUPEPSY EUPEPSIA

DIGIT TOE UNIT DOIGT POINT THUMB DACTYL FIGURE FINGER HALLUX MEDIUS NUMBER DEWCLAW DIGITAL

DIGNIFIED GRAND LOFTY MANLY NOBLE STAID AUGUST LORDLY SEDATE SOLEMN COURTLY EXALTED STATELY ELEVATED ENNOBLED MAJESTIC

DIGNIFY DUB ADORN CROWN EXALT GRACE HONOR RAISE ELEVATE ENNOBLE PROMOTE

DIGNITARY DON WIG BABA RAJA CANON PRIEST DIGNITY PRELATE PROVOST ALDERMAN

DIGNITY DOG CHIC FACE RANK BENCH HONOR PRIDE STATE AFFAIR LAUREL REPOSE BEARING DECORUM DUKEDOM EARLDOM FITNESS GRAVITY MAJESTY SHAHDOM STATION WORSHIP CHIVALRY EARLSHIP GRANDEUR NOBILITY

DIGRESSION ASIDE VAGARY EPISODE PASSAGE TANGENT EXCURSUS SIDESLIP PARENTHESIS

DIKE BAR RIB BANK BUND POND POOL DITCH LEVEE CAUSEY CHANNEL ABOIDEAU CAUSEWAY ESTACADE SPREADER

DILAPIDATED BAD BEATEN CREAKY RAGGED RUINED SHABBY WRECKY RUINOUS DESOLATE TATTERED WOBEGONE

DILAPIDATION RUIN DECAY DECREPITY DISREPAIR

DILATE TENT DELAY PLUMP SWELL WIDEN EXPAND EXTEND SPREAD AMPLIFY BROADEN DIFFUSE DISTEND ENLARGE INFLATE PROLONG STRETCH DISPERSE INCREASE LENGTHEN PROTRACT DISCOURSE

DILATORY LATE SLOW SLACK SPARE TARDY REMISS LAGGARD TEDIOUS BACKWARD DELAYING INACTIVE SLUGGISH

DILEMMA FIX FORK LOCK NODE CHOICE JEOPARDY QUANDARY

DILETTANTE LOVER ADMIRER AMATEUR DABBLER DABSTER ESTHETE AESTHETE

DILIGENT BUSY HARD TIDY ACTIVE STEADY CAREFUL EARNEST HEEDFUL OPEROSE PAINFUL PATIENT WORKFUL CAUTIOUS CONSTANT LABOROUS SEDULOUS STUDIOUS

DILUTE CUT FUSE LEAN THIN WEAK ALLAY BLUNT DELAY WATER RAREFY REDUCE WEAKEN DIMINISH LENGTHEN WATERISH
(— LIQUOR) BREW SPLIT
(— WINE) GALLIZE
(VERY —) SMALL

DIM WAN BLUR DARK DULL FADE GRAY HAZY MIST PALE PALL VEIL BEDIM BLEAK BLEAR BLIND DUSKY DUSTY FAINT FOGGY MISTY STAIN UNLIT BEMIST BLEARY CLOUDY DARKEN GLOOMY OBTUSE SHADOW TWILIT BECLOUD DARKISH ECLIPSE OBSCURE SHADOWY TARNISH DARKLING OVERCAST

DIMENSION BODY BULK SIZE SCOPE WIDTH ASSIZE DEGREE EXTENT HEIGHT LENGTH BREADTH PROPORTION MEASUREMENT

DIMINISH GO CUT EBB SAP BATE BURN CHOP DAMP DROP EASE FADE FAIL FINE FRET MELT PARE PINK SINK WANE WEAR ABATE ALLAY BREAK CLOSE DRAFT DWARF ERODE LOWER MINCE PETER SLACK SMALL TAPER DAMPEN DEBATE DECOCT DEDUCT DILUTE IMPAIR LESSEN REBATE REDUCE SLOUGH VANISH WITHER ABRIDGE ASSUAGE CORRODE CURTAIL DEGRADE DEPLETE DEPRESS DETRACT DWINDLE FRITTER INHIBIT QUALIFY REFRACT RELIEVE TARNISH ADMINISH CONDENSE DECREASE DISCOUNT MITIGATE MODERATE RETRENCH

DIMINUTIVE TOY WEE BABY TINY BANTY DWARF PETTY RUNTY SMALL YOUNG BANTAM LITTLE MIDGET PETITE POCKET MINIKIN EXIGUOUS

DIMNESS DIM HAZE MIST SLUR GLOOM CALIGO DARKNESS

DIN REEL RIOT ALARM BABEL BRUIT CHIME CLANG NOISE ALARUM CLAMOR FRAGOR HUBBUB RACKET RANDAN RATTLE STEVEN TUMULT UPROAR CLANGOR CLATTER DISCORD TURMOIL

DINAH (BROTHER OF —) LEVI SIMEON
(FATHER OF —) JACOB
(MOTHER OF —) LEAH

DINE EAT SUP FARE FEAST REGALE

DINER EPICURE GOURMAND

DINGY DUN DARK BLACK DIRTY DUSKY GRIMY OURIE SMOKY FUSCOUS SUBFUSC SMIRCHED

DINNER HALL KALE MEAL MEAT NOON BEANO FEAST DINING REPAST BANQUET PUCHERO FUNCTION

DIOCESE SEE EPARCHY DISTRICT BISHOPRIC

DIONYSUS BACCHUS BROMIOS BROMIUS LENAEUS LIKNITES

DIP DAP DIB DOP SOP BAIL DROP DUCK DUNK LADE LAVE SINK SOAK BATHE DELVE LADLE LOWER MERSE PITCH SCOOP SLOPE SOUSE SWOOP TAINT CANDLE HOLLOW PLUNGE BAPTIZE DECLINE IMMERGE IMMERSE INCLINE MOISTEN DIPSTICK SUBMERGE GUACAMOLE

DIPLOMA DEGREE CHARTER CODICIL PARCHMENT SHEEPSKIN

DIPLOMACY TACT POLICE TREATY

DIPLOMAT DEAN ENVOY CONSUL ATTACHE MINISTER

DIPLOMATIC SUAVE FETIAL

DIPPER BAIL GAWN PIET PLOW GOURD HANDY LADLE SCOOP SPOON BUCKET DUNKER PIGGIN PLOUGH TUNKER DUNKARD PICKLER CALABASH

DIRE DERN EVIL FELL AWFUL FATAL DEADLY DISMAL DREARY TRAGIC WOEFUL DOLEFUL DRASTIC FEARFUL DREADFUL HORRIBLE TERRIBLE ULTIMATE

DIRECT AIM BID CON KEN SAY SET BEAM BEND BOSS CAST DEAD EDIT EVEN FLAT FULL GAIN HEAD HELM HOLD LEAD NEAR NIGH OPEN REIN SEND SOON SWAY TELL TURN WAFT WEND WILL WISE APPLY BLANK INDEX BURLY COACH DRESS ETTLE FLUSH FRAME FRANK GUIDE HIGHT INDEX LEVEL ORDER PLUMP POINT REFER RIGHT SPEED STEER TEACH TRAIN UTTER WRITE DEVOTE ENJOIN ENSIGN FASTEN GOVERN GRAITH HANDLE HOMELY HONEST IMPART INDITE INFORM INTEND LINEAL MANAGE MASTER REFORM SQUARE STEADY TEMPER ADDRESS APPOINT COMMAND CONDUCT CONTROL CONVERT DEICTIC DESTINE EXECUTE EXPRESS FRONTAL GENERAL INSTANT MARSHAL OFFICER PRESIDE ABSOLUTE ADMONISH CONVERSE DEDICATE DIRECTOR HOMESPUN INSTRUCT INTIMATE MINISTER OUTRIGHT REGULATE STRAIGHT
(— AGAINST) LAUNCH
(— ATTENTION) ATTEND
(— BLOW) MARK
(— DOGS) BLOW
(— FALL OF TREE) GUN
(— HELMSMAN) CON CONN
(— HORSE) HUP
(— ITSELF) TENT
(— ONE'S COURSE) HIT
(— PROCEEDINGS) PRESIDE
(— SECRETLY) STEAL

(— SIDEWAYS) SKLENT
(— TO GO) ADDRESS
(— UPWARD) MOUNT

DIRECTION (ALSO SEE MUSICAL DIRECTION) AIM RUN WAY BENT CARE DUCT EAST GATE HAND LEFT PART ROAD RULE WEST WORD YARD AEGIS ANGLE COAST DRIFT NORTH ORDER PARTY POINT RANGE ROUTE SENSE SOUTH TENOR TREND ASPECT COURSE DESIGN ADDRESS BEARING BIDDING CHANNEL COMMAND CONDUCT CONTROL COUNSEL DICTATE HEADING HELMAGE MANDATE PRECEPT STRETCH BEARINGS CALENDAR DIAGONAL GUIDANCE STEERAGE STEERING TENDENCY ORDINANCE ORIENTATION PRESCRIPTION
(— OF CURRENT) AXIS
(— OF FLOW) SET
(— OF ROCK CLEAVAGE) GRAIN
(— OF WIND) EYE CORNER
(— OUTWARD) BEAM
(—S FOR DELIVERY) ADDRESS
(DANCE —) CALL
(HORIZONTAL —) COURSE AZIMUTH
(OBLIQUE —) SKEW
(OPPOSITE —) EYE COUNTER
(SINGING —) GIMEL GYMEL
(PREF.) PHORO

DIRECTLY DUE BANG BOLT DEAD FLAT GAIN JUST MEAN PLAT SLAP SOON PLAIN PLUMB PLUNK POINT ROUND SHEER SMACK SOUSE SPANG CLEVER SIMPLY SQUARE RIGHTLY SHEERLY OUTRIGHT PROMPTLY SLAPDASH STRAIGHT PRESENTLY

DIRECTOR BOSS HEAD COACH GUIDE PILOT STAFF ARCHON BISHOP LEADER MASTER RECTOR WARDEN CURATOR MANAGER PREFECT TRAINER DISPOSER GOVERNOR PRODUCER

DIRGE KEEN SONG ELEGY HEARSE LAMENT MONODY REQUIEM CORONACH THRENODY ULLAGONE

DIRIGIBLE BLIMP AIRSHIP

DIRT FEN MUD DUST GORE GUCK MOOL MUCK NAST SOIL SUMP CROCK EARTH FILTH GRIME GROUT TRASH GRAVEL GROUND REFUSE MULLOCK SLOTTER MUCKMENT

DIRTY LOW RAY BASE CLAT DIRT FOUL MOIL MUSS SOIL WORY BAWDY BLACK CABBY DINGY FOGGY GRIMY GUSTY MUDDY NASTY SULLY BEMIRE CLARTY DEFILE DIRTEN FILTHY GREASY GRUBBY IMPURE MUSSED SLURRY SMIRCH SMUTTY SOILED SORDID STORMY BEGRIME CLOUDED MUDDIED PIGGISH ROYNOUS SCRUFFY SMUTCHY SQUALID SULLIED TARNISH UNCLEAN

DISABLE OUT HOCK LAME MAIM BREAK CHINK CROCK GRUEL UNFIT WRECK BRUISE DISMAY UNABLE WEAKEN CRIPPLE
(— CANNON) SPIKE
(— HORSE) NOBBLE
(— TANK) BELLY

DISABLED LAME INVALID

DISADVANTAGE HURT MISS RISK LURCH WORRY DAMAGE DENIAL INJURY STRIKE DICKENS PENALTY DISFAVOR HANDICAP

DISAGREE VARY ARGUE CLASH DIFFER DISCEPT DISCORD DISSENT QUARREL CONFLICT

DISAGREEABLE BAD ILL ACID EVIL FOUL PERT SOUR UGLY VILE AWFUL CROSS HARSH NASTY STIFF GREASY PUTRID ROTTEN SNUFFY STICKY UNEASY UNGAIN BEASTLY CHRONIC COMICAL GHASTLY HATEFUL INGRATE IRKSOME NAUGHTY UNLUSTY CHISELLY KINDLESS TERRIBLE UNGENIAL UNLIKELY UNLOVELY UNSAVORY

DISAGREEMENT BREE CLASH CROSS FIGHT BREACH FRATCH DISCORD DISGUST DISLIKE DISSENT FISSURE MISLIKE QUARREL WRANGLE ARGUMENT CLASHING DISTANCE DIVISION FRICTION SQUABBLE VARIANCE MISUNDERSTANDING

DISAPPEAR DIE FLY DROP FADE FALL FLEE LIFT PASS SINK WEND WHOP BREAK CLEAR FAINT LAPSE SLIDE SLOPE SNUFF REMOVE RETIRE VANISH EVANISH IMMERGE DISSOLVE EVANESCE
(— GRADUALLY) ELY FADE DRAIN EVANESCE
(— SUDDENLY) COOK DUCK BURST MIZZLE
(— UNEXPECTEDLY) LEVANT

DISAPPOINT BALK BILK FAIL FALL MOCK SOUR UNDO CHEAT SNAPE BAFFLE DEFEAT DELUDE OUTWIT THWART BEGUILE DECEIVE DESTROY FALSIFY NULLIFY DISPOINT

DISAPPOINTMENT RUE BALK SUCK BAULK LURCH DENIAL LETDOWN COMEDOWN

DISAPPROVAL BAN BOOH HISS VETO CATCALL CENSURE DISFAVOR DISGRACE

DISAPPROVE NIX GROAN REJECT RESENT CENSURE CONDEMN DISLIKE MISTAKE PROTEST DISALLOW DISPROVE HARRUMPH

DISARRANGE MESS MUSS DEFORM GARBLE RUFFLE TIFFLE UNTIDY UNTUNE CLUTTER CONFUSE DERANGE DISTURB RUMMAGE SLATTER TROUBLE COCKBILL DISHEVEL DISORDER UNSETTLE

DISARRAY MESS TASH RIFLE STRIP CADDLE DESPOIL UNDIGHT DISHEVEL DISORDER

DISASTER ILL WOE BALE BLOW EVIL FATE RUIN GRIEF MISHAP STROKE REVERSE ACCIDENT CALAMITY CASUALTY EXIGENCY FATALITY

DISASTROUS BAD ILL FATAL WEARY SINISTER

DISAVOW DENY ABJURE DISOWN RECANT REFUSE DECLINE RETRACT ABNEGATE DISCLAIM RENOUNCE

DISBAND BREAK REDUCE REFORM ADJOURN CASHIER DISMISS RELEASE SCATTER DISSOLVE

DISBURDEN RID EASE CLEAR UNLOAD DELIVER DISLOAD RELIEVE

DISBURSE SPEND DEFRAY EXPEND OUTLAY DEBURSE

DISC (ALSO SEE DISK) DIAL DISK BLANK MEDAL PATEN PLATE QUOIT COLTER RECORD RONDEL SQUAIL COULTER DISCOID PLATTER TROCHUS
(— FOR PRESSING HERRINGS) DAUNT
(FLOPPY —) DISKETTE

DISCARD CAST DECK DEFY JILT JUNK MOLT OMIT OUST SHED CHUCK DITCH FLING SCRAP SHUCK SLUFF THROW TRASH CHANGE DECARD DISUSE DIVEST EXCUSS REJECT SLOUGH ABANDON CASHIER DISMISS EXPUNGE FORSAKE ABDICATE JETTISON

DISCERN KEN SEE SPY WIT DEEM ESPY KNOW READ SCAN JUDGE SIGHT BEHOLD DESCRY DETECT DEVISE NOTICE PIERCE DISCOVER PERCEIVE

DISCERNIBLE EVIDENT VISIBLE APPARENT MANIFEST OBSERVABLE

DISCERNING SAGE WISE NASUTE SHREWD SUBTLE SAPIENT SAGACIOUS PERCEPTIVE PERCIPIENT PENETRATING

DISCERNMENT EYE DOOM GOUT TACT FLAIR SENSE SKILL TASTE ACUMEN INSIGHT ELECTION JUDGMENT SAGACITY SAPIENCE PERCEPTION PENETRATION

DISCHARGE AX DO CAN GUN RUN BOLT BOOT DUMP EMIT FIRE FLOW FLUX FREE GIVE KICK PASS POUR QUIT SACK SEND SHOT VENT VOID BLAST BLEED BRUSH CLEAR DRAIN EJECT EMPTY EXPEL EXUDE ICHOR ISSUE LOOSE PURGE RHEUM SHOOT SPEED START VOMIT WHIFF YIELD ACQUIT BOUNCE EFFECT EXCERN EXEMPT EXHALE FEEDER TICKET UNLOAD ABSOLVE CASHIER DEBOUCH DELIVER DISBAND DISMISS EXCRETE EXHAUST MISSION PAYMENT PERFORM QUIETUS RELEASE RELIEVE SATISFY CATAPULT COMPOUND DEFECATE DESPATCH DISGORGE DISPATCH DISPLACE EMISSION EVACUATE SOLUTION STREAMER
(— ARROW) TWANG
(— BULLET) DRIVE
(— CARGO) STRIKE
(— DEBT) MEET CLEAR ACQUIT LOOSING
(— DUTY) SERVE
(— FROM HORSE'S FOOT) FRUSH
(— FROM RESERVOIR) HUSHING
(— MATTER) WEEP
(— OF DEBT) SETOFF
(— OF GAS) FEEDER
(— OF STREAM) FALL SPOUT
(— SUDDENLY) HIKE
(BLOODY —) SHOW SANIES
(CANNON —) TIRE CANNON
(CONCENTRATED —) BARRAGE
(DISHONORABLE —) BOBTAIL

(ELECTRIC —) ARC SPARK LEADER
EFFLUVE STREAMER LIGHTNING
(ELECTRIC —S) STATIC
(HEAVY —) STORM
(SIMULTANEOUS —) SALVO
BROADSIDE FUSILLADE
DISCIPLE SON JOHN MARK JUDAS PETER
PUPIL ANANDA DORCAS HEARER
APOSTLE AUDITOR MATTHEW OVIDIAN
SCHOLAR SECTARY STUDENT ADHERENT
FOLLOWER SECTATOR
DISCIPLINE WHIP BREAK DRILL INURE
TEACH TRAIN TUTOR ETHICS GOVERN
INFORM PUNISH SEASON VIRTUE
CHASTEN CORRECT CULTURE EDUCATE
NURTURE SCOURGE DOCTRINE EXERCISE
INSTRUCT LEARNING MATHESIS
PEDAGOGY REGULATE RESTRAIN
TEACHING TRAINING TUTORING
PHILOSOPHY CASTIGATION
DISCLAIM DENY ABJURE DISOWN
REFUSE DISAVOW ABDICATE ABNEGATE
DISALLOW RENOUNCE
DISCLOSE OPE RIP BARE BLOW CALL
KNOW OPEN TELL BREAK UTTER BETRAY
BEWRAY DESCRY DIVINE EXPOSE
IMPART REVEAL UNBURY UNCASE
UNHASP UNROLL UNSHUT
UNVEIL UNWRAP CONFESS DEVELOP
DISCUSS DISPLAY DIVULGE EXHIBIT
EXPLAIN MANTLE UNCOVER DISCOVER
INDICATE MANIFEST
DISCOLOR FOX BURN FADE SPOT BLACK
SMOKE STAIN TINGE SMIRCH STREAK
TARNISH BESMIRCH
DISCOLORATION CORN BLEED SCALD
SPECK STAIN TINGE FOXING MILDEW
BURNING MELASMA BROWNING
CHLOASMA CYANOSIS DYSCHROA
SCALDING
(— OF FRUIT) SUNBURN
(— OF TURKEYS) BLUEBACK
(— ON CHOCOLATE) BLOOM
(— ON CURED FISH) RUST
(SMALL —) FRECKLE
DISCONCERT BASH BOWL FAZE FUSS
HACK ABASH BLANK DAUNT UPSET
WORRY BAFFLE PUZZLE RATTLE SQUASH
CONFUSE DISTURB FLUMMOX NONPLUS
PERTURB SQUELCH BROWBEAT
DISORDER
DISCONCERTED BLANK ASHAMED
RATTLED CONFUSED
DISCONCERTING BAFFLING
DISCONNECT UNDO SEVER DIVIDE
UNYOKE DISJOIN DISSOLVE DISUNITE
SEPARATE UNCOUPLE
DISCONNECTED LOOSE ABRUPT
BROKEN CHOPPY CURSORY RAMBLING
STACCATO
DISCONSOLATE SAD GLOOMY WOEFUL
DOLEFUL FORLORN UNCOUTH DEJECTED
DESOLATE DOWNCAST HOPELESS
DISCONTENT ENVY DISQUIET
SOURNESS
DISCONTENTED DUMPY RESTLESS
MALCONTENT

DISCONTINUE END DROP HALT QUIT
STOP BREAK CEASE CLOSE LETUP
DESIST DISUSE SUNDER DISRUPT
SUSPEND INTERMIT SURCEASE
DISCORD DIN JAR BROIL JANGLE
SCHISM STRIFE DISLIKE FISSURE
CONFLICT DIVISION FRACTION MISCHIEF
VARIANCE CACOPHONY
DISCORDANT AJAR RUDE CRONK
HARSH FROWZY HOARSE JANGLY
JARRING SQUAWKY ABSONANT
CONTRARY JANGLING
DISCOURAGE CARP DAMP CHILL DAUNT
DETER FROST DAMPEN DEJECT DISMAY
FREEZE STIFLE DEPRESS FLATTEN
INHIBIT DISPIRIT DISSUADE
DISCOURAGEMENT COLD DAMP CHILL
DAUNT REBUFF LETDOWN PUTBACK
DISCOURAGING CHILL DREARY
DISCOURSE RANT READ TALE TALK TELL
WORD FABLE ORATE SPEAK SPELL
THEME TRACT DILATE EULOGY HOMILY
PARLEY PREACH REASON SERMON
THESIS TONGUE TREATY ACCOUNT
ADDRESS COMMENT CONTEXT DECLAIM
DELIVER DISCUSS ENTREAT EXPOUND
GRAMMAR LECTURE NARRATE ORATION
PARABLE PRATING RECITAL TALKING
ARGUMENT COLLOQUY CONVERSE
LOCUTION PARLANCE SPEAKING
TRACTATE TREATISE PHILIPPIC
(— OF LITTLE VALUE) STUFF
(LAUDATORY —) PANEGYRIC
(LONG —) SCREED
(PROLONGED —) DIATRIBE
(RAMBLING —) RHAPSODY
(SERIOUS —) HOMILY
(SIMPLE —) PAP
(UNIMAGINATIVE —) PROSE
(PREF.) LOG(O)
DISCOURTEOUS RUDE SCURVY UNCIVIL
CAVALIER IMPOLITE UNGENTLE
DISCOURTESY CUT SLIGHT
DISCOVER RIP SEE SPY ESPY FEEL FIND
PICK CATCH LEARN SPELL DEFINE
DESCRY DETECT DIVINE EXPOSE IMPART
INVENT LOCATE REVEAL STRIKE DISCERN
DIVULGE EXHIBIT EXPLORE UNCOVER
UNEARTH CONTRIVE DECIPHER DESCRIBE
MANIFEST
DISCOVERY FIND TROVE DESCRY ESPIAL
STRIKE DESCRIAL
DISCREDIT FOUL SLUT DECRY DOUBT
DEFACE DEFECT ASPERSE BLEMISH
DESTROY IMPEACH SCANDAL SUSPECT
BELITTLE DISGRACE DISHONOR
DISTRUST REPROACH UNCREDIT
DISCREET SAGE WARY WISE CIVIL
HUSHED POLITE SILENT CAREFUL
GUARDED POLITIC PRUDENT CAUTIOUS
RESERVED RETICENT
DISCRETE ETERNAL DISTINCT
DISCRETION TACT OPTION WISDOM
CONDUCT COURTESY JUDGMENT
PRUDENCE
DISCRIMINATING GOOD NICE ACUTE

SHARP ASTUTE CHOICE NASUTE SELECT
CHOOSEY CRITICAL EXPLICIT
DISCRIMINATION EYE DOOM TACT
TASTE ACUMEN CHOICE FINESSE
RESPECT DELICACY SAPIENCE
DISCUSS AIR MOOT TALK ARGUE COVER
TREAT CONFER DEBATE DICKER PARLEY
BESPEAK CANVASS COMMENT CONSULT
DESCANT DISCANT DISCEPT DISCUTE
DISPUTE DISSERT EXAMINE NARRATE
TRAVERSE
(— AT LENGTH) BAT
(— CASUALLY) MENTION
(— EXCITEDLY) AGITATE
(— LIGHTLY) BANDY
(— QUICKLY) SKIP
(— TERMS) CHAFFER
(— THOROUGHLY) EXHAUST
(— TO EXCESS) VEX
DISCUSSION MOOT FORUM COMMON
CONFAB DEBATE HOMILY HUDDLE
PARLEY TREATY BARGAIN CANVASS
COMMENT COUNSEL DISCUSS DISPUTE
MOOTING PALAVER ARGUMENT
CAUSERIE CHINFEST COLLOQUY
DIATRIBE ENTREATY EXCURSUS
QUESTION
DISDAIN DAIN DEFY PRIDE SCORN SPURN
SLIGHT CONTEMN DESPISE CONTEMPT
DISDAINFUL COY DIGNE PROUD SAUCY
SLIGHT SNIFFY SNUFFY HAUGHTY
ARROGANT PROUDFUL SCORNFUL
SNIFFISH TOPLOFTY
DISEASE BUG FLU MAL ROT BATS CRUD
EVIL FLAW GOUT GRIP PEST SORE
AGROM BEJEL BENDS CAUSE CROUP
DECAY DOLOR FEVER GRIEF LUPUS
PINTA SHAKE SPRUE SURRA ANGINA
CANCER CARATE CORYZA DENGUE
GRAVEL GRIPPE HERPES MALADY
MORBUS PALMUS PIEDRA POPEYE
SCURVY SICKEN SURRAH UROSIS
ZOOSIS AILMENT CHOLERA DECLINE
ENDEMIC ENTASIA LANGUOR LEPROSY
MALEASE MISLIKE MYCOSIS MYIASIS
PATHEMA RAPHANY SCOURGE SEQUELA
SERPIGO SIBBENS SORANCE SYCOSIS
XERASIA ZYMOTIC ALASTRIM ATHEROMA
BERIBERI COXALGIA CRIPPLER
CYNANCHE DIAMONDS ENZOOTIC
JAUNDICE LEUKEMIA PALUDISM
PANDEMIC PELLAGRA RAPHANIA
SCABBADO SICKNESS SMALLPOX
SORRANCE STAGGERS SYPHILIS
UNHEALTH XANTHOMA ZOONOSIS
(— OF ANIMALS, GENERAL) ROT CLAP
CORE FIRE GOUT HUSK LICK WEED
APTHA CLEFT CLING CLOSH COTHE
CROOK DRUSE FARCY FLAPS NENTA
NGANA PAINS SPEED SWEAT TAINT
APHTHA AVIVES BROSOT CANKER
CARNEY CREEPS FARCIN GARGET
GRAPES LAMPAS NAGANA ROUGET
SPAVIN SURRAH WOBBLE ANTHRAX
BIGHEAD CALCINO CALORIS CARCEAG
DOURING EARWORM EQUINIA FASHION
FISTULA FOUNDER FROUNCE KETOSIS

LAMPERS MURRAIN MURRINA QUITTER
QUITTOR SLOBBER SOLDIER TAKOSIS
BULLNOSE CRATCHES CRIPPLES
FERNSICK FOOTHALT HORSEPOX
HYSTERIA MAWBOUND SLOBBERS
SNUFFLES THWARTER VACCINIA
EPIZOOTIC
(— OF APPLES) CORK BLOTCH
(— OF BANANAS) SIGATOKA SQUIRTER
(— OF BARLEY) STRIPE
(— OF BEES) SACBROOD
(— OF BEETS) HEARTROT
(— OF BIRDS) GOUT
(— OF BLUEBERRY) BLUESTEM
(— OF CABBAGE) ANBURY CLUBROOT
(— OF CATERPILLARS) WILT
FLACHERY
(— OF CATS) PANLEUCOPENIA
(— OF CATTLE) PUCK TURN BARBS
BLAIN CLOSH FARCY HOOVE HOOZE
SLOWS COWPOX GARGET GRAPES
HAMMER HEAVES ANTHRAX BLACKLEG
BLOATING
(— OF CEREALS) BRAND ERGOT
(— OF CHICKEN) PIP CORYZA
(— OF CHILDREN) PROGERIA
(— OF COTTON) HYBOSIS CYRTOSIS
STENOSIS
(— OF DUCKLING) KEEL
(— OF EYES) WALL GLAUCOMA
SYNECHIA TRACHOMA
(— OF FIGS) SMUT
(— OF FINGERNAILS) FLAW
(— OF FLAX) BROWNING
(— OF FOWLS) PIP CRAY ROUP GAPES
SOREHEAD
(— OF GRAIN) ILIAU ICTERUS
(— OF GRAPES) COLEUR ERINOSE
ROUGEAU ROUGEOT SHELLING
(— OF HAWKS) RYE CRAY CROAK
CROAKS FROUNCE FILANDER
(— OF HORSES) HAW CLAP CURB
MOSE MULE WEED FARCY LEUMA VIVES
APHTHA SCALMA THRUSH BARBELS
DOURINE QUITTOR SARCOID AZOTURIA
GLANDERS HORSEPOX STRANGLES
(— OF INSECTS) POLYHEDROSIS
(— OF LAMB) SWAYBACK
(— OF LETTUCE) STUNT
(— OF NARCISSUS) SMOLDER
SMOULDER
(— OF ONION) SMUDGE
(— OF ORANGE) LEPROSIS
(— OF PALMS) KOLEROGA
(— OF PLANTS, GENERAL) POX ROT
BUNT DROP FIRE GOUT KNOT PULP
SMUT DWARF EDEMA FLECK GRUBS
SCALD SCALE SCURF SPIKE TUKRA
TWIST AUCUBA BLIGHT BLUING BRAUNE
CALICO CANKER GIRDLE OEDEMA OIDIUM
PETECA STREAK VIROSE BLISTER
BLUEING BRINDLE CRINKLE DIEBACK
EYESPOT FROGEYE MEASLES PRURIGO
ROSETTE SHATTER STIPPEN TIPBURN
TOMOSIS VIRUELA WALLOON BREAKING
BUCKSKIN DARTROSE EXANTHEM
FLYSPECK GUMMOSIS MELANOSE

MELAXUMA POLEBURN PSOROSIS
RAPHANIA SMOULDER STENOSIS
VIROSITY WHIPTAIL WILDFIRE
CHLOROSIS
(— OF POTATO) CURL HAYWIRE
(— OF RABBITS) SNUFFLES
(— OF RICE) BLAST SPECK
(— OF SHEEP) CAW COE GID MAD RAY
ROT BANE BELT CORE HALT SHAB WIND
BLAST BLOOD BRAXY GILLAR OVINIA
PINING STURDY ANTHRAX BRADSOT
DAISING RUBBERS SCRAPIE THWARTER
WILDFIRE BREAKSHARE
(— OF SILKWORM) UJI CALCINO
GATTINE PEBRINE FLACHERY
(— OF SUGARCANE) ILIAU SEREH
EYESPOT
(— OF SWINE) GARGET
(— OF TOBACCO) ETCH CALICO
BRINDLE FROGEYE
(— OF TOMATO) FERNLEAF GRAYWALL
(— OF TONGUE) AGROM
(— OF TREES) KNOT CANKER
(— OF TULIPS) SHANKING
(— OF UNKNOWN ORIGIN) AINHUM
ACRODYNIA
(CAISSON —) CHOKES
(FATAL — OF NERVOUS SYSTEM)
KURU
(FOOT-AND-MOUTH —) AFTOSA
(FUNGUS —) PECK MYCOSIS
(KIDNEY —) RIPPLE
(LUNG —) CON
(MUSHROOM —) FLOCK
(PINK —) ACRODYNIA
(SKIN —) ACNE SCAB FAVUS HIVES
LEPRA MANGE PSORA RUPIA SCALL
TINEA ECZEMA LICHEN TETTER EXORMIA
PORRIGO PRURIGO PURPURA SERPIGO
VERRUGA CHLOASMA IMPETIGO
MILIARIA MYCETOMA SHINGLES
VERRUGAS VITILIGO PEMPHIGUS
(VENEREAL —) BURNING SYPHILIS
(WINE —) GRAISSE
(WOOLSORTER'S —) ANTHRAX
DISEASED BAD EVIL SICKLY MORBOSE
PECCANT VICIOUS MORBIFIC
DISENCUMBER RID FREE UNCUMBER
DISENGAGE FREE EDUCE UNTIE
DETACH EVOLVE LOOSEN CUTOVER
RELEASE UNRAVEL LIBERATE UNCLUTCH
DISENTANGLE CARD COMB FREE CLEAR
LOOSE RAVEL TEASE EVOLVE SCUTCH
UNMESH RESOLVE UNRAVEL UNTWINE
UNTWIST UNTANGLE
DISFAVOR DUTCH ODIUM DISLIKE
OFFENCE OFFENSE UMBRAGE MALGRACE
DISFIGURE MAR BLUR FOUL MAIM SCAR
TASH AGRISE DEFACE DEFEAT DEFORM
INJURE MANGLE BLEMISH DISGRACE
DISGUISE MUTILATE
DISGRACE BLOT FOIL FOUL HISS SLUR
SOIL SPOT ABASE CRIME ODIUM SCORN
SHAME SPITE STAIN TAINT BAFFLE
BEFOUL HUMBLE INFAMY REBUKE
STIGMA VILIFY AFFRONT ATTAINT
DEGRADE OBLOQUY OFFENSE REPROOF

SCANDAL SLANDER UMBRAGE
CONTEMPT DISHONOR IGNOMINY
REPROACH VILLAINY OPPROBRIUM
DISGRACEFUL MEAN SOUR FILTHY
INDIGN IGNOBLE CRIMINAL DEFAMOUS
INHONEST SHAMEFUL
DISGUISE DAUB HIDE MASK VEIL BELIE
CLOAK COLOR COUCH COVER FEIGN
GUISE SHADE VISOR COVERT MANTLE
MASQUE CONCEAL OBSCURE PRETEND
PURPORT COLORING PRETENSE
UMBRELLA
DISGUST IRK CLOY PALL LOATH REPEL
SHOCK STALL HORROR NAUSEA OFFEND
REVOLT SICKEN SURFEIT AVERSION
DISTASTE LOATHING NAUSEATE
DISGUSTING FOUL PERT VILE LOUSY
MUCKY NASTY FILTHY SICKLY BEASTLY
CLOYING FULSOME HATEFUL MAWKISH
NOISOME OBSCENE NAUSEOUS
SHOCKING
DISH CAP CUSH DISC MOLD PLAT SOLE
BASIN BATEA COMAL DEVIL NAPPY
PATEN PINAX PLATE CHINA BASQUE
BASSIE BICKER BLAZER BUTTER CHAFER
ENTREE FONDUE PANADA PHIALE
SAUCER SUNDAE TUREEN BOBOTIE
CEVICHE CHARGER COCOTTE COMPOTE
CRESSET DOUBLER EPERGNE PAPBOAT
PATELLA PLATEAU PLATTER RAMEKIN
SCUTTLE SUPREME TERRINE TIMBALE
COQUILLE GALATINE MAZARINE
ENTREMETS
(— IN PYRAMID STYLE) BUISSON
(— OF MEAT AND EGGPLANT)
MOUSSAKA
(BAKING —) SCALLOP
(BRAISED —) HASLET
(CHAFING —) CHAFER SCALDINO
(CONE-SHAPED —) BOMBE
(EXQUISITE —) AMBROSIA
(FANCY —) SURPRISE
(FLAT —) ASHET COMAL CHARGER
(HIGH-FLAVORED —) HOGO
(JAPANESE —) SUSHI TERIYAKI
(JEWISH —) CHOLENT
(PHILIPPINE —) BURO
(PIE —) COFFIN
(PILE OF —S) BUNG
(ROMAN —) LANX PATERA PATINA
(SAILOR'S —) BURGOO SCOUSE
(SCOTTISH —) BROSE
(SIDE —) OUTWORK
(SWEET —) JUNKET FLUMMERY
(TASTY —) MORSEL
(WOODEN —) CUP CAUP BOWIE
GOGGAN LUGGIE KICKSHAW
(PREF.) LECO
DISHEARTEN DAUNT FAINT DEJECT
DEPRESS FLATTEN UNNERVE DISPIRIT
DISHEARTENED DULL GLOOMY
DOWNCAST DEPRESSED
DISHEARTENING GLOOMY DESOLATE
DISHEVEL MUSS TOWSE RUFFLE TOUSLE
TUMBLE TRACHLE DISARRAY DISORDER
DISHEVELED BLOUSY FROWZY

TUMBLED UNKEMPT FROWZLED
SLIPSHOD TATTERED

DISHONEST FOUL LEWD CRONK CROSS
FALSE LYING QUEER SNIDE TWISTY
UNFAIR UNJUST CORRUPT CROOKED
JACKLEG KNAVISH INDECENT INDIRECT
SHAMEFUL SINISTER UNCHASTE
UNHONEST MENDACIOUS

DISHONOR FILE FOUL ABASE ABUSE
ODIUM SHAME SPITE STAIN WRONG
DEFAME DEFILE DEFORM INFAMY VILIFY
DEGRADE SLANDER VIOLATE DISGRACE
IGNOMINY REPROACH VILLAINY

DISHONORABLE BASE FOUL MEAN
BLACK NASTY SHABBY YELLOW DISLEAL
IGNOBLE SHAMEFUL UNHONEST
UNWORTHY

DISINFECT SCRUB SEASON CLEANSE
SWEETEN

DISINTEGRATE BEAT DUST MELT BREAK
DECAY ERODE GRUSH SLAKE SPLIT
MOLDER CRUMBLE DISBAND RESOLVE
SHATTER COLLAPSE DISSOLVE
SEPARATE

DISINTEGRATION DECAY BREAKUP
EROSION BIOLYSIS COLLAPSE HEARTROT
SOLUTION

DISINTERESTED FAIR CANDID
APATHETIC IMPARTIAL

DISK (ALSO SEE DISC) EYE NOB ORB
PAN SAW WAX WEB BURR CHAD DIAL
DISC FLAN FLAT KNOB PALM PUCK STAR
TUFT PATEN PLATE ROUND SABLE
SABOT SPILL TOKEN TRUCK WAFER
WHEEL BUMPER BUTTON CACHET
CARTON CORONA DISCUS HARROW
PALLET RECORD RONDEL SEQUIN
SHEAVE SQUAIL WASHER WEIGHT
CHECKER CHIPPER KNICKER MEDALET
PHALERA ROSETTE TONDINO EYEPIECE
RONDELLE ROUNDLET ZECCHINO
(— FOR BARRELING HERRING)
DAUNT
(— FOR CHEESE) FOLLOWER
(— FOR STRIKING HOURS) GHURRY
(— OF JELLYFISH) BELL
(— OF WAX) AGNUS
(— ON WOODEN ROD) SPILL
(BULL'S-EYE —) CARTON
(COIN-MAKING —) FLAN PLANCHET
(ECCENTRIC —) SHEAVE
(FLESHY —) SARCOMA
(HANDLED —) RIFFLE
(MEDICATED —) LAMELLA
(METAL —) SLUG MEDAL
(ORNAMENTAL —) BANGLE SPANGLE
(PADDED IRON —) SPINNER
(PAPER —S) CONFETTI
(POTTER'S —) BAT
(REVOLVING —) WAFTER
(ROTATING —) SCANNER
(SOLAR —) ATEN ATON

DISLIKE HATE LUMP MIND LOATH SPITE
DETEST PHOBIA REGRET SPLEEN DESPISE
QUARREL AVERSION DESPISAL DISFAVOR
DISTASTE DYSPATHY

DISLOYAL FALSE FELON UNTRUE
DISLEAL

DISMAL SAD WAN BLUE DARK DIRE DULL
GLUM GRAY GREY BLACK BLEAK DREAR
EERIE LURID SABLE SORRY SURLY
SWART WISHT DREARY GLOOMY LENTEN
SULLEN TRISTE DIREFUL DOLEFUL
FUNERAL GHASTLY JOYLESS OMINOUS
STYGIAN UNCOUTH UNHAPPY DESOLATE
DOLOROUS FUNEREAL LONESOME
SOLITARY MELANCHOLY

DISMAY FEAR RUIN ALARM DAUNT
DREAD FLUNK APPALL FRIGHT SUBDUE
TERROR DEPRESS DEPRIVE FOUNDER
HORRIFY TERRIFY AFFRIGHT CONFOUND
CONSTERNATION

DISMISS AX CAN BOOT BUMP BUST
CAST DROP DRUM FIRE KICK OUST QUIT
SACK SEND SHAB BREAK BRUSH CHUCK
DEMIT DITCH EJECT EXPEL FLUNK
SCOUT BANISH BOUNCE DISOWN
REJECT REMOVE SHELVE CASHIER
DISCARD DISPATCH RELEGATE
WITHDRAW

DISMISSAL AX BOOT SACK CHUCK
SHAKE BOUNCE REMOVAL DISPATCH

DISOBEDIENT BAD FORWARD FROWARD
NAUGHTY UNBUXOM UNGODLY
WAYWARD MUTINOUS

DISORDER ILL PIE CRUD FLAW MESS
MUSS RIOT STIR CHAOS CRACK DERAY
GRIME HAVOC REVEL SNAFU SPLIT
TOUSE UPSET BURBLE HUDDLE JUMBLE
LITTER MALADY MASTIC MUCKER
MUDDLE RUFFLE TOUSLE TROPPO
TUMULT UNTIDY AILMENT CLUTTER
COBWEBS CONFUSE DERANGE DISEASE
DISTURB EMBROIL FERMENT FLUTTER
GARBOIL ILLNESS MISDEED MISRULE
OUTRAGE PERTURB SHATTER TROUBLE
UNRAVEL UNSHAPE DISARRAY DISHEVEL
EPILEPSY NEUROSIS ROWDYISM
SICKNESS UNSETTLE COMMOTION
CONFUSION
(— OF BIRDS) PIP
(— OF EYES) HIPPUS
(— OF VISION) DIPLOPIA
(— OF WINES) CASSE
(COMPLETE —) CHAOS ANARCHY
(MENTAL —) INSANITY PARANOIA
(SPEECH —) LALOPATHY

DISORDERED ILL SICK WILD CRAZY
GAUMY LIGHT MESSY UNRID BLOTTO
FROWZY INCULT INSANE MUSSED
TURBID CHAOTIC CLOUDED FORLORN
TUMBLED UNSIDED CONFUSED
DERANGED DISEASED FEVERISH
FLURRIED INCHOATE

DISORDERLY RANDY ROWDY RABBLE
UNRULY BUNTING LAWLESS ROARING
CONFUSED FAROUCHE LARRIKIN
SLIPSHOD SLOVENLY SLUTTISH
SLATTERNLY

DISORGANIZE SHOCK UPSET CONFUSE
CONTUSE DERANGE DISBAND DISRUPT
DISORDER DISSOLVE

DISOWN DENY REJECT DISAVOW

RETRACT ABDICATE DISALLOW
DISCLAIM RENOUNCE REPUDIATE

DISPARAGE SLUR ABUSE DECRY LOWER
TRASH DEBASE LESSEN SLIGHT
DEGRADE DEMERIT DEPRESS DETRACT
DISABLE DOWNCRY IMPEACH BELITTLE
DEROGATE DIMINISH DISCOUNT
DISHONOR MINIMIZE VILIPEND

DISPARAGING SNIDE SLIGHTING
PEJORATIVE

DISPASSIONATE CALM COOL FAIR
STOIC SEDATE SERENE CLINICAL
COMPOSED MODERATE

DISPATCH RID FREE KILL MAIL NOTE
POST SEND SLAY WING BRIEF ENVOY
FLASH HASTE HURRY SHOOT SPEED
DIRECT EMPLOY HASTEN ADDRESS
COMMAND DELIVER EXPRESS CELERITY
CONCLUDE EXPEDITE TELEGRAM

DISPEL FRAY SHOO CHASE ASSOIL
BANISH DISCUSS SATISFY SCATTER
DISPERSE

DISPENSE DEAL DOLE EFFUSE EXEMPT
FOREGO SPREAD ABSOLVE ARRANGE
DISPEND DRIBBLE MINISTER

DISPERSE DOT SOW MELT ROUT SHED
LOOSE SCALE SEVER STREW DEFEAT
DILATE DISPEL SPARSE SPREAD UNKNIT
VANISH WINNOW DIFFUSE DISBAND
DISJECT DISMISS FRITTER SCATTER
SPARKLE DISSOLVE DISTRACT SEPARATE
SQUANDER

DISPIRITED LETDOWN SHOTTEN
DOWNCAST SACKLESS WOBEGONE

DISPLACE BUMP EDGE MOVE STIR
BANISH DEPOSE REMOVE DERANGE
UNHINGE UNPLACE ANTEVERT DISLODGE
DISPLANT MISPLACE SUPPLACE
SUPPLANT UNSETTLE

DISPLACEMENT BUMP SLIP HEAVE
SCEND SHIFT START OFFSET EVECTION
(— OF STAR) ABERRATION
(DOWNWARD —) PTOSIS
(OPTICAL —) PARALLAX

DISPLAY ACT AIR BRAG DASH ORGY
POMP SHOW SIGN STAR WEAR AGONY
ARRAY BINGE BLAZE BOAST DERAY
ECLAT EMOTE FLASH PRIDE SCENE
SHINE SIGHT SPLAY SPORT STAGE
VAUNT BLAZON DEPLOY DESCRY ESTATE
EVINCE EXPOSE EXTEND FLAUNT
MUSTER OSTENT OUTLAY PARADE
REVEAL RUFFLE SETOUT SPLASH
SPRANK SPREAD UNCASE APPROVE
BALLOON BRAVERY ETALAGE EXHIBIT
EXPRESS FANFARE FLUTTER PAGEANT
PRESENT SHOWING SPLURGE TRADUCE
UNCOVER BEEFCAKE BLAZONRY
BOOKFAIR CEREMONY DISCLOSE
DISCOVER EMBLAZON EQUIPAGE
EVIDENCE EXERCISE EXPOSURE
FLOURISH INDICATE MANIFEST
PARAFFLE SPLENDOR TINSELRY
(— EXCITEMENT) FAUNCH
(— OF COMPUTER TASKS) MENU
(— OF EMOTION) GUSH
(— OF SKILL) APPERTISE

(BOASTFUL —) JACTATION
(DARING —) BRAVURA
(EMPTY —) GAUD EYEWASH
(EXCESSIVE —) OSTENTATION
(FLORAL —) BLOW BLANKET
(IMPRESSIVE —) SWELL
(LAVISH —) PROFUSION
(OSTENTATIOUS —) DOG GAUDERY
SWAGGER
(RADAR —) SCAN

DISPLEASE VEX MIFF ANGER ANNOY
PIQUE OFFEND DISLIKE PROVOKE
IRRITATE

DISPLEASURE IRE ANGER MUMPS PIQUE
INJURY STRUNT UNWILL DISLIKE
OFFENSE TROUBLE UMBRAGE DISFAVOR
DISGRACE DISTASTE

DISPORT PLAY AMUSE FRISK SPORT
DIVERT FROLIC GAMBOL DISPLAY

DISPOSAL SALE CLEANUP BESTOWAL
DEVOTION DISPATCH

DISPOSE SET BEND CAST DUMP GIVE
MIND TRIM ARRAY ORDER PLACE POSIT
ADJUST ATTIRE BESTOW SETTLE
TEMPER APPOINT ARRANGE GESTURE
INCLINE PREPARE RESOLVE DISPATCH
REGULATE
(— OF) JOB SELL SCRAP FINISH HANDLE

DISPOSED APT FIT SET LIEF GIVEN
PRONE READY MINDED MINDFUL
WILLING ADDICTED TALENTED

DISPOSITION BENT BIAS MAKE MIND
MOOD RACE SORT TRIM TURN DRIVE
ETHOS FRAME HABIT HEART HUMOR
SPITE ANIMUS GENIUS HEALTH KIDNEY
NATURE SPIRIT TALENT TEMPER
CONCEPT FACULTY STOMACH APTITUDE
ATTITUDE PERSONALITY
(— OF DRAPERIES) CAST
(— OF PAWNS) SKELETON
(— TO ANGER) CHOLER
(— TO RESIST) DEFIANCE
(GENEROUS —) HEART
(GENIAL —) BONHOMIE
(KINDLY —) CHARITY HUMANITY
(NATURAL —) KIND GRAIN TARAGE
INDOLES
(ORNAMENTAL —) DECOR
(ULTIMATE —) FATE

DISPOSSESS OUST EJECT EVICT EXPEL
DEPOSE DIVEST BEREAVE CASHIER
DEPRIVE SEPARATE

DISPROVE BREAK REBUT NEGATE
REFUTE CONFUTE EXPLODE DISALLOW

DISPUTATION POLEMIC PROBLEM
WRANGLE ARGUMENT DEBATING
QUODLIBET

DISPUTE JAR ROW CALL CHOP DENY
FEUD FRAY FUSS HOLD RIOT SAKE SPAR
SPAT TILT ARGUE BRAWL BROIL CABAL
CHEST PLEAD ARGUFY BARNEY BICKER
DEBATE DIFFER FRATCH HAGGLE HASSLE
IMPUGN NAGGLE SQUALL BRABBLE
CONTEND CONTEST DERAIGN DISCUSS
FACTION GAINSAY QUARREL WRANGLE
ARGUMENT CATFIGHT QUESTION
SKIRMISH SQUABBLE

DISQUIET VEX FEAR FRET PAIN TOSS EXCITE UNEASE UNREST AGITATE ANXIETY DISTURB PERTURB SOLICIT TROUBLE TURMOIL

DISREGARD SIT OMIT PASS BELAY WAIVE FORGET HUBRIS IGNORE SLIGHT UNHEED CASHIER DESPISE NEGLECT OVERSEE DISCOUNT DISVALUE EASINESS OVERLOOK

DISREPUTABLE LOW BASE HARD GAMEY SEAMY SEEDY SHADY TOUGH SHODDY RAFFISH SHAMEFUL UNHONEST

DISREPUTE DISFAME DISFAVOR DISHONOR REPROACH

DISRESPECT AFFRONT CONTEMPT RUDENESS

DISRESPECTFUL SAUCY UNCIVIL IMPOLITE IMPUDENT INSOLENT

DISROBE STRIP CHANGE DIVEST DESPOIL UNDRESS

DISRUPT GASH REND TEAR BREAK CROSS HAMPER DISRUMP DISTRACT

DISRUPTION BREACH BREAKUP DEBACLE RUPTURE SOLUTION

DISSATISFACTION PAIN DISTASTE VEXATION
(FEELING OF —) BLAHS

DISSATISFIED UNEASY MALCONTENT

DISSEMBLE ACT FOX HIDE MASK CLOAK FEIGN BOGGLE CONCEAL DISGUISE SIMULATE

DISSEMINATE SOW BEAR BLAZE STREW EFFUSE SPREAD DIFFUSE PUBLISH SCATTER DISPERSE

DISSENSION JAR ODDS DEBATE STRIFE DISCORD DISLIKE DISSENT FACTION MISLIKE BROILERY DISUNITY DIVISION FRACTION FRICTION SEDITION

DISSENT VARY DIFFER HERESY CONTEND PROTEST DISAGREE

DISSENTER HERETIC SECTARY RECUSANT SEPARATE RASKOLNIK

DISSERTATION ESSAY THEME TRACT DEBATE MEMOIR SCREED THESIS DESCANT LECTURE MEMOIRS EXCURSUS EXERCISE TRACTATE TREATISE

DISSIMILAR UNLIKE DIVERSE

DISSIPATE BURN FRAY SPEND WASTE BANISH DISPEL EXPEND CONSUME DIFFUSE FRITTER RESOLVE SCATTER SHATTER DISPERSE DISSOLVE EMBEZZLE EVANESCE SQUANDER

DISSIPATED FAST HIGH LOST SPORTY OUTWARD RACKETY

DISSOLUTE LAX LEWD WILD LOOSE SLACK RAKISH UNTIED WANTON IMMORAL LAWLESS VICIOUS DESOLATE RAKEHELL RECKLESS UNCURBED

DISSOLUTION END RUIN DECAY BREAKUP DECEASE DIVORCE DIALYSIS
(PREF.) LYS(I)

DISSOLVE CUT END FADE FUSE MELT THAW BREAK LOOSE SOLVE UNFIX DIGEST RELENT UNBIND UNGLUE UNKNIT ADJOURN DESTROY DISBAND DISJOIN DISTILL DIVORCE LIQUEFY DISUNITE SEPARATE

DISTANCE WAY GAIT PIPE SPAN STEP DEPTH DRAFT RANGE SPACE GROUND LENGTH SPREAD STANCE STITCH BOWSHOT BREADTH FARNESS JOURNEY MILEAGE RESERVE STRETCH YARDAGE COLDNESS DIAMETER FOOTSTEP HANDSPAN LATITUDE OFFSCAPE OUTSTRIP
(— ALONG TRACK) LEAD
(— BETWEEN BATTENS) GAG
(— BETWEEN GEAR TEETH) PITCH
(— BETWEEN MASTS) INTERVAL
(— BETWEEN RAILS) GAUGE
(— BETWEEN RIVET-HEADS) GRIP
(— FOR PUTTING COAL) RENK
(— FROM BELLY TO BACK) BODY
(— FROM EQUATOR) HEIGHT
(— FROM LOCK FACE) BACKSET
(— FROM THE EYE) DEPTH
(— IN ADVANCE) START
(— OF ARCHERY RANGE) BUTT
(— OF BOW SHOT) CAST
(— OF HAUL) LEAD LEADAGE
(— OF TURNING SHIP) ADVANCE
(— OF VISION) KEN
(— ON FISHHOOK) BITE
(— ON GEAR WHEEL) ADDENDUM
(— OVER WHICH WIND BLOWS) FETCH
(ANGULAR —) ANOMALY
(AT A —) LARGE
(GREAT —) INFINITY
(INTERVENING —) GAP
(PERPENDICULAR —) DROP CAMBER ALTITUDE
(SAFE —) BERTH
(SEA —) OUTING STEAMING
(SHOOTING —) SHOOT
(SHORT —) INCH SPIT STEP SPELL BITTIE FOOTSTEP
(SHORT — AWAY) OUTBYE
(SMALL —) HAIR STEP

DISTANT COY FAR OFF AFAR AWAY BACK COLD YOND ALOOF HENCE REMOTE YONDER FARAWAY FOREIGN REMOVED STRANGE RESERVED

DISTASTE HATE DISGUST DISLIKE AVERSION MISTASTE
(— FOR FOOD) APOSITIA

DISTASTEFUL SOUR AUGEAN BITTER BEASTLY HATEFUL BRACKISH NAUSEOUS SHOCKING UNSAVORY REPUGNANT

DISTEND BAG BLOW FILL GROW HEFT BLOAT PLUMP STRUT SWELL WIDEN DILATE EXPAND EXTEND SPREAD BALLOON ENLARGE INFLATE STRETCH

DISTENDED BIG FULL PENT TAUT TRIG WIDE BLOWN POOCH TUMID GRAVID BLOATED SWOLLEN INFLATED

DISTINCT HOT FAIR FREE BRISK CLEAR PLAIN SHARP VIVID PROPER SUNDRY ANOTHER ASUNDER DIVERSE EVIDENT LEGIBLE OBVIOUS PRECISE SPECIAL APPARENT DISCRETE PALPABLE PECULIAR SEPARATE

DISTINCTION MARK NOTE RANK TEST CLASS GLORY HONOR FIGURE LAUREL

LUSTER RENOWN QUALITY SUBTLETY
REFINEMENT

DISTINCTIVE JUICY DIRECT PROPER
SIGNAL PECULIAR PHONEMIC SEPARATE
SPANKING TALENTED

DISTINCTLY CLEAR REDLY FAIRLY
CLEARLY

DISTINGUISH DEEM MARK SORT BADGE
JUDGE LABEL SKILL STAMP DEFINE
DESCRY DEVISE DIVIDE ENSIGN
CONCERN DISCERN DESCRIBE PERCEIVE
SEPARATE

DISTINGUISHED CLEAR GREAT NOTED
SWELL BANNER FAMOUS GENTLE
MARKED SOLEMN EMINENT NOTABLE
SPECIAL TOPPING DISTINCT ESPECIAL
LAUREATE RENOWNED SPLENDID
CONSPICUOUS

DISTORT WRY SKEW WARP CLOUD
COLOR FUDGE SCREW TWIST WREST
WRING CRINGE DEFACE DEFORM GARBLE
MANGLE WRENCH WRITHE CONTORT
FALSIFY GRIMACE PERVERT

DISTORTED WRY AWRY ASKEW CRANK
SKEWED WARPED CROOKED GNARLED
LOXOTIC DEFORMED DEGRADED
STRAINED PERVERTED

DISTORTION FIB SAG WREST STRAIN
FLUTTER GRIMACE GARBLING
SKEWNESS

(— IN WOOD) WARP DIAMONDING

DISTRACT AMUSE CRAZE BEMUSE
DIVERT HARASS MADDEN PUZZLE
TWITCH AGITATE CONFUSE DETRACT
DISTURB EMBROIL PERPLEX SCATTER
BEWILDER CONFOUND

DISTRACTED WILD CRAZY FRANTIC
FRENETIC

DISTRACTION ALARM BLIND ESCAPE
FRENZY TUMULT ECSTASY

DISTRAUGHT MAD CRAZED FRANTIC
DERANGED

DISTRESS AIL ILL MAR VEX BITE GNAW
HURT MOAN NEED PAIN PUSH TEAR
AGONY ANGER ANNOY DOLOR GRATE
GRIEF GRILL GRIPE LABOR PINCH PRESS
SMART TWEAK WORRY WOUND WRING
DANGER DURESS GRIEVE GRUDGE
HARASS HARROW LAMENT MISERY
SORROW STRESS AFFLICT ANGUISH
ANXIETY CHAGRIN DESTROY DISEASE
OPPRESS PASSION PENANCE PERPLEX
TORMENT TORTURE TRAVAIL TROUBLE
AGGRIEVE CALAMITY DARKNESS
DISTASTE EXIGENCE FORHAILE
PRESSURE SORENESS STRAITEN
GRIEVANCE

DISTRESSING BAD HOT SAD GRIM HARD
SORE BLEAK CHARY CRUEL DIRTY SHARP
BITTER SEVERE SHREWD THORNY
FEARFUL GRIPING PAINFUL GRIEVOUS

DISTRIBUTE DOT SOW CAST DEAL DOLE
GRID METE SEED SORT TAME ALLOT
CLASS DIVVY ISSUE PLACE SHARE SHIFT
SPEND ASSIGN ASSORT DEPART DEVISE
DIGEST DIVIDE EXPEND IMPART PARCEL
SPREAD ARRANGE DISPOSE PRORATE

SCATTER ALLOCATE CLASSIFY DESCRIBE
DISBURSE DISPENSE DISPERSE
SEPARATE SPRINKLE

DISTRICT AMT WAY WON AREA COIL
FARM HUNT PALE PART SIDE TEMA
WARD WICK WOON ANNEX EXURB
OKRUG PARTY SHIRE TRACT VICUS
AGENCY BARRIO BOWERY CANTON
CIRCLE COUNTY FOREST MEMBER
PARISH REGION SIRCAR STAPLE STREET
COMMUNE COUNTRY DEMESNE ENCLAVE
FREEDOM LIBERTY MAYFAIR MISSION
PIMLICO PURLIEU QUARTER SEASIDE
UPRIVER CHAPELRY DIVISION FAUBOURG
LEGATION PRECINCT PROVINCE
REGIMENT MAGISTRACY PREFECTURE
(— BORDERING RIVER) WATER
(— OF COURT) LEET
(— OF JAPAN) DO KEN
(BROTHEL —) STEW
(BURNED —) QUEMADO
(CHINESE —) HIEN
(COASTAL —) RIVIERA
(ECCLESIASTICAL —) SYNOD CLASSIS
DIOCESE
(HUNTING —) WALK
(ICELANDIC —) SYSSEL
(JUDICIAL —) CIRCUIT
(OUTWARD —) END
(POOR —) SLUM SLUMS
(POSTAL —) RAYON
(RURAL —) WAYBACK
(RURAL —S) STICKS
(RUSSIAN —) OBLAST STANITSA
(TENANT —) THIRL
(TRIBAL —) GAU
(TURKISH —) ORDU SANJAK

DISTRUST FEAR DOUBT DREAD STRIFE
SUSPECT DEFIANCE MISTRUST
QUESTION

DISTRUSTFUL SHY LEERY JEALOUS

DISTURB VEX BUSY FAZE FRET FUSS
JOLT RILE ROCK ROIL STIR TOSS ALARM
ANNOY KNOCK ROUSE SHAKE STEER
UPSET AFFRAY BOTHER HARASS JOSTLE
MOLEST RUFFLE SQUEAK AGITATE
COMMOVE CONCUSS DERANGE DISREST
FRAZZLE GARBOIL PERTURB SCUFFLE
SOLICIT STURBLE CONVULSE DISORDER
DISQUIET DISTRACT DISTRESS FRIGHTEN
(— BY HANDLING) TOUCH
(— SUDDENLY) START
(— THE PEACE) RIOT INQUIET

DISTURBANCE VEX BOIL CAIN COIL
DUST RIOT ROUT STIR WIND WORK
ALARM BRAWL BROIL FUROR HURRY
SHOCK STEER STORM AFFRAY BOTHER
BREEZE FRACAS FURORE HUBBUB
KICKUP POTHER RUCKUS RUMBLE
RUMPUS SHINDY SQUALL STATIC
TUMULT UPROAR BLUNDER BOBBERY
CHAGRIN CLATTER CLUTTER DISTURB
EMOTION FERMENT MADNESS RUCTION
TROUBLE TURMOIL BROILERY BUSINESS
DISORDER FOOFARAW INCIDENT
STRAMASH

DISUNITE RIP PART SEVER UNTIE

DETACH DIVIDE SUNDER UNKNIT
DISBAND DISJOIN DISSENT DIVORCE
UNRAVEL ALIENATE DISSEVER DISSOLVE
ESTRANGE SEPARATE UNSOLDER

DISUNITY DISCORD DISUNION DIVISION

DITCH RUT SAP SOW DELF DIKE GOUT
GRIP LEET MOAT SINK TRIG CANAL
DELVE FENCE FLEAM FOSSA FOSSE
GRAVE GULLY RHINE RIGOL SEWER
SLONK SLUIT STELL ZANJA GUTTER
HOLLOW TRENCH ZANJON ABANDON
CHANNEL

DITTO SAME REPEAT LIKEWISE

DITTY LAY POEM SING SONG THEME
VERSE SAYING VINETTA

DIVAN SOFA OTTOMAN SOCIABLE

DIVE BAR DEN DASH DUMP JOINT SOUSE
GAINER HEADER PLUNGE SALOON
BROTHEL JACKNIFE SUBMERGE
(KIND OF —) SWAN TWIST GAINER
JACKKNIFE

DIVERSE MOTLEY SUNDRY UNLIKE
VARIED ADVERSE SEVERAL VARIOUS
DISTINCT SEPARATE VARIETAL

DIVERSION GAME MASK PLAY FEINT
HOBBY SPORT SCHEME SOLACE DISPORT
PASTIME ESCAPISM PLEASURE
SIDESHOW

DIVERSITY CHANGE DISCORD DISSENT
VARIETY CONTRAST
(PREF.) POLY

DIVERT SWAY AMUSE RELAX SHUNT
DERAIL SIPHON SWITCH BEGUILE
DECEIVE DEFLECT DISPORT DISSUADE
DISTRACT ESTRANGE RECREATE

DIVEST BARE DOFF EMPTY SHEAR SPOIL
STRIP DENUDE DEPOSE DEPRIVE DESPOIL
DISROBE UNCOVER UNDRESS UNCLOTHE

DIVIDE CUT LOT CAST DEAL FORK PART
RIFT SHED SLIP TEAR ZONE BREAK
CARVE CLEFT DIVVY SCIND SEVER
SHARE SHIFT SLICE SPACE SPLIT BISECT
BRANCH CLEAVE DEPART DEVISE DIFFER
INDENT PARCEL RAMIFY SUNDER
ANALYZE ATOMIZE DISSECT DIVERGE
FISSURE FRITTER PRORATE ALLOCATE
CLASSIFY DISSEVER DISTRACT DISUNITE
FRACTION FRAGMENT GRADUATE
SEPARATE STRATIFY

DIVINE HOLY ATMAN AUGUR GUESS
PIOUS DEIFIC DETECT GODFUL PRIEST
SACRED BLESSED FORESEE GODLIKE
PORTEND PREDICT PRESAGE ARIOLATE
CONTRIVE FOREBODE FORETELL
HEAVENLY IMMORTAL MINISTER
SPIRITUAL

DIVISION BOX CUT DAG FIT JAG LEG
CHAP CLAN DOLE FARM FAUN FORK
HOLD LITH NEAT PACE PANE PART RANK
RIFT CHASM CLASS CLEFT CURIA DIVVY
FIELD FIGHT GRANT GROUP REALM
SHARD SHARE TAXIS THEME BARONY
CANTON COHORT DECADE DECURY
DEGREE DIVIDE SCHISM SEASON SECTOR
SUNDER BREAKUP CUSTODY DIOCESE
DUALISM FISSURE FURLONG KINGDOM
PARTING SECTION SEGMENT CATEGORY

CLEAVAGE DISTRICT PRECINCT SCISSION
SCISSURE SQUADRON
(— BETWEEN PIERS) BAY
(— BETWEEN STALLS) BAIL
(— FOR TAXATION) GELD
(— IN DENMARK) AMT
(— IN HUNGARY) COMITAT
(— IN MINING BED) CLEAVE
(— OF ANGELS) CHOIR
(— OF ARMY) BATTLE LOCHUS
(— OF BEJA) BISHARIN
(— OF BOOK) CHAPTER FASCICLE
(— OF BUILDING) STORY
(— OF CHARIOTEERS) FACTION
(— OF CHURCH) AISLE
(— OF CONTEST) HEAT INNING
(— OF COUNTY) RAPE BARONY
HUNDRED
(— OF CROPLAND) FLAT
(— OF DISCOURSE) HEADING
(— OF DRAMA) ACT SCENE
(— OF FAMILY) BRANCH
(— OF FIELD) RIG
(— OF FOOT) SEMEION
(— OF FOREST) WARD
(— OF GEOLOGICAL TIME) ERA EPOCH
PERIOD
(— OF GRASS) SPRIG
(— OF HEADLINE) BANK DECK
(— OF HERALDIC SHIELD) POINT
(— OF ISLE OF MAN) SHEADING
(— OF KENT) LATHE
(— OF LAND) LAINE KONOHIKI
(— OF LEGION) COHORT HASTATI
MANIPLE TRIARII
(— OF LOG LINE) KNOT
(— OF MANCHU ARMY) BANNER
(— OF MANKIND) RACE
(— OF MEAL) COURSE
(— OF NIGHT) WATCH
(— OF ORANGE) LITH
(— OF POEM) FIT DUAN CANTO
STANZA STROPHE
(— OF PROCESS) STAGING
(— OF ROCKS) SYSTEM
(— OF ROSARY) DECADE CHAPLET
(— OF SOCIETY) CASTE ATOMISM
(— OF SONG) FIT
(— OF STOPE) FLOOR
(— OF STRUCTURE) STAGE
(— OF SUSSEX) RAPE
(— OF TREF) RANDIR
(— OF UTTERANCE) COLON
(— OF WINDOW) DAY
(— OF YORKSHIRE) RIDING
(— OF ZILLAH) PARGANA
(— OF ZODIAC) SIGN DECAN
(— OVER ISSUE) BREACH
(ADMINISTRATIVE —) FU LATHE
CHARGE CIRCLE COUNTY EYALET
CUSTODY DIOCESE TOWNSHIP
(ANTHROPOLOGICAL —) STOCK
(ARMY —) MORA
(ASTROLOGICAL —) FACE
(CELL —) MITOSIS AMITOSIS
(ECCLESIASTICAL —) SCHISM SOCIETY
PRECINCT

(GEOLOGICAL —) ERA LIAS MALM
BUNTER KEUPER LUDIAN SERIES
LARAMIE ARNUSIAN RICHMOND
(HINGED —) LEAF
(ISLE OF MAN —) SHEADING
(MUSICAL —) ALLEGRO
(NUCLEAR —) FISSION
(PHILIPPINE —) ATO
(POLICE —) TANA THANA
(POLITICAL —) ATO CITY LATHE STATE
COUNTY PARISH BOROUGH HUNDRED
SURPLUS DISTRICT PURCHASE
WAPENTAKE
(POPULATION —) STRATUM
(SOCIAL —) HORDE
(TRIBAL —) CLAN
DIVULGE BARE CALL SHOW TELL BLURT
SPILL UTTER VOICE BABBLE IMPART
REVEAL SPREAD UNFOLD PUBLISH
UNCOVER DISCLOSE PROCLAIM
DIZZY CRAZY FAINT GIDDY LIGHT TOTTY
WOOZY FICKLE STUPID FOOLISH
SWIMMING UNSTEADY
DO ACT TRY BILK COME DEAL MAKE PASS
SUIT CHEAT EXERT SERVE TRICK
ANSWER COMMIT RENDER ACHIEVE
EXECUTE PERFORM PRODUCE SATISFY
SUFFICE TRANSACT
DOCILE CALM MEEK TAME FACILE
GENTLE DUCTILE DUTIFUL OBEDIENT
TOWARDLY
DOCK BOB CUT PEN CLIP MOOR PIER
QUAY SCUT BASIN SHORE WHARF
MARINA BOBTAIL CURTAIL SHORTEN
SHIPSIDE
DOCTOR (ALSO SEE PHYSICIAN) DOC
DOPE DOSE FAKE PILL HAKIM LEECH
SUGAR TREAT HAIKUN HEALER INTERN
MEDICATE PHYSICIAN MANIPULATE
DOCTOR'S DILEMMA
(AUTHOR OF —) SHAW
(CHARACTER IN —) LOUIS RALPH
CULLEN COLENSO DUBEDAT PATRICK
RIDGEON WALPOLE JENNIFER
BONINGTON BLENKINSOP
DOCUMENT BILL BOND BOOK CALL
CHOP DEED FORM SEAL WRIT CHART
DEMIT DIMIT LEASE PAPER PROOF SCRIP
TARGE TEACH TITLE BILLET BREVET
CEDULA DOCKET PATENT SCRIPT
SOURCE SURVEY TICKET VOLUME
ARCHIVE CONDUCT DIPLOMA ESCRIPT
EXHIBIT INQUEST LICENSE MISSIVE
PRECEPT WARRANT WAYBILL WRITING
CITATION CONTRACT COVENANT
MORTGAGE SCHEDULE SECURITY
BORDEREAU
DODECANESE (— ISLAND) KOS SYME
KASOS LEROS TELOS KHALKE LIPSOS
PATMOS NISYROS KALYMNOS
DODGE RIG SHY BILK DUCK GAME RUSE
AVOID CHEAT ELUDE EVADE FENCE
FUDGE GLOSS LURCH PARRY PLANT
SHIFT SHIRK SHUNT STALL TRICK
ESCAPE FIDDLE PALTER RACKET WHEEZE
DECEIVE EVASION PROFFER ARTIFICE
CROTCHET SIDESTEP

DOE ROE TEG FAUN HIND NANNY
ALMOND BISCUIT
(— IN 1ST YEAR) FAWN
(BLUE —) FLIER
DOER ACTOR AGENT MAKER AUTHOR
FACTOR FEASOR WORKER FACIENT
MANAGER ATTORNEY EXECUTOR
DOG PUG PUP CHOW FAUS GOER KIYI
MUTT PAWL STAG TRAY TYKE ARGOS
BEDOG BESET BOXER CALEB CANID
CORGI DERBY DODGE HOUND LIMER
PELON POOCH PUPPY RAKER SILKY
SLING SPITZ STALK WHELP AFGHAN
BARBET BARKER BAWTIE BEAGLE
BELTON BORZOI BOSTON BOWWOW
BRIARD BUFFER CANINE COCKER
COONER DANCER DETENT ESKIMO
FINDER GUNDOG HEADER HEELER
JOWLER MISSET POODLE RANGER
RATTER SIRIUS SUSSEX TALBOT VIZSLA
YAPPER YELPER BULLDOG CRAMPON
CREEPER GRIFFON LURCHER MALTESE
MONGREL SCOTTIE SKIRTER SLEUGHI
SPORTER STARTER TERRIER TUMBLER
WHIPPET YAPSTER ABERDEEN AIREDALE
ALEUTANT ALSATIAN CERBERUS
COACHDOG CYNHYENA DOBERMAN
ELKHOUND FISSIPED FOXHOUND
KEESHOND LABRADOR LANDSEER
LONGTAIL MALEMUTE SAMOYEDE
SEALYHAM SHEPHERD SIBERIAN
SPRINGER TURNSPIT VERMINER
WATCHDOG WATERRUG PEKINGESE
POMERANIAN AFFENPINSCHER
(— OF INDIA) PARIAH
(— OF LATHE) DRIVER
(— TRAINED AS DECOY) TOLLER
(BELGIAN —) SCHIPPERKE
(BIRD —) BOLTER
(CHAINED —) BANDOG
(CHINESE —) SHIHTZU
(DECOY —) PIPER
(ESKIMO —) HUSKY SIWASH
(FARM —) KOMONDOR
(FEMALE —) GYP SLUT BITCH DOGGESS
(FOXLIKE —) COLPEO
(GERMAN —) ROTTWEILER
(HUNGARIAN —) PULI KUVASZ
(HUNTING —) ALAN BRACH RACHE
RATCH BASSET HUNTER KENNET LUCERN
SALUKI SEIZER SETTER SLOUGH
COURSER DROPPER HARRIER POINTER
STRIKER
(JAPANESE —) AKITA
(LAP —) MESSAN SHOUGH
(LARGE —) DANE TOWSER MASTIFF
KOMONDOR
(LONG-HAIRED —) ALCO SHOCK
(MONGREL —) CUR BRAKJE DEMIWOLF
(NON-BARKING —) BASENJI
(PARTI-COLORED —) PIE PYE
(PET —) MINX LAPDOG MOPPET
(PUG —) MOPS
(PUNCH'S —) TOBY
(SHAGGY —) RUG OWTCHAH
(SHEEP —) CUR COLLIE KELPIE BEARDIE
MALINOIS SHEPHERD

(SMALL —) TOY FICE FIST DOGGY FEIST LAIKA PIPER DOGGIE AMERTOY SPANIEL PAPILLON PEKINESE
(VICIOUS —) TAEPO
(WATCH —) CUR GARM GARMR
(WILD —) ADJAG DHOLE DINGO GUARA JACKAL AGOUARA CIMARRON
(YELPING —) WAPPET
(PREF.) CYN(O)
DOGCART GADDER TUMTUM BOUNDER GADABOUT
DOG COLLAR TRASH
DOGFISH DOG HOE HOUND MANGO TOPER DAGGAR GALEID MORGAY BONEDOG GABBACK SPURDOG GRAYFISH SEAHOUND
DOGGED DOUR SULLEN DOGLIKE STUBBORN OBSTINATE
DOGGEREL NOMINY TRIVIA SINGSONG
DOGIE LEPPY STRAY
DOGMA CREED TENET DICTUM DOCTRINE DOCUMENT
DOGMATIC THETIC PONTIFIC POSITIVE ARBITRARY CONFIDENT PONTIFICAL
DOG SALMON CHUM KETA MORGAY DOGFISH
DOGWOOD OSIER SUMAC CORNEL CORNUS GAITER WIDBIN BARBASCO FISHWOOD
DOILY MAT TIDY NAPKIN
DOING ACT DEED FACT STIR EVENT ACTION FUNCTION PRACTIVE
DOLE LOT ALMS DEAL DOOL GIFT GOAL METE PART VAIL ALLOT FRAUD GRIEF GUILE MOURN POGEY SHARE DECEIT GRIEVE RELIEF SORROW CHARITY DEALING DESTINY HANDOUT PAYMENT PORTION BOUNDARY DIMENSUM DISPENSE DIVISION GRATUITY LANDMARK PITTANCE
DOLEFUL SAD DREAR HEAVY DISMAL DREARY RUEFUL FLEBILE DOLOROUS MOURNFUL TRAGICAL
DOLL TOY BABE MABY MOLL DOLLY KEWPIE MAIDEN MAUMET MOPPET MUNECA POPPET POUPEE PUPPET KACHINA
(— UP) SWANK
(PASTEBOARD —) PANTINE
(PREF.) PUPI
DOLLAR BALL BEAN BONE BUCK CASE FISH ROCK SCAD SKIN SPOT ADOBE BERRY DALER EAGLE WHEEL GOURDE PATACA DAALDER SMACKER FROGSKIN PATACOON SIMOLEON
(ONE MILLION —S) MEGABUCK
(SILVER —) SINKER
(SPANISH —) COB DURO COBBE
(THOUSAND —S) GEE THOU GRAND
DOLL'S HOUSE (AUTHOR OF —) IBSEN
(CHARACTER IN —) NORA RANK HELMER LINDEN TORVALD KROGSTAD CHRISTINA
DOLMEN SENAM TOLMEN CROMMEL CROMLECH MEGALITH
DOLOMITE ANKERITE PEARLSPAR

DOLOR GRIEF SORROW ANGUISH SADNESS DISTRESS MOURNING
DOLOROUS SAD DISMAL DOLEFUL GRIEVOUS PATHETIC
DOLPHIN INIA SUSU BOUTO WHALE DORADO TURSIO BOLLARD COWFISH SNUFFER CETACEAN MAHIMAHI PORPOISE
DOLT ASS OAF CALF CHUB CLOD FOOL MOKE PEAK POOP STUB BOOBY CHUMP CLUNK DUMMY DUNCE IDIOT NUMPS THICK BEFOOL OXHEAD BLUNTIE DAWCOCK DULLARD JACKASS SAPHEAD SCHNOOK BONEHEAD BOSTHOON CLODPATE DUMBBELL IMBECILE LUNKHEAD MACAROON MOONCALF NUMSKULL LAMEBRAIN
DOLTISH DULL STUPID FOOLISH PEAKISH SOTTISH TOMFOOL BESOTTED BLOCKISH DOLTLIKE
DOMAIN LAND BOUND BOURN REALM SCOPE STATE WORLD BARONY BOURNE COUNTY EMPIRE ESTATE SPHERE DEMESNE EARLDOM DOMINION LORDSHIP PROVINCE SEIGNORY STAROSTY
(— OF SULTAN) SOLDAN
(— OF THE UNCONSCIOUS) SHADOWLAND
(MATHEMATICAL —) FIELD
(NETHER —) HELL
(TRANSCENDENT —) HEAVEN
(WOMAN'S —) DISTAFF
DOMBEY AND SON (AUTHOR OF —) DICKENS
(CHARACTER IN —) GAY PAUL EDITH CARKER CUTTLE DOMBEY WALTER GRANGER FLORENCE
DOME CAP CIMA TYPE CROWN VAULT COCKLE CUPOLA EDIFICE CIMBORIO HEMIDOME
(— OVER TOMB) WELI
(BUDDHIST —) TOPE
(OBSERVATION —) BLISTER
(ROUND —) THOLUS
(SNOW-CAPPED —) CALOTTE
DOMESTIC HIND HOME MAID TABBY FAMILY HOMELY HOMISH INLAND INMATE MENIAL NATIVE SCALDER SERVANT FAMILIAR HOMEMADE
DOMESTICATE TAME ENTAME AMENAGE RECLAIM CIVILIZE
DOMESTICATED CADE TAME GENTLE INWARD DOMESTIC FAMILIAR
DOMICILE CRIB HOME SHED ABODE HOUSE MENAGE DWELLING RESIDENCE
DOMINANT BOSSY CHIEF FIFTH TENOR MASTER RULING SOVRAN CENTRAL REGNANT SUPREME DOMINULE SUPERIOR PARAMOUNT OVERBEARING PREPONDERANT
DOMINATE TOP HAVE RULE CHARM REIGN COERCE DIRECT GOVERN VASSAL BEWITCH COMMAND CONTROL ENVELOP POSSESS BESTRIDE DOMINEER OVERRIDE OVERSWAY OVERTONE
DOMINEER BOSS BRAG LORD RULE

BULLY FEAST REVEL TOWER COMPEL
COMMAND SWAGGER DOMINATE
OVERBEAR OVERLORD
(— OVER) RIDE HECTOR
DOMINEERING SURLY LORDLY
HAUGHTY ARROGANT DESPOTIC
MASTERLY MASTERFUL

DOMINICAN REPUBLIC
BAY: OCOA YUMA NEIBA RINCON SAMANA
ISABELA CALDERAS ESCOCESA
CAPE: BEATA FALSO CABRON ENGANO
CAUCEDO ISABELA MACORIS
CAPITAL: SANTODOMINGO
COIN: ORO PESO
INDIAN: TAINO
ISLAND: BEATA SAONA ALTOVELO
CATALINA HISPANIOLA
LOWLAND: CIBAO
MEASURE: ONA TAREA FANEGA
MOUNTAIN: TINA GALLO DUARTE
MOUNTAINS: NEIBA BAHORUCO
ORIENTAL
RIVER: YUNA OZAMA
TOWN: AZUA BANI MOCA PENA POLO
BONAO COTUI NAGUA NEIBA NIZAO
SOSUA HIGUEY OVIEDO SANCHEZ
BARAHONA SANTIAGO
VALLEY: REAL NEYBA

DOMINION RULE SWAY CROWN REALM
REIGN DOMAIN EMPIRE REGNUM
CONTROL DYNASTY KHANATE MASTERY
REGENCY CALIFATE IMPERIUM LORDSHIP
SEIGNORY SOVRANTY OBEDIENCE
DOMINO DIE BONE MASK TILE BLANK
JETON STONE DOUBLE MATADOR
VENETIAN
DON WEAR ARRAY DRESS ENDUE INDUE
THROW ASSUME CLOTHE INVEST
DONATE GIVE BESTOW PRESENT
DONATION GIFT GRANT PRESENT
BENEFACTION
DONE OVER BAKED ENDED GIVEN
COOKED THROUGH
(— BY WORD OF MOUTH) PAROL
(— CARELESSLY) SCAMBLING
(— FOR) GONE SUNK KAPUT FINISHED
(— IN PLAIN SIGHT) BRAZEN
(— POORLY) BOTCHY
(— TOGETHER) CONCERTED
(— WITHOUT DELIBERATION) SNAP
(— WRONG WAY) AWK
DON GIOVANNI (CHARACTER IN —)
ANNA ELVIRA MASETTO OTTAVIO
ZERLINA GIOVANNI LEPORELLO
(COMPOSER OF —) MOZART
DON PASQUALE (CHARACTER IN —)
NORINA ERNESTO PASQUALE SOFRONIA
MALATESTA

(COMPOSER OF —) DONIZETTI
DON QUIXOTE (AUTHOR OF —)
CERVANTES
(CHARACTER IN —) PANZA PEDRO
PEREZ ALONZO DAPPLE SAMSON
SANCHO TOBOSO GUINART QUIXOTE
CARRASCO DULCINEA NICHOLAS
ROSINANTE
DOOM LAW LOT DAMN FATE RUIN CURSE
DEATH JUDGE ADDEEM DECREE DEVOTE
CONDEMN DESTINE DESTINY FORTUNE
STATUTE DECISION SENTENCE
DOOMED FEY DEAD DONE LORN FATAL
DAMNED FORLORN ACCURSED FINISHED
DOOR LID DROP EXIT FOLD GATE SHUT
TRAP ENTRY HATCH JANUA VALVE
DAMPER JIGGER PORTAL RADDLE
WICKET BARRIER DOORWAY INGRESS
OPENING PASSAGE POSTERN ANTEPORT
ENTRANCE POSTICUM
(— IN MINE) STOPPING
(— OF ASH PIT) ARCH
(— OF MASONIC LODGE) TILE
(AIRPLANE —) CLAMSHELL
(HALF —) HECK HATCH
(ROMAN —S) FORES
(SLIDING —) SHUT SHOJI FUSUMA
TRAVERSE
(STORM —) DINGLE
(STRONG —) OAK
(TRAP —) SLOT SCRUTO VAMPIRE
DOORMAN FOOTMAN HALLMAN
DOORWARD
DOORWAY DOOR EXIT PORTAL OPENING
DOPE HOP LUG BOOB DRUG GOFF GOON
GOOP INFO BOOBY OPIUM PASTE STUPE
HEROIN INSIDE OPIATE LOWDOWN
PREDICT STUPEFY NARCOTIC
DORIS
(BROTHER AND HUSBAND OF —)
NEREUS
(FATHER OF —) OCEANUS
(MOTHER OF —) TETHYS
DORMANT FIXED INERT ASLEEP LATENT
TORPID RESTING INACTIVE SLEEPING
CONNIVENT
DORMER WINDOW LUCOMB MEMBER
DORMANT EYEBROW LUCARNE LUTHERN
DORMITORY DORM HALL HOUSE
HOSTEL BULLPEN CUBATORY QUARTERS
DOSE BOLE SHOT BROMO DRAFT STORE
TREAT DATION DOCTOR DOSAGE
DRENCH POTION BOOSTER BROMIDE
CAPSULE QUANTITY
DOT SET CLOT LUMP MOTE PECK SPOT
STAR TICK COVER POINT PRICK PUNTO
SPECK BULLET CENTER PERIOD STIGME
TITTLE TOCHER PUNCTUM PUNCTUS
SPECKLE STIPPLE FLYSPECK PARTICLE
SPRINKLE
(— IN CODE) DIT
(— ON FOREHEAD) BOTTU
(— ON PATCH OF DIFFERENT
COLOR) ISLET
(BLACK —) DARTROSE
DOTAGE FOLLY DRIVEL SENILITY
TWICHILD

DOTE ROT DOZE FOND LIKE LOVE TIRE
ADORE DECAY ENDOW BESTOW DRIVEL
DOTING FOND GAGA PAWING
DOUBLE BOW PLY DUAL FOLD SORE
TWIN CRACK DUPLE ROUND BIFOLD
BINARY BINATE DUPLEX MIDDLE DIPLOID
DOUBLET TWOFOLD BIVALENT
GEMINATE BIFARIOUS SIMILITUDE
(— IMPRESSION) MACKLE
(— IN POKER) STRADDLE
(— MUSICAL NOTES) AUGMENT
(— UP) BUCK JACKKNIFE
(PHANTOM —) FETCH
DOUBLECROSS BITCH CHEAT BETRAY
DECEIVE SWINDLE BUSINESS
DOUBLE-CROSSER RAT HEEL
DOUBLE-DEALING DECEIT DUPLICITY
DOUBLE-TALK NEWSPEAK RAZZMATAZZ
DOUBT FEAR DEMUR DREAD QUERY
WAVER BALANCE DUBIETY SCRUPLE
SKEPSIS SUSPECT SWITHER UMBRAGE
DISTRUST DUBITATE HESITATE
MISTRUST QUESTION STAGGERS
MISLIPPEN
DOUBTER CYNIC SKEPTIC DUBITANTE
DOUBTFUL JUBUS UNSURE DUBIOUS
FEARFUL JEALOUS PERHAPS WILSOME
BOGGLISH DREADFUL PERILOUS
WAVERING QUESTIONABLE
PROBLEMATICAL
DOUGH CASH DUFF MASA CRUST MONEY
PASTE CHANGE HALLAH NOODLE
SPONGE BRIOCHE MANDLEN TEIGLACH
(BISCUIT —) CAKE
(BREAD —) SPONGE
(FERMENTING —) LEAVEN
(FRIED —) SPUD
(NOODLE —) FARFEL
DOUGHNUT NUT SINK DONUT SINKER
CRULLER FATCAKE NUTCAKE OLYKOEK
SIMBALL TWISTER BISMARCK FASNACHT
DOUGHTY FELL TALL BRAVE VALIANT
INTREPID
DOUR GLUM GRIM HARD SOUR ROUGH
STERN GLOOMY MOROSE SEVERE
STRONG SULLEN OMINOUS TACITURN
DOUSE BEAT BLOW DUCK QUIT STOW
CEASE DOWSE RINSE SOUSE DRENCH
PLUNGE SLUICE STRIKE STROKE
IMMERSE DOWNPOUR
DOVE DOW KUKU JONAH CULVER
CUSHAT JEMIMA PIGEON COLUMBA
LAUGHER NAMAQUA SLUMBER
RINGDOVE
(— SOUND) CURR
(GROUND —) ROLA
(RING —) TOOZOO
(ROCK —) SOD
(SCALE —) INCA
DOVETAIL COG JAG MESH MERGE
TENON
DOWDY POKY FRUMP MOPSY TACKY
BLOWZY SHABBY STODGY UNTIDY
FRUMPISH SLOVENLY
DOWEL NOG PEG PIN STUD SPRIG
JOGGLE PINTLE
DOWN OFF CAST FELL FLUE FUZZ HILL
LINT MOXA PILE SOUR BELOW EIDER
FLOOR FLUFF FRIEZE LANUGO PAPPUS
HANDOUT HILLOCK PLUMAGE
DOWNLAND
(— AND OUT) QUISBY
(— AT THE HEEL) SLIPSHOD
(— THE LINE) ALONG
DOWNCAST BAD SAD DOWN ABJECT
GLOOMY HANGING DEJECTED HOPELESS
DOWNFALL PIT FALL FATE RUIN TRAP
ABYSS DECAY FINISH DESCENT ECLIPSE
UNDOING COLLAPSE DOWNCOME
DOWNPOUR RAIN BRASH DOUSE FLOOD
PLASH SPILL SPOUT DELUGE TORRENT
CATARACT AVALANCHE
DOWNRIGHT FAIR FLAT PURE RANK
BLANK BLUNT PLAIN PLUMB PLUMP
ROUND SHEER STARK ARRANT DIRECT
FAIRLY STURDY REGULAR ABSOLUTE
POSITIVE THOROUGH
DOWNWARD BELOW LOWER PRONE
DOWNWITH
DOWNY SOFT MOSSY NAPPY PILAR
PLUMY QUIET CALLOW FLOSSY FLUFFY
PILARY PLACID COTTONY CUNNING
KNOWING SOOTHING
(PREF.) HEBE
DOWRY DOS DOT GIFT DOWER SULKA
LOBOLA TALENT PORTION
DOXOLOGY GLORIA KADDISH
DOXY WENCH HARLOT
DOZE NAP NOD DORM DOTE DECAY SLEEP
SLOOM CATNAP DROWSE MUDDLE
SNOOZE SLUMBER STUPEFY
DRAB DAW FOX SAD DULL BLEAK DINGY
GRAVE HEAVY TRULL WENCH FRUMPY
ISABEL MALKIN POISON STODGY
PROSAIC PUCELLE EVERYDAY POMPLESS
DRAFT NIP SIP CHIT DOSE DRAG DRAM
DRAW GLUT GULF GUST ITEM LEVY PLAN
PLOT SUCK SWIG TOOT WORK BLAST
CHECK DRINK EPURE SLOCK SWILL
SWIPE TAPER WRITE DESIGN DRENCH
POTION PROJET REDACT RETURN
SCHEME SCROLL SKETCH ABBOZZO
DRAUGHT DRAWING OUTLINE PATTERN
PHILTER PROJECT BEVERAGE POTATION
(— OF A VESSEL) GAUGE
(— OF AIR) COOKE
(— OF COMPOSITION) SCORE
(— OF LAW) BILL
(— OF PATTERN) STRIP
(— OFF) SHED
(HEAVY —) WHITTER
(LARGE —) SCOUR CAROUSE
(MIDDAY —) NOONING
(ORIGINAL —) PROTOCOL
(ROUGH —) EBAUCHE BROUILLON
SCANTLING
(SLEEPING —) DORTER
(SMALL —) NIP SIP SUCK TIFF TIFT
DRAG DOG LAG HALE HOOK RASH SHOE
SLUR TOLL DEVIL DRIFT FLOAT LURRY
PLUCK RALLY SLIDE SNAKE SWEEP
TEASE TRAIL TRAIN TRAWL TRICE
DAGGLE DROGUE LINGER REMORA
SCHOOL TAIGLE DRAGBAR GRAPNEL

GRAPPLE SCHLEPP SKIDPAN ARRASTRA
DRAGSHOE
(— ALONG) LUG CRAWL SHOOL
TRAYNE
(— CARELESSLY) HIKE
(— DOWN) DEGRADE
(— FEET) SLODGE
(— FORCIBLY) SNAKE
(— HOME CARCASS OF GAME) TUMP
(— IN DEEP WATER) CREEP
(— JERKILY) SNIG
(— LOGS) SKID
(— OFF) HARRY
(— OUT) DRAWL
(PLANK —) RUBBER

DRAGON AHI LUNG WORM DRAKE
RAHAB NIDHOG VRITRA WYVERN
BASILISK DRAGONET NIDHOGGR
NITHHOGG
(— WITH 7 HEADS) HYDRA
(SEA —) QUAVIVER
(WINGLESS —) LINDWORM

DRAIN DRY FRY GAN GAW SAP SEW TOP
BUZZ COUP DALE DELF DIKE DRAG DRAW
GOUT GRIP LODE MILK SIKE SINK SOAK
SUMP TILE BLEED CANAL DRAFT DRILL
EMPTY GULLY LEECH RHINE SEWER
SHORE EMULGE FILTER FURROW GUZZLE
RIGGOT SIPHON SPONGE TRENCH
TROUGH ZANJON ACEQUIA ALBERCA
CARRIER CHANNEL CULVERT DEPLETE
EXHAUST SCUPPER SINKHOLE
(— DRY) JIB
(— IN FEN) LEAM
(— IN MINE) SOUGH
(— IN STABLE) GROOP
(COVERED —) THURROCK
(OPEN —) SIVER STELL
(SMALL —) TRONE

DRAM NIP MITE SLUG TIFF DRAFT DRINK
SOPIE CALKER CHASSE DRACHM JIGGER
SNIFTER MERIDIAN POTATION QUANTITY
(— OF LIQUOR) TOT SLUG SNIFTER
(— OF SPIRITS) NOBBLER

DRAMA MIME PLAY LEGIT OPERA
COMEDY NATAKA SOAPER TRAGIC
COMEDIA HISTORY THEATRE TRAGEDY
DUODRAMA MONODRAM PASTORAL
(DANCE —) KATHAKALI
(JAPANESE —) NO KABUKI
(MUSICAL —) OPERA SAYNETE
OPERETTA

DRAMATIC WILD VIVID SCENIC
THESPIAN

DRAPE HANG PALL VEST ADORN COVER
CRAPE WEAVE CURTAIN FESTOON

DRAPERY SWAG BAIZE DRAPE SCENE
CURTAIN REREDOS VALANCE MOURNING
(— ON BEDSTEAD) PAND
(PIECE OF —) HANGING

DRASTIC DIRE HARSH EXTREME RADICAL
RIGOROUS
(NOT —) BLAND

DRAW LUG TIE TOW TUG DRAG HALE
HAUL LADE LIMN LINE LURE PUFF PULL
RAKE SPAN TILL TIRE TOLL TREK VENT
CATCH DRAFT DRILL EDUCE ENDUE

EXACT HEAVE PAINT TRACE ALLURE
BUCKET DEDUCE DEPICT DERIVE DESIGN
DEVISE ELICIT ENGAGE ENTICE INDUCE
INHALE SELECT SKETCH STRIKE
ATTRACT BEGUILE CONTOUR DETRACT
DOGFALL EXTRACT INSPIRE PORTRAY
INSCRIBE INVEIGLE STANDOFF
(— A CARD) CUT
(— AIR) BREATHE
(— ALONG) TRACK TRAIN
(— APART) REAM DIVEL DIDUCE
DIVERGE
(— AWAY) DRAFT ABDUCT ENTRAIN
ABSTRACT DISTRACT
(— AWKWARDLY) SCRAWL
(— BACK) FADE REVEL START WINCE
ARREAR RETIRE REVOKE SHRINK
CRINKLE RECLAIM
(— BACK FROM) BLENCH FLINCH
RESILE TORFEL TORFLE
(— BACK LIPS) GRIN
(— BOLT) SLOT
(— BY SUCTION) ASPIRATE
(— DEEP BREATH) SUSPIRE
(— DRINK) BIRL
(— EARTH AROUND) HILL
(— FIRST FURROW) FEER
(— FORTH) EDUCE EVOKE FETCH ELICIT
DEPROME EXHAUST
(— IN) PINK
(— OFF) BROACH
(— ON) INDUE INDUCE SOLICIT
(— OUT) MILK SLUB EXACT SKINK
TRACT ELICIT EXHALE EXTEND
(— TIGHT) FRAP THRAP STRAIN
(— TOGETHER) COWL LACE COART
GATHER CRIMPLE
(— UP) FORM MAKE HUCKLE INKNIT
UPWALE

DRAWBACK OUT LETDOWN TAKEOFF
DISCOUNT PULLBACK

DRAWER TILL LIMNER LOCKER TILLER
ENTERER INTAKER SHUTTLE
(— OF WATER) GIBEONITE
(COAL —) PUTTER
(TYPEWRITER —) BED

DRAWERS PANTS SHORTS LININGS
PANTIES SHALWAR CALZONS
SHINTYAN PANTELETS

DRAWING CHALK DRAFT ENVOI EPURE
SEPIA CRAYON DESIGN DETAIL FIGURE
FUSAIN SKETCH CAMAIEU CARTOON
CROQUIS DIAGRAM HAULING ISOTYPE
PULLING RETRAIT CHARCOAL CROSSING
DOODLING FREEHAND FROTTAGE
HATCHING LINEWORK SANGUINE
SLUBBING SPECULUM TRACTION
TRANSFER TRICKING
(— BACK) ABDUCENT
(— IN) INDRAFT
(— OF LOTS) BALLOT
(— OUT) BATTUE
(COMIC —) CARTOON DROLLERY
(PREHISTORIC —) PICTOGRAM
PICTOGRAPH
(SIDEWALK —) SCREEVE

(PREF.) GRAMO
(SUFF.) GRAM
DRAY CART LORRY SCOOT SLOOP
  WAGON CAMION JIGGER SLOVEN
  WHEERY
DREAD AWE DREE FEAR FRAY FUNK
  WARD ANGST AWFUL DOUBT GRISE
  TIMOR AGRISE DISMAY ESCHEW HORROR
  TERROR ANXIETY DISMISS DRIDDER
  AFFRIGHT TERRIBLE
DREADFUL DERN DIRE AWFUL CRUEL
  DISMAL GRISLY HORRID AWESOME
  CAREFUL DIREFUL DRIDDER FEARFUL
  GHASTLY GRIMFUL HIDEOUS UNCOUTH
  DOUBTFUL HORRIBLE HORRIFIC
  PERILOUS SHOCKING TERRIBLE TERRIFIC
DREAM METE MOON MUSE REVE FANCY
  SWEVEN VISION AISLING AVISION
  CHIMERA FANTASY IMAGINE NIRVANA
  REVERIE ROMANCE CHIMAERA
  DAYDREAM PHANTASM SOMNIATE
  (FRIGHTENING —) NIGHTMARE
  (PREF.) ONEIR(O) ONIR(O)
DREAMER POET METER MUSARD
  FANTAST IDEALIST PHANTAST
DREAMINESS LANGUOR
DREAMY SOFT MOONY VAGUE POETIC
  FARAWAY LANGUID MUSEFUL ONEIRIC
  PENSIVE DREAMFUL FANCIFUL
  SOOTHING
DREARY SAD DIRE DREE DULL FLAT
  GLUM BLEAK CRUEL DRURY OURIE
  WASTE DISMAL ELENGE GLOOMY
  LONELY DOLEFUL HOWLING WILSOME
  GRIEVOUS WEARIFUL
DREDGE MOP DRAG SIFT SCOOP TRAIN
  DEEPEN SCRAPE SPONGE TANGLE
  SCALLOP EXCAVATE SPRINKLE
DREGS LAG MUD FAEX LEES SCUT SILT
  SUDS TAIL DRAFF DROSS DRUGS FOOTS
  GROUT JAUPS MAGMA BOTTOM DRAINS
  DUNDER FECULA MOTHER REFUSE
  SORDES SORDOR ULLAGE GROUNDS
  HEELTAP OUTWALE RESIDUE RINSING
  REMNANTS SEDIMENT SETTLING
  (— OF LIQUOR) TAPLASH
  (— OF MOLTEN GLASS) DRIBBLE
  (— OF SOCIETY) WASH LEGGE
  CANAILLE
  (— OF TALLOW) GREAVES
DRENCH DOSE HOSE SOAK BLASH
  DOUSE DRAFT DRINK DROWN SLUSH
  SOUSE STEEP SWILL BUCKET DELUGE
  DOUCHE IMBRUE INFUSE POTION SLUICE
  EMBATHE IMMERSE PERMEATE
  SATURATE SUBMERGE
DRESS AX BED DUB DUB FIG FIT HOE KIT
  RAG RAY RIG TOG BARB BEGO BOWN
  BUSS CLAY COAT COMB DESK GALA
  GARB GEAR GORE GOWN HONE HUKE
  MIDI MILL MINI RAIL ROBE SUIT TIFF
  TRIM TUBE TUCK VEST WEAR BIGAN
  BRAWS CLEAN CLOTH CRUMB CRUSH
  CURRY DIGHT DIZEN EQUIP FLOAT
  FROCK GUISE HABIT IHRAM MAGMA
  PREEN PRICK PRUNE SHAPE THING TRICK
  AGUISE ATTIRE ATTRAP BETRIM BROACH

CLOTHE ENROBE FANGLE FRAISE GRAITH
INVEST JELICK JUMPER KIRTLE MAGPIE
MULLET MUUMUU OUTFIT PLIGHT
REVEST SARONG SHEATH TOILET
ADDRESS AFFAITE APPAREL BEDIZEN
CHEMISE CLOTHES COSTUME DALLACK
DUBBING GARMENT GARNISH HARNESS
HATCHEL RAIMENT TOGGERY VESTURE
ACCOUTER ACCOUTRE CLEADING
CLOTHING DECORATE FEATHERS
HANDMADE ORNAMENT SUNDRESS
TAILLEUR VESTMENT EMBELLISH
(— A SKIN) WHEEL
(— DOWN) BRACE
(— ELEGANTLY) DINK
(— FISH) CALVER
(— FLAX) TED
(— FLINT) NAP KNAP
(— FOOD) SAUCE
(— FOR FELTING) CARROT
(— HAIR) TIRE TRUSS BARBER
(— HIDES) BEAM
(— HURRIEDLY) HUDDLE
(— IN FINE CLOTHES) DIKE BRANK
(— MEAT) LARD SHROUD
(— NEGLIGENTLY) MOB
(— ORE) VAN
(— OVER) STOP
(— SHEEPSKINS) TAW
(— SMARTLY) DALLACK
(— STONE) DAB NIG DAUB DRAG FACE
GAGE HACK GAUGE NIDGE POINT
SCABBLE SCAPPLE
(— TAWDRILY) BEDIZEN
(— UNTIDILY) MAB
(— UP) BUSK DILL ADORN ARRAY
PRANK PRIMP PRINK SPICK WATER
FETTLE TOGGLE BECLOUT BEDRESS
TITIVATE
(— VULGARLY) DAUB
(— WITH CHISEL) DROVE
(— WITH TROWEL) STRIKE
(— WORN BY MAN) DRAG
(— WOUND) PANSE BANDAGE
(COAT —) SIMAR
(EVENING —) FORMAL
(FESTIVE —) GALA
(INCOMPLETE —) DISARRAY
(LONG —) MAXI
(LOOSE —) SACK SACQUE
(MORNING —) PEIGNOIR
(ONE-PIECE —) CAGE
(PECULIAR —) LIVERY
(POPLIN —) TABINET
(RUSSIAN NATIONAL —) SARAFAN
(SHOWY —) BRAVERY
(SLEEVELESS —) SKIMMER
(STYLE OF —) GETUP
(SUFF.) ESTHES
DRESSED CLAD DONE BOUND BECLAD
  COATED COMBED HABITED GOFFERED
  (— GAILY) FRESH SPARKISH
  (— IN WHITE) CANDIDATE
  (LOOSELY —) DISCINCT
  (RICHLY —) BROCADED
  (ROUGHLY —) HEWN
  (SHOWILY —) BEPRANKED

(STYLISHLY —) SMART
(WELL —) BRAW GASH
DRESSER AMBRY ROBER TAWER BUREAU
FRAMER MODISTE CUPBOARD
DRESSING CAST GRAVY BEATING
BLANKET IODOFORM RAVIGOTE
REMOLADE SCOLDING STUFFING
MAYONNAISE
(— FOR WOUNDS) LINT SPONGE
(— OF STONE) SKIFFLING
DRESSMAKER SEWER SEAMER
MODISTE STITCHER COUTURIER
TIREWOMAN
DRESSY SHARP
DRIED SEAR SERE ADUST GIZZEN TORRID
WIZENED GIZZENED
DRIFT FAN JET SAG DUNE FORD HERD
PLOT RACK SILT TIDE TILL DRIVE DROVE
FLEET FLOAT FLOCK SENSE SLIDE
SLOOM TENOR TREND BROACH COURSE
DESIGN DRIBBLE GALLERY HEADING
IMPETUS IMPULSE LATERAL OUTWASH
PURPORT SETBOLT DILUVIUM DRIFTPIN
TENDENCY
(— LANGUIDLY) SWOON
(— OF CLOUDS) CARRY
(— OF SAND OR SNOW) WREATH
(— SIDEWISE) CRAB
(— WITH ANCHOR DOWN) CLUB
(DOWNWARD —) DROOP
(GLACIAL —) CARY TILL IOWAN
(RUBBLE —) HEAD
DRILL GAD JAR JIG RIG SOW TAP BORE
CORE SPUD AUGER BORER CHARK
CHURN DECOY PADDY THIRL TRAIN
TUTOR TWIRL WHIRL ALLURE BROACH
ENTICE FURROW JUMPER PIERCE
SCHOOL SEEDER SINKER CHANNEL
DRIFTER PLUGGER STARTER EXERCISE
INSTRUCT
DRINK GO ADE ALE BIB BUM FIX GIN
HUM LAP MOP PEG POT RUM RYE SIP
SUP TEA TOT BALL BEER BEND BOLL
BOZA BREW BULL BUMP CHIA COKE
COLA DRAG FIZZ FLIP HAVE HORN JAKE
LUSH NOGG PULL PURL SIND SLUG SOPE
SWIG TIFF AIRAH BEVER BINGE BOUSE
BOZAH BUBUD CIDER DAISY DRAFT
FLOAT GLOGG HAOMA JULEP LAGER
MORAT NEGUS PUNCH QUAFF ROUSE
SKINK SLOCK SMACK SMASH SMILE
SMOKE SNIFF SOPIE SWATS THING
TOAST VODKA ZOMBI ABSORB BRACER
BRANDY BUMPER BURTON CASIRI
CATLAP CAUDLE CHASER COFFEE
COOPER DIBBLE DRENCH EGGNOG
FUDDLE GIMLET GODOWN GUGGLE
HOOKER IMBIBE MESCAL POSSET
POTION RICKEY SCREED SHANDY SIPPLE
SIRPLE SWANKY TACKLE
TAMPOY TIPPLE VELVET WAUCHT
WAUGHT ZOMBIE BRAGGET BRIMMER
CHEERER CHIRPER COBBLER COLLINS
CONSUME CORDIAL DILUENT DRAUGHT
FLANNEL GUARANA INHAUST MORNING

NOONING PROPOMA SHERBET SIDECAR
SNEEZER SUCTION SUPPAGE SWALLOW
TANKARD TRILLIL APERITIF BEVERAGE
BRIDECUP COCKTAIL LIBATION
MAHOGANY POTATION QUENCHER
REFRESCO RUMBARGE SANGAREE
SPRITZER SYLLABUB TEQUILA
PHOSPHATE
(— AT DRAFT) TOP
(— EXCESSIVELY) TOPE BIBLE SOUSE
BEZZLE BIBBLE SWIZZLE
(— FROM FERMENTED MILK) AIRAN
KEFIR
(— GREEDILY) SLOP SWACK SWILL
GUTTLE GUZZLE
(— HEAVILY) TOOT SWINK
(— LIQUOR) TIP DRAM SOAK BOOZE
PAINT
(— NOISILY) SLURP
(— OF BEER) BUTCHER
(— OF BEER AND BUTTERMILK)
BONNY CLABBER
(— OF BEER AND GINGERALE)
SHANDYGAFF
(— OF IMMORTALITY) SOMA
(— OF INDIA) SHRAB
(— OF LIQUEUR) FRAPPE
(— OF LIQUOR) WET DRAM JOLT SHOT
SPOT TASS WHET SETUP WHIFF CALKER
JIGGER TASTER WETTING HIGHBALL
NIGHTCAP
(— OF MOLASSES) SWITCHEL
(— OF THE GODS) AMRITA NECTAR
(— OF VINEGAR AND WATER) POSCA
(— OFF) COUP
(— SOCIALLY) BIRL HOBNOB
(— SPARINGLY) BLEB
(— TO LAST DROP) BUZZ
(— UP) CRUSH EPOTE CAROUSE
EXHAUST
(— WITHOUT PAUSE) CHUGALUG
(ADDITIONAL —) EIK EKE
(ALCOHOLIC —) BENO BINO MIST NIPA
BOMBO BUDGE BUMBO DRAIN JOUGH
SHRAB SLING SNORT SNIFTER
(AUSTRALIAN —) BEAL
(BRAZILIAN —) ASSAI ASSAHY
(BUTTERMILK AND WATER —) BLAND
(CURRANT —) CASSIS
(DRUGGED —) HOCUS
(FARINACEOUS —) PTISAN
(FERMENTED —) BOSA MEAD BALCHE
MUSHLA PULQUE CASSIRI GUARAPO
(FREE —) SHOUT
(GREAT —) JORUM
(HALF-SIZED —) CHOTAPEG
(HEADY —) HUFFCAP
(HOT —) COPUS SALOP TODDY BISHOP
EGGHOT PLOTTY SALOOP CARDINAL
(INSIPID —) SLUM
(INTOXICATING —) AVA GROG SUCK
BOOZE KUMISS SCOTCH DRAPPIE
PAIWARI SWIZZLE SKOKIAAN
(INTOXICATING —S) SAUCE BOTTLE
(LONG —) SWIPE HIGHBALL
(MEAN —) LAP
(MEDICINAL —) ADVOCAAT

(MIDDAY —) NOONING MERIDIAN
(NARCOTIC —) KAVA
(NON-ALCOHOLIC —) GAZOZ COOLER
(PALM —) ASSAI
(PARTING —) BONAILIE
(POISONOUS —) DRENCH
(RUSSIAN —) OBARNE OBARNI
(SACRED —) HOMA AMRIT HAOMA
AMRITA
(SACRIFICIAL —) HOMA SOMA
(SMALL —) PEG DRAM SOPIE DALLOP
WETTING
(SOUR —) ALEGAR
(STRONG —) BUB HUM BENO SICER
FUDDLE SHICKER
(TASTELESS —) SLOP
(THIN —) SLOSH
(WEAK —) LAP BOOL BULL CATLAP
DRINKER SOT LUSH TANK POTER TOAST
TOPER BARFLY BENDER CUPMAN
LUSHER SOAKER SPONGE IMBIBER
INTAKER QUAFFER DRUNKARD
(EXCESSIVE — OF TEA) THEIC
(HEAVY —) JUICEHEAD
(WATER —) HYDROPOT
DRIP LIP DROP LEAK SILE WEEP DRILL
EAVES DRIBBLE LARMIER TRICKLE
DRIVE CA CAW COT FOG HOY JOG AUTO
BANG BEAR BEAT BUTT CALL CRAM
DING DRUB DRUM FLOG GOAD HACK
HERD HUNT HURL JASM JEHU KICK LASH
MOVE PICK PILE POSS PUSH RACK RIDE
SERR SINK SLOG SPUR STAB TOOL TURN
URGE BRAWL CHASE CHECK COACT
CROWD DRIFT DROVE FLAIL FORCE
HORSE HURRY IMPEL INFER LODGE
MOTOR PEDAL POACH PRESS PULSE
PUNCH ROUST SHOVE SLASH SMITE
SPANK TEASE ATTACK BATTER BEETLE
BENSEL CHARGE COMPEL CUDGEL
DEDUCE DERIVE FERRET HAMMER
HASTEN IMPACT JARVEY JOSTLE
PLUNGE PROPEL BLUSTER ENFORCE
IMPULSE OVERTAX SETDOWN TRAVAIL
CATAPULT CONATION SHEPHERD
TENDENCY MOTIVATION
(— A BALL) LACE SEND
(— A HORSE ONWARD) WHIG
(— AIR) BLOW
(— ANIMALS) HAZE
(— AT TOP SPEED) BARREL CAREER
(— AWAY) RID FIRK HUSH SHOO
BANDY EXILE FEEZE FLEME HOOSH
REPEL SMOKE SWEEP AROINT BANISH
DEFEND DISPEL ENCHASE DISPLACE
EXORCISE
(— BACK) RUSH REBUT REPEL CULBUT
DEFEND REBATE REBUFF RETUND
REPULSE REFRINGE
(— BACK AND FORTH) TENNIS
(— BEFORE STRONG WIND) SPOON
(— BRISKLY) JUNE
(— CLOSE BEHIND WHILE RACING)
DRAFT
(— CRAZY) BUG
(— DISTRACTED) BEDEVIL
(— FORTH) ISH

(— HARD) SWEAT HACKNEY
(— HOME) CLINCH
(— HURRIEDLY) BUM BUCKET
(— IN) CRAM DINT PILE TAMP INJECT
(— IN A PARK) TOUR
(— INTO THE GROUND) STUB
(— INTO WATER) ENEW
(— LOGS) SPLASH
(— OFF) KEEP LIFT EXCOCT
(— OFF STAGE) EXPLODE
(— OUT) BOLT FIRE DEPEL DROWN
EJECT EXPEL KNOCK WREAK AROINT
EXTURB ABANDON DISLODGE EXORCISE
PROPULSE
(— RECKLESSLY) COWBOY
(— ROUGHLY) CHOUSE
(— SLANTINGLY) TOE
(— TO BAY) EMBOSS
(— TO MADNESS) FRENZY
(— VIOLENTLY) THUD SMASH HURTLE
(— WITH BLOWS) SKELP COURSE
(— WITH SHOUTS) HOY HUE
(FREE GOLF —) MULLIGAN
DRIVER MUG HACK MUSH WHIP DRABI
URGER CABMAN CALLER COWBOY
FLYMAN HAULER JARVEY JOCKEY
MALLET MIZZEN MUSHER PONIER
STAGER VANMAN WAINER CATCHER
COCHERO FLANKER HACKMAN HOODLUM
HURRIER JITNEUR PHAETON SPANKER
TOPSMAN TRUCKER WHIPMAN
BANDYMAN BULLOCKY CALESERO
COACHMAN DRAGSMAN ENGINEER
GALLOWAY GOADSMAN IMPULSOR
JITNEUSE MOTORMAN OVERSEER
REINSMAN TEAMSTER WHIPSTER
(— OF ANIMALS) DROVER SKINNER
(— OF ELEPHANT) MAHOUT
(— OF OMNIBUS) PIRATE
(CAMEL —) SARWAN CAMELEER
(FAST —) JEHU SPEEDER
(FIELD —) HAYWARD
(PACK-HORSE —) SUMPTER
(SKILLFUL —) REINSMAN
(TOWPATH —) HOGGY HOGGEE
(PREF.) ELATRO
DRIZZLE DANK DRIP HAZE RAIN STEW
MIZZLE SCOUTHER SPRINKLE
(— OF RAIN) SKEW
DROLL ODD RUM COMIC FUNNY MERRY
QUEER WITTY JESTER JOCOSE AMUSING
BUFFOON COMICAL JOCULAR STRANGE
WAGGISH FARCICAL HUMOROUS
DROLLERY WIT JEST FARCE HUMOR
DROMEDARY OONT CAMEL DELOUL
MEHARI CAMAILE CAMELUS
DRONE BEE HUM DRUM IDLER SNAIL
THRUM BUMBLE BURDEN CHORUS
LUBBER BAGPIPE HUMMING SHIRKER
SLEEPER SOLDIER SPEAKER LOITERER
SLUGGARD
DROOL DRIVEL SLAVER DRIBBLE
SLOBBER SALIVATE

DROOP FAG LOB LOP SAG BEND DROP
FADE FLAG HANG LAVE LOLL PEAK PINE
SINK SWAG WEEP WILT MOURN BLOUSE
DANGLE DEPEND NUTATE SLOUCH
CURTAIN DECLINE FLITTER LANGUISH
PENDENCY

DROP DIP BEAD BLOB CAST DRIP DUMP
FALL GLOB GOUT OMIT SHED SILE SINK
SPOT STOP TEAR BREAK CLOTH DROOP
FLUMP GUTTA LAPSE LOWER MINIM
PEARL PLUMP PLUNK SLUMP SWOOP
CANCEL FUMBLE GOBBET PLUNGE
SINKER SLOUGH TUMBLE ABANDON
CURTAIN DESCENT DISCARD DISMISS
DISTILL DRIBBLE DROPLET EXPUNGE
FORSAKE GLOBULE GUTTULE INCURVE
PLUMMET RELEASE SPATTER DECREASE
(— ANCHOR) SLIP
(— AWAY) DESERT
(— BAIT IN WATER) DAP
(— BY DROP) DROPWISE GUTTATIM
(— DOWN) VAIL
(— IN) STOP HAPPEN INSTIL INSTILL
(— OF GIN) DAFFY
(— OUT) FLOUNCE
(CHOCOLATE —) DRAGEE
(THEATRICAL —) TAB SCRIM
(UNEXPECTED —) DOYST

DROPSY EDEMA ASCITES ANASARCA

DROUGHT THIRST ARIDITY DRYNESS

DROVE MOB ATAJO CROWD DRIFT FLOCK
MANADA DRIFTWAY

DROWN DEAFEN DRENCH STIFLE
INUNDATE OVERTONE

DROWSE NOD DOZE DRONE SLEEP
SNOOZE SLUMBER

DROWSY DOZY DULL LOGY HEAVY
NODDY SLEEPY SNOOZY STUPID SUPINE
SWOONY DORMANT LULLING NODDING
COMATOSE SLUGGISH LETHARGIC

DRUDGERY FAG MOIL SLOG TOIL WORK
LABOR SWEAT FAGGERY SLAVERY
TURMOIL

DRUG (ALSO SEE NARCOTIC) HOP ACID
ALOE ALUM CURE DOPE DULL HEMP
LOAD NUMB JALAP OPIUM RUTIN SALOL
SENNA SPEED SULFA TRUCK DEWTRY
HEROIN IPECAC MYOTIC OPIATE PEYOTL
POTION SIMPLE ANODYNE ASPIRIN
ATEBRIN BOTANIC DAMIANA DAPSONE
ECBOLIC ETHICAL HASHISH JAMBOOl
PHILTER QUASSIA STUPEFY STYPTIC
SURAMIN ZEDOURY ASPIDIUM ATARAXIC
BANTHINE HYPNOTIC KOROMIKO
LAXATIVE MEDICATE MEDICINE
NARCOTIC NEPENTHE PEMOLINE
SALIVANT SEDATIVE SPECIFIC TOXICANT
ZERUMBET ATARACTIC PAINKILLER
(— DOSE) HIT
(— IN TABLET OF VARIOUS COLORS)
RAINBOW
(— USER) ACIDHEAD JOYPOPPER
(BITUMINOUS —) MUMMY
(DEPRESSANT —) DOWNER
(ONE WHO USES A —) HEAD
(ONE WHO USES ILLICIT —S) FREAK
(STIMULANT —) UPPER

(STRENGTHENING —) ROBORANT
(VEGETABLE —) FINGER
(PL.) DRUGGERY
(PREF.) PHARMACO

DRUGGIST CHEMIST GALLIPOT

DRUM GIN BOWL DRUB ROUT SKIN SPOT
TOPH TRAP BONGO CONGA CRAWL
DRONE SNARE SWASH TABOR THRUM
ATABAL BARREL CROCUS RIGGER
TABRET TUMBLE TYMPAN BUBBLER
CROAKER FRUSTUM GRUNTER REDFISH
SNUBBER TAMBOUR TIMBREL TUMBLER
BAMBOULA BARBUKKA CANISTER
CYLINDER MOULINET TYMPANUM
(— AS SHIP'S SIGNAL) SHAPE
(— FOR WINDING ROPE) CAGE
(— IN WINCH) GYPSY
(— MADE FROM HOLLOW TREE)
GUMBY
(— OF CAPSTAN) RUNDLE MOULINE
(— ON WINDLASS) WILDCAT
(— UP BUSINESS) HUSTLE
(— UP INTEREST) BALLYHOO
(HEATED —) DRIER
(IGOROT —) GANGSA
(PAIR OF HINDU —S) TABLA
(REVOLVING —) GURDY RATTLER
(SUMERIAN —) ALA ALAL

DRUMS ALONG THE MOHAWK
(AUTHOR OF —) EDMONDS
(CHARACTER IN —) HON JOHN LANA
MARK YOST BRANT JURRY NANCY
WOLFF ARNOLD GAHOTA JOSEPH
MARTIN DEMOOTH GILBERT MCLONIS
SCHUYLER MAGDELANA MCKLENNAR

DRUNK CUT FAP WET GONE HIGH LUSH
NASE PAID RIPE SOSH BLIND BOSKY
LUMPY LUSHY MALTY MOPPY OILED
QUEER SHICK STIFF TIGHT TIPSY
BAGGED BLOTTO BOILED BOMBED
BUZZED CANNED FLUFFY GROGGY
JAGGED LOADED LOOPED MORTAL
POTTED SLOPPY SODDEN SOSHED
SOUSED SOZZLY SPONGY SPRUNG
STEWED STINKO STONED TIDDLY
ZONKED BLOTTER BONKERS BOTTLED
CROCKED PICKLED SHICKER SLOPPED
SMASHED SOZZLED SQUIFFY SWACKED
COCKEYED SQUIFFED STINKING
PIXILATED

DRUNKARD SOT LUSH SOAK BLOAT
DIPSO DRUNK RUMMY SOUSE TOPER
LUSHER SPONGE SHICKER STEWBUM
TIPPLER TOSSPOT BORACHIO SWILLTUB

DRY KEX SEC TED ARID BAKE BLOT BRUT
DULL KILN PINE SOUR WELT WIPE AREFY
CORKY DRAIN JUSKY MEALY PARCH
PROSY SANDY SWEAT VAPID WIZEN
BARREN BORING GIZZEN JEJUNE
SCORCH BRUSTLE INSIPID SAPLESS
SICCATE STERILE THIRSTY XEROTIC
TIRESOME
(— HERRINGS) DEESE
(— IN SUN) RIZZAR
(— PARTLY) SAMMY
(— UP) SERE WELK WITHER AREFACT
FORWELK SKELLER

(— WOOD) BEATH SWEAT SEASON
(NOT —) SWEET
DRYNESS ARIDITY DROUGHT SICCITY
XEROSIS HASKNESS AREFACTION
DUBIOUS FISHY DOUBTFUL DOUBTING
JUBEROUS PRECARIOUS QUESTIONABLE
(NOT —) EXPRESS
DUCK AIX BOB BOW CAN DIG DIP DOP
MIG PET WIO CHAP COLK COOT DIVE
DOGY DOKE JOUK LADY LORD SMEE
SMEW TEAL BOOBY BUNTY DILLY DODGE
DOUSE EIDER MOMMY NODDY PADDY
RODGE ROUEN SCAUP SHIRK SOUSE
SPIKE SPRIG STOOL BOBBER CANARD
FELLOW GARROT PEKING PLUNGE
QUANDY RUNNER SCOTER BARWING
BLACKIE BUMMALO DABBLER DRABBET
DUNBIRD FIDDLER FLAPPER GADWALL
GEELBEC GREASER MALLARD OLDWIFE
PINKEYE PINTAIL POCHARD REDHEAD
REDLEGS REDWING SCOOTER WADDLER
WIDGEON YAGUAZA BALDPATE BLUEBILL
BLUEWING BOATBILL BULLNECK
GARGANEY HARDHEAD IRONHEAD
MOONBILL MORILLON PIKETAIL
REDSHANK RINGBILL RINGNECK
SHOVELER SHUFFLER SQUEALER
WIRETAIL BERGANDER
(— AT CRICKET) BLOB
(MALE —) DRAKE
(STUFFED —) DUMPOKE
(YOUNG —) CANETON FLAPPER
FLOPPER
DUCT VAS MAIN PIPE TUBE VEIN CANAL
ALVEUS MEATUS URETER CHANNEL
CONDUIT PASSAGE TRACHEA AQUEDUCT
CALIDUCT EFFERENT
(PREF.) RHYN(O) VAS(I) VAS(O)
DUCTILE SOFT DOCILE FACILE PLIANT
PLASTIC PLIABLE TENSILE FLEXIBLE
TRACTILE
(PREF.) ELAST(O)
DUD FLOP LEMON STUMER FAILURE
DUDE FOP DANDY COXCOMB JACKEEN
DUDGEON PIQUE OFFENSE
DUE LOT OWE DEBT FAIR FLAT JUST
MEED OWED TOLL DROIT FATED MERIT
OWING COMING CUSTOM DESERT
EXTENT LAWFUL MATURE PROPER
UNPAID FITTING ADEQUATE DIRECTLY
RIGHTFUL SUITABLE
DUEL TILT FENCE FIGHT COMBAT
MENSUR CONTEST MEETING CONFLICT
DUFFER DUB MUFF SHAM CHEAT BUFFER
HAWKER RABBIT SHICER PEDDLER
DUGOUT ABRI CAVE BANCA BONGO
CANOE SHELL BAROTO BUNKER CAYUCO
CORIAL TROUGH BANTING PIROGUE
DULL DIM DOW DRY FAT LAX SAD ARID
BLAH CLOD COLD DAMP DEAD DILL DRAB
DRUG DUMB FLAT GRAY GREY LOGY
POKY SLOW TAME THIN BLACK BLAND
BLEAR BLUNT CRASS DENSE DINGY
DREAR DUSTY FISHY FOGGY GLAZY
GRAVE GROSS HEAVY INERT MATTE
MOSSY MUDDY MUSTY POKEY PROSY
SHADE SLACK SOGGY STILL SULKY

THICK UNAPT VAPID WASTE BARREN
BLEARY BOVINE CLOUDY DAMPEN
DARKEN DEADEN DISMAL DREARY
DROWSY FRIGID FRUMPY GLASSY
HEBETE JEJUNE LEADEN MUFFLE
OBTUSE OPAQUE PALLID SLEEPY
SODDEN SOMBER STODGY STOLID
STUFFY STUPID SULLEN TIMBER TORPID
TRISTE TURBID WOODEN BLUNTED
CONFUSE DOLTISH DRAINED DUMPISH
HUMDRUM INSIPID IRKSOME LANGUID
LUMPISH MUMPISH PROSAIC SOTTISH
STUPEFY TEDIOUS VACUOUS BACKWARD
BEFUDDLE BROMIDIC COMATOSE
DISCOLOR EDGELESS FRUMPISH
HEBETATE LIFELESS LISTLESS OVERCAST
PLODDING SLUGGISH STAGNANT
TIRESOME PINHEADED PONDEROUS
SATURNINE
(— EDGE OF) ABATE
(— IN MOTION) LOGY
(— WITH LIQUOR) SEETHE
(MENTALLY —) DOPY DOPEY BARREN
(PREF.) AMBLY(O) BRADY
DULLARD DOLT BOOBY DUNCE IDIOT
MORON BROMIDE DASTARD DOLDRUM
POTHEAD
DULLNESS HAZE CLOUD TORPOR
DIMNESS DOLDRUM FATUITY LANGUOR
OPACITY DUMBNESS HEBETUDE
SLOWNESS VAPIDITY STOLIDITY
DUMB DULL MUTE STONY SILENT STUPID
DUMBBELL DUMMY DUNCE HALTER
KNOTHEAD
DUMBFOUND DAZE STUN AMAZE
CONFUSE CONFOUND SURPRISE
DUMMY COPY DOLT MUTE SHAM FAGOT
EFFIGY PONTIC SHADOW
(SWORDSMAN'S —) PEL
DUMP TIP COUP FALL HOLE JAIL MUSE
NAIL EMPTY SHOOT GRIEVE PLUNGE
TIPPLE UNLOAD BOGHOLE COUNTER
DEPOSIT REVERIE SADNESS STORAGE
(MINE —) BURROW
(PL.) SUDS MOPES SADNESS
DUNCE ASS DOLT GONY BOOBY IDIOT
NINNY HOBBIL PEDANT DULLARD
SOPHIST NUMSKULL
DUNE BAR DENE MEAL MOUND TOWAN
TWINE BARKAN BARCHAN BARKHAN
(SAND —) DRAB SAIF SEIF
DUNGEON PIT CELL HELL HOLE VAULT
CACHOT DONJON PRISON CONFINE
REVOLVER OUBLIETTE
DUNK DIP SOP SOAK STEEP IMMERSE
MOISTEN
DUPE APE FOB MUG BOOB COAX CONY
CULL FOOL GULL HOAX LAMB ROOK
TOOL CHEAT CHUMP CONEY MOUTH
TRICK BEFOOL BUBBLE COUSIN DELUDE
MONKEY PIGEON SQUARE SUCKER
VICTIM CATSPAW CHICANE CULLION
DECEIVE MISLEAD SAPHEAD SWINDLE
HOODWINK
DUPLICATE COPY ALIKE DITTO SPARE
TALLY DOUBLE FLIMSY REPEAT COUNTER

ESTREAT MISLEAD REPLICA TWOFOLD
LIKENESS

DUPLICITY ART GUILE DECEIT TRICKERY

DURABLE FIRM HARD STOUT STABLE
STAPLE LASTING CONSTANT ENDURING
LIVELONG

DURATION AGE DATE LIFE SPAN TERM
TIME WHEN SPACE LENGTH PERIOD
LASTING INFINITE LIFETIME STANDING

DURESS FORCE DANGER CRUELTY
DURANCE COERCION HARDNESS
PRESSURE

DURING IN ON AMID OVER AMONG INTRA
WHILE AMIDST WHILST WITHIN
AMONGST PENDING
(PREF.) DIA INTRA

DUSK DIM EVE DARK GLOOM DIMNESS
DARKNESS GLOAMING OWLLIGHT
TWILIGHT NIGHTFALL

DUSKY DIM DUN SAD WAN DARK BLACK
BROWN DINGY GRIMY MOORY TAWNY
GLOOMY PHAEIC SMUTTY SOMBER
OBSCURE SUBFUSC SWARTHY BLACKISH
(PREF.) PERCNO PHAEO

DUST DIRT FOGO MUCK MULL SMUT
CLEAN FLOUR STOUR DREDGE POLLEN
POWDER SMEECH EBURINE REMAINS
SMEDDUM TURMOIL ANTELOPE
PUMICITE
(— IN FLOUR MILLS) STIVE
(— IN QUARTZ MILL) SLICKENS
(BLOOD —) HEMOCONIA
(CHOKING —) POTHER
(COAL —) COOM CULM DUFF
(COKE —) BREEZE
(COSMIC —) STARDUST
(DIAMOND —) SEASONING
(FIBER —) FLOCK
(FLAX —) POUCE
(THICK —) SMOTHER

DUSTY ADUST MOTTY POUCEY STOURY
POWDERY

DUTIFUL PIOUS DOCILE LAWFUL
OBEDIENT OFFICIAL REVERENT
OFFICIOUS

DUTY JOB LOT TAX CALL CARE ONUS
PART PROW ROLE TASK TASK TOLL
CHORE DEVER LADLE OUGHT RIGHT
STINT BLANCH BURDEN CHARGE DEVOIR
DHARMA EXCISE EXITUS IMPOSE IMPOST
OFFICE TARIFF AVERAGE ROYALTY
SCAVAGE SERVICE STATION TRIBUTE
BUSINESS FUNCTION OBLIGATION
(— FOR LEAD ORE) COPE
(CUSTOMS —) OCTROI
(FEUDAL —) HERIOT
(IMPORT —) ERMIN INDULTO
(MILITARY —) STABLES
(TIRING —) FATIGUE

DWARF ELF PUG URF AETA GRIG NANA
RUNT GNOME KNURL MIDGE PYGMY
SCRUB STUNT TROLL MIDGET SHRIMP
MANIKIN OVERTOP ALBERICH BELITTLE
HOMUNCIO

DWELL COT DIG SIT BIDE LIVE STAY
WONT ABIDE BOWER BROOD BUILD
DELAY HOUSE LODGE PAUSE SHACK

STALL TARRY LINGER REMAIN RESIDE
TENANT INHABIT

DWELLER TENANT DENIZEN DOWNSMAN
HABITANT OCCUPANT RESIDENT

DWELLING DAR HUT INN SEE WON CASA
FARM FLAT FORT HAFT HALL HOME NEST
ROOF SLUM TENT WIKE ABODE CABIN
DOMUS HOOCH HOUSE HOVEL
JOINT MANSE MOTEL PLACE CASTLE
DUGOUT DUPLEX HOMING MALOCA
TEEPEE WIGWAM COTTAGE LODGING
MANSION SALTBOX TRAILER TRIPLEX
BUILDING BUNGALOW DOMICILE
TENEMENT PENTHOUSE RESIDENCE
(— IN UNDERWORLD) CHTHONIC
(ATTRACTIVE —) BOWER
(CRUDE —) SHED SHEBANG
(LAKE —) CRANNOG PALAFITTE
(MEAN —) SHANTY
(MISERABLE —) BURROW DOGHOLE
(NAVAJO —) HOGAN
(NEOLITHIC —) TERRAMARA
(ONE-ROOM —) CELL
(PORTABLE —) CAMPER
(RAMSHACKLE —) HUMPY
(RUDE —) BOTHY
(SMALL —) CRIB
(SUBTERRANEAN —) WEEM
(SWISS —) CHALET

DWINDLE FADE FAIL MELT PINE WANE
DECAY DRAIN PETER TAPER TRAIL
WASTE MOLDER SHRINK CONSUME
DECLINE FRITTER DECREASE DIMINISH

DYE DIP ANIL COLOR FUCUS IMBUE STAIN
TINCT VENOM IMBRUE INFECT MADDER
TINGER ENGRAIN LOGWOOD PUCCOON
COLORANT DYESTUFF FUGITIVE
TINCTURE
(— FUR) FEATHER
(— NOT FAST) FUGITIVE
(BLACK —) GUAKO
(BLUE —) RUM ROOM SAXE WOAD
CYANINE DICYANINE
(BROWN —) CACHOU
(GENERAL —S) NIL AZINE BROWN
GREEN DIANIL ISAMIN ORANGE PURPLE
VIOLET CYANINE METANIL PONCEAU
PRIMULA ALIZARIN AURANTIA CIBACRON
DICYANIN EURHODOL FUCHSINE
HYPERNIC INDULINE NIGROSIN
TURNSOLE VIRIDINE NIGROSINE
SAFRANINE
(HAIR —) RASTIK
(KIND OF —) SRA
(ORANGE —) KAMALA ROUCOU
(PURPLE —) CASSIUS GALLEIN
TURNSOLE
(RED —) AAL AURIN EOSIN GRAIN
HENNA RUBIN AURINE CERISE RELBUN
RUBINE ALKANET ANNATTO CORINTH
CRIMSON MAGENTA PONCEAU SAFFLOR
ALIZARIN AMARANTH BORDEAUX
CORALLIN CROCEINE
(SCARLET —) TULY GRAIN
(VIOLET —) MAUVE ARCHIL ORCHIL
LACMOID

(YELLOW —) ARUSA FLAVIN CHRYSIN
FISETIN LAWSONE WONGSHY AURAMINE
DYING FEY DEATH MORENDO PARTING
MORIBUND
(— AWAY) CALANDO DILUENDO
MANCANDO PERDENDO SMORZATO
DYNAMIC POTENT DRIVING KINETIC
FORCEFUL

DYNAMITE BLAST SAWDUST RENDROCK
GELIGNITE
DYNAMO EXCITER TORNADO
(PART OF —) BRUSH FIELD FRAME
RIGGING ARMATURE COUPLING
COMMUTATOR
DYSENTERY FLUX SCOUR MENISON
TOXEMIA DIARRHEA

E

E EASY ECHO

EACH A EA UP ALL ILK THE ILKA EVERY APIECE EITHER EVERYONE

EAGER HOT RAD YAN ACID AGOG AVID EDGY FAIN FELL FOND FREE GAIR HIGH KEEN RATH SOUR TARE THRO VAIN WARM WAVE YARE YERN AFIRE AGASP ANTSY BRIEF FIRST FRACK FRECK HASTY ITCHY PRIME READY SHARP SNELL YIVER ARDENT FIERCE GREEDY HETTER INTENT STRONG TIPTOE ANXIOUS ATHIRST BRITTLE BURNING EXCITED FERVENT FORWARD ITCHING PROVOKE DESIROUS SPIRITED VIGOROUS YEARNING SOLICITOUS

EAGERLY FAST FELL YERN HOTLY BELIVE TIPTOE YARELY YEPELY PRESTLY HUNGRILY INTENTLY

EAGERNESS GOG ELAN GARE ZEAL ARDOR DESIRE FERVOR ARDENCY AVIDITY ALACRITY CUPIDITY DEVOTION FAINNESS FERVENCY

EAGLE AAR CROW GIER TERN HARPY AQUILA BERGUT EAGLET FALCON FORMAL FORMEL RAPTOR ALLERION BATELEUR BEARCOOT BERGHAAN RINGTAIL

(SEA —) ERN ERNE PYGARG

(PREF.) AET(O)

(SUFF.) AETUS

EAGLE OWL KATOGLE

EAGLESTONE AETITES

EAGLEWOOD AGAR AGILA ALOES AGALLOCH AQUILARI

EAR LUG NEB CLIP HEAR HEED HOOK LIST OBEY PLOW TILL AURIS BRACE PINNA SENSE SOUSE SPIKE CANNON CONCHA CROSET EARLET LISTEN AURICLE HEARING SENSORY AUDIENCE PAVILION RECEPTOR

(— OF BELL) CANNON

(— OF CORN) COB ICKER MEALIE NUBBIN CORNCOB

(— OF GRAIN) RISOM SPIKE RIZZOM

(— OF WHEAT) SPICA WHEATEAR

(—S OF GRAIN) CAPES EARHEAD

(PART OF —) LOBE TUBE CANAL HELIX INCUS PINNA CONCHA MEATUS SCAPHA STAPES TRAGUS COCHLEA MALLEUS MEMBRANE TYMPANUM ANTIHELIX ANTITRAGUS

(UNRIPE — OF CORN) TUCKET

EARACHE OTALGY OTALGIA

EARL EORL GRAF JARL LORD PEER COMES NOBLE CONSUL SIWARD

(— OF COVENTRY) SNIPSNAPSNORUM

EARLIER ERE OLD ERST FORE ELDER UPPER BEFORE FORMER HITHER RATHER

SOONER FIRSTER FURTHER PIONEER PREMIER PREVIOUS

EARLIEST ERST FIRST ELDEST MAIDEN PIONEER PREMIER RATHEST FURTHEST PRIMROSE ABORIGINAL

(PREF.) EO

EARLY AIR ERE OLD GOOD HIGH RARE RATH SOON FORME PRIMY RATHE VERTY REARLY SUDDEN TIMELY ANCIENT BETIMES ERLICHE FORWARD YOUTHFUL MATUTINAL

EARMARK BIT CROP SPLIT LUGMARK OVERBIT SLEEPER ALLOCATE OVERCROP UNDERBIT

EARN GET WIN FANG GAIN TILL VANG ADDLE ETTLE MERIT GARNER HUSTLE OBTAIN ACHIEVE ACQUIRE CHEVISE DEMERIT DESERVE

(— BY LABOR) ADDLE SWINK BESWINK

EARNEST ARRA DEAR DERN HARD PAWN ARLES EAGER GRAVE SMART SOBER STAID ARDENT ENTIRE HEARTY INTENT SEDATE SOLEMN EMULOUS ENGAGED FERVENT FORWARD HANDSEL INTENSE SERIOUS SINCERE ZEALOUS DILIGENT EMPHATIC STUDIOUS

EARNESTLY HARD DEARLY WISHLY DEVOUTLY ENTIRELY HEARTILY INTENTLY INWARDLY

EARNESTNESS GLOW FERVOR WARMTH GRAVITY DEVOTION DILIGENCE

EARNINGS GET MAKING PICKING ADDLINGS

EARRING DROP GRIP EARBOB EARLET PENDLE EARCLIP EARDROP PENDANT EARSCREW

EARSHOT SOUND HEARING EARREACH

EARTH ERD ORB SET BALL BANK BURY CLAY CLOD DIRT DUST FLAG GRIT LAND MARL MASS MEAL MOLD ROCK SOIL STAR VALE ADOBE GLEBE GLOBE INTER LOESS MOULD REGUR TERRA WORLD CENTER COARSE GROUND YACATA MIDGARD TERRENE TIERRAS TOPSOIL TRIPOLI MAGNESIA MIDGARTH

(— FOR RAMPART) REMBLAI

(— PROVIDING OCHER) KOKOWAI

(— SUITABLE FOR CULTIVATION) LAYER

(BLACK —) MUCK SORY KILLOW AMPELITE CHERNOZEM

(BLUE —) KIMBERLITE

(BROWN —) UMBER

(CLAYEY —) LAME LOAM

(DRY —) MOOL GROOT

(FULLER'S —) CRETA CIMOLITE SMECTITE

(GEM-BEARING —) BYON

(HEAVY —) BARYTA

(LOOSE —) CRUMB GEEST
(MOIST —) SLAB SLIME
(POOR —) RAMMEL
(RAMMED —) PISE
(RED —) RUDDLE
(REFUSE —) MURGEON
(RIVER-BANK —) GREWT
(SMALL —) TERRELLA
(SOAP —) SOAPROCK
(STRAW-YELLOW —) BISMITE
(SUN-DRIED —) SWISH
(VITRIFIED —) FLOSS
(VOLCANIC —) TRASS TARRASS

EARTHEN FICT DIRTEN EARTHLY

EARTHENWARE PIG POT DELF CHINA
CLOAM CROCK DELFT CLAYEN JASPER
ASTBURY BISCUIT FAIENCE POTTERY
TICKNEY BUFFWARE CROCKERY
MAJOLICA TALAVERA
(BROKEN PIECE OF —) CROCK

EARTHLY LAIRY CARNAL EARTHY
MORTAL EARTHEN GLEBOUS MUNDANE
SECULAR TERRAIN TERRENE WORLDLY
SUBLUNAR TELLURIC TEMPORAL

EARTHQUAKE QUAKE SEISM SHAKE
SHOCK TEMBLOR SEAQUAKE

EARTHWORK BANK RATH AGGER
CASTLE SCONCE RAMPART TERRACE
(PL.) PARADOS

EARTHWORM ESS MAD WORM ANNELID
DEWWORM IPOMOEA MADDOCK
ANGLEDOG BRANDLIN EACEWORM
FISHWORM RAINWORM TWATCHEL
BRANDLING LUMBRICID OLIGOCHATE

EARTHY GROSS SALTY WORMY CLODDY
VULGAR EARTHLY TERRENE BARNYARD
TERREOUS VISCERAL

EAR TRUMPET CORNET AEROPHONE

EARWIG GOLACH TOUCHBELL

EASE CALM COZY EASY REST ALLAY
KNACK PEACE QUIET RELAX SLAKE
LOOSEN PACIFY REDUCE RELIEF REPOSE
SAUGHT SMOOTH SOFTEN SOOTHE
APPEASE ASSUAGE COMFORT CONTENT
FACULTY FLUENCY FREEDOM LEISURE
LIBERTY LIGHTEN RELIEVE SLACKEN
SUBSIDE DIMINISH FACILITY MITIGATE
MODERATE PALLIATE PLEASURE
SECURITY UNBURDEN
(— OFF) FLOW CHECK START SLOUGH
(APATHETIC —) INDOLENCE
(AT —) OTIOSE
(CAREFREE —) ABANDON

EASEL FRAME SUPPORT SCAFFOLD

EASEMENT EASE EASING RELIEF
HERBAGE TURBARY SERVITUS
WAYLEAVE

EASILY EASY EATH WELL LIGHT EATHLY
GENTLY GLIBLY HANDILY LIGHTLY
READILY SLIGHTLY SMOOTHLY
(PREF.) EU

EASINESS GRACE FACILITY

EAST ASIA MORN LEVANT ORIENT
SUNRISE EASTWARD

EASTERN LEVANT ORTIVE AURORAL
ORIENTAL

EASTERNER DUDE

EAST GERMANY

CAPITAL: EASTBERLIN
DISTRICT: GERA SUHL HALLE ERFURT
ROSTOCK
RIVER: ELBE ODER HAVEL SAALE SPREE
TOWN: GERA SUHL HALLE ERFURT
COTTBUS DRESDEN LEIPZIG POTSDAM
ROSTOCK SCHWERIN MAGDEBURG

EASY CALM COZY CRIP EATH EITH GAIN
GLIB MILD RIFE SNAP SOFT CUSHY
JAMMY LARGE LIGHT PLAIN PRONE
ROYAL SUAVE YEZZY CASUAL COMODO
FACILE FLUENT FRUITY GENTLE GENTLY
SECURE SIMPLE SMOOTH UNHARD
ARTLESS GRADUAL LENIENT NATURAL
CAREFREE CARELESS CAVALIER
EXPEDITE FAMILIAR GRACEFUL
HOMELIKE MODERATE TRANQUIL
UNFORCED
(— IN MIND) SECURE
(— TO HANDLE) HANDSOME
(— TO UNDERSTAND) PELLUCID
(— TO USE) CLEVER

EASYGOING LAX QUIET DEGAGE

EAT FOG KAI SUP BITE CHOP CHOW DINE
FARE FEED FRET HAVE HEYT MAKE PECK
RUST FEAST GRAZE MANGE MUNCH
TASTE WASTE ABSORB BEGNAW
DEVOUR INGEST NIBBLE RAVAGE
CONSUME DESTROY SWALLOW VICTUAL
(— A MEAL) GRUB
(— A SNACK) NOSH
(— AS HOGS) SLUICE
(— AWAY) GNAW ERODE RANKLE
CORRODE
(— BETWEEN MEALS) NOSH
(— BIG MEAL) STOKE
(— CRUNCHINGLY) GROUZE
(— GLUTTONOUSLY) GUDGE STUFF
(— GREEDILY) GAMP GAWP SLAB SLOP
TUCK CHAUM MOOCH SCOFF GOBBLE
GOFFLE GUTTLE GUZZLE RAUNGE
GLUTTON GOURMAND
(— HEARTILY) THORN
(— IN GULPS) LAB
(— MINCINGLY) PICK PICKLE PIDDLE
(— NOISILY) SLOP GULCH SLURP
GUTTLE SLOTTER
(— OUT) EXEDE
(— RUDELY) TROUGH
(— SLOVENLY) SLUP MUMMICK
(— SPARINGLY) DIET
(— TO EXCESS) COLF BEZZLE
(— UP) DEMOLISH
(— VORACIOUSLY) CRAM WORRY
(— WITH GUSTO) SMOUSE
(— WITHOUT CHEWING) BOLT

EAVESDROP DARK HARKEN LISTEN
HEARKEN

EAVESDROPPER COWAN EARWIG
DRAWLATCH

EBB FAIL FALL SINK WANE ABATE DECAY
RECEDE REFLOW REFLUX RETIRE TIDING

DECLINE REFLOAT SUBSIDE DECREASE DIMINISH
(— AND FLOW) ESTUS AESTUS FLUIDITY
EBONY EBON BLACK GABOON WAMARA HEBENON IRONWOOD
EBULLIENCE OVERFLOW ELEVATION
EBULLIENT BRASH FERVID BOILING
EBULLITION SEETHE FERMENT OUTBURST
ECCENTRIC FEY ODD OFF CARD DOER NUTS CRANK DOTTY KINKY OUTRE QUEER WIPER CRANKY LOCOED OUTISH PSYCHO SCREWY SHAGGY BIZARRE CURIOUS DEVIOUS ERRATIC STRANGE TOUCHED ABNORMAL FITIFIED PECULIAR SINGULAR
ECCENTRICITY KINK FERLY ODDITY ANOMALY CROTCHET QUIDDITY
(— OF CURVE) E
ECCLESIASTES KOHELETH
ECCLESIASTIC ABBE ABBOT CLERK VICAR ARCHON FATHER LECTOR LEGATE PRIEST KIRKMAN PRELATE SECULAR EPISTLER SUBDEACON
ECCLESIASTICAL CHURCH CANONIC CHURCHLY CHRISTIAN SPIRITUAL
ECHIDNA NODIAK ANTEATER EDENTATE MONOTREME PORCUPINE
ECHO RING SING CHORUS REPEAT REVERB SECOND IMITATE ITERATE RESOUND RESPEAK RESPOND REVOICE REDOUBLE RESPONSE
(RADAR —) ANGEL
ECLAT FAME GLORY RENOWN ACCLAIM SCANDAL APPLAUSE FACILITY PRESTIGE SPLENDOR
ECLECTIC BROAD LIBERAL
ECLIPSE DIM BIND BLOT HIDE BLIND CLOUD SHADE STAIN SULLY DARKEN DAZZLE DEFECT EXCEED OCCULT DEFAULT OBSCURE PRODIGY TRAVAIL OUTRIVAL OCCULTATION
ECOLOGIST BIONOMIST
ECOLOGY BIOLOGY BIONOMY MESOLOGY
ECONOMICAL WARY CHARY FENDY FRUGAL SAVING CAREFUL PRUDENT SPARING THRIFTY SCREWING
ECONOMICS PLUTONOMY
ECONOMIST HUSBAND MANAGER PHYSIOCRAT
ECONOMIZE HAIN SAVE SKIMP STINT SCRIMP HUSBAND UTILIZE RETRENCH
ECONOMY SPARE SAVING SYSTEM THRIFT MANAGERY PARSIMONY
ECSTASY JOY BLISS POWER SWOON TRANCE DELIGHT EMOTION MADNESS RAPTURE RHAPSODY
ECSTATIC HOT RAPT PYTHIAN GLORIOUS

ECUADOR

ANCIENT NAME: QUITO
CAPE: ROSA PASADO PUNTILLA
CAPITAL: QUITO
COIN: SUCRE CONDOR CENTAVO

INDIAN: CARA INCA PALTA CANELO JIVARO
ISLAND: PUNA WOLF MOCHA PINTA BALTRA CHAVES DARWIN PINZON WENMAN ISABELA
ISLANDS: COLON GALAPAGOS
MEASURE: CUADRA FANEGA
MOUNTAIN: ANDES SANGAY CAYAMBE ANTISANA COTOPAXI
NATIVE: MONTUVIO
PROVINCE: LOJA AZUAY CANAR COLON ELORO CARCHI GUAYAS MANABI BOLIVAR LOSRIOS COTOPAXI IMBABURA
RIVER: COCA MIRA NAPO DAULE PINDO TIGRE GUAYAS TUMBES ZAMORA CURARAY PASTAZA AGUARICO BOBONAZA CONONACO NARANJAL PUTUMAYO
TOWN: JAMA LOJA MERA NAPO PUYO TENA CANAR GUANO MANTA PAJAN PINAS PIURA QUITO YAUPI AMBATO CUENCA IBARRA PUJILI TULCAN ZARUMA AZOGUES CAYAMBE GUAMOTE MACHALA PELILEO PILLARO SALINAS BABAHOYO GUARANDA RIOBAMBA
WATERFALL: AGOYAN
WEIGHT: LIBRA

ECUMENICAL LIBERAL CATHOLIC
ECZEMA TETTER EARWORM MALANDERS
EDDA SAGA
EDDO TARO COCOYAM
EDDY CURL CURL PURL WASH WEEL WELL ACKER GURGE SHIFT SWIRL TWIRL WHIRL SWOOSH VORTEX WIRBLE BACKSET WREATHE
(PREF.) DINO
EDDYING WALE
EDEMA BRAXY TUMOR DROPSY BIGHEAD HYDROPS ANASARCA SWELLING
EDEMATOUS BLOATED HYDROPIC
EDEN HEAVEN UTOPIA ARCADIA ELYSIUM PARADISE
EDENTATE SLOTH AARDVARK ANTEATER
EDGE AGE BIT HEM JAG LIP RIM BANK BERM BRIM BROW CURB DRAW KANT LIMB LIST SIDE TRIM WELL WHET BEVEL BLADE BOARD BRINK CHIMB CHIME CREST EAVES KNIFE LABEL LEDGE MARGE PEARL RULER SHARP SIDLE SPLAY VERGE BORDER CANTLE FLANGE FORAGE IMPALE LABRUM MARGIN NOSING PLANGE MARGENT SELVAGE SHARPEN VANDYKE BOUNDARY EMBORDER KEENNESS MAJORITY OUTSKIRT SELVEDGE STICKING UMSTROKE
(— FORWARD) CREEP
(— IN MINING DRIFT) ARRAGE
(— OF BASKET) FOOT
(— OF BED) STOCK
(— OF BIRD'S BILL) TOMIUM
(— OF BOOK) FERRULE BACKBONE
(— OF BOOK COVER) FLAP
(— OF BRILLIANT) GIRDLE
(— OF CASK) CHIME CHINE

(— OF COAL PILE) RUN
(— OF DAM) CREST
(— OF DUMP) TOE
(— OF FLAG) HOIST
(— OF MESA) CEJA
(— OF MINERAL VEIN) APEX
(— OF ROADWAY) SHOULDER
(— OF RUDDER) BEARDING
(— OF RUFFLE) HEADING
(— OF SAIL) FOOT HEAD LEECH
(— OF SAW) SAFE
(— OF SHELL) HINGE
(— OF STRATUM) BASSET
(— OF STREAM) HAG
(— OF TOOL) BEZEL
(— OF TOOTH) SCALPRUM
(— OF TROUSERS) CREASE
(— OF VAULT) GROIN
(— OF WOOD) WOODRIME
(—S OF COAT) LAP
(BEVELED —) CHAMFER
(CUTTING —) SHOE
(DOUBLE —) FLAT
(EMBROIDERED —) SURFLE
(EXTERIOR —) AMBITUS
(FRONT — OF BOOK) FACE
(ORNAMENTAL —) FRILL
(RAGGED —) RAG
(ROCKY —) ARETE
(ROUGH —S) FASH
(SHARP —) ARRIS BEARD
(UNPLOWED — OF FIELD) RAND
(UNTRIMMED —) DECKLE
(PREF.) AMBO
EDGED EDGY EROSE SHARP CRENATE
CUTTING
(— BY ARCS) INVECTED
EDGING HEM CURB EDGE LACE LIST
FILET FRILL LEDGE PICOT BORDER FILLET
FRINGE LIMBUS BEADING BINDING
GIMPING HAMBURG COQUILLE FRILLING
PUNTILLA RICKRACK SKIRTING
SURROUND PASSEMENTERIE
EDGY EAGER SHARP ANGULAR CRITICAL
SNAPPISH
EDIBLE EDULE EATABLE ESCULENT
EDICT ACT BAN LAW BULL FIAT TYPE
ARRET BANDO BULLA IRADE ORDER
SANAD UKASE ASSIZE DECREE DICTUM
NOTICE COMMAND EMBARGO PLACARD
PROCESS PROGRAM STATUTE ECTHESIS
RESCRIPT
EDIFICE DOME CHURCH TURBEH
BUILDING ERECTION TETRAGON
EDIFY GROW BUILD FAVOR TEACH
BENEFIT IMPROVE PROSPER CONVINCE
INSTRUCT ORGANIZE
EDIFYING HIGH SAVORY ELEVATED
EDIT CUT EMEND DIRECT REDACT REVIEW
REVISE ARRANGE COMPILE CORRECT
PREPARE PUBLISH REWRITE COPYREAD
EDITION KIND EXTRA FINAL FIRST ISSUE
PRINT STAMP ALDINE DIGLOT SOURCE
AUSGABE BULLDOG HEXAPLA OCTAPLA
VERSION PRINCEPS VARIORUM
(FIRST —) PRINCEPS
EDITOR AUTHOR OVERSEER REDACTOR

EDITORIAL LEADER
EDUCATE REAR BREED TEACH TRADE
TRAIN EXPAND INFORM SCHOOL
DEVELOP NURTURE INSTRUCT
EDUCATED BRED CIVIL TAUGHT
TRAINED INFORMED LETTERED LITERATE
EDUCATION CLERGY NURTURE
BREEDING LEARNING NORTELRY
PEDAGOGY TRAINING
(LIBERAL —) HUMANITY
(PHYSICAL —) GYM
EDUCATOR TEACHER
EDUCE DRAW EVOKE ELICIT EVOLVE
EXTORT EXTRACT
EEL GRIG LING OPAH SNIG TUNA ELVER
MORAY SIREN APODAN CARAPO CONGER
FAUSEN MOREIA MURENE CONGRIO
KWATUMA LAMPREY MURAENA SNIGGLE
WRIGGLE CONGEREE GYMNOTID
KINGKLIP
(YOUNG —) ELVER OLIVER YELVER
(25 —S) STICK SWARM
EELGRASS DREW WRACK ENALID
EELPOUT BARD LING POUT QUAB
BURBOT CONGER GUFFER YOWLER
LYCODOID
EERIE EERY SCARY TIMID WEIRD WISHT
CREEPY DISMAL GLOOMY GOUSTY
SPOOKY AWESOME GHOSTLY GOUSTIE
MACABRE STRANGE UNCANNY ELDRITCH
GHOULISH POKERISH
EFFACE BLOT DASH DELE RAZE WEAR
ERASE CANCEL DEFACE SPONGE STRIKE
DESTROY DISLIMN EXPUNGE NULLIFY
UNPAINT
EFFECT DO SEE DENT DOES FECK HAVE
PRAY PREY TEEM WORK CAUSE CLOSE
ENACT ETTLE EVENT FORCE FRUIT ISSUE
STAMP ACTION ENERGY GROWTH
INDUCE INTENT OBTAIN RESULT SECURE
SEQUEL STEREO UPSHOT ACHIEVE
ACQUIRE ARRANGE COMPASS CONDUCE
EMOTION EXECUTE FULFILL IMPRESS
IMPRINT OPERATE OUTCOME PERFORM
PROCURE PRODUCE PURPORT REALIZE
CAUSATUM COMPLETE CONCLUDE
CONTRIVE FRUITAGE CONSEQUENT
(— OF PAST EXPERIENCE) MNEME
(BLURRED —) FUZZ
(COUNTERBALANCING —) STANDOFF
(DAZZLING —) ECLAT
(DECORATIVE —) CHIPPING
(ELECTRICAL —) STRAY
(ESTHETIC —) ATMOSPHERE
(FALSE —) FACADE
(FINAL —) AMOUNT
(ILL —) EVIL
(INTENSE —) STRESS
(MOTTLED —) SPRINKLE
(MUSICAL —) BEND SHADING
(OPTICAL —) PHANTASMAGORIA
(PAINFUL —) JAR
(PAINTING —) STIPPLE
(PENETRATING —) SEARCH
(PERNICIOUS —) BLAST
(PERSONAL —S) DUNNAGE
(SECONDARY —) OVERTONE

(SHATTERING —) BRISANCE
(THEATRICAL —) CURTAIN
(TOTAL —) ENSEMBLE
(TOXIC —S) THEISM
(TREMOLO —) BEBUNG
(VISIBLE —) TOUCH
(SUFF.) ERGATE ERGY
EFFECTIVE ABLE HOME MEAN REAL
ALIVE GREAT HAPPY PITHY SIKER SOUND
VALID ACTIVE ACTUAL CAUSAL DEADLY
DIRECT FRUITY POTENT SEVERE SICKER
SOVRAN CAPABLE FECKFUL OPERANT
TELLING VIRTUAL ADEQUATE FORCEFUL
POWERFUL SMASHING STRIKING
VIGOROUS TRENCHANT
EFFECTIVELY NAITLY
EFFECTIVENESS AIM BANG CHIC EDGE
VOLTAGE EFFICACY LEVERAGE
EFFECTUAL ACTUAL TOOTHY ADEQUATE
POWERFUL MAGISTRAL
EFFECTUATE FULFILL COMPLETE
EFFEMINATE NICE SOFT MILKY MISSY
SAPPY SISSY BITCHY FEMALE LYDIAN
NIMINY PRISSY SILKEN TENDER WANTON
WEAKLY CITIZEN EPICENE MEACOCK
WOMANLY FEMINATE FEMININE
LADYLIKE OVERSOFT WOMANISH
EFFERVESCE FIZZ HUFF KNIT BUBBLE
SPARKLE
EFFERVESCENCE FRET CRACKLE
SPARKLE
EFFERVESCENT UP BRISK FIZZY QUICK
BUBBLY ABUBBLE ELASTIC BUBBLING
EFFERVESCING BRISK
EFFETE SERE PASSE SPENT BARREN
DECADENT ETIOLATE MORIBUND
EFFICACIOUS VALID MIGHTY POTENT
FORCIBLE POWERFUL SINGULAR
VIGOROUS VIRTUOUS OPERATIVE
EFFICACY DINT FECK DEVIL FORCE
GRACE MIGHT POWER DEGREE VIRTUE
POTENCY VALIDITY OPERATION
EFFICIENCY POWER SKILL AGENCY
ABILITY FACULTY DISPATCH EFFICACY
PERFORMANCE
EFFICIENT ABLE GOOD SMART VALID
POTENT CAPABLE FECKFUL POWERFUL
SPEEDFUL
EFFIGY GUY IDOL POPE SIGN DUMMY
IMAGE LIKENESS MONUMENT
EFFLORESCE GERMINATE
EFFLORESCENCE RASH BLOOM
BLOSSOM ROSEOLA ANTHESIS ERUPTION
WHITEWASH
EFFLUENCE ISSUE EFFLUX ELAPSE
EMANATE
EFFLUVIA SCENT
EFFLUVIUM AURA MIASMA FLUXION
SPECIES APORRHEA EMISSION
OUTGOING EMANATION
EFFLUX OUTGO OUTFLOW EFFUSION
EFFORT JOB TRY TUG DINT FIST HUMP
JUMP MINT PASS SHOT TOIL BRUNT
BURST CRACK DRIVE ESSAY FLING
LABOR NISUS PAINS POWER REACH
TRIAL ANIMUS DEVOIR FAVORS FIZZLE
FUFFLE PINGLE STRAIN STROKE THRIFT

ATTEMPT CONATUS MOLIMEN NITENCY
SPLURGE STRETCH TENSURE TROUBLE
WORKING ENDEAVOR EXERTION
GOODWILL INDUSTRY MOLITION
REACHING STRIVING STRUGGLE
(— FOR ONESELF) FEND
(ABORTIVE —) FIZZLE
(AGONIZED —) THROE
(ARTICULATIVE —) ACCENT
(EARNEST —) STUDY
(EFFECTIVE —) LICK
(FINAL —) CHARETTE
(INITIAL —) ASSAY
(MAXIMUM —) BEST
(SALVATIONIST —) ATTACK
(SINGLE —) HEAT TRICE
(STRENUOUS —) HASSLE
(UNSUCCESSFUL —) ATTEMPT
(UTMOST —) DEVOIR BUSINESS
(VIOLENT —) BURST STRAIN OUTRAGE
STRUGGLE
EFFORTLESS EASY
EFFRONTERY BROW FACE GALL BRASS
FRONT BRONZE AUDACITY BOLDNESS
CHUTZPAH FOREHEAD TEMERITY
EFFULGENCE BLAZE GLORY RADIANT
RADIANCE SPLENDOR
EFFULGENT BRIGHT FULGENT RADIANT
SHINING
EFFUSE GUSH SHED FLING EFFUND
EMANATE DISPENSE
EFFUSION EFFLUX FOISON SCREED
SPILTH STREAM
EFFUSIVE GOOEY GUSHY LAVISH SLOPPY
GUSHING BUBBLING
EFFUSIVENESS SLOP
EFT ASK EVET NEWT LIZARD TRITON
EGG ABET GOOG OVUM PROD SEED SPUR
CHECK HUEVO OVULE SPORE DARNER
INCITE OOCYTE PEEWEE ZYGOTE
ACTUATE COCKNEY COKENEY OOPLAST
OOSPERM PROTOVUM
(— CASE) POD
(— CLUTCH) LAUGHTER
(— OF FISH OR LOBSTER) BERRY
(— ON) HAG EDGE GOAD URGE
(— PRODUCT) ZOON
(— WITH BACON) COLLOP
(—S OF BEES) BROOD
(—S OF SILKWORM) GRAINE
(ACID —) SLOWCASE
(CRACKED —) CHECK CRACK LEAKER
(DRIED —S) AHUATLE
(DUCK —S) PIDAN
(FLY'S —) BLOW FLYBLOW
(FOSSIL —) OVULITE
(GOLDEN —S) SUNCUP
(GOOSE —) BLOB
(INFERTILE —) CLEAR
(INSECT —) BLOW
(PART OF —) YOLK SHELL WHITE
ALBUMEN CHALAZA MEMBRANE
BLASTODISC
(SMALL —) OVULE OVULUM
EGGFRUIT LUCUMA CANISTEL
EGGHEAD HIGHBROW INTELLECTUAL
EGGNOG NOG CAUDLE ADVOCAAT

EGGPLANT BRINJAL SOLANUM
BRINGELA EGGFRUIT
EGLANTINE (FATHER OF —) PEPIN
(HUSBAND OF —) VALENTINE
EGO I ATTA SELF ATMAN EGOITY FYLGJA
CONCEIT SUBJECT
EGOCENTRIC INSEEING
EGOISM PRIDE ONEISM VANITY CONCEIT
EGOTISM OWNHOOD SELFNESS
NARCISSISM
EGOIST (AUTHOR OF —) MEREDITH
(CHARACTER IN —) DALE LUCY CLARA
HARRY OXFORD VERNON DECRAYE
CROSSJAY DARLETON LAETITIA
PATTERNE WHITFORD MIDDLETON
CONSTANTIA WILLOUGHBY
EGOTISM EGO PRIDE EGOISM VANITY
CONCEIT EGOMANIA
EGREGIOUS FINE GROSS CAPITAL
EMINENT FLAGRANT PRECIOUS
SHOCKING
EGRESS EXIT ISSUE OUTGO OUTLET
EXITURE OUTCOME OUTGATE PASSAGE
REGRESS OUTGOING
EGRET HERON PLUME GAULIN KOTUKU
AIGRETTE GAULDING

EGYPT

BAY: FOUL
CANAL: SUEZ
CAPE: BANAS RASBANAS
CAPITAL: CAIRO ELQAHIRA
COIN: FILS DINAR GIRSH POUND DIRHAM
GUINEA JUNAYH PIASTER MILLIEME
DAM: ASWAN
DESERT: LIBYAN
GULF: AQABA
ISTHMUS: SUEZ
KING: AY IB KA ITI ITY TUT DJER DJET
HUNY PAMI PEPI SETI TEOS TETI UNIS
ARSES BEBTI FOUAD ITETI KEBEH KHUFU
KNIAN MENES NEBKA NECHO NEFER
UDIMU ZEMTI ZOSER CHEOPS DARIUS
FAROUK KHAFRE NARMER RANSES
SENEDJ XERXES MENKURE PHARAOH
PTOLEMY RAMESES SALADIN CHEPHREN
THUTMOSE
LAKE: EDKU IDKU MARYUT MOERIS
MANZALA BURULLUS MAREOTIS
LAKES: BITTER
MEASURE: APT DRA HEN PIK ROB DRAA
KHET ROUB THEB ABDAT ARDAB CUBIT
FARDE KELEH KILAH SAHME ARTABA
AURURE FEDDAN KEDDAH ROBHAH
SCHENE CHORYOS DARIBAH MALOUAH
ROUBOUH TOUMNAH KASSABAH
KHAROUBA
MOUNTAIN: SINAI GHARIB KATHERINA
NATIVE: ARAB COPT NILOT BERBER
MUSLIM NUBIAN
OASIS: SIWA DAKHLA KHARGA FARAFRA
BAHARIYA
PENINSULA: SINAI
PORT: TOR SUEZ ATTUR DUMYAT QUSEIR
RASHID SAFAGA SALLUM ROSETTA

DAMIETTA HURGHADA PORTSAID
ALEXANDRIA
PROVINCE: GIZA QENA QINA ASWAN
ASYUT MINYA SOHAG DUMYAT FAIYUM
SAWHAJ TAHRIR ALJIZAH BEHEIRA
BENISUEF DAMIETTA GHARBIYA
MINUFIYA SHARQIYA
RESERVOIR: ASWAN
RIVER: NILE
RUINS: ABYDOS THEBES MEMPHIS
PYRAMIDS
TOWN: NO MUT DUSH GIZA IDFU ISNA
QENA SAIS SIWA SUEZ ZOAN ASWAN
ASYUT BENHA BULAQ CAIRO ELTUR
FAYID GIRGA GIZEH LUXOR NAKHL
SALUM SOHAG TAHTA TANIS TANTA
ABYDOW AKHMIN DUMYAT ELQASR
HELWAN RASHID THEBES BURSAID
ROSETTA ZAGAZIG BENISUEF DAMIETTA
ISMAILIA
WEIGHT: KAT KET OKA OKE HEML KHAR
OKIA ROTL ARTAL ARTEL DEBEN KERAT
MINAE MINAS OKIEH POUND RATEL
UCKIA HAMLAH KANTAR DRACHMA
QUINTAL

EGYPTIAN ARAB COPT TASIAN PHARIAN
BADARIAN MEMPHIAN
EIDER COLK WAMP DIVER EDDER DUCKER
SHOREYER
EIDOLON ICON GHOST IMAGE IDOLUM
PHANTOM LIKENESS
EIGHT ETA ECHT AUGHT CHETH OCTAD
OCTET OCTAVE OGDOAD OCTONARY
EIGHTH NOTE UNCA CROMA CHROMA
QUAVER
EIRE (SEE IRELAND)
EITHER ANY EDDER ITHER OTHER
WHETHER
EJACULATE BELCH BLURT EJECT FLING
EXCLAIM EMISSION
EJACULATION HOW COADS ZOWIE
BEGORRA CRIMINE UTTERING
(MYSTIC —) OM
EJECT OUT BLOW BOOT CAST EMIT FIRE
HOOF OUST SHED SPAT SPEW SPIT VOID
WARP AVOID BELCH CHUCK ERUCT
ERUPT EVICT EXPEL SHAKE SHOOT
SPOUT SPURT VOMIT BANISH BOUNCE
REJECT SQUIRT DEFORCE DISMISS
EXCLUDE EXTRUDE OBTRUDE DISGORGE
OUTBRAID
EJECTION BLOW OUSTER OUTING
EVICTION
EKE IMP ALSO AUGMENT ENLARGE
HUSBAND STRETCH APPENDIX INCREASE
LENGTHEN LIKEWISE UNDERLAY
ELABORATE LUSH FIKIE GREAT LABOR
DELUXE DRESSY ELABOR ORNATE
QUAINT REFINE CURIOUS DEVELOP
ENLARGE LABORED PERFECT
(OVERLY —) NIGGLING
ELABORATED WROUGHT
ELABORATELY FANCILY
ELAH (FATHER OF —) UZZI CALEB
BAASHA

(SLAYER OF —) ZIMRI
(SON OF —) HOSHEA
ELAINE (FATHER OF —) PELLES
BRANDEGORIS
(SON OF —) GALAHAD
ELAN DASH ARDOR DRIVE GUSTO VERVE
SPIRIT WARMTH POTENCY
ELAND ORYX IMPOFO
ELAPSE GO RUN PASS ROLL SLIP GLIDE
SPEND EXPIRE
ELAPSING CURRENT
ELASTIC QUICK GARTER RUBATO
SPONGY BUOYANT SPRINGY STRETCH
CHEVEREL FLEXIBLE STRETCHY
VOLATILE
ELASTICITY GIVE LIFE ELATER SPRING
STRETCH
ELATE PUFF CHEER EXALT EXULT FLUSH
LOFTY RAISE EXCITE PLEASE THRILL
ELEVATE GLADDEN INFLATE SUBLIME
SUCCESS ELEVATED HEIGHTEN INSPIRIT
JUBILATE
ELATED RAD HIGH RADE CHUFF HAPPY
PROUD VAUDY VOGIE WLONK CHUFFY
JOVIAL UPPISH UPPITY EXCITED
EXULTED JOCULAR SUBLIME EXULTANT
GLORIOUS INFLATED JUBILANT PRIDEFUL
UPLIFTED
ELATER BEETLE CRINULA SKIPJACK
ELATION JOY GLEE RUFF BUOYANCY
ELBOW ELL BEND ANCON JOINT NUDGE
SHOVE CROSET ELBUCK JOSTLE JUSTLE
SPRING PIERDROP
(PREF.) CUBITO ULNO
ELDER AIN IVA AINE WITE ELLER OLDER
PRIOR MAHANT PRIMUS SENIOR
ANCIENT NEGUNDO STAROST TRAMMON
ANCESTOR BOURTREE CARELESS
DANEWORT ELDERMAN PRESBYTER
ELDERLY AGED GRAY ALDER ELDERN
SENILE BADGERLY
ELDEST AYNE EIGNE OLDEST PRIMUS
ELEAZAR (BROTHER OF —) ABIHU
NADAB ITHAMAR
(FATHER OF —) AARON ELIUD MAHLI
PAROSH ABINADAB PHINEHAS
(GRANDFATHER OF —) MERARI
ELECT CALL PICK VOICE ASSUME CHOOSE
CHOSEN DECIDE ISRAEL PREFER SELECT
ELECTION PROXY CHOICE LECTION
PRIMARY
ELECTIVE OPTION OPTIONAL
ELECTOR VOTER ELISOR CHOOSER
ELIGENT INTRANT ELECTANT
ELECTORATE PEOPLE COUNTRY
ELECTRA LAODICE
(BROTHER OF —) ORESTES
(DAUGHTER OF —) IRIS AELLO
OCYPETE
(FATHER OF —) ATLAS OCEANUS
AGAMEMNON
(HUSBAND OF —) PYLADES THAUMAS
(MOTHER OF —) ERATO TETHYS
PLEIONE CLYTEMNESTRA
(SON OF —) IASION DARDANUS
ELECTRICIAN GAFFER JUICER
BOARDMAN

ELECTRICITY JUICE POWER PYROGEN
ELECTRIC GALVANISM
ELECTRIFY EXCITE THRILL STARTLE
ELECTROCUTE BURN EXECUTE
ELECTRODE GRID ANODE PLATE DYNODE
CATHODE IGNITER CROWFOOT
REOPHORE
ELECTRON ION NEGATON POLARON
NEGATRON POSITRON CORPUSCLE
ELECTRONIC RADIONIC
ELECTROTYPE PATCH CLICHE WORKER
ELECTRO
ELECTRYON (DAUGHTER OF —)
ALCMENE
(FATHER OF —) PERSEUS
(MOTHER OF —) ANDROMEDA
ELEGANCE CHIC GARB LUXE TONE
CLASP GRACE STYLE SWANK TASTE
FINERY GAIETY GAYETY LUXURY NICETY
POLISH COURTESY EUPHUISM FINENESS
FRIPPERY GRANDEUR SPLENDOR
ELEGANT CHIC DINK FAIR FEAT FINE FIXY
GENT JIMP POSH CIVIL COMPT FANCY
NOBBY RITZY SHARP SLEEK SWANK
SWISH CHOICE CLASSY DAINTY DELUXE
DRESSY FACETE MINION POLITE PRETTY
QUAINT SUPERB SWANKY URBANE
VENUST CAPITAL CLEANLY COURTLY
FEATISH FEATOUS GENTEEL MINIKIN
REFINED SMICKER DEBONAIR DELICATE
GINGERLY GRACEFUL GRAZIOSO
HANDSOME POLISHED TASTEFUL
CONCINNOUS
ELEGANTLY FINE TALLY FAIRLY GENTLY
GINGERLY
ELEGIAC MOURNFUL EPICEDIAL
ELEGY POEM SONG DIRGE KINAH QINAH
LAMENT MONODY EPICEDE
ELEMENT AIR ATOM DIAD DYAD RECT
WOOF BEARD ETHER FIBER FIBRE METAL
MONAD PUNCT STUFF AETHER ARTIAD
COSTAL FACTOR HEPTAD LOSSER
MATTER MOMENT SIMPLE ACTINON
ADAPTER BUNCHER CARRIER CATCHER
ESSENCE FEATURE ACTINIDE BACKBONE
CEREBRAL EQUATION PERISSAD
RUDIMENT SELECTOR THERBLIG
(— IN GRAPH) SPIKE
(— IN WAVE) DART
(— IN WORD GROUP) KOINON
(— OF ALCHEMIST) AIR FIRE EARTH
WATER
(— OF EXISTENCE) DHARMA
(— OF MACHINE) HORN SPIDER
(— OF WEALTH) COMMODITY
(ALIEN —) ALLOY
(ARCHITECTURAL —) SLAB
(BINDING —) CEMENT
(CHARACTERISTIC —) PARAMETER
(CHEMICAL —) TIN GOLD IRON LEAD
NEON ZINC ARGON BORON RADON
XENON BARIUM CARBON CERIUM
CESIUM COBALT COPPER CURIUM
ERBIUM HELIUM INDIUM IODINE MURIUM
NICKEL OSMIUM OXYGEN RADIUM
SILVER SODIUM SULFUR ARSENIC
BISMUTH BROMINE CADMIUM CALCIUM

FERMIUM GALLIUM HAFNIUM HOLMIUM
IRIDIUM KRYPTON LITHIUM MERCURY
NIOBIUM RHENIUM RHODIUM SILICON
TERBIUM THORIUM THULIUM URANIUM
WOLFRAM YTTRIUM ACTINIDE ACTINIUM
ANTIMONY ASTATINE CHLORINE
CHROMIUM EUROPIUM FLUORINE
FRANCIUM HYDROGEN LUTETIUM
MASURIUM NITROGEN NOBELIUM
NONMETAL PLATINUM POLONIUM
RUBIDIUM SAMARIUM SCANDIUM
SELENIUM TANTALUM THALLIUM
TITANIUM TUNGSTEN VANADIUM
METALLOID PALLADIUM PLUTONIUM
(COMMUNION —) GIFT
(CRIMINAL —) GANGLAND
(DECORATIVE —S) ART
(DOMINANT —) CAPSHEAF
(ELECTRIC —) IMPEDOR
(ESSENTIAL —) CORPUS
(EUCHARISTIC —S) HAGIA SPECIES
(FATAL —) BANE
(FUNDAMENTAL —) STAMEN
KEYSTONE
(GLOOMY —) PALL
(HEATING —) CALANDRIA
(HYPOTHETICAL —) CORONIUM
(INTERFERING —) CRIMP
(LAMP —) GLOWER
(LEADING —) HEAD
(LINGUISTIC—) SERVILE INTENSIVE
(MILITARY —) SUPPORT
(MODIFYING —) LEAVENING
(MORAL —) DAENA
(MOST IMPORTANT —) CAPSTONE
(PRIMAL —) GUNA SALT ARCHE
(PRINCIPAL —) STAPLE
(SKELETAL —) SCLERE
(STRUCTURAL —) ARCUALE
(SUPPOSED —) PROTYLE WELSIUM
VICTORIUM
(SUSTAINING —) BREAD STAPLE
(TRACE —) MICRONUTRIENT
(TRANSITORY —S) SKANDHAS
(UNITING —) BOND
ELEMENTAL PURE BASIC PRIMAL SIMPLE
PRIMARY ULTIMATE PRIMITIVE
ELEMENTARY PRIMAL SIMPLE INITIAL
PRIMARY INCHOATE ULTIMATE
RUDIMENTARY
ELEPHANT COW BULL CALF HINE PUNK
HATHI HATTY JUMBO ROGUE MUCKNA
TUSKER KOOMKIE AIRAVATA LOXODONT
MASTODON OLIPHANT PROBOSCIDEAN
ELEPHANTIASIS TYRIASIS
ELEPHANTINE HUGE ENORMOUS
ELEPHANT'S-EAR TARO
ELEVATE HAIN JUMP LIFT REAR RISE
EDIFY ELATE ENSKY ERECT EXALT EXTOL
GRIMP HEAVE HOIST MOUNT RAISE
TOWER REFINE UPLIFT ADVANCE
DIGNIFY ENHANCE ENNOBLE GLORIFY
PROMOTE SUBLIME UPRAISE HEIGHTEN
INSPIRIT
ELEVATED EL FINE HIGH GREAT LOFTY
NOBLE RISEN STEEP AERIAL AMOTUS
ELATED RAISED RISING WINGED

BULLATE ELEVATO EXALTED MOUNTED
STILTED SUBLIME MAJESTIC UPLIFTED
(— IN CHARACTER) HIGH
(NOT —) COMICAL
ELEVATION UP ARM BAND BANK DOME
DRUM GLEE HIGH HILL HUMP LIFT RISE
SPUR TOFT TOOT UMBO AGGER BULLA
GRADE KNOLL MOUND PITCH RAISE
RIDGE SHOAL SWELL TOWER WHEAL
CONULE CRISTA HEIGHT PAPULE UPLIFT
DIGNITY FURCULA MAJESTY UPRIGHT
ALTITUDE EMINENCE EVECTION
HIGHNESS LEVATION MOUNTAIN
SWELLING MONTICULE
(— OF CARTILAGE) ANTHELIX
(— OF CUTICLE) BLEB
(— OF SKIN) BLISTER
(— ON TOOTH) STYLE
(— SEPARATING CREEKS) BUGOR
(GUN —) RANDOM
(TURRET —) HOOD
(PREF.) ORO
ELEVATOR BIN CAGE LIFT SILO HOIST
BRIDGE LIFTER TEAGLE HOISTER
STACKER UPTAKER UPLIFTER UPRAISER
ELF FAY HAG HOB IMP OAF PUG DROW
FANE OUPH PERI PUCK DWARF FAIRY
GNOME OUPHE PIGMY PIXIE ELFKIN
GOBLIN SPIRIT SPRITE URCHIN BLASTIE
BROWNIE INCUBUS SUCCUBUS
ELFIN ELF FEY CHILD ELFIC ELFISH
URCHIN
ELFISH ELFIN ELVAN ELVISH IMPISH
URCHIN ELFLIKE TRICKSY
ELFRIDA (HUSBAND OF —) EDGAR
(SON OF —) AETHELRED
ELIAB (BROTHER OF —) DAVID
(DAUGHTER OF —) ABIHAIL
(FATHER OF —) HELON NAHATH
(SON OF —) ABIRAM DATHAN
ELICIT DRAW MILK PUMP CLAIM EDUCE
EVOKE EXACT FETCH WREST WRING
DEDUCE DEMAND ENTICE EXTORT
INDUCE EXTRACT PROVOKE SOLICIT
ELIDE OMIT SKIP ANNUL IGNORE
DESTROY NULLIFY DEMOLISH SUPPRESS
ELIGIBLE FIT ACTIVE WORTHY SUITABLE
(— IN POKER) ACTIVE
ELIMINATE FAN COMB EDIT KILL EDUCE
EXPEL PURGE SCRUB DELETE EFFACE
EXCEPT IGNORE REMOVE SCREEN
WINNOW BLANKET BRACKET DIVULGE
EXCLUDE EXCRETE RELEASE SCISSOR
SILENCE SUBLATE SEPARATE
ELISABETH (HUSBAND OF —)
ZACHARIAS
(SON OF —) JOHN
ELISHA (FATHER OF —) SHAPHAT
ELISION SYNCOPE
ELISSA (BROTHER OF —) PYGMALION
(FATHER OF —) BELUS METGEN
(HUSBAND OF —) ACERBAS SYCHAEUS
SICHARBAAL
(SISTER OF —) ANNA
ELITE BEST LITE PINK CREAM CHOICE
CIRCLE FLOWER GENTRY SELECT
PERFECTI

ELIXIR DAFFY AMRITA SPIRIT AMREETA ARCANUM CORDIAL CUREALL ESSENCE PANACEA MEDICINE

ELK ALCE DEER LAMA LOSH ALAND ELAND LOSHE MOOSE CERVID SAMBAR WAPITI SAMBHUR WAMPOOSE
(— HIDE) LOSH
(YOUNG —) DEACON

ELL ULNA ELBOW ALNAGE ADDITION

ELLIPSE OVAL

ELLIPSOID CONOID ELLIPTIC SPHEROID

ELLIPTICAL OVAL OVATE OBLONG

ELM ULME ELVEN ULMUS WAHOO MEZCAL CHEWBARK ORHAMWOOD

ELOCUTION SPEECH DICTION ORATORY

ELOCUTIONIST READER RECITER

ELOIGN CONVEY REMOVE ABSCOND CONCEAL

ELONGATE EXTEND REMOVE STRETCH LENGTHEN PROTRACT

ELONGATED LANK LONG LINEAR OBLONG PROLATE SLENDER HAIRLIKE PRODUCED

ELOPE DECAMP ESCAPE ABSCOND

ELOQUENCE FACUND FLUENCY ORATORY

ELOQUENT VOCAL DISERT FACUND FERVID FLUENT SILVER RENABLE SPEAKING ORATORICAL

EL SALVADOR

CAPITAL: SANSALVADOR
COIN: PESO COLON CENTAVO
DEPARTMENT: LAPAZ CABANAS MORAZAN SONSONATE
GULF: FONSECA
INDIAN: PIPIL
LAKE: GUIJA ILOPANGO
MEASURE: VARA CAFIZ CAHIZ FANEGA TERCIA BOTELLA CAJUELA CANTARO MANZANA
POINT: REMEDIOS
PORT: CUTUCO ACAJUTLA
RIVER: JIBOA LAPAZ LEMPA
RUINS: TAZUMAL
TOWN: CUTUCO IZALCO CORINTO METAPAN ACAJUTLA USULUTAN SONSONATE AHUACHAPAN
VOLCANO: IZALCO
WEIGHT: BAG CAJA LIBRA

ELSE OR ENS ENSE OTHER BESIDES INSTEAD

ELSEWHERE ALIBI EXCEPT THENCE

ELUCIDATE CLEAR LUCID EXPLAIN SIMPLIFY

ELUDE BEAT FLEE FOIL JINK MISS MOCK SLIP AVOID DODGE EVADE BAFFLE BEFOIL DELUDE DOUBLE ESCAPE BEGUILE DECEIVE HEDGEHOP

ELUSIVE EELY LUBRIC SHIFTY SUBTLE TRICKY TWISTY EVASIVE BAFFLING FUGITIVE SLIPPERY

ELYSIUM EDEN ANNWFN PARADISE

EMACIATED LEAN POOR EMPTY GAUNT MEAGER PEAKED SKINNY WASTED TABETIC WASTREL MARASMIC SKELETAL WANTHRIVEN

EMACIATION NITON TABES MACIES ATROPHY POVERTY ASTHENIA MARASMUS

EMANATE FLOW ARISE EMANE EXUDE ISSUE DERIVE EFFUSE EXHALE OUTRAY SPRING BREATHE OUTCOME PROCEED RADIATE

EMANATING EFFLUENT

EMANATION FUG AURA BEAM BLAS GLORY NITON AZILUT BREATH EFFLUX ELAPSE EIDOLON MOFETTE OUTCOME PROCESS SEPHIRA EMISSION PROCESSION
(— FROM A MEDIUM) ECTOPLASM
(SENSED —) KARMA

EMANCIPATE FREE MANUMIT RELEASE LIBERATE UNFETTER

EMANCIPATION FREEDOM RELEASE
(FINAL —) NIRVANA

EMBALM BALM CERE MUMMY SPICE BALSAM SEASON CONDITE MUMMIFY

EMBANKMENT BAY BANK BANK BUND DIKE FILL QUAY ARGIN DIGUE LEVEE MOUND REVET BUNKER STAITH BACKING BANKING PARADOS PILAPIL RAMPART RAMPIRE SEAWALL APPROACH STRENGTH REVETMENT

EMBARGO EDICT ORDER IMBARGE BLOCKADE STOPPAGE

EMBARK BANK SAIL SHIP ENGAGE ENLIST INSHIP INVEST LAUNCH IMBARGE

EMBARRASS SET CHAW CLOG FAZE HACK LAND POSE ABASH ANNOY SHAME UPSET BOGGLE CUMBER GRAVEL HAMPER HINDER HOBBLE IMPEDE PLUNGE PUZZLE RATTLE CONFUSE ENTRIKE FLUMMOX INVOLVE NONPLUS BEWILDER CONFOUND DUMFOUND ENCUMBER ENTANGLE HANDICAP IMPESTER OBSTRUCT STRAITEN

EMBARRASSED AWKWARD FLURRIED SHEEPISH

EMBARRASSING STICKY AWKWARD HIDEOUS

EMBARRASSMENT FIX GENE LURCH SHAME STAND CADDLE CUMBER HOBBLE PUZZLE NONPLUS CONFUSION

EMBASSY SAND ERRAND MESSAGE MISSION INBASSAT LEGATION

EMBELLISH GEM DECK GILD TRIM ADORN DRESS FUDGE GRACE BEDECK BETRIM BLAZON EMBOSS ENRICH FIGURE FLOWER APPAREL BEDRAPE EMBLAZE GARNISH MYSTIFY VARNISH BEAUTIFY DECORATE FLOURISH ORNAMENT

EMBELLISHED FLORID GESTED ORNATE COLORED FUCUSED BROCADED SPLENDID

EMBELLISHMENT FILIP GRACE FILLIP RELISH AGREMEN GARNISH GILDING WINDING AGREMENT FLOURISH MOUNTING ORNAMENT PARERGON TRAPPING TRICKING PASSAGGIO

(MUSICAL —) MELISMA ROULADE
ARABESQUE
(PL.) FIXINGS

EMBER ASH COAL AIZLE GLEED IMBER
CINDER
(RED-HOT —S) BAGA

EMBEZZLE STEAL PECULATE SQUANDER

EMBEZZLEMENT THEFT PLUNDERAGE

EMBITTER SOUR BITTER CURDLE ACIDIFY
ENVENOM ACERBATE EMPOISON
VERJUICE

EMBITTERED SOURED ACERBATE
ENFESTED

EMBLAZON LAUD ADORN EXTOL
BLAZON DISPLAY EMBLAZE EXHIBIT
GLORIFY

EMBLAZONED CLOUE CRINED CRESTED
BRISTLED
(— WITH ANTLERS) ATTIRED
(— WITH BEARD) BARBED

EMBLAZONMENT HERALDRY

EMBLEM BAR ANKH LOGO MACE
ORLE SEAL SIGN STAR TYPE AWARD
BADGE CREST CROSS EAGLE FAVOR
IMAGE TIARA TOKEN DEVICE DIADEM
ENSIGN FIGURE KAHILI SABCAT SHIELD
SIGNAL SYMBOL TRISUL CHARACT
IMPRESA IMPRESE SCEPTER SCEPTRE
ALLEGORY CADUCEUS COLOPHON
INSIGNIA
(— OF CUCKOLD) HORN
(— OF IMMORTALITY) AMARANTH
(— OF IRELAND) SHAMROCK
(— OF WALES) LEEK
(AUTOMOBILE —) MARQUE
(PRINTING —) COLOPHON
(SACRED —) HIEROGRAM

EMBLEMATIC TYPAL FIGURAL TYPICAL
SYMBOLIC

EMBODIMENT MAP SON SELF AVATAR
GENIUS EPITOME IMAGERY BODIMENT

EMBODY BODY UNITE INBODY CONTAIN
EXPRESS COALESCE ORGANIZE

EMBOLDEN BOLD BIELD BRAVE ERECT
NERVE ASSURE BOWDEN ENHARDY
HEARTEN STOMACH

EMBOSS BOSS HIDE KNOB KNOT ADORN
BLOCK CHASE GOFFER INDENT POUNCE
ANTIQUE CONCEAL ENCLOSE EXHAUST
GAUFFER INFLATE ORNAMENT

EMBOSSED BOSSED RAISED ANTIQUE
CHAMPED MATELASSE

EMBOSSING CELATURE

EMBOUCHURE LIP CHOPS LIPPING

EMBRACE ARM HUG CLIP COLL FOLD
LOVE NECK PLAT SIDE ZONE ADOPT
BOSOM BRACE CHAIN CLASP CLING
CRUSH ENARM GRASP HALCH HALSE
INARM OXTER PRESS TWINE ABRAZO
ACCEPT ACCOLL AMPLEX BECLIP
CARESS CLINCH COMPLY CUDDLE
ENFOLD FATHOM HUDDLE INCLIP INFOLD
PLIGHT SHRINE AMPLECT CHERISH
CONTAIN ENCLOSE ESPOUSE INCLUDE
INVOLVE ACCOLADE AMPLEXUS
CANOODLE COMPLECT COMPRESS
COMPRISE CONCLUDE ENCIRCLE

EMBRASURE LOOP PORT VENT CRENEL
CRENELLE PORTHOLE

EMBROCATION ARNICA EMBROCHE
LINIMENT

EMBROIDER RUN TAT DARN FRET LACE
BROUD COUCH FAGOT PANEL SMOCK
BEWORK EMBOSS FAGGOT FRIEZE
NEEDLE PURFLE STITCH SURFLE TISSUE
BROIDER TAMBOUR ORNAMENT

EMBROIDERED BRODEE BROWDEN
BROCADED

EMBROIDERER SPRIGGER

EMBROIDERY KANT LACE OPUS WORK
BREDE ASSISI BONNAZ CREWEL EDGING
HEDEBO APPAREL CHICKEN CUTWORK
ORPHREY SETWORK TAMBOUR
ARRASENE BRODERIE BROIDERY
COUCHING FAGOTING LISTWORK
PHULKARI SMOCKING TAPESTRY
CREWELLERY NEEDLEPOINT

EMBROIL BROIL JUMBLE INVOLVE
PERPLEX TROUBLE DISORDER DISTRACT
ENTANGLE

EMBRYO GERM CADET FETUS OVULE
FOETUS EMBRYON NEURULA PLANULA
ACANTHOR BLASTULA GASTRULA
PRINCIPE
(PREF.) BLAST(O)

EMBRYONIC GERMINAL

EMCEE HOST

EMERALD BERYL GREEN EMRAUD
EMERANT PRASINE SMARAGD

EMERGE BOB DIP BOLT LOOM PEER RISE
BREAK ERUPT EXUDE ISSUE START
APPEAR BECOME PLUNGE SPRING
DEBOUCH EXTRUDE
(— FROM EGGSHELL) HATCH ECLOSE
(— FROM SLEEP) AWAKE
(— SLOWLY) PEEK

EMERGENCE NEED BIRTH PINCH EGRESS
GROWTH PRICKLE BECOMING DEBOUCHE
ECLOSION EMERSION ERUPTION
EXIGENCE TENTACLE
(— FROM DARKNESS) BREAK

EMERGENCY NEED PEND PUSH PINCH
CRISIS STRAIT SUDDEN EMERGENT
EXIGENCY JUNCTURE

EMERGENT RISING ONCOMING

EMERY EMERIL SMIRIS ABRASIVE
CORUNDUM

EMETIC ALUM PICK PUKE PUKER VOMIT
EVACUANT VOMITIVE VOMITORY

EMIGRANT EMIGRE EXODIST PATARIN
SETTLER COLONIST PATERINE STRANGER
(— FROM MECCA) COMPANION

EMIGRATE MOVE REMOVE MIGRATE

EMIGRATION EXODUS HEGIRA HEJIRA
SWARMING

EMINENCE DUN NAB BALL BERG CRAG
KNOT MONS MOTE NOTE POLE RANK
RISE SCAR TOOT CHIEF HOYLE KNOLL
PERCH STATE WHEAL WORTH ASCENT
HEIGHT KRANTZ RENOWN RIDEAU
ALTITUDE GRANDEUR TUBERCLE
(— OF HAND) SUBVOLA

EMINENT BIG ARCH HIGH CHIEF GRAND
GREAT LOFTY NOBLE NOTED FAMOUS

MARKED SIGNAL EXCELSE SUBLIME
TOPPING GLORIOUS RENOWNED
SINGULAR TOWERING PROMINENT
CONSPICUOUS

EMIR AMIR AMEER NOBLE RULER LEADER
PRINCE ADMIRAL GOVERNOR

EMISSARY SPY AGENT SCOUT LEGATE
DELEGATE

EMISSION FUME GUST VENT

EMIT RUN BARK BEAM CAST DRIP GIVE
GUSH HURL LASH MOVE OOZE PASS
POUR REEK SEND SHED SPIT VENT VOID
WARP AVOID BELCH EJECT ERUCT EXERT
EXUDE FLASH FLING ISSUE UTTER YIELD
DECANT DONATE EVOLVE EXHALE
EXPIRE SPREAD BREATHE DISTILL
EMANATE EXHAUST OUTSEND RADIATE
REFLAIR ERUCTATE TRANSMIT
(— COHERENT LIGHT) LASE
(— FOAM) SPURGE
(— FORCEFULLY) FIRE
(— IN PUFFS) PLUFF
(— LIGHT) GLOW
(— ODOR) REEK STEAM
(— OUTCRIES) CHUNNER CHUNTER
(— PLAY OF COLORS) OPALESCE
(— RAYS) RADIATE IRRADIATE
(— SMOKE) SMEECH
(— SOUND) BUFF MOVE
(— SPARKS) SNAP

EMMA (AUTHOR OF —) AUSTEN
(CHARACTER IN —) EMMA JANE
BATES ELTON FRANK SMITH GEORGE
MARTIN ROBERT WESTON FAIRFAX
HARRIET CHURCHILL KNIGHTLEY
WOODHOUSE

EMMET ANT ENEMY PISMIRE FORMICID

EMOLLIENT LENIENT ICHTHYOL LENITIVE
MALACTIC MOLLIENT SUPPLING

EMOLUMENT FEES WAGES INCOME
PROFIT SALARY BENEFIT STIPEND

EMOTION IRE LOVE ONDE PANG STIR
AGONY ANGER CHORD GRIEF HEART
SHAME AFFECT EFFECT MOTION RAPTUS
SNIVEL SPLEEN ECSTASY FEELING
PASSION VULTURE GRAMERCY
MOVEMENT SURPRISE SENTIMENT
(CONTROLLING —) LEITMOTIF
LEITMOTIV
(EVIL —) DEMON DAEMON

EMOTIONAL MUSHY DRIPPY EMOTIVE
AFFECTIVE
(UNDULY —) SPOONY RHAPSODIC

EMOTIONLESS COLD

EMPATHY SYMPATHY

EMPEROR CZAR INCA KING TSAR AKBAR
RULER TENNO CAESAR DESPOT KABAKA
KAISER SULTAN BAGINDA MONARCH
VIKRAMA AUGUSTUS IMPERIAL
PADISHAH

EMPHASIS ANGLE ACCENT STRESS
WEIGHT EMPIRISM SALIENCE

EMPHASIZE HIT CLICK PINCH PRESS
ACCENT BETONE CHARGE STRESS

EMPHATIC LOUD STRONG EARNEST
MARCATO SERIOUS ENFATICO FORCIBLE
MARCANDO POSITIVE RESOUNDING

EMPHATICALLY FLATLY STRONGLY
POINTEDLY

EMPHYSEMA HEAVES

EMPIRE RULE SWAY POWER REALM
REIGN STATE DIADEM DOMAIN EMPERY
CONTROL KINGDOM IMPERIUM

EMPIRIC QUACK IMPOSTOR

EMPIRICAL POSITIVE

EMPIRICIST VIRTUOSO

EMPLACEMENT BATTERY GALLERY
PLATFORM

EMPLOY FEE PAY USE BUSK BUSY HIRE
PLOY TAKE WAGE WISE ADOPT APPLY
BESET IMPLY SPEND BESTOW ENGAGE
ENLIST INFOLD INVOKE OCCUPY SUPPLY
CONCERN CONDUCT ENCLOSE IMPROVE
INVOLVE SERVICE UTILIZE PRACTICE
(— FLATTERY) COLLOGUE
(— ONESELF ABOUT) TOSS
(— SHIFTS) CHICANE

EMPLOYED APPLIED ENGAGED

EMPLOYEE HAND HELP BOOTS CLERK
FACTOR LEADER BELLBOY BOOTBOY
CALLBOY CARRIER SERVANT CHASSEUR
CIVILIAN FLOORMAN IMPROVER
(— WHO RUNS ERRANDS) GOFER
GOPHER

EMPLOYER BOSS JOSS BLOKE GAFFER
ENGAGER MANAGER PADRONE
GOVERNOR
(SMALL —) CORK

EMPLOYMENT FEE JOB USE CALL HIRE
NOTE TASK TOIL USER WORK CRAFT
TRADE TREAD USAGE MISTER THRIFT
CALLING PURPOSE PURSUIT SERVICE
USAUNCE BUSINESS EXERCISE POSITION
RETAINER VOCATION
(CASUAL —) GRASS

EMPORIUM MART SHOP BAZAR STORE
BAZAAR EMPORY MARKET STAPLE
MONOPOLE

EMPOWER POWER ENABLE ENTITLE
DELEGATE DEPUTIZE

EMPTIED DRAINED

EMPTINESS VAIN VOID INANE ANEMIA
VACUUM VANITY ANAEMIA INANITY
VACANCY VACUITY LEERNESS
(— OF SPIRIT) ENNUI

EMPTY DRY FAT RID TIM AIRY BARE
BOSS BUZZ CANT DEAF DUMP EMPT
FALL FARM FREE GLIB HOWE IDLE LEER
NEAR POUR ROOM TEEM TOOM VAIN
VIDE VOID ADDLE AVOID BLANK BLEED
CLEAN CLEAR DRAIN EQUAL EXPEL
HUSKY INANE LEERY MOUTH SCOOP
SHOOT SKAIL STARK START STRIP
SWAMP TINNY WINDY BARREN BUBBLE
CHAFFY DEVOID GOUSTY HOLLOW
JEJUNE STRIKE SWASTY UNEMPT
UNLOAD VACANT VACATE DELIVER
DEPLETE EXHAUST EXPRESS UNTAKEN
VACUATE VACUOUS VIDUOUS DISGORGE
EVACUATE EVANESCE NEGATION
UNFILLED
(— AN EGG) BLOW

EMPYREAN ETHER HEAVENS EMPYREUM

EMU RHEA RATITE

EMULATE APE VIE COPY EMULE EQUAL EXCEL RIVAL COMPETE IMITATE

EMULATION STRIFE CONTEST PARAGON RIVALRY

EMULATOR RIVAL

EMULSION PAP LATEX

ENABLE ABLE EMPOWER ENTITLE QUALIFY INHABILE

ENACT LIVE MAKE PASS ADOPT DECREE EFFECT ORDAIN ACTUATE APPOINT PERFORM PORTRAY

ENACTMENT LAW DOOM ENACT NOVEL ASSIZE DECREE MEASURE PASSAGE STATUTE ENACTION ENACTURE

ENAMEL AMEL FLUX SLIP EMAIL GLAZE GLOSS PAINT SLUSH AUMAIL SHIPPO SMALTO DENTINE LIMOGES SCHMELZ

ENAMOR LOVE CHARM SMITE CAPTIVE

ENAMORED FOND EPRIS EPRISE MASHED AMOROUS CHARMED SMITTEN (VAINLY —) FOOLISH

ENCAMP TELD TENT LODGE PITCH INCAMP LAAGER BIVOUAC LEAGUER

ENCAMPMENT CAMP DOUAR ETAPE SIEGE LAAGER BIVOUAC CASTRUM HUTMENT TOLDERIA

ENCASE CASE HOUSE SHELL INCASE ENCHASE INCLOSE SURROUND ENCAPSULE

ENCEPHALON CEREBRUM

ENCHANT CHARM DELUDE GLAMOR INCANT ATTRACT BECHARM BESPELL BEWITCH DELIGHT GLAMOUR BEDAZZLE ENSORCEL CAPTIVATE

ENCHANTED RAPT HAGGED CAPTIVE

ENCHANTER MAUGIS CHARMER MAGICIAN MALAGIGI ARCHIMAGE

ENCHANTING ORPHIC WIZARD HEAVENLY SPELLFUL

ENCHANTMENT HEX TAKE CHARM FAIRY MAGIC SPELL SPOKE CARACT CHANTRY DEVILRY GRAMARY SORCERY SORTIARY WITCHERY

ENCHANTRESS CIRCE FAIRY MEDEA ACRASIA URGANDA

ENCIPHER CODE CIPHER ENCRYPT

ENCIRCLE ORB BAND BELT BIND CLIP COIL GIRD GIRT HALO HOOP PALE RING RINK STEM WIRE ZONE BELAY BESET BRACE CLASP CROWN EMBAY EMBOW GIRTH HEDGE INORB ROUND TWINE TWIST BECLIP CIRCLE EMBALL ENGIRT ENLACE ENRING ENWIND FATHOM GIRDLE IMPALE SWATHE WRITHE BETREND COMPASS EMBRACE ENCLAVE ENCLOSE ENTWINE ENVIRON ENWHEEL SERPENT WREATHE CINCTURE CORSELET ENSPHERE IMMANTLE SURROUND

ENCIRCLED GIRT CINCT BELTED SUCCINCT

ENCIRCLEMENT EMBRACE

ENCIRCLING AROUND EMBRACE CORONARY ENCYCLIC (PREF.) AMPLEXI

ENCLOSE IN BAY BOX CAN HEM LAP MEW ORB PAR PEN PIN RIM BANK BUNG CAGE CASE COOP FORT GIRD HAIN HOOP PALE SPAR TINE WALL WARD WOMB YARD BOSOM BOUND BOWER BRICK CHEST CLOSE DITCH EMBAR EMBED EMBOX FENCE FRAME GARTH GRIPE HEDGE HOUSE IMBED INURN BOUGHT CARTON CASTLE CAVERN CIRCLE CORDON CORRAL EMBANK EMBOSS EMPALE EMPARK EMPLOY ENCASE ENCYST ENFOLD ENGULF ENLOCK FASTEN IMMURE IMPALE IMPARK INCASE INCLIP INHOOP INSACK INWALL JACKET PICKET POCKET TACKLE APPROVE CAPSULE COMPASS CONFIDE CONTAIN CURTAIN EMBOSOM EMBOWEL EMBOWER EMBRACE ENCHASE ENCLAVE ENGLOBE ENHEDGE ENVELOP HARNESS IMBOSOM IMMERSE IMPOUND INBOUND INCLUDE INFIELD PARROCK PINFOLD SHEATHE BULKHEAD COMPRISE COMPRIZE CONCLUDE CONVOLVE EMBORDER ENCIRCLE ENSHRINE ENSPHERE IMPRISON LANDLOCK PALISADE PARCLOSE SURROUND (— IN ARMOR) EMPANOPLY (— LOGS) CRIB

ENCLOSED BOUND CLOSED OBTECT INGROWN INTERNAL

ENCLOSURE HAG HAW HOK MEW PAR PEN REE STY TYE BOMA BYTH CAGE CAVE CELL COOP DOCK FOLD HAIN HOCK HOPE KILN LIST PALE PEEL SEPT SKIT SLOT TIGH TOWN WALL WEIR YARD ALTIS ATAJO BASIN BLIND BOOLY BOOTH BOSOM CAROL CLOSE COURT CRAWL CREEP CUBBY FENCE FRANK GARTH GOTRA KRAAL LOBBY MARAI PLECK POUND REEVE STALL STELL AVIARY BOOLEY BOXING CANCHA CARREL CORRAL COWPEN CRUIVE DRYLOT GARDEN HURDLE INTAKE KENNEL OUTSET PALING PRISON SERAIL TAMBOR TEOPAN TINING VIVARY WARREN BELLOWS BOROUGH BULLPEN CLOSURE COCKPIT EMBRACE GALLERY GONDOLA HAINING HENNERY HOUSING HUMIDOR LANTERN PADDOCK PIGHTLE PUDDOCK SEVERAL STUFFER TAMBOUR AEDICULA CASEMATE CHIPYARD CINCTURE CLAPNEST CLAUSURE CLOISTER COMPOUND DELUBRUM ENCEINTE ENCHASER PARADISE POUNDAGE PRECINCT PURPRISE SEPIMENT SERAGLIO SKIRTING STOCKADE VIVARIUM (— ABOUT ALTAR) BEMA (— FOR BOWLING) ALLEY (— FOR COCKPIT) CANOPY (— FOR FISH) CROY YAIR YARE KENCH SPILLER SPILLET (— FOR JURY) BOX (— FOR KNIGHTLY ENCOUNTERS) BARRACE (— FOR LIGHT) LANTERN (— FOR ROASTING ORE) STALL (— OF HOUSE) BAWN (— SURROUNDED BY DITCH) COP (ELEPHANT —) KEDDAH

(OBLONG —) CIRCUS
(PORTABLE —) PLAYPEN
(POULTRY —) HENNERY
(SACRED —) SECOS SEKOS
ENCOMIUM ELOGE ENCOMY EULOGY
PRAISE PLAUDIT TRIBUTE PANEGYRIC
ENCOMPASS BEGO BELT CLIP GIRD
PALE RING SPAN WALL WRAP BELIE
BERUN BESET BIGAN BRACE CLOSE
CROWN ROUND BEGIRD BEGIRT CIRCLE
ENGIRD BESEIGE COMPASS EMBOWEL
EMBRACE ENCLOSE ENVIRON INCLUDE
SUBSUME UMBESET CINCTURE
ENCIRCLE ENGIRDLE PURPRISE
SURROUND
(— WITH ARMS) FATHOM
ENCOMPASSED AMID BAYED AMIDST
BEGIRT
ENCOMPASSING ROUND AMBIENT
CINCTURE PROFOUND INCLUSIVE
ENCORE BIS AGAIN ANCORA RECALL
REPEAT
ENCOUNTER BIDE BUMP COIL COPE
FACE FIND KEEP MEET MOOT RINK
BRUSH CLOSE FIGHT FORCE GREET
INCUR OCCUR ONSET SHOCK STOUR
VENUE ACCOST AFFRAY ANSWER ASSAIL
ATTACK BATTLE BREAST CAREER
COMBAT JOSTLE JUSTLE OPPOSE
RUFFLE ADDRESS AFFRONT CONTEST
COUNTER DISPUTE HOSTING JOINING
PASSAGE CONFLICT CONFRONT
CONGRESS REANSWER RECONTER
SKIRMISH COLLISION
(— HOSTILELY) CROSS
(HOSTILE —) CLOSE
(PUGILISTIC —) MILL
ENCOURAGE DAW EGG ABET BACK
FIRM URGE BOOST CHEER ERECT FAVOR
FLUSH HEART IMPEL NERVE SERVE
STEEL ADVISE ASSURE EXHORT FOMENT
FOSTER HALLOO HARDEN INCITE INDUCE
INVITE NUZZLE REHETE SECOND SPIRIT
UPHOLD ADVANCE ANIMATE CHERISH
COMFORT CONFIRM CONSOLE ENFORCE
ENLIVEN FLATTER FORTIFY FORWARD
HEARTEN INSPIRE PROMOTE STOMACH
UPCHEER UPRAISE EMBOLDEN INSPIRIT
REASSURE
ENCOURAGED BUCKED CONFIRMED
ENCOURAGEMENT BOOST FLUSH
HURRAH COMFORT FOMENTO IMPETUS
BLESSING SANCTION
ENCOURAGING HELPFUL FAVORING
ENCROACH PINCH POACH IMPOSE
INVADE TRENCH IMPINGE INTRUDE
SHINGLE ENTRENCH INFRINGE TRESPASS
ENCROACHING INVASIVE
ENCROACHMENT BREACH INROAD
INVASION
ENCRUST CAKE CANDY BARKEN BARKLE
ENCUMBER CLOG LOAD PACK BESET
CHECK CROWD TRASH ACCLOY BEMOIL
BURDEN FELTER HAMPER HINDER
IMPEDE LUMBER MITHER MOIDER
RETARD SADDLE WEIGHT BEPAPER
INVOLVE OPPRESS ACCUMBER

ENTANGLE HANDICAP OBSTRUCT
OVERCOME OVERLOAD
ENCUMBERED HEAVY CONGESTED
ENCUMBRANCE CLOG LIEN LOAD
CLAIM BURDEN CHARGE CUMBER
TROUBLE MORTGAGE ALBATROSS
ENCYCLICAL PASCENDI
END AIM DAG EAR FAG TIP BUTT DATE
DOUP FACE FATE FINE FOOT GOAL HALT
HEEL LAST MAN MARK SAKE STOP TAIL
TERM VIEW AMEND ARTHA BLOCK
BREAK CAUSE CEASE CLOSE DEATH
ENSUE EVENT FINIS ISSUE LIMIT LOOSE
NAPOO OMEGA POINT PRICK RAISE
SCOPE SCRAP SHANK START STASH
THULE DECIDE DEFINE DESIGN DOMINO
EFFECT EFFLUX ENDING EXITUS EXPIRE
EXPIRY FINALE FINISH INTENT NAPOOH
OBJECT PERIOD RESULT THIRTY UPSHOT
UTMOST WINDUP ABOLISH ACHIEVE
CLOSURE CURTAIN DESTROY FANTAIL
FINANCE LINEMAN MEANING OUTGIVE
PURPOSE REMNANT BOUNDARY
COMPLETE CONCLUDE DESITION
DISSOLVE FINALITY SURCEASE
TERMINAL TERMINUS ULTIMATE
(— DEBATE) CLOTURE
(— OF ANTENNA) CLAVA
(— OF ANVIL) BICKIRON
(— OF ARCHERY PILE) STOPPING
(— OF ARROW) NOCK
(— OF BEEF LOIN) BUTT
(— OF BLANKET) DAGON
(— OF BONE) EPIPHYSIS
(— OF BOOM) JAW
(— OF BOW) EAR
(— OF BRICK) HEADING
(— OF BRISTLE) FLAG
(— OF BUILDING) GABLE
(— OF CAN) BREAST
(— OF CANE) FRAZE
(— OF CART) TIB
(— OF CRESCENT) HORN
(— OF EAR CANAL) AMPULLA
(— OF EGG) DOUP
(— OF EXISTENCE) DEMISE
(— OF FABRIC) FENT
(— OF FISHHOOK) SPEAR
(— OF FLAG) FLY
(— OF FROG) TOE
(— OF HALTER) CAPITULUM
(— OF HAMMER) CLAW POLL
(— OF HAMMERHEAD) PEEN
(— OF HORSE-COLLAR) GULLET
(— OF INGOT) CROP
(— OF KEEL) GRIPE
(— OF LEVER) FORK
(— OF LOAF) HEEL
(— OF MINE TUNNEL) FACE
(— OF MINERAL LODE) SLOVAN
(— OF MINING LEVEL) DEAN
(— OF MUZZLE) MUFFLE
(— OF NAIL) CLENCH
(— OF ONE'S LIFE) DOOM
(— OF PIER) CUTWATER
(— OF PIPE) TAFT SPIGOT

(— OF POCKETKNIFE HANDLE) BOLSTER
(— OF RAILROAD CAR) BEND
(— OF ROAD) ROADHEAD
(— OF ROD) FORKHEAD
(— OF SHEEP SHEARING) CUTOUT
(— OF SHIP) STERN
(— OF SPINE) ACRUMION
(— OF TENON) HAUNCH
(— OF TOOL) BUTT
(— OF UTERUS) FUNDUS
(— OF WORLD) PRALAYA
(— OF YARD) ARM YARDARM
(— ON) ABUT
(— ON POND) FOREBAY
(—S OF RIBBONS) FATTRELS
(—S OF SATURN'S RINGS) ANSA
(CANDLE —) DOUP SNUFF
(DOMINO —) ACE
(FAG —) RUMP
(HANGING —) DAG DAGGE
(JAGGED —) SHRAG
(NARROWED —) NEB
(NORTH — OF COMPASS NEEDLE) LILY
(POINTED —) APEX
(POSTERIOR —) BOTTOM
(REEF —) DEADMAN
(ROPE'S —) COLT FEAZE PIGTAIL FEAZINGS
(SPECIAL —) SAKE
(TAPERING —) POINT
(TATTERED —) FRAZZLE
(ULTIMATE —) SUM TELOS
(UNPLEASANT —) GRIEF
(UPPER —) HEAD
(WARP —S) ACCIDENTAL
(PREF.) ACR(O) FINI TEL(IO)
ENDANGER HAZARD IMPERIL SCUPPER
ENDANGERED BESTEAD FRAUGHT
ENDEARMENT LOVE CARESS
ENDEAVOR DO AIM PUT TRY WIN BEST MINT SEEK WORK ASSAY ESSAY ETTLE EXERT OFFER STUDY TEMPT TRIAL AFFAIR ASSAIL EFFORT INTEND STRIFE STRIVE AFFORCE ATTEMPT CONATUS CONTEND CULTURE EMPRISE EMULATE IMITATE MOLIMEN NITENCY WORKING EXERTION PURCHASE STRUGGLE
(— TO CONCLUSION) STUDY
(BEST —) DEVOIR
(EARNESTLY —) FEND
ENDED DONE OVER PAST FINISHED
ENDEMIC LOCAL
ENDING END CLOSE DEATH GRAVE FINALE BREAKUP FINANCE DESITION.
(NERVE —) SPINDLE
ENDIVE CHICORY WITLOOF ESCAROLE SCARIOLE
ENDLESS ANANTA ETERNE ETERNAL FOREVER UNDYING UNENDED UNENDLY DATELESS FINELESS IMMORTAL INFINITE UNENDING
ENDORSE BACK SIGN ADOPT BOOST DOCKET ENDOSS SECOND APPROVE CERTIFY INDORSE SPONSOR SUPPORT ADVOCATE SANCTION RECOMMEND

ENDORSEMENT FIAT FORM VISA RIDER BACKING APPROVAL HECHSHER SANCTION
ENDOW DOW DUE DOTE GIFT RENT VEST BLESS CROWN DOWER ENDUE EQUIP FOUND INDUE SEIZE STATE STUFF ASSIGN CLOTHE DOTATE ENABLE ENRICH ENSOUL ESTATE INVEST CHARTER ENLARGE FURNISH INSTATE APPANAGE BENEFICE BEQUEATH ENTALENT
(— WITH FORCE) DYNAMIZE
ENDOWED ABLE GIFTED FAVORED
ENDOWMENT CLAY FINE GIFT WAKF DOWER DOWRY GRACE CORPSE GENIUS TALENT APANAGE CHANTRY CHARISM FACULTY APPANAGE DOTATION PATRIMONY BENEFACTION
(NATURAL —S) BUMP DOTES TALENT
(PL.) ALTARAGE
ENDUE DUE ENDOW TEACH CLOTHE INVEST INSTRUCT
ENDURABLE LIVABLE BEARABLE LIVEABLE PORTABLE
ENDURANCE GAME LAST TACK PLUCK BOTTOM BEARING COMFORT DURANCE GRANITE LASTING STAMINA BEARANCE DURATION GAMENESS HARDSHIP PATIENCE STRENGTH
ENDURE GO SIT VIE ABYE BEAR BIDE DREE DURE HOLD KEEP LAST TAKE TIDE WEAR ABEAR ABIDE ALLOW BROOK CARRY DRIVE POUCH SPARE STAND STICK STOUT THOLE TOUGH WIELD ABROOK ACCEPT DRUDGE HARDEN REMAIN SUFFER ABROOKE COMFORT FORBEAR PERSIST STOMACH SUPPORT SUSTAIN SWALLOW TOUGHEN UNDERGO WEARING CONTINUE FOREBEAR TOLERATE
ENDURING FAST SURE STOUT BIDING DURING STABLE STURDY ABIDING DURABLE ETERNAL LASTING PATIENT IMMORTAL REMANENT STUBBORN PERENNIAL
ENDYMION (DAUGHTER OF —) EURYDICE
(FATHER OF —) ZEUS JUPITER AETHELIUS
(MOTHER OF —) CALYCE
(SON OF —) EPEUS PAEON AETOLUS
(WIFE OF —) CROMIA ASTERODIA HYPARIPPE
ENEMA CLYSMA CLYSTER LAVEMENT
ENEMY FOE AXIS BOYG FEID DEVIL FIEND SATAN FOEMAN HOSTILE CONTRARY OPPONENT
(— OF MANKIND) DEVIL FIEND SATAN
(PERSONAL —) HATER
ENEMY OF THE PEOPLE
(AUTHOR OF —) IBSEN
(CHARACTER IN —) KIIL PETER MORTEN HORSTER HOVSTAD ASLAKSEN STOCKMANN
ENERGETIC BUSY FAST FELL HARD LIVE RASH BRISK DASHY LUSTY PITHY STOUT TIGHT VITAL YAULD ZIPPY ACTIVE HEARTY HUSTLE LIVELY SPROIL ACTIOUS

ANIMOSO ARDUOUS DASHING DRIVING
DYNAMIC ENERGIC FURIOUS NERVOUS
PUSHFUL PUSHING VIBRANT EMPHATIC
ENERGICO FORCEFUL FORCIBLE
HUSTLING VIGOROUS
ENERGETICALLY MANLY FURIOUSLY
ENERGIZE EXCITE ANIMATE
ENERGIZING KINETIC VIRTUAL
ENERGY GO PEP VIM ZIP BANG BENT
DASH EDGE LIFE SNAP TUCK ZING
ARDOR ECLAT FORCE INPUT NERVE
POWER STEAM VIGOR EFFORT FOISON
INTAKE ORGONE OUTPUT SPIRIT SPRAWL
SPRING SPROIL STARCH VIRTUE
POTENCY SPIRITS ACTIVITY AMBITION
DYNAMISM ENERGEIA MOTIVITY
PRAKRITI STRENGTH VIVACITY
(— PEAK) NUCLEUS
(EMOTIONAL —) LIBIDO
(LIBINAL —) CATHEXIS
(LIFE —) JIVA SAKTI SHAKTI
(LIGHT —) RAD
(MENTAL —) DOCITY PSYCHURGY
(POTENTIAL —) ERGAL
(QUANTUM OF —) PLASMON
(RADIANT —) SOUND ACTINISM
EINSTEIN
(VITAL —) HORME PANZOISM
ENERVATE SAP COOK FLAG MELT
SOFTEN WEAKEN MOLLIFY UNNERVE
UNSINEW ENFEEBLE
ENERVATED BEDRID EFFETE LANGUID
BEDRIDDEN
ENERVATING MUGGY DREARY
ENFEEBLE NUMB FAINT SHAKE APPALL
DEADEN FEEBLE IMPAIR SOFTEN
WEAKEN DEPRESS UNSINEW AFFEEBLE
ENERVATE IMBECILE UNSTRONG
ENFEEBLED FEY NUMB
ENFOLD (ALSO SEE INFOLD) LAP FURL
ROLL WRAP CLASP COVER DRAPE ENROL
IMPLY COMPLY ENLACE ENROLL ENWIND
ENWRAP INCLIP INFOLD INWIND
SHADOW SWATHE WATTLE EMBRACE
ENCLOSE ENVIRON INCLUDE
INVOLVE UMBELAP CONVOLVE
ENFORCE BULL LEVY EXACT FORCE
PRESS COERCE COMPEL EFFECT FOLLOW
INVOKE EXECUTE IMPLANT
ENFORCED COMPULSORY
ENFORCER EXECUTOR MUSCLEMAN
ENGAGE DIP WED BOOK BUSY GAGE
HAVE HIRE JOIN LIST MESH RENT SIGN
TAKE WAGE AGREE AMUSE CATCH
ENTER LEASE PITCH TRADE TRYST
ABSORB ARREST EMBARK EMPLOY
ENLIST INDUCE OBLIGE OCCUPY PLEDGE
PLIGHT BESPEAK BETROTH CONCERN
CONDUCE CONSUME ENGROSS IMMERSE
INVOLVE PROMISE AFFIANCE CONTRACT
COVENANT ENTANGLE INTEREST
INTRIGUE PERSUADE PREOCCUPY
(— DEEPLY) DROWN
(— IN) GO CUT SUE HAVE JOIN LEAD
PROSECUTE
(— IN ARGUMENT) BALK BAULK

(— IN COMBAT) DEBATE STRIKE
(— IN DEBATE) STONEWALL
(— IN DISCUSSION) CONTEND
(— IN PRANKS) LARK
(— IN TILT) JUST JOUST
(— WHOLLY) ABSORB CONSUME
IMMERSE
ENGAGED BENT BUSY FAST GONE HIRED
ACTIVE BONDED BOOKED MESHED
ASSURED BESPOKE EARNEST ENTERED
PLEDGED TOKENED VERSANT ABSORBED
ATTACHED EMBEDDED EMPLOYED
INSERTED INTEREST INVOLVED
OCCUPIED PROMISED
(— IN) ABOUT
(— IN CONTROVERSY) DISPUTANT
(MENTALLY —) VERSANT
(WARMLY —) ZEALOUS
ENGAGEMENT AVAL DATE COWLE
SPURN ACTION AFFAIR BATTLE COMBAT
ESCROW PLIGHT STANZA SURETY
BARGAIN BOOKING DUSTING SERVICE
CONFLICT RETAINER SKIRMISH
WARRANTY
(— TO MARRY) TRYST
(MILITARY —) DO SHOW
(SHORT —) SNAP
(SINGLE —) GIG
(THEATRICAL —) SHOP
(WRITTEN —) COWLE
ENGAGING SOFT SAPID SWEET TAKING
ENGENDER BEGET BREED CAUSE EXCITE
GENDER DEVELOP PRODUCE GENERATE
INGENDER OCCASION
ENGINE GAS JET SIX FOUR GOAT TANK
EIGHT JINNY MOTOR OILER STEAM
BANKER DIESEL JORDAN KICKER PUFFER
RADIAL ROADER YARDER MACHINE
POACHER SKIDDER STEAMER TRACTOR
TURBINE BULLGINE COMPOUND
EXPANDER GASOLINE IMPULSOR
(— FOR HAULING LOGS) DUDLER
DUDLEY
(— FOR THROWING MISSILES) GIN
PETRARY SPRINGAL
(— OF TORTURE) GIN RACK
(— OF WAR) RAM SWEEP HELEPOLE
(AIRPLANE —) SCRAMJET
(DONKEY —) DOCTOR
(FIRE —) TUB
(JET —) ATHODYD
(MILITARY —) BOAR TOWER BRICOL
FABRIC TREPAN BRICOLE DONDINE
PERRIER PETRARY TORMENT WARWOLF
BALLISTA DONDAINE MANGONEL
MARTINET SCORPION
(RAILROAD —) HOG GOAT YARDER
SWITCHER
(REACTION —) THRUSTER THRUSTOR
(ROCKET —) ARCJET VERNIER
ENGINEER PLAN GUIDE DRIVER FANNER
HOGGER MANAGE SAPPER HOGHEAD
PLANNER PLOTTER CONTRIVE DESIGNER
INGENIER INVENTOR MANEUVER
ENGINEMAN HOISTER HOISTMAN
ENGIRDLED CINCT

ENGLAND HOME ALBION LOGRIA
BLIGHTY BRITAIN LOEGRIA HOMELAND

ENGLAND

BAY: TOR LYME WASH START MOUNTS
BIGBURY BIDEFORD CARDIGAN
FALMOUTH TREMADOC WEYMOUTH
CAPITAL: LONDON
CHANNEL: SOLENT BRISTOL ENGLISH
SPITHEAD
CHANNEL ISLAND: HERM SARK JERSEY
ALDERNEY GUERNSEY
COIN: ORA RIAL RYAL ACKEY ANGEL
CROWN GROAT NOBLE PENCE PENNY
POUND SPRAT UNITE BAWBEE FLORIN
GUINEA SESKIN TESTON ANGELET
CAROLUS HAPENNY TUPPENY FARTHING
SHILLING SIXPENCE TUPPENCE
COUNTY: KENT DEVON ESSEX HANTS
NOTTS SALOP WIGHT DORSET DURHAM
LONDON SURREY SUSSEX NORFOLK
RUTLAND SUFFOLK CHESHIRE
CORNWALL SOMERSET
HILLS: MENDIP BRENDON CHEVIOT
MALVERN CHILTERN COTSWOLD
ISLAND: HOLY LUNDY WIGHT COQUET
MERSEA THANET TRESCO WALNEY
BARDSEY HAYLING IRELAND SHEPPEY
ANGLESEA ANGLESEY FOULNESS
HOLYHEAD
ISLANDS: FARNE SCILLY CHANNEL
KING: HAL LUD BRAN BRUT CNUT COLE
KNUT LEAR HENRY JAMES SWEYN
ALFRED BLADUD BRUTUS CANUTE
EDWARD EGBERT GEORGE ARTEGAL
ELIDURE RICHARD WILLIAM GORBODUC
LAKE: CONISTON
MEASURE: CUT ELL LEA MIL PIN ROD RUN
TON TUN VAT ACRE BIND BOLL BUTT
CADE COMB COOM CRAN FOOT GILL
GOAD HAND HANK HEER HIDE INCH LAST
LINE MILE NAIL PACE PALM PECK PINT
PIPE POLE POOL ROOD ROPE SACK SEAM
SPAN TRUG TYPP WIST YARD YOKE
BODGE CABOT CHAIN COOMB CUBIT
DIGIT FLOAT FLOOR FLUID HUTCH
JUGUM MINIM OUNCE PERCH POINT
PRIME QUART SKEIN STACK TRUSS
BARREL BOVATE BUSHEL CRANNE
FATHOM FIRKIN GALLON HOBBET
HOBBIT LEAGUE MANENT OXGANG
POTTLE RUNLET SECOND SQUARE
STRIKE SULUNG THREAD TIERCE
AUCHLET FURLONG KENNING QUARTER
RUNDLET SEAMILE SPINDLE TERTIAN
VIRGATE CARUCATE CHALDRON
HOGSHEAD LANDYARD PUNCHEON
QUADRANT QUARTERN STANDARD
MOUNTAIN: PEAK SCAFELL SKIDDAW
SNOWDON
MOUNTAINS: BLACK PENNINE SNOWDON
CAMBRIAN CUMBRIAN
PENINSULA: PORTLAND
POINT: NAZE LYNAS MORTE SALES

DODMAN LIZARD PRAWLE HARTLAND
LANDSEND GIBRALTAR
RIVER: CAM DEE DON ESK EXE LEA NEN
URE WYE AIRE AVON EDEN LUNE NENE
NIDD OUSE PENK TAME TEES TILL TYNE
WEAR YARE ANKER COLNE DEBEN
STOUR SWALE TAMAR TAWAR TRENT
TWEED HUMBER KENNET MERSEY
RIBBLE ROTHER SEVERN THAMES
WENSUM WHARFE WITHAM DERWENT
PARRETT WAVENEY WELLAND TORRIDGE
ROYAL HOUSE: YORK TUDOR STUART
HANOVER WINDSOR LANCASTER
PLANTAGENET
STRAIT: DOVER
TOWN: ELY BATH DEAL HULL RYDE WARE
YORK BLYTH BRENT DERBY DOVER ERITH
FLINT LEEDS RIPON TRURO WIGAN
BARNET BOLTON BOOTLE CAMDEN
DURHAM EALING EXETER HANLEY
JARROW LEYTON LONDON OLDHAM
OXFORD YEOVIL BRISTOL BROMLEY
BURNLEY CHELSEA CROYDON ENFIELD
GRIMSBY HALIFAX HORNSEY IPSWICH
LAMBETH NEWPORT NORWICH PRESTON
SALFORD SEAFORD WESTHAM
BRADFORD BRIGHTON CORNWALL
COVENTRY DEWSBURY HASTINGS
PLYMOUTH ROCHDALE WALLASEY
WALLSALL GREENWICH LIVERPOOL
SHEFFIELD BIRMINGHAM MANCHESTER
TRIBE: ICENI
VALLEY: COOM EDEN TEES TYNE COMBE
COOMB COQUET
WEIGHT: BAG KIP TOD TON KEEL LAST
MAST MAUN BARGE FAGOT GRAIN
MAUND POUND SCORE STAND STONE
TRUSS BUSHEL CENTAL FANGOT FIRKIN
FOTHER FOTMAL POCKET QUARTER
QUINTAL SARPLER

ENGLISH SAXON AUSTRAL BRITISH
ENGLAND SAXONISH SOUTHRON
STANDARD
(— MIXED WITH SPANISH)
SPANGLISH
ENGLISHMAN SAXON BRITON BRONCO
GODDAM GRINGO JOHNNY ROOINEK
MACARONI SOUTHRON ENGLISHER
ENGLISHWOMAN INGLESA
ENGORGE GLUT GORGE DEVOUR
SWALLOW
ENGRAFT INSET
ENGRAVE CUT ETCH RIST CARVE CHASE
GRAVE HATCH PRINT SCULP CHISEL
INCISE SCULPT CRIBBLE ENCHASE
EXARATE IMPRESS IMPRINT INSCULP
STIPPLE INSCRIBE ORNAMENT
ENGRAVED GRAVEN GRAPHIC INCISED
(PREF.) GRAPTO
ENGRAVER POINT CHASER ETCHER
GRAVER ARTISAN INSCULP BURINIST
MEDALIST SCULLION WRIGGLER
(— OF STONES) LAPIDARY
ENGRAVING CUT PRINT SCULP STAMP
GRAVERY GRAVING GRAVURE WOODCUT

AQUATINT DRYPOINT HATCHING
INTAGLIO LINEWORK MEZZOTINT
(PREF.) GLYPHO GLYPT(O)
ENGROSS BURY SINK SOAK AMASS
GROSS ABSORB ENGAGE ENROLL
ENWRAP OCCUPY SCROLL COLLECT
CONSUME IMMERSE INVOLVE
PREOCCUPY
ENGROSSED DEEP FULL RAPT INTENT
BEMUSED WRAPPED ABSORBED
IMMERSED PREOCCUPIED
ENGULF GULF ABYSM ABYSS SOUSE
SWAMP WHELM ABSORB DEVOUR
INVADE QUELME SLOUGH ENGORGE
SWALLOW SUBMERGE
ENHANCE FOIL LIFT BUILD ENARM
ENDOW EXALT RAISE DEEPEN AUGMENT
ELEVATE ENLARGE EXHANCE GREATEN
IMPROVE SHARPEN HEIGHTEN INCREASE
ENHANCEMENT SAKE
ENID (HUSBAND OF —) GERAINT
ENIGMA WHY EGMA GRIPH REBUS
PUZZLE RIDDLE SPHINX GRIPHUS
MYSTERY PROBLEM PROVERB
ENIGMATIC HUMAN MYSTIC CRYPTIC
OBSCURE ELLIPTIC MYSTICAL ORACULAR
PUZZLING RIDDLING
ENJOIN BID JOIN WILL ENIUN ORDER
CHARGE DECREE DIRECT FORBID
COMMAND DICTATE REQUIRE ADMONISH
PROHIBIT
ENJOY GO JOY FAIN HAVE LIKE BROOK
FANCY PROVE SAVOR TASTE WIELD
ADMIRE DEVOUR GROOVE RELISH
DELIGHT
(— ONESELF) FEAST LAUGH
ENJOYABLE GOOD FRUITY AMIABLE
BLESSED CAPITAL GLORIOUS SAVOROUS
SPLENDID
ENJOYING FRUITIVE
ENJOYMENT FUN JOY USE BANG BASK
BOOT EASE GUST KAMA PLAY ZEST
FEAST GUSTO LIKING RELISH COMFORT
DELIGHT JOLLITY JOYANCE JOYANCY
FELICITY FRUITION PLEASURE SKITTLES
(— FROM OTHERS' TROUBLES)
SCHADENFREUDE
ENKINDLE WARM INCENSE INFLAME
ENLARGE ADD EKE BORE GROW HONE
HUFF OPEN REAM ROOM BUILD FARCE
LARGE SWELL WIDEN BIGGEN BRANCH
BROACH DIDUCE DILATE EXPAND
EXTEND FRAISE GATHER LARGEN
OMNIFY SPREAD AMPLIFY AUGMENT
DISTEND ENHANCE GREATEN IMPROVE
INGREAT MAGNIFY STRETCH AMPLIATE
CUMULATE FLOURISH INCREASE
ENLARGED TUMID BLOATED CLUBBED
SWELLED SWOLLEN AMPLIATE CAPITATE
EXPANDED EXTENDED VARICOSE
ACCRESCENT
ENLARGEMENT BULB DISC DISK KNOP
NODE CLAVA SWELL BLOWUP BUNION
GIBBER GROWTH SCYPHA ENLARGE
FOOTING SCYPHUS STATION ANEURYSM
INCREASE SWELLING PROPAGATION
(— IN MINE SHAFT) STATION

(— IN MUSCLE) KNOT
(— OF GLAND) GOITER
(— OF GULLET) CROP
(— OF MOLD) RAPPAGE
(— OF NERVE FIBER) BOUTON
(— OF ORGAN) STRUMA
(BONY —) SPAVIN SPAVINE
ENLIGHTEN OPEN CLEAR EDIFY TEACH
ILLUME INFORM UNSEEL EDUCATE
LIGHTEN CIVILIZE ENKINDLE INSTRUCT
ENLIGHTENED WISE LUMINOUS
ENLIGHTENMENT BODHI LIGHT SATORI
WISDOM CULTURE INSIGHT SAMADHI
AUFKLARUNG
ENLIST DRUM JOIN LEVY SOUD ENROL
ENTER HITCH PREST ENGAGE ENROLL
INDUCT IMPRESS RECRUIT REGISTER
ENLISTMENT LEVY HITCH PREST
LISTING
ENLIVEN DASH JAZZ WARM BRACE
BRISK CHEER QUICK RAISE ROUSE
KITTLE REVIVE ANIMATE COMFORT
INSPIRE REFRESH SMARTEN BRIGHTEN
INSPIRIT RECREATE
ENLIVENING GENIAL LIVELY VIVIFIC
CHIRPING
ENMESH TRAP CATCH SNARL IMMESH
ENSNARE ENTANGLE
ENMITY WAR FEUD SPITE WRAKE
ANIMUS HATRED MALICE RANCOR
STRIFE FOEHOOD AVERSION
ENNOBLE LORD EXALT HONOR NOBLE
RAISE GENTLE UPLIFT DIGNIFY ELEVATE
GLORIFY GREATEN NOBLIFY SUBLIME
ENNUI BORE TEDIUM ACCIDIE BOREDOM
DOLDRUM
ENOCH (FATHER OF —) CAIN JARED
(SON OF —) METHUSALEH
ENOCH ARDEN (AUTHOR OF —)
TENNYSON
(CHARACTER IN —) LEE RAY LANE
ANNIE ARDEN ENOCH MIRIAM PHILIP
ENORMITY GRAVITY
ENORMOUS BIG GOB HUGE REAM VAST
ENORM GREAT HEROIC MIGHTY UNRIDE
IMMENSE ABNORMAL COLOSSAL
FLAGRANT GIGANTIC WHAPPING
WHOPPING
ENOS (FATHER OF —) SETH
(GRANDFATHER OF —) ADAM
(SON OF —) CAINAN
ENOUGH BAS ENOW WELL WHEN AMPLE
ASSAI BASTA BELAY ANEUCH PLENTY
APLENTY SUFFICE ADEQUATE
(HARDLY —) SKIMP
ENOUNCE STATE UTTER AFFIRM
DECLARE PROCLAIM
ENRAGE RAGE ANGER GRIEVE MADDEN
INCENSE INFLAME STOMACH
ENRAGED MAD ASHY WODE WOOD
ANGRY IRATE LIVID SAVAGE AGRAMED
BERSERK CHOLERIC INCENSED
MADDENED
ENRAPTURE RAVISH TRANCE ECSTASY
ENCHANT ENRAVISH ENTRANCE
ENRAPTURED RAPT ENRAPT TRANCED
ECSTATIC

ENRICH FAT BOOT FEED FRET LARD RICH
ADORN CROWN ENDOW GUANO BATTEN
FATTEN INVEST FEATHER FORTIFY
FURNISH GUANIZE INCREASE ORNAMENT
TREASURE
(— A GAS) CARBURET
(— A MINE) SALT
(— FUEL MIXTURE) CHOKE
ENRICHED FLORID
ENRICHMENT DITATION
ENROLL BEAR JOIN LIST POLL ENROL
ENTER WRITE ATTEST BILLET ENFOLD
ENLIST INDUCT MUSTER RECORD
ASCRIBE IMPANEL INITIATE INSCRIBE
REGISTER
ENROLLMENT LISTING REGISTRY
ENSCONCE HIDE COVER SETTLE
CONCEAL SHELTER
ENSEMBLE CORPS DECOR WHOLE
COSTUME PANTSUIT
(— OF ARMS) ARMORY
(WOMAN'S —) PANTSUIT
ENSHRINE SAINT SHRINE ENCHASE
ENTEMPLE
ENSHROUD WRAP
ENSIFORM ENSATE XIPHOID GLADIATE
ENSIGN FLAG IAGO SIGN BADGE COLOR
SENYE AQUILA BANNER BEACON
PENNON PISTOL SIGNAL SYMBOL
ALFEREZ ANCIENT INSIGNE DANEBROG
GONFALON ORIFLAMB PAVILION
STANDARD
(—S ARMORIAL) ARMS
(IMPERIAL —) TUT
(JAPANESE —) SUNBURST
(PL.) ENSIGNRY HERALDRY
ENSLAVE THEW CHAIN SLAVE THIRL
NESLAVE SLAVISH ENTHRALL
ENSNARE NET WEB GIRN LACE LIME
MESH TOIL TRAP WRAP BENET CATCH
NOOSE SNARE SNARL ALLURE ATTRAP
ENGINE ENMESH ENTOIL ENTRAP
TANGLE TREPAN BEGUILE DECEIVE
ENGLEIM SNIGGLE SPRINGE BIRDLIME
INVEIGLE OVERTAKE SURPRISE
ENSNARL ENTANGLE
ENSUE FOLLOW RESULT SUCCEED
ENSUING NEXT SEQUENT
ENSURE ASSURE INSURE SECURE
BETROTH ESPOUSE WARRANT AFFIANCE
ENTABLATURE (PART OF —) CORONA
FRIEZE TAENIA CORNICE CYMATIUM
ARCHITRAVE
ENTAIL INCUR IMPOSE CONTAIN INVOLVE
REQUIRE TAILZIE
ENTANGLE ELF LAP MAT TAT WEB BALL
CAST COLL FOUL HARL KNIT KNOT LIME
MESH MIRE TOIL WRAP BROIL CATCH
HALCH RAVEL SNAFU SNARE SNARL
TWIST BEFOUL COMMIT COTTER
ENGAGE ENLACE ENMESH ENTRAP
ENWRAP FANKLE FELTER HAMPER
HANKLE HATTER INMAZE INMESH
PESTER PUZZLE RAFFLE RANGLE TACKLE
TAIGLE TANGLE WRAPLE CONFUSE
EMBRAKE EMBROIL ENSNARL ENTRIKE
IMBRIER INVOLVE PERPLEX TRAMMEL

BEWILDER ENCUMBER IMPESTER
INTRIGUE STRAPPLE
ENTANGLED DEEP FOUL COTTY TANGLY
COMPLEX KNOTTED IMPLICIT
ENTANGLEMENT FOUL KNOT TWIT
HITCH BUNKER COBWEB ENTRAIL
HEDGEHOG OBSTACLE PERPLEXITY
ENTENTE TREATY ALLIANCE
ENTER BOX DIP SET BEAR BOOK JOIN
POST ADMIT BEGIN BOARD BREVE ENROL
INCUR PROBE SHARE START ACCEDE
APPEAR BILLET ENGAGE ENLIST ENROLL
ENTRER INCEPT INVADE PIERCE RECORD
SPREAD INGRESS INTRUDE COMMENCE
ENCROACH INITIATE INSCRIBE
NOMINATE REGISTER PENETRATE
(— BY FORCE) BREAK IRRUPT INTRUDE
(— DATA) INPUT
(— HASTILY) BULGE
(— IN ATTACK) FORCE
(— IN BOOK) ACCESS
(— IN BOOKS) ACCRUE
(— INFORMATION INTO COMPUTER)
WRITE
(— INTO) JOIN INTERN
(— PROGRAM INTO COMPUTER)
LOAD
(— SLOWLY) SEEP
(— UNNOTICED) CREEP
(— UPON CAREER) INCEPT
(— UPON DUTIES) ASSUME
(— WITHOUT RIGHT) ABATE
ENTERPRISE FIRM IRON PUSH TOGT
DRIVE ESSAY ACTION EMPIRE SPIRIT
VOYAGE ATTEMPT EMPRISE HOLDING
PROJECT VENTURE BUSINESS CARNIVAL
GUMPTION VIRITOOT
(CRIMINAL —) JOB
(HARD —) DIFFICULTY
(REMEDIAL —) CRUSADE
(SPECULATIVE —) ADVENTURE
(UNPROFITABLE —) SINKHOLE
ENTERPRISING BOLD FORTHY PUSHFUL
PUSHING
ENTERTAIN INN BEAR BUSK EASE FETE
HAVE HOLD HOST AMUSE ENJOY FEAST
GUEST SPORT TREAT DIVERT FROLIC
GESTEN HARBOR JUNKET RECULE
REGALE RETAIN SOLACE TICKLE
ACCOURT BEGUILE CHERISH DISPORT
KITCHEN CONSIDER INTEREST RECREATE
(— WITHOUT CHARGE) DEFRAY
ENTERTAINER BHAT HOST ACTOR
AMUSER ARTIST BUSKER DANCER
FIDDLE HARLOT SINGER ACTRESS
ARTISTE DISEUSE GLEEMAN HETAERA
HOSTESS REGALER SPEAKER BEACHBOY
COMEDIAN HOSTELER MAGICIAN
MINSTREL
ENTERTAINING GOOD RICH TREAT
PRETTY AMUSING BEDSIDE GUESTING
SPORTFUL
ENTERTAINMENT BASH BILL FARE FETE
GALA GLEE PLAY SHOW BOARD CHEER
FEAST GAUDY OPERA REVUE SPORT
CIRCUS DIVERT DOMENT GAIETY GAYETY
HOSTEL INFARE KERMIS NAUTCH

SETOUT SHIVOO WATTLE BANQUET
BENEFIT BUMMACK BUMMOCK BURLESK
CEILIDH CONCERT COSHERY FESTINE
FESTINO JOLLITY KERMESS PASTIME
RIDOTTO TAMASHA CAKEWALK
CARNIVAL COMMORTH DROLLERY
EASEMENT ENTREATY ENTREMES
FUNCTION GESTNING GESTONIE
GUESTING HOGMANAY JONGLERY
MUSICALE WAYZGOOSE
(FAREWELL —) FOY

ENTHRALL SEND CHARM THIRL THRALL
ENSLAVE CAPTIVATE

ENTHRONE CROWN EXALT STALL
ENSEAT THRONE THRONIZE

ENTHUSIASM BUG ELAN FIRE FURY
ZEAL ZEST ZING ARDOR ESTRO FEVER
FLAME HEART OOMPH VERVE FERVOR
HURRAH SPIRIT WARMTH ABANDON
ARDENCY AVIDITY MADNESS MUSTARD
DEVOTION LYRICISM
(— IN BATTLE) EARNEST
(CONTAGIOUS —) FUROR FURORE
(EXCESSIVE —) MANIA
(WILD —) DELIRIUM

ENTHUSIAST BUG FAN NUT BUFF BIGOT
FREAK ROOTER VOTARY ZEALOT
DEVOTEE EUCHITE FANATIC FANCIER
FOLLOWER VOTARESS VOTARIST
(PL.) ARDITI

ENTHUSIASTIC GAGA KEEN NUTS
WARM HAPPY NUTTY RABID ARDENT
HEARTY CRACKED FERVENT GLOWING
CRACKERS PASSIONATE
(BECOME —) FLIP
(EXCESSIVELY —) FANATIC
(VAINLY —) FOOLISH

ENTICE COG COY PUT WIN BAIT COAX
DRAW DRIB LEAD LOCK LURE TICE
TOLL WILE CHARM DECOY DRILL LATHE
SIREN SLOCK STEAL TEMPT TRAIN TROLL
TULLE ALLECT ALLURE ATTICE CAJOLE
ENLURE INCITE INDUCE INVITE SEDUCE
ATTRACT BEWITCH SOLICIT SUGGEST
INVEIGLE PERSUADE

ENTICEMENT BAIT CORD LURE TICE

ENTICING SIREN ALLURING

ENTIRE ALL DEAD EVEN FULL HALE MEAR
MERE SOLE CLEAN EVERY GROSS PLAIN
QUITE ROUND SOUND STARK TOTAL
TUTTO UTTER WHOLE VERSAL PERFECT
PLENARY ABSOLUTE COMPLETE
ENDURING GLOBULAR INTEGRAL
LIVELONG OUTRIGHT TEETOTAL
UNBROKEN

ENTIRELY DEAD DEIN FAIR FULL PURE
CLEAN CLEAR FULLY PLAIN QUITE STARK
WHOLE BODILY WHOLLY EXACTLY
QUITELY THROUGH CLEVERLY
ABSOLUTELY

ENTIRETY WHOLE ENTIRE TOTALITY
(PREF.) PAM PAN

ENTITLE DUB CALL NAME TERM AFFIX
STYLE ENABLE CAPTION EMPOWER
QUALIFY INTITULE NOMINATE

ENTITLED APPARENT ELIGIBLE

ENTITY ENS BODY FORM UNIT BEING

HABIT OUSIA SPACE THING ENERGY
ESSENCE INTEGER TOTALITY

ENTOMB BURY TOMB INTER INURN
ENCAVE HEARSE IMMURE INHUME
SHRINE

ENTOMBMENT BURIAL

ENTRAILS GUT GUTS DRAFT TRIPE
FIBERS GIBLET HALLOW HASLET
INWARD JAUDIE MUGGET PAUNCH
QUARRY QUERRE UMBLES INSIDES
NUMBLES CHAWDRON GRALLOCH
PURTENANCE

ENTRANCE DOOR GATE HALL PEND
BOCCA CHARM ENTER ENTRY FOYER
GORGE INLET MOUTH PORCH STULM
THIRL TORAN ACCESS ATRIUM ENTREE
INFAIR INGANG INGATE PORTAL RAVISH
TORANA TRANCE ZAGUAN DELIGHT
GATEWAY HALLWAY INGOING INGRESS
INITIAL INTRADO INTROIT PASSAGE
ENTRESSE FOREGATE VOMITORY
PROPYLAEUM
(— TO SEWER) JAWHOLE
(— TO VALLEY) CHOPS
(ASTROLOGICAL —) CUSP
(CELLAR —) ROLLWAY
(FORCIBLE —) INROAD
(FORMAL —) DEBUT
(HARBOR —) BOCA
(HOSTILE —) INVASION
(HURRIED —) BOUT
(MINE —) EYE ADIT
(PRIVATE —) POSTERN

ENTRANCED RAPT CHARMED TRANCED
ECSTATIC

ENTRANCEMENT SPELL

ENTRANCING ORPHIC

ENTRANT STARTER BEGINNER

ENTRAP BAG EBB NET HOOK SNIB TOIL
TRAP CATCH CRIMP DECOY NOOSE
SNARE ALLURE AMBUSH ATTRAP
CAJOLE ENGAGE ENTOIL TAIGLE TANGLE
TREPAN BEGUILE ENSNARE PITFALL
ENTANGLE INVEIGLE

ENTREAT ASK BEG BID SUE WOO PRAY
PRIG SEEK URGE CRAVE HALSE PLEAD
PRESS TREAT ADJURE APPEAL DESIRE
INVOKE BESEECH CONJURE EXORATE
IMPLORE PREVAIL PROCURE REQUEST
SOLICIT PERSUADE PETITION

ENTREATING TREAT CRAVING

ENTREATY DO CRY PLEA SUIT APPEAL
PRAYER TREATY BESEECH BIDDING
PURSUIT REQUEST URGENCY PETITION
PLEADING

ENTRENCH INVADE SCONCE TRENCH
ENCROACH TRESPASS

ENTRUST ARET FIDE GIVE STOW BEKEN
TRUST CHARGE COMMIT CREDIT LIPPEN
ADDRESS BEHIGHT COMMEND CONFIDE
CONSIGN DEPOSIT INTRUST BEQUEATH
DELEGATE ENCHARGE RECOMMEND
(— TO DEPUTY) DEVIL

ENTRY ADIT HALL ITEM STET BREAK
CLOSE DEBIT AUTHOR CREDIT DOCKET
ENTREE PORTAL POSTEA RECORD
RINGER TRANCE ENTRADA INGRESS

INTRADO PASSAGE ENTRANCE ENTRESSE
ENTRYWAY NOTANDUM REGISTER
VOCATION
(— IN CHRONICLE) ANNAL
ENTWINE FOLD LACE WIND BRAID CLASP
IMPLY PLASH TWINE TWIST WEAVE
ENLACE INWIND ENTWIST INVOLVE
SERPENT WREATHE
ENTWINED ACCOLLE BRAIDED INWOVEN
ACCOLLEE
ENUMERATE POLL TELL COUNT SCORE
DETAIL NUMBER RECITE RECKON RELATE
COMPILE COMPUTE ITEMIZE RECOUNT
ESTIMATE REHEARSE
ENUMERATION LIST TALE COUNT
SCORE CENSUS ACCOUNT CATALOG
RECITAL CITATION
ENUNCIATE SAY UTTER DECLARE
DELIVER ENOUNCE ANNOUNCE
PROCLAIM
ENUNCIATION DICTION DELIVERY
(IMPERFECT —) LALLATION
ENVELOP BUR FOG LAP LOT POD WEB
BURR CASE COMA FOLD HUSK MAIL
ROLL BRACE CLOUD COVER KNIFE
ROUND BEGIRD BEGIRT BEMIST BINDLE
CLOTHE COCOON CUPULE ENFOLD
ENGIRT ENTIRE ENWRAP FARDEL FOLDER
INFOLD INVEST MANTLE MUFFLE POCKET
SHEATH SHROUD STIFLE SWATHE
WRIXLE CALYMMA CAPSULE CHORION
ENCLOSE ENVIRON INVOLVE SWADDLE
SWALLOW VESTURE WRAPPER
ENSPHERE ENVELOPE MANTLING
PERIANTH PERIDIUM POCHETTE
SURROUND WRAPPAGE
(— IN SMOKE) ENFUME
(GLASS —) BULB
(LUMINOUS —) CORONA
(NEBULOUS —) CHEVELURE
(OPEN —) JACKET
(PAY —) PACKET
(STAMPED —) ENTIRE
(VEGETABLE —) COD
ENVELOPING AMBIENT
ENVIOUS YELLOW EMULOUS JEALOUS
ENVIRON HEM BEGO GIRD BIGAN LIMIT
GIRDLE SUBURB COMPASS ENVELOP
INCLOSE INVOLVE PURLIEU DISTRICT
ENCIRCLE SURROUND
(PL.) SKIRT UMLAND BANLIEU SUBURBS
PRECINCT
ENVIRONMENT HOTBED MEDIUM
MILIEU AMBIENT CONTEXT ELEMENT
HABITAT SETTING TERRAIN AMBIANCE
CINCTURE PRECINCT
(— OF NURTURE) LAP
(ACADEMIC —) ACADEME
(DOMESTIC —) INTERIEUR
(NORMAL —) HOME
ENVISAGE FACE CONFRONT ENVISION
ENVOY AGENT ELCHI ENVOI DEPUTY
ELCHEE LEGATE LENVOY NUNCIO
EMBASSY TORNADA ABLEGATE
LEGATION METATRON
ENVY CHAW ONDE COVET GRUDGE

EMULATE BEGRUDGE GRUDGERY
JEALOUSY
ENWRAP FOLD ROLL CLASP IMPLY
ENFOLD INFOLD KIRTLE ENGROSS
ENVELOP OBVOLVE CONVOLVE
ENVELOPE INSWATHE
ENZYME ASE ZYM ZYMO LYASE RENIN
CYTASE KINASE LIGASE LIPASE LOTASE
MUTASE OLEASE PAPAIN PEPSIN RENNIN
UREASE ZYMASE ACYLASE ADENASE
AMIDASE AMINASE AMYLASE APYRASE
CASEASE EMULSIN ENOLASE EREPSIN
FERMENT GUANASE HYDRASE INULASE
LACCASE LACTASE MALTASE MYROSIN
OXIDASE PECTASE PEPSINE PHYTASE
PLASMIN PRUNASE TANNASE TRYPSIN
ALDOLASE ARGINASE BROMELIN
CATALASE CATALYST CYTOLIST
DIASTASE ELASTASE EREPTASE
ESTERASE FUMARASE INVERTIN
LYSOZYME NUCLEASE PERMEASE
PROTEASE RACEMASE SEMINASE
SYNTHASE THROMBIN TRYPTASE
EOS MORNING
EPAULET KNOT SWAB SWOB WING
SCALE SHELL
EPHEMERAL BRIEF VAGUE HORARY
DIURNAL FUNGOUS PASSANT PASSING
EPISODAL EPISODIC FUGITIVE
MUSHROOM STAYLESS MOMENTARY
EPHEMERIS DIARY TABLE RECORD
ALMANAC JOURNAL CALENDAR
EPHRAIM (FATHER OF —) JOSEPH
(MOTHER OF —) ASENATH
EPIC EDDA EPOS SAGA GRAND ILIAD
NOBLE BYLINA EPOPEE HEROIC LUSIAD
BEOWULF EPYLLION KALEVALA
RAMAYANA
EPICENE SEXLESS
EPICURE FRIAND FEASTER GLUTTON
GOURMET GOURMAND PALATIST
EPICUREAN APICIAN SENSUOUS
EPIDEMIC FLU PLAGUE POPULAR
PANDEMIA PANDEMIC
EPIDERMIS SKIN CUTICLE ECDERON
VELAMEN
EPIGLOTTIS FLAP WEEZLE
EPIGRAM POEM ENGLYN EPITAPH
EPIGRAMMATIC LACONIC POINTED
EPILEPTIC FITIFIED
EPILOGUE CLOSE APPENDIX
EPIPHANY TWELFTH
EPISCOPAL PRELATIC
EPISODE GAG EPOCH EVENT SCENE
STORY AFFAIR INCIDENT SEQUENCE
OCCURRENCE
(COMIC —) BURLA
(MUSICAL —) COUPLET
EPISTLE CANON JAMES LETTER MISSIVE
WRITING DECRETAL
EPISTLER SUBDEACON
EPITHET AKAL GOOD NAME TERM LABEL
SMEAR TITLE BYWORD MONETA PHRASE
AGNOMEN JAPHETIC MULCIBER
EPITOME MAP SUM FLETA DIGEST
PRECIS SCHEME COMPEND SUMMARY
SUMMULA ABSTRACT BREVIARY

LANDSKIP SYLLABUS SYNOPSIS
ABRIDGMENT CONSPECTUS
EPITOMIZE RESUME ABRIDGE CURTAIL
ABSTRACT COMPRESS CONDENSE
CONTRACT DIMINISH
EPOCH AGE ERA DATE ECCA TIME
DWYKA EVENT EOCENE PERIOD CLINTON
OLIGOCENE
EQUAL AEQ PAR TIE COPE EGAL EVEN
FERE JUST LIKE MAKE MATE MEET PEEL
PEER SAME ALIKE LEVEL MATCH PARTY
RIVAL TOUCH DOUBLE EQUATE EVENLY
FELLOW MARROW PAREIL ABREAST
BALANCE COMPEER EMULATE EQUABLE
IDENTIC PARAGON PAREGAL UNIFORM
ADEQUATE EQUALIZE EVENHAND
PATCHING TRANQUIL
(— IN MEANING) BE
(— QUANTITY) ANA
(— TO) ANOTHER
(NOT —) UNMEET UNMETE
EQUALITY PAR TIE EQUITY OWELTY
PARAGE PAREIL PARITY BALANCE
EGALITE EGALITY ISOTELY EQUATION
EVENHAND EVENNESS FAIRNESS
(— BEFORE THE LAW) ISONOMY
(— OF ELEVATION) ISOMETRY
(— OF POWER) ISOCRACY
(— OF RATIOS) ANALOGY
EQUALIZE EVEN KNOT EQUAL LEVEL
EQUATE BALANCE ADEQUATE
EQUALIZER EVENER
EQUALLY AS BOTH LIKE ONCE SAME
ALIKE EGALLY EVENLY JUSTLY EMFORTH
EQUANIMITY POISE PHLEGM TEMPER
BALANCE EGALITY CALMNESS EVENNESS
SERENITY SANGFROID
EQUATE EQUAL BALANCE EQUALIZE
EQUATION CUBIC IDENTITY
EQUATOR LINE GIRDLE EQUINOX
EQUATORIAL GUINEA
(CAPITAL OF —) MALABO
(RIVER OF —) MUNI CAMPO BENITO
(TOWN OF —) BATA NSOK
SANTAISABEL
EQUIDISTANT CENTRAL HALFWAY
EQUILIBRIUM POISE APLOMB BALANCE
STATION EQUATION EVENHAND
ISOSTASY
(— OF FLUID) LEVEL
EQUINE COLT FOAL MARE FILLY HORSE
ZEBRA EQUOID EQUINAL HORSELY
EQUIP ARM FIT IMP KIT RAY RIG ABLE
BEAM DECK FEAT FIND GEAR GIRD GIRT
HEEL REEK TRIM ARRAY DIGHT DRESS
ENARM ENDOW POINT SPEED STUFF
AGUISE ATTIRE BUCKLE ORDAIN OUTFIT
SUBORN APPAREL APPOINT BEDIGHT
FORTIFY FRAUGHT FURNISH GARNISH
HARNESS PLENISH PREPARE QUALIFY
ACCOUTER ACCOUTRE ACCOMPLISH
(— FOR ACTION) ARM
EQUIPAGE RIG CREW SAMAN SUITE
TRAIN SUPPLY RETINUE TURNOUT
UNICORN CARRIAGE
EQUIPMENT KIT FARE GEAR TIRE STOCK
STUFF ATTIRE CONREY DUFFEL DUFFLE

FITOUT GRAITH OUTFIT SETOUT TACKLE
APPAREL BAGGAGE FITMENT HARNESS
PANOPLY ARMAMENT EQUIPAGE
MATERIAL MATERIEL MOUNTING
SUPELLEX
(— FOR CATCHING FISH) CRAFT
(— FOR JOURNEY) FARE
EQUIPOISE POISE BALANCE
EQUIPOTENTIAL LEVEL
EQUIPPED SEEN ARMED BODEN THERE
EQUIPT ARMORED INSTRUCT WEAPONED
(FULLY —) SUMMED
(INADEQUATELY —) HAYWIRE
(LIGHTLY —) EXPEDITE
EQUITABLE EVEN FAIR JUST EQUAL
RIGHT EVENLY HONEST EQUABLE
UPRIGHT BONITARY RATIONAL RIGHTFUL
EQUIVALENT KIND SAME EQUAL
COUSIN UNISON ANALOGUE EVENHAND
(— IN MONEY) CHANGE
(— OF TWO BUSHELS) HUTCH
EQUIVOCAL FISHY SHADY DOUBLE
FORKED DUBIOUS EVASIVE HALFWAY
OBSCURE DOUBTFUL HAVERING
PUZZLING SIBYLLIC
EQUIVOCATE LIE DODGE EVADE SHIFT
BOGGLE ESCAPE PALTER TRIFLE WAFFLE
WEASEL QUIBBLE SHUFFLE SCRAFFLE
PREVARICATE
EQUIVOCATION QUIP QUIRK EVASION
QUIBBLE SHUFFLE EQUIVOKE
ERA AGE AEON DATE TIME EPOCH STAGE
PERIOD CENOZOIC PROTEROZOIC
(EMPEROR'S —) KIMIGAYO
(HINDU —) SAMVAT
(MUSLIM —) HEGIRA
ERADICATE DELE ROOT SLAY WEED
CROSS ERASE STAMP DELETE EFFACE
REMOVE UPROOT ABOLISH DESTROY
EXPUNGE OUTROOT SUPPLANT
(— HAIR) EPILATE
ERASE BLOT DASH DELE DELE RACE RASE
RASH RAZE ANNUL PLANE CANCEL
DEFACE DELETE EFFACE EXCISE REMOVE
SCRAPE SPONGE DESTROY EXPUNGE
OUTRAZE SCRATCH UNWRITE
OBLITERATE
ERASER RASER RUBBER
ERASURE ERASION DELETION EXCISION
ERE OR AIR SOON EARLY PRIOR BEFORE
EREWHILE FORMERLY
EREBUS (FATHER OF —) CHAOS
(SISTER OF —) NOX
(SON OF —) CHARON
ERECHTHEUS (DAUGHTER OF —)
CREUSA PROCRIS CHTHONIA ORITHYIA
(FATHER OF —) PANDION
(SLAYER OF —) JUPITER
(SON OF —) MERION CECROPS
PANDORUS
(WIFE OF —) PRAXITHEA
ERECT BIG SET BIGG LEVY REAR RECT
STEP STEY SWAY TELD AREAR BRANT
BUILD DRESS EXALT FRAME MOUNT
RAISE SETUP STAND ARRECT UPLIFT
UPREAR ADDRESS ATROPAL BRISTLE

ELEVATE STATELY UPRAISE UPRIGHT
UPSTART STANDING STRAIGHT VERTICAL
(— TENT) PITCH
(NOT —) LAZY COUCHED
ERELONG ANON SOON
EREMITE HERMIT ASCETIC RECLUSE
ANCHORET
EREWHILE ERE WHILOM
EREWHON (AUTHOR OF —) BUTLER
(CHARACTER IN —) HIGGS GEORGE
STRONG ZULORA CHOWBOK AROWHENA
NOSNIBOR
ERGO SO ARGAL HENCE
ERGOT SPUR CLAVUS ECBOLIC
ERIGONE (FATHER OF —) ICARIUS
AEGISTHUS
(MOTHER OF —) CLYTEMNESTRA
ERMINE VAIR VARE STOAT WEASEL
ERMELIN FUTERET FUTTRAT MINIVER
CLUBSTER WHITRACK WHITTRET
ERNANI (CHARACTER IN —) CARLO
GOMEZ SILVA ELVIRA ERNANI
(COMPOSER OF —) VERDI
ERODE EAT COMB ETCH GNAW GULL
WEAR CLIFF GULLY SCOUR ABRADE
DENUDE CORRODE DESTROY
EROS AMOR CUPID AENGUS POTHOS
EROSE ERODED UNEVEN
EROSION PIPING CHIMNEY NIVATION
SCOURING
(MECHANICAL —) PLANATION
EROTIC LOVING AMATORY AMOROUS
CURIOUS LESBIAN THERMAL
EROTICA CURIOSA FACETIAE
ERR MAR SIN BOOT FAIL MISS SLIP ABERR
LAPSE MISGO STRAY BUNGLE FORVAY
WANDER BLUNDER DEVIATE MISPLAY
MISTAKE SCRITHE STUMBLE MISCARRY
MISJUDGE
ERRAND CHORE ENVOY JOURNEY
MISSION LEGATION
ERRANT STRAY ASTRAY ERRING
DEVIOUS PRICKANT
ERRATIC WILD CRAZY HUMAN LOONY
QUEER WACKY CRANKY STRANGE
TANGENT VAGRANT ACROSTIC
ERRABUND FITIFIED PLANETAL PLANETIC
TRAVELED VAGABOND PLANETARY
ERRATUM ERROR
ERRONEOUS AMISS FALSE WRONG
UNTRUE ERRATIC MISTAKEN STRAYING
WRONGFUL
(PREF.) PSEUD(O)
ERROR HOB SIN BAN BALK BUBU BULL FLUB
HELL MUFF SLIP TRIP BEARD BEVUE
BONER DEVIL FAULT FLUFF LAPSE SCAPE
BOBBLE BOOBOO FUMBLE GARBLE
HOWLER LAPSUS MISCUE NAUGHT
SPHALM BLOOMER BLUNDER DEFAULT
ERRATUM FALLACY FALSITY LITERAL
MISPLAY MISSTEP MISTAKE OFFENSE
RHUBARB SNAPPER STUMBLE DELUSION
HAMARTIA MISPRINT MISSMENT
SOLECISM OVERSIGHT MISPRISION
ERST ONCE FORMERLY RECENTLY
ERSTWHILE ONCE FORMER FORMERLY
ERUDITE LEARNED CLERGIAL DIDACTIC

ERUDITION WIT LORE WISDOM LETTERS
LEARNING
ERUPT BOIL BELCH BURST EJECT IRRUPT
ERUPTION ITCH RASH REEF RUSH AGRIA
BLAIN BRASH BURST RUPIA SALLY
SALVO STORM BLOTCH HYDROA NIRLES
ACTERID BLOWOUT ECTHYMA MORPHEA
MORPHEW PUSTULE SAWFLOM
SUDAMEN SYCOSIS EMPYESIS
ENANTHEM EXANTHEM MALANDER
OUTBREAK OUTBURST
(— ON CHIN) MENTAGRA
(CUTANEOUS —) HUMOR
ERYSIPELAS POX ROSE BLAST WILDFIRE
ESAU EDOM
(BROTHER OF —) JACOB
(FATHER OF —) ISAAC
(MOTHER OF —) REBEKAH
(SON OF —) JEUSH KORAH REUEL
JAALAM ELIPHAZ
(WIFE OF —) ADAH BASHEMATH
ESCAPADE CAPER PRANK SALLY
SCHEME SPLORE RUNAWAY FREDAINE
ESCAPE GUY LAM RUN BAIL BALE BEAT
BLOW BOLT FLEE GATE HISS JINK JUMP
LEAK MISS SKEW SLIP VENT AVOID
BREAK CHAPE DODGE ELOPE EVADE
FLANK ISSUE SCAPE SHIFT SKIRT SMOKE
SPILL ASTERT DECAMP ESCHEW OUTLET
POWDER SQUEAK AVOLATE BLOWOUT
ELUSION EXHAUST GETAWAY LEAKAGE
MISTAKE OUTFLOW SCRITHE SQUEEZE
WILDING BLOWBACK ESCAPADE
ESCAPAGE EXSHEATH OUTSCAPE
OVERSLIP RIDDANCE WITHSLIP
(— FROM) FLY SHUN ILLUDE
(— FROM WORK) SNIB
(— LEGAL PROCESS) ABSCOND
(— NOTICE) ELUDE
(— OF FLUID) EFFUSION
(NARROW —) SHAVE
ESCARGOT SNAIL
ESCARPMENT EDGE
ESCHEW SHUN ABHOR AVOID FORGO
ESCAPE FOREGO ABSTAIN
ESCORT MAN SEE SET TRY BEAR BEAU
COND LEAD SHOW TEND WAIT BRING
CARRY GUARD USHER ATTEND CONVEY
CONVOY FOLLOW SQUIRE COLLECT
CONDUCT CONSORT ESQUIRE GALLANT
CAVALIER CHAPERON SHEPHERD
SAFEGUARD
(PAID —) GIGOLO
ESCRITOIRE DESK BUREAU LECTERN
ESCULENT EDIBLE EATABLE
ESCUTCHEON CREST SHIELD
(CENTER OF —) NOMBRIL
ESKIMO ITA HUSKY INNUIT AGOMIUT
AMERIND ANGAKOK KUNMIUT OKOMIUT
ORARIAN AGLEMIUT ESQUIMAU
IKOGMIUT KIDNELIK KINIPETU
MAGEMIUT MALEMIUT NUGUMIUT
SINIMIUT
ESOPHAGUS GULLET SWALLOW
WEASAND
ESOTERIC INNER MYSTIC ORPHIC

SECRET PRIVATE ABSTRUSE RAREFIED
RARIFIED

ESPALIER CORDON LATTICE RAILING
TRELLIS PALISADE

ESPECIAL VERY CHIEF SPECIAL
PECULIAR UNCOMMON

ESPECIALLY SUCH EXTRA RATHER
CHIEFLY OVERALL SPECIAL

ESPIONAGE SPYING

ESPLANADE BUND WALK DRIVE MAIDAN
MARINA

ESPOUSAL CEREMONY SPOUSAGE
BETROTHAL

ESPOUSE WED AFFY MATE ADOPT
MARRY DEFEND ENSURE SPOUSE
BETROTH EMBRACE HUSBAND SUPPORT
ADVOCATE MAINTAIN

ESPOUSED HANDFAST

ESPY SEE SPOT SIGHT WATCH BEHOLD
DESCRY DETECT LOCATE NOTICE
DISCERN OBSERVE DESCRIBE DISCOVER

ESQUIRE RADMAN ARMIGER ESCUDERO
SERGEANT

ESSAY TRY SEEK ASSAY CHRIA OFFER
PAPER PROVE TASTE THEME TRACT
TRAIL CASUAL EFFORT MEMOIR SAILYE
SATIRE SCREED THESIS ARTICLE
ATTEMPT PROFFER VENTURE WRITING
CAUSERIE ENDEAVOR EXERCISE
EXERTION TRACTATE TREATISE
TURNOVER

ESSENCE ENS NET ALMA BASE BONE
CORE CRUX ESSE GIST GUTS KIND ODOR
PITH QUID RASA SUUL YOLK ATTAR
BASIC BASIS BEING EIDOS FIBER HEART
JUICE OUSIA STUFF BOTTOM EFFECT
ENTITY FLOWER INWARD MARROW
NATURE SPRITE ALCOHOL ELEMENT
EXTRACT GODHEAD INBEING MEDULLA
PERFUME RATAFIA BERGAMOT ESSENTIA
(— OF BEING) SAT
(— OF FLOWERS) CONCRETE
(— OF GOD) SPIRIT DIVINITY
(— OF MEAT) BLOND
(— OF TEA) DRAW
(— OF VITAL MATTER) GLAME
(INNERMOST —) ATMAN
(UNIVERSAL —) FORM
(VITAL —) STAMINA

ESSENTIAL KEY REAL BASAL BASIC
VITAL ENTIRE FORMAL INWARD CENTRAL
CRUCIAL NEEDFUL CARDINAL CRITICAL
INHERENT MATERIAL NECESSARY

ESTABLISH BED FIX PUT SET BASE FAST
FIRM FOOT MAKE REAR REST ROOT SEAT
BUILD DEFIX EDIFY ENACT ERECT EVICT
FOUND PLANT PROVE RAISE SEIZE SETUP
START STATE STELL ATTEST AVOUCH
BOTTOM CEMENT CLINCH CREATE
ENROOT FASTEN FICCHE GROUND
INVENT INVEST LOCATE ORDAIN RATIFY
SETTLE STABLE VERIFY ACCOUNT
APPOINT APPROVE CONFIRM ENSTATE
INSTALL INSTATE INSTRESS POSSESS
PREEMPT SUSTAIN COLONIZE CONSTATE
CONTRACT ENSCONCE ENTRENCH
IDENTIFY INITIATE INSTRUCT RADICATE

REGULATE STABLISH VALIDATE
ASCERTAIN
(— FACT) APPROVE
(— FIRMLY) HAFT INDURATE
(— MORALS) ETHIZE
(— TRUMP) PITCH

ESTABLISHED FAST FIRM SURE LEGAL
ROOTED SEATED STABLE STAPLE
STATED STRONG CERTAIN SETTLED
STANDING

ESTABLISHMENT HONG MILL SHOP
STAB DAIRY FORGE JOINT PLANT POWER
SALON STORE AGENCY CAISSE CENOBY
LAYOUT SCHOOL ARSENAL BROTHEL
CONCERN FACTORY FOUNDRY FUNDUCK
SHEBANG AQUARIUM AVERMENT
BUSINESS ERECTION HACIENDA
(— IN NEW HABITAT) ECESIS
(— OF COLONY) DEDUCTION
(BATHING —) THERM
(DOMESTIC —) MENAGE
(DRINKING —) STUBE SALOON
BARROOM SHEBEEN
(GAMBLING —) HOUSE TRIPOT
(HORSE-BREEDING —) HARAS
(MONASTIC —) CLOISTER

ESTATE FEE ALOD COPY FEOD FIEF HOME
LAND POMP RANK UDAL ACRES DAIRA
DOWRY ETHEL FINCA FUNDO HABIT
HOUSE MANOR STATE TALUK ABBACY
BARONY DEMISE DOMAIN ENTAIL
GROUND LIVING MISTER QUINTA TALUKA
ALODIUM CHATEAU COMMONS
DEMESNE DIGNITY DISPLAY FORTUNE
HAVINGS MAJORAT ALLODIUM BENEFICE
COPYHOLD DOMINION EXECUTRY
FREEHOLD HACIENDA JOINTURE
LIFEHOLD LONGACRE MESNALTY
POSITION PROPERTY SENATORY
STANDING STAROSTY PATRIMONY
PERPETUITY
(— OF REBEL) FISC
(— WITH SERFS) HAM
(CATTLE —) ESTANCIA
(HINDU —) CHAK
(PORTION OF —) LEGITIM
(REAL —) FUNDUS
(PL.) AMANI

ESTEEM AIM LET USE DEEM HOLD RATE
TALE ADORE COUNT FAVOR HONOR
PRICE PRIDE STEEM THINK VALUE WEIGH
WORTH ADMIRE CREDIT EXTIME REGARD
REPUTE REVERE TENDER WONDER
ACCOUNT CONCEIT OPINION RESPECT
SUSPECT APPRAISE CONSIDER ESTIMATE
VENERATE

ESTEEMED DEAR PRECIOUS

ESTHER (COUSIN OF —) MORDECAI
(FATHER OF —) ABIHAIL
(HUSBAND OF —) AHASUERUS

ESTIMABLE GOOD SOLID WORTH
GENTLE HONEST WORTHY THRIFTY
VALUABLE

ESTIMATE AIM SET CALL CAST RANK
RATE READ RECK ASSAY AUDIT CARAT
CENSE COUNT GAUGE GUESS JUDGE
MOUNT PLACE PRIZE SCALE STOCK

TALLY VALUE WEIGH ASSESS BUDGET ESTEEM RECKON REGARD SURVEY ACCOUNT AVERAGE BALANCE CENSURE COMPUTE CONCEIT MEASURE APPRAISE CONSIDER CRITIQUE CALCULATE
(— OF ONE'S SELF) OPINION
(— TOO HIGHLY) OVERRATE
(LOW COST —) LOWBALL
ESTIMATION AIM EYE CESS FAME NAME ODOR PASS RATE COUNT HONOR PRICE SIEGE VALUE CHOICE ESTEEM REGARD REPUTE ACCOUNT OPINION JUDGMENT PRESTIGE
(— OF STRAIGHTNESS) BONING
(HIGH —) CONCEIT
(LOW —) DISREPUTE

ESTONIA

CAPITAL: TALLINN
COIN: SENT KROON ESTMARK
ISLAND: DAGO MUHU OESEL SAARE VORMSI HIIUMAA SAAREMAA
LAKE: PEIPUS
MEASURE: TUN ELLE LIIN PANG SUND TOLL TOOP FADEN VERST SAGENE VERSTA KULIMET VERCHOC TONNLAND
NATIVE: ESTH AESTI
PROVINCE: SAARE
RIVER: EMA NARVA PARNU KASARI
TOWN: NARVA PARNU REVAL TARTU TALLINN
WEIGHT: LOOD NAEL PUUD

ESTONIAN ESTH
ESTRANGE PART WEAN AVERT DIVERT ALIENATE DISUNITE
ESTUARY PARA WASH CREEK FIRTH FLEET INLET LIMAN ESTERO
ETCH BITE FROST ENGRAVE AQUATINT INSCRIBE
ETCHER POINT
ETCHING AQUATINT
ETEOCLES (BROTHER OF —) POLYNICES
(FATHER OF —) OEDIPUS
(MOTHER OF —) JOCASTA
ETERNAL ETERNE TARNAL AGELESS ENDLESS LASTING UNAGING ENDURING IMMORTAL TIMELESS UNCAUSED
ETERNALLY AKE EER EVER ALWAYS ETERNE FOREVER
ETERNITY AGE EON AEON GLORY ETERNE EWIGKEIT INFINITY PERPETUITY
ETESIAN ANNUAL PERIODIC
ETHAN FROME (AUTHOR OF —) WHARTON
(CHARACTER IN —) ETHAN FROME ZEENA MATTIE PIERCE SILVER ZENOBIA
ETHEREAL AERY AIRY SKYEY AERIAL SKYISH AIRLIKE FRAGILE SLENDER DELICATE HEAVENLY SUPERNAL VAPOROUS
ETHICAL ETHIC MORAL HONORABLE
ETHICS HEDONICS PHILOSOPHY

ETHIOPIA

ANCIENT CAPITAL: AXUM AKSUM
CAPITAL: ADDISABABA
COIN: BESA BIRR AMOLE GIRSH DOLLAR TALARI ASHRAFI PIASTER
DEPRESSION: DANAKIL
LAKE: ABE TANA ABAYA SHOLA ZEWAY RUDOLF STEFANIE
MEASURE: TAT KUBA SINJER SINZER FARSAKH FARSANG
MOUNTAIN: BATU GUGE GUNA TALO
MOUNTAINS: AHMAR CHOKE
NAME: ABYSSINIA
NATIVE: AFAR GALLA ABIGAR AMHARA ANNUAK HAMITE SEMITE SOMALI TIGRAI CUSHITE DANAKIL FALASHA
PORT: ASSAB MASSAWA
PROVINCE: BALE KEFA WELO ARUSI GOJAM HARER SHEWA TIGRE SIDAMO ERITREA
RIVER: OMO WEB BARO DAWA GILA ABBAI AKOBO AWASH FAFAN TAKKAZE
TOWN: EDD DESE GOBA GORE JIMA THIO ADOLA ADUWA AKSUM ASSAB AWASH DIMTU HARAR HARER JIMMA MOJJO ASMARA DESSYE DUNKUR GONDAR MAKALE MEKELE GARDULA MASSAWA NAKAMTI NEKEMTE DIREDAWA LALIBALA MUSTAHIL
WATERFALL: FINCHA DALVERME TESISSAT
WEIGHT: KASM NATR OKET ALADA NETER WAKEA WOGIET FARASULA

ETHIOPIAN SIDI HAMITE HARARI AETHIOP CUSHITE FALASHA
ETHOS MANNER
ETIQUETTE FORM DECORUM MANNERS
(— OF DRINKING TEA) CHANOYU
ETUDE STUDY
ETYMOLOGY ORIGIN DERIVATION
EUCALYPT GUM YATE APPLE BIMBIL CARBUN JARRAH MALLEE MYRTAL CARBEEN CUTTAIL COOLABAH IRONBARK MESSMATE WHITETOP YERTCHUK
EUCALYPTUS BLUEGUM EUCALYPT WHIPSTICK
EUCHARIST HOUSEL MAUNDY SUPPER MYSTERY VIATICUM
EUCHITE SATANIST ADELPHIAN MESSALIAN
EUGENE ONEGIN (CHARACTER IN —) OLGA GREMIN LARINA ONEGIN OLENSKY TATYANA TRIQUET
(COMPOSER OF —) TCHAIKOVSKY
EULOGIST PRAISER LAUREATE PANEGYRIST
EULOGISTIC EULOGIC EPENETIC MAGNIFIC LAUDATORY
EULOGY PRAISE TONGUE ADDRESS ELOGIUM ORATION ENCOMIUM PANEGYRE
EUNUCH CAPON SPORUS WETHER GELDING HALFMAN CASTRATE

EUPHEMISM DEE FIB GEE GOR DASH GOSH GOLES GOLLY LAWKS DIANTRE DICKENS GRACIOUS
EUPHEMUS (FATHER OF —) NEPTUNE POSEIDON
(MOTHER OF —) EUROPA
(SON OF —) BATTUS
EUPHONIOUS TUNEFUL
EUPHORIA ELATION
EUPHROSYNE JOY
EUPHUISM GONGORISM
EUROPA (BROTHER OF —) CILIX CADMUS THASUS PHINEUS PHOENIX
(FATHER OF —) AGENOR
(HUSBAND OF —) ASTERIUS
(MOTHER OF —) TELEPHASSA
(SON OF —) MINOS SARPEDON RHADAMANTHYS
EUROPEAN FRANK SAHIB BOHUNK EUROPE FRINGE INDIAN FERINGI TOPIWALA
(— IN INDIES) BLIJVER
(WESTERN —) FRANK
EURYANTHE (CHARACTER IN —) ADOLAR LYSIART EGLANTINE EURYANTHE
(COMPOSER OF —) WEBER
EURYNOME (DAUGHTERS OF —) GRACES CHARITES
(FATHER OF —) CHAOS OCEANUS
EUTERPE (FATHER OF —) JUPITER
(MOTHER OF —) MNEMOSYNE
EVACUATE PASS VENT VOID AVOID EMPTY EXPEL STOOL VACATE DEPRIVE EXCRETE EXHAUST NULLIFY VACUATE PERSPIRE
EVACUATION OFFICE DUNKIRK
EVADE BEG GEE DUCK FLEE FOIL JUMP SHUN SLIP VOID AVERT AVOID BLINK DALLY DODGE ELUDE FENCE FLANK PARRY SHIRK SKIVE BAFFLE BLENCH BYPASS COPOUT DELUDE ESCAPE ILLUDE BEGUILE FINESSE OUTSLIP QUIBBLE HEDGEHOP LEAPFROG SIDESTEP
(— LEGAL PROCESS) ABSCOND
(— PAYMENT) BILK
(— WORK) JOUK BLUDGE
EVALUATE RATE ASSESS PONDER RECKON DISSECT APPRAISE ESTIMATE
EVALUATION STOCK ESTIMATE
EVANDER (FATHER OF —) HERMES
(MOTHER OF —) CARMENTA
EVANESCE FADE VANISH
EVANESCENCE ANICCA
EVANESCENT FLEET EVANID BRITTLE CURSORY EVASIVE FRAGILE DELICATE FLEETING FLITTING FUGITIVE STAYLESS
EVANGELICAL GOSPEL SIMEONITE
EVANGELIST LUKE MARK EVANGEL GOSPELER SALVATIONIST
EVAPORATE DRY EXHALE AVOLATE CONDENSE VAPORIZE
EVASION JINK SLIP DODGE QUIRK SALVE SHIFT AMBAGE ESCAPE SNATCH ELUSION OFFCOME SHUFFLE TWISTER ARTIFICE ESCAPISM VOIDANCE

EVASIVE SLY EELY DODGY SHIFTY SUBTLE TWISTY ELUSIVE ELUSORY TRICKSY SLIPPERY SLIPSKIN
EVE DUSK EREB EVEN VIGIL SUNSET SUNDOWN
(NEW YEAR'S —) HAGMENA HOGMANAY
EVEN ALL DEN EEN TIE YET FAIR HUNK JUST PAIR TIED TILL ALINE CLEAN EQUAL EVERY EXACT FLUSH GRADE HUNKY LEVEL MATCH PLAIN RIVAL STILL SUANT SUENT SWEET DIRECT ITSELF PLACID SILKEN SMOOTH SQUARE STEADY ABREAST BALANCE EQUABLE FLATTEN REGULAR UNIFORM UPSIDES EQUALIZE MODERATE PARALLEL
(— OFF) LEVEL
(— THOUGH) IF ALTHO ALBEIT ALTHOUGH
EVENING DEN EVE EREB EVEN ABEND TARDE SUNSET VESPER EVENTIDE VESPERAL
(— OF SONG) CEILIDH
(YESTERDAY —) STREEN
EVENING STAR VENUS HESPER VESPER EVESTAR HESPERUS
EVENLY FAIR PLAIN FLATLY EQUALLY
EVENNESS EQUALITY
EVENT HAP CASE FACT FATE FEAT TILT CASUS DOING EPOCH FRAME ISSUE THING ACTION EFFECT FACTUM RESULT TIDING TIMING EPISODE FIXTURE PORTENT TRAGEDY INCIDENT OCCASION OCCURRENCE
(AMUSING —) COMEDY
(CHANCE —) ACCIDENT FORTUITY
(EXTRAORDINARY —) MIRACLE
(FORTUITOUS —) HAZARD
(GRAVE —) CALAMITY
(HAPPY —) GODSEND
(IMPORTANT —) ACE ERA
(PAST —S) HISTORY
(SET OF —S) EPISODE
(SIGNIFICANT —) CRISIS
(SKI —) DOWNHILL
(SOCIAL —) BENEFIT
(SPORTING —) STAKE
(THEATRICAL —) DRAW
(TURNING-POINT —) LANDMARK
(UNEXPECTED —) STUNNER ACCIDENT AFTERCLAP
(UNPLEASANT —) BUMMER
(YEARLY —) ANNUAL
EVENTFUL LIVELY NOTABLE
EVENTIDE VESPER EVENING
EVENTUAL LAST FINAL ULTIMATE
EVENTUALITY EVENT
EVENTUALLY YET FINALLY
EVENTUATE GO LEAD ISSUE RESULT SUCCEED ULTIMATE
EVER AY SO AYE EER ONCE STILL ALWAYS ETERNE FOREVER
EVERGREEN BOX FIR IVY YEW ASIS BAGO ILEX PINE TAWA BOLDO CAROB CEDAR HEATH HOLLY LARCH SAVIN THUYA TOYON BAUERA COIGUE DAHOON LAUREL MASTIC SPRUCE BANKSIA

BARETTA BEBEERU BILIMBI GOWIDDE
HEMLOCK JASMINE TARATAH
BOXTHORN CALFKILL CARAUNDA
IRONWOOD TILESEED
(PL.) CHRISTMAS
EVER-INCREASING ACCRESCENT
EVERLASTING ETERNE AEONIAL
AGELONG DURABLE ENDLESS ETERNAL
FOREVER LASTING TEDIOUS ENDURING
IMMORTAL INFINITE TIMELESS
PERPETUAL
EVERT UPSET EVERSE SUBVERT
OVERTURN
EVERY ALL ANY ILK PER THE EACH EVER
ILKA ENTIRE EVERICH COMPLETE
EVERYBODY ALL EACH EVERYMAN
EVERYONE
EVERYDAY USUAL HOMELY PROSAIC
ORDINARY WORKADAY
EVERY MAN IN HIS HUMOUR
(AUTHOR OF —) JONSON
(CHARACTER IN —) EDWARD KITELY
BOBADIL BRIDGET CLEMENT KNOWELL
MATTHEW WELLBRED BRAINWORM
EVERYTHING ALL ATHING
EVERYWHERE PASSIM UBIQUE
ALGATES OVERALL ALLWHERE
EVICT OUST EJECT EXPEL
EVIDENCE MARK SHOW SIGN TEST
PROOF SCRIP SMOKE TOKEN TRACE
TRIAL ATTEST AVOUCH BETOKE RECORD
REVEAL CHARTER EXHIBIT HEARSAY
SHOWING SUPPORT ARGUMENT
DISPROOF DOCUMENT EVICTION
INDICATE MANIFEST MONUMENT
MUNIMENT WARRANTY ADMINICLE
(— OF DISEASE) SYMPTOM
(— OF FRESHNESS) BLOOM
(— OF WRONGDOING) GOODS
(POSITIVE —) CONSTAT
EVIDENT LOUD OPEN PERT APERT BROAD
CLEAR FRANK GROSS NAKED PLAIN
EXTANT LIQUID PATENT WITTER
EMINENT GLARING OBVIOUS PROBATE
VISIBLE APPARENT DISTINCT FLAGRANT
LUCULENT MANIFEST PALPABLE
(PREF.) DELO
EVIL BAD DAR DER ILL SIN BALE BASE DIRE
HARM LEWD PAPA POOR SORE VICE VILE
WICK YELL CRIME CURSE DEVIL FELON
FOLLY HYDRA MALUM QUEDE SORRY
WATHE WRONG CANCEL DIVERS INJURY
MALIGN NAUGHT PLAGUE ROTTEN
SHREWD SINFUL UNFEEL UNFELE
UNGOOD UNWELL WICKED WONDER
ADVERSE BALEFUL CORRUPT DISEASE
DIVERSE HEINOUS HURTFUL IMMORAL
MISDEED NOXIOUS SATANIC UNHAPPY
UNSOUND VICIOUS CALAMITY
DEPRAVED DEVILISH DISASTER
GANGRENE IMPROPER INIQUITY
MISCHIEF QUEDSHIP SINISTER
NEFARIOUS
(— OF MANY PHASES) HYDRA
(IMAGINARY —) WINDMILL
(IMPENDING —) MENACE IMMINENCE
(SOCIAL —) SCOURGE

(SPIRITUAL —) SCAB
EVIL EYE DROCHUIL MALOCCHIO
EVINCE SHOW ARGUE PROVE SUBDUE
BREATHE CONQUER DISPLAY EXHIBIT
EVIDENCE INDICATE MANIFEST
EVOCATION SADHANA
EVOCATIVE REDOLENT
EVOKE FIT MOVE STIR EDUCE AROUSE
ELICIT SUMMON EVOCATE PROVOKE
SUGGEST
EVOLUTION DRIFT GROWTH BIOGENY
DIOECISM HOROTELY MANEUVER
BRADYTELY
EVOLVE COOK EMIT EDUCE DERIVE
UNFOLD UNROLL BLOSSOM DEVELOP
EVOLUTE CONCEIVE UNPLIGHT
EWE KEB TEG DRAPE SHEEP GIMMER
LAMBER RACHEL CHILVER
(— AND LAMB) COUPLE
(OLD —) BIDDY CROCK CRONE BIDDIE
(YOUNG —) THEAVE
EWER JUG CREW LAIR BASIN UDDER
PITCHER URCEOLE
EXACERBATE SOUR ENRAGE FERMENT
EMBITTER IRRITATE
EXACERBATION PAROXYSM
EXACT ASK DUE DEAD EVEN FINE FLAT
HAVE JUMP JUST LEVY NEAT NICE TRUE
VERY PRESS SCREW WREAK WREST
COMPEL DEMAND ELICIT EVINCE EXTORT
FORMAL GRAITH MINUTE NARROW
PROPER SEVERE SQUARE STRAIT STRICT
CAREFUL CERTAIN COLLECT COMMAND
CORRECT ENFORCE EXPRESS EXTRACT
LITERAL PARTILE PERFECT POINTED
PRECISE PRECISO REFINED REGULAR
REQUIRE ACCURATE CRITICAL EXPLICIT
FAITHFUL RIGOROUS SPECIFIC
(— BY FINE) ESTREAT
(— SATISFACTION) AVENGE
(NOT —) PLATIC
(PREF.) ORTH(O)
EXACTING NICE HARSH PICKY STERN
STIFF TIGHT SCREWY SEVERE STRAIT
STRICT ARDUOUS EXIGENT FINICKY
ONEROUS CRITICAL IMPOSING IRONCLAD
PRESSING SCREWING PARTICULAR
PERSNICKETY
EXACTION TAX MART GOUGE GRIPE
EXACTLY DUE BANG DEAD EVEN FLAT
FLOP FULL JUMP JUST VERY PLUMB
PLUNK QUITE RIGHT SHARP SPANG
TRULY ARIGHT EVENLY ITSELF JUSTLY
NICELY PERFECT SLAPDAB DIRECTLY
MINUTELY SMACKDAB
EXACTNESS RIGOR TRUTH NICETY
ACCURACY DELICACY DISPATCH
FIDELITY IDENTITY JUSTNESS SAPIENCE
SEVERITY PRECISION PARTICULARITY
(FUSSY —) FIKE
EXAGGERATE GAB MORE COLOR
BOUNCE CHARGE COLOUR EXTEND
OVERDO AMPLIFY ENHANCE ENLARGE
MAGNIFY OUTLASH ROMANCE STRETCH
INCREASE OVERDRAW OVERLASH
OVERPLAY OVERTELL OVERSTATE
OVERCHARGE

(— OPENING OF MOUTH) CHINK
EXAGGERATED CAMP SLAB TALL
COLORED FUSTIAN FABULOUS INFLATED
OVERDONE OVERSHOT OVERWEENING
EXAGGERATING ARROGANT
EXAGGERATION BLAH REACHER
HYPERBOLE
EXALT HAUT REAR AREAR BUILD DEIFY
ELATE ERECT EXTOL HEAVE HEEZE
HONOR MOUNT RAISE TOWER ALTIFY
ASCEND EXHALE PREFER REFINE THRONE
UPREAR WORTHY ADVANCE AUGMENT
DIGNIFY ELEVATE ENHANCE ENNOBLE
FEATHER GLORIFY GREATEN INSPIRE
MAGNIFY PROMOTE SUBLIME DIVINIZE
ENTHRONE GRADUATE HEIGHTEN
INHEAVEN PEDESTAL
EXALTATION LAUD AVATAR ANAGOGE
ELATION RAPTURE
EXALTED HAUT HIGH ELATE GRAND
LOFTY NOBLE SHEEN SKYEY SOARY
ASTRAL TIPTOE TOPFUL HAUGHTY
SUBLIME ELEVATED EXALTATE MAGNIFIC
EXAMINATION EXAM FACE QUIZ TEST
ASSAY AUDIT BOARD CHECK FINAL
GREAT POINT PROBE STUDY TRIAL
BIOPSY EXAMEN NOTICE REVIEW
SCHOOL SEARCH SURVEY TRIPOS
AUTOPSY BEARING CANVASS CHECKUP
DIVVERS EXAMINE HEARING INQUEST
INQUIRY MIDYEAR OPPOSAL TUGGERY
ANALYSIS CRITIQUE DOCIMASY
EXERCISE NECROPSY PHYSICAL
RESEARCH SCANNING SCRUTINY
PRACTICAL PRELIMINARY
EXAMINE ASK CON FAN SEE SPY TRY
BOLT CASE COMB FEEL LAIT LINE LOOK
OGLE QUIZ RIPE SEEK TEST VIEW ASSAY
AUDIT CHECK ENTER GROPE PROBE
QUEST QUOTE SAMEN SENSE SOUND
STUDY VISIT APPOSE BEHOLD CANDLE
DEBATE PERUSE REVIEW SCREEN
SEARCH SURVEY ANALYZE CANVASS
COLLATE DISCUSS EXPLORE INQUIRE
INSPECT OVERSEE RUMMAGE COGNOSCE
CONSIDER OVERHAUL TRAVERSE
(— BY TOUCH) PALPATE
(— CAREFULLY) SCAN SIFT PONDER
(— LAND) SOUM
EXAMINER POSER TRIER CENSOR
CONNER SABORA ANALYST APPOSER
AUDITOR CORONER PROBATOR
SEARCHER
EXAMPLE CASE CAST COPY LEAD NORM
TYPE BEAUT ESSAY LIGHT MODEL PIECE
EMBLEM PRAXIS SAMPLE BOUNCER
LEADING LECTURE PATTERN PURPOSE
SAMPLER THEATER CALENDAR
ENSAMPLE EXEMPLAR EXEMPLUM
FORBYSEN FOREGOER INSTANCE
PARADIGM SPECIMEN
(DISGRACEFUL —) BYZEN
MONSTROSITY
(EXTREME —) CAUTION
(FINEST —) PEARL
(INFERIOR —) EXCUSE
(INSTRUCTIVE —) LESSON

(OLDEST —) DOYEN
(PERFECT —) APOTHEOSIS
(STANDARD —) PROTOTYPE
(SUPERLATIVE —) BLINGER
EXASPERATE IRE IRK MAD BAIT GALL
HEAT URGE ANNOY BLOOD ENRAGE
EXCITE NETTLE INFLAME PROVOKE
ROUGHEN ACERBATE IRRITATE
EXASPERATED SNAKY WROTH
EXASPERATION GALL HEAT WRATH
EXCAVATE CUT DIG PIT HOLE HOWK
MINE MOLE MUCK PION SINK DELVE
DRILL DRIVE GRAVE NAVVY SCOOP
STOPE BURROW DREDGE EXCAVE
GULLET HOLLOW QUARRY
EXCAVATION CUT DIG PIT HOLE MINE
REDD SINK SUMP BERRY DELFT DELPH
DITCH GRAFT GRAVE HEUGH PILOT
STOPE BURROW CAVITY DUGOUT
GROOVE TRENCH BREAKUP CUTTING
PADDOCK TUTWORK WORKING
DENEHOLE SLUSHPIT
EXCAVATOR DIG BILDAR CLEOID
DIGGER DIPPER DRIFTER HATCHET
PIONEER
EXCEED COW TOP BEST PASS EXCEL
OUTDO OUTGO BETTER OUTRUN OUTVIE
OVERDO OVERGO ECLIPSE OUTPASS
OVERRUN OVERTAX PRECEDE SURPASS
OUTRANGE OUTREACH OUTSTRIP
OVERCOME OVERGANG OVERSTEP
OVERWEND SURMOUNT PREPONDERATE
(— IN IMPORTANCE) OVERSHADOW
(— THE RESOURCES) BEGGAR
EXCEEDING VILE
EXCEEDINGLY ALL DONE PURE TRES
VERY AMAIN BLAME BLAMED MASTER
PROPER PURELY AWFULLY LICKING
PARLOUS PASSING HEARTILY HEAVENLY
HORRIBLE PROPERLY
(PREF.) PRE ULTRA
EXCEL CAP COB TOP BANG BEAT BEST
DING FLOG MEND PASS STAR BLECK
OUTDO OUTGO SHINE TRUMP BETTER
EXCEED MASTER OUTRAY OVERDO
OVERGO PRECEL ECLIPSE EMULATE
OUTPEER SURPASS OUTCLASS
OUTRANGE OUTRIVAL OUTSHINE
OUTSTRIP OVERPEER SUPERATE
SURMOUNT
EXCELLENCE ARETE MERIT PRICE VIRTU
WORTH BEAUTY DESERT HEIGHT VIRTUE
DIGNITY PROWESS GOODNESS
SPLENDOR BRILLIANCE PREROGATIVE
(— OF QUALITY) STRIKE
(MORAL —) GRACE
(PL.) SANCTITIES
EXCELLENT FAB GAY RUM BEST BOSS
BRAW COOL FINE GOOD HEND HIGH
PURE RARE RIAL SLAP TALL TRIM ATHEL
BONNY BONZA BRAVE BULLY BURLY
CRACK GREAT JAMMY JOLLY LUMMY
PIOUS PRIME SOLID SUPER SWELL
TOUGH TRIED WALLY BONNIE BONZER
BOSKER BUMPER CHEESY CHOICE
CLASSY FAMOUS FREELY GENTLE
GOODLY PRETTY PROPER SELECT SPIFFY

WICKED WIZARD WORTHY YANKEE
BLIGHTY BOSHTER CAPITAL CORKING
CURIOUS ELEGANT GALLANT IMMENSE
QUALITY SNIFTER STAVING TOPPING
CLIPPING COLOSSAL EXIMIOUS
GENEROUS KNOCKOUT SPIFFING
STUNNING SUPERIOR VALUABLE
VIRTUOUS WAUREGAN YNGOODLY
(— IN QUALITY) FRANK
(MOST —) BEST

EXCELLENTLY BRAWLY CLEVER FINELY
FREELY PROUDLY DIVINELY FAMOUSLY

EXCELLING BEST PASSANT

EXCEPT BAR BUT CEP NOT BATE BOUT
OMIT ONLY SAVE ABATE FORBY SEVER
EXEMPT FORBYE NOBBUT SAVING
SCUSIN UNLESS BARRING BESIDES
EXCLUDE OUTCEPT OUTSIDE OUTTAKE
OUTWITH RESERVE WITHOUT FORPRISE
OUTTAKEN RESERVED
(PREF.) PRETER

EXCEPTING BATING EXCEPT SAVING
UNLESS BARRING

EXCEPTION DEMUR SALVO SAVING
DISSENT OFFENSE DEMURRER INSTANCE

EXCEPTIONAL RARE EXEMPT ROUSING
STRANGE UNUSUAL ABERRANT
ABNORMAL ESPECIAL SINGULAR
UNCOMMON

EXCEPTIONALLY AMAZING SPANKING

EXCERPT CITE PATCH QUOTE SCRAP
EXTRACT
(— FROM SONG) SNATCH

EXCESS OVER PLUS RIOT FLOOD INORD
LUXUS PRIDE ACRASY SPILTH BALANCE
DEBAUCH EXTREME MISRULE NIMIETY
OUTRAGE OVERAGE OVERSET PROFUSE
RIOTISE SURFEIT SURPLUS GLUTTONY
INTEREST OVERLASH OVERMUCH
OVERPLUS PLEONASM PLETHORA
PLEURISY SATURNALIA
OVERABUNDANCE
(— OF ACTION) OVERKILL
(— OF LOGS) BANK
(— OF METAL) FEEDHEAD
(— OF SOLAR MONTH) EPACT
(— OF VOTES) PLURALITY

EXCESSIVE TOO OVER RANK ENORM
FANCY STEEP STIFF THICK UNDUE
DEADLY DEUCED WOUNDY BURNING
EXTREME FURIOUS NIMIOUS OVERDUE
SURFEIT ABNORMAL CRIMINAL DEVILISH
ENORMOUS HORRIBLE INSOLENT
OVERMUCH TERRIBLE TERRIFIC
PLETHORIC

EXCESSIVELY TOO SUPER DEADLY
OVERLY STRONG UNDULY PARLISH
PARLOUS PASSING PLAGUEY WOUNDLY
DEVILISH PLAGUILY
(PREF.) HYPER

EXCHANGE RAP SET CASH CAUP CHOP
CODE COPE COUP KULA MART SELL
SWAP SWOP BANDY BOARD BOLSA
CORSE SHIFT STORE TRADE TROKE
TRUCK BARTER BOURSE CAMBIO
CHANGE DICKER EXCAMB MARKET
NIFFER RESALE RIALTO SCORSE SHOPPE

TOLSEL TOLZEY VALUTA WISSEL WRIXLE
BARROOM CAMBIUM COMMUTE
CONVERT DEALING PERMUTE TRAFFIC
COMMERCE TRUCKAGE
(— IN CHECKERS) CUT SHOT
(— OF BLOWS) HANDPLAY
(— OF PRISONERS) CARTEL
(— OF SYLLABLES) ANACLASIS
(— SMALL TALK) CHAFFER
(— THOUGHTS) CONVERSE
(— VISITS) GAM
(DANCE —) CROSSOVER
(FAIR —) GIFFGAFF
(FOREIGN —) DEVISE
(POETICAL —) FLYTING
(POST —) CANTEEN
(TELEPHONE —) CENTRAL

EXCISE CUT TAX CROP DUTY GELD TOLL
SLASH EXCIDE EXSECT IMPOST RESECT
EXSCIND ALCABALA RETRENCH

EXCITE HOT CITE FIRE HEAT HYPO SEND
SPUR STIR URGE WAKE WHET WORK
YERK ALARM AMOVE ANGER CHAFE
ELATE ERECT FLAME FLUSH IMPEL PIQUE
RAISE ROUSE SCALD SPOOK AROUSE
AWAKEN BOTHER DAZZLE DECOCT
FLURRY FOMENT GROOVE IGNITE INCEND
INCITE INVOKE JANGLE KINDLE LATHER
PROMPT SALUTE TICKLE UPREAR
WECCHE AGITATE ANIMATE COMMOVE
ENCHAFE FERMENT INCENSE INFLAME
PHILTER PROVOKE QUICKEN STARTLE
WHITTLE DISQUIET ENGENDER EXCITATE
IRRITATE
(— MIRTH) DIVERT

EXCITED UP GAY HOT AGOG GYTE PINK
ABOIL AGLOW CADGY EAGER PROUD
RANTY SKEER BLEEZY ELATED HEATED
STEAMY ATHRILL FEVERED HAYWIRE
SKEERED WAKENED AGITATED
ATWITTER ELEVATED FEVERISH
FLURRIED FRENETIC STARTLED
OVERWROUGHT
(EASILY —) KITTLE
(INTENSELY —) MAD

EXCITEMENT ADO GOG BUZZ FUME
FUSS GLOW HEAT KICK RUFF STIR TOSS
UNCO FEEZE FUROR KICKS LARRY MANIA
SETUP STOUR FRENZY SPLASH WARMTH
FERMENT FRISSON NERVISM TAMASHA
BROUHAHA DELIRIUM INTEREST
RACKETRY
(GREAT —) FEVER
(MENTAL —) WIDDRIM
(PLEASANT —) SUSPENSE
(VIOLENT —) GARE

EXCITING HOT HIGH ZINGY HECTIC
AGACANT BURNING PARLOUS RACKETY
ROUSING EXCITANT EXCITIVE PATHETIC
STIRRING TERRIFIC

EXCLAIM CRY HOWL BLURT ESCRY
SNORT CLAMOR OUTCRY BESPEAK

EXCLAMATION
(ALSO SEE INTERJECTION) O AH AY BO
EH EY HI HO LA LO MY OH SO ST YO AHA
BAH BAM BOO FEN GEE GRR GUP HAI
HAW HAY HEM HEP HEY HIC HOY HUH

NOW OCH OFF OHO OUF OUT PEW POH
POX ROT SEE SUZ TCH TCK TUT VOW
WEE WOW YAH YOW ALAS BUFF DEAR
DRAT EGAD EVOE FAST GARN GOOD
HAIL HECH HECK HIST HOLA HUFF HUSH
HYKE OONS OUGH PHOO PHUT PIFF PISH
POOH PRUT RATS RIVO SCAT SIRS SOFT
SOHO TCHU TUSH WALY WEEK WEET
WELL WHAM WHAT WHEE WHEW WHIR
WHIT WUGG YOOP YULE ALACK BRAVO
EWHOW FAINS FANCY GLORY GOODY
HEIGH HELLO HOLLA HUFFA HULLO
HUZZA JOSSA OHONE RIGHT SALVE
SHISH SKOAL SORRY SUGAR TEREU
WAUGH WHING WHISK WHIST WHOOP
WIRRA WOONS CARAJO CLAMOR
ENCORE HALLOO HEYDAY HOOTAY
HURRAH OUTCRY PERFAY QUOTHA
RATHER RIGHTO SHUCKS STEADY
WHOOSH CARAMBA DOGGONE GODSAKE
HOSANNA JEEPERS JIGGERS KERCHOO
KERWHAM NICHEVO PRITHEE RUBBISH
SALAMAT TANTIVY THUNDER WELCOME
WHOOPEE FAREWELL WAESUCKS
WELLAWAY
(— OF DISGUST) AUH FIE FOH PAH
UGH AUGH AVOY PHEW PISH POOT PSHA
PUGH FAUGH FEICH FEIGH PSHAW
WELOO
(— OF DISTRESS) AI AIE HARO
HARROW
(— OF DOUBT) HUM HUMPH
(— OF IMPATIENCE) GIP PHEW
(— OF INCREDULITY) AHEM INDEED
WALKER
(— OF REPUGNANCE) UGH
(— OF SURPRISE) HA OW GIP LAW
HEIN HUNH LACK LAND LAWK LORD
ODSO BABAI HEUGH LAWKS MARRY
CRIMINE CRIMINY HEAVENS JUCKIES
GORBLIMY GRAMERCY
(— OF TRIUMPH) AH IO GRIG HEUCH
HOOCH HURRAH
(PROFANE —) BAN
EXCLAMATION POINT BANG SHOUT
SCREAMER
EXCLUDE BAR SHUT SINK CLOSE DEBAR
EJECT EXPEL FENCE BANISH DISBAR
EXCEPT EXEMPT FORBAR FORBID REJECT
BLANKET DEFAULT EXPUNGE FOREBAR
FOREIGN OUTTAKE OUTWALL REPULSE
SECLUDE SUSPEND OSTRACIZE
EXCLUDING BAR BUT LESS BARRING
EXCLUSION OSTRACISM
EXCLUSIVE ALL ONLY RARE SOLE VERY
ALONE ELECT WHOLE NARROW SELECT
CLIQUISH ENTIRELY RECHERCHE
EXCLUSIVELY ALL ONLY ALONE SINGLY
ENTIRELY
EXCOMMUNICATE CURSE UNCHURCH
EXCOMMUNICATION BAN CURSE
HEREM EXCISION
EXCORIATE FLAY GALL SCORE STRIP
ABRADE SCATHE SCORCH BLISTER
LAMBASTE
EXCRESCENCE NOB PIN WEN BURL
BURR GALL HORN KNOB KNOT KNUR

LUMP SCAB WART FUSEE KNURL THORN
EXCESS HURTLE MORULA NUBBLE
PIMPLE BOLSTER PUSTULE RATTAIL
SPINACH CARUNCLE EPITHEMA
TUBERCLE
(— ON HORSE'S FOOT) FIG TWITTER
(— ON WHALE'S HEAD) BONNET
EXCRUCIATE RACK GRIND AGONIZE
TORMENT TORTURE
EXCRUCIATING GRINDING
EXCULPATE FREE CLEAR REMIT ACQUIT
EXCUSE PARDON ABSOLVE FORGIVE
JUSTIFY RELEASE PALLIATE
EXCURSION DIP HOP ROW DIET RIDE
SAIL SPIN TOUR TRIP ESSAY JAUNT
RANGE SALLY START TRAMP AIRING
CANTER CRUISE FLIGHT JUNKET OUTING
PASEAR RAMBLE SASHAY VAGARY
VOYAGE JOURNEY OUTLOPE OUTRIDE
OUTROAD CAMPAIGN ESCAPADE
EXCUSE FAIK PLEA ALIBI COLOR GLOSS
PLANE REMIT SALVO SCUSE ACQUIT
ESSOIN EXEMPT PARDON REASON
REFUGE SCONCE SECURE SUNYIE
ABSOLVE APARDON APOLOGY CONDONE
ESSOIGN EVASION EXCUSAL FORGIVE
OFFCOME PRETEXT DISPENSE OCCASION
OVERLOOK PALLIATE PRETENCE
(CONSCIENTIOUSLY —) SCRUPLE
EXCRATE BAN DAMN ABHOR CURSE
DEVOTE
EXECRATION CURSE ANATHEMA
MALEDICTION
EXECUTE DO ACT CUT TOP BURN DASH
FILL GIVE HANG HAVE KILL OBEY PASS
PLAY SLAY FRAME GANCH LYNCH SCRAG
YIELD DESIGN DIRECT EFFECT FINISH
FULFIL GARROT GIBBET MANAGE
ACHIEVE CONDUCT ENFORCE FULFILL
GAROTTE PERFORM STRETCH COMPLETE
DISPATCH EXPEDITE PRACTICE PRACTISE
(— BOW) WREATHE
(— POORLY) DUB
(— SUCCESSFULLY) COMPLETE
EXECUTION GANCH TOUCH EFFECT
FACTURE GARROTE HANGING TECHNIC
CARRIAGE PRACTICE PERFORMANCE
(— BY BURNING) STAKE
(— BY DROWNING) NOYADE
(— OF WILL) FACTUM
EXECUTIONER BURRIO HEADER TORTOR
BUTCHER HANGMAN HEADMAN
LOCKMAN CARNIFEX EXECUTOR
HEADSMAN CRUCIFIER
EXECUTIVE BOSS DEAN MAYOR
WARDEN CHAIRMAN MANAGER PODESTA
PREMIER GOVERNOR OFFICIAL
EXECUTOR DOER AGENT ALBACEA
SECUTOR ENFORCER MINISTER
EXEMPLARY LAUDABLE
EXEMPLIFICATION SOUL SAMPLE
CONSTAT EXAMPLE
EXEMPLIFY SAMPLE SATISFY ENSAMPLE
MODELIZE
EXEMPT EXON FREE FRANK SEVER
SPARE EXPERT FIDATE IMMUNE

EXCLUDE RELEASE DISPENSE EXCEPTED
    PRIVILEGE

EXEMPTION GRACE CHARTER FREEDOM
    LIBERTY SWEATER BLOODWIT IMMUNITY
    IMPUNITY

EXERCISE ACT AIR DIP PLY URE USE
    BEAR HAVE DRILL ETUDE EXERT HALMA
    LATIN LONGE SWEAT AIRING BREATH
    CAREER EMPLOY EXERCE LESSON
    MANUAL PARADE PRAXIS SCHOOL
    AUFGABE BREATHE DISPLAY ENHAUNT
    JOGGING PROBLEM ACTIVITY EXERTION
    FORENSIC PALESTRA PRACTICE
    PRACTISE
    (— CONTROL) BOSS PRESIDE
    (— HORSE) BREEZE
    (—S TO REDUCE WEIGHT)
    SLIMNASTICS
    (ACADEMIC —) PRACTICUM
    (CAVALRY —) MELEE
    (DEVOTIONAL —) ANGELUS
    (MUSICAL —) ETUDE SOLFEGE
    VOCALISE
    (PRELIMINARY —) WARMUP
    PROLUSION
    (PUNISHMENT —) PENSUM
    (STRONG —) INTENSION
    (SYSTEM OF —) AEROBICS
    (UNWARRANTED —) STRETCH

EXERT DO PLY PUT DRAW EMIT HUMP
    STIR DRIVE SPEND SWING BESTIR
    EXTEND REVEAL STRAIN AFFORCE
    ENFORCE IMPRESS CHARETTE ENDEAVOR
    EXERCISE
    (— A SPELL) TAKE
    (— POWER) ACT BEAR
    (— PRESSURE) PRESS SQUEEZE
    (— TRACTION) HAUL

EXERTION DINT HEFT BURST ESSAY
    LABOR TRIAL WHILE ACTION EFFORT
    MOTION PINGLE STRESS STRIFE
    ATTEMPT TROUBLE ENDEAVOR EXERCISE
    STRUGGLE
    (EXCESSIVE —) STRAIN
    (STRENUOUS —) HUMP

EXHALATION AURA FUME REEK STEAM
    BREATH EXPIRY MIASMA HALITUS
    MALARIA FUMOSITY MEPHITIS

EXHALE CAST EMIT REEK EXUDE STEAM
    WHIFF EXPIRE BREATHE FURNACE
    REFLAIR RESPIRE EXHALATE PERSPIRE

EXHAUST DO FAG SAP BEAT BURN COOK
    COWL EMIT FAIL FLAG FLOG JADE KILL
    MATE SOAK TIRE TUCK BLAST BREAK
    CLEAN DRAFT DRAIN EMPTY FORDO
    GRUEL LEECH PETER SHOOT SPEND
    SWINK WASTE WEARY ABRADE BETOIL
    BOTTOM BUGGER EMBOSS FINISH
    FOREDO HARASS HATTER OVERDO
    TAIGLE TUCKER BREATHE CONSUME
    DEPLETE DEPRIVE DRAUGHT EXTRACT
    FATIGUE OUTWEAR SCOURGE SURREIN
    TRACHLE DISTRESS EDUCTION
    EVACUATE FORSPEND FORSWINK
    FORWEARY OVERWEAR OVERSPEND

EXHAUSTED TAM BEAT DEAD DONE
    DUNG GONE WEAK WORN BLOWN

EMPTY JADED SPENT STANK TIRED
    BARREN BEATEN BUSHED EFFETE
    GROGGY MARCID PLAYED TOILED TRAIKY
    ATTAINT DRAINED EMPTIED FORDONE
    FORSUNG FORWORN TEDIOUS WHACKED
    BANKRUPT CONSUMED FOREDONE
    FOREWORN FORFAIRN FORSPENT
    FOUGHTEN HARASSED OUTSPENT
    OVERWORN

EXHAUSTING ARDUOUS IRKSOME
    PREYING

EXHAUSTION FATIGUE SELLOUT
    DISTRESS GONENESS PROSTRATION

EXHAUSTIVE FULL MINUTE THOROUGH

EXHIBIT AIR PEN FAIR HAVE SHEW SHOW
    TURN WEAR CARRY SPORT STAGE
    BLAZON DEMEAN EVINCE EXPOSE
    OPPOSE OSTEND PARADE REVEAL
    APPROVE CONCENE DIORAMA DISPLAY
    EXPRESS MONSTER PERFORM PRESENT
    PRODUCE PROJECT PROPOSE TRADUCE
    BOOKFAIR BRANDISH CONCEIVE
    DISCLOSE DISCOVER EMBLAZON
    EVIDENCE FORTHSET MANIFEST
    SHOWCASE
    (— ALARM) GLOFF
    (— DOGS) BENCH

EXHIBITION EXPO FAIR SALE SHOW
    DROLL ENTRY SALON SIGHT ANNUAL
    PARADE SALARY ACADEMY DISPLAY
    EXHIBIT PAGEANT PENSION PRESENT
    SHOWING STAGERY EXERCISE
    PERFORMANCE
    (— OF DOGS) BENCH
    (— ON STAGE) STAGERY
    (PUBLIC —) SPECIES
    (RIDING —) CAROUSEL

EXHIBITOR SHOWER

EXHILARATE AMUSE CHEER ELATE
    ANIMATE ELEVATE ENLIVEN GLADDEN

EXHILARATED RAD GLAD HAPPY HEADY
    ELEVATED

EXHILARATING SAPID

EXHILARATION GAIETY JOLLITY
    GLADNESS HILARITY

EXHORT URGE WARN CHARM ADHORT
    ADVISE CHARGE DEHORT ENGAGE INCITE
    PREACH CAUTION ADMONISH DISSUADE

EXHORTATION ADVICE EXHORT HOMILY
    COUNSEL PROPHECY PREACHMENT

EXHORTER HORTATOR PREACHER

EXHUME DIG DELVE UNBURY UNTOMB
    UNEARTH DISINTER EXHUMATE

EXIGENCY NEED PUSH WANT EXIGENT
    URGENCY JUNCTURE OCCASION
    PRESSURE

EXIGENT DIRE VITAL URGENT CRITICAL
    EXACTING PRESSING

EXILE POOR RUIN THIN EXPEL WREAK
    BANISH DEPORT GALUTH OUTLAW
    SCANTY WRETCH EXULATE GERSHOM
    OUTCAST PILGRIM REFUGEE SLENDER
    DIASPORA FUGITIVE OUTLAWRY
    OSTRACIZE

EXILED FOREIGN FUGITIVE

EXIST AM BE IS ARE LIE COME GROW

LIVE MOVE PASS DWELL CONSIST
SUBSIST
EXISTENCE ENS ESSE LIFE SEIN BEING
DASEIN ENTITY IDEATE ESSENCE
IDEATUM REALITY ENERGEIA IDENTITY
STANDING SURVIVAL PERSONALITY
(— AFTER DEATH) AFTERLIFE
(DULL —) DEATH
(ETERNAL —) SAT
(EVER-CHANGING —) SAMSARA
(INDEPENDENT —) ASEITY PERSEITY
(PERMANENT —) INHERENCE
(WAKING —) JAGRATA
EXISTENT HARD REAL ALIVE BEING
ACTUAL EXTANT EXISTING
EXISTING GOING ACTUAL EXTANT
PRESENT EXISTENT
(— IN NAME ONLY) DUMMY
EXIT ISH DOOR GATE VENT GOING ISSUE
LEAVE EGRESS EXITUS OUTLET OUTWAY
EXITION OUTGATE OUTPORT PASSAGE
DEBOUCHE
EXODUS EXITUS HEGIRA EXODIUM
EXONERATE FREE ALIBI CLEAR ACQUIT
EXCUSE EXONER UNLOAD ABSOLVE
RELIEVE
EXORBITANT STEEP UNDUE ABNORMAL
EXOTIC ALIEN FOREIGN STRANGE
ADVENTIVE RECHERCHE
EXPAND OPE WAX BLOW BULK FLAN
FLUE FOAM GROW HUFF OPEN FARCE
FLASH RETCH SPLAY SWELL WIDEN
DIDUCE DILATE EXTEND INTEND SPREAD
SPROUT UNFOLD UNFURL AMPLIFY
BALLOON BLOSSOM BOLSTER BROADEN
BURGEON DEVELOP DIFFUSE DISPAND
DISPLAY DISTEND EDUCATE ENLARGE
EXPANSE EXPLAIN INFLATE STRETCH
DISPREAD INCREASE LENGTHEN
OUTREACH
(— AS A VESSEL) FLAN
(— FEATHERS) PRIDE
(— INTO PODS) KiD
EXPANDED NOWY OPEN OVERT DILATE
PATENT SPREAD DILATED SWOLLEN
INFLATED PATULENT PATULOUS
EXPANSE AREA ROOM BOSOM BURST
FIELD REACH TRACT EXTENT LENGTH
SPREAD COUNTRY STRETCH DISTANCE
EXPANSUM SEPARATE
(— OF ICE) SHEET
(— OF SEA ICE) FIELD
(BROAD —) ACRE MAIN
(FLAT —) LEVEL
(IMMEASURABLE — OF TIME)
ETERNITY
(IMMENSE —) OCEAN
(INDEFINITE —) VAGUE
(VAST —) SEA
(WIDE —) BREADTH
EXPANSION ALA BULB WING FLUSH
SPLAY GROWTH SPREAD ECTASIA
ECTASIS EXPANSE HASTULA ACROCYST
COQUILLE DIASTOLE DILATION INCREASE
SWELLING
(— IN SEEDS) ALA WING
(— OF RIVER) BROAD

(FOLIOSE —) LAMINA
(LITURGICAL —) EMBOLISM
EXPANSIVE FREE WIDE BROAD GENIAL
ELASTIC LIBERAL GENEROUS SPACIOUS
SWELLING
EXPATIATE DWELL DILATE EXPAND
SPREAD AMPLIFY BROADEN DESCANT
DIFFUSE ENLARGE SATISFY
EXPATRIATE EXILE EXPEL BANISH
OUTLAW OUTCAST
EXPECT ASK DEEM HOPE LOOK STAY
TEND TROW WAIT WEEN ABIDE AWAIT
THINK ATTEND DEMAND INTEND RECKON
PRESUME REQUIRE SUPPOSE SUSPECT
CALCULATE
EXPECTANT ATIPTOE CHARGED
HOPEFUL INCHOATE
EXPECTATION HOPE VIEW WAIT WEEN
TRUST EXPECT FUTURE ESPEIRE OPINION
SUPPOSE THOUGHT WEENING PROSPECT
EXPECTED DUE NATURAL SUPPOSED
EXPECTORATE SPIT
EXPEDIENT FIT WISE ATAJO CRAFT
DODGE JOKER KNACK SALVO SHIFT
DEVICE RESORT STRING DODGERY
POLITIC STOPGAP ARTIFICE RESOURCE
DESIRABLE MAKESHIFT
EXPEDITE HIE EASY FREE HURRY SPEED
EXPEDE GREASE HASTEN QUICKEN
DISPATCH
EXPEDITION CAMP FARE PLOY ROAD
TREK HASTE HURRY RANGE SCOUT
TRADE VOYAGE CARAVAN ENTRADA
OUTLOPE SERVICE COMMANDO
HEADHUNT PROGRESS
(FISHING —) DRAVE
(HUNTING —) SAFARI
(MILITARY —) HARKA CRUSADE
HOSTING JOURNEY WARPATH
EXPEDITIOUS FAST HASTY QUICK RAPID
READY SHORT PROMPT SPEEDY
EXPEL CAN OUT USH BLOW BOLT DRUM
DUMP FIRE OUST VOID WARP AVOID
CHASE CHECK DEPEL EJECT ERUPT
EVICT EXILE KNOCK SPURT BANISH
BOUNCE DEBOUT DEPORT DEVOID
DISBAR DISOWN OUTPUT OUTRAY
REFUSE ABANDON EXCLUDE EXPULSE
EXTRUDE OBTRUDE SCRATCH SECLUDE
SUSPEND DISLODGE DISPLACE
EVACUATE FORJUDGE
(— AIR) COUGH
(— FROM MEMBERSHIP) HAMMER
(— GAS) BELCH
(— SUDDENLY) SLIRT
(PREF.) DIS
EXPEND USE LEND SPEND SPORT WASTE
WREAK DEFRAY IMPEND OCCUPY
OUTLAY PONDER CONSUME DISPEND
EROGATE EXHAUST OVERUSE DISBURSE
SQUANDER
EXPENDITURE COST MISE OUTGO
PENSE CHARGE OUTLAY EXPENSE
PENSION SPENDING
(— OF ENERGY) EFFORT
EXPENSE EX COST GAFF LOSS BATTA
PRICE

EXPENSIVE DEAR HIGH SALT PRICY STIFF COSTLY LAVISH PRICEY APICIAN LIBERAL THRIFTY

EXPERIENCE SEE TRY FEEL FIND HAVE HENT HOLD KNOW LIVE TEST ASSAY EVENT PROOF PROVE SKILL TASTE TRIAL USAGE BEHOLD EXPERT FRAIST SAMPLE SUFFER APPROVE CONTACT FEELING FURNACE KNOWING REALIZE SUSTAIN UNDERGO ESCAPADE
(— GOOD OR ILL FORTUNE) SPEED
(— OF INTENSE SUFFERING) CALVARY
(— WITH BITTERNESS) BEAR
(CALAMITOUS —) ADVERSITY
(DRUG —) TRIP
(ENJOYABLE —) GROOVE
(EXCITING —) TRIP
(FIRST —) TIROCINIUM
(HALLUCINATORY —) TRIP
(ORDINARY —) USE
(PAINFUL —) FIT
(PARTIAL —) GUST
(TRYING —) ORDEAL

EXPERIENCED HAD MET OLD SEEN USED SALTY EXPERT TRADED ANCIENT PRACTIC THRIVEN VETERAN WEIGHED SEASONED
(— INTENSIVELY) ACUTE
(ACTUALLY —) SPECIOUS

EXPERIMENT SHY TRY TEST ASSAY ESSAY TRIAL ATTEMPT CONTROL

EXPERT ACE DAB DEFT FULL GOOD PERT ADEPT CRACK FLASH MAVEN MAVIN READY SHARP SWELL ADROIT ARTIST CLEVER FACILE HABILE KAHUNA MASTER PANDIT PERTLY QUAINT SUBTLE WIZARD ARTISTE ATTACHE CAPABLE DABSTER PERFECT PERITUS SKILLED DEXTROUS GAINSOME SKILLFUL SPEEDFUL VIRTUOSO PROFESSED PROFICIENT
(— IN JEWISH LAW) DAYAN
(— ON DRIVING LOGS) LAKER
(BANK —) SHROFF
(GREAT —) ONER
(SCIENTIFIC —) BOFFIN

EXPERTNESS SAVVY SKILL FACILITY HABILITY

EXPIRATION END DEATH BREATH EFFLUX ELAPSE EXPIRE EXPIRY

EXPIRE DIE END EMIT FALL EXPEL GHOST LAPSE ELAPSE EXHALE OUTRUN PERISH

EXPLAIN OPEN REDE SAVE SCAN UNDO WISE AREAD AREED CLEAR GLOSS GLOZE PLANE RECHE SOLVE SPEED TOUCH DEFINE EXPAND EXPLAT EXPONE REMENE RIDDLE UNFOLD ABSOLVE ACCOUNT AMPLIFY CLARIFY COMMENT CONTRUE DECLARE DEVELOP DISCUSS EXHIBIT EXPOUND JUSTIFY RESOLVE CONSTRUE DESCRIBE MANIFEST SIMPLIFY UNPLIGHT UNWONDER

EXPLANATION KEY NOTE FARSE GLOSS SALVE SALVO ANSWER CAVEAT ACCOUNT APOLOGY ADDENDUM EXEGESIS INNUENDO NOTATION SOLUTION

EXPLETIVE GEE BOSH EGAD GOSH OATH BEGAD BEHEAR SDEATH TUNKET DAMMISH MORBLEU GOODYEAR GRACIOUS

EXPLICATE OPEN CLEAR EXPAND UNFOLD ACCOUNT EXPLAIN

EXPLICIT OPEN CLEAR EXACT FIXED PLAIN EXPRESS PRECISE ABSOLUTE DEFINITE IMPLICIT POSITIVE PUNCTUAL SPECIFIC

EXPLICITLY BARELY DIRECT FORMALLY

EXPLODE POP BLOW FIRE BELCH BLAST BURST CRUMP ERUPT PLUFF SHOOT SQUIB SPRING BACKFIRE DETONATE DISPLODE

EXPLOIT ACT DEED FEAT GEST JEST MILK WORK GOUGE STUNT PERFORM SUCCESS CHIVALRY PARERGON PROPERTY
(— FINANCIALLY) RIPOFF
(— SUCCESSFULLY) PARLAY

EXPLORATION SPY PROBE SEARCH EXPLORE

EXPLORATORY FRONTIER PROBATIVE PROBATORY

EXPLORE DO DIP MAP SPY DIVE DRAG FEEL VIEW CHART COAST DELVE RANGE SCOUT SOUND SEARCH EXAMINE PALPATE BOTANIZE DISCOVER
(— FOR MINERALS) PROSPECT

EXPLORER CAVEMAN PIONEER COLUMBUS

EXPLOSION POP BANG BLOW BLAST BURST CRUMP SALVO BLOWUP BOUNCE REPORT PLOSION INCIDENT OUTBURST
(FUEL —) BACKFIRE
(SLIGHT —) PLUFF

EXPLOSIVE EGG TNT MINE AMVIS AMATOL JOVITE LIMPET POWDER TETRYL TONITE TORPEX TOUCHY TRITON ABELITE AMMONAL AZOTINE DUNNITE LIGNOSE LYDDITE PLOSIVE PRIMING PUDDING SHIMOSE THORITE AMMONITE CHEDDITE DYNAMITE ECRASITE ERUPTIVE GELATINE MAXIMITE MELINITE PYROLITE ROBURITE SABULITE SAXONITE SECURITE RACKAROCK SAMSONITE
(CHARGE OF —) TULIP RESPONDER

EXPONENT INDEX POWER

EXPORT OUTCARRY

EXPOSE AIR BARE GIVE OPEN RISK SHOW STRIP BEWRAY DEBUNK DETECT EXPONE GIBBET OBJECT OPPOSE REVEAL UNHUSK UNMASK DISPLAY EXHIBIT EXPOUND PILLORY PROPINE PUBLISH SUBJECT UNCOVER UNEARTH UNTRUSS BRANDISH DISCLOSE DISCOVER MUCKRAKE RIDICULE SATIRIZE UNCLOTHE UNSHROUD
(— FOR BLEACHING) CROFT
(— ORE) HUSH
(— PLAYING CARD) BURN
(— SELF TO) WAGE
(— SUDDENLY) FLASH
(— TO AIR) AERATE
(— TO DANGER) JUMP COMMIT SUBMIT

(— TO HEAT) AIR
(— TO INFAMY) GIBBET
(— TO MOISTURE) RET
(— TO SCORN) PILLORY
(— TO SULFUR DIOXIDE) STOVE
(— TO SUN) INSOLATE SOLARIZE
(— TO SUN AND AIR) FIELD
EXPOSED AIRY BARE OPEN BLEAK
LIABLE PUBLIC UNSAFE SUBJECT
VEILLESS
(— TO) AGAINST
(— TO DANGER) INSECURE
EXPOSITION FAIR GECK SHOW ZEND
TRACT APERCU EXPOSE METHOD
SURVEY ACCOUNT EXPOSAL MIDRASH
ANALYSIS EXEGESIS EXPOSURE
EXTHESIS HAGGADAH TREATISE
(— OF FEAST) SYNAXARY
EXPOSTULATE ARGUE OBJECT DISCUSS
EXAMINE PROTEST
EXPOSURE ASPECT EXPOSE EXPOSAL
FLASHING FRONTAGE PROSPECT
(— OF CARDS) SPREAD
(— OF KING) CHECK
(— TO AIR) AERATE AIRING
(BODY —) FLASH
EXPOUND OPEN REDE UNDO GLOZE
SENSE TREAT DEFINE EXPONE EXPOSE
COMMENT DEVELOP DISCUSS EXPLAIN
EXPOSIT EXPRESS CONSTRUE SIMPLIFY
PHILOSOPHIZE
EXPOUNDER MUFTI MULLAH EXPRESS
EXPONENT HERMETIC
(— OF THEORY) ALFAQUI
PHILOSOPHER
EXPRESS AIR BID PUT SAY CAST EMIT
PASS POST VENT COUCH EMOTE FRAME
OPINE SPEAK STATE UTTER VOICE WIELD
BROACH DEMEAN DENOTE DIRECT
EVINCE IMPORT PHRASE ABREACT
BREATHE DECLARE DICTATE EXPOUND
EXTREME TESTIFY DEFINITE DESCRIBE
DISPATCH EXPLICIT INTIMATE MANIFEST
(— APPROVAL) AGREE ACCEDE
APPLAUD
(— AS LANGUAGE) LAY
(— BY GESTURE) BECK
(— BY LAUGHTER) LAUGH
(— CONCERN) CLUCK
(— DISAPPROVAL) BOO CHIDE DECRY
GROAN CATCALL
(— DISDAIN) TUT
(— EFFERVESCENTLY) CHORTLE
(— FOLLY) EXPAND
(— GRATITUDE) THANK AGGRATE
(— GRIEF) DEPLORE
(— IN WORDS) SAY DRAW SPEAK
PHRASE
(— NUMERICALLY) EVALUATE
(— ONE'S FEELINGS) FLOW
(— SORROW) LAMENT COMPLAIN
(— WILLINGNESS) CONSENT
EXPRESSION DIT HIT SAY CAST EUGE
FACE FORM POSE SHOW SIGN TERM
VULT WORD ADIEU GLIFF IDIOM SNEER
TOKEN VOICE BYWORD DILOGY DIVERB
EFFECT FACIES ORACLE PHRASE SPEECH
SYMBOL COMMENT DESCANT EPITHET
EXPRESS GRIMACE ALLEGORY
AUSDRUCK DANICISM FELICITY
LACONISM MONOMIAL
(— IN FEW WORDS) BREVITY
(— OF ANNOYANCE) SOH
(— OF APPROVAL) EUGE PLACET
(— OF ASSENT) CONTENT
(— OF BEAUTY) ART
(— OF CHOICE) VOTE
(— OF CONTEMPT) COBLOAF
(— OF DISPLEASURE) FROWN
(— OF DISTASTE) FACE
(— OF HOMAGE) OVATION
(— OF JOY) GREETING
(— OF OPINION) EDITORIAL
(— OF RESPECT) DUTY
(— OF SADNESS) SHADE
(— OF SCORN) GECK
(— OF SINGLE IDEA) RHEME
(APT —) FELICITY
(CHEMICAL —) EQUATION
(COMMONPLACE —) BROMIDE
(CORRECT —) SUMPSIMUS
(CURT —) LACONIC
(FACIAL —) GRIN CHEER SCOWL SMILE
(INCONGRUOUS —) BULL
(LOUD —) CLAMOR
(MATHEMATICAL —) INDEX SERIES
BINOMIAL EQUATION FUNCTION
INTEGRAL
(MOCKING —) SCOFF
(PECULIAR —) IDIOM
(PET —) CANT
(PUERILE —) BOYISM
(SARCASTIC —) GIBE JIBE
(SERIOUS —) EARNEST
(SINCERE —) CANDOR
(SYMBOLIC —) FORMULA
(TENDER —) LANGUISH
(TRITE —) CLICHE
(UNRESTRAINED —) EFFUSION
(VERBAL —) LETTER
(VULGAR —) SOLECISM
(WISE —) ORACLE
EXPRESSIONLESS BLANK STONY
LEADEN SODDEN VACANT WOODEN
TONELESS
EXPRESSIVE POETIC TONGUED
ELOQUENT EMPHATIC SPEAKING
EXPRESSIVENESS DICTION DELICACY
TOURNURE ELOQUENCE
EXPRESSWAY FREEWAY SPEEDWAY
EXPULSION EXILE BOUNCE OUSTER
BANNIMUS EJECTION EXCISION
EXPUNGE BLOT DELE ERASE SLASH
CANCEL DELETE EFFACE EXCISE SCRAPE
DESTROY SCRATCH DISPUNGE
EXPURGATION BOWDLERISM
EXQUISITE FOP DUDE FINE NICE PERT
PINK RARE DANDY EXACT CHOICE
DAINTY CAREFUL ELEGANT GEMLIKE
PERFECT REFINED AFFECTED DELICATE
ETHEREAL MACARONI RECHERCHE
EXTANT ALIVE BEING LIVING VISIBLE
EXISTING MANIFEST

EXTEND GO EKE LIE RUN BEAR BUSH COME DATE DRAW GROW LAST OPEN PASS PUSH RISE ROLL SPIN BREDE BULGE CARRY FARCE REACH RENEW RETCH SEIZE SHOOT STENT VERGE WIDEN AMOUNT DEEPEN DEPLOY DILATE EXPAND INTEND OUTLIE SPREAD SPRING STRAIN STREAK THRUST TRENCH AMPLIFY BROADEN DIFFUSE DISPLAY DISTEND ENLARGE OVERRUN PORRECT PORTEND PRODUCE PROFFER PROJECT PROLONG PROMOTE PROTEND RADIATE STRETCH CONTINUE ELONGATE INCREASE LENGTHEN OUTREACH PROROGUE PROTRACT PROTRUDE OUTSPREAD PROPAGATE OUTSTRETCH
(— ACTIVITIES) BRANCH
(— AROUND) GIRTH
(— HAND) RAX
(— IN SPACE) DURE
(— IRREGULARLY) TRAIL
(— OVER) SPAN COVER CROSS CONTAIN OVERLAP OVERRIDE
(— SAIL) SHEET
(— THE FRONT) DEPLOY
(— TO) LINE REACH

EXTENDED FAT LONG OPEN BROAD EXTENT SPREAD EXTENSE LENGTHY PROLATE SPLAYED EXPANDED INTENDED

EXTENSION ARM EKE ELL AREA CAPE SCOPE POCKET SATTVA SPHERE SPREAD BREADTH STRETCH ADDENDUM ADDITION DURATION INCREASE PROTENSE
(— OF BUILDING MATERIAL) APRON
(— OF CREDIT) DATING
(— OF MINERAL VEIN) FLAT
(— OF RACE TRACK) CHUTE
(— OF SHELL) LAPPET
(— OF TIME) RESPITE
(— OF WAGON FRAME) THRIPPLE
(BALLET) BATTEMENT

EXTENSIVE HUGE VAST WIDE AMPLE BROAD LARGE IMMENSE EXPANDED INFINITE SWEEPING

EXTENT DUE RUN TAX AREA BODY BULK DEAL GAGE LEVY PASS SIZE WRIT AMBIT DEPTH FIELD GAUGE LIMIT RANGE REACH SCOPE SPACE STENT SWEEP TRACK AMOUNT ASSIZE ATTACK DEGREE LENGTH SPREAD STREEK ACREAGE ASSAULT BREADTH COMPASS CONTENT EXPANSE PURVIEW SEIZURE STRETCH VARIETY DISTANCE INCREASE LATITUDE OUTREACH QUANTITY STRAIGHT
(— OF FRONT) FRONTAGE
(— OF LAND) HEIGHT CONTINENT
(— OF SPACE) ROOM
(BROAD —) SWEEP MAGNITUDE
(RELATIVE —) SCALF
(SOME —) BIT
(UNLIMITED —) INFINITY
(UTMOST —) FULL
(VAST —) DEEP
(VERTICAL —) ALTITUDE

EXTERIOR CRUST ECTAD ECTAL OUTER SHELL EXTERN OUTSIDE OUTWARD SURFACE EXOTERIC EXTERNAL OUTLYING

EXTERMINATE WIPE EXPEL UPROOT ABOLISH DESTROY

EXTERNAL OUT OUTER EXTERN OUTSIDE OUTWARD STRANGE EXOTERIC EXTERIOR INCIDENT PHYSICAL PERIPHERAL
(PREF.) ECT(O) OUT

EXTINCT DEAD BYGONE DEFUNCT QUENCHED

EXTINCTION DOOM FINE DEATH EXPIRY DELETION

EXTINGUISH OUT DAMP DOUT REDD STUB ANNUL CHOKE CRUSH DOUSE DROWN QUELL REPEL SLAKE SNUFF STAMP ASLAKE QUENCH STANCH STIFLE ABOLISH BLANKET DESTROY ECLIPSE EXPIATE EXTINCT OBSCURE OPPRESS SLOCKEN SUPPRESS
(— BY CRUSHING) DINCH
(— CIGARETTE) SNUB

EXTINGUISHED OUT DEAD EXTINCT

EXTIRPATE DELE ROOT STUB ERASE EXPEL STAMP STOCK EXCISE UPROOT DESTROY OUTROOT

EXTOL CRY FETE HYMN LAUD BLESS CRACK EXALT KUDOS SPEAK PRAISE ADVANCE APPLAUD COMMEND ELEVATE ENHANCE GLORIFY MAGNIFY RESOUND UPRAISE EMBLAZON EULOGIZE PROCLAIM

EXTORT PEEL PILL RAMP BLEED BRIBE EDUCE EXACT FORCE PINCH WREST WRING COMPEL ELICIT SPONGE STRAIN WRENCH WRITHE EXTRACT OUTWREST

EXTORTION CHOUT GOUGE EXTORT HOLDUP SCOTAL BRIBERY PILLAGE CHANTAGE EXACTION RAPACITY SHAKEDOWN

EXTORTIONER BRIBER POLLER SHAVER BLEEDER VAMPIRE

EXTRA ODD GASH MORE ORRA OVER PLUS ADDED SPARE SPECIAL SURPLUS SUPERIOR LAGNIAPPE
(PREF.) HYPER SUPER

EXTRACT DIG PRY CITE COPY DRAW KINO KOLA PULL SOAK ANIMA BLEED CUTCH DRAFT EDUCE ELUTE EXACT KUTCH KYPOO QUOTE RENES SCRAP STEEP WRING CORTIN CURARE DEDUCE DERIVE DEWTRY DISTIL ELICIT ELIXIR EXTORT GOBBET GUACIN MULIUM OVARIN REMOVE RENDER TRIPOS UZARON ABORTIN ARCANUM DESCENT DISTILL ERGOTIN ESSENCE ESTREAT EXCERPT EXHAUST FUMARIA INTRAIT LIMBECK MONESIA PASSEWA SUMMARY VANILLA ACETRACT AMBRETTE GINGERIN HYPERNIC INFUSION LICORICE PERICOPE SEPARATE TIKITIKI TINCTURE WITHDRAW
(— BY BOILING) DECOCT ELIXATE
(— BY DIGGING) GRUB
(— DATA FROM COMPUTER) READ
(— FORCIBLY) EVULSE

(— FROM ACACIA) KATH CASHOO
CATECHU
(— FROM BERBERIS) RUSOT RUSWUT
(— OF BARK) EUONYMIN
(— OF GINGER) JAKE JAKEY
(— ORE) STOPE
(TANNING —) AMALTAS
EXTRACTION KIN BIRTH BROOD STOCK
ORIGIN DESCENT EDITION ESSENCE
EXTRACT EXTREAT BREEDING TINCTURE
(— OF ROOTS) EVOLUTION
(— OF STEAM) BLEEDING
EXTRADITE BANISH
EXTRANEOUS ALIEN OUTER EXOTIC
FOREIGN OUTLYING SPURIOUS
EXTRAORDINARY ODD FREM ONCO
RARE BYOUS ENORM SMASH DAMNED
EXEMPT MIGHTY RAGING SIGNAL
CORKING CURIOUS HUMMING NOTABLE
SPECIAL STRANGE UNUSUAL ABNORMAL
EXIMIOUS FORINSEC SINGULAR
SMASHING UNCOMMON PHENOMINAL
PRODIGIOUS
EXTRAVAGANCE CAMP FRILL PRIDE
WASTE LUXURY EXPENSE RAMPANCY
SQUANDER UNTHRIFT WILDNESS
PROFUSION SATURNALIA
(MENTAL —) MADNESS
EXTRAVAGANT MAD HIGH LUSH WILD
FANCY FISHY FOLLE LARGE OUTRE
COSTLY GOTHIC HEROIC LAVISH SHRILL
WANTON BAROQUE BIZARRE COSTLEW
FANATIC FLAMING FURIOUS NIMIOUS
PROFUSE RAMPANT VAGRANT INSOLENT
PRODIGAL RECKLESS ROMANTIC
UNTHRIFT WANDERER WASTEFUL
BOMBASTIC PROFLIGATE
EXTREME NTH BLUE DEEP DIRE HIGH
LAST RANK SORE VILE ACUTE BLACK
CLOSE CRUEL DENSE DIZZY FINAL GREAT
LIMIT PITCH STEEP ULTRA UNDUE UTTER
ARDENT ARRANT BRAZEN DEADLY
FAROUT FIERCE HEROIC LENGTH
MORTAL SAVAGE SEVERE STRONG
UTMOST WOUNDY ABYSMAL DRASTIC
FEARFUL FORWARD FRANTIC HOWLING
INTENSE OUTWARD PROFUSE RADICAL
SURFEIT VICIOUS VIOLENT ALMIGHTY
DEVILISH DREADFUL EGYPTIAN
ENORMOUS FABULOUS FARTHEST
GREATEST MERCIFUL SPENDFUL
TERRIBLE TERRIFIC ULTIMATE EXQUISITE
(PL.) PASO
(PREF.) ACR(O) ARCH
EXTREMELY SO BIG DOG TOO WAY
BONE DEAD EVER FULL MAIN RANK SELI
THAT UNCO VERY AWFUL BLACK BULLY
BYOUS CRAZY CRUEL EXTRA HEAPS
RIGHT SELLE SOWAN SUPER BITTER
DAMNED DEADLY DEUCED HIGHLY
MIGHTY NATION POISON SORELY SURELY
UNCOLY APLENTY AWFULLY BOILING
CRUELLY EXTREME GALLOWS HOPPING
INNERLY SOPPING STAVING ALMIGHTY
ENORMOUS MORTALLY PRECIOUS
PROPERLY

EXTREMITY END TIP HEAD NEED PUSH
TAIL CLOSE LIMIT SHIFT START VERGE
BORDER FINGER EXIGENT EXTREME
ACROSTIC ALTITUDE DISASTER
JUNCTURE OUTRANCE TERMINAL
(— OF MOON) HORN
(— OF TENDRIL) HOLDFAST
(— OF TOOTH ROOT) APEX
(REMOTEST —) CORNER
EXTRICATE FREE HELP WIND CLEAR
LOOSE RESCUE SQUIRM OUTWIND
EXPEDITE LIBERATE UNTANGLE
(— ONESELF) WANGLE
EXTRINSIC ALIEN EVERY FOREIGN
OUTWARD EXTERNAL OUTLYING
EXTROVERT SYNTONIC
EXTRUDE BEAR SPEW EJECT EXPEL
SHOOT PROJECT PROTRUDE
EXUBERANCE PRICE EXCESS LUXURY
PLENTY ABANDON LAUGHTER
OVERFLOW
EXUBERANT RANK BOUNCY FEISTY
LAVISH COPIOUS FERTILE GLOWING
PROFUSE RAMPANT EFFUSIVE
EXUDE GUM DRIP EMIT OOZE REEK SPEW
BLEED STILL SWEAT EXTILL STRAIN
STREAM EXUDATE GUTTATE SCREEVE
SECRETE SWELTER PERSPIRE
EXULT JOY CROW LEAP BOAST GLOAT
GLORY INSULT SPRING MAFFICK REJOICE
TRIUMPH
EXULTANT PROUD ELATED PRIDEFUL
EXULTATION JOY PAEAN OVATION
RAPTURE
EYE ORB SPY DISC GAZE GLIM LAMP LOOP
MIEN SCAN UVEA VIEW GLARE GLASS
GLENE NAVEL OPTIC SENSE SHANK
SIGHT TOISE WATCH BEHOLD EUCONE
EYELET GOGGLE OCULAR OCULUS OILLET
PEEPER POPEYE REGARD ROLLER SHINER
VISION WINDOW WINKER BLINKER
EUCONIC EXOCONE EYEBALL EYEHOLE
OBSERVE OCELLUS PIERCER PIGSNEY
PINKANY PINKENY SENSORY WITNESS
LATCHING NOISETTE OMMATEUM
RECEPTOR
(— AMOROUSLY) OGLE
(— FORMED BY ROPE) TONGUE
(— IN BIGHT) COLLAR
(— IN EGYPTIAN SYMBOLISM) UT.
(— OF BEAN) HILUM
(— OF FRUIT) NOSE
(— OF HINGE) GUDGEON
(— OF INSECT) STEMMA
(— OF RA) SEKHET
(BLACK —) KEEK MOUSE SHINER
(EVIL —) DROCHUIL MALOCCHIO
(JERKY — MOVEMENT) SACCADE
(METAL —) HONDA
(PART OF —) IRIS LENS FOVEA PUPIL
CORNEA MACULA SCLERA CHAMBER
CHOROID LIGAMENT CONJUNCTIVA
EYEGLASSES GLIMS SPECS LENSES
GLASSES LORGNON NIPPERS BIFOCALS
EYELASH BREE LASH CILIUM WINKER
EYEBREE
EYELET MAIL PINK AGRAFE OILLET

POUNCE AGRAFFE CRINGLE GROMMET
PEEPHOLE
EYELID HAW LID BREE WINDOW EYEBREE
PALPEBRA
EYESHADE VISOR OPAQUE
EYESHOT RANGE REACH EYESIGHT

EYESIGHT VIEW LIGHT SIGHT
EYETOOTH CUSPID DOGTOOTH
EYEWASH COLLYRIE EYEWATER
COLLYRIUM
EZEKIEL (FATHER OF —) BUZI
EZRA (SON OF —) EPHER

F

F EFF FOX DIGAMMA FOXTROT
FABLE MYTH TALE FEIGN STORY LEGEND
    FICTION PARABLE UNTRUTH ALLEGORY
    APOLOGUE
    (— OF GOLD COAST) NANCY
    (MORAL —) EMBLEM
    (PREF.) MYTHO
FABRIC BAN CORD GOLD HAIR TAPA
    TARS TUKE CHECK CREPE DHOTI DOBBY
    DYNEL FANCY MOIRE NINOW PRINT
    SPLIT STUFF SURAT TAMMY TARSE
    TEWKE WEAVE ALACHA BENGAL BYSSUS
    CAFFOY CARPET CYPRUS DACRON
    DAMASK DOBBIE EPONGE ESTRON
    FLEECE HARDEN LAPPET LUSTER LUSTRE
    MARBLE MASHRU MURREY POODLE
    SENNIT STRIPE TAMINY TANJIB TARTAN
    TUSSAH VELURE VELVET WINCEY
    ZENANA ACETATE ALEPINE ALLOVER
    BANDALA BANDING BELTING BEWPERS
    BINDING CANILLE CHALLIS CHEKMAK
    CYPRESS DOESKIN EDIFICE FACONNE
    FUSTIAN MIXTURE MORELLA PAISLEY
    PLUMBET SAYETTE SEGATHY SILESIA
    SUITING TABARET TABINET TAFFETA
    TEXTILE TIFFANY VESSETS AGABANEE
    BARRACAN BOURETTE CANNELLE
    CASEMENT CHAMBRAY DUCHESSE
    HAIRLINE HANDMADE HARATEEN
    JACQUARD KNITTING LUSTRINE
    MATERIAL MOLESKIN OSNABURG
    SHANTUNG SHIRTING SICILIAN SKIRTING
    SWANSKIN TAPESTRY TARLATAN
    VALENCIA
    (— CONTAINING GOLD OR SILVER
    THREAD) ACCA TASH TASS KINCOB
    (— FOR STIFFENING) WIGAN
    (— OF TWO OR MORE MATERIALS)
    UNION
    (— RESEMBLING TOWELING) AGARIC
    (— WITH INWOVEN SCENES) ARRAS
    (ABSORBENT —) HUCK
    (BROCADED —) LAME LAMPAS
    (CARPET —) DURRIE
    (COARSE —) TAT BAFT CRASH HAIRE
    DUFFEL RATINE STAMIN BAGGING
    BOCKING DRABBET SACKING STAMMEL
    DAGSWAIN
    (CORDED —) REP PIQUE DUCAPE
    POPLIN OTTOMAN BENGALINE
    (COTTON —) CREA DUCK JEAN LENO
    LINO SUSI BAIZE BASIN DENIM DRILL
    RUMAL SUPER SWISS VICHY WIGAN
    BURRAH CALICO CANVAS CATGUT
    CHILLO CHINTZ COUTIL COVERT DIMITY
    MADRAS MUSLIN PENANG SATEEN
    BLANKET BUSTIAN CANTOON DAMASSE
    ETAMINE FLANNEL GALATEA GINGHAM
    HICKORY HOLLAND JACONET ORLEANS

PERCALE TICKING BOCASINE BUCKSKIN
COTELINE COUTILLE CRETONNE DRILLING
DUNGAREE INDIENNE SHEETING
SILKALINE MARSEILLES
    (DECORATED —) DIAMANTE
    (DELICATE —) HUSI JUSI
    (DURABLE —) SCRIM SERGE
    (ELASTIC —) GORING ELASTIC
    (EMBOSSED —) CLOKY CLOQUE
    (EMBROIDERED —) BALDAQUIN
    (FIGURED —) BROCADE BROCATEL
    (FINE —) PIMA SILK SUSI LINEN DIMITY
    MERINO MOHAIR BATISTE PERCALE
    (GAUZELIKE —) BAREGE GOSSAMER
    (GLAZED —) CIRE
    (GLOSSY —) SATIN GLORIA SATEEN
    PERCALINE
    (GOAT'S-HAIR —) ABA TIBET
    (HEAVY —) GROS CRASH DENIM DRILL
    BURLAP CATGUT FRIEZE LINENE TOBINE
    WHITNEY
    (JUTE —) BALINE BURLAP
    (KNITTED —) SUEDE BOUCLE JERSEY
    TRICOT CHIFFON
    (LIGHTWEIGHT —) GLORIA BUNTING
    DELAINE FORTISAN PARAMATTA
    SEERSUCKER
    (LINEN —) HARN SINDON BEWPERS
    BUCKRAM CAMBRIC DRABBET HOLLAND
    NACARAT CRETONNE
    (MOTTLED —) CHINE
    (MOURNING —) ALMA
    (MUSLIN —) TANJIB
    (OPENWORK —) LACE SKIPDENT
    (ORNAMENTAL —) GIMP LACE LAMPAS
    GALLOON
    (PEBBLY-SURFACED —) ARMURE
    (PILED —) TERRY BOLIVIA KRIMMER
    CHENILLE
    (PRINTED —) BATIK CALICO ALLOVER
    PERCALE TOURNAY
    (RAFFIA —) RABANNA
    (RIBBED —) CORD GROS PIQUE COTELE
    FAILLE SOLEIL DROGUET CORDUROY
    MAROCAIN MOGADORE WHIPCORD
    (RICH —) SAMITE
    (ROUGH —) TERRY HOPSACK
    HOMESPUN
    (SATIN —) CAMLET ETOILE CHARMEUSE
    (SHEER —) LAWN NINON SHEER SWISS
    BAREGE DIMITY BATISTE SOUFFLE
    VALENCE GOSSAMER MOUSSELINE
    MARQUISETTE
    (SHORT-NAPPED —) RAS
    (SILK —) ACCA ALMA FUGI FUJI GROS
    IKAT MOFF RASH ATLAS CARDE NINON
    PEKIN RAJAH RUMAL SATIN SHIKH
    SURAH TIRAZ ARMURE BROCHE CAMACA
    CHAPPE CREPON DIAPER DUCAPE FAILLE

KHAIKI MANTUA PONGEE SENDAL
ALACHAH ALAMODE BROCADE EPINGLE
GROGRAM SCHAPPE YESTING BARATHEA
DUPPIONI EOLIENNE IMPERIAL
ORMUZINE SHAGREEN SIAMOISE
MARCELINE MESSALINE BROCATELLE
(SOFT SILK —) KASHA BARATHEA
(SOFT-NAPPED —) PANNE DUVETYN
(STRIPED —) ABA STRIPE BAYADERE
MERALINE
(THIN —) CRISP GAUZE VOILE PONGEE
TAMISE HERNANI MARABOU PERSIAN
(TWILLED —) REP SAY DENIM KASHA
SERGE SURAH COUTIL RUSSEL BOLIVIA
ESTAMIN FLANNEL ZANELLA CAMELINE
CASHMERE CORDUROY DIAGONAL
MARCELLA SHALLOON VENETIAN
(UNBLEACHED —) DRABBET
(UNGLAZED —) CRETONNE
(UPHOLSTERY —) FRISE FRIEZE
BROCATEL MOQUETTE
(VELVETY —) TRIPE DUVETYN
(WATERPROOF —) MACINTOSH
MACKINTOSH
(WOOLEN —) REPP BAIZE DOILY OSSET
SERGE TAMIS TWEED BUFFIN BURNET
COTTON DJERSA DUFFEL FRISCA
MANTLE MOREEN MOTLEY PERPET
SAXONY SHAYAK SHODDY STAMIN
TAMISE VICUNA WADMAL WITNEY
BATISTE BOCKING BOLIVIA CHEVIOT
CHEYNEY CRYSTAL DELAINE DRUGGET
FRISADO HEATHER RATTEEN STAMMEL
ALGERINE BATSWING BURBERRY
CASHMERE CATALOON CHIVERET
HARATEEN LAMBSKIN PRUNELLA
RATTINET SHALLOON SHETLAND
WOOLENET ZIBELINE
(WORSTED —) TABBY COBURG
ESTAMIN ETAMINE SAGATHY BARATHEA
(WOVEN —) LENO TWEED TWILL
SOLBIL TISSUE GROGRAM TEXTURE
VALENCIA
FABRICATE COIN COOK FAKE FORM
MAKE MINT VAMP WARP BUILD FORGE
FRAME FRUMP WEAVE DEVISE FANGLE
INVENT CONCOCT FASHION IMAGINE
PRODUCE CONTRIVE
FABRICATION LIE WEB TRIFLE CHIMERA
FICTION FINGURE FORGERY UNTRUTH
BASKETRY PRETENSE
FABULOUS FEIGNED MYTHICAL
ROMANTIC
FACADE FACE FRONT FUCUS
FACE JIB MAP MUG NEB PAN BIDE CHIV
CLAD COPE DARE DEFY GIZZ HEAD LEER
LINE MEET MOUE MUNS PHIZ PUSS SIDE
ABIDE BEARD BRAVE BRICK BRUNT
CASTE CHECK CHEER COVER FACET
FAVOR FRONT GUARD INDEX REVET
STAND STONE VISOR VIZOR ASPECT
BRAZEN FACADE FACIES KISSER
MAZARD MUZZLE OPPOSE PHIZOG
VENEER VISAGE AFFRONT BAZOOKA
COMMAND DIGLYPH FASHION FEATURE
GRIMACE GRUNTLE PROPOSE RESPECT
REVERSE SURFACE UPRIGHT CONFRONT

ENVISAGE EXTRADOS FEATURES
FROGFACE FRONTAGE FRONTIER
PROSPECT SEMBLANT PERPENDICULAR
(— DOWN) DEFACE
(— IN DEFIANCE) AFFRONT
(— OF ANIMAL) MASK
(— OF CUBE) SQUARE
(— OF CUTTING TOOL) BEZEL
(— OF GLACIER) SNOUT
(— OF STUMP) SCARF
(— ON DOOR KNOCKER) MASCARON
(— ONE'S DANCING PARTNER) SET
(— THE EAST) ORIENTATE
(— TO FACE) AFRONT BEFORE FACIAL
DIRECTLY
(— WITH MARBLE) PIN
(— WITH STONE) BATCH
(CLOCK —) DIAL TABLE WATCH
(CRYSTAL —) PINAKOU
(CURVED —) EXTRADOS INTRADOS
(DIE —) ACE
(FANTASTIC —) ANTIC
(HALF DOMINO —) END
(INNER —) CONCAVE
(MADE-UP —) MOP
(MINING —) BANK BREAST FOREHEAD
LONGWALL
(MOCKING —) MOE MOWE
(QUARRY —) HEUGH
(ROCK —) CLIFF
(UPPER —) BROW
(WRY —) MOUTH GRIMACE
FACEPLATE FRONT DOGPLATE
FACET PANE STAR BEZEL CULET PHASE
COLLET STEMMA FACETTE LOZENGE
TEMPLET
FACETIOUS FUNNY MERRY SMART
WITTY FACETE JOCOSE JOCULAR
HUMOROUS POLISHED
FACILE PAT ABLE EASY QUICK READY
EXPERT FLUENT GENTLE AFFABLE
DUCTILE LENIENT
FACILITATE AID EASE HELP FAVOR
SPEED ASSIST GREASE EXPEDITE
FACILITY ART EASE FEEL HELP ECLAT
KNACK SKILL ADDRESS COMMAND
FREEDOM PROWESS EASINESS
FACING DADO HARL FRONT LAPEL LINER
PANEL SKIRT BEFORE TOWARD VENEER
AGAINST FORNENT SURFACE BLACKING
CAMPSHOT CONFRONT COVERING
FACEWORK FORNENST OPPOSITE
PITCHING
(— AGAINST GLACIER) STOSS
(— AHEAD) FULL
(— APEX) ACROSCOPIC
(— AUDIENCE OBLIQUELY) EFFACE
(— EACH OTHER) AFFRONTE
(— FOR WALLS) CASE
(— INWARD) INTRORSE
(— OUTWARDS) EXTRORSE
(PREF.) OB
FACSIMILE FAX COPY MODEL REPLICA
AUTOTYPE
FACT CASE DEED FAIT DATUM EVENT
SOOTH TRUTH DONNEE EFFECT FACTUM
VERITY COMPERT FORMULA GENERAL

INDICIA KEYNOTE LOWDOWN REALITY
PARTICULAR
(CONCLUSIVE —) CRUSHER
(DECISIVE —) CLINCHER
(FUNDAMENTAL —) KEYNOTE
(TRUE —S) STRENGTH
(PL.) DATA FEAT

FACTION BLOC NERI PART SECT SIDE
WING CABAL JUNTO PARTY BRIGUE
CLIQUE SCHISM BIANCHI DISPUTE
PINFOLD QUARREL INTRIGUE SPLINTER
(— OF SECEDERS) CAVE
(PARTY —) STASIS

FACTOR DOER ITEM AGENT CAUSE
MAKER ALLELE AUTHOR CENTER DETAIL
BAILIFF CONTROL COUCHER CUSHION
ELEMENT ENTROPY FACTRIX ISOLATE
STEWARD ADHERENT AUMILDAR
COFACTOR DOMINANT EQUATION
GOMASHTA INCIDENT INCITANT
PARAMETER
(—S IN EVOLUTION) ANTICHANCE
(CYTOPLASMIC —) KAPPA
(DECISIVE —) CAPSTONE
(ECOLOGICAL —) INFLUENT
(ENVIRONMENTAL —) GEOGEN
(HEREDITY —) GENE INSTINCT
(HINDERING —) CRIMP
(PERSONALITY —) SURGENCY
(RESTRICTIVE —) BARRIER

FACTORY HONG MILL SHOP PLANT
USINE FABRIC SUGARY CANNERY
HATTERY HOSIERY OFICINA SOAPERY
BUILDING COMPTOIR FABRIQUE
FILATURE HACIENDA OFFICINA
STAMPERY WORKSHOP MANUFACTORY

FACTUAL HARD REAL TRUE ACTUAL
BEDROCK EARTHLY EMPIRIC LITERAL
PROSAIC

FACULTY ART WIT EASE GIFT WILL
FANCY POWER SENSE BREATH BUDDHI
SEEING TALENT ABILITY COLLEGE
COUNSEL HABITUS APTITUDE CAPACITY
FELICITY
(— OF EXPRESSION) LANGUAGE
(CRITICAL —) JUDGMENT
(MENTAL —) HEADPIECE
(POETIC OR CREATIVE —) IDEALITY
PRINCIPLE
(REASONING —) DISCOURSE

FAD BUG CULT RAGE WHIM CRAZE
HOBBY FOIBLE MAGGOT CROCHET
FASHION WRINKLE

FADE DIE DIM FLY WAN CAST FLAT GIVE
PALE PEAK PINE PINK WILT BLANK
DAVER DECAY FLEET PASSE PETER
QUAIL SWING SWOON DARKLE PERISH
VANISH WITHER DECLINE INSIPID
LIGHTEN DIMINISH DISCOLOR DISSOLVE
EVANESCE LANGUISH

FADED PASSE SHABBY EXOLETE
SHOPWORN

FAERIE QUEENE (AUTHOR OF —)
SPENSER
(CHARACTER IN —) UNA GUYON IRENE
TALUS ACRASY AMORET ARTHUR
DUESSA TIMIAS ASTRAEA MALEGER

ARTEGALL CALIDORE GLORIANA
ORGOGLIO RADIGUND ARCHIMAGO
BELPHOEBE BRITOMART FLORIMELL
GRANTORTO SCUDAMOUR

FAFNIR (FATHER OF —) HREIDMAR
(SLAYER OF —) SIGURD

FAG FLAG JADE TIRE TOIL DROOP WEARY
DRUDGE HARASS MENIAL EXHAUST
FATIGUE FRAZZLE

FAGOT KID BUNT PILE PIMP BAVIN
FADGE NICKY KNITCH GARBAGE

FAIL GO CUT EBB ERR PIP BANK BUST
CONK FALL FLAG FLOP FOLD LACK LOSE
MISS SKEW SPIN WANE APPAL BURST
CRACK FAULT FLUFF FLUKE FLUNK
PETER QUAIL SLAKE SMASH SPILL VAILE
APPALL BETRAY DEFAIL DEFECT DESERT
FALTER FIZZLE REPINE WINDER DECLINE
DEFAULT EXHAUST FALSIFY FLICKER
FLUMMOX FOUNDER MISFARE MISGIVE
SCANTLE LANGUISH
(— AT) FLUB
(— IN DUTY) LAPSE
(— IN EARLY STAGES) ABORT
(— IN HEALTH) SINK BREAK
(— IN STUDIES) BILGE
(— ON RIFLE RANGE) BOLO
(— TO GAIN ALTITUDE) MUSH
(— TO GROW) MISS

FAILING BAD ILL BLOT FAULT FOIBLE
BLEMISH FAILURE FRAILTY ABORTIVE
WEAKNESS

FAILURE DUD BALK BOMB BUST FAIL
FLOP FLUB FOIL LACK LOSS MISS MUFF
TRIP BILGE CRASH DECAY ERROR FAULT
FLUKE FLUNK FROST GRIEF GUILT LAPSE
LEMON PLUCK SMASH BRODIE FIASCO
FIZZLE OUTAGE STUMER BLOOMER
CROPPER DEBACLE DECLINE DEFAULT
FLIVVER FLUMMOX NEGLECT STUMBLE
ABORTION COLLAPSE DISASTER
FLOPEROO OMISSION
(— OF DAM) BLOW
(— OF FIREARM) STOPPAGE
(— OF MUSCLE) ACHALASIA
(— OF PAVEMENT) BLOWUP
(— OF PRIMER) HANGFIRE
(— OF VITALITY) DELIQUIUM
(— TO RAISE OAR) CRAB
(COMPUTER —) CRASH
(FLAT —) DUD
(RIDICULOUS —) FIASCO

FAINT GO DIM LOW WAN COLD CONK
COOL DARK PALE PALL SOFT THIN WEAK
LIGHT QUEAL QUEER SHADY SWELT
SWOON TIMID WAUGH WERSH EVANID
FEEBLE REMISS REMOTE SICKLY
WAMBLY FEIGNED FORGONE LANGUID
OBSCURE SWITHER SYNCOPE WEARISH
COWARDLY DELICATE LANGUISH
LISTLESS SLUGGISH TIMOROUS
(— FROM HEAT) SWELTER
(— FROM HUNGER) LEERY
(— OF SCENT) COLD WAUGH

FAINTHEARTED TIMID COWARD
CRAVEN COWARDLY UNHEARTHY

FAIR GAY MOP BEAU BELL CALM EVEN

FINE GAFF GALA GOOD JUST MART PLAY
TIDE TIDY BAZAR BLOND CLEAN CLEAR
EQUAL FERIA HENDE LARGE RIGHT
ROUND SHEER TRYST WHITE AONACH
BAZAAR BLONDE CANDID COMELY
DECENT HONEST KERMIS PRETTY
SERENE SQUARE EXHIBIT STRAIGHT
STATUTE BOOKFAIR DISTINCT FESTIVAL
MIDDLING RATIONAL STRAIGHT
UNBIASED OBJECTIVE REASONABLE
(— AND CALM) SETTLED
(— AND SQUARE) DINKUM
(HINDU —) MELA
(VILLAGE —) WALK

FAIRLY WELL GAILY GEYAN EVENLY
JUSTLY MEANLY HANDILY PLAINLY
RIGHTLY MIDDLING PROPERLY SUITABLY

FAIRNESS FAIR CANDOR EQUITY
HONESTY JUSTICE EQUALITY EVENNESS

FAIRY ELF FAY FEE HOB IMP FAIN PERI
PUCK SHEE VILA OUPHE PECHT PIXIE
SIDHE WIGHT COURIL FAERIE HATHOR
KEWPIE SPIRIT SPRITE YAKSHA ARGANTE
BANSHEE ORIANDA SHEOGUE SYLPHID
URGANDA FOLLETTO MELUSINA
(IRISH —) SHEE SIDHE
(TRICKSY —) PUCK

FAITH DIN FAY FOY LAW LAY VAY FACK
FAIX FEGS SLAM TROW CERTY CREED
HAITH STOCK TOUCH TROTH TRUST
TRUTH BELIEF CERTIE CREDIT GOSPEL
CREANCE FACKINS AFFIANCE RELIANCE
RELIGION
(BAD —) DUPLICITY

FAITHFUL FAST FEAL FIRM GOOD JUST
LEAL LIKE REAL TRIG TRUE FALSE
HEMAN LIEGE LOYAL PIOUS SOOTH
SWEER TIGHT TREST TRIED AEFALD
ARDENT ENTIRE FIDELE HONEST LAWFUL
PISTIC STANCH STEADY TRUSTY
DEVOTED SINCERE STAUNCH ACCURATE
CONSTANT RESOLUTE SPEAKING
RELIGIOUS

FAITHFULNESS HSIN FEALTY VERITY
LOYALTY FIDELITY TRUENESS

FAITHLESS FALSE PUNIC FICKLE
HOLLOW ROTTEN UNJUST UNTRUE
ATHEIST APOSTATE DELUSIVE DISLOYAL
SHIFTING UNSTABLE NIDDERING
PERFIDIOUS

FAITHLESSNESS FALSITY PERFIDY
UNTRUTH

FAKE DUD DUFF FEKE HOAX HOKE SHAM
BOGUS CHEAT FALSE FEIGN FLAKE
FRAUD FUDGE PHONY WANGLE DUFFING
FALSIFY FURBISH GUNDECK PRETEND
SWINDLE SIMULATE SPURIOUS
ADULTERINE
(— OF STOWED ROPE) FLEET
(FOOTBALL —) JUKE
(PREF.) PSEUD(O)

FAKER QUACK HUMBUG CAMELOT
PEDDLER
(— OF ART) TRUQUEUR

FALCON EYAS HAWK SORE BESRA SAKER
STOOP GENTLE JAGGER JUGGER LUGGAR
LUGGER MUSKET PREYER RAPTOR

SHAHIN SAKERET BERIGORA BOCKEREL
FALCONET PEREGRIN SOREHAWK
(— IN FIRST YEAR) SORE SOREHAWK
(FEMALE —) FORMAL FORMEL LANNER
(MALE —) TASSEL TERCEL SAKERET
(SMALL —) HOBBY MERLIN KESTREL
(WHITE —) ICELANDER

FALCONER HAWKER OSTREGER

FALL GO SYE TIP BACK BAND COME COUP
DIVE DROP DUNT HANG PICK RASH RUIN
RUSE SHED SILE SINK SWAK SWAY
SWOP TILT WHAP WHOP ABATE CHUTE
CRASH DROOP HANCE INCUR JABOT
LIGHT LODGE PLUMB RAPID SHAKE
SHOOT SKITE SLIPE SPILL SQUAB
THROW TRACE TWINE ALIGHT AUTUMN
BRODIE DEVALL DOUNCE DRYSNE
FOOTER HAPPEN HEADER JOUNCE
PERISH PLUNGE SEASON SLOUGH
STREEK STRIKE TOPPLE TUMBLE
CASCADE CROPPER CROWNER DECLINE
DEGRADE DEPRESS DESCEND DEVOLVE
ESCHEAT ILLAPSE PLUMMET RELAPSE
RETREAT SQUELCH SUBSIDE CATARACT
COMMENCE DECREASE DOWNCOME
PRECIPITATE
(— ABRUPTLY) DUMP
(— APART) BREAK SHIVER COLLAPSE
DISUNITE
(— AWAY) DEFECT
(— BACK) RECEDE RESORT
(— BEHIND) LAG
(— DIZZILY) SPIN
(— DOWN) CAVE FLOP SWAP SLUMP
REVERSE SWITHER
(— DUE) ACCRUE BEFALL
(— FAST) HOP
(— FLAT) PLAT FLIVVER
(— FORWARD) PECK PITCH PROLAPSE
(— FROM A HORSE) PURL VOLUNTARY
(— FROM SURFBOARD) WIPEOUT
(— FROM UNDERMINING) CALVE
(— FROM VIRTUE) LAPSE
(— GRADUALLY) EBB SAG
(— HEAVILY) DING LUMP SOSS CLOIT
CLYTE GULCH PLOUT PLUMP SOUSE
SWACK THROW
(— ILL) TRAIK
(— IN) CAVE FOUNDER
(— IN DROPS) DRIP STILL DRIBBLE
(— IN FLURRIES) SPIT
(— IN FOLDS) BLOUSE
(— IN RIVER) SAULT
(— IN WITH) INCUR
(— INTO) STRIKE
(— INTO ERROR) SLIP STUMBLE
(— INTO FAINT) DWALM
(— INTO RUIN) DECAY
(— INTO SLUMBER) DROWSE
(— INTO TRAP) DECOY
(— INTO WATER) DOP
(— OF DEW) SEREIN SERENE
(— OF RAIN) SKIFF SKIFT ONDING
SHOWER
(— OF SNOW) SKIFF SKIFT ONCOME
SCOUTHER SNOWFALL
(— OF WICKETS) ROT

(— OFF) BATE SLIP SLACK
(— ON BACK) BACKER
(— ON SUCCESSIVE DAYS) CONCUR
(— ON THE NOSE) NOSER
(— OUT) BREAK LIGHT FORTUNE
QUARREL
(— PRONE) GRABBLE
(— RAPIDLY) SKID
(— SHORT) DROP FAIL FAULT
(— SLOWLY) SETTLE
(— SUDDENLY) BOLT PLOP SLUMP
(— THROWING HORSE AND RIDER)
CRUMPLER
(— TO NOTHING) DISSOLVE
(— TO PIECES) BUCKLE CRUMBLE
(— UPON) WARP
(— VIOLENTLY) BEAT
(BAD —) BUSTER
(HEAVY —) PASH POUR SWAG BLASH
CLOIT GULCH SKELP SOUSE SQUAT
MUCKER
(INCOMPLETE WRESTLING —) FOIL
(SOFT —) SCLAFF
(SUDDEN —) HANCE SQUAT SQUASH
FALLACIOUS SLY WILY ABSURD CRAFTY
UNTRUE DELUSIVE GUILEFUL ILLUSORY
FALLACY IDOL ERROR IDOLUM SOPHISM
EQUIVOKE ILLUSION
FALLIBLE HUMAN ERRANT ERRABLE
FALLING SIT CADENT CAVING PROLAPSE
WINDFALL
(— BACK) ESCHEAT
(— DOWN) RUIN
(— INTO) INFALL
(— OF MINE ROOF) SIT
(— OF RAIN) SPIT
(— OFF) CADUCE LEEWAY CADUCOUS
(— ON SOMETHING) INCIDENT
(— OUT) DIFFICULTY
(— SHORT) DEFICIT
FALLOW LEA PALE HOBBY BARREN
VALEWE
FALSE DEAD FAKE FLAM SHAM BOGUS
FAUSE LYING PASTE PHONY WRONG
FICKLE HOLLOW LUTHER PSEUDO
UNTRUE ASSUMED BASTARD CROOKED
FEIGNED APOSTATE DISLOYAL ILLUSIVE
RECREANT RENEGADE SPECTRAL
SPURIOUS MENDACIOUS
(PREF.) PSEUD(O)
FALSEHOOD COG FIB LIE BUNG CRAM
FLAM TALE CRACK ERROR FABLE STORY
FALSET UNFACT YANKER CRAMMER
CRETISM FALSAGE FALSERY FALSITY
FIBBERY FICTION LEASING PERFIDY
PHANTOM ROMANCE UNTRUTH
ROORBACK STRAPPER
FALSIFY LIE COOK FAKE WARP ABUSE
BELIE FEINT FORGE BETRAY DOCTOR
FIDDLE GUNDECK VIOLATE EMBEZZLE
MISREPRESENT
FALSTAFF (CHARACTER IN —) MEG
FORD JOHN PAGE ALICE BROOK CAIUS
FENTON QUICKLY FALSTAFF NANNETTA
(COMPOSER OF —) VERDI
FALTER FAIL HALT PAUSE WAVER

BOGGLE FLINCH TOTTER FRIBBLE
STAMMER STUMBLE TREMBLE HESITATE
FAME BAY CRY LOSE NAME STAR WORD
BRUIT ECLAT GLORY HONOR KUDOS
PRICE RUMOR VOICE ESTEEM LAUREL
RENOWN REPORT REPUTE TONGUE
HEARSAY WORSHIP
FAMED RIFE KNOWN NOTED EMINENT
RENOMEE RENOWNED
FAMILIAR FLY BAKA BOKO BOLD COZY
EASY FREE FULL TAME TOSH CLOSE
CONNU GREAT HOMEY KNOWN PRIVY
THICK USUAL BEATEN CHUMMY
COMMON ENTIRE FOLKSY GERMAN
HOMELY INWARD KENNED STRAIT
THRONG VERSED AFFABLE POPULAR
FREQUENT HABITUAL INTIMATE
SOCIABLE STANDARD
FAMILIARITY HABIT FREEDOM LIBERTY
PRIVACY PRIVITY TRAFFIC HABITUDE
INTIMACY CONSUETUDE
FAMILIARIZE HAFT VERSE ACCUSTOM
ACQUAINT FREQUENT
FAMILY ILK KIN AIGA CLAN GING KIND
LINE NAME RACE TEAM TRIP CINEL
CLASS FLESH GOTRA GROUP HOUSE
MEINY STIRP STOCK CLETCH FAIMLY
PARAGE STEMMA STIRPS STRAIN ZEGRIS
DYNASTY KINDRED LINEAGE ORLEANS
PROGENY CATEGORY FIRESIDE
FAMINE LACK PINE WOLF DEARTH
HUNGER SCARCITY
FAMISH KILL STARVE DESTROY
ENFAMISH
FAMOUS MERE BREME FAMED GRAND
NOBLE NOTED FAMOSE NAMELY
EMINENT NAMABLE NOTABLE
RENOWNED
FAN ONE RUN VAN BEAT BLOW BUFF
COOL WASH WHIFF BASKET BLOWER
CHAMAR COLMAR FANNER FLABEL
FLIGHT PUNKAH ROOTER SHOVEL
SPREAD VENTOY WINNOW ADMIRER
DEVOTEE FLABRUM FLYFLAP WHISKER
FOLLOWER RHIPIDION
(— FOR BLOWER) WAFTER
(ALLUVIAL —) CONE APRON DELTA
(FEMALE — OF ROCK MUSICIAN)
GROUPIE
(FOOTBALL —) GRIDDER
(JAZZ —) CAT
(WINNOWING —) SAIL LIKNON
FANATIC MAD BIGOT CRAZY FIEND
RABID ULTRA ZEALOT DEVOTEE FURIOSO
PHANTIC FRENETIC
FANATICAL RABID ULTRA EXTREME
FURIOUS
FANCIED UNREAL DREAMED AFFECTED
FANCIFUL ODD ANTIC FAIRY IDEAL
QUEER VIEWY DREAMY QUAINT UNREAL
BIZARRE CURIOUS FANCIED LAPUTAN
STRANGE WHIMSIC CHIMERIC FANCICAL
FILIGREE NOTIONAL ROMANTIC
FANCY BEE FAD GIG IDEA ITEM LIKE
LOVE TROW WEEN WHIM BRAID BRAIN
DREAM FREAK GUESS HUMOR SHINE
AFFECT BEGUIN FANGLE FIGURE FLOSSY

IDEATE LIKING MAGGOT MEGRIM NOTION
ORNATE SHINDY VAGARY VISION
WHIMSY CAPRICE CONCEIT CONCEPT
CROCHET FANCIED FANCIFY FANTASY
PROPOSE ROMANCE SUSPECT THOUGHT
WRINKLE CONCEIVE DAYDREAM
ILLUSION PHANTASM PHANTASY
(FOOLISH —) CHIMERA
(PASSING —) FIKE
(PERVERSE —) CROTCHET
(WILD —) TOY MAZE

FANFARE TUSCH HOORAY HURRAH
TUCKET TANTARA FANFARON FLOURISH

FANG FAN EARN FALX TAKE TANG TUSK
VANG BEGIN PRONG SEIZE SNARE
TOOTH ASSUME OBTAIN PANGWE
CAPTURE PAHOUIN PROCURE

FANTASTIC ODD WILD ANTIC LUCIO
OUTRE QUEER ABSURD GOTHIC ROCOCO
TOYISH UNREAL ANTICAL BAROQUE
BIZARRE WHIMSIC FANCIFUL FREAKISH
ROMANTIC SINGULAR

FANTASY IDEA DREAM FANCY DESIRE
VISION CAPRICE CHIMERA PHANTOM
ROMANCE PHANTASM PHANTASY

FAR AWAY LONG MUCH ROOM SIDE WELL
WIDE CLEAN SIZES WIDEN REMOTE
DISTANT FARAWAY ROOMWARD
(— OFF) OUTBYE
(— ON) ADVANCED

FARCE MIME DROLL EXODE FORCE STUFF
COMEDY GARLIC SOTTIE EXODIUM
MOCKERY TEMACHA BURLETTA
DROLLERY FARCETTA

FARE DO GO EAT TRY COME DIET FEND
FOOD PATH RATE TIME WEND CHEER
CHEFE CHIVE FRAME GOING LIGHT PRICE
TABLE TOKEN TRACK VIAND COMMON
FARING FETTLE HAPPEN TRAVEL
CARFARE JOURNEY PASSAGE PROCEED
PROSPER WAFTAGE WAYFARE
PROGRESS
(— FOR FERRY) NAULUM FERRYAGE
(— WELL) SPEED
(COARSE —) HAWEBAKE

FAREWELL AVE VALE ADIEU ADIOS
ALOHA CONGE FINAL LEAVE CHEERO
BONALLY CHEERIO GOODBYE LEAVING
LULLABY PARTING

FAREWELL TO ARMS
(AUTHOR OF —) HEMINGWAY
(CHARACTER IN —) HENRY BARKLEY
RINALDI FREDERIC CATHERINE

FARFETCHED FORCED DEVIOUS
STRAINED EXQUISITE

FAR FROM THE MADDING CROWD
(AUTHOR OF —) HARDY
(CHARACTER IN —) OAK TROY FANNY
ROBIN GABRIEL BOLDWOOD EVERDENE
BATHSHEBA

FARINA MEAL FLOUR POLLEN STARCH

FARM FEU PEN CROP TACK TILL TORP
TOWN WALK CROFT DAIRY EMPTY FIRMA
MAINS MILPA PLACE RANGE STEAD
BOWERY ESTATE FURROW GRANGE
RANCHO TYDDEN CLEANSE HENNERY
POTRERO POULTRY SOVKHOS VACCARY
HACIENDA HATCHERY LABORING
LOCATION STEADING TOWNSHIP
(— OUT) DIMIT ARRENT
(COLLECTIVE —) KIBBUTZ KOLKHOZ
(COMMUNAL —) KVUTZAH
(DAIRY —) WICK
(LARGE —) RANCH BARTON
(RENTED —) MAILING
(SMALL —) CHACRA
(STOCK —) ESTANCIA
(STUD —) STUD HARAS

FARMER HOB CARL FARM HOBB KHOT
KYLE RUBE RYOT TATE AUMIL BOWER
CEILE CLOWN COLON HODGE KISAN
GROWER HOGMAN JIBARO TILLER
YEOMAN BUCOLIC BUSHMAN BYWONER
COTTIER CROFTER GRANGER HAYSEED
HUSBAND LANDMAN METAYER PLANTER
PLOWMAN RANCHER SCULLOG TILLMAN
TRUCKER COCKATOO PRODUCER
PUBLICAN RURALIST SELECTOR
(AUSTRALIAN —) SELECTOR
(NORWEGIAN —) BONDER
(POOR —) PIKE
(PROSPEROUS —) KULAK
(SMALL —) BOOR COCKIE
(TENANT —) AILLT GEBUR SIRDAR
COLONUS SHAREMAN SHARECROPPER

FARMHOUSE FARM TOWN ONSET
GRANGE QUINTA CASERIO ONSTEAD
STEADING

FARMLAND ACREAGE

FARMYARD WERF CLOSE BARTON
RICKYARD

FARO MONTE STUSS TIGER PHARAOH

FARROW PIG ROW RAKE DRAPE LITTER

FARSIGHTED SHREWD SIGHTY

FARTHER YOND AHEAD STILL LONGER
FURTHER REMOTER THITHER

FARTHEST ULTIMA ENDMOST EXTREME
FARMOST LONGEST OUTMOST
DOWNMOST FURTHEST REMOTEST
ULTIMATE

FARTHING RAG GRIG JACK QUAD FADGE
FERLING QUARTER QUADRANS
QUADRANT
(HALF —) CUE
(THREE —S) GILL

FASCINATE DARE CHARM SEIZE WITCH
ALLURE ENAMOR ATTRACT BEWITCH
ENCHANT ENGROSS GLAMOUR PHILTER
ENSORCEL ENTRANCE INTEREST
INTRIGUE SIRENIZE CAPTIVATE

FASCINATED BESOTTED

FASCINATING NUTTY ORPHIC TAKING
SIRENIC CHARMING FETCHING
MESMERIC

FASCINATION CHARM SPELL WITCHERY

FASHION GO CRY CUT FAD LAT TON
WAY CHIC FEAT FORM GARB GATE KICK
MAKE MODE MOLD RAGE RATE SORT
TURN TWIG WEAR WISE BUILD CRAZE
FEIGN FORGE FRAME GUISE MODEL
MOULD SHAPE STYLE VOGUE WEAVE
AGUISE ASSIZE BUSTLE CAMBER CREATE
CUSTOM DESIGN FANGLE INVENT

MANNER METHOD ALAMODE COMPOSE
IMAGERY PORTRAY QUALITY CONTRIVE
(LATEST —) KICK
(PREVAILING —) CRY
(SPECIAL —) TOUCH
FASHIONABLE CHIC PINK POSH TONY
DASHY DOGGY DOSSY NOBBY RITZY
SMART SWELL SWISH VOGUE GIGOLO
JAUNTY MODISH TIMISH TONISH
TRENDY DASHING GALLANT GENTEEL
STYLISH SWAGGER BELGRAVIAN
(NOT —) DEMODE
FAST HOT HUT COLD FIRM HARD LENT
SOON SURE WIDE AGILE APACE BRISK
CHEAP FIXED FLASH FLEET HASTY QUICK
RAPID ROUND SADLY STUCK SWIFT
TIGHT TOSTO CARENE ESTHER FASTLY
LIVELY SECURE SPEEDY SPORTY STABLE
STARVE ABIDING EXPRESS HOTSHOT
HURRIED PROVISO RASPING SETTLED
SIKERLY STATION TAANITH ENDURING
FAITHFUL SPINNING SPORTING WIKIWIKI
FASTEN BAR DOG FAY FIX GAD GIB KEY
LAG PEN PIN SEW TIE YOT BELT BEND
BIND BITT BOLT BRAD CLIP FRET GIRD
GIRT GLUE GRIP HANG HANK HASP HOOK
HOOP HORN KILT KNIT KNOT LACE LASH
LINK LOCK MOOR NAIL ROPE SEAL SNIB
SOUD SPAN SPAR STAY WELD WIRE
AFFIX ANNEX BELAY BIGHT BRACE
CABLE CATCH CHAIN CHOCK CINCH
CLAMP CLASP CLING COPSE CRAMP
DEFIX GIRTH HALSH HITCH INFIX LATCH
PASTE RIVET SCREW SLOUR SNECK
STEEK STICK STRAP TRUSS WITHE
ANCHOR ATTACH BATTEN BUCKLE
BUTTON CEMENT CLINCH COTTER
COUPLE ENGAGE ENTAIL FATHER
GARTER HAMPER HANKLE INKNOT
PICKET SECURE SKEWER SOLDER STAPLE
STITCH STRAIN TETHER BRACKET
CONFINE EMBRACE GRAPPLE GROMMET
PADLOCK BARNACLE FORELOCK
INTERTIE OBLIGATE TRANSFIX
(— A SAIL) CROSS
(— ABOUT) THRAP
(— ANCHOR) SCOW
(— AS SPURS) SPEND
(— IN) EMBAR
(— PROMPTLY) CLAP
(— TO) TAG
(— TOGETHER) COAPT SEIZE SPLICE
CONNECT
(— WINGS ON) IMP
(— WITH A GIRTH) WARRICK
(— WITH NOTCHES) GAIN
(PREF.) HAPT(O)
FASTENED FAST SHUT BOUND FIXED
BOUNDEN
FASTENER BAR GIB GIN NUT PIN AGAL
BOLT DOME FAST FROG HASP LOCK NAIL
SNAP TACK CATCH CLAMP CLASP LATCH
RIVET SCREW SPIKE STRAP TATCH
THONG BUCKLE BUTTON HATPIN STAPLE
ZIPPER FIXATOR LATCHET PADLOCK
SNAPPER TENDRIL FASTNESS STAYLACE
FASTENING TEE TIE FROG HASP SEAL

SNAP SNIB STAY TACK TACHE BUCKLE
CLINCH LACING MUZZLE STRIKE TINGLE
BINDING CLOSURE LATCHET MOUSING
PINNING SEIZING FORELOCK KNITTING
(— FOR HAWK'S WING) BRAIL
(— OF COPE) MORSE
(— ON HARPOON IRON) HITCH
(HOOK AND LOOP —) AGRAFE
FASTIDIOUS FINE NEAT NICE CHARY
DONCY FEST FUSSY NAISH NATTY
PAWKY PICKY CHOICE CHOICY CHOOSY
DAINTY DONSIE MOROSE PICKED QUAINT
QUEASY SPRUCE CHOOSEY CURIOUS
ELEGANT FINICAL FINICKY HAUGHTY
PICKING REFINED TAFFETA TAFFETY
CRITICAL DELICATE EXACTING GINGERLY
OVERNICE PICKSOME PRECIOUS
SCORNFUL SQUEAMISH PARTICULAR
PERSNICKETY SCRUMPTIOUS
FAT GHI OIL TUB FOZY GHEE LIPA MORT
RICH BROSY CETIN CHUFF COCUM
FOGGY GROSS JUICY KEDGE KOKUM
LARDY LIPID LIPIN LUSTY OBESE PLUMP
PODGY PORKY PUDDY PUDGY PURSY
SAAME SPICK SQUAB STOUT SUMEN
THICK WASTY AXUNGE BLOWSY CHOATY
CHUBBY CHUFFY DEGRAS FATTED FINISH
FLESHY LIPIDE LIPOID PLUFFY PORTLY
PUBBLE PUNCHY PYKNIC ROTUND
STOCKY STUFFY UCUUBA ADIPOSE
BLOATED BLUBBER CEROTIN FATNESS
FERTILE FLESHLY FULSOME LANOLIN
OPULENT PINGUID PURSIVE REPLETE
EXTENDED FRUITFUL MARROWED
MURUMURU PALMITIN UNCTUOUS
(— AROUND WHALE'S NECK) KENT
(— OF HIPPOPOTAMUS) SPECK
(ANIMAL —) GLOR SAIM SUET ADEPS
GLORE GREASE TALLOW
(FLOATING —) FLOT
(LARD —) FLARE FLECK FLICK
(LUMP OF —) KEECH
(NATURAL —) ESTER
(POULTRY —) SCHMALTZ
(SOLID —) LARD KIKUEL STEARIN
FATAL FEY DIRE MORT FERAL VITAL
DEADLY DISMAL DOOMED LETHAL
MORTAL TRAGIC CAPITAL DEATHLY
FATEFUL KILLING OMINOUS RUINOUS
BASILISK DESTINED MORTIFIC
FATALITY DOOM ACCIDENT CALAMITY
DISASTER
FATE DIE END KER LOT CAST DOLE DOOM
EURE NORN RUIN SORT STAR CAVEL
EVENT GRACE KARMA MOIRA MORTA
WEIRD WHATE WRITE ANANKE CHANCE
KISMET DESTINY FORTUNE OUTCOME
PORTION DOWNFALL FATALITY
FATED DUE FEY FATAL DOOMED DECREED
DESTINED
FATEFUL FATAL FATED DEADLY
DOOMFUL OMINOUS DOOMLIKE
FATES MOERAE PARCAE
(ONE OF —) URD NONA PARCA SKULD
CLOTHO DECUMA ATROPOS LACHESIS
VERDANDE
FATHER BU DA PA ABU AMA DAD POP

TAT ABBA ABOU AMBA ANBA ATEF
BABA BAPU DADA PAPA PERE SIRE
ADOPT BABBO BEGET DADDY FRIAR
PADRE PATER VADER PARENT PRIEST
SUBORN ELKANAH GENITOR TATINEK
BEAUPERE GENERATE GOVERNOR
PATRIARCH PATERFAMILIAS
(CHURCH —) APOLOGIST
(SEMIDIVINE —) PITRI
FATHERLAND KITH HOMELAND
FATHERS AND SONS
(AUTHOR OF —) TURGENEV
(CHARACTER IN —) KATYA PAVEL
ARKADY VASILY NIKOLAI BAZAROFF
FENICHKA KIRSANOFF ODINTZOFF
SITNIKOFF
FATHOM BRACE BRASS DELVE FADME
PLUMB SOLVE SOUND TOUCH BOTTOM
MEASURE PLUMMET
FATIGUE FAG HAG TEU BEAT BORE COOK
JADE TASH TIRE TRAY SPEND STALL
TARRY THRIE TRAIK TRASH WEARY
HARASS OVERDO TAIGLE TUCKER
EXHAUST LANGUOR TRACHLE FATIGATE
VEXATION
FATIGUED BEAT GONE JADED TIRED
WEARY TASKIT OUTWORN WEARIED
FATIGATE HARASSED OVERDONE
TUCKERED
FATIGUING HARD IRKSOME
FATNESS BLOOM GREASE
FATTEN FAT BEEF LARD SOIL BRAWN
FARCE FLESH FRANK PROVE SMEAR
STALL BATTEN BATTLE ENRICH FINISH
TALLOW THRIVE PINGUEFY SAGINATE
FATTY SUETY BACONY GREASY ADIPOSE
ADIPOUS FATLIKE PINGUID SEBIFIC
LIPAROID LIPAROUS UNCTUOUS
ALIPHATIC
FATUOUS DOPY GAGA DOPEY INANE
SILLY SIMPLE STUPID UNREAL FATUATE
FOOLISH IDIOTIC WITLESS DEMENTED
ILLUSORY IMBECILE
FAUCET BIB TAP COCK QUILL SPOUT
VALVE CUTOFF OFFLET SPIGOT BIBCOCK
HYDRANT PETCOCK TURNCOCK
(WOODEN —) HORSE
FAULT BUG RUB SIN BEAM CLAG COUP
DEBT FAIL FLAW FLUB GALL HOLE LACK
LAST MOLE SAKE SLIP SPOT VICE WANT
WITE ABUSE AMISS BLAME BREAK
CULPA ERROR FLUFF GUILT LAPSE SCAPE
SHIFT SLIDE SWICK TACHE BLOTCH
DEFECT FOIBLE RUNNER THRUST VICETY
VITIUM BLEMISH BLISTER BLUNDER
DEFAULT DEMERIT EYELAST FAILING
FAILURE FRAILTY MISTAKE NEGLECT
OFFENSE FAULTING PECCANCY
WEAKNESS
(— IN BADMINTON) SLING
(MINING —) COUP LEAP CHECK HITCH
FAULTFINDER MOMUS CARPER CRITIC
MOMIST CAPTION KNOCKER NAGSTER
FAULTFINDING CARPING CAPTIOUS
CRITICAL
FAULTLESS PURE CLEAN RIGHT
CORRECT PERFECT PRECISE FLAWLESS

FAULTY BAD ILL SICK AMISS UNFIT
WRONG FLAWED FAULTED PECCANT
VICIOUS BLAMABLE CULPABLE
SPURIOUS
FAUN SATYR WOODMAN WOODWOSE
FAUST (AUTHOR OF —) GOETHE
(CHARACTER IN —) FAUST HELEN
SIEBEL WAGNER GRETCHEN VALENTINE
HOMUNCULUS MARGUERITE
MEPHISTOPHELES
(COMPOSER OF —) GOUNOD
FAUX PAS SLIP BONER ERROR GAFFE
BLOOMER FLOATER MISSTEP MISTAKE
SNAPPER
FAVOR AID FOR ORE PRO BOON ESTE
FACE GREE HEAR HELP LIKE MAKE BLESS
BRIBE GRACE LEAVE MENSK SERVE
SPARE SPEED THANK TREAT ASSIST
ERRAND ESTEEM LETTER NOTICE PENCEL
UPHOLD ADVANCE BENEFIT FEATURE
FORWARD GRATIFY INDULGE RESPECT
SUPPORT ADVOCACY BEFRIEND
COURTESY GOODWILL KINDNESS
RESEMBLE SYMPATHY ACCEPTANCE
FAVORABLE HOT BOON FAIR FREE GOOD
HIGH KIND ROSY TIDY CIVIL CLEAR
HAPPY LARGE MERRY TRINE WHITE
WILLY BENIGN DEXTER GENIAL GOLDEN
KINDLY TOWARD BENEFIC EXALTED
OPTIMAL POPULAR PRESENT FAVONIAN
FRIENDLY GRACIOUS PLEASING
PROPENSE SPEEDFUL TOWARDLY
BENIGNANT PROPITIOUS PROSPEROUS
FAVORITE BOY PET POT PEAT CHALK
GREAT INGLE WHITE MINION DARLING
FANCIED MINIKIN POPULAR SPECIAL
GRACIOSO WHITEBOY
FAVORITISM BIAS FAVOR NEPOTISM
FAWN COG BUCK CLAW DEER JOUK
ROOT COWER CRAWL CREEP GLOZE
HONEY SMARM TOADY WHELP CRINGE
CROUCH GROVEL KOWTOW SHRINK
SLAVER ADULATE FLATTER HANGDOG
SERVILE SPANIEL TOADEAT TRUCKLE
WHEATEN BOOTLICK
FAWNING SLEEK CRINGE GREASE
MENIAL SMARMY SUPPLE FLETHER
GLOZING HANGDOG SERVILE SPANIEL
FLATTERY
FAZE DAUNT WORRY
FEALTY FEE HOMAGE LOYALTY SERVICE
TREWAGE FIDELITY
FEAR UG AWE DREE FLAY FUNK WARD
ALARM DOUBT DREAD JELLY PANIC
AFFRAY ALARUM DANGER DISMAY
FRIGHT HORROR PHOBIA TERROR
ANXIETY SUSPECT AFFRIGHT DISQUIET
DISTRUST EERINESS MISDOUBT
VENERATE
FEARFUL ARGH DIRE AWFUL FERLY
PAVID TIMID WINDY WROTH AFRAID
COWISH FRIGHTY GHASTLY NERVOUS
PANICKY WORRIED CAUTIOUS
DOUBTFUL DREADFUL GRUESOME
HORRIBLE HORRIFIC SHOCKING SKITTISH
TERRIBLE TERRIFIC TIMOROUS

FEARLESS BOLD BRAVE DARING HEROIC
AWELESS IMPAVID INTREPID
FEASIBLE FIT LIKELY POSSIBLE
PROBABLE SUITABLE
FEAST (ALSO SEE FESTIVAL) EAT PIG
SUP DINE FARM FETE LUAU MEAL TUCK
UTAS AZYME CHEER CHOES CITUA
FESTA FESTY GAUDY REVEL TREAT
ARTHEL AVERIL BRIDAL DEVOUR DINNER
DOUBLE INFARE ISODIA JUNKET
MAUNDY REGALE REPAST SIMPLE
SMOUSE SPREAD AHAAINA BRIDALE
DELIGHT FESTINO GRATIFY GREGORY
LAMBALE LEMURIA SYNAXIS ANALEPSY
CAROUSAL DOMINEER EPIPHANY
FESTIVAL GESTNING GESTONIE
HANUKKAH KOIMESIS PASSOVER
POTLATCH VESTALIA
(— BEFORE JOURNEY) FOY
(— OF BOOTHS) SUKKOTH
(— OF LANTERNS) HON
(— OF LOTS) PURIM
(— OF WEEKS) SHEVUOS SHABUOTH
(— PLACE) IDGAH
(DRINKING —) BANQUET
(FUNERAL —) ARVAL ARVEL DIRGIE
(HARVEST —) BUSK
(JEWISH —) SENDAH
(RELIGIOUS —) CANAO KANYAW
PENTECOST
(VILLAGE —) TANSY
FEAT ACT KIP DEED FATE WORK GESTE
SPLIT STUNT TRICK CRADDY CUTOFF
EXPLOIT MASTERY MIRACLE WORSHIP
DEXTROUS PERFORMANCE
(— IN SURFING) SPINNER QUASIMODO
(CRICKETER'S —) DOUBLE
(TUMBLING —) SCISSORS
FEATHER PEN TAB DECK DOWN FLAG
HERL SETA STUB VANE ADORN AXIAL
PENNA PINNA PLUMA PLUME QUILL
REMEX CLOTHE COVERT CRINET FLEDGE
FLETCH FLIGHT HACKLE MANUAL PINION
SQUAMA TIPPET TONGUE AXILLAR
BRISTLE FLEMISH IMPLUME PRIMARY
REMICLE TECTRIX TERTIAL TOPPING
AXILLARY SCAPULAR STREAMER
TERTIARY
(BRISTLELIKE —) VIBRISSA
(HAWK'S —S) BRAIL BRAILS
(HORSE —) SPEAR
(NEW —) STIPULE
(OSTRICH TAIL —) BOO
(PINION —) SARCEL
(TAIL —) SICKLE RECTRIX
(YELLOW —S) HULU
(PL.) GIG BOOT CAPE DOWN FLUE MAIL
BRAIL CRISSUM CUSHION FLIGHTS
PLUMAGE REMIGES SPURIAE
FEATURE WAY FACE ITEM NOTE STAR
BREAK FAVOR GRACE MOTIF TOKEN
TRACT TREAT ASPECT CACHET SPLASH
OUTLINE SALIENCE
(— OF WORD FORM) ASPECT
(ATTRACTIVE —) AMENITY
(DETERMINING —) LIMIT

(DISTINGUISHING —) TRAIT STROKE
HALLMARK
(ESSENTIAL —) CHARACTER
(FATAL —) BANE
(LINGUISTIC —) ISOGLOSS SURVIVAL
(MAIN —) CRUX
(MOST COGENT —) BEAUTY
(OBJECTIONABLE —) DISCOUNT
DRAWBACK
(SALIENT —) MOTIF
(TOPOGRAPHIC —) ARC
(TOPOGRAPHIC —S) LIE
FECKLESS WEAK FEEBLE
FECUND FERTILE FRUITFUL PROLIFIC
FEDERATION BUND CROM UNION
LEAGUE NATION COUNCIL ALLIANCE
FEDERACY TRIALISM
FEE FEU DUES DUTY FEAL FEUL FIEF FIER
HIRE RATE WAGE CAULP EXTRA PRICE
RIGHT ALNAGE AMOBER BARONY
CHARGE EMPLOY EXCISE REWARD
SALARY SHEKEL BUOYAGE DASTURI
DUMPAGE DUSTOOR FALDAGE FIRNAGE
FURNAGE GAOLAGE GARNISH GRATIFY
GUIDAGE HALLAGE HOUSAGE JAILAGE
MULTURE PAYMENT PINLOCK PREFINE
STIPEND STORAGE TALLAGE TRIBUTE
VANTAGE BOOTHAGE BOUNTITH
CHUMMAGE EXACTION FAREWELL
GRATUITY MALIKANA POUNDAGE
REREFIEF RETAINER SHIPPAGE
WHARFAGE
(— TO LANDOWNER) TERRAGE
(— TO TEACHER) MINERVAL
(CUSTOMARY —) DASTUR
(CUSTOMS —) LOT
(ENTRANCE —) HANSA HANSE INCOME
(GRINDING —) THIRLAGE
(INITIATION —) FOOTING
(PHYSICIAN'S —) SOSTRUM
(ROAD —) PIKE
(UNAUTHORIZED —) GARNISH
(PL.) EXHIBITS
FEEBLE LOW WAN FLUE LAME MEAN
PALE POOR PUNY SOFT WEAK DONCY
DOTTY FAINT SEELY SILLY SOBER UNORN
WANKY WASHY WERSH WONKY CADUKE
DEBILE DONSIE DOTAGE FAINTY FLABBY
FLIMSY FOIBLE INFIRM PAULIE PUISNE
SCANTY SEMMIT SICKLY SIMPLE TANGLE
UNFIRM WANKLE WEANLY DWAIBLY
DWEEBLE FRAGILE INVALID LANGUID
QUEECHY RICKETY SAPLESS SHILPIT
SLENDER SLIMPSY THREADY UNWIELD
UNWREST WEARISH DECREPIT
DROGHLIN FEATLESS IMBECILE
IMPOTENT INFERIOR LUSTLESS
MALADIVE RESOLUTE SACKLESS
THEWLESS THOWLESS UNSTRONG
UNWIELDY WATERISH YIELDING
NERVELESS
FEEBLE-MINDED ANILE DOTTY DOTTLE
FOOLISH MORONIC WANTING IMBECILE
FEEBLENESS DOTAGE FEEBLE POVERTY
CADUCITY DEBILITY WEAKNESS
FEED EAT HAY BAIT BEET CROP DIET DINE
FILL FOOD GLUT GRUB MEAL MEAT OATS

SATE AGIST FLESH FLUSH GORGE GRASS
GRAZE NURSE TABLE BROWSE FOSTER
INFEED NOODLE REFETE REPAST SUCKLE
SUPPLY BLOWOUT FURNISH GRATIFY
HERBAGE INDULGE KEEPING NOURISH
NURTURE PASTURE PROVENT SATISFY
SUBSIST SURFEIT SUSTAIN VICTUAL
PROVENDER
(— ABUNDANTLY) STOKE
(— ANIMAL) SORT SERVE
(— AT NIGHT) SUP
(— CATTLE) SOIL
(— FOR CATTLE) FODDER STOVER
TACKLE
(— FORCIBLY) CRAM
(— GLUTTONOUSLY) BATTEN
(— HIGH) FRANK
(— IN STUBBLE) SHACK
(— ON FLIES) SMUT
(— RAVENOUSLY) FRAUNCH
(— STOCK) FOG SOIL SOILING
(— TO REPLETION) ENGORGE
(— TO THE FULL) SATIATE
(— WELL) BATTLE
(GROUND —) CHOP
(POULTRY —) SCRATCH
(RED —) HAYSEED
(STOCK —) BRAN
(WHALE —) GRIT
FEEL FIND FIMB SENSE THINK TOUCH
FIMBLE FINGER HANDLE RESENT
EXAMINE EXPLORE FEELING SENSATE
PERCEIVE
(— ACUTELY) SUFFER
(— AVERSION FOR) HATE LOATHE
(— CHILLY) CREEM
(— COMPASSION) PITY YEARN
(— DEJECTION) REPINE
(— FEAR) GRUE TREMBLE
(— GRIEF) GRIEVE DEPLORE
(— HAPPY OR BETTER) LIGHT
(— NAUSEA) WAMBLE
(— OF CLOTH) HAND
(— ONE'S WAY) GROPE FUMBLE
GRAMMEL
(— OUT) SOUND
(— PAIN) URN
(— REPUGNANCE) ABHOR
(— SHAME) BLUSH
(— WANT OF) MISS
FEELER DRAW KITE PALP SNIFF PALPUS
TACTOR ANTENNA SMELLER PROPOSAL
TENTACLE
FEELING FEEL PITY TACT VIEW CHEER
HEART HUMOR SENSE SORGE TOUCH
AFFECT CEMENT MORALE CONSENT
EMOTION OPINION PASSION VELUNGE
ATTITUDE SENTIENT SENSATION
PRESENTIMENT
(— ILL) HOWISH
(— MIRTH) JOCUND
(— OF ACCORD) SYMPATHY
(— OF AMUSEMENT) CHARGE
(— OF ANTIPATHY) ALLERGY
(— OF ANXIETY) ANGST
(— OF CONTEMPT) DISDAIN
(— OF DISGUST) UG

(— OF DOUBT) SCRUPLE
(— OF HORROR) CREEP CREEPS
(— OF HOSTILITY) ANIMUS
(— OF JOY) GLOAT
(— OF OPPOSITION) KICK
(— OF RESENTMENT) GRUDGE
(— OF ROMANCE) STARDUST
(— OF UNEASINESS) MALAISE
(— OF WEARINESS) ENNUI
(— OF WELL-BEING) EUPHORIA
(— PRODUCED BY DRUG) RUSH
(ANGERED —) DUDGEON
(BODILY —) TABET
(CONCEITED —) SWELLING
(ILL —) HARDNESS
(INTUITIVE —) HUNCH
(KINDLY —) GOODWILL
(REPRESSION OF —) STOICISM
(STRONG —) STAB
(STRONG, POSITIVE —) SOUL
FEIGN ACT FAKE MINT MOCK SEEM SHAM
AVOID FABLE FALSE FORGE PAINT SHAPE
SHIRK AFFECT ASSUME GAMMON
INVENT POSSUM CONCEAL FALSIFY
FASHION IMAGINE POETIZE PRETEND
ROMANCE DISGUISE SIMULATE
(— ASSENT) COLLOGUE
(— IGNORANCE) CONNIVE
(— ILLNESS) MALINGER
FEIGNED SHAM FALSE FEINT POETIC
PSEUDO ASSUMED COLORED FICTIVE
FICTIOUS SIMULATE
FEINT FAKE MINT RUSE SHIFT SPOOF
TRICK FALSIFY FINCTURE PRETENSE
REVIRADO
FELDSPAR ALBITE AMBITE GNEISS
CELSIAN SYENITE ADULARIA ANDESINE
FELSPATH PERTHITE PETUNTZE
SANIDINE MOONSTONE
FELICITOUS FIT HAPPY
FELICITY JOY BLISS SONSE HEAVEN
FELLOW BO BOY COD EGG FOX GUY JOE
LAD MAC MAN MUN NUT WAG WAT YOB
BALL BEAN BEAU BIRD BOZO CHAL CHAP
COVE CUSS DEAN DICK DUCK DUDE
DULL GENT GILL GINK HUSK JOHN LOON
MATE NABS PEER PRIG SNAP BILLY
BIMBO BLOKE BUDDY CHIEL COVEY
CULLY FRUIT GROOM GUEST JOKER
MATCH PARTY SCOUT SKATE SLAVE
SPORT SPRIG SWIPE BEGGAR BILLIE
BIRKIE BOHUNK BOOGER BUDDIE BUFFER
BUGGER BUSTER CALLAN CHIELD CUFFIN
CUTTER FELLER FOOTER GAZABO
HOMBRE JOCKEY JOHNNY JOSSER
KIPPER PERSON SHAVER SINNER SIRRAH
SISTER SOCIUS TURNIP BASTARD
BROTHER CALLANT CHAPPIE COMRADE
CULLIES CUSTRON KNOCKER PARTNER
SCROYLE SNOOZER BLIGHTER CONFRERE
DOTTEREL MERCHANT NEIGHBOR
SYNODITE
(AWKWARD —) JAY OAF CLUB GAWK
CLOWN LOOBY GALOOT SLOUCH
(BASE —) CARL CULLION
(BASHFUL —) SHEEP
(BOLD —) HEARTY

(BRUTAL —) CLUBFIST
(CLOWNISH —) COOF BAYARD LOBLOLLY
(CLUMSY —) BOOB FILE CAMEL FARMER LUBBER PALOOKA
(COMMON —) JACK LOUT
(CONCEITED —) JEMMY DALTEEN PRINCOX
(CONTEMPTIBLE —) DOG SCUT SMAIL SNAKE RABBIT SMATCH PEASANT
(CONTENTIOUS —) SQUARER
(CORPULENT —) POMPION
(COUNTRY —) JAKE JASPER
(CRUDE —) STIFF
(DASHING —) BUCK BLADE
(DASTARDLY —) HOUND
(DESPICABLE —) FOUTER FOUTRA HANGDOG SMATCHET
(DIRTY —) SCAB BROCK
(DISAGREEABLE —) GLEYDE
(DISSOLUTE —) RAKE ROUE RAKEHELL
(DROLL —) CARD
(DROWSY —) LUNGIS
(DRUNKEN —) BORACHIO
(DULL —) BUFF DRIP FOGY CHUFF SUMPH LUNGIS HUMDRUM
(FAT —) HIND GULCH GLUTTON
(FIERCE-LOOKING —) KILLBUCK
(FINE —) BAWCOCK
(FOOLISH —) SOP GABY GOFF ZANY GANDER JACKSON WIDGEON
(GAY —) GALLIARD
(GOOD —) BRICK BULLY TRUMP HEARTY TROJAN
(GOOD-FOR-NOTHING —) JACKEEN
(GREEDY —) SLOTE
(IDLE —) FANION FOOTER STOCAH LOLLARD SKULKER
(IGNORANT —) GOBBIN
(ILLBRED —) LARRIKIN
(IMPERTINENT —) JACK WHISK
(INSIGNIFICANT —) SQUIB
(JOLLY —) VAVASOR
(LAZY —) BUM LUSK TOOL LENTO
(LOW —) RAG WAFF SWEEP LIMMER VARLET MECHANIC WHORESON
(MEAN —) CAD DOG BOOR BOUCH BUCKO CAVEL CHURL SCURF RASCAL CULLION BEZONIAN COISTREL SNEAKSBY SPALPEEN STINKARD
(NIGGARDLY —) SNUDGE
(NOISY —) MOUTH
(OLD —) GLYDE GAFFER GEEZER
(OLD-FASHIONED —) FOGY
(OVERBEARING —) GRIMSIR
(PROSAIC —) PRUNE
(PUNY —) SMAIK
(QUARRELSOME —) HECTOR
(QUEER OLD —) CODGER GEEZER
(RESIDENTIAL —) DON
(ROGUISH —) DOG
(RUDE —) BOOR JACK ROUGH
(SHABBY —) SHAB SQUEEF
(SHEEPISH —) SUMPH
(SHIFTLESS —) PROG SHACK PROGGER
(SHREWD —) COLT

(SILLY —) TOT GUMP ZANY SHEEP SMAIK BUFFER DOTTEREL MUSHHEAD
(SIMPLE —) DOODLE
(SLOVENLY —) SLUTE
(SLY —) FOX COON
(SNEAKING —) SNUDGE
(SORDID —) HUNKS
(SOUTH AFRICAN —) KEREL
(SPIRITED —) BRICK
(SPORTY —) PLAYBOY
(STRANGE —) CODGER
(STRAPPING —) SWANKY SWANKIE
(STUPID —) ASS BOOB CLOD COOF DAFF DOLT GUMP HASH MUFF SIMP BOOBY CUDDY DUNCE MORON STIRK BAYARD BUFFER FARMER FOOZLE GANDER ASINOCO DOWFART HUMDRUM CLODPOLL CODSHEAD SOCKHEAD
(SULLEN —) GLUMP
(SURLY —) CHUFF CHOUGH
(TRICKISH —) HUMBUG
(TRICKY —) ROOK GREEK KNAVE SCAMP DODGER RASCAL
(UNCIVIL —) RUDESBY
(UNCOUTH —) JAKE KEMP TIKE
(VILE —) RAT SNAKE
(VULGAR —) TIGER
(WORTHLESS —) BUM CUR DOG HASH PROG RAFF WAFF ROGUE SCAMP SHOAT SNAKE STUMER BROTHEL BUDMASH PROGGER VAURIEN TARTARET
(WRETCHED —) DEVIL DOGBOLT
(YOUNG —) BILLY BUCKO CADIE CADDIE
FELLOWSHIP GUILD HAUNT UNION FAMILY COMPANY ALLIANCE SODALITY
(CHRISTIAN —) KOINONIA
FELON WILD CRUEL FETLOW FIERCE WICKED CONVICT CULPRIT PANARIS VILLAIN WHITLOW PHLEGMON RUNROUND MALEFACTOR
FELONY ARSON CRIME OFFENSE
FEMALE DOE EWE HEN HER SHE SOW DAME GYNE LADY MORT ADULT JENNY SMOCK SQUAW WOMAN WAHINE WEAKLY DISTAFF FEMINAL WOMANLY DAUGHTER FEMININE GYNAECIC LADYLIKE WOMANISH PETTICOAT
(— ANCESTOR) TAPROOT
(IMPERFECT —) FREEMARTIN
(PARTHOGENETIC —) AMAZON
FEMININE FAIR SOFT WEAK WOMAN FEMALE TENDER WAHINE FEMINAL WOMANLY WOMANISH PETTICOAT
(SUFF.) INA INE
FEMININITY MUSLIN FEMINITY MULIEBRITY
FEMUR THIGH
FEN BOG CARR FAIN FELL FOWL MERE MOOR WASH BROAD MARSH SNIPE SWAMP VENTS MORASS QUAGMIRE
FENCE BAR HAW HAY BAWN DIKE DUEL HAHA HAIN PALE PLAY STUB WALL WIRE BEARD DODGE FRITH GUARD HEDGE MOUND PALIS DUTCH DETENT FENDER FRAISE GLANCE HURDLE PALING PICKET RADDLE RASPER SCHERM

SCRIME TIMBER BARRIER BULWARK
CYCLONE DEFENSE ENCLOSE FENCING
FENSURE IMPALER PASSAGE SWAGMAN
BACKSTOP ENCHASER ENCLOSER
GRAFFAGE HOARDING PALISADE
PALISADO SEPIMENT SKIRMISH
BRANDRETH BRANDRITH
(— AROUND BULLRING) BARRERA
(— AROUND MACHINERY) BRATTICE
(— CLOSING DITCH) WOLF
(— OF LOCK) STUB
(— OF LOGS) GLANCE
(CATTLE —) OXER WIPE SKERM
SCHERM
(FISH —) WEIR KIDDLE LEADER
(METAL —) RAIL RAILING
FENCER DUELIST IMPALER PARRIER
PROVOST SCRIMER SWORDER FOILSMAN
BACKSWORD
FEND WARD PARRY SHIRK DEFEND
FORBID RESIST SUPPORT
FENDER SKID WING CAMEL GUARD
SKATE BUFFER BUMPER SHIELD DOLPHIN
PUDDING BOWGRACE MUDGUARD
SPLASHER
(— FOR FIREPLACE) CURB KERB
(— NEAR HOLE) TELLTALE
(ROPE —) PUDDENING
FER-DE-LANCE BONETAIL JARARACA
FERMENT FRY LOB BARM FRET HEAT
SOUR TURN WORK FEVER SWEAT
YEAST DANDER ENZYME FLOWER
FOMENT SEETHE SIMMER TUMULT
UPROAR AGITATE QUICKEN TURMOIL
DISORDER
(PREF.) ZYM(O)
(SUFF.) ZYME
FERMENTATION SWEAT CUVAGE
FERMENT MOWBURN WORKING ZYMOSIS
FERN HEII NITO PULU TARA WEKI BRAKE
DUGAL EKAHA FROND NARDO PITAU
PONGA ULUHI WHEKI AMAMAU DOODIA
NARDOO OSMUND PTERIS ACROGEN
ATERACH BOGFERN BRACKEN OSMUNDA
SYNANGE WOODSIA ADIANTUM
ASPIDIUM BAROMETZ BUCKHORN
BUNGWALL CETERACH DAVALLIA
DENDRITE FERNWORT FILICITE
GOLDBACK HARDFERN KOLOKOLO
MOONWORT MULEWORT PARAREKA
PILLWORT POLYPODY SPOROGEN
STAGHORN MAIDENHAIR
FEROCIOUS ILL FELL GRIM RUDE WILD
BRUTE CRUEL FERAL BLOODY BRUTAL
FEROCE FIERCE GOTHIC RAGING SAVAGE
ACHARNE INHUMAN OMINOUS VIOLENT
WOLFISH PITILESS RAVENOUS
RUTHLESS
FEROCITY FERITY SAVAGERY VIOLENCE
ACHARNEMENT
FERRET MONK TAPE PADOU MONACH
WEASEL POLECAT
(— OUT) FOSSICK
(FEMALE —) GIL GILL JILL BITCH
(MALE —) HOB
FERRULE CAP TIP CUFF RING SHOE VIRL

COLLET PULLEY RUNNER VERREL VIROLE
ARMGARN BUSHING CRAMPET
FERRY FORD PASS PONT SCOW PASSAGE
TRAJECT TRANECT TRANSFER
FERRYBOAT BAC PONT SCOW FERRY
FERRYMAN CHARON FERRIER
WATERMAN
FERTILE FAT GOOD RANK RICH GLEBY
BATFUL BATTLE FECUND HEARTY
STRONG TEEMING ABUNDANT BATTABLE
FRUITFUL GENEROUS PREGNANT
PROLIFIC SPAWNING
FERTILITY HEART FATNESS
FERTILIZE FAT DUNG FISH LIME MARL
CHALK BATTEN ENRICH FRUCTIFY
FERTILIZER FAT MARL GUANO HUMUS
ALINIT FLOATS MANURE POLLEN
POTASH CARRIER COMPOTE HUMOGEN
KAINITE NITRATE TANKAGE AMMONITE
CINEREAL NITROGEN
FERULE ROD RULER COLLET FENNEL
FERULA PALMER
FERVENT HOT KEEN WARM EAGER FIERY
ARDENT BITTER FERVID FIERCE INWARD
RAGING SAVAGE BOILING BURNING
GLOWING INTENSE PECTORAL
ROMANTIC VEHEMENT RELIGIOUS
FERVID HOT ARDENT TROPIC BOILING
BURNING FERVENT GLOWING ZEALOUS
UNCTUOUS VEHEMENT
FERVOR FIRE HEAT RAGE SOUL ZEAL
ARDOR WARMTH PASSION CANDENCY
DEVOTION STRENGTH VIOLENCE
FESTIVAL (ALSO SEE FEAST) ALE BON
PWE BUSK FAIR FEIS FETE GALA HOLI
MELA PUJA TIDE UTAS WAKE DELIA
FEAST FERIA FESTA GAUDY HALOA
PURIM REVEL ROUSE SEDAR ADONIA
BAIRAM BRIDAL CARNEA DEWALI DIASIA
DIPALA FIESTA HOHLEE HUFFLE KERMIS
LAMMAS LENAEA OPALIA PONGOL
POOJAH POSADA SUCCOS AGONIUM
AGRANIA BANQUET BELTANE DASAHRA
EQUIRIA FESTIAL HILARIA KERMESS
MATSURI PALILIA SUKKOTH THIASOS
TOXCATL UPHELYA VINALIA AGRIONIA
AIANTEIA APATURIA ATHENAEA
BEALTINE BRUMALIA CARNIVAL
COTYTTIA DASAHARA DIIPOLIA DIONYSIA
DUSSERAH ENCAENIA FASNACHT
FLORALIA HANUKKAH HIGHTIDE
KALENDAE LUPERCAL MARYMASS
MATRALIA MITHRIAC MUHARRAM
MUNYCHIA NATIVITY NEOMENIA
POTLATCH STAMPEDE TAARGELIA
SATURNALIA
(HIGHLAND —) MOD
(MUSICAL —) EISTEDDFOD
FESTIVE GAY GALA JOLLY FESTAL
GENIAL JOYOUS FEASTLY HOLIDAY
JOCULAR MIRTHFUL SPORTIVE
CONVIVIAL
FESTIVITY GALA GAUD UTAS UTIS
BEANO FEAST MIRTH RANDY REVEL
GAIETY GAYETY SPLORE HOLIDAY
JOLLITY JOYANCE PATTERN FESTIVAL
FUNCTION MERRIMENT MERRYMAKING

FESTOON SWAG WREATH GARLAND DECORATE

FETCH FET FESH GASP GIVE SHAG TACK TAKE TEEM WAIN BRING SWEEP TRICK DOUBLE STROKE WRAITH ACHIEVE ATTRACT ARTIFICE FETCHING INTEREST

FETCHING SWEET CRAFTY CUNNING ALLURING PLEASING SCHEMING

FETE FAIR GALA FEAST HONOR BAZAAR FIESTA HOLIDAY

FETISH OBI IDOL JUJU OBIA ZEME ZEMI ZOGO ANITO ASCON CHARM GUACA HUACA OBEAH TOTEM AMULET NAGUAL VOODOO SHINTAI SORCERY FETISHRY TALISMAN

FETTER BAND BEND BOLT BOND FIND GYVE IRON SPAN BASIL BEWET BILBO CHAIN SLANG SWATH ANKLET GARTER HALTER HAMPER HOBBLE HOPPLE IMPEDE LANGEL RACKAN SWATHE CLINKER CONFINE ENCHAIN FETLOCK GARNISH MANACLE SHACKLE SPANCEL TRAMMEL RESTRAIN (PL.) IRONS LINKS DARBIES GARNISH GARTERS

FEUD FIEF FRAY BROIL AFFRAY ENMITY FEODUM FEUDUM STRIFE CONTEST DISPUTE QUARREL VENDETTA

FEVER AGUE FIRE ARDOR CAUMA DANDY LEUMA OCTAN CAUSUS DENGUE FEBRIS HECTIC SEPTAN SEXTAN SODOKU TYPHIA TYPHUS VOMITO AMAKEBE FERMENT FEVERET HELODES MALARIA PINKEYE PYREXIA QUARTAN TERTIAN TYPHOID SYNOCHUS TERTIANA TYPHINIA CALENTURE (— OF HORSE) WEED SCALMA (— OF PERU) VERRUGA (— OF SHEEP) BRAXY (BRAIN —) PHRENITIS (HAY —) RHINITIS (MALARIAL —) TAP (MARSH —) HELODES (TEXAS —) TRISTEZA

FEVERISH HOT FIERY FEVERY HECTIC EXCITED FEBRILE FRANTIC RESTLESS

FEW LIT CURN LESS SOME SCANT THREE WHEEN WHONE CURRAN PICKLE LIMITED SEVERAL EXIGUOUS

FEY DEAD DYING ELFIN FATAL UNLUCKY PIXILATED

FEZ TARBOOSH

FIANCE TRUST SPOUSE FIANCEE PROMISE AFFIANCE

FIASCO CRASH FLASK FROST FIZZLE FAILURE DISASTER

FIAT EDICT ORDER UKASE DECREE COMMAND ORDER DECISION SANCTION

FIB LIE YED FLAW WHID SLANT STORY FITTEN PUMMEL SKLENT TARADIDDLE

FIBER TAL ADAD BASS FERU FLAX HARL HEMP IMBE JUTE LINE PITA SILK SUNN TULA ABACA AGUST AZLON CAJUN CAROA CHOEL ERIZO FIBRE HARLE ISOTE ISTLE IXTLE IZOTE KENAF KITUL MURVA OAKUM RAMIE RAPHE SIMAL SISAL STRAW TERAP TOSSA TUCUM VIVER AMIRAY ARGHAN BINDER BUNTAL BURITI CABUYA CATENA DACRON EMBIRA FIBRIL FIMBLE HINOKI KANAFF KENDIR KOHEMP MUCUNA NYTRIL RAFFIA SALAGO STRAND STRING SUTURE THREAD TUCUMA TURURI VINYON YACHAN ZAPUPE ACETATE ACRYLIC ANONANG ARAMINA BASSINE CANTALA CASCARA CHANDUL CHINGMA COQUITA ESPARTO FILASSE FUNICLE GEBANGA GRAVATA GUAXIMA GUMIHAN HUARIZO KERATTO KITTOOL MOCMAIN PALMITE PANGANE PAUKPAN POCHOTE SABUTAN CANAPINA CURRATOW FILAMENT HARAKEKE HENEQUEN PIASSAVA TOQUILLA TRONADOR (— FROM PEACOCK FEATHERS) MARL (— OF PALM) DOH LIF ERUC COYOL COROZO GOMUTI KITTUL COQUITA GEBANGA (—S OF FLAX) HARE (CLUSTER OF —S) NEP (COARSE —) KEMP (COCONUT —) COIR KYAR (COTTON —) LINT STAPLE (FLAX —) TOW (KNOT OF —) NOIL (MANUFACTURED —) DYNEL ORLON ESTRON ACRILAN SPANDEX (MATTED —) SHAG (MINERAL —) ASBESTOS (MUSCLE —) RHABDIUM (NERVE —) EFFERENT DEPRESSOR (PULVERIZED —) FLOCK (SILKY —) PULU KAPOK KUMBI YACHAN CASTULI (TWISTED —S) STRAND (WASTE —) FLY GOUT (WASTE —S) FLOSS (WOODY —) BAST GRAIN SCUTCH

FICKLE GERY DIZZY FALSE GIDDY LIGHT UNSAD HARLOT KITTLE MOBILE PUZZLE SHIFTY VOLAGE WANKLE WANKLY CASALTY FLATTER MOONISH MOVABLE MUTABLE VAINFUL VARIANT VOLUBLE GOSSAMER MOVEABLE SKITTISH STIRRING UNSTABLE UNSTEADY VARIABLE VOLATILE WAVERING

FICTION BAM TALE FABLE FALSE NOVEL ROMAN STORY DECEIT DEVICE FABULA FITTEN LEGEND COINAGE FANTASY FIGMENT FORGERY MARCHEN NOVELRY ROMANCE ROMANZA KAILYARD PHANTASY PRETENCE PRETENSE

FICTITIOUS MADE BOGUS DUMMY FALSE PHONY FABLED POETIC ASSUMED FEIGNED PHANTOM FABULOUS FICTIOUS MYTHICAL ROMANTIC SIMULATE SPURIOUS LEGENDARY

FIDDLE BOW BOX GIG SAW VIOL CHEAT CROWD GEIGE GIGUE GUDOK CHORUS FITHEL POTTER TRIFLE URHEEN VIOLIN CHROTTA SARANGI SWINDLE HUMSTRUM (— STRING) THAIRM (— WITH) TWIDDLE

FIDELIO (CHARACTER IN —) ROCCO
FIDELIO LEONORE PIZARRO JACQUINO
FLORESTAN MARZELLINE
(COMPOSER OF —) BEETHOVEN
FIDELITY TRUE ARDOR FAITH PIETY
TROTH TRUTH FEALTY HONESTY
LOYALTY ADHESION DEVOTION RELIGION
VERACITY CONSTANCY
FIDGET MOP FIKE FIRK FUSS RIDGE
FITCH HOTCH SHRUB SHRUG WORRY
BREVIT FIGGLE FISSLE FRIDGE HIRSEL
JIFFLE JIGGET NESTLE NIBBLE NIGGLE
TIDDLE TRIFLE RESTLESS
(— ABOUT TRIFLES) SPOFFLE
FIDGETY FIKIE FUSSY ITEMY FEISTY
FIGENT FLISKY KITTLE UNEASY RESTIVE
TWITCHY RESTLESS
FIEF FEE HAN FEUD FEOFF TIMAR ZIAMET
SATSUMA SUBFIEF BENEFICE
FIELD LOT ACRE AREA BENT CAMP FELL
FLAT HADE INAM LAND LIST PALE PARK
RAND WONG BRECK CAMPO CHAMP
CLOUR EARTH GLEBE INNAM LAYER
MILPA NILPA PADDY RANGE TILTH VELDE
ARRISH CAMPUS CAREER CHAMPE
GARDEN MACHAR MATTER PADANG
PINGLE SHIELD SPHERE CHARMEL
COMPASS CULTURE DIAMOND FERRING
INFIELD MOWLAND NEWTAKE PADDOCK
PARROCK PIGHTLE PURVIEW QUILLET
THWAITE TILLAGE CLEARING PROVINCE
(— ADJOINING HOUSE) CROFT
(— AT CRICKET) SCOUT
(— OF ACTIVITY) GAME ARENA
BARONY SPHERE TERRAIN
(— OF BATTLE) PLAIN
(— OF BLOODSHED) ACELDAMA
AKELDAMA
(— OF CONTROL) DOMAIN
(— OF ENDEAVOR) BUSINESS
(— OF SNOW) NEVE SNOWPACK
(— OF STUDY) GROUND
(— ON WHICH GRASS IS GROWN)
MEAD MEADOW
**(— SOWN FOR TWO SUCCESSIVE
YEARS)** HOOK
(ENCLOSED —) AGER TOWN CLOSE
CROFT
(FOOTBALL —) GRIDIRON
(FRUITFUL —) CHARMEL
(GRASSY —) LEA PEN GARSTON
(HOP —) HOPYARD
(LAVA —) PEDREGAL
(LITTLE-KNOWN —) BYWAY
(NEW GOLD —) RUSH
(PLOWED —) FURROW
(RICE —) SAWAH
(SMALL —) HAW CLOSE CROFT
PADDOCK
(SPORTS —) ARENA PITCH
(STUBBLE —) HIRSH ROWEN ARRISH
GRATTEN
(TILTING —) LISTS
(TOBACCO —) VEGA
(UNEXPLOITED —) FRONTIER
(UNPLOWED EDGE OF —) RAND
FIELDER GLOVEMAN

(CRICKET —) SLIP COVER FIELD GULLY
POINT SCOUT GULLEY INFIELDER
FIEND FEN FOE PUG DEMON DEVIL ENEMY
SATAN TRULL WIZARD SHAITAN TITIVIL
BARBASON SUCCUBUS
FIENDISH CRUEL WICKED DEMONIC
FIENDLY SATANIC DEMONIAC DEVILISH
DIABOLIC INFERNAL
FIERCE ILL BOLD FELL GRIM KEEN RUDE
THRO WILD WOOD ASPER BREME CRUEL
EAGER FELON HATEL ORPED RETHE
SHARP SMART STARK STERN STOUT
STOUT WROTH ARDENT FEROCE GOTHIC
HETTER IMMANE LUPINE RAGING
RUGGED SAVAGE STURDY UNMEEK
UNMILD WICKED BRUTISH FERVENT
FURIOSO FURIOUS GRIMFUL INHUMAN
MANKIND RABIOUS RAMPANT SCADDLE
VICIOUS VIOLENT STERNFUL TIGERISH
(PREF.) LABRO
FIERCENESS FURY FEROCITY
FIERY HOT RED ADUST FIRED QUICK
SHARP ARDENT FLASHY IGNITE BURNING
FERVENT FLAMING FURIOUS GLOWING
HOTHEAD IGNEOUS PARCHED PEPPERY
VIOLENT ADUSTIVE CHOLERIC FEVERISH
FRAMPOLD INFLAMED PHRAMPEL
SPIRITED SPITFIRE VEHEMENT
FIGHT BOX MIX WAP WAR WIN BEAT
BEEF BLUE BOUT CAMP CLEM COCK
COPE COWP CRAB CUFF FLOG FRAY
LAKE MEET MELL MILL SHOW SLUG
SPAR TILT WAGE YOKE BANDY BRAWL
CLASH FIELD FLOLT HURRY JOUST
MATCH MELEE RAMMY SCRAP SHINE
SPURN STOUR TOUSE AFFAIR AFFRAY
BARNEY BATTLE BICKER BLOWUP
COMBAT DEBATE FEUCHT FRACAS
FRAISE HASSLE IMPUGN MEDDLE
OPPOSE RELUCT PEPUGN RESIST RUFFLE
SHOWER STOUSH STRIFE STRIKE STRIVE
TOUSEL BARGAIN BRABBLE CONTEND
CONTEST COUNTER JOURNEY QUARREL
RUCTION SIMULTY TUILYIE WARFARE
CONFLICT DOGFIGHT DUOMACHY
FINISHER GUNFIGHT MILITATE SKIRMISH
SLUGFEST SQUABBLE STRUGGLE
TIRRIVEE TIRRWIRR TRAVERSE
(— AGAINST) BUCK OPPUGN
(— BETWEEN TWO) DUEL DUOMACHY
(— FOR) SERVE CHAMPION
(— WITH CLUB) TIMBER
(FIST —) RIPPIT TURNUP
(SEA —) NAUMACHY
(STREET —) HABBLE
FIGHTER PUG VAMP BOXER COCKER
BATTLER DUELIST SLUGGER SOLDIER
WARRIOR ANDABATA BARRATOR
CHAMPION GUERILLA PUGILIST
SCRAPPER
(FIRE —) EXEMPT HOTSHOT
(GUERILLA —) MAQUIS
FIGHTING BLOW ACTION AFFRAY
DEBATE WARLIKE CONFLICT MILITANT
FIGMENT IDEA FICTION
FIGURATIVE FLORID FIGURAL FIGURED
FLOWERY TYPICAL ALLUSIVE TROPICAL

FIGURE FIG HUE VOL BOSH DOLL FORM
IDEA SIGN STAR ANGLE ANTIC DATUM
DIGIT FLIRT FRAME MAGOT MOTIF
SHAPE SPADE SPRIG AUMAIL BABOON
CHANGE CIPHER COCKUP CUTOUT
DEVICE EFFIGY EMBLEM ENTAIL FIGGER
GOOGOL INCUSE NUMBER PERSON
SCHEME SYMBOL TAILLE TATTOO
CHASSIS CHEVRON CHIFFER CHIFFRE
COMPUTE CONTOUR DRAWING GESTALT
IMPRESS NUMERAL OUTLINE STATURE
DIHEDRAL FIGURATE GRAFFITO
HEXAGRAM LIKENESS SEMBLANT
MARIONETTE
(— FORMED BY INTERSECTING
LINES) KNOT
(— IN PRAYER) ORANT
(— IN WOOD GRAIN) BURL FLAKE
(— MADE OF CORN) KNACK
(— MADE OF 3 LINES) TRIGRAM
TRIANGLE
(— OF SPEECH) IMAGE IRONY TROPE
APORIA CLIMAX FLOWER SCHEME SIMILE
VISION ZEUGMA ANALOGY IMAGERY
CHIASMUS DIALLAGE METAPHOR
METONYMY OXYMORON SYLLEPSIS
ABSCISSION
(— OUT) BOTTOM
(— UP) ITEM
(— USED AS COLUMN) ATLAS
TELAMON CARYATID
(— USED AS MAGIC SYMBOL)
PENTACLE
(—S OF SPEECH) COLORS
(ANATOMICAL —) ECORCHE
(ARTIFICIAL —) GOLEM
(BIBLICAL —) ANGEL CHERUB
(CARVED —) GLYPH FIGURINE
(CENTRAL —) HERO
(CIRCULAR —) HOOP
(COMIC —) BILLIKEN
(CONSPICUOUS —) MARK
(CRESCENT-SHAPED —) LUNE
(DANCE —) SWING TRACE SQUARE
PURPOSE ASSEMBLE PROMENADE
(DOMINANT —) CAPTAIN
(FEMALE —) ORANTE
(FOLDED PAPER —) FLEXAGON
(GEOMETRICAL —) BODY CONE CUBE
LUNE PRISM RHOMB SOLID CIRCLE
GNOMON ISOGON ISOGON OBLONG
SECTOR SQUARE DIAGRAM ELLIPSE
LOZENGE PELCOID RHOMBUS SECTION
HEXAFOIL SPHEROID
(GREEK —) KOUROS
(GROTESQUE —) MAGOT BABOON
MAXIMON
(IDEAL —) EIDOLON
(IMAGINARY —) BOGEYMAN
(INCISED —) INTAGLIO
(JAPANESE — ON GRAVE) HANIWA
(MUMMYLIKE —) USHABTI
(MUSICAL —) IDEA LICK OSTINATO
(ODD —) MAUMET
(OVAL —) SWASH ELLIPSE
(PREHISTORIC —) CHACMOOL
(QUADRILLE —) POULE

(QUEER —) GIG
(RHETORICAL —) COLOR COLOUR
(RHYTHMIC —) SNAP
(SCULPTURED —) CANEPHOR
(SHADOW —) SKIAGRAM
(SKATING —) SPIRAL BRACKET
COUNTER
(SPINDLE-SHAPED —) FUZEE
(STUFFED —) DUMMY
(SYLLOGISTIC —) SCHEMA
(SYMBOLIC —) MORAL EMBLEM
(TAILOR'S —) MANNEQUIN
(TRIANGULAR —) TRIQUET
(UNDRAPED —) NUDE
(WINGED —) ANGEL EIDOLON
(PREF.) EID(O)
(SUFF.) HEDRON
FIGUREHEAD DUMMY FRONT SCROLL

FIJI

BAY: MBYA NATEWA NGALOA SAVUSAVU
CAPITAL: SUVA
EASTERN GROUP: LAU
ISLAND: ELD KIA ONO AIWA KIOA KORO
MALI NGAU VIWA WAIA AGATA MANGO
MOALA NAIAU RAMBI MAMOLO MATUKU
MBENGA MBULIA NAIRAI NAVITI
NGAMEA OVALAU TOTOYA YASAWA
YENDUA KAMBARA KANDAVU LAKEMBA
TAVEUNI VITILEVU
MOUNTAIN: NARARU MONAVATU
TOWN: BA MAU MBA MOMI NADI REWA
SUVA TUVU NANDI THUVU ETUMBA
LABASA NALOTO NAMOLI NARATA
NASALA NAVOLA SAGARA LAUTOKA
VATUKOULA

FILAMENT DOWL HAIR NEMA PILE SILK
CHIVE CHORD FIBER FILUM TWIRE
CIRRUS ELATER HEATER MANTLE
STRAND THREAD FIMBRIA FLIMMER
RHIZOID TEXTILE PARANEMA PHACELLA
STERIGMA PARAPHYSIS
(— OF FEATHER) BARB DOWL DOWLE
(— OF MINERAL) STRINGER
(— OF SILK) BRIN
(—S OF FLAX OR HEMP) HARL
(TWISTED —S) STRAND
FILCH BOB FUB NIM ROB BEAT DRIB FAKE
PILK PRIG SMUG SNIP SNIP LURCH
PILCH SNAKE SNEAK STEAL CLOYNE
PILFER SMOUCH STRIKE CABBAGE
PURLOIN
FILE ROW BARB DECK LINE LIST RANK
RASP RATE RISP ROLL SLIP STUB EMERY
ENTER FLOAT FOUND INDEX LABEL RIFLE
TRACK TRAIN ACCUSE ANSWER BEFOUL
CARLET FILACE RASCAL RUBBER STRING
ARCHIVE ARRANGE CHOILER CONDEMN
DOSSIER EXHIBIT QUANNET TICKLER
DRAWFILE
(— DOWN SAW TEETH) JOINT
(— OF SIX SOLDIERS) ROT
(— OFF) DEFILE

(— USED BY COMBMAKERS) GRAIL
TOPPER GRAILER
(— WITH COURT OF LAW) BOX
(COARSE —) RAPE
(CURVED —) RIFFLER
FILL EKE HIT PAD BUNG CLOY CRAM FEED
GLUT HOLD LADE LINE MEET PANG QUAR
SATE TEEM BELLY BLOAT BULGE FLOCK
GORGE KEDGE PITCH PRIME STORE
CHARGE INFUSE OCCUPY QUERRE
SUPPLY AGGRADE DISTEND ENLARGE
EXECUTE FILLING FRAUGHT FULFILL
IMPLETE INFLATE INVOLVE PERFECT
PERFORM PERVADE SATIATE SATISFY
SUFFUSE COMPLETE COMPOUND
FREQUENT PERMEATE
(— COMPLETELY) SATURATE
(— CUP TO BRIM) BRIM CROWN
BUMPER
(— FULL) FARCE STUFF
(— HORSES' TEETH) BISHOP
(— IN) NOG KILL STOP SLUSH INFILL
BALLAST
(— IN CHINKS) LIP
(— IN WITH RUBBLE) HEART
(— INTERSTICES) BLIND
(— LEATHER WITH OIL) FAT
(— OUT) BUNCH SWELL
(— TO EXCESS) CROWD FLOOD
CONGEST SURFEIT
(— TO OVERFLOWING) FLOW
THWACK
(— UP) STOP BRICK CHOKE CLOSE
ESTOP STOAK IMPACT STODGE PLENISH
(— UP HOLE) STIFLE
(— WITH) SWILL
(— WITH ALE) RACK
(— WITH ANXIETY) ALARM ALARUM
(— WITH CARGO) STOW
(— WITH CLAY) CAT PUG
(— WITH FEAR) APPAL APPALL
(— WITH HORROR) ABHOR
(— WITH LIGHT) GLUT
(— WITH LIQUOR) TUN SKINK
(— WITH METAL) BACK
(— WITH MORTAR) GROUT
(— WITH ODORS) EMBALM
(— WITH RUBBISH) BASH
(— WITH TERROR) AMAZE
(ONE'S —) SLITHERS
FILLET BAND BONE GIRT LIST ORLE ORLO
SOLE TAPE AMPYX CROWN FACET FILET
GORGE LABEL LEDGE MITER MITRE
QUIRK SCROD SNOOD STRAP STRIA
TIARA VITTA ANADEM BENDEL BINDER
CIMBIA COMBLE CORONA DIADEM
FASCIA INFULA LISTEL NORSEL POTONG
QUADRA REGLET REGULA RIBBON
ROLLER TAENIA TURBAN TURBOT
ANNULET BANDAGE BANDEAU CLOISON
CORONET EYEBROW FACETTE FRONTAL
GARLAND LAMBEAU MOLDING TRESSON
TRINGLE BANDELET CINCTURE FRONTLET
HAIRLACE HEADBAND PLATBAND
TRESSOUR TRESSURE UNDERCUT
FILLING GOB FILL MODE PLUG WEFT

WOOF INLAY STUFF FILLER STOPPING
STUFFING
(— OF GAPS) CONFAB
(— UP) CLOSURE RIPIENO
(BASKET —) SLEW
(DENTAL —) INLAY
(SILK —) SHIKII
FILM HAZE HULL KELL MIST SCUM SKIM
SKIN VEIL WEFT BLEAR COVER FLAKE
FLICK GLAZE LAYER PEARL PLATE SHOOT
SHORT BUBBLE MOTHER SCRUFF
CUTICLE FEATURE PHILOME TAFFETA
TOPICAL TRAILER FIRECOAT NEGATIVE
PELLICLE MICROFILM MONOLAYER
(— OF AIR) PLASTRON
(— OF ICE) VERGLAS
(— OF OIL) SLICK
(— OF TARTAR) SCALE PLAQUE
(— ON COPPER) PATINA
(— ON PORRIDGE) BRAT
(— ON WINE) BEESWING
(— OVER EYE) WEB
(DISCARDED —) OUTTAKE
(POLYESTER —) MYLAR
(X-RAY —) BITEWING
FILMY FINE HAZY GAUZY MISTY SHEER
WISPY CLOUDY CLOUDED TIFFANY
FILMLIKE GOSSAMER
FILTER CLAY RAPE SIFT SILE DRAIN SEITZ
SIEVE BOUGIE CANDLE COLATE CONTEX
LAUTER MEDIUM PURIFY REFINE STRAIN
BAGHOUSE COLATURE FILTRATE
INFILTER STRAINER
FILTHINESS MUCOR SQUALOR SULLAGE
CENOSITY
FILTHY LOW FOUL MIRY VILE BAWDY
DIRTY DROVY DUNGY GROSS LAIRY
MUCKY NASTY AUGEAN BAWDRY
CRUMBY CRUMMY CRUSTY DIRTEN
IMMUND IMPURE SORDID BEASTLY
BESTIAL HOGGISH OBSCENE PIGGISH
SQUALID UNCLEAN ORDUROUS
SLUTTISH
FIN ARM RAG RIB ANAL BURR FANG HAND
KEEL SAIL FLASH PINNA CAUDAL FINLET
ACANTHA FEATHER FLIPPER PINNULE
VENTRAL FORELIMB PECTORAL
(BOMB —) VANE
FINAL LAST UTTER LATTER RUNOFF
ULTIMA UTMOST DERNIER EXTREME
OUTMOST FAREWELL SUPREME ABSOLUTE
DECISIVE DEFINITE EVENTUAL FAREWELL
ULTIMATE
FINALE END CODA FINIS ENDING
CLOSING
FINALLY YET LAST AFINE LASTLY
FINANCE TAX BACK BANK FUND GOODS
REVENUE TAXATION TREASURE
FINANCIAL FISCAL MONETARY
PECUNIARY
FIND GET RUG MEET VAIL CATCH INVENT
LOCATE STRIKE ADJUDGE FINDING
DISCOVER SCROUNGE
(— FAULT) CARP BARGE BLAME CAVIL
GRONT KNOCK PINCH SCOLD NATTER
ARRAIGN
(— GUILTY) ATTAINT CONVICT

FINE

(— OUT) AFIND CHECK ESSAY LEARN
SPELL TROVE DETECT CONTRIVE
DECIPHER DISCOVER
(— REFUGE) BIEL BIELD
(— SOLUTION) SOLVE
(— THE SUM) SUMMATE

FINE CRO GAY RUM TAX BEIN BIEN BRAW
CAIN CROP DIRE FAIR GENT GOOD HUNK
JAKE LEVY MOOI NICE PURE RARE SEPT
SLAP TALL TEAR TINE TRIM ABWAB
BONNY BRAVE BULLY CHECK DAISY
DANDY DELIE DUCKY FRAIL GRAND
GREAT HUNKY ISSUE KELTY MULCT
NIFTY NOBLE RORTY SHARP SHEER
SMALL SPALE SWANK SWEET UNLAW
WALLY WHITE AMENDE AMERCE BONNIE
BONZER BRAWLY BRIGHT CHEESY
CHOICE CLEVER COSTLY CRAFTY DAINTY
FACETE FINISH FLUTED GERSUM HERIOT
HUNGRY INCONY ORNATE PEACHY
PRETTY PROPER QUAINT RANSOM
SARAAD SCONCE SERENE SILKEN SLIGHT
SPIFFY TENDER CLARIFY CONDEMN
CORKING CREANCE CUNNING ELEGANT
ESTREAT FERDWIT FINICAL FORFEIT
FRAGILE GALANAS GALLANT GALLOWS
GRADELY GRASSUM IMMENSE MARCHET
MERCHET MURDRUM ORFGILD PENALTY
PERFECT REFINED SCUTAGE STAVING
TENUOUS TOPPING VALIANT WERGILD
ABSOLUTE BLOODWIT BUDGEREE
CAVALIER CLINKING DELICATE DUSTLIKE
FLITWITE FOOTGELD HANDSOME
LASHLITE MARITAGE PENALIZE
PESHKASH PINPOINT PLEASANT
SKILLFUL SUPERIOR WARDWITE
WIRESPUN MAGNIFICENT
(— AGAINST SERVANTS) CHECK
(— FOR KILLING) BOTE
(— IN LIEU OF FLOGGING) HIDE
(BLOOD —) ERIC WITE
(OSTENTATIOUSLY —) GAUDY
(PRINTING OFFICE —) SOLACE
(VERY —) BUNKUM SPLENDID
(PREF.) LEPT(O)

FINERY GAUD ARRAY BRAWS WALLY
BAUBLE BAWDRY BEAUTY GAIETY
TAWDRY BRAVERY GAUDERY REGALIA
ELEGANCE FINENESS FOLDEROL
FOOFARAW FRIPPERY ORNAMENT
RIBANDRY

FINESSE ART CHEAT SKILL TRICK PURITY
SERENE CUNNING ARTIFICE DELICACY
SUBTLETY THINNESS

FINGER TOY PAUT PLAY DIGIT DACTYL
HANDLE MEDDLE MEDIUS PADDLE PILFER
POLLEX DIGITAL PURLOIN DIGITIZE
THRIMBLE
(— INFECTION) FELON
(FORE —) INDEX
(LITTLE —) PINKIE PIRLIE MINIMUS
AURICULAR
(RING —) ANNULAR RINGMAN
ANNULARY

FINGERPRINT DAB ARCH LOOP WHORL
LATENT

FINICKY NICE DINKY FIKIE PRISSY
FINICAL FINIKIN PRECISE

FINISH DO DIE END CHAR EDGE FACE
FINE MILL OVER PASS SINK SNUG STOP
BLOOM BOUND CEASE CHARE CHEVE
CLOSE CROWN FEEZE GLACE GLAZE
LIMIT SPEED UPPER BOTTOM BUSHEL
FULLDO PLISSE POLISH SETTLE WINDUP
ABSOLVE ACHIEVE DEPETER EXECUTE
FLUTING FULFILL PERFECT SURFACE
COMPLETE CONCLUDE DEPRETER
DRESSING FINALIZE FROSTING TERMINAL
(— CAREFULLY) NEATEN
(— CLOTH) BURL CONVERT
(— METAL) PLANISH
(— OF FABRIC) CIRE HOLLAND
(— OF PAPER) STIPPLE
(— OFF) DASH CRUSH ABSOLVE
ACCOMPLISH
(— STONE) COMB BOAST DROVE
(— WITH A SEAM) FELL
(— WORK) FLOOR
(CALENDERED —) CHASING
(DULL —) MAT MATTE
(GLAZED —) GLACE LACQUER
(STUCCO —) SPATTER
(SUPERFICIAL —) BLAZONRY

FINISHED BY DID OER PAU ARCH DONE
DOWN GONE OVER RIPE SHOT ENDED
EXACT KAPUT NAPOO ROUND CLOSED
ORNATE PERFECT REFINED ROUNDED
STOPPED THROUGH BANKRUPT
CLIMAXED GOFFERED LUSTERED
POLISHED
(— IN NATURAL COLOR) FAIR
(— WITH NAP) BRUSHED
(ABSOLUTELY —) SUNK
(HIGHLY —) SUAVE
(IMPERFECTLY —) RUDE

FINITE LIMITED

FINLAND

CAPITAL: HELSINKI HELSINGFORS
DIVISION: IJORE VILLIPURI
ISLAND: ALAND KARLO AALAND HAILUTO
VALLGRUND
ISTHMUS: KARELIA
LAKE: JUO MUO KEMI KIVI NASI OULO
PURU PYHA SIMO ENARE HAUKI INARI
KALLA LAPPA LESTI PUULA LENTUA
SAIMAA SOUNNE SYVARI KOITERE
NILAKKA PIELINEN
MEASURE: KANNU TUNNA VERST
FATHOM SJOMIL OTTINGER SKALPUND
TUNNLAND
MOUNTAIN: HALTIA
NAME: SUOMI
PROVINCE: HAME KYMI OULU LAPPI
VAASA KUOPIO MIKKELI UUSIMAA
RIVER: II KALA OULU SIMO TENO IVALO
LOTTA OUNAS SIIKA IIJOKI LAPUAN
MUONIO PASVIK TORNIO KITINEN
KOKEMAKI
TOWN: ABA ABO KEM KEMI OULU PORI
VASA ENARE ESPOO KOTKA LAHTI

TURKU VAASA IMATRA KUOPIO MIKKELI
TAMPERE HELSINKI
TRIBE: HAME VEPS VEPSE UGRIAN
KARJALAISET SUOMALAISET

FIR VER LARCH SAPIN BAUMIER LASHORN
PINABETE
FIRE CAN FEU LOW AGNI APOY BALE BRIO
BURN HEAT KILN LOWE POOP SWAP
SWOP ZEAL ARDOR ARSON BLAST BLAZE
BREAK BURST EMPTY FEVER GLEED
INGLE LIGHT LOGHE LOOSE LOUGH
PLUFF SERVE SHOOT SQUIB STOKE
AROUSE ENGHLE EXCITE FERVOR IGNITE
INCITE KINDLE SMUDGE SPIRIT SPLEEN
VULCAN ANIMATE BONFIRE BURNING
BURNOUT CHIMNEY DISMISS EMITTER
EXPLODE FURNACE GLIMMER INFLAME
INSPIRE SMOLDER BACKFIRE BALEFIRE
CAMPFIRE DETONATE HELLFIRE
ILLUMINE IRRITATE NEEDFIRE VIVACITY
PORCELAINIZE
(— A REVOLVER) FAN
(— ON) AFIRE
(— THE CHARGE) HIT
(— TWO ROUNDS) DOUBLE
(— UPON) GUN SPRAY
(CROSS —) GAUNTLET
(DAMPENED —) SMOTHER
(FOREST —) BREAK
(LITTLE —) SPONK SPUNK
(MASSED —) ARTILLERY
(PEAT —) GREESAGH
(RUNNING-OUT —) DANDY
(SIGNAL —) BALE BEACON BALEFIRE
FIREARM ARM GUN IRON SHOT TUBE
FIRER ORGAN PIECE RIFLE JEZAIL
MAGNUM MAUSER MUSKET PISTOL
POPPER BOMBARD CARBINE CURRIER
DEMIHAG HANDGUN PINFIRE SHOOTER
SPANNER ARQUEBUS BROWNING
CULVERIN EXPELLER EXPLODER
PETRONEL REVOLVER
(PL.) HARDWARE ARTILLERY
FIRECRACKER DEVIL SQUIB BANGER
PETARD SALUTE CRACKER SNAPPER
FIREWORK WHIZBANG
FIRE ENGINE RIG TUB MANUAL
FIRE EXTINGUISHER SQUIRT
EXTINCTOR
FIREFLY CUCUYO FIREBUG GLOWFLY
LAMPFLY FIREWORM GLOWWORM
LAMPYRID
FIREMAN VAMP FIRER FUELER STOKER
TEASER TIZEUR FIREBOY HOSEMAN
BAKEHEAD FURNACER
FIREPLACE FOCUS FOGON FORGE FOYER
GRATE INGLE TISAR HEARTH CHIMNEY
(— AND CHIMNEY) STACK
(— STONE) MANTEL
(PORTABLE —) BARBECUE BARBEQUE
FIREPLUG PLUG HYDRANT
FIRESIDE SMOKE HEARTH
FIREWOOD FIRE LENA SLAB WOOD
CHUNK FAGOT BILLET BILLOT ELDING
FIRING FIREBOTE TALSHIDE

FIREWORK JET SUN DEVIL GERBE PEEOY
SAXON SHELL WHEEL FIZGIG MAROON
PETARD ROCKET SALUTE SHOWER
TRACER CASCADE SERPENT TORPEDO
FOUNTAIN SPARKLER
FIRM HUI PAT BUFF FAST HARD IRON
NASH SURE TAUT TRIG TRIM CHAMP
CORKY CRISP DENSE FIRMA FIXED
HARDY HOUSE LOYAL RIGID SOLID
SOUND STARK STIFF STITH STOUT
SWITH TIGHT TOUGH HARDEN HEARTY
SECURE SETTLE SINEWY STABLE
STANCH STEADY STEEVE STOLID
STRONG STURDY TRUSTY ADAMANT
CERTAIN COMPACT COMPANY CONCERN
CONFIRM CONTEXT DECIDED DURABLE
UNMOVED CONSTANT FAITHFUL
FIDUCIAL OBDURATE RESOLUTE
SUBSTANT UNSHAKEN
FIRMAMENT SKY DEEP POLE CARRY
CANOPY HEAVEN EXPANSE EMPYREAN
FIRMLY BUFF FAST FIRM HARD SADLY
STARK TIGHT HARDLY SQUARE SURELY
SOLIDLY SECURELY STRONGLY
FIRMNESS BODY GRIT IRON ETHAN
PROOF FIXURE COURAGE FIRMITY
GRANITE BACKBONE DECISION
FASTNESS SECURITY SOLIDITY
STRENGTH TENACITY
FIRST GULE HEAD HIGH MAIN ALPHA
CHIEF FORME NIEVE PRIMA PRIME PRIMO
MAIDEN PRIMAL PRIMUS VIRGIN
HIGHEST INITIAL LEADING PREMIER
PRIMARY EARLIEST FOREHAND
FOREMOST FORMERLY ORIGINAL
PREMIERE PRINCEPS
FIRST-CLASS GAY TOP BOSS POSH
FLASH PRIME PUKKA BUNKUM
STUNNING
FIRST-RATE BOSS BRAG GOOD JAKE
MAIN SLAP BULLY DANDY LUMMY PRIME
SLEEK SLICK SUPER SWELL BONZER
CHEESY FAMOUS TIPTOP BLIGHTY
CAPITAL SKOOKUM STELLAR TOPPING
CHAMPION CLINKING CLIPPING
TOPNOTCH
FISH ID AKU AWA AYU BIB CAT COD DAB
DAP DIB EEL FIN GAR GIG GOO HEN IDE
IHI JIG JUG ORF RAY SAR TAI UKU BANK
BARB BASS BLAY BOCE BOGA CARP
CAST CERO CHUB CHUG CHUM CLOD
CRAB CUSK DACE DORY DRAG DRAW
DRUM ERSE FUGU GADE GHOL GOBY
GRIG HAKE HIND HUCH HUSO JACK
JUNK LINE LING LOTE MADO MERO
MOLA OPAH PEAL PEGA PIKE POOR POUT
PRIM QUAB RAIL RUDD RUFF SCAD SCUP
SEER SHAD SOLE SPET SPIN SPOT TILE
TORO TUNA ACARA AHOLE AKULE ANGLE
ATULE BEGTI BETTA BINNY BLAIN BLEAK
BOLTI BOLTY BREAM BULLY BULTI CABIO
CATLA CHIRO CISCO COBIA CONEY
DANIO DORAB DRAIL DRIFT DRIVE ELOPS
ERIZO FLOAT FLUKE FOGAS FRIAR GADID
GRUNT GUPPY HILSA HUCHO JUREL
KILLY LAKER LANCE MANTA MIDGE
MINIM MORAY OTTER PERCH PIABA

PLATY PORGY POWAN POWER REINA
ROACH SAIDE SARGO SAURY SEINE
SHARK SKATE SMELT SNOEK SNOOK
SPRAT SQUID SULEA SWEEP TENCH
TETRA TRABU TROLL TROUT TUNNY
UMBRA VIUVA VORAZ WAHOO WHIFF
AIMARA ALEVIN ANABAS ANGLER
BARBEL BARBER BENNET BICHIR BISKOP
BLENNY BONITO BOWFIN BUMPER
BURBOT CALLOP CANDIL CAPLIN
CARANX CARIBE COELHO COTTID
CREOLE CUCHIA CUNNER DARTER
DASSIE DENTEX FISHET GANOID GINNEL
GULPER GUNNEL HAMLET HAPUKU
HILSAH HUSSAR INANGA KOKOPU
LAUNCE LEDGER LIGGER LOUVAR
MAIGRE MARLIN MENISE MILTER
MINNOW MOLLIE MOLOID MULLET
NONNAT PHOEBE PLAICE POMPON
PUFFER PUNECA REDFIN REMORA
ROBALO ROUGHY RUNNER SABALO
SALELE SALEMA SALMON SAPSAP
SARDEL SAUGER SAUREL SERRAN
SHINER SIERRA SIMARA SPARID SUCKER
TAILER TAIMEN TANDAN TARPON
TAUTOG TESTAR TETARD TINOSA
TOMCOD TURBOT VENDIS WALLER
WEAVER WIRRAH WRASSE ZINGEL
ALEWIFE ALFIONA ANCHOVY BACALAO
BARBUDO BATFISH BEARDIE BERGYLT
BERYCID BOXFISH BRAGGLE BUFFALO
BUMMALO CABEZON CANDIRU CAPELIN
CAPLING CATFISH CAVALLA CAVALLY
CHIMERA CHROMID CICHLID CLUPEID
CONVICT CORVINA COWFISH CRAPPIE
CROAKER CTENOID CUTLIPS CYCLOID
DRABBLE DREPANE DRUMMER EELPOUT
ESCOLAR FATHEAD FINFISH GALJOEN
GEELBEC GEELBEK GOBIOID GOGGLER
GOLDEYE GOURAMI GRAYSBY GROUPER
GRUNION GRUNTER GUAPENA GUAVINA
GUDGEON GULARIS GURNARD GWYNIAD
HADDOCK HAGFISH HALIBUT HARMOOT
HERRING HINALEA HOGFISH HOUTING
ICEFISH ICHTHUS INCONNU JAWFISH
JEWFISH JUGULAR LABROID LAGARTO
LONGFIN MACHETE MAHSEER MAYFISH
MOJARRA MOONEYE MORWONG
OARFISH OLDWIFE OQUASSA PEGASUS
PIGFOOT PINTADO PIRANHA POISSON
POLLACK POMFRET POMPANO PUPFISH
RONQUIL SANCORD SARDINE SAUROID
SAVELHA SAWFISH SCALARE SCAROID
SCHELLY SCULPIN SENNETT SILURUS
SLEEPER SMUTTER SNAPPER SOLDIER
SPAWNER STERLET SUNFISH TELEOST
TOMTATE TOPKNOT TORPEDO TUBFISH
UMBRANA UNICORN VENDACE VIAJACA
WAREHOU WAUBEEN WHAPUKA
WHAPUKU WHITING
(— BY TROLLING) DRAIL
(— FOR EELS) GRIG SNIGGLE
(— FOR SALMON) SNIGGER
(— NETTED) LIFT
(— NOT UNDERSIZED) COUNT KEEPER
(— TAPE) SNAKE
(— THROUGH ICE) CHUG

(— UNDERWATER) GOGGLE
(— WITH HANDS) GUMP GUDDLE
(AQUARIUM —) GUPPY RASBORA
(BLIND —) PINKFISH
(CURED —) DUNFISH
(FABLED —) MAH
(FEMALE —) RAUN SPAWNER
(FIGHTING —) PLAKAT
(HAWAIIAN —) AU
(HERALDIC —) CHABOT
(INDIAN —) ROHU
(NUMBER OF —) SCHOOL
(OLD —) MOSSBACK
(PULPED —) POMACE
(RAW —) SASHIMI
(REFUSE —) CHUM SHACK
(SALTED —) COR
(SMOKED —) FUMADO
(SPLIT —) KLIPFISH
(STEWED —) MATELOTE
(THIN —) RACER
(YOUNG —) FRY ALEVIN
(25 LBS. OF —) STICK
FISHERMAN (ALSO SEE ANGLER) TOTY
EELER ANGLER GIGMAN GILLER KEDGER
MAIMUL SEINER WORMER ADMIRAL
DORYMAN DRAGMAN DRIFTER PRAWNER
RODSTER SHANKER SMELTER STRIKER
TRAWLER TROTTER TROWMAN
PETERMAN PISCATOR SEASONER
SHRIMPER
FISHHOOK FLY GIG HOOK LARI ANGLE
DRAIL KIRBY LARIN SLEEK ANGULE
SPROAT KENDALL ABERDEEN BARBLESS
CARLISLE LIMERICK
FISHLINE GIMP TROT SNELL TRAWL
DIPSEY LIGGER BOULTER GANGION
OUTLINE SETLINE TRIMMER HAIRLINE
TROTLINE
FISHPOND STEW VIVER PISCINA
VIVARIUM
FISHY DULL FUNNY GLASSY VACANT
FISSION BREAKING CLEAVAGE CLEAVING
GAMOGENY SCISSION
FISSURE GAP CHAP CONE FLAW GOOL
GULL LEAK LOCH LODE RENT RIFT RIMA
RIME SEAM SLIT TEAR VEIN VENT
CHASM CHINE CHINK CLEFT CRACK
FLAKE GRIKE PIPER PORTA SHAKE SPLIT
ZYGON CLEAVE CRANNY DIVIDE LESION
RICTUS RIMULA SPRING SULCUS
BLEMISH CREVICE FISSURA MOFETTE
OPENING SWALLET APERTURE
BLOWHOLE CLEAVAGE COLOBOMA
CREVASSE INCISURE QUEBRADA
SCISSURA TRAVERSE
(— IN BUILDING STONE) DRY
(— IN HEEL) GAUG
(— IN MAST) SPRING
(— IN PLATEAU) ABRA
FIT APT JAG PAN RIG SET SIT ABLE BOUT
FEAT FURY GOOD HARD MEET PANG RIPE
SORT SUIT TRIM TURN WELL WHIM
ADAPT ADEPT APPLY BESIT CHINK CLICK
DIGNE EXIES FADGE FANCY FITLY FRAME
FRISK FUROR HAPPY ICTUS MATCH
PITCH QUEME QUIRK READY RIGHT

SERVE SPASM SPELL START STOUR
SWOON TALLY ACCESS ADJUST
ANSWER ATTACK BECOME BEHOVE
BESORT DUEFUL FINISH FITTEN HABILE
HEPPEN LIABLE PROPER SEASON SEEMLY
SQUARE STREAK STROKE STRONG
SUITED WORTHY ADAPTED BEHOOVE
CAPABLE CONCENT CONDIGN CONFORM
CORRECT DESPAIR FASHION FITTING
HEALTHY PREPAIR QUALIFY SEIZURE
WIDDRIM ADEQUATE BECOMING
DOVETAIL ELIGIBLE GLOOMING
IDONEOUS OUTBREAK PAROXYSM
PASSABLE SUITABLE SYNCOPES
(— CLOSELY) FAY CHOCK
(— CORNER TO CORNER) BUTT
(— FOR THE GALLOWS) WIDDIFOW
(— IN) GO
(— INTO SOCKET) FANG
(— LOOSELY) SLOP
(— OF ANGER) WAX FRAP FUME HUFF
RAGE TIFF FLING RAVERY SPLEEN
(— OF DEPRESSION) HUMP
(— OF ILL HUMOR) DOD PET TIG FUNK
POUT TOUT GRUMPS
(— OF ILL TEMPER) MAD TANTRUM
(— OF ILLNESS) DROW TOUT FLING
(— OF LAUGHTER) GIRD KINK
(— OF NERVOUSNESS) TWITCHET
(— OF RESENTMENT) PIQUE SNUFF
(— OF SHIVERING) AGUE GROOSE
(— OF STUBBORNNESS) REEST
(— OF SULKS) GEE STRUM
(— OF SULLENNESS) DOD
(— OF TEMPER) WAX BAIT BIRSE
HISSY PADDY TETCH GROUCH SPLEEN
SQUALL BRAINGE
(— OF WEEPING) CRY
(— OF YAWNING) GAPE
(— ONE WITHIN ANOTHER) NEST
(— OUT) ARM BUSK BEFIT EQUIP
ASTORE CLOTHE OUTFIT APPAREL
APPOINT FURNISH HABILLE ACCOUTER
(— RIFLE BARREL) BED
(— TIGHTLY) STUFF
(— TO BE DRUNK) SORBILE
(— TOGETHER) MESH NEST COAPT
JOINT COHERE ASSEMBLE
(— UP) RIG
(— WITH COMPACTNESS) BOX
(— WITH FETTERS) GARNISH
(RITUALLY —) KOSHER
FITNESS FORM APTNESS DECENCY
DECORUM DIGNITY APTITUDE CAPACITY
IDONEITY JUSTNESS PROPERTY
CONGRUITY
FITTING TO APT CAP DUE LUG PAT BUTT
FAIR FEAT FORK HARP JUMP JUST KIND
MEET CLEAT HAPPY QUEME WORTH
BECOME CLENCH CLEVIS LEADER
PROPER SADDLE SEEMLY WASHER
ADAPTER CONGRUE PENDANT SERVING
SHACKLE SUCTION TACTFUL CONDULET
DECOROUS GRACEFUL RIGHTFUL
SUITABLE RECEPTACLE
(— TIGHTLY) CLOSE
(PIPE —) CROSS ELBOW

FIVE CINQ FUNF CINQUE EPSILON
QUINQUE
(— CENTS) JITNEY NICKEL
(— HUNDRED DOLLARS, POUNDS)
MONKEY
(— IN CRAPS) PHOEBE
(— OF TRUMPS) PEDRO
(— YEARS) LUSTRUM
(TWO —S) QUINAS
FIX BOX JAM PEG PIN SET CLEW CLUE
FAST FIRM GAFF GLUE HOLD HOLE JAMB
LOCK MEND MOOR PICK RELY SPOT STAY
ALLOT DEFIX FOUND GRAFT GRAVE
IMBED INFIX LIMIT PLACE PLANT POINT
POSIT SEIZE STATE STEEK STELL STICK
TRYST ADJUST ANCHOR ARREST ASSIGN
ATTACH CEMENT CLINCH DEFINE
ENROOT ENTAIL FASTEN FICCHE FIXATE
GROUND IMPALE REPAIR REVAMP
SQUARE TEMPER APPOINT ARRANGE
CALCIFY CONFIRM DELIMIT DESTINE
DILEMMA GRAPPLE IMPLANT IMPRESS
IMPRINT PREPARE STATION PINPOINT
RENOVATE TRANSFIX
(— AMOUNT) AFFEER
(— ATTENTION) NAIL
(— FIRMLY) SEAL FREEZE IMPACT
INCUBE RAMPIRE
(— PRICE) ASSIZE CHARGE SETTLE
(— UPON) CHAP AFFIX
FIXED PAT PUT SAD SET SOT FAST FIRM
FLAT HARD GIVEN STAID UPSET FINITE
FROZEN INTENT MENDED SICKER STABLE
STATED STEADY STRONG CERTAIN
DORMANT EMPIGHT HABITED LIMITED
SETTLED SITFAST STATARY STATIVE
STELLED ACCURATE ARRANGED
ATTACHED CONSTANT DEFINITE
EXPLICIT FASTENED IMMOBILE
IRONCLAD MOVELESS RESIDENT
RESOLUTE STANDING STUBBORN
(NOT —) FLUID SHIFTY FUGITIVE
FIXTURE ANNEX EVENT GUARD FAUCET
SHIELD BRACKET CREEPER KNOCKER
THIMBLE
(LIGHTING —) SCONCE
(STORE —) GONDOLA
FIZZLE FLOP FUSS BARNEY FAILURE
FLIVVER
FLABBY LAX FOZY LASH LIMP WEAK
BAGGY FLASH FOGGY FRUSH SAPPY
WOOZY CASHIE DOUGHY FEEBLE FLAGGY
FLAPPY LIMBER QUAGGY WATERY
FLACCID YIELDING
FLACCID LIMP WOOZY FLABBY FLAGGY
EMARCID FLACKED YIELDING
FLAG FAG LAG SOD FAIL FANE FLAT
HOOK JACK JADE LECK PINE TURF WAIF
WILT CREST DROOP FAINT FLAKE SEDGE
SLAKE UNION VEXIL WHEFT WHIFF
BANNER BOUGEE BURGEE COLORS
CORNET EMBLEM ENSIGN FANION
GUIDON LEVERS PENCEL PENNON
SIGNAL TABARD WIMPLE ANCIENT
BEEWORT CALAMUS CATTAIL CURTAIN
DECLINE DRAPEAU FANACLE LABARUM
PENDANT PENNANT SCOURGE

BANDEROL BRATTACH GONFALON
HANDFLAG LANGUISH PAVILION
STREAMER TRICOLOR VEXILLUM
WATCHMAN
(— CORNER) UNION
(— OF DENMARK) DANEBROG
(— OF TRANSVAAL) VIERKLEUR
(— OF TRUCE) KARTEL
(— OF U.S.) GRIDIRON
(— ON LANCE) PAVON
(BLUE — WITH WHITE SQUARE)
PETER
(CAVALRY —) STANDARD
(KNOTTED —) WAFT
(PIRATE —) ROGER BLACKJACK
(SERPENT-LIKE —) DRACO ANGUIS
(SHIP'S —) DUSTER
(TURKISH —) ALEM
(WATER —) SAG
FLAG BEARER GUIDON ANCIENT
FLAGEOLET PIPE ZUFOLO BASAREE
LARIGOT SIBILUS MONAULOS
FLAGGING WEAK LANGUID
FLAGITIOUS WICKED CORRUPT HEINOUS
CRIMINAL FLAGRANT GRIEVOUS
FLAGON GUN STOUP BOTTLE VESSEL
FLACKET FLAGONET REHOBOAM
FLAGRANT BAD RED RANK GROSS
ODIOUS STRONG WANTON WICKED
BLATANT GLARING HATEFUL HEINOUS
SCARLET VIOLENT SHAMEFUL
FLAGSHIP FLAG ADMIRAL
FLAGSTONE FLAG LECK SLAB FAVUS
FLAIL BEAT FLOG WHIP DRASH FRAIL
THRAIL THRASH THRESH SWINGLE
SWIPPLE STRICKLE THRESHEL
FLAIR RAY BENT NOSE ODOR SMELL
GENIUS LEANING
FLAKE CHIP FILM FLAW RACK SNOW
FLANK FLECK FLOCK LAMIN SCALE
SLATE SPALL STRIP APHTHA HURDLE
LAMINA PALING FLAUGHT SHAVING
FLOCCULE FRAGMENT
(— OF METAL) FLITTER
(— OF SNOW) FLAG
FLAKY SCALY SHIVERY
FLAMBOYANCE BLARE PANACHE
FLAMBOYANT FLORID GARISH ORNATE
BAROQUE BUCKEYE FLAMING GORGEOUS
FLAME LOW FIRE GLOW LUNT ARDOR
BLAZE FLARE FLASH GLARE GLEED INGLE
LIGHT RESEPH TONGUE BURNING
INKINDLE
(ACETYLENE —) CALCIUM
(SMALL —) SPUNK FLAMELET
FLAMMULE
FLAMING LIVE AFIRE FIERY FLAMY VIVID
AFLAME ARDENT BLAZING BURNING
FLARING FLAGRANT
FLANGE BEAD BOSS BEZEL COLLAR
COLLET FLANCH SHROUD FEATHER
DUCKBILL FOLLOWER
(— OF GIRDER) BOOM
(WITHOUT —) BALD
FLANK LEER LISK SIDE WING CHEEK
SKIRT THIGH BORDER FLITCH

FLANNEL LANA DOMETT SAXONY
STAMIN WHITTLE MOLLETON SWANSKIN
FLAP FAN LUG ROB TAB TAG TAP WAP
BATE BEAT BLOW CLAP FLIP FLOP LOBE
LOMA SLAM WAFF WELT ALARM APRON
FLACK FLAFF FLICK BALLUP BANGLE
LAPPET LIBBET STRIKE TONGUE WAFFLE
WALLOP WINNOW AILERON BLINDER
CLICKET FLACKER FLAPPET FLICKER
FLUTTER SWINDLE AVENTAIL BACKFLAP
COATTAIL CODPIECE TURNOVER
AGITATION COMMOTION CONFUSION
(— OF BOOTEE) FLY
(— OF GARMENT) LAP
(— OF HAT OR CAP) VALANCE
(— OF HINGE) LEAF
(— ON HOLSTER) FLOUNCE
(— ON SADDLE) SKIRT JOCKEY
(— VIOLENTLY) FLOG SLAT
(CARDIAC —) CUSP
(FLESHY —) GILL
(MUD —) BOOT
(TROUSERS' —) FALL
FLARE BELL FLUE BLAZE FLAME FLASH
FLECK FUSEE LIGHT SPIRT TORCH
FLANCH SIGNAL SPREAD FLICKER
TRUMPET OUTBURST
(— ON SHIPBOARD) DUCK
(— UP) KINDLE
FLARING BELL FLUE EVASE GAUDY
AFLARE FLAMING GLARING SWAGGER
BOUFFANT DAZZLING
FLASH DOT DASH DASH LAIT LAMP LASH
LEAM POOL SHOT STAB WINK BLASH
BLAZE BURST FLAME FLARE FLOSH
FLUFF GLADE GLAIK GLEAM GLENT
GLINT LEVIN MARSH SPARK STEAM
BOTTLE FILLIP GLANCE QUIVER BLUETTE
FLAUGHT FOULDRE GLIMMER GLIMPSE
GLISTEN GLITTER INSTANT LIGHTEN
QUICKEN SHIMMER SPARKLE TWINKLE
SPLINTER SUNBURST CORUSCATE
SCINTILLATION
(— FORTH) OUTRAY
(HOT —) FLUSHING
(NEWS —) FUDGE
FLASHING CURB FLASH STEEP ARDENT
BRIGHT FLASHY FORWARD LAMPING
SHINING CREASING METEORIC SLASHING
SNAPPING
FLASHLIGHT BUG GLIM FLASH TORCH
PENLITE PENLIGHT
FLASHY GAY FLAT GAUD LOUD BAVIN
FIERY GAUDY NOBBY SHOWY SLEEK
FLOSSY FROTHY GARISH SLANGY
SPORTY STUNTY INSIPID RAFFISH
TINHORN DAZZLING FLASHING SPORTING
TIGERISH VEHEMENT
FLASK BOX PIG BODY HEAD HELM JACK
OLPE SNAP BETTY BULGE FRAME GIRBA
GOURD BOTTLE FIASCO FLACON GUTTUS
HELMET LAGENA AMPULLA BOMBOLA
CANTEEN FLASKET MATRASS TICKLER
WARBURG CHRISMAL CUCURBIT
(POCKET —) TICKLER
FLAT DEAD DOWD DULL EVEN FADE FLUE
TAME ABODE AFLAT BANAL BLAND

BLUNT DUSTY HAUGH LEVEL MUSTY
PLAIN PLANE PRONE ROOMS SEBKA
VAPID WALSH AGRUFE BORING CALLOW
DREARY FLASHY JEJUNE LEADEN
PLANAR QUATCH SEBKHA SILENT
SIMOUS DECIDED FLIPPER INSIPID
INSULSE PLATOID PROSAIC SHILPIT
TABULAR UNIFORM DIRECTLY LIFELESS
UNBROKEN WATERISH CHAMPAIGN
POINTLESS PROSTRATE
(— AND CIRCULAR) DISCOID
(— AND SHORT) CAMUS
(— IN MUSIC) BEMOL MOLLE
(— OF SWORD) PLAT
(MUD —) SLOB SLAKE CORCASS
(NOT —) BRISK
(SALT —) SALINA
(THEATRICAL —) JOG
FLATBOAT ARK SCOW PULLBOAT
FLATCAR FLAT IDLER LORRY
FLATFISH DAB RAY BUTT DACE KITE SLIP
SOLE TONG BREAM BRILL FLUKE QUIFF
RHINA WHIFF ACEDIA CARTER PLAICE
TURBOT HALIBUT SUNFISH TORPEDO
FLOUNDER MARYSOLE
FLATIRON IRON GOOSE STEEL SADIRON
FLATNESS BATHOS SILENCE EVENNESS
KURTOSIS
(— OF NOSE) SIMITY
FLATTEN BEAT COMB DECK EVEN PLAT
CRUSH LEVEL PLUSH SPLAT BEETLE
CLINCH DEJECT SMOOTH SPREAD
SQUASH DEPRESS EXPLAIN PANCAKE
PLANISH SUBSIDE SURBASE COMPRESS
DISPIRIT
FLATTENED ECRASE OBLATE DILATED
PLANATE TABULAR
FLATTER BULL CLAW COAX DAUB FAGE
FUME PALP SOAP WORD CHARM FLOAT
GLOZE HONEY PAINT ROOSE SLEEK
SMALM BECOME BUTTER CAJOLE
CRINGE FICKLE FLEACH FRAISE GLAVER
KITTLE PEPPER PHRASE SAWDER SLAVER
SMOOGE SOOTHE STROKE ADULATE
BEGUILE BEHONEY BLARNEY FLETHER
FLUTTER INCENSE PALAVER SOOTHER
SWEETEN WHEEDLE BESLAVER
BLANDISH BOOTLICK COLLOGUE
FLATTERER FLOIT COGGER DAUBER
EARWIG GLOZER JENKINS PRONEUR
SOOTHER BOOTLICK CLAWBACK
COURTIER DAMOCLES INCENSER
LOSENGER SLAVERER SMOOTHER
FLATTERING SOAPY SMARMY SMOOTH
BUTTERY CANDIED COURTLY GLAVERING
FLATTERY BULL BUNK DAUB FLUM
MUSH SOAP FRAIK GLOZE SALVE TAFFY
BUTTER CARNEY FLEECH GREASE
PHRASE SAWDER SLAVER BLARNEY
DAUBING EYEWASH FAWNING FLETHER
INCENSE PALAVER CAJOLERY
ADULATION
FLATWARE SILVER
FLAUNT BOSH SHOW WAVE BOAST
SKYRE STOUT VAUNT PARADE DISPLAY
FLUTTER TRAIPSE BRANDISH FLOURISH

FLAUNTING GAUDY PURPLE SKYRIN
FLAGGERY
FLAVOR GAMY GOUT MASK ODOR RASA
SALT TANG ZEST AROMA ASSAI CURRY
DEVIL SAPID SAPOR SAUCE SAVOR
SCENT SMACK SPICE TASTE TINGE
ASARUM ASSAHY INFUSE RANCIO
RELISH SEASON TARAGE FLAVOUR
PERFUME SUPTION HAUTGOUT
PIQUANCY
(HIGH —) HOGO
(SPECIAL —) GUST
(UNPLEASANT —) TACK
FLAVORED SPICY TINCT SPICED
FLAVORLESS BLAND STALE SILENT
WATERISH
FLAW BUG FIB GAP LIE MAR RUB WEM
BANE BLOT CHIP FLEE GALL HOLE RASE
RIFT SPOT WIND BOTCH BURST CHICK
CLEFT CRACK CRAZE FAULT FLAKE
PLUME SPECK BLOTCH BREACH DEFECT
FOIBLE LACUNA LESION BLEMISH
BLISTER DEFAULT EYELAST FISSURE
NULLIFY SUNSPOT VIOLATE WHITLOW
FRACTURE FRAGMENT WINDFLAW
(— IN CASTING) BUCKLE
(— IN CLOTH) BRACK
(— IN DIAMOND) GENDARME
(— IN MARBLE) TERRACE
(— IN METAL) SNAKE
(— IN PRECIOUS STONE) FEATHER
(— IN STEEL) STAR
(— IN STONE) DRY
(— IN WICK) THIEF
(MORAL —) SMIRCH
FLAWED CRACKED
FLAWLESS CLEAN SOUND PERFECT
FLAX LIN POB TOW CARD HARL LINE LINT
ROCK GRAIN HURDS BREADS BYSSUS
KORARI PEANUT PEBBLE SCUTCH
LINSEED FLAXWORT HARAKEKE
FLAY SKIN SCULP STRIP FLEECE UNCASE
CENSURE PILLAGE REPROVE SCARIFY
FLEA LOP SCUD PULEX TUNGA CHIGOE
VERMIN PULICID SANDBOY
FLEDERMAUS, DIE
(CHARACTER IN —) ADELE FALKE
FRANK ALFRED ORLOFSKY ROSALINDE
EISENSTEIN
(COMPOSER OF —) STRAUSS
FLEDGLING SQUAB NESTER FLIGGER
BIRDLING
FLEE FLY LAM RUN BOLT FLEG LOUP
SHUN TURN ELOPE ELUDE SKIRR SPEED
ESCAPE VANISH ABANDON ABSCOND
FORSAKE SCAMPER LIBERATE
SKEDADDLE
FLEECE JIB KET TEG BUCK CAST FELL
GAFF MORT PLOT ROOK SKIN FLICK
PASHM PLOAT SHAVE SHEAR SHEEP
SWEAT PIGEON TOISON SHEARING
(— OF MEDIUM GRADE) SUPER
(POOREST PART OF —) ABB
FLEEING FUGIENT HOTFOOT RUNNING
FUGITIVE
FLEET BAY FAST FLIT NAVY SAIL SKIM
SWIM CREEK DRAIN DRIFT EVAND FLOAT

FLOTA HASTY INLET POWER QUICK
RAPID SWIFT ARGOSY ARMADA FLIGHT
HASTEN NIMBLE SPEEDY CARAVAN
COMPANY FLOTILLA NAVARCHY
WARCRAFT

FLEETING BRIEF BUBBLE CADUCE FLYING
VOLAGE CURSIVE FLIGHTY PASSING
POSTING SHADOWY VOLATIC CADUCOUS
FUGITIVE VOLATILE

FLESH KIN BEEF BODY GAME LAMB LIRE
MEAT RACE WEED SLATE STOCK FAMILY
MUSCLE SEASON CARNAGE KINDRED
MANKIND NATURAL HUMANITY
MOONLIGHT

  (— ABOUT CHIN AND JAWS) GILL
  (— OF CALF) SLINK
  (— OF GOAT) CHEVON
  (— OF KID) CABRITO
  (— OF SHEEP) TRAIK
  (— ON LOWER JAW) CHOLLER
  (— OUT) CLOTHE
  (— UNDER SKIN) FELL
  (ANIMAL —) BRAWN
  (DEAD —) MURRAIN
  (HORSE —) JACK
  (LIFELESS —) MUMMY
  (PUTREFYING —) CARRION
  (SUN-DRIED —) TAPA
  (SUPERFLUOUS —) LUMBER

FLESHLY CARNAL FLESHY SENSUAL
SARKICAL

FLESHY FAT BEEFY LUSTY OBESE PLUMP
PULPY STOUT ANIMAL BODILY BRAWNY
CARNAL BUNTING CARNOSE SARCOUS
CARNEOUS

FLEX BEND

FLEXIBILITY WHIP FLUIDITY

FLEXIBLE LIMP LUSH SOFT BUXOM
LIMSY LITHE WANDY WITHY FLOPPY
LIMBER LITHER PLIANT SUPPLE DUCTILE
ELASTIC FINGENT FLEXILE FLEXIVE
LISSOME PLIABLE SPRINGY WILLOWY
WINDING WRIGGLE BENDSOME YIELDING

FLEXURE ARCH BEND BENT CURL FOLD
CURVE TWIST SIGMOID WINDING

FLICKER FAIL FLIT LICK WINK BLINK
FLAME FLARE FLICK FLUNK WAVER
BICKER FITTER SHIVER YUCKER BLINTER
FLIMMER FLITTER FLUTTER SKIMMER
TREMBLE TWINKLE WHIFFLE FLICHTER
HIGHHOLE

FLICKERING FLICKY FLUTTER LAMBENT
FLEXUOUS UNSTEADY

FLIER ACE BIRD KIWI FLYER PILOT
AIRMAN AVIATOR

FLIGHT FLY GUY HOP LAM BOLT BUNK
LAKE PAIR ROUT WING CHEVY FLOCK
GLIDE GRICE SCRAP VOLEE CHIVVY
EXODUS FUGACY HEGIRA JOYHOP
SPIRAL BOUQUET EVASION FLAUGHT
FLYOVER MIGRATE MISSION SCAMPER
STEPWAY REGIFUGE STAMPEDE
SWARMING

  (— OF BALL) HOOK DRIVE SLICE
  (— OF BIRDS) VOLARY VOLLEY
  (— OF FANCY) SALLY
  (— OF GEESE) SKEIN

  (— OF SNIPE) WISP
  (— OF STEPS) RISE TRAP GRECE PITCH
SCALE STOOP PERRON STAIRS STEPWAY
STAIRWAY
  (— OF WILD FOWL) SKEIN
  (— OF WOODCOCK) RODING
  (ABORTIVE —) ABORT
  (HASTY —) TIFT
  (HAWK'S —) CAREER
  (HIGH —) TOWER
  (IN —) ALOFT
  (SUDDEN —) START STAMPEDE
  (UNAUTHORIZED —) BUGOUT
  (UPWARD —) SOAR

FLIGHTY ANILE BARMY GIDDY LIGHT
SWIFT FITFUL GARISH UNFIRM VOLAGE
WHISKY FLYAWAY FOOLISH GIGGISH
MOONISH ROCKETY FLEETING FREAKISH
HELLICAT

FLIMSY LIMP THIN VAIN WEAK FRAIL
GAUDY JERRY FEEBLE PALTRY SLEAZY
SLIGHT SLIMSY HAYWIRE SHALLOW
TENUOUS TIFFANY GIMCRACK
GOSSAMER JIMCRACK TWITTERY

FLINCH FUNK GAME JARG BLUNK BUDGE
FEIGN QUAIL SHUNT START WINCE
WONDE BLANCH BLENCH FALTER
FLENSE RECOIL SHRINK SCRINGE
SCUNNER SQUINCH

FLING SHY BUZZ CAST DART DASH DING
EMIT FLAP FLEG GIBE HURL KICK LASH
PECK PICK SLAT TOSS WARP BRAID
CHEAT DANCE FLIRT LANCE PITCH
SHOOT SLING SNEER SWING THROW
WHANG BAFFLE EFFUSE HURTLE
LAUNCH PLUNGE REBUFF SPIRIT
ENFORCE FLOUNCE REPULSE SARCASM
SCATTER SWINDLE SHYLANCE
SPANGHEW

  (— MISSILES) CHUNK
  (— UPWARD) HAUNCH
  (HIGHLAND —) WALLOCH

FLINT CORE BLANK CHERT MISER SILEX
EOLITH QUARTZ REJECT ESLABON
FURISON SCRAPER GRATTOIR GUNFLINT

FLIP SKY TAP FLAP SNAP TOSS TRIP
FLANK FLICK FLIRT SLIRT SMART FILLIP
FLITCH LIMBER NIMBLE PLIANT PROPEL

FLIPPANT AIRY FLIP GLIB FLUENT
LIMBER NIMBLE

FLIPPER ARM FIN PAW HAND SWELL
PADDLE FLAPPER SPRINGER

FLIRT TOY FIKE FLIP MASH TICK VAMP
FLICK ROVER SLIRT JILLET MASHER
TRIFLE GALLANT PICKEER TWINKLE
COQUETTE PHILANDER

FLIRTATION FIKE PASSADE COQUETRY
PHILANDER

FLIT DART FLOW SCUD FLECK FLEET
FLICK FLIRT FLOAT FLURR HOVER QUICK
SCOOT SKIFF SWIFT NIMBLE FLICKER
FLUTTER

FLOAT FLY KIT SEA BOOM BUOY DRAG
FLOW FLUX HAWK HONE HOVE LIVE
PONT RAFT RIDE SAIL SCOW SOAR SWIM
TILT WAFT WAVE BALSA BLADE CAMEL
DERBY FLEET FLOOD FLUSH GRAIL

HOVER LADLE QUILL SHOAD SWOON
BILLOW BUCKET BUNGEY CANNEL
PADDLE PONTON RADEAU STREEL
TOPPER CAISSON DRINGLE FLATTER
FLOTTER FRESHEN OROPESA PAGEANT
PLANKER PLUMMET PONTOON SLICKER
LEVITATE PICKOVER
(— AIMLESSLY) DRIFT
(— DELIGHTFULLY) COWD
(— FOR HERRING NET) BOWL
(— FOR RING BUOY) LEMON
(— LOGS) DRIVE
(— OF REEDS) KELEK LIGGER
(— PAST) GLACE
(— PROPERLY) WATCH
(CANOE —) AMA
(FISHLINE —) BOB CORK BOBBER
DOBBER TRIMMER
(PLASTERER'S —) DARBY
FLOATING FREE WAFT AWASH LOOSE
ADRIFT AFLOAT FLYING NATANT
BUOYANT FLYAWAY PENDENT DRIFTING
FLUITANT SHIFTING UNFUNDED
FLOCK MOB BAND BEVY GANG MANY
PACK ROUT SAIL SORT TRIP BROOD
BUNCH CROWD DRIFT DROVE FLAKE
FLECK GROUP PLUMP SHOAL SWARM
TROOP COVERT FLIGHT HIRSEL MANADA
MEINIE RAFTER SCHOOL SCURRY
COMPANY GOOSERY THICKEN
(— OF BIRDS) POD BANK HERD TEAM
WISP BROWN COVEY SEDGE SIEGE TRIBE
FLIGHT VOLERY
(— OF BITTERNS) SEDGE SIEGE
(— OF DUCKS) PADDLING
(— OF FINCHES) CHARM CHIRM
(— OF GEESE) SKEIN GAGGLE
(— OF HERONS) SEDGE SIEGE
(— OF LARKS) EXALTATION
(— OF LIONS) PRIDE
(— OF MALLARDS) SORD SUTE
(— OF NIGHTINGALES) WATCH
(— OF PARTRIDGE) COVEY
(— OF PEACOCKS) MUSTER
(— OF PIGEONS) KIT LOFT
(— OF PLOVER) WING
(— OF ROOKS) ROOKERY
(— OF SANDPIPERS) FLING
(— OF SHEEP) FOLD HIRSEL
(— OF SHELDRAKE) DOPPING
(— OF SNIPE) WISP
(— OF SWANS) BANK GAME MARK
(— OF TURTLE-DOVES) DOLE
(— OF WIDGEONS) COMPANY
(— OF WILDFOWL) SCRY SKEIN
(— TOGETHER) RAFT
(SMALL —) SPRING
FLOE PAN
FLOG CAT TAN TAW BEAT CANE CHOP
HIDE LASH LICK LUMP TOCO WALE
WARM WELK WHIP YANK BIRCH EXCEL
FIGHT FLAIL HORSE KNOUT LINGE QUILT
SAUCE SKEEG SWISH WHANG BREECH
COTTON LARRUP LATHER STRIKE
SWITCH THRASH WALLOP WATTLE
BALEISE BELABOR COWHIDE SCOURGE
SJAMBOK TROUNCE CARTWHIP

CHAWBUCK SLAISTER URTICATE
VAPULATE
FLOGGING TOCO TANNING BIRCHING
WHIPPING
FLOOD SEA BORE BUOY FLOW FLUX
POUR TIDE EAGRE FLOAT FLUSH SPATE
SWAMP SWILL WATER DELUGE EXCESS
RAVINE SLUICE SPLASH DEBACLE
FLOTTER FRESHET NIAGARA TORRENT
ALLUVION CATARACT INUNDATE
OVERFLOW SURROUND
FLOODED AWASH AFLOAT
FLOODLIGHT OLIVET
FLOOR BECK DROP FLAT LAND LOFT
PAVE SEAT BOARD FLOAT GRASS PIANO
PIECE SOLAR STAGE STORY BELFRY
FLIGHT GROUND SOLLAR PLANCHE
BARBECUE FLOORING HALFPACE
PAVEMENT SUBFLOOR
(— OF COAL MINE) SOLE THILL
(— OF COAL SEAM) SILL
(— OF FORGE) HEARTH
(— OF GLASS FURNACE) SIEGE
(— OF OCEAN) SEABED
(— OF SPORTS RING) CANVAS
(— OF WOOLSHED) BOARD
(FOREST —) SEEDBED
(GROUND —) TERRENO BASEMENT
(OPENWORK —S) GRATINGS
(RAISED —) LEEWAN HALFPACE
(THRESHING —) MOWSTEAD
FLOP DOG BOMB SWOP WHOP SQUAB
BUMMER TURKEY TRAGEDY
FLORID FINE HIGH BUXOM FRESH RUDDY
ORNATE ROCOCO RUBIED ASIATIC
FLOWERY TAFFETA BLOOMING FIGURATE
RUBICUND SANGUINE SPLENDID
VIGOROUS

FLORIDA

BAY: BISCAYNE APALACHEE
WACCASASSA
CAPITAL: TALLAHASSEE
COUNTY: BAY LEE DADE GULF LEON POLK
BAKER DIXIE HARDEE HENDRY NASSAU
ORANGE ALACHUA BREVARD BROWARD
MANATEE OSCEOLA VOLUSIA PINELLAS
SARASOTA
INDIAN: AIS OCALE UTINA CALUSA
CHATOT POTANO TIMUCUA SEMINOLE
KEY: WEST LARGO BISCAYNE
LAKE: DORA APOPKA HARNEY JESSUP
NEWNAN LEDWITH ARBUCKLE
KISSIMMEE OKEECHOBEE
NATIVE: CONCH CRACKER
RIVER: BANANA INDIAN AUCILLA
MANATEE SCAMBIA SUWANEE
OCHLAWAHA
STATE BIRD: MOCKINGBIRD
STATE NICKNAME: SUNSHINE
STATE TREE: PALMETTO
TOWN: TICE COCOA MIAMI OCALA TAMPA
ORLANDO PALATKA SEBRING SARASOTA
PENSACOLA

FLOSS FLUFF SKEIN WASTE CADDIS
SLEAVE CADDICE
FLOUNCE FLAP HUFF SKIT SLAM FLING
FRILL RUCHE PEPLUM RIPPLE ROBING
ROUNCE RUFFLE VOLANT FALBALA
FALBELO FROUNCE RUCHING FLOUNDER
FURBELOW STRUGGLE
FLOUNDER DAB GAD BUTT KEEL POLE
ROLL TOSS BREAM FLUKE SLOSH WITCH
WRELE GADOID GROVEL MEGRIM
MUDDLE PLAICE TOLTER TURBOT
WALLOP WALLOW WARSLE BLUNDER
FLASKER FLOUNCE PLOUNCE STUMBLE
SUNFISH TOPKNOT VAAGMAR
ANACANTH FLATFISH FOOLFISH
PLUNTHER SANDLING
FLOUR AMYL DUST HOVIS BINDER
CLEARS FARINA FLOWER PATENT
POLLEN SICKEN TSAMBA WHITES
BRAVURA CANAILLE
(— OF MALT) SMEDDUM
(COARSE —) THIRD CHISEL BOXINGS
CRIBBLE
(FINE —) CONES SUJEE
(LOW-GRADE —) TAIL
(PARTICLE OF —) CHOP
(POTATO —) FROW
(UNSORTED —) ATTA
FLOURISH TAG WAG BOOM BRAG FUSS
GROW LICK RIOT RISE SHOW TUCK
WAVE ADORN BLOOM BOAST CHEVE
GLOSS QUIRK REIGN SHAKE SWASH
SWING SWISH TUSCH VAUNT CATTER
PARADE PARAPH QUAVER SQUIRL
THRIVE BLOSSOM BURGEON CADENZA
DISPLAY ENLARGE FANFARE GAMBADE
GAMBADO PASSAGE PROSPER ROULADE
SUCCEED TRIUMPH WAMPISH ARPEGGIO
BRANDISH CURLICUE INCREASE
ORNAMENT SKIRMISH
(— OF BAGPIPE) WARBLER
(— OF TRUMPET) MORT SENNE₁
TUCKET
FLOURISHING FAR FRIM FRUM PERT
GREEN PALMY PEART VITAL BLOOMY
FLORID GOLDEN FLORENT HEALTHY
VERNANT THRIVING VEGETOUS
PROSPEROUS
FLOWER (ALSO SEE PLANT AND HERB)
BUD GAY BEST BLOW FLAG IRIS IXIA
PINK POLE POSY ROSE ARROW ASTER
BLOOM BLUET BREAK DAISY ELITE
FANCY FLOOR GOWAN LILAC PANSY
PHLOX TRUSS TULIP TUTTY AZALIA
CHOICE CORYMB CROCUS CYMULE
DAHLIA DATURA FLORET MAYPOP
ORCHID SCILLA SEASON SHOWER
SINGLE STEVIA UNFOLD AMELLUS
ANEMONE ARBUTUS BLETHIA BLOSSOM
BOSTRYX CAMPANA DEVELOP ESSENCE
FLEURET FLOSCLE GAZANIA GENTIAN
GERBERA IPOMOEA PETUNIA PICOTEE
TORENIA BELAMOUR CAMELLIA
CYCLAMEN DAFFODIL DIANTHUS
GARDENIA GERANIUM HEPATICA
HIBISCUS HYACINTH PRIMROSE
SPARAXIS

(— WITH 6 SEGMENTS) SEXFOIL
(COTTON —) SQUARE
(DEFORMED —) BULLHEAD
(DOUBLE —) BURSTER
(DRIED —S) BRAYERA
(IMAGINARY —) AMARANTH
(PART OF —) OVARY PETAL SEPAL
STALK STYLE ANTHER PISTIL STAMEN
STIGMA PEDICEL FILAMENT PEDUNCLE
PERIANTH RECEPTACLE
(SHOWY —) ORCHIS
(STRIPED —) BIZARRE
(UNFADING —) AMARANTH
FLOWERING AFLOWER FLOWERY
ANTHESIS BLOOMING
FLOWERY BLOWN BLOOMY FLORID
POSIED FLORENT PRIMROSE
FLOWING FAIR FLUX LAVE SIDE AFLOW
FLOAT FLUID FLUOR QUICK TIDAL
AFFLUX DEFLUX FLUENT FUSILE LIVING
COPIOUS CURRENT CURSIVE EMANANT
FLUXING FLUXION FLUXIVE RUNNING
SLIDING DEFLUENT DILUENDO FLUVIOSE
(— AT LOW SPEED) SLACK
(— BACK) EBB
(— IN) INFLUX INFLUENT INFLUXION
(— OF GLAZE) STREAMING
(— OF TIDE) FLOOD
(— OUT) ELAPSE EFFLUENT
(— SMOOTHLY) PROFLUENT
FLUCTUATE SWAY VARY VEER FLEET
SWING WAVER BALANCE VIBRATE
WAMPISH UNDULATE UNSTEADY
VACILLATE
FLUCTUATING WAVY HECTIC LABILE
RUBATO ERRATIC FLUXIVE WAYWARD
UNSTABLE UNSTEADY
FLUCTUATION CYCLE FADING JIGGLE
FLICKER FLUTTER VIBRATO OSCILLATION
(— IN LAKES) SEICHE
FLUE NET BARB DOWN OPEN PIPE THIN
VENT FLARE FLUFF FLUKE TEWEL
FUNNEL TUNNEL UPTAKE CHIMNEY
OUTTAKE PASSAGE DOWNTAKE
FLUENCY SKILL
FLUENT GASH GLIB FLUID READY FACILE
LIQUID SMOOTH STREAM COPIOUS
CURRENT FLOWING FLUIDIC RENABLE
VERBOSE VOLUBLE ELOQUENT FLIPPANT
FLUFFY SOFT DOWNY DRUNK FILMY
FLUEY FUZZY LIGHT LINTEN PLUFFY
FEATHERY UNSTEADY
(NOT —) CLOSE
FLUID INK SAP MASS RASA BLOOD FLUOR
HUMOR JUICE LATEX SPERM SWEAT
WATER FLUENT LIQUID WATERY
COOLANT FLOWING FLUIDE FLUXILE
GASEOUS SYNOVIA EMULSION FLOATING
FLUXIBLE FORESHOT PERSPERATION
(ANIMAL —) SERUM
(BODY —) CHYLE
(EAR —) PERILYMPH
(EGYPTIAN PRIMEVAL —) NU NUN
(ELECTRIC —) VRIL
(ETHEREAL —) ICHOR
(LIVER —) BILE
(LUBRICATING —) SYNOVIA

(MAMMARY —) MILK
(SOLDERING —) FAKE
(THICK VISCOUS —) GRUME
(WATERY —) LYE SANIES SEROSITY
(WORKING —) AIR
(PREF.) SERO
FLUNK BUST FAIL SKEW SPIN FLICKER
FLUNKY SNOB TOADY COOKEE JEAMES
   LACKEY FOOTMAN SERVANT STEWARD
FLURRY ADO FIT FACT FRET GUST PIRR
   SPIT STIR TEAR HASTE SKIFF SKIRL
   BOTHER BUSTLE SCURRY SQUALL
   CONFUSE FLUSKER FLUSTER FLUTTER
   FOOSTER SWITHER WHITHER SPITTING
FLUSH JET EVEN GLOW HUSH JUMP
   POOL ROSE BLOOM BLUSH COLOR ELATE
   FLASH FLUSK FRESH KNOCK LEVEL
   RAISE ROUGE SCOUR START VIGOR
   AFLUSH EXCITE HECTIC LAVISH MANTLE
   MORASS REDDEN RUDDLE SLUICE
   SPRING THRILL ANIMATE BOBTAIL
   CRIMSON SUFFUSE ABUNDANT
   AFFLUENT PRODIGAL ROSINESS
   (— GAME) SERVE
   (— IN SKY) SUNGLOW
   (NOT —) FLAT
FLUSHED RED ROSY BEAMY FIERY
   FLOWN FLORID FLUSHY HECTIC
   CRIMSON RUBICUND
FLUSTER PAVIE SHAKE BOTHER FLURRY
   FUDDLE MUDDLE POTHER RATTLE
   CONFUSE FLUSKER FOOSTER SWITHER
   BEFUDDLE FLOWSTER FLUSTRUM
FLUTE FIFE PIPE AULOS CRIMP CUENA
   PUNGI QUENA STICK STYKE TIBIA TWILL
   CANNEL DOUCET FLAUTO GEWGAW
   ZUFOLO CHAMFER DIAULOS FLAMFEW
   FLUTING HEMIOPE PICCOLO SIBILUS
   SIFFLOT TONETTE TRANGAM WHISTLE
   FLAUTINO MONAULOS RECORDER
   (— OF A COLUMN) STRIGA CHANNEL
   (CHINESE —) TCHE
   (EAST INDIAN —) MATALAN
   (EUNUCH —) KAZOO
   (JAPANESE —) FUYE SHAKUHACHI
   (LYDIAN —) MAGADIS
   (MOSLEM —) NAY
   (PHOENICIAN —) GINGRAS
   (PREF.) AUL(O)
FLUTTER BAT FAN FUG BATE BLOW
   BUZZ FLAP FLIT FLOW FLUE OOZE PLAY
   WAFF WAVE FLACK FLAFF FLARE FLECK
   FLICK FLOSS FLURR HOVER SHAKE
   WAVER BANGLE FLAUNT FLURRY RUFFLE
   SWIVEL WAFFLE WALLOP WINNOW
   FLACKER FLAFFER FLASKER FLATTER
   FLAUGHT FLICKER FLITTER FLUSKER
   SKIMMER WAGTAIL WHIFFLE FLICHTER
   SQUATTER VOLITATE
FLY FAG FAN HOP RUN FIRK FLEA FLEE
   FLEG FLIT FRIT KITE KIVU LASH LEAP
   MELT RACK SAIL SOLO WHEW WHIR
   WHIZ WIND WING ZIMB AGILE ALERT
   EMPID FLEET FLIER FLOAT FLURR FLUSH
   FLYER GLIDE LATCH MIDGE MUSCA
   OXFLY PERLA PHORA PILOT QUICK
   SHARP SKIRL STOUR WHAME WHIRR

ZEBUB ASILID AVIATE BLOWER BOTFLY
BREEZE DAYFLY ESCAPE FLIGHT FLYBOY
GADFLY GORFLY JARFLY LEPTID MOTUCA
NIMBLE PALMER PHORID PUNKIE
RANDON ROBBER SEPSID SEROOT
SPRING TIPULA TSETSE VANISH VERMIN
WINNOW AVIGATE AVOLATE BROMMER
CANOPID CHALCID CONOPID FORMATE
GRANNOM KNOWING LOVEBUG ORTALID
PYRALIS SCIARID TYRPHID AIRPLANE
BIBIONID BRACONID COACHMAN
DIPTERAN DROPPING EPHYDRID
EULOPHID GLOSSINA HOUSEFLY
HOUSEFLY RUBYTAIL SIMULIID TACHINID
TATUKIRA VOLITATE
(— AFTER GAME) RAKE
(— AIMLESSLY) BANGLE
(— ALOFT) SOAR TOWER
(— AWAY) CARRY
(— CLUMSILY) FLIGHTER
(— ERRATICALLY) GAD
(— INTO RAGE) FUFF RARE
(— LOW) DICE DRAG HEDGEHOG
(— NEAR THE GROUND) ACCOST
(— OUT) EXPIRE
(— RAPIDLY) SKIRR
(— TOO HIGH) SCUD
(— WIDE) MISS
(BITING —) PIUM
(FISHING —) BEE DUN OAK BUZZ GNAT
HARL HERL SMUT WASP ZULU ABBEY
ALDER BAKER FAIRY NYMPH SEDGE
BADGER BOBFLY CADDIS CAHILL
CANARY CLARET DOCTOR HACKLE
MILLER ORIOLE WILLOW BABCOCK
BUTCHER CADDICE COLONEL DROPPER
DUBBING GRANNOM HUZZARD SPINNER
WATCHED WATCHET BUCKTAIL
CATSKILL COACHMAN FERGUSON
GOVERNOR STREAMER WOODRUFF
WRENTAIL
(MAY —) DUN DRAKE
(SHEEP —) FAG KED
(STONE —) SALLY
FLYING DUTCHMAN, THE
   (CHARACTER IN —) ERIK SENTA
   DALAND
   (COMPOSER OF —) WAGNER
FLYING FISH SKIPPER VOLADOR
FLYING SQUIRREL TAGUAN ASSAPAN
FOAL CADE COLT FILLY PODDY SLEEPER
FOAM FOB SUD BARM BEES BOIL FUME
   HEAD KNIT REAM SCUD SCUM SUDS
   WORK CREAM FROST FROTH SPUME
   YEAST BUBBLE FLOWER FLURRY FREATH
   IMBOST LATHER SEETHE BLUBBER
   DESPUME MELDROP
FOAMY BARMY BEADY SPUMY SUDSY
   FROTHY SPUMOSE
FOCUS FIX PUT POINT PURSE TRAIN
   CENTER CLIMAX DIRECT FASTEN FIXATE
   HEARTH TEMPLE NUCLEUS CONVERGE
   FOCALIZE GANGLION
FODDER HAY FEED FOOD SOIL VERT
   GOOMA MANGE EATAGE FORAGE
   FOTHER PODDER SILAGE STOVER

FARRAGE PODWARE PROVAND
BROWSING ENSILAGE ROUGHAGE
FOE ENEMY FIEND RIVAL FOEMAN
HOSTILE OPPOSER OPPONENT
WRANGLER
FOG DAG RAG DAMP DAZE HAZE MIST
MOKE MOSS MURK PRIG RACK ROKE
SMOG SMUR SOUP BEDIM BRUME
CLOUD GRASS HUMOR MUDDY SMIRR
SPRAY STOUR VAPOR MUDDLE NEBULA
SALMON STUPOR FOGGAGE OBSCURE
POGONIP SMOTHER BEWILDER
MOISTURE
(— OF THE NILE) QOBAR
(FROZEN —) BARBER
(LIGHT —) GAUZE
(SEA —) HAAR
FOGGY DIM DULL HAZY MIRK MOKY
MURK ROKY DENSE DIRTY GROSS MISKY
MISTY MURKY ROOKY ROUKY SPEWY
CLOUDY GREASY GROGGY MARSHY
MILKEN SMURRY BRUMOUS MUDDLED
OBSCURE CONFUSED NUBILOUS
VAPOROUS
FOGHORN SIREN TYFON RIPPER
MEGAFOG
FOIBLE VICE FAULT FERLY FEEBLE
FAILING FRAILTY WEAKNESS
FOIL BACK BALK FILE FOIN SOIL BLADE
BLANK CHEAT ELUDE EVADE FALSE
STAIN STUMP SWORD TRACK TRAIL
BAFFLE BLENCH BOGGLE CHATON
DEFEAT DEFILE OFFSET OUTWIT STIGMA
STOOGE THWART BEGUILE FAILURE
FOILING FOLIATE LAMETTA PAILLON
POLLUTE REPULSE STONKER TRAMPLE
DISGRACE
(FENCING —) EPEE BLUNT FLORET
FLEURET
(PART OF —) END TIP BELL GRIP HILT
BLADE FORTE GUARD POINT BUTTON
FOIBLE HANDLE POMMEL MOUNTING
(POINTED —) TANG
(TIN —) TAIN
FOIST WISH FUDGE FATHER SUBORN
FOISTER SHOEHORN
FOLD BOW FLY LAP PEN PLY SET WAP
BEND COTE CREW CRUE DART FAIL FALX
FAUN FELD FLAP FURL HANK HOOD LIRK
LOOP RUCK RUGA SWAG TUCK WRAP
BREAK CLASP CRIMP CRISP CROZE
DRAPE FAULD FLAKE FLOCK FLYPE FRILL
GROIN LAYER PARMA PINCH PLAIT PLEAT
PLICA PRANK QUILL SINUS YIELD
BOUGHT BUCKLE COLLOP CREASE
CUTTLE DOUBLE ENFOLD FORNIX
FRENUM FURDLE GATHER GUSSET
HURDLE INFOLD LABIUM MANTLE PIPING
PLIGHT PUCKER RIMPLE RUMPLE WIMPLE
CAPSIZE CRINKLE CRUMPLE EMBRACE
ENVELOP FLEXION FLEXURE PINFOLD
PLACATE PLICATE REVERSE ROLLING
ROULEAU TURNING VALVULA CRIMPING
FLECTION FLITFOLD QUILLING SCAPULET
SPLENIUM SURROUND PLICATION
REPLICATE REFLECTION
(— CLOTH) RAG

(— DOWN) COLLAPSE
(— FOR CATTLE) BAWN
(— IN HOOD) SHOVE
(— INWARD) CRIMP
(— OF MEMBRANE) CRISTA
(— OF SKIN) APRON DEWLAP SHEATH
OMENTUM FORESKIN MESENTERY
(— ROCKS) DEFORM
(—S OF TOGA) SINUS
(CARDIAC —) CUSP
(GEOLOGICAL —) DIAPIR CLOSURE
EXOCLINE SYNCLINE MONOCLINE
(LOOSE —) LAPPET
(RESTRAINING —) FRENUM
(SHEEP —) REEVE
FOLDER KIT BOOK FILE FOLD ATLAS
COVER FOLIO BINDER CLEANER
HANDOUT LEAFLET STROKER PAMPHLET
FOLIAGE HERB SHADE GREENS LEAVES
SHROUD BOSCAGE GILLERY LEAFAGE
LEAFERY UMBRAGE FRONDAGE
GREENERY
FOLIO CASE ATLAS FOLIUM
FOLKSONG SON TONADA VOLKSLIED
FOLKSY HOMEY HOMESPUN
FOLLOW GO PAD SUE TAG COME COPY
HUNT NEXT SEEK SHAG TAIL TAKE TOUT
ADOPT AFTER CHASE DODGE ENSUE
SNAKE SPOOR TRACE TRACK TRAIL
TREAD ADHERE ATTEND DANGLE FOLLER
OCCUPY PURSUE RESULT SECOND
SHADOW SUIVEZ TAGGLE HOTFOOT
IMITATE OBSERVE PROFESS REPLACE
SUCCEED VALOUWE PRACTICE
SUPPLANT
(— A POINTER'S LEAD) BACK
(— IN SUCCESSION) VARY
(— INSIDIOUSLY) DOG
(— SCENT) ROAD CARRY
(— SLOWLY) DRAGGLE
(— THROUGH) PRESS
(— TRACK) SLEUTH
(— UP) SUE ATTEND
(— UPON) WAIT
FOLLOWER FAN IST SON APER BEAU
ZANY ADEPT CHELA GILLY BILDAR
COHORT DRIVEN ENSUER GILLIE GUDGET
KNIGHT LACKEY SEQUEL SUITOR SULTER
VOTARY ACACIAN ACOLYTE CARRIER
DEVOTEE EPIGONE FLATTER GRIFTER
POLIGAR PURSUER RETINUE SECTARY
SEQUENT SPANIEL SUPPOST TRAILER
ADHERENT DISCIPLE FAITHFUL FAVORITE
HENCHMAN MYRMIDON OBSERVER
OFFSIDER PARTISAN RETAINER
SECTATOR SERVITOR SATELLITE
PURSUIVANT
(— OF ART) BOHEMIAN
(— OF CELEBRITY) GROUPIE
(CAMP —) BUMMER GUDGET LASCAR
(CRANE —) SPOTTER
(SERVILE —) SLAVE LACKEY ANTHONY
(PL.) FOLK SECTA SEQUACES
FOLLOWING LAST NEXT SECT SUIT
AFTER FIRST SUANT TRACE TRAIN
BEHIND SEQUEL ENSUANT ENSUING
SEQUENT AUDIENCE BUSINESS

SECUNDUM SEGUENDO TRAILING
VOCATION

FOLLY ATE SIN RAGE LAPSE MORIA SOTIE
BETISE DOTAGE LUNACY NICETY
WANWIT DAFFERY DAFFING FOOLERY
FOPPERY IDIOTCY MADNESS MISTAKE
SOTTAGE UNSKILL FONDNESS
FOOLHEAD IDLENESS LEWDNESS
MOROLOGY NONSENSE RASHNESS
SURQUIDY UNTHRIFT UNWISDOM
WILLNESS WOODNESS SIMPLICITY

FOND TID DAFT DEAR DOTE FAIN FOOL
FUND KIND VAIN WEAK CRAZY SILLY
STOCK STORE ARDENT BEFOOL CARESS
CHOICE DEARLY DOTING FONDLE
FONDLY LOVING SIMPLE TENDER
AMATORY AMOROUS BEGUILE BROWDEN
FONDISH FOOLISH INSIPID PARTIAL
DESIROUS ENAMORED SANGUINE
TRIFLING UXORIOUS

FONDLE PET BABY BILL CLAP COAX
DAUT FOND NECK TICK DAUNT INGLE
NURSE WALLY CARESS COCKER CODDLE
COSSET CUDDLE CUTTER DANDLE
GENTLE KIUTLE MUZZLE PAMPER
SLAVER STROKE TANTLE TIDDLE
CHERISH FLATTER SMUGGLE TWATTLE
BLANDISH CANOODLE

FONDNESS GRA LOVE FANCY FOLLY
TASTE DOTAGE NOTION FEELING
DEARNESS WEAKNESS

FONT BILL FUND PILA BASIN FOUNT
SOURCE SPRING LAVACRE PISCINA
BENITIER DELUBRUM

FOOD BIT KAI SAP BAIT BITE BUNK CATE
CHIH CHOP CHOW CRAM DIET DISH EATS
FARE FARM FUEL GRUB HASH JOCK KAIL
KALE MEAT NOSH PECK PLAT PROG SALT
SOCK STEW TACK TOKE TUCK BREAD
BROMA CHUCK FLUFF FORAY GRILL
SCAFF SCOFF SCRAN TABLE THING
TREAT TRIPE APPAST BUTTER DODGER
DOINGS EATING FOSTER LIVING MAIGRE
MORSEL MUKTUK REFETE STOVER
SUNKET VIANDS VIVERS WRAITH
ALIMENT FAUSTER HANDOUT INGESTA
KEEPING NURTURE PABULUM PASTURE
PECKAGE PROVANT PULTURE EATABLES
FLUMMERY GRUBBERY NUTRIENT
PEMMICAN PROVIANT TRENCHER
VICTUALS PROVENDER NOURISHMENT
(— AND DRINK) BOUGE CHEER
LOWANCE
(— AND LIQUOR) GEAR
(— AND LODGING) FOUND EASEMENT
(— BANNED DURING PASSOVER)
HAMETZ
(— EATEN AS RELISH) KITCHEN
(— EATEN BETWEEN MEALS)
BAGGING
(— FOR ANIMALS) FODDER FORAGE
(— FOR CATTLE) BROWSE TACKLE
(— FROM KELP) KOMBU
(— IN SLICES) LEACH
(— IN STOCK) LARDER
(— NOT RITUALLY CLEAN) TEREPHAH
(— OF DUCK EGGS) BALUT

(— OF RUMINANTS) CUD
(— OF THE GODS) AMRITA AMBROSIA
(— OF WHALE) KRILL
(— OF WORKMEN) TOMMY
(— ON TABLE AT ONE TIME) MESS
(ASIATIC —) TEMPEH
(BEE —) CANDY
(COOKED —) CURY BAKEMEAT
(DAILY —) TUCKER
(EXTRA —) GASH
(FILLING —) STODGE
(FLAVORLESS —) HOGWASH
(GROUND —) DUST
(HAWAIIAN —) POI
(INDIGESTIBLE —) STODGE
(JAPANESE —) TERIYAKI
(LIQUID —) LAP SLOP SOUP GRUEL
LEBEN SUPPING
(LUXURIOUS —) CATE CATES JUNKET
(MIRACULOUS —) MANNA
(RICH —) CHEER
(SEMILIQUID —) SWILL
(SOFT —) PAP
(STARCHY —) AMYLOID
(TAPIOCA-LIKE —) SALEP
(WATERY —) SLIPSLOP

FOOL APE ASS BAM BOB COD CON DAW
DOR FON FOP FOX FUN GIG KID MUG NIT
NUP POT RIG SAP SOT TOY BULL BUTT
CAKE CHUB CLOT COLT DOLT DUPE
FOND GECK GOER GOFF GOOP GOWK
GYPE HARE HAVE HOIT JAPE JEST JOKE
JOSH MOME MUCK NIZY POOP RACA
RACH SIMP TONY TOOT TWIT ZANY
BLIND BLUFF BUFFO CHUMP CLOWN
DALLY FUNGE GALAH GLAIK GOOSE
GREEN HORSE IDIOT KNAVE MORON
NINNY NIZEY NODDY PATCH PATSY
SAMMY SCREW SILLY SNIPE SPOOF
STICK STIFF STIRK TOMMY TRICK
BUFFLE COUSIN CUCKOO CUDDEN
DELUDE DIMWIT DISARD DOTARD
DOTTLE FOLEYE FOOTER GAMMON
JESTER MOTLEY MUCKER MUSARD
NIDGET NIMSHI NINCOM NUPSON
SAWNEY SHMUCK STRING TAMPER
WITTOL ASINEGO BECASSE BUFFOON
COXCOMB DAGONET DECEIVE DIZZARD
FATHEAD FOOLISH FRIBBLE GOMERAL
GOMERIL HAVERAL JACKASS LACKWIT
MADLING MISLEAD NATURAL OMADAWN
PINHEAD PLAYBOY SCHMUCK STOOKIE
TOMFOOL WANTWIT WITLING ABDERITE
BADINAGE DRIVELER FONDLING
HOODWINK IMBECILE MONUMENT
OMADHAUN TOMNODDY NINCOMPOOP
(— AROUND) JIVE SKYLARK LALLYGAG
(— AWAY) FRIBBLE
(BORN —) MOONCALF
(LEARNED —) MOROSOPH
(NATURAL —) INNOCENT

FOOLHARDY RASH BRASH FOOLATUM

FOOLISH FAT SOT BETE DAFT DUMB
FOND FOOL GAGA GYPE IDLE MADE NICE
RASH SOFT VAIN VOID WEAK ZANY
BALMY BARMY BATTY BOGGY BUGGY
DILLY DIPPY DIZZY DOILT EMPTY FONNE

GAWKY GOOFY GOOSY INANE INEPT
JERKY LOONY NODDY POTTY SILLY
SAWNY SCREW SEELY SILLY YAPPY
ABSURD CUDDEN DOTISH DOTTLE
FONDLY GLAKED GOTHAM GOWKIT
HARISH INSANE MOMISH MOPISH
SHANNY SIMPLE SLIGHT SOFTLY
SPOONY STOLID STULTY STUPID TAWPIE
UNWISE VACANT ASININE DAMFOOL
DOLTISH ETOURDI FANGLED FATUOUS
FLIGHTY FOLLIAL FOPPISH GLAIKIT
GOOSISH GULLISH IDIOTIC PEEVISH
PUERILE SOTTISH TOMFOOL UNWITTY
WANTWIT WITLESS ABDERIAN FOOTLING
FOPPERLY HEADLESS HEEDLESS
HIGHLAND IMBECILE SENSELESS
(PREF.) STULT(I)
FOOLISHNESS JAZZ PUNK FOLLY
BARNEY BUNKUM FADDLE LEVITY
LUNACY RUBBLE VANITY FATUITY
PORANGI BUNCOMBE FONDNESS
INSANITY TOMMYROT ABSURDITY
SAPPINESS
FOOT FIT PAT PEG PES BASE COOT FUSS
GOER HEEL PIED SOLE TAIL BASIS PIECE
BOTTOM CLUTCH GAMMON PATTEN
PODIUM RHYTHM TOOTSY TRILBY
WALKER FOOTING GAMBONE MEASURE
METREME PEDICEL FOREFOOT
(— OF ANIMAL) PAD PAW HOOF
TROTTER
(— OF APE) HAND
(— OF INSECT) TARSUS
(— OF WINE GLASS) MULE
(CHINESE —) CHEK CHIH
(HALF —) SEMIPED
(LARGE AWKWARD —) CAVE
(METRIC —) IAMB BASIS DIAMB IONIC
PAEAN CHOREE DACTYL DIIAMB IAMBUS
SYZYGY ANAPEST BACCHIC PYRRHIC
SPONDEE TROCHEE ANAPAEST
BACCHIUS CHORIAMB DOCHMIUS
EPITRITE MOLOSSUS TRIBRACH
TRIMACER
(STEWED OX —) COWHEEL
(TUBE —) SUCKER
FOOTING PAR FOOT TROD BASIS EARTH
TRACK HEADING PIECING TOEHOLD
FOOTHOLD
FOOTMAN SKIP FLUNKY JEAMES
LACKEY VARLET DOORMAN FOOTPAD
BOTTOMER CHASSEUR HIRCARRA
WAGONMAN
FOOTPATH LANE TROD JETTY SENDA
TRAIL FOOTWAY HIGHWAY PARAPET
RAMPIRE SIDEWALK TROTTOIR
(— TO A PASTURE) DRUNG
(RAISED —) CLAPPER
FOOTPRINT PAD PUG STEP TROD PRICK
SPOOR TRACE TRACK TRADE TREAD
FOOTING ICHNITE PUGMARK FOOTMARK
FOP ADON BEAU BUCK DUDE DUPE FOOL
KNUT PRIG TOFF DANDY FLASH PUPPY
MASHER MOPPET VANITY COXCOMB
JESSAMY GIMCRACK MACARONI
MACAROON MUSCADIN POPINJAY
SKIPJACK

FOPPISH APISH DANDY FOPPY SAPPY
SILLY DAPPER PRETTY SPRUCE STUPID
BEAUISH BUCKISH FANGLED FINICAL
FOOLISH DANDYISH SKIPJACK
FOR IN TO PRO VER TILL SINCE FORWHY
BECAUSE FORNENT FAVORING
(— A LONG TIME) YORE
(— CASH) SPOT
(— EXAMPLE) EG VG
(— FEAR THAT) LEST
(— INSTANCE) AS SAY
(— THE EMERGENCY) PRN
(— THE MOST PART) FECKLY
GENERALLY
(— TIME BEING) ACTUALLY
FORAGE ERS OAT RYE CORN GUAR MAST
PROG RAID ETAPE FORAY BREVIT
RUSSUD ZACATE GOITCHO HAYLAGE
PICKEER BOOTHALE SCROUNGE
FORAY RAID MELEE CREAGH FURROW
INROAD MARAUD RAVAGE RAZZIA
SORTIE CHAPPOW HERSHIP PILLAGE
SPREAGH SPREATH
FORBID BAN BAR NIX DEFY DENY FEND
TABU VETO WARN DEBAR TABOO
BANISH DEFEND ENJOIN IMPEDE OPPOSE
REFUSE SHIELD FORFEND FORWARN
GAINSAY INHIBIT WITHSAY DISALLOW
FORSPEAK PRECLUDE PROHIBIT
PROSCRIBE
FORBIDDING DOUR GRIM HARD BLACK
GAUNT STERN FIERCE GLASSY GLOOMY
GRISLY ODIOUS STRICT FORBODE
GRIZZLY REPULSIVE
FORCE GAR GUT HAP JAM LID VIM VIS
ZIP BANG BEAR BEAT BEND BIRR BODY
CLIP CRAM DINT DOOM DRAG EDGE FECK
FOSS GRIP GUTS HEAD JAMB JINX MAIN
MAKE MANA SNAP SOCK ABATE AGENT
ARDOR BRAWL BRING BRUSH CLAMP
COACT CRAFT CROWD CRUSH DEMON
DRAFT DRIVE EXACT EXERT FOHAT
GAVEL IMPEL KARMA MIGHT PAINT
PEISE POACH POINT POWER PRESS PRIZE
PUNCH REPEL SHEAR SHOVE SINEW
STEAM STUFF THROW WAKAN WREST
CHARGE COERCE COMPEL CUDGEL
DURESS EFFECT EFFORT ENERGY EXTORT
HIJACK HOTBED IMPACT IMPOSE JOSTLE
OBLIGE POWDER RAVISH SHAKTI STRAIN
STRESS WRENCH ABILITY AFFORCE
BLUSTER CASCADE COGENCY CONCUSS
DYNAMIC IMPETUS IMPRESS IMPULSE
LASHKAR OPPRESS REQUIRE SQUEEZE
TORMENT VIOLATE WAKANDA ACTIVITY
ADHESION AFFINITY BULLDOZE
COACTION COERCION DYNAMISM
EFFICACY HOTHOUSE MOMENTUM
PRESSURE STRENGTH VALIDITY
VIOLENCE VIRILITY NECESSITATE
(— AIR UPON) BLOW
(— AN ENTRANCE) RANDOM THRUST
(— APART) SUNDER DISPART
(— BACK) REPEL RAMBARRE
(— BY THREAT) SWAGGER
(— DOWN) CLEW CLUE DETRUDE
DISMOUNT

(— IN) INJECT INTRUDE
(— OPEN) BURST JIMMY SPORT RANFORCE
(— OUT) SPEW EJECT ERUPT EVICT EXPEL KNOCK WRING EXTUND EXPRESS
(— PASSAGE) SQUEEZE
(— WAY) CROWD WREST WRING
(— WITH LEGAL AUTHORITY) POSSE
(ALLEGED —) OD
(ARMED —) CREW HEAD POWER CONREY ARMAMENT BATTALIA
(CONCENTRATED —) PITH
(CONFINING —) LID
(CONSTRAINING —) STRESS
(COSMIC —) EVIL
(CREATIVE —) NATURE
(DRIVING —) STEAM SWINGE
(EVOLUTIONARY —) BATHMISM
(EXPLOSIVE —) MEGATON
(HYPOTHETICAL —) FORTUNE
(LIFE —) SHAKTI
(MAIN —) BRUNT
(MILITANT —) SWORD
(MILITARY —) FYRD LEGION WERING BAYONET OCCUPATION
(NAVAL —) FLEET
(PHYSICAL —) NERVE
(PREPONDERATING —) SWAY
(PROTECTIVE —) CONVOY
(RELIGIOUS —) SANCTITY
(SACRED —) KAMI
(SPIRITUAL —) SOUL
(UNRESTRAINED —) FURY
(UPWARD —) BUOYANCY
FORCEFUL RUDE GREAT GUTSY PITHY STIFF STOUT MIGHTY PUNCHY STRONG VIRILE DYNAMIC STHENIC VIOLENT BRUISING ELOQUENT EMPHATIC ENFATICO FORCIBLE VIGOROUS TRENCHANT
FORD PASS RACK RIFT WADE WATH DRIFT STREAM CURRENT FORDING PASSAGE PASSING CROSSING
FORE VAN WAY AFORE AHEAD FRONT PRIOR FORMER FURTHER
FOREBODE BODE GIVE OMEN ABODE AUGUR CROAK BETIDE DIVINE BETOKEN MISBODE OMINATE PORTEND PREDICT PRESAGE FORETELL
FOREBODING OMEN BLACK FATAL AUGURY BODING DISMAL GLOOMY ANXIETY BALEFUL BANEFUL DRUTHER OMINOUS PRESAGE BODEMENT SINISTER ABODEMENT PROGNOSTICATION
FORECAST BODE CAST SCHEME CAUTION FORESEE FORESET PREDICT FOREDEEM FOREDOOM FORETELL PROPHESY ADUMBRATE PREVISION PROGNOSIS PREDICTION PROGNOSTICATION
FOREFATHER AYEL SIRE ELDER PITRI PARENT ANCESTOR FOREBEAR PROGENITOR PRIMOGENITOR
FOREGOING PAST ABOVE ANTERIOR PREVIOUS PRECEDING
FOREHEAD BROW FRONS FRONT FRONTLET SINCIPUT

FOREIGN UNCO ALIEN FREMD WELSH ALANGE EXILED EXOTIC FRENCH REMOTE UNKIND DISTANT ECDEMIC EPIGENE EXCLUDE FRAMMIT HEATHEN OUTBORN OUTLAND OUTWARD STRANGE BARBARIC EPIGENIC EXTERIOR EXTERNAL FORINSEC OVERSEAS PEREGRIN STRANGER BARBAROUS OUTLANDISH TRAMONTANE
FOREIGNER ALIEN HAOLE ALLTUD GRINGO PAKEHA GREENER OUTBORN OUTLAND PARDESI ETRANGER OUTSIDER PEREGRIN PORTUGEE STRANGER OUTLANDER
FOREMAN BOSS BULL CORK JOSS LUNA PUSH CHIEF DOGGY BUNTER GAFFER GANGER LEADER RAMROD SIRDAR TENTER CAPATAZ CAPORAL CAPTAIN FOUNDER HEADMAN MANAGER MANDOER OVERMAN SHOOFLY SKIDDER STEWARD FOREHAND GANGSMAN OVERSEER
(— OF JURY) CHANCELLOR
FOREMOST TOP HEAD HIGH MAIN CHIEF FIRST FORME FRONT GRAND BANNER FORMER LEADING RANKING SUPREME VANMOST CHAMPION
FORERUNNER OMEN SIGN USHER AUGURY HERALD ANCESTOR FOREGOER FOURRIER OUTRIDER PRODROME MESSENGER PRECURSOR
FORESEE SEE READ DIVINE PURVEY PREVISE PROVIDE ENVISAGE ENVISION FORECAST FOREKNOW PROSPECT PREFIGURE
FORESHADOW HINT FIGURE HERALD FORERUN PATTERN PRELUDE PRESAGE UMBRATE FORETYPE ADUMBRATE
FORESIGHT FEAR VISION FOREWIT FORECAST FORELOOK PROSPECT PRUDENCE
FOREST BUSH GAPO MATA RUKH WOLD WOOD GLADE GUBAT MATTO MONTE SYLVA TAIGA WASTE WEALD JUNGLE TIMBER BOSCAGE CALYDON COPPICE WOODLAND
(— FOR DEER) FIRTH
(IMMENSE —) MONTANA
(RAIN —) SELVA
(SIBERIAN —) URMAN
(STUNTED —) CAATINGA KRUMMHOLZ
FORESTALL BEAT HELP LURCH STALL DEVANCE FORERUN OBVIATE PREVENE PREVENT FORSTEAL ANTICIPATE
FORETASTE GUST TEASER EARNEST HANDSEL ANTEPAST PROSPECT PRELIBATION
FORETELL BODE ERST READ SPAE AUGUR INSEE WEIRD WRITE DIVINE HALSEN HERALD BESPEAK FORESAY PORTEND PREDICT PRESAGE ANNOUNCE FOREBODE FORECAST FORESHOW PROPHESY SOOTHSAY
FORETHOUGHT CAUTION FORECAST PREPENSE PRUDENCE
FORETOKEN OMEN AUGUR PORTEND

PROMISE FORECAST FORESHOW
FORESIGN
FOREVER AY AKE AYE EVER ETERN
ALWAYS ETERNE ENDLESS ETERNITY
EVERMORE
FOREWORD PROEM PREFACE PREAMBLE
FORFEIT WED FINE LOSE TINE WITE
CHEAT CRIME DEDIT FORGO LAPSE
FOREGO SCONCE DEFAULT ESCHEAT
FORWORK PENALTY FORFAULT
FORFEITURE FINE BLIND MULCT TINSEL
ESCHEAT FORFEIT PENALTY
FORGE MINT TILT WELL CLICK FALSE
FEIGN SMITH STOVE HAMMER SMITHY
STEADY STITCH STITHY SWINGE
CHAFERY FALSIFY FASHION BLOOMERY
FORGED BOGUS SPURIOUS
FORGER SMITH FALSER FALSARY
LEVERMAN
FORGERY SHAM FALSUM FICTION
BLOOMERY
FORGET LOSE OMIT WANT FLUFF BILEVE
UNKNOW UNMIND NEGLECT OVERLOOK
FORGETFUL OBLIVIOUS
FORGETFULNESS SWIM FLUFF LETHE
AMNESIA AMNESTY OBLIVION
(PREF.) LETHO
FORGIVE REMIT SPARE ASSOIL EXCUSE
PARDON ABSOLVE CONDONE OVERLOOK
FORGIVING GRACE HUMANE CLEMENT
MERCIFUL MAGNANIMOUS
FORGOTTEN DERELICT UNMINDED
FORK CROC EVIL HOOK TANG TINE CLEFT
CLOFF FURCA GLACK GRAIN GRAIP
PRONG TWIST BISECT BRANCH CLITCH
CROTCH DIVIDE FEEDER GAFFLE HACKER
OFFSET TWISEL BIPRONG FOURCHE
FRUGGIN HAYFORK TOASTER CROTCHET
EQUULEUS GRAINING PITCHFORK
(— OF BODY) SHARE
(— OF PENNON) FANON
(— OF WINDPIPE) BRONCHUS
(MEAT —) TORMENTOR
(THATCHER'S —) GROM
(TUNING —) DIAPASON
(PREF.) FURCI
FORKED BIFID FORKY FURCAL PRONGY
DIVIDED FURCATE LITUATE BIFORKED
BIRAMOUS BRANCHED FOURCHEE
SUBBIFID
FORLORN LORN LOST REFT ALONE
ABJECT FORFAIRN FORSAKEN HELPLESS
HOPELESS PITIABLE WITLOSEN
FORM AME DIG FIG HEW HUE SET BLEE
BODY CASE CAST CAUL DOME FLOW
GARB IDEA KERN KITE MAKE MODE
MOLD PLAN RITE SEAT THEW TURN
BENCH BLANK BLOCK BOARD BUILD
BUNCH CHART CHECK CRUSH DUMMY
EIDOS ERECT FORGE FORMA FORME
FRAME GALBE GUISE IMAGE MATCH
MEUSE MODEL SHAPE SPELL STAMP
THROW USAGE ADJUST CHALAN
COUPON CREATE CUSTOM DEVISE
DOCKET FIGURE FILLER HANGER INVENT
MANNER REMOVE RITUAL SCHEMA
SCHOOL SPONGE STRIKE SYSTEM TAILLE

AGENDUM ARRANGE COMPOSE CONFECT
CONTOUR DEVELOP FASHION FEATURE
FORMULA GESTALT IMPANEL INVOICE
LITURGY MAKEDOM OUTLINE PATTERN
PORTRAY PORTURE PRODUCE PROFILE
SPECIES STATURE BILLHEAD CEREMONY
COMPOUND CONCEIVE CONTRIVE
FORMWORK INSTRUCT LIKENESS
MODALITY ORGANIZE SEMBLANCE
(— A HEAD) POME
(— A NETWORK) PLEX
(— A RING) ENVIRON
(— ASSUMED AFTER DEATH)
KAMARUPA
(— BRANCHES) BREAK
(— BY CUTTING OFF) ABJOINT
(— CONNECTION) ALLY
(— FOR BELL FOUNDING) SWEEP
(— FOR CONCRETE) BOXING
(— FOR HOLDING BARREL) SQUAW
(— FOR MOLD) JACKET
(— FOR PRESSING VENEERS) CAUL
(— FRUIT) KNIT
(— INTO A CHAIN) CATENATE
(— INTO BALL) CONGLOBE
(— INTO RINGLETS) CRISP
(— LEATHER) CRIMP
(— MOUND) TUMP
(— OF GOVERNMENT) ESTATE
KINGSHIP
(— OF PREDICATION) CATEGORY
(— POLITICAL SUCCESSION) CAVE
(— WITH PLASTER) RUN
(— YARN INTO THREAD) CABLE
(ANCESTRAL —) BLASTAEA STEMFORM
(CONVENTIONAL —) AMENITY
(DEXTROROTATORY —) CAMPHOR
(DISPLAY —) MANNEQUIN
(IMPERFECT —) SEMIFORM
(IRREGULAR —) PSEUDOMORPH
(ISOMETRIC —) DIPLOID
(LINGUISTIC —) FOSSIL GERUND
(LITERARY —) KNACK
(LYRICAL —) SESTINA
(MUSICAL —) RAGA SUITE
(POETIC —) CINQUAIN
(POINTED —) ANGLE
(SCHOOL —) SHELL
(SHOE —) LAST FILLER
(SHORTENED —) ABBREVIATION
(SONG —) BAR
(SPECTRAL —) SHADOW
(SPEECH —) LEXEME IDIOLECT
(SPIRAL OR CIRCULAR —) GYRE
(STRUCTURE —) MORPHOLOGY
(TOP —) GROOVE
(VERB —) FUTURE CONATIVE DEFINITE
DURATIVE
(VERSE —) EPODE BALLAD PANTUM
SONNET KYRIELLE LIMERICK
(VISIBLE —) RUPA
(WILD —) AGRIOTYPE
(WORD —) ETYMON ANOMALY
FORMAL DRY SET BOOK PRIM BUDGE
CHILL COURT EXACT STIFF SOCIAL
SOLEMN STOCKY ANGULAR BOOKISH
LOGICAL NOMINAL ORDERLY OUTWARD

PRECISE REGULAR SOLWARD STARCHY
STATELY STILTED ABSTRACT ACADEMIC
AFFECTED ELEVATED FORMULAR
OFFICIAL PUNCTUAL STARCHED

FORMALITY FORM SASINE STARCH
BUCKRAM DECENCY WIGGERY
CEREMONY PHARISAISM

FORMAT SIZE GETUP SHAPE STYLE

FORMATION FORM RANK SPUR BIOME
FLIGHT GROWTH HARROW MASSIF
SPREAD POTENCE BOTRYOID
(— ENCLOSING MINE WORKING)
GROUND
(— ENCOUNTERED IN DRILLING)
STRAY
(— OF BRAIN) FORNIX
(— OF BRANCHES) CANOPY
(— OF CRYSTAL) SHOOT
(— OF JOINT) ANKYLOSIS
(— OF PLANES) JAVELIN
(— ON TOAD) SPADE
(— RESEMBLING ICICLE) STIRIA
(BATTLE —) HERSE
(CLOUD —) NUBECULA
(DANCE —) SET
(DIAGONAL —) HARROW
(DRIPSTONE —) COLUMN
(ECOLOGICAL —) BIOME
(FLIGHT —) SQUADRON
(FOOTBALL —) SHOTGUN WISHBONE
(GEOLOGIC —) BOEL CULM CHICO
STRAY MARKER MEDINA CURTAIN
MANLIUS MATAWAN POTOMAC TERRAIN
AQUIFUGE FERNANDO KOOTENAI
LOCKPORT TOPATOPA YORKTOWN
(HABIT —) FIXATION
(INDENTED —) CLEFT
(INFANTRY —) TERTIA ECHELON
(LAND —) BOOTHEEL
(MILITARY —) SNAIL FLIGHT
(NAVAL —) SCREEN
(POINTED —) BEAK

FORMER DIE OLD ERER ERST FERN FORE
LATE ONCE PAST ELDER FORME GAUGE
GUIDE MAKER OTHER PRIOR BYGONE
RATHER WHILOM ANCIENT ANOTHER
CREATOR EARLIER FIRSTER FURTHER
ONETIME PRIDIAN QUONDAM TEMPLET
UMWHILE PRETERIT PREVIOUS PRISTINE
SOMETIME STRICKLE UMQUHILE
PRECEDING

FORMERLY ERE NEE OLD ERST FORE
ONCE THEN YORE GRAVE WHILOM
WHILST ONETIME QUONDAM SOMETIME
UMQUHILE

FORMIDABLE MEAN FEARFUL
ALARMING DREADFUL MENACING
TERRIBLE FEROCIOUS REDOUBTABLE

FORMLESS ARUPA DOUGHY ANIDIAN
CHAOTIC DEFORMED INDIGEST

FORMOSA (SEE TAIWAN)

FORMULA LAW MIX DATE FIAT FORM
RULE CANON CREED DHIKR GRAPH INDEX
LURRY KEKULE MANTRA METHOD RECIPE
THEORY RECEIPT APOLYSIS CLAUSULE
DOXOLOGY EXORCISM
(— OF FAITH) KELIMA

(MAGICAL —) CARACT
(WORD —) PATERNOSTER

FORMULATE PUT CAST DRAW FRAME
DEVISE CAPSULE COMPOSE FORMULE
PLATFORM

FORSAKE DENY DROP FLEE QUIT SHUN
ABAND AVOID LEAVE WAIVE DEFECT
DEPART DESERT FOREGO FORHOO
FORLET REFUSE REJECT ABANDON
DISCARD FORLESE DESOLATE RENOUNCE
WITHDRAW

FORSAKEN LORN FORLORN DESERTED
DESOLATE

FORSYTE SAGA (AUTHOR OF —)
GALSWORTHY
(CHARACTER IN —) JON VAL JUNE
MONT FLEUR HOLLY IRENE JOLLY MONTY
DARTIE JOLYON PHILIP SOAMES
ANNETTE FORSYTE LAMOTTE MICHAEL
PROFOND PROSPER SWITHIN TIMOTHY
BOSINNEY WINIFRED

FORT PA DUN PAH LISS PEEL SPUR WORK
COTTA REDAN CASTLE SANGAR SCHERM
SCONCE STRONG BASTION BULWARK
CITADEL CLOSURE REDOUBT BASTILLE
CASTILLO FASTHOLD FASTNESS
FORTRESS MARTELLO PRESIDIO
(FAIRY —) LIS LIOS LISS SHEE SIDHE
(HILL —) RATH
(RUINS OF —) ZIMBABWE
(SMALL —) GURRY FORTIN BASTIDE
FORTLET FORCELET

FORTHRIGHT BALD BURLY GUTTY
CANDID

FORTHWITH EFT NOW ANON AWAY
BEDENE DIRECT BETIMES FORTHON
DIRECTLY

FORTIFICATION BAWN BOMA FORT
MOAT WALL REDAN TOWER ABATIS
CASHEL CASTLE GLACIS LAAGER
BASTION BULWARK CITADEL DEFENCE
DEFENSE PARAPET PILLBOX RAMPART
RAVELIN REDOUBT FORTRESS MUNITION
RONDELLE STRENGTH
(LINE OF —S) TROCHA
(PART OF —) BERM MOAT ANGLE
DITCH FLANK GORGE SCARP SLOPE
COVERT ESCARP GLACIS PARADE
BASTION CURTAIN PARAPET RAMPART
SALIENT BANQUETTE TERREPLEIN
COUNTERSCARP.

FORTIFY ARM MAN BANK FORT LINE
WALL WARD FENCE SPIKE STANK
BATTLE IMMURE MUNIFY MUNITE
BULWARK COMFORT DEFENSE GARNISH
RAMPIRE BASTILLE EMBATTLE FORTRESS
RAMFORCE STOCKADE

FORTITUDE GRIT GUTS SAND FIBER
NERVE PLUCK METTLE BRAVERY
COURAGE HEROISM STAMINA BACKBONE
PATIENCE STRENGTH

FORTRESS (ALSO SEE FORT) BURG
KEEP PIECE PLACE ROCCA CASBAH
CASTLE ALCAZAR BARRIER BOROUGH
CASTRUM CHATEAU CITADEL KREMLIN
ZWINGER ALCAZAVA BASTILLE
FASTNESS STRENGTH

FORTUITOUS CASUAL CHANCE RANDOM
  FORTUNEL
FORTUNATE EDI FAT HAP SRI GOOD
  WELL CANNY FAUST HAPPY LUCKY
  RIGHT WHITE DEXTER EUROUS BLESSED
  FAVORED WEIRDLY GRACIOUS
FORTUNE DIE HAP LOT URE BAHI FALL
  FARE FATE HAIL LUCK PILE SEEL STAR
  EVENT GRACE ISSUE LINES WEIRD
  WHATE CHANCE ESTATE MISHAP RICHES
  WEALTH DESTINY SUCCESS THEEDOM
  VENTURE ACCIDENT CASUALTY FELICITY
  STOCKING
  (GOOD —) SELE SONSE SPEED THRIFT
  FURTHER GOODHAP BONCHIEF FELICITY
  (ILL —) DOOM THRAW
FORTUNE-TELLER SEER SIBYL
  SPAEMAN SORTIARY SPAEWIFE
FORUM COURT PLATFORM TRIBUNAL
FORWARD ON TO AID BOG BUG GAY
  ABET BAIN BOLD FORE FREE HELP PERT
  SEND SHIP STEP AHEAD ALONG AVANT
  BARDY BRASH CAGER EAGER FAVOR
  FORTH FRACK FRECK FRONT HASTY
  PAWKY PUSHY RANDY READY RELAY
  REMIT SAUCY SERVE SPACK ULTRA
  AFFORD ARDENT AVAUNT BEFORE
  BRIGHT COMING DEVANT FORRIT
  FORTHY HASTEN NUZZLE ONWARD
  PROMPT ROUDAS SECOND TOWARD
  ADVANCE BETIMES EARNEST EXTREME
  FURTHER PROMOTE PUSHING RADICAL
  SOLICIT ADELANTE ARROGANT
  FROMWARD IMMODEST IMPUDENT
  MALAPERT ONCOMING PERVERSE
  PETULANT TELLSOME TOWARDLY
  TRANSMIT OBTRUSIVE
FOR WHOM THE BELL TOLLS
  (AUTHOR OF —) HEMINGWAY
  (CHARACTER IN —) MARIA PABLO
  PILAR JORDAN ROBERT ANSELMO
FORZA DEL DESTINO, LA
  (CHARACTER IN —) CARLO ALVARO
  LEONORA CALATRAVA
  (COMPOSER OF —) VERDI
FOSTER REAR NURSE COCKER HARBOR
  NUZZLE SUCKLE CHERISH DEPOSIT
  EMBOSOM GRATIFY INDULGE NOURISH
  NOURSLE NURTURE BEFRIEND
  CULTIVATE
FOUL BAD BASE EVIL HORY RANK ROIL
  VILE BAWDY BLACK DIRTY DITCH FUNKY
  GRIMY GURRY HORRY KETTY LOUSY
  MUDDY MUSTY NASTY RUSTY SULLY
  WEEDY CLARTY DEFAME DIRTEN DREGGY
  FILTHY GREASY IMPURE MALIGN ODIOUS
  PUTRID ROTTEN SOILED SORDID UNFAIR
  VIROSE ABUSIVE BEASTLY DEFACED
  FULSOME HATEFUL ILLEGAL IMBROIN
  NOISOME OBSCENE PROFANE SLOTTER
  SMEARED SQUALID TETROUS UNCLEAN
  VICIOUS AMURCOUS ENTANGLE
  FECULENT INDECENT MEPHITIC
  SLOTTERY STAGNANT STINKING
  TRAUCHLE WRETCHED
FOULMOUTHED RIBALD ROUDAS
  ABUSIVE OBSCENE PROFANE

FOUNDATION BED BASE BODY FIRM
  FOND FUND GIST ROOT SILL SOLE BASIS
  FOUND STOCK STOOL ANLAGE BOTTOM
  CRADLE GROUND LEGACY MATRIX
  PODIUM RIPRAP BEDDING BEDROCK
  CHANTRY COLLEGE MORTISE PINNING
  RADICAL ROADBED SUBBASE WARRANT
  BACKBONE DONATION MATTRESS
  MIREPOIX PEDESTAL PLATFORM
  STANDARD UNDERLAY
  (— FOR WIG) CAUL
  (— OF BASKET) SLATH
  (FLOATING —) CRIB
  (LACE —) RESEAU
  (PRECARIOUS —) STILT
FOUNTAIN URN AQUA FOND HEAD KELD
  PANT PILA SYKE WELL DIRCE FOUNT
  GURGE QUELL SURGE ORIGIN PHIALE
  PIRENE SOURCE SPRING BUBBLER
  CONDUIT SPRUDEL AGANIPPE SALMACIS
  UPSPRING WELLHEAD
  (INK —) DUCT
  (SODA —) SPA
  (PREF.) PEGO
  (SUFF.) CRENE
FOUR MESS CATER DELTA DALETH
  FEOWER TETRAD QUARTET QUATRAL
  MURNIVAL QUADRATE
  (— OF ANYTHING) GUNDA
  (— OF TRUMPS) TIDDY
  (— TIMES A DAY) QD QID
  (— YEAR PERIOD) PYTHIAD
  (GROUP OF —) TETRAD
FOUR HORSEMEN OF APOCALYPSE
  (AUTHOR OF —) IBANEZ
  (CHARACTER IN —) JULIO CHICHI
  MARCELO DESNOYER HARTROTT
FOWL HEN RED COCK GAME GRIG JAVA
  ROCK SLIP BIDDY CHUCK CLUCK COPPY
  DUMPY MALAY MANOC MARAN SILKY
  ANCONA ASHURA BANTAM BRAHMA
  CAMBAR COCHIN HOUDAN LAMONA
  LEGBAR POLISH REDCAP SULTAN
  SUSSEX BUFFBAR CAMPINE CHICKEN
  CORNISH DORKING FRIZZLE HAMBURG
  LEGHORN MINORCA OKLABAR POULTRY
  ROOSTER SPANISH SUMATRA COCKEREL
  CUBALAYA DELAWARE DUCKWING
  DUNGHILL GAMECOCK LANGSHAN
  SHANGHAI SHOWBIRD VOLAILLE
  (AGGREGATION OF —) RAFT
  (CASTRATED —) CAPETTE
  (CRESTED —) TOPKNOT
  (GUINEA —) KEEL COMEBACK
  (MALE —) STAG
  (STUFFED —) FARCI
  (TAILLESS —) RUMKIN
  (5-TOED —) SILKY SILKIE
FOX DOG KIT PUG TOD ASSE FOOL STAG
  WILD ADIVE BRANT CAAMA SWIFT TRICK
  VIXEN ZORRO ARCTIC BAGMAN CANDUC
  COLFOX CORSAC FENNEC LOWRIE
  OUTWIT RENARD RUSSEL BEGUILE
  CHARLEY CHARLIE KARAGAN REYNARD
  STUPEFY VULPINE CUSTOMER
  MUSKWAKI OUTAGAMI PLATINUM

FOXY SLY WILY COONY SHREWD CUNNING VULPINE DEXTROUS

FOYER HALL LOBBY ANTEROOM

FRACAS BOUT BRAWL MELEE MUSIC BICKER RUMPUS SHINDY UPROAR QUARREL SHINDIG FRACTION INCIDENT

FRACTION BIT CUT PYO FLUX PART BREAK PIECE SCRAP BREACH LITTLE MOIETY DECIMAL GLUTOSE WETNESS
(— OF RADIATION) ALBEDO
(NAPHTHA —) LIGROIN

FRACTURE BUST FLAW REND BILGE BREAK CLEFT CRACK FAULT JOINT BREACH DEFORM HACKLE DIACOPE FISSURE RUPTURE DIACLASE FRACTION

FRAGILE FINE WEAK FRAIL LIGHT SWACK FEEBLE INFIRM SLIGHT TENDER BRICKLE BRITTLE SLENDER TIFFANY DELICATE EGGSHELL ETHEREAL SLATTERY BREAKABLE

FRAGILITY DELICACY

FRAGMENT BIT ORT ATOM BLAD CHIP DRIB FLAW GROT MOIT MOTE PART RUMP SHED SNIP WISP ANGLE BLAUD BRACK BREAK BROKE CATCH CHUNK CLOUT CRUMB FRUST GIGOT PIECE RELIC SCRAP SHARD SHERD SHIVE SHRED SPALL SPELL SPLIT FARDEL FILING GOBBET MORSEL REMAIN SCREED SHIVER SIPPET SLIVER CANTLET EXCERPT FLINDER FLITTER FRITTER FRUSTUM MACERAL MAMMOCK REMANIE REMNANT SEGMENT SHATTER SHAVING SNIPPET AVULSION CHIPPING DETRITUS FRACTION OARTICLE POTSHERD SCANTLET SKERRICK SPLINTER
(— CUT OFF) CANTLE
(— OF BONE) SEQUESTER
SEQUESTRUM
(— OF BRICK) BRICKBAT
(— OF DIAMOND) CLEAVAGE
(— OF ICE) CALF
(— OF LAVA) FAVILLA LAPILLUS
(— OF MELODY) LAY
(— OF ROCK) CRAG AUTOLITH
LAPILLUS
(— OF SAIL) HULLOCK
(— OF SOD) TAB
(— OF STONE) SCABBLING
(— OF UNFINISHED WORK) TORSO
(— OF VEIN MATERIAL) SHOAD
(—S OF CLOUD) SCUD
(-S OF DIAMOND) BORT
(—S OF SAND) FINES
(CAST IRON —) POTLEG
(ICE —S) BRASH
(JAGGED —) BROCK
(LITERARY —) ANALECTA
(MASS OF —S) BRASH
(PLANT —) SHIVE
(SHELL —) SHRAPNEL
(WOODY —S FOUND IN FOOD) CHAD

FRAGMENTARY HASHY SNIPPY SCRAPPY DIVIDUAL

FRAGRANCE BALM ODOR AROMA SCENT SMELL SWEET BREATH FLAVOR FRAGOR BOUQUET INCENSE PERFUME SUAVITY

FRAGRANT NOSY RICH BALMY OLENT SPICY SWEET SAVORY SPICED ODORANT ODOROUS PERFUMY SCENTED AROMATIC FLAGRANT NECTARED ODORIFIC REDOLENT

FRAIL FINE POOR PUNY WEAK CRAZY REEDY SEELY SILLY BASKET BROTEL CROCKY FLIMSY INFIRM SICKLY SINGLE SLIGHT SLIMSY SQUEAL TICKLE TOPNET BRITTLE BRUCKLE FRAGILE SLENDER SLIMPSY UNHARDY DELICATE PINDLING

FRAILTY FAULT FOIBLE INVENT FAILING DELICACY WEAKNESS
(HUMAN —) ADAM

FRAME BED BIN BOW BOX FLY GYM MAT SET BULK BUNK CASE CAUM CELL CLAM CRIB CURB DESK DRAG FORM FROG GATE HARP HECK JACK MOLD PORT RACK SASH SOLE STEP ANGLE BANJO BLADE BLIND BLOCK BUILD CADRE CLEAT CROOK CROOK DRAFT EASEL FLAKE FLASK FLEAK FLOAT GRATE HORSE MOUNT OXBOW PERCH SCRAY SHAPE STAND STATE STEAD STOCK STOOL TRAIL BARROW BINDER BUCKET CASING CHEVAL COFFIN CRADLE CRATCH CRUTCH DECKLE FABRIC FENDER GRILLE HANGER HARROW HOTBED HURDLE PERSON PILLAR QUADRA REDACT REEDER SCREEN SETTLE SPIDER STAPLE TESTER ARMRACK BREAKER CABINET CARRIER CASEBOX CHASSIS COAMING COASTER CRAMPON CRIMPER DRAUGHT DROSSER FASHION FRAMING FRISKET GALLOWS GARLAND GATEWAY GIGTREE GRATING HAYRACK HOUSING ICEBOAT MACHINE MONTURE OXBRAKE PORTRAY SETTING TRANSOM TRESTLE TRIBBLE BARBECUE BOWGRACE CARRIAGE CASEMENT CONCEIVE CONTRIVE DOORCASE GRAFFAGE GRIDIRON GRILLAGE HALBERDS HOGFRAME PLOWHEAD RAILROAD RECEIVER RETAINER SKELETON THRIPPLE TRIANGLE TURNPIKE BRANDRITH OUTRIGGER
(— FOR ARCH) COOM
(— FOR BEEHIVE) SECTION
(— FOR CANDLES) HEARSE
(— FOR CARRYING STRAW) KNAPE
(— FOR CASK) GANTRY STALDER
(— FOR CATCHING FISH) HATCH
(— FOR CLOTHES DRYING) AIRER
(— FOR CONFINING HORSE) TRAVE
TRAVAIL
(— FOR COW'S HEAD) BAIL
(— FOR DRYING FISH) HACK
(— FOR DRYING SKINS) HERSE
(— FOR FISHING LINE) CADAR CADER
(— FOR GLAZING LEATHER) BUCK
(— FOR HAWKS) CADGE
(— FOR KILLING PIGS) CREEL
(— FOR LENS) BOW
(— FOR ROLLER BEARINGS) CAGE
(— FOR SMOKING MEAT) BUCCAN

(— FOR STACK) HAYRACK STADDLE
(— FOR WASHING ORE) BUDDLE
(— OF A VESSEL) HULL
(— OF MIND) HAZE SPITE SPIRIT
TEMPER FEELING POSTURE
(— OF PIER) JETTY
(— OF SAW) HUSK
(— OF SPINNING MULE) SQUARE
(— OF STRAW) SIME
(— OF TINWORK) MARQUITO
(— ON STAGE) CEILING
(— TO CATCH STARFISH) TANGLE
(— TO CLEAN SHIP'S BOTTOM) HOG
(— TO DRY CLOTHES) AIRER
(BELL —) SWEEP
(BOBBIN —) BANK
(CARRIAGE —) BRAKE BREAK
(COUNTING —) ABACUS
(DIVING —) LUNETTE
(EMBROIDERY —) TENT TABORET
TAMBOUR
(FISHING —) DREDGE
(GLAZIER'S —) FRAIL
(HARNESS —) HEALD
(LOOM —) SLAY SLEY LATHE BATTEN
SLEIGH
(MINING —) APRON
(PHOTOGRAPHY —) BUTTERFLY
(PORTABLE —) BIER CACAXTE
(PRINTING —) CHASE PRESS
(SHIP'S —) CANT
(SLUBBING —) BILLY
(STRETCHING —) TENT SLEDGE
TENTER
(TANNING —) BEAM
(WINDOW —) CHESS
(2-WHEELED —) GILL
FRAMEWORK BED BENT BIER BONE
BUCK BULK CRIB DURN GRID RACK SASH
BONES CADRE CHUTE COPSE CREEL
FLAKE SHELL STOCK BELFRY BRIDGE
CABANE CRADLE DESIGN FABRIC
GOCART GUARDS HARROW HEARSE
REBATO SHIELD STROMA WATTLE
CABINET CARCASS CLIMBER COMMODE
DERRICK FRAMING FULCRUM JACKBOX
LATTICE REBATER RETABLE STADDLE
TRESTLE BARBECUE BEDSTEAD
BULKHEAD CARRIAGE CRADLING
CRIBWORK GRIDIRON GRILLAGE
OSSATURE SCAFFOLD SHELVING
SHOWCASE SKELETON
(— AROUND HATCHWAY) FIDDLEY
(— FOR CORNSTACK) HOVEL
(— FOR PEAL OF BELLS) CAGE
(— OF REFERENCE) SCHEMA
(— TO EXPAND SKIRTS) BUSTLE
PANNIER
(EMPTY —) HUSK
(SCULPTOR'S —) ARMATURE

FRANCE

BAY: BISCAY ARACHON
CAPE: HAGUE
CAPITAL: PARIS

COIN: ECU SOL SOU GROS AGNEL BLANC
BLANK FRANC LIARD LIVRE LOUIS OBOLE
SAIGA SCUTE BLANCA BLANCO DENIER
DIZAIN TESTON AGNEAUX CENTIME
TESTOON CAVALIER NAPOLEON
DEPARTMENT: AIN LOT VAR AUBE AUDE
CHER EURE GARD GERS JURA NORD OISE
ORNE TARN AISNE INDRE ISERE LOIRE
RHONE YONNE ARIEGE CANTAL CREUSE
LOZERE NIEVRE CORREZE GIRONDE
MOSELLE
ISLAND: RE YEU CITE CORSE GROIX HYERE
OLERON USHANT CORSICA
KING: ODO EUDES PEPIN CLOVIS LOTHAIR
LAKE: ANNECY CAZAUX
MEASURE: POT SAC AUNE LINE MINE
MUID PIED VELT ARPEN CARAT LIEUE
LIGNE MINOT PERCH PINTE POINT POUCE
TOISE VELTE ARPENT HEMINE LEAGUE
QUARTE SETIER CHOPINE HEMINEE
POISSON SEPTIER BOISSEAU QUARTAUT
ROQUILLE QUARTERON
MOUNTAIN: PUY DORE BLANC CINTO
FOREZ PELAT COTEDOR MOUNIER
VENTOUX VIGNEMALE CHAMBEYRON
MOUNTAIN RANGE: ALPS ECRINS
VOSGES CEVENNES PYRENEES
MARITIMES
NATIVE: CELT GAUL FRANK BASQUE
BRETON GASCON NORMAN PICARD
CATALAN GALLOIS LORRAIN FRANCIEN
LIGURIAN PROVENCAL BURGUNDIAN
PORT: CAEN BREST CALAIS TOULON
LEHAVRE BORDEAUX CHERBOURG
DUNKERQUE MARSEILLE
PROVINCE: FOIX ANJOU AUNIS BEARN
ALSACE ARTOIS COMTAT POITOU
AUVERGNE BRETAGNE BRITTANY
LIMOUSIN LORRAINE PROVENCE
TOURAINE
RIVER: AIN LOT LUY LYS VAR AIRE AUBE
AUDE CHER DRAC EURE GARD GERS LOIR
OISE ORNE TARN VIRE ADOUR AISNE
AULNE DROME INDRE ISERE LOIRE
MARNE MEUSE RHONE RISLE SAONE
SEINE SOMME VIAUR YONNE ALLIER
ARIEGE ESCAUT SAMBRE SCARPE
VEZERE VIENNE DURANCE GARONNE
GIRONDE MAYENNE MOSELLE CHARENTE
DORDOGNE
TOWN: AY EU AIX DAX GEX PAU AGDE
AGEN ALBI AUBY AUCH BRON CAEN
LAON LOOS METZ NICE OPPY ORLY RIOM
SENS SETE STLO TOUL UZES VAUX VIMY
VIRE ARLES ARRAS BLOIS BREST DIJON
DINAN DOUAI ERNEE LAVAL LILLE LISLE
LYONS NANCY NERAC NESLE NIMES
ORNES PARIS REIMS ROUEN SEDAN
TOURS TULLE VICHY AMIENS ANGERS
CALAIS LEMANS LONGWY NANTES
PANTIN RENNES RHEIMS SARLAT SENLIS
SEVRES TARARE TARBES TOULON
TROYES TULLUM VALOIS VERDUN
BAREGES CASTRES LIMOGES ORLEANS
ROUBAIX VALENCE BORDEAUX
CLERMONT GRENOBLE MULHOUSE

ROCHELLE TOULOUSE MARSEILLE
STRASBOURG
TRIBE: REMI AEDUI ARVERNI SALUVII
ALLOBROGES
WEIGHT: GROS MARC ONCE CARAT LIVRE
POUND TONNE TONNEAU ESTERLIN

FRANCESCA DA RIMINI
(CHARACTER IN —) PAOLO
FRANCESCA GIANCIOTTO MALATESTINO
(COMPOSER OF —) ZANDONAI
FRANCHISE SOKE VOTE CHASE FERRY
HONOR INFANG CHARTER FREEDOM
LIBERTY CONTRACT FREELAGE
SUFFRAGE TENEMENT
FRANCISCAN MINOR MINORITE
FRANK FREE OPEN RANK BLUFF BLUNT
BURLY LUSTY NAIVE PLAIN BRAZEN
CANDID DIRECT FORTHY HONEST SALIAN
ARTLESS GENUINE LIBERAL PROFUSE
SINCERE CAREFREE CAVALIER
GENEROUS STRAIGHT VIGOROUS
OUTSPOKEN OPENHEARTED
PLAINSPOKEN
FRANKENSTEIN (AUTHOR OF —)
SHELLEY
(CHARACTER IN —) HENRY ROBERT
VICTOR WALTON CLERVAL JUSTINE
WILLIAM ELIZABETH FRANKENSTEIN
FRANKLY FREELY OPENLY PLAINLY
CANDIDLY
FRANKNESS CANDOR FREEDOM
OPENNESS
FRANTIC MAD WOOD RABID INSANE
MANIAC FURIOUS LUNATIC VIOLENT
DERANGED FEVERISH FRENETIC
FRENZIED MANIACAL
FRATERNAL BROTHERLY DIZYGOTIC
NONIDENTICAL
FRATERNITY FRAT FRARY HOUSE ORDER
FRATRY QUALITY SOCIETY SODALITY
FRAUD GYP DOLE FAKE GAFF GAUD GULL
JAPE JUNT LURK RUSE SHAM SKIN WILE
CHEAT COVIN CRAFT DOLUS FAKER
FAVEL GLAIK GUILE HOCUS LURCH
SHARK SHIFT SHUCK SWICK SWIKE
TRICK BROGUE DECEIT FIDDLE FULLAM
HUMBUG INTAKE STUMER WRENCH
FLIVVER KNAVERY ROGUERY STUMOUR
SWINDLE BOODLING COZENAGE
IMPOSTER OPERATOR SUBTLETY
TRUMPERY
FRAUDULENT SKIN WILY CRONK
COGGED CRAFTY QUACKY ABUSIVE
CROOKED CUNNING KNAVISH CHEATING
COVINOUS FRAUDFUL GUILEFUL
QUACKISH SINISTER SPURIOUS
FRAY FRET BROIL BROOM FEAZE MELEE
RAVEL AFFRAY BUSTLE CHAUVE FRIDGE
TIFFLE CONTEST FRAZZLE
FREAK FIRK FLAM WHIM FANCY HUMOR
LUSUS MOODS SCAPE SPORT MEGRIM
SPLEEN WHIMSY CAPRICE CROTCHET
ESCAPADE FLIMFLAM WHIMWHAM
MONSTROSITY
FREE LAX LET MOD RID BOLD EASE LISS

OPEN PERT SHED SHUT CLEAN CLEAR
FLUID FRANK LARGE LISSE LOOSE READY
SCOUR SLAKE SPARE DEGAGE EXEMPT
FACILE FLUENT FREELY GRATIS IMMUNE
LOOSEN SOLUTE UNSLIP VACANT
VAGILE CLEANSE DELIVER GRIVOIS
INEXACT LASKING LIBERAL MANUMIT
RELEASE SCIOLTO UNBOUND UNSLAVE
UNTWIST WILLING ABSOLUTE AUTARKIC
BUCKSHEE EASINESS EXPEDITE FACILITY
FREEHAND GRIVOISE INDIGENT
LAXATIVE LIBERATE UNBRIDLE
(— AND EASY) GLIB CAVALIER
FAMILIAR
(— BROOK OF WEEDS) RODE
(— FROM) EX REDD DEVOID DISPATCH
(— FROM ABIGUITY) HOMELY DECIDED
(— FROM ACCUSATION) SACKLESS
(— FROM ACIDITY) DULCIFY
(— FROM ANXIETY) CONTENT
(— FROM ARTIFICIAL) ARTLESS
(— FROM BIAS) CANDID
(— FROM CARE) EASY CARELESS
(— FROM CHARGE) PURGE FRANCO
(— FROM CONSTRAINT) CASUAL
(— FROM DEDUCTIONS) NET
(— FROM DEFECT) HALE SOUND
(— FROM DIRT) BRIGHT
(— FROM DOUBT) RESOLVE
(— FROM ELECTRICAL CHARGE)
DEAD
(— FROM ERROR) LEAL SOUND
CORRECT ACCURATE
(— FROM EVIL) RESCUE
(— FROM EXTREMES) EQUABLE
(— FROM FLAWS) GOOD
(— FROM FROST) FRESH
(— FROM IMPURITIES) FINE DRESS
DEFECATE DEPURATE
(— FROM KNOTS) ENODE ENODATE
(— FROM MARKS) BLANK
(— FROM MICROORGANISMS)
ASEPTIC STERILE
(— FROM OBLIGATION) ACQUIT
EXCUSE
(— FROM PENALTY) ABSOLVE
(— FROM RESTRAINT) ABANDONED
(— FROM STONES) CHESSOM
(— OF DIFFICULTIES) AFLOAT
(— OF FAT) ENSEAM
(— OF OVERTONES) PURE
(— OF TAR) WRECK
(— ONE'S SELF) SOLVE
FREEBOOTER TORY RIDER ROVER THIEF
PIRATE BRIGAND CATERAN CORSAIR
PINDARI PILLAGER RAPPAREE
SNAPHANCE
FREEDOM RUN EASE FRITH LARGE
UHURU ACCESS STREET APATHIA
BREADTH LEISURE LIBERTY LICENCE
LICENSE RELEASE AUTONOMY FREELAGE
FREENESS IMMUNITY IMPUNITY
LARGESSE WITGATE
(— FROM BIAS) CANDOR
(— FROM CONSTRAINT) ABANDON
(— FROM DANGER) SECURITY
(— FROM ERROR) ACCURACY

(— FROM GUILT) SHRIVE
(— OF ACCESS) ENTREE
(— OF ACTION) SWINGE LATITUDE
(— OF SPEECH) PARISIA
(— TO PROCEED) HEAD
(CARELESS —) ABANDON
FREEMAN BUR AIRE BARON CEORL
HAULD BONDER CITIZEN FRANKLIN
ROTURIER
(POOR —) THETE
FREEZE ICE RIME CATCH CHILL FROST
CURDLE FRAPPE HARDEN STARVE
STEEVE CONGEAL GLACIATE
FREEZING COLD FREEZY FRIGID FROSTY
GLACIAL CRYONICS GELATION
FREIGHT LOAD CARGO GOODS ASTRAY
BURDEN LADING FRAUGHT HOTSHOT
PLUNDER PORTAGE TRUCKAGE
(— CAR) TRUCK
FREISCHUTZ, DER
(CHARACTER IN —) MAX CUNO
AGATHE HERMIT KASPAR SAMIEL
AENNCHEN
(COMPOSER OF —) WEBER
FRENCH GUIANA (CAPE OF —)
ORANGE
(CAPITAL OF —) CAYENNE
(RIVER OF —) MARONI
(TOWN OF —) MANA KOUROU
FRENCHMAN GAUL PICARD FRENCHY
MONSIEUR PARLEYVOO
FRENZIED MAD MUST RABID RAMAGE
BERSERK FANATIC FRANTIC MADDING
FRENETIC FURIBUND POSSESSED
FRENZY AMOK FURY GERE MOON RAGE
AMUCK FUROR MANIA MUSTH FURORE
RAVING MADNESS OESTRUS SWIVVET
DELIRIUM INSANITY
FREQUENCY HERTZ PITCH CREBRITY
FREQUENT USE BANG KEEP HAUNT
HOWFF OFTEN THICK AFFECT COMMON
HOURLY INFEST RESORT ENHAUNT
OFTTIME CREBROUS FAMILIAR PRACTICE
ACCUSTOMED
FREQUENTLY OFT OFTEN HOURLY
UNSELDOM
FRESH HOT NEW WET FLIP GOOD
RACY GAY SMUG WARM BRISK CRISP GREEN
MOIST QUICK RUDDY SASSY SMART
SOUND SWEET VIVID CALLER CALVER
FLORID LIVELY MAIDEN STRONG UNUSED
VERNAL VIRENT VIRGIN ANOTHER
NOUVEAU UNFADED VERDANT
NOUVELLE ORIGINAL SPANKING
YOUTHFUL
(PREF.) CENO
(SUFF.) CENE
FRESHEN BRACE FRESH RENEW BREEZE
REVIVE CHOUNCE PEARTEN REFRESH
SWEETEN
FRESHMAN FOX BEJAN FROSH GREENY
PENNAL FRESHER
FRESHNESS DEW VERD NOVELTY
VERDURE VIRIDITY ORIGINALITY
FRET DIK NAG ORP RUB RUX VEX CARK
FASH FRAY FUSS GALL GNAW RAGE
STEW YIRM CHAFE CRAKE CRISP FLISK

GRATE PIQUE WORRY WREAK ABRADE
CORSIE CRYSAL HARASS MUCKLE
NETTLE PLAGUE REPINE RIPPLE RUFFLE
CHRYSAL GRECQUE GRIZZLE MEANDER
SCRUPLE SQUINNY ALIGREEK IRRITATE
FREY FREYR YNGVI
(FATHER OF —) NJORD
(SISTER OF —) FREYA
FREYA (BROTHER OF —) FREY
(FATHER OF —) NJORD
(HUSBAND OF —) ODIN
FRIAR FRATE FREER MINIM MINOR
BHIKKU FRATER GELONG GOSAIN LISTER
BHIKSHU JACOBIN LIMITER SERVITE
BREVIGER CAPUCHIN JACOBITE
MINORIST MINORITE PREACHER
AUGUSTINE CARMELITE CORDELIER
MENDICANT BENEDICTINE
FRICTION BUZZ DRAG HISS CHAFE
WINDAGE
FRIEND AME AMI AMY BOR CAD EME PAX
BHAI CHUM NABS OPPO PARD WINE
AMIGO BRICK BUDDY INGLE NETOP
TROUT AIKANE BELAMY COUSIN GOSSIP
INWARD KIMMER PRINCE QUAKER
ACHATES COMRADE SOCIETY COCKMATE
DEMOPHIL FEDERATE HICKSITE
INTIMADO INTIMATE TILLICUM
(— OF BRIDEGROOM) PARANYMPH
(—S NOT SPEAKING) CUTS
(CLOSE —) PRIVY COBBER COMPADRE
(DIVINE —) SOCIUS
(FAMILIAR —) CRONY GREMIAL
SPECIAL
(GIRL —) DOXY DRAG DONEY STEADY
(INTIMATE FEMALE —) CUMMER
(PRIVATE —) PRIVADO
(WOMAN —) GIMMER
FRIENDLINESS AMITY AFFINITY
BONHOMIE GOODWILL
FRIENDLY COSH GOOD HOLD HOMY KIND
TOSH CADGY CHIEF COUTH GREAT
HOMEY MATEY THICK AMICAL CHATTY
CHUMMY FOLKSY FORTHY HOMELY
KINDLY SMOOTH AFFABLE AMIABLE
AMICOUS COUTHIE AMICABLE HOMELIKE
INTIMATE SOCIABLE NEIGHBORLY
FRIENDSHIP PAX AMITY AMOUR
FRIGGA (HUSBAND OF —) ODIN
(SON OF —) BALDER
FRIGHT COW BOOF FEAR FLEG FRAY
ALARM GHAST GLIFF GLOFF PANIC
SCARE AFFRAY GASTER GLIFFY SCHRIK
TERROR STARTLE SWITHER FRIGHTEN
GASTNESS GLIFFING
FRIGHTEN AWE COW FLY SHY SOB BAZE
BREE DARE DOSS FEAR FLEG FLEY FRAY
FUNK HARE HAZE SHOO AFEAR AFLEY
ALARM ALARUM BLUFF GALLY GHOST
GLIFF HAZEN SCARE SHORE SPOOK
AFFRAY ALARUM APPALL BOGGLE
BOOGER COWARD FLAITE FLIGHT FRIGHT
GALLEY GALLOW AFFREUX FRECKEN
SCARIFY STARTLE TERRIFY AFFRIGHT
MISTRYST
FRIGHTENED RAD FRIT GAST EERIE

GHAST WINDY AFRAID AGHAST SCARED
SCAREY STURTIN GHASTFUL
(EASILY —) TIMID SKITTISH
FRIGHTENING DREAD EERIE GOURY
HAIRY FRIGHTY GHASTLY SHIVERY
DREADFUL FLEYSOME
FRIGHTFUL WAN GRIM UGLY AWFUL
FERLY HORRID UGSOME AFFREUX
DIREFUL FEARFUL GASHFUL GHASTLY
HIDEOUS ALARMING DREADFUL
ELDRITCH FEARSOME GHASTFUL
HORRIBLE HORRIFIC TERRIBLE TERRIFIC
FRIGID DRY ICY COLD BLEAK FISHY
ARCTIC FROSTY FROZEN WINTRY
GLACIAL FREEZING SIBERIAN
FRILL DIDO PURL JABOT RUCHE RUFFLE
ARMILLA FLOUNCE SPINACH CHITLING
CRIMPING FRILLERY FURBELOW
(— OF HAIR) APRON
FRINGE WLO EDGE GILL LOMA RUFF
WELT BEARD THRUM BORDER EDGING
MARGIN PELMET TASSEL BULLION
CREPINE EYELASH FEATHER FIMBRIA
MACRAME SELVAGE TRAILER VALANCE
WHISKER CILIELLA FRISETTE INDUSIUM
PENUMBRA SELVEDGE TRIMMING
(— OF TEETH) PERISTOME
(SOFT —S) THRUM
FRINGED JUBATE CILIATE LACINIATE
FRISK COLT FISK PLAY ROLL SKIP WHID
BOUND CAPER SKICE CAREER CAVORT
CURVET FROLIC TITTUP WANTON
FRISKLE
FRISKY GAY PERT FRISK CROUSE FEISTY
KIPPER LIVELY WANTON BUCKISH
COLTISH JIGGISH PLAYFUL SKITTISH
SPORTIVE
FRIVOLITY LEVITY FRIBBLE INANITY
ITEMING FUTILITY NONSENSE NUGACITY
FRIVOLOUS GAY DAFT VAIN GIDDY
INANE LIGHT PETTY SILLY WASHY
FLIMSY FRILLY FRIVOL FROTHY FUTILE
TOYISH YEASTY FATUOUS FRIBBLE
LIGHTLY NIDGETY SHALLOW TRIVIAL
GIMCRACK JIMCRACK SKITTISH TRIFLING
FROCK DUD JAM GOWN JUMP SLIP SLOP
WRAP LAMMY SMOCK TRUSS TUNIC
CLERIC JERSEY LAMMIE MANTLE
ROCHET SUKKENYE
FROG PAD POD KICK FROSH FROSK
FROUD PADDO PADDY RANID RONCO
ANURAN PEEPER TOGGLE CHARLIE
CRAWLER CREEPER CROAKER CUSHION
FRESHER FROGLET PADDOCK PODDOCK
QUILKIN BULLFROG FERREIRO FROGGING
PLATANNA REPLACER
(— IN LOOM) HEATER
(— OF HORSE'S HOOF) FRUSH
CUSHION
(TREE —) NOTOTREMA
FROGS (AUTHOR OF —) ARISTOPHANES
(CHARACTER IN —) AEACUS CHARON
BACCHUS DIONYSUS HERCULES
XANTHIAS AESCHYLUS EURIPIDES
FROLIC BUM GAY RIG BLOW COLT GAME
GELL HAZE JINK LAKE LARK ORGY PLAY
PLOY RANT REEK ROMP TEAR CAPER

FREAK FRISK MERRY PRANK RANDY
ROUSE SALLY SPORT SPREE BUSTER
CAVORT CURVET FRATCH GAMBOL
PLISKY POWWOW PRANCE ROLLIX
SHINDY SPLORE VAGARY WANTON
DISPORT GAMMOCK MARLOCK PLISKIE
ROLLICK SCAMPER SKYLARK SPANIEL
STASHIE WASSAIL CAROUSAL
JAMBOREE
FROLICSOME GAY DAFT ROID ANTIC
BUXOM CADGY FRISK GILPY LARKY
FRISKY LIVELY WANTON ANTICAL
JOCULAR LARKING LARKISH PLAYFUL
WAGGISH ESPIEGLE FRISKFUL FROLICKY
GAMESOME LARKSOME PRANKISH
SPORTFUL SPORTIVE
FRONT BOW VAN BROW FACE FORE
HEAD PROW THIN AFORE VAUNT BEFORE
DEVANT FACADE FACING FORMER
OPPOSE SECTOR VAWARD ADVANCE
FORWARD FRONTAL FURTHER OBVERSE
PALATAL PREFACE RESPECT SLENDER
FOREHEAD FOREMOST FOREPART
FORESIDE FRONTAGE
(— OF ASTROLABE) WOMBSIDE
(— OF BARN) FOREBAY
(— OF BIRD'S NECK) GUTTUR
(— OF BODY) GROUF
(— OF HEAD) VISAGE FORETOP
(— OF HELMET) VENTAIL
(— OF SHIRT) BOSOM
(— OF WATERWHEEL BUCKET)
START
(— UPON) AFFRONT
FRONTIER BOUND COAST FRONT MARCH
BORDER BARRIER FRONTURE OUTLYING
(FORTIFIED —) LIMES
FRONT PAGE (AUTHOR OF —) HECHT
MACARTHUR
(CHARACTER IN —) EARL BURNS
GRANT HILDY PEGGY WALTER HARTMAN
JOHNSON WILLIAMS
FROST ICE COLD HOAR RIME RIND
FROSTING ICING DIVINITY
FROSTY ICY COLD RIMY CHILL CRISP
FRORE GELID GLARY HUNCH BOREAL
FRIGID FROREN CHILLING INIMICAL
PRUINOUS
FROTH FOB BARM FOAM HEAD REAM
SCUM SUDS WORK CREAM SPUME
YEAST FLOWER FREATH LATHER SPURGE
FROWN GLUM GLOM GLOUT GLOUT
GLUMP LOWER SCOWL GLOWER
GLUNCH FROUNCE FRONTLET
FROWZY BLOWSY RAFFISH FROWZLED
SCABROUS SLOVENLY
FROZEN FAST FIXED FRORE FRORY GELID
GLARY FRAPPE FROREN
FRUGAL EASY MILD CANNY CHARY
ROMAN SCANT SPARE SAVING SCARCE
SCOTCH CAREFUL PRUDENT SLENDER
SPARING THRIFTY PROVIDENT
PARSIMONIOUS
FRUGALITY SPARE THRIFT ECONOMY
PARCITY MANAGERY
FRUIT BEL FIG HAW UVA AKEE ATTA
BAEL BITO COYO DATE DIKA DROP GEAN

JACK LIME NOOP PEAR PLUM POME
SEED SLOE SNAP SORB ANISE APPLE
BERRY CLING COUMA DRUPE GENIP
GOURD GRAPE GUAVA HAZEL ILAMA
LEMON LIMON MANGO MELON OLIVE
PAPAW PEACH RIPER SORVA TRYMA
ACHENE ACINUS ALMOND BANANA
BUTTON CEDRON CEREZA CHERRY
CITRON CITRUS COBNUT COCHAL
COCONA DAMSON DURIAN EMBLIC
EMBOLO GUARRI JUJUBE KEEPER
LEGUME LONGAN LOQUAT MAMMEE
MARANG MAYPOP MUYUSA NARRAS
ORANGE PAPAYA PAWPAW PELLAS
POMATO RESULT SAPOTA SQUASH
UVALHA WAMPEE WESTME ZAPOTE
APRICOT ATEMOYA AVOCADO AZAROLE
BILIMBI BLOATER CARAWAY CHAYOTE
CHECKER CIRUELA COCONUT CURRANT
DESSERT GEEBUNG GENIPAP GHERKIN
KUMQUAT MURCOTT PIGFACE PRODUCT
RIPENER SERVICE SHALLON SOROSIS
SOURSOP TANGELO ACHENIUM
BAYBERRY BELLERIC BILBERRY
CALABASH CANISTEL CAPSICUM
CARDAMUM CITRANGE COCOPLUM
CUCUMBER DEWBERRY DOGBERRY
EGGFRUIT FOLLICLE FRUITAGE FRUITERY
FRUITLET GOLKAKRA INKBERRY
LIMEQUAT OSOBERRY PIEPRINT
PODOCARP RAMBUTAN SEBESTEN
SEEDBALL SHADDOCK SWEETSOP
SYCONIUM CARYOPSIS NECTARINE
PINEAPPLE SAPODILLA CHERIMOYER
MANGOSTEEN
(— OF CACTUS) SABRA
(— OF CAPER) CAPOT
(— OF CITRON) ETHROG
(— OF HEMLOCK) CONIUM
(— OF OAK) ACORN
(— OF PALM) SALAK PUPUNHA
(— OF ROSE) HIP BUTTON
(— ON TREES) HANG
(—S COOKED IN SYRUP) COMPOTE
(AGGREGATE —) ETAERIO DRUPETUM
(ASTRINGENT —) GAB GAUB CHEBULE
(AVOCADO-LIKE —) ANAY
(CANDIED —) CONSERVE
(CARMINATIVE —) BADIAN
(COILED —) STROMBUS
(COLLECTIVE —) SYNCARP
(DRIED —) PASA CUBEB MUMMY SABAL
OREJON CAPSULE EMBELIA
(EARLY —) PRIMEUR HASTINGS
(FALLEN —) SHEDDER WINDFALL
(FIRST —S) ANNATES BIKKURIM
PRIMICES
(FLESHY —) SYCONIUM SARCOCARP
(GOURD —) PEPO
(GRAPEFRUIT-LIKE —) SUHA
(GRAPELIKE —) WAMPEE
(HAWTHORN —) PEGGLE
(IMPERFECT —) SPECH NUBBIN
(MASHED —) FOOL
(MEDICINAL —) AIWAIN AJOWAN
EMBELIA
(ONE-SEEDED —) ACHENE

(PALMYRA —) PUNATOO
(PLUMLIKE —) CARISSA CIRUELA
(PRESERVED —) SUCCADE CONFITURE
(PRICKLY —) HEDGEHOG
(SELF-FERTILIZED —) AUTOCARP
(SLICED DRIED —) SCHNITZ
(SPURGE —) TAMPOE
(SUPERIOR —) TOPPER
(UNRIPE OAK —) CAMATA
(WINGED —) SAMARA
(WOODY —) XYLOCARP
FRUITFUL FAT FOODY BATTEL FECUND
FRUITY GRAVID FERTILE TEEMFUL
UBEROUS ABUNDANT CHILDING
FRUITIVE PREGNANT PROLIFIC
PLENTEOUS
FRUITLESS DRY GELD VAIN ADDLE
BARREN FUTILE STERILE USELESS
ABORTIVE BOOTLESS
FRUSTRATE BALK BEAT BILK CRAB
DASH DISH FOIL LAME BAULK BLANK
BLOCK CHECK CROSS ELUDE SMEAR
THRAW WRECK BAFFLE BLIGHT BUGGER
DEFEAT DELUDE KIBOSH OUTWIT
SCOTCH THWART ANIENTE DECEIVE
FALSIFY PREVENT CONFOUND INFRINGE
STULTIFY
FRUSTRATED DISHED MANQUE
FRUSTRATION FOIL SUCK DEFEAT
FIASCO
FRY SILE BROOD FRIZZ KRILL SAUTE
FRIZZLE GREYFISH
FRYING PAN FRYPAN SPIDER CREEPER
SKILLET
FUDGE HUNCH SNUDGE PENUCHE
DIVINITY
FUEL GAS OIL POB COAL COKE FIRE PEAT
UPLA ARGOL ACETOL BUNKER ELDING
FIRING SHRUFF TIMBER COALITE
PABULUM SYNTHOL FIREBOOT FIREBOTE
GASOGENE GAZOGENE TRIPTANE
(JELLED —) NAPALM
(ROCKET —) HYDYNE
FUGITIVE HOT FLEME FLYER FUGIE
SCAMP OUTLAW FLEEING LAMSTER
REFUGEE RUNAWAY FLEETING
RUNAGATE UNSTABLE
FULFILL FILL FULL KEEP MEET HONOR
ANSWER COMPLY REDEEM ACHIEVE
PERFORM SATISFY COMPLETE
ACCOMPLISH
(— A TERM) EXPIRE
FULFILLMENT PASS EFFECT FUNCTION
PERFORMANCE
(— OF GOD'S WILL) KINGDOM
(IMAGINARY —) FANTASY
FULL BAD BIG FAT FOW COOL DEEP FAIR
GOOD JUST PANG RANK TRIG TUCK
AMPLE AWASH BROAD CLEAR FLUSH
LARGE LUCKY PIENO PLAIN PLENY
ROUND SATED SOLID TIGHT TOTAL
WHOLE ENTIRE GOGGLE HONEST
STRONG BAPTIZE BRIMFUL COPIOUS
DESTROY DIFFUSE FULFILL FULSOME
LIBERAL OROTUND PERFORM PLENARY
REPLETE TEEMING TRAMPLE WEALTHY
ABSOLUTE ADEQUATE BOUFFANT

BRIMMING CHOCKFUL COMPLETE
EXTENDED FREQUENT PREGNANT
RESONANT THOROUGH
(— CLOTH OR YARN) WALK
(— OF AIR) LIGHT
(— OF BLANKS) LACUNOSE
(— OF CHINKS) RIMOSE
(— OF DELAY) MOROSE
(— OF DEVILTRY) HEMPY HEMPIE
(— OF DIRT) FOUL
(— OF EGGS) GRAVID
(— OF ENERGY) STOUT SWANK
(— OF FLAWS) CRAZY
(— OF FUN) FROLIC
(— OF HAPPINESS) SUNSHINY
(— OF INTEREST) AGOG
(— OF IRON) SIDEROSE
(— OF LIFE) SPUNKY ANIMATE
(— OF LOOPS) KINKY
(— OF MATTER FOR THOUGHT)
MEATY
(— OF RUSHES) SPRITTY
(— OF SAND) ARENOSE
(— OF SLEEP) SOPOROSE
(— OF SMALL OPENINGS) POROUS
(— OF SPIRIT) GENEROUS
(— OF VIGOR) FLUSH GREEN LUSTY
ANIMATED SPIRITED
(— OF ZEST) RACY
FULL-GROWN RIPE GROWN MATURE
SEEDED
FULLNESS BODY FLAIR FLARE FULTH
PLENUM PLEROMA SATIETY
FULLY ALL DOWN EVEN INLY WELL
AMPLY LARGE ENOUGH FAIRLY THRICE
WHOLLY CLEARLY LARGELY UTTERLY
CLEVERLY ENTIRELY INWARDLY
MATURELY
FUMBLE BOOT MUFF MULL PIRL BOBBLE
BOGGLE FAFFLE MUMBLE PRODDLE
MISFIELD THRUMBLE
FUME FUFF RAGE REEK EWDER SMOKE
STIFE STORM SNUFFLE FUMIGATE
FUMIGATE SMEEK SMOKE CYANIDE
PASTILLE
FUN GIG GAME GELL JEST JOKE LAKE
PLAY BORAK BOURD HUMOR KICKS
MIRTH MUSIC SPORT FROLIC GAIETY
DAFFERY DAFFING GAMMOCK WHOOPEE
FUNCTION ACT JOB RUN USE DUTY
ROLE WORK POWER ACTION AGENCY
MATRIX MISTER OFFICE SQUASH
CONCEPT FACULTY ISOLATE PERFORM
SERVICE WORKING ACTIVITY BUSINESS
MINISTRY PROVINCE
(— EFFECTIVELY) AVAIL
(—S OF JUDGES) ERMINE
(APPARENT —) STUDY
(CHEMICAL —) PARACHOR
(ECCLESIASTICAL —) DIET
(ESSENTIAL —) DHARMA
(MATHEMATICAL —) DEL FORM
METRIC INVERSE QUARTIC
(SPECIAL —) CEREMONY
FUNCTIONAL DYNAMIC
FUND BOX BANK FOND MASS CHEST
KITTY MOUNT SLUSH STOCK STORE

ESCROW CHALUKA JACKPOT RESERVE
HALUKKAH PECULIUM
(COMMON —) POT POOL
(POLITICAL —S) BARREL
(PL.) CAJA PURSE COFFER
FUNDAMENTAL NET BASE BASAL
BASIC KLANG PRIME VITAL BOTTOM
PRIMAL SIMPLE BASILAR BEDROCK
ORGANIC PRIMARY RADICAL ABSOLUTE
CARDINAL ORIGINAL RUDIMENT
SUBSTRAT ULTIMATE PRIMORDIAL
RUDIMENTARY
FUNDAMENTALLY AUFOND
FUNDUS FORNIX
FUNERAL TANGI BURIAL EXEQUY
BURYING CORTEGE FUNEBRE FUNERARY
MORTUARY
FUNEREAL BLACK FERAL DISMAL
SOLEMN FUNEBRE FUNERAL DIRGEFUL
EXEQUIAL MOURNFUL SEPULCHRAL
FUNGICIDE MANEB NABAM ZINEB
FERBAM CALOMEL BORDEAUX DICHLONE
FUNGUS BUNT MOLD SMUT BLACK
BRAND ERGOT FUNGE HYPHO MOREL
MOULD PHOMA SPUNK SWARD TRUFF
VALSA VERPI AGARIC BOLETE FUNGAL
MILDEW OIDIUM AMANITA BOLETUS
CHYTRID FUNGOID GEASTER LEPIOTA
TRUFFLE AECIDIUM CLATHRUS
CORNBELL EUMYCETE FUSARIUM
HELVELLA MUCEDINE MUSHROOM
OOMYCETE OTOMYCES PHALLOID
POLYPORE PUFFBALL RHIZOPUS
SAPROGEN SPOROGEN TREMELLA
TUCKAHOE NEUROSPORA PENICILLIUM
(UNICELLULAR —) BEES EAST YEAST
FUNNEL CAST STACK TEWEL TRUNK
FILLER FUMMEL HOPPER SIPHON TUNNEL
TUNNER TRUMPET TUNDISH HYPONOME
WINDSAIL
FUNNY ODD GOOD COMIC DROLL MERRY
QUEER COMICAL JOCULAR RISIBLE
STRANGE HUMOROUS
(VERY —) SPLITTING SIDESPLITTING
FUR FOX BEAR CALF COON FLIX FLUE
MINK PEAN PELF PELL PILE SEAL VAIR
COYPU CROSS FITCH FLICK GENET GRISE
OTTER PAHMI SABLE SCARF SHUBA
BADGER BEAVER COUGAR DESMAN
ERMINE FISHER GALYAC GENET MARTIN
NUTRIA PELAGE POTENT RABBIT SPRING
SUSLIK CALABER CARACAL FITCHET
FITCHEW FURRURE MINIVER TOPCOAT
CACOMIXL ERMINOIS KOLINSKI
(— OF LAMBSKIN AND WOOL)
BUDGE
(— RESEMBLING PERSIAN LAMB)
KRIMMER
(BEAVER —) WOOM CASTOR
(GRAY —) GRAY GREY GRIS GRISE
CRIMMER LETTICE
(LAMB —) CARACUL KARAKUL
(NUMBER OF — SKINS) TIMBER
TIMMER
(RABBIT —) SCUT CONEY FLICK LAPIN
HATTER SEALINE ERMILINE

(SQUIRREL —) CALABAR
(SQUIRREL OR MARTIN —) AMICE
POPEL
(STONE MARTEN'S —) FOIN
FURBISH DO FIG RUB FAKE FINE VAMP
CLEAN SCOUR FINIFY POLISH BURNISH
VARNISH RENOVATE
FURIES ALECTO ERINYS MEGAERA
TISIPHONE
FURIOUS MAD GRIM WOOD YOND ANGRY
BRAIN GIDDY IRATE LIVID RABID SHARP
FIERCE FURIAL FURIED INSANE RENISH
STORMY ACHARNE FRANTIC HOPPING
MADDING MANKIND PELTING RAGEOUS
REDWOOD RUSHING TEARING VIOLENT
FRENZIED MAENADIC TOWERING
VEHEMENT VESUVIAN WRATHFUL
FURL FOLD HAND ROLL STOW WRAP
FRESE TRUSS FARDEL FURDLE
FURLOUGH LEAVE BLIGHTY
FURNACE ARC KILN OVEN TANK BENCH
CUPEL DRIER DRYER FORGE MOUTH
BURNER CALCAR COCKLE CUPOLA
HEATER ATHANOR CHAFERY FIREPOT
PUDDLER ROASTER BESSEMER
BLOOMERY CALCINER CHAUFFER
FIREWORK IRONCLAD LIMEKILN
PRODUCER REFINERY TRYWORKS
(— DOOR) TWEEL
(ALMOND —) ALMAN
(ARC —) HEROULT
(GLASS-HEATING —) TISAR
(PORTABLE —) DANDY CRESSET
FURNISH ARM SOW DECK FEAT FEED
FILL FRET FRUB GIVE LEND TRIM VEST
ARRAY BESEE ENDOW EQUIP FRAME
INDUE PITCH POINT SERVE SPEED STOCK
STORE STUFF AFFORD GRAITH INSURE
INVEST OUTFIT RENDER SUPPLY
ADVANCE APPAREL APPOINT BRACKET
GARNISH INSTORE PERFORM PLENISH
PRESENT PRODUCE PROVIDE SUFFICE
ACCOUTER DECORATE FRUBBISH
MINISTER ACCOMMODATE
(— ABUNDANTLY) FREQUENT
(— ANALYSIS) ACCOUNT
(— FULLY) CHARGE
(— REFRESHMENT) EASE
(— WITH) BESEE
(— WITH DRINK) BIRL BYRL
(— WITH MEALS) BOARD
(— WITH NEW PARTS) RETROFIT
(— WITH STEEP SLOPE) ESCARP
(— WITH STRENGTH) MAN
(— WITH WINGS) IMP
FURNITURE ADAM BUHL TIRE SAMAN
STOOL STUFF GRAITH FITMENT INSIGHT
MEUBLES MOVABLE EQUIPAGE
ORNAMENT SUPELLEX TACKLING
(CHEAP —) BORAX
(SHIP'S —) HARNESS
(STORED —) LUMBER

FURROW FUR GAP GAW RIB RUT FURR
GRIP HINT LINE PLOW RAIN RILL ROUT
RUCK SEAM SULK CHASE DRAIN DRILL
EARTH FIELD RIGOL SCORE SEUGH STRIA
GROOVE GUTTER INDENT SULCUS
SUTURE TRENCH BREAKER CHAMFER
CHANNEL CRUMPLE FEERING PLOWING
QUILLET SCRATCH WINDROW WRINKLE
CARRIAGE NOTAULIX THOROUGH
VALLECULA
FURTHER MO AID YET ALSO HELP YOND
ADDED AGAIN FRESH SPEED SUPRA
BEYOND EXTEND SECOND ADVANCE
DEVELOP FARTHER FORWARD PROMOTE
MOREOVER REMANENT ULTERIOR
FURTHERMORE BESIDES FURTHER
OVERMORE
FURTIVE SLY PRIVY CLAMMY SECRET
SHIFTY SNEAKY HANGDOG MEACHING
MYSTICAL SNEAKING STEALTHY
THIEVISH CLANDESTINE
FURY HAG IRE MAD WAX BURN RAGE
ANGER BRETH DREAD FUROR IRISH
RIGOR WRATH ALECTO BELDAM CHOLER
FRENZY FURORE MADNESS MEGAERA
WIDDRIM DELIRIUM FEROCITY VIOLENCE
WOODNESS TISIPHONE
FUSE RUN CAKE FLOW FLUX FRIT FUZE
MELT BLEND FOUND FUSEE FUZEE QUILL
SMELT SQUIB SWAGE TRAIN UNITE
MINGLE SPITTER COALESCE CONCRETE
CONFLATE COPULATE PORTFIRE
SAUCISSE COLLIQUATE
FUSION ZYG FLUX FUSURE CHIASMA
FLUXION CYTOGAMY MITAPSIS
PLASMOGAMY
FUSS DO ADO ROW TEW COIL FAFF FIKE
FIRK FIZZ FRET ROUT SONG STIR TIME
TOUSE TOWSE TRADE WHAUP BOTHER
CADDLE DIRDUM FANTAD FETTLE FISSLE
FISTLE FIZZLE FRAISE FUFFLE FUSTLE
HOORAY HURRAH PHRASE POTHER
RACKET SETOUT STROTH TURNUP
FOOSTER FRIGGLE FUSSIFY NAUNTLE
POOTHER SPUFFLE SPUTTER TAMASHA
BUSINESS FOOFARAW SCRONACH
FUSSINESS DAINTY FADDLE FIKERY
FOOSTER
FUSSY BUSY FIKY FIXY FUDGY PICKY
CHICHI FIDFAD PROSSY SPOFFY SPRUCE
STICKY FIDGETY NIGGLING NOTIONAL
SPOFFISH SQUEAMISH PERSNICKETY
FUSTIAN HOLMES PILLOW BOMBAST
TWADDLE CORDUROY MOLESKIN
FUTILE IDLE TOOM VAIN OTIOSE USELESS
BOOTLESS FECKLESS FOOTLESS
FUTILOUS HELPLESS NUGATORY
FUTILITY VANITY NUGACITY VAINESSE
FUTURE LATER SKULD AVENIR COMING
ONWARD OPTION TOCOME TOWARD
LAVENIR FUTURITY ONCOMING
FUZZY LOUSY MUZZY WOOLY WOOLLY

G

G GEE GOLF GEORGE

GAB YAP BLAB CHIN

GABBLE CANK CHAT BABBLE GAGGLE
PATTER TATTER YABBLE CLATTER
JAUNDER TWADDLE TWITTER SLIPSLOP
SLUMMOCK

GABLE DETAIL DORMER GABLET KENNEL
PINION AILERON PEDIMENT

GABON (CAPITAL OF —) LIBREVILLE
(LAKE OF —) ANENGUE AZINGUO
(MOUNTAIN OF —) MPELE IBOUNDJI
(NATIVE OF —) FANG ADOUMA ECHIRA
OKANDE
(RIVER OF —) ABANGA IVINDA OGOOUE
NGOUNIE
(TOWN OF —) OYEM BONGO KANGO
MITZIC OMVANE MAKOKOU

GAD RUN FISK JAZZ RAKE JINKET
TRAIPSE VIRETOT
(— ABOUT) HAIK ROLL STRAM
GALLANT TROLLOP
(BROTHER OF —) ASHER
(FATHER OF —) JACOB
(MOTHER OF —) ZILPAH

GADFLY GAD CLEG BRIZE STOUT WHAME
BOTFLY BREEZE GADBEE OESTRID
TABANID HORSEFLY

GADGET GIZMO DINGUS DOODAD GILGUY
HICKEY JIGGER JIMJAM WIDGET
CONCERN DOFUNNY GIMMICK BUSINESS
GIMCRACK CONTRAPTION

GAEL CELT SCOT GOIDEL GAEDHEAL

GAELIC ERSE IRISH

GAFF CLIP SPAR SPUR YARD GAFFLE
GABLOCK GAFFLET SLASHER GAVELOCK

GAFFER STAGEHAND

GAG BOFF JOKE PONG SCOB HEAVE
KEVEL AGUAJI MUZZLE WHEEZE

GAGE (ALSO SEE GAUGE) LAY PAWN
WAGE GAUGE JEDGE NORMA WAGER
FEELER PLEDGE SPIDER SCANTLE
STANDARD

GAIETY JOY GALA JEST RANT CHEER
MIRTH BAWDRY FROLIC LEVITY
BAUDERY BEGONIA DAFFING GAYNESS
JOLLITY JOYANCE ROLLICK BUOYANCY
FESTIVAL HILARITY VIVACITY

GAILY GAY BRAVELY LIGHTLY

GAIN BAG DAP GET NET POT WIN BEAR
BOOT GROW HAVE LAND MAKE PELF
SACK TILL ADDLE BOOTY CATCH LATCH
LUCRE REACH SCORE ARRIVE ATTAIN
CHIEVE DERIVE GATHER INCOME OBTAIN
PROFIT STRAIN CAPTURE CONQUER
EMBRACE GAYMENT GETTING HARVEST
POSSESS PROCURE REALIZE VANTAGE
WINNING CLEANING CONQUEST
PURCHASE PERQUISITE
(— ADMISSION) ENTER

(— ADVANTAGE) GLEEK
(— ASCENDANCY) PREVAIL
(— BY EXTORTION) SQUEEZE
(— BY FORTUNE) DRAW HAZARD
(— COMMAND OF) MASTER
(— IN FAVOR) PROPITIATE
(— KNOWLEDGE) EDIFY LEARN
(— OVER) ENGAGE
(— UNDERSTANDING) SMOKE
(— WITHOUT DEDUCTION) CLEAR
(DISHONEST —) MEED
(ESTIMATED —) ESTEEM
(ILL-GOTTEN —) PELF BOODLE
(ILLICIT —) SPLOSH
(MATERIAL —) PUDDING
(UNEXPECTED —) BUNCE

GAINSAY DENY FORBID IMPUGN OPPOSE
REFUTE RESIST DISPUTE RECLAIM
WITHSAY

GAIT BAT JOG GANG LOPE PACE RACK
SKIP STEP TROT VOLT WALK AUBIN
GOING STALK TRAIN ALLURE CANTER
GALLOP LOUNGE SLOUCH SWINGE
TODDLE WADDLE WALLOW WAMBLE
WOBBLE DOGTROT HICKORY PIAFFER
SAUNTER SCUTTLE SHAMBLE SHUFFLE
WALKING WAUCHLE
(— OF ILL-BROKEN HORSE) CHACK
(DEFECTIVE —) WINDING
(LIMPING —) HIRPLE
(UNSTEADY —) STAGGER
(4-BEAT —) AMBLE

GAITER SPAT VAMP STRAD BONNET
BRAGAS COCKER GASKIN GUETRE
HOGGER PUTTEE GAMBADE GAMBADO
LEGGING STARTUP BOOTIKIN CUTTIKIN
(PL.) UPPERS GASKINS GAMASHES
GRAMOCHES

GALATEA (DAUGHTER OF —)
LEUCIPPUS
(FATHER OF —) NEREUS
(HUSBAND OF —) PYGMALION
(LOVER OF —) ACIS
(MOTHER OF —) DORIS
(SON OF —) PAPHUS METHARME

GALAXY NEBULA SPIRAL
(KIND OF —) SEYFERT

GALE BLOW GELL HELM WIND GAGEL
PERRY STOUR BUSTER EASTER BAYBUSH
BURSTER GALEAGE TEMPEST FLEAWOOD
GALEWORT NORWESTER

GALL BAIT FELL FRET NERVE WRING
ANBURY COCKLE HARASS ANBERRY
CHUTZPA GALLNUT KNOPPER NUTGALL
BEDEGUAR CECIDIUM CHUTZPAH
FLEASEED IRRITATE OAKBERRY
SEEDGALL SPURGALL TACAHOUT
(SAND —) SALT NATRON SANDIVER

GALLANT GAY BEAU PROW BLADE

BRAVE BULLY CIVIL JOLLY LOVER NOBLE
PREUX SHOWY SPARK SWAIN DONZEL
ESCORT HEROIC POLITE RUTTER SPARKY
SQUIRE SUITOR AMATORY AMORIST
AMOROSO AMOROUS CONDUCT
GALANTE GREGORY SPARKER STATELY
TOPPING YOUNKER BELAMOUR
CAVALIER CICISBEO FEMALIST GALLIARD
HANDSOME POLISHED
GALLANTRY GAME DRURY DRUERY
BRAVERY COURAGE PROWESS CHIVALRY
PARAMOUR
GALLERY POY SAP COOP JUBE LOFT
PAWN ALURE BOYAU ORIEL PRADO
ARCADE BURROW DEDANS NARROW
PIAZZA SCHOOL SOLLAR SUBWAY
TUNNEL BALCONY GALERIE HEADWAY
MIRADOR TERRACE VERANDA BARTISAN
BRATTICE CANTORIA CORRIDOR
HOARDING PARADISE PERAMBLE
SCAFFOLD TRAVERSE BLINDSTORY
(— IN BAZAAR) PAWN
(— IN HOUSE OF COMMONS)
VENTILATOR
(— MADE BY INSECT) MINE
(— OF FORT) CASEMATE
(CHURCH —) JUBE LOFT
(MINE —) BORD BROW SLOVAN
(MINSTREL'S —) ORIEL
(OPEN —) LOGGIA
(UNDERGROUND —) HYPOGEUM
GALLEY FUST CUDDY DRAKE FOIST STICK
BIREME HEARTH ZYGITE BASTARD
CABOOSE DROMOND GALLIOT HEXERIS
LYMPHAD TRIREME UNIREME CAMBOOSE
COOKROOM CROMSTER GALLEASS
RAMBERGE
(CHIEFTAIN'S —) BIRLING
(PHILIPPINE —) CALAN
(VIKING —) AESC DRAKE
GALLIVANT KITE ROAM ROVE GALLANT
GALLON GAWN CONGIUS
(— OF ORE) DISH
(EIGHTH —) OCTARIUS
(HALF —) POTTLE
(128 —S) LEAGUER
GALLOP FOG RUN AUBIN PRICK CANTER
CAREER COURSE TITTUP WALLOP
TANTIVY
GALLOWS NUB CRAP DROP FORK TREE
BOUGH CHEAT FURCA WIDDY GIBBET
WOODIE DERRICK FORCHES JUSTICE
POTENCE STIFLER WARYTREE
GALVANIZE ZINCIFY SHERADISE
GAMBIA (CAPITAL OF —) BANJUL
(COIN OF —) BUTUT DALASI
(LANGUAGE OF —) JOLA WOLOF
FULANI MALINKE
(MONEY OF —) DALASI
(NATIVE OF —) JOLA PEUL WOLOF
DIOLAS FULANI MANDINGO SERAHULI
(TOWN OF —) KAUUR MANSA FATOTO
BINTANG BRIKAMA KUNTAUR KUNTAUR
GAMBIT MANEUVER
GAMBLE BET DICE GAFF GAME NICK
PLAY PUNT RISK SPORT STAKE WAGER

CHANCE GAMMON HAZARD PLUNGE
FLUTTER
(— AGAINST) BUCK
GAMBLER PIKER SPORT CARROW
DEALER PLAYER PUNTER HUSTLER
PLAYMAN PLUNGER SLICKER THROWER
BLACKLEG GAMESTER HAZARDER
GAMBLING HOUSE HELL TRIPOT
GAMBOL HOP PLAY CAPER FRISK KEVEL
PRANK CAREER CAVORT FROLIC PRANCE
GAMBADO CAPRIOLE
GAME COB FUN JEU JIG GAMY LAKE
MAIL PLAY DANCE GAMEY PARTY SPIEL
SPORT WATHE BATTUE MORRIS QUARRY
RAMSCH VENERY JENKINS KNICKER
BREATHER FIGHTING FOREGAME
(— FOR FISHERMEN) SKISH
(— LIKE HANDBALL) FIVES
(— LIKE HOCKEY) DODDART
(— NARROWLY WON) SQUEAKER
(— OF CAT) BILLET
(— OF FOOTBALL) BOWL CAMP
(— OF FORFEITS) KEN
(— OF HOCKEY) BANDY SHINNY
(— OF INSULTS) DOZENS
(— OF MARBLES) TAW BOWL BONCE
GULLY KEEPS KNUCKS MIGGLES
(— OF MENTAL SKILL) GO CHESS
CHECKERS
(— OF NINEPINS) KAILS
(— OF PRISONER'S BASE) CHEVY
CHIVVY
(— WITH BOOMERANG) BRIST
(— WITH COUNTERS) DUMPS GOOSE
(— WITH SHUTTLECOCK) TAHYING
(BACKGAMMON —) HIT IRISH
(BALL —) CAT TUT SNOB CATCH RUGBY
SOCCER SQUASH TENNIS CRICKET
KNAPPAN BASEBALL FOOTBALL
HANDBALL SLUGFEST SOFTBALL
(CARD —) AS HOC LOO MAW NAP PAM
PIT PUT SET BRAG CENT FARO FISH
FROG GRAB JASS LANT PINK POOL POPE
POST RUFF SANT SKAT SLAM SNAP
SOLO STUD VINT BEAST BUNCO BUNKO
CARDS CARIE CHICO CINCH COMET
CRIMP DECOY GILET GLEEK GRAND
LEAST MONTE NODDY OMBER OMBRE
PEDRO PITCH POKER PRIME RUMMY
SCOPA SLAMM STOPS STUSS TRUMP
WHIST BANKER BASSET BIRKIE BOODLE
BOSTON BRIDGE CASINO CHEMMY
COMMIT ECARTE EIGHTS EUCHRE
FARMER FLINCH HEARTS HOWELL
LOADUM PANFIL PIQUET QUINZE
RAMSCH ROUNCE SLOUGH SMUDGE
SPIDER TOURNE AUCTION AUTHORS
BELOTTE BEZIQUE CANASTA CASSINO
CAYENNE CHICAGO COONCAN GARBAGE
HUNDRED JACKPOT PLAFOND PONTOON
PRIMERO REVERSI SCOPONE SETBACK
TRIUMPH VINGTUN VITESSE BACCARAT
BASEBALL BRISCOLA COMMERCE
CONQUIAN CONTRACT CRIBBAGE
FREAKPOT HANDICAP IMPERIAL
NAPOLEON PATIENCE PENCHANT
PENNEECH PINOCHLE SHOWDOWN

SKINBALL SKINNING SLAPJACK TREDILLE
TRESILLO VERQUERE VIDERUFF
(CARNIVAL —) HOOPLA
(CHILDREN'S —) TAG DIBS JACKS
KICKBALL PEEKABOO
(CONFIDENCE —) RAMP BIGMITT
(COURT —) PELOTA SQUASH TENNIS
HANDBALL
(DICE —) FARE TRAY BINGO CRAPS
NOVUM RAPHE HAZARD BARBUDI
ADDITION BARBOTTE CAMEROON
HOOLIGAN
(DRAWN —) SPOIL REFAIT
(DRINKING —) HIJINKS
(EGYPTIAN —) SENT SENIT
(GAMBLING —) EO TAN FARO HAND
PICO BOULE CRAPS MACAO MONTE
POKER PROPS RONDO STUSS BRELAN
HAZARD RONDEAU ROULETTE
(GENERAL —) HEI HIM HIT HOB TAG TIG
BALL BASE BULL BUNT BUZZ CENT DIBS
DUCK FARE GOLF HOLE JOWL KENO
MALL POLO POOL SLAM SNOB TICK
BANDY BINGO BONCE BOULE CHESS
CHUBA CHUNK CLOSH DARTS DOLOS
FIVES GOOSE HALMA HOUSE IRISH
JACKS LOTTO LURCH NOVUM NULLO
PITCH PUSSY RUGBY SALTA SALVO
SCRUB TROCO WHOOP BEAVER BEETLE
CAROMS CHIVVY CHUNKY CLUMPS
COBNUT COCKAL COOTIE CRAMBO
FEEDER GOBANG GRACES HAZARD
HOOPLA HUBBUB JEREED KAYLES
MERELE PELOTA PLUMPS RAGMAN
RINGER SEESAW SHINNY SIPPIO SKILLO
STICKS TENNIS TIGTAG TIPCAT TIVOLI
TRIGON TRUCKS BALLOON BEANBAG
BEEBALL BOWLING COBBLER CONKERS
CROQUET CURLING DIABOLO DODDART
DOUBLES DREIDEL ENDBALL GOGGANS
HANGMAN HURLBAT LOGGATS
MAHJONG MATADOR MUGGINS NETBALL
PALLONE PASSAGE PEEVERS PUSHPIN
QUINTET RINGTAW SARDINE SQUAILS
STATUES TENPINS TOMBOLA ANAGRAMS
BALKLINE BASEBALL CHARADES
CHECKERS CHOUETTE DOMINOES
DOUBLETS DRAUGHTS DUCKPINS
FIVEPINS FOOTBALL FORFEITS
GIVEAWAY HARDHEAD KICKBALL
KORFBALL LEAPFROG PURCHASE
PEEKABOO PETANQUE PURPOSES
PUSHBALL PYRAMIDS RINGTOSS
ROULETTE ROUNDERS SCRABBLE
SKITTLES STOBBALL STOWBALL
TRAPBALL VERQUERE PARCHEESI
PHILOPENA SHUFFLEBOARD
(GUESSING —) LOVE MORA CANUTE
(INDIAN —) CHUNKY HUBBUB
(INFERIOR —) CHECK
(JAPANESE —) GO
(MEXICAN —) FRONTENIS
(NUMBERS —) BUG
(OUTDOOR —) GOLF POLO HURLY
ROQUE RUGBY SOCCER CROQUET
HURLING BASEBALL FOOTBALL
LACROSSE

(PROGRESSIVE —) DRIVE
(PUZZLE —) GLAIK
(REHEATED —) SALMI
(SWISS —) JASS
(THREE BOWLING —S) SERIES
(TRAPSHOOTING —) SCOOT
(WAR —) BARRIERS
(WORD —) GHOST ANAGRAMS
(PREF.) LUDI
GAMECOCK STAG
GAMEKEEPER GAMIE KEEPER WALKER
WARNER VENERER WARRENER
GAMESTER DICER PLAYER GAMBLER
PLAYMAN SHARPER HAZARDER
TABLEMAN
GAMETE SPERM OOCYTE ZYGOTE
GAMETOID OOGAMETE OOSPHERE
GAMIN TAD ARAB URCHIN GAVROCHE
GAMUT GAMME RANGE SCALE SERIES
COMPASS DIAGRAM
GANDER STEG STAIG GANNER
(— AND GEESE) SET
GANG MOB SET BAND BUND CORE CREW
GING PACK PAIR PUSH TEAM BATCH
BUNCH GROUP HORDE SPELL SQUAD
CHIURM COFFLE GAGGLE LAYOUT
MOHOCK SCHOOL COMPANY
(— MEMBER) WHYO
(— OF FISHHOOKS) PULLDEVIL
(— OF MINERS) CORE
(— OF WITCHES) COVEN
(ROWDY —) TRIBULATION
GANGLING GAWKY GANGLY
GANGLION TUMOR CEREBRUM
GANGPLANK BROW GANGWAY
GANGSTER HOOD PUNK WHYO APACHE
BANDIT COWBOY CHOPPER
GANGWAY BROW ROAD SLIP LOGWAY
TUNNEL CATWALK COULOIR GATEWAY
GANNET BOOBY GAUNT SOLAN PIQUERO
SEAFOWL ALCATRAS
GANYMEDE (BROTHER OF —) ILUS
ASSARACUS
(FATHER OF —) TROS
(MOTHER OF —) CALLIRRHOE
GAP SAG FLAW GAPE GOWL GULF MUSE
NICK SLAP SLOP WANT BREAK BRECK
CHASM CHAUM CHAWN CLOVE FRITH
MEUSE MUSET NOTCH SHARD SHERD
VUIDE BREACH GULLET HIATUS LACUNA
SPREAD THROAT VACUUM CLOSING
OPENING VACANCY VACUITY APERTURE
DIASTEMA ENTREFER INTERVAL
MULTIGAP QUEBRADA
(— IN BANK OF STREAM) GAT
(— IN FOOTBALL LINE) SLOT
(— IN MEMORY) AMNESIA
(— SERVING AS PASS) COL
GAPE GAN GAP GANT GAUP GAWK GAZE
GOVE GRIN YAWN CHAUN GERNE HIATE
STARE RICTUS DEHISCE INHIATE
GAPING GALP AGAPE HIANT CHAPPY
CHASMA GAWISH MOUTHED RINGENT
ADENOIDAL
GAR HOUND SNOOK AGUJON CHERNA
GARFISH GARPIKE BILLFISH GOREFISH

GURDFISH HORNBEAK HORNFISH
HORNKECK LONGJAWS LONGNOSE
GARAGE HANGAR LOCKUP SIDING
(ROW OF —S) MEWS
GARB
(ALSO SEE APPAREL AND DRESS)
COWL GEAR TOGA VEST DRESS GUISE
HABIT APPAREL CLOTHES COSTUME
RAIMENT
(UNIVERSITY —) ACADEMICALS
GARBAGE GASH SLOP OFFAL TRASH
WASTE GIBLET REFUSE SCRAPS
GARBLE GELD JUMBLE MANGLE DISTORT
GARBLING MUTILATE MISREPRESENT
GARDEN HAW EDEN KNOT YARD ARBOR
GARTH CIRCLE POMACY POMARY
QUINTA ROSARY SHAMBA VERGER
VIHARA ACADEMY HERBARY OLITORY
ORCHARD ROCKERY TOPIARY CHINAMPA
FLORETUM HORTYARD KALEYARD
LEIGHTON PARADISE PARTERRE
POTAGERE ROSARIUM
(BEER —) BRASSERIE
(SECLUDED —) PLEASANCE
GARDENER MALI PONICA CROPPER
PLANNER BOSTANGI
GARGANTUA AND PANTAGRUEL
(AUTHOR OF —) RABELAIS
(CHARACTER IN —) JOHN BRIDE
BACBUC TRIPPE BADEBEC PANURGE
ANARCHUS JOBERLIN GARGANTUA
TRIBOULET GARGAMELLE GRANGOSIER
HOLOFERNES PANTAGRUEL PICROCHOLE
PONOCRATES ENTOMMEURES
TROUILLOGAN RAMINAGROBIS
GARGANTUAN HUGE VAST GIANT
HOMERIC TITANIC ENORMOUS GIGANTIC
HOMERIAN
GARGLE GURGLE COLLUTORY
GARGOYLE BOSS
GARISH GAUDY GIDDY SHOWY CRIANT
GLARING
GARLAND BAY LEI CROWN TORAN VITTA
ANADEM CORONA CRANTS ROSARY
WREATH CHAPLET CORANCE CORONAL
FESTOON
GARLIC AJO MOLY RAMP CHIVE ALLIUM
PORRET RAMSON
GARMENT DUD TOG BACK BRAT COAT
GOWN PELL PELT RAIL ROBE SARK SHAG
SILK SLIP SLOP SULU VEST WEED ABAYA
BUREL BURKA CENTO CLOAK CLOTH
COTTE CYMAR DRESS FROCK HABIT
HAORI JOSEY JUPON KHAKI MANGA
NABOB SHAWL SHIFT SHIRT SIMAR
SKIRT STOLE WRIEL ALPACA ATTIRE
BARROW BLOUSE BURKHA CAFTAN
CAMLET CAPOTE CHAMMA COTTON
CYCLAS ERMINE EXOMIS FECKET HUIPIL
JACKET JERSEY JUMPER KERSEY KIRTLE
MOHAIR MOTLEY SARONG SHORTY
SHROUD STROUD TAMEIN ZIZITH
AMICTUS BROIGNE BUNTING CAMBLET
CASSOCK CHIRIPA CRAWLER CUCULLA
CULOTTE DOUBLET FALDING FLOCKET
GROGRAM PALETOT PELISSE RAIMENT
SHORTIE SURCOAT SWEATER VESTURE

WRAPPER BATHROBE CAMELINE
CAPUCHIN CHAUSSES COLOBIUM
CORSELET COVERALL DEERSKIN
EPIBLEMA GAMBESON GUERNSEY
HIMATION INDUMENT PADUASOY
PULLOVER SCAPULAR SEALSKIN
SLIPOVER SNOWSUIT VESTMENT
WEARABLE PETTICOAT REDINGOTE
STROUDING
(— OF DERVISH) KHIRKAH
(— OF HERALD) TABARD
(— OF HIGH PRIEST) EPHOD
(— OF PATCHES) CENTO
(ARABIAN —) ABA
(BABY'S —) BARROW CRAWLER
CREEPER
(BADLY-MADE —) DRECK
(BLUE —) MAZARINE
(BURIAL —) SHROUD
(COARSE —) BRAT STROUD
(DEFENSIVE —) JACK BROIGNE
GAMBESON
(ECCLESIASTICAL —) STOLE RHASON
ROCHET CASSOCK
(ETHIOPIAN —) CHAMMA
(HINDU —) SARI SAREE
(INFANT'S —) BARRY BARROW DIAPER
BUNTING SLEEPER PANTYWAIST
(JAPANESE —) HAORI
(LEATHER —) BUFF
(LINEN —) LINE
(LONG —) JIBBA KANZU STOLE JIBBEH
MANDYAS PELISSE HIMATION
(MEDIEVAL —) ROCHET CHAUSSES
DALMATIC GAMBESON
(MONK'S —) SCAPULAR
(MOURNING —) SABLE
(ONE-PIECE —) BODYSUIT
(ONE-PIECE WOMAN'S —) CATSUIT
(OUTER —) BRAT COAT GOWN HAIK
HYKE SLOP WRAP FROCK HAORI NABOB
PALLA PILCH SMOCK DOLMAN ROCHET
CHEMISE GALABIA PALETOT SURCOAT
SWEATER HIMATION OVERSLOP
(PADDED —) TRUSS
(PENITENTIAL —) CILICE
(PULLOVER —) DASHIKI
(SLEEVELESS —) ABA CAPE COWL
VEST MANTLE CUCULLA GANDURAH
(SQUARE —) KAROSS
(SYRIAN —) ABAYA
(THIN —) GOSSAMER
(TIGHT-FITTING —) HOSE COTTE
TRICOT LEOTARD
(WOMAN'S —) IZAR BURKA CYMAR
NABOB SIMAR BURKHA CHITON JOSEPH
PEPLOS PEPLUM VISITE BLOUSON
BURNOUS
(PREF.) RHACO
GARNER REAP STORE GATHER IMBARN
COLLECT
GARNET GRENAT PYROPE ANTHRAX
GRANATE OLIVINE VERMEIL ESSONITE
MELANITE ROSOLITE YANOLITE
CARBUNCLE RHODOLITE UVAROVITE
GARNISH LARD TRIM ADORN DRESS
EQUIP MENSE STICK FURNISH PARSLEY

TOPPING CHUMMAGE DECORATE
DUXELLES ORNAMENT
GARNISHED GARNI
GARRET ATTIC SOLAR MANSARD
COCKLOFT
GARRISON WARD STUFF PRESIDY
WARNISON
GARROTE STRANGLE
GARRULITY POLYLOGY
GARRULOUS GABBY TALKY WORDY
BABBLY TONGUY VOLUBLE
GARTER GARTEN LEGLET ELASTIC
STRAPPLE
GAS DAMP XENON FLATUS GENAPP
LEAVEN OXYGEN PETROL EXHAUST
KRYPTON YPERITE AFTERGAS ETHERION
FIREDAMP HYDROGEN STANNANE
VESICANT
(COLORLESS —) OXANE KETENE
GERMANE STIBINE
(EXPLOSIVE —) METHYLAMINE
(NERVE —) SARIN
(NONCOMBUSTIBLE —) INERT
(POISONOUS —) ARSINE ADAMSITE
AQUINITE CYANOGEN PHOSGENE
BRETONITE PHOSPHINE
(TEAR —) ACROLEIN
(VOLCANIC —) MOFETTE
GASEOUS AERIFORM GASIFORM
VOLATILE
GASH CUT CHOP LASH BLASH CRIMP
GANCH GRIDE SCORE SLASH SLISH
SCOTCH SLUICE TRENCH INCISION
INCISURE
GASKET LUTE CASKET GASKIN GROMMET
SCISSIL
GASOLINE AVGAS JUICE PETROL
BENZINE NATURAL
GASP FOB BLOW GAPE KINK PANK PANT
CHINK CROAK FETCH THRATCH
GASPING CHINK
GASTRONOME EPICURE
GASTROPOD SLUG DRILL HARPA OLIVA
SNAIL BUCKIE NERITE ABALONE
MOLLUSK TOXIFER UNIVALVE VELUTINA
PULMONATE PROSOBRANCH
GATE BAB JET HEAD LIFT PORT SLAP
YATE YETT ENTRY JANUA SALLY SPRAY
STICK TORAN ENAJIM ESCAPE FENDER
HARROW INGATE LIGGAT PADDLE
PORTAL RUNNER TORANA TORANA
WICKET ZAGUAN CLICKET FIVEBAR
GATEWAY LIDGATE SHUTTER ABOIDEAU
ANTEPORT DECUMANA ENTRANCE
FOREGATE GURDWARA PENSTOCK
TOLLGATE TOWNGATE TRIMTRAM
TURNPIKE
(— OF CASTLE) BAR
(— OF DRYDOCK) CAISSON
(BACK —) POSTERN
(CUSTOMS —) BARRIER
(IRRIGATION —) CHECK TAPPOON
(LICH —) SCALLAGE TRIMTRAM
(RUNNING —) FUNNEL
(SAW —) FRAME
(SAWMILL —) SASH
(SLALOM —S) HAIRPIN

(SLUICE —) HATCH VALVE
(TEMPLE —) VIMANA
(TIDE —) ABOIDEAU ABOITEAU
(WATER —) SLUICE
GATEHOUSE BAR LODGE
GATEKEEPER WARDEN CERBERUS
GATEWARD PORTITOR STILEMAN
GATEPOST DURN HARR HEEL PIER POST
SHAFT POSTEL
GATEWAY DAR DOOR GATE LOKE PORT
PYLON TORAN TORII BARWAY GOPURA
TORANA PROPYLON
GATHER GET LEK POD WIN BAND BREW
CLAN CLOT CROP CULL FURL HERD HIVE
PICK REAP RELY TUCK AMASS BANGE
BROOM BUNCH FLOCK GLEAN GUESS
INFER LEASE PLUCK RAISE SWEEP
ACCRUE COMPEL CORRAL DECERP
DERIVE GARNER HUDDLE HUSTLE
IMBARN MUSTER RAMASS SCRAPE
CLUSTER COLLATE COLLECT COMPILE
CONGEST CONVENE CONVOKE HARVEST
RAMMASS RECRUIT ASSEMBLE
CUMULATE SHEPHERD
(— AS ARMY) HOST
(— BY SCRAPING) SCRATCH
(— GRASS SEED) STRIP
(— HEADWAY) SET
(— HERBS) SIMPLE
(— IN A HEAP) HATTER
(— IN RAGS) TAT
(— SEWING) GAUGE
(— UP) KILT
(SUFF.) LEGE
GATHERED KILTED CUMULATE
GATHERER GEDDER TUCKER RUFFLER
CHICLERO PLICATOR PUCKERER
GATHERING HUI LED LEK SUM FAIR
FEST KNOT SING SIVA LEVEE SHINE
TRYST AFFLUX INDABA MUDDLE PLISSE
POWWOW RUELLE COLLECT COMMERS
COMPANY FUNFEST HARVEST HUSKING
JOLLITY MEETING MOOTING NYMPHAL
ROCKING TURNOUT ASSEMBLY
CONCLAVE FUNCTION PANIONIA
POTATION RECOURSE SINGSONG
SOCIABLE STAMPEDE
(— OF ANIMALS) DRIVE
(— OF ARMED MEN) HOSTING
(— OF CLOTH) SHIRR SHIRRING
(— OF FILM) CISSING
(— OF SCOUTS) CAMPOREE JAMBOREE
(— PLACE) LESCHE
(BASUTO —) PITSO
(FORMAL —) HALL
(RELIGIOUS —) SHOUT
(SOCIAL —) BEE FRY BAKE BALL CLUB
DRUM STAG WINE BAILE BINGE BINGO
DANCE MIXER SHIVOO SMOKER CANTICO
KLATSCH SHINDIG SQUEEZE BARBECUE
CAMPFIRE CLAMBAKE TALKFEST
RECEPTION SYMPOSIUM
(STUDENTS' —) KOMMERS
GAUCHE CLUMSY AWKWARD
GAUD GAY GAUDY FANGLE VANITY
TRINKET
GAUDINESS GLARE GLITTER

GAUDY GAY LOUD CHEAP FLARY SHOWY
VAUDY BRAZEN FLASHY FLIMSY FLORID
GARISH GAWISH SKYRIN TAWDRY
TINSEL BRANKIE CHINTZY FLARING
GAUDISH GLARING MERETRICIOUS

GAUGE (ALSO SEE GAGE) BORE GAGE
MOOT PLUG SIZE TRAM GADGE NORMA
RANGE DENTIN FEELER FORMER GABARI
DEPTHEN TEMPLET TRAMMEL ESTIMATE
INDICANT MEASURER STANDARD
SURFACER TEMPLATE MANOMETER
(— FOR SLATES) SCANTLE
(RAIN —) UDOMETER

GAUGER SURVEYOR

GAUNT BONY GRIM LANK LEAN SLIM
THIN PINED SPARE THIRL BARREN
HAGGED HOLLOW MEAGER SHELLY
HAGGARD SLENDER DESOLATE
RAWBONED CADAVEROUS

GAUNTLET TOP CUFF GLOVE GANTLET
GAINPAIN GANTLOPE

GAUZE LISSE MARLI UMPLE CYPRESS
TIFFANY CARBASUS

GAUZY FILMY

GAVEL HAMMER GAVELAGE

GAVOTTE MUSETTE

GAWK GAWKY GAWNEY LUMPKIN
RAMMACK

GAWKY GOWKIT ANGULAR AWKWARD
GAWKISH

GAY MAD AIRY BOON DAFT GLAD GLEG
HIGH RORY TRIM WILD BONNY BUXOM
GAUDY JOLLY LIGHT MERRY NITID RIANT
RORTY SUNNY VAUDY WLONK ALEGER
BLITHE CHEERY FLASHY FRISKY FROLIC
GARISH JOCUND JOVIAL JOYFUL
JOYOUS KIPPER LIVELY SOCIAL SPORTY
WANTON BOBBISH CHIPPER FESTIVE
GALLANT GIOJOSO GLEEFUL LARKING
RACKETY SMICKER SMILING TITTUPY
WINSOME CAVALIER DEBONAIR
FROHLICH GAMESOME PLEASANT
PRIMROSE SPARKISH SPLENDID
SPORTIVE

GAZE EYE PRY CAPE GAPE GOWK LEER
LOOK MOON OGLE PEER PORE SCAN
TOOT GLAIK GLARE GLOAT GLORE SIGHT
STARE TWIRE VISIE WLITE ASPECT
GLOWER REGARD AFTEREYE

GAZELLE AHU GOA ADMI AOUL CORA
DAMA MOHR ADDRA ARIEL KORIN
MHORR DZEREN GROUSE ALGAZEL
CHIKARA CORINNE DIBATAG TABITHA
CHINKARA

GAZETTE COURANT JOURNAL
(— OF CRIMES) HUE

GEAR KIT SPUR TACK TRIM IDLER TOOTH
FOURTH GRAITH HYPOID PINION TACKLE
CLOBBER GEARING HARNESS REVERSE
RIGGING SEGMENT TRILOBE BACKPACK
HEADGEAR OVERDRIVE
(— OF DIVER) ARMOR
(CHAFING —) SCOTCHMAN
(DEFENSIVE —) ARMORY
(RUNNING —) CARRIAGE
(TRANSMISSION —) HIGH FIRST SPEED
FOURTH SECOND REVERSE

GEARED GIRT

GEARWHEEL UNILOBE WOBBLER

GEL JELL JELLY LIVER GELATE ALCOGEL

GELATIN AGAR GLUE COLLIN GLUTIN
GLUTOID HAITSAI NORGINE ISINGLASS

GELATINOUS COLLOID MUCULENT
JELLYLIKE

GELD LIB GELT ALTER CASTRATE

GELDING HORSE SPADE SPADO

GEM GIM JADE ONYX OPAL RUBY AGATE
BERYL BIJOU JAZEL JEWEL PEARL SPARK
STONE TOPAZ ZIMME AMULET BAGUET
CRUSTA GARNET IOLITE JASPER PEBBLE
PYROPE RONDEL ZIRCON CITRINE
DIAMOND DOUBLET EMERALD JACINTH
KUNZITE ONEGITE PERIDOT SPARKLE
ACHROITE AMATRICE AMETHYST
BAGUETTE HYACINTH MARQUISE
ORIENTAL RONDELLE SAPPHIRE
SARDONYX HIDDENITE MOONSTONE
RUBICELLE
(— CARVED IN RELIEF) CAMEO
INTAGLIO
(— ENGRAVED WITH CHARM)
ABRAXAS
(— OF IMPERFECT BRILLIANCY)
LOUPE
(— REFLECTING LIGHT IN 6 RAYS)
ASTERIA
(IMITATION —) PASTE
(UNCUT —) ROUGH CABOCHON

GEMSBOK ORYX KOKAMA GEMSBUCK

GEMSTONE JADE STAR CHEVEE PYROPE
SPINEL EMERALD FISHEYE CROSSCUT
HYALITHE MORGANITE
(PART OF —) BEZEL CROWN CULET
FACET TABLE GIRDLE PAVILION

GENDER SEX KIND CLASS FEMININE

GENE GEN ALLEL AMORPH FACTOR
LETHAL PRIMER CYTOGENE MODIFIER
POLYGENE RECESSIVE

GENERAL (ALSO SEE SOLDIER) MAIN
MOST BROAD GROSS ATAMAN COMMON
HETMAN PUBLIC VULGAR CURRENT
GENERIC MARSHAL SUMMARY AUFIDIUS
CANIDIUS CATHOLIC ECUMENIC
ENCYCLIC OVERHEAD PANDEMIC
PUFIDIUS STRATEGE BRIGADIER

GENERALITY CREDO GENERALE

GENERALIZATION LAW AXIOM
BROMIDE

GENERALIZE WIDEN EXTEND SPREAD
BROADEN

GENERALIZED GROSS GLOBAL

GENERALLY BROADLY LARGELY
OVERALL ROUNDLY MOSTWHAT

GENERATE MAKE SIRE TEEM BEGET
BREED IMPEL SPAWN STEAM CREATE
FATHER GENDER IMPOSE KITTLE
DEVELOP INBREED PRODUCE ENGENDER

GENERATION AGE KIND TIME WORLD
STRAIN STRIND DESCENT DIPLOID
GETTING KINDRED GAMOBIUM GENITURE
SAECULUM THEOGONY TRIPLOID
UPSPRING OFFSPRING
(FUTURE —S) POSTERITY
(SPONTANEOUS —) ABIOGENESIS

GENERATOR KIPP BUZZER DYNAMO RULING ELEMENT DIPHASER GENERANT OSCILLATOR

GENEROSITY GRACE LARGE BOUNTY GENTRY BREADTH FREEDOM HONESTY COURTESY GOODNESS KINDNESS LARGESSE

GENEROUS BIG FREE OPEN SOFT FRANK HEFTY LARGE NOBLE LIBERAL GRACIOUS HANDSOME INSORDID LARGEOUS MAGNIFIC OPENHANDED

GENEROUSLY LUCKY MANLY KINDLY FRANKLY

GENESIS BIRTH ORIGIN BERESHIT GENETICS

GENIAL BIEN WARM DOUCE SONSY DOULCE FORTHY FURTHY HEARTY KINDLY MELLOW MENTAL CHEERFUL GRACIOUS PLEASANT

GENIALITY BONHOMIE

GENIE GENIUS HATHOR SANDMAN

GENII XIN JANN

GENIUS KA FIRE GIFT HAPI KALI TURN ANGEL BRAIN DEMON GENIO NUMEN DAEMON INGENY INGINE TALENT WIZARD DUSTMAN DUAMUTEF EINSTEIN FRAVASHI SILVANUS

(— OF LANGUAGE) IDIOM

GENRE EPIC KIND SORT TYPE CLASS STYLE FABLIAU SPECIES CATEGORY

GENTEEL NICE GENTY GENTIL JAUNTY POLITE STYLISH GRACEFUL

GENTIAN BIT FELWORT AGUEWEED GALLWEED BALDMONEY PENNYWORT

GENTILITY POLISH CIVILITY GENTRICE NICENESS

GENTLE MOY CALM DEFT DEWY FAIR HEND KIND MEEK MILD MURE NESH SLOW SOFT SOOT TAME BLAND CANNY LIGHT LITHE MILKY QUIET SMALL SOBER SWEET BENIGN BONAIR CADISH DOCILE FACILE LYDIAN MODEST PLACID REMISS SILKEN SILVER SOFTLY TENDER AFFABLE AMIABLE CLEMENT GRADUAL SOAKING SUBDUED DEBONAIR DELICATE DOVELIKE EGGSHELL LAMBLIKE LENITIVE MAIDENLY MANSUETE MODERATE PEACEFUL SARCENET TOWARDLY TRANQUIL

(— AS OF THE WIND) LOOM

GENTLEMAN NIB SIR BABU GENT TOFF BABOO CURIO DORAY SAHIB SENOR GEMMAN MILORD SENHOR SIGNOR YONKER BRAVERY GALLANT GENTMAN MYNHEER CAVALIER MIRABELL SEIGNEUR SEIGNIOR SQUIREEN

(— COMMONER) HAT

(— TRAINING FOR KNIGHTHOOD) DONZEL

(COUNTRY —) SQUIRE

(GIPSY —) RYE

(MILITARY —) CADET

(POOR —) BUCKEEN

(WOULD-BE —) SHONEEN

(PL.) HERREN CHIVALRY

GENTLEMANLY JAUNTY

GENTLENESS FLESH LENITY AMENITY DOUCEUR CLEMENCY KINDNESS MANSUETUDE

GENTLY SOFT CANNY SOAVE EASILY FAIRLY LIGHTLY EASYLIKE PRETTILY TENDERLY

GENTRY COUNTY GENTRICE SQUIRAGE SZLACHTA

GENUINE ECHT GOOD LEAL PURE REAL TRUE VRAI PLAIN PUKKA SOLID ACTUAL ARRANT DINKUM DIRECT HONEST KOSHER PISTIC CURRENT GERMANE GRADELY SINCERE VERIDIC GRAITHLY STERLING

(NOT —) TIN SHAM BOGUS PLASTIC PRETENDED

(SEEMINGLY —) COLORABLE

GENUINENESS VERIDITY

GENUS KIND CLASS ANALOG GENDER GENERAL

(— OF ALGAE) DASYA FUCUS BANGIA CHORDA CODIUM HYPNEA NOSTOC PADINA DIATOMA LEMANEA LIAGORA PTILOTA VALONIA ZYGNEMA

(— OF AMOEBA) CHAOS

(— OF AMPHIBIAN) HYLA RANA SIREN PROTEUS

(— OF ANT) ATTA ECITON LASIUS PONERA TERMES FORMICA

(— OF ANTELOPE) ORYX KOBUS BUBALIS GAZELLA MADOQUA REDUNCA

(— OF APE) PAN PONGO SIMIA

(— OF APHID) ADELGES CHERMES

(— OF ARACHNID) ACARUS GALEODES

(— OF ARMADILLO) DASYPUS XENURUS

(— OF BACTERIA) VIBRIO EIMERIA ERWINIA GAFFKYA PROTEUS SARCINA

(— OF BADGER) MELES ARCTONYX HELICTIS

(— OF BARNACLE) LEPAS BALANUS ELMINIUS

(— OF BAT) EUDERMA PETALIA

(— OF BEAN) ABRUS

(— OF BEAR) URSUS

(— OF BEAVER) CASTOR

(— OF BEE) APIA APIS BOMBUS ANDRENA TRIGONA

(— OF BEETLE) AMARA FIDIA HISPA LAMIA LARIA LYTTA MELOE SAGRA ALTICA ASILUS CLERUS ELATER LYCTUS PTINUS SILPHA ACILIUS ADELOPS AGRILUS ANOBIUM ANOMALA BRUCHUS CARABUS CASSIDA EPITRIX PRIONUS SAPERDA SITARIS

(— OF BIRD) ARA ALCA APUS CRAX CREX GYPS JYNX MIRO MITU MOHO OTIS PICA RHEA SULA TYTO XEMA AJAJA ANOUS ANSER ARDEA ARGUS ASTUR BUCCO FALCO GAVIA GOURA GUARA GYGIS IRENA JUNCO LARUS LERWA LOXIA MIMUS MITUA MUNIA PIPRA PITTA SITTA TODUS UPUPA VIDUA VIREC ALAUDA ALCEDO ANHIMA ANTHUS AQUILA BONASA BRANTA CAPITO CIRCUS COLIUS CORVUS DACELO ELANUS FULICA GALLUS JACANA LANIUS LEIPOA LIMOSA MARECA

MENURA MEROPS MILVUS MONASA
NESTOR NUMIDA PASSER PASTOR
PERDIX PERNIS PROGNE QUELEA RALLUS
SAPPHO SCOPUS SIALIA SPINUS STERNA
SYLVIA TETRAO TRERON TRINGA
TROGON TURDUS TURNIX VULTUR
ANHINGA APTERYX ARTAMUS BUCEROS
CACICUS CAPELLA CARIAMA CERTHIA
CHIONIS CICONIA CINCLUS COLINUS
COLUMBA COTINGA CUCULUS ELAENIA
GALBULA GARRUPA HALCYON HIRUNDO
IBYCTER ICTERUS KAKATOE LAGOPUS
LOPHURA LYRURUS MALURUS MANACUS
MESITES MILVAGO MOMOTUS ORIOLUS
PANDION PAROTIA PIRANGA PITYLUS
PLAUTUS PLOCEUS PORZANA REGULUS
SEIURUS SERINUS STURNUS TANAGRA
TIMALIA TOTANUS XENICUS ZENAIDA
(— OF BIVALVES) MYA PINNA ANOMIA
MACTRA NUCULA ETHERIA MYTILUS
PANDORA
(— OF BOWFIN) AMIA
(— OF BUG) ANASA CIMEX EMESA
CORIXA TINGIS
(— OF BUTTERFLY) CALIGO COLIAS
DANAUS MORPHO PIERIS THECLA
EURYMUS JUNONIA KALLIMA LYCAENA
PAPILIO STRYMON VANESSA ARGYNNIS
HESPERIA LEMONIAS MELITAEA
SPEYERIA
(— OF CABBAGE) COS
(— OF CACTUS) CEREUS NOPALEA
OPUNTIA
(— OF CANTELOUPE) CUCUMIS
(— OF CAT) FELIS ACINONYX HEMIGALE
(— OF CATTLE) BOS NEAT TAURUS
(— OF CEPHALOPOD) SEPIA SPIRULA
(— OF CETACEAN) INIA
(— OF CHINK) LACUNA
(— OF CHIPMUNK) EUTAMIAS
(— OF CILIATE) COLPODA CHILODON
EUPLOTES
(— OF CIVET) FOSSA PAGUMA
(— OF CLAM) ENSIS GEMMA SOLEN
SPISULA
(— OF COCKLE) CHIONE
(— OF COCKROACH) BLATTA
(— OF CODFISH) GADUS
(— OF CORAL) ASTREA FUNGIA
MAENDRA OCULINA PORITES ACROPORA
TUBIPORA
(— OF CRAB) UCA MAIA BIRGUS
CANCER GRAPSUS OCYPODE PAGURUS
LITHODES PORTUNUS
(— OF CRANE) GRUS
(— OF CRAYFISH) CAMBARUS
(— OF CRICKET) ACHETA GRYLLUS
(— OF CRUSTACEAN) APUS HIPPA
JASUS LIGIA MYSIS CYPRIS LIGYDA
SELLUS TRIOPS ARGULUS ARTEMIA
ASTACUS BOPYRUS CALAPPA CHELURA
DAPHNIA EMERITA HOMARUS IDOTHEA
LERNAEA NEBALIA SQUILLA
(— OF CTENOPHORE) BEROE CESTUM
(— OF CUCUMBER) CUCUMIS
(— OF CURASSOW) CRAX

(— OF DEER) AXIS DAMA PUDU RUSA
CERVUS MAZAMA MOSCHUS RUCERVUS
(— OF DOG) CUON CANIS LYCAON
(— OF DORMOUSE) GLIS
(— OF DRAGONFLY) AESCHNA
(— OF DUCK) AIX ANAS AYTHYA
MERGUS NYROCA NETTION SPATULA
(— OF EAGLE) AQUILA
(— OF EDENTATE) MANIS
(— OF EEL) CONGER ECHIDNA
MURAENA ANGUILLA GYMNOTUS
MORINGUA
(— OF FERN) FILIX TODEA ANEMIA
AZOLLA DOODIA CYATHEA ISOETES
ONOCLEA OSMUNDA PELLAEA WOODSIA
(— OF FIREFLY) LAMPYRIS
(— OF FISH) AMIA ESOX HURO LOTA
MOLA RAJA ZEUS ALOSA BADIS BERYX
BETTA DORAS ELOPS GADUS GOBIO
HUCHO LATES MANTA MUGIL PERCA
SALMO SARDA SOLEA UMBRA ALBULA
ANABAS APOGON BAIGRE BARBUS
BELONE CARANX CLUPEA COTTUS
DIODON GERRES GOBIUS HIODON
KUHLIA LABRUS LATRIS MOBULA
MYXINE NOMEUS PAGRUS PSETTA
REMORA SCARUS SPARUS TRIGLA
TRUTTA TURSIO WEEVER ABRAMIS
ALOPHAS ALOPIAS ARACANA ASPREDO
BROTULA CARAPUS CLARIAS DREPANE
ECHIDNA GARRUPA GIRELLA GYMNORA
LEPOMIS LIMANDA LUCANIA LYCODES
OSMERUS PEGASUS PRISTIS SCIAENA
SCOMBER SEPIOLA SERIOLA SIGANUS
SILLAGO SILURUS SPHYRNA SQUALUS
SYNODUS THUNNUS TORPEDO TOXOTES
TRIODON XIPHIAS ZOARCES
(— OF FLAGELLATE) COCOS GONIUM
OPHION SYNURA VOLVOX ATTALEA
CARYOTA EUGLENA GIARDIA
(— OF FLEA) PULEX BOSMINA
(— OF FLY) DACUS MUSCA MYMAR
PERLA PHORA ASILUS CEPHUS FANNIA
PIMPLA RHYSSA SCIARA TIPULA
CALIROA CHALCIS DIOPSIS EPHYDRA
HYLEMYA MIASTOR ORTALIS OSCINIS
PANORPA TACHINA THEREVA
(— OF FLYING SQUIRREL) BELOMYS
(— OF FOSSIL) AMPYX ERYON ADAPIS
ATRYPA BAIERA ERYOPS GEIKIA HYENIA
KLUKIA MAMMUT OLENUS ORTHIS
RHYNIA ANDRIAS ANTEDON APTIANA
ASAPHUS DICERAS EXOGYRA GANODUS
HAMITES HYBODUS KNORRIA LESKEYA
LESLEYA LOXOMMA MESONYX MOROPUS
MYLODON OTOZOUM PHACOPS PHIOMIA
PROAVIS PROETUS WALCHIA
(— OF FOX) ALOPEX VULPES UROCYON
(— OF FROG) RANA ANURA HYLODES
(— OF FUNGUS) FOMES IRPEX PHOMA
TUBER VALSA VERPA ALBUGO BREMIA
CAEOMA EMPUSA FOMAGO HYDNUM
ISARIA OIDIUM PEZIZA TORULA ZYTHIA
ACRASIA AMANITA BOLETUS CANDIDA
CHALARA CYATHUS ELSINOE ERYSIBE
FABRAEA GEASTER LEPIOTA MONILIA
NECTRIA OZONIUM PACHYMA PYTHIUM

RHIZINA RUSSULA SIMBLUM STEREUM
STICTIS STILBUM TYPHULA XYLARIA
(— OF GALLFLY) CYNIPS
(— OF GASTROPOD) FICUS HARPA
LIMAX OLIVA EBURNA PATELLA TENEBRA
SCYLLAEA STROMBUS
(— OF GEESE) CHEN ANSER NETTAPUS
(— OF GNAT) SCIARA
(— OF GOAT) IBEX CAPRA OREAMNOS
(— OF GRASS) POA ZEA AIRA COIX
AVENA BRIZA ORYZA STIPA APLUDA
ARUNDO BROMUS ELYMUS HOLCUS
LOLIUM LYGEUM MELICA MILIUM
NARDUS PHLEUM SECALE UNIOLA
ZOYSIA BAMBUSA BUCHLOE CHLORIS
CYNODON FESTUCA HILARIA HORDEUM
LAGURUS LEERSIA MELINIS MOLINIA
PANICUM SETARIA SORGHUM ZIZANIA
(— OF GRASSHOPPER) LOCUSTA
(— OF GUAN) CRAX
(— OF GULL) XEMA LARUS
(— OF HAWK) BUTEO CIRCUS
(— OF HERB) GYP IVA AMMI ARUM
BETA GEUM GLAX HEBE LENS MEUM
MUSA OLAX RUTA SIDA SIUM ADOXA
AJUGA APIOS APIUM CALLA CANNA
CAREX CARUM CICER DALEA DRABA
ERUCA ERVUM FEDIA GALAX GAURA
GILIA GLAUX HOSTA INULA LAPPA LAVIA
LAYIA LEMNA LINUM LOASA LOTUS
LUFFA MADIA MALVA NAPEA PANAX
PARIS PHACA PHLOX PILEA RHEUM
RHOEO RUBIA SEDUM TACCA URENA
VICIA VIGNA VINCA VIOLA ZIZIA ACAENA
ACNIDA ACORUS ACTAEA ADONIS
ALISMA ALLIUM ALSINE AMOMUM
ANOGRA ARABIS ARALIA ARNICA
ASARUM ATROPA BACOPA BAERIA
BASSIA BELLIS BIDENS BLITUM BLUMEA
BORAGO CAKILE CALTHA CASSIA CELSIA
CICUTA CISTUS CLEOME CNICUS
COLEUS CONIUM COPTIS COSMOS
CRAMBE CREPIS CRINUM CROCUS
CROTON CUNILA CYNARA DAHLIA
DATURA DAUCUS DIODIA DONDIA
ECHIUM ELODEA ELODES EMILIA EUCLEA
FILAGO GALEGA GALIUM GIFOLA
GYNURA ISATIS ISMENE KOCHIA KRIGIA
KUHNIA LAMIUM LECHEA LUZULA
MALOPE MENTHA MIMOSA MONTIA
MUCUNA MUILLA NERINE NERIUM
NESLIA ONONIS OTHAKE OXALIS PICRIS
PISTIA PYROLA RESEDA RESTIO RHEXIA
RIVINA RUPPIA SAGINA SALVIA SCILLA
SESBAN SESELI STEVIA SUAEDA THALIA
TULIPA VIORNA ZINNIA ABRONIA
ADLUMIA AETHUSA ALEGRIA ALETRIS
ALKANNA ALPINIA ALTHAEA ALYSSUM
AMORPHA AMSONIA ANCHUSA
ANEMONE ANETHUM ANYCHIA APHANES
ARACHIS ARCTIUM ARNEBIA ARUNCUS
BABIANA BARTSIA BEGONIA BOEBERA
BUTOMUS CACALIA CAJANUS CALYPSO
CARLINA CELOSIA CHELONE CIRCAEA
CIRSIUM CLARKIA COMARUM CROOMIA
CURCUMA CUSCUTA CYTINUS DATISCA
DECODON DERINGA DIASCIA DROSERA

ELATINE EOMECON EPISCIA ERODIUM
FELICIA FICARIA FRASERA FREESIA
FUMARIA GAZANIA GERBERA GLECOMA
GLYCINE GUNNERA HALENIA HECHTIA
HEDEOMA HOMERIA HUGELIA HYPOXIS
IRESINE JASIONE KICKXIA KNAUTIA
KOELLIA LACTUCA LAPPULA LAPSANA
LEWISIA LIATRIS LINARIA LINNAEA
LOGANIA LOPEZIA LUNARIA LUPINUS
LYCHNIS LYTHRUM MARANTA MEDEOLA
MIMULUS MITELLA MOLLUGO MONESES
MUSCARI NEMESIA NIGELLA OTHONNA
PAEONIA PAPAVER PAVONIA PEGANUM
PETUNIA PLUCHEA PRIMULA RORIPPA
ROTALIA RUELLIA SALSOLA SAMOLUS
SCANDIX SENECIO SESAMUM SHORTIA
SILYBUM SINAPIS SOLANUM SONCHUS
STACHYS STATICE SUCCISA SWERTIA
TAGETES TALINUM TELLIMA THAPSIA
THESIUM THLASPI THURNIA TORENIA
TORILIS TOVARIA TRILISA URGINEA
VALLOTA VERBENA ZEBRINA
(— OF HERON) ARDEA EGRETTA
(— OF HORSE) EQUUS CALIPPUS
EOHIPPUS
(— OF HYDROZOAN) DIPHYES
PHYSALIA
(— OF HYENA) HYAENA CROCUTA
(— OF INSECT) NEPA APHIS EMESA
JAPYX SIREX BOREUS CICADA COCCUS
CORIXA EMPUSA ICERYA KERMES
MANTIS PHASMA PODURA SIALIS THRIPS
CHALCIS FORMICA FULGORA LEPISMA
ORYSSUS RANATRA STYLOPS VEDALIA
(— OF ISOPOD) IDOTEA IDOTHEA
CIROLANA
(— OF JAY) GARRULUS
(— OF JELLYFISH) CYANEA AURELIA
AEQUOREA
(— OF JERBOA) DIPUS
(— OF KELP) AGARUM
(— OF LANGUR) SIMIAS
(— OF LEAFHOPPER) AGALLIA
EMPOASCA
(— OF LEECH) HIRUDO HAEMOPIS
(— OF LEMUR) INDRI GALAGO
(— OF LIANA) BAUHINIA
(— OF LICE) APHIS PSYLLA ARGULUS
ONISCUS BOVICOLA ERIOSOMA
GONIODES LIPEURUS
(— OF LICHEN) CORA USNEA STICTA
EVERNIA GRAPHIS LECIDEA LOBARIA
PHYSCIA CETRARIA CLADONIA
LECANORA PARMELIA ROCCELLA
STRIGULA
(— OF LIMPET) ACMAEA
(— OF LIZARD) UTA AGAMA DRACO
GEKKO AMEIVA ANGUIS ANOLIS IGUANA
EUMECES LACERTA PYGOPUS SCINCUS
ACONTIAS CHIROTES COLEONYX
LYGOSOMA RHINEURA
(— OF LOCUST) TETRIX TETTIX
(— OF MACAW) ARA
(— OF MAMMAL) BOS SUS HOMO
LAMA ALCES BISON CAPRA TAYRA
DUGONG FRISON AELURUS AILURUS
BUBALUS GALIDIA GYMNURA LINSANC

OTOCYON AUCHENIA CYCLOPES
CYNOGALE SURICATA TRAGULUS
(— OF MAPLE) ACER
(— OF MARSUPIAL) DASYURUS
MACROPUS POTOROUS TARSIPES
(— OF MARTEN) MARTES MUSTELA
(— OF MILDEW) ERYSIPHE UNCINULA
(— OF MILLIPEDE) JULUS
(— OF MINT) ICIMUM NEPETA MELISSA
PERILLA PHLOMIS ORIGANUM
(— OF MITE) ACARUS ACERIA LEPTUS
DEMODEX ACARAPIS
(— OF MOLD) MUCOR FULIGO MELIOLA
(— OF MOLE) TALPA SCALOPS
SCALOPUS
(— OF MOLLUSK) ARCA DOTO LEDA
LIMA CHAMA DONAX EOLIS FICUS
HARPA LIMAX MUREX OLIVA VENUS
AEOLIS ANOMIA BANKIA CASSIS CHITON
LEPTON LUCINA OSTREA PECTEN
PHOLAS PYRULA SEMELE TEREDO
TETHYS ACTAEON ASTARTE ATLANTA
CARDITA CARDIUM CYPRAEA CYPRINA
DOSINIA ETHERIA EXOGYRA LINGULA
TELLINA BUCCINUM GRYPHAEA HALIOTIS
LIMACINA LUTRARIA MODIOLUS
NAUTILUS PINCTADA SCYLLAEA
STROMBUS
(— OF MONGOOSE) GALIDIA
(— OF MONKEY) AOTES AOTUS CEBUS
ATELES MACACA CACAJAO COLOBUS
NASALIS SAIMIRI PITHECIA
(— OF MOOSE) ALCES
(— OF MOSQUITO) AEDES CULEX
(— OF MOSS) BRYUM CHILO EUXOA
MNIUM SAMIA SESIA TINEA ACTIAS
ALYPIA ARCTIA BOMBYX COSSUS
DATANA HYPNUM LESKEA PLUSIA
PSYCHE SPHINX THYRIS URANIA
AGROTIS ALABAMA APATELA ARCHIPS
ATTACUS BARBULA CRAMBUS FUNARIA
GRIMMIA PHASCUM PRONUBA PYRALIS
SESAMIA TORTRIX ZEUZERA ZYGAENA
(— OF MOTH) CHILO ABRAXAS
(— OF MOUSE) MUS APODEMUS
(— OF MUSKMELON) CUCUMIS
(— OF MUSKRAT) FIBER ONDATRA
(— OF NARWHAL) MONODON
(— OF NEMATODE) ACUARIA ALAIMUS
ANGUINA NECATOR
(— OF OATS) AVENA
(— OF OPOSSUM) MARMOSA
(— OF ORCHID) DISA VANDA BLETIA
LAELIA PHAJUS ACINETA AERIDES
ANGULOA BRASSIA CORDULA EUCOSIA
IBIDIUM ISOTRIA LIPARIS LISTERA
MALAXIS POGONIA VANILLA ANGRECUM
ARETHUSA BLETILLA CALANTHE
CATTLEYA CYTHEREA FISSIPES
GOODYERA MILTONIA ONCIDIUM
PERAMIUM SERAPIAS SOBRALIA
TRIPHORA
(— OF OTTER) LUTRA
(— OF OWL) BUBO NINOX STRIX
KETUPA NYCTEA AEGOLIUS SPEOTYTO
(— OF OXEN) BIBOS
(— OF OYSTER) OSTREA AVICULA

(— OF PALM) NIPA ARECA ASSAI
COCOS HOWEA SABAL ARENGA ELAEIS
INODES KENTIA RAPHIA RHAPIS ATTALEA
BACTRIS CALAMUS CARYOTA CORYPHA
ERYTHEA EUTERPE GEONOMA LATANIA
LICUALA PHOENIX SERENOA THRINAX
(— OF PARASITE) STRIGA CUSCOTA
CUSCUTA NIDPHORA
(— OF PARRAKEET) ARATINGA
(— OF PARROT) NESTER AMAZONA
KAKATOE
(— OF PEACOCK) PAVO
(— OF PENGUIN) EUDYPTES
(— OF PHALANGER) DROMICIA
(— OF PIGEON) GOURA DUCULA
COLUMBA
(— OF PLANT) ALOE ARUM COLA DION
FABA IRIS IXIA PUYA SOJA ADOXA
AGAVE ASTER BATIS CANNA CHARA
DIOON DRYAS INULA NAIAS PIPER
RUMEX TRAPA TYPHA XYRIS YUCCA
ZILLA ABROMA ACACIA AIZOON ALBUCA
ANANAS CACTUS CUPHEA DATURA
EXACUM FERULA IBERIS JAMBOS
JUNCUS LICHEN LILIUM MAYACA
MORAEA NUPHAR PHRYMA RICCIA
SILENE SMILAX STRIGA URTICA VISCUM
ALONSOA ASTILBE BALLOTA CABOMBA
CUCUMIS CYPERUS DIONAEA DROSERA
ENCELIA EPACRIS EPIGAEA EURYALE
FAGELIA GLYCINE GODETIA HELXINE
HOOKERA ISOETES ISOLOMA KARATAS
LYCOPUS MANIHOT MONARDA NELUMBO
NITELLA RAOULIA RICINUS STEMONA
SYRINGA TRIURUS TURNERA WOLFFIA
WYETHIA ZOSTERA
(— OF POPLAR) ALAMO
(— OF PORCUPINE) COENDOU
HYSTRIX
(— OF PORPOISE) INIA PHOCAENA
(— OF PRAWN) PALAEMON
(— OF RABBIT) LEPUS
(— OF RACCOON) OLINGO
(— OF RAT) ANISOMYS
(— OF RODENT) MUS CAVIA DIPUS
LEPUS ZAPUS GEOMYS LEMMUS SPALAX
CYNOMYS DINOMYS ECHIMYS LEGGADA
MERINES NESOKIA ZYZOMYS ALACTAGA
ARVICOLA CAPROMYS CITELLUS
CRICETUS HAPLODON HYDROMYS
LAGIDIUM MICROTUS MYOTALPA
ORYZOMYS
(— OF RUST) UREDO HEMILEIA
UROMYCES
(— OF SALAMANDER) ANDRIAS
EURYCEA SIREDON TRITURUS
(— OF SCALLOP) HINNITES
(— OF SCORPION) BUTHUS SCORPIO
CHELIFER
(— OF SEA ANEMONE) MINYAS
ACTINIA
(— OF SEA FAN) GORGONIA
(— OF SEA OTTER) ENHYDRA
(— OF SEA SLUG) ELYSIA
(— OF SEA URCHIN) ARBACIA CIDARIS
DIADEMA ECHINUS

(— OF SEAL) PHOCA HYDRURGA MIROUNGA ZALOPHUS
(— OF SEAWEED) ULVA ALARIA
(— OF SHARK) LAMNA GALEUS ISURUS ACRODUS ALOPIAS SPHYRNA SQUALUS CLADODUS MENASPIS SQUATINA
(— OF SHEEP) OVIS
(— OF SHELL) PUPA LAMBIS EXOGYRA LATIRUS MALLEUS TROCHUS HAMINOEA MACLUREA OLIVELLA TRIGONIA UMBRELLA
(— OF SHREW) SOREX BLARINA
(— OF SHRIMP) CRAGO CRANGON
(— OF SHRUB) IVA ACER BIXA BRYA HOYA ILEX INGA ITEA MABA OLEA RHUS ROSA SIDA THEA ULEX ALNUS ANONA BIOTA BUTEA BUXUS CATHA DALEA DIRCA ERICA EURYA FICUS HAKEA IXORA LEDUM MALUS OCHNA PADUS RIBES RUBUS SABIA SALIX TAXUS THUJA TREMA UNONA URENA VITEX ABELIA ACAENA ADELIA ALHAGI AMYRIS ANNONA ARALIA AUCUBA AZALEA BAPHIA BAUERA BETULA BLUMEA BYBLIS CANTUA CASSIA CELTIS CERCIS CISTUS CITRUS CLEOME CLUSIA COFFEA CORDIA COREMA CORNUS CORREA CROTON DAPHNE DATURA DERRIS DIOSMA DONDIA DRIMYS ECHIUM EVODIA FATSIA FEIJOA GARRYA GNETUM GREWIA GUAREA KALMIA KERRIA LARREA LIPPIA LITSEA LUCUMA LYCIUM MIMOSA MYRCIA MYRICA MYRTUS OCOTEA OLINIA OPILIA PENAEA PERSEA PIERIS PROTEA PTELEA PUNICA QUIINA RAMONA RANDIA ROCHEA ROYENA RUSCUS SALVIA SAPIUM SCHIMA SELAGO SESBAN SORBUS STEVIA STYRAX SUAEDA TECOMA AECULUS AMORPHA ARBUTUS ARDISIA ARMERIA ASIMINA ASSONIA BANKSIA BAROSMA BENZOIN BORONIA BUMELIA BURSERA CALLUNA CARISSA CASASIA CERASUS CESTRUM CLETHRA CNEORUM COLUTEA CORYLUS COTINUS CUNONIA CYRILLA CYTISUS DEUTZIA DOMBEYA DURANTA EHRETIA ENCELIA EPACRIS EPHEDRA EUCHLEA EUGENIA EURSERA FABIANA FUCHSIA GENISTA GMELINA GYMINDA HAMELIA HOVENIA KARATAS LAGETTA LANTANA MAHONIA MERATIA MONIMIA MORINDA MUTISIA MYRRHIS NANDINA NEMESIA OLEARIA OTHONNA PAVETTA PAVONIA PENTZIA PIMELEA PISONIA PURSHIA QUASSIA QUERCUS RAPANEA REMIJIA RHAMNUS RHODORA ROBINIA ROMNEYA RUELLIA SALSOLA SENECIO SKIMMIA SOLANUM SOPHORA SPIRAEA SURIANA SYRINGA TAMARIX TELOPEA XIMENIA XYLOPIA XYLOSMA ZELKOVA
(— OF SILKWORM) BOMBYX
(— OF SKUNK) MEPHITIS
(— OF SLOTH) BRADYPUS
(— OF SLUG) DOTO ARION DORIS LIMAX ELYSIA GLAUCUS
(— OF SNAIL) HUA PILA CONUS FUSUS

GALBA HELIX MITRA OVULA PHYSA THAIS TURBO CERION EULIMA NATICA NERITA RISSOA TRITON ANCYLUS BITTIUM BULINUS BUSYCON CYMBIUM LATIRUS LITIOPA LYMNARA MELANIA MODULUS PURPURA RANELLA VALVATA VERTIGO VITRINA ZONITES
(— OF SNAKE) BOA ERYX NAIA NAJA ASPIS BITIS BOIGA ECHIS ELAPS CAUSUS DABOIA ELAPHE HURRIA ILYSIA LIGUUS NATRIX PYTHON VIPERA ATHERIS BOAEDON COLUBER ECHIDNA MEHELYA OPHIDIA ZAMENIS
(— OF SPIDER) ARANEA LYCOSA MYGALE AGALENA ARGIOPE ATTIDAE NEPHILA PHOLCUS LINYPHIA ULOBORUS
(— OF SPONGE) SYCON GEODIA SCYPHA ASCETTA CHALINA GRANTIA SPONGIA SYCETTA LEUCETTA
(— OF SQUID) LOLIGO SEPIOLA
(— OF SQUIRREL) SCIURUS
(— OF SWAN) OLOR CYGNUS
(— OF TAPEWORM) BERTIA LIGULA DAVAINEA HARRISIA
(— OF TERN) GYGIS STERNA
(— OF THISTLE) CNICUS CARDUUS
(— OF TICK) ARGAS ARGUS IXODES HYALOMMA
(— OF TOAD) BUFO HYLA PIPA ALYTES XENOPUS ASCAPHUS
(— OF TREE) ACER BIXA BRYA COLA HURA ILEX INGA MABA OLAX OLEA RHUS THEA ABIES AEGLE ALNUS ANIBA BIOTA BUTEA BUXUS CARYA CEIBA CYCAS DURIO EURYA FAGUS FICUS HAKEA HEVEA HOPEA IXORA KHAYA LARIX MALUS MELIA MESUA MORUS NYSSA OCHNA PADUS PICEA PINUS PYRUS SALIX TAXUS THUJA TILIA TOONA TREMA TSUGA ULMUS UNONA VITEX XYLIA ABROMA ACHRAS AKANIA AMOMIS AMYRIS ANDIRA ANNONA ARALIA AUCUBA AZALEA BAPHIA BETULA BOMBAX CANTUA CARAPA CARICA CASSIA CEDRUS CELTIS CERCIS CITRUS CLUSIA COFFEA CORDIA CORNUS DATURA DRIMYS EPERUA EPERVA EUCLEA EVODIA FEIJOA GARRYA GENIPA GINKGO GNETUM GREWIA GUAREA IDESIA ILLIPE LAURUS LITCHI LITSEA LUCUMA LYCIUM MAMMEA MIMOSA MYRCIA MYRICA OCOTEA OLNEYA OSTRYA OWENIA PAPPEA PARITI PERSEA PRUNUS PTELEA QUIINA RANDIA ROYENA SAPIUM SAPOTA SCHIMA SENCIO SESBAN SHOREA SIMABA SORBUS STYRAX TECOMA AGATHIS ARBUTUS ARDISIA ASIMINA ASSONIA BANKSIA BUMELIA BURSERA CANANGA CANELLA CASASIA CATALPA CEDRELA CERASUS CLETHRA COPAIVA CORYLUS COTINUS CUNONIA CYDONIA CYRILLA DOMBEYA ECHINUS EHRETIA EPACRIS EUGENIA FERONIA GMELINA GUAZUMA GYMINDA HAGENIA HALESIA HICORIA HOVENIA HUMIRIA JUGLANS KADELIA KOKOONA LAGETTA LICANIA

LINGOUM MACLURA MICONIA MORINDA
MORINGA MURRAYA OCHROMA OLEARIA
PANGIUM PIMENTA PISONIA PLANERA
POPULUS PROTIUM PSIDIUM QUASSIA
QUERCUS RAPANEA REMIJIA RHAMNUS
ROBINIA SCHINUS SENECIO SEQUOIA
SLOANEA SOLANUM SOPHORA SURIANA
SYRINGA TAMARIX TECTONA TELOPEA
TORREYA TROPHIS VATERIA XIMENIA
XYLOPIA XYLOSMA ZELKOVA
(— OF TUNICATE) SALPA ASCIDIA
DOLIOLUM
(— OF TURTLE) EMYS AMYDA CHELUS
CHELYS CARETTA CHELONE CLEMMYS
TESTUDO TRIONYX ARCHELON CHELONIA
CHELYDRA PELUSIOS
(— OF TWINER) STEMONA
(— OF UNIVALVE) DOLIUM
(— OF VINE) ROSA ABRUS ABUTA
PISUM TAMUS UNONA VIGNA VITIS
AKEBIA CISSUS COBAEA DERRIS ENTADA
HEDERA MUCUNA PETREA POTHOS
SICANA SICYOS SOLLYA VIORNA
ARAUJIA BASELLA BOMAREA BRYONIA
ECHITES EMBELIA EPACRIS FALCATA
HUMULUS IPOMOEA MIKANIA PISONIA
SECHIUM UNCARIA ZANONIA ANAMIRTA
ATRAGENE BIGNONIA CLEMATIS
COCCULUS DEGUELIA DOLICHOS
EUONYMUS JASMINUM KENNEDYA
PANDOREA PUERARIA SECAMONE
SERJANIA TACSONIA WISTARIA
(— OF WALRUS) ODOBENUS
(— OF WASP) SPHEX VESPA BEMBEX
CYNIPS SCOLIA TIPHIA CHRYSIS
EUMENES MASARIS MUTILLA ANDRICUS
CHLORION ODYNERUS POLISTES
POMPILUS SPHECIUS
(— OF WEASEL) MUSTELA
(— OF WEED) CAPSELLA
(— OF WEEVIL) APION HYPERA SITONA
CLEONUS CALANDRA CALENDRA
CURCULIO
(— OF WHALE) CETE ARETA KOGIA
BALAENA ORCINUS ZIPHIUS PHYSETER
(— OF WOLVERINE) GULO
(— OF WORM) DERO SPIO ALARIA
EUNICE KERRIA MERMIS NEREIS SYLLIS
ACHAETA ACHOLOE ASCARIS DUGESIA
EISENIA FILARIA GLYCERA GORDIUS
HESIONE LEODICE POLYNOE SABELLA
SAGITTA SERPULA SETARIA SPIRURA
TUBIFEX
GEODE DRUSE
GEOMETRIC CUBIST CUBISTIC
GEOMETRY EUCLID SPHERICS

GEORGIA

CAPITAL: ATLANTA
COUNTY: BIBB CLAY COBB COOK HALL
TIFT WARE BANKS BRYAN BUTTS DOOLY
EARLY FLOYD GRADY PEACH RABUN
TROUP WORTH COFFEE COWETA DEKALB
ECHOLS ELBERT FANNIN FULTON JASPER
LANIER OCONEE TWIGGS WILKES
CATOOSA LAURENS LUMPKIN GWINNETT
MUSCOGEE
INDIAN: GUALE YUCHI CHIAHA OCONEE
YAMASEE
LAKE: LANIER MARTIN HARDING NOTTELY
BANKHEAD HARTWELL SINCLAIR
MOUNTAIN: STONE KENNESAW
NATIVE: CRACKER
RIVER: PEA FLINT ETOWAH OCONEE
PIGEON CONECUH SATILLA ALTAMAHA
OCMULGEE
STATE BIRD: THRASHER
STATE NICKNAME: PEACH
STATE TREE: LIVEOAK
TOWN: JESUP MACON JASPER OCILLA
AUGUSTA CONYERS DECATUR ELLIJAY
GRIFFIN VIDALIA MARIETTA MOULTRIE
SAVANNAH VALDOSTA WAYCROSS
UNIVERSITY: EMORY GATECH MERCER

GERAINT (WIFE OF —) ENID
GERANIUM DOVEFOOT FLUXWEED
SHAMEFACE
GERBIL JIRD
GERM BUG CHIT SEED SPARK SPAWN
SPERM GERMEN GERMULE MICROBE
SEMINAL RUDIMENT SEEDLING
SEMINARY SEMINIUM
(— CELL) GONE
GERMAN BALT HANS ALMAN HEINE
JERRY ALMAIN DUTCHY HEINIE TEUTON
TEDESCO COTILLON GERMANIC
TUDESQUE
(PREF.) TEUTO
GERMANE GERMAN RELEVANT
PERTINENT
GERMANIC GOTHIC TEUTONIC
GERMAN SHEPHERD ALSATIAN

GERMANY

ANCIENT TRIBESMAN: JUTE TEUTON
VISIGOTH OSTROGOTH
CANAL: KIEL WESER LUDWIG
CAPITAL: BONN BERLIN
COIN: MARK KRONE TALER GULDEN
KRONEN THALER PFENNIG GROSCHEN
HANSEATIC CITY: KOLN LUBECK
COLOGNE HAMBURG LUEBECK
ISLAND: USEDOM WOLLIN FEHMARN
FRISIAN
LAKE: DUMMER WURMSEE AMMERSEE
BODENSEE CHIEMSEE MURITZEE
CONSTANCE
LANGUAGE: DEUTSCH
MOUNTAIN: FELDBERG WATZMANN
MOUNTAIN RANGE: ORE ALPS HARZ
RHON HARDT HUNSRUCK
NAME: REICH ASHKENAZ GERMANIA
DEUTSCHLAND
NATIVE: GOTH SAXON TEUTON
PORT: EMDEN BREMEN HAMBURG
ROSTOCK STETTIN
RIVER: ALZ EMS INN EDER EGER ELBE ISAR
LAHN LECH MAIN NAAB NAHE ODER
OKER REMS RUHR SAAR SIEG ALLER

DONAU EIDER FULDA HAVEL HUNTE
ILLER LEINE LIPPE MOSEL MULDE PEENE
REGEN RHEIN RHINE SAALE SAUER
SPREE UCKER VECHT WERRA WESER
DANUBE ELSTER KOCHER NECKAR
NEISSE RANDOW TAUBER WARNOW
ALTMUHL JEETZEL PEGNITZ SALZACH
UNSTRUT
STATE: BADEN HESSE LIPPE BAYERN
BREMEN HESSEN SAXONY BAVARIA
HAMBURG PRUSSIA SAARLAND
BRUNSWICK
TOWN: AUE EMS HOF ULM BONN GERA
GOCH HAAR HAMM JENA KIEL KOLN
LAHR AALEN AHLEN EMDEN ESSEN
FURTH GOTHA HAGEN HALLE HERNE
MAINZ MOLLN NEUSS PIRNA TRIER
AACHEN ALTENA ALTONA BARMEN
BERLIN BREMEN CASSEL DACHAU
DESSAU ERFURT KASSEL LINDEN
LUBECK MUNICH PLAUEN TREVES
BAMBERG BRESLAU COBLENZ COLOGNE
CREFELD DRESDEN GORLITZ HAMBURG
HANOVER LEIPZIG MAYENCE MUNCHEN
MUNSTER POTSDAM ROSTOCK SPANDAU
ZWICKAU AUGSBURG CHEMNITZ
DORTMUND DUISBURG FREIBURG
LIEGNITZ MANNHEIM NURNBERG
WURSELEN WURZBURG DARMSTADT
KARLSRUHE MAGDEBURG NUREMBERG
OSNABRUCK STUTTGART WUPPERTAL
DUSSELDORF HEIDELBERG OBERHAUSEN

GERMICIDE KRELOS MERBROMIN
GERMINATE BUD HIT CHIP CHIT GERM
SHOOT SPIRE SPRIT BRAIRD SPROUT
STRIKE PULLULATE
GESTATION GOING BREEDING
PREGNANCY
GESTICULATE GESTURE
GESTURE CUT FIG BECK BERE GEST SIGN
FILIP GESTE HONOR SANNA ACTION
BECKON BREATH CUTOFF FILLIP MOTION
SALUTE SIGNAL CURTSEY FASHION
FLICKER MURGEON ACCOLADE
CEREMONY
(— OF DERISION) SNOOK
(AFFECTED —) GAATCH
(HINDU —) NAMASTE
(OBSCENE —) BIRD
(OSTENTATIOUS —) POMP
(USELESS —) FUTILITY
GET COP GIT WIN EARN FALL GAIN GRAB
HAVE HENT TAKE TILL AFONG ANNEX
CATCH COVER FETCH LATCH DERIVE
OBTAIN PUZZLE SECURE ACQUIRE
COMPARE CONQUER PROCURE PRODUCE
RECEIVE PERCEIVE
(— ABOARD) FLIP
(— ABOUT) BEGO NAVIGATE
(— ALONG) DO GEE FARE FEND AGREE
FADGE FODGE SPEED FETTLE
(— AROUND) BYPASS COMPASS
FINESSE FLUMMER OUTFLANK
(— AT) ATTAIN

(— AWAY) LAM RYNT SLIP EVADE
CHEESE ESCAPE
(— BACK) REDEEM RETIRE RECOVER
(— BETTER OF) WAX BEST DING DOWN
DAUNT FLING SHEND SHENT STICK
STING JOCKEY OVERGO RECOVER
OVERCOME SURMOUNT
(— BY ARTIFICE) WIND
(— BY ASKING) KICK
(— BY CUNNING) WHIZZLE
(— BY EXTORTION) GRATE
(— BY FLATTERY) COG
(— CLEAR OF) STRIP
(— DISHONESTLY) FIRK
(— DOWN) ALIGHT
(— ON) FARE BOARD CHEFE CHEVE
FRAME SHIFT EXPLOIT
(— ON WELL) LIKE
(— OUT) LEAK SCRAM CHEESE OUTWIN
VOETSAK
(— PAST) BEAT HURDLE
(— POSSESSION) CARRY
(— READY) GET BOUN PARE RANK
BOWNE BRACE FRAME FETTLE ORDAIN
APPAREL
(— RID) CAST DISH DUMP FREE JUNK
SHAB TOSS ERASE SHAKE SHIFT SHOOT
SLOUGH UNLOAD DELIVER DISCARD
EXTRUDE DISPATCH DISSOLVE
(— SURREPTITIOUSLY) SNEAK
(— THE POINT) SAVVY
(— TO BOTTOM OF) FATHOM
(— UNDER CONTROL) RAIM
(— UP) ARISE HUDDUP UPRISE HAIRPIN
GET-TOGETHER DO DRINK HOBNOB
BAMBOCHE POTLATCH
GEWGAW DIE TOY WALY KNACK WALLY
BAUBLE FANGLE FEGARY JIGGER
FLAMFEW TRANGAM TRINKET FOLDEROL
GIMCRACK JIMCRACK TRIMTRAM
GEYSER BORE JETTER

GHANA

CAPITAL: ACCRA
COIN: PESEWA
DAM: AKOSOMBO
LAKE: VOLTA BOSUMTWI
MONEY: CEDI NEWCEDI
MOUNTAIN: AFADJATO
NATIVE: GA EWE AHAFO BRONG FANTI
ASHANTI DAGOMBA MAMPRUSI
RIVER: OTI PRA DAKA TANO AFRAM
VOLTA ANKOBRA KULPAWN
TOWN: HO WA ODA AXIM FIAN KETA TALA
TEMA ACCRA BAWKU ENCHI LAWRA
LEGON SAMPA YAPEI DUNKWA KARAGA
KPANDU KUMASI NSAWAM OBUASI
SWEDRU TAMALE TARKWA WASIPE
ANTUBIA DAMONGO MAMPONG PRESTEA
SEKONDI SUNYANI WINNEBA
AKOSOMBO KINTAMPO TAKORADI

GHASTLY WAN GASH GRIM PALE BLATE
GHAST LURID UNKET UNKID DISMAL
GOUSTY GRISLY PALLID CHARNEL

GHASTLY DEATHLY FEARFUL GASHFUL GRIZZLY GRUGOUS HIDEOUS MACABRE DREADFUL GRUESOME HORRIBLE SHOCKING TERRIBLE

GHETTO JEWRY JUDAISM

GHOST HAG KER BHUT HANT JUBA WAFF BUGAN CADDY DUFFY DUPPY FETCH GAIST GUEST HAUNT JUMBY LARVA PRETA SHADE SPOOK UMBRA CHUREL SOWLTH SPIRIT SPRITE TAISCH ANTAEUS ANTAIOS BOGGART BUGGANE GYTRASH PHANTOM SPECTER SPECTRE VAMPIRE BARGHEST GUYTRASH PHANTASM REVENANT

GHOSTLY EERY EERIE GOUSTY SHADOWY UNCANNY WEIRDLY CHTHONIC GHASTFUL SPECTRAL

GHOSTS (AUTHOR OF —) IBSEN
(CHARACTER IN —) HELEN JACOB ALVING OSWALD REGINA MANDERS ENGSTRAND

GHOULISH SATANIC

GIANNI SCHICCHI
(CHARACTER IN —) BUOSO DONATI LAURETTA RINUCCIO SCHICCHI
(COMPOSER OF —) PUCCINI

GIANT ORC ETEN HUGE OGRE OTUS WATE YMER YMIR AFRIT BALOR CACUS HYMIR JOTUN MIMAS MIMER THRYM TITAN TROLL AFREET ALBION FAFNIR GIGANT GOEMOT PALLAS THJAZI THURSE TITYUS WARLOW ANTAEUS GOLIATH WARLOCK ASCOPART BELLERUS COLBRAND GIGANTIC GOEMAGOT GOGMAGOG MASTODON MORGANTE ORGOGLIO TYPHOEUS PROCRUSTES
(1-EYED —) CYCLOPS
(100-HANDED —) GYGES COTTUS BRIAREUS
(1000-ARMED —) BANA

GIANTESS NORN ARGANTE

GIBBER CHAT CHATTER

GIBBERISH GREEK JABBER JARGON CHOCTAW ABRACADABRA

GIBBET STOB TREE CROOK JEBAT GALLOWS POTENCE EQUULEUS

GIBBON LAR WAWA UNGKA WUYEN CAMPER HULOCK HOOLOCK SIAMANG HYLOBATE

GIBBOUS CONVEX HULCHY HUMPED SACCATE

GIBE (ALSO SEE JIBE) BOB RUB GIRD JAPE JEST JIBE PROG QUIB QUIP SKIT WIPE FLEER FLING FLIRT FRUMP GLEEK KNACK SCOFF SCOMM SCORN SLANT SNEER DERIDE GLANCE HECKLE BROCARD SARCASM RIDICULE

GIBING SNASH

GIDDINESS LUNACY SOORAWN

GIDDY BARMY GLAKY LIGHT WESTY GIGLET GLAKED GOWKED GOWKIT SHANNY STURDY VOLAGE GLAIKET LARKING HALUCKET HELLICAT

GIDEON (FATHER OF —) JOASH

GIFT BOX FOY QUO SOP BENT BOON DASH ENAM MEED SAND BONUS BRIBE CAULP CUDDY DONUM GRANT KNACK TOKEN BEFANA CADEAU DASHEE DONARY GENIUS GERSUM GIFTIE GIVING HANSEL LEGACY RECADO REGALO TALENT XENIUM APTNESS BEFFANA BENEFIT CHARISM CHARITY DEODATE DONATIO DOUCEUR ETRENNE FACULTY FAIRING GIFTURE HANDSEL PRESENT PROPINE REGALIO SUBSIDY TASHRIF TRIBUTE AMATORIO APTITUDE BENEFICE BESTOWAL BLESSING COURTESY DONATION DONATIVE GARRISON GIVEAWAY GRATUITY MORTUARY OBLATION OFFERING POTLATCH SPORTULA BENEFACTION REMEMBRANCE PHILANTHROPY PRESENTATION
(— FROM HUSBAND TO WIFE) ARRAS
(— OF GOD) GRACE
(— OF MONEY) POUCH BAKSHISH
(— OF NATURE) DOWER DOWRY
(— TO ROMAN PEOPLE) CONGIARY
(CHARITABLE —) ALMS ENAM PITTANCE
(COMPULSORY —) SIXENIA
(LIBERAL —) LARGESSE
(NATURAL —) TALENT
(NEW YEAR'S EVE —) ETRENNE HAGMENA HOGMANAY
(SPIRITUAL —) CHARISM CHARISMA

GIG TUB MOZE BANDY BUGGY CHAIR GIGGE CHAISE CLATCH DENNET WHISKY CALESIN TILBURY STANHOPE

GIGANTIC HUGE GIANT MAMMOTH TITANIC COLOSSAL ENORMOUS GIGANTAL ATLANTEAN MONSTROUS BROBDINGNAGIAN

GIGGLE KECKLE NICKER TEEHEE TITTER SNICKER TWITTER

GIL BLAS (AUTHOR OF —) LESAGE
(CHARACTER IN —) GIL BLAS LEWIS PEREZ AURORA MENCIA SCIPIO ANTONIA ARSENIA ROLANDO ALPHONSO DOROTHEA FABRICIO MATTHIAS OLIVAREZ SANGRADO

GILD GILT BEGILD ENGILD ORFGILD

GILDED GILT AURATE INAURATE

GILEAD (FATHER OF —) MACHIR
(SON OF —) JEPHTHAH

GILL JILL QUAD GHYLL PLICA GILLIE LAMELLA BRANCHIA QUADRANT
(—S OF BIVALVE) BEARD

GIMCRACK QUIP BAUBLE FIZGIG GEWGAW JIMJAM TRIFLE TRANGAM TRINKET WHIMWHAM

GIMLET SCREW WIMBLE PIERCEL PIERCER

GIMMICK GAFF

GIN MAX CRAB GRIN LACE RUIN TAPE CLEAN JACKY SNARE SNARL DIDDLE GENEVA JAMBER JAMMER SPRINGE TITTERY TWANKAY EYEWATER HOLLANDS SCHIEDAM SCHNAPPS
(DROP OF —) DAFFY

GINGER PEPPER RATOON AROMATIC ZINZIBER COLTSFOOT

GINGERBREAD SPICE PARKIN

GINGERLY GINGER WARILY CHARILY
EDGINGLY
GINGHAM CHAMBRAY
GINSENG SANG FATIL PANAX ARALIA
IVYWORT REDBERRY
GIOCONDA, LA (CHARACTER IN —)
ENZO CIECA LAURA ALVISE BARNABA
GIOCONDA GRIMALDO
(COMPOSER OF —) PONCHIELLI
GIRAFFE OONT CAMEL DAPPLE KAMEEL
SERAPH CAMAILE RUMINANT
GIRD BELT BIND GIRR GIRT HASP YERK
CLOSE SCOFF ENGIRD FASTEN GIRDLE
SECURE ACCINGE ENVIRON CINCTURE
SURROUND
GIRDER BEAM GIRD GIRT GIRTH TABLE
TRUSS BINDER SUMMER WARREN
GIRDING TWISTER BUCKSTAY STRINGER
GIRDLE OBI ZON BARK BELT GIRD SASH
ZONA ZONE CEINT GIRTH MITER PATTE
SARPE WAIST BODICE CINGLE CIRCLE
MOOCHA TISSUE ZODIAC ZONULA
ZOSTER BALDRIC BALTEUS CENTRUM
CENTURE COMPASS GIRDING SHINGLE
CEINTURE CINCTURE CINGULUM
SURROUND
(— FOR HELMET) TISSUE
(— OF DIATOM) HOOP
(BRIDE'S —) CEST CESTUS
(LITTLE —) ZONULE ZONELET
(ROYAL —) MALO
(SACRED —) KUSTI
GIRL BIT GAL HER KIT POP SHE SIS TIB
TID TIT BABE BABY BINT BIRD CHIT
DAME DEEM DELL GILL JANE JILL JUDY
LASS MARY MOPS MORT PERI PUSS
SLUT WREN BEAST FILLY FLUFF GUIDE
KITTY LUBRA QUEAN SISSY SKIRT TIDDY
TITTY TOOTS TRULL BURDIE CALICO
CLINER CUMMER DALAGA DAMSEL
DEEMIE FEMALE FIZGIG GEISHA GIRLIE
LASSIE LOVELY MAGGIE NUMBER
PIGEON SHEILA SISTER SUBDEB TOMATO
CAMILLA COLLEEN CRUMPET DAMOSEL
MADCHEN MAUTHER TENDREL BONNIBEL
FARMETTE FEMININE GRISETTE
MUCHACHA
(AGILE —) YANKER
(AWKWARD —) HOIT
(BEATIFIED —) BEATA
(BEAUTIFUL —) BELLE
(BOLD —) HOYDEN
(CAMP FIRE —) ARTISAN
(CHORUS —) CHORINE CORYPHEE
(CLUMSY —) TAWPIE
(COUNTRY —) MEG JOAN
(DANCING —) ALMA DASI ALMAH
KISAENG BAYADERE DEVADASI
(DANCING —S) GHAWAZI
(DEAR —) PEAT
(DUMPY —) CUTTY
(FLIGHTY —) GOOSECAP
(FLIRTATIOUS —) JADE JILLET
(FLOWER —) NYDIA
(FORWARD —) STRAP
(FROLICSOME —) GILPY
(GIDDY —) GIG GIGLET GIGLOT JILLET

(GREEK —) HAIDEE
(GYPSY —) GITANA
(HIRED —) BIDDY BIDDIE
(IMPUDENT —) STRAP
(JAPANESE —) GEISHA
(LITTLE —) SIS COOKY SISSY COOKIE
LASSOCK
(MISCHIEVOUS —) CUTTY HUSSY
(MODEST —) BLUSHET
(NAIVE —) INGENUE
(NON-JEWISH —) SHIKSE SHICKSA
(PERT —) MINX HUSSY
(PRETTY —) PRIM BUNNY CUTEY CUTIE
(ROMPING —) STAG TOMBOY
(SAUCY —) SNIP
(SERVANT —) SLUT
(SHIFTLESS —) MYSTERY
(SILLY —) SKIT
(SINGING —) ALMA ALMEH
(SLENDER —) SYLPH
(SMALL —) PINAFORE
(SPIRITED —) FILLY
(UNATTRACTIVE —) FRUMP
(UNMARRIED —) MOUSME TOWDIE
MUSUME MADEMOISELLE
(WANTON —) GIG FILLOCK
(WILD —) BLOWZE
(WORKING —) ORISETTE
(WORTHLESS —) HUSSY
(YOUNG —) BUD MODER TITTY MAIDEN
MOTHER BAGGAGE COLLEEN FLAPPER
GIRLEEN ROSEBUD
GIRL OF THE GOLDEN WEST
(CHARACTER IN —) DICK JACK RANCE
MINNIE JOHNSON RAMERREZ
(COMPOSER OF —) PUCCINI
GIRT CINCT
GIRTH GIRD GIRT TAPE CINCH GARTH
GIRSE GRETH WANTY CINGLE WARROK
COMPASS GIRDING SHINGLE WEBBING
GIST JET NET NUB SUM CHAT CORE GITE
KNOT MEAT PITH GREAT HEART JOIST
POINT SENSE BURDEN KERNEL PURPORT
SUMMARY STRENGTH
GIVE ADD GIE HOB TIP BEAR DEAL DOLE
HAND METE SELL TAKE WEVE WHIP
YEVE ALLOW AWARD COUGH GRANT
REFER YIELD ACCORD AFFORD BESTOW
CONFER DEMISE DOTATE IMPART
IMPART IMPOSE IMPUTE RENDER SUPPLY
CONSIGN DELIVER FORGIVE FURNISH
PRESENT PROPINE BEQUEATH DISPENSE
(— A BOOST) BOLSTER
(— A PLACE TO) SITUATE
(— A REASON) ACCOUNT
(— A REMEDY) MINISTER
(— ADHERENCE) ASSENT
(— ADMITTANCE) ACCEPT
(— ADVICE) READ ADVISE
(— AN ACCOUNT) TELL RELATE
REPORT
(— AND TAKE) GIFFGAFF
(— ANYTHING NAUSEOUS TO) DOSE
(— APPROVAL) CONSENT
(— AS CONCESSION) YETTE
(— AS EXPLANATION) ASSIGN
(— ASSURANCE) EFFRONT

(— ATTENTION TO) HEED
(— AUTHORITY) ENABLE EMPOWER
ACCREDIT
(— AWAY) PART
(— BACK) REFUND RETURN RESTORE
(— BIRTH) KIT BEAR BORN DROP FIND
MAKE BEGET BREED ISSUE WORLD
FARROW KINDLE LITTER DELIVER
FRESHEN
(— BY WILL) DEVISE
(— CARE) NURSE
(— CLAIM TO) REMISE
(— COUNSEL) AREAD AREED
(— CREDIT FOR) FRIST
(— CURRENCY TO) PASS
(— EAR) HARK HARKEN LISTEN
HEARKEN
(— EXPRESSION TO) EMOTE FRAME
VOICE
(— FORM) CUT
(— FORTH) WARP YIELD AFFORD
CONCEIVE
(— GROUND) RETIRE
(— HEED) LOOK ATTEND
(— IN) BOW CONCEDE COLLAPSE
(— IN EXCHANGE) SWAP SWOP
(— IN MARRIAGE) BESTOW SPOUSE
(— INFORMATION) WARN
(— INSTRUCTION) LEAR
(— NAME TO) BAPTIZE
(— NOTICE) WARN HERALD APPRISE
PUBLISH ANNOUNCE INTIMATE
(— NOTICE TO APPEAR) GARNISH
(— OBLIQUE EDGE) CANT
(— OFF) EMIT SEND SHED EXUDE FLING
DIVIDE EFFUSE EVOLVE EXHALE EXPIRE
EXCRETE SEPARATE
(— ONE'S SELF OVER TO) ADDICT
(— ONE'S WORD) PROMISE
(— OUT) BOOM LEAK EXUDE ISSUE
PETAL EVOLVE EMANATE OUTGIVE
(— OVER) LIN
(— PAIN) AGGRIEVE
(— PLACE) VAIL BACCARE
(— PLEDGE) GAGE
(— PROMINENCE TO) FEATURE
(— RELUCTANTLY) BEGRUDGE
(— SATISFACTION) ABY ABYE ABEGGE
(— SPARINGLY) INCH
(— STRENGTH TO) NERVE
(— SUPPORT) ASSIST ANIMATE
(— TEMPORARILY) LEND
(— TIP) TOUT
(— TONGUE) CRY YEARN
(— UP) PUT BURY DROP PART CHUCK
DEMIT DEVOW FORGO LEAVE RAISE
REMIT SHOOT SPARE SPEND ABJURE
ADDICT BETRAY DESERT DEVOTE
FOREGO MIZZLE REFUSE RELENT RENDER
RESIGN VACATE ABANDON DEPOSIT
DESPAIR FLUMMOX FORBEAR FORGIVE
REFRAIN RELEASE ABDICATE RENOUNCE
(— VENT TO) EMIT ISSUE DISCHARGE
(— VOICE) BOLT ACCENT
(— WARNING) ALERT
(— WAY) GO FAIL FOLD KEEL SINK VAIL
BREAK BUDGE BURST FAINT SLAKE

YIELD BUCKLE FALTER RELENT SWERVE
FOUNDER RECLAIM SUCCUMB
(— WITNESS) DEPOSE
GIVER DONOR
(— OF LIFE) APHETA
(NAME —) EPONYM
GIVING DOLE BOUNTY DATION REMISE
(— HELP) ADJUTANT
(— MILK) FRESH
(— NO MILK) YELD YELL
(— TROUBLE) CUMBROUS
GLACIER BRAE ICECAP STREAM CALOTTE
ICEBERG PIEDMONT
GLAD GAY FAIN LIEF VAIN CANTY HAPPY
PROUD BLITHE FESTUS GLADLY JOCUND
JOYFUL JOYOUS GLADFUL GLEEFUL
JOCULAR ANIMATED CHEERFUL
CHEERING FESTIVAL GLADSOME
PLEASING
GLADDEN JOY GLAD BLESS BLISS CHEER
EXULT MIRTH BLITHE COMFORT GLADIFY
LIGHTEN REJOICE
GLADE LAWN LAUND SLADE SHRADD
SUNGLADE SUNSCALD
GLADIATOR THRAX RETIARY SAMNITE
SECUTOR ANDABATA
GLADLY GLAD LIEF FAINLY LIEFLY
LOVELY HAPPILY
GLADNESS JOY GLAD GLEE BLISS MIRTH
BLITHE FAINNESS GLADSHIP PLEASURE
GLAMOR SCRY UTIS OOMPH BRABBLE
PIZZAZZ BALLYHOO
GLAMORIZE POT GLORIFY
GLAMOROUS EXOTIC ALLURING
CHARMING
GLANCE EYE RAY SEE BEAM CAST GLIM
LEER PEEK SCRY SKEG VIEW WINK
BLENK BLINK BLUSH CAROM FLASH
GLEEK GLENT GLIDE GLIFF GLINT GLISK
GRAZE PRINK SCREW SIGHT SKIME
SLANT SQUIZ TWIRE APERCU ASPECT
CARROM GANDER REGARD SCANCE
STRIKE VISION EYEBEAM EYESHOT
EYEWINK GLIMPSE BELAMOUR GLIFFING
OEILLADE
(— OFF) GLACE
(— THROUGH) SAMPLE
(LOVE —) AMORET
(MELANCHOLY —) DOWNCAST
(SHARP —) DART
(SIDELONG —) SHEW SLENT SKLENT
(SLY —) GLEG GLIME GLOAT
GLAND MILT NOIX SETA CLYER CRYPT
GONAD LIVER MAMMA ACINUS BREAST
KERNEL THYMUS ADRENAL CRUMENA
NECTARY PAROTID PAROTIS TEARPIT
THYROID CONARIUM ENDOCRIN
FOLLICLE FOLLOWER GANGLION
GLANDULA GLANDULE HOOFWORM
PROSTATE SCIRRHUS SPERMARY
GLARE BEAT GAZE BLARE BLAZE BLOOM
FLAME GLAZE STARE GLITTER ICEBLINK
RADIANCE
GLARING HARD RANK GLARY AGLARE
GARISH BURNING FLARING STARING
FLAGRANT
GLASS CUP VER CALX FLAT FLUX FRIT

JENA MOIL PONY VITA CHARK FACER
FLINT GLAZE STOOP STOUP VERRE VITRE
CALGON CEMENT CULLET RUMMER
SPECKS VITRUM ALEYARD BIFOCAL
BRIMMER CHIRPER CRYSTAL PERLITE
SCHMELZ TALLBOY VITRITE FROSTING
OBSIDIAN SCHOPPEN PERSPECTIVE
(— IN STATE OF FUSION) METAL
(— OF A MIRROR) STONE
(— OF BEER) BREW
(— OF BRANDY) SNEAKER
(— OF SPIRITS) CHASSE
(— OF WHISKY) KELTY RUBDOWN
(— OF WINE) APERITIF
(— STICKING TO PUNTY) COLLET
(BEER —) SHELL SEIDEL PILSNER
(BELL-SHAPED —) CUP CLOCHE
(BURNING —) SUNGLASS
(CHEVAL —) PSYCHE
(COLORED —) SMALT SMALTO TINTER
SCHMELZ
(COLORED —S) GOGGLES
(CUPPING —) VENTOSE
(CURVED —) LENS
(DESSERT —) COUPE
(DRINKING —) GOBLET RUMKIN
PILSNER PIMLICO SCUTTLE TUMBLER
SCHOONER
(EUROPEAN ORNAMENTAL —)
PELOTON
(EXAMINATION —) SLIDE
(FULL —) BUMPER
(FUSIBLE —) FLUX
(HALF —) SPLIT
(ICE CREAM —) SLIDER
(LEAD —) STRASS
(LIQUEUR —) PONY PONEY
(LIQUOR —) GUN
(MAGNIFYING —) LOUPE
(MASS OF MOLTEN —) PARISON
(METEORITIC —) MOLDAVITE
(OPALESCENT —) OPALINE
(OPAQUE —) HYALITHE
(PIECE OF HOT —) BIT
(PULVERIZED —) FROSTING
(REFUSE —) CALX CULLET
(RUBY —) SCHMELZE
(RUSSIAN —) CHARK
(SHERBET —) SUPREME
(SHERRY —) COPITA
(SMOKED —) SHADE
(STAINED —) VITRAIL
(TALL —) RUMMER
(THIN —) MOUSSELINE
(VOLCANIC —) PUMICE PERLITE
(WINDOW —) PANE
(WINE —) FLUTE
GLASSBLOWER MUMBLER
GLASS MENAGERIE (AUTHOR OF —)
WILLIAMS
(CHARACTER IN —) TOM JAMES
LAURA AMANDA OCONNOR
GLASSWARE AGATA AURENE BURMESE
FAVRILE OPALINE STEUBEN VITRICS
AMBERINA
GLASSY GLIB FILMY GLAZY GLAZEN

GLASSEN HYALINE HYALOID VITREAL
VITREOUS
GLAZE DIP LEAD SIZE SLIP GLASS SLEET
SMEAR ENAMEL QUARRY CELADON
COPERTA EELSKIN GLASSEN GLAZING
GLIDDER COUVERTE TIGEREYE
(— OF ICE) GLARE
GLAZED FILMY GLACE GLASSEN
GLOSSED
GLEAM RAY BEAM GLOW LEAM WAFT
WINK BLENK BLINK BLUSH FLASH GLAIK
GLEEN GLENT GLINT GLISK GLIST GLOSE
SHINE SKIME SPUNK STARE STEEM
TWIRE GLANCE SCANCE FOULDRE
GLIMMER GLITTER SHIMMER CORUSCATE
SCINTILLA
(— FAINTLY) SHIMMER
(— OF LIGHT) LEAM PINK GLAIK
SCANCE
(FAINT —) SCAD
GLEAMING FAW GLOW CLEAR GLINT
STEEP ABLAZE BRIGHT GLEAMY ADAZZLE
SHINING GLOOMING
GLEAN CULL EARN REAP LEASE GATHER
COLLECT SCRINGE
GLEANER STIBBLER
GLEBE SOD CLOD LAND SOIL TERMON
KIRKTOWN
GLEE GLY JOY SONG MIRTH SPORT
GAIETY DELIGHT ELATION WASSAIL
HILARITY MADRIGAL
GLEEFUL GAY MERRY JOYOUS JOCULAR
GLEESOME
GLEEMAN SONGMAN MINSTREL
GLEN DEN GILL GLYN GRIFF HEUCH
HEUGH KLOOF SLACK SLADE TEMPE
CANADA DINGLE POCKET
GLIB PAT FLIP SLICK CASUAL GLOSSY
OFFHAND RENABLE SHALLOW VOLUBLE
FLIPPANT
GLIDE GO SKI FLOW SAIL SILE SKIM SLIP
SLUR SOAR SWIM COAST CREEP DANCE
FLEET GLACE GRAZE LAPSE MERGE
PLANE SCOOP SHIRL SKATE SKIFF SKIRR
SKITE SLADE SLEEK SLICK SLIDE SLIPE
STEAL GLANCE GLIDER SASHAY SNOOVE
ILLAPSE SCRIEVE SCRITHE SKITTER
SLITHER AIRPLANE GLISSADE VOLPLANE
SEMIVOWEL
(— AWAY) ELAPSE
(— BY) PASS FLEET
(— OFF) EXIT
GLIDER BIPLANE SCOOTER SAILPLANE
GLIDING LAPSE TRAIL SLIDING
(— OF THE VOICE) DRAG
(— OVER) LAMBENT
GLIMMER FIRE GLIM GLOW LEAM STIM
BLINK FLASH GLEAM GLOOM STIME
SIMPER BLINTER FLIMMER GLIMPSE
GLITTER SHIMMER SPARKLE TWINKLE
SUNBLINK
GLIMMERING GHOST AGLIMMER
GLOOMING
GLIMPSE IDEA WAFF WAFT BLINK BLUSH
FLASH GLIFF GLINT GLISK SIGHT STIME
TINGE TRACE WHIFF GLANCE GLEDGE
LUSTER SCANCE GLIMMER INKLING

(BRIEF —) APERCU
(FLEETING —) SHIM SNATCH
GLINT PEEP FLASH GLEAM GLENT
GLANCE SPARKLE
GLISTEN FLASH GLISK GLISS GLIST
SHINE GLISTER GLITTER SHIMMER
SPANGLE SPARKLE RUTILATE
GLITTER FLASH GLARE GLEAM GLEIT
GLINT GLORE SHEEN SHINE SKYRE
STARE BICKER LUSTER SCANCE
GLIMMER GLISTEN GLISTER SKINKLE
SPANGLE SPARKLE TWINKLE BRANDISH
RADIANCE RUTILATE CORUSCATE
(FALSE —) GILT
GLITTERING GEMMY SHEEN SHINY
STEEP FULGID SPANGLY AGLITTER
GLITTERY RUTILANT BRILLIANT
CLINQUANT
GLOAMING EVE DUSK GLOAM
GLOOMING TWILIGHT
GLOAT GAZE GLUT TIRE EXULT PREEN
GLOBAL PLANETARY
GLOBE ORB BALL BOWL CLEW CLUE
POME AGGER GEOID MONDE MOUND
ROUND SPHERE COMPASS GEORAMA
GLOBULE GRENADE AQUARIUM
ROUNDURE
GLOBULE BEAD BLOB DROP GLOB PEARL
BUBBLE BUTTON REGULUS GLOBULET
SPHERULE
(— OF TAPIOCA) FISHEYE
GLOCKENSPIEL BELL LYRA CARILLON
GLOOM DAMP DUSK MURK CLOUD
DREAR FROWN SOMBER DESPAIR
DIMNESS GLOOMTH SADNESS
DARKNESS MIDNIGHT
GLOOMY DUN SAD WAN BLUE COLD
DARK DOUR DREE DULL EERY GLUM
MIRK MURK ADUSK ADUST BLACK
BROWN DOWFF DREAR DUSKY EERIE
FERAL GUMLY HEAVY LURID MOODY
MORNE MUDDY MUNGY MUSTY MUZZY
ROOKY SABLE SORRY STERN SULKY
SURLY SWART TRIST CLOUDY DISMAL
DREARY DREICH DROOPY DRUMLY
GLUMMY MOROSE SOLEMN SOMBER
SULLEN TETRIC THRAWN OBSCURE
STYGIAN THESTER DARKSOME DESOLATE
DOLESOME DOWNBEAT DOWNCAST
FUNEREAL GLOOMING LOWERING
OVERCAST TRISTFUL PESSIMISTIC
GLORIFY HERY LAUD BLESS DEIFY EXALT
EXTOL HERSE HONOR PRIDE WURTH
KUDIZE PRAISE CLARIFY ELEVATE
MAGNIFY DIVINIZE EMBLAZON EULOGIZE
PROCLAIM STELLIFY
GLORIOUS SRI DEAR DERE MERE GRAND
PROUD BRIGHT EMINENT RENOWNED
GLORY JOY ORE SUN FACE FAME HALO
HORN BLAZE BOAST EXULT HONOR
KUDOS PRIDE WULDER AUREOLA
CLARITY GARLAND GLORIFY RADIANCE
SPLENDOR WORTHING
GLOSS GILL COLOR DUNCE GLASS GLAZE
GLOZE JAPAN SHEEN SHINE BLANCH
LUSTER POSTIL REMARK VENEER

BURNISH EXPOUND VARNISH FLOURISH
PALLIATE POLITURE
(— OVER) FARD HUSH SALVE SLEEK
SOOTHE
GLOSSY GLOZE NITID SHINY SILKY SLEEK
SLICK SATINY SMOOTH
GLOVE KID CUFF GAGE MITT COFFE
BERLIN MITTEN CHEVRON DANNOCK
GANTLET GOMUKHI GAUNTLET
(— FOR RUBBING SKIN) STRIGIL
(BISHOP'S —) GWANTUS
(BODY OF —) TRANK
(BOXING —) MUFFLE
(HEDGER'S —) DANNOCK
(HUSKING —) HUSKER
(PART OF —) THUMB TRANK GUSSET
BINDING FOURCHETTE
GLOW ARC LOW AURA BURN FIRE LEAM
LOOM LOWE BLAZE BLOOM BLUSH
FLAME FLASH FLUSH GLAZE GLEAM
GLEED GLORY GLOSS GLOZE SHINE
STEAM CORONA KINDLE WARMTH
FLUSTER LIGHTEN
(— OF PASSION) ESTUS AESTUS
(— WITH INTENSE HEAT) IGNITE
GLOWER GAZE GLOW GLARE GLOOM
GLORE
GLOWING HOT LIVE WARM AGLOW
FIERY LIGHT QUICK RUDDY VIVID ABLAZE
ARDENT ORIENT BURNING CANDENT
FERVENT RADIANT SHINING FLAGRANT
RUTILANT
GLOWWORM FIREFLY FIREWORM
GLOWBIRD LAMPYRID
GLUE PAD EPOXY MOUNT STICK BEGLEW
CEMENT FUNORI STICKER STICKUM
TAUROCOL
(BEE —) PROPOLIS
GLUEY GLUISH STICKY STRINGY VISCOUS
ADHESIVE
GLUM CLUM DOUR GRUM SURLY GLOOMY
GLUMPY MOROSE SULLEN DEJECTED
GLUT CLOY FILL GULP QUAT SATE CHOKE
DRAFT GORGE BATTEN ENGLUT EXCESS
MARROW PAMPER PAUNCH ENGORGE
GLUTTON SATIATE SURFEIT SWALLOW
OVERFEED SAGINATE SATURATE
GLUTTED QUAT GORGED SATIATED
GLUTTON HOG PIG GLUT GORB GUTS
GULCH MIKER GLOTUM HELLUO MACCUS
EPICURE GUTLING LURCHER MOOCHER
RAVENER SWILLER CARCAJOU
DRAFFMAN GOURMAND GULLYGUT
(STUPID —) GRUB
GLUTTONY GULE EDACITY SURFEIT
GNARL NOB KNOB KNUR KNARL KNURR
SNIRL WARRE DEFORM
GNARLED GNARLY KNARRY KNOTTY
CRABBED KNOTTED KNURLED
GNAT KNAW SMUT MIDGE PUNKY STOUT
KNATTE SCIARA SCIARID SCINIPH
BLACKFLY DIPTERAN GNATLING
GNAW EAT NAB BITE FRET TIRE CHELE
GNARL MOUSE SHEAR ARRODE BEFRET
BEGNAW CANKER CHAVEL NATTLE
NIGGLE ROUNGE CHIMBLE CHUMBLE
CORRODE

GNAWING EATING RODENT FRETFUL ARROSION ROSORIAL

GNOME NIS NISSE PECHT PYGMY KOBOLD VAKSHA YAKSHI GNOMIDE GREMLIN HODEKEN ERDGEIST

GNU KOKOON BRINDLE

GO BE DO ACT GAE HOP ISH LAY NIM PEP TEE WAG BANG BEAR BING BOWN BUSK DRAW FAND FARE FOND GANG HARK HAUL HUMP MOVE QUIT RAIK ROAM ROLL SEEK SHOT SILE SLAP SNAP STAB STEP TAKE TEEM TOUR WADE WANE WEAR WEND WEVE WIND WISE WORK YEAD YEDE AMBLE BOUND CARRY CHEVE DEMON DRESS FETCH FRAME HAUNT KNOCK LEAVE MOSEY PLUCK REACH SCRAM SHAKE SLOPE SPEED TOUCH TRACE TRACK TRENE TRINE TRUSS WHIZZ YONGE BECOME BETAKE CHIEVE CRUISE DEPART EXTEND QUATCH QUETCH REPAIR RESORT RESULT RETIRE SASHAY STRAKE STRIKE TODDLE TRAVEL WEAKEN JOURNEY SCRITHE DIMINISH WITHDRAW

(— ABOUT) JET BEGO BIGAN
(— ABOUT DEJECTEDLY) PEAK
(— ABOUT GOSSIPING) COURANT
(— AHEAD) HOLD
(— AIMLESSLY) ERR BUMMLE
(— ALONG) PATH
(— ALONG WITH) ACCOMPANY
(— AROUND) SKIRT BYPASS CIRCUE
(— ASHORE) LAND
(— ASTRAY) ERR MAR WRY MANG WILL MISGO DELIRE FORVAY MISWEND DEROGATE MISCARRY
(— AWAY) AGO HOP OFF BEAT BUNK HIKE NASH PART SHOO VADE CLEAR HENCE IMSHI LEAVE SCRAM SHIFT BEGONE BUGGER DEPART REMOVE VACATE SKIDDOO ELONGATE
(— BACK IN TIME) MOUNT
(— BAD) SOUR
(— BEFORE) LEAD FOREGO PRECEDE ANTECEDE PREAMBLE
(— BEYOND) SURPASS FOREPASS
(— BRISKLY) JUNE
(— BROKE) BUST
(— COURTING) WENCH
(— DOWN) SET SINK VAIL DROOP SOUND DESCEND
(— EASILY) AMBLE
(— ERRATICALLY) KICK
(— FAST) HURRY SPLIT BARREL BEELINE
(— FORTH) AGO DEPART FORTHGO
(— FORWARD) HUP HUPP ADVANCE AGGRESS PROCEED
(— FOWLING) AUCUPATE
(— FURTIVELY) SLINK SNEAK STEAL
(— HANG) SNICK
(— HEAVILY) LOB LAMPER
(— IN) ENTER INGRESS
(— IN A HURRY) SCUFFLE
(— IN HASTE) LEN LAMMAS
(— IN PURSUIT) SUE
(— INTO BUSINESS) EMBARK
(— LAME) FOUNDER

(— LEISURELY) BUMMEL JIGGET JIGGIT
(— LIGHTLY) TIPTOE
(— MAD) CRAZE MADDLE
(— NEAR) APPROACH
(— NOISILY) LARUM
(— OFF) MOG DISCHARGE
(— ON) DO GARN LAST PASS PERGE FURTHER PROCEED
(— ON BOARD) BOARD EMBARK ENTRAIN
(— ON FOOT) SHANK
(— ON TO SAY) ADD
(— OUT) EXIT ISSUE SLOCK EGRESS EXEUNT QUENCH SORTIE
(— OVER) KNEE REVOLT SURPASS OVERGANG
(— OVER AGAIN) RENEW REVISE RETRACE
(— PROSPEROUSLY) COTTON
(— QUICKLY) GET HIE BUZZ LAMP PIKE SCAT SPEED
(— RAPIDLY) LAMP SPLIT
(— SHARES) SNACK
(— SLOWLY) CRAWL CREEP
(— SLUGGISHLY) SHACK
(— SMOOTHLY) SLIP
(— STEALTHILY) SHIRK SLINK SNEAK GUMSHOE
(— SUDDENLY) CLAP SCOOT
(— SWIFTLY) SKISE STRIP HIGHBALL
(— THE ROUNDS) PATROL
(— THROUGH) SUFFER
(— THROUGH WATER) SQUATTER
(— THROUGHOUT) COAST
(— TO BED) KIP DOSS FLOP SNUG
(— TO EXCESS) DEBORD
(— TO HARBOR) VERT
(— TO PIECES) SNURP
(— TO SCHOOL) SCOLEY
(— TO SLEEP) HUSHABY
(— TO WAR) RISE
(— TOO FAR) OUTREACH
(— UP) CLIMB AMOUNT ASCEND
(— WEARILY) HAGGLE
(— WITH EFFORT) HIKE
(— WRONG) MISS FAULT CURDLE MISFARE BACKFIRE

GOAD EGG GAD GIG HAG BAIT BROD BROG DARE EDGE GAUD LASH MOVE PROD SPUR URGE WHIP YERK ANKUS HARRY IMPEL PIQUE PRICK PROGG PUNGE STING VALET INCITE NEEDLE OXGOAD ANKUSHA HOTFOOT INFLAME PROVOKE IRRITATE SLAPJACK STIMULUS

GOAL BYE DEN END BASE BUTT DOLE DOOL HAIL HALE MARK METE PORT BOURN FINIS IDEAL SCOOP SCOPE SCORE STING DESIGN OBJECT SIGHTS DESTINY HORIZON TERMINUS OBJECTIVE
(— IN GAMES) HUNK
(FIELD —) BASKET
(REMOTE —) THULE
(UNATTAINABLE —) STAR

GOAT BOK TUR IBEX TAHR BEDEN BILLY BOVID EVECK SEROW ALPINE ANGORA AOUDAD CAPRID CHAMAL JEMLAH MAZAME NUBIAN PASANG SAANEN

WETHER CHAMOIS AEGAGRUS CAPRIPED
MARKHOOR BOUQUETIN
(DOMESTIC —) HIRCUS
(FEMALE —) NANNY DOELING
(MALE —) BUCK BUCKLING
(YOUNG —) KID KIDDY TICCHEN
GOATLING

GOB CLOT GOAF SWAB SWOB WASTE
GOBBET SWABBY

GOBBLE MOP BOLT SLOP GOFFLE
GORBLE

GOBBLEDYGOOK PEDAGESE

GO-BETWEEN BAWD FIXER MEANS
BROKER DEALER PANDAR CONTACT
MEDIATOR

GOBLET DINOS GLASS HANAP POKAL
SKULL STOOP STOUP BUMPER HOLMOS
RUMKIN CHALICE SCYPHUS SNIFTER
TALLBOY JEROBOAM STANDARD
STEMWARE

GOBLIN (ALSO SEE HOBGOBLIN) COW
HAG NIS PUG BHUT MARE PUCK BOGEY
NISSE OUPHE POOKA BODACH BOGGLE
BOOGER CHUREL EMPUSA FOLIOT
SPRITE BOGGART BROWNIE BUGBEAR
KNOCKER PADFOOT BARGHEST
BOGEYMAN FOLLETTO

GOD (ALSO SEE DEITY) AS EA EL VE BES
COG DAD DES DEV DOD EAR GAR GAW
GOG GOL GOM GUM ING LOK MEN MIN
ODD SUN ULL AITU AMEN ASUR ATEO
ATUA BEER BURE CHAC COCK DEUS
DEVA DIEU ESUS FONS FREY GAWD
GOSH HAPI HOLY INTI JOVE KANE KING
LIFE LOKE LOKI LOVE LUGH MIND NABU
NEBO NUDD PTAH SHEN SHIN SOMA
SOUL TANE TIKI ULLR VAYU XIPE ZEUS
ARAWN ASHUR ASURA ATTES COMUS
DAGDA DEITY DEOTA DUVEL DYLAN
EBISU ELOAH FREYR GHOST GOLES
GOLLY GRAVE GUACA HESUS HIEMS
HUACA HYMEN INDRA JUDGE KINGU
LADON LIBER LLUDD MENTU MIDER
MOMUS NJORD NUMEN PALES TAMUZ
TINIA TRUTH TYCHE WAKEA WODIN
WOTAN ZOMBI ADITYA ADONAI ADONAY
ANSHAR ANUBIS ASEITY AUTHOR
CHAMOS CONSUS DEVATA DHARMA
ELATHA ELOHIM FATHER GANESA
HEAVEN HERMES HOENIR MEZTLI
MILCOM MITHRA NEREUS NERGAL
OSIRIS PATRON PENEUS PLUTUS
PUSHAN SESHAT SOCIUS SOURCE SPIRIT
SUTEKH SYLENE TAAROA TAMMUZ
TARTAK TERAPH TRITON TRIVIA VARUNA
VEDUIS VERITY VISHNU WISDOM
YAKSHA YAKSHI ZOMBIE ABRAXAS
ADRANUS ALPHEUS ANTEROS BELENUS
CHEMOSH DAIKOKU DELLING ETERNAL
GODHEAD HANUMAN IAPETUS JEHOVAH
JUPITER KANALOA MITHRAS MUTINUS
NJORTHR PRYDERI REMPHAN ROBIGUS
SAVITAR SERAPIS TRIGLAV VATICAN
VEJOVIS ZAGREUS ALMIGHTY ASTRAEUS
BISHAMON CAMAXTLI DEMIURGE
DEVOTION DIVINITY GUCUMATZ INFINITE
JIUROJIN KUKULKAN MIXCOATL

MORPHEUS SABAZIOS SUMMANUS
TANGAROA TERMINUS TUTELARY
VEDIOVIS ZEPHYRUS OMNIPOTENT
(— OF AGRICULTURE) PICUS URASH
FAUNUS AMAETHON NINGIRSU
(— OF ARTS) SIVA
(— OF ATMOSPHERE) HADAD
(— OF COMMERCE) MERCURY
(— OF CORN) CAT
(— OF DAY) HORUS
(— OF EARTH) BEL GEB KEB SEB
DAGAN
(— OF EVIL) SET FOMOR FOMORIAN
ZERNEBOCK
(— OF FERTILITY) SHANGO
(— OF FIRE) AGNI GIRRU NUSKU RUDRA
VULCAN
(— OF FLOCKS) PAN
(— OF HAPPINESS) HOTEI JUROJIN
(— OF HEAVENS) ANU JUMALA
(— OF JUSTICE) FORSETE FORSETI
(— OF LEARNING) IMHOTEP
(— OF LOVE) AMOR ARES EROS KAMA
BHAGA CUPID AENGUS
(— OF MOON) SIN ENZU NANNAR
(— OF NATURE) MARSYAS
(— OF POETRY) BRAGE BRAGI
(— OF RAIN) PARJANYA
(— OF SEA) LER VAN AEGIR DYAUS
NEPTUNE PROTEUS PALAEMON
POSEIDON
(— OF SKY) ANU GWYDION
(— OF SLEEP) HYPNOS HYPNUS
MORPHEUS
(— OF SOUTHEAST WIND) EURUS
(— OF STORM) ZU ADAD ADDA ADDU
MARUT RUDRA TESHUP
(— OF SUN) RA RE SHU SOL TEM TUM
UTU AMON ATMU ATUM BAAL LLEU
UTUG SAMAS SEKER SURYA APOLLO
HELIOS SOKARI KHEPERA PHOEBUS
SHAMASH PHAETHON TONATIUH
(— OF THUNDER) THOR DONAR PERUN
PERKUN PEROUN SHANGO TLALOC
HURAKAN TARANIS
(— OF UNDERWORLD) DIS BRAN
GWYN YAMA HADES ORCUS PLUTO
(— OF VEGETATION) ATYS ATTIS
(— OF WAR) ER IRA ORO TIU TYR ARES
COEL IRRA MARS MENT ODIN THOR
MONTU NINIB MEXITL SKANDA
CAMULUS MEXITL NINURTA ENYALIUS
NINGIRSU QUIRINUS
(— OF WEALTH) BHAGA KUBERA
KUVERA PLUTUS
(— OF WIND) ADAD ADDA ADDU VAYU
MARUT AEOLUS BOREAS EECATL
(— OF WISDOM) TAT THOTH
(BLIND —) HOTH HOTHR
(FALSE —) BAAL IDOL MAUMET
(FEMALE —) GODDESS
(HAWAIIAN —) AUMAKUA
(IMMORTAL —) AKAL
(INFERIOR —) PANISK
(PAGAN —) DEMON
(RAM-HEADED —) AMON KHNUM
KHNEMU

(TIMELESS —) AKAL
(TUTELARY —) LAR
(UNKNOWN —) KA
(WOOD —) SILEN SILENUS
GODDESS (ALSO SEE DEITY) AI NU ANA
ANU AYA DEA DON NUT UNI VAC ANTA
BADB BODB CACA DANA DANU ERUA
FRIA JORD JUNO MAIA MEDB NONA PELE
SATI TARA UPIS ALLAT AMENT ANTUM
BAUBO CHLOE DEESS DIANE DIRGA
DOLMA DOMNU EPONA FRIGG HYBLA
IAMBE ISTAR KOTYS MAEVE NANAI
NINTU PAKHT PALES PARCA SALUS
SEDNA SKADI TANIT ADEONA AESTAS
ANATUM ANUKIT APHAIA BELILI BENDIS
BOOPIS BRIGIT CYRENE EOSTRE FRIGGA
GEFJON HELENA INNINA KISHAR LIBERA
MOTHER NINGAL PEITHO PHOBOS
POMONA PRORSA RUMINA SEKHET
SKATHI SOTHIS TANITH TEFNUT TRIVIA
URANIA YDGRUN ANAHITA ANAITIS
ASHERAH DERCETO FERONIA FJORGYN
GODHEAD KOTYTTO LARENTA LARUNDA
MAJAGGA MAJESTA MORNING MORRIGU
MYLITTA NEKHEBT PALATUA PARBATI
PARVATI SALACIA ADRASTEA AGLAUROS
ANGERONA BELISAMA CARMENTA
CENTEOTL COCAMAMA DESPOINA
DICTYNNA GULLVEIG MORRIGAN
NEPHTHYS PARBUTTY PRAKRITI
RHIANNON SEFEKHET THOUERIS
VICTORIA
(— OF AGRICULTURE) BAU OPS
DEMETER CENTEOTL
(— OF AIR) AURA
(— OF BEAUTY) VENUS LAKSHMI
(— OF BURIAL) LIBITINA
(— OF CHILDBIRTH) LEVANA LUCINA
(— OF DAWN) EOS USAS USHAS
AURORA MATUTA
(— OF DEW) HERSE
(— OF DISCORD) ATE ERIS
(— OF EARTH) GE LUA SEB ERDA GAEA
GAIA TARI ARURU DIONE JORTH TERRA
SEMELE TELLUS THEMIS DAMKINA
PERCHTA
(— OF FERTILITY) MA ISIS MAMA
NERTHUS
(— OF FLOWERS) FLORA CHLORIS
(— OF FORTUNE) TYCHE FORTUNA
(— OF GRAIN) CERES
(— OF HEALING) EIR GULA
(— OF HEALTH) DAMIA HYGEIA
VALETUDO
(— OF HEARTH) VESTA HESTIA
(— OF HISTORY) SAGA
(— OF HOPE) SPES
(— OF INFATUATION) ATE
(— OF JUSTICE) DIKE MAAT THEMIS
ASTRAEA NEMESIS JUSTITIA
(— OF LEGISLATION) EUNOMIA
(— OF LOVE) ATHOR FREYA VENUS
FREYJA HATHOR
(— OF MAGIC) HECATE
(— OF MARRIAGE) HERA
(— OF MATERNITY) APET
(— OF MERCY) KWANNON

(— OF MOTHERHOOD) ISIS
(— OF NIGHT) NOX NYX
(— OF OCEAN) NINA
(— OF OVENS) FORNAX
(— OF PEACE) PAX IRENE NERTHUS
(— OF PLEASURE) BES
(— OF RAINBOW) IRIS
(— OF SEASONS) DIKE HORA
(— OF THE DEAD) HEL HELA
(— OF THE HUNT) DIANA VACUNA
ARTEMIS
(— OF THE MOON) LUNA MOON DIANA
SELENA TANITH ARTEMIS
(— OF THE SEA) INO RAN DORIS
BRANWEN EURYNOME
(— OF TRUTH) MAAT
(— OF VEGETATION) OPS CERES
COTYS COTYTTO
(— OF VENGEANCE) ARA NEMESIS
(— OF VICTORY) NIKE
(— OF WAR) ENYO ANATH ANATU
ANUNIT BELLONA
(— OF WATER) ANAHITA
(— OF WEALTH) LAKSHMI
(— OF WISDOM) ATHENA MINERVA
(— OF YOUTH) HEBE JUVENTAS
(COW-HEADED —) ISIS
(ESKIMO —) SEDNA
(FERTILITY —) ASTARTE
(MARRIAGE —) VOR
(SUBORDINATE —) DEMIURGE
(THUNDER-SMITTEN —) SEMELE
KERAUNIA
(3-HEADED —) HECATE
GODFATHER GOSSIP GODPAPA PADRINO
SPONSOR GODPHERE
GODHEAD DEITY GODHOOD DIVINITY
GODLESS WICKED ATHEIST IMPIOUS
PROFANE UNGODLY
GODLESSNESS ATHEISM
GODLIKE DEIFIC DIVINE IMMORTAL
OLYMPIAN
GODLINESS PIETISM SANCTITY
GODLING DEVATA GENIUS GODKIN
GODLET PANISC DEMIGOD PANISCUS
GODLY HOLY WISE PIOUS DEVOUT
GRACIOUS
GODMOTHER CUMMER GOSSIP
SPONSOR GODMAMMA MARRAINE
GODPARENT SPONSOR
GOING FARE GAIT BOUND AGOING
WAYING PASSADO SLEDDING
(— ABOUT) AROUND
(— BEYOND OTHERS) ULTRA
(— IN) INEUNT INFARE INGOING
(— ON) FARE AGATE TOWARD
(— OUT) EGRESS
(— UP) ANABASIS
(SUFF.) GRESS
GOITER WEN GLANS GOITRE STRUMA
BRONCHOCELE
GOLD OR ORO RED SOL DORE GILT GULL
ALTUN AURUM GUILD METAL OCHER
RIDGE SHINY GOLDEN OBRIZE ORMOLU
YELLOW BULLION SPANKER
(— PIECE) TALI
(GREENISH —) AENEOUS

(IMITATION —) PINCHBECK
GOLDEN RED DORE GOLD BLEST DURRY
GOLDY SUNNY AUREAL BLONDE GILDEN
GILTEN AUREATE AUREOUS HALCYON
AURULENT DEAURATE
GOLDEN ASS (AUTHOR OF —)
APULEIUS
(CHARACTER IN —) ISIS MILO FOTIS
LUCIUS CHARITES PAMPHILE SOCRATES
BYRRHAENA LEPOLEMUS THRASILLUS
ARISTOMENES
GOLDEN BOWL (AUTHOR OF —)
JAMES
(CHARACTER IN —) ADAM STANT
MAGGIE VERVER AMERIGO CHARLOTTE
GOLDENROD BONEWORT SOLIDAGO
JIMMYWEED
GOLDFINCH JACK FINCH GOLDY GOWDY
CANARY REDCAP FLAXBIRD GRAYPATE
GOLDFISH FUNA MOOR COMET CALICO
FANTAIL CYPRINID VEILTAIL
GOLDSMITH SONAR AURIFEX
GONE AWAY LOST NAPOO
(— BY) AGO DONE PAST AGONE PASSE
BEHIND BYGONE
(— OUT OF USE) EXTINCT
(— TO PIECES) HAYWIRE
GONE WITH THE WIND
(AUTHOR OF —) MITCHELL
(CHARACTER IN —) FRANK OHARA
RHETT ASHLEY BUTLER WILKES
CHARLES KENNEDY MELANIE HAMILTON
SCARLETT
GONG BELL CLOCK GANGSA DOORBELL
(SERIES OF —S) BONANG
GOOD BON GAY TOP TRY ABLE BEAU
BEIN BIEN BOON BRAW FINE GAIN HEND
NICE NOTE PROW SAKE BONNY BONUM
BRAVE BULLY CANNY FRESH GWEED
JELLY KAPAI PAKKA PUKKA SEELY
SOUND VALID BENIGN BRAWLY BUCKRA
DIVINE EXPERT FACTOR FORBYE HONEST
MABUTI PRETTY PROFIT PROPER
WEALTH BENEFIT COPIOUS CORKING
FAIRISH FORTHBY GODLIKE GRADELY
HELPFUL LIBERAL SNIFTER STAVING
TRAINED UPRIGHT BUDGEREE GRAITHLY
INTEREST LAUDABLE PLEASING
SALUTARY SKILLFUL SUITABLE
(EXCEPTIONALLY —) SLAMBANG
(EXTREMELY —) SLICK
(HOLD —) BEAR
(INFINITELY —) HOLY
(MIGHTY —) SKOOKUM
(NO —) DUFF NAPOO
(PRETTY —) FAIR TIDY
(RELATIVELY —) SMOOTH
(SUPERLATIVELY —) BRAG BEAUTIFUL
(SUPREMELY —) IMMENSE GORGEOUS
(SURPASSINGLY —) SUPERIOR
(VERY —) HOT TOP DANDY DICTY
GRAND NIFTY BONZER BOSHTA BOSKER
BOSHTER NAILING SPLENDID SWINGING
GOOD-BYE BY BYE TATA ADDIO ADIEU
ADIOS LULLABY FAREWELL SAYONARA
GOOD EARTH (AUTHOR OF —) BUCK
(CHARACTER IN —) LIU LUNG NUNG

OLAN PEAR WANG CHING HWANG
LOTUS
GOOD-FOR-NOTHING BUM ORRA SLIM
SLINK DONNOT KEFFEL RIBALD STUMER
BRETHEL FUSTIAN SCROYLE SHOTTEN
SKEEZIX SKELLUM SKYBALD VAURIEN
WOSBIRD VAGABOND
GOOD-HUMORED SONSY
GOOD-LOOKING BRAW FAIR FOXY MOOI
BONNY GAWSY COMELY PRETTY SEEMLY
EYESOME GRADELY WINSOME GOODLIKE
HANDSOME STUNNING
GOODLY BOON PROPER GOODLIKE
GOOD-NATURED SONSY CLEVER
AMIABLE
GOODNESS BONTE BONUM MENSK
PROOF BONITY BOUNTY SATTVA VIRTUE
KINDNESS
GOODS FEE BONA GEAR KIND PELF
CARGO STUFF TRADE WORLD WRACK
ADVANCE CAPITAL CHATTEL EFFECTS
FINANCE HAVINGS INSIGHT TRAFFIC
CHAFFERY HIGGLERY PROPERTY
(— BARTERED) DICKER
(— CAST OVERBOARD) JETSAM
(— SUNK IN SEA) LAGAN
(DRY —) DRAPERY
(HOUSEHOLD —) INSIGHT
(IMPERFECT —) FENT
(INFERIOR —) BRACK
(PIECE —) CUTTANEE
(SECONDHAND —) BROKERY
(SLOW-SELLING —) JOBS
(STOLEN — THROWN AWAY) WAIF
(SURPLUS —) OVERAGE
(VALUABLE —) SWAG
GOODWILL GREE PHILANTHROPY
GOOEY CLARTY
GOOF BOOB GOOFER
GOON MUSCLEMAN
GOOSE ELK LAMA NENE ROUT BRANT
BRENT EMDEN HANSA HOBBY ROMAN
SOLAN WAVEY CAGMAG CANADA
EMBDEN GALOOT GANDER GOSLET
HISSER HONKER SOLAND AFRICAN
BLACKIE BUSTARD GAGGLER GOSLING
GRAYLAG GREASER GREYLAG OUTARDE
WIDGEON BALDHEAD BARGOOSE
BARNACLE BERNICLE SPURWING
TOULOUSE
(MYTHICAL —) GANZA
GOOSEBERRY BLOB FABE FAPE POHA
BRAGAS GOBLIN GOZILL GROZER
DOWNING GASKINS GROZART CARBERRY
CATBERRY DOGBERRY EATBERRY
FEABERRY GOOSEGOG HOUGHTON
INDUSTRY
(PL.) THAPES
GOPHER TUZA GAUFFRE GEOMYID
MUNGOFA QUACHIL SALAMICH
TUCOTUCO
GORE CLY CLOY GARE HIKE HIPE HOOK
HORN PICK PIKE SHOT CRUOR GODET
STICK GORING GUSSET
GORGE GAP JAM FILL GASH GAUM GLUT
JAMB KHOR RENT BREAK CAJON CANON
CHASM CHINE CLUSE DRAFT FARCE

FLUME GULLY GURGE KLOOF PONGO
POUCH STECH STRID STUFF TANGI
CANYON DEFILE NULLAH RAVINE
STODGE STRAIT THROAT COULOIR
DATIATE DRAUGHT ENGORGE SATIATE
SLABBER BARRANCA QUEBRADA
GORGED ACCOLLE
GORGEOUS VAIN GRAND SHOWY
COSTLY DAZZLING GLORIOUS SPLENDID
GORGON MEDUSA STHENO EURYALE
GORILLA APE PYGMY
GORMANDIZER HELLUO GLUTTON
GORSE ULEX WHIN FURZE GORST
GORY BLOODY
GOSHAWK GOS ASTUR TERCEL
GOSLING GULL
GOSPEL SPELL DHARMA EVANGEL
KERUGMA KERYGMA SYNOPTIC
(— OF REDEMPTION) CROSS
GOSSAMER MOUSEWEB STARDUST
GOSSIP EME GUP PIE AUNT BLAB BUZZ
CANT CLAT CONK COZE DIRT NEWS
TALK CAUSE CLACK CLASH CLYPE
COOSE CRACK FERLY FRUMP GOSSY
SIEVE YENTA BABBLE CACKLE CADDLE
CALLET CAMPER CLAVER CUMMER
FERLIE JANGLE KIMMER NORATE TATTLE
TITTLE CLATTER COMPERE GOSTHER
HASHGOB NASHGAB SCANDAL TATTLER
TRATTLE CAUSERIE CHITCHAT GOSSIPRY
QUIDNUNC SCHMOOZE NEWSMONGER
GOSSIPY BUZZY NEWSY CHATTY
GOTH GOTHIAN SUIOGOTH VISIGOTH
GOTHAM ABDERA
GOTHAMITE ABDERITE
GOTHIC OGIVAL
GOTTERDAMMERUNG
(CHARACTER IN —) HAGEN GUNTHER
GUTRUNE SIEGFRIED WALTRAUTE
BRUNNHILDE
(COMPOSER OF —) WAGNER
GOUGE DIG PUG BENT SCUFF CHISEL
FLUKAN GOUGER HOLLOW SCRIBE
FLOOKAN SCORPER SELVAGE SELVEDGE
STICKING
(— OUT) BULLDOZE
(V-TYPE —) VEINER
GOUGER CHISELLER
GOURD MATE PEPO LUFFA ABOBRA
JICARA PATOLA ANGURIA DISHRAG
HECHIMA CALABASH CUCURBIT
PEPONIDA PEPONIUM
GOURMAND EPICURE GLUTTON
GORMAND
GOURMET PALATE EPICURE GOURMAND
GOUT GUT CLOT DROP SPLASH PODAGRA
PODAGRY CHIRAGRA ARTHRITIS
GOVERN RUN WIN CURB KING LEAD
REDE REIN RULE SWAY WALD WARD
WIND YEME GUIDE JUDGE REGLE STEER
TREAT WIELD BRIDLE DIRECT MANAGE
ORDAIN POLICE POLICY TEMPER
COMMAND CONDUCT CONTROL PRESIDE
REFRAIN DISPENSE DOMINATE IMPERATE
MODERATE OVERRULE OVERSWAY
POLICIZE REGULATE RESTRAIN
GOVERNED BENT

GOVERNESS ABBESS DUENNA FRAULEIN
MISTRESS MADEMOISELLE
GOVERNING REGENT REGITIVE
GOVERNMENT LAND RULE KREIS
METRO POWER STATE STEER DURBAR
HAVANA POLICY RULING CABINET
CZARISM DYARCHY RECTION REGENCY
REGIMEN TSARISM CIVILITY ENDARCHY
GOBIERNO HEGEMONY ISOCRACY
ISOCRYME KINGSHIP STEERING
ABSOLUTISM
(— BY FEW) OLIGARCHY
(— BY GOD) THEONOMY
(— BY MOB) OCHLOCRACY
(— BY WEALTHY) PLUTOCRACY
(— BY WOMEN) GYNARCHY
(— BY 10) DECARCHY
(— BY 2) DIARCHY DUARCHY
(— OF CEYLON) DISSAVA
(— OF TURKEY) GATE PORTE
(ARBITRARY —) ABSOLUTISM
(CHURCH —) PRELACY
(INDIAN —) SIRCAR
(MALAYSIAN —) KOMPENI
GOVERNMENTAL ARCHICAL
GOVERNOR BAN EARL KAID LORD NAIK
TUTU VALI BANUS CLEON DEWAN
DIWAN HAKIM NABOB NAZIM SHEIK
SUBAH TUPAN AUTHOR DYNAST GRIEVE
MOODIR MYOWUN NAIGUE NAIQUE
PATESI PENLOP RECTOR REGENT SATRAP
SHEIKH SHERIF TUCHUN WARDEN
DAROGHA LEONATO PODESTA RECTRIX
SERKALI SHEREEF TOPARCH TSUNGTU
VICEROY WIELDER AUTOCRAT
BURGRAVE ETHNARCH HOSPODAR
MISTRESS RESIDENT SUBAHDAR
TETRARCH CASTELLAN PRESIDENT
PROCONSUL
(— OF ALGIERS) DEY DISAWA
(— OF BURMA) WOON
(— OF EGYPT) MUDIR
(— OF FORTRESS) ALCAIDE
(— OF SHIRE) ALDERMAN
(— OF TAMMANY) SACHEM
(BYZANTINE —) EXARCH CATAPAN
(CEYLON —) DISAWA
(GERMAN —) LANDVOGT
(GREEK —) ETHNARCH
(JAPANESE —) SHOGUN TYCOON
(PAPAL —) LEGATE
(ROMAN —) TETRARCH
(SELJUK —) ATABEG
(SPARTAN —) HARMOST
(TURKISH —) BEY WALI MUDIR KEHAYA
GOVERNOR-GENERAL VALI
GOWN GOR SAC GITE GORE HUKE JAMA
RAIL SACK SILK TOGA BANIA DRESS
FROCK GOUND HABIT JAMAH MANTO
TABBY TOOSH BANIAN BANIYA CAFTAN
CAMISE CANDYS CHITON JESUIT
JOHNNY KIMONO KIRTLE KITTEL LEVITE
MANTUA ARISARD CASSOCK GARMENT
JOHNNIE SLAMKIN SULTANA SULTANE
WRAPPER CAMISOLE GANDOURA
MAZARINE PEIGNOIR
(HAWAIIAN —) MOLOKU MUUMUU

GRAB NAB NAP RAP GLAM GOPE GLAUM
SCRAB CLUTCH COLLAR CRATCH DIPPER
NIPPER NOBBLE SNATCH CRAPPLE
GRABBLE GRAPNEL GRAPPLE NIPPERS

GRACE EST ORE BEAT ESTE GARB HELD
SWAY ADORN COULE FAVOR HONOR
MENSE MERCY SLIDE THANK VENUS
BEAUTY BECOME BEDECK CHARIS
POLISH RELISH THALIA AGGRACE
CHARISM COMMEND DIGNITY FINESSE
GRATIFY MELISMA MORDENT BACKFALL
BEAUTIFY BLESSING DECORATE
EASINESS ELEGANCE FELICITY GRATUITY
LEVATION ORNAMENT
(— OF FORM) FLOW SWAY TOURNURE

GRACEFUL AIRY FEAT GENT BONNY
GENTY GRATE COMELY FEATLY FELINE
FLUENT GAINLY QUAINT SEEMLY SILKEN
VENUST ELEGANT FITTING GENTEEL
GRACILE SYLPHID WILLOWY CHARMING
DELICATE GRACIOUS LEGGIERO
MACEVOLE SWANLIKE SYLPHISH

GRACEFULLY FAIR FEATLY HAPPILY
LEGGIERO

GRACEFULNESS JOLLITY ELEGANCE

GRACELESS AWKWARD

GRACES CHARITES

GRACIOUS GOOD HEND HOLD KIND MILD
CIVIL GODLY HAPPY LUCKY SUAVE
WINLY BENIGN GENIAL GENTLE GOODLY
KINDLY AFFABLE CORDIAL WINSOME
BENEDICT DEBONAIR GENEROUS
HANDSOME MERCIFUL PLEASING
SOCIABLE BENIGNANT

GRACIOUSLY FAIR SWEETLY

GRACIOUSNESS GRACE MENSK
FACILITY GRATUITY

GRADATION HUE CLINE ABLAUT
CLIMAX NUANCE GEOCLINE STRENGTH

GRADE CUT BANK CHOP EVEN FORM
MARK RANK SIZE STEP GLIDE LEVEL
ORDER PLANE SCORE SIEGE STAGE
ASCENT DEGREE RATING STAPLE TRIAGE
FAILURE INCLINE INSPECT DEMISANG
GRADIENT GRADUATE MERIDIAN
STANDARD
(— DOWN) FAULT
(— LUMBER) SURVEY
(— OF BEEF) GOOD CUTTER
(— OF LUMBER) CULL
(— OF OAK) WAINSCOT
(— OF OFFICER) CORNET
(— ROAD) IMPROVE
(ABLAUT —) SUPER
(SUPERIOR —) SUPER
(THIRD —) FAIR

GRADIENT GRADE LAPSE SLOPE ASCENT
INCLINE DOWNHILL

GRADUAL EASY FLAT SLOW GRAIL
GENTLE LENTOUS STEPWISE PIECEMEAL

GRADUALLY GENTLY EDGINGLY
GRADATIM INCHMEAL PIECEMEAL

GRADUATE GRAD GRADE ALUMNA
DIVIDE FELLOW ALUMNUS GRADATE
BACHELOR
(EISTEDDFOD —) OVATE

GRADUATED SCALAR MEASURED

GRADUATION CLICK

GRAFT BUD IMP PIE CION WORK GRAFF
GRAVY INEYE SCION BOODLE INARCH
PAYOLA SPLICE ENGRAFT IMPLANT
JOBBERY SQUEEZE TOPWORK APPROACH
BOODLING GRAFTING INSITION

GRAFTED ENTE

GRAFTER BOODLER

GRAIL CUP GRAAL CHALICE SANGRAAL

GRAIN JOT RUN RYE WAY CORN CURN
DANA KERN PILE RICE SAND SEED WALE
WOOD EMMER FIBER FIBRE FUNDI GLEBE
PANIC SCRAP SPARK STUFF TRACE
WHEAT ANNONA BARLEY BRAINS
CEREAL CURRAN GROATS KERNEL
FRUMENT GRANULE PANICLE VICTUAL
GRAINING PARTICLE STRAIGHT
SWEEPAGE
(— FOR MUSH) KASHA
(— FROM MASH TUN) DRAINS
(— LEFT AFTER HARVEST) GAVEL
SHACK
(— MEASURE) THRAVE
(— OF BOARD) BEAT
(— OF CORN) PICKLE
(— OF GOLD) PIPPIN
(— OF WOOD) BATE
(CHAFF OF —) BRAN
(COARSE —) THIRD
(COARSELY GROUND —) MEAL GRITS
KIBBLE
(DAMAGED —) SALVAGE
(EAR OF —) SPIKE RISSOM RIZZON
(GERMINATED —) MALT
(GROUND —) GRIST
(HANDFUL OF —) REAP
(HULLED —) GRITS GROUT GROATS
SHELLING
(HUSKED —) SHEALING
(MILLET —) CUSCUS
(MIXED —) MASLIN
(MIXED —S) DREDGE
(PARCHED —) GRADDAN
(REFUSE —) SHAG DRAFF
(SACRIFICIAL —) ADOR
(SHOCK OF —) COP
(STACK OF —) HOVEL
(STORED —) MOW
(STREAKED —) ROEY

GRAMMAR DONAT SYNTAX GRAMARY
PRISCIAN
(TYPE OF —) TAGMEMIC

GRAMMARIAN PRISCIAN

GRANARY GOLA GUNJ SILO GOLAH
GUNGE LATHE GARNER GIRNEL GRANGE
HORREUM RESERVE CORNLOFT
GRAINERY

GRAND OLD AIRY BRAW EPIC MAIN TALL
CHIEF GREAT LOFTY NOBLE PROUD
SHOWY SWELL WLONK ANDEAN
AUGUST COSMIC EPICAL FAMOUS
GLOBAL KINGLY LORDLY SIGHTY SUPERB
SWANKY EXALTER IMMENSE STATELY
SUBLIME COSMICAL FOREMOST
GLORIOUS GORGEOUS IMPOSING
MAJESTIC SPLENDID MAGNIFICENT
(PREF.) BEL

GRANDEUR POMP STATE ESTATE FIGURE PARADE MAJESTY ELEGANCE GRANDEZA HAUTESSE NOBILITY SPLENDOR VASTNESS

GRANDFATHER AIEL NONO BOBBY GRAMP ATAVUS GRAMPS BELSIRE GRANDAD GRANDPA GRANDFER GUIDSIRE
(GREAT —) NONO
(GREAT-GREAT-GREAT —) QUATRAYLE

GRAND HOTEL (AUTHOR OF —) BAUM
(CHARACTER IN —) ANNA OTTO FLAMM GAIGERN PREYSING ELISAVETA FLAEMMCHEN KRINGELEIN GRUSINSKAYA OTTERNSCHLAG

GRANDIOSE GRAND COSMIC TURGID SUBLIME COSMICAL IMPERIAL

GRANDMOTHER GRAM GRAN LUCKY NANNY GRANNY GUDAME LUCKIE BELDAME NOKOMIS BABUSHKA GRANDAME

GRANITE MOYITE RUNITE GREISEN SYENITE ALASKITE RAPAKIVI PEGMATITE
(DECOMPOSED —) GROWAN

GRANT AID BOOK BOON CEDE GIFT GIVE HEAR LEND LOAN MISE SEND STOW YARK ADMIT ALLOT AWARD BONUS CHART FLOAT FUERO LEASE SEIZE SPARE TITHE YETTE YIELD ACCEDE AFFORD ASSENT BESTOW BETAKE BETEEM BOUNTY CONFER DESIGN EXTEND FIRMAN IMPART NOVATE OCTROI PATENT PERMIT REMISE ADJUDGE APPOINT COLLATE CONCEDE CONSENT DISPONE INDULGE LICENSE PRESENT PROMISE SUBSIDY TRIBUTE APPANAGE BESTOWAL CONTRACT DONATION EXCHANGE MONOPOLY PITTANCE TRANSFER CONCESSION ACKNOWLEDGE
(— AS PROPER) ACCORD
(— OF LAND) FEU ENAM GALE PATA SASAN CASATE
(— PERMISSION) ALLOW DISPENSE
(— RELIEF) FORGIVE
(— TIME) FRIST
(INDIAN —) ENAM COWLE SASAN JAGEER JAGHIR

GRANULAR CORN OPEN GRAINY

GRANULATE CORN KERN GRAIN SUGAR

GRANULE GRIT GRANUM LUCULE NODULE BIOBLAST GONIDIUM GRANULET
(ALTMANN'S —S) BIOPLAST
(ICE —S) FRAZIL
(SUFF.) PLAST

GRAPE UVA VINE BERRY GRAIN PINOT TOKAY ACINUS AGAWAM ISABEL MALAGA MONICA MUSCAT RAISIN VERDEA WORDEN CATAWBA CONCORD HAMBURG MALMSEY MISSION NIAGARA SULTANA CABERNET DELAWARE GRAPELET HANEPOOT ISABELLA LABRUSCA MALVASIA MORILLON MOUNTAIN MUSCATEL NUCULANE RIESLING SLIPSKIN SYLVANER THOMPSON VINIFERA MUSCADINE

GRAPEFRUIT POMELO TORONJA

GRAPES OF WRATH (AUTHOR OF —) STEINBECK
(CHARACTER IN —) AL JIM TOM JOAD NOAH ROSE CASEY MULEY CONNIE GRAVES RUTHIE WINFIELD

GRAPH CHART CURVE OGIVE TRACE CONTOUR DIAGRAM PROFILE ISOPLETH

GRAPHIC PICTORIAL PICTURESQUE

GRAPHITE WAD KISH LEAD PENCIL PLUMBAGO MODERATOR

GRAPNEL CROW DRAG GRAB CREEP CREEPER GRABBLE GRAPPLE SNIGGER GRABHOOK

GRAPPLE DOG CLOSE GRASP GRIPE LATCH BUCKLE CLINCH GRABBLE GRAPNEL GRIPPLE SNIGGER SNIGGLE WRESTLE
(— QUARRY) BIND

GRASP HUG NAP SEE CLAM CLAW CLUM FAKE FANG FIST GLAM GRAB GRIP HAND HENT HOLD SNAP SPAN TAKE VICE CATCH CINCH CLAMP CLASP CLAUT CLEUK GRIPE GROPE LATCH SAVVY SEIZE SENSE SHAKE SPEND CLENCH CLINCH CLUTCH COLLAR FATHOM GOUPEN RUMBLE SNATCH CLAUGHT COMPASS ENCLOSE GRAPPLE GRIPPLE SMITTLE CONCEIVE HANDFAST HOLDFAST
(— FULLY) SWALLOW
(— MENTALLY) ENVISAGE
(— OF REALITY) EPIPHANY

GRASPING HARD NIPPY SNACK GRABBY GREEDY GRIPPY HAVING TAKING BROKING MISERLY PUGGING COVETOUS HANDGRIP AVARICIOUS

GRASS BON RAY COIX GAMA HERB ICHU KANS KUSA MUNJ MUSK RAGI TARE USAR ANKEE BARIT BROME COUCH CROFT DRINN FLAWN FUNDI GARSE GIRSE GLAGA GRAMA HARIF HAVER HICHU ILLUK KOGON KUSHA MELIC MUHLY PANIC QUILA ROOSA SEREH SPIRE STIPA SUDAN ZORRA BARLEY BHABAR BHARTI DARNEL EMOLOA FESCUE FIORIN GLUMAL KIKUYU RAGGEE REDTOP RIPGUT TOETOE TWITCH ZACATE AMOURET CANNACH ESPARTO EULALIA FESTUCA FINETOP FOXTAIL GALLETA GOLDEYE HERBAGE HORDEUM JARAGUA MATWEED MUSCOVY PANICLE PASTURE PIGROOT SETARIA SORGHUM TIMOTHY TOCUSSO TUSSOCK VETIVER ZACATON AEGILOPS BLUESTEM BROWNTOP CALFKILL CAMALOTE CELERITY COCKSPUR DOGSTAIL DRAWLING DROPSEED EELGRASS ELEUSINE FINEBENT GAMELOTE MANGRASS MATGRASS PASPALUM SANDBURR SANDSPUR SANDSTAY SPANIARD SPARTINA SPINIFEX SWEEPAGE TEOSINTE WHITETOP MARIJUANA
(— AMONG GRAIN) DRAWK
(— FOR STOCK) EATAGE
(— FOR THATCHING) BANGO
(— ON BORDER OF FIELD) RAND
(— READY FOR REAPING) SWATH

(AROMATIC —) KHUS KHUSKHUS
(BEACH —) STAR
(BERMUDA —) DOOB SCUTCH
(COARSE —) FAG RISP TATH COGON
 REESK LALANG SNIDDLE
(COUCH —) CUTCH KWEEK QUITCH
 SCUTCH STROIL SQUITCH
(CURED —) HAY
(DEAD —) FOG FOGGAGE
(DITCH —) ENALID
(GOOSE —) CLEAVERS
(MEADOW —) POA
(NUT —) COCO COCOA
(ORCHARD —) DOGFOOT
(PASTURE —) TORE GRAMMA
(POVERTY —) HEATH
(QUAKING —) SHAKER
(REED —) CARRIZO
(REEDLIKE —) BENT DISS
(SUDAN —) GARAWI
(SWEET —) SORGO
GRASSHOPPER GRIG CICADA HOPPER
 QUAKER SAWYER TETTIX ACRIDID
 CRICKET KATYDID SKIPPER ACRIDIAN
 LANGOSTA
GRASSLAND HAM LEA RAKH VELD
 VELDT BOTTOM MEADOW PATANA
 LEYLAND PASTURE SAVANNA
 (TRACT OF —) PRAIRIE
GRATE JAR FRET GRIT RASP CHARK
 CHIRK DEVIL GRIDE GRIND RANGE STOVE
 ABRADE CHAFER SCRAPE SCREAR
 SCREEK SCROOP GRATING MANGRATE
 (FALSE —) DANDY
GRATEFUL KIND SAPID WELCOME
 THANKFUL
GRATIFICATION GLUT GUST LUXURY
 RELISH REWARD SATIETY DELICACY
 GRATUITY PLEASURE TICKLING
 SATISFACTION
GRATIFIED GLAD PROUD CHARMED
 CONTENT PLEASED
GRATIFY PAY BABY FEED LUST AMUSE
 FEAST FLESH GRACE HUMOR MIRTH
 QUEME SAVOR SERVE STILL WREAK
 ARRIDE FOSTER OBLIGE PAMPER PLEASE
 REGALE SALUTE TICKLE AGGRATE
 CONTENT DELIGHT FLATTER GLADDEN
 INDULGE SATISFY PLEASURE
GRATIFYING GOOD COMELY DELICATE
 GRATEFUL
GRATING GRID HACK HARP HECK JACK
 RACK CRATE CRUDE GRILL HARSH
 RANGE RASPY TRAIL BAFFLE CRATCH
 BAFFLER ECHELLE ECHELON BABRACOT
 CATAPULT GRIDIRON METALLIC
 SCRANNEL STRIDENT PORTCULLIS
GRATIS FREE FREELY BUCKSHEE
GRATITUDE THANK THANKS GRATUITY
GRATUITOUS FREE WANTON BASELESS
 NEEDLESS
GRATUITY FEE TIP BOON DASH VAIL
 PILON SPIFF SPILL BOUNTY CUMSHAW
 DASTURI DOUCEUR PRESENT PRIMAGE
 BAKSHISH BONAMANO BUCKSHEE

COURTESY DUSTOORI GRATUITO
 REAPDOLE PERQUISITE
(CHRISTMAS —) BOX
GRAVE BED DRY LOW PIT SAD URN BALK
 BASS BIER CELL CIST DEEP DELF FOSS
 GRIT HIGH HOME KIST LAIR LAKE MOLD
 MOOL RUDE SADE SAGE TOMB URNA
 DELFT FOSSE GRAFF GROVE HEAVY
 MOULD SHEOL SOBER STAID STIFF
 SUANT VAULT BURIAL DEMURE GRIEVE
 HEARSE SEDATE SEVERE SOLEMN
 SOMBER SOMBRE STEADY AUSTERE
 EARNEST FUNERAL PITHOLE SERIOSO
 SERIOUS SOBERLY CATONIAN
 DECOROUS MATRONAL SERMONIC
 SATURNINE
GRAVEL GRIT GEEST GRAIL CHESIL
 RANGLE SAMMEL SHILLA BALLAST
 CALICHE CHANNEL RATCHEL SHINGLE
 STANNER BLINDING
 (— AND SAND) DOBBIN
 (— DEPOSIT) LEAD
 (— IN KIDNEYS) ARENA
 (LOOSE —) SLITHER
 (SCREENED —) HOGGINS
GRAVITY WEIGHT DIGNITY EARNEST
 SOBRIETY
GRAVY JUS SOP BREE FOND LEAR BLANC
 BUNCE JIPPER
GRAY ASH BAT FOG ASHY BEAR BLAE
 BLUE DOVE DUSK GREY GRIS GULL HOAR
 IRON LEAD SALT ACIER CAMEL CRANE
 HOARY LYART MOUSE STEEL WHIFF
 CASTOR CINDER DENVER FROSTY
 FRUSTY GREIGE GRISLY ISABEL LEADEN
 NICKEL NUTRIA PEWTER QUAKER STRING
 BLUNKET CRUISER GRANITE GRIZARD
 GRIZZLE GRIZZLY HUELESS MURINUS
 NEUTRAL PELICAN PILGRIM SARKARA
 SPARROW ALUMINUM BLONCKET
 CHARCOAL CINEREAL CINEROUS
 EVENGLOW FELDGRAU PLATINUM
 PLYMOUTH
 (DARKEST —) BLACK
 (GOOSE —) LAMA
 (MOLE —) TAUPE
 (MOTH —) SHEEPSKIN
 (STREAKED WITH —) LYARD
 (VIOLET —) GRIDELIN
GRAZE BITE CROP FEED SCUR SKIM
 AGIST BRUSH GRASS GRIDE RANGE
 SCAMP SCUFF SHAVE SKIFF SKIRR
 STOCK BROWSE CREASE FODDER
 GLANCE RIPPLE SCRAPE SCRAZE
 PASTURE
GRAZING BIT FEED GRASS COLLOP
 RASANT FOLDING PASCUAGE
GREASE COOM SAIM SEAM ADEPS BLECK
 SMEAR SPICK ARMING AXUNGE CREESH
 ENSEAM LIQUOR POMATE ALEMITE
 SAINDOUX
 (— IN HARD CAKES) SEAK
 (PIG'S —) MORT
 (WOOL —) YOK DEGRAS LANOLIN
 (PREF.) SEBI
GREASY FAT GLET OILY RICH FATTY

PORKY YOLKY SMEARY TRAINY CREESHY
PINGUID TALLOWY UNCTUOUS
GREAT BIG FAR FAT FIT OLD BARO DEEP
DREE FELL FINE GONE GURT HUGE KEEN
MAIN MUCH RIAL SOME TALL UNCO
VAST VILE AMPLE BURRA CHIEF FELON
GRAND LARGE MEKIL STOUR SWEET
SWELL TOUGH YEDER FIERCE GAPING
HEROIC MICKLE NATION STRONG
CAPITAL EMINENT EXTREME GALLOWS
HOWLING IMMENSE INTENSE STAVING
TITANIC VIOLENT VOLUMED ALMIGHTY
CRACKING ELEVATED ENORMOUS
FAVORITE GALACTIC GALAXIAN
GIGANTIC HORRIBLE INFINITE PRECIOUS
TERRIFIC MONSTROUS MAGNIFICENT
GREAT BRITAIN (SEE ENGLAND)
GREATEST UTMOST EXTREME MAXIMAL
(— POSSIBLE) ALL SUPREME
GREAT EXPECTATIONS
(AUTHOR OF —) DICKENS
(CHARACTER IN —) JOE PIP ABEL
BIDDY DOLGE SARAH ORLICK PHILIP
PIRRIP POCKET PROVIS BENTLEY
DRUMMLE ESTELLA GARGERY HERBERT
JAGGERS MATTHEW HAVISHAM
MAGWITCH COMPEYSON PUMBLECHOOK
GREAT GATSBY (AUTHOR OF —)
FITZGERALD
(CHARACTER IN —) JAY TOM NICK
BAKER DAISY MCKEE GATSBY GEORGE
JORDAN MYRTLE WILSON BUCHANAN
CARRAWAY CATHERINE WOLFSHIEM
GREAT-GRANDCHILD IEROE
GREAT GRANDFATHER NONO BESAIEL
GRANDSIR
GREAT LAKE ERIE HURON ONTARIO
MICHIGAN SUPERIOR
GREATLY FAR MUY FELL MUCH AMAIN
SWITH FINELY MAINLY STRONG SWYTHE
SWEETLY WOUNDLY MIGHTILY
GREATNESS FORCE GRANDEUR
GRANDEZA MUCHNESS

GREECE

BAY: ELEUSIS SALAMIS PHALERON
CAPE: KRIOS MALEA SPADA AKRITAS
MATAPAN SIDEROS DREPANON
GRAMBYSA TAINARON
CAPITAL: ATHENS ATHENAI
COIN: OBOL HECTE DIOBOL LEPTON
STATER DRACHMA DIOBOLON
DISTRICT: ARTA ELIS CANEA CHIOS
CORFU CRETE DRAMA EVROS KHIOS
PELLA SAMOS ZANTE ACHAEA ACHAIA
ATTICA EPIRUS EUBOEA KILKIS KNANIA
KOZANE LARISA LESBOS LEUKAS PHOCIS
PIERIA SERRAI THRACE XANTHE AETOLIA
ARCADIA ARGOLIS BOEOTIA CORINTH
KAVALLA LACONIA LARISSA LASETHI
MTATHOS PREVEZA RHODOPE CYCLADES
IOANNINA KARDITSA KASTORIA
MAGNESIA MESSENIA PHLORINA
RETHYMNE SALONIKA THESSALY
TRIKKALA MACEDONIA

GULF: VOLOS ATHENS MESARA PATRAI
PATRAS ARGOLIS CORINTH KAVALLA
KNANION LACONIA LEPANTO MESSINI
RENDINA SARONIC STRIMON MESSENIA
SALONIKA SINGITIC THERMAIC
TORONAIC
ISLAND: DIA IOS KEA KOS NIO CEOS KEOS
MILO SYME SYRA CHIOS CORFU CRETE
DELOS KASOS KHIOS LEROS MELOS
MILOS NAXOS PAROS PAXOI PAXOS
PSARA RODOS SAMOS SARIA SYROS
TELOS TENOS THERA THIRA TINOS
ZANTE ANAPHE ANDROS CANDIA CERIGO
CHALKE EUBOEA EVVOIA GAVDOS
IKARIA ITHACA ITHAKI LEMNOS LESBOS
LEUKAS LEVKAS PATMOS RHENEA
RHODES SIFNOS SKYROS THASOS
AMORGOS CIMOLUS CYTHERA KERKYRA
KIMOLOS KYTHERA KYTHNOS LEVITHA
MYKONOS NISYROS SALAMIS SIPHNOS
KALYMNOS MYTILENE SANTORIN
SERIPHOS
LAKE: KARLA VOLVE COPAIS KOPAIS
PRESPA TOPOLIA KASTORIA TACHINOS
VISTONIS
MEASURE: PIK BEMA PIKI POUS BARIL
CADOS CHOUS CUBIT DIGIT MARIS
PEKHE PODOS PYGON XYLON ACAENA
BACHEL BACILE BARILE COTULA DICHAS
GRAMME HEMINA KOILON ORGYIA
PALAME PECHYS SCHENE AMPHORA
CHENICA CHOENIX CYATHOS DIAULOS
HEKTEUS METRETA STADION STADIUM
STREMMA CONDYLOS DAKTYLOS
DEKAPODE DOLICHOS MEDIMNOS
METRETES PALAISTE PLETHRON
PLETHRUM SPITHAME STATHMOS
MOUNTAIN: IDA IDHI OSSA ATHOS PAROS
ELIKON PARNON PELION PILION WITSCH
HELICON OLYMPUS VURANON
KRAGNOVO SMOLIKAS TAYGETOS
PARNASSUS
PENINSULA: ACTE AKTE AKTI MOREA
SITHONIA PELOPONNESE
PORT: SYRA CORFU PYLOS SYROS VOLOS
MEGARA PATRAI PATRAS KAVALLA
KERKYRA PIRAEUS SALONIKA
RIVER: IRI ARDA ARTA AURO AXIOS
DOONA EVROS LERNA ALFIOS NESTOS
PENEUS PINIOS STRUMA VARDAR
ALPHEUS EUROTAS EVROTAS ILISSOS
PENEIOS ROUFIAS SARANTA STRIMON
ACHELOUS AKHELOOS ALIAKMON
KEPHISOS RHOUPHIA
SEA: CRETE AEGEAN IONIAN MIRTOON
STATE: PHOCIS
TOWN: IOS KEA KOS ARTA ELIS KYME
PETA SYME YDRA ADREA AGYIA ARGOS
CANEA CHIOS CORFU DRAMA KARYA
MELOS NAXOS NEMEA PELLA POROS
PSARI PYLOS PYRGI SAMOS SYROS
TENOS VAMOS VATHY VOLOS VYRON
ZANTE ACTIUM ATHENS CANDIA DAPHNI
DELPHI EDESSA ITHACA JANINA KOZANE
LARISA MEGARA NIKHIA PATRAS
RHODES SERRAI SERRES SPARTA THEBES
TIRYNS XANTHE ATHENAI CORINTH

ELEUSIS KERKYRA LARISSA MYCENAE
PIRAEUS IOANNINA KOMOTINE
MARATHON PHARSALA SALONIKA
TRIKKALA PERISTERI

GREED AVARICE AVIDITY HOGGERY
CUPIDITY
GREEDINESS AVARICE AVIDITY
GULOSITY
GREEDY AVID GAIR GORB YELP EAGER
GUTTY YIVER GRABBY GUNDIE KITISH
STINGY GLUTTON GRIPPLE HOODOCK
MISERLY PIGGISH COVETOUS ESURIENT
GRASPING RAVENOUS LICKERISH
(PREF.) LICHNO
GREEK GREW ATTIC HADJI KOINE METIC
ARGIVE IONIAN KLEPHT ACHAIAN
AEOLIAN GRECIAN GRIFFON HELLENE
GRECANIC HELLADIC HELLENIC ITALIOTE
SICELIOT
GREEN (ALSO SEE COLOR) LEEK VERD
VERT CRUDE FRESH CALLOW VIRENT
NOUVEAU SINOPLE UNFIRED VERDANT
BAYBERRY IMMATURE NOUVELLE
VAGABOND VIRIDIAN WEDGWOOD
WOODLAND
(COOKED —S) SALAD
(NILE —) BOA
(PALE —) ALOE ALOES
(YELLOWISH —) GLAUZY ABSINTHE
GLAUCOUS
GREENHOUSE STOVE GREENERY
HOTHOUSE ORANGERY COOLHOUSE

GREENLAND

AIR BASE: THULE
BAY: DISKO BAFFIN MELVILLE
CAPE: JAAL GRIVEL WALKER BISMARCK
BREWSTER FAREWELL LOWENORN
CAPITAL: GODTHAAB
MOUNTAIN: FOREL PAYER KHARDYU
GUNNBJORN
STRAIT: DAVIS DENMARK
TOWN: ETAH NORD THULE UMANAK
GODHAVN IVIGTUT GODTHAAB
JULIANEHAB EGEDESMINDE
SUKKERTOPPEN HOLSTEINSBORG

GREEN MANSIONS (AUTHOR OF —)
HUDSON
(CHARACTER IN —) ABEL RIMA NUFLO
GREET CRY JOY CROW HAIL HALSE
ACCOST HERALD SALAAM SALUTE
ADDRESS RECEIVE WELCOME
GREETING HOW CIAO HIYA ALOHA
GREET HELLO HOWDY KOMBO ACCOST
CHEERO SALAAM SALUTE SHALOM
ADDRESS CHEERIO COMMEND SLAINTE
WELCOME REMEMBRANCE
GREGARIOUS GREGAL SOCIAL
GREYHOUND GREW SALUKI BANJARA
SAPLING TUMBLER WHIPPET
GRIDDLE CAKE AREPA LATKE

CHAPATTY CORNCAKE FLAPJACK
SLAPJACK
GRIDIRON GRID GRILL TRAIL BRANDER
BROILER GRIDDLE
GRIEF VEX WOE CARE DILL DOLE DOOL
DREE HARM HURT MOAN MOOD PAIN
RUTH SORE TEEN TINE AGONY DOLOR
GRAME RUING TRIAL WRONG BARRAT
DESIRE MISHAP REGRET SORROW
STOUND WONDER ANGUISH CHAGRIN
EMOTION FAILURE OFFENSE SADNESS
THOUGHT TROUBLE WAESUCK
WAYMENT DISASTER DISTRESS
HARDSHIP
GRIEVE VEX CARE DOLE DUMP EARN
ERME HONE HURT PAIN PINE SIGH WAIL
GRAME GRIPE MOURN SORRY WOUND
YEARN ATHINK CORSIE LAMENT REPINE
SORROW AFFLICT CHAGRIN CONDOLE
GRIZZLE TROUBLE WAYMENT COMPLAIN
DISTRESS
GRIEVOUS SAD DEAR DEEP DERF HARD
SORE CHARY DIRTY GRIEF HEAVY SORRY
WEARY BITTER DREARY SEVERE SHREWD
CAREFUL HEINOUS WEIGHTY DOLOROUS
ATROCIOUS
GRIM DOUR GASH SOUR BLEAK CRUEL
GAUNT STERN GRIMLY GRISLY HORRID
SULLEN TORVID GHASTLY GRIZZLY
HIDEOUS MACABRE TORVOUS PITILESS
RUTHLESS
GRIMACE MOP MOW MUG POT FACE
GIRN IRPE MOUE MUMP YIRN FLEER
MOUTH SNEER SNOOT GIMBLE SHEYLE
STITCH MURGEON SIMAGRE
GRIME DIRT SMUT COLLY SMOUCH
SMUTCH
GRIMY DINGY GRUBBY SCABROUS
GRIN DRAD GIRN MUMP FLEER RISUS
SNEER SIMPER GRIZZLE
GRIND DIG SAP BONE CHEW FILE GRUN
MILL MULL MUZZ SMUG SWOT CRUSH
FLOAT FLOUR GRIDE GRIST QUERN
CRUNCH DRUDGE POWDER EMERIZE
GRISTLE SWOTTER LEVIGATE
(— COARSELY) KIBBLE
(— DIAMONDS) SKIVE
(— SMALL) BRAY
(— TEETH) GNASH GRATE GRINT
GRISBET
GRINDSTONE MANO PAVER STONE
GRIP BITE BURR CLIP FANG FIST HOLD
HOLT TAKE VICE CHOKE CINCH CLAMP
CLASP GRASP GRIPE PINCH SALLY SEIZE
BARREL CLINCH CLUTCH CRADLE FREEZE
EMBRACE HANDBAG HOLDING SEIZURE
ADHESION FOOTLOCK HANDFAST
HANDGRIP HANDHOLD STAGEHAND
(— OF A SWORD) FUSEAU
(— OF BELL ROPE) SALLY
(— TO A SPAR) DOG
GRIPE CRAB FRIB BITCH CREATE GROUSE
HOLLER KVETCH NATTER SNATCH
GRIZZLE COMPLAIN
GRISLY GRIM GHASTLY GRIZZLY HIDEOUS
GRUESOME
GRIT SAND GRIND PLUCK BOTTOM

BRAVERY DECISION GRITROCK
RUBSTONE
(PL.) CUTLINGS
GROAN MOAN ROME GRANK GRUNT
STECH COMPLAIN
GROCER SPICER EPICIER PEPPERER
GROCERY BODEGA PULPERIA
GROGGY SHAKY UNSTEADY WAVERING
GROOM LAD MAFU NEAT SYCE CURRY
DRESS MAFOO STRAP SWIPE TIGER
BARBER BATMAN FETTLE FOGGER
GUINEA MEHTAR OSTLER HOSTLER
MARSHAL COISTREL COISTRIL
GROOMLET STRAPPER
GROOVE RUT BEAD DADO GAIN KERF
LUCE PORT RAKE SLOT CANAL CHASE
GLYPH GOUGE GUIDE JOINT QUIRK
REGAL RIFLE RIGOL SCORE STRIA SWAGE
CREASE CULLIS FULLER FURROW
GUTTER KEYWAY RABBET RAGLET
REBATE RIFFLE RUNNER SULCUS
THROAT TRENCH CHAMFER CHANNEL
GARLAND KEYHOLE PLOWING SULCATE
BOTHRIUM GROOVING PHILTRUM
CANNELURE VALLECULA
(— IN AUGER) POD
(— IN COLUMN) FLUTE
(— IN MASONRY) RAGGLE
(— IN STAVES) CROZE
(— IN STONE) JAD
(— IN TIRE) SIPE
(— ON UPPER LIP) PHILTRUM
(— ON WEEVIL) SCROBE
(— ON WHALE) SCARF
(— UNDER COPING) GORGE
(— S ON ROCK) LAPIES
(RECTANGULAR —) REGLET
GROPE CLAM CLAW FEEL POKE RIPE
GLAUM GRAIP FUMBLE GUDDLE
GRABBLE GRAPPLE GROPPLE GRUBBLE
SCRABBLE
GROSS FAT DULL FOUL LUMP RANK
BROAD CRASS FOGGY GREAT GUTTY
LARGE MACRO SLUMP THICK WHOLE
ANIMAL COARSE EARTHY FILTHY GREASY
SORDID STRONG BLOATED FULSOME
CLODDISH FLAGRANT INDECENT
SLUTTISH
GROTESQUE ANTIC WOOZY ROCOCO
BAROQUE BIZARRE CROTESCO FANCIFUL
GROTTO CAVE GROT ANTRE SPEOS
CAVERN LUPERCAL
GROUCH SULK CRANK GROUSE
SOURBALL SOURPUSS
GROUND SEW SOD SUE BASE CLOD DIRT
FOLD GIST LAND MOLD REST ROOT SOIL
STAY WOLD EARTH FIRTH FOUND
MOULD PLACE SCORE SOLUM TRAIN
TUTOR VENUE CREASE MATTER REASON
SMACKED FORELAND INITIATE
(— AT TOP OF SHAFT) BANK
(— COVERED WITH RUBBLE) TITI
(— FOR COMPLAINT) BEEF
(— OF FLAG) FIELD
(— OF LACE) FOND
(— OVERLYING TIN DEPOSIT)
BURDEN

(BOGGY —) SOG CARR SNAPE
(BROKEN —) HAG
(BURYING —) CEMETERY
(CAMPING —) AUTOCAMP
(COLLEGE —S) CAMPUS
(DUMPING —) TIP TOOM
(FALLOW —) BRISE
(FEEDING —) HAUNT
(FIRM-HOLDING —) LANDFANG
(FISHING —) HAAF
(FROZEN —) TJAELE
(GRASSY —) LAWN CLOWRE
(GRAZING —) HERDWICK
(HARD —) HARDPAN
(HUNTING —) CHASE
(LOW —) INCH SWALE TALAO
(MIDDLE —) LIMBO
(MUDDY —) SLOB
(NEW ENCLOSED —) TINING
(ORIGINAL —) URGRUND
(PARADE —) MAIDAN
(PASTURE —) HIRSEL
(RECREATION —) PARK
(RISING —) HURST HYRST
(SLOPING —) CLEVE
(SOLID —) HILL
(SPONGY —) BOG
(SWAMPY —) PUXY CRIPPLE
(UNCULTIVATED —) JUNGLE
(UNUSED —) AREA
(WET WASTE —) MOOR REESK
GROUNDLESS IDLE FALSE BASELESS
GROUP MOB SET BAND BEVY BODY
CREW DECK FOLD GANG KNOT PAIR RING
SECT SORT STEW TREF ARRAY BREED
CLASS CLUMP COVEY FIRCA FLOCK
GENUS GLOBE PLUMP SABHA SKULK
SQUAD STACK TALLY WHEEN CIRCLE
CLUTCH COHORT FAMILY GRUPPO
PARCEL RUBRIC AGGROUP BATTERY
BOILING BOUROCK BRACKET CLASSIS
CLUSTER COLLEGE COMMUNE COMPANY
CONSORT FELLOWS FLUTTER QUOTITY
SECTION SEVERAL SOCIETY ALLIANCE
CATEGORY CLASSIFY DIVISION FAISCEAU
FLOTILLA GROUPING
(— OF ANGELS) FLIGHT
(— OF ARTIFACTS) CACHE
(— OF BADGERS) CETE
(— OF BUILDINGS) BLOCK
(— OF CASTINGS) SPRAY
(— OF CATS) CLOWDER
(— OF CELLS) GLAND ISLET LAURA
CENTER CORONA EPITHEM SEMILUNE
(— OF COMPUTER JOBS) BATCH
(— OF DECOYS) STOOL
(— OF DEITIES) CABEIRI
(— OF DIALECTS) AEOLIC
(— OF EELS) SWARM
(— OF EIGHT) OCTAD OCTET
(— OF FAMILIES) FINE
(— OF FIVE) PENTAD CINQUAIN
(— OF FOUR) MESS QUARTET
(— OF FRIENDS) BUNCH
(— OF FURNISHINGS) ENSEMBLE
(— OF HAITIANS) COMBITE
(— OF HOUSES) BOROUGH

(— OF HUTS) KRAAL BUSTEE
(— OF ILLUSTRIOUS PERSONS) PANTHEON
(— OF INDIAN STATES) AGENCY
(— OF ISOGLOSSES) BUNDLE
(— OF KINDRED) SIOL
(— OF KINSMEN) AHL
(— OF LAYMEN) COFRADIA
(— OF LIONS) PRIDE
(— OF LISTENERS) AUDIENCE
(— OF MARTENS) RICHESSE
(— OF MILITARY VEHICLES) DEADLINE
(— OF MOLDINGS) DANCETTE
(— OF NINE) ENNEAD NONARY
(— OF NUCLEONS) SHELL
(— OF OFFSPRING) CLUTCH
(— OF ORGANISMS) FORM STRAIN
(— OF PARACHUTISTS) STICK
(— OF PERSONS) BAG CLUB KNOT SWAD CROWD DROVE CIRCLE GAGGLE KENNEL
(— OF RETORTS) BENCH SETTING
(— OF RUFFIANS) PUSH
(— OF SCHOLARS) ULAMA
(— OF SCULPTURE) MORTORIO
(— OF SEVEN) HEPTAD SEPTET HEBDOMAD
(— OF SIX) HEXAD SENARY
(— OF SLAVES) COFFLE
(— OF SOILS) LATERITE
(— OF SOLDIERS) DRAFT COHORT
(— OF STARS) ASTERISM
(— OF STRATIFIED BEDS) FACIES
(— OF STUDENTS) SEMINAR
(— OF SYLLABLES) FOOT
(— OF SYMBOLS) FORMULA
(— OF SYMPTOMS) SYNDROME
(— OF TEN) DECADE DENARY
(— OF TENTS) CAMP CANVAS
(— OF THEATERS) CIRCUIT
(— OF THREE) TRIO GLEEK TRIAD TRINE
(— OF TRAITS) COMPLEX
(— OF TROUT) HOVER
(— OF VERSES) SYSTEM
(— OF WEAPONS) NEST
(— OF WINGS) RUFFLE
(— OF WIRES) DROP
(— OF WORDS) ACCENT GENITIVE
(— OF 10 NOTES) DECUPLET
(— OF 1000) CHILIAD
(— OF 12) DOZEN
(— OF 2 VOWELS) DIGRAM DIGRAPH
(— OF 40 THREADS) BEER BIER
(— OF 60 PIECES) SHOCK
(ASSISTANCE —) AINI
(ATOMIC —) LIGAND
(AUTHORITATIVE —) CONCLAVE
(AVANT-GARDE —) UNDERGROUND
(CONFUSED —) SNARL
(CORE —) CADRE
(CRIME SYNDICATE —) FAMILY
(ECOLOGICAL —) GUILD
(ETHNIC —) LI ACHANG BALAHI BATTAK ETHNOS CHINGPAW
(ETHNOLOGICAL —) ISLAND
(EXCLUSIVE —) ELECT

(FAMILY —) GWELY
(HARMONIOUS —) DOVECOTE
(INTIMATE —) COTERIE
(KINSHIP —) SUSU
(LANGUAGE —) ATALAN
(LARGE —) PASSEL
(LINKED —) NEXUS
(LIVELY —) GALA
(NON-MOSLEM —) MILLET
(PAGAN —) BATAK BATANGAN
(PHILOSOPHICAL —) CENACLE
(POLITICAL —) BLOC PARTY FASCIO COMMONS MACHINE
(SEGREGATED —) GHETTO
(SMALL —) PLUMP
(SOCIAL —) KITH SEPT TRIBE FAMILY INGROUP

GROUSE CRAB BITCH GANGA PEEVE GORHEN GROUCH HOOTER ATTAGEN CHEEPER GAZELLE GORCOCK PINTAIL COMPLAIN MOORBIRD MOORFOWL PTARMIGAN
(YOUNG —) POULT SQUEALER

GROVE HEWT MOTT TOFT WONG BLUFF COPSE GLADE HURST HYRST GARDEN GREAVE GROVET ISLAND OLIVET SCROBE SPRING ACADEMY ARBORET BOSCAGE COPPICE SPINNEY THICKET WOODING SERINGAL WODELEIE
(— OF ALDERS) CARR
(— OF MANGO TREES) TOPE
(— OF OAKS) ENCINAL
(— OF OSIERS) HOLT
(— OF SUGAR MAPLES) CAMP
(SACRED —) ALTIS SARNA
(SMALL —) SHAW

GROVEL FAWN ROLL CREEP CRINGE TUMBLE WALLOW WELTER GRABBLE FLOUNDER

GROW AGE BUD GET HIT ICH WAX BOLL COME CROP ECHE ITCH MAKE RISE SEED THEE THRO WEAR EDIFY ISSUE PLANT PROVE RAISE SHOOT SWELL ACCRUE BECOME DOUBLE EXPAND EXTEND GATHER SPRING SPROUT AUGMENT BROADEN BURGEON DEVELOP DISTEND ENLARGE NOURISH ADOLESCE FLOURISH HEIGHTEN INCREASE THRODDEN PROLIFERATE
(— ANGRY) STIVER
(— BETTER) IMPROVE
(— DARK) GLOAM GLOOM NIGHT DARKEN DARKLE
(— FAINT) DIE APPAL APPALL
(— FAT) FEED BATTEN
(— IN LENGTH) ELONGATE
(— IRREGULARLY) SCRAMBLE
(— LESS) ABATE SLAKE ASSUAGE DECREASE
(— LIGHT) DAWN
(— LUXURIANTLY) THRIVE
(— MAD) WOOD
(— MILD) GIVE
(— OLD) AGE OLD SENESCE
(— OVER) INVADE
(— PLUMP) PLIM
(— RICH) FATTEN

(— SOUND) HEAL
(— SPIRITLESS) FLAG
(— STILL) HUSH
(— STRONG) FORTIFY STORKEN
(— THIN) PEAK
(— TO HEAD) CABBAGE
(— TO STALK) SPINDLE
(— TOGETHER) KNIT ACCRETE
CONCREW COOSIFY COALESCE
(— UNDER GLASS) GLASS
(— UP) STEM ACCRUE
(— WEAK) FAINT
GROWL YAR GNAR GURL GURR NARR
RASE ROIN ROME WIRR YARR YIRR
GARRE GNARL GNARR GROIN SNARL
GOLLAR HABBLE GRUMBLE MAUNDER
GROWN-UP ADULT GROWN MATURE
GROWTH FUR WAX BUSH COAT CORN
GROW JUBA RISE SPUR DUVET GUMMA
MAQUI STAND STOCK STOOL SWELL
CALLUS CANCER CLAVUS EATAGE
EPULIS FRINGE FUNGUS SCREEN SPROUT
TYLOSE UPCOME WASTME AUXESIS
BRACKEN COPPICE ERINEUM FUNGOID
MACCHIE SARCOID STATURE TYLOSIS
BEARDING CARUNCLE ENDOGENY
INCREASE SETATION SWELLING
UPSPRING ACCRETION
(— IN EYE) FILM
(— OF BEARD) DOWN
(— OF HAIR) SUIT
(— OF HORN) BUTTON SPIDER
(— OF PLANKTON) BLOOM
(— OF TREES) MOTTE BOSQUE
BOSCAGE COPPICE SHINNERY
(— ON HORSE'S LEG) FUSEE
(— ON VESSEL'S BOTTOM) GARR
(ABUNDANT —) FLUSH
(DENSE —) BRUSH FOREST SHINNERY
(DOWNY —) LANUGO
(GREEN —) GREENTH
(HARD —) STONE
(LUXURIANT —) FLOURISH
(ROUGH —) STUBBLE
(RUDIMENTARY —) STUB STUMP
(SIDE —) SPRIG
(SPARSE —) SCRAGGLE
(SUPERFICIAL —) MILDEW
(TRANSPARENT —) DRUSE
(VIGOROUS —) THRIFT
(WOODY —) BURL
(2ND — OF GRASS) FOG
GRUB BOB DIG EATS HUHU MOIL MOOT
ROUT STUB WORM CHUCK GROUT
MATHE SCRAN SNOUT WROTE ASSART
ESSART GRUGRU MAGGOT MUZZLE
ROOTLE NEASCUS PIGROOT FLAGWORM
GRUBWORM MUCKWORM SKINWORM
GRUDGE DOWN ENVY DERRY PEEVE
SCORE SPITE ANIMUS GROUCH GRUNCH
GRUTCH MALICE MALIGN SPLEEN
DESPITE EYELAST SIMULTY
GRUEL SLOP BLEERY BURGOO CAUDLE
CONGEE CROWDY SKILLY SOFKEE
BROCHAN CROWDIE LOBLOLLY
WANGRACE

GRUESOME UGLY GRISLY GROOLY
HORRID SORDID FEARFUL GHASTLY
HIDEOUS MACABRE
GRUFF BLUFF ROUGH CLUMSE SULLEN
AUSTERE BEARING BRUSQUE CLUMPST
GRUMBLE CARP GIRN GREX HONE KREX
ROIN BLEAT BROCK CROAK DRUNT
GROIN GROWL GRUMP GRUNT MUNGE
GROUCH GROUSE GRUDGE GRUNCH
MUMBLE MUNGER MURMUR MUTTER
NOLLER PEENGE REPINE RUMBLE
SQUEAL TARROW YAMMER CHANNER
CHUNNER CHUNTER GNATTER GRIZZLE
GRUNTLE MAUNDER MURGEON QUADDLE
SWAGGER COMPLAIN
GRUMBLING BITCH DRUNT GRIPE GROIN
GRUDGE MURMUR MURGEON
GRUMPY ILL CROSS GLUMPY GLUMPISH
GRUMPISH
GRUNT OINK BURRO GROIN HUMPH
RONCO SARGO GRUMPH RONCHO
BURRITO CROAKER GRUNTER GRUNTLE
PIGFISH PINFISH TOMTATE KNORHAAN
KOORHAAN PORKFISH REDMOUTH
RONCADOR
GUAM (BAY OF —) AGAT YLIG CETTI
AJAYAN UMATAC
(CAPITAL OF —) AGANA
(HARBOR OF —) APRA
(ISLAND OF —) CABRAS
(MOUNTAIN OF —) TENJO LAMLAM
(PENINSULA OF —) OROTE
(TOWN OF —) UPI ARRA ASAN TOTO
YONA AGANA LUPOG MAGUA MERIZO
UMATAC MALOLOS
GUANO OSITE
GUARANTEE (ALSO SEE GUARANTY)
BAIL BAND SEAL CINCH COVER AVOUCH
ENGAGE ENSURE INSURE RATIFY SECURE
SURETY CAUTION CERTIFY HOSTAGE
WARRANT AWARRANT GUARANTY
PRESTATE SECURITY WARRANTY
GUARANTEED ASSURED CERTIFIED
FOOLPROOF
GUARANTY (ALSO SEE GUARANTEE)
ANDI AVAL PAWN SEAL CAUTIO PLEDGE
WARRANT SECURITY WARRANTY
GUARD LEG NIT PAD SEE CARE CURB
HERD HOLD KEEP KNOW LOOK REDE
SAVE STOP STUB TENT TILE WAIT WEAR
WERE WITE YEME ASKAR AWARD BLESS
BLOCK CHECK COVER FENCE FORAY
HEDGE HINGE PILOT SKIRT TUTOR
WAKEN WATCH ASKARI BANTAY BASKET
BRIDLE BUMPER CONVOY DEFEND
DRAGON ESCORT FENDER GHAFIR
GUNMAN KEEPER MIDDLE POLICE
SCREEN SECURE SENTRY SHIELD
SHROUD WAITER WARDER YEMING
BULWARK CHERISH ESGUARD FRONTAL
GHAFFIR GHATWAL GUARDER KEEPING
PANDOUR PRESIDY PROTECT SOULACK
TRABANT WARDAGE WARRANT
CHAPERON GARRISON MUDGUARD
OUTGUARD PEDESTAL PILOTMAN
PRESERVE SECURITY SENTINEL

SHEPHERD SPLASHER WARDSMAN
WATCHMAN
(— ON FOIL) BUTTON
(— WHILE IN TRANSIT) RIDE
(AXLE —) HOUSING
(COACH —) SHOOTER
(CONSULAR —) KAVASS
(IMPERIAL —) BOSTANJI
(KEYHOLE —) LAPPET
(MOUNTED —) SHOMER
(NECK —) CAMAIL
(ON —) AWARE EXCUBANT
(PRISON —) HACK SCREW CHASER
JAILER
(STIRRUP —) TAPADERA
(SWORD —) BOW TSUBA
(WRIST —) BRACER
GUARDED WARY IMMUNE MANNED
GUARDEDLY GINGERLY
GUARDHOUSE BRIG CLINK BULLPEN
HOOSEGOW
GUARDIAN HERD ANGEL ARGUS TUTOR
YEMER CUSTOS KEEPER MIMING PASTOR
PATRON SHOMER WARDEN CORONER
CURATOR GARDANT GARDEEN GRIFFIN
BARTHOLO BELLERUS CERBERUS
CREANCER DEFENDER ECKEHART
FRAVASHI GOVERNOR GUARDANT
PROTUTOR TUTELARY
(— OF HOME) SIF
(WORLD —) LOKAPALA MAHARAJA
GUARDIANSHIP WARD TUTELA
CUSTODY KEEPING TUITION WARDAGE
WARDING CUSTODIA GUARDAGE
TUTELAGE WARDENRY WARDSHIP

GUATEMALA

CAPITAL: GUATEMALA
COIN: PESO CENTAVO QUETZAL
DEPARTMENT: PETEN IZABAL JALAPA
QUICHE SOLOLA ZACAPA JULIAPA
ESCUINTLA
GULF: HONDURAS
INDIAN: MAM CHOL ITZA IXIL MAYA
XINCA CARIBE QUICHE POKOMAM
LAKE: DULCE GUIJA PETEN IZABAL
ATITLAN
MEASURE: VARA CUARTA FANEGA TERCIA
CAJUELA MANZANA
MOUNTAIN: AGUA FUEGO PACAYA
TACANA ATITLAN TOLIMAN TAJAMULCO
PORT: OCOS BARRIOS LIVINGSTON
RIVER: AZUL BRAVO DULCE LAPAZ BELIZE
CHIXOY NEGINO PASION SAMALA
CHIAPAS MOTAGUA SARSTUN POLOCHIC
TOWN: OCOS COBAN VIEJA CHAHAL
CHISEC CUILCO FLORES IZTAPA JALAPA
SALAMA SOLOLA TACANA TECPAN
YALOCH ZACAPA ANTIGUA CUILAPA
JUTIAPA SANJOSE PROGRESO
VOLCANO: AGUA FUEGO PACAYA TACANA
ATITLAN TAJUMULCO
WEIGHT: CAJA LIBRA

GUAVA ARACA MYRTAL GUAYABA
GUAYABO GOIABADA
GUERRILLA COWBOY GORILLA
JAYHAWK SKINNER BUSHWACK
FELLAGHA KOMITAJI
GUESS AIM CALL HARP REDE SHOT WEEN
AREAD COUNT ETTLE FANCY INFER
TWANG DEVISE DIVINE RECKON IMAGINE
SURMISE SUSPECT
(— CORRECTLY) TOUCH
GUEST COME GOER HOST DINER INVITEE
VISITOR SYMPHILE VISITANT
(— AT RANCH) DUDE
(UNINVITED —) SHADOW
GUIDANCE AIM DUCT EGIS AEGIS STEER
CONDUCT GUIDAGE HELMAGE LEADING
WISSING AUSPICES ENGINERY REGIMENT
STEERAGE
GUIDE GUY LAY TIP AIRT BEAD CURB
GAGE GATE LEAD PASS REIN RULE SWAY
WISE CARRY CHARM DRESS FRAME
GAUGE LIGHT MAHDI MOROC PILOT
STEER TEACH WEISE ADALID BARKER
BEACON BEDWAY CONVOY DIRECT
ESCORT FORMER GILLIE GOVERN INFORM
LEADER MANAGE POPPET CONDUCE
CONDUCT COURIER GHILLIE INSPIRE
MARSHAL MERCURY PIONEER SHIKARI
STERNER TRACKER CALENDAR CICERONE
DIRECTOR DRAGOMAN ENGINEER
FAIRLEAD LODESMAN PEDESTAL
POLESTAR PRACTICO REPEATER
SHIKAREE SIGNPOST
(MORAL —) LABARUM
(RAILWAY —) ABC BRADSHAW
(SPIRITUAL —) PIR GURU BISHOP
DIVINE
(TRAFFIC —) MUSHROOM
GUIDEBOOK ABC GUIDE WAYBOOK
BAEDEKER HANDBOOK ROADBOOK
GUIDELINE SLUG PARAMETER
GUIDEPOST GUIDE PARSON WAYMARK
WAYPOST SIGNPOST
GUILD HUI GILD HOEY HONG YELD CRAFT
HANSA HANSE GREMIO GUIDRY SCHOLA
BASOCHE COLLEGE COMPANY MYSTERY
GUILE DOLE WILE CHEAT CRAFT FRAUD
TRAIN CAUTEL DECEIT HUMBUG
CUNNING FALLACY ARTIFICE
GUILELESS PLAIN CANDID HONEST
ARTLESS ONEFOLD IGNORANT INNOCENT
SACKLESS UNNOOKED
GUILT SIN SAKE WITE BLAME CULPA
FAULT PIACLE PLIGHT NOCENCE
OFFENSE HAMARTIA INIQUITY
GUILTLESS FREE PURE CLEAN UNSAKED
INNOCENT SACKLESS
GUILTY FAULTY NOCENT WICKED
CORREAL HANGDOG NOXIOUS PECCANT
BLAMEFUL CRIMINAL CULPABLE
GUILTFUL
(— OF ERROR) LAPSED
GUINEA MEG BEAN QUID QUEED GEORGE
SHINER GEORDIE
(HALF —) SMELT SMELT

GUINEA

CAPE: VERGA
CAPITAL: CONAKRY
COIN: FRANC
ISLAND: TOMBO TRISTAO
ISLAND GROUP: LOS
MEASURE: JACKTAN
MOUNTAIN: TAMGUE
MOUNTAINS: LOMA NIMBA
NATIVE: SUSU TOMA KISSI FULANI
  GUERZI MALINKE KOURANKE LANDUMAN
RIVER: NIGER BAFING FALEME SENEGAL
  KONKOURE TINKISSO
TOWN: BOKE FRIA KADE LABE BENTY
  BEYLA COYAH KOULE MAMOU DABOLA
  DALABA DOUAKO FABALA KANKAN
  KINDIA BOFOSSO CONAKRY DUBREKA
  FARANAH KONFARA KOUMBIA OUASSOU
  SIGUIRI KEROUANE
WEIGHT: AKEY PISO UZAN BENDA SERON
  QUINTO AGUIRAGE

GUINEA PIG CAVY
  (MALE —) BOAR BUCK
GUISE HUE FORM GARB COLOR COVER
  SHAPE MANNER PERSON APPAREL
  CLOTHES GUISARD LIKENESS
GUITAR AX AXE BOX KIT PIPA DOBRO
  JAMON KITAR SITAR TIPLE GIMBRI
  KITTAR SANCHO SATTAR CITHERN
  CITTERN MACHETE UKULELE CHARANGO
  CHITARRA
  (PART OF —) KEY NUT PEG BASE BODY
  BONE FRET HEAD HEEL HOLE NECK
  BRACE GUARD WAIST BRIDGE SADDLE
  STRING ROSETTE FINGERBOARD
GULCH GULLY SLUIT CANYON COULEE
  RAVINE
GULF SINE CHAOS GULPH VORAGE
  VORAGO
  (BOTTOMLESS —) ABYSM ABYSS
GULL COB COX MEW COBB CONY COOT
  CULL DUPE FOOL GOLL LARI MALL PINT
  PIRR SELL SKUA XEME ALLAN ALLEN
  ANNET BOSUN CHEAT CHUMP COBBE
  COKES CROCK CULLY HOODY JAGER
  LARID LARUS PEWIT SCULL SMELT
  YAGER BONXIE BUBBLE CHOUSE COUSIN
  JOCKEY PEEWIT PIGEON SIMPLE TEASER
  TULIAC VICTIM WAGGEL WHILLY
  CROCKER DECEIVE MEDRICK PICKMAW
  POPELER SCAURIE SEABIRD SEAFOWL
  SWARBIE TARROCK TRUMPIE BLACKCAP
  DIRTBIRD DOTTEREL DUNGBIRD
  SEEDBIRD
GULLET MAW GULE LANE GORGE GARGLE
  PECHAN THROAT KEACORN STOMACH
  SWALLOW WEASAND GURGULIO
GULLIBLE GOOFY GREEN SIMPLE
  CULLIBLE
GULLY BOX GEO GUT DRAW GULL RAIK
  RAKE SICK SIKE DONGA DRAFT GOYLE
  GULCH SLAKE SLUIT ZANJA ARROYO

GULLET GULLEY GUTTER NULLAH RAVINE
  SHEUCH SHEUGH CHIMNEY COULOIR
  DRAUGHT BARRANCA
GULP BOLT GAUP GLUT GULL POOP SOPE
  SWIG GULCH QUILT SLOSH SWIPE
  ENGLUT GLUTCH GOBBLE GOLLOP
  PAUNCH SLABBER SWALLOW SWATTLE
  SLUMMOCK
  (— NOISILY) SLORP
GUM ASA AMRA BLOB FILL GOOM LOAD
  TUNO ALGIN AMAPA BABUL CUMAY
  DHAVA ACAJOU ANGICO BARRAS CHICLE
  KARAYA TOUART TUPELO CARANNA
  CARAUNA GINGIVA GUMWOOD PERRIER
  BORRACHA CARABEEN DEXTRINE
  DRESSING FEVERGUM CALENDULIN
  (ACACIA —) GEDDA
  (AROMATIC —) MYRRH
  (ASTRINGENT —) KINO
  (CHEWING —) WAX
  (FRAGRANT —) BUMBO
  (RED —) JARRAH
  (UNGRADED —) SORTS
  (WOOD —) XYLAN
GUM ARABIC KIKAR ACACIA ACACIN
GUMBO OKRA
GUN GAT POP BREN HAKE PIAT ROER
  STEN TUBE BARIL FIFTY FIRER FUSEE
  FUZEE RAKER REWET RIFLE ARCHIE
  BERTHA CANNON CHASER CULVER
  DUCKER INCHER JEZAIL MINNIE QUAKER
  RANDOM SPIGOT SWIVEL TUPARA
  CALIVER FIREARM HACKBUT HANDGUN
  JINGALL LANTACA MUZZLER AMUSETTE
  ARQUEBUS CHAUCHAT CULVERIN
  FIRELOCK GALLOPER OERLIKON
  PEDERERO SHAGBUSH TROMBONE
  (BOAT —) BASE
  (LOWER-DECK —) BARKER
  (MACHINE —) CHOPPER GATLING
  (SPRING —) STEL
  (TOY —) SPARKLER
GUNBOAT SKIP BARCA GONDOLA
  TINCLAD
GUNMAN HOOD GUNSEL GUNSMAN
  TORPEDO ENFORCER GANGSTER
GUNNER GUN POPPER FIREMAN
  SHOOTER ENGINEER
GUNNY TAT BURLAP BAGGING SACKING
GUNNYSACK CORNSACK
GUNPOWDER SULFUR SULPHUR
GUNSIGHT VISIE HAUSSE
GUNSTOCK BLANK TIPSTOCK
GUNTHER (SISTER OF —) KRIEMHILD
  (WIFE OF —) BRUNEHILDE
GUNWALE GUNNEL PORTOISE
GURGLE GLOX BRAG CLUNK QUARK
  SLOSH BICKER BUBBLE BULLER BURBLE
  GOLLER GUGGLE RUCKLE
GUSH JET BOIL FLOW FOAM HUSH RAIL
  SLOP WALM BELCH SLUSH SMALM
  SMARM SPIRT SPURT STOUR SWOSH
  BURBLE PHRASE SWOOSH WALLOW
  WHOOSH SLOBBER
  (SENTIMENTAL —) SLOSH
GUSHING SLOPPY SMARMY EFFUSIVE

GUSSET GORE MITER MITRE QUIRK
  PIECETTE
GUST BUB WAFF WAFT WIND FRESH
  SLANT FLURRY HUFFLE FLAUGHT
  WILLIWAW
  (— OF RAIN) SKIT
  (— OF WIND) FLAM FLAN FUFF GALE
  GUSH PIRR SCUD TIFT BERRY BLAST
  BLORE FLAFF THODE SQUALL WINDFLAW
GUSTO GUST ZEST VERVE RELISH
  UNCTION
GUSTY DIRTY PUFFY BLASHY BLASTY
  FRETFUL GUSTFUL SQUALLY
GUTTER GRIP REAN SIKE GRIPE GULLY
  RIGOL SIVER SPOUT SWEAL CANNEL
  CULLIS GROOVE GUZZLE RIGGOT
  RUNNEL STRAND TROUGH VENNEL
  CHANNEL CHENEAU GRIZZLE
  (— OF STREET) KENNEL
  (MINING —) BOTTOM HASSING
  (ROOF —) RONE
  (PL.) LIMBERS
GUTTURAL GRUM BURRY HARSH THICK
GUY BOD CAT EGG JOE NUT BIRD BOZO
  DUDE GENT GINK HUSK JACK JOHN
  BLOKE COOKY JOKER SCOUT SPOOF
  BUFFER COOKIE GAZABO GAZEBO
  GAZOOK GILGUY HOMBRE JASPER
  JIGGER MALKIN MAUMET MAWKIN
  KNOCKER BLIGHTER
GUYANA (CAPITAL OF —)
  GEORGETOWN
  (RIVER OF —) CUYUNI BERBICE
  DEMERARA MAZARUNI ESSEQUIBO

  (TOWN OF —) ITUNI BILOKU ISSANO
  MACKENZIE
  (WATERFALL IN —) MARINA KAIETEUR
GUY MANNERING (AUTHOR OF —)
  SCOTT
  (CHARACTER IN —) GUY MEG LUCY
  BROWN DANDY HARRY JULIA BERTRAM
  DINMONT GLOSSIN SAMPSON
  MANNERING MERRILIES ELLANGOWAN
  HATTERAICK
GUZZLE BUM GUM SOT TUN BEND GULL
  SLOSH SWILL GOOZLE GUDDLE SWATTLE
  SWIZZLE
GYMKHANA AUTOCROSS
GYMNASIUM GYM PALESTRA TURNHALL
  PALAESTRA
GYMNAST SOKOL BENDER TURNER
  ACROBAT TUMBLER
GYPSUM GYP GYPS YESO GESSO LUDIAN
  PARGET GYPSITE SATINITE SELENITE
  ALABASTER
GYPSY FAW CALO APTAL CAIRD GIPSY
  ROMNI BOSHAS GITANO ROMANY
  TINKER AZUCENA CZIGANY MOONMAN
  TINKLER TZIGANE ZINCALO ZINGARO
  BOHEMIAN EGYPTIAN FLAMENCO
  ZIGEUNER
  (NON —) GORGIO
  (SEA —) BAJAU
  (PL.) ROMANESE
GYRATE GYRE SPIN TURN TWIRL WHIRL
  CURVET INGYRE ROTATE REVOLVE
  SQUIRREL
GYRATION PRECESSION

H

H AITCH HOTEL
HABERDASHER OUTFITTER
HABERDASHERY TOGGERY
HABIT LAW PAD SET USE WON COAT
GARB GATE SUIT THEW WONT FROCK
HAUNT TACHE TRADE TRICK USAGE
CUSTOM GROOVE MANNER PRAXIS
TALENT CLOTHES FOLKWAY HABITUS
WONTING CROTCHET HABITUDE
PHYSIQUE PRACTICE PRACTISE
ASSUETUDE CONSUETUDE
(— OF GRINDING TEETH) BRUXISM
(BAD —) HANK VICE MISTETCH
CACOETHES
(DEPRAVED —) CACHEXY
(SPEECH —S) ACCENT
HABITATION HOLD TELD TENT ABODE
BIELD HABIT HOUSE BIDING WONING
DOMICILE DWELLING PANTHEON
TENEMENT RESIDENCE
(— SITE) YACATA
(QUIET —) SHADE
(UNDERGROUND —) HOLE
HABITUAL USUAL COMMON HECTIC
CHRONIC REGULAR FREQUENT ORDINARY
HABITUATE USE HOWF ENURE FLESH
HABIT INURE ADDICT SEASON HACKNEY
ACCUSTOM ACQUAINT OCCASION
HABITUE DENIZEN COURTIER
HACK HAG HEW BOLO CHIP HAKE HATCH
DRUDGE FIACRE HACKLE HAGGLE
HODMAN JOBBER MANGLE SCOTCH
HACKNEY MATTOCK VETTURA MUTILATE
(LITERARY —) GRUB DEVIL
HACKNEY CARRIAGE MIDGE FIACRE
JARVEY VETTURA
HACKNEYED HACK WORN BANAL
HOARY TRITE CANNED CLICHE COMMON
FOREWORN
HADDOCK GADE GADID SCROD DICKEY
HADDIE
(DRIED —) CRAIL RIZZAR SPELDING
SPELDRIN
HADES PIT HELL ORCUS PLUTO SHEOL
SHADES TARTAR ACHERON AIDONEUS
TARTARUS
(FATHER OF —) SATURN
(WIFE OF —) PROSERPINA
HAG ATE MARE REBEC RUDAS SIBYL
VECKE WITCH BELDAM HECATE ROUDAS
BELDAME HAGGARD HELLCAT HARRIDAN
HAGAR (MISTRESS OF —) SARAH
(SON OF —) ISHMAEL
HAGGARD PALE THIN GAUNT WISHT
HAGGED
HAGGLE CHOP PRIG DODGE BADGER
BANTER BOGGLE DICKER HACKER
HIGGLE HUCKLE NAGGLE NIFFER PALTER

SCOTCH THREEP BARGAIN CHAFFER
HUCKSTER
HAGGLER DODGER
HAGGLING BARGAIN CHAFFER
HAIL AVE HOY HALE GREET SALVE SPEAK
STORM ACCOST BAYETE HAGGLE
HALLOO HERALD SALUTE ACCLAIM
(SOFT —) GRESIL GRAUPEL
HAIR FAX JAG RIB BARB CROP FLUE HEAD
PILE SETA WIRE BEARD CRIMP CRINE
FRONT PILUS QUIFF ANGORA BRILLS
BRUTUS CRINET FIBRIL MERKIN SETULA
THATCH TRAGUS TOPKNOT WHISKER
CAPILLUS PALPOCIL TENTACLE
TRICHODE TRICHOME
(— BROWN) ARGALI
(— OF ANIMALS) FUR PELF
(— OF HORSES OR COWS) CERDA
(— OF TERRIER) FALL
(— ON HORSE'S HOOF) CRONET
(— ON LEAF) GLAND
(— ON TEMPLES) HAFFET
(— ON THIGHS) CULOTTE
(— OVER EYES) BROW GLIB EYELASH
(BARBED —) GLOCHIS
(BRAID OF —) QUEUE PIGTAIL
(BUNDLE OF —) LEECH
(CAMEL'S —) DEER
(COARSE —) KEMP BRISTLE
(CURLED —) FRIZZ
(CUTDOWN —) STUMPS
(FALSE —) WIG JANE FRONT PERUKE
(FRIZZED —) FROWZE
(GRAY —) GRIZZLE
(LOCK OF —) TUZ FEAK TATE FLOCK
TRESS
(LONG HEAVY —) MANE
(LOOSE —) COMBINGS
(MATTED —) SHAG ELFLOCK
(MOP OF —) TOUSLE
(NOSE —) VIBRISSA
(PLANT —) COLLETER
(ROOT —) FIBRIL
(SNARL OF —) TANGLE
(SOFT —) DOWN LANUGO
(STINGING —) STING STIMULUS
(STINGING —S) COWHAGE
(STRAY LOCK OF —) TAG
(STYLE —) CORNROW
(TUFT OF —) PLUME KROBYLOS
(WAVING LOCK OF —) WIMPLER
(WHITE —) SNOW SNOWS
HAIRBREADTH HERMELE WHISKER
HAIRCUT BOB CUT CROP BUTCH
SHINGLE DUCKTAIL
HAIRDO AFRO FRISURE
HAIRDRESSER WAVER FRISEUR
COIFFEUR
HAIRDRESSING FRISURE BANDOLINE

HAIRLESS BALD PELON CALLOW ATRICHIC DEPILOUS GLABROUS
HAIRY FAXED MOSEY PILAR ROUGH COMATE COMOUS PILARY PILINE CRINITE CRINOSE HIRSUTE PILEOUS VILLOUS UNSHAVEN

HAITI

CAPE: FOUX
CAPITAL: PORTAUPRINCE
CHANNEL: SUD STMARC
COIN: GOURDE
GULF: GONAVE
INDIAN: TAINO
ISLAND: VACHE GONAVE TORTUE NAVASSA TORTUGA
ISLAND GROUP: CAYMITES
LAKE: SAUMATRE
MOUNTAIN: NORD CAHOS NOIRES LAHOTTE LASELLE TROUDEAU
PLAIN: NORD CAYES JACMEL LEOGANE ARCAHAIE CULDESAC GONAIVES
PRIEST: BOCOR HOUNGAN
RIVER: GUAYAMOUC ARTIBONITE
SPIRIT: LOA BAKA BOKO
TOWN: AQUIN CAYES FURCY LIMBE HINCHE JACMEL JEREMIE LEOGANE SALTROU GONAIVES KENSCOFF

HALCYON CALM ALCYON GOLDEN
HALE YELL FRACK FRECK TRAIL ROBUST STRONG HEALTHY VIGOROUS
HALF ARF ELF DEMI HAUF HOVE SEMI SIDE MEDIO HALFEN HALFLY MOIETY MEDIETY
 (— GALLON) POTTLE
 (— OF DRAW) BRACKET
 (— OF EM) EN
 (— OF INNING) BOTTOM
 (— OF MOLD) VALVE
 (FRUIT —S) SLABS
HALF-BLOOD DEMISANG
HALF-BREED BREED METIF METIS SAMBO MUSTEE RAMONA CABOCLO MESTIZO METISSE DEMISANG HARRATIN MIXBLOOD
HALF HITCH ROLLING
HALF-MOON LUNETTE DEMILUNE
HALF NOTE MINIM
HALFPENNY OB MAG MEG GREY MAIK MAIL MAKE MEKE OBOL SOUSE STAMP BAUBEE BAWBEE MAILLE HAPENNY PATRICK STUIVER
 (COUNTERFEIT —) RAP GRAY
 (THICK —) DUMP
HALF-PINT CUP JACK CUPFUL
HALF REST SOSPIRO
HALF SOLE TAP
HALF STEP CHROMA
HALFTONE DROPOUT
HALF TURN DEMIVOLT
HALF-WIT DOLT DUNCE HAVEREL TOMFOOL STAUMREL UNDERWIT
HALF-WITTED SOFT DOTTY SIMPLE HALUCKET IMBECILE STAUMREL

HALIBUT BUT BUTT FLITCH TURBOT FLATFISH
HALL HA AULA HELL IWAN SALA AIWAN ATRIO BALAI BURSA CURIA DIVAN ENTRY FOYER HOUSE OECUS SALLE SALON ATRIUM CAMERA DURBAR EXEDRA GARDEN LESCHE SALOON SCHOOL SENATE TOLSEY TRANCE APADANA CHAMBER DANCERY GALLERY HALLWAY KURHAUS KURSAAL MEGARON PASSAGE VINGOLF ANTEROOM ARCHEION ASSEMBLY BASILICA CHOULTRY COLISEUM CORRIDOR FOREHALL HASTROND HOSPITAL RAADZAAL TOLBOOTH VALHALLA
 (— FOR PERFORMANCES) ODEUM
 (— OF JUSTICE) COURT
 (— WITH STATUES) VALHALLA
 (DINING —) COMMON REFECTORY
 (LECTURE —) SCHOLA
 (MISSION —) CITADEL
 (MUSIC —) GAFF
 (TOWN —) CABILDO RATHAUS TRIBUNAL
 (UNIVERSITY —) BURSA
HALLMARK CROWN SHOPMARK
HALL OF FAME (AVIATION —) ELY SIX BYRD LAHM LEAR LINK LUKE MOSS POST RYAN WADE EAKER GLENN LEMAY PIPER REEVE ARNOLD BOEING CESSNA FOKKER HUGHES LEVIER MARTIN ROGERS SPAATZ SPERRY TOWERS TRIPPE TURNER WALDEN WRIGHT YAEGER CHANUTE EARHART GRUMMAN LANGLEY LOENING SHEPARD TWINING MITCHELL NORTHROP SIKORSKY ARMSTRONG LINDBERGH MCDONNELL RICKENBACKER
 (BASEBALL —) OTT COBB DEAN FORD FOXX HOYT KELL KLEM MACK MAYS MIZE RUTH WYNN AARON BANKS BERRA COMBS EVERS FRICK GOMEZ GROVE HAFEY KINER LEMON LOPEZ LYONS PAIGE PLANK RUSIE SPAHN TERRY VANCE WALSH WANER WHEAT YOUNG ALSTON CHANCE CRONIN CUYLER FELLER FRISCH GEHRIG GOSLIN KALINE KOUFAX LAJOIE LANDIS MANTLE MANUSH MCGRAW MUSIAL RICKEY SISLER TINKER WAGNER WILSON WRIGHT YAWKEY APPLING AVERILL BURKETT HORNSBY HUBBARD HUGGINS JOHNSON PENNOCK RUFFING SIMMONS SPEAKER STENGEL TRAYNOR BOUDREAU COMISKEY DIMAGGIO GRIFFITH MACPHAIL MARICHAL MCCARTHY ROBINSON WILLIAMS COVELESKI BRICKHOUSE MARANVILLE
 (BASKETBALL —) GALE GOLA PAGE REED WEST COUSY FULKS GREER HAGAN HYATT LUCAS MIKAN ARIZIN BARLOW BAYLOR COOPER FOSTER HANSON HOLMAN KRAUSE MURPHY PETTIT PHILIP RAMSEY ROOSMA SEDRAN TWYMAN WOODEN BECKMAN BRADLEY BRENNAN DEHNERT GRUENIG KURLAND POLLARD SCHAYES SCHMIDT SHARMAN WACHTER BORGMANN ENDACOTT LAPCHICK

LUISETTI MACAULEY SCHOMMER
MCCRACKEN STEINMETZ VANDIVIER
DEBERNARDI DEBUSSCHERE
(BUSINESS —) FORD HAAS LUCE OCHS
VAIL GARST HEINZ ROUSE SLOAN
BATTEN DISNEY DORIOT DUPONT HILTON
KAISER LASKER MELLON MORGAN
OGILVY PENNEY SCHIFF SCHWAB
EASTMAN SARNOFF WHITNEY CARNEGIE
FRANKLIN MCCORMICK VANDERBILT
ROCKEFELLER WESTINGHOUSE
WEYERHAEUSER
(FOOTBALL —) MIX RAY BELL HEIN
HUFF LARY MARA OTTO FEARS GROZA
GUYON HALAS HAYES LAYNE LILLY
LYMAN MUSSO NEALE RINGO ROYAL
BADGRO BLANDA BUTKUS GRANGE
HINKLE KINARD MATSON MCAFEE
ROONEY THORPE TITTLE TRIPPI UNITAS
ALWORTH GILLMAN LUCKMAN MILLNER
LOMBARDI MITCHELL WARFIELD
JURGENSEN PARSEGHIAN
(GOLF —) BERG FORD HOPE BOROS
BURKE DUTRA EVANS HAGEN HOGAN
JONES SHAW SMITH SNEAD GOLDEN
COOPER DIEGEL GHEZZI LITTLE NELSON
OUIMET PALMER PICARD RUNYAN
TRAVIS DEMARET GULDAHL HARBERT
MANGRUM REVOLTA SARAZEN
ZAHARIAS DEVICENZO
(THEATER —) DREW KERR BROOK
HECHT KELLY SIMON PRINCE DUNNOCK
CHAMPION KINGSLEY LANSBURY
MCARTHUR MEREDITH SONDHEIM
STRASBERG YOUNGMANS
BLOOMGARDEN
HALLOW BLESS HALWE DEDICATE
SANCTIFY
HALLOWED HOLY SACRED BLESSED
HALLUCINATION DWALE ACOASMA
ACOUASM ACOUSMA FANTASY
PHONEME DELUSION ILLUSION
PHANTASY ZOOSCOPY
HALLUCINOGEN ACID
HALLWAY ENTRY FOYER TRANCE
HALO DOG BURR GLOR NIMB GLORY
SHINE AREOLA CIRCLE CORONA GLORIA
NIMBUS SUNDOG AREOLET AUREOLE
BOROUGH CINCTURE
HALT HO HOP ALTO BAIT BALK HOLD
LIMP SKID STAY STOP TRIP WAIT BAULK
BLOCK BREAK CEASE CHECK HILCH
HITCH STAND STICK ARREST BARLEY
SCOTCH STANCE CONTAIN CRIPPLE
STATION STOPPAGE
(— GAME) CALL
(— TO DOGS) TOHO
HALTER EVIL SOLE BRANK TRASH
WANTY WIDDY WITHE POISER CAUSSON
CAVESON JAQUIMA POINTEL BALANCER
NECKLACE
HALTING BODE LAME ZOPPA CRIPPLE
LIMPING
HAM PIG GAMMON JAMBON JARRET
PESTLE GAMBONE PROSCIUTTO
(BROTHER OF —) SHEM JAPHET
(FATHER OF —) NOAH

(PICNIC —) CALA CALI
(SON OF —) CUSH PHUT CANAAN
MIZRAIM
HAMLET KOM DORP TOON TOWN TREF
VILL ALDEA CASAL HAMEL SITIO STEAD
THORP VICUS ALDEIA BUSTEE THORPE
CLACHAN KAMPONG KIRKTON
KIRKTOWN
(AUTHOR OF —) SHAKESPEARE
(CHARACTER IN —) OSRIC HAMLET
HORATIO LAERTES OPHELIA BERNARDO
CLAUDIUS GERTRUDE POLONIUS
REYNALDO CORNELIUS FRANCISCO
MARCELLUS VOLTIMAND FORTINBRAS
ROSENCRANTZ GUILDENSTERN
HAMMER AX AXE BIT PEG SET CALL
DROP HORN MALL MASH MAUL MELL
SETT TILT CAVIL KNOCK POUND SMITE
THUMP BEETLE BUCKER CLOYER DRIVER
FALLER FULLER MALLET MARTEL NOPPER
OLIVER PLEXOR SLEDGE TACKER TILTER
KNAPPER KNOCKER MALLEUS PLESSOR
STRIKER CRANDALL MALLEATE
MJOLLNIR SCUTCHER TREMBLER
(— FOR DRESSING STONE) KEVEL
(— OF GUNLOCK) DOG COCK DOGHEAD
(— OUT) ANVIL
(LEADEN —) MADGE
(MINER'S —) BULLY
(PART OF —) BELL CLAW FACE GRIP
HEAD NECK PEEN POLL CHEEK HANDLE
(PAVING —) REEL
(PNEUMATIC —) GUN BUSTER
(SLATE-CUTTER'S —) SAX
(STEAM —) IMPACTOR
(TUNING —) KEY
HAMMOCK SACK HUMMOCK
(— CARRIED BY BEARERS) DANDY
(— SLUNG ON POLE) MACHILA
(WOODEN —) KATEL KARTEL
HAMPER BIN COT MAR PED TUB BEAT
BIND CLOG CURB FLAT HURT LOAD
SLOW TUCK BLOCK CABIN CRAMP
CRATE MAUND RUSKY SERON BASKET
BURDEN FETTER HALTER HINDER
HOBBLE HOPPLE IMPEDE TANGLE
BUFFALO CONFINE HANAPER MANACLE
PANNIER PERPLEX SHACKLE TRAMMEL
ENCUMBER ENTANGLE OBSTRUCT
RESTRAIN RESTRICT STRAITEN
HAMPERING STIFLING DIFFICULT
HAMSTER CRICETID
HAMSTRING HOX HOCK LAME HOUGH
ENERVATE
HAND CAT DAB FAM FIN HAN PAW PUD
CLAW DEAL DUKE GIVE GOLL HALF JACK
LOOF MAIN MANO MITT PART PASS
SPAN CAMAY CLAUT CLEUK FLUSH
GLAUM GRASP GRIPE INDEX MANUS
NIEVE POWER SHARE STIFF STOCK
BRIDGE CLUNCH CLUTCH DADDLE
DOUBLE FAMBLE GOWPEN HANDLE
MAULEY MINNIE STAGER WORKER
CLAWKER FAMELEN FLAPPER FLIPPER
POINTER WORKMAN GRAPPLER
MORTMAIN
(— COUNTING ZERO) BACCARAT

(— DOWN) DEVOLVE TRADUCE
BEQUEATH TRANSMIT
(— IN POKER) FULL SKIP BLAZE FLUSH
SKEET TIGER BICYCLE JACKPOT SKIPPER
IMMORTAL STRAIGHT
(— IN WHIST) MORT TENACE
(— ON) BUCK SPREAD
(— ON HIP) AKIMBO
(— OVER) GIVE REACH BETEACH
BITECHE DELIVER
(— UP STRAW) SERVE
(— WITH 5 HIGHEST TRUMPS)
JAMBOREE
(BABY'S —) SPUD
(BIG AND UNGAINLY —) MAIG
(BRIDGE —) BID DUMMY DOUBLE
CHICANE LAYDOWN
(CLENCHED —) FIST
(COLD —S) SHOWDOWN
(CURSIVE —) CIVILITE
(DECK —) HAWSEMAN
(DUMMY —) BOARD
(ELDEST —) EDGE SENIOR
(EUCHRE —) JAMBONE
(EXTRA — IN LOO) MISS
(FRENCH —) COULEE
(GRASPING —) CLAUT
(GREEN —) FARMER JACKEROO
(LEFT —) SINISTRA
(LONE —) JAMBONE
(PERSIAN —) SHIKASTA
(POKER —S) BOARD
(RANCH —) COWBOY
(REEL —) SPINDLER
(RIGHT —) DEXTER
(ROUND —) RONDE
(SECTION —) SNIPE
(SKILLFUL —) DAB
(SPARE — IN CARDS) CAT JAMBOREE
(UNSKILLED —) DABSTER
(UPPER —) BULGE EMINENCE
(WEAK CARD —) BUST
HANDBAG BAG CABA NEIF CABAS
PURSE SATCHEL ENVELOPE GRIPSACK
POCHETTE RETICULE POCKETBOOK
HANDBILL BILL FLIER FLYER LIBEL
DODGER
HANDCART PRAM DANDY HURLY TRUCK
GOCART TROLLY TROLLEY
HANDCUFF CUFF STAY LINKER NIPPER
STAYER MANACLE TRAMMEL WRISTER
BRACELET HANDBOLT HANDLOCK
LIGAMENT SNITCHER WRISTLET
(PL.) IRONS SNAPS DARBIES NIPPERS
HANDFUL OF DUST (AUTHOR OF —)
WAUGH
(CHARACTER IN —) JOCK JOHN LAST
TODD TONY BEAVER BRENDA MENZIES
MESSINGER
HANDICAP START BURDEN DENIAL
HAMPER HINDER IMPEDE STRIKE
PENALTY ENCUMBER PENALIZE
HANDICAPPED CRIMP CRIMPED
HANDICRAFT MYSTERY ARTIFICE
MECHANIC HANDCRAFT
HANDICRAFTSMAN ARTISAN
HANDKERCHIEF WIPE CLOUT FOGLE

HANKY ROMAL STOOK WIPER HANKIE
MADRAS NAPKIN SUDARY TIGNON
BANDANA BELCHER FOULARD KERCHER
MANIPLE ORARIUM SNEEZER BANDANNA
KERCHIEF MOCKETER MONTEITH
MOUCHOIR SUDARIUM VERNACLE
VERONICA
HANDLE BOW EAR FAN LUG NIB NOB
PAD PIN PLY USE ANSA BAIL BALE BUTT
FEEL FIST GRIP HAND HANK KNOB LIFT
RAPE RUNG STOP GRIPE GROPE MOUNT
SHAFT SPOKE STAIL STEAL STELE STOCK
SWING TREAT WIELD BECKET FETTLE
FINGER FUSEAU HANGER LIFTER
MANAGE MANURE POMMEL CONDUCT
WOOLDER BEERPULL BELLPULL
BITSTALK BITSTOCK DISPENSE
HANDGRIP HANDHOLD HANDLING
MOPSTICK STAGHORN PENHOLDER
MANIPULATE
(— AWKWARDLY) FUMBLE THUMBLE
(— BADLY) ILLGUIDE
(— CLUMSILY) PAW FUMBLE
(— IMPROPERLY) GAUM
(— MODISHLY) GALLANT
(— OF AXE) HELVE
(— OF BENCH PLANE) TOAT TOTE
(— OF CANNON) MANIGLION
(— OF DAGGER) DUDGEON
(— OF KETTLE) BAIL
(— OF LADLE) SHANK
(— OF OAR) GRASP
(— OF PLOW) HALE STAFF START STILT
PLOWTAIL
(— OF PRINTING PRESS) ROUNCE
(— OF RAKE) STALE
(— OF SCYTHE) TACK SNATH SNEAD
THOLE SNATHE SNEATH
(— OF SWORD) HAFT HILT
(— OF WHIP) CROP
(— RECKLESSLY) FOOL
(— ROUGHLY) MALL MAUL TOWSE
MUZZLE GRABBLE MANHANDLE
(— VIOLENTLY) BOUNCE
(CRANK —) WINK
(CROSSBOW —) TILLER
(CURVED —) BOOL BOUL
(DETACHABLE —) KILP
(LIFTING — OF GUN) DOLPHIN
(PUMP —) BRAKE SWIPE
(ROPE —) SHACKLE
(WOODEN —) TREE
HANDMAID ANCILLA
HANDRAIL BAR RAIL MANROPE
BANISTER EASEMENT MOPSTICK
TOADBACK
HANDSOME BRAW FAIR FINE MOOI NICE
PERT TALL BONNY FITTY FUSOM
LUSTY ADONIC BRAWLY CLEVER COMELY
FARAND GOODLY HEPPEN LIKELY PROPER
SEEMLY ADONIAN AVENANT ELEGANT
FEATISH FEATOUS FEWSOME GALLANT
LIBERAL SMICKER GOODLIKE STUNNING
VENEREAN WEELFARD
HANDWRITING PAW FIST HAND WRITE
DUCTUS NESHKI NIGGLE SCRIPT SCRIVE

BATARDE WRITING BACKHAND
HANDWRIT

HANDY DAB DEFT GAIN NEAT WEME
JEMMY LUSTY QUEME READY TIGHT
ADROIT CLEVER HEPPEN KNACKY
DEXTROUS EXPEDITE HANDSOME
SKILLFUL

HANDYMAN MOZO JUMPER GREASER
SWAMPER

HANG NUB TOP CRAP DRAG FALL HANK
KILT PEND TREE TUCK DRAPE KETCH
NOOSE SCRAG SWING TRINE TRUSS
TWIST ANHANG APPEND GIBBET HALTER
IMPEND SLOUCH STRING TALTER
DOGGONE HANGING LANTERN STRETCH
SUSPEND
(— ABOUT) DRING HOVER
(— AROUND) KNOCK HANKER SLINGE
(— BACK) LAG BOGGLE
(— BEHIND) PLOD
(— CRIMINAL) STRAP TOTTER
(— DOWN) DIP LOP LAVE DROOP
DEPEND FESTOON PROPEND
(— HEAVILY) SWAG
(— LOOSELY) BAG SAG FLAG FLOW
LOLL BANGLE DANGLE PAGGLE
(— ONE'S HEAD) SLINK
(— OUT) LILL
(— OVER) WAUVE IMPEND WHAUVE
(— PICTURE NEAR CEILING) SKY
(— SOGGILY) TROLLOP
(— WITH TAPESTRY) TAPIS

HANGAR DOCK GARAGE AIRDOCK

HANGER-ON BUR CAD BURR SPIV LEECH
TOADY CLIENT HANGBY HEELER LACKEY
SPONGE LACQUEY PENDING PARASITE
(— OF CELEBRITY) GROUPIE

HANGING FLAG HEMP TURN ARRAS
BAGGY DRAPE SWING CELURE DORSEL
DOSSER DERRICK DRAPERY PENDENT
PENSILE ANTEPORT HANGMENT
PARAMENT
(— LOOSE) LOPPY BAGGED
(— LOW) SIDE
(— THREATENINGLY) IMMINENT
(LIMPLY —) FLAGGY SLIMPSY
(WALL —) CEILING TENTURE
KAKEMONO

HANGMAN KETCH HANGER HANGIE
TOPMAN DERRICK GREGORY TOPSMAN
VERDUGO CARNIFEX SCRAGGER

HANGNAIL AGNAIL

HANGOUT NEST JOINT SCATTER

HANGOVER HOLDOVER RESIDUUM

HANK HASP SKEIN BOBBIN SELVAGEE
(— OF FLAX) HEAD
(— OF TWINE) RAN
(— OF YARN) SLIP

HANKER HANK LONG LINGER

HANKERING ITCH HANKER

HANNAH (HUSBAND OF —) ELKANAH
(SON OF —) SAMUEL

HANS BRINKER (AUTHOR OF —)
DODGE
(CHARACTER IN —) HANS RAFF GLECK
HILDA GRETEL BOEKMAN BRINKER
MEVROUW

HAPHAZARD CASUAL CHANCE CHANCY
RANDOM BUCKEYE SCRATCH CARELESS
SCRAMBLY SLAPDASH TUMULTUARY

HAPHAZARDLY ANYHOW

HAPLESS POOR UNLUCKY

HAPPEN BE DO GO HAP COME COOK
FALL FARE GIVE LUCK PASS RISE TIDE
TIME BREAK EVENE EVENT LIGHT OCCUR
SHAPE ARRIVE BECOME BEFALL BETIDE
CHANCE TUMBLE FORTUNE STUMBLE
SUCCEED BECHANCE OVERCOME
(— TOGETHER) CONCUR

HAPPENING HAP FACT EVENT THING
CHANCE TIDING TIMING INCIDENT
OCCASION OCCURRENCE
(ACTUAL —) FACT
(UNEXPECTED —) ACCIDENT

HAPPILY FAIN FITLY GLADLY JOYOUSLY

HAPPINESS JOY WIN GLEE SELE SONS
WEAL BLISS GLORY MIRTH SOOTH
FELICE WEALTH DELIGHT ECSTASY
FELICIA RAPTURE UTILITY FELICITY
GLADNESS HILARITY

HAPPY FIT COSH FAIN GLAD GLEG SELI
WELY BONNY FAUST FELIX LIGHT LUCKY
MERRY PROUD SEELY SONSY SUNNY
WHITE BLITHE BONNIE BRIGHT JOYFUL
COMICAL GLEEFUL HALCYON JOCULAR
PERFECT SEELFUL WEALFUL WEIRDLY
BLISSFUL CAREFREE DISPOSED
FROHLICH GRACIOUS SUNSHINE
(PREF.) FELICI

HARA-KIRI SEPPUKU

HARANGUE ORATE CONCIO PATTER
SERMON SPEECH TIRADE ADDRESS
DECLAIM EARBASH DIATRIBE PERORATE

HARASS FAG GIG HAG HOX MAG NAG
RAG TAW VEX BAIT CARK FRAB FRET
GALL GNAW HAKE HALE HARE HAZE
HOCK JADE PAIL PUSH RIDE SEEK TIRE
TOIL TOSS WORK ANNOY BESET BULLY
CHAFE CHASE CHEVY CHIVY CURSE
FLISK GRIND GRIPE HARRY HURRY PRESS
TARGE TEASE TRASH WEARY WORRY
BADGER BOTHER CHIVVY CHOUSE
CUMBER FERRET HASSLE HATTER
HECKLE HECTOR HESPEL HOORAY
HURRAH INFEST MOLEST MURDER
OBSESS PESTER PINGLE PLAGUE POTHER
PURSUE AFFLICT AGITATE BEDEVIL
DRAGOON HAGRIDE HARRAGE OPPRESS
PERPLEX PROVOKE TERRIFY TORMENT
TRAVAIL TROUBLE TURMOIL BULLYRAG
DISTRACT DISTRESS EXERCISE FORHAILE
IRRITATE SPURGALL SUPPRESS
PERSECUTE
(— MENTALLY) GRUDGE

HARBINGER ANGEL USHER HERALD
FORAGER FORAYER FURRIER OUTRIDER
PRODROME
(— OF SUMMER) SWALLOW

HARBOR REE BEAR DOCK HOLD PIER
PORT BASIN BAYOU CHUCK CREEK
HAVEN HITHE SLADE BREACH BUNDER
COTHON FOSTER REFUGE OUTPORT
PORTLET SEAPORT SHELTER CARENAGE
ENHARBOR SHIPRADE

(— A CRIMINAL) RESET
(SUBMARINE —) PEN
HARD DRY FIT ILL COLD DEAR DOUR
DURE FAST FIRM IRON MEAN NASH OPEN
CHAMP CLOSE CORKY HARSH HORNY
ROCKY SMART SNELL SOLID SOUND
STEEL STERN STIFF STONY STOOR
STOUT TIGHT BOARDY BRAWNY COARSE
FLINTY GLASSY KITTLE KNOBBY KNOTTY
ROBUST RUGGED SEVERE STARKY
STINGY STRICT STRONG STURDY
UNEATH UNNETH WOODEN ADAMANT
ARDUOUS AUSTERE CALLOUS HARDWAY
HORNISH ONEROUS SUBDUE
CORNEOUS DILIGENT HARDBACK
HARDENED IRONHARD OBDURATE
PETROSAL RIGOROUS SCLEROID
SCLEROSE TOILSOME
(— BY) FORBY FORTHBY
(— TO BEAR) FIERCE
(— TO MANAGE) SALTY
(— TO PLEASE) FINICKY CONCEITY
(— TO REACH) CUMBROUS
(— TO READ) BLIND
(— TO SATISFY) EXIGENT EXIGEANT
(— TO SELL) STICKY
(— TO UNDERSTAND) DIFFUSE
HARD-BITTEN GNARLED
HARDEN SET TAW BAKE BEEK CAKE
FIRM HARN KERN SEAR BRAZE ENURE
FLESH INURE STEEL STONE BRONZE
ENDURE FREEZE OBDURE OSSIFY
POTASH SEASON TEMPER CALCIFY
EMBRAWN PETRIFY STIFFEN THICKEN
CONCRETE ENHARDEN INDURATE
SOLIDIFY
(— QUILL) DUTCH
HARDHEARTED STERN STONY
OBDURATE
HARDLY ILL SCANT BARELY RARELY
SCARCE UNEATH SCARCELY
HARDNESS SEG GRAIN PROOF RIGOR
STEEL DURESS DURITY ADAMANT
HARDSHIP SEVERITY SOLIDITY
(— OF CHARACTER) HEART
HARD-OF-HEARING DULL DUNCH
DEAFISH
HARDSHIP HARD GRIEF PINCH RIGOR
STOUR THRONG UNWEAL SQUEEZE
ASPERITY HARDNESS
HARDTACK PANTILE
(— AND MOLASSES) BURGOO
HARD TIMES (AUTHOR OF —)
DICKENS
(CHARACTER IN —) JUPE JAMES
SISSY JOSIAH LOUISA SLEARY THOMAS
SPARSIT STEPHEN GRAGRIND
BLACKPOOL BOUNDERBY HARTHOUSE
MCCHOAKUMCHILD
HARDY DOUR HARD WIRY LUSTY MANLY
STOUR STOUT TOUGH GARDEN INURED
RUGGED STURDY SPARTAN STUBBED
GAILLARD GALLIARD STUBBORN
HARE PUG WAT BAWD CONY PUSS SCUT
BAWTY CUTTY LEPUS PUSSY MALKIN
MAUKIN BELGIAN LEPORID POUSSIE

VENISON BAUDRONS KLIPHAAS
LEPORINE
(— IN FIRST YEAR) LEVERET
(FEMALE —) DOE
(GREAT —) MANABOZHO
(LITTLE CHIEF —) CONY PIKA
(MALE —) BUCK
(PATAGONIAN —) MARA
(SIBERIAN —) TOLAL
HAREBRAINED GIDDY WINDY
HARELIP LAGOSTOMA
HAREM SERAI ZENANA ANDERUN
HAREMLIK SERAGLIO
HARLOT PUG DRAB LOON SLUT HIREN
PAGAN QUEAN RAHAB STRAP TWEAK
WHORE RIBALD TOMBOY DELILAH
MERMAID WAGTAIL MERETRIX
MISWOMAN STRUMPET
HARLOTRY PUTAGE BITCHERY
HARM NEY NOY NYE WEM ARME BALE
BANE DERE HURT SCAT SORE TEEN
WERD ANNOY GRAME HERME LOATH
QUALM SHEND SPOIL TOUCH WATHE
WEMMY WOUGH WOUND WRAKE
WREAK WRONG DAMAGE DAMNUM
DANGER GRIEVE INJURE INJURY SCATHE
SORROW WONDER DESPITE DISEASE
FORFEIT IMPEACH TROUBLE UNQUERT
BUSINESS DISAVAIL DISSERVE
ENDAMAGE MISCHIEF NOCUMENT
NUISANCE
HARMFUL BAD EVIL HARM NASTY
NOXAL NOCENT NOCIVE NOYFUL UNSELY
BANEFUL HURTFUL NOISOME NOXIOUS
DAMAGING INIMICAL SINISTER
PERNICIOUS
HARMFULNESS VICE MALICE
HARMLESS SAFE TAME CANNY SEELY
SILLY WHITE DOVISH FEARLESS
HURTLESS INNOCENT SACKLESS
UNHARMED
HARMONIC OVERTONE
HARMONICA HARP EUPHON SYRINX
AEOLINE PANPIPE ARMONICA
ZAMPOGNA
HARMONIOUS HAPPY SWEET COSMIC
SILKEN UNITED MUSICAL SPHERAL
TUNEFUL BALANCED CHARMING
HARMONIC PEACEFUL ACCORDING
CONCINNOUS CONCORDANT
(PREF.) SYMPHO
HARMONIZE GO FIT GEE KEY JIBE SORT
TUNE AGREE ATONE BLEND CHORD
GROUP HITCH RHYME ACCORD ASSORT
COTTON COMPORT CONCENT CONCORD
CONSORT ORDINATE ACCOMMODATE
HARMONY SUIT TUNE CHIME CHORD
UNITY ACCORD ATTUNE COSMOS
HEAVEN MELODY UNISON BALANCE
CONCENT CONCERT CONCORD CONSENT
CONSORT KEEPING RAPPORT DIAPASON
FABURDEN SYMPATHY SYMPHONY
CONGRUITY
HARNESS TUG GEAR HAME LEAF REIN
BRACE CROWN DRAFT FRONT GEARS
SLING TRACE COLLAR FETTLE GULLET
INSPAN TACKLE DRAUGHT GEARING

GIGTREE LORMERY SIMBLOT TOGGERY
DRAWGEAR ENCLOSER HEADGEAR
TACKLING TURNBACK
(— FOR LOOM) LEAF HEALD MOUNTING
(— FOR PULLING GUNS) BRICOLE
(DECORATIVE —) CAPARISON
(WEAVING —) HEDDLE

HARP ARPA FORK LYRE VINA NABLA
NANGA HARPER SABECA CHROTTA
DECHORD SAMBUKE AUTOHARP
CLARSACH
(CELTIC —) TELYN CLARSACH
(FINNISH —) KANTELE
(ICELANDIC —) LANGSPIL
(JAPANESE —) KOTO
(JEW'S —) TRUMP
(PART OF —) BASE BODY FOOT NECK
BOARD PEDAL PILLAR STRING
(PERSIAN —) SANG
(TRIANGULAR —) TRIGON

HARPOON IRON FIZGIG GRAINS FISHGIG
HARPAGO STRIKER HARPAGON

HARPSICHORD SPINET CEMBALO
CLAVIER CLAVECIN HASPICOL

HARPY HAG AELLO CELAENO OCYPETE
PODARGE

HARROW COG CHIP DISC DISK DRAG
HARO TINE BRAKE BREAK HERSE DREDGE
DRUDGE FALLOW LADDER SPADER
CUTAWAY LACERATE OXHARROW

HARSH ILL ACID BULL DOUR FOUL HARD
HASH HASK IRON RUDE SOUR ACERB
ACRID ASPER BRUTE CRONK CRUDE
GRILL GRUFF HEAVY HUSKY RASPY
ROUGH ROUND RUVID SHARP SNELL
STARK STERN STIFF STOUR STOUT
BRUTAL COARSE FLINTY GRAVEL GRISLY
HOARSE RAGGED RASPED RUGGED
SEVERE SHREWD STURDY SULLEN
TETRIC UNKIND UNRIDE AUSTERE
CRABBED RASPING RAUCOUS SQUAWKY
VIOLENT ABRASIVE ACERBATE
ASPERATE ASPEROUS CATONIAN
CLASHING DRACONIC GRAVELLY
GRINDING GUTTURAL JANGLING
OBDURATE RIGOROUS SCABROUS
SCRANNEL STRIDENT STROUNGE
STUBBORN TETRICAL UNGENTLE
UNKINDLY

HARSHLY HARD HARSH SHORTLY

HARSHNESS WOLF RIGOR DURESS
CATOISM CRUDITY CRUELTY DUREZZA
RAUCITY ACERBITY ACRIMONY ASPERITY
FELLNESS HARDNESS HASKNESS
MORDANCY SEVERITY

HARVEST IN WIN CROP HEAP RABI REAP
SLED SNAP FOISON GATHER HAIRST
RUBBEE COMBINE GRABBLE INGATHER
SHEARING

HARVESTER COMBINE

HASH RAPE MINCE HACHIS MUDDLE
RAGOUT

HASSOCK TUT BOSS PESS POUF TOIT
TRUSH BUFFET TUFFET

HASTE HIE POST RACE RAGE RAPE CHASE
FEVER HASTY HURRY SPEED BUSTLE

FLURRY SWIVET DISPATCH RAPIDITY
STROTHER PRECIPITATION
(HEADLONG —) SPURN
(IN —) HOTFOOT
(IN GREAT —) AMAIN

HASTEN HIE RAP RUN BUSK DUST FIRK
PELL PLAT POST RACE RAPE RUSH SPUR
URGE CATCH CHASE DRIVE FLEET HASTE
HURRY PRESS PREST SLATE SPEED
STEER EXPEDE SCURRY STREAK SWITHE
ADVANCE FORWARD HACKNEY HOTFOOT
PREVENT QUICKEN SLITHER SWIFTEN
WITHHIE DISPATCH EXPEDITE
ACCELERATE
(— AWAY) FLEE SHERRY SQUIRR

HASTILY HOTLY RAPELY RASHLY
FOOTHOT HOTFOOT HYINGLY HEADLONG

HASTY FAST RAPE RASH BRASH FLEET
QUICK FLYING RAPELY CURSORY
HOTHEAD HURRIED PEPPERY TEARING
HASTEFUL HEADLONG SUBITANE
(TACTLESSLY —) BRASH

HAT DIP FEZ LID NAB ATTE COIF DISC
DISK FELT HIVE KNAB MOAB SLOP
BEANY BERET BOXER CADDI CORDY
DICER MILAN MITER MITRE SHELL TRUSH
ABACOT BEANIE BRETON BUMPER
CADDIE CASQUE CLOCHE COCKUP
COIFFE FEDORA HELMET PILEUS RAFFIA
SLOUCH TURBAN VIGONE BANDEAU
BANGKOK BLOOMER BRIMMER BYCOKET
CAUBEEN CHAPEAU FANTAIL HATTING
HATTOCK HOMBURG PETASOS PILLBOX
PLATEAU PLATTER SALACOT SHALLOW
SKIMMER BONGRACE CAPELINE
GOSSAMER HEADGEAR JIPIJAPA
MONTABYN MUSHROOM NABCHEAT
RAMILIES REHOBOAM ROUNDLET
SOMBRERO
(— BLOCKER) ROPER
(— OF MERCURY) PETASUS
(BEAVER —) CASTOR
(CLERGYMAN'S —) SHOVEL
(COCKED —) BICORNE RAMILIE
SCRAPER
(COWBOY —) STETSON
(FABRIC —) TOQUE
(FELT —) DERBY JERRY TERAI ALPINE
BOWLER TRILBY BILLYCOCK
(HIGH —) KYL PLUG TILE TOPPER
(IRON —) GOSSAN
(MILITARY —) BUSBY BEARSKIN
(OILSKIN —) SQUAM
(OPERA —) GIBUS CLAQUE
(PITH —) TOPEE
(SILK —) KYL BEAVER SHINER CATSKIN
(STIFF —) TILE DERBY KELLY BOATER
BOWLER SAILOR
(STOVEPIPE —) CAROLINE
(STRAW —) BAKU FLAT HOOD KADY
KATY TOYO BENJY BENNY CADDY
STRAW BASHER BOATER PANAMA
LEGHORN
(TOP —) PLUG TOPPER
(UNBLOCKED —) CONE
(WATERPROOF —) TARPAULIN

(WIDE-BRIMMED —) FLAT BENJY
TARAI SMASHER SUNDOWN
(3-CORNERED —) TRICORN
HATCH HECK BREED BROOD CLECK
CLOCK COVEY GUICHET UNSHELL
DISCLOSE INCUBATE
HATCHET MOGO HACHE GWEEON THIXLE
FRANCISC TOMAHAWK
HATE FIRE TEEN ABHOR SPITE DETEST
HATRED LOATHE UNLOVE DESPITE
HATEFUL FOUL LOTH BLACK CURST
DIRTY HATEL LOATH CURSED ODIOUS
HEINOUS HIDEOUS ACCURSED
FLAGRANT ABOMINABLE
HATRED DOSA ENVY HATE HELL ONDE
HAINE ODIUM SPITE ENMITY RANCOR
AVERSION ABHORRENCE
(— OF CHILDREN) MISOPEDIA
(— OF MARRIAGE) MISOGAMY
(— OF MEN) MISANDRY MISANTHROPY
(— OF NEW IDEAS) MISCAINEA
(— OF REASONING) MISOLOGY
(— OF WOMEN) MISOGYNY
(PREF.) MIS(O)
HAUGHTINESS AIR PRIDE HEIGHT
MORGUE ORGUIL DISDAIN HAUTEUR
STOMACH HAUTESSE
HAUGHTY DAIN HIGH RANK STAY DIGNE
DORTY HUFFY LOFTY LUSTY POTTY
PROUD STOUT SURLY TAUNT FEISTY
FIERCE HAUGHT QUAINT DISTANT
HAUTAIN HONTISH PAUGHTY STATELY
SUBLIME ARROGANT CAVALIER
DEIGNOUS FASTUOUS GLORIOUS
IMPERIAL INSOLENT ORGULOUS
PRIDEFUL SCORNFUL SNIFFISH SUPERIOR
TOPLOFTY PEREMPTORY
HAUL KEP LUG RUG TEW TOW TUG DRAG
DRAW DRAY HALE HURL JUNK PULL SKID
TAKE TOTE TRAM BOUSE DRAVE HEAVE
LIGHT ROUSE SNAKE TRACT TRICE
TRAVOY DRAUGHT SCHLEPP CORDELLE
HANDBANK
(— AFT) TALLY
(— DOWN) STRIKE
(— IN) GATHER
(— LOGS) TODE SLOOP SWAMP
SIWASH HANDBANK
(— OF FISH) TACK DRAVE
(— OF NET) LIFT
(— SAIL) BUNT CLEW CLUE
(— SHIP) SPRING
(— TO DECK) BOARD
(— UP AND FASTEN) TRICE
(— WITH TACKLE) BOUSE
HAUNT DEN HANT HOME HOWF KEEP
NEST WALK GHOST HOWFF SPOOK
STALK INFEST KENNEL OBSESS OUTLAY
PURSUE REPAIR PURLIEU FREQUENT
PRACTICE
(— OF ANIMALS) LIE HOME
(FAMILIAR —) SLAIT
HAUNTED SPOOKY
HAUNTING BESETTING
HAVE A AN OF OWN HOLD BOAST ENJOY
OUGHT WIELD POSSESS

HAVEN ARK HOPE PIER PORT HITHE
HARBOR HAVENET
HAVOC HOB HELL WASTE RAVAGE

HAWAII

BAY: POHUE HALAWA KIHOLO MAMALA
KAMOHIO KANEOHE WAIAGUA
KAWAIHAE MAUNALUA
BEACH: WAIKIKI
CAPITAL: HONOLULU
CHANNEL: AUA KAIWI KALOHI PAILOLO
COUNTY: MAUI KAUAI HAWAII HONOLULU
HARBOR: PEARL
HEAD: DIAMOND
ISLAND: MAUI OAHU KAUAI KAULA LANAI
NIIHAU MOLOKAI
MOUNTAIN: KAALA KOHALA KAMAKOU
MAUNAKEA LANAIHALE
MOUNTAIN RANGE: KOHALA KOOLAU
WAIANAE
NATIVE: KANAKA
STATE BIRD: GOOSE
STATE FLOWER: HIBISCUS
STATE NICKNAME: ALOHA
STATE TREE: CANDLENUT
TOWN: EWA AIEA HANA HILO LAIE PAIA
KAPAA KEAAU LIHUE MAILI KAILUA
KEKAHA PAHALA HONOKAA KAHULUI
KANEOHE WAHIAWA WAIANAE WAILUKU
HONOLULU PAPAIKOU
VALLEY: MANOA
VOLCANO: KILAUEA HUALALAI
MAUNAKEA MAUNALOA

HAWK IO EYAS KITE ALLAN BATER
BUTEO CADGE EYESS HOICK HOUGH
REACH RIVER STOOP BAWREL FALCON
FOOTER HIGGLE KEELIE MERLIN MUSKET
OSPREY PALLET PEDDLE RAMAGE
RAPTOR RIFLER SHIKRA VERMIN
BUZZARD GOSHAWK HAGGARD HARRIER
HERONER KESTREL LENTNER STANIEL
SWOOPER BRANCHER CARACARA
HARROWER LENTINER PASSAGER
ROUGHLEG SPARHAWK TALENTER
TARTARET MORTARBOARD
(CROP OF —) GORGE
(FEMALE —) FORMAL FORMEL
(MALE —) JACK TASSEL TERCEL
(YOUNG —) EYAS NIAS BOWET
BOWESS BRANCHER
HAWSER FAST WARP HEADLINE
HAWTHORN HAW MAY QUICK THORN
AIGLET MAYBUSH COCKSPUR
MAYBLOOM MAYTHORN QUICKSET
(FRUIT OF —) HAZEL PEGGLE
HAY HEI RIP MATH RAKH RISP FETTLE
STOVER WINDLIN SWEEPAGE
(— CUT FINE) CHAFF
(— PUT IN BARN) END
(BUNDLE OF —) TRUSS
(PILE OF —) TUMBLE
(ROW OF —) WINDROW
(SECOND-GROWTH —) EDDISH
(SMALL LOAD OF —) HURRY

(SMALL PIECE OF —) TATE
HAYLOFT LOFT TALLET SCAFFOLD
HAYMOW GOAF HAYLOFT OVERDEN
OVERHEAD
HAYSTACK COB PIKE RICK HOVEL
HAYRICK STACKAGE
HAZARD DIE LAY LOT JUMP PAWN RISK
WAGE JENNY LOSER PERIL CHANCE
DANGER NIFFER BALANCE IMPERIL
VENTURE ENDANGER JEOPARDY
HAZARDOUS NICE NASTY RISKY
CHANCY QUEASY UNSAFE
UNSURE PARLOUS PERILOUS
HAZE FOG URE FILM GLIN MIST REEK
SMOG TRUB DEVIL GAUZE HAZLE
SMEETH
(— AND SMOKE) SMAZE
HAZY DIM FOGGY MISTY MUZZY SMOKY
THICK VAGUE CLOUDY DREAMY
OBSCURE SMUISTY NEBULOUS
HEAD BIT BUT COP DON FAT MIR NAB
NOB PEN POW TOP BEAN BOSS CAPE
COCO CONK COSP CROP DATU DEAN
DOME HELM JOLE JOWL KAID KNOB
LEAD MAKE MASK NOLL PASH PATE
POLL RAIS TURN YEAD ALDER ATTIC
BLADE BLOCK BONCE CHIEF CHUMP
CROWN DATTO MAZER ONION RISER
SCALP SHODE SKULL START TIBBY
TROPE BELFRY BLANCH CABEZA CENTER
CHAULE COBBRA COCKER DAROGA
EXARCH GARRET GATHER HEADER
KAISER MAHANT MAZARD NAPPER
NODDLE PALLET RUBRIC SCONCE
CAPITAL CAPTAIN COCONUT COSTARD
COSTREL COXCOMB CRUMPET CUPHEAD
GENARCH HEADING HEGUMEN NUCLEUS
PRELATE TOPKNOT CALABASH
CEPHALON DECURION DIRECTOR
DUFFADAR FOUNTAIN HEADLINE
INITIATE PHYLARCH POINTING TOPPIECE
CAPERNOITIE
(— IN PARTICULAR DIRECTION)
STEM
(— OF ABBEY) ABBOT
(— OF ALEMBIC) MITER MITRE
(— OF BEAR, WOLF OR BOAR) HURE
(— OF CABBAGE) LOAF
(— OF CEREAL) EAR
(— OF CHAIR) MAKER
(— OF CLOVER) COB SUCKER
(— OF COLUMN) CHAPITER
(— OF COMET) COMA
(— OF CONVENT) ABBESS SUPERIOR
(— OF CRIME SYNDICATE) CAPO
(— OF DANDELION) BLOWBALL
(— OF DRILL BRACE) CUSHION
(— OF FAMILY) ALDER COARB COMARB
GOODMAN
(— OF FISH) JOWL
(— OF GANG) TINDAL
(— OF GOVERNMENT) MUKHTAR
(— OF GRAIN) ICKER
(— OF GUILD) ALDERMAN
(— OF HAIR) SUIT CRINE FLEECE
CHEVELURE
(— OF HARPOON) BOMB

(— OF HERRING) COB
(— OF JEWISH ACADEMY) GAON
(— OF LANCE) MORNE MOURNE
(— OF LOOM) JACQUARD
(— OF MONASTERY) HEGUMEN
(— OF MUSHROOM) BUTTON
(— OF MUSICAL INSTRUMENT)
SCROLL
(— OF NUNNERY) DAME
(— OF ORDER) MURSHID
(— OF PROJECTILE) OGIVE
(— OF RING) CHATON
(— OF RIVET) BULLHEAD FLATHEAD
SNAPHEAD
(— OF SEPT) COARB COMARB
(— OF STATE) CAUDILLO PRINCEPS
(— OF TAPEWORM) SCOLEX
(— OF TREE) COMA
(— OF 10 MONKS) DEAN
(— ON) SQUARE
(— PREMATURELY) BUTTON
(— USED AS TARGET) SARACEN
(BAKED SHEEP'S —) JAMES JEMMY
(BALD —) PILGARLIC
(BARBED —) FLUKE
(DRAGON'S —) RANU
(FLOWER —) DAISY ARNICA BUTTON
PINBALL
(FLOWER —S) CURD ANTHEMIS
(FROM — TO FOOT) CANAPE
(LATHE —) POPPET
(NAIL —) ROSEHEAD
(POPPY —) POST
(PRINTED —) BOXHEAD
(SEED — OF FLAX) HOPPE
(SHRUNKEN —) TSANTSA
HEADACHE HEAD SODA BUSTHEAD
HEADWARK MIGRAINE CEPHALALGY
HEADDRESS FLY TOP TOY APEX COIF
FRET HEAD HORN KELL PARE POUF TETE
TIRE TOUR AEGIS AMPYX CROWN GABLE
LAUTU PASTE POLOS PSHEM SHAKO
TIARA VITTA ALMUCE ATTIRE ATTOUR
BONNET CASQUE CORNET FAILLE
HENNIN KENNEL KULLAH MOBCAP
TIRING TUINGA COMMODE FLANDAN
MORTIER PSCHENT TABLITA THERESE
TRESSON TUTULUS BILIMENT BINNOGUE
BYCOCKET CAPRIOLE COIFFURE
HEADGEAR HEADTIRE KAFFIYEH
MASKETTE STEPHANE TRESSURE
(— OF DOGES) TOQUE
(— OF GODS) MODIUS
(— OF POPE) REGNUM
(— WITH LONG LAPPET) PINNER
(HIGH —) TOWER STEEPLE FONTANGE
(WIDOW'S —) BANDORE
HEADHUNTER LAKHER TAIYAL ATAIYAL
QUIANGAN
HEADING END HEAD STOW LEMMA
PILOT TROPE WICKET CAPTION DIPHEAD
HEADILY STENTON WITCHET FOREHAND
STENTING
HEADLAND KOP PEN RAS BILL CAPE
HEAD MULL NAZE NESS NOOK NOUP
PEAK SCAW THRUM FORELAND
PROMONTORY

HEADLINE HEAD LABEL BANNER CAPTION DROPLINE SCREAMER STREAMER SCAREMONGER

HEADLONG FULL RANK AHEAD HASTY PRONE STEEP SUDDEN RAMSTAM TANTIVY GADARENE HEADLING RECKLESS PRECIPITATE

HEADMAN BAAS JARL CHIEF DATTO MALIK PATEL POMBO VIDAN ATAMAN CABEZA HETMAN INDUNA LOWDAH LULUAI POTAIL TOPMAN KOMARCH ALDERMAN CABOCEER CAPITANO HEADSMAN KONOHIKI MALGUZAR MOKADDAM PENGHULU PRINCEPS STAROSTA TENIENTE

HEADMASTER HEAD RECTOR REGENT PRECEPTOR

HEADQUARTERS BASE DEPOT YAMEN AGENCY FONDACO EXCHANGE BATTALION

HEADSTRONG RASH COBBY RACKLE STOCKY UNRULY HOTSPUR RAMSTAM VIOLENT WAYWARD PERVERSE STUBBORN

HEADWAITER CAPTAIN

HEADWAY WAY DENT SEAWAY WAYGATE HEADROOM

HEAL CURE HALE MEND SAIN AMEND COVER LEECH SALVE SOUND WHOLE PHYSIC RECURE SUPPLE TEMPER WARISH CLEANSE GUARISH RECOVER REDRESS RESTORE MEDICATE
(— OVER) INCARN

HEALING IATRIC POWWOW BALSAMIC CURATION IATRICAL SANATION

HEALTH SAP HAIL HEAL SONS QUART SALEW LIKING PLEDGE SALUTE SANITY EUCRASY SLAINTE EUCRASIA TONICITY VALETUDE VALIDIT'
(GOOD —) PLIGHT VERDURE
(ILL —) SICKNESS
(NORMAL —) USUAL

HEALTHFUL HEALTHY HYGIENIC SALUTARY SANATORY SANITARY

HEALTHY FIT FIER FIRM HALE IRON SAFE SANE TIDY WELL BONNY HODDY QUART SOUND STOUT VALID ENTIRE HEARTY ROBUST BOUNCING LAUDABLE SALUTARY SANITARY VEGETOUS VIGOROUS
(PREF.) SANI

HEAP COP CUB HOT MOW PIE SOW TON BALE BULK DECK DESS HILL LEET PILE POKE POOK RAFF REEK RUCK SESS TASS TUMP AMASS CLAMP CLUMP COUCH CROWD SHOCK SORUS STACK WOPSE HIPPLE HOTTER ISLAND JALOPY MEILER OODLES RICKLE RUCKLE SCRAPE SORITE TOORIE BOUROCK CUMULUS ENDORSE HAYCOCK HAYRICK TOOROCK TUMMELS WINDROW CONGERIES ACCUMULATE ACCUMULATION
(— HAY) UNCOCK
(— OF DEAD BODIES) CARNAGE
(— OF GAME) QUARRY
(— OF GRAIN) BING
(— OF MORTAR) BINK

(— OF ORE) PANEL MONTON
(— OF PRODUCE) BURY CLAMP
(— OF REFUSE) BURROW BASURAL
(— OF RUBBISH) GAGING
(— OF SILVER ORE) TORTA
(— OF STONES) AHU MAN CAIRN SCRAE SCREE HURROCK MONTJOY
(— OF VEGETABLES) HOG
(— REPROACHES) KICK
(— TOGETHER) AGGEST HOWDER LUMBER CUMULATE
(— UP) HILL SACK AGGEST ACERVATE AGGERATE OVERHEAP
(COMBUSTIBLE —) PYRE
(MANURE —) HOTT MIXEN
(PROMISCUOUS —) RAFF

HEAR EAR LIST OYES OYEZ LEARN LITHE HARKEN LISTEN HEARKEN
(— DIRECTLY) IMPINGE

HEARER AUDIENT AUDITOR

HEARING EAR LIST OYER AUDIT SOUND ASSIZE AUDIENCE AUDITION

HEARKEN HARK HEAR HEED LIST TEND LITHE ATTEND HARKEN INTEND

HEARSAY REPORT ACCOUNT

HEART AB COR CORE GIST HATI PUMP RAAN SOUL YOLK BOSOM BOWEL CHEER JARTA QUICK BREAST CENTER CENTRE DEPTHS HASLET MIDDLE NATURE TICKER VISCUS COURAGE EMOTION ESSENCE FEELING
(— OF DIXIE) ALABAMA
(— OF ROTTEN TREE) DADDOCK
(DEAR —) DILIS

HEARTACHE SORROW

HEARTBREAK HOUSE
(AUTHOR OF —) SHAW
(CHARACTER IN —) DUNN ELLIE MANGAN HESIONE MAZZINI HUSHABYE SHOTOVER UTTERWORD

HEARTBURN PYROSIS

HEARTFELT DEAR DEEP REAL TRUE INFELT INWARD CORDIAL GENUINE SINCERE

HEARTH EARD SOLE TEST ASTRE CUPEL EARTH FOCUS FOGON FOYER SMOKE CHIMNEY

HEARTILY INLY AGOOD DEARLY FREELY WARMLY SHEERLY DINGDONG INWARDLY STRONGLY

HEART OF MIDLOTHIAN
(AUTHOR OF —) SCOTT
(CHARACTER IN —) MEG JOHN DAVID DEANS EFFIE MADGE BUTLER GEORGE JEANIE REUBEN GEORDIE PORTEUS STAUNTON ROBERTSON MURDOCKSON

HEARTY REAL WARM BUXOM COBBY FRECK HEAVY STOUT DEVOUT ENTIRE ROBUST STANCH BOBBISH CORDIAL EARNEST HEALTHY RAFFING SINCERE HEARTFUL VIGOROUS BOISTEROUS

HEAT HET HOT RUT SUN TAP BOIL FIRE GLOW SALT WARM ARDOR BEATH BROI' CALOR CAUMA CHAFE FEVER PRIDE PROUD STECH TEPOR TRIAL ACHAFE ANNEAL DEGREE DIGEST FERVOR HEATEN IGNITE SCORCH SEASON SIZZLE

SPARGE WARMTH CALCINE CALORIC
ENCHAFE FERMENT FLUSTER INCENSE
INFERNO PASSION SWELTER UPERIZE
CALIDITY
(— GENTLY) SOAK
(— OF BATTLE) PRESS
(— SCRAP IRON) BUSHEL
(— SWEETEN, AND SPICE) MULL
(— TOBACCO) SAP
(ROWING —) REPECHAGE
(SCORCHING —) EWDER
HEATED WARM FIERCE STEAMY
HEATER GAT GUN FIRE COCKLE PISTOL
SMOKER CHAFFER CHOFFER LATROBE
HEATH BENT YETH BESOM BRIAR BRIER
ERICA ERICAD COMMONS HEATHER
RHODORA CRAKEBERRY
(PREF.) ERICO
HEATHEN AKKUM PAGAN ETHNIC
PAYNIM GENTILE PROFANE SARACEN
GENTILIC
HEATHER BENT GRIG LING BROOM ERICA
HEATH HADDER
HEAVE GAG BUNG HEFT HOVE KECK LIFE
QUAP FETCH HOIST SCEND SURGE
BUCKLE KECKLE POPPLE ESTUATE
HEAVEN SKY HIGH ABOVE BLISS DYAUS
ETHER GLORY ASGARD CANAAN HIMMEL
SVARGA SWARGA URANUS WELKIN
KINGDOM OLYMPUS DEVALOKA
EMPYREAL EMPYREAN PARADISE
SVARLOKA
(12TH PART OF —) HOUSE
HEAVENLY ABOVE DIVINE ANGELIC
BLESSED URANIAN ETHEREAL OLYMPIAN
AMBROSIAL
HEAVEN'S MY DESTINATION
(AUTHOR OF —) WILDER
(CHARACTER IN —) BAT HERB BRUSH
COREY EFRIM LOUIE MCCOY BURKIN
CROFUT GEORGE JESSIE MARGIE MORRIE
DOREMUS QUEENIE ROBERTA BLODGETT
ELIZABETH
HEAVILY SOSS CLOIT CLYTE HEAVY
PLUMP SADLY SOUSE SWACK
HEAVINESS DOLE HEFT GLOOM POISE
WEIGHT GRAVITY
HEAVY FAT HOT SAD CLIT DEEP DOWF
DULL HARD BEEFY BURLY DENSE DUNCH
GRAVE GREAT GROSS HEFTY HOGGY
STIFF THARF THICK WROTH CHARGE
CLUMPY CLUMSY DOUGHY DRAGGY
HEARTY LEADEN LIVERY LOGGER
SODDEN STODGY STRONG STUPID
WOODEN INSIPID LABORED LIVERED
LUMPING MASSIVE ONEROUS OUTSIZE
PESANTE WEIGHTY CUMBROUS
GRIEVOUS PREGNANT THUMPING
PONDEROUS SATURNINE
HEBE (FATHER OF —) JUPITER
(HUSBAND OF —) HERCULES
(MOTHER OF —) JUNO
HECATE TRIVIA
(FATHER OF —) PERSES
(MOTHER OF —) ASTERIA
HECKLE BAIT GIBE HACK BADGER
HARASS HECTOR HATCHEL

HECTIC ETIK SEPTIC HECTIVE FEVERISH
FRENETIC FRENZIED
HECTOR BAIT HUFF BULLY HARRY TEASE
WORRY HARASS HECKLE BLUSTER
BRAVADO BROWBEAT
(FATHER OF —) PRIAM
(MOTHER OF —) HECUBA
(SLAYER OF —) ACHILLES
(WIFE OF —) ANDROMACHE
HECUBA (DAUGHTER OF —) POLYXENA
(FATHER OF —) DYMAS CISSEUS
(HUSBAND OF —) PRIAM
(SON OF —) PARIS HECTOR HELENUS
POLYDORUS
HEDDA GABLER (AUTHOR OF —)
IBSEN
(CHARACTER IN —) THEA BRACK
DIANA HEDDA EILERT GABLER GEORGE
TESMAN ELVSTED JULIANA LOVBERG
HEDGE BAR HAW HAY HYE OXER SAVE
BEARD EDDER FENCE FRITH FUDGE
HOVER MOUND QUICK COPPER FRIGHT
RADDLE ENCLOSE QUICKSET RUFFMANS
SEPIMENT SURROUND THICKSET
HEDGEHOG ORCHEN URCHIN ECHINUS
ERICIUS YLESPIL HEDGEPIG HERISSON
HEED CARK COME CURE GAUM HEAR
KEEP LOOK MIND NOTE RECK TEND TENT
VISE WARE YEME AWAIT TASTE VALUE
ATTEND INTENT NOTICE REGARD
REMARK REWARD CAUTION OBSERVE
RESPECT SUSPECT THOUGHT
OBSERVATION
HEEDFUL WARE ATTENT DILIGENT
VIGILANT REGARDFUL
HEEDLESS RASH BLIND DIZZY GIDDY
BLITHE REMISS UNWARY LANGUID
UNHEEDY CARELESS LISTLESS MINDLESS
RECKLESS WISTLESS NEGLECTFUL
HEEL TIP BUTT CALX FROG HIELD SPIKE
TALON DOTTLE INCLINE BOOTHEEL
(— IN) SHOUGH
(— OF GATE) HARR
(— OF HORSESHOE) SPONGE
(— OF SWORD BLADE) TALON
RICASSO
(— OVER) SEEL TILT CAREEN
HEFT WEIGHT
HEFTY HEAVY
HEIFER IO QUEY BULLER STOCKER
(— IN 2ND YEAR) STIRK
(YEARLING —) BURLING
HEIGHT SUM ACME ALTO APEX FELL
HIGH LOFT MOTE PINK TUNE CREST
HICHT STATE ALTURE INCHES CEILING
COMMAND HEIGHTH STATURE SUPREME
ALTITUDE EMINENCE HAUTESSE
SIDENESS VERTICAL ACROPOLIS
(— OF FASHION) GO
(— OF PROSPERITY) GLORY
(— OF ROOM) STUD STUDDING
(— OF SAIL) HOIST
(GREATEST —) NOON SUMMIT ZENITH
(ROCKY —) KNOT
HEIGHTEN ENDOW EXALT FORCE RAISE
ACCENT BOLSTER ENHANCE SUBLIME
(— FLAVOR) PETUNE

HEINOUS SWART CRYING WICKED
SCARLET FLAGRANT GRIEVOUS
HEIR SCION SPRIG COHEIR HERITOR
APPARENT PARCENER
(— APPARENT) ATHELING
(CELTIC —) TANIST
(FEMALE —) DISTAFF
HEIRESS BEGUM PORTIA FORTUNE
HERITRIX
HELENUS (FATHER OF —) PRIAM
(MOTHER OF —) HECUBA
(SON OF —) CESTRINUS
(WIFE OF —) ANDROMACHE
HELICOPTER HOVER COPTER CHOPPER
WINDMILL
(— TO REMOVE CASUALTIES)
DUSTOFF
(ARMED —) GUNSHIP
HELIOS HYPERION PHAETHON
(DAUGHTER OF —) CIRCE PASIPHAE
(FATHER OF —) HYPERION
(MOTHER OF —) THEIA
(SISTER OF —) EOS SELENE
(SON OF —) AEETES PHAETHON
HELIX COIL SPIRAL
HELL PIT HECK PAIN ABYSS AVICI
BLAZE DEUCE HADES SHEOL BLAZES
NARAKA TARTAR TOPHET TUNKET
ABADDON GEHENNA HELLBOX INFERNO
TORMENT TARTARUS BARATHRUM
PERDITION PANDEMONIUM
HELM KEY STEER STERN TIMON HELMET
TIMBER STEERAGE
HELMET CAP POT CASK HELM HOOD
ARMET CREST GALEA MAZER MOUND
BARBEL BEAVER CASQUE CASTLE
GALERA HEAUME MORION PALLET
SALADE SALLET TESTER BASINET
CASQUET GALERUM GALERUS AVENTAIL
BURGANET BURGONET HEADGEAR
KNAPSCAP SCHAPSKA SKULLCAP
TARNHELM TESTIERE
HELMSMAN PILOT STEER GLAUCUS
TIMONEER
HELP AID BOT ABET BACK BOOT CAST
LIFT STOP AVAIL BOOST FAVOR FRITH
HEEZE RESET SPEED START STEAD
YELDE ASSIST HELPER RELIEF REMEDY
SECOND SUCCOR UPTAKE BENEFIT
BESPEED BESTEAD CHEVISE COMFORT
FORWARD HELPING IMPROVE PRESIDY
PROMOTE REDRESS RELIEVE SUPPORT
SUSTAIN ADJUMENT BEFRIEND
SUFFRAGE
(— FORWARD) FRANK FURTHER
(— ON) ADVANCE
(— ONWARD) FORWARD
(— OUT) FIRK
(HIRED —) LABOR
HELPER AID CAD FOAL HELP MATE PAGE
ANSAR AIDANT BARBOY COOKEE DIENER
FLUNKY JUMPER NIPPER TENTER WAITER
ADJOINT ADJUNCT ADJUTOR ANCILLA
CASHBOY GALOPIN SUMPMAN
SWAMPER HELPMATE OFFSIDER
SCULLION TROUNCER
(— IN GLASSWORKS) SNAPPER

(BLACKSMITH'S —) STRIKER
(CHIMNEY SWEEP'S —) CHUMMY
(COOK'S —) SLUSHY
(COOPER'S —) TUBBIE
(HORSESHOER'S —) FLOORMAN
(PICKPOCKET'S —) BULKER
(YOUNG —) FOAL
HELPFUL GOOD AIDANT AIDFUL HELPLY
SECOND SPEEDY USEFUL ADJUVANT
HELPSOME OBLIGING SINGULAR
SERVICEABLE
HELPLESS NUMB SILLY ABJECT UNABLE
AIDLESS FORLORN FECKLESS HAVELESS
REDELESS
HELTER-SKELTER TAGRAG PELLMELL
HEM HUM WLO FELL SLIP WELT HEDGE
SPLAY PURFLE TURNUP HEMMING
TURNING SURROUND
(— AND HAW) HAVER
(— GLOVE) WRIST
(— IN) BOX LAP BEBAY BESET IMPALE
BESIEGE COMPASS ENCLOSE ENVIRON
STRAITEN SURROUND
(— IN FISH) EBB
(— OF SAIL) TABLING
(— OF TROUSERS) CUFF
HEMLOCK BUNK CASH KELK BENNET
CICUTA COWBANE DEATHIN SHINWOOD
HEMORRHAGE STAXIS APOPLEXY
BLEEDING HEMOPTOE PETECHIA
HEN FOWL BIDDY CHUCK LAYER BROODY
MABYER PULLET CLOCKER HOVERER
PARTLET LANGSHAN
(— THAT HAS NOT LAID) TOWDIE
(— WITH CHICKENS) CLUCK
(— WITH SHORT LEGS) GRIG
(BROODY —) SITTER
(FATTENED —) POULARD
(1-YEAR-OLD —) YEAROCK
HENCHMAN FELLOW SATRAP SERVANT
FOLLOWER RETAINER UNDERLING
HENPECK NAG
HENRY ESMOND (AUTHOR OF —)
THACKERAY
(CHARACTER IN —) HOLT FRANK
HENRY JAMES MOHUN ESMOND RACHEL
STUART BEATRIX FRANCIS
HENRY IV-PART I (AUTHOR OF —)
SHAKESPEARE
(CHARACTER IN —) JOHN OWEN PETO
BLUNT HENRY PERCY POINS EDMUND
SCROOP THOMAS VERNON WALTER
DOUGLAS HOTSPUR MICHAEL QUICKLY
RICHARD BARDOLPH FALSTAFF
GADSHILL MORTIMER ARCHIBALD
GLENDOWER LANCASTER
WESTMORELAND
HENRY IV-PART II (AUTHOR OF —)
SHAKESPEARE
(CHARACTER IN —) DAVY DOLL FANG
JOHN PETO WART BLUNT GOWER HENRY
POINS RUMOR SNARE FEEBLE MORTON
MOULDY PISTOL SCROOP SHADOW
SURREY THOMAS MOWBRAY QUICKLY
SHALLOW SILENCE TRAVERS WARWICK
BARDOLPH BULLCALF CLARENCE
FALSTAFF HARCOURT HASTINGS

HUMPHREY COLEVILLE LANCASTER
TEARSHEET WESTMORELAND
NORTHUMBERLAND
HENRY V (AUTHOR OF —)
SHAKESPEARE
(CHARACTER IN —) NYM GREY JAMY
YORK ALICE BATES COURT GOWER
HENRY LEWIS EXETER ISABEL PISTOL
SCROOP THOMAS BEDFORD BOURBON
CHARLES MONTJOY ORLEANS WARWICK
BARDOLPH BURGUNDY FLUELLEN
GRANDPRE RAMBURES WILLIAMS
ERPINGHAM KATHARINE MACMORRIS
SALISBURY GLOUCESTER
WESTMORELAND
HENRY VIII (AUTHOR OF —)
SHAKESPEARE
(CHARACTER IN —) ANNE VAUX
BUTTS DENNY HENRY SANDS BULLEN
LOVELL SURREY THOMAS WOLSEY
ANTHONY BRANDON CRANMER NORFOLK
SUFFOLK CAMPEIUS CAPUCIUS
CROMWELL GARDINER GRIFFITH
NICHOLAS PATIENCE GUILDFORD
KATHARINE BUCKINGHAM
ABERGAVENNY
HENRY VI-PART I (AUTHOR OF —)
SHAKESPEARE
(CHARACTER IN —) JOAN JOHN LUCY
HENRY BASSET EDMUND TALBOT
THOMAS VERNON ALENCON BEDFORD
CHARLES RICHARD SUFFOLK WARWICK
WILLIAM BEAUFORT BURGUNDY
FASTOLFE GARGRAVE MARGARET
MORTIMER REIGNIER GLANSDALE
LAPUCELLE SALISBURY WOODVILLE
GLOUCESTER PLANTAGENET
HENRY VI-PART II (AUTHOR OF —)
SHAKESPEARE
(CHARACTER IN —) SAY CADE DICK
HUME IDEN JOHN VAUX HENRY
GOFFE HENRY PETER SMITH EDWARD
GEORGE HORNER SCALES ELEANOR
HOLLAND MATTHEW MICHAEL RICHARD
SIMPCOX STANLEY SUFFOLK WARWICK
BEAUFORT CLIFFORD HUMPHREY
JOURDAIN MARGARET SOMERSET
STAFFORD ALEXANDER SALISBURY
SOUTHWELL BUCKINGHAM
BOLINGBROKE PLANTAGENET
HENRY VI-PART III (AUTHOR OF —,
SHAKESPEARE
(CHARACTER IN —) BONA HUGH JOHN
HENRY LEWIS MARCH EDMUND EDWARD
EXETER GEORGE OXFORD RIVERS
BOURBON NORFOLK RICHARD RUTLAND
STANLEY WARWICK CLIFFORD HASTINGS
MARGARET MONTAGUE MORTIMER
PEMBROKE SOMERSET STAFFORD
MONTGOMERY PLANTAGENET
WESTMORELAND NORTHUMBERLAND
HEPHAESTUS LEMNIAN
(FATHER OF —) ZEUS
(MOTHER OF —) HERA
(WIFE OF —) CHARIS
HERA JUNO
(FATHER OF —) KRONOS

(HUSBAND OF —) ZEUS
HERALD BODE LYON USHER BEADLE
DECLARE FORERUN PREFACE STENTOR
BLAZONER PRECURSE PROCLAIM
ROTHESAY MESSENGER
HERB ANU APE PIA RUE UDO WAD ALOE
ANET ANYU ARUM COUS DILL HEMP IRID
POLY RAPE SAGE SOLA WOAD WORT
YAMP YARB AWIWI BLITE BRUSH CHIVE
CREAT CROUT DAGGA DAISY DRABA
GALAX GAURA GILIA GRASS HOSTA
LOASA LUFFA MEDIC MUNGO NANCY
SEDGE SOLAH STOCK SULLA THYME
ZIZIA ARALIA ARNICA AXSEED BAGPOD
BAMBAN BANANA BLINKS BORAGE
CATGUT CENIZO CICELY CISTUS CLOVER
COCASH COLEUS COWISH COWPEA
ELODEA ENDIVE ERYNGO FENNEL
GALAXY GINGER HARMEL HYSSOP
KOCHIA KRIGIA KRIGLA LOOFAH LOVAGE
RAMTIL RATTLE ROBERT SESAME SESELI
SHEVRI WASABI ABRONIA ALPINIA
ALTHAEA ALYSSUM AMORPHA AMSONIA
ANCHUSA ANEMONE ANGELON ARACHIS
BABROOT BARTSIA BIRDEYE BLINKER
BONESET BUGSEED BUGWEED CHICORY
CUDWEED CULVERS DEWDROP DYEWEED
EPISCIA ERODIUM FREESIA FUMMORY
GERBERA GINSENG GOSMORE GOUAREE
GUAYULE GUNNERA HARMALA HEDEOMA
HENBANE HERBLET IRESINE ISOLOMA
JONQUIL LABIATE LEWISIA LINNAEA
MARANTA MIMULUS MUDWEED
MUDWORT MULLEIN MUSTARD NAILROD
NEMESIA NIEVETA PAVONIA PETUNIA
PINESAP PINWEED PUCHERA ROSELLE
SAFFLOR SALSIFY SEEDBOX SKIRRET
SOWBANE SPIGNEL STACHYS
(— COUNTERACTING POISON)
CANCER
(— OTHER THAN GRASS) FORB
(AROMATIC —) MINT ANISE CLARY
CATNIP CAAPEBA CHERVIL DITTANY
(BIENNIAL —) LEEK PARSLEY ANGELICA
(BULBOUS —) LILY CANNA ALLIUM
CRINUM GARLIC NERINE SQUILL
BABIANA SHALLOT DOGTOOTH
SLANGKOP
(FABULOUS —) MOLY PANAX PANACE
(FLOATING —) FROGBIT
(FORAGE —) FITCHES GOITCHO
(MEDITERRANEAN —) CRAMBE
(POISONOUS —) CONIUM HEMLOCK
MONKSHOOD
HERBAGE HAY BITE GRASS GRAZE PICHI
ADONIS SACATE ZACATE GRAZING
HERBICIDE IPE DIURON SILVEX DALAPON
MONURON PARAQUAT PICLORAM
PROPANIL SIMAZINE
HERCULES ERCLES ALCIDES HERSHEF
OETAEUS OVILLUS HERAKLES
(BROTHER OF —) IPHICLES
(CAPTIVE OF —) IOLE
(FATHER OF —) JUPITER
(MOTHER OF —) ALCMENA
(WIFE OF —) HEBE MEGARA DEIANIRA
HERD BOW MOB BAND CREW GAME

GANG HEAD ROUT RUCK TEAM TRIP
DROVE FLOCK HEARD TROOP CAVIYA
CHOUSE HIRSEL HUDDLE MANADA
MEINIE REMUDA SPREAD THRAVE
CREAGHT RANGALE SHEPHERD
(— CATTLE) TAIL WRANGLE
(— OF CATTLE) FLOTE
(— OF COLTS) RAG
(— OF HORSES) RACE HARRAS
(— OF SEALS) PATCH
(— OF WHALES) GAM
(— OF WILD SWINE) SOUNDER
HERDSMAN AMOS SENN GAUCHO
HERDER LOOKER PASTOR HERDBOY
LLANERO THYRSIS VAQUERO BEASTMAN
DAMOETAS GARTHMAN NEATHERD
PASTORAL PASTURER RANCHERO
SWANHERD WRANGLER
HERE ADSUM READY WHERE HEREAT
HITHER PRESENT
(— AND THERE) ABOUT ABROAD
AROUND PASSIM SPARSIM
HEREAFTER BEYOND
HEREDITARY INBORN INNATE KINDLY
LINEAL PATERNAL
HERESY DOCETISM KETZEREI MISBELIEF
HERETIC BUGGER KETZER ZINDIQ
LOLLARD PATARIN PROFANE SECTARY
JUDAIZER MISCREANT SABELLIUS
MISBELIEVER
HERMES MERCURY AGORAIOS
CYLLENIUS
(FATHER OF —) ZEUS
(MOTHER OF —) MAIA
HERMIA (BELOVED OF —) LYSANDER
(FATHER OF —) EGEUS
HERMIONE (FATHER OF —) MENELAUS
(HUSBAND OF —) PYRRHUS
(MOTHER OF —) HELEN
HERMIT ARME MUNI HANIF MINIM
ANCHOR SANTON SULLEN ASCETIC
EREMITE RECLUSE TAPASVI ANCHORET
MARABOUT SOLITARY
HERO CID KIM RAB AJAX EGIL IDAS KAMI
MAUI NALA NATA OFFA RINK YIMA
ADAPA BERNE DEBON ETANA FAUST
GHAZI HODER HOTHR IRAYA KIPPS
MARKO ORSON TASSO TIMON VOTAN
EGMONT FIGARO GIDEON GOLIAS HEROIC
IASION IOLAUS MAUGIS MINYAS OSSIAN
PELHAM PENROD RIENZI ROLAND
RUSTAM SIGURD TARZAN USHEEN
VATHEK ALCESTE BOGATYR DEMIGOD
FAUSTUS GLUSKAP INGOMAR JAMSHID
MACBETH MANRICO MARMION MAZEPPA
ORLANDO OTHELLO PALADIN RAFFLES
TANCRED THALABA THESEUS TROILUS
ULYSSES VOLPONE WERTHER WIDSITH
WIELAND ACADEMUS ARGONAUT
CHAMPION FANSHAWE FERUMBAS
FRITHJOF GAEDHEAL GILGAMES
LAMMIKIN MALAGIGI MORGANTE
OROONOKO PALMERIN PARSIFAL
PERICLES RASSELAS RODOMONT
SUPERMAN TRISTRAM WAVERLEY
(LOVER OF —) LEANDER
(TRIBAL —) JUDGE

HEROIC EPIC FELL GREAT NOBLE EPICA,
FEATLY EXTREME GALLANT VALIANT
FEARLESS HEROICAL HOMERIAN
INTREPID SPLENDID
HEROIN JUNK SCAG SKAG SNOW HORSE
SMACK
HEROINE AIDA EMMA MIMI RUTH JULIE
MEDEA NORMA SEDNA THAIS ESTHER
FEDORA GUDRUN HELENA JUDITH JULIET
MARTHA MIGNON PAMELA PHEDRE
RAMONA ROMOLA SALOME SILVIA
TRILBY UNDINE ERMINIA EVELINA
GALATEA GINEVRA GRAINNE HEROESS
MONIMIA SHIRLEY ZENOBIA ZULEIKA
ATALANTA ISABELLA MARGARET
PATIENCE POMPILIA ROSMUNDA
SOFRONIA
HEROISM VALOR BRAVERY COURAGE
PROWESS
HERON QUA POKE SOCO CRAIG CRANE
EGRET FRANK HERNE PADDY QUAWK
YABOA AIGRET GAULIN KIALEE KOTUKU
QUAKER SQUAWK BITTERN CRABIER
GOLIATH HANDSAW QUABIRD SQUACCO
BOATBILL GAULDING HERONSEW
UMBRETTE
HERRING ALEC CHUB BLOAT DORAB
HILSA MARAY KIPPER POLLAN TAILOR
BLOATER CLUPEID NAILROD ROLLMOP
SHADINE BLUEBACK BRISLING BUCKLING
CROPSHIN GRAYBACK QUODDIES
SCUDDAWN STRADINE
(FEMALE —) RAUN
(LAKE —) KIYI CISCO
(RED —) CAPON SOLDIER
(SMOKED —) BLOATER
(YOUNG —) COB BRIT SILD SILE SILL
SOIL WILE MATIE SPRAT SARDINE
SPERLING
(2, 3 OR 4 —S) WARP
HESITANT SHY CAGY CHARY GROPING
HALTING SUSPENSE
(NOT —) FACILE
HESITATE COY HEM STAY STOP CHECK
CRANE DEMUR DOUBT FORCE PAUSE
STAND STICK SUSSY WAVER BOGGLE
FALTER HANKER LINGER MAMMER
RELUCT SCOTCH TARROW TARTLE
BALANCE PROFFER SCRUPLE STAGGER
STAMMER SWITHER THRIMBLE
(— IN SPEAKING) HACKER
HESITATION HANG HINK WAND PAUSE
STAND STICK SUSSY SWITHER
HETEROGENEOUS MIXED MOTLEY
UNLIKE DIVERSE PIEBALD ASSORTED
HEW CUT HAG CHIP SNAG STUB SHRED
SLICE
(— OUT) CARVE
(— STONE) CHAR
HIATUS GAP BREAK CHASM BREACH
HIATAL LACUNA
HIBERNATE SHACK WINTER SLUMBER
HIBERNATING LATITANT
HICCUP YEX YOX HICK HOCKET HOQUET
SINGULTUS
HICK BOOR HIND JAKE BACON BUSHMAN
CORNBALL

HICKORY NOGAL PIGNUT BULLNUT SHAGBARK

HIDDEN HID SHY DEEP DERN LOST TECT BLIND CLOSE DOGGO DUSKY PERDU PRIVY ARCANE BURIED COVERT INNATE LATENT MASKED MYSTIC OCCULT SECRET VEILED BOSOMED CLOUDED COVERED CRYPTIC OBSCURE RECLUSE SUBTILE ABDITIVE ABSTRUSE CRYPTOUS HIDEAWAY PALLIATE SCREENED SECLUDED SNEAKING CRYPTICAL RECONDITE

HIDE HOD WRY BUFF BURY CASE CROP DARK DERN FELL FELT HILL HOOD JOUK LEAN MASK PELL PELT SCAB SKIN SKUG SNUG STOW VEIL WELL BELIE BELLY BLIND CACHE CLOAK CLOUD COUCH COVER DITCH EARTH FLANK GLOSS LAYNE LOSHE MANSE PLANT SHADE SPOIL STASH STEER TAPIS BURROW BUSHEL CASATE EMBOSS ENCAVE ENWOMB FOREST HUDDLE IMBOSK MANENT PELAGE SCREEN SHADOW SHIELD SHROUD ABSCOND CONCEAL COWHIDE EMBOWEL FLAUGHT OBCLUDE OVERLAY SECLUDE SECRETE SPREADY TAPPICE CARUCATE DISGUISE ENSCONCE HIDELAND HOODWINK PALLIATE PLOWLAND SQUIRREL SUPPRESS CLANDESTINE
(— AS AN EEL) MUD
(— IN WOODS) WOOD BUSHWACK
(— UNDER) BUSHEL
(CALF'S —) DEACON
(DRESSED —S) LEATHER
(HALF OF —) BEND
(HAVING SOFT —) MELLOW
(SHEEP'S —) SLAT
(TANNED —) CROP
(THICKEST —S) BACKS
(UNDRESSED —) KIP
(PL.) JUFTI JUFTS

HIDEOUS FELL GASH GRIM UGLY AWFUL TOADY DEFORM GRIMLY GRISLY HORRID ODIOUS OGRISH GHASTLY DEFORMED DREADFUL FIENDISH GRUESOME HORRIBLE SHOCKING TERRIBLE MONSTROUS

HIGH UP AIRY DEAR MAIN RANK TALL ALOFT BRENT CHIEF CLOSE FIRST GREAT LOFTY MERRY NOBLE SHARP STEEP BOMBED COSTLY SHRILL ZONKED EMINENT EXALTED HAUGHTY STICKLE SUBLIME TOPPING VIOLENT ELEVATED FOREMOST PIERCING TOWERING
(— AND MIGHTY) HOGEN
(— IN CHROMA) STRONG
(— IN PITCH) ALT ACUTE
(— IN RANK) MUCH
(— PITCH) ORTHIAN
(MOST —) SERENE
(PRETTY —) STIFFISH
(VERY —) TAUNT RAREFIED

HIGHBROW EGGHEAD
HIGH-CLASS CLASSY UPSTAGE
HIGH-HANDED CAVALIER
HIGHLAND RAND CERRO

HIGHLANDER GAEL TARTAN NAINSEL PLAIDMAN REDSHANK TREWSMAN UPLANDER
(PL.) TREWS TARTAN

HIGHLIGHT ADORN HEIGHTEN PINPOINT SALIENCE

HIGH-SPIRITED CRANK FIERY FIERCE LIVELY GALLANT GINGERY RAMPANT CAVALIER VASCULAR

HIGH-STRUNG TENSE NERVOUS

HIGHWAY VIA WAY BELT ITER PATH PIKE ROAD TOBY BOLOS ARTERY CAUSEY COURSE RUMPAD SKYWAY STREET BELTWAY CALZADA FREEWAY RAMPIRE THRUWAY ARTERIAL AUTOBAHN BROADWAY CAUSEWAY CHAUSSEE HIGHROAD MOTORWAY SPEEDWAY

HIGHWAYMAN PAD RIDER SCAMP BANDIT CUTTER PADDER RODMAN BRIGAND FOOTPAD LADRONE PRANCER RODSMAN TOBYMAN BIDSTAND DAMASTES HIGHTOBY HIJACKER LANCEMAN OUTRIDER BANDOLERO

HIKE MUSH MARCH TRAMP RAMBLE

HILARIOUS MAD RORTY JOVIAL JOCULAR RAUGHTY CHIRPING GLORIOUS

HILARITY GIG JOY GLEE LAUGH MIRTH GAIETY GAYETY DEVILRY JOLLITY WHOOPEE MERRIMENT

HILL BEN DEN DUN HOE KOP LOW PUY VAN ALTO BANK BERG BRAE BULT BUMP COTE DAGH DOWN DRUM FELL HIGH LUMP MESA MOOR MOTE NOUP PAHA ZION CERRO CLIFF COAST HEUGH KNOCK MORRO MOUND MOUNT SWELL TELLE WATCH ASCENT BARROW BEACON COBBLE COLLIS COPPLE CUESTA HEIGHT HEUVEL LOMITA SPRUNT CAELIAN CAPITOL COLLINE DRUMLIN NUNATAK PICACHO VIMINAL AREOPAGY DRUMLOID FOOTHILL MONTICLE QUIRINAL MONADNOCK
(— OF SAND) DENE DUNE
(— OF STRATIFIED DRIFT) KAME
(— UP) MOLD
(BROAD-TOPPED —) LOMA
(CONICAL —) LAW LAP PINGO
(CRAGGY —) TOR
(FORTIFIED —) RATH
(HIGH —) BEN
(ISOLATED —) HUM TOFT BARGH BUTTE
(LAST —) STRONE
(LOW —) HOW BAND WOLD KOPPIE SOWBACK
(NIPPLELIKE —) PAP
(NORTH AFRICAN —) DJEBEL
(RESIDUAL —) CATOCTIN
(ROUNDED —) DODD HONE MAMELON
(SHARP-POINTED —) KIP KIPP PIKE
(SMALL —) KNAP KNOLL KOPJE KOPPIE HILLOCK MOLEHILL
(STEEP —) BREW BROW STILL
(STONY —) ROACH
(SUGAR-LOAF —) SPITZKOP
(WOODED —) HOLT HURST
(PREF.) BUNO

HILLOCK HOW LOW NOB BOSS BULT DOWN KAME KNAP KNOB TERP TOFT TUMP BERRY HEAVE HURST KNOCK KNOLL KOPJE MOUND TOMAN BARROW BURROW COPPET HILLET HUMMOCK MAMELON TUMMOCK TUMULUS MOLEHILL

HILLSIDE BENT BRAE COTE EDGE CLEVE FALDA SLADE FELLSIDE SIDEHILL

HILLTOP DOD NAB PIKE RISE KNOLL

HILT HAFT BASKET POIGNET HANDGRIP
(— OF DAGGER) DUDGEON

HIND ROE CONY HINE HINT CONEY HEARST HINDER VENISON CABRILLA

HINDER BAR DAM KEP LET MAR ROB CLOG HELP SLOW SLUG STAY STOP TENT WARN AFTER BLOCK CHEAT CHECK CHOKE CRAMP DEBAR DELAY DETER EMBAR ESTOP HEDGE SLOTH THROW TRASH ARREST CUMBER DETAIN FORBID FORLET HAMPER HARASS HINNER IMPEDE IMPEND INJURE RETARD RETRAL SCOTCH TAIGLE UNHELP ABSTAIN DEPRIVE FORELAY IMPEACH INHIBIT OCCLUDE PREVENT TRACHLE ENCUMBER HANDICAP IMPEDITE OBSTRUCT PRECLUDE PROHIBIT POSTICOUS

HINDRANCE BAR LET RUB BALK CURB REIN SLUG STAY STOP BLOCK CHECK DELAY HITCH TRASH ARREST CUMBER DENIAL HINDER OBJECT UNHELP SHACKLE UNSPEED DISCOUNT DRAWBACK HOLDBACK OBSTACLE PULLBACK

HINDU BABU BABOO SUDRA BABHAN BANIAN BANYAN GENTOO JAJMAN KALWAR KHATRI NAYADI SHUDRA THAKUR VAISYA MUSAHAR VAIRAGI

HINGE RUN BAND BUTT FLAP HARR TRIM TURN CROOK GEMEL JOINT MOUNT NODUS SKELL SKEWL TWIST DEPEND GARNET GEMMEL GIMMER HANGLE JIMMER SNIBEL COXCOMB FULCRUM HOLDBACK
(— OF BIVALVE SHELL) CARDO
(— OF HELMET) CHARNEL
(— TOGETHER) SCISSOR
(HALF OF —) FLAP
(PHILATELIC —) STICKER

HINT CUE ASTE ITEM MINT TANG WIND WINK CHEEP IMPLY INFER POINT SPELL STEER TOUCH TRACE WHIFF ALLUDE GLANCE OFFICE SMATCH TIPOFF WHEEZE INKLING LEADING MEMENTO POINTER SUGGEST UMBRAGE WHISPER WRINKLE ALLUSION INDICATE INNUENDO INTIMATE TELLTALE

HIP HEP COXA HUCK PITCH HAUNCH HUCKLE HIPBERRY
(— JOINT) THURL
(— OF ROSE) BERRY SHOOP
(— OF TARGET) SPOT

HIPBONE FINBONE PINBONE EDGEBONE SIDEBONE

HIPPOLYTUS (FATHER OF —) THESEUS
(MOTHER OF —) HIPPOLYTE
(STEPMOTHER OF —) PHAEDRA

HIPPOPOTAMUS HIPPO ZEEKOE BEHEMOTH BUNODONT

HIRE FEE JOB HAVE MEED RENT SIGN WAGE PREST WAGES EMPLOY ENGAGE RETAIN SALARY BESPEAK CHARTER CONDUCE CONDUCT FREIGHT STIPEND
(— CATTLE) TACK

HISS BLOW FUFF HISH HIZZ QUIZ SISS SIZZ GOOSE WHISS FISSLE FIZZLE SIFFLE WHOOSH WHISTLE SIBILATE
(— OF SWORD) SOUGH

HISSING BIRD AFFLATUS SIBILANT

HISTORIAN MORONI STORIER ANNALIST

HISTORICAL GENETIC

HISTORIOGRAPHER SKALD

HISTORY STORY ANNALS LEGEND RECORD SURVEY ACCOUNT ANCESTRY PROPHECY RELATION
(— OF EXPERIENCES) MEMOIRS
(— OF JAPAN) KOJIKI
(LIFE —) COURSE
(TRIBAL —) PHYLOGENY

HISTRIONIC ACTORY ACTORISH ACTRESSY

HIT BAT BOP BOX DOT GET HAT JOB PEG PIP WOW BASH BEAT BELT BIFF BLOW BOFF BUST CHOP CONK DONG FOUR GOLD NAIL PINK POKE PUCK PUNK RUFF SLAM SOCK SWAT SWIP TAKE TANK TUNK WART WIPE ANGLE CHECK CLOUT CLUNK CROWN FIVER FLICK GOUFF KNOCK POTCH PRANG PUNTA PUNTO SCORE SLASH SLOSH SMASH SMITE SWIPE TAINT TOUCH VENUE SCLAFF VOLLEY ATTAINT BOFFOLA CONNECT MUZZLER SANDBAG WHERRE BLUDGEON BOUNDARY LENGTHER STRICKEN
(— A KEY) STRIKE
(— BALL) CUR FLY DINK DRIVE SHOOL SKITE SNICK
(— BUNT) DRAG
(— GAME) STOP
(— GENTLY) BABY
(— GOLF BALL) CAN BLAST EXPLODE
(— HARD) DUMP SLOG SLUG PASTE SKELP SOUSE DEVVEL STOUSH STONKER
(— IN BOXING) LEADOFF
(— IN FIELD HOCKEY) CORNER
(— IN TILTING) TAINT
(— IT OFF) CLICK
(— LIGHTLY) KISS
(— ON BULL'S-EYE) GOLD
(— POORLY) DUB
(— SHARPLY) CLIP
(— SUDDENLY) ZAP
(— TOGETHER) CLASH
(— UPON) FIND
(— WITH FOOT) KICK SPURN
(BASE —) BINGLE DOUBLE SAFETY SINGLE TRIPLE SCRATCH SMOTHER
(CRICKET —) SLOG BOUNDARY
(EASILY —) SITTING
(FENCING —) HAI HAY VENUE
(SHARP —) LICK
(SMASH —) SOCKEROO

HIT-OR-MISS CASUAL CHANCE HOBNOB CARELESS

HIVE GUM BIKE SKEP PYCHE STAND STATE STOCK SWARM APIARY ALVEARY BEEHIVE SWARMER

(— PLACED OVER ANOTHER) SUPER

HOARD HEAM POSE SAVE AMASS HUTCH MISER STOCK COFFER MAGPIE MUCKER STOUTH GENIZAH HUSBAND SQUIRREL TREASURE

HOARDER MUCKER STORER HUSBAND

HOARFROST RAG HOAR RIME RIND

HOARSE RAW FOGGY GRUFF HEAZY HUSKY RAWKY ROKEY ROUGH ROUPY STOUR CROAKY CROUPY RASPED ROUPIT GRATING RAUCOUS

HOARSENESS FROG ROUP QUACK RAUCITY HASKNESS BARYPHONIA

HOARY AGED GRAY GREY HOAR WHITE FROSTY ANCIENT HOARISH INCANOUS

HOAX BAM COD FUN GAG HUM KID RAG RIG BILK DUPE FAKE GAFF GEGG GUNK JOSH QUIZ RAMP RUSE SELL SHAM SKIT CHEAT FRAUD GREEN SHAVE SPOOF TRICK WINDY CANARD DIDDLE HUMBUG STRING BLAFLUM DECEIVE FLIVVER ARTIFICE

HOBBLE GIMP LOCK SPAN BUNCH HILCH HITCH STILT STUMP HABBLE HIRPLE HOPPLE LANGLE LANKET TOLTER CRAMBLE CRAMMEL CRIPPLE SHACKLE SHAFFLE SPANCEL STAGGER TRAMMEL SIDELINE

HOBBY BUG FAD HOBBLER AVOCATION

HOBGOBLIN (ALSO SEE GOBLIN) COW HAG HOB PUG PUCK BOGEY BUCCA BUGAN POKER SCRAT SPOOK BOODIE BOWSIE EMPUSA SPOORN BUGABOO RAWHEAD BOGGLEBO COLTPIXY POPLEMAN PUCKEREL WORRICOW

HOBNAIL HOB HUB PUNCH TACKET

HOBO BO BUM STIFF

HOCK HAM HOX HEEL HOUGH HUXEN SINEW SKINK JARRET CAMBREL GAMBREL HOCKSHIN SUFFRAGO

HOCKEY HURLY HORKEY HURLEY SHINNY CAMMOCK HURLBAT

HOCUS-POCUS FAKERY HUMBUG FLIMFLAM QUACKERY

HODGEPODGE CHOW HASH MESS OLIO RAFF SALAD BOLLIX JUSSEL MAGPIE MEDLEY MELANGE CHIVAREE CHOWCHOW HOTCHPOT KEDGEREE MISHMASH PASTICHE PORRIDGE SCRAMPUM PATCHWORK

HOE BROD CHIP CLAT HACK HOWE SHIM CLAUT LARRY THIRD CHONTA HACKER PAIDLE PECKER SARCLE GRUBBER PULASKI SCRAPER SCUFFLE GRIFFAUN

(— HANDLE) STAIL

(HORSE —) NIDGET NIGGET

HOG BEN SOW BOAR GALT GILT PORK DUROC GRUNT SHOAT BARROW HOGGET HOGGIE PORKER PORKET YORKER BACONER BUTCHER GRUNTER HOGLING MONTANA BABIRUSA BUNODONT HEREFORD LANDRACE VICTORIA RAZORBACK

HOGSHEAD CASK CARDEL

HOGWASH DRAFF SWASH SWILL PIGWASH

HOIST FID HEFT KILT LIFT SWAY SWIG WHIM WHIP CRANE ERECT HEAVE HEEZE HEIST HOICK HOOSH HORSE RAISE WEIGH JAMMER LAUNCH LIFTER TUGGER WHIMSY DERRICK

(— A LOG) CANNON

(— ANCHOR) CAT

(— FISH) BRAIL

(— FLUKES) FISH FANCIER

HOLD HOD OWN BULK DEEM FEEL FILL GAUM GIVE GRIT HANK HAVE HELD HEND HILT HOLE HOLT HOOK KEEP LOCK NAIL RELY SOFT STOW AFONG AHOLD AHOLT CARRY CINCH CLAMP GRASP GRIPE LATCH LEASE PAUSE POISE ROCCA STORE WOULD ADHERE ADSORB ARREST CLUTCH HANDLE INTERN MANURE OCCUPY REGARD REPUTE RETAIN ADJUDGE CAPTURE CLAUGHT CONFINE ENCLOSE FERMATA GRAPPLE HOLDING RECEIVE SEIZURE SUBSIST SUSPEND COMPRISE FOOTHOLD FOREHOLD HANDFAST HANDHOLD HEADLOCK HOLDFAST PURCHASE THURROCK

(— A BELIEF) SUPPOSE

(— AS PRECIOUS) TREASURE

(— AS TRUE) ACCEPT

(— AT BAY) DOMPT

(— BACK) STOP WELL BELAY LAYNE BOGGLE DETAIN FLINCH HINDER RETIRE SHRINK CONTAIN DETRACT FORBEAR RECLAIM REFRAIN SLACKEN HESITATE SUPPRESS WITHDRAW

(— BACK ON LEASH) TRASH

(— CLOSELY) CRADLE CUDDLE

(— CONSULTATION) ADVISE

(— CORONER'S INQUEST) CROWN

(— DEAR) CHERISH

(— DOWN) PINION CONTAIN

(— FAST) FIX BAIL BITE CLING SNARL CLENCH CLINCH SECURE STABLE

(— FIRMLY) CLIP INSIST

(— FORTH) SPIEL

(— FROM) ABSTAIN

(— GOOD) APPLY SERVE

(— IN CHECK) REIN GOVERN REPRESS COMPESCE

(— IN CONTEMPT) SMILE DISPRIZE

(— IN PLACE) ANCHOR

(— OF PLASTER) KEY

(— ON COURSE) STEM FETCH STAND

(— ON FINAL NOTE) TENOR

(— ON SHORE) LANDFAST

(— OUT) DREE LAST STAY OFFER EXTEND PROTEND STRETCH SUSTAIN

(— PROTECTIVELY) LAP

(— TIGHTLY) CLIP STICK

(— TOGETHER) BOND COHERE CONSIST

(— UP) BEAR HALT STAY ERECT HEIST IMPEDE UPHOLD RUMPADE SUPPORT SUSTAIN TRADUCE

(— UP BY LEADING STRINGS) DADE
(— UP TO CONTEMPT) FLEER
(— UP TO PUBLIC NOTICE) GIBBET
(SHIP'S —) HOLE HOLL FISHHOLD
(WRESTLING —) CROTCH KEYLOCK
CHANCERY HEADLOCK SCISSORS
SIDEHOLD
HOLDER WYE HAVER STOCK DIPPER
SOCKET CRACKER CASSETTE JAGIRDAR
(— FOR CARRYING GLASS) FRAIL
(— FOR COIL) SPOOL
(— FOR CUP) ZARF
(— FOR FLOWERS) FROG
(— FOR TOOLS) TURRET
(— FOR WHIP) BUCKET
(— OF GRANT) ENAMDAR
(ALLOTMENT —) CLERUCH
(CANDLE —) SPIDER GIRANDOLE
(LAMP —) BODY
HOLDING HAL COPY HOLD TAKE
GRASP HONOR HADDIN POFFLE TENANT
TENURE TENANCY COMMENDA
(— DIFFERENT OPINIONS) APART
(— FAST) IRON
(— OF OFFICE) OCCUPATION
(— OF SECURITIES) CARRY
HOLDUP HEIST STICKUP
HOLE CAN CUP EYE GAP PIT TAP BORE
BURY LEAK MAIL MUSE PECK PINK POCK
PUKA WANT CHINK DITCH FLOSS FOSSE
MEUSE SINUS SLACK SQUAT TEWEL
THIRL THURL BURROW CAVITY CENTER
CENTRE CRANNY CRATER EYELET
HOLLOW LACUNA OBTAIN OILLET PIERCE
POCKET POUNCE WEEPER BLOWOUT
BOGHOLE BOTHROS DIBHOLE EYEHOLE
KEYHOLE MORTICE MORTISE OILHOLE
OPENING PINHOLE POTHOLE SCUTTLE
SWALLET VENTAGE ACCEPTER
APERTURE BLOWHOLE BOREHOLE
COALHOLE CRABHOLE FUMAROLE
HANDHOLE KNOCKOUT KNOTHOLE
OVERTURE PEEPHOLE POSTHOLE
PUNCTURE WELLHOLE WINDHOLE
PERTUSION PERFORATION
(— CAUSED BY LEAK) GIME
(— FOR WIRE) HUB
(— IN BANK OF STREAM) GAT
(— IN GARMENT) FRACK
(— IN GUILLOTINE) LUNETTE
(— IN HEDGE) SMEUSE
(— IN HIDE) BOTHOLE
(— IN KEEL) LIMBER RUFFLE
(— IN KIVA) SIPAPU
(— IN ONE STROKE) ACE
(— IN STREAM BED) DUMP
(— IN WIND INSTRUMENT) LILL
(— INTO MOLD) GEAT SPRUE
(— THREE BELOW PAR) ALBATROSS
(AIR —) SPIRACLE
(BREATHING —) SUSPIRAL
(DEEP —) POT GOURD
(FOX —) KENNEL
(GOLF —) CUP DOGLEG
(MELON —) GILGAI
(RABBIT —) CLAPPER
(SAND —) BUNKER

(SINK —) SOAKAWAY
(SPY —) JUDAS
(TO —) GOBBLE HAZARD
(VOLCANIC —) FUMAROLE
(WATER —) DUB CHARCO
(WELL-LIKE —) CASCAN
HOLIDAY HOL PLAY TIDE WAKE FERIE
FESTA MERRY FIESTA JOVIAL FESTIVE
HALEDAY PLAYDAY YEARDAY PASSOVER
SHABUOTH WAYGOOSE
(HALF —) REMEDY
HOLINESS PIETY HALIDOM SANCTITY
SANCTIMONY
HOLLOW DEN DIP KEX BOSS BOWL CAVE
COMB COVE DALK DELL DENT DINT DISH
DOCK DOKE FOLD GORE HOLE HOLL
HOWE KEXY KHUD SINK SLOT THIN VOID
WAME BASIN BIGHT CAVUM CHASE
CLEFT CUPPY DELVE DOWFF EMPTY
GAUNT GOYLE GULCH HEUCH LAIGH
NOTCH SCOOP SINUS SWAMP WOMBY
ARMPIT BULLAN CAVITY CORRIE DIMPLE
HOLLER INDENT KETTLE MATRIX POCKET
RECESS SOCKET SUNKEN VACANT
WALLOW BOXLIKE CONCAVE UNSOUND
VACUITY CAVITARY CHELIDON CORELESS
CRUCIBLE FISTULAR FOSSETTE
NOTCHING SPECIOUS
(— AMONG HILLS) SWAG SLOCK
(— IN COIL OF CABLE) TIER
(— IN HILL) CLASH COMBE CORRIE
(— IN TILE) KEY
(— OF ARM) LEAD ARMPIT
(— OF EAR) ALVEARY
(— OF HANDS) GOWPEN
(— OF HORSE'S TOOTH) MARK
(— OF KNEE) HAM
(— OF ROOF) VALLEY
(— OUT) CUT DIG BORE HOWK KERF
CAVERN EXCISE
(LONG —) GROOVE
(NOT —) SOLID FARCTATE
(PASSING —) CRESCENT
(ROUND —) CIRQUE
(SECLUDED —) GLEN
(SPRINGY —) GAW
(WOODED —) GULLY
HOLLY HOLM HULL ILEX MATE DAHOON
HOLLIN HULVER TOLLON YAUPON
CATBERRY INKBERRY MILKMAID
HOLLYHOCK HOCK ALTHEA MALLOW
HOLY SRI HUACA SAINT SANTO DEVOUT
DIVINE SACRAL SACRED BLESSED
PERFECT SAINTLY SINLESS BLISSFUL
INNOCENT REVEREND SPIRITUAL
SANCTIMONIOUS
(— MAN) SADHU
(— OF HOLIES) ADYT ADYTUM
(ALL —) PANAGIA
HOMAGE FEE COURT HONOR YMAGE
FEALTY MANRED INCENSE LOYALTY
MANRENT MANSHIP OVATION SERVICE
TREWAGE EMINENCE OBEISANCE
(SUPREME —) LATRIA
HOME BYE DEN HAM BASE HAME HUNK
WIKE ABODE ASTRE BEING DOMUS

FOYER HAUNT SMOKE HEARTH BLIGHTY
SHELTER DOMICILE FIRESIDE ROOFTREE
(— FOR THE POOR) HOSPICE
(— OF THE BLESSED) GIMLE
(FUNERAL —) CHAPEL
(HARVEST —) KERN KIRN MELL HOCKEY
(REST —) FARM HOSTEL
HOMELAND HAVAIKI
HOMELESS ROOFLESS VAGABOND
HOMELY FOUL UGLY PLAIN DUDGEN
RUGGED PLAINLY EVERYDAY FAMILIAR
HOMELIKE
HOME PLATE RUBBER
HOMESICKNESS HEIMWEH NOSTALGIA
HOMESPUN KERSEY RUSSET RAPLOCH
HOMESTEAD TOFT TREF ONSET PLACE
WORTH TYDDYN FARMERY ONSTEAD
STEADING
HOMICIDE DEATH MORTH KILLING
HOMILY PRONE OMELIE POSTIL SERMON
HOMINY SAMP NASAUMP
HOMOGENEOUS LIKE SOLID GLOBAL
SIMPLE COMPACT MASSIVE SIMILAR
HOMOGENOUS ENTIRE

HONDURAS

CAPITAL: TEGUCIGALPA
COIN: PESO CENTAVO LEMPIRA
DEPARTMENT: YORO COLON COPAN
VALLE OLANCHO
GULF: FONSECA
INDIAN: MAYA PAYA SUMO ULVA CARIB
LENCA PIPIL TAUIRA JICAQUE MISKITO
MOSQUITO
ISLAND: ROATAN
ISLANDS: BAY BAHIA
LAKE: CRIBA YOJOA BREWER
MEASURE: VARA MILLA MECATE TERCIA
CAJUELA MANZANA
MOUNTAINS: PIJA AGALTA CELAQUE
PORT: LACEIBA TRUJILLO
RIVER: COCO SICO ULUA AGUAN LEMPA
NEGRO TINTO WANKS PATUCA SULACO
GUAYAPE OLANCHO SEGOVIA SANTIAGO
RUINS: TENAMPUA
TOWN: TELA YORO COPAN LAPAZ ROATAN
GRACIAS LACEIBA TRUJILLO YUSCARAN
JUTICALPA
WEIGHT: CAJA LIBRA

HONE HO STROP STROKE STRICKLE
HONEST FAIR GOOD JAKE TRUE AFALD
FRANK ROUND SOUND WHITE CANDID
DEXTER DINKUM ENTIRE PROPER RUSTIC
SINGLE SQUARE SINCERE UPRIGHT
RIGHTFUL STRAIGHT
HONESTLY TRULY DINKUM HONEST
INDEED SINGLY SQUARE SQUARELY
HONESTY FAITH HONOR SATIN EQUITY
LUNARY REALTY VERITY JUSTICE
LUNARIA PROBITY BOLBONAC FAIRNESS
FIDELITY MOONWORT SATINPOD
YEOMANRY
HONEY MEL MELL HINNY HONEYBUN
(— BEVERAGE) MULSE

(ROSE-FLAVORED —) RODOMEL
HONEYBEE (ALSO SEE BEE) BEE GYNE
KING DRANE DRONE QUEEN DINGAR
DRONER EGATES CYPRIAN DEBORAH
DESERET KOOTCHA MELISSA STINGER
ACULEATE ANGELITO
HONEYSUCKLE VINE SUCKLE WEIGELA
BINDWEED SUCKLING WOODBINE

HONG KONG

BAY: SHEKO REPULSE
CAPITAL: VICTORIA
COIN: CENT DOLLAR
DISTRICT: WANCHAI
ISLAND: LANTAO
MOUNTAIN: CASTLE VICTORIA
PENINSULA: KOWLOON
TOWN: KOWLOON

HONK KONK YANG CRONK
HONOR BAY ORE FAME FETE HORN KUDO
ADORE CROWN GLORY GRACE HERRY
IZZAT MENSE SPEAK TREAT CREDIT
DECORE ENHALO ESTEEM HOMAGE
HONOUR LAUREL PRAISE REVERE
SALUTE WORTHY DIGNITY EMBLAZE
GLORIFY HONESTY MANSHIP RESPECT
WORSHIP ACCOLADE DECORATE
GRANDEZA TASHREEF
HONORABLE DEAR FREE GOOD DIGNE
NOBLE OPIME WHITE GENTLE HONEST
HONORA LORDLY SQUARE UPRIGHT
GENEROUS HANDSOME HONORARY
HONORARIUM SALARY DOUCEUR
ALTARAGE HONORARY
HONORED GOOD FAMOUS LAUREL
LAURELED PRESTIGIOUS
HONORIFIC MAGNIFIC
HOOD HOW HUDE JACK AMICE ALMUCE
BIGGIN BONNET BURLET CALASH
CANOPY CUTOFF DOMINO FUNNEL
MANTLE RAFFIA BANGKOK BASHLYK
CALOTTE CAPUCHE BLINDAGE CALYPTRA
CAPUCCIO CAPUTIUM CHAPERON
CUCULLUS FOOLSCAP LIRIPIPE LIRIPOOP
MAZARINE TROTCOZY NITHSDALE
(— AND CAPE COMBINED) FALDETTA
(— FOR EVENING WEAR) CAPELINE
(— OF BOILER) VOMIT
(— OF CARRIAGE) HEAD
(— OF MAIL) COIF CAMAIL COIFFE
(— OF VEHICLE) TOP CAPOTE
(— ON CUPBOARD) TREMOR
(— ON HORSES) BLINKER
(— OVER DOOR) MARQUISE
(LENS —) SUNSHADE
(MONK'S —) COWL
(STIRRUP —) TAPADERO
(STRAW —) JAVA
(WOMAN'S —) SURTOUT VOLUPER
HOODED COWLED GALEATE CUCULLATE
HOODLUM HOOD PUNK BADDIE SKOLLY
LURCHER HOOLIGAN LARRIKIN
HOODOO JINX
HOODWINK MOP DUPE FOOL SEEL

BLEAR BLIND BLUFF CHEAT BAFFLE
CLOYNE DELUDE GAMMON WIMPLE
AVEUGLE BEGUILE BLINKER DECEIVE
MISLEAD INVEIGLE
HOOEY BUSHWAH
HOOF CLOOF CLOOT COFFIN UNGUIS
UNGULA CLOOTIE HOOFLET FOREHOOF
HOOK DOG GAB JIG PEW TUG CLIP DRAG
GAFF HAKE HUCK NOCK PEVY PRIN PUGH
SETT SKID STAY TACK CATCH CHAPE
CLEEK CLICK CRAMP CROME CROOK
HAMUS ONCIN PEAVY PREEN SPOON
TACHE UNCUS BECKET DETENT HINGLE
PINTLE TENTER AGRAFFE GAMBREL
GRUNTER HAMULUS HITCHER HOOKLET
KNUCKLE NUTHOOK PELICAN PINHOOK
RAMHEAD SPERKET UNCINUS
BOATHOOK CROTCHET GRABHOOK
PORTHOOK PULLBACK VULSELLA
WEEDHOOK
(— FISH) FOUL HANG SNAG DRAIL
HITCH STRIKE SNIGGLE FISHHOOK
(— FOR BACON) COMB
(— FOR KETTLE) KILP HANGLE
TRAMMEL
(— FOR POT) DRACKEN POTHOOK
SLOWRIE
(— FOR TWISTING HEMP) WHIRL
WHIRLER
(BENCH —) JACK
(BOAT —) HITCHER
(BOXING —) CROSS
(COUPLING —) JIGGER
(LONG-HANDLED —) HOCK MEAK
(MUSICAL —) FLAG PENNANT
(PRUNING —) SARPE CALABOZO
(REAPING —) HINK TWIBILL
(SAFETY —) CLEVIS
(SKIDDING —S) GRAB
(2 —S FASTENED AT SHANKS)
DOUBLES
HOOKAH KALIAN CHILLUM
HOOKED ADUNC UNCATE UNCOUS
ADUNCAL FALCATE HAMATED HAMULAR
ADUNCATE ADUNCOUS AQUILINE
HAMIFORM UNCINATE
HOOLIGAN ROUGH ROWDY TOUGH
APACHE GOONDA LARRIKIN
HOOP RIB BAND BOOL CLIP GIRR PASS
RING TIRE GARTH HOOPLE LAGGIN
WICKET CIRCLET GARLAND TROCHUS
TRUNDLE
(— FOR A SPAR) BANGLE
(— FOR BARREL) BAND GIRD GIRTH
(— FOR LAMPSHADE) HARP
(— FOR ORE BUCKET) CLEVIS
(— FOR WINNOWING GRAIN) WEIGHT
(— NET) TRUNK
(— OF WHEEL) STRAKE
(— TO STRENGTHEN GUN) FRETTE
(HALF —) BAIL BALE
HOOPSKIRT TUBTAIL
HOOSIER SCHOOLMASTER
(AUTHOR OF —) EGGLESTON
(CHARACTER IN —) BUD PETE JONES
MEANS RALPH SMALL WHITE HANNAH
MARTHA SANDER SHOCKY WALTER

HAWKINS JOHNSON MATILDA PEARSON
THOMSON
HOOT CURR WHOO WHOOP WHOOT
EXPLODE ULULATE
HOP HIP NIP FLIP JUMP LEAP BOUND
HITCH SWINE FLIERS GAMBOL SPRING
TITTUP CROWHOP HOPBIND HOPVINE
LUPULUS SKIPPER
HOPE WON DEEM SPES TROW COMBE
THINK TRUST DESIRE EXPECT PERDUE
ESPEIRE THOUGHT SPERANZA VELLEITY
(VAIN —) PIPE WANHOPE
HOPEFUL FOND BUOYANT SANGUINE
WENLICHE
HOPELESS DULL ABJECT FORLORN
DOWNCAST
HOPELESSNESS ANOMIE DESPAIR
HOPPER CURB JACK BUNKER CLOSET
HAPPER MACARONI
HOPSCOTCH POTSY HOPPERS PALLALL
PEEVERS
HORDE ARMY CAMP CLAN PACK CROWD
GROUP SWARM LEGION THRONG
(INNER —) BUKEYEF
HORIZON LAYER VERGE COMPASS
FINITOR ORTERDE SKYLINE
HORIZONTAL LEVEL LINEAR NAIANT
ACLINAL STRAIGHT
HORIZONTALLY FLATLY BARWAYS
BARWISE ENDLONG FESSWAYS
FESSWISE
HORMONE CORTIN LUTEIN EQUILIN
ESTRIOL ESTRONE GASTRIN INSULIN
RELAXIN STEROID THEELIN THEELOL
ANDROGEN ENDOCRIN ESTROGEN
FLORIGEN GALACTIN LACTOGEN
OESTRIOL SECRETIN CORTISONE
HORN BEAK BATON BUGLE CONCH
CORNO CORNU ANTLER CLAXON KLAXON
OXHORN TOOTER ALPHORN ALTHORN
ANTENNA BUFFALO CLARONE FOGHORN
HELICON HUTCHET OUTHORN PRICKET
SHOPHAR UNICORN BEAKIRON
BUCKHORN CLAVICOR CORNICLE
OLIPHANT SLUGHORN STAGHORN
WALDHORN NOISEMAKER
(— OF COW) SCUR
(— OF CRESCENT MOON) CUSP
(— OF DILEMMA) PIKE
(— OF DRINK) SLOSH
(— OF YOUNG STAG) BUNCH
(BUDDING —) SHOOT
(DRINKING —) RHYTON
(ENGLISH —) CA
(FRENCH —) CORNO
(GREY —) COLUMN
(HUNTER'S —) HUTCHET WALDHORN
(INSECT'S —) ANTENNA
(IVORY —) OLIFANT
(RAM'S —) SHOPHAR
(RUDIMENTARY —) SLUG
(STUNTED —) SCUR
(PREF.) CORNEO CORNI CORNU
(SUFF.) CERA(S) CEROS CEROUS CERUS
CORN
HORNET VESPA VESPID STINGER
HORNPIPE MATELOTE

HOROSCOPE SCOPE THEME FIGURE GENESIS NATIVITY
HORRIBLE DIRE GRIM UGLY AWFUL BLACK GREAT GRISLY HORRID GEARFUL GHASTLY HIDEOUS HORRENT UNSLOGH DREADFUL GRUESOME HORRIFIC SHOCKING TERRIBLE MONSTROUS
HORRID GRIM UGLY AWFUL ROUGH RUGGED SNUFFY UGSOME WICKED HIDEOUS DREADFUL GRUESOME HORRIBLE SHOCKING
HORRIFIC FEARFUL
HORRIFIED AGHAST GHASTLY HORRENT
HORRIFY APPAL AGRISE DISMAY ENHORROR
HORROR FEAR DREAD TERROR CONSTERNATION
(PL.) JIMJAMS
HORS D'OEUVRE CANAPE RELISH OUTWORK ZAKUSKA
HORSE BAY CUT DUN GEE GRI POT RIP AVER BARB DOON GOER GROG HOSS MOKE PRAD QUAD RACK RIDE ROAN SKIN STUD TEAM TURK WEED YAWD ARION ARVAK BEAST BLACK BROCK CAPLE CAPUL CHUNK CREAM DUMMY EQUID GLYDE GRANI HOBBY MILER MOREL PACER PIPER POLER RACER ROGUE RUNSY SHIER SOMER STEED STIFF TACKY WALER WIDGE ALEZAN AMBLER BANKER BOLTER BRONCO BUCKER BUSSER CABBER CALICO CASTER CHASER CHEVAL COLLOP CURTAL CUSSER DAPPLE DRIVER ENTIRE EQUINE FENCER FILLER GRULLA HUNTER JUMPER LEADER MAIDEN MORGAN NUBIAN ORLOFF PELTER POSTER PULLER RACKER ROARER ROUNCY RUNNER SAVAGE SORREL STAGER TRACER TURKEY VANNER WARPER WEAVER ALSVINN ALSVITH BARBARY BOARDER CABALLO CHARGER CLICKER CLIPPER COACHER COCOTTE COURSER CRIBBER CRIOLLA CRITTER DRAFTER FLEMISH GALATHE GIGSTER GRUNTER HACKNEY KNACKER LEEFANG MONTURE MUSTANG NEIGHER PACOLET PALFREY PIEBALD PRANCER RATTLER REESTER REFUSER RUNAWAY SADDLER SLEDDER SLEEPER SPANKER STAGGIE STEPPER TRAPPER TRESTLE TROOPER TROTTER WHEELER ARDENNES BATHORSE BUCKSKIN CHESTNUT CHEVALET COCKTAIL COLICKER CREATURE CYLLAROS DEMISANG DESTRIER EOHIPPUS FOOTROPE FRIPPERY GALLOPER HRIMFAXI KADISCHI MACHINER OUTSIDER PALOMINO RIDGLING ROADSTER SKEWBALD STIBBLER TRIPPLER WHISTLER YARRAMAN
(— CERTAIN NOT TO WIN) STIFF
(— LOSING FIXED RACE) STUMER
(— OF UNIFORM DARK COLOR) ZAIN
(— THAT WON'T START) STICK
(—S RUNNING BEHIND) RUCK
(ARABIAN —) ARAB KOHL ARABIAN

(BALKY —) JIB JIBBER
(BROKEN-DOWN —) JADE CROCK SCREW DURGAN
(CALICO —) PINTO
(CASTRATED —) GELDING
(CLUMSY —) STAMMEL
(DECREPIT —) SKATE GLEYDE
(DRAFT —) HAIRY PUNCH SHIRE BEETEWK BELGIAN SUFFOLK PERCHERON
(DROVE OF —S) ATAJO
(EASY-PACED —) PAD
(FALLOW —) FAVEL
(FAMILY —) DOBBIN
(FAST —) GANGER
(FEMALE —) MARE FILLY
(FLEMISH —) ROIL
(GRAY —) SCHIMMEL
(HIGH-SPIRITED —) STEPPER
(IMAGINARY —) AULLAY
(IMMUNIZED —) BLEEDER
(INFERIOR —) PLUG CAYUSE PLATER
(JUMPING —) LEPPER
(MALE —) STALLION
(NEAR —) HAND
(OLD —) JADE PROD YAUD AIVER CROCK
(PACK —) BIDET SUMPTER
(RANGE —) FANTAIL
(ROAN —) SCHIMMEL
(SADDLE —) MOUNT
(SHAFT —) SHAFTER THILLER
(SHAGGY —) ALTAI
(SLUGGISH —) HOG
(SMALL —) NAG TIT BIDET GENET HOBBY CANUCK JENNET GALLOWAY
(STOCKY —) COB
(TEAM OF —S) CARTWARE
(TEAM OF 3 —S WITH LEADER) UNICORN
(TRICK —) SIMON
(UNBROKEN —) BRONCO
(VICIOUS —) LADINO
(WILD —) FUZZY BRUMBY KUMRAH OUTLAW TARPAN JUGHEAD BANGTAIL FUZZTAIL WARRIGAL
(WINGED —) PEGASUS
(WORN-OUT —) HACK GARRAN KNACKER CROWBAIT
(WORTHLESS —) JADE SHACK KEFFEL
(YOUNG —) TIT COLT FOAL STAG STOT STAGGIE
(2-YEAR OLD —) TWINTER
(3 —S ABREAST) TROIKA
(3 —S ONE BEHIND ANOTHER) RANDEM
(4 —S ABREAST) QUADRIGA
(PREF.) HIPP(O)
(SUFF.) HIPPUS
HORSE DEALER COPER CHANTER COURSER
HORSEFLY BOT GAD CLEG CLEGG STOUT BOTFLY BREEZE GADBEE GADFLY BULLDOG DEERFLY TABANID
HORSEMAN RIDER CHARRO COWBOY HUSSAR KNIGHT RUTTER COURIER PICADOR PRICKER CAVALIER GALLOPER

HORSEPOWER SOUP
HORSESHOE TIP SHOE PLATE HOBBER
  LUNETTE
HORUS SEPT SOPT SEPTI HORMAKHU
  (FATHER OF —) OSIRIS
  (MOTHER OF —) ISIS
HOSE LINE VAMP HOSEN GASKIN
  BROGUES BULLION HOSIERY CHAUSSES
  HANDLINE HOSEPIPE
HOSEA (FATHER OF —) BEERI
HOSIERY HOSE KNITWEAR
HOSPICE IMARET DIACONIA HOSPITAL
HOSPITABLE DOUCE CLEVER DOULCE
  SOCIAL CORDIAL FRIENDLY
HOSPITAL BEDLAM CRECHE SPITAL
  COLLEGE LAZARET PESTHOUSE
  POLYCLINIC
HOSPITALITY SALT MENSE XENODOCHY
HOST SUM ARMY FYRD WARE CROWD
  JASON MAKER POWER SWARM WERED
  LEGION LODGER NATION THRONG
  BALEBOS COMPANY FYRDUNG SACRING
  VIANDER LANDLORD PARTICLE
  MULTITUDE
  (— OF INVADERS) HERE
  (EUCHARISTIC —) LAMB SACRING
HOSTAGE BORROW PLEDGE SURETY
  RANSOMER
HOSTEL INN ENTRY HOSTAGE KINGDOM
  HOSPITAL
HOSTELRY AUBERGE
HOSTESS TAUPO LANDLADY CHATELAINE
HOSTILE FOE HARD ALIEN BLACK ENEMY
  FREMT HATEL STOUT DEADLY FRIGID
  INFEST ADVERSE ASOCIAL FIENDLY
  OPPOSED UNQUERT WARLIKE CONTRARY
  INIMICAL OPPOSITE
HOSTILITY WAR FEID FEUD HATE
  ANIMUS ENMITY HATRED RANCOR
  SCHISM DAGGERS RUPTURE
HOT WARM ADUST CALID EAGER FIERY
  ARDENT ESTIVE FERVID IGNITE SULTRY
  TORRID ANIMOSE ANIMOUS BOILING
  BURNING CANDENT FERVENT PEPPERY
  THERMAL CAYENNED FEVERISH
  SEETHING SIZZLING
HOTBED BED NEST HOTHOUSE
HOT-BLOODED VASCULAR
HOTEL INN SPA FLOP FONDA HOUSE
  HYDRO HOSTEL HOTTLE POSADA
  FLEABAG FONDACO FUNDUCK GASTHOF
  HOSTELRY
  (— NEAR AIRPORT) AIRTEL
  (WATERSIDE —) BOATEL
HOTELKEEPER HOTELIER
HOTHOUSE STEW STOVE PINERY
  FRUITERY
HOT ROD DRAGSTER
HOT-TEMPERED PEPPERY CHOLERIC
  SPITFIRE
HOUND DOG PIE BAIT HARL HUNT MUTE
  BRACE ENTRY HARRY LEASH LIMER
  SLATE AFGHAN BASSET BEAGLE HUNTER
  JOWLER LEAMER LUCERN SLEUTH
  TUFTER CURTISE ENTRADA GELLERT
  REDBONE SKIRTER BARUKHZY BLUETICK
  BRATCHET COURSING FOXHOUND

  (BITCH —) BRACH
  (EXTINCT —) TALBOT
  (RELAY OF —S) VANLAY
  (SLEUTH —) TALBOT
  (SPECTRAL —) SHUCK
  (PL.) RACHES
HOUR URE TIDE TIME CURFEW GHURRY
  (CANONICAL —) NONE SEXT PRIME
  MATINS TIERCE ORTHROS VESPERS
  COMPLINE EVENSONG
  (HALF —) BELL
  (KILOWATT —) KELVIN
  (LAST —S) DEATHBED
  (STUDY —) PREP
  (6 —S) QUADRANT
  (PREF.) HORO
HOUSE BOX CASA DOME DUMP FIRM
  FLET HOLE HOME RACE ROOF
  STOW ABODE AERIE BAHAY COVER
  DOMUS HOOCH HOOSE JACAL LODGE
  MEESE STAGE WHARE BESTOW BIGGIN
  BOTTLE CAMARA CASTLE CHEMIS
  CLOTHE DUPLEX FAMILY HEARTH
  HOOTCH MAISON PALACE PARISH
  SINGLE STABLE WIGWAM BIGGING
  CABOOSE CASSINE EUDEMON FAZENDA
  HOGGERY HOUSING MESUAGE QUARTER
  SHELTER AEDICULA BARADARI
  BUNGALOW DOMICILE DOVECOTE
  DWELLING MEDSTEAD MESSUAGE
  TENEMENT NOVITIATE
  (— AND LAND) DEMESNE
  (— AND 5 ACRES) COTE
  (— FOR DOGS) KENNEL
  (— FOR WOMEN) HAREM
  (— IN BOROUGH) HAW
  (— OF A MARABOUT) KOUBA
  (— OF CORRECTION) BRIDEWELL
  (— OF KNIGHTS TEMPLARS)
  PRECEPTORY
  (— OF LEGISLATURE) SEANAD
  CHAMBER ASSEMBLY
  (— OF PARLIAMENT) COMMONS
  LAGTING
  (— OF PROSTITUTION) CRIB BAGNIO
  BORDEL
  (— OF REFUGE) MAGDALEN
  (— OF THIEVES) KEN
  (— OF WORSHIP) BETHEL CHURCH
  (— WITH TRIANGULAR FRONT)
  AFRAME
  (APARTMENT —) INSULA
  (ASTROLOGICAL —) ANGLE
  (AUSTRALIAN —) HUMPY
  (CHANGE —) DRY
  (CHAPTER —) CABILDO
  (CLAY —) ADOBE TEMBE
  (COACH —) REMISE
  (COMMUNAL —) MORONG
  (COUNTRY —) PEN DACHA CASINO
  GRANGE QUINTA BASTIDE CHATEAU
  (COW —) VACCARY
  (DAIRY —) WICK
  (EATING —) COOKSHOP
  (ESKIMO —) IGLOO TOPEK KASHGA
  KASHIMA
  (FIJI —) BURE

(FORTIFIED —) GARRISON
(GAMBLING —) BANK HELL RIDOTTO
(GOVERNMENT —) KONAK
(GRINDING —) HULL
(GROUP OF —S) CLUSTER
(HAWAIIAN —) HALE
(LODGING —) INN KIP HOST ENTRY
HOTEL HOSTEL
(LOG —) TILT
(MANOR —) HAM HALL COURT PLACE
SCHLOSS SEIGNEURY
(PLANETARY —) TOWER
(POULTRY —) ARK HENNERY
(PUBLIC —) INN HOSTEL SHANTY
CANTEEN SNUGGERY
(RANCH —) HUT
(RELIGIOUS —) CELL CONVENT
KELLION MONASTERY PRESBYTERY
(RENTED —) LET
(REST —) DAK KHAN SERAI
(RETREAT —) CENACLE
(ROOMING —) DOSS FLOP FLEABAG
(ROYAL —) AERIE
(SENATE —) CURIA
(SMALL —) COT HUT BACH CELL CABIN
HOVEL SHACK CASITA COTTAGE
MAISONETTE
(SOD —) SODDY
(STILT —) CHIKEE CHICKEE
(SUMMER —) TRELLIS
(TENEMENT —) LAND CHAWL
(THATCHED —) BANDA
(TOY —) COBHOUSE
(TURKISH —) KONAK
HOUSEHOLD HIRED HOUSE FAMILY
HOUSAL MEINIE MENAGE FIRESIDE
MAINPAST
HOUSEHOLDER ASTRER GOODMAN
GUIDMAN NAUKRAR FRANKLIN
HOUSEKEEPER HUSSY MATRON
HOUSE OF SEVEN GABLES
(AUTHOR OF —) HAWTHORNE
(CHARACTER IN —) MAULE PHOEBE
VENNER JAFFREY CLIFFORD HEPZIBAH
HOLGRAVE PYNCHEON
HOUSEWIFE DAME FRAU FROW WIFE
HUSSY VROUW BUSHWIFE HAUSFRAU
(MEAN —) NIP
HOUSING BOX CASE DRUM TRAP BANJO
BLIMP GLOBE HOUSE KIOSK BARREL
RADOME SHIELD HOUSAGE SHELTER
DOGHOUSE PADCLOTH PECTORAL
PEDESTAL SHABRACK
(HORSE'S —) BASE
(RADAR —) BLISTER
HOVER BAIT FLIT HANG HOVE BROOD
POISE FLUTTER HOVERER
HOW GREEN WAS MY VALLEY
(AUTHOR OF —) LLEWELLYN
(CHARACTER IN —) HUW BETA DAVY
IVOR OWEN EVANS IANTO GWILYM
IESTYN MARGED MORGAN BRONWEN
ANGHARAD GRUFFYDD
HOWL WAP WOW BAWL GOWL GURL
HURL RAVE WAUL WAWL YAWL YOLL
YOUT YOWL TIGER WHEWL WRAWL
BEHOWL STEVEN ULULATE

(— VOCIFEROUSLY) TONGUE
HUB HOB BOSS NAVE STOCK CENTER
CENTRE FAUCET HUBBLE SOCKET SPIDER
OMPHALOS
(— AND SPOKES) SPEECH
HUBBUB DIN COIL STIR CLAMOR FRAISE
HUBBLE RABBLE RACKET TUMULT
BOBBERY CLUTTER BROUHAHA
HUBBABOO ROWDYDOW SPLATTER
HUCKLEBERRY FINN (AUTHOR OF —)
TWAIN CLEMENS
(CHARACTER IN —) JIM TOM DUKE
FINN HUCK JANE KING POLLY SALLY
SUSAN WILKS JOANNA PHELPS SAWYER
WATSON DOUGLAS GRANGERFORD
SHEPHERDSON
HUCKSTER BADGER CADGER KIDDER
HAGGLER KIDDIER TRUCKER OUTCRIER
HUDDLE RUCK HUNCH CRINGE CROUCH
FUMBLE HOWDER HURTLE SCRUMP
SHRIMP SHRINK CROODLE SCRINCH
SCROOCH SCRUNCH SHUFFLE
HUDIBRAS (AUTHOR OF —) BUTLER
(CHARACTER IN —) RALPHO
CROWDERO HUDIBRAS SIDROPHEL
HUE RUD RAB BLEE BLUE COND CHLOR
COLOR GREEN LEMON SHOUT TAINT
TINCT CHROMA
(DULL —) DRAB
(SOMBER —) DARK
HUG CLIP COLL COUL MOLD CREEM
CRUSH HALSE PRESS CUDDLE HUDDLE
HUGGLE STRAIN CHERISH EMBRACE
SQUEEZE
HUGE BIG FELL MAIN VAST ENORM GIANT
GREAT JUMBO LARGE STOUR HEROIC
IMMANE BANGING BUMPING DECUMAN
HIDEOUS IMMENSE MASSIVE MONSTER
TITANIC COLOSSAL ENORMOUS
GALACTIC GIGANTIC MOUNTAIN
PYTHONIC SLASHING SWAPPING
THUMPING THWACKING MOUNTAINOUS
HUGENESS ENORMITY
HULL HUD HOD POD BODY BULK HULK HUSK
PILL BURSE CASCO SWELL
(— OF COTTON BOLL) BUR BURR
(— OF SHIP) BODY HULK BOTTOM
(PART OF —) BEAM DECK KEEL RAIL
BATTEN RABBET CEILING FUTTOCK
KEELSON GARBOARD PLANKING
STRINGER WATERWAY STANCHION
SHELFPIECE SPIRKETING
HULLABALOO DIN FLAP CLAMOR
HUBBUB RACKET BROUHAHA
HUM BUM BLUR BRUM BUZZ HUSS TUNE
CHIRM CROON DRONE FEIGN SOUGH
SOWFF HUMBLE TEEDLE FREDDON
TRUMPET
HUMAN BEING MANLY FINITE FLESHY
HUMANE MORTAL MANNISH HOMININE
HUMANIST
HUMAN COMEDY (AUTHOR OF —)
SAROYAN
(CHARACTER IN —) BESS MARY
ARENA HOMER KATEY TOBEY ACKLEY
GEORGE GROGAN HUBERT LIONEL

MARCUS THOMAS BYFIELD ULYSSES
MACAULEY SPANGLER

HUMANE CIVIL KINDLY TENDER
MERCIFUL

HUMANITY FLESH MENSK WORLD
MANHEAD MANHOOD MANSHIP SPECIES
ADAMHOOD HUMANISM KINDNESS
LENITUDE

HUMBLE LOW BASE HOWE MEAN MEEK
MILD MURE POOR TAME VAIL ABASE
ABATE BUXOM DEMIT DIMIT LOWER
LOWLY PLAIN SILLY SMALL SOBER
WORMY ATTERR DEJECT DEMEAN
DEMISS EMBASE HONEST MASTER
MODEST REDUCE SIMPLE SLIGHT
UNPUFF AFFLICT DEGRADE DEPRESS
FOOLISH IGNOBLE MORTIFY OBSCURE
CONTRITE DISGRACE
(— ONESELF) STOOP GROVEL

HUMBUG GAS GUM HUM KID BUNK
FLAM GAFF GAME GUFF JAZZ SHAM
CHEAT FRAUD FUDGE GUILE JOLLY
SPOOF SPOOK TRICK BARNEY BLAGUE
GAMMON BLARNEY FLUMMER VERNEUK
FLIMFLAM FLUMMERY HUCKMUCK
IMPOSTER NONSENSE

HUMDINGER LULU ONER DOOZY DINGER
HUMMER SNORTER RIPSNORTER

HUMDRUM IRKSOME PROSAIC
BOURGEOIS

HUMID WET DAMP DANK MOIST SOGGY
STICKY SULTRY WETTISH HUMOROUS

HUMILIATE ABASE ABASH SCALP
SHAME NIDDER NITHER DEGRADE
MORTIFY UNPLUME DISGRACE

HUMILIATED SMALL ASHAMED

HUMILIATION DUST COMEDOWN
DISGRACE

HUMILITY MODESTY MEEKNESS
MILDNESS

HUMMINGBIRD RUBY STAR MANGO
SYLPH TENUI TOPAZ AMAZON COQUET
HERMIT HUMMER ROSTER SAPPHO
COLIBRI EMERALD HUMBIRD JACOBIN
RAINBOW SNOWCAP TROCHIL WARRIOR
CALLIOPE COQUETTE FIRETAIL
FROUFROU MIMOTYPE PICARIAN
SAPPHIRE WHITETIP

HUMMOCK HUMP CHENIER HAMMOCK
TUSSOCK

HUMOR CUE PIN TID WIT BABY CANT
COAX MOOD TIFF VEIN WHIM FRAME
IRONY TUTOR MEGRIM PAMPER PHLEGM
SANIES SOOTHE SPLEEN SPRITE TEMPER
FOOLING GRATIFY INDULGE VITREUM
VITRINA ARCHNESS DISHUMOR
DROLLERY EYEWATER FUMOSITY
SANGUINE VITREOUS
(BAD —) BATS THROW
(ILL —) BILE DUDGEON
(QUIET —) DRYNESS
(SLIMY —) HIPPOMANES

HUMORIST JOKER FUNSTER FUNMAKER
FUNNYMAN
AUSTRIAN SAPHIR
CANADIAN LEACOCK
ENGLISH PAIN WARD SEAMAN
FRENCH RABELAIS
GERMAN RICHTER

HUMOROUS DROLL FUNNY PAWKY
QUEER JOCOSE COMICAL GIOCOSO
PLAYFUL WAGGISH PLEASANT
SARDONIC

HUMP BOSS HUNK BULGE BUNCH CROUP
CRUMP HULCH HUNCH GIBBER GIBBUS
HUMMIE GIBBOUS

HUMPBACK LORD CRUMP PUNCH
KYPHOSIS

HUMPBACKED HUMPED HUMPTY
GIBBOSE GIBBOUS
(PREF.) CYPH(O) HYB(O)

HUMPHRY CLINKER (AUTHOR OF —)
SMOLLETT
(CHARACTER IN —) JERRY LYDIA
GEORGE WILSON BRAMBLE CLINKER
HUMPHRY JENKINS MATTHEW MELFORD
OBADIAH TABITHA DENNISON WINIFRED
LISMAHAGO

HUNCHBACK OF NOTRE DAME
(AUTHOR OF —) HUGO
(CHARACTER IN —) CLAUDE FROLLO
PHOEBUS ESMERALDA GRINGOIRE
QUASIMODO CHATEAUPERS

HUNDRED RHO CENT CENTUM HUNDER
HUNNER CANTRED CANTREF CENTARY
(— THOUSAND) LAC LAKH
(NINE —) SAN SAMPI
(5 —) D

HUNGARY

CAPITAL: BUDAPEST

COIN: GARA BALAS LENGO FILLER FORINT
KORONA

COUNTY· VAS PEST ZALA BEKES FEJER
HEVES TOLNA NOGRAD SOMOGY
BARANYA

FOREST: BAKONY

KING: BELA GEZA IMRE ARPAD ISTVAN
KALMAN MATTHIAS

LAKE: FERTO BALATON VELENCE
BLATENSEE

MEASURE: AKO HOLD JOCH YOKE ANTAL
ITCZE MAROK METZE HUVELYK MERFOLD

MOUNTAIN: KEKES BAKONY MECSEK
BORZSONY KORISHEG'

MOUNTAIN RANGE: BUKK MATRA
MECSEK CARPATHIAN

NATIVE: HUN SERB CROAT GYPSY
MAGYAR SLOVAK UGRIAN

RIVER: DUNA MURA RAAB RABA SAJO
ZALA BODVA DRAVA DRAVE IPOLY
KAPOS KOROS MAROS RABCA TARNA
TISZA DANUBE HENRAD POPRAD
SZAMOS THEISS ZAGYVA VISTULA
BERRETYO

TOWN: ABA ACS OZD VAC BUDA EGER
GYOR MAKO PAPA PECS PEST TATA ZIRC
KOMLO CEGLED MOHACS SOPRON
SZEGED DBRECEN MISKOLC SZENTES
DEBRECEN SZEGEDIN

WEIGHT: VAMFONT VAMMAZSA

HUNGER BELL CLEM WANT ACORIA
DESIRE FAMINE CRAVING
HUNGRY YAP HOWE KEEN LEER YAUP
EMPTY THIRL HOLLOW JEJUNE PECKISH
YAPPISH ANHUNGRY ESURIENT
HUNK DAD DAUD JUNK MOUNTAIN
(— OF BREAD) TOMMY
HUNT DOG GUN JAG MOB RUN GREW
JACK LARK PUMP SEAL SEEK SHOP
CHASE CHEVY DRIVE HOUND REVAY
TRACK TRAIL BATTUE BEAGLE BREVIT
CHEVVY COURSE FALCON FERRET
SEARCH SHIKAR VANLAY ENCHASE
AUCUPATE PIGSTICK SCROUNGE
VENATION
(— BIG GAME) GHOOM
(— DEER) FLOAT
(— DOWN) QUARRY
(— DUCKS) TOLL
(— FOX) CUB
(— WITH HAWK) FLY
(— WITH SPEAR) STICK
HUNTER GUN HUNT PINK JAGER BIRDER
CHASER GUNNER JAEGER NIMROD
THERON ACTAEON BUSHMAN CATCHER
COURSER MONTERO SHIKARI SHOOTER
SKIRTER STALKER TRAILER VENERER
CEPHALUS CHASSEUR FIELDMAN
HUNTSMAN TRAILMAN
(— ON SNOW) CRUSTER
(BUFFALO —) CIBOLERO
(MYTHOLOGICAL —) GWYN ORION
(RING OF —S) TINCHEL TINCHILL
HUNTING DRAG HANK AHUNT WATHE
SHIKAR VENERY CUBBING GUNNING
BEAGLING PURCHASE SHOOTING
SURROUND VENATION
(— SIGNAL) SEEK
HUNTSMAN WHIP HUNTER JAEGER
ACTAEON CATCHER COURSER MONTERO
SCARLET VENATOR VENERER CHASSEUR
HURDLE TRAY FLAKE FRITH PANEL STALE
STICK DOUBLE RADDLE SLEDGE WATTLE
HURDY-GURDY LIRA ROTA LANTUM
VIELLE SAMBUKE HUMSTRUM
SYMPHONY
HURL BUM BUN CAST CLOD DASH DUST
FIRE PASH PELT PICK SLAT SOAK SOCK
DRIVE FLING HEAVE LANCE PITCH SLING
SMITE SPANG SWING THIRL THROW
WHIRL THRILL HURLBAT SWITHER
WHITHER JACULATE PRECIPITATE
HURRAH HAIL HUZZA HOORAY HURRAY
BRAVISSIMO
HURRICANE BAGUIO PRESTER
FURACANA FURICANE WILDWIND
HURRIED HASTY RAPID THRONG
HASTEFUL SNATCHED
HURRY ADO FOG NIP RAP RUB RUN BUSK
DUST HUMP PELL PLAT POST RAPE RESE
RUSH STIR TIFT TROT URGE WHIR CHASE
CROWD HASTE HYPER LURRY MOSEY
PRESS SESSA SKIRT SPEED STAVE
STOUR WHIRL BUCKET BUNDLE BUSTLE
HASTEN HUSTLE POWDER STROTH
TATTER WHORRY HOTFOOT QUICKEN
SCUDDLE SKELTER SLITHER WHITHER

DISPATCH EXPEDITE SPLUTTER
ACCELERATE
(— A HORSE) SPUR
(— ABOUT) SCOUR
(— AWAY) FLEE BUNCH SCREW SKIRT
(— CLUMSILY) TAVE TEAVE
(— NOISILY) SPLUTTER
(— OFF) DUST
(— UP) BUSK
HURT CUT HOT NOY DERE FIKE GALL
HARM PAIN SCAT ABUSE BLAME GRIEF
GRIPE PINCH SORRY SPITE THORN
WATHE WOUND BRUISE DAMAGE GRIEVE
IMPAIR INJURE INJURY LESION MIFFED
MITTLE PAINED PUNISH SCATHE STRAIN
STROKE WINGED AFFLICT HURTING
OFFENCE OFFENSE SCADDLE MISCHIEF
NUISANCE
(— EASILY) FROISSE
(— FEELINGS) CUT TOUCH
(— REPUTATION) LIBEL
(— SEVERELY) KILL
(EASILY —) GINGER
(PREF.) NOCI
HURTFUL BAD ILL EVIL MALIGN NOCENT
NOCIVE NOUGHT SHREWD TAKING
BALEFUL BANEFUL HARMFUL MALEFIC
NOCUOUS NOXIOUS SCADDLE UNQUERT
GRIEVOUS HURTSOME SCATHFUL
HURTLE HURL FLING THIRL
HUSBAND EKE MAN WER BOND CHAP
FERE KEEP LORD MAKE MATE SAVE SIRE
BARON CHURL HOARD HUBBY MATCH
STORE MANAGE MASTER MISTER
SPOUSE CONSORT GOODMAN GUIDMAN
HENPECK PARTNER CONSERVE
(— OF ADULTRESS) CUCKOLD
(AFFIANCED —) FUTURE
(SUPPLEMENTARY —) PIRRAURU
HUSHED QUIET STILL GENTLE WHISHT
HUSK BUR COD HUD KEX SID ARIL BARK
BURR COAT COSH HOSE HUCK HULK PILL
SEED SHIV SKIN HOOSE SCALE SHALE
SHAUP SHELL SHILL SHUCK SHUDE
COLDER DEHUSK SLOUGH CARCASS
CASCARA
(— OF NUT) SHACK BOLSTER
(— OF OATS) SHUD SHOOD FLIGHT
(CORN —) HOJA
HUSKY HUSK CODDY FOGGY THICK
FURRED BUIRDLY HULKING BOUNCING
SIBERIAN
HUSSY MINX SLUT BESOM CUTTY GIPSY
GYPSY MADAM STRAP HIZZIE LIMMER
DROSSEL
HUSTLE FAN PEG HUMP JUMP BLITZ
SKELP BUCKET BUNDLE BUSTLE JOSTLE
RABBLE RUSTLE SCUFTER
HUT COT BARI BUTT COSH COTE CREW
CRIB HALE HULL HULL ISBA IZBA SHED
TENT TILT BASHA BENAB BOHIO BOOTH
BOTHY CABIN CHAWL CHOZA HOVEL
HUMPY HUTCH JACAL KRAAL LODGE
SCALE SETER SHACK SHIEL TOLDO
TOPEK WHARE BOHAWN BOTHAN
CANABA CHALET GUNYEH PONDOK

RANCHO REFUGE SAETER SCONCE
SHANTY SHELTY WIGWAM WIKIUP
BALAGAN BARRACK BOUROCK CAMALIG
COTTAGE GOONDIE HUDDOCK HUTMENT
SHEBANG YAKUTAT BARABARA
CHANTIER RONDAWEL SHIELING
THOLTHAN TUGURIUM
(— FOR TEMPORARY USE) CORF
(— IN VIETNAM) HOOCH
(— OVER MINING SHAFT) COE
(ABORIGINAL —) MIMI GUNYAH
MIAMIA WURLEY GOONDIE
(FISHERMAN'S —) SKEO
(HEATED —) HOTHOUSE
(HERMIT'S —) CELL
(NAVAJO —) HOGAN
(POULTRY —) IGLOO
(SAMOYED —) CHUM
(SENTRY —) BOX
(SIBERIAN —) JURT
(SOUTH AFRICAN —) STRUIS
HUTCH ARK BUDDLE RABBITRY
HYACINTH LILY MUSK LILIUM CROWTOE
FLOATER GREGGLE JACINTH BLUEBELL
CROWFOOT HAREBELL JACOUNCE
HYBRID DZO ZHO MULE ZOBO CROSS
GRADE HINNY LIGER COYDOG GALYAK
MOSAIC MULISH SPLAKE TURKEN
BASTARD BIGENER CATTALO JERSIAN
MONGREL PLUMCOT ZEBRASS ZEBRULA
ZEBURRO CARIDEER CITRANGE KAFERITA
LIMEQUAT ZEBRINNY
HYDRANT CHUCK FIREPLUG
HYDROCARBON ARENE CUMOL FREON
GUTTA IDRYL INDAN IRENE TOLAN XYLOL
ALKANE ALKYNE ALLENE BUTANE
BUTYNE CARANE CETANE CETENE
CYMENE DECANE ETHANE ETHENE
HEXINE INDANE INDENE MELENE
NONENE OCTANE OCTENE OCTINE
PICENE PINENE PYRENE RETENE TOLANE
TOLUOL XYLENE AMYLENE AZULENE
BENZENE CHOLANE CYCLENE DECALIN
ETHERIN FULVENE HEPTANE HEPTENE
HEPTYNE LYCOPIN MUCKITE MYRCENE

OLEFINE PENTINE PENTYNE PHYTANE
PROPANE STYRENE TETROLE TOLUENE
HYDROGEN HYDRO PROTIUM
HYDROPHOBIA LYSSA RABIES
HYENA HINE DABUH SIMIR HYAENID
HYGIENIC SANITARY
HYMN ODE FUGE LAUD SING DIRGE
GATHA PAEAN PSALM YASHT YMPNE
ANTHEM CARVAL CHORAL HIMENE
HIRMOS MANTRA ORPHIC THEODY
VESPER CHORALE EXULTET HEIRMOS
INTROIT CANTICLE CATHISMA
DOXOLOGY ENCOMIUM PSALMODY
SEQUENCE TRISAGION TROPARION
(— COLLECTION) MENAION
(MEXICAN —) ALABADO
HYMNAL HYMNARY HYMNBOOK
HYPERBOLE AUXESIS
HYPERCRITICAL NICE CAPTIOUS
CRITICAL
HYPERION (DAUGHTER OF —) AURORA
(FATHER OF —) URANUS
(MOTHER OF —) GAEA
(WIFE OF —) THEA
HYPNOTIC AMYTAL BROMAL CHLORAL
SECONAL BARBITAL NARCEINE
SOPORIFIC
HYPNOTISM DEVIL BRAIDISM HYPNOSIS
MESMERISM
HYPNOTIST OPERATOR SVENGALI
HYPOCRISY SHAM POPEHOLY
PHARISAISM
HYPOCRITE CANT BIGOT CHEAT FACER
FRAUD BLIFIL CAFARD HUMBUG MUCKER
MAWWORM SIMULAR CHADBAND
DECEIVER TARTUFFE
HYPOCRITICAL FALSE SLAPE DOUBLE
CANTING PLASTER POPEHOLY SPECIOUS
HYPOTHESIS SYSTEM THEORY PREMISE
WEGENER SUPPOSAL POSTULATE
HYPOTHETICAL IDEAL
HYSTERIA NERVES PIBLOKTO TARASSIS
(PRONE TO —) VAPORISH
(RELIGIOUS —) LATA
HYSTERICAL NERVOUS SHRIEKY

I

I A ICH SHE ITEM
IAPETUS (FATHER OF —) URANUS
  (MOTHER OF —) GAEA
  (SON OF —) ATLAS MENOETIUS
  (WIFE OF —) ASIA CLYMENE
IBEX KYL TEK TUR ZAC KAIL BEDEN
  EVECK IZARD JAELA EVICKE SAKEEN
IBIS GUARA GANNET HADADA JABIRU
  TURKEY CICONIID IRONHEAD
ICARUS (FATHER OF —) DAEDALUS
  (MOTHER OF —) NAUCRATE
ICE GEAL FROST GLACE CRYSTAL
  VERGLAS
  (— IN ROUGH BLOCKS) RUBBLE
  (ANCHOR —) FRAZIL
  (DRIFTING FRAGMENT OF —) PAN
    CALF
  (PATCH OF —) RONE
  (PINNACLE OF —) SERAC
  (RIDGE OF —) HAMMOCK HUMMOCK
  (SEA —) GLACON SLUDGE
  (SHORE —) FAST
  (SLUSHY —) SISH
  (SOFT —) SLOB LOLLY
  (THIN NEW —) DISH PANCAKE
  (THIN OR FLOATING —) FLOE GRUE
    BRASH
  (WATER —) SHERBET
ICEBERG BERG GROWLER FLOEBERG
ICEBOAT SKEETER
ICE CREAM CREAM GLACE AUFAIT
  BISQUE NOUGAT TASTER SPUMONI
  TORTONI
ICED COLD GLACE FRAPPE
ICEFISH SALANGID

ICELAND

BAY: FAXA HUNA
CAPITAL: REIKJAVIK REYKJAVIK
COIN: AURAR EYRIR KRONA
EPIC: EDDA SAGA
FJORD: BREIDHA
GEYSER: GRYLA
GLACIER: HOFSJOKULL LANGJOKULL
  VATNAJOKULL
LAKE: MYVATN THORISVATN
MEASURE: SET ALIN LINA ALMUD TURMA
  ALMENN ALMUDE FERFET POTTUR
  FATHMUR FERALIN FERMILA OLTUNNA
  SJOMILA
MOUNTAIN: JOKUL
PARLIAMENT: ALTHING
RIVER: HVITA JOKULSA THJORSA
TOWN: AKRANES AKUREYRI KEFLAVIK
  KOPAVOGUR
VOLCANIC ISLAND: SURTSEY
VOLCANO: LAKI ASKJA HEKLA ELDFELL

WATERFALL: GULL DETTI GULLFOSS
  DETTIFOSS
WEIGHT: PUND POUND

ICHABOD (FATHER OF —) PHINEHAS
  (GRANDFATHER OF —) ELI
ICHNEUMON URVA NYMSS MEERKAT
  VANSIRE
ICHU HICHU STIPA
ICICLE ICARY ICKLE YOKEL TANGLE
  SHOGGLE COCKBELL
ICINESS GLARE
ICING ICE PIPING ALCORZA FROSTING
  MERINGUE
ICON IKON EIKON IMAGE DEESIS
ICONOCLAST DEBUNKER
ICY GELID BOREAL FRIGID WINTRY
  GLACIAL
ID ES ORF GARDON SYPHILID

IDAHO

CAPITAL: BOISE
COUNTY: ADA GEM BUTTE CAMAS LATAH
  LEMHI POWER TETON BLAINE BONNER
  CARNAS CASSIA JEROME OWYHEE
  BENEWAH KOOTENAI
DAM: OXBOW BROWNLEE
INDIAN: BANNOCK KALISPEL NEZPERCE
  SHOSHONI
LAKE: BEAR GRAYS PRIEST
MOUNTAIN: RYAN BORAH RHODES
  TAYLOR BIGBALDY BLUENOSE
MOUNTAIN RANGE: CABINET SELKIRK
NICKNAME: GEM
RIVER: SNAKE LOCHSA SALMON PAYETTE
SPRINGS: SODA HOOPER LAVAHOT
STATE BIRD: BLUEBIRD
STATE FLOWER: SYRINGA
TOWN: BUHL MALAD NAMPA BURLEY
  DRIGGS DUBOIS MOSCOW WEISER
  CASCADE CHALLIS ORIFINO REXBURG
  POCATELLO

IDEA EGG GIG KINK EIDOS IMAGE THING
  ANONYM DHARMA ECTYPE FIGURE
  INTENT NOTICE NOTION RECEPT THREAP
  THROPE BEGRIFF CONCEIT CONCEPT
  GIMMICK GLIMPSE MAROTTE OPINION
  PROJECT SPECIES SURMISE THOUGHT
  GIMCRACK NOTIONAL PRECONCEPTION
  (—S OF LITTLE VALUE) STUFF
  (CENTRAL —) ARGUMENT
  (COMMONPLACE —) SHIBBOLETH
  (CONSERVATIVE —S) FOGYISM
  (DOMINANT —) CLOU
  (DULL STUPID —S) STODGE

(FAINT —) GLIMMER
(FALSE —) FALLACY
(FANTASTIC —) VAPOR MAGGOT
(FAVORITE —) HORSE
(FIXED —) TICK
(FUNDAMENTAL —) KEYNOTE
(IRRATIONAL —) FOLLY
(MAIN —) POINT
(MUSICAL —) SENTENCE
(ODD —) FREAK
(OVERWORKED —) CLICHE
(PLATONIC —) ESSENCE
(RECURRING —) BURDEN
(STALE —S) BILGE
(SUPERSTITIOUS —) FREIT
(TRANSCENDENT —) FORM
(PL.) EIDE THOUGHT
(PREF.) IDEO
IDEAL ISM IDEA DREAM AERIAL BEAUTY
DOMNEI DREAMY MENTAL UNREAL
PATTERN PERFECT UTOPIAN ABSTRACT
FANCIFUL IDEALITY NOTIONAL
QUADRATE ORIFLAMME
(— OF BEAUTY) KALON
IDEALISM IDEOLOGY
IDEALIST IDEIST UTOPIAN FICHTEAN
UTOPIAST
IDEALIZE PLATONIZE
IDEALIZED POETICAL
IDENTICAL LIKE SAME SELF VERY ALIKE
EQUAL EVENLY PROPER CORRECT
IDENTIC NUMERIC SELFSAME
IDENTIFICATION DOCUMENT EQUATION
RECOGNITION
IDENTIFY PEG TAB MARK NAME RANK
SPOT IDENT PLACE TALLY FINGER
DISCERN DIAGNOSE PINPOINT
IDIOCY ANOIA ANOESIA FATUITY IDIOTRY
MOROSIS IDIOTISM
IDIOM CANT ARGOT JUANG DORISM
IFUGAO JARGON MEDISM SPEECH
AEOLISM ANOMALY GRECISM PEHLEVI
TURKISM DANICISM DORICISM IDIOTISM
IONICISM LANGUAGE LOCALISM
PARLANCE RURALISM
IDIOSYNCRASY WAY IDIASM RUMNESS
IDIOT FON OAF SOT DAFF DOLT FOOL
AMENT BOOBY DUNCE FONNE CRETIN
HOBBIL NIDGET NIDIOT DULLARD
NATURAL OMADAWN PINHEAD IMBECILE
INNOCENT SLAVERER
(AUTHOR OF —) DOSTOEVSKI
(CHARACTER IN —) LEF GANYA
AGLAYA PARFEN MYSHKIN NATASYA
EPANCHIN ROGOZHIN FILIPOVNA
ARDALIONOVITCH
IDIOTIC DAFT ZANY IDIOT FATUOUS
FOOLISH WANTWIT IMBECILE
IDLE COLD DEAD HACK HAKE HANG HULL
JAUK LAKE LAZE LAZY LUSK MUZZ SOFT
SORN TICK VAIN VOID DALLY EMPTY
SHOOL SLIVE THOKE WASTE COOTER
DAIDLE DANDER DREAMY FOOTER
GAMMER LOUNGY OTIANT OTIOSE
SLIMSY TEETER TIDDIE TIFFLE TRIFLE
TRUANT UNUSED VACANT DRONISH
IDLEFUL IDLESET LOAFING SAUNTER

SHACKLE SLUMBER SLUTHER UNLUSTY
VACUOUS WHIFFLE BASELESS
BOOTLESS FAINEANT INACTIVE
INDOLENT SHAMMOCK SLAISTER
SLOTHFUL TRIFLING WORKLESS
IDLENESS LAZE RUST SLOTH IGNAVIA
VACANCY VACUITY FLANERIE INACTION
IDLER BUM GAUM HAKE JAUK KERN
LOON DRONE BADAUD BUMBLE DONNOT
IDLEBY LUBBER PLAYER QUISBY RODNEY
STALKO TRUANT BLELLUM BUCKEEN
DAWDLER FAITOUR FRANION IDLESBY
LOLLARD LOUNGER LOUTHER LURDANE
SLOUNGE TRIFLER DOLITTLE FAINEANT
IDLESHIP LAYABOUT LAZARONE
UNWORKER WHIFFLER
IDLY TOOMLY VAGUELY
IDOL GOD BAAL ICON JOSS TIKI WOOD
ZEMI ANITO BESAN EIKON GUACA
HOBAL HUACA IMAGE STOCK SWAMI
MAUMET MINION PAGODA POPPET
PUPPET TERAPH EIDOLON MAHOMET
BAPHOMET MAUMETRY PANTHEUM
IDOLATRY BAALISM IMAGERY ADULTERY
MAUMETRY
IDOLIZE GOD IDOL ADORE ADMIRE
WORSHIP
IDYL IDYLL BUCOLIC ECLOGUE
IDYLLIC HALCYON PASTORAL
THEOCRITEAN
IDYLLS OF THE KING
(AUTHOR OF —) TENNYSON
(CHARACTER IN —) BORS ENID BALAN
BALIN ISOLT ARTHUR ELAINE GARETH
GAWAIN MERLIN MODRED VIVIEN
ETTARRE GALAHAD GERAINT LYNETTE
PELLEAS BEDIVERE LANCELOT TRISTRAM
GUINEVERE PERCIVALE
IF AN AND GIN SOBEIT THOUGH PROVIDED
(— EVER) ONCE
(— NOT) BUT ELSE NISI
IGNEOUS PLUTONIC
IGNIS FATUUS WISP SPUNKIE WILDFIRE
IGNITE TIND FLASH LIGHT SHOOT ILLUME
KINDLE CALCINE LIGHTEN
IGNITED LIVING BURNING
IGNITER SPARKER
IGNITION FIRE LIGHTING
IGNOBLE LOW BASE MEAN VILE ABJECT
GRUBBY SORDID CURRISH SERVILE
UNNOBLE BASEBORN SHAMEFUL
IGNOMINIOUS BASE VILE INFAMOUS
SHAMEFUL
IGNOMINY SHAME REBUKE SCANDAL
DISGRACE DISHONOR
IGNORAMUS IDIOT IGNARO SIMPLE
AMHAAREZ
IGNORANCE TAMAS AGNOSY AVIDYA
BETISE NICETY RUDITY UNSKILL
DARKNESS IDIOTISM NESCIENCE
(BOLD —) BAYARD
(FEIGNED —) IRONY
IGNORANT LAY DARK NICE RUDE VAIN
GREEN GROSS SILLY INGRAM SIMPLE
ARTLESS SECULAR UNAWARE UNCOUTH
UNKNOWN IMPERITE INNOCENT

INSCIENT INSCIOUS NESCIENT UNTAUGHT BENIGHTED

IGNORE BALK BLOW SINK SNUB VAIN BLINK ELIDE BYPASS MISKEN SLIGHT DESPISE MISKNOW NEGLECT CONFOUND OVERJUMP OVERLEAP OVERLOOK OVERPASS

ILIAD (AUTHOR OF —) HOMER (CHARACTER IN —) AIAS HELEN PARIS PRIAM ATHENA HECTOR NESTOR ACHILLES DIOMEDES MENELAUS ODYSSEUS PANDARUS AGAMEMNON APHRODITE PATROCLUS ANDROMACHE

ILK KIN

ILL BAD EVIL SICK AEGER CRONK CROOK DONCY FUNNY WISHT GROGGY INJURY POORLY SICKLY UNWELL SICKISH VICIOUS MISCHIEF PHYSICAL (— AT EASE) ASHAMED AWKWARD FAROUCHE (PREF.) MAL(E) MIS

ILL-ADVISED FOOLISH

ILL-BRED HOYDEN CADDISH CHURLISH PLEBEIAN MISLEARED

ILL-CONSIDERED HASTY

ILL-DEFINED BLIND VAGUE MONGREL

ILLEGAL BLACK LAWLESS UNLAWFUL ADULTERINE

ILLEGITIMATE BASE BASTARD BOOTLEG NATURAL NOTHOUS MISBEGOT NAMELESS UNLAWFUL WRONGFUL MISBEGOTTEN (PREF.) NOTH(O)

ILL-HUMORED FOUL GLUM CROOK DUDDY GRUMPY MOROSE STUFFY SULLEN CROOKED FRETFUL PEEVISH

ILLIBERAL LITTLE NARROW INSULAR BANAUSIC GRUDGING

ILLICIT SLY BLACK ILLEGAL UNLAWFUL

ILLINOIS

CAPITAL: SPRINGFIELD

COLLEGE: AURORA EUREKA OLIVET QUINCY SHIMER

COUNTY: BOND CASS COOK KANE OGLE COLES MACON BUREAU DUPAGE GRUNDY HARDIN MASSAC PEORIA IROQUOIS MACOUPIN SANGAMON

LAKE: MICHIGAN

NICKNAME: SUCKER PRAIRIE

RIVER: OHIO ROCK WABASH ELKHORN MACKINAW SANGAMON

STATE BIRD: CARDINAL

STATE FLOWER: VIOLET

STATE TREE: OAK

TOWN: PANA ALEDO ALTON CAIRO CARMI DIXON FLORA LACON OLNEY PARIS PEKIN ALBION CANTON EUREKA GALENA HARDIN HAVANA HERRIN JOLIET OTTAWA PEORIA QUINCY SKOKIE URBANA VIENNA CHICAGO DECATUR GENESEO MENDOTA NOKOMIS TAMPICO ROCKFORD

ILLITERATE UNREAD IGNORANT MUSELESS UNTAUGHT

ILL-NATURED ACID UGLY NASTY SURLY CRABBY SNARLY SULLEN THWART CANKERY PEEVISH

ILLNESS TOUT BRASH CHILL TRAIK MORBUS PLUNGE DISEASE SICKNESS (MENTAL —) MONOMANIA (MINOR —) HURRY (MOMENTARY —) DROW (SUDDEN —) WEED SWEAM

ILL-NOURISHED SHELLY

ILLOGICAL MAD SPURIOUS

ILL-OMENED DISMAL UNLUCKY

ILL-SMELLING FUSTY STINKING

ILL-TEMPERED ILL FESS MEAN PUXY ACRID CHUFF NURLY RATTY CAMMED CHUFFY CURSED GIRNIE SHRILL SNAGGY RAMPANT ROPABLE VICIOUS CAMSHACH LUNGEOUS SHREWISH VIXENISH MALODOROUS

ILL-TREAT FOB HOIN MISDO AFFRONT

ILLUMINATE FIRE LIMN CLEAR LIGHT ENLIMN ILLUME KINDLE BESHINE CLARIFY EMBLAZE LIGHTEN MINIATE RADIATE EMBRIGHT FLOURISH ILLUMINE LUMINATE

ILLUMINATION GLIM GLORY LIGHT SHINE LIGHTING LUMINARY

ILLUMINE SUN FIRE LAMP CLEAR LUMINE ENLIGHT

ILL-USAGE ABUSE

ILLUSION MAYA DEATH ERROR FAIRY FANCY FLESH TRICK MATTER CHIMERA FALLACY FICTION MOCKERY PHANTOM RAINBOW ZOLLNER DELUSION PHANTASM PRESTIGE

ILLUSORY FALSE EVANID FATUOUS PHANTOM TRICKSY APPARENT SPECTRAL

ILLUSTRATION CUT GAY ICON SHOW SPOT INSET FIGURE COMPARE DISIMILE EXEMPLUM INSTANCE VIGNETTE

ILLUSTRIOUS GRAND NOBLE NOTED SHEEN BRIGHT CANDID HEROIC EMINENT EXALTED GLORIED SHINING GLORIOUS HEROICAL LUCULENT MAGNIFIC PRECLARE RENOWNED SPLENDID STARLIKE BRILLIANT REDOUBTABLE

ILL WILL SPITE ENMITY GRUDGE MALICE MAUGRE RANCOR DESPITE AMBITION

IMAGE DAP GOD MAP FORM ICON IDOL JOSS MAKE SEAL SIGN SPIT TIKI AGNUS DITTO EPHOD HERMA MEDAL MORAL PAINT PRINT SAMMY SHAPE SIGIL SWAMY TOTEM AGALMA ALRAUN EFFIGY EMBLEM FIGURE MAUMET MODULE POPPET REFLEX SHRINE SPHINX STATUE TERAPH VISAGE WEEPER EIDOLON EXPRESS IMAGERY KATCINA PICTURE PROPOSE CONCEIVE DAIBUTSU OPTOGRAM PORTRAIT SURPRINT ZOOMORPH SEMBLANCE SIMILITUDE SIMULACRUM RESEMBLANCE (— IN CHINESE COSTUME) MANDARIN (— OF CHRIST) SUDARIUM (— OF DEITY) SWAMI GODKIN SVAMIN GODLING

(— OF SAINT) BULTO SAINT SANTO
GEORGE SANTON
(— OF WOOD) XOANON
(— RECALLED BY MEMORY) IDEA
(CULT —) JOSS
(FALSE —) GHOST
(GOOD-LUCK —) ALRAUN ALRUNA
(HEAVENLY —) FRAVASHI
(LINGERING —) SHADE
(MENTAL —) FANCY IMAGO RECEPT
CONCEPT FANTASY SPECIES PHANTASM
(RADAR —) BLIP
(REFLECTED —) SHADOW SPECIES
(SEQUENCE OF —S) REVERIE
(VAGUE —S) FRINGE
IMAGERY ICONISM
IMAGINARY IDEAL AERIAL FEIGNED
FICTIVE SHADOWY CHIMERAL CHIMERIC
FANCIFUL FICTIOUS MYTHICAL
NOTIONAL QUIXOTIC ROMANTIC
SCENICAL VISIONAL BARMECIDE
IMAGINATION CHIC BRAIN FANCY
FLAME NOTION FANTASY PROJECT
THOUGHT
(DROLL —) HUMOR
IMAGINATIVE FORMFUL CREATIVE
FANCIFUL POETICAL
IMAGINE SEE WIS REDE WEEN DREAM
FANCY FEIGN FRAME GUESS IMAGE
THINK DEVISE FIGURE IDEATE INVENT
RECKON COMPASS CONCEIT CONJURE
FANCIFY FANTASY FEATURE PICTURE
PORTRAY PROJECT PROPOSE SUPPOSE
SURMISE SUSPECT CONCEIVE
DAYDREAM JEALOUSE
IMBECILE MAD DOTE FOOL AMENT ANILE
DAFFY IDIOT CRANKY DOTARD DOTING
DOTISH CONGEON FATUOUS
IMBECILITY AMENTIA FATUITY
IMBIBE DRINK SMACK ABSORB SPONGE
INHAUST SWALLOW IRRIGATE
IMBUE SOAK STEW COLOR CROWN
INDUE SCENT STEEP TINCT ENSOUL
IMBIBE INFUSE LEAVEN SEASON
ANIMATE INGRAIN INSENSE INSTILL
SATURATE TINCTURE
IMBUED INSTINCT REDOLENT
IMITATE APE COPY ECHO MIME MOCK
ZANY ENSUE FORGE IMAGE MIMIC
AFFECT ANSWER FOLLOW SEMBLE
COPYCAT EMULATE PAGEANT PATTERN
PASTICHE RESEMBLE SIMULATE
(PREF.) MIMO
IMITATION COPY FAKE SHAM DUMMY
IMAGE MIMIC ALPACA ANSWER BUMPER
ECTYPE SHADOW CAMBLET FOULARD
IMITANT MIMESIS MOCKAGE MOCKERY
CHENILLE PARROTRY PASTICHE
POSTIQUE
(— OF COIN) COUNTER
(BURLESQUE —) TRAVESTY
(COTTON —) CAMBRIC
(EXAGGERATED —) BURLESQUE
(UNSUBSTANTIAL —) GHOST
IMITATOR APE MIME ZANY MIMIC
COPIER COPYIST EPIGONE EMULATOR
EPIGONUS HOMERIST

IMMACULATE CLEAN CANDID CHASTE
BLOTLESS SPOTLESS UNSOILED
IMMATERIAL MENTAL SLIGHT
ETHEREAL FORMLESS SEPARATE
TRIFLING
IMMATURE RAW CRUDE GREEN SAPPY
SMALL VEALY YOUNG BOYISH CALLOW
JEJUNE LARVAL NEANIC TENDER
GIRLISH HALFLIN IMPUBIC LADDISH
NOUVEAU PUERILE UNBAKED JUVENILE
NEPIONIC UNWEANED SHIRTTAIL
IMMATURITY NONAGE
IMMEASURABLE UNTOLD ABYSMAL
INFINITE
IMMEDIATE DIRECT MODERN PARATE
SUDDEN INSTANT PRESENT PROXIMAL
SYNECTIC POSTHASTE
IMMEDIATELY PDQ TIT ANON AWAY
FAST JUST ONCE SOON PLUMB RIGHT
ASTITE DIRECT PRESTO PRONTO SUBITO
DIRECTLY HEREUPON OUTRIGHT
STRAIGHT
IMMEMORIAL DATELESS
IMMENSE HUGE VAST GRAND GREAT
LARGE UNMEET UNRIDE TITANIC
ENORMOUS GIGANTIC INFINITE
SLASHING WHOOPING PLANETARY
IMMERSE DIP SINK SOAK COVER DOUSE
MERGE MERSE SOUSE STEEP DRENCH
PLUNGE BAPTIZE BOWSSEN DEMERGE
EMBATHE ENSTEEP IMMERGE DISSOLVE
IMMERSED DEEP INNATE
IMMINENT TOWARD PENDING
PROXIMATE
IMMOBILE FIXED STILL FROZEN
DORMANT GLACIAL TRANCED MOVELESS
(PREF.) ANKYL(O)
IMMOBILIZE FREEZE SPLINT STIFFEN
IMMOBILIZED STIFF
IMMODERATE FREE DIZZY UNDUE
LAVISH UNMETH EXTREME
OVERWEENING
IMMODERATENESS EXCESS
IMMODEST FREE BRAZEN OBSCENE
INDECENT PETULANT UNCHASTE
IMMORAL BAD ILL EVIL IDLE LOOSE
WRONG WANTON CORRUPT VICIOUS
CULPABLE DEPRAVED INDECENT
SLIPPERY
IMMORTAL DIVINE ENDLESS ETERNAL
GODLIKE UNDYING ENDURING UNDEADLY
IMMORTALITY AMRITA ATHANASY
ETERNITY
IMMOVABLE PAT SET FAST FIRM FIXED
RIGID ADAMANT SITFAST CONSTANT
IMMOBILE IMMOTIVE OBDURATE
IMMUNE FREE SALTED REFRACTORY
IMMUNITY SOC CHARTER FREEDOM
LIBERTY WOODGELD PROTECTION
IMMUTABLE ETERNAL
IMP PUG LIMB DEMON DEVILET DEVILING
DEVILKIN FOLLETTO
IMPACT HIT JAR BEAT BITE BLOW BUMP
DASH DUSH JOLT SLAM BRUNT CLASH
FEEZE PEISE POISE PULSE SHOCK SKITE
GLANCE STROKE CONTACT IMPULSE
COLLISION

IMPAIR MAR BLOT HARM HURT MAIM MANK SOUR WEAR ALLOY CLOUD CRACK CRAZE DECAY ERODE QUAIL SPOIL TAINT ACRAZE DAMAGE DEADEN DEFACE HINDER INJURE LABEFY LESSEN REDUCE SICKEN WEAKEN WORSEN BLEMISH CRIPPLE DISABLE IMPEACH REFRACT SHATTER STRETCH VITIATE DECREASE ENFEEBLE IMBECILE IMPERISH INFRINGE LABEFACT
(— BY INACTIVITY) RUST
(— ESSENTIALLY) RUIN

IMPAIRED HURT STALE CROCKY FLYBLOWN
(— BY AGE) FUSTY
(— IN TONE) BREATHY
(PREF.) DYS

IMPAIRMENT ALLAY FAULT SPOIL DOTAGE IMPAIR INJURY LESION BEATING DEFICIT DISEASE EROSION WEARING AKINESIA PAIRMENT

IMPALE BAIT SPIT GANCH SPEAR SPIKE STAKE STICK STING SKIVER TRANSFIX

IMPART GIVE SHED TELL BREAK DRILL SHARE YIELD BESTOW COMMON CONFER CONVEY DIRECT IMPUTE INSTIL PARTEN REVEAL DELIVER DIVULGE PURPORT DISCOVER INSTRUCT INTIMATE

IMPARTIAL EVEN FAIR JUST EQUAL LEVEL CANDID NEUTER UNBIASED

IMPARTIALITY CANDOR EQUITY EQUACITY EVENNESS

IMPASSABLE WICKED INVIOUS PASSLESS ROADLESS TRACKLESS

IMPASSE LOGJAM DEADLOCK

IMPASSIVE FROZEN STOLID PASSIVE STOICAL PHLEGMATIC

IMPASSIVENESS APATHY MORGUE STOICISM

IMPATIENT HOT ANTSY EAGER HASTY SHARP TESTY FRETFUL PEEVISH RESTIVE TIDIOSE CHOLERIC PETULANT

IMPEACH CALL ACCUSE CHARGE INDICT ARRAIGN CENSURE IMPLEAD TRAVERSE

IMPEDE BOG DAM GUM JAM LET MAR CLOG GRAB JAMB KILL SLUG SNAG ANNOY BLOCK CHECK CHOKE DELAY EMBAR ESTOP HITCH SLOTH SPOKE BAFFLE FETTER FORBID FORSET HAMPER HARASS HINDER HOBBLE PESTER RETARD STYMIE IMPEACH PREVENT SHACKLE ENCUMBER HANDICAP OBSTRUCT PRECLUDE

IMPEDIMENT BAR RUB CLOG SNAG STOP BLEAR BLOCK HITCH SPOKE STICK BURDEN RUBBER SCOTCH BLINDER EMBARGO OBSTACLE OBSTANCY
(— IN SPEECH) HAAR HALT

IMPEL PAT PUT BEAR BEAT CALL CAST GOAD HURL MOVE SEND URGE WHIP CARRY DRIVE FEEZE FORCE KNOCK PRESS PRICK PULSE COMPEL EXCITE INCITE INDUCE PROPEL ACTUATE DESTINE INSPIRE INSTINCT MOTIVATE

IMPEND BREW HANG DEPEND OVERHANG

IMPENDING TOWARD PENDENT PENDING IMMINENT MENACING

IMPENETRABLE HARD DENSE MURKY PROOF THICK AIRTIGHT HARDENED

IMPENITENT OBDURATE

IMPERATIVE VITAL PRESSING MASTERFUL

IMPERCEPTIBLE OCCULT SUBTLE

IMPERFECT ILL HALF POOR AMISS BLIND FUZZY ROUGH BOTCHY FAULTY PLATIC ATELENE STICKIT UNWHOLE VICIOUS INPARFIT MUTILOUS

IMPERFECTION BUG RUB WEN FLAW KINK MOLE SLUR VICE ERROR FAULT BLOTCH DEFECT FOIBLE BLEMISH CRUDITY DEFAULT DEMERIT FAILING FRAILTY WEAKNESS
(— IN BOTTLE) HEELTAP
(— IN GLASS) STRIA STREAK
(— IN LEATHER) FRIEZE
(— IN SILK) CORKSCREW
(— IN WICK) THIEF WASTER

IMPERIAL TUFT ROYAL KINGLY PURPLE MAJESTIC

IMPERIL RISK EXPONE EMPERIL ENDANGER JEOPARDY

IMPERIOUS SURLY LORDLY HAUGHTY DESPOTIC IMPERIAL MASTERLY PRESSING MASTERFUL

IMPERISHABLE ETERNAL UNDYING ENDURING IMMORTAL

IMPERMANENT FLEETING

IMPERSONAL COLD DEADPAN INHUMAN ABSTRACT

IMPERSONATE POSE TYPIFY PERSONIFY

IMPERTINENCE PAWK SNASH AUDACITY

IMPERTINENT GAY FREE PERT RUDE FRESH SASSY SAUCY PUSHING IMPERENT IMPUDENT OBTRUSIVE OFFICIOUS MEDDLESOME

IMPERTURBABLE COOL PLACID GLACIAL TRANQUIL UNFLAPPABLE

IMPERVIOUS DEAD GASTIGHT HARDENED HERMETIC MOTHPROOF

IMPETUOUS HOT RAMP RUDE BRASH EAGER FIERY FRECK HASTY HEADY SHARP ARDENT BROTHE FIERCE FLASHY LAVISH RACKLE STRONG BUCKISH FURIOUS HOTHEAD HOTSPUR RAMSTAM VIOLENT BRAINISH EMPRESSE HEADLONG SLAPDASH VEHEMENT PRECIPITATE

IMPETUS BIRR FARD SEND DRIFT GRACE SWING YMPET BENSEL IMPACT POWDER RAVINE SWINGE SWOUGH IMPULSE MOMENTUM

IMPINGE FALL IMPACT ASSAULT CROSSCUT

IMPIOUS UNHOLY ATHEIST ATHEOUS GODLESS UNGODLY DOWNWEED HOARWORT NEFANDOUS NEFARIOUS

IMPLACABLE STOUT DEADLY MORTAL

IMPLEMENT (ALSO SEE TOOL) AX AXE BAT CARD DISC DISK FORK GRAB HACK HONE HOOK LOOM PLOW SPUD SPUR TOOL CROOK DRILL FLINT LANCE SCRUB

SHEAR SLICK SPADE SPOON STEEL STICK
TRIER AMGARN BEAMER BLADER
BROACH COLLAR COOLER DIBBLE
DREDGE DRIVER DUSTER EOLITH FLUTER
HACKER HARROW INVOKE LADDER
LIPPER LUNATE MARKER MEALER
PACKER PADDLE PESTLE PLOUGH
RIMMER SCREEN SCYTHE SEATER
SERVER SHEARS SHOVEL SLICER
(— FOR CUTTING CHEESE) HARP
(— FOR HANGING POT) HALE
(— TO PREVENT MALT FROM
OVERFLOWING) STROM
(—S OF HUSBANDRY) WAINAGE
(ANCIENT —) POINT SLICE AMGARN
EOLITH NEOLITH RACLOIR PALEOLITH
(BAKER'S —) PEEL
(CLIMBING —) CREEPER
(ESKIMO —) ULU
(GARDENING —) HOE RAKE SEEDER
SICKLE
(HEDGING —) TRAMP
(IRRIGATION —) CROWDER
(LOGGING —) TODE
(POTTER'S —) PALLET SPATTLE
(PREHISTORIC —) CELT FLAKER
(SHOVEL-LIKE —) SCOOP
(SOLDERING —) DOCTOR
(TORTURE —) ENGINE
(UPROOTING —) MAKE
(WINNOWING —) FAN
IMPLICATE DIP ENWRAP CONCERN
EMBROIL INCLUDE INVOLVE
IMPLICIT COVERT
IMPLIED TACIT IMPLICIT
IMPLORE ASK BEG CRY PRAY CHARM
CRAVE PLEAD INVOKE OBTEST BESEECH
CONJURE ENTREAT SOLICIT PETITION
IMPLY HINT ARGUE CARRY COUCH INFER
EMPLOY ENTAIL IMPORT INDUCE
CONNOTE CONTAIN INCLUDE INVOLVE
PRESUME SIGNIFY SUGGEST SUPPOSE
PREDICATE
IMPOLITE RUDE UNCIVIL
IMPOLITENESS CRUDITY
IMPONDERABLE FRIGORIC
IMPORT SAY WIT BEAR BODY TOUR
DRIFT FORCE IMPLY MORAL SCOPE
SENSE SOUND SPELL VALOR AMOUNT
CHARGE DENOTE INGATE INTENT
MATTER SPIRIT BETOKEN MEANING
PRETEND SIGNIFY CARRIAGE INDICATE
IMPORTANCE BORE MARK PITH FORCE
POISE WORTH CHARGE IMPORT MATTER
MOMENT REMARK STRESS STROKE
WEIGHT ACCOUNT ESSENCE GRAVITY
VALENCY EMPHASIS MAGNITUDE
SIGNIFICANCE
IMPORTANCE OF BEING EARNEST
(AUTHOR OF —) WILDE
(CHARACTER IN —) JACK ALGIE PRISM
CECILY EARNEST ALGERNON WORTHING
BRACKNELL GWENDOLEN MONCRIEFF
IMPORTANT BIG DEAR DREE HIGH MAIN
REAL GRAVE GREAT GAPING NEEDLE
STRONG URGENT CAPITAL CENTRAL
CRUCIAL EMINENT PIVOTAL SERIOUS

EVENTFUL MATERIAL PRESSING
MOMENTOUS OVERBEARING
SIGNIFICANT
IMPORTUNE BEG WOO BEAT BONE PRIG
TOUT PRESS TEASE BESEECH BESIEGE
INSTANT SOLICIT TERRIFY INSTANCE
IMPOSE SET TOP CLAP GIVE LEVY MUMP
POLE SORN ABUSE APPLY CLAMP INPUT
STAMP TRUMP BURDEN CHARGE ENJOIN
ENTAIL FASTEN FATHER IMPONE IMPUTE
BLAFLUM DICTATE INFLICT IRROGATE
(— UPON) FOB GAG HUM LAY DUPE
SELL CULLY TRAIL BLUDGE DELUDE
EXCISE HUMBUG NUZZLE CULLION
DECEIVE HOODWINK
IMPOSING BIG EPIC BUDGE BURLY
GRAND HEFTY NOBLE PROUD AUGUST
EPICAL FEUDAL PORTLY HAUGHTY
POMPOUS STATELY HANDSOME
MAGNIFIC SONORANT SONOROUS
IMPOSITION BAM COD HUM LEVY SELL
TAIL GOUGE IMPOT CHOUSE GAMMON
INTAKE TAILLE IMPOSAL ARTIFICE
IMPOSURE
(MILITARY —) CESS
(SCHOOL —) PENSUM
IMPOSSIBLE OUT HOPELESS
IMPOST LAY TAX CAST LEVY TAIL TASK
TOLL EXCISE GABELLE POUNAMU
TALLAGE TONNAGE TRIBUTE CHAPTREL
SPRINGER
IMPOSTOR FOB FAKE GULL IDOL CHEAT
FAKER FRAUD GOUGE QUACK BUNYIP
FOURBE HUMBUG MUMPER EMPIRIC
FAITOUR PROCTOR SHAMMER
PHANTASM
IMPOSTURE BAM GAG FAKE HOAX
SHAM CHEAT FRAUD TRICK DECEIT
HUMBUG JUGGLE ARTIFICE DELUSION
JUGGLERY
IMPOTENCE ACRATIA UNMIGHT
WEAKNESS
IMPOTENT WEAK FRIGID PAULIE UNABLE
STERILE UNMIGHTY
IMPOVERISHED POOR OBOLARY
BANKRUPT INDIGENT
IMPRACTICAL CRAZY FECKLESS
IMPRECATION DASH OATH PIZE WISH
BLAME CURSE ANATHEMA
IMPREGNABLE FAST PROOF
IMPREGNATE BIG HOP DOPE FILL LIME
MILT BREED IMBUE STOCK STUFF TINCT
AERATE CHARGE INFORM INFUSE
LEAVEN SEASON SETTLE ENVENOM
CONCEIVE FRICTION FRUCTIFY
MEDICATE PERMEATE SATURATE
SILICATE
IMPRESS FIX BITE COIN DING DINT ETCH
MARK AFFIX BRAND CLAMP CRIMP DRIVE
GRAVE GRILL INFIX PRESS PRINT REACH
SEIZE STAMP STEAD WRITE AFFECT
ENSEAL FASTEN INCUSE INDENT SALUTE
STRIKE ANTIQUE ENSTAMP IMPLANT
IMPREST IMPRINT INSENSE AUTOTYPE
INSCRIBE NEGATIVE
(— DEEPLY) DELVE ENGRAVE
(— SUDDENLY) SMITE

(— WITH FEAR) AFFRIGHT

IMPRESSION CUT HIT AURA CAST CHOP
DENT DINT IDEA MARK MOLD SEAL STEP
STIR FANCY GOUGE IMAGE MOULD PRINT
STAMP STATE ECTYPE EFFECT ENGRAM
FIGURE INCUSE OFFSET SIGNET STRIKE
EOPHYTE ETCHING FANTASY IMPRESS
MOULAGE OPINION SEALING SQUEEZE
STENCIL TOOLING BLANKING
ENGRAMMA NEGATIVE PRESSION
PRESSURE STAMPAGE TOOLMARK
PHOTOGENE
(— OF DIE) CLICHE
(— ON COIN) CROSS
(— WITHOUT INK) ALBINO
(AUDITORY —) SOUND
(DOUBLE —) MACKLE MACULE
(IMMEDIATE —) APERCU
(LUMINOUS —) PHOSPHENE
(MAKE AN — ON) GRAB
(MENTAL —) GRAVING
(STRONG —) HUNCH
(TRANSITORY —) SNAPSHOT
(VIVID —) SPLASH

IMPRESSIONABLE SOFT WAXY WAXEN
TENDER PLASTIC PASSIBLE

IMPRESSIVE BIG FAT EPIC AWFUL
GRAND NOBLE PROUD EPICAL SOLEMN
STATELY TEARING TELLING WEIGHTY
FORCIBLE IMPOSING SMASHING
SONORANT SONOROUS STUNNING
MAGNIFICENT

IMPRINT DINT ETCH SIGN STEP PRESS
STAMP CUTOFF FASTEN STRIKE
ENGRAVE ENSTAMP IMPRESS COLOPHON
EPIGRAPH PRESSURE

IMPRISON JUG LAG NUN BOND GAOL
HULK JAIL QUOD SEAL SHOP WARD
CROWD EMBAR GRATE COMMIT IMMURE
JIGGER PRISON SLOUGH CONFINE
INTOWER BASTILLE

IMPROBABLE FISHY UNLIKE UNLIKELY

IMPROMPTU GLIB MAGGOT SUDDEN
OFFHAND

IMPROPER BAD AMISS SPICY UNDUE
UNJUST ILLICIT INDECENT PERVERSE
TORTIOUS UNSEEMLY MALODOROUS

IMPROPERLY AMISS

IMPROVE FIX GAIN GOOD GROW HELP
MEND AMEND EDIFY EMEND GRADE
SMART TOUCH BETTER ENRICH PROFIT
ADVANCE BENEFIT CORRECT CULTURE
ELEVATE PERFECT PROMOTE RECTIFY
UPSWING
(— APPEARANCE OF HORSE) BISHOP
(— APPEARANCE OF TEA) FACE
(— CONDUCTIVITY) AGE

IMPROVEMENT AMENDS PICKUP
POLICY PROFIT REFORM REDRESS
UPSWING

IMPROVIDENT PRODIGAL WASTEFUL

IMPROVISE COOK PONG VAMP ADLIB
FANTASY
(— MUSICALLY) JAM FAKE NOODLE

IMPRUDENT FESS RASH FALSE UNWARY
FOOLISH RECKLESS

IMPUDENCE GALL BRASS CHEEK MOUTH
NERVE SLACK BRONZE PUPPYISM

IMPUDENT BOLD COXY RUDE BANTY
BRASH FRESH GALLY LIPPY SASSY
SAUCY BRASSY BRAZEN CHEEKY STOCKY
BIGGETY FORWARD INSOLENT
MALAPERT AUDACIOUS BAREFACED

IMPULSE FIT BIAS SEND URGE DRIVE
NISUS SPEND START DESIRE MOTIVE
SIGNAL SPLEEN CALLING IMPETUS
INSTINCT MOVEMENT STIRRING
(BLIND —) ATE
(ELECTRICAL —) KICK
(SPONTANEOUS —) ACCORD
(SUDDEN —) SPLEEN
(SUPERNATURAL —) AFFLATUS

IMPULSIVE QUICK FITFUL HEADLONG

IMPURE DRY FOUL LEWD GROSS MUDDY
FILTHY TURBID UNPURE MONGREL
SCABBED UNCLEAN VICIOUS INDECENT
MACULATE PRURIENT

IMPURITY CRUD DONOR DROSS FEDITY
ACCEPTOR FOULNESS
(— IN LINT) SHALE
(— IN MINERAL) GANGUE

IN AT TO INTO UPON ALONG
(— A FAINT) AWAY
(— A SERIES) SERIATIM
(— A STATE OF ACTION) ENERGIC
(— ACCORDANCE) AFTER
(— ADDITION) EKE TOO ALSO ABOVE
AGAIN ALONG FORBY STILL BEYOND
BESIDES FARTHER FURTHER MOREOVER
OVERPLUS THERETIL
(— ADVANCE) AHEAD FORTH BEFORE
(— ANY CASE) EVER HOWEVER
(— BEHALF OF) PRO
(— CASE THAT) AUNTERS
(— CIRCULATION) ABROAD
(— CONNECTION WITH) FORNENT
FERNINST
(— EARNEST) AGOOD
(— EXCESS OF) OVER
(— FACT) SOOTH TRULY INDEED ITSELF
MERELY VERILY ACTUALLY VERAMENT
(— FAITH) IVADS EFECKS YFACKS
(— FRONT) FORE AFACE FORNE
AGAINST PARAVANT
(— FULL) ALONG
(— GOOD SEASON) BETIMES
(— GOOD SPIRITS) BOBBISH
(— GRACEFUL MANNER) ADAGIO
(— JEST) AGAME
(— NO MANNER) NOWISE NAEGATES
(— ONE DIRECTION) ANON
(— ORDER) FOR ATAUNT ATAUNTO
(— PLACE OF) FOR WITH INSTEAD
(— POSSESSION) WITHIN
(— PROGRESS) AFOOT TOWARD
(— PROPER MANNER) DULY
(— RESPECT TO) ANENT
(— RETURN FOR) AGAINST
(— ROTATION) ABOUT
(— SO FAR AS) AS QUA
(— SOLE CONTROL) ABSOLUTE
(— SOOTH) PARFEY PERFAY

(— SPITE OF) FOR ALTHO MALGRE AGAINST DESPITE MALGRADO
(— SUSPENSE) PENDING
(— THE DOING OF) WITH
(— THE FIELD) ABROAD
(— THE FIRST PLACE) IMP IMPRIMIS
(— THE FUTURE) HENCE
(— THE MORNING) MANE
(— THE REAR) AREAR ASTERN
(— THE SAME PLACE) IBID IBIDEM
(— THE SAME WAY) AS
(— TOWARD) INOWER
(— TRUTH) MARRY SOOTH CERTES INDEED VERILY SOOTHLY FORSOOTH
(— VAIN) WASTELY
(— VIEW OF THE FACT THAT) SEEING
(— WHAT MANNER) HOW QUOMODO
(NOT —) OUT

INACCESSIBLE COY REMOTE WICKED SHADOWY

INACCURATE SOUR FALSE LOOSE FAULTY UNJUST INEXACT IMPROPER SLIPSHOD

INACTION RUST

INACTIVATE MOTHBALL

INACTIVE LAX DEAD DRUG FLAT IDLE LAZY SLOW HEAVY INERT NOBLE SLACK SULKY ASLEEP STATIC SUPINE TORPID CESSANT DORMANT PASSIVE RESTIVE COMATOSE COMATOUS DILATORY SLOTHFUL SLUGGISH THEWLESS QUIESCENT

INACTIVITY SLOTH ANERGY TORPOR ANERGIA ABEYANCE IDLENESS CESSATION SEGNITUDE

INADEQUATE BAD BARE POOR THIN INEPT SCANT SHORT SLACK FEEBLE STRAIT FOOLISH INVALID SLENDER HIGHLAND INFERIOR MISERABLE

INADVERTENT CARELESS

INANE DIZZY EMPTY JERKY SILLY VAPID JEJUNE VACANT FATUOUS FOOLISH INSIPID VACUOUS IMBECILE SLIPSLOP TRIFLING

INANIMATE DEAD DULL BRUTE INERT DEADLY STOLID STUPID LIFELESS

INAPPROPRIATE INEPT UNAPT UNDUE FOREIGN UNHAPPY

INARTICULATE DUMB LAME THICK

INATTENTION ABSENCE NEGLECT APROSEXIA

INATTENTIVE DEAF SLACK ABSENT REMISS SUPINE DREAMSY CARELESS DISTRAIT HEEDLESS MINDLESS

INAUGURATE AUGUR BEGIN HANDSEL INITIATE

INAUSPICIOUS BAD ILL EVIL FOUL ADVERSE OBSCENE OMINOUS UNHAPPY UNLUCKY SINISTER

INCA INGUA OREJON

INCALCULABLE UNTOLD SUMLESS UNKNOWN

INCANDESCENT BRIGHT

INCANTATION CHARM DAWUT SPELL CARMEN FETISH MANTRA CANTION CHANTRY GREEGREE

INCAPABLE DEAD NUMB UNABLE HANDLESS

INCAPACITATE NAPOO UNFIT NOBBLE UNABLE DISABLE

INCAPACITATED FLAT DISABLED STRICKEN

INCARCERATE IMMURE CONFINE IMPRISON

INCARNATE BODIED EMBODY CARNATE ENFLESH HUMANIFY PERSONIFY

INCARNATION RAMA IMAGE ADVENT AVATAR GENIUS TERTON EPIPHANY

INCENDIARY FIREBUG ARSONIST BOUTEFEU

INCENSE CENSE INFLAME KETURAH PROVOKE IRRITATE THYMIAMA

INCENSED RAW IRATE WROTH WRATHFUL

INCENTIVE BROD GOAD SPUR PRICK MOTIVE IMPETUS IMPULSE INCITIVE STIMULUS MOTIVATION

INCESSANT STEADY ENDLESS CONSTANT

INCH PRIME UNCIA
(ABOUT 7 —S) FISTMELE
(100TH OF —) POINT
(4 —S) HANDFUL
(48TH OF —) IRON
(9 —S) SPAN

INCIDENT GO EVENT LIABLE CAUTION EPISODE PASSAGE SUBJECT ACCIDENT CASUALTY OCCASION OCCURRENCE
(AMUSING —) BAR BREAK
(LITERARY —) BIT

INCIDENTAL BY SIDE STRAY CASUAL EPISODIC GLANCING INCIDENT OCCURRENT

INCIDENTALLY BYHAND OBITER APROPOS

INCINERATE COMBUST CREMATE

INCINERATOR BURNER SALAMANDER

INCISION CUT GASH SLIT SNIP ISSUE SCORE BROACH SCOTCH STREAK CUTDOWN DIACOPE APLOTOMY CECOTOMY COLOTOMY
(SUFF.) TOMY

INCISIVE ACID KEEN CRISP SHARP BITING BRUTAL CUTTING ACULEATE PIERCING TRENCHANT

INCITE EGG HIE HOY PUT SIC TAR ABET BEET BUZZ EDGE FIRE GOAD LASH MOVE PROD SICK SNIP SPUR STIR URGE WHET AWAKE CHIRK IMPEL PRICK PROKE SPARK SPURN STING TEMPT AROUSE BESTIR ENTICE EXCITE EXHORT FILLIP FOMENT HALLOO INDUCE KINDLE NETTLE PROMPT UPSTIR ACTUATE ANIMATE COMMOVE INCENSE INSPIRE PROMOVE PROVOKE QUICKEN SOLICIT INCITATE MOTIVATE
(— SECRETLY) SUBORN
(— TO ATTACK) SET HIRR SOOL

INCLEMENT RAW HARD RUDE SOUR GURLY STARK COARSE RUGGED SEVERE UNFINE UNKINDLY

INCLINATION GEE MAW PLY SET BENT BIAS BROO CANT CARE DRAG DRAW

EDGE FALL GUST HANG LEAN LIKE LIST
LOVE LUST MIND SLEW TURN VEIN WILL
BEVEL BOSOM DRAFT DRIFT FANCY
GRAIN HABIT HIELD HUMOR KNACK
LURCH PITCH POISE SLANT SLOPE
STUDY SWING TASTE THEAT TREND
AFFECT ANIMUS ANLAGE ASCENT
DESIRE DEVICE GATHER GENIUS INTENT
LIKING MOTION NOTION PONDUS RELISH
SQUINT TALENT YETZER APTNESS
CONATUS COURAGE CURRENT DRAUGHT
FANTASY INKLING LEANING STOMACH
VERSANT WILLING APPETITE APTITUDE
CLINAMEN DEVOTION GRADIENT
PENCHANT TENDENCY VELLEITY
VERGENCY WOULDING PROCLIVITY
PROPENSITY
(— DOWNWARD) DIP DESCENT
HANGING
(— OF OARSMAN'S BODY) LAYBACK
(INWARD —) BATTER
(PREDOMINATE —) STRENGTH
INCLINE APT BOW DIP KIP TIP WRY BEAR
BEND BIAS BREW CANT CAST DOCK
DOOK DOOR DROP GIVE HANG HEEL
HELD HILL LEAN LIKE LIST PECK PEND
RAKE SEEL STAY SWAY TILT TURN
BEVEL CLIMB CLINE DROOP FLECT HIELD
JINNY OFFER PITCH SHAPE SLANT SLOPE
SOUND VERGE AFFECT GLACIS INTEND
SHELVE STEEVE UPBROW DECLINE
DESCEND GANGWAY PROPEND PROCLINE
PROCLIVE
INCLINED APT SIB BENT CANT FAIN LIEF
RIFE VAIN ARAKE GIVEN PRONE READY
COUCHE MINDED PROMPT SLOPED
SUPINE FORWARD HANGING OBLIQUE
PRONATE STUDIED AFFECTED DISPOSED
ENCLITIC PREGNANT PROPENSE
SIDELING TALENTED
INCLUDE ADD LAP HAVE TAKE ANNEX
COUCH COVER IMPLY EMPLOY ENSEAM
RECKON BELOUKE COLLECT CONNOTE
CONTAIN EMBRACE IMMERSE INVOLVE
RECOUNT SUBSUME COMPRISE
CONCLUDE
INCOHERENT FUZZY BROKEN RAVING
INCHOATE
INCOME GAIN PORT RENT LIVING
PEWAGE PROFIT SALARY FACULTY
INTRADO PRODUCE REVENUE STIPEND
INTEREST PROCEEDS POCKETBOOK
(— OF BENEFICE) ANNAT
(ANNUAL —) RENTE
(UNFORESEEN —) GRAVY
INCOMPARABLE ALONE
INCOMPATIBLE ALIEN REPUGNANT
INCOMPETENT INEPT UNFIT SLOUCH
UNABLE UNMEET FECKLESS HANDLESS
HELPLESS SPLITTER
INCOMPLETE WANE BLIND ROUGH
BROKEN UNDONE DIVIDED LACKING
PARTIAL IMMATURE INCHOATE
SEGMENTAL
INCOMPREHENSIBLE PARTIAL
COCKEYED
INCONCLUSIVE FUZZY

INCONGRUOUS ALIEN ABSURD
ANOMALOUS
INCONSIDERATE RASH UNKIND
ASOCIAL RECKLESS
INCONSISTENT ALIEN REPUGNANT
INCONSPICUOUS OBSCURE
INCONSTANT FICKLE BRUCKLE FLUXILE
MOONISH MUTABLE SLIDING VARIOUS
FLUXIBLE MOVEABLE STRUMPET
VARIABLE CHAMELEON MERCURIAL
VERSATILE
INCONVENIENCE FASH BOTHER
CUMBER STRESS SQUEEZE DISQUIET
INCONVENIENT UNKED CLUMSY
UNBANE UNGAIN AWKWARD UNHANDY
ANNOYING UNCHANCY UNTOWARD
INCORPORATE MIX FOLD FUSE JOIN
ANNEX KNEAD MERGE UNITE ABSORB
EMBODY ENGRAIN ENTRAIN INWEAVE
INCORPSE
INCORRECT BAD ILL OFF FALSE WRONG
PECCANT UNRIGHT UNSOUND VICIOUS
PERVERSE
INCORRIGIBLE HARD
INCREASE UP ADD EKE IMP WAX BUMP
GAIN GROW HIKE ITCH JACK JUMP
MEND MORE MUCH PLUS PUSH RISE
SOAR THEE THRO BOOST BUILD BULGE
CLIMB CROWD FLUSH FRESH HEAVE
LARGE RAISE SPURT SWELL ACCENT
ACCESS ACCRUE BETTER BIGGEN
CHANGE DEEPEN DOUBLE EXPAND
EXTEND EXTENT GATHER GROWTH
SPREAD SPRING ADVANCE AMPLIFY
AUCTION AUGMENT AUXESIS BALLOON
DISTEND ELEVATE ENGROSS ENHANCE
ENLARGE GREATEN IMPROVE INFLATE
MAGNIFY STEEPEN SURCRUE ACCRESCE
ADDITION COMPOUND FLOURISH
HEIGHTEN LENGTHEN MAJORATE
MAXIMATE MAXIMIZE MULTIPLY
THRODDEN PROPAGATE PROLIFERATE
(— AT USURY) OCKER
(— GREATLY) ACCUMULATE
(— HEAT OF KILN) RUSTLE GLISTER
(— IN BUSINESS) UPBEAT
(— IN PAY) FOGY
(— IN STRENGTH) FRESHEN
(— KNOWLEDGE) ENRICH
(— POWER) SOUP
(— PRICE BY BIDDING) CANT
(— SPEED) JAZZ ACCELERATE
(— STITCHES) FASHION
(— SUDDENLY) LEAP
(PRICE —) RIST
(SHORT-TERM —) BOOMLET
INCREASING GROWING CRESCENT
CRESCIVE DILATANT SWELLING
INCREDIBLE TALL STEEP DAMNED
FABULOUS
INCRUSTATION CRUD MOSS CRUST
SCALE TARTAR FOULING FURRING
INCULCATE BREED INFIX INCULK INFUSE
IMPLANT IMPRESS INSTILL
INCUR RUN BEAR GAIN WAGE CONTRACT
INCURABLE BOOTLESS HOPELESS
INCURSION RAID ROAD FORAY INFALL

INROAD RAZZIA DESCENT HOSTING
INBREAK INCURSE ANABASIS INVASION
INDECENT PAW BLUE FOUL LEWD RANK
BAWDY GROSS NASTY SAUCY GREASY
IMPURE PAWPAW SMUTTY CURIOUS
GRIVOIS IMMORAL OBSCENE IMMODEST
IMPROPER SHAMEFUL UNCOMELY
INDECISION DEMUR DOUBT MAYBE
POISE SWITHER
INDECOROUS RUDE COARSE FORWARD
UNCIVIL IMMODEST IMPOLITE IMPROPER
INDECENT UNSEEMLY UNTOWARD
INDEED SO TOO YEA EVEN JUST SURE
MARRY TIENS ITSELF PARDIE SURELY
FAITHLY FRANKLY FORSOOTH VERAMENT
INDEFINITE HAZY FUZZY GROSS LOOSE
VAGUE DIVERS INEXACT AORISTIC
INDELIBLE FAST FIXED
INDELICATE RAW FREE WARM BROAD
GROSS ROUGH COARSE GREASY
IMPOLITE IMPROPER UNSEEMLY
INDEMNIFY PAY RECOUP SATISFY
WARRANT
INDENT JAG BRIT DENT GIMP MUSH NICK
CHASE DELVE NOTCH STAMP TOOTH
WHEEL BRUISE CRENEL ENGRAIL
GAUFFER
INDENTATION CHOP DENT DINT DOKE
FOIL KINK SCAR BOSOM BULGE CLEFT
CRENA DINGE NOTCH SINUS DIMPLE
FURROW GROOVE INDENT RECESS
IMPRESS CRENELLE TOOTHING
(— IN BOTTLE) KICK
(— IN DOG'S FACE) STOP
(— IN SHELL) EYE
INDEPENDENCE AUTARKY FREEDOM
(— OF GOD) ASEITY
(POLITICAL —) SWARAJ
INDEPENDENT FREE PROUD SEEKER
BIGGITY DIVIDED MUGWUMP SECTARY
ABSOLUTE PECULIAR POSITIVE
SEPARATE
(STATISTICALLY —) ORTHOGONAL
INDEX PIE FIST HAND ARNETH ELENCH
PIGNET TONGUE POINTER ALPHABET
EXPONENT REGISTER

INDIA

CAPE: COMORIN
CAPITAL: NEWDELHI
COIN: LAC PIE ANNA FELS LAKH PICE
TARA ABIDI CRORE PAISA RUPEE
DESERT: THAR
DISTRICT: SIBI NASIK PATNA SIMLA
ZILLAH MALABAR NELLORE MOFUSSIL
GULF: KUTCH CAMBAY MANNAR
ISLAND: CHILKA
LAKE: WULAR CHILKA COLAIR DHEBAR
SAMBAHR
MEASURE: ADY DHA GAZ GUZ JOW KOS
LAN SER BYEE COSS DAIN DHAN HATH
JAOB KUNK MOOT PARA RAIK RATI SEIT
TAUN TENG TOLA ANNA BIGHA CAHAR
COVID CROSA DANDA DRONA GARCE
GIREH HASTA PALLY PARAH RATTI

SALAY YOJAN ADHAKA ANGULA COVIDO
CUDAVA CUMBHA GEERAH LAMANY
MOOLUM MUSHTI PALGAT PARRAH
ROPANI TIPREE UNGLEE YOJANA
ADOULIE DHANUSH GAVYUTI KHAHOON
NIRANGA PRASTHA VITASTI OKTHABAH
MOUNTAIN: MERU GHATS KAMET
MASTUJ TANKSE KALAHOI SIWALIK
VINDHYA SULEIMAN
MOUNTAIN RANGE: SATPURA VINDHYA
ARAVALLI HIMALAYA
NATIVE: TODA HINDU TAMIL
PROVINCE: HAR ASSAM BIHAR ANDHRA
BENGAL KERALA MADRAS MYSORE
ORISSA PUNJAB GUJARAT HARYANA
KASHMIR MANIPUR
REGION: MALABAR
RIVER: AI DOR SON TEL KOSI KUSI NIRA
REHR SIND BETWA BHIMA DAMOH
GOGRA INDUS JAWAI RAPTI SANKH
SONAR TAPTI TUNGA CHENAB GANGES
KISTNA PENNER SUTLEJ WARDHA
CAUVERY CHAMBAL IRAWADI KRISHNA
NARMADA NERMEDA HEMAVATI
HYDASPES MAHANADI NERBUDDA
VINDHYAS
SEAPORT: DAMAN BOMBAY COCHIN
MADRAS CALCUTTA
STATE: ASSAM BIHAR KERALA MYSORE
ORISSA PUNJAB GUJARAT MANIPUR
TOWN: DIU AGRA DAMA GAYA PUNA
REWA ADONI AKOLA ALWAR ARCOT
BHERA DACCA DATIA DELHI GIROT KALPI
PATAN PATNA POONA SALEM SIMLA
SURAT TEHRI AJMERE AMBALA BARELI
BARODA BHOPAL BOMBAY CHAMBA
COCHIN DUMDUM HOWRAH INDORE
JAIPUR KANPUR LAHORE MADIRA
MADRAS MADURA MEERUT MULTAN
MUTTRA MYSORE NAGPUR RAMPUR
UJJAIN ALIGARH BENARES BIKANER
CALICUT CAWNPUR DINAPUR GWALIOR
JODHPUR KARACHI KURNOOL LASWARI
LUCKNOW RANGOON RANGPUR
AMRITSAR BHATINDA BHATPARA
CALCUTTA DINAPORE JABALPUR
KOLHAPUR MANDALAY MIRZAPUR
PESHAWAR SHOLAPUR SRINAGAR
VARANASI
WATERFALL: JOG GOKAK CAUVERY
WEIGHT: MOD PAI SER VIS DHAN DRUM
KONA MYAT PALA PANK PICE RAIK RATI
RUAY SEER TANK TOLA YAVA ADPAD
BAHAR CANDY CATTY HUBBA MASHA
MAUND PALLY POUAH RATTI RETTI
RUTEE TICAL TICUL TIKAL ABUCCO
DHURRA KARSHA CHITTAK PEIKTHA

INDIAN LO RED ROJO INJUN TAWNY
ABNAKI INDISH BHARATI HOSTILE
REDSKIN LONGHAIR
(AMERICAN —) FOX KAW OTO REE SAC
UTE COOS CREE CROW DOEG ERIE EYAK
HANO HOPI HUPA IOWA KATO MONO
OTOE PIMA SAUK TANO TAOS TEWA
TIOU TOAG UTAH WACO YUMA ZUNI

ACOMA ALSEA BANAK CADDO CREEK
HANIS HOOPA HUECO HURON KANIA
KANSA KIOWA KOROA LIPAN MIAMI
MINGO MODOC MOQUI NAMBE OMAHA
OSAGE OSTIC OZARK PECOS PINAL PIUTE
PONCA SIOUX SITKA SLAVE SNAKE
TETON TEXAS TONTO UINTA WASCO
WASHO YAZOO AGAWAM APACHE
ATSINA ATUAMI BILOXI CAYUGA CAYUSE
CHERAW COOSUC CUPENO DAKOTA
DIGGER GILENO HAINAI HAISLA ISLETA
KAIBAB KAINAH KANSAS KICHAI KUITSH
LAGUNA LENAPE MANDAN MAUMEE
MICMAC MOHAVE MOHAWK MUNSEE
NASHUA NATICK NAUSET NAVAHO
NAVAJO NOOTKA OGLALA ONEIDA
OREJON OTTAWA PAIUTE PAPAGO
PAWNEE PEORIA PEQUOD PEQUOT
PODUNK PUEBLO QUAPAW SALISH
SAMISH SANTEE SATSOP SENECA
SHASTA SILETZ SIOUAN SIWASH SKAGIT
TOHOME TUNICA UMPQUA WAXHAW
WIKENO YAKIMA ZUNIAN ABENAKI
ALABAMA AMERIND ANDARKO ARIKARA
ATAKAPA AYAHUCA BANNOCK CAHOKIA
CALOOSA CATAWBA CHILCAT CHINOOK
CHOCTAW CHUMASH CHUMAWI
CLALLAM CLATSOP COWLITZ DWAMISH
HIDATSA HUICHOL INGALIK JUANENO
KANAWHA KLAMATH KUNESTE KUTCHIN
KUTENAI LUISENO MASHPEE MOHEGAN
MOHICAN MONACAN MONTAUK
NANAIMO NASCAPI NATCHEZ NIANTIC
OJIBWAY PADUCAH PAMLICO PICURUS
QUAITSO SALINAN SANPOIL SERRANO
SHAPTAN SHAWANO SHAWNEE SIKSIKA
SIUSLAW SONGISH SPOKANE TAMAROA
TESUQUE TLINGIT TONKAWA TULALIP
WAMESIT WASHAKI WEWENOC WICHITA
WITUMKI WYANDOT YANKTON YAVAPAI
YONKALA
(BRAZILIAN —) BUGRE
(CANADIAN —) DENE COMOX HAIDA
SLAVE TINNE DOGRIB HAISLA LASSIK
MICMAC SARSEE BEOTHUK GOASILA
KHOTANA KOYUKON
(FEMALE —) SQUAW KLOOCH
(MALE —) BUCK SANNUP SIWASH
(MEXICAN —) MAM OVA CHOL CORA
JOVA MAYA MAYO ROTO SERI TECA
TECO XOVA AZTEC CHIZO CHORA HUABI
HUAVE KAMIA NAHUA OPATA OTOMI
YAQUI ZOQUE CAHITA CHOCHO CONCHO
EUDEVE KILIWI NEVOME OTONIA
PAKAWA TARASC TOLTEC ZOTZIL
ACOLHUA AKWAALA AMISHGO CHATINO
CHINCHA CHINIPA CHONTAL COTONAM
COUHIMI GUASAVE HUASTEC HUAXTEC
MAZATEC MISTECA MIXTECA NAYARIT
SINALOA TEGUIMA TEHUECO TEPANEC
TEPEHUA TZENTAL TZOTZIL ZACATEC
ZAPOTEC
(OTHER —) ONA URU YAO AGAZ ANDE
ANTA ANTI AUCA BABU CAME CANA
CARA CHUJ COTO CUNA DENE DIAU DUIT
INCA ITEN ITZA IXIL MOJO MOXO MURA
MUSO MUZO PEBA PIRO RAMA TAMA

TAPE TATU TOBA TRIO TUPI TUPY ULUA
ULVA ACROA ARARA ARAUA ARUAC
AUETO BAURE BETOI BRAVO BUGRE
CAITE CAMPA CANCA CARIB CHANE
CHIMU CHITA CHOCO CHOKO CHOLA
CHOLO CHONO COCTO COLAN CUEVA
DIRIA GUANA GUATO HUARI JAVAH
KASKA LENCA MOCOA MOZCA OPATA
OYANA PALTA PAMPA PASSE PETEN
PINTO PIOJE PIOXE PIPIL POKAN POKOM
QUITU SENCI SIUSI SMOOS TAINO
UAUPE UMAUA VEJOZ WAURA XINCA
YAGUA YAMEO YUNCA YUNGA AGUANO
AIMARA AKAVAI AKAWAI AMORUA
ANDOKE ANTISI APANTO APARAI APIACA
ARAWAK AROACO ATORAI AYMARA
BABINE BANIVA BETOYA BORORO BRIBRI
BRUNKA CAHETE CAIGUA CANCHI
CANELO CARAHO CARAJA CARAYA
CARIRI CAUQUI CAVINA CAYAPA CHAIMA
CHARCA CHAYMA CHICHA CHISCA
CHOCOI CHORTI COCAMA COCOMA
COCORA COFANE COLIMA COTOXO
CUCAMA CULINO CUMANA DOGRIB
DORASK GALIBI GOYANA GUAIMI
GUAQUE GUAYMI HUARPE HUBABO
IGNERI INCERI IXIAMA JIVARO JUCUNA
JUMANA JURUNA KARAYA KEKCHI
KUCHIN LENGUA LUCAYO MACUSI
MAKUSI MANGUE MANIVA MIRANA
MUYSCA NAHANE NASCAN OMAGUA
OTOMAC PAPAGO PKOMAM PURUHA
QUICHE SABUJA SACCHA SALIBA
SALIVA SAMUCU SEKANE SETIBO SIPIBO
SUERRE TACANA TAGISH TAHAMI
TAMOYO TAPAJO TAPUYA TARUMA
TECUNA TICUNA TIMOTE TOTORO
TUCANO TUNEBO UIRINA UITOTO VILELA
WAIWAI WITOTO WOOLWA YAHGAN
YAHUNA YARURO YURUNA ZAPARA
ACHAGUA ACKAWOI AKAMNIK ANDAQUI
ANGAITE APALAII APINAGE ARECUNA
ARHUACO BEOTHUK BILQULA CACHIBO
CAINGUA CALIANA CAMACAN CARANGA
CARIBAN CARIBEE CARRIER CASHIBO
CHARRUA CHIBCHA CHIMANE CHIMILA
CHIRINO CHONCHO CHOROTE CHUMULU
CHUNCHO CHURAPA CHUROYA CIBONEY
CJACOGO COROADO FRENTON FUEGIAN
GITKSAN GOAHIVO GOAJIRA GUAHIVO
GUARANI GUARANY GUARANY GUARRAU
GUARUAN GUATUSO GUETARE
HUANUCO HUATUSO ITONAMA JACUNDA
JICAQUE KALIANA KOPRINO KULIANA
LUCAYAN MAIPURE MISKITO MONGOYO
MORCOTE NICARAO PAMPERO PAYAGUA
PEDRAZA PIARROA POKOMAM PUELCHE
PUQUINA QUECHUA QUEKCHI RANQUEL
SARIGUE SATIENO SHUSWAP SINSIGA
SIRIONE TAHLTAN TALUCHE TALUHET
TAMANAC TARIANA TARRABA TAYRONA
TELEMBI TIMBIRA TIRRIBI TSONECA
UARAYCU UCAYALE VOYAVAI WOYAWAY
YUSTAGA ZUTUHIL
(SPANISH-AMERICAN —) CHOLO

INDIANA

CAPITAL: INDIANAPOLIS
COUNTY: JAY CASS CLAY KNOX OWEN
   PIKE RUSH VIGO BOONE FLOYD WELLS
   JASPER TIPTON DAVIESS PULASKI
LAKE: MONROE MANITOU WAWASEE
   MICHIGAN
NATIVE: HOOSIER
RIVER: OHIO WHITE WABASH
STATE BIRD: CARDINAL
STATE FLOWER: PEONY
STATE TREE: TULIP
TOWN: GARY PERU PAOLI VEVAY ALBION
   ANGOLA BRAZIL GOSHEN JASPER
   KOKOMO MUNCIE SHOALS WABASH

INDIAN BREAD TUCKAHOE
INDIAN HEMP KEF KIF SANA DAGGA
   SABZI AMYROOT DOGBANE
INDIAN PIPE FITROOT EYEBRIGHT
   WAXFLOWER
INDIAN TOBACCO GAGROOT LOBELIA
   PUKEWEED SOURBUSH
INDICATE RUN SAY BODY CITE HINT
   LOOK MAKE MARK READ SHOW ARGUE
   INDEX INFER POINT PROVE SPEAK
   ALLUDE ATTEST BETRAY DENOTE DESIGN
   EVINCE FINGER IMPORT NOTIFY REVEAL
   BESPEAK BETOKEN CONNOTE DECLARE
   DISPLAY PORTEND SIGNIFY SPECIFY
   ADMONISH ANNOUNCE DECIPHER
   DISCLOSE EVIDENCE MANIFEST
   OUTPOINT REGISTER SIGNALIZE
INDICATION BECK CLEW CLUE HINT
   LEAD MARK NOTE SHOW SIGN CURVE
   INDEX PROOF SCENT TOKEN AUGURY
   BEACON INDICE REMARK SAMPLE
   SIGNAL AUSPICE MENTION PROFFER
   SYMPTOM ALLUSION ARGUMENT
   EVIDENCE MONITION MONUMENT
   NOTATION SIGNANCE TELLTALE
   (— OF APPROVAL) CACHET
   (— OF CONTROL) COLLAR
   (— OF LIGHT) AUREOLE
   (— OF OFFICE) SEAL
   (OBSCURE —) SHADOW
   (VAGUE —) GLIMMER
INDICATOR PIN HAND SIGN FLOAT
   INDEX LITMUS SHOWER STYLUS TARGET
   LACMOID POINTER DETECTOR TELLTALE
   (— OF BALANCE) COCK
   (— OF HOUR) GNOMON
   (ECONOMIC —) LAGGER LEADER
INDICTMENT CHARGE DITTAY
INDIFFERENCE APATHY PHLEGM
   ATARAXY DISDAIN COLDNESS EASINESS
   FROIDEUR
INDIFFERENT COLD COOL DEAD DRAM
   EASY SOSO ALOOF BLASE EQUAL SOBER
   CASUAL DEGAGE FRIGID SUPINE
   CALLOUS LANGUID NEUTRAL DETACHED
   LISTLESS LUKEWARM MEDIOCRE
   RECKLESS SUPERIOR UPSITTEN
   APATHETIC

INDIGENOUS NATIVE DOMESTIC
   HOMEBORN ABORIGINAL
INDIGENT POOR BEGGARLY
INDIGESTIBLE STUDGY
INDIGNANT ANGRY WROTH ANNOYED
   UPTIGHT INCENSED
INDIGNATION IRE ANGER WRATH
   DESPITE DISDAIN DUDGEON JEALOUSY
INDIGNITY CUT SLUR SCORN INSULT
   SLIGHT AFFRONT OFFENCE CONTUMELY
INDIGO ANIL NILL SHOOFLY
INDIRECT SLY SIDE DEVIOUS OBLIQUE
   CIRCULAR GLANCING OVERHEAD
   SIDELONG SIDEWAYS SIDEWISE
   ROUNDABOUT
INDISCREET RASH HASTY SILLY
   WITLESS CARELESS HEEDLESS
INDISCRETION FOLLY FREDAINE
INDISCRIMINATE MIXED MINGLED
   SWEEPING PROMISCUOUS
INDISPENSABLE NEEDFUL CRITICAL
INDISPOSED ILL MEAN SICK UNWELL
INDISPUTABLE SURE CERTAIN EVIDENT
   MANIFEST POSITIVE APODICTIC
INDISTINCT DIM DARK DULL HAZY FAINT
   FUZZY INNER LIGHT MISTY MUDDY
   SHADY THICK VAGUE BLEARY CLOUDY
   DREAMY INWARD SLURRY WOOLLY
   BLEARED BLURRED OBSCURE SHADOWY
   UNCLEAR NEBULOUS
INDIVIDUAL MAN ONE HEAD SORT UNIT
   BEING MONAD THING PROPER SINGLE
   SPIRIT VERSAL BIONTIC DIPLOID EIDETIC
   ISOLATE MONADIC NUMERIC SEVERAL
   SPECIAL EVERYONE IDENTITY SEPARATE
   SINGULAR SOLITARY SPECIMEN
   PERSONAGE
INDIVIDUALITY SEITY QUALITY
   SELFDOM HECCEITY IDENTITY SELFHOOD
INDIVIDUALLY APART APIECE SINGLY
   PROPERLY
INDOCTRINATE BRIEF INSTRUCT
INDOLENT IDLE LAZY FAINT INERT
   SWEER DROWSY OTIOSE SUPINE
   DRONISH WILSOME FAINEANT INACTIVE
   LISTLESS LOUNGING SLOTHFUL
   SLUGGISH PICKTOOTH

INDONESIA

CAPITAL: DJAKARTA
COIN: RUPIAH
GULF: BONE TOLO TOMINI
ISLAND: ALOR BALI BURU JAVA CERAM
   IRIAN SUMBA WETAR BAWEAN BORNEO
   BUTUNG FLORES KOMODO LOMBOK
   MADURA PELENG CELEBES SALAJAR
   SUMATRA SUMBAWA SULAWESI
LAKE: RANAU TOWUTI
LANGUAGE: BAHASA MALAYAN
MOUNTAIN: BULU NIUT RAJA DEMPO
   MURJO NIAPA LEUSER SLAMET
   MENJAPA OGOAMAS SAMOSIR
   KATOPASA KERINTJI MAHAMERU
   RINDJANI TALAKMAU

MOUNTAINS: MULLER BARISAN QUARLES SCHWANER
NATIVE: BUGI
PROVINCE: RIAU ATJEH DJAMBI MALUKU LAMPUNG BENGKULU
RIVER: HARI MUSI DIGUL KAJAN PAWAN BARITO KAMPAR KAPUAS MAHAKAM
SEA: JAVA BANDA CERAM TIMOR FLORES ARAFURA CELEBES
STRAIT: SUNDA LOMBOK MAKASSAR
TOWN: PALU MEDAN MALANG MANADO BANDUNG KENDARI MAKASAR SEMARANG SURABAJA PALEMBANG SURAKARTA
VOLCANO: GEDE AGUNG DEMPO RAUNG MARAPI MERAPI SINILA SLAMET SUNDORO TAMBORA KERINTJE RINDJANI
WEIGHT: CATTY OUNCE THAIL

INDOORS WITHIN
INDUBITABLE SURE EVIDENT APPARENT MANIFEST UNIVOCAL
INDUCE GET DRAW LEAD MOVE URGE WORK ARGUE BRIBE BRING CAUSE IMPEL INFER TEMPT WEIGH ADDICT ADJURE ALLURE ENGAGE ENTICE IMPORT INCITE INVITE OBTAIN REDUCE SEDUCE SUBORN ACTUATE PREVAIL PROCURE PROVOKE SOLICIT MOTIVATE PERSUADE WIREDRAW
INDUCEMENT MOTIVE REASON FEATURE PERSUASION
INDULGE PET BABY CADE CANT FEED GLUT ALLOW HUMOR JOLLY SPOIL TUTOR WALLY WREAK COCKER FOSTER PAMPER PETTLE DEBAUCH GRATIFY
INDULGENCE LAW BINGE FAVOR FOLLY MERCY SPREE EXCESS INDULT PARDON PATENT JUBILEE QUIENAL SURFEIT COURTESY DELICACY EASINESS GLUTTONY POCULARY
INDULGENT FOND GOOD MEEK MILD SPOONY LENIENT TOLERANT
INDUSTRIOUS BUSY DEEDY EIDENT STEADY OPEROSE PAINFUL DILIGENT SEDULOUS VIRTUOUS WORKSOME
INDUSTRY TOIL LABOR SCREEN VIRTUE CERAMICS SEDULITY
INEFFECTIVE DUD WEAK CLUMSY DREEPY FLABBY FUTILE FLACCID HALTING STERILE BUMBLING
INEFFECTUAL WAN DEAD IDLE TAME VAIN VOID JERKY FUTILE SPINDLY USELESS BOOTLESS FAINEANT FIDDLING NUGATORY
INEFFICIENT ILL LAME POOR CLUMSY DOLESS ROTTEN UNABLE SLOUCHY USELESS FECKLESS HANDLESS
INEPT INAPT ABSURD AWKWARD FOOTLESS MALADROIT
INERT DEAD DULL LAZY SLOW HEAVY NOBLE SULKY LEADEN SODDEN STUPID SUPINE TORPID PASSIVE INACTIVE INDOLENT LIFELESS SLOTHFUL SLUGGISH STAGNANT THEWLESS

INEVITABLE DUE SURE DIRECT CERTAIN FATEFUL
INEXPENSIVE LOW CHEAP REASONABLE
INEXPERIENCED RAW PUNY CRUDE FRESH YOUNG UNSEEN KITLING STRANGE INEXPERT INSOLENT PRENTICE UNTRADED
INFAMOUS BASE RUDDY BLOODY ODIOUS BLEEDING FLAGRANT SHAMEFUL NEFARIOUS OPPROBRIOUS
INFAMY STAIN DISHONOR IGNOMINY OPPROBRIUM
INFANCY CRADLE BABYHOOD
INFANT BABE BABY TINY CHILD MINOR PREMIE CHRISOM MILKSOP PREEMIE BALDLING BANTLING
(NAKED —) SCUDDY
(NEWLY-BORN —) NEONATUS
(VORACIOUS -) KILLCROP
INFANTILE BABYISH
INFANTRYMAN ASKAR ZOUAVE DOGFACE DRAGOON DOUGHBOY PIOUPIOU SOREFOOT VOETGANGER
INFATUATED MAD FOND GONE ASSOT CRAZY DOTTY ENTETE ENGOUEE FOOLISH BESOTTED
INFECT SMIT TAINT CANKER DEFILE EMPEST ENTACH INFEST POISON CORRUPT DISEASE POLLUTE SMITTLE CONTAMINATE
INFECTION COLD DOSE SMIT FELON TAINT FUNGUS
INFER DRAW PICK TAKE GUESS JUDGE DECIDE DEDUCE DEDUCT DERIVE DIVINE GATHER INDUCE REASON COLLECT INCLUDE PRESUME SURMISE CONCLUDE CONSTRUE
INFERIOR BAD BUM DOG ILL JAY LOW OFF SAD EVIL LESS MEAN POOR PUNK SLIM SOUR WAFF BASER BAUCH BELOW CHEAP DOGGY GROSS LOUSY LOWER PETTY PLAIN SCALY SCRUB WORRY BEHIND CAGMAG COARSE COMMON CRAPPY FEEBLE FEMALE IMPURE LESSER MEASLY PALTRY PEDARY PUISNE PUISNY ROTTEN SECOND SHABBY SHODDY WOODEN BADDISH CRIPPLE HUMBLER NAGGISH POPULAR SCRUBBY SUBJECT ABNORMAL ANTERIOR DEROGATE ORDINARY PARAVAIL TERRIBLE
INFERNAL BLACK AVERNAL BLASTED ETERNAL HELLISH SATANIC SHEOLIC STYGIAN CHTHONIC DAMNABLE DEVILISH PLUTONIAN
INFEST COE VEX BESET INFECT PESTER PLAGUE OVERRUN TORMENT
INFIDEL DEIST KAFIR GIAOUR PAYNIM ATHEIST SARACEN SKEPTIC AGNOSTIC MISCREANT MISBELIEVER
INFIDELITY PERFIDY ADULTERY
INFINITE CHAOS COSMIC ENDLESS ETERNAL IMMENSE
INFINITY OLAM ANANTA ETERNITY
INFIRM LAME WEAK ANILE CRAZY CRONK SHAKY CRANKY FEEBLE SICKLY UNFIRM UNSURE CASALTY CRAICHY DOWLESS DWAIBLE FRAGILE INVALID SAPLESS

UNFEARY DODDERED FIRMLESS
INSECURE RESOLUTE UNSTRONG
INFIRMITY WOE CRAZE DOTAGE FOIBLE
UNHEAL DISEASE FAILING FRAILTY
UNMIGHT DEBILITY SICKNESS
WEAKNESS
INFLAME BURN FIRE GOAD HEAT STIR
ANGER BLAIN FLAME SCALD SHAME
AROUSE ENAMOR EXCITE FESTER IGNITE
INCEND KINDLE MADDEN RANKLE
EMBRASE FLUSTER INCENSE ESCHAUFE
INFLAMMATION ACNE FIRE ANGER
FELON GLEET SCALD SEBEL AGNAIL
ANCOME BLIGHT CANKER DEFLUX
GREASE IRITIS CATARRH CHAFING
FISTULA QUITTOR SUNBURN SHINGLES
INFLATE HOVE HUFF KITE PLIM PUFF
BLOAT BOLNE HEAVE SWELL DILATE
EMBOSS EXPAND HUFFLE INBLOW
TUMEFY BLADDER BOMBAST DISTEND
FORBLOW OUTSWELL SUFFLATE
INFLATED TRIG BLOWN FLOWN GASSY
PUFFY TUMID TURGID BOMBAST
BULLATE FUSTIAN OROTUND STILTED
SWOLLEN TURGENT BLADDERY
OUTBLOWN TOPLOFTY TUMOROUS
VANITOUS BOMBASTIC OVERBLOWN
PLETHORIC
INFLEXIBLE ACID DOUR FIRM HARD IRON
EAGER SOLID STERN STIFF STONY
STOUR SEVERE STRICT STUFFY
ADAMANT RESTIVE GRANITIC IRONCLAD
OBDURATE PREFRACT RESOLUTE
RIGOROUS STIFFISH STUBBORN
ADAMANTINE
INFLICT DO ADD PUT SET GIVE SEND
INFER YIELD IMPOSE RAMROD STRIKE
INFLUENCE IN WIN BEND BIAS COAX
DRAG DRAW HAND HANK HEFT LEAD
MOVE PULL PUSH RULE SUCK CHARM
CLOUT COLOR ENACT FORCE GRACE
IMPEL MOYEN POWER REACH SPELL
VAPOR VOGUE WEIGH AFFECT ALLURE
CREDIT EFFECT GOVERN IMPORT INDUCE
INFLOW INFLUX MOTIVE PONDUS
SALUTE SHADOW STROKE WEIGHT
ACTUATE ATTINGE ATTRACT BEARING
BEWITCH BLARNEY BOSSDOM CAPTURE
CONCUSS CONTROL DISPUTE ENCHANT
GRAVITY IMPRINT INCLINE INSPIRE
MASTERY SUASION TENDRIL DOMINION
HEGEMONY INTEREST LEVERAGE
MEDICINE PRESTIGE SANCTION
STRENGTH CAPTIVATE
(— BY GIFTS) GREASE
(— CORRUPTLY) BRIBE
(— OF GODS) MANA
(— OF THE STARS) BLAS
(— UNREASONABLY) OBSESS
(ATTEMPT TO —) JAWBONE
(BENIGN —) UNCTION
(CONTROLLING —) SWAY
(CORRUPTING —) SMOUCH SMUTCH
(DEPRESSING —) CHILL
(DIABOLICAL —) DEVILDOM
(DISRUPTIVE —) GREMLIN
(DOMINANT —) GENIUS STREAM

(DULLING —) DAMPER
(ELEVATING —) LIFT
(HARMFUL —) UPAS GRUDGE
(INJURIOUS —) RUST
(MALEVOLENT —) DISASTER
(MALIGN —) TAKING
(PERNICIOUS —) BALE BLAST
(SINISTER —) MALICE
(SOOTHING —) SALVE
(SURROUNDING —) AIR AMBIENCE
INFLUENTIAL BIG GRAVE POWERFUL
INFLUENZA FLU LEUMA GRIPPE PINKEYE
INFORM KEN BEEF BLOW FINK NOSE
POST SHOP SHOW TELL WARN WISE
LEARN PEACH ADVISE ASSURE DELATE
DETECT NOTIFY PREACH SNITCH WITTER
APPRISE EDUCATE IMPEACH INSENSE
PARTAKE POSSESS RESOLVE SIGNIFY
SUGGEST ACQUAINT DENOUNCE
INFORMED INSTRUCT SPARSILE
INFORMAL BREEZY CASUAL CHATTY
COMMON FOLKSY TWEEDY INTIMATE
SLIPSHOD SOCIABLE NEGLIGENT
INFORMATION AIR WIT CLEW CLUE
DOPE INFO LORE NEWS NOTE TALE WIRE
WORD DATUM SCOOP SKILL ADVICE
INSIDE LIGHTS NOTICE APPRISE
READOUT TIDINGS WITTING BRIEFING
NOTITION
INFORMED UP HEP WISE AWARE WITTY
KNOWING LEARNED
INFORMER FINK NARK NOSE PIMP SPIV
STAG RUSTY SNEAK SPLIT BEAGLE
CANARY FINGER SETTER SNITCH TELLER
DELATOR STOOLIE TANQUAM APPROVER
PROMOTER SQUAWKER SQUEAKER
SQUEALER TELLTALE
INFREQUENT RARE SELDOM FUGITIVE
UNCOMMON
INFRINGE IMPOSE INVADE TRENCH
IMPINGE INFRACT INTRUDE ENCROACH
TRESPASS
INGENIOUS SLY CUTE FAST FEAT FINE
ACUTE SHARP SMART WITTY ADROIT
BRAINY CLEVER CRAFTY DAEDAL GIFTED
KNACKY PRETTY QUAINT SUBTLE
CUNNING POLITIC SKILLFUL
INGENUITY ART WIT ENGINE ADDRESS
COMPASS ARTIFICE CONTOISE INDUSTRY
QUENTISE
INGENUOUS FREE FRANK NAIVE PLAIN
CANDID HONEST SUBTLE ARTLESS
NATURAL SINCERE INNOCENT
INGENUOUSNESS NAIVETE
INGOT GAD SOW WEDGE LINGOT NIGGOT
CROPHEAD
(— OF BRASS) STRIP
(— OF SILVER) SHOE TING SCHUYT
(SILVER —S) SYCEE
(SOAKING —S) HEAT
INGRATIATE FLATTER
INGRATIATING BLAND SILKY SLEEK
SLICK SOAPY SILKEN SMOOTH
INGREDIENT FACTOR AMALGAM
BINDING ELEMENT ADJUVANT
(ACTIVE —) ANIMA
(FUNDAMENTAL —) BASIS

(FUSIBLE —) BOND
(MAIN —) BASE
INHABIT BIG COVER DWELL HABIT OCCUPY BEDWELL INDWELL POSSESS POPULATE
INHABITANT INMATE BURGHER CITIZEN DENIZEN DWELLER PEOPLER BORDERER CONFINER DEMESMAN HABITANT
(— OF ALASKA) SOURDOUGH
(— OF BORDER REGION) MARCHER
(— OF CITY) CIT CITIZEN
(— OF INDIA) BHARATA
(— OF JUNGLE) JUNGLI
(— OF SWISS ALPS) GRISON
(— OF TORRID ZONE) ASCIAN
(— OF VIRGINIA) COOHEE
(— OF WISCONSIN) BADGER
(EARTH —) TERRAN
INHALE DRAW TAKE SMOKE SNIFF SNUFF ATTRACT BREATHE INSPIRE RESPIRE ASPIRATE
(— A DRUG) SNORT
INHERENT KIND INBORN INNATE INWARD NATIVE PROPER HABITUAL IMMANENT INTEGRAL INTERNAL RESIDENT
INHERIT HEIR SUCCEED
INHERITANCE KIND ENTAIL HEIRDOM HEIRSHIP HEREDITY HERITAGE LANDFALL VACANTIA
INHERITED INBORN INNATE CONGENITAL
INHIBIT COOP CURB SNUB CRIMP DETER FORBID STIFLE SUPPRESS
INHUMAN FELL CRUEL BRUTAL FIERCE SAVAGE BESTIAL DEVILISH KINDLESS
INHUMANITY CRUELTY
INIMICAL BAD FROSTY HOSTILE
INIQUITOUS ILL DARK WRONG SINFUL WICKED NEFARIOUS
INIQUITY SIN EVIL VICE CRIME GUILT DARKNESS MISCHIEF
INITIATE HEAD OPEN ADEPT ADMIT BEGIN BREAK ENTER FOUND START GROUND INDUCE INDUCT INVENT LAUNCH ORPHIC BAPTIZE INSTALL INSTATE OPERATE ORPHEAN COMMENCE INCHOATE ORIGINATE
INITIATIVE PEP LEAD GETUP ACTION AMBITION GUMPTION OVERTURE
INJECTION JAG HYPO SHOT BOOSTER CLYSTER INSERTION
INJUNCTION HEST BEHEST CHARGE IMPOSE RUBRIC BIDDING DICTATE EXPRESS MANDATE PRECEPT
INJURE DO GAS ILL MAR BURN CHEW DERE ENVY GALL HARM HURT MAUL TEAR TEEN WERD ABUSE BLAST CRAZE DIRTY MISDO RIFLE SCALD SHEND SMITE SPOIL STEER WOUND WRONG BRUISE DAMAGE DEFACE DEFECT DEPAIR GRIEVE HINDER IMPAIR INJURY MANGLE NOBBLE PUNISH RANKLE SCATHE SCOTCH STRAIN AFFLICT AFFRONT CONTUSE DAMNIFY DESPITE FORWORK MISBEDE TERRIFY AGGRIEVE DISASTER DISSERVE FORSLACK IMPERISH INTERESS MISCHIEF

MISGUIDE MUTILATE PREJUDGE SPURGALL
INJURIOUS BAD ILL EVIL NOCENT NOYANT NOYFUL SHREWD ABUSIVE HARMFUL HURTFUL NOXIOUS SCADDLE DAMAGING GRIEVOUS SINISTER TORTIOUS TORTUOUS WRACKFUL WRONGFUL PERNICIOUS
INJURY ILL JAM MAR BALE BANE BURN EVIL HARM HURT JEEL LOSS RUIN SCAT TEEN TORT WITE ABUSE BLAME CHAFE CRUSH GRIEF SCALD SCORE SPITE SPOIL TOUCH WATHE WRACK WRONG BREACH BRUISE DAMAGE DANGER IMPAIR LESION SCATHE STRAIN STROKE TRAUMA BEATING DESPITE EXPENSE OFFENSE OUTRAGE PAYMENT SCADDLE SCRATCH SORANCE BUSINESS CASUALTY CREPANCE INTEREST MISCHIEF NUISANCE
INJUSTICE WRONG INJURY HARDSHIP INEQUITY
(GROSS —) INIQUITY
INKLING HINT ITEM SCENT GLIMMER GLIMPSE UMBRAGE
INLAY PICK PIKE COUCH HATCH INLET PIQUE SPELL CRUSTA ENAMEL IMPAVE INDENT NIELLO TARSIA ENCHASE ENCRUST INCRUST COMMESSO
INLET ARM BAY CUT GEO RIA VOE COVE DOCK HOPE MERE SLEW WICK BAYOU BRACE CHUCK CREEK FIORD FJORD FLEET HAVEN LOGAN LOUGH STOMA ESTERO HARBOR INFALL SLOUGH TONGUE DOGHOLE INDRAFT SUCTION CALANQUE SEAPOOSE
INN PUB KHAN STOP VENT ANGEL HOTEL MESON TAMBO VENTA CABACK HARBOR HOSTEL IMARET POSADA PUBLIC SHANTY AUBERGE BOLICHE CAFENEH FONDOUK LOCANDA SOJOURN SURAHEⁱ CHOULTRY GASTHAUS HOSTELRY ORDINARY SERAGLIO WAYHOUSE ROADHOUSE
INNATE BORN KIND INBORN INBRED CONNATE INGRAIN NATURAL INSTINCT
INNER ENTAL INSIDE INWARD MENTAL INTERIOR INTERNAL PECTORAL
INNKEEPER HOST DUENA TAPPER VENTER GOODMAN HOSTESS HOSTLER PADRONE BONIFACE
INNOCENCE BLUET WHITE CANDOR PURITY SIMPLICITY
INNOCENT SOT FREE NAIF PURE CANNY CLEAR NAIVE SEELY SILLY WHITE CHASTE DOVISH HONEST SIMPLE CHRISOM LAMBKIN UPRIGHT ARCADIAN HARMLESS IGNORANT PASTORAL PRIMROSE SACKLESS UNGUILTY ZACCHEUS
INNOCUOUS HARMLESS INNOCENT
INNUENDO HINT SLUR SLIPE
INNUMERABLE MYRIAD NUMBERLESS
INO (BROTHER OF —) POLYDORUS
(FATHER OF —) CADMUS
(HUSBAND OF —) ATHAMAS
(MOTHER OF —) HARMONIA

(SISTER OF —) AGAVE SEMELE
AUTONOE
(SON OF —) LEARCHUS PALAEMON
MELICERTES

INOFFENSIVE HARMLESS

INORDINATE WILD UNDUE ENORMOUS

INQUEST CROWN QUEST ASSIZE OFFICE
INQUIRY

INQUIRE ASK SEEK QUERY DEMAND
FRAYNE SEARCH EXAMINE QUESTION

INQUIRY PROBE QUERY TRIAL DEMAND
EXAMEN TRACER DOCIMASY QUESTION
RESEARCH SCRUTINY

INQUISITIVE NOSY PEERY PRYING
CURIOUS MEDDLING QUIZZICAL

INSANE MAD WUD DAFT BALMY BATTY
BUGGY CRAZY DIPPY QUEER WRONG
CRANKY LOCOED SCREWY FLIGHTY
FRANTIC FURIOUS LUNATIC WITLESS
BUGHOUSE DEMENTED DERANGED

INSANITY RAGE CRACK CRAZE FOLIE
MANIA FRENZY LUNACY MADNESS
DELIRIUM DEMENTIA PSYCHOSIS

INSATIABLE GREEDY

INSCRIBE DELVE ENTER WRITE BLAZON
DOCKET INDITE LEGEND LETTER SCRIBE
SCRIVE SCROLL ASCRIBE ENDORSE
ENGROSS DEDICATE DESCRIBE
EMBLAZON ENSCROLL INTITULE

INSCRIPTION HEAD ELOGY CACHET
LEGEND LETTER EPIGRAM EPITAPH
MENTION TITULUS WRITING COLOPHON
EPIGRAPH GRAFFITO INSCRIPT SCRIBING

INSCRUTABLE EQUIVOCAL MYSTERIOUS

INSECT ANT BEE BUG DOR DUN ELF FLY
NIT ANER FLEA GNAT GOGO GYNE MOTH
PELA PEST PUPA SPIT WASP WETA ZIMB
APHID APHIS BICHO BORER FLYER
GOGGA GUEST IMAGO LOUSE MINER
ROACH SCALE BEETLE BLIGHT CALLOW
CICADA CIXIID EARWIG EMBIID HAWKER
HOPPER INSTAR MANTIS NITTER PODURA
PSOCID SAPPER SAWFLY THRIPS VERMIN
WALKER WEEVIL ATTACUS BLATTID
BOATMAN BRUMMER BUZZARD
CRAWLER CREEPER CRICKET CYNIPID
DEALATE DRUMMER EARWORM FIREBUG
FIREFLY GALLFLY GIRDLER GRAYFLY
HEXAPOD JAPYGID KATYDID PHASMID
SANDBOY SCINIPH SKIPPER SPECTRE
STAINER STYLOPS TERMITE VAGRANT
WEBWORM ALDERFLY ALKERMES
BLACKFLY BRACONID DIPTERAN
FIREBRAT FULGORID GLOWWORM
HOMOPTER HORNTAIL LACEWING
LECANIUM MEALYBUG PRONYMPH
SEMIPUPA SEXUPARA SPHECOID
STINKBUG STYLOPID SYMPHILE

INSECTIVORE AGOUTA DESMAN
MOONRAT ALAMIQUI

INSECURE DICKY LOOSE SHAKY INFIRM
TICKLE UNFAST UNSAFE UNSURE

INSENSIBLE DEAR DULL LOST NUMB
BRUTE DENSE MARBLE SEARED WOODEN
DATELESS APATHETIC

INSENSITIVE DEAD BLUNT STONY
OBTUSE STUPID BOORISH

INSERT SLIP SPUD STOP BOTCH DICKY
ENROL ENTER FUDGE IMMIT INFER INFIX
INLET INSET STUFF COLLET GUSSET
INWORK INWEAVE GATEFOLD INTROMIT
SANDWICH SLASHING SUBTRUDE
THROWOUT

INSIDE IN INNER INWITH KEYHOLE
INTERIOR
(— OF ANGLE BAR) BOSOM
(— OF OUTER EAR) BUR BURR

INSIDIOUS SLY SNARY COVERT SUBTLE
GUILEFUL

INSIGHT KEN SIGHT APERCU THEORY
NOSTRIL

INSIGNIA TYPE ORDER SIGNS COLLAR
GEORGE CADUCEUS COMMENDA
HERALDRY OPINICUS PONTIFICALS

INSIGNIFICANT NULL POOR PUNY
DINKY FOOTY PETIT PETTY POTTY SCRUB
SMALL HUMBLE NAUGHT PALTRY PUISNE
SIMPLE SLIGHT FOOLISH NOMINAL
PELTING SCRUBBY TENUOUS TRIVIAL
INFERIOR PEDDLING PITIABLE SNIPPING
TRIFLING TRIPENNY

INSINCERE FALSE DOUBLE FEIGNED
ARTIFICIAL

INSINCERITY ARTIFICE DISGUISE

INSINUATE HINT MINT WIND CRAWL
SCREW TWIST ALLUDE GLANCE INFUSE
INSTIL WRITHE IMPLANT

INSINUATION HINT INKLING

INSIPID DRY DEAD FLAT FOND FOZY
LASH TAME BANAL BLAND FLASH INANE
PROSY STALE VAPID FLASHY FRIGID
JEJUNE SWASHY THREEP WALLOW
EXOLETE FATUOUS MAWKISH PROSAIC
SAPLESS SHILPIT WEARISH LIFELESS
UNSAVORY WATERISH

INSIST AVER PRESS THREAP CONSIST

INSISTENT LOUD ADAMANT INSTANT
EMPHATIC FRENZIED IMPOSING

INSOLENCE GUM CHEEK PRIDE SNASH
HUBRIS DISDAIN AUDACITY SURQUIDY
CONTUMELY PETULANCE

INSOLENT FACY PERT RUDE WISE BARDY
BRASH LUSTY PROUD CHEEKY LORDLY
WANTON ABUSIVE DEFIANT PAUGHTY
ARROGANT IMPUDENT PETULANT
SCORNFUL AUDACIOUS

INSOLUBLE HOPELESS

INSPECT SEE VET CASE ESPY LOOK
BRACK CHECK SIGHT VISIT INLOOK
PERUSE SURVEY EXAMINE OVERSEE
CONSIDER OVERLOOK OVERVIEW
(— CASUALLY) BROWSE
(— COINS) SHROFF
(— MERCHANDISE IN BALTIC) BRACK

INSPECTION EYE PRY VIEW CHECK
SIGHT REVIEW SURVEY BEDIKAH
CHECKUP INSIGHT INSPECT PERUSAL
VIDIMUS OVERHAUL OVERVIEW
SCRUTINY
(— OF CLOTH) ALNAGE

INSPECTOR SAYER SNOOP BISHOP
CENSOR CONNER JUMPER LOOKER
VIEWER GRAINER MOOCHER PERCHER

SAMPLER SNOOPER VEADORE EXAMINER
SEARCHER
(— OF COAL) KEEKER
(— OF COTTON LOOMS) TACKLER
(— OF ELECTRIC LAMPS) AGER
(ECCLESIASTICAL —) EXARCH

INSPIRATION FIRE SIGH POESY ANIMUS
SPIRIT SPRITE IMPULSE MADNESS
PEGASUS AFFLATUS AGANIPPE
INFLATUS

INSPIRE FIRE MOVE CHEER ELATE EXALT
SPARK BEACON INBLOW INCUSS INDUCE
INFORM INFUSE KINDLE PROMPT
ACTUATE ANIMATE EMBRAVE ENFORCE
ENLIVEN HEARTEN IMPLANT PREMOVE
QUICKEN SUGGEST CATALYZE ENTALENT
INSPIRIT MOTIVATE SUFFLATE

INSPIRED VATIC AFFLATED DAEMONIC
ENTHEATE VISIONED

INSPIRING INFUSIVE SPLENDID STIRRING

INSTALL SEAT CHAIR STALL INDUCT
INVEST ENSTOOL POSSESS ENTHRONE
INITIATE

INSTALLATION INDUCTION

INSTALLMENT KIST SERIAL EARNEST
CONTRACT
(— OF SERIAL) HEFT
(— OF WAGES) COMPO
(— SELLER) TALLYMAN
(FIRST —) HANDSEL
(NEXT —) SEQUEL

INSTANCE CASE PINK SAMPLE EXAMPLE
PURPOSE ENSAMPLE EXEMPLAR
(EXTREME —) CAPSHEAF

INSTANT POP HINT WHIP WINK BLICK
CLINK CRACK FLASH GLENT GLIFF GLISK
JIFFY POINT SHAKE SOUND START TRICE
WHIFF WIGHT BREATH FLIFFY MINUTE
MOMENT SECOND PRESENT CLIFFING
(PRECISE —) TIME

INSTANTANEOUS PRESTO DIRECTLY

INSTANTLY SLAP SWITH PRONTO
SWITHE DIRECTLY MOMENTLY

INSTEAD EITHER

INSTIGATE EGG ABET GOAD MOVE SPUR
URGE IMPEL ATTICE ENTICE EXCITE
FOMENT INCITE INDUCE INVOKE PROMPT
SPIRIT SUBORN ACTUATE INCENSE
INSTINCT

INSTIGATOR AUTHOR MOTIVE SOURCE
MONITOR

INSTILL GRAFT INFIX IMPART INFUSE
INSTIL BREATHE IMPLANT

INSTINCT KIND FILLED NATURE
CHARGED IMPULSE CAPACITY TENDENCY

INSTINCTIVE INNATE NATURAL
INHERENT ORIGINAL

INSTITUTE BEGIN BRING ERECT FOUND
RAISE STUDY FOMENT INVENT KINDLE
ORDAIN ACTIVATE

INSTITUTION BANK CAMP FOLD CLINIC
FRIARY SCHOOL ACADEMY CHARITY
COLLEGE GALLERY JUBILEE LIBRARY
SHELTER STATION VERITAS SEMINARY
ORPHANAGE OBSERVATORY
PENITENTIARY

(— FOR HOMELESS CHILDREN)
PROTECTORY
(— FOR INSANE) ASYLUM
(CHARITABLE —) SPITTLE DEACONRY
HOSPITAL
(DRUIDICAL —) GORSEDD

INSTRUCT KEN REAR SHOW WISE BREED
COACH DRILL EDIFY ENDUE GUIDE TEACH
TRAIN CHARGE DIRECT GROUND INDUCE
INFORM LESSON PREACH REFORM
SCHOOL COMMAND EDUCATE INSENSE
POSSESS ADMONISH DOCUMENT
(— BEFOREHAND) PRIME

INSTRUCTION LORE ADVICE ASSIZE
CHARGE LESSON COUNSEL PRECEPT
TUITION WISSING COACHING DOCTRINE
DOCUMENT MONITION PEDAGOGY
PROPHECY TEACHING TUTELAGE

INSTRUCTIVE DOCENT DIDACTIC

INSTRUCTOR DON SOAK SCREW TUTOR
MENTOR REGENT ACHARYA CRAMMER
MONITOR TEACHER BEACHBOY
CHAIRMAN ELDERMAN

INSTRUMENT
(ALSO SEE MUSICAL INSTRUMENT)
DEED TOOL WRIT AGENT SLANG THEME
FACTUM UTENSIL SYNGRAPH
(— FOR ACQUIRING KNOWLEDGE)
ORGANON
(— NOT UNDER SEAL) PAROL
(— OF DESTRUCTION) SWORD
(— OF DIVINATION) EPHOD
(— OF TORTURE) BOOT RACK BRAKE
BRANK FURCA GADGE WHEEL TUMBREL
BARNACLE SQUEEZER SCARPINES
PILLIWINKS
(—S OF WAR) ENGINERY
(CALCULATING —) ABACUS
(FINANCIAL —) ITEM
(LEGAL —) DEED GRANT FACTUM
SASINE SCRIPT CHARTER CODICIL
DUPLICATE
(METEOROLOGICAL —) LIDAR
(NEGOTIABLE —) HUNDI HOONDEE
(OFFICIAL —) SLANG
(PREHISTORIC —) CELT
(SCIENTIFIC OR OTHER —) AWL FAN
HOE KEY MET RAX SAX BROG CLAM
COMB DIAL DRAG FILE FORK GAGE HOOK
PALM PLOW RACK RING SPAR ARMIL
BEVEL BLADE BRACE BRAKE CHAIN
CLAMP CORER DATER DOLLY DRILL FLAIL
FLOAT FLUKE GAUGE GLASS INDEX
KNIFE LADLE LEVER METER MISER PILOT
RAZOR SCALE SCOPE SLATE SLICE SLING
SPADE SPEAR SPRAY STAMP STEEL
SWIFT THROW TONGS TUNER WHISK
ABACUS BEATER BEETLE BODKIN BRIDGE
CHOWRY CIRCLE DOUCHE ENGINE
ERASER FERULE FOLDER GRATER LEAPER
MORTAR NEEDLE PALLET PESTLE PICKER
PLOUGH PULLER PUMPER RAMMER
RASPER RATTLE RUBBER SCALER
SCORER SCRIBE SCUTCH SCYTHE
SHEARS SQUARE SQUIRT STADIA STRAIK
STROBE STYLET STYLUS TACKLE TICKER
WIMBLE ALIDADE BELLOWS BREAKER

CADRANS CLEAVER COMPASS DIOPTER
DOLABRA DOUBLER FISTUCA GRAFTER
GRAINER GRAPPLE HATCHEL LAYOVER
MASSEUR MEASURE OOMETER OOSCOPE
PAVIOUR PELORUS PIERCER PINCERS
PRICKER PRINTER PYROPEN QUADRAT
SCRAPER SEXTANT SHOCKER SHUTTLE
SLITTER SOUNDER SPLAYER SPRAYER
STRIGIL SUNDIAL SWINGLE TRAMMEL
TRIMMER WHISTLE
(SURGICAL OR MEDICAL —) GAG
HOOK SPUD FLEAM PROBE SCALA
SCOOP SNARE SOUND STAFF STYLE
BILABE BOUGIE BROACH GORGET
LANCET SEEKER TREPAN TROCAR
UNGULA VECTIS XYSTER AGRAFFE
AIRDENT DILATER FORCEPS HARPOON
LEVATOR LIGATOR MYOTOME PELICAN
PLUGGER RONGEUR SCALPEL SOUNDER
SYRINGE TRACTOR TRILABE TURNKEY
INSUBORDINATE FACTIOUS MUTINOUS
UNWIELDY
INSUBORDINATION MUTINY
INSUBSTANTIAL AIRY INANE FROTHY
SLENDER SPECTRAL
INSUFFICIENT POOR WANE SHORT
SCANTY
INSULATION LAGGING ISOLATION
INSULATOR KNOB CLEAT TAPLET
VITRITE MEGOHMIT STANDOFF
(PL.) STRING
INSULT CAG FIG JOEY RUMP SLAP SLUR
ABUSE CHECK FLOUT FRUMP SLANG
INJURE INJURY OFFEND RUFFLE SCRAPE
ABUSION AFFRONT OFFENCE OUTRAGE
BRICKBAT DISHONOR CONTUMELY
INSULTING RUDE ABUSIVE ARROGANT
INSOLENT
INSURANCE LINE CHOMAGE COVERAGE
INDEMNITY
INSURE COVER ASSURE ENSURE FURNISH
INSURGENT REBEL RISER CHOUAN
OAKBOY TAIPING BARRABAS CAMISARD
STEELBOY
INSURRECTION RIST MUTINY REVOLT
UPROAR OUTBREAK SEDITION UPRISING
REBELLION
INTACT SOUND WHOLE ENTIRE MAIDEN
INTANGIBLE VAGUE SUBTLE AERIFORM
SLIPPERY
INTEGER SUM NORM TOTITIVE
INTEGRAL FLUX NEEDFUL
INTEGRATE FUSE PIECE COMBINE
FULFILL ORGANIZE
INTEGRATION BALANCE HARMONY
INTEGRITY HONOR TRUTH HONESTY
JUSTICE PROBITY CHASTITY STRENGTH
SINCERITY
INTEGUMENT KEX ARIL PILL SKIN TESTA
TUNIC SWATHE CUTICLE ENVELOP
EPIDERM EXODERM PRIMINE TUNICLE
VELAMEN EPISPERM PERISARC
SCABBARD SECUNDINE
INTELLECT MIND NOUS HEART INWIT
MAHAT SKILL BRAINS NOTICE REASON
SPIRITS THINKING
INTELLECTUAL BLUE GAON IDEAL

BOOKSY MENTAL NOETIC SOPHIC
BRAHMIN EGGHEAD GNOSTIC CEREBRA
LONGHAIR SOPHICAL DIANOETIC
SPIRITUAL
INTELLIGENCE AIR CIT SAT CHIT KNOW
MIND NEWS NOTE NOUS WORD AGIEL
SAVVY SENSE ADVICE BRAINS ESPRIT
INGENY NOTICE PSYCHE WITTING
MENTALITY
INTELLIGENT APT GASH PERT ACUTE
ALERT SMART SPACK BRAINY BRIGHT
CLEVER MENTAL SHREWD KNOWING
INFORMED LUMINOUS RATIONAL
SKILLFUL
INTELLIGIBLE CLEAR PLAIN LUMINOUS
PELLUCID PERVIOUS REVELANT
PERCEIVABLE
INTEND GO AIM FIX CAST MEAN MIND
MINT PLAN PLOT TEND ALLOT ALLOW
TIGHT ATTEND DESIGN RECKON BEHIGHT
DESTINE PRETEND PROPOSE PURPORT
PURPOSE MEDITATE
INTENSE HOT ACID COLD DEEP HARD
HIGH KEEN BLANK DENSE GREAT HEAVY
QUICK SHARP TENSE VIVID ARDENT
BRAZEN FIERCE INTENT PITCHY SEVERE
STRONG BURNING CHARGED CHRONIC
CUTTING EXTREME FERVENT FRANTIC
FURIOUS VICIOUS VIOLENT EGYPTIAN
GRIEVOUS POWERFUL PROFOUND
SEETHING TERRIFIC VEHEMENT
INTENSIFY RISE URGE EXALT RAISE
ACCENT DEEPEN BOLSTER ENFORCE
ENHANCE IMPROVE INFLAME MAGNIFY
SHARPEN THICKEN CONDENSE HEIGHTEN
INCREASE REDOUBLE
INTENSITY EDGE HEAT ARDOR DEPTH
DRIVE FEVER FIELD VIGOR ACCENT
DEGREE DOSAGE FERVOR FRENZY
STRESS CURRENT FEROCITY STRENGTH
VIOLENCE
INTENT SET DEEP FELL HENT MIND RAPT
TENT BEADY CAUSE DRIFT ETTLE FIXED
HEART PRICK SCOPE TENOR TENSE
EFFECT SPIRIT COUNSEL INTENSE
PRESENT PURPOSE STUDIED WISTFUL
(CRIMINAL —) DOLE
(EVIL —) DOLUS
INTENTION AIM END GOAL HENT MIND
VIEW WILL HEART SCOPE ANIMUS
DESIGN DEVICE EFFECT INTENT OBJECT
REGARD EARNEST FORESET MEANING
PROPOSE PURPORT PURPOSE SUPPOSE
THOUGHT PRETENSE OBJECTIVE
INTENTIONAL SET WILLFUL WILLING
WITTING INTENDED
INTER BURY EARTH ENTER GRAVE PLANT
ENTOMB INHUME INEARTH
INTERCEPT KEP HEAD KEEP STOP CATCH
NORMAL ABSCISS TRAMMEL GAINCOPE
INTERPEL RETRENCH
INTERCHANGE CHANGE ANAGRAM
COMMUTE PASSAGE PERMUTE
COMMERCE EXCHANGE
(— OF OPINION) COUNSEL
(— OF WORDS) SPEECH
INTERCOURSE GAM DEAL MANG MONG

TRADE TRUCK HOBNOB COITION DEALING MIXTURE QUARTER SOCIETY TRAFFIC BUSINESS COMMERCE CONVERSE RECOURSE RELATIONS

INTERDICT BAN TABOO FORBID INHIBIT PROHIBIT SUPPRESS

INTEREST BUG DIP FAD USE BENT GOOD HAND HOLD PART CLOSE COLOR DRIVE FAVOR FETCH GAVEL HOBBY RENTE RIGHT STAKE STUDY USAGE USURA USURY BEHALF ENGAGE EQUITY ESTATE FAENUS FERVOR FINGER INCOME USANCE ATTRACT CONCERN RESPECT USAUNCE CONTANGO INCREASE VIGORISH
(— OF HUSBAND) CURTESY
(— ON LAND) CLOSE
(ACTIVE —) SYMPATHY
(EXORBITANT —) JUICE
(LEGAL —) EASEMENT
(POLITICAL —) FENCE
(SECURITY —) LIEN
(SPECIAL —) MEAT ANGLE

INTERESTING FRUITY CURIOUS PIQUANT STORIED ABSORBING

INTERFERE CUT MAKE ANNOY BLOCK CHECK HITCH POACH BAFFLE HAMPER HINDER HOBBLE IMPEDE MEDDLE STRIKE TAMPER INTRUDE INTROMIT
(— SLIGHTLY) BRUSH
(— WITH) AIL JOLT MESS CROSS HECKLE BLANKET DISTURB

INTERFERENCE BALK CHOKE THUMP HINDER JOSTLE MEDDLE CONFLICT FREINAGE

INTERIOR BELLY BOSOM INNER INLAND INWARD MIDDLE GIZZARD ENTRAILS INTERNAL
(— OF CUPOLA) CALOTTE
(— OF TEMPLE) CELLA
(— OF VESSEL) HOLD

INTERJECTION (ALSO SEE OATH) AW ER HA LO BAH COO FIE GEE HAH HEH HEY OOH AHEM AHOY ALAS EGAD FORE GOSH JOVE OOPS OUCH ADIOS ALACK GOODY MARRY PSHAW TENEZ BARLEY CRIKEY CRIPES EUREKA OUTCRY PHOOEY PROSIT CARAMBA LACKADAY

INTERLACE LACE WARP BRAID WEAVE ENLACE INWEAVE WREATHE

INTERLACED BRACED FRETTED

INTERLOCK KNIT LOCK MESH PITCH ENGAGE FINGER TANGLE DOVETAIL

INTERLUDE JIG JEST LETUP COMEDY VERSET TEMACHA TRIUMPH ANTIMASK ENTRACTE ENTREMES RITORNEL VERSETTE PARENTHESIS

INTERMEDIARY MEAN AGENT MOYENER MEDIATOR TRAMPLER MIDDLEMAN

INTERMEDIATE MEAN MESNE FILLER ISATIN MEDIAL MEDIUM MIDDLE NEUTRAL MIDDLING

INTERMINABLE ETERNAL INFINITE TIMELESS UNENDING

INTERMINGLE MIX BRAID COALESCE IMMINGLE INTERMIT INTERMIX

INTERMISSION REST WAIT BREAK DWELL PAUSE DEVALL RECESS NOONING RELACHE RESPITE INTERVAL SURCEASE VACATION

INTERMITTENT BROKEN FITFUL PERIODIC

INTERNAL INNER INLAND INNATE INSIDE INWARD DOMESTIC

INTERPOSE BAR CHOP POKE DEMUR OBJECT THRUST THWART MEDIATE

INTERPRET MAKE OPEN READ SCAN TAKE AREAD AREED FANCY GLOSS GLOZE DEFINE DIVINE INTEND CLARIFY COMMENT DECLARE EXPLAIN EXPOUND CONSTRUE DECIPHER SIMPLIFY

INTERPRETATION REDE GLOSS SENSE GOSPEL STRAIN ANAGOGE COMMENT MEANING CABALISM EXEGESIS INNUENDO MOONSHEE SOLARISM SOLUTION

INTERPRETER BROKER DUBASH UNDOER EXEGETE LATINER MUNCHEE CABALIST DRAGOMAN EXPONENT LINKSTER TRUCHMAN

INTERROGATE ASK TARGE DEBRIEF EXAMINE INQUIRE

INTERRUPT CUT MAR NIP CHOP STOP TAKE BREAK CHECK CRACK EMBAR ARREST DERAIL DERANGE DISRUPT FORBREAK INTERMIT INTERPEL OBSTRUCT

INTERRUPTION CESS JUMP STOP BLOCK BREAK CHECK DWELL LAPSE PAUSE BREACH HIATUS HOCKET ISLAND OUTAGE CAESURA CUTBACK DIASTEM BLOCKING BREAKAGE SOLUTION STOPOVER

INTERSECT CUT CROSS BISECT INCISE CROSSCUT

INTERSECTION LEET CHINE CROSS CURVE CHIASMA CROSSING CROSSWAY JUNCTION

INTERSPERSE DOT SALT SHED MEDDLE THREAD CHECKER INTERSOW SPRINKLE

INTERSTICE PORE SEAM CHINK GRATE SPACE AREOLA AREOLE RIFFLE CELLULE VACUITY

INTERTWINE KNIT LACE WARP TWINE FELTER TANGLE WAMPLE WARPLE WRITHE ENSNARL COMPLECT IMPLEACH INTERTEX

INTERVAL GAP LAG CENT GULF REST SAND SEXT SPOT STEP BLANK BREAK COMMA CYCLE FIFTH LAPSE PRIME QUINT SIXTH SPACE SWING TENTH THIRD BREACH DECIMA DEGREE DIESIS DITONE FOURTH MERLON SECOND SLATCH SYSTEM ADVANCE DIASTEM DISCORD HEADWAY HEMIOLA INTERIM PASTIME RESPITE SCHISMA SETTIMO STADIUM TRITONE DIAPASON DIAPENTE DISTANCE ELEVENTH ENTRACTE FONTANEL INTERACT MICROTONE PARENTHESIS
(— BETWEEN FINGERS) SUBVOLA
(— BETWEEN ROPE STRANDS) CONTLINE
(— OF BRIGHTNESS) FLICKER

(— OF FAIR WEATHER) SLATCH
(— OF HARSH WEATHER) SNAP
(— OF SEMITONE) APOTOME
(— OF TIME) WINDOW
(REST —) SOB
(SHORT —) STREAK
(TIME —) HEADWAY

INTERVENE CHOP STEP STRIKE MEDIATE
OBVIATE STICKLE INTERCUR

INTERVIEW BUZZ CONTACT AUDIENCE
CONGRESS

INTERWEAVE MAT PLAT CRISP PLAIT
PLASH PLEACH RADDLE TANGLE WATTLE
ENTWINE TEXTURE TRELLIS COMPLECT
ENTANGLE IMPLEACH INTERTEX

INTIMATE SIB BOON GRIT HINT HOME
HOMY KIND NEAR NEXT PACK TOSH
BOSOM CHIEF CLOSE GREAT HOMEY
PALLY PRIVY THICK ALLUDE ENTIRE
FRIEND HOMELY INTIME INWARD NOTICE
SECRET STRAIT STRICT THRANG THRONG
CHAMBER CLOSEUP GREMIAL INNERLY
INNUATE KEYHOLE PRIVADO PRIVATE
SIGNIFY SPECIAL SUGGEST COCKMATE
ESPECIAL FAMILIAR FREQUENT FRIENDLY
INDICATE INTIMADO

INTIMIDATE COW HAZE ABASH BULLY
COWER DAUNT DETER PSYCH HECTOR
TERRIFY BROWBEAT BULLDOZE
BULLYRAG FRIGHTEN

INTOLERANT CLOSED BIGOTED

INTONE CANT SING TONE CHANT
ENTUNE MODULATE CANTILLATE

INTOXICATE FOX TIP TOX CORN FLAW
GOOF SOAK TODDY FUDDLE MUDDLE
SOZZLE SPRING TIPSIFY DISGUISE
OVERTAKE SPRINKLE

INTOXICATED CUT FAP LIT WET HIGH
LUSH RIPE SHOT SOSH TOFT TOSY
BOSKY BUFFY DRUNK FRESH FRIED
FUNNY HEADY LACED NAPPY PIPED
TIGHT BLOTTO BOILED GROGGY LOADED
LOOPED MELLOW PIPPED QUAINT
SCREWY SKEWED SLEWED SLOPPY
SODDEN SOSHED SOZZLE STEWED
TANKED UPPISH UPPITY ZONKED
EBRIATE EXALTED FLECKED JINGLED
POTSHOT SCREWED SLOPPED SMASHED
SPIFFED SQUIFFY UNSOBER BESOTTED
COCKEYED DELEERIT ELEVATED
OVERSEEN OVERSHOT PLEASANT
SQUIFFED TEMULENT TOXICATE

INTRACTABLE BAD HARD SALTY STACK
SURLY FIERCE KITTLE SULLEN THWART
UNRULY CRABBED HAGGARD RESTIVE
ROPABLE WAYWARD CHURLISH
INDOCILE MUTINOUS OBDURATE
PERVERSE SHREWISH

INTREPID BOLD BRAVE HARDY HEROIC
PRETTY SAVAGE DOUGHTY VALIANT
RESOLUTE

INTRICATE HARD MAZY BLIND DAEDAL
KNOBBY KNOTTY SUBTLE TANGLY
TRICKY COMPLEX CRABBED CURIOUS
GORDIAN PUZZLED SINUOUS INVOLUTE
INVOLVED

INTRIGUE PLOT ANGLE CABAL CLOAK
STORY AFFAIR AMOUNT DECEIT SCHEME
CONNIVE FACTION FINAGLE TRINKET
TRINKLE ARTIFICE CHEATING COLLOGUE
PRACTICE STRATEGY

INTRIGUING EXCITING SCHEMING

INTRINSIC REAL TRUE INBORN INBRED
INNATE INWARD NATIVE GENUINE
NATURAL ABSOLUTE IMMANENT
INHERENT INTERNAL INTIMATE

INTRODUCE READ DEBUT ENTER FRONT
INFER PLANT START USHER BROACH
HERALD INDUCE INDUCT INFUSE INJECT
INSERT INVECT INVOKE LAUNCH PREFER
FORERUN IMPLANT INSTILL INVEIGH
PRECEDE PREFACE PRELUDE PRESENT
SPONSOR ACQUAINT INNOVATE

INTRODUCTION LASSU PROEM PRONE
INTRADA INTROIT ISAGOGE MENTION
PREFACE ENTRANCE EXORDIUM
PREAMBLE PROLOGUE PRELUSION

INTRUDE JET ABATE BARGE CRASH
POACH BOTHER CHISEL INGYRE INJECT
INVADE IRRUPT THRUST AGGRESS
OBTRUDE ENCROACH INFRINGE
TRESPASS

INTRUDER INTRUS INCOMER INVADER
STRANGER

INTRUSION INVASION

INTRUSIVE NOSY FRESH SPURIOUS

INTUITION HUNCH PRESAGE INSTINCT

INUNDATE FLOW DROWN FLOOD
SWAMP DELUGE OVERFLOW SUBMERGE
SURROUND

INUNDATION FLOW FLOOD WATER
DELUGE ALLUVIO FRESHET ALLUVION
FLOODAGE OVERFLOW

INURE BREAK STEEL HARDEN SCHOOL
SEASON ACCUSTOM INDURATE
ACCLIMATIZE

INVADE ASSAIL INTRUDE ENCROACH
INTRENCH TRESPASS

INVALID BAD BUM NULL CHRONIC
NUGATORY

INVALIDATE UNDO AVOID BREAK
CANCEL INFIRM IMPROVE INVALID
VITIATE

INVALUABLE COSTLY PRECIOUS
PRICELESS

INVARIABLE STEADY UNIFORM
CONSTANT

INVARIABLY EVER ALWAYS

INVASION RAID INROAD DESCENT
INBREAK

INVECTIVE ABUSE HOKER SATIRE
RAILING DIATRIBE REPROACH

INVEIGH RANT INVECT DECLAIM
DENOUNCE

INVEIGLE COAX ROPE WILE CHARM
DECOY SNARE ALLURE ENTICE SEDUCE

INVENT COIN FIND FORM MINT VAMP
FEIGN FRAME FRUMP CREATE DESIGN
DEVISE IDEATE CONCOCT CONJURE
CONTRIVE DISCOVER

INVENTION FANCY DEVICE NOTION
FANTASY FICTION FIGMENT FORGERY
WITCRAFT

INVENTIVE ADROIT FERTILE CREATIVE MECHANIC ORIGINAL PREGNANT

INVENTOR TALOS COINER FINDER FRAMER MINTER CREATOR MINTMAN ENGINEER ARTIFICER

INVENTORY BILL LIST STOCK ACCOUNT INVOICE ANAGRAPH DATABASE REGISTER SCHEDULE

INVERT CANT TURN REVERT REVERSE

INVERTED AWKWARD

INVEST DON DUB PUT BELT FUND GARB GIFT GIRD GIRT GOWN LOCK SINK VEST WRAP BELAY BLOCK ENDOW ENDUE FEOFF INDUE CLOTHE EMBODY ENROBE FORSET OCCUPY ORDAIN BESIEGE COMPASS ENFEOFF ENVELOP INSTATE OBSERVE BENEFICE BLOCKADE SURROUND
(— ONESELF) COVER ASSUME
(— WITH) INFEFT
(— WITH AUTHORITY) SCEPTER ACCREDIT
(— WITH ENERGY) CATHECT
(— WITH SOVEREIGN DIGNITY) ENTHRONE

INVESTIGATE SPY SIFT CHECK PROBE SOUND STUDY EXCUSS FATHOM SEARCH DISCUSS EXAMINE EXPLORE INQUIRE INDAGATE SCRUTATE

INVESTIGATION CHECK PROBE TRIAL EXAMEN PILPUL SEARCH DELVING INQUEST INQUIRY LEGWORK ZETETIC ANALYSIS QUESTION RESEARCH SCRUTINY SOUNDING

INVESTIGATOR SNOOP TRIER SLEUTH GUMSHOE SPOTTER FIELDMAN

INVETERATE BLACK SWORN ROOTED CHRONIC HARDENED

INVIDIOUS ENVIOUS HATEFUL

INVIGORATE PEP BRACE CHEER RAISE RENEW VIGOR VIVIFY COMFORT ENFORCE ENLIVEN FORTIFY INNERVE INSINEW REFRESH INSPIRIT

INVIGORATING BRISK CRISP FRESH TONIC VITAL HEARTY LIVELY BRACING CORDIAL VEGETANT

INVISIBLE HID BLIND SECRET UNSEEN VIEWLESS SIGHTLESS

INVITATION BID CALL CARD INVITE BIDDING CALLING

INVITE ASK BID WOO BEAR CALL LURE PRAY TOLL CLEPE COURT LATHE TEMPT TRYST ALLURE DESIRE ENTICE INDITE ATTRACT CONVITE PROVOKE REQUEST SOLICIT

INVOICE BILL BRIEF CHALAN FACTURE MANIFEST BORDEREAU

INVOKE WISH CLEPE EVOKE APPEAL ATTEST OBTEST CONJURE ENTREAT PROVOKE SOLICIT INVOCATE

INVOLVE DIP LAP MIX MIRE WRAP BROIL CARRY COUCH IMPLY RAVEL DIRECT EMPLOY ENGAGE ENTAIL INWRAP TANGLE COMPORT CONCERN CONNOTE EMBRACE EMBROIL ENSNARE ENTWINE IMMERSE INCLUDE ENCUMBER ENTANGLE INTEREST

INVOLVED DEEP BLIND KNOTTY COMPLEX ENGAGED PLAITED IMPLICIT INVOLUTE CONCERNED

IO (BROTHER OF —) PHORONEUS
(FATHER OF —) INACHUS
(SON OF —) EPAPHUS

ION ACID ADION ANION CATION ISOMER KATION LIGAND AMPHION HYDRION OXONIUM SPECIES ZWITTERION

IOTA JOT WHIT GHOST TITTLE SCRUPLE

IOU MARKER

IOWA

CAPITAL: DESMOINES

COLLEGE: COE DORDT LORAS CORNELL PARSONS GRINNELL WARTBURG

COUNTY: IDA LEE SAC CASS LINN PAGE POLK TAMA ADAIR BOONE CEDAR EMMET FLOYD LUCAS SIOUX BREMER KEOKUK OBRIEN DUBUQUE KOSSUTH MAHASKA OSCEOLA

LAKE: CLEAR STORM SPIRIT

NICKNAME: HAWKEYE

RIVER: CEDAR SKUNK BIGSIOUX MISSOURI

STATE BIRD: GOLDFINCH

STATE FLOWER: WILDROSE

STATE TREE: OAK

TOWN: ADEL AMES LEON ALBIA MASON ONAWA OSAGE PERRY SIOUX ALGONA ELDORA KEOKUK LEMARS MARION SIBLEY VINTON ANAMOSA OTTUMWA WATERLOO DAVENPORT

IPHIGENIA (BROTHER OF —) ORESTES
(FATHER OF —) AGAMEMNON
(MOTHER OF —) CLYTEMNESTRA
(SISTER OF —) ELECTRA

IRAN

CAPE: HALILEH

CAPITAL: TEHRAN TEHERAN

COIN: PUL ASAR CRAN LARI RIAL BISTI DARIC DINAR LARIN SHAHI TOMAN STATER ASHRAFI KASBEKE PAHLAVI

DESERT: KERMAN

LAKE: NIRIS NIRIZ TASHT TUZLU URMIA SAHWEH SISTAN MAHARLU NEMEKSER URUMIYEH

LANGUAGE: ZEND PAHLAVI

MEASURE: GAZ GUZ MOV ZAR ZER CANE FOOT GAREH JERIB KAFIZ MAKUK QASAB ARTABA CHARAC CHEBEL GARIBA GHALVA OUROUB CAPICHA CHENICA FARSAKH FARSANG MANSION MISHARA PAIMANEH PARASANG SABBITHA STATHMOS

MOUNTAIN: CUSH KUSH HINDU KHOSF ARARAT HAMUNT BINALUD KHORMUJ SABALAN DEMAVEND

MOUNTAIN RANGE: ELBURZ SIAHAN ZAGROS JAGATAL

PEOPLE: LUR KURD MEDE SART KAJAR MUKRI PERSE TAJIK HADJEMI PERSIAN

PORT: JASK BUSHIRE PAHLEVI
PROVINCE: FARS GILAN KERMAN TEHRAN
ESFAHAN KHORASAN KORDESTAN
RIVER: MAND MUND SHUR ARAKS JAGIN
KARUN RABCH SEFID BAMPUR GORGAN
HALIRI TIGRIS KARKHEH MASHKEL
SAFIDRUD ZAYENDEH EUPHRATES
STRAIT: HORMUZ
TOWN: FAO KOM AMOL SARI YAZD AHVAZ
KHVOY NIRIZ RASHT RESHT ABADAN
DEZFUL GORGAN KASVIN KERMAN
MASHAD MESHED SHIRAZ TABRIZ
TAURIS HAMADAN ISFAHAN SANANDAJ
WEIGHT: SER DRAM DUNG ROTL SANG
SEER ABBAS ARTEL MAUND PINAR
RATEL BATMAN DIRHEM GANDUM
KARWAR MISCAL NAKHOD NIMMAN
ABBASSI TCHEIREK

IRAQ

CAPITAL: BAGDAD BAGHDAD
COIN: DINAR DIRHAM
DISTRICT: BASRA KURDISTAN
FORMER NAME: MESOPOTAMIA
MOUNTAINS: ZARGOS KURDISTAN
OASIS: MANIYA
PEOPLE: ARAB KURD
PORT: FAO BASRA
RIVER: ZAB TIGRIS EUPHRATES
TOWN: ANA HIT AFAQ AMARA BAIJI
BASRA ERBIL HILLA MOSUL NAJAF
HILLAH KIRKUK TIKRIT KARBALA

IRASCIBILITY BILE CHOLER
IRASCIBLE WARM ANGRY CROSS FIERY
GASSY HASTY IRATE SHARP TECHY
TESTY CRANKY IREFUL SPUNKY TETCHY
TOUCHY ANGULAR BILIOUS FRETFUL
IRACUND PEEVISH TINDERY TOUSTIE
WASPISH CAPTIOUS CHOLERIC
PETULANT SNAPPISH STOMACHY
IRATE ANGRY HEATED CHOLERIC
WRATHFUL
IRE FURY ANGER WRATH
IREFUL ANGRY JEALOUS

IRELAND

BAY: MAL CLEW SLIGO BANTRY DINGLE
GALWAY TRALEE DONEGAL DUNDALK
KILLALA BLACKSOD DROGHEDA
CAPE: CLEAR
CAPITAL: TARA DUBLIN BELFAST
COUNTY: CORK DOWN LEIX MAYO CAVAN
CLARE KERRY LOUTH MEATH SLIGO
ANTRIM ARMAGH CARLOW GALWAY
OFFALY TYRONE ULSTER DONEGAL
KILDARE LEITRIM WEXFORD WICKLOW
KILKENNY LIMERICK MONAGHAN
FERMANAGH LONDONDERRY
ISLAND: ARAN TORY SALTEE RATHLIN
LAKE: DOO KEY REE TAY CONN DERG ERNE
MASK CARRA GOWNA LEANE RAMOR

BODERG COOTER ENNELL DROMORE
OUGHTER SHEELIN
MEASURE: MILE BANDLE
MOUNTAIN: OX CAHA ANTRIM GALTEE
KEEPER MOURNE MULREA DONEGAL
ERRIGAL KENNEDY KIPPURE WICKLOW
LEINSTER
PEOPLE: CELT ERSE GAEL CELTIC
HIBERNIAN
POINT: CAHORE CARNSORE
PORT: COBH
PROVINCE: ULSTER MUNSTER LEINSTER
CONNAUGHT
RIVER: LEE BANN DEEL ERNE NORE SUIR
BOYNE CLARE FEALE FLESK FOYLE
LAUNE BANDON BARROW LIFFEY
KENMARE MUNSTER SHANNON
TOWN: CORK NAAS TRIM ADARE CAVAN
ENNIS OMAGH SLIGO ARMAGH CARLOW
DUBLIN GALWAY LURGAN TRALEE
LIMERICK TIPPERARY

IRENIC CALM HENOTIC PEACEFUL
IRIDESCENT SHOT IRISED IRIDINE
IRISATE OPALINE PAVONINE
IRIS EYE SET FLAG LILY LUCE LUCY SEGG
AZURE IREOS ORRIS SEDGE FLAGON
LEVERS LILIAL LILIUM SHADOW
SUNBOW ALCAZAR BABIANA FLAGGER
GLADDON FLAGLEAF
(FATHER OF —) THAUMAS
(MOTHER OF —) ELECTRA
(PREF.) IRID(O) IRIDICO IRIDIO
IRISHMAN MAC PAT CELT GAEL KELT
SCOT IRISH PADDY TEAGUE IRISHER
MILESIAN ORANGEMAN
IRK BORE ITCH ANNOY WEARY BOTHER
IRKSOME DULL WARM WEARY
HUMDRUM OPEROSE PAINFUL TEDIOUS
ANNOYING TIRESOME
IRON BIT DOG IRE AIRN MARS WIRE
ANGLE ANVIL BASIL BRAND DRAIL FLOSS
NEGRO PRESS SPIKE STEEL WAVER
ANCONY CALKER CAUTER FERRUM
GAGGER GOFFER JAGGER OSMUND
CAUTERY CRAMPER FERRITE FURISON
GAMBREL GAUFFER PRICKER SADIRON
FLATIRON TRICOUNI
(— FOR CLOSING STAVES) HORSE
(— OF MILLSTONE) RIND
(— SUPPORTING SPIT) COBIRON
(— TO SUPPORT BEAM) TORSEL
(ANGLE —) LATH STIFFENER
(BASKETWORK —) BEATER
(BOOM —) WITHE
(BRANDING —) BURN
(CAST —) METAL SPIEGEL YETLING
PROMETAL SEMISTEEL
(CLIMBING —) GAFF SPUR CREEPER
(CRUDE CASTING OF —) PIG
(DRIVING —) CLEEK
(GLASSBLOWING —) BAIT
(GOLF —) JIGGER
(GRAPPLING —) CRAMPON
(HATTER'S —) SLUG
(MASS OF WROUGHT —) BLOOM

(METEORIC —) SIDERITE
(PASTY —) SPONGE
(PIG —) SPIEGEL KENTLEDGE
(PRIMING —) DRIFT
(PUDDLING —) RABBLE
(RUSSIAN —) SABLE
(SHEET —) TERNE
(SOLDERING —) COPPER
(SPECULAR —) HEMATITE
(TAILOR'S —) GOOSE
(TAMPING —) DRIVER
(8 PIGS OF CAST —) FODDER
IRONIC ACERB ACERBIC SATIRIC
  SARCASTIC
IRONICAL BLAND CRUEL PAWKY
IRONY SATIRE ASTEISM SARCASM
  RIDICULE
IROQUOIS HURON MINGO CAYUGA
  MENGWE
IRRATIONAL MAD REE SURD WILD
  BRUTE SILLY ABSURD RAVING STUPID
  BESTIAL FOOLISH
IRRECONCILABLE HOSTILE FRONDEUR
IRREGULAR ODD DUMB WILD BUMPY
  EROSE FANCY MIXED WOPSY ATYPIC
  CATCHY FITFUL PATCHY RAGGED
  RUGGED SPOTTY UNEVEN UNLIKE
  WEEWAW ANAXIAL ATACTIC BAROQUE
  CATERAN CRABBED CROOKED CURSORY
  DEVIOUS DIFFORM ERRATIC FRECKET
  MUTABLE SCRAWLY SNATCHY UNEQUAL
  WAYWARD ABNORMAL ATYPICAL
  DOGGEREL INFORMAL PINDARIC
  SCRAGGLY SCRAMBLY UNLAWFUL
  UNSTABLE UNSTEADY VARIABLE
  AMORPHOUS PROMISCUOUS
IRREGULARITY SNAG DEFECT RUFFLE
  ANOMALY ACCIDENT
  (— IN YARN) SNICK
IRRESISTIBLE MESMERIC OPPOSELESS
IRRESOLUTE FICKLE INFIRM UNSURE
  WANKLE DOUBTFUL UNSTABLE
IRRESPONSIBLE WILDCAT CAREFREE
  FECKLESS SKITTISH
IRREVERENCE IMPIETY
IRREVERENT ATHEIST AWELESS
  IMPIOUS PROFANE
IRREVOCABLE DEAD
IRRIGATE FLOAT WATER SYRINGE
IRRITABILITY BATE NERVES SPLEEN
  ERETHISM SORENESS VAGOTONY
  SENSITIVITY
IRRITABLE BAD EDGY BIRSY CROOK
  FIERY FUSSY HASTY HUFFY JUMPY
  MUSTY NAGGY RASPY TETTY TILTY
  TOITY CRANKY GROWLY NETTLY PATCHY
  SNUFFY SPUNKY STOCKY TEETHY
  TETCHY TOUCHY CRABBED FRATCHY
  FRETFUL HORNETY HUFFISH KICKISH
  PECKISH PEEVISH SPLEENY TEDIOUS
  TWITCHY WASPISH LIVERISH PETULANT
  SNAPPING SNAPPISH STOMACHY
  SPLENETIC
IRRITATE BUG EAT GET IRE IRK NAG RUB
  TAR TEW TRY VEX BURN CRAB FIRE FRET
  GALL GOAD GRIG GRIT ITCH NARK RILE
  ROIL SOUR TEEN ANGER ANNOY CHAFE

EAGER FRUMP GRATE GRILL GRIPE PEEVE
  PIQUE STING TARRY ABRADE BOTHER
  FRIDGE GRAVEL HARASS HECTOR
  NETTLE RUFFLE AFFRONT INCENSE
  INFLAME NERVOUS PROVOKE STOMACH
  ACERBATE
IRRITATED RILY SORE HUFFY RAGGY
  MUFFED SHIRTY EMPORTE FRATCHED
  SOREHEAD
  (EASILY —) TESTY
IRRITATING ACRID HARSH CORSIE
  ELVISH GRAVEL FRETFUL GALLING
  IRKSOME PUNGENT RASPING ANNOYING
  FRETSOME GRAVELLY NETTLING
  SCRATCHY SPITEFUL STINGING
  TIRESOME MADDENING NETTLESOME
IRRITATION FRET TEEN BIRSE PIQUE
  STEAM NEEDLE RUFFLE TEMPER
  WARMTH ANTPRICK FLEABITE PINPRICK
  VEXATION
ISAAC (FATHER OF —) ABRAHAM
  (MOTHER OF —) SARAH
  (SON OF —) ESAU JACOB
  (WIFE OF —) REBEKAH
ISAIAH ESAY ESAIAS
  (FATHER OF —) AMOZ
ISEULT (FATHER OF —) HOEL ANGUISH
  (HUSBAND OF —) MARK
  (LOVER OF —) TRISTAN
ISHMAEL (FATHER OF —) AZEL
  ABRAHAM JEHOHANAN NETHANIAH
  (MOTHER OF —) HAGAR
  (SON OF —) ZEBADIAH
ISINGLASS AGAR LEAF MICA PIPE
  KANTEN CARLOCK
ISIS (BROTHER OF —) OSIRIS
  (FATHER OF —) SATURN
  (MOTHER OF —) RHEA
ISLAND CALF CAYO HOLM INCH ISLE
  JAVA POLO ENNIS MALTA MAYDA
  AVALON ITHACA OGYGIA REFUGE RIALTO
  CIPANGO JAMAICA MADEIRA TOWHEAD
  BLEFUSCU CALAURIA DOMINICA
  GUERNSEY LILLIPUT LUGGNAGG
  (— IN EVERGLADES) HAMMOCK
  (— OF REIL) INSULA
  (ARTIFICIAL —) CRANNOG
  (CORAL —) ATOLL
  (FABLED —) MERU UTOPIA
  (FLOATING —) HOVER
  (FLYING —) LAPUTA
  (FORTIFIED —) CRANNOG
  (LEGENDARY —) BRAZIL OBRAZIL
  (LITTLE —) AIT KAY KEY ISLET
  (LOW —) KEY
  (ROCKY —) SKERRY
  (SANDY —) BEACH BARRIER
  (SMALL —) CAY ISLE ISLET NUBBLE
  SANDKEY
ISLANDER KANAKA ISLEMAN INSULARY
ISLE IZLE ISLET SKERRY
ISLET OE AIT CAY KEY EYOT HAFT HOLM
  ILOT MOTU ROCK ISLOT STACK NUBBLE
ISOLATE SPORE ENISLE LANDS DISSECT
  SECLUDE COLONIZE INSULATE PRESCIND
  SEPARATE SEQUESTER

ISOLATED LONE POCKET UNIQUE OUTLYING SOLITARY STRANDED SECESSIVE
ISOLATION HERMITRY LONENESS SOLITUDE SEQUESTER

ISRAEL

CAPITAL: JERUSALEM
DESERT: NEGEV
GULF: AQABA
LAKE: HULEH TIBERIAS
MEASURE: CAB HIN KOR LOG BATH EPHA EZBA OMER REED SEAH CUBIT EPHAH HOMER KANEH QANEH
MOUNTAIN: NAFH SAGI HARIF MERON RAMON ATZMON CARMEL
PLAIN: ESDRAELON
RIVER: FARIA MALIK SOREQ JORDAN QISHON SARIDA YARKON LAKHISH
SEA: DEAD GALILEE
SEAPORT: EILAT ELATH ASHDOD TELAVIV
TOWN: ACRE RAMA HAIFA HOLON JAFFA JENIN JOPPA RAMLE SAFAD BATYAM HEBRON NABLUS JERICHO NATANYA TELAVIV TULKARM NAZARETH

ISRAELI SABRA
ISSUE END ISH COME EMIT FALL FLOW GIVE GUSH HEAD MISE REEK TERM VENT ARISE COUNT EVENT FRUIT LOOSE OUTGO SETON SOURD UTTER EFFECT EFFUSE EGRESS EMERGE ESCAPE EXITUS MUTTON RESULT SEQUEL SETTER SPRING UPPING BALLOON DEBOUCH DESCENT DRIZZLE EMANATE ESSENCE EXSURGE OUTCOME PROCEED PROGENY REDOUND REFLAIR SUCCESS EXPEDITE FONTANEL INCREASE ISSUANCE KINDLING OUTGOING
(— AND ORDER) BID
(— SLOWLY) EXUDE
(— SPASMODICALLY) BELCH
(— SUDDENLY) SALLY
(— WITH FORCE) SPOUT
(BOND —) CONSOL
(FAVORABLE —) SPEED FORTUNE
(FINAL —) FATE UPSHOT UTMOST
(NUMEROUS —) SPAWN
(REAL —) CRUX
ISSUING EMANANT JESSANT MANATION
ISTHMUS BALK STRAIT TARBET
ISTLE PITA IXTLE JUAMAVE GUAPILLA
ITALIANA IN ALGIERI, L'
(CHARACTER IN —) ELVIRA TADDEO LINDPRO ISABELLA MUSTAPHA
(COMPOSER OF —) ROSSINI

ITALY

CAPE: TESTA CIRCEO LICOSA LINARO COLONNE FALCONE PASSERO RIZZUTO SANVITO TEULADA VATICANO
CAPITAL: ROMA ROME

GULF: GAETA GENOA OROSEI SALERNO TARANTO CAGLIARI ORISTANO
ISLAND: ELBA LERO CAPRI LEROS PONZA GIGLIO ISCHIA LINOSA SALINA SICILY USTICA ALICUDI ASINARA CAPRAIA GORGONA LEVANZO PANAREA PIANOSA SICILIA VULCANO FILICUDI SARDINIA
ISLANDS: EGADI LIPARI TUSCAN PELAGIE PONTINE TREMITI
LAKE: COMO ISEO NEMI GARDA ALBANO LESINA LUGANO VARANO BOLSENA PERUGIA MAGGIORE BRACCIANO
MEASURE: PIE ORNA CANNA PALMA PALMO PIEDE PUNTO SALMA STAIO STERO BARILE MIGLIE MIGLIO MOGGIO RUBBIO TAVOLA TOMOLO BOCCALE BRACCIO SECCHIO GIORNATA POLONICK QUADRATO
MOUNTAIN: ETNA ROSA VISO AMARO BLANC CORNO SOMMA CIMONE BERNINA VESUVIUS
MOUNTAIN RANGE: ALPS ORTLES APENNINES MARITIMES
NATIVE: ITALO LATIN OSCAN ROMAN SABINE TIRANO TUSCAN LOMBARD SIENESE LIGURIAN VENETIAN
PASS: FREJUS BERNINA BRENNER SPLUGEN
PORT: BARI POLA ZARA GENOA TRANI ZADAR RIMINI SALERNO TRIESTE
PROVINCE: ASTI COMO ENNA PISA AOSTA CUNEO FORLI LECCE NUORO PARMA PAVIA RIETI SIENA UDINE FOGGIA MATERA MODENA PADOVA RAGUSA TRENTO VERONA BRESCIA PISTOIA SASSARI VITERBO
REGION: CARSO APULIA LATIUM MARCHE MOLISE PUGLIA SICILY UMBRIA ABRUZZI LIGURIA TUSCANY VENETIA CALABRIA CAMPANIA LOMBARDY PIEMONTE SARDINIA
RIVER: PO ADDA AGRI ANIO ARNO LIRI NERA RENO SELE TARO ADIGE CRATI MANNU OGLIO PARMA PIAVE SALSO STURA TIBER TIRSO ANIENE BELICE MINCIO OFANTO PANARO RAPIDO SANGRO SIMETO TANARO TEVERE TICINO BIFERNO BRADANO CHIENTI METAURO MONTONE OMBRONE PESCARA RUBICON SECCHIA TREBBIA VOLTURNO
SEA: IONIAN ADRIATIC LIGURIAN
STRAIT: MESSINA OTRANTO BONIFACIO
TOWN: BRA RHO ACRI ALBA ASTI BARI COMO DEGO ELEA ENNA ESTE FANO GELA IESI LODI NARO NOLA PISA POLA ROMA ROME ACQUI ANZIO AOSTA ASOLA AVOLA CAPUA CUNEO EBOLI FIUME FORLI GENOA IMOLA LECCE LUCCA MASSA MILAN MONZA OSTIA PADUA PARMA PAVIA SIENA TEANO TRENT TURIN UDINE VELIA ALCAMO AMALFI ANCONA ANDRIA AREZZO CEFALU FAENZA FOGGIA GENOVA MANTUA MESTRE MILANO MODENA NAPLES NAPOLI NOVARA RIVOLI SPEZIA TRENTO VARESE VENICE VERONA

BERGAMO BOLOGNA BOLZANO BRESCIA CARRARA CASERTA CATANIA COSENZA CREMONA FERRARA FIRENZE GORIZIA IMPERIA LEGHORN LIVORNO MARSALA MESSINA PALERMO PERUGIA PISTOIA POMPEII RAVENNA TARANTO TRIESTE BRINDISI CAGLIARI FLORENCE PIACENZA SORRENTO SYRACUSE
VOLCANO: ETNA SOMMA VULCANO VESUVIUS STROMBOLI
WATERFALL: FRUA TOCE

ITCH EACH REEF RIFF PSORA TICKLE ITCHING SCABIES PRURITUS CACOETHES VANILLISM
ITCHING ITCHY PRURIENT PRURITUS URTICANT
ITEM ANA JOB TOT ENTRY POINT THING DETAIL PARCEL ARTICLE SEVERAL PARTICULAR
  (— IN SERIES) COURSE
  (— OF PROPERTY) CHATTEL
  (— OF VALUE) ASSET
  (APPENDED —) ADDENDUM
  (COLLECTOR'S —) SPOIL
  (DECORATIVE —) CONCEIT
  (LUXURY —) BOUTIQUE
  (NEWS —) DISPATCH
  (UNPUBLISHED —S) ANECDOTE
  (VALUELESS —) BEAN
ITEMIZE DETAIL
ITERATION PLEONASM

ITINERANT ERRANT AMBULANT STROLLING PERIPATETIC
ITINERARY DIET JOURNAL WAYBILL
  (— OF ROYAL PROGRESS) GEST
IVANHOE (AUTHOR OF —) SCOTT
  (CHARACTER IN —) JOHN BRIAN GIRTH ISAAC LUCAS ROBIN WAMBA CEDRIC ROWENA ULRICA MAURICE REBECCA RICHARD WILFRED REGINALD BEAUMANOIR
IVORY EBURE DENTINE ELEPHANT
  (DUST OF —) EBURINE

IVORY COAST

CAPE: PALMAS
CAPITAL: ABIDJAN
DAM: BANDAMA
MOUNTAIN: NIMBA
PEOPLE: ABE AKAN ATLE KOUA KROU MANDE ABOURE LAGOON MALINKE VOLTAIC
RIVER: KOMOE BANDAMA CAVALLY SASSANDRA
TOWN: MAN DALOA TABOU BOUAKE GAGNOA KORHOGO SASSANDRA

IVY TOD GILL HOVE IVIN JILL PICRY ARALIA HEDERA HIBBIN ALEHOOF ARALIAD IVYWORT BINDWEED FOALFOOT
IWW WOBBLY

J

J JAY
JAB GAG GIG JAG JOB POKE STAB STICK
JABAL (BROTHER OF —) JUBAL
 (FATHER OF —) LAMECH
 (MOTHER OF —) ADAH
JABBER CHAT JAVER BURBLE GABBER
 GABBLE JOBBER YABBER YATTER
 CHATTER
JABOT RUFFLE
JACINTH LIGURE
JACK DIB FLAG JACA CRICK DICKY
 NANCA COLORS KATHAL SCALET SETTER
 MATADOR BLOCKING JACKFISH
 POLIGNAL SOURJACK TURNSPIT
 UPLIFTER
 (— IN BOWLS) BABY MARK KITTY
 MASTER MISTRESS
 (— IN CARDS) PAM PUR TOM BOWER
 CNAFE KITTY KNAPE KNAVE MAKER
 KNIGHT VARLET WENZEL VARLETTO
 (— OF CLUBS) NODDY BRAGGER
 MATADOR
 (— OF SAME SUIT) NOB
 (— OF TRUMPS) TOM JASS JASZ
 BOWER HONOR PLAYBOY
 (PIANO —) HOPPER STICKER
 SAUTEREAU
 (SPINNING —) BEAT
JACKAL DIEB JACK KOLA THOS CANID
 CANINE DRAGON SILVER THOOID
 SIACALLE
JACKASS JACK
JACKDAW DAW KAE JACK SHELL
 CADDOW CARDER CHOUGH KADDER
 CADESSE DAWCOCK DAWPATE GRACKLE
JACKET SAC COAT ETON JACK JUMP
 JUPE SACK VEST COVER DICKY JUPON
 PARKA POLKA SHRUG WAMUS BASQUE
 BIETLE BLAZER BOLERO CARACO CORSET
 DOLMAN FECKET GANSEY JERKIN
 JERSEY JUMPER RAILLY REEFER SACQUE
 SADDLE SLEEVE SLIVER TABARD TEMIAK
 WAMPUS WARMUS ZOUAVE BEDGOWN
 CANEZOU LOUNGER NORFOLK PALETOT
 PALTOCK PEACOAT RISTORI SPENCER
 SURCOAT SWEATER CAMISOLE
 CARDIGAN CHAQUETA HANSELIN
 JIRKINET MACKINAW OVERSLOP
 PENELOPE SEALSKIN CARMAGNOLE
 ROUNDABOUT
 (— FOR TURKEY) APRON
 (— LINED WITH STEEL) PLACCATE
 (— OF INDIA) BANIAN BANIYA
 (— UNDER ARMOR) ACTON TRUSS
 HAQUETON
 (CROCHETED —) SONTAG
 (HOODED —) GREGO ANORAK
 (HUSSAR'S —) PELISSE
 (KIND OF —) MAO NEHRU

 (LADY'S —) BRUNSWICK
 (LOOSE —) VAREUSE
 (MALAY —) BAJU KABAYA
 (PEASANT'S —) SAYON
 (UNDRESS MILITARY —) SHELL
 (WORK —) BAWNEEN
JACKHAMMER SINKER PLUGGER
JACKKNIFE JACK PIKE BARLOW
JACK-OF-ALL-TRADES DOCTOR TINKER
 GIMCRACK
JACOB ISRAEL
 (BROTHER OF —) ESAU
 (DAUGHTER OF —) RACHEL DEBORAH
 (FATHER OF —) ISAAC
 (MOTHER OF —) REBEKAH
 (SON OF —) JOSEPH
JADE YU DUN TIT HACK JAUD MINX PLUG
 SLUT TIRE HUSSY QUEAN TRASH BEJADE
 HARASS RANNEL AXSTONE HILDING
 POUNAMU
 (DIRTY —) SLAISTER
JADED FORGONE SHOPWORN DISJASKIT
JAG BUN JOG BARB GIMP JAUG LOAD
 SOSH TOOT SKATE TOOTH INDENT
JAGGED JAGGY HACKLY RAGGED
 RUGGED SCRAGGY SHAGGED SNAGGED
 INDENTED SCRAGGLY TATTERED
JAGUAR CAT OUNCE TIGER PANTHER
 UTURUNCU
JAI ALAI PELOTA
 (— COURT) FRONTON
JAIL CAN GIB JUG BOOB CAGE COOP CRIB
 DUMP GAOL HELL HOLD HOLE KEEP LAKE
 LOCK NICK STIR WARD CHOKY CLINK
 GRATE KITTY LIMBO LODGE POKEY
 TENCH TRONK BUCKET CARCEL COOLER
 ENJAIL JIGGER LIMBUS LOCKUP TOLZEY
 FREEZER FURNACE GEHENNA KIDCOTE
 PINFOLD SLAMMER TOLLERY BASTILLE
 CALABOZO HOOSEGOW IMPRISON
 MILLDOLL TOLLHALL BRIDEWELL
 CALABOOSE
JAILBIRD LAG
JAILER ADAM GAOLER KEEPER WARDEN
 ALCAIDE TURNKEY INCLUDER
JALOPY HEAP CLUNKER
JAM DIP CRAM JAMB BLOCK CHOKE
 CROWD STICK KONFYT THRONG
 JACKPOT
JAMAICA (CAPITAL OF —) KINGSTON
 (RIVER OF —) BLACK COBRE MINHO
 (TOWN OF —) MAYPEN PORTANTONIO
 SPANISHTOWN
JAMB DURN ALETTE HAUNCH REVEAL
 DOORPOST
 (PL.) COVING
JAMES JEM JIM JIMMY SEAMAS
 SHAMUS
 (BROTHER OF —) JOHN JESUS JOSES

(COUSIN OF —) JESUS
(FATHER OF —) CLOPAS
(MOTHER OF —) MARY SALOME
JANE EYRE (AUTHOR OF —) BRONTE
(CHARACTER IN —) EYRE JANE JOHN
MARY REED ADELE DIANA ELIZA GRACE
POOLE BERTHA BESSIE EDWARD ELLIOT
INGRAM LEAVEN RIVERS TEMPLE
VARENS BLANCHE FAIRFAX GEORGIANA
ROCHESTER
JANGLE CLAM SQUABBLE
JANGLING HARSH JANGLY AJANGLE
JANITOR DURWAN PORTER SERVITOR
JAPAN NIPPON YAMATO CIPANGO

JAPAN

BAY: ISE MUTSU OTARU ARIAKE ATSUMI
SENDAI SURUGA TOYAMA WAKASA
UCHIURA
CAPE: TOI ESAN MINO NOMA SHIO SOYA
SUZU ERIMO KYOGA RURUI MUROTO
NOJIMA TODOGA SHIRIYA ASHIZURI
SHAKOTAN
CAPITAL: TOKIO TOKYO
COIN: BU RIN SEN YEN OBAN KOBAN
OBANG TEMPO ICHEBU ITZEBU KOBANG
ISLAND: IKI SADO AWAJI BONIN HONDO
KURIL REBUN HONSHU KIUSHU KURILE
KYUSHU RYUKYU CIPANGO LOOCHOO
RISHIRI SKIKOKU HOKKAIDO IKISHIMA
OKIGUNTO OKUSHIRI TSUSHIMA
YAKUJIMA
ISLAND GROUP: OKI GOTO BONIN
VOLCANO
LAKE: BIWA TOYA TOWADA CHUZENJI
KUTCHAWA SHIKOTSU INAWASHIRO
MEASURE: BU JO SE BOO CHO KEN TAN
HIRO SHAKU TSUBO
MOUNTAIN: ZAO FUJI ASAHI ASAMA
YESSO ASOSAN ENASAN HIUCHI KIUSIU
YARIGA FUJISAN HAKUSAN KUJUSAN
TOKACHI FUJIYAMA
PORT: OTARU YAHATA YAWATA
PREFECTURE: MIE GIFU NARA OITA SAGA
AICHI AKITA CHIBA EHIME FUKUI
GUMMA HYOGO IWATE KOCHI KYOTO
SHIGA AOMORI KAGAWA MIYAGI
NAGANO TOYAMA NIIGATA OKINAWA
SAITAMA TOTTORI NAGASAKI
WAKAYAMA YAMAGATA TOKUSHIMA
SEA: SUO AMAKUSA
STRAIT: KII BUNGO OSUMI NEMURO
TANEGA TOKARA TSUGARU TSUSHIMA
TOWN: OME TSU GIFU KOBE KURA MITO
NAHA NARA OITA OTSU SAGA UEDA
AKITA ATAMI CHIBA FUKUI KIOTO KOCHI
NIKKO OSAKA OTARU SAKAI UJINA
URAWA CHOSHI MATSUE NAGOYA
SASEBO SENDAI TAKADA TOYAMA
FUKUOKA NIIGATA OKAYAMA OKAZAKI
SAPPORO HAKODATE KAMAKURA
KANAZAWA KAWASAKI KUMAMOTO
NAGASAKI YOKOHAMA YOKOSUKA
HIROSHIMA

VOLCANO: ASO USU FUJI ASAMA
ASOSAN HAKUSAN FUJIYAMA
WATERFALL: KEGON
WEIGHT: MO FUN KIN KON RIN SHI KATI
KWAN NIYO CARAT CATTY MOMME
PICUL KWAMME HIYAKKIN

JAPANESE CHERRY SAKURA
JAPE GAUD JOKE BEGUNK
JAPHETH (BROTHER OF —) HAM SHEM
(FATHER OF —) NOAH
(SON OF —) JAVAN
JAR TUN CELL JANG JARG JOLT JURR
BOCAL CADUS CRUSE KADOS SHOCK
DOLIUM HUSTLE IMPACT JUDDER KALPIS
PANKIN PINATA TINAJA CANOPUS
CONCUSS POTICHE PSYKTER STAMNOS
MARTABAN STINKPOT
(BELL —) CLOCHE
(BULGING —) OLLA
(EARTHENWARE —) CAN NAN CROCK
GAMLA PIPKIN PITHOS TERRINE
(POROUS —) GURGLET
(SQUAT —) KORO
(STONE —) STEEN STONE CROPPA
(WATER —) KANG BANGA CHATTI
CHATTY GUMLAH HYDRIA
(2-HANDLED —) AMPHORA
JARGON CANT JIVE RANE SLUM ARGOT
LINGO SLANG LINGUA LINSEY PATOIS
PATTER PIDGIN SHELTA SIWASH
CHINOOK CHOCTAW DIALECT JARGOON
PALAVER BARRIKIN KEDGEREE
PARLANCE POLYGLOT SCHMOOZE
SHOPTALK
(THIEVES' —) FLASH
(TINKER'S —) KENNICK
(UNINTELLIGIBLE —) BARAGOUIN
JARRING JARG RUDE SOUR HARSH
ROUGH DARING STRIDENT
JASMINE BELA MALATI PIKAKE JESSAMY
WOODBINE
JASPER JASPIS MORLOP DIASPER
BASANITE CREOLITE
JAUNDICE AURIGO GULSACH ICTERUS
JANDERS YELLOWS JAUNDERS
GRASSERIE
JAUNDICED ICTERODE
JAUNT TRIP SALLY JAUNCE VAGARY
JOURNEY
JAUNTILY AIRILY BOUNCILY
JAUNTING CAR SIDECAR OUTSIDER
JAUNTY PERK PERT TRIM COCKY PERKY
SASSY DAPPER JANTEE SHANTY FINICAL
PERKING DEBONAIR

JAVA

INDONESIAN NAME: DJAWA
ISLAND: BALI LOMBOK MADURA
MEASURE: PAAL
MOUNTAIN: GEDE MURJO RAOENG
SEMERU SLAMET SEMEROE SOEMBING
PORT: BATAVIA SURABAJA TJILATJAP
RIVER: SOLO LIWUNG BRANTAS
TOWN: BOGOR DESSA KEDIRI MALANG

BANDUNG BATAVIA JAKARTA
SEMARANG SURABAJA
WEIGHT: POND TALI

JAVA HEAD (AUTHOR OF —)
HERGESHEIMER
(CHARACTER IN —) TAOU YUEN
RHODA EDWARD GERRIT JEREMY NETTIE
VOLLAR AMMIDON DUNSACK WILLIAM
JAVELIN COLP DART PILE ACLYS PILUM
JARED LANCET ASSAGAI HARPOON
HURLBAT JAVELOT ACONTIUM
GAVELOCK
JAW JIB CHAW CHOP JOWL WANG ANVIL
CHAFT CHEEK CHOKE SCOLD CHAWLE
FEELER JAWBONE MAXILLA MANDIBLE
(— OF FORCEPS) BEAK
(— OF SPIDER) FANG
(— OF VISE) CHAP
(—S OF BIRD) BILL
(FALSE —) CLAMP
**(RECEDING NOSE AND UNDERSHOT
—)** LAYBACK
JAWBONE JOWL WANG MAXILLA
CHAWBONE
JAY JAYPIET SIRGANG BLUECOAT
MEATBIRD
JAZZ BOP JIVE HOTCHA
JEALOUS YELLOW EMULOUS ENVIOUS
JEALOUSY ENVY YELLOWS EMULATION
ZELOTYPIA
JEEP PEEP SEEP BANTAM
JEER BOB BOO MOB GECK GIBE GIRD
JAPE JEST JIBE MOCK SKIT WIPE FLIRT
FLOUT FLUTE FLYTE FRUMP GLAIK
LAUGH SCOFF SCOMM SNEER TAUNT
CHIACK DERIDE BARRACK RIDICULE
JEERING BIRD FLOUT DERISIVE
JEHOIAKIM (FATHER OF —) JOSIAH
(SON OF —) JEHOIACHIN
JEHOVAH JAH LORD JAHVE YAHWEH
(— WITNESS) PIONEER
JEHU (FATHER OF —) HANANI JOSIBIAH
JEHOSHAPHAT
(SON OF —) JEHOAHAZ
(VICTIM OF —) JEHORAM
JEJUNE DRY ARID MEAGER INSIPID
JELL COME FIRM
JELLY GEAL JEEL JELL GELEE CULLIS
JUJUBE ALCOGEL FISNOGA GELATIN
JELLIFY FLUMMERY HYDROGEL
QUIDDANY MARMALADE
(AGAR-AGAR —) KANTEN
(CALF'S-FOOT —) SULZE
(FRUIT —) ROB
(MEAT —) ASPIC
JELLYFISH JELLY QUARL CARVEL
MEDUSA ACALEPH AURELIA BLUBBER
MEDUSAN SLOBBER SUNFISH SCYPHULA
SEACROSS STROBILA
(PART OF —) ARM BELL MOUTH
MARGIN STOMACH TENTACLE UMBRELLA
MANUBRIUM
JELLYLIKE SLABBY
JENNY MULE BETTY JINNY

JEOPARDIZE STAKE EXPOSE HAZARD
IMPERIL ENDANGER
JEOPARDY RISK PERIL DANGER HAZARD
JEREMIAD TRAGEDY
JEREMIAH (DAUGHTER OF —)
HAMUTAL
(FATHER OF —) HILKIAH
(SON OF —) JAZANIAH
JERK BOB GAG JET NUD TIT BOUT CANT
FIRK GIRD HIKE JERT JIRT JOLT JOUK
KICK PECK SNAP SNIG YANK YERK BRAID
CHUCK FLIRT HITCH HOICK SCHMO SLIRT
SNAKE SPANG SURGE TWEAK TWICK
FILLIP JIGGER SWITCH TWITCH WRENCH
FLOUNCE SACCADE SCHMUCK
SPANGHEW
JERKIN SAYON JACKET
JERKY NERVY SHARP CHOPPY ELBOIC
FLICKY FLINGY HITCHY JIGGETY
CHOPPING PALMODIC RATCHETY
SACCADIC
JEROBOAM REHOBOAM
(FATHER OF —) JOASH NEBAT
(WIFE OF —) ANO
JERSEY FROCK SHIRT GANSEY TRICOT
ZEPHYR MAILLOT SINGLET CAMISOLE
GUERNSEY
JERUSALEM ZION ARIEL SOLYMA
AHOLIBAH
JERUSALEM ARTICHOKE TUBER
CANADA GIRASOL
JERUSALEM DELIVERED
(AUTHOR OF —) TASSO
(CHARACTER IN —) HUGH OTHO
SWENO ARMIDA OLINDO ALADINE
ERMINIA GODFREY RINALDO TANCRED
ARGANTES BOUILLON CLORINDA
SOLIMANO SOPHRONIA
JESSE (FATHER OF —) OBED
(SON OF —) DAVID
JESSICA (FATHER OF —) SHYLOCK
(HUSBAND OF —) LORENZO
JEST BAR BOG COD COG FUN GAB JOE
TAX BULL GAME GAUD GIRD JAPE JOKE
JOSH PLAY QUIP QUIZ RAIL SKIT BOURD
BREAK CHAFF CLOWN DROLL FLIRT
GESTE SLEEK SPORT THING BANTER
GLANCE JAPERY RAILLY TRIFLE DICTERY
GAMMOCK JOLLITY WAGGERY DROLLERY
RAILLERY
(— SPITEFULLY) SLENT
JESTER FOOL MIME BUFFO CLOWN
DROLL IDIOT JAPER JOKER PATCH
WAMBA DISOUR MOTLEY YORICK
BADCHAN BOURDER BUFFOON DIZZARD
DROLLER JOCULAR JUGGLER PICADOR
SCOFFER SCOGGIN TOMTRAM
MERRYMAN OWLGLASS PLEASANT
RAILLEUR TRINCULO
JESTING DROLL JAPERY SCOPTIC
WAGGISH
(RUDELY —) INFICETE
JESUIT PAULIST TERTIAN IGNATIAN
LOYOLITE
JESUS GEE GIS JESU WISDOM
JET BOLT TAIL TANG DUMBY DUMMY
JETTO SALLY SCOOT SPOUT SPRAY

SPURT CANDLE DELUGE DOUCHE
GAGATE SQUIRT FANTAIL JETTEAU
SPATTER SPURTER FOUNTAIN SOFFIONE
UPSPRING
(— OF FLAME) TONGUE
(— OF METAL) BREAK
(— OF VOLCANIC STEAM) STUFA
(SMALL —) SQUIB
(SUBSONIC —) AIRBUS
JET-BLACK BUGLE
JETHRO (DAUGHTER OF —) ZIPPORAH
(SON-IN-LAW OF —) MOSES
JETTISON DUMP JETSAM
JETTY JET PEN DIKE GROIN JUTTY
BRIDGE OVERHANG
JEW SAINT ESSENE JUDEAN LITVAK
SEMITE SMOUCH SMOUSE TOBIAD
BARABAS GRECIAN KARAITE MARRANO
APIKOROS CONVERSO GALICIAN
JUDAHITE LANDSMAN SEPHARDI
(—S OUT OF ISRAEL) DIASPORA
(BALKAN —) LADINO
JEWEL GEM JOY DROP OUCH BIJOU
REGAL STONE BROOCH GEORGE TRIFLE
CRAPAUD GARLAND POUNDER
JEWELER GEMMARY LAPIDARY
JEWELRY ICE JUNK OUCH PARURE
COLLARET LAPIDARY
(MOCK —) LOGIE
(PIECE OF —) GAUD
JEWELS OF THE MADONNA
(CHARACTER IN —) GENNARO
MALIELLA RAFFAELE
(COMPOSER OF —) WOLFFERRARI
JEW OF MALTA (AUTHOR OF —)
MARLOWE
(CHARACTER IN —) JACOMO MARTIN
ABIGAIL BARABAS MATHIAS CALYMATH
ITHAMORE LODOWICK BELLAMIRA
BERNARDINE
JEW'S-HARP HARP TROMP TRUMP
GEWGAW FLAMFEW TRANGAM
GUIMBARD
JEZEBEL GILLIVER
(FATHER OF —) ETHBAAL
(HUSBAND OF —) AHAB
(SLAYER OF —) JEHU
JIB GIB BALK BAULK DEMUR GIGUE STICK
GIBBET SPITFIRE
JIBE (ALSO SEE GIBE) GEE KAY GAFF
GIBE JAPE JERK MOCK SKIT AGREE FLIRD
MARCH SNACK THRUST
JIFFY JIFF BRAID FLISK WHIFF GLIFFY
GLIFFING
JIG BUCK FRISK GIGUE SQUID GARLIC
JIGGER JIGGET JITTER LOCATOR
(— FOR WASHING ORE) HUTCH
(FISHING —) PILK
JIGGER SHOT DANDY PIQUE DOODAD
GADGET JIGMAN VATMAN CHIGGER
JIGGLE DIDDLE JUGGLE TEETER
JILT GUNK KICK SACK BEGOWK BEGUNK
MITTEN
JINGLE TUNE CHIME CHINK CHINK CLINK
DINGLE RICKLE TINKLE CHINKLE
CLERIHEW DINGDONG JINGLING
(MEANINGLESS —) SPORT

JINGLING SMIT JANGLE RIGADIG
TINKLING
JINGO WARRIOR WARMONGER
JINGOISM CHAUVINISM
JINN DJIN JANN AFRIT EBLIS GENIE
AFREET DJINNI SHAITAN
(PL.) JINNI
JINNI MARID AFREET ALUKAH GENIUS
YAKSHA YAKSHI JINNIYEH
JINRIKISHA GOCART KURUMA
RICKSHAW
JINX HEX JONAH HOODOO
JITTERBUG TRUCKING
JITTERY EDGY JUMPY TENSE SPOOKY
AJITTER
JOAB (BROTHER OF —) ASAHEL
ABISHAI
(MOTHER OF —) ZERUIAH
(SLAYER OF —) BENAIAH
(UNCLE OF —) DAVID
(VICTIM OF —) ABNER
JOAN JUG JONE
(— OF ARC) PUCELLE
JOASH (FATHER OF —) AHAB BECHER
AHAZIAH SHEMAAH JEHOAHAZ
(SON OF —) GIDEON
(VICTIM OF —) ZECHARIAH
JOB LAY TUT CHAR CRIB FIST SHOP TURN
BERTH CHORE FIRST PLACE BILLET
HOBJOB HUSTLE JOBSITE SWEATER
BUSINESS POSITION
(EASY —) BLUDGE
(FATHER OF —) ISSACHAR
(SMALL —) CHORE JOBBLE
JOBBER BRAGER DEALER FLUNKY
BROGGER COURSER
(— FOR POSITION) DICE
(DISC —) DEEJAY
JOCOSE JOCO LEPID JOCULAR
JOCULAR GAY AIRY GLAD JOKY DROLL
FUNNY HAPPY JOLLY MERRY WITTY
BLITHE ELATED JAPISH JOCOSE JOCUND
JOKISH JOVIAL JOYFUL JOYOUS LIVELY
BUOYANT COMICAL FESTIVE GLEEFUL
PLAYFUL WAGGISH ANIMATED
CHEERFUL DEBONAIR GLADSOME
HUMOROUS JOCATORY JOKESOME
LAUGHING MIRTHFUL BURLESQUE
JOCULARITY FUN WAGGERY
JOCUND BUDGE MERRY JOCANT
JOCULAR
JOG BOB HOD JAG JIG JOT MOG KICK
POKE SHOG SPUD STIR TROT WHIG
HOTCH MOSEY NUDGE TWEAK DIDDLE
JITTER JOGGLE JUNDIE
(— ALONG) FADGE FODGE
(— AWKWARDLY) DODGE
(— WITH ELBOW) DUNCH
JOGGER LAYBOY
JOGGLE HOTCH JUGGLE SHOGGLE
SHOOGLE
JOHN IAN JEAN JOCK JONE JUAN SEAN
JOHANN SEAGHAN GIOVANNI
(BROTHER OF —) JAMES
(FATHER OF —) ZEBEDEE ZACHARIAS

(MOTHER OF —) SALOME ELISABETH
JOHN BROWN'S BODY
(AUTHOR OF —) BENET
(CHARACTER IN —) CLAY JACK LUCY
LUKE DUPRE SALLY SOPHY SPADE VILAS
ELLYAT MELORA SHIPPY WINGATE
WEATHERBY BRECKINRIDGE
JOHNNYCAKE CORNCAKE
JOIN ADD COP FAY OUP PAN TAG TIE UNY
ALLY COPE FAIR FUSE GAIN GLUE KNIT
LINK MEET MELL SEAM SOUD TAIL TEAM
YOKE ANNEX BLEND ENTER JOINT
MERGE TENON UNITE WRING ACCEDE
ADJECT ADJOIN ASSIST ATTACH
CEMENT COCKET COMMIT CONCUR
INDENT JOGGLE MARROW MINGLE
PIECEN RELATE RELIDE SPLICE STRIKE
COMBINE CONJOIN CONNECT CONTACT
INJOINT JOINING SHACKLE ACCOUPLE
COMPOUND COPULATE DOVETAIL
JUNCTION ACCOMPANY
(— BATTLE) JOUST ENGAGE
(— BY SEWING) STITCH SUTURE
(— CLOSELY) FAY AFFY WELD GRAFT
(— IN COMBAT) BUCKLE
(— IN MARRIAGE) WED TACK HITCH
COUPLE
(— THE PARTS OF) PIECE
(— TOGETHER) CLOSE COAPT FRANK
HITCH COUPLE ENGLUE ENJOIN
ASSEMBLE COAGMENT COALESCE
(— UP) ACCEDE
(PREF.) ARTIO
JOINED JOINT ALLIED DIRECT SEAMED
ACCOLLE ADJUNCT APPINED EMBOITE
ADJUGATE COMBINED CONJUNCT
COPULATE INTEGRAL
JOINER SNUG WRIGHT JOINTER
JOINING BAR JOIN SEAM BRIDE CLOSE
SPLICE BETWEEN JOINDER ADDITION
JUNCTION JUNCTIVE JUNCTURE
SYNECTIC
JOINT BED HAR HIP BUTT FISH HEAD
HELL HOCK JOIN KNEE LITH LOCK SEAL
SEAM TUCK ANKLE BRAZE CARDO
ELBOW MITER MITRE PLACE SCAPE
SCARF SPALD UNION UNITE WRIST
COMMON HAUNCH MUTUAL SCARPH
SPLICE SUTURE TOGGLE UNITER
ARTHRON ARTICLE COGGING DIGITAL
FETLOCK ISCHIUM JOINING KNUCKLE
SCATTER SHIPLAP SIAMESE CONJOINT
CONJUNCT COUPLING DIACLASE
DOVETAIL FLASHING JOINTURE
JUNCTURE SUBJOINT SUFFRAGO
TROCHOID VARIATOR
(— ABOVE HOCK) STIFLE
(— OF BIRD'S WING) FLEXURE
(— OF FLAIL) CAPEL
(— OF MEAT) BARON SADDLE
(— OF SHIP) CHASE
(— OF STEM) NODE
(ANKLE —) COOT
(ELBOW —) NOOP
(FLEXIBLE —) HINGE
(GROOVED —) RABBET
(HIP —) COXA THURL

(MASONRY —) JOGGLE
(MINING —) CLEAT SLINE
(QUARRYING —) CUTTER
(SCARF —) BOXING
(UNIVERSAL —) CARDAN
(VERTICAL —) BUILD
(WHEEL-LIKE —) TROCHITE
JOINTED ARTHROUS
JOIST GEEST LEDGE BRIDGE RAGLIN
DORMANT SLEEPER CARRIAGE
JOKE DOR GAB GIG JOE KID ROT WIT
FOOL GAFF GAME GAUD GEGG JAPE
JEST JOSH LICE NOTE QUIP QUIZ TYPE
BREAK CRACK FLIRT GLEEK GRIND
LAUGH PRANK RALLY SPORT TRICK
BANTER JAPERY PLISKY WHEEZE
JOKELET WAGGERY CHESTNUT
(PRACTICAL —) BAR FUN GAG RIG
HOAX REAK SHAVIE HOTFOOT
(STALE —) CHESTNUT
(PL.) JAPERY
JOKER BUG DOR WAG CARD CLOWN
GRIND SLAVE FARCER FOOLER GAGGER
JOKIST FARCEUR GIMMICK FUNNYMAN
HUMORIST JOKESTER
JOKESTER WAG WIT
JOKING JOSH BANTER JOCOSE
(PRACTICAL —) GAME
JOLLIFICATION RAG RANT BEANO
JOLLY SINDIG
JOLLITY MIRTH GAIETY HILARITY
JOLLITRY
JOLLY GAY KID BOON BUXOM GAWSY
MERRY RORTY SONSY WALLY BLITHE
CROUSE JOVIAL STRING JOCULAR
RAUGHTY DISPOSED
JOLLY BOAT YAWL DANDY
JOLT JET JIG JOG JOT JUT BELT BUMP
DIRD DIRL HIKE JOWL JUMP KICK SHOG
JAUNT HOTTER IMPACT JOGGLE JOSTLE
JOUNCE JUMBLE
JOLTING JERKY BUMPITY HOTTERY
JONAH JINX JONAS HOODOO
(FATHER OF —) AMITTAI
JONATHAN (BROTHER OF —)
JOHANAN
(COMPANION OF —) DAVID
(FATHER OF —) SAUL ASAHEL JOIADA
KAREAH ABIATHAR
(SON OF —) MEPHIBOSHETH
JONQUIL JONK LILY DAFFODIL

JORDAN

CAPITAL: AMMAN
GULF: AQABA
MOUNTAIN: BUKKA DABAB ATAIBA
MUBRAK
REGION: PEREA BASHAN PERAEA
RIVER: JORDAN YARMUK
TOWN: AQABA ARIHA IRBID KARAK ZARQA
ZERKE NABLUS JERICHO

JOSEPH JOSEY GIUSEPPE
(FATHER OF —) HELI JACOB JUDAH
MATTATHIAS

(MOTHER OF —) RACHEL
(SON OF —) IGAL JESUS
(WIFE OF —) MARY ASENATH
JOSEPH ANDREWS (AUTHOR OF —) FIELDING
  (CHARACTER IN —) ADAMS BOOBY FANNY PETER JOSEPH PAMELA POUNCE THOMAS WILSON ANDREWS GOODWILL SLIPSLOP
JOSH ACE GUY KID RIB JOKE CHAFF STRING
JOSHUA JESUS
  (FATHER OF —) NUN JOZADAK
JOSIAH (FATHER OF —) AMON ZEPHANIAH
  (MOTHER OF —) JEDIDAH
JOSTLE JOG JOLT JOSS PUSH SHOG CROWD ELBOW HUNCH JUNDY SHOVE HURTLE HUSTLE JOGGLE JUNDIE JUSTLE SHOULDER
JOSTLING SCRAMBLE
JOT ACE DOT ATOM IOTA MARK MITE TARE WHIT GRAIN MINIM POINT TWINT WIGHT TITTLE SCRUPLE SYLLABLE
  (— DOWN) NICK
JOTTING TOT
JOUNCE HIKE JOLT JAUNT
JOURNAL TOE BOOK DIARY PAPER BLAZER SERIAL DAYBOOK DIURNAL GAZETTE GUDGEON JOURNEY CASHBOOK NOCTUARY TRUNNION
  (SEA —) LOGBOOK
JOURNAL BEARING RHODING
JOURNALISM NEWSWRITING
JOURNALIST SCRIBE WRITER BYLINER DIARIAN
JOURNEY BE GO JOG RUN WAY DIET EYRE FARE FORE GAIT GANG GATE HIKE JUMP RACE RAIK RIDE ROAD STEP TOUR TREK TRIP TURN WENT BROAD COVER DRIVE JAUNT REISE SITHE TRAIK TRAIL TURUS WEENT COMINO ERRAND FLIGHT HEGIRA JUNKET TRAVEL VAGARY EMBASSY ENTRADA EXCURSE JORNADA JOURNAL MEANDER PASSAGE STRETCH TRAVAIL TROUNCE WALKING WAYFARE GODSPEED PROGRESS PILGRIMAGE
  (— BY SEA) VOYAGE
  (— DOWNSTREAM) DESCEND
  (DAY'S —) DIET
  (DESERT —) JORNADA
  (FATIGUING —) TRAIK
  (LONG —) TREK
  (TEDIOUS —) TRANCE
  (PL.) PERIPATETICS
JOURNEYING CRUISE
JOURNEYMAN YEOMAN
JOUST PLAY TILT JOSTLE JUSTLE TOURNEY
JOUSTER TILTER
JOVIAL GAY BOON JOVY BULLY JOLLY MERRY GENIAL HEARTY MELLOW WANTON BACCHIC HOLIDAY JOCULAR CONVIVIAL RANTIPOLE
JOVIALITY JOLLITY ROLLICK HILARITY
JOWL CHOW CHAULE
  (PL.) CHOPS

JOY JO WIN GLEE LIST PLAY BLISS CHEER DREAM EXULT MIRTH REVEL GAIETY HEYDAY DELIGHT ECSTASY ELATION JOYANCE RAPTURE REVELRY FELICITY GLADNESS HILARITY PLEASURE
JOYFUL GAY GLAD BEAMY JOLLY BLITHE FESTUS JOCUND JOVIAL JOYANT JOYOUS GAUDFUL GLADFUL GLEEFUL JOCULAR GLADSOME
JOYFULLY FAIN FAINLY GLADLY JOYOUSLY
JOYLESS DESOLATE LUSTLESS UNBLITHE
JOYOUS GAY GLAD JOLLY MERRY YOUSE BLITHE JOVIAL FESTIVE GIOJOSO GLEEFUL JOCULAR SMILING FRABJOUS FROHLICH SUNSHINY
JOYOUSNESS HILARITY
JUBAL (FATHER OF —) LAMECH
  (MOTHER OF —) ADAH
JUBILANT ELATED JOYFUL EXULTANT
JUBILATION JOY JOYANCE JUBILEE
JUDAH (FATHER OF —) JACOB
  (MOTHER OF —) LEAH
JUDE THE OBSCURE (AUTHOR OF —) HARDY
  (CHARACTER IN —) SUE DONN JUDE FAWLEY RICHARD ARABELLA DRUSILLA BRIDEHEAD PHILLOTSON
JUDGE (ALSO SEE JURIST) DAN JUS SEE WIG CADI CAID CAZY DEEM DOOM HOLD IMAM JUEZ JURY KAZI QADI RATE RULE SCAN AWARD COUNT COURT DAYAN GAUGE HAKIM INFER JUDEX MINOS OPINE PUNEE TRIER WEIGH BREHON CENSOR CRITIC DANIEL DECERN DEEMER DICAST DOOMER INTEND JUDGER JURIST OPINER PUISNE SAMSON SAMUEL SETTLE SQUIRE ACCOUNT ADJUDGE ALCALDE ARBITER BENCHER BRIDOYE CENSURE DISCERN FLAGMAN FOUJDAR HELIAST JURYMAN JUSTICE MUNSIFF PODESTA REFEREE SCABINE SHAMGAR SUPPOSE APPRAISE CENTENAR CONCLUDE CONSIDER DEEMSTER DEMPSTER DIRECTOR DOOMSMAN DOOMSTER ESTIMATE FOREDEEM JEPHTHAH JUDGMENT JUDICATE LINESMAN MINISTER MITTIMUS ORDINARY QUAESTOR RECORDER REGICIDE SCABINUS STRADICO
  (— OF UNDERWORLD) AEACUS
  (PREF.) KRIT(O)
JUDGMENT ACT EYE BOOK DEEM DOME DOOM REDE VIEW ARRET AWARD FANCY JUISE SENSE SIGHT SKILL TASTE ADVICE ASSIZE DECREE ESTEEM JUWISE OUSTER STEVEN ACCOUNT CENSURE CONCEIT HOLDING OPINION THOUGHT VERDICT WITTING DECISION ESTIMATE JUDICIAL JUDICIUM SAGACITY SAPIENCE SENTENCE THINKING PREJUDICE OBSERVATION
  (PREF.) GNOMO
JUDICATORY SYNOD
JUDICIOUS SAGE WISE POLITIC

PRUDENT CRITICAL JUDICIAL MODERATE SENSEFUL SENSIBLE WISELIKE

JUDITH (FATHER OF —) BEERI
(HUSBAND OF —) ESAU

JUG CAN EWER JACK JUST ASCUS ASKOS BUIRE GAMLA GOTCH JORUM JUBBE STEAN BOGGLE CROUKE GOGLET GOMLAH HYDRIA CREAMER PITCHER CRUISKEN LECYTHOS LEKYTHOS OENOCHOE PROCHOOS
(— WITH SPOUT) BUIRE DOLLIN
(ALE —) TOBY
(BEER —) BOCK
(BULGING —) GOTCH
(LEATHER —) JACK BOMBARD
(ONE-HANDLED —) URCEUS
(SPOUTLESS —) OLPE

JUGGLE TRICK BAFFLE FUMBLE CONJURE SHUFFLE

JUGGLER HARLOT CONJURER JONGLEUR TREGETOUR

JUICE JUS SEW BREE BROO FOND OOZE SUCK ANIMA BLOND BLOOD GRAVY HUMOR LASER MOBBY PERRY CASIRI CREMOR JIPPER SUCCUS CAMBIUM AGUAMIEL HYPOCIST VERJUICE
(— OF COCONUT) MILK
(— OF TREE) SAP LYCIUM JELUTONG
(— OF UNRIPE FRUIT) OMPHACY
(APPLE —) CIDER
(CANE —) SLING
(CASSAVA —) CASSAREEP CASSARIPE
(CONCENTRATED —) SIRUP SYRUP
(DRIED —) ALOE KINO
(FERMENTED —) SURA GRAPE
(FRUIT —) ROB ROHOB
(GRAPE —) MUST SAPA STUM
(INSPISSATED —) HYPOCIST
(INTOXICATING —) SOMA
(LETTUCE —) THRIDACE
(MEAT —) BLOND
(POPPY —) CHICK MECONIUM
(TOBACCO —) AMBEER AMBIER
(PL.) ESSENCE HUMIDITY

JUICY FAT FRIM FRUM NAISH SAPPY FRUITY SUCCOSE WATERISH

JUJUBE BER ELB TSAO LOTUS LOTEBUSH LOTEWOOD ZIZYPHUS

JUKEBOX PICCOLO NICKELODEON

JULIUS CAESAR (AUTHOR OF —) SHAKESPEARE
(CHARACTER IN —) CATO CASCA CINNA CLITO PORTA VARRO BRUTUS CAESAR CICERO CIMBER DECIUS JULIUS LUCIUS MARCUS STRATO CASSIUS FLAVIUS LEPIDUS MESSALA PUBLIUS ANTONIUS CLAUDIUS LIGARIUS LUCILIUS MARULLUS METELLUS OCTAVIUS PINDARUS POPILIUS TITINIUS CALPURNIA DARDANIUS TREBONIUS VOLUMNIUS ARTEMIDORUS

JUMBLE PI PIE ROG HASH MESS MUSS RAFF BOTCH BOLLIX BUMBLE FUDDLE GARBLE HUDDLE JABBLE JUMPER JUNGLE MEDLEY MOMBLE MUDDLE PALTER RAFFLE WELTER WUZZLE CLUTTER CONFUSE EMBROIL GOULASH SHUFFLE DISORDER MISHMASH PASTICHE RHAPSODY SMACHRIE
(— OF SOUNDS) LURRY

JUMBLED CRAZY HASHY JUMBLY MEDLEY HUDDLING MACARONIC

JUMP HOP LEP NIP DART JETE LEAP LUTZ SKIP STEN STOT TUMB BOUND FENCE HALMA SALTO SAULT SPANG SPEND START STOIT VAULT DOUBLE FOOTER HURDLE INSULT LAUNCH SPRING SPRUNT STARRE WALLOP CISEAUX CROWHOP SALTATE SKYLARK BALLONNE
(— ABOUT) SKIT CAPER
(— FROM AIRCRAFT) BAIL BALE
(— IN FENCING) BALESTRA
(— ON HORSEBACK) LARK
(— ON SKATES) AXEL SALCHOW
(— TO CONCLUSION) SALTUS

JUMPER LAMMY SWAGE BARKER LEPPER HANDYMAN

JUMPING SALIENT SALTANT

JUMPING JACK PANTINE

JUMPY ITCHY NERVOUS

JUNCO SNOWBIRD

JUNCTION HIP FROG JOIN CLOSE CROWN RAPHE UNION FILLET INFALL CONTACT JOINING MEETING UNITION ABUTMENT JUNCTURE CONSERTION
(— OF EARTH AND SKY) HORIZON
(— OF STREAMS) GRAINS
(— OF THREADS) FELL STOP
(— ON TOOTH) CERVIX

JUNCTURE PASS PINCH CRISIS STRAIT ARTICLE BRACKET JOINING OPHRYON EXIGENCY JOINTAGE JOINTURE OCCASION QUANDARY

JUNE BUG BUZZARD DUMCLOCK

JUNGLE BUSH RUKH SHOLA BOONDOCK
(AUTHOR OF —) SINCLAIR
(CHARACTER IN —) ONA JACK DUANE JONAS CONNOR JURGIS MARIJA RUDKUS ANTANAS ELZBIETA STANISLOVAS

JUNGLE BOOK (AUTHOR OF —) KIPLING
(CHARACTER IN —) KAA KHAN AKELA BALOO HATHI SHERE BULDEO MESSUA MOWGLI TABAQUI BAGHEERA BANDARLOG

JUNIOR PUNY CADET YOUNG PUISNE YOUNGER

JUNIPER CADE EZEL GORSE GORST RETEM SAVIN SABINE

JUNK CRAM GEAR GOOK TOPE DRECK REFUSE SCULCH DISCARD PLUNDER TONGKANG
(WORTHLESS —) SLUM

JUNKET TRIP KNACK JINKET SAFARI

JUNKMAN TATTER SCRAPMAN SCAVENGER

JUNO MONETA PRONUBA

JUNO AND THE PAYCOCK
(AUTHOR OF —) OCASEY
(CHARACTER IN —) JACK JUNO MARY BOYLE JERRY JOXER DEVINE JOHNNY BENTHAM CHARLIE TANCRED

JUPITER JOVE STATOR FORTUNE
MUSHTARI TERMINUS
JURGEN (AUTHOR OF —) CABELL
(CHARACTER IN —) LISA HELEN
JURGEN MERLIN SEREDA ANAITIS
CHLORIS DESIREE DOLORES DOROTHY
KOSHCHEI GUENEVERE
JURISDICTION SOC BAIL SOKE FUERO
HONOR REALM VERGE ABBACY BANDON
BEYLIK DANGER DIWANI RIDING SPHERE
DEANERY DEWANEE DROSTDY EMIRATE
FOUDRIE KHANATE BAILIERY CHAPELRY
FOUJDARY LIGEANCE PASHALIC
PROVINCE
(— OF BISHOP) SEE
(COERCIVE —) SWORD
(MORMON —) KEYS
(SUFF.) DOM
JURISPRUDENCE LAW BYRLAW
REPORTS
JURIST JUDGE MUFTI BREHON LAWYER
DOTTORE
JUROR JURAT ASSIZER JURYMAN
CENTUMVIR
JURY ARRAY PANEL QUEST ASSIZE
JURATA COUNTRY EMPANEL INQUEST
(— COUNTY) VISNE
JURYMAN DICAST JURIST ASSIZER
JURY-RIGGED HAYWIRE
JUST ALL DUE EVEN FAIR FLOP LEAL
ONLY TRUE EQUAL FIRST LEVEL NOBUT
ROUND VALID ZADOC CANDID GIUSTO
HONEST JUSTIN JUSTUS MERELY
SQUARE EQUABLE LEESOME UPRIGHT

ACCURATE LIEFSOME RATIONAL
RIGHTFUL SKILLFUL UNBIASED
(— AS) AFTER
(— HOVE CLEAR) ATRIP
(— IN TIME) SONICA
(ONLY —) HARDLY SCARCELY
JUSTICE LAW DOOM RIGHT SKILL
DHARMA EQUITY REASON HONESTY
SHALLOW SILENCE DEEMSTER
JUDGMENT JUSTITIA JUSTNESS
RECORDER
(— OF PEACE) BEAK SQUIRE
JUSTIFIABLY FAIRLY
JUSTIFICATION CALL COLOR EXCUSE
APOLOGY DEFENCE WARRANT APOLOGIA
JUSTIFIED FAIR JUST
JUSTIFY AVOW CLEAR PROVE SALVE
DEFEND EXCUSE HONEST EXPLAIN
RECTIFY SUPPORT WARRANT DARRAIGN
MAINTAIN SANCTION UNDERPIN
VINDICATE
JUSTLY WELL TRULY EVENLY FAIRLY
EQUALLY HANDILY SQUARELY
JUSTNESS SQUARE FITNESS JUSTICE
ACCURACY
JUT HANG BULGE JETTY JUTTY BEETLE
EXTEND IMPEND EXTRUDE
JUTE PAT DESI PAUT DAISEE ARAMINA
CHINGMA
JUTTING HANGING
JUVENILE TEEN YOUNG JEJUNE PUERILE
YOUTHFUL
JUXTAPOSITION CONTACT CONTRAST
NEARNESS

K

K KAY KING

KAFFIR KATI XOSA FINGO TEMBU CAFFRE
 INFIDEL TAMBUKI WAIGULI
 (— BOY) UMFAAN

KALE COLE KAIL COLLARD SPROUTS
 BORECOLE

KALEVALA (AUTHOR OF —) UNKNOWN
 (CHARACTER IN —) KULLERVO
 ILMARINEN VAINAMOINEN
 LEMMINKAINEN

KALI (HUSBAND OF —) SIVA SHIVA

KAMA (DAUGHTER OF —) TRISHA
 (FATHER OF —) DHARMA
 (MOTHER OF —) LAKSHMI SHRADDHA
 (SON OF —) ANIRUDDHA
 (WIFE OF —) RATI PRITI

KANGAROO ROO EURO BILBI FLIER
 FLYER TUNGO BOOMER FOSTER WOILIE
 DIDELPH POTOROO WALLABY BETTONGA
 BOONGARY FILANDER FORESTER
 WALLAROO
 (FEMALE —) DOE GIN
 (YOUNG —) JOEY

KANGAROO RAT JERBOA BETTONG
 POTOROO

KANSA (FATHER OF —) UGRASENA
 (SLAYER OF —) KRISHNA

KANSAN JAYHAWK

KANSAS

CAPITAL: TOPEKA
COLLEGE: BAKER TABOR BETHANY
 STERLING WASHBURN
COUNTY: ELK GOVE LINN LYON NESS
 RENO GEARY PRATT ROOKS TREGO
 BARTON COFFEY NEMAHA NEOSHO
 BOURBON LABETTE ATCHISON
LAKE: CHENEY KIRWIN NEOSHO MILFORD
MOUNTAIN: SUNFLOWER
NICKNAME: JAYHAWKER SUNFLOWER
RIVER: SALINE SOLOMON ARKANSAS
 MISSOURI
STATE BIRD: MEADOWLARK
STATE FLOWER: SUNFLOWER
STATE TREE: COTTONWOOD
TOWN: ALMA GOVE HAYS IOLA COLBY
 DODGE HOXIE LAKIN LEOTI SEDAN
 LARNED SALINA ABILENE CHANUTE
 LIBERAL ULYSSES WICHITA

KAPOK CEIBO FLOSS
KARMA FATE
 (BAD —) DEMERIT
KATHERINE (HUSBAND OF —)
 PETRUCHIO
KAW AKHA

KAZOO BAZOO GAZOO ZARAH HEWGAG
 MIRLITON

KEEL FIN BACK SEEL BARGE CARINA
 CRISTA RADDLE SERRULA
 (— OF BIRD'S MANDIBLE) GONYS

KEEN DRY FLY FLY GAY SHY YAP ACID DEAR
 FINE GAIR GLEG HIGH HOWL NUTS PERT
 TART TEEN WAIL WARM WILD ACUTE
 BREME BRIEF BRISK EAGER QUICK
 SHARP SMART SNELL SPICY VIVID
 ARGUTE ASTUTE BITTER CAOINE GREEDY
 LIVELY SEVERE SHREWD SHRILL
 CUNNING HAWKING MORDANT PARLISH
 PARLOUS PUNGENT SERIOUS THIRSTY
 OBSERVANT SAGACIOUS TRENCHANT
 PERSPICACIOUS
 (PREF.) OXY

KEENER HOWLER

KEENLY KEEN FELLY DEARLY ACUTELY

KEENNESS EDGE ACUITY ACUMEN
 PUNGENCY
 (— OF SIGHT) ACIES

KEEN-SCENTED NASUTE NOSEWISE

KEEN-SIGHTED EAGLE

KEEP HUG HAVE HOLD SALT SAVE WAIT
 WITE BLESS ROCCA WITIE COFFER
 DETAIN REDUIT CONFINE CONTAIN
 DEFORCE HUSBAND KEEPING OBSERVE
 RESERVE CONSERVE MAINTAIN
 PRESERVE RESTRAIN WITHHOLD
 (— A COURSE) CAPE
 (— A SMALL SHOP) CRAME
 (— A WOUND OPEN) TENT
 (— ABREAST) FOLLOW
 (— AFLOAT) BUOY
 (— AN EYE ON) STAG
 (— APART) DOTTLE ISOLATE SEPARATE
 (— AT A DISTANCE) ESTRANGE
 (— AWAY) ABSENT
 (— AWAY FROM) ABHOR AVOID
 (— BACK) DAM HAP ROB STAY ARREAR
 DETAIN RETARD RESERVE
 (— COMPANY WITH) GANG MOOP
 CONSORT
 (— FREE) ESCHEW
 (— FROM BOILING OVER) KEEL
 (— FROM BURNING) REDD
 (— HIDDEN) HOARD SECRETE
 (— IN) CAGE
 (— IN CIRCULATION) WIND
 (— IN EXCITEMENT) ALARM ALARUM
 (— IN MIND) RETAIN
 (— IN ORDER) TARGE
 (— IN STOCK) CARRY
 (— IN THE TRACK) GATHER
 (— OFF) FEND WEAR EXPEL SHIELD
 (— OUT) BAR EXPEL
 (— POSSESSION) HARBOR

(— SCORELESS) BLANK
(— SECRET) HUSH WHIST
(— STRAIGHT) DIRECT
(— TABS ON) FINGER
(— TIME) GO
(— TO ONESELF) BOSOM
(— UNTIL YEAR OLD) HOG
(— UP) SUBSIST SUSTAIN CONTINUE
(— WAITING) DELAY
(— WARM) STIVE STOVE FOSTER
(— WATCH) BARK TOUT WAIT BEWAKE
KEEPER NAB KEEP SCREW TUTOR YEMER
CUSTOS LIFTER LOOKER PARKER PASTOR
RAHDAR RANGER BAILIFF CURATOR
GEARMAN PIKEMAN BEARWARD
DEERHERD DOLLYMAN ELDERMAN
GUARDANT GUARDIAN HOUNDMAN
TRAITEUR WARRENER
(— OF CATTLE) HAYWARD
(— OF DOGS) FEWTERER
(— OF ELEPHANT) MAHOUT
(— OF PRISON) GAOLER JAILER
WARDEN ALCAIDE PROVOST
(DOOR —) DURWAN
KEEPING CARE WARD TRUST CHARGE
CUSTODY DETAINER
KEEPSAKE DRURY TOKEN GIFTBOOK
SOUVENIR
KEG CAG PIN TUB CADE CASK KNAG
WOOD ANKER BARRICO COSTREL
KELP KILP LEAG VAREC WRACK GIRDLE
SEAWEED BELLWARE
KELPIE NIX BARB
KENILWORTH (AUTHOR OF —) SCOTT
(CHARACTER IN —) AMY HUGH TONY
GILES JANET SMITH ALASCO DICKIE
DUDLEY EDMUND FOSTER SLUDGE
SUSSEX VARNEY WALTER GOSLING
MICHAEL RALEIGH RICHARD ROBSART
WAYLAND DOBOOBIE ELIZABETH
LAMBOURNE LEICESTER TRESSILIAN
FLIBBERTIGIBBET
KENNEL STALL VENERY VENISON
DOGHOUSE

KENTUCKY

CAPITAL: FRANKFORT
COLLEGE: BEREA ASBURY CENTRE
BRESCIA URSULINE
COUNTY: BATH BELL BOYD HART TODD
ADAIR BOYLE TRIGG WOLFE ESTILL
MENIFEE MAGOFFIN
LAKE: CUMBERLAND
RIVER: DIX OHIO SALT BARREN
STATE BIRD: CARDINAL
STATE FLOWER: GOLDENROD
STATE NICKNAME: BLUEGRASS
STATE TREE: TULIP
TOWN: INEZ BEREA CADIZ DIXON HYDEN
MCKEE PARIS CORBIN HARLAN HAZARD
GLASGOW GREENUP PADUCAH DANVILLE
COVINGTON LEXINGTON OWENSBORO

KENYA

BAY: FORMOSA
CAPITAL: NAIROBI
LAKE: MAGADI RUDOLF NAIVASHA
VICTORIA
MEASURE: WARI
MOUNTAIN: ELGON KENYA KULAL NYIRU
MATIAN LOGONOT
PEOPLE: LUO MERU BANTU KAMBA KISII
LUHYA MASAI NANDI KIKUYU OGADEN
BALUHYA HAMITIC HILOTIC TURKANA
KIPSIGIS
RIVER: LAK ATHI TANA KEIRO TURKWELL
TOWN: MERU KITUI NAROK KIPINI KISUMU
MOYALE NAKURU NAYUKI ELDORET
MALINDI MOMBASA

KERCHIEF CURCH ROMAL RUMAL
ANALAV CYPRUS MADRAS NAPKIN
PEPLUM CYPRESS KERCHER PANUELO
THERESE BABUSHKA BANDANNA
HEADRAIL KAFFIYEH KINGSMAN
KERF CARF SKAFF GROOVE UNDERCUT
KERNEL NUT BUNT CORE KERN MEAT
PITH BERRY GOODY GROAT ACINUS
ALMOND CARNEL PICKLE NUCLEUS
PICHURIM
(CORN —S) HOMINY
(UNHUSKED —S) CAPES
(PL.) NIXTAMAL
(PREF.) CARY(O) KARY(O)
KEROSINE PARAFFIN
KESTREL FANNER KEELIE STANIEL
STANNEL STANCHEL WINDHOVER
KETCH SAIC
KETONE IRONE ACETOL ARMONE CARONE
CARVOL COTOIN HEXONE IONONE
QUINOL ACETOIN ACETONE ACYLOIN
BENZOIN CAMPHOR CARVONE DYPNONE
FLAVONE JASMONE MUSCONE PHORONE
SHOGAOL THUJONE ACRIDONE
ANTHRONE BAECKEOL BUTANONE
BUTYRONE CHALCONE CHALKONE
CHROMONE DEGUELIN EXALIONE
FENCHONE MENTHONE PROPIONE
PULEGONE ROTENONE STEARONE
TAGETONE THIENONE VALERONE
XANTHONE
KETTLE LEAD STEW DIXIE BOILER
CANNER FESSEL MARMIT MASLIN
TRIPOD VESSEL CALDRON SKILLET
STEWPOT CALABASH FLAMBEAU
KETTLEDRUM NAKER ATABAL KETTLE
TIMBAL
KEYBOARD CLAVIER PEDALIER
KEYHOLE KEY LOCKHOLE
KEYSTONE KEY QUOIN VERTEX SAGITTA
VOUSSOIR
KICK BOOT FICK FLEG FLIG FOOT FUNK
HEEL HOOF LASH PORR POTE PUNT SHIN
TURF YERK ANGLE BUNCH KEVEL PAUSE
PUNCH SKELP SPANG CHARGE FITTER
KICKER KICKUP OBJECT SPIRAL VOLLEY

DROPOUT FOUETTE KICKOFF DROPKICK
PLACEKICK
(— ABOUT) SPARTLE
(— AS A HORSE) FLING WINCE
(— HEELS UP) SPURN
(— ON SHINS) HACK SHINNER
(BALLET —) BRUSH
(SOCCER —) CORNER
(SWIMMING —) THRASH

KID COD FUN POD TUB FAWN FOOL JIVE
JOKE CHILD FAGOT HORSE JOLLY KIDDY
SPOOF KIDLET SQUIRT DECEIVE EANLING
FATLING TICCHEN YOUNGER CHEVEREL
YEANLING

KIDDING JOKE SPOOFERY

KIDNAP STEAL ABDUCT PANYAR SPIRIT

KIDNAPER PLAGIARY SNATCHER
SPIRITER

KIDNAPING SNATCH PLAGIUM PLAGIARY

KIDNAPPED (AUTHOR OF —)
STEVENSON
(CHARACTER IN —) ALAN BRECK
COLIN DAVID RIACH SHUAN BALFOUR
RANSOME CAMPBELL EBENEZER
HOSEASON RANKEILLOR

KIDNEY NEER REIN TYPE NEPHRON
(PL.) REINS ROGNONS

KIDNEY BEAN FRIJOLE
(PL.) FASELS

KILL DO BAG END GET MOW OFF OUT PIP
ZAP BANE BOLO COOK COOL DOWN FELL
MORT NECK SLAY TAME WING BLAST
BRAIN CROAK CULLE FETCH FORDO
GANCH MISDO NAPOO QUELL SABER
SCRAG SHOOT SMITE SNUFF SPEED
SPEND SPILL SPOIL STALL STICK SWELT
SWORD WASTE CORPSE DEADEN DIDDLE
FAMISH FINISH HANDLE IMPALE MARTYR
MURDER POISON STARVE UNLIVE
ACHIEVE BUTCHER DESTROY EXECUTE
FLATTEN HATCHET KILLING MORTIFY
SMOTHER STONKER SUICIDE DEATHIFY
DISPATCH DISSOLVE IMMOLATE
JUGULATE STILETTO
(— ANIMALS) CONTROL
(— BY STONING) LAPIDATE
(— BY SUBMERSION) STIFLE
(— CALF AFTER BIRTH) DEACON
(— CATTLE) PITH
(— EVERY TENTH) DECIMATE
(— GAME) SATCHEL
(— OFF) ENECATE
(— SMALL GAME) BARK
(— TIME) GOOF
(— WITH GRENADE) FRAG

KILLED KILT WINGED SKITTLED
(FRESHLY —) GREEN

KILLER GUN BRAVO GUNMAN SLAYER
TORPEDO MURDERER THRESHER

KILLER WHALE ORCA DOLPHIN
GRAMPUS

KILLING FELL KILL MORT QUELL TUANT
MURDER CLEANUP HANGING CLEANING
DISPATCH FELICIDE HOMICIDE
MANSLAUGHTER
(MERCY —) EUTHANASIA

KILLJOY NARK GLOOM LEMON
SOURPUSS

KILN BING KEEL LEHR OAST CULLE DRIER
GLAZE STOVE TILER COCKLE CUPOLA
TILERY FURNACE CALCINER LIMEKILN

KIM (AUTHOR OF —) KIPLING
(CHARACTER IN —) ALI KIM OHARA
ARTHUR HURREE LURGAN MAHBUB
BENNETT KIMBALL CREIGHTON
MOOKERJEE

KIN SIB KATI KITH CATTY CUNNE FLESH
FAMILY AFFINITY RELATION

KIND ILK KIN LOT BOON CAST FAIR FORM
GOOD HAIR HEND LIKE MAKE MEEK MILD
MODE MOLD NICE RATE SELY SOFT SORT
SUIT TRIM TYPE WING BREED BROOD
CLASS GENRE GENUS GESTE ORDER
SPICE STAMP BENIGN BLITHE FACILE
GENDER GENTLE GOODLY HUMANE
KIDNEY KINDLY MANNER MISTER
NATURE SPEECE STRAIN STRIPE TENDER
CLEMENT EDITION FASHION FEATHER
FLESHLY LENIENT QUALITY REGIMEN
SPECIAL SPECIES SPECKLE FRIENDLY
GENEROUS MANSUETE OBLIGING
BENIGNANT INDULGENT OFFICIOUS
PERSUASION
(— OF) A
(— OF PEOPLE) FOLK
(DIFFERENT IN —) DIVERS
(DISTINCTIVE —) BRAND
(OF EVERY —) ALKIN

KINDLE BEET BLOW FIRE LUNT MOVE
TAKE TEND TIND FLAME LIGHT QUICK
SPUNK ACCEND ALIGHT DECOCT ENFIRE
EXCITE IGNITE ILLUME EMBLAZE ESPRISE
INCENSE INFLAME SOLICIT KINDLING

KINDLINESS CANDOR

KINDLING FIRE BAVIN FAGOT TINDER
IGNITION

KINDLY FAIR GAIN KIND NESH AGREE
COUTH HENDE NAISH BENIGN BLITHE
COUTHY GENIAL HOMELY AMIABLE
BENEFIC INNERLY FAVOROUS GENEROUS
GRACIOUS QUEMEFUL TOWARDLY

KINDNESS LOVE ALOHA FAVOR BOUNTY
CANDOR LENITY BENEFIT SERVICE
CLEMENCY EASINESS GOODNESS
HUMANITY LENITUDE MILDNESS

KINDRED KIN SIB KIND KITH BLOOD
FLESH HOUSE FAMILY KOBONG NATION
STRIND COGNATE KINFOLK KINSMEN
RELATED SIBSHIP AFFINITY COGNATION
CONGENIAL CONGENEROUS

KING SO BAN DAM LOT LUD PUL REX REY
ROY AGAG AMON ATLI BALI BELI BIJA
BORS BRAN BRES CRAL CZAR JEHU KRAL
LEIR MARK NUDD NUMA OMRI OTTO
PHUL RAJA RIAL TSAR TZAR WANG YIMA
BALOR BELUS CONOR CREON DAGDA
DAHAK EGLON ETZEL GYGES HIRAM
HOGNI HOSEA IPHIS IXION JOASH LAIUS
LLUDD LYCUS MESHA MIDAS MINOS
NADAB NEGUS NORSE NUADA PEKAH
PRIAM RAJAH SAMMY SWAMI ZIMRI
ZOHAK AEOLUS AGENOR AILILL ALBOIN
ALONSO ALOROS ARIOCH BLADUD

CODRUS DIOMED DUNCAN ELATHA
FINGAL FRODHI FROTHI GOEMOT INKOSI
KABAKA LEMUEL MEMNON MINYAS
NESTOR NODONS OENEUS OGYGES
PELEUS PELIAS SAUGHT SHESHA
SVAMIN TEUCER URIENS UZZIAH VASUKI
ADMETUS AHAZIAH AMAIMON AMYCLAS
ANGEVIN ARDRIGU ARTEGAL ATHAMAS
BAGINDA BELINUS BUSIRIS CACIQUE
CEPHEUS CROESUS ELIDURE EPAPHUS
EPOPEUS ETHBAAL EURYTUS GUNTHER
HYGELAC INACHUS JAMSHID JEHOASH
JEHORAM KINGLET LAERTES LATINUS
LEONTES MENAHEM MONARCH PANDION
PHINEUS POLYBUS REGULUS ROMULUS
ROYALET SMERDIS SOLOMON VOLSUNG
ACRISIUS ADRASTUS AEGYPTUS
AMRAPHEL ASNAPPER BAHMANID
BRENNIUS CLAUDIUS COPHETUA
ELDORADO ETEOCLES GILGAMES
GOEMAGOT GOGMAGOG GORBODUC
HEZEKIAH HROTHGAR JEHOAHAZ
JEROBOAM KINGLING LAOMEDON
LISUARTE MANASSEH MELIADUS
MENELAUS ODYSSEUS ORCHAMUS
OSNAPPAR OVERKING PADISHAH
PEKAHIAH PENTHEUS RAMESSID
REHOBOAM RODERICK RODOMONT
ROITELET SARPEDON SHEPHERD
SISYPHUS TANTALUS
  (— AND QUEEN OF TRUMPS) BELLA
  (— CHANGED TO WOLF) LYCAON
  (— OF ARMS) GARTER NORROY
  (— OF BEASTS) LION
  (— OF DWARFS) ALBERICH
  (— OF FAIRIES) OBERON
  (— OF TRUMPS) HONOR
  (IRISH —) RI RIG ARDRI ARDRIGH
  (POLYNESIAN —) ALII ARII ARIKI
  (PREF.) REGI
KINGDOM WEI REALM REIGN WORLD
  ESTATE MONERA MORVEN REGION
  SAXONY MITANNI
KINGFISHER HALCYON PODITTI
  TOROTORO
KING JOHN (AUTHOR OF —)
  SHAKESPEARE
  (CHARACTER IN —) JOHN BIGOT
  ESSEX HENRY JAMES LEWIS MELUN
  PETER ARTHUR BLANCH ELINOR GURNEY
  HUBERT PHILIP ROBERT DEBURGH
  LYMOGES BRETAGNE PANDULPH
  PEMBROKE CHATILLON CONSTANCE
  SALISBURY FAULCONBRIDGE
KING LEAR (AUTHOR OF —)
  SHAKESPEARE
  (CHARACTER IN —) KENT LEAR CURAN
  EDGAR REGAN ALBANY EDMUND
  OSWALD GONERIL BURGUNDY CORDELIA
  CORNWALL GLOUCESTER
KINGLY REGAL ROYAL REGNAL BASILIC
  IMPERIAL MAJESTIC PRINCELY
KINGSHIP STOOL THRONE KINGDOM
  ROYALTY DEVARAJA KINGHOOD
KING SOLOMON'S MINES
  (AUTHOR OF —) HAGGARD
  (CHARACTER IN —) GOOD JOHN JOSE

ALLAN HENRY KHIVA TWALA CURTIS
GAGOOL GEORGE IGNOSI UMBOPA
FOULATA SCRAGGA INFADOOS
SILVESTRE VENTVOGEL QUATERMAIN
KING'S ROW (AUTHOR OF —)
  BELLAMANN
  (CHARACTER IN —) DRAKE ELISE
  JAMIE NOLAN RANDY RENEE TOWER
  CASSIE GORDON LOUISE MCHUGH
  PARRIS SANDOR PERDOFF MONAGHAN
  CASSANDRA WAKEFIELD
KING'S SCHOLAR TUG
KINKY NAPPY ENCOMIC KINKLED
KINSHIP SIB BLOOD NASAB STOOL
  ENATION KINDRED SIBNESS SIBSHIP
  AFFINITY AGNATION RELATION
  PROPINQUITY
KINSMAN KIN SIB ALLY BLOOD AFFINE
  AGNATE COUSIN FRIEND BROTHER
  GOTRAJA KINDRED WINEMAY
  BANDHAVA RELATION RELATIVE
  COLLATERAL
KINSWOMAN SISTER KINDRED
  RELATIVE
KISH (FATHER OF —) JEHIEL
  (SON OF —) SAUL
KISS BA LIP NEB BASS BUSS PECK PREE
  MOUTH POGUE SLAKE SMACK BEKISS
  CARESS SALUTE SLAVER SMOOCH
  SMOUCH OSCULATE
  (— OF PEACE) PAX
  (— WETLY) SLOBBER
  (STOLEN —) SMOORICH
KIT CHIT DUFFEL KITTEN OUTFIT
  POCHETTE
  (LUMBERMAN'S —) TURKEY
  (MESS —) CANTEEN
KITCHEN BUT GALLEY CABOOSE CUISINE
  KITCHIE COOKROOM
KITE LAP CHIL CYTE HAWK GLEDE CHILLA
  DRACHE DRAGON ELANET FALCON
  PREYER SENTRY MILVINE PUDDOCK
  PUTTOCK FORKTAIL HELLKITE
KITTEN KIT KITTY KITTLE CATLING
  KITLING
KITTIWAKE GULL WAEG ANNET KITTY
  PICKUP HACKLET TARROCK TIRRLIE
KNACK ART FEAT FEEL GATE GIFT HANG
  CATCH QUIRK SKILL TRICK SLEIGHT
  WRINKLE INSTINCT
KNAPSACK WALLET MOCHILA MUSETTE
  SNAPBAG SNAPSACK
KNAVE BOY ELF LAD NOB PAM PUR TOM
  JACK BOWER CHEAT DROLE MAKER
  NODDY ROGUE TIGER COQUIN FRIPON
  HARLOT KNIGHT PICARO RASCAL VARLET
  WENZEL CAMOOCH CUSTREL PEASANT
  VILLAIN BEZONIAN COISTREL SWINDLER
  VARLETTO
KNAVERY ROPERY CATZERIE PATCHERY
  RASCALITY
KNAVISH ROGUISH SCAMPISH
KNEAD ELT TEW MOLD POST BRAKE
  PETRIE MASSAGE
  (— HIDES) STOCK
KNEE GENU HOCK CROOK KNAPPER
  SLEEPER SUFFRAGO

KNEE
(— HOLLOW) HAM
(— OF COMPOSING STICK) SLIDE
KNEECAP CAP ROTULA PATELLA
KNEEL SIT KNEE COUCH SHIKO KOWTOW
KNELL BELL RING TOLL KNOLL STROKE
KNICKKNACK TOY KNACK TRICK
GEWGAW NOTION PRETTY BIBELOT
GIMCRACK
KNIFE DIE SAX BOLO BUCK MOON SAEX
SHIM SHIV SPUD TANG BOWIE BURIN
CHIVE CUTTO FACON GULLY KNIVE
KUKRI PANGA SHANK SHAVE SKEAN
SLICE BARLOW BARONG CAMPIT CARVER
COLTER COUTEL CUTTLE CUTTOE
DAGGER JIGGER PANADE PARANG
PAVADE PORKER PULLER RIMMER SICKLE
SLICER TREVET TRIVAT WORKER
BREAKER CHOPPER COUTEAU FIPENNY
KIOTOME MACHETE PALETTE SEVERER
SKINNER SLASHER SNICKER STICKER
SUNDANG TICKLER WHITTLE BELDUQUE
BILLHOOK CALABOZO JOCTELEG
SERPETTE THWITTLE YATAGHAN
SNICKERSNEE
(— FOR BREAKING FLAX) BEATER
(— FOR LEATHER) PIN
(— FOR RUBBER DOUGH) DOCTOR
(BLACKSMITH'S —) BUTTERIS
(BURMESE —) DAH
(CURRIER'S —) CLEANER
(ENGRAVER'S —) CRADLE
(ESKIMO —) ULU
(MORO —) BARONG
(PART OF —) NEB TIP WEB BACK EDGE
HEEL HILT BLADE CHOIL GUARD POINT
RIVET FULLER HANDLE POMMEL
BOLSTER QUILLON ROCASSO
(SHOEMAKER'S —) BUTT
(SURGICAL —) CATLING SCALPEL
BISTOURY EXSECTOR
(TANNER'S —) GRAINER
KNIGHT ELF SIR ADUB GANO TULK
EQUES LANCE RIDER THANE TOLKE
CABALL ERRANT KEMPER PENCEL RITTER
ROGERO GENILON PALADIN YOUNKER
ALMANZOR BACHELOR BANNERET
CAVALIER COLVILLE GANELONE
IRONCLAD ISENBRAS PALMERIN
RUGGIERO
(— IN CHESS) HORSE
(— OF ROUND TABLE) GAN BORS
OWEN GARETH GAWAIN MODRED
CARADOC CRADOCK GALAHAD GANELON
EGLAMORE LANCELOT PALMERIN
PERCIVAL TRISTRAM
(CARPET —) DAMMARET
KNIT SET BIND KNOT PLAIT PURSE UNITE
WEAVE COMPACT CONNECT WRINKLE
CONTRACT
(— STOCKINGS) SHANK
KNOB BOB BUR NOB NUB BEAD BOLL
BOSS BURR CLUB DENT HEAD HEEL
KNOP KNOT KNUB LIFT NODE NOOP PULL
SNUG STUD TORE BULLA BUNCH FORTE
GEMMA KNURL NATCH ONION PLOOK
PLUKE BUTTON EMBOSS NOBBLE
NUBBLE PIMPLE PISTON FERRULE

HORNTIP KNOBBLE BELLPULL
DOORKNOB DRAWSTOP OMPHALOS
(— OF HAIR) TOORIE
(— OF ROCK) BUHR BURR KNUCKLE
(— ON BILL OF SWAN) BERRY
(— ON BUTT OF CANNON) GRAPE
(— ON CHAIR) POMMEL
(— ON DEER'S ANTLER) OFFER
CROCHE
(— ON ROPE) MOUSE
KNOBBED NODOSE TOROSE BULLATE
TUBEROUS TYLOTATE
KNOBBY GOUTY KNOTTY TOROSE
WHELKY GOUTISH KNOBBLY SCRAGGED
KNOCK CON DAD HIT JOW JUT POP PUN
RAP WAP BANG BASH BEAT BUMP CALL
CHAP CHOP DASH DAUD DING DUNT
HACK JOLT JOWL KNAP NOCK NOIT PINK
PLUG POLT POSS PUSH ROUT SLAM
SLAY SNOP TANK TIRL WHAP WHOP
CLOUR CLUMP KNOIT POUND SNOCK
STAVE STRAM THUMP BOUNCE DUNTLE
KNATCH KNETCH STOTER CANVASS
PINKING
(— ABOUT) RUMBLE
(— DOWN) MOW DROP DUMP FELL
FLOOR GRASS LEVEL SMITE SOUSE
HURTLE RAFFLE UNPILE
(— OFF) SECURE
(— ON HEAD) MAZER MAZARD
(— OUT) OUT SAP CONK COOL KAYO
FLATTEN STIFFEN
(— UNCONSCIOUS) COLDCOCK
(— WITH THE HORNS) DISH
(IGNITION —) PING
KNOCKER CROW RISP WHACKER
(DOOR —) CROW HAMMER RAPPER
KNOLL NOB HIGH KNAP KNOB KNOW
TOFT HEAVE HURST HYRST MOUND
SHOAL COPPLE BOUROCK HUMMOCK
KNOT NIB NOB NUB TIE BEND CHOU
CLOD CLOT HARL KILL KNOB NODE NOIL
NURL TRUE WALL BUNCH CROWN
DUNNE GNARR HALCH HALSH HATCH
HITCH MOUSE NODUS NOEUD SNARL
SWIRL TWIST WARRE BOUGHT BUTTON
CLINCH CROCHE FINIAL GRANNY
MASCLE SORTIE TANGLE BOWKNOT
BOWLINE COCKADE GORDIAN MAYBIRD
CICISBEO DRAWKNOT GRAYBACK
KNITTING SLIPKNOT TRUELOVE
SHEEPSHANK
(— IN CLOTH) FAG NEP BURL
(— IN COTTON FIBERS) NEP
(— IN SIGNAL FLAG) WAFT WEFT
(— IN WOOD) PIN BURL BURR KNAG
KNAR SNUB GNARL KNAUR KNURL
(— IN YARN) SLUG SNICK
(— OF HAIR) BOB BUN COB PUG CLUB
KNURL CHIGNON
(— OF RIBBONS) FAVOR
(EMBROIDERY —) PICOT
(LOVE —) AMORET
(ORNAMENTAL —) BOW
(SHOULDER —) WING
(WALL —) WALE
KNOTTED KNIT NOUE TIED NOWED

NODOSE SWIRLY CRABBED NODATED SCRAGGY

KNOTTY HARD CRAMP GOUTY NODAL COMMON CRAGGY GNARLY KNAGGY KNOBBY KNURRY NODOSE NODOUS COMPLEX GNARLED GOUTISH JOINTED KNARRED KNOTTED SCABROUS

KNOW CAN CON KEN WIS WIT WOT CITE HAVE SABE WEET WIST WOTH SAVVY SKILL COGNIZE

KNOW-HOW SAVVY SKILL

KNOWING FLY HEP HIP SLY FOXY GASH SPRY WISE AWARE CANNY DOWNY JERRY LEERY SPACK WITTY EXPERT SCIENT SCIOUS SHREWD WITFUL WITTER GNOSTIC SAPIENT
(— SUPERFICIALLY) SCIOLOUS

KNOWLEDGE CAN WIT BOOK KITH KNOW LAIR LEAR LORE NOTE INWIT JNANA SKILL VIDYA ADVICE AVIDYA CLERGY NOESIS NOTICE WISDOM CUNNING DIANOIA HEARING KNOWING MEANING SCIENCE WITTING DAYLIGHT DOCTRINE EPISTEME LEARNING LETTRURE NOTITION PRUDENCE SAPIENCE SCIENTIA COGNIZANCE
(— OF SPIRITUAL TRUTH) GNOSIS
(FAMILIAR —) HANG
(LATER —) AFTERWIT
(MYSTERIOUS —) ARCANUM
(PIECEMEAL —) SMATTER
(PRIVATE —) PRIVITY
(PUBLIC —) LIGHT
(SLICK —) ANGLE
(SLIGHT —) INKLING SMATTER

(SUPERFICIAL —) SCIOLISM
(SUPERIOR —) MASTERY
(SUPREME —) PRAJNA
(SYSTEMATIZED —) SCIENCE
(UNIVERSAL —) PANSOPHY

KNOWLEDGEABLE KNOWING SKILLED STUDIED

KOBOLD NIS GNOME NISSE HODEKEN HUTCHEN

KORAN KITAB QURAN ALCORAN
(SECTION OF —) SURA SURAH

KOWTOW KNEEL SHIKO

KRAAL CRAW MANYATTA ZIMBABWE

KREUTZER SONATA (AUTHOR OF —) TOLSTOY
(CHARACTER IN —) LIZA VASYLA POZDNISHEF TRUKHASHEVSKY

KRIEMHILD (BROTHER OF —) GERNOT GUNTHER GISELHER
(FATHER OF —) GIBICH
(HUSBAND OF —) ATTILA SIEGFRIED

KRISHNA VASUDEVA
(BROTHER OF —) BALARAMA
(FATHER OF —) VASUDEVA
(FOSTER FATHER OF —) NANDA
(FOSTER MOTHER OF —) YASHODA
(MOTHER OF —) DEVAKI
(UNCLE OF —) KANSA

KUMQUAT NAGAMI

KUWAIT (CAPITAL OF —) ALKUWAIT
(OIL FIELD OF —) WAFRA BAHRAH BURGAN SABRIYA MINAGISH RAUDHATAIN
(TOWN OF —) MAGWA AHMADI HAWALLI ABDULLAH FAHAHEEL

L

L EL LIMA
LABAN (DAUGHTER OF —) LEAH RACHEL
(FATHER OF —) BETHUEL
(SISTER OF —) REBEKAH
LABEL TAG BILL FILE MARK FICHE STAMP TALLY TITLE DIRECT DOCKET TICKET ENDSEAL LAMBEAU STICKER
(— ON SUIT OF CLOTHES) ETIQUET
LABOR ADO FAG TUG WIN CARK MOIL TASK TAVE TILL TOIL WORK DELVE GRAFT GRIND HEAVE PAINS SWEAT SWINK TEAVE TREAD WHILE YAKKA DRUDGE EFFORT HAMMER STRIVE BULLOCK FATIGUE MANUARY OPIFICE PROCURE SERVICE SLAVERY TRAVAIL TROUBLE TURMOIL BUSINESS DRUDGERY EXERTION GROANING INDUSTRY LABORAGE STRUGGLE
(— ARDUOUSLY) BILDER
(— HARD) THRASH THRIPPLE
(— UNDER) SUFFER
(DAY'S —) DARG JOURNEY
(DIFFICULT —) DYSTOCIA
(EXCESSIVE —) STRAIN
(FORCED —) BEGAR CORVEE
(HARD —) HARD BULLWORK
(HIRED —) TOGT
(IMPOSED —) TASKAGE
(MENTAL —) HEADWORK
(SEVERE —) AGON
(UNPAID —) CORVEE
LABORATORY LAB SHOP KITCHEN OFFICINA WORKSHOP
LABORED HEAVY FORCED SWEATY STRAINED
LABORER
(ALSO SEE WORKER AND WORKMAN) BOY BHAR ESNE HIND JACK JOEY MOZO PEON TOTY BAGDI CHURL GUASO HUNKY NAVVY PALLI PINER STIFF BALAHI BEGARI BOHUNK COALER COOLIE DAYMAN DILKER DOCKER FELLAH FLUNKY FOGGER HEAVER HODMAN HOLEYA JIBARO LUMPER RAFTER TASKER WAYMAN WORKER BRACERO BYWONER CREWMAN DAYSMAN DIGGORY DIRGLER DRAINER DVORNIK GRECIAN HOBBLER MANUARY MAZDOOR PICKMAN PIONEER PIPEMAN PLOWMAN SANDHOG SCOURER SHIPPER SMASHER SOUGHER SPALLER STOCKER SWINKER TOTYMAN WORKMAN BIJWONER CHAINMAN COTTAGER DOLLYMAN FARMHAND FLOORMAN GANGSMAN HOLDSMAN SPADEMAN SPALPEEN STRAPPER TIDESMAN ROUSTABOUT
(INEXPERIENCED —) GREENER
LABORIOUS HARD HEAVY STIFF TOUGH SWEATY UPHILL ARDUOUS OPEROSE SLAVISH TOILFUL DILIGENT LABOROUS TOILSOME
LABYRINTH MAZE CIRCUIT MEANDER
LACE VAL BEAT BEST FOND GOTA LASH PEAK FILET LACIS LIVEN ORRIS POINT SCREW SPRIG WEAVE BLONDE CADDIS CORDON DEFEAT EDGING GRILLE LACING LASHER THRASH TUCKER VENISE ALENCON ALLOVER BULLION CURRAGH CUTWORK FOOTING GALLOON GUIPURE HONITON LATCHET MACRAME MALINES MECHLIN MELANGE NANDUTI TAMBOUR TATTING TORCHON TROLLEY ARGENTAN BOBBINET BONEWORK BOOTLACE BRUSSELS DENTELLE ILLUSION LACEWORK LIMERICK PEARLING STAYLACE COLBERTINE NEEDLEPOINT
LACERATE REND TEAR GANCH ENGORE HARROW MANGLE SCARIFY FRACTURE
LACERATION RIP TEAR WOUND
LACK FAIL LANK LIKE LOSS MAIM MISS NEED VOID WANE WANT FAULT MINUS DEARTH DEFECT INLAIK ABSENCE BLEMISH DEFAULT FAILURE PAUCITY VACANCY SCARCITY SOLITUDE WANTROKE
(— CONFIDENCE) DOUBT
(— FAITH) DIFFIDE
(— HARMONY) DISAGREE
(— OF APPETITE) ANOREXIA
(— OF CLARITY) DARKNESS
(— OF CONFIDENCE) MISTRUST
(— OF COORDINATION) ASYNERGY DYSERGIA
(— OF DEVELOPMENT) AGENESIS
(— OF EARNESTNESS) ITEMING
(— OF EFFUSIVENESS) RESERVE
(— OF EMOTION) APATHY
(— OF ENERGY) ATONY ANERGY ATONIA
(— OF FLAVOR) SILENCE
(— OF FORESIGHT) MYOPIA
(— OF HARMONY) DISCORD DISUNITY
(— OF INTENTION) ACCIDENT
(— OF INVOLVEMENT) DISTANCE
(— OF ORDER) ATAXY ATAXIA DISARRAY
(— OF PATRIOTISM) INCIVISM
(— OF REFINEMENT) CRUDITY
(— OF SENSE) FOLLY
(— OF SENSE OF SMELL) ANOSMIA
(— OF STEADINESS) LEVITY
(— OF SYMPATHY) DYSPATHY
(— OF VIGOR) LANGUOR
(— OF VITALITY) ANEMIA ADYNAMIA
(— OF WIND) CALM
(— OF WORTH) IMMERIT
(— STRENGTH) DROOP

LACKADAISICAL LANGUID LISTLESS
LACKEY SKIP SLAVE LACQUEY STAFFIER
LACKING BUT SHY BARE FREE SANS
WANT ALACK GNEDE MINUS SHORT
ABSENT BARREN DEVOID WITHIN
WANTING DESOLATE INDIGENT
LACKLUSTER DULL FISHY CLOUDY
GLASSY
LACONIC CURT SHORT CONCISE
POINTED SPARTAN SUCCINCT
LACQUER LAC DOPE DUCO JAPAN
CHATON LACKER URUSHI VARNISH
LAD BOY BUB MAN BOYO CARL CHAP
DICK HIND JOCK LOON SNAP BILLY
BUCKO CADDY CHIEL GROOM YOUTH
BURSCH CADDIE CALLAN FELLOW
LADDIE LADKIN MANNIE NIPPER SHAVER
CALLANT MUCHACHO SPRINGER
STRIPLING
(AWKWARD —) GRUMMET
(MISCHIEVOUS —) GAMIN
(MY —) AVICK
(SERVING —) GILLIE GOSSOON
LADDER STY STEE JACOB SCALE AERIAL
BANGOR ESCAPE PULEYN GANGWAY
POLEYNE POMPIER
(FIREMAN'S —) STICK
(FISH —) FISHWAY
(JACOB'S —) CHARITY
(REVOLVING —) POTENCE
(ROPE —) ETRIER
LADEN HEAVY BELAST LOADED FRAUGHT
FREIGHT GESTANT
LADLE DIP JET GAWN SKEP CLATH
KEACH STOOP DIPPER LADING CUVETTE
POTSTICK
(— OUT SOUP) SLEECH
(— WITH HANDLES) CYATH SHANK
CYATHUS KYATHOS SKIPPET
(BRINE —) LOOT
(LARGE —) SCOOP
LADY BIBI BURD DAME RANI DONNA
HANUM BEEBEE DOMINO FEMALE
KADINE KHANUM RAWNIE SAHIBA
SENORA LADYKIN MADONNA SENHORA
BELAMOUR SINEBADA
(— OF HIGH RANK) BEGUM
(— OF HOUSE) GOODWIFE
(BEAUTIFUL —) CLEAR
(LEADING —) PREMIERE
(TURKISH —) KHANUM
LADYLIKE FEMALE
LADY WINDERMERE'S FAN
(AUTHOR OF —) WILDE
(CHARACTER IN —) LORTON ERLYNNE
AUGUSTUS MARGARET DARLINGTON
WINDERMERE
LAERTES (FATHER OF —) ARCESIUS
(MOTHER OF —) CHALCOMEDUSA
(SON OF —) ULYSSES
(WIFE OF —) ANTICLEA
LAG DRAG DRAW SLOG DELAY TRAIL
HOCKER LAGGER LINGER LOITER STRING
DRIDDLE LAGGING
(— IN PRODUCTION) SLIPPAGE
LAGGARD SLOW TARDY LAGGER
TORTOISE

LAGGING TARDY JACKET DEADING
LAGGARD CLEADING DRAWLING
FOREPOLE
LAGNIAPPE TIP GIFT BONUS PILON
PRESENT
LAGOON HAFF POOL BAYOU LIMAN
LAGUNA SALINA
LAIR DEN LAY FORM HOLD SHED COUCH
EARTH HAUNT LODGE MEUSE SQUAT
HARBOR KENNEL SPELUNK
(— OF FOX) KENNEL
(— OF OTTER) HOLT HOVER
(— OF WILD BOAR) SOUNDER
LAITY FOLK LAYMEN PEOPLE
LAKE LAY SEA VLY BAHR JAIL JHIL LAGO
LLYN LOCH MERE MOAT SHOR TANK VLEI
VLEY BAYOU CHOTT JHEEL LERNA LIMAN
LOUGH SPARK TUBIG LAGOON NYANZA
STROND ANCYLUS CARMINE LAKELET
TURLOUGH
(DRY —) PLAYA
(FENNY —) BROAD
(MOUNTAIN —) TARN
(SMALL —) GURGES MARIGOT
(TEMPORARY —) PINAG
LAKME (CHARACTER IN —) LAKME
GERALD NILAKANTHA
(COMPOSER OF —) DELIBES
LAMB BUM PET PUR CADE DEAR DUPE
LOME SOCK YEAN AGNUS PESAH PODDY
AGNEAU COSSET HIEDER LAMBIE
LAMKIN PESACH SUCKER WASTER
WEANER CHILVER EANLING FATLING
HOGLING PASCHAL PERSIAN RUFFIAN
TWAGGER BAAHLING LAMBLING
PASSOVER YEANLING
(— AND WHEAT) KIBBE
(SCYTHIAN —) BAROMETZ
(SHOULDER OF —) BANJO
(SIDE OF —) CONCERTINA
LAMBASTE CREAM SQUABASH
LAME BUM GAME HALT LAHN GAMMY
GIMPY GRAVEL TINSEL CRIPPLE CRIPPLY
HALTING HIPHALT GORGERIN SPAVINED
(— A HORSE) STUB NOBBLE
(— WITH HORSESHOE NAIL) ACCLOY
LAMECH (DAUGHTER OF —) NAAMAH
(SON OF —) NOAH JABAL JUBAL
TUBALCAIN
(WIFE OF —) ADAH ZILLAH
LAMENT CRY WEY CARE DOLE HONE
HOWL KEEN MEAN MOAN PINE SIGH
TEAR WAIL WALY WEEP CROON DUMKA
GREET KINAH MOURN PLAIN QINAH
BEHOWL BEMOAN BEWAIL BEWEEP
COMMOS KOMMOS PLAINT REGRET
REPINE SORROW SQUAWK THREAP
YAMMER BEMOURN CONDOLE DEPLORE
EJULATE ELEGIZE GRIZZLE REGRATE
THRENOS WAYMENT COMPLAIN
CORONACH MOURNING THRENODY
ULLAGONE WELLAWAY
LAMENTABLE YEMER FUNEST RUEFUL
DOLEFUL PITIFUL PITIABLE PLAINFUL
YAMMERLY
LAMENTATION KEEN MOAN WAIL
DOLOR LINOS RUING TANGI LAMENT

PLAINT REGRET SORROW THRENE PLANGOR TRAGEDY WAYMENT WILLAWA CORONACH MOURNING PATHETIC WAILMENT WELLAWAY LAMENTING

LAMP ARC EYE SEE DAVY GLIM INKY JACK SLUT ALDIS ARGAND ASTRAL BULLET HELION LAMPAD TARGET ILLUMER LAMPION LAMPLET LANTERN LUCERNE LUCIGEN SUNLAMP SUNSPOT AEOLIGHT CIRCLINE GASLIGHT SIDELAMP TORCHERE PHOTOFLASH PHOTOFLOOD
(— FOR FIREPLACE) KYLE
(CHIMNEYLESS —) TORCH
(DARKROOM —) SAFELIGHT
(IRON —) CRUSIE
(MAKESHIFT —) BITCH
(NIGHT —) VEILLEUSE
(SAFETY —) DAVY GEORDIE
(STAGE —S) BATTEN
(4-CORNERED —) CHILL

LAMPBLACK LINK SOOT

LAMPOON PIPE SKIT GESTE LIBEL SQUIB IAMBIC SATIRE BERHYME PASQUIN COCKALAN RIDICULE SATIRIZE PASQUINADE

LANCE PIC CANE DART SHAFT SPEAR STAFF BROACH ELANCE GLAIVE GLEAVE LANCET ROCKET LANCELET SPICULUM
(KING ARTHUR'S —) RON

LAND ERD ERF NOD RIB AGER DIRT FOLD GALE GISH GORE JODO MARK SITE SOIL EARTH EJIDO FIELD GLEBE JUGER PLANT SHORE SOLUM ALIGHT FUNDUS GROUND COMMONS COUNTRY DEMESNE ELLASAR HOLDING LANDING LIBRATE QUILLET TERRENE ALLODIAL BOOKLAND COMMONTY FARMLAND FLEYLAND FOLKLAND POMERIUM PRAEDIUM
(— A PLANE) GREASE
(— BETWEEN FURROWS) SELION
(— BETWEEN RIVERS) DOAB
(— CONVERTED TO TILLAGE) THWAITE
(— HAVING VALUE OF POUND PER YEAR) LIBRATE
(— IN CONACRE) MOCK
(— IN GRASS) LAYER
(— LEFT FALLOW) ARDER
(— OF BLISS) GOKURAKU
(— OF GIANTS) UTGARTHAR
(— OF PLENTY) GOSHEN
(— OF REGION) MOLD
(— PLOWED IN A DAY) JORNADA
(— RECOVERED FROM SEA) INTAKE INNINGS
(— REGULARLY FLOODED) SALTING
(— SURROUNDED BY WASTE) HOPE
(ALLUVIAL —) BATTURE
(ANCESTRAL —) ETHEL
(ARABLE —) LEA
(ARID —) DESERT STEPPE
(BOTTOM —) SLASH CALLOW STRATH
(CHURCH —) GLEBE TERMON
(CHURCH —S) CROSS
(CLEARED —) ASSART
(COMMON —) EJIDO STRAY
(CONTINENTAL —) MAIN

(CULTIVATED —) FARM ARADA TILTH
CULTURE FEERING WAINAGE LABORAGE METAIRIE
(ENCLOSED —) CLOSE INTAKE
(FREEHOLD —) MULK
(GRAVELLY —) GEEST GRAVES
(GRAZING —) GRASS HIRSEL FEEDING
(HEATHY —) ROSLAND
(HERITABLE —) ODAL
(IMAGINARY —) FAERIE COCKAYNE LILLIPUT
(LEASED —) TACK
(LONG STRIP OF —) SLANG SPONG
(LOW —) BOG FEN GALL INKS CARSE BOTTOM
(LOW RICH —) CARSE
(NATIVE —) SOD KITH BLIGHTY BIRTHDOM HOMELAND
(OBDURATE —) TILL
(PARCEL OF —) FEU LOT MOCK
(PASTURE —) HA ALP FEED HOGA WALK GRASS VELDT LEASON SCATHOLD SCATLAND
(PLATEAU —) HIGHVELD
(PLOWED —) ARADA FALLOW FURROW BREAKING
(PRIVATE —) SEVERAL
(PROMISED —) CANAAN
(PURE —) JODO SUKHAVATI
(RECLAIMED —) POLDER
(RESOWN —) HOOKLAND
(ROUGH —) BRAKE
(SAVANNAH —S) LALANG
(SCRUBBY —) SCROG SCROGS
(SMALL PARCEL OF —) SUERTE
(SWAMPY —) WOODSERE
(TIMBER —S) STICKS
(WASTE —) HEATH
(WESTERN —) HESPERIA
(WET —) SOAK SWAMP SWANG
(WOODED —S) STICKS

LANDING BANK YARD STAITH LANDAGE ARRIVAGE FOOTPACE HALFPACE LANDFALL
(ABRUPT —) PANCAKE
(CRASH —) PRANG
(SMOOTH —) GREASER

LANDING PLACE GHAT HARD SCALE PALACE ARRIVAGE

LANDLADY WIFE DUENA PADRONA GOODWIFE

LANDLORD HOST LESSOR GOODMAN PADRONE ZAMINDAR

LANDMARK COPA DOLE DOOL MARK MERE BAKEN BOUND CAIRN MARCH MEITH SENAL CIPPUS SEAMARK

LANDOWNER THANE BONDER SQUIRE CACIQUE EFFENDI FREEMAN BHUMIDAR FRANKLIN ZAMINDAR

LANDSCAPE VIEW BOCAGE PAYSAGE SCENERY LANDSKIP

LANE GUT WAY GANG LOAN LOKE PASS RACE VEIN WIND WYND ALLEY CHASE DRANG DRONG ENTRY VENNEL LANEWAY LOANING TWITTEN DRIFTWAY
(AIR TRAFFIC —) CORRIDOR

(NARROW —) CHARE TEWER BOREEN RUELLE
(OCEAN —) SEAWAY
LANGUAGE (ALSO SEE DIALECT) BAT LIP CHIB CODE LEED RUNE TALE TESO LEDEN LINGO SLANG LANGUS LINGUA SPEECH TONGUE YABBER ACCENTS CABLESE DIALECT IDIOLECT LEGALESE PARLANCE PILIPINO
(— THAT CONDEMNS) ABUSE
(ARTIFICIAL —) RO IDO NEO ARULO NOVIAL VOLAPUK ESPERANTO
(BANTU —) KIRUNDI
(COMPUTER —) BAL ALGOL BASIC COBOL SNOBOL FORTRAN
(FIGURATIVE —) IMAGERY
(FLORID —) SILLABUB
(FOOLISH —) STUFF FLUMMERY
(FOUL —) SMUT ORDURE
(GYPSY —) CALO
(IMPUDENT —) SNASH
(INCOMPREHENSIBLE —) CHOCTAW
(INTERNATIONAL —) ANGLIC
(LATIN —) GRAMMAR HUMANITY
(NONSENSICAL —) BANTER
(OBSCENE —) BAWDY BAWDRY
(ORDINARY —) PROSE
(OVERPRETENTIOUS —) BOMBAST
(PERT —) SAUCE
(PIDGIN —) SABIR CAVITENO FANAKALO
(PLAIN —) CLEAR
(PROPAGANDISTIC —) NEWSPEAK
(SECRET —) ARGOT
(SHOWY —) FLUBDUB
(SPECIFIC —) GA GE HO MO VU AIS AKA ATA EDO EFE EPE EVE EWE FAN FON FOX FUL GEG HET ICA IJO ILA KAI KAU KOL KOT KRU KUI LAB LAI LAZ MON MRU SIA TWI UDI YAO ZIA AFAR AGAO AGAU AGNI AHOM AINU AKAN AKIM ALUR AMBO ANDI ANTA ARUA AVAR BARI BEJA BIAK BODO BONI BORA BUBE BUGI BULU CARA CHAM CHIN CHOL CHUJ COOS CORA COTO CREE CROW CUNA DENE DOBU DYAK EFIK EKOI ERIE EYAK FANG FIJI FULA FUNG GARO GEEZ GHEG GOLA GOLD HARE HEHE HOPI HOVA HULA HUPA IBAN IDJO IJAW IXIL KADU KAFA KAMI KAVI KAWI KELE KOCH KOMI KONO KOTA KUKI KURI LAHU LAKH LAPP LASI LATI LAZI LESU LETT LUBA MANX MAYA MOLE MORO NAGA NAMA NIAS NIUE NUBA NUPE OGOR PALA PALI PEGU PEUL PUME RAMA SAHO SERB SERI SGAW SHAN SIUS SORB SULU SUMO SUMU SUSU TAAL TIAM TIBU TINO TODA TSHI TUPI TUPY VEPS VOTE XOSA ZULU ALEUT ALSEA ARAUA AUETO AZTEC BAJAU BALTI BANTU BASSA BATAK BATTA BAURE BEMBA BHILI BICOL BILIN BONNY CAMPA CARIB CAYUA CHANE CHIMU CHOCO CHOPE COFAN COIBA COMAN CUEVA CUMAN CUNZA CZECH DAFLA DAYAK DIERI DINKA DUALA DUTCH DYULA EMPEO FANTI FINGO FUNJI GAFAT GALLA GANDA GETAN

GETIC GOLDI GONDI GREBO GREEK GUAMO GUATO GURMA GYPSY HABAB HAIDA HAKKA HATSA HAUSA HINDI HUABI HUARI HURON HUSKY HYLAM IGALA ILOKO IRAYA IRISH JAKUN JATKI JUANG JUTIC KABYL KAMBA KAMIA KANDH KAREN KAROK KHASI KHMER KHOND KHUZI KIOWA KISSI KIWAI KOINE KOLIS KONDE KONGO KORKU KORWA KOTAR KUMUK KUMYK KUSAN KWOMA LAMBA LAMUT LANGO LATIN LENCA LENDU LHOKE LHOTA LIMBA LIMBU LUIAN LUNDA MAGHI MAHRA MAHRI MALAY MALTO MAORI MAZUR MBUBA MEDIC MENDI MIKIR MODOC MOSSI MUONG MURMI MURUT NAHUA NOGAI NORSE NYORO ORAON ORIYA OROMO OSAGE OSCAN PALAU PAMIR PELEW PEUHL PLATT PUNIC RONGA SAKAI SAMAL SANTO SAXON SCOTS SERER SHILH SHINA SHONA SICEL SIKEL SLAVE SOTHO SOYOT SUOMI SWAZI TAINO TAMIL TELEI TONGA TURKI UDISH UIGUR URIYA UZBEK VOGUL WAYAO WELSH WOLOF YAKUT YUNCA ZERMA ABIPON ABKHAS ACAWAI ACHOLI ADIGHE ADZHAR AFGHAN AHTENA ALTAIC ANDAKI ANDHRA ANDOKE ANGAMI APACHE APANTO APIACA ARABIC ARANDA ARAONA ARAWAK ARUNTA ATAROI AVANTI AYMARA BAGOBO BAHASA BAITSI BAKELE BANIVA BASQUE BASUTO BEAVER BHOTIA BHUMIJ BIHARI BILAAN BILOXI BOHUNK BONTOC BORORO BRAHUI BRETON BRIBRI BUKAUA BULGAR BURIAT CAGABA CANITA CANUBA CARIAN CARIRI CAUQUI CAVINA CAYAPA CAYUGA CAYUSE CEBUAN CHAGGA CHAIMA CHANGO CHOCHO CHOKWE COCAMA CONIBO COPTIC CREOLE DAKOTA DANISH DOGRIB DYERMA ESKIMO EUDEVE FRENCH FULANI FULNIO FUTUNA GADDAN GALCHA GALIBI GATHIC GENTOO GERMAN GILAKI GILIAK GILYAK GOTHIC GUAIMI GUETAR GUINAU GULLAH GURIAN HAINAN HANTIK HARARI HATTIC HEBREW HERERO HIBITO IBANAG IBIBIO IFUGAO IGNERI IGOROT INDIAN INDOIS INNUIT INUPIK ISINAI ISLETA IVATAN KABARD KACHIN KAFFIR KAIBAL KALMUK KAMASS KANAKA KANURI KATIRI KEKCHI KHALKA KHAMTI KHARIA KHOWAR KIKUYU KILIWA KODAGA KODAGU KOIARI KOIBAL KOLAMI KOREAN KORYAK KOTIAK KPELLE KUNAMA KURNAI KURUKH KYURIN LADINO LAGUNA LAHNDA LAHULI LENAPE LEPCHA LIBYAN LIUKIU LIVIAN LUSHAI LUVIAN LUWIAN LYCIAN LYDIAN MAGAHI MAGYAR MANCHU MANOBO MBONDO MBUNDA MEDIAN MEGREL MICMAC MINOAN MISHMI MISIMA MOHAWK MONTES MUYSCA MYSIAN NEPALI NEWARI NINGPO NOOTKA NUBIAN NYANJA OJIBWA ONEIDA OORIVA OSTIAK OTOMAC

OVAMPO PAHARI PAIUTE PALAIC
PAPAGO PAPUAN PASHTO PAZAND
POLISH PUSHTO PUSHTU RASHTI
REJANG ROMANY SAFINE SAKIAN
SALISH SAMOAN SANGIL SANGIR
SARCEE SASSAK SAVARA SEDANG
SEKANI SELKUP SELUNG SEMANG
SENECA SENUFO SESUTO SHARRA
SHASTA SILETZ SINDHI SLOVAK SOMALI
SONRAI SUBIYA SURHAI SUSIAN TARTAR
TAVGHI TELEGU TELEUT TETTUM
THONGA TIPURA TUNGUS VANNIC
VOTYAK YANKEE YARURA YORUBA
ZAREMA ABENAKI ACHAGUA AEQUIAN
AKWAALA AKWAPIM ALABAMA ALTAIAN
AMANAYE AMHARIC AMORITE AMUESHA
APINAYE ARAMAIC ARAPAHO ARAUCAN
ARECUNA ARGOBBA ARICARA ARMORIC
ASHANTI ASURINI ATACAMA ATAKAPA
AUSTRAL AVESTAN AXUMITE BAGHELI
BAGIRMI BAINING BAKONGO BALANTE
BALUCHI BAMBARA BANGALA BANNACK
BASHKIR BENGALI BEOTHUK BERBERI
BHOTIYA BHUTANI BOSNIAN BRITISH
BULANDA BUNDELI BUNYORO BURMESE
BUSHMAN CALINGA CALINGA CARRIER
CASHIBO CATALAN CATAWBA CAWAHIB
CHACOBO CHARRUA CHATINO CHEBERO
CHECHEN CHIBCHA CHIMILA CHINOOK
CHIRINO CHIWERE CHONTAL CHOROTI
CHUKCHI CHUMASH CHUROYA CHUVASH
CIBONEY CIMBRIC CLALLAM COCHIMI
CORNISH COTONAM COWLITZ CYMRAEG
DAGBANE DAGOMBA DANAKIL DANKALI
DARGHIN DEUTSCH DHEGIHA DRAVIDA
ENGLISH ESCUARA ESSELEN EUSKERA
FINNISH FLEMISH FOOCHOW FRIESIC
FRISIAN GAULISH GOAJIRO GUAHIBO
GUARANI GUAYAKI GURUNSI GYARUNG
HAITIAN HANUNOC HIDATSA HITTITE
HUASTEC HUCHNOM HUICHOL HURRIAN
IBERIAN ILOKANO ILONGOT INGALIK
IPURINA ITALIAN ITELMES ITONAMA
JACUNDA JAGATAI KAKHYEN KALINGA
KALMUCK KAMASIN KANAUJI KANNADA
KASHUBE KASSITE KIKONGO KIPCHAK
KIRANTI KIRGHIZ KIRUNDI KLAMATH
KOASATI KONKANI KOYUKON KUBACHI
KULAMAN KURDISH KUTCHIN KUTENAI
LAMPONG LATVIAN LESGHIN LINGALA
LOATUKO LUGANDA MAGADHI MAHICAN
MALINKE MALTESE MAPUCHE MARATHI
MASKOKI MERCIAN MEXICAN MINAEAN
MINGREL MISKITO MITANNI MOABITE
MOCHICA MONUMBO MORATTY
MORISCO NAHUATL NICOBAR OJIBWAY
OSMANLI OSSETIC PAHLAVI PALAUNG
PANJABI PARBATE PERMIAK PERMIAN
PERSIAN PICTISH PRAKRIT PUNJABI
PUQUINA QUECHUA QUERCHI SABAEAN
SALINAN SAMBALI SAMNANI SAMNITE
SAMOYED SANDAWE SANTALI SANTANA
SEMITIC SERBIAN SHAWANO SHAWNEE
SHILLUH SHIPIBO SHUSWAP SIAMESE
SIRIONO SIUSLAW SOGDIAN SONGHAI
SONGISH SORBIAN SPANIOL SPANISH
STIKINE SUBANUN SVANISH SWAHILI

SWEDISH TAGALOG TIBETAN TUAMOTU
TURKISH UMBRIAN UMBUNDU VISAYAN
WALLOON WENDISH YENISEI YIDDISH
ZABERMA ZONGORA
(SWAHILI —) KISWAHILI
(UNCLEAN —) SEWERAGE
(UNIVERSAL —) PASILALY
(WELSH —) CYMRAEG
LANGUID WAN LANK DOWIE FAINT
DREAMY FEEBLE SICKLY SUPINE TORPID
CARELESS FLAGGING HEEDLESS
INDOLENT LISTLESS SLUGGISH
LANGUISH DIE FADE FALL FLAG PINE
WILT DROOP DWINE FAINT QUAIL
SWOON SICKEN WITHER DECLINE
LANKY LEAN RENKY SLINK GANGLY
GANGLING
LANTERN (ALSO SEE LAMP) BOUET
CROWN LIGHT CUPOLA LOUVER SCONCE
THOLUS CIMBORIO LANTHORN
(— ON ROOF) FEMEREIL
(DARK —) DARKY ABSCONCE
ABSCONSA
(ELEVATED —) PHAROS
(OPTICAL —) EPISCOPE

LAOS

CAPITAL: VIENTIANE
COIN: KIP
MEASURE: BAK
MOUNTAIN: BIA LAI LOI SAN COPI KHAT
ATWAT KHOUNG TIUBIA
PEOPLE: LU KHA LAO MEO YAO THAI
RIVER: NOI DONE KHONG MEKONG
NAMHOU SEBANG
TOWN: NAPE PAKSE XIENG PAKLAY
THAKHEK SAVANNAKHET
LUANGPRABANG
WATERFALL: MEKONG

LAP LEP LIP BARM FOLD GORE LICK SLAP
SLOD SOSS SUCK WASH WELT SKIVE
LAPPER LAPPET SHOVEL INTERLAP
(— IN STEEL) SPILL
(— OF STRAKES) LAND
LAPEL LAPPET REVERE REVERS
LAPSE DROP FADE FALL HALT SLIP ERROR
FAULT FOLLY SPACE TRACT EFFLUX
HIATUS LAPSUS DELAPSE ESCHEAT
FAILURE PASSAGE PROCESS RELAPSE
RESOLVE SLIDING ABEYANCE CADUCITY
(— OF MEMORY) BLACKOUT
(MENTAL —) ABERRATION
(PL.) LACHES
LARCENY THEFT FELONY ROBBERY
BURGLARY STEALAGE
LARCH ALERCE LARICK JUNIPER
EPINETTE TAMARACK
LARD MORT SAIM ADEPS DAUBE ENARM
FLARE FLECK FLICK AXUNGE NEUTRAL
SAINDOUX
LARDER CAVE PANTRY SPENCE BUTTERY
LARDINER
LARGE BIG BULL FEAT GOOD LONG MAIN
ROOM TALL AMPLE BULKY BURLY GRAND

GREAT GROSS HUSKY JOLLY LARGY
MACRO MAXIM RENKY ROUND SMART
SPACY WALLY GAWSIE GOODLY HEROIC
MAXIMA STRONG TRABAL BOWERLY
CAPITAL COPIOUS FAIRISH FEARFUL
HEALTHY HULKING LASKING LIBERAL
MASSIVE OUTSIZE SIZABLE BOUNCING
CHOPPING OUTSIZED PLUMPING
SENSIBLE SWACKING
(— AND HOLLOW) CAVAL
(— AND ROUND) SIDE
(— IN DIAMETER) STOUT
(APPALLINGLY —) HIDEOUS
(EXTRA —) MAXI
(EXTREMELY —) GIANT DECUMAN
GIGANTIC
(FAIRLY —) SMART
(INDEFINITELY —) NTH INFINITE
(MODERATELY —) FAIR TIDY PRETTY
(UNUSUALLY —) HEAVY SKELPIN
SKELPING
(VERY —) HUGE JUMBO ROYAL BOXCAR
BUMPER INGENT NATION GOLIATH
INTENSE BEHEMOTH SLAPPING
SPANKING SWINGING WHACKING
LARGENESS BULK MICKLE BREADTH
FREEDOM GIANTISM LARGEOUR
LARGEST BEST MAXIMUS
LARIAT ROPE LASSO RIATA CABESTRO
LARK GAME ROMP FROLIC PEEWEE
SCHEME GAMMOCK LAVROCK LAYROCK
SKYLARK CALANDER LAVEROCK
LARVA BOT BLOW BOTT CRAB GRUB
HUHU SLUG TURK WOLF WORM ALIMA
ASCON BARDY BRUKE ERUCA LEECH
OTTER REDIA SYCON CORBIE COSSID
DRAGON EPHYRA GRUGRU HOPPER
LEPTUS LEUCON LOOPER MAGGOT
MEASLE NIGGER PEDLAR TORCEL
WABBLE WORMIL WOUBIT ATROCHA
BUDWORM CADELLE CREEPER DIPORPA
FIGWORM FLYBLOW GORDIAN HYDATID
HYPOPUS PEDDLER PLANULA PLUTEUS
PREPUPA VELIGER WIGGLER
LARYNGITIS CROUP
LASCIVIOUS LEWD NICE SALT HORNY
LUBRIC WANTON BLISSOM FLESHLY
GOATISH PAPHIAN PRURIENT SALACIOUS
LASCIVIOUSNESS LECHERY ASELGEIA
LUXURITY LUBRICITY
LASH CUT BEAT FIRK FLOG JERK LACE
WELT WHIP WIRE YERK LEASE LEASH
SCORE SKEEG SLASH THONG TRICE
WHALE CANVAS CILIUM LAINER LAUNCH
STRIPE SWINGE SWITCH FLYFLAP
KURBASH SCOURGE
(— BOWSPRIT) GAMMON
(— TOGETHER) RACK
LASHING YARK YERK GAMMON LISTING
MOUSING SEIZING SLATING FRAPPING
LASS TIB GILL PRIM TRULL DAMSEL
KUMMER LASSIE DAMOZEL LASSIKY
TENDREL MUCHACHA
LASSO LASH LAZO ROPE RIATA LARIAT
CABESTRO
LAST ABY LAG DURE HOLD KEEP RIDE
SAVE ABIDE FINAL SERVE ABEGGE

ENDURE LATEST LATTER REMAIN ULTIMA
UTMOST DARREIN DERNIER EXTREME
PERDURE SUPREME CONTINUE
EVENTUAL HINDMOST LATEMOST
REARMOST TERMINAL ULTIMATE
AFTERMOST
(— BUT ONE) PENULT
(— OUT) SPIN STAY
(AT —) FINALLY
(THE —) OMEGA
LAST DAYS OF POMPEII
(AUTHOR OF —) BULWER LYTTON
(CHARACTER IN —) IONE BURBO
JULIA NYDIA DIOMED ARBACES CLODIUS
GLAUCUS SALLUST APAECIDES
LASTING FIXED LASTY DURANT DURING
STABLE ABIDING DURABLE DUREFUL
CONSTANT ENDURING LIVELONG
REMANENT STANDING
(— FOR LONG PERIOD) AEONIC
AEONIAL
(— FOR ONE DAY) DIARY DIURNAL
LAST OF THE MOHICANS
(AUTHOR OF —) COOPER
(CHARACTER IN —) CORA WEBB ALICE
DAVID GAMUT MAGUA MUNRO NATTY
UNCAS BUMPPO DUNCAN HAWKEYE
HEYWARD MONTCALM CHINGACHGOOK
LAST PURITAN (AUTHOR OF —)
SANTAYANA
(CHARACTER IN —) JIM IRMA ROSE
ALDEN BOBBY EDITH MARIO PETER
WEYER BOWLER OLIVER DARNLEY
HARRIET SCHLOTE BUMSTEAD
LAST SUPPER CENA COENA MAUNDY
LATCH FLY PIN HASP RISP CATCH CHAIR
CLICK CLINK SNECK SNICK KEEPER
CLICKET
LATE LAG NEW DEEP RIPE SLOW TARDY
ADVANCED LATEWARD SOMETIME
(— IN DEVELOPING) SEROTINOUS
LATE GEORGE APLEY
(AUTHOR OF —) MARQUAND
(CHARACTER IN —) JOHN MARY APLEY
AMELIA GEORGE ELEANOR HORATIO
MONAHAN OREILLY WILLIAM WILLING
BOSWORTH PRENTISS CATHARINE
LATENT HIDDEN MASKED ABEYANT
DORMANT PASSIVE LATITANT
QUIESCENT
LATER ANON POST SYNE AFTER ELDER
BEHIND FUTURE LATTER PUISNE
ANOTHER INFERIOR
LATERAL SIDE
LATEST LAST LATTER FARTHEST
FURTHEST
LATH BAT LAG SLAT SPALE SWALE
SPLINT LATHING FOREPOLE LATHWORK
LATHE SLEY BEATER WISKET
(— FOR CYLINDERS) BROAD
(— OF LOOM) LAY
(TURNING —) THROW
(WATCHMAKER'S —) TURN MANDREL
LATHER FOAM SUDS FROTH FREATH
SAPPLES
LATHERED SOAPY

LATIN ROMAN HISPERIC LATINITY
SCATTERMOUCH
LATITUDE SCOPE WIDTH EXTENT HEIGHT
(HELIOCENTRIC —) LIMIT
LATONA (DAUGHTER OF —) DIANA
(FATHER OF —) COEUS
(MOTHER OF —) PHOEBE
(SON OF —) APOLLO
LATRINE BOG REAR PRIVY TOILET
BOGGARD
LATTER LAST FINAL RECENT SECOND
PRESENT
LATTICE GRATE HERSE TWINE PINJRA
UMBREL GRATING CANCELLI
(— OF POINTS) SATIN
(MOVING —) APRON
(PREF.) CLATHR
LATTICEWORK ARBOR GRATE GRATING
ESPALIER TUKUTUKU

LATVIA

CAPITAL: RIGA
COIN: LAT RUBLIS KAPEIKA SANTIMS
MEASURE: STOF KANNE STOFF STOOF
VERST ARSHIN KULMET SAGENE
VERCHOC KROUCHKA POURVETE
PEOPLE: LETT
RIVER: AA OGRE DVINA GAUJA VENTA
SALACA LIELUPE
TOWN: CESIS LIBAU DVINSK LIBAVA
TUKUMS JELGAVA LIEPAJA REZEKNE
DUNABURG VALMIERA DAUGAVPILS
WEIGHT: LIESPFUND

LAUD EXTOL PRAISE ADVANCE APPLAUD
COMMEND GLORIFY MAGNIFY
EMBLAZON EULOGIZE MACARIZE
LAUDATORY SNEER EPENETIC PRAISING
LAUGH GAFF CHUCK RISUS ARRIDE
NICKER TITTER CHORTLE GRIZZLE
SNICKER SNIGGER TWITTER LAUGHTER
(— CONTEMPTUOUSLY) SNORT
DERIDE
(— GLEEFULLY) CHECKLE
(— HYSTERICALLY) CHECKLE
(— IN AFFECTED MANNER) GIGGLE
(— IN COARSE MANNER) FLEER
GUFFAW
(— LIKE HEN) CACKLE
(— LOUDLY) GAFF GUFFAW
(— QUIETLY) GULE SMUDGE CHUCKLE
SNIRTLE
(BELLY —) BOFF BOFFOLA
(LOUD —) GAUSTER
LAUGHABLE ODD RICH COMIC DROLL
FUNNY MERRY QUEER WITTY AMUSING
COMICAL RISIBLE STRANGE WAGGISH
FARCICAL HUMOROUS LAUGHING
PLEASANT SPORTIVE RIDICULOUS
LAUGHING RIANT RIDENT IRRISION
LAUGHINGSTOCK GUY BUTT JEST
JOKE SONG SPORT DERISION RIDICULE
LAUGHTER JOKE MIRTH RISUS SNIRT
CACKLE LAWTER SPLEEN HILARITY
RISIBILITY

(HYSTERICAL —) CACHINNATION
LAUNCH PUT BURST DRIVE STRIKE
BAPTIZE PINNACE PROMOTE STEAMER
VIBRATE CATAPULT
(— HOSTILELY) DIRECT
LAUNDER TYE WASH TRUNK SLUICE
STRAKE LAUNDRY
LAUNDRESS TRILBY LAVENDER
LAUNDRY WASH LAVATORY
LAUREL BAY IVY LAURY UNITE WICKY
DAPHNE KALMIA MALLET MYRTLE
CAJEPUT IVYWOOD WOEVINE BREWSTER
CALFKILL
(GROUND —) ARBUTUS
LAVA ASHES SPINE COULEE LATITE
VERITE FAVILLA LAPILLO MALPAIS
ASPERITE ORENDITE PAHOEHOE
(MUD —) MOYA LAHAR
(SCORIACEOUS —) AA SLAG
(SLAGGY —) SCORIA
LAVATORY BASIN CHALET CLOSET
LAVETTE WASHROOM CLOAKROOM
LAVE LIP WASH BATHE SPLASH
LAVENDER ASPIC BEHEN SPICK SPIKE
INKROOT STICHADO
LAVINIA (FATHER OF —) LATINUS
(HUSBAND OF —) AENEAS
(MOTHER OF —) AMATA
LAVISH FREE LASH LUSH FLUSH LARGE
SPEND SPORT WASTE COSTLY WANTON
COPIOUS OPULENT PROFUSE GENEROUS
LUCULLAN PRODIGAL SQUANDER
WASTEFUL REDUNDANT MUNIFICENT
LAVISHNESS WASTE FINERY LAVISH
LAW ACT FAS JUS LAY LEX DOOM JURE
RULE CANON DROIT NOMOS TORAH
BYELAW DECREE DHARMA EQUITY
BROCARD DANELAW DERECHO HALAKAH
JUSTICE PRECEPT SETNESS STATUTE
JUDGMENT ROGATION TANISTRY
ORDINANCE
(—S OF MANU) SUTRA
(BEDOUIN —) THAR
(DIETARY —S) KASHRUTH
(ISLAMIC —) ADA BAI ADAT SHARIA
(MARRIAGE —) LEVIRATE
(OPPOSING —) ANTINOMY
(PROPOSED —) BILL
(UNIVERSAL —) HEAVEN
LAWFUL DUE LEAL TRUE VERY LEGAL
LICIT LOYAL VALID KINDLY ENNOMIC
LEESOME INNOCENT LIEFSOME
RIGHTFUL
LAWGIVER MINOS MOSES SOLON
LAWYER LAWMAKER
LAWLESS LEWD UNRULY ILLEGAL
MOBBISH ANARCHIC
LAWLESSNESS ANOMY ANOMIE
ANARCHY
LAWN ARBOR GRASS LINON SWARD
UMPLE CYPRUS BATISTE QUINTIN
TIFFANY
LAWSUIT LIS CASE SAKE SECTA ACTION
BRABBLE
LAWYER (ALSO SEE JURIST) JET PEAT
AVOUE PATCH SHARK BREHON JURIST
LAWMAN LEGIST SQUIRE WRITER

COUNSEL MUKHTAR TEMPLAR DEFENDER
LEGISTER TRAMPLER BARRISTER
MOUTHPIECE PETTIFOGGER
LAX DULL FREE LASH LAZY LINK SLOW
SWAG WIDE LARGE LOOSE RELAX SLACK
TARDY REMISS BACKWARD INACTIVE
DISSOLUTE NEGLIGENT
LAY LIE SET CLAP LAIC LEWD SLEY SONG
WAGE BIGHT CIVIL COUCH DITTY LATHE
LEDGE QUIET STAKE STILL COMMON
HAZARD IMPOSE IMPUTE APPEASE
ASCRIBE LAYDOWN POPULAR SECULAR
SIRVENTE TEMPORAL
(— ASIDE) DOFF DOWN DUMP SHUCK
DEPOSE DIVEST DEPOSIT PIGEONHOLE
(— AWAY) STORE
(— BARE) BARE NAKE TIRL TIRVE
DENUDE DETECT OPPOSE UNCOVER
DENUDATE
(— CLAIM) ASSERT BESPEAK
ARROGATE
(— CROSSWISE) COB
(— DOWN) ABDICATE PRESCRIBE
(— EGGS) BLOW WARP LEDGE OVIPOSIT
(— FLAT) SQUAT ADPRESS
(— HOLD OF) FANG GRIP HENT TAKE
GRIPE LATCH ATHOLD ATTACH COLLAR
COMPRISE
(— IN BIGHTS) JAG
(— IN COIL) FLEMISH
(— IN PLEATS) FOLD
(— LOW) STREW STRIKE
(— OF LOOM) BEATER
(— ON) APPLY INFLICT
(— OPEN) BREAK CHINE EXPOSE
UNMASK
(— OUT) FRAY PLAT RANGE SPELD
SPEND BEWARE DESIGN EXTEND SPREAD
STREEK CHECKER DEVELOP STRETCH
CONTRIVE
(— PRONE) LEVEL
(— RUBBLEWORK) SNECK
(— SIEGE) INVEST
(— SMOOTH) EVEN
(— SNARE FOR RABBITS) HAY
(— STONE) PAVE
(— STRAIGHT) COMB
(— TYPE) CASE
(— UP) HEAP HIVE ADDLE HOARD
HUTCH STOCK TREASURE
(— WASTE) PEEL WEST HARRY HAVOC
HARASS RAVAGE DESTROY DESOLATE
FORWASTE
LAYER BED LAY BARK CAKE COAT DASS
FACE FILM FLAP FOLD LAIR LOFT RIND
SEAM SKIN WEFT ZONA CHESS COUCH
COVER CRUST CUTIS FLAKE FLASH
LEDGE SCALE CARPET COURSE FASCIA
FILLER FOLIUM INTINE LAMINA LISSOM
STREAK BLANKET COATING CUTICLE
FEATHER PACKING PROVINE STRATUM
SUBCOAT SUPPORT INTERBED MOLLISOL
PERIOPLE SUBCRUST
(— OF BLOOD VESSEL) EXTIMA
EXTERNA
(— OF CELLS) EXINE CORTEX CAMBIUM
PHELLEM TAPETUM PERICYCLE

(— OF CLAY) GLEY VARVE SELVAGE
(— OF EARTH) SPIT
(— OF FAT) LEAF FINISH
(— OF FELT) BAT
(— OF FIBER) LAP
(— OF FUEL) FIREBED
(— OF GLASS) CASING
(— OF IRIS) UVEA
(— OF MORTAR) SCREED
(— OF ORGANIC MATTER) FLOOR
(— OF ROCK) CAP SHELF SHELL SLATE
FOLIUM SEPTUM BLISTER SKULLCAP
(— OF ROOTS) SOLE
(— OF SEDIMENT) WARP
(— OF SHALE) BONE
(— OF SILT) VARVE
(— OF SKIN) DERM DERMA EPIDERM
(— OF SOIL) SOLUM CALLOW CASING
HARDPAN HORIZON
(— OF STONES) DASS DESS
(— OF TURF) FLAW KERF
(— OF WOOD) CORE
(BONY —) LAMELLA CEMENTUM
(BOTTOM —) BEDDING
(FLAT —) BED FLAP FLAKE
(FROZEN —) PERMAFROST
(IMPERVIOUS —) LINING
(OUTER —) HUSK
LAYOFF FURLOUGH
LAZY IDLE DOXIE DRONY FAINT INERT
SLOAN SLOTH CLUMSY LIMPSY INERT
ORNERY DRONISH PEAKISH DROGHLIN
FAINEANT FECKLESS INDOLENT
OSCITANT SLOTHFUL SLUGGARD
TRIFLING SHIFTLESS
LEAD GO TEE VAN WIN BEAR GIVE GROW
HAVE HEAD HERD LEED SLIP TAKE TEEM
WORK BLAZE BOUND BRING CARRY
GREBE GUIDE MAYNE PILOT PRESA
SOUND START TRAIN TREAT CONVEY
DEDUCE DIRECT ESCORT INDUCE INDUCT
LEADER SATURN BEGUILE CAPTAIN
CONDUCE CONDUCT LEADING MARSHAL
PIGTAIL PIONEER PLUMBUM PLUMMET
LEADSMAN MANUDUCE MANUDUCT
SQUIRREL
(— A BAND) BATON
(— AND SUPPORT) DADE
(— ASIDE) CHAR SINGLE
(— ASTRAY) ERR MANG TURN WARP
BEFOOL BETRAY ENTICE WANDER
WILDER DEBAUCH MISLEAD MISWEND
PERVERT SOLICIT TRADUCE BEWILDER
INVEIGLE MISGUIDE
(— AWAY) CHAR ABDUCT DIVERGE
(— BACK) REDUCT
(— FORCIBLY) ESCORT
(— IN CARD GAME) SNEAK
WHITECHAPEL
(— IN RACE) LAP
(— IN SINGING) PRECENT
(— INTO ERROR) ABUSE DELUDE
(— MONOXIDE) MASSICOT
(— ON) TRAIL
(— PASSIVE EXISTENCE) VEGETATE
(— POISONING) PLUMBISM
(BLACK —) WAD GRAPHITE

(MOCK —) BLENDE
(PLUMBING —) BLUEY
(WHITE —) KREMS CERUSE
LEADER BO COB DUX HOB MIR CAST
COCK DUCE DUKE HEAD HOBB JEFE NAIG
NAIK OMDA SOUL TYEE CHIEF DOYEN
ELDER FIRST MAHDI MOSES OMDEH
PILOT SEYID TRACE ARCHON CALIPH
DESPOT HEADER HONCHO RECTOR
SAYYID TYCOON ACREMAN ADVISER
CAPTAIN CONDUCT DEMAGOG DRUNGAR
FOREMAN FUEHRER INDUCER PRIMATE
ACCENTOR CAUDILLO DIRECTOR
FUGLEMAN HEADSMAN HERETOGA
LODESMAN PANDARUS STRATEGE
PENDRAGON PROTAGONIST
(— OF ARMY) VOIVODE
(— OF DACOITS) BOH
(— OF GUISERS) SKUDLER
(— OF MINING GANG) CORPORAL
(— OF MUTINEERS) ELECTO
(— OF REVOLT) ANARCH
(BAND —) BATONEER
(CHOIR —) CANTOR PRECENTOR
(CHORUS —) CHORAGUS
(COSSACK —) HETMAN
(FASCIST —) RAS
(INTELLECTUAL —) BRAIN
(MOB —) MOBOCRAT
(POLITICAL —) SACHEM
(PRAYER —) IMAM
(RELIGIOUS —) AGA SHEIKH
(SCOUT —) AKELA SIXER
(SPIRITUAL —) GURU SADDIK
GUARDIAN
LEADERSHIP LEAD AEGIS MANRED
CONDUCT IMAMATE LEADING MANRENT
CHIEFDOM GUIDANCE HEADSHIP
HEGEMONY
LEADING BIG BEST COCK DUCT HEAD
LEAD MAIN CHIEF FIRST BANNER
PREMIER STELLAR PROMINENT
LEAF PAD BACK BUYO FLAP FOIL FOLD
PAGE PALM STUB BLADE BLANK FLIER
FROND GRASS GUARD LEAVE SCALE
SEPAL SIGHT SPILL TEPAL BONNET
CADJAN CARPEL COUPON FOLIUM
FRAISE FULZIE NEEDLE PEPPER DAMIANA
FOLDOUT HARNESS LEAFLET TREFOIL
WITNESS PHYLLADE PHYLLOME
MICROPHYLL
(— FAT) FLICK
(— FROM AXIL) BRACT
(— OF BOOK) PAGE FOLIO INSET PLATE
FLYLEAF
(— OF CALYX) BARB
(— OF CORN) HUSK
(— OF COROLLA) PETAL
(— OF DOOR) VALVE
(— OF HEDDLES) GEAR
(— OF PALM) FAN PAN CHIP OLLA
FROND LATANIER
(— OF SPRING) BACK
(BETEL —) PAN SIRIH
(BIBLE —) COSTMARY
(DEAD —) FLAG
(HOLLOW —) PHYLLODE

(SPRING —) WRAPPER
(STRAWBERRY —) FRAISE
(THIN —) LAMELLA
(TOBACCO —) LUGS STRIP CUTTER
WRAPPER
(WASTE GOLD —) SKEWING
LEAFY GREEN LEAVY FOLIATE FOLIOSE
FRONDOSE
LEAGUE BOND BUND BANDY BOARD
GUEUX HANSA PARTY UNION WHEEL
CIRCUIT COMPACT ALLIANCE SYSTASIS
COALITION
LEAH (DAUGHTER OF —) DINAH
(FATHER OF —) LABAN
(HUSBAND OF —) JACOB
(SISTER OF —) RACHEL
(SON OF —) LEVI JUDAH REUBEN
SIMEON ZEBULUN ISSACHAR
LEAK BLOW SEEP WEEP SPUNK SIGGER
SPRING ZIGGER LEAKAGE SCREEVE
LEAKY UNTIGHT GIZZENED
LEAN BEAR BEND BONY HANG HEEL LANK
PEND POOR PRIN RACY RELY REST SEEL
STAY SWAY THIN TOOM EMPTY GAUNT
HIELD LANKY LEANY SLANK SOUND
SPARE STOOP HOLLOW MEAGER
RECUMB SKINNY SPRING UPLEAN
ANGULAR FATLESS HAGGARD INCLINE
SCRAGGY SCRAWNY SLUNKEN STRINGY
MACILENT SCRAGGED SCRANNEL
(— FOR SUPPORT) ABUT
(— FORWARD) PROCLINE
(— OVER) WHAUVE
LEANDER (LOVE OF —) HERO
LEAN-TO SHED LINTER OUTSHOT
SKILLION
LEAP FLY HOP POP BEND DART DIVE FALL
GIVE JUMP LOPE LOUP RAMP RISE SKIT
WIND BOUND BREAK DANCE FLIER FLYER
FRISK LUNGE PRIME SALTO SAULT
SCOPE SCOUP SPANG STEND VAULT
BOUNCE INSULT LAUNCH SPRENT
SPRING WALLOP REBOUND SALTARY
SALTATE SUBSULT BUCKJUMP
LEAPFROG SPANGHEW UPSPRING
(— BACK) RESULT SPRUNT
(— FOR JOY) EXULT
(— IN DANCING) STOT
(— LIGHTLY) SKIP
(— OF HORSE) CURVET BALOTADE
CAPRIOLE CROUPADE
(— OF WHALE) BREACH
(— OUT) SALLY
(— OVER) FREE OVER SKIP CLEAR
HURDLE
(— UPON) ASSAIL
(BALLET —) JETE ASSEMBLE CABRIOLE
(FROLICSOME —) CAPER
(SUICIDAL —) BRODIE
LEARN DO CON GET SEE FIND HAVE HEAR
LEAR LERE EDIFY GLEAN STUDY RECORD
REALIZE RECEIVE DISCOVER ASCERTAIN
LEARNED BLUE SEEN LERED LORED
DUCTUS BOOKISH CLERKLY CUNNING
ERUDITE STUDIED TUITIVE ACADEMIC
CLERGIAL LETTERED OVERSEEN
POLYMATH PROFOUND SCIENCED

LEARNER PUPIL NOVICE SCHOLAR
TRAINEE PRENTICE ABECEDARIAN
LEARNING ART WIT BOOK LEIR LERE
LORE CLERGY WISDOM APPRISE
CUNNING GRAMMAR INSIGHT LETTERS
WISTING BOOKLORE DOCTRINE
HUMANISM LETTRURE MATHESIS
PEDANTRY
(SUFF.) MATHY
LEASE FEU LET SET FARM HIRE RENT
TACK COWLE DIMIT FIRMA LISSE DEMISE
POTTAH RENTAL ASSEDAT CHARTER
SETTING BACKTACK SUBLEASE
LEASH LEAD LYME LEASE COUPLE
STRING SWINGE
(— OF HOUNDS) HARL
(DOG —) SLIP TRASH TIRRET
(HAWK'S —) LOYN LUNE TIRRET
CREANCE
LEATHER ELK KID BEND CALF CAPE HIDE
NAPA SEAL ADUST BALAT FLANK NIGER
RETAN SUEDE CASTOR CHROME LIZARD
ORIOLE OXHIDE PEBBLE RUSSET SKIVER
TURKEY BELTING BUFFING CANEPIN
CHAMOIS COWHIDE COWSKIN DEGRAIN
DOGSKIN DONGOLA HEADCAP HOGSKIN
KIDSKIN MURRAIN PANCAKE PECCARY
PERSIAN SAFFIAN ANTELOPE BUCKSKIN
BULLNECK CABRETTA CALFSKIN
CAPESKIN CHEVEREL COLTSKIN
DEERSKIN GOATSKIN KANGAROO
LAMBSKIN SHAGREEN SHEEPSKIN
(— FOR DRESSING FLAX) RIBSKIN
(— FROM SHEEPSKIN) ROAN
(— SHREDS) MOSLINGS
(— STRIP) RAND
(ARABIAN —) MOCHA
(ARTIFICIAL —) KERATOL PEGAMOID
(CORDOVAN —) CORDOBAN
CORDWAIN
(GRAINED —) ROAN
(MOROCCO —) LEVANT MAROQUIN
(PATCH OF —) CLOUT
(PRUSSIAN —) SPRUCE
(RUSSIAN —) YUFT BULGAR RUSSIA
JUCHTEN
(SHEEPSKIN —) BOCK BUCK MOCHA
(SOFT —) OOZE ALUTA
(SUPERIOR —) BUFF
(THICK —) BUTT
(WASH —) LOSH
LEAVE GO GET LET BUNK DROP FADE
FLEE HOOK LEAF PART QUIT VADE VOID
WALK AVOID CONGE FAVOR FORGO
GRACE SHOVE WAIVE BUGGER BUGOFF
DEPART DESERT DEVOID FORLET PERMIT
RETIRE SECEDE STRAND VACATE
FORLEIT FORLESE FORSAKE LARGESS
LIBERTY LICENSE FAREWELL PATIENCE
UNTENANT PERMISSION SABBATICAL
(— ALONE) FORBEAR DESOLATE
(— BEHIND) LET PLANT DISTANCE
OUTSTRIP
(— BRIGHT TRAIL) STREAM
(— BY WILL) BEQUEATH
(— COVER) BREAK
(— HASTILY) SKIRR

(— HURRIEDLY) CUT BLOW FLEE JUMP
SCAT SKIP
(— IN ISOLATION) MAROON
(— IN SAFEKEEPING) CHECK
(— NOTHING TO BE DESIRED)
SATISFY
(— OF ABSENCE) ABSIT EXEAT
LIBERTY FURLOUGH
(— OFF) CEASE DEVAL PETER BILEVE
CHEESE DESIST SURCEASE
(— OUT) BATE OMIT SKIP SLIP ELIDE
(— PORT) CLEAR
(— QUICKLY) SCREW
(— SECRETLY) STEAL
(— SUDDENLY) KITE
(— UNDONE) PRETERMIT

LEBANON

CAPITAL: BEIRUT BEYROUTH
COIN: LIVRE PIASTRE
MOUNTAIN: ARUBA HERMON SANNINE
KENISSEH
PLAIN: ELBIKA
RIVER: JOZ LYCOS DAMOUR LITANI
HASBANI LEONTES ORONTES KASEMIEH
SEAPORT: TYRE SAIDA SIDON BEIRUT
TOWN: SUR TYRE ALEIH HALBA SAIDA
SIDON ZAHLE JUNIYE ZAHLAH QARTABA
TRIPOLI MERJUYUN
VALLEY: BEQAA

LECHEROUS LEWD SALT PRIME RANDY
WANTON BOARISH CODDING GOATISH
LUSTFUL LIKEROUS SCABROUS
SPORTIVE STUPROUS SALACIOUS
(PREF.) LUBRI
LECTERN DESK EAGLE LUTRIN LATERAN
LATTERIN
LECTURE JOBE CREED FORUM HOMILY
LECTOR LESSON SERMON ADDRESS
EARBASH HEARING PRELECT READING
JOBATION ORDINARY
LEDA (DAUGHTER OF —) HELEN
CLYTEMNESTRA
(FATHER OF —) THESTIUS
(HUSBAND OF —) TYNDAREUS
(SON OF —) CASTOR POLLUX
LEDGE BEAD BERM DESS LINE STEP
ALTAR BENCH CLINT LINCH SHELF
SNOUT BEARER OFFSET SETTLE STANCE
CHANNEL LEDGING RETABLE
LEDGER BOOK SLAB JOURNAL OVERLIER
LEER LOOK OGLE FLEER LEERY SKIME
SMIRK TWIRE
LEES LAGS ADDLE DRAFF DREGS DROSS
GROUT AMURCA BOTTOM DUNDER
MOTHER ULLAGE GROUNDS EMPTINGS
SEDIMENT WINEDRAF
LEFTHANDED CAR GAUCHE AWKWARD
DUBIOUS OBLIQUE KITHOGUE
SOUTHPAW
LEG GAM PIN CRUS GAMB JAMB LIMB
TRAM BOUGH JAMBE REACH SHANK
STICK BENDER GAMBON GAMMON
LEGLET MOGGAN OVIGER PLANTA

PROLEG WALKER FORELEG TRESTLE
FORELIMB
(— OF CRUSTACEAN) PODITE
(— OF HAWK) ARM
(— OF LAMB) GIGOT WOBBLER
(— OF TABLE) BALUSTER
(— OF WHEELBARROW) STILT
(— USED FOR FOOD) PESTLE
(—S OF ARTIFICIAL FLY) HACKLE
(ARTIFICIAL —) PYLON
(FURNITURE —) CABRIOLE
(MILK —) WEED
(TROUSER —) SLOP
(WIRE —S) SLING
(WOODEN —) PEG STUMP TIMBER
LEGACY ENTAIL BEQUEST HERITAGE
WINDFALL
LEGAL LICIT SOUND VALID LAWFUL
SQUARE JURIDIC RIGHTFUL
LEGATE ENVOY DEPUTY EXARCH
LEGATUS CONSULAR LEGATARY
PANDULPH
LEGEND EDDA MYTH POSY SAGA TALE
FABLE STORY TITLE THREAP CAPTION
CUTLINE HAGGADA
(MAP —) KEY
LEGENDARY FABLED FICTIOUS
LEGERDEMAIN PRESTIDIGITATION
LEGERDEMAIN HOST TERZO TERZIO
LEGISLATOR SOLON LAWGIVER
LAWMAKER
LEGISLATURE DIET COURT THING
LAGTING RIKSDAG LANDRATH RIGSRAAD
LEGITIMATE JUST TRUE VERY LEGAL
LEGIT LOYAL HONEST KINDLY KOSHER
LAWFUL REABLE SQUARE NATURAL
LEGITIME
LEGITIMATELY FAIRLY
LEISURE TIME TOOM VOID OTIUM
RESPITE VACANCY VACATION
LEISURELY SLOW SOODLY TIMELY
TOOMLY GRADUAL PICKTOOTH
LEMON DOG DUD CEDRA CHLOR
CEDRATE FAILURE KUMQUAT
LEMUR MAKI VARI AVAHI INDRI KOKAM
LORIS POTTO SIFAC ADAPID COBEGO
COLUGO GALAGO KUBONG MACACO
MAHOLI MONKEY SIFAKA APOSORO
MEERKAT NATTOCK PRIMATE SEMIAPE
TARSIER AMPONGUE BABAKOTO
MONGOOSE PRIMATAL TARSIOID
LEND OCKER PREST SECOND ADVANCE
IMPREST
(— AT INTEREST) GAVEL
(— ITSELF) ALLOY
LENGTH LUG DREE TOWT PITCH SCOPE
SIDTH COURSE EXTENT TOWGHT
FOOTAGE DISTANCE LEGITUDE SIDENESS
(— ATHWARTSHIP) ABURTON
(— OF BRIDGE) BAY
(— OF CABLE) SCOPE SHACKLE
(— OF CHAIN) SHOT
(— OF CLOTH) CUT
(— OF FIBER) STAPLE
(— OF FISHING LINE) CAST
(— OF GEAR TOOTH) FACE
(— OF HAIR) KNOT

(— OF HAIR IN FISHING LINE) IMP
(— OF LINE) LOYN
(— OF METAL) SHAPE
(— OF MOUTH) GAPE
(— OF NET) LEAD
(— OF PISTON STROKE) TRAVEL
(— OF ROPE) DRIFT SPOKE BRIDLE
COURSE STOPPER
(— OF SERVICE) STANDING
(— OF SHOEMAKER'S THREAD) END
(— OF THREAD) STITCH
(— OF TILE) GAUGE
(— OF TIMBER) BALK FLITCH
(— OF TRIP) GATE
(— OF WINDMILL ARM) WHIP
(— OF YARN) KNOT TAPE CHASE SKEIN
(— UNIT) FERMI
(AT FULL —) ALONG
(CONTINUOUS —) STRETCH
(FOCAL —) FOCUS
(UTMOST —) EXTREME
LENGTHEN EKE LONG DILATE EXPAND
EXTEND LENGTH AMPLIFY DISTEND
PRODUCE PROLONG STRETCH ELONGATE
INCREASE PROTRACT
(— BY INTERPOLATION) FARSE
LENGTHWISE ALONG ALENGTH
ENDLONG ENDWAYS ENDWISE VERTICAL
LENGTHY LONG LARGE PROLIX LONGFUL
EXTENDED
LENIENCY FAVOR MERCY LENITY
CHARITY CLEMENCY LENIENCE
LENIENT LAX EASY KIND MILD SOFT
FACILE GENTLE HUMANE LENITIVE
LENITY MERCY HUMANITY KINDNESS
LENITUDE
LENS EYE CROWN GLASS OPTIC FLASER
PEBBLE READER APLANAT BIFOCAL
CONCAVE CONTACT DOUBLET
ACHROMAT EYEGLASS EYEPIECE
HYPERGON LENTICLE LUNETTES
MENISCUS MAGNIFIER
LENT CAREME IMPREST
LEONORE (GUARDIAN OF —) ARISTE
(SISTER OF —) ISABELLE
LEOPARD PARD TIGER PARDAL WAGATI
LIBBARD PAINTER PANTHER
CATAMOUNT
(SNOW —) IRBIS OUNCE
LEPRECHAUN ELF SPRITE LURACAN
LEPROSY LEPRA MESEL SCALL ALPHOS
LAZARY MESELRY
LESION PIT GALL HIVE SORE CRATER
ESCHAR LEPRID ANTHRAX CHANCRE
FISSURE LEPROMA BEESTING ERUPTION
LEUKEMID TERTIARY

LESOTHO

CAPITAL: MASERU
COIN: RAND
FORMER NAME: BASUTOLAND
LANGUAGE: SOTHO SESOTHO
MOUNTAINS: MALUTI
PEOPLE: BASOTHO
RIVER: ORANGE CALEDON

TOWN: LERIBE MASHAI MORIJA PITSENG QUTHING SEKAKES MAFETENG
WATERFALL: MALETSUNYANE

LESS FEW MIN MENO FEWER MINOR LESSER SMALLER WANTING
LESSEN CUT EBB BATE DOCK EASE FAIK FRET KILL LESS SINK WANE ABATE BREAK LOWER MINCE SMALL TAPER BUFFER DEADEN DEJECT IMPAIR INLESS MINIFY MINISH NARROW REBATE REDUCE WEAKEN AMENUSE ASSUAGE CURTAIL DEPLETE DEPRESS ELEVATE LIGHTEN RELIEVE SHORTEN CONTRACT DECREASE DEROGATE DIMINISH DISCOUNT EMBEZZLE MITIGATE MODERATE PALLIATE
(— **FORCE**) GELD
(— **IN VALUE**) SHRINK CHEAPEN
(— **SENSITIVITY**) DULL
(— **STRENGTH**) WEAR
(— **TENSION**) RELAX
(— **VELOCITY**) DEADEN
LESSER PETIT MINUTE SMALLER INFERIOR
LESSON TAX LEAR TASK STUDY EXAMPLE LECTURE PRECEPT READING DOCUMENT LIRIPOOP
(**DIFFICULT** —) SOAK
(**TORAH** —) PARASHAH
LET. SET HIRE ALLOW LEASE LEAVE PERMIT SUFFER TENANT
(— **BAIT BOB**) DIB
(— **BECOME KNOWN**) SPILL
(— **BURN**) BISHOP
(— **CONTINUE**) DRILL
(— **DOWN**) VAIL DEMIT DIMIT LOWER STOOP STRIKE SUBMIT
(— **DOWN ROCK FACE**) ABSEIL
(— **FALL**) DROP VAIL AVALE AWALE DEPOSE
(— **FLY**) PEG BOLT FIRE WING
(— **GO**) DROP FAIK QUIT DEMIT BILEVE DEMISE DISMIT UNHAND DISCARD UNSEIZE
(— **HIM TAKE**) SUM
(— **IN**) IMMIT INLET IMMISS ADHIBIT
(— **IT BE REPEATED**) REPET
(— **IT STAND**) STET
(— **KNOW**) ACQUAINT
(— **LAND**) GAVEL
(— **LOOSE**) FREE SLIP LIBERATE
(— **OUT**) BLAB TEAM WAGE BREAK SPILL ARRENT BROACH
(— **SLIP**) BALK BAULK CHECK FOREGO
LETHAL FATAL DEADLY MORTAL
LETHARGIC INERT DROWSY SLEEPY TORPID DORMANT PASSIVE COMATOSE COMATOUS SLUGGISH SLUMBROUS
LETHARGY COMA SLOTH STUPOR TORPOR SLUMBER HEBETUDE INACTION SOPITION
LETTER EF EL EM EN EX HE PE AIN AYN BEE CEE CHI DAK DEE ESS ETA GEE HET JAY KAY LIL MEM NUN PEE SIN TAV TAW TEE VEE WAW YOD YOK ZED ZEE ALEF

ALIF AYIN BETA BETH BILL DEAD HETH IOTA KAPH RESH SHIN SORT TETH YODH YOGH AITCH ALEPH BLIND CAPON DELTA DEMIT FAVOR GAMMA GIMEL GRAPH KAPPA KNOWN KOPPA SADHE SIGMA STAVE STIFF ZAYIN ACCENT ADVICE ANSWER CADJAN CHARTA COCKUP DALETH FAVVER ITALIC LAMBDA LAMEDH MEDIAL SAMEKH SCRIPT SIGLUM SUNNUD SYMBOL VERSAL CODICIL CONTROL DIGAMMA DIPLOMA EPISTLE EPSILON KAREETA MISSIVE SPECIAL AEROGRAM ASCENDER ENCYCLIC MONITORY NUNDINAL PASTORAL
(— **OF DEFIANCE**) CARTEL
(— **OF PERMISSION**) EXEAT
(—**S DIMISSORY**) APOSTOLI
(—**S OF MARQUE**) MART
(**ANGLO-SAXON** —) EDH ETH THORN
(**AUTHORIZING** —) BREVE
(**BEGGING** —) SCREEVE
(**BLACK** —) GOTHIC
(**BREAD AND BUTTER** —} COLLINS
(**CAPITAL** —) CAP UNCIAL CAPITAL FACTOTUM MAJUSCULE
(**FRIENDLY** —) SCREED
(**INITIAL** —) BLOOMER
(**LOVE** —) POULET
(**LOWERCASE** —) MINISCULE
(**OBSOLETE** —) EPISEMON
(**OFFICIAL** —) BRIEF
(**PAPAL** —) BULL TOME BREVE ENCYCLIC
(**PRIVATE** —) BOOK
(**SHORT** —) CHIT LINE NOTE BILLET LETTERET
(**SILENT** —} MUTE
(**SMUGGLED** —) KITE
(**SUBSCRIPT** —) SUBFIX
(**WORD** —) LOGOGRAM
LETTUCE COS BIBB GRASS SALAD KARPAS SALLET ICEBERG ROMAINE FIREWEED MILKWEED
LEUKEMIA CHLOROMA LEUKOSIS
LEVANT EASTERN WORMSEED
LEVEE DIKE WALL WEIR DURBAR STOPBANK
LEVEL BONE EVEN FAIR FLAT GLAD LUTE PLAT RAZE SHIM VIAL COUCH EQUAL FLUSH GRADE PLAIN PLANE POINT SLICK SOLID CHARGE DOUBLE EVENLY FIELDY NIVEAU SLIGHT SMOOTH STRIKE TUNNEL FLATTEN GALLERY GANGWAY REGULAR DEMOLISH LEVELLER SUBGRADE
(— **A RAFTER**) EDGE
(— **AFTER PLOWING**) BUSH
(— **AND SCATTER**) GELD
(— **OF SOCIETY**) STRATUM
(— **OF STAGE**) STUDY
(— **OFF**) HAMMER BULLDOZE
(**COMMON** —) PAR
(**ENERGY** —) SINGLET
(**EYE** —) EYELINE
(**HIGHER** —**S**) BRASS
(**HIGHEST** —) SUMMIT
(**LOWEST** —) FLOOR BOTTOM HARDPAN

(MINING —) KIP HEAD GALLERY GANGWAY
(STRATIGRAPHIC —) HORIZON
(TOP —) HIGH CEILING
LEVER KEY PRY BEAM GAUL HOOK HORN
SWAY TREE BRAKE FLAIL FLIRT HELVE
PEDAL PINCH PLUTO PRIZE SPOON
STANG STANK SWIPE THROW CLUTCH
COUPER DETENT FEELER HAMMER
HEAVER HOPPER LOWDER PORTER
ROCKER TAPPET TILLER BALANCE
POINTER RAMHEAD SHIPPER TREADLE
TRIGGER TUMBLER GAVELOCK SELECTOR
THROTTLE
(— FOR CROSSBOW) GAFFLE GARROT
(— FOR TURNING RUDDER) HELM
TILLER
(— IN KNITTING MACHINE) JACK
(— IN TIMEPIECE) PALLET
(— LIKE CANTHOOK) PEAVY
(— OF GIN) START
(GEARSHIFT —) STICK
(ORGAN —) BACKFALL
(SPINNING —) BOOTLEG
(SPOKELIKE —) SWINGLE
(THROTTLE —) GUN
(WEAVING —) LAM SWELL BINDER
TIPPLER
LEVI (FATHER OF —) JACOB ALPHAEUS
(MOTHER OF —) LEAH
(SON OF —) KOHATH MERARI GERSHON
LEVITY FOLLY HUMOR GAIETY
WHIFFLERY
LEVY CUT TAX CESS MISE REAR LEVEL
RAISE ASSESS EXTEND EXTENT IMPOSE
IMPOST UPTAKE IMPRESS TRIBUTE
DISTRAIN DISTRESS SHIPPAGE
(— A TAX) GELD GELT TAIL STENT
(— DISTRESS) DRIVE
(IRISH —) MART
LEWD NICE BAWDY FOLLY PRIME RANDY
HARLOT IMPURE LACHES LUBRIC RAKISH
WANTON HIRCINE LEERING LUSTFUL
OBSCENE RAMMISH RIGGISH SCARLET
SENSUAL WHORISH PRURIENT SLUTTISH
UNCHASTE SALACIOUS
LEWDNESS FOLLY RAKERY LECHERY
HARLOTRY PUTANISM LUBRICITY
SCULDUDDERY
LEXICON CALEPIN WORDBOOK
LIABILITY DEBT DEBIT CHARGE TRIBUTE
OBLIGATION
LIABLE APT ABLE OPEN GUILTY EXPOSED
OBVIOUS ONEROUS SUBJECT AMENABLE
INCIDENT
LIAISON BOND AFFAIR AFFAIRE LINKING
INTIMACY INTRIGUE
LIAR LEAR ANANIAS BOUNCER CRACKER
CRAMMER PROCTOR WARLOCK
WERNARD FABULIST
LIBEL DEFAME MALIGN VILIFY SLANDER
LIBELOUS FAMOUS SCANDALOUS
LIBERAL FAIR FREE GOOD OPEN WHIG
BROAD FRANK LARGE NOBLE SOLUTE
JANNOCK PROFUSE ADVANCED
CATHOLIC GENEROUS HANDSOME
LARGEOUS PRODIGAL SEPARATE
MUNIFICENT

(CANADIAN —) GRIT
(NOT —) CHARY SPARE
LIBERATE FREE QUIT FRITH REMIT
UNGYVE UNWRAP DELIVER MANUMIT
RELEASE UNSLAVE UNFETTER UNTHRALL
LIBERATION FREEDOM RELEASE
DELIVERY KAIVALYA DISCHARGE

LIBERIA

CAPITAL: MONROVIA
HILLS: BOMI
MEASURE: KUBA
MOUNTAIN: UNI NIETE NIMBA WUTIVI
MOUNTAINS: BONG SATRO
PEOPLE: GI KRU KWA VAI VEI GOLA KROO
KROU TOMA BASSA GIBBI GISSI GREBO
KPELLE KROOBY KRUMAN KROOBOY
MANDINGO
RIVER: CESS LOFA MANO LOFFA MANNA
MORRO CESTOS DOUOBE STJOHN
STPAUL CAVALLY SANPEDRO
TOWN: GANTA GRIBO REBBO HARPER
ZORZOR NANAKRU TAPPITA BUCHANAN
MARSHALL SASSTOWN

LIBERTINE ROUE PUNKER PANURGE
STRIKER LOTHARIO LOVELACE STRINGER
LIBERTY MAY SOC EASE LARGE LEAVE
SCOPE ACCESS SCOUTH STREET
FREEDOM LARGESS LICENSE WITHGANG
(— OF ACTION) PLAY SWING
(— OF ENTRANCE) INGRESS
(— OF GOING OUT) ISH
(— OF TURNING PIGS INTO FIELDS)
SHACK
(— TO BUY AND SELL) TOLL
(— TO HUNT) CHASE
(PARTIAL — OF HAWK) HACK
(SEXUAL —) INTIMACY
(UNDUE —) HEAD
LIBRARY AMBRY BIBLE MUSEUM
BHANDAR BOOKERY ATHENEUM

LIBYA

CAPITAL: BENGASI BENGAZI TRIPOLI
COIN: DIRHAM
DESERT: FEZZAN MURZUK MURZUCH
GULF: SIDRA SIRTE
MEASURE: SAA BOZZE DONUM JABIA
TEMAN BARILE MISURA MATTARO
MOUNTAIN: BETTE
OASIS: JALO KUFRA SEBHA FEZZAN
GIOFRA TAZERBO GIARABUB
SEAPORT: HOMS DERNA SIDRI TOBRUK
BENGAZI
TOWN: BRAK DERJ HOMS BARKA DERNA
SEBHA SIDRI UBARI ZAWIA ELMARJ
GARIAN MURZUQ REMADA TOBRUK
MISURATA
WEIGHT: KELE UCKIA GORRAF TERMINO
KHAROUBA

LICENSE CHOP GALE HEAD EXEAT LEAVE SWING BANDON CAROON FIRMAN INDULT PATENT PERMIT READER TICKET CERTIFY CROTTLE FACULTY FREEDOM INDULTO LIBERTY LICENCE PLACARD WARRANT ESCAMBIO IMMUNITY MORTMAIN PASSPORT TEZKIRAH
(— FOR CART) CAROOME
(PEDDLER'S —) SLANG
LICENTIOUS GAY LAX FREE LEWD WILD FRANK LARGE LOOSE FILTHY RIBALD UNRULY WANTON CYPRIAN FLESHLY IMMORAL LAWLESS LIBERAL UNYOKED
LICIT LEGAL LAWFUL LEEFUL
LICK LAP LIKE SUCK MOUTH SLAKE CONQUER
LICORICE POMFRET SWEETROOT
LID DIP BRED DECK TYMP COVER BRIDLE EYELID POTLID CLAPPER CLICKET CLOSURE SCUTTLE SHUTTER COVERCLE OPERCULUM
LIE FIB GAB KIP LAY LIG LIN SIT YED CRAM FLAW FLIGG LIGG REST RIDE WHID DEVIL DWELL FABLE FEIGN LEASE STAND STORY FITTEN PALTER RAPPER RESIDE SPRAWL VANITY YANKER BOUNCER CONSIST CRACKER CRAMMER CRUMPER FALSITY GRABBLE LEASING PLUMPER TWISTER UNTRUTH WHACKER WHISKER WHOPPER MENDACITY TARADIDDLE PREVARICATE
(— ALONGSIDE) ACCOST
(— AROUND) COMPASS
(— AT ANCHOR) HOVE
(— AT FULL LENGTH) STRETCH
(— CONCEALED) DARKLE
(— CONTIGUOUS) CONFINE
(— DORMANT) SLEEP
(— DOWN) LEAN COUCH CHARGE
(— FLAT ON BELLY) GROVEL
(— HEAD TO WIND) TRY
(— HIDDEN) LURK MICHE TAPPISH
(— IN AMBUSH) HUGGER
(— IN BED) KIP THOKE
(— IN WAIT) AWAIT LOWER AMBUSH FORELAY
(— IN WATER) DOUSE DROWN
(— LOW) TAPPICE
(— NEXT TO) ADJOIN
(— OPPOSITE TO) SUBTEND
(— OVER) COVER
(— PRONE) GROVEL GRABBLE
(— PROSTRATE) STREEK
(— QUIET) SNUDGE
(— SNUG) CUDDLE
(— UNEVENLY) SAG
(— WITH SAILS FURLED) HULL
(BIG —) CAULKER
(IMPUDENT —) BOUNCE
(MONSTROUS —) STRAMMER

LIECHTENSTEIN
CAPITAL: VADUZ
CASTLE: GUTEMBURG
MOUNTAIN: RHATIKON

RIVER: RHINE SAMINA
ROMAN NAME: RHAETIA
TOWN: HAAG BALZER SCHAAN NENDELN

LIED BALLAD
LIEUTENANT LUFF ZANY LOUEY JAYGEE KEHAYA CAIMAKAM QAIMAQAM TENIENTE WOODVILE
LIFE IT VIE ZOE HIDE JIVA PUFF SNAP TUCK VALE ANIMA BEING BLOOD DEMON HEART LIFER QUICK SWEAT BIOSIS BREATH CANDLE COURSE ENERGY SPIRIT SPRITE LIFELET LIFEWAY VITALITY VIVACITY
(— AFTER DEATH) FUTURITY
(— IN HEAVEN) GLORY
(— IN SOCIETY) SAMSARA
(— OF FURNACE LINING) CAMPAIGN
(— OF THE SEA) HALIBIOS
(ACADEMIC —) ACADEMIA
(ANIMAL —) FLESH
(ANIMAL AND PLANT —) BIOS BIOTA BIOLOGY EDAPHON
(CLOISTERED —) VEIL
(INTELLECTUAL —) JIVATMA
(MONASTIC —) CLOISTER
(MORAL —) DAENA
(MOSS —) BRYOLOGY
(PLANT —) FLORA BOTANY
(ROBUST —) JUICE
(SINGLE —) CELIBACY
(TERRESTRIAL —) GEOBIOS
(WAY OF —) BAG SCENE
(WITHOUT —) AZOIC
LIFELESS ARID DEAD DULL FLAT AMORT HEAVY INERT VAPID ANEMIC TORPID SAPLESS DESOLATE GRIPLESS INACTIVE
(PREF.) ABIO
LIFELIKE VIVE QUICK EIDETIC NATURAL ANIMATED SPEAKING
LIFE PRESERVER FLOAT NEDDY
LIFETIME AGE DAY WORLD LIVING LIFEDAY DURATION LIFELONG
LIFE WITH FATHER (AUTHOR OF —) DAY
(CHARACTER IN —) DELIA GULICK CLARENCE MARGARET
LIFT WIN BOOM BUOY CAST COCK HEFT JACK REAR TOSS WEVE ARSIS BOOST BREAK ELATE HEAVE HITCH HOICK HOIST HOOSH MOUNT PRESS RAISE SPOUT STEAL WEIGH BUCKET CLEECH SNATCH ELEVATE ENHANCE HEELTAP NAUNTLE BOOKLIFT CHAIRWAY ELEVATOR LEVITATE
(— HAT) DOFF
(— IN VEHICLE) SETDOWN
(— OF WAVE) SCEND
(— ONESELF) SOAR
(— QUICKLY) PERK
(— UP) HOVE CRANE ERECT EXALT EXTOL HORSE WEIGH ADVANCE ELEVATE NAUNTLE
(— WITH BLOCK AND TACKLE) BOUSE

LIFTER GAGGER SERVER HOISTER
HOISTMAN
LIGAMENT BAND BOND ARTERY FRENUM
PAXWAX STRING ZONULE ARMILLA
LIGATURE
LIGHT DAY GAY HAP LAW SHY SUN AIRY
EASY FAIR FALL FINE FIRE FLIT FLUX
GLIM LAMP LEET LUNT MILD SLUT SOFT
BAVIN BLAZE CORKY FILMY FLAME
FLEET FUFFY LEGER LOUGH MERRY
PITCH QUICK SHEER SPILL WHITE
BEACON BRIGHT CHAFFY FLOATY
FLOSSY FLUFFY FROTHY GENTLE HAPPEN
KINDLE LUSTER LUSTRE MARKER PASTEL
PHAROS SIGNAL SLUSHY STINGY SUTTLE
VOLAGE BENGOLA BUOYANT CRESSET
FRAGILE GLITTER SFOGATO SMITHER
SUMMERY TORTAYS TRIVIAL UNGRAVE
BACKFIRE DAYLIGHT DELICATE
DIAPHANE ELECTRIC EXPEDITE
FEATHERY GASLIGHT GOSSAMER
LEGGIERO LUMINARY PALOUSER
SUNLIGHT SUNSHINE
(— AND BRILLIANT) LAMBENT
(— AND FIRE ON HORSE'S MANE)
HAG
(— AND FREE) FLYAWAY
(— AND QUICK) VOLANT
(— CANDLES) TOLLY
(— FROM NIGHT SKY) AIRGLOW
(— IN WINDOW) LANCET
(— OF MORNING) AURORA
(— ON TV SCREEN) SNOW
(— UP) FLASH GLOZE ILLUME RELUME
GLORIFY
(— UPON) STRIKE
(BRIGHT —) GLARE GLEAM
(BURST OF —) FLASH
(CIRCLE OF —) HALO NIMBUS
(FAINT —) GLIMMER SCARROW
(FEEBLE —) TAPER GLIMMER
(FITFUL —) SHIMMER
(HARBOR —) BUG
(INDICATOR —) BEZEL
(INNER —) SEED
(NEBULOUS —) CHEVELURE
(NEW —) SEPARATE
(NIGHT —) MORTAR
(PARKING —S) DIMMERS
(REFLECTED —) SKYME
(SHIP'S —) FANAL
(SMALL —) TAPER
(TRAFFIC —) BLINKER
(WAVERING —) FLICKER
LIGHTEN ALAY CLEAR LEVIN LIGHT RAISE
ALLEGE BLEACH ENCLEAR FOULDRE
MOLLIFY SWEETEN THUNDER LEVIGATE
LIGHTER KEEL SCOW ACCON BARGE
CASCO PRAAM WHERRY DROGHER
GABBARD GONDOLA PONTOON
CHOPBOAT
LIGHT-HEADED IDLE BARMY LIGHT
LIVELY CARRIED GLAIKET SKITTISH
LIGHT-HEARTED GAY GLAD GIDDY
BUOYANT WINSOME CAREFREE
DEBONAIR VOLATILE
LIGHTHEARTEDNESS BUOYANCY

LIGHTHOUSE FANAL LIGHT MINAR
BEACON PHAROS LANTERN
LIGHTNESS CHEER VALUE GAIETY
LEVITY AIRINESS BUOYANCY LEGERETE
LEGERITY
(— OF MOVEMENT) BALLON
LIGHTNING BOLT FIRE LAIT LEVIN
FULMEN METEOR FOULDRE SULPHUR
THUNDER FIREBALL FIREBOLT WILDFIRE
LIKE AS DIG DOTE LIST LOVE ALIKE ENJOY
EQUAL FANCY SAVOR TASTE ADMIRE
AFFECT BELIKE LIKELY MATTER PLEASE
SEMBLE SIMILE CONCEIT SIMILAR
SEMBLANT SUITABLE SEMBLABLE
(— A GLAND) ADEMOSE ADENOUS
(— BETTER) PREFER
(— HAIR) CRINITE
(VERY —) SIAMESE
LIKELIHOOD APTNESS
LIKELY APT FAIR LIKE READY LIABLE
PROOFY SEEMLY GRADELY SMITTLE
APPARENT FEASIBLE POSSIBLE
PROBABLE PROSPECTIVE
(MOST —) BELIKE
LIKEN EVEN LIKE REMENE SEMBLE
COMPARE ASSEMBLE CREDIBLE
RESEMBLE SIMILIZE
LIKENESS DAP BLEE ICON IDOL MAKE
SECT BLUSH DUMMY GLIFF IMAGE
MORAL SHAPE EFFIGY FIGURE STATUE
ANALOGY KINSHIP PATTERN PICTURE
RETRAIT EQUALITY HOMOLOGY
PARALLEL PORTRAIT SEMBLANCE
SIMILARITY
(PERFECT —) SPIT
LIKEWISE EKE TOO ALSO ITEM EITHER
EQUALLY LIKEWAYS
(— NOT) NOR
LIKING GOO GRA PAY GOUT GUST LIKE
LIST LUST FANCY FLAIR GUSTO HEART
SHINE SKILL SMACK TASTE THEAT
SWALLOW AFFINITY APPETITE
FONDNESS PENCHANT
(ECCENTRIC —) FOIBLE
LILIOM (AUTHOR OF —) MOLNAR
(CHARACTER IN —) WOLF JULIE
MARIE FICSUR LILIOM LOUISE MUSKAT
LINZMAN HOLLUNDER
LILY ALOE IXIA KELP SEGO AZTEC CALLA
CLOTE AUGUST LILIUM VALLEY COCUISA
MONOCOT ASPHODEL LILYWORT
MARTAGON NENUPHAR
(AFRICAN —) AGAPANTHUS
(CLIMBING —) GLORIOSA
(PALM —) TI
(SEA —) CRINOID
(WATER —) CANDOCK CAMALOTE
LILY OF THE VALLEY LILIUM MUGUET
LILYWORT SHINLEAF
LIMB ARM LEG CLAW FOOT KNOT LITH
TRAM WING ARTUS BOUGH SPALD
SPAUL SWAMP BRANCH MEMBER
PODITE FEATURE FLIPPER FORCEPS
PLEOPOD NECTOPOD
(PREF.) MEL
LIMBER BAIN FLIP LIMP LUSH LINGY
LITHE LISSOM SEMMIT SUPPLE SWANKY

BRUSHER BRUTTER KNOTTER LIMMOCK
PLIABLE FLEXIBLE FLIPPANT
LIME CALX LIMA CEDRA CEDRAT CHUNAM
CITRON FUSTIC
(— IN BRICK) BOND
(WILD —) COLIMA
LIMESTONE CAM HUM CALP CAUK
CAUM LIAS MALM POROS ROACH
CLUNCH KUNKUR OOLITE CIPOLIN
SCAGLIA PISOLITE TRAVERTINE
(DECOMPOSED —) ROTTENSTONE
LIMIT END FIX BIND BUTT FINE HOLD LINE
LIST MARK MERE PALE TAIL BLOCK
BOUND COAST GAUGE HEDGE SCANT
STENT STINT VERGE BORDER BOURNE
DEFINE EFFLUX EXTENT FINISH FINITE
HAMPER LENGTH MODIFY NARROW
PALING SCRIMP TROPIC UPSHOT
ASTRICT CLOSURE COMPASS CONFINE
CONTENT HORIZON MAXIMUM MEASURE
OUTSIDE BOUNDARY CONTRACT
DEADLINE IMPRISON LIMINARY LIMITATE
OUTGOING OUTREACH RESTRAIN
RESTRICT SOLSTICE TERMINUS
PARAMETER
(— EFFECT) ALLAY
(— IN A FOREST) BAIL
(— MOTION) HOLD
(— OF STATUTE) PURVIEW
(— OF VISION AT SEA) KENNING
(EXTREME —) HEIGHT
(LOWER —) FLOOR
(UPPER —) CEILING
(UTTER —) EXTREME
LIMITATION TAIL FRAME STINT DENIAL
CLOTURE RESERVE
LIMITED MILD TAIL BORNE BRIEF SHORT
SMALL FINITE NARROW STINTY STRAIT
BOUNDED SPECIAL CONFINED DEFINITE
LIMITARY PAROCHIAL SECTARIAN
MEASURABLE PROVINCIAL RESTRICTED
LIMOUSINE BERLIN SALOON SUBURBAN
LIMP HIP HOP GIMP HALT HIMP
HOIT SOFT THIN HENCH HILCH HITCH
LINGY LOOSE LOPPY SLAMP STILT
FLABBY FLIMSY HAMBLE HIRPLE HOBBLE
LENNOW LIMBER LIMPSY FLACCID
LIMMOCK SHAFFLE UNSMART DRAGGLED
DROOPING
LIMPID PURE CLEAR LUCID BRIGHT
CRYSTAL PELLUCID
LINE BAR BOX RAY ROW TAW BOFF CASE
CEIL COLA CRIB DASH FACE FILE GAME
GAPE LACE LARD LATH LING MAIN MARK
RACE RANK RULE STOP TAUM WHIP
AGONE FAINT FEINT FLEET HATCH LIGNE
LINEA METER RANGE SCORE STRIA
TOUCH TRAIL TRAIN TWIST
BINDER CABURN CEVIAN CREASE
DEGREE DOUBLE EARING GASKET
ISOBAR ISOHEL ISOPAG ISOTAC METIER
NETTLE SECANT SECOND SPRING STRIPE
AZIMUTH BABBITT CATLINE CONTOUR
CREANCE ENVELOP GUNLINE HIPLINE
ISOCHOR ISOGRAM ISOTOME KNITTLE
MARLINE NACARAT SCRATCH WINDROW
BALKLINE BISECTOR BOUNDARY

BUSINESS CHAMPAIN DATELINE
DEADLINE DIAGONAL DIAMETER
DRAGLINE DRUMLINE FISHBACK
GANTLINE GEODESIC GIRTLINE HAIRLINE
HANDLINE HEXAPODY ISOGLOSS
ISOGONIC ISOPHANE ISOPHENE
ISOPLERE ISOTHERE ISOTHERM
LANDWIRE LIFELINE MARTINET
SLIPBAND STRINGER SUBCLONE
SUBSTILE SUBSTYLE UPSTROKE
(— AROUND STAMP) FRAME
(— AS CENTER FOR REVOLVING)
AXIS
— HEARTH) FIX FETTLE
(— IN GLASS) STRING
(— IN HAT) HEADLINE
(— MINESHAFT) TUB
(— OF ACTION) LAY
(— OF BATTLE) FRONT
(— OF BUSINESS) WAY
(— OF CELLS) ANNULUS
(— OF CLIFFS) SCARP BREAKS
(— OF COLOR) SLASH STREAK
(— OF DANCERS) CHAIN
(— OF DESCENT) SIDE STEM STIRP
STOCK PHYLUM STRAIN ANCESTRY
BREEDING
(— OF DETERMINANT) COLUMN
(— OF DEVELOPMENT) STREET
(— OF DEVOLUTION) ENTAIL
(— OF FIBERS) CHRYSAL
(— OF FIRE HOSE) LEAD
(— OF FLOTATION) BEARINGS
(— OF FORTIFICATION) LIMES
ENCEINTE
(— OF HAY) WAKE WALLOW
(— OF HEALTH) HEPATICA
(— OF HIGH TIDE) LANDWASH
(— OF HOUSES) BLOCK
(— OF INTERSECTION) GROIN
BUTTOCK
(— OF JUNCTION) MEET SEAM
(— OF MERCHANDISE) NAMEPLATE
(— OF MERCURY) HEPATICA
(— OF PERSONS) QUEUE CORDON
STICKLE
(— OF PORES) HATCHING
(— OF SOLDIERS) RAY FILE RANK
WAVE CORDON
(— OF STITCHING) BASTING
(— OF TIMBERS) BOOM STOCKADE
(— OF TREES) SCREEN
(— OF TYPE) SLUG KICKER
(— OF UNION) SUTURE
(— ON A LETTER) SERIF
(— ON BOOK COVER) BAND
(— ON COAT) GORGE
(— ON DOLPHIN) STOP
(— ON HIGHWAY) BARRIER
(— THAT CUTS ANOTHER) SECANT
(— TO BIND CABLES) CABURN
(— TO FASTEN SAIL) EARING GASKET
(— TO RAISE FLAG) LANIARD LANYARD
(— TO START RACE) TRIG
(— TOUCHING ARC) TANGENT
(— UP) LAY
(— WITH BRICKS) GINGE

(— WITH PANELLING) WAINSCOT
(— WITH STONES) STEEN STEYN
(— WITH TIMBER) CRIB
(ANCHOR —) RODING
(BEARING —) CUT
(BOUNDARY —) MERE FENCE BORDER ISOGLOSS
(BOUNDING —) SIDE BOUNDARY PERIMETER
(BRIEF —) ITEM
(COASTAL —) SEAMARK
(CONNECTING —) LIGATURE
(CONTINUOUS —) STRETCH
(CURVED —) ARC SLUR SWEEP
(DEMARCATION —) BOMBLINE
(DIAGONAL —) BIAS
(DIVIDING —) EDGE MIDRIB DIVISION FRONTIER
(ELECTRIC —) HIGHLINE
(FACIAL —) TRAIT
(FINISHING —) TAPE WIRE
(FISHING —) TOME TROT FLEET SNELL SNOOD LEADER LEDGER NORSEL BACKING BOULTER OUTLINE SPILLER SPILLET TRIMMER BLOWLINE CORKLINE FISHLINE SNAGLINE TROTLINE
(HORIZONTAL —) LEVEL
(INCLINED —) CANT
(LONGITUDINAL —) MERIDIAN
(MEDIAN —) RAPHE
(METRICAL —) EIGHT STAFF STICH DIMETER SAPPHIC STICHOS MONOMETER OCTAMETER PENTAMETER
(MINESHAFT —) BRATTICE
(MUSICAL —) ACCOLADE
(NAUTICAL —) EARING LACING GESWARP MARLINE PAINTER RATLINE DOWNHAUL MESSENGEI
(ONE-TENTH OF —) GRY
(PERPENDICULAR —) CATHETUS
(PLOTTED —) ADIABAT
(RADIATING —) BEAM
(RAILROAD —) STEM STUB
(RAISED —) RIDGE
(SPECTRUM —) GHOST DOUBLET SINGLET TRIPLET MULTIPLET
(STARTING —) SCRATCH
(STRAIGHT —) CHORD BEELINE STRAIGHT
(SUPPLY —) AIRLIFT UMBILICAL
(SURVEYING —) WAD BASE CHAIN
(THEATRICAL —S) FAT
(TOW —) CORDELLE
(TRANSPORTATION —) FEEDER CARRIER
(WAVY —) SQUIGGLE
(ZIGZAG —) DANCETTE
(42 —S) LENGTH
LINEN LIN BUCK LAWN CRASH IRISH TOILE BARRAS DAMASK DIAPER RAINES SENDAL BATISTE DORNICK HOLLAND LOCKRAM TABLING BARANDOS OSNABURG PLATILLA
(— FOR SHIRTS) SARKING
(— TO COVER CHALICE) PALL
(CHINESE —) KOMPOW
(COARSE —) HARN BARRAS

(FINE —) LAKE LAWN BYSSUS DAMASK DIAPER RAINES
(HOUSEHOLD —) NAPERY TABLING
(SCRAPED —) LINT
(SPANISH —) CREA
LINER SHIP BASKET SCRIBER STEAMER
LINGER LAG HANG HOVE LING STAY CLING DALLY DELAY DEMUR DWELL HAUNT HOVER PAUSE TARRY DRETCH HANKER LOITER TAIGLE TARROW DRINGLE
LINGERIE FRILLIES PRETTIES
LINGERING SLOW DELAY MOROSE TARDANT DRAGGING
LINGO BAT CANT JARGON LINGUA PATTER DIALECT
LINGUISTICS GRAMMAR PHILOLOGY
LINING FUR BACK COAT BAIZE BRASS FACING PANNEL BABBITT BUSHING CEILING FURRING FURRURE THIMBLE TINNING TUBBING CLEADING DOUBLING DOUBLURE FIREBACK SHEETING UNDERLAY WAINSCOT PERCALINE
(— FOR WELL) STEENING
(— OF BEARING) JEWEL
(— OF CYLINDER) BUSH
(— OF FURNACE) BASQUE FIREBACK
(— OF HAT) TIP
(— OF SMELTING LADLE) SCULL
(MINESHAFT —) CRIB
(WOODEN —) LAG BRATTICE
LINK JAR TIE TOW JOIN KNIT LUNT SHUT YOKE COMMA NEXUS COPULA COUPLE FASTEN FETTER TOUGHT CODETTA CONNECT COUPLER ENCHAIN INVOLVE LIAISON SHACKLE CATENATE IDENTIFY VINCULUM COLLIGATE
(— ARMS) CLEEK
(— IN NETWORK) LEG
(COMPOUND —) SWIVEL
(WOODEN —) LAG
LINTEL CAP CLAVY HANCE CLAVEL DARNER SUMMER SQUINCH TRANSOM BRESSUMMER
LION CAT LLEW MORNE SHEDU SIMBA LIONEL LIONET LEOPARD
(MOUNTAIN —) PUMA COUGAR
LIP BLOB EDGE MASK PUSS APRON CHOPS GROIN MOUTH SPOUT TUTEL LABIUM LABRUM ROUTER CHILOMA LABELLUM UNDERLIP
— DISEASE) PERLECHE
— OF BELL) SKIRT
(— OF COROLLA) GALEA
(— OF FLOWER) HELM
(— OF ORCHID) SLIPPER
(— OF PITCHER) BEAK
(—S OF MOOSE) MUFFLE
(FLAT —) APRON
(LOWER —) JIB FIPPLE
LIQUEFY RUN FUSE MELT RELENT LIQUATE DISSOLVE ELIQUATE
LIQUEUR EAU OUZO RAKI AURUM CREM... NOYAU CHASSE GENEPI KUMMEL PASTIS PERNOD RACKEE STREGA ANESONE CORDIAL CURACAO PERSICO RATAFIA RATIFIA ABSINTHE ADVOCAAT

ALKERMES ANGELICA ANISETTE
CALVADOS MANDARIN PRUNELLE
VESPETRO MARASCHINO BENEDICTINE
LIQUID AQUA BLASH DRINK FLUID LEACH
MOIST ACETAL FLUENT FURANE
AEROSOL BUCKING CINEOLE EYEWASH
FLOWAGE VINASSE BLACKING EFFLUENT
EFFUSION EXCITANT FURFURAN
LEACHATE LIBATION SOLUTION
(— AFTER SALT CRYSTALLIZATION)
BITTERN
(— IN CELL) EXCITANT
(ACID-RESISTANT —) GROUND
(COLORING —) HENNA
(COOKING —) BREE BROO BROTH
STOCK
(DISABLING —) MACE
(DISTILLED —) SPIRIT
(FILTHY —) ADDLE
(REFUSE —) SCOURAGE
(SIZING —) GLAIK
(STERILIZED —) JOHNIN
(STINKING —) CACODYL
(SYRUPY —) HONEY
(TANNING —) LIME
(THICK —) DOPE SYRUP
(THICK, STICKY —) GLOP
(VISCOUS —) TAR SCHRADAN
(VOLATILE —) ETHER ALCOHOL
DILUENT LIGROIN
(WEAK —) BLASH SLIPSLOP
LIQUOR GAS LAP OKE PAD POT RUM SUP
TAP WET BREE FIRE FIZZ GEAR PURL
SUCK SWIG TIFF BOGUS CEBUR DRINK
GLASS JUICE KEFIR NAPPY PISCO SAUCE
SHRAB SHRUB SICER SKINK STICK
BOTTLE CASSIS CHICHA DIDDLE FOGRAM
FUDDLE GATTER GENEVA HYDROL
KIRSCH MASTIC MESCAL POTTLE
ROTGUT TIPPLE WHISKY BRACKET
BRAGGET GROCERY PHLEGMA SPUNKIE
SUCTION TAPLASH TEQUILA WHISKEY
ABSINTHE BRAGWORT EYEWATER
HYDROMEL MEDICINE OKOLEHAO
POTATION RUMBOOZE FIREWATER
(— FROM MUST) ARROPE
(— FROM PEARS) PERRY
(— FROM WOOL-SCOURING) SUDS
(— MIXED WITH WINE) DOCTOR
(— TAKEN IN SODA WATER) CINDER
(ACID —) VERJUICE
(ALCOHOLIC —) GIN HOOCH ARRACK
BRANDY SAMSHU AQUAVIT BITTERS
SNOOTFUL
(BITTER —) TIRE
(CHEAP —) SMOKE
(CRAB APPLE —) WHERRY
(DISTILLED —) DEW SOTOL GRAPPA
PHLEGM SCHNAPPS
(DRUGGED —) HOCUS
(HARD —) BOOZE
(INTOXICATING —) GROG LOAD LUSH
TAPE BUDGE GUZZLE KUMISS HASHISH
MOONSHINE
(MALT —) ALE BUB BEER STOUT ENTIRE
PORTER STINGO
(MOTHER —) HYDROL BITTERN

(POT —) BREWIS
(RICE —) SAMSHU
(SPIRITUOUS —) DEW GROG MOBBY
STRUNT WAIPIRO KAOLIANG
(STRAIGHT —) SHORT
(STRONG —) RUG TUBA VINO HOGAN
RUMBO STINGO
(TAN —) OOZE
(TANNING —) LAYAWAY TAILING
(WATERED —) BLASH
(WEAK —) BULL SLIPSLOP
LISSOME LITHE LIMBER NIMBLE SUPPLE
SVELTE FLEXIBLE
LIST TIP BILL FILE HEEL NOTE POLL ROLL
ROON ROTA SWAG BRIEF GISTS INDEX
PANEL SCORE SCRIP SCROW AGENDA
CENSUS COLUMN DETAIL DOCKET
ERRATA HUDDLE LEGEND PURREL
RAGGER RAGMAN RECORD ROSTER
SCREED SCROLL SERIES CATALOG
CITATOR COMPILE DIPTYCH ITEMIZE
LISTING NOTITIA WAYBILL CALENDAR
CINCTURE HANDLIST PLATBAND
REGISTER SCHEDULE SYNONYMY
TITULARY
(— OF BOOKS) CANON
(— OF CANDIDATES) LEET SLATE
TERNA
(— OF CONTESTANTS) DRAW SEEDING
(— OF DISEASES) NOSOLOGY
(— OF JURORS) TALES
(— OF MAP SYMBOLS) LEGEND
(— OF PASSERS WITHOUT HONORS)
GULF
(— OF RATES) TARIFF
(— OF THEATRICAL PARTS) CAST
(GENEALOGICAL —) BEGATS
(IMPRESSIVE —) ARRAY
(LEGAL —) TABLEAU
(PRAYER —) BEADROLL
(WINE —) CARD
LISTEN LIST TEND TENEZ HARKEN
INTEND WHISPER
(— TO) DIG EAR HARK HEAR CATCH
ATTEND
LISTENER AUDITOR OTACUST
LISTLESS DOPY DULL WOFF DOWFF
FAINT DONSIE SUPINE LANGUID UNLISTY
UNLUSTY CARELESS INDOLENT
THOWLESS TONELESS UNHEARTY
LITERAL VERBAL TEXTUAL
LITERATURE FICTION LETTERS
CLAPTRAP
(— CLANDESTINELY DISTRIBUTED)
SAMIZDAT
(SACRED —) VEDA SRUTI
LITHE BAIN SWACK CLEVER LIMBER
SILKEN SUPPLE SVELTE WANDLE
LISSOME FLEXIBLE

LITHUANIA

CAPITAL: VILNA WILNA VILNIUS
PEOPLE: BALT LETT ZHMUD LITVAK
YATVYAG

RIVER: NEMAN NERIS RUSNE VENTA DUBYSA LIELUPE NEMUNAS PREGOLYA
TOWN: MEMEL VILNA JELGAVA VILNIUS KAPSUKAS KLAIPEDA SIAULIAI

LITIGATION LAW LIS MOOT SUIT LAWING PLEADING PLEASHIP
LITTER DIG PIG BIER RAFF REDD BREED CABIN CLECK DOOLY DRECK HAULM MULCH SEDAN DOOLIE GOCART KINDLE KITTEN MAHMAL REFUSE CLUTTER LETTIGA LOUSTER MAMMOCK NORIMON RUBBISH RUMMAGE SCAMBLE BRANCARD CARRIAGE KINDLING MUNCHEEL PAVILION STRETCHER
(— FOR LIVESTOCK) BEDDING
(— OF PIGS) FAR FARE FARROW
(— ON PACK ANIMAL) CACOLET
(CAMEL —) KAJAWAH
(FOREST —) DUFF
LITTLE FEW LIL WEE CURN LITE TINY VEEN CHOTA CRUMB SMALL TASTE WHONE BITTIE DAPPER LEETLE MINUTE PETITE PICKLE PUSILL KENNING MODICUM THOUGHT FRACTION SNIPPING
(— BY LITTLE) EDGINGLY INCHMEAL
(— LESS THAN) ABOUT
(— MUSICALLY) POCO
(— ONE) BUTCHA POPPET
LITTLE DORRIT (AUTHOR OF —) DICKENS
(CHARACTER IN —) AMY JOHN CASBY FANNY FLORA ARTHUR DORRIT EDWARD PANCKS CHIVERY CLENNAM MEAGLES WILLIAM BLANDOIS PLORNISH BARNACLES
LITTLE MINISTER (AUTHOR OF —) BARRIE
(CHARACTER IN —) DOW ROB ADAM GAVIN MICAH NANNY BABBIE OGILVY DISHART MCQUEEN RINTOUL WEBSTER MARGARET
LITTLE WOMEN (AUTHOR OF —) ALCOTT
(CHARACTER IN —) JO AMY MEG BETH DEMI JOHN BHAER DAISY FRITZ KIRKE MARCH BROOKE CARROL LAURIE MARMEE LAURENCE THEODORE
LITURGY FORM RITE ABODAH MAARIB MINHAG NEILAH MINCHAH MYSTERY HIERURGY SHAHARIT
LIVE BE USE WIN KEEP LEAD STAY ALERT ALIVE DWELL EXIST GREEN HABIT LEEVE QUICK SHACK VITAL HARBOR LIVELY LIVING REMAIN RESIDE BREATHE INHABIT SUBSIST CONTINUE CONVERSE VIGOROUS
(— AT ANOTHER'S EXPENSE) COSHER
(— BY BEGGING) CADGE SKELDER
(— BY STRATAGEMS) SHARK
(— FROM DAY TO DAY) EKE
(— IN CONTINENCE) CONTAIN
(— IN LUXURY) STATE
(— IN PEACE) COEXIST
(— IN SAME PLACE) STALL

(— ON) SURVIVE
(— RIOTOUSLY) JET
(— TEMPORARILY) CAMP
(— THROUGH) PASS TIDE
(— TOGETHER) AGREE COHABIT
(— WELL) BATTEN
LIVELINESS PEP BRIO FIRE FIZZ LIFE PUNCH SPUNK BOUNCE ESPRIT GAIETY SPIRIT ENTRAIN SPARKLE ACTIVITY VITALITY VIVACITY
LIVELY GAY TID AIRY BRAG CANT FAST FESS GLEG KECK LIVE PERT RACY TAIT TRIG VITE VIVE WARM YARE AGILE ALERT ALIVE BONNY BRISK BUXOM CANTY CHIRK COBBY CORKY CRISP DESTO FRESH FRISK JAZZY KEDGE KINKY MERRY PAWKY PEART PEPPY POKEY RUDDY SASSY SMART VIVID WHICK ACTIVE BLITHE BOUNCY BRIGHT CHEERY CHIRPY COCKET CROOSE CROUSE DAPPER FIERCE FRISCH GINGER JOCUND KIPPER LIVING NIMBLE QUIVER SEMMIT SPARKY SPRACK TROTTY VEGETE WHISKY WIMBLE ALLEGRO ANIMATE ANIMOSE BOBBISH BUCKISH BUOYANT GIGGISH GIOCOSO JOCULAR KINETIC LEBHAFT POINTED ROUSING SPIRITY SPRINGY TITTUMY TITTUPY WINCING ANIMATED BOUNCING CHIRRUPY FRISKFUL FRISKING GALLIARD SANGUINE SKITTISH SMACKING SPANKING SPIRITED SPORTIVE STEERING STIRRING TRIPSOME VEGETOUS VOLATILE SPARKLING
LIVERY SUIT CLOTH UNIFORM CLOTHING
LIVESTOCK FEE WARE STOCK STORE STUFF CHATTEL BESTIALS FATSTOCK
LIVING KEEP ALIVE BEING BREAD GOING QUICK VITAL WHICK AROUND LIVELY VIABLE ZOETIC ANIMATE SUPPORT ANIMATED
(— IN THE WORLD) SECULAR
(— IN WAVES) LOTIC
(— NEAR THE GROUND) EPIGEAN
(— ON BANKS OF STREAMS) RIPAL RIPARIAN
(BARE —) CRUST
(ECCLESIASTICAL —) BENEFICE
LIZARD DAB EFT GOH UMA UTA DABB GILA IBIT SEPS TEGU TEJU URAN AGAMA ANOLE BLUEY DRACO GECKO GUANO SKINK SNAKE SWIFT TEIID TOKAY TWEEG VARAN AMEIVA ANGUID ARBALO DRAGON GOANNA HARDIM IGUANA LACERT LEGUAN MOLOCH TEIOID WORRAL MONITOR REPTILE SAURIAN SCINCID SCINCUS TUATARA BASILISK SCORPION CHAMELEON
LLAMA ALPACA VICUNA GUANACO
LO SEE ECCE
LOAD LUG TON BUCK CARK CRAM DRAW FILL HAUL LADE LAST LUMP PACK RAKE SEAM STOW TOTE TURN BARTH CARGO DRAFT PITCH PRIME STACK TRUSS TURSE BURDEN CHARGE COMBLE FODDER FOTHER HAMPER LADING LOADEN THRACK BALLAST CARLOAD DERRICK DRAUGHT FRAUGHT FREIGHT

ONERATE OPPRESS BACKPACK CARRIAGE
HEADLOAD SHIPLOAD PLANELOAD
(— A DIE FOR CHEATING) COG
(— FABRICS) WEIGHT
(— OF COAL) KEEL
(— OF HAY OR CORN) HURRY
(— OF LAMBS) DECK
(— OF LOGS) PEAKER BUNKLOAD
(— OF WOOL) TOD
(— ON BACK) ENDORSE
(— SHIP) STEM
(— TO CAPACITY) SATURATE
(— TO EXCESS) ENCUMBER
(ELECTRIC —) DEMAND
(HORSE —) SEAM SUMAGE
(LAST — OF GRAIN) WINTER
(SMALL —) JAG JOBBLE

LOAF BUM AZYM HACK HAKE LAKE MIKE
SLIM SORN BANGE BREAD BRICK DRING
MOUCH SHOOL SLIVE BLUDGE BROGUE
CADDLE DIDDLE SLINGE WASTEL
HOOSIER MANCHET SHACKLE SLOUNGE
SOLDIER OBLATION PANHAGIA
QUARTERN SHAMMOCK
(— AROUND) HULL HOWFF SLOSH
RODNEY
(— OF BREAD) COB BATON FADGE
MICHE TOMMY HALLAH TAMMIE
(BROWN —) GEORGE
(ROUND —) BUN COBURG
(SMALL —) BAP COB NACKET
(SUGAR —) TITLER

LOAFER BUM CAD YOB BEAT GRUB STIFF
BUMBLE BUMMER CADGER KEELIE
SLOUCH SLOVEN BLUDGER COASTER
FAITOUR HOODLUM SLINKER SOLDIER
COBERGER HOOLIGAN LARRIKIN
LAYABOUT SEASONER

LOAN DHAN LEND LENT PREST CREDIT
DONATE MUTUUM ADVANCE FIXTURE
IMPREST

LOATHE UG HATE SHUN ABHOR LAITH
WLATE AGRISE DETEST DESPISE
SCUNDER SCUNNER NAUSEATE

LOATHING NAUSEA REVOLT DISGUST
SCUNNER

LOATHSOME FOUL UGLY VILE POCKY
LAIDLY UNLIEF HATEFUL LOATHLY
MAWKISH OBSCENE TETROUS WLATFUL
DEFORMED NAUSEOUS WLATSOME
NEFANDOUS ABOMINABLE

LOBBY HALL FOYER NARTHEX PASSAGE
TAMBOUR ANTEROOM COULISSE

LOBSTER CRAY HOMARD DECAPOD
SHEDDER CRAWFISH CRAYFISH
LANGOSTA MACRURAN
(— LESS THAN 10 INCHES LONG)
JOE
(FEMALE —) HEN
(NORWAY —) SCAMPO
(SMALL —) PAWK NANCY
(UNDERSIZED —) SHORT

LOCAL HOME NATIVE LIMITED TOPICAL
VICINAL REGIONAL EPICHORIC
(NOT —) AZONIC

LOCALE SITE LOCAL PLACE SCENE

LOCALITY SPA HAND PLAT SPOT LOCUS

PLACE POINT SITIO SITUS STEAD
HABITAT LATITUDE POSITURE SITUATION
(BARREN —) GALL
(BEAUTIFUL —) XANADU
(GUARDED —) POST

LOCATE SITE SPOT PITCH PLACE
BESTOW BILLET SETTLE SITUATE
PINPOINT
(— AT INTERVALS) SPOT
(— WATER) DIVINE

LOCATED SET FIXED SEATED SITUATED

LOCATION FALL HOME PLOT PLACE
SITUS WHERE UBIETY AMENITY STATION
HOMESITE STANDING
(ESSENTIAL —) EYE
(FOREST —) CHANCE
(GEOGRAPHIC —) SEAT
(MINING —) MYNPACHT
(NATURAL —) HABITAT

LOCK COT KEY FEAK FRIB HOLD TRIM
YALE CHUBB CLASP SASSE DUBBEH
ENLOCK LUCKEN DAGLOCK EARLOCK
KEYLOCK PINLOCK SPANNER DEADLOCK
FORELOCK
(— IMPROPERLY) BIND
(— IN RIVER) SASSE
(— OF HAIR) COT TAG TUZ COTT CURL
FEAK TATE FLAKE FLOCK FLUKE QUIFF
TRESS TANGLE COWLICK EARLOCK
FRIZZLE SERPENT WIMPLER FORELOCK
SIDELOCK
(— OF WOOL) TAG COTT FRIB FLOCK
STAPLE HASLOCK
(— UP) JAIL STOW CABINET
(CANAL —) COFFER CHAMBER
(DIRTY —) FRIB
(MATTED —) COT COTT DAGLOCK
(MUSKET —) ROWET
(PART OF —) REWET STRIKE
(WHEEL —) REWET

LOCKET BRELOQUE

LOCKJAW TETANUS TRISMUS

LOCKUP JUG GAOL JAIL LOCK LOGS
CHOKY CLINK TRONK COOLER
HOOSEGOW ROUNDHOUSE

LOCOMOTIVE HOG PIG PUG BOGY GOAT
HOGG MULE SHAG TANK BOGIE DINKY
DUMMY MOGUL PILOT DIESEL DOCTOR
DOLLIE DONKEY ENGINE LOADER PUSHER
SMOKER YARDER BOBTAIL BOOSTER
SHUNTER STEAMER CALLIOPE
CHOOCHOO COMPOUND DOLLBEER
(— WITHOUT CARS) WILDCAT
(EXTRA —) HELPER

LOCUS PLACE EVOLUTE SURFACE
SYNAPSE CONCHOID ENVELOPE
HOROPTER

LOCUST WETA BRUKE HONEY CICADA
QUAKER SKIPPER TETRIGID VOETGANGER

LOCUST TREE CAROB ACACIA LOCUST
ROBINIA ALGAROBA

LODE LEAD REEF VEIN LEDGE COURSE
FEEDER QUARRY SCOVAN COUNTER

LODESTONE MAGNET SIDERITE
TERRELLA

LODGE DIG HUT INN LIE BEAT CAMP
HOST KEEP ROOM STAY STOW TENT

BOWER CABIN COUCH COURT GROVE
GUEST HOGAN HOTEL HOUSE HOWFF
LAYER LOGIS STICK TARRY ALIGHT
BESTOW BILLET BURROW COSHER
GESTEN GRANGE HOSTEL RESIDE SETTLE
BARRACK LODGING QUARTER SOJOURN
EMBOLIZE HARBINGE
(— AND EAT) COSHER
(— FOR SAFEKEEPING) DEPOSIT
(— IN COURT) BOX
(LOCAL —) COURT
(SPORTSMAN'S —) SHEAL
LODGER INMATE ROOMER TENANT
LODGING BED CRIB FERM GIST HAFT
HOST NEST GEAST LOGIS HARBOR
HOSTEL LIVERY HOSPICE HOUSING
COUCHANT GUESTING
(— FOR SOLDIERS) CASERN
(— OF MARABOUT) KOUBA
(VILE —) KENNEL
LOFT BALK FLAT GOLF JUBE LAFT ATTIC
SOLAR GARRET SOLLAR HAYLOFT
COCKLOFT SCAFFOLD TRAVERSE
(HAY —) TALLET
LOFTY AIRY HIGH LOFT TALL BRENT
ELATE GRAND GREAT NOBLE PROUD
SKYEY STEEP WINGY AERIAL ANDEAN
HAUGHT TOPFUL TOWERY UPWARD
WINGED ANDESIC ARDUOUS EMINENT
EXCELSE HAUGHTY SUBLIME ARROGANT
ELEVATED GENEROUS MAJESTIC
OLYMPIAN TOWERING
LOG BUNK CLOG SKID CHOCK CHUCK
CHUNK PIECE STICK STOCK BILLET
PEAKER PEELER SADDLE SAWLOG
BACKLOG DAYBOOK DEGRADE JOURNAL
LOGBOOK
(— AS ANCHOR) DEADMAN
(— AS RAFTER) VIGA
(— BINDING A RAFT) SWIFTER
(— FASTENED TO TRAP) DRAG
(— SUPPORTING MINE ROOF) NOG
(— WITH SPIKES IN END) DEADENER
(— WITHOUT BARK) BUCKSKIN
(ENCLOSED —S) BOOM
(FLOATING —S) DRIVE
(LOAD OF —S) PEAKER
(PILE OF —S) DECK ROLLWAY
(SAWED —) BOULE
(SLABBED —) CANT
(SMALL —) LOGGET
(SPLIT —) PUNCHEON
(STRIPPED —) BATTEN
(SUNKEN —) DEADHEAD
LOGIC NYAYA LOGICS CANONIC
WITCRAFT
LOGICAL SANE RAISONNE RATIONAL
LOGO EMBLEM
LOHENGRIN (CHARACTER IN —) ELSA
HENRY ORTRUD FREDERICK GOTTFRIED
LOHENGRIN TELRAMUND
(COMPOSER OF —) WAGNER
(FATHER OF —) PARSIFAL
(WIFE OF —) ELSA
LOIN LEER LISK ALOYAU LUNYIE
(PORK —) GRISKIN
(2 UNCUT —S) BARON

LOINCLOTH IZAR MALO MARO DHOTI
LUNGI PAGNE PAREU MOOCHA PANUNG
DHOOTIE
LOITER LAG CLUG FOOL HAKE HANG
HAWM HAZE HOVE LOUT MIKE MUCK
SLUG COOSE DELAY DRAWL KNOCK
MOUCH SHOOL SIDLE TARRY COOTER
DAWDLE LAGGER LINGER MUCKER
STRAKE TAIGLE PROJECT SHAFFLE
LALLYGAG LOLLYGAG SCOWBANK
LOITERING SLIMSY LAGGARD
LOKI (DAUGHTER OF —) HEL
(FATHER OF —) FARBAUTI
(MOTHER OF —) NAL LAUFEY
ANGRBODHA
(SLAYER OF —) HEIMDALL
(WIFE OF —) SIGYN ANGURBODA
LOLL FUG LOUT FROWST LOLLUP LOUNGE
SOZZLE SPRAWL RECLINE SCAMBLE
SCOWBANK
LOLLIPOP LOLLY SUCKER SUCKABOB
LONDON SMOKE COCKAGNE
(BRIDGE IN —) TOWER ALBERT PUTNEY
CHELSEA WATERLOO
(DISTRICT OF —) SOHO ACTON
ADELPHI ALSATIA BRIXTON CHELSEA
MAYFAIR
(MONUMENT IN —) GOG MAGOG
NELSON CENOTAPH VICTORIA
(RIVER OF —) THAMES
(STREET OF —) BOND FLEET CANNON
SAVILE DOWNING WARDOUR
HAYMARKET
(SUBURB OF —) KEW FINCHLEY
LONE LANE SOLE ALONE APART SINGLE
SOLITARY
LONELINESS ONENESS VACANCY
SOLITUDE
LONELY LORN ONLY SOLE VAST ALONE
UNKET UNKID WISHT ALANGE DEAFLY
SULLEN DEAVELY FORLORN LONEFUL
SOLEYNE DESOLATE SECLUDED
SOLITARY
LONESOME ALONE DOLEY LONELY
LANESOME SOLITARY
LONG HO HOE DIE FAR FIT YEN ACHE DREE
HANK LANG SIDE TALL WILN WISH
YAWN DREAM GREEN LATHY LONGA
MOURN STARK WEARY YEARN ARIGUE
DREICH HANKER HUNGER LINGER
LONGUS PROLIX STOUND THIRST
LENGTHY TEDIOUS WEILANG GEMINATE
INFINITE
(— AGO) FERN LANGSYNE
(— AND SLENDER) REEDY SQUINNY
(— AND UNIFORM IN WIDTH) LINEAR
(— FOR) CARE HONE COVET CRAVE
TASTE ASPIRE DESIRE SUSPIRE
(— RESTLESSLY) ITCH
(— SINCE) YORE
(EXTRA —) MAXI
(TEDIOUSLY —) MORTAL
LONGBOAT SLOOP
LONGING YEN ENVY ITCH LUST PINE
WISH BRAME YEARN DESIRE HANKER
TALENT THIRST ATHIRST CRAVING
THIRSTY WILLING WISHFUL WISTFUL

APPETENT APPETITE CUPIDITY
HOMESICK PRURIENT
LONGSHOREMAN DOCKER HOBBLER
WHARFIE DOCKHAND ROUSTABOUT
LONG-STANDING OLD
LONG-SUFFERING MEEK PATIENT
ENDURING PATIENCE
LONG-WINDED PROLIX PROSAIC
LOOK LA LO AIR EYE KEN SPY CAST
GAWK GIVE HEED KEEK LATE LUCK
MARK MIEN POKE SEEM SWAP WAIT
ACIES BLUSH DEKKO FAVOR FLASH
GLEAM GLEER GLIFF SCREW SIGHT
SQUIZ VIZZY WLITE APPEAR ASPECT
EYEFUL GANDER GLANCE VISION
EYESHOT EYEWINK INSIGHT SEEMING
DISCOVER LANGUISH OEILLADE
(— ABOUT) BELOOK SPECTATE
(— AFTER) TENT ATTEND FATHER
FETTLE PROCURE
(— ASKANCE) GLIM LEER SKEW BAGGE
GLENT GLEDGE SKLENT
(— AT) DIG SEE GLOM LAMP VIEW VISE
GLISK ADVISE BEHOLD REGARD REWARD
CONSIDER SPECTATE
(— CLOSELY) PRY ESPY SCAN
(— CROSS-EYED) SHEYLE
(— DOWN UPON) SNOB DESPISE
(— DULLY) BLEAR
(— FIXEDLY) GAZE KYKE GLORE STARE
(— FOR) SPY FOND SEEK GROPE EXPECT
PROPOSE RESPECT
(— FORWARD) EXPECT FORESEE
ENVISAGE ENVISION
(— GLANCINGLY) BLINK
(— IN SNEAKING MANNER) SNOOP
(— INTENTLY) GLOSE VISIE GLOWER
EYEBALL
(— INTO) SOUND SEARCH
(— OBLIQUELY) GLIME GOGGLE
SQUINT
(— OF DERISION) FLEER
(— OF PLANETS) ASPECTS
(— OUT) FEND MIND CHEESE JIGGERS
OUTLOOK
(— OVER) SCAN TOISE BROWSE
SURVEY EXAMINE
(— SEARCHINGLY) PEER PORE TOOT
(— SLYLY) PEEP GLINK
(— SOUR) GLUNCH
(— STEADFASTLY) GLOAT
(— SULKY) LUMP
(— SULLEN) LOUR LOWER
(— UPON AS) ACCOUNT
(— WILDLY) GLOP WAUL WHAWL
(— WITH FAVOR) SMILE
(AMOROUS —) SMICKER
(ANGRY —) SCOWL
(BRIEF —) GLIM GLINT GLIMPSE
(LOVING —) BELGARD
(QUICK —) SCRY GLENT
(SEARCHING —) SCRUTINY
(SEVERE —) FROWN
(SIDELONG —) GLEE GLIME
(SLY —) GLEG GLIME TWIRE
(SULLEN —) GLOOM GLOUT GLUNCH
(TENDER —) LANGUISH

(WANTON —) LEER
LOOK HOMEWARD ANGEL
(AUTHOR OF —) WOLFE
(CHARACTER IN —) BEN GANT LUKE
DAISY ELIZA HELEN JAMES LAURA
EUGENE GROVER OLIVER LEONARD
MARGARET
LOOKING BACKWARD
(AUTHOR OF —) BELLAMY
(CHARACTER IN —) WEST EDITH
LEETE JULIAN BARTLETT PILLSBURY
LOOKOUT HUER TOUT SCOUT WATCH
BANTAY CONNER TOOTER FUNERAL
OUTLOOK ATALAYAN BANTAYAN
BARTIZAN COCKATOO PROSPECT
TOWERMAN WATCHOUT OBSERVATORY
LOOM BEAM BULK HULK LEEM DOBBY
FRAME GLOOM BEETLE DRAWLOOM
HANDLOOM JACQUARD OVERPICK
LOOP BOW EYE LUG NOB TAB TAG ANSA
BEND COIL HANK KNOB KNOP LEAF LINK
LOUP PURL CHAPE COQUE GUIDE LACET
LATCH PEARL PICOT SHANK STRAP
TERRY WITHY BILLET BUCKLE FOLIUM
HANGER HOLDER KEEPER SPIRAL STAPLE
STITCH TWITCH COCKEYE COUPURE
CRINGLE CRUPPER GROMMET LATCHET
SEGMENT ANTINODE COURONNE
(— AND THIMBLES) CLEW CLUE
(— BY ICESKATER) SPOON
(— IN KNITTING) STEEK
(— IN MINER'S ROPE) SLUG
(— IN NEEDLEWORK) BRIDE
(— OF INTESTINES) KNUCKLE
(— OF IRON) OOLLY
(— OF ROPE) FAKE BIGHT FLAKE KINCH
NOOSE ANCHOR BECKET PARRAL
SNORTER SNOTTER
(— OF SCABBARD) FROG
(— OF TUBING) SCROLL
(— ON ARMOR) VERVELLE
(— ON SAIL) LASKET
(— ON SPINNING FRAME) BAND
(— ON SWORD BELT) HANGER
(HANGING —) FESTOON
(HEDDLE —) DOUP
(ORNAMENTAL —) PICOT
(SHOULDER —) EPAULET
(SURGICAL —) CURET CURETTE
(TIGHT —) KINK KINKLE
LOOPHOLE LOOP CHINK MEUSE EYELET
OILLET WICKET BARBICAN PORTHOLE
LOOSE GAY LAX EMIT FREE GLAD LASH
LIMP OPEN SOFT UNDO WIDE WILD
BAGGY CRANK FRANK LARGE LIGHT
RELAX SLACK VAGUE WASHY ADRIFT
FLUFFY LIMBER SLOPPY SOLUTE SPORTY
SUBURB UNBIND UNGIRT UNLASH
WOBBLY ABSOLVE CHESSOM FLYAWAY
IMMORAL MOVABLE RELAXED SHOGGLY
STRINGY UNBOUND UNHITCH UNTIGHT
DIFFUSED DISCINCT FLOATING INSECURE
LAXATIVE SHATTERY UNSTABLE
LOOSEN LAX BREAK SLACK UNTIE
LAXATE LIMBER UNBEND RESOLVE
SLACKEN UNGRIPE UNLOOSE UNSCREW
DISHEVEL UNSTRING

LOOSENESS SLACK LAXITY LATITUDE
LOOT SACK SWAG BOOTY HARRY SPOIL
STEAL THEFT BOODLE MARAUD HERSHIP
PILLAGE PLUNDER SNAFFLE
LOP LAP CLIP OCHE SNED SNIG TRIM
SHRAG SHRED SHRUB STUMP TRASH
TWINE SHROUD SNATHE TRASHIFY
TRUNCATE
(— OFF) COW DOD CROP HEAD SNAG
PRUNE TRUNK DEFALK AMPUTATE
LOPE SHAG
LOQUACIOUS GABBY FUTILE
LORD BEL DAM DEN DON GOD HER LOR
MAR SID SIR DION DOMN EROS HERR
LAUK LOSH NAIK SIRE TUAN ANGUS
ARAWN BARON LAFEU LIEGE LUDDY
NIGEL OMRAH RABBI SAHIB SWAMI
DOMINE DUMAIN KYRIOS PRABHU
SAYYID SIGNOR TANIST THAKUR
CAMILLO CERIMON JACQUES JEHOVAH
MARCHER OGTIERN VAVASOR
BHAGAVAT DESPOTES DRIGHTEN
GRANDPRE LORDLING MARGRAVE
OVERLORD PALATINE SEIGNEUR
SEIGNIOR SUPERIOR SUZERAIN
THALIARD
(— OF DARKNESS) HYLE
(— OF WORLD) LOKINDRA
(FEUDAL —) DAUPHIN VAVASOR
SUZERAIN
(JAPANESE —) KAMI
LORD CHANCELLOR WOOLPACK
LORD JIM (AUTHOR OF —) CONRAD
(CHARACTER IN —) JIM DAIN BROWN
STEIN WARIS MARLOW DORAMIN
LORDLY PROUD SUPERB ARROGANT
DESPOTIC
LORE LEAR LORUM MASTAX LEARNING
LORGNETTE STARER
LORNA DOONE (AUTHOR OF —)
BLACKMORE
(CHARACTER IN —) FRY TOM ALAN
JOHN RIDD ANNIE DOONE DUGAL ENSOR
LORNA CARVER FAGGUS JEREMY
REUBEN BRANDIR STICKLES HUCKABACK
LORRY DRAG RULLY CAMION ROLLEY
LOSE LET TIN AMIT DROP TINE WANT
FORGO LAPSE LEASE TRAIL GAMBLE
MISLAY FORBEAR FORFEIT FORLESE
SLATTER
(— AT CARDS) BUST
(— BET) WRONG
(— BRILLIANCE) FAINT
(— BY DEATH) BURY
(— BY GAMING) GAME
(— BY STUPIDITY) BLUNDER
(— CONTROL) BLOW CRACK
(— COURAGE) DREEP TAINT
(— FLAVOR) FOZE APPAL APPALL
(— FORCE) COLLAPSE
(— FRESHNESS) FADE WILT WITHER
(— HEART) JADE FAINT QUAIL
COLLAPSE
(— HOPE) DESPAIR DESPOND
(— LUSTER) TARNISH
(— MOISTURE) GUTTATE
(— NERVE) CHICKEN

(— OFFICE) FALL
(— ONE'S BREATH) CHINK
(— ONE'S WAY) STRAY
(— POWER) FAIL DISSOLVE
(— SELF-POSSESSION) ABASH
(— SPIRIT) JADE
(— STRENGTH) GO FADE FAIL PALL
WEAKEN LANGUISH
(— VISION) DAZZLE
(— WARMTH) COOL CONGEAL
(— WEIGHT) ENSEAM
LOSS ACE COST HARM LEAK LOST MISS
LAPSE QUALM WASTE BURIAL DAMAGE
DAMNUM DEFEAT INJURY TINSEL
AVERAGE DEBACLE DEFICIT EXPENSE
JACTURE LEAKAGE LEESING MISTURE
REPRISE AMISSION BREAKAGE CLEANING
MISSMENT PERDITION SACRIFICE
(— BY EVAPORATION) ULLAGE
(— BY SIFTING) ULLAGE
(— IN WORKING) SLIPPAGE
(— OF ABILITIES) COLLAPSE
(— OF ACTIVITY) AKINESIA
(— OF APPETITE) ASITIA ANOREXIA
(— OF CONSCIOUSNESS) SWOON
ABSENCE APOPLEXY BLACKOUT
FAINTING
(— OF ELASTICITY) SET
(— OF ELECTRICITY) EFFLUVE
(— OF EXPRESSION) AMIMIA
(— OF HAIR) DEFLUX ALOPECIA
PTILOSIS
(— OF HONOR) ATIMY
(— OF HOPE) DESPAIR
(— OF MEMORY) AMNESIA BLACKOUT
(— OF PRESTIGE) DISHONOR
(— OF SCENT) CHECK
(— OF SENSE OF SMELL) ANOSMIA
(— OF SIGHT) ANOPSY ANOPSIA
(— OF SIZE) WANE
(— OF SOUND) APOCOPE SYNCOPE
APHERESIS
(— OF SPEECH) ALALIA APHASIA
APHONIA
(— OF VOICE) ANAUDIA APHONIA
(— OF VOWEL) APHESIS
(— OF WILL POWER) ABULIA
(CONTRACT —) LESION
(SUFF.) ZEMIA
LOST ASEA GONE LORN TINT STRAY
WASTE ASTRAY BUSHED HIDDEN
NAUGHT FORFEIT FORLORN MISSING
CONFUSED OBSCURED BENIGHTED
(— IN THOUGHT) PREOCCUPIED
LOST HORIZON (AUTHOR OF —)
HILTON
(CHARACTER IN —) HUGH BRIAC
CHANG HENRY CONWAY LOTSEN
BARNARD CHARLES ROBERTA BRINKLOW
MALLISON PERRAULT RUTHERFORD
LOT CUT HAP PEW CHOP CROP DEAL DOLE
DOOM DRAW FALL FATE HEAP PACK
PART PILE REDE SKIT SLEW SLUE SORS
SORT BATCH BLOCK BUNCH CAVEL
FIELD GRACE GRIST GROSS LINES SHARE
SHOOT SIGHT SITHE STAND TEEMS
TROOP WEIRD AMOUNT BARREL BUNDLE

CHANCE DICKER FARDEL OODLES
PARCEL TICHEL BOILING DESTINY
FEEDLOT FORTUNE OODLINS PORTION
SANDLOT BACKYARD CABOODLE
JINGBANG MOUTHFUL RIMPTION
WOODLAND
(— OF PERSONS) BOODLE
(— OF TEA) BREAK
(— OF 60 PIECES) SHOCK
(BUILDING —) ERF
(BURIAL —) LAIR
(FATHER OF —) HARAN
(GREAT —) SWAG
(MISCELLANEOUS —) RAFT
(SISTER OF —) ISCAH MILCAH
(UNCLE OF —) ABRAHAM
(VACANT —) COMMON COMMONS
LOTION WASH EYEWASH EYEWATER
LAVATORY
LOTS HEAPS TEEMS BUSHEL HODFUL
LOTTERY AMBO LOTTO TERNO RAFFLE
TOMBOLA
LOTUS LOTE LOTOS PADMA NELUMBO
WANKAPIN
LOUD HARD HIGH MAIN CRUDE FORTE
GAUDY GREAT HEAVY SHOWY STARK
STOUR WIGHT BRASSY BRAZEN COARSE
CRIANT FLASHY GARISH HOARSE
VULGAR BLATANT CLAMANT HAUTAIN
VIOLENT BIGMOUTH FRENZIED PIERCING
SLAMBANG STREPENT STRIDENT
VEHEMENT STREPITANT
LOUDSPEAKER WOOFER SPEAKER
TWEETER BULLHORN SQUAWKER

LOUISIANA

CAPITAL: BATONROUGE
COLLEGE: LSU TULANE DILLARD
GRAMBLING
INDIAN: ADAI WASHA ATAKAPA
LAKE: IATT CLEAR LARTO BORGNE SALINE
DARBONNE MAUREPAS
MOUNTAIN: DRISKILL
NATIVE: CAJUN CREOLE ACADIAN
NICKNAME: CREOLE PELICAN
PARISH: WINN CADDO ACADIA IBERIA
SABINE TENSAS ORLEANS RAPIDES
OUACHITA CALCASIEU
RIVER: RED AMITE BOEUF SABINE TENSAS
OUACHITA
STATE BIRD: PELICAN
STATE FLOWER: MAGNOLIA
STATE TREE: CYPRESS
STREAM: BAYOU
TOWN: JENA MANY HOMER HOUMA
EDGARD GRETNA MINDEN MONROE
RUSTON BASTROP VIDALIA BOGALUSA
TALLULAH NEWORLEANS

LOUNGE HAWM LOAF LOLL SORN SOSS
BANGE TRAIK DACKER FROUST FROWST
GLIDER LOLLUP LOPPET RIZZLE SLINGE
SOZZLE LAMMOCK SAUNTER SLOUNGE
LOUNGER IDLER SLOUNGER

LOUSY SEEDY CRAPPY CRUMMY
PEDICULOUS
LOUT HOB LOB LUG YOB BOOR CHUB
COOF GAUM GAWK JAKE LOON NOWT
SWAB SWAD BOOBY CHUMP CUDDY
GNOFF LOOBY LOURD ROBIN THRUM
WHAUP YAHOO BOHUNK CLUNCH
GOBBIN HOBLOB LOURDY LUBBER
LUNGIS SLOUCH TRIPAL GROBIAN
HALLION HAWBUCK LOBCOCK PALOOKA
LOBLOLLY
(COUNTRY —) KERN BUMPKIN
LOUTISH SWAB HULKY SLOOMY
BOORISH HULKING VILLAIN BOEOTIAN
CLOWNISH
LOVABLE CUDDLY AMIABLE ADORABLE
DOVELIKE LOVESOME
LOVE GRA LOO AMOR EROS KAMA LIKE
ALOHA AMOUR CUPID DRURY FANCY
HEART MINNE AFFECT TENDRE EMBRACE
FEELING PASSION DEVOTION KINDNESS
LOVEHOOD PARAMOUR
(— IN RETURN) REDAME
(— OF COUNTRY) PATRIOTISM
(— OF MARVELOUS) TERATISM
(— TO EXCESS) IDOLIZE
(— TOWARD DEITY) BHAKTI
(CHRISTIAN —) CHARITY
(INTENSE —) FIRE
(NATURAL —) STORGE
(SELF-GIVING —) AGAPE
(UNLAWFUL —) LEMANRY
LOVED DEAR BELOVED
(MUCH —) SWEET
LOVE FEAST AGAPE
LOVELINESS BEAUTY
LOVELY DREAMY LOVING TENDER
AMIABLE AMOROUS ADORABLE
LOVESOME
LOVER GRA LAD MAN BEAU CHAP AMANT
AMOUR DRURY LEMAN ROMEO SPARK
SWAIN AMADIS AMANTE MARROW
MINION SQUIRE ADMIRER AMORIST
AMOROSO CELADON GALLANT PATRIOT
SPARKER SPECIAL SPRUNNY AMORETTO
BELAMOUR CASANOVA CICISBEO
PARAMOUR STREPHON
(MODEL —) LEILAH
(SILLY —) SPOON
LOVE'S LABOR'S LOST
(AUTHOR OF —) SHAKESPEARE
(CHARACTER IN —) DULL MOTH
BOYET MARIA ARMADO DUMAIN
ADRIANO BEROWNE COSTARD MERCADE
ROSALINE FERDINAND KATHERINE
NATHANIEL HOLOFERNES JAQUENETTA
LONGAVILLE
LOVING DEAR FOND TENDER AMATORY
AMOROUS
LOW BAS BOO LAW MOO BASE BASS
KEEN MEAN NEAP ORRA ROUT SLOW
VILE WEAK BLORE DIRTY GROSS LAICH
PUTID SHORT SMALL SNIDE THIRD
CALLOW EARTHY FILTHY GENTLE
GRUBBY HARLOT HUMBLE LIMMER
MENIAL ORNERY RASCAL RIBALD SECRET
SHABBY SILKEN TURPID VULGAR

BESTIAL IGNOBLE RAFFISH REPTILE
SLAVISH IGNOBLE SOUTERLY
(— AS OF A VOWEL) OPEN
(— DOWN) SIDE
(— IN LIGHTNESS) DULL
(— IN PERCEPTION) CRUDE
(— IN PITCH) GRAVE
(— IN PRICE) MODERATE
(— IN QUALITY) HEDGE
(— IN SATURATION) GRAYISH
(— IN SPIRITS) BLUE DOWN GLOOMY
DOWNCAST
(— IN TONE) SOFT SUBMISS
(— IN WATER) RACE
(IMMEASURABLY —) ABYSMAL
LOWER CUT DIP LOW BASE BATE DOWN
DROP DUCK FELL ABASE ABATE ALLOY
AVALE BELOW BLAME COUCH COWER
DECRY SCOWL DEBASE DEJECT DEMEAN
LEVEL SCOWL DEBASE DEJECT DEMEAN
EMBASE GLOWER HUMBLE JUNIOR
LESSEN MODIFY NETHER REDUCE SETTLE
STRIKE SUBDUE SUBMIT BENEATH
DECLASS DEGRADE DEPRESS SHORTEN
DIMINISH DOWNWARD INFERIOR
MODERATE
(— BANNER) VAIL
(— BY HALF STEP) FLAT
(— IN ESTEEM) CHEAPEN DEROGATE
(— IN PITCH) FLAT SHADE
(— ONESELF) SINK BEMEAN DESCEND
(— PRICES) BEAR
(— SAIL) AMAIN
(— THE HEAD) STOOP
LOWEST LAST LEAST EXTREME
LOWMOST PRIMARY PARAVAIL
NETHERMOST
LOWLY LOW BASE SILLY HUMBLE
BASEBORN
LOYAL FAST FEAL FIRM HOLD LEAL REAL
TRUE LIEGE PIOUS SOUND ARDENT
HEARTY LAWFUL SECRET STANCH
CONSTANT FAITHFUL STALWART
YEOMANLY
LOYALIST TORY
LOYALLY SURELY
LOYALTY ARDOR FAITH FEALTY HOMAGE
LEALTY REALTY SPIRIT REALITY
DEVOTION FIDELITY CONSTANCY
NATIONALISM
LOZENGE TAB JUBE COIGN QUOIN
CACHOU JUJUBE MASCLE PASTIL
QUARRY ROTULA RUSTRE TABLET
TABULE TROCHE CREMULE DIAMOND
TABELLA PASTILLE ROSEDROP
(— OF CEMENT) WAFER
LSD ACID
LUBRICANT DOPE GREASE AQUADAG
UNGUENT
LUBRICATE OIL DOPE GLIB GREASE
LUBRIFY
LUCIA DI LAMMERMOOR
(CHARACTER IN —) LUCY EDGAR
HENRY ARTHUR ASHTON BUCKLOW
RAVENSWOOD
(COMPOSER OF —) DONIZETTI

LUCID SANE CLEAR AERIAL BRIGHT
LIMPID CRYSTAL DILUCID LITERATE
LUCULENT LUMINOUS
LUCIDITY SANITY CLARITY
LUCIFER DEVIL PHOSPHOR
LUCK HAP CESS EURE SONS SPIN GRACE
ISSUE CHANCE THRIFT FORTUNE
HANDSEL SUCCESS VENTURE HAMINGJA
(BAD —) ACE DOLE DEUCE HOODOO
UNLUCK AMBSACE MISCHANCE
(GOOD —) HAP FORTUNE THEEDOM
(ILL —) UNHAP DIRDUM DISGRACE
MISHANTER
(UNEXPECTED —) BUNCE
LUCKY HOT CANNY HAPPY JAMMY SEELY
SONSY CHANCY LUCKLY LUCKFUL
GRACIOUS PROVIDENTIAL
LUCRATIVE FAT GOOD GAINFUL
LUCRE SWAG DROSS
LUDICROUS AWFUL COMIC DROLL
ABSURD COMICAL FOOLISH HIDEOUS
RISIBLE FARCICAL BURLESQUE
LUG EAR HUG TUG WAG SNUG SPUD TOTE
ZULU PATCH WALTZ
LUGGAGE SWAG TRAPS HATBOX
BAGGAGE TRUSSERY
LUGUBRIOUS BLACK TEARY BALEFUL
DOLEFUL DOLOROUS
LUKEWARM LEW LUKE TEPID WLACH
LULL CALM DRUG FODE HUSH ROCK
CROON HUSHO LETUP SLACK STILL
SOPITE HUSHABY HUSHEEN
LULLABY LULL BALOO BALOW LULLAY
HUSHABY HUSHEEN ROCKABY
LUMBER BURR DEAL RAFF NANMU
STOCK STRIP CUMBER FINISH FLITCH
RAFFLE REFUSE SAMCHU SHORTS
TIMBER DEGRADE DUNNAGE GUMWOOD
RUMMAGE TRUNDLE STEPPING
(INFERIOR —) SAPS SCOOT
LUMBERING AWKWARD LUMBERLY
LUMBROUS
LUMBERJACK JACK LOGGER TOPPER
TIMBERER
LUMBERMAN PINER DOGGER SCORER
CHOPPER GIRDLER TIMBERER
LUMINARY LIGHT CANDLE PLANET
LUMINESCENCE FLAME
LUMINOSITY FIRE GLOW LIGHT VALUE
LUMINOUS LIGHT LUCID SHINY BRIGHT
LUMINANT
LUMMOX LOBSTER PALOOKA
LUMP BOB COB CUB DAB DAD FID GOB
JOB LOB NIB NOB NUB WAD BLOB CLAG
CLAM CLOT COOL COWL DUNT JUNK
KNOB KNOT NIRL PONE SWAD TOKE
BUNCH CHUCK CHUNK CLAUT CLUMP
CLUNK GLEBE HUNCH KNOLL KNURL
MOUSE SLUMP STONE WEDGE WODGE
CLUNCH DOLLOP GOBBET HUBBLE
HUDDLE LUMPET NUBBLE NUGGET
CLUMPER CLUNTER PUMPKNOT
(— IN CLOTH) BURL
(— IN GLASS) YOLK
(— OF BLACK LEAD) SOP
(— OF BLOOD) CLOD

(— OF CLAY) BAT
(— OF COAL) NUBBLING
(— OF DOUGH) DIP
(— OF FAT) KEECH
(— OF GLASS) BLOOM
(— OF IRON) OOLLY
(— OF LAVA) BOMB
(— OF LINT) SLUG
(— OF MEAT) OLIVE
(— OF METAL) MASS SLUG
(— OF ORE) ROCK HARDHEAD
(— OF RUBBER) THIMBLE
(— OF SALT) SALTCAT
(— OF WOOD) CHUMP
(— OF YEAST) BEE
(— ON HORSE'S BACK) SITFAST
(— ON SKIN) MILIUM
(LARGE —) BLAD DOLL HUNK
(LITTLE —) NODULE KNOBBLE
(ROUNDED —) CLOT
LUMPY GOBBY CHUNKY CLOGGY CLUNCH
COBBLY STODGY BUNCHED
LUNACY MOON FOLLY MADNESS
DELIRIUM INSANITY
LUNATIC GELT LOONY BEDLAM MADMAN
MANIAC FANATIC FRANTIC CRACKPOT
MOONLING MOONSICK
LUNCH CUT BAIT CRIB TIFF BEVER PIECE
SNACK BRUNCH NACKET TIFFIN UNDERN
BAGGING ELEVENS DEJEUNER DRINKING
ELEVENER LUNCHEON NUNCHEON
COLLATION
(DAIRY —) CREMERIE
(MINER'S —) SNAP
LUNCHEON CRIB LUNCH STULL TIFFIN
DEJEUNE DINETTE NOONMEAT
LUNCHROOM EATERY
LUNGE FOIN PASS SPAR POINT VENUE
CHARGE ALLONGE
LUNGS LIGHTS VISCUS BELLOWS
LURCH JOLL STOT SWAG PITCH STOIT
CAREEN STOITER STUMBLE SWAGGER
LURE CON JAY BAIT HOOK ROPE TOLL
WISE DECOY DRILL FEINT SLOCK SNARE
SNOOK SPOON SQUID STALE TEMPT
TROLL ALLURE CAPPER CLARET ENTICE
ENTRAP RABATE SEDUCE TREPAN
VELURE GUDGEON INVEIGH PHANTOM
PITFALL WOBBLER BUCKTAIL INVEIGLE
LUREMENT
(— INTO GAMBLING) HUSTLE
(— OF CARRION) TRAIN
(— WILDFOWL) STOOL
LURID RED PURPLE SULTRY CRIMSON
GHASTLY
LURK DARE LOUT COUCH LOWER SKULK
SLINK SNEAK AMBUSH DARKLE
LURKING LURKY GRASSANT LATITANT
LUSCIOUS FOND RICH SWEET CREAMY
DULCET DELICATE
LUSH RICH GREEN LUSTY MOIST SAVORY
FERTILE OPULENT PROFUSE THRIVING
LUST HELL KAMA BLOOD PRIDE DESIRE
LIBIDO LIKING LUXURY NICETY PASSION
COVETISE CUPIDITY CARNALITY
LUSTER NAIF GLASS GLINT GLOSS SHEEN

SHINE WATER LUSTRE POLISH REFLET
BURNISH GLIMPSE GLISTER LUSTRUM
NITENCY FULGENCE LUSTRATE
RADIANCY SPLENDOR
(— OF FIBER) BLOOM
(BRONZE-LIKE —) SCHILLER
LUSTFUL HOT GAMY GOLE LEWD RANK
SALT CADGY LUSTY PRIME RANDY RUTTY
WANTON BEASTLY CODDING FLESHLY
FULSOME GOATISH JEALOUS RAMMISH
RUTTISH LIKEROUS SALACIOUS
LUSTROUS CLEAR DOGGY NITID BRIGHT
GLOSSY ORIENT SHEENY SILKEN SILVER
SHINING SPLENDID
LUSTY BRAG CANT BURLY CRANK FLUSH
FRANK GUTSY HARDY JUICY RANDY
STIFF STOUT ROBUST STURDY LUSTFUL
BOUNCING PHYSICAL SPORTIVE
VIGOROUS
LUTE TAR BIWA LAUD DOMRA NABIA
NABLE REBAB REBEC SAROD CITOLE
ENLUTE LORICA LUTING SCREED VIELLE
ANGELOT BANDORE DICHORD DYPHONE
MANDOLA MANDORE MINIKIN PANDORE
THEORBO VIHUELA ANGELICA ARCHLUTE
PENORCON TAMBOURA TEMPLATE
TRICHORD

LUXEMBOURG

CAPITAL: LUXEMBOURG
HIGHEST POINT: BURGPLATZ
LOWLAND: BONPAYS GUTLAND
MEASURE: FUDER
MOUNTAIN RANGE: ARDENNES
PLATEAU: ARDENNES
RIVER: OUR SURE SAUER ALZETTE
MOSELLE
TOWN: BOUS EICH ROODT WILTZ
PETANGE VIANDEN DIEKIRCH
DUDELANGE ETTELBRUCK DIFFERDANGE

LUXURIANT LUSH RANK RICH FRANK
PROUD LAVISH WANTON OPULENT
PROFUSE RAMPANT TEEMING PAMPERED
PRODIGAL
LUXURIATE BASK REVEL WALLOW
LUXURIOUS HIGH LUSH NICE POSH
RANK SOFT GAUDY PLUSH SWANK
CAPUAN DELUXE GILDED PALACE SILKEN
SWANKY WANTON ELEGANT DELICATE
LUCULLAN PRODIGAL SENSUOUS
TRYPHENA TRYPHOSA
LUXURY FRILL FINERY OUTRAGE
DELICACY ELEGANCE PLEASURE
RICHNESS PRINCELINESS
LYCANTHROPE WEREWOLF
LYCEUM PLATFORM
LYE BOUK BUCK STRAKE LESSIVE
LIXIVIUM SOAPLEES
LYING FLAT FALSE LEASE CRETISM
LEASING MENTERY ACCUBATION
MENDACIOUS
(— APART) DISSITE

(— AT BASE OF MOUNTAINS)
PIEDMONT
(— CLOSE) QUAT
(— DOWN) DOWN LODGED CUMBENT
DORMANT COUCHANT
(— HID) LATITANT
(— IDLE) INACTIVE
(— ON BACK) SUPINE
(— ON FACE) PRONE PROCUMBENT
(— OVER) JACENT
(— UNDER GRASS) LEA
LYMPH CHYLE VIRUS
LYNCH HANG DEWITT

LYNX LOSSE OUNCE PISHU BOBCAT
GORKUN LUCERN CARACAL LUCIVEE
WILDCAT CARCAJOU
LYRE ASOR HARP LYRA SHELL CHELYS
KINNOR KISSAR TRIGON CITHARA
TESTUDO BARBITON PHORMINX
TRICHORD TRIGONON
LYRIC LAY LIED HOKKU LAEAN MELIC
GHAZEL TENSON CANCION CHANSON
DESCORT MADRIGAL
**(HAVING — AND DRAMATIC
QUALITIES)** SPINTO
(LOVE —) ALBA

M

M EM EMMA MIKE
M-1 GARAND
MA'AM MARM MISTRESS
MACABRE SICK HORRIBLE
MACAO (CHINESE NAME OF —)
 AOMEN
 (ISLAND OF —) TAIPA COLOANE
MACAQUE KRA BROH BRUH MACAC
 TOQUE MACHIN RHESUS RILAWA
 WANDEROO
MACARONI DITALI
MACARONIC SKEW
MACAW ARA ARARA PARROT MARACAN
 ARACANGA COCKATOO
MACBETH (AUTHOR OF —)
 SHAKESPEARE
 (CHARACTER IN —) ROSS ANGUS
 BANQUO DUNCAN HECATE LENNOX
 SEYTON SIWARD FLEANCE MACBETH
 MACDUFF MALCOLM MENTEITH
 CAITHNESS DONALBAIN
MACE CROC MAUL POKER VERGE MALLET
 SPARTH CATTAIL
 (PART OF —) HEAD HILT SPIKE FLANGE
 HANDLE
 (REED —) DOD
 (ROYAL —) SCEPTER
MACE-BEARER BEADLE VERGER
 MACEMAN
MACERATE RET SOUR STEEP
MACHETE GULOC PARANG CURTAXE
 CUTLASS
MACHIAVELLIAN CRAFTY CUNNING
 GUILEFUL
MACHINATION ARTIFICE INTRIGUE
 SCHEMERY
MACHINE
 (ALSO SEE DEVICE AND ENGINE) GIN
 HOG JIG SAW COMB GEAR JACK LIFT
 MULE PUMP RASP TRAY WHIM WINK
 ADDER AWNER BALER BENCH BILLY
 BOARD BRAKE BREAK COPER CRANE
 DEVIL EDGER FRAME JENNY JERRY
 JOLLY LATHE LAYER METER MIXER
 MOWER RAKER ROVER SCREW SETUP
 SIZER STAMP SULKY WILLY BARKER
 BEADER BEAMER BEATER BEETLE
 BENDER BILLER BINDER BOLTER BUCKLE
 BUMPER BUTTER CANTER CAPPER
 CARDER COOLER DONKEY DRAPER
 DREDGE DUSTER ENGINE FLAKER FOLDER
 FOOTER FORMER GADDER GAPPER
 GLAZER GRADER GRATER GUMMER
 HEADER HEMMER HOGGER HOOPER
 HULLER HUSKER IRONER JIGGER KICKER
 LEGGER LIFTER LINTER LOGGER MAILER
 MANGLE MILLER MITRER NAPPER NETTER
 NIBBER NIPPER PACKER PEGGER PINNER
 PLATER PUMPER RIPPER ROSSER ROTARY
 ROUTER SANDER SCUTCH SEALER
 SEAMER SHAKER SHAPER SHAVER
 SINGER SLICER SORTER SPACER STOKER
 TEDDER TENTER TWINER WASHER
 WELDER ABRADER BACKHOE BATCHER
 BELLOWS BLENDER BOTTLER BREAKER
 CAPSTAN CHIPPER COMBINE CRUSHER
 DRESSER EMULSOR ENCODER ENROBER
 ERECTOR FLANGER FLOSSER FREEZER
 GLASSER GRAINER GRINDER GROOVER
 GROUTER HUMIDOR IRONMAN JOINTER
 KNITTER KNOTTER MANGLER MATCHER
 MITERER PRINTER QUILLER RIVETER
 ROASTER SCALPER SHEARER SHEETER
 SLABBER SLASHER SLITTER SLOTTER
 SLUBBER SLUGGER SMASHER SPEEDER
 SPINNER SPONGER SPOOLER SPRAYER
 STACKER STAMPER STAPLER STEAMER
 STICKER TENONER TRAMPER TREATER
 TRIMMER TRUSSER TWILLER TWISTER
 TYPOBAR WHIPPER WHIZZER AERIFIER
 BROACHER CALENDER CANCELER
 CARTONER CLINCHER COLLATOR
 COMPRESS EXPLODER EXTRUDER
 FINISHER FORKLIFT GATHERER
 HARDENER HAYMAKER IMPACTER
 MORTISER PULSATOR SCUTCHER
 SHREDDER SOFTENER SPLITTER
 SPREADER SQUEEZER STITCHER
 STRANDER STRIPPER SURFACER
 TEMPERER THREADER THRESHER
 TRAVELER TUNNELER UPSETTER
 WINNOWER ADDRESSER
MACHINE GUN STINGER CHAUCHAT
MACHINERY MINT TOPCAP SUCCULA
 APPARATUS
MACHINIST FRILLER THINNER
 MACHINER
MACHISMO MACHO
MACKEREL CHAD PETO SCAD TINK
 BLINK OPELU SNOEK TUNNY BONITO
 SAUREL TINKER BLINKER BLOATER
 SCOMBER TASSARD ALBACORE
 HARDHEAD SCOMBRID SEERFISH
 (— ABOUT 8 OR 9 INCHES) TINK
 TINKER
 (PICKLED —) SCALPEEN
 (POOR BONY —) SLINK SLINKER
 (YOUNG —) SPIKE
MACROSCOPIC GROSS
MAD FEY AWAY GYTE HYTE WOOD YOND
 ANGRY BATTY BRAIN CRAZY DIPPY
 FOLLE RABID BEDLAM INSANE MANIAC
 BERSERK BONKERS FANATIC FRANTIC
 FURIOUS LUNATIC MADDING WITLESS
 DELIRANT DEMENTED DISTRACT
 INFORMAL MANIACAL MINDLESS
 RAVENING POSSESSED

MADAGASCAR

CAPITAL: ANTANANARIVO
ISLAND GROUP: ALDABRA
LAKE: ITASY ALAOTRA
MEASURE: GANTANG
NATIVE: HOVA SAKALAVA
PEOPLE: HOVA COTIER MARINA
RIVER: IKOPA MANIA SOFIA MANGOKY
MANGORO ONYLAHY
TOWN: IHOSY MANJA TULEAR MAJANGA
NOSSIBE TSIVORY TAMATAVE
ANTISIRABE

MADAM MEM MUM BAWD MAAM PANI
DONNA MADAME SENORA SENHORA
SIGNORA GOODWIFE MISTRESS
SINEBADA
MADAMA BUTTERFLY
(CHARACTER IN —) SUZUKI
CIOCIOSAN PINKERTON SHARPLESS
(COMPOSER OF —) PUCCINI
MADAME BOVARY (AUTHOR OF —)
FLAUBERT
(CHARACTER IN —) EMMA LEON
BOVARY DUPUIS HOMAIS CHARLES
HELOISE ROUAULT LHEUREUX RODOLPHE
BOULANGER
MADDEN ENRAGE INCENSE INFLAME
DISTRACT
MADDENED ENRAGED FRENZIED
MADDER GAMENE LIZARY ALIZARI
GARANCE MUNJEET TANAGRA
GARANCIN SPURWORT WOODRUFF
MADE SET BUILT COMPACT PREPARED
TIMBERED
(— FLUID BY HEAT) FUSILE
(— OF DISSIMILAR PARTS) MIXED
(— OF FLAX) LINEN
(— OF GRAIN) OATEN CEREAL
(— OF IVORY) EBURNEAN
(— OF SILVER) ARGENT
(— OF STONE) STONEN
(— OF TWIGS) VIRGAL
(— SHORT) CURTAL
(— TART) EUCHRED
(— TO ORDER) BESPOKEN
(— TRANSLUCENT) AJOURE
(— UP) ACCRETE
(— WITH CEDAR) CEDARN
MADEIRA ISLANDS (ISLAND OF —)
GRANDE DEZERTE
(TOWN OF —) FUNCHAL
(WINE OF —) BUAL TINTA MALMSEY
SERCIAL VERDELHO
MADHOUSE ASYLUM BEDLAM
MADLY WOOD CRAZY
MADMAN GELT BEDLAM MANIAC
FURIOSO LUNATIC WOODMAN
MADNESS MAD FURY MOON WOOD
FOLIE FOLLY FUROR MANIA BEDLAM
FRENZY LUNACY DEWANEE ECSTASY
MOONERY WIDDRIM DELIRIUM
DEMENTIA PIBLOKTO WILLNESS
WOODNESS WOODSHIP

MADONNA LADY VIRGIN
MADRIGAL ENSALADA
MAENAD FROW BASSARID BACCHANTE
(PL.) BACCHAE
MAGAZINE BOOK DRUM FLAT IGLOO
SLICK STORE RETORT ALMACEN
JOURNAL CASSETTE
MAGGOT MAD GRUB MAWK WORM
METHE GENTLE WARBLE WORMIL
MADDOCK SKIPPER MUCKWORM
MAGIC JUJU MAYA RUNE CRAFT FAIRY
GOETY SPELL TURGY GOETIC TREGET
VOODOO ALCHEMY CANTRIP CONJURY
DEVILRY GLAMOUR GRAMARY MAGICAL
SORCERY BRUJERIA HECATEAN
WIZARDRY NECROMANCY
(BLACK —) GOETY GOETIC MALEFICE
(WHITE —) TURGY
MAGICAL WIZARD WONDER HERMETIC
NUMINOUS THEURGIC
MAGIC FLUTE, THE
(CHARACTER IN —) PAMINA TAMINO
PAPAGENA PAPAGENO SARASTRO
MONOSTATOS
(COMPOSER OF —) MOZART
MAGICIAN MAGE BOKOR MAGUS UTHER
CUNJAH GOETIC GOOFER MAGIAN
MERLIN WABENO WIZARD CHARMER
GWYDION KOSCHEI WARLOCK WIELARE
WISEMAN CONJURER FETISHER
SORCERER THEURGIC TROLLMAN
ARCHIMAGE
MAGIC MOUNTAIN (AUTHOR OF —)
MANN
(CHARACTER IN —) HANS NAPHTA
BEHRENS CASTORP CAUCHAT CLAVDIA
JOACHIM ZIEMSSEN KROKOWSKI
PEEPERKORN SETTEMBRINI
MAGISTERIAL LOFTY PROUD AUGUST
CURULE LORDLY HAUGHTY STATELY
ARROGANT DOGMATIC
MAGISTRATE BEAK FOUD EPHOR JUDGE
MAYOR PRIOR REEVE AMTMAN ARCHON
AVOYER BAILIE BAILLI CENSOR CONSUL
FISCAL KOTWAL SYNDIC ALCALDE
BAILIFF BURGESS DUUMVIR ECHEVIN
EPHORUS JUSTICE NOMARCH PODESTA
PRAETOR PREFECT SUFFETE TRIBUNE
ALABARCH ALDERMAN CAPITOUL
DEFENSOR DEMIURGE DICTATOR
GOVERNOR MITTIMUS PHYLARCH
PRYTANIS RECORDER STRADICO
STRATEGE HUNDREDER CORREGIDOR
(— IN CHANNEL ISLANDS) JURAT
(— OF ANCIENT ROME) EDILE
(— OF VENICE AND GENOA) DOGE
(MOHAMMEDAN —) CADI CADY
SHERIF
(SCOTCH —) PROVOST STEWARD
MAGNANIMITY HEIGHT FREEDOM
MAGNANIMOUS BIG FREE GREAT
LARGE LOFTY NOBLE HEROIC EXALTED
GENEROUS
MAGNATE BARON MOGUL BASHAW
TYCOON
MAGNESIA PULVIL

MAGNET FIELD ADAMAS MAGNES ADAMANT SOLENOID TERRELLA
MAGNETISM IT DEVIL OOMPH
MAGNIFICENCE GITE POMP FLARE GLORY STATE PARADE JOLLITY ROYALTY GRANDEUR SPLENDOR
MAGNIFICENT RIAL GRAND NOBLE PROUD ROYAL AUGUST LAVISH IMMENSE POMPOUS STATELY SUBLIME GLORIOUS GORGEOUS MAGNIFIC PALATIAL PRINCELY SPLENDID
MAGNIFICENT OBSESSION (AUTHOR OF —) DOUGLAS (CHARACTER IN —) BRENT HELEN JOYCE NANCY WAYNE DAWSON HUDSON ROBERT ASHFORD MERRICK
MAGNIFY LAUD BLESS ERECT EXALT PRAISE ADVANCE DISTEND ENLARGE GLORIFY GREATEN INCREASE MAXIMIZE MULTIPLY
MAGNITUDE BULK MASS SIZE DATUM LEVEL SOLID EXTENT FIGURE PERIOD EXTREME CONSTANT FUNCTION INFINITE
MAGNOLIA YULAN BIGBLOOM CUCUMBER MAURICIO
MAGPIE MAG PIE PIET PYAT CISSA KOTRI MADGE NINUT MARGET NANPIE PIANET PIEMAG SIRGANG HAGISTER MARGARET PHEASANT PIENANNY
MAHATMA SAGE ARHAT
MAH-JONGG WOO
MAHOGANY SIPO ALMON CAOBA CEDAR ROHAN ACAJOU AGUANO SAPELE THITKA ALBARCO AVODIRE BAYWOOD GUNNUNG MADEIRA RATTEEN TABASCO BANGALAY HARDTACK TANGUILE (INDIAN —) TOON (PHILIPPINE —) BAGTIKAN
MAIA (FATHER OF —) ATLAS (MOTHER OF —) PLEIONE (SON OF —) MERCURY
MAID MAY GIRL LASS MEDE SLUT CHINA WENCH WOMAN MAIDEN TWEENY VIRGIN ANCILLA GENERAL MAIDKIN PHYLLIS PUCELLE WENCHEL BONIBELL BRANGANE HANDMAID TIREMAID (— IN WAITING) DAMSEL DAMOZEL (— OF HONOR) MARIE (— OF-ALL-WORK) SLAVEY GENERAL (KITCHEN —) SCOGIE (LADY'S —) AYAH ABIGAIL TIREMAID (NURSE —) BONNE (OLD —) TABBY SPINSTER (WAITING —) ABIGAIL SUIVANTE
MAIDEN MAY BIRD BURD DAME GIRL MAID DALAGA DAMSEL FROKIN MEISJE COLLEEN CYDIPPE DAMOZEL MADCHEN DAUGHTER
MAIDSERVANT LASS BIDDY BONNE SKIVVY ANCILLA LISETTE
MAIL BAG DAK HOOD POST MATTER AIRMAIL JACKPOT MAILBAG ORDINAR POSTAGE POSTBAG SEAPOST TAPPALL ORDINARY
MAILMAN POSTMAN BREVIGER
MAIM LAME BREAK TRUNK HAMBLE MANGLE MAYHEM SCOTCH CRIPPLE MUTILATE TRUNCATE (— AN ANIMAL) LAW MANK
MAIMED GAMMY SPAVINED (PREF.) PERO
MAIN HIGH LINE MOST CHIEF GRAND GREAT PRIME SHEER MIGHTY CAPITAL LEADING CARDINAL FOREMOST

MAINE

CAPITAL: AUGUSTA
COLLEGE: BATES COLBY BOWDOIN
COUNTY: KNOX WALDO KENNEBEC AROOSTOOK PENOBSCOT SAGADAHOC PISCATAQUIS
INDIAN: ABNAKI
LAKE: GRAND SEBEC SEBAGO RANGELEY SCHOODIC MOOSEHEAD CHESUNCOOK
MOUNTAIN: BIGELOW CADILLAC KATAHDIN
RIVER: SACO KENNEBEC AROOSTOOK KENNEBAGO PENOBSCOT
STATE BIRD: CHICKADEE
STATE FLOWER: PINECONE
STATE NICKNAME: LUMBER PINETREE
STATE TREE: PINE
TOWN: BATH ORONO AUBURN BANGOR BELFAST HOULTON KITTERY MACHIAS BOOTHBAY LEWISTON OGUNQUIT PORTLAND SKOWHEGAN

MAINLY BROADLY CHIEFLY LARGELY
MAINSTAY KEY ATLAS SINEW STOOP PILLAR BACKBONE RELIANCE
MAIN STREET (AUTHOR OF —) LEWIS (CHARACTER IN —) ERIK HUGH WILL CAROL MILFORD VALBORG KENNICOTT
MAINTAIN AVOW BEAR FEND FIND HOLD KEEP LAST SAVE ADOPT ARGUE CARRY CLAIM ESCOT SALVE ADHERE ALLEGE ASSERT AVOUCH DEFEND INTEND RETAIN THREAP UPHOLD UPKEEP CONFIRM CONTEND DECLARE DISPUTE JUSTIFY NOURISH SUBSIST SUPPORT SUSTAIN CONTINUE PRESERVE
MAINTENANCE KEEP LIVING UPKEEP ALIMONY CUSTODY FINDING KEEPING PREBEND SERVICE
MAIZE CORN GRAIN CEREAL INDIAN JAGONG STAPLE MEALIES DJAGOONG (— CRUSHED WITH PESTLE) STAMP
MAJESTIC HIGH AWFUL GRAND LOFTY REGAL ROYAL AUGUST KINGLY SUPERB STATELY SUBLIME ELEVATED IMPERIAL MAESTOSO SPLENDID
MAJESTY DIGNITY AUGUSTUS GRANDEUR KINGSHIP
MAJOR BEY DUR DURUM SHARP CAPITAL GREATER MAGGIORE
MAJOR BARBARA (AUTHOR OF —) SHAW (CHARACTER IN —) LOMAX SARAH CUSINS BARBARA CHARLES STEPHEN ADOLPHUS BRITOMART UNDERSHAFT

MAJORITY BODY BULK FECK CORPSE
SUBSTANCE
(ABSOLUTE —) QUORUM
MAKE DO CUT GAR LET MAY FORM GIVE
LEVY BRAND BUILD CAUSE COVER FETCH
FORGE FRAME SEIZE SHAPE STAMP
AUTHOR COBBLE CREATE GRAITH
INDUCE RENDER CONFECT FASHION
IMAGERY IWURCHE PERFORM PRODUCE
CONTRIVE GENERATE
(— A DIFFERENCE) SKILL
(— A MESS OF) PIE
(— A RUG) HOOK
(— A VISIT) COSHER
(— ACKNOWLEDGMENT) CONFESS
(— ACTIVE) ENERGIZE
(— AMENDS) ABYE ATONE ABEGGE
ANSWER REDEEM EXPIATE REDRESS
(— ANGRY) GRAMY WRATH
(— ATTRACTIVE) GILD
(— AWAY WITH) ABOLISH EMBEZZLE
(— BARE) STRIP DENUDE
(— BELIEVE) LET PRETEND
(— BETTER) AMEND HEIGHTEN
(— BLUE) HIP
(— BRIGHT) ENGILD ILLUME CLARIFY
(— BRISK) PERK
(— BROWN) TAN
(— BY STAMPING) MINT
(— CANDLE) DIP DRAW
(— CERTAIN) ASSURE ENSURE
(— CHANNEL IN) THROAT
(— CHEERFUL) SOLACE
(— CHOICE) OPT CHOOSE SELECT
(— CLAMMY) ENGLEIM
(— CLEAR) DECLARE DEVELOP DISCUSS
EXHIBIT EXPOUND LIGHTEN DESCRIBE
(— COLD) REFREID
(— COMPLETE) SPHERE
(— CONSPICUOUS) ENNOBLE
(— CONTENT) SATISFY
(— CULTIVABLE) EMPOLDER
(— CUT PRIOR TO LAYERING)
TONGUE
(— DESTITUTE) BEREAVE
(— DIFFERENT) ALTER CHANGE
(— DIRTY) MOIL GRIME
(— DISPLAY OF) AFFECT DISCOVER
(— DRUNK) FOX SOUSE FUDDLE
SOZZLE
(— DRY) HAZLE HAZZLE
(— EARLIER) ADVANCE
(— EFFERVESCENT) AERATE
(— EFFIGY) GUY
(— END OF) SNIB FETCH
(— ENDURING) ANNEAL
(— EQUAL) WEIGH EQUATE
(— EVEN) GLAZE LEVEL WEIGH SQUARE
(— FACES) GIMBLE MURGEON
(— FALSE PRETENSES) SHAM
(— FAST) FIX BAIL FAST GIRD KNIT
MAKE STOP BELAY HITCH BUCKLE
FASTEN SECURE
(— FAT) BATTEN
(— FIRM) FIX BRACE FASTEN
(— FIT) APTATE STRIKE

(— FOOL OF) DOR BORE DOLT DORRE
BEGOWK DOODLE
(— FOOLISH) DAFF GREEN NUGIFY
STULTIFY
(— FOOTSORE) SURBATE
(— FROTHY) MILL
(— FULL) FARCE FULFILL
(— FUN OF) GUY KID GAFF JAPE JEST
JOSH RIDE DROLL GLAIK SCOUT SMOKE
(— FUSS OVER NOTHING) FAFF
(— GLAD) FAIN
(— GLASS) FOUND
(— GLOSSY) SLEEK
(— GLOW) FURNACE
(— GOLDEN) ENDORE
(— GOOD) ABET
(— GRINDING NOISE) GRINCH
(— GURGLING SOUND) CROOL
(— HAPPY) BLESS ENJOY REFORM
BEATIFY SATISFY FELICIFY
(— HARD) TAW STEEL ENDURE
HORNIFY
(— HARDY) FASTEN
(— HEADWAY) STEM WALK ENFORCE
(— HELPLESS) STAGGER
(— HOLY) BLESS SACRE HALLOW
SANCTIFY
(— HORSE SEEM YOUNGER) BISHOP
(— ILL) MORBIFY
(— IMMOBILE) FREEZE
(— IMPACT) ASSAIL
(— INCURSION) HARRY
(— INSIGNIFICANT) MICRIFY
(— INTO BUNDLE) FARDEL
(— INTO LAW) ENACT
(— INVALID) DAMASK
(— JOINT) SYPHER
(— KNOWN) BID OUT GIVE WISE AREAD
BEKEN BREAK KITHE SOUND SPEAK
BEWRAY BROACH COUTHE DENOTE
DESCRY EXPOSE INFORM REVEAL
SPREAD CONFESS DECLARE DELIVER
DIVULGE PUBLISH SIGNIFY UNCOVER
ANNOUNCE DECIPHER DISCLOSE
DISCOVER INDICATE PROCLAIM
PROMULGE
(— LESS DENSE) THIN RAREFY
(— LESS SEVERE) MITIGATE
(— LIABLE) DANGER
(— LOVE) WOO COURT SPOON GALLANT
(— LUKEWARM) WLECCHE
(— LUSTERLESS) FLATTEN
(— MANIFEST) EVINCE EXPLAIN
(— MELANCHOLY) HYP
(— MELODIOUS) ATTUNE
(— MELODY) DREAM
(— MENTION) SPEAK
(— MERRY) JET GAUD CHEER SPORT
FROLIC SHROVE DISPORT REHAYTE
(— METALLIC SOUND) CHINK
(— MISTAKE) ERR BOOB GOOF
(— MONOTONOUS NOISE) DRONE
(— MORAL) ETHICIZE
(— MUCH OF) DAWT DANDLE
(— MURMURING NOISE) BUM
(— NEAT) FEAT SMUG TIDY GROOM
(— NEST) TIMBER

(— NONMAGNETIC) DEGAUSS
(— NUMB) DAZE ETHERIZE
(— OFF) BAG BOLT HOOK ANNEX HEIST MOSEY SLOPE SPIRIT SCARPER
(— ONE) UNE
(— ONE'S WAY) AIRT BORE TRADE
(— OPEN) AIR PATEFY
(— OUT) FARE FILL GLEAN SKILL DISCERN DECIPHER
(— OVER) TURN ALIEN CHANGE RECOCT DELIVER REFORGE
(— PALE) CHALK
(— PLEASANT) SWEETEN
(— POIGNANT) SAUCE
(— PREGNANT) ENWOMB
(— PROGRESS) GAIN STEM GATHER
(— PROUD) WLENCH
(— PUBLIC) BLOW BLAZE BREAK BLAZON DELATE DIVULGE FANFARE PUBLISH BULLETIN
(— QUIET) ALLAY QUIET APPEASE
(— RATTLING NOISE) TIRL
(— READY) DO BUN GET BOUN BOWN BUSK YARK BELAY BOWNE DRESS PREST PRIME FETTLE GRAITH ADDRESS APPAREL DISPOSE PREPARE
(— RECORD OF) REFER
(— REFERENCE) MENTION
(— RESISTANCE) REBEL
(— RESOLUTE) STEEL
(— RETURN FOR) REQUITE
(— RICH) FREIGHT IMBURSE
(— ROSY) FLUSH
(— RUSTLING SOUND) FISSLE FISTLE
(— RUTTING CRY) FREAM
(— SCANTY LIVING) EKE
(— SERIES OF NOTES) TINKLE
(— SHIFT) SCAMBLE
(— SIGN OF CROSS) BLESS
(— SMALL) MICRIFY BELITTLE
(— SMALLER) MINIFY COMPRESS
(— SMOOTH) SLAB GLAZE SLEEK GENTLE HAMMER SCRAPE LEVIGATE
(— SOFT) NESH GENTLE
(— SOGGY) SOP
(— SOUR) FOX WIND
(— SPIRITLESS) MOPE
(— SPORT OF) LARK
(— SPRUCE) PERK SMARTEN
(— STRAIGHT) ADDRESS
(— STRONG) STEEL FASTEN FORTIFY
(— STUPID) MOIDER STULTIFY
(— SUITABLE) ADAPT
(— SURE) SEE INSURE
(— TIPSY) FLUSTER
(— TRANSITION TO) MODULATE
(— UP) UP COOK FORM SPELL INDITE SETTLE ANALYZE COMPACT COMPOSE COMPUTE CONCOCT CONFECT FASHION COMPOUND COMPRISE DISPENSE
(— UP ACCOUNTS) BREVE
(— USE OF) FEE BUSK APPLY AVAIL BROOK SERVE SPEND EMPLOY EXECUTE IMPROVE UTILIZE
(— VIBRANT SOUND) CHIRR
(— VOID) ABATE ANNUL
(— WAR) WARRAY

(— WET) DRAGGLE
(— WHISTLING NOISE) WHEW
(— WHITE) BLANCH BLEACH CANDIFY
(— WORSE) IMPAIR PEJORATE
MAKER DOER JACK KNAVE SMITH FACTOR FORGER FORMER WORKER WRIGHT CREATOR DECLARER OPERATOR
(— OF ARROWS) FLETCHER
(— OF BARRELS) COOPER
(— OF POTS) POTTER
(— OF SADDLETREES) FUSTER
(— OF SONGS) BULBUL
(— OF TALLOW) CHANDLER
MAKESHIFT JURY RUDE JERRY TOUSY BEWITH KUTCHA JACKLEG STOPGAP RESOURCE
MAKEUP FACE BUILD GETUP HABIT PAINT ROUGE SETUP SHAPE FORMAT ANATOMY CONSIST FEATURE EYELINER PHYSIQUE
MALADROIT ILL INEPT AWKWARD UNHANDY BUNGLING
MALADY AMOK EVIL MORB GRIEF AILMENT DISEASE ILLNESS DISORDER MISCHIEF SICKNESS
MALARIA AGUE MIASMA SHAKES QUARTAN PALUDISM

MALAWI

CAPITAL: LILONGWE
COIN: KWACHA TAMBALA
FORMER CAPITAL: ZOMBA
FORMER NAME: NYASALAND
LAKE: NYASA
LANGUAGE: YAO CEWA BANTU NGONI TONGA NYANJA TUMBUKA
MOUNTAIN: MLANJE
PEOPLE: YAO BANTU CHEWA NGURU NYANJA
RIVER: SHIRE
TOWN: DOWA CHOLO MZUZU NCHEU ZOMBA KARONGA BLANTYRE LILONGWE

MALAY ASIL BAJAU ILOCO JAKUN MANOBO ILOKANO

MALAYSIA

CAPITAL: KUALALUMPUR
COIN: TRA TRAH
ISLAND: ARU GOA KAI OBI OMA ALOR BALI GAGA JAVA MUNA MURU SULU AMBON BANDA BOHOL BUTON CERAM LUZON MISOL PANAY SANGI SUMBA TIMOR WETAR BANGKA BOEFON BOEROE BORNEO BUTUNG FLORES LOMBOK MADURA PELENG SANGIR TALAUR WAIGEU AMBOINA CELEBES JAMDENA MINDORO MOROTAI PALAWAN SALAJAR SALWATI SUMATRA SUMBAWA BELITONG DJAILOLO TANIMBAR
ISTHMUS: KRA
LANGUAGE: TAGALOG
MOUNTAIN: BULU NIUT RAJA MURJO

NIAPA LEUSER SLAMET BINAIJA
RINDJANI
PEOPLE: ATA BAJAU SEMANG BISAYAN
TAGALOG VISAYAN
RIVER: KUTAI PERAK BARITO PAHANG
STATE: KEDAH PERAK SABAH JOHORE
PAHANG PENANG PERLIS MALACCA
SARAWAK
TOWN: IPOH DAVAO ILOILO KANGAR
KUPANG MANADO KUANTAN KUCHING
MALACCA SANDAKAN SEREMBAN
WEIGHT: TAEL WANG TAMPANG

MALE HE DOG HIM MAN BUCK BULL
COCK JACK ADULT MANLY SPEAR
JOHNNY MANFUL MASCLE VIRILE
LALAQUI MANLIKE MANNISH PURUSHA
(— OF ANIMALS) TOM BUCK BULL
JACK STUD STALLION
(EFFEMINATE —) NANCE
(GELDED —) GALT
(YOUNG —) GROOM
MALEDICTION BAN WISH CURSE
MALISON ANATHEMA
MALEFACTOR FELON BADDIE CULPRIT
CRIMINAL EVILDOER
MALEVOLENCE SPITE ENMITY GRUDGE
HATRED MALICE RANCOR SPLEEN
MALIGNITY
MALEVOLENT ILL EVIL FELL MALIGN
HATEFUL HOSTILE SPITEFUL
RANCOROUS
MALFEASANCE MISCONDUCT
MALPRACTICE
MALFORMATION CURL ERROR
HEMITERY MONSTROSITY
MALFUNCTION GLITCH

MALI

ANCIENT CITY: TIMBUKTU
CAPITAL: BAMAKO
FORMER NAME: FRENCHSUDAN
LAKE: DO DEBO GAROU KORAROU
LANGUAGE: DOGON DYULA MANDE
MARKA PEULH BAMBARA MALINKE
SENOUFO SONGHAI
MOUNTAIN: MINA MANDING
PEOPLE: MOOR PEUL TUAREG BAMBARA
MALINKE SONGHAI SENOULFO
RIVER: BANI BAGOE BAKOY NIGER
BAOULE AZOUAK SENEGAL
TOWN: GAO SAN KATI KITA NARA BAMBA
KAYES MOPTI NIONO NIORO SEGOU
SIKASSO

MALICE DOLE ENVY HAIN PIQUE SPITE
VENOM VIRUS ENMITY GRUDGE RANCOR
SPLEEN DESPITE AMBITION MALIGNITY
MALICIOUS BITTER DOGGED MALIGN
WANTON HATEFUL HEINOUS LEERING
VICIOUS CANKERED SINISTER SPITEFUL
VENOMOUS VIPEROUS
MALIGN FOUL ABUSE LIBEL WRONG
BEWRAY DEFAME REVILE VILIFY

ASPERSE DEPRAVE SLANDER
BLASPHEME
MALIGNANT EVIL BLACK FELON FERAL
SWART MALIGN BALEFUL ENVIOUS
HATEFUL HELLISH PEEVISH REPTILE
VICIOUS CANKERED SHREWISH SPITEFUL
VENOMOUS VIPEROUS VIRULENT
WRATHFUL RANCOROUS
MALIGNITY GALL LIVER VENOM VIRUS
HATRED MALICE RANCOR
MALINGER MIKE DODGE SKULK
MALLEABLE MILD SOFT DUCTILE
PLASTIC
MALLET MALL MAUL GAVEL BEETLE
DRIVER HAMMER DRESSER FLOGGER
STRIKER PLOWMELL
(— FOR BREAKING CLODS) BILDER
(CURRIER'S —) MACE
(HATTER'S —) BEATER
(PAVER'S —) TUP
MALTA (ANCIENT NAME OF —)
MELITA
(CAPITAL OF —) VALLETTA
(ISLAND OF —) GOZO COMINO
(TOWN OF —) QORMI RABAT HAMRUN
SLIEMA XAGHRA ZABBAR BIRKIRKARA
MALTREAT MAUL ABUSE DIGHT DEFOUL
DEMEAN MISUSE BEDEVIL MISGUIDE
MANHANDLE
MAMMAL OX ASS BAT CAT COW DOG
FOX PIG YAK BEAR BOAR COON DEER
GOAT HARE LION LYNX MINK MOLE
PUMA SEAL ZEBU BEAST BISON CAMEL
COATI COYPU GENET HORSE HYENA
LEMUR LLAMA MOOSE OKAPI OTTER
PANDA RATEL SABLE SHEEP SHREW
SKUNK SLOTH SWINE TAPIR TIGER
WHALE ZORIL ALPACA ANIMAL BADGER
COUGAR CULPEO DESMAN DUGONG
FISHER FOUSSA GOPHER GRISON
JAGUAR MARTEN MONKEY OCELOT
TENREC VICUNA WALRUS WOMBAT
BUFFALO CARIBOU DOLPHIN ECHIDNA
GIRAFFE GLUTTON GUANACO HIPPOID
HUANACO MANATEE OPOSSUM PECCARY
POLECAT PRIMATE RACCOON SUCKLER
SURICAT TARSIER TYLOPOD WILDCAT
AARDVARK AARDWOLF ANTELOPE
BANXRING CACOMIXL CREODONT
ELEPHANT FALANAKA HEDGEHOG
KINKAJOU MAMMIFER PANGOLIN
PINNIPED REINDEER SQUIRREL
PRONGHORN RHINOCEROS
MAMMOTH HUGE LARGE GIGANTIC
GIGANTIC
MAN BO HE BOY GEE GUY HIM LAD TAO
WAT WER BUCK CHAL CHAP COVE DICK
EARL GENT GOME HOMO JACK JONG
MALE RINK TULK BERNE BIMBO BIPED
BLOKE CHURL COVEY CULLY FORCE
FREKE GROOM GUEST HEART HOMME
HORSE JOKER SEGGE SWAIN WIGHT
BIMANE CHIELD CUFFIN FELLOW
HOMBRE MANTZU WEPMAN BIMANUS
HOMINOID KINSMAN MANKIND
(— DRESSED AS WOMAN) BESSY
MALINCHE

(— OF ALL WORK) MOZO
(— OF BRASS) TALOS
(— OF GREAT WEALTH) NABOB
(— OF HIGH RANK) CHAM KHAN
THAKUR GRANDEE
(— OF WAR) ANDREW CARAVEL
CRUISER
(ARTIFICIAL —) GOLEM
(BALD —) PILGARLIC
(BEST —) BRIDEMAN PARANYMPH
(BIG —) COB BRUISER MUGWUMP
(CHURLISH —) NABAL BODACH
(CLEANING —) BUSBOY
(COMMON —) CARL STREET YEOMAN
(CRAFTY —) FOX
(CRUEL —) OGRE BRUTE
(DISAGREEABLE —) GLEYDE
(DISSOLUTE —) RAKE
(ECCENTRIC —) GEEZER
(EDUCATED —) EFFENDI
(EFFEMINATE —) DILDO FAIRY NANCE
PUNCE SISSY JESSIE COCKNEY
MEACOCK MIDWIFE MILKSOP ANDROGYN
MOLLYCODDLE
(FASHIONABLE —) TOUPET ELEGANT
FOPLING GALLANT
(FIRST —) ASK ADAM ASKR TIKI
(FLASHILY-DRESSED —) LAIR
(FOPPISH —) BLOOD
(FREE —) LIBER
(HOLY —) SADHU SAINT SANNYASI
(IDEAL —) SUPERMAN
(IMMORAL —) REP
(INSANE —) FURIOSO
(LADY'S —) FOPLING DAMMARET
(LEARNED —) ULEMA LAMDAN OLLAMH
PUNDIT SAVANT SOPHIST
(LECHEROUS —) SATYR
(LIAISON —) COURIER
(LITERARY —) GIGADIBS
(LITTLE —) MANNET SHRIMP MANNIKIN
(LUSTFUL —) GOAT
(MARRIED —) HUSBAND BENEDICT
(MEDICINE —) PEAI DOCTOR SHAMAN
ANGAKOK
(MIGHTY —) SAMSON
(OLD —) HAG OLD BOOL CUFF GAFF
CRONE DOBBY UNCLE BODACH DUFFER
FATHER GAFFER NESTOR GERONTE
STARETS ECKEHART VELYARDE
PATRIARCH
(PRIMITIVE —) URMENSCH
(PRINCIPAL —) HERO TOPARCH
(RICH —) DIVES CROESUS
(RIGHTEOUS —) SADDIK
(RIGHT-HAND —) HENCHMAN
(SERVING —) GARCON
(STRAIGHT —) STOOGE
(STRONG-ARM —) HOOD GORILLA
(THICKSET —) GRUB KNAR SPUD
(TOUGH —) KNAR
(UNEMPLOYED —) BATLAN
(VICIOUS —) YAHOO
(WHITE —) BOSTON BUCKRA PAKEHA
CACHILA
(WILD —) WOODMAN WOODWOSE
(WISE —) NAB HAKAM SABIO SOLON

SOPHY NESTOR WIZARD SOLOMON
TOHUNGA
(WRETCHED —) CAITIFF
(YOUNG —) BOY LAD JONG PUNK
YOUTH BOCHUR DAMSEL EPHEBE
KNIGHT BOUCHAL BUCKEEN YOUNKER
COCKEREL SPRINGAL
MAN-ABOUT-TOWN FLANEUR
MANACLE BAND BOND DARBY HAMPER
TIRRET SHACKLE HANDCUFF HANDLOCK
(PL.) IRONS CHAINS
MANAGE DO GET MAN RUN BEAR BOSS
CURB FEND HACK HOLD KEEP LEAD
MAKE RULE TEND TOOL WIND WORK
BROOK CARRY DIGHT FORTH FRAME
GUIDE MAYNE ORDER SHIFT SPEND
STEER SWING WIELD CONVEY DEMEAN
DEVISE DIRECT FETTLE GOVERN HANDLE
INTEND MANURE TEMPER AGITATE
CONDUCT DISPOSE EXECUTE FINAGLE
HUSBAND MINSTER OFFICER OPERATE
SOLICIT STEWARD CONTRIVE ENGINEER
NEGOTIATE
MANAGEABLE EASY YARE BANTAM
DOCILE WIELDY DUCTILE FLEXIBLE
YIELDING
MANAGEMENT CARE HEEL WORK
CHARGE CONDUCT CONTROL ECONOMY
GESTION RUNNING CARRIAGE
DEMEANOR ENGINERY MANAGERY
MANEUVER REGIMENT STEERAGE
STEERING
(DOMESTIC —) MENAGE HUSBANDRY
(GOOD —) EUTAXY
(SKILLFUL —) PRACTICE
MANAGER BOSS DOER AGENT DAROGA
DEPUTY PURSER SYNDIC AMILDAR
CURATOR ERENACH HUSBAND STEWARD
WIELDER AUMILDAR DIRECTOR
DISPOSER ENGINEER HERENACH
INSTITOR
MAN-AT-ARMS KNIGHT
MANATEE COWFISH HOGFISH MERMAID
LAMANTIN MUTILATE SIRENIAN
MANCHURIA
(CHINESE NAME FOR —) MANCHOW
(PENINSULA OF —) LIAOTUNG
(PROVINCE OF —) JILIN LIAONING
HEILONGJIANG
(RIVER OF —) AMUR LIAO YALU ARGUN
USSURI SUNGARI
MANDARIN TOWKAY
MANDARIN ORANGE SATSUMA
MANDATE BREVE ORDER BEHEST
CHARGE DECREE FIRMAN BIDDING
COMMAND PRECEPT PROCESS
MANDAMUS MANDATUM WARRANTY
(— OF GOD) JUDGMENT
MANDATORY OBLIGATORY
MANDOLIN OUD MANDORA
MANE JUBA MONE CREST PITRI
ENCLOURE
MANEUVER PLAY TURN WISE GAMBIT
JOCKEY MANURE PESADE VRILLE
FINAGLE FINESSE ARTIFICE DEMARCHE
ENGINEER EXERCISE STRATEGY
WINDLASS

(— IN AUTO RACING) SLINGSHOT
(— IN SPACE) DOCK
(— IN SURFING) CUTBACK
(— OF MOTORCYCLE OR BICYCLE) WHEELIE
(- GENTLY) EASE
(AERIAL —) BUNT LOOP SPIN FISHTAIL WINGOVER
(BULLFIGHTING —) VERONICA
(ILLEGAL —) GAME
(ROCK-CLIMBING —) LAYBACK
(SKIING —) SNOWPLOW
(WRESTLING —) ESCAPE BUTTOCK
MANGE ITCH REEF SCAB CANKER DARTARS SCABIES
MANGER BIN BUNK CRIB HECK STALL CRATCH
MANGLE MAR HACK MOUTH BRUISE GARBLE HACKLE IRONER MAGGLE MURDER MAMMOCK LACERATE MUTILATE
MANGO DIKA AMHAR AMINI BAUNO AMCHOOR CARABAO PAHUTAN
MANGROVE BACAO GORAN MANGLE MYRTAL BACAUAN CERIOPS COURIDA HANGALAI LANGARAI
MANHANDLE MESS ROUGH SCRAG
MANIA RAGE CRAZE FUROR FRENZY DELIRIUM HYSTERIA INSANITY CACOETHES
MANIAC KILLER MADMAN FANATIC LUNATIC
MANIFEST HAVE NUDE OPEN RIFE SHOW CLEAR FRANK GROSS NAKED OVERT PLAIN PROVE SPEAK ARRANT ATTEST EVINCE EXTANT LIQUID OSTEND PATENT APPROVE BETOKEN CONFESS DECLARE EVIDENT EXHIBIT EXPRESS OBVIOUS SIGNIFY VISIBLE APPARENT DISCLOSE DISCOVER INDICATE PALPABLE PROCLAIM
(NOT —) LATENT
MANIFESTATION ACT BEAM SIGN GLINT AVATAR COMING EFFECT OSTENT ADVANCE DISPLAY EXPRESS OUTSIDE SHOWING EPIPHANY MANIFEST
(BARELY PERCEPTIBLE —) SCINTIL
(BRIEF —) GLEAM
(DIVINE —) SPIRIT SHEKINAH
(HORRIBLE —) CHIMAERA
(MORAL —) SOUL
(VAGUE —) GLIMMER
MANIFOLD MANY TURRET VARIOUS MULTIPLE MULTIPLEX REPLICATE
(SUFF.) PLOID
MANIKIN ECORCHE PANTINE PHANTOM HOMUNCIO HOMUNCLE MANNIKIN
MANILA HEMP ABACA
MANIPULATE COG COAX COOK DIAL FAKE HAND STIR TOOL CROOK HUMOR KNEAD SHAPE TREAT WIELD GOVERN HANDLE JOCKEY MANAGE WANGLE SHUFFLE
(— BY DECEPTIVE MEANS) RIG
MANITOBA (CAPITAL OF —) WINNIPEG
(RIVER OF —) RED SEAL SWAN NELSON

ROSEAU SOURIS PEMBINA CHURCHILL SASKACHEWAN
(TOWN OF —) CARMAN BRANDON DAUPHIN KILLARNEY SWANRIVER
MANKIND MAN FLESH SHEEP WORLD BIMANA SPECIES HUMANITY UNIVERSE MORTALITY
MANLINESS ARETE VIRTUS
MANLY BOLD MALE HARDY DARING VIRILE MANLIKE
MAN-MADE CULTURAL SYNTHETIC
MANNER BAT JET LAT WAY FORM GARB GATE KIND MAKE MIEN MODE RATE SORT THEW WISE WONE GUISE LATES SHAPE STYLE TENUE TRICK COURSE CUSTOM METHOD MISTER STRAIN ADDRESS AMENITY FASHION QUALITY QUOMODO CARAPACE DEMEANOR LANGUAGE
(— OF APPROACH) ABORD
(— OF DOING) ACTION
(— OF HANDLING) HAND
(— OF MAKING ANYTHING) FACTURE
(— OF SITTING) ASANA
(— OF SPEAKING) SLUR SOUGH ACCENT GRAMMAR PARLANCE
(— OF WALKING) STEP
(AFFECTED —) AIR
(AMUSING —) DROLLERY
(ARROGANT —) BRAG HAUTEUR
(FORBIDDING —) SHELL
(FORMAL —) STARCH
(HABITUAL —) SONG
(OUTWARD —) TOUR FRONT
(SMOOTH —) JAPAN
(SWAGGERING —) SIDE PANACHE
(UNUSUAL —) SINGULARITY
(USUAL —) HABIT
MANNERISM POSE TRICK IDIASM
(PL.) DAPS
MANNERLY CIVIL POLITE
MANNERS MORES HAVANCE HAVINGS BEAUETRY BREEDING
MAN-OF-WAR CARAVEL
MANON (CHARACTER IN —) MANON GRIEUX LESCAUT BRETIGNY
(COMPOSER OF —) MASSENET
MANON LESCAUT
(CHARACTER IN —) MANON GRIEUX GERONTE
(COMPOSER OF —) PUCCINI
MANOR HAM HOF BURY HALL TOWN VILL BARONY COMMOTE MANSION LORDSHIP TOWNSHIP
MANPOWER BRAWN LABOR
MANSERVANT (ALSO SEE SERVANT) LAD MOZO GROOM VALET ANDREW BUTLER TEABOY
MANSION DOME SEAT HOTEL HOUSE MANSE SIEGE TOWER CASTLE HARBOR HOSTEL CHATEAU
(— OF THE MOON) ALNATH
MANSLAUGHTER BLOOD FELONY HOMICIDE
MANTELPIECE BRACE PAREL CLAVEL MANTEL MANTLING
MANTLE CAPA HOSE PALL REAM ROBE

CLOAK CREAM FROCK JABUL LAMBA PALLA TUNIC CAMAIL CAPOTE KHIRKA KIRTLE ROCHET SLAVIN SOLMAN TABARD CHLAMYS CHRISOM CHUDDAR FERIDJI MANTEAU PAENULA PALLIUM SLEEVES WHITTLE WRAPPER BARRACAN CHRYSOME MANTELET REGOLITH RICINIUM STOCKING

MANUAL VADY COACH GREAT TUTOR PORTAS CAMBIST CEMBALO DIDACHE MANUARY BOMBARDE HANDBOOK KEYBOARD ORDINARY PORTHORS SYNOPSIS
(MAGICIAN'S —) GRIMOIRE
(NAVIGATION —) BOWDITCH

MANUFACTURE COIN FAKE MAKE FORGE PERFORM PRODUCE WORKING BOOKWORK

MANUFACTURER BRAND MAKER WRIGHT SPINNER SUPPLIER

MANURE HOT MIG DUNG LIME MUCK SAUR SOIL TATH FECES GUANO MIXEN FULZIE SEASON SLEECH COMPOST FOLDING GOODING POUDRET DRESSING WORTHING

MANUSCRIPT CODEX FLIMSY MATTER SCRIPT UNCIAL CURSIVE PANDECT PAPYRUS PINTURA WITNESS EXEMPLAR PARCHMENT

MANY TEN MUCH SERE FORTY GREAT OODLES TWENTY ENDLESS JILLION SEVERAL VARIOUS MANIFOLD COUNTLESS
(GOOD —) HANTLE
(GREAT —) MORT RAFF SWITH

MAP KEY CARD DICE PLAT PLOT CARTE CENTO CHART DRAFT INSET STILL GRAPHIC GATEFOLD

MAPLE MAZER DOGWOOD SYCAMORE WINGSEED
(FLOWERING —) ABUTILON
(GROVE OF —) SAPBUSH

MAR BLOT SCAR SNIT SNIP BLOOM BOTCH SHEND SPILL SPOIL BLOTCH DEFACE DEFEAT DEFORM EFFACE IMPAIR INJURE MANGLE BLEMISH DISGRACE

MARAUD RAID DACOIT PICKEER PILLAGE

MARAUDER TORY BANDIT BUMMER LOOTIE PIRATE CATERAN LADRONE

MARBLE MIB MIG PEA POT TAW BOOL BOWL DUCK DUMP MARL AGATE AGGIE ALLEY BONCE COMMY IMMIE IVORY LINER PUREY RANCE DOGGLE MARMOR MARVEL MIGGLE PARIAN PEEWEE STEELY CARRARA CIPOLIN GLASSIE GRIOTTE KNICKER PARAGON PITCHER SHOOTER BROCATEL DOLOMITE KNUCKLER
(BLACK —) JET
(IMITATION —) SCAGLIOLA
(SIENA —) BROCATELLO

MARCH FILE HIKE MARK MUSH SLOG ROUTE TRACE TROOP DEFILE DOUBLE PARADE REVIEW DEBOUCH STRETCH FOOTSLOG PROGRESS
(— BEHIND) COVER
(— IN FRONT OF) LEAD
(— OBLIQUELY) INCLINE
(DAY'S —) ETAPE

MARE SEA YAUD GILLIE GILLOT GRASNI HUNTRESS

MARGIN HEM RIM VAT BANK BRIM BROW CURB EDGE FOLD HAIR INCH LIMB LIST RAND BRINK EAVES MARGE VERGE BORDER FRINGE LACING CUSHION DRAUGHT MARGENT SELVAGE HAIRLINE
(— OF CARAPACE) DOUBLURE
(— OF CIRCLE) LIMB
(— OF LIP) PROLABIUM
(— OF PAGE) BACK
(— OF SAFETY) LEEWAY
(— OF SHELL) LABRUM LIMBUS
(— OF SUPERIORITY) LEAD
(— OF WING) TERMEN
(—S OF HERD) SWING
(NARROW —) ACE NECK

MARIGOLD GOLD GULL SAMH AZTEC BOOTS GOOLS HELIO BACLIN BUDDLE GOLDCUP GOLDING GOLLAND KINGCUP MARYBUD TAGETES

MARIJUANA BOO POT WEED DAGGA GRASS MOOCAH LOCOWEED MARYJANE
(ONE OUNCE OF —) LID
(ONE WHO TAKES —) POTHEAD
(OUNCE OF —) CAN
(PUFF ON — CIGARETTE) TOKE

MARINE JOLLY GALOOT GULPIN GYRENE TOPMAN HALIMOUS MARITIME NAUTICAL THALASSIC

MARINER MARINE SAILOR SEALER SEAMAN BUSCARLE SEAFARER WARRENER

MARIONETTE POPPET PUPPET

MARITAL INTIMATE HUSBANDLY

MARITIME MARINE HALIMOUS NAUTICAL

MARJORAM AMARACUS

MARK AIM END HOB HUB POP BLOT BUOY BUTT CHOP CLIP DELE DINT FAZE FIST GOAL LINE MIND NOTE RIST SCAR SEAR SIGN SMOT SMUT SPOT TEND TEXT TICK VIRE WAND WIND BADGE BOTTU BRAND CHANT CHECK CLOUD DITTO DRAFT FLECK FRANK GHOST GRADE HILUM KNIFE LABEL MARCH MARCO NOKTA PRINT PRINT PROOF SCART SCOPE SCORE SCUFF SPOOR STAMP SWIRL TOKEN TRACE TRACK TRACT WATCH ACCENT ALPIEU BEACON BESPOT BLOTCH BUTTON CARACT DAGGER DAPPLE DENOTE DIRECT INDICE LETTER MARKER NOTICE OBJECT SMUTCH STREAK STROKE SUCKER SYMBOL TARGET UPSHOT WICKER WITTER BETOKEN CHARBON COCKSHY DEMERIT DIAMOND DRAUGHT EROTEME EXCUDIT FINMARK IMPRESS IMPRINT KENMARK SCARIFY SERRATE SIGNARY SPECKLE STRIATE SYMPTOM VESTIGE WAYMARK BRACELET CROWFOOT DATEMARK DIASTOLE DISPUNCT EVIDENCE FOOTMARK FOOTSTEP IDENTIFY IDEOGRAM MONUMENT NOTATION

(— A BIRD) BAND
(— AFTER ASSAY) TOUCH
(— AS SPURIOUS) ATHETIZE
(— BY BURNING) CHAR
(— BY CUTTING) SCRIBE
(— BY PLOWING) STRIKE
(— CROSSWISE) CRANK
(— DENOTING CORRUPT PASSAGE) OBELUS
(— DIRECTIONS) ADDRESS
(— IN ARCHERY) CLOUT HOYLE ROVER WHITE
(— IN BOOK) PRESSMARK
(— IN CANON) LEAD
(— IN CURLING) TEE COCK
(— IN QUOITS) MOT
(— INDICATING CONTRACTION) CORONIS
(— INDICATING DIRECTION) ARROW
(— OF ACKNOWLEDGEMENT) ACCOLADE
(— OF DISGRACE) STAIN STIGMA
(— OF DISHONOR) ABATEMENT
(— OF DISTINCTION) BELT
(— OF ESTEEM) LAUREL GARLAND
(— OF OFFICE) SEAL
(— OF OWNERSHIP) SWANMARK
(— OF PURITY) HALLMARK
(— OF REFERENCE) OBELISK
(— OF SIGNATURE) CROSS
(— OF SUPERIORITY) BELL
(— OF WEAVER) KEEL
(— OFF) SUBTEND
(— OFF LAND) FEER PHEER
(— ON ANIMAL'S FACE) BLAZE STRIPE
(— ON CHART) VIGIA
(— ON FEATHER) BAR SPANGLE
(— ON FOREHEAD) KUMKUM
(— ON PENNSYLVANIA BARNS) HEXAFOOS
(— ON SHEEP) SMIT BUIST
(— ON SHIP) SURMARK
(— ON SKIN) PLOT CREASE
(— ON STAMP) CONTROL
(— OUT) RUN CANCEL DELINE AIRMARK APPOINT COMPART DESCRIBE
(— OVER GERMAN VOWEL) UMLAUT
(— OVER LETTER N) TILDE
(— OVER LONG VOWELS) MACRON
(— TIME) BEAT COUNT
(— TO BE ATTAINED) BOGEY BOGIE
(— TO GUIDE VESSELS) MYTH
(— TO SCARE DEER) SHEWEL
(— TRANSVERSELY) LADDER
(— UNDER LETTER C) CEDILLA
(— WITH LINES) HATCH CAMLET
(— WITH POINTED ROLLER) GRILL
(— WITH RIDGES) RIB
(— WITH STRIPES) WALE STREAM
(— WITH TAR) BASTE
(ACCENT —) VERGE
(ANGULAR —) HOOK
(BALLOT —) SCRATCH
(BOUNDARY —) DOOL MERE TERM WIKE MEITH STAKE LANDMARK
(CADENCY —) BRISURE
(CANCELLATION —) BUMPER KILLER

(DIACRITICAL —) TIL TILDE TITTLE
(DIRTY —) SMIRCH
(DISTINCTIVE —) BADGE INDICIA
(DISTINGUISHING —) ITEM COCARDE EARMARK INSIGNE
(DOUBLE-DAGGER —) DIESIS
(EASY —) YAP SMELT PIGEON
(EIGHTH —) URE
(EXACT —) NICK
(EXCLAMATION —) SCREAMER
(IDENTIFICATION —) MOLE CREST SPLIT SIGNET WATTLE EARMARK KENMARK LUGMARK COLOPHON
(LOW-WATER —) DATUM
(MAGICAL —) SIGIL
(MERIDIAN —) MIRE
(MUSICAL —) PRESA CORONA
(PARAGRAPH —) PILCROW
(PROOFREADER'S —) STET CARET
(PUNCTUATION —) DASH STOP BRACE BREVE COLON COMMA HYPHEN PERIOD BRACKET DIERESIS ELLIPSIS DIACRITIC SEMICOLON PARENTHESIS
(RED —) HICKEY
(SECTARIAN —) BOTTU TILAKA
(SKATE —) CUSP
(SMALL ROUND —) DOT
(TRAMP'S —) MONICA MONNIKER
(WHITE —) RACHE
MARKED FAR GREAT SCORED SEVERE SPOTTY COLORED EMINENT MARCATO POINTED SCARRED SPECKED SPOTTED
MARKER HOB HUB IOU DOLE FLAG MARK SPAD STUMP TYPER BUTTON GUIDON HOBBLE HUBBLE TABBER DAYMARK SCRIBER
MARKET CURB GUNJ MART PORT SALE SOOK VEND VENT CHEAP CROSS GUNGE HALLE PASAR PRICE TRONE TRYST BAZAAR BOURSE MERCAT OUTLET PARIAN RIALTO STAPLE POULTRY CHEAPING DEBOUCHE EMPORIUM EXCHANGE MACELLUM
(CATTLE —) TRISTE
(MEAT —) SHAMBLES
MARKETPLACE SUQ TRON AGORA CHOWK HALLE PLAZA BAZAAR RIALTO EMPORIUM
MARKSMAN SHOT MARKER PLUFFER SHOOTER SHOTMAN SHOOTIST
MARLINESPIKE FID JAEGER PRICKER STABBER
MARMOSET MICO TITI SAGOIN JACCHUS OUITITI QUIRCAL SAIMIRI TAMARIN WISTITI ORABASSU
MARMOT BOBAC PAHMI GOPHER SUSLIK SCIURID SIFFLEUR WHISTLER
MAROON AZTEC PICNIC CIMARRON
MARQUEE CANOPY
MARRIAGE MUTA DAIVA HYMEN KARAO BEENAH BRIDAL BUCKLE SPLICE SPOUSE EXOGAMY NUPTIAL PUNALUA SPOUSAL WEDDING WEDLOCK CONUBIUM LEVIRATE OPSIGAMY
(— AFTER DEATH OF FIRST SPOUSE) DIGAMY
(— AT ADVANCED AGE) OPSIGAMY

(— BELOW POSITION) HYPOGAMY
(— OUTSIDE FAMILY) EXOGAMY
(— PORTION) TOCHER
(— WITH AN INFERIOR) MESALLIANCE
(— WITHIN A GROUP) ENDOGAMY
(PREF.) GAMO
MARRIED COVERT WEDDED ESPOUSED
(NOT —) SOLE
MARRY TIE WED FAST WIFE WIVE CLEEK
MATCH BUCKLE CROTCH ENSURE
MARROW SPLICE HUSBAND NUPTIAL
WEDLOCK DESPOUSE
(— OFF) BESTOW
MARS ARES MAMERS MARMAR MAVORS
MASPITER TEUTATES
(FATHER OF —) JUPITER
(MOTHER OF —) JUNO
(SON OF —) REMUS ROMULUS
MARSH BOG FEN HAG CARR DANK FELL
FLAM FLAT HOPE MASH MIRE OOZE
QUAG ROSS SOIL SUDS TARN VLEI
WASH WHAM FLASH GLADE JHEEL
LIMAN SLACK SLASH SLUMP SWAMP
MORASS PALUDE PUDDLE CIENAGA
CORCASS POCOSIN PONTINE QUAGMIRE
STROTHER TURLOUGH
(SALT —) SALT SEBKA SALINA SALINE
MARSHAL ARRAY ORDER MUSTER
PARADE JERONIMO MARECHAL MOBILIZE
MARSH MARIGOLD BOOTS CAPER
CRAZY GOOLS DRAGON GAMOND
GOWLAN COWSLIP ELKSLIP GOLDCUP
KINGCOB KINGCUP MARYBUD
DRUNKARD
MARSHY BOGGY FOGGY MOORY MOSSY
PONDY SNAPY SPEWY CALLOW MARISH
PLASHY QUAGGY QUASHY SLUMPY
HELODES MOORISH PALUDAL QUEACHY
PALUDINE WATERISH
MARSUPIAL KOALA QUOLL CUSCUS
POSSUM WOMBAT BETTONG DASYURE
OPOSSUM KANGAROO BANDICOOT
PETAURIST
MARTEN FOIN PEKAN SABLE SOBOL
FISHER MARTRIX MUSTELID MUSTELIN
(GROUP OF —S) RICHESSE
MARTHA (CHARACTER IN —) JULIA
NANCY LIONEL MARTHA HARRIET
PLONKETT
(COMPOSER OF —) FLOTOW
MARTIAL BELLIC WARLIKE WARRIOR
BELLICAL MILITARY
MARTIN CHUZZLEWIT
(AUTHOR OF —) DICKENS
(CHARACTER IN —) GAMP MARK
MARY SETH JONAS MERCY SARAH
GRAHAM MARTIN TAPLEY ANTHONY
CHARITY PECKSNIFF CHUZZLEWIT
MARTYR STEPHEN WITNESS SUFFERER
MARVEL MARL MUSE FERLY SELLY
ADMIRE WONDER MAGNALE MIRACLE
MONSTER PORTENT PRODIGY SELCOUTH
ADMIRATION
MARVELOUS FAB EPATANT MIRIFIC
STRANGE FABULOUS WONDROUS
MIRACULOUS

MARYLAND

CAPITAL: ANNAPOLIS
COLLEGE: HOOD GOUCHER STJOHNS
COUNTY: KENT CECIL TALBOT CALVERT
HARFORD ALLEGANY SOMERSET
INDIAN: CONOY NANTICOKE
LAKE: PRETTYBOY
MOUNTAIN: BACKBONE
NATIVE: WESORT TERRAPIN
RIVER: CHESTER POTOMAC CHOPTANK
PATUXENT
STATE BIRD: ORIOLE
STATE TREE: OAK
TOWN: BELAIR DENTON EASTON ELKTON
TOWSON LAPLATA ABERDEEN BETHESDA
POCOMOKE BALTIMORE

MASCULINE MALE BUTCH DOGGY
MACHO RUDAS VIRILE LALAQUI MANLIKE
MASH PAP PEER CHAP MASA MASK
MESH SLOP CHAMP CREEM SMASH
SMUSH MUDDLE STILLAGE
MASK FACE HIDE JEST LOUP SLUR VEIL
BLOCK BLOOP CLOAK COVER GUISE
LARVE POINT VIZOR DOMINO GRILLE
MUZZLE SCREEN VEILER VIZARD
BECLOUD CONCEAL CURTAIN MASKOID
ANTEMASK DEFILADE DISGUISE
MASCARON PRETENSE
(— OUT) CROP
(GAS —) CANARY
(HALF —) LOO LOUP DOMINO
MASKED BALL (CHARACTER IN —)
HORN ANGRI AMELIA RENATO TOMASI
ULRICA ARMANDO RIBBING SAMUELE
ARVIDSON GUSTAVUS RICCARDO
ANCKERSTROEM
(COMPOSER OF —) VERDI
MASON LAYER BUILDER MASONER
COMACINE KNOBBLER LAMMIKIN
SCUTCHER
MASONRY ASHLAR MANTLE BACKING
BLOCAGE MOELLON NOGGING ISODOMUM
QUOINING ROCKWORK RUBBLEWORK
MASQUERADE MASK GUISE DOMINO
MASQUE PARADE MASKERY DISGUISE
MASS BAT BED GOB SOP WAD BODY
BULK CLOD GOUT HEAP HEFT KNOT
LEAD LUMP MOLE OBIT STOW SWAD
AMASS BATCH BLOOM CLAMP CLASH
CLUMP CROWD CRUST DIRGE GLOBE
GORGE GROSS MATTE MISSA PRESS
SLUMP SOLID SPIRE STORE WODGE
COMMON GOBBET NUGGET PROPER
VOLUME WEIGHT BOUROCK CONGEST
DENSITY MASKINS MESKINS MYSTERY
REQUIEM SALOMON CALAPITE CONGERIE
ENDOSOME FLOCCULE MOUNTAIN
MYCETOMA SOULMASS ACCUMULATION

MASSACHUSETTS

CAPE: ANN COD
CAPITAL: BOSTON

COLLEGE: SMITH AMHERST SIMMONS WHEATON WILLIAMS RADCLIFFE WELLESLEY
COUNTY: DUKES ESSEX BRISTOL NORFOLK SUFFOLK BERKSHIRE NANTUCKET BARNSTABLE
INDIAN: NAUSET POCOMTUC
ISLAND: DUKES NANTUCKET
LAKE: ONOTA QUABBIN ROHUNTA WEBSTER
MOUNTAIN: BRODIE POTTER ALANDER EVERETT GREYLOCK
MOUNTAIN RANGE: BERKSHIRE
POND: WALDEN
RIVER: NASHUA CHARLES CONCORD QUABOAG TAUNTON CHICOPEE DEERFIELD MERRIMACK
STATE BIRD: CHICKADEE
STATE FLOWER: MAYFLOWER
STATE TREE: ELM
TOWN: AYER LYNN OTIS ATHOL BARRE LENOX AGAWAM DEDHAM GROTON LOWELL NAHANT NATICK REVERE SAUGUS WOBURN HOLYOKE IPSWICH PEABODY TAUNTON BROCKTON CHICOPEE COHASSET SCITUATE UXBRIDGE YARMOUTH CAMBRIDGE NANTUCKET WORCESTER PITTSFIELD SPRINGFIELD
UNIVERSITY: CLARK TUFTS HARVARD BRANDEIS

MASSACRE SLAY POGROM CARNAGE SCUPPER BUTCHERY SLAUGHTER
MASSAGE WISP KNEAD FACIAL PETRIE SHAMPOO TRIPSIS LOMILOMI ANATRIPSIS
MASSIVE BIG BEAMY BULKY GROSS HEAVY LUSTY MASSY SOUND STERN STRONG HEALTHY HULKING VOLUMED TIMBERED MONUMENTAL
MAST BUCK MAIN POLE SPAR OVEST STICK STING DRIVER JIGGER MIZZEN PANNAGE SPANKER FOREMAST JURYMAST MAINMAST MIZZENMAST
MASTER DON HER JOE MAS RAB SAB SIR ARCH BAAS BEAK BOSS COCK FACE HERR JOSS KING LORD MIAN SIRE TUAN BWANA MARSE MASSA RABBI SAHIB SWAMI SWAMY SWELL BRIDLE BUCKRA CASTER DEACON DOMINE HUMBLE MAITRE PATRON RECTOR RHETOR SIRCAR WAFTER CAPTAIN CONQUER DOMINIE DOMINUS EFFENDI MAESTRO NAKHODA OGTIERN PADRONE RABBONI AMAISTER BARGEMAN BEMASTER KINGFISH LANDLORD MAGISTER OVERCOME SLOOPMAN SURMOUNT VANQUISH
MASTERFUL BOSSY LORDLY VIRILE HAUGHTY ARROGANT MAGERFUL PEREMPTORY
MASTER OF BALLANTRAE (AUTHOR OF —) STEVENSON (CHARACTER IN —) CHEW DASS BALLY BURKE HENRY JAMES TEACH ALISON DURRIE GRAEME FRANCIS SECUNDRA MACKELLAR DURRISDEER
MASTERPIECE TOPPIECE
MASTERY GREE GRIP COMMAND MAISTRY OVERHAND
MASTICATE GUM CHEW
MASTIFF ALAN MASTY BANDOG TIEDOG
MASTURBATION ONANISM FROTTAGE
MAT COT RUG TOD FLET FOOT HAIR MOSS NIPA PACE RAFT SHAG TAUT DOILY KILIM TATTY COTTER FELTER PAUNCH PETATE TARGET COASTER CUSHION DOORMAT KAITAKA MATTING FOOTPACE FROSTING MATTRESS SPANDREL
(BOWLING —) FOOTER
(FIBER —) BASS
(PALM-LEAF —) YAPA
(PICTURE-FRAME —) FLAT
(POLYNESIAN —) LAUHALA
(SCOURING —) BEAR
(TABLECLOTH —) GARDNAP
MATADOR MAT ESPADA CAPEADOR
MATCH GO CAP VIE BOUT COPE EVEN FERE MAKE MATE MEET MILL MOTE PAIR PEEL PEER SIDE SUIT AMATE EQUAL FIRER FUSEE FUZEE MOUSE PARTY RIVAL SPUNK TALLY VENUE VESTA ASSORT BESORT CANCEL COMMIT FELLOW KIPPIN MARROW QUADER RUBBER SAMPLE SWATCH COMPEER EXAMPLE IGNITER ILLUMER KINDLER KIPPEEN LIGHTER LUCIFER PARAGON PAREGAL PATTERN PENDANT SINGLES APPROACH BREATHER CONGREVE EUPYRION INFLAMER LOCOFOCO PARALLEL PORTFIRE REANSWER VESUVIAN VESUVIUS SEMIFINAL PREMINIARY QUARTERFINAL
(— AT DICE) MAIN
(BOXING —) SPAR FIGHT PRELIM SLUGFEST
(CURLING —) SPIEL BONSPIEL
(DANCING —) KANTIKEY
(DISHONEST —) CROSS
(GOLF —) NASSAU FOURSOME
(SCOLDING —) FLYTE
(SHOOTING —) TIR SHOOT
(SLOW —) LUNT SMIFT SQUIB
(TILTING —) CAROUSEL
MATCHLESS ALONE UNIQUE NONESUCH PEERLESS
MATCHMAKER SHADCHAN
MATE CAWK FERE METE PAIR PEER BILLY BREED BUDDY BULLY CHINA CLASP CULLY DICKY MATCH PARTY TALLY YERBA BUNKIE COBBER FELLOW FUTURE MARROW PAREIL BROTHER COMPEER COMRADE CONSORT HUSBAND PARAGON NEIGHBOR PIRRAURA
MATERIAL FINE MOLD GAUZE GOUGE HYLIC METAL MOULD PASTE PLASS STUFF THING TRADE BORROW CARNAL CYANUS FABRIC GRAITH HOGGIN MATTER PAPREG PUBLIC THINGY APPAREL FOOTING SUBJECT TEXTILE

UNIDEAL WEIGHTY ADDITIVE CORPORAL
ECONOMIC EQUIPAGE RELEVANT
SENSIBLE SNOODING TANGIBLE
THINGISH OBJECTIVE PHENOMENAL
MATERIALISM HYLISM SOMATISM
MATERIALISTIC SENSATE SENSUAL
BANAUSIC
MATERIALIZE REIFY DESCEND
MATHEMATICIAN ALGORIST
GEOMETER
MATHEMATICS MATHESIS
MATING NICK COUPLE DIALLEL
BREEDING HOMOGAMY PANMIXIA
(RANDOM —) PANGAMY
MATRIMONIAL MARITAL NUPTIAL
SPOUSAL CONJUGAL
MATRIMONY WEDLOCK MARRIAGE
MATRIX PI BED MAT SORT PLASM SHELL
SLIDE DYADIC MASTER MOTHER STRIKE
STROMA CALYMMA FORMULA MATRICE
PATTERN PROPLASM
MATRON DAME
MATTED COTTY FELTY PINNY FELTED
TAGGED TAUTED WAUKIT STRINGY
FELTLIKE CESPITOSE
MATTER RES BONE CASE GEAR HYLE
ITEM RECK WHAT AMPER FORCE PARTY
SKILL STUFF THEME TOPIC AFFAIR
ARGUFY BEHALF DITTAY IMPORT
ARTICLE CONCERN MATERIA SHEBANG
SIGNIFY SUBJECT BUSINESS COMETHER
MATERIAL
(— ADDED TO BOOK) APPENDIX
(— AROUND THE TEETH) TOPHUS
(— CONSTITUTING PERFUME)
ESSENCE
(— IN DISPUTE) ISSUE
(— OF BUSINESS) SHAURI
(— OF CONCERN) FUNERAL
(— OF INTEREST) GRIST
(— TO) CONCERN
(ALLUVIAL —) GEEST
(BRAIN —) ALBA
(CARTILAGINOUS —) GRISTLE
(COLORING —) DYE COLOR CROCK
EOSIN MORIN PIURI ALNEIN BUTEIN
FUSTIC INDIGO ORCEIN PIOURY CARMINE
CASTORY CUDBEAR LIGULIN OENOLIN
PIGMENT PUNICIN XANTHIN ALGOCYAN
ALIZARIN BRAZILIN FUSTERIC LAPACHOL
SCOPARIN TINCTION
(CORRUPT —) PUS ATTER
(DECAYED ORGANIC —) DUFF
(ESSENTIAL —) POINT
(EXPLANATORY —) HAGGADA
(FATTY —) SEBUM
(FECAL —) SIEGE
(FILTHY —) GUNK
(FOREIGN —) SOIL DROSS
(FOUL —) FILTH SORDES
(FRONT —) FOREWORD
(GELATINOUS —) BREAK SPAWN
(GRAY —) GLIOSA CINEREA
(HYPOTHETICAL —) PROTYLE
(INANIMATE —) AJIVA
(INFECTIOUS —) MIASMA
(MINERAL —) FLOAT FLOATS

(NERVE —) CINEREA
(POTENTIAL —) PRAKRITI
(PRIMARY —) PRADHANA
(PRINTED —) BOX DISPLAY
(PULVERIZED —) ATTRITUS
(READING —) BODY
(SLIMY —) GLAIR
(SMALL —) MINUTIA
(SOFT —) PASH
(SUBJECT —) SCOPE CONTENT
(SUPPURATIVE —) PUS
(TRIVIAL —) JOKE
(TYPESET —) CHASE
(WASTE —) DIRT DRAFF DROSS
RAMMEL SEWAGE EXCRETA
(WORTHLESS —) SLAG CHAFF
GARBAGE
(WRITTEN —) SCRIVE
(PL.) HARNESS SQUARES
(PREF.) HYL(O)
MATTER-OF-FACT DRY LITERAL
PROSAIC
MATTHEW (FATHER OF —) ALPHAEUS
MATTING MAT TAT BAST BEAR BUMP
SIRKI TATTY SAWALI TATAMI COCOMAT
RABANNA
MATTOCK MAT BILL HACK MATAX
PICKAX TUBBAL TWIBIL GRUBBER
MATTRESS BED MAT TICK DIVAN QUILT
REZAI PALLET BISCUIT MATRACE
PALLIASSE
MATURE AGE OLD BOLD FULL GRAY RIPE
ADULT MANLY RIPEN SHOOT ACCRUE
AUTUMN DECOCT DIGEST MELLOW
SEASON SEEDED CONCOCT DEVELOP
FURNISH PERFECT PROVECT MATURATE
(PREF.) TEL(E) TEL(O)
MATURED ADULT GROWN FORMED
HEADED MELLOW SEEDED HOMOGAMY
MATURITY AGE RIPENESS
MAUDLIN BEERY MOIST FUDDLED
MAUL FAN PAW TUG MALL MELL GAVEL
GLAUM BEATER BEETLE BEMAUL
MUZZLE SCAMBLE
MAURITANIA (CAPITAL OF —)
NOUAKCHOTT
(MONEY OF —) OUGUIYA
(RIVER OF —) SENEGAL
(TOWN OF —) ATAR NEMA AGMAR
KAEDI OUJAF
MAURITIUS (CAPITAL OF —)
PORTLOUIS
(CHANNEL OF —) QUOIN
(ISLAND OF —) AGALEGA GABRIEL
RODRIGUEZ
(RIVER OF —) GRAND POSTE REMPART
(TOWN OF —) VACOAS TRIOLET
CUREPIPE SOUILLAC
MAUSOLEUM MOLE TOMB SHRINE
TURBEH BARADARI
MAW CROP GORGE THROAT
MAWKISH CUTE SAPPY SOPPY SOUPY
WALSH DRIPPY SICKLY VANILLA
MAXIM SAW SAY DICT ITEM NORM RULE
TEXT WORD ADAGE AXIOM GNOME
LARGE MOTTO DICTUM SAYING SYMBOL
BROCARD DICTATE IMPRESA PRECEPT

PROVERB APHORISM APOTHEGM
DOCTRINE MORALISM PROTASIS
SENTENCE
(PL.) LOGIA

MAXIMUM FULL MOST PEAK CREST
EXTREME OUTSIDE SUMMARY ULTIMATE

MAY CAN MUN MOTE MOWE MUST PRIME
SHALL HEYDAY HAWTHORN SYCAMORE

MAYA PRAKRITI

MAYBE MEBBE HAPPEN PERHAPS
POSSIBLY

MAY DAY BELTANE

MAYONNAISE MAYO GOULASH
DRESSING
(GARLIC —) AIOLI

MAYOR MAIRE BAILIFF DEMARCH
PODESTA PROVOST PALATINE
(BULGARIAN —) KMET
(SPANISH —) ALCALDE

MAYOR OF CASTERBRIDGE
(AUTHOR OF —) HARDY
(CHARACTER IN —) JOPP SUSAN
DONALD NEWSON FARFRAE LESUEUR
LUCETTA MICHAEL RICHARD HENCHARD
ELIZABETH TEMPLEMAN

MAZE JUNGLE WARREN CONFUSE
BEWILDER LABYRINTH

MEADOW LEA MEAD VEGA WISH WONG
FIELD GRASS LEASE MARSH SWALE
CALLOW PARAMO SMOOTH POTRERO
(ARTIFICIAL —) CHINAMPA
(IRISH —) BAAN
(LOW —) ING INCH HAUGH CALLOW

MEADOWLARK ACORN MEDLAR

MEAGER BALD BARE LANK LEAN NICE
POOR THIN GAUNT NAKED SCANT SILLY
SKIMP SOBER SPARE JEJUNE LEEPIT
LENTEN NARROW PILLED SCANTY
SLIGHT SPARSE STINGY SCRAGGY
SCRANNY SCRIMPY SCRUBBY SLENDER
SPARING STARVED STERILE MARGINAL
SCRANNEL SCRATCHY MISERABLE

MEAGERNESS ECONOMY EXILITY
TENUITY SPARENESS

MEAL AMYL BAKE CENA CHOW FARM
FEED HASH KAIL MEAT MONG NOSH
TUCK COENA FLOUR MANGE SCOFF
BUFFET COMIDA DINNER FARINA
MANGER POLLEN REPAST SPREAD
SQUARE SUPPER UNDERN BLOWOUT
COOKOUT MELTITH NAGMAAL NOONING
SETDOWN CORNMEAL EVENMETE
MEALTIME ORDINARY TRENCHER
(— AND WATER) DRAMMOCK
(— FROM CASSAVA ROOT) FARINE
FARINHA
(— GROUND BY HAND) GRADDAN
(— OF FELLOWSHIP) AGAPE
(— STIRRED WITH MILK) STUROCH
(ACORN —) RACAHOUT
(COARSE —) GRIT GROUT KIBBLE
CRIBBLE GURGEONS
(CORN —) MASA ATOLE NOCAKE
(ELABORATE —) FEAST BANQUET
(FIRST —) ALMUERZO
(FULL —) GORGE
(HASTY —) SNAP CHACK

(HEARTY —) AIT
(IMPROMPTU —) BITE CHECK
(LIGHT —) BAIT BEVER CHACK CHECK
FOURS NUNCHEON
(MIDDAY —) NOON
(MORNING —) BRUNCH
(PERTAINING TO —) PRANDIAL
(PURIM —) SEUDAH
(SCANTY —) PICK
(SMALL —) SNAP MORSEL
(SOLITARY —) SULLEN
(UNSORTED —) ATTA
(PL.) TUCKER
(PREF.) ATHERO

MEAN LOW BASE CLAM HARD LEAN MIDS
NICE POKY POOR SLIM VILE AGENT
ARGUE DINGY DIRTY DUSTY FOOTY
GRIMY KETTY LOUSY MANGY MESNE
MEZZO MIDST MINGY MOYEN MUCKY
NASTY PETIT PETTY RATTY RUNTY
SCALD SCALL SCALY SCRUB SEEDY
SILLY SMALL SNIDE SNIVY SORRY
SOUND SPELL ABJECT BEMEAN
COMMON DENOTE DESIGN DIRTEN
FEEBLE FROWZY FRUGAL GRUBBY
HUMBLE HUNGRY IMPORT INSECT
INTEND LEADEN LITTLE MEASLY MEDIAL
MEDIUM MENIAL MIDDLE NARROW
ORNERY PALTRY PEANUT PILLED POKING
RASCAL SCABBY SCREWY SCUMMY
SCURVY SHABBY SLIGHT SNIFTY SNIPP
SORDID SQUALL STRAIT TEMPER
YELLOW AVERAGE CAITIFF CHANNEL
CHETIVE COMICAL CONNOTE HACKNEY
HILDING IGNOBLE MESQUIN MISERLY
MOTETUS OBSCURE PEAKING PELTING
PIGGISH PIMPING PITIFUL PORTEND
REPTILE ROINISH SCABBED SHABBED
SIGNIFY VICIOUS BEGGARLY CHURLISH
DOGGEREL MEDIOCRE MIDDLING
NIGGLING PICAYUNE PITIABLE RASCALLY
RIFFRAFF SHAMEFUL SNEAKING
TWOPENNY WRETCHED

MEANDER WIND STRAY TWINE CIRCLE
SERPENT STRAGGLE

MEANING WIT HANG DRIFT SENSE
SOUND IMPORT INTENT SEMEME
PURPORT PURPOSE CARRIAGE INNUENDO
SENTENCE STRENGTH REFERENCE
SIGNIFICANCE

MEANINGFUL RICH PREGNANT

MEANINGLESS BANAL ABSURD
FECKLESS SENSELESS

MEANS MIDS AGENT DRIVE MESNE
MOYEN PURSE THEME AGENCY AVENUE
ENGINE MATTER MIDDES POCKET
STRING WRENCH BALANCE BENEFIT
DEMESNE FACULTY FASHION QUOMODO
COURTESY

MEASLES RUBEOLA MORBILLI
(BLACK —) ESCA APOPLEXY

MEASURE
(ALSO SEE UNIT AND WEIGHT) AR BU
EM EN HO KO LI MO RI SE TU AAM ARE
AUM BAG CAB CHO DRA ELL FAT FEN FIT
FOU FUN GAD GAZ GUZ HIN HOB IMI KAB
KAN KIP KOR KOS LEA LOG LUG MAU MIL

MOY PIK RIG RIN ROD SAA SHO TON TUN
VAT VOG WEY ACRE ALMA AUNE BARN
BATH BEKA BOLL BOUW BUTT CADE
CENT CHIH COOM COSS DEPA DOSE
DRAA DRAM DYNE EPHA EPHI FALL FANG
FOOT FULL GAGE GERA GILL GIRT GOAD
GRAM GREX HAND HATT HIDE HOOP
HOUR IMMI INCH KNOT KOKU LAST
MEAL METE MILE MUID NAIL NOOK
OMER PACE PINT PIPE POLL REAM RIME
ROOD ROPE ROTL SAAH SACK SALM
SEAH SEAM SIZE SKEP SPAN STEP TAKT
TAPE TIME TRAM TRUG TSUN VARA
WIST YARD ALMUD AMBER ANKER
ARDAB ARDEB ARURA BEKAH BIGHA
BLANK BODGE BRASS CABAN CABLE
CABOT CARAT CARGA CATTY
CAVAN CHAIN CHANG CHING CLOVE
COOMB CRANS CUBIT CUMAL CUNIT
DENUM DEPOH DIGIT DRAFT DUNAM
DUNUM EPHAH GAUGE GERAH GIRTH
HOMER HUTCH JUGER LABOR LAGEN
LIANG LIBRA LIGNE LIPPY LITER LITRE
MEITH METER METRE MINIM MODEL
OUNCE PEISE PERCH PLANK POUND
QUIRE RASER RHYME SALMA SCALE
SCORE SHAKU SHENG SHING SIEVE
SLEEP STACK STERE STONE STOOP
STOUP THERM TOISE TOVET TRACE
VERST YOJAN APATAN ARCHIN ARPENT
ARSHIN ASSIZE BARREL BATMAN
BEMETE BOVATE BUNDLE BUSHEL
CANADA CANTAR CHOMER CHOPIN
COLLOP COUDEE COVIDO CUERDA
DAVACH DAVOCH DECARE DEGREE
DENIER DIPODY DIRHAM DRACHM
ENGLER EXTENT FANEGA FATHOM
FEDDAN FINGER FIRKIN FIRLOT FLAGON
FODDER FORPET FOTHER GALLON
GRAMME HALEBI HIDAGE KISHEN
LEAGUE MICRON MODIUS MODULE
MOGGIO MORGEN NUMBER OITAVA
OUROUB OXHIDE QANTAR REASON
SAZHEN SETIER SQUARE STERAD STRIKE
SULUNG TERMIN THRAVE WINDLE
YOJANA ADOULIE AMPHORA ANAPEST
ARSHINE BATTUTA BRACCIO BREADTH
CADENCE CALIPER CALORIE CENTARE
CENTNER CENTRAD CHITTAK COMPASS
CONGIUS CONTAIN DECIARE DIOPTER
DRACHMA DRAUGHT ENTROPY FARSAKH
FARSANG FRUNDEL FURLONG HECTARE
HEMINEE KILIARE NOCKTAT QUARTAN
QUARTER SCHEPEL SCRUPLE SECCHIO
SKEPFUL SKIPPLE SPANGLE SPINDLE
STADION STATION TERTIAN VIRGATE
ALQUEIRE CAPACITY CARUCATE
CENTIARE CHETVERT CRANNOCK
DACTYLIC DECAGRAM DECIGRAM
DESIATIN DIAPASON HOGSHEAD
INNOCENT LANDYARD METEWAND
MUTCHKIN PARASANG PLOWGANG
PLOWGATE SCHOONER SCHOPPEN
STANDARD PRECAUTION
MEASURE FOR MEASURE
(AUTHOR OF —) SHAKESPEARE
(CHARACTER IN —) ELBOW FROTH

LUCIO PETER ANGELO JULIET POMPEY
THOMAS CLAUDIO ESCALUS MARIANA
VARRIUS ABHORSON ISABELLA
OVERDONE FRANCISCA VINCENTIO
BARNARDINE
MEASURELESS ENDLESS INFINITE
MEASUREMENT GAGE DEPTH GAUGE
LEVEL MEITH METAGE DIALING MEASURE
SOUNDING
(— FOR TAXATION) HIDE HIDAGE
(— OF CLOTH) ALNAGE
(— OF FINENESS) SET SETT
(LUMBER —) LAST
MEAT BEEF FISH FOOD LAMB LEAN LIFT
PORK FLESH STEAK VIFDA VIVDA
BUCCAN CAGMAG FLEECE MATTER
NUTTON TARGET PECKAGE
(— AND FISH) LAULAU
(— COOKED WITH SKEWERS)
SASSATIE
(— DRIED IN SUN) JERKY CHARQUI
PEMMICAN
(— OF CONCH) SCUNGILI
(— OF KID) CAPRETTO
(— WITH VEGETABLES) STEW
MULLIGAN
(BOILED —) SOD SODDEN BOUILLI
(BROILED —) GRISKIN GRILLADE
(BUFFALO —) FLEECE
(CANNED —) SPAM
(CHOPPED —) BURGER
(COCONUT —) COPRA
(CURED —) HAM
(CUT OF —) ARM
(DRIED —) MUMMY
(FAT —) SPECK
(FROZEN —) FRIGO
(INFERIOR —) CAGMAG STICKING
(JERKED —) BILTONG CHARQUI
(LEAN —) MUSCLE
(MINCED —) CHUET JIGOTE RISSOLE
SANDERS
(POTTED —) RILLETT
(RABBIT —) LAPAN
(RAGOUT OF —) HARICOT
(ROAST —) BREDE CABOB
(ROLLED —) BIRD
(SALTED —) JUNK MART
(SIDE —) SOWBELLY
(SMOKED —) BUCCAN
MEAT JELLY ASPIC
MEATY PITHY
MECHANIC JOINER WRIGHT ARTISAN
FELTMAN SHOPMAN WORKMAN
BANAUSIC OPERATIVE
MECHANICAL FROZEN INHUMAN
METALLIC AUTOMATIC
(NOT —) HORMIC
MECHANISM FAN BOND FEED GEAR
KITE LIFT MOTE APRON CATCH CROWD
FORCE ORGAN SHAKE SLIDE SPARK
STEER ACTION BOTTOM CUTOFF INFEED
MOTION SICKLE STRIKE AUTOVAC
BUILDER CHANNEL CONTROL EJECTOR
GIGBACK GRIPPER GUNLOCK HOLDOUT
SETTING TRIPPER ACTUATOR ELEVATOR
KINETICS RACKWORK SELECTOR

SETWORKS SIGNALER STEERING STOPWORK THROWOUT

MECONIN OPIANYL

MEDAL STAR AWARD STAMP PLAQUE MEDALET OSCELLA VERNICLE MEDALLION

MEDALLION CAMEO TONDO PADUAN PATERA PANHAGIA

MEDDLE TIG FOOL MELL MESS MIRD POKE TOUCH DABBLE FIDDLE FINGER HECKLE POTTER PUTTER TAMPER TANGLE TINKER

MEDDLER SNOOP SNOOPER BUSYBODY KIBITZER STICKLER STIFFLER BUTTINSKY

MEDDLESOME FRESH NEBBY

MEDDLING BUSY

MEDEA (BROTHER OF —) ABSYRTUS APSYRTUS
(FATHER OF —) AEETES
(HUSBAND OF —) JASON AEGEUS
(MOTHER OF —) IDYIA
(SISTER OF —) CHALCOPE CHALCIOPE

MEDIATOR MEANS MEDIUM DAYSMAN MIDDLER PLACATER STICKLER MODERATOR

MEDICAL IATRIC PHYSIC IATRICAL PAEONIAN

MEDICINAL IATRIC PHYSIC MEDICAL THERIAL PHYSICAL SALUTARY THERICAL OFFICINAL

MEDICINE DRUG MUTI PEAI DROPS GRUEL STEEL STUFF TONIC TRADE AMULET ECLEGM ELIXIR MAGUAL PHYSIC POWDER REMEDY SIMPLE ALOETIC ANODYNE ANTACID CORDIAL HEPATIC LUCHDOM MIXTURE OPORICE PLACEBO POROTIC PYROTIC SPLENIC AROMATIC DIAPENTE DIGESTER DRUGGERY EARDROPS ECCRITIC EMULGENT LAXATIVE LEECHDOM LENITIVE LOBLOLLY PECTORAL PHARMACY PULMONIC RELAXANT SPECIFIC STOMATIC PRESCRIPTION
(CHINESE —) SENSO
(QUACK —) NOSTRUM
(SYSTEM OF —) AYURVEDA
(UNIVERSAL —) PANACEA

MEDICINE MAN PEAI DOCTOR KAHUNA PIACHE POWWOW SHAMAN SINGER ANGEKOK TOHUNGA CONTRARY POWWOWER

MEDIEVAL OLD GOTHIC

MEDIOCRE HACK MEAN SUCH MEDIUM AVERAGE INFERIOR MIDDLING MODERATE PASSABLE

MEDITATE CAST CHEW MUSE BROOD GLOAT STUDY THINK WEIGH PONDER RECORD BETHINK COMMENT IMAGINE PREPEND REFLECT REVOLVE COGITATE CONSIDER PURPENSE RUMINATE

MEDITATION MOYEN STUDY THINK DHYANA MUSING REVERIE THOUGHT HIGGAION

MEDITATIVE MUSING MUSEFUL PENSIVE RUMINANT

MEDIUM BATH EVEN LENS MEAN ETHER JUICE MIDST MOYEN ORGAN BALIAN

BISTER DIGEST MIDDLE MIDWAY ORACLE SLUDGE TEMPER PSYCHIC VEHICLE MEDIOCRE SHOWCASE CONTINUUM
(— OF EXCHANGE) CURRENCY
(— OF TRANSMISSION) AIR AIRWAVE
(CULTURE —) AGAR STAB BROTH HYRAX SLANT CULTURE BOUILLON
(ENVELOPING —) SWATH
(REFINING —) ALEMBIC

MEDLEY OLIO BABEL REVUE JUMBLE CHIVARI CLANGOR FARRAGO GOULASH MELANGE MIXTURE BROUHAHA KEDGEREE MACARONI MISHMASH RHAPSODY SLAMPAMP VARIORUM CHARIVARI MACEDOINE

MEDUSA JELLY QUARL GORGON BLUBBER GERYONID
(FATHER OF —) PHORCYS
(MOTHER OF —) CETO
(SLAYER OF —) PERSEUS

MEEK LOW DAFT MURE LOWLY GENTLE HUMBLE PACIFIC LAMBLIKE YIELDING

MEEKNESS MANSUETUDE

MEERSCHAUM PIPE GRAVEL KIEFEKIL SEPIOLITE

MEET FIT KEP SEE COPE FACE FILL HENT NOSE ABIDE CLOSE CROSS FRONT GREET INCUR OCCUR PIECE TOUCH ANSWER BATTLE BEMEET COMBAT CONCUR FULFIL INVENT SEMBLE CONTACT CONVENE CONVENT COUNCIL FULFILL SATISFY ASSEMBLE CONFRONT CONVERGE GAINCOPE
(— A BET) SEE
(— A NEED) SUFFICE
(— AT END) BUTT
(— FACE TO FACE) AFFRONT
(— SQUARELY) ENVISAGE
(— VIOLENTLY) CHECK HURTLE
(— WITH) GET SEE BUMP FIND STRIKE
(ATHLETIC —) GALA GYMKHANA

MEETING MOD FEIS MOOT CLOSE FORUM SABHA SHINE STOUR SYNOD TRYST ACCESS AUMAGA CAUCUS CHAPEL CLINIC HUDDLE POWWOW SEANCE CABINET CHAPTER COLLEGE CONTACT CONVENT COUNCIL JOLLITY MOOTING OCCURSE REVIVAL SEMINAR SITTING SYNAXIS ASSEMBLY CONGRESS CONSULTA DELEGACY ECCLESIA EXERCISE JUNCTION OSCULANT TERTULIA WARDMOTE CONCOURSE COLLOQUIUM
(— OF BARDS) GORSEDD
(— OF NEIGHBORS) HUSKING
(— OF SCHOLARS) LEVY
(— OF WITCHES) ESBAT
(— OF WORSHIPERS) SERVICE
(ANGLO-SAXON —) GEMOTE
(GENERAL —) PRIME
(NOT —) PARALLEL
(POLITICAL —) CAUCUS
(SECRET —) CABAL CONSULT CONCLAVE
(SOCIAL —) CLUB JOLLY HOBNOB
(TOWN —) TUNMOOT

MEETINGHOUSE MORADA

MEISTERSINGER VON NURNBERG, DI (CHARACTER IN —) EVA HANS VEIT DAVID FRITZ SACHS POGNER KOTHNER WALTHER STOLZING MAGDALENE BECKMESSER

(COMPOSER OF —) WAGNER

MELANCHOLY LOW SAD WOE BLUE DRAM DULL DUMP MARE ADUST BLUES DEARN DOWIE DREAR DUSKY GLOOM SORRY WISHT GLOOMY SOMBER SOMBRE SORROW SPLEEN SULLEN YELLOW CHAGRIN DOLEFUL DUMPISH ELEGIAC SADNESS SPLEENY THOUGHT ATRABILE LIVERISH TRISTFUL

MELANESIAN DOBUAN KANAGA KANAKA EFATESE

MELEAGER (FATHER OF —) OENEUS

(MOTHER OF —) ALTHAEA

MELEE BRAWL MEDLEY DOGFIGHT PELLMELL WINGDING

MELLIFLUOUS SUGARED HYBLAEAN

MELLOW AGE OMY HAZE LUSH MALM PLUM RICH RIPE SOFT FRUSH RIPEN FLUTED GOLDEN MATURE

MELODIOUS SOFT SOOT TUNY SWEET TUNED ARIOSO DULCET MELODIC MUSICAL SIRENIC SONGFUL TUNABLE TUNEFUL CANOROUS CHARMING NUMEROUS SOUNDFUL

MELODRAMA HAM TANK

MELODY AIR HUM LAY ARIA NOTE TUNE CANTO CHANT CHARM DREAD MELOS MIRTH NIGUN CANTUS CHORAL GHAZEL MONODY NIGGUN STROKE CANZONE CHORALE DESCANT HARMONY MEASURE MELISMA PLANXTY ROSALIA CARILLON CAVATINA DIAPASON VOCALISE

MELON PEPO GOURD MANGO CASABA CITRON DUDAIM MAYCOCK CUCURBIT HONEYDEW PEPONIDA PEPONIUM

MELT FLY RIN RUN BLOW FADE FLOW FLUX FUSE THAW FOUND LEACH SMELT SWELT TOUCH GUTTER RELENT SOFTEN DISTILL FORMELT RESOLVE DISCANDY DISSOLVE ELIQUATE COLLIQUATE

(— AWAY) SWEAL

(— DOWN) RENDER

(— IRREGULARLY) DROZE

MEMBER LIMB LITH PART BRANCH FELLOW FILLET GIRDER SOCIUS AMANIST COMPART ERANIST FAIRING ALBRIGHT AULARIAN BRIDLING

(— OF ANSAR) HELPER

(— OF BALLET) FIGURANT

(— OF BAND) SIDEMAN

(— OF BODYGUARD) HUSCARL

(— OF BROTHERHOOD) ESSENE SENUSSI

(— OF CLAN) CHILD CALEBITE

(— OF CLERGY) DEFENSOR

(— OF COAST GUARD) SPAR

(— OF COUNCIL) CONSUL HEEMRAAD

(— OF COURT) DICAST EPHETE

(— OF CREW) HAND IDLER LAYER DRIVER STROKE BOWSMAN FORETOP BRAKEMAN SHAREMAN

(— OF CULT) ANGEL AMIDIST

(— OF FACULTY) COUNSEL LECTURER

(— OF FAMILY) FETII

(— OF FRATERNAL ORDER) ELK SHRINER FORESTER KIWANIAN

(— OF FRATERNITY) GREEK

(— OF FRENCH ACADEMY) IMMORTAL

(— OF GANG) HENCHMAN

(— OF GENTRY) SEIGNEUR

(— OF GIRL SCOUTS) BROWNIE

(— OF GREEK ARMY) EVZONE

(— OF GUILD) COMACINE HOASTMAN

(— OF HOUSEHOLD) FAMILIAR

(— OF HUNTING PARTY) STANDER

(— OF INN OF COURT) ANCIENT BENCHER

(— OF ITALIAN ARMY) ALPINO

(— OF KNOW-NOTHING PARTY) SAM

(— OF LEGISLATURE) SOLON DEPUTY DELEGATE

(— OF LITERARY GROUP) FELIBRE

(— OF MIDDLE CLASS) BURGHER

(— OF PARLIAMENT) CONTENT THINGMAN

(— OF PRIMROSE LEAGUE) KNIGHT

(— OF RELIGIOUS ORDER) DAME FRIAR EUDIST FRAILE FRATER HERMIT JESUIT SISTER ALEXIAN BEGUINE BRINSER DERVISH HUSSITE SEPARTE SERVANT SERVITE CENOBITE EXORCIST HUMANIST SALESIAN

(— OF RETINUE) SEQUEL SEQUENT

(— OF RUSSIAN ARISTOCRACY) BOIAR BOYAR BOYARD

(— OF SAME GENUS) CONGENER

(— OF SECRET ORGANIZATION) DEMOLAY

(— OF SECRET SOCIETY) BOXER DANITE

(— OF SECT) BABI BABEE DRUSE HASID KHOJA AUDIAN BEREAN BRAHMO CATHAR DIPPER DOPPER IBADHI JUMPER KHLYST SMARTA AISSAWA AJIVIKA AUDAEAN CAINITE CHASSID DREAMER EMPIRIC EUCHITE IBADITE ISAWIYA ISMAILI RAPPIST SENUSSI SEVENER AQUARIAN CALIXTIN DARBYITE DUKHOBOR EBIONITE FAMILIST GLASSITE LABADIST MANDAEAN SADDUCEE SEVERIAN SHAFIITE SIMONIAN

(— OF STAFF) ATTACHE

(— OF STATE) CITIZEN

(— OF STOCK EXCHANGE) BOARDMAN

(— OF TEAM) SPARE BOBBER KICKER

(— OF TRIBE) LEVITE JUDAHITE LAMANITE

(— OF UPPER CLASS) EFFENDI

(— OF VARNA) SUDRA SHUDRA

(— OF WHITE RACE) HAOLE

(— OF WINDOW) APRON

(—S OF CLASS) FRY

(—S OF PROFESSION) FACULTY

(—S OF SECT) SKOPTSY

(—S OF TRIBUNAL) ACUERDO

(ARCHITECTURAL —) FAN ARCH FLAT

SILL SPAN GABLE SOCLE STILE STILT
CORBEL FASCIA CONSOLE CORNICE
(CHURCH —) GREEK LATIN DANITE
DUNKER KIRKER TUNKER AZYMITE
BAPTIST BEGHARD BROTHER DUNKARD
KIRKMAN SECEDER ARMENIAN BRYANITE
CATHOLIC DISCIPLE DOWIEITE JACOBITE
(CHURCH —S) FAITHFUL
(EVERY —) ALL
(FEEBLEST —) WRIG
(FULL —) GREMIAL
(OLDEST —) FATHER
(OVERHANGING —) BRACKET
(POLITICAL —) CADET ENDEK SHIRT
GUELPH HUNKER LEADER APRISTA
LEFTIST LIBERAL ABHORRER BUCKTAIL
DEMOCRAT HERODIAN LABORITE
(PROJECTING —) TENON
(SECRET —) CRYPTO
(SENIOR —) DOYEN
(TENSION —) HANGER
(TERMINAL —) TOE
MEMBRANE RIM WEB CAUL COAT DURA
FELL HEAD TELA GALEA HYMEN VELUM
AMNION AMNIOS EXTINE INTINE MENINX
MOTHER MUCOSA PLEURA RETINA
SEPTUM SEROSA TIMBAL TUNICA
TYMPAN BLANKET CAPSULE CHORION
CHOROID CUTICLE DECIDUA EPICYTE
HYALOID OOLEMMA PUTAMEN STRATUM
VELAMEN ECTODERM ENDOCYST
ENVELOPE EPENDYMA EPISPORE
EXOLEMMA INDUSIUM INTEXINE
LABELLUM PATAGIUM PELLICLE
STRIFFEN ALLANTOIS PERIPLAST
PERITONEUM
MEMENTO RELIC TOKEN MEMORY
TROPHY KEEPSAKE REMINDER SOUVENIR
MEMOIR ELOGE RECORD HISTORY
MEMORIAL
MEMORABLE GRAND SIGNAL CLASSIC
NOTABLE MEMORIAL NAMEABLE
NOTEWORTHY
MEMORANDUM BILL CHIT NOTE SLIP
BRIEF JURAT CAHIER CIPHER DOCKET
MEMOIR MINUTE TICKET JOTTING
MEMORIAL NOTANDUM PROTOCOL
BORDEREAU
MEMORIAL AHU AGALMA CAHIER
FACTUM MEMOIR MEMORY RECORD
TROPHY DENKMAL MEMENTO MENTION
EBENEZER MONUMENT REMEMBRANCE
MEMORIZE LEARN MANDATE REMEMBER
MEMORY MIND HEART IMAGE STORE
RECALL RECORD MEMENTO STORAGE
MEMORIAL SOUVENIR
(— ON COMPUTER CHIP) RAM ROM
(— SUBDIVISION) PAGE
(COMPUTER —) STACK
(OF POOR —) FLUFFY
(PAINFUL —) SCAR
(SMALL COMPUTER —) SCRATCHPAD
MENACE BOAST IMPEND THREAT
BOGEYMAN MINATORY THREATEN
MENACING STOUT SURLY FIERCE
TOWARD MINATORY MINACIOUS
MEND DO FIX DARN HEAL HELP STOP

TINK AMEND CLOUT EMEND GRAFT
COBBLE DOCTOR FETTLE REFORM
REPAIR SOLDER IMPROVE INWEAVE
REDRESS RIGHTLE
(— BY ADDING FEATHERS) IMP
(— CLUMSILY) BOTCH
(— MEN'S CLOTHES) BUSHEL
MENDACIOUS FALSE DISHONEST
MENDACITY LYING DECEIT FALSITY
UNTRUTH
MENDICANT NAGA DANDI FAKIR FRIAR
UDASI BEGGAR BHIKKU FRATER GOSAIN
AJIVIKA BAIRAGI EUCHITE VAIRAGI
PANDARAM SANNYASI PASSIONIST
MENELAUS (BROTHER OF —)
AGAMEMNON
(FATHER OF —) ATREUS PLISTHENES
(MOTHER OF —) AEROPE
(SISTER OF —) ANAXIBIA
(WIFE OF —) HELEN
MENIAL FAG BASE LOON PAGE KNAVE
DRIVEL HARLOT POTBOY VARLET
SERVILE SLAVISH BANAUSIC SCULLION
SERVITOR
MENTAL IDEAL GENIAL INWARD MINDLY
PHRENIC PSYCHIC CEREBRAL
MENTALITY MIND SENSE ACUMEN
REASON SPIRIT PSYCHISM
MENTHOL CAMPHOR
MENTION CALL CITE HINT MIND MING
MINT NAME CHEEP CLEPE SPEAK TOUCH
MEMBER NOTICE SPEECH MEANING
SPECIFY SUGGEST CITATION INSTANCE
MEMORATE REHEARSE REMEMBER
REFERENCE REPETITION
(— CASUALLY) DROP
(HONORABLE —) ACCESSIT
MENTOR TEACHER CICERONE
MENU CARD CARTE
MEPHISTOPHELIAN SATANIC
MERCENARY HACK VENAL JACKAL
HESSIAN PINDARI HIRELING WAGELING
MERCHANDISE CARGO CHEAP GOODS
STUFF WARES ARTWARE CHAFFER
SHIPPER TRAFFIC CHAFFERY SALEWARE
(CHEAP SHODDY —) BORAX
(RETURNED —) COMEBACK
MERCHANT ARAB SETH SETT TELI
WALLA BADGER FACTOR KITELY
NEPMAN RETAIL TAIPAN TRADER
ANTONIO CHAPMAN GOLADAR HANSARL
HOWADJI CHANDLER HUCKSTER
MARCHAND POVINDAH SOUDAGUR
(GRAIN —) LAMBADI
(GREAT —) TAIPAN
(HINDU —) BUNNIA
(WINE —) VINTNER
MERCHANT OF VENICE
(AUTHOR OF —) SHAKESPEARE
(CHARACTER IN —) GOBBO TUBAL
PORTIA ANTONIO JESSICA LORENZO
NERISSA SALANIO SALERIO SHYLOCK
BASSANIO GRATIANO LEONARDO
SALARINO STEPHANO BALTHASAR
LAUNCELOT
MERCIFUL KIND MILD HUMANE RUEFUL

TENDER CLEMENT LENIENT MILDFUL
PITIFUL SPARING GRACIOUS QUEMEFUL
MERCILESS GRIM CRUEL SHARP BLOODY
FIERCE SAVAGE WANTON PITILESS
MERCURY HG AZOTH DRAGON HERMES
SPIRIT CHIBRIT MARKERY TEUTATES
QUICKSILVER
(FATHER OF —) JUPITER
(MOTHER OF —) MAIA
MERCY LAW ORE HORE PITY RUTH
GRACE GRITH BLITHE LENITY CHARITY
CLEMENCY LENIENCY COMPASSION
MERE BARE NUDE ONLY PURE PUTE SOLE
VERY NAKED SHEER SINGLE
(PREF.) PSIL(O)
MERELY BUT JUST ONLY BARELY PURELY
SIMPLY SINGLY SOLELY ALONELY
UTTERLY ENTIRELY SCARCELY
MERETRICIOUS CHEAP GAUDY GILDED
TAWDRY PUNKISH
MERGANSER SMEE SMEW HARLE
SNOWL SPIKE HERALD SAWNEB WEASER
BRACKET GARBILL JACKSAW RANTOCK
SAWBILL TADPOLE TOWHEAD TWEEZER
WHEEZER EARLDUCK MOSSHEAD
SHELDRAKE
MERGE FUSE JOIN MELD BLEND ENTER
GLIDE UNIFY VERGE MINGLE COALESCE
COMMERGE CONFLATE LIQUESCE
MERIT DUE EARN MEED PUNY BROOK
FOUND THANK WORTH DESERT PRAISE
VIRTUE WRIHTE DEMERIT DESERVE
PUDDING
(— CONSIDERATION) COUNT
(POSSESSING —) WORTHY
MERITED JUST
(NOT —) INDIGN
MERITORIOUS CAPITAL MERITORY
THANKFUL VALOROUS
MERMAID NIXIE SIREN MERROW
MERWOMAN
MERMAN SEAMAN MANFISH
MERRILY GAILY GAMELY LIGHTLY
LUSTICK JOYOUSLY
MERRIMENT FUN JOY GALE GLEE JEST
UTAS DERAY MIRTH FROLIC SPLEEN
DAFFERY DAFFING FESTIVE JOLLITY
WAGGERY HILARITY
MERRY GAY BOON CANT GLAD GOLE
BONNY BUXOM CADGY CRANK DROLL
JOLLY LIGHT LUSTY MURRY SUNNY
VOGIE VOKIE BLITHE COCKET FROLIC
JOCANT JOCOSE JOCUND JOVIAL
JOYOUS LIVELY FEASTLY GLEEFUL
HOLIDAY JOCULAR LUSTICK RAFFING
WINSOME CHIRPING DISPOSED FESTIVAL
GAMESOME GLEESOME LAUGHING
PLEASANT SPANKING SPORTFUL
SPORTIVE CONVIVIAL
(UNREASONABLY —) DAFT
MERRY-ANDREW AIRY ZANY ANTIC
DROLL JESTER BUFFOON
MERRY-GO-ROUND CAROUSEL
TURNABOUT ROUNDABOUT
MERRYMAKING ALE MAY RAG KIRN
PLOY REVEL GAIETY JUNKET RACKET
SPLORE CARNIVAL

MERRY WIDOW (CHARACTER IN —)
ZETA HANNA MIRKO DANILO GLAWARI
(COMPOSER OF —) LEHAR
MERRY WIVES OF WINDSOR
(AUTHOR OF —) SHAKESPEARE
(CHARACTER IN —) NYM ANNE FORD
HUGH JOHN PAGE CAIUS EVANS ROBIN
RUGBY FENTON PISTOL SIMPLE QUICKLY
SHALLOW SLENDER WILLIAM BARDOLPH
FALSTAFF
MESA HILL LOMA BENCH MESILLA
PLATEAU TERRACE CARTOUCH
MESH MASK MOKE CHAIN PITCH SHALE
ACCRUE ENGAGE MASCLE SCREEN
INTERLOCK SCREENING
(— IMPROPERLY) BUTT
(IN —) DIRECT
MESQUITE HONEY KEAWE PACAY
CASHAW ALGAROBA HONEYPOD
IRONWOOD MOSQUITO
MESS JAG JAM MIX MUX PIE SOP CLAT
FIST HASH JAMB MUCK MULL MUSS
SLUB SOSS STEW SUSS BOTCH CAUCH
JAKES STREW SWILL BOLLIX BUNGLE
CADDLE CLATCH JUMBLE MUCKER
PICKLE PUDDLE SOZZLE TUMBLE
MAMMOCK MULLOCK SCAMBLE SLOTTER
COUSCOUS DISORDER LOBLOLLY
SHAMBLES SLAISTER
(— AROUND) JUKE
(— OF FOOD) SAND
(GREASY —) GAUM
(SLOPPY —) SLOBBER SLAISTER
MESSAGE CHIT MODE SAND SEND WIRE
WORD RUMOR BREVET CIPHER ERRAND
GOSPEL LETTER SCROLL BLINKER
BODWORD DEPECHE EMBASSY MISSION
SENDING TIDINGS AEROGRAM CREDENCE
DISPATCH
(— BY FLAGS) HOIST
(— FROM GOD) ANGEL
(CHRISTIAN —) EVANGEL
(CIPHER —) SCYTALE
(COMPLIMENTARY —) RECADO
(SEQUENCE OF —S) QUEUE
MESSENGER BODE PEON POST SAND
SEND TOTY VAUX ENVOY VISOR BEADLE
BROKER CHIAUS HERALD LEGATE
NUNCIO PIGEON RUNNER CARRIER
CASHBOY CONTACT COURANT COURIER
EXPRESS FORAGER FORAYER MALACHI
MESSAGE MISSIVE PATAMAR TOTYMAN
TROTTER TRUMPET EMISSARY FOREGOER
HIRCARRA LOBBYGOW NUNCIATE
ORDINARY PORTATOR APPARITOR
(— OF APSU AND TIAMAT) MUMMU
(— OF GOD) ANGEL
(— OF SHAMASH) BUNENE
(— OF THE GODS) HERMES MERCURY
(MOUNTED —) COSSID ESTAFET
(RELIGIOUS —) APOSTLE
(UNDERWORLD —) NAMTARU
MESSIAH CHRIST WOVOKA
(MUSLIM —) MAHDI
MESSY GOOEY SLOPPY SOZZLY STICKY
METAL ORE TIN BODY DIET GOLD IRON
LEAD ZINC BARIUM CESIUM CHROME

COBALT COPPER INDIUM LATTIN NICKEL
ORMOLU OSMIUM RADIUM SILVER
SODIUM BISMUTH CADMIUM CALCIUM
HAFNIUM IRIDIUM LITHIUM RHENIUM
RHODIUM THORIUM TUTANIA URANIUM
YTTRIUM ALUMINUM ANTIMONY
CHROMIUM DEADHEAD PLATINUM
RUBIDIUM SCANDIUM TANTALUM
TINCTURE TITANIUM TUNGSTEN
VANADIUM
(— IN MASS) BULLION
(— IN SHEETS) LEAF PLATE
(BABBITT —) LINING
(BASE —) BILLON
(DECORATED —) TOLE
(GROUND —) BRONZING
(HEAVIEST —) OSMIUM
(IMPURE MASS OF —) REGULUS
(LIGHTEST —) LITHIUM
(LIQUID —) MERCURY
(MASS OF —) INGOT
(MOLTEN —) TAP SQUIRT
(OLD POT —) POTIN
(PERFORATED —) STENCIL
(PIECE OF CRUDE —) SLUG
(POINTED —) NAIL
(POROUS —) SPONGE
(SEMIFINISHED —) SEMIS
(SHEET —) LATTEN DOUBLES KALAMEIN
(WASTE —) GATE
METALLIC HARD THIN TINNY
METALWARE TOLE LORMERY
GRAYWARE PONTYPOOL
METAMORPHOSIS METABOLE
PETALODY PHYLLODY SEPALODY
METAPHOR IMAGE TROPE FIGURE
KENNING
METE DEAL DOLE GIVE ALLOT AWARD
MATCH SERVE MEASURE APPORTION
METEOR STAR ARGID CETID COMID
DRAKE LUPID LYRID URSID ANTLID
AUGUST BOLIDE BOOTID CORVID CYGNID
DRAGON HYDRID LIBRID LYNCID LYRAID
PHASMA PISCID TAURID AQUARID
AQUILID ARIETID AURIGID CAMELID
CANCRID CEPHEID CORONID GEMINID
MEATURE ORIONID PEGASID PERSEID
POLARID PRODIGY COLUMBID CRATERID
DRACONID ERIDANID FIREBALL
FORNAXID HERCULID LACERTID SAGITTID
SCORPIID SHOTSTAR TOUCANID
VIRGINID
(SUFF.) ID
METEORITE BAETYL BOLIDE ANDRITE
ATAXITE EUCRITE AEROLITE AEROLITH
BAETULUS BAETYLUS IREOLITE SIDERITE
SKYSTONE
METEOROLOGY AEROLOGY
METER IONIC METRE SEVEN ALCAIC
RHYTHM CADENCE GAYATRI MEASURE
SUBMETER VIAMETER YAWMETER
(CUBIC —) STERE
(MILLIONTH OF —) MICRON
(NETHERLANDS —) ELL
(SQUARE —) CENTIARE
(VEDIC —) GAYATRI
(10 CUBIC —S) DEKASTERE

(10,000 —S) GREX
METHOD ART WAY DART FORM GARB
GATE KINK LINE MIDS MODE REDE RULF
SORT ORDER STYLE TRACK USAGE
COURSE ENGINE MANNER STEREO
SYSTEM FASHION PROCESS TACTICS
WRINKLE ADJUVANT STANDARD
(— OF ANGLING) HARLING
(— OF APPEALING) DHARNA DHURNA
(— OF COLORING TEA) FACING
(— OF CONSTRUCTION) JACAL
(— OF CULTIVATION) JUM JOOM
STUMPING
(— OF DIETING) BANTING
(— OF DISTILLATION) DESCENT
(— OF ELECTION) SCRUTINY
(— OF FATTENING POULTRY)
GAVAGE
(— OF INDUCTION) CANON
(— OF MILKING) NIEVLING
(— OF MURAL DECORATION) KHASI
(— OF PROCEDURE) GAME
(— OF SELECTING POPE) SCRUTINY
(— OF TRACKING) DOVAP
(— OF TREATMENT) SCOPE
(CLEVER —) KINK KINKLE
(FIXED —) FORMULA
(MEDICAL —) CUSHION
(OUTMODED —) ARCHAISM
(PAINTING —) GOUACHE
(PRINTING —) AQUATONE
(SCIENTIFIC —) BACONISM
(SURVEYING —) STADIA
(USUAL —) COURSE PRACTICE
METHODICAL TRIG EXACT FORMAL
SEVERE ORDERLY REGULAR ORDINARY
ORDINATE
METHODIST JUMPER WESLEYAN
SWADDLING
METHODIZE ORDER REGULATE
METHUSELAH (FATHER OF —) ENOCH
METRONOME (PART OF —) BOX KEY
CASE PIVOT SCALE SHAFT WEIGHT
PENDULUM
METROPOLIS CITY SEAT CAPITAL
METTLE PITH SAUL PRIDE SPUNK GINGER
SPIRIT COURAGE SMEDDUM
METTLESOME FIERY PROUD SKEIGH
SPUNKY STUFFY FLIGHTY GINGERY
SPIRITED
MEW PEN WOW CAGE CAST COOP GULL
MEWL MOLT SHED MEUTE MIAOU
MIAOW HIDEAWAY INTERMEW SEEDBIRD
CONFINEMENT
MEXICAN CHOLO LEPERO WETBACK
(AMERICAN OF — DESCENT) CHICANO
MEXICAN-AMERICAN PACHUCO

MEXICO

CAPITAL: MEXICOCITY
COIN: PESO TLAC ADOBE CLACO TLACO
AZTECA CENTAVO PIASTER
LAKE: CHAPALA
MEASURE: PIE VARA ALMUD BARIL JARRA

LABOR LEGUA LINEA SITIO FANEGA
PULGADA
MOUNTAIN: BUFA BLANCO CUPULA
PEROTE ORIZABA
PENINSULA: BAJA YUCATAN
PEOPLE: MAM CHOL CORA MAYA MIXE
PIMA SERI TECO XOVA AZTEC NAHUA
OPATA OTOMI ZOQUE EUDEVE MIXTEC
TOLTEC NAYARIT TEPANEC TOTONAC
ZACATEC ZAPOTEC TEZCUCAN
TOTONACO ZACATECO
RIVER: BRAVO LERMA BALSAS GRANDE
PANUCO TABASCO GRIJALVA SANTIAGO
STATE: LEON NUEVO COLIMA OAXACA
SONORA CHIAPAS DURANGO HIDALGO
NAYARIT SINALOA TABASCO YUCATAN
CAMPECHE QUINTANA VERACRUZ
TOWN: LEON LAPAZ TEPIC ARIZPE COLIMA
JALAPA JUAREZ MERIDA OAXACA
PARRAL POTOSI PUEBLA CANANEA
DURANGO GUAYMAS MORELIA ORIZABA
PACHUCA TAMPICO TORREON CULIACAN
MAZATLAN MONCLOVA SALTILLO
TLAXCALA VERACRUZ
VOLCANO: COLIMA TOLUCA JORULLO
PARICUTIN POPOCATEPETL
WEIGHT: BAG ONZA CARGA LIBRA MARCO
ADARME ARROBA OCHAVA TERCIO
QUINTAL

MEZZANINE ENTRESOL
MIASMA REEK MALARIA MAREMMA
MICA DAZE TALC GLIST SLUDE BIOTITE
GLIMMER ALURGITE FUCHSITE PHENGITE
PHLOGOPITE
MICAH (FATHER OF —) UZZIEL
MERIBBAAL
   (SON OF —) ABDON
MICHAEL MIKE MICKY MICHEL MIGUEL
   (FATHER OF —) IZRAHIAH
JEHOSHAPHAT
   (SLAYER OF —) JEHORAM
   (SON OF —) OMRI SETHUR
MICHAH (FATHER OF —) UZZIEL
MICHAL (FATHER OF —) SAUL
   (HUSBAND OF —) DAVID PHALTI

MICHIGAN

BAY: SAGINAW THUNDER KEWEENAW
STURGEON
CAPITAL: LANSING
COLLEGE: ALMA WAYNE ADRIAN ALBION
CALVIN OLIVET OWOSSO OAKLAND
COUNTY: BAY CASS IRON LUCE CLARE
DELTA IONIA IOSCO ALCONA OCEANA
OGEMAW OSCODA OTSEGO GOGEBIC
OSCEOLA TUSCOLA KALKASKA
INDIAN: OTTAWA
LAKE: BURT TORCH HOUGHTON
MOUNTAIN: CURWOOD
RIVER: CASS BRULE HURON DETROIT
SAGINAW STCLAIR ESCANABA
MONTREAL MENOMINEE
STATE BIRD: ROBIN
STATE FLOWER: APPLEBLOSSOM

STRAIT: MACKINAC
TOWN: MIO ALMA CARO HART FLINT
IONIA LANSE ADRIAN ALPENA BADAXE
OWOSSO PAWPAW WARREN DETROIT
LANSING LIVONIA PONTIAC SAGINAW
ANNARBOR CADILLAC ESCANABA
KALKASKA MANISTEE MUNISING
MUSKEGON CHEBOYGAN KALAMAZOO

MICROBE GERM
MICRONESIAN KANAGA NAURUAN
   (— ISLAND) NUI GUAM ROTA TRUK
MAKIN NAURU WOTHO MAJURO
MICROORGANISM BUG GERM AZOFIER
BUTYRIC MICROBE BACILLUS
MYCOPLASMA
MICROPHONE BUG MIKE PARABOLA
MICROSCOPE GLASS SCOPE
   (PART OF —) ARM BASE CLIP KNOB
LENS LIMB TUBE STAGE FILTER HOLDER
APERTURE EYEPIECE CONDENSER
DIAPHRAGM NOSEPIECE OBJECTIVE
ADJUSTMENT
MICROSCOPIC SMALL MINUTE
MIDDAY NOON UNDERN MIDNOON
NOONDAY MERIDIAN NOONTIME
MIDDLE MEDIO MESNE NAVEL CENTER
MEDIAL MEDIAN CENTRAL MEDIATE
MEDILLE
   (— OF SAIL) BUNT
   (— OF SHIP) WAIST
   (— OF WINTER) HOLL HOWE
MIDDLEMAN BUTTY BROKER DEALER
FOGGER JOBBER LUMPER BUMAREE
BUMMAREE BUTTYMAN HUCKSTER
REGRATER
MIDDLING FAIR MEAN SOSO NEUTRAL
MEDIOCRE MEETERLY
MIDGE GNAT SMUT MIDGET MINGIE
PUNKIE WEEVIL
MIDPOINT BASION PORION STOMION
GNATHION
MIDRIFF APRON SKIRT
MIDSHIPMAN WART MIDDY PLEBE
REEFER SNOTTY OLDSTER
MIDST DEPTH CENTER MIDDLE MIDWARD
MIDSUMMER DAY JOHNSMAS
MIDSUMMER NIGHT'S DREAM
   (AUTHOR OF —) SHAKESPEARE
   (CHARACTER IN —) MOTH PUCK SNUG
EGEUS FLUTE SNOUT BOTTOM COBWEB
HELENA HERMIA OBERON QUINCE
THESEUS TITANIA LYSANDER DEMETRIUS
HIPPOLYTA STARVELING MUSTARDSEED
PHILOSTRATE PEASEBLOSSOM
MIDWAY MEDIO GAYWAY HALFWAY
MIDWIFE BABA DHAI GAMP LUCKY
COMMER CUMMER GRANNY HOWDIE
KIMMER LUCINA GRANNIE HEBAMME
MIEN AIR BROW PORT VULT ALLURE
ASPECT DEMEAN MANNER OSTENT
BEARING DEMEANOR PORTANCE
MIGHT ARM BULK MOTE FORCE MOUND
POWER SHOULD STRENGTH
MIGHTY FELL HIGH KEEN MAIN MUCH
RANK RICH VAST FELON GREAT HEFTY

STERN STOOR POTENT STRONG VIOLENT
ENORMOUS FORCEFUL POWERFUL
PUISSANT SAMSONIC
MIGNON (CHARACTER IN —) MIGNON
MEISTER SPERATA WILHELM LOTHARIO
(COMPOSER OF —) THOMAS
MIGRAINE MEGRIM
MIGRATE RUN FLIT TREK DRIFT FLIGHT
COLONIZE
MIGRATION TREK EXODUS FLIGHT
EELFARE EMOTION PASSAGE DIASPORA
MIGRATORY PEREGRINE
MIKADO DAIRI
MILD CALM COLD EASY FAIR LENT MEEK
SOFT TAME WARM BALMY BLAND
BUXOM GREEN LIGHT LITHE MELCH
MILKY QUIET BENIGN FACILE GENIAL
GENTLE HUMBLE KINDLY REMISS
SMOOTH AFFABLE AMIABLE CLEMENT
LENIENT VELVETY BENEDICT DOVELIKE
FAVONIAN LENITIVE MERCIFUL
SARSENET SOOTHING TRANQUIL
(PREF.) LENI
MILDNESS LENITY SUAVITY CLEMENCY
HUMILITY KINDNESS
MILE (NAUTICAL —) KNOT KAIRI
(ONE-EIGHTH —) FURLONG
(SEA —) NAUT
(SIXTY —S) DEGREE
(3 —S) HOUR LEAGUE
MILIEU CLIMATE TERRAIN AMBIENCE
MILITANT WARRISH FIGHTING
(ONE WITH — ATTITUDE) HAWK
MILITARISTIC PRUSSIAN
MILITARY MARTIAL WARLIKE MILITANT
SOLDIERY
MILITIA FYRD ARRAY MILICE
MILITIAMAN CHOCO UHLAN LUMPER
TRAINER FENCIBLE SHIRTMAN
(TURKISH —) TIMARIOT
MILK COW LAC FUZZ LAIT PAIL SKIM
BLEED JUICE MILCH MULCT BOTTLE
ELICIT STROKE SUCKLE EXPLOIT
(— CLOSELY) JIB
(— DRY) STRIP
(— OUT) EMULGE
(— PRODUCT) GALACT(O)
(BREAST —) SUCK DIDDY
(COW'S —) MESS
(CURDLED —) SKYR TYRE TAYER
LOPPER CLABBER TATMJOLK
(FERMENTED —) KUMISS MATZOON
(NEW —) RAMMEL
(SOUR —) SKYR WHIG BONNY BLEEZE
BLINKY CLABBER JOCOQUE
(WATERY —) BLASH
(PREF.) GALACT(O) LACT(I) LACT(O)
MILKFISH AWA BANGOS SABALO
SAVOLA BANDENG SABALOTE
MILKMAN KITTER CHALKER
MILK PAIL TRUG LEGLEN
MILK SHAKE FRAPPE
MILKSOP SOP MOLLY COCKNEY
MEACOCK
MILKY MILCHY LACTARY LACTEAL
OPALOID LACTEOUS
MILL FULL MILN STAR BREAK FLOUR

KNURL QUERN CHERRY FANNER STAMPS
BLOOMER PUGMILL SMUTTER ARRASTRA
BUHRMILL SPINNERY WALKMILL
(CHOCOLATE —) MOLINET
(FULLING —) STOCKS
(SHINGLING —) FORGE
(SUGAR —) CENTRAL TRAPICHE
MILLENIUM CHILIAD
MILLER MILLMAN STOCKER MULTURER
NILLWARD
MILLET BUDA KODA KOUS MOHA ARZUN
BAJRA CHENA CUMBU DUKHN DURRA
GRAIN HIRSE KODRA MILLY PANIC
PROSO TENAI WHISK BAJREE HUREEK
JONDLA JOWARI MILIUM RAGGEE
DAGASSA PANICLE ZABURRO BIRDSEED
KADIKANE
MILLINER ARTISTE MODISTE
MILLION CONTO QUENT
(10 —) CRORE
(1000 —) MILLIARD
(PL.) GUPPY
(PREF.) MEGA
MILLIPEDE JULID POLYPOD DIPLOPOD
PILLWORM RINGWORM WIREWORM
MILL ON THE FLOSS (AUTHOR OF —)
ELIOT
(CHARACTER IN —) BOB TOM KENN
LUCY DEANE GLEGG GUEST JAKIN
WAKEM MAGGIE PHILIP PULLET STEPHEN
STELLING TULLIVER
MILLPOND DAM MILLDAM BINNACLE
MILLPOOL
MILLRACE LADE LEAT FOREBAY
TAILRACE MILLSTREAM
MILLSTONE RYND STONE BEDDER
LEDGER LIGGER RUNNER
(LOWER —) METATE
(UPPER —) MANO
MILLSTREAM DAM LADE FLEAM
MILQUETOAST CASPAR
MIME ACTOR MIMER MIMIC
MIMIC APE HIT COPY MIME MINT MOCK
MOCKER MONKEY BUFFOON COPYCAT
IMITATE PAGEANT
MIMICRY APERY MIMESIS MOCKAGE
MOCKERY
MIMOSA AROMA CASSIE ALBIZZIA
HUISACHE TURMERIC
MINCE CHOP SHEAR FINICK
MINCED HACHE
MINCEMEAT GIGOT MINCE
MINCING NIMINY FINICAL MINIKIN
MIGNIARD SKIPJACK
MIND CIT CHIT HEAD HEED MOOD NOTE
NOUS RECK SOUL BESEE BRAIN PHREN
SENSE SKULL WATCH ANIMUS MATTER
NOTICE PSYCHE REGARD COURAGE
SENSORY SUBJECT THINKER THOUGHT
(CONSCIOUS —) SENTIENT
(INFINITE —) GOD
(RIGHT FRAME OF —) TUNE
(STATE OF —) BAG
MINDFUL HEEDY MINDLY HEEDFUL
OBSERVANT
MIND READER MENTALIST
MINE DIG PIT DELF HOLE BARGH METAL

STOPE WHEAL COYOTE GROOVE RESCUE
BONANZA OPENCUT TORPEDO
MYNPACHT PROSPECT
(— BY BLASTING) SHOOT
(— IRREGULARLY) GOPHER
(COAL —) ROB COALPIT COLLIERY
(MILITARY —) FOUGADE FOUGASSE
CAMOUFLET
(OLD —) GWAG
(RICH —) GOLCONDA
(TIN —) STANNARY
(UNPRODUCTIVE —) DUFFER SHICER
BORASCA
MINER PECK PICK PYKE BARER DOGGY
ARTIST BUCKER CUTTER DAMMER
DELVER DIGGER GANGER GETTER
HAGGER JUMPER MATTER PELTER
REEFER SNIPER STOPER TINNER TOPMAN
VANNER COLLIER CRUTTER DIRGLER
FEIGHER GEORDIE GROOVER HITCHER
HUTCHER LEADMAN PICKMAN PIKEMAN
PIONEER PLUGMAN ROCKMAN SNUBBER
ENTRYMAN HEADSMAN STRIPPER
WINZEMAN
(— WHO WORKS ALONE) HATTER
MINERAL JET GEET HOST MINE SPAR
BERYL BLOOM EARTH FLUOR GLEBE
GUEST LENAD SQUAT TRONA ACMITE
ALAITE AUGITE BARITE BARYTE BLENDE
CASTOR CERITE COCKLE CURITE DAVYNE
EGERAN EHLITE ERRITE GALENA GARNET
GLANCE GYPSUM HALITE HAUYNE
HELVIN HUMITE ILLITE IOLITE LABITE
MIXITE NATRON NOSEAN NOSITE PINITE
RUTILE SALITE SILICA SPHENE SPINEL
ADAMINE ADAMITE ADELITE ALTAITE
ALUMITE ALUNITE AMOSITE ANATASE
APATITE ATOPITE AXINITE AZORITE
AZULITE AZURITE BAUXITE BAZZITE
BELLITE BIOTITE BISMITE BITYITE
BOHMITE BOLEITE BORNITE BRUCITE
CALCITE CELSIAN CYANITE DIAMOND
DICKITE DUFTITE EDENITE EPIDOTE
ERIKITE ERINITE EUCLASE FLOKITE
GAGEITE GAHNITE GEDRITE GLADITE
GOTHITE GUMMITE HELVITE HESSITE
HOPEITE HOWLITE HULSITE IHLEITE
ILVAITE INESITE INYOITE ISERITE
JADEITE JARLITE JOSEITE KEMPITE
KERNITE KOPPITE KOTOITE KYANITE
LANGITE LARNITE LAURITE LAUTITE
LEHIITE LEIFITE LEONITE LEPTITE
LEUCITE LOWEITE MARTITE MELLITE
MULLITE OKENITE OLIVINE PALAITE
PENNINE PETZITE PYRITES RATHITE
REALGAR RETZIAN RHAGITE RINKITE
ROMEITE ROSSITE SENAITE SODDITE
SVABITE SYLVITE THORITE TURGITE
ULEXITE UTAHITE UVANITE VAUXITE
VOGLITE VRBAITE WARBITE WIIKITE
ZEOLITE ZINCITE ZOISITE ZORGITE
ZUNYITE
(BLACK —) JET GEET CERINE YENITE
KNOPITE NIOBITE ALLANITE GRAPHITE
HIELMITE ILMENITE ONOFRITE
MAGNETITE SAMARSKITE
(BLUE —) MOLYBDENITE

(BRIGHT —) BLENDE
(BROWN —) CERINE EGERAN GUILDITE
JAROSITE
(FIBROUS —) ASBESTOS
(GRAY-WHITE —) TRONA HOPEITE
(GREEN —) AMESITE GAHNITE ILESITE
PRASINE PREHNITE SMECTITE
(MOTTLED —) SERPENTINE
(ORANGE —) SANDIX
(RADIATED —) ASTROITE
(RADIOACTIVE —) CURITE
(RARE —) CYMRITE EUCLASE TYCHITE
BARYLITE
(RED —) GARNET RHODOCHROSITE
(SOFT —) TALC KERMES
(TRANSPARENT —) MICA POLLUX
ABRAZITE SODALITE
(WHITE —) BARITE HOWLITE STILBITE
(YELLOW —) TOPAZ PYRITES
PENTLANDITE
(YELLOWISH-GREEN —) EPIDOTE
ECDEMITE
MINERAL TAR MALTHA
MINERAL WATER SELTZER
MINESWEEPER ALGERINE
MINGLE MIX FUSE JOIN MELL MOLD
MONG MOOL ADMIX BLEND MERGE
TWINE COMMIX FELTER HUDDLE JUMBLE
MEDDLE MEDLEY COMBINE COALESCE
CONFOUND
(PREF.) MISCE
MINGLED FUSED MEDLEY CONFUSED
MINIATURE BABY SMALL LITTLE POCKET
MINIKIN
MINIMAL BASAL LIMINAL MARGINAL
MINIMIZE DECRY MINCE LESSEN MINIFY
SMOOTH SCISSOR BELITTLE DISCOUNT
MINIMUM BARE BEDROCK
MINING WORK MINERY SPATTER
GROOVING
MINION PEAT SATAN MIGNON DARLING
MINIKIN CREATURE SATELLITE
MINISTER PRIG CLERK ELDER ENVOY
HAMAN PADRE VIZIR ATABEG DEACON
DIVINE GALLAH HELPER PANDER PARSON
PASTOR PESHWA PRIEST VIZIER
BROTHER DOMINIE OFFICER PESHKAR
PREFECT PALATINE PREACHER
(— OF FINANCE) DEWAN
(— TO) TEND SERVE INTEND
(— WITHOUT SETTLEMENT) STIBBLER
(PRIME —) PADRONE
MINISTRY SERVICE
MINK FAG HURON NORSE VISON
JACKASH KOLINSKY MUSTELIN
PLATINUM

MINNESOTA

WILKIN CHISAGO WABASHA CROWWING
HENNEPIN OTTERTAIL
INDIAN: SIOUX OJIBWA CHIPPEWA
LAKE: LEECH ITASCA BEMIDJI SUPERIOR
MOUNTAIN: EAGLE MISQUAH
MOUNTAIN RANGE: CUYUNA MESABI
MISQUAH
RIVER: RAINY STCROIX
STATE BIRD: LOON
STATE TREE: REDPINE
TOWN: ADA ELY MORA ANOKA EDINA
FOLEY AUSTIN CHASKA DULUTH MILACA
NEWULM WADENA WASECA WINONA
BEMIDJI FOSSTON HIBBING IVANHOE
MANKATO BRAINERD PIPESTONE

MINNESOTAN GOPHER
MINNOW PINK BANNY GUPPY HITCH
MINIM MINNY BAGGIE MENNON DOGFISH
FATHEAD GULARIS PHANTOM PINHEAD
PINKEEN BONYTAIL CYPRINID FLATHEAD
GAMBUSIA MOONFISH SATINFIN
MINOR FLAT LESS MOLL WARD PETIT
PETTY INFANT LESSER SLIGHT
MINORITY FEW NONAGE INFANCY
MINOS (DAUGHTER OF —) ARIADNE
PHAEDRA
(FATHER OF —) JUPITER LYCASTUS
(MOTHER OF —) EUROPA
(SLAYER OF —) COCALUS
(SON OF —) ANDROGEOS DEUCALION
(WIFE OF —) PASIPHAE
MINSTREL BARD LUTER HARPER JOCKEY
BADCHAN GLEEMAN JOCULAR PARDHAN
PIERROT SONGMAN JONGLEUR
MINT COIN NANA SAGE AJUGA BASIL
ORGAN THYME HYSSOP SAVORY STRIKE
ALLHEAL BALLOTA CAPMINT LABIATE
MONARDA OLITORY OREGANO PERILLA
PHLOMIS POTHERB STACHYS BERGAMOT
CALAMINT IRONWORT LAMPWICK
LAVENDER MARJORAM SAGELEAF
SELFHEAL SKULLCAP PATCHOULI
PATCHOULY PENNYROYAL PEPPERMINT
MINUS LESS WANTING
MINUTE FINE NICE TINY CLOSE MINIM
PRIME SMALL ATOMIC MOMENT
NARROW INSTANT SCRUPLE DETAILED
(24 —S) GHURRY
(PL.) ACTA
MINX JADE PEAT SLUT SNIP HUSSY
LIMMER SNICKET
MIRACLE SIGN ANOMY MARVEL
WONDER PRODIGY THEURGY
MIRACLE PLAY GUARY
MIRACULOUS MARVELOUS
MIRAGE SERAB CHIMERA FLYAWAY
LOOMING ILLUSION TOWERING
MIRANDA (FATHER OF —) PROSPERO
(LOVER OF —) FERDINAND
MIRE BOG DUB CLAY LAIR MOIL SLOB
SLUB SLUE SLUR ADDLE CLART EMBOG
FANGO GLAUR LATCH SEUGH SLAKE
SLOSH SLUSH SQUAD STALL SLOUGH
SLUDGE SLUTCH CLABBER GUTTERS
SLUBBER LOBLOLLY WORTHING

MIRIAM (BROTHER OF —) MOSES
MIRROR FLAT BERYL GLASS IMAGE
STEEL STONE PEEPER PSYCHE REFLEX
SHINER SHOWER CONCAVE HORIZON
REFLECT DIAGONAL SPECULUM
MIRTH GLEE CHEER DREAM GAIETY
BAUDERY DISPORT JOLLITY HILARITY
(CONTEMPTUOUS —) SPORT
(VIOLENT —) SPLEEN
MIRTHFUL CADGY MERRY RIANT FESTIVE
GLEEFUL JOCULAR DISPOSED LAUGHFUL
CONVIVIAL
MIRY OOZY PUXY LAIRY MUCKY SLAKY
CLAGGY CLASHY LUTOSE MIRISH
POACHY SLABBY GUTTERY SLOUGHY
MISADVENTURE GRIEF ACCIDENT
CALAMITY CASUALTY DISASTER
MISHANTER
MISANTHROPE CYNIC TIMON
(AUTHOR OF —) MOLIERE
(CHARACTER IN —) ORONTE ALCESTE
ARSINOE ELIANTE CELIMENE PHILINTE
MISANTHROPIC CYNICAL
MISANTHROPY CYNICISM TIMONISM
MISAPPLY ABUSE CROOK WREST
DISUSE MISUSE
MISAPPREHENSION ILLUSION
MISBEHAVE MISUSE MISBEAR MISFARE
MISHAVE MISLEAD MISGUIDE
MISCALCULATE DUTCH MISCAST
MISCOUNT
MISCARRIAGE FAIL MISHAP FAILURE
ABORTION
MISCELLANEOUS CHOW ORRA SUNDRY
ASSORTED CHOWCHOW
MISCELLANY VARIA MEDLEY WHATNOT
CHOWCHOW GIFTBOOK
MISCHANCE CALAMITY CASUALTY
DISASTER
MISCHIEF HOB ILL BALE BANE EVIL
HARM HURT JEEL WRACK INJURY
MURCHY SORROW WONDER DEVILRY
KNAVERY MALICHO SCADDLE DEVILTRY
MALLECHO
MISCHIEVOUS BAD SLY ARCH IDLE PIXY
ROYT ELFIN HEMPY PIXIE ROYET ELFISH
ELVISH GALLUS HEMPIE IMPISH NOCENT
NOYANT SHREWD SULLEN WICKED
GALLOWS HARMFUL KNAVISH LARKISH
MOCKING NAUGHTY PARLISH PLISKIE
PUCKISH ROGUISH SCADDLE UNHAPPY
UNLUCKY WAGGISH LITHERLY
LUNGEOUS SPORTIVE SPRITISH
VENOMOUS WANSONSY
MISCONCEPTION DELUSION ILLUSION
MISCONDUCT CULPA DOLUS OFFENCE
OFFENSE DISORDER MALFEASANCE
MISCONSTRUE MISJUDGE
MISCREANT KNAVE
MISDEED ILL MISS SLIP AMISS UNWORK
DEFAULT FORFEIT OFFENCE OFFENSE
DISORDER
MISDEMEANOR SIN CRIME FAULT
DELICT OFFENCE OFFENSE DISORDER
MISDIRECT PERVERT MISGUIDE
MISER CUFF SKIN CHUFF CHURL FLINT
GRIPE HAYNE HUNKS NABAL SCRAT

SCRIB CODGER HUDDLE NIPPER PELTER
SCRIMP SNUDGE WRETCH DRYFIST
GOBSECK NIGGARD SCRAPER CHINCHER
GATHERER HAPTERON HARPAGON
HOLDFAST MUCKERER MUCKWORM
PINCHGUT CURMUDGEON
MISERABLE WOE EVIL GRAY PUNK SOUR
DAWNY DEENY DUSTY MISER WOFUL
YEMER ABJECT CHETIF CRUMBY
CRUMMY ELENGE FEEBLE PRETTY
UNSELY WOEFUL BALEFUL FORLORN
PITIFUL SCRUFFY UNHAPPY WANSOME
FORSAKEN PITIABLE SCRANNEL
UNTHENDE WRETCHED
MISERABLES, LES (AUTHOR OF —)
HUGO
(CHARACTER IN —) JEAN JAVERT
MARIUS COSETTE EPONINE FANTINE
VALJEAN JONDRETTE MADELEINE
PONTMERCY THENARDIER
FAUCHELEVANT
MISERY WOE BALE RUTH WREAK THREAT
ANGUISH MISEASE TRAGEDY CALAMITY
DISTRESS
MISFIRE SKIP SNAP
MISFORTUNE ILL BLOW DOLE EVIL
HARM CROSS CURSE HYDRA TRAIK
DAMAGE DIRDUM MISERY MISHAP
RUBBER SCATHE SORROW UNHEAL
UNLUCK AMBSACE MALHEUR MISCARE
MISFALL REVERSE TRAGEDY TROUBLE
CALAMITY DISASTER DISGRACE
DISTRESS MISCHIEF ADVERSITY
MISCHANCE
MISGIVING DOUBT QUALM
MISHANDLE BUNGLE
MISHAP SLIP GRIEF SHUNT FORTUNE
MISTIDE ACCIDENT CASUALTY MISCHIEF
PRATFALL
(MINOR —) GLITCH
MISHMASH BOTCH GOULASH
MISINTERPRET WARP WREST WRITHE
MISREAD PERVERT MISCOUNT
MISLEAD COG ERR BUNK DUPE GULL
HOAX HYPE JIVE BLUFF CHEAT FALSE
SHUCK BETRAY DELUDE SEDUCE WILDER
CONFUSE DEBAUCH DECEIVE MISLEAR
INVEIGLE MISGUIDE BAMBOOZLE
MISLEADING JIVE BLIND FALSE
CIRCEAN TORTIOUS
MISPLAY BLOW DUFF ERROR FLUFF
FUMBLE
MISREPRESENT SKEW ABUSE BELIE
COLOR MISUSE DISTORT FALSIFY
SLANDER MISCOLOR
MISREPRESENTATION FRAUD
CALUMNY DAUBERY GARBLING
MISS ERR HIP FAIL LACK LOSE SKIP SLIP
SNAB FORGO HANUM MISSY PANNA
SKIRT DESIRE KUMARI FRAULEIN
MISTRESS OVERLOOK OVERSLIP
SENORITA
(CLOSE —) SHAVE
MISSHAPEN UGLY BLOWN DEFORMED
MALFORMED
MISSILE GUN BALL BIRD BOLT DART NIKE
SHOT PLUMB SHAFT STONE BULLET

SEEKER BOMBARD GRENADE MISSIVE
OUTCAST AERODART BRICKBAT
PROJECTILE
(DEFECTIVE —) DUD
MISSING LACK WANT ABSENT WANTING
MISSION SAND TASK CHARGE ERRAND
SORTIE VISITA MESSAGE BUSINESS
DEVOTION LEGATION
MISSIONARY APOSTLE COLPORTER

MISSISSIPPI

CAPITAL: JACKSON
COLLEGE: RUST ALCORN BELHAVEN
MILLSAPS TOUGALOO
COUNTY: TATE HINDS JONES LAMAR
LEAKE PERRY YAZOO ALCORN ATTALA
COPIAH JASPER PANOLA TIPPAH TUNICA
CHOCTAW NESHOBA NOXUBEE
ITAWAMBA YALOBUSHA
INDIAN: TIOU BILOXI TUNICA CHOCTAW
NATCHEZ CHICKASAW
LAKE: ENID SARDIS BARNETT GRENADA
OKATIBBEE
MOUNTAIN: WOODALL
RIVER: LEAF PEARL YAZOO BIGBLACK
STATE BIRD: MOCKINGBIRD
STATE FLOWER: MAGNOLIA
STATE TREE: MAGNOLIA
TOWN: IUKA MARKS BILOXI HELENA
LAUREL PURVIS TUNICA TUPELO
WINONA BELZONI CORINTH GRENADA
NATCHEZ WIGGINS BOGALUSA
GULFPORT MERIDIAN KOSCIUSKO

MISSIVE NOTE BILLET LETTER EPISTLE
MESSAGE MISSILE

MISSOURI

CAPITAL: JEFFERSONCITY
COLLEGE: AVILA DRURY TARKIO LINCOLN
WEBSTER STEPHENS
COUNTY: RAY COLE DENT IRON LINN
ADAIR BARRY HENRY MACON RALLS
TANEY GRUNDY PETTIS PLATTE DAVIESS
NODAWAY
INDIAN: OSAGE
LAKE: OZARKS TABLEROCK
MOUNTAIN: TAUMSAUK
RIVER: OSAGE
STATE BIRD: BLUEBIRD
STATE FLOWER: HAWTHORN
STATE TREE: DOGWOOD
TOWN: AVA EDINA ELDON HAYTI LAMAR
MACON MILAN ROLLA BUTLER GALENA
KAHOKA NEOSHO POTOSI BETHANY
BOLIVAR CAMERON LEBANON MOBERLY
PALMYRA SEDALIA STLOUIS HANNIBAL
SIKESTON

MIST DAG FOG MUG URE DAMP DRIP FILM
HAAR HAZE MOKE RACK ROKE SCUD
BRUME CLOUD GAUZE STEAM MIZZLE
NEBULE SEREIN SERENE SMEETH

(COLD —) DROW BERBER
(DRIZZLING —) SMUR DRISK
(SMOKY —) SMOG
(WHITE —) HAG
MISTAKE ERR BALK GOOF MISS SLIP
TRIP ERROR FAULT FLUFF GAFFE LAPSE
BARNEY BOBBLE ESCAPE MISCUE SLIPUP
STUMER BLOOMER BLUNDER CONFUSE
DEFAULT JEOFAIL CONFOUND MISPRINT
MISPRISE
(STUPID —) BUBU BONER CLANGER
(PL.) ERRATA
MISTAKEN WRONG ASTRAY OVERSHOT
TORTIOUS
MISTER DON REB HERR SENOR SENHOR
SIGNOR GOODMAN SIGNIOR GOVERNOR
MISTREAT BANG VIOLATE
MISTRESS MRS PUG TOY AMIE BIBI
DAME DOLL DOXY LADY MISS PURE
AMIGA AMOUR DOLLY DONNA DUENA
FANCY LEMAN LUCKY MADAM NANCY
WOMAN BEEBEE MINION MISSIS MISSUS
NEAERA PARNEL SAHIBA SENORA
TACKLE WAHINE BEDMATE DELILAH
HERSELF HETAERA KITTOCK LEVERET
METREZA PADRONA SENHORA SIGNORA
SULTANA CAMPASPE DESPOINA
DULCINEA FARMWIFE GOODWIFE
GUDEWIFE HAUSFRAU LADYLOVE
LANDLADY MIGNIARD PARAMOUR
PECULIAR SINEBADA TIMANDRA
COURTESAN
(— OF CEREMONIES) FEMCEE
MISTRUST SURMISE DISTRUST
JEALOUSY MISDOUBT
MISTY HAZY MOKY BLEAR DAGGY FILMY
FOGGY MISKY MOCHY MOOTH MURKY
RAWKY ROKEY ROUKY BLURRY CLOUDY
GREASY MIZZLY SMURRY STEAMY
BRUMOUS OBSCURE NEBULOUS
NUBILOUS VAPOROUS
MISUSE ABUSE ABUSION PERVERT
MALTREAT
MITE BIT ATOM CENT DITE DRAM ATOMY
BICHO SPECK ACARID ACARUS CHIGOE
LEPTUS MINUTE SMIDGE ACARIAN
BDELLID CHIGGER DEMODEX SMIDGEN
ARACHNID DIBRANCH FARTHING
HANDWORM ORIBATID SANDMITE
MITIGATE BALM COOL EASE HELP ABATE
ALLAY DELAY MEASE RELAX REMIT
SLAKE ASLAKE LENIFY LESSEN MODIFY
PACIFY SOFTEN SOOTHE SUCCOR
TEMPER ASSUAGE COMMUTE CUSHION
ELEVATE MOLLIFY QUALIFY RELEASE
RELIEVE SWEETEN PALLIATE ALLEVIATE
(— PAIN) PLASTER
MITTEN BOOT CUFF MITT MUFF LOOFIE
MUFFLE NIPPER MUFFLER
MIX BEAT CARD DASH FUSE JOIN KNIT
MELL MENG MESS STIR ADMIX ALLOY
BLEND BRAID IMMIX KNEAD MISCE
TWINE BLUNGE CAUDLE COMMIX
CRUTCH GARBLE JUMBLE MEDDLE
MEDLEY MINGLE MUDDLE PERMIX
STODGE TEMPER WUZZLE BLUNDER

SHUFFLE SWIZZLE CONFOUND LEVIGATE
SCRAMBLE
(— AND STIR WHEN WET) PUG
(— CONFUSEDLY) BROIL
(— FLOCKS) BOX
(— LIQUORS) BREW
(— PLASTER) GAGE GAUGE
(— TEA) BLEND
(— WINE) PART
(— WITH YEAST) BARM
(— WOOL OF DIFFERENT COLORS)
TUM
(CONCRETE —) SOUP
MIXED CHOW IMPURE MEDLEY MOTLEY
PIEBALD STREAKY CHOWCHOW
MIXTURE AIR MIX BODY BREW DASH
FEED HASH MANG MONG MULL OLIO
PUER SOAP STEW ALGIN ALLOY BLEND
BLENT BROMO DOUGH GUMBO SALAD
STUFF FOURRE GARBLE GUNITE LIGNIN
MASLIN MEDLEY MELLAY MINGLE
MOTLEY TEMPER AMALGAM COMPOST
CUSTARD FARRAGO FILICIN FORMULA
GOULASH HEADING KOGASIN MELANGE
MISTION MISTURA MIXTION MONGREL
OLLAPOD RECEIPT TIMBALE ALKYLATE
BLENDURE DRAMMOCK EMULSION
POSSODIE POWSOWDY SOLUTION
MACEDOINE MENAGERIE MISCELLANY
SALMAGUNDI SMORGASBORD
MNEMONIC MEMORIAL
MOAN HONE MOON REEM WAIL CROON
GROAN MOURN MUNGE QUIRK SOUGH
MUNGER
MOANING SOUGH DIRGEFUL
MOAT FOSS DITCH FOSSE GRAFF RUNDEL
MOB CREW HERD RAFF ROUT COHUE
CROWD HURRY PLEBE PLEBS MOBILE
RABBLE TUMULT VOULGE DOGGERY
CANAILLE RIFFRAFF VARLETRY
CLAMJAFRY
(PREF.) OCHLO
MOBILE THIN FLUID ROVING MOVEABLE
MOBSTER HOODLUM
MOBY DICK (AUTHOR OF —) MELVILLE
(CHARACTER IN —) AHAB STUBB
ISHMAEL FEDALLAH QUEEQUEG
STARBUCK
MOCCASIN PAC CONGO TEGUA
SHOEPACK
(— WITH LEGS) LARRIGAN
MOCK BOB BOR DOR GAB MOW COPY DEFY
GECK GIBE GIRD JAPE JEER JEST JIBE
PLAY QUIZ BOURD DORRE ELUDE FLEER
FLIRT FLOUT FRUMP HOKER KNACK
MIMIC RALLY SCOFF SCORN SCOUT
SLEER SPORT TAUNT BEMOCK DELUDE
DERIDE ILLUDE NIGGLE IMITATE
MURGEON RIDICULE
MOCKER MOWER GIRDER BOURDER
FLOUTER SCORNER RAILLEUR
MOCKERY DOR GAB MOW GLEE JEER
BOURD DORRE FARCE FLOUT GLAIK
SCOFF SPORT TAUNT BISMER HETHING LUDIBRY
MOCKADO MOCKAGE DERISION ILLUSION
RIDICULE SCOFFERY
MOCKING GAB ACID SPORT SCOPTIC

IRRISORY NARQUOIS SARDONIC
TRUMPERY
MOCKINGBIRD MIMUS MOWER
MOCKER
MODE CUT JET TON WAY FORM GATE
MOOD RAGA TONE TWIG WISE FERIO
FINAL GENUS MODUS STATE STYLE
ACTING BAROCO CESARE COURSE DATISI
FAKOFO FANGLE FESAPO MANNER
METHOD BAMALIP CALEMES CAMENES
DABITIS DARAPTI DIBATIS DIMARIS
DIMATIS DISAMIS FAPESMO FASHION
FERISON FESTINO CELARENT DOKMAROK
FELAPTON FRESISON TONALITY
(— OF BEHAVIOR) THEW HABITUDE
(— OF BEING) CATEGORY
(— OF CONDUCT) LAW
(— OF DRESS) HABIT TENUE
(— OF DRESSING HAIR) MADONNA
(— OF EXPRESSION) IRONY
(— OF MORAL ACTION) CONDUCT
(— OF PARTITIONING) CANT
(— OF PROCEDURE) ORDER SYSTEM
(— OF RULE) REGIME
(— OF SPEECH) ACCENT LATINISM
PARLANCE
(— OF STANDING) STANCE
(— OF STRUCTURE) BUILD
(PREVAILING —) GARB
(TEMPORARY —) VOGUE
MODEL WAX COPY FORM MOLD NORM
CANON DUMMY IDEAL LIGHT MOULD
NORMA SHAPE DESIGN FUGLER GABARI
MODULE PRAXIS SOURCE BOZZETO
DIORAMA EXAMPLE GABARIT MODULET
PARAGON PATTERN PICTURE SAMPLER
CALENDAR ENSAMPLE EXEMPLAR
EXEMPLUM FORMULAR FUGLEMAN
MAQUETTE MODELLER MODULIZE
PARADIGM PROPLASM SPECIMEN
TYPORAMA MANNEQUIN PLANETARIUM
(— OF HUMAN BODY) FORM MANIKIN
(— OF STATUE) ESQUISSE
(PRELIMINARY —) MAQUETTE
PROPLASM
MODERATE BATE COOL CURB EASE
EASY EVEN MEEK SOFT ABATE ALLAY
ALLOY LIGHT LOWER MEZZO REMIT
SLACK SOBER SWEET ARREST
BRIDLE DECENT GENTLE LESSEN MEANLY
MIDWAY MODEST MODIFY REMISS
SEASON SOFTEN SUBMIT TEMPER
CENTRAL CHASTEN CONTROL SLACKEN
ATTEMPER CENTRIST MIDDLING
MITIGATE ORDINATE PALLIATE
PASSABLE CONTINENT ABSTEMIOUS
MEASURABLE REASONABLE
MODERATELY GEY FAIR MEAN MEANLY
MEETLY PRETTY MIDWISE MIDDLING
MODERATION MEAN STAY MINCE
SPARE MANNER MEDIUM REASON
COMPASS MEDIETY MODESTY SOBRIETY
ABATEMENT IMMODESTY
MODERN NEW LATE RECENT NEOTERIC
MODEST COY SHY DEFT MURE NICE
PURE SNUG BLATE DOUCE LOWLY QUIET
SMALL CHASTE DEMURE HUMBLE

PUDENT SIMPLE VIRGIN CLERKLY
PUDICAL DISCREET MAIDENLY PUDIBUND
RESERVED RETIRING SHAMEFUL
VERECUND VIRTUOUS
MODESTY AIDOS PUDOR NICETY
DECENCY PUDENCY SHYNESS CHASTITY
FOREHEAD HUMILITY PUDICITY
MODICUM DROP BREAK SPICE
SCANTLING SEMBLANCE
MODIFICATION BOB ECAD FORM SALT
CHANGE ENGRAM FACIES SANDHI
SINGLE UMLAUT ENGRAMMA
MODIFY EDIT VARY ALTER AMEND HEDGE
TOUCH BUFFER CHANGE DOCTOR
MASTER TEMPER ARABIZE COMPARE
FASHION QUALIFY ATTEMPER DENATURE
GRADUATE MODERATE FAUCALIZE
MODISH CHIC MODY SOIGNE TIMISH
TONISH STYLISH
MODRED (FATHER OF —) ARTHUR
(MOTHER OF —) MARGAWSE
MODULATE SINK INFLECT QUALIFY
MODULATION ACCENT CHANGE
CADENCE BUNCHING PASSAGIO
MOIST WET DAMP DANK DEWY GREEN
HUMID JUICY SAMMY SAPPY SLACK
SOAKY SPEWY SWACK WASHY WEEPY
CLAMMY STICKY WETTISH HUMOROUS
MUCULENT
MOISTEN DIP WET DAMP MOIL BASTE
BATHE BEDEW JUICE LATCH LEACH
STEEP DABBLE DAMPEN HUMIFY IMBRUE
SPARGE TEMPER HUMIDIFY IRRIGATE
MOISTURE DEW WET BREE DAMP DANK
ROKE HUMOR MOIST WATER PHLEGM
AQUOSITY HUMIDITY
(— DEFICIENT) XERIC
(— IN STONE) SAP
(CONDENSED —) BREATH
MOLAR WANG FORMAL MOLARY
GRINDER
MOLASSES DIP LICK CLAGGUM THERIAC
TREACLE LONGLICK
MOLD DIE PIG PLY CALM CAST CURB
FORM MULL MUST SOIL TRAP BLOCK
CHAPE CHILL FRAME INGOT MODEL
MOULD MUCOR PLASM PRINT SHAPE
SHARE STENT STINT VALVE COFFIN
GABARI INFORM LINGET MATRIX SQUARE
BASTARD FASHION FESTOON MATRICE
RILLETT SANDBOX TEMPLET COQUILLE
FUMAGINE HOODMOLD PROPLASM
TEMPLATE WHISKERS PENICILLIUM
(— FOR METAL) SOW SKILLET
(— OF ASPIC) DARIOLE
(— OF SHIP) SWEEP
(— THAT ATTACKS HOPS) FEN
(CHEESE —) CHESSEL
MOLDING BEAD COVE CYMA DADO GULA
KEEL LIST OGEE OVAL FILET LABEL
LEDGE ROVER STAFF BANDLE BILLET
CASING COLLAR COVING FILLET LISTEL
MULLER REGLET SQUARE ZIGZAG
ANNULET BEADING CABLING CHAPLET
CORNICE DOUCINE ECHINUS EYEBROW
FINGENT HIPMOLD LOZENGE MOULAGE
NECKING SURBASE TONDINO TRINGLE

BAGUETTE BANDELET CASEMATE
CASEMENT CINCTURE CYMATION
CYMATIUM DANCETTE DOGTOOTH
HOODMOLD KNURLING MOULDING
NAILHEAD NECKMOLD ARCHIVOLT
BOLECTION
(CONCAVE —) GORGE CONGEE SCOTIA
CAVETTO
(CONVEX —) REED CABLE OVOLO
THUMB TORUS BASTON REEDING
ASTRAGAL FUSAROLE
(OGEE —) TALON
(OUTSIDE —) BACKBAND
MOLDY FUSTY HOARY MUCID MUGGY
MUSTY VINNY FOISTY MOULDY FOUGHTY
MOLE COB UNT COBB MAIL OONT PIER
PILE TAPE WANT JUTTY MOODY NEVUS
TALPA TAUPE ANICUT MOUDIE HYDATID
TALPOID MOLDWARP MOONCALF
SORICOID STARNOSE UROPSILE
ZANDMOLE
MOLECULE ACID ATOM BASE AMMINE
DIPOLE HYDROL LIGAND PRIMER
HYDRONE SPECIES TEMPLATE
MOLEST GALL HAUNT TEASE BOTHER
HARASS HECKLE INFEST PESTER
TROUBLE
MOLL FLANDERS (AUTHOR OF —)
DEFOE
(CHARACTER IN —) MOLL JEMMY
ROBIN FLANDERS
MOLLIFY HUSH RELAX GENTLE PACIFY
RELENT SOFTEN SOOTHE TEMPER
ASSUAGE DULCIFY SWEETEN ATTEMPER
MITIGATE UNRUFFLE
MOLLUSK ARK CLAM CONE PIPI SPAT
BORER CHAMA CHANK CHINK CLAMP
CONCH COWRY DORIS DRILL MUREX
PINNA SNAIL VENUS AEOLID BAILER
BUBBLE CERION CHITON COCKLE COURIE
DOLIUM JINGLE LEPTON LIMPET MUSSEL
NERITA OYSTER PECTEN PHOLAD PURPLE
SEMELE STROMB ABALONE ADMIRAL
ASTARTE BIVALVE CARDITA DECAPOD
JUNONIA MOLLUSC PIDDOCK SALPIAN
SCALLOP TOHEROA TREPANG TROPHON
DUCKFOOT FIGSHELL HALIOTIS
NAUTILUS PTEROPOD SAXICAVA
STROMBUS UNIVALVE VERMETUS
SHELLFISH NUDIBRANCH PERIWINKLE
MOLT MEW CAST MUTE SHED MOULT
DISCARD EXUVIATE INTERMEW
MOLUCCAS (ISLAND OF —) ARU KAI
OBI BURU LETI SULA AMBON BABAR
BANDA CERAM WETAR BATJAN TIDORE
MOROTAI TERNATE TANIMBAR
HALMAHERA
MOMENT MO GIRD HINT SAND TICK
AVAIL BLINK BRAID CLINK CRACK GLIFF
GLISK JIFFY SHAKE SNIFT SPURT STOUN
TRICE VALUE FILLIP GLIFFY MINUTE
PERIOD SECOND STOUND WEIGHT
YAWING ARTICLE INSTANT INSTANCE
MOMENTUM TWINKLING
(— FOR LEGERDEMAIN ACTION)
TEMPS
(— OF STRESS) CRISE

(APPROPRIATE —) PLACE
(CRITICAL —) BIT INCH CORNER
(DECISIVE —) CRISIS
(EXACT —) BIT POINT
(OPPORTUNE —) KAIROS
(SCHEDULED —) TIME
MOMENTARY TRANSIENT
MOMENTOUS FELL GRAVE EPOCHAL
FATEFUL WEIGHTY EVENTFUL PREGNANT
MOMENTUM WAY FORCE SPEED
IMPETUS

MONACO

ANCIENT NAME: MONOECUS
CAPITAL: MONACO MONACOVILLE
LANGUAGE: FRENCH
PEOPLE: MONEGASQUES
PRINCE: LOUIS ALBERT HONORE ANTOINE
CHARLES RAINIER FLORESTAN
RIVER: VESUBIE
SECTION: MONTECARLO LACONDAMINE
MONACOVILLE

MONARCH KING QUEEN DANAID DIADEM
PRINCE DANAINE EMPEROR AUTOCRAT
MONARCHY KINGDOM
MONASTERY WAT ABBEY BADIA LAURA
FRIARY MANDRA VIHARA CONVENT
MINSTER MONKERY CLOISTER
(ALGERIAN —) RIBAT
(BUDDHIST —) TERA KYAUNG BONZERY
LAMASERY
(CARTHUSIAN —) CERTOSA
(HINDU —) MATH
(MOSLEM —) TEKKE TEKYA KHANKAH
MONASTIC MONKLY MONKISH
ABBATIAL CENOBIAN MONACHAL
MONEY (ALSO SEE COIN) AES BOX DIB
FAT FEE FEI GET OOF ORO SAP TIN WAD
COAT COIN COLE CRAP CUSH DUBS
DUST FUND GATE GELT GILT GOLD HOOT
JACK JAKE KALE LOOT LOUR MALI MINT
MOSS MUCK PELF ROLL SALT SAND
SHAG SWAG BEANS BLUNT BRASH
BRASS BREAD BUNCE BUNTS CHINK
CHIPS CLINK DIMES DOUGH DUMPS
FUNDS GRIGS IMPUT LOLLY LUCRE
MEANS MOOLA MOPUS OCHER PURSE
RHINO ROCKS ROWDY SCADS SHINY
SMASH SPUDS STIFF SUGAR ARGENT
BARATO BARREL CHANGE CUNYIE
DANARO DINERO FARLEU FARLEY
FEUAGE FLIMSY FUMAGE GRAITH
HANSEL KELTER MAZUMA POCKET
SHEKEL SILLER SILVER SPENSE SPLOSH
STAMPS STEVEN TALENT WISSEL
ADVANCE CHATTEL CHINKER COUNTER
CRACKER CRUSADE DEPOSIT FALDAGE
GUNNAGE OOFTISH SCRATCH SPANKER
SPECIES STOCKER CRIMPAGE DEMIMARK
INCOMING INTEREST SPENDING
STERLING STOCKING XERAPHIN
(— DUE) DEVOIRS
(— FOR LIQUOR) WHIP
(— LENT) LUMBER.

(— OF ACCOUNT) ORA
(— PAID TO BIND BARGAIN) ARLES
(ADDITIONAL —) BONUS
(AVAILABLE —) CAPITAL
(BAR —) BONK TANG
(BASE —) SHICE
(BRIBE —) SOAP BOODLE
(COUNTERFEIT —) BOGUS QUEER
BOODLE DUFFER SHOWFUL SLITHER
(EARNEST —) ARLES ARRHA DEPOSIT
HANDSEL HANDGELD HANDSALE
(FERRY —) NAULUM
(HARD —) SPECIE
(HAT —) TAMPANG
(INVESTED —) STOCK
(PAPER —) GREEN CABBAGE CURRENCY
FROGSKIN
(PASSAGE —) SHIPHIRE
(PRIZE —) PEWTER
(PROTECTION —) ICE
(PUSH —) SPIFF
(READY —) CASH DARBY PREST READY
STUFF STUMPY
(SHELL —) PEAG HAWOK WAKIKI
WAMPUM
(SILVER —) SYCEE
(SMALL SUM OF —) SPILL
(STANDARD BANK —) BANCO
(SUBSISTENCE —) BATTA
(TRAVELLING —) VIATICUM
(WIRE —) LARI LARIN LARREE
MONEY-CHANGER SARAF SHROFF
CAMBIST ARGENTER
MONEYLENDER BANYA CHETTY
USURER LOMBARD MAHAJAN MARWARI
SHYLOCK BUMMAREE
MONGOL HUN KALKA BALKAR BURIAT
DAGHUR SHARRA BERBERI KALMUCK
KHALKHA SILINGAL
MONGOLIA (CAPITAL OF —)
ULAANBAATAR
(DESERT IN —) GOBI
(MONEY OF —) TUGHRIK
(RIVER OF —) ORHON DZAVHAN
KERULEN SELENGE
(TOWN OF —) ONON MUREN DARHAN
BULAGAN CHOIREN TAMTSAK
ULANBATOR CHOYBALSAN
MONGREL CUR DOG FICE MUTT CROSS
FEIST LIMER POOCH SCRUB HYBRID
PYEDOG BASTARD CURRISH PIEBALD
DOGGEREL
MONITOR CRT MARKER MENTOR
LANTERN PREFECT
MONITOR LIZARD IBID IBIT URAN
VARAN WARAL GOANNA WORRAL
MONITOR KABARAGOYA
MONK BO FRA COWL LAMA MARO ARHAT
BONZE CLERK FRATE FRIAR PADRE
YAHAN ARAHAT BHIKKU CULDEE GALLAH
GETSUL GOSAIN MONACH SANTON
VOTARY CALOYER CLUNIAC GALLACH
JACOBIN STARETS STUDITE ATHONITE
BACHELOR BASILIAN MARABOUT
MONASTIC OLIVETAN SANNYASI
TALAPOIN TRAPPIST BALDICOOT

CELESTINE THELEMITE BERNARDINE
CISTERCIAN
MONKEY APE CAY ORA PUG SAI TUP
BEGA BROH BRUH DOUC KAHA MONA
MONK MONO SAKI SIME TITI TOTA
WAAG ZATI ARABA CEBID DIANA JACKO
JOCKO KAHAU MUNGA OATAS PATAS
PONGO PUGGY SAJOU TOQUE UNGKA
BANDAR COAITA COUXIA GRISON
GRIVET GUENON HOWLER LANGUR
MACACO MARTEN MIRIKI MONACH
NISNAS OUBARI PINCHE RILAWA SAMIRI
SIMIAN SIMPAI TEETEE VERVET WARINE
WEEPER WISTIT BHUNDER COLOBIN
GUARIBA GUEREZA HANUMAN KALASIE
LUNGOOR MACAQUE MEERKAT
MOUSTOC OUAKARI PRIMATE ROLOWAY
SAIMIRI SAPAJOU STENTOR TAMARIN
ARAGUATO CAIARARA CAPUCHIN
DURUKULI ENTELLUS LEONCITO
MANGABEY MARMOSET MARTINET
MUSTACHE ORABASSU PRIMATAL
TALAPOIN TCHINCOU WANDEROO
BRACHYURA MALBROUCK
MONOCLE QUIZ LORGNON EYEGLASS
MONOGRAM CIPHER HERALD
CHRISMON
MONOGRAPH STUDY MEMOIR BULLETIN
DISCOURSE
MONOLITH MENHIR PILLAR
(CIRCLE OF —S) CROMLECH
MONOPOLIZE LURCH ABSORB
CONSUME ENGROSS
MONOPOLY REGIE TRUST CARTEL
APPALTO
MONOTONOUS ARID DEAD DULL FLAT
WASTE DREARY SAMELY SODDEN
ADENOID HUMDRUM INSIPID IRKSOME
TEDIOUS BORESOME DRUDGING
SAMESOME SINGSONG UNVARIED
VEGETABLE
MONOTONY DRAB DRYNESS HUMDRUM
DULLNESS SAMENESS
MONSIEUR BEAUCAIRE
(AUTHOR OF —) TARKINGTON
(CHARACTER IN —) BEAU MARY NASH
VALOIS CARLISLE MIREPOIX PHILLIPE
MOLYNEUX WINTERSET CHATEAURIEN
MONSOON VARSHA
MONSTER OGRE BILCH LARVA MORMO
RAHAB TERAS UNMAN ELLOPS GERYON
MAKARA SHRIMP TYPHON BICORNE
CHIMERA CYCLOPS DIDYMUS DIPYGUS
ECHIDNA GRENDEL GRIFFIN GRIFFON
PRODIGY SLAPPER UNBEAST WARLOCK
JANICEPS LINDWORM MOONCALF
TARASQUE TYPHOEUS UROMELUS
LEVIATHAN
(— WITH 100 EYES) ARGUS
(— WITH 100 HANDS) BRIAREUS
(FABULOUS —) KRAKEN TANIWHA
(FEMALE —) HARPY LAMIA SCYLLA
(HALF-BULL HALF-MAN —) MINOTAUR
(INVISIBLE —) BUNYIP
(MAN-DEVOURING —) OGRE LAMIA
(MYTHICAL —) HARPY SCYLLA SPHINX
CHIMERA WARLOCK MINOTAUR

(SEA —) BELUE PHOCA KRAKEN PISTRIX
    ZIFFIUS WASSERMAN
(SUPERNATURAL —) LARVA
(TWO-BODIED —) DISOMUS
(WATER —) NICKER
(9-HEADED —) HYDRA
MONSTROUS VAST ENORM GIANT
    FIENDLY FLAMING HIDEOUS TITANIC
    BEHEMOTH COLOSSAL DEFORMED
    ENORMOUS FLAGRANT GIGANTIC
    PYTHONIC SLAPPING NEFARIOUS
    PRODIGIOUS

MONTANA

CAPITAL: HELENA
COLLEGE: CARROLL
COUNTY: HILL TETON TOOLE CARBON
    CUSTER FERGUS MCCONE WIBAUX
    BIGHORN PONDERA RAVALLI CHOUTEAU
    FLATHEAD MISSOULA
INDIAN: CROW ATSINA SALISH ARAPAHO
    KUTENAI SIKSIKA SHOSHONE
LAKE: HEBGEN FLATHEAD FORTPECK
    MEDICINE
MOUNTAIN: AJAX BALDY COWAN SPHINX
    TORREY GRANITE HILGARD TRAPPER
    GALLATIN PENTAGON SNOWSHOE
MOUNTAIN RANGE: CRAZY LEWIS POCKY
    BIGBELT
RIVER: MILK TONGUE KOOTENAI MISSOURI
STATE BIRD: MEADOWLARK
STATE FLOWER: BITTERROOT
TOWN: BUTTE HAVRE MALTA TERRY
    CIRCLE CONRAD HARDIN HELENA
    HYSHAM SCOBEY BOZEMAN CHINOOK
    CHOTEAU EKALAKA FORSYTH GLASGOW
    ROUNDUP BILLINGS MISSOULA

MONTENEGRO

CAPITAL: CETINJE
COIN: PARA FLORIN PERPERA
LAKE: SCUTARI SHKODER
MOUNTAIN: DURMITOR
PORT: BAR ULCINJ ANTIVARI DULCIGNO
RIVER: IBAR ZETA DRINA MORACA
TOWN: NIKSIC CETINJE TITOGRAD
    PODGORICA

MONTH AB AV BUL MAY PUS SOL ZIF
    ZIW ABIB ADAR AHET APAP ASIN ELUL
    IYAR JETH JULY JUNE KUAR MAGH
    MOON TYBI AGHAN APRIL ASARH CHAIT
    IYYAR MAIUS MARCH NISAN PAYNI
    RABIA RAJAB SAFAR SAWAN SEBAT
    SHVAT SIVAN SIWAN TEBET THOTH
    TIZRI UINAL AUGUST BHADON CHOIAK
    JUMADA LUNAR KARTIK KISLEV KISLEW
    KISLEY MECHIR MESORE NISSAN NIVOSE
    PAOPHI PHAGUN SAPHAR SHABAN
    SHABAT TAMMUZ TEBETH TISHRI
    VEADAR ABAGHAN APRILIS BAISAKH
    BYSACKI CHAITRA CHISLEV ETHANIM

FLOREAL HESHVAN JANUARY MARTIUS
    OCTOBER PACHONS PHALGUN RAMADAN
    SARAWAN SHAABAN SHAWWAL
    THAMMUZ VENTOSE BRUMAIRE
    DECEMBER DULKAADA FEBRUARY
    FERVIDOR FRIMAIRE GAMELION
    GERMINAL MESSIDOR MUHARRAM
    NOVEMBER PLUVIOSE POSEIDON
    PRAIRIAL SEXTILIS ZULKADAH
    SEPTEMBER
(IN PRECEDING —) ULTIMO
(PRESENT —) INSTANT
(SIX —S) SEMESTER
(PREF.) MENO
MONTHLY MENSAL
MONUMENT VAT WAT LECH TOMB
    CROSS STONE TABUT TITLE BILITH
    DOLMEN HEARSE HEROON MEMORY
    RECORD TROPHY ARCHIVE CHAITYA
    CHHATRI CHORTEN DENKMAL FUNERAL
    TRILITH BILITHON CENOTAPH MEMORIAL
    MONOLITH TROPAION
(— IN CHURCH) SACELLUM
(— OF BALEARIC ISLES) TALAYOT
(— OF HEAPED STONES) CAIRN
(PILLARLIKE —) SHAFT STELA STELE
MOO LOW
MOOCH BUM CADGE SPONGE
MOOCHER MIKER CADGER GRAFTER
    SKELDER
MOOD CUE FIT TID MIND TIFF TIFT TONE
    TUNE VEIN WHIM DEVIL FRAME FREAK
    HEART HUMOR SPITE PLIGHT SPIRIT
    SPLEEN SPRITE STRAIN TALENT TEMPER
    CAPRICE FANTASY FEATHER JUSSIVE
    ATTITUDE OPTATIVE
(— IN LOGIC) BARBARA
(— OF BAD TEMPER) MAD DORTS
(— OF DEPRESSION) LETDOWN
(CROSS —) FRUMPS
(FRIVOLOUS —) JEST
(GROUCHY —) DODS
(IRRITABLE —) GRIZZLE
(PENSIVE —) MELANCHOLY
(SULKY —) PET
(SULLEN —) STRUNT SULLENS
MOODY SAD GLUM SULKY BROODY
    GLOOMY MOROSE SULLEN MOODISH
    PENSIVE
MOON BUAT LAMP LUNA MAHI DIANA
    LUNET LUCINA PHOEBE CHANDRA
    CYNTHIA LEWANNA LUNETTE MOONLET
    FOGEATER MENISCUS SATELLES
(FULL —) PLENILUNE
(NEW —) PRIME
(WANING —) WANIAND
MOON AND SIXPENCE
(AUTHOR OF —) MAUGHAM
(CHARACTER IN —) AMY ATA DIRK
    TIARE BLANCHE CHARLES COUTRAS
    STROEVE STRICKLAND
MOONSHINE MOON SHINE SHINNY
    BOOTLEG BLOCKADE
MOONSTONE (AUTHOR OF —)
    COLLINS
(CHARACTER IN —) CUFF EZRA JOHN
    BLAKE BRUFF CANDY LUKER RACHEL

GABRIEL GODFREY ROSANNA FRANKLIN JENNINGS SPEARMAN VERINDER ABLEWHITE BETTEREDGE HERNCASTLE MURTHWAITE

MOOR FEN BENT FELL MOSS POST BEACH BERTH HOVEL TURCO COMONTE MARRANO MOGRABI MOORMAN MORESCO MORISCO COMMONTY (INFERTILE —) LANDE

MOOSE BELL ELAND CERVID ORIGNAL (YOUNG —) CALF

MOP BOB SOP SWAB MOPPET SCOVEL (— FOR CLEANING CANNON) MERKIN (— OF HAIR) TOUSLE (BAKER'S —) MALKIN MAWKIN

MOPE MUMP PEAK POUT SULK BOODY BROOD GLOOM

MORAL TAG PURE CIVIL ETHIC EPIMYTH ETHICAL UPRIGHT HONORARY

MORALITY MORALS VIRTUE

MORASS BOG FLOW MOSS ROSS SUMP FLUSH MARSH SLACK POLDER SLOUGH QUAGMIRE

MORAY PUSI ELGIN HAMLET MURAENA

MORBID SICK MORBOSE PECCANT

MORDANT HANDLE SPIRIT CAUSTIC STRIKER SCATHING

MORDECAI (FATHER OF —) JAIR (WARD OF —) ESTHER

MORE PIU OTHER HELDER (— OR LESS) HALFWAY (— THAN) BUT OVER ABOVE RISING PLUSQUAM (— THAN ADEQUATE) AMPLE (— THAN ENOUGH) TOO (— THAN HALF) BETTER (— THAN ONE) SEVERAL (— THAN ONE OR TWO) SUNDRY (— THAN SUFFICIENT) ABUNDANT (— THAN THIS) YEA (LITTLE —) ADVANTAGE

MOREOVER EFT EKE TOO ALSO MORE AGAIN EITHER BESIDES FARTHER FURTHER THERETO LIKEWISE OVERMORE

MORMON COHAB SAINT DANITE PATRIARCH

MORNING GAY MORN MATIN MORROW UNDERN COCKCROW MORNTIME

MORNING GLORY NIL KOALI TWINER GAYBINE IPOMOEA MANROOT PILIKAI BINDWEED SCAMMONY MOONFLOWER (— GROWING AMONG GRAIN) BEAR

MORNING STAR VENUS DAYSTAR LUCIFER MERCURY BARTONIA

MORO LUTAO SAMAL YAKAN ILLANO JOLOANO MARANAO

MOROCCO

CAPE: NUN NOUN
CAPITAL: RABAT
COIN: OKIA RIAL OKIEH DIRHAM MOUZOUNA
FRENCH NAME: MAROC
MEASURE: KALA SAAH FANEGA IZENBI TOMINI

MOUNTAIN: TOUBKAL
MOUNTAIN RANGE: RIF ATLAS
PEOPLE: MOOR BERBER KABYLE MOSLEM MUSLIM
PORT: SAFI CEUTA RABAT SAFFI AGADIR TETUAN LARACHE MAZAGAN MELILLA MOGADOR TANGIER
PROVINCE: CEUTA MELILLA
RIVER: DRA SOUS WADI SEBOU TENSIFT MOULOUYA
TOWN: FES FEZ SAFI OUJDA RABAT AGADIR MEKNES KENITRA TANGIER TETOUAN MARRAKECH CASABLANCA
WEIGHT: ROTL ARTAL ARTEL GERBE RATEL KINTAR QUINTAL

MORON FOOL AMENT IMBECILE

MOROSE ACID GLUM GRUM SOUR MOODY RUSTY SURLY CRUSTY GLOOMY SEVERE STINGY SULLEN CRABBED CROOKED PEEVISH STROUNGE SATURNINE SPLENETIC

MORSEL BIT NIG ORT TIT BITE GNAP SNAP SCRAN BUCKONE MORCEAU NOISETTE PARTICLE SKERRICK (— OF CHEESE) TRIP (— OF CHOCOLATE) BUD (— OF SEASONED MEAT) GOBBET (CHOICE —) TIDBIT TITBIT

MORTAL BEING DYING FATAL HUMAN VITAL DEADLY FINITE LETHAL BRITTLE DEATHLY DEATHFUL (FIRST —) YAMA

MORTAR DAB COMPO DAGGA GROUT LARRY ROYAL SORKI SWISH CANNON CEMENT HOLMOS MINNIE POTGUN BEDDING COEHORN DAUBING PERRIER POUNDER PUGGING SOORKEE (— AND PESTLE) DOLLY DOLLIE (— EXTRUDED BETWEEN LATHS) KEY (— FOR ROCKETS) TROMBE (— FOR SALUTES) CHAMBER (— MADE WITH STRAW) BAUGE (INFERIOR —) SLIME (SMALL —) HOBIT ROYAL TINKER (THIN —) LARRY

MORTGAGE DIP LAY BOND LIEN ENGAGE MONKEY OBLIGE WADSET THIRLAGE

MORTIFICATION ENVY SHAME SPITE CHAGRIN GANGRENE NECROSIS VEXATION

MORTIFIED ASHAMED

MORTIFY ABASE ABASH SHAME SPITE HUMBLE CHAGRIN CRUCIFY MACERATE

MORTUARY MORGUE FUNERARY SAWLSHOT SEPULCHRAL

MOSAIC AUCUBA EMBLEM MUSIVE SCREEN FRISOLEE INTARSIA TERRAZZO

MOSLEM MOOR HADJI HAFIZ HANIF ISLAM MALAY SALAR PAYNIM SHIITE TURBAN ISLAMIC MOORMAN SANGGIL SARACEN ISLAMITE SANGUILE

MOSQUE JAMI MOSCH DURGAH MASJID MESKED

MOSQUITO GNAT AEDES CULICID GAMBIAE SKEETER ANOPHELE DIPTERAN

MOSS FOG MNIUM USNEA HYPNUM
MUSKEG AEROGEN FOXFEET GULAMAN
HAIRCAP PILIGAN TORTULA CROWFOOT
MOSSWORT SPHAGNUM STAGHORN
(— HANGING FROM TREE) WEEPER
MOST BEST MOSTLY FARTHEST
MOTH GEM NUN PUG DART HAWK MOTE
PAGE ACREA APPLE ATLAS EGGAR
EGGER FLAME GAMMA IMAGO MORMO
PISKY PLUME SAMIA SWIFT THORN
USHER WITCH ANTLER BAGONG
BUGONG BURNET COSSID DAGGER
DATANA HERALD HUMMER JUGATE
LACKEY LAPPET MILLER MOODER
MUSLIN PLUSIA PRALID QUAKER RUSTIC
SPHINX THISBE TINEID TISSUE TUSSUR
VENEER ARCTIAN ARCTIID BAGWORM
BUDWORM CRAMBID CRININE DELTOID
DRINKER EMERALD EMPEROR EUCLEID
FESTOON FIGWORM FOOTMAN FRENATE
HOOKTIP NOCTUID PEGASUS PSYCHID
PYRALIS SLICKER STINGER SYLINID
TINEOLA TORTRIX TUSSOCK URANIID
VAPORER ZYGENID
MOTHER INA MOM DAME MAMA MADRE
MAMMA MAMMY MATER MINNY MODUR
MITHER MULIER VENTER GENETRIX
(— OF THE GODS) RHEA
(DIVINE —) MATRIGAN
(GREAT —) AGDISTIS
(NOURISHING — OF MAN) CYBELE
(SEVEN —S) MATRIS
MOTHERLAND COUNTRY
MOTHERLY MATERNAL MATRONAL
MOTHER-OF-PEARL NACRE PEARL
MOTIF SPRIG DESIGN DEVICE MOTIVE
SCALLOP APPLIQUE MORESQUE
MOTION WAY FARD FEED GIRD MOVE
SIGN WHID HURRY PAVIE APPORT
MOMENT MOTIVE TRAVEL UNREST
IMPULSE ACTIVITY MOVEMENT
OVERTURE
(— OF AIR) AIRFLOW
(— OF CONTEMPT) FICO
(— OF HORSE) AIR
(— TO) ALLATIVE
(ABRUPT —) CHOP
(CAM —) COULIER
(CIRCULAR —) GYRE COMPASS
(CONFUSED —) GURGE
(DANCE —) CAPER
(DIZZY —) SWIMBEL
(EXPRESSIVE —) GESTURE
(FORWARD —) HEADWAY
(GLIDING —) SWIM SKITTER
(HEAVING —) ESTUS AESTUS
(HURRIED —) HUSTLE
(ILLEGAL —) BALK BAULK
(IRREGULAR —) SWAG
(JERKING —) BOB LIPE JIGGLE
(LATERAL —) DRIFT
(QUIVERING —) TREMOR
(RAPID —) SCOUR BRATTLE
(REARING —) PESADE
(RECIPROCATING —) SEESAW
(ROTARY —) SWAY BACKSPIN
SIDESPIN

(SHOWY —) FANFARE
(SIDEWAYS —) CRAB
(SLOW —) CRAWL
(SPINNING —) ENGLISH
(SUNWISE —) DEASIL
(SWIMMING —) FLUTTER
(UPWARD —) HEAVE
(VIGOROUS —) SKELP
(VIOLENT —) JERK RAPT BENSEL
(WAVERING —) SHAKE
(WAVING —) WAFF
(WHIRLING —) SWIRL
MOTIONLESS DEAD ASLEEP STATIC
IMMOBILE STAGNANT STIRLESS
MOTION PICTURE PIC CINE FILM FLICK
MOVIE BIOPIC CINEMA TALKIE CHEAPIE
SMELLIE FLICKERS
MOTIVATE PROPEL ACTUATE ANIMATE
INSPIRE
MOTIVE GOAD SAKE SPUR CAUSE MOTIF
SCORE ACTUAL DESIRE OBJECT REASON
REGARD SPRING ATTACCO IMPULSE
PATTERN RESPECT RINCEAU SUBJECT
INSTANCE STIMULUS
(ALLEGED —) PRETEXT
(CHIEF —) MAINSPRING
MOTLEY MIXED MEDLEY RAGTAG
MOTTLED PIEBALD
MOTOR AUTO TOOT TOUR MOVER
ENGINE BOOSTER ROTATOR TURBINE
EFFERENT OUTBOARD
MOTORBIKE MOPED
MOTORBOAT KICKER LAUNCH
AUTOBOAT RUNABOUT HYDROFOIL
MOTORCAR MOTOR DOODLEBUG
(MINIATURE — FOR RACING) KART
MOTORCYCLE BIKE CYCLE MOTOR
STEED TRICAR CHOPPER AUTOETTE
MINIBIKE TRICYCLE
(SMALL —) MINIBIKE
MOTORTRUCK DRAY LORRY CAMION
BOBTAIL FLATBED
MOTTLED JAZZ PIED CHINE PINTO
TABBY MARLED MOTLEY RUMINATE
SPLASHED
MOTTO MOT WORD AXIOM POESY
CACHET DEVICE EUREKA LEGEND
REASON IMPRESA EPIGRAPH
MOUND AHU COP HOW BALK BANK
BOSS BUND BUTT GOAL HILL HUMP
KNOW MOLE POME TELL TEPE TERP TUFT
AGGER DHERI ESKAR ESKER KNOLL
MONDE MOUNT PINGO RAISE STUPA
TOMAN CAUSEY MEILER RIDEAU ANTHILL
BOUROCK HILLOCK MAMELON
BACKSTOP SNOWBANK TEOCALLI
(— ABOUT A PLANT) TUMP
(— FOR MEMORIAL) CAIRN
(— IN BUILDING MATERIAL) DIMPLE
(— OF DETRITUS) WASH
(— OF ICE) DOME
(— OF WOOD TO BE CHARRED)
MEILER
(BURIAL —) LAW LOW TOR TOLA BERRY
GUACA HUACA BARROW KURGAN
TUMULUS
(FORTIFIED —) DUN

(GLACIAL —) KAME
(MILITARY —) BARBETTE
(PALISADED —) MOTTE
(VOLCANIC —) HORNITO
(PREF.) BUNO

MOUNT BEN STY BACK HEAD RIDE RISE
SCAN ARISE BIPOD BOARD CLIMB HEAVE
HINGE SPEEL SPIRE SWARM ASCEND
ASPIRE BREAST MORIAH CHARGER
COLLINE HAIRPIN HARNESS BESTRIDE
MOUNTAIN MOUNTING MOUNTURE
SURMOUNT

MOUNTAIN BEN KOP BERG CIMA DAGH
FELL KLIP MONS MONT NEBO PICO PIKE
JEBEL MOUNT RANGE BARROW BUNDOC
GILEAD GUNONG HEIGHT PISGAH
HELICON MONTURE NUNATAK
MONADNOCK
(— INHABITED BY SPIRIT) HUACA
(— MASS) OROGEN
(— PASS) GHAT
(— TRACT) DUAR
(FABLED —) KAF MERU
(GREEK —) OSSA PELION HELICON
OLYMPUS MAENALUS
(HIGH —) ALP
(ROUND —) REEK
(SMALL —) NOB KNOB BUTTE
(SNOW —) JOKUL
(SUBMARINE —) GUYOT SEAMOUNT

MOUNTAINEER WAZIR HEIDUC
HAYDUCK HILLMAN ORESTES MONTESCO
TIERSMAN

MOUNTAIN GOAT IBEX MAZAME

MOUNTAIN LAUREL IVY HEATH
ERICAD KALMIS LAUREL IVYWOOD
CALFKILL

MOUNTAIN LION PUMA COUGAR

MOUNTAINOUS RANGY VICIOUS

MOUNTEBANK ANTIC BALADINE
IMPOSTOR OPERATOR

MOUNTED CARDED SADDLE EASELED
EQUITANT

MOUNTING MOUNT SCAPE ASCENT
FLIGHT MONTANT SOAKING ASPIRANT
INCABLOC MOUNTURE
(— OF GEM) CHASE
(STYLE OF —) SETTING

MOURN DOLE KEEN SIGH WAIL PLAIN
GRIEVE LAMENT SORROW GRIZZLE

MOURNER WAILER WEEPER
(HIRED —) SAULIE
(PROFESSIONAL —) MUTE BLACK
KEENER

MOURNFUL SAD BLACK MINOR SORRY
WEEPY RUEFUL DERNFUL FUNEBRE
SIGHFUL WAILFUL DEJECTED DIRGEFUL
ELEGIOUS FUNEREAL MAESTIVE
MESTFULL PLANTFULL YEARNFUL
PLAINTIVE

MOURNING DOLOR SHIVA DISMAL
SORROW WIDOWED

MOURNING BECOMES ELECTRA
(AUTHOR OF —) ONEILL
(CHARACTER IN —) ADAM EZRA ORIN
BRANT DAVID HAZEL NILES PETER
MANNON LAVINIA CHRISTINE

MOUSE MURINE MYGALE RODENT
VERMIN ARVICOLE CRICETID MYOMORPH
(MEADOW —) VOLE
(STRIPED —) KUSU

MOUTH OS GAB GAM GOB JIB MUG MUN
NEB ORF ROW YAP BEAK HEAD MUSS
PUSS SHOP TRAP YAWN BAZOO CHOPS
STOMA TUTEL GEBBIE KISSER MUZZLE
RABBLE RICTUS SUCKER THROAT
CLAPPER FLUMMER ORIFICE STOMACH
LORRIKER PAVILLON
(— AND THROAT) COPPER WHISTLE
(— OF CANYON) ABRA
(— OF GLASS FURNACE) BOCCA
(— OF HARBOR) BOCA
(— OF PERITHECIUM) OSTIOLE
(— OF RIVER) BEAL BOCA LADE ENTRY
FIRTH INFLUX OSTIUM ESTUARY
OSTIARY OUTFALL
(— OF SHAFT) BRACE
(— OF TRUMPET) BELL CODON
PAVILLON
(KILN —) KILNEYE KILNHOLE
(SORE — OF SHEEP) ECTHYMA
(WRY —) MURGEON

MOUTHFUL GAG GOB SUP GNAP GOLEE
GOBBET

MOUTHPIECE BAR BEAK BOCAL MOUTH
FIPPLE SYRINX PROPHET
(— OF BAGPIPE) MUSE
(— OF PIPE) STEM

MOVABLE FREE LOOSE MOBILE
PORTABLE REMUABLE

MOVE GO ACT FIG GEE GET WAG BOOM
BORE BUCK BUMP CALL DRAW FIRK FLIT
GOAD HEAT KNEE MAKE PIRL ROLL SILE
SPUR STEP STIR SWAY WORK ANKLE
BLITZ BUDGE CARRY CAUSE CROWD
DRAFT HEAVE IMPEL LIGHT MARCH
MUDGE QUECH REMUE ROUSE SHAKE
SHIFT TOUCH GAMBIT HANDLE HUSTLE
INCITE INDUCE KINDLE MOTION PROMPT
QUITCH REMBLE SASHAY STRAKE
ACTUATE AGITATE ANIMATE DISTURB
DRAUGHT FLUTTER INSPIRE MIGRATE
PROVOKE AMBULATE BULLDOZE
CATAPULT DEMARCHE DISLODGE
DISPLACE MOTIVATE
(— ABOUT) ROLL WEND DISPACE
SHUFFLE CONVERSE LOCOMOTE
(— ACROSS) THWART
(— AIMLESSLY) POKE BOGUE
(— ALONG) SHOG
(— ASIDE) SKEW
(— AT TOP SPEED) LICK
(— AWAY) CUT MOG DECAMP RECEDE
(— AWKWARDLY) HODGE HIRSEL
LARRUP SHAMBLE SLUMMOCK
(— BACK) FADE ARSLE RECUR RECEDE
RETIRE RETREAT
(— BRISKLY) FAN HALE STIR FRICK
FRIKE FRISK KNOCK SQUIRT TRANCE
TRAVEL WHIPPET
(— CLUMSILY) HOIT JOLL PAUT BARGE
KEVEL HIRSEL LUMBER TOLTER
GALUMPH STUMBLE

(— DOWN) SILE STOOP DECLINE
DESCEND
(— FORWARD) BREAK ADVANCE
PROGREDE
(— FURTIVELY) LEER GLIDE SLINK
SLIVE SNEAK STEAL
(— GRADUALLY) EDGE
(— JERKILY) JAG BUCK FLIP KICK FLIRT
BUCKET TWITCH
(— LAZILY) HULK
(— LEISURELY) AMBLE
(— LIGHTLY) BRUSH FLUFF
(— NERVOUSLY) DITHER
(— NIMBLY) KILT LINK WHIP DANCE
(— OFF) FIRK RYNT MOSEY MORRIS
(— ON) MOG VAMP AVAUNT SUCCEED
WHIGFARE
(— QUICKLY) BOB FIG CLIP DUCK FIRK
FLAX FLIT GIRD JINK KITE SCUR WHAP
WHEW WHID WHOP YANK FLASH GLENT
SKEET SKIRR SKITE SPANK SQUIB STAVE
STOUR THROW NIDDLE STRIKE WALLOP
SKIMMER
(— QUIETLY) SLIP
(— RAPIDLY) BANG BOLT BUZZ HEEL
HURL SKIR THUD CHASE GLINT SCOUR
CAREER GIGGIT HURTLE WHIRRY
AGITATE CLATTER HIGHTAIL
(— RESTLESSLY) FIG GAD FIKE ITCH
CHURN SQUIB JIFFLE KELTER
(— SIDEWISE) CRAB EDGE SIDLE SLENT
(— SLOWLY) LAG MOG INCH PANT
PAUT SLUG BOGUE CRAWL CREEP
DRAWL FUDGE SHLEP SLOOM SNAIL
HAGGLE LINGER SCHLEP SCHLEPP
TRINTLE
(— SMOOTHLY) SLIP DRIFT FLOAT
GLIDE SLEEK GLISSADE
(— STEALTHILY) GLIDE SLINK SMOOT
SNAKE
(— SUDDENLY) BOLT LASH YERK
GLENT START FLOUNCE STARTLE
(— SWIFTLY) CUT FLY BOOM HARE
LEAP RAKE SCUD SPIN BREEZE COURSE
WUTHER SWIFTEN
(— TO AND FRO) FAN FLOP DODGE
SHAKE WIGWAG AGITATE
(— UNSTEADILY) BICKER BUMBLE
FALTER HOBBLE WABBLE WAMBLE
WELTER WOBBLE BLUNDER STAGGER
STUMBLE
(— UP AND DOWN) BOB HOWD
SEESAW TEETER
(— UPWARD) ARISE ASCEND
GRADUATE
(— VIOLENTLY) DASH FLOG HURL LASH
LEAP SWASH AGITATE COMMOVE
(CHESS —) KEY COOK NECK PLOY
GAMBIT KEYMOVE
(SUDDEN —) GAMBADE
MOVED MOSSO ANIMATE FRANTIC
INSTINCT
MOVEMENT EDDY MOTO PLAY STIR
CARRY CAUSE FLICK FLISK FLOAT FRONT
GESTE MUDGE TREND UKIYO ACTION
CURSUS ENTREE MOMENT MOTION

PIAFFE SPRAWL STROKE CURRENT
FURIANT GAMBADO GESTURE KINESIS
PIAFFER UKIYOYE BUSINESS CHARTISM
FEMINISM FUTURISM HASKALAH
STIRRING PERIPATETICS
(— FROM POINT TO POINT) PASSAGE
(— IN BULLFIGHT) SUERTE
(— OF HORSE) LEVADE PIAFFE
(— OF TIDE) LAKIE
(— OF TROOPS) LIFT
(— TOWARD GOAL) STRIDE
(AGITATED —) WORKING
(ART —) CUBISM
(BACKWARD —) BACKUP BACKLASH
BACKWASH
(BALLET —) PLIE FRAPPE FOUETTE
FLICFLAC
(BOWEL —) LAXATION
(BROWNIAN —) PEDESIS
(DANCE —) FRIS BRISE CLOSE GIGUE
GLIDE LASSU SPIRAL BATTERIE
(DARTING —) FLIRT
(DOWNWARD —) DECLINE
(EXPANSION —) BOOM
(FENCING —) VOLT
(FORWARD —) SWEEP ADVANCE
PROGRESS INCESSION PROCESSION
(GYMNASTIC —) KIP SWING
DISMOUNT
(INVOLUNTARY —) REFLEX
(JAPANESE ART —) YAMATO
YAMATOE
(JERKY —) SNATCH
(LATERAL —) LEEWAY
(MASS —) STAMPEDE
(MILITARY —) BOUND MANEUVRE
(MUSICAL —) AIR DUET BURLA DUMKA
LARGO ADAGIO ENTREE FINALE PRESTO
SARABAND SYMPHONY
(OSCILLATING —) HUNT
(PAINTING —) FAUVISM TACHISM
VORTICISM
(POETRY —) IMAGISM
(POLITICAL —) LEFTISM GAULLISM
(QUICK —) PAW DART WHID WHIP
YERK GLENT SHAKE GLANCE
(RELIGIOUS —) JOCISM BABIISM
PIETISM STUNDISM
(RETURN —) BACKHAUL
(RHYTHMIC —) DANCE
(SKATING —) MOHAWK CHOCTAW
(SPASMODIC —) JUMP HICCUP
SPRUNT HICCOUGH
(SPRINGY —) LILT
(STEALTHY —) SLINK
(SUDDEN —) HITCH SPANG START
FLICKER
(SWAYING —) SWAG
(SWEEPING —) SWINGE
(SWIFT —) SWOOSH
(THEOLOGICAL —) ARIANISM
(TUMULTUOUS —) HORROR EMOTION
(UP AND DOWN —) SEESAW
(UPWARD —) BULGE SCEND
(WALKING —) AMBLE
(WATCH —) EBAUCHE BAGUETTE

(ZIGZAG —) TACK MEANDER
MOVING WAY HIGH ASTIR GOING QUICK
AFLOAT MOVENT ANIMATE CURRENT
AMBULANT FLITTING PATHETIC
POIGNANT TOUCHING AFFECTING
MOW CUT BARB GOAF SKIM CRADLE
SCYTHE SICKLE DESECATE
(— BEANS) THROAT
(— FOR STORING GRAIN) TOSS
(— OF CORN) CANSH
(HAY —) TASS
MOZAMBIQUE (CAPE OF —) DELGADO
(CAPITAL OF —) MAPUTO
(LAKE OF —) CHUALI NHAVARRE
(MONEY OF —) METICAL
(RIVER OF —) SAVE MSALU RUVUMA
LIMPOPO LUGENDA ZAMBEZI
(TOWN OF —) MAUA TETE BEIRA
MAPAI ZUMBO CHEMBA MANICA
NAMAPA PAFURI CHIMOIO NAMPULA
**MRS WARREN'S PROFESSION
(AUTHOR OF —)** SHAW
(CHARACTER IN —) FRANK PRAED
VIVIE CROFTS GEORGE SAMUEL WARREN
GARDNER
MUCH FAR FELE MICH REAL WELL GREAT
HEAPS MOLTO MOULT SIZES MICKLE
MUCHLY ABUNDANT MUCHWHAT
(— CALLED FOR) LEEFTAIL
(PRETTY —) GAILY GAYLY
(SO —) ALL SUCH TANTO INSOMUCH
(TOO —) TROP TROPPO
(VERY —) ALL BADLY GREAT HEAPS
LOADS SWITHE SWYTHE APLENTY
GEYLIES GREATLY
**MUCH ADO ABOUT NOTHING
(AUTHOR OF —)** SHAKESPEARE
(CHARACTER IN —) HERO JOHN
PEDRO URSULA VERGES ANTONIO
CLAUDIO CONRADE FRANCIS LEONATO
BEATRICE BENEDICK BORACHIO
DOGBERRY MARGARET BALTHASAR
MUCILAGE GUM MUCUS MUCAGO
MUD DAB FEN CLAY DIRT DUBS FANC
GLAR LAIR MIRE MOIL SAUR SIND SLAB
SLEW SLOB SLOP SLUB SLUD SLUE SLUR
SUMP CLART FANGO GLAUR GUMBO
SLAKE SLIME SLOSH SLUSH SPOSH
SQUAD WAISE PELOID SLOUGH SLUDGE
CLABBER GUTTERS MURGEON SLOBBER
SLODDER SLUDDER SLUTHER SULLAGE
MUDDLE MIX BALL DOZE HASH MASH
MESS MULL MUZZ SOSS ADDLE SNAFU
BEMUSE BURBLE FANKLE FOITER
FUDDLE HUDDLE JUMBLE MAFFLE
MIZZLE MOFFLE MUCKER POTHER
PUDDLE TANGLE BECLOUD BEDEVIL
BLUNDER CONFUSE EMBROIL FLUSTER
POOTHER STUPEFY BEFUDDLE BEWILDER
CONFOUND DISORDER FLIUNDER
MUDDLED ADDLE BEERY FOGGY FUZZY
MUSED MUZZY DRUMLY GROGGY
BESOTTED CONFUSED
MUDDY DEEP FOUL GLET OOZY ROIL
SICK DIRTY DROVY DUBBY GUMLY ROILY
SLAKY CLAGGY CLARTY CLASHY DREGGY

DROUMY DRUMLY GROUTY LIMOUS
PUDDLY SALLOW SLABBY SLOBBY
SLOPPY SLUBBY SLUDGY TURBID
CLATCHY GUTTERY MUDDIFY MUDDISH
SLOUGHY CLABBERY LUTULENT
SLOBBERY
(— BY STIRRING) STUDDLE
MUDHOLE PULK SLOUGH LOBLOLLY
MUFF BLOW BOBBLE MUFFLE SNUFFKIN
MUFFIN COB GEM SINK HAZEL SINKER
MANCHET PIKELET POPOVER
MUFFLE MOB MOP PAD DAMP DULL
MUTE NOSE WRAP BUMBLE DEADEN
MUZZLE SHROUD STIFLE ENVELOP
(— A BELL) CLAM
(— THE HEAD) MOBLE
MUFFLED DEAD DEAF DULL CLOSE THICK
HOLLOW INWARD MOBBED WRAPPED
MUFFLER SCARF SILENCER
MUFTI JURIST CIVVIES
MUG TOT BOCK CANN FACE STEIN
NOGGIN PEWTER SCONCE SEIDEL
CANETTE GODDARD BLACKPOT PANNIKIN
SCHOPPEN
(ALE —) TOBY
(LIQUOR —) CAN GUN
MUGGY FOZY MUNGY PUGGY STICKY
MUGGISH PUTHERY
MULBERRY AL AAL ACH AUTE KOZO
MORE WAUKE ALROOT MURREY
MORELLO SOURBUSH SYCAMINE
MULE BUCKER HYBRID ACEMILA
IRONMAN JARHEAD JUGHEAD RATTAIL
SUMPTER CENCERRO HARDTAIL
QUADROON QUATERON
(DROVE OF —S) ATAJO MULADA
(MOHAMMED'S —) ALBORAK
MULISH BALKY STUPID STUBBORN
OBSTINATE
MULL CHAW BOSOM FETTLE MULMUL
STEATIN
MULLET BOBO LISA LIZA BOURI GARAU
KANAE MOLET HARDER MULLOID
GOATFISH MUGILOID SPRINGER
MULTIPLE DECUPLE PARALLEL SEPTUPLE
MULTIPLEX
MULTIPLICATION INCREASE
DUPLATION
MULTIPLICITY MULTEITY
MULTIPLY VIE BREED LAYER DOUBLE
INVOLVE ENGENDER INCREASE
MANIFOLD PROPAGATE PROLIFERATE
MULTITUDE ARMY CRAM HEAP HIVE
HOST ROUT RUCK CLOUD CROWD FLOTE
MEINY POWER SHOAL SWARM HIRSEL
HOTTER LEGION MAMPUS MEINIE
NATION THRONG SMOTHER PLURALITY
MULTITUDINOUS LEGION MYRIAD
MANIFOLD NUMEROUS
MUMBLE CHEW MOUP MUMP BROCK
CHELE MOUTH CHAVEL FAFFLE FUMBLE
HOTTER MAMMER MAFFLE MOFFLE
PALTER DRUMBLE FLUMMER GRUMBLE
MUMMER ACTOR GUISER GUISARD
MUMMERY MORRIS HODENING
PUPPETRY

MUMMY CASE SLEDGE
MUMPS BRANKS PAROTITIS
MUNCH CHEW NOSH CHUMP MANGE
MUNGE
MUNDANE WORLD EARTHLY FLESHLY
SECULAR TERRENE SUBSOLAR
MUNICIPALITY CITY TOWN CABILDO
CABILDO
MUNIFICENCE BOUNTY ROYALTY
MUNIFICENT ROYAL LIBERAL MUNIFIC
PROFUSE MAGNIFIC PRINCELY
OPENHANDED
MURAL TOPIA FRESCO
MURDER OFF BANE KILL SLAY BLOOD
BURKE DEATH SCRAG FELONY KILLING
MURDRUM MURTHER THUGGEE
HOMICIDE MASSACRE THUGGERY
THUGGISM PATRICIDE
(PREMEDITATED —) HIT
MURDERER BANE CAIN KILLER
ASSASSIN
MURDEROUS FELL GORY CRUEL FELON
BLOODY CARNAL SAVAGE DEATHFUL
SANGUINARY
MURKINESS GLOOM
MURKY DARK BLACK DIRTY MIRKY
MUDDY CLOUDY PUDDLY
MURMUR HUM BRUM BURR CLUM HUZZ
MUSE BRAWL GRANK INKLE MOURN
RUMOR SOUCH SOUGH BURBLE GRUDGE
GRUTCH HUMMER MUTTER PIPPLE
REPINE RUMBLE CROODLE MURGEON
WHIMPER WHISPER WHITTER COMPLAIN
(— AGREEABLY) CHIRM
(— OF STREAM) PURL
(CONFUSED —) BABBLE
(DEEP —) BROOL
MURMURING BUZZ BRABBLE MURGEON
RUMOROUS
MUSCLE EYE BOWR LIRE THEW FLESH
MOUSE PSOAS SINEW BENDER BICEPS
CORACO FLEXOR LACERT PENNON
RECTUS SOLEUS TENSOR AGONIST
AMBIENS CANINUS DELTOID DILATOR
ERECTOR EVERTOR FLECTOR GLUTEUS
ILIACUS LEVATOR MUSCULE NASALIS
OBLIQUE ROTATOR SCALENE SCALLOP
TRICEPS VAGINAL ABDUCTOR
ADDUCTOR ADJUSTER ANCONEUS
ARRECTOR ATOLLENT BIVENTER
DIDUCTOR EXTENSOR GEMELLUS
GRACILIS INVERTOR MASSETER
MENTALIS OBLIQUUS OMOHYOID
OPPONENS PALMARIS PATHETIC
PECTORAL PERONEUS PROCERUS
PRONATOR RETENTOR SCALENUS
SERRATUS SPINALIS SPLENIUS
TEMPORAL TIBIALIS OBTURATOR
SARTORIUS
MUSCULAR ROPY HEFTY HUSKY THEWY
BRAWNY ROBUST SINEWY STRONG
TOROSE NERVOUS ATHLETIC
MUSE CLIO DUMP MESE MULL NETE REVE
AMUSE AOIDE DREAM ERATO MNEME
STUDY THINK HYPATE MELETE PONDER
THALIA URANIA EUTERPE REFLECT
CALLIOPE COGITATE CONSIDER

MEDITATE POLYMNIA RUMINATE
MELPOMENE POLYHYMNIA TERPSICHORE
(— OF ASTRONOMY) URANIA
(— OF COMEDY) THALIA
(— OF EPIC POETRY AND
ELOQUENCE) CALLIOPE
(— OF HISTORY) CLIO
(— OF LOVE POETRY) ERATO
(— OF MIMIC ART) POLYHYMNIA
(— OF POETRY AND DANCE)
TERPSICHORE
(— OF THE FLUTE) EUTERPE
(— OF TRAGEDY) MELPOMENE
(PL.) PIERIDES
MUSEUM MUSEE
MUSHROOM FAT CEPE FLAT DEATH
MITRA MOREL AGARIC BEAVER BUTTON
FUNGUS BLEWITS BOLETUS BROILER
LEPIOTA MUSHRUMP WHITECAP
CHAMPIGNON SHAGGYMANE
CHANTERELLE
(PART OF —) CAP GILL RING STEM
STALK STIPE VOLVA PILEUS ANNULUS
MYCELIUM
(PREF.) MYC(O) MYCET(O)
MUSHY SOFT SOPPY
MUSIC RAG DRAG GLEE JAZZ NOME
BEBOP CANOR CHIME GIMEL GYMEL
MURKY NOISE SWING DREHER MUSICA
DESCANT FORLANA LANCERS LANDLER
MUSICAL MUSICRY FALSETTO
FANDANGO GUARACHA
(CALYPSO —) GOOMBAY
(CONCERTED —) ENSEMBLE
(COUNTRY —) BLUEGRASS
(EVENING —) DREAM SERENA
(IDENTIFYING —) SIG
(JAPANESE COURT —) GAGAKU
(JAZZ OR FOLK —) SKIFFLE
(LIVELY —) GALOP FURLANA
(MORNING —) AUBADE
(PATTERN OF HINDU —) TALA
(RECORDED BACKGROUND —)
MUZAK
(RESOUNDING —) HIGGAION
(ROCK —) BIGBEAT BUBBLEGUM
(SAD —) MESTO
(SENTIMENTAL —) SCHMALZ
SCHMALTZ
(STACCATO —) SECCO
(UNSOPHISTICATED —) FUNK
(WEST INDIAN —) REGGAE
(ZULU —) KWELA
MUSICAL LYRIC SWEET LIQUID LYRICAL
TUNABLE TUNEFUL CANOROUS
HARMONIC NUMEROUS
MUSICAL INSTRUMENT AX AXE GLY
GUE KIN OUD QIN TAR UKE ZEL ALTO
ASOR BELL CRUT DRUM GLEE GLEW
GORA HARP HORN KOTO LIRA LUTE LYRE
OBOE ROTE SANG SAWM TAAR TUBA
VINA VIOL ANVIL AULOS BANJO BLOCK
BUGLE CELLO CHENG CRWTH CUICA
DOMRA FLUTE GORAH GOURA GUDOK
GUIRO GUSLA GUSLE KAZOO MBIRA
NABLA ORGAN RAMKI REBAB REBEC

ROCTA RUANA SAROD SHAWM SHELL
SHENG TARAU TELYN TRUMP VIOLA
ZANZE ZINKE BALAFO BONANG CABASA
CITOLE CORNET CROUTH CYMBAL
DOUCET FIDDLE GENDER GLARIN GUITAR
GUSLEE JARANA RAPPEL REBECK RIBIBE
SABECA SANCHO SANTIR SPINET
TABRET TREBLE TYMPAN URHEEN
VIOLET VIOLIN ZITHER ALTHORN
ANGELOT ANKLONG ARGHOOL BAGPIPE
BANDORE BANDURA BASSOON BAZOOKA
CELESTA CHEKKER CHIKARA CITHARA
CLARINA CLAVIER CLAVIOL DICHORD
DOLCIAN DOLCINO DULCIAN FISTULA
FLUTINA GAMELIN GITTERN HELICON
KANTELE MAGADIS MARIMBA OCARINA
PANDURA PIBCORN RACKETT SAMISEN
SARANGI SARINDA SAXHORN SERPENT
SISTRUM SORDONO THEORBO TRUMPET
UKULELE URANION ADIAPHON AKALIMBA
AUTOHARP AUTOPHON BARBITON
BOUSOUKI BOUZOUKI CALLIOPE
CASTANET CLARINET CORNPIPE
CRESCENT DULCIMER DYOPHONE
EUPHONON FIDICULA FLAUTINO
HORNPIPE HUMSTRUM KRUMHORN
LAPIDEON MARTENOT MELODION
NEGINOTH NEHILOTH PENORCON
PHONIKON PSALTERY SCHWEGEL
SERINGHI SOURDINE SYMPHONY
TAMBOURA TAROGATO TRIANGLE
TRICHORD TROMBONE VIRGINAL
ZAMBOMBA ACCORDION BOMBARDON
SAXOPHONE MELLOPHONE
MUSIC HALL GAFF MELODEON
MUSICIAN BARD WAIT ASAPH LINOS
VIOLA BOPPER BUSKER MUSICO PLAYER
VIOLER VIOLIN BANDMAN BOPSTER
CELLIST GAMBIST ORPHEUS TWANGER
VIOLIST KORAHITE MARIACHI MINSTREL
MUSICKER THRUMMER TWANGLER
CITYBILLY MINNESINGER
(PL.) ENSEMBLE WAITSMEN
MUSING PENSIVE MUSARDRY
MUSK MOOST CATTAIL MIMULUS
AMBRETTE FIXATIVE
MUSK DEER CERVID KASTURA
MUSKET FUSIL MATCH DRAGON JINGAL
BUNDOOK CALIVER ENFIELD GINGALL
BANDHOOK BISCAYAN CULVERIN
ESCOPETA SNAPHAAN TOPHAIKE
MUSKMELON MANGO ATAMON
WUNGEE SPANSPEK CANTALOUPE
MUSKRAT SQUASH ONDATRA
MUSQUASH
MUSLIM LAZ ALIM SIDI SWAT TURK
ARAIN HAFIZ IBADHI KAZAKH TURBAN
ABBADID AYYUBID BAGIRMI BASHKIR
IBADITE KHAKSAR MUDEJAR SUNNITE
ALAOUITE ISLAMIST ISLAMITE QADARITE
SIFATITE
MUSLIN BAN MULL DORIA SWISS
GURRAH MULMUL SHALEE SHILLA
TANJIB BETEELA FACTORY JAMDANI
ORGANDY STENTER COTELINE SEERHAND
TARLATAN

MUSS FUFFLE RUMPLE GLOMMOX
UNDRESS
MUSSEL CLAM UNIO NAIAD ANODON
JINGLE LACERT MUCKET PALOUR
BIVALVE GLOCHID MYTILID UNIONID
BULLHEAD DEERHORN
MUST BIT BUD BUT MAN MAY MUN BOOD
MAUN MOTE SAPA STUM DULCE SHALL
MUSTACHE WALRUS VALANCE
WHISKER
MUSTANG PONY BRONCO SPHINX
MUSTARD CRESS SENVY SINEWY
AWLWORT CADLOCK KEDLOCK SINAPIS
CHADLOCK CHARLOCK FLIXWEED
AUBRIETIA
MUSTARD GAS YPERITE
MUSTARD PLASTER SINAPISM
MUSTER LEVY ENROL RAISE SPUNK
GATHER HOSTING MARSHAL RECRUIT
MUSTY HOAR FUNKY FUSTY HOARY
MOLDY MUCID RAFTY VINNY FOISTY
FROWZY RANCID FOUGHTY FROWSTY
COBWEBBY
MUTATION SHIFT SPORT CHANGE
MUANCE SILKIE ANAGRAM VARIANT
SALTATION
MUTE PAD DUMB ECHO LENE SURD
BLACK MEDIA WHIST DAMPER MUFFLE
SILENT STIFLE TENUIS SORDINE
SOURDINE
(— AT FUNERAL) SALLIE
(— FOR TRUMPET) DERBY
MUTED DULL SORDO STILL DISCREET
SOURDINE
MUTILATE MAR HACK MAIM BREAK
GARBLE HAMBLE INJURE MANGLE
MARTYR MITTLE CONCISE CASTRATE
EMBEZZLE
MUTILATION STRIP CONCISION
MUTINEER PANDY MUTINADO
MUTINOUS UNRULY
MUTINY REVOLT STRIFE REBELLION
MUTINY ON THE BOUNTY
(AUTHOR OF —) HALL NORDHOFF
(CHARACTER IN —) BYAM BLIGH
PEGGY ROGER GEORGE ROBERT TEHANI
BURKITT ELLISON MAIMITI STEWART
TINKLER WILLIAM FLETCHER MILLWARD
MORRISON MUSPRATT CHRISTIAN
MUTTER CROOL MOTRE HOTTER
HUMMER MURMUR PATTER
THROAT CHANNER CHUNTER GRUMBLE
MAUNDER TOOTMOOT MUSSITATE
MUTTON BRAXY VIFDA VIVDA MOUTON
BRAXIES
MUTUAL COMMON RECIPROCAL
MUZZLE NOSE MOUTH SNOUT FOREFACE
(— FOR FERRET) COPE
(— OF CANNON) CHOPS
MYRIAD HOST TOMAN COUNTLESS
MYRRH STACTE
MYRTLE MYRT LILAC BALTIC JAROOL
ARRAYAN JAPONICA RAMARAMA
MYSTERIES OF UDOLPHO
(AUTHOR OF —) RADCLIFFE
(CHARACTER IN —) EMILY DUPONT

MORANO MONTONI LUDOVICO STAUBERT VILLEFORT LAURENTINI VALANCOURT
MYSTERIOUS DIM DARK DEEP EERY SELI EERIE SABLE WAKON ARCANE EXOTIC MYSTIC OCCULT SECRET CRYPTIC PUCKISH UNCANNY UNCOUTH ABSTRUSE ESOTERIC NUMINOUS SIBYLLIC CRYPTICAL
MYSTERIOUSLY DARKLY EERILY HEIMLICH

MYSTERY MIST RUNE CABALA ENIGMA SECRET ARCANUM PROBLEM SECRECY
MYSTIC SUFI OCCULT ORPHIC SECRET EPOPTIC ESOTERIC
MYSTICAL MISTY MYSTIC ANAGOGIC TELESTIC
MYSTIFY BEAT BEFOG BOTHER MUDDLE PUZZLE BECLOUD CONFUSE BEWILDER
MYTH SAGA FABLE LEGEND MYTHOS ALLEGORY
MYTHICAL FABLED FABULOUS FICTIOUS

N

N EN NU NOVEMBER

NAB HAT NIB GRAB HEAD KNAB NAIL
CATCH SEIZE ARREST CLUTCH COLLAR
NIBBLE NOBBLE SNATCH CAPTURE
APPREHEND

NABOB DIVES NAWAB NOBOB DEPUTY
VICEROY GOVERNOR PLUTOCRAT

NACELLE CAR BOAT BASKET CHASSIS
COCKPIT SHELTER

NADIR BATHOS BEDROCK
(OPPOSED TO —) ZENITH

NAG CUT RAG TIT BAIT FRAB FRET FUSS
GNAW JADE MOKE PLUG PONY PROD
SNAG TWIT YAFF ANNOY COBRA HOBBY
HORSE SCOLD SKATE SNAKE STEED
TEASE BADGER BERATE BOTHER DOBBIN
GARRAN GLEYDE HAGGLE HARASS
HECKLE HECTOR KEFFEL PADNAG
PESTER PLAGUE ROUNCY WANTON
HACKNEY HENPECK TORMENT
DINGDONG HARANGUE IRRITATE
PARAMOUR

NAGGING NIGGLING

NAHOR (BROTHER OF —) HARAN
ABRAHAM
(FATHER OF —) SERUG
(SON OF —) TERAH
(WIFE OF —) MILCAH

NAIL CUT FIX HOB NAB PIN TEN BOSS
BRAD BRAG BROD CLAW CLOY DUMP
HOOF PILE SLUG STUD TACK TRAP AFFIX
CATCH DRIVE GROPE PLATE SCALE SEIZE
SPICK SPIKE TALON BULLEN CLENCH
CLINCH COOLER CORKER DETAIN FASTEN
GARRON HAMMER SECURE SINKER
TACKET TINGLE UNGUIS UNGULA
CAPTURE CLINKER FASTENER HOLDFAST
ROSEHEAD SPIKELET TENPENNY
TRICOUNI
(HEADLESS —) SPRIG
(HOOKED —) TENTER TENTERHOOK
(INGROWN —) ONYXIS ACRONYX
(MARKING —) SPAD SPEED
(OLD HORSESHOE —) STUB
(SHOEMAKER'S —) CLOUT SPARABLE
(TOED —) TOSHNAIL

NAIVE OPEN RACY FRANK GREEN CANDID
JEJUNE SIMPLE ARTLESS NATURAL
CHILDISH INNOCENT UNTAUGHT
CHILDLIKE GUILELESS INGENUOUS
PRIMITIVE UNTUTORED UNWORLDLY

NAIVETE GREENNESS SIMPLICITY

NAKED BALD BARE MERE NUDE OPEN
CLEAR EXACT PLAIN STARK ADAMIC
BARREN CUERPO SCUDDY SIMPLE
EXPOSED LITERAL OBVIOUS MANIFEST
STARKERS STRIPPED SMOCKLESS
UNADORNED UNCLOTHED UNCOVERED
(PREF.) GYMN(O) NUDI

NAMBY-PAMBY INANE SILLY VAPID
CODDLE INSIPID KEEPSAKE

NAME DUB FIX NOM SET CALL CITE FAME
NAIL NOMB NOUN TERM CLAIM CLEPE
COUNT ETHIC NEVEN NOMEN POINT
QUOTE STYLE TITLE ADDUCE APPEAL
GOSSIP MONICA REPUTE SELECT
ALLONYM APPOINT BEHIGHT DECLARE
ENTITLE EPITHET MENTION MONIKER
SPECIFY VOCABLE CATEGORY CHRISTEN
COGNOMEN IDENTIFY IDENTITY INDICATE
ENUMERATE PATRONYMIC
(— WRITTEN BACKWARDS) ANANYM
(ADDED —) AGNAME AGNOMEN
(ALTERNATIVE —) BUNCH
(ANCESTOR'S —) EPONYM
(ANOTHER —) ALIAS
(ASSUMED —) PEN ALIAS ONOMASTIC
PSEUDONYM SOBRIQUET
(BAD —) CACONYM
(DAY —) AHAU
(FIRST —) FORENAME PRAENOMEN
(GOOD —) HONOR CREDIT
(PEN —) PSEUDONYM
(REGISTERED —) AFFIX
(TECHNICAL —) ONYM
(WELL-SUITED —) EUONYM

NAMED DIT CITED HIGHT NEMPT DUBBED
YCLEPT ONYMOUS

NAMELY FOR VIZ SCIL NOTED TOWIT
FAMOUS SCILICET

NAMEPLATE MASTHEAD
(AUTOMOBILE —) MARQUE

NAMESAKE EPONYM JUNIOR HOMONYM

NAMIBIA (BAY OF —) WALVIS
(CAPITAL OF —) WINDHOEK
(DESERT OF —) KALAHARI
(PEOPLE OF —) NAMAS BANTUS
BUSHMEN OVAMBOS

NANA (AUTHOR OF —) ZOLA
(CHARACTER IN —) NANA ROSE
HUGON LOUIS SATIN FONTAN GEORGE
HECTOR MIGNON MUFFAT SABINE
XAVIER ESTELLE STEINER BEUVILLE
DAGUENET FAUCHERY PHILIPPE
DECHOUARD

NAOMI MARA
(DAUGHTER-IN-LAW OF —) RUTH

NAP GIG KIP NOD RAS CALK CAMP DOWN
DOZE FUZZ LINT OOZE PILE RUFF SHAG
WINK COVER DOVER FLUFF GRASP SEIZE
SLEEK SLEEP STEAL CATNAP DROWSE
SIESTA SNOOZE EMERIZE SLUMBER

NAPE NOD CUFF NECK NUKE POLL NUCHA
NUQUE SCRAG SCUFT SCURF TURNIP
NODDLE SCRUFF NIDDICK

NAPERY LINEN DAMASK DOILIES
NAPKINS

NAPHTHA NEFTE PETROLEUM

NAPKIN CLOTH DOILY TOWEL DIAPER
NAPERY KERCHIEF SUDATORY
HANDCLOTH SERVIETTE
NAPOLEON (— III) LOUIS BOUSTRAPA
(BATTLE OF —) ULM ACRE JENA
WATERLOO
(BIRTHPLACE OF —) CORSICA
(BROTHER-IN-LAW OF —) MURAT
(GAME LIKE —) PAM
(ISLAND OF —) ELBA HELENA CORSICA
(MARSHALL OF —) NEY
(MOTHER OF —) HORTENSE
(PLACE OF VICTORY FOR —) LODI
LIGNY
NARCISSUS LILY PLANT CRINUM EGOIST
FLOWER LILIUM JONQUIL POLYANTHUS
(FATHER OF —) CEPHISSUS
(LOVED BY —) ECHO
(MOTHER OF —) LIRIOPE
(TRUMPET —) DAFFODIL
NARCOTIC (ALSO SEE DRUG) KAT KEF
DOPE DRUG HEMP JUNK BHANG DAGGA
ETHER OPIUM HEROIN OPIATE ANODYNE
COCAINE CODEINE HASHISH METOPON
NARCEIN HYPNOTIC MORPHINE
TAKROURI DIACODION MARIJUANA
SOPORIFIC CHLORODYNE
NARK SPY VEX NOTE ANNOY TEASE
OBSERVE INFORMER IRRITATE
NARRATE SPIN TELL BRUIT STATE
STORY DEPICT DETAIL DEVISE RECITE
RELATE REPORT DISCUSS RECOUNT
STORIFY DESCRIBE REHEARSE
NARRATION TALE FABLE STORY DETAIL
ACCOUNT HAGGADA RECITAL SYNAXAR
ALLEGORY DELIVERY DIEGESIS
HAGGADAH
NARRATIVE EPIC JOKE MYTH SAGA
TALE CONTE DRAMA FABLE PROSE
STORY COMEDY JATAKA LEGEND
ACCOUNT EPISODE HISTORY MEMOIRS
MIDRASH NOVELLA PARABLE RECITAL
ALLEGORY ANECDOTE APOLOGUE
ARETALOGY HAGIOLOGY
(— OF VOYAGE) PERIPLUS
(BRIEF —) ANECDOTE
(PL) ACTA EXEMPLA
NARRATOR TESTO TELLER RELATOR
SAGAMAN TALESMAN RACONTEUR
NARROW JERK LEAN MEAN NEAR POKY
SLIT TRUE BORNE CLOSE CRAMP PINCH
RIGID SCANT SHARP SMALL SOUND
TAPER ANGUST BIASED LINEAR LITTLE
MEAGER STRAIT STRICT TWITCH
BIGOTED ERICOID LIMITED PRIMARY
SLENDER THRIFTY CONDENSE CONTRACT
PAROCHIAL PROVINCIAL
(— DOWN) CONFINE
(— DOWN STAVES) BUCK
(NOT —) CATHOLIC
(VERY —) HAIRBREADTH
NARROWED LISTED INSWEPT
CONTRACT ANGUSTATE
NARROWLY WIDE STRAITLY
NARROW-MINDED BORNE PETTY
NARROWNESS BIAS BIGOTRY
LOCALISM PAROCHIALISM

NARWHAL MONODON
NASAL NOSY NARINE RHINAL TWANGY
ADENOID STRINGY
NASTURTIUM CAPUCINE NOSEWORT
RADICULA STURSHUM STURTION
NASTY BAD PAH FOUL MEAN UGLY DIRTY
SNIDE FILTHY HORRID ODIOUS RIBALD
BAGGAGE BEASTLY DEFILED HARMFUL
OBSCENE SQUALID UNCLEAN INDECENT
NAUSEOUS DANGEROUS MALICIOUS
OFFENSIVE
NATAL INBORN INNATE NATIVE GLUTEAL
CONGENIAL
NATION BENI FOLK GEAT HOST LAND
LEDE RACE VOLK AEDUI CASTE CLASS
FANTE FANTI REALM STATE TRIBE
FANTEE GEATAS PEOPLE WAGOGO
ARVERNI COUNTRY SOCIETY LANGUAGE
COMMUNITY MANDATORY MINISTATE
MULTITUDE
(HEBREW —) JACOB
(LARGE —) COLOSSUS
NATIONAL CITIZEN FEDERAL GENTILE
GENTILIC
NATIONALISM JINGOISM PHYLETISM
NATIONALIST CHINA (SEE TAIWAN)
NATIONALITY FLAG
NATIVE (ALSO SEE PEOPLE AND TRIBE)
ABO ITE RAW SON TAO BORN FREE
GOOK HOME KIND LIVE NEIF WILD INNER
NATAL PUNTI EPIROT GENIAL INBORN
INNATE KINDLY MOTHER NORMAL
SIMPLE VIRGIN CITIZEN DENIZEN
DZUNGAR ENDEMIC GENUINE NATURAL
PAISANO POLISTA DOMESTIC GRASSCUT
HABITUAL HOMEBORN HOMEMADE
INHERENT LANDSMAN ORIGINAL
PRIMEVAL PRISTINE RESIDENT
YAMMADJI ABORIGINE CONGENIAL
INGRAINED INHERITED INTRINSIC
ORIGINARY TAWNYMOOR ABORIGINAL
(— OF ALBANIA) SKIPETAR
(— OF BENGAL) KOL
(— OF CHINA) CELESTIAL
(— OF FENS) SLODGER
(— OF FLORIDA KEYS) CONK CONCH
(— OF ILLINOIS) SUCKER
(— OF IRELAND) BOGTROTTER
(— OF LONDON) COCKNEY
(— OF LOW CLASS) TAO
(— OF MADAGASCAR) HOVA
(— OF MALAYA) INFIEL
(— OF MANCHESTER) MANCUNIAN
(— OF MARITIME PROVINCES)
BLUENOSE
(— OF N. CAROLINA) TARHEEL
(— OF NEW GUINEA) BOONG
(— OF NEW SOUTH WALES)
CORNSTALK
(— OF PHILIPPINES) GUGU
(— OF SCOTLAND) GEORDIE
(— OF SOUTHERN ILLINOIS)
EGYPTIAN
(— OF W. AUSTRALIA) GROPER
(— WHO TEACHES) CATECHIST
(FREE —) TIMAWA
(UNCIVILIZED —) MYALL

NATIVE SON (AUTHOR OF —) WRIGHT
(CHARACTER IN —) JAN MAX MARY
BORIS MEARS BESSIE BIGGER DALTON
ERLONE THOMAS BRITTEN BUCKLEY
NATIVITY BIRTH JATAKA GENESIS
GENITURE HOROSCOPE
NATTY CHIC NEAT POSH TIDY TRIG TRIM
NIFTY SMART SPICY DAPPER JAUNTY
SPRUCE FOPPISH VARMINT
NATURAL RAW BORN EASY FOOL HOME
KIND OPEN RACY REAL WILD NAIVE
USUAL CANCEL CASUAL COMMON
CONJON CRETIN DIRECT HOMELY
INBORN INBRED INNATE KINDLY MOTHER
NATIVE NORMAL PHYSIC ARTLESS
GENUINE QUADRUM REGULAR INHERENT
LIFELIKE ORDINARY PHYSICAL UNCOINED
PRIMITIVE REALISTIC UNASSUMED
UNFEIGNED
NATURALIZE ADAPT ADOPT ACCUSTOM
ACCLIMATE ENDENIZEN HABITUATE
NATURALLY SN KINDLY GENIALLY
NATURALNESS EASE NAIVETE
NATURE ILK BENT BIOS CAST CLAY
FORM HAIR KIND MAKE MOOD RACE
SORT TRIM TYPE COLOR OUSIA SHAPE
STATE TENOR ANIMAL DHARMA FIGURE
HEAVEN KIDNEY PHYSIS STRIPE ESSENCE
FEATHER INBEING QUALITY SPECIES
PRAKRITI UNIVERSE CHARACTER
QUALIFICATION
(— DIVINITY) NYMPH
(— GOD) PAN
(— GODDESS) CYBELE ARTEMIS
(— OF GOD) DIVINITY
(— PRINT) PHYTOGRAPH
(— SPIRIT) NAT
(— WORSHIP) PHYSIOLATRY
(APPARENT —) STUDY
(CONCEALED —) LATENCY
(DIVINE —) DEITY
(EMOTIONAL —) HEART
(ESSENTIAL —) ESSE FORM GENIUS
(GOOD —) BONHOMIE
(HUMAN —) FLESH MANHEAD
MANKIND
(INHERENT —) GENIUS
(INTRINSIC —) BOTTOM
(MORAL —) ETHNOS
(OF THE SAME —) HOMOGENEOUS
(ORGANIC —) BIOS
(ROUGH —) SPINOSITY
(SPECIAL —) IDIOM
(SPIRITUAL —) INTERNAL
(TRUE —) PROPRIETY
(ULTIMATE —) ESSENCE
(UNREGENERATE —) ADAM
NAUGHT NIL EVIL ZERO AUGHT NAGHT
OUGHT CIPHER NOUGHT WICKED
NOTHING USELESS WORTHLESS
NAUGHTY BAD PAW SAD EVIL WRONG
PAWPAW SHREWD WICKED OBSCENE
WAYWARD IMPROPER
NAURU (CAPITAL OF —) YAREN
(DISTRICT OF —) BOE EWA AIWO IJUW
BAITI BUADA NIBOK UABOE YAREN
ANABAR ANETAN MENENG ANIBARE

(FORMER NAME OF —)
PLEASANTISLAND
(TOWN OF —) ANNA ORRO ANABAR
RONAWI YANGOR
NAUSEA PALL QUALM DISGUST NAUSITY
LOATHING SICKNESS ANTIPATHY
DIZZINESS
NAUSEATE TURN TWIST WLATE REVOLT
SICKEN DISGUST SCUNNER STOMACH
DISTASTE SCOMFISH
NAUSEATED ILL SICKISH QUALMISH
SQUEAMISH
NAUSEATING NASTY WAUGH QUEASY
BILIOUS FULSOME BRACKISH
STAWSOME LOATHSOME REVOLTING
SICKENING
NAUSEOUS OFFENSIVE
NAUTICAL (ALSO SEE NAVIGATION)
NAVAL MARINE MARINAL OCEANIC
TARRISH MARITIME NAVIGABLE
NAUTILUS MOLLUSK ARGONAUT
ARGONAUTA
(— COMMANDER) NEMO
NAVAHO DINE NAVAJO LONGHAIR
(— GROUP) OUTFIT
(— RITE) WAY
NAVAL SEA MARINE NAUTICAL
NAVIGABLE
NAVE HOB HUB NEF APSE BODY FIST
PACE AISLE NATHE NIEVE CENTER
NAVEL NOMBRIL OMPHALOS UMBILICUS
NAVIGABLE BOATABLE PORTABLE
NAVIGATE KEEL SAIL DRIVE GUIDE SKIFF
STEER AVIATE COURSE CRUISE DIRECT
MANAGE TRAVEL CONDUCT CONTROL
JOURNEY OPERATE TRAVERSE
ASTROGATE
NAVIGATION HOMING VOYAGE NAUTICS
PASSAGE SAILING TRAFFIC CABOTAGE
SHIPPING
NAVIGATOR FLYER NAVVY PILOT
AIRMAN AVIATOR COPILOT LABORER
AERONAUT SEAFARER SPACEMAN
NEPTUNIAN NEPTUNIST
NAVY FLEET SHIPFERD
(— BOARD) ADMIRALTY
(— OFFICER) CPO AIDE MATE BOSUN
CHIEF ENSIGN ADMIRAL ARMORER
CAPTAIN COMMANDER COMMODORE
(— RADIO OPERATOR) SPARKS
(— VESSEL) PT SUB CARRIER CRUISER
FLATTOP DESTROYER SUBMARINE
TRANSPORT
NAY NO NAI NEI NOT DENY EVEN NYET
FLUTE NEVER DENIAL REFUSE REFUSAL
NEGATIVE
NAZI BROWN HITLERITE
(— SYMBOL) FYLFOT SWASTIKA
NAZIM VICEROY GOVERNOR
NEANDERTHAL CAVEMAN
NEAR AD AT BY IN GIN KIN NAR AKIN
BAIN DEAR FAST GAIN HARD HEND INBY
NEXT NIGH ABOUT ANEAR ANENT ASIDE
CLOSE EWEST FORBY HANDY HENDE
JUXTA MATCH NUDGE ROUND SHORT
TOUCH ALMOST AROUND BESIDE
CLIMAX HEREBY NARROW STINGY

TOWARD WITHIN ADVANCE AGAINST
FORTHBY SIMILAR THRIFTY VICINAL
ADJACENT APPROACH IMMINENT
INTIMATE CONTIGUOUS
(— AKIN) HANDSOME
(— THE BEGINNING) EARLY FORMER
(— THE EQUATOR) LOW
(— THE MOUTH) ADORAL
(— THE SURFACE) EBB FLEET
(— THE WIND) HIGH AHOLD
(CONVENIENTLY —) HANDSOME

NEARBY AROUND GAINLY LOCALLY
ADJACENT

NEAREST NEXT EWEST CLOSEST
NEARMOST PROCHAIN PROXIMAL
IMMEDIATE PROXIMATE
(— THE STERN) AFTERMOST

NEARLY GAIN JUST LIKE MOST MUCH
ABOUT CLOSE ALMOST FECKLY
PRACTICALLY

NEARNESS AFFINITY VICINITY
PROPINQUITY

NEARSIGHTED MYOPIC PURBLIND

NEAT GIM NET COSH COWS DEFT DINK
FEAT FEEL FEIL GENT JIMP MACK NICE
OXEN PRIM PURE SMUG SNOD SNUG
TIDY TOSH TRIG TRIM BULLS CLEAN
CLEAR COMPT CRISP DINKY DONCY
DONSY DOUCE EXACT FEATY FETIS
GENTY JEMMY NATTY NIFTY PREST
QUEME SMART SMIRK SPICK TERSE
TIGHT ADROIT BOVINE CATTLE CLEVER
DAINTY DAPPER DIMBER DONSIE HEPPEN
MINION POLITE QUAINT SPANDY SPRUCE
BANDBOX CONCISE FEATOUS ORDERLY
PERJINK PRECISE REFINED SHAPELY
TRICKSY UNMIXED MENSEFUL SKILLFUL
STRAIGHT TASTEFUL DEXTEROUS
SHIPSHAPE UNDILUTED WHOLESOME

NEATLY SNUG DEFTLY FAIRLY FEATLY
SMARTLY SPRUCELY

NEATNESS MENSE DEFTNESS ELEGANCE
SPRUCERY

NEBRASKA

CAPITAL: LINCOLN
COLLEGE: DANA DOANE DUCHESNE
HASTINGS
COUNTY: GAGE LOUP OTOE DEUEL DUNDY
KEITH SARPY CHERRY COLFAX FURNAS
HOOKER NEMAHA VALLEY BUFFALO
ANTELOPE BOXBUTTE KEYAPAHA
INDIAN: OTO OMAHA PONCA PAWNEE
RIVER: LOGAN DISMAL PLATTE ELKHORN
NIOBRARA
STATE BIRD: MEADOWLARK
STATE FLOWER: GOLDENROD
STATE TREE: ELM
TOWN: ORD ALMA COZAD OMAHA PONCA
TRYON WAHOO GERING MULLEN NELIGH
PENDER TEKAMAH OGALLALA REDCLOUD
THEDFORD
UNIVERSITY: CREIGHTON

NEBULA SKY CRAB SPOT VAPOR BALAXY
GALAXY SPIRAL PLANETARY

NEBULOUS DIM DARK HAZY FOGGY
MISTY MUDDY VAGUE CLOUDY MYSTIC
TURBID CLOUDED EVASIVE SHADOWY
UNCLEAR DREAMLIKE

NECESSARILY NEEDS NEEDLY
PERFORCE

NECESSARY NEEDY PRIVY VITAL FRIEND
TOILET KINSMAN NEEDFUL FORCIBLE
INTEGRAL OBLIGATE BEHOVEFUL
ESSENTIAL INTRINSIC

NECESSITATE FORCE IMPEL COMPEL
DEMAND ENTAIL OBLIGE REQUIRE
CONSTRAIN

NECESSITY USE CALL DUTY FATE FOOD
LACK MUST NEED TASK WANT DRINK
ANANKE BEHOOF BESOIN MISTER
MUSCLE NEEDBE URGENCY PERFORCE
REQUIREMENT
(— OF MOVING) ZUGZWANG
(BY —) PRESENTLY

NECK COL NUB PET CAPE CRAG CROP
HALS KISS WAKE BEARD CHOKE CRAIG
HALSE SCRAG SPOON SWIRE TRAIL
BEHEAD CARESS CERVIX COLLET
COLLUM FONDLE STRAIT CHANNEL
EMBRACE ISTHMUS SQUEEZE TUBULUS
LALLYGAG
(— OF BOTTLE) THROTTLE
(— OF LAMB) TARGET
(— OF VOLCANO) CORE
(BACK OF —) NOD NAPE NUCH NUQUE
SCRUFF NIDDICK
(BOW —) HAWSE
(PERT. TO —) JUGULAR CERVICAL
(RED —) ROOINEK

NECK AND NECK TIE EVEN CLOSE

NECKBAND BAND COLLAR COLLET
SHIRTBAND

NECKCLOTH BOA TIE RUFF AMICE
CHOKE SCARF STOLE CHOKER CRAVAT
BURDASH NECKTIE PANUELO STARCHER
BARCELONA SOLITAIRE STEINKIRK

NECKERCHIEF GIMP RAIL FOGLE
BELCHER FOULARD NECKLET KERCHIEF
NECKATEE NECKCLOTH NECKENGER

NECKLACE BEE LEI BEADS CHAIN NOOSE
CARCAN CHOKER COLLAR GORGET
SANKHA TAWDRY TORQUE BALDRIC
CHAPLET RIVIERE SAUTOIR LAVALIER
NEGLIGEE ESCLAVAGE

NECKLINE COWL SCOOP

NECKTIE BOW TIE ASCOT SCARF CHOKER
CRAVAT GRAVAT OVERLAY

NECROMANCER GOETIC MAGICIAN

NECROMANCY GOETY MAGIC GRAMARY
SORCERY WIZARDRY EGROMANCY

NECROPOLIS CEMETERY

NECROPSY AUTOPSY

NECTAR HONEY AMRITA AMBROSIA

NEED ASK LACK TAKE WANT CRAVE
DRIVE BEHOOF BEHOVE BESOIN DEMAND
DESIRE MISTER STRAIT BEHOOVE
NEEDHAM POVERTY REQUIRE URGENCY
DISTRESS EXIGENCY MISCHIEF
EMERGENCE EXTREMITY NECESSITY

NEEDED NECESSARY
NEEDFUL VITAL INTEGRAL ESSENTIAL
NECESSARY REQUISITE
NEEDLE SEW VEX YEN ACUS DARN GOAD
TIER WIRE ANNOY BLUNT POINT SHARP
SPIKE STRAW STYLE BODKIN DARNER
STYLUS OBELISK PRICKER PROVOKE
SPICULE TUMBLER
(— SORTER) HANDER
(PART OF —) EYE HOLE CROWN POINT
SHANK
(PINE —) SPILL
(PINE —S) PININGS
NEEDLEFISH GAR SNOOK AGUJON
BELONID LONGJAW
NEEDLELIKE ACUATE ACERATE ACEROSE
ACEROUS ACIFORM ACICULAR BELONOID
SPLINTERY
NEEDLESS AMOK
NEEDLEWORK SEWING SAMPLER
SEAMING TATTING KNITTING
WOOLWORK HEMSTITCH INSERTION
NEEDY BARE POOR INDIGENT NEEDSOME
HUNGARIAN PENNILESS PENURIOUS
NECESSITOUS
NE'ER-DO-WELL BUM PELF LOSEL
SKELLUM SCHLEMIEL SHIFTLESS
WORTHLESS RAPSCALLION
NEFARIOUS WICKED HEINOUS IMPIOUS
FLAGRANT HORRIBLE INFAMOUS
ATROCIOUS
NEGATE DENY SUBLATE
NEGATION NAY NOT EMPTY DENIAL
REFUSAL ANNULMENT NONENTITY
(PREF.) DIS
NEGATIVE NA NE NO CON NAE NAY NIT
NIX NON NOR NOT NUL DENY FILM VETO
MINUS NEVER NAYWARD STAMPER
APOPHATIC PRIVATIVE
(— PRINCIPLE) YIN
(PHOTOGRAPHIC —) CLICHE
NEGLECT DEBT FAIL HANG OMIT SHUN
SLIP FAULT FORGO SHIRK SLOTH WAIVE
BYPASS CESSER FOREGO FORGET
IGNORE LACHES LOITER PERMIT SLIGHT
DEFAULT DISOBEY FAILURE OVERSEE
RESPECT FORSLACK OMISSION
OVERLOOK OVERSLIP RECKLESS
DISREGARD MISLIPPEN OVERSIGHT
PRETERMIT MISPRISION
(— OF DUTY) INCIVISM
NEGLECTED TACKY SHABBY UNDONE
DORMANT OBSOLETE
NEGLECTFUL LAX REMISS CARELESS
DERELICT HEEDLESS RECKLESS
DISSOLUTE NEGLIGENT
NEGLIGEE ROBE MANTEAU MATINEE
UNDRESS PEIGNOIR NIGHTGOWN
DISHABILLE
NEGLIGENCE CULPA LACHES DEFAULT
LASCHETY DISREGARD OVERSIGHT
NEGLIGENT LAX LASH SOFT SLACK
CASUAL OVERLY REMISS CARELESS
DERELICT DISCINCT RECKLESS
SLOVENLY YEMELESS DISSOLUTE
NEGLECTFUL
NEGOTIATE DEAL SELL BROKE FLOAT

TREAT TROKE TRUCK TRYST ADVISE
ASSIGN CONFER DICKER DIRECT
MANAGE PARLEY SETTLE ARRANGE
BARGAIN CHAFFER CONDUCT CONSULT
DISCUSS ENTREAT CONCLUDE ENTREATY
TRANSACT TRANSFER TEMPORIZE
NEGOTIATION DEAL DICKER PARLEY
TREATY PASSAGE ENTREATY PRACTICE
NEGRO FON JUR LUO LWO SUK AKIM
ALUR BENI BINI BONI EGBA FONG IRON
MADI MOKE NUBA NUPE SIDI BENIN
BLACK BONGO CUFFY DINKA DJUKA
FULUP FUZZY HATSA MUNGO SEPIA
SEREC SMOKE TEMNE GULLAH HUBSHI
AKWAPIM DAHOMAN GEECHEE QUASHIE
SANDAWE SHELLUH SHILLUK BECHUANA
ETHIOPIAN MANGBATTU
(GOLD COAST —) GA FANTI
(LIBERIAN —) KRU VAI VEI GREBO
ICROO KRUMAN KROOBOY
NEHEMIAH (FATHER OF —) AZBUK
HACHALIAH
NEIGH NIE NVE WHI HINNY NICKER
WHINNY WIGHER WHICKER
NEIGHBOR BOR ADJOIN BORDER
FELLOW NEIPER ACCOLENT BORDERER
CONFINER UCALEGON
NEIGHBORHOOD WAY AREA HAND
VENUE BARRIO LOCALE REGION PURLIEU
SECTION DISTRICT ENVIRONS PRESENCE
PROCINCT VICINAGE VICINITY BAILIWICK
COMMUNITY PROXIMITY TERRITORY
VOISINAGE
NEIGHBORING NIGH NEARBY CONFINE
VICINAL ACCOLENT ADJACENT
NEIGHBORLY FOLKSY AMICABLE
NEMESIS BANE FATE UPIS AGENT
AVENGER PENALTY
NEOPHYTE TYRO EPOPT NOVICE
AMATEUR CONVERT BEGINNER
PROSELYTE YOUNGLING
NEOPLASM TUMOR GROWTH TUMOUR
SARCOMA NEWGROWTH

NEPAL

CAPITAL: KATMANDU KATHMANDU
COIN: MOHAR RUPEE
MOUNTAIN: EVEREST
MOUNTAIN RANGE: HIMALAYA
NATIVE: AOUL LIMBU MURMI NEWAR
GURKHA GORKHALI
RIVER: KALI KOSI MUGU SETI BABAI BHERI
RAPTI SARDA GANDAK KARNALI
NARAYANI
TOWN: ILAM MUGU GALWA JUMLA
PATAN BIRGANJ POKHARA BHADGAON
LALITPUR BHAKTAPUR BIRATNAGAR

NEPENTHE DRUG PLANT POTION
ANODYNE
NEPHEW OY OYE NEVE VASU NEFFY
NEVOY NIECE NEPOTE BENVOLIO
NEPHRITE YU JADE AXSTONE POUNAMU
TREMOLITE

NEPTUNE LER PAN SEA GREEN OCEAN
PLATE SEAGOD
(BROTHER OF —) PLUTO JUPITER
(CONSORT OF —) SALACIA
(DISCOVERER OF —) GALLE
(EMBLEM OF —) TRIDENT
(FATHER OF —) SATURN
(MOTHER OF —) RHEA
(SISTER OF —) JUNO
NEREID NYMPH NEREIS THALIA THETIS
CYMODOCE
NEREIDES (FATHER OF —) NEREUS
(MOTHER OF —) DORIS
NERO TYRANT FIDDLER
(MOTHER OF —) AGRIPPINA
(SUCCESSOR TO —) GALBA
(VICTIM OF —) LUCAN SENECA
(WIFE OF —) OCTAVIA
NERVE RIB BEND CORD GALL GRIT GUTS
LINE SAND VEIN CHEEK CHORD CRUST
PLUCK PUDIC SINEW SPUNK STEEL
TENON VAGUS VIGOR APLOMB COSTAL
DARING DENTAL ENERGY FACIAL HUTZPA
LUMBAR RADIAL SACRAL STRING
AXILLAR CHUTZPA COELIAC COURAGE
HUTZPAH SAPHENA SCIATIC SPINDLE
ABDUCENS AUDACITY BOLDNESS
CERVICAL CHUTZPAH COOLNESS
EFFERENT EMBOLDEN STRENGTH
TEMERITY AUTONOMIC ENCOURAGE
EYESTRING ACCELERATOR
(— CELL) ANAXON NEURON DIAXONE
DENDRAXON
(— CENTER) BRAIN CORTEX PLEXUS
(— FIBERS) PONS
(— NETWORK) RETIA PLEXUS
(— SLEEP) NEURO HYPNOTISM
NERVELESS DEAD WEAK BRAVE INERT
UNNERVED FOOLHARDY POWERLESS
NERVOUS EDGY TOEY FUSSY GOOSY
JUMPY TENSE TIMID WINDY FIDGET
SINEWY SPOOKY TOUCHY UNEASY
FEARFUL FRETFUL JITTERY RESTIVE
SCADDLE NEUROTIC TIMOROUS
EXCITABLE SENSITIVE TREMULOUS
TWITTERLY
(— MALADY) APHASIA NEURITIS
(— SEIZURE) TIC ANEURIA
NERVY BOLD RASH JERKY PUSHY
BRAZEN SINEWY STRONG FORWARD
JITTERY IMPUDENT INTREPID VIGOROUS
EXCITABLE
NEST DEN EST JUG WEB AERY BIKE BINK
DRAY DREY EYRY HOME LAIR NIDE REDD
SHED TRAP ABODE AERIE BROOD EYRIE
HAUNT HOUSE NIDUS SWARM COLONY
CUDDLE HOTBED RESORT WURLEY
CABINET LODGING RETREAT VESPIARY
WITHYPOT LARVARIUM PENDULINE
RESIDENCE TERMITARY
(— OF ANIMALS) BED
(— OF ANT) FORMICARY
(— OF BOXES) INRO
(— OF EGGS) CLUTCH
(SQUIRREL'S —) CAGE
NESTLE JUG LAP LIE PET NEST SNUG
NICHE SPOON BURROW CUDDLE FIDGET

NUZZLE PETTLE SETTLE SNUDGE
CHERISH SHELTER SNUGGLE SNUZZLE
NESTLING BABY BIRD EYAS NEST POULT
SQUAB CUDDLE RETREAT BIRDLING
NIDULATE FLEDGLING
NESTOR SAGE SOLON LEADER ADVISER
ADVISOR COUNSELOR PATRIARCH
(FATHER OF —) NELEUS
(MOTHER OF —) CHLORIS
(SON OF —) ANTILOCHUS
(WIFE OF —) ANAXIBIA EURYDICE
NESTORIAN WISE
NET BAG GIN HAY LAM POT WEB CAUL
FIKE FLAN FLEW FLUE FYKE GAIN HAAF
KELL LACE LAUN LAWN LEAD LEAP
MESH MOKE NEAT PURE RETE SALE
SEAN TOIL TRAP TRIM WEIR BRAIL
CATCH CLEAN CLEAR DRIFT GAUZE
LACIS PITCH POUND SCOOP SEIZE
SNARE SNOOD TRAWL TRINK TULLE
YIELD BAGNET BASKET BRIGHT COBWEB
ENTRAP FABRIC GROUND LEADER
MALINE MASILE PANTER PROFIT RAFFLE
SAGENE SAPIAO TOWNET TUNNEL
DRAGNET ENSNARE FLYTAIL LAMPARA
MALINES NETWORK PROTECT RETICLE
RINSING SCRINGE SHELTER SPILLER
STALKER TRAINEL TRAMMEL MESHWORK
SALAMBAO BUCKSTALL RETICULUM
NETHANIAH (FATHER OF —) ASAPH
ELISHAMA
(SON OF —) JEHUDI ISHMAEL
NETHER DOWN BELOW LOWER UNDER
NEDDER DOWNWARD INFERIOR
INFERNAL

NETHERLANDS

CANAL: ORANJE JULIANA DRENTSCH
CAPITAL: AMSTERDAM
COIN: CENT DOIT RYDER FLORIN GULDEN
STIVER DUCATON ESCALIN GUILDER
STOOTER
ISLAND: TEXEL MARKEN AMELAND
VLIELAND
MEASURE: EL AAM AHM AUM ELL KAN
MUD VAT ZAK DUIM LOOD MIJL ROOD
ROPE VOET ANKER CARAT ROEDE STOOP
WISSE BUNDER KOPPEN LEGGER MAATJE
MUDDLE MUTSJE STREEP SCHEPEL
MINGELEN OKSHOOFD STEEKKAN
PROVINCE: DRENTHE LIMBURG UTRECHT
ZEELAND FRIESLAND GRONINGEN
GELDERLAND OVERIJSSEL
RIVER: EEMS LECK MAAS WAAL YSEL
DONGE HUNSE YSSEL DINTEL DOMMEL
KROMME MEAUSE SCHELDT
TOWN: EDE ASSEN BREDA HAGUE AALTEN
ARNHEM LEIDEN ZWOLLE HAARLEM
TILBURG UTRECHT AALSMEER ENSCHEDE
NIJMEGEN AMSTERDAM EINDHOVEN
GRONINGEN ROTTERDAM
WEIGHT: ONS LAST LOOD POND BAHAR
GREIN KORREL WICHTJE ESTERLIN

NETHERWORLD HADES SHADES
NETTING BAR CAUL LING MESH SCREEN
DEEPING FISHNET FOOTING BOBBINET
WIREWORK
NETTLE VEX FRET LINE ANNOY CNIDA
ETTLE PEEVE PIQUE STING HENBIT
ORTIGA RUFFLE SPLICE URTICA AFFRONT
BLUBBER BLUETOP KNITTLE PROVOKE
STINGER IRRITATE CLOWNHEAL
GLIDEWORT PELLITORY SMARTWEED
(— RASH) HIVES UREDO URTICARIA
(— TREE) LOTUS GYMPIE
(WHITE DEAD —) ARCHANGEL
(PREF.) CNID(O)
NETWORK WEB CAUL FRET GRID KELL
MAZE MESH MOKE RETE CHAIN LACIS
BRIDGE COBWEB CRADLE PLEXUS
RESEAU SAGENE SYSTEM DRAGNET
DIPLEXER GRIDIRON KNITTING
WATTLING RETICULUM
(— OF BLOOD VESSELS) TOMENTUM
(— OF CRACKS) CRACKLE
(— ON MAP) GRATICULE
(NUCLEAR —) SKEIN
(PL.) RETIA
NEURALGIA SCIATICA COSTALGIA
NEUROTIC DRUG NERVOUS
(— CONDITION) NERVOSITY
NEUTRAL GRAY INERT SWEET AMORAL
MIDDLING NEGATIVE UNBIASED
COLORLESS IMPARTIAL
(— IN COLOR) SOBER
(OPTICALLY —) INACTIVE
NEUTRALIZE KILL ANNUL BLUNT ERASE
CANCEL ABOLISH BALANCE CORRECT
DESTROY NULLIFY VITIATE NEGATIVE
OVERRIDE SATURATE FRUSTRATE

NEVADA

CAPITAL: CARSONCITY
COUNTY: NYE ELKO LANDER STOREY
WASHOE MINERAL PERSHING
INDIAN: WASHO PAIUTE
LAKE: MUD MEAD RUBY TAHOE WALKER
PYRAMID WINNEMUCCA
PEAK: BOUNDARY
RIVER: REESE TRUCKEE HUMBOLDT
STATE BIRD: BLUEBIRD
STATE FLOWER: SAGEBRUSH
STATE NICKNAME: SILVER SAGEBRUSH
STATE TREE: ASPEN
TOWN: ELY ELKO RENO EUREKA FALLON
NELLIS PIOCHE SPARKS TONOPAH
LASVEGAS LOVELOCK

NEVER NAY NIE NOT NARY NARRA NIVER
NOWHEN
NEVERTHELESS BUT YET STILL ALWISE
THOUGH ALGATES HOWBEIT HOWEVER
WHETHER NATHELESS NONETHELESS
NEW NEO NEU RAW LATE NOVA FRESH
GREEN MOIST NOVEL YOUNG MODERN
RECENT UNUSED VIRGIN ANOTHER
FOREIGN STRANGE UNTRIED UPSTART
INITIATE NEOTERIC ORIGINAL YOUTHFUL
BEGINNING
(— BUT YET OLD) NOVANTIQUE
(BRAND —) SPICK
NEWBORN YEANLING
NEW BRUNSWICK (CAPITAL OF —)
FREDERICTON
(COUNTY OF —) KINGS QUEENS
SUNBURY MADAWASKA
(MOUNTAIN OF —) CARLETON
(TOWN OF —) BURTON MONCTON
BATHURST GAGETOWN
NEW CALEDONIA (— BIRD) KAGU
(CAPITAL OF —) NOUMEA
(ISLAND OF —) HUON BELEP DEPINS
LOYALTY WALPOLE
(SEAPORT OF —) NOUMEA
NEWCOMER CADET SETTLER COMELING
FRESHMAN JACKEROO MALIHINI
RINGNECK GREENHORN IMMIGRANT
KIMBERLIN
NEWCOMES (AUTHOR OF —)
THACKERAY
(CHARACTER IN —) ANN KEW JOHN
BRIAN CLARA CLIVE ETHEL JAMES
ROSEY ALFRED BARNES BINNIE HOBSON
RIDLEY THOMAS NEWCOME PULLEYN
FARINTOSH MACKENZIE
NEWEL POST VICE SPINDLE
NEWFOUNDLAND (— CAPE) RAY RACE
BAULD
(— HOUSE) TILT
(— INHABITANT) OUTPORTER
(CAPITAL OF —) STJOHNS
(ISLAND OF —) BELL FOGO GROAIS
MIQUELON
(RIVER OF —) GANDER HUMBER
EXPLOITS
(TOWN OF —) GANDER HOWLEY
WABANA CORNERBROOK

NEW GUINEA

BAY: ORO MILNE HOLNICOTE
GOODENOUGH COLLINGWOOD
CAPITAL: PORTMORESBY
GULF: HUON PAPUA
ISLAND: BUKA MANUS MUSSAU
ISLAND GROUP: CRETIN NINIGO SAINSON
SOLOMON
MOUNTAIN: ALBERT VICTORIA
NATIVE: ARAU BOONG KARON PAPUAN
PORT: LAE DARU WEWAK MADANG
RIVER: FLY HAMU SEPIK KIKORI PURARI
AMBERNO
TOWN: LAE WAU DARU SORON AITAPE
KIKORI RABAUL SAMARAI

NEW HAMPSHIRE

CAPITAL: CONCORD
COLLEGE: DARTMOUTH
COUNTY: COOS BELKNAP GRAFTON
MERRIMACK

LAKE: SQUAM OSSIPEE SUNAPEE
  UMBAGOG WINNIPESAUKEE
MOUNTAIN: MORIAH PAUGUS WAUMBEK
  CHOCORUA MONADNOCK
MOUNTAIN RANGE: WHITE
NOTCH: CRAWFORD FRANCONIA
RIVER: SACO ISRAEL BELLAMY SOUHEGAN
  MERRIMACK PISCATAQUA
TOWN: DOVER KEENE EXETER NASHUA
  HANOVER LACONIA OSSIPEE

NEW HEBRIDES (CAPITAL OF —) VILA
  (ISLAND OF —) EPI TANA EFATE
  MAEWO MABRIM MALEKULA

NEW JERSEY

CAPITAL: TRENTON
COLLEGE: UPSALA
COUNTY: ESSEX OCEAN SALEM UNION
  BERGEN CAMDEN MERCER MORRIS
  SUSSEX WARREN PASSAIC MONMOUTH
INDIAN: DELAWARE
RIVER: DENNIS HAYNES MANTUA RAMAPO
  MULLICA PASSAIC RARITAN COHANSEY
  TUCKAHOE
STATE BIRD: GOLDFINCH
STATE FLOWER: VIOLET
STATE NICKNAME: GARDEN
STATE TREE: REDOAK
TOWN: LODI SALEM CAMDEN NEWARK
  NEWTON NUTLEY RAHWAY TOTOWA
  BAYONNE CLIFTON HOBOKEN HOHOKUS
  MATAWAN NETCONG ORADELL
  PARAMUS PASSAIC TEANECK TENAFLY
  TRENTON WYCKOFF CARTERET
  FREEHOLD METUCHEN PATERSON
  SECAUCUS WATCHUNG HACKENSACK
UNIVERSITY: RUTGERS PRINCETON

NEWLY ANEW AGAIN AFRESH LATELY
  FRESHLY NEWLINS RECENTLY
NEWMARKET MICHIGAN SARATOGA
  GRABOUCHE

NEW MEXICO

CAPITAL: SANTAFE
COUNTY: LEA EDDY LUNA MORA QUAY
  TAOS OTERO CATRON CHAVES DEBACA
  HIDALGO SOCORRO VALENCIA
INDIAN: SIA TANO TEWA TIWA ZUNI
  JEMEZ PECOS APACHE NAVAHO NAVAJO
  PUEBLO
MOUNTAIN: WHEELER
RIVER: UTE GILA PECOS SANJOSE
STATE BIRD: ROADRUNNER
STATE FLOWER: YUCCA
STATE TREE: PINON PINYON
TOWN: JAL MORA AZTEC BELEN RATON
  CLOVIS DEMING GALLUP GRANTS
  ARTESIA SANTAFE SOCORRO CARLSBAD
  LASVEGAS TUCUMCARI ALAMOGORDO

NEWNESS NOVITY
NEWS BUZZ DOPE UNKO WORD CLASH
  ADVICE BUDGET CRACKS FERLIE GOSPEL
  NOTICE REPORT EVANGEL KHUBBER
  TIDINGS WITTING NOUVELLE
  KNOWLEDGE SPEERINGS
NEWSBOY NEWSY CAMELOT CARRIER
  PAPERBOY
NEWSCASTER ANCHORMAN
NEWSMONGER GOSSIP TATTLER
  NOVELANT NOVELIST QUIDNUNC
  REPORTER
NEWSPAPER RAG NEWS DAILY ORGAN
  PAPER PRESS SHEET TIMES ARRIBA
  HERALD SERIAL SUNDAY COURANT
  DIURNAL GAZETTE JOURNAL MERCURY
  TABLOID TRIBUNE NEWSPRINT
NEWSSTAND BOOTH KIOSK STALL
  STAND BOOKSTALL
NEWT ASK EFT ESK EVET EBBET EFFET
  LIZARD TRITON AXOLOTL CRAWLER
  CREEPER REPTILE MANKEEPER
NEW YEAR'S EVE HAGMENA
  HOGMANAY

NEW YORK

BAY: JAMAICA PECONIC MORICHES
BOROUGH: BRONX KINGS QUEENS
  BROOKLYN MANHATTAN
CANAL: ERIE GOWANUS
CAPITAL: ALBANY
COLLEGE: BARD CCNY IONA PACE FINCH
  UNION HUNTER VASSAR WAGNER
  ADELPHI BARNARD CANISIUS HAMILTON
  SKIDMORE
COUNTY: ERIE BRONX ESSEX KINGS
  TIOGA WAYNE YATES BROOME CAYUGA
  NASSAU ONEIDA OSWEGO OTSEGO
  PUTNAM QUEENS SENECA ULSTER
  CHEMUNG GENESEE NIAGARA STEUBEN
  SUFFOLK CHENANGO DUTCHESS
  HERKIMER ONONDAGA RICHMOND
  ROCKLAND SARATOGA SCHUYLER
INDIAN: CAYUGA MOHAWK ONEIDA
  SENECA MOHICAN MONTAUK IROQUOIS
  ONONDAGA
ISLAND: FIRE LONG ELLIS STATEN
  FISHERS LIBERTY SHELTER GOVERNORS
  MANHATTAN
LAKE: ERIE CAYUGA GEORGE ONEIDA
  OTISCO OTSEGO OWASCO PLACID
  SENECA CONESUS HONEOYE ONTARIO
  SARANAC SCHROON SUCCESS
  SARATOGA
MOUNTAIN: BEAR MARCY
MOUNTAINS: TACONIC CATSKILL
  ADIRONDACK
RIVER: TIOGA HARLEM HOOSIC HUDSON
  MOHAWK OSWEGO GENESEE NIAGARA
STATE BIRD: BLUEBIRD
STATE FLOWER: ROSE
STATE TREE: SUGARMAPLE
TOWN: RYE OVID ROME DELHI ILION ISLIP
  NYACK OLEAN OWEGO UTICA ATTICA
  AUBURN CARMEL COHOES ELMIRA

GOSHEN ITHACA MALONE ONEIDA
OSWEGO TAPPAN WARSAW ARDSLEY
BABYLON BATAVIA BUFFALO CONGERS
ENDWELL GENESEO HEWLETT MAHOPAC
MASSENA MERRICK MINEOLA MONTAUK
ONEONTA PENNYAN POTSDAM SUFFERN
SYOSSET WANTAGH YAPHANK YONKERS
BETHPAGE CATSKILL HERKIMER
KINGSTON OSSINING SYRACUSE
TUCKAHOE ROCHESTER
UNIVERSITY: LIU NYU ADELPHI COLGATE
CORNELL FORDHAM HOFSTRA YESHIVA
COLUMBIA
WATERFALL: NIAGARA

NEW ZEALAND

BAY: OHUA HAWKE LYALL AWARUA
CLOUDY GOLDEN FITZROY PEGASUS
POVERTY RANGAUNU
CAPE: EGMONT FAREWELL PALLISER
CAPITAL: WELLINGTON
GULF: HAURAKI
ISLAND: OTEA STEWART PUKETUTU
LAKE: OHAU HAWEA TAUPO PUKAKI
PUPUKE TEANAU TEKAPO WANAKA
BRUNNER ROTORUA WAKATIPU
MOUNTAIN: COOK FLAT OWEN CHOPE
LYALL MITRE OTARI EGMONT STOKES
AORANGI PIHANGA TUTAMOE TYNDALL
ASPIRING EARNSLAW
NATIVE: ATI ARAWA MAORI RINGATU
PENINSULA: MAHIA OTAGO
RIVER: MOKAU ORETI WAIPA CLUTHA
TAIERI TAMAKI WAIHOU WAIROA
MATAURA WAIKATO WAITAKI CLARENCE
MANAWATU WANGANUI RANGITIKEI
STRAIT: COOK FOVEAUX
TOWN: LEUIN ORETI OTAKI TAUPO
CLUTHA FOXTON NAPIER NELSON
OAMARU PICTON TIMARU DUNEDIN
MANUKAU RAETIHI ROTORUA AUCKLAND
HAMILTON KAWAKAWA CHRISTCHURCH
VOLCANO: RUAPEHU NGAURUHOE
TONGARIRO
WATERFALL: BOWEN HELENA STIRLING
SUTHERLAND

NEXT POI NEAR SYNE THEN UNTO WISE
AFTER EWEST FIRST LATER NEIST RIGHT
BESIDE COMING SECOND TIDDER
TOTHER CLOSEST NEAREST DIRECTLY
PROCHAIN PROCHEIN ADJOINING
IMMEDIATE
(— AFTER) THEN FOLLOWING
(— IN ORDER) EKA
(— MONTH) PROXIMO
(— OF KIN) GOEL
(— TO LAST) PENULT
(PREF.) (— IN ORDER) EKA
NIBBLE EAT NAB NIB NIP BITE GNAW
KNAB KNAP MOOP MOUP NOSH PECK
PICK CHAMP GNARL MOUSE PIECE
SHEAR ARRODE BROWSE CHAVEL

NATTLE PICKLE PILFER CHIMBLE
GNABBLE GNATTER KNABBLE SNAGGLE
NIBELUNGENLIED (AUTHOR OF —)
UNKNOWN
(CHARACTER IN —) UTA ETZEL HAGEN
IRING GERNOT HUNOLD LUDGER
BLOEDEL GUNTHER ORTLIEB BRUNHILD
DANKWART DIETRICH GISELHER
KRIEMHILD SIEGFRIED HILDEBRAND
NIBLICK BLASTER

NICARAGUA

CAPITAL: MANAGUA
COIN: PESO CENTAVO CORDOBA
DEPARTMENT: LEON BOACO RIVAS
CARAZO ESTELI MADRIZ MASAYA
ZELAYA MANAGUA
ISLAND: OMETEPE
LAKE: MANAGUA
MEASURE: VARA CAHIZ MILLA SUERTE
TERCIA CAJUELA ESTADAL MANZANA
MOUNTAIN: MADERA MOGOTON
PORT: CORINTO
RIVER: COCO TUMA WANKS GRANDE
ESCONDIDO
TOWN: LEON BOACO RIVAS MASAYA
OCOTAL SOMOTO GRANADA MANAGUA
JINOTEGA MATAGALPA CHINANDEGA
WEIGHT: BAG CAJA TONELADA

NICE APT FIT FEAT FINE GOOD JUMP KIND
NEAT NYCE PURE TRIM CANNY EXACT
FUSSY NIECE SWEET BONITA BONITO
DAINTY GENTIL MINUTE PEACHY QUAINT
QUEASY SPICED STRICT SUBTLE TICKLE
CORRECT ELEGANT FINICAL GENTEEL
MINCING PERJINK PICKING PRECISE
PRUDISH REFINED DECOROUS DELICATE
EXACTING PLEASANT PLEASING
TICKLISH PARTICULAR SCRUMPTIOUS
(TOO —) SUPERFINE
NICETY HAIR DELICACY JUSTNESS
CRITICISM CURIOSITY PRECISION
NICHE BAY APSE CANT COVE NOOK SLOT
AMBRY HOVEL PLACE ALCOVE ANCONA
BOXING COVERT CRANNY EXEDRA
GROOVE MIHRAB RECESS RINCON
EDICULE HOUSING RETREAT ROUNDEL
AEDICULA CREDENCE TOKONOMA
HABITACLE TABERNACLE
NICHOLAS NICKLEBY
(AUTHOR OF —) DICKENS
(CHARACTER IN —) BRAY HAWK KATE
FRANK GRIDE NOGGS RALPH SMIKE
NEWMAN SQUEERS VINCENT CRUMMLES
MADELINE MULBERRY NICHOLAS
NICKLEBY WACKFORD CHEERYBLE
MANTALINI
NICK CUT JAG MAR NAG NOB CHIP DENT
DINT HACK NACK SLAP SLIT CHEAT
CHICK GOUGE NITCH NOTCH PRICK
SCORE SLACK SNICK TALLY TRICK
ARREST RECORD DEFRAUD
(— OF TIME) GODSPEED
NICKEL JIT COIN JITNEY NIMBUS

(ALLOY OF —) INVAR KONEL MONEL
(SYMBOL OF —) NI
NICKELODEON JUKEBOX
NICKNAME DUB DOEG NICK ALIAS
AGNAME BYWORD HANDLE MONICA
TONAME CRACKER EKENAME MISNAME
MONIKER NICKERY COGNOMEN
MONARCHO MONICKER TARTUFFE
SOBRIQUET
NICKNAMING PROSONOMASIA
NICTATE WINK BLINK CLOSE TWINK
TWINKLE NICTITATE
NIECE OY OYE NEPHEW
NIFTY FINE GOOD KEEN SMART STYLISH
NIGER JOLIBA KWORRA RAMTIL
(CAPITAL OF —) NIAMEY
(MOUTH OF —) NUN
(NATIVE OF —) PEUL HAUSA DJERMA
FULANI SONGHA TOUBOU TUAREG
(OASIS IN —) KAOUAR
(REGION OF —) AIR
(RIVER OF —) DILLIA
(TOWN OF —) SAY GAYA TERA BAGAM
FACHI GOURE MADAMA MARADI
TAHOUA ZINDER

NIGERIA

CAPITAL: LAGOS
COIN: KOBO NAIRA
NATIVE: ARO EBO EDO IBO IJO VAI BENI
EBOE EFIK EJAM EKOI NUPE BENIN
HAUSA FULANI YORUBA
PLATEAU: JOS
PORT: LAGOS CALABAR
PROVINCE: ISA OYO KANO NUPE ONDO
IJEBU OGOJA WARRI OWERRI ADAMAWA
RIVER: OLI GANA YOBE BENUE NIGER
KADUNA SOKOTO GONGOLA HADEJIA
KOMADUGU
STATE: IMO OYO KANO OGUN ONDO
BENUE BORNO KWARA LAGOS BAUCHI
SOKOTO ANAMBRA GONGOLA
TOWN: ABA ADO EDE ISA IWO JOS BIDI
BUEA KANO OFFA YOLA AKURE ENUGU
IKEJA LAGOS MINNA ZARIA BAUCHI
IBADAN ILESHA ILORIN KADUNA MUSHIN
OWERRI TAKOBA CALABAR ONITSHA
OSHOGBO ABEOKUTA
TREE: AFARA

NIGGARD CARL CHURL CLOSE MISER
NIGON PIKER SCART TIGHT NIGGER
SCRIMP SCRUNT STINGY CHINCHE
DRYFIST NITHING PUCKFIST SCRIMPER
EARTHWORM PINCHBECK PINCHFIST
PUCKFOIST SKINFLINT
NIGGARDLY MEAN CLOSE STINT
NARROW NIGHLY SCANTY SCREWY
SKIMPY SORDID STINGY STRAIT CHINCHE
MISERLY PARSIMONIOUS
NIGGLING PETTY PICAYUNE
NIGH AT NEAR ANEAR ANIGH CLOSE
ALMOST NEARLY ADJACENT
NIGHT PM EVE DARK NUIT DARKY DEATH
NACHT NOCHE SLEEP DARKNESS

(— AND DAY) NYCHTHEMERON
(CHILDREN OF —) ERINYS FURIES
ERINNYES
(DEPTH OF —) HOLL
(GODDESS OF —) NOX NYX
(LAST —) YESTREEN
(NORSE —) NATT NOTT
(STAY OUT ALL —) PERNOCTATE
NIGHT BLINDNESS NYCTALOPIA
NIGHTCAP HOW COWL DOWD HOUVE
PIRNY BIGGIN PIRNIE DORMEUSE
SUNDOWNER
NIGHTCLUB CAFE CLUB SPOT AGOGO
BOITE BISTRO NITERY CABARET
DANCERY NIGHTERY
NIGHTDRESS SLOP WYLIECOAT
NIGHTFALL EEN EVE DARK DUSK EVEN
SHUTTING TWILIGHT
(OCCURRING AT —) ACRONICAL
NIGHTGOWN SLOP TOOSH NIGHTY
BEDGOWN NIGHTIE WYLIECOAT
NIGHTHAWK PISK CUIEJO BULLBAT
NIGHTINGALE JUG BULBUL FLORENCE
PHILOMEL ROSSIGNOL
(— SOUND) JUG
(SWEDISH —) LIND JENNY
NIGHTJAR PUCK POTOO EVEJAR
DERHAWK SPINNER WHEELER
MOREPORK POORWILL NIGHTHAWK
NIGHTMARE ALP HAG MARA MESS
DREAM FANCY FIEND VISION INCUBUS
CACODEMON CAUCHEMAR EPHIALTES
NIHILIST ANARCHIST SOCIALIST
NIKE (BROTHER OF —) BIA ZELUS
CRATOS
(FATHER OF —) PALLAS
(MOTHER OF —) STYX
NIL ZERO NILGAI IPOMOEA NOTHING
NIMBLE FLY DEFT FLIP FLIT GLEG LISH
SPRY SWAK YALD YARE AGILE BRISK
FLEET LIGHT NIPPY QUICK SWACK TRICK
WIGHT YAULD ACTIVE ADROIT CLEVER
FEIRIE LIMBER LISSOM LIVELY PROMPT
QUIVER SPRACK SUPPLE VOLANT
WANDLE DELIVER LISSOME SWIPPER
FLIPPANT TRIPPING CITIGRADE
SENSITIVE SPRIGHTLY
(PREF.) PRESTI
NIMBLENESS HASTE AGILITY SLEIGHT
LEGERITY DEXTERITY LIGHTNESS
NIMBUS AURA HALO NIMB CLOUD GLORY
SHINE VAPOR GLORIA AUREOLA
AUREOLE
NINCOMPOOP ASS DOLT FOOL POOP
NINNY NINCOM WITLING BLOCKHEAD
SIMPLETON
NINE IX NIE NYE TEAM COMET POTHOOK
(— A.M.) UNDERN MIDMORN
(— ANGLED FIGURE) NONAGON
(— DAYS DEVOTION) NOVENA
(— FOLD) NONUPLE
(— HEADED MONSTER) HYDRA
(— HUNDRED) SAN
(— INCHES) SPAN
(— OF CLUBS OR DIAMONDS) COMET
(— OF DIAMONDS) BRAGGER
(— OF TRUMPS) DIX MENEL SANCHO

(— YEAR CYCLE) JUGLAR
(GROUP OF —) ENNEAD
(MUSIC FOR —) NONET
NINEPIN KAIL SQUAIL SKITTLE SKITTLES
(PL.) BOWLS KEELS KAYLES NINEPEGS
NINNY DOLT FOOL LOUT DUNCE IDIOT
NONNY PATCH SAMMY SPOON FONDLE
NOODLE SAPHEAD FONDLING
BLOCKHEAD NIDDICOCK PEAKGOOSE
SIMPLETON
NIOBE HERB HOSTA FUNKIA
(BROTHER OF —) PELOPS
(FATHER OF —) TANTALUS
(HUSBAND OF —) AMPHION
(SISTER-IN-LAW OF —) AEDON
NIP CUT SIP VEX BITE BUMP CLIP DRAM
GIVE KNIP NIPE PECK SNUB TANG TAUT
TUCK BLAST CHEAT CHECK CHILL CLAMP
DRAFT FROST PINCH SEIZE SEVER SNAPE
SNEAP THIEF BENUMB BLIGHT CATNIP
TIPPLE TWITCH WITHER SARCASM
SQUEEZE WETTING COMPRESS
FROSTBITE VELLICATE
NIPPER BOY LAD CLAW CRAB GRAB
HAND BITER CHELA MISER THIEF
CUNNER URCHIN GRIPPER INCISOR
BRAKEMAN
NIPPERS DOG NIP BITS NIPS TONGS
GRATER PLIERS TURKIS FORCEPS
PINCERS OSTEOTOME
NIPPLE BUD DUG PAP TIT BEAN TEAT
DIDDY DUMMY SPEAN NIBBLE PILLAR
MAMILLA PAPILLA THELIUM
(— POINT) THELION
NIPPY BOLD SHARP
NITER NITRE PETER PETRE POTASH
SALTPETER
NITRIC AZOTIC
NITROGEN GAS AZOTE ALKALIGEN
NITROGLYCERIN TNT SOUP NITRO
SIRUP SYRUP GLONOIN
NITWIT DAW NIT DOLT DOPE DRONGO
DIZZARD SIMPLETON
NIX NO HARD NECK NICKER NOBODY
SPIRIT SPRITE UNDINE NOTHING
**NJORD (DAUGHTER OF —) FREYA
(SON OF —) FREY
(WIFE OF —) SKADHI
NO NA NE NAE NAH NAW NAY NIT NIX
NUL BAAL BAIL BALE NONE NYET NAPOO
AIKONA NAPOOH NOGAKU
NOAH NOE
(DOVE OF —) COLUMBA
(FATHER OF —) LAMECH ZELOPHEHAD
(GRANDFATHER OF —) METHUSALEH
(GRANDSON OF —) ARAM
(GREAT-GRANDSON OF —) HUL
(MEXICAN —) COXCOX
(RAVEN OF —) CORVUS
(SON OF —) HAM SEM SHEM JAPHETH
(WINE CUP OF —) CRATER
NOBEL PRIZE (— IN CHEMISTRY)
BERG HAHN HOFF KUHN TODD UREY
ALDER ASTON BOSCH CURIE DEBYE
DIELS EIGEN FLORY FUKUI HABER LIBBY
NATTA PREGL SODDY SYNGE TAUBE
CALVIN HARDEN HASSEL KARRER LELOIR

NERNST PERUTZ PRELOG RAMSAY
SANGER SUMNER WERNER WITTIG
BERGIUS BUCHNER GIAUQUE GILBERT
KENDREW MOISSAN NORRISH ONSAGER
OSTWALD RUZICKA SEABORG SEMENOV
WALLACH WIELAND WINDAUS
LANGMUIR MULLIKEN TISELIUS
(— IN ECONOMICS) ARROW KLEIN
OHLIN SIMON TOBIN DEBREU FRISCH
MYRDAL KUZNETS SCHULTZ STIGLER
FRIEDMAN LEONTIEF
(— IN LITERATURE) BOLL BUCK GIDE
MANN SHAW AGNON BUNIN CAMUS
ELIOT HESSE HEYSE LEWIS PERSE SACHS
YEATS ANDRIC BELLOW ELYTIS EUCKEN
FRANCE MILOSZ NERUDA ONEILL SARTRE
SINGER TAGORE BECKETT CENETTI
GOLDING KIPLING LAXNESS MAURIAC
MISTRAL MONTALE ROLLAND RUSSELL
BJORNSON CARDUCCI FAULKNER
LAGERLOF CHURCHILL HEMINGWAY
PASTERNAK STEINBECK LAGERKVIST
MAETERLINCK
(— IN MEDICINE) DAM CORI DALE
HESS KATZ KOCH ROSS ROUS WALD
ARBER BLOCH BOVET BUMET CHAIN
CRICK CURIE DOISY EULER GOLGI HENCH
HUBEL KREBS KROGH LOEWI LURIA
LYNEN MINOT MONIZ MONOD OCHOA
SNELL TATUM YALOW BARANY BEADLE
BEKESY BORDET CARREL CLAUDE
DOMAGK ECCLES ENDERS FLOREY
GASSER GRANIT HOLLEY HUXLEY
KOCHER KOSSEL LORENZ PALADE
PAVLOV RICHET SPERRY WIESEL
AXELROD BEHRING FIBIGER HERSHEY
HODGKIN KHORANA LAVERAN NATHANS
NICOLLE SCHALLY THELLER DELBRUCK
MCCLINTOCK
(— IN PEACE) ORR THO HULL KING
MOTT PIRE ROOT SATO ASSER BAJER
BALCH BEGIN DAWES FRIED GOBAT
LANGE PASSY SADAT ADDAMS ANGELL
BRANDT BRIAND BUNCHE BUTLER
CASSIN CREMER DUNANT MONETA
NANSEN QUIDDE WALESA WILSON
BORLAUG BUISSON JOUHAUX KELLOGG
LUTHULI PAULING RENAULT THERESA
BRANTING CORRIGAN ESQUIVEL
SAKHAROV KISSINGER ROOSEVELT
SODERBLOM SCHWEITZER
HAMMARSKJOLD
(— IN PHYSICS) LEE BOHR BORN HESS
LAMB LAUE MOTT NEEL RABI RYLE
TAMM TING WIEN YANG BASOV BETHE
BLOCH BOTHE BRAGG BRAUN CURIE
DALEN DIRAC ESAKI FERMI GABOR
HERTZ KUSCH PAULI SEGRE ALFVEN
BARKLA CRONIN FOWLER GLASER
HEWISH LANDAU PERRIN PLANCK
STRUTT TOWNES WIGNER YUKAWA
BARDEEN GLAEVER GLASHOW KAPITSA
LORENTZ MARCONI RICHTER EINSTEIN
ROENTGEN CHANDRASEKHAR
NOBILITY RANK ELITE GRACE GENTRY
STATUS DIGNITY KWAZOKU PEERAGE

QUALITY STATION BARONAGE SZLACHTA
ELEVATION

NOBLE DON ALII DOGE DUKE EARL EDEL
EPIC FAME FREE GENT GOOD GRAF HIGH
JARL JUST KAMI KUGE LORD PEER PURE
RIAL ARIKI ATHEL BARON BROAD BURLY
COUNT DUCAL ERECT ETHEL FURST
GRAND GREAT HIRAM KHASS LOFTY
MANLY MORAL MURZA PROUD ROYAL
STATE AUGUST COUSIN DAIMIO EPICAL
FLAITH GENTLE GESITH HAUGHT HEROIC
JUNKER KINGLY LORDLY LUCUMO
MANFUL SIRDAR SUPERB THAKUR
WORTHY YONKER ACERBAS CACIQUE
GALLANT GLAUCUS GLORIED GRANDEE
HIDALGO LIBERAL MAGNATE MARQUIS
PATRICK STAROST STATELY STEWARD
SUBLIME TOISECH VOLPONE PANGLIMA
PRINCELY
(MINOR —) VIDAME

NOBLEMAN DUKE EARL EMIR LORD PEER
SOUL BARON COUNT PARIS THANE
COUSIN MILORD ORLOFF THAKUR
GRANDEE HIDALGO MAGNATE MARQUIS
STAROST VOLPONE YOUNKER ADELIGER
ALDERMAN ALMAVIVA BELARIUS
MARCHESE MARQUESS LANDGRAVE
MAGNIFICO

NOBLENESS HONOR DIGNITY
(— OF BIRTH) EUGENY

NOBLEWOMAN LADY MILADY DUCHESS
PEERESS BARONESS COUNTESS

NOBODY NIX NEMO NONE NADIE NOMAN
SCRUB SCARAB NOTHING JACKSTRAW

NOCTURNAL NIGHT NOXIAL NIGHTLY
NIGHTISH MOONSHINE

NOCTURNE LULLABY UHTSONG
PAINTING SERENADE

NOD BOB BOW ERR NAP NID NIP BECK
BEND DOZE NAPE SIGN SLIP SWAY WINK
DROOP LAPSE ASSENT BECKON DODDLE
DROWSE NODDLE NUTATE SALUTE
SIGNIFY

NODDING DROWSY NUTANT ANNUENT
CERNUOUS DROOPING NUTATION

NODE BOW BUMP KNOB KNOT LUMP
PLOT JOINT NODUS POINT TUMOR
BULBIL NODULE DILEMMA GRANULE
KNUCKLE FOLLICLE PHYTOMER
SWELLING TUBERCLE

NODULE BOB AUGE BUMP KNOT LUMP
MASS NODE YOLK FLINT GEODE PHYMA
MILIUM BLISTER CATHEAD GRANULE
LEPROMA NABLOCK SARCOID AMYGDALE
AMYGDULE COALBALL TUBERCLE
WHITEHEAD
(— OF FLINT) CORE
(CHALCEDONY —) ENHYDROS

NOEL XMAS CAROL NATALIS CHRISTMAS

NOISE (ALSO SEE SOUND) ADO AIR BUM
DIN GIG HUM POP ROW BANG BOOM
BRAY BUMP BURR CLAM COIL HOOT
KLOP MUSH PEAL RALE RASH REEL RERD
ROTE ROUT SLAM ZING ALARM BABEL
BLARE BLAST BLOOP BRAWL BRUIT
BURLE CHANG CHIRM CLICK DREAM

GRASS JERRY KNOCK LARRY LARUM
LEDEN PLASH QUONK REERE RERDE
RUMOR SLORP SNORE SOUND STEER
SWISH WHANG BICKER CACKLE CLAMOR
DUNDER GOBBLE GOSSIP HUBBUB
NORATE OUTCRY PUDDER RACKET
RANTAN RATTLE REPORT SPLASH
SQUAWK STEVEN STRIFE TUMULT
UPROAR BLUSTER BRATTLE CLITTER
CLUTTER CRACKLE ORATION SCANDAL
SPATTER STREPOR STRIDOR FLICFLAC
QUONKING TINTAMAR CONFUSION

NOISELESS QUIET STILL SWEET TACIT
SILENT APHONIC CATLIKE

NOISY LOUD CLASHY CREAKY BLATANT
DINSOME FRANTIC MOILING RACKETY
RIOTOUS ROUTOUS BRAWLING
CLATTERY SONOROUS STREPENT
HILARIOUS RATTLEBAG SCAMBLING
BOISTEROUS

NOMADIC ERRATIC VAGRANT
VAGABOND FOOTLOOSE ITINERANT

NOM DE PLUME PENNAME TELONISM
PSEUDONYM

NOMENCLATURE LIST NAME TERM
ONYMY NAMING GLOSSARY REGISTER
CATALOGUE

NOMINAL PAR BASIC PAPER FORMAL
SLIGHT UNREAL TITULAR TRIVIAL
PLATONIC TRIFLING

NOMINATE CALL LEET NAME ELECT
NEVEN SLATE SELECT APPOINT ENTITLE
PRESENT PROPOSE SPECIFY DESIGNATE
POSTULATE

NONBELIEVER PAGAN ATHEIST
AGNOSTIC

NONCE NANES NONES NOANCE PRESENT
PURPOSE OCCASION

NONCHALANT COOL GLIB ALOOF
CASUAL JAUNTY CARELESS DEBONAIR
NEGLIGENT

NONCOMMITTAL NEUTRAL

NONCONFORMIST REBEL NONCON
BEATNIK DEVIANT FANATIC HERETIC
SECTARY BOHEMIAN RECUSANT
DISSENTER
(— IN ART) FAUVE

NONCONFORMITY HERESY ADHARMA
DISSENT NEGLECT REFUSAL RECUSANCE
RECUSANCY

NONESSENTIAL CASUAL FRILLY
UNNEEDED EXTRINSIC

NONESUCH APPLE MODEL PARAGON
PATTERN PARADIGM MATCHLESS
NONPAREIL UNRIVALED

NONEXISTENT NULL NAPOOH NOUGHT
NONBEING BARMECIDE

NONPAREIL BEST POPE TYPE PARAGON
PERFECT SUPREME UNEQUAL NONESUCH
PEERLESS UNRIVALED

NONPLUS SET FAZE POSE STOP BLANK
FLOOR POSER STICK STUMP TRUMP
BAFFLE GRAVEL PUZZLE RATTLE
CONFUSE MYSTIFY PERPLEX STAGGER
QUANDARY DULCARNON EMBARRASS

NONPLUSSED BLANK FOOLISH

NONPROFESSIONAL BUM LAY LAIC
AMATEUR
NONSENSE BAH GAS GUP PAH ROT BILK
BLAA BLAH BOSH BUFF BULL BUNK
COCK CRAP FLAM FLUM GAFF GOOK
GUFF JIVE JUNK PISH POOH PUNK TOSH
BALLS BILGE BLASH DROOL FOLLY
FUDGE HAVER HOOEY NERTS SPOOF
STITE STUFF TRASH TRIPE WAHOO
BABBLE BETISE BLAGUE BUNKUM
DRIVEL FADDLE FOLDER FOOTLE KIBOSH
LINSEY NAVERS PIFFLE RUBBLE SQUISH
TRIVIA BLARNEY BLATHER EYEWASH
FARRAGO INANITY LOCKRAM RHUBARB
RUBBISH TOSHERY TRIFLES TWADDLE
BUNCOMBE CLAPTRAP COBBLERS
DISHWASH FALDEROL FLIMFLAM
FLUMMERY GALBANUM MACARONI
MOROLOGY PISHPOSH PISHTOSH
SKITTLES SPLUTTER TOMMYROT
TRUMPERY ABSURDITY FRIVOLITY
MOONSHINE POPPYCOCK SILLINESS
BALDERDASH CODSWALLOP
NONSENSICAL ABSURD
NOOK IN BAY OUT WRO CANT COVE
GLEN HERN HOLE NALK ANGLE HALKE
HERNE NICHE ALCOVE CANTLE CORNER
CRANNY RECESS CREVICE NOOKERY
RETREAT
NOON M APEX DINE NOWN SEXT DINNER
MIDDAY UNDERN MIDNOON MERIDIAN
NOOSE TIE TOW BOND FANK GIRN HEMP
LACE LOOP ROPE TRAP BIGHT CATCH
GRANE HITCH HONDA LASSO LATCH
LEASH SNARE SNARL WIDDY CAUDLE
CLINCH ENTRAP HALTER LARIAT SPRING
TETHER TIPPET TWITCH ENSNARE
EXECUTE LANIARD LANYARD SPRINGE
NECKLACE TWITCHEL
(— FOR HAULING LOG) CHOKER
CHOCKER
(— FOR SNARING FISH) DULL
(— IN A CORD) KINCH
(HANGMAN'S —) SQUEEZER
NORMAL PAR FULL HOME JUST MEAN
SANE WISE CLEAR ERECT USUAL
FORMAL NATIVE SCHOOL AVERAGE
NATURAL NEUTRAL REGULAR TYPICAL
ORDINARY STANDARD CUSTOMARY
NORN FATE URTH WURD WYRD NORNA
SKULD URDHR URTHR VERDHANDI
VERTHANDI

NORTH CAROLINA

CAPE: FEAR LOOKOUT HATTERAS
CAPITAL: RALEIGH
COLLEGE: ELON CATAWBA DAVIDSON
COUNTY: ASHE DARE HOKE HYDE NASH
PITT WAKE AVERY DAVIE GATES ROWAN
SURRY BERTIE BLADEN CRAVEN
ONSLOW YADKIN YANCEY CATAWBA
PAMLICO CURRITUCK
INDIAN: ENO COREE CHERAW MORATOK
PAMLICO CHOWANOC HATTERAS
MOUNTAIN: HARRIS MITCHELL

RIVER: HAW TAR NEUSE CHOWAN
LUMBER PEEDEE YADKIN ROANOKE
SOUND: BOGUE CROATAN PAMLICO
STATE BIRD: CARDINAL
STATE FLOWER: DOGWOOD
STATE TREE: PINE
TOWN: BOONE SYLVA BURGAW DOBSON
DURHAM LENOIR SHELBY SPARTA
EDENTON HICKORY ROXBORO TARBORO
GASTONIA CHARLOTTE
UNIVERSITY: DUKE DUKE

NORTH DAKOTA

CAPITAL: BISMARCK
COLLEGE: JAMESTOWN
COUNTY: DUNN EDDY SLOPE STARK
WELLS DICKEY DIVIDE GRIGGS KIDDER
OLIVER TRAILL PEMBINA ROLETTE
INDIAN: MANDAN ARIKARA HIDATSA
MOUNTAIN: WHITEBUTTE
RIVER: RUSH CEDAR HEART JAMES
SOURIS DESLACS SHEYENNE WILDRICE
STATE BIRD: MEADOWLARK
STATE FLOWER: ROSE PRAIRIE
STATE TREE: ELM
TOWN: MOTT CANDO FARGO MINOT
ROLLA AMIDON LAKOTA LINTON MOHALL
BOWBELLS NAPOLEON

NORTHERN PIKE ARCTIC BOREAL
NORLAND NORTHEN

NORTH KOREA

CAPITAL: PYONGYANG
COIN: JUN WON HWAN
PROVINCE: CHAGANG KANGWON
TANGGANG
RIVER: NAM YALU IMJIN TUMEN TAEDONG
TOWN: HAEJU HEIJO KEIJO ANDONG
ANTUNG HYESAN JUSHIN POCHON
SAINNI WONSAN HAMHUNG HUICHON
HUNGNAM KAESONG KANGGYE
SARIWON SINUIJU CHONGJIN

NORTH VIETNAM

CAPITAL: HANOI
COIN: XU DONG
GULF: TONKIN TONKING
MOUNTAIN: FANSIPAN
NATIVE: HOA MAN MEO TAY KINH NUNG
THAI MUONG
PORT: BENTHUY HONGGAI HAIPHONG
REGION: ANNAM TONKIN
RIVER: BO CA DA LO MA CHU GAM KOI
CHAY NHIHA
TOWN: VINH BACNINH CAOBANG
DONGHOI NAMDINH VIETTRI HAIPHONG
THANHHOA

NORWAY

CAPE: NORDKYN NORDKAPP
CAPITAL: OSLO
COIN: ORE KRONE
COUNTY: AMT OSLO FYLKE TROMS
BERGEN TROMSO FINMARK HEDMARK
OPPLAND OSTFOLD NORDLAND
ROGALAND OSTFOLD NORDLAND
ROGALAND TELEMARK VESTFOLD
FJORD: OSLO SOGNE HARDANGER
TRONDHEIM
INLET: IS KOB RAN ALST ANDS BOKN
NORD OFOT SALT SUNN TYRI VEST
FIORD FJORD FOLDA LAKSE SOGNE
BJORNA HADSEL HORTENS TRONDHEIM
ISLAND: VEGA BOMLO DONNA FROYA
HITRA HOPEN SENJA SMOLA ALSTEN
AVEROY BOUVET HINNOY KARMOY
KVALOY SOLUND SOROYA VANNOY
GURSKOY LOFOTEN MAGEROY SEILAND
JANMAYEN SVALBARD RINGVASSOY
LAKE: ALTE ISTER MJOSA SNASA FEMUND
ROSTAVN TUNNSJO ROSTVATN
MOUNTAIN: SOGNE KJOLEN NUMEDAL
BLODFJEL SNOHETTA TELEMARK
USTETIND
PLATEAU: DOURE FJELD HARDANGER
RIVER: OI ENA ALTA OTRA RANA TANA
BARDU BEGNA GLAMA LAGEN ORKLA
OTTER RAUMA REISA GLOMMA LOUGEN
NAMSEN PASVIK DRAMSELVA
TOWN: GOL NES BODO MOSS ODDA OSLO
VOSS BJORT FLORO HAMAR MOLDE
SKIEN SKJAK BERGEN HORTEN LARVIK
NARVIK ALESUND ARENDAL DRAMMEN
SANDNES STAVANGER
WATERFALL: VETTI SKYKJE VORING

NOSE CAP NEB NIZ PRY PUG SPY BEAK
BOKO CONK NASE GROIN LORUM NASUS
SCENT SMELL SNIFF SNOOP SNOUT
TRUNK BEEZER CYRANO DETECT
GNOMON MUFFLE MUZZLE NOZZLE
PECKER ROOKIE SEARCH SNITCH SOCKET
ADVANCE PERFUME SMELLER DISCOVER
INFORMER OLFACTOR PERCEIVE
PROBOSCIS SCHNOZZLE
(— A LOG) SNIPE
(— OF ANIMAL) GROIN
(— OPENING) NARE
(— PARTITION) VOMER
(BLUNT —) SNUB
(FLAT —) PUG SNUB
NOSEBLEED EPISTAXIS RHINORRHAGIA
NOSEGAY BOB ODOR POSY SCENT
TUTTY BOUQUET CORSAGE PERFUME
NOSTALGIA LONGING YEARNING
NOSTRIL ALA NARE NARIS THIRL THRILL
BLOWHOLE
NOSY BEAKY PRYING CURIOUS
FRAGRANT INTRUSIVE
NOT NA NE NAE NAY NOR PAS BAAL BAIL
BALE NICHT SHORN SORRA NOUGHT
POLLED SHAVEN NEITHER HORNLESS
NEGATIVE

(— ANY) NO NUL NANE NARY NONE
NAIRY NOKIN STEAD
(— AT ALL) NEVER LITTLE NOWAYS
NOWHIT NOWISE
(— FINAL) NISI
(— THE SAME) OTHER ANOTHER
DIFFERENT
(— TO BE REPEATED) NR
(— WANTED) DETROP SUPERFLUOUS
(ALMOST —) SCARCELY
(COULD —) NOTE
NOTABLE VIP FINE FABLED FAMOUS
GIFTED NOTARY SIGNAL UNIQUE
EMINENT STORIED SUBLIME DISTINCT
ESPECIAL EVENTFUL HISTORIC
MEMORABLE NOTORIOUS NOTEWORTHY
NOTARY NOTAR GRAFFER GREFFIER
NOTEBOOK OBSERVER OFFICIAL
SCRIVENER
NOTARY PUBLIC TABELLION
NOTATION HOLD MEMO NOTE ENTRY
SYSTEM MARKING
(PHONETIC —) ROMIC
NOTCH CUT DAG DAP GAP HAG JAG JOG
PEG COPE DENT DINT GAIN GIMP KERF
MUSH NICK NOCK SLOT SNIP STEP
WARD CRENA GABEL GRADE HILUM
SCORE SHARD SHERD SWICK TALLY
CRENEL CROTCH DEFILE DEGREE
HOLLOW INDENT JOGGLE RAFFLE
RECORD SCOTCH CRENATE GUDGEON
SERRATE INCISION
(— BETWEEN HILLS) SLAP
(— ON VERTEBRAE) HYPANTRUM
(— TO FELL TREE) UNDERCUT
NOTCHED EROSE JAGGY RAGULY
SERRATE CRENATED
NOTE BON DOG IOU JOT SEE TEN UNE
BILL CARD CENT CHIT ESPY FAME FLAT
HEED MARK MEMO NAME NOIT SIGN
SOLE SONG TENT TONE TUNE VIEW
CHECK FIVER GLOZE LABEL PRICK SHORT
SIXTH SOUND STIFF TENTH TOKEN
TWANG ATTEND BILLET DEGREE EXCUSE
FIGURA FLIMSY LETTER MELODY MINUTE
NOTICE POLICY RECORD REGARD
REMARK RENOWN REPORT SECOND
STRAIN TENNER BETOKEN COMMENT
DISCORD MESSAGE MISSIVE NATURAL
OBSERVE PUNCTUS REDBACK ANNOTATE
BLUEBACK BRADBURY BREVIATE
DISPATCH EMINENCE MARGINAL
PERCEIVE POSTFACE TREASURY
GREENBACK POSTSCRIPT
(— FROM TRAIN) BUTTERFLY
(— OF ASSAULT) WARISON
(— OF HUMOR) TRAIT
(— OF SCALE) DO FA LA MI RE SI SO TI
UT ARE SOL
(— OF SNIPE) SCAPE
(— OF WARNING) WATCHWORD
(— ON SHOPHAR) TEKIAH
(— TO RECALL DOG) FORLOIN
(—S ON HUNTING HORN) SEEK
(ALTERED —) ACCIDENTAL
(BANK —S) CABBAGE
(BASS —) DRONE

(BIRD'S —) JUG CHIRP
(BUGLE —) MOT
(EIGHTH —) UNCA QUAVER
(EMBELLISHING —) ORNAMENT
(ESCAPE —) ECHAPPEE
(EXPLANATORY —) ANAGRAPH
SCHOLIUM ANNOTATION
(FUNDAMENTAL —) ROOT
(GRACE —) NACHSCHLAG
(HALF —) MINIM
(HARSH —) BLOB
(HIGHEST —) ELA
(HIGH-PITCHED —) BEEP
(LEADING —) SUBTONIC
(LONG —) LARGE
(LOVE —) POULET
(LOWEST —) KEY GAMUT
(MARGINAL —) TOT QUOTE POSTIL
APOSTIL
(MUSICAL —) ALT RAY MESE MIND
BREVE GAMUT SHARP ALAMIRE
MEDIANT PUNCTUS LICHANOS
PARAMESE PIZZICATO
(NONHARMONIC —) CAMBIATA
(POUND —) BRADBURY
(PROMISSORY —) DOG GOOD HUNDI
CEDULA ASSIGNAT
(QUARTER —) CROTCHET SEMIMINIM
(SIXTEENTH —) DEMIQUAVER
SEMIQUAVER
(SIXTY-FOURTH —)
HEMIDEMISEMIQUAVER
(THIRTY-SECOND —) SUBSEMIFUSA
DEMISEMIQUAVER
(TWO —S) DUPLET
(WARBLING —) CHIRL
(WHOLE —) SEMIBREVE
(100-POUND —) CENTURY
NOTEBOOK LOG DIARY NOTARY RECORD
STREET JOURNAL
NOTECASE WALLET POCKETBOOK
NOTED COUTH FAMED GREAT NAMELY
EMINENT INSIGNE RENOWNED
DISTINGUE
NOTEWORTHY BIG SOLEMN EMINENT
NOTABLE SALIENT SPECIAL BODACIOUS
MEMORABLE OBSERVABLE
NOTHING NIL NIX FREE LUKE NILL WIND
ZERO AUGHT BLANK NIHIL ZILCH CIPHER
NAUGHT NOBODY NOUGHT TRIFLE
NULLITY SCRATCH USELESS BAGATELLE
NOTICE AD BAN SEE ESPY CALL ESPY
GAUM GOME HEED IDEA KEEP MARK
MIND NEWS NOTE PIPE RIDE SIGN SPOT
TWIG ALARM AWAIT COUNT FLOAT
NOTAM ORDER QUOTE ADVICE ALLUDE
BILLET ESPIAL NOTION PERMIT READER
REGARD REMARK REWARD AFFICHE
ARTICLE DISCERN MENTION OBSERVE
PLACARD PROGRAM WARNING
MONITION PERCEIVE WITTERING
(— UNEXPECTEDLY) CATCH
(ADVANCE —) HERALDRY
PREMONITION
(COMMENDATORY —) PUFF BLURB
(DEATH —) OBIT OBITUARY
(FAVORABLE —) RAVE

(LEGAL —) CAVEAT
(MARRIAGE —) BANS BANNS
(OFFICIAL —) EDICT SUMMONS
BULLETIN CITATION
(PUBLIC —) BAN EDICT BULLETIN
SPOTLIGHT
NOTICEABLE CRUDE GROSS FLASHY
MARKED SIGNAL EVIDENT NOTABLE
POINTED SALIENT HANDSOME PALPABLE
STRIKING OBTRUSIVE PROMINENT
CONSPICUOUS OUTSTANDING
NOTIFY ALL BID CRY JOG CITE PAGE TELL
WARN ADVISE INFORM NOTICE SIGNAL
APPRISE DECLARE FRUTIFY PUBLISH
ACQUAINT INTIMATE
NOTION BEE GEE BUZZ IDEA IDEE KINK
MAZE OMEN VIEW WHIM FANCY IMAGE
SENSE THING WARES BELIEF CEMENT
DESIRE DONNEE GADGET MAGGOT
NOTICE THEORY VAGARY BROMIDE
CONCEIT CONCEPT FANTASY INKLING
MAROTTE OPINION THOUGHT WRINKLE
CATEGORY FOLKLORE PHANTASY
SUPPOSAL WHIMWHAM INTENTION
SENTIMENT WHIRLIGIG
(FALSE —) IDOL
(FIXED —) TICK
(FOOLISH —) VAPOR
(PUERILE —) BOYISM
(SUPERSTITIOUS —) FREIT
(VISIONARY —) ABSTRACTION
NOTORIETY FAME ECLAT GLORY HONOR
RUMOR RENOWN REPUTE PUBLICITY
NOTORIOUS BIG KNOWN ARRANT
COMMON CRYING FAMOUS NOTARY
STRONG EVIDENT NOTABLE NOTOIRE
APPARENT FLAGRANT INFAMOUS
MANIFEST EGREGIOUS
NOTWITHSTANDING BUT FOR THO
YET EVEN WITH MAUGER MAUGRE
AGAINST DESPITE HOWBEIT HOWEVER
ALTHOUGH
NOUGHT BAD NIL NOT NOWT ZERO
NOCHT WRONG NOTHING USELESS
WORTHLESS
NOUN MANE WORD THING SUPINE
NOMINAL CONSTRUCT INCREASER
(INDECLINABLE —) APTOTE
(KIND OF —) COMMON PROPER
DIPTOTE REGULAR TRIPTOTE
MONOPTOTE
(QUOTATION —) HYPOSTASIS
(VERBAL —) GERUND
NOURISH AID FEED FOOD GROW BREED
NORSH NURSE TRAIN BATTLE BREAST
FOISON FOSTER NORICE REFETE SUCCOR
SUCKLE SUPPLY CHERISH DEVELOP
EDUCATE NURTURE NUTRIFY PROVIDE
SUPPORT SUSTAIN MAINTAIN
CULTIVATE REPLENISH STIMULATE
NOURISHING ALMA RICH ALIBLE
BATTLE HEARTY STRONG NUTRIENT
ALIMENTAL HEALTHFUL NUTRITIVE
WHOLESOME NUTRITIOUS
NOURISHMENT DIET FARE CIBE FOOD
KEEP MEAT MANNA FOISON FOSTER

ALIMENT PABULUM PASTURE
NUTRIMENT REFECTION

NOVA SCOTIA (CAPITAL OF —)
HALIFAX
(COUNTY OF —) DIGBY HANTS PICTOU
(STRAIT OF —) CANSO
(TOWN OF —) TRURO PICTOU SYDNEY
ARICHAT BADDECK DARTMOUTH

NOVA SCOTIAN ACADIAN BLUENOSE

NOVEL HOT NEW BOOK EPIC RARE FRESH
PROSE RECIT ROMAN STORY DARING
RECENT SERIAL THRILL FICTION
ROMANCE STRANGE UNUSUAL NEOTERIC
ORIGINAL THRILLER UNCOMMON
NARRATIVE PAPERBACK
(BRIEF —) CONTE

NOVELTY FAD NEWEL RENEW CHANGE
NEWNESS PRIMEUR WRINKLE CURIOSITY
FRESHNESS

NOVICE DUB HAM BOOT COLT PUNK
PUNY TIRO TYRO CHELA GOYIN PUPIL
YOUTH DRONGO RABBIT ROOKIE
ACOLYTE AMATEUR CONVERT GRIFFIN
LEARNER STARTER STUDENT YOUNKER
BACHELOR BEGINNER FRESHMAN
INEXPERT NEOPHYTE ARCHARIOS
GREENHORN NOVITIATE ABECEDARIAN

NOW NOO YET HERE ARRAH NONCE
SINCE TODAY EVENOO EXTANT
ANYMORE CURRENT INSTANT PRESENT
FORTHWITH PRESENTLY
(— AND THEN) SOMETIMES
STOUNDMEAL
(BUT —) ERSTWHILE
(JUST —) ENOW FRESH

NOXIOUS BAD ILL EVIL FETID DEADLY
NOCENT NOYOUS PUTRID BALEFUL
BANEFUL DAMPISH HARMFUL HURTFUL
NOCUOUS NOISOME SCADDLE TEDIOUS
VICIOUS INFAMOUS VIRULENT
INJURIOUS MIASMATIC OFFENSIVE
PESTILENT POISONOUS PERNICIOUS

NOZZE DI FIGARO, LE
(CHARACTER IN —) FIGARO BARTOLO
BASILIO SUSANNA BARBARINA
CHERUBINO MARCELLINA
(COMPOSER OF —) MOZART

NOZZLE BIB JET TIP BEAK BIBB NOSE
ROSE VENT GIANT SNOUT SPOUT TWEER
GROVEL OUTLET MONITOR NIAGARA
ORIFICE SHUTOFF ADJUTAGE ROSEHEAD
VERMOREL NOSEPIECE
(BLAST FURNACE —) TUYERE
(MINING —) GIANT

NUANCE SHADE NICETY FINESSE
GRADATION VARIATION

NUB EAR HUB JAB JAG KEY NOB CORE
CRUX GIST HANG KNOB KNOT KNUB
LUMP NECK PITH SNAG HEART NUDGE
POINT KERNEL NUBBIN EXECUTE

NUBBIN EAR STUB STUMP

NUCLEOSIDE VICINE INOSINE CYTIDINE
ADENOSINE

NUCLEUS HUB CELL CORE GERM KERN
PITH ROOT SEED CADRE FOCUS HEART
MIDST SPERM CENTER COLONY DEUTON

KERNEL MIDDLE ISOTOPE NIDULUS
HABENULA MEROCYTE MESOPLAST
(— OF CELL) KARYON
(— OF STARCH GRAIN) HILUM
(— OF SUNSPOT) UMBRA
(ATOMIC —) SPECIES
(CELL —) SYNCARYON HEMIKARYON

NUDE BARE LOOSE NAKED NAKED
SEASAN STATUE UNCLAD DENUDED
EXPOSED PICTURE PAINTING STARKERS
STRIPPED UNDRESSED

NUDGE JOG NOG NUB WAG GOAD JOLT
KNUB LUMP POKE POTE PROD PUSH
BLOCK CHUCK DUNCH ELBOW

NUDIST ADAMITE NUDIFIER GYMNOSOPH

NUGGET EYE LOB GOLD HUNK LUMP
MASS SLUG PRILL YELLOW

NUISANCE BANE BORE EVIL HARM HURT
PAIN PEST STING INJURY PLAGUE
TERROR VEXATION ANNOYANCE

NULL NIL VOID EMPTY INEPT IRRITE
INVALID NULLIFY USELESS VACUOUS
NUGATORY FRUSTRATE

NULLIFY BEAT FLAW LAME NULL UNDO
VETO VOID ABATE ANNUL ELIDE ERASE
LAPSE CANCEL DEFEAT NEGATE OFFSET
REPEAL REVOKE ABOLISH COUNTER
DESTROY ABROGATE EVACUATE
STULTIFY FRUSTRATE

NUMB DEAD DRUG DULL DAZED FUNNY
STONY ASLEEP BENUMB CLUMSY
DEADEN STUPID TORPID STUPEFY
ENFEEBLE HEBETATE HELPLESS
RIGESCENT TABETLESS

NUMBER SUM BAND BODY COPY DRAW
LOTS MANY MESS TALE TELL COUNT
DATUM DIGIT FOLIE GRIST GROUP INDEX
ISSUE SCORE STAND TOTAL WHOLE
ADDEND AMOUNT BUNDLE CIPHER
ENCORE FACTOR FIGURE FILLER POLICY
RECKON SCALAR TICHEL CHIFFER
COMPUTE DECIMAL DIVISOR FOLIATE
NUMERIC SEVERAL CARDINAL FRACTION
NUMERATE QUANTITY CALCULATE
MAGNITUDE MULTITUDE MULTIPLIER
MULTIPLICAND
(— BETWEEN 4 AND 10) MAIN
(— OF ARROWS) END
(— OF ATOMS) CHAIN
(— OF BEASTS) HERD
(— OF BOMBS) STICK
(— OF BRICKS) CLAMP
(— OF CATTLE) SOUM
(— OF FUR SKINS) TIMBER
(— OF HANKS OF YARN TO POUND)
COUNT
(— OF HAWKS) CAST
(— OF HONEYBEES) CLUSTER
(— OF NEEDLES) GAGE GAUGE
(— OF POEMS) EPOS
(— OF SHEARERS) BOARD
(— OF TEA CHESTS) BREAK
(— OF THREADS PER INCH) PITCH
(— OF TRICKS) BOOK
(— OF WORDS) FOLIO
(— THROWN IN CRAPS) POINT
(COMPLEX —) IMAGINARY

(CONSIDERABLE —) WHEEN HATFUL
FISTFUL
(EXCESS —) ADVANTAGE
(EXCESSIVE —) SPATE
(EXTRA —) ENCORE
(GOLDEN —) PRIME
(GOOD —) THRAVE
(GREAT —) HEAP HOST LAKH MORT
BREAK HIRST MEINY POWER SHOAL
SIGHT SWARM LEGION MYRIAD INFINITE
INFINITY THOUSAND MULTITUDE
MULTIPLICITY
(GREAT —S) FLOCKS
(INDEFINITE —) STEEN SUNDRY
THRAVE JILLION SEVERAL UMPTEEN
(IRRATIONAL —) SURD
(LARGE —) ARMY FECK HERD HOST
LUMP PECK SLEW ARRAY CROWD FORCE
POWER SCADS SHEAF SPATE STACK
STORE WORLD GALLON GOOGOL HIRSEL
LEGION MELDER BILLION JILLION
PLURALITY
(LARGE —S) STRENGTH
(LEAF —) FOLIO
(LEAST WHOLE —) UNIT
(ODD —S) IMPAIR
(OPPOSITE —) COUSIN
(SMALL —) FEW CURN HANDFUL
PAUCITY SPATTER
(TOTAL —) AMOUNT
(VAST —) HORDE
(WHOLE —) ALL DIGIT INTEGER
NUMBNESS STUPOR TORPOR STUPIDITY
NUMERAL (ALSO SEE NUMBER) SUM
WORD DIGIT CIPHER FIGURE LETTER
CHAPTER NUMERIC
(CLOCK —) CHAPTER
NUMEROUS BIG LOTS MANY RANK RIFE
GREAT LARGE STOUR DIVERS GALORE
LEGION MYRIAD SUNDRY UNRIDE
COPIOUS CROWDED ENDLESS FEARFUL
FERTILE PROFUSE SEVERAL TEEMING
UMPTEEN ABUNDANT FREQUENT
MANIFOLD MULTIPLE POPULOUS
THRONGED EXTENSIVE MULTIFOLD
NUMBERFUL PLENTIFUL
(— AND POWERFUL) MAIN
(MODERATELY —) FAIR
(VERY —) EXCESSIVE
(PREF.) MYRI
NUMSKULL NUM DAFF DOLT FLAT
BOOBY DUNCE LACKWIT BONEHEAD
BLOCKHEAD LAMEBRAIN
NUN BIRD SMEW CLARE CLERK MONIAL
PIGEON SISTER TERESA VESTAL VOWESS
CLUNIAC CONFINE DEANESS DEVOTEE
EXTERNE MINCHEN MONKESS RECLUSE
THEATIN BASILIAN CHAPLAIN CLARISSE
PRIORESS TITMOUSE URBANIST
URSULINE VISITANT VOTARESS
ANGELICAL CARMELITE LORETTINE
PRIESTESS RELIGEUSE
(CHIEF —) ABBA ABBESS MOTHER
(LATIN —) VESTA
NUNNERY ABBEY NUNRY CONVENT
CLOISTER MINCHERY

(HEAD OF —) ABBESS
NUPTIAL BRIDAL GENIAL THORAL
MARITAL WEDDING ESPOUSAL
HYMENEAL MARRIAGE
NURSE AMAH AYAH BABA CARE FEED
NANA NUSS REAR SUCK TEND BONNE
MAMMY NANNY NORSH ATTEND
BAYMAN CRADLE FOMENT FOSTER
GRANNY KEEPER NANNIE NORICE
NUZZLE SISTER SITTER SUCKLE UMFAAN
CHERISH FURTHER NOURISH NURTURE
PROMOTE CULTIVATE ENCOURAGE
NURSEMAID
(— A GRIEVANCE) SULK
(— OF HIAWATHA) NOKOMIS
(— OF ULYSSES) EURYCLEA
(— OF ZEUS) AMALTHEA CYNOSURA
(GULLIVER'S —) GLUMDALCLITCH
(WET —) DHAI DHOLL
NURSERY RACE CRECHE BROODER
FOSTERAGE
NURTURE CARE DIET FEED FOOD REAR
TEND BREED NURSE TRAIN COCKER
CRADLE FOSTER NUZZLE CHERISH
EDUCATE SUPPORT BREEDING NORTELRY
TRAINING EDUCATION ESTABLISH
NUTRIMENT
(PREF.) TROPH(O)
NUT ACA BEN BUR COB GUY JOU NIT TAP
ANTA BURR COLA CORE DOLT FOOL
HEAD KOLA LORE MAST NITE PILI PITH
SEED TASK ACORN BETEL BONGA
BUNGA CRANK FLAKE FRUIT GLANS
HAZEL HICAN JUVIA PECAN TRYMA
ALMOND BONDUC BRAZIL CASHEW
FELLOW HICCAN ILLIPE KERNEL PEANUT
PINION PYRENE CASTANA FILBERT
HICKORY PROBLEM APPLENUT
BEECHNUT BREADNUT CHESTNUT
GOORANUT LARRIKIN CAPOTASTO
CHINKAPIN ECCENTRIC MACADAMIA
PHILOPENA
(— OF VIOLIN BOW) FROG
(— PINE) PIGNON PINOON PIGNOLIA
(CASHEW —) SEDGE ANACARD
(CONSORT OF —) GEB KEB SET
(DAUGHTER OF —) ISIS NEPHTHYS
(FALLEN —S) SHACK
(PALM —) BETEL LICHI BABASSU
COCOANUT COQUILLA
(RIPE —) LEAMER
(RUSH —) CHUFA
(SON OF —) RA OSIRIS
NUTHATCH SITTA TOMTIT XENOPS
JARBIRD SITTINE TITMOUSE NUTJOBBER
NUTRIMENT DIET FOOD KEEP VIANDS
ALIMENT PABULUM SU'PPORT
NOURISHMENT
NUTRITION EUTROPHY TROPHISM
(IMPERFECT —) DYSTROPHY
DYSTROPHIA
(PREF.) TROPH(O)
(SUFF.) TROPHIA TROPHIC TROPHY
NUTRITIOUS BAITTLE TROPHIC
NUTTY GAGA LOCO NUTS RACY ZANY
BUGGY CRAZY QUEER SPICY FRUITY

LOVING SPRUCE AMOROUS FOOLISH
PIQUANT ZESTFUL DEMENTED PLEASANT
ECCENTRIC FLAVORFUL
NUZZLE DIG PET ROOT NURSE SNUFF
BURROW CARESS FONDLE FOSTER
NESTLE NUDDLE NURTURE SNOOZLE
SNUGGLE SNUZZLE
NYMPH FLY GIRL MAIA MITE MUSE PINK
PIXY PUPA TICK AEGLE HOURI LARVA
NIXIE SYLPH BYBLIS CYRENE DAMSEL
DAPHNE HELICE HESTIA KELPIE MAIDEN
SPRITE CORYCIA ERYTHEA HESPERA
LIRIOPE CALLISTO CYNOSURA EURYDICE
MARPESSA PROSOPON BUTTERFLY
HAMADRYAD
(— BELOVED BY PAN) SYRINX
(— BELOVED OF NARCISSUS) ECHO
(— OF FOUNTAIN) EGERIA SALMACIS
(— OF HILLS) OREAD
(— OF MEADOWS) LIMONIAD

(— OF MESSINA STRAIT) SCYLLA
(— OF MT. IDA) OENONE
(CITY —) POLIAD
(LAKE —) NAIAD LIMNIAD
(OCEAN —) SIREN GALATEA OCEANID
SEAMAID
(QUEEN OF —S) MAB
(RIVER —) NAIS NAIAD
(SEA —) MERROW NEREID CALYPSO
GALATEA MERMAID
(WATER —) NAIS EGERIA LURLEI
UNDINE APSARAS HYDRIAD JUTURNA
RUSALKA EPHYDRIAD
(WOOD —) DRYAD NAPEA ARETHUSA
NYX NIGHT
(— PERSONIFIED) NIGHT
(BROTHER OF —) EREBUS
(DAUGHTER OF —) DAY ERIS LIGHT
(HUSBAND OF —) CHAOS
(SON OF —) CHARON

O

O HO OH OCH ZERO CIPHER OMICRON

OAF BOOR DOLT FOOL LOUT CLOWN DUNCE IDIOT YOKEL MUCKER NASHGAB PALOOKA POMPION BLOCKHEAD FOUNDLING SCHLEMIEL SIMPLETON

OAK CLUB CORK HOLM ILEX BRAVE BRIAR EMORY HOLLY ROBUR ACAJOU BAREEN CERRIS ENCINA KERMES STRONG TOUMEY VALOMA BELLOTA BELLOTE DURMAST EGILOPS KELLOGG PALAYAN TURTOSA BEEFWOOD BLUEJACK CHAMPION CHAPARRO WAINSCOT BLACKJACK CHINKAPIN QUERCITRON
(JERUSALEM —) AMBROSE
(WHITE —) ROBLE
(YOUNG —) FLITTERN

OAR AIR BOW PLY ROW POLE ALOOF BLADE RANGE SPOON SWAPE SWEEP YULOH PADDLE PALLET PROPEL OARSMAN PROPELLER
(— BLADE) PALM PEEL WASH
(— FULCRUM) LOCK THOLE OARLOCK ROWLOCK
(BOW —) GOUGER
(HANDLE OF —) GRASP
(INBOARD PORTION OF —) LOOM

OARLOCK LOCK THOLE ROWLOCK

OARSMAN OAR REMEX ROWER BOWMAN STROKE BENCHER SCULLER WATERMAN

OASIS BAR OJO SPA MERV SIWA WADI SPRING

OAT AIT WOT FEED FOOD PIPE POEM SKEG SONG AUCHT CHEAT GRAIN HAVER PEARL ANGORA EGILOPS
(EDIBLE PORTION OF —) GROATS
(FALSE WILD —S) FATUOID
(HUSKED —) SHEALING
(NAKED —) PILLAS PILCORN
(UNTHRASHED —) OATHAY
(WILD —S) HAVERGRASS

OATH OD ADS BAN DAD DOD GAD GAR GOL GOR GUM ODD SAM VOW BOND CRUM CUSS DARN DRAT ECOD EGAD GEEZ GOSH HECK JEEZ JING NIGS OONS SANG SLID SLUD WORD BEDAD BEGAD BEGOB BLIMY CURSE DAMME DEUCE GOLLY HOKEY MORDU PARDY SACRE SFOOT SLIFE SNIGS SWEAR YERRA ADSBUD APPEAL CRACKY CRIKEY CRIPES CRUMBS FEALTY JABERS JERNIE NEAKES PARDIE PLEDGE RAPPER SBLOOD SLIGHT STRUTH ZOUNDS BEGORRA BEGORRY BEJESUS BYRLADY CORBLEU GADSLID GEEWHIZ GEEWIZZ JEEPERS JIMMINY MORBLEU ODSFISH ODZOOKS PROMISE THUNDER ANATHEMA BEJABERS BODYKINS CRICKETY GADZOOKS JURAMENT PITIKINS SANCTION SEREMENT SNIGGERS SPLUTTER AFFIDAVIT BEJABBERS BLASPHEMY DODGASTED EXPLETIVE PROFANITY SACRAMENT SLIDIKINS SWEARWORD

OATMEAL OATS STODGE YELLOW POTTAGE DRAMMOCK PORRIDGE

OBADIAH ABDIAS
(FATHER OF —) AZEL JEHIEL SHEMAIAH
(SON OF —) ISHMAIAH

OBDURATE FIRM HARD BALKY HARSH INERT ROCKY ROUGH STARK STONY DOGGED INURED MULISH RUGGED SEVERE STURDY SULLEN ADAMANT CALLOUS HARDENED PERVERSE STUBBORN IMPASSIVE UNBENDING

OBED (FATHER OF —) BOAZ JARHA SHEMAIAH
(MOTHER OF —) RUTH
(SON OF —) JESSE AZARIAH

OBEDIENCE ORDER FEALTY CONTROL SERVICE DOCILITY OBEISANCE

OBEDIENT BENT RULY TALL TAME BUXOM DOCILE PLIANT DEVOTED DUTEOUS DUTIFUL HEEDFUL MINDFUL ORDERLY SUBJECT AMENABLE BIDDABLE YIELDING ATTENTIVE OBSERVING SERVIABLE TRACTABLE

OBEISANCE BOW LEG JOUK BINGE CONGE HONOR SALAM CONGEE CRINGE CURTSY FEALTY HOMAGE SALAAM CURTSEY DEFERENCE HUMBLESSO REFERENCE

OBELISK MARK PYLON SHAFT DAGGER GUGLIA GUGLIO NEEDLE OBELUS PILLAR AGUGLIA MONUMENT HAGIOLITH

OBERON KING POEM FAIRY OPERA SATELLITE
(CHARACTER IN —) HUON PUCK FATIMA OBERON TITANIA SHERASMIN
(COMPOSER OF —) WEBER
(WIFE OF —) TITANIA

OBESE FAT FOZY PLUMP PUDGY PUFFY PURSY STOUT FLESHY PORTLY PYKNIC ROTUND TURGID ADIPOSE PORCINE PURSIVE BLUBBERY LIPAROUS CORPULENT

OBESITY FAT FATNESS LIPOSIS ADIPOSIS FOZINESS ADIPOSITY

OBEY EAR HEAR HEED MIND DEFER YIELD COMPLY FOLLOW SUBMIT CONFORM EXECUTE OBSERVE
(— HELM) STEER

OBJECT AIM END TAP BALK BEEF CARE CARP FINE GOAL IDEA ITEM KICK MIND PASS SAKE WHAT ARGUE CAVIL DEMUR GRIPE PINCH POINT SCOPE SIGHT TELOS THING AFFAIR DESIGN EMBLEM ENTITY FIGURE GADGET INTENT MATTER MOTIVE

OPPOSE TARGET ARTICLE DINGBAT
DISLIKE DISSENT MEANING PROTEST
PURPOSE QUARREL REALITY RECLAIM
NOUMENON TENDENCY CHALLENGE
INTENTION SPECTACLE
(— OF AMBITION) MAIN
(— OF ART) VASE CURIO VIRTU
ANTIQUE BIBELOT FIGURINE
(— OF CRITICISM) BUTT
(— OF DEVOTION) IDOL TOTEM FETISH
(— OF DISGUST) UG
(— OF DREAD) BOGEY BUGBEAR
(— OF PURSUIT) SHADOW
(— OF RELIANCE) STAY
(— OF RIDICULE) FUN GAME
(— OF SCORN) GECK SCOFF BYWORD
HISSING DERISION
(— OF TERROR) BUG
(— OF THOUGHT) CONSTRUCT
(— OF WONDER) ADMIRATION
(BELOVED —) MINION DARLING
MISTRESS
(BULKY —) WODGE
(CONICAL —) ACORN
(CONSPICUOUS —) LANDMARK
(CURVED —) BELLY
(CYLINDRICAL —) BOLE
(DECORATIVE —) BIBELOT
(DESIRABLE —) GRAIL
(FACTORY-MADE —S) ARTWORK
(MINUTE —) ATOM MITE
(ROUND —) COB RONDEL TRINDLE
TRUNDLE
(SACRED —) URIM ZOGO GUACA
HUACA SHRINE CHURINGA
(SILLY —) INANITY
(SMALL —) PIRLIE
(TRANSCENDENTAL —) ENTITY
(ULTIMATE —) TELOS
(UNIDENTIFIED FLYING —) BOGEY
(VILE —S) SCUM
(WORTHLESS —) SPLINTER
OBJECTION BAR BUT BEEF CRAB FUSS
KICK CAVIL DEMUR DOUBT BOGGLE
QUARREL QUIBBLE SCRUPLE QUESTION
CHALLENGE CRITICISM EXCEPTION
OBJECTIONABLE VILE AWFUL HORRID
GHASTLY UNLIKELY FRIGHTFUL
OBNOXIOUS OFFENSIVE
OBJECTIVE AIM END FAIR GAME GOAL
HOME REAL SAKE OUTER ACTUAL
AMORAL ANIMUS DESIGN MOTIVE
TARGET PURPOSE DETACHED TANGIBLE
UNBIASED DIRECTION INTENTION
POSITIVAL QUAESITUM ULTIMATUM
OBLATION CORBAN OFLETE SACRED
CHARITY ANAPHORA DEVOTION
OFFERING SACRIFICE
OBLIGATE COMMIT STRICT
OBLIGATED BOUND LIABLE BEHOLDEN
OBLIGATION DUE IOU TIE VOW BAIL
BAND CALL DEBT KNOT LOAD LOAN
MUST NOTE OATH ONUS SEAL CHECK
OUGHT SCORE ARREAR BURDEN CHARGE
CONSOL CORVEE FEALTY PLEDGE
ANNUITY BONDAGE PROMISE TRIBUTE

CONTRACT HYPOTHEC SECURITY
WARRANTY AGREEMENT LIABILITY
(— NOT TO MARRY) CELIBACY
(— TO RENDER RENT) CUSTOM
(MORAL —) BOND DUTY
(PL.) STRINGS
OBLIGATORY BINDING BOUNDEN
FORCIBLE IMPOSING LIGATORY
INCUMBENT MANDATORY
OBLIGE PUT HOLD PAWN DRIVE FAVOR
FORCE COMPEL ENGAGE PLEASE
GRATIFY REQUIRE CONCLUDE
MORTGAGE OBLIGATE CONSTRAIN
ACCOMMODATE
OBLIGED FAIN BOUND DEBTED BOUNDEN
DEBTFUL FAVORED PLEASED PLEDGED
BEHOLDEN GRATEFUL OBSTRICT
BEHOLDING OBLIGATED
OBLIGING KIND BUXOM CIVIL CLEVER
TOWARD AMIABLE FAVOROUS
AGREEABLE COURTEOUS FAVORABLE
OFFICIOUS
OBLIQUE AWRY BIAS SIDE SKEW ASKEW
BEVEL CROSS SLANT ASLANT ASWASH
LOUCHE SQUINT THWART ASKANCE
AWKWARD CROOKED EMBELIF EVASIVE
SCALENE SIDLING SLOPING DIAGONAL
INCLINED INDIRECT SIDELONG SIDEWAYS
SIDEWISE SLANTING TORTUOUS
INDICULAR UNDERHAND
(— IN MINING) CLINIC
(— STROKE) SLASH SOLIDUS
OBLITERATE INK BLOT DELE RASE RAZE
WIPE ANNUL BLACK COVER ERASE
SMEAR CANCEL DELETE EFFACE SPONGE
ABOLISH DESTROY EXPUNGE OUTRAZE
SCRATCH OVERSCORE
OBLIVION LETHE LIMBO PARDON
AMNESTY NIRVANA SILENCE
OBLIVIOUS AMORT BLISSFUL HEEDLESS
FORGETFUL
OBNOXIOUS FOUL PERT VILE CURST
CURSED FAULTY HORRID LIABLE ODIOUS
RANCID SEPTIC HATEFUL INVIDIOUS
OFFENSIVE REPUGNANT VERMINOUS
OBOE PIPE REED WAIT AULOS SHAWM
SURNAY HAUTBOY MUSETTE PIFFERO
CHIRIMIA HAUTBOIS SCHALMEY
SZOPELKA CHALUMEAU
OBSCENE FOUL LEWD BAWDY GROSS
NASTY ROCKY COARSE FILTHY IMPURE
RIBALD SMUTTY VULGAR KNAVISH
PROFANE IMMODEST INDECENT
LOATHSOME OFFENSIVE REPULSIVE
SALACIOUS
OBSCURE DIM FOG BLOT BLUR DARK
DEEP HARD HART HAZY HIDE PALE SLUP
BEDIM BEFOG BLACK BLANK BLEND
BLIND CLOUD COVER DUSKY FAINT
FOGGY GLOOM INNER LOWLY MIRKY
MISTY MUDDY MURKY SHADE SMEAR
STAIN VAGUE BEMIST CLOUDY DARKEN
DARKLE DEADEN DELUDE GLOOMY
HUMBLE MYSTIC OCCULT OPAQUE
REMOTE SHADOW SOMBER SUBTLE
BECLOUD BENIGHT CLOUDED CONCEAL
CONFUSE CRABBED CRYPTIC ECLIPSE

ENCRUST ENVELOP OBLIQUE OVERLAY OVERTOP SHADOWY SLUBBER TARNISH UNCLEAR UNKNOWN UNNOTED ABSTRUSE DARKLING DISGUISE DOUBTFUL FAMELESS MYSTICAL NAMELESS NUBILOUS OBSTRUSE ORACULAR OVERSILE CALIGINOUS

OBSCURED HAZY HIDDEN BLINDED CLOUDED DUSKISH DARKSOME DISGUISED INFUSCATE

OBSCURITY FOG MIST CLOUD GLOOM SHADE SHADOW DIMNESS OPACITY PRIVACY SILENCE DARKNESS TENEBRES BLINDNESS SECLUSION

OBSEQUIOUS MENIAL SUPPLE COURTLY DEVOTED DUTEOUS DUTIFUL FAWNING SERVILE SLAVISH CRINGING OBEDIENT OBEISANT TOADYING COMPLIANT

OBSERVANCE ACT FORM RITE RULE FREET HONOR CUSTOM REGARD KEEPING CEREMONY PRACTICE ADHERENCE ATTENTION DEFERENCE INDICTION SOLEMNITY
(— OF PROPRIETIES) DECORUM BREEDING ETIQUETTE
(RELIGIOUS —) NOVENA SACRAMENT
(REVERENTIAL —) PUJA

OBSERVANT ALERT EYEFUL CAREFUL HEEDFUL MINDFUL DILIGENT VIGILANT WATCHFUL REGARDFUL PERCEPTIVE

OBSERVATION EYE SPY HEED IDEA NOTE VIEW SIGHT WATCH ESPIAL NOTICE REGARD REMARK AUSPICE AUTOPSY COMMENT CONTACT DESCANT OPINION EYESIGHT ASSERTION ATTENTION ESPIONAGE COGNIZANCE PERCEPTION
(— BY BALLOON) PIBAL
(ECOLOGICAL —S) ANNUATION
(PRELIMINARY —) PROEM

OBSERVATORY LICK TOWER LOOKOUT PALOMAR

OBSERVE LO EYE SEE SPY ESPY HEED HOLD KEEP LOOK MAKE MARK MIND NARK NOTA NOTE OBEY SPOT TENT TOUT TWIG WAIT YEME ABIDE QUOTE STUDY UTTER WATCH ADHERE ADVERT ATHOLD BEHOLD DETECT DEVISE FOLLOW NOTICE NOTIFY REGARD REMARK SURVEY COMMENT DISCERN EXPRESS MENTION PROFESS RESPECT WITNESS PERCEIVE PRESERVE SPECTATE ADVERTISE CELEBRATE SOLEMNIZE
(— CLOSELY) SMOKE
(— DULLY) BLEAR

OBSERVER WATCHER AUDIENCE INFORMER ONLOOKER BYSTANDER SCRUTATOR SPECTATOR

OBSESS RIDE BESET HAUNT HARASS INVEST BESIEGE HAGRIDE POSSESS PREOCCUPY

OBSESSED CRAZY DOTTY HAPPY HIPPED BESOTTED

OBSESSION TIC CRAZE MANIA SIEGE MAGGOT ECSTASY FIXATION

OBSOLETE OLD DEAD PAST DATED PASSE BYGONE EFFETE ANCIENT ARCHAIC CLASSIC DISUSED EFFACED EXTINCT OUTWORN OUTDATED OUTMODED OVERWORN DISCARDED

OBSTACLE BAR DAM LET BUMP DRAG JUMP SNAG STAY STOP BLOCK CHECK CLAMP CRIMP FENCE HITCH SPOKE STICK STILE ABATIS BUNKER HURDLE LOGJAM OBJECT RETARD BARRIER STOPPER BLOCKADE MOLEHILL BARRICADE CONDITION HINDRANCE ROADBLOCK

OBSTETRICS TOCOLOGY MAIEUTICS MIDWIFERY

OBSTINACY BRASS CONTUMACY

OBSTINATE SET SOT DOUR FIRM SULY BALKY FIXED ROWDY RUSTY STIFF STOUT TOUGH ASSISH CUSSED DOGGED KNOBBY MULISH STEEVE STUFFY STUPID STURDY SULLEN UNRULY ASININE BULLISH CRABBED FROWARD PEEVISH RESTIVE WILLFUL CROTCHED OBDURATE PERVERSE STUBBORN PIGHEADED STONEWALL TENACIOUS

OBSTREPEROUS LOUD WILD NOISY UNRULY CLAMOROUS

OBSTRUCT BAR DAM GAG JAM CLOG COOP CRAB FILL FOUL JAMB STOP TRIG TRIP BESET BLANK BLOCK CHAIN CHECK CHOKE CROSS DELAY HEDGE THROW ARREST CUMBER FORBAR HAMPER HOBBLE IMPEDE OPPOSE PESTER RETARD STIFLE THWART WAYLAY BARRIER FORELAY OCCLUDE BLOCKADE EMBOLIZE ENCUMBER FLOUNDER BARRICADE EMBARRASS INCOMMODE

OBSTRUCTION BAR DAM LET RUB BOOM BUMP CLOG SLUG SNAG STAY STOP BLOCK CHOKE HITCH HAMPER THWART BARRAGE BARRIER BLINDER CHOKAGE OBSTACLE STOPPAGE OCCLUSION
(— IN OILWELL) BRIDGE
(— IN RIVER) GORGE
(— IN VALVE) GAG
(— OF BLOOD VESSEL) EMBOLISM
(— OF PINE LEAVES) TAPPEN
(INNER —) LOAD

OBTAIN BEG BUM BUY EKE GET WIN EARN FANG FIND GAIN ANNEX CADGE CATCH ETTLE REACH ARRIVE ATTAIN BORROW DERIVE EXPEDE SECURE SPONGE ACHIEVE ACQUIRE CAPTURE CHEVISE COMPASS DEMERIT EXTRACT POSSESS PREVAIL PROCURE RECEIVE SUCCEED PURCHASE SCROUNGE
(— BY CHANCE) DRAW
(— BY REQUEST) IMPETRATE
(— BY THREAT) EXTORT
(— CONTROL) ENGROSS
(— DISHONESTLY) CROOK SHARP FLEECE NOBBLE SKELDER
(— MONEY FROM) BLEED
(— PERMISSION) CLEAR

OBTRUDE DIN JET EJECT EXPEL GLARE FLAUNT IMPOSE MEDDLE THRUST INTERFERE

OBTRUSIVE FRESH PUSHY GARISH BLATANT FORWARD PUSHING BUMPTIOUS INTRUSIVE

OBTUSE DIM DULL BLINK BLUNT CRASS DENSE THICK BOVINE OPAQUE STUPID STUBBED BOEOTIAN HEBETATE PURBLIND
(NOT —) ACUTE

OBVIOUS LOUD OPEN BROAD CLEAR CRUDE FRANK GROSS NAKED OVERT PLAIN SLICK STARK LIABLE PATENT BLATANT EVIDENT EXPOSED GLARING SHALLOW SUBJECT VISIBLE APPARENT DISTINCT MANIFEST PALPABLE BAREFACED PROMINENT
(NOT —) DEEP INNER ARCANE HIDDEN MASKED OCCULT SECRET SUBTLE DELICATE DOUBTFUL PROFOUND INEVIDENT

OCARINA CAMOTE

OCCASION SEL BOUT CALL GIVE HINT NEED SELE SITH TIME TURN BREAK BREED CASUS CAUSE CHARE EVENT INFER NONCE RAISE SITHE SLANT STOUR WHILE YIELD AFFAIR AUTHOR CHANCE COURSE EXCUSE PERIOD REASON STOUND CHESOUN INSPIRE OPENING PRETEXT QUARREL CEREMONY ENGENDER EXIGENCY FUNCTION INCIDENT INSTANCE CONDITION ENCHEASON HAPPENING
(DEFINITE —) TIDE
(EXCITING —) BLAST
(FAVORABLE —) ADVANTAGE
(FESTIVE —) UTAS BEANO HOLIDAY SHINDIG BEANFEAST MERRYMAKING
(HAPPY —) SIMHAH
(SOCIAL —) COFFEE
(SPECIAL —) CEREMONY

OCCASIONAL ODD STRAY CASUAL SCARCE POPPING EPISODIC FUGITIVE SPORADIC IRREGULAR

OCCASIONALLY EVERY BETIMES SOMETIME SOMETIMES

OCCULT MAGIC ARCANE HIDDEN LATENT MYSTIC SECRET VOODOO ALCHEMY CRYPTIC ECLIPSE UNKNOWN ESOTERIC MYSTICAL SIBYLLIC CONCEALED RECONDITE SIBYLLINE

OCCUPANT HOLDER INMATE RENTER TENANT CITIZEN DWELLER RESIDENT INCUMBENT
(— OF THEATER GALLERY) GOD
(SUFF.) ITE

OCCUPATION ART JOB LAY USE CALL GAME LINE NOTE PLOY TOIL WORK BERTH GRAB GRAFT TRADE BILLET CAREER EMPLOY METIER RACKET SPHERE TENURE THRIFT CALLING CONCERN CONTROL MYSTERY PURSUIT QUALITY SERVICE ACTIVITY BUSINESS FUNCTION INDUSTRY INVASION PLUMBING VOCATION

OCCUPIED BUSY FULL HELD KEPT RAPT TOOK ACTIVE INTENT ENGAGED ABSORBED CAPTURED
(FULLY —) ENGROSSED

OCCUPY LIE SIT USE BUSY FILL HAVE HOLD KEEP TAKE WARM AMUSE BELAY BESET DWELL ABSORB BETAKE EMPLOY ENGAGE EXPEND FULFIL OBTAIN TENANT COHABIT CONCERN CONTAIN ENGROSS ENTREAT IMPROVE INHABIT INVOLVE OVERSIT PERVADE POSSESS SWALLOW DISSOLVE GARRISON INTEREST POPULATE POURPRISE

OCCUR BE GO COME COOK FALL GIVE MAKE MEET PASS RISE SORT ARISE BREAK CLASH EXIST INCUR APPEAR ARRIVE BEFALL BETIDE CHANCE HAPPEN PROCEED TRANSPIRE
(— AGAIN) RECUR REPEAT
(— BY CHANCE) LIGHT
(— TO) CROSS ENTER STRIKE

OCCURRENCE GO HAP CASE FACT ITEM NOTE REDE EVENT WEIRD EPISODE PASSAGE INCIDENT JUNCTURE OCCASION ENCOUNTER FREQUENCE HAPPENING
(CHANCE —) ADVENTURE CONTINGENT
(COMMON —) USE FREQUENCY
(FREQUENT —) COMMUNITY
(SIMULTANEOUS —) COINCIDENCE
(SUDDEN —) ZAP
(SUPERNATURAL —) MIRACLE
(UNEXPECTED —) SUDDEN BLIZZARD BOMBSHELL
(UNFORTUNATE —) CASUALTY
(UNUSUAL —) ODDITY

OCEAN SEA BLUE BRIM DEEP MAIN POND BRINE DRINK ARCTIC INDIAN EXPANSE NEPTUNE PACIFIC ATLANTIC ANTARCTIC
(— FLOATING MATTER) ALGAE LAGAN FLOTSAM
(— ROUTE) LANE
(— SPRAY) IRONWOOD CREAMCUPS
(— SWELL) SEA
(ON THE —) ASEA
(RELATING TO — BELOW 6000 METERS) HADAL

OCEANIA MALAYA AUSTRALIA MELANESIA POLYNESIA

OCEANIC NAVAL MARINE PELAGIC NAUTICAL AEQUOREAL

OCEANUS TITAN
(DAUGHTER OF —) DORIS OCEANID EURYNOME
(FATHER OF —) URANUS OURANOS
(MOTHER OF —) GAEA GAIA
(SISTER OF —) TETHYS
(SON OF —) NEREUS
(WIFE OF —) TETHYS

OCELOT CAT LEOPARD WILDCAT

OCTAVE UTAS EIGHT EIGHTH OTTAVA HUITAIN DIAPASON SHEMINITH
(— FLUTE) FLAUTINO
(— OF THE SEVENTH) FOURTEENTH
(— SINGING) MAGADIZE
(DIMINISHED —) SEMIDIAPASON

OCTAVIA (BROTHER OF —) AUGUSTUS
(HUSBAND OF —) ANTONY

OCTOPUS HEE POLYP POULP PREKE SQUID CUTTLE CATFISH POLYPOD

POLYPUS SCUTTLE DIBRANCH
OCTOPEAN DEVILFISH
(AUTHOR OF —) NORRIS
(CHARACTER IN —) DYKE TREE HILMA
LYMAN HOOVEN MAGNUS SARRIA
BEHRMAN CARAHER DELANEY DERRICK
PRESLEY RUGGLES VANAMEE ANNIXTER
SHELGRIM CEDARQUIST GENSLINGER
(SECRETION OF —) INK

ODD OUT RUM FELL LEFT LONE ORRA
RARE ANTIC CRAZY DIPPY DROLL EXTRA
FLAKY FUNKY FUNNY IMPAR KINKY
OUTRE QUEER UNKET UNKID WEIRD
FLAKEY IMPAIR QUAINT SINGLE UNEVEN
UNIQUE BAROQUE BIZARRE COMICAL
CURIOUS ERRATIC STRANGE UNEQUAL
UNUSUAL FANCIFUL FREAKISH PECULIAR
SINGULAR UNPAIRED BURLESQUE
ECCENTRIC FANTASTIC GROTESQUE
LAUGHABLE SQUIRRELY UNMATCHED
WHIMSICAL

ODDITY GIG QUIP JIMJAM RUMNESS
QUIZZITY PECULIARITY
(PL.) PURLICUES

ODDS BISK EDGE CHALK PRICE BISQUE
DISCORD DISPUTE QUARREL HANDICAP
VARIANCE ADVANTAGE DISPARITY
(— AND ENDS) ORTS BROTT REFUSE
SCRAPS GIBLETS SECONDS FEWTRILS
REMNANTS SHAKINGS ETCETERAS
FRAGMENTS

ODE HYMN POEM SONG LYRIC PAEAN
PSALM MONODY ODELET CANZONE
EPICEDE CANTICLE PALINODE PINDARIC
SERENATA STASIMON EPICEDIUM
EPINICION PARABASIS

ODIN OTHIN WODAN WODEN WOTAN
(BROTHER OF —) VE VILI
(CREATED BY —) ASK EMBLA
(DAUGHTER-IN-LAW OF —) NANNA
(DESCENDANT OF —) SCYLD
(FATHER OF —) BOR BORR
(HALL OF —) VALHALLA
(HORSE OF —) SLEIPNER SLEIPNIR
(MANSION OF —) GLADSHEIM
(MOTHER OF —) BESTLA
(PALACE OF —) SYN
(RAVEN OF —) HUGIN MUNIN
(RING OF —) DRAUPNIR
(SHIP OF —) NAGLFAR SKIDBLADNIR
(SON OF —) TYR THOR VALI BALDR
BALDER
(SPEAR OF —) GUNGNIR
(SWORD OF —) GRAM
(THRONE OF —) HLIDSKJALF
(WIFE OF —) FRIA RIND FRIGG RINDR
FRIGGA
(WOLF OF —) GERI FREKI

ODIOUS FOUL UGLY VILE LOATH
HATABLE HATEFUL HEINOUS HIDEOUS
DAMNABLE FLAGRANT INFAMOUS
ABHORRENT INVIDIOUS OBNOXIOUS
OFFENSIVE REPUGNANT

ODOR AIR FUNK OLID TANG WAFF WAFT
AROMA FETOR FLAIR NIDOR SCENT
SMACK SMELL SNUFF BREATH FLAVOR
HODURE REPUTE BOUQUET ESSENCE

FUMETTE NOSEGAY PERFUME VERDURE
PUNGENCE EFFLUVIUM EMPYREUMA
FRAGRANCE REDOLENCE
(— FROM FLOWERS) FUME
(— OF GAME) FUMET
(— OF HAY) NOSE
(BAD —) EWDER FROWST STENCH
(DISGUSTING —) STINK
(FOUL —) FIST MEPHITIS
(PUNGENT —) SPICE
(SPICY —) BALM
(STUDY OF —S) OSMICS

ODOROUS FOUL BALMY OLENT SMELLY
ODORANT AROMATIC FRAGRANT
NIDOROSE NIDOROUS PERFUMED
REDOLENT SCENTFUL SMELLFUL

ODYSSEUS ULYSSES
(DOG OF —) ARGOS
(FATHER OF —) LAERTES SISYPHUS
(FRIEND OF —) MENTOR
(ISLAND OF —) ITHACA
(SON OF —) TELEGONUS TELEMACHUS
(WIFE OF —) PENELOPE

ODYSSEY (AUTHOR OF —) HOMER
(CHARACTER IN —) ARETE CIRCE
HELEN AEOLUS NESTOR EUMAEUS
ALCINOUS MENELAUS NAUSICAA
ODYSSEUS PENELOPE DEMODOCUS
EURYCLEIA TEIRESIAS POLYPHEMUS
TELEMACHUS

OEDIPUS OEDIPAL
(BROTHER-IN-LAW OF —) CREON
(DAUGHTER OF —) ISMENE ANTIGONE
(FATHER OF —) LAIUS
(FOSTER MOTHER OF —) PERIBOEA
(MOTHER OF —) JOCASTA
(SON OF —) ETEOCLES POLYNICES
(WIFE OF —) JOCASTA

OF BY DE OFF VAN VON FROM HAVE TILL
WITH ABOUT
(— AGE) AE
(— ALL) AVA ALDER ALLER
(— COURSE) NATCH
(— EACH) ANA PER SING
(— THIS DAY) HODIERNAL

OFF BY AFF FAR ODD WET AFAR AGEE
AWAY DOFF DOWN GONE ALONG ASIDE
RIGHT WONKY WRONG ABSENT CUCKOO
DEPART REMOTE FURTHER REMOVED
SEAWARD TAINTED ABNORMAL
OPPOSITE
(— GUARD) TARDY
(— THE PATH) ASTRAY
(— THE SUBJECT) AFIELD
(— THE WIND) ROOM ROOMWARD
(FAR —) DISTANT

OFFAL WASTE REFUSE CARRION
DOGMEAT GARBAGE LEAVING RUBBISH
GRALLOCH
(— OF FISH) GURRY STOSH
(MILLING —S) GRIT

OFF-BEAT KOOKY

OFFEND CAG ERR PET SIN VEX GALL
HARM HUFF HURT MIFF RASP RASS
ABUSE ANGER ANNOY GRATE GRILL
PIQUE SHOCK SPITE TOUCH WRONG
ATTACK GRIEVE INJURE INSULT NETTLE

REVOLT AFFRONT DEFAULT DISDAIN
MORTIFY OUTRAGE PROVOKE REGRATE
STOMACH UMBRAGE VIOLATE
CONFRONT DISTASTE IRRITATE
TRESPASS DISOBLIGE DISPLEASE
OFFENDED HUFF MIFF SORE AVERTED
FROISSE INJURED INSULTED
OFFENDER SINNER CULPRIT MISDOER
PECCANT HABITUAL OFFENDANT
OFFENSE PET SIN HUFF LACK SLIP WITE
ABUSE CRIME ERROR FAULT GRIEF GUILT
PIQUE SNUFF ATTACK BIGAMY FELONY
PIACLE PRITCH REATUS STRUNT
AFFRONT DEFAULT DEMERIT DUDGEON
LARCENY MISDEED OUTRAGE SCANDAL
UMBRAGE PECCANCY TRESPASS
EXTORTION INDECORUM INDIGNITY
THEFTBOTE
(— AGAINST LAW) MALUM DELICT
DELICTUM
(— AGAINST MORALITY) EVIL CRIME
(SLIGHT —) PECCADILLO
OFFENSIVE BAD ACID EVIL FOUL HARD
UGLY CRUDE DIRTY FETID GROSS NASTY
SLIMY COARSE FROWZY GARISH HORRID
RANCID RIBALD ROTTEN ABUSIVE
BEASTLY FULSOME HATEFUL HIDEOUS
NOISOME PECCANT RASPING SCARLET
DREADFUL INVADING MEPHITIC
SHOCKING STINKING UNSAVORY
LOATHSOME OBNOXIOUS REPUGNANT
REVOLTING SCANDALOUS
OFFER GO BID PUT BODE GIVE HAND
LEND PLEA SHOW TAKE TEND DEFER
HEAVE PARTY SHORE START ADDUCE
AFFORD ALLEGE DELATE INJECT OBLATE
OPPOSE PREFER SUBMIT SUPPLY TENDER
ADVANCE BIDDING COMMEND EXHIBIT
PRESENT PROFFER PROPINE PROPOSE
SUGGEST OVERTURE PROPOSAL
VOLUNTEER
(— EXCUSE) ALIBI
(— FOR SALE) HAWK EXPOSE
(— IN SACRIFICE) IMMOLATE
(— PROOF) APPROVE
(— PUBLICLY) JACTITATE
(— TO VERIFY) AVER
(— UP) APPEAL
(LAST —) ULTIMATUM
(SOLEMN —) PLEDGE
(UNACCEPTED —) POLLICITATION
OFFERING BID ALMS DALI DEAL GIFT
HOST SOMA DOLLY ENTRY NUZZER
OFLETE PIACLE PRESENT RETABLO
TRIBUTE ANATHEMA DEVOTION
DONATION LIBATION PESHKASH
PIACULUM SACRIFICE
(— TO GOD) CORBAN DEODATE
(— TO HOUSEHOLD DEITIES) BALI
(EUCHARISTIC —) ANAPHORA
(PEACE —S) PACIFICS
(RELIGIOUS —) OBLATION
(SACRIFICIAL —) HOLOCAUST
(THEATRICAL —) FLUFF
OFFHAND AIRY CURT GLIB SOON ADLIB
BLUSH HASTY ABRUPT BREEZY CASUAL
BRUSQUE READILY CARELESS CAVALIER

GLANCING INFORMAL EXTEMPORE
IMPROMPTU UNSTUDIED
OFFICE HAT JOB SEE BOMA DUTY NONE
PART POST ROLE ROOM SHOP TASK
TOGA WIKE WORK PLACE STINT TRUST
WIKEN YAMEN ABBACY AGENCY BUREAU
CHARGE DAFTAR DIWANI DUFTER
METIER MISTER BULLPEN CAMARIN
CENTRAL DEWANEE DROSTDY EDILITY
MYSTERY SERVICE STATION SURGERY
AEDILITY CAPACITY CUTCHERY
ENSIGNCY FUNCTION KINGSHIP
MINISTRY POSITION PROVINCE
WOOLPACK BAILIWICK BANKSHALL
SITUATION
(— OF BISHOP) LAWN
(— OF JUDGE) BENCH ERMINE
(— OF PROFESSOR) CHAIR
(— OF ROMAN CURIA) DATARY
DATARIA
(— OF RULER) REGENCY
(— OF THE DEAD) DIRGE
(BRANCH —) WING
(CASHIER'S —) CAISSE
(CLERICAL —) CASSOCK
(DIVINE —) AKOLUTHIA
(ECCLESIASTICAL —) FROCK BENEFICE
EXORCIST
(HIGH —) DIGNITY
(LITURGICAL —) SEXT SERVICE
(MAGISTRATE'S —) KACHAHRI
(MORNING —) ORTHRON ORTHROS
(NAVAL —S) BEACH
(PAY —) WANIGAN
(POLICE —) NICK
(PRIESTLY —) SACERDOCY
(PRINTING —) CHAPEL IMPRIMERY
(RECORD —) CHANCERY
(RESIGN AN —) DEMIT
(TIMEKEEPER'S —) PENNYHOLE
OFFICER (ALSO SEE OFFICIAL) COP TAB
EXEC EXON FLAG HOLD VOGT AGENT
CHIEF CRIER DIWAN GRAND GRAVE
GROOM JURAT SEWER TAXOR USHER
ALCADE BEADLE BEDRAL BUTLER
CENSOR DEPUTY DIRECT GAILLI GEREFA
HERALD KOTWAL LAWMAN MANAGE
ORATOR SYNDIC TINDAL ADJOINT
ALNAGER ASSIZER COMMAND CONDUCT
CORONER DUUMVIR EPAULET FEDERAL
GAVELER KLEAGLE LOBSTER NAPERER
PANTLER PATROON REGIDOR SANCTUM
SCHEPEN SHERIFF SPEAKER WHIPPER
WOODMAN ALDERMAN ALGUACIL
ANDREEVE BANNERET CHAFFWAX
COFFERER DOORWARD FORESTER
GOVERNOR GRASSMAN MERESMAN
MINISTER PALATINE QUESTEUR
REPORTER TIPSTAFF VISCOUNT
WOODWARD CONSTABLE DIKEGRAVE
FINANCIER INTENDANT MODERATOR
PAYMASTER SCHOOLMAN TAHSILDAR
(— OF CHURCH) ABBOT ELDER
DEACON SEXTON ANTISTES DEFENSOR
LAMPADARY SACRISTAN
(— OF COURT) MACER MASTER BAILIFF
FEODARY FILACER CURSITOR DEMPSTER

EXAMINER SERGEANT ASSOCIATE
BYRLAWMAN SURROGATE
(— OF FORESTS) AGISTER
(— OF KING'S STABLES) AVENER
(BARDIC —) DRUID
(CAVALRY —) CORNET
(CHIEF —) NASI DEWAN DAROGA
PARNAS PRESIDENT
(CUSTOMS —) GAGER SHARK GAUGER
JERQUER DOUANIER SEARCHER
SURVEYOR TIDESMAN
(GREEK —) STRATEGUS
(JAPANESE —) SHIKKEN
(MASONIC —) EAST KING DEACON
STEWARD
(MILITARY —) NAIG NAIK COMES
MAJOR SUBAH ENSIGN NAIQUE RANKER
SARDAR SIRDAR CAPTAIN COLONEL
GENERAL JEMADAR MARSHAL SUBADAR
WARRANT COMMANDER RABSHAKEH
SHAVETAIL
(MINOR —) CHINOVNIK
(MONASTERY —) CELLARER
(MUNICIPAL —) SCHOUT
(NAVAL —) CPO EXON MATE SWAB
BOSUN ENSIGN PURSER YEOMAN
ADMIRAL CAPTAIN MUSTANG SPOTTER
YOUNKER SUNDOWNER
(PAPAL —) DATARY
(POLICE —) PIG PEON RURAL EXEMPT
JAVERT KOTWAL RUNNER SBIRRO
ALYTARCH SEARCHER THANADAR
DETECTIVE ROUNDSMAN
(PRESIDING —) CHAIRONE
CHAIRPERSON
(PUBLIC —) JUDGE FISCAL NOTARY
PODESTA
(ROMAN —) LICTOR
(SHERIFF'S —) FANG BEAGLE BAILIFF
BULLDOG HUISSIER
(SHIP'S —) MATE FANTOD
(STAFF —) TAB AIDE REDTAB
ADJUTANT
(TURKISH —) AGA AGHA MUTE VIZIR
VIZIER BIMBASHI BINBASHI
(UNIVERSITY —) DEAN PROVOST
(WARRANT —) MACHINIST
OFFICIAL (ALSO SEE OFFICER) AGA BEG
DEY VIP AMIN BOSS KUAN KWAN TRUE
AGENT AHONG AMALA AMBAN AMEEN
AMLAH CLERK EDILE EPHOR GYANI
HAJIB HOMER JURAT LIMMU LINER
MAYOR NAZIR REEVE SAHIB AEDILE
ARCHON ATABEG BASHAW CENSOR
CONSUL EPARCH EPONYM FISCAL
FORMAL GABBAI GRIEVE HAZZAN
HERALD LAWMAN MASTER NOTARY
PANDIT PREVOT RABMAG SATRAP
SCRIBE SEALER SINGER TAOTAI TAOYIN
TRONER VERGER WARDEN WEDANA
ALMONER APOSTLE ASIARCH BURGESS
CERTAIN JEMADAR LANDRAT MARSHAL
MOORMAN PRISTAW REFEREE STALLAR
STARTER SUBASHI ALDERMAN
APPROVED CARDINAL CELLARER
CUSTOMER DOGBERRY GOVERNOR
LINESMAN MANDARIN PRYTANIS

VESTIARY WHIFFLER EXECUTIVE
MAJORDOMO OMBUDSMAN SELECTMAN
MAGISTRATE
(BLUNDERING —) DOGBERRY
(EISTEDDFOD —) DRUID
(PALACE —) PALADIN
(POMPOUS —) BUMBLE
(PRETENTIOUS —) PANJANDRUM
OFFICIATE ACT FILL SERVE SUPPLY
PERFORM CELEBRATE
OFFICIOUS BUSY COOL PERT SAUCY
FORMAL FORTHY PUSHING ARROGANT
IMPUDENT INFORMAL MEDDLING
OFFICIAL INBEARING PRAGMATIC
OFFING OFF FUTURE PICTURE
OFFSET SLAB STEP ALTAR CRIMP ERASE
POISE CANCEL CONTRA JOGGLE REDEEM
SETOFF BALANCE COUNTER LATERAL
RETREAT SETBACK PROPAGULE
(— ON BULB) SPLIT
OFFSHOOT GET PUP ROD SON LIMB
SPUR BOUGH ISSUE SCION SHOOT SPRIG
BRANCH FILIAL GROWTH MEMBER
OFFSET SPROUT ADJUNCT APOPHYSIS
FILIATION OUTGROWTH RAMIFICATION
(— OF LAKE) BAYOU
OFFSPRING BOY FRY IMP KID KIN SON
BRAT BURD CHIT HEIR SEED SLIP BIRTH
BREED BROOD CHILD FRUIT ISSUE SCION
SPAWN BEGATS DUSTEE EMBRYO
FOSTER GRIQUA JUMART PROLES
RESULT STRAIN STRIND MORISCO
NISHADA OUTCOME PRODUCE PRODUCT
PROGENY YOUNGER CHILDREN
DAUGHTER DEMISANG GENITURE
INCREASE KINDLING BAIRNTEAM
MUSTAFINA
(— OF FAIRIES) CHANGELING
(— OF NEGRO AND MULATTO)
GRIFFE
(— OF WITCH) HAGSEED HOLDIKEN
(PREMATURE —) CASTLING
OF HUMAN BONDAGE
(AUTHOR OF —) MAUGHAM
(CHARACTER IN —) CAREY EMILY
ERLIN FANNY NORAH PRICE SALLY
WEEKS LAWSON LOUISA NESBIT PHILIP
ROGERS THORPE ATHELNY CLUTTON
HAYWARD MILDRED WILLIAM
CRONSHAW WILKINSON
OF MICE AND MEN (AUTHOR OF —)
STEINBECK
(CHARACTER IN —) SLIM CANDY
SMALL CROOKS CURLEY GEORGE LENNIE
MILTON
OFTEN OFT AFTEN OFTLY COMMON
EFTSOONS FREQUENT REPEATED
(VERY —) CONTINUALLY
OF TIME AND THE RIVER
(AUTHOR OF —) WOLFE
(CHARACTER IN —) ANN GANT JOEL
WANG BASCOM ELINOR EUGENE PIERCE
ROBERT WEAVER COULSON FRANCIS
HATCHER MORNAYE PENTLAND
OGLE EYE GAZE LEER LOOK MASH STARE
GLANCE EXAMINE MARLOCK SMICKER
OEILLADE

OGRE ORC BOYG BRUTE DEMON GHOUL GIANT HUGON TYRANT YAKSHA BUGABOO BUGBEAR MONSTER WINDIGO

OHIO

CAPITAL: COLUMBUS
COLLEGE: KENT HIRAM KENYON XAVIER ANTIOCH OBERLIN DEFIANCE
COUNTY: ERIE PIKE ROSS DARKE MIAMI STARK GALLIA HARDIN SUMMIT LICKING CUYAHOGA HAMILTON
INDIAN TRIBE: ERIE WYANDOT
NATIVE: BUCKEYE
RIVER: MIAMI MAUMEE SCIOTO CUYAHOGA MUSKINGUM
STATE BIRD: CARDINAL
STATE FLOWER: CARNATION
STATE TREE: BUCKEYE
TOWN: ADA LIMA TROY ADENA AKRON BEREA CADIZ NILES XENIA CANTON DAYTON LORAIN MENTOR TOLEDO CHARDON COLUMBUS SANDUSKY CLEVELAND

OIL BEN FAT ILE ULE BALM CHIA DIKA FUEL ZEST BRIBE CRUDE JUICE OLEUM SMEAR STOCK TRAIN ULYIE ULZIE ACEITE ANOINT BINDER BUTTER CARDOL CHRISM CREESH EUPION GREASE LIQUOR SAFROL SMOOTH ZACHUN CEDRIUM ESSENCE LANOLIN MYRRHOL PHLOROL RETINOL VETIVER BERGAMOT COUMARAN ERIGERON GINGEROL PHTHALAN SDRAVETS TETRALIN CARVACROL LUBRICATE PETROLEUM
OILSKIN OIL OILER SQUAM OILCASE OILCOAT SLICKER
OILY FAT GLIB BLAND FATTY LOEIC OLEIC SLEEK SOAPY SUAVE GREASY OILISH OLEOSE OLEOUS SMARMY SMOOTH SUPPLE PINGUID SERVILE SLIPPERY UNCTUOUS COMPLIANT PLAUSIBLE
(PREF.) LIPAR(O)
OINTMENT UNG BALM MULL NARD PASTE SALVE SMEAR BALSAM CERATE CEROMA CHARGE CHRISM GREASE POMADE REMEDY UNGUENT EYESALVE POPULEON REMOLADE SPIKENARD WHITFIELD
(— OF GODS) AMBROSIA

OKLAHOMA

CAPITAL: OKLAHOMACITY
COLLEGE: CAMERON LANGSTON PHILLIPS
COUNTY: KAY COAL LOVE ADAIR ATOKA CADDO GREER OSAGE ALFALFA OKFUSKEE OKMULGEE
INDIAN TRIBE: WACO WICHITA TAWAKONI
LAKE: EUFAULA OOLOGAH
MOUNTAINS: OUACHITA
RIVER: RED GRAND WASHITA ARKANSAS CANADIAN CIMARRON

STATE FLOWER: MISTLETOE
STATE TREE: REDBUD
TOWN: ADA JAY ALVA ENID HUGO ALTUS MIAMI PONCA TULSA ELRENO GUYMON IDABEL LAWTON MADILL TALOGA VINITA ANTLERS SAPULPA SHAWNEE ANADARKO FORTSILL MUSKOGEE

OLD AGY ELD AGED AULD COLD WOLD YALD ANILE HOARY STALE WOULD FORMER FOROLD INFIRM MATURE SENILE SHABBY VETUST AGEABLE ANCIENT ANTIQUE ARCHAIC ELDERLY FORWORN OGYGIAN UMWHILE DECREPIT MEDIEVAL OBSOLETE DODDERING HACKNEYED SENESCENT VENERABLE
(— AND MELLOW) CRUSTY
(— BAILEY) GAOL JAIL PRISON
(BEING LESS THAN 13 YEARS —) PRETEEN
(GROWING —) SENESCENT
(OF —) WHILOM ERSTWHILE
OLD CURIOSITY SHOP
(AUTHOR OF —) DICKENS
(CHARACTER IN —) KIT DICK FRED NELL BRASS QUILP SARAH CODLIN JARLEY MARTON THOMAS BARBARA NUBBLES SAMPSON SWIVELLER CHRISTOPHER
OLDER MORE ALDER ELDER SENIOR ANCESTOR
OLD-FASHIONED CORNY DOWDY FUSTY PASSE FOGRAM FOGRUM QUAINT STODGY ANCIENT ANTIQUE ARCHAIC ARRIERE ELDERLY VINTAGE FRUMPISH OBSOLETE CRINOLINE PRIMITIVE RINKYDINK OLDFANGLED
OLD WIVES' TALE (AUTHOR OF —) BENNETT
(CHARACTER IN —) JOHN CYRIL POVEY BAINES CHIRAC GERALD SAMUEL SCALES SOPHIA HARRIET FAUCAULT CONSTANCE CRITCHLOW
OLIO STEW MEDLEY MELANGE MIXTURE MISHMASH MACEDOINE PASTICCIO POTPOURRI
OLIVE OLEA MORON BRUNET LIERRE OLIVER OXHORN PIMOLA RESEDA BAROUNI CITRINE MISSION MORILLON OLEASTER
(AMERICAN —) DEVILWOOD
(OVERRIPE —) DRUPE
(PREF.) (—OIL) ELAEO ELAIO ELEO
OLIVER NOLL HAMMER HOLLIPER
(BROTHER OF —) ORLANDO
(WIFE OF —) CELIA
OLIVER TWIST (AUTHOR OF —) DICKENS
(CHARACTER IN —) BILL JACK NOAH ROSE TOBY BATES FAGIN HARRY MONKS NANCY SALLY SIKES TWIST BEDWIN BUMBLE CORNEY EDWARD MAYLIE OLIVER CHARLEY CRACKIT DAWKINS GRIMWIG LEEFORD BROWNLOW CLAYPOLE LOSBERNE SOWERBERRY
OLLA JAR JUG POT PUCHERA PUCHERO

OMAN (CAPITAL OF —) MUSCAT
(LANGUAGE OF —) ARABIC BALUCHI
(MOUNTAIN OF —) SHAM HAFIT
HARIM NAKHL TAYIN AKHDAR
(NATIVE OF —) ADNAN QAHTAN
BALUCHI
(TOWN IN —) SUR NIGWA MASQAT
MATRAH SALALAH

OMEGA END LAST

OMEN BODE LUCK SIGN ABODE AUGUR
BODER FREIT GUEST TOKEN WEIRD
AUGURY HANSEL AUSPICE PORTENT
PRESAGE PRODIGY WARNING CEREMONY
FOREBODE SOOTHSAY HARBINGER

OMINOUS DIRE DOUR GRIM BLACK
FATAL BODING DISMAL SHREWD
AUGURAL BALEFUL BANEFUL BODEFUL
DIREFUL DOOMFUL FATEFUL MENACING
SINISTER THUNDERY PROPHETIC
PORTENTOUS

OMISSION OUT BALK CHASM SALTUS
DEFAULT FAILURE MISPICK NEGLECT
SILENCE PASSOVER OVERSIGHT
(— OF A LETTER) APOCOPE
(— OF SYLLABLES) SYNCOPE
(TACIT —) SILENCE

OMIT CUT LET BALK BATE DROP EDIT KILL
MISS PASS SKIP SLIP ABATE ELIDE
OBMIT SPARE BELEVE CANCEL DELETE
EXCEPT FORGET IGNORE DISCARD
EXPUNGE NEGLECT DISCOUNT OVERLEAP
OVERLOOK OVERSKIP OVERSLIP
DISREGARD PRETERMIT

OMNIBUS BUS BUSS BARGE HERDIC
JOGGER PIRATE AUTOBUS MOTORBUS
KITTEREEN

OMNIPOTENT GOD ABLE DEITY GREAT
ARRANT MIGHTY ALMIGHTY POWERFUL
UNEQUALED UNLIMITED

ON IN TO ONE SUR ATOP AWAY OVER
UPON ABOUT ABOVE AHEAD ALONG
ANENT WITHIN FORWARD

ONAGER ASS GOUR KULAN KOULAN
ONAGRA ALACRAN CATAPULT SCORPION

ONCE ANE EEN ERST AINCE ONCET WHILE
YANCE FORMER WHILOM QUONDAM
UMWHILE FORMERLY SOMETIME
UMQUHILE WHENEVER ERSTWHILE
(— MORE) YET AGAIN ENCORE ITERUM
(AT —) PRESTO

ONE J AE AN HE UN ACE AIN ANE ANY EIN
MAN OON TAE UNA UNE WON YAE YAN
YEN YIN YOU SAME SOLE SOME TANE
TEAN THIS TONE TOON UNAL UNIT
WHON WONE ALONE ALPHA UNITY
WOONE ABOARD FELLOW PERSON
SINGLE UNIQUE UNITED CERTAIN
NUMERAL PRONOUN SIMPLUM
UNBROKEN SINGLETON UNDIVIDED
UNMARRIED

ONEROUS HARD HEAVY ARDUOUS
ONEROSE WEIGHTY EXACTING GRIEVOUS
LABORIOUS

ONETIME FORMER FORMERLY
ERSTWHILE

ONION BOLL CEPA LEEK LILY SYBO CIBOL
INGAN PEARL ALLIUM LILIUM PORRET
BERMUDA CEBOLLA HOLLEKE PICKLER
SHALLOT AYEGREEN RARERIPE SCALLION
VALENCIA
(ROPE OF —S) REEVE
(SEASONED WITH —S) LYONNAISE
(STRING OF —S) TRACE

ONLOOKER BOOK GAZER WITNESS
AUDIENCE BEHOLDER OVERSEER
BYSTANDER SPECTATOR

ONLY ALL BUT JUST LONE MERE ONCE
SAVE SOLE AFALD ALONE ARRAH FIRST
MERED NOBUT OLEPY ANERLY BARELY
MERELY NOBBUT SIMPLE SINGLE SINGLY
SOLELY ALLENARLY EXCEPTING
(— THIS) MERE

ONOMATOPOEIC ECHOIC IMSONIC
MIMETIC IMITATIVE

ONSET DASH DINT FALL FARD RESE RUSH
BRAID BREAK BRUNT FAIRD FRUSH
START STORM STOUR VENUE ACCESS
AFFRET ATTACK CHARGE COURGE
IMPACT INSULT ONDING ONFALL
POWDER THRUST ASSAULT BRATTLE
BEGINNING ENCOUNTER ONSLAUGHT

ONSLAUGHT LASH BLAST ONSET
ATTACK ASSAULT DESCENT SISERARA
SALIAUNCE

ONTARIO (CANAL IN —) TRENT RIDEAU
(CAPITAL OF —) TORONTO
(LAKE IN —) SIMCOE
(TOWN IN —) EMO GALT LONDON
OTTAWA WINDSOR HAMILTON
KINGSTON KITCHENER

ONTO ATOP ABOARD

ONUS DUTY LOAD BLAME BURDEN
CHARGE WEIGHT INCUBUS

ONWARD AWAY AHEAD ALONG FORTH
UPWARD FORTHON FORWARD TOWARDS
FORERIGHT

ONYX NICOLO TECALI JASPONYX
SARDONYX
(MEXICAN —) ALABASTER

OODLES HEAP LOTS MANY RAFTS SCADS
SLEWS LASHINGS SLITHERS
ABUNDANCE

OOZE OZ BOG MUD SEW SOP DRIP EMIT
LEAK MIRE SEEP SLEW SLOB SLUE WEEP
EXUDE GLEET MARSH SLIME SWEAT
WEEZE EXHALE SICKER SLEECH SLOUGH
SLUDGE SQUASH SQUDGE STRAIN
SCREEVE TEICHER PERCOLATE
(— OUT) SEW SPEW SPUE

OOZING WEEPY SQUDGY SEEPAGE
SPEWING WEEPING

OOZY OASY SEEPY WASHY SLEECHY
ULIGINOUS

OPAL GEM NOBLE RESIN FIORITE GIRASOL
HYALITE ISOPYRE JASPOPAL MENILITE
SEMIOPAL CACHOLONG GEYSERITE

OPAQUE DIM DARK DULL DENSE MUDDY
SHADY THICK VAGUE OBTUSE STUPID
CLOUDED OBSCURE ABSTRUSE
EYESHADE

OPEN GO DUP LAX OPE AIRY AJAR BARE
FAIR FREE FERT UNDO VIDE
AGAPE APERT BEGIN BLOWN BREAK
BROAD BURST CHINK CLEAR CRACK

FLARE FRANK FRESH LANCE LOOSE
MUSHY NAKED OVERT PLAIN RELAX
SPALD SPLAT SPLAY START UNBAR
UNPEG UNTIE APPERT CANDID DIRECT
ENTAME EXPAND EXPOSE FACIAL
FORTHY GAPING HONEST LIABLE
OUVERT PATENT PUBLIC SINGLE SPREAD
UNBOLT UNFOLD UNFURL UNGLUE
UNLOCK UNROLL UNSEAL UNSHUT
UNSPAR UNSTOP UNTINE UNWINK
VACANT ARTLESS BLOSSOM DISPART
FIELDEN OBVIOUS OUTLINE SINCERE
THROUGH UNCLOSE UNHINGE APPARENT
COMMENCE DISCLOSE EXPLICIT
EXTENDED INITIATE MANIFEST PERVIOUS
RESERATE UNFASTEN CHAMPAIGN
OSTENSIBLE
(— A VEIN) BROACH
(— AIR) ALFRESCO
(— AND CLEANSE) WILLOW
(— CLOTH) SCUTCH
(— COUNTRY) VELDT WEALD
(— EYES OR LIPS) SEVER
(— THE WAY) INVITE PIONEER
(— TO PURSUIT) FAIR
(— UP) START DEVELOP DISPART
DISCLOSE
(— VIOLENTLY) SPORT
(— WIDE) YAWN EXPAND STRETCH
(— WIDELY) GAPE
(FULLY —) WIDE AGAPE YAWNING
(HALF —) MID AJAR
(TOO —) OVERBARISH
OPENER KEY KNOB LATCH SESAME
APERIENT
(— IN POKER) PAIR JACKS
(FURROW —) SHOE STUBRUNNER
(OYSTER —) HUSKER
OPENHANDED FREE LIBERAL GENEROUS
RECEPTIVE
OPENING OS CUT EYE GAP YAT ANUS
BOLE BORE DAWN DOOR DROP FENT
FLUE GATE HOLE LOOP PASS PORE PORT
PYLA RIFT RIMA SLAP SLIT SLOT SPAN
VENT VOID YAWN YEAT BLEED BRACK
BREAK CHASM CHINK CLEFT CROSS
DEBUT GRILL HILUM INLET LIGHT MOUTH
SCOOT SINUS START THIRL WIDTH
ADITUS AVENUE BREACH CASING
CHANCE GRILLE HIATUS INTAKE LACUNA
MEATUS OILLET OUTLET PORTAL SLUICE
SPREAD AIRPORT CREVASS CREVICE
DISPLAY FISSURE ORIFICE OUTCAST
SWALLET APERIENT APERTURE
BUNGHOLE CREVASSE ENTRANCE
OVERTURE PLUGHOLE SCISSURE
TEASEHOLE
(— BELOW PENTHOUSE) GALLERY
(— FOR ESCAPE) MUSE MEUSE
(— FROM SEA) INDRAFT
(— IN ANTHER) STOMIUM
(— IN DECK) SCUTTLE
(— IN EARTH) MOFETTE
(— IN FLOOR OR ROOF) HATCH
SKYLIGHT
(— IN GARMENT) FENT ARMHOLE
(— IN LOCK TUMBLER) GATING

(— IN MINE) EYE ADIT RAISE SHAFT
WINZE WINNING
(— IN MOLD) POUR
(— IN PICTURE FRAME) SIGHT
(— IN PILLAR OF COAL) JENKIN
JUNKING
(— IN ROCK) GRIKE
(— IN SALMON TRAP) SLAP
(— IN SEA CAVE) GLOUP
(— IN SKIRT) PLACKET
(— IN SPONGE) APOPYLE
(— IN STAGE) DIP
(— IN TENNIS COURTS) GRILLE
HAZARD GALLERY
(— IN TROUSERS) SPARE
(— IN VAULT) LUNET LUNETTE
(— IN WALL) BOLE DREAMHOLE
(— OF BALL) PROMENADE
(— OF BUD) ANTHESIS
(— OF EAR) BUR BURR
(— OF ESOPHAGUS) CARDIA
(— OF GEYSER) CRATER
(— OF HOCKEY GAME) BULLY
(— OF PRAIRIE) BAY
(— OF SHELL) GAPE
(— THROUGH BULWARKS) GANGWAY
GUNPORT SCUPPER
(— TO ASH PIT) GLUT
(— WIDE) DEHISCENT
(— WITH LID) SCUTTLE
(— WITHOUT TREES) BLANK
(— IN EARTH) GROTTO CHIMNEY
SWALLOW
(ARCHED —) ALCOVE ARCADE
(CHECKERS —) ALMA DYKE FIFE CROSS
CENTER SOUTER BRISTOL GLASGOW
PAISLEY WHILTER DEFIANCE SWITCHER
(CHESS —) DEBUT GAMBIT DEFENCE
DEFENSE
(EROSIONAL —) FENSTER
(FUNNELLIKE —) CHOANA
(GRILL —) GUICHET
(JAR —) PITHOIGIA
(MOUTHLIKE —) STOMA OSTIUM
(SMALL —) PORE SLOT CHINK STOMA
CRANNY EYELET LACUNA CATHOLE
CREVICE DOGHOLE FORAMEN GUICHET
PINHOLE QUARREL FENESTRA
(WINDOWLIKE —) SPLITE FENESTRA
OPENLY BARELY FREELY BROADLY
FRANKLY PUBLICE ROUNDLY STRAIGHT
OPEN-MINDED LIBERAL
OPENNESS FREEDOM PATENCY
DAYLIGHT FRANKNESS ROUNDNESS
OPERA AIDA FAUST LAKME MANON
NORMA THAIS TOSCA BOHEME CARMEN
DAPHNE ERNANI LOUISE MIGNON
OTELLO RIENZI SALOME ELEKTRA
FIDELIO BURLETTA FALSTAFF IOLANTHE
LOKACOLO PARSIFAL TRAVIATA
WALKYRIE LOHENGRIN PAGLIACCI
RHEINGOLD RIGOLETTO SIEGFRIED
TROVATORE
(— DIVISION) SCENA
(— GLASS) GLASS JUMELLE LORGNET
LORGNETTE
(— HAT) GIBUS CLAQUE

(— SONG) ARIA
(— STAR) DIVA
(COMIC —) BUFFA BURLETTA
(HORSE —) WESTERN
(SPANISH —) ZARZUELA
(TV OR RADIO —) SOAP
(16TH CENTURY —) PASTORALE

OPERATE GO ACT CUT MAN RUN PUSH
TAKE WORK DRIVE MULES AFFECT
EFFECT MANAGE CONDUCT PROCEED
FUNCTION
(— BY HAND) MANIPULATE
(— GUNS) SERVE
(— MINE) FLUSH
(— RADIO) BLOOP

OPERATION DEED PLAY BLAST ACTION
AGENCY EFFECT VIRTUE PROCESS
CREATION EXERCISE FUNCTION
PRACTICE EXECUTION INFLUENCE
PROCESSUS

OPERATIVE EYE HAND ARTIST LIVING
ARTISAN OUVRIER MECHANIC DETECTIVE
EFFECTIVE

OPERATOR DEL DOER AGENT BAKER
DEWER NABLA PILOT QUACK BEAMER
BILLER BOLTER BUMPER BUSMAN
CAPPER DEALER DEGGER DRIVER
DUNGER DYADIC GAGGER JOCKEY
KICKER RAGGER TRADER AVIATOR
BREAKER CENTRAL CHEESER DENTIST
FACIENT GLASSER JOGGLER MANAGER
OPERANT SURGEON IDENTITY
MOTORMAN CONDUCTOR
(INFERIOR —) PLUG
(RADIO —) HAM SPARKS SPARKER
(TRUCK —) GYPSY

OPHELIA (BROTHER OF —) LAERTES
(FATHER OF —) POLONIUS

OPIATE DOPE DRUG HEMP DWALE OPIUM
DEADEN ANODINE HYPNOTIC NARCOTIC
SEDATIVE DORMITARY PAREGORIC
SOPORIFIC

OPINE DEEM JUDGE THINK PONDER
BELIEVE SUPPOSE OPINIATE

OPINION CRY EYE MOT BOOK DOXY
FAME IDEA MIND VIEW WEEN DOGMA
FANCY FUTWA GUESS HEART SENSE
SIGHT TENET THINK VARDI VARDY VOICE
ADVICE ASSENT BELIEF DEVICE DICTUM
ESTEEM GROUND NOTION REPUTE
SCHISM CENSURE CONCEIT CONCEPT
CONSENT COUNSEL DIANOIA FEELING
HOLDING MEASURE SEEMING THINKSO
THOUGHT TROWING VERDICT DECISION
DOCTRINE JUDGMENT SUFFRAGE
PREJUDICE SENTIMENT PERSUASION
(COLLECTION OF —S) SYMPOSIUM
(EXAGGERATED —) BIGHEAD
(EXPRESSION OF —) VOTE
(FAVORABLE —) BROO ESTEEM
(MOHAMMEDAN —) FUTWA
(SET OF PROFESSED —S) CREDO
(UNORTHODOX —) HERESY
(WRONG —) CACODOXY
(PREF.) DOXO
(SUFF.) DOX(Y)

OPINIONATED DOGMATIC CONCEITED
OBSTINATE PRAGMATIC

O PIONEERS (AUTHOR OF —) CATHER
(CHARACTER IN —) LOU CARL EMIL
IVAR FRANK MARIE OSCAR AMEDEE
BERGSON SHABATA TOVESKY
ALEXANDRA LINDSTRUM

OPIUM HOP MUD DOPE DRUG OPIE POST
CHANDU MECONIUM TOXICANT
(— ALKALOID) CODEIN CODEINE
MORPHINE NARCOTIN NARCOTINE
PAPAVERIN
(— POPPY) NEPENTHE
(OF —) THEBAIC
(TINCTURE OF —) LAUDANUM

OPOSSUM QUICA POSSUM YAPOCK
MARMOSE SARIGUE VULPINE
MARSUPIAL PHILANDER TACUACINE

OPPONENT FOE ANTI ENEMY PARTY
RIVAL ALOGIAN NEMESIS OPPOSER
ADVERSARY ASSAILANT
(— OF WAR) PEACENIK
(BOORISH —) BOEOTIAN
(IMAGINARY —) WINDMILL

OPPORTUNE FIT PAT HAPPY LUCKY
READY TIMELY APROPOS FITTING
TIMEFUL SUITABLE FAVORABLE

OPPORTUNELY TIMELY APROPOS
HAPPILY

OPPORTUNITY GO MAY OPE EASE HENT
MEAN MINT ROOM SELE SHOT TIDE TIME
SIGHT SLANT SPACE ACCESS CHANCE
SEASON SQUEAK LEISURE OPENING
RESPITE VANTAGE APPROACH FACILITY
OCCASION ADVANTAGE
(— TO PROCEED) WAY
(FAVORABLE —) SHOW TIME

OPPOSE PIT VIE WAR BUCK COPE DEFY
FACE HEAD MEET NOSE STEM WARN
WEAR ARGUE BLOCK CHECK CLASH
CROSS FIGHT FRONT OCCUR REPEL
BATTLE BREAST COMBAT DEFEND
NAYSAY OBJECT OBTEND OPPUGN
REPUGN RESIST THWART WITHER
CONTEST COUNTER GAINSAY OBVIATE
REVERSE WITHSET CONFLICT CONFRONT
CONTRARY CONTRAST FRONTIER
OBSTRUCT TRAVERSE ENCOUNTER
WITHSTAND ANTAGONIZE
(— BY ARGUMENT) REBUT
(— ONE IN AUTHORITY) REBEL
DEFORCE

OPPOSED ANTI ALIEN AVERSE ADVERSE
AGAINST COUNTER HOSTILE CONTRARY
ABHORRENT ANTARCTIC REPUGNANT
(PERSISTENTLY —) RENITENT

OPPOSITE TO ANENT POLAR ACROSS
ANENST AVERSE FACING WITHER
ADVERSE COUNTER FORNENT INVERSE
OBVIOUS REVERSE ANTIPODE CONTRARY
CONTRAST CONVERSE ANTIPODAL
REPUGNANT RECIPROCAL
(— MIDDLE OF SHIP'S SIDE) ABEAM
(— OF TRUTH) DEVIL
(— THE ALTAR) WEST

OPPOSITION CON FLAK ATILT CLASH
STOUR THWART DISCORD CLASHING

CONTRAST OBSTACLE POLARITY ANIMOSITY COLLISION HOSTILITY RENITENCY

OPPRESS SIT HOLD LADE LOAD PEIS RACK RAPE RIDE SWAY THEW CROWD CRUSH GRIND GRIPE HEAVY PEISE POISE PRESS WEIGH WRONG BETOIL BURDEN DEFOIL DEFOUL EXTORT HARASS HARROW NIDDER NITHER RAVISH SUBDUE THREAT AFFLICT DEPRESS INGRATE OVERLAY REPRESS SQUEEZE TRAMPLE CONFRONT DISTRESS ENCUMBER PRESSURE SUPPRESS OVERPOWER OVERTHROW OVERWEIGH OVERWHELM
(— WITH DREAD) HAGRIDE
(— WITH HEAT) SWELTER

OPPRESSED SERVILE

OPPRESSION ROD GRIPE PRESS BURDEN THRALL MIZRAIM DULLNESS PRESSURE EXTORTION GRIEVANCE LASSITUDE

OPPRESSIVE HOT DIRE HARD CLOSE DOWIE FAINT HARSH HEAVY BITTER LEADEN SCREWY SEVERE SMUDGY SULTRY TORRID URGENT WEIGHT ONEROUS SLAVISH GRIEVOUS GRINDING RIGOROUS

OPPRESSOR CSAR CZAR NERO TSAR TZAR EGLON TYRANT INCUBUS

OPPROBRIUM ENVY ABUSE ODIUM SCORN SHAME INFAMY INSULT CALUMNY DISDAIN OFFENSE SCANDAL DISGRACE DISHONOR REPROACH CONTUMELY

OPS (ASSOCIATE OF —) CONSUS
(CONSORT OF —) SATURN
(DAUGHTER OF —) CERES
(FESTIVAL OF —) OPALIA
(PERSONIFICATION OF —) FAUNA TERRA TELLUS

OPT CULL PICK WISH ELECT CHOOSE DECIDE OPTATE SELECT

OPTIC EYE OCULAR VISUAL

OPTIMISTIC GLAD ROSY SUNNY JOYOUS BULLISH HOPEFUL ROSEATE EUPEPTIC SANGUINE EXPECTANT

OPTION UP CALL DOWN CHOICE SPREAD REFUSAL STRADDLE PRIVILEGE

OPTIONAL ELECTIVE VOLUNTARY PERMISSIVE

OPULENT FAT LUSH RICH AMPLE FLUSH PLUSH SHOWY LAVISH MONEYED PROFUSE WEALTHY ABUNDANT AFFLUENT LUXURIANT PLENTIFUL SUMPTUOUS

OPUS WORK ETUDE STUDY

ORACLE SEER TRIP SIBYL TRIPOD TRIPOS DIVINER AUTOPHONE

ORACULAR OTIC VATIC ORPHIC DELPHIC VATICAL DELPHIAN PYTHONIC PROPHETIC

ORAL ALOUD PAROL VOCAL BUCCAL PAROLE SONANT SPOKEN VERBAL UTTERED UNWRITTEN NONCUPATIVE

ORANGE KING MOCK CERES CHILE CHILI CHINO FLAME GENIP HEDGE JAFFA NAVEL OSAGE TENNE AURORA BODOCK BRAZIL COPPER MIKADO NAVAHO SUNTAN TEMPLE TITIAN UVALHA COWSLIP FLORIDA LEATHER MACLURA NARTJIE PAPRIKA PONCEAU PUMPKIN RANGPUR SEVILLE TANGELO TANGIER BERGAMOT BIGARADE CHINOTTI CLAYBANK FLAMINGO HONEYDEW JACINTHE MANDARIN MARATHON MOROCCAN POMANDER SUNBURST VALENCIA BUCCANEER CARNELIAN PERSIMMON TANGERINE
(— MEMBRANE) ZEST
(— PIECE) LITH SEGMENT
(— SEED) PIP
(— TREE) SATSUMA
(BROWNISH —) SPICE
(LARGE —) KING
(MOCK —) SERINGA
(OSAGE —) HEDGE BODOCK
(SOUR —) CURACAO BIGARADE CHINOTTO
(SWEET —) CHINA CHINO

ORANGUTAN APE MIAS ORANG PONGO SATYR SATIRE SATURY PRIMATE SALTIER SATYRUS WOODMAN WOODSMAN

ORATE PLEAD SPEAK SPIEL SPOUT ADDRESS DECLAIM LECTURE BLOVIATE HARANGUE DISCOURSE SPEECHIFY

ORATION EULOGY HESPED SERMON ADDRESS CONCION HARANGUE SUASORIA OLYNTHIAC PANEGYRIC
(— OF CICERO) PHILIPPIC
(FUNERAL —) ELOGE ELOGY MONODY ELOGIUM ENCOMIUM

ORATOR RHETOR DEMAGOG SPEAKER STUMPER CICERONE BOANERGES DEMAGOGUE PLAINTIFF SPOKESMAN

ORATORICAL ELOQUENT RHETORICAL

ORATORY CHAPEL SACRARY ORACULUM SPEAKING ELOCUTION ELOQUENCE PROSEUCHE
(EXAGGERATED —) RHETORIC

ORB EYE SUN BALL MOON STAR EARTH GLOBE MOUND ORBIT CIRCLE PLANET SPHERE CIRCUIT ENCLOSE ENCIRCLE SURROUND FIRMAMENT

ORBIT AUGE PATH APSIS CYCLE TRACK CIRCLE SOCKET SPHERE CIRCUIT ELLIPSE EYEHOLE ECCENTRIC
(POINT IN —) APSIS APOGEE EPIGEE SYZYGY PERIGEE

ORCHARD HOLT TOPE ARBOR GROVE ARBOUR GARDEN HUERTA OLIVET VERGER ARBUSTUM FRUITERY PEACHERY POMARIUM SUGARBUSH

ORCHESTRA BAND GROUP CHAPEL CAPELLE CONSORT GAMELAN KAPELLE ENSEMBLE GAMELANG SYMPHONY SINFONIETTA PHILHARMONIC
(SECTION OF —) BRASS WINDS WOODS STRINGS WOODWINDS PERCUSSION

ORCHID FAAM FAHAM PETAL VANDA CYMBID DUFOIL LAELIA PURPLE AERIDES ANGULOA BOATLIP CALYPSO CULLION FLYWORT LYCASTE POGONIA VANILLA ARETHUSA CALANTHE DENDROBE

GYNANDER LABELLUM ONCIDIUM RAMSHEAD SATYRION CORALROOT HABENARIA PUTTYROOT TWAYBLADE SNAKEMOUTH

ORDAIN LAW PUT DEEM DOOM LOOK MAKE SEND WILL WITE ALLOT ENACT JAPAN ORDER SHAPE WIELD WRITE DECREE PRIEST ADJUDGE APPOINT ARRANGE BEHIGHT COMMAND DESTINE DICTATE FORTUNE INSTALL PREPARE PRESCRIBE

ORDEAL FIRE GAFF TEST AGONY TRIAL CALVARY GAUNTLET

ORDEAL OF RICHARD FEVEREL (AUTHOR OF —) MEREDITH (CHARACTER IN —) TOM LUCY BERRY CLARE MOUNT ADRIAN AUSTIN BLAIZE CAROLA HARLEY RIPTON FEVEREL RICHARD BAKEWELL THOMPSON GRANDISON DESBOROUGH MONTFALCON

ORDER BAN BID RAY SAY TAX BOON CALL CASE CHIT FIAT FORM ORDO RANK RULE SAND SECT STOP SUIT TELL TIFF TRIM WILL WORD ALIGN ARRAY CHIME CLASS DIGHT EDICT GENUS GRADE GUIDE HAVOC PRESS QUIET RANGE SHIFT STATE TAXIS WHACK ASSIGN AVAUNT BEHEST BILLET CEDULA CHARGE COSMOS CURFEW DECREE DEGREE DEMAND DIRECT ENJOIN FIRMAN FOLLOW GRAITH HOOKUM INDENT KILTER MANAGE METHOD NATURE ORDAIN POLICE POTENT SERIES SETTLE SYNTAX SYSTEM ADJUDGE ARRANGE BESPEAK BIDDING BOOKING COMMAND COMPOSE DISPOSE EMBARGO FLOATER MANDATE PRECEPT PROCESS SOCIETY CATEGORY KODASHIM METHODIZE ORDINANCE PRESCRIBE (— OF ANGELS) CHOIR QUIRE MIGHTS THRONES DOMINIONS PRINCIPALITIES (— OF BATTLE) BATTALIA (— OF BELLS) CHANGE (— OF COURT) SIST VACATUR (— OF HOLY BEINGS) HIERARCHY (— OF WORSHIP) AGODUM (— OFF) TURN (CIVIL —) EUNOMY (COSMIC —) TAO RITA (GOOD —) EUTAXY (KNIGHTHOOD —) DANNEBROG (LEGAL —) SIST STET WRIT DAYWRIT SUMMONS SENTENCE SUBPOENA (LOWER — OF MAN) ALALUS (MINOR CHURCH —) BENET (MONASTIC —) SANGHA ACOEMETI (PROPER —) TRAIN (TRAIN —) FLIMSY (TURKISH —) MEDJIDIE (UNIVERSAL —) KIND (WRITTEN —) CHECK DRAFT BILLET DRAUGHT

ORDERED BANDBOX BESPOKE REGULAR SCRAPED COHERENT (WELL —) TRIM

ORDERLINESS METHOD SYSTEM CLARITY DECORUM

ORDERLY AIDE DULY NEAT PEON RULY SNOD TIDY TRIM CRISP SOWAR BATMAN BURSCH COSMIC FORMAL MODEST ORDENE GRADELY REGULAR SHAPELY DECOROUS GALLOPER GRAITHLY OBEDIENT PEACEABLE SHIPSHAPE

ORDINANCE LAW DOOM FIAT RITE BYLAW EDICT ASSIZE DECREE RECESS CONTROL MANDATE SETNESS STATUTE WORKING DECRETUM JUDICIAL REGIMENT TAKKANAH DIRECTION

ORDINARY LAY LOW SOS BEND FESS LALA MEAN PALE PALL RUCK BANAL CHIEF CROSS NOMIC PLAIN PROSE USUAL CANTON COMMON FILLET FLANCH MODERN NORMAL PAIRLE SIMPLE VULGAR AVERAGE MUNDANE NATURAL PROSAIC ROUTINE SALTIRE SAUTIER TRIVIAL VULGATE EVERYDAY FAMILIAR HABITUAL MEDIOCRE MIDDLING PLEBEIAN RUMTYTOO WORKADAY QUOTIDIAN SHAKEFORK

ORDNANCE LAW GUNS ARMOR ORGUE FALCON MINION PETARD PEDRERO RABINET SERPENT WEAPONS BASILISK PETERERO ARTILLERY

ORE (ALSO SEE MINERAL) TIN CHAT DISH DRAG FELL GOLD IRON LEAD MINE POST PULP ROCK CRAZE CRUDE FAVOR GLORY GRACE HONOR MANTO MERCY METAL PRILL COPPER CUPRITE FLOATER RESPECT SEAWEED SMEDDUM CLEMENCY KNOCKING CARBONATE REVERENCE (— DEPOSIT) LODE SCRIN BONANZA (— LAYER) SEAM STOPE (— MASS) SQUAT (— NOT DRESSED) WORK (— WITH STONE ADHERING) CHAT CHATS (BEST —) CROP (BROKEN —) DIRT (COPPER —) HORNITE ATACAMITE MALACHITE (CRUDE —) HEADS (CRUSHED —) SCHLICH (CUBE —) SIDERITE (EARTHY-LOOKING —) PACO (HORSEFLESH —) BORNITE (IMPURE —) SPEISS HALVANS (IRON —) OCHER OCHRE MINION IRONMADE LIMNITE MINETTE OLIGIST TURGITE HEMATITE TACONITE JACUTINGA (LEAD —) BOOZE GALENA ARQUIFOUX (LUMP OF —) HARDHEAD (MERCURY —) GRANZA CINNABAR (SOLID —) RIB (TIN —) ROWS CRAZE SCOVE WHITS FLORAN TINSTUFF (WORTHLESS —) SLAG DROSS MATTE (ZINC —) SMITHSONITE

OREAD PERI NYMPH

OREGON

CAPITAL: SALEM
COLLEGE: REED
COUNTY: LINN CROOK CURRY WASCO
CLATSOP KLAMATH MALHEUR
WALLOWA YAMHILL UMATILLA
INDIAN: ALSEA MODOC WASCO CAYUSE
CHETCO KUITSH TENINO KLAMATH
TAKELMA YAQUINA
LAKE: ABERT WALDO CRATER HARNEY
KLAMATH MALHEUR
MOUNTAIN: HOOD WALKER WILSON
GRIZZLY JACKASS TIDBITS
MOUNTAIN RANGE: BLUE COAST
CASCADE
RIVER: ROGUE IMNAHA OWYHEE POWDER
UMPQUA BLITZEN KLAMATH SILVIES
COLUMBIA DESCHUTES
STATE BIRD: MEADOWLARK
STATE FLOWER: GRAPE
STATE TREE: FIR
TOWN: BEND MORO VALE NYSSA CONDON
EUGENE FOSSIL MADRAS ASTORIA
HEPPNER COQUILLE PORTLAND
CORVALLIS

OREGON TRAIL (AUTHOR OF —)
PARKMAN
(CHARACTER IN —) SHAW HENRY
QUINCY FRANCIS PARKMAN CHATILLON
DESLAURIERS
ORESTES (COMPANION OF —)
PYLADES
(FATHER OF —) AGAMEMNON
(FRIEND OF —) PYLADES
(MOTHER OF —) CLYTEMNESTRA
(SISTER OF —) ELECTRA IPHIGENIA
(WIFE OF —) HERMIONE
ORGAN CUP GILL LIMB PART CHELA
FLOAT GREAT HEART MEANS PAPER
REGAL SERRA ELATER FEEDER FEELER
HAPTOR MEDIUM SPLEEN SUCKER
CLASPER CONSOLE JOURNAL ARMATURE
EFFECTOR ISOGRAFT MAGAZINE
MELODEON MELODICA MYCETOME
OOGONIUM EQUIPMENT HARMONIUM
NEWSPAPER PORTATIVE
(— GALLERY) LOFT
(— OF HEARING) EAR
(— OF SCORPION) PECTEN
(— OF SENSE) SENSE SENSORY
(— OF SILKWORM) FILATOR
(— OF TOUCH) TACTOR TACTUS
(— PIPE) REED FLUTE SCHWEGEL
(— VIBRATO) TREMOLO
(BRISTLELIKE —) SETA
(CHINESE —) SANG CHENG
(HAND —) SERINETTE
(OLFACTORY —) NOSE
(RESPIRATORY —) LUNG
(SMALL —) REGAL
(SWIMMING —) CTENE
(VOCAL — OF BIRDS) SYRINX
(WASTE —) KIDNEY

ORGANIC VITAL INBORN NATURAL
INHERENT
ORGANISM WOG BODY ECAD GERM
GUEST PLANT AEROBE ANIMAL EMBRYO
SYSTEM DIPLONT DISEASE MACHINE
PLANONT SUSCEPT HEMAMEBA
PATHOGEN PLANKTER MESOPHILE
POLYMORPH
(COLD-BLOODED —) POIKILOTHERM
(COMPOUND —) STOCK
(FOSSIL —) EOZOON
(MINUTE —) AMEBA MONAD SPORE
(MODIFIED —) ECAD
(PELAGIC —S) NEKTON
(POLITICAL —) LEVIATHAN
(SIMPLE —) MONAD
ORGANIZATION ART BIG ITO CLUB
FIRM KLAN CADRE FIDAC FORUM HOUSE
MAFIA SETUP CHURCH OUTFIT SURVEY
SYSTEM CHARITY CONCERN DEMOLAY
ECONOMY GIDEONS MENORAH SOCIETY
CONGRESS PATRONAGE STRUCTURE
(— OF ACTORS) COMPANY
(— OF DEALERS) AUCTION
(— OF EXPERIENCE) SCHEMA
(— WITH MANY BRANCHES)
OCTOPUS
(ARMY —) LANDSTORM
(AUXILIARY —) AID SYNODICAL
(COLLEGE —) FRAT ALUMNA ALUMNI
ALUMNUS SORORITY
(HARMONIOUS —) ORCHESTRATION
(JEWISH —) ITO MENORAH
(MUSICAL —) BAND COMBO CAPELLE
KAPELLE ENSEMBLE ORCHESTRA
(POLICE —) GESTAPO
(POLITICAL —) PARTY VEREIN
HETAERIA HETAIRIA APPARATUS
(SAMOAN —) AUMAGA
(SECRET —) WOW BPOE ELKS MOOSE
MASONS MIDEWIN
(SOCIAL —) POLICE
(WAR VETERANS —) AVC DAV GAR
SAR VFW FIDAC AMVETS
(WOMEN'S —) DAR WAF WRC WCTU
SORORITY
(YOUTH —) KOMSOMOL
ORGANIZE FORM EDIFY FOUND MODEL
ORDER RALLY DESIGN EMBODY ARRANGE
MODULIZE REGIMENT UNIONIZE
BLUEPRINT INSTITUTE INTEGRATE
STRUCTURE
ORGANIZED FORMED ORGANIC
TOGETHER
(BADLY —) INCONDITE
ORGY LARK RITE ROMP BINGE REVEL
SPREE FROLIC SHINDY REVELRY
WASSAIL CAROUSAL CEREMONY
SATURNALIA
ORIENT DAWN EAST ADAPT BUILD PEARL
PLACE SHEEN ADJUST LEVANT LOCATE
LUSTER RISING GLOWING INCLINE
RADIANT SUNRISE LUSTROUS
SPARKLING
ORIENTAL ASIAN PEARL BRIGHT INDIAN
ORTIVE RISING EASTERN SHINING

INDOGEAN LUSTROUS PELLUCID PRECIOUS BRILLIANT LEVANTINE

ORIENTATION ASPECT PHORIA STRIKE COLORING LOCALITY

ORIFICE BUNG HOLE PORE PORT VENT INLET MOUTH STOMA TREMA CAVITY OUTLET RICTUS SIPHON THROAT CHIMNEY EARHOLE FORAMEN OPENING OSCULUM OSTIOLE APERTURE INTROITUS
(— IN VOLCANIC REGION) FUMAROLE
(— OF INFUNDIBULUM) LURA
(BREATHING —) SPIRACLE
(VOLCANIC —) BLOWER

ORIGIN NEE GERM KIND RISE ROOT SEED BIRTH CAUSE RADIX START STOCK FATHER GROWTH NATURE PARENT SOURCE SPRING EDITION GENESIS LINEAGE UPSTART NASCENCE UPSPRING BEGINNING INCEPTION OFFSPRING PARENTAGE PROVENANCE
(— ON EARTH) EPIGENE
(FOREIGN —) ECDEMIC

ORIGINAL NEW HOME SEED FIRST FRESH NOVEL PRIME STOCK FONTAL MASTER MOTHER NATIVE PRIMAL PRIMER SAMPLE PIONEER PRIMARY RADICAL SEMINAL NASCENCY PRISTINE AUTHENTIC AUTOGRAPH BEGINNING INVENTIVE OFFSPRING PRIMITIVE
(NOT —) DERIVED

ORIGINALITY INGENUITY

ORIGINATE COIN COME DATE GROW HEAD MAKE MOVE OPEN REAR RISE SIRE ARISE BEGIN BIRTH BREED CAUSE ENDOW FOUND HATCH RAISE START AUTHOR CREATE DERIVE DESIGN DEVISE FATHER INVENT PARENT SPRING CAUSATE DESCEND EMANATE PIONEER PROCEED PRODUCE COMMENCE CONCEIVE CONTRIVE DISCOVER GENERATE INITIATE INSTITUTE

ORIGINATION DESCENT GENESIS BREEDING ORIGINAL COSMOGONY ETYMOLOGY

ORIGINATOR AUTHOR FATHER CREATOR INVENTOR GENERATOR PROGENITOR

ORIOLE PIROL BUNYAH LARIOT LORIOT CACIQUE FIGBIRD PEABIRD FIREBIRD GOLDBIRD HANGBIRD HANGNEST TROUPIAL

ORION RIGEL ALGEBAR
(BELT OF —) ELLWAND
(FATHER OF —) HYRIEUS POSEIDON
(GUIDE OF —) CEDALION
(HOUND OF —) ARATUS
(SLAYER OF —) ARTEMIS

ORKNEY ISLANDS (CAPITAL OF —) KIRKWALL
(ISLAND OF —) HOY POMONA ROUSAY SANDAY STRONSAY

ORLANDO (BELOVED OF —) ROSALIND

ORNAMENT DUB FLY FOB JOY PIN POT TAG TEE TOY URN BALL BOSS CURL CUSP DICE ETCH FALL FRET GAUD GEAR HUSK KNOP LEAF NULL OUCH RULE STAR TOOL TRIM WALY WING ADORN BRAID CHASE CROSS CROWN DECOR EXORN FUSEE GRACE GUTTA HELIX HONOR INLAY KNOSP LUNET MENSK MENSO OVOID PATCH POPPY PRUNT SPANG SPRAY SPRIG STALK TRAIL TRICK WALLY AMULET ANKLET ATTIRE BEDAUB BEDECK BILLET BRANCH BROOCH BUTTON CIMIER COLLAR DIAPER DOODAD EDGING EMBOSS ENRICH FALLAL FINERY FLORET FLOWER GORGET INSERT LABRET LUNULA NIELLO OFFSET PAMPRE PARURE PATERA ROCOCO ROSACE RUNTEE SETOFF TABLET TAHALI TIRADE AGREMEN AKROTER AMALAKA BIBELOT BUCRANE CIRCLET COCARDE CORBEIL CROCKET DIGLYPH EARPLUG ECHINUS EMBLEMA ENGRAVE ENHANCE FRIGGER FURNISH GADROON GARNISH NETSUKE RINCEAU SEXFOIL STRIGIL TREFOIL TRINKET ACCOLADE ANAGLYPH APPLIQUE BRELOQUE DECORATE FLOURISH GIMCRACK LAVALIER MORESQUE PALMETTE ROCAILLE SWASTIKA POPPYHEAD
(— FOR HEAD) MIND TARGET
(— ON SHIP) BADGE APLUSTRE
(CHILD'S —) GAY
(CLAW-LIKE —) GRIFFE
(DRESS —) FROG LACE JABOT SEQUIN SPANGLE
(FANTASTIC —) ANTIC
(HAIR —) TETTIX
(HEAD —) TIARA TEMPLE
(HORSE COLLAR —) HOUNCE
(MUSICAL —) TURN MORDENT BACKFALL PRALLTRILLER
(PENDANT —) BOB BULLA ANADEM BANGLE TASSEL EARRING LAVALIER
(ROOF —) ANTEFIX
(SHOULDER —) EPAULET
(TAWDRY —) GINGERBREAD

ORNAMENTAL FANCY CHICHI FRILLY LILYTURF BLUEBEARD NASTURTIUM SEMPERVIVUM

ORNAMENTATION BOSS FOIL ACORN DECOR ADORNO BABERY CHICHI CILERY DICING BARBOLA CUSPING ECHELLE LACWORK STYLING ACANTHUS APPLIQUE FROUFROU HEADWORK PURFLING ROCAILLE STAFFAGE TRESSURE
(CHEAP —) TINSEL
(EXTRAVAGANT —) ROCOCO
(MUSICAL —) GRUPPO GRUPPETTO SCHLEIFER

ORNAMENTED FIGURY FOILED ORNATE TAWDRY ADORNED FLOUNCY FROSTED TREFLEE WROUGHT GOFFERED SINNOWED ELABORATE STELLATED

ORNATE GAY FINE FANCY FUSSY GIDDY SHOWY DRESSY FLORID FLOSSY PURPLE SUPERB AUREATE BAROQUE FLOWERY TAFFETA MANDARIN OVERRIPE SPLENDID ELABORATE UNNATURAL
(EXTREMELY —) GIDDY

ORNITHOLOGIST AUDUBON BIRDMAN

OROTUND FULL CLEAR SHOWY MELLOW

STRONG POMPOUS RESONANT SONOROUS BOMBASTIC

ORPHAN PIP WARD FOUNDLING STEPCHILD

ORPHANED ORBATE

ORPHEUS (BIRTHPLACE OF —) PIERIA
(FATHER OF —) APOLLO OEAGRUS
(MOTHER OF —) CALLIOPE
(WIFE OF —) EURYDICE

ORTHODOX GOOD GREEK SOUND USUAL PROPER CANONIC CORRECT ACCEPTED CATHOLIC STANDARD CUSTOMARY

ORTHODOXY PIETY TRUTH SOUNDNESS

ORTHOPTERON WALKER

ORTNIT (BROTHER OF —) WOLFDIETRICH

ORTOLAN BIRD RAIL SORA BUNTING BOBOLINK WHEATEAR

ORTSTEIN HARDPAN

ORYX BEISA PASANG PASENG GAZELLE GEMSBOK ANTELOPE LEUCORYX

OS BONE ESKAR ESKER MOUTH OPENING ORIFICE

OSCILLATE LOG WAG HUNT ROCK SWAY VARY SQUEG SWING WAVER WEAVE SHIMMY FEATHER VIBRATE FLUCTUATE

OSCILLATION HOWL WAVE SHOCK SEICHE SHIMMY SQUEAL FLUTTER LIBRATION VIBRATION
(— OF EARTH'S AXIS) NUTATION

OSCULATE BUSS KISS

OSCULATION TACNODE

OSIER ROD WAND EDDER SALIX SKEIN SPLIT WITHY BASKET SALLOW WICKER WILLOW DOGWOOD WILGERS REDBRUSH

OSIRIS HERSHEF UNNEFER
(BROTHER OF —) SET SETH
(CROWN OF —) ATEF
(FATHER OF —) GEB KEB SEB
(MOTHER OF —) NUT
(SISTER OF —) ISIS
(SON OF —) HORUS ANUBIS
(WIFE OF —) ISIS

OSPREY GLED HAWK OSSI GLEDE PYGARG BALBUSARD OSSIFRAGE

OSSIFICATION OSTOSIS UROSTEON METOSTEON SIDEBONES

OSTENSIBLE NOMINAL SEEMING APPARENT SPECIOUS

OSTENTATION DOG POMP PUFF SHOW CLASS ECLAT FLARE PRIDE STRUT SWANK VAUNT PARADE VANITY DISPLAY FLUTTER PAGEANT PORTENT PRESAGE FLOURISH FRIPPERY PRETENCE PRETENSE SHOWINESS SPECTACLE

OSTENTATIOUS ARTY LOUD VAIN GAUDY SHOWY SWANK FLASHY SPORTY SWANKY TURGID FLAUNTY GLARING OBVIOUS POMPOUS SPLASHY SPLURGY FASTUOUS ELABORATE

OSTRACIZE BAN BAR CUT SNUB EXILE BANISH PUNISH REJECT ABOLISH BOYCOTT CENSURE EXCLUDE BLACKBALL PROSCRIBE

OSTRICH EMU RHEA NANDU BREVIPEN STRUCION

OSWALD (FATHER OF —) ETHELFRITH
(SLAYER OF —) PENDA

OTHELLO MOOR
(AUTHOR OF —) SHAKESPEARE
(CHARACTER IN —) IAGO BIANCA CASSIO EMILIA MONTANO OTHELLO GRATIANO LODOVICO RODERICO BRABANTIO DESDEMONA
(ENSIGN OF —) IAGO
(FRIEND OF —) IAGO
(LIEUTENANT OF —) CASSIO
(WIFE OF —) DESDEMONA

OTHER MO ELSE MORE ALTER FORMER NOTHER SECOND TIDDER TOTHER ALTERUM FURTHER DISTINCT DIFFERENT
(— THAN) SAVE

OTHERWISE OR NOT ELSE ENSE ALIAS SECUS ALITER EXCEPT BESIDES ELSEHOW ELSEWAYS

OTIOSE IDLE LAZY VAIN ALOOF FUTILE OTIANT REMOTE STERILE USELESS INACTIVE INDOLENT REPOSING

OTTER DOG FUR PUP FISH NAIR PELT BITCH HURON LOUTRE SIMUNG TACKLE ANNATTO PERIQUE MAMPALON MUSTELIN PARAVANE
(DEN OF — S) HOLT
(SEA —) KALAN

OTTOMAN (ALSO SEE TURKEY) POUF SEAT TURK COUCH DIVAN SQUAB STOOL FABRIC OTHMAN POUFFE SULTANE FOOTSTOOL

OUGHT BIT BUD BUT MOW BOOD BOOT MOTE MUST ZERO SHALL BELONG CIPHER NAUGHT NOUGHT SHOULD BEHOOVE

OUNCE URE OKET OKIA ONCA ONCE ONZA OKIEH UNCIA CHEETAH LEOPARD WILDCAT
(CHINESE —) LIANG
(EIGHT —S) CUPFUL
(HALF —) SEMUNCIA
(ONE-16TH OF —) DRAM
(ONE-20TH OF —) EASTERLING
(ONE-8TH OF —) DRAM

OUR UR UR ORE URE WIR WIR HORE NOTRE UNSER

OUR TOWN (AUTHOR OF —) WILDER
(CHARACTER IN —) JOE WEBB EMILY GIBBS HOWIE SIMON WALLY GEORGE CROWELL NEWSOME REBECCA STIMSON GORUSLOWSKI

OUST BAR BUMP FIRE SACK CHUCK EJECT EVICT EXPEL BANISH DEBOUT REMOVE CASHIER DISCARD DISMISS SUSPEND DISSEIZE FORJUDGE ELIMINATE

OUT EX AWAY DOWN HORS FORTH ABSENT BEGONE ISSUED OOTWITH OUTWARD EXTERNAL PUBLISHED
(— AT ELBOWS) SCRUFFY
(— LOUD) BOST
(— OF) EX FROM DEHORS OUTWITH
(— OF BREATH) BLOWN
(— OF COMMISSION) BUNG
(— OF DATE) OLD DOWDY PASSE OUTWORN TIMEWORN OVERDATED

(— OF DOORS) ABROAD FOREIGN THEREOUT
(— OF EXISTENCE) AWAY
(— OF KILTER) ALOP AWRY CRANK BROKEN
(— OF ONE'S MIND) FEY DAFT DELEERIT
(— OF ORDER) AMISS KAPUT FAULTY DEFICIENT
(— OF PLACE) AMISS INEPT
(— OF PLAY) DEAD FOUL
(— OF SIGHT) DOGGO INVISIBLE
(— OF SORTS) CROOK CROSS HUMPY NOHOW COMICAL PEEVISH
(— OF THE WAY) BY BYE ASIDE BLIND CLEAR CLOSE AFIELD GEASON REMOTE
(— OF THIS LIFE) HYNE
(— OF TUNE) FALSE SCORDATO
(FARTHER —) UTTER

OUT-AND-OUT GROSS PLUMB SHEER SWORN UTTER ARRANT DIRECT WHOLLY REGULAR ABSOLUTE COMPLETE CRASHING OUTRIGHT

OUTBREAK FIT ROW RASH RIOT BURST SALLY EMEUTE PLAGUE REVOLT RUCKUS TUMULT UPROAR BOUTADE OUTCROP RUCTION BLIZZARD ERUPTION OUTBURST EXPLOSION
(— OF DISEASE) PANDEMIC
(— OF EMOTIONALISM) HYSTERIA
(— OF TEMPER) MOORBURN
(REVOLUTIONARY —) PUTSCH
(SUDDEN —) SPURT

OUTBUILDING BARN SHED LODGE PRIVY BARTON GARAGE HEMMEL OUTHOUSE SKEELING SKILLING BACKHOUSE

OUTBURST BOUT CROW FLAW FUME GALE GUST RAGE TEAR TIFF AGONY BLAST BLAZE BLURT BREAK BRUNT BURST FLARE FLASH GEARE SALLY SPATE START STORM ACCESS BLOWER BLOWUP ESCAPE FANTAD FANTOD GOLLER TIRADE TUMULT BLOWOUT BOUTADE OUTCROP PASSION TANTRUM TORRENT ERUPTION EXPLOSION
(— OF ANGER) FIT GERE GEARE TATTER
(— OF ORATORY) SQUIRT
(— OF SPEECH) STRAIN
(— OF TEMPER) FUFF TIFF BLOWOUT

OUTCAST EXILE LEPER RONIN SHREW ABJECT PARIAH WRETCH AOUTLET ISHMAEL MISSILE OUTWALE CASTAWAY CHANDALA REJECTED VAGABOND DIALONIAN
(HOMELESS —) ARAB
(JAPANESE —) ETA RONIN
(PYRENEES —) CAGOT

OUTCOME END OUT FATE TERM CLOSE EDUCT EVENT HATCH ISSUE LOOSE PROOF UPSET BROWST EFFECT EXITUS OUTLET PERIOD RESULT SEQUEL UPSHOT EMANATE PROGENY SUCCESS FATALITY AFTERMATH

OUTCROP CROP REEF LEDGE BASSET INLIER BLOSSOM BLOWOUT OUTBREAK OUTBURST

OUTCRY CAW CRY HUE YIP BAWL BRAY DITE GAFF HOWL REAM ROAR SCRY UTAS YARM YELL ALARM BOAST DITTY NOISE OUTAS SHOUT STINK WHAUP BELLOW CLAMOR HOLLER RACKET SCREAM SHRIEK STEVEN TUMULT CALLING EXCLAIM PROTEST SCREECH SHILLOO COMPLAINT PHILLILEW

OUTDISTANCE DROP SKIN OUTGO SURPASS OUTSTRIP

OUTDO CAP COB COP COW POT TOP BANG BEAT BEST FLOG WHIP EXCEL OUTGO REVIE TRUMP WORSE DEFEAT EXCEED OUTACT NONPLUS OUTPACE SURPASS OUTMATCH OUTSHINE OVERCOME

OUTDOORS FORTH OUTBY OUTBYE OUTSIDE

OUTER BUT OVER ALIEN ECTAD ECTAL UPPER UTTER FOREIGN OUTSIDE OUTWARD EXTERIOR EXTERNAL FORINSEC

OUTERMOST FINAL UTTER UTMOST EVEREST EXTREME OUTWARD FARTHEST REMOTEST

OUTFIT KIT RIG GANG GARB REAR REEK SUIT TEAM UNIT DRESS EQUIP GETUP HABIT TROUP ATTIRE CONREY DUFFEL FITOUT LAYOUT CLOTHES FURNISH SHEBANG EQUIPAGE FURNITURE GRUBSTAKE
(INFANT'S —) LAYETTE
(SPARE —) CHANGE

OUTGO EXIT EXCEL ISSUE OUTDO EFFLUX EGRESS EXCEED OUTLAY OUTLET OUTRUN OUTCOME PRODUCT SURPASS OUTSTRIP

OUTGROWTH ALA BUD JAG ARIL FOOT HAIR LEAF MOSS SPUR CLAMP FRUIT HILUM HYPHA SCALE SPINE ACULEA COCKLE CUPULE FIBRIL ENATION FEATHER ISIDIUM APPENDIX CARUNCLE EPIDERMA HAPTERON INDUSIUM OFFSHOOT CARBUNCLE EMERGENCE OSTEOPHYTE

OUTHOUSE SHED SKEO BIFFY LODGE PRIVY BIGGIN LINHAY OUTHUT LATRINE SKEELING SKILLION

OUTING OUT SKIP STAY TRIP JUNKET PICNIC COOKOUT HOLIDAY CLAMBAKE VACATION EXCURSION WAYZGOOSE

OUTLANDISH ALIEN KINKY EXOTIC REMOTE BIZARRE FOREIGN STRANGE UNCOUTH PECULIAR BARBAROUS FANTASTIC GROTESQUE UNEARTHLY

OUTLAST ELAPSE SURVIVE OVERBIDE

OUTLAW BAN BAR CACO HORN TORY EXILE EXLEX FLEME RONIN ARRANT BADMAN BANDIT BANISH BRUMBY COWBOY DACOIT UNLEDE BANDIDO ISHMAEL FUGITATE FUGITIVE PROHIBIT PROSCRIBE PROSCRIPT
(IRISH —) WOODKERN
(JAPANESE —) RONIN
(PL.) MANZAS

OUTLAWED ILLEGAL ILLICIT LAWLESS

OUTLAY COST MISE OUTGO EXPENSE PENSION

OUTLET BORE DRIP EXIT VENT ISSUE
EGRESS ESCAPE EXITUS FUNNEL
OUTAGE OPENING FUMEDUCT
OVERFLOW SINKHOLE AVOIDANCE
(— FOR COASTAL SWAMP) BAYOU
(— FOR SMOKE) FEMERALL
(— OF CARBURETOR) BARREL
(— OF SPRING) EYE
(AIR —) GRILL GRILLE
(ELECTRIC —) POINT

OUTLINE MAP BOSH ETCH FLOW FORM
LINE PLAN PLAT BRIEF CHALK CHART
DRAFT FRAME MODEL SHAPE TRACE
AGENDA APERCU DESIGN DOODLE
FIGURE FILLET LAYOUT SCHEMA SCHEME
SCROLL SKETCH SURVEY CAPSULE
CONTOUR CROQUIS DRAUGHT ELEMENT
EXTRACT FEATURE GABARIT ISOTYPE
PROFILE SUMMARY CONTORNO
DESCRIBE ESQUISSE SKELETON
SYLLABUS SYNOPSIS GUIDELINE
TREATMENT
(— HASTILY) SPLASH
(— OF A SCIENCE) GRUNDRISS
(— OF ANIMAL'S BODY) UNDERLINE
(— OF COLUMN) ENTASIS
(— OF PLAY) SCENARIO
(— SHARPLY) ITALICIZE
(CURVING —) SWING
(DOUBLE —) FRINGE
(SHADOWY —) GHOST

OUTLIVE OUTLAST OUTWEAR SURVIVE
OVERBIDE

OUTLOOK MIND VIEW FRONK FRONT
VISTA ASPECT CLIMATE LOOKOUT
PURVIEW FRONTAGE OUTSIGHT
PROSPECT MENTALITY
(BRASH —) FACE
(MEDICAL —) PROGNOSIS
(SELF-CONFIDENT —) SWAGGER

OUTMANEUVER HAVE OUTPLAY

OUTMODED COLD DATED PASSE RUSTY
BYGONE EFFETE ANTIQUE ELDERLY
VINTAGE OBSOLETE

OUTPOST STATION FOREPOST
OUTGUARD

OUTPOURING FLOW GALE GUSH FLOOD
RIVER SPATE EARFUL LAVISH STREAM
OUTFLOW FUSILLADE

OUTPUT CUT GET CROP MAKE EXPEL
GRIST POWER YIELD ENERGY UPCOME
TURNOUT

OUTRAGE RAPE ABUSE INSULT OFFEND
RAVISH AFFRONT OFFENSE VIOLATE
VIOLENCE INDIGNITY

OUTRAGEOUS DAMNED HEINOUS
OBSCENE UNGODLY FLAGRANT
INFERNAL SHAMEFUL SHOCKING
ATROCIOUS DESPERATE MONSTROUS

OUTRE ODD BIZARRE STRANGE
ECCENTRIC

OUTRIGGER BOOM PROA BUMKIN
RIGGER SPIDER

OUTRIGHT RUN BALD CLEAN TOTAL
WHOLE DIRECT ENTIRE OPENLY WHOLLY
ABSOLUTE COMPLETE DIRECTLY
ENTIRELY

OUTRUN BEAT COTE NICK PASS OUTGO
EXCEED ATRENNE FORERUN OUTFOOT
PREVENT

OUTSET START OFFSET SETOUT
BEGINNING THRESHOLD

OUTSIDE BUT OUT BOUT FREE RIND
OUTBY UTTER AFIELD OUTFACE
SURFACE EXTERIOR EXTERNAL
(— BOUNDS) ALOGICAL
(— OF) BESIDE

OUTSIDER ALIEN OUTMAN BOUNDER
ISHMAEL EXOTERIC STRANGER
EXTRANEAN FOREIGNER PHILISTER

OUTSKIRTS SIDE SKIRTS PURLIEU
OUTSHIFTS

OUTSPOKEN BOLD FREE LOUD APERT
BLUFF BLUNT BROAD FRANK NAKED
PLAIN ROUND CANDID DIRECT ARTLESS
EXPRESS EXPLICIT

OUTSTANDING ACE BIG ARCH RARE
SOME AMONG FAMED NOTED SMASH
BANNER FAMOUS GIFTED HEROIC
MARKED SIGNAL SNAZZY UNPAID
EMINENT PALMARY SALIENT STELLAR
SUBLIME SUPREME TOPPING FABULOUS
INSPIRED PREMIERE SEASONED
SKELPING SLAMBANG SMACKING
STANDOUT TOWERING BEAUTIFUL
PRINCIPAL PROMINENT UNSETTLED
MONUMENTAL NOTICEABLE PREEMINENT

OUTWARD ECTAD OUTER OVERT
DERMAD EXODIC EXTERN FORMAL
EXTREME VISIBLE APPARENT EXTERIOR
EXTERNAL OBSOLETE OUTFORTH
EXTRINSIC

OUTWEIGH WEIGH OUTPOISE OVERBEAR
OVERSHADE PREPONDERATE

OUTWIT FOX POT BALK BEST DISH FOIL
HAVE BLOCK CHECK CROSS BAFFLE
EUCHRE FICKLE JOCKEY OVERGO
THWART STONKER OUTGUESS
OUTSHARP CROSSBITE OVERREACH
CIRCUMVENT

OVAL ELLIPSE STADIUM VESICAL
VULVATE AVELONGE NUMMULAR
VULVIFORM

OVATION HAND APPLAUSE

OVEN OON UMU KILN LEAR LEER LEHR
OAST BAKER BENCH GLAZE GLOOM
HANGI KOHUA TANUR TILER CALCAR
MUFFLE CABOOSE FURNACE KITCHEN

OVER BY BYE OER TOO ALSO ANEW ATOP
BACK DEAD DONE GONE UPON ABOVE
AGAIN ALOFT ATOUR ATURN CLEAR
ENDED EXTRA VAULT ABROAD ACROSS
AROUND BEYOND DESSUS EXCESS
UPWARD SURPLUS THROUGH FINISHED
(— AGAINST) FORNENT
(— AND ABOVE) ATOP ATOUR BESIDES
(ALL —) NAPOO SURTOUT

OVERABUNDANCE WASTE EXCESS
SURPLUS PLETHORA

OVERALLS SLIP CHAPS JEANS TONGS
DENIMS

OVERBEARING HIGH PROUD LORDLY OVERLY HAUGHTY ARROGANT BULLYING DOGMATIC INSOLENT PRUSSIAN SNOBBISH IMPERIOUS MASTERFUL

OVERCAST DIM SEW BIND DARK DULL GLUM WHIP CLOUD HEAVY SERGE CLOUDY DARKEN GLOOMY LOWERY CLOUDED NUBILOUS

OVERCOAT MINO BENNY GREGO JEMMY SHUBA BANGUP CAPOTE RAGLAN SLIPON TABARD TOPPER ULSTER PALETOT SPENCER SURTOUT TOPCOAT BENJAMIN COONSKIN TAGLIONI COTHAMORE GREATCOAT INVERNESS

OVERCOME DO AWE GET MOW WAR WIN BEAT BEST DING LICK LOCK MATE POOP SACK SUNK TAME WAUR CHARM CRUCH DAUNT DROUK DROWN FORDO STILL STOOP THROW APPALL BEATEN BUSHED CRAVEN DEFEAT EXCEED EXPUGN FOREDO HURDLE MASTER MOIDER OUTRAY PLUNGE SUBDUE VICTOR CONFUTE CONQUER DEPRESS ENFORCE RECOVER SMOTHER CONVINCE OUTSTRIP SUPERATE SURMOUNT SURPRISE PROSTRATE
(— DIFFICULTIES) SWIM
(— WITH FATIGUE) FORDO
(— WITH WEARINESS) HEAVY
(BE — BY HEAT) SWELTER

OVERCONFIDENT SECURE POSITIVE

OVERDO EXCEED EXHAUST FATIGUE PERCOCT OVERCOOK OVERWORK BURLESQUE

OVERDUE BACK LATE TARDY UNPAID ARREARS BELATED DELAYED EXCESSIVE

OVEREAT GORGE SLOFF SATIATE GOURMAND

OVERFLOW REE COME FLUX REAM SLOP SWIM TEEM VENT BRIME FLOAT FLOOD SPATE SPILL ABOUND DEBORD OUTLET SPILTH OVERRUN REDOUND BOILOVER EXUNDATE INUNDATE OUTSWELL SUBMERGE CATACLYSM

OVERFLOWING FLOW AWASH FLOAT DELAVY DELUGE ALLUVIO COPIOUS FRESHET PROFUSE INUNDANT EXUBERANT LANDFLOOD SUPERFLUX

OVERGROWN FOZY RANK GAWKY BRANCHY FULSOME SPRATTY SPRITTY

OVERHANG JUT BEND EAVE RAKE BULGE JETTY BEETLE SHELVE TOPPLE FANTAIL OVERLAP PROJECT SUSPEND

OVERHANGING BEETLE SHELVY HANGING PENDENT PENSILE BEETLING IMMINENT OBUMBRANT PENTHOUSE PRECIPITOUS

OVERHAUL EXAMINE OVERHAIL RENOVATE FOREREACH

OVERHEAD COST ABOVE ALOFT BURDEN ONCOST UPKEEP EXPENSE OVERTOP

OVERLAP LAP RIDE SYPHER SHINGLE IMBRICATE INTERSECT

OVERLAPPING JUGATE RIDING EQUITANT OBVOLUTE IMBRICATE

OVERLAY CAP LAP CEIL COAT WHIP APPLY COUCH COVER GLAZE PATCH PLATE CEMENT CRAVAT SPREAD STUCCO VENEER ENCRUST OPPRESS OVERLIE SMOTHER APPLIQUE TEMPLATE
(— WITH GOLD) BEAT GILD

OVERLOOK BALK MISS OMIT PASS SKIP SLIP WINK BLINK FORGO ACQUIT EXCUSE FOREGO FORGET IGNORE MANAGE OVERGO ABSOLVE COMMAND CONDONE FORGIVE INSPECT MISKNOW NEGLECT CONFOUND DOMINATE DISREGARD DISSEMBLE

OVERLORD LIEGE DESPOT ISWARA SATRAP TYRANT ISHVARA SUZERAIN TYRANNIZE

OVERNICE FEAT FUSS SAUCY DAINTY QUAINT SPRUCE FINICKY PRECISE DENTICAL PRECIOUS SQUEAMISH

OVERPOWER AWE BEAT ROUT RUSH CRUSH DROWN QUELL SWAMP WHELM COMPEL DEFEAT DELUGE ENGULF MASTER OVERGO SUBDUE WRIXLE CONQUER CONTROL OPPRESS REPRESS CONVINCE OUTSCOUT SCUMFISH SURPRISE
.(— WITH HEAT) SWELT
(— WITH LIGHT) DAZZLE

OVERPOWERING DIRE FIERCE KILLING DAZZLING STUNNING DESPERATE MONSTROUS

OVERREACH DO POT DUPE GRAB CHEAT COZEN CHOILE GREASE NOBBLE OUTWIT OVERGO DECEIVE

OVERRUN TEEM BESET CRUSH SWARM DELUGE EXCEED INFEST INVADE OVERGO RAVAGE SPREAD DESTROY

OVERSEE TEND WATCH DIRECT HANDLE MANAGE SURVEY EXAMINE INSPECT NEGLECT DISREGARD SUPERVISE

OVERSEER BAAS BOSS CORK JOSS EPHOR GRAVE REEVE BISHOP CENSOR DRIVER GAFFER GRIEVE KEEKER MIRDHA TINDAL WARDEN BAILIFF CAPATAZ CAPORAL CURATOR FOREMAN HEADMAN KANGANI MANAGER MANDOER MAYORAL OVERMAN PRISTAW TAPSMAN BANKSMAN CHAPRASI DECURION MARTINET SURVEYOR VILLICUS
(— OF MACHINERY) TENTOR
(— OF MINE) CAPTAIN
(SPIRITUAL —) PASTOR PRIEST

OVERSHADOW DIM CLOUD COVER DWARF SHADE TOWER DARKEN EFFACE ECLIPSE OBSCURE UMBRAGE BESCREEN DOMINATE OVERCAST

OVERSHOE GUM BOOT GUME ARCTIC GAITER GALOSH PATTEN RUBBER SANDAL FLAPPER EXCLUDER FOOTHOLD PANTOFLE

OVERSIGHT EYE CARE HOLE SLIP ERROR FAULT GAFFE LAPSE WATCH CHARGE BLUNDER CONTROL JEOFAIL MISTAKE OMISSION TUTELAGE DIRECTION
(LEGAL —) JEOFAIL

OVERT OPEN PATENT PUBLIC OBVIOUS APPARENT MANIFEST

OVERTAKE PASS ATAKE CATCH ATTAIN
BEFALL DETECT ENSNARE OVERHIE
FOREHENT OVERHAUL
OVERTHROW TIP CAST DASH DOWN
FALL FELL FOIL FOLD HURL RAZE ROUT
RUIN RUSH WALT WEND ALLAY CRUSH
EVERT FLING LEVEL QUASH UPSET
WORST WRACK WRECK DEFEAT DEJECT
DEPOSE REPUTE SLIGHT TOPPLE TUMBLE
UNSEAT WRITHE AFFLICT CONQUER
CONVELL DESTROY DISMISS RUINATE
SUBVERT UNDOING UNHORSE WHEMMLE
CONFOUND DEMOLISH OVERCOME
OVERTURN REVERSAL SUPPLANT
VANQUISH CHECKMATE CONFUSION
OVERWHELM
(— BY TRIPPING) CHIP
OVERTURE OFFER PROEM ADVANCE
OPENING PRELUDE APERTURE PROPOSAL
SINFONIA VORSPIEL
(INDECENT —) ASSAULT
OVERTURN TIP CAVE COUP KEEL TILT
WALT WELT TERVE THROW UPEND
UPSET WELME WHALM WHELM SLIGHT
TIPPLE TOPPLE WELTER CAPSIZE
DESTROY PERVERT REVERSE SUBVERT
WHEMMLE
(— A WATCHMAN) BOX
OVERWHELM BOWL BURY SINK SLAY
AMAZE COVER CRUSH DROOK DROUK
DROWN FLOOD SEIZE SPATE SWAMP
CUMBER DEFEAT DELUGE ENGULF
OBRUTE PLUNGE QUELME QUENCH
ASTOUND BOMBARD CONFUTE CONQUER
ENGROSS FLATTEN IMMERSE INFLOOD
OPPRESS SMOTHER ASTONISH DISTRESS
INUNDATE OVERCOME SUBMERGE
AVALANCHE
OVERWORK HOIN TIRE TOIL SWEAT
STRAIN SURMENAGE
OVULE EGG NIT GERM SEED EMBRYO
OVULUM GEMMULE SEEDLET
OVUM EGG OVAL SEED SPORE OOSPERM
OOSPHERE
OWE DUE OWN REST AUGHT OUGHT
SHALL POSSESS ATTRIBUTE
OWL ULE BUBO LULU MOMO RURU SURN
TYTO UTUM JENNY MADGE NINOX
PADGE SCOPS STRIX TAWNY WEKAU
AZIOLA HOOTER HOWLET KETUPA
MUCARO RAPTOR STRICH VERMIN
WHEKAU BOOBOOK HARFANG KATOGLE
WAPACUT WOOLERT BILLYWIX
COQUIMBO MOREPORK
(YOUNG —) UTUM OWLET
(PREF.) STRIGI
OWN AIN OWE AVOW FESS HAVE HOLD
HOWE MEET NAIN SELF ADMIT AUGHT
OUGHT MASTER CONCEDE CONFESS
POSSESS PROSPER ACKNOWLEDGE

OWNER BEL MALIK WALLA HOLDER
DOMINUS HERITOR ODALLER
PROPRIETOR
(— OF ESTATE) ALIRD
(— OF FISHING PLANT) PLANTER
(— OF SLAVES) PATRON
(— OF YACHT) AFTERGUARD
(PLANTATION —) COLON
(SHEEP —) NABAL
OWNERSHIP UDAL AUGHT TITLE
CORNER SEIZIN SEIZURE SEVERAL
TENANCY DOMINIUM PROPERTY
COMMUNITY POSSESSION
OX YAK AVER BEEF BULL MUSK NAWT
NEAT NEWT NOWT OWSE ZEBU AIVER
GAYAL SANGA STEER TOLLY TSINE
BOVINE MITHAN ROTHER TWINTER
TALLOWER
(CAMBODIAN —) KOUPREY
(HORNLESS —) MOIL
(SMALL —) RUNT
(TAME —) COACH
(WILD —) URE ANOA BUFF GAUR REEM
URUS BISON BUGLE BANTIN BANTENG
BUFFALO SELADANG
(YEARLING —) STIRK
(YOUNG —) STOT
OXBOW INCIDENT (AUTHOR OF —)
CLARK
(CHARACTER IN —) GIL DREW ROSE
CANBY CROFT GRIER JOYCE MAPEN
TYLER CARTER DAVIES DONALD GERALD
MARTIN OSGOOD RISLEY TETLEY
FARNLEY KINKAID
OXFORD DOWN SHOE CLOTH OXONIAN
SLIPPER
OXIDATION RUST
OYSTER COPIS COPIS COUNT PINNA PLANT
SHELL COTUIT HUITRE NATIVE REEFER
BIVALVE MOLLUSK PANDORE RATTLER
SHARPER BLUEPOINT GREENGILL
LYNNHAVEN
(— BED) PARK STEW LAYER SCALP
CLAIRE SCALFE OYSTERAGE
(— CATCHER) OLIVE PYNOT TIRMA
KROCKET PIANNET REDBILL SCOLDER
SHELDER PILWILLET SKELDRAKE
(— CRAB) PINNOTERE
(— FOSSIL) OSTRACITE
(— MEASURE) WASH
(— PLANT) SALSIFY
(— SHELL) HUSK TEST SHUCK
(— SMALLER THAN QUARTER)
BLISTER
(— SOLD BY POUND) COUNT
(IRISH —) POWLDOODY
(ROCK —) CHAMA
(VEGETABLE —) SALSIFY
(YOUNG —) SET SPAT
(2,3, OR 4 —S) WARP

P

P PAPA PETER
PA DAD PAW PAPA DADDY FATHER
PACE FIG PAD RIP WAY CLIP GAIT LOPE
PASS PELT RACK RATE STEP TEAR TROT
WALK AMBLE SLINK SPACE SPEED STEEK
SWING TEMPO TRACE TREAD CANTER
GALLOP STRAIT STRIDE STILL CHANNEL
CHAPTER DOGTROT MEASURE PASSAGE
SCUTTLE
PACER HORSE AMBLER SPANKER
TRIPPLER
PACHYDERM HIPPO RHINO ELEPHANT
PACIFIC CALM MEEK MILD IRENE IRENIC
PLACID SERENE PEACEFUL TRANQUIL
PEACEABLE
PACIFY CALM EASE LULL STAY ABATE
ALLAY QUELL QUIET STILL PECIFY
SERENE SETTLE SOFTEN SOOTHE
APPEASE ASSUAGE MOLLIFY PLACATE
QUALIFY STICKLE MITIGATE ALLEVIATE
RECONCILE
PACK JAM WAD BALE CRAM DECK FILL
GANG JAMB LADE LOAD ROUT STOW
SWAG TAMP TOTE TUCK COUCH CROWD
FLOCK HORDE SKULK SOMER STEVE
STORE STUFF TRUSS BARREL BOODLE
BUDGET BUNDLE CARTON DUFFLE
EMBALE ENCASE HAMPER IMPACT
PARCEL THWACK TURKEY WALLET
PANNIER PORTAGE RUMMAGE
KNAPSACK
PACKAGE PAD BALE BOLT PAIR DUMMY
TRUSS BINDLE BUNDLE PACKET PARCEL
SAMPLE SEROON DORLACH
(— OF CIGARETTES) DECK
(— OF GOLDBEATER'S SKINS)
SHODER
(— OF LEAF) BOOK
(— OF PEPPERS) ROBBIN
(— OF STAMPS) KILOWARE
(— OF VELLUM) KUTCH
(— OF VENEER) FLITCH
(— OF WOOL) BAG PAD BUTT FADGE
(YARN —) CONE CHEESE
PACKET BOAT BOOK DECK ROLL SCREW
BUNDLE PARCEL SACHET
PACKHORSE SOMER JAGGER PACKER
SUMPTER
PACT MISE ACCORD CARTEL PACTUM
TREATY BARGAIN COMPACT LOCARNO
ALLIANCE CONTRACT COVENANT
AGREEMENT CONCORDAT
PAD MAT WAD WAY BLAD BOSS FROG
LURE MUTE PATH PUFF ROAD ROLL SHOE
WALK WASE BLOCK INKER PERCH PILCH
QUILT STENT STINT STUFF TABBY
TRAMP BASKET BUFFER BUSTLE DAUBER
HOLDER JOCKEY NUMNAH PADDLE

PADNAG PANNEL PILLOW SPONGE
TABLET TRUDGE VELURE WREATH
BOLSTER BOMBAST CUSHION FOOTPAD
SASHOON
(— IN CRIB) BUMPER
(— OF ROPE) PUDDING PUDDENING
(— OF STRAW) SUNK WASE
(— ON HORSE'S FOOT) FROG
(ETCHER'S —) DABBER
(FENCING —) PLASTRON
(HAIR —) RAT MOUSE TOQUE
(INKING —) INKER TOMPION
(MEDICAL —) PLEDGET
(PERFUMED —) SACHET
(SADDLE —) PANEL PILLOW PILLION
(PREF.) TYL(O)
PADDLE OAR ROW SPUD WADE CANOE
DABBLE STRIKE TODDLE SPANKER
PADRE MONK CLERIC FATHER PRIEST
CHAPLAIN
PAGAN ATA BUID BATAK BUKID APAYAO
BAGOBO BANGON BILAAN BONTOC
ETHNIC PAYNIM SABIAN ALANGAN
DUMAGAT GENTILE HEATHEN INFIDEL
SARACEN SUBANUN UNGODLY
IDOLATOR
PAGE BOY CALL LEAF MOTH SIDE CHILD
FACER FOLIO GROOM SHEET DONZEL
ERRATA SUMMON VARLET BUTTONS
CALLBOY FUNNIES PAVISER SERVANT
CHASSEUR HENCHMAN ICHOGLAN
(— BOTTOM) TAIL
(BLANK —S) CANCEL
(FACING —S) SPREAD
(LADY'S —) ESCUDERO
(LAST FEW —S) BACK
(LEFTHAND —) VERSO
(RIGHTHAND —) RECTO OUTPAGE
(TITLE —) UNWAN RUBRIC
PAGEANT POMP SHOW PARADE RIDING
TABLEAU TAMASHA TRIUMPH
AQUACADE CAVALCADE SPECTACLE
WATERWORK
PAGEANTRY POMP PARADE HERALDRY
SPLENDOR
PAGLIACCI (CHARACTER IN —) BEPPE
CANIO NEDDA TONIO SILVIO
(COMPOSER OF —) LEONCAVALLO
PAGODA PON TAA HOON WATT TEMPLE
VARELLA
PAIL CAN PAN BEAT BOWK GAWN MEAL
STOP BOWIE CRUCK SKEEL STOOP
BUCKET COGGIE HARASS KETTLE
NOGGIN SITULA THRASH COLLOCK
(MILK —) KIT SOE TRUG ESHIN LEGLEN
(ON WHEELS) DANDY
(SMALL —) KIT BLICKY

(WOODEN —) COG COGUE LUGGIE PIGGIN

PAIN GYP ACHE AGRA BALE CARE CARK DOLE FRET GRUE HARM HURT PANG SITE SORE TEEN TINE WARK AGONY BEANS CRAMP DOLOR GRIEF GRIPE PINCH PINSE SCALD SMART STING STOUN THRAW THROE WOUND WRING BARRAT GRIEVE MISERY SHOWER STITCH TWINGE AFFLICT ALGESIS ANGUISH EARACHE HURTING MYALGIA OFFENCE PENALTY TORTURE TRAVAIL TROUBLE AGGRIEVE DISTRESS FLEABITE

PAINFUL BAD ILL DIRE EVIL FELL SORE SOUR TART ANGRY CRUEL SHARP SORRY BITTER STICKY TENDER THORNY BALEFUL GRIPING HURTFUL IRKSOME LABORED PENIBLE PUNGENT EXACTING TERRIBLE TORTUOUS DIFFICULT HARROWING
(PREF.) MOGI

PAINT BICE BLOT COAT DAUB DRAW FARD GAUD LIMN PENT PICT SOIL COLOR FEIGN FUCUS GRAIN ROUGE STAIN BEDAUB DAZZLE DEPICT ENAMEL FRESCO OPAQUE SHADOW SKETCH BESMEAR PORTRAY PRETEND SCUMBLE AIRBRUSH DECORATE DEPEINCT DESCRIBE DISGUISE URFIRNIS CALCIMINE

PAINTER BRUSH FAUVE ARTIST DAUBER PICTOR PANTHER SIGNIST SIGNMAN WORKMAN BRUSHMAN LUMINIST MURALIST NAZARENE STIPPLER DECORATOR TACTILIST

PAINTING ART OIL PAT DAUB PATA DRAFT MURAL PIECE TABLE WATER CANVAS CROUTE FRESCO MINERY TITIAN BODEGON CAMAIEU CARTOON COMBINE DAUBING GRADINO GRAPHIC HISTORY PAYSAGE FROTTAGE PREDELLA SEAPIECE SYMPHONY AQUARELLE MINIATURE
(— IN COLLOIDAL MEDIUM) TEMPERA
(— OF EVERYDAY LIFE) GENRE
(— ON PLASTER) SECCO FRESCO
(— WITH OPAQUE COLORS) GOUACHE
(CIRCULAR —) TONDO
(PREHISTORIC —) PICTOGRAM PICTOGRAPH
(RELIGIOUS —) PIETA TANKA
(SCENIC —) SCAPE
(SMALL —) TABLET
(THREE PANEL —) TRIPTYCH

PAIR DUO TWO CASE DUAD DUAL DYAD MATE SIDE SPAN TEAM TWIN YOKE BRACE MARRY MATCH TWAIN UNITE COUPLE GEMINI COUPLET DOUBLET JUMELLE TWOSOME
(— OF FILMS) BIPACK
(— OF MILLSTONES) RUN
(— OF SHOTS) BRACKET
(— OF TONGS) GRAMPUS GRAPPLE
(— OF WINGS) SHEARS
(— ROYAL) PARIAL

PAJAMAS SHALWAR SLEEPER

PAKISTAN

BAY: SOYMIANI
CAPE: FASTA JADDI JIWANI
CAPITAL: ISLAMABAD
COIN: ANNA RUPEE
LANGUAGE: URDU PUSHTU SINDHI BALUCHI BENGALI PUNJABI
MOUNTAIN: TIRICHMIR
MOUNTAIN RANGE: MAKRAN KIRTHAR HIMALAYA SULAIMAN
NATIVE: BENGAL PATHAN SINDHI BALUCHI PUNJABI
PORT: CHALNA KARACHI
PROVINCE: SIND PUNJAB
RIVER: NAL BADO RAVI ZHOB DASHT INDUS CHENAB GANGES JAMUNA JHELUM KUNDAR PORALI
STATE: DIR SWAT KALAT KHARAN CHITRAL KHAIRPUR
TOWN: DACCA CHALNA KHULNA LAHORE MULTAN QUETTA KARACHI SIALKOT LYALLPUR PESHAWAR SARGODHA
WEIGHT: SEER TOLA MAUND

PAL BO ALLY CHUM JACK PARD BILLY BUDDY BUTTY CRONY COBBER COPAIN DIGGER FRIEND COMRADE PARTNER COMPANION

PALACE SALE CHIGI COURT SERAI STEAD CASTLE ELYSEE LOUVRE PALAIS ALCAZAR EDIFICE LATERAN MANSION PALAZZO TRIANON VATICAN ZWINGER BASILICA SERAGLIO WHITEHALL

PALATABLE SAPID SPICY TASTY DAINTY SAVORY MOREISH DELICATE LUSCIOUS PLEASING SAPOROUS AGREEABLE DELICIOUS TOOTHSOME

PALATIAL LARGE ORNATE STATELY SPLENDID

PALE DIM WAN ASHY BLOC FADE GREY GULL LILY PALL SICK THIN WHEY ASHEN BLAKE BLATE BLEAK CLOSE FAINT FENCE GREEN LIGHT LINEN LIVID LURID MEALY STAKE STICK VERGE WHITE ANEMIC BLANCH CHALKY CHANGE DOUGHY FALLOW FEEBLE PALLID PASTEL PICKET REGION REMISS SICKLY SILVER WATERY WHITEN DEFENSE GHASTLY HAGGARD INSIPID OBSCURE SHILPIT DELICATE WATERISH

PALENESS WAN PALLOR ACHROMA

PALISADE HAY BOMA PALE PEEL CLIFF FENCE RIMER STAKE FRAISE PICKET BARRIER ENCLOSE FORTIFY HURDIES STACKET TAMBOUR ESPALIER
(MILITARY —) CIPPUS
(PL.) BAIL BARRIER

PALL FOG BORE CLOY PALE SATE CLOAK CLOTH FAINT QUALM STALE WEARY MANTLE NAUSEA SHROUD DISGUST SATIATE ANIMETTA MORTCLOTH

PALLET BED COT PAD COUCH QUILT PADDLE BLANKET MATTRESS PLANCHER

PALLIATE EASE HIDE MASK VEIL ABATE

CLOAK COLOR COVER GLOSS GLOZE LITHE BLANCH LESSEN REDUCE SMOOTH SOFTEN SOOTHE CONCEAL CUSHION SHELTER DISGUISE MITIGATE

PALLID WAN ASHY PALE PALY BLEAK MEALY WASHY WAXEN WHITE SALLOW GHASTLY BLOODLESS COLORLESS INNOCUOUS

PALLOR ASH WAN PALE ASHES PALENESS

PALM ADY DOM ITA ATAP BRAB BURI BUSU COCO DATE DOUM HIDE JARA KOKO NIOG NIPA PAWN SAGO SLIP TARA ARCHA ARENG ASSAI BUNGA CARRY COCOA COYOL CURUA DATIL INAJA JAGUA LOULU MACAW MERUS NIKAU SABAL SALAK TECUM TUCUM UNAMO YAGUA YARAY ANAHAO ASSAHY BACABA BURITI CHONTA COHUNE COROJO COROZO GEBANG JAMBEE JUPATI KENTIA KITTUL LAWYER LONTAR NIBONG PACAYA RAFFIA ROTANG TOOROO TROPHY APRICOT BABASSU BACTRIS CARANDA CONCEAL COQUITO ERYTHEA GEONOMA MORICHE PALMYRA PUPUNHA SAGWIRE TALIPOT TROOLIE JACITARA LATANIER MACAHUBA PIASSAVA
(— OF HAND) FLAT LOOF VOLA TABLE THENAR
(— OFF) COG FOB TOP SHAB FOIST TRUMP
(— OUT) APPAUME
(BETEL —) ARECA BONGA PUGUA PINANG
(CLIMBING —) RATTAN
(FEATHER —) HOWEA GOMUTI URUCURI
(SPINY —) PEACH GRIGRI GRUGRU

PALMISTRY CHIROMANCY

PALPABLE BALD RANK PLAIN PATENT AUDIBLE EVIDENT OBVIOUS TACTILE APPARENT DISTINCT MANIFEST TANGIBLE CORPOREAL

PALPITATE PANT QUAP THROB FLACKER FLICKER FLUTTER PULSATE

PALPITATION BEAT DUNT PANT FLICKER FLUTTER PULSATION SALTATION THROBBING
(— OF HEART) THUMB

PALSY PARLESIE PARALYSIS

PALTRY BALD BARE BASE MEAN ORRA PUNY SCAB VILE WAFF CHEAP FOOTY MINOR PETTY SCALD SCALL SCRUB SILLY TRASH CHETIF FLIMSY JITNEY SHABBY SLIGHT TRASHY WOEFUL HILDING PELTING PIMPING PITEOUS PITIFUL ROYNISH RUBBISH SCABBED SCRUBBY TRIVIAL PICAYUNE PICKLING PIDDLING TRIFLING

*AMPER PET BABY CRAM DELT GLUT POMP HUMOR SPOIL TUTOR WALLY CARESS COCKER CODDLE COSHER COSSET CUDDLE CUITER DANDLE FONDLE MAUNGE POSSET TIDDLE CHERISH COCKNEY FORWEAN GRATIFY INDULGE SATIATE SMOODGE SAGINATE

PAMPHLET JACK LEAD QUIRE SHEET TRACT FOLDER BOOKLET CATALOG LEAFLET NOVELET BROCHURE CHAPBOOK WORKBOOK CATALOGUE NEWSLETTER

PAN FIT TAB MELL PART PRIG VLEI WASH AGREE BATEA GRAND SHEET UNITE CENSER FRACHE LAPPET PANKIN PATINA SPIDER VESSEL CRANIUM CREAMER HARDPAN PORTION ROASTER SKILLET SUBSOIL PANNIKIN RIDICULE
(— FOR COALS) BRAZIER
(— OF BALANCE) BOWL BASIN SCALEPAN
(— WITH 3 FEET) POSNET
(EARTHENWARE —) PANCHEON
(EVAPORATING —) ROOM COVER TACHE SALTPAN
(IRON —) YET FRACHE
(LONG-HANDLED —) PINGLE
(MILK —) LEAD
(OIL —) SUMP

PANACEA CURE BEZOAR ELIXIR REMEDY SOLACE CUREALL GINSENG HEALALL NEPENTHE CATHOLICON

PANACHE STYLE

PANAMA

CAPITAL: PANAMA
COIN: BALBOA
COUNTY: DARIEN HERRERA
GULF: DARIEN SANBLAS CHIRIQUI MOSQUITO
ISLAND: COIBA
LAKE: GATUN
MEASURE: CELEMIN
MOUNTAIN: CHICO GANDI COLUMAN SANTIAGO
MOUNTAIN RANGE: VERAGUA
PENINSULA: AZUERO
PORT: CRISTOBAL
PROVINCE: COCLE COLON CHIRIQUI VERAGUAS
RIVER: CHEPO SAMBU TUIRA BAYANO PANUGO CHAGRES
TOWN: COLON DAVID AZUERO BALBOA PANAMA PENONOME SANTIAGO

PANCAKE BLIN FLAM AREPA CREPE FADGE FLAWN KISRA LEFSE TOURT BLINTZ FRAISE CRUMPET FLAPPER FRITTER HOTCAKE CORNCAKE FLAPJACK

PANDEMONIUM DIN HELL CHAOS NOISE TUMULT UPROAR DISORDER CONFUSION

PANDORA BANDORE
(BROTHER OF —) PROMETHEUS
(HUSBAND OF —) EPIMETHEUS

PANE GLASS GLAZE LOZEN PANEL QUIRK SHEET SHOCK SLASH QUARRY QUARREL SECTION PORTLIGHT

PANEL FIN PAN JURY SKIN BOARD GROUP LABEL TABLE ABACUS ASSIZE COFFER HURDLE MIRROR PADDLE PILLOW ROSACE TABLET TYMPAN CAISSON

CONSOLE FLIPPER LACUNAR DECORATE
MANDORLA MEDALLION
(— IN FENCE) LOOP
(— IN GARMENT) LAP STEAK
(CIRCULAR —) ROUNDEL
(GAUZE —) SCRIM
(GLAZED —) LAYLIGHT
(LEGAL —) ARRAY
(RECESSED —) ORB COFFER LACUNAR
(SUNKEN —) CAISSON
(3-PART —) TRIPTYCH
PANG ACHE CRAM FILL GIRD PAIN STAB
TANG AGONY PINCH PRONG SPASM
STANG STUFF THROE SHOWER STOUND
TWINGE ANGUISH TRAVAIL
PANIC FEAR FRAY FUNK WILD ALARM
AMAZE CHAOS SCARE FRIGHT SCHRIK
TERROR SWITHER
PANOPLY POMP ARMOR UNIFORM
PANORAMA VIEW RANGE SCENE SWEEP
VISTA NEORAMA PICTURE SCENERY
CYCLORAMA POLYORAMA
PANSY FANCY VIOLA KISSES PENSEE
VIOLET TRINITY FANTASQUE HEARTEASE
PANT FAB ACHE BEAT BLOW FUFF GAPE
GASP HECH LONG PANK PINE PUFF
HEAVE QUIRK THROB YEARN ASPIRE
PULSATE
PANTAGRUEL (COMPANION OF —)
PANURGE
(FATHER OF —) GARGANTUA
(MOTHER OF —) BADEBEC
PANTHEON TEMPLE ROTUNDA
VALHALLA
PANTHER CAT PARD PUMA COUGAR
JAGUAR LEOPARD PAINTER
PANTRY CAVE AMBRY COVEY CUDDY
CLOSET LARDER SPENCE BUTLERY
BUTTERY PANNIER SERVERY SPICERY
CUPBOARD
PANTS JEANS LEVIS BRIEFS SLACKS
DRAWERS JODHPUR BREECHES
BRITCHES KNICKERS SNUGGIES
TROUSERS
(— WITH WIDE BOTTOMS) BELLS
(LEATHER —) CHAPS LEDERHOSEN
(WIDE-LEGGED —) PALAZZO
PAPER LIL WEB BILL BOND BLANK ESSAY
STUDY THEME ASTHMA BINDLE CARTEL
PAPIER REPORT VESSEL CHEVIOT
EXHIBIT JOURNAL WRITING YOSHINO
MONOGRAPH NEWSPRINT PARCHMENT
VALENTINE
(ABSORBENT —) BLOTTER TOWELLING
(BUILDING —) FELT
(BUNDLE OF —S) DUFTER DOSSIER
(CHINESE —) INDIA
(COMMERCIAL —) PORTFOLIO
(DAMAGED —) BROKE CASSE SALLE
RETREE
(DRAWING —) TORCHON
(GLOSS —) GILL
(HARD —) PELURE
(NEGOTIABLE —) STIFF
(OFFICIAL —) TARGE HOOKUM
DOCUMENT
(PARCHMENT —) VELLUM PERGAMYN

(PHOTOGRAPHIC —) SEPIA
(STRIP OF —) TAPE
(THIN —) FLIMSY TISSUE ONIONSKIN
(TOILET —) BUMF
(UNCUT —) BOLT
(WATERMARKED —) BATONNE
(WRAPPING —) SKIP KRAFT SEALING
SCREENING
(WRITING —) FLAT LINEN WEDDING
PAPUA (BAY OF —) DYKE MILNE
ACLAND HOLNICOTE
(CAPITAL OF —) PORTMORESBY
(MONEY OF —) KINA
(RIVER OF —) FLY KIKORI PURARI
(TOWN OF —) LAE BUNA DARU WEWAK
GOROKA KIKORI MADANG SAMARAI
PAR BY NORM EQUAL NORMAL AVERAGE
EQUALITY
(ONE OVER —) BOGIE
(ONE UNDER —) BIRDIE
(TWO UNDER —) EAGLE
PARABLE MYTH TALE FABLE STORY
BYWORD MASHAL SAMPLE BYSPELL
PROVERB ALLEGORY APOLOGUE
LIKENESS
PARACHUTE SILK CHUTE BROLLY
DROGUE PATAGIUM STREAMER
(SMALL —) BALLUTE
PARADE JET TOP POMP SHOW WALK
MARCH STRUT FLAUNT MUSTER REVIEW
STROLL CORTEGE DISPLAY EXHIBIT
MARSHAL CEREMONY EXERCISE
FLOURISH GRANDEUR SPLENDOR
PAGEANTRY
(— OF BULLFIGHTERS) PASEO
PARADISE EDEN JODO BLISS JENNA
AIDENN GOLOKA HEAVEN PARVIS
ELYSIUM NIRVANA
(— OF INDRA) SVARGA
PARADOX KOAN ANTINOMY
PARAGON GEM HERO PINK TYPE IDEAL
MODEL PEARL APERSEE PATTERN
PEROPUS PHOENIX NONESUCH
NONPARIEL
(— OF KNIGHTHOOD) PALADIN
PARAGRAPH ITEM SIGN CAPUT PAUSE
CLAUSE NOTICE RUBRIC ARTICLE INITIAL
PILCROW SECTION CAUSERIE MATERIAL
PERSONAL SUBLEADER
(UNIMPORTANT —S) BALAAM

PARAGUAY

CAPITAL: ASUNCION
COIN: GUARANI
DEPARTMENT: GUAIRA ITAPUA OLIMPO
CAAZAPA BOQUERON
LAKE: VERA YPOA YPACARAI
MEASURE: PIE LINE LINO VARA LEGUA
LINEA CORDEL CUADRA CUARTA FANEGA
PLAIN: CHACO
RIVER: YPANE ACARAY PARANA CONFUSO
TOWN: LUQUE PILAR CAACUPE CAAZAPA
TRINIDAD CONCEPCION VILLARRICA
WEIGHT: QUINTAL

PARAKEET CONURE PARROT WELLAT ROSELLA ARATINGA KAKARIKI POPINJAY ROSEHILL GREENLEEK

PARALLEL EVEN LIKE ALONG EQUAL MATCH SECOND EXAMPLE FRONTAL PARAGON PENDANT ANALOGUE LIKENESS MULTIPLE QUANTITY

PARALYZE DARE DAZE STUN PALSY SCRAM ASTONY BENUMB CONGEAL IMPALSY PETRIFY TORPEDO TORPEFY

PARALYZED NUMB PALSIED CRIPPLED

PARAMOUNT ABOVE CHIEF RULER CAPITAL SUPREME DOMINANT SUPERIOR SUZERAIN SOVEREIGN

PARAMOUR DOLL PRIM PURE LEMAN LOVER WOMAN WOOER AMORET FRIEND MASTER MINION GALLANT HETAERA SERVANT SULTANA

PARAPET BUTT WALL BAHUT REDAN BARBET BONNET FLECHE PARPEN TRENCH BULWARK PLUTEUS RAILING RAMPART BARTIZAN ENVELOPE TRAVERSE

PARAPHERNALIA GEAR EQUIPAGE APPARATUS EQUIPMENT TRAPPINGS

PARASITE BUG BUR FLY BURR MOSS DRONE LEECH SHARK TOADY VIRUS FEEDER FUNGUS SHADOW SPONGE SUCKER BLEEDER SPONGER TAGTAIL EPIPHYTE HANGERON SLAVERER INFESTANT SPARGANUM SYCOPHANT TOADEATER

PARASOL SHADE SHADOW ROUNDEL TIRESOL KITTYSOL SUNSHADE UMBRELLA

PARCEL DAK DAWK DEAD DEAL DOLE METE PACK PART WISP BUNCH GROUP BUNDLE DIVIDE FARDEL PACKET PACKAGE PORTION
(— OF DIAMONDS) SERIES
(— OF GROUND) LOT PICK CLOSE SOLUM SUERTE CONACRE PENDICLE
(— OF HEMP FIBER) PIG
(— OF JEWELS) BULSE
(— OUT) ALLOT

PARCH DRY FRY BURN COOK SEAR ROAST TOAST RIZZER SCORCH BRISTLE GRADDAN SHRIVEL TORREFY

PARCHED ARID HUSK SERE ADUST FIERY GIZZEN TORRID THIRSTY SCORCHED

PARDON FREE CLEAR COVER GRACE MERCY REMIT SPARE ACQUIT ASSOIL EXCUSE SHRIVE ABSOLVE AMNESTY CONDONE FORGIVE OVERLOOK REPRIEVE TOLERATE EXCULPATE

PARDONABLE VENIAL EXCUSABLE

PARE CUP CHIP COPE FLAY PEEL SKIN FRIZZ SHAVE SKELP SLIPE SPADE CHISEL REDUCE REMOVE RESECT CURTAIL FLAUGHT WHITTLE
(— LEATHER) SKIVE
(— SOD) BURNBEAT
(— STAVES) BUCK
(— STONE) BOAST

PARENTAGE KIND BIRTH BROOD FAMILY ORIGIN PROGENY ENGENDURE

PARENTHESIS HOOK ASIDE PAREN BRACKET TOENAIL INNUENDO INTERVAL INTERLUDE
(PL.) HOOKS CURVES

PARIS ALEXANDER
(FATHER OF —) PRIAM
(MOTHER OF —) HECUBA
(WIFE OF —) OENONE

PARISH CURE HOUSE TITLE CHARGE SOCIETY PECULIAR

PARISIAN LUTETIAN

PARITY ANALOGY EQUALITY LIKENESS GRAVITY

PARK HAY PEN HOLE STOP WAIT GREEN LEAVE CIRCLE DAPHNE GARDEN PRATER COMMONS DIAMOND PADDOCK TERRACE PARADISE TETRAGON

PARKA ANORAK JACKET PULLOVER

PARLEY DODGE SPEAK TREAT UTTER CONFER DISCUSS PALAVER PARLANCE DISCOURSE NEGOTIATION

PARLIAMENT DIET RUMP TING COURT SENAT CORTES FANTAN MAJLIS SAEIMA COUNCIL ESTATES KNESSET LAGTING RIKSDAG TYNWALD CONGRESS CONVERSE STORTING VOLKSRAAD
(GREEK —) BOULE
(SCAND. —) THING

PARLOR BEN BOOR HALL FOREROOM LOCUTORY SNUGGERY SOLARIUM
(COUNTRY —) SPENCE
(MILKING —) BAIL

PARLOUS KEEN RISKY CLEVER SHREWD CUNNING CRITICAL PERILOUS DANGEROUS HAZARDOUS

PAROCHIAL PETTY NARROW PAROCHIAN SECTARIAN

PARODY RIB SKIT SPOOF SATIRE TRAVESTY BURLESQUE IMITATION

PAROLE FAITH PLEDGE LICENSE PROMISE

PAROXYSM FIT KINK PANG AGONY COLIC QUIRK SPASM STORM STOUR THROE ACCESS ATTACK FRENZY ORGASM RAPTUS SHOWER RAPTURE EPITASIS AGITATION

PARROT ARA HIA KEA COPY ECHO JAKO KAKA LORO LORY POLL VAZA ARARA CAGIT MACAW MIMIC POLLY AMAZON CAIQUE CONURE KAKAPO REPEAT TIRIBA CORELLA GRASSIE ITERATE LORILET COCKATOO LORIKEET LOVEBIRD PARAKEET PICARIAN POPINJAY BROADTAIL COCKATEEL

PARRY FEND STOP WARD AVOID BLOCK DODGE EVADE FENCE PRIME QUART SIXTE OCTAVE PARADE QUINTE SECOND THWART TIERCE COUNTER DEFLECT EVASION

PARSIFAL (CHARACTER IN —) KUNDRY TITUREL AMFORTAS KLINGSOR PARSIFAL GURNEMANZ
(COMPOSER OF —) WAGNER

PARSIMONIOUS GARE MEAN NEAR NIGH CLOSE MINGY NIPPY SCANT SPARE TIGHT FRUGAL NARROW SCARCE SCOTCH SKIMPY SORDID STINGY STRAIT

MISERLY SCRIMPY SPARING COVETOUS
GRASPING GRUDGING SCREWING
WRETCHED MERCENARY NIGGARDLY
PENURIOUS RETENTIVE ABERDONIAN

PARSON RECTOR CROAKER PATRICO
PERSONA MINISTER PREACHER
GUIDEPOST
(COUNTRY —) RUM

PARSONAGE GLEBE MANSE RECTORY
PASTORATE PASTORIUM

PART DEL END LOT PAN DEAL DOLE FECK
GRIN HAET HALF HAND NECK PANE ROLE
ROVE SECT SHED SIDE SOME TEAR TWIN
AUGHT PARTY PIECE QUOTA SEVER
SHARE SHODE SNACK SPLIT TWAIN
BEHALF CANTON CLEAVE DEPART
DETAIL DIVIDE FEEDER FINGER MEMBER
MINUTE MOIETY PARCEL PORTIO
QUORUM SECTOR SINGLE SUNDER
UNYOKE DISJOIN ELEMENT FEATURE
FRUSTUM PORTION SECTION SEGMENT
SEVERAL ALIENATE DISSEVER DIVISION
ELIQUATE FRACTION LIRIPIPE

PARTAKE BITE PART DIVIDE
PARTICIPATE
(— OF) USE HAVE SHARE TASTE TOUCH
IMPART

PARTIAL HALF PART SEMI BIASED
UNFAIR COLORED HALFWAY UNEQUAL
HARMONIC INCLINED PARTISAN
PROPENSE SKELETON FAVORABLE
SEGMENTAL PARTICULAR RESPECTIVE

PARTIALITY FAVOR RESPECT AFFECTION
SPECIALTY

PARTICIPANT BOOK ACTOR PARTY
MEMBER PARTNER DUETTIST PARTABLE
PARTISAN
(SUBORDINATE —) STOOGE

PARTICIPATE SIDE ENTER SHARE
ENGAGE ENLIST IMPART COMPETE
PARTAKE
(— IN) GO HAVE JOIN STAY STAND
TASTE COMMON STICKLE

PARTICIPATION HAND PLOT SOCIETY
INTEREST
(COMMON —) COMMUNITY

PARTICLE ACE BIT DOT FIG GRU JOT RAY
ATOM BETA CORN CROT DUST IOTA KNIT
MITE MOTE SNIP SPOT WHIT ALPHA
BOSON FLAKE FLECK GHOST GRAIN
MESON OMEGA POINT QUARK SHRED
SIGMA SPECK THRUM FILING LEPTON
MOMENT RIZZOM SMIDGE SMITCH
TITTLE VIRION AMICRON FERMION
GEMMULE GRANULE NUCLEUS PSYCHON
SINGLET SMIDGIN TACHYON ACCEPTER
NEUTRINO SMIDGEON SYLLABLE
MICROSOME POSITRINO SCINTILLA

PARTICULAR AND ATOM FIXY ITEM
NICE SELF SOME FUSSY PARTY POINT
THING CHOOSY DAINTY DETAIL MINUTE
MOROSE REGARD SINGLE STICKY
ARTICLE CAREFUL CERTAIN CORRECT
FINICKY PRECISE PRIVATE RESPECT
SEVERAL SPECIAL UNUSUAL CLERKISH
CONCRETE ESPECIAL PECULIAR

PICKSOME PRECIOUS SINGULAR
SUBALTERN RESPECTIVE
(NOT —) INCURIOUS

PARTING DEATH GOODBYE FAREWELL
(— AS OF HAIR) SHED

PARTITION BAR CUT DAM FIN FLAG
SEPT WALL SHOJI DIVIDE PARPAL
PARPEN SCONCE SCREEN SEPTUM
BARRIER CLOISON ENCLOSE GRATING
PINFOLD PORTION SCANTLE BULKHEAD
CLEAVAGE DIVISION TRAVERSE
DASHBOARD DAYABHAGA ICONOSTAS
MESENTERY STOOTHING
(— BETWEEN STALLS) TRAVIS
(— IN CHIMNEY) WITH
(— IN CORAL) TABULA
(— IN COTTAGE) SPEER HALLAN
(— IN FRUIT) REPLUM
(— IN LOUDSPEAKER) BAFFLE
(— IN WATERWHEEL) WREST
(— OF LATH AND PLASTER)
STOOTHING
(HORIZONTAL —) STAGE
(MINING —) SOLLAR BRATTICE
STOPPING
(PL.) CANCELLI

PARTNER BOY PAL ALLY HALF MATE
PARD WIFE BUDDY BUTTY PARTY
FELLOW MARROW SHARER COMRADE
CONSORT HUSBAND CAMARADA
COPEMATE SIDEKICK YOKEMATE
(— OF DUMMY) VIVANT
(DANCING —) GIGOLO CAVALIER
(PREF.) CO

PARTNERSHIP HUI AXIS FIRM HOUSE
FUSION CAHOOTS COMPANY CONSORT
SOCIETY SOCIETEIT

PARTY DO BAL BEE CAMP CLAN GALA
SECT SIDE BINGE BLAST BRAWL BUNCH
CABAL COVEY CRUSH GROUP LEVEE
COMITE FIESTA FROLIC INFARE JUNKET
PERSON SETOUT SHINDY COMPANY
FACTION PATARIA SHINDIG DRINKING
POTLATCH POUNDING MERRIMENT
(— GIVEN AT HOME) HUDDLE
(AFTERNOON —) TEA RECEPTION
(BEACH —) CLAMBAKE
(BOISTEROUS —) JAMBOREE
(BRIDAL —) SEND SHOWER
(DANCING —) HOP GERMAN CANTICO
HOEDOWN RIDOTTO FANDANGO
(DRINKING —) KNEIPE MOLLIE
POTATION SYMPOSIUM
(DRUNKEN —) BLIND
(EVENING —) BALL SOIREE GREGORY
ROCKING TERTULIA
(FISHING —) HUKILAU
(HUNTING —) FAID
(INFORMAL —) SOCIABLE TERTULIA
(IRISH —) HOOLEY
(LARGE —) ROUT
(MASQUERADE —) GUISE
(MEN'S —) STAG SMOKER
(POLITICAL —) SAM SIDE WAFD HOOKS
LABOR CAUCUS FRONDE SWARAJ
ZENTRUM MINSEITO KENSEIKAI
SQUADRONE OPPOSITION

(POPULAR —) HOOKS
(ROWDY —) BLOWOUT
(SCOUTING —) ESPIAL
(SUPPLY —) BRIGADE
(TEA —) DRUM TEMPEST
(THIRD —) STRANGER
PASS BY GO END FIG USE BEAL CEDE
CHIT COMP COVE DROP FALL FARE FLIT
HALS HAND HAVE JARK LANE LEAD PACE
RIDE ROLL SEEK SILE SLAP STEP WADE
WALK WEAR WIND ALLOW CANTO
ENACT GORGE HURRY LAPSE LITHE
NOTCH OCCUR ORDER PAPER REACH
RELAY SHAKE SHOOT SMITE SPEND
STRIP TRADE UTTER WASTE WHELM
YODEL BILLET CHALAN CONVEY COUPON
DEMISE ELAPSE EXCEED HAPPEN
PASSUS PERMIT RAVINE SPIRAL TICKET
TRAVEL TWOFER ABSOLVE APPROVE
BREATHE DESCEND DEVOLVE DIFFUSE
ENTREAT LATERAL PASSAGE UNDERGO
JUNCTURE
(— ALONG) BANDY DERIVE
(— AWAY) DIE SET FLEE VADE WING
DEPART EXPIRE PERISH FORFARE
(— BACK AND FORTH) FIG
CRISSCROSS
(— BY) COTE OMIT SKIP VADE WEND
APASS CLEAR FORGO FOREGO IGNORE
OVERGO
(— GRADUALLY) FADE
(— IN BULLFIGHT) SUERTE
(— JUDGMENT ON) DEEM DECERN
SENTENCE
(— LIGHTLY) BRUSH SKATE SKITTER
(— OFF) SHAM FOIST
(— ON) LEAK PACE DELATE
(— OUT) CONK DEBOUCH EXHAUST
(— OVER) DO HIP BALK FREE SKIM SKIP
SLIP COVER CROSS ELIDE FLEET SCOUR
SWEEP TRANCE INTERMIT OVERLOOK
TRAVERSE
(— QUICKLY) FLIT SPIN SPEED STRIKE
(— THROUGH) CROSS REEVE TRACE
DIVIDE OVERGO PIERCE SUFFER
EXCURSE PERVADE OVERPASS OVERRIDE
PERMEATE PROGRESS PENETRATE
(— TIME) DRIVE SPEND TRADE
(— UNHAPPILY) DREE
(— UP) REJECT DECLINE DISREGARD
(CUSTOMS —) CARNET
(FENCING —) FOIN BOTTE LUNGE
PUNTA
(FOOTBALL —) FLY FLARE FORWARD
LATERAL PITCHOUT
(FORWARD —) AERIAL
(HOCKEY —) CENTER
(LONG — IN FOOTBALL) BOMB
(MOUNTAIN —) COL GAP NEK SAG
GATE GHAT SLAY CLOVE KLOOF KLOOT
KOTAL POORT SWIRE SWIRL BEALACH
(NARROW —) ABRA GULF CLOSE SLYPE
DEFILE
(SUDDEN —) LUNGE
PASSABLE FIT FAIR SOSO TOLLOL
GENUINE ADEQUATE MEDIOCRE

MODERATE POSSIBLE TRAVELED
PERMEABLE TOLERABLE
PASSAGE CUT GAT ROW VIA WAY WRO
BELT BORD DOOR EXIT FARE FORD GANG
GATE HALL LANE PACE PASS RACE RAMP
SLIP VENT WELL AISLE ALURE BAYOU
BEARD BOGUE CANAL CHOPS CHUTE
CLOSE CREEK CRUSH DRAFT DRIFT
ENTRY FLYBY GLADE GOING INLET
MEUSE PATCH PORCH SHUNT SOUND
ACCESS ADITUS ARCADE ATRIUM
AVENUE BRIDGE BURROW BYPASS
CAREER COURSE EGRESS ELAPSE
FAUCES HIATUS MEATUS PARODE RELIEF
SCREEN SLUICE TRAJET TRANCE TRAVEL
TUNNEL VOYAGE ARCHWAY BALTEUS
CHANNEL CHAPTER CHIMNEY CONDUIT
COULOIR COUPURE DIAZOMA DOGTROT
DRAUGHT ESTUARY FISTULA FRAUGHT
GALLERY GANGWAY GATEWAY ISTHMUS
JOURNEY MANHOLE OFFTAKE OUTTAKE
PARADOS PROCESS TRANSIT APPROACH
AQUEDUCT CITATION CLOISTER
COMMERCE DEBOUCHE DELETION
PARADIGM PERICOPE SENTENCE
SHIPPING SINUSOID SPILLWAY
(— TO TOMB) DROMOS SYRINX
(AIR —) FLUE THIRL WINDWAY
THIRLING
(ANATOMICAL —) ITER
(CENSORED —) CAVIAR
(CONTINUOUS —) LAPSE
(COVERED —) OPE PAWN PEND
(DIFFICULT —) APORIA
(LITERARY —) TEXT QUOTE EXCERPT
SNIPPET QUOTATION
(MINE —) RUN ADIT HEAD ROOF SLUM
DRIVE LEVEL SHAFT THIRL AIRWAY
STENTON
(MUSICAL —) CUE CODA LINK BREAK
FORTE STAVE ARIOSO FUGATO LEGATO
PRESTO REPEAT CADENZA CODETTA
FANFARE STRETTO FLOURISH SPICCATO
STACCATO SYMPHONY
(NARROW —) GUT HASS ALLEY CREEP
GORGE JETTY NOTCH SLYPE SMOOT
DEFILE GULLET NARROW STRAIT
(SUBTERRANEAN —) POSTERN
(SWIFT —) FLIGHT
(VAULTED —) PEND
PASSAGE TO INDIA (AUTHOR OF —)
FORSTER
(CHARACTER IN —) AZIZ ADELA CECIL
MOORE RONALD STELLA GODBOLE
HEASLOP QUESTED FIELDING
PASSAGEWAY (ALSO SEE PASSAGE)
BORD FLUE GANG HALL LANE PACE PASS
PEND PORT RACE SHED SLIP WENT
YAWN AISLE ALLEY CHUTE DRIFT DRONG
ENTRY GOING LUMEN RAISE SHOOT
SMOOT STULM ACCESS AIRWAY AVENUE
COURSE DINGLE FUNNEL GUTTER INTAKE
MANWAY RUNWAY TRANCE ZAGUAN
DOORWAY GALLERY SLIPWAY TWITTEN
WALKWAY WAYGATE CALLEJON
CORRIDOR HATCHWAY

PASSENGER FARE INSIDE FERRYMAN
TRAVELER WAYFARER
(— WHO AVOIDS PAYING FARE) NIP
STOWAWAY
(— WITHOUT TICKET) HARE
(AIRPLANE —) BIRDMAN
(UNBOOKED —) CAD
PASSING DEATH DYING ELAPSE
CURSORY DIADROM PASSADO RUNNING
SLIDING ELAPSING FLEETING
ENACTMENT EPHEMERAL WAYFARING
PASSION IRE WAX BATE FIRE FURY HEAT
LOVE LUST RAGE TEAR TIDE WILL ZEAL
ANGER ARDOR BLOOD CHAFE DEVIL
ERROR FLAME LETCH MANIA SPUNK
WRATH CHOLER DESIRE FERVOR PELTER
SATTVA SPLEEN TALENT WARMTH
EARNEST EMOTION EROTISM FEELING
OUTRAGE VULTURE APPETITE DISTRESS
VIOLENCE PADDYWACK
PASSIONATE HOT FOND WARM WILD
FIERY GUTSY QUICK WHITE ARDENT
FERVID FIERCE FUMOUS IREFUL STORMY
SULTRY TORRID AMOROUS FLAMING
PEPPERY THERMAL VIOLENT CHOLERIC
FRENETIC VASCULAR VEHEMENT
WRATHFUL DIONYSIAN IRASCIBLE
PASSIVE INERT STOIC PATHIC STOLID
PATIENT FEMININE INACTIVE SIGNLESS
YIELDING APATHETIC
PASSWORD SIGN WORD TOKEN
DUSTUK TESSERA WATCHWORD
PAST BY AGO WAS GONE YOND YORE
AFTER AGONE APAST ASIDE ENDED
SINCE BEHIND BYGONE FOREBY PRETER
ANOTHER FOREGONE PRETERIT
COMPLETED
PASTE HIT PAP BEAT BLOW DIKA DUFF
GLUE MISO PACK CREAM DOUGH FALSE
GESSO PUNCH STICK ATTACH BATTER
CERATE FASTEN GROUND PANADA
RASTIK STRASS CLOBBER COLOGNE
DRAWOUT FILLING STICKUM BADIGEON
(— FOR CAULKING) BLARE
(— FOR LINING HEARTHS) BRASQUE
(— FOR SHOES, BOOTS) CLOBBER
BLACKING
(— OF CLAY) BATTER
(— TO FILL HOLES IN WOOD AND
STONE) BADIGEON
(ALIMENTARY —) FEDELINI SCUNGILLI
SPAGHETTI
(AROMATIC —) PASTILE
(COLORING —) HENNA
(DRIED —) GUARANA
(EARTHY —) ENGOBE
(FISH —) BAGOONG
(MEDICATED —) ELECTUARY
(PORCELAIN —) PATE
(POTTER'S —) BARBOTINE
(TOBACCO —) GORACCO
(WEAVER'S —) SOWENS BUCKETY
PASTIME GAY TOY GAME PLOY HOBBY
SPORT GOSSIP OLEARY SAILING
PASTANCE AMUSEMENT DIVERSION
PASTOR HERD ANGEL RABBI CURATE

KEEPER PRIEST RECTOR DOMINIE
VICAIRE GUARDIAN MINISTER SHEPHERD
PASTORAL POEM DRAMA RURAL RUSTIC
BUCOLIC CROSIER IDYLLIC NOMADIC
ROMANCE ARCADIAN THEOCRITEAN
PASTRY PIE FLAN PUFF TART CORNET
DANISH ECLAIR ABAISSE BRIOCHE
STRUDEL BAKEMEAT NAPOLEON
TURNOVER APPLEJACK
PASTURE ALP FOG HAG HAM ING LEA
PEN FEED GANG GATE GIST HAFT HALF
KEEP PARK RAIK AGIST DRIFT EJIDO
GRASS GRAZE LAYER LEASE RANGE
VELDT INTAKE MEADOW OUTRUN
GRAZING HERBAGE LEALAND POTRERO
VACCARY VICTUAL HERDWICK OUTFIELD
(— IN STUBBLE) SHACK
(HILL —) HOGA
(MOUNTAIN —) SAETER SHIELING
(SHEEP —) HEAF EWELEASE
(WET —) SLINK
PAT APT DAB DIB TAP TIG BLOW CLAP
GLIB JUMP PALP TICK CHUCK FITLY
FIXED IMPEL THROW CARESS DABBLE
PRETTY SMOOGE SOOTHE STRIKE
STROKE TIMELY APROPOS CHERISH
FITTING PATAPAT READILY SUITABLE
PERTINENT SEASONABLE
PATCH BIT EKE FLY BOUT LAND SKIP
SPOT SWAB SWOB VAMP BLAZE BODGE
CLUMP COVER FRIAR PIECE SAVER
SCRAP SPLAT BLOTCH COBBLE COOPER
DOLLOP GORGET PARCEL REVAMP
SOLDER SPETCH SWATCH TINKLE
CLOBBER INWEAVE REMNANT
(— AS ORNAMENT) MOUCHE
(— CLUMSILY) BOTCH CLOUT CLAMPER
(— OF COLOR) CLOUP DAPPLE SPLASH
SPECULUM
(— OF DARK HAIR) SMUT
(— OF DIRT) MIRE
(— OF FEATHERS) BIB CAP PTERYLA
(— OF ICE) RONE
(— OF LAND) RODHAM
(— OF LEATHER) SPECK
(— OF LIGHT) GLADE
(— OF PRINT) FUDGE
(— OF RUFFLED WATER) ACKER
(— OF SALIVA) SIXPENCE
(— OF TIRE) BOOT
(— ON BOAT) TINGLE
(— ON PRINTED PAGE) FRIAR
(— ON THROAT) GORGET
(— TOGETHER) CONSARCINATE
(— UP) HEAL MEND
(BALD —) AREA
(LIVID —) PELIOMA
(OOZY —) SPEW SPUE
(OPEN — IN FOREST) CAMPO
(SHOULDER —) FLASH
PATENT ARCA BALD OPEN BERAT BROAD
OVERT PLAIN SUNNUD CHARTER
EVIDENT LICENSE OBVIOUS APPARENT
ARCHIVES MANIFEST PALPABLE
PRIVILEGE
PATH ARC PAD RIG RUN RUT TAN WAY
FARE GATE LANE LEAD LINE LODE RACE

ROAD TROD WALK ALLEY BYWAY GOING
JETTY PISTE ROUTE SPACE TRACK
TRACT TRADE TRAIL BYPASS CAMINO
CASAUN CIRCLE COMINO COURSE
GROOVE SLEUTH SPHERE TRENCH
CHANNEL FAIRWAY FOOTWAY HIGHWAY
LANDWAY MEANDER PASSAGE RODDING
SIDEWAY TARIQAT TOWPATH TRAFFIC
TRUNDLE WAYGATE BORSTALL
CENTRODE CROSSCUT DRIFTWAY
TRAILWAY CROSSWALK
(— BETWEEN HEDGES) TWITCHEL
(— CUT IN MOWING) SWATH
(— FOLLOWED BY ENERGY) ERGODIC
(— MADE BY ANIMAL) PISTE
(— OF CELESTIAL BODY) ORBIT
(— OF CLOUDS) RACK
(— OF MOVING POINT) CURVE LOCUS
(— OF RACE) STRIP
(— UP STEEP HILL) BORSTAL
(BRIDLE —) SPURWAY
(CLOSED —) CIRCUIT
(FORTIFICATION —) RELAIS
(GARDEN —) ALLEE
(NARROW —) BERM RACK TRIG RODDIN
TROCHA
(PHILIPPINE FOOT —) SENDA
(STONE-PAVED —) STEEN
(SUFI —) TARIQAT
(WINDING —S) AMBAGES
(PREF.) HODO ODO
PATHETIC SAD SILLY TEARY TENDER
FORLORN PITIFUL DOLOROSO PATETICO
PITIABLE POIGNANT STIRRING TOUCHING
AFFECTING
PATHFINDER (AUTHOR OF —) COOPER
(CHARACTER IN —) CAP DAVY MUIR
MABEL NATTY BUMPPO DUNHAM
JASPER MACNAB CHARLES WESTERN
SANGLIER ARROWHEAD CHINGACHGOOK
PATHOS BATHOS SNIVEL POIGNANCY
PATHWAY (ALSO SEE PATH) RUN LANE
PATH RACK SLADE COURSE RAMBLA
RAMBLE RODDIN BORSTAL RODDING
(RAISED —) CAUSEY CAUSEWAY
PATIENCE CALM BEARANCE STOICISM
COMPOSURE ENDURANCE FORTITUDE
PATIENT CASE MEEK SOBER BOVINE
PASSIVE ENDURING THOLEMOD
SUFFERANT
(— OF ASYLUM) BEDLAM
(BE —) BEAR
(HYDROPATHIC —) WATERER
(MEDICAL —) CURE
PATOIS CANT GOMBO GUMBO CREOLE
JARGON PATTER DIALECT GUERNSEY
(FRENCH —) JOUAL
PATRIARCH JOB ABBA ENOS LEVI NASI
NOAH PAPA POPE ALDER ELDER JACOB
PITRI DESPOT JOSEPH NESTOR
ABRAHAM ANCIENT VETERAN
VENERABLE
(ETHIOPIAN —) ABUNA
PATRICIAN NOBLE EMPEROR PATRICK
NOBLEMAN GENTLEMAN
PATROL GUARD SCOUT WATCH STOOGE
PROTECT

PATRON BUYER GUEST STOOP AVOWRY
CLIENT FATHER FAUTOR JAJMAN
ACCOUNT PADRONE PATROON PROCTOR
SPONSOR ADVOCATE CHAMPION
CUSTOMER DEFENDER GUARDIAN
MAECENAS
PATRONAGE AEGIS FAVOR AVOWRY
CUSTOM FAVOUR ACCOUNT AUSPICE
FOMENTO HEARING AUSPICES BUSINESS
PADROADO
(— AND CARE) AUSPICE
(POLITICAL —) PAP
PATRONIZE USE DEIGN FAVOR DEFEND
FATHER PROMOTE PROTECT EMPATRON
FREQUENT
PATTER CANT TALK LINGO HAPPER
JARGON BLATHER BLATTER CHATTER
DIALECT
PATTERN CUT FUR SET BASE CAST
COMB COPY FORM GIMP IDEA LAUE
MOLD NORM PLAN SEME STAR WAVE
BISON BYSEN CHECK DECOR DISME
DRAFT EPURE GUIDE IDEAL INLAY MODEL
MOIRE MOULD NOTAN PLAID SEMEE
SHAPE WATER BASKET BURELE CANVAS
CHECKS DESIGN DIAPER ENTAIL ETOILE
FABRIC FIGURE FLORAL FORMAT
FORMER LACERY MAGPIE MATRIX
MIRROR MODULE MUSTER ONDULE
PATRON POUNCE RANDOM RECIPE
SAMPLE SQUARE STRIPE SYSTEM
ALLOVER CHEVRON EXAMPLE FACONNE
FILLING FOLKWAY GESTALT GRIZZLE
HOBNAIL MEANDER MEANING MULLION
PARAGON PROJECT SAMPLER SLEIGHT
STENCIL TEMPLET CALENDAR DENTELLE
DYNAMICS FILIGREE HATCHING ILLUSION
OVERSHOT PARADIGM PLATFORM
STRICKLE PROTOTYPE
PAUCITY LACK DEARTH FEWNESS
EXIGUITY SCARCITY
PAUNCH TUN KYTE BELLY RUMEN
ABDOMEN STOMACH GUNDYGUT
POTBELLY
PAUPER BEGGAR INDIGENT ROUNDSMAN
PAUSE HEM MAUL HANG HOLD LULL REST
STAY STOP WAIT ABIDE BREAK CEASE
CHECK COMMA DELAY DEMUR DWELL
HOVER LETUP LIMMA POISE TARRY
TENOR BREACH BREATH CUTOFF FALTER
HANKER HIATUS PERIOD STANCE
CAESURA FERMATA RESPITE VIRGULE
BREATHER INTERVAL
PAVE LAY TAR PATH STUD TILE COVER
FLOOR CAUSEY COBBLE QUARRY
SMOOTH OVERLAY PREPARE RUDERATE
PAVEMENT SARN SLAB HEARTH
TELFORD FLAGGING FLOORING
PEDIMENT SIDEWALK TROTTOIR
WASHBOARD
PAVILION BASE FLAG TENT KIOSK ROYAL
CANOPY ENSIGN HOWDAH LITTER
COVERING GLORIETTE
PAW PAT PUD TOE CLAW FOOT GRAB
HAND MAUL PORT FLAIL TRICK CLUTCH
FUMBLE HANDLE PATTEE FLIPPER
FOREFOOT

PAWN DIP POP WED FINE GAGE HOCK
SOAK VAMP WAGE SPOUT SWEAT
ENGAGE LUMBER OBLIGE PIGNUS
PLEDGE WADSET COUNTER HOSTAGE
PEACOCK CHESSMAN MOSKENEER
TRIBULATION
PAWNBROKER MOUNT UNCLE BROKER
LUMBERER MONEYLENDER
PAY DO FEE TIP ANTE FOOT FORK GIVE
MEET RENT SOLD WAGE CLEAR COUGH
PLANK SHEPE SOUND WAGES YIELD
ANSWER BETALL DEFRAY IMPEND
REWARD SALARY SETTLE COMMUTE
DEADRAY HALVANS IMBURSE REQUITE
SATISFY SOULDIE STIPEND TRIBUTE
RECOMPENSE
(— ATTENTION) DIG SEE COME GAUM
HARK HEED TENT ADVERT REGARD
(— COURT TO) NUT SUE GALLANT
(— DOWN) DOUSE
(— FLIRTATIOUS ADVANCES) QUEEN
(— FOR) ABY BUY COUP COVER ESCOT
STAND
(— FOR LIQUOR) BIRL
(— HEAVY PENALTY) SMART EXPIATE
(— HOMAGE) CHEFE CHEVE CHIVE
SALAAM ADULATE
(— IN ADVANCE) IMPRESS
(— MONEY) PINGLE
(— OF SOLDIER) SAWDEE
(— OFF) LIFT SINK ACQUIT
(— OUT) VEER BLEED SPEND STUMP
EXPEND DISBURSE
(— PENALTY) ABY
(— TAXES) GILD
(— UP) ANTE QUIT SETTLE LIQUIDATE
(— WITH IOU) VOWEL
(ADVANCE —) IMPREST
(DAILY —) DIET
(EXTRA —) BATTA BONUS KICKBACK
(SMALL —) SCREW
PAYMENT CRO DUE FEE TAX BILL CENS
DOES DOLE DUTY ERIC FEAL FINE GALE
GILD HIRE LEVY MAIL MISE TACK TOLL
BONUS CANON CLAIM GAVEL MAILL
MENSE MODUS PREST PRICE YIELD
ANGILD BOUNTY CHARGE LINAGE
LOBOLA OUTLAY PAYOLA PLEDGE
REBATE RETURN REWARD TARIFF
ADVANCE ALIMONY ANNUITY BENEFIT
CUSTOMS DEPOSIT FOOTAGE GARNISH
PANNAGE PENSION PRIMAGE SOLUTIO
STIPEND SUBSIDY SUBSIST TREWAGE
TUITION CASUALTY FOREGIFT GRATUITY
KICKBACK MALIKANA MARITAGE
MONEYAGE TREASURY WOODGELD
HEADPENNY MALGUZARI
PAYOFF FIX BRIBE CLIMAX PROFIT
REWARD DECISIVE RECKONING
PEACE PAX CALM EASE FINE REST AMITY
QUIET TRUCE REPOSE SHALOM
CONCORD HARMONY REQUIEM
(— OF MIND) ATARAXIA
PEACEFUL CALM SOBER STILL IRENIC
PLACID HALCYON ORDERLY PACIFIC
PEACOCK MAO PAON PAWN POSE
STRUT PAVONE PHASIANID

PEAK BEN NAB NOB PAP PIC TOP TOR
ACME APEX BEAK CIMA CUSP DENT
DOLT KNOB KNOT BLOOM CREST CROWN
PITCH PITON POINT SLINK SNEAK SPIRE
STEAL STUMP CLIMAX SHASTA SUMMIT
ZENITH EPITOME MAXIMUM CENTROID
(— OF ANCHOR) PEE
(— OF CAP) SCOOP
(— OF ENERGY) NUCLEUS
(ICE —) SERAC
(ISOLATED —) TOLT
(SHARP —) HORN AIGUILLE
(SNOW-CAPPED —) DOME CALOTTE
(PREF.) ACR(O)
PEAKED WAN PALE THIN DRAWN SHARP
SICKLY POINTED
PEAL CLAP RING TOLL CHIME CRACK
SHOVEL RESOUND SUMMONS THUNDER
CARILLON
PEARL GEM MABE TERN GRAIN NACRE
ONION PICOT BOUTON ORIENT BAROQUE
BLISTER PARAGON CATARACT
MOONBEAM MARGARITE
(IMITATION —) OLIVET
(IRREGULAR —) SLUG
(PIERCED —) WIDOW
(SEED —) ALIOFAR
(SMOKED —) MITRAILLE
PEARL FISHERS, THE
(CHARACTER IN —) LEILA NADIR
ZURGA NOURABAD
(COMPOSER OF —) BIZET
PEARLSIDES ARGENTIN
PEARLWEED SAGINA POVERTY
SEALWORT
PEARLY NACRY NACROUS MARGARIC
PRECIOUS
PEARLY EVERLASTING LIVELONG
MOONSHINE
PEASANT TAO BOND BOOR HIND PEON
RAYA SERF BOWER CHURL KNAVE
SWAIN CARLOT COTMAN COTTAR
FARMER RUSTIC BONDMAN LABORER
PAISANO VILLAIN CHOPSTICK
CONTADINO
(— OF INDIA) RYOT KISAN
(ARABIC —) FELLAH
(IRISH —) KERN
(RUSSIAN —) KULAK MUZHIK
PEAT GOR PET SOD VAG COOM FUEL
MIST MOOR MUCK MULL TURF YARFA
LAWYER MINION YARPHA DARLING
FAVORITE
PEBBLE DIB FLAX JACK PLUM CHUCK
SCREE STONE BANTAM COGGLE GIBBER
GRAVEL QUARTZ SHILLA SYCITE
CHUCKIE CRYSTAL SHINGLE STANNER
JACKSTONE
PECCADILLO FAULT OFFENSE MISCHIEF
PECK DAB DOT JOB NIP BEAK BILL CARP
FOOD GRUB HOLE JERK KISS PYKE PITCH
PRICK STOCK THROW HATFUL NIBBLE
PEGGLE PICKLE PIERCE STROKE CHIMBLE
PECULIAR ODD VERY QUEER WEIRD
PROPER QUAINT UNIQUE CURIOUS
PRIVATE SEVERAL SPECIAL STRANGE
UNUSUAL SEPARATE SINGULAR SPECIFIC

PECULIARITY KINK IDIOM QUIRK TRAIT TRICK TWIST IDIASM ODDITY AEOLISM FEATURE IRISHRY CROTCHET HEADMARK MANNERISM PROPRIETY SINGULARITY

PECUNIARY POCKET MONETARY FINANCIAL

PEDAGOGUE TUTOR PEDANT DOMINIE SQUEERS TEACHER THWACKUM

PEDAL LEVER SWELL TREADLE FOOTFEED THROTTLE
(PIANO —) CELESTE

PEDANT PRIG DUNCE TUTOR DORBEL PURIST TASSEL ACADEME PEDAGOG GAMALIEL DRYASDUST OLOFERNES

PEDANTIC BLUE STODGY BOOKISH DONNISH ERUDITE INKHORN TEACHING SCHOLASTIC

PEDDLE HAWK SELL CADGE SHOVE TRUCK MEDDLE PIDDLE RETAIL

PEDDLER ARAB BADGER CRAMER JAGGER JOWTER MUGGER STROLL WALKER NIGGLER PACKMAN ROADMAN SANDBOY SWADDER TROGGER TRUCKER HUCKSTER BOXWALLAH DUSTYFOOT
(— OF DOPE) FIXER
(— OF DRESS PIECES) DUDDER
(— OF FISH) RIPIER
(— OF SHAM JEWELRY) DUFFER
(BOOK —) COLPORTEUR
(ITINERANT —) SMOUS STROLLER
(MOHAM. —) BORA
(STREET —) CAMELOT

PEDESTAL ANTA BASE BASIS BLOCK SOCLE STAND PILLAR PODIUM SUPPORT

PEDESTRIAN DULL FOOT SLOW HIKER FOOTER HOOFER WALKER FOOTMAN PROSAIC PLODDING PONDEROUS

PEDIGREE STEMMA DESCENT LINEAGE ANCESTRY PUREBRED

PEEK PEEP GLANCE GLIMPSE

PEEL BARK HULL HUSK PARE RIND SKIN SCALE SLIPE STRIP CORTEX SHOVEL UNDRESS
(— OFF) HARL CRAZE FLAKE SHUCK
(BAKER'S —) PEEL SPITTLE

PEEP PRY SPY KEEK KOOK PEEK PEER PINK PULE SKEG STEP TOOT TOTE TOUT CHEEP CHIRP DEKKO GLINT PIPIT SNOOP TWEET GLANCE SQUEAK SQUINNY

PEER PRY DUKE EARL FEAR GAZE LOOK LORD MATE PEEP PINK TOOT TOUT BARON EQUAL GLINT GLOZE MATCH NOBLE RIVAL STARE THANE FELLOW COMPERE

PEER GYNT (AUTHOR OF —) IBSEN
(CHARACTER IN —) ASE BOYG GYNT PEER ANITRA HEGSTAD SOLVEIG

PEERLESS SUPREME MATCHLESS NONPAREIL UNRIVALED

PEEVE IRK ANNOY GRUDGE NETTLE IRRITATE

PEEVISH SOUR CROSS TECHY TESTY TIFFY CRUSTY GIRNIE HIPPED PATCHY SNARLY SNUFFY SULLEN TOUCHY UPPISH UPPITY VAPORY CRABBED FRETFUL FROWARD GROUCHY PETTISH SPLEENY TEDIOUS TIFFISH WASPISH CAPTIOUS PERVERSE

PEEWEE BOOT RUNT TINY MARBLE LAPWING

PEG FIX HOB HUB NOB NOG PIN KING KNAG PLUG SCOB SHAG SKEG STEP CLEAT DOWEL DRINK NOTCH PERCH PRONG SPILE SPILL STAKE THOLE THROW TOOTH WADDY DEGREE FAUCET MARKER NORMAN PICKET REASON SPIGOT TIPCAT PRETEXT SCOLLOP SUPPORT TRENAIL
(— FOR PLAYING GAME) CAT SPILIKIN
(— OF STRINGED INSTRUMENT) CHEVILLE
(BELAYING —) KEVEL
(IRON —) PITON
(THATCH —) SCOB

PEGASUS QUAVIVER HYPOSTOME

PELEUS (BROTHER OF —) TELAMON
(FATHER OF —) AEACUS
(HALF-BROTHER OF —) PHOCUS
(MOTHER OF —) ENDEIS
(SON OF —) PELIDES ACHILLES
(WIFE OF —) THETIS ANTIGONE

PELIAS (BROTHER OF —) NELEUS
(DAUGHTER OF —) ALCESTIS
(FATHER OF —) POSEIDON
(MOTHER OF —) TYRO
(SON OF —) ACASTUS
(WIFE OF —) ANAXIBIA PHYLOMACHE

PELLEAS ET MELISANDE
(CHARACTER IN —) ARKEL GOLAUD YNIOLD PELLEAS ALLEMONDE GENEVIEVE MELISANDE
(COMPOSER OF —) DEBUSSY

PELLET BB WAD BALL CAST PILL SHOT BOLUS STONE BEEBEE BULLET FECULA CASTING GRANULE BUCKSHOT GUNSTONE HAILSTONE
(SNOW —S) GRAUPEL
(PL.) SHOT

PELLINORE (SLAYER OF —) GAWAIN
(SON OF —) TORRE DORNAR LAMEROK PERCIVAL AGGLOVALE

PELOPS (FATHER OF —) TANTALUS
(SON OF —) ATREUS TROEZEN PITTHEUS THYESTES
(WIFE OF —) HIPPODAMIA

PELT FUR KIT BEAR BEAT BLOW CAPE CAST CLOD COON DASH FELL HIDE HURL PUSH RACK SKIN BESET CHUNK FITCH HURRY SABLE SLASH SPEED STONE WHACK BADGER BEAVER FISHER PELTER PEPPER SERVAL SPRING BETHUMP COONSKIN
(— OF SEAL, WITH BLUBBER) SCULP
(— WITH MISSILES) BUM SQUAIL
(— WITH STONES) LAPIDATE
(BEAVER —) BLANKET

PEN COT GET MEW STY BOLT CAGE COOP CROW FOLD JAIL STUB WALK YARD CREEP CUBBY HUTCH POINT QUILL STYLE WRITE BOUGHT CORRAL FASTEN FLIGHT HURDLE INDITE RECORD STYLUS ZAREBA CONFINE
(— CATTLE) STANCE

(— FOR CATTLE) CUB LOT CREW CRUE
LAIR REEVE
(— FOR ELEPHANTS) KRAAL
(— FOR HOGS OR SLAVES) CRAWL
(— OF CUTTLEFISH) GLADIUS
(— UP) FRANK STIVE
(FOUNTAIN —) STICK
(MUSIC —) RASTRUM
(REED —) CALAMUS
PENALIZE CHECK
PENALTY BETE CAIN DOOM FINE LOSS
PAIN BEAST JUISE MULCT AMENDE
AMERCE SOLACE FORFEIT NEMESIS
SURSIZE BLOODWIT HARDSHIP
SCAFFOLD
(DRINKING —) KELTIE
PENCIL PEN RED WAD BLUE LEAD LINER
SHEAF SKETCH STYLUS POINTEL
CHARCOAL KEELIVINE
PENDANT BOB JAG DROP FLAG JAGG
PEND TAIL AGLET BULLA GUTTA POINT
LUSTER PLAYER TABARD TARGET
TASSEL EARDROP LANGUET SUPPORT
LAVALIER
PENDENNIS (AUTHOR OF —)
THACKERAY
(CHARACTER IN —) BELL AMORY
EMILY FANNY FOKER HELEN HENRY
LAURA ARTHUR BOLTON GEORGE
JEMIMA BLANCHE FRANCIS ALTAMONT
COSTIGAN CLAVERING PENDENNIS
WARRINGTON THISTLEWOOD
PENDULOUS LOP SLOUCH HANGING
NODDING PENSILE CERNUOUS DROOPING
PENDULUM SWING PENDLE SWINGEL
SWINGLE VIBRATILE
(INVERTED —) NODDY
PENELOPE (FATHER OF —) ICARIUS
(FATHER-IN-LAW OF —) LAERTES
(HUSBAND OF —) ULYSSES ODYSSEUS
(MOTHER OF —) PERIBOEA
(SON OF —) TELEMACHUS
(SUITOR OF —) AGELAUS
PENETRATE CUT DIG DIP BITE BORE
DIVE GORE PASS PINK SINK STAB WADE
BREAK DRILL DRIVE ENTER IMBUE PROBE
SEIZE CLEAVE FATHOM GIMLET INVADE
PIERCE RIDDLE SEARCH STRIKE WIMBLE
DISCERN PERVADE PERFORATE
PENETRATING ACID KEEN ACUTE LEVEL
NASAL SHARP ASTUTE DEADLY SHREWD
SHRILL SUBTLE INGOING KNOWING
PUNGENT PIERCING TRENCHANT
PENETRATION DEPTH ACUMEN FATHOM
INROAD INSIGHT SEEPAGE INCISION
INVASION SAGACITY
PENGUIN ISLAND (AUTHOR OF —)
FRANCE
(CHARACTER IN —) MAEL CLENA
CRRES DRACO OLIVE PYROT TALPA
AGARIC KRAKEN TRINCO VISIRE EVELINE
BOSCENOS CLARENCE GREATANK
JOHANNES OBEROSIA CHATILLON
MARBODIUS
PENINSULA CAPE MULL NECK BYLAND
PENILE CHERSONESE

PENITENT RUER SORRY HUMBLE WEEPER
MOURNER STANDER CONTRITE
(— OF 3RD STAGE) KNEELER
PENITENTIARY JUG PEN JAIL STIR
TENCH PRISON PENITENT
PENNANT FANE FLAG WHIP COLOR
ROGER BANNER CORNET ENSIGN PENCIL
PENNON STREAMER
PENNILESS POOR BROKE NEEDY
BANKRUPT INDIGENT STRAPPED
PLACKLESS
PENNON FLAG VANE WING ANVIL
BANNER PENCIL PENOUN PINION
FEATHER GONFANON

PENNSYLVANIA

CAPITAL: HARRISBURG
COLLEGE: JUNIATA URSINUS LYCOMING
COUNTY: ELK ERIE PIKE YORK BERKS
BUCKS PERRY TIOGA LEHIGH CAMBRIA
JUNIATA LUZERNE VENANGO WYOMING
LYCOMING
MOUNTAIN RANGE: POCONO ALLEGHENY
RIVER: LEHIGH CLARION JUNIATA LICKING
TOWANDA CALDWELL LEHIGH CAMBRIA
SCHRADER ALLEGHENY SCHUYLKILL
MONONGAHELA SUSQUEHANNA
STATE BIRD: GROUSE
STATE FLOWER: LAUREL
STATE TREE: HEMLOCK
TOWN: ERIE ETNA PLUM YORK AVOCA
MEDIA EASTON EMMAUS SHARON
ALTOONA EPHRATA HERSHEY READING
TOWANDA BRYNMAWR SCRANTON
SHAMOKIN BETHLEHEM CHARLEROI
GETTYSBURG PITTSBURGH
UNIVERSITY: PITT DREXEL LEHIGH
TEMPLE BUCKNELL DUQUESNE
VILLANOVA

PENNY AES MEG RED SOU WIN GILL
WING WINN BROWN PENCE COPPER
FOLLIS SALTEE BROWNIE STERLING
(DUTCH —) STIVER
(HALF —) HALFLIN
(OLD SCOTCH —) TURNER
PENNY-PINCHING STINGY
PENROD (AUTHOR OF —) TARKINGTON
(CHARACTER IN —) CRIM JONES
SARAH PENROD MARJORIE SCHOFIELD
PENSION WAGE PAYMENT STIPEND
SUBSIDY TRIBUTE GRATUITY MALIKANA
PENSIVE MOODY SOBER DREAMY
MUSING WISTFUL THOUGHTY
MELANCHOLY
PENTATEUCH TORAH
PENTECOST SHABUOTH WHITSUNDAY
PENTHOUSE CAT PENT ROOF SHED
AERIE ANNEX HANGAR LOOKUM
SHADOW PLUTEUS BULKHEAD SKEELING
APPENTICE
PENURIOUS MEAN POOR BARREN
SCANTY STINGY MISERLY WANTING
INDIGENT HIDEBOUND NIGGARDLY
PENURY WANT BEGGARY BORASCO

POVERTY SCARCITY INDIGENCE PRIVATION

PEON HAND PAWN SERF SLAVE PELADO THRALL FOOTMAN LABORER PEASANT SOLDIER CONSTABLE

PEOPLE (ALSO SEE NATIVE AND TRIBE) ARO FUL LOG MEN PUL TAT VAI YAO AKRA ASHA BENI BUGI CHIN CHUD EMIM FOLK FULA GARO GENS HERD HIMA HUMA IRON LAND LEDE LUBA LURI PHUD PHUL PHUT RACE RAIS REMI SAFI SARA SEBA SERE TEMA THEY TODA TOMA TULU USUN VITI VOLK WARE AFIFI AVARS BENIN BONGO CATTI CHAGA COURS DEMOS DUALA EDONI ELYMI FOLKS FULAH GENTE GOMER HAUSA JACKS KAREN LAITY LANAO LENDU LUREM MARSI NOGAI ORANG PUNAN QUADI RAMBO ROTSE SACAE SALAR SAURA SHAKA STOCK TAURI VOLTA WARUA WORLD ABABUA ACHUAS AFSHAR AISSOR ANGAMI ANGLES ARUNTA AVIKOM BAHIMA BAKELE BAKUBA BALUBA BELTIR BOSHAS BULLOM CIMBRI COMMON DAOINE GENTRY GILAKI GILEKI HAUSSA HERERO HERULI KANWAR KPUESI KRUMAN MANTZU MINYAE MOSCHI NATION OVAMPO PAMIRI PUBLIC RAMUSI RUTULI SAFINI SAMBAL SATRAE SEMANG SHARRA TADJIK TAGAUR TELUGU TUNGUZ TURSHA VENETI VOLCAE WACAGO WAHIMA YNDOYS YUECHI ZAMBAL

PEP GO VIM DASH MOXIE VERVE VIGOR ENERGY GINGER ANIMATE QUICKEN ACTIVITY

PEPPER CAVA ITMO KAVA SIRI BETEL CHILI MANGO MATICO TOPEPO CAYENNE PAPRIKA PIMENTA RELIENO JALAPENO KAVAKAVA
(JAVA —) CUBEB
(RED —) LADYFINGER

PEPPERY HOT FIERY SAUCY SPICY TOUCHY PIQUANT PUNGENT SPIRITED STINGING

PEPPY GINGERY

PER BY THE EACH THROUGH

PERAMBULATOR BUGGY WAGON BASSINET VIAMETER WAYWISER PEDOMETER

PERCEIVE SEE ESPY FEEL FIND HEAR KNOW LOOK MIND NOTE SCAN SCENT SENSE SMELL TASTE TOUCH BEHOLD DESCRY DIVINE FIGURE NOTICE REMARK SURVEY DISCERN OBSERVE REALIZE DESCRIBE RECOGNIZE

PERCENTAGE CUT AGIO PART SHARE PROFIT PORTION SCALAGE CONTANGO PROPORTION
(MINING —) LEY

PERCEPTIBLE PUBLIC NOTABLE TACTILE VISIBLE APPARENT PALPABLE SENSIBLE TANGIBLE TRACTABLE PERCEIVABLE

PERCEPTION RAY BUMP TACT SAVOR SCENT SENSE SIGHT ACUMEN VISION CLOSURE FEELING GLIMMER NOSTRIL DELICACY COGNITION SENSATION SENTIMENT

PERCH BAR LUG PEG ROD SIT BASS JOUK MADO OKOW PERK PIKE POLE POPE RUFF SEAT BEGTI BLOCK LIGHT REACH ROOST STAFF ALIGHT BUGARA CALLOP COMBER PERCID SAUGER SETTLE ZANDER ZINGEL ALFIONE HOGFISH STATION ROCKFISH

PERCHANCE HAPLY MAYBE FORTUNE PERHAPS POSSIBLY

PERCOLATE MELT OOZE PERK SEEP SIFT SILT SOAK WEEP DRILL EXUDE LEACH FILTER STRAIN

PERCUSSION BLOW IMPACT STROKE PNEUMATIC

PERDITION HELL LOSS RUIN BALLYWACK DAMNATION

PEREMPTORY FLAT FINAL UTTER EXPRESS HAUGHTY ABSOLUTE DECISIVE DOGMATIC POSITIVE ESSENTIAL MASTERFUL

PERENNIAL HERB CAREX LIANA PEONY SEDUM BANANA CENTRO BLUEWEED CONSTANT ENDURING KNAPWEED TOADFLAX CONTINUAL EVERGREEN PENNYWORT PERPETUAL RECURRENT

PERFECT ALL BACK BORN CURE FILL FINE FULL HOLY PURE SURE EXACT FINAL FULLY IDEAL PLAIN RIGHT RIPEN SHEER SOUND TOTAL UTTER WHOLE ENTIRE EXPERT FINISH MATURE POLISH REFINE SPHERE CERTAIN CONCOCT CONTENT CORRECT CROWNED DEVELOP GEMLIKE IMPROVE PLENARY PRECISE SINLESS SPHERAL TYPICAL COMPLETE COPYBOOK FLAWLESS INFINITE INTEGRAL REPLENISH

PERFECTION ACME BEST PINK BLOOM IDEAL BEAUTY FINISH PLENTY

PERFIDIOUS FALSE SNAKY DISLEAL SNAKISH DISLOYAL SPITEFUL FAITHLESS

PERFIDY DECEIT TREASON FALSEHOOD FALSENESS TREACHERY

PERFORATE EAT DOCK HOLE DRILL PRICK PUNCH SIEVE THIRL PIERCE POUNCE RIDDLE PINHOLE PUNCTURE PENETRATE

PERFORATION BORE HOLE THIRL BROACH EYELET STIGMA FORAMEN PINHOLE STENCIL FENESTRA DIABROSIS PERTUSION

PERFORM DO ACT CUT FILL HAVE KEEP LAST MAKE PLAY SHOW STEP DIGHT ENACT EXERT FETCH ACQUIT COMMIT EFFECT FULFIL RENDER ACHIEVE EXECUTE EXHIBIT EXPLOIT FURNISH OPERATE PRESENT PROSECUTE
(— AWKWARDLY) BOGGLE
(— BADLY) BOLLIX
(— BRILLIANTLY) STAR SPARKLE
(— CLUMSILY) THUMB BUNGLE
(— FULLY) END
(— HASTILY) SKIMP SCAMP,
(— HURRIEDLY) SLUR
(— IN DANCING) FIGURE
(FAIL TO — EFFECTIVELY) CHOKE

PERFORMANCE ACT JOB DEED FEAT

HAND SHOW TEST WORK CAPER SLANG
SPORT STUNT ACTING ACTION BALLET
EFFECT MASQUE ACCOUNT BENEFIT
BOOKING CONCERT EXPLOIT MATINEE
MUMMERY RELEASE SHOWING
FAREWELL FUNCTION PRACTICE
OPERATION
(— FOR ONE) SOLO
(— OF DUTY) FEASANCE
(— OF OBLIGATION) SOLUTIO
(ARAB —) FANTASIA
(BRILLIANT —) BRAVURA
(CHRISTMAS EVE —) GOMBAY
(CLUMSY —) BUNGLE
(DRAMATIC —) TOPENG PANTOMIME
(FIRST —) OPENING PREMIERE
(INEPT —) BOMB
(PAST —) FORM
(TRIAL —) AUDITION
(VULGAR —) BLOWOFF
(WRONG —) MISPRISION
PERFORMER ACT DOER GEEK STAR
ACTOR ARTIST DANCER LEADER PLAYER
WORKER ACROBAT ARTISTE HOTSHOT
SOLOIST EXECUTOR HAMFATTER
HEADLINER
(— ON SEVERAL INSTRUMENTS)
MOKE
(BURLESQUE —) GRINDER
(CIRCUS —) LEAPER
(INFERIOR —) HAM SHINE
(SUFF.) ANT ENT
PERFUME BALM FUME MUSK NOSE OTTO
AROMA ATTAR CENSE CIVET MYRRH
SCENT SMELL SPICE EMBALM FLAVOR
BOUQUET ESSENCE INCENSE JASMINE
NOSEGAY ODORIZE SWEETEN BERGAMOT
PERFUNCTORY CURSORY CARELESS
SLIPSHOD SLOVENLY APATHETIC
PERHAPS MAYBE BELIKE HAPPEN
MAYHAP LIGHTLY POSSIBLY PERCHANCE
PERICLES (AUTHOR OF —)
SHAKESPEARE
(CHARACTER IN —) BOULT CLEON
DIANA GOWER MARINA THAISA
CERIMON DIONYZA ESCANES LEONINE
PERICLES PHILEMON THALIARD
ANTIOCHUS HELICANUS LYCHORIDA
SIMONIDES LYSIMACHUS
(FATHER OF —) XANTHIPPUS
(MISTRESS OF —) ASPASIA
(MOTHER OF —) AGARISTE
(SON OF —) PARALUS XANTHIPPUS
(TEACHER OF —) ZENO DAMON
PERIL RISK CRISIS DANGER HAZARD
MENACE SCYLLA THREAT TRANCE
DISTRESS JEOPARDY CHARYBDIS
PERILOUS KITTLE DOUBTFUL DREADFUL
INFAMOUS DANGEROUS HAZARDOUS
PERIMETER RIM CIRCUIT OUTLINE
BOUNDARY PERIPHERY
PERIOD DOT END ERA DATE LIFE RACE
STOP TERM TIDE TIME YEAR AVAIL
CLOSE EPACT LABOR LAPSE PATCH
POINT SPACE CUTOFF GHURRY HEMERA
PARODY PICTUN SEASON STOUND
ACCOUNT DICOLON FLORUIT PASTIME

STADIUM STRETCH DURATION INDUCIAE
INSTANCE LIFETIME SENTENCE
(— IN DEVELOPMENT) STAGE
(— OF ACTION) GO BOUT
(— OF DECLINE) SUNSET EVENING
(— OF DRYNESS) DROUGHT
(— OF FAIR WEATHER) SLATCH
(— OF FESTIVITY) WAKES
(— OF GLOOM) DEAD
(— OF GRACE) DAY
(— OF HEAT) CALLING
(— OF HUMID WEATHER) SIZZARD
(— OF IMMATURITY) SWADDLE
(— OF INSTRUCTION) LESSON
(— OF LIFE) AGE ELD SPAN
(— OF MILITARY SERVICE) HITCH
(— OF MOURNING) SHIBAH
(— OF PLAY) HALF CHUKKER QUARTER
(— OF RECREATION) HOLIDAY
VACATION
(— OF REMISSION) JUBILEE
(— OF REST) SMOKO BREATHER
(— OF REVOLUTION OF HEAVENLY
BODY) ORB
(— OF TIME) DAY HOUR WEEK YEAR
MONTH DECADE MINUTE SECOND
(— OF WORK) SHIFT SPELL STINT
(— OF 10 YEARS) DECADE
(— OF 100 YEARS) AGE CENTURY
(— OF 1000 YEARS) CHILIAD MILLIAD
(— OF 14 MINUTES, 24 SECONDS)
CENTIDAY
(— OF 2 MONTHS) DIMESTER
(— OF 2 YEARS) BIENNIUM
(— OF 20 YEARS) KATUN
(— OF 260 DAYS) TONALMATL
(— OF 4 YEARS) QUADRENNIUM
(— OF 5 DAYS) PENTAD
(— OF 5 YEARS) LUSTRE LUSTRUM
(— OF 50 YEARS) JUBILEE
(— OF 7 DAYS) HEBDOMAD
(— OF 7 YEARS) SEPTENARY
(— PRECEDING IMPORTANT EVENT)
EVE
(CLASS —) HOUR
(CULTURAL —) HORIZON
(DEFINITE —) MOMENT
(DISTINCTIVE —) EPOCH
(DULL —) SLACK
(EVOLUTIONAL —) HEMERA
(GEOLOGICAL —) JURA KAROO
EOCENE ALGOMAN HORIZON NEOCENE
CAMBRIAN DEVONIAN JURASSIC
SILURIAN TERTIARY TRANSVAAL
(HAPPY —) MILLENIUM
(HYPOTHETICAL —) ACME
(JAPANESE CULTURAL —) JOMON
(LONG —) EON AEON CYCLE
(MEETING —) SESSION
(MENSTRUAL —) TERMS
(OCCASIONAL —) SNATCH
(PENITENTIAL —) LENT
(RECURRING —) EMBER
(SHORT —) BIT FIT BLINK SHAKE SPELL
SPURT SNATCH
(WAITING —) MORATORIUM
(WET —) PLUVIAL

PERIODIC ERAL ANNUAL CYCLIC ETESIAN REGULAR FREQUENT SEASONAL

PERIODICAL DAILY ORGAN PAPER SHEET ANNUAL DIGEST REVIEW ETESIAN JOURNAL REGULAR TABLOID DREADFUL EXCHANGE MAGAZINE EPHEMERIS PICTORIAL

PERIPATETIC ROVING RAMBLING ITINERANT

PERIPHERAL DEEP OUTER DISTAL DISTANT EXTERNAL MARGINAL

PERIPHERY LIP RIM BRIM DOME EDGE AMBIT LIMIT SKIRT AREOLA BORDER BOUNDS FRINGE AMBITUS CONTOUR SUBURBS SURFACE CONFINES PERIMETER

PERISH DIE FADE FALL RUIN QUAIL SPILL WASTE DEPART EXPIRE STARVE DESTROY MISCARRY
(— GRADUALLY) FADE

PERISHABLE SOFT DYING BRITTLE FUGITIVE

PERJURE FORSWEAR

PERKY AIRY PERT COCKY JAUNTY CHIPPER

PERMANENCE STAY STABILITY

PERMANENT FIXED STABLE ABIDING DURABLE LASTING CONSTANT ENDURING STANDING INDELIBLE

PERMANENTLY KEEPS

PERMEATE FILL SEEP SOAK BATHE IMBUE DRENCH INFORM INVADE ANIMATE PERVADE DOMINATE SATURATE PENETRATE

PERMISSIBLE FREE VENIAL POSSIBLE CONGEABLE
(NOT —) NEFAS

PERMISSION FIAT LIEF PASS CONGE DARST FAVOR GRACE GRANT LEAVE ACCESS ACCORD PERMIT CONSENT LIBERTY LICENSE SANCTION

PERMISSIVE TOLERANT CONCESSORY

PERMIT LET CHIT CHOP GIVE PASS ADMIT ALLOW CONGE EXEAT FAVOR GRACE GRANT LEAVE SERVE ACCORD BETEEM CEDULA ENDURE ENTREE SUFFER CONCEDE CONSENT FACULTY LICENSE WARRANT

PERMITTED FREE LICIT ALLOWED INNOCENT SUPPOSED
(— BY LAW) LEGAL

PERNICIOUS BAD ILL EVIL FATAL QUICK SWIFT DEADLY MALIGN WICKED BALEFUL BANEFUL HARMFUL HURTFUL NOISOME NOXIOUS RUINOUS

PERPENDICULAR ERECT PLUMB SHEER ABRUPT NORMAL APOTHEM UPRIGHT CATHETUS VERTICAL
(MUTUALLY —) ORTHOGONAL

PERPETRATE DO PULL COMMIT EFFECT PERFORM

PERPETUAL ETERN ENDLESS ETERNAL CONSTANT INFINITO UNENDING CONTINUAL PERENNIAL

PERPETUALLY EVER ALWAYS FOREVER

PERPETUATE CONTINUE ETERNIZE MAINTAIN

PERPLEX CAP MAR SET VEX BEAT CLOG DOZE MAZE STUN AMAZE BESET STUMP TWIST BAFFLE BOGGLE BOTHER DARKEN HAMPER HARASS HOBBLE KITTLE MUDDLE PLAGUE POTHER POTTER PUTTER PUZZLE RIDDLE BEDEVIL BUMBAZE CONFUSE DIFFUSE EMBROIL FLUMMOX MYSTIFY NONPLUS STAGGER STUMBLE TORMENT BEWILDER CONFOUND SURPRISE BAMBOOZLE

PERPLEXED MAZY ANXIOUS PUZZLED CONFUSED TROUBLED INTRICATE

PERPLEXING HARD MAZY SPINY CRABBY KNOBBY KNOTTY COMPLEX CRABBED BAFFLING

PERPLEXITY FOG KNOT BRAKE HOBBLE PUZZLE TAKING TANGLE ANXIETY TROUBLE SURPRISE CONFUSION LABYRINTH PUZZLEMENT
(MENTAL —) STUDY

PERQUISITE FEE TIP LOCK PERK VAIL GOWPEN INCOME ADJUNCT APANAGE VANTAGE GRATUITY

PERSECUTE VEX BAIT ANNOY CHASE HARRY HOUND WRACK WRONG HARASS PESTER PURSUE AFFLICT CRUCIFY DRAGOON OPPRESS TORMENT TORTURE

PERSEPHONE KORE DESPOINA PRAXIDIKE
(DAUGHTER OF —) CORA KORE
(FATHER OF —) ZEUS JUPITER
(HUSBAND OF —) HADES PLUTO
(MOTHER OF —) CERES DEMETER

PERSEUS RESCUER CHAMPION
(FATHER OF —) ZEUS JUPITER
(GRANDFATHER OF —) ACRISIUS
(MOTHER OF —) DANAE
(VICTIM OF —) MEDUSA
(WIFE OF —) ANDROMEDA

PERSEVERANCE GRIT MOXIE STAMINA INDUSTRY PATIENCE TENACITY CONSTANCY PERSISTENCE

PERSEVERE PEG KEEP PLUG ABIDE STICK INSIST REMAIN PERSIST CONTINUE

PERSEVERING BUSY HARD STILL PATIENT RESOLUTE SEDULOUS ASSIDUOUS INSISTENT

PERSIA (SEE IRAN)

PERSIST HOLD KEEP LAST URGE ADHERE ENDURE INSIST REMAIN PREVAIL SUBSIST CONTINUE PERSEVERE

PERSISTENCE GUTS

PERSISTENT SET DREE FIRM HARD GREAT STOUT TOUGH DOGGED GRITTY HECTIC DURABLE RESTIVE CONSTANT ENDURING OBDURATE RESOLUTE SEDULOUS STUBBORN ASSIDUOUS OBSTINATE PERENNIAL RELENTLESS

PERSON BOD CAT EGG EGO GUY MAN ONE BABY BODY CHAP COVE DUCK FISH FOOD FORM GINK LIFE PRIG SELF SOUL BEING BOSOM CHILD COOKY GHOST HEART HUMAN PARTY PIECE STICK THING WATCH WIGHT ANIMAL BUGGER ENTITY FELLOW GALOOT GAZABO

JOHNNY KIPPER NUMBER SINNER SISTER SPIRIT SPRITE ARTICLE SPECIMEN

PERSONABLE COMELY SHAPELY HANDSOME

PERSONAL SELF PRIVY DIRECT PRIVATE CHATTELS CORPORAL INTIMATE

PERSONALITY EGO AURA DRAW SELF SOUL BEING ETHOS HEART EGOITY FIGURE CONTROL FACULTY DEMIURGE PRESENCE SELFHOOD SELFNESS

PERSONIFICATION SOUL GENIUS
(— OF DIVINE VIRTUE) EON
(— OF JUSTICE) THEMIS

PERSONIFY EMBODY INCARNATE PERSONIZE

PERSONNEL BLOOD STAFF KITCHEN PHYSIQUE

PERSPECTIVE OPTICS DISTANCE TELESCOPE

PERSPICACIOUS KEEN ACUTE ASTUTE SHREWD

PERSPICACITY WIT ACUMEN

PERSPIRATION DEW SUDOR SUINT SWEAT HIDROSIS OLIGIDRIA SUDORESIS

PERSPIRE PUG MELT BREAN SWEAT SWELTER TRANSPIRE

PERSUADE CON GET WIN COAX GAIN MOVE RULE SNOW URGE ARGUE BRING EDUCE ADVISE ARGUFY ASSURE CAJOLE ENGAGE ENTICE INDUCE SUBORN CONVERT DISPUTE ENTREAT IMPRESS PREVAIL SATISFY INFLUENCE

PERSUASION KIND SORT BELIEF OPINION JUDGMENT

PERSUASIVE COGENT WINNING INDUCTIVE PLAUSIBLE

PERT BOLD CHIC FLIP SPRY TRIM ALERT ALIVE BRISK COCKY PEART PERKY QUICK SASSY SAUCY SMART CHEEKY CLEVER COMELY DAPPER FRISKY BOBBISH INSOLENT PETULANT

PERTAIN BE LIE BEAR COME LONG BELIE TOUCH BEFALL BELONG RELATE RETAIN CONCERN
(— TO) RINE

PERTINACIOUS FIRM STIFF DOGGED ADHERING STUBBORN OBSTINATE

PERTINENCE RELEVANCE

PERTINENT APT FIT PAT HAPPY COGENT PROPER TIMELY ADAPTED APROPOS GERMANE POINTED TELLING INCIDENT MATERIAL RELATIVE RELEVANT

PERTURB BITE GRATE UPSET WORRY DISMAY AGITATE CONFUSE DERANGE DISTURB TROUBLE

PERU

CAPITAL: LIMA
COIN: SOL LIBRA DINERO CENTAVO
DEPARTMENT: ICA LIMA PUNO CUSCO CUZCO JUNIN PIURA TACNA ANCASH LORETO TUMBES
DESERT: SECHURA
ISLAND: CHINCHA
LAKE: TITICACA

MOUNTAIN: HUAMINA COROPUNA HUASCARAN
RIVER: NAPU RIMAC SANTA TIGRE MORONA YAGUAS YAVARI CURARAY MARANON PASTAZA UCAYALI AMAZONAS APURIMAC HUALLAGA URUBAMBA
TOWN: ICA LIMA PUNO CUZCO PAITA PISCO PIURA TACNA CALLAO TUMBES IQUITOS AREQUIPA CHICLAYO TRUJILLO
VOLCANO: MISTI YUCAMANI

PERUSE CON READ SCAN STUDY HANDLE SEARCH SURVEY EXAMINE INSPECT

PERVADE FILL BATHE IMBUE DRENCH OCCUPY THREAD INSTILL PERMEATE TRAVERSE

PERVASIVE POIGNANT

PERVERSE AWK CAM AWRY CROSS GAMMY THRAW WROTH CUSSED DIVERS THWART WICKED WILFUL AWKWARD CRABBED CROOKED DIVERSE FORWARD FROWARD OBLIQUE PEEVISH WAYWARD CRANKISH STUBBORN

PERVERT WRY DRAW RACK RUIN SKEW TURN WARP ABUSE CROOK GLOSS TWIST UPSET WREST DEBASE DIVERT GARBLE INVERT MISUSE POISON VOYEUR WRENCH WRITHE CONTORT CORRUPT DEGRADE DEPRAVE DEVIATE DISTORT MISTURN SUBVERT TRADUCE VITIATE

PERVERTED BAD WICKED ABUSIVE AWKWARD CORRUPT TWISTED VICIOUS

PESKY VERY PLAGUY ANNOYING DEVILING EXTREMELY

PESSIMIST ALARMIST JEREMIAH WORRYWART

PESSIMISTIC GLOOMY ALARMED BEARISH CYNICAL DOWNBEAT

PEST BOT BANE TICK WEED MOUSE INSECT MENACE PLAGUE SORROW VERMIN NUDNICK SCOURGE MEALYBUG SANDMITE BUTTINSKY

PESTER DUN HOX NAG RIB TIG HAKE ANNOY DEVIL TEASE WORRY BADGER BOTHER HARASS INFEST MOLEST BEDEVIL TORMENT TROUBLE OBSTRUCT PERSECUTE

PESTILENCE PEST DEATH QUALM PLAGUE MURRAIN EPIDEMIC MORTALITY

PESTILENT FATAL DEADLY VEXING NOXIOUS

PESTLE MIX CADE BRAY GRIND STAMP BEETLE BRAYER MULLER CHAPPER POUNDER STAMPER

PET TOY CADE COAX DEAR DUCK LAMB NECK SOCK SULK TIFF DUCKY HUMOR QUIET SPOIL SPOON TETCH CARESS CODDLE COSHER COSSET CUDDLE DANDLE FANTOD FONDLE GENTLE PAMPER PETKIN SMOOCH SQUALL STROKE WANTON CHERISH DARLING INDULGE TANTRUM UMBRAGE CANOODLE FAVORITE

PETAL ALA HELM LEAF WING BANNER
(— IN PEA FLOWER) VEXILLUM

(— OF IRIS) STANDARD
(UPPER —) HOOD BANNER
PETER GRIMES (CHARACTER IN —)
ELLEN PETER GRIMES ORFORD
BALSTRODE
(COMPOSER OF —) BRITTEN
PETER IBBETSON (AUTHOR OF —)
DUMAURIER
(CHARACTER IN —) DEANE MADGE
MIMSY PETER LINTOT GREGORY
PLUNKET IBBETSON PASQUIER
PETER PAN (AUTHOR OF —) BARRIE
(CHARACTER IN —) PAN HOOK JOHN
NIBS SMEE PETER WENDY TINKER
DARLING MICHAEL TOOTLES MARGARET
SLIGHTLY
PETITE SMALL LITTLE MIGNON
PETITION ASK BEG SUE BILL BOON PLEA
PRAY SUIT VOTE WISH APPLY ORATE
PLEAD APPEAL DESIRE INVOKE MOTION
PRAYER ADDRESS BESEECH ENTREAT
IMPLORE ORATION SOLICIT ROGATION
SUFFRAGE
PETITIONER BEGGAR ORATOR SUITOR
BEADSMAN APPLICANT ENTREATER
PLAINTIFF
PETRIFY DAZE DEADEN STONIFY
STUPEFY LAPIDIFY FOSSILIZE
GORGONIZE
PETROL GAS GASOLINE
PETROLATUM VASELINE
PETROLEUM OIL CRUDE PETROL
NAPHTHA
PETTICOAT GORE KILT SLIP DICKY
JUPON PAGNE SOUSE KIRTLE LUHINGA
PLACKET BALMORAL BASQUINE
PETTINESS NAGGLE PARVINIMITY
PETTISH HUFFY FRETFUL PEEVISH
PLAINTIVE
PETTY TIN BASE JERK MEAN ORRA PUNY
VAIN BANAL GRIMY MINOR PETIT SMALL
MEASLY MINUTE PALTRY PEANUT
POKING PUISNE SNIFTY TRIVIAL
TWATTLE CHILDISH FIDDLING INFERIOR
NIGGLING NUGATORY PEDDLING
PICAYUNE SNIPPETY TRIFLING
PAROCHIAL
PETULANT PERT CROSS SAUCY SHORT
TESTY TIFFY FEISTY SULLEN WANTON
WILFUL CRABBED FRETFUL FROWARD
HUFFISH PEEVISH WASPISH PERVERSE
SNAPPISH
PEW BOX BOUT DESK SEAT SLIP BENCH
STALL BOUGHT
PEYOTE HIKULI
PHAEDRA (AUTHOR OF —) RACINE
(CHARACTER IN —) ARICIA OENONE
PHAEDRA THESEUS HIPPOLYTUS
THERAMENES
(FATHER OF —) MINOS
(HUSBAND OF —) THESEUS
(MOTHER OF —) PASIPHAE
(SISTER OF —) ADRIADNE
(SON OF —) ACAMAS DEMOPHON
PHANTASM DREAM FANCY GHOST
VAPOR FIGURE SHADOW SPIRIT
FANTASY PHANTOM SPECIES SPECTER

PHANTOM IDOL BOGEY DUMMY GHOST
IMAGE SHADE SHAPE UMBRA BOGGLE
DOUBLE SHADOW SPIRIT BUGBEAR
EIDOLON ELUSIVE FANTASY FEATURE
SPECIES SPECTER ILLUSORY
PHARISEE MUGWUMP NICODEMUS
PHASE END LEG SIDE ANGLE FACET
GRADE STAGE ASPECT AVATAR
BACKLASH PASSOVER DICHOTOMY
(INITIAL —) BUD
(LOWEST —) BATHOS
(TRANSITORY —) STREAK
PHENOMENON FIRE ANOMY COLOR
EVENT IMAGE ARTHUS EFFECT METEOR
MIRAGE SHADOW ISOTOPY MIRACLE
PARADOX PROCESS SYMPTOM ASTERISM
PRAKRITI SIDERISM SUNQUAKE
LANDSPOUT
PHIAL CUP VIAL CRUET BOTTLE VESSEL
PHILANTHROPIC HUMANE
PHILANTHROPIST ALTRUIST
HUMANITARIAN
PHILANTHROPY CHARITY ALMSGIVING
PHILIPPIC SATIRE SCREED TIRADE
ABUSIVE DIATRIBE

PHILIPPINES

ARCHIPELAGO: SULU
CAPITAL: BAGUIO MANILA
COIN: PESO PESETA CENTAVO SENTIMO
ISLAND: CEBU BATAN BOHOL LEYTE
LUZON PANAY SAMAR NEGROS
MASBATE MINDORO PALAWAN
ROMBLON MINDANAO
LAKE: TAAL LANAO
MOUNTAIN: APO IBA MAYON PULOG
BANAHAO
NATIVE: ATA ATI ITA TAO AETA ATTA
ETAS MORO SULU BICOL TAGAL VICOL
IGOROT TIMAUA BISAYAN TAGALOG
FILIPINO
PROVINCE: ABRA CEBU SULU ALBAY
CAPIZ DAVAO LANAO RIZAL BATAAN
CAVITE IFUGAO ILOILO TARLAC SURIGAO
RIVER: ABRA AGNO MAGAT PASIG
AGUSAN LAOANG CAGAYAN MINDANAO
PAMPANGA
TOWN: IBA AGOA BOAC CEBU JOLO MATI
ALBAY DAVAO DIGOS LAOAG PASAY
VIGAN APARRI BAGUIO CAVITE ILAGAN
ILOILO MANILA BACOLOD BASILAN
DAGUPAN CALOOCAN
VOLCANO: APO TAAL MAYON BULOSAN
CANLAON

PHILISTINE BOOB GIGMAN MUCKER
BABBITT GITTITE BOEOTIAN BARBARIAN
BOURGEOIS HYPOCRITE
PHILOMELA (FATHER OF —) PANDION
(RAVISHER OF —) TEREUS
(SISTER OF —) PROCNE
(VICTIM OF —) ITYS
PHILOSOPHER WIT SAGE CYNIC STOIC
ARTIST IONIAN LEGIST DOTTORE
ELEATIC ERISTIC SCHOLAR SOPHIST

SUMMIST THINKER ZETETIC ACADEMIC
EPOCHIST MAGICIAN VIRTUOSO
ACADEMIST ALCHEMIST DIALECTIC
PHYSICIAN SCHOOLMAN

PHILOSOPHER'S STONE ADROP
MICROCOSM

PHILOSOPHY ETHICS GOSPEL MAGISM
SYSTEM TAOISM APRISMO COSMISM
DUALISM INQUIRY MIMAMSA SANKHYA
SCEPSIS ACTIVISM HINDUISM
HUMANISM IDENTISM IDEOLOGY
LEGALISM OCCAMISM STOICISM
ABSURDISM NOUMENISM SOCRATISM
VEDANTISM

PHINEUS (BROTHER OF —) CADMUS
CEPHEUS
(FATHER OF —) BELUS AGENOR
(MOTHER OF —) ANCHINOE
TELEPHASSA
(SISTER OF —) EUROPA
(WIFE OF —) IDAEA CLEOPATRA

PHLEGMATIC CALM COOL DULL SLOW
INERT MUCOID SLEEPY WATERY
VISCOUS COMPOSED SLUGGISH
APATHETIC IMPASSIVE

PHLOX CYME ALBION BEACON COBAEA

PHOEBE FIVE MOON DIANA PEWEE
ARTEMIS
(BROTHER OF —) CASTOR POLLUX
POLYDEUCES
(DAUGHTER OF —) LETO
(FATHER OF —) URANUS LEUCIPPUS
TYNDAREUS
(MOTHER OF —) GAEA LEDA
(SISTER OF —) HELEN CLYTEMNESTRA

PHOENICIA (COLONY OF —)
CARTHAGE
(GODDESS OF —) TANIT BALTIS
TANITH ASTARTE
(KING OF —) AGENOR
(TOWN OF —) ACRE TYRE SIDON
SAREPTA

PHOENIX (BROTHER OF —) CILIX
CADMUS THASUS PHINEUS
(FATHER OF —) AGENOR AMYNTOR
(MOTHER OF —) CLEOBULE
TELEPHASSA
(PUPIL OF —) ACHILLES
(SISTER OF —) EUROPA

PHONOGRAPH VIC PHONO VICTROLA

PHONY FAKE JIVE SHAM BOGUS FAKER
FALSE BRUMMY PLASTIC IMPOSTOR
SPURIOUS

PHOSPHATE EHLITE FLOATS APATITE
CABOCLE CACOXENE GRIPHITE
MONAZITE

PHOSPHORESCENCE BRIMING
MARFIRE

PHOTOGRAPH MUG PIC FILM LENS
SNAP CARTE IMAGE PANEL PHOTO PINUP
SHOOT STILL CANDID GLOSSY MOSAIC
RETAKE SCENIC STEREO AIRVIEW
PICTURE TINTYPE LIKENESS PORTRAIT
POSITIVE SNAPSHOT TABLETOP
CYCLOGRAM MAMMOGRAM

PHOTOGRAPHER PHOTOG LENSMAN
CAMERAMAN PAPARAZZO SHUTTERBUG

PHRASE CRY HIT MOT SET CRIB FUSS
HAVE IDEA TERM WORD COMMA COUCH
IDIOM LABEL LEMMA POINT STATE
STYLE TOPIC TROPE BYWORD CLAUSE
CLICHE HOBNOB NOTION PNEUMA
PRAISE SAVING SLOGAN DICTION
EPITHET PASSAGE CONCEIVE DIVISION
DORICISM FLATTERY IDEOGRAM
IRISHISM LATINISM LEITMOTIV
(— DIFFERENTLY) TURN
(— UNCTUOUSLY) DROOL
(MUSICAL —) RIFF POINT ATTACCO
SUBJECT
(PET —) SHIBBOLETH
(REDUNDANT —) CHEVILLE
(STOCK —) CANT
(TRITE —) CLICHE
(WELL-TURNED —) STROKE

PHYSIC CURE HEAL PURGE TRADE
REMEDY MEDICAL NATURAL RELIEVE
DRUGGERY

PHYSICAL LUSTY SOMAL BODILY
CARNAL DISTAL NATURAL SOMATIC
CORPORAL CURATIVE EXTERNAL
MATERIAL CORPOREAL

PHYSICIAN ASA DOC PILL CURER GALEN
HAKIM LEECH MEDIC QUACK ARTIST
BAIDYA DOCTOR FELLOW HEALER
INTERN MEDICO DOTTORE EMPIRIC
SURGEON ALIENIST RESIDENT
SAWBONES SUNDOWNER
(— OF THE GODS) PAEAN

PHYSICIST HYLOZOIST

PHYSIOGNOMY MUG FACE PHIZ
VIZNOMY PORTRAIT VISENOMY

PHYSIOLOGY BIONOMY ZOONOMY

PHYSIQUE BODY BUILD COOST HABIT
FIGURE STRENGTH

PIANO SOFT FLOOR GRAND STORY
FLUGEL GENTLY SOFTLY SPINET SQUARE
CLAVIAL CLAVIER GIRAFFE PIANOLA
QUIETLY UPRIGHT MELOTROPE
(AFRICAN —) KALIMBA

PIAZZA PORCH SQUARE BALCONY
GALLERY PORTICO VERANDA PIAZZETTA

PICAYUNE PETTY MEASLY PALTRY
TRIVIAL

PICCOLO BUSBOY JUKEBOX FLAUTINO
OTTAVINO

PICK NIB OPT BILL GAFF HACK LIFT PIKE
SHOT WALE ADORN BREAK CAVIL ELECT
LEASE PLUCK PRIDE PRIME CHOICE
CHOOSE GATHER PICKAX TWITCH
BARGAIN DIAMOND DRESSER MANDREL
(— APART) TOW
(— KNOTS FROM) BURL
(— OUT) CULL SPOT TAKE WELE CRONE
GLEAN GARBLE SELECT
(— POCKETS) FIG FILE FOIST TOUCH
(— TOBACCO) STRIP

PICKED TRIM CHOSEN DAINTY SELECT
ADORNED POINTED
(PREF.) LECTO

PICKEREL JACK SNAKE DUNLIN SAUGER
SLINKER WALLEYE

PICKET PEG PALE POST TERN FENCE

STAKE FASTEN PALING TETHER ENCLOSE
FORTIFY OUTPOST PALISADE
PICKLE BOX ALEC DILL MESS PECK
ACHAR BRINE GRAIN MANGO SAUCE
SOUSE CAPERS DAWDLE MUDDLE
NIBBLE PLIGHT TRIFLE CONFECT
GHERKIN TROUBLE VITRIOL MARINADE
PICKLED DRUNK MURIATED POWDERED
MARINATED
PICKPOCKET DIP FIG GUN NIP BUNG
FILE WIRE DIVER FILER FOIST BULKER
BUZZER CANNON DIPPER FIGBOY
HOOKER NIPPER RATERO FOISTER
MOBSMAN CLYFAKER CUTPURSE
KNUCKLER BUZZGLOAK
(HELPER OF —) STALL BULKER
PICKWICK PAPERS (AUTHOR OF —)
DICKENS
(CHARACTER IN —) BOB SAM MARY
ALLEN EMILY TRACY ALFRED HUNTER
JINGLE PERKER SAWYER TUPMAN
WARDLE WELLER WINKLE BARDELL
RACHAEL SLAMMER ARABELLA
AUGUSTUS CLUPPINS ISABELLA
PICKWICK NATHANIEL SMORLTORK
SNODGRASS
PICNIC FRY BALL GYPSY BURGOO FROLIC
JUNKET MAROON OUTING SHOULDER
SQUANTUM SUMMERING WAYZGOOSE
PICTORIAL GRAPHIC
PICTURE MAP OIL COPY DAUB ICON LIMN
SIGN VIEW DECAL FRAME IMAGE PAINT
PHOTO PIECE PINAX PRINT CHROME SHAPE
STAMP STORY TABLE CACHET CANVAS
CHROMO CUTOUT DEPICT EMBLEM
MARINE PASTEL SHADOW STEREO
TABLET CUTAWAY DIORAMA DIPTYCH
EMBLEMA ETCHING EXHIBIT FASHION
FEATURE GOUACHE GRAPHIC HISTORY
PORTRAY RETRAIT SCENERY TABLEAU
VANDYKE AIRSCAPE AUTOTYPE
DESCRIBE ENVISION IDEOGRAM
LANDSKIP LIKENESS MONOTINT
OVERDOOR PAINTING PANORAMA
PORTRAIT PROSPECT RITRATTO
SEASCAPE SKYSCAPE VIGNETTE
ENCAUSTIC
(— IN BOOK) GAY
(— IN 3 COMPARTMENTS) TRIPTYCH
(— OF MONKEYS) SINGERIE
(— ON ROLLER) KAKEMONO
MAKIMONO
(—S IN BOOKS) BABY
(COMIC —) DROLLERY
(RELIGIOUS —) TANKA
(STEREOSCOPIC —) ANAGLYPH
(THREE-DIMENSIONAL —) HOLOGRAM
(PREF.) PINAC(O)
PICTURE OF DORIAN GRAY
(AUTHOR OF —) WILDE
(CHARACTER IN —) ALAN GRAY VANE
BASIL HENRY JAMES SIBYL DORIAN
WOTTON CAMPBELL HALLWARD
PICTURESQUE VIVID EXOTIC QUAINT
SCENIC GRAPHIC IDYLLIC ROMANTIC
PICTORIAL
PIDDLING JERK PALTRY TRIVIAL

USELESS FOOTLING TRIFLING
JERKWATER
PIE FLAN HEAP MESS PATE PILE TART
DOWDY PASTY PATTY TORTA AFFAIR
BRIDLE CHEWET MAGPIE PASTRY
COBBLER SMASHER STRUDEL BAKEMEAT
CRUSTADE FLAPJACK PANDOWDY
SURPRISE TURNOVER
PIECE BAT COB CUT JOB LAB LOG MAN
TUT GIRL MIND PART PISE PLAY DRAMA
DWANG FLOOR PEZZO SHARD SHERD
SHRED SLICE SNODE STEEK STUCK
THROW COLLOP FARDEL FUGATO
GOBBET PARCEL STITCH CANTLET
EXAMPLE FLINDER FLITTER MORCEAU
OPINION PICTURE PORTION SEGMENT
EMBOLIUM FANDANGO PAINTING
(— AT END) HEELPIECE
(— FOR TWO) DUET DUOLOGUE
(— IN CHECKERS) DAM
(— IN ORGAN) THUMPER
(— OF ARMOR) JAMB JAMBE
(— OF BAD LUCK) DIRDUM
(— OF BLANKET) DAGON
(— OF BLUBBER) BIBLE
(— OF DECEPTION) BEGUNK
(— OF DECORATED METAL) NIELLO
(— OF FALSE HAIR) JANE
(— OF FIBER) NOIL
(— OF FIRED CLAY) TILE
(— OF GROUND SURROUNDED BY
WASTE) HOPE
(— OF HARD WOOD) MOOT
(— OF LAND) ERF HAM LOT BUTT GORE
LEASE SPONG SQUAT HUERTA RINCON
SECTION CLEARAGE SOLIDATE
(— OF LIGHT ORDNANCE) ASPIC
(— OF LINEN) AMIT AMICE
(— OF LOG) SLAB
(— OF MAST) TONGUE
(— OF MEAT) EYE HEEL RAND COLLOP
EPIGRAM
(— OF METAL) JAG COIN JAGG SPRAG
(— OF MONEY) COG SOU SHINER
(— OF NEEDLEWORK) SAMPLER
(— OF NONSENSE) FUDGE TRIMTRAM
(— OF ORE) CHAT
(— OF PROPERTY) CHOSE
(— OF SAIL) HULLOCK
(— OF SKIN) BLYPE
(— OF SKIN FOR GLOVE) TRANK
(— OF SLATE) SLAT
(— OF SOAP) BALL
(— OF SOMETHING EDIBLE) STULL
(— OF TIMBER) FISH COULISSE
FOREHOOK
(— OF TOAST) SLINGER
(— OF TOBACCO) FIG
(— OF TRACK) LEAD RUNBY
(— OF TRICKERY) CROOK CANTRIP
(— OF TURF) FLAG DIVOT SCRAW
SHIRREL
(— OF WOOD) KIP LATH APRON BOARD
CHUMP CHUNK PLANK SPOON WADDY
BILLET COMMON STOWER TIMBER
LIPPING
(— OF WORK) JOB CHAR TURN

(— OF WRITING) SCREED SCREEVE
(— OUT) EKE
(— SPLIT OFF) SPLINT
(— TO PREVENT SLIPPING) CLEAT
(ARTILLERY —) DRAKE SAKER
LANTACA
(BACKGAMMON —) BLOT STONE
(BROAD —) SHEET
(BROKEN —) BRACK MAMMOCK
FRACTION
(BUTTING —) HURTER
(CHESS —) PIN KING PAWN ROOK
QUEEN BISHOP CASTLE KNIGHT OFFICER
(DREAMY —) REVERIE
(END — OF BUCKET) CANT
(FLAT —) FLAP FLAKE
(FUR —) PALATINE
(GOLD —) SLUG TALI
(IRREGULAR —) SNAG
(LARDED — OF MEAT) DAUB
(LARGE —) HUNK MOLE STULL DOLLOP
(LITERARY —) CAMEO
(LITTLE —) STNEKI SCANTLING
(LONG —) STRIP
(MUSICAL —) ITEM CHORO DANCE
ETUDE CHASER LESSON ALLEGRO
ANDANTE BLUETTE CONCERTO
DUOLOGUE ENTRACTE OVERTURE
INVENTION
(NARROW —) LABEL STAVE STRIP
(ROTATING —) CAM ROTOR SPINDLE
(SAMPLE —) SWATCH
(SHAPELESS —) DUMP MAMMOCK
(SIDE —) RIB JAMB JAMBE
(SINGLE —) LENGTH
(SLENDER —) SPILL SLIVER
(SMALL —) BIT BOB NOB PEA CHIP
SNIP TATE CRUMB PATCH PRILL SCRAP
SPECK MORSEL SIPPET DRIBLET FLITTER
PALLION SPLINTER
(STRENGTHENING —) DWANG HURTER
(TAPERING —) GORE GUSSET
(THICK —) JUNK HUNCH
(THIN —) SHIM FLAKE SHIVE SLICE
PIECEWORK SETWORK TUTWORK
TASKWORK
PIED PINTO SHELD MAGPIED PIEBALD
PIER COB ANTA BELT COBB DOCK MOLE
PILE QUAY TILT GROIN JETTY JOWEL
JUTTY LEVEE STILT WHARF BRIDGE
BUNDER MULLION STAGION PIEDROIT
STELLING
PIERCE CUT DAG DIG JAB JAG BARB
BEAR BITE BORE CLOY DART GORE HOLE
HOOK LACE PASS PINK POKE PROG RIVE
STAB TANG WHIP BREAK DRIFT DRILL
ENTER GOUGE LANCE PERCH PITCH
POACH PROBE PRONG SHEAR SNICK
SPEAR SPIKE STICK STING THIRL
BROACH CLEAVE DAGGER GIMLET
IMPALE LAUNCH PRITCH RIDDLE SEARCH
SKEWER STITCH STRIKE THRUST
LACERATE PUNCTURE PENETRATE
PIERCING FELL HIGH KEEN LOUD TART
ACUTE CLEAR SHARP SNELL ARROWY
BITTER BORING SHREWD SHRILL
CUTTING GIMLETY POINTED PUNGENT

DRILLING INCISIVE POIGNANT STABBING
STICKING
PIETY HONOR LOYALTY DEVOTION
SANCTION GODLINESS
PIG (ALSO SEE HOG, SWINE) FAR HAM
HOG SLIP BACON BONAV BROCK CHEAT
CHUCK GRICE INGOT PIGGY SHOAT
BONHAM COCHON FARROW GUSSIE
HOGGIE PORKET PORKIN SUCKER
WEANER GLUTTON GRUMPHY
PIGEON DOO NUN OWL TOY BARB CLAY
DOVE JACK KING KITE LUPE RUFF RUNT
SPOT BALDY HOMER PIPER SQUAB
CULVER CUSHAT DODLET DRAGON
FEEDER HELMET MAGPIE MANUMA
MAUMET MODENA POUTER PRIEST
ROCKER SHAKER TURBIT TURNER
WATTLE ANTWERP CARNEAU CARRIER
CROPPER FANTAIL JACINTH JACOBIN
MALTESE PINTADO SWALLOW TIPPLER
TUMBLER BALDHEAD CAPUCHIN
MANUTAGI RINGDOVE SASSOROL
SQUABBER SQUEAKER SQUEAKER
PIGEONHOLE BOX SLOT LABEL SHELVE
ANALYZE CELLULE CLASSIFY
CUBBYHOLE
PIGHEADED WILLFUL PERVERSE
STUBBORN OBSTINATE
PIGMENT (ALSO SEE DYE, COLOR)
BLUE BROWN COLOR EARTH GREEN
HUMIN MORIN PAINT STAIN TONER
BRONZE CEROID CERUSE IDAEIN LITHOL
MALVIN ORANGE PURPLE VIOLET
BEZETTA GOUACHE PAINTRY STAINER
COLORANT EXTENDER GOSSYPOL
MELANOID PAINTURE TINCTURE
UROPHEIN
(— IN BUTTERFLY WING) PTERIN
(BLACK —) ABAISER MELANIN
(BLUE —) BICE SMALT CYANIN ALTHEIN
CERULEUM MARENNIN
(BLUE-GREEN —) LEUCOCYAN
(BROWN —) MUMMY SEPIA UMBER
BISTER FUSCIN ASTERIN SINOPIA
(BROWNISH-YELLOW —) SIENNA
(GRAPE —) OENIN
(GREEN —) VERDITER
(MADDER-ROOT —) RUBIATE
(ORANGE-RED —) REALGAR
(PLANT —) CYANIN
(RED —) HAEM LAKE ARUMIN PATISE
SANDYX AMATITO KOKOWAI PUCCOON
SCARLET SINOPIA CAPSUMIN URORUBIN
URRHODIN VERMILION
(RED-VIOLET —) TURACIN
(WHITE —) CERUSE ANATASE
LITHOPONE
(YELLOW —) FLAVIN PURREE ETIOLIN
FISETIN GAMBOGE PUCCOON CAROTENE
DIATOMIN GALANGIN GENTISIN
MASSICOT ORPIMENT UROBILIN
PIGSTY FRANK CRUIVE HOGCOTE
HOGGERY PIGGERY SWINESTY
PIGTAIL PLAIT QUEUE COLETA
PIKE GED DORY GADE JACK LUCE TANG
TOUG TUCK HAKED LUCET SNAKE
SNOOK STING VOUGE SALMON SAUGER

JAVELIN WALLEYE BLOWFISH GLASSEYE
JACKFISH NORTHERN PARTISAN
PICKEREL POULAINE TURNPIKE
MUSKELLUNGE

PIKER TRAMP VAGRANT TELLTALE
TIGHTWAD VAGABOND

PILASTER ANTA PIER RIDGE ALETTE
RESPOND TELAMON

PILE COP FUR LOT NAP PIE TIP BALE
BANK BING BURR DOWN HAIR HEAP
LEET LOAD PEEL PIER POLE POOK REEK
RUCK SHAG SPUD AMASS CROWD
FAGOT POINT SPILE SPIRE STACK STILT
TOWER CASTLE FENDER FILLER GALGAL
PILLAR RUCKLE FORTUNE JAVELIN
PYRAMID REACTOR CROWBILL INCREASE
SANDPILE
(— CROSSWISE) COB
(— CURD) CHEDDAR
(— OF BRICKS) HACK CLAMP
(— OF CLOTH) LAY
(— OF HAY) RICK SHOCK DOODLE
HAYCOCK HAYRICK
(— OF ICE) HUMMOCK
(— OF LOGS) DECK
(— OF PLATES) BUNG
(— OF REFUSE) DUSTHEAP
(— OF SALT FISH) BULK
(— OF SEALSKINS) PAN
(— OF SHEAVES) SESS
(— OF SHEETS) LIFT
(— OF STONES) ISLAND STONAGE
WARLOCK
(— OF TOBACCO) BULK
(— OF WOOD) STRAND
(— TO BE BURNT) PYRE
(— UP) BIG BULK CORD RICK COMPILE
ACCUMULATE
(— WHEAT SHOCKS) STITCH
(IRON —) SPINDLE
(LITTLE —) HOT
(LOOSE —) RICKLE
(ROCK —) HOODOO
(SMALL —) COCK CANCH
(PL.) FIG DRIFT

PILFER NIM NIP ROB CRIB HOOK PELF
PICK PRIG SNIG FILCH MOOCH PROWL
SHARP SLOCK STEAL SWIPE FINGER
MAGPIE NIBBLE SMOUCH SNITCH
CABBAGE PLUNDER PURLOIN SNAFFLE
PETTIFOG SCROUNGE

PILGRIMAGE TRIP TURUS VOYAGE
JOURNEY
(— TO MECCA) HADJ
(BRETON —) PARDON

PILGRIM'S PROGRESS
(AUTHOR OF —) BUNYAN
(CHARACTER IN —) POPE PAGAN
PIETY SLOTH PLIANT SIMPLE CHARITY
DESPAIR HOPEFUL SINCERE APOLLYON
FAITHFUL GOODWILL PRUDENCE
WATCHFUL CHRISTIAN FORMALISM
HYPOCRISY IGNORANCE KNOWLEDGE
OBSTINATE DISCRETION EVANGELIST
EXPERIENCE PRESUMPTION

PILL ROB BARK GOLI CREEK EXTORT
UNHAIR DESPOIL DIURNAL GLOBULE

GRANULE PARVULE PILLULE BASEBALL
GOOFBALL BLACKBALL
(AROMATIC —) CACHOU
(LARGE —) BALL BOLUS
(LITTLE —) PILULE

PILLAGE LOOT PREY SACK BOOTY FORAY
HARRY REAVE RIFLE SPOIL HARROW
MARAUD RAPINE RAVAGE DESPOIL
PICKEER PLUNDER RANSACK ROBBERY
SPOLIATE DEVASTATE

PILLAR COG HERM JAMB PACK PIER PILE
POST PROP STUD TERM JAMBE NEWEL
SHAFT STELA STELE STOCK STONE
COLUMN PILLER STAPLE BEDPOST
TRESTLE BOUNDARY PEDESTAL
STANCHION
(— CAPPED WITH SLAB) BILITH
(— IN LARGE DOORWAY) TRUMEAU
(— IN MINE) STUMP
(— OF COAL) SPURN STOOK STOOP
(— SUPPORTING ARCH) RESPONSE
(— SURMOUNTED BY HEAD) HERMES
(—S OF HERCULES) ABILA CALPE
(BUDDHIST —) LAT
(EARTH —) HOODOO
(SACRED —) ASHERAH
(SEMITE —) MASSEBAH
(STONE —) CIPPUS
(TEMPORARY —) DEADMAN
(4-SIDED —) OBELISK

PILLORY THEW JOUGS TRONE CANGUE
CRUCIFY HALSFANG

PILLOW COD BOTT DAWN PILE REST
FLOAT BOLSTER CUSHION FUSTIAN
HEADING PULVINAR

PILLOWCASE COD BEAR PILL SHAM
PILLIVER

PILOT ACE SPY KIWI COACH GUARD
GUIDE STEER AIRMAN ESCORT MANAGE
THAMUS AVIATOR CAPTAIN CONDUCT
HOBBLER LODEMAN SHIPMAN WINGMAN
AIREDALE GOVERNOR HELMSMAN
WHEELSMAN
(AUTHOR OF —) COOPER
(CHARACTER IN —) TOM GRAY ALICE
JONES MERRY COFFIN DILLON EDWARD
HOWARD MANUAL MUNSON CECILIA
PLOWDEN RICHARD GRIFFITH
DUNSCOMBE KATHERINE BARNSTABLE
CHRISTOPHER BORROUGHCLIFFE

PIMPLE GUM NOB NOB PAP BURL KNOB PUSH
QUAT SPOT BLAIN BOTCH HICKY PLOUK
WHELK BLOTCH BOUTON BUTTON
PAPULE TETTER PUSTULE

PIN FID FIX HUB LAG LEG NOG PEG PEN
ACUS APEX AXLE BANK BOLT MOOD
PEEN POST PRIN PYNE RUNG STUD
HUMOR KAYLE POINT PREEN SPILL
BOBBIN BODKIN BROACH BROOCH
CALIGO CURLER FASTEN HATPIN JOGGLE
NORMAN PINNET SKEWER SPIGOT
TEMPER TENPIN TOGGEL TONGUE TRIFLE
CONFINE ENCLOSE GUDGEON HAIRPIN
IMPOUND LOCKPIN PUSHPIN SPINDLE
TAMPION TUMBLER WOODLER PINNACLE
(— FOR FITTING PLANKS) SETBOLT
(— IN AXLETREE) LINCHPIN

(— IN RIFLE) TIGE
(— OF DIAL) STYLE GNOMON
(— OF LANTERN PINION) RUNDLE
(— OF WATCH) DART
(— ON CLAVICHORD KEY) TANGENT
(— TO HOLD BEDCLOTHES) BEDSTAFF
(— USED AS TARGET) HOB
(BELAYING —) CAVIL
(BOWLING —) DUCKPIN HEADPIN KINGPIN SLEEPER
(CARPENTRY —) DOWEL
(COUPLING —) DRAWBOLT
(ENGAGING —) BAYONET
(HAIR —) BARRETTE
(HEADED —) RIVET
(JEWELED —) PROP
(OAR —) THOLE
(ORNAMENTAL —) AGLET
(PIVOT —) PINTLE
(SMALL —) LILL MINIKIN MICROPIN
(SPLIT —) COTTER FORELOCK
(SURVEYOR'S —) ARROW
(TAPERED —) DRIFT
(TIRLING —) RISP
(WOODEN —) SPILE TRENAIL
(PL.) LEGS KAILS DEADWOOD
(PREF.) PERONEO PERONO
PINAFORE BRAT SLIP TIDY TIER DAIDLY PINNER SAVEALL SLIPPER GABERDINE
PINCERS TEW CLAM CHELA PLIERS FORCEPS MULLETS NIPPERS PINSONS TWEEZERS
PINCH NIP TOP VEX WRY BITE CLAM HURT STOP TUCK CRIMP GRIPE PUGIL SNUFF SQUAT STEAL STINT TAPER THEFT TWEAK WRING ARREST CLUTCH EXTORT HARASS NARROW SNITCH STRAIT STRESS TWITCH SQUEEZE PRESSURE SHORTAGE
PINCHPENNY CARL MISER NIGGARD NIGGARDLY
PINE ARA LIM CHIL CHIR FADE FLAG WANT GRIEF KAURI MATAI MATSU MOURN OCOTE PINON WEARY WRIST YEARN APACHE AROLLA DUSTER FAMINE GRIEVE HUNGER LAMENT PANDAN SHRINK SORROW STARVE WITHER CYPRESS DAISING DWINDLE TARWOOD TORMENT TORTURE AUSTRIAN LANGUISH LOBLOLLY LONGLEAF PINASTER STAGHORN
(— AWAY) PEAK DROOP DWINE SNURI WANZE WINDER
(AUSTRALIAN —) BEEFWOOD
(GROUND —) FOXTAIL
(PITCH —) THYME
(PREF.) PINI PITYO
PINEAPPLE BOMB NANA PINA PINO PITA ANANA ANANAS ABACAXI GRENADE
PINION NOIL WING QUILL PENNON SARCEL SECURE LANTERN PINACLE SHACKLE TRUNDLE
PINK JAG PIP CYME DAWN DECK FADE STAB WINK ADORN BLINK CORAL ELITE SWELL WOUND AURORE BISQUE CHERUB FIESTA SHRIMP SILENE TATTOO ZEPHYR ANNATTO ARBUTUS BEGONIA

BERMUDA BLOSSOM CAMPION EXTREME PARAGON SANDUST COQUETTE DIANTHUS GILLIVER LIMEWORT RADIANCE RECAMIER
PINNACE BARK CROWN BARQUE MISTRESS
PINNACLE IT TOP ACME APEX CREST CROWN SPIRE THUMB FINIAL HEIGHT SUMMIT
(ICE —) SERAC
(ROCKY —) TOR HOODOO AIGUILLE GENDARME
PINPOINT ISOLATE
PINT GULL PINNET SWIGGER OCTARIUS
(FOURTH —) GILL JACK
(HALF —) CUP NIP GILL JACK CUPFUL NIPPERKIN
(9-10THS —) MUTCHKIN
PIONEER BLAZE GUIDE MINER GROPER HALUTZ SETTLE EXPLORE EARLIEST EMIGRANT ORIGINAL RAWHIDER VOORTREKKER
PIONEERS (AUTHOR OF —) COOPER
(CHARACTER IN —) JOHN GRANT HIRAM JONES NATTY BUMPPO LOUISA OLIVER TEMPLE EDWARDS RICHARD DOOLITTLE EFFINGHAM ELIZABETH CHINGACHGOOK
PIOUS HOLY WISE GODLY MORAL SEELY DEVOUT DIVINE INWARD PIETIC CANTING DUTIFUL SAINTED SAINTLY FAITHFUL RELIGIOUS
PIPE BIN TAP TEE BUTT CALL CANE DALE DRIP DUCT HOSE LINE MAIN MUTE PULE TILE TUBE WEEP WORM BLAST CANAL CANEL CINCH CRANE CROSS PROBE QUILL RIDER RISER SPOUT STAND TEWEL TRUMP TRUNK VOICE BRANCH BURROW CALEAN CASING DUCTUS FAUCET FILLER NIPPLE NOTICE NOZZLE OFFLET OFFSET POOGYE RANKET SLEEVE SLUICE SUCKER TROWEL TUBULE TUNNEL UPTAKE WEEPER CHANNEL CONDUIT DUCTURE HYDRANT SERVICE SPARGER SUCTION TALLBOY TWEEDLE WHISTLE DOWNTAKE GALOUBET LAMPHOLE MIRLITON NARGHILE NARGILEH PENSTOCK SEMIDOLE SUSPIRAL TELLTALE THRIBBLE
(— AS NAVIGATION AID) SPINDLE
(— FOR CONDUCTING WATER) LEADER
(— OF ORE) BUNNY
(— OF PAN) SYRINX
(— OF QUEEN BEE) TEET
(— ON BAGPIPE) DRONE CHANTER
(— USED IN WELL) STRING
(— WITH SOCKET ENDS) HUB
(CEREMONIAL —) CALUMET
(CLAMMING —) BRAIL
(CONNECTING —) HOGGER
(HEATING —) CALIDUCT
(MUSICAL —) BODY GEWGAW FISTULA SORDINE HORNPIPE SCHWEGEL
(OATEN —) OAT
(ORGAN —) FLUE KINURA LABIAL ERZAHLER SCHWEGEL TREMOLANT
(ORGAN —S) MONTRE

(PEACE —) CALUMET
(PROJECTING —) BRACKET
(SEWER —) SLANT
(SHEPHERD'S —) REED LARIGOT CHALUMEAU
(SNAKE-CHARMER'S —) PUNGI
(TOBACCO —) GUN CLAY BRIAR BRIER CUTTY STRAW CALEAN DUDEEN HOOKAH BULLDOG CHIBOUK CHILLUM CORNCOB BILLIARD CALABASH MEERSCHAUM
(TOY —) HEWGAG
(VERTICAL —) STACK LAMPHOLE
(WATER — FOR ENGINE) SLOUCH
(4 LENGTHS OF —) FOURBLE
PIQUANT BOLD RACY JUICY NUTTY SALTY SHARP SPICY TASTY ZESTY LIVELY SEVERE CUTTING PEPPERY PUNGENT POIGNANT STINGING
PIQUE FRET GOAD TICK ANNOY SPITE STING HARASS MALICE NETTLE OFFENSE PROVOKE UMBRAGE IRRITATE
PIRATE CAPER ROVER ROBBER VIKING CATERAN CORSAIR PICKEER SCUMMER ALGERINE MAROONER PICAROON BUCCANEER SEALEEMAN
PISTOL DAG GAT GUN POP ROD BULL COLT IRON STICK BARKER BUFFER CANNON DRAGON HEATER POTGUN RIFFLE ROSCOE BULLDOG TICKLER DERINGER PETRONEL REVOLVER PEPPERBOX
PISTON BUCKET FORCER PALLET SUCKER EMBOLUS PLUNGER
PIT PET POT PUT BURY DELF DELL DISC DISK FOSS HELL HOLE KHUD LAKE MINE PLAY PUTT SINK SUMP SWAG TURN WEEM WELL ABYSM CRYPT DELFT DITCH FOSSA FOVEA FROST GRAVE MATCH PITCH PORUS SLACK TREAD BORROW KERNEL OPPOSE RADDLE WALLOW ALVEOLA AMPULLA CHARPIT FOSSULA FOXHOLE LATRINE PINHOLE VARIOLE CESSPOOL DOWNFAL FAVEOLUS FENESTRA POCKMARK PUNCTULE WELLHOLE
(— FOR BAKING) UMU
(— FOR OFFERINGS) BOTHROS
(— OF STOMACH) MARK WIND
(— OF THEATER) GROUND PARTERRE
(— ON COCKROACH HEAD) FENESTRA
(— ON LICHENS) LACUNA CYPHELLA
(— SACRED TO DEMETER) MEGARON
(BITTER —) STIPPEN
(BOTTOMLESS —) ABYSS ABADDON BARATHRUM
(COAL —) HEUGH WINNING
(FODDER —) SILO
(MAORI —) RUA
(MIRY —) SLUIG
(RIFLE —) SANGAR
(ROOFED —) CIST
(SALT —) VAT PEZOGRAPH
(SAND —) BUNKER
(SMALL —) AREOLE LACUNA STAPLE

(TANNING —) LIME LAYER LEACH HANDLER LAYAWAY SUSPENDER
PITCH DIP FIT KEY LAB MEL PIC BUCK CANT CHAT CODE COOK DING FALL FORK HURL PECK PICK PLUG RAKE TELL TONE TOSS ABODE BOOST BUNCH CHUCK FLING LABOR LURCH PLANT SLENT SLOPE SPIEL THROW TWIRL BINDER DIRECT ENCAMP FILLER LENGTH MALTHA MANJAK PLUNGE SQUARE TOTTER TUMBLE VOLLEY WICKET CURRENT NARRATE ALKITRAN OVERHANG
PITCHER JUG JACK OLLA PILL PRIG BUIRE CROCK CRUET GALON AFTABA CROUKE GALLON HURLER POURIE STRAIN CANETTE CHUCKER FLINGER STARTER STOPPER TWIRLER ASCIDIUM SOUTHPAW MOUNDSMAN
(— AND CATCHER) BATTERY
(— FOR BEER) GROWLER
(— OF ORCHID) BUCKET
(— SHAPED LIKE MAN) TOBY
(— WITH ONE HANDLE) URCEUS
(BULGING —) GOTCH
(EARTHEN —) GORGE
(RELIEF —) FIREMAN
(RELIEF —S) BULLPEN
(REMOVE — FROM BASEBALL GAME) DERRICK
(WIDEMOUTHED —) EWER
PITEOUS MEAN PALTRY PITIFUL MERCIFUL MOURNFUL PIERCING
PITFALL PIT FALL TRAP SNARE DANGER TRAPFALL
PITH JET SAP CORE GIST MEAT PULP HEART VIGOR ENERGY KERNEL MARROW ESSENCE EXTRACT MEDULLA NUCLEUS STRENGTH
PITH HELMET TOPI TOPEE
PITHY CRISP MEATY SAPPY TERSE STRONG CONCISE LACONIC MARROWY
PITIFUL MEAN MEEK RUTH SILLY SORRY PALTRY RUEFUL TENDER HANGDOG RUESOME RUTHFUL MERCIFUL PATHETIC
PITILESS GRIM CRUEL STERN STONY BRASSY SAVAGE RUTHLESS MERCILESS
PITTANCE BIT ALMS DOLE GIFT MITE SONG TRIFLE BEQUEST
PITY RUE MEAN MOAN RUTH MERCY PIETY SCATH BEMOAN PATHOS MERCIFY REMORSE CLEMENCY SYMPATHY COMPASSION
PIVOT TOE CRUX SLUE TURN HEART CENTER GUDGEON TRAVERSE TRUNNION
PIVOTAL POLAR CENTRAL TROCHOID
PIXY ELF FAIRY PYGMY ROGUE IMPISH RASCAL SPRITE PUCKISH ROGUISH
PLACARD BILL POST TITLE POSTER TICKET AFFICHE REDLINE
PLACATE CALM GENTLE PACIFY PLEASE SOOTHE APPEASE FORGIVE
PLACE DO BIT FIX PUT SET AREA HOLE LIEU PLAT PLOT POSE POST RANK ROOM SEAT SITE SITU SPOT STEL STEP STOW TEXT VICE YARK BEING ESTER ESTRE HOUSE JOINT LOCUS PLAZA POINT POSIT SCENE SITUS STALL STATE STEAD

STELL STOUR WHERE BESTOW CHARGE
GROUND IMPOSE INVEST LAYOUT
LOCALE LOCATE OFFICE POSSIE ROOMTH
ALLODGE ARRANGE DEPOSIT KITCHEN
STATION ABDITORY ALLOCATE DIGGINGS
EMPORIUM LOCATION POSITION

PLACID CALM COOL EVEN MEEK MILD
SOFT DOWNY QUIET SUENT GENTLE
SEDATE SERENE SMOOTH PACIFIC
TRANQUIL

PLACKET FENT SPARE WOMAN CLOSING
PETTICOAT

PLAGIARIZE CRIB LIFT STEAL

PLAGUE DUN IMP POX VEX FRAB FRET
GNAW PEST TWIT BESET CURSE DEATH
DEUCE HARRY QUALM TEASE WEARY
WORRY WOUND BOTHER BURDEN
HAMPER HARASS INFEST PESTER
SORROW DESTROY MURRAIN PERPLEX
SCOURGE TORMENT TORTURE TROUBLE
BEPESTER HANDICAP OUTBREAK
PESTILENCE

PLAIN DRY LOW BALD BARE EASY EVEN
FLAT OPEN PLAT RIFE VEGA WOLD
BLUNT BROAD CAMPO FIELD FRANK
GREEN GROSS LEVEL LLANO MOURN
NAKED PROSE ROUND SECCO SILLY
SMALL SOBER BEMOAN BEWAIL CHASTE
GRAITH HOMELY HONEST HUMBLE
LENTEN MAIDAN PARAMO RUSTIC
SEVERE SIMPLE SINGLE SMOOTH
ARTLESS EVIDENT GENUINE LEGIBLE
OBVIOUS POPULAR TERRACE APPARENT
CAMPAIGN DISTINCT EVERYDAY
EXPLICIT FAMILIAR HOMEMADE
HOMESPUN PALPABLE PIEDMONT
STRAIGHT
(— AMONG TREES) LAUND
(— OF ARGENTINA) PAMPA
(— OF RUSSIA) STEPPE
(ALKALI —S) USAR
(ALLUVIAL —) APRON CARSE HAUGH
(ARCTIC —) TUNDRA
(DESOLATE —) CHOL
(HEATHY —) LANDE
(LOW-LYING —) MACHAIR
(MARSHY —) BLAIR
(SALINE —) SEBKHA
(SALT —) SALADA
(SLOPING —) HOPE CUESTA
CONOPLAIN
(SMALL GRASSY —) CAMAS
(TREELESS —) BLED TUNDRA SAVANNA
(UNOCCUPIED —) DESERT
(PL.) VIZCACHA
(PREF.) LITI PEDI(O) PLAN(I)

PLAINTIFF SUER ACTOR ORATOR
PURSUER QUERENT

PLAINTIVE SAD CROSS PINING DOLENTE
ELEGIAC FRETFUL MOANFUL PEEVISH
PETTISH DOLOROSO MANGENDO
PETULANT WAILSOME SORROWFUL

PLAIT CUE PLY KNIT PAIR PLAT RUFF
TURN WALE WAND BRAID CRIMP FITCH
PEDAL PINCH QUEUE QUILL QUIRK
TRACE TRESS WEAVE BORDER DOUBLE
GATHER GOFFER PLIGHT RUMPLE

TUSCAN WIMPLE WRITHE CRIMPLE
FROUNCE PIGTAIL

PLAN AIM ART LAY WAY CARD CAST
COUP DART FOOT GAME HANG IDEA
MIND MOOD PLAT PLOT ALLOW BRIEF
CHART DARTY DRAFT DRIFT ETTLE
FRAME HOBBY MODEL REACH SHAPE
ADVICE AGENDA BUDGET CIPHER
DECOCT DESIGN DEVISE ENGINE FIGURE
INTEND LAYOUT METHOD MODULE
ORDAIN SCHEMA SCHEME SURVEY
THEORY ARRANGE CONCOCT COUNSEL
DRAWING NOSTRUM OUTLINE PATTERN
PROJECT PURPOSE THOUGHT COGITATE
CONSPIRE CONTRIVE ENGINEER
LANDSKIP MEDITATE PLATFORM
PRACTICE SCHEDULE SKELETON
STRATEGY CALCULATE
(— AHEAD) FORECAST
(— OF FUTURE PROCEDURE)
PROGRAM
(— ON A FLOOR) EPURE
(— TOGETHER) CONCERT
(CUNNING —) WHEEZE
(GROUND —) TRACE GRUNDRISS
(INSURANCE —) TONTINE
(5-YEAR —) PIATILETKA

PLANE BEAD DADO FACE FLAT MILL
AXIAL CHUTE FACET GLIDE LEVEL
MESON SHOOT STICK WHISK BEADER
REEDER ROUTER SMOKER COURIER
INSHAVE JOINTER NONSKED SURFACE
WITCHET BULLNOSE DECLINER
LEEBOARD MERIDIAN RECLINER
SYCAMORE TRAVERSE
(— OF CLEAVAGE) BACK
(— OF EARTH'S ORBIT) ECLIPTIC
(— OF ROCK) BED
(—S OF GUNNERY FIRE) SHEAF
(ENEMY —) BANDIT
(INCLINED —) RAMP SLIP
(MOLDING —) HOLLOW
(PERSPECTIVE —) TABLE
(RABBET —) PLOW RABAT PLOUGH
REBATE FILLETER
(SLOPING —) CUESTA

PLANET SUN IRIS JOVE MARS MOON
STAR EARTH GLOBE PLUTO VENUS
WORLD SATURN SPHERE URANUS
BENEFIC JUPITER MERCURY NEPTUNE
PRIMARY CHASUBLE LUMINARY
RECEPTOR WANDERER
(— IN A NATIVITY) ALMUTEN
(BENEVOLENT —) FORTUNE
(CONTROLLING —) LORD
(HYPOTHETICAL —) VULCAN
(MALEFICENT —) SHREW
(RULING —) DOMINATOR
(SMALL —) IRIS ASTEROID TERRELLA

PLANETARIUM ORRERY

PLANE TREE CHINAR PLATAN COTONIER
PLANTAIN SYCAMORE

PLANK HOOD PATA PLAT RAIL SOLE
BOARD CLAMP PATTA SWALE DAGGER
FLITCH ROOFER STRAKE CLAPPER
CROSSER DEPOSIT STEALER STRINGER
(— AS PROTECTION) SHOLE

(— OVER BROOK) CLAM
(— 6 FT. X 1 FT.) WARE
(—S IN BRIDGE) CHESS
(—S LESS THAN 6 FT.) DEAL
(CURVED —) SNYING
(ROUGHHEWN —) SLAB
PLANKING GORE RACK HATCH SWALE
CEILING LAGGING BERTHING BRATTICE
GARBOARD WATERWAY
PLANKTON KRILL SESTON
PLANT AJI BED SET SOW ACHE ALGA
ARUM BURY CROP FAST HIDE MORE
SALT SEED SLIP TREE WORT ABACA
AGAVE AJWAN ARGEL CAROA CHIVE
CLOTE CLOVE EARLY FANCY GRAFT
HEATH INTER INULA JALAP KEIKI ORACH
PITCH SEDUM SHRUB YERBA ACACIA
AJOWAN AKELEY ALASAS ANNUAL
BEDDER CACOON CALALU CARROT
COKERY COTTON DERRIS DIBBLE ESCAPE
FICOID FORCER GALAXY GROWTH
KARREE LENTIL LIGGER MANUKA MEDICK
MESCAL ORPINE PEPINO SETTLE SPRING
YARROW ABANDON ALKANET ALYSSUM
BREWERY CARDOON CONCEAL CUTTING
DAGGERS ENCELIA HAEMONY IMPLANT
JIKUNGU LETTUCE PALMIET PICKERY
RAMBONG SAWMILL ABUTILON
AGERATUM AGRIMONY ANGLEPOD
BIENNIAL BLUEBELL CONSOUND
DRAWLING DYEHOUSE EMERGENT
ENGINERY FUMEROOT GASWORKS
GROMWELL HONEWORT KNAPWEED
LARKSPUR
(— BY SPADING) SPIT
(— DEEPLY) HEEL
(— FIRMLY) BRACE
(— IN ROWS) DRILL
(— OF THE DEAD) ASPHODEL
(— ROOTED IN GROUND) LIANA
(— SUPPORTING PARASITES)
SUSCEPT
(— 2ND CROP) ETCH
(ANCIENT —) CYCAD
(AQUATIC —) ALISMA NUPHAR
SUGAMO TAWKEE AMBULIA AWLWORT
FROGBIT DUCKWEED PONDWEED
(AROMATIC —) MINT NARD BASIL
CUMIN TANSY THYME AMOMUM
CARAWAY DITTANY ALBAHACA
CALAMINT LAVENDER SPIKENARD
(BULBOUS —) GALTONIA
(CENTURY —) PITA
(CLIMBING —) VETCH LAWYER ULLUCU
CORALITA
(COMPOSITE —) SUCCORY HAWKWEED
SNEEZEWEED
(CONSECRATED —) HAOMA
(CROSSBRED —) HYBRID
(DYE —) ANIL WOAD WOLD MADDER
(FIBER —) ALOE FLAX HEMP PITA
CAJUN RAMIE SISAL
(FLOWERING —) HOP ROSE DAISY
HOLLY POPPY ORCHID VIOLET
HAWTHORN LARKSPUR POLYGALA
PRIMROSE SNOWDROP
(FORAGE —) RAPE ALFALFA DAINCHA

(GRAIN —) TEFF
(HEDGE —) ESPINO
(LEAFLESS —) ULEX DODDER RESTIAD
TRIURID
(MARSH —) FERN CALLA JUNCUS
CATTAIL BUCKBEAN
(MEDICINAL —) ALOE HERB ERICA
ARNICA CATNIP IPECAC SIMPLE ACONITE
BONESET GENTIAN LOBELIA CAMOMILE
(POISONOUS —) COWBANE DEATHIN
SAMNITIS
(POTTED —) BONSAI LANTANA
(PRICKLY —) BRIAR BRIER CACTUS
NETTLE TEASEL TEAZEL PRICKFOOT
(PUNGENT —) PEPPER
(SUCCULENT —) ALOE HERB GASTERIA
HAWORTHIA HOUSELEEK
(TWINING —) SMILAX WINDER
CLIMBER BINDWEED SCAMMONY
PLANTATION PEN HOLT WALK FINCA
GROVE BOSKET BOWERY COLONY
ESTATE SHAMBA SPRING YERBAL
CAFETAL FAZENDA NOPALRY PINETUM
THICKET ARBUSTUM HACIENDA
TRAPICHE VINEYARD
PLAQUE CHIP PINAX PLATE PLATEAU
SARCOID NAMEPLATE STOMACHER
PLASTER CAST DAUB HARL LOCK TEER
CLEAM GATCH PARGE SLICK SMALM
STAFF CHUNAM CLATCH GAGING
MORTAR PARGET SPARGE STOOTH
STUCCO BLISTER MALAGMA DIACULUM
DIAPALMA VESICANT CATAPLASM
(— BETWEEN LATHS) CAT
(— OF PARIS) GESSO GYPSUM
(— WITH COW DUNG) LEEP
(COARSE —) GROUT
(MEDICAL —) SALVE TOPIC TREAT
CHARGE SPARADRAP
(MUSTARD —) SINAPISM
(2 COATS OF —) RENDERSET
PLASTIC FOAM RICH SIRUP LABILE
PLIANT ACETATE CATALIN CRYSTAL
DUCTILE FICTILE ORGANIC CREATIVE
FLEXIBLE LAMINATE MELAMINE
PHENOLIC TECTONIC UNCTUOUS
FORMATIVE
PLATE CAP CUT DIP EAR FIN GIB WEB
ANAL BACK BRIN CASE CAST CURB DIAL
DISK FISH GILL GONG GULA HOME HOOF
LEAF MOLD NAIL ORAL RETE ROSE SHOE
SOLE STUD TACE TRAY AMPYX ANODE
BASAL BELLY CHAIR CLAMP CLEAT
FENCE FLOOR FLUKE FORCE GLAND
GUARD LAMEL PYGAL SCALE SCUTE
SHEET SHOLE SLICE STAMP STRAP
TABLE TASSE TERNE TRAMP UNCUS
WATER ADORAL BAFFLE BRIDGE BUCKLE
CASTER CIRCLE CLICHE COLLAR COPPER
COSTAL CRUSTA DAMPER EPIGNE
FASCIA FILLER FOLIUM FRIZEL GENIAL
GORGET GUSSET LABIAL LOREAL
MASCLE MATRIX MENTAL MENTUM
MOTHER PALLET PATTEN PLATEN RADIAL
SCREEN SCUTUM SEPTUM SERVER
SHEATH STAPLE TARSUS TURTLE
TYMPAN VESSEL BESAGNE BOLSTER

BRACKET BUCCULA BUCKLER CHARGER
CLYPEUS COASTER CORNULE CORONET
CRYSTAL ETCHING FRIZZLE FRONTAL
GRAVURE HUMERAL INKBLOT MORDANT
MYOTOME NEPTUNE PETALON PRIMARY
ROSTRAL ROUNDEL SPANGLE STEALER
STEELER TERGITE TESSERA VENTRAL
ASSIETTE BEDPLATE BIQUARTZ
BRACHIAL CELLOCUT DIASCOPE
DRAWBACK ELECTRUM EPIGYNUM
EPIPROCT EPISTOME FIREBACK
FLOUNDER STAPLING STRINGER
SUBPLATE SURPRINT
(— COVERING KEYHOLE) DROP
(— COVERING MIDDLE EAR) TEGMEN
(— IN BATTERY) GRID
(— IN ORGAN PIPE) LANGUET
(— IN STEAM BOILER) SPUT DASHER
(— OF BALEEN) BLADE
(— OF BLAST FURNACE) TYMP
(— OF CTENOPHORE) COMB
(— OF GELATIN) BAT
(— OF GLASS) SLIDE
(— OF JAW) AURICLE
(— OF PRECIOUS METAL) BRACTEA
(— OF SOAP FRAME) SESS
(— OF SUNDIAL) GNOMON
(— ON FIREPLACE) BLOWER
(— ON LANCE SHAFT) VAMPLATE
(— ON PLOW) MOLDBOARD
(— ON SADDLE) SIDEBAR
(— ON SATCHEL STRAP) OLIVE
(— ON THROAT OF FISH) GULAR
(— ON WATERWHEEL) SHROUD
(—S OF CARDING MACHINE) ARCH
(—S OF GUN CARRIAGE) FLASK
(ARMOR —) SPLINT AILETTE PALLETTE
(COLLECTION —) BROD
(COMMUNION —) PATEN
(DEEP —) MAZARINE
(DORSAL —) ELYTRUM ALINOTUM
(EARTHEN —) MUFFIN
(FASHION —) SWELL
(FIREPLACE —) IRONBACK
(FLAT —) APRON
(GUARD —) SHELL
(HINGED —) SHUT
(HOME —) DISH
(IRON —) CLOUT STAVE LATTEN
MARVER LAPSTONE SKEWBACK
MOLDBOARD TURNPLATE TURNSHEET
(LARGE —) DOUBLER
(LOCK —) SELVEDGE
(NAME —) FACIA
(PERFORATED —) DOD GRID WORTLE
PINNULE
(PITCHER'S —) SLAB MOUND
(RIMLESS —) COUPE
(SIEVE —) LATTICE
(SIFTING —) TROMMEL
(THIN —) LAME LAMP LAMINA LAMELLA
(THIN TIN —) TAIN LATTEN TAGGERS
(WALL —) PAN RASEN TORSEL
(WOODEN —) TRENCHER
PLATEAU PUNA FJELD KAROO KARST
TABLE CAUSSE HAMADA MESETA

NIVEAU PARAMO SABANA UPLAND
ANASAZI
PLATFORM TOP BANK BEMA DAIS DECK
DUCK FLAT GHAT PACE STEP WING
APRON BENCH BLIND BLOCK CHAIN
FLOAT SOLEA STAGE STAND STOOL
STOOP STULL STUMP ARBOUR BRIDGE
DESIGN GANTRY HURDLE ISLAND
MACHAN PALLET PERRON PILLAR
PODIUM PULPIT RUNWAY SETTLE
SLEDGE BALCONY CATWALK ESTRADE
FORETOP GALLERY LANDING LOGEION
PADDOCK ROLLWAY ROSTRUM SKIDWAY
SOAPBOX TRIBUNE BARBETTE FOOTPACE
HUSTINGS SCAFFOLD
PLATITUDE TRUISM BROMIDE DULLNESS
STALENESS TRITENESS
PLATOON SQUAD VOLLEY PELOTON
PLOTTON
PLATTER DISH DISK LANX ASHET GRAIL
PLATE RECORD CHARGER TRENCHER
PLAUSIBLE FAIR OILY SLEEK GLOSSY
SMOOTH AFFABLE POPULAR CREDIBLE
PROBABLE PROVABLE SUITABLE
OSTENSIBLE
PLAY FUN JEU JIG RUN RUX TOY AUTO
BEAR COME DAFF DEAL DICE DRAW FAIR
GAME JEST LAKE MOVE MUCK PLEE
PUNT ROMP SPIN TUNE WAKE CARRY
CHARM DALLY DRAMA ENACT FLIRT
FROST HORSE SHOOT SOTIE SOUND
SPIEL SPORT STUCK WREAK YEDDE
ACTION COMEDY COQUET DANDLE
DIVIDE FILLER FROLIC GAMBLE GAMBOL
GAMING GHOSTS MUSERY NUMBER
PIDDLE ROLLIX TRIFLE CUTBACK
CUTBACK DISPORT EXECUTE EXPLOIT
GUIGNOL HISTORY HOLIDAY MIRACLE
PAGEANT PASSION PERFORM PRELUDE
STAGERY VENTURE BURLETTA MORALITY
SKITTLES MELODRAMA
PLAYBOY OF THE WESTERN
WORLD (AUTHOR OF —) SYNGE
(CHARACTER IN —) QUIN KEOGH
MAHON SHAWN PEGEEN CHRISTY
FLAHERTY MARGARET CHRISTOPHER
PLAYER IT CAP END BACK SIDE ACTOR
COLOR GUARD BANKER BUSKER FEEDER
STAGER STROLL TENTER ALTOIST
FORWARD GAMBLER STRIKER TRIFLER
TURQUET BUDGETER GAMESTER
HORNSMAN STROLLER
(— IN CHESS) BLACK WHITE
(— IN CHOUETTE) CAPTAIN
(— OF JAZZ) CAT
(— WHO CUTS CARDS) PONE
(— WHO IS IT) HE
(— WHO SCORES ZERO) DUCK
(— WITH LOWEST SCORE) BOOBY
(BACKGAMMON —) TABLER
(BASEBALL —) SHORT SACKER
CATCHER FIELDER LEADOFF PITCHER
BACKSTOP
(BASKETBALL —) CAGEMAN HOOPMAN
HOOPSTER
(BOWLING —) LEAD
(CARD —) EAST HAND PONE WEST

BLIND DUMMY NORTH OMBRE SOUTH
JUNIOR SENIOR BRAGGER DECLARER
(CRICKET —) LEG BOWLER INNING
(CROQUET —) MALLET
(DICE —) SHOOTER
(FLUTE —) AULETE
(FOOTBALL —) END GUARD SLANT
BUCKER CENTER TACKLE BLOCKER
FLANKER GRIDDER SNAPPER FULLBACK
HALFBACK SCATBACK SLOTBACK
(KEY —) PIVOT
(LACROSSE —) HOME COVER POINT
ATTACK STICKMAN
(LEAPFROG —) BACK
(POKER —) AGE
(RUGBY —) SCRUM HOOKER
(SOCCER —) CAP INNER BOOTER
(STUPID —) HAM
(TENNIS —) SMASHER
(TWO OR MORE —S) PLATOON
(UNSKILLFUL —) DUB
(VOLLEYBALL —) SPIKER
(WEAK —) RABBIT

PLAYFUL SLY ELFIN MERRY FRISKY
GAMBOL JOCOSE LUSORY TOYISH
WANTON COLTISH JIGGISH JOCULAR
TOYSOME GAMESOME HUMOROUS
LARKSOME SPORTFUL SPORTIVE
KITTENISH

PLAYTHING DIE TOY HOOP KNACK PLAIK
SPORT BAUBLE LAKING SUCKER TRIFLE
PLAYOCK

PLAYWRIGHT AUTHOR DRAMATIST
PLAYMAKER

PLAZA PLACE PLEIN SQUARE ZOCALO

PLEA BAR BID MOOT NOLO SUIT ALIBI
CLAIM PLEAD ABATER APPEAL EXCUSE
REFUGE APOLOGY CONTEND DEFENCE
LAWSUIT PRETEXT QUARREL DILATORY
ENTREATY PLACITUM PRETENSE

PLEAD BEG SUE MOOT PLEA PRAY URGE
ORATE ALLEGE APPEAL ASSERT PURSUE
ENTREAT IMPLORE SOLICIT WRANGLE
ADVOCATE LITIGATE
(— FOR) SOLICIT PETITION

PLEASANT FUN GAY BEEN BIEN BRAW
FAIR FINE GLAD GOOD HEND JOLI NEAT
TRIM WEME AMENE BIGLY BONNY
CANNY COUTH CUSHY DOUCE DRUNK
DUCKY GREEN HAPPY HENDE HODDY
JOLLY LEPID LISTY LUSTY MERRY NUTTY
QUEME SMIRK SUAVE SWEET TIPSY
WALLY WETHE COMELY DAINTY DULCET
GENIAL KINDLY PRETTY SAVORY
SMOOTH AFFABLE ELEGANT FARRAND
JANNOCK LEESOME WINSOME DELICATE
GLORIOUS GRATEFUL HEAVENLY
LIEFSOME LIKESOME LOVESOME
THANKFUL TOWARDLY GEMUTLICH

PLEASANTNESS GAIETY AMENITY
SUAVITY JOCUNDITY

PLEASANTRY WIT JEST JOKE SPORT
BANTER JESTING JOLLITY WAGGERY

PLEASE PAY GAME LIKE LIST LUST SUIT
WANT WISH AGREE AMUSE BITTE
CHARM ELATE FANCY HUMOR QUEME
SAVOR TASTE ARRIDE KITTLE OBLIGE
REGALE SOOTHE TICKLE AGGRATE
APPLESE CONTENT DELIGHT GLADDEN
GRATIFY PLACATE REJOICE SATISFY

PLEASED FAIN FOND GLAD APAID HAPPY
PROUD BUCKED CONTENT GLADSOME

PLEASING AMEN COOL GLAD GOOD LIEF
NICE SOFT AMENE DICTY NIFTY SOOTH
SWEET CLEVER COMELY DREAMY FACILE
FLASHY GAINLY LIKING LUSTLY MELLOW
PRETTY AMIABLE BLESSED CORKING
DARLING LIKABLE LIKEFUL TUNABLE
WELCOME CHARMING DELICATE
FAVOROUS FETCHING GRACEFUL
GRACIOUS GRATEFUL HEAVENLY
INVITING LIKESOME PLACABLE PLAUSIVE
SPECIOUS PLAUSIBLE PERSONABLE

PLEASURABLE GOOD JOLLY ANIMAL
MIRTHFUL

PLEASURE FUN JOY BANG BOOT EASE
GREE KAMA LIST LUST PLAY WILL BLISS
KICKS MIRTH SAVOR SOOTH TASTE
DAINTY GAIETY LIKING LUXURY NICETY
VOLUPT COMFORT DELIGHT GRATIFY
JOLLITY JOYANCE DELICACY FRUITION
GLADNESS HILARITY

PLEAT SET FOLD KILT POKE RUCK FLUTE
FRILL PINCH PLAIT PRANK GUSSET
SUNRAY

PLEBEIAN LOW BASE COMMON HOMELY
VULGAR IGNOBLE LOWBORN POPULAR
BASEBORN EVERYDAY HOMESPUN
INFERIOR MECHANIC ORDINARY

PLEDGE LAY VOW AFFY BAND CLAP EARL
GAGE HAND HEST HOCK PASS PAWN
WAGE WORD FAITH STAKE SWEAR
SWEAT TOKEN TROTH TRUTH WAGER
ARREST BORROW COMMIT ENGAGE
IMPONE LUMBER PAROLE PLEVIN PLIGHT
VADIUM WADSET BARGAIN BETROTH
CAUTION CREANCE EARNEST HOSTAGE
PROMISE MORTGAGE SECURITY
VADIMONY
(— IN DRINKING) PROPINE

PLEDGED HIGHT SWORN ASSURED
ENGAGED PIGNORATE
(— TO MARRY) SURE

PLEIADES MAIA MEROPE ALCYONE
CELAENO ELECTRA STEROPE TAYGETA

PLENTEOUS RICH COPIOUS FERTILE
AFFLUENT FRUITFUL GENEROUS
ABOUNDING EXUBERANT

PLENTIFUL OLD FULL RANK RICH RIFE
AMPLE HEFTY LARGE STORE ENOUGH
FOISON GALORE LAVISH COPIOUS
FERTILE LIBERAL OPULENT PROFUSE
UBEROUS ABUNDANT FRUITFUL
NUMEROUS EXUBERANT

PLENTY WON BAIT COPY MANY RAFF
AMPLE CHEAP PRICE TEEMS FOISON
SCOUTH UBERTY LASHINGS

PLETHORA RASH EXCESS PLENUM
FULLNESS PLEURISY POLYEMIA
PROFUSION REPLETION

PLIABLE WAXY WEAK LITHY WAXEN
DOCILE LIMBER PLIANT SEMMIT SUPPLE
BOWABLE FICTILE FINGENT FLEXILE

PLASTIC WINDING CUSHIONY FLEXIBLE COMPLIANT

PLIANT APT FLIP AGILE BUXOM LITHE SWACK YOUNG DOCILE LIMBER SUPPLE DUCTILE PLASTIC PLIABLE SLIPPER WILLOWY FLEXIBLE SUITABLE WORKABLE

PLIGHT PLY FOLD ARRAY BRAID DRESS PLAIT POINT STATE WOVEN ATTIRE ENGAGE PICKLE PLEDGE STRAIT TAKING BETROTH MISCHIEF QUANDARY

PLOD JOG GRUB PLOT SLOG TROG VAMP POACH TRAMP TRASH DRUDGE SLOUCH TRUDGE PLUNTHER

PLOT BREW CAST MARK PACK PLAN CABAL DRIFT FRAUD GLEBE GRAPH GREEN HATCH MODEL SCALD STORY STUDY WATCH ACTION BRIGUE CLIQUE DESIGN DEVISE GARDEN MALIGN SCHEME TAMPER AGITATE COLLUDE COMPACT COMPASS CONJECT CONNIVE CONTOUR DRAUGHT FEEDLOT MACHINE PRETEND QUADRAT SWIDDEN ARGUMENT COGITATE CONSPIRE CONTRIVE INTRIGUE PRACTICE PROTRACT MACHINATE
(— OF GRASS) SONK
(— OF LAND) ERF LOT PLAT SHOT FORTY MILPA PATCH PLECK SPLAT COMMON SCHERM SHAMBA HAGGARD LAZYBED SEVERAL
(— SECRETLY) WHISPER
(GARDEN —) BED ERF QUINTA QUARTER
(UNPRODUCTIVE —) HIRST

PLOTTER PACKER HATCHER JACOBIN SCHEMER DESIGNER ENGINEER

PLOW EAR BOUT DISK FOIL HINT MOLE PLOD RIVE ROVE SLUG STIR SULK SULL TILL BREAK FLUNK SPLIT SULKY THROW ARAIRE BUSTER DIGGER FALLOW FURROW GOPHER JUMPER LISTER PLOUGH RAFTER ROOTER RUTTER BACKSET BREAKER HUSBAND SCOOTER SULCATE TWISTER FIREPLOW FURROWER GANGPLOW SNOWPLOW TURNPLOW
(— CROSSWISE) THORTER
(— LIGHTLY) SKIM RIFFLE

PLOWSHARE LAY SLIP SOCK LAVER REEST SHARE JUMPER

PLUCK GO PUG ROB TUG BOUT CROP CULL DRAG GAME GRAB GRIT PELT PICK PILL POOK PULL RACE RASE RASH SAND TUCK BREAK DRAFT MOXIE NERVE PLUME SMITE SPUNK STEAL STRIP AVULSE FLEECE GATHER PIGEON PLOUGH QUARRY SNATCH SPIRIT TWINGE TWITCH COURAGE DEPLUME PLUNDER BOLDNESS DECISION GAMENESS
(— AS A STRING) TIRL PINCH
(— FEATHERS) STUB
(— LEAVES) BLADE
(— OF SHEEP OR CALF) RACE GATHER
(— UP COURAGE) CHEER
(— WOOL BY HAND) ROO

PLUCKY GAMY SANDY BANTAM GRITTY SPUNKY FIGHTING

PLUG PEG PIN TAP TOP WAD BLOW BONE BUNG FILL JADE ROOT SHOT SLOG SWAT BOOST DOWEL DUMMY PILOT PUNCH SHACK SKATE SPILE STUFF SWEAT BOUCHE BOXING BULLET COMEDO DOSSIL DOTTLE FIDDLE SPIGOT BUSHING CHAMBER CHUGGER FERRULE STOPPER DRIVECAP STOPCOCK
(— FOR CANNON) TAMPION
(— IN GRENADE) BOUCHON
(— IN ORGAN PIPE) STOPPLE TAMPION
(— OF CLAY) BOTT
(— OF OAKUM) FID
(— OF VOLCANO) CORE
(— TO HOLD NAIL) DOOK
(— UP) CLAM STOP ESTOP RAMFORCE
(FISHING —) BUG
(LIP —) LABRET
(NOSE —) TEMBETA TEMBETARA
(WASTE —) WASHER
(WATER —) HYDRANT

PLUMAGE ROBE RUFF FLUFF HACKLE SHROUD FEATHER FLOCCUS JUVENAL PENNAGE FEATHERS PARADISE PTILOSIS

PLUMB BUNG SHEER BOTTOM BULLET SINKER EXACTLY PLUMMET UTTERLY ABSOLUTE COMPLETE DIRECTLY ENTIRELY VERTICAL

PLUMBAGO LUSTER LUSTRE GRAPHITE LEADWORT

PLUME PEN TIP TUFT EGRET PRIDE PRUNE DEPRIVE DESPOIL FEATHER AIGRETTE
(— ON HELMET) CREST PANACHE
(— ON HORSE) PLUMADE
(— ON TURBAN) CULGEE
(EGRET —) OSPREY

PLUMP FAT BOLD FAIR FULL PLOP SLAP TIDY BLUNT BONNY BUXOM CLUMP FUBBY FUBSY GROUP JOLLY SAPPY SLEEK SMACK SONSY SQUAB STOUT THICK BONNIE CHUBBY DIRECT FATTEN FLATLY FLESHY PUBBLE ROTUND BLUNTLY BUNTING CLUSTER DISTEND FULSOME RIBLESS

PLUNDER GUT ROB BOOT FANG JUNK LOOT PILL POLL PREY RAPE RIPE SACK SWAG BEROB BOOTY CHEAT GAINS HARRY PLUCK RAVEN RIFLE SCOFF SHAVE SPOIL STRIP BEZZLE BOODLE FLEECE FORAGE HARROW MARAUD PROFIT RAPINE RAVAGE DESPOIL ESCHEAT FREIGHT PILFERY PILLAGE RANSACK SACKAGE FREEBOOT

PLUNDERER THIEF BANDIT BUMMER PEELER POLLER RAPTOR ROBBER VANDAL ROUTIER SPOILER MARAUDER RAPPAREE

PLUNDERING PREY SACK MARAUD RAPINE ESCHEAT HERSHIP PURCHASE SPECHERY SPOILFUL SPOILING PREDATORY

PLUNGE BET DIG DIP DIVE DUCK DUMP JUMP PURL PUSH RAKE RISK SINK BURST DOUSE FLING PITCH PLUMP

SOUSE SWOOP GAMBLE HEADER
LAUNCH SPLASH THRUST WALLOP
DEMERGE IMMERSE SUBMERGE
(— INTO) CLAP ENGULF IMMERGE
(— INTO WATER) ENEW
(GAMBLING —) RAKER

PLURALITY MAJORITY MORENESS
TRIALITY

PLUS AND GAIN WITH EXTRA SURPLUS
ADDITION INCREASE POSITIVE

PLUSH EASY BEAVER VELOUR SUPERIOR

PLUSHY SWANK SWANKY

PLUTO DIS HADES ORCUS
(BROTHER OF —) JUPITER NEPTUNE
(FATHER OF —) SATURN
(WIFE OF —) PROSERPINE

PLUTOCRAT NABOB RICHARD

PLY RUN BEAT BEND BIAS CORD CORE
DRAM FOLD MOLD SAIL URGE ADAPT
APPLY EXERT LAYER STEER TWIST
WIELD YIELD COMPLY DOUBLE HANDLE
TRAVEL EXERCISE
(— WITH DRINK) BIRL ROSIN
(— WITH DRUGS) HOCUS

PNEUMONIA PULMONITIS

POACH PUG ROB COOK DROP POKE PUSH
SINK BLACK DRIVE FORCE POTCH STEAL
BLEACH PLUNGE INTRUDE

POACHER BLACK POGGE SPOACH
LURCHER STALKER WIDGEON BALDPATE
BULLHEAD

POCKET BOX CLY PIT KICK POKE BASIN
BURSE MEANS POUCH PURSE STEAL
ACCEPT CASING CANTINA PLACKET
SWALLOW TROUSER ENVELOPE
ISOLATED SUPPRESS CONDENSED
MINIATURE
(— IN BOOK BINDER) STATION
(— OF NET) BOWL
(BILLIARD —) POT HOLE HAZARD
(MAGICIAN'S —) PROFONDE
(NOODLE —S) KREPLACH
(ORE —) CHURN BONANZA
(SMALL —) FOB
(TROUSER —) PRAT BECKET
(WATER —) TINAJA ALBERCA
(PREF.) PERO

POCKETBOOK BAG KICK SKIN PURSE
INCOME READER WALLET HANDBAG
LEATHER BILLFOLD NOTECASE

POCKETKNIFE BARLOW PENKNIFE
PIGSTICKER

POD BAG COD GAM POP SAC BALL BEAN
BOLL HUSK POKE BURSE CAROB FLOCK
POUCH SHAUP SHELL SHUCK SNAIL
CHILLI LEGUME SCHOOL HARICOT
PEASCOD SILIQUA PEASECOD PODOCARP
POTBELLY SEEDCASE TAMARIND
(— OF LEGUME) KID
(— OF MESQUITE) HONEYPOD
(EXPLOSIVE —) SANDBOX
(SUBTERRANEAN —) EARTHNUT
(UNRIPE —) SQUASH

PODIUM DAIS FOOT WALL LECTERN

POEM GEM DUAN EPIC POSY RUNE SONG
CENTO DIRGE METER STAFF VERSE
BALLAD CACCIA CARMEN CYCLIC

HEROID MELODY MONODY SESTET
TERCET BUCOLIC CANTARE CANTATA
DESCORT ELEGIAC SOTADIC TRIOLET
VIRELAY VOLUSPA ACROSTIC CANTICLE
DINGDONG DOGGEREL INVICTUS
LIMERICK MADRIGAL TELESTIC
THEOGONY TRISTICH TROCHAIC
VERSICLE MONORHYME ROUNDELAY
(— ABOUT DEBATE) ESTRIF
(— ABOUT SHEPHERDS) ECLOGUE
(— GREETING DAWN) AUBADE
(— OF LAMENTATION) ELEGY
(— OF RETRACTION) PALINODE
(— OF 10 LINES) DIZAINE
(— OF 14 LINES) SONNET
(AMATORY —) EROTIC SONNET
(EPIC —) EPOS EPOPEE LUSIAD THEBAID
(HOMELY —) DIT
(IRISH —) AMHRAN
(JAPANESE —) HAIKU TANKA
(LITURGICAL —) VIDDUI SELIHOTH
(LOVE —) AMORETTO
(LYRIC —) LAI LAY ODE ALBA EPODE
GHAZEL RONDEL CANZONA PARTIMEN
(PART OF —) PASSUS
(PASTORAL —) IDYL IDYLL BUCOLIC
(PERSIAN —) GHAZAL
(RELIGIOUS —) HYMN
(RURAL —) GEORGIC
(SACRED —) PSALM YIGDAL
(SATIRICAL —) IAMBIC KASIDA
(SHORT —) DIT DITTY EPILOG SONNET
CANZONE EPIGRAM EPILOGUE EPYLLION
(TONE —) BALLADE
(WELSH —) CYWYDD
(SUFF.) STICH

POET OG BARD LARK MUSE SWAN ARION
LINUS LYRIC MAKER ODIST RISHI SAYER
SKALD FINDER GNOMIC IBYCUS LAKIST
LYRIST SHAPER SINGER DICHTER
ELEGIAC EPICIST IDYLIST IMAGIST
MUSAEUS ORPHEUS FERAMORZ
GEORGIAN LAUREATE LUTANIST
MINSTREL SONGSTER TROUVERE
MINNESINGER
(IRISH —) FILI
(MEDIOCRE —) RIMER RHYMER
(MINOR —) BARDIE

POETIC ODIC LYRIC STILTED PEGASEAN

POETRY SONG BLANK MELIC POEMS
VERSE EPOPEE POESIS DOGGREL
KALEVALA
(FINNISH —) RUNES
(GOD OF —) BRAGI
(HEROIC —) EPOS
(MUSE OF —) ERATO THALIA EUTERPE
CALLIOPE

POIGNANT APT HOME KEEN ACUTE
SHARP SMART BITING BITTER MOVING
SEVERE URGENT CUTTING POINTED
PUNGENT SATIRIC INCISIVE PIERCING
PRESSING STINGING STRIKING
TOUCHING

POINT AIM DOT JOT NAK NEB NIB NUB
PEG PIN RES WAY BOCK BOKE CHAT
CUSP GAFF GAME GOOD HOLD ITEM
KNOT LACE LOOK NAIL PICK PILE PINT

SPOT STOP WHET CHALK FOCUS INDEX
LEVEL MUCRO PITCH PUNCH PUNCT
PUNTA PUNTO REFER STAND TEACH
THING TOOTH ALLUDE BROACH CUSPIS
CUTOFF DEGREE FLECHE JUGALE
MATTER NOSING THESIS TITTLE ZYGION
APICULA ARTICLE BENEFIT CACUMEN
CRUNODE ESSENCE GATEWAY PUNCTUM
PUSHPIN SHARPEN TANJONG TRAGION
ANNOUNCE PUNCTULE STRIPPER
PARTICULAR
(— AT ISSUE) BEEF CRUX
(— BEHIND EAR) ASTERION
(— IN CAPSTAN) STRIPPER
(— IN CONSONANT) DAGHESH
(— IN ORBIT OF PLANET) AUGE APSIS
APOGEE SYZYGY APOJOVE PERIGEE
APASTRON APHELION
(— IN QUESTION) ISSUE
(— NEAREST EARTH) PERIGEE
(— OF ANCHOR) BILL
(— OF ANTLER) PRONG
(— OF ANVIL) HORN
(— OF CELESTIAL SPHERE) ANTAPEX
(— OF CHIN) BUTTON
(— OF CRESCENT MOON) CUSP
(— OF DECLINE) EBB
(— OF DIVERGENCE) AXIL
(— OF ECLIPTIC) LAGNA SOLSTICE
(— OF EPIGRAM) STING
(— OF FAITH) ARTICLE
(— OF HONOR) PUNDONOR
(— OF INTERSECTION) FOOT
STAURION
(— OF JAVELIN) SAGAIE
(— OF JUNCTION) MEET BREGMA
LAMBDA
(— OF LAND) ODD CAPE SPIT MORRO
HEADLAND
(— OF LEAF) MUCRO
(— OF LIGHT) GLINT SPANGLE
(— OF LIGHTNING ROD) AIGRETTE
(— OF LIPS) CHEILION
(— OF PEN) NEB NIB
(— OF REFERENCE) STYLION
(— OF ROCK) NUNATAK
(— OF STAG'S HORN) START
(— OF SUPPORT) BEARING
(— OF TIME) DATE INSTANT JUNCTURE
(— OF TOOTH) CUSP
(— OF VIEW) EYE ANGLE FRONT SLANT
COLORS CORNER GROUND RESPECT
(— ON AUGER OR BIT) SPUR
(— ON BACKGAMMON BOARD)
FLECHE
(— ON CURVE) TACNODE
(— ON JAW) GONION
(— ON SUNDIAL) NODE
(— OUT) SHOW DIGIT INFER ASSIGN
DIRECT ENSIGN FINGER MUSTER NOTIFY
REMARK PRESAGE INDICATE
(APPROPRIATE —) PLACE
(ASTROLOGICAL —) INGRESS
(BARBED —) FORK
(BLUNT —) MORNETTE
(CARBON —) CRAYON

(CARDINAL —) EAST WEST HINGE
NORTH SOUTH
(CARDINAL —S) CARDINES
(CENTRAL —) OMPHALOS
(CHRONOLOGICAL —) ERA EPOCH
(COMPASS —) E N S W NE NW SE SW
ENE ESE NNE NNW SSE SSW WNW WSW
AIRT AIRTH RHUMB COURSE
(CRITICAL —) JUMP
(CROWNING —) CAPSHEAF CAPSTONE
(CRUCIAL —) CRUX
(CULMINATING —) HEAD COMBLE
(DOUBLE — OF CURVE) ACNODE
CRUNODE
(ESSENTIAL —) MAIN
(EXACT —) TEE
(EXCESS —S) LAP
(EXCLAMATION —) BANG SCREAMER
(EXTREME —) END
(FARTHEST —) APOGEE SOLSTICE
(FINAL —) UPCOME
(FIXED —) ABUTMENT
(GLAZIER'S —) SPRIG
(HIGHEST —) TIP ACME APEX AUGE
NOON PEAK CREST FLOOD APOGEE
CLIMAX CULMEN HEIGHT PERIOD
SUMMIT VERTEX ZENITH EVEREST
MAXIMUM MERIDIAN SOLSTICE
(KNOTTY —) CRUX NODUS
(LAST —) END
(LATERAL —) ALARE
(LOWEST —) NADIR BOTTOM BEDROCK
(LOWEST — OF HULL) BILGE
(MAIN —) JET SUM GIST
(MEDIAN —) HORMION
(NO —S) LOVE
(PEDAL —) DRONE
(PIVOTAL —) KNUCKLE
(PRECISE —) NICK
(PROJECTING —) CRAG PEAK BEARD
(SHARP —) JAG PRICK PRICKLE
(SIGNIFICANT —) MILESTONE
(SINGLE —) ACE
(SKULL —) TYLION
(SORE —) NERVE
(STARTING —) BASE
(STATIONARY —) SPINODE
(STRIKING —) SALIENCE
(STRONG —) FORTE
(TAPERING —) ACUMEN
(TENNIS —) LET CHASE BISQUE
(TENTH OF —) MOMENT
(TERMINAL —) GOAL BOURN BREAK
AIRPORT
(TO THE —) COGENT
(TOP —) TUFT
(TURNING —) CARDO EPOCH CRISIS
(UNIPLANAR —) UNODE
(UTMOST —) EXTREME SUBLIME
(VANTAGE —) TOWER
(VOWEL —) SERE SEGOL SEGHOL
(WEAK —) BLOT
POINT COUNTER POINT
(AUTHOR OF —) HUXLEY
(CHARACTER IN —) JOHN LUCY MARK
BURLAP ELINOR GILRAY PHILIP RACHEL
SIDNEY WALTER WEBLEY BIDLAKE

CARLING EVERARD QUARLES RAMPION BEATRICE MARJORIE SPRANDRELL TANTAMOUNT

POINTED TIP YAD COCK HAND WAND SET ERDE HOME ACUTE EXACT FIXED PEAKY PIKED TANGY TERSE LIVELY PEAKED PECKED PICKED SPIRED ANGULAR FITCHEE LACONIC PRECISE SPICATE ZESTFUL ACICULAR ACULEATE CULTRATE DIACTINE PUNCTUAL STELLATE ACUMINATE
(PREF.) OXY

POINTER TIP YAD COCK HAND WAND INDEX POINT FINGER GUNDOG INDICE STYLUS FLUSHER INDICANT SIGNITOR
(— IN GREAT BEAR) DUBHE
(— ON ASTROLABE) ALMURY
(— ON GAUGE) ARM
(BUILDER'S —) RAKER
(TEACHER'S —) FESCUE

POINTLESS DRY ILL DULL FLAT INANE SILLY VAPID FRIGID STUPID INSIPID WITLESS MUTICOUS

POISE CALM HEAD REST SWAY TACT BRACE APLOMB OFFSET PONDER BALANCE BEARING DIGNITY OPPRESS DELIVERY EASINESS SERENITY

POISED SET FACILE HOVERING NERVELESS

POISON FIG GAS BANE DRAB DRUG GALL TUBA VERY ATTER TAINT TOXIN VENOM VIRUS INFECT RANKLE TOXIFY TOXOID ACONITE CORRUPT ENVENOM FLYBANE MINERAL PERVERT PHALLIN VITIATE ACQUETTA DELETERY RATSBANE VENENATE SAXITOXIN
(— IN DEATH CUP) PHALLIN
(ARROW —) HAYA INEE URALI URARI ANTIAR ANTJAR CURARE DERRIS OURARI OUABAIN
(FISH —) AKIA CUBE TIMBO DERRIS HAIARI BARBASCO
(RAT —) ANTU
(VIRULENT —) BIKH TANGHIN
(PREF.) PHARMACO VENENI VENENO VIRU

POISONED BUCKEYED TOXICATE VENENATE VENOMOUS

POISONOUS ATTRY TOXIC ATTERY VENENE VIROSE VIROUS BANEFUL NOISOME NOXIOUS DELETERY MEPHITIC TOXICANT VENENATE VENOMOUS VIRULENT MALIGNANT

POKE BAG DAB DIG DUB HIT JAB JOG PUG PUR WAD BROD PROD RUCK SACK SOCK STAB STIR NIDGE POACH PUNCH ROUSE STEER STOKE COWBOY DAWDLE INCITE PIERCE POCKET POUNCE WALLET
(— ABOUT) ROKE ROUT RUMMAGE
(— AROUND) ROOT SCROUNGE
(— FUN) COD
(— LIGHTLY) POTTER PUTTER
(— WITH FOOT) SCUFF
(— WITH NOSE) SNUZZLE

POKER DART DRAW FLIP POIT PORR POTE STUD BLUFF BOGIE CURATE GOBLIN STOKER ACEPOTS FRUGGAN LOWBALL PASSOUT POCHARD SHOTGUN BASEBALL COALRAKE JACKPOTS MISTIGRI SHOWDOWN

— POLAND

CAPITAL: WARSAW
COIN: DUCAT GROSZ MARKA ZLOTY FENNIG HALERZ KORONA
LAKE: GOPLO MAMRY SNIARDWY
MEASURE: CAL MILA MORG PRET LINJA SAZEN STOPA VLOKA WLOKA CWIERK KORZEC KWARTA LOKIEC GARNIEC
MOUNTAIN: RYSY TATRA SUDETEN
NATIVE: SLAV MARUR SILESIAN
PROVINCE: OPOLE KIELCE
RIVER: BUG SAN ALLE BRDA GWDA LYNA NYSA ODER STYR BIALA BZURA DRANA DWINA NOTEC SERET WARTA WISTA NEISSE NIEMEN PILICA PRIPET PROSNA STRYPA WIEPRZ VISTULA WISTOKA DNIESTER
TOWN: LWO KOLO LIDA LODZ LVOV OELS BREST BYTOM CHELM POSEN RADOM SRODA TORUN VILNA GDANSK GDYNIA GRODNO KRACOW KRAKOW LUBLIN POZNAN TARNOW WARSAW ZABRZE BEUTHEN BRESLAU CHORZOW GAROCIN GLIWICE LEMBERG LITOUSK WROCLAW GLEIWITZ KATOWICE SZCZECIN TARNOPOL
WEIGHT: LUT FUNT UNCYA KAMIAN CENTNER SKRUPUL

POLAR ARCTIC EMANANT PIVOTAL DIRECTRIX

POLARIS ALRUCABA

POLE BAR LAT LEG LUG ROD SKY XAT BEAM BIND BROG COPE FALL HOOK PALO PERK PIKE PROP SKID SPAR TREE FOCUS MASUR MAZUR PERCH SHAFT SPEAR STAFF STANG STILT STING STODE SWAPE SWIPE BEACON FLOWER IMPOSE RISSLE SPONGE TONGUE BARLING HEAVENS TOWMAST FLAGPOLE FOOTPICK POLANDER STANDARD
(— AS EMBLEM OF SOVEREIGNTY) KAHILI
(— AS HOLDFAST FOR BOATS) RYPECK
(— FOR BEARING COFFIN) SPOKE
(— FOR PROPELLING BOAT) POY
(— FOR TOSSING) CABER
(— HOLDING SAIL) BOOM MAST SPRIT
(— MARKING SAND DUNE) BALIZE
(— OF TIMBER WAGON) NIB JANKER
(— OF VEHICLE) NEAP
(— SEPARATING HORSES) BAIL
(— USED AS SIGN) ALEPOLE ALESTAKE
(— WITH BIRD DECOY) STOOL
(CARRIAGE —) NIB BEAM
(COUPLING —) REACH
(FIR —) UFER
(FISHING —) WAND
(FORKED —) CROTCH
(LOGGING —) JANKER KILHIG

(LONG —) PEW
(MANGROVE —) BORITY
(MINE —S) LAGGING
(NEGATIVE —) CATHODE
(PUNT —) QUANT STOWER
(RANGE —) FLAG
(SACRED —) ASHERAH
(SHEPHERD'S —) KENT
(SPRINGY —) BINDER
(STABLE —) BAIL
(STOUT —) KILHIG RICKER
(WATER-RAISING —) SWEEP
(SUFF.) KONT

POLICE MAN HEAT GUARD WATCH
GOVERN CONTROL JEMADAR OCHRANA
POLIZEI PROTECT TOXOTAE OPRICHNIK
(SECRET —) CHEKA

POLICEMAN COP JOE KID NAB PIG BOGY
BULL FLIC FUZZ GRAB JACK JOHN PEON
SLOP TRAP ZARP BOBBY BOGEY BULKY
BURLY GAZER PEACE RURAL SCREW
SEPOY ASKARI BADGER BOBBIE COPPER
FISCAL FLATTY HARMAN JOHNNY
PEELER REDCAP ROZZER RUNNER
SHAMUS CRUSHER FOOTMAN GHAFFIR
GUMSHOE JEMADAR OFFICER SHOOFLY
TROOPER ZAPTIAH ZAPTIEH BARGELLO
BLUECOAT DOGBERRY FLATFOOT
GENDARME MINISTER PATROLMAN

POLICE STATION THANA BARGELLO
KOTWALEE

POLICY WIT DEAL FRONT ORDER GOVERN
NUMBER TICKET WISDOM AUTARKY
COUNSEL CUNNING FLOATER LEFTISM
LOTTERY TONTINE VOUCHER ACTIVISM
ARTIFICE SAGACITY STATEWAY
PLURALISM
(CHOSEN —) COURSE

POLISH BOB LAP MOP RUB BUFF DUCO
FILE POLE CLEAN GLAZE GLOSS GRACE
RABAT ROUND SHINE SLICK STONE
AFFILE BARREL LUSTER REFINE SLIGHT
SMOOTH STREAK BEESWAX BURNISH
CHAMOIS FURBISH LACQUER PERFECT
PLANISH VARNISH ELEGANCE SIMONIZE

POLISHED FINE COMPT ROUND SHINY
SLICK TERSE BUFFED FACETE GLOSSY
INLAND POLITE SMOOTH ELEGANT
GALLANT GENTEEL POLITIC REFINED
CULTURED

POLITE NEAT TIDY TRIM BLAND CIVIL
SUAVE GENTLE SMOOTH URBANE
COURTLY GALLANT GENTEEL DELICATE
DISCREET LUSTROUS ATTENTIVE
COURTEOUS

POLITENESS FINISH TASHRIF CIVILITY
COURTESY ELEGANCE URBANITY

POLITIC WARY WISE SUAVE CRAFTY
CUNNING TACTFUL DISCREET
PROVIDENT

POLITICIAN BOSS STATIST WARWICK
PIPELAYER STATESMAN

POLLEN DUST MEAL FLOUR FARINA
POWDER BEEBREAD

POLLINATE SELF FECUNDATE
FECUNDIZE FERTILIZE

POLLUTE FOIL FOUL SOIL BLEND DIRTY

SMEAR TAINT BEFOUL DEFILE INFECT
MUDDLE RAVISH ADULTER DEBAUCH
PROFANE SLOTTER VIOLATE

POLLUTED FOUL DRUNK TURBID
CORRUPT

POLLUTION STAIN SULLAGE FOULNESS
IMPURITY

POLLUX POL HERCULES
(BROTHER OF —) CASTOR
(MOTHER OF —) LEDA

POLONIUS CORAMBIS
(DAUGHTER OF —) OPHELIA
(SON OF —) LAERTES

POLTROON IDLER COWARD CRAVEN
WRETCH DASTARD COWARDLY
SLUGGARD

POLYDORUS (FATHER OF —) PRIAM
CADMUS HIPPOMEDON
(MOTHER OF —) HECUBA HARMONIA
(SLAYER OF —) POLYMNESTOR
(SON OF —) LABDACUS
(WIFE OF —) NYCTEIS

POLYGON DECAGON HEXAGON
NONAGON HEPTAGON PENTAGON
CHILIAGON MULTANGLE

POLYNESIA

ISLAND: COOK LINE SAMOA TONGA
EASTER ELLICE PHOENIX
ISLE: MOTU
LANGUAGE: UVEA TAGALOG
NATIVE: ATI MAORI KANAKA NIVEAN
TONGAN NESOGAEAN

POLYNESIAN MAORI KANAKA TONGAN
FUTUNAN

POLYNICES (BROTHER OF —)
ETEOCLES
(FATHER OF —) OEDIPUS
(MOTHER OF —) JOCASTA
(WIFE OF —) ARGIA

POMADE CIDER POMATUM LIPSTICK
OINTMENT

POMERANIA (CAPITAL OF —) STETTIN
(CITY IN —) THORN TORUN ANKLAM
(ISLAND IN —) RUGEN USEDOM
(PROVINCE IN —) POMORZE

POMP BRAG FARE WEAL BOAST PRIDE
STATE ESTATE PAMPER PARADE RIALTY
SCHEME SPRUNK BOBANCE DISPLAY
PAGEANT PANOPLY SPLURGE CEREMONY
EQUIPAGE GRANDEUR SEMBLANT
SPLENDOR

POMPOSITY TUMOR BIGHEAD BIGNESS
BOMBAST

POMPOUS BIG BUG BUDGE JELLY LARGE
SHOWY TUMID WIGGY ASTRUT AUGUST
TURGID BLOATED BOMBAST FUSTIAN
OROTUND STILTED SWOLLEN TURGENT
BEWIGGED INFLATED MAGNIFIC
SWELLING TOPLOFTY IMPORTANT
PONTIFICAL PORTENTOUS

POND (ALSO SEE POOL) LAY LUM DELF
DIKE MOAT PULK SLEW TANK VLEI VLEY
CANAL DECOY DELFT LACHE LETCH

STANK WAYER CLAIRE LAGOON LOCHAN
PUDDLE SALINA SLOUGH SPLASH
STAGNE MULLETRY
(— FOR OYSTERS) CLAIRE
(ARTIFICIAL —) AQUARIUM
(DIRTY —) SOAL
(FISH —) VIVER GURGES PISCINA
(FISH STORING —) STEW
(SMALL —) KHAL
(STAGNANT —) DUB
(PREF.) LACO LIMN(I) LIMN(O)
PONDER CON CAST CHAW MUSE PORE
ROLL TURN BROOD STUDY VOLVE WEIGH
ADVISE EXPEND REASON RECORD
REMORD BALANCE COMPASS EXAMINE
IMAGINE PERPEND REFLECT REVERIE
REVOLVE APPRAISE COGITATE CONSIDER
MEDITATE
PONDEROUS DULL SLOW BULKY GRAVE
HEAVY SOGGY AWKWARD WEIGHTY
UNWIELDY IMPORTANT
PONE CAKE LUMP WRIT PAUNE PUDDING
SWELLING
PONTIFF POPE BISHOP PRIEST PONTIFEX
PONY CAB RAW TAT CAVY TROT YABU
BIDET DALES GRIFF PAINT PINTO POWNY
TACKY TRICK WELCH WELSH BASUTO
BHUTIA BRONCO CAYUSE EXMOOR
GARRAN SHELTY TANGUN TATTOO
ENGLISH HACKNEY MANIPUR MUSTANG
SHELTIE FORESTER GALLOWAY
SHETLAND
(STUDENT'S —) CRIB TROT BICYCLE
POOL (ALSO SEE POND) CAR DIB DUB
LAY PIT POT BANK BOOK CARR DIKE
DUMP FARM FLOW LAKE MERE POND
RING SINK SLEW SOIL SWAG TANK
BAYOU BOWLY DECOY FLASH FLUSH
FRESH KITTY LOUGH PLASH PLUMB
SLACK STANK STILL THERM CARTEL
CHARCO FLODGE LAGOON LASHER
PLUNGE PUDDLE SILOAN SPLASH
STABLE CARLINE CATHOLE JACKPOT
PLASHET SNOOKER INTERLOT QUINIELA
(— AT JERUSALEM) BETHESDA
(— BELOW WATERFALL) LINN LLYN
(— IN BOG) HAG
(— WITH SALMON NETS) STELL
(— WITHOUT OUTLET) STAGNUM
(ARTIFICIAL —) CUSHION
(AUCTION —) CALCUTTA
(BETTING —) EXACTA PERFECTA
TRIFECTA
(DIRTY —) SUMP
(FISH —) TRUNK STEWPOND
(MOUNTAIN —) TARN
(MUDDY —) LETCH
(SWIMMING —) BATH LIDO PISCINA
NATATORY NATATORIUM
(PREF.) LIMN(I) LIMN(O) STAGNI
POOR BAD OFF SAD BASE EVIL FOUL
LEAN LEWD PUNK SICK SOUR THIN
DINKY GROSS SCALY SILLY SOBER
SORRY UNORN FEEBLE HUMBLE HUNGRY
LEADEN MEAGER MEASLY SCANTY
SHABBY STREET CODFISH HAPLESS
NAUGHTY SCRAWNY SCRUBBY SQUALID

TRIVIAL UNLUCKY INDIGENT ORDINARY
PRECIOUS SCRANNEL SNEAKING
TERRIBLE PENNILESS PENURIOUS
POORHOUSE MEASONDUE
POORLY ILL BADLY SADLY BARELY
FEEBLY SIMPLY SLIGHT SHABBILY
POP GO DOT GUN HIT TRY BLOW DART
HOCK JUMP PAWN SODA BREAK CLOOP
CRACK KNOCK SHOOT ATTACK EFFORT
FATHER POPPER STROKE THRUSH
ASSAULT ATTEMPT CONCERT EXPLODE
INSTANT REDWING BACKFIRE SUDDENLY
POPE PAPA RUFF BISHOP PUFFIN SHRIKE
PONTIFEX FISHERMAN
POPLAR ABELE ALAMO ASPEN BAHAN
LIARD BALSAM POPPLE BAUMIER
ABELTREE WHITEBARK
POPPY HEAD BLAVER CANKER COPROSE
EARACHE PONCEAU REDWEED
ARGEMONE BALEWORT BOCCONIA
HEADACHE DANNEBROG SQUATMORE
COQUELICOT
POPPYCOCK BOSH FOLLY STUFF
HAVERS
POPULACE MOB MASS CROWD DEMOS
PLEBS MASSES PEOPLE PUBLIC
COUNTRY MULTITUDE
(PREF.) DEM(O) OCHLO
POPULAR LAY POP COMMON GOLDEN
PUBLIC SIMPLE VULGAR CROWDED
DEMOTIC VULGATE APPROVED FAVORITE
PEOPLISH PLEBEIAN
POPULARITY VOGUE CLAPTRAP
POPULATE MAN BREED PLANT WORLD
PEOPLE INHABIT
POPULATION DEME COLONY FLOTSAM
KINDRED TOPODEME UNIVERSE
PORCELAIN JU KO CHINA MURRA SPODE
BISQUE MURRHA NANKIN BISCUIT
CELADON DRESDEN NANKEEN NANKING
MANDARIN STEATITE
(JAPANESE —) KUTANI
(VARIETY OF —) CAEN KUAN ARITA
HIZEN IMARI KYOTO AMSTEL PARIAN
SEVRES BUDWEIS DRESDEN LIMOGES
MEISSEN SWANSEA COALPORT
HAVILAND KAKIEMON CHANTILLY
PORCH HOOD STOA LANAI STOOP
PARVIS PIAZZA PORTAL RAMADA
BALCONY GALERIE NARTHEX PASSAGE
PORTICO VERANDA ANTENAVE
SOLARIUM TRANSEPT
PORCUPINE QUILL URSON CAWQUAW
COENDOU ERECTER ERICIUS PORKPEN
HEDGEHOG HEDGEPIG
PORE GAZE GLOZE STARE STOMA STUDY
TRYPA BROWSE PONDER ALVEOLA
CINCLIS OSTIOLE TUBULUS BAJONADO
JOLTHEAD LENTICEL POROSITY
PORK HAM HOG PIG LARD BRAWN
MONEY SWINE BALDRIB LARDOON
MIDDLING
(— AND SALMON) LAULAU
(— CHOP) BALDRIB GRISKEN
(— SHOULDER) HAND
(FRIED CUBE OF —) CUCHIFRITO
(SALT —) BACON SPECK SOWBELLY

PORNOGRAPHIC LEWD CURIOUS OBSCENE

POROUS OPEN LIGHT LEACHY CELLULAR

PORPOISE WHALE PALACH PUFFER COWFISH DOLPHIN HOGFISH SNUFFER CETACEAN GAIRFISH

PORRIDGE KHIR POBS SAMP ATOLE BROSE GROUT GRUEL BURGOO CROWDY SEPAWN SKILLY SOWENS TARTAN BROCHAN OATMEAL POBBIES POLENTA POTTAGE FLUMMERY SAGAMITE

PORT GATE GOAL LEFT MIEN WICK WINE CARRY CREEK HAVEN SALLY SCALE STATE HARBOR REFUGE AIRPORT BEARING DIGNITY LIBERTY DEMEANOR LARBOARD PORTHOLE

PORTABLE MOBILE MOVABLE BEARABLE

PORTAL DOOR GATE ENTRY PORCH DOORWAY ENTRANCE

PORTEND BODE AUGUR DIVINE EXTEND BESPEAK BETOKEN PREDICT PRESAGE DENOUNCE FOREBODE FORECAST FORETELL

PORTENT AYAH LUCK SIGN SOUND TOKEN AUGURY MARVEL OSTENT WONDER AUSPICE PREDICT PRESAGE PRODIGY CEREMONY DISASTER SOOTHSAY PROGNOSTIC

PORTENTOUS AWFUL GRAVID BODEFUL DOOMFUL FATEFUL OMINOUS POMPOUS DOOMLIKE DREADFUL INFLATED SINISTER

PORTER ALE BEER MOZO CADDY HAMAL STOUT BADGER BEARER CADDIE COOLIE DURWAN ENTIRE KHAMAL REDCAP SUISSE DROGHER DVORNIK JANITOR BUMMAREE CARGADOR CHAPRASI LODGEMAN PORTITOR RECEIVER
(— AND STOUT) COOPER
(JAPANESE —) AKABO
(MEAT —) PITCHER
(MEXICAN —) TAMEN

PORTIA (HUSBAND OF —) BRUTUS
(LOVER OF —) BASSANIO
(MAID OF —) NERISSA

PORTICO STOA WALK ORIEL PORCH EXEDRA PARVIS PIAZZA SCHOOL XYSTUS BALCONY DISTYLE GALLERY NARTHEX PRONAOS TERRACE VERANDA VERANDAH

PORTION CUP CUT LAB LOT PAN BLAD DALE DEAL DOLE DOSE FATE FECK PART SIZE WHAT DOWER PIECE RATIO SHARE SLICE SNACK WHACK CANTLE CANTON COLLOP DETAIL MATTER PARCEL EXCERPT PARTAGE SECTION SEGMENT TODDICK TRANCHE FRACTION FRAGMENT PITTANCE QUANTITY SCANTLET FODDERING
(— DRUNK) DRAFT DRAUGHT
(— OF BIRD SONG) TOUR
(— OF BREAD OR BEER) CUE
(— OF CITRUS RIND) ALBEDO
(— OF ESTATE) LEGITIM
(— OF FARMLAND) BEREWICK
(— OF FLOODPLAIN) BANCO
(— OF FODDER) JAG
(— OF FOOD) HELP GOBBET HELPING

(— OF HIDE) HEAD
(— OF LAND) BLOCK PATTI INTAKE DIVISION DONATION
(— OF LIQUOR) STICK DIVIDEND
(— OF LITURGY) ANAPHORA
(— OF MAST) HOUSING HOUNDING
(— OF PASTURE) BREAK
(— OF POEM) STRAIN
(— OF RUG) GRIN
(— OF SERPENT'S BODY) TRAIN
(— OF STEM) BOON
(— OF STORY) SNATCH
(— OF STREAM) LAVADERO
(— OF TEA) DRAWING
(— OF TIME) SPAN DISTANCE
(— OF TOBACCO) CUD
(ADDITIONAL —) RASHER
(ALLOTTED —) MOIRA SCANTLING
(BRIDE'S —) DOWRY
(CLOTTED — OF BLOOD) CRUOR
(COARSER —) BOLTINGS
(EARLY —) SPRING
(INHABITED — OF EARTH) ECUMENE
(LARGE —) SKELP
(LATTER —) AUTUMN EVENING
(MAIN —) CORPSE
(MARRIAGE —) DOT DOTE TOCHER
(MINUTE —) GRAIN
(MOST VALUABLE —) CHIEF
(PERCEPTIBLE —) KENNING
(REPRESENTATIVE —) SAMPLE
(SIGNIFICANT —) CHAPTER
(SIZABLE —) DUNT
(SMALL —) BIT DAB DOT DRAM DROP SOSH TATE CHACK SPICE SPUNK SHADOW KENNING MODICUM REMNANT SCANTLE SMIDGEN SOUPCON SCANTLET
(SMALL — OF LIQUOR) DOLLOP HEELTAP
(TRIFLING —) SMACK

PORTLY FAT FULL AMPLE STOUT GOODLY STATELY SWELLING OVERBLOWN

PORTMANTEAU BAG HOOK VALISE POCKMANKY

PORTRAIT BUST ICON IMAGE MODEL PIECE KITKAT STATUE VISAGE PORTRAY RETRAIT LIKENESS RITRATTO VERONICA MINIATURE
(— ON COIN) EFFIGY

PORTRAIT OF A LADY
(AUTHOR OF —) JAMES
(CHARACTER IN —) MERLE PANSY RALPH ARCHER CASPAR EDWARD GEMINI ISABEL OSMOND ROSIER GILBERT BANTLING GOODWOOD TOUCHETT HENRIETTA STACKPOLE WARBURTON

PORTRAY GIVE LIMN LINE BLAZE ENACT IMAGE PAINT CIPHER CLOTHE DEPICT FIGURE SHADOW FEATURE IMITATE PICTURE DECIPHER DESCRIBE RESEMBLE

PORTUGAL

BAY: SETUBAL
CAPE: ROCA MONDEGO ESPICHEL

CAPITAL: LISBON
DISTRICT: BEJA FARO BRAGA EVORA HORTA PORTO VISEU LEIRIA LISBOA
ISLAND: TIMOR
ISLANDS: MADEIRA
MOUNTAIN: ACOR GEREZ MARAO MOUSA PENEDA ESTRELA MONCHIQUE
RIVER: SOR TUA LIMA MINO MIRA SADO SEDA TAGO TEJO DOURO MINHO SABAR TAGUS VOUGA ZATAS CAVADO CHANCA TAMEGA ZEZERE MONDEGO GUADIANA
TOWN: BEJA FARO OVAR BRAGA EVORA HORTA PORTO VISEU GUARDA OPORTO COIMBRA FUNCHAL SETUBAL BRAGANCA
UNIVERSITY: COIMBRA
WEIGHT: GRAO ONCA LIBRA MARCO ARROBA OITAVA ARRATEL QUINTAL
WINE: PORT

POSE SET SIT HOARD MODEL OFFER PLANT STICK BAFFLE NONPLUS PEACOCK POSTURE PRESENT PROPOSE POSITION PRETENSE PROPOUND QUESTION MANNERISM
POSEIDON NEPTUNE EARTHSHAKER
(BROTHER OF —) ZEUS
(FATHER OF —) KRONOS
(MOTHER OF —) RHEA
(WIFE OF —) AMPHITRITE
POSER FACER POSEUR PUZZLE STAYER STICKER STUMPER TWISTER EXAMINER STICKLER BANDARLOG
POSH RITZY SWAGGER
POSITION LAY LIE HANG LINE POSE SITE CENSE PLANT POINT POSTE SIEGE SITUS STAND STEAD ASSIZE FIGURE OFFICE STANCE UBIETY POSTURE STATION ATTITUDE CAPACITY DOCTRINE VOCATION PLACEMENT
(— OF AFFAIRS) STATUS
(— OF FEAR) GAZE
(— OF HEAVENLY BODY) HARBOR
(— OF VESSEL) GAUGE HEIGHT
(— WITH NO ESCAPE) IMPASSE
(— WITH NO RESPONSIBILITY) SINECURE
(BALLET —) POINTE
(CHESS —) ZUGZWANG
(COMMANDING —) PRESTIGE
(DEFENSIVE —) OUTWORK
(DISTINGUISHED —) HONOR
(EMBARRASSING —) FIX HOLE LURCH CORNER
(FENCING —) CARTE SIXTE SIXTH QUARTE TIERCE SACCOON SECONDE SEPTIME
(FOREMOST —) HEAD LEAD STEM
(INITIAL —) ANLAUT
(MEDIAL —) INLAUT
(RELATIVE —) RANK PLACE TERMS BEARING FOOTING STANDING
(SOCIAL —) CASTE STATE VALOUR
(SYMBOLIC —) HASTA
(SUFF.) TOPE TOPY
POSITIVE COOL DOWN FLAT PLUS SURE BASIC SHEER UTTER ACTIVE DIRECT

GENUINE HEALTHY ABSOLUTE CONCRETE DECISIVE DEFINITE DOGMATIC EXPLICIT INHERENT RESOLUTE
POSITIVELY BUT FLAT PLUS QUITE FAIRLY INDEED STRICTLY
POSSESS GET OWE OWN HAVE HOLD BOAST BROOK OUGHT REACH WIELD MASTER OBTAIN OCCUPY BEDEVIL ENVELOP FURNISH INHABIT INHERIT INSTALL INSTATE ACQUAINT DOMINATE INSTRUCT
POSSESSED MAD CALM COOL CRAZED ENTHEATE
(— BY EVIL SPIRIT) DEMONIAC
POSSESSION HAND HOLD AUGHT GRASP STATE CLUTCH CORNER SEISIN WEALTH CONTROL COUNTER DEMESNE FINGERS KEEPING MASTERY SEIZURE CONQUEST DEFIANCE PROPERTY
(— OF COMMON FEATURES) AFFINITY
(BURDENSOME —) ELEPHANT
(LOST — OF BALL) TURNOVER
(RELIGIOUS —) POWER
(TEMPORAL —S) WORLD
(TEMPORARY —) LEND
POSSIBILITY MAY MAYBE POSSE CHANCE PROSPECT QUESTION
POSSIBLE ABLE RIFE MAYBE LIKELY EARTHLY ELIGIBLE FEASIBLE PROBABLE PROBABLY POTENTIAL CONTINGENT PRACTICABLE
(BARELY —) OUTSIDE
POSSIBLY MAPPEN LIGHTLY PERHAPS PERCHANCE PERADVENTURE
POST SET TIE BOMA CAMP CRIB DOLE MAIL POLE ROOM SPOT SPUD STOB STUD TREE BERTH CHEEK CRANE NEWEL PLACE SPILE SPRAG STAKE STAND STILT STING STOCK STODE STUMP BILLET CIPPUS COLUMN CROTCH FENDER INFORM OFFICE PICKET PILLAR SCREEN STAPLE TRUNCH COURIER PLACARD POSTAGE POSTBOX QUARTER STATION UPRIGHT BANISTER LEGPIECE MAKEFAST PRESIDIO PUNCHEON QUINTAIN STRADDLE STANCHION
(— AS RACE MARKER) META
(— ON PIER) FAST BOLLARD DEADHEAD
(BOUNDARY —) TERM STOOP TERMINUS
(CHIMNEY —) SPEER
(CUSTOMS —) CHOKEY
(DECK —) BITT
(DOOR OR GATE —) DURN
(ECCLESIASTIC —) BENEFICE
(FENCE —) DROPPER
(HANGING —) GIBBET
(INDIAN MILITARY —) THANA
(MILITARY —) FORT GARRISON
(MOORING —) BITT DOLPHIN
(OBSERVATORY —) CUPOLA
(SACRED —) ASHERAH
(SIGN —) PARSON
(PREF.) STELO
POSTER BILL CLAP SNIPE AFFICHE PLACARD SHOWING STICKER STREAMER

POSTERIOR BACK REAR CAUDAL DORSAL POSTIC RETRAL ADAXIAL BUTTOCKS

POSTERITY SEQUEL KINDRED FUTURITY

POSTPONE OFF STAY WAIT DEFER DELAY REFER REMIT WAIVE FUTURE LINGER RETARD ADJOURN DEGRADE OVERSET PROLONG RESPECT SUSPEND CONTINUE PROROGUE REPRIEVE WITHHOLD

POSTPONEMENT MORA STAY DELAY RESPECT RESPITE

POSTURE SET POSE SEAT SITE FRONT HEART PLACE SHAPE SQUAT STATE LOUNGE SLOUCH STANCE BEARING CROWHOP STATION STATURE ATTITUDE CARRIAGE POSITION
(— OF DEFENSE) GUARD
(DANCE —) HOLD
(KNEELING —) SHIKO

POSY POESY TUTTY FLOWER BOUQUET NOSEGAY ANTHOLOGY

POT BAG FOOL JUST LEAD PINT POOL RUIN CREWE CRUSE KITTY SHOOT CHYTRA KETTLE MARMIT MONKEY OUTWIT POCKET BRAISER CHAMBER CUVETTE DECEIVE POTSHOT SEETHER SKILLET YETLING FAVORITE PRESERVE MARIJUANA
(— FOR CATCHING FISH) COOP
(— OF BRASS) LOTA MASLIN
(— OF DRINK) SHANT
(— WITH 3 FEET) POSNET
(BULGING —) OLLA
(BUSHMAN'S —) JACKSHAY
(CHAMBER —) JERRY JORDAN COMMODE JEROBOAM
(CHIMNEY —) CAN TUN
(EARTHEN —) OLLA CROCK CHATTY PIPKIN
(LEATHER —) GISPIN
(LOBSTER —) COY TRUNK
(LONG-HANDLED —) PINGLE
(MELTING —) CREVET CRUCIBLE
(PEAR-SHAPED —) ALUDEL
(SMALL ROUND —) LOTA
(TEA —) TRACK
(12-GALLON —) DIXIE

POTABLE DRINK BEVERAGE POTATORY

POTATION POT DRAM DRAFT DRINK LIBATION

POTATO PAP YAM CHAT PAPA SPUD YAMP FLUKE IDAHO RURAL TATER TUBER BATATA CAMOTE KUMARA LUMPER MURPHY PRATEY SKERRY BURBANK EPICURE SOLANUM BLUENOSE
(— SLICES) LATTICE
(—S AND CABBAGE) COLCANNON
(FRENCH FRIED —) CHIP
(FRENCH FRIED —S) GAUFRETTES
(JAPANESE —) IMO
(STEWED —S) STOVIES
(WITH —S) PARMENTIER

POTBELLIED KEDGE PODDY STOMACHY ABDOMINOUS

POTENCY FORCE POWER VIGOR ORENDA

VIRTUE EFFICACY STRENGTH VITALITY OPERATION

POTENT ABLE MAIN RICH STAY STIFF CAUSAL COGENT CRUTCH MIGHTY STRONG DYNAMIC SUPPORT WARRANT FORCIBLE POWERFUL PUISSANT VIGOROUS VIRTUOUS VIRULENT

POTENTATE KING RULER POTENT PRINCE DICTATOR DOMINION SOVEREIGN

POTENTIAL LATENT VIRTUAL IMPLICIT INCHOATE POSSIBLE PREGNANT

POTION DOSE DRUG DRAFT DRINK DWALE STUFF DRENCH POISON AMATORY MIXTURE PHILTER PHILTRE NEPENTHE

POTPOURRI HASH OLIO STEW MASLIN MEDLEY POTPIE RAGOUT FANTASIA PASTICHE JAMBALAYA SALMAGUNDI

POTTAGE SEW SOUP STEW BROTH BRUET BREWIS OATMEAL PULMENT

POTTER FAD FUSS MUCK POKE ANNOY TRUCK BOTHER DABBLE DACKER DIDDLE DISHER DODDER FIDDLE FOOTLE JOTTER KUMHAR MUDDLE NANTLE NIGGLE PETTLE POUTER TIDDLE TIFFLE TRIFLE CLOAMER DISTURB FOSSICK HANDLER NAUNTLE PERPLEX THROWER TROUBLE CERAMIST

POTTERY POT BANK CHUN WARE CROCK DELFT ROUEN SPODE FICTIL KASHAN MIMPEI ASTBURY BELLEEK BOCCARO BRISTOL DIPWARE FIGMENT JETWARE POTWARE POTWORK REDWARE SATSUMA TICKNEY TZUCHOU CERAMICS SANTORIN SLIPWARE BROWNWARE
(— DECORATED WITH SCRATCHING) GRAFFITO
(ANCIENT —) KAMARES GRAYWARE
(BLACK —) BASALT BUCCHERO
(CHINESE —) KUAN YIHSING
(CRUSHED —) GROG
(HINDU —) UDA
(RICHLY COLORED —) MAJOLICA
(UNGLAZED —) BISCUIT

POUCH BAG COD JAG POD SAC CYST POCK POKE BULGE BURSA PURSE BUDGET CAECUM GIPSER PACKET POCKET PURSET SACHET ALFARGA ALFORJA CANTINA GIPSIRE MAILBAG MOCHILA OVICYST SCROTUM SPORRAN SWALLOW BURSICLE PROTRUDE SPEUCHAN MARSUPIUM
(— OF FLY) AEROSTAT
(— ON DEER'S NECK) BELL
(PILGRIM'S —) SCRIP
(TOBACCO —) DOSS

POULTRY FOWL HENS DUCKS GEESE PULLEN PEAFOWL PIGEONS PULLERY TURKEYS CHICKENS PULLAILE VOLAILLE

POUNCE NAB NOG CLAP JUMP POKE SWAP SWOP FLECK PRICK PUNCH SOUSE SWOOP TALON EMBOSS PIERCE TATTOO BOBCOAT DESCEND SPRINKLE
(— UPON) TIRE STOOP

POUND BUM DAD LIB PIN PUN SOV BEAT CHAP DRUB FRAM PELT PIND POON POSS PUND QUID SKIT THUD TRAP TUND

CRUSH FRAME KNOCK LABOR LIVRE
NEVEL STAMP THUMP TRAMP WEIGH
BATTER BRUISE HAMMER LUMBER
NICKER POUNCE PRISON THRASH
CONTUND CONTUSE PINFOLD THUNDER
LAMBASTE RESTRAIN
(— FINE) BRAY
(FISH —) KEEP MADRAGUE
(100 —S) CENTAL CENTURY
(12 —S OF BUTTER) GAUN
(1-8TH OF —) HANDFUL
(25 —S) PONY PONEY
(32, 56, OR 75 —S OF RAISINS) FRAIL
(500 —S) MONKEY
POUR JAW RUN TUN YET BREW DROP
EMIT FLOW GOSH GUSH HELD LAVE RAIN
TEEM FLOOD FLUSH SLIDE SOUSE SPILL
SPOUT SWARM TRILL CASCADE
CHANNEL SUFFUSE
(— AWAY) STAVE
(— BACK) REFUND
(— BEER OR WINE) BIRL
(— CLUMSILY) SLOSH
(— COPIOUSLY) HALE
(— DOWN) RASH SILE SHOWER
DESCEND DISPUNGE
(— FORTH) SHED TIDE VENT WELL
DISTILL OVERFLOW
(— FREELY) SWILL
(— FROM ONE VESSEL TO
ANOTHER) DECANT JIRBLE TRANSFUSE
(— IN) INFUSE INFOUND INHELDE
(— IN DROP BY DROP) INSTILL
(— LIKE RAIN OR TEARS) LASH
(— MELTED WAX) BASTE
(— MOLTEN LEAD) YOTE
(— OFF) SLUICE
(— OIL UPON) ANOINT
(— OUT) FILL SEND SHED SKINK STOUR
UTTER EFFUSE LIBATE DIFFUND DIFFUSE
(— UPON) AFFUSE
POURBOIRE TIP GRATUITY TRINKGELD
POUT BIB MOP MAID MOUE PUSS SULK
BLAIN BOODY GROIN BRASSY BRASSIE
CATFISH EELPOUT BULLHEAD PROTRUDE
POVERTY LACK NEED WANE WANT
DEARTH PENURY BEGGARY DEFAULT
MISEASE TENUITY DISTRESS POORTITH
SCARCITY NECESSITY
POVERTY-STRICKEN POOR NAKED
NEEDY SQUALID SHIRTLESS
POWDER BRAY MILL MULL SAND CHALK
CURRY FLOUR GRIND HEMOL PICRA
STOUR CEMENT CHARGE DECAMP
ESCAPE FARINA KERMES RACHEL
SMEETH BESTREW SCATTER SPACKLE
SPODIUM ALGAROTH CATAPASM
DYNAMITE PALEGOLD
(— A SHIELD) GERATE
(— FOR BRONZING) BROCADE
(— OBTAINED BY SUBLIMATION)
FLOWERS
(— TO MASK SWEAT ODOR) EMPASM
EMPASMA
(— USED IN CHOCOLATE) PINOLE
(ABRASIVE —) EMERY
(ANTHELMINTIC —) KOSIN

(ANTIMONY —) KOHL
(ASTRINGENT —) BORAL
(BLEACHING —) CHEMIC CHLORIDE
(BROWNISH —) LIGNIN
(CATHARTIC —) KAMALA
(COLORING —) HENNA
(FINE —) DUST POUNCE ALCOHOL
(FLUORESCENT —) FLUMERIN
(GOA —) ARAROBA
(GOLD —) VENTURINE
(GRAPHITIC —) KISH
(GRAY —) ANTU
(HAIR —) MUST
(MALT —) SMEDDUM
(PERFUMED —) ABIR PULVIL SACHET
(PINK —) CALAMINE
(POISONOUS —) ROBIN
(PURPLE —) CUDBEAR
(REDDISH —) ABIR KUMKUM SIMMON
(ROSE-COLORED —) ERBIA
(SACHET —) PULVIL
(SILICEOUS —S) SILEX
(SMOKELESS —) FILITE PEYTON
CORDITE AMBERITE INDURITE SOLENITE
(WHITE —) CHINOL YTTRIA HYPORIT
SCANDIA HALAZONE LANTHANA
PARAFORM
(YELLOW —) KOSIN DERMOL MELLON
LUPULIN MALARIN SAMARIA TANNIGEN
POWDERY MEALY PRUINOSE
POWER ARM ART JUS ROD SAY SUN VIS
BEEF BULK DINT GIFT GRIP HAND HANK
HEAP HORN IRON MAIN SOUP SWAY
WILL AGENT CROWN DEMON DEVIL
FORCE GRACE HUACA HYDRO INPUT
LURCH MIGHT SINEW SKILL STEAM
VALUE VIGOR WIELD AGENCY APPEAL
BREATH CLUTCH CREDIT DANGER
DEGREE DOUGHT EFFORT ENERGY
FOISON IMPACT STROKE SWINGE
TALENT VIRTUE WEIGHT ABILITY
BALANCE BOSSDOM COMMAND
CONTROL DEMESNE DESTINY DYNAMIS
ENTHEOS FACULTY POTENCY VALENCY
VOLTAGE ACTIVITY AUTONOMY
CAPACITY CLUTCHES COERCION
DELEGACY DEMIURGE DISPOSAL
DOMINION INTEREST LEVERAGE
LORDSHIP SEIGNORY STRENGTH
PUISSANCE PREROGATIVE
POWERFUL BIG FAT ABLE DEEP HIGH
MAIN RANK RICH VERY FORTE HEFTY
HUSKY LUSTY STARK STOUT VALID
VIVID COGENT HEROIC MIGHTY POTENT
SEVERE STRONG CAPABLE FECKFUL
INTENSE POLLENT VALIANT FORCIBLE
PUISSANT VIGOROUS
(PREF.) MEGA
POWERLESS WEAK FEEBLE UNABLE
HELPLESS IMPOTENT
PRACTICABLE AGIBLE DOABLE USABLE
VIABLE FEASIBLE OPERABLE POSSIBLE
PRACTICAL HARD UTILE ACTIVE ACTUAL
USEFUL OPERARY VIRTUAL WORKING
HOMESPUN PRACTIVE
PRACTICALLY ALMOST NEARLY REALLY
VIRTUALLY

PRACTICE ACT ISM SUE TRY USE KEEP
LIVE PLAN PLOT ADOPT APPLY ASSAY
DRILL FOUND GUISE HABIT HAUNT
TRADE TRAIN USAGE CUSTOM EMPLOY
FOLLOW GROOVE OCCUPY RECORD
BRUSHUP KNOCKUP OPERATE PROCEED
PROFESS ACTIVISM ALARMISM EXERCISE
FREQUENT OBSERVANCE
(— CHEATING) FOIST
(— DECEPTION) DEACON
(— DILIGENTLY) PLY
(— FRAUD) SHARK
(— HYPOCRISY) CANT
(— OF AN ART) PRAXIS
(— OF MEDICINE) GALENISM
(— ROWING) TUB
(— WITCHCRAFT) HEX
(BINDING —) LAW
(CEREMONIAL —) RITE
(COMMUNAL —) SUNNA SCHEME
INTRIGUE
(CORRUPT —) ABUSE WHORE
(DIPLOMATIC —) ALTERNAT
(DISHONEST —S) CROSS
(HORTICULTURAL —) CUTTAGE
(MEDICAL —) ALLERGY
(RELIGIOUS —) CULT CULTUS
(SUPERSTITIOUS —) FREET
(UNDERHAND —) JUGGLING
(VICIOUS —) MOLOCH
PRACTITIONER DOCTOR HEALER
LAWYER NOVICE LEARNER EXERCENT
FELDSHER HUMANIST HERBALIST
HOMEOPATH NATUROPATH
PRAGMATIC BUSY BUSYBODY
DOGMATIC MEDDLING OFFICIOUS
PRACTICAL
PRAIRIE BAY BLED CAMAS PAMPA PLAIN
MEADOW PLATEAU
PRAISE CRY FUME LAUD LOVE ADORE
ALLOW BLESS CAROL CHANT CRACK
DEIFY EXTOL GLORY HONOR KUDOS
PLAUD PRIZE SALVE VALUE ANTHEM
BELAUD EULOGY HILLEL KUDIZE LOVING
ORCHID SALUTE TONGUE ACCLAIM
ADULATE APPLAUD COMMEND FLATTER
GLORIFY MAGNIFY NOSEGAY PLAUDIT
PUFFING TRIBUTE WORSHIP ACCOLADE
APPLAUSE BLESSING DOXOLOGY
ENCOMIUM EULOGIZE PROCLAIM
(— IN THANKSGIVING) JOY
(— INORDINATELY) FUME
(— OF ANOTHER'S FELICITY)
MACARISM
(EFFUSIVE —) FUSS
(EXAGGERATED —) PUFFERY
(EXCESSIVE —) FLATTERY ADULATION
PANEGYRIC
(EXTRAVAGANTLY —) PUFF
(INSINCERE —) CLART DAUBING
(PUBLIC —) PRECONY
PRAISEWORTHY WORTHY AMIABLE
GLORIOUS LAUDABLE SPLENDID
EXEMPLARY
PRANCE STIR CAPER DANCE JAUNT
PRANK CAREER CAVORT CURVET

GAMBOL JAUNCE TITTUP TRANCE
SWAGGER CAKEWALK
PRANK JIG RAG RIG DECK DIDO FOLD
GAME JEST LARK PLOY ADORN ANTIC
CAPER FREAK SHINE SKITE TRICK
CURVET FROLIC GAMBOL VAGARY
ESCAPADE MONKEYSHINE
PRATTLE CHAT CLACK BABBLE BURBLE
CACKLE YATTER BLATTER CHATTER
CLATTER TWADDLE CHITCHAT
PRAY ASK BEG BID BLESS CRAVE VOUCH
INVITE BESEECH ENTREAT IMPLORE
REQUEST WRESTLE INVOCATE
PRAYER AVE CRY VOW BEAD BENE
BOON PLEA SUIT VOTE AGNUS SHEMA
APPEAL ERRAND LITANY MANTRA
MATINS ORISON STEVEN VESPER
BIDDING MEMENTO ORATION PREFACE
ANAPHORA DEVOTION MISERERE
PETITION SUFFRAGE
(— OF DISMISSAL) APOLYSIS
(CANONICAL —S) BREVIARY
(CHIEF MOHAMMEDAN —) NAMAZ
(HINDU —) GAYATRI
(INWARD —) ACT
(JEWISH —) ALENU ABODAH GEULLAH
HOSHANA KADDISH
(LAST — OF DAY) COMPLIN
(LONG —) CATHISMA
(LORD'S —) PATERNOSTER
(MUSLIM —) SALAH SALAT KHUTBAH
(OPENING —) COLLECT
(SHORT —) GRACE
(SILENT —) SECRET
PREACH EDIFY SOUGH TEACH EXHORT
GOSPEL SERMON DELIVER HOMILIZE
PREDICATE
PREACHER PARSON TUBMAN LOLLARD
MARTEXT PROPHET ROUNDER TEACHER
EXHORTER KOHELETH MINISTER
PARDONER PULPITER QOHELETH
SERMONER SWADDLER BOANERGES
PRECARIOUS NEAR DICKY RISKY SHAKY
CASUAL INFIRM NARROW UNSURE
DUBIOUS TRICKLE CATCHING DELICATE
INSECURE PERILOUS UNSTABLE
DANGEROUS UNCERTAIN
PRECAUTION CARE GUARD CAUTEL
SAFEGUARD
PRECEDE LEAD FOREGO HERALD
FORERUN PREFACE PREVENT ANTECEDE
PREAMBLE
PRECEDENT LEAD SIGN MODEL TOKEN
USAGE INSTANCE ORIGINAL SPECIMEN
STANDARD AUTHORITY
PRECEDING OLD FORE BEFORE FORMER
LEADING ADJACENT PREVIOUS
(PREF.) ANTE
PRECEPT LAW LINE RULE WRIT ADAGE
AXIOM BREVE MAXIM ORDER SUTRA
SUTTA TORAH BEHEST DICTATE
MANDATE WARRANT DOCTRINE
DOCUMENT LANDMARK
PRECIOUS CUTE DEAR FINE LIEF RARE
VERY CHARY CHERE GREAT HONEY
CHICHI CHOICE COSTLY DAINTY GOLDEN
PEARLY POSING SILVER TENDER PRECISE

AFFECTED ORIENTAL OVERNICE VALUABLE WORTHFUL PRICELESS
PRECIPICE KHUD LINN CLIFF SHEER STEEP DOWNFALL HEADWALL
PRECIPITATE GEL CURD HURL RASH HASTY HURRY SHOOT SPEED STEEP ABRUPT HASTEN SLUDGE SUDDEN TUMBLE UNWARY DISTILL SUBSIDE TRIGGER CATALYZE HEADLONG PROCLIVE SEDIMENT SETTLING
PRECIPITATION HAIL MIST RAIN SNOW HASTE SLEET VIRGA
PRECIPITOUS FULL RASH BRENT HASTY STEEP ABRUPT CHICHI STEEPY SUDDEN HEADLONG
PRECIS JUNONIA SUMMARY ABSTRACT
PRECISE DRY SET FLAT HARD JUMP JUST NEAT NICE TIDY TRIG TRIM TRUE VERY CLEAN CLOSE EXACT PRESS SOUND FORMAL NARROW STRICT CAREFUL CERTAIN CLERKLY CORRECT EXPRESS PERFECT STARCHY ABSOLUTE ACCURATE DEFINITE EXPLICIT HAIRLINE PINPOINT PUNCTUAL RIGOROUS
PRECISELY BUT EVEN JUST CLEAN SHARP FINELY JUSTLY STRAIT EXACTLY
PRECISION NICETY CLARITY ACCURACY DELICACY ELEGANCE JUSTNESS
PRECLUDE BAR DENY STOP CLOSE CROSS DEBAR ESTOP FORBID HINDER IMPEDE OBVIATE PREVENT SILENCE CONCLUDE PROHIBIT
PREDATORY HUNGRY HARMFUL RAVENOUS
PREDECESSOR ANCESTOR FOREGOER
PREDICAMENT BOX FIX JAM SOUP SPOT LURCH STATE STEAD PICKLE PLIGHT SCRAPE DILEMMA IMPASSE QUANDARY
PREDICT LAY BODE CALL DOPE READ AUGUR FORESAY PRESAGE FOREBODE FORECAST FORETELL PROPHESY SOOTHSAY PROGNOSTICATE
PREDICTION DOPE AUGURY BODING PORTENT PRESAGE FORECAST PROPHECY
PREDOMINANT GREAT RULING CAPITAL REIGNING SUPERIOR
PREDOMINATE RULE DOMINE EXCEED GOVERN PREVAIL
PREEMINENT BIG TOP ARCH HIGH STAR FIRST GRAND GREAT STELLAR SUPREME FOREMOST SPLENDID SUPERIOR PARAMOUNT
PREEN PIN PERK PICK TRIM WHET DRESS GLOAT PLUME PRINK PRUNE SWELL TRICK SMOOTH
PREFACE FRONT PROEM USHER HERALD PRESAY EPISTLE PRECEDE PREPOSE EXORDIUM FOREWORD PREAMBLE PROLOGUE
PREFER LAY LIKE LOVE ELECT EXALT FAVOR OFFER CHOOSE SELECT OUTRANK PRESENT PROMOTE PROPOSE SURPASS
PREFERENCE LIKE FAVOR CHOICE DESIRE LIKING RATHER DRUTHERS FAVORITE PRIVILEGE PRECEDENCE
PREGNANT BIG GONE OPEN GREAT

HEAVY QUICK READY BAGGED CAUGHT COGENT GRAVID ENCEINT FERTILE GESTANT TEEMING WEIGHTY GERMINAL PRESSING
PREJUDICE BIAS DOWN HARM HURT KINK TURN DAMAGE IMPAIR INJURY SEXISM SCUNNER JAUNDICE
PREJUDICED BIGOTED INSULAR PARTIAL
PREJUDICIAL BIASED HURTFUL CONTRARY DAMAGING INIMICAL SINISTER
PRELATE CHIEF LEADER PRIEST HIERARCH ORDINARY SUPERIOR MONSIGNOR
PRELIMINARY PRIOR PRELIM PREFACE PRELUDE PREAMBLE PREVIOUS PREFATORY
PRELUDE PROEM DESCANT FORERUN INTRADA PREFACE ANTELUDE OVERTURE RITORNEL VERSETTE
PREMIER CHIEF FIRST OLDEST LEADING EARLIEST
PREMISE LEMMA MAJOR ASSUME GROUND REASON SUMPTION
PREMIUM AGIO BACK AWARD BONUS FANCY PRIZE SHAVE USURY BOUNTY DEPORT REWARD GIVEAWAY
PREMONITION OMEN HUNCH NOTICE PRESAGE WARNING
PREOCCUPIED DEEP LOST·RAPT CRAZY ABSENT FILLED INTENT CRACKED ABSORBED ENGROSSED
PREPARATION BALM DOPE PREP CREAM GLAZE JELLY READY ACETUM BLEACH BLUING DERRIS FACIAL LOTION PEPSIN SIMPLE ADDRESS CLEANER DIPPING ESSENCE EXTRACT FITNESS FONDANT PLACEBO VARNISH ABSTRACT CONSERVE COSMETIC INHALANT MEDICINE TRAINING MAKEREADY PROVISION
(— CONTAINING HONEY) MELLITE
(— FOR COLORING LIQUORS) FLASH
(— OF GRAPEJUICE) DIBS
(AROMATIC —) ELIXIR
(CHEESE —) FONDU
(CHEESELIKE —) YOGURT CROWDIE
(COSMETIC —) HENNA
(ENZYME —) KOJI
(EYELID —) KOHL
(IMPURE RADIOACTIVE —) EMANIUM
(INTOXICATING —) BOZA GANJA
(MEDICAL —) STUFF
(OPIUM —) LAUDANUM
(SALINE —) LICK
(SLOPPY —) SLIBBERSAUCE
(SWEET —) DULCE
(UNCTUOUS —) CERATE
PREPARE DO FIT FIX GET LAY ABLE COOK GIRD MAKE PARE PLOT PREP TILL BLEND BOWNE BRACE DIGHT DRAFT DRESS EQUIP FRAME ORDER PREDY READY TRAIN ADJUST DESIGN GRAITH ORDAIN ADDRESS AFFAITE APPAREL APPOINT CONCOCT CONFECT DISPOSE

EDUCATE PRODUCE PROVIDE QUALIFY
INSTRUCT

PREPARED UP APT FIT SET GIRT RIPE
ALERT BOUND PREST READY GRAITH
CURRIED EQUIPPED TOGETHER

PREPONDERANCE MAJORITY
DOMINANCE

PREPOSSESSION BENT BIAS FETICH
FANTASY PREJUDICE

PREPOSTEROUS RICH INEPT ABSURD
FOOLISH LAPUTAN GROTESQUE
RIDICULOUS

PREROGATIVE GRACE HONOR RIGHT
REGALE FACULTY PECULIAR PRIVILEGE

PRESAGE BODE HINT OMEN SIGN AUGUR
TOKEN AUGURY BETIDE BETOKEN
FORESEE PORTEND PREDICT FOREBODE
FORECAST FOREDOOM FORETELL
INDICATE PREAMBLE PROPHESY

PRESCRIBE SET TAX ALLOT GUIDE LIMIT
ORDER ASSIGN DEFINE DIRECT ENJOIN
INDITE ORDAIN APPOINT CONFINE
CONTROL DICTATE RESTRAIN

PRESCRIBED SET BASIC THETIC
POSITIVE THETICAL FORMULARY

PRESCRIPTION RX BILL FORM CIPHER
RECIPE DICTATE FORMULA RECEIPT

PRESENCE EYE FACE SELF BEING
ASPECT BEARING COMPANY ASSEMBLY
INSTANCE

PRESENT AIM BOX NOW BILL BOON GIFT
GIVE HAND HERE MEED NEAR NIGH
SHOW BEING DOLLY ENTER GRANT
NONCE OFFER PLACE RAISE READY
STAGE THERE ACCUSE ACTUAL ADDUCE
ALLEGE AROUND BESTOW BOUNTY
BROACH CLOTHE DONATE LATTER
MODERN NEARBY PREFER REGALE
RENDER COMMEND DISPLAY DOUCEUR
EXHIBIT EXPOUND FURNISH INSTANT
LARGESS PERFORM PRETEND RELEASE
BLESSING DONATION GRATUITY
INSTANCE OFFERING RESIDENT
(— AS GIFT) DASH
(— FOR ACCEPTANCE) TENDER
(— FROM PUPIL TO TEACHER)
MINERVAL
(— IN DETAIL) DISCUSS
(— IN MIND) DEAR
(— ONESELF) APPEAR
(— TO SOLDIERS) CONGIARY
(— TO STRANGER) XENIUM
(— TO VIEW) YIELD
(— WITHOUT WARRANT) OBTRUDE
(ALWAYS —) CHRONIC
(BRIDEGROOM'S —) HANDSEL
(CEREMONIAL —) KHILAT
(NOT —) ABSENT

PRESENTATION BILL GALA GIFT SHOW
DROLL IMAGE MUSTER SCHEMA BILLING
DISPLAY EPITOME MUSICAL ANALYSIS
BESTOWAL DELIVERY DONATION
EXPOSURE PERFORMANCE

PRESENTLY NOW ANON ENOW SOON
SHORTLY DIRECTLY

PRESERVATION FILING SAVING
KEEPING

PRESERVATIVE SALT BORAX SPICE
SUGAR CONSERVE TREATMENT

PRESERVE CAN JAR HOLD KEEP SAVE
BLESS GUARD SERVE SPARE SWEET
BOTTLE COMFIT DEFEND EMBALM
FREEZE POWDER RETAIN SECURE SHIELD
UPHOLD CONDITE FORFEND PROTECT
RESERVE SUCCADE SUSTAIN
CHOWCHOW CONSERVE ENSHRINE
MAINTAIN MOTHBALL
(— BY BOILING WITH SUGAR) CANDY
(— BY SALTING) CORN CURE SALT
(— OF GRAPES) RAISINE
(— WOOD) KYANIZE PAYNISE
(GAME —) MOOR SHIKARGAH
(HUNTING —) WALK

PRESERVED WET CONFECT BRANDIED
POWDERED

PRESIDE RULE GUIDE DIRECT MODERATE

PRESS FLY HUG JAM SIT BEAR BEND
CRAM DOME DROP HORN HUSH IRON
KISS PLOT THEW TUCK URGE VICE
ARGUE BESET CHAFE CRIMP CROWD
CRUSH DRIVE EXACT FORCE KNEAD
MIDST SCREW SMASH STAMP STUFF
TWIST WEIGH WRING ASSAIL CHISEL
CLOSET CRUNCH HARASS MANGLE
SQUASH STRESS THREAT
THRONG THRUST AFFLICT ARMOIRE
ATTEMPT BESEECH BESIEGE CRUMPLE
EMBRACE ENVIRON OPPRESS SCRUNGE
SQUEEZE CALENDER COMPRESS
SCROUNGE SQUEEGEE SURROUND

PRESSING RASH ACUTE CRYING URGENT
CLAMANT EARNEST EXIGENT INSTANT
CRITICAL PREGNANT NECESSITOUS

PRESSURE JAM HEAT PUSH SWAY DRIVE
FORCE PINCH STAMP BURDEN DURESS
STRESS THRONG WEIGHT BEARING
MERCURY PUSHING SQUEEZE TENSION
URGENCY EXACTION EXIGENCY
(— OF CIRCUMSTANCE) NECESSITY
(— OF 1 DYNE) BARAD
(— ON INSTRUMENT STRING) STOP
(LIQUID —) HEAD
(MANUAL —) TAXIS
(VAPOR —) FUGACITY

PRESTIGE FACE MANA CASTE KUDOS
PLACE STATUS STATURE ILLUSION
INFLUENCE

PRESUME BEAR DARE GROW IMPLY
INFER ASSUME EXPECT DARESAY
SUPPOSE ARROGATE

PRESUMING ARROGANT FAMILIAR

PRESUMPTION GALL JOLLITY OUTRAGE
AUDACITY

PRESUMPTUOUS BOLD PERT FRESH
PROUD WICKED WILFUL FORWARD
HAUGHTY ARROGANT ASSUMING
FAMILIAR INSOLENT FOOLHARDY

PRETEND ACT FAKE MAKE MOCK SHAM
CLAIM FEIGN AFFECT ASPIRE ASSERT
ASSUME INTEND RECKON SEMBLE
ATTEMPT PRESUME PROFESS SUPPOSE
VENTURE SIMULATE

PRETENDER FOP FAKE IDOL CHEAT
FAKER FRAUD QUACK PSEUDO SEEMER

CLAIMANT IMPOSTOR TARTUFFE
MOUNTEBANK
(— TO LEARNING) SCIOLIST
PRETENSE ACT AIR FACE MASK MIEN
RUSE SHAM SHOW SIGN WILE CLOAK
COLOR COVER FEINT GLOSS GLOZE
EXCUSE HUMBUG CHARADE FICTION
GRIMACE PRETEXT PURPOSE UMBRAGE
ARTIFICE DISGUISE
PRETENTIOUS BIG BRAG HIGH FLASH
GAUDY PUFFY SHOWY BRAGGY CHICHI
GEWGAW GLOSSY PUFFED ROCOCO
TINSEL BOMBAST POMPOUS STILTED
TINHORN OVERBLOWN
PRETEXT FLAM MASK VEIL CLOAK
COLOR COVER GLOSS STALL EXCUSE
REFUGE APOLOGY UMBRAGE OCCASION
PRETENCE
PRETTY APT PAT ABLE BRAW CUTE DEFT
FAIR FEAT FINE GAIN GOOD MILD TRIM
BONNY JOLIE QUITE SWEET FINELY
MINION RATHER CLEMENT CUNNING
DOLLISH GENTEEL PRECIOUS
PREVAIL WIN BEAR BEAT REIGN WIELD
CONQUER PERSIST SUCCEED TRIUMPH
DOMINATE
(— UPON) GET FOLD LEAD ARGUFY
ENTICE INDUCE OBTAIN ENTREAT
OVERSWAY
PREVAILING RIFE GOING USUAL
CURRENT DOMINANT
PREVALENT UP RIFE BRIEF COMMON
POTENT VULGAR CURRENT GENERAL
POPULAR RAMPANT REGNANT CATHOLIC
EPIDEMIC POWERFUL
PREVARICATE LIE EVADE STRAY
WANDER QUIBBLE SHUFFLE WHIFFLE
PREVENT BAR LET HELP KEEP SHUN
STAY STOP WARN AVERT CHECK DEBAR
DETER ESTOP ARREST DEFEND FORBID
HINDER FORFEND INHIBIT OBVIATE
PRECEDE PARALYZE PRECLUDE PROHIBIT
WITHHOLD
PREVIOUS HASTY PRIOR BEFORE
FORMER RATHER EARLIER LEADING
FOREGONE PRECEDING
PREY ROB FEED GAME BOOTY SPOIL
QUARRY RAVAGE RAVINE VICTIM
PILLAGE PLUNDER ROBBERY
PRIAM (DAUGHTER OF —) CREUSA
POLYXENA CASSANDRA
(GRANDFATHER OF —) ILUS
(SLAYER OF —) PYRRHUS
(SON OF —) PARIS HECTOR TROILUS
(WIFE OF —) HECUBA
PRICE ANTE COST FARE FOOT ODDS RATE
BRIBE CHEAP CLOSE VALUE WORTH
CHARGE FIGURE TARIFF EXPENSE
STORAGE CARRIAGE FERRIAGE INTEREST
PRICELESS RARE COSTLY UNIQUE
UNSALABLE
PRICK DOT JAB JAG BROD BROG GOAD PECK
PROG SPUR STAB TANG URGE ERECT
POINT PREEN PUNCH BROACH LAUNCH
POUNCE SKEWER TARGET THRUST
TWINGE POINTED
PRICKLE PIKE SETA BRIAR SPEAR SPINE

THORN BASKET ACANTHA ACULEUS
SPICULA STICKLE STIMULUS
PRICKLY BURRY JAGGY SHARP SPINY
URCHIN BEARDED SPINOSE SPINOUS
STICKLY THISTLY ACULEATE ECHINATE
MURICATE SCRATCHY SPICULAR
STICKERY STINGING VEXATIOUS
PRIDE LUST POMP RUFF ADORN CREST
GLORY PLUME PREEN PRIME HUBRIS
METTLE NOSISM VANITY COMPANY
CONCEIT DISDAIN EGOTISM GLORIFY
HAUTEUR STOMACH
PRIDE AND PREJUDICE
(AUTHOR OF —) AUSTEN
(CHARACTER IN —) JANE MARY
DARCY KITTY LUCAS LYDIA BENNET
GEORGE BINGLEY COLLINS WICKHAM
CAROLINE DEBOURGH GARDINER
CATHERINE CHARLOTTE ELIZABETH
FITZWILLIAM
PRIEST ABBE DEAN EZRA IMAM MAGA
CLERK COHEN IMAUM ISIAC MOBED
PADRE PATER SABIO VICAR ZADOK
ABACES BISHOP DIVINE FALMEN FATHER
GALLAH JETHRO LEVITE POWWOW
SHAMAN ANANIAS CASSOCK CHANTER
GALLACH LAOCOON PAPALOI PATENER
PRESTER STOLIST TEACHER HANANIAH
MINISTER PENANCER SACERDOS
SEMINARY SOGGARTH VARDAPET
ZADOKITE
(— OF APOLLO) CALCHAS CHRYSEIS
(— OF CYBELE) CORYBANT
(— OF RAMA) KASHYAPA
(— OF RHEA) CURETE
(BABYLONIAN —) BEROSSOS
(BUDDHIST —) LAMA BHIKKU GELONG
POONGHIE TALAPOIN
(CHIEF —) SYRIARCH
(CHIEF — OF SHRINE) EN
(EGYPTIAN —) ARBACES CHOACHYTE
(ETRUSCAN —) LUCUMO
(EUNUCH —) GALLUS
(FRENCH —) PERE SULPICIAN
(GYPSY —) PATRICO
(HIGH —) ELI SARIP DASTUR KAHUNA
DESTOUR PHINEAS PONTIFF PRELATE
CAIAPHAS HIERARCH JEHOIADA
PONTIFEX
(HINDU —) PANDARAM
(INCA —) AMAUTA
(LAMAIST —) GETSUL
(MAORI —) TOHUNGA
(MORO —) SARIP PANDITA
(MOSLEM —) ALFAQUI TALISMAN
(PAGAN —) BABAYLAN
(PARISH —) CURA CURE PAPA POPE
PARSON PERSON SECULAR
(ROMAN —) EPULO FLAMEN
(TIBETAN —) LAMA
(VAISHNAVA —) GOSAIN
(VOODOO —) BOCOR
PRIESTESS NUN MAMBO MAMBU
DIOTIMA MAMALOI PHITONES
PYTHONESS
(— OF APOLLO) PYTHIA PHOEBAD
(— OF THE BOTTLE) BACBUC

(BABYLONIAN —) ENTUM
(VOODOO —) HORSE
PRIESTLY LEVITIC SACERDOTAL
PRIG BEG FOP BUCK DANDY FILCH STEAL
THIEF FELLOW HAGGLE PILFER TINKER
PURITAN QUIBBLE
PRIM NEAT TRIG TRIM DEMURE FORMAL
MIMSEY PRISSY PROPER STUFFY
MISSISH PRECISE STARCHY
PRIMA DONNA DIVA STAR
PRIMARY BASIC CHIEF FIRST PRIME
CAUCUS DIRECT FONTAL ARCHICAL
CARDINAL HYPOGENE ORIGINAL
PRIMEVAL PRINCIPAL
PRIMATE BISHOP GALAGO LEADER
PREMAN PRINCE
PRIME MAY FANG FILL LOAD MAIN CHIEF
COACH FIRST PRIDE TONIC YOUTH
CHOICE FLOWER SPRING CENTRAL
LEADING LUSTFUL PREPARE DOMINEER
ORIGINAL YOUTHFUL PRINCIPAL
PRIMER ABC CAP DONAT WAFER READER
CORDERY HORNBOOK
PRIMEVAL OLD NATIVE ANCIENT
OGYGIAN PRIMARY PRISTINE PRIMITIVE
PRIMITIVE DARK CRUDE EARLY FIRST
GROSS NAIVE PLAIN PRIME GOTHIC
PRIMAL SAVAGE SIMPLE ANCIENT
ARCHAIC PRIMARY PRISCAN BARBARIC
EARLIEST IGNORANT ORIGINAL PRISTINE
ABORIGINAL PRIMORDIAL
PRINCE MIN DUKE EARL EMIR KHAN KING
LORD NASI RIAL ALDER EMEER GEBIR
MIRZA ARJUNA DESPOT DYNAST
MONARCH TOPARCH ARCHDUKE
CARDINAL HOSPODAR MAMILIUS
PENDRAGON
(— OF ABYSSINIA) RAS RASSELAS
(— OF APOSTATE ANGELS) DEVIL
EBLIS
(— OF BOHEMIA) FLORIZEL
(— OF DARKNESS) DEVIL SATAN
(— OF DEMONS) BEELZEBUB
(— OF DYFED) PWYLL
(— OF SALERNO) TANCRED
(— OF SCOTLAND) ZERBINO
(— SOLD INTO SLAVERY) OROONOKO
(— WITH CHARLEMAGNE) ASTOLFO
(ANGLO-SAXON —) ATHELING
(ARAB —) SHERIF
(CHINESE —) WANG
(ETRUSCAN —) LUCUMO
(GERMAN —) FURST ELECTOR
(INDIAN —) RAJA RANA RAJAH
BHARATA AHLUWALIA
(LYCIAN —) GLAUCUS SARPEDON
(MOSLEM —) IMAM SAID SAYID SAYYID
SHEIKH SOLDAN
(PETTY —) SATRAP VERGOBRET
(SERVIAN —) CRAL
(SLAVIC —) KNEZ
(TROJAN —) HELENUS
PRINCELY NOBLE ROYAL KINGLY
STATELY SOVEREIGN
PRINCESS AIDA ELSA RANI PALLA RANEE
SARAH MADAME PSYCHE DRAUPADI
MAHARANI
(— CHANGED INTO CROW) CORONIS
(— MOTHER OF ZEUS) ANTIOPE
(— OF ARGOS) DANAE
(— OF CORINTH) CREUSA GLAUKE
(— WHO SLEW ATTILA) ILDICO
(MOHAMMEDAN —) BEGUM
(THRACIAN —) PHYLLIS
(TYRIAN —) DIDO
PRINCIPALITY ZUPA ARZAVA ARZAWA
ORANGE SATRAPY APPANAGE DESPOTAT
PRINCEDOM
PRINCIPLE JUS LAW TAO BASE FATE
RULE SEED YANG AGENT AXIOM BASIS
CANON CAUSE DATUM SPARK STUFF
TENET ANIMUS COGITO ELIXIR EMBRYO
GOSPEL BROCARD CLYSSUS ELEMENT
FORMULA GENERAL PRECEPT THEOREM
DOCTRINE LANDMARK SANCTION
SPECIFIC TINCTURE
PRINT CUT GUM RUN MARK TYPE FUDGE
PRESS SEPIA STAMP BANNER BORDER
CARBON ENFACE LETTER STRIKE
DUOTYPE ENGRAVE GRAPHIC GRAVURE
IMPRESS PUBLISH TRACING VANDYKE
VESTIGE WOODCUT AQUATONE
CALOTYPE CHLORIDE DRYPOINT
HALFTONE INSCRIBE MONOTYPE
POSITIVE
PRINTER TYPO TWICER PRESSMAN
IMPRIMENT
(AID TO —) DEVIL
PRIOR ERE OLD FORE PAST ELDER
FORMER RATHER ALREADY EARLIER
FARTHER ANTERIOR FOREHAND
HITHERTO PREVIOUS PRECEDING
PRIORITY PRIVILEGE PRECEDENCE
PREFERMENT
PRIORY ABBEY NUNNERY CLOISTER
PRIORATE
PRISON GIB JUG BRIG COOP GAOL HELL
HOCK HOLD HOLE JAIL KEEP NICK QUOD
SHOP STIR WARD CLINK FLEET LIMBO
POUND TENCH VAULT BAGNIO BAILEY
BUCKET CARCER COOLER JIGGER
BASTILE BOCARDO BULLPEN CONFINE
DUNGEON FREEZER GEHENNA LUDGATE
NEWGATE SLAMMER DARTMOOR
HOOSEGOW TRIBUNAL CALABOOSE
PENITENTIARY
PRISONER CON POW LIFER DETENU
INMATE REMAND CAITIFF CAPTIVE
CONVICT GAOLBIRD JAILBIRD
LONGTIMER
PRISONER OF ZENDA
(AUTHOR OF —) HOPE
(CHARACTER IN —) ROSE SAPT FRITZ
FLAVIA RUDOLF MICHAEL DEMAUBAN
BURLESDON ANTOINETTE RASSENDYLL
TARLENHEIM

PRISSY PRIM FUSSY DAINTY FINICKY PRUDISH PRIGGISH SISSIFIED

PRIVACY RECESS SECRET PRIVITY RETREAT SECRECY DARKNESS INTIMACY SOLITUDE SECLUSION

PRIVATE SNUG ALONE CLOSE GUIDE PRIVY SHARE CLOSET COVERT INWARD POCKET SECRET SECRECY SEVERAL SOLDIER CIVILIAN DOMESTIC ESOTERIC HOMEFELT INTERNAL INTIMATE PERSONAL SINGULAR

PRIVATEER CAPER MARQUE PIRATE ALABAMA CORSAIR CRUISER DUNKIRK PICKEER

PRIVILEGE SOC BOTE HAND STAR TEAM CLAIM ENTRY FAVOR FRANK GRACE HONOR RIGHT EXCUSE OPTION PATENT CHARTER FREEDOM LIBERTY PASSAGE PERQUISITE PREROGATIVE

PRIZE CUP GEM PRY BELL BEND GAME PALM PRIX RATE RISK AWARD BACON BOOTY LEVER PLATE PLUME PURSE STAKE VALUE WAGER ESTEEM PRAISE TROPHY BENEFIT GARLAND PREMIUM ESTIMATE LEVERAGE PURCHASE TREASURE

PRIZED DEAR CHARY

PRIZEFIGHT GO BOUT MILL MATCH SCRAP BARNEY

PRIZEFIGHTER BOXER BLEEDER FIGHTER SLUGGER PUGILIST

PROBABILITY ODDS SHOW CHANCE PERCENTAGE

PROBABLE MAYBE LIKELY APPARENT FEASIBLE POSSIBLE

PROBATION TEST PROOF TRIAL PAROLE EVIDENCE

PROBE PICK SEEK SIFT ENTER GROPE SOUND FATHOM SEARCH SEEKER STYLET THRUST TRACER ACCOUNT EXAMINE INQUIRY

PROBLEM NUT WHY CRUX KNOT HYDRA POSER APORIA ENIGMA BUGBEAR DILEMMA GORDIAN TICKLER EXERCISE HEADACHE JEOPARDY QUESTION STICKLER SITUATION
(CHESS —) DUAL MOVER SUIMATE MINIATURE

PROBLEMATICAL DUBIOUS DOUBTFUL PUZZLING UNCERTAIN UNDECIDED

PROBOSCIS NOSE SNOUT TRUNK LINGUA SIPHON TONGUE ROSTRUM

PROCEDURE FORM VEIN DRAFT ORDER TENOR TRACK AFFAIR COURSE METHOD POLITY SYSTEM DRAUGHT PROCESS PRODUCT ACTIVITY PROTOCOL OPERATION
(PRESCRIBED —S) CEREMONY
(ROUNDABOUT —) CIRCUITY
(SECRET —) STEALTH
(STANDARDIZED —) BIT
(UNWISE —) FOLLY

PROCEED DO GO BEAR FARE FLOW MAKE MARK MOVE PASS ROAM ROLL SEEK STEP TAKE TOOL TOUR WEAR WEND WIND AMBLE ARISE DRESS ISSUE MARCH REACH TRACE BREEZE PURSUE RESULT SPRING TRAVEL ADVANCE AGGRESS CONTINUE PROGRESS
(— AIMLESSLY) CIRCLE
(— ALONE) SINGLE
(— AWKWARDLY) SCHLEPP
(— CLUMSILY) FLOUNDER
(— OBLIQUELY) CUT
(— RAGGEDLY) HALT
(— RAPIDLY) RAKE STRETCH
(— UNSTEADILY) DRIDDLE
(— WITH DIFFICULTY) STRUGGLE

PROCEEDING ACT DEED FARE PLOY STEP AFFAIR COURSE ISSUANT MEASURE ONGOING PASSANT INSTANCE PRACTICE
(— BY THREES) TERNARY
(— FROM GOD) DIVINE
(— FROM THE EARTH) TELLURIC
(COURT —S) TRIAL ACTION
(INDIRECT —S) AMBAGES
(PARLIAMENTARY —S) HUSTINGS
(RECORDED —S) ACTA

PROCESS RUN FOOT WRIT CREST FURCA SPINA CALCAR CILIUM COURSE FEELER HABEAS METHOD REPORT ACCOUNT BARBULE FURCULA LAMELLA MANDATE SPATULA SUMMONS ACROMION ACTIVITY APPENDIX FILAMENT INSTANCE MANUBRIUM OPERATION

PROCESSION POMP WALK DRIVE TRACE TRAIN BRIDAL EXEQUY LITANY PARADE STREAM CORTEGE FUNERAL TRIUMPH ENTRANCE PROGRESS MOTORCADE
(BOISTEROUS —) SKIMMITY
(IRISH CIVIC —) FRINGES
(SUFF.) CADE

PROCLAIM BID CRY BAWL DEEM OYEZ SING TOOT TOUT BLARE BLAZE BOAST CLAIM KNELL SOUND SPEAK BLAZON HERALD INDICT OUTCRY CLARION DECLARE DIVULGE PROTEST PUBLISH TRUMPET ANNOUNCE DENOUNCE RENOUNCE
(— ALOUD) ROAR
(— PUBLICLY) PRECONIZE
(— WITH BIG TALK) BOUNCE

PROCLAMATION CRY HUE FIAT OYEZ BANDO BANNS BLAZE EDICT UKASE PLACARD PROGRAM

PROCRASTINATE LAG TIME DEFER DELAY LINGER ADJOURN POSTPONE TEMPORIZE

PROCTOR LIAR PROG ACTOR AGENT PROXY BEGGAR RECTOR MONITOR PROCUTOR

PROCURE GET WIN FIND GAIN HALE BRING INFER TOUCH EFFECT INDUCE OBTAIN ACHIEVE ACQUIRE COMPARE CONQUER CONTRIVE PURCHASE

PROD DAB EGG GIG JAB JOG BROD BROG GOAD POKE PROG GOOSE HURRY NUDGE PROBE INCITE JOSTLE THRUST IRRITATE

PRODIGAL FLUSH LARGE COSTLY LAVISH WANTON WASTER PROFUSE SPENDER PROFLIGATE

PRODIGIOUS HUGE VAST GIANT AMAZING IMMENSE STRANGE

ABNORMAL ENORMOUS GIGANTIC
MONSTROUS PORTENTOUS

PRODIGY OMEN SIGN MARVEL OSTENT
WIZARD WONDER MIRACLE MONSTER
PORTENT CEREMONY

PRODUCE DO GO BEAR FORM GIVE
GROW MAKE REAR SHOW WAGE BEGET
BIRTH BREED BRING BROOD BUILD
CAUSE DRIVE FORGE FRAME HATCH
ISSUE RAISE SPAWN THROW TRADE
YIELD CREATE EFFECT GROWTH INCOME
INVENT SECURE ADVANCE ANIMATE
COMPOSE INSPIRE PRODUCT PROLONG
CONCEIVE ENGENDER GENERATE
INCREASE LENGTHEN OFFSPRING
(— A COPY OF) TYPE
(— AN EFFECT) ACT AFFECT
(— AUDIBLE EFFECT) SOUND
(— CROPS) CARRY
(— DULL APPEARANCE) CHILL
(— FREELY) PULLULATE
(— FRUIT) TEEM
(— HEAT) ENRAGE
(— IN SPECIFIED FORM) FORMAT
(— PAID FOR RENT) CAIN
(— SHARP NOISE) CRINK
(AGRICULTURAL —) PODWARE
(FARM —) HUSBANDRY
(MINING —) LEY

PRODUCT HEIR ITEM BRAND CHILD
FRUIT GROSS OUTGO SPAWN FABRIC
GROWTH RESULT UPCOME FALLOUT
OUTTURN PRODUCE PROGENY TURNOUT
OUTBIRTH OFFSPRING

PRODUCTIVE FAT RICH LOOSE QUICK
ACTIVE BATTLE STRONG CAUSING
FERTILE GAINFUL HEALTHY TEEMING
CREATIVE FRUITFUL GERMINAL
PLENTEOUS

PROFANE BLUE FOUL ABUSE COARSE
DEBASE DEFILE UNHOLY VULGAR
WICKED GODLESS IMPIOUS POLLUTE
SECULAR UNGODLY VIOLATE WORLDLY
TEMPORAL UNHALLOW

PROFANITY OATH CURSE CURSING
LANGUAGE BLASPHEMY

PROFESS OWN AVOW ADMIT CLAIM
AFFIRM ALLEGE ASSERT ASSUME
FOLLOW PRESUME PRETEND PURPORT
PRACTICE

PROFESSION ART BAR LAW FEAT GAME
WALK CRAFT FAITH FORTE TRADE
CAREER CHURCH EMPLOY METIER
CALLING FACULTY QUALITY SERVICE
ADVOCACY BUSINESS FUNCTION
PEDAGOGY SOLDIERY VOCATION
(SUFF.) SHIP

PROFESSIONAL PRO COLT PAID HIRED
EXPERT SKILLED TRAINED FINISHED

PROFESSOR DON ESTOP HANIF KHOJA
LAWYER REGENT ADJOINT ACADEMIC
CIVILIAN EMERITUS

PROFFER BID GIVE TEND DEFER ESSAY
OFFER EXTEND TENDER ATTEMPT
PRESENT

PROFICIENCY SIGHT SKILL ABILITY
APTNESS

PROFICIENT ADEPT EXPERT MASTER
SALTED VERSED PERFECT SKILLED
SKILLFUL

PROFILE FORM FLANK PURFLE SKETCH
CONTOUR OUTLINE SECTION

PROFIT AID GET NET WIN BOOT GAIN
SKIN VAIL AVAIL EDIFY GRIST LUCRE
SCALP BEHOOF INCOME MAKING PAYOFF
RETURN ACCOUNT ADVANCE BENEFIT
CLEANUP FURTHER IMPROVE REVENUE
VANTAGE WINNING INCREASE INTEREST
PERCENTAGE

PROFITABLE FAT GOOD UTILE GOLDEN
PLUMMY GAINFUL HELPFUL PAYABLE
BEHOVELY ECONOMIC PROVABL
REPAYING VAILABLE REWARDING

PROFLIGATE ROUE DEFEAT CORRUPT
IMMORAL RIOTOUS SPENDER VICIOUS
WASTREL DEPRAVED FLAGRANT
RAKEHELL WASTEFUL

PROFOUND DEEP HARD WISE HEAVY
SOUND THICK STRONG ABYSMAL
INTENSE ABSTRUSE COMPLETE
PREGNANT REACHING THOROUGH

PROFUNDITY ABYSS DEPTH FATHOM
DEEPNESS

PROFUSE FREE LUSH FRANK GALORE
LAVISH COPIOUS LIBERAL OPULENT
ABUNDANT GENEROUS PRODIGAL
WASTEFUL REDUNDANT

PROFUSION WASTE EXCESS LAVISH
FLUENCY OPULENCE REDUNDANCY

PROGNOSTICATE BODE AUGUR SPELL
BETOKEN CONJECT PREDICT PRENOTE
FOREBODE FORESHOW FORETELL
PROPHESY

PROGNOSTICATOR SEER DOOMER
PROPHET HARUSPEX

PROGRAM CARD SHOW FORUM AGENDA
DESIGN SCHEME PREFACE CLAMBAKE
FESTIVAL GIVEAWAY GUIDANCE
JAMBOREE PLAYBILL SCHEDULE
SEQUENCE SYLLABUS

PROGRESS WAY FARE GAIN GROW
MOVE RACE RISE STEP TOUR WEND
BUILD DRIFT FORGE GOING MARCH
SWING ASCENT BUFFET COURSE
GROWTH ADVANCE DEVELOP FOOTING
HEADWAY IMPROVE JOURNEY PASSAGE
PROCESS PROFICIENCY

PROGRESSION WAY SWING COURSE
GALLOP ADVANCE PASSAGE PROGRESS
SEQUENCE
(— OF CHORDS) SWIPE
(MUSICAL —) SKIP
(SMOOTH —) SLIDE

PROGRESSIVE ACTIVE ONWARD
FORWARD GRADUAL LIBERAL

PROHIBIT BAN BAR STOP VETO BLOCK
DEBAR ESTOP DEFEND ENJOIN FORBID
HINDER OUTLAW FORFEND FORWARN
INHIBIT PREVENT DISALLOW PRECLUDE
SUPPRESS PROSCRIBE

PROHIBITED HOT TABU TABOO ILLEGAL
ILLICIT UNLAWFUL VERBOTEN

PROJECT JET JUT LAP BEAM CAST
GAME IDEA PLAN POKE PUSH SAIL SWIM

BULGE CHART DRAFT DRIVE IMAGE SETUP SHOOT STICK THROW BEETLE DESIGN DEVICE ESTATE EXTEND FILLIP OUTJUT PROPEL SCHEME SCREEN SHELVE EXTRUDE IMAGINE OUTCROP PATTERN BUSINESS CONTRIVE OUTREACH OUTSHOOT OVERHANG PROPOSAL PROTRUDE

PROJECTILE BALL BOLT CASE SHOT SHAFT TRACER FIREBALL SHRAPNEL
(— DESIGNED TO SET FIRE TO HOUSES) CARCASS
(EXPLOSIVE —) BOMB SHELL
(SUBMARINE —) TORPEDO

PROJECTING BEETLE EMINENT JUTTING PENDENT SALIENT PROMINENT OUTSTANDING

PROJECTION ARM CAM COG DOG EAR FIN JET JOG JUT NUT TOE BEAK BOSS BROW COCK CUSP HEEL HORN KEEL KINK KNAG KNOB LOBE SAIL SNUG SPUD SPUR TEAT WING BULGE CLEAT ELBOW SCRAG SHANK SHOOT SPIKE TOOTH BRANCH CALCAR CORBEL FUSULA HEARTH ICICLE NOSING PALATE RELISH TAPPET BREAKER CONSOLE DRAWING EPAULET KNUCKLE LANGUET ORILLON PRICKER PRICKLE RESSAUT AJUTMENT EMINENCE OVERHANG SALIENCE SHOULDER PROMINENCE
(— CONNECTING TIMBER) COAK
(— EXTENDING BACKWARD) BARB
(— FROM CASTING) SPRUE
(— FROM SHIP'S KEEL) SPONSON
(— IN CLOCK) SQUARE
(— IN ORCHIDS) MENTUM
(— OF FOREHEAD) ANTINION
(— OF JAW) GNATHISM
(— OF PEAT) HAG
(— OF RAFTER) SALLY
(— OF TERRITORY) PANHANDLE
(— ON CANNON) CASCABEL
(— ON CHURCH SEAT) MISERICORD
(— ON GUN) CROC LUMP
(— ON HARNESS) HAME
(— ON HORSE'S LEG) FETLOCK
(— ON HORSESHOE) STICKER
(— ON LOCK) FENCE STUMP
(— ON MAST) STOP
(— ON OVARY) STIGMA
(— ON POCKETKNIFE) KICK
(— ON SALMON JAW) GIB
(— ON WHEEL) GUB GROUSER GROUTER
(— OVER AIR PORT) EYEBROW
(FIREPLACE —) HOB
(JAGGED —) SNUG
(SHARP —) BARB FANG
(SUBMERGED —) KNOLL

PROLIFIC BIRTHY BREEDY FECUND FERTILE PROFUSE TEEMING ABUNDANT FRUITFUL SPAWNING

PROLOGUE BANNS INDEX PREFACE

PROLONG LONG SPIN DEFER DELAY DRIVE DILATE EXTEND LINGER SPREAD PRODUCE RESPITE SUSTAIN CONTINUE LENGTHEN POSTPONE PROTRACT

PROLONGED GREAT PROLIX DELAYED EXTENDED SOSTENUTO

PROMENADE BUND MALL PIER PROM WALK CORSO FRONT PASEO PRADO MARINA PARADE ALAMEDA GALLERY FRESCADE BOULEVARD

PROMETHEUS (BROTHER OF —) ATLAS MENOETIUS EPIMETHEUS
(FATHER OF —) IAPETUS
(MOTHER OF —) CLYMENE

PROMINENCE BUR BOSS BURR CUSP KNOB UMBO AGGER BULLA CREST SWELL TUBER ACCENT NODULE BUTTOCK CONDYLE FASHION HAMULUS KNUCKLE LINGULA AMYGDALA EMINENCE EMPHASIS SALIENCE PROMONTORY

PROMINENT BIG BOLD GREAT STEEP BEETLE MARKED SIGNAL BLATANT BOLTING CAPITAL EMINENT JUTTING LEADING NOTABLE OBVIOUS SALIENT AQUILINE BEETLING MANIFEST STRIKING NOTICEABLE CONSPICUOUS

PROMISCUOUS LIGHT CASUAL RANDOM CARELESS

PROMISE VOW AVOW BAND HOPE PASS SURE WORD FAITH GRANT HIGHT TRUTH ASSURE BEHEST ENGAGE FIANCE INSURE PAROLE PLEDGE PLIGHT WARRANT CONTRACT COVENANT GUARANTY BETROTHAL OBLIGATION
(— IN MARRIAGE) BETROTH ESPOUSE AFFIANCE
(— TO PAY) NOTE ACCEPT
(— TO TAKE IN MARRIAGE) AFFY

PROMISING APT FAIR BRIGHT LIKELY TOWARD

PROMONTORY BEAK BILL HEAD NESS NOOK PEAK ELBOW MORRO POINT REACH SNOUT SALIENT FORELAND HEADLAND

PROMOTE AID HELP LOFT PUSH AVAIL BOOST EXALT NURSE RAISE SERVE SPEED ASSIST EXCITE FOMENT FOSTER LAUNCH PREFER ADVANCE DIGNIFY ELEVATE FORWARD FURTHER IMPROVE PREFECT PRODUCE SUCCEED SUPPORT INCREASE

PROMOTION LIFT REMOVE ADVANCE PROMOVAL

PROMPT APT CUE MOVE URGE ALERT QUICK READY SERVE SWIFT EXCITE INDITE NIMBLE SPEEDY SUDDEN ANIMATE FORWARD PROVOKE SUGGEST PUNCTUAL REMINDER

PROMPTLY UP PAT TID SOON PRONTO PRESTLY QUICKLY DIRECTLY SPEEDILY

PROMPTNESS ALACRITY CELERITY DISPATCH

PROMULGATE SPREAD DECLARE PUBLISH PROCLAIM

PRONE APT BENT EASY FLAT FREE BUXOM GIVEN LIABLE SUPINE BEASTLY BESTIAL DORMANT SUBJECT ADDICTED COUCHANT DISPOSED DOWNWARD

PRONG NEB NIB PEG BILL FANG FORK HOOK SPUR TANG SPADE FOURCHE

(— FOR EXTRACTING BUNG) TICKLER
(— FOR FISH) PEW PUGH
(— OF ANTLER) KNAG TIND TINE POINT
(— OF FORK) SPEAN

PRONOUN HE IT ME MY WE YE ANY HER
HIM HIS ONE OUR SHE THY WHO YOU
OURS THAT THEM THEY THOU WHAT
WHOM THINE WHICH WHOSE
ITSELF MYSELF HERSELF HIMSELF
OURSELF WHOEVER YOURSELF
OURSELVES
(GENDERLESS —) THON

PRONOUNCE SAY PASS SPEAK UTTER
PREACH RECITE TONGUE ADJUDGE
CENSURE ASPIRATE

PRONOUNCED HIGH MARKED DECIDED
HOWLING INTENSE MOVABLE
(— AS FRICATIVE) GRASSEYE
(— PALATALLY) MOUILLE
(NOT —) SOFT

PRONOUNCEMENT FIAT CURSE
DICTUM DICTAMEN

PRONUNCIATION BROGUE DICTION
ETACISM LIAISON DELIVERY ENCLISIS
(BAD —) CACOEPY CACOLOGY
LABDACISM
(BROAD —) PLATEASM
(CORRECT —) ORTHOEPY
(ROUGH —) BUR BURR

PROOF SAY MARK PULL SLIP TEST ESSAY
TOKEN TOUCH TRIAL GALLEY ORDEAL
REASON RESULT REVISE ATTEMPT
OUTCOME PROBATE SHOWING UTTERLY
VOUCHER WARRANT ANALYSIS
DOCUMENT EVIDENCE GOODNESS
MONUMENT
(— OF WRONGDOING) GOODS
(ABSOLUTE —) APODIXIS
(INDIRECT —) APAGOGE

PROP LEG BUNT POST REST SPUR STAY
STUD BRACE PERCH SHORE SHOVE
SPRAG SPURN STAFF STOOP STULL
COLUMN CROTCH CRUTCH PILLAR
SHORER STAYER UPHOLD BOLSTER
FULCRUM PINNING STUDDLE SUPPORT
SUSTAIN BUTTRESS CROTCHET
(— FOR CART) NEAP
(— FOR ROOF OF MINE) GIB
(— UP) CUSHION SCAFFOLD

PROPAGANDA BOLOISM AGITPROP
BALLYHOO

PROPAGATE BREED HATCH EXTEND
SPREAD DIFFUSE PRODUCE PUBLISH
ENGENDER GENERATE INCREASE
MULTIPLY POPULATE TRANSMIT
PROCREATE

PROPEL ROW CALL CAST FIRE FLIP PUSH
SEND URGE DRIVE FLICK IMPEL KNOCK
RANGE SPANK THROW HURTLE LAUNCH
PROJECT
(— BALL) STROKE
(— BOAT) OAR ROW SET KENT POLE
SCULL BUSHWACK
(— BOAT WITH FEET) LEG
(— ONESELF) HAUL
(— PUCK) CARRY
(— SUDDENLY) ZAP

PROPELLER FAN HELIX SCREW
AIRSCREW WINDMILL

PROPENSITY YEN BENT ITCH APTNESS
IMPULSE LEANING APPETITE FONDNESS
INTEREST TENDENCY

PROPER FIT OWN GOOD JUST MEET
TRUE WELL RIGHT COMELY DECENT
HONEST LAWFUL MODEST SEEMLY
CAPITAL CORRECT FITTING GRADELY
SEEMING SKILFUL ABSOLUTE BECOMING
DECOROUS RIGHTFUL SUITABLE
VIRTUOUS

PROPERLY DULY WELL FITLY TRULY
ARIGHT FAIRLY FEATLY GLADLY MEETLY
RIGHTLY

PROPERTY AVER TOOL ASSET AUGHT
GRANT MOYEN STATE STOCK THING
WORTH APPEAL HAVIOR LIVING REALTY
TALENT USINGS WEALTH ACQUEST
APANAGE ESCHEAT ESSENCE FACULTY
FITNESS HARNESS HAVINGS QUALITY
ALLODIAL PECULIUM POSSESSION
(— BELONGING TO WOMAN)
STRIDHAN
(— FROM WIFE TO HUSBAND) DOS
(— GIVEN BY WILL) DEVISE
(— SECURED DISHONESTLY) HARL
(— SEIZED BY FORCE) SPOIL
(ABSOLUTE —) ALODIUM
(ENEMY —) HEREM
(LANDED —) DOMAIN ESTATE DEMESNE
PRAEDIUM
(MOVABLE —) GEAR CHATTEL EFFECTS
CATALLUM
(PERSONAL —) FEE BONA GOODS
STUFF INSIGHT PLUNDER
(PRIVATE —) SEVERAL
(RURAL —) FINCA
(STOLEN —) PELF MAINOR STEALTH
(THEATRICAL —S) PROPS

PROPHECY WEIRD EXHORT PREACH
PREDICT BODEMENT FORECAST
SOOTHSAY

PROPHESY AUGUR DIVINE EXHORT
PREACH OMINATE PORTEND PREDICT
FORETELL

PROPHET GAD AMOS JOEL SEER ANGEL
AUGUR DRUID ELIAS HOSEA JONAH
MICAH MOSES NAHUM SILAS SYRUS
ARIOLE BALAAM DANIEL ELIJAH HAGGAI
ISAIAH MERLIN MORONI NATHAN
PYTHON SAMUEL EZEKIEL MALACHI
HABAKKUK JEREMIAH

PROPHETESS ANNA ANNE HULDA SIBYL
PYTHIA DEBORAH SEERESS VOLUSPA
DRUIDESS CASSANDRA PYTHONESS

PROPHETIC FATAL VATIC MANTIC
FATEFUL MANTIAN DELPHIAN ORACULAR
SIBYLLIC

PROPITIOUS FAIR KIND HAPPY LUCKY
BENIGN KINDLY HELPFUL FRIENDLY
GRACIOUS MERCIFUL TOWARDLY
FAVORABLE PROMISING AUSPICIOUS

PROPORTION LOT SIZE FRAME QUOTA
RATIO SCALE SHARE ACCORD DEGREE
EXTENT FORMAT QUOTUM BALANCE

MEASURE EURYTHMY SYMMETRY PERCENTAGE

PROPOSE FACE MOVE PLAN POSE SHOW WISH OFFER ALLEGE DESIGN INJECT INTEND MOTION ADVANCE EXHIBIT IMAGINE PURPOSE SUPPOSE CONFRONT

PROPOSITION FACT AXIOM MODAL OFFER THEME AFFAIR MEMBER GENERAL INVERSE PROBLEM PURPOSE THEOREM IDENTITY JUDGMENT NEGATION OVERTURE PROPOSAL SINGULAR SUPPOSAL

PROPRIETOR LORD LAIRD OWNER MASTER PATRON YEOMAN ESQUIRE PATROON BONIFACE

PROPRIETY GRACE ESTATE NATURE REASON DECENCY DECORUM ESSENCE FITNESS HOLDING MODESTY CIVILITY PROPERTY ETIQUETTE

PROSAIC DRAB DULL FLAT PROSY PROLIX STODGY STOLID STUPID FACTUAL HUMDRUM INSIPID LITERAL TEDIOUS SOULLESS TIRESOME WORKADAY

PROSE CHAT GOSSIP PROSAIC TEDIOUS SEQUENCE ELOQUENCE

PROSECUTE SUE HOLD URGE CARRY ENSUE ACCUSE CHARGE DEDUCE FOLLOW INDICT INTEND PURSUE IMPLEAD PROCESS

PROSELYTE CONVERT NICOLAS NEOPHYTE PURSUANT
(JEWISH —) GER

PROSPECT HOPE VIEW SCENE VISTA CHANCE FUTURE REGARD SEARCH SURVEY COMMAND EXPLORE HORIZON LOOKOUT OUTLOOK PROJECT
(— FOR GOLD) SPECK
(— WITHOUT SYSTEM) GOPHER
(FORBIDDING —) DESERT

PROSPER DO LIKE RISE EDIFY FRAME SPEED BATTEN THRIVE BLOSSOM SUCCEED FLOURISH

PROSPERITY HAP GLEE GOOD WEAL HEALTH THRIFT FORTUNE SUCCESS WELFARE FLOURISH

PROSPEROUS UP FAT BIEN GOOD FELIX FLUSH HAPPY LUCKY PALMY GILDED HALCYON HEALTHY THRIFTY SUNSHINE THRIVING WEALSOME

PROSTITUTE CAT COW DOG AUNT BAWD DOXY DRAB PUNK SLUT TART PAGAN WHORE BULKER CHIPPY GIRLIE HARLOT HOOKER MUTTON TOMATO BAGGAGE CRUISER CYPRIAN HETAERA HUSTLER PUCELLE BERDACHE MAGDALEN MERETRIX SLATTERN STRUMPET COURTESAN

PROSTRATE LOW FELL FLAT RAZE PRONE THROW FALLEN REPENT WEAKEN FLATTEN DEJECTED HELPLESS OVERCOME DEPRESSED

PROTAGONIST HERO ACTOR LEADER PALADIN ADVOCATE CHAMPION

PROTECT CAP BANK DIKE FEND FORT KEEP SAVE WARD WEAR CHAIN CLOUT COVER FENCE GRATE GUARD HEDGE SHADE SHEND BORROW DEFEND SCREEN SHADOW BULWARK CHERISH CUSHION FORFEND SECLUDE SHELTER SUPPORT WARRANT CHAMPION DEFILADE PRESERVE SAFEGUARD
(— AGAINST RAIN) FLASH
(— BY COVERING) HILL
(— BY WINDING WITH WIRE) GANGE
(— FROM INTRUSION) TILE
(— IRON OR STEEL) BARFF

PROTECTION LEE EGIS WARD AEGIS ARMOR BIELD COVER GUARD SHADE TOWER AMULET ASYLUM CONVOY ESCORT FENDER REFUGE SAFETY SCREEN SHADOW SHROUD AUSPICE CUSTODY DEFENCE HOUSING SHELTER UMBRAGE WARRANT COVERAGE DEFILADE PASSPORT SECURITY WARDSHIP SAFEGUARD
(— FOR SAILOR) HORSE
(— FROM LOSS) INDEMNITY
(— FROM RAIN) OMBRIFUGE
(— FROM SUN) HAVELOCK
(— FROM WEATHER) LEWTH
(— RIGHT) MUND

PROTECTOR BIB GUARD BRACER KEEPER PATRON REGENT WARRANT DEFENDER GUARDIAN

PROTEST AVER BEEF FUSS HOWL KICK CROAK DEMUR AFFIRM ASSERT BOWWOW EXCEPT HOLLER OBJECT PLAINT SQUAWK SQUEAL CONTEST INVEIGH RHUBARB HARRUMPH

PROTOCOL PROCEDURE

PROTOTYPE IDEAL MODEL FATHER EXAMPLE PATTERN ANTITYPE EXEMPLAR

PROTRACT DRAG DRAW SPIN DEFER DELAY DRIVE TRAIL TRAIN DILATE EXTEND LINGER SPREAD PROLONG CONTINUE LENGTHEN PROROGUE

PROTRACTED LONG PROLIX LENGTHY DRAGGING EXTENDED

PROTRUDE BUG JUT POKE POUT BULGE POUCH SHOOT START STICK STRUT SWELL EXSERT EXTEND EXTRUDE PROJECT OUTREACH

PROTUBERANCE BUD NOB NUB BOLL BOSS BULB BUMP HEEL HUMP KNAP KNOB KNOP KNOT LUMP NODE SNAG STUB BULGE BUNCH CAPUT GLAND GNARL HUNCH KNURL SWELL TORUS TUBER TUMOR BREAST CALLUS HUBBLE CRANKLE EXTANCY PAPILLA MAMELEON NODOSITY SWELLING APOPHYSIS PROJECTION
(— AT BASE OF BIRD'S BILL) CERE SNOOD
(— BEARING SPINE) UMBO
(— FROM SWELLING) PUFF
(— IN SIDE OF DEER) FLANKARD
(— ON A CASTING) SCAB
(— ON BONE) CONDYLE EMINENCE
(— ON HORSE'S HOOF) BUTTRESS
(— ON MANDIBLE OF GEESE) BEAN
(— ON SADDLEBOW) POMMEL
(— ON SALAMANDER) BALANCER
(— ON TONGUE) PAPILLA

(KNOBLIKE —) CAPUT
(OCCIPITAL —) INION
(RAGGED —) JAG
(ROUGH —) HUB
(SKIN —) WEN MOLE WART PIMPLE
PROTUBERANT BULGY BUMPY PROUD
TUMID BUCKED GOGGLE BULGING
BUNCHED EMINENT GIBBOUS SALIENT
SWOLLEN PROMINENT PROTRUSIVE
PROUD GLAD HIGH RANK VAIN CHUFF
GREAT JELLY LOFTY NOBLE SAUCY
STEEP STIFF STOUT WINDY ELATED
FIERCE LORDLY UPPISH UPPITY VAUNTY
HAUGHTY SUBLIME SWOLLEN TOPPING
ARROGANT EXULTANT GLORIOUS
IMPOSING INSOLENT SPLENDID
TOPLOFTY OVERBEARING
PROVE TRY SHOW TEST ARGUE ASSAY
TAINT TASTE TEMPT ARGUFY EVINCE
SUFFER VERIFY CONFESS CONFIRM
CONVICT IMPROVE JUSTIFY CONCLUDE
CONVINCE INDICATE INSTRUCT
MANIFEST
(— FALSE) BELIE BETRAY FALSIFY
(— GUILTY) ATTAINT
(— ONESELF) ACQUIT
(— OUT) SERVE
(— TITLE) DEDUCE
(— VALID) DEFEND
PROVERB SAW SAY WORD ADAGE
AXIOM CREED GNOME SOOTH BALLAD
BYWORD DITTON SAYING WHEEZE
BYSPELL IMPRESA PARABLE APHORISM
PAROEMIA SCHOLIUM
PROVIDE DO FIT SEE FEND FILL FIND
GIRD LEND CATER ENDOW ENDUE EQUIP
SPEED STOCK STORE AFFORD PURVEY
SUPPLY COMPARE EXHIBIT FORESEE
FURNISH PREPARE ACCOUTER
APPANAGE DISPENSE PURCHASE
PROVIDED IF BODEN FIXED READY
SOBEIT PROVISO INSTRUCT PREPARED
PROVIDENCE THRIFT ECONOMY
PRUDENCE
PROVIDENT WARY WISE FRUGAL
SAVING CAREFUL PRUDENT THRIFTY
PROVINCIAL HICK CRUDE NARROW
RUSTIC STUFFY INSULAR MOFUSSIL
SUBURBAN PAROCHIAL
PROVISION BOARD CARE GRIST
FODDER MATTER PURVEY UNLESS
CAUTION CODICIL DOWNSET KEEPING
SLEEPER VICTUAL
(—S FOR JOURNEY) VIATICUM
(BOUGHT —S) ACATES ACATERY
(SUBORDINATE —) ITEM
PROVISO SALVO CAVEAT CLAUSE
CAUTION CONDITION
PROVOCATIVE GUTTY SALTY PIQUANT
IRRITANT APPEALING
PROVOKE EGG GIG IRE TAR VEX DARE
HUFF MOVE PICK STIR TEEN URGE WORK
ANGER ANNOY EVOKE PIQUE TAUNT
TEMPT APPEAL ELICIT EVINCE EXCITE
GRIEVE HARASS INCITE KINDLE NETTLE
PROMPT SUMMON TICKLE AFFRONT

ILLICIT INCENSE INFLAME INSPIRE
IRRITATE
PROW BOW BEAK SPUR STEM SNOUT
SPERON STEVEN GALLANT VALIANT
(— OF GONDOLA) FERRO
PROWESS FEAT VALOR BRAVERY
COURAGE
PROWL OWL ROAM LURCH MOOCH
MOUSE RAVEN RAMBLE
PROXIMITY SHADOW NEARNESS
PRESENCE VICINITY PROPINQUITY
NEIGHBORHOOD
PRUDENCE CARE ADVICE WISDOM
CAUTION COUNSEL SLEIGHT FORELOOK
PRUDENT FIT SAFE SAGE WARY WISE
CANNY SOLID FRUGAL QUAINT POLITIC
CAUTIOUS DISCREET PROVIDENT
PRUDISH NICE PRIM MIMSEY PRIGGISH
PUDIBUND
PRY NOSE NOTE PEEK PEEP PEER JIMMY
LEVER PRIZE SNOOP FERRET PUTTER
CROWBAR GUMSHOE
(— ABOUT) OWL MOUSE SNOOK
SCROUNGE
(— INTO) BREVIT
PRYING NOSY PEERY CURIOUS PEEPING
PSALM ODE HYMN SONG DIRGE GATHA
TRACT ANTHEM CHORALE INTROIT
MISERERE
(100TH —) JUBILATE
(95TH —) VENITE
(98TH —) CANTATE
PSEUDONYM ALIAS ANONYM JUNIUS
PSYCHE MIND SELF SOUL
PSYCHIATRIST SHRINK ALIENIST
PSYCHOSIS INSANITY PARANOIA
SENILITY MELANCHOLIA
PSYCHOTIC MAD CRAZY INSANE
PUB BAR INN BISTRO BOOZER LOUNGE
SHANTY TAVERN
PUBLIC OPEN TOWN CIVIC OVERT
WORLD COMMON SOCIAL VULGAR
GENERAL OMNIBUS POPULAR EXTERNAL
MATERIAL NATIONAL MULTITUDE
PUBLICATION BOOK ORDO BIBLE FOLIO
ISSUE SHEET ANNUAL SERIAL WEEKLY
ALMANAC BOOKLET JOURNAL MONTHLY
WRITING BIWEEKLY BULLETIN
DOCUMENT EMISSION PERIODICAL
PUBLICITY AIR BLAZE ECLAT BUILDUP
PUFFERY BALLYHOO BROUHAHA
PROMOTION
PUBLICIZE CRY PLUG BLURB BRUIT
HERALD BALLYHOO HEADLINE
PROPAGATE
PUBLIC SQUARE PLAZA PLEIN ZOCALO
PUBLISH AIR BLOW EDIT EMIT VEND
VENT CARRY ISSUE PRINT SPEAK UTTER
BLAZON BROACH EVULGE EXPOSE
SPREAD DECLARE DIFFUSE DIVULGE
PROTEST RELEASE DISCLOSE PROCLAIM
PROMULGE
PUBLISHER CRIER EDITOR PRINTER
STATIONER
PUCKER DRAW RUCK PURSE REEVE
COCKLE COTTER FURROW RUCKLE

WRINKLE CONTRACT AGITATION
CONSTRICT
PUCKERED PURSY BULLATE COCKLED
ROUCHED WRINKLED BULLIFORM
PUDDING DICK SAGO BOMBE DOWDY
KUGEL BURGOO HAGGIS SPONGE
TANSEY DESSERT BLOODING PANDOWDY
WHITEPOT CHARLOTTE
(— CONTAINING KALE) TARTAN
(— OF FLOUR) DUFF
(BOILED —) HOY
(FRUIT —) HEDGEHOG
(HASTY —) MUSH SEPON SUPAWN
(HAWAIIAN —) HAUPIA
(MEAT —) ISING CHEWET HACKIN
HACKING
(SUET —) KUGEL
PUDDLE POOL ROIL SLAB SLOP SOSS
SUMP FLUSH PLANT PLASH CHARCO
KENNEL MUDDLE SPLASH TAMPER
CONFUSE PLASHET BEFUDDLE
PUDGY MIRY BULKY MUDDY SQUAT
CHUBBY
PUERILE WEAK SILLY BOYISH JEJUNE
TRIVIAL CHILDISH IMMATURE YOUTHFUL

PUERTO RICO

BAY: SUCIA RINCON BOQUERON
AQUADILLA
CAPITAL: SANJUAN
ISLAND: MONA CULEBRA VIEQUES
LAKE: LOIZA CARITE CAONILLAS
MEASURE: CUERDA CABALLERIA
RIVER: CAMUY CANAS YAUCO ANASCO
TANANA FAJARDO
TOWN: CAYEY COAMO PONCE ANASCO
DORADO MANATI ARECIBO BAYAMON
FAJARDO GUAYAMA HUMACAO
MAYAGUEZ

PUFF POP BRAG DRAG GUFF HUFF PANT
SHOW WAFT BLURB BLURT ELATE ERUPT
EXTOL FLUFF SWELL WHIFF CAPFUL
EXPAND BLUSTER EXPLODE GRATIFY
WHIFFET BRAGGART OVERRATE
(— FROM SHELL BLAST) BURST
(— OF WIND) FLAM TIFT SCART SLANT
FLATUS HUFFLE
(— ON MARIJUANA CIGARETTE)
TOKE
(— OUT) BELL BLUB VENT BLOUSE
BLUBBER EFFLATE INFLATE
(— OUT SMOKE) EFFUME
(— UP) BLOW HUFF RISE BLOAT HEAVE
BLADDER
(— VIOLENTLY) BLAST
(SUDDEN —) FLAN FLAW GUST
PUFFY SOFT BAGGY BLOAT GUSTY PURSY
CHUBBY FLUFFY PURFLY PURSIVE
SWOLLEN BLADDERY BOUFFANT
DROPSICAL
PUGNACIOUS BELLICOSE
PULCHRITUDE GRACE BEAUTY
PULL IN EAR LUG RUG TOW CHUG CLAW
DRAG DRAW DUCT HALE HAUL HOOK

SWIG TIRE TREK BREAK CLOUT DRAFT
HEAVE HITCH IMPEL PLUCK PROOF
TWEAK ASSUME COMMIT GATHER
OBTAIN SECURE TWITCH UPROOT
WRENCH ATTRACT EXTRACT
(— A BELL) SET
(— ABOUT) TEW SOOL TOSE TOZE
MOUSLE
(— APART) RAVE REND TEAR DIVULSE
(— AWAY) AVEL AVELL WREST
REVULSE
(— BY EARS) SOLE SOWL
(— DOWN) UNPILE DESTROY DEMOLISH
(— HERE AND THERE) TOUSLE
(— NOSE) SNITE
(— OF DRUM) EAR
(— OFF) CROP DRAW STRIP AVULSE
(— ON FISHING ROD) STRIKE
(— ON ROPE) BOWSE
(— OUT) RAX EXTRACT OUTBRAID
(— QUICKLY) YANK
(— ROUGHLY) WAP TOWSE WOUSE
(— SUDDENLY) TRICE
(— THE LEG) STRING
(— TOGETHER) KNOT ATTRACT
(— TRIGGER) SQUEEZE
(— UP) LOUK
(— UP BY THE ROOTS) ARACE
(— WITH JERK) HOICK SWITCH
PULLEY RIM CONE DRUM BLOCK FUSEE
FUZEE IDLER WHEEL JOCKEY RIGGER
SHEAVE CAPSTAN FERRULE TRUCKLE
PURCHASE
PULLOVER JERSEY SWEATER
PULP PAP CHUM MUSH JELLY NERVE
SLUSH STOCK STUFF MARROW SQUEEZE
SQUELCH
(FOOD —) CHYME
PULPIT PEW TUB AMBO BEMA DESK
CHAIR PREACH ROSTRUM TRIBUNE
(— FOR CHOIR BOOKS) ANALOGION
(MOSLEM —) MINBAR
(OPEN-AIR —) TENT
PULPY SOFT FLABBY FLESHY BACCATE
SQUELCHY
PULSATE BEAT BRIM FLAP PANT PUMP
THROB COURSE STRIKE PALPITATE
PULSE DAL BEAT WAVE POUCE STUFF
THROB IMPULSE SPHYGMUS VITALITY
PULSING VIBRANT
PULVERIZE BRAY BUCK DRAG FINE MEAL
MULL CRUSH FLOUR GRIND POUND
BRUISE POWDER ATOMIZE DEMOLISH
VANQUISH COMMINUTE MICRONIZE
PUMA COUGAR PAINTER PANTHER
PUMMEL BEAT DRUB SLAT POUND
SLATE THUMP POUNCE
PUMP GIN JACK FORCE HEART PLUMB
SLUSH FORCER SINKER BOOSTER
EJECTOR SLUDGER SYRINGE BEERPULL
ELEVATOR INFLATER INJECTOR
PULSATOR
(— ON SHIPS) DOWNTON
(GAS —) BOWSER
(HAND —) GUN
(MINE —S) SET
(SET OF —S) LIFT

PUN NICK WHIM ALLUDE QUIBBLE EQUIVOKE PARAGRAM CALEMBOUR PARANOMASIA

PUNCH DIG JAB SET BASH BELT BLOW BOFF BUST DING PLUG POKE SOCK TIFF BUMBO DOUSE DRIFT FORCE PASTE SLOSH CANCEL PATRIX SHAPER STINGO STRIKE PERLOIR SANGRIA STARTER EMBOSSER GROUNDER PUNCTURE
(CHASING —) TRACER
(DOG OF —) TOBY
(ETCHER'S —) MATTOIR
(HORSESHOE —) PRITCHEL
(OVAL —) PLAISHER
(WIFE OF —) JUDY

PUNCTILIOUS NICE EXACT STIFF FORMAL CAREFUL POINTED PRECISE PUNCTUAL

PUNCTUAL DUE EXACT PROMPT CAREFUL PRECISE ACCURATE DEFINITE DETAILED EXPLICIT

PUNCTUATE MARK STOP POINT EMPHASIZE

PUNCTUATION MARK DOT DASH STOP BRACE COLON COMMA PRICK SLASH HYPHEN PERIOD STIGME BRACKET VIRGULE ELLIPSIS SEMICOLON

PUNCTURE HOLE PICK PINK PROD STAB DRILL POINT PUNCH STICK NEEDLE PIERCE DEFLATE DESTROY PUNCTUM CENTESIS PINPRICK

PUNDIT SAGE SWAMI CRITIC PANDIT TEACHER

PUNGENT HOT BOLD FELL KEEN RACY RICH SALT TART ACRID ACUTE BRISK NIPPY QUICK SHARP SMART SPICY TANGY BITING BITTER SHRILL SNAPPY CAUSTIC MORDANT PEPPERY PIQUANT POINTED TELLING CAYENNED PIERCING POIGNANT STABBING STINGING

PUNISH FIX PAY CANE COOK FLOG SORT WIPE ABUSE BIRCH CURSE SCOUR SLATE SPILL STOCK STRAP TWINK WREAK AVENGE CAMPUS FERULE IMMURE REFORM STRAFE STRIKE CHASTEN CORRECT CORRIGE REQUITE SCOURGE CARTWHIP CHASTISE CASTIGATE
(— BY BLOW ON PALM) PANDY
(— BY COMPENSATION) FINE AMERCE
(— BY CONFINEMENT) GATE
(— BY FINE) MULCT
(— BY LASHING WRISTS) BUCK

PUNISHMENT GIG FINE LASH PAIN RACK SACK YARD GRUEL LIBEL SMART WRACK WREAK DESERT FERULE LESSON EXAMPLE GALLOWS GANTLET PAYMENT PENALTY PENANCE REVENGE SCOURGE JUDGMENT PUNITION EXECUTION
(CAPITAL —) SCAFFOLD
(MILITARY —) JANKERS

PUNK BAD BOY MUG POOR AMADOU BUNKUM NOVICE HOODLUM RUFFIAN BEGINNER GANGSTER INFERIOR NONSENSE STRUMPET TERRIBLE TOUCHWOOD

PUNT BET HIT POY KENT KICK QUANT GAMBLE GARVEY SKERRY

PUNY WEAK DWARF FRAIL PETTY WEARY JUNIOR MAUGER NOVICE PUISNE SICKLY MANIKIN PIMPING QUEECHY YOUNGER INFERIOR RECKLING

PUP PUPPY WHELP

PUPA EGG NYMPH PUPPET TUMBLER WIGGLER FLAXSEED WRIGGLER CHRYSALIS

PUPIL BOY GYTE TYRO WARD CADET CHILD ELEVE ALUMNA GRADER INFANT JUNIOR SENIOR LEARNER PAULINE SCHOLAR STUDENT ABSENTEE BLUECOAT DISCIPLE RUGBEIAN SCHOOLER
(— AT HEAD OF CLASS) DUX
(— IN STUDIO) RAPIN
(— OF EYE) BLACK PEARL SIGHT
(ANGLO-INDIAN —) CHELA
(BOARDED —) SOJOURN
(GERMAN —) ABITURIENT

PUPPET BABY DOLL DUPE IDOL MOTE DROLL DUMMY MAUMET POPPIN STOOGE GUIGNOL DROLLERY MARIONETTE

PUPPY FOP PUP DOLL DOUGH WHELP PUPPET
(FEMALE —) GYP
(GREYHOUND —) SAPLING

PURCHASE BUY WIN EARN FISH GAIN BOOTY HEDGE PRIZE EFFECT TACKLE ACQUIRE BARGAIN EMPTION PILLAGE PROCURE BARRATRY

PURCHASER BUYER EMPTOR VENDEE CHAPMAN POULTER SHOPPER CUSTOMER

PURE NET EVEN FAIR FINE FREE FULL GOOD HOLY MERE NEAT TRUE CLEAN CLEAR FRESH MORAL NAKED SHEER STARK UTTER WHITE WHOLE CANDID CHASTE ENTIRE LIMPID SIMPLE VESTAL VIRGIN ANGELIC GENUINE PERFECT SINCERE ABSOLUTE ABSTRACT COMPLETE DOVELIKE INNOCENT PRISTINE SERAPHIC SPOTLESS VIRGINAL VIRTUOUS SPIRITUAL

PUREE DAL SOUP CREAM

PURGATIVE PURGE SENNA CALOMEL DRASTIC TURPETH ALOEDARY APERIENT CLEANSER EVACUANT CATHARTIC

PURGE RID FIRE FLUX SOIL CLEAR RHEUM SCOUR DRENCH PHYSIC REMOVE SHRIVE CLEANSE DETERGE ABSTERGE

PURIFICATION BAPTISM ELUTION LUSTRUM VASTATION

PURIFY TRY BOLT FINE PURE WASH CLEAN PURGE BLEACH DISTIL FILTER REFINE SETTLE WINNOW BAPTIZE CHASTEN CLEANSE EXPIATE LAUNDER MUNDIFY SUBLIME SWEETEN EXORCISE FILTRATE LUSTRATE SANCTIFY SPRINKLE
(— ORE) DILVE
(— SUGAR) CLAY

PURITAN PRIG SAINT CROPPY BLUENOSE CATHARAN GOSPELER PRECISIAN ROUNDHEAD

PURITANICAL BLUE STRICT GENTEEL PRECISE

PURITANI, I (CHARACTER IN —)
ARTHUR ELVIRA TALBOT WALTON
HENRIETTA
(COMPOSER OF —) BELLINI

PURITY ASSAY HONOR WHITE CANDOR
VIRTUE FINESSE CHASTITY FINENESS
PURENESS
(— OF BREED) PEDIGREE

PURLOIN CAB CRIB WEED ANNEX BRIBE
FILCH STEAL SWIPE FINGER PILFER
PIRATE CABBAGE SNAFFLE SURREPT
SCROUNGE

PURPORT GIST DRIFT SENSE TENOR
DESIGN EFFECT IMPORT INTEND INTENT
BEARING MEANING PROFESS PURPOSE
STRENGTH

PURPOSE AIM END GOAL IDEA MAIN
MEAN MIND PLAN SAKE TALK TEND
VIEW WILL CAUSE POINT SCOPE STUDY
THINK DESIGN DEVICE EFFECT INTEND
INTENT REASON SCHEME COMPASS
COUNSEL DESTINE EARNEST IMAGINE
MEANING PROPOSE THOUGHT DEVOTION
FUNCTION PLEASURE PROPOUND
DISCOURSE
(ALLEGED —) PRETEXT
(FIXED —) HEART
(INSIDIOUS —) CAUTEL
(MORAL —) ETHOS

PURSE BAG CLY BUNG FISC KNIT POKE
SKIN BURSE DUMMY FUNDS MEANS
POUCH COMMON POCKET PUCKER
READER ALMONER LEATHER SPORRAN
BUCKSKIN BURSICLE CRUMENAL
POCKETBOOK

PURSUE RUN SUE HUNT SEEK CHASE
CHIVY HOUND QUEST STALK TRADE
COURSE FOLLOW GALLOP TRAVEL
BEDEVIL HOTFOOT CONTINUE PRACTICE
(— ZIGZAG COURSE) TACK

PURSUER FOLLOWER PLAINTIFF
QUESTRIST

PURSUIT FAD HUNT SUIT CAPER CAUSE
CHASE CHEVY CRAFT HOBBY COURSE
SEARCH ACTIVITY

PUSH JAM JOG PUT BANG BOIL BOOM
BORE DING FLOG PICK PING POTE STOP
BLITZ BRUSH BUNCH CROWD CRUSH
DRIVE DUNCH GOOSE PINCH POACH
SHOVE STICK STOVE HURTLE JOGGLE
JOSTLE POTTER PROPEL THRONG
THRUST ASSAULT IMPETUS IMPULSE
PERPLEX SHUFFLE INCREASE SHOULDER
(— ALONG) TUSH
(— APART) SPREAD
(— ASIDE) SHOG
(— BY STICK) KENT POLE
(— FORWARD) BUCKET ADVANCE
(— GENTLY) NUDGE
(— INTO) INVADE
(— MONEY) SPIFF
(— ON) BEAR YERK
(— OUT) DEBOUT LAUNCH
(— RUDELY) BARGE HORSE HUSTLE
(— TO FULL STRIDE) EXTEND
(— TOGETHER) CONTRUDE
(— UP) BOOST

(— WITH ELBOW) ELBOW HUNCH
(— WITH FEET) DIG SCAUT
(— WITH HEAD) BUNT BUTT
(STRONG —) BEVEL

PUT BET PIT SET BANG BUTT FILL GIVE
GROW PILT REST URGE ADAPT DRIVE
FOCUS PLACE STALL STATE STEAD
STEEK STELL WAGER ASSIGN BESTOW
DECAMP IMPOSE INVEST PHRASE
REPOSE SPROUT THRUST DEPOSIT
EMPLACE EXPRESS INFLICT SUBJECT
(— AN END TO) DATE SNIB ABATE
SNUFF SPIKE STASH STILL STINT
STANCH ABOLISH ASSUAGE EXPIATE
SATISFY ABROGATE DEMOLISH
SURCEASE
(— ASIDE) BLOW SAVE SHUNT REJECT
SHUFFLE
(— AT REST) HUSH
(— AWAY) STOW COVER HUTCH SHIFT
DIVORCE
(— BACK) REMIT REMISE
(— DOWN) LAY DEMIT QUASH QUELL
DEPOSE SQUASH DEPRESS OPPRESS
REPRESS SILENCE DIMINISH SUPPRESS
(— FORTH) GEM BLOW CAST GIVE
PUSH EXERT LANCE PROFER STRETCH
(— IN) ENTER INSERT INTROMIT
(— IN MOTION) AROUSE
(— IN OPERATION) LAUNCH
(— IN ORDER) DO SET SIDE SORT TRIM
DIGHT MENSE SHIFT TRICK ADJUST
GRAITH ORDAIN SETTLE ARRANGE
CLARIFY DISPOSE REDRESS INSTRUCT
(— IN PLACE) POSE
(— OFF) DAFF DOFF HAFT DEFER DELAY
DEMUR FOIST PARRY REMIT SHIFT
TARRY THROW LINGER RETARD SHELVE
ADJOURN PROLONG RESPITE POSTPONE
PROROGUE PROCRASTINATE
(— ON) DON HYPE APPLY CRACK DRAPE
ENDUE MOUNT STAGE ASSUME INVEST
ADDRESS
(— OUT) GET OUT OUST DOWSE EVICT
EXERT SLAKE RETIRE DISMISS EXCLUDE
EXTINCT FORJUDGE
(— TO FLIGHT) AFLEY FEAZE FLEME
GALLY
(— TO RIGHTS) SORT DIGHT
(— TO SHAME) DASH ABASH SHEND
UPBRAID
(— TO SLEEP) OPIATE SOPITE
SOPORATE
(— TO USE) STOW APPLY BESTOW
(— TOGETHER) ADD JOIN BUILD
COMPILE COMPOSE CONCOCT CONFECT
PREPARE ASSEMBLE COMPOUND
(— UP) ANTE ERECT FLUSH DISPENSE
(— UP WITH) GO BEAR BIDE HACK
ABIDE BROOK ENDURE SUFFER COMPORT
STOMACH SWALLOW TOLERATE

PUTREFY ROT ADDLE DECAY SWEAT
FESTER POLLUTE PUTRESCE

PUTRID FOUL RANK SOUR VILE LOUSY
ADDLED RANCID ROTTEN CORRUPT
DECAYED FRIABLE VICIOUS DEPRAVED
MALODOROUS

PUTTER FUSS MESS MUCK POKE TRUCK
CADDLE DAWDLE MUCKER MUCKLE
PIDDLE TINKER FRIGGLE
PUZZLE CAP GET SET BEAT CRUX LICK
POSE BEFOG POSER QUEER REBUS STICK
BAFFLE BOTHER ENIGMA FICKLE FOITER
JIGSAW KITTLE RIDDLE CONFUSE
MYSTERY MYSTIFY NONPLUS PERPLEX
STICKER TANGRAM ACROSTIC BEFUDDLE
BEWILDER CONFOUND DISTRACT
DUMFOUND ENTANGLE INTRIGUE
CROSSWORD
PUZZLED ASEA PERPLEXED
PUZZLING KNOTTY CURIOUS KNOTTED
RIDDLING DIFFICULT PROBLEMATIC
PYCNOGONID SPIDER
PYGARG ADDAX OSPREY
PYGMALION (AUTHOR OF —) SHAW
(BELOVED OF —) GALATEA
(CHARACTER IN —) HILL LIZA CLARA
HENRY ALFRED FREDDY HIGGINS
EYNSFORD DOOLITTLE PICKERING
(FATHER OF —) BELUS MUTGO
AGENOR

(MURDERED BY —) SICHAEUS
(SISTER OF —) DIDO
(STATUE FASHIONED BY —) GALATEA
PYGMY ELF AKKA AMBA DOKO ACHUA
AFIFI ATOMY BATWA DWARF GNOME
PIXIE WOCHUA ACHANGO ASHANGO
MANIKIN DWARFISH VAALPENS
DANDIPRAT
PYRAMID BENBEN HOPPER TEOCALLI
(— OF CRAYFISH) BUISSON
(DOUBLE —) TWIN ZIRCONOID
(INVERTED —) HOPPER
PYRAMIDAL HUGE ENORMOUS
IMPOSING
PYRE BALE PILE TOPHET BONFIRE
BALEFIRE
PYROMANIAC FIREBUG ARSONIST
PYRRHUS (FATHER OF —) AEACIDES
(MOTHER OF —) PHTHIA
(SON OF —) PTOLEMY SOPATER
(WIFE OF —) ANTIGONE
PYTHON ADJIGER PEROPOD ANACONDA
PYX BOX CAPSA CASKET CHRISM VESSEL
BINNACLE CHRISMAL CIBORIUM

Q

Q CUE QUEEN QUEUE QUEBEC
QATAR (CAPITAL OF —) DOHA
(TOWN OF —) RUWAIS UMMSAID
QUACK PUFF WHACK CROCUS SALVER
SUBTLE EMPIRIC IMPOSTOR SANGRADO
CHARLATAN
QUACKERY HUMBUG
QUADRAGESIMA LENT
QUADRANT BOW RADIAL SQUARE
QUARTER TETRANT ALTIMETER
QUADRILLE CONTREDANSE
(PL.) LANCERS
QUADROON QUATERON TERCERON
QUAFF TOOT DRINK CAROUSE TRILLIL
QUAGMIRE BOG FEN HAG SOG LAIR
MARSH MIZZY SWAMP MORASS PUDDLE
SLOUGH BOGMIRE
QUAHOG CLAM VENUS BULLNOSE
QUAINT DRY ODD NAIVE BIZARRE
STRANGE FANCIFUL HANDSOME
PICTURESQUE
(— IN APPEARANCE) FUNKY
QUAKE JAR CHILL QUAIL SHAKE DITHER
QUIVER SHIVER WAMBLE FLUTTER
SHUDDER TREMBLE
(PREF.) PALLO
QUAKER ASPEN HERON FRIEND OBADIAH
WHACKER HICKSITE TREMBLER
BEACONITE BROADBRIM SHADBELLY
QUAKING ASPEN TREPID SHAKING
TREMBLING
QUALIFICATION NATURE RESERVE
SHADING CAPACITY
QUALIFIED FIT ABLE MEET FITTED
LIKELY CAPABLE ELIGIBLE SUITABLE
AUTHENTIC
(NOT —) INAPT INHABILE
QUALIFY FIT ADAPT ALLAY ALLOY EQUIP
HEDGE ENABLE MODIFY SOFTEN TEMPER
ABSOLVE CERTIFY ENTITLE LICENSE
PREPARE GRADUATE MODERATE
RESTRAIN RESTRICT
QUALITY BRAN BUMP CHOP COST FEEL
GUNA LEAD SORT COLOR GRACE STATE
TRAIT ASSIZE BARREL FABRIC STRAIN
THREAD TIMBER TIMBRE ADJUNCT
CALIBER KINSHIP STATURE ACCIDENT
MOVEMENT PROPERTY TONEBRAND
QUALITY STREET (AUTHOR OF —)
BARRIE
(CHARACTER IN —) BROWN LIVVY
PATTY SUSAN BLADES PHOEBE
THROSSEL VALENTINE
QUALM DROW PALL NAUSEA SQUEAM
SCRUPLE
QUANDARY FIX PUXY PUZZLE TANGLE

DILEMMA NONPLUS SWITHER
DOLDRUMS JUNCTURE
QUANTITY BAG JAG SUM SUP BODY
DISH DOSE LIFT MASK SOME SOUD
WARE BATCH BREAK CLASH KITTY SIEGE
TROOP WHEEN ACTION ADDEND
AMOUNT BAGFUL BOTTLE BUDGET
EFFECT FOTHER HANTLE NUMBER
PARCEL THRAVE CONTENT FOOTAGE
PORTION QUANTUM GLASSFUL KNIFEFUL
LADLEFUL PARAMETER
(— OF ARROWS) SHEAF
(— OF BUTTER) CHURNING
(— OF CLOTHES) BUCKING
(— OF COTTONSEED) CRUSH
(— OF CUT TREES) FALL
(— OF DRINK) HOOP DRAFT DRAUGHT
(— OF ELECTRICITY) FARADAY
(— OF EXPLOSIVE) CHARGE
(— OF FISH OR GAME) TAKE CATCH
(— OF GRAIN) GAVEL
(— OF HAY) LOCK TRUSS
(— OF IRRIGATION WATER) DUTY
(— OF LIQUID) DROP JAUP SLASH
GOBBET JABBLE
(— OF LIQUOR) HEELTAP
(— OF LUMBER) RUN
(— OF MEAL) MELDER
(— OF METAL) BLOW
(— OF MUD) CLASH
(— OF NARCOTICS) BINDLE
(— OF PAPER) TOKEN
(— OF PRODUCE) BURY
(— OF RAISINS) FRAIL
(— OF THREAD) LEASE
(— OF WOOD) HAG FATHOM
(ESTIMATED —) WEY
(EXCESSIVE —) GLUT SPATE
(FIXED —) CONSTANT
(GREAT —) HOST MORT MUCH SHOAL
SIGHT STORE BARREL FOREST SLATHER
TUMMELS
(LARGE —) ACRE BOLT DEAL FECK
HEAP MASS PECK SCAD SLEW FLOOD
FORCE GRIST JORUM POWER SCADS
SHEAF STACK STORE BUCKET BUSHEL
DICKER DOLLOP GALLON MATTER
MELDER CLUTHER SKINFUL HECATOMB
MOUNTAIN PLURALITY
(LEAST —) BEDROCK
(MINUTE —) DRAM DROP SHADE
SCRUPLE PARTICLE
(NOTEWORTHY —) CHUNK
(RELATIVE —) DEGREE
(SETTLED —) SIZE
(SIZABLE —) SCUMP

(SMALL —) ACE BIT SUP CURN DASH DUST HAIR HARL IOTA PEAK SOSH SPOT CANCH PRILL SMACK SPICE SQUIB TOUCH JOBBLE MORSEL PICKLE SAMPLE SONGLE STIVER CAPSULE CURTSEY DRIBBLE DRIBLET EPSILON HANDFUL MODICUM SMICKET SPATTER TODDICK FARTHING MOUTHFUL PENNORTH SCANTLET PENNYWORTH
(UNDIRECTED —) SCALAR
(VARYING —) SKID

QUARANTINE DETAIN ISOLATE SANCTION

QUARREL JAR BEEF CHIP DEAL FEUD FRAY FUSS JARL JOWL MIFF NIFF ODDS PICK PLEA BRACK BRAWL BROIL FLITE GRUFF HURRY NOISE PIQUE SCOLD SCRAP SHINE STOUR UPSET AFFRAY BARNEY BLOWUP BREACH BREEZE BRIGUE DEBATE DIFFER DUSTUP FRATCH GARROT MATTER QUARRY SQUARE SQUEAL STRIFE THWART BRABBLE BRATTLE DISGUST DISPUTE FACTION OUTCAST RUCTION STASHIE SWAGGER TUILZIE WRANGLE DISAGREE SPLUTTER SQUABBLE TRAVERSE
(— IN WORDS) JANGLE
(NOISY —) ROW FRACAS KICKUP
(PETTY —) MIFF SPAT TIFF

QUARRELSOME UGLY FEISTY CURRISH SCRAPPY DRAWLING FRAMPOLD FRATCHED PETULANT BELLICOSE BUMPTIOUS FRACTIOUS LITIGIOUS CONTENTIOUS
(NOT —) AMICABLE

QUARRY DELF GAME LODE MEAT CHASE PLUCK LATOMY REWARD LATOMIA LOZENGE
(HAWK'S —) MARK

QUART SHANT WHART
(METRIC —) LITER
(ONE-HALF —) PINT
(TWO —S) MAGNUM
(1-8TH —) GILL
(2 —S) FLAGON
(4 —S) GALLON

QUARTER AIRT PART STUD EAVER TRACT BARRIO BEHALF BESTOW COLONY FARDEL HARBOR SECTOR CONTRADA FAUBOURG STANDARD
(— IN BATTLE) GRITH
(— OF A POUND) TRIPPET
(— OF BEEF OR MUTTON) BOUT
(— OF CITY) BLOCK GHETTO
(— OF COMPASS) PLAGE
(— OF FLAG) CANTON
(— OF HOUR) POINT
(— OF HUNDRED) FIERDING
(— OF YEAR) RAITH
(— ONESELF) SORN
(— UPON) LAY
(JEWISH —) ALJAMA

QUARTERS BOTHY BILLET LIVERY MENAGE FARDELS CHUMMERY DIGGINGS LODGMENT

(— FOR IMMIGRANTS) HOSTEL
(— OF SALVATION ARMY) BARRACKS
(HIGH —) AERIE
(JUNIOR OFFICERS' —) GUNROOM
(MEN'S —) SELAMLIK
(MONASTERY —) FRATRY

QUARTET FOURSOME

QUARTZ IRIS ONYX SARD AGATE CHERT FLINT PRASE TARSO TOPAZ JASPER MORION PEBBLE PLASMA SILICA ALENCON CITRINE CRYSTAL RUBASSE SINOPLE AMETHYST BASANITE SARDONYX SIDERITE YENTNITE BUHRSTONE

QUASH CRUSH QUELL SPIKE PEREMPT SUPPRESS

QUAVER CROMA SHAKE TRILL WAVER CHROMA FALTER QUIVER WOBBLE VIBRATE

QUAY KEY POW QUAI LEVEE BUNDER STRAND

QUEASINESS KECK SICKNESS

QUEASY NICE SICK SQUEEZY DELICATE NAUSEATED SQUEAMISH

QUEEN REG DAME FERS LADY AEDON FIERS RANEE ATOSSA REGINA ROXANA TAILTE JOCASTE PHEARSE STATIRA BRUNHILD GUINEVERE
(— AND KING OF TRUMPS) BELLA
(— IN CHESS) FERS LADY FIERS
(— OF CLUBS) SPADILLA
(— OF DENMARK) GERTRUDE
(— OF ETHIOPIA) CANDACE
(— OF FAIRY LAND) MEDB GLORIANA
(— OF GEORGIA) TAMARA
(— OF GOTHS) TAMORA
(— OF HEARTS) ELIZABETH
(— OF HEAVEN) HERA
(— OF JUDAH) ATHALIA
(— OF LYDIA) OMPHALE
(— OF SHEBA) BALKIS
(— OF SPADES) BASTA LIZZY
(— OF THE ADRIATIC) VENICE
(— OF THE ANTILLES) CUBA
(— OF THE EAST) ZENOBIA
(— OF THEBES) JOCASTA
(— OF TRUMPS) HONOR
(FAIRY —) MAB ARGANTE TITANIA
(INDIAN —) RANI SUNK MAHARANI
(MOHAMMEDAN —) BEGUM

QUEER HEX ODD RUM HARM DICKY DIPPY DROLL FAINT FUNNY GIDDY NUTTY RUMMY COCKLE FIFISH HIPPED QUEASY UNIQUE AMUSING COMICAL CURIOUS DISRUPT ERRATIC STRANGE TOUCHED FANCIFUL OBSESSED PECULIAR

QUELL DIE CALM FLOW HUSH KILL SLAY ABATE ALLAY CRUSH QUASH QUIET YIELD PACIFY PERISH REDUCE SOOTHE SPRING STANCH STIFLE REPRESS SQUELCH SUPPRESS

QUENCH COOL DAMP ALLAY CHECK CRUSH SLAKE STILL STANCH STIFLE ASSUAGE

QUENTIN DURWARD
  (AUTHOR OF —) SCOTT
  (CHARACTER IN —) CARL CROYE
  LOUIS LESLEY PHILIP PIERRE TOISON
  BALAFRE CHARLES DURWARD EBERSON
  HERMITE LAMARCK LUDOVIC QUENTIN
  TRISTAN WILLIAM CRAWFORD HAMELINE
  ISABELLE HAYRADDIN JAQUELINE
  MAUGRABIN CREVECOEUR

QUERULOUS WHINY FRETFUL PEEVISH
  NATTERED PETULANT IRRITABLE

QUERY ASK DOUBT DEMAND INQUIRE
  INQUIRY QUESTION

QUEST ASK HOW POSE QUIZ TALK
  EXAMINE PURSUIT SEEKING VENTURE

QUESTION ASK HOW POSE QUIZ TALK
  ARGUE DOUBT DREAD QUERY ACCUSE
  CHARGE DEMAND LEADER MATTER
  PONDER REASON EXAMINE INQUIRE
  INQUIRY PROBLEM PURPOSE SCRUPLE
  OVERTURE RELEVANT RESEARCH
  STICKLER CATECHISE
  (— AMBIGUOUSLY WORDED) RIDDLE
  (— FRETFULLY) RAME
  (BAFFLING —) POSER
  (PERPLEXING —) STUMPER
  (RHETORICAL —) EROTEMA
  (UNSOLVED —) CRUX
  (ZEN —) KOAN

QUESTIONABLE FISHY QUEER SHAKY
  UNSAFE BATABLE CLOUDED DUBIOUS
  DOUBTFUL PROBLEMATIC
  (NOT —) DECENT

QUESTIONNAIRE POLL INVENTORY

QUEUE CUE COLA LINE BRAID PIGTAIL
  CROCODILE

QUIBBLE COG PUN BALK CARP QUIP
  CAVIL DODGE EVADE QUIRK SALVO
  AMBAGE BAFFLE BICKER PALTER
  BRABBLE CAPTION CHICANE SHUFFLE
  PETTIFOG CONUNDRUM

QUICK RAD FAST FLIT KECK KEEN LISH
  LIST PERT RIFE SNAP SOON WHIT WICK
  AGILE ALIVE APACE BRISK FLEET HASTY
  MERRY NIFTY NIPPY PREST RAPID READY
  SHARP SHORT SWIFT TRICK ACTIVE
  CLEVER FACILE KITTLE NIMBLE PROMPT
  PRONTO SNAPPY SPEEDY SUDDEN
  DARTING SCHNELL SHUTTLE DEXTROUS
  (— AND NEAT) DEFT
  (— AS A FLASH) WHIP
  (— IN PERCEPTION) ACID
  (— IN RESPONSE) GNIB
  (— TO DETECT) SMOKY
  (— TO FLARE UP) GASSY
  (— TO LEARN) APT
  (— TO MOVE) YARE
  (LIGHT AND —) VOLANT

QUICKEN PEP MEND STIR WHET HURRY
  SPEED ACUATE AROUSE HASTEN INCITE
  KINDLE REVIVE VIVIFY ANIMATE ENLIVEN
  PROVOKE REFRESH SHARPEN EXPEDITE
  INSPIRIT ACCELERATE

QUICKLY TID FAST RIFE SOON WHIP
  YARE NEWLY SHARP SNELL SWITH TIGHT

BELIVE HOURLY PRESTO PRONTO
  RASHLY EFTSOON PRESTLY READILY
  SPEEDILY

QUICKNESS HASTE SPEED ACUMEN
  AGILITY SMEDDUM ACTIVITY CELERITY
  DISPATCH KEENNESS SAGACITY
  (MENTAL —) NOUS SLEIGHT LEGERITY

QUICKSAND FLOW SYRTIS SWALLOW

QUICKSILVER OREMIX MERCURY
  TIERRAS HEAUTARIT

QUICK-TEMPERED DONSY PEPPERY
  IRASCIBLE

QUICK-WITTED APT SHARP SMART
  NIMBLE KNOWING

QUIESCENT QUIET LATENT STATIC
  RESTING INACTIVE

QUIET QT COY LAY CALM COSH DEAD
  DUMB EASE EASY HUSH LULL REST
  ROCK SNUG SOFT WEME CANNY CIVIL
  DOWNY LEVEL PEACE QUELL SALVE
  SHADY SILKY SLEEP SOBER SQUAT STILL
  SUANT WHIST DREAMY GENTLE PACIFY
  PLACID RETIRE SEDATE SERENE SETTLE
  SILENT SMOOTH SOFTLY SOOTHE
  STEADY HUSHFUL ORDERLY REQUIEM
  RESTFUL SILENCE COMPOSED
  DECOROUS PEACEFUL TRANQUIL
  UNRUFFLE

QUIETLY LOW FAIR CANNY STILL WINLY
  EVENLY GENTLY SOFTLY TIPTOE

QUIETNESS REST REPOSE SERENITY

QUILL RIB PIRN FLOAT STALK BOBBIN
  FESCUE PINION SLEEVE BRISTLE
  CALAMUS PRIMARY TRUNDLE
  (— FOR WINDING THREAD) COP
  (— OF FEATHER) BARREL
  (PORCUPINE —) PEN

QUILT BEAT GULP WELT WHIP DUVET
  REZAI CADDOW CHALON PALLET
  THRASH SWALLOW MATTRESS POULTICE
  COMFORTER

QUINSY ANGINA PRUNELLA

QUINTESSENCE CREAM ELIXIR
  CLYSSUS OSMAZOME

QUIP GIBE JAPE JEST JOKE CRACK QUIRK
  SALLY SCOFF TAUNT CONCEIT QUIBBLE

QUIRK BEND KINK QUIP TURN CLOCK
  CROOK TWIST CONCEIT QUIBBLE
  FLOURISH PAROXYSM MANNERISM
  PECULIARITY

QUIT GO DROP NASH PART AVOID BELAY
  CEASE DOUSE LEAVE SHIFT SHOOT
  STASH BEHAVE DESERT DESIST FOREGO
  RESIGN SECEDE VACATE ABANDON
  FORSAKE RELEASE

QUITE SO ALL BUT GEY BRAW EVEN FAIR
  FREE FULL JUST PLAT WELL CLEAR
  CLOSE FULLY SHEER STARK CLEVER
  DAMNED ENOUGH JUSTLY MERELY
  TOTALLY PERFECTLY
  (NOT —) HARDLY
  (PREF.) DE

QUITTER SLAG PIKER COWARD JUMPER
  SHIRKER TURNBACK

QUIVER DIRL QUAG BEVER NIDGE QUAKE

SHAKE TRILL WAVER BICKER COCKER
DIDDER SHEATH SHIMMY SHIVER
TREMOR WAMBLE FLUTTER SHUDDER
TREMBLE TWIDDLE TWINKLE TWITTER
VIBRATE
(PREF.) PALLO
QUIVERING ASPEN AGUISH DIDDER
DITHER QUAGGLE QUAKING AGITATED
ATREMBLE
QUIXOTIC ERRANT IMAGINARY
VISIONARY
QUIZ ASK GUY HOAX MOCK CHAFF QUEER
EXAMINE QUESTION RIDICULE
QUIZZICAL ODD QUEER QUIZZY CURIOUS
WHIMSICAL
QUOIT CIST DISC DISH DISK LINER
DISCUS HOBBER CROMLECH

QUONDAM OLD ONCE WHILE FORMER
ONETIME SOMETIME
QUOTA PART BOGEY SHARE QUOTIENT
PROPORTION
QUOTATION TAG PRICE QUOTE
EXTRACT SNIPPET EPIGRAPH
(— DEVELOPED INTO ESSAY) CHRIA
QUOTE CITE MARK NAME NOTE ADDUCE
ALLEGE RECITE REPEAT EXCERPT
EXTRACT OBSERVE REHEARSE
(— SARCASTICALLY) FLOUT
QUO VADIS (AUTHOR OF —)
SIENKIEWICZ
(CHARACTER IN —) ACTE NERO PAUL
CHILO LYGIA PETER URSUS CROTON
EUNICE GLAUCUS VINICIUS PETRONIUS
TIGELLINUS

R

R ROGER ROMEO

RABBET CHECK GROOVE BACKJOINT
FILLISTER

RABBI AMORA HAKAM TANNA MASTER
SABORA TEACHER GAMALIEL

RABBIT BUN REX TAN BUNT CONY JACK
POLE RACK BUNNY DUTCH FRIER LAPIN
ANGORA ASTREX HAVANA OARLOP
PARKER POLISH BEVEREN CONYNGE
FLEMISH LEPORID SNOWSHOE
(CASTRATED —) CAPON
(FEMALE —) DOE
(MALE —) BUCK
(YOUNG —) KITTEN
(PL.) FLICK WARREN

RABBLE MOB TAG HERD RAFF ROUT
SCUM SCUFF TRASH MEINIE RAFFLE
RAGTAG DOGGERY PUDDLER TRAFFIC
BRAGGERY CANAILLE RIFFRAFF
VARLETRY RASCALITY CLAMJAMFRY

RABBLE-ROUSER DEMAGOG

RABID MAD RAGING FRANTIC FURIOUS
FRENZIED RAVENING VIRULENT

RABIES LYSSA MADNESS PIBLOKTO
RAVENING

RACCOON COON COATI GUARA TEJON
AGOUARA RINGTAIL CRABEATER

RACE CAP CUP LOG ROD RUN DRAG KIND
LINE NAME RING RINK TEAM TRAM
BLOOD BREED BROOD CASTE CHEVY
CORSO FLESH HOUSE ISSUE PURSE
RATCH ROUTE SPEED STAKE COURSE
FAMILY NATION PEOPLE PHYLON
RUNOFF SPRING STIRPS STRAIN BIOTYPE
CENTURY CLAIMER CLASSIC HACKNEY
KINDRED LINEAGE NURSERY PROGENY
PROSAPY RACEWAY STADIUM HANDICAP
MARATHON OFFSPRING
(— A HORSE) CAMPAIGN
(— AT WEDDING) BROOSE
(— FOR BALL-BEARINGS) CONE
(— OF BARLEY) BENT
(— OF GODS) VANIR
(— OF UNDERGROUND ELVES) DROW
(— OF WINDMILL) CURB
(HORSE —) AGON DERBY PLATE SPRINT
MATINEE FUTURITY WALKOVER
(HUMAN —) MAN MANKIND SPECIES
MORTALITY
(IMPROMPTU —) BRUSH
(JUMPING —) SCURRY
(LENTEN —S) TORPIDS
(LONG —) ENDURO
(MILL —) LADE
(MOTORCYCLE —) SCRAMBLE
MOTOCROSS
(PRELIMINARY —) HEAT
(ROWING —) SCULLS REGATTA

(RUNNING —) MILE RELAY SPRINT
HUNDRED HURDLES
(SHORT —) BICKER
(SHORT-DISTANCE —) DASH SCURRY
SPRINT
(SKI —) SLALOM DAUERLAUF
(TIDAL —) ROOST

RACECOURSE OVAL RING TURF EPSOM
CIRCUS DROMOS STADIE STRETCH
GYMKHANA SPEEDWAY
(PREF.) DROM(O)
(SUFF.) DROME

RACEHORSE PONY PACER RACER
CHASER SLEEPER TROTTER BANGTAIL
(— THAT HAS NEVER WON) MAIDEN
(INFERIOR —) PLATER HAYBURNER
(2-YEAR OLD —) JUVENILE

RACHEL POWDER
(FATHER OF —) LABAN
(HUSBAND OF —) JACOB
(SISTER OF —) LEAH
(SON OF —) JOSEPH BENJAMIN

RACK GIN TUB BUCK CASE SHOG TACK
AMBLE DRIER FRAME POKER THROW
TRAIN WRING CIRCLE CUDGEL ENGINE
NIPPER PULLEY WRENCH AFFLICT
AGONIZE POTTARO TORMENT TORTURE
BARBECUE PINEBANK SAWHORSE
(— ATTACHED TO WAGON)
SHELVING OUTRIGGER
(— FOR BARRELS) JIB
(— FOR CHINAWARE) FIDDLE
(— FOR DISHES) BINK
(— FOR FEEDING) HACK HAYRACK
(— FOR FODDER) HECK CRATCH
(— FOR PLATES) CREEL
(— FOR STORAGE) FLAKE
(— IN THRESHER) SHAKER
(DRYING —) CRIB TREBLE
(WOODEN —) BUCAN

RACKET BAT DIN GAME BANDY MUSIC
RAZOO CLAMOR CROSSE DRIVER
HUBBUB HUSTLE RAQUET RATTLE
BUSINESS REVELING STRAMASH

RACKETEER HOOD HUSTLER GANGSTER

RACY GAMY LEAN SEXY JUICY SALTY
SMART SPICY LIVELY RISQUE PIQUANT
PUNGENT ZESTFUL SPIRITED

RADIANCE RAY GLOW GLARE GLEAM
GLINT GLORY LIGHT SHINE LUSTER
AUREOLA GLITTER SPLENDOR

RADIANT BEAMY SHINY ABLAZE BRIGHT
GOLDEN LUCENT SHEENY AURORAL
BEAMFUL BEAMING FULGENT LAMBENT
GLORIOUS LUSTROUS RELUCENT
SPLENDID BRILLIANT

RADIATE RAY BEAM POUR SHED SHINE
EFFUSE SPREAD EFFULGE EMANATE

RADIATION AURA LIGHT INFRARED

RADIATOR HEATER EMANATOR
RADICAL KEY SURD BASAL GROUP
RADIX ROUGE ULTRA HEROIC CAPITAL
DRASTIC EXTREME FORWARD HERETIC
JACOBIN LEFTIST LEVELER LIBERAL
PRIMARY CARDINAL LOCOFOCO
RADICALISM EXTREMISM JACOBINISM
RADIUS RAYON SPOKE SWEEP THROW
ADRADIUS
RAFFISH RAKISH TAWDRY UNKEMPT
RAFFLE MOVE RAFF JUMBLE RABBLE
REFUSE RUBBISH
RAFT MOKI BALSA FLOAT TABLE DINGHY
JANGAR PIPERY RADEAU JANGADA
ZATTARE
(— OF INVERTED POTS) GHARNAO
(— OF LOGS) BOOM CRIB
(— WITH CABIN) COW
(BAMBOO —) RAKIT
(FIRE —) CATAMARAN
(LUMBER —) BATCH
RAFTER HIP BALK BLAD FIRM SILE SOIL
SPAR VIGA BLADE CABER RIDGE BULKER
COUPLE CARLINE CHEVRON SLEEPER
RAG JAG LAP TAT HAZE HOAX SAIL
ANNOY CLOUT PRANK SCOLD SCRAP
SHRED WIPER LIBBET RAGGLE TAGRAG
TATTER FLITTER REMNANT TORMENT
RAGSTONE STRAGGLE NEWSPAPER
(CURLING —) CRACKER
(FLAPPING —) WALLOP
(TARRED —) HARDS
RAGAMUFFIN MUFFLIN BEGGARLY
SHABROON TITMOUSE
RAGE AWE FAD RAG WAX BAIT BEEF
FARE FOAM FRET FUFF FUME FURY
GLOW GRIM HEAT PELT RAMP TEAR
ANGER CHAFE CRAZE FUROR PADDY
STORM VOGUE WRATH FRENZY FURORE
BLUSTER FASHION MADNESS PASSION
RUFFIAN TEMPEST INSANITY
RAGGED DUDDY HARSH FRAYED JAGGED
SCOURY UNEVEN SHAGRAG SHREDDY
TATTERY SCRAGGLY SCRATCHY
TATTERED
RAGING HOT GRIM WILD RABID FIERCE
FERVENT MADDING PELTING VIOLENT
FLAGRANT WRATHFUL
RAGOUT SALMI GOULASH HARICOT
TERRINE SALPICON CHIPOLATA
PULPATONE
RAID TALA FORAY HARRY PINCH FORAGE
HARASS INROAD MOLEST RAZZIA
DESCENT JAYHAWK OUTRAKE OUTRIDE
OUTROAD COMMANDO SPOILING
(— ORCHARDS) SCRUMP
(AIR —) BLITZ
(BOMBING —) PRANG
(CATTLE —) SPREAGH SPREATH
(MAKE A — ON) BUST
(WARLIKE —) HERSHIP
RAIL BAR BULL COOT GIRD LIST MOHO
RANT RAVE SKID SORA TRAM WING
CRAKE EASER FENCE GUARD PLATE
SCOLD STEEL SWEAR BANTER BEDWAY
CALLET FENDER RUNNER COURLAN
INVEIGH OARCOCK RACKWAY TOPRAIL

BULLHEAD CORNBIRD PORTLAST
TOADBACK VIGNOLES
(— AT) JEST CURSE SCOFF RATTLE
REVILE BETONGUE
(— OF BED) STOCK
(— OF RAILWAY SWITCH) TONGUE
(— ON GUN PLATFORM) TRINGLE
(— ON HAY VEHICLE) THRIPPLE
(— ON SHIP) FIFE
(ALTAR —) SEPTUM
(ARCHED —) HOOPSTICK
(CHAIR —) LEDGE
(FENCE —) RIDER
RAILING BAR SEPT GRATE FENDER
FIDDLE BARRIER GALLERY PARAPET
CANCELLI ESPALIER HANDRAIL
PARCLOSE TRAVERSE
RAILLERY GAFF HASH JEST JOKE RAGE
CHAFF RALLY SPORT BANTER HOORAY
HURRAH SATIRE TRIFLE MOCKERY
BADINAGE RABULOUS RIDICULE
PERSIFLAGE
RAILROAD EL ROAD YARD STEEL
COALER FEEDER GRANGER TRAMWAY
CEINTURE ELEVATED
RAILWAY ROAD TUBE COGWAY SUBWAY
COGROAD INCLINE TRANVIA WIREWAY
ASCENSOR PLATEWAY TRAMROAD
FUNICULAR
RAIMENT GARB CLOTH APPAREL
CLOTHES VESTURE CLOTHING DRESSING
WARDROBE
(SPLENDID —) SHEEN
(SUFF.) ESTHES
RAIN WET ISLE ULAN WEET BLASH
STORM DELUGE MIZZLE SOAKER DRIZZLE
DOWNPOUR
(— AND SNOW) SLEET
(— HEAVILY) TEEM
(— LIGHTLY) SMUR SPIT SPRINKLE
(DRIZZLING —) DAG
(FINE —) MIST SEREIN
(GOD OF —) PARJANYA
(HEAVY —) PASH SPOUT
(LIGHT —) SEREIN WEATHER
HEATDROPS
(SHORT —) SHOWER
(SUDDEN —) SKEW
(WHIRLING —) SKIRL
(WIND-DRIVEN —) SCAT
RAINBOW ARC BOW ARCH IRIS GAMUT
METEOR SUNBOW ILLUSION
(BROKEN —) WINDDOG WINDGALL
RAINCOAT MAC MACK MINO PONCHO
BURSATI OILSKIN SLICKER GOSSAMER
MACKINTOSH
RAINFALL PLOUT SKIFT ONDING
STEMFLOW
RAINY WET FRESH JUICY SAPPY WEETY
BLASHY DRIPPY HYETAL SPONGY
PLUVIAL SHOWERY WEEPING PLUVIOUS
RAISE END SET WIN BUMP GROW HEFT
HIGH HIKE JACK KICK LIFT MAKE OVER
REAR ROOF STIR TOSS BLOCK BOOST
BREED BUILD CAIRN CHOCK CRANE
DIGHT ERECT FORCE GREET HEAVE
HOIST HORSE LEAVE MOUND MOUNT

PRICK RISER ROUSE VOICE ASSIST
BETTER CREATE DOUBLE EMBOSS
GATHER LEAVEN MUSTER PREFER
REMOVE RISING UPHOLD UPLIFT
ADDRESS ADVANCE COLLECT ENHANCE
LIGHTEN NOURISH PRESENT PROMOTE
RECRUIT UPSHOOT ANGELIZE HEIGHTEN
INSPIRIT
(— A BUMP) CLOUR
(— A NAP) MOZE TEASE TEASEL
(— ALOFT) SPHERE
(— ANCHOR) CAT
(— BY ASSESSMENT) LEVY
(— BY HAND) NOB
(— CLAMOR) BRAWL
(— IN PITCH) SHARP
(— OBJECTIONS) CAVIL BOGGLE
(— ONESELF) CHIN
(— TO HIGH DEGREE) STRAIN
(— TO 3RD POWER) CUBE
(— UP) BUOY AREAR ELATE EXALT
EXTOL ELEVATE CIVILIZE
RAKE HOE RIP WAY COMB PATH RACK
REAP ROAM ROUE ROVE BLOOD PITCH
SULKY TIGER PLUNGE RABBLE ROLLER
SEARCH RANSACK SCRATCH LOTHARIO
(— GRAIN) GAVEL
(— UP IN ROWS) HACK
(— WITH GUNFIRE) SCOUR STRAFE
ENFILADE
(— WITHOUT TEETH) LUTE
(BUCK —) SWEEP
(CRANBERRY —) SCOOP
(OYSTER —) GLEANER
RAKISH SLANG JAUNTY SPORTY
WANTON DASHING CARELESS DEVILISH
RALLY KID DRAG JOKE MOCK STIR BULLY
JOLLY QUEER BANTER DERIDE REVIVE
COLLECT CAMPOREE CLAMBAKE
RIDICULE
RAM PUN TIP TUP BUCK CRAM PACK
STEM ARIES CHOKE CRASH POACH
ROGER SLIDE BEETLE CHASER RANCID
ROSTRUM BULLDOZER
(— OF WAR VESSEL) SPUR
(CASTRATED —) WETHER
RAMA MELCHORA
(FATHER OF —) DASHARATHA
(MOTHER OF —) KAUSHALYA
(WIFE OF —) SITA
RAMBLE RAKE ROAM ROVE SKIR WALK
JAUNT PROWL RANGE TRACE TROLL
DODDER STROLL VAGARY WANDER
SAUNTER TROUNCE SCRAMBLE
(— AIMLESSLY) HAZE
RAMBLING GAD VAGARY CURSORY
DEVIOUS WINDING DESULTORY
SCATTERED
RAMBUNCTIOUS RUDE WILD ROUGH
UNRULY UNTAMED VIOLENT
RAMIFICATION ARM RAMUS BRANCH
OFFSHOOT OUTGROWTH
RAMP RUN BANK EXIT HOAX RAGE RANK
SLIP CREEP STORM EASING FROLIC
GARLIC FOOTPAD SLIPWAY SWINDLE
GRADIENT

RAMPAGE RAGE ROMP BINGE SPRAY
SPREE STORM RANDAN
RAMPANT RANK PROFUSE SALIENT
RAMPART LINE WALL AGGER ABATIS
VALLUM BULWARK DEFENSE PARAPET
BARBICAN BARRICADE
RAMROD FORMAL GUNSTICK
RAMSHACKLE RUDE UNRULY RICKETY
UNSTEADY
RANCH RUN FARM TEAR FINCA CHACRA
OUTFIT SPREAD STATION ESTANCIA
HACIENDA
RANCHER COWMAN GRAZIER SHEEPMAN
CATTLEMAN
RANCID RAM RANK SOUR RAFTY RASTY
REEST RESTY FROWZY ODIOUS ROTTEN
MALODOROUS
RANCOR GALL HATE SPITE ENMITY
GRUDGE HATRED MALICE ACRIMONY
RANCOROUS ACRID VENOMOUS
MALIGNANT ACRIMONIOUS
RANDOM LOOSE STRAY CASUAL
CHANCE CHANCY AIMLESS SHOTGUN
UNAIMED VAGRANT ALEATORIC
(AT —) HOBNOB
(SOMEWHAT —) LONG
RANGE ROW AREA BEAT GATE LINE RAKE
RANK ROAM ROVE SCUM SHOT TOUR
WALK ALIGN BLANK FIELD GAMUT HILLS
ORBIT REACH SCOPE SCOUR SHOOT
SPACE STAND START SWING VERGE
DANGER EXTEND EXTENT LENGTH
RADIUS RAMBLE SPHERE STROLL
WANDER BOWSHOT COMPASS DEMESNE
EARSHOT HABITAT HORIZON PURVIEW
CLASSIFY DIAPASON LATITUDE
PANORAMA
(— FOR FOOD) FORAGE
(— OF ARROW) FLIGHT
(— OF BRICK) COURSE
(— OF FOOD) FARE
(— OF FREQUENCIES) SPECTRUM
(— OF GOVERNANCE) DOMAIN
(— OF GUN) CARRY RANDOM GUNSHOT
(— OF HILLS) GHAT HUMP TIER CHAIN
RIDGE SIERRA SAWBACK BACKBONE
(— OF ORGANISM) BIOZONE
(— OF PASTURE) GANG
(— OF PLANKS) STRING
(— OF PRINTING TYPES) SERIES
(— OF SIGHT) KEN SCAN EYESHOT
KENNING
(— OF TONES) KEY SCALE GRADATION
(— OF WAVELENGTH) BAND
(— OVER) SWEEP
(— TOP) COOKTOP
(ARCHERY —) BUTTS GREEN
(COOKING —) KITCHENER
(SHOOTING —) MES GALLERY
(TEMPERATURE —) CONE
RANK RAY ROW SEE DANK FOOT FORM
FOXY GOLE GREE LINE RAMP RATE ROOM
SEED SOUR STEP TIER CENSE FETID
FRANK FUSTY GROSS HONOR LEVEL
MARCH ORDER PLACE RANGE SIEGE
SPACE STALL STAND STATE TRAIN
AFFAIR DEGREE ERMINE ESTEEM FIGURE

LAVISH RATING SPHERE STATUS
STRONG CALIBER CALLING DUKEDOM
EARLDOM FOOTING GLARING RAMPANT
STATION WORSHIP ABSOLUTE EARLSHIP
ENSIGNCY EQUIPAGE FLAGRANT
LADYSHIP STINKING MALODOROUS
(— AND FILE) RUCK RANGALE
(— OF GENTLEMEN) GENTRY
GENTILITY
(— OF SERGEANT-AT-LAW) COIF
(ACADEMIC —) AGREGE
(BOTTOMMOST —) CELLAR
(HIGH —) PURPLE DIGNITY EMINENCE
(LOWEST —) SCOURING
(MILITARY —) GRADE AIRMAN CORNET
CHAOUSH
(NOBLE —) ADELAIDE
(ONE HIGHEST IN —) SUPREMO
(SAME —) KIND
(SOCIAL —) CLASS ESTATE HERALDRY
POSITION
(SUFF.) CY HEAD HOOD
RANKLE FRET CHAFE FESTER INJURE
RANCOR DESTROY INFLAME
RANSACK DRAG RAKE SACK SEEK RIFLE
SEARCH PLUNDER RUMMAGE
RANSOM FINE REDEEM RESCUE EXPIATE
RANT HUFF RAIL MOUTH REVEL ROUSE
SCOLD SPOUT STEVEN BOMBAST
CAROUSE DECLAIM FROTHING
RODOMONTADE
RAP BOB BON BLOW CHAP GRAB KNAP
TIRL TUNK CLICK CLINK FLIRT KNOCK
STEAL TOUCH BARTER HANDLE YANKER
RAPACIOUS CRUEL GREEDY TAKING
RAVENING RAVENOUS
RAPACITY RAVEN RAVIN CUPIDITY
EXTORTION VULTURISM
RAPE OF THE LOCK (AUTHOR OF —)
POPE
(CHARACTER IN —) ARIEL BETTY
PETRE PLUME SPLEEN BELINDA UMBRIEL
CLARISSA THALESTRIS
RAPID GAY FAST CHUTE HASTY QUICK
ROUND SHARP SHOOT TOSTO SPEEDY
WINGED CURSIVE SCHNELL SKELPIN
TANTIVY SLAPPING
(—S IN RIVER) SAULT DALLES RIFFLE
STICKLE CATARACT
(MORE —) STRETTO
RAPIDITY HASTE SPEED RADEUR
CELERITY VELOCITY
RAPIDLY APACE CHEAP FLEETLY
HASTILY SPEEDILY QUICKFOOT
RAPIER TUCK BILBO ESTOC SHARP
STOCK VERDUN TOASTER
RAPINE FORCE RAVIN PILLAGE PLUNDER
VIOLENCE
RAPT LOST TENSE INTENT CARRIED
ENGAGED ABDUCTED ABSORBED
ECSTATIC
RAPTURE JOY BLISS DELIGHT ECSTASY
PAROXYSM RHAPSODY
RARE FINE REAL THIN ALONE EARLY
GREAT CHOICE SCARCE SELDOM SPARSE
SUBTLE SULLEN UNIQUE CURIOUS

TENUOUS UNUSUAL CRITICAL SINGULAR
UNCOMMON RECHERCHE
RAREFIED HIGH THIN SUBTILE
ABSTRUSE AETHERED ESOTERIC
RARITY SWAN CURIO RELIC TENUITY
(PL.) CURIOSA
RASCAL BOY CAD DOG IMP BASE DUCK
KITE LOON MEAN SHAG GANEF KNAVE
ROGUE SCAMP THIEF BEGGAR BUGGER
COQUIN RABBLE RIBALD TINKER
BLEEDER CULLION GLUTTON HALLION
HESSIAN PEASANT SKEEZIX SKELLUM
VILLAIN BEZONIAN BLIGHTER PALLIARD
PICAROON RAKEHELL SKALAWAG
SPALPEEN VAGABOND RAPSCALLION
RASH BRASH HARDY HASTY HEADY
SLASH DARING SUDDEN UNWARY
URGENT HOTSPUR RAMSTAM ROSEOLA
BLIZZARD CARELESS ERUPTION
EXANTHEM HEADLONG HEEDLESS
PRESSING RECKLESS TEMEROUS
RASHNESS RAGE HASTE ACRISY
TEMERITY HEADINESS
RASP RUB FILE RAPE ERUCT GRATE
TOOTH RUBBER RIFFLER
(SHOEMAKER'S —) FLOAT
RASPING HARSH ROUGH STOUR HOARSE
RAZZLY GRATING RAUCOUS GUTTERAL
RASSELAS (AUTHOR OF —) JOHNSON
(CHARACTER IN —) IMLAC PEKUAH
NEKAYAH RASSELAS
RAT BUCK DAMN DRAT HEEL SCAB VOLE
LOUSE SELVA ZEMMI MURINE RODENT
VERMIN CUSHION CONFOUND INFORMER
MYOMORPH
RATCHET DOG PAWL DETAIL DETENT
RATE LAY SET CESS CHOP DEEM GAIT
GIVE HAND KIND RANK RATA ABUSE
CURVE PRIZE RATIO REBUT SCOLD
STENT STYLE VALUE ASSIZE GALLOP
ACCOUNT BESHREW DESERVE FASHION
MILLAGE REPROVE CLASSIFY ESTIMATE
QUANTIFY
(— HIGHLY) PRICE
(— OF ASCENT) GRADE
(— OF DRAINAGE) FREENESS
(— OF EXCHANGE) BATTA
(— OF INTEREST) COUPON DISCOUNT
(— OF MOVEMENT) PACE TEMPO
(— OF RECKONING) FOOT
(— OF SPEED) BAT AGOGE
(— OF TAX) CENSE
(— OF TRANSFER) FLUX
(— OF TUITION) CULET
(BIRTH —) NATALITY
RATHER BUT LIKE SOON QUITE BEFORE
FAIRLY KINDLY PRETTY SEEMLY EARLIER
INSTEAD SOMEWHAT
RATIFY AMEN PASS SEAL SIGN VISA
ENSEAL FASTEN OBSIGN APPROVE
CONFIRM SANCTION VALIDATE
RATING RANK CENSE CLASS GRADE
STANDING
RATIO PI GAIN RATE SINE INDEX SETUP
SHEAR ASPECT CAMBER QUOTUM
SECANT AVERAGE PORTION CONTRAST
PROPORTION

RATION DOLE RATIO ALLOCATE
(— OF BREAD) TOMMY
(ANIMAL —) CHOW
(EXTRA —S) BUCKSHEE
(HOG —) SWILL
RATIONAL SANE LUCID SOBER LOGICAL
SENSIBLE THINKING
RATIONALIZE THOB EXPLAIN
RATTLE DIN BIRL BURL RICK TIRL CHINK
CLACK CROTAL HURTLE MARACA RIFFLE
CLACKER CLAPPER CLATTER CLICKET
CREAKER GNATTER SISTRUM CAIXINHA
CHOCALHO NOISEMAKER
(CRIER'S —) CLAPPER
(IRON —) SKELLAT
RATTLESNAKE BELLTAIL CASCABEL
CROTALID MASSASAUGA SIDEWINDER
RATTLETRAP GEWGAW TRIFLE RICKETY
RAUCOUS LOUD HARSH COARSE
HOARSE SQUAWKY STRIDENT
RAVAGE EAT PREY RIOT RUIN SACK
FORAY HARRY HAVOC SPOIL WASTE
FORAGE DESPOIL DESTROY OVERRUN
PILLAGE PLUNDER DESOLATE SPOLIATE
RAVE RAGE BLURB CRUSH RATHE ROUSE
STORM WANDER
RAVEL FAG RUN FRAY FRET SNARL
LADDER RUNNER TANGLE CONFUSE
INVOLVE PERPLEX UNWEAVE
RAVEN CRAKE RALPH CORBIE FORAGE
WAYBIRD
RAVENOUS GREEDY LUPINE TOOTHY
WOLFISH RAPACIOUS VORACIOUS
RAVINE GAP GUT DELL DRAW KHOR LINN
WADI BREAK CHASM FLUME GHYLL
GORGE GULCH GULLY KLOOF ARROYO
CLOUGH COULEE DINGLE GULLET
HOLLOW NULLAH STRAIT BARRANCA
QUEBRADA
RAVISH ROB RAPE ABUSE CHARM FORCE
HARRY SPOIL ABDUCT ATTACK DEFILE
CORRUPT DELIGHT ENFORCE OPPRESS
OUTRAGE OVERJOY PLUNDER POLLUTE
VIOLATE VITIATE DEFLOWER ENTRANCE
RAW BRUT LASH RUDE BLEAK CHILL
CRUDE FRESH GREEN HARSH NAKED
SHARP BITTER CALLOW COARSE UNRIPE
VULGAR NATURAL NOUVEAU UNBOUND
VERDANT IMMATURE UNCOOKED
UNEDITED VISCERAL
RAWBONED RAW BONY LEAN GAUNT
LANKY SCRAG SCRAWNY
RAY BEAM BETA WIRE ALPHA BRAND
DRESS EQUIP FLAIR FLAKE GLEAM
ORDER SKATE BATOID OBISPO RADIAL
RADIUS STREAM TRYGON BATFISH
COWFISH DEWBEAM FIDDLER HOMELYN
TORPEDO BRACHIUM MOONBEAM
NUMBFISH PLOWFISH
(— OF LIGHT) GLINT SPEAR GLANCE
SUNRAY SUNBEAM
(— OF STARFISH) ARM
(FEMALE —) MAID
(FIN —) SPINE
RAZE CUT FLAT RUIN LEVEL EFFACE
UNPILE DESTROY SCRATCH SUBVERT
UNBUILD DEMOLISH

REACH GO GET HIT WIN BEAT COME FIND
GAIN HAWK MAKE PUSH SHOT SPIT
TEND BRACE CROSS FETCH GRASP
RANGE TOUCH ARRIVE FATHOM LENGTH
OBTAIN SNATCH ACHIEVE COMPASS
CONTACT GUNSHOT
(— ACROSS) SPAN OVERSTRIDE
(— AN END) STAY
(— BY EFFORT) ATTAIN
(— BY FIGURING) STRIKE
(— FORTH) EXTEND
(— GOAL) HAIL
(— OF WATER) LODE
(— OUT) UTTER SPREAD STRETCH
(— TO) LINE
(— TOTAL) AMOUNT
(— UNDERSTANDING) AGREE
(— WITH END) ABUT
(EXTREME —) PITCH STRETCH
(TRY TO —) ASPIRE
(ULTIMATE —) PITCH
REACTION BUZZ START RECOIL
BLOWOFF EMOTION FEELING SETBACK
BACKLASH BACKWASH EXCHANGE
KICKBACK
REACTIONARY BOURBON BACKWARD
READ GO CON CALL TURN JUDGE SOLVE
PERUSE RELATE FORESEE LEARNED
PREDICT ABOMASUM DECIPHER
FORETELL INDICATE OVERLOOK
(— ALOUD) LINE DEACON
(— HERE AND THERE) BROWSE
(— MECHANICALLY) RETINIZE
(— OF) SEE
(— OFF) DICTATE
(— PROOF) HORSE
(— RAPIDLY) DIP SKIM GOBBLE
(— SLOWLY) SPELL
(— SYSTEMATICALLY) FREQUENT
(— WITH PROFOUND ATTENTION)
PORE STUDY
READER LECTOR MAFTIR GRANTHI
PISTLER DEVOURER
READILY PAT LIEF APTLY PREST EASILY
GAINLY PROBABLY SPEEDILY
READINESS ART EASE GIFT PRESS SKILL
BELIEF FLUENCY FREEDOM ALACRITY
FACILITY
READY UP APT FIT BOON FREE GIRT GLIB
RIPE TALL APERT EAGER HANDY HAPPY
PREST QUICK SWIFT THERE TIGHT
ADROIT APPERT FACILE HEARTY PROMPT
PREPARE PRESENT WILLING CHEERFUL
DEXTROUS HANDSOME PREGNANT
PREPARED PROVIDED SKILLFUL
(— A COMPUTER) BOOT
(— FOR ACTION) ARM EXPEDITE
(— WITH WORDS) FLUENT
REAL BODY FAIR GOOD PURE TRUE VERY
PUKKA RIGHT ROYAL SOLID SOOTH
ACTUAL DINKUM ENTIRE HONEST
GENUINE GRADELY SINCERE CONCRETE
DEFINITE EXISTENT POSITIVE
(EXTERNALLY —) TANGIBLE
REALISTIC HARD SOBER VIVID EARTHLY
LIFELIKE PROBABLE
REALITY FEAT BEING SOOTH THING

TRUTH ACTUAL EFFECT VERITY EARNEST
SUBJECT IDENTITY REALNESS TRUENESS
REALIZE GAIN KNOW FETCH LEARN
SENSE EFFECT FULFIL ACQUIRE
CONCEIVE RECOGNIZE
REALLY JUST TRULY FINELY INDEED
SIMPLY SURELY VERILY ACTUALLY
REALM LAND SOIL BOURN CLIME RANGE
REIGN CIRCLE EMPIRE HEAVEN REALTY
REGION SPHERE DEMESNE KINGDOM
TERRENE DOMINION GHOSTDOM
(— OF DARKNESS) PO
(— OF FABULOUS RICHNESS)
ELDORADO
(MARINE —) NOTALIA TROPICALIA
(VISIONARY —) CLOUDLAND
REAMER BURR SPUD DRIFT BROACH
WIDENER
REAP BAG CUT CROP GLEAN SHEAR
GARNER GATHER SICKLE HARVEST
REAR AFT BACK HIND JUMP LIFT TOSS
BREED BUILD CARVE ERECT AROUSE
CRADLE FOSTER NURSLE SUCKLE
ARRIERE EDUCATE ELEVATE NOURISH
NURTURE UPBRING BUTTOCKS
HINDMOST REARWARD
(— CAREFULLY) TIDDLE
(NEARER THE —) AFTER
(TO THE —) BACK BEHIND
(TO THE — OF) ABAFT
REASON PEG WAY NOUS SAKE TALK
ARGUE CAUSE COLOR COUNT LOGOS
PROOF RATIO SCORE SENSE SKILL THINK
TOPIC EXCUSE GROUND MANNER
MATTER MOTION NOESIS ACCOUNT
PREMISE SUBJECT ARGUMENT
REASONABLE FAIR JUST SANE SOBER
NATURAL SKILFUL FEASIBLE MODERATE
RATIONAL SENSIBLE
REASONING LOGIC THOUGHT ERGOTISM
RATIONAL
(CLUMSY —) ARGAL
(FALLACIOUS —) CIRCLE SOPHISTRY
PARALOGISM
REBATE BLUNT CHECK LESSEN DIMINISH
DISCOUNT KICKBACK
REBECCA (AUTHOR OF —) DUMAURIER
(CHARACTER IN —) JACK BAKER
FRANK GILES MAXIM FAVELL JULYAN
CRAWLEY DANVERS BEATRICE
DEWINTER
(FATHER OF —) ISAAC
REBEKAH (BROTHER OF —) LABAN
(FATHER OF —) BETHUEL
(HUSBAND OF —) ISAAC
(SON OF —) ESAU JACOB
REBEL REB KICK RISE TURN BRAND
ANARCH CROPPY MUTINE REVOLT
MALCONTENT
REBELLION MUTINY PUTSCH REVOLT
MISRULE UPRISING
REBELLIOUS RUSTY ANARCHIC
MUTINOUS AUDACIOUS INSURGENT
REBOUND DAP HOP HANG KISS CAROM
BOUNCE CANNON RECOIL RESILE RESULT
BRICOLE REDOUND RICOCHET SNAPBACK
REBUFF SLAP SNUB CHECK FLING REPEL

DEFEAT DENIAL REBUKE REFUTE
REPULSE
REBUKE NIP BAWL RATE SNUB TRIM
BARGE BLAME CHECK CHIDE DRESS
SCOLD LESSON RATING RATTLE
CENSURE CHIDING CORRECT LECTURE
REPROOF REPROVE SARCASM CHASTISE
KEELHAUL REPROACH CASTIGATE
REBUT REPEL RECOIL REFUTE REPULSE
RETREAT DISPROVE
RECALCITRANT UNRULY OBSTINATE
RESISTANT
RECALL CITE BRING REMIND RETURN
REVOKE BETHINK RECLAIM RETRACE
RETRACT REVIVAL REMEMBER
WITHDRAW
RECANT UNSAY ABJURE REVOKE
DISAVOW RETRACT SWALLOW
RENOUNCE
RECAPITULATE SUM REPEAT RECOUNT
REITERATE SUMMARIZE
RECEDE DIE EBB BACK FADE RECUR
DEPART DIFFER RETIRE SHRINK DECLINE
DIGRESS RETREAT CONTRACT DIMINISH
ELONGATE WITHDRAW
RECEIPT CHIT BINDER RECIPE WARRANT
RECEIVE GET GAIN HAVE HOLD TAKE
ADMIT CATCH GUEST LATCH ACCEPT
ASSUME BORROW DERIVE GATHER
HARBOR BELIEVE CONTAIN EMBRACE
INHERIT SUSTAIN PERCEIVE
(— A CRIMINAL) RESET
(— AS GUEST) FANG HOST VANG
GREET
(— AS MEMBER) INCEPT
(— AS REWARD) REAP
(— FROM LOTTERY) DRAW
(— SHEETS) FLY
(— WITH PLEASURE) GRATIFY
(PREF.) RECIPIO
RECENT HOT NEW LATE FRESH GREEN
HOURLY LATELY LATTER MODERN
CURRENT NEOTERIC
RECENTLY ANEW JUST LATE NEWLY
LASTLY LATELY FRESHLY LATTERLY
RECEPTACLE ARK BIN BOX CAN CUP DIP
TIN TUB URN VAT BATH BOAT BOWL
CASE CELL CIST DROP HOLD INRO LOOM
SAFE CARRY CREEL KIOSK SCOOP TORUS
BASKET BUCKET BUTLER CARTON
CUPULE DIPPER DRAWER HAMPER
HOPPER POCKET TROUGH ASHTRAY
CAPSULE CARRIER CORBULA DUSTBIN
ENVELOP OMNIBUS RECEIPT SANDBOX
SETTLER SOAPBOX STOWAGE TRAVOIS
CANISTER CESSPOOL HONEYPOT
OVERFLOW SPITTOON STOCKPOT
(— FOR ABANDONED INFANTS) TOUR
(— FOR BONES) OSSUARY OSSARIUM
(— FOR BROKEN TYPE) HELL
(— FOR BUTTER) RUSKIN
(— FOR COAL) BUNKER
(— FOR CONVEYING) APRON
(— FOR DRY ARTICLES) FAT
(— FOR FOUL THINGS) SINK
(— FOR GLASS BATCH) ARBOR
(— FOR HOLY WATER) FONT

(— FOR ORE-CRUSHING) MORTAR
(— FOR POKER CHIPS) KITTY
(— FOR SACRED RELICS) TABLE
SHRINE TABLET SEPULCHRE
(— FOR SAVINGS) SOCK
(— FOR SEWING MATERIALS) TIDY
(— FOR TREASURE) HANAPER
(— FOR TYPE CASES) RACK
(— FOR VOTES) SITULA
(— IN BOTTLE-MAKING MACHINE)
PARISON
(— OF CLAY OR STONE) STEAN STEEN
(— OF FLOWER) THALAMUS
(— ON WEIGHING SCALES) PAN
(— OVER ALTAR) DOVE
(CLAY —) BOOT
(DILATED —) GYNOBASE
(ELECTRICAL —) BASEPLUG
(INCENSE —) ACERRA
(OPEN —) TRAY
(PURSELIKE —) BURSICLE
(TAILOR'S —) HELL
(WOODEN —) SEBILLA
RECEPTION TEA COURT CRUSH TREAT
ACCOIL RUELLE SOIREE MATINEE
OVATION PASSAGE RECEIPT ASSEMBLY
FUNCTION GREETING SOCIABLE
ACCEPTANCE
(— AT BEDTIME) COUCHEE
(— OF NATIVE PRINCES) DURBAR
(— OF SOUND) AUDIO
(ARABIC —) DIFFA
(CORDIAL —) WELCOME
(CROWDED —) SQUASH
(FASHIONABLE —) LEVEE SALON
(WEDDING —) INFARE
RECEPTIVE OPEN SENSORY
OPENHANDED
RECESS ARK BOX COD CUP BUNK COVE
DEEP HOLE NOOK TRAP BOWER CANAL
CAVUM CLEFT CREEK HAVEN INLET
ORIEL PRESS SINUS CAVERN CENTER
CHAPEL CLOSET COFFER CRANNY
EXEDRA GROTTO INDENT RABBET
BEDSITE CONCAVE CREVICE LOCULUS
MANHOLE RETREAT INTERVAL LOCKHOLE
OVERTURE TRAVERSE VACATION
PIGEONHOLE
(— BETWEEN CAPES) BAY
(— FOR FAMILY RECORDS)
TABLINUM
(— FOR HINGE LEAF) PAN
(— FOR PIECE OF SCULPTURE)
ANCONA
(— IN CHURCH WALL) AMBRY
(— IN COLON) HAUSTRUM
(— IN JAPANESE HOUSE) TOKONOMA
(— IN MOUNTAIN) CIRQUE
(— IN ROCK) HITCH
(— IN SIDE OF HILL) CORRIE
(— IN SIDE OF ROOM) ALA
(— IN WALL) BOLE NICHE ALCOVE
(— ON STAGE) CANOPY
(INMOST —) BOSOM
RECHERCHE RARE CHOICE EXOTIC
CURIOUS PRECIOUS UNCOMMON
EXQUISITE

RECIPE RX FORM RULE FORMULA
RECEIPT
RECIPIENT HEIR DONEE ALMSMAN
DONATEE DONATORY LAUREATE
RECIPROCAL CROSS COMMON MUTUAL
SECANT SEESAW
RECIPROCATE REPAY RETURN REQUITE
RETROACT
RECITAL STORY EXPOSE LITANY PARADE
REPEAT READING RELATION REPETITION
(— OF PRAYER) GEULAH HAMOTZI
KEDUSHAH
(UNTRUE —) TALE
RECITATION READING RECITAL
RHAPSODY
RECITE SAY CARP TELL STATE RECKON
RELATE RENDER REPEAT DECLINE
DICTATE NARRATE RECOUNT REHEARSE
(— AS ELOCUTION EXERCISE)
DECLAIM
(— IN MONOTONE) INTONE
(— METRICALLY) SCAN
(— MONOTONOUSLY) CHANT
(— NUMBERS) COUNT
(— PRAYERS) BENSH DAVEN
(— TIRESOMELY) THRUM
(— WITH GREAT EASE) RUSH
RECKLESS RASH WILD BLIND MADCAP
SAVAGE RAMSTAM CARELESS
HEADLONG HEEDLESS BLINDFOLD
RECKLESSLY FAST BLIND RAMSTAM
HEADLONG HEADFIRST
RECKON CAST DATE ITEM RATE RECK
RELY TELL TOTE ALLOT AUDIT CLAIM
CLASS COUNT JUDGE PLACE SCORE
TALLY THINK ASSIGN FIGURE IMPUTE
NUMBER REPUTE ACCOUNT ASCRIBE
COMPUTE INCLUDE PRETEND RECOUNT
SUPPOSE CONSIDER ESTIMATE
RECKONING TAB BILL NICK POST TALE
COUNT SCORE TALLY REASON ACCOUNT
(TAVERN —) LAWING
RECLAIM TAME RECALL REDEEM
REFORM RESCUE SUBDUE PROTEST
RECOVER RESTORE
(— FROM SAVAGE STATE) CIVILIZE
RECLINE LIE LEAN LOLL REST COUCH
ACCUMB RECUMB UPLEAN DISCUMB
(— LANGUIDLY) GAULSH
RECLUSE NUN MONK HERMIT REMOTE
ASCETIC EREMITE ANCHORET SECLUDED
SOLITARY SCIOPHYTE SOLITAIRE
RECOGNITION FAME SPUR HONOR
SENSE CREDIT STATUS FEELING
KENNING KNOWING AGNITION SANCTION
(— OF ACHIEVEMENT) LAUREL
CITATION
RECOGNIZE KEN SEE WIT ESPY FACE
KNOW SPOT TELL ADMIT ALLOW BLINK
HONOR ACCEPT AGNIZE BEKNOW
DISCERN REALIZE ACCREDIT
RECOGNIZED GOOD CLEAR KNOWN
CLASSIC FAMILIAR
RECOIL SHY BALK KICK TURN REBUT
SHRUG SHUCK START BLENCH BOUNCE
FLINCH RETORT SHRINK REBOUND
REDOUND REVERSE BACKLASH

RECOLLECT RECALL RECORD RETAIN
BETHINK COMPOSE RECOVER REMEMBER
RECOLLECTION MIND MEMORY RECALL
RECORD MINDING THOUGHT MEMORIAL
SOUVENIR
RECOMMEND MOVE PLUG TOUT WISH
ADVISE COMMIT PRAISE PREFER
COMMEND CONSIGN COUNSEL ENTRUST
ADVOCATE
RECOMMENDATION CHIT COUNSEL
TESTIMONY
RECOMPENSE PAY MEED MEND QUITS
REPAY YIELD AMENDS BOUNTY RECOUP
REWARD SALARY GUERDON PAYMENT
PREMIUM REQUITE RESTORE SATISFY
SERVICE
RECONCILE ADAPT AGREE ATONE
ACCORD ADJUST SETTLE REUNITE
HARMONIZE
RECONCILIATION ACCORD REUNION
IRENICON
RECONNOITER SCOUT SURVEY
EXAMINE DISCOVER REMEMBER
RECORD CAN CUT BOOK CARD DATE
MARK NICK PAGE ROLL SING SLIP
ALBUM CHART ENTER ENTRY
GRAPH PRICK QUIPU SLATE STYLE TITLE
ANNALS CHARGE DOCKET LEGEND
MEMOIR SCROLL SPREAD WARBLE
ACCOUNT DUBBING LEXICON MENTION
SHOWING TICKLER TRACING ARCHIVES
CYLINDER ENTRANCE INSCROLL
JUDGMENT MEMORIAL MONUMENT
PRESSING REGISTER REMEMBER
SCHEDULE STUDBOOK
(— BY NOTCHES) SCORE
(— OF CAR MOVEMENTS) JUMBO
(— OF DOCUMENT) PROTOCOL
(— OF EVENTS) FASTI
(— OF FOOTPRINTS) STIBOGRAM
(— OF HUMANITY'S FATE) SIJILL
(— OF JOURNEY) JOURNAL ITINERARY
(— OF LOAN) CHARGE
(— OF MUHAMMAD'S SAYINGS)
HADIT
(— OF PROCEEDINGS) ACTA ITER
JOURNAL MINUTES
(COMPUTER —) PRINTOUT
(COURT —) EYRE
(DAILY —) DIARY
(FORMAL —) ACT
(MAGNETIC —) DISK FLOPPY
(PHONOGRAPH —) DISC DISK MONO
SINGLE BISCUIT SHELLAC
(SHIP'S —) LOG
RECOUNT TELL COUNT DEVISE RECITE
REGARD RELATE REPEAT SPREAD
EXPRESS HISTORY NARRATE CONSIDER
DESCRIBE
RECOURSE SUIT ACCESS APPEAL
REFUGE RESORT REGRESS
RECOVER DOW CURE FIRM HEAL RALLY
REACH UPSET BOUNCE RECURE REGAIN
RESCUE RESUME RETAKE RETIRE REVERT
REVOKE DELIVER OVERSET RECLAIM
RECRUIT REPRISE RESTORE RETRIEVE

RECOVERY CURE REMEDY RETURN
SALVAGE COMEBACK SNAPBACK
RECREATION PLAY SPORT SOLACE
RENEWAL ACTIVITY DIVERSION
RECRUIT BOOT FRESH RAISE GATHER
INTAKE MUSTER REPAIR REVIVE
RECOVER REFRESH RESTORE BEZONIAN
CONSCRIPT
(RAW —) ROOKIE
RECTIFY AMEND EMEND RIGHT ADJUST
BETTER REFORM REMEDY CORRECT
IMPROVE REDRESS REGULATE
RECTITUDE DOOM EQUITY JUSTICE
PROBITY
RECTOR RULER LEADER PARSON
PERSONA INCUMBENT
RECUPERATE MEND RALLY REGAIN
RECOVER
RECUR CYCLE REPEAT RESORT RETURN
REVOLVE REAPPEAR
(— CONSTANTLY) HAUNT
RECURRENCE RESORT RETURN
ATAVISM REPRISE ITERANCE ITERANCY
RECOURSE
RECURRENT CYCLIC FREQUENT
PERENNIAL
RECURRING ROLLING CONTINUAL
(— ANNUALLY) ETESIAN
(— EVERY THIRD DAY) TERTIAN
(— EVERY 72 HOURS) QUARTAN
(— ON NINTH DAY) NONAN NONANE
(— ON SEVENTH DAY) SEPTAN
(CONSTANTLY —) ETERNAL
(CONTINUALLY —) CONSTANT
RED (ALSO SEE COLOR) GOYA PINK
PUCE ROSY RUBY ANGRY CORAL FIERY
ROUGE RUDDY RUFUS ARCHIL AZALEA
BLOODY CERISE FLORID GARNET ORCHIL
ORIENT RUBRIC TITIAN VERMIL CARMINE
GLOWING PIMENTO RADICAL RUBIOUS
ARMENIAN AUBUSSON BORDEAUX
CARDINAL CHOLERIC FLAGRANT
MANDARIN RUBICUND SANGUINE
RED AND THE BLACK
(AUTHOR OF —) STENDHAL
(CHARACTER IN —) SOREL FOUQUE
JULIEN PIRARD DERENAL VALENOD
MATHILDE
RED BADGE OF COURAGE
(AUTHOR OF —) CRANE
(CHARACTER IN —) JIM HENRY
WILSON CONKLIN FLEMING
REDEEM BUY WIN SAVE CLEAR BORROW
OFFSET RANSOM DELIVER FULFILL
JUSTIFY RECLAIM LIBERATE
REDNESS RED GLOW HEAT RUBOR
ERYTHEMA
(— OF SKY) AURORA
REDOLENT RICH ODOROUS SCENTED
AROMATIC FRAGRANT SMELLING
REDOUND TURN ACCRUE BILLOW
REFLECT OVERFLOW
REDRESS HEAL AVENGE OFFSET REFORM
RELIEF REMEDY REPAIR CORRECT
RECTIFY RELIEVE
REDUCE CUT BATE CLIP DOCK DROP
EASE PARE PULL THIN ABASE ABATE

ALLAY APPAL DRAFT ELIDE LOWER
QUELL SCANT SHAVE SLAKE SLASH
SMELT DEJECT DELETE DEPOSE DILUTE
HUMBLE LESSEN REBATE REDUCT
SHRINK SUBDUE WEAKEN ABANDON
ABRIDGE ASSUAGE CONQUER CURTAIL
DEFLATE DEPLETE DWINDLE ECLIPSE
RESOLVE RETREAT SCISSOR SHORTEN
ABSTRACT CONDENSE DECREASE
DIMINISH MINIMIZE
(— ACCORDING TO FIXED RATIO)
SCALE
(— ANGLE) CHAMFER
(— BULK) BLEND
(— LUMBER) SIZE
(— PROFITS) SQUEEZE
(— PURITY) ALLOY
(— STONE BLOCKS) SPALL
(— THE VALUE) DECRY BEGGAR
DEPRAVE
(— TO A MEAN) AVERAGE
(— TO ASHES) CREMATE
(— TO CARBON) CHAR
(— TO FINE PARTICLES) ATOMIZE
MICRONIZE
(— TO FLAT SURFACE) LEVEL
(— TO INSIGNIFICANCE) DROWN
(— TO LOWER GRADE) BREAK
DEMOTE DEGRADE
(— TO NIL) CLOSE
(— TO NOTHING) ANNUL
(— TO PASSIVITY) CHINAFY
PROSTRATE
(— TO POWDER) GRIND PULVERIZE
(PREF.) DE
REDUCTION BUST LETUP SLASH
CUTBACK CUTDOWN DOCKAGE SHAVING
ANALYSIS DILUTION DISCOUNT
ABATEMENT SHRINKAGE
REDUNDANCY EXCESS NIMIETY
SURPLUS PLEONASM PLETHORA
VERBIAGE TAUTOLOGY
REDUNDANT WORDY LAVISH PROFUSE
SURPLUS VERBOSE SWELLING
EXCESSIVE
REED RIX SAG BENT JUNK PIPE SLEY
TULE ARROW DONAX SPEAR TWILL
RADDLE SAGGON CALAMUS FISTULA
WHISTLE
REEDY THIN WEAK FRAIL TWILLED
REEF CAY KEY LODE SCAR VEIN ATOLL
LEDGE SHELF STICK BOILER SADDLE
SKERRY BALANCE
REEK FOG EMIT FUME HEAP MIST PILE
RICK RISE VENT EQUIP EXUDE ISSUE
NIDOR SMEEK SMOKE STEAM VAPOR
EXHALE OUTFIT EMANATE
(— WITH CORRUPTION) FESTER
REEL PIRN RANT ROCK SPIN SWIM TURN
SPOOL TRULL WAVER WHEEL WHIRL
WINCH BOBBIN RECOIL SWERVE TOTTER
TUMULT WAGGLE WINDER STAGGER
TITUBATE
REFER DEFER LEAVE POINT ADVERT
ALLUDE APPEAL ASSIGN CHARGE
COMMIT DELATE DIRECT IMPUTE SUBMIT
ASCRIBE RELEGATE

(— TO) SEE CITE INTEND CONCERN
CONSULT MENTION INTIMATE
REFEREE BREHON UMPIRE ARBITER
AUDITOR
REFERENCE TAB FOLIO REMIT SIGIL
APPEAL REGARD MEANING RESPECT
ALLUSION HANDBOOK INNUENDO
RELATION
REFINE RUN TRY BOLT EDIT CUPEL EXALT
PLAIN SLICK SMELT DECOCT FILTER
SMOOTH CONCOCT ELEVATE PERFECT
SUBLIME SWEETEN CIVILIZE HUMANIZE
URBANIZE
(— AS GOLD) TEST CARAT
(— PULP) JORDAN
(— SUGAR) CLAY
(— WINE) FORCE
REFINED FINE GENT NEAT NICE EXACT
TERSE CHASTE NIMINY POLITE QUAINT
SUBTLE COURTLY ELEGANT GENTEEL
PRECISE AUGUSTAN DELICATE ELEVATED
HIGHBRED PRECIEUX PRECIOUS
REFINEMENT GRACE NICETY POLISH
CULTURE FINESSE DELICACY ELEGANCE
POLITURE SUBTLETY URBANITY
PRECIOSITY
REFLECT CHEW MUSE PORE SHOW
BLAZE FLASH GLASS GLINT IMAGE SHINE
STUDY THINK ADVISE DAZZLE DEBATE
MIRROR PONDER RECORD REFLEX
RETORT RETURN REVISE PERPEND
REDOUND REFRACT SHIMMER COGITATE
CONSIDER MEDITATE RUMINATE
(— IRREGULARLY) SCATTER
(— UPON) SPECULATE
REFLECTION ECHO IDEA GHOST GLARE
DEBATE MUSING RETURN SHADOW
COUNSEL THOUGHT THINKING
(— OF SELF IN ANOTHER'S EYES)
BABY
REFORM MEND AMEND EMEND PRUNE
BETTER REBUKE REPAIR CENSURE
CORRECT RECLAIM RECTIFY REDRESS
REFRACTORY TOUGH SULLEN UNRULY
WANTON FROWARD RESTIVE VICIOUS
WAYWARD MUTINOUS PERVERSE
STUBBORN REBELLIOUS
REFRAIN CURB KEEP SHUN AVOID SPARE
DESIST FOREGO RETAIN ABSTAIN
FORBEAR LULLABY REPRISE RESTRAIN
WITHDRAW
(— FROM) CAN HELP AVOID SPARE
WAIVE FOREGO RESIGN ABSTAIN
(— FROM TELLING) LAYNE
(— FROM USING) BOYCOTT
(— OF SONG) BOB TAG DOWN FOOT
WHEEL BURDEN CHORUS FALDEROL
(MEANINGLESS —) DERRY DUCDAME
REFRESH FAN COOL REST CHEER FRESH
SLAKE REGALE REPOSE REVIVE
COMFORT FORTIFY FRESHEN QUICKEN
IRRIGATE RECREATE
REFRESHING DEWY BALMY FRESH
TONIC LIVING BRACING COOLING
REFUGE ARK DIVE HOME PORT ROCK
HAVEN OASIS ASYLUM COVERT HARBOR
RESORT ALSATIA RETREAT SHELTER

UMBRAGE FORTRESS HIDEAWAY
MAGDALEN SAFEHOLD

REFUSE ASH NAY ORT BALK DENY DUST
JUNK PELT REDD SCUM SKIM SOIL SUDS
DEADS EXPEL OFFAL REPEL STENT
STUFF SWASH SWILL TRADE TRASH
WAIVE WASTE DANDER DEBRIS FORBID
LITTER LUMBER MIDDEN PALTRY
RAMMEL REJECT SCRUFF SHORTS
SORDOR SPILTH BAGGAGE DECLINE
DISAVOW DISOBEY FORSAKE GARBAGE
OUTCAST PRUNING RUBBISH SOILAGE
SULLAGE DISALLOW DISCLAIM
LEAVINGS RIFFRAFF SWEEPAGE
WITHHOLD
(— ADMISSION) CLOSE
(— FROM CHARCOAL OR COKE)
BREEZE
(— FROM COFFEE BERRIES) TAILINGS
(— FROM CUTTING UP WHALE)
GURRY
(— FROM MELTING METALS) SLAG
DROSS SCORIA
(— FROM SIFTING COFFEE-BEANS)
TRIAGE
(— FROM THRESHING) HUSK COLDER
(— OF MINE) DEAD
(— OF CROP) STOVER
(— OF FLAX) PAB POB HURDS
(— OF FRUITS) MUST
(— OF GRAIN) PUG BRAN
(— OF GRAPES) MARC
(— OF INSECT) FRASS
(— OF MINE) BING
(— OF OIL MILLS) SHODE
(— OF PLANTS) ROSS
(— OF SILK) STRASS
(— OF SPICES) GARBLE
(— OF WHALE) FENKS GURRY TWITTER
(— OF WOOL) BACKINGS
(— TO APPROVE) VETO
(— TO COMPLY) STONEWALL
(— TO GO) JIB BALK
(— TO RECOGNIZE) CUT
(— TO SUPPORT) BOLT
(— TO TALK) DUMMY
(BREWERY —) DRAFF
(FISH —) CHUM GUBBINS
(FOOD —) SWILL
(LEATHER —) SPETCHES
(PLANT —) SCROFF
(STREET —) FULLAGE SCAVAGE

REGAIN RECOVER RETRIEVE
(— SOMETHING LOST) RECOUP

REGAL REAL ROYAL KINGLY PURPLE
STATELY IMPERIAL MAJESTIC PRINCELY
SPLENDID

REGALE FETE FEAST TREAT PLEASE
DELIGHT REFRESH

REGALIA KIT ROYALTY

REGARD CON CARE DEEM FIND GAZE
HEED HOLD LIKE LOOK MARK MIND RATE
SAKE TELL ADORE COUNT FAVOR HONOR
TREAT WEIGH ADMIRE ASPECT BEHOLD
ESTEEM FIGURE GLANCE HOMAGE
INTEND LIKING MOTIVE NOTICE RECKON
REWARD SURVEY ACCOUNT ADJUDGE

CONCERN OBSERVE RESPECT CONSIDER
ENVISAGE ESTIMATE

REGARDING ABOUT ANENT APROPOS

REGARDLESS DEAF CARELESS
HEEDLESS RECKLESS
(— OF THAT) BUT

REGENERATE RENEW REFORM REVIVE
RECLAIM GRACIOUS RENOVATE

REGENT RULER RULING WARDEN
SHIKKEN GOVERNOR PROTECTOR

REGIMENT BUFF RULE COLOR GUIDANCE
INFANTRY
(BRITISH —) GRAYS GREYS
(COSSACK —) PULK
(FRAMEWORK OF —) CADRE
(INDIA —) PULTON
(SPANISH —) TERCIO
(TURKISH —) ALAI
(28TH —) SLASHERS

REGION END ERD EYE GAU WON AREA
BELT KITH KNOT NECK PART SOIL WONE
WOON ZONE CLIME COAST EARTH
EXURB INDIA PAGUS PLACE PLAGE
REALM SHIRE TRACT TROAD ALKALI
BORDER CENTER DESERT DOMAIN
EXTENT GILEAD GROUND GUIANA
TATARY CLIMATE CONFINE DEMESNE
ENCLAVE IMAMATE KINGDOM MALABAR
STATION TARTARY CHIEFDOM CLUBLAND
DEMERARA DISTRICT ENVIRONS
FLATLAND FORTRESS FRONTIER
KRATOGEN LAKELAND LATITUDE
NAPHTALI PROVINCE REGIMENT
SERICANA STANNARY TERRITORY
(— ABOVE MOUTH) EPISTOME
(— ADJACENT TO BOUNDARY)
MARCH
(— BEYOND ATMOSPHERE) SPACE
(— BEYOND DEATH) CANAAN
(— BORDERING ON HELL) LIMBO
(— FAR AWAY) STRAND
(— IN FIBER) MICELLE
(— NEAR EQUATOR) DOLDRUMS
(— NOTED FOR MANY CONFLICTS)
COCKPIT
(— OF AMPLITUDE) ANTINODE
(— OF COLD AND DARKNESS)
NIFLHEL NIFLHEIM
(— OF DEAD) AMENTI UTGARTHAR
(— OF JAPAN) DO
(— OF MARS) LIBYA
(— OF OCEAN) COUNTRY
(— OF ORIGIN) CRADLE
(— OF PHOTOSPHERE) FACULA
(— OF SIMPLE PLEASURE) ARCADY
ARCADIA
(— OF SOURCE OF GOLD) OPHIR
(— OF TISSUE) FIELD
(— WITHOUT LAW) ALSATIA
(— WITHOUT WOODS) WOLD WEALD
(CELESTIAL —S) LANGI
(COASTAL —) LITTORAL
(CULTIVATED —) GARDEN
(DARKISH —S ON MARS) MARE
(DESERT —) ERG HAMADA
(DESERTED —) WASTE
(DESOLATE —) PUNA

(DISTANT —) THULE
(E. INDIAN —) DESH
(ELEVATED —) ALTITUDE
(FOREST —) TAIGA
(FORESTED —) MONTANA
(GEOGRAPHICAL —) BOWL SIDE
(HEAVENLY —) SPHERE
(IDEAL —) JINNESTAN
(INFERNAL —S) ABYSS TARTAR
TARTARUS
(LARGE —) COMPAGE
(LIMESTONE —) KARST
(MOUNTAINOUS —) SIERRA
(OPEN —) SAVANNAH
(ORIENTAL —) INDOGAEA
(STAGNANT —) EDDY
(SUPERIOR —) HIGH
(TREELESS —) HIGHMOOR
(UPPER —) HIGH LOFT
(UPPER —S) ETHER
(WOODED —) FOREST
(PL.) DIGGINGS
REGISTER BEAR BOOK LIST MARK PILE
POLL READ ROLL ALBUM DIARY ENROL
ENTER GRILL SLATE ANNALS BEHAVE
ENROLL LEDGER MUSTER RECORD
ALMANAC ASCRIBE CALENDS CATALOG
INDORSE ARCHIVES CALENDAR INDICATE
INSCRIBE PEDIGREE TOLLBOOK
REGRET RUE RUTH GRIEF DESIRE RELENT
REPENT SORROW DEPLORE REMORSE
REGRETFUL BAD SORRY REPINING
REGRETTABLE DIRTY DOLOROUS
REGULAR DUE SET EVEN FULL JUST
SOBER SUANT USUAL FORMAL NORMAL
SQUARE STATED STEADY CANONIC
CERTAIN CORRECT NATURAL ORDERED
ORDERLY ORDINAL PERFECT TYPICAL
UNIFORM COMPLETE CONSTANT
DECOROUS FORMULAR HABITUAL
ORDINARY ORDINATE TESSERAL
(PREF.) SYM
REGULARITY METHOD SQUARE SYSTEM
EVENNESS SYNAPHEA
(— OF NATURE) LAW
REGULATE SET RATE RULE WIND FRAME
GUIDE ORDER RIGHT SHAPE ADJUST
BEHAVE DIRECT GOVERN MASTER
SETTLE SQUARE TEMPER ARRANGE
CONTROL MEASURE RECTIFY MODERATE
REGULATION LAW RULE BYLAW ORDER
CURFEW CONTROL PRECEPT STATUTE
DISPOSAL
REHEARSAL CALL PREVIEW CLAMBAKE
NARRATION
REHEARSE TELL TRAIN DETAIL RECITE
RELATE DECLINE NARRATE RECOUNT
DESCRIBE PRACTICE
REIGN RULE REALM EMPIRE GOVERN
KINGDOM PREVAIL REGNANCY
(— IN INDIA) RAJ
REIMBURSE PAY REPAY DEFRAY RECOUP
REFUND INDEMNIFY
REIN CURB STOP CHECK THONG GOVERN
LEATHER PLOWLINE RESTRAIN
REINFORCE BAR GUY BACK FACE STAY
BRACE INLAY STUFF CRADLE DOUBLE

HARDEN SUPPLY BOLSTER BULWARK
GROMMET STIFFEN SUPPORT
REINFORCEMENT CREW FUEL STAY
BRACE SPLICING STRAINER
REJECT ORT CAST DEFY FAIL JILT KICK
SPIN ABHOR BANDY BELIE BRUSH CHECK
EJECT REPEL SCOUT SPURN WAIVE
ABJURE DELETE DESERT IGNORE REFUSE
REFUTE RETORT ABANDON CASHIER
CONTEMN DECLINE DISCARD DISMISS
FORSAKE REPULSE ABNEGATE
DISALLOW FORSWEAR RENOUNCE
REJECTION SACK BRUSH SPURN DENIAL
REBUFF REFUSAL REPULSE DEFIANCE
TURNDOWN
REJOICE FAIN GAME CHEER ENJOY
EXULT GLORY PLEASE DELIGHT GLADDEN
JUBILATE
REJOICING GLEE MIRTH OVATION
FESTIVITY
REJOINDER REPLY ANSWER COUNTER
RESPONSE
RELATE SAY ALLY BEAR JOIN READ TELL
PITCH REFER SPELL STATE TOUCH
ALLUDE ASSERT DETAIL DEVISE RECITE
REPORT CONCERN DECLARE INVOLVE
NARRATE PERTAIN RECOUNT REHEARSE
RELATED KIN SIB AKIN ALLIED AFFINED
(— BY FATHER'S SIDE) AGNATE
(— INVERSELY) RECIPROCAL
(— ON MOTHER'S SIDE) ENATE
ENATIC COGNATE
RELATION TALE BLOOD REGARD
ACCOUNT BEARING HISTORY KINSHIP
KINSMAN RAPPORT RESPECT TELLING
HABITUDE RELATIVE TENDENCY
REFERENCE PROPORTION
(— BETWEEN SPECIES) AFFINITY
(— OF LIKENESS) ANALOGY
(BLOOD —) KIN SIB
(FIXED —) RATIO
(FRIENDLY —S) AMITY
(SYNTACTIC —) FUNCTION
(WORKING —) GEAR
RELATIONSHIP KIN BLOOD AGENCY
AMENITY ANALOGY BEARING KINDRED
KINSHIP LIAISON RESPECT SOCIETY
AFFINITY AGNATION CONTRAST
COGNATION FILIATION
(BUSINESS —) ACCOUNT
(CLOSE —) BOSOM AFFIANCE INTIMACY
BELONGING
(INHARMONIOUS —) OUTS
(MARITAL —) BED
(MATHEMATICAL —) PARITY
(MUTUAL —) TERMS SYMMETRY
(SEXUAL —) AFFAIR
(SOCIAL —) FOOTING
RELATIVE KIN ALLY BLOOD AGNATE
ALLIED COUSIN GERMAN KINDRED
KINSMAN APPOSITE RELATION
RELEVANT PERTINENT
RELAX GIVE REST ABATE BREAK LOOSE
REMIT SLACK DIVERT SOFTEN UNBEND
UNKNIT RELEASE RESOLVE SLACKEN
UNPURSE MITIGATE UNCLENCH
RELAXATION EASE LAZE REST LETUP

SOLACE DETENTE LETDOWN BREATHER DIVERSION

RELAXED LAX LOOSE SLACK REMISS INFORMAL RESOLVED UNBRACED

RELEASE LET BAIL DROP EMIT FREE SHED SLIP TRIP UNDO ERUPT LOOSE REMIT SLAKE ACQUIT DEMISE EXCUSE EXEMPT LAUNCH UNTACK ABSOLVE DELIVER LIBERATE DISCHARGE
(— AS DOGS) UNLEASH
(— DANCING PARTNER) BREAK
(— EMOTION) ABREAST
(— FROM CONFINEMENT) UNMEW UNPEN SPRING STREET
(— FROM DEBT) FREITH
(— FROM MILITARY) INVALID
(— FROM SLAVERY) MANUMIT
(— ON ONE'S WORD) PAROLE
(PRESS —) HANDOUT

RELENT COME MELT ABATE YIELD REGRET REPENT LIQUEFY MOLLIFY SLACKEN

RELENTLESS GRIM HARD HARSH STERN STONY BITTER SAVAGE STRICT AUSTERE PITILESS RIGOROUS

RELEVANT APT VALID APROPOS GERMANE MATERIAL PERTINENT

RELIABLE GOOD HARD SAFE SURE TRUE PUKKA SOLID SOUND TRIED WHITE DINKUM STEADY TRUSTY CERTAIN FAITHFUL STRAIGHT

RELIANCE HOPE TRUST CREDIT MAINSTAY

RELIC REMAIN ANTIQUE LEAVING MEMENTO VESTIGE SOUVENIR

RELIEF AID EASE HELP RELAY SCRUB SPELL SWING ESCAPE REMEDY SUCCOR COMFORT REDRESS EASEMENT

RELIEVE ROB EASE FREE HELP ALLAY RIGHT SLAKE SPARE SPELL ASSIST LESSEN REMEDY REMOVE RESCUE SOOTHE SUCCOR ASSUAGE COMFORT DELIVER DEPRIVE FRESHEN LIGHTEN REDRESS REFRESH SUCCEED SUPPORT SUSTAIN SWEETEN MITIGATE

RELIGION LAW SECT BONBO CREED FAITH OBEAH PIETY SOPHY DHARMA SHINTO SYSTEM TAOISM ELOHISM JAINISM JUDAISM ORPHISM PERSISM SIKHISM BUDDHISM CAODAISM HINDUISM MAZDAISM PEYOTISM SHAMANISM
(— OF ABRAHAM) HANIFIYA
(— OF TIBET) BON
(CHRISTIAN —) WAY
(UNORTHODOX —) CULT

RELIGIOUS HOLY EXACT GODLY PIOUS RIGID DEVOUT DIVINE SACRED FERVENT GHOSTLY ZEALOUS SPIRITUAL

RELINQUISH LAY LET CEDE DROP QUIT DEMIT FORGO GRANT LEAVE WAIVE YIELD CANCEL DESERT RESIGN ABANDON FORSAKE RELEASE ABDICATE ABNEGATE RENOUNCE

RELISH CHOW DASH EDGE GUST LIKE TANG ZEST ACHAR ENJOY GUSTO SAVOR SPICE TASTE TRACE ATSARA FLAVOR LIKING PALATE BOTARGO STOMACH APPETITE FONDNESS

RELUCTANT SET SHY CAGY CHARY LOATH AFRAID AVERSE DAINTY FORCED ASHAMED HALTING BACKWARD GRUDGING

RELY BANK BASE LEAN REST STAY COUNT TRUST DEPEND CONFIDE
(— ON) LIPPEN VENTURE

REMAIN LIE SIT BIDE REST STAY STOP ABIDE CLING DWELL LEAVE STAND TARRY ENDURE RESIDE SUBSIST SURVIVE CONTINUE

REMAINDER NET REST ARREAR EXCESS RELIEF BALANCE REMNANT RESIDUE SURPLUS LEAVINGS LEFTOVER RESIDUAL RESIDUUM

REMARK SAY SEE HEED NOTE WORD GLOSS STATE TOKEN EARFUL NOTICE REGARD COMMENT OBSERVE PERCEIVE
(— BRIEFLY) GLANCE
(AMIABLE —) DOUCEUR
(AMUSING —) GAG
(BANAL —) PLATITUDE
(BITING —) BARB
(CLEVER —) NIFTY
(CONCLUDING —S) ENVOI
(CUTTING —) DIG SPINOSITY
(DULL —) BROMIDE
(EMBARRASSING —) BREAK
(EXPLANATORY —) SCHOLION SCHOLIUM
(FOOLISH —) INANITY
(ILL-TIMED —) CLANGER
(INSULTING —) SLUR
(JEERING —) JEST SKIT
(LAUGH-PROVOKING —) GAG
(SARCASTIC —) HIT GIRD SLANT
(SATIRICAL —) JEST SKIT
(SHARP —) GANSEL STINGER
(SILLY —) FADAISE
(STALE —S) BILGE
(UNCOMPLIMENTARY —) BRICKBAT
(WITTY —) JEST CRACK ZINGER

REMARKABLE SOME GREAT SIGNAL STRONG NOTABLE STRANGE UNUSUAL FABULOUS SINGULAR SPANKING STRIKING UNCOMMON BODACIOUS PHENOMENAL

REMEDY AID BOOT CURE GAIN HALE HEAL HELP SHERE PHYSIC RECURE RELIEF REPAIR URETIC ANTACID CORRECT DRASTIC OTALGIC PLASTER RECTIFY REDRESS RELIEVE MEDICINE PHARMACY RECOVERY REMEDIAL SPECIFIC
(— COUNTERACTING POISON) TREACLE ANTIDOTE
(— FOR ALL DISEASES) PANACEA CATHOLICON
(— FOR DIZZINESS) DINIC
(— FOR JAUNDICE) ICTERIC
(— TO REDUCE FEVER) FEBRIFUGE
(CHINESE —) SENSO
(EXTERNAL —) TOPIC

(FAVORITE —) NOSTRUM
(SECRET —) ARCANUM
(TAPEWORM —) EMBELIA
(TOOTHACHE —) TONGA
(UNIVERSAL —) AZOTH CATHOLICON
(WITHOUT —) BOOTLESS
REMEMBER MIND IDEATE RECALL
RECORD REMIND RETAIN BETHINK
RECOLLECT
REMEMBRANCE OF THINGS PAST
(AUTHOR OF —) PROUST
(CHARACTER IN —) MOREL SWANN
MARCEL ODETTE RACHEL ROBERT
VEDURIN GILBERTE VINTEUIL ALBERTINE
DECHARLUS GUERMANTES
REMIND JOG MIND PROMPT REMEMBER
REMISS LAX LAZY MILD FAINT SLACK
TARDY BEHIND DILUTED LANGUID
CARELESS DERELICT DILATORY
HEEDLESS NEGLIGENT
REMIT SEND COVER LOOSE RELAX
CANCEL EXCUSE PARDON REMAND
ABSOLVE FORGIVE RELEASE SUSPEND
ABROGATE
REMNANT END TAG BUTT DREG REST
RELIC STUMP TRACE LEAVING REMAINS
(— OF CLOTH) FENT
(— OF FOOD) CRUST
(— OF ROCK MASS) KLIPPE
(— OF VEIL) ANNULUS
(—S OF FILLETS) SCISSEL
(—S OF VEIL) CORTINA
(VESTIGIAL —) SHADOW
REMORSE HELL PITY RUTH REGRET
PENITENCE
REMOTE FAR OFF BACK DEEP HIGH LONG
ALOOF UTTER EXEMPT SECRET DEVIOUS
DISTANT EXTREME FARAWAY FOREIGN
OBSCURE OUTSIDE ABSTRUSE INTERIOR
OUTLYING SECLUDED SOLITARY
REMOVE GET RID COMB DELE FILE FREE
LIFT MOVE PARE PEEL QUIT RAZE VOID
WEED AVOID BLAST BRUSH CLEAR
ERASE HOIST LIGHT RAISE SHIFT SHUCK
SWEEP WAIVE BANISH CANCEL CHANGE
CONVEY DEDUCT DEPART EFFACE
EXEMPT EXPORT SPIRIT DEPRIVE
DESCENT DISPOST DIVORCE EXCERPT
RESCIND RETRACT REVERSE STRANGE
SUBDUCT SUBLATE ASPIRATE DISPLACE
DISPLANT ESTRANGE EVACUATE
SUPPLANT TRANSFER WITHDRAW
(— A STITCH) DECREASE
(— BARK FROM LOG) ROSS
(— BIT BY BIT) SCAMBLE
(— BY CUTTING) ABLATE
(— BY DEATH) SNATCH
(— CLOTHING) DOFF STRIP
(— COLOR) BLEACH
(— COVER) UNCAP
(— DEFECTS) SCARF
(— DIRT) BLADE GARBLE
(— EXCESS METAL) CUT
(— FROM CHECKER BOARD) HUFF
(— FROM OFFICE) DEPOSE RECALL
DISMISS
(— FROM REMEMBRANCE) COVER

(— GILLS) BEARD
(— HAIR) DEPILATE
(— HUSKS AND CHAFF) GELD
(— INSIDES OF FISH) GIB GIP
(— JUDGE) ADDRESS
(— LOWER BRANCHES) BRASH
(— MAST) UNSTEP
(— ORE) EXTRACT
(— PARTICLES OF GOLD LEAF) SKEW
(— PITCHER FROM BASEBALL
GAME) DERRICK
(— POTATOES) GRABBLE
(— QUEEN BEE) DEMAREE
(— QUIETLY) ABSTRACT
(— ROOTS) GRUB
(— SEED FROM FLAX) RIBBLE
(— SEEDS) STONE
(— SKIN) HULL HUSK
(— SOUND FROM TAPE) BLIP
(— SPROUTS FROM) CHIT
(— STALK FROM) STRIG
(— STAMENS) CASTRATE
(— TABLECLOTH) DRAW
(— THE TOP OF) COP
(— TO AVOID TAX) SKIM
(— TROUSERS) DEBAG
(— WASTE TO FIBER) GARNETT
(— WOOL) BELLY
(— WORKS OF STOLEN WATCH)
CHURCH
REMUNERATE PAY REWARD GRATIFY
SATISFY CONSIDER REIMBURSE
REND PULL RIVE TEAR TOIL BREAK BURST
SEVER SPLIT WREST CLEAVE WRENCH
RUPTURE FRACTURE LACERATE
SPLINTER
RENDER DO PAY PUT BEAR DRAW ECHO
EMIT MAKE DEFER REPAY YIELD RECITE
REPEAT RETURN DELIVER REFLECT
REQUITE RESTORE SERVICE TRANSMIT
(— ACID) PRICK
(— AGREEABLE) DULCIFY
(— AS LARD) TRY
(— ASSISTANCE TO SHIP) FOY
(— CAPABLE) ACTIVATE
(— CLEAR) OPEN
(— FIT) ADAPT
(— GODLIKE) DEIFY
(— HEAVY WITH FOOD) STODGE
(— HOMAGE) ATTORN
(— IMMUNE) FRANK VASTATE
(— INEFFECTIVE) VITIATE
(— KNOTTY) GNARL
(— OBLIQUE) SPLAY
(— OBSCURE) DARKLE
(— QUIET) ACCOY
(— SENSELESS) STUN ASTONISH
(— TURBID) ROIL
(— UNFIT) DENATURE
(— UNSTABLE) UNHINGE
(— VERDICT) PASS
(— VOID) CASS DEFEAT
(SUFF.) EN
RENDEZVOUS DATE HAUNT TRYST
REFUGE HANGOUT MEETING RETREAT
(— FOR SHIPS) DOWN

RENDITION ACCOUNT CONDUCT
DELIVERY
RENEGADE PERVERT TRAITOR APOSTATE
RECREANT TURNCOAT
RENEW REST RECALL REFORM REPEAT
RESUME REVIVE REBUILD REFRESH
REPLACE RESTORE OVERHAUL
REJUVENATE
(— MORTAR) REPOINT
(— WINE) STUM
RENOUNCE CEDE DEFY DENY QUIT
FORGO WAIVE ABJURE DISOWN RECANT
REFUSE REJECT RENEGE RESIGN REVOKE
ABANDON DECLARE FORSAKE RETRACT
WITHSAY ABDICATE ABNEGATE
DISCLAIM FORSWEAR RELINQUISH
RENOVATE DUST RENEW REVIVE
FURBISH REFRESH RESTORE OVERHAUL
RENOWN BRAG FAME ECLAT GLORY
KUDOS RUMOR ESTEEM LUSTER REPORT
SWAGGER PRESTIGE NOTORIETY
RENOWNED FAMED NOBLE NOTED
FAMOUS EMINENT GLORIOUS MAGNIFIC
RENT LET TAX FARM GAPE HIRE MAIL
RACK RIVE SLIT TEAR TOLL WAGE BREAK
ENDOW SPLIT BREACH BROKEN CRANNY
CUSTOM INCOME SCHISM SCREED
CHARTER CORNAGE CRACKED CREVICE
FISSURE REVENUE RUPTURE TRIBUTE
STALLAGE
(— BY BOAR'S TUSK) GANCH
(— IN LIEU OF SUPPER) CUDDY
(— OF LAND PAID IN KIND) CAIN
(ANNUAL —) CANON
(EARTHQUAKE —) SCARPLET
(GROUND —) CENSO CENSUS
(OATS IN LIEU OF —) AVENAGE
REPAIR DO EKE FIX HEAL HELP MEND
HAUNT RALLY RENEW COBBLE COOPER
DOCTOR FETTLE RECURE REFORM
REMEDY RESORT RETURN UPKEEP
CORRECT REDRESS RESTORE SERVICE
OVERHAUL REVIVIFY
(— BOAT) CAREEN
(— CLUMSILY) BOTCH
(— FENCE) MOUND
(— ROAD) SKID
(— SHOE) FOX TAP
REPAST FEED FOOD MEAL FEAST TREAT
DRINKING COLLATION
REPAY MEED TALLY YIELD ACQUIT
ANSWER REFUND RETORT RETURN
REWARD IMBURSE REQUITE
REPEAL ANNUL CANCEL RECALL REVOKE
ABANDON ABOLISH RESCIND REVERSE
ABROGATE DEROGATE RENOUNCE
REPEAT SAY ECHO SHOW TELL DITTO
QUOTE RECUR RENEW RESAY THRUM
ANSWER RESUME SECOND DIVULGE
ITERATE PRESENT REPLICA REPRISE
REPLICATE
(— BY ROTE) PARROT
(— GLIBLY) SCREED
(— MONOTONOUSLY) CUCKOO
DINGDONG
(— OF PATTERN) GAIT
(— TIRESOMELY) DIN

REPEL FEND TURN WARD FENCE REBUT
DEFEND REBUFF REFUSE REFUTE REJECT RESIST
REVOLT REPULSE
REPENT RUE MOURN GRIEVE REGRET
FORTHINK
REPENTANCE RUE PITY RUTH RUING
REGRET SORROW PENANCE REMORSE
REPETITION BIS COPY ECHO REPEAT
MENTION RECITAL REPLICA REPRISE
ITERANCE ITERANCY PARROTRY
RECOVERY REHEARSAL
(— OF SPEECH FORMS) ROTE
(NEEDLESS —) REDUNDANCY
(UNINSPIRED —) STENCIL
REPLACE SWAP RENEW REPAY SHIFT
STEAD CHANGE REFUND REMISE SUPPLY
FRESHEN PREEMPT RESTORE SUCCEED
DISPLACE SUPPLANT REPLENISH
REPLENISH REFIT RENEW SUPPLY
NOURISH PERFECT REPLETE RESTORE
REPLICA COPY IDEA CHARM IMAGE
FACSIMILE
REPLY CAP RESAY ANSWER REJOIN
RETORT RETURN RESOUND RESPOND
REPARTEE RESPONSE
REPORT POP SAY ITEM NOTE TELL VENT
WORD AUDIT BRUIT CRACK NOISE REFER
ROUND SOUND STORY DETAIL GOSSIP
RECITE RELATE RENOWN REPUTE
STEVEN SURVEY ACCOUNT HEARING
HEARSAY INKLING NARRATE OPINION
PROCESS RECITAL ADVISORY DESCRIBE
VERBATIM
(— NEWS) COVER
(— OF GUN) CLAP
(— OF INFRACTION) GIG
(— OF PROCEEDINGS) CAHIER
(— OF TIMBER SURVEYOR) CRUISE
(ABSURD —) CANARD
(BELIEVED —) CREDIT
(CASUAL —) FABLE
(COMMON —) CRY FAME SPEECH
(FALSE —) SHAVE CANARD FURPHY
SLANDER
(FLYING —) SOUGH
(HONORABLE —) TONGUE
(LAW —) CASE
(MILITARY —) STATE SITREP
(NEWS —) FLASH SCOOP
(NOISY —) RUMBLE
(OFFICIAL —) HANSARD
(POPULAR —) RUMOR
(UNFAVORABLE —) SKIN
(UNVERIFIED —) VOICE GRAPEVINE
(VAGUE —) BREEZE
REPORTER LEGMAN PISTOL CREEPER
NEWSMAN NEWSHAWK PRESSMAN
STRINGER PAPARAZZO
REPOSE BED LIE PUT CALM EASE REST
PEACE PLACE POISE QUIET SLEEP
RECLINE EASINESS QUIETUDE SERENITY
REPOSITORY ARK AMBRY DEPOT HOARD
VAULT ARMORY CASKET MUSEUM
VESTRY CABINET CAPSULE GRANARY
HANAPER ARCHIVES MAGAZINE
TREASURY SEPULCHER
REPRESENT GIVE LIKE LIMN SHOW

SHADE DEPICT TYPIFY DISPLAY EXHIBIT
FASHION PICTURE PORTRAY DESCRIBE
RESEMBLE PERSONATE
(— CONCRETELY) THING
(— IN LANGUAGE) ACT BODY DRAW
ENACT SPEAK BLAZON EMBODY FIGURE
EXPRESS

REPRESENTATION SUN BUST FORM
ICON IDEA IDOL SHOW ANGLE DRAFT
INSET MEDAL AVOWAL EFFIGY FIGURE
MODULE SCHEME SKETCH ANATOMY
DIORAMA DRAWING EPITOME EXTRACT
SCENERY TABLEAU BLAZONRY EXTERIOR
IDIOGRAM LIKENESS SIMULACRUM
RESEMBLANCE
(— OF SERPENT) BASIL DRAGON
BASILISK
(— OF SHRINE OF HUSAIN) TABUT
(— OF VISION) AISLING
(DIPLOMATIC —) DEMARCHE
(FACSIMILE —) TYPORAMA
(FAINT —) SHADOW
(GRAPHIC —) CHART BISECT
(HERALDIC —) LEOPARD LIONCEL
(MENTAL —) FANCY IMAGE
(MINIATURE —) MODEL
(SYMBOLIC —) ALLEGORY

REPRESENTATIVE REP TYPE AGENT
ENVOY COMMON DEPUTY EMBLEM
LEDGER SAMPLE VAKEEL BURGESS
TRIBUNE TYPICAL DELEGATE EMISSARY
EXPONENT FIELDMAN OBSERVER
SALESMAN SPECIMEN

REPRESS CURB HUSH BLUNT CHAIN
CHECK CHOKE CRUSH DAUNT DROWN
QUELL BRIDLE COERCE DEADEN REBUKE
STIFLE SUBDUE CONTROL DEPRESS
INHIBIT SILENCE COMPRESS OVERBEAR
RESTRAIN RESTRICT STRANGLE
SUPPRESS WITHHOLD

REPRIMAND WIG BAWL CALL CHEW
JACK SKIN SLAP TASK CHECK SPANK
BOUNCE CARPET EARFUL REBUKE
STRAFE CENSURE LECTURE REPROOF
REPROVE DRESSING

REPROACH ILL TAX BLOT GIBE NOTE
RAIL SLUR SPOT TWIT ABUSE BLAME
BRAID BRAND CHIDE SCOLD TAUNT
INFAMY REBUKE REVILE VILIFY BLEMISH
CENSURE CONDEMN REPROOF REPROVE
SLANDER UPBRAID DISHONOR
CONTUMELY OPPROBRIUM

REPROBATE HARD LOST SCAMP RASCAL
SINNER ABANDON CENSURE CORRUPT
REPROVE DEPRAVED HARDENED
SCALAWAG

REPRODUCE BUD COPY BREED RECITE
REPEAT PORTRAY MULTIPLY REFIGURE
PROCREATE

REPRODUCTION CAST COPY IMAGE
PRINT ECTYPE RECALL STEREO EDITION
ELECTRO REPLICA REVIVAL LIKENESS

REPROVE RAG TAP BAWL FLAY RATE
BLAME CHECK CHIDE CRAWL SCOLD
BERATE REBUKE REFORM CENSURE
CONDEMN CORRECT IMPROVE LECTURE
UPBRAID ADMONISH CHASTISE
KEELHAUL REPROACH

REPTILE LOW MEAN WORM SNAKE VIPER
GAVIAL LIZARD MOLOCH TURTLE
CRAWLER CREEPER SAURIAN SERPENT
TUATARA BASILISK DINOSAUR TORTOISE
ALLIGATOR CROCODILE
(PREF.) HERPET(I)

REPUBLIC STATE SOVIET POBLACHT
(FRENCH —) MARIANNE
(IDEAL —) ICARIA
(IMAGINARY —) OCEANA

REPUDIATE DEFY ABJURE DISOWN
RECANT REFUTE REJECT DECLINE
DISAVOW DISCARD DIVORCE RETRACT
DISCLAIM RENOUNCE

REPUGNANCE ENMITY HATRED HORROR
DISGUST DISLIKE DISTASTE LOATHING

REPUGNANT ALIEN DIRTY NASTY
ADVERSE HATEFUL OPPOSED INIMICAL
OPPOSITE ABHORRENT OBNOXIOUS
REPULSIVE

REPULSE FOIL ROUT CHECK REBUT
REPEL DEFEAT DENIAL REBUFF REFUSE
REJECT

REPULSIVE COLD EVIL UGLY VILE
GREASY FULSOME HATEFUL LOATHLY
SQUALID SCABROUS

REPUTABLE GOOD HONEST WORTHY
CREDIBLE ESTIMABLE

REPUTATION FAME NAME NOTE ODOR
GLORY HONOR NOISE RUMOR SAVOR
VOICE CREDIT ESTEEM RECORD RENOWN
SHADOW LAURELS OPINION RESPECT
WORSHIP
(EVIL —) INFAMY
(GOOD —) STANDING

REPUTE FAME ODOR RANK WORD NOISE
SAVOR THINK RECKON REGARD STATUS
OPINION RESPECT WORSHIP ESTIMATE
JUDGMENT POSITION

REQUEST ASK BEG BOON CALL PLEA
PRAY SEEK SUIT TELL WISH CLAIM LIBEL
YEARN APPEAL DESIRE DIRECT ENCORE
INVITE MOTION BESPEAK COMMAND
ENTREAT INQUIRY REQUIRE SOLICIT
ENTREATY PETITION
(— FOR HELP) SOS
(STRONG —) DUN DEMAND

REQUIRE ASK HAVE LACK NEED TAKE
WANT CLAIM CRAVE EXACT FORCE
COMPEL DEMAND DEPEND DESIRE
ENJOIN ENTAIL EXPECT GOVERN OBLIGE
BEHOOVE DICTATE INVOLVE SOLICIT

REQUIRED DUE SET SUPPOSED
NECESSARY OBLIGATORY

REQUIREMENT CALL NEED ORDER
BEHEST DEMAND NECESSITY

REQUISITION ORDER DEMAND INDENT
EMBARGO REQUEST

RESCIND LIFT ANNUL CANCEL REMOVE
REPEAL REVOKE ABOLISH RETRACT
ABROGATE

RESCUE RID FREE HELP SAVE BORROW
RANSOM REDEEM SUCCOR DELIVER
RECLAIM RECOVER RELEASE SALVAGE
DELIVERY LIBERATE RECOURSE

RESEARCH ARBEIT SEARCH INQUIRY
RESEMBLANCE SWAP PARITY SIMILE
ANALOGY AFFINITY LIKENESS PARALLEL
VICINITY SIMILARITY
RESEMBLE AGREE FAVOR IMAGE LIKEN
APPEAR DEPICT FIGURE RECALL
COMPARE IMITATE PORTRAY SIMULATE
RESENT HATE MALIGN STOMACH
RESENTFUL HARD HURT BITTER SULLEN
ENVIOUS JEALOUS
RESENTMENT HURT PIQUE SPITE
CHOLER ENMITY GRUDGE HATRED
MALICE RANCOR DISDAIN DUDGEON
OFFENSE UMBRAGE JEALOUSY
RESERVATION DIBS SPACE SAVING
UNLESS BOOKING CAUTION PROVISO
RESERVE
(MENTAL —) SALVO SCRUPLE
RESERVE BOOK FUND HOLD KEEP SALT
SAVE SPARE BACKUP NICETY SEPOSE
BACKLOG CAUTION CONTROL DIGNITY
SHYNESS COLDNESS DISTANCE
FALLBACK WITHHOLD STOCKPILE
RESERVED COY DRY SHY COLD ALOOF
CHARY SAVED BOOKED CLOSED DEMURE
MODEST SILENT DISTANT STRANGE
RETICENT RETIRING STANDOFF
TACITURN
RESERVOIR DAM FONT KEEP LAKE SUMP
TANK BASIN FOUNT STORE SOURCE
CISTERN PISCINA AFTERBAY FOUNTAIN
MAGAZINE
RESIDE WIN BIDE HOME LIVE STAY
WONT ABIDE DWELL LODGE REMAIN
CONSIST SOJOURN HABITATE
RESIDENCE WON HALL HOME SEMI
WONE ABODE COURT HOUSE BIDING
DUKERY HOSTEL MANOIR TENSER
DROSTDY EMBASSY SOJOURN DOMICILE
DWELLING LEGATION RESIDUUM
(— FOR STUDENTS) INN
(— OF CHIEF OF VILLAGE) TATA
(— OF ECCLESIASTIC) MANSE
DEANERY CURATAGE
(— OF FRENCH PRESIDENTS) ELYSEE
(— OF MIKADO) DAIRI
(— OF SOVEREIGN) PALACE
(FORTIFIED —) DUN
(HILL —) RATH
(OFFICIAL TURKISH —) KONAK
(RURAL —) SEAT FARMSTEAD
(SUMMER —) MAHAL
(TEMPORARY —) STAY
RESIDENT FIXED LEGER LIVER INMATE
STABLE CITIZEN DENIZEN DWELLER
PRESENT RESIANT RESIDER HABITANT
INHERENT MINISTER OCCUPANT
(— AT A UNIVERSITY) GREMIALE
(— OF HAWAII) KAMAAINA
(— OF NEWFOUNDLAND) LIVYER
(— OF WEST. AUSTRALIA) GROPER
(ALIEN —) GER METIC
(CHINESE — OF TIBET) AMBAN
(FOREIGN-BORN —) ALIEN
(OLD —) STANDARD
(SUFF.) ESE ITE
RESIDUE DREG FOOT GUNK HEEL LEES

REST SILT SLAG SHARD SHERD GRUFFS
RELICS BAGASSE CINDERS REMAINS
LEAVINGS LEFTOVER REMANENT
RESIDUUM TAILINGS
(— FROM FAT) CRAP
(— FROM OLIVES) SANZA
(— FROM REFINING TIN) HARDHEAD
(— IN STILL) BOTTOM BOTTOMS
(— OF COAL) COKE SEMICOKE
(— OF COKE) BREEZE
(— OF COMBUSTION) ASH
(— OF HONEYCOMB) SLUMGUM
(— OF PETROLEUM) MAZUT ASTATKI
(— OF SHINGLES) SPALT
(FRIABLE —) CALX
(INSOLUBLE —) MARC
(PL.) TANKAGE
RESIGN LAC DEMIT FORGO REMIT YIELD
SUBMIT ABANDON DELIVER ABDICATE
RENOUNCE RELINQUISH
RESIGNATION PATIENCE DEMISSION
SURRENDER
RESILIENT TOUGH BOUNCY LIVELY
SUPPLE WHIPPY ELASTIC SPRINGY
FLEXIBLE
RESIN LAC BALM BATU BREA TOLU
ANIME COPAL CUMAR ELEMI EPOXY
KAURI PITCH ROSET SYRUP BINDER
CONIMA DAMMAR GUACIN HARTIN
MASTIC STORAX TAMANU ACOUCHI
ACRYLIC BENZOIN FLUAVIL SAGAPEN
SHELLAC ALKITRAN BAKELITE CACHIBOU
CANNABIN GALLIPOT GUAIACUM
MALAPAHO MELAMINE OPOPANAX
PHENOLIC SANDARAC SCAMMONY
(— DRAWN FROM TREES) CHIP
(— FROM HEMP) CHARAS
(— FROM NORWAY SPRUCE) THUS
(— OF FIR TREE) BLOB
(FOSSIL —) AMBER AMBRITE HARTITE
GEDANITE GLESSITE RETINITE
(GRADE OF —) SORTS
(GUM —) GUGUL LASER MYRRH ANTIAR
BISABOL GAMBOGE BDELLIUM
SAGAPENUM
(TURPENTINE —) ALK GALIPOT
COLOPHONY
RESIST BUCK DEFY FACE STAY REPEL
STAND DEFEND IMPUGN OPPOSE
CONTEST DISPUTE GAINSAY KNUCKLE
OUTBRAVE
RESISTANCE LOAD OHMAGE REBUFF
BALLAST BLOCKAGE FASTNESS
FRICTION HARDNESS OBSTACLE
SEDITION
(— OF COTTON FIBERS) DRAG
(— OF KEYS) ACTION
(— THAT EXPLOSIVE MUST
OVERCOME) BURDEN
(— TO ATTACK) DEFENSE
(— TO CHANGE) INERTIA
(— TO COLOR CHANGE) FASTNESS
(— TO DISEASE) PREMUNITION
(— TO SLIPPING) BOND
RESOLUTE BOLD FIRM GRIM BRAVE
FIXED HARDY MANLY STERN STIFF
STOUT GRITTY MANFUL PLUCKY STABLE

STANCH STEADY STURDY DECIDED
CONSTANT FAITHFUL INTREPID POSITIVE
STALWART STUBBORN UNSHAKEN

RESOLUTION VOW SAND THEW NERVE
PLUCK POINT STARCH COURAGE
MANHEAD MANHOOD PURPOSE RESOLVE
THOUGHT ANALYSIS DECISION
STRENGTH CONSTANCY

RESOLVE ACT MELT UNDO LAPSE RELAX
SOLVE UNTIE VOUCH ADJUST DECIDE
DECREE REDUCE SETTLE ABSOLVE
APPOINT BETHINK PURPOSE CONCLUDE
DISSOLVE UNRIDDLE UNTANGLE
RECONCILE
(— GRAMMATICALLY) PARSE
(— INTO ELEMENTS) ANALYZE

RESOLVED BENT BOUND INTENT
CERTAIN INTENSE RESOLUTE

RESONANT BIG BRASS OROTUND
RINGING SILVERY VIBRANT CANOROUS
PLANGENT SONORANT SONOROUS
SOUNDING

RESORT GO RUN SPA BEAT DOME LIDO
TEEM TOUR TURN CAUSE FRAME HAUNT
JOINT VISIT ESCORT FINISH REPAIR
RETURN REVERT THRONG COMPANY
PIMLICO RECOURSE RESOURCE
(— TO) SEEK
(— TO DEVIOUS METHODS) FINAGLE
(BATHING —) PLAGE
(DRINKING —) DOGGERY
(EVIL —) ROOKERY
(LOW —) KEN DIVE STEW SPITAL
(WORKINGMEN'S —) TEETOTUM

RESOUND DIN ECHO PEAL RING REECHO
EXPLODE REBOUND VIBRATE

RESOUNDING BRASS EMPHATIC
FORCEFUL PLANGENT RESONANT
RUMOROUS

RESOURCE BOOT FUND MEANS SHIFT
REFUGE RESORT STOPGAP PURCHASE

RESOURCEFUL APT SHARP SMART
ADROIT CLEVER FACILE SHIFTY

RESPECT WAY DUTY FACE HEED LOOK
MARK DEFER FRONT HONOR PARTY
VALUE ASPECT BEHALF DETAIL ESTEEM
HALLOW HOMAGE NOTICE REGARD
CONCERN OBSERVE RESPITE WORSHIP
CONSIDER HABITUDE RELATION
VENERATE

RESPECTABLE GOOD NICE SMUG
DOUCE DECENT PROPER

RESPECTFUL AWFUL CIVIL CAREFUL
DUTEOUS DUTIFUL HEEDFUL REVERENT

RESPITE REST STAY DELAY LETUP PAUSE
BREATH LAYOFF REMISE LEISURE
RESPECT INTERVAL REPRIEVE SURCEASE

RESPLENDENT LUCID BRIGHT GILDED
ORIENT SILVER AUREATE SHINING
GLORIOUS GORGEOUS LUSTROUS
SPLENDID SUNSHINY

RESPOND REACT REPLY ANSWER
RETURN
(— TO LURE) STOOL
(— WARMLY) RISE

RESPONSE AMEN ECHO CHORD REPLY
ANSWER EARFUL VOLLEY INTROIT

ANTIPHON BEHAVIOR INSTINCT
REACTION REANSWER RECEPTION
(— OF KEYS) ACTION
(— OF SHIP) STEERING
(— TO GRAVITY) GEOTAXIS

RESPONSIBILITY BALL CARE DUTY
ONUS BLAME GUILT TRUST CHARGE

RESPONSIBLE GOOD SOLID DIRECT
LIABLE AMENABLE

RESPONSIVE OPEN SOFT WARM
MUTUAL NIMBLE SUPPLE TENDER
MEETING AMENABLE SENSIBLE
(— TO BEAUTY) ESTHETIC
(NOT —) IMMUNE

REST BED LAY LIE PUT SET SIT BASE
BLOW CALM CAMP EASE HEEL LAIR
LEAN PROP RELY RIDE STAY STOP
COUCH FOUND PAUSE PEACE POISE
QUIET RENEW ROOST SLEEP SPELL
TRUST ANCHOR GROUND REMAIN
REPOSE SETTLE BALANCE BREATHE
CAESURA CLARION COMFORT NOONING
RECLINE REFRESH REMNANT REQUIEM
RESIDUE RESPITE SILENCE SLUMBER
SOJOURN SUPPORT SURPLUS INTERVAL
QUIETUDE STANDOFF VACATION
(— FOR SPEAR OR LANCE) QUEUE
FAUCRE FEWTER
(— FOR SUPPORT) ABUT
(— FOR TYMPAN) GALLOWS
(— HORSE) WIND
(— IDLY) SLUG
(— LAZILY) FROWST
(— ON PLANER) SIDEHEAD
(— ON SUPPORT) BOTTOM
(— UPRIGHT) STAND
(HALF —) MINIM
(LATHE —) STEADY
(LEG — ON SADDLE) CRUTCH
(MUSKET —) GAFFLE
(NOONDAY —) NAP SIESTA
(QUARTER —) SOSPIRO

RESTAURANT CAFE DINER GRILL HOUSE
PLACE BISTRO BUFFET EATERY
AUTOMAT BEANERY CABARET CANTEEN
TEAROOM HIDEAWAY BRASSERIE
CHOPHOUSE TRATTORIA

RESTFUL COOL SOFT QUIET PLACID
RELAXED SOOTHFUL TRANQUIL

RESTLESS ANTSY FUDGY ITCHY FITFUL
HECTIC ROVING UNEASY AGITATO
FIDGETY FLIGHTY FRETFUL INQUIET
TOSSING UNQUIET UNRESTY VARIANT
WAKEFUL FEVERISH

RESTORE FIX AMEND BLOCK COVER
RENEW REPAY STORE YIELD DOCTOR
REDEEM REFORM REFUND RENDER
REVERT REVIVE CONVERT REBUILD
RECLAIM RECOVER REFRESH REPLACE
RECREATE
(— CONFIDENCE) REASSURE
(— TO CIVIL RIGHTS) INLAW
(— TO HEALTH) CURE HEAL MEND
(— TO ORDER) STILL

RESTRAIN BIT DAM BATE BIND BOLT
COOP CRIB CURB DAMP GRAB GYVE
KEEP REIN SHUT SINK STAY STEM STOP

BRANK CHAIN CHECK CRAMP DETER
GUARD LEASH SHUNT STILL STINT
ARREST BOTTLE BRIDLE COERCE DETAIN
ENJOIN FETTER FORBID GOVERN HALTER
HAMPER HINDER KENNEL RETAIN RETIRE
REVOKE STIFLE STRAIN TEMPER
ABRIDGE ABSTAIN CHASTEN CONFINE
CONTAIN CONTROL ENCHAIN EXCLUDE
INHIBIT QUALIFY REPRESS RETRACT
SHACKLE SNAFFLE COMPRESS
HANDCUFF IMPRISON RESTRICT
WITHHOLD
(— BY FEAR) OVERAWE
(— HAWK'S WING) BRAIL
(— MOTION) SNUB
(PREF.) ISCH(O)

RESTRAINED SOBER CHASTE MODEST
SEVERE ASHAMED DISCREET RESERVED

RESTRAINT BIT CLOG CURB STAY STOP
CHECK CRAMP FORCE LEASH SPARE
STINT ARREST BRIDLE DURESS FETTER
BONDAGE CONTROL DURANCE MANACLE
RESERVE SNAFFLE TRAMMEL SOBRIETY

RESTRICT TIE CURB HOLD BOUND CHAIN
FENCE HEDGE STINT COERCE CORRAL
CORSET HAMPER NARROW QUALIFY
REPRESS SWADDLE CONTRACT DIMINISH
RESTRAIN STRAITEN

RESTRICTED CLOSE LOCAL CLOSED
FINITE NARROW STRAIT STRICT
PAROCHIAL

RESTRICTION STINT BURDEN DENIAL
BARRIER CONFINE RESERVE

RESULT END OUT ECHO FATE GROW RISE
TAKE BACON BRING ENSUE EVENT FRUIT
ISSUE PROOF EFFECT EFFORT ENDING
EVOLVE FINISH FOLLOW GROWTH
RECOIL REVERT SEQUEL UPSHOT
FALLOUT FINDING OUTCOME PURPOSE
REBOUND SUCCESS SEQUENCE
OFFSPRING
(— FAVORABLY) SUCCEED
(— FROM) SUE
(ALGEBRAIC —) DUAL EXPANSION
(INCONCLUSIVE —) DOGFALL
(INEVITABLE —) NEMESIS
(REWARDING —) HAY
(SECONDARY —) SEQUELA

RETAIN HAVE HEFT HOLD KEEP SAVE
CATCH CONTAIN RESERVE CONTINUE
MAINTAIN PRESERVE

RETALIATE REPAY AVENGE RETORT
REQUITE RECIPROCATE

RETARD LAG DAMP DRAG SLOW STEM
BRAKE DEFER DELAY TARRY BELATE
DEADEN DETAIN HINDER INHIBIT
SLACKEN ENCUMBER OBSTRUCT
PROTRACT RESTRAIN

RETARDED DARK BEHIND LAGGED
SIMPLE

RETCH GAG BOKE KECK HEAVE VOMIT

RETENTION MEMORY HOLDING KEEPING
RETINUE

RETICENT DARK SNUG CLOSE SECRET
SILENT SPARING

RETINUE CREW SUIT TAIL COURT MEINY

SUITE TRAIN FAMILY COMPANY CORTEGE
EQUIPAGE BODYGUARD
(— OF CAVALRY) SOWARRY
(VILLAINOUS —) BLACKGUARD

RETIRE GO GET DRAW GIVE AVOID LEAVE
DEPART RECALL RECEDE RECESS RECOIL
SHRINK PENSION RETRACT RETREAT
WITHDRAW

RETIRED QUIET SECRET DEVIOUS
OBSCURE PRIVATE SHADOWY EMERITUS
SECLUDED SOLITARY

RETIREMENT SHADE RECESS SECESS
PRIVACY RETREAT FIRESIDE SOLITUDE

RETIRING SHY TIMID DEMURE MODEST
RESERVED RECESSIVE

RETORT MOT QUIP RISE SNAP QUIRK
REPAY REPLY ANSWER RETURN RIPOST
CRUSHER REFLECT SQUELCH BACKWORD
COMEBACK REPARTEE

RETRACT BACK UNSAY ABJURE DISOWN
RECALL RECANT RECEDE REVOKE SHRINK
RESCIND RETREAT SWALLOW RENOUNCE
WITHDRAW

RETREAT DEN END DROP FADE GIVE LAIR
NEST ROUT ARBOR AVOID BOWER
LODGE NICHE QUAIL QUIET SHADE
ASYLUM CASTLE RECEDE RECESS
REFUGE RETIRE REVOLT DESCEND
PRIVACY RETRACT SHELTER ANABASIS
FASTNESS SOLITUDE STAMPEDE
WITHDRAW
(— FOR FISH) HOD
(— FORTIFIED) REDUIT
(RELIGIOUS —) ASHRAM
(SECURE —) STRENGTH
(SHADY —) ALCOVE

RETRIEVE RECALL RECURE REGAIN
REPAIR RESCUE REVIVE CORRECT
RECOVER RESTORE SALVAGE

RETURN EBB COME VAIL RECUR REFER
REPAY REPLY VISIT YIELD ANSWER
HOMING REMISE RENDER REPAIR RESORT
RETIRE RETORT REVERT PAYMENT
REBOUND REDOUND REFLECT REPRISE
REQUITE RESTORE REVENUE DIVIDEND
FEEDBACK RECOURSE RECOVERY
RECIPROCATE
(— FROM DEATH) ARISE
(— OF MERCHANDISE) COMEBACK
(— TENNIS BALL) RALLY

RETURN OF THE NATIVE
(AUTHOR OF —) HARDY
(CHARACTER IN —) VYE CLYM VENN
DAMON CANTLE JOHNNY DIGGORY
NUNSUCH WILDEVE EUSTACIA
THOMASIN CHRISTIAN YEOBRIGHT

REUBEN (FATHER OF —) JACOB
(MOTHER OF —) LEAH

REVEAL BARE BLAB HINT OPEN SHOW
TELL WRAY BREAK EXERT UTTER YIELD
APPEAR DETECT EVINCE IMPART OSTEND
UNLOCK UNMASK UNVEIL UNWRAP
CLARIFY CONFESS DEVELOP DISPLAY
DIVULGE UNCLOAK UNCOVER DISCLOSE
DISCOVER MANIFEST UNSHADOW
(— BY SIGNS) EXHIBIT

(— SECRETS) BABBLE
(— UNINTENTIONALLY) BETRAY
REVEL JOY MASK RIOT COMUS FEAST GLORY FROLIC WALLOW WANTON CAROUSE DELIGHT ROISTER CAROUSAL FESTIVAL
REVELATION TORAH EXPOSE ORACLE SHOWING OVERTURE APOCALYPSE
REVELRY JOY ORGY RIOT WASSAIL CARNIVAL CAROUSAL FESTIVAL
REVENGE HELL WREAK AVENGE REQUITE REQUITAL
REVENUE RENT JAGIR MANSE YIELD INCOME ENTRADA FINANCE PROFITS INCOMING
(— FROM WATER RIGHTS) JALKAR
(— REVENUE PAID TO POPE) ANNAT
(STATE —) HACIENDA
REVERBERATE ECHO RING RETORT REBOUND REDOUND REFLECT RESOUND
REVERE ADORE HONOR ADMIRE ESTEEM HALLOW RESPECT WORSHIP VENERATE
REVERENCE AWE FEAR DREAD HONOR PIETY HOMAGE REGARD WORSHIP DEVOTION VENERATE
REVERENT DEVOUT STRONG AWESOME DUTIFUL
REVERENTIAL PIOUS SOLEMN
REVERIE MUSE DREAM DWALM STUDY PONDER MEMENTO MOONING DAYDREAM
REVERSE BACK DOWN FACE FLOP ANNUL CHECK UPSET CHANGE DEFEAT INVERT REPEAL RETURN REVERT REVOKE COUNTER INVERSE PUTBACK RETREAT SETBACK SUBVERT CONTRARY CONVERSE OPPOSITE OVERRULE OVERTURN TRAVERSE WATERLOO
(— OARS) SHEAVE
(— OF COIN) PILE TAIL WOMAN
(— PAGE OF BOOK) VERSO REVERSO
REVERT ANNUL RESORT RESULT RETURN REVOKE ESCHEAT RESTORE RECOURSE BACKSLIDE
REVIEW HASH VIEW NOTICE REVISE SURVEY BRUSHUP CRITIQUE REVISION
REVILE CALL RAIL ABUSE BRAWL SCOLD SLANG MISSAY MISUSE VILIFY INVEIGH MISCALL MISNAME BACKBITE DISGRACE EXECRATE REPROACH
REVISE EDIT ALTER REDACT REFORM REVIEW CORRECT OVERHAUL
REVISION REVIEW SURVEY REVISAL EPANAGOGE
REVIVE WAKE FETCH QUICK RALLY RENEW ROUSE EXHUME GINGER RECALL RELIVE REVERT REVOKE ENLIVEN FRESHEN FURBISH QUICKEN REFRESH RESPIRE RESTORE RECREATE REKINDLE RENOVATE
REVOKE LIFT ADEEM ANNUL CANCEL RECALL RECANT RENEGE REPEAL REVERT ABOLISH COMMUTE RESCIND REVERSE ABROGATE
REVOLT ARISE REBEL REPEL START MUTINY OFFEND UPROAR OUTBREAK

SEDITION UPRISING JACQUERIE REBELLION
REVOLTING GARISH HORRID BILIOUS FEARFUL HATEFUL HIDEOUS DREADFUL
REVOLUTION RIOT TURN CYCLE WHEEL CHANGE ANARCHY CIRCUIT REVOLVE GYRATION MUTATION ROTATION SEDITION REBELLION
REVOLUTIONARY RED RADICAL MUSCADIN ROTATING BOLSHEVIK
REVOLVE BIRL GYRE ROLL SPIN TURN ORBIT PIVOT THROW TREND TROLL TWINE WHEEL WHIRL CENTER CIRCLE GYRATE ROTATE AGITATE OVERTURN REVOLUTE
REVOLVER GAT GUN ROD STICK CANNON HOGLEG PISTOL BULLDOG DUNGEON
REWARD FEE PAY MEED RENT SPUR WAGE AMEED BOOTY BRIBE MERIT PLUME YIELD BOUNTY PAYOFF SALARY TROPHY GUERDON PREMIUM STIPEND DIVIDEND EXACTION REQUITAL
(— FOR INFORMATION ON CATTLE THIEVES) TASCAL
(— OF VICTORY) CROWN
(— TO HOUNDS) HALLOW
(ILLUSORY —) CARROT
(UNEXPECTED —) JACKPOT
RHAPSODY JUMBLE MEDLEY BOMBAST ECSTASY RAPTURE REVERIE
RHEA EMU EMEU NANDU OSTRICH AGDISTIS AVESTRUZ
(DAUGHTER OF —) JUNO CERES VESTA
(FATHER OF —) URANUS
(HUSBAND OF —) SATURN
(MOTHER OF —) GAEA
(SON OF —) PLUTO NEPTUNE
RHEINGOLD, DAS (CHARACTER IN —) ERDA LOGE FREIA WOTAN FAFNER FASOLT FRICKA HUNDING ALBERICH SIEGMUND SIEGLINDE
(COMPOSER OF —) WAGNER
RHETORIC SPEECH BOMBAST PROSAIC ELOQUENCE
RHETORICAL FLORID PURPLE AUREATE FORENSIC SWELLING
RHINOCEROS FOW ABADA BADAK RHINO BORELE KEITLOA UNICORN UPEYGAN NASICORN

RHODE ISLAND

CAPITAL: PROVIDENCE
COLLEGE: BROWN BRYANT
COUNTY: KENT BRISTOL NEWPORT
MOTTO: HOPE
NICKNAME: LITTLERHODY
RIVER: PAWTUXET PAWCATUCK BLACKSTONE
STATE FLOWER: VIOLET
STATE TREE: MAPLE
TOWN: BRISTOL NEWPORT WARWICK CRANSTON KINGSTON PAWTUCKET

RHODESIA (SEE ZIMBABWE)

RHYME CHIME VERSE CRAMBO POETRY
RHYTHM TINKLE MEASURE

RHYTHM BEAT TIME CHIME METER
PULSE SWING CADENCE RAGTIME
BACKBEAT MOVEMENT SEQUENCE

RIB FIN KID CORD DIKE JOKE PURL SLAT
WALE COSTA GROIN NERVE OGIVE
PEARL RIDGE VITTA BRANCH NEEDLE
PARODY SCROLL TIMBER TONGUE
BRISTLE NERVURE STRATUM SIDEBONE
(— IN GROINED ROOF) SPRINGER
(— OF INSECT WING) VEIN
(— OF SHIP) WRONG
(— OF VIOLIN) BOUT
(—S OF UMBRELLA) FRAME
(SHORT —S) CROP
(STRENGTHENING —) FEATHER

RIBBON BAR BOW BEND BRAID FILET
LABEL PIECE SHRED BENDEL FILLET
RIBAND SHOWER STRING TAENIA TISSUE
BANDING TORSADE BANDEROL
BOOKMARK FRAGMENT
(— AS BADGE OF HONOR) CORDON
(— AS HEADDRESS) TRESSOUR
TRESSURE
(— FOR BORDER) LISERE
(— HANGING FROM CROWN) JESS
(— USED FOR GARTERS) CADDIS
(COLORED —S) DIVISA
(END OF —S) FATTRELS
(FLOATING —) PAN
(KNOT OF —S) SORTIE
(LINGUAL —) TONGUE
(SILK —) CORSE PADOU TASTE
(WATERED —) PADS

RICE RISE SELA TWIG ARROZ BATTY
GRAIN MACAN PATNA BRANCH CEREAL
CONGEE SIDDHA ANGKHAK
(— BOILED WITH MEAT) PILAF
(— COOKED WITH MEAT) RISOTTO
JAMBALAYA
(— FIELD) SAWAH
(— IN HUSK) PALAY
(— OF 2ND OR 3RD GRADE) CHITS
(BOILED —) CANIN
(HUSKED —) CHAL
(INFERIOR —) PAGA
(LONG-STEMMED —) AMAN
(MOUNTAIN —) SMILO
(SHORT-STEMMED —) AUS
(SPRING —) BORO
(UNCOOKED —) BIGAS
(UNMILLED —) PADI PADDY
(WILD —) MANOMIN

RICH FAT ABLE DEEP FAIR HIGH LUSH
OPIME PLUMP RITZY ROUND VIVID
BATFUL COSTLY DAEDAL FRUITY HEARTY
PLUMMY PLUSHY SUPERB AMUSING
COPIOUS FERTILE MONEYED OPULENT
WEALTHY ABUNDANT AFFLUENT
GENEROUS HUMOROUS LUSCIOUS
(— IN GIFTS) PREMIOUS
(— IN INTEREST) JUICY
(— IN MALT) HEAVY
(— IN SILICA) ACID
(— IN TIMBRE) GOLDEN

(— OF SOIL) PINGUID
(NOT —) PLAIN

RICHARD CARVEL (AUTHOR OF —)
CHURCHILL
(CHARACTER IN —) FOX JONES
CARVEL DOROTHY MANNERS RICHARD
WALPOLE

RICHARD II (AUTHOR OF —)
SHAKESPEARE
(CHARACTER IN —) JOHN ROSS YORK
BAGOT BUSHY GAUNT GREEN HENRY
PERCY EDMUND PIERCE SCROOP SURREY
THOMAS AUMERLE HOTSPUR LANGLEY
MOWBRAY NORFOLK RICHARD BRANDON
BERKELEY HEREFORD FITZWATER
LANCASTER SALISBURY WILLOUGHBY
BOLINGBROKE NORTHUMBERLAND

RICHARD III (AUTHOR OF —)
SHAKESPEARE
(CHARACTER IN —) ANNE JOHN YORK
DERBY HENRY JAMES LOVEL BLOUNT
DORSET EDWARD GEORGE MORTON
OXFORD RIVERS ROBERT SURREY
THOMAS TYRREL WALTER BRANDON
CATESBY HERBERT NORFOLK RICHARD
STANLEY TRESSEL URSWICK VAUGHAN
BERKELEY CLARENCE HASTINGS
MARGARET RATCLIFF RICHMOND
BOURCHIER ELIZABETH ROTHERHAM
BRAKENBURY BUCKINGHAM
GLOUCESTER CHRISTOPHER

RICHES GOLD PELF WEAL LUCRE WORTH
MAMMON TALENT WEALTH FORTUNE
OPULENCE RICHESSE TREASURE

RICKETY SHAKY UNSOUND RACHITIC
SHATTERY UNSTABLE TOTTERING
RAMSHACKLE

RID FREE QUIT SHED SHUT CLEAR SCOUR
ACQUIT REMOVE DELIVER
(— OF INSECTS) BUG
(— OF LICE) CHAT
(— OF WEEDS) CLEAN
(— ONESELF OF) DOFF DEPOSIT
DISPATCH

RIDDLE SIFT GRIPH REBUS ENIGMA
PUZZLE SCREEN CORRUPT CRIBBLE
EXPLAIN GRIDDLE GRIPHUS MYSTIFY
PERPLEX PROBLEM PERMEATE

RIDE RIB BAIT HACK HURL LAST LIFT PRIG
SAIL TOOL CROSS DRIVE TEASE BANTER
CANTER DEPEND GALLOP SADDLE
HAYRIDE JOYRIDE OVERLAP SURVIVE
TANTIVY
(— FAST) PRICK POWDER
(— HARD) POUND BUCKET
(— IN HIRED VEHICLE) JOB
(— ON A WAVE) BODYSURF
(— ON HORSE) BOOT LARK BURST
JOCKEY SCHOOL
(— RECKLESSLY) BRUISE
(— TO HOUNDS) GO
(AMUSEMENT PARK —) SWING

RIDER TACK ANNEX HAZER LABEL
COWBOY JOCKEY SITTER CODICIL
PRICKER CAVALIER HORSEMAN
(DUKEY —) BRAKEMAN
(DUMMY —) CROSS

RIDERS TO THE SEA (AUTHOR OF —)
SYNGE
(CHARACTER IN —) NORA MAURYA
BARTLEY MICHAEL

RIDGE AAS ARM BAR FIN RIB RIG BALK
BAND BANK BARB BROW BURR BUTT
COMB DRUM FRET HILL KEEL LINK LIST
RAIN ROLL SHIN SPUR WAVE WELT
BARGH CHINE COSTA CREST EARTH
EAVES JUGUM KNURL LEDGE LINCH
SHANK SPINE TORUS VARIX BRIDGE
CARINA CREASE CUESTA CULMEN DIVIDE
DORSUM FRENUM RAFTER RIDEAU
SADDLE SUMMIT ANNULET APODEMA
BREAKER EYEBROW HOGBACK
HUMMOCK SOWBACK WINDROW
WRINKLE CINGULUM HEADLAND
SHOULDER

RIDICULE FUN GUY MOB PAN RIG TAX
GAME GIBE JEER JEST MOCK PLAY QUIZ
RAZZ TROT TWIT CHAFF CLOWN HORSE
IRONY MIMIC QUEER RALLY SCOFF
SCOUT SMOKE SNEER TAUNT BANTER
DERIDE EXPOSE SATIRE BUFFOON
LAMPOON MOCKERY SARCASM DERISION
RAILLERY SATIRIZE SPOOFERY
BURLESQUE

RIDICULOUS DOTTY DROLL FUNNY SILLY
ABSURD INSANE COMICAL FOOLISH
MOCKING DERISIVE FARCICAL INDECENT
COCKAMAMY MONSTROUS

RIFFLE REEF WAVE RAPID RIPPLE
SHUFFLE WATERFALL

RIFFRAFF MOB RAFF SCUM SCAFF
TRASH RABBLE REFUSE RUBBISH
CANAILLE POPULACE RAGABASH

RIFLE RIG ROB KRAG LOOT PIECE JEZAIL
SNIDER ARISAKA BUNDOOK CARBINE
DESPOIL ENFIELD MARTINI PILLAGE
PLUNDER RANSACK REPEATER STRICKLE
CHASSEPOT

RIFT RIVE BELCH CHASM CRACK SPLIT
CLEAVE DIVIDE BLEMISH FISSURE
CREVASSE
(— IN TIMBER) LAG

RIG FIG HOAX JEST JOKE REEK WIND
DRESS RADIO GETUP PRANK SPORT
STORM TRICK BANTER CLOTHE ROTARY
SADDLE SCHEME SWINDLE BACKSTAY
RIDICULE SEMITRAILER

RIGGING NET GEAR ROOF RIDGE TACKLE
APPAREL CLOTHING JACKSTAY
TACKLING

RIGHT DUE FEE FIT OFF SAY SOC DUTY
FAIR GOOD HAND JUST LIEN REAL SANE
SLAP TRUE WELL CLAIM DRESS ENTRY
EXACT FAVOR FERRY LEGAL SOUND
STRAY ACTUAL BALLOT DEMAND
DEXTER EQUITY PROPER ANNUITY
APANAGE BENEFIT CORRECT DESIRED
FACULTY FITTING FOLDAGE FREEDOM
GENUINE HAYBOTE LIBERTY LICENSE
PRENDER RECTIFY RELIEVE SLAPDAB
UPRIGHT WARRANT BLOODWIT HEIRSHIP
SEIGNORY STALLAGE STRAIGHT
SUFFRAGE SUITABLE PREROGATIVE
(— AND LEFT) HAY HEY

(— AS COMMAND TO HORSES) REE
(— IN A THING) INTEREST
(— IN WIFE'S INHERITED PROPERTY)
CURTESY
(— OF CHOICE) OPTION
(— OF EXIT) ISH
(— OF FREE QUARTERS) CORODY
(— OF HOLDING COURT) TEAM
(— OF INQUIRY) SOKEN
(— OF OWNERSHIP) TITLE COMMONTY
(— OF PASTURAGE) FEED STINT
EATAGE COWGATE COMMONAGE
HORSEGATE
(— OF PRECEDENCE) PAS
(— OF PRESENTATION) ADVOWSON
(— OF PROTECTION) MUND
(— OF USING ANOTHER'S
PROPERTY) EASEMENT
(— TO COMMAND) IMPERIUM
(— TO CUT WOOD) VERT GREENHEW
(— TO DRAW WATER) HAUSTUS
(— TO DRIVE BEAST) ACTUS
(— TO PASS OVER LAND) ITER
(— TO SEIZE PROPERTY) ANGARY
(— TO SHOOT FIRST) CAST
(— TO WORK IN MINE) BEN
(ALL —) HUNK JAKE HUNKY
(FEUDAL —) CUDDY THIRL THIRLAGE
(FISHING —) PISCARY
(INDIAN LEGAL —) HAK HAKH
(LEGAL —) IUS JUS JURE DROIT
ACCESS APPEAL COMMON FISHERY
HYPOTHEC
(LEGAL —S) JURA
(MILLER'S —) SOKEN
(MINING —) GALE
(NOT —) ACUTE
(PROPERTY —) DOMINIUM
(WIDOW'S —) TIERCE
(PL.) DIBS JURA

RIGHTEOUS GOOD JUST GODLY MORAL
DEVOUT FITTING PERFECT SKILFUL
UPRIGHT INNOCENT VIRTUOUS

RIGHTEOUSNESS DOOM DHARMA
EQUITY JUSTICE HOLINESS JUDGMENT
JUSTNESS MORALITY RECTITUDE

RIGHTFUL DUE JUST TRUE LEGAL
KINDLY LAWFUL PROPER FITTING

RIGHTLY FITLY ARIGHT FAIRLY JUSTLY
HANDILY SUITABLY

RIGID SET FIRM HARD HIGH FIXED SOLID
STARK STERN STIFF STONY STOUT
TENSE TOUGH FORMAL FROZEN MARBLY
SEVERE STRICT AUSTERE IRONCLAD
RIGOROUS STRAIGHT INELASTIC
STRINGENT

RIGIDITY FROST RIGOR SETNESS
HARDNESS STIFFNESS

RIGOLETTO (CHARACTER IN —) GILDA
MANTUA MADDALENA RIGOLETTO
SPARAFUCILE
(COMPOSER OF —) VERDI

RIGOROUS FIRM HARD CLOSE CRUEL
EXACT HEFTY RIGID STERN STIFF TOUGH
BITTER FLINTY SEVERE STRAIT STRICT
STRONG AUSTERE DRASTIC PRECISE

RIGOROUS SPARTAN DRACONIC EXACTING IRONCLAD STRAIGHT
(MORALLY —) PURITANIC
(NOT —) INEXACT
(UNDULY —) HARSH

RILE VEX ANGER PEEVE IRRITATE

RILL PURL RUNLET RILLOCK RIVULET BROOKLET TRICKLET

RIM HEM LIP BEAD BRIM CURB EDGE SHOE BRINK EAVES FRAME SKIRT BORDER FILLET MARGIN
(— HOLDING WATCH CRYSTAL) BEZEL
(— OF BASKET) HOOP
(— OF COROLLA) ANNULUS
(— OF CRATER) SOMMA
(— OF EAR) HELIX
(— OF GEM) GIRDLE
(— OF HORSESHOE) WEB
(— OF INSECT'S WING) TERMEN
(— OF JELLYFISH) VELUM
(— OF SANIO) CRASSULA
(— OF TIN) LIST
(— OF WHEEL) FELLY FELLOE STRAKE
(— ON CASK) CHIME
(— ON CLOG) CALKER
(— SURROUNDING FLAGELLUM) CHOANA
(EXTERNAL —) FLANGE
(PROTECTIVE —) BANK
(RAISED —) BOSS
(PREF.) AMBO

RINALDO (BELOVED OF —) ANGELICA
(COUSIN OF —) ORLANDO
(FATHER OF —) AYMON
(HORSE OF —) BAYARD

RIND BARK PEEL CRUST FROST SWARD SWARTH
(— OF HAM) SKIN
(— OF MEAT) SPINE
(— OF POMEGRANATE) GRANATUM
(— OF ROASTED PORK) CRACKLING

RING GO BEE CUP DIE FAM ORB PIT RIM AMBO BAIL BAND BONG CURB DING DIRL ECHO GYRE HOOP LOOP PASS PEAL RACE RINK SHUT SING TANG TOLL ANLET ARENA CHIME CHINK CLANG CYCLE GRAIN GROUP GUARD GUIDE JEWEL KNELL ROUND ROWEL TORUS VERGE WITHE BANGLE CIRCLE CIRCUS CIRQUE CLIQUE COLLAR COLLET EYELET GIRDLE KEEPER LEGLET RUNDLE SIGNET WASHER CIRCLET CIRCUIT CLAPPER COMPASS COUPLER CRINGLE DIAMOND FERRULE NUCLEUS PACKING RESOUND ROWLOCK SHACKLE STIRRUP VIBRATE BRACELET BULLRING CINCTURE DINGDONG DUSTBAND ENCIRCLE FAIRLEAD PACIFIER SONORITY SURROUND
(— A TREE) FRILL
(— AROUND ARTICULAR CAVITY) AMBON
(— AROUND MOON) BROCH
(— AROUND NIPPLE) AREOLA
(— AT EACH END OF CINCH) LARIGO
(— ATTACHED TO JIB) HANK

(— BELLS) FIRE
(— FOR CARRYING SHOT) LADLE
(— FOR SECURING BIRD) VERVEL
(— FOR TRAINING HORSES) LONGE
(— FORMING HANDLE OF KEY) BOW
(— OF ANNULATED COLUMN) BAGUE
(— OF BOILER) STRAKE
(— OF COLOR) STOCKING
(— OF DOTS AROUND EDGE OF COIN) GRAINING
(— OF LIGHT) GLORY
(— OF ODIN) DRAUPNIR
(— OF PILES) STARLING
(— OF RIDING SCHOOL) PISTE
(— OF ROPE) HANK BECKET GARLAND GROMMET SNORTER SNOTTER
(— OF SPINES) CORONULE
(— OF STANDING STONES) CAROL
(— OF TWO HOOPS) GEMEL
(— OF WAGONS) CORRAL LAAGER
(— ON BATTLEAX) BUR BURR
(— ON BIRD'S TIBIA) ARMILLA
(— ON DECK) CRANCE
(— ON GUN CARRIAGE) LUNETTE
(— ON HINGE) GUDGEON
(— ON LAMP) CRIC
(— ON UMBRELLA ROD) RUNNER
(— SUPPORTING LAMPSHADE) GALLERY
(— SURROUNDING BUGLE) VIROLE
(— SUSPENDING COMPASS) GIMBAL
(— TO ENCLOSE DEER) TINCHEL
(— UNDER BEEHIVE) EKE
(— USED AS MONEY) MANILLA
(— USED AS VALVE) WAFER
(— WITH GROOVED OUTER EDGE) THIMBLE
(— WITH VIBRATION) DIRL
(BLACKSMITH'S —) BOLSTER
(BRIGHT —) HALATION
(CERVICAL —) TORQUE
(CURTAIN —) EYE
(FINGER —) HOOP
(FLESHY —) ANNULUS
(HARNESS —) DEE BUTTON LARIGO TERRET
(HAWK'S —) VERVEL
(INTERLINKED METAL —S) MAIL
(JOINED —) GIMMER
(LITTLE —) ANNULET
(LUMINOUS —) BROUGH
(MOUNTAINEER'S —) KARABINER
(NOSE —) PIRN
(OIL —) WIPER
(PACKING —) LUTE
(PLAITED —) RUSH WISP
(SURGICAL —) CURETTE
(TAPERING SHANK —) BELCHER
(TARGET —) SOUS
(TOOTHED IRON —) HARROW

RINGING BELL BRIGHT FERVID JANGLE CLANGOR OROTUND SINGING DECISIVE RESONANT SONORANT SONOROUS TINNITUS

RINGWORM TINEA KERION TETTER SERPIGO

RINK ALLEY GLACIARIUM

RINSE NET WASH RANGE SCIND SCOUR SWILL BLUING DOUCHE CLEANSE

RIOT DIN HURL BRAWL REVEL ATTACK CLAMOR EXCESS JUMBLE MEDLEY RANTAN TUMULT ANARCHY CONFUSE DESPOIL REVELRY CAROUSAL

RIOTOUS WILD NOISY RANDY STORMY WANTON BACCHIC PROFUSE ROARING

RIP TEAR BREAK SHRED UNSEW BASKET UNSEAM

RIPE FIT BOLD LATE DRUNK READY MATURE MELLOW FINISHED SUITABLE

RIPEN AGE ADDLE MELLOW CONCOCT DEVELOP PERFECT COMPLETE MATURATE

RIPENESS MATURITY

RIPPLE CURL FRET PURL WAVE ACKER TWINE COCKLE DIMPLE RUFFLE CRINKLE WAVELET WRINKLE

RISE COME FLOW GROW HEAD HIGH HIKE LIFT SOAR ARISE BEGIN CHEER CLIMB ERECT HOIST MOUNT OCCUR PITCH PROVE RAISE ROUSE SCEND STAND START SURGE YEAST ASCENT ASPIRE BILLOW EMERGE GROWTH HAPPEN HEIGHT ORIGIN RESULT RETORT SOURCE THRIVE UPREAR ADVANCE HUMMOCK UPHEAVE UPSHOOT EMINENCE HEIGHTEN INCREASE LEVITATE
(— ABOVE) OVERLOOK SURMOUNT
(— ABRUPTLY) SKYROCKET
(— AGAIN) RESURGE
(— AND FALL) LOOM HEAVE WELTER
(— AS PRICE) MEND
(— GRADUALLY) LOOM
(— IN BLISTERS) YAW
(— IN CLOUDS) STOOR
(— IN MINE FLOOR) HOGBACK
(— IN PRICES) BULGE
(— IN VALUE) IMPROVE
(— OF CURVE) CAMBER
(— OF HAWK AFTER PREY) MOUNTY
(— OF SHIP'S LINES) FLIGHT
(— OF WATER) FLOOD
(— PRECIPITOUSLY) SKY
(— RAPIDLY) KITE
(— SHARPLY) BREAK
(— SUDDENLY) BOOM SPRING
(— SWIFTLY) BOIL
(— TO BAIT) TAKE
(— TO GREAT HEIGHT) TOWER
(— TO PEAK) SWELL
(— UP) FUME REAR ASCEND INSURRECT
(CURVED —) HANCE
(SHARP —) HOGBACK

RISING BOIL ARISE ORIENT PUTSCH SOURCE MONTANT PUSTULE SURGENT EMERGENT INCREASE NAISSANT ONCOMING EXCEEDING

RISK GO RUN GAGE JUMP LUCK PAWN PERIL STAKE THROW WAGER CHANCE DANGER GAMBLE HAZARD THREAT BALANCE IMPERIL VENTURE ENDANGER EXPOSURE

RISKY BOLD CHANCY DARING PARLOUS TECHOUS TICKLISH

RISQUE BLUE RACY BROAD DARING SCABROUS

RITE FORM BRITH HONOR RIGHT AUGURY EXEQUY FETISH OFFICE RITUAL BAPTISM FUNERAL LITURGY MYSTERY OBSEQUY CEREMONY HIERURGY OBSERVANCE

RITUAL FORM RITE SOLEMN HAGGADA LITURGY OBSEQUY SERVICE CEREMONY

RIVAL VIE EVEN PEER MATCH COMPETE EMULATE PARAGON CORRIVAL EMULATOR OPPONENT

RIVALRY VIE GAME STRIFE JEALOUSY STRIVING EMULATION

RIVALS (AUTHOR OF —) SHERIDAN (CHARACTER IN —) BOB JACK LUCY ACRES JULIA LYDIA LUCIUS ANTHONY ABSOLUTE BEVERLEY LANGUISH MALAPROP MELVILLE OTRIGGER FAULKLAND

RIVE RIP PLOW REND STAB TEAR CRACK SEVER SPLIT WEDGE CLEAVE SUNDER SHATTER FRACTURE

RIVER LEE RIO AVON ILOG KILL WADI CREEK FLOOD GLIDE GUTTER STRAIT STREAM CHANNEL ESTUARY RUBICON AFFLUENT ERIDANUS
(— NEAR GATE OF HEL'S ABODE) GJOLL
(— OF ATTICA) ILISSUS
(— OF DAMASCUS) PHARPAR
(— OF LYDIA) PACTOLUS
(— OF PARADISE) GEON GIHON
(— OF UNDERWORLD) STYX LETHE ACHERON COCYTUS FLEGETON
(FULL —) BANKER
(MINOR —) BAYOU
(SACRED —) ALPH GANGA
(SMALL —) BACHE TCHAI

RIVET STUD CLINK PANHEAD FLATHEAD
(— ATTENTION) GRIP

RIVULET RUN BURN GILL RILL BACHE BAYOU BOURN BROOK RUNLET RUNNEL STREAM CHANNEL RIVERET BROOKLET

ROAD LEG PAD VIA WAY BELT DRAG FARE GANG LINE PASS PAVE PIKE SPUR BLAZE BYWAY CLOSE DRIFT ROUTE TRACE TRACK BYROAD CAMINO CAREER CHEMIN COURSE DUGWAY FEEDER RIDING RUNWAY STREET TARMAC TRAJET BEELINE CARTWAY ESTRADA GANGWAY HIGHWAY LANDWAY PACKWAY PASSAGE RAILWAY ROADWAY ROLLWAY AUTOBAHN BLACKTOP BROADWAY CORDUROY HORSEWAY OVERPASS SPEEDWAY TRAMROAD TRAVERSE TURNPIKE WAGONWAY ROADSTEAD
(— BORDERING SHORE) PRAYA
(— FOR LOGGING) SKIDWAY CROSSHAUL
(— IN COAL MINE) BORD BOARD FOOTRILL
(— ON CLIFF) CORNICHE
(CEMENT OR CONCRETE —) SLAB
(COUNTRY —) BOREEN DRIFTWAY
(DESCENDING —) BAJADA
(IMPASSABLE —) SLOUGH IMPASSE

(IMPROVISED —) CASH
(NARROW —) DRANG RODDIN
(PAVED —) CALZADA CHAUSSEE
(PRINCIPAL —) ARTERY
(PRIVATE —) LOKE DRIVE DRIVEWAY
(RAISED —) AGGER RAMPIRE
CAUSEWAY
(ROMAN —) ITER CAUSEY
(SIDE —) BRANCH SHUNPIKE
(STEEP —) BRAE PATH BARGH SPRUNT
(TEMPORARY —) SHOOFLY
(UNIMPROVED —) DROVE
(ZIGZAG —) SWITCHBACK
(PREF.) ODO VIA
ROAM GO ERR RUN RAKE ROLL ROVE
WALK GYPSY RANGE SPACE STRAY
WAVER RAMBLE STROLL SWERVE
VAGARY WANDER PROCEED VAGABOND
(— FURTIVELY) PROWL
ROAR CRY BAWL BELL BOOM BRAY
HOWL ROOP ROUT YELL BLARE CRACK
SHOUT BELLOW BULLER CLAMOR
SCREAM SHRIEK BLUSTER ULULATE
(— AS BOAR) FREAM
(— LIKE WIND) HURL
(— LOW OF SURF) ROTE
(LOW —) BROOL
ROAST RAZZ ROTI SOAK BROWN PARCH
TORREFY BARBECUE RIDICULE
(— IN ASHES) BRY
(STUFFED —) FARCI
ROB COP PAD FAKE FLAP NICK PEEL PELF
PICK PILL POLL PREY PULL RAMP TOBY
BRIBE HARRY HEIST PINCH PLUCK
PROWL RIFLE ROIST SPOIL STEAL TOUCH
HARROW HIJACK HUSTLE PILFER RAVISH
RIPOFF STRIKE THIEVE DEPRIVE DESPOIL
PLUNDER DEFLOWER SPOLIATE
ROBBER THIEF BANDIT BRIBER HOLDUP
RIFLER BRIGAND CATERAN HEISTER
LADRONE PANDOUR PRANCER RAVENER
SPOILER BARABBAS PILLAGER
BANDOLERO
(— ON HIGH SEAS) PIRATE
(— WHO USES VIOLENCE) RABIATOR
(GRAVE —) GHOUL
(HIGHWAY —) PAD FOOTPAD
TOBYMAN
(INDIAN MURDEROUS —) DACOIT
(IRISH —) WOODKERN
(MOUNTAIN —) CHOAR
(NIGHT —) MOONMAN
(SEA —) FOMOR FOMORIAN
(WANDERING —) ROUTIER
(PREF.) LESTO
ROBBERY JOB JUMP HEIST SCREW
FELONY HOLDUP DACOITY LARCENY
PILLAGE PLUNDER STICKUP THUGGEE
SPOLIATION
ROBE GOWN VEST KANZU STOLA
KIMONO MANTLE PEPLOS REVEST
ARISAID BUFFALO GALABIA SURCOAT
VESTURE PARAMENT WOLFSKIN
(— FOR THE DEAD) HABIT
(— OF MONARCH) PLUVIAL
(— PRESENTED BY DIGNITARY)
KHALAT

(— REACHING TO ANKLES) TALAR
(ACTOR'S —) SYRMA
(BAPTISMAL —) CHRISOM
(BISHOP'S —) CHIMER
(CIRCULAR —) CYCLAS
(CORONATION —) COLOBIUM
DALMATIC
(DERVISH'S —) KHIRKA KHIRKAH
(EMPEROR'S —) PURPLE
(FUNERAL —) SABLE
(JEWISH —) KITTEL
(LOOSE —) MANT CAMIS SIMAR
MANTUA MANTEAU
(MASQUERADE —) VENETIAN
(MEXICAN —) MANGA
(MONK'S —) HAPLOMA
(OLD-FASHIONED —) SAMARE
(OUTER —) JAMA
(TARTAN —) ARISAID
(TURKISH —) DOLMAN
ROBOT GOLEM AUTOMAT TELEVOX
ROB ROY (AUTHOR OF —) SCOTT
(CHARACTER IN —) ROB OWEN DIANA
FRANK ANDREW MACFIN MORRIS
VERNON TRESHAM WILLIAM CAMPBELL
FREDERICK INGLEWOOD MACVITTIE
RASHLEIGH HILDEBRAND FAIRSERVICE
OSBALDISTONE
ROBUST ABLE FIRM HALE HARD IRON
BONNY HARDY HUSKY LUSTY SOUND
STARK STIFF STOUT TOUGH VALID
HEARTY RUGGED SINEWY STRONG
STURDY HEALTHY VALIANT MUSCULAR
STALWART VIGOROUS STRAPPING
ROCK CAP LOG PAY DAZE HOST KLIP
REEL SWAY TOSS BRACK CLIFF FLOOR
HORSE LEDGE SHAKE SKARN STONE
TRILL CRADLE GROUND PELITE TOTTER
BRECCIA PHYLLITE SILTSTONE
(— AROUND DRILL HOLE) COLLAR
(— CHUNK) KNUCKLE
(— IN ANOTHER ROCK) XENOLITH
(— IN MINE) CAPPING
(— IN SEA) STACK
(— VIOLENTLY) STAGGER
(ARTIFICIAL —) GRANOLITH
(BALD —) SCALP
(BANDED —) BAR
(BARE —) SCARTH
(COMPACT —) BASEMENT
(CONGLOMERATE —) PSEPHITE
(COUNTRY —) RIDER
(CRUSHED —) GREET
(CRYSTALLINE —) ELVAN DUNITE
SCHIST DIORITE GREISEN ECLOGITE
(DECOMPOSED —) GOSSAN
(DENSE —) ADINOLE
(DISINTEGRATED —) SAPROLITE
(EXTRUSIVE —) DACITE SPILITE
ANDESITE CIMINITE
(FELDSPATHIC —) PETUNTSE
(FISSILE —) SHALE
(FLUID —) LAVA
(GABBROITIC —) EUCRITE
(GLASSY —) PITCHSTONE
(GRANULAR —) GABBRO OOLITE

DIORITE IJOLITE KOSWITE MYLONITE
PSAMMITE QUARTZITE
(GRANULATED —) GRUSS
(GREEN —) OPHITE
(HARD —) WHIN KIMGLE WHINSTONE
NOVACULITE
(HIGH —) SCOUT
(IGNEOUS —) BOSS SIAL SIMA TRAP
BASALT DUNITE GABBRO URTITE FELSITE
GRANITE MINETTE PICRITE SYENITE
DOLERITE ESSEXITE RHYOLITE TONALITE
(IMPURE —) CHERT
(INSULATED —) SKERRY
(INTRUSIVE —) HORTITE MINETTE
MAENAITE
(IRON-BEARING —) GAL
(ISOLATED —) SCAR SCARR SCAUR
(JUTTING POINT OF —) KIP
(MANTLE —) REGOLITH
(METAMORPHIC —) SKARN GNEISS
SCHIST BUCHITE GONDITE LEPTITE
ECLOGITE HORNFELS LIMURITE
(MICA-BEARING —) DOMITE
(MOLTEN —) MAGMA
(MOTTLED —) SERPENTINE
(PLUTONIC —) TAWITE HOLLAITE
TURJAITE
(POROUS —) TUFA TUFF ARSOITE
(PROJECTING —) CLINT
(PULVERIZED —) FLOUR
(RARE —) ALNOITE
(ROUGH —) CRAG KNAR SCARTH
(ROUNDED —) ROGNON SHEEPBACK
(SEDIMENTARY —) CRAG IRONSTONE
SANDSTONE
(SHARP —) NEEDLE AIGUILLE
(SLATY —) PLATE SCHALSTEIN
(SOFT —) MALM
(SOLID —) GIBBER
(STUDY OF —S) LITHOLOGY
(SUBMERGED —) SHELF
(UNDERLYING —) FLOOR
(VOLCANIC —) TUFA TUFF BASALT
DACITE DOMITE LATITE TAXITE PEPERIN
ANDESITE ASHSTONE EUTAXITE
RHYOLITE TEPHRITE TRACHYTE
(WASTE —) MULLOCK
(WORTHLESS —) GANG GANGUE
ROCKET DRAKE REBUKE STREAK
SKYLIGHT STARSHIP FIREDRAKE
ROCKY DAFT HARD STONY PETROUS
UNCOUTH OBDURATE UNSTABLE
DIFFICULT
ROCOCO ORNATE QUAINT BAROQUE
OUTMODED
ROD BAR BOW CUE GUY LUG PIN TIE
BOLT CANE CORE FALL GONG LINK MACE
POLE STEM STUD WAND WHIP ARBOR
BIRCH CATCH DOWEL PERCH POWER
PUNCH REACH ROUND SHOOT SPILL
SPOKE SPRAG STAFF STANG STEEL
STICK STING BROACH CENTER FINGER
HANGER PISTOL RAMMER SPRING
SWITCH WICKER FEATHER PLUNGER
POINTER POTHOOK PRICKER SCEPTER
STICKER TYRANNY WHISKER BACKSTAY

BOWSTAVE DIPSTICK KINGBOLT
REVOLVER
(— AS SYMBOL OF OFFICE) VERGE
(— BEARING TRAFFIC SIGNAL)
STANCHION
(— FOR ALIGNING HOLES) PODGER
(— FOR CARRYING GLASS) FORK
(— FOR DISCIPLINE) YARD FERULE
(— FOR FASTENING THATCH) SPELK
SPRINGLE
(— FOR FIREARM BORE) WIPER
(— FOR GLASS-MAKING) PUNTY
FASCET PONTIL CROPPIE
(— FOR HOLDING MEAT) SPIT
(— FOR TRANSMITTING MOTION)
TRACE
(— IN ARC LAMP) CARBON
(— IN CRICKET) STUMP
(— IN INTERFEROMETER) ETALON
(— IN MINE PUMP) SPEAR
(— IN NERNST LAMP) GLOWER
(— IN SPINNING WHEEL) SPINDLE
(— OF FOUNDRY MOLD) LANCE
(— OF LOOM) SHAFT
(— OF WOOD) SCOB
(— ON LOGGING TRUCK) RAVE
(— POINTED AT BOTH ENDS) SKEWER
(— SYMBOLIZING AUTHORITY)
BACULUS
(— TO BIND A CONTRACT) FESTUCA
(— TO FASTEN SAILS) JACKSTAY
(— TO IMMERSE SHEEP) CRUTCH
(— TO URGE BEAST) GOAD PROD
(— UPSET AT ONE END) SETUP
(— USED AS KEY) TOMMY
(— WITH ENDS AT RIGHT ANGLES)
STRAINER
(— WITH SPONGE ON END) PROBANG
(— WITH T-HEAD) TOGGLE
(AXIAL —) VIRGULA AXOSTYLE
(BASKETRY —) OSIER SLATH
(BUNDLE OF —S) DRIVER
(CARTILAGINOUS —) LYTTA
COLUMELLA
(CLAMMING —) BRAIL
(CONNECTING —) PITMAN
(CURTAIN —) TRINGLE
(DANCER'S —) CROTALUM
(DIVINING —) TWIG DOWSER
(FISHING —) GAD CALCUTTA
(FLEXIBLE —) RADDLE WATTLE
(FORKED —) CRUTCH
(GEM-CUTTING —) SETTER
(GRADUATED —) STADIA STADIUM
(IRON —) SNAP BETTY
(KNITTING —) NEEDLE
(LEAD —) CAME
(LOGGING —) CANARY
(MEASURING —) JUDGE SPILE STADIA
ELLWAND METEWAND METEYARD
(PLIABLE —) WINDING
(SMALL —) LANCE
(STRENGTHENING —) RIB
(SUPPLE —) SWABBLE
(TETHERING —) STAKE
(THIN —) TEYNE SCALLOM
(TIE —) ANCHOR

(UMBRELLA —) STRETCHER
(WITHE —) BILBERRY
RODENT RAT DEGU HARE MOLE PACA
PIKA VOLE CONEY COYPU HUTIA LEROT
MOUSE AGOUTI BEAVER BITING GERBIL
GNAWER GOPHER JERBOA MARMOT
MURINE RABBIT GEOMYID GNAWING
HAMSTER LEMMING LEVERET MUSKRAT
CAPIBARA DORMOUSE LEPORIDE
SEWELLEL SQUIRREL VIZCACHA
PORCUPINE
ROGUE BOY IMP NYM KEMP KITE LOON
CATSO CRANK GREEK GYPSY HEMPY
KNAVE SCAMP BEGGAR BUGGER CANTER
CHOUSE COQUIN CURTAL LIMMER
PICARO RASCAL TINKER ERRATIC
FOISTER HALLION LADRONE PANURGE
SHARPER SKELLUM SWINGER VILLAIN
PICAROON SCALAWAG SWINDLER
ROGUISH SLY ARCH HEMPY WICKED
KNAVISH TRICKSY VAGRANT WAGGISH
DISHONEST
ROISTER REVEL SCOUR CAROUSE
GALRAVAGE
ROISTERER GREEK HUZZA BUSTER
HECTOR RIOTER SCOURER EPHESIAN
ROLAND (BETROTHED OF —) AUDE
(COMPANION OF —) OLIVER
(HORN OF —) OLIVANT
(SWORD OF —) DURANDAL
(UNCLE OF —) CHARLEMAGNE
ROLE BIT JOB LEAD PART HEAVY FIGURE
FUNCTION
(SMALL —) CAMEO
ROLL BUN ROW WEB BOLT COIL CURL
FILE FLOW FURL LIST MILL PASS REEL
ROAM ROTA SWAG WIND WRAP BAGEL
BIALY BREAD DANDY TRILL WHELM
BILLOW BUNDLE CIRCLE ELAPSE ENFOLD
GROVEL MUSTER RECORD ROSTER
ROTATE SCROLL UPWIND WANDER
BISCUIT BRIOCHE CROCKET ENVELOP
MANCHET REVOLVE STRETCH TRUNDLE
TWISTER BROTCHEN CANNELON
CRESCENT LAMINATE REGISTER
ROLLER FLY BOWL BRAY DRUM JACK
LEAD MILL PUCK DANDY INKER RIDER
SHELL WAVER WINCH BRAYER DOFFER
FASCIA MANGLE RUNNER CARRIER
TRUCKLE STRIPPER
ROLLICKING GAY WILD MERRY JOVIAL
LIVELY
ROLLING CURL GOGGLE WHEELY
SWAYING TRILLED LURCHING VOLUTION
ROMANCE WOO GEST FANCY FEIGN
NOVEL STORY UTOPIA FANTASY FICTION
ROMANZA

ROMANIA

CAPITAL: BUCHAREST
COUNTY: OLT ARAD CLUJ DOLJ GORJ IASI
ARGES BACAU BIHOR BUZAU ILFOV
MURES NEAMT SALAJ SIBIU TIMIS
DISTRICT: ALBA BANAT BIHOR DOBRUJA
DOBROGEA MARAMURES

LAKE: SINOE
MOUNTAIN: BIHOR NEGOI CODRUL
RODNEI CALIMAN PIETROSU
PROVINCE: ARDEAL MOLDAVIA
WALACHIA
RIVER: ALT OLT JIUL PRUT ALUTA ARGES
BUZDU MOROS MURES OLTUL SCHYL
SIRET TIMIS TISZA VEDEA CRASNA
DANUBE ARGESUL MURESUL SOMESUL
BISTRITA IALOMITA
RIVER PORT: BRAILA GALATI GALATZ
TOWN: ARAD CLUJ IASI BACAU CERNA
JASSY NEAMT SIBIU TURNU BRAILA
BRASOV GALATI GALATZ LUPENI
CRAIOVA FOCSANI PLOESTI SEVERIN
CERNAVTI KISHENEF TEMESVAR
KOLOZSVAR

ROMANTIC AIRY WILD IDEAL ARDENT
DREAMY GOTHIC POETIC UNREAL
FERVENT FABULOUS FANCIFUL
ROME HAUL (AUTHOR OF —)
EDMONDS
(CHARACTER IN —) BEN DAN JOE RAE
SOL LUCY BERRY JACOB KLORE MOLLY
WAMPY CALASH GURGET HARROW
HECTOR JOTHAM JULIUS SAMSON
TINKLE WEAVER WILSON FORTUNE
LARKINS TURNESA WILLIAM FRIENDLY
CASHDOLLAR BUTTERFIELD
ROMEO AND JULIET (AUTHOR OF —)
SHAKESPEARE
(CHARACTER IN —) JOHN PARIS PETER
ROMEO JULIET TYBALT ABRAHAM
CAPULET ESCALUS GREGORY SAMPSON
BENVOLIO LAURENCE MERCUTIO
MONTAGUE BALTHASAR
ROMOLA (AUTHOR OF —) ELIOT
(CHARACTER IN —) DINO LUCA TITO
BARDO CALVO LILLO MONNA PIERO
TESSA MELEMA ROMOLA BRIGIDA
NICCOLO BERNARDO BALDASARRE
ROMP RIG LARK PLAY ROIL FRISK SPORT
FROLIC GAMBOL HOORAY HOYDEN
HURRAH COURANT RAMMACK
ROOF TOP BACK DECK DOME FLAT COVER
HOUSE RAISE RISER SHELL BONNET
CUPOLA SUMMIT TECTUM CRICKET
GAMBREL MANSARD RIGGING TECTURE
BULKHEAD HOUSETOP SEMIDOME
PENTHOUSE
ROOK GYP CROW DUPE CHEAT CRAKE
JUDGE TOWER BLACKY CASTLE
DEFRAUD
ROOKIE COLT DRONGO NOVICE RECRUIT
BEGINNER
ROOM PAD WON AULA CAFE FARM HALL
KILN LIEU PLAY SALA SLUM LODGE
PLACE SCOPE SHACK SPACE STALL
STUDY CHAPEL MARGIN SCOUTH SINGLE
SMOKER STANCE STUDIO CABINET
CHAMBER HOLDING KITCHEN LAUNDRY
LIBRARY SEMINAR SMOKERY SURGERY
ASSEMBLY BASEMENT CAPACITY
DRYHOUSE HOTHOUSE LAVATORY

PLAYROOM SCULLERY SWEATBOX
PRESSROOM
(— ADJOINING SYNAGOGUE)
GENIZAH
(— BEHIND FACADE) ATTIC
(— BETWEEN KITCHEN AND DINING
ROOM) SERVERY
(— CONTAINING FOUNTAIN)
NYMPHEUM
(— DUG IN CLIFF) HYPOGEE
HYPOGEUM
(— FOR ACTION) LEEWAY
(— FOR BATHING) HAMMAM
(— FOR CONVERSATION) EXEDRA
LOCUTORY
(— FOR FAMILY RECORDS)
TABLINUM
(— FOR KEEPING FOOD) LARDER
PANTRY
(— FOR PAINTINGS) GALLERY
(— FOR PRIVATE DEVOTIONS)
ORATORY
(— FOR PUBLIC AMUSEMENTS)
CASINO THEATER
(— FOR STOWAGE) LASTAGE
(— FOR TABLE LINEN) EWERY
(— IN COAL MINE) BREAST
(— IN HAREM) ODA
(— IN KEEP) DUNGEON
(— IN PREHISTORIC BUILDING) CELL
(— IN REAR OF TEMPLE) EPINAOS
(— IN SIDE OF LARGER ROOM) ALA
(— IN TOWER) BELFRY
(— OF STUDENTS' SOCIETY) HALL
(— ON SHIP) CABIN STOKEHOLD
(— OVER CHURCH PORCH) PARVIS
(— OVER STAGE) SHADOW
(— TOGETHER) CHUM
(— UNDER BUILDING) CELLAR
(CHILDREN'S —) NURSERY
(COTTAGE —) END
(DINING —) CENACLE DINETTE
REFECTORY TRICLINIUM
(DRAWING —) SALON SALOON
(DRESSING —) SHIFT BOUDOIR
CAMARIN VESTUARY WARDROBE
TIREHOUSE
(ESKIMO ASSEMBLY —) KASHGA
(EXHIBITION —) THEATER
(GRINDING —) HULL
(HEATED —) STEW
(HIGH —) AERIE
(INNER —) BEN INBY INBYE SPENCE
(INSULATED —) FREEZER
(LECTURE —) AUDITORY
(LIVING —) HOUSE LANAI SALON
SERDAB SOLARIUM VOORHUIS
(MONASTERY —) CELL LAVABO
(NARROW —) CRIB
(OCTAGONAL —) TRIBUNA
(PRIVATE —) SNUG SCHOLA CONCLAVE
(PUEBLO ASSEMBLY —) ESTUFA
(READING —) ATHENEUM
(RECEPTION —) DIVAN PARLOR
KURSAAL MANDARAH
(REFRIGERATED —) COOLER
(RETIRING —) RECAMERA

(ROMAN —) ATRIUM AEDICULA
FUMARIUM
(ROUND —) ROTUNDA
(SEA —) BERTH
(SECLUDED —) DEN
(SERIES OF —S) SWEEP
(SITTING —) SEAT SITTER BOUDOIR
(SLEEPING —) DORMER BEDROOM
DORMITORY
(SMALL —) ALA CELL SNUG STEW ZETA
CUBBY CUDDY LOBBY CLOSET CUBICLE
SNUGGERY
(SMOKING —) DIVAN DIWAN TABAGIE
(SORTING —) SALLE
(STEAM —) STOVE
(STORAGE —) CAMARIN MAGAZINE
THALAMUS
(SWEATING —) SUDARIUM SUDATORY
LACONICUM
(THRONE —) AIWAN
(TOP —) GARRET IMPERIAL
(UPPER —) SOLAR
(VAULTED —) CAMERA
ROOMY WIDE LARGE RANGY SPACY
SPACIOUS CAPACIOUS COMMODIOUS
ROOST SIT TIDE PERCH GARRET HARBOR
LODGING ROOKERY SHELTER
ROOSTER COCK GAME GALLO MANOC
GAMECOCK
ROOT DIG PRY TAP BASE BULB CHOY
GRUB MOOR MORE PLUG PULL RACE
SPUR TAIL CHEER FIBER FRUIT GROUT
HEART RADIX STOCK BOTTOM CARROT
GROUND ORIGIN SETTLE CHICORY
CRAMPON GINSENG IMPLANT IPOMOEA
RADICAL RUMMAGE
(— CONTAINING STARCH) KOONTI
(— DEEPLY) SCREW
(— OF GINGER) RACE
(— OF ORCHID) CULLIONS
(— OF TARO) EDDO
ROOTED FIXED CHRONIC
(DEEPLY —) BESETTING
ROPE GUY TOW TUG CORD FALL FAST
LINE ROOD SPAN TACK TAIL TAUM TOME
WARP CABUL CHECK CHORD LASSO
SWEEP TWIST WIDDY WITHE CABLET
LARIAT LISSOM LIZARD MECATE RAPEYE
RUNNER SLATCH STRAND STRING
TETHER WARROK BEDCORD ENTRAIL
HAYBAND LASHING SERPENT SERVICE
FOREFOOT INHAULER LIFELINE
NECKLACE SEQUENCE THRAMMLE
BREECHING
(— A STEER) HEEL
(— CONNECTING NETS) BALK BAULK
(— FOR FASTENING GATE) CRINGLE
(— FOR FISH) STRINGER
(— FOR TRAINING HORSE) LONGE
(— FOR TYING CATTLE) CEEL SEAL
AWEBAND
(— HOLDING RAFT TOGETHER) BRAIL
(— OF HAIR) CABESTRO
(— OF ONIONS) REEVE
(— OF STRAW) GAD SIME VINE SIMON
SUGAN FETTLE SIMMON SOOGAN
(— OF 10 OR MORE INCHES) CABLE

(— ON DERRICK) TELEGRAF
(— ON FISHING NET) PINION SEAMING
(— PASSING AROUND DEADEYE)
STRAP STROP
(— STOLEN FROM DOCKYARD)
RUMBO
(— WITH HOOK AND TOGGLE)
PROLONGE
(— WITH SWIVEL AND LOOP)
TOGGEL TOGGLE
(— WOUND AROUND CABLE)
KECKLING
(—S IN RIGGING) CORDAGE
(ANCHOR —) RODE VIOL VOYAL
(BELL —) TYALL HANGER
(CIRCUS —) JEFF
(DRAFT —) SOAM
(DRAG —) GUSS
(FLAG-RAISING —) HALYARD
(FOOT —) HORSE
(GRASS —) SOGA
(GUIDE —) DRAGLINE
(HANGMAN'S —) HEMP TIPPET
(HARNESS —) TRACE HALTER
(HARPOON —) FOREGOER
(MOORING —) HEADFAST
(NAUTICAL —) TIE TYE COLT FANG LIFT
STAY VANG BRACE BRAIL SHEET SLING
STRAP STROP GILGUY HAWSER INHAUL
LACING RATLIN SHROUD BOBSTAY
BOWLINE CATFALL GESWARP LANYARD
LEEFANG OUTHAUL PAINTER PAZAREE
PENDANT PENNANT PIGTAIL RATLINE
SNORTER SNOTTER STIRRUP STOPPER
SWIFTER BACKBONE BACKSTAY
BUNTLINE DOWNHAUL FORETACK
JACKSTAY PASSAREE ROUNDING
SELVAGEE WOOLDING TIMENOGUY
(SHORT —) SHANK
(SHORT CART —) WANTY
(SMALL HANDMADE —) FOX
(SMUGGLER'S —) LINGTOW
(TALLOWED —) GASKET
(TETHERING —) SPANCEL
(TOW —) CORDELLE
(WIRE —) HAULBACK JACKSTAY
(WORN OR POOR —) JUNK
ROSARY BEADS CORONA TASBIH
BEADING PSALTER BEADROLL
(MOHAMMEDAN —) COMBOLOIO
ROSE ASH KNOT MOSS BRIAR BRIDE
BUCKY FLUSH CANKER POMPON
BOURBON LOZENGE MANETTI OPHELIA
RAMBLER AGRIMONY COLUMBIA
DOGBERRY PEDELION
ROSENKAVALIER, DER
(CHARACTER IN —) OCHS SOPHIE
FANINAL MARIANDL OCTAVIAN
MARSCHALLIN
(COMPOSER OF —) STRAUSS
ROSETTE CHOU KNOT ROSACE ROSULA
COCKADE
ROSEWOOD BUBINGA MOLOMPI
JACARANDA PALISANDER
ROSTRUM PEW AMBE BEAK BEMA
GUARD SNOUT PULPIT TRIBUNE

ROSY ROSEN BLUSHY AURORAL HEALTHY
AUROREAN BLOOMING RUBICUND
ROT DOTE DROP POKE SOUR DECAY SPOIL
TEASE BLUING FESTER CORRUPT
PUTREFY NONSENSE STAGNATE
(— BY EXPOSURE) RET
(— OF GRAPES) SLIPSKIN
(APPLE —) FROGEYE
(FOOT —) FOUL
(FRUIT —) LEAK
(LIVER —) COE
ROTARY CIRCLE GYRATORY
ROUNDABOUT
ROTATE RUN BIRL GYRE ROLL SPIN TURN
PIVOT SCREW WHEEL GYRATE REVOLVE
TRUNDLE ALTERNATE
ROTATION SPIN TURN ROUND TWIRL
GYRATION SPINNING WHIRLING
ROTTEN BAD FOUL PUNK SOUR ADDLED
AMPERY MOOSEY PUTRID DECAYED
SPOILED DEPRAVED UNSTABLE
(HALF —) DOTED
(PARTIALLY —) DRUXY
ROTUND FAT PLUMP ROUND STOUT
CHUBBY
ROUE RAKE RAKEHELL DEBAUCHEE
ROUGE RED BLUSH PAINT FUCATE
REDDEN RUDDLE SCRIMMAGE
ROUGH ROW BEAT FOUL HARD RUDE
THUG WILD ACRID BLUFF BLUNT BRUTE
CHURL CRUDE DIRTY GOBBY HAIRY
HARSH HEFTY JAGGY LUMPY ROWDY
RUGGY STARK STERN STOUR TOUGH
BROKEN CHOPPY COARSE COBBLY
CRABBY CRAGGY HISPID HOARSE
HORRID INCULT JAGGED KNAGGY
KNOTTY RAGGED RASPED ROBUST
RUFFLE RUGGED SEVERE SHAGGY
SKETCH STICKY TRYING UNEVEN UNKIND
ABUSIVE AUSTERE BOORISH BRISTLY
CRABBED HIRSUTE INEQUAL INEXACT
JARRING RAUCOUS RUFFLED STICKLY
UNCOUTH UNKEMPT VICIOUS ABRASIVE
ASPERATE CHURLISH IMPOLITE LARRIKIN
OBDURATE SCABROUS SCRAGGED
STUBBORN UNGENTLE UNTENDER
MANHANDLE
ROUGHEN FRET HACK EMERY FLOCK
FROST TOOTH ABRADE STIVER CRIZZLE
ENGRAIL SCRATCH ASPERATE
ROUGHING IT (AUTHOR OF —) TWAIN
CLEMENS
(CHARACTER IN —) HANK MARK
SLADE TWAIN YOUNG BRIGHAM
ERICKSON
ROUGHNECK ROWDY TOUGH MUCKER
UNCOUTH BANGSTER
ROUGHNESS GAFF GRAIN SCUFF TOOTH
RUFFLE CRIZZLE CRUDITY ACRIMONY
ASPERITY
(— OF SEA) LIPPER
(— OF SKIN) GOOSESKIN GOOSEFLESH
(— OF WALL) KEY
ROUND BALL BEND BOLD BOUT FAST
FULL GIRO HEAD RICH ROTA TOUR WALK
ABOUT AMPLE BEADY CATCH DANCE
GLOBE HAMBO LARGE MOONY ORBED

ROMAN RONDO SPOKE TUBBY CIRCLE
COURSE ENTIRE MELLOW NEARLY
ROTUND SPHERY SPIRAL STREAK ZODIAC
ANNULAR CIRCUIT SHAPELY CIRCULAR
COMPLETE CROSSBAR ENCIRCLE
GLOBULAR SONOROUS
(— EDGES OF TIMBER) BEARD
(— END OF LOG) SNIPE
(— FREQUENTLY GONE OVER) BEAT
(— IN BOWLING) FRAME
(— IN CARDS) GRAND
(— IN ROLLER DERBY) JAM
(— OF ACTIVITIES) SWING
(— OF APPLAUSE) HAND JOLLY SALVO
PLAUDIT
(— OF CHAIR) BALUSTER
(— OF KNITTING) BOUT
(— OF LADDER) STAVE
(— OF PLAY) LAP
(— OFF) TOP CROWN FILLET
(— OUT) ORB BELLY INTEGRATE
(— UP) CORRAL WRANGLE SCROUNGE
(PLUMP AND —) CHUBBY
(SWEDISH —) HAMBO
ROUNDABOUT DETOUR ROTARY
CURVING DEVIOUS CAROUSEL CIRCULAR
INDIRECT TORTUOUS
ROUNDED FULL BOMBE BOWLY CONVEX
MELLOW ROTUND CONCAVE GIBBOUS
SHAPELY COMPLETE FINISHED
SONOROUS
ROUSE GIG HOP JOG BAIT CALL DRAW
GOAD MOVE RANT RAVE STIR WAKE
WHET ERECT MOUNT RAISE START
STEER UPSET WAKEN ABRADE EXCITE
FOMENT KINDLE NETTLE RATTLE REVIVE
RUFFLE AGITATE ANIMATE DISTURB
ENLIVEN HEARTEN INFLAME STARTLE
INSPIRIT IRRITATE
(— TO ACTION) HIE ALARM ALARUM
BESTIR ALACRIFY
ROUSING LIVELY
ROUT MOB MOW DRUM FUSS HERD
CHASE CROWD EJECT FLOCK LURCH
SMEAR SMITE CLAMOR DEFEAT FLIGHT
RABBLE THRONG UPROAR CONFUSE
CONQUER DEBACLE SCATTER
CONFOUND DISTRESS VANQUISH
(BACCHIC —) THIASUS
ROUTE WAY BELT GATE LINE PASS PATH
SEND TRACE TRACK AIRWAY CAREER
COURSE CUTOFF SKYWAY CHANNEL
CIRCUIT LANDWAY PASSAGE SHUTTLE
CORRIDOR LIFELINE SHORTCUT
TRAVERSE
(— MARKED OUT) ITER
(— TO DEFEAT) SKIDS
(CIRCUITOUS —) DETOUR
(MIGRATION —) FLYWAY
(OCEAN —) LANE
(PREF.) ODO
ROUTINE RUT ROTA DRILL GRIND
GROOVE HARNESS EVERYDAY ORDINARY
(COMPUTER —) BOOTSTRAP
(DOMESTIC —) HOMELIFE
(THEATRICAL —) SCHTICK
(WEARISOME —) TREADMILL

ROVE RUN ROAM GUESS RANGE SCOUR
SPACE STRAY FORAGE MARAUD RAMBLE
STROLL WANDER STRAGGLE
ROVER FLIRT STRAY MASHER RANGER
VIKING GANGREL MARAUDER TRAVELER
WANDERER
ROVING NOMAD VAGUE ERRANT
DEVIOUS NOMADIC VAGRANT
GADABOUT RAMBLING RESTLESS
VAGABOND MIGRATORY
ROW LAY OAR SET FILE LINE MUSS PULL
RANK RULE TIER ALLEY BRAWL FIGHT
NOISE ORDER RANGE SCOLD SCRAP
TRAIN BARNEY BERATE COURSE PADDLE
POTHER RACKET RUCKUS RUMPUS
SHINDY STREET STROKE QUARREL
RUCTION SHINDIG OUTBURST SQUABBLE
(— BACKWARD) STERN
(— OF BENCHES) STACK
(— OF CASKS) LONGER
(— OF CORN, BARLEY, ETC.) RIG
(— OF DRY HAY) STADDLE
(— OF GRAIN) SWATH
(— OF GRASS) HACK SWATH
(— OF GUNS) TIRE
(— OF HOUSES) CRESCENT
(— OF LAMPS) BATTEN
(— OF SEATS) BARRERA
(— OF SEED) DRILL
(— OF STAKES) ORGUE
(— OF STONES) CORDON
(— OF TREES) ESPALIER
(— OF VEGETABLES) RINGE
(-S OF BALCONY) MEZZANINE
(DISORDERLY —) RAG
ROWBOAT GIG BARK BARIS COBLE
SCULL SKIFF BARQUE CAIQUE DINGHY
WHERRY SCULLER
(CLINKER-BUILT —) FUNNY
(FLAT-BOTTOMED —) DORY
(SMALL —) COG
ROWDY BHOY ROUGH TOUGH TOMBOY
UNRULY VULGAR HOODLUM RAFFISH
LARRIKIN ROUGHNECK
ROWENA (FATHER OF —) HENGIST
(GUARDIAN OF —) CEDRIC
(HUSBAND OF —) IVANHOE
VORTIGERN
ROYAL EASY ELITE REGAL AUGUST
KINGLY REGIUS SOVRAN SUPERB
GLORIOUS IMPERIAL IMPOSING
MAJESTIC PRINCELY
ROYALIST TORY ULTRA REGIAN TANTIVY
CAVALIER MUSCADIN
ROYALTY LOT BONUS CROWN REGAL
REALTY MAJESTY LORDSHIP NOBILITY
REGALITY
RUB BILL FILE FRAY FRET FRIG CHAFE
DIGHT FEEZE LABOR SMEAR STONE
RUBBER BEESWAX FURBISH MASSAGE
(— AS A ROPE) SNUG
(— AS ANIMALS) SHAB
(— AWAY) ERODE ABRADE
(— BOOT) BONE
(— DOWN) WIPE STRAP
(— ELBOWS) JOSTLE
(— GENTLY) STROKE

(— HARD) SCOUR SCRUB
(— HARSHLY) GRIND
(— LIGHTLY) GRAZE
(— OFF) CROCK ABRADE ABRASE
(— OUT) ERASE EFFACE EXPUNGE
(— ROUGHLY) GRATE
(— SNUFF) DIP
(— THE SKIN OFF) SHAW
(— TOGETHER) FIDDLE
(— VELVET FROM ANTLERS) BURNISH
(— WITH GREASE) DUB
(— WITH OIL) ANOINT

RUBBER BUNA FOAM PARA BUTYL CREPE
CAUCHO ERASER BISCUIT EBONITE
ELASTIC RAMBONG NEOPRENE

RUBBISH BUNK CRAP FLAM GEAR MUSH
PUNK RAFF BILGE OFFAL SLUSH STUFF
TRASH TRUCK WASTE DEBRIS GARBLE
KELTER LITTER PIFFLE RAFFLE REFUSE
RUBBLE SPILTH BAGGAGE RUMMAGE
TRAFFIC NONSENSE RIFFRAFF TRUMPERY

RUBRIC RED NAME CANON CLASS TITLE
CONCEPT CATEGORY

RUBY AGATE BALAS RUBIN PYROPE
ANTHRAX SPARKLE VERMEIL

RUDDER HELM STEER STERN STEERER
STEERAGE GOVERNAIL

RUDDY RED FRESH VIVID BLOWSY
FLORID LIVELY GLOWING BLUSHFUL
RUBICUND SANGUINE

RUDE ILL RAW BOLD LEWD WILD BLUFF
BLUNT CRUDE GREEN GROSS PLUMP
ROUGH SURLY ABRUPT BITTER BRASSY
CALLOW CHUFFY CLUMSY COARSE
GOTHIC HOMELY HOYDEN RIBALD
ROBUST RUGGED RUSTIC SAVAGE
SHAGGY SIMPLE VULGAR ABUSIVE
ARTLESS BOORISH CARLISH INCIVIL
LOUTISH HOMESPUN NATURAL UNCOUTH
CHURLISH HOMESPUN IMPOLITE
INSOLENT PETULANT STUBBORN

RUDIMENTARY BASIC ABORTIVE
INCHOATE ABECEDARY ELEMENTAL
EMBRYONIC PRIMITIVE

RUE MOURN REGRET REPENT SORROW

RUFF SET FURY POPE CREST PRIDE TEASE
TRUMP COLLAR RABATO RUFFLE TIPPET
ELATION PARTLET PASSION

RUFFIAN PIMP PUNK THUG TORY BRAVO
BULLY DEVIL ROUGH ROWDY TIGER
TOUGH APACHE BRUTAL COARSE
CUTTER MOHOCK NICKER PANDER
HOODLUM HOOLIGAN

RUFFLE VEX BAIT FRET BULLY CRISP
FRILL JABOT PLEAT SHIRR ABRADE
ATTACK GATHER NETTLE PEPLUM RIPPLE
BLUSTER BRISTLE DERANGE FLOUNCE
FLUTTER SWAGGER DISHEVEL DISORDER
DISTRACT FURBELOW IRRITATE
SKIRMISH

RUG BAKU COZY SNUG WRAP HERAT
HEREZ KAZAK KONIA LADIK MECCA
MOSUL SENNA USHAK YURUK KANARA
KASHAN KIRMAN MOGHAN NAMMAD
PERGAM RUNNER SHIRAZ SMYRNA
TABRIZ TOUPEE WILTON BALUCHI
BERGAMA BOKHARA FERAHAN GOREVAN
ISPAHAN YARKAND AUBUSSON
DOMESTIC SEDJADEH

RUGGED RUDE WILD HAIRY HARDY
ROUGH STIFF COARSE CRAGGY HORRID
JAGGED KNAGGY KNOTTY ROBUST
SAVAGE STRONG STURDY UNEVEN
GNARLED OBDURATE VIGOROUS

RUIN DO MAR BANE COOK DAMN DOOM
FALL FATE FELL HELL KILL LOSS RAZE
SINK BLAST BOTCH BREAK CRUSH
DECAY EXILE SHOOT SMASH SPEED
SPILL SPLIT SPOIL SWAMP TRASH
WRACK WRECK BEDASH BLIGHT CANCEL
DAMAGE DEFACE DEFEAT DISMAY
INJURY MANGLE RAVAGE CORRUPT
DESTROY FLATTEN PERVERT SHATTER
SUBVERT TORPEDO UNDOING BANKRUPT
COLLAPSE DEMOLISH DESOLATE
DISASTER DOWNFALL

RUINED FLAT GONE LORN BROKE KAPUT
BROKEN FALLEN NAUGHT FORLORN
BANKRUPT DESOLATE

RULE LAW RAJ KING NORM SWAY WARD
YARD AXIOM CANON GUIDE JUDGE
MAXIM NORMA ORDER POWER REGLE
REIGN RIGHT RULER STAFF SUTRA WIELD
DECIDE DECREE DOMINE EMPIRE
GNOMON GOVERN MANAGE MASTER
METHOD REGNUM REGULA SQUARE
COMMAND CONTROL COUNSEL DICTATE
DIETARY FORMULA PRECEPT PRESIDE
REGENCY REGIMEN THEOREM DOCTRINE
DOMINATE FUNCTION LEGALISM
ORDINARY REGNANCY STANDARD
OBSERVANCE
(— BY UPSTARTS) NEOCRACY
(— OUT) EXCLUDE
(— TYRANNICALLY) HORSE
(—S OF CONDUCT) ETIQUETTE
(—S OF DUELING) DUELLO
(ABSOLUTE —) AUTARCHY
(MOB —) OCHLOCRACY
(OPPOSING —) ANTINOMY

RULER
(ALSO SEE CHIEF, TITLE, LEADER) DEY
CZAR DAME DUKE EMIR INCA KING LORD
TSAR TZAR AMEER EMEER HAKIM MPRET
MWAMI NAWAB ARCHON AUTHOR
CAESAR DESPOT DYNAST EPARCH
ISWARA KABAKA KAISER MASTER
RECTOR REGENT SHERIF SULTAN
TYRANT BOURBON KHEDIVE MONARCH
PTOLEMY RECTRIX REGULUS REIGNER
TOPARCH TRIARCH WIELDER AUGUSTUS
GOVERNOR HEPTARCH INTERREX
OLIGARCH OVERLORD PADISHAH
PENTARCH PHYLARCH
(— IN A NATIVITY) APHETA
(— OF ENCLOSURE) HENRY
(CURVED —) SWEEP
(ELF —) AUBREY
(INCA —) CURACA
(JEWISH —) EXILARCH
(MONGOLIAN —) HUTUKTU
(MOSLEM —) SOLDAN
(STRONG —) REGINALD
(TATAR OR MOGUL —) CHAM

(WHITE —S) SERKALI
RULING CALL CHIEF REGENT SOVRAN
CURRENT HOLDING
RUM ODD QUEER RUMBO TAFIA BACARDI
CACHACA JAMAICA PECULIAR
EXCELLENT
RUMBLE GROWL RUMOR SNORE BUMBLE
HOTTER LUMBER GRUMBLE QUARREL
RUMINANT OX COW YAK BULL DEER
GOAT CAMEL LLAMA MOOSE SHEEP
STEER ALPACA VICUNA GIRAFFE
ANTELOPE
RUMINATE CHEW MULL MUSE PONDER
CONCOCT REFLECT CONSIDER
RUMMAGE GRUB POKE ROOT SEEK
BUSTLE FORAGE TOUSLE UPROAR
RANSACK DISORDER SKIRMISH
UPHEAVAL
RUMOR CRY SAW BUZZ FAMA FAME
TALK WORD BRUIT NOISE STORY VOICE
BREEZE CANARD GOSSIP MURMUR
RENOWN REPORT HEARSAY INKLING
OPINION WHISPER GRAPEVINE
SCUTTLEBUTT
RUMP ASS ARSE DOCK CROUP NATCH
STERN BOTTOM CRUPPER HURDIES
KEISTER BUTTOCKS DERRIERE
RUMPLE FOLD MUSS TOUSE CRUMPLE
SCRUNCH WRINKLE
RUMPUS RAG ROW BRAWL CLAMOR
FRACAS HUBBUB RUCKUS SHINDY
UPROAR BOBBERY RUCTION ROWDYDOW
RUN GO HOP JOG LAM PLY URN
BUNK CALL FLOW FUSE HEEL HUNT
LEAD MELT PASS PLAY RACE ROAM
ROVE TEND TRIG TRIP TROT TURN WALK
WORK ASSAY BLEND BREAK BRUSH
COAST HURRY POINT SPEED SPEND
STAND TABLE TRACE COURSE ELAPSE
EXTEND GALLOP HASTEN MANAGE
RESORT ROTATE STREAM TUMBLE
CONDUCT CONTAIN LIQUEFY OPERATE
PASSAGE RETREAT SKELTER TRANSCUR
(— ABOUT) TIG FISK DISCURRE
(— ACROSS) STRIKE
(— AGAINST) JOSTLE
(— AGROUND) BEACH GRAVEL HURTLE
STRAND STRIKE
(— ALONG EDGE OF) SKIRT
(— AS STOCKING) LADDER
(— AT HIGH SPEED) SCORCH
(— AT THE NOSE) WALK
(— AT TOP SPEED) SPRINT
(— AWAY) FLY GUY FLEE HIKE JINK
JUMP SMUG ELOPE SCRAM SMOKE
DECAMP SCAMPER SCARPER FUGITATE
SKEDADDLE
(— AWAY FROM DEBTS) LEVANT
(— AWAY IN PANIC) STAMPEDE
(— BEFORE A GALE) SCUD
(— BEFORE A JUMP) FEEZE
(— BETWEEN) INTERCUR
(— BLINDLY) SKITTLE
(— CLUMSILY) LOPPET TUMBLE
(— COUNTER) BELIE CROSS
(— DOWN) SLUR TRASH OVERRUN
(— HARD) DIG

(— HIGH) FLOOD
(— IN CRICKET) BYE WIDE EXTRA
NOTCH
(— IN DROPS) WEEP
(— INTO) INCUR
(— ITS COURSE) LAPSE
(— OBLIQUELY) SQUINT
(— OF CLAPBOARDING) STRAKE
(— OF MULE CARRIAGE) DRAW
(— OF SHAD) SPURT
(— OF STAIRS) GOING
(— OFF) BOLT SCADDLE
(— ON SKIS) SCHUSS
(— OUT) EXCUR ISSUE PETER
(— OVER) HEAT TRAMP OVERFLOW
(— RAPIDLY) KITE RAKE SCUR SCOUR
SKIRR SPLIT CAREER
(— SOAP) FRAME
(— SPEEDILY) CHASE CAREER
(— SWIFTLY) HARE LEAP SCUD CHEVY
CHIVY
(— THROUGH) PIERCE DISCURRE
(— TO) ACCURRE
(— TO EXERCISE HORSE) HEAT
(— TOGETHER) HERD MUDDY CLUTTER
(— TRAINS) BLOCK
(— WILD) GAD ESCAPE STARTLE
(— WILDLY) STARTLE
(— WITH AFFECTED PRECIPITATION)
SCUTTLE
(— WITH SKIPS) SCOUP
(— WITH VELOCITY) DART
(BRIEF —) STREAK FLUTTER
(COMMON —) RUCK
(END —) SWEEP
(GLASS FURNACE —) BLAST
(MUSICAL —) TIRADE
(OBSTACLE —) GYMKHANA
(RAPID MUSICAL —) TIRADE VOLATA
(SAILING —) STRETCH
(SHEEP —) SLAIT STATION
(SHORT —) FAIL BICKER SCURRY
FLUTTER RAMRACE SCUTTLE
(SKI —) PISTE SCHUSS LANGLAUF
(WILD —) LAMP
RUNG ROUND SCALE STAFF STAIR STAVE
STEAL TREAD DEGREE RUNDLE STOWER
CROSSBAR TRAVERSE
(— OF CHAIR) SPELL
(— OF LADDER) RIME STEP RANGE
SPOKE STALE RONDLE STREAK
(— OF ROPE WALK) STAKE
RUNNER GOER POST SCUD SHOE SKID
BLADE FLOAT RACER SABOT SCARF
SKATE SLIDE SPRAY CURSOR STOLON
TOUTER CHANNEL COURIER HARRIER
CURSITOR SKIPJACK TRAILING
(— FOR GRINDING STONE) MARTIN
(— WHO SETS PACE) RABBIT
(BOOKMAKER'S —) SPIV
(ERRAND —) CAD
(FLUME —) HERDER
(PAIR OF —S) SLOOP
(RACE —) SCUTTLER
(SLED —) BOB
(SLEDGE —S) SLIPES
RUNNING CARE EASY RACE FLUID QUICK

COURSE LIVING COURANT CURRENT
CURSIVE FLOWING SLIDING FUGITIVE
RUNT BOOR SCRUB SLINK STEER STUMP
STUNT HEIFER PEEWEE SHARGAR
SLINKER RECKLING
RUPTURE BLOW REND RENT BREAK
BURST CRACK SPLIT BREACH HERNIA
RHEXIS DISRUPT RUPTION FRACTURE
HERNIATE
RURAL RUSTIC BUCOLIC COUNTRY
AGRESTIC ARCADIAN LANDWARD
PASTORAL PLEASANT PRAEDIAL
VILLATIC
RUSE HOAX SHIFT STALL TRICK ARTIFICE
TRICKERY
RUSH FLY RIP RIX SAG BANG BENT BOLT
CLAP DASH GIRD HUSH JUNK LASH LEAP
RACE RACK RASH ROUT SCUD SLUR
SPUR TEAR TILT WHIP WIND CHASE
CHUTE DRIVE FEEZE FLASH FRUSH
HURRY ONSET SCOUR SPART SPRAT
SPRIT START STAVE STORM WHIRL
DELUGE FESCUE HURTLE JUNCUS
POWDER RAMACK RANDOM RAVINE
STREAK THRESH ASSAULT BULRUSH
DEBACLE JUNCITE RAMRACE SKELTER
SWITHER TANTIVY TORNADO VIRETOT
DEERHAIR SALTWEED
(— ABROAD) FLUSH
(— AGAINST) CHARGE
(— AWAY) BOLT FLEE SCUTTLE
(— DOWN) TRACE
(— FOR WEAVING) FRAIL
(— HEADLONG) BOIL RUIN SPURN
STAMPEDE
(— OF LIQUID) HEAD FLUSH
(— OF WATER) FRESH SHOOT SPOUT
SWASH
(— OF WORDS) SPATE
(— ON PASSER IN FOOTBALL) BLITZ
(— OUT) SALLY
(CLUMP OF —S) RASHBUSS
(COMMON —) FLOSS
(DOWNWARD —) HURL
(FLAT —) SHALDER
(FORCEFUL —) JET
(NOISY —) SCUTTER
(ONWARD —) BIRR SURGE

RUSSIA

CAPITAL: MOSCOW
COIN: KOPEK RUBLE GRIVNA KOPECK
DISTRICT: KARELIA
LAKE: ARAL NEVA SEGO CHANY ELTON
ILMEN ONEGA BAYKAL LADOGA SELETY
TAYMYR TENGIZ ZAYSAN BALKHASH
MEASURE: FUT LOF DUIM FASS LOOF
STOF FOUTE KOREC LIGNE OSMIN PAJAK
STOFF VEDRO VERST ARSHIN CHARKA
LINIYA PALETZ SAGENE TCHAST
BOTCHKA CHKALIK GARNETZ VERCHOC
BOUTYLKA CHETVERT KROUSHKA
MOUNTAIN: POBEDA BELUKHA
MOUNTAIN RANGE: ALAI URAL
CAUCASUS

PENINSULA: KOLA CRIMEA KARELIA
KAMCHATKA
PORT: EISK ANAPA ODESSA
REPUBLIC: UZBEK KAZAKH KIRGIZ LATVIA
ARMENIA ESTONIA GEORGIA TADZHIK
TURKMEN UKRAINE MOLDAVIA
LITHUANIA BYELORUSSIA
AZERBAIDZHAN
RIVER: IK OB DON ILI KET NER OKA ROS
TAZ TYM UFA USA AMGA AMUR KARA
LENA NEVA OREL SURA SVIR URAL
LOVAT MEZEN NADYM ONEGA TEREK
TOBOL VOLGA ABAKAN DONETS IRTYSH
DNIEPER PECHORA
SEA: ARAL AZOV KARA BLACK BAIKAL
OKHOTSK
TOWN: BAKU KIEV OMSK OREL PERM RIGA
GOMEL KASAN KAZAN KYZYL MINSK
PENSA PSKOV TOMSK FRUNZE IGARKA
KERTCH KURGAN NIZHNI ODESSA
ROSTOV SARTOV URALSK ALMAATA
BATAISK DONETSK IRKUTSK IVANOVO
KALININ KHARKOV RYBINSK TALLINN
KOSTROMA ORENBURG SMOLENSK
TAGANROG TASHKENT VLADIMIR
VORONEZH YAROSLAV
VOLCANO: ALAID SHIVELUCH TOLBACHIK

RUST DROSS UREDO AERUGO CANKER
CORRODE FERRUGO OXIDIZE
RUSTIC HOB JAY BOOR CARL CHAW HICK
HIND JOCK RUBE RUDE BACON CHUFF
CHURL COLIN DAMON DORIC HODGE
ROUGH RURAL SILLY YOKEL AGREST
COARSE FARMER GAFFER HONEST
JOBSON RUSSET SAVAGE STURDY
SYLVAN UPLAND ARTLESS BOORISH
BUCOLIC BUMPKIN BUSHMAN COUNTRY
DAPHNIS GEORGIC HAYSEED HOBNAIL
HOOSIER LANDMAN PAISANO PEASANT
PLOWMAN THYRSIS AGRESTIC
ARCADIAN BACKVELD LANDWARD
MOSSBACK CLODHOPPER
(NOT —) CIVIL
(UNCOUTH —) JAKE
(YOUTHFUL —) SWAIN
RUSTLE STEAL FISSLE HIRSEL BRUSTLE
CRINKLE SKITTER WHISTLE
(— OF SILK) SCROOP
(— UP) SNAVVLE
RUSTLER THIEF WADDY DUFFER
HUSTLER
RUSTLING CRINKLY FROUFROU
SOUGHING FRICATION SUSURROUS
RUSTY HOARY MOROSE SULLEN
CANKERY OUTMODED
RUT BRIM RACK RUCK TRACK TREAD
CREASE FURROW GROOVE STRAKE
CHANNEL WRINKLE
(— IN PATH) GAY
RUTH PITY MERCY MISERY REGRET
SORROW CRUELTY REMORSE SADNESS
SYMPATHY
(HUSBAND OF —) BOAZ MAHLON
(MOTHER-IN-LAW OF —) NAOMI
(SON OF —) OBED JESSE

RUTHLESS FELL GRIM CRUEL BRUTAL
PITILESS CUTTHROAT

RWANDA

CAPITAL: KIGALI
LAKE: KIVU
LANGUAGE: KIRUNDI SWAHILI

MOUNTAIN: KARISIMBI
MOUNTAIN RANGE: MITUMBA
PEOPLE: TWA HUTU TUTSI
RIVER: KAGERA AKANYARU LUVIRONZA
TOWN: BUTARE GABIRO NYANZA GISENYI
TRIBE: BATWA BAHUTU WATUSI BATUTSI

RYE ERAY SPELT WHISKY GENTLEMAN

S

S ESS SUGAR

SABER KUKRI SABRE BANCAL BASKET
TULWAR ATAGHAN SCIMITAR

SAC BAG GUT POD CYST SACK ASCUS
BURSA FLOAT POUCH THECA AMNION
VESICA AMPULLA BLADDER CAPSULE
CISTERN VESICLE FOLLICLE

SACCHARIN SWEET STICKY SUGARY
GLUCOSE

SACERDOTAL HIERATIC PRIESTLY

SACK BAG BED MAT SAC LOOT POKE
HARRY POUCH SPOIL BUDGET POCKET
RAVAGE DISMISS PILLAGE PLUNDER
RANSACK
(— OF PALM LEAVES) BAYONG
(— OF WOOL) SARPLAR
(MAIL —) BUM
(PACK —) KYACK

SACRAMENT RITE BAPTISM MYSTERY
PENANCE

SACRED HOLY PIOUS SACRE TABOO
DIVINE SACRAL HALLOWED HEAVENLY
REVEREND SACROSANCT

SACRIFICE GIVE LOSS OFFER SPEND
FOREGO VICTIM EXPENSE CHILIOMB
IMMOLATE OBLATION OFFERING

SACRILEGIOUS IMPIOUS

SAD LOW DARK BLACK DREAR DUSKY
MOODY SOBER SORRY WEARY DREARY
SOLEMN SULLEN TRISTE WOEFUL
BALEFUL DOLEFUL FORLORN UNHAPPY
DEJECTED MOURNFUL PATHETIC
PITIABLE MELANCHOLY

SADDLE PAD RIG SAG TAG LOAD CHINE
PANEL SELLE STICK BURDEN
(— FOR ONE-LEGGED RIDER)
SOMERSET
(— STUFFED WITH STRAW) SODS
(— WITH) STICK
(LIGHT —) PILCH PILLION
(MOTORCYCLE —) PILLION
(PACK —) BAT
(STRAW —) SUNK SUGGAN
(PREF.) SELLI

SADDLEBAG ALFORJA CANTINA
SUMPTER TEETSOOK

SADNESS DREAR DUMPS GLOOM GRIEF
SORROW

SAFE CRIB PETE SURE WELL AMBRY
SOUND SECURE HEALTHY COCKSURE

SAFEGUARD SAVE WARD GUARD HEDGE
DEFEND SAFETY SECURE BASTION
BULWARK WARRANT PRECAUTION

SAFEKEEPING CUSTODY STORAGE

SAFETY REFUGE SALUTE SURETY
WARRANT SECURITY

SAG BAG DIP CREEP DROOP SLUMP
DEFLATE

SAGA EDDA EPIC MYTH TALE RIMUR
LEGEND

SAGACIOUS DEEP ACUTE CANNY SHARP
ASTUTE SHREWD POLITIC PRUDENT
SAPIENT

SAGE WISE HAKAM RISHI SOLON
DHARMA SHREWD WIZARD MAHATMA
SAPIENT SOPHIST

SAIL LUG RAG BEAT MAIN SCUN SWAN
SWIM WING DANDY FLOAT JUMBO
SHEET CANVAS CRUISE DRIVER MIZZEN
MUSLIN SINGLE LUGSAIL SKYSAIL
SPANKER TRYSAIL FORESAIL GAFFSAIL
HEADSAIL MAINSAIL MOONSAIL
NAVIGATE STAYSAIL
(— ALONG COAST) COAST ACCOST
(— AROUND) TURN DOUBLE
(— BEFORE THE WIND) SPOON
(— BRISKLY) SPANK
(— BY THE WIND) STRETCH
(— CLOSE TO WIND) PINCH
(— DOWN) AVALE
(— FASTER) FOOT
(— IN SPECIFIED DIRECTION) STAND
(— OF WINDMILL) ARM AWE EIE FAN
VAN FLIER SWEEP SWIFT
(— ON COURSE) HAUL WORK
(— QUIETLY) GHOST
(— RAPIDLY) SKIRR
(— SWIFTLY) RAMP
(— TO WINDWARD) THRASH
(— WITH WIND ABEAM) LASK
(LIGHT —) SHADOW
(LOWEST —) COURSE
(SMALL —) ROYAL
(TRIANGULAR —) RAFFE LATEEN
BENTINCK
(WIND —) BADGIR
(3-CORNERED —) JIB TRINKET

SAILBOAT SCOW BULLY DANDY NABBY
SCOUT SHARP SKIFF SLOOP SNIPE
DINGHY QUODDY SAILER CATBOAT
SCOOTER SHALLOP SHARPIE KEELBOAT
SKIPJACK TRIMARAN

SAILFISH BOHO WOOHOO GUEBUCU
LONGJAW VOILIER VOLADOR BILLFISH

SAILOR (ALSO SEE NAVAL OFFICER)
GOB TAR JACK LAKER LIMEY DECKIE
HEARTY MARINE SEAMAN TARPOT
TOPMAN COLLIER MARINER SHIPMAN
SWABBER YARDMAN COXSWAIN
DECKHAND SHIPMATE
(EAST INDIAN —) LASCAR
(OLD —) SALT SHELLBACK
(SCANDINAVIAN —) KLOSH

SAINT HOLY ARHAT SANTO BHAGAT
HALLOW PATRON CANONIZE

SAINT JOAN (AUTHOR OF —) SHAW

(CHARACTER IN —) JOAN DUNOIS
ROBERT WARWICK BAUDRICOURT
SAINT LUCIA (CAPITAL OF —)
CASTRIES
(MOUNTAIN OF —) GIMIE
(MOUNTAINS OF —) PITONS CANARIES
(VOLCANO OF —) SOUFRIERE
SAINTLY DEVOUT ANGELIC BEATIFIC
SAINT VINCENT (CAPITAL OF —)
KINGSTOWN
(PART OF —) UNION BEQUIA
GRENADINES
SALAD SALLET COLESLAW SILLSALLAT
(CORN —) FETTICUS
SALAMANDER OLM NEWT TWEEG
LIZARD TRITON AXOLOTL CRAWLER
CREEPER
SALARY PAY HIRE WAGES INCOME
PENSION STIPEND
SALE FAIR HEDGE TOUCH BOURSE
(— BY AUCTION) CANT ROUP BLOCK
VENDUE OUTROOP
(— BY OUTCRY) ROUP HAMMER
(— OF OFFICE) BARRATRY
(— OF TOBACCO) BREAK
(PUBLIC —) AUCTION
(RUMMAGE —) JUMBLE
SALESMAN CLERK BAGMAN RUNNER
SELLER BOOKMAN DRUMMER PITCHMAN
SALIENT SPUR BULGE CHIEF BASTION
SALIVA SPIT DROOL WATER DRIVEL
SLAVER SPUTUM SPITTLE
SALLOW WAN SICK MUDDY PALLID
YELLOW
SALMON DOG LOX KETA MASU PINK
COHOE HADDO HOLIA SMOLT TECON
ALEVIN KIPPER LAUREL SILVER
ANADROM BLUECAP BOTCHER CHINOOK
DOGFISH GILLING KOKANEE NEWFISH
QUINNAT REDFISH RUNFISH SHEDDER
SOCKEYE BLUEBACK HUMPBACK
SPRINGER
SALOME (FATHER OF —) HEROD
(HUSBAND OF —) PHILIP ZEBEDEE
ARISTOBULUS
(MOTHER OF —) HERODIAS
SALON HALL SALOON GALLERY
SALOON CAFE DIVAN SALON BARROOM
CANTINA RUMSHOP DEADFALL DRINKERY
BRASSERIE
SALT SAL CORN KERN BRINY AMIDOL
GAMMON MALATE OLEATE SALINE
MALEATE BRACKISH HALINOUS
(— OUT) CUT GRAIN
(DOUBLE —) ALUM
(HAIR —) ALUNOGEN
(LUMP OF —) SALTCAT
(METAL —) SILICATE
(MIXTURE OF —S) REH USAR
(ROCK —) PIG HALITE
SALTPETER NITER NITRE PETER
ANATRON CALICHE PRUNELLA
SALUTARY GOOD BENIGN HEALTHY
HELPFUL BENEDICT
SALUTATION AVE HAIL ALOHA MIZPAH
SALAAM SALUTE SLAINTE WELCOME
GREETING

(DRINKING —) SKOAL PROSIT PROFACE
WASSAIL
SALUTE CAP HAIL HEIL KISS CHEER
DRINK GREET HONOR SALVO COLORS
SALAAM EMBRACE
SALVATION BODAI MOKSHA SAFETY
NIRVANA KAIVALYA SOULHEAL
SALVE TAR NERVAL SUPPLE PLASTER
UNGUENT OINTMENT
SAME ID ILK ONE IDEM LIKE SELF VERY
DITTO EQUAL SELFSAME
SAMOA (CAPITAL OF —) APIA
PAGOPAGO
(COIN OF —) SENE TALA
(ISLAND OF —) OFU TAU ROSE MANUA
UPOLU SAVAII OLOSEGA TUTUILA
(MOUNTAIN OF —) FITO SAVAII
MATAFAO MATAFAO
SAMPLE SIP CAST CHECK ESSAY TASTE
TRIAL CHANCE COUPON MUSTER
SWATCH EXAMPLE EXCERPT PATTERN
INSTANCE SPECIMEN
SAMSON (FATHER OF —) MANOAH
SAMSON ET DALILA
(CHARACTER IN —) PRIEST SAMSON
DELILAH
(COMPOSER OF —) SAINTSAENS
SAMUEL (FATHER OF —) ELKANAH
(MOTHER OF —) HANNAH
SANCTIFY BLESS SACRE DEDICATE
SANCTION AMEN ALLOW ASSENT
RATIFY APPROVE ENDORSE JUSTIFY
SUPPORT ACCREDIT APPROVAL
CANONIZE SUFFRAGE
SANCTITY HALIDOME HOLINESS
SANCTUARY BEMA FANE ABBEY ALTAR
ADYTUM ASYLUM CHAPEL REFUGE
SHRINE SACRARY SHELTER HALIDOME
HOLINESS
(— FOR LAWBREAKERS) ALSATIA
SAND DIRT GRIT GRAIL GRAVEL ASBESTIC
BLINDING
(— FOR STREWING ON FLOORS)
BREEZE
(— IN KIDNEYS) ARENA
(— MIXED WITH GRAVEL) GARD
DOBBIN
(— ON SEA BOTTOM) PAAR
(BRAIN —) SABULUM ACERVULUS
(COLORED —) SMALT
(VOLCANIC —) SANTORIN
SANDAL TIP FLAT SOCK TEGUA CALIGA
PATTEN SCUFFER GUARACHE HUARACHO
SANDBAR BALK LOOP BARRA SHOAL
TOMBOLO TOWHEAD
SANDPIPER JACK KNOT PEEP RUFF STIB
WEET OXEYE SNIPE TEREK DUNLIN
OXBIRD PLOVER REDLEG TRINGA
CHOROOK FATBIRD HAYBIRD PEETWEET
REDSHANK
SANDSTONE FLAG GRIT HAZEL ARKOSE
KINGLE ARENITE HASSOCK CARSTONE
GANISTER
(BLOCK OF —) SARSEN
SANDWICH BUTTY HOAGY BURGER
HOAGIE GRINDER WESTERN

SANDY GINGER ARENOSE PSAMMOUS SABULINE SABULOUS
SANE WISE LUCID RIGHT NORMAL HEALTHY PERFECT RATIONAL SENSIBLE
SANGUINE FOND MURREY HEMATIC HOPEFUL
SANITARY HYGIENIC
SANITY SENSE REASON WISDOM BALANCE MARBLES LUCIDITY
SAP MUG GOON MINE OOZE LYMPH WEAKEN
(— COURAGE) DAUNT
(PALM —) TODDY
(POISONOUS —) UPAS
(SUGAR MAPLE —) HUMBO
SAPLING SCOB PLANT SPIRE RUNNEL TILLER STADDLE SEEDLING SPRINGER
(— AMONG FELLED TREES) WAVER
SARAH ATOSSA
(FATHER OF —) ASHER
(HUSBAND OF —) ABRAHAM
(SON OF —) ISAAC
SARCASM RUB GIBE WIPE IRONY TAUNT SATIRE BROCARD RIDICULE
SARCASTIC ACID WITTY BITING IRONIC ACERBIC CUTTING MORDANT PUNGENT INCISIVE SARDONIC SATIRICAL

SARDINIA
CAPITAL: CAGLIARI
COIN: CARLINE
GULF: OROSEI ASINARA CAGLIARI ORISTANO
MOUNTAIN: RASU FERRY LINAS GALLURA LIMBARA SERPEDDI VITTORIA
PROVINCE: NUORO SASSARI CAGLIARI
RIVER: MANNU TIRSO LASCIA SAMASSI COGHINAS FLUMENDOSA
STRAIT: BONIFACIO
TOWN: NUORO SASSARI THATARI CAGLIARI CARBONIA IGLESIAS

SARDONIC SARCASTIC
SARGO ZEBRA
SARI PATOLA TAMEIN
SARONG PAU KAIN COMBOY KIKEPA
SARSAPARILLA NUNNARI SHOTBUSH
SASH BAR BELT TOBE SCARF TAPIS TOWEL VITTA FASCIA GIRDLE BALDRIC BURDASH CASEMENT CORSELET WAISTBAND
(JAPANESE —) OBI
(WINDOW —) CHESS
SASSY KICKY LIPPY
SATAN DEVIL EBLIS FIEND SHREW BELIAL LUCIFER SHAITAN DIABOLUS
SATCHEL SCRIP HANDBAG KEESTER
SATE GLUT ACCLOY SATIATE SATISFY SATURATE
SATELLITE MOON ARIEL DEIMOS OBERON PHOBOS ACOLYTE LUNETTE ORBITER SPUTNIK TELSTAR UMBRIEL FOLLOWER
(— OF JUPITER) IO EUROPA CALLISTO GANYMEDE

(— OF SATURN) RHEA DIONE MIMAS TITAN PHOEBE TETHYS IAPETUS HYPERION
SATIATE CLOY FILL GLUT PALL SATE GORGE SERVE SATISFY SURFEIT SATURATE
SATIATED SICK JADED SATED
SATIN ATLAS PANNE CYPRUS MUSHRU COOTHAY CYPRESS SATINET
SATIRE WIT IRONY LAMPOON SARCASM SOTADIC RIDICULE
SATIRIC BITTER IRONIC ABUSIVE CAUSTIC CUTTING POIGNANT SLASHING
SATIRIST NIPPER JUVENAL PASQUIN
SATIRIZE SKIN GRIND EXPOSE LAMPOON PASQUIN RIDICULE
SATISFACTION CRO PAY EASE TREAT AMENDS CHANGE REASON COMFORT CONTENT DELIGHT GLADNESS PLEASURE
SATISFACTORY PAT FAIR GOOD JAKE WELL DUCKY HUNKY CLEVER DECENT NOMINAL ADEQUATE LAUDABLE
SATISFIED FAIN FULL GLAD PAID VAIN PROUD ASSURED CONTENT PERFECT
SATISFY PAY EVEN FEED FILL MEET SATE SUIT AGREE SERVE SLAKE ANSWER DEFRAY PLEASE SUPPLY ASSUAGE CONTENT FULFILL GRATIFY SATIATE SUFFICE SATURATE
SATISFYING DUE COOL AMPLE SQUARE PERFECT REWARDING
SATURATE SOG GLUT SATE SOAK IMBUE SOUSE STEEP DRENCH IMBIBE SEETHE INGRAIN SATIATE
SATURATED SOGGY SOPPY SODDEN SPONGY DRUNKEN
SATURN (FATHER OF —) URANUS
(MOTHER OF —) GAEA
(SATELLITE OF —) RHEA DIONE MIMAS TITAN TETHYS JAPETUS HYPERION ENCELADUS
(SON OF —) JUPITER
SATURNINE SULLEN SATANIC
SATYR FAUN LECHER WOODMAN
SAUCE SASS BERCY CHILI CREAM CREME CURRY GRAVY PESTO SALSA CATSUP MORNAY PANADA KETCHUP MARENGO SOUBISE SUPREME TABASCO VELOUTE BECHAMEL CHAWDRON DUXELLES MATELOTE REMOLADE
(CURRY —) SAMBAL
(FISH —) ALEC BAGOONG
(GARLIC —) AIOLI
(SALAD —) DRESSING
(SAVORY —) DIP
(THICK —) LEAR
SAUCEPAN CHAFER GOBLET POSNET SKILLET STEWPAN PANNIKIN
SAUCER BIRD PATERA PHIALE CAPSULE PANNIKIN
SAUCY ARCH BOLD PERT BRASH FRESH LIPPY POKEY SASSY SMART BANTAM THWART FORWARD MALAPERT PETULANT
SAUDI ARABIA: (CAPITAL OF —) JIDDAH RIYADH
(COIN OF —) RIYAL HALALA HALALAH

(DESERT REGION OF —) NEFUD
DAHANA ALNAFUD
(PLATEAU OF —) NEJD
(TOWN OF —) HAIL HOFUF JIDDA
MECCA MEDINA ALHOFUF
(WEIGHT OF —) OKE OKE
SAUL (FATHER OF —) KISH
(SON OF —) JONATHAN
SAUNTER IDLE ROAM ROVE AMBLE
RANGE SIDLE STRAY DANDER LINGER
LOITER LOUNGE POTTER PUTTER
RAMBLE STROLL TODDLE WANDER
SAUSAGE POT LINK COPPA GIGOT
BANGER POLONY SALAMI BOLOGNA
BOLONEY BOTARGO CHORIZO PUDDING
SAVELOY CERVELAT KIELBASA
SAVAGE ILL FELL GRIM RUDE WILD
BRUTE CRUEL FELON FERAL STERN
BRUTAL FIERCE GOTHIC BRUTISH
FERVENT HOWLING INHUMAN UNCIVIL
VIOLENT CANNIBAL PITILESS
(PREF.) AGRIO
SAVAGERY FURY FEROCITY
SAVE BAR WIN HELP KEEP STOP SPARE
SPELL DEFEND EXCEPT RESCUE SCRIMP
BARRING DELIVER HUSBAND SALVAGE
WARRANT CONSERVE PRESERVE
(PREF.) SOZ(O)
SAVIOR LORD SAVER SOTER REDEEMER
SAVOR EDGE SALT SAPOR SMACK TASTE
DEGUST FLAVOR RELISH SEASON
SAPIDITY
SAVORY MERRY SAPID TASTY DAINTY
GUSTABLE TASTEFUL
SAW SEY ADAGE GNOME SPOKE JIGSAW
PITSAW RIPSAW SAYING SCRIBE
BACKSAW BUCKSAW DRAGSAW
FRETSAW HACKSAW HANDSAW
HEADSAW PROVERB WHIPSAW
CROSSCUT
(— INTO LOGS) BUCK
(— LENGTHWISE OF GRAIN) RIP
(— OF SAWFISH) SERRA
(— WITH TWO BLADES) STADDA
(CIRCULAR —) BURR EDGER DAPPER
TRIMMER
(CROSSCUT —) BRIAR
(CYLINDER —) CROWN TREPAN
TREPHINE
SAWHORSE BUCK JACK SETTER
SAWBUCK TRESTLE
SAY MEAN MOVE TAKE TELL SPEAK SPELL
AUTHOR RELATE REMARK
(— A BLESSING) BENSH
(— FOOLISHLY) BLABBER
(— FURTHER) ADD
(— GLIBLY) SCREED
(— NO TO) NAIT NICK
(— OVER AGAIN) REPEAT
(— SPITEFUL THINGS) BACKBITE
(— TOO MUCH) OVERSAY
(— UNDER OATH) DEPOSE
SAYING DIT SAW TAG ITEM TEXT WORD
ADAGE AXIOM CHRIA MAXIM SPEAK
BYWORD LOGION DICTION PROVERB
APOTHEGM SENTENCE SPEAKING
(— LITTLE) DUMB

(—S OF JESUS) AGRAPHA
(—S OF RELIGIOUS TEACHER) LOGIA
(CLEVER —) QUIP
(COMMON —) CANT
(CURRENT —) DICTUM
(OBSCURE —) ENIGMA
(QUICK —) JERK
(SILLY —) FADAISE
(TERSE —) EPIGRAM
(WISE —) SCHOLIUM
(WITTY —) MOT SALLY DICTERY
WITNESS
(WITTY —S) FACETIAE
SCAB RAT ROIN CRUST SCALD CANKER
ESCHAR BLACKLEG
(— ON HORSE'S HEEL) MELLIT
SCAFFOLD CAGE PEGMA STAGE BRIDGE
CATASTA HAYLOFT STAGING HOARDING
(MOVABLE —) GANTRY
SCALD BURN BLAST PLOUT BLANCH
SCALE PIP LEAF PILL STEP TAPE CLIMB
FLAKE GULAR PALEA PELTA POISE SCUTE
SHALE SHELL ASCEND CAUDAL CINDER
FORNIX KELVIN LABIAL LADDER LAMINA
LIGULE NUCHAL OCULAR RAMENT
SHIELD SQUAMA STRIGA BALANCE
CLINKER ELYTRON FRONTAL FULCRUM
HUMERAL LATERAL REAUMUR ROSTRUM
VENTRAL VERNIER BRACHIAL INDUSIUM
RAMENTUM SCRAMBLE
(— DOWN) DEGRADE
(— OF CORNSTALK) SHIVE
(— OF 7 TONES) SEPTAVE
(— ON BUTTERFLY) PLUMULE
(— ON MOTH) PATAGIUM
(— USED BY TAILORS) LOG
(GRADUATED —) RETE
(GREAT —) GAMUT
(SHAD —) CENIZO
SCALY SCABBY SQUAMY LEPROSE
PALEATE SCABROUS SQUAMOSE
SCAMP LAD RIP ROGUE THIEF BOOGER
BUGGER NICKUM RASCAL SINNER
HALLION PEASANT RAMMACK SLUBBER
BLIGHTER SCALAWAG SLYBOOTS
SPALPEEN VAGABOND
SCAMPER CHEVY SCOUP SCOUR
BRATTLE SKITTER
SCAN PIPE GLASS METER DEVISE SURVEY
EXAMINE
SCANDAL CRACK SHAME CALUMNY
OFFENSE SLANDER
SCANDALOUS UNHOLY SHAMEFUL
SCANDINAVIAN DANE LAPP NORSE
SWEDE VIKING LOCHLIN NORSEMAN
NORTHMAN SCANDIAN VARANGIAN
SCANT SHY LEAN MEET POOR THIN
SHORT SKIMP BARISH LITTLE MEAGER
SCANTY SKINNY STINGY SLENDER
SCANTY BARE LANK LEAN POOR SLIM
SCANT SHORT SILLY SPARE FRUGAL
MEAGER MEASLY SKIMPY SLIGHT
SPARSE SCRIMPY SLENDER SPARING
EXIGUOUS PENURIOUS
SCAR EYE WEM FESTER KELOID RADDLE
STIGMA TRENCH CHELOID SCARIFY
CICATRIX

(— ON SAWED STONE) STUN
(— ON SEED) HILUM
(— ON TREE) CATFACE
SCARCE DEAR RARE THIN SLACK DAINTY
UNCOMMON
SCARCELY ILL SCANT BARELY HARDLY
MERELY SCANTLY
SCARCITY LACK WANT FAULT SCANT
DEARTH FAMINE RARITY PAUCITY
SCARE COW FAZE FEAR GAST HUSH
SHOO ALARM APPAL PSYCH SPOOK
AFFRAY FRIGHT STARTLE TERRIFY
AFFRIGHT FRIGHTEN
SCARECROW BUCCA MOGGY SEWEL
BOGGLE MALKIN MAUMET BUGABOO
DEADMAN HODMADOD
SCARF HOOD SASH ASCOT CLOUD
CYMAR FICHU LUNGI PAGRI SHADE
STOCK STOLE THROW CRAVAT PEPLOS
REBOZO SCREEN SQUARE TIPPET
BURDASH FOULARD MANIPLE MUFFLER
NECKTIE ORARIUM PUGGREE SAUTOIR
LIRIPIPE MANTILLA
(— ON KNIGHT'S HELMET) COINTISE
(ARABIAN —) CABAAN
(FEATHER —) BOA
(PRAYER —) TALLIS TALLITH
SCARLET LAC RED PINK TULY GRAIN
KERMES
SCARLET LETTER (AUTHOR OF —)
HAWTHORNE
(CHARACTER IN —) PEARL ROGER
ARTHUR HESTER PRYNNE BELLINGHAM
DIMMESDALE CHILLINGWORTH
SCATHING MORDANT SCALDING
SCATTER SOW TED FLEE SALT SEED
SHED SPEW VOID FLING SCALE SHAKE
SPRAY STREW STROW DISPEL PEPPER
SHOWER SPARGE SPREAD WINNOW
DIFFUSE FRITTER SKITTER SPARKLE
SPATTER DISPERSE SEPARATE SPRINKLE
SQUANDER
(— BAIT FOR FISH) TOLE TOLL
(— OVER) BESTREW
(— WATER) SPLASH
SCAVENGER RAKER MEHTAR REMOVER
HALALCOR
SCENE SET CODA FLAT SITE VIEW ARENA
VISION EPISODE PAGEANT COULISSE
EXTERIOR INTERIOR PROSPECT
(— IN OPERA) SCENA
(— OF ACTION) STAGE
(— OF ACTIVITY) BEEHIVE
(— OF CONFUSION) BABEL BEDLAM
(CLOSING —) FINALE
(FINAL —) CURTAIN EPILOGUE
SCENT AIR NOSE ODOR VENT WIND
CIVET FLAIR FUMET SAVOR SMELL SNIFF
SPOOR TASTE ESSENCE INCENSE
ODORIZE VERDURE FUMIGATE PASTILLE
REDOLENCE
(— OF ANIMAL FOLLOWED BY
HOUNDS) FEUTE
(— OF COOKING) NIDOR
(— OF FOX) DRAG
(FALSE —) RIOT
(LOST —) FAULT

SCEPTER ROD WAND VERGE BAUBLE
FERULA WARDER
SCHEDULE BOOK CARD HOLD LIST TIME
PANEL SETUP SLATE TABLE SCROLL
CATALOG TABLEAU CALENDAR REGISTER
(— OF DUTIES) TARIFF
(— OF GAMES) SEASON
SCHEHERAZADE (HUSBAND OF —)
SCHAHRIAH
(SISTER OF —) DINARZADE
SCHEME AIM WAY WEB CAST GAME
PLAN PLAT PLOT REDE ANGLE DODGE
DRAFT DRIFT KNACK REACH SCALE
SETUP TABLE THINK TRAIN CIPHER
DESIGN DEVICE DEVISE FIGURE POLICY
TAMPER THEORY COUNSEL DRAUGHT
GIMMICK IMAGINE KNAVERY PROJECT
PURPOSE CONSPIRE CONTRIVE
FORECAST IDEOLOGY INTRIGUE
MANEUVER PLATFORM PRACTICE
MACHINATE
(— OF RANK) LADDER
(ABORTIVE —) SOOTERKIN
(BETTING —) SYSTEM
(DECEITFUL —) SHIFT
(DELUSIVE —) BUBBLE
(DIAGRAMMATIC —) PINAX
(FANCIFUL —) WINDMILL
(FAVORITE —) NOSTRUM
(VISIONARY —) BABEL
SCHEMING PLANFUL SPIDERY FETCHING
PRACTICE
SCHOLAR IMAM CLERK PUPIL DIVINE
DOCTOR FELLOW MASTER PANDIT
SABORA SAVANT SCOLOG BOOKMAN
LEARNER STUDENT BOURSIER DISCIPLE
HUMANIST
(— OF QUEENS COLLEGE) TABERDAR
SCHOLARLY CLERKLY ACADEMIC
SCHOOL PREP AGGIE BOOKS ECOLE
TEACH TRADE TRAIN TUTOR CAMPUS
CHURCH SCHOLA SCHULE TRIPOS
ACADEME ACADEMY PENSION STUDIUM
AUDITORY SEMINARY
(— FOR JUDO OR KARATE) DOJO
(— FOR SINGERS) MAITRISE
(— OF FISH) HERD SCALE SCULL
(— OF PAINTING) GENRE
(— OF WHALES) GAM POD
(ART —) BAUHAUS LUMINISM
(DAY —) EXTERNAT
(ELEMENTARY —) GRADES
(HIGH —) HIGH ACADEMY COLLEGE
(REFORM —) BORSTAL
(RELIGIOUS —) ALJAMA YESHIVA
(RIDING —) MANEGE
(SCOTCH —) SQUEEL
(SECONDARY —) LYCEE LYCEUM
COLEGIO
(WRESTLING —) PALESTRA
SCHOOL FOR SCANDAL
(AUTHOR OF —) SHERIDAN
(CHARACTER IN —) MARIA MOSES
PETER JOSEPH OLIVER ROWLEY TEAZLE
CANDOUR CHARLES PREMIUM SURFACE
SNEERWELL
SCHOOLMASTER BEAK CAJI AKHUN

KHOJA MASTER PEDANT DOMINIE PEDAGOG
SCHOONER JACK TERN QUART QUINT PUNGEY BALLAHOO
SCIENCE ART OLOGY SOPHY MATHESIS SCIENTIA
SCIMITAR SEAX TURK KHEPESH TULWAUR
SCINTILLATE SNAP FLASH GLEAM GLANCE GLITTER SPARKLE TWINKLE
SCION IMP ROD CION ROOT SLIP GRAFT SPRIG BRANCH SPROUT
SCISSORS SHEARS CLIPPER SECATEUR
SCOFF GALL GECK GIBE JEER MOCK RAIL CURSE FLEER FLOUT SCORN SCOUT SNEER TAUNT DERIDE REPROVE RIDICULE
SCOLD JAW MAG NAG RAG ROW YAP BAWL CALL CANT FLAY FUSS HAZE JUMP RAIL RANT RATE SNAG SNUB YAFF ABUSE BASTE CHIDE DRESS FLITE PRATE SCALD SCORE SHREW STORM VIXEN BERATE BOUNCE CARPET HAMMER MAGPIE RATTLE REVILE TATTER TONGUE REPROVE TROUNCE UPBRAID BALLYRAG CHASTISE
SCOLDING HURL DIRDUM JAWING RAKING RATTLE SISERA FLITING LECTURE RAGGING CARRITCH JOBATION
SCOOP BAIL DRAG ROUT GOUGE BUCKET DIPPER DISHER SHOVEL WIMBLE SCRAPER SKIMMER SKIPPET
(— FOR CANNON) LADLE
(— FOR DAMPENING CANVAS) SKEET
(— FOR GRAIN) WECHT
(— UP) LAP LAVE GATHER
(CHEESE —) PALE
(GLASSMAKING —) PADDLE
(JAI ALAI —) CHISTERA
(LONG-HANDLED —) DIDLE
(SURGICAL —) CURET CURETTE
SCOPE AIM AREA AMBIT POWER RANGE REACH ROUND SCALE SWEEP VERGE SPHERE BREADTH CIRCUIT COMPASS PURVIEW CONFINES LATITUDE
SCORCH BURN CHAR SCAM SEAR ADUST BROIL PARCH SCALD SINGE SWELT BIRSLE BISHOP DEGREE SWINGE SWITHE BLISTER BRISTLE FRIZZLE SWITHER TORRIFY
SCORE ACE CUT RUN CARD DEBT DROP GAME GOAL HOLE MAKE MARK NICK POST RIDE CHASE COUNT EXTRA NOTCH OPERA TALLY FURROW SAFETY SCOTCH SCRIVE SPADES STRING TARGET TICKET TWENTY CONVERT SCRATCH SQUEEZE
(— FOR ALE) ALESHOT
(— HEAVILY AGAINST) SHELL
(— IN BRIDGE) BOARD BONUS SWING
(— IN CRIBBAGE) GO PEG FIFTEEN
(— IN CRICKET) BLOB CENTURY
(— IN PIQUET) CAPOT
(— OF NOTHING) DUCK
(APTITUDE —) STANINE
(BASKETBALL —) HOOP
(BOWLING —) PINFALL
(GOLF —) DEUCE EAGLE BIRDIE BUZZARD
(PINOCHLE —) LAST
(TENNIS —) CALL FIVE LOVE DEUCE FORTY FIFTEEN
(THREE —) SHOCK
(TIE —) HALVE DEADLOCK
SCORN LOUT SPURN SLIGHT CONTEMN DESPISE DESPITE DISDAIN CONTEMPT DERISION
SCORNFUL SAUCY SNIFFY HAUGHTY FRUMPISH INSOLENT SARDONIC
SCOT (ALSO SEE SCOTSMAN) CELT JOCK KELT SANDY SAXON SCOTTY BLUECAP SCOTSMAN

SCOTLAND

BAY: SCAPA
CAPITAL: EDINBURGH
COIN: DEMY BODLE GROAT PLACK RIDER BAWBEE
COUNTY: AYR BUTE FIFE ROSS ANGUS BANFF MORAY NAIRN PERTH ARGYLL LANARK ORKNEY BERWICK KINROSS PEEBLES RENFREW SELKIRK WIGTOWN ABERDEEN AYRSHIRE CROMARTY DUMFRIES ROXBURGH SHETLAND STERLING
FIRTH: LORN CLYDE FORTH MORAY SOLWAY PENTLAND
ISLAND: RUM BUTE IONA JURA MULL RHUM SKYE ARRAN BARRA ISLAY LEWIS HARRIS ORKNEY SHETLAND
ISLANDS: ORKNEY HEBRIDES SHETLAND
LAKE: TAY NESS MORAR LAGGAN LINNHE LOMOND KATRINE RANNOCH
LANGUAGE: ERSE LALLAN LALLAND
MEASURE: COP BOLL CRAN FALL MILE PECK PINT ROOD ROPE SPAN CRANE LIPPY FIRLOT AUCHLET CHALDER CHOPPIN MUTCHKIN STIMPART
MOUNTAIN: HOPE ATTOW DEARG NEVIS TINTO WYVIS CHEVIOT MACDHUI
NATIVE: GAEL PICT SCOT
REGION: FIFE BORDERS GRAMPIAN
RIVER: AYR DEE DON ESK TAY DOON GLEN NITH NORN SPEY AFTON ANNAN CLYDE FORTH GARRY TWEED YTHAN AFFRIC TEVIOT TUMMEL DEVERON FINDHORN
SEAPORT: ALLOA LEITH DUNDEE ABERDEEN
TOWN: AYR DUNS OBAN WICK ALLOA BRORA CUPAR ELLON LEITH NAIRN PERTH SALEN TROON DUNDEE GIRVAN HAWICK DUNKELD GLASGOW PAISLEY ABERDEEN DUMFRIES GREENOCK KIRKWALL STIRLING

SCOTSMAN SANDY SAWNY BLUECAP
SCOUNDREL PIMP SCAB VILE KNAVE SHREW SWEEP THIEF BRIBER LIMMER SLOVEN VARLET HALLION SKELLUM VILLAIN BEZONIAN
SCOUR ASH BEAT RAKE SEEK SCRUB SWEEP DRENCH SLUICE FURBISH

SCOURGE LASH CURSE FLAIL KNOUT SLASH SWING PLAGUE SCORPION
SCOUT SPY BEAR LION SKIP ROVER MARINER PIONEER SCOURER WATCHER EMISSARY OUTRIDER
(BOY —) CUB BOBCAT SCOUTER WEBELOS EXPLORER
SCOWL LOUR FROWN GLARE GLOOM LOWER GLOWER
SCRAMBLE MUSS SPRAWL CLAMBER SCRAFFLE
SCRAP BIT END JAG ORT ITEM JUNK BRAWL PATCH SHRED WASTE DISCARD REMNANT FRACTION SKERRICK
(— FOR PATCHING) SPETCH
(— OF PAPER) SCRIP
(— OF SONG) CATCH
(— OF WRITING) SCRAPE
(FOOD —S) BROCK
(LITERARY —S) ANA
(RAGGED —) SCART
SCRAPE RUB CLAW COMB RAZE ERODE GRATE GRAZE SCUFF SHAVE ABRADE HOBBLE CURETTE SCRATCH SCRABBLE
(— ALONG) HARL SHOOL
(— GOLF CLUB ON GROUND) SCLAFF
(— OFF) SPUD
(— OUT) ERASE HOLLOW
(— SKINS) MOON SCUD FLESH HARASS
(— TOGETHER) RAKE GLEAN MUCKER SCAMBLE
(— WITH FEET) SCAUT
SCRAPER PIG HARL SLIP GLOVE RASER SPOON GRADER GRATER RASPER CURETTE FLANGER LEVELER STRIGIL GRATTOIR
SCRATCH RAT CLAW CRAB RAKE RAZE RISP STUN CHALK CURRY GRAZE SCART SCORE SCRAB SCRUB TEASE TOUCH BRUISE CANCEL RASURE SCORCH SCOTCH SCRAPE SCRAWL EMERIZE EXPUNGE SCARIFY SCRABBLE SCRIBBLE
(— OUT MORTAR) POINT
SCRAWNY BONY LEAN SCRAGGY SCRANNY
SCREAM CRY YAUP YAWL YAWP SKIRL SHRIEK SHRILL SQUAWL YAMMER SCREECH
SCREEN TRY HARP HIDE LAWN MASK SEPT SIFT TENT VEIL BLIND CLOAK CLOSE COVER GAUZE HOARD SHADE SIEVE TATTY BAFFLE BASKET BORDER CANVAS DEFEND ESCORT PURDAH RESEAU SCONCE SHAKER SHIELD SHROUD VOIDER CONCEAL CURTAIN FLYWIRE SECLUDE SHELTER SHUTTER BACKSTOP COVERING ECLIPSER EXCLUDER PARAVENT STRAINER TRAVERSE
(— ALONGSIDE SHIP) PAVISADE
(— BEHIND ALTAR) REREDOS
(— FOR BATTING PRACTICE) CAGE
(— FOR SHIP'S COMBATANTS) FIGHT
(— FOR SIZING ORE) GRATE TROMMEL
(— FOR THEATER LIGHT) JELLY MEDIUM
(— IN BASKETBALL) PICK

(— OF BAMBOO SLIPS) CHEEK CHICK
(— OF BRUSHWOOD) SCHERM
(— OF FIRE) BARRAGE
(— OF SHIELDS FOR TROOPS) TESTUDO
(— OF TAPESTRY) ARRAS CEILING
(— ON AUTOMOBILE) GRILLE
(— TO PROTECT LOOKOUTS) DODGER
(— USED BY ARCHERS) PANNIER
(BULLETPROOF —) MANTA MANTEL MANTELET
(CHANCEL —) JUBE
(FIRE —) FENDER
(MECHANICALLY ACTUATED —) GRIZZLY
(PAPER —) SHOJI
SCREW HOB VISE WORM WREST TEMPER TOGGLE COCHLEA FLATHEAD SETSCREW WINDMILL
SCREWBALL KOOK ZANY FLAKE ECCENTRIC NONSENSICAL
SCRIBBLE SQUIB DOODLE SCRAWL SCRATCH SQUIGGLE
SCRIBE EZRA CLERK THOTH BOOKER PENMAN WRITER MASORET SCRIPTOR
SCRIMMAGE MAUL BULLY ROUGE SCRAP BICKER SKIRMISH
SCRIPTURE WRIT AGAMA CHING SUTRA
SCROLL BEND ROLL LABEL LEGEND VOLUME VOLUTE PAPYRUS RINCEAU BANDEROL CARTOUCH MAKIMONO
SCRUB FILE CLEANSE YANNIGAN
SCRUPULOUS NICE SPICED TENDER CAREFUL FINICKY PRECISE DELICATE QUALMISH
SCRUTINIZE PRY SEE SPY SCAN VIEW AUDIT PROBE SIGHT SOUND VISIT PERUSE SURVEY EXAMINE INSPECT TRAVERSE
SCRUTINY EYE SEARCH CANVASS PERUSAL
SCUFFLE CUFF BUSTLE CLINCH TUSSLE BRULYIE SHAMBLE
SCULPTOR CARVER GRAVER IMAGER MARBLER PLASTIC
SCULPTURE CAMEO GRAVE BRONZE SCULPT CARVING DRAUGHT ENGRAVE STABILE PORTRAIT PREDELLA
SCUM FOAM GALL HEAD SCUD SILT SKIN DROSS FROTH SCURF SLUSH SPUME FLURRY MANTLE MOTHER REFUSE
SCURRILOUS LOW FOUL VILE DIRTY GROSS RIBALD VULGAR ABUSIVE INDECENT
SCURRY CRAB SKIN HURRY SCUFFLE SCUTTLE SKELTER SKITTER
SCUTTLE HOD SKEP BEETLE SCUTTER SCRATTLE
SEA ZEE BLUE BRIM FOAM GULF HOLM MAIN RACE TIDE WAVE BRINE BRINY FLOOD LOUGH OCEAN STRAND CHANNEL NEPTUNE DEEPNESS
(HEAVY —) POPPLE
(MODERATE —) SEAWAY
SEA GULL COB GOR MEW ANNET POPELER
SEA HOLLY ERYNGO ERYNGIUM

SEAL CAN FIX FOB CHOP CORK HARP
HOOD JARK LUTE CLOSE PHOCA SIGIL
STAMP THONG WAFER CACHET ENSIGN
FASTEN GASKET PHOCID SECURE SIGNET
CONFIRM CONSIGN HOODCAP IMPRESS
SIGNARY WEDDELL ADHESIVE CYLINDER
PINNIPED SECRETUM SIGILLUM
SIGNACLE VALIDATE
(— FOR WATCH CHAIN) ONION
BRELOQUE
(— OFF) CAP
(— OVER CORK) CAPSULE
(BEARDED —) URSUK MAKLUK
(EARED —) OTARY
(FEMALE —) MATKA
(GOLD —) BEZEL
(HARBOR —) DOTARD RANGER
TANGFISH
(HERD OF —S) PATCH
(IMMATURE —) BEDLAMER
(MALE —) WIG SADDLER BACHELOR
SEECATCH
(NEWFOUNDLAND —) SWILE RANGER
(PAPAL —) BULL BULLA
(SHETLAND —) SILKIE
(YEARLING —) HOPPER
(YOUNG —) PUP BEATER JACKET
BLUEBACK
(3-YEAR OLD —) TURNER
SEAM BAND DART PURL REND PEARL
SPILL FAGGOT INSEAM SUTURE
JUNCTURE
(— IN INGOT) SPILL
(— IN SHIP'S HULL) DEVIL
(— OF COAL) RIDER SPLIT STREAK
(IRREGULAR —) FASH
SEAMAN SALT JACKY CALASH LUBBER
SAILOR MARINER MASTMAN SHIPMAN
WAISTER
SEAPORT PARA PORT GROIN NATAL
HARBOR ENTREPOT
SEAR BURN FIRE SERE FLAME FRIZZ
SCORCH SIZZLE FRIZZLE
SEARCH FAN SPY BEAT DRAG GAPE RAKE
ROUT SEEK SIFT WAIT PROBE SNOOP
VISIT DREDGE FUMBLE SLEUTH ENQUIRE
EXPLORE INQUEST INQUIRE INSPECT
RANSACK SCROUNGE SHAKEDOWN
(— ABOUT) GRUB PROG GROPE
(— DEEPLY) TENT
(— EVERYWHERE) BUSK
(— FOR) FORK HUNT LAIT SNOOK
REQUIRE
(— FOR FOX'S TRAIL) CIPHER
(— FOR GAME) DRAW GHOOM QUEST
(— FOR GOLD) FOSSICK
(— FOR KNOWLEDGE) OUTREACH
(— FOR PROVISIONS) FORAGE
(— FOR SMUGGLED GOODS) DACKER
JERQUE
(— FOR STOLEN GOODS) RANZEL
(— FOR WEAPONS) FRISK
(— GROPINGLY) GLAMP
(— OUT) FERRET INVENT ROOTLE
EXQUIRE INDAGATE
(— SHIP) RUMMAGE
(— SYSTEMATICALLY) COMB

(— THROUGH) TURN
(— UNDERWATER) FISH
(SYSTEMATIC —) SWEEP
SEARCHING HARD CLOSE SHREWD
CURIOUS GROPING
SEASHORE RIPE CLEVE COAST PLAYA
MARINE SEASIDE SEABEACH SEABOARD
SEACOAST
SEASICKNESS HILO NAUPATHIA
SEASON CORN DASH FALL SALT TIDE
TIME INURE SAUCE SAVOR SPICE
AUTUMN EASTER FLOWER HARDEN
MASTER SPRING SUMMER WINTER
BUDTIME FLYTIME HARVEST SEEDTIME
(— FOR HERRING FISHING) DRAVE
(— HIGHLY) DEVIL
(— IN THE SUN) HAZE
(— OF JOY) JUBILEE
(— OF MERRYMAKING) CARNIVAL
(CLOSED —) SHUTOFF
(DULL —) SLACK
(EGYPTIAN —) AHET PERT SHEMU
(HAYING —) HAYING HAYSEL
(LENTEN —) CAREME
(RAINLESS —) DRY
(RAINY —) KHARIF VARSHA
(REGULARLY RECURRING —) EMBER
(SPRING —) WARE APRIL GRASS
(THE RIGHT —) TID
SEASONABLE PAT TIDY TIMELY
VETERAN TOWARDLY OPPORTUNE
SEAT CAN SET FLOP ROOM SILL SLIP
SUNK TOIT ASANA CHAIR SELLA SLIDE
BOUGHT EXEDRA HUMPTY RUMBLE
SADDLE SEATER SEGGIO SETTEE SETTLE
BUTTOCK CUSHION GRADINE INSTALL
OTTOMAN TABORET BLEACHER
ENTHRONE SEGGIOLA SUBSELLA
WOOLPACK
(— AT PUBLIC SPECTACLE) PULVINAR
(— FOR GRINDER) HORSING
(— FOR PLANE IRON) FROG
(— NEAR ALTAR) SEDILIUM
(— OF BIRTH) SIDE
(— OF CHAIR) BOTTOM
(— OF EMOTIONS) CHEST SPLEEN
(— OF FEELINGS) STOMACH
(— OF HARE) FORM
(— OF INTELLECT) HEAD
(— OF KNOWLEDGE) RUACH
(— OF ORACLE) DODONA
(— OF PITY) BOWEL
(— OF POWER) SEE
(— OF REAL LIFE) SOUL
(— OF RESPONSIBILITY) SHOULDER
(— OF RULE) OGDOAD
(— OF TURF) SUNK
(— OF UNDERSTANDING) SKULL
(— ON ELEPHANT'S BACK) TOWER
CASTLE HOWDAH
(— ONESELF) LEAN PITCH
(— SLUNG ON POLES) HORSE
(— WITH BRAZIER BELOW) TENDOUR
(— WITHIN WINDOW OPENING)
CAROL
(AIRPLANE —) DORMETTE
(BACKLESS —) STOOL HASSOCK

(BISHOP'S —) APSE BISHOPRIC
(CANOPIED —) COZY
(CHIMNEY —) SCONCE
(CHURCH —) PEW DESK STALL SEDILE
(COACH —) BOOT POOP
(COUNTRY —) TOWER GRANGE QUINTA
(DILIGENCE —) BANQUETTE
(DRAPED —) MUSNUD
(DRIVER'S —) BOX DICKY COCKPIT
FORETOP
(ELEVATED —) PERCH
(FIXED —) DAIS
(GARDEN —) ALCOVE
(KEY —) KEYWAY
(LONG —) BANK FORM BENCH
(OARSMAN'S —) TAFT
(PORCH —) GLIDER
(RECLINING —) DORMEUSE
(ROWER'S —) THWART
(ROYAL —) SIEGE STEAD THRONE
(STAGECOACH —S) BASKET
(STRAW —) BOSS
(TIER OF —S) TENDIDO
(TURF —) BUNKER
(UNRESERVED —S) BLUES
(PREF.) EDRI(O)
(SUFF.) HEDRAL
SEAWEED ORE AGAR ALGA KELP LIMU
MOSS NORI REIT TANG WARE DRIFT
DULSE KOMBU LAVER SLOKE VRAIC
WRACK FUCOID FUNORI HAITSAI
OARWARE SEAWARE CARAGEEN
GULFWEED HEMPWEED SARGASSO
SEABEARD
SEA WOLF (AUTHOR OF —) LONDON
(CHARACTER IN —) HUMP MAUD
WOLF DEATH LEACH LOUIS LARSEN
JOHNSON BREWSTER HUMPHREY
JOHANSEN MUGRIDGE VANWEYDEN
SECLUDE TACKLE ENCLOSE ISOLATE
RECLUSE CLOISTER SEQUESTER
SECLUDED COY SHY DEEP CLOSE QUIET
HIDDEN REMOTE SECRET PRIVATE
RETIRED HIDEAWAY MONASTIC
SEPARATE SOLITARY
SECLUSION RECESS SHADOW PRIVACY
PRIVITY RETREAT SECRECY SOLITUDE
(— OF WOMEN) PURDAH
SECOND AID ABET BACK BETA TICK
OTHER VOUCH ASSIST LATTER MOMENT
ANOTHER INSTANT SUPPORT SUSTAIN
(— IN COMMAND) DEPUTY
(— IN HORSE RACE) PLACE
(— PERSON USE) TUISM
(MAJOR —) TONE
(1000TH OF A —) SIGMA
(60TH OF A —) THIRD
SECONDARY BYE SUB CUBITAL
DERIVED INFERIOR MIDDLING
SECOND-RATE COMMON SHODDY
INFERIOR
SECRECY HUSH HIDING PRIVACY PRIVITY
SILENCE DARKNESS
SECRET SLY DARK BLIND CABAL CLOSE
PRIVY QUIET ARCANE CLOSET COVERT
HIDDEN INWARD POCKET STOLEN
ARCANUM COUNSEL CRYPTIC FURTIVE

MYSTERY PRIVACY PRIVATE PRIVITY
RESERVE RETIRED UNKNOWN HIDLINGS
MYSTICAL SNEAKING STEALTHY
SECRETARY CLERK BARUCH MUNSHI
SCRIBE FAMULUS
SECRETE HIDE CACHE SECERN CONCEAL
SECLUDE
SECRETION INK LAC LERP MILT SPIT
HUMOR MUCUS SEPIA SLIME SALIVA
CERUMEN FLOCOON HORMONE
ENDOCRIN
SECRETIVE SLY DARK SNUG CAGEY
CLOSE COVERT SECRET SILENT
INVOLVED
SECTION CUT END AREA PACE PART
UNIT PIECE SHARE BILLET BRANCH
CANTON LENGTH MEMBER SECTOR
ARTICLE CUTTING HEADING SEGMENT
ADDENDUM DIVISION FRACTION
SECURE FID GET GIB KEY POT RUG SEW
WIN BAIL BOLT BOND COCK COLD EASY
FAST FIRM GAIN GIRD HOOK LAND MOOR
NAIL SAFE SEAL SNUG STAY SURE
WARM BELAY BLOCK CINCH CLEAT
SOUND STRAP TIGHT ANCHOR ASSURE
BECKET BUTTON CLINCH DEFEND
ENSURE FASTEN OBTAIN PLEDGE SETTLE
STABLE ACQUIRE BULWARK CONFINE
FORTIFY WARRANT GARRISON PRESERVE
(— A SAIL) TRICE
(— AGAINST INTRUSION) TILE
(— AID OF) ENLIST
(— BAIT) EBB
(— FROM LEAKING) COFFER
(— WITH BARS) GRATE
SECURITY BAIL BAND EASE GAGE SEAL
GUARD QUIET STOCK CEDULA EQUITY
PLEDGE REFUGE SAFETY SCREEN SEVERE
SURETY VADIUM BULWARK CAUTION
CUSTODY DEFENSE DEPOSIT HOSTAGE
SHELTER SLEEPER WARRANT COVENANT
FASTNESS GUARANTY STRENGTH
MUNICIPAL
SEDATE CALM COOL QUIET SOBER STAID
SERENE EARNEST SERIOUS SETTLED
COMPOSED DECOROUS
SEDIMENT LEES SILT WARP DREGS
FOOTS MAGMA BOTTOM FECULA
SLUDGE GROUNDS SETTLING
(— OF BEER OR ALE) CRAP
(IRON —) CARR
(REDDISH —) SIMMON
SEDITION REVOLT TREASON
SEDITIOUS RIOTOUS FACTIOUS
MUTINOUS
SEDUCE DRAW LOCK DECOY TEMPT
WRONG ALLURE BETRAY ENTICE
DEBAUCH ENSNARE MISLEAD SUGGEST
TRADUCE INVEIGLE
(— WITH THE EYE) LEER
SEDULOUS BUSY INTENT STUDIED
DILIGENT UNTIRING
SEE LO EYE KEN SPY ESPY LOOK MIND
NOTE PIPE SPOT VIEW CATCH CHAIR
SIEGE SIGHT STOOL WATCH ATTEND
BEHOLD DESCRY NOTICE REMARK

SURVEY DISCERN GLIMPSE OBSERVE
WITNESS CATHEDRA PERCEIVE
SEED NIB PIP BOIL CORN DIKA GERM
KOLA LIMA MOTE TARE BEHEN BERRY
CACAO CARAT GRAIN LUPIN SEMEN
SPAWN SPERM SPORE STONE ACHENE
BONDUC FENNEL KERNEL LEGUME
LENTIL NICKER NUTLET PIGNON PIPPIN
ACHIOTE ANISEED BUCKEYE HARICOT
HAYSEED SEMINAL DILLSEED FLAXSEED
HEMPSEED PRINCIPE PISTACHIO
(AROMATIC —S) ANISE
(EDIBLE —) PEA BEAN
(GRAPE —) ACINUS
(IMMATURE —) OVULE
(MUSTARD —) SENVY SINEWY
(NUTLIKE —) PEANUT
(OILY —) ARGAN ABILLA
(PALM —) COROZO
(POPPY —) MAW MOHNSEED
SEEK ASK BEG BUSK FEEL FISH HUNT
LOOK SIFT COURT DELVE ESSAY FETCH
SCOUR BOTTOM FERRET FOLLOW
PURSUE SEARCH INQUIRE RANSACK
REQUIRE RUMMAGE SOLICIT ENDEAVOR
(— AFTER) SUE SUIT ENSUE EXPLORE
(— AIMLESSLY) PROG
(— FAVOR) WISH
(— FOR) APPETE
(— IN MARRIAGE) WOO PRETEND
(— OUT) COMB ENSEARCH
(— TO ATTAIN) ASPIRE
(— URGENTLY) PRESS
SEEM BID EYE FARE LOOK PEER SOUND
APPEAR BESEEM REGARD
SEEMING GUISE QUASI LIKELY SEEMLY
APPARENT SEMBLANT
SEEMLY FIT TALL CIVIL COMELY DECENT
LIKELY MODEST BECOMING DECOROUS
GRACEFUL
SEEP LEAK OOZE EXUDE PERCOLATE
SEER SWAMI MOPSUS SCRYER PROPHET
CHALDEAN
SEERESS SAGA SIBYL VOLVA PHOIBAD
SEESAW PUMP TILT DANDLE TEETER
TIDDLE TOTTER
SEETHE FRY BOIL ITCH STEW WALM
HOTTER SIMMER BLUBBER FERMENT
SEGMENT CUT HAND LITH PART BLANK
CHORD ELITE FURCA SHARE SLICE
CANTLE GLOSSA LENGTH SAMPLE
ARTICLE ISOMERE MYOMERE BRACHIUM
DIVISION HYPOMERE INTERVAL
(— OF CASK) CANT
(— OF CAULIFLOWER) FLOWERET
(— OF CIRCLE) SECTION
(— OF COMMUNITY) FACIES
(— OF EARTH'S CRUST) GRABEN
(— OF FIBER) BAND
(— OF IRIS) FALL
(— OF LEAF) LACINIA
(— OF MAXILLA) STIPES SUBGALEA
(— OF RATTLESNAKE'S RATTLE)
BUTTON
(— OF SPEECH) DOMAIN
(HERALDIC —) FLANCH
(INSTRUCTIONAL —) LESSON

(MERE —) SNAPSHOT
SEGREGATE SHED SEVER INTERN
ISOLATE CLASSIFY INSULATE SEPARATE
SEIZE BAG CAP GET NAP BEAK CLAW
FANG GLOM GRAB GRIP HAND HENT
HOOK JUMP KEEP LEVY NAIL RAMP SNAP
TAKE TIRE YOKE CATCH CLASP CRIMP
DRIVE GRASP GRIPE LATCH PINCH REACH
SNACK ARREST ASSUME ATTACH
CLUTCH EXTEND FASTEN GOBBLE
QUARRY SECURE CAPTURE ENCLASP
ENCLOSE GRAPPLE IMPOUND POSSESS
PREEMPT SWALLOW ARROGATE
SURPRISE
(— AND HOLD FIRMLY) TRUSS
(— BAIT) STRIKE
(— BY NECK) SCRAG COLLAR SCRUFF
(— PREY) CHOP
(— SUDDENLY) NAB NIP SWOOP
SNATCH
(— UPON) ATTACK INFECT
(— WITH CLAWS) STRAIN
(— WITH TEETH) BITE
(— WITH WHOLE HAND) GLAUM
(— WITHOUT RIGHT) USURP
SEIZURE PIT BITE HOLD GRIPE ICTUS
SPELL ARREST PRISAL RAPTUS TAKING
CONCEIT DISTRESS
SELECT TAP TRY CULL PICK SIFT SORT
TAKE DRAFT ELECT ELITE TRIED ASSIGN
BALLOT CHOICE CHOOSE DECIDE PREFER
SAMPLE SINGLE WINNOW EXCERPT
EXTRACT
(— BY LOT) DRAW
(— BY PATTERN) SWATCH
(— JURY) STRIKE
SELECTION CHAP CULL ITEM PICK
CHOICE CHOOSE EXCERPT EXTRACT
ELECTION
(— OF PSALMS) HALLEL
(VERSE —) BLAUD SINGSONG
SELF EGO JIVA SOUL DAENA NATURE
PERSON PSYCHE
(INNER —) ANIMA
(SUPREME UNIVERSAL —) ATTA
ATMAN
SELF-ASSERTIVE BRASH PERKY CHESTY
BLUSTERY BUMPTIOUS
SELF-ASSURANCE CHEEK APLOMB
COOLNESS
SELF-ASSURED CALM PERKY
CONFIDENT
SELF-CENTERED SELFISH
SELF-CONFIDENCE CREST HUBRIS
HUTZPA CHUTZPA HUTZPAH OPINION
SELF-CONSCIOUS GAWKY BASHFUL
SELF-CONTROL STAY WILL MODESTY
PATIENCE
SELF-DETERMINATION FREEDOM
AUTONOMY
SELF-ESTEEM EGO PRIDE CONCEIT
SELFNESS
SELF-EVIDENT MANIFEST
SELF-IMPORTANT COXY PURDY CHESTY
BIGGETY POMPOUS BUMPTIOUS
SELF-INDULGENCE NICETY PLEASURE
SELF-INDULGENT WANTON

SELFISH PIGGISH SELFFUL DISSOCIAL
SELFISHNESS EGO SELF EGOTISM
SUICISM SELFHOOD
(MORBID —) PLEONEXIA
SELF-POSSESSION COOL POISE
APLOMB COOLNESS SANGFROID
SELF-RESTRAINT HOO ASCESIS
CONTROL RESERVE
SELF-WILLED SET SENSUAL WAYWARD
CONTRARY PERVERSE
SELL GIVE VEND PITCH SHAVE TRADE
BARTER MARKET AUCTION
(— A HORSE) CHANT
(— AT LOW PRICE) DUMP
(— BELOW COST) FOOTBALL
(— BY AUCTION) CANT ROUP
(— DRUGS ILLEGALLY) PUSH
(— FOR) BRING FETCH
(— IN SMALL QUANTITIES) RETAIL
(BUY AND —) CHOP
SEMBLANCE SHOW SIGN COLOR GUISE
IMAGE VISAGE PRETEXT LIKENESS
SIMULACRUM
(— OF DIGNITY) FACE
(— OF REALITY) DREAM
(FALSE —) COLORING
SEMINARY YESHIVA JUVENATE
SEMIRAMIS (HUSBAND OF —) NINUS
(MOTHER OF —) DERCETO
SEMITE JEW ARAB HARARI SYRIAN
SHEMITE ARAMAEAN ASSYRIAN
CHALDEAN
SENATE BOULE COUNCIL GEROUSIA
SENATORY
SEND PACK SHIP ENVOY THROW RENDER
ADDRESS CHANNEL CONSIGN DELIVER
FORWARD DISPATCH TRANSMIT
(— ABOUT) TROLL
(— ALOFT) CROSS
(— AWAY) MAND SHIP BANISH
DISBAND DISMISS RELEGATE
(— BACK) ECHO TURN WISE REMIT
REMAND REMISE RENVOY RESEND
RETURN REFRACT
(— BY MAIL) DROP
(— DOWN) DEMIT DIMIT STRIKE
(— FOR) SUMMON
(— FORTH) BEAM BEAR CAST EMIT
MAND DIMIT FLING EFFUSE OUTSEND
(— OFF) WING
(— OUT) BEAM EMIT AMAND SHOOT
SPEED DEDUCE DEPORT LAUNCH
DIFFUSE EXPEDITE

SENEGAL

CAPITAL: DAKAR
MOUNTAIN: GOUNOU
NATIVE: PEUL SOCE DIOLA FOULA LAOBE
SERER WOLOF FULANI SERERE BAMBARA
MALINKE TUKULER MANDINGO
RIVER: FALEME GAMBIA SALOUM
SENEGAL CASAMANCE
TOWN: BAKEL LOUGA MATAM THIES
DAGANA KAOLACK RUFISQUE

SENILITY DOTAGE CADUCITY PROGERIA
SENIOR AINE DEAN SIRE DOYEN ELDER
ANCIENT SUPERIOR
SENNACHERIB (FATHER OF —)
SARGON
(SON OF —) ESARHADDON
SENSATION FEEL ITCH SOUR SENSE
TASTE FEELING ESTHESIS
(— OF COLD) RHIGOSIS
(— OF FRIGHT) FRISSON
(— OF HEAT) HOTNESS
(— OF PAIN) ALGESIS
(ANTICIPATORY —) FOREFEEL
(BURNING —) ARDOR
(DARTING —) SHOOT
(STRONG —) CREEP
(SUBJECTIVE —) AURA
(TASTE —) GUST BITTER
(TINGLING —) DIRL
(VIBRATING —) FREMITUS
(VISUAL —) PHOSE PHOTOMA
SENSATIONAL GORY BOFFO LURID
YELLOW SAFFRON SPLASHY TABLOID
STUNNING
SENSE WIT SMELL MATTER REASON
WISDOM FEELING HEARING MARBLES
MEANING JUDGMENT
(— OF APPREHENSION) ANXIETY
(— OF HEARING) EAR
(— OF HUMOR) MUSIC
(— OF ONENESS) KINSHIP
(— OF OUTRAGE) SHOCK
(— OF PANIC) JITTERS
(— OF RIGHT) GRACE
(— OF SIGHT) VISION
(— OF SMELL) SCENT
(— OF SUPERIORITY) EGOTISM
(— OF TOUCH) FEEL TASTE
(— ON ONE'S WORTH) PRIDE
(— THE MEANING OF) READ
(COMMON —) NOUS SALT BALANCE
GUMPTION
(DISCRIMINATING —) FLAIR
(LACKING —) INEPT
(PLAIN —) ENGLISH
(SOUND —) MATTER
SENSE AND SENSIBILITY
(AUTHOR OF —) AUSTEN
(CHARACTER IN —) JOHN LUCY
EDWARD ELINOR STEELE BRANDON
FERRARS MARIANNE WILLOUGHBY
SENSELESS MAD COLD DUMB SILLY
FRIGID STUPID UNWISE WANTON
FOOLISH IDIOTIC POINTLESS
REASONLESS
SENSIBLE SANE WISE AWARE PRIVY
WITTY ACTUAL MATERIAL PASSIBLE
RATIONAL SENTIENT
SENSITIVE FINE KEEN SORE ALIVE QUICK
NIMBLE TENDER TETCHY FEELING
NERVOUS PRICKLY ALLERGIC DELICATE
(— TO PAIN) TART
(NERVOUSLY —) TOUCHY
(TOO —) OVERSTRUNG
SENSITIVITY FLESH DELICACY FINENESS
SENSUAL LEWD BRUTE CARNAL FLESHY

SULTRY WANTON BEASTLY BESTIAL BRUTISH SWINISH

SENSUOUS SOFT LYDIAN FLESHLY LUSCIOUS

SENTENCE BAN DIT SAW DAMN DOOM TIME AWARD ARREST COMMIT DECREE DEPORT ADJUDGE CENSURE CONDEMN JUDGMENT
(— CONTAINING EACH LETTER) PANGRAM
(— INDICATING CHARACTER) MOTTO
(CONCISE —S) LACONICS
(IMPRISONMENT —) LAG RAP LIFE LAGGING STRETCH
(MUSICAL —) PERIOD
(SHORT —) CLAUSE
(WITTY —) ATTICISM

SENTIMENT MIND POSY ETHNOS GENIUS NOTION PLEDGE FEELING OPINION
(EXCESSIVE —) SCHWARMEREI
(FALSE —) FALSETTO
(SLOPPY —) DRIP

SENTIMENTAL SOFT CORNY GOOEY GUSHY MUSHY SAPPY SOPPY SOUPY FRUITY SLUSHY SPOONY SUGARY SYRUPY INSIPID MAUDLIN MAWKISH ROMANTIC SCHMALZY MOONSTRUCK

SENTIMENTALITY GOO HAM MUSH BLURB SYRUP BATHOS

SENTINEL GUARD WATCH PICKET SENTRY WARDEN WATCHMAN
(MOUNTED —) VEDETTE

SEPARATE CUT COMB CULL DEAL FALL FREE PART SIFT SORT TEAR ASIDE BREAK CALVE FENCE HEDGE SCALE SEVER SIEVE SKILL SPLIT TWAIN TWIST ABDUCT ASSORT BISECT CLEAVE DEPART DETACH DIGEST DIVIDE FILTER REMOTE SCREEN SETTLE SPREAD SUNDER SUNDRY WINNOW ABSCISE CONCERN DIALYZE DISJOIN DIVERSE EXPANSE ISOLATE SCATTER SEVERAL ABSTRACT DETACHED DISCRETE DISSOLVE DISTINCT FRACTION LAMINATE LEVIGATE LIBERATE PECULIAR RESPECTIVE

SEPARATION GAP GULF PART RENT BREAK CHASM SPLIT SCHISM BARRIER PARTING ANALYSIS DIALYSIS DISTANCE DIVISION SOLUTION SEQUESTER
(— OF LEAF) CHORISIS
(— OF MAN AND WIFE) ZIHAR DIVORCE
(— OF METALS) DEPART
(— OF PIGMENT) FLOATING
(— OF WORD PARTS) TMESIS
(— OF YEAST IN BEER) BREAK

SEPULCHER BIER GRAVE CENOTAPH MONUMENT MORTUARY

SEPULCHRAL HOLLOW CHARNEL TUMULARY

SEQUENCE ROPE SUIT TRACT TRAIN SEQUEL SERIES STRING CADENCE SPECTRUM STRAIGHT
(— IN MELODY) AGOGE
(— OF BEHAVIOR) ACT
(— OF BILLIARD SHOTS) BREAK

(— OF CARDS) QUART TENACE STRINGER
(— OF CHESS MOVES) DEFENSE
(— OF EVENTS) CYCLE SCENARIO
(— OF MELODRAMA) CHASE
(— OF ROCK UNITS) SECTION
(— OF SOUNDS) AFFIX
(CUSTOMARY —) COURSE
(LITURGICAL —) CANON

SEQUESTERED LONELY PRIVATE RECLUSE RETIRED SECLUDED SOLITARY

SERAPHIC ANGELIC BEATIFIC

SERENADE AUBADE HORNING ALBORADA NOCTURNE SERENATA
(MOCK —) SHIVAREE

SERENE CALM EVEN CLEAR SEDATE SMOOTH HALCYON DECOROUS

SERENITY CALM PEACE REPOSE

SERF BOND CHURL HELOT SLAVE THRALL BONDMAN COLONUS PEASANT

SERGEANT TOP SARGE CHIAUS SERVANT TOPKICK HAVILDAR

SERIES RUN SET RANK SUIT TIRE CHAIN ORDER SUITE TALLY TRACE COURSE STRING SYSTEM BATTERY CASCADE CATALOG SEQUENCE PROGRESSION
(— OF ABSTRACTS) SYLLABUS
(— OF ARCHES) ARCADE
(— OF BALLET TURNS) CHAINE
(— OF BOAT RACES) REGATTA
(— OF CELLS) FILAMENT
(— OF CHARACTERS) CLINE
(— OF CHESS MOVES) COOK
(— OF CLASHES) CLATTER
(— OF COMMUNITIES) SERE
(— OF DANCE MOVEMENTS) ADAGIO
(— OF DRAIN TILES) FIELD
(— OF EVENTS) EPOS ACTION
(— OF FORTIFICATIONS) CEINTURE
(— OF LEGENDS) SAGA
(— OF MEETINGS) SESSION
(— OF METAL DISKS) PILE
(— OF MILITARY OPERATIONS) CAMPAIGN
(— OF NEIGHBORING LOTS) COTE
(— OF NOTES) GAMUT GLISSADE
(— OF PASSES) FAENA
(— OF PILES) DRIFT
(— OF POEMS) DIVAN
(— OF PRAYERS) COURSE SYNAPTE
(— OF RACES) CIRCUIT
(— OF REASONS) ARGUMENT
(— OF RINGS) COIL GIMMAL
(— OF ROOMS) SWEEP
(— OF SHOTS) BURST
(— OF SIMILAR STRUCTURES) STROBILA
(— OF SLALOM GATES) FLUSH
(— OF STAIRS) FLIGHT
(— OF STAMPS) SET
(— OF STITCHES) STAY
(— OF STRAPS) LADDER
(— OF STRATA) KAROO
(— OF THREADS) BINDER STUFFER
(— OF TONES) SCALE
(— OF TRAVELS) ODYSSEY
(— OF VERSES) ANTIPHON

(CARD —) CORONET
(CONNECTED —) CATENA
(CONSECUTIVE —) STREAK
(DANCE —) DOUBLE
(IMPRESSIVE —) ARRAY
SERIOUS RUM SAD DEEP ACUTE GRAVE
HEAVY SOBER SOLID STAID DEMURE
SEDATE SEVERE SOLEMN SOMBER
SULLEN AUSTERE EARNEST WEIGHTY
GRIEVOUS
SERMON SPELL HOMILY POSTIL
ADDRESS FUNERAL
SERPENT (ALSO SEE SNAKE) WORM
ABOMA ADDER APEPI OPHIS SIREN
SNAKE TRAIN CHITAL DIPSAS DRAGON
GERARD PYTHON APOPHIS JARARACA
OPHIDIAN
(FEATHERED —) GUCUMATZ
KUKULKAN
(HERALDIC —) REMORA
(NORSE —) GOIN
(SACRED —) AWANYU
(SKY —) AHI
SERPENTINE SNAKY OPHITE SNAKISH
BOWENITE METAXITE
SERVANT KID MAN TAG HELP HIND LUCE
MATY BAGOT BOOTS BOULT GROOM
HAMAL SLAVE SOSIA USHER BEARER
EWERER FEEDER FERASH FLUNKY
GRUMIO HAIDUK KHAMAL MENIAL
SLAVEY TEABOY VARLET VASSAL
BOOTBOY COURIER FEODARY FLUNKEY
FOOTMAN GENERAL PAPELON CHAPRASI
FOLLOWER HENCHMAN HOUSEBOY
MANCIPLE MINISTER OUTRIDER
SERGEANT STANDARD
(— IN CHARGE OF BREAD) PANTLER
(— IN CHARGE OF DAIRY) DEY
(— IN OFFICE) DUFTERY
(— OF SCHOLAR OR MAGICIAN)
FAMULUS
(— WHO CARVES) TRENCHER
(— WHO CLEARS TABLE) VOIDER
(— WHO RUNS BEFORE CARRIAGE)
PIQUEUR
(— WHO SERVES TABLE) SEWER
(ARMED —) PANDOUR
(ARMY —) BATMAN LASCAR
(BENGAL —) MEHTAR SIRCAR
(BODY —) VALET SIRDAR
(BOY —) BOY KNAVE CHOKRA BOUCHAL
(CAMP —) BILDAR
(CLOWNISH —) SPEED LAUNCE
(COLLEGE —) GYP SKIP SCOUT
(FEMALE —) NAN AMAH DASI GIRL
LASS MAID MAMMY NURSE WENCH
PAMELA SKIVVY ANCILLA HANDMAID
MUCHACHA WARDMAID
(GENERAL —) FACTOTUM
(HEAD —) BUTLER TINDAL
(HIGH PRIEST'S —) MALCHUS
(HINDU —) DASI
(HOUSE —) COOK SEWER DOMESTIC
MATRANEE SCULLION
(KITCHEN —) COOK WASHPOT
(LORD OR KING'S —) THANE
(LYING —) FAG

(MAN —) BOY JACK MOZO SWAIN
VALET ANDREW GILLIE KNIGHT GHILLIE
KHANSAMA MUCHACHO SERVITOR
(MISCHIEVOUS —) TEAGUE
(NON-RESIDENT —) DAILY
(PETULANT —) DORINE
(PHILIPPINE —) BATA ALILA
(SCOTTISH —) JURR
(TRUSTY —) TROUT
SERVE DO ACT AID GIVE HELP SHEW
SLAP TEND TOSS WAIT COVER FRAME
HORSE STAND ANSWER ASSIST INTEND
SETTLE SPREAD SUCCOR ADVANCE
FORWARD FURTHER FUNCTION
SERVICE AID FEE DUTY HELP RITE YOKE
FAVOR STEAD EMPLOY ERRAND FACTOR
OFFICE BENEFIT BONDAGE CORNAGE
FUNERAL LITURGY OBSEQUY RETINUE
BREEDING EQUIPAGE FUNCTION
KINDNESS MINISTRY
(ASSIGNED —) MYSTERY
(BODYGUARD —) INWARD
(CHURCH —) LAUDS CHAPEL CHURCH
HEARING STATION SYNAXIS ASPERGES
EVENSONG
(COFFEE —) CABARET
(COMPULSORY —) ANGARIA
(DOMESTIC —) CHAKARI
(FEUDAL —) BOON AVERA ARRIAGE
HEADWARD
(MILITARY —) ARMS CAMP DUTY
ESCUAGE
(MILITIA —) COMMANDO
(RELIGIOUS —) AHA SEDER COMMON
(SECRET —) OGPU
(TENNIS —) ACE LET
SERVICEABLE USEFUL DURABLE
THRIFTY FRIENDLY VAILABLE
SERVILE BASE ABJECT MENIAL SUPINE
CAITIFF SLAVISH CRAWLING CRINGING
SERVIENT
SERVITUDE USE YOKE BONDAGE
SERVICE SLAVERY THIRLAGE
SESSION DAY BOUT DIET HOUR SEAT
COURT SCHOOL SEANCE HEARING
SEMINAR SITTING CONGRESS SEMESTER
(COURT —) HILARY
(JAM —) CLAMBAKE
SET DO DIP FIX GEL KIT LAY LOT MOB PUT
SIC SIT SOT CASE CREW CUBE GAGE
GIVE JELL KNIT KNOT NEST PAIR PICK
PILT POSE REST SETT SORT STEP STOW
BATCH CLACK CLOCK COVEY CROWD
FIXED GAUGE GLADE GROUP INFIX
PAVER PLACE POSIT STACK STAID
STAND STEAD STEEK STICK SUITE
ADJUST CIRCLE CLIQUE DEFINE FASTEN
FINALE FORMAL GLAZED GROUND
HARDEN IMPOSE PARCEL SERIES SETTLE
SPREAD SQUARE STATED BATTERY
BOILING COMPANY COMPOSE CONFIRM
COTERIE DEPOSIT DISPOSE ENCHASE
FACTION IMPLANT INSTATE PLATOON
SERVICE STATION STIFFEN STRATUM
EQUIPAGE PANTALON SEQUENCE
SOLIDIFY STANDARD

(— ABOUT) FALL FANG GANG BEGIN ADDRESS

(— APART) MARK DESIGN DEVOTE EXEMPT SACRED ISOLATE RESERVE ALLOCATE DEDICATE INSULATE SEPARATE SEQUESTER

(— ASIDE) BAR DROP SINK SLIP KAPUT BRACKET EARMARK RESERVE SUSPEND ABROGATE DISPENSE OVERRIDE OVERRULE REVERSED

(— DOWN) JOT LAY GIVE LAND EXPONE DEPOSIT

(— FORTH) DRAW ETCH SHOW GIVEN STATE DEPART DEPICT EXPOSE SPREAD DISPLAY EXHIBIT EXPOUND PRESENT PROPOSE PURPOSE PROPOUND

(— FREE) BAIL EASE REMIT SOLVE ACQUIT ABSOLVE DELIVER UNLOOSE DISSOLVE EXPEDITE

(— IN ORDER) ARRAY PITCH ADIGHT FETTLE ADDRESS

(— OF BELLS) RING CHIME CARILLON

(— OF BOOKS) PLENARY

(— OF CARS) DRAG

(— OF CIRCUMSTANCES) CASE EGIS FRAME

(— OF DISHES) GARNISH SERVICE CUPBOARD

(— OF FURNITURE) SUITE DINETTE

(— OF IDEAS) SYSTEM

(— OF MUSICAL INSTRUMENTS) CONSORT

(— OF NOTES) ACCORD

(— OF OPINIONS) CREDO

(— OF RULES) CODE EQUITY DECALOG

(— OF SHELVES) STAGE BUFFET DRESSER WHATNOT

(— OF STEPS) LADDER

(— OF THREE) BALE LEASH

(— OFF) FOIL SEVER SHOOT ACCENT BALANCE COMMEND EMBLAZE CONTRAST DECORATE EMBLAZON

(— ON) TAR

(— ON FIRE) SPIT TIND LIGHT IGNITE KINDLE ENFLAME ENKINDLE

(— OUT) MAKE FOUND SALLY START INTEND

(— RIGHT) REDD ADJUST SCHOOL SQUARE CORRECT REDRESS

(— UP) AREAR ERECT RAISE INSTALL UPDRESS ACTIVATE

(— UPON) BESET ATTACK AGGRESS BROWDEN

SETBACK DASH JOLT KNOCK LURCH BLIGHT LICKING REVERSE COMEDOWN

SETH (BROTHER OF —) ABEL CAIN
(FATHER OF —) ADAM
(MOTHER OF —) EVE
(SON OF —) ENOS

SETTING FALL PAVE VAIL CHASE MIDST SETUP MILIEU MONTURE INTERIOR MARQUISE MOUNTING SHOWCASE

SETTLE BED FIT FIX PAY SAG SET SIT BANK BIND CALM DAIS FAST FIRM NEST REST ROOT SEAT SINK AGREE CLEAR COUCH LIGHT LODGE ORDER PLACE PLANT QUIET SQUAT STILL ACCORD ADJUST ALIGHT ASSIGN CLINCH DECIDE ENCAMP LOCATE NESTLE RESIDE SCREEN SECURE SOOTHE SQUARE ACCOUNT APPEASE APPOINT ARRANGE BALANCE CLARIFY COMPOSE CONCERT CONFIRM DEPOSIT INHABIT PIONEER RESOLVE SUBSIDE COLONIZE REGULATE RECONCILE

(— A FINE) AFFEER

(— AMICABLY) COMPOUND

(— DOWN) CAMP SLUMP STEADY DESCEND

(— ITSELF) INVEST

(— LANDS ON A PERSON) ENTAIL

(— ON) POINT

(— UPON) AFFIX AGREE TIGHT

(— VERTICALLY) SQUASH

SETTLED SET FIRM FIXED QUIET STAID FORMED SEATED SEDATE SQUARE CERTAIN DECIDED DECOROUS RESOLVED STANDING

SETTLEMENT DEAL FINE FORK POST BARRIO COLONY WINDUP ACCOUNT BIVOUAC MAABARA OUTPOST STATION DECISION DISPATCH PRESIDIO SHOWDOWN TOWNSHIP PLANTATION

(— OF MONKS) SKETE

(— OF SHACKS) FAVELLA

(COLLECTIVE —) KVUTZA MOSHAV KIBBUTZ

(HARSH —) DIKTAT

(INDIAN —) BUSTEE

(MARRIAGE —) MAHR ARRAS DOWNSET

(NEW ZEALAND —) PA

(RAPID —) BOOM

(UPLAND —) BOOLEY

SETTLER SAHIB NESTER PEOPLER PILGRIM PIONEER FINISHER HABITANT

(— IN AUSTRALIA) GROPER

SEVENTEEN (AUTHOR OF —) TARKINGTON

(CHARACTER IN —) MAY JANE PRATT BAXTER GEORGE JOHNNY WATSON GENESIS PARCHER WILLIAM CLEMATIS

SEVER AX CUT BITE HACK REND SLIT SHEAR SHRED CLEAVE DEPART DETACH DIVIDE SUNDER DISJOIN SEPARATE

(PREF.) TEMNO

SEVERAL ODD TEN DIVERS SUNDRY DIVERSE VARIOUS MULTIPLE

SEVERE BAD DRY ACID DOUR FIRM HARD IRON KEEN RUDE SORE TART TAUT ACUTE CRUEL GRUFF HARSH RIGID ROUGH SHARP SMART SOBER STARK STERN STIFF TOUGH BITING BITTER BRUTAL COARSE SIMPLE SOLEMN STRICT UNKIND ACERBIC ASCETIC AUSTERE CAUSTIC CHRONIC CUTTING DRASTIC SERIOUS SPARTAN VICIOUS VIOLENT ACULEATE CATONIAN EXACTING GRIEVOUS GRINDING HORRIBLE RIGOROUS SCATHING STRINGENT

SEVERITY FROST RIGOR CRUELTY TYRANNY ACRIMONY ASPERITY RIGIDITY SORENESS VIOLENCE

SEW FELL SEAM SLIP PREEN NEEDLE
STITCH OVERSEW THIMBLE OVERCAST
(— A CORPSE) SOCK
(— LOOSELY) BASTE
(— TO REINFORCE) BAR
(— WAVED PATTERN) DICE
SEXTON SAXON WARDEN SACRIST
SHAMASH SACRISTAN
SEYCHELLES (CAPITAL OF —)
VICTORIA
(ISLAND OF —) MAHE LADIGUE
PRASLIN
SHABBY BASE MEAN WORN DINGY
DOWDY MANGY RATTY SEEDY SORRY
TACKY CHEESY FROWZY GRUBBY
SCUFFY SCURVY SHODDY SLEAZY
TAGRAG SCRUFFY SQUALID SLIPSHOD
SHACK HUT CRIB HUMPY HUTCH SHANTY
SHACKLE TIE BAND BIND BOLT BOND
GYVE LOCK STAY BILBO CLAMP CRAMP
FETTER HAMPER PINION STAYER
COUPLER MANACLE TRAMMEL RESTRAIN
SHADE DULL VEIL BLEND COLOR GHOST
GLOOM TASTE TINCT TINGE TRACE
UMBER UMBRA DEGREE FRESCO
SHADOW SHIELD SHROUD SPRITE
STRAIN TONING CURTAIN ECLIPSE
GRADATE HACHURE PROTECT UMBRAGE
HALFTONE UMBRELLA
(— OF COLOR) EYE CAST TONE
(— OF DIFFERENCE) NUANCE
(— OFF) GRADUATE
(EYE —) UGLY
(OVERHANGING —) CANOPY
(WINDOW —) STORE
(PREF.) UMBRI
SHADOW BLOT TAIL CLOUD SHADE
UMBER UMBRA DARKEN SHROUD TAILER
PHANTOM SUGGEST UMBRAGE
PENUMBRA PHANTASM
SHADOWS ON THE ROCK
(AUTHOR OF —) CATHER
(CHARACTER IN —) LAVAL CECILE
HECTOR PIERRE AUCLAIR BLINKER
CHARRON EUCLIDE SAINTCYR
FRONTENAC
SHADOWY MISTY VAGUE GLOOMY
GHOSTLY OBSCURE
SHADY DARK BOSKY BOWERY CLOUDY
SHADOWY UMBROSE ADUMBRAL
SHAFT BAR NIB BOLT HOLE PILE POLE
WELL QUILL SHANK SHOOT SPRAG
STAFF STILT STING TRUNK COLUMN
GNOMON TILLER TUNNEL UPRISE
CHIMNEY MANDREL SPINDLE CAMSHAFT
STANDARD WELLHOLE
(— CONNECTING WHEELS) AXLE
(— IN GLACIER) MOULIN
(— IN WATCH) STEM
(— OF CANDLESTICK) BALUSTER
(— OF CARRIAGE) FILL SILL THILL
(— OF CART) ROD TRAM SHARP STANG
(— OF CAVERN) DOME
(— OF CHARIOT) BEAM
(— OF CLUSTERED PIER) BOLTEL
(— OF COLUMN) FUST TIGE SCAPE
VERGE

(— OF FEATHER) SCAPE SCAPUS
(— OF MINE) PIT WORK GRUFF HEUGH
RAISE SLOPE STULM WINZE GROOVE
STAPLE INCLINE WINNING
(— OF PADDLE) LOOM ROUND
(— OF SPEAR OR LANCE) TREE STALE
(— OF WAGON) STAVE THILL LIMBER
(HARNESS —) HEALD
(HOLLOW —) CANNON
(MAIN —) ARBOR
(ORNAMENTAL —) VERGE
(SCYTHE —) SNEAD
(STAIRWAY —) VICE
(TWISTED —) TORSO
(VENTILATION —) UPCAST UPTAKE
WINDHOLE
SHAGGY HARSH NAPPY ROUGH TATTY
TOUSY BRUSHY COMATE RAGGED
HIRSUTE SQUALID VILLOUS TATTERED
SHAKE BOB JAR JOG WAG JOLT PLUM
ROCK STIR SWAY WHOP KNOCK QUASH
SHOCK SWING TRILL DITHER DODDLE
GOGGLE HUSTLE JOGGLE JOUNCE
QUAVER QUIVER RUFFLE SHIMMY
SHIVER TOTTER WAMBLE WARBLE
WOBBLE AGITATE CONCUSS SHUDDER
STAGGER TREMBLE TWITTER BRANDISH
CONVULSE
(— LIGHTLY) LIFT
(— OFF) ARISE EXCUSS
(— TO SEPARATE) HOTCH
(— UP) JABBLE JUMBLE RATTLE
SHAKY QUAKY ROCKY TIPSY TOTTY
WOOZY AGUISH CRANKY GROGGY
INFIRM PALSIED RICKETY TITTUPY
TOTTERY INSECURE
SHALE BAT BASS BONE CLOD FLAG
PLATE KILLAS MUDSTONE TORBANITE
SHALLOW EBB BANK FLAT GLIB FLEET
INANE SHOAL SILLY SMALL FLIMSY
FROTHY LITTLE RIFFLE SLIGHT CURSORY
TRIVIAL
SHAM FOB FOX GIG FAKE HOAX MOCK
PUFF BLUFF BOGUS CHEAT DUMMY
FALSE FEIGN FRAUD QUEER ASSUME
DECEIT DUFFER HUMBUG PSEUDO
FALSITY FORGERY PRETEND PRETENSE
SPURIOUS
(PREF.) PSEUD(O)
SHAME ABASH SPITE ASHAME REBUKE
MORTIFY PUDENCY SCANDAL SLANDER
CONTEMPT DISGRACE DISHONOR
REPROACH VITUPERY
SHAMEFUL BASE FOUL MEAN GROSS
IGNOBLE FLAGRANT IMPROPER
INFAMOUS
SHAMELESS HARD BRASH ARRANT
BRAZEN IMMODEST IMPUDENT
SHANK BODY JAMB TANG CANNON
TARSUS KNUCKLE
SHANTY BOIST HUMPY HUTCH SHACK
SHEBANG
SHAPE AX ADZ CUT DIE HUE BEAT BEND
CAST DRAW FACE FAIR FORM HACK
MOLD NICK BEVEL BLOCK COLOR DRAPE
DRESS FORGE FRAME GUISE LATHE
MODEL MOULD CHISEL CUTOUT FIGURE

FORMER HAMMER JIGGER CONFORM
CONTOUR FASHION FEATURE INCLINE
OUTLINE PATTERN TONNEAU LIKENESS
(— BY HAMMERING) SMITH
(— DIAMOND) BRUTE
(— GARMENTS) BOARD
(— METAL) SWAGE EXTRUDE
(— OF BUST) TAILLE
(— ON POTTER'S WHEEL) THROW
(— ONE'S COURSE) ETTLE
(— RIGHTLY) FIT
(— ROUGHLY) BOAST SCABBLE
SCAPPLE
(— STONE) BROACH SCABBLE
(CLAY —) FLOATER
(CONICAL —) BEEHIVE
(GLOVE —) TRANK
(SPIRALLING —) SWIRL
(SURFACE —) GEOMETRY
(UNBLOCKED —) HOOD
SHAPED BUILT FITTED BLOCKED
FEATURED
SHAPELESS DUMPY INFORM FORMLESS
INDIGEST UNSHAPED
SHAPELY GENT TIDY TRIM CLEAN TIGHT
DECENT FORMAL GAINLY
SHARE CUT END LOT DEAL HAND PART
PLOT RENT SNIP DIVVY PARTY RATIO
SLICE SNACK SPLIT WHACK COMMON
COPART DIVIDE IMPART RATION
PARTAKE PORTION DIVIDEND DIVISION
INTEREST PERCENTAGE PROPORTION
(— A BED) BUNK
(— EQUALLY) HALVE
(— IN ACTIVITY) PIECE
(— OF EXPENSES) LAW CLUB
(— OF LAND) DAIL DALE FREEDOM
RUNDALE
(— OF PROFIT) LAY
(— OF STOCK) STOCK ACTION
(— QUARTERS) CHUM
(— SECRETS) CONFIDE
(ALLOTED) DOLE
(ANCESTRAL —) PATTI
(FULL —) SKINFUL
(GREATER —) FECK
(LEGAL —) HAK
(ONE'S —) AFFERE
(PROPORTIONAL —) QUOTA
(SMALL —) MOIETY
SHARED JOINT BETWEEN
(PREF.) CO
SHARK GATA SAKO MAKO TOPE HOUND LAMIA
TIGER BEAGLE GALEID REQUIN DOGFISH
PLACOID SLEEPER TIBURON BULLHEAD
SEAHOUND THRASHER PORBEAGLE
SHARP DRY ACID CUTE EDGY FINE HIGH
KEEN PERT SALT TART ACERB ACRID
ACUTE ALERT BRASH BRISK CRISP
EAGER EDGED FALSE HARSH NASAL
NIPPY PEERY QUICK SMART STEEP STIFF
VIVID ACIDIC ACUATE ARGUTE ASTUTE
BITING BITTER BRIGHT CRISPY JAGGED
SEVERE SHREWD SHRILL SNELLY
ANGULAR AUSTERE BRITTLE CAUSTIC
CUTTING GINGERY NIPPING PIQUANT

POINTED PUNGENT SLICING VIOLENT
INCISIVE POIGNANT
SHARPEN EDGE FILE FINE HONE KEEN
WHET FROST GRIND POINT RAISE STROP
ACCENT ENHANCE QUICKEN SMARTEN
HEIGHTEN
SHARPNESS WIT EDGE SALT WHET
PLUCK ACRITY ACUITY ACUMEN ACIDITY
ACERBITY ACRIDITY ACRIMONY
ASPERITY EDGINESS PUNGENCY
SHARPSHOOTER JAGER VOLTIGEUR
TIRAILLEUR BERSAGLIERE
SHARP-WITTED ACUTE CANNY SNELL
SHREWD
SHATTER BLOW DASH BLAST BREAK
BURST CRASH SMASH SPLIT WRECK
SHIVER SPIDER EXPLODE TORPEDO
DEMOLISH DYNAMITE SPLINTER
SHAVE BARB BITE DRAW PARE RAZE
GRAZE SKIVE SCRAPE FLATTEN
SHAWL WRAP MANTA PATTU RUMAL
SCARF AFGHAN ANGORA PEPLUM
PUTTOO SERAPE TAPALO ZEPHYR
PAISLEY WRAPPER ALGERINE CASHMERE
KAFFIYEH
(COARSE —) KAMBAL
(COTTON —) FARDA
(PLAID —) MAUD
(TASSELED —) TALLITH
SHEAF TIE BUNG GERB OMER GERBE
BATTEN DORLACH CAPSHEAF
(— LEVIED AS TAX) CORNBOLE
(— OF ARROWS) FLASH
(— OF FLAX OR HEMP) BEAT BEET
GLEAN
(— OF GRAIN) GAIT GARB HOSE
GARBAGE
(LAST — OF CORN) NECK
(LAST — OF HARVEST) KIRN
(PROTECTING —) HATTOCK
(UNBOUND —) REAP GAVEL
SHEAR CUT CLIP CROP TRIM BREAK
STRIP FLEECE
SHEARS LEWIS SNIPS SECATEUR
SHEATH COT BOOT CASE CYST HOSE
ARMOR OCREA SHEAF THECA COCOON
OCHREA QUIVER SCABBARD
(— FOR BOOK) FOREL
(— FOR FINGER) STALL
(— FOR GAMECOCK'S SPUR) HOT
(— OF CIGARETTE) SPILL
(— OF PLOW) STANDARD
(— OF TISSUE) PERIBLEM
(MEDULLARY —) CORONA
(PREF.) COLE(O) COLI(O) ELYTR(O)
(SUFF.) LEMMA THECA THECIUM
SHEATHING SKIN ARMOR COPPER
FACING SHEATH SHIPLAP
SHED BOX ABRI CAST COTE DROP MOLT
PEEL POUR SLIP BOOTH HOVEL MOULT
SCALE SPILL THROW VINEA EFFUSE
GARAGE HANGAR SLOUGH COTTAGE
DIFFUSE DISCARD RADIATE WOODSHED
(— BLOOD) BROACH
(— DROPS) DRIZZLE
(— FEATHERS OR HORNS) MEW
(— FOR LIVESTOCK) SHIPPEN

(— FOR SHEEP) SHEALING
(— OVER MINE SHAFT) COE
(— TEARS) GIVE
(— TO PROTECT SOLDIERS) TESTUDO
(CATTLE —) CUB HELM LAIR BELFRY
(MOVABLE —) SOW BAIL MUSCULE
(TEMPORARY —) PANDAL
(WEATHER —) DINGLE
SHEEN GLAZE SHINE LUSTER LUSTRE
SHIMMER
SHEEP DOWN LAMB ZENU ANCON BOVID
HUNIA MUGGS OVINE SAIGA TAGGE
AOUDAD BHARAL BIDENT CHURRO
DORPER DORSET EXMOOR HIRSEL
MERINO MUTTON OXFORD ROMNEY
WETHER WOOLIE WOOLLY BIGHORN
BLEATER CHEVIOT DELAINE JUMBUCK
KARAKUL LINCOLN POLLARD SUFFOLK
COTSWOLD DARTMOOR LONGWOOL
(— DIFFICULT TO HANDLE) COBBLER
(— IN 2ND YEAR) HOB TAG TEG
TWINTER
(— THAT HAS SHED PORTION OF
WOOL) ROSELLA
(— TO BE SHEARED) BOARD
(DEAD —) MORT BRAXY MORLING
(FEMALE —) EWE GIMMER SHEDER
(HORNLESS —) NOT
(LOST —) WAIF
(MALE —) RAM TUP BUCK HEDER
DINMONT
(MOUNTAIN —) IBEX
(OLD —) GUMMER
(THICK-WOOLED —) MUG
(WILD —) SHA ARGAL RASSE URIA
AOUDAD ARGALI BHARAL SHAPOO
BURRHEL MOUFLON
(YOUNG —) HOG HOGGEREL
(3-YEAR-OLD —) THRINTER
SHEEPFOLD REE FANK KRAAL REEVE
STELL BOUGHT BARKARY SHEPPEY
SHEER BOLD FINE MAIN MERE PURE
BLANK CRUDE FRANK NAKED STARK
STEEP SIMPLE
SHEET FIN CARD FINE FOIL LEAF BLANK
CANVAS DOUBLE FLIMSY SHROUD
BLANKET CHUDDER PAPYRUS WRAPPER
EIGHTEEN INTERLAY
(— ATTACHED TO INVOICE) APRON
(— FOR BRIDGE SCORES) FLOGGER
(— OF CLOUDS) PALLIUM
(— OF DOUGH) STRUDEL
(— OF FIBER) LAP BATT
(— OF ICE) GLARE GLAZE
(— OF IRON) CRAMPET
(— OF LAVA) COULEE
(— OF LEAD) SOAKER
(— OF LEATHER) BUFFING
(— OF MICA) FILM
(— OF MUSCLE) PLATYSMA
(— OF PAPER) FLAT FOLIO FRISKET
LEAFLET HANDBILL
(— OF PARCHMENT) SKIN FOLLOWER
(— OF RUBBER) DAM
(— OF STAMPS) PANE
(— OF STRAW) YELM
(— OF SUGAR) SLAB

(— OF TISSUE) FASCIA
(— OF TOBACCO) BINDER
(— OF WATER) NAPPE
(— USED FOR MATRIX) FLONG
(HEATED —) CAUL
(METAL —S) LATTENS
(NEWS —) GAZETTE
(ORGANIZATION —) BILL
(PERFORATED —) SIEVE
(PROTECTIVE —) CURTAIN
(THEATRICAL —) SIDE
(THIN —S OF IRON) DOUBLES
(TRANSPARENT —) GELATINE
(WINDING —) SINDON SUDARY
SHELF BANK DECK STEP BENCH LEDGE
STAGE STOOL MANTEL SCONCE SETTLE
BRACKET COUNTER PLATEAU CREDENCE
CUPBOARD
(— BEFORE STOVE) HEARTH
(— BEHIND ALTAR) GRADINE RETABLE
(— IN MINE) BUNNING
(— OF ROCK) CAR LENCH LENCHEON
(CONTINENTAL —) PLATFORM
(FIREWORKS —) BALLOON
(RAISED —) SETTLE
SHELL PEN POD BAND CASK CLAM CONE
HARD HULL HUSK MAIL OBUS PILL PUPA
SKIN UMBO UNIO BALAT CHANK CONCH
CRUST FRITZ GOURD MITRA MUREX
ORMER SHARD SHERD SHOCK SHUCK
TESTA TROCA TURBO VALVE VENUS
ARCHIE BULLET CERION COCKLE COWRIE
CRUSTA DOLIUM ECLAIR LORICA
NUCULA PULLET PURPLE SANKHA
STROMB TRITON TURBAN VOLUTE
WINKLE BALANUS CARACOL CARCASS
COCONUT DISCINA GLADIUS PROJECT
SCALLOP SPONDYL TEREBRA THIMBLE
TOHEROA TROCHID TRUMPET UNICORN
BACULITE CARAPACE COQUILLE
ENVELOPE ESCALLOP MERINGUE
OLIVELLA PUPARIUM SOLARIUM
STROMBUS UNIVALVE
SHELLFISH ORM COCK BUCKY NACRE
PIROT BUCKIE LIMPET WIGGLE MOLLUSK
PERIWIG ASTACIAN
SHELTER CAB HUT LEE ABRI BURY HERD
HIDE HIVE ROOF BARTH BIELD BOIST
BOOTH BOTHY BOWER CLOAK COVER
EMBAY HAVEN HOARD HOUSE HOVEL
SHADE ASYLUM AWNING BURROW
COVERT CRADLE DEFEND DUGOUT
GABION HANGAR HARBOR PANDAL
REFUGE SCREEN SHADOW SHIELD
SHROUD CABINET CARPORT DEFENSE
EMBOSOM HOUSING NACELLE QUARTER
RETREAT ROOFING UMBRAGE WICKIUP
DOGHOUSE ENSCONCE PALLIATE
SECURITY
(— FOR CATTLE) HELM BOOLY STELL
HEMMEL
(— FOR CROP WATCHERS) KISI
(— FOR DANCES) ENRAMADA
(— FOR SENTRY) GUERITE
(— FROM WEATHER) LEWTH
(— OVER BEEHIVE) HOOD

(BULLETPROOF —) MANTLET
MANTELET
(CONCRETE-AND-STEEL —) PILLBOX
(CRAMPED —) HUTCH
(FISH —) CROY
(LEAFY —) LEVESEL
(MINING —) TALPA
(PORTABLE —) MANTA CABANA
(ROCK —) KRAPINA
(ROUGH —) JACAL
(TEEPEELIKE —) CHUM
(TEMPORARY —) HALE HOLD CABIN
BIVOUAC
SHEM (BROTHER OF —) HAM JAPHET
(FATHER OF —) NOAH
SHEPHERD HERD SHEP COLIN CORIN
GYGES SWAIN PASTOR CORYDON
DAPHNIS KURUMBA THYRSIS TITYRUS
MELIBEUS PASTORAL SHEEPMAN
STREPHON
SHEPHERDESS DELIA MOPSA PHEBE
DORCAS BERGERE GALATEA PASTORA
PERDITA AMARYLLIS
SHERBET ICE GLACE SHRAB SORBET
GRANITA SOUFFLE
SHERIFF DEPUTY GRIEVE SCHOUT
BAILIFF SHRIEVE ALGUACIL HUISSIER
SHIREMAN
SHERRY FINO CLOVE XERES SOLERA
OLOROSO MONTILLA MANZANILLA
SHE STOOPS TO CONQUER
(AUTHOR OF —) GOLDSMITH
(CHARACTER IN —) KATE TONY
MARLOW CHARLES LUMPKIN NEVILLE
HASTINGS PEDIGREE CONSTANCE
HARDCASTLE
SHIELD ECU EGIS HIDE AEGIS BOARD
CLOAK COVER FENCE GUARD PAVIS
PELTA PYGAL SCUTE SHEND TARGE
CASQUE DEFEND FENDER OCULAR
RONDEL SCREEN SCUTUM SECURE
TARGET BUCKLER CLYPEUS CONCEAL
PAVISSE PROTECT ROTELLA ROUNDEL
SHELTER SUPPORT CARTOUCH INSULATE
PRESERVE SUNSHADE
(— BELOW A DAM) APRON
(— FOR ARCHERS) PANNIER
(— FOR HORSE) BIB
(— FOR LAMP) BONNET CHIMNEY
(— OF A STIRRUP) HOOD
(— OF ABORIGINES) MULGA HIELAMEN
(— OF CONTINENT) CORE
(— OF HIDE) SKILDFEL
(— OF SOMITE) STERNITE
(— OF TRILOBITE) CEPHALON
(— ON MAST) PAUNCH
(— ON THROAT OF FISH) GULAR
(— OVER BASE OF FAN) CANOPY
(— WITHOUT ARMS) ALBERIA
(BONY —) CARAPACE
(BULLETPROOF —) MANTA MANTLET
MANTELET
(HERALDIC —) BLAZON
(KING ARTHUR'S —) PRIDWIN
(LEATHER —) CHAFE
(SACRED —) ANCILE
(SIBERIAN —) ANGARA

(WICKERWORK —) SCIATH
(PREF.) ASPID(O) CLYPEI CLYPEO PELTATI
PELTATO SCUT(I) SCUTATI SCUTELLI
(SUFF.) ASPIS
SHIELDBEARER SQUIRE ESQUIRE
PELTAST ESCUDERO SCUTIFER
SHIFT BACK FEND FLIT HAUL MOVE RUSE
TACK TURN VARY VEER WEND BREAK
BUDGE CREEP CYMAR DRIFT SHUNT
SIMAR SLIDE SMOCK SPELL TRICK
CHANGE DENIAL DEVICE PALTER
SWERVE SWITCH CHEMISE EVASION
SHUFFLE ARTIFICE DISLODGE DISPLACE
DOGWATCH MUTATION TRANSFER
TURNOVER
(— ABOUT AS THE WIND) LARGE
(— ABRUPTLY) JUMP
(— IN DANCING) BALANCE
(— IN TACKING) JIB
(— ORDER OF BELLS) HUNT
(— RAILROAD EQUIPMENT) DRILL
(— SUDDENLY) FLY CHOP JIBE
(— WEIGHT) WING
(MINING —) CORE
SHIFTING FLUID QUICK AMBULANT
CHOPPING DRIFTING FLOATING SLIPPAGE
VARIABLE VEERABLE
SHIFTY GREASY DEVIOUS EVASIVE
HANGDOG SLIDING SLIPPERY
SHILLING BOB HOG CHIP PREST DEENER
HARPER TESTON
(20 —S) POUND
(21 —S) GUINEA
(5 —S) CROWN DECUS
SHIMMER FLASH GLIMMER SKIMMER
SHIN SHANK SKINK SWARM CNEMIS
SHINE RAY SUN BEAM BUFF GLOW LAMP
STAR BLARE BLINK BLOOM EXCEL GLARE
GLEAM GLINT GLORY GLOSS SHEEN
STARE BEACON DAZZLE LUSTER LUSTRE
EFFULGE GLIMMER GLISTEN GLITTER
RADIATE REFLECT SHIMMER SPARKLE
RUTILATE
SHINGLE SHIM BEACH SHAKE SLATE
CHESIL KNOBBLE
SHINING GLAD NEAT CLEAR GLARY LIGHT
LUCID NITID SHEER WHITE ARDENT
ARGENT BRIGHT FULGID GLOSSY
GOLDEN LUCENT NITENT SHEENY
STARRY ADAZZLE BURNING FULGENT
GLARING GLIMMER FLASHING GLEAMING
LUCULENT LUSTRANT LUSTROUS
NITIDOUS RUTILANT SPLENDID
SUNBEAMY SUNSHINY
SHIP (ALSO SEE BOAT AND VESSEL)
ARK CAT COG HOY BARK BOAT HAND
NAVY PAHI PINE PINK SAIL SEND LAKER
OILER PINTA PRORE RAZEE SCOUT SKIFF
ARGOSY BARQUE BOTTOM CASTLE
CHASER COALER CODMAN DIESEL
GALIOT GALLEY HOLCAD HOPPER
LATEEN MISTIC MOTHER PACKET PUFFER
RUNNER SAILER SEALER TRAVEL VESSEL
CARRACK CLIPPER COLLIER CONSORT
FELUCCA FRIGATE FRUITER GALLEON
GUNBOAT INVOICE MULETTA PATAMAR
PINNACE POLACRE SHALLOP STEAMER

BILANDER CUNARDER DRUMBLER FLAGSHIP GALLEASS INDIAMAN SCHOONER SMUGGLER SPANIARD MERCHANTMAN
(— FITTED AS CHURCH) BETHEL
(— IN LIQUOR TRADE) COPER
(— OF ARGONAUTS) ARGO
(— OF NORSEMEN) KEEL
(CLUMSY) HULK
(DEPOT —) TENDER
(ESCORT —) CORVETTE
(FLEET OF —S) ARMADA
(JAPANESE —) MARU
(MALAY —) COUGNAR
(NOVA SCOTIAN —) BLUENOSE
(PIRATE —) GALLIVAT
(PRIZE —) CAPTURE
(QUARANTINE —) LAZARET
(RECEIVING —) GUARDO
(REMOTE-CONTROLLED —) DRONE
(SLOW —) BUCKET
(STORE —) FLUTER
(SUPPLY —) COOPER
(UNTRIM —) BALLAHOO
(VIKING —) DRAKE
SHIPMENT CARLOT RAILING DISPATCH SHIPPAGE
SHIPSHAPE NEAT TIDY TRIM CIVIL ORDERLY
SHIRK BALK FUNK GOOF MIKE BLINK DODGE EVADE FEIGN FUDGE SKULK SLACK FINAGLE SHACKLE SHAMMOCK
SHIRKER FUNK PIKER ROTTER BLUDGER SLACKER SLINKER SUGARER COBERGER SCOWBANK
SHIRT SARK TOBE BLUEY JUPON KAMIS SHIFT BANIYA CAMISE PALAKA PARTLET VAREUSE
(HAIR —) CILICE
(SLEEVELESS —) FECKET
(WORKMAN'S —) FROCK
(WORNOUT —) DICKY
SHIVER JAR BREAK CHILL CREEP QUAKE SHRUG DITHER DUDDER HOTTER NIDDER QUIVER TREMOR FLICKER FRISSON SHATTER SHUDDER TREMBLE
SHOAL BAJO BANK FLAT REEF SPIT BARRA SHELF SHALLOW
SHOCK JAR BLOW BUMP DINT JOLT RACK STUN TURN APPAL BRUNT GAVEL SHAKE DISMAY FRIGHT IMPACT JOSTLE STRIKE ASTOUND HORRIFY STAGGER STARTLE STUPEFY TERRIFY SURPRISE
(— OF CORN) STOOK STOUT STITCH
(MENTAL —) TRAUMA
SHOCKING GRIM AWFUL LURID HORRID UNHOLY BURNING FEARFUL GHASTLY HIDEOUS DREADFUL ENORMOUS HORRIBLE SCANDALOUS
SHODDY SOFT CHEAP MUNGO TACKY SLEAZY
SHOE BAL BOOT CLOG FLAT HALF BLAKE DERBY MOYLE ROMEO SLING SPIKE STOGA STRAP BROGAN BROGUE CHOPIN CRAKOW CREOLE DORSAY GAITER GALOSH SADDLE SANDAL BLUCHER BOTTINE CALCEUS CHOPINE COWHIDE

OXONIAN SHOEPAC SNEAKER BALMORAI CALCEATE SABOTINE SLIPSLOP
(— FOR GRINDING) MULLER
(— FOR MULE) PLANCHE
(— IN TRUSS OR FRAME) SKEWBACK
(— NOT FASTENED ON) PUMP
(— OF A SLEDGE) HOB
(— OF AN OX) CUE
(— OF COMIC ACTOR) BAXA
(— OF SUBWAY CAR) PAN
(— TO CHECK WHEEL) DRAG SKID
(— USED AS BRAKE) SKATE
(— WORN ON EITHER FOOT) STRAIGHT
(ARMORED —) SABBATON
(BABY'S —) CACK
(DOWN-AT-HEEL —) SHAUCHLE
(HOBNAILED —) TACKET
(LARGE —S) GUNBOATS
(LOW-CUT —) SOCK GILLY ANKLET BUSKIN SLIPPER COLONIAL
(MILITARY —) CALIGA
(OLD —) BAUCHLE
(PIKED —) BEAKER
(RAWHIDE —) HIMMING VELSKOEN
(STEEL —) SOLLERET
(THIN —) PINSON SCLAFF
(WINGED —S) TALARIA
(WOODEN —) KLOMP SABOT PATTEN RACKET RACQUET
(WORN —) SCRAE
SHOOT DAG GUN PAY POT ROD TIP BANG BOLT CANE CION DRAW LEAF PLUG SLIP ARROW BLAST BLAZE DRILL DRIVE EXPEL FROND GEMMA LAYER PLUFF SCION SPEAR SPRAY SPRIG SPRIT SQUIB STICK STOOL TUBER VIMEN FLIGHT FLOWER GERMEN GROWTH HEADER HURTLE LAUNCH RATOON SPRING SPROUT STOLON STOUND SUCKER TILLER BUDLING SCOURGE TENDRIL THALLUS
(— A MARBLE) LAG TAW KNUCKLE
(— A WHALE) STRIKE
(— ASIDE FROM MARK) DRIB
(— AT LONG RANGE) SNIPE
(— DOWN) SPLASH
(— DUCKS) SKAG
(— FORTH) JET GLEAM SPIRE
(— FROM DEER'S ANTLER) SPELLER
(— INDISCRIMINATELY) BROWN
(— MOOSE OR DEER) YARD
(— OF A TREE) STOW WHIP LANCE BRANCH
(— OUT) JUT CHIT DART ERADIATE
(— SEAL) SWATCH
(— UP) SPIRE SPURT
(—S USED AS FODDER) BROWSE
(FIRST —S) BRAIRD
(FLEXIBLE —) BINE
(LATERAL —) ARM
(PAWNBROKER'S —) SPOUT
(SUGARCANE —) LALO
(TENDER —) FLUSH
(WILLOW —) SALLOW
SHOOTING STAR METEOR COWSLIF SHOOTER PRIMWORT

SHOP CRIB BOOTH BURSE STORE TRADE SHOPPE TIENDA ALMACEN BOTTEGA CABARET MERCERY SPICERY TABERNA TURNERY BOUTIQUE COOKSHOP CREMERIE EMPORIUM EXCHANGE SLOPSHOP WAREROOM
(BARBER —) BARBERY
(BLACKSMITH —) SMITHY
(LIQUOR —) SALOON
(OLD CLOTHES —) FLIPPERY
(PAWNBROKER'S —) LUMBER SPROUT
(REPAIR —) GARAGE
(SUTLER'S —) CANTEEN

SHORE GIB BANK RIPE RIVE SAND SIDE BEACH BENCH COAST MARGE RIVAGE STRAND BUTTRESS SEACOAST

SHORT LAG LOW SHY CURT NEAR NIGH SOON BLUFF BRIEF CLOSE CRISP FUBSY SQUAB UNDER ABRUPT SCANTY SCARCE STUNTY SUDDEN BRUSQUE CURTATE LACONIC STUBBED SUMMARY SNAPPISH SUCCINCT
(— AND FLAT) CAMUS
(— AND THICK) CHUNKY STOCKY STUBBY STUMPY TRUNCH TRUNCHED
(— AND THICKSET) NUGGETY
(— AS OF WOOL) FRIBBY
(BRIEF —S) MONOKINI
(STOUT AND —) BUNTY CHUFFY PLUGGY THICKSET

SHORTAGE FAMINE DROUGHT WANTAGE UNDERAGE

SHORTEN CUT CLIP ELIDE SLASH REDUCE ABRIDGE CURTAIL EXCERPT CONTRACT DIMINISH RETRENCH ABBREVIATE
(— AND THICKEN IRON) JUMP
(— GRIP) CHOKE

SHORTNESS BREVITY CURTNESS

SHORT-TEMPERED CRUSTY SNIPPY SNUFFY

SHOT POP SET JOLT PLUG SLUG BLANK FLIER FLING OUTER PLUFF SHOOT CENTER REBOTE BOMBARD DEADEYE GUNSHOT LANGREL BUCKSHOT SCORCHER
(— BEYOND TARGET) OVER
(— FOR CULVERIN) PELICAN
(— IN FIFTH CIRCLE) WHITE
(— IN FOURTH CIRCLE) BLACK
(— IN THIRD CIRCLE) BLUE
(— OF NARCOTIC) FIX
(— STRIKING BULL'S-EYE) CARTON
(— THAT HITS) CLOUT
(ARCHERY —) GREEN
(BADMINTON —) CLEAR
(BASKETBALL —) BOMB JUMPER
(BILLIARD —) DRAG STAB CAROM MASSE SCREW FOLLOW SAFETY SPREAD BRICOLE SCRATCH
(BOW —) DRAFT
(CAMERA —) INTERCUT
(CROQUET —) SPLIT FOLLOW
(CURLING —) INWICK OUTWICK
(FINAL —) UPSHOT
(GOOD —) SCREAMER
(PISTOL —) BARK

(POOL —) BREAK
(SIZE OF —) F T BB FF TT BBB DUST BUCKSHOT
(SMALL —) PELLET
(SNOOKER —) POT
(TENNIS —) ACE LOB DINK SERVE SMASH
(VOLLEY OF —S) BLIZZARD

SHOULDER AXLE CLOD HUMP STEP BOUGH PITCH SPALL VERGE AXILLA EPAULE KNUCKLE
(— AROUND TENON) RELISH
(— OF BOLT) NAB
(— OF FIREARM STOCK) RIMBASE
(— OF FLY) CHEEK
(— OF LAMB) BANJO
(— OF PORK) HAND PICNIC CUSHION
(— OF RABBIT OR HAM) WING
(— OF ROAD) BERM HAUNCH QUARTER
(BEVELED —) GAIN

SHOUT BAY BOO CRY HOY HUE BAWL CALL CROW HAIL HOOT ROOT YELL CHEER CRACK HAVOC HOLLO HUZZA WHOOP BOOHOO CLAMOR HALLOO HOLLER HURRAH YAMMER ACCLAIM
(— AS CHILDREN) BELDER
(— FOR OR AGAINST) BARRACK
(— OF APPROVAL) BRAVO
(— OF ENCOURAGEMENT) HARK
(— OF HIGHLAND DANCER) HOOCH
(— OF JOY) IO
(HUNTING —) CHEVY

SHOVE JUT PUT BUNT FEND PICK PUSH SHUN BOOST CROWD ELBOW HUNCH SHUNT HUSTLE JOSTLE MUSCLE THRUST
(— CARELESSLY) BUNG
(— IN MARBLES) FULK

SHOVEL FAN SPUD SCOOP SPADE SPOON BLUNGER SCOPPET SLUDGER
(— FOR COIN) MAIN
(— FOR DRESSING ORE) VAN
(BRICKMAKING —) CUCKHOLD
(CASTING —) SCUTTLE
(CHARCOAL BURNER'S —) RABBLE
(FIRE —) PEEL SLICE
(GRATED —) HARP
(MINER'S —) BANJO
(PERFORATED —) SKIMMER

SHOW DO SAY CALL DASH HAVE MARK MIEN SEEM VIEW WEAR ASSAY EXERT GLOSS PRIDE PROVE SHINE SIGHT TEACH ACCUSE ASSIGN BETRAY BLAZON CHICHI DENOTE DETECT DEVICE DIRECT ESCORT EVINCE EXPOSE FIGURE FLAUNT GAIETY LAYOUT MUSTER REVEAL SPREAD VANITY ADVANCE ANALYZE BALLOON BESPEAK BETOKEN BRAVURA BREATHE DECLARE DIVULGE EXHIBIT EXPRESS FASHION PRESAGE PRODUCE PROPOSE SELLOUT SIGNIFY TRIUMPH EVIDENCE FLOURISH INDICATE MANIFEST PRETENCE PROCLAIM
(— APPROVAL) CLAP APPLAUD
(— CONTEMPT) SCOFF
(— DISCONTENT) GROUCH
(— DISPLEASURE) POUT
(— DOGS) BENCH

(— ENTHUSIASM) DROOL
(— FORTH) BLAZE CIPHER
(— IN PUBLIC CELEBRATION)
PAGEANT
(— ITSELF) APPEAR
(— MERCY) SPARE
(— OF LEARNING) SCIOLISM
(— OF LIGHT) BLINK
(— OF REASON) COLOR
(— OF VANITY) AIR
(— OFF) FLASH PRANK SPORT SWANK
HOTDOG PARADE
(— ONESELF) BE
(— PROMISE) FRAME SHAPE
(— RESPECT FOR) REGARD
(— REVERSE TREND) REACT
(— SIGNS OF GIVING WAY) WAVER
(— SIGNS OF ILLNESS) GRUDGE
(— THE BOTTOM) KEEL
(— THE SIGHTS) LIONIZE
(— THE WAY) LEAD CONDUCT
(— TO BE FALSE) BELIE DISPROVE
(— UNKINDNESS) WAIT
(— WITHOUT SUBSTANCE) FORM
(ARTFUL —) GRIMACE
(FALSE —) COLOR FUCUS BUBBLE
TINSEL ILLUSION PRETENCE
(FLOOR —) CABARET
(GAUDY —) HOOPLA BRAVERY
(MERE —) PHANTOM
(MOMENTARY —) FLASH
(ORNATE —) FLUBDUB
(OSTENTATIOUS —) SPRUNK DISPLAY
(OUTSIDE —) VARNISH
(OUTWARD —) FUCUS VISAGE
(PUBLIC —) EXPO
(PUPPET —) DROLL MOTION WAYANG
GUIGNOL
(RIDICULOUS —) FARCE
(RUDIMENTARY —) SATURA
(SPECIOUS —) GLOZE
(STREET —) RAREE
(SUPERFICIAL —) GLOSS VENEER
(TRAVELLING —) SLANG
SHOW BOAT (AUTHOR OF —) FERBER
(CHARACTER IN —) KIM ANDY ELLY
HAWKS JULIE PARTHY GAYLORD
RAVENAL MAGNOLIA SCHULTZY
SHOWER WET HAIL RAIN BLASH SOUSE
FLURRY PELTER PEPPER DRIBBLE
WEATHER
(CONCENTRATED —) BARRAGE
(HEAVY —) SUMP
(RAIN —) RASH
(SUDDEN —) SCUD SKIT BRASH PLUMP
SHOWINESS DASH GLARE PIZAZZ
GLITTER PIZZAZZ FLOURISH SPLENDOR
SHOWY GAY FINE LOUD NICE VAIN
FLASH GAUDY GIDDY GRAND JAZZY
SPICY SWANK BRAZEN CHICHI DRESSY
FLASHY FLOSSY GARISH GLOSSY
JAUNTY SPORTY TAWDRY DASHING
GALLANT HOTSHOT POMPOUS SPLASHY
CLAPTRAP FASTUOUS GORGEOUS
SPECIOUS SPLENDID
(NOT —) CIVIL LENTEN DISCREET
SHRED DAG JAG RAG SNIP TEAR WISP

CLOUT PATCH SLIVER FRAZZLE FRITTER
FILAMENT
(— FISH) SCROD
(— OF CLOTHES) TACK
(— OF FLESH) TAG AGNAIL
(— OF HAIR) TAIT
SHREW ERD NAG PRESS SOREX VIXEN
CALLET MIGALE TARTAR VIRAGO
HELLCAT PENTAIL SCYTALE XANTHIPPE
SHREWD SLY ACID ARCH CUTE FELL
SAGE TIDY WARE WISE ACUTE CAGEY
CANNY HEADY SHARP SMART ARGUTE
ARTFUL ASTUTE CLEVER CRAFTY SUBTLE
CUNNING KNOWING PARLOUS POLITIC
SAPIENT
SHREWDNESS SAVVY ACUMEN
SLYNESS PRUDENCE SAGACITY
SHRIEK CRY YIP YELL SKIRL SCREAM
SHRIKE
SHRILL HIGH KEEN THIN ACUTE SHARP
BRASSY GLASSY PIPING SQUEAK TREBLE
PIERCING STRIDENT
SHRINE NAOS HUACA ISEUM SEKOS
STUPA ADYTUM DAGOBA DURGAH
HALLOW HIERON MEMORY SAMADH
ZIARAT FANACLE SACRARY THESEUM
AEDICULA PANTHEON VALHALLA
RELIQUARY
SHRINK COY SHY DARE DUCK GIVE
ABHOR COWER QUAIL RELAX SHRUG
START WINCE BLANCH BLENCH CRINGE
FLINCH LESSEN RECOIL SETTLE WEAZEN
CRUMPLE DWINDLE SHRIVEL COLLAPSE
CONTRACT
SHRIVEL SEAR BLAST CLING PARCH
SHRAM WIZEN BLIGHT GIZZEN SCORCH
SHRINK WITHER
SHROUD HIDE CLOAK CRAPE DRAPE
HABIT SHEET HEARSE MUFFLE SCREEN
SHADOW SUDARY CONCEAL CURTAIN
CEREMENT
SHRUB TI BAY HAW KAT MAY QAT TOD
AKIA ALEM BUSH COCA HOYA INGA ITEA
KARO KEUR KHAT MUSK ULEX AKALA
AKELA ALDER ALISO ARUSA BOCCA
BROOM BUAZE CEIBO CUMAY ELDER
GOOMA GOUMI HAZEL HENNA IXORA
LEDUM LEMON LILAC MAQUI MARIA
MUDAR RETEM SALAL SHROG SUMAC
TOYON ZILLA ABELIA AGRITO AKONGE
AMULLA ANAGUA ANILAO ARALIA
ARUSHA AUCUBA AUPAKA AZALEA
BLOLLY CENIZO CHEKAN CHERRY CISTUS
CORREA DAPHNE DRAURI DRIMYS
FEIJOA FRUTEX JACARO JOJOBA
KARAMU KOWHAI LABRUM LARREA
LAUREL MATICO MYRTLE NARRAS
PENAEA PITURI RAETAM SAVINE STORAX
STYRAX ACEROLA AFERNAN AGARITA
AMORPHA ARBORET ARRAYAN ARRIMBY
AZAROLE BANKSIA BORONIA BUCKEYE
BULLACE CANTUTA CHACATE CHAMISE
CHANCHE DEUTZIA EHRETIA ENCELIA
EPACRID EPHEDRA FUCHSIA GUMWOOD
GUTWORT HOPBUSH HOPSAGE JASMINE
JETBEAD JEWBUSH JOEWOOD
KUMQUAT LANTANA MAHONIA NUNNARI

PAVONIA PEABUSH PEARHAW PIMELEA
RHODORA SPIRAEA TARBUSH THEEZAN
SHUDDER GRUE CREEP QUAKE SHRUG
HOTTER SHIVER FRISSON TREMBLE
SHUFFLE JANK MAKE SLUR MOSEY
SCUFF SHIFT JUGGLE RIFFLE SCLAFF
DRAGGLE DRIBBLE SHAMBLE
(— DISHONESTLY) PACK
SHUN SHY BALK FLEE TABU VOID ABHOR
AVOID EVADE SHUNT TABOO ESCAPE
ESCHEW REFUSE SHRINK DECLINE
FORBEAR FORSAKE
SHUT FAST HASP MAKE SEAL SHOT SLAM
SLOT SPAR TAKE TEEN TINE CLOSE
LATCH STEEK STICK CLOSED CABINET
OCCLUSE UPCLOSE
(— EYES) WINK
(— IN) BAR LAP CAGE EMBAY ENCLAVE
(— OFF) SCREEN SECLUDE
(— OUT) BAR DEBAR REPEL SKUNK
DEPRIVE EXCLUDE PRECLUDE
(— TOGETHER) CLASP
(— UP) MEW PENT STOP CHOKE CLOSET
ENJAIL IMMURE CONDEMN CONFINE
DUNGEON ENCLOSE IMPOUND INCLUDE
OPPRESS SECLUDE CONCLUDE
PRECLUDE
SHUTTER LID DROP BLIND CUTOFF
DAMPER SLUICE JALOUSIE
(— IN ORGAN) SHADE
(— OF TRIPTYCH) VOLET
SHUTTLE FLY FLUTE SHUNT LOOPER
SWIVEL
SHY COY MIM SHUN WILD CAGEY CHARY
DEMUR FLING SCARE SHUNT TIMID
UNCOW DEMURE MODEST BASHFUL
GAWKISH RABBITY STRANGE TREMBLY
BACKWARD RETIRING SHEEPISH
SKITTISH
SHYNESS COYNESS MODESTY RESERVE
TIMIDITY
SIAM (SEE THAILAND)
SIBERIA (GULF IN —) OB
(MOUNTAIN RANGE IN —) URAL
ALTAI
(RIVER IN —) OB ILI KET PUR TAZ TYM
AMGA AMUR LENA MAYA ONON UCUR
ALDAN ISHIM NADYM SOBOL TOBOL
ANGARA IRTYSH OLEKMA VILYUY
(TOWN IN —) OMSK CHITA KYZYL
TOMSK IGARKA KURGAN BARNAUL
IRKUTSK LENINSK YAKUTSK

SICILY

CAPE: BOEO FARO PASSARO
CAPITAL: PALERMO
GULF: NOTO CATANIA
ISLAND: EGADI LIPARI USTICA
MEASURE: SALMA CAFFISO
MOUNTAIN: EREI ETNA MORO SORI IBREI
NEBRODI
PROVINCE: ENNA RAGUSA CATANIA
MESSINA PALERMO TRAPANI SIRACUSA
RIVER: SALSO TORTO BELICE SIMETO
PLATANI

SEAPORT: ACI CATANIA MARSALA
MESSINA PALERMO TRAPANI
TOWN: ENNA NOTO RAGUSA CATANIA
MARSALA MESSINA TRAPANI SYRACUSE
VOLCANO: ETNA

SICK BAD ILL BADLY CRONK CROOK
MORBID UNWHOLE STREAKED
SICKEN TIRE TURN WEARY SUNDER
WEAKEN DISGUST SURFEIT NAUSEATE
SICKENING FELL SICKLY FULSOME
MAWKISH NAUSEOUS
SICKLY WAN FOND PALE PUKY SICK
FAINT GREEN PEAKY SILLY WEARY
ANEMIC CLAMMY CRANKY FEEBLE
INFIRM PULING WEAKLY INVALID
LANGUID MAWKISH DELICATE DISEASED
MALADIVE
SICKNESS (ALSO SEE DISEASE) SORE
AILMENT DISEASE ILLNESS SURFEIT
DISORDER
(MILK —) SLOWS TIRES
(MOTION —) KINETOSIS
(MOUNTAIN —) PUNA SOROCHE
(SUDDEN —) DWALM
SIDE CAMP COST EDGE FACE HALF HAND
LEAF PANE PART BOARD CHEEK FLANK
LATUS PARTY PHASE BEHALF PENDANT
SIDELONG
SIDESTEP BEG AVOID DODGE
SIDEWALK WALKWAY PAVEMENT
TROTTOIR BANQUETTE
SIDLE EDGE PASSAGE SAUNTER
SIEGE BOUT SEDGE JOURNEY LEAGUER
SIEGFRIED (CHARACTER IN —) MIME
WOTAN FAFNER SIEGFRIED BRUNNHILDE
(COMPOSER OF —) WAGNER
(SLAYER OF —) BRUNHILD
(WIFE OF —) KRIEMHILD

SIERRA LEONE

CAPITAL: FREETOWN
COIN: LEONE
MEASURE: LOAD KETTLE
MOUNTAIN: LOMA
NATIVE: VAI KONO LOKO SUSU KISSI
LIMBA MENDE TEMNE FULANI GALLINA
SHERBRO MANDINGO
RIVER: MOA JONG SEWA MONGO ROKEL
ROKKEL SCARCY WAANJE
SEAPORT: HEPEL BONTHE SULIMA
TOWN: BO DARU MANO KISSI LUNGI
KENEMA MAKENI

SIEVE BOLT BUNT HARP LAWN SCRY SIFT
SIZE GRATE SCALP BOLTER RANGER
RIDDLE SEARCH SIFTER CRIBBLE
STRAINER
SIFT TRY BOLT DUST SCRY RANGE SIEVE
DREDGE RIDDLE SCREEN WINNOW
CANVASS DRIBBLE
(— FLOUR) DRESS
(— IN) INFILTER
(— IN MINING) LUE

(— MEAL) BUNT
(— SHOT) TABLE
(— WHEAT) SCALP
SIGH SOB WIND MOURN SIGHT SOUGH
BEMOAN BEWAIL SORROW DEPLORE
SUSPIRE
SIGHT AIM EYE KEN RAY ESPY FACE GAZE
VIEW SCENE TRACK BEHOLD DESCRY
OBJECT TICKET DISCERN DISPLAY
EYESHOT GLIMPSE CONSPECT DISCOVER
EYESIGHT
(— FOR GUN) BEAD LEAF PEEP SCOPE
VISIE VIZZY HAUSSE GUNSIGHT
(— OF COMPASS) VANE
(— ON SURVEYOR'S STAFF) TARGET
(— TO SEE IF LEVEL) BONE
(—S OF CITY) LIONS
(AMAZING —) STOUND
(IMAGINARY —) VISION
(PITIFUL —) RUTH
(SECOND —) TAISCH
(SORRY —) BYSEN
SIGN INK DASH HINT MARK NOTE OMEN
TYPE BADGE COLON GHOST INDEX SIGIL
SPOOR STAMP TOKEN TRACE AUGURY
CARACT ENGAGE ENSIGN NOTICE
PARAPH REMARK SIGLUM SIGNAL
SYMBOL TITTLE AUSPICE EARMARK
ENDORSE INDICIA INSIGNE PORTENT
PRESAGE SHINGLE SYMPTOM VESTIGE
WARNING INDICANT INSTANCE
PROCLAIM TELLTALE
(— DOCUMENT) FIRM
(— FOR KEYNOTE) ISON
(— OF ALEHOUSE) LATTICE
(— OF AN IDEA) EMBLEM
(— OF APPROVAL) CACHET
(— OF CONTEMPT) FIG
(— OF DANGER) SEAMARK
(— OF GLOTTAL STOP) HAMZA
(— OF MULTIPLICATION) DOT
(— OF ZODIAC) LEO RAM BULL CRAB
GOAT LION ARIES HOUSE LIBRA TWINS
VIRGO ARCHER CANCER FISHES GEMINI
PISCES TAURUS VIRGIN BALANCE
SCORPIO AQUARIUS SCORPION
(— ON MAP) ICON
(ASTROLOGICAL —) CIPHER
(MATHEMATICAL —) NAME FUNCTOR
(MUSICAL —) GUIDA NEUME PRESA
SEGNO SWELL SIMILE FERMATA
(OUTWARD —) EVIDENCE
(SANSKRIT —) ANUSVARA
(SHILLING —) SOLIDUS
(SHORTHAND —) DIPHONE
(SLIGHT —) SURMISE
(SUBSCRIPT —) SUBFIX
(SUPERSTITIOUS —) GUEST
(TAVERN —) BUSH ALEBUSH ALEPOLE
CHECKER CHEQUER ALESTAKE
(TRAMP'S —) MONIKER
(VOWEL —) SEGOL SEGHOL
(SUFF.) SEME
SIGNAL GUN WAG BECK BELL BUZZ CALL
FLAG SIGN WAVE WINK ALERT BLINK
LIGHT SHORT SPEAK TOKEN WHIFF
ALARUM BANNER BEACON BECKON

BUZZER ENSIGN HERALD MARKER
BLINKER EMINENT NOTABLE RETREAT
STANDARD STRIKING
(— FISHERMEN) BALK
(— FOR A PARLEY) CHAMADE
(— FOR WHALERS) WAIF
(— IN WHIST) ECHO PETER
(— OF DISTRESS) SOS
(— ON RADARSCOPE) BLIP
(— TO ATTACK) CHARGE
(— TO BEGIN ACTION) CUE
(— WITH FLAGS) WIGWAG
(AUDIO —) HUM
(BOAT'S —) WAFF WAFT
(DEATH —) KNELL
(FOG —) FOGHORN TORPEDO DIAPHONE
(HUNTER'S —) SEEK PRIZE GIBBET
STRAKE
(MILITARY —) FLARE TURNOUT
ASSEMBLY
(NAVAL —) SECURE
(RADIO —) BEAM
(RAILROAD —) BANJO BOARD FUSEE
FUZEE TARGET HIGHBALL SEMAPHORE
(TRAFFIC —) ROBOT
(WARNING —) ALARM KLAXON TOCSIN
SIGNATURE FIRM HAND VISA FRANK
SHEET SIGIL THEME SIGNUM SIGNATOR
SIGNIFICANCE WIT BODY PITH SOUND
AMOUNT IMPORT INTENT STRESS
WEIGHT BEARING CONTENT GRAVITY
MEANING STRENGTH
(HIDDEN —) HYPONOIA
(MORAL —) ETHOS
SIGNIFICANT REAL RICH GREAT MEATY
EPOCHAL OMINOUS POINTED SERIOUS
PERTINENT
SIGNIFY SAY BEAR GIVE MEAN NOTE
WAVE AUGUR IMPLY SOUND SPEAK
SPELL TOKEN UTTER AMOUNT ASSERT
DENOTE IMPORT INTEND MATTER
BESPEAK CONNOTE DECLARE EXPRESS
PORTEND PRETEND INDICATE INTIMATE
MANIFEST
SIGURD (HORSE OF —) GRANI
(SLAIN BY —) FAFNIR
(SLAYER OF —) HOGNI
(VICTIM OF —) FAFNIR
(WIFE OF —) GUDRUN
SIKKIM (CAPITAL OF —) GANGTOK
(NATIVE OF —) RONG BHOTIA LEPCHA
(RIVER OF —) TISTA
SILAS MARNER (AUTHOR OF —)
ELIOT
(CHARACTER IN —) CASS AARON
DOLLY EPPIE NANCY SILAS MARNER
DUNSTAN GODFREY LAMMETER
WINTHROP
SILENCE GAG MUM HIST HUSH REST
CHOKE FLOOR PEACE QUIET SHUSH
STILL MUFFLE SETTLE STIFLE CONFUTE
SQUELCH DUMBNESS PRECLUDE
SUPPRESS
SILENT MUM HUSH MUTE SNUG CLOSE
MUTED STILL TACIT SULLEN TIPTOE
APHONIC ASPIRATE RESERVED RETICENT
TACITURN

SILHOUETTE SHADE ISOTYPE OUTLINE
SILK SOY ERIA MUGA FLOSS GREGE
TABBY CULGEE DUCAPE MANTUA
SENDAL SOUPLE TUSSAH CHIFFON
HABUTAI SCHAPPE TIFFANY TUSSORE
LUSTRINE MILANESE
(— FOR LININGS) SARCENET
(CORDED —) PADUASOY
(HEAVY —) CRIN ARMOZINE
(RAW —) GREIGE MARABOU TAYSAAM
TSATLEE
(REFUSE —) BURR
(TWILLED —) SURAH TOBINE FOULARD
LOUSINE
(UNDYED —) CORAH
(UNTWISTED —) SLEAVE
(UPHOLSTERY —) TABARET
(WASTE —) KNUB NOIL FRISON
SILL SOLE PLATE PATTEN SADDLE
MUDSILL DOORSILL
SILLINESS BOSH FOLLY BETISE INANITY
IDLENESS NONSENSE ABSURDITY
SILLY DAFT FOND FOOL NICE VAIN APISH
BALMY BATTY BUGGY DENSE DIZZY
GOOFY INANE KOOKY LOONY SAPPY
CRANKY CUCKOO DAWISH DOTARD
FRUITY SIMPLE SLIGHT SPOONY VACANT
ASININE FATUOUS FOOLISH FOPPISH
PUERILE SHALLOW ANSERINE FEATLESS
SILT DREGS DEPOSIT RESIDUE SULLAGE
SILVER LUNA MOON DIANA PLATE SYCEE
WHITE ARGENT BULLION STERLING
ARGENTINE
(DEBASED —) VELLON
(GERMAN —) ALBATA
(GILDED —) VERMEIL
(NICKEL —) PAKTONG
SIMEON (FATHER OF —) JACOB
(MOTHER OF —) LEAH
SIMILAR LIKE SAME SUCH ALIKE EVENLY
LIKELY COGNATE KINDRED SELFLIKE
SIMILARITY SIMILE ANALOGY
HOMOLOGY LIKENESS PARALLEL
SAMENESS
SIMMER FRY STEW SIMPER
SIMON ZELOTES
(BROTHER OF —) JESUS
(FATHER OF —) MATTATHIAS
(SON OF —) JUDAS
SIMPER MINCE SMIRK BRIDLE
SIMPLE LOW BALD BARE EASY FOND
MERE NICE ONLY PURE RUDE SNAP VERY
WEAK AFALD BLEAK DIZZY GREEN NAIVE
NAKED PLAIN SEELY SILLY SMALL SOBER
AEFALD CHASTE GLOBAL HOMELY
HONEST HUMBLE NATIVE OAFISH
RUSTIC SEMPLE SEVERE SINGLE STUPID
VIRGIN ARTLESS ASININE AUSTERE
BABYISH FATUOUS FOOLISH ONEFOLD
POPULAR SIMPLEX SPECIES ARCADIAN
EXPLICIT HOMEMADE INNOCENT
INORNATE SACKLESS SEMPLICE
SOLITARY
SIMPLETON DAW OAF SAP SOT BOOB
COOT CULL FOOL GAWP ROOK SOFT
ZANY GOOSE IDIOT NINNY NODDY
SAMMY SNIPE SPOON BADAUD DAUKIN

GANDER GREENY GULPIN NOODLE
SAWNEY DAWPATE ABDERITE FLATHEAD
INNOCENT KNOTHEAD MOONCALF
SOFTHEAD WISEACRE NINCOMPOOP
SIMPLICITY NICETY PURITY MODESTY
NAIVETE ELEGANCE
SIMPLIFY CLARIFY EXPOUND
SIMPLY JUST ALONE FONDLY MERELY
CRUDELY QUIETLY
SIMULATE ACT FAKE MOCK FEIGN MIMIC
AFFECT ASSUME
SIMULATED FAINT FAKED ERSATZ
FICTIOUS
SIMULATION ACTING PRETENSE
SIMULTANEOUSLY ONCE TOGETHER
SIN ERR DEBT EVIL HELL VICE BLAME
CRIME ERROR FAULT FOLLY GUILT SLOTH
WRONG FELONY OFFEND PLIGHT FRAILTY
OFFENSE INIQUITY PECCANCY TRESPASS
(DEADLY —) ACEDIA
(ORIGINAL —) ADAM
SINCE AS AGO FOR NOW GONE SYNE
WHERE BECAUSE WHEREAS INASMUCH
SINCERE GOOD REAL TRUE FRANK
DEVOUT HEARTY HONEST SIMPLE
CORDIAL EARNEST GENUINE UPRIGHT
FAITHFUL
SINCERELY TRULY SIMPLY DEVOUTLY
ENTIRELY HEARTILY
SINCERITY FAITH HEART VERITY
HONESTY REALITY
SINEWY WIRY NERVY THEWY ROBUST
FIBROUS STRINGY
SINFUL BAD EVIL VILE WRONG WICKED
PECCANT UNGODLY VICIOUS PIACULAR
SING HUM LIP CANT HYMN TUNE CAROL
CARRY CHANT DIRGE LYRIC RAISE
TOUCH CHAUNT CHORUS INTONE
RECORD RELISH STRAIN WARBLE
CHORTLE DESCANT TWEEDLE VOCALIZE
(— ABOVE TRUE PITCH) SHARP
(— AS A BEGGAR) GRIDDLE
(— BRISKLY) KNACK
(— CHEERFULLY) LILT
(— FLORIDLY) DIVIDE
(— HARSHLY) SCREAM
(— IN A CRACKED VOICE) CRAKE
(— IN CHORUS) CHOIR
(— IN LOW VOICE) CROON
(— IN SWISS MANNER) YODEL
(— LOUDLY) BELT TROLL TROLLOL
(— PRAISES) LAUD
(— ROMANCES) GESTE
(— SECOND PART) SURCENT
(— SOFTLY) SOWF
(— WITH FLOURISHES) ROULADE
SINGE GAS BURN SCORCH SCOWDER
SINGER ALTO BARD DIVA LARK SWAN
BASSO BUFFA BUFFO SKALD VOICE
BULBUL CANARY CANTOR LYRIST
CHANTER CROONER SOLOIST SONGMAN
SOPRANO TROLLER WARBLER CHANTEUR
FALSETTO MELODIST VOCALIST
(— OF FOLK SONGS) CANTADOR
(— OF ROCK MUSIC) ROCKER
(— OF THE GODS) GANDHARVA
(FEMALE —) SONGBIRD

(MENDICANT —) BUSKER
(PRINCIPAL —) PRIMOMO
(PROVENCAL —) MUSAR
SINGING CANT SCAT CHANT LYRIC
HYMNODY CANOROUS JONGLERY
(— CAROLS) PLYGAIN HODENING
(CANTORIAL —) HAZANUTH
(SIMULTANEOUS —) CHORUS
SINGLE ODD ONE LAST ONLY SOLE UNAL
SIMPLE UNIQUE ONEFOLD SIMPLEX
PECULIAR SEPARATE SINGULAR
SOLITARY PARTICULAR
SINGULAR ODD RARE QUEER QUAINT
SINGLE CURIOUS STRANGE PECULIAR
SINISTER DARK DIRE FELL GRIM DISMAL
MALIGN AWKWARD OBLIQUE OMINOUS
SINK DIP EBB SAG BORE DROP FADE FAIL
FALL KILL SWAG DRAIN DROOP DROWN
LAPSE LOWER SQUAT SWAMP CLOACA
GUTTER PLUNGE PUDDLE SETTLE
COMMODE DESCEND FOUNDER IMMERSE
RELAPSE SCUTTLE SUBSIDE DECREASE
(— A WELL) DRILL
(— AND FALL) TWINE
(— AS IN MUD) LAIR
(— DOWN) BOG AVALE STOOP DECLINE
(— FANGS INTO) STRIKE
(— INTO OOZE) WASEL
(— NAILHEAD) SET
(— SUDDENLY) SLUMP
(— UNDER TRIAL) QUAIL
SINUOUS WAVY SNAKEY SINUATE
SNAKISH WINDING INDENTED
SIP BIB NIP SUP SUCK TIFF WHIFF TIPPLE
DELIBATE
SIPHON CRANE THIEF VALINCH FLINCHER
SIR DAN DON AZAM BAAS HERR TUAN
BWANA SAHIB SENOR SAYYID SIGNOR
EFFENDI SIGNORE
SIREN HOOTER ENTICER LORELEI
MERMAID
SIRUP LICK GOLDY SYRUP GOWDIE
ORGEAT RUNOFF LIQUEUR MOLASSES
QUIDDANY
SISSY SISTER CHICKEN PANTYWAIST
SISTER NUN SIB SIS GIRL NURSE SISSY
WOMAN
(YOUNGER —) CADETTE
SISTERHOOD BEGUINES SORORITY
SISYPHUS (BROTHER OF —) ATHAMAS
SALMONEUS
(FATHER OF —) AEOLUS
(MOTHER OF —) ENARETE
(SON OF —) SINON GLAUCUS
ORNYTION
(WIFE OF —) MEROPE
SIT SET SEAT BENCH ROOST SQUAT
WEIGH BESTRIDE
(— ABRUPTLY) CLAP
(— ASTRIDE) CROSS HORSE STRADDLE
(— ERECT LIKE A DOG) BEG
(— FORCIBLY) DOSS
(— IN JUDGMENT) DEEM
(— ON) BROOD COVER
(— OVER EGGS) RUCK BROOD CLOCK
SITE AREA PLOT SEAT SITU SPOT TOFT

FIELD PLACE STAND STANCE BIVOUAC
HABITAT STEADING
SITUATE PLACE POSITION
SITUATED SET SEATED STATURED
SITUATION JOB LIE CASE CRIB PASS
PLOT POST SEAT SITE SPOT BERTH
SIEGE SITUS STATE STEAD ASSIZE
CHANCE ESTATE OFFICE PLIGHT STATUS
EPISODE PICTURE PORTENT POSTURE
STATION INCIDENT INSTANCE POSITURE
STANDING UBIQUITY
(— BESET BY DIFFICULTIES) SCRAPE
(— IN FARO) CATHOP
(— IN OMBRE) CODILLE
(— OF PERPLEXITY) HOBBLE STRAIT
(AMUSING —) BAR
(AWKWARD —) SCRAPE JACKPOT
(CRITICAL —) CLUTCH
(DIFFICULT —) BOX BOGGLE
PREDICAMENT
(DISTRESSING —) STYMIE
(FAVORABLE —) BREAK
(PAINFUL —) DISTRESS
(RELATIVE —) BEARING
(TIGHT —) CRUNCH
(UNPLEASANT —) BUMMER
(UNSATISFACTORY —) DILEMMA
SIXPENCE HOG PIG BEND KICK ZACK
SIMON SPRAT TIZZY BENDER FIDDLE
TANNER TESTON CRIPPLE FIDDLER
SIZABLE SNUG HEFTY LARGE HANDSOME
SIZE WAX AREA BIND BULK MARK MASS
DRESS GIRTH MOUND PLANK SCALE
EXTENT FORMAT GROWTH MICKLE
MOISON PICNIC SIZING BIGNESS
CONTENT CORSAGE FITTING THIRTEEN
TWELVEMO
(— OF BOOK) FOLIO
(— OF HOLE) BORE
(— OF HOSIERY) POPE
(— OF PARTICLE) GRIND
(— OF ROPE) GRIST
(— OF SLATE) PEGGY IMPERIAL
(— OF TYPE) GEM PICA RUBY AGATE
CANON ELITE PEARL MINION PRIMER
BREVIER DIAMOND EMERALD ENGLISH
PARAGON COLUMBIAN
(CLOTHING —) LONG SHORT STOUT
JUNIOR PETITE
(EXTRA LARGE —) SUPER
(GREAT —) MAGNITUDE
(RELATIVE —) SCALE
SKATE BOB RAY RINK SKIT FLAIR SCULL
BATOID PATTEN ROCKER ROLLER
RUNNER TINKER CHOPINE FLAPPER
SKELETON CAGE MORT ATOMY BONES
FRAME ANATOMY CARCASS RAWBONE
ARMATURE OSSATURE
SKEPTIC DOUBTER INFIDEL ZETETIC
APIKOROS APORETIC
SKEPTICAL ACADEMIC APORETIC
DOUBTFUL
SKEPTICISM HUMISM UNBELIEF
SKETCH BIT DASH DRAW LIMN PLAN
VIEW PAINT TRACE APERCU DESIGN
DOODLE SCHEME SPLASH BOZZETO

SKETCH DRAUGHT DRAWING EBAUCHE OUTLINE
MONOGRAM PROSPECT VIGNETTE
(— BEFOREHAND) INDICATE
(AUTOBIOGRAPHICAL —) VITA
(BIOGRAPHICAL —) ELOGY
(HERALDIC —) TRICK
(OUTDOORS —) LANDSKIP
(PRELIMINARY —) DRAFT ABBOZZO
MAQUETTE
(ROUGH —) NOTE CROQUIS POCHADE
ESQUISSE
(SATIRICAL —) SKIT
SKEWER PROG SPIT PRICK TRUSS
BROCHETTE
SKID DOG DRAG SLUE DRIFT SLOUGH
SLIPPER SIDESLIP
(— LOGS) SNAKE TRAVOY TWITCH
(— ON RAIL) SKATE
(AUTOMOBILE —) SPINOUT
(FENDER —) GLANCER
(IRON —) SABOT
SKIFF CANOE SHELL CAIQUE DINGHY
SAMPAN
SKILL ART WIT FEAT FEEL HAND CRAFT
KNACK TRICK ENGINE ABILITY ADDRESS
APTNESS CUNNING FINESSE MASTERY
PROWESS SCIENCE ARTIFICE CAPACITY
DEFTNESS FACILITY INDUSTRY LEARNING
SKILLED OLD WISE ADEPT ASTUTE
MASTER VERSED HOTSHOT EDUCATED
SKILLFUL APT SLY ABLE DEFT FEAT FINE
GOOD PERT TIDY WISE ADEPT CANNY
HANDY SLICK ADROIT ARTFUL CLEVER
CRAFTY DAEDAL EXPERT SUBTLE
CUNNING DEXTROUS PROFICIENT
SKIM TOP SCUD SKIP FLEET GRAZE SCALE
SKIRR BROWSE SAMPLE SKITTER
SKIMPY CHARY SPARE MEAGER SCANTY
STINGY
SKIN KIP BARK CASE DERM FELL FLAY
HIDE PEAU PELT RIND BALAT FLOAT
GENET SLUFF STRIP CORIUM PELTRY
CUTICLE DOESKIN KIDSKIN LEATHER
PELLAGE BUCKSKIN LAMBSKIN
SEALSKIN TEGUMENT
(— FOR BOOKBINDING) BASAN
(— FOR HOLDING WATER) KIRBEH
(— OF BACON) SWARD
(— OF BOARDS) CARPET
(— OF FRUIT) PEEL
(— OF GOOSE) APRON
(— OF INSECT) CAST
(— OF POTATO) JACKET
(— OF POULTRY NECK) HELZEL
(— OF RABBIT) RACK CONEY
(— OF SEAL) SCULP
(— OF THE HEAD) SCALP
(— OF WALNUT) ZEST
(— OF YOUNG CALF) SLINK DEACON
(— WITH WOOL REMAINING ON IT)
WOOLFELL
(BARE —) BUFF
(BEAVER —) PLEW
(BOAR'S —) SHIELD
(CAST —) SPOIL SLOUGH EXUVIAE
(CHAFED OR SORE —) IRE
(CHAMOIS —) FURWA

(DEEP LAYER OF THE —) CUTIS
(FAWN —) NEBRIS
(INNER PART OF THE —) DERMA
(LAMB — PREPARED LIKE FUR)
BUDGE
(OUTER —) HUSK
(PENDULOUS FOLD OF —) DEWLAP
(ROUGHTANNED —) CRUST
(SHARK —) SHAGREEN
(SHEEP —) BASIL
(SQUIRREL —) VAIR
(THICKENED —) BRAWN
(THIN —) FILM PELLICLE STRIFFEN
(60 —S) TURN
SKINNY BONY LEAN THIN SLINK
SKIP DAP HIP BALK FOOT JUMP LEAP SLIP
TRIP BOUND CAPER DANCE FRISK SALTO
SKITE VAULT GAMBOL GLANCE LAUNCH
SPRING SALTATE SKITTER RICOCHET
SKIRMISH FRAY BRUSH CLASH MELEE
BICKER HASSLE
SKIRT CUT HUG LAP COAT JUPE MIDI
MINI TUBE TUTU JUPON STRIP TREND
TWIST DIRNDL HOBBLE JUMPER KIRTLE
PEPLUM SARONG TAMEIN BASQUINE
(ARMOR —) TASSES LAMBOYS
(DIVIDED —) CULOTTE
(HOOP —) CRINOLINE
(LONG —) MAXI
(TARTAN —) KILT ARISAID
SKITTISH SHY GOOSY FLISKY SPOOKY
FLIGHTY SCADDLE BOGGLISH SKITTERY
SKULDUGGERY JOUKERY PAWKERY
SKULK LURK MOOCH SCOUT
SKULL BEAN POLL SCALP VAULT MAZARD
SCONCE CRANIUM HARNPAN PANNICLE
(BACK OF —) OCCIPUT
(INCOMPLETE —) CALVARIA
(UPPER HALF OF —) SINCIPUT
SKULLCAP COIF PIXIE VAULT BEANIE
CALOTTE CAPELINE
(ARABIAN —) CHECHIA
(JEWISH —) YARMULKE
(STEEL —) SECRET
SKUNK ATOC ATOK PUSS HURON ZORIL
CHINCHA POLECAT SMELLER MUSTELID
ZORRILLO
(JAVANESE —) TELEDU
SKY BLUE HIGH LIFT LOFT AZURE ETHER
VAULT CAELUS CANOPY HEAVEN
WELKIN HEAVENS OLYMPUS
SLAB CANT PARE SLAT BLADE BOARD
LINER PANEL SLATE TABLE FLITCH
MARVER PAVIOR RUNNER FLAPPET
PLANCHE PORPHYRY
(— BY SINK) BUNKER
(— OF CLAY) BAT
(— OF COAL) SKIP SLIP
(— OF ICE) SCONCE
(— OF LIMESTONE) BALATTE
(— OF MARBLE) DALLE
(— OF PEAT) SCAD
(— OF SANDSTONE) COMAL
(— OVER BROOK) CLAM
(BROKEN-OFF —) BLAUD
(GRINDING —) MULLER
(HOPSCOTCH —) PEEVER

(MEMORIAL —) LEDGER
(PAINTER'S —) SLANT
(PLASTERER'S —) HAWK
(STONE —) PLANK STELA STELE
INKSTONE

SLACK LAX OFF CULM LASH SLOW SOFT
VEER CHECK FLOWN LOOSE TARDY
ABATED FLABBY FLAPPY REMISS
RELAXED CARELESS DILATORY INACTIVE
NEGLIGENT
(— IN TRIGGER) CREEP
(— OF ROPE) SLATCH
(— SHEET OF SAIL) FLOW

SLACKEN LAG EASE FLAG SLOW DELAY
LOOSE QUAIL RELAX EXOLVE RELENT
UNBEND

SLAG SCAR DROSS CINDER DANDER
SCORIA

SLAM CLAP DASH SLOG CLASH GRAND
PLANK SLOSH FLOUNCE

SLANDER CANT BELIE LIBEL NOISE
SMEAR BEFOUL DEFAME INJURE MALIGN
MISSAY VILIFY ASPERSE CALUMNY
SCANDAL TRADUCE BACKBITE
DEROGATE ASPERSION

SLANG CANT ARGOT FLASH DIALECT

SLANT TIP CANT SKEW TILT BEVEL
SLOPE SPLAY STOOP DIAGONAL

SLANTING AWRY BIAS CANT SKEW
BEVEL SLOPE ASLANT ASLOPE SQUINT
OBLIQUE SLOPING SIDELONG

SLAP BOX DAB BLOW CLAP CUFF FLAP
LICK SNUB SPAT CLINK CLOUT CRACK
POTCH SKITE SMACK SPANK TWANG
BUFFET SLIGHT STRIKE TINGLER
(— HARD) BLAD
(RANDOM —) FLAY

SLASH CUT JAG COUP GASH SLIT KNIFE
MINCE SCORE SCORCH STREAK SLITTER

SLAT LAG FLAT PALE WAND BLADE
STAVE SPLINE BEDSTAFF

SLATE RAG SLAT FRAME KILLAS TABLET
SHALDER

SLATTERN DAW FROW SLUT DOLLY
FAGOT MAWKS MOPSY DOLLOP MALKIN
SLOVEN TROLLOP SLUMMOCK

SLAUGHTER FELL KILL SLAM SLAY
BUTCH MURDER BUTCHER CARNAGE
KILLING SHAMBLE BUTCHERY MASSACRE
(— ACCORDING TO MOSLEM LAW)
HALAL
(— OF LARGE NUMBER) HECATOMB
(WHOLESALE —) QUELL

SLAUGHTERHOUSE ABATTOIR
BUTCHERY MATADERO SHAMBLES

SLAVE BOY BOND DUPE ESNE SERF
HELOT ABJECT CUMHAL GUINEA
MAMLUK THRALL VASSAL BONDMAN
CAPTIVE CHATTEL HACKNEY SERVANT
BONDMAID MAMELUKE MANCIPLE
PRAEDIAL ODALISQUE
(— IN TEMPLE) HIEROS
(— WHO WHIPS OTHERS) LORARIUS
(DEFORMED —) CALIBAN
(FREED —) CLIENT
(FUGITIVE —) MAROON CIMMARON

(GALLEY —) FORSAR FORSADO
SFORZATO
(HINDU —) DAS DASI

SLAVEDRIVER RUSHER

SLAVERY YOKE THRALL BONDAGE
HELOTRY MIZRAIM THRALDOM
SERVITUDE

SLAY KILL SMITE SPILL MURDER STRIKE
BUTCHER EXECUTE STRANGLE
SLAUGHTER

SLED LUGE TODE JUMBO SCOOT SLIDE
SLEDGE SLEIGH BOBSLED CLIPPER
COASTER DOGSLED KOMATIK MONOSKI
SLIPPER TRAVOIS TOBOGGAN

SLEDGE DRAG DRAY LUGE SLED GURRY
SLIDE TRAIN TROLL SLEIGH KOMATIK
TROLLEY
(— FOR CRIMINALS) HURDLE
(— FOR STRAIGHTENING RAILS) GAG
(LOG —) SLOOP TIEBOY
(MINER'S —) MALLET

SLEEK SOFT JOLLY SILKY SLICK TRICK
SILKEN SLIGHT SMARMY SMOOTH
SVELTE SOIGNEE SLIPPERY

SLEEP BED LIE CAMP DORM DOZE REST
WINK CRASH ROOST DROWSE SOMNUS
SLUMBER WINKING
(— BROKEN BY SNORING) GRUFF
(— ON A PERCH) JOUK
(DEEP —) SWOON
(LIGHT —) SLOOM
(PRETENDED —) DOGSLEEP
(PROFOUND —) SOPOR
(SHORT —) NAP SIESTA SNOOZE

SLEEPY DOZY HEAVY NODDY DROWSY
GROGGY MORPHIC SLUMBERY SOMNIFIC

SLEEVE ARM ARMLET MANCHE BUSHING
HOUSING THIMBLE
(— ON A SHAFT) CANNON
(— ON GUN) BAND
(CANVAS —) DROGUE
(HANGING —) TAB
(LEG-OF-MUTTON —) GIGOT
(LONG —) POKE
(TAPERED —) SKEIN

SLEIGH PUNG SLED TRAIN BERLIN
CUTTER SLEAD CARIOLE

SLENDER FINE HAIR LANK LEAN SLIM
THIN FAINT LATHY REEDY SLEEK SMALL
SPIRY WISPY SCANTY SLIGHT STALKY
SVELTE TENDER GRACILE LISSOME
SLIVERY THREADY ACICULAR ETHEREAL
HAIRLIKE

SLICE CUT BITE CHOP FLAP JERK GIGOT
SHARE SHAVE SKELB CANTLE CULPON
SLIVER TARGET TRENCH SHAVING
COSSETTE
(— CUT IN PLOWING) FLAG
(— OF BACON) BARD LARDON RASHER
(— OF BREAD) BUTTY WHANG CROUTE
TRENCHER
(— OF CHEESE) KEBBOC
(— OF COAL) SKIP
(— OF FISH) COBBIN
(— OF MEAT) STEAK COLLOP CUTLET
SCALLOP TAILZIE
(— OF MEAT OR FISH) PAUPIETTE

(— OF SMOKED SALMON) CORNET
(— OF TOAST) ROUND
(— REMOVED FROM ROADWAY)
CANCH
(— WITH MOTIONS) SAW
(—S OF APPLES) CHOPS
(LARGE —) BLAD DODGE
(THICK —) SLAB WHANG
(THIN —) CHIP WAFER SECTION
SLIDE SLEW SLIP CHUTE COAST CREEP
GLIDE HURRY SCOOT SHIRL SLOUGH
SLITHER GLISSADE SCHLEIFER
(— A DIE) SLUR
(— CARDS) SKIN
(— DOWN) RUSE SLUMP
(— FOR LOWERING CASKS) POLEYNE
(— ON DRUMHEAD) BRACE
(— SIDEWISE) SKID
(TENT —) EUPHROE
SLIGHT CUT OFF EASY FINE HURT POOR
SLAP SLIM SLUR SNUB THIN WEAK
FILMY GAUZY LIGHT MINOR SCANT
SMALL FLIMSY FORGET LITTLE MINUTE
REMOTE TWIGGY FRAGILE NEGLECT
NOMINAL SHALLOW SKETCHY SLENDER
DELICATE OVERLOOK
SLIGHTER LESS
SLIGHTEST FIRST LEAST
SLIGHTINGLY LIGHTLY
SLIGHTLY FAINTLY SOMEWHAT
(PREF.) MI(O)
(SUFF.) ESCENT ULOUS
SLIM THIN GAUNT SLIGHT SLENDER
TENUOUS
SLIME GORE OOZE SLAB SLIP GLEET
SLUDGE SCHLICH SLUBBER
SLIMY OOZY SLAB MUCID GLAIRY
MUCOUS SLEECHY
SLING LOOP FLING BRIDGE BRIDLE
HALTER
(— FOR HAULING GAME) TUMPLINE
(— OF BRAIDED FIBERS) MA
SLINGSHOT SLAPPY TWEAKER
CATAPULT SHANGHAI
SLINK SLY CAST LEER LURK PEAK SHIRK
SNEAK
(— AWAY) SHAG SLOKE FLINCH MIZZLE
SHRINK
SLIP DIP NOD BALK CARD CHIT FALL RUSE
SKEW SKID SLUR BONER CHECK ERROR
FLIER GLIDE LABEL LAPSE SCION SHIFT
SKATE SLICK SLIDE SLUMP STALK
COUPON MISCUE SLURRY TICKET
FOUNDER MISSTEP MORTISE STUMBLE
GLISSADE
(— AWAY) GO BILK SKIN WISE EVADE
ELAPSE
(— FROM A PLANT) STALLON
(— OF FISH) RAND
(— OF PAPER) ALLONGE
(— OF PARCHMENT) PANEL
(— OF WOOD) SPILL REGLET
(— OFF COURSE) SLEW SLOUGH
(— ON CARELESSLY) SLIVE
(— OUT) TIB
(— SECRETLY) CREEM
(— SMOOTHLY) SWIM

(— UP) BLUNDER
(CERAMICS —) SLOP ENGOBE
(INFANT'S —) GERTRUDE
(PILLOW —) BIER
(PREF.) CLAD(O)
SLIPPER FLAT MULE PUMP SOCK GLAVE
MOYLE SCUFF BALLET BOOTEE DORSAY
JULIET PANTON SANDAL CRAKOWE
SCUFFER BABOUCHE PANTOFLE
SLIPPERY GLIB GLARY SLEEK SLICK
SOAPY CRAFTY GREASY LUBRIC SHIFTY
ELUSIVE EVASIVE GLIBBERY
SLIPSHOD JERRY RAGGED SLOPPY
UNKEMPT SLAPDASH SLOVENLY
SLIT CUT EYE GATE NICK PORT RACE
RENT SCAR SLOT VENT CRACK CRANNY
OSTIUM FISSURE PLACKET APERTURE
BOTHRIUM
(— HIND LEG) HARL
(— IN EDGE OF SHIELD) BOUCHE
(— IN ORGAN PIPE) MOUTH
(— IN STONE) GRIKE
(— MADE BY CUT) KERF
(ORNAMENTAL —) SLASH
SLIVER SHAVE SKELF SLICE SHIVER
SPLINTER
(— OF WOOL) ROLL ROVE
(SPINNING —) END RIBBON DELIVERY
SLOBBER SLOP SLUP SMARM SLAVER
SLATHER
SLOGAN CRY CACHET PHRASE
CATCHCRY CATCHWORD SHIBBOLETH
SLOOP STAR BOYER COMET SMACK
SCHUIT HOOGAARS
SLOPE UP DIP LIE BANK BENT BRAE CANT
CAST DROP FALL HILL LEAN RAMP RISE
SINK TILT BEVEL CLIFF COAST PITCH
SCARP SLANT SPLAY STEEP TALUS
VERGE ASCENT BAJADA BREAST
BROACH ESCARP SHELVE TUMBLE
UPRISE DOWNSET INCLINE LEANING
PENDANT UPGRADE BANKSIDE GLISSADE
GRADIENT SHOULDER SNOWBANK
(— BACK) BATTER
(— DOWN) SHED
(— OF CUESTA) INFACE
(— OF ROOF) CURB
(— OF STERNPOST) RAKE
(— UPWARD) CLIMB ASCEND BATTER
(DOWNWARD —) HANG DEVALL
DECLINE DESCENT HANGING DOWNHILL
(GENTLE —) GLACIS
(MARGINAL —) CESS
(MOUNTAIN —) ADRET
(SKIING —) SCHUSS
(STEEP —) BROW HEADWALL
SLOPING CANT ASLOPE SHELVY
SCARPED DOWNHILL SIDELING
SLOPPY JUICY SOPPY SOZZLY SLAPDASH
SLATTERN SLIPSHOD
SLOT COVE DROP SPLINE KEYHOLE
GUIDEWAY
SLOTHFUL FAT IDLE LAZY INERT
INDOLENT SLUGGISH
SLOUCH LOLLOP LOUNGE TROLLOP
SHAMMOCK

SLOUGH CORE SHED SLEW SLUE BAYOU SHUCK SLUFF SPOIL SWAMP DISCARD

SLOVENLY DOWDY MESSY BLOWZY FROWZY GRUBBY SHABBY SLOPPY SLOVEN UNTIDY SLOUCHY CARELESS SLIPSHOD SLUBBERY SLUTTISH

SLOW LAG LAX WET DULL LATE LAZY SULK BLUNT HEAVY POKEY TARDY UNAPT ARREST HINDER RETARD SLOOMY SOODLY TRAILY COSTIVE DRONISH HALTING LANGUID TEDIOUS INACTIVE SLUGGISH
(— DOWN) SEIZE
(— IN BURNING) SOFT
(— IN MOVEMENT) GRAVE INERT SULKY
(— OF MIND) STUPID
(— TO LEARN) BACKWARD
(— TO RESPOND) GROSS
(— UP) SLACK SLACKEN
(MODERATELY —) ANDANTE
(MUSICALLY —) LENTO
(PLEASANTLY —) SOFT
(VERY —) LARGO

SLOWLY DULLY GRAVE LENTO ADAGIO GENTLY HEAVILY

SLUG BUST LINE MILL PLOW SHOT SNAG CLUMP SNAIL STRIKE TREPANG GEEPOUND

SLUGGARD DAW DRONE BUZZARD SLOWBACK SLUGABED

SLUGGISH DOZY DULL FOUL LATE LAZY LOGY SLOW DOPEY FAINT HEAVY INERT SULKY BOVINE DRAGGY DROWSY LEADEN SLEEPY SUPINE TORPID COSTIVE DORMANT LAGGARD LANGUID LUMPISH RESTIVE INACTIVE INDOLENT SLOTHFUL

SLUICE GOOL GOUT TRUNK CLOUGH FENDER LAUNDER PENSTOCK WASTWEIR

SLUMBER DORM DOZE REST SLEEP DROWSE

SLUMP FALL FLOP SLOUCH LETDOWN

SLUR BIND COULE GLIDE SCRUFF SLIGHT LIGATURE
(— IN PRINTING) SHAKE

SLUSH MIRE SLOP SLOSH STUFF SWASH LOPPER SLUDGE SLOBBER

SLUT MAUX BITCH QUEAN DOLLOP MALKIN DROSSEL PUCELLE SLATTERN

SLY ARCH FOXY SLIM CANNY LEERY LOOPY PAWKY SNAKY ARTFUL ASTUTE CRAFTY FELINE SUBTLE SUPPLE CUNNING EVASIVE FURTIVE POLITIC SUBTILE GUILEFUL SNEAKING STEALTHY THIEVISH CLANDESTINE

SMACK BANG BARK BIFF BUSS KISS SLAP TANG SAVOR SPICE TASTE TWANG BARQUE FLAVOR SPANKER SLAPDASH

SMALL BIT SMA BABY MEAN SEED SLIM WEAK BIJOU BITTY DINKY ELFIN PETIT PETTY WEENY BANTAM GRUBBY LITTLE MIDGET NARROW PEANUT PETITE SCANTY SLIGHT CAPSULE PICCOLO SCRIMPY SLENDER THRIFTY MINIATURE MINISCULE
(— AND NUMEROUS) MILIARY
(— AND THICK) DUMPY DUMPTY

(— BUT TANGIBLE) CERTAIN
(CONTEMPTIBLY —) MEASLY
(DAINTILY —) MIGNON
(EXCESSIVELY —) BOXY
(VERY —) WEE FINE TINY DWARF MICRO PUSIL PYGMY TEENY MINUTE MINIKIN TIDDLEY DWARFISH

SMALLEST FIRST LEAST MINIM MINIMUS

SMALL-MINDED PETTY PICAYUNE

SMALLNESS NANISM EXILITY FEWNESS PAUCITY EXIGUITY SCARCITY

SMALLPOX POX VARIOLA ALASTRIM

SMART NIP BRAW FLIP FOXY NICE POSH RACY SNAP SPRY SWAG TRIG ACUTE BRISK CLEAN FLASH HEADY NIFTY PEERT RITZY SASSY SAUCY SHARP SLEEK SLICK SPICY SPRIG STING SWANK TRICK BRIGHT CLEVER DAPPER JAUNTY PERTLY SHREWD SPIFFY SPRUCE SWANKY KNOWING PUNGENT SWAGGER VOGUISH

SMASH BASH BUMP CAVE DASH BREAK CRACK CRASH SOCKO STAVE WRECK SHATTER DEMOLISH STRAMASH

SMEAR DAB RUB BLOT BLUR DAUB GLOB MOIL SLARE SMARM SULLY BEDAUB BESLAB DEFILE SLAVER SLURRY SMIRCH SMUDGE STREAK BESMEAR PLASTER POLLUTE SPLOTCH
(— OVER) ENGLUTE
(— WITH BLOOD) GILD
(— WITH EGG WHITE) GLAIR
(— WITH MUD) CLART SLIME
(— WITH SOMETHING STICKY) GAUM GORM LIME
(— WITH TAR) PAY
(— WITH WAX) CERE

SMELL NOSE ODOR VENT AROMA SAVOR SCENT SMACK SNIFF SNUFF TASTE OLFACT BREATHE PERFUME
(— AFTER PREY) BREVIT
(— OFFENSIVELY) REEK
(DAMP FUSTY —) RAFT
(DISAGREEABLE —) GOO PONG STENCH
(MUSTY —) FUST
(OFFENSIVE —) FUNK FETOR STINK MEPHITIS
(STRONG —) HOGO
(SWEET —) SWEET

SMILE BEAM GRIN FLASH SMUDGE SMIRKLE
(— AMOROUSLY) SMICKER
(AFFECTED —) SMIRK
(SELF-CONSCIOUS —) SIMPER

SMILING GOOD BONNY RIANT SMILY BONNIE RIDENT SMIRKY TWINKLY

SMIRCH SOIL SMEAR SULLY SLURRY TARNISH

SMITE FRAP GIRD SLAY FLING STRIKE
(— WITH LIGHTNING) LEVEN

SMITH MIMIR REGIN BOSSER FORGER SMITHY FARRIER WAYLAND FORGEMAN

SMITHY FORGE STITHY STUDDIE FARRIERY

SMOCK BRAT SLOP KAMIS JIBBAH JUMPER CHEMISE

SMOKE PEW USE BLOW FOGO FUME

NAVE PIPE REEK REECH SMEEK STIVE
VAPOR WHIFF BREATH BUCCAN SMUDGE
INCENSE SMOLDER SMOTHER
(FROST —) BARBER
(HAZE AND —) SMAZE
(OFFENSIVE —) FUNK
(TOBACCO —) BLAST

SMOKESTACK STACK FUNNEL TUNNEL
CHIMNEY

SMOKY HAZY DINGY FUMID FUMOSE
REECHY SMUDGY

SMOOTH DUB FAT COMB DRAG EASE
EASY EVEN FACE FAIR FILE FLAT GLAD
GLIB HONE IRON SOFT TRIM BLAND
CLEAR COIN DIGHT DOLCE DRESS
EMERY FLOAT LEVEL LITHE NAKED PLAIN
PLANE PRESS QUIET SILKY SLICK SOAPY
SUANT SUAVE TERSE BUFFED CREAMY
FLUENT GLOSSY GREASE GREASY
LEGATO LIMBER MANGLE POLITE SILKEN
SLIGHT STROKE SVELTE FLATTEN
GLABROUS GRAZIOSO LEVIGATE
UNRUFFLE
(— BY BREAKING LUMPS) BILDER
(— MARBLE) GRIT
(— ONESELF UP) PREEN
(— OVER) GLOZE PLASTER
(— TYPE) KERN
(HYPOCRITICALLY —) SLEEK
(PHONETICALLY —) LENE LENIS

SMOOTHLY SLICK EASILY EVENLY
GLIBLY SWEETLY POLITELY

SMOTHER BURKE CHOKE SMOKE
SMUDGE STIFLE OPPRESS SMOLDER

SMUDGE BLUR GAUM SLUR SMUT SOIL
SOOT SMEAR SMOKE SOILURE

SMUG SLEEK SUAVE

SMUGGLE RUN STEAL BOOTLEG
SHUFFLE

SMUGGLER OWLER RUNNER SPOTSMAN
(— OF DRUGS) MULE

SMUT BLACK BLECK COOMB GRIME
SMUTCH SMATTER

SMUTTY BAWDY DIRTY SOOTY SULTRY
BARNYARD

SNACK BIT CUT BAIT BITE NOSH SNAP
BUTTY NACHO SHARE TASTE SNATCH

SNAG KNAG STUB POINT SNAGGLE

SNAKE
(ALSO SEE SERPENT AND REPTILE)
ASP BOA BOMA NAJA ABOMA COBRA
CRIBO JIBOA KRAIT MAMBA RACER
VIPER BONGAR CHITAL DABOIA ELAPID
HISSER PYTHON ROLLER RUNNER
WENONA BOKADAM CAMOODI CRAWLER
CREEPER CULEBRA DIAPSID LANGAHA
RATTLER REPTILE SCYTALE SERPENT
ANACONDA BONETAIL BUNGARUM
CROTALID EGGEATER FLATHEAD
MOCCASIN OPHIDIAN RINGHALS

SNAP ZIP BARK BITE CHOP HUFF JERK
PIPE BREAK CLACK FLICK GANCH KNACK
PHOTO SMACK BLUDGE SNATCH
FASTENER PUSHOVER
(— AT) HANCH
(— LIGHTLY) KNICK
(— OFF) SNIP

(— TOGETHER) CRASH
(— UP) SNUP SNAFFLE
(— WITH FINGER) LIRP FILIP THRIP
FILLIP

SNAPPY CRISP JEMMY NIPPY ZIPPY

SNARE GIN NET PIT SET BAIT FANG HOOK
LACE LIME TOIL TRAP WIRE BRAKE
CATCH FRAUD LATCH LEASH SNARL
TRAIN COBWEB SNATCH MANTRAP
PITFALL SNIGGLE SPRINGE BIRDLIME
INVEIGLE MOUSETRAP
(— DEER) WITHE
(— FOR ELEPHANTS) KEDDAH
(FISH —) WEEL

SNARL ARR BITE GIRN GNAR TWIT WAFF
GNARL GRILL KNURL RAVEL TWINE
BOWWOW BUMBLE MUCKER TANGLE
GRIZZLE GRUMBLE

SNATCH NAB NIP GRAB HINT SNAP SNIP
CATCH CLICK GRASP PLUCK SWIPE
SWOOP TWEAK WREST SNITCH TWITCH
WRENCH GRABBLE

SNEAK GRUB LURK PIMP LURCH MOOCH
SCOUT SHARK SHIRK SKULK SLIDE SLINK
MICHER WEASEL SNIGGLE

SNEER SHY GIBE GIRN JEER MOCK FLEER
FLOUT SCOFF SCOUT GIZZEN WRINKLE
RIDICULE

SNICKER TITTER SMIRKLE SNIGGER
SNIGGLE

SNIDE ORNERY

SNIFF NOSE VENT WIND SMELL SNUFF
SNIVEL SNIFFLE

SNIP CUT CLIP CROP MINX NICK SHRED
SNICK SCISSOR

SNIVEL BUBBLE SNIFFLE SNUFFLE

SNOB SNOOT FLUNKY SHONEEN

SNOBBISH RITZY DICKTY SNOOTY
UPSTAGE

SNOOP PRY PEEK PEEP SNEAK GUMSHOE

SNORT BLOW ROUT TOOT VENT BLURT
SNEER SNORE WHOOF EXCLAIM

SNOUT NEB BEAK BILL NOSE SERRA
SNOOT MUZZLE NOZZLE ROSTRUM

SNOW CORN DRIP GRUE COVER SPOSH
STORM SUGAR WHITE POWDER
SCOUTHER
(— PELLETS) GRAUPEL
(— SLIGHTLY) SPIT
(DISSOLVING —) FLUSH
(DRIFTED —) WINDLE
(GLACIER —) FIRN NEVE BLIZZ
(HEAVY FALL OF —) PASH
(MUSHY —) SLOB
(NEW-FALLEN —) MANNA
(PARTLY MELTED —) SLUSH
(WHIRLING —) SKIRL

SNOWFALL PASH SKIFT FLURRY ONDING

SNUB AIR RITZ SLAP SWANK REBUFF
SLIGHT SETDOWN

SNUFF TOP VENT SNIFF TABAC COHOBA
PULVIL RAPPEE STIFLE BERGAMOT
MACCABOY

SNUG LEW COZY NEAT TAUT CANNY
CLOSE QUEME TIGHT

SNUGGLE BURROW CUDDLE CROODLE

SO SAE SUCH THAT THIS THUS
INSOMUCH SUCHWISE

SOAK SOB SOD SOG WET BUCK BINGE
DROWN SOUSE STEEP TOAST DRENCH
IMBRUE SEETHE SPONGE SWELTER
SATURATE
(— A CASK) GROG
(— FLAX) RET
(— IN) SOP FEATHER

SOAKED SOGGY SOPPY SODDEN WATERY
DRUNKEN DRAGGLED

SOAP SAPO SUDS CHIPS CASTILE
SAVONETTE
(CAKE OF —) TABLET TABULATE
(LIQUID —) FIT

SOAR FLY FLOAT MOUNT PLANE
SPIRE TOWER ASCEND ASPIRE

SOB YEX SOUGH BLUBBER SINGULT

SOBER SAD CALM COOL SAGE CIVIL
FRESH GRAVE QUIET STAID SEDATE
SEVERE SOLEMN SOMBER STEADY
EARNEST PENSIVE REGULAR SERIOUS
DECOROUS MODERATE

SOBRIETY DRYNESS GRAVITY
ABSTINENCE

SOCIABLE COSY CHUMMY CLUBBY
FOLKSY SOCIAL AFFABLE AMIABLE
INNERLY FAMILIAR INFORMAL

SOCIAL DISTAL PUBLIC SUPPER
SOCIABLE SOCIETAL CONVIVIAL

SOCIETY BUND HERD GUILD SAMAJ
MENAGE PARISH SYSTEM VEREIN
ACADEMY COLLEGE COMPANY COUNCIL
KINGDOM SOCIETE EXCHANGE PRECINCT
SODALITY SORORITY
(— OF RELIGIOUS FANATICS)
COLORUM
(CHORAL —) CHOIR
(CLOWN —) KOSHARE KOYEMSHI
(CRAFT —) ARTEL
(DEBATING —) POP
(GYMNASTIC —) SOKOL
(HIGH —) SWELLDOM
(LITERARY —) HALL
(POLITICAL —) TAMMANY
(RELIGIOUS —) CHURCH
(SECRET —) HUI EGBO HOEY PORO
TONG LODGE MAFIA OGBONI PURRAH
CAMORRA
(STUDENT —) CORPS
(UTOPIAN —) ANARCHY

SOCK BOP BIFF BUST HOSE VAMP
ANKLET ARGYLE VAMPEY STOCKING
(— OF GOAT'S HAIR) UDO
(INFANT'S —) BOOTEE
(JAPANESE —) TABI

SOCKET BOX CUP LEAD NOSE SHOE
CHAIR POINT SHANK BUCKET EYEPIT
POCKET SCONCE ALVEOLE FERRULE
GUDGEON THIMBLE ALVEOLUS
(— FOR GEM) OUCH
(— FOR LANCE) PORT
(— FOR LENS) CELL
(— FOR MAST) TABERNACLE
(— FOR MOUTHPIECE) BIRN
(— IN GOLF CLUB HEAD) HOSE HOSEL
(— OF BONE) POT

(— OF HINGE) PAN
(— OF MILLSTONE) INK COCKEYE
(— OF WATER PIPE) BELL
(BIT —) POD

SOD BEAT DELF FLAG TURF DELPH GLEBE
SWARD TERRON

SOFA BOIST COUCH DIVAN LOUNGE
SETTEE SOCIABLE

SOFT COY TID LASH LIMP LUSH MILD
MURE NASH NESH PLUM WAXY WEAK
BALMY BLAND CUSHY DOLCE DOWNY
FAINT LENIS LIGHT MALMY MEALY
MUSHY PAPPY PIANO SILKY SLACK
SMALL SOAPY SOOTH SWEET WAXEN
CREAMY EFFETE FLOSSY FLUFFY GENTLE
LYDIAN MELLOW PLACID SILKEN SLOPPY
SMOOTH SPONGY SPOONY TENDER
CLEMENT COTTONY CRUMBLY DUCTILE
LENIENT SQUASHY CUSHIONY FEMININE
FLEXIBLE LADYLIKE TRANQUIL

SOFTEN MELT SOAK TAME LITHE TOUCH
DIGEST LENIFY PACIFY RELENT SOOTHE
SUBDUE SUBMIT TEMPER WEAKEN
APPEASE ASSUAGE CUSHION LENIATE
MOLLIFY QUALIFY SWEETEN MITIGATE
MODULATE PALLIATE
(— BY BOILING) CREE
(— BY KNEADING) MALAX MALAXATE
(— BY STEEPING) MACERATE
(— COLOR) CUT SCUMBLE
(— FIBERS) BREAK
(— GRADUALLY) SQUAT
(— JUTE) BATCH
(— LEATHER) BREY FRIZZ
(— METAL) ALLAY
(— TONE) SURD

SOFTLY LOW BAJO HOOLY FAIRLY
GENTLY SWEETLY CREAMILY TENDERLY

SOGGY SAD DUNCH SODDEN SPONGY
WATERY

SOIL DAG MUD SOD BLOT CLAY CLOD
DAUB DIRT DUST FOUL GRIT LAND MIRK
MUCK MURK MUSS SILE SLUR SMUT
SOOT CROCK EARTH GLEBE GRIME
LAYER MUCKY SLUSH SMEAR SOLUM
STAIN SULLY BEDAUB BEFOUL BEMIRE
GROUND SLURRY SMIRCH SPLASH
BEGRIME BESMEAR POLLUTE TARNISH
ALLUVIAL BESMIRCH FLYSPECK
CONTAMINATE
(— ABOVE CLAY) KELLY
(— DEPOSITED BY WIND) ELUVIUM
(— FORMED BY DECAY) GEEST
(— INTERMEDIATE BETWEEN SAND
AND CLAY) ROSEL
(— PREPARED FOR SOWING) TILTH
(— REMOVED FROM ORE) BARING
(— WITH GREASE) LARD
(AGGREGATE —) PED
(ALKALINE —) SOLONETZ
(ASHLIKE —) PODZOL
(CLAYEY —) GALT MALM MAUM ADOBE
SOLOD SOLOTH
(COTTON —) REGUR
(DRY —) GROOT
(FRIABLE —) CRUMB
(GRAVELLY —) ROACH GROWAN

(HARD —) RAMMEL
(INFERTILE —) GALL
(LEACHED —S) LATOSOL
(PEATY —) YARPHA
(PLUMBER'S —) SMUDGE
(POROUS —) SPONGE
(POTTING —) COMPOST
(PRAIRIE —) BRUNIZEM
(SILTY —) GUMBO
(SPRINGY —) WOODSERE
SOILED FOUL BLACK DINGY DIRTY MUSSY
SOOTY TARRY SMUDGY SMUTTY
DRAGGLED SHOPWORN
SOJOURN LIE BIDE STAY STOP ABIDE
ABODE TARRY RESIDE STATION
SOLACE CHEER COMFORT CONSOLE
SWEETEN
SOLDER BRAZE FLOAT SPELTER
SOLDIER SON BLEU BOLO LEVY TULK
BERNE KHAKI LANCE LINER
PERDU PIKER POILU SAMMY TOLKE
TOPAS BONAGH BUMMER DARTER
GALOOT GUNNER HAIDUK HOSTER
MARKER REITER SENTRY SOLDAT
SWADDY WEAPON ZOUAVE BAYONET
BRIGAND CARABIN CORSLET DARTMAN
DOGFACE FEDERAL FIGHTER HOBBLER
INVALID MATROSS ORDERLY PAVISOR
PELTAST PIKEMAN PRIVATE REGULAR
SCARLET SLINGER SOLDADO STRIKER
VETERAN WARRIOR ARQUEBUS
BLUECOAT BUFFCOAT CAMELEER
DESERTER FUSILIER GALLOPER
GENDARME GRAYCOAT IRONSIDE
JANIZARY LANCEMAN MILITANT
SENTINEL SERVITOR SPEARMAN
SWORDMAN WARFARER YARDBIRD
(— OF MUSCOVITE GUARD) STRELITZ
(— WITH SIDE WHISKERS) BADGER
(ALBANIAN —) PALIKAR
(ALGERIAN —) ARBI
(ANT —) MAXIM
(AUSTRALIAN —) ANZAC DIGGER
BILLJIM
(BOMBAY —S) DUCKS
(BRITISH —) LIMEY TOMMY BLIGHTY
LOBSTER REDCOAT ROOINEK
(BRUTAL —) PANDOUR
(CAREER —) LIFER
(COWARDLY —) CAPITANO
(FEMALE —) AMAZON
(FILE OF 6 —S) ROT
(FILIPINO —) GUGU
(FOOT —) KERN PAGE PEON GRUNT
PIETON FOOTMAN TOLPATCH
(GERMAN —) HUN FRITZ HEINE KRAUT
HEINIE
(GREEK —) EVZONE HOPLITE
(INCOMPETENT —) BOLL
(INDIAN —) PEON JAWAN SEPOY
GURKHA
(INVALID —) FOGY
(IRREGULAR —) CROAT CATERAN
JAYHAWK SEBUNDY MIQUELET
RAPPAREE SILLADAR
(MERCENARY —) RUTTER HESSIAN
(MOROCCAN —) ASKARI

(MOUNTED —) LANCER DRAGOON
GENETOR LOBSTER TROOPER VEDETTE
CAVALIER
(OLD —) GROGNARD
(PROFESSIONAL —) SAMURAI
(REVOLUTIONARY —) REDCOAT
BUCKSKIN
(ROMAN —S OF THIRD LINE) TRIARY
TRIARII
(RUSSIAN —) IVAN
(SCOTTISH —) JOCK
(SMALL —) BANTAM
(TURKISH —) NIZAM REDIF
SOLE MERE ONLY SLIP SOCK ALONE
CLUMP LEMON WHOLE INSOLE PLANTA
SINGLE TONGUE UNIQUE FLATFISH
SINGULAR SOLITARY
(— A SHOE) SPECK
(— FOR WALKING OVER SAND)
BACKSTER
(— OF BIRD'S FOOT) PTERNA
(— OF FOOT) PLAT VOLA PELMA PLANT
(— OF PLANE) FACE
(— OF PLOW) SLADE
(— WITH WOOD) CLOG
(HALF —) SHOULDER
(TOWARD THE —) PLANTAD
SOLEMN DEEP SAGE AWFUL SOBER
DEVOUT FORMAL RITUAL EARNEST
SERIOUS WEIGHTY FUNEREAL
SOLEMNITY OBIT RITE SACRE GRAVITY
SEVERITY
SOLICIT ASK BEG SUE WOO DRUM MOVE
SEEK TOUT URGE APPLY COURT CRAVE
TREAT ACCOST HUSTLE INVITE INVOKE
BESEECH CANVASS ENTREAT IMPLORE
PROCURE REQUEST APPROACH PETITION
SOLICITATION SUIT QUEST CANVASS
SOLICIT ENTREATY
SOLICITOR AVOUE LAWYER WRITER
ADVOCATE ATTORNEY TRAMPLER
SOLICITOUS URGENT CAREFUL CURIOUS
JEALOUS DESIROUS CONCERNED
SOLICITUDE CARE FEAR HEED HEART
WORRY ANXIETY CONCERN JEALOUSY
SOLID DRY CONE CUBE FAST FIRM FULL
HARD CUBIC MEATY SOUND STIFF
STOUT THICK TIGHT SECURE STABLE
STRONG STURDY COMPACT UNIFORM
CONSTANT MATERIAL
(GEOMETRICAL —) CONE CUBE PRISM
FRUSTUM POLYHEDRON
SOLIDIFY DRY SET JELL HARDEN
COMPACT CONGEAL STIFFEN CONCRETE
SOLIDITY SADNESS FASTNESS
FIRMNESS HARDNESS
SOLITARY ODD LONE ONLY SOLE ALONE
LONELY SINGLE EREMITE PRIVATE
RECLUSE WIDOWED DESOLATE EREMITIC
ISOLATED LONESOME SECLUDED
SEPARATE
SOLITUDE PRIVACY RETREAT SOLITARY
SOLO ARIA ARIOSO CAVATINA SPADILLA
SOLOMON SAM KOHELETH
(BROTHER OF —) ADONIJAH
(FATHER OF —) DAVID
(MOTHER OF —) BATHSHEBA

SOLOMON ISLANDS (CAPITAL OF —) HONIARA
(ISLAND OF —) BUKA GIZO SAVO TULAGI FLORISA MALAITA RENDOVA RUSSELL CHOISEUL GUADALCANAL BOUGAINVILLE
SOLON SAGE GNOMIST SENATOR LAWMAKER
SOLUTION LYE AQUA STAIN TINCT ACETUM ANSWER SALINE EXTRACT EYEWASH LACQUER ANALYSIS LEACHATE TINCTURE
(— ADDED FOR GOOD MEASURE) INCAST
(— OF CHESS PROBLEM) COOK
(— OF FERMENTED BRAN) DRENCH
(— OF GUM TRAGACANTH) BED
(ALCOHOLIC —) ESSENCE
(CORROSIVE —) OLEUM
(PICKLING —) SOUSE
(PRESERVING —) BOLIN
(SALINE —) BRINE
(SOAP —) NIGRE
(STERILE —) JOHNIN
(VISCOUS —) GLUE
(WATERY —) EAU SAP
SOLVE DO FIX READ UNDO WORK BREAK CRACK ANSWER CIPHER FIGURE REDUCE RIDDLE RESOLVE UNRAVEL DECIPHER
SOLVENT ETHER ELUENT SPIRIT ACETONE ALCOHOL BENZINE DILUENT REMOVER SPOTTER CARBITOL PICOLINE STRIPPER TEREBENE
(UNIVERSAL —) ALKAHEST
SOMALIA (CAPITAL OF —) MOGADISHU
(COIN OF —) BESA
(DIVISION OF —) HAWIYA
(MEASURE OF —) TOP CABA CHELA DARAT TABLA CUBITO
(MOUNTAIN OF —) SURUDAD
(MOUNTAIN RANGE OF —) GUBAN
(NATIVE OF —) GALLA HAWIYA ISBAAK SOMALI DANAKIL
(RIVER OF —) JUBA NOGAL SCEBELI
(TOWN OF —) MERCA BERBERA KISMAYU HARGEISA
(WEIGHT OF —) PARSALAH
SOMBER SAD DULL GRAVE SOBER GLOOMY LENTEN SOLEMN SOMBRE SULLEN AUSTERE SERIOUS
SOME ANY ODD THIS CERTAIN
SOMERSAULT FLIP TOPPLE TWISTER BACKFLIP SOMERSET
SOMETHING WHAT ALIQUID WHATNOT SOMEWHAT
SOMETIME FORMER ANCIENT QUONDAM SOMEWHEN
SOMETIMES NOW TOO WHILE UMQUHILE OCCASIONALLY
SOMEWHAT BIT POCO SOME PRETTY RATHER SLIGHT
SON BEN BOY LAD FILS FITZ CHILD FILIUS JUNIOR EPIGONUS
(— OF CHIEF) OGTIERN
(— OF KING OF FRANCE) DAUPHIN
(— OF NISEI) SANSEI

(— OF PEER) MASTER
(— OF SUDRA) CHANDALA
(DAVID'S FAVORITE —) ABSALOM
(FOURTH —) MARTLET
(ILLEGITIMATE —) NEPHEW
(YOUNG —) MOPSY
(YOUNGER —) CADET
(YOUNGEST —) BENJAMIN
SONG AIR DIT CANT GATO NOTE RANT TUNE CHANT CHARM CROON DITTY MELOS MOLPE OLDIE VOCAL CANTIC CANZON CARMEN CHORUS JINGLE MELODY STRAIN WARBLE BALLATA CANTION CHANSON COMIQUE DESCANT MELISMA MELODIA ROMANCE SCOLION SONGLET THRENOS BIRDSONG CANTICLE FLAMENCO PALINODE RHAPSODY ROUNDELAY
(— ACCOMPANYING TOAST) BRINDISI
(— FOR TWO VOICES) GYMEL
(— OF BASQUES) ZORTZICO
(— OF BIRD) LAY KOLLER
(— OF JOY) CAROL PAEAN JUBILATE
(— OF MINSTREL) YEDDING
(— OF OCEANIA) HIMENE
(— OF PRAISE) HYMN CAROL ANTHEM CHORALE
(— UNACCOMPANIED) GLEE
(— WITH MONOTONOUS RHYME) VIRELAY
(—S OF BIRDS) RAMAGE
(ANDALUSIAN —) SAETA
(BOAT —) JORRAM
(CEREMONIAL —S) AREITO
(CRADLE —) HUSHO
(CUBAN —) GUAJIRA COMPARSA
(DANCE —) BALLAD BAMBUCO
(DRINKING —) BACCHIC SCOLION WASSAIL
(EVENING —) SERENA EVENSONG SERENATA
(FOLK —) SON FADO FOLK BLUES DOINA BYLINA CANTIGA JUBILEE STORNELLO
(FUNERAL —) DIRGE MONODY EPICEDE THRENODY
(FUNEREAL —) ELEGY
(GAY —) LILT
(GERMAN —) LIED
(HAWAIIAN —) MELE
(HEBREW —) ELIELI HATIKVAH
(IMPROMPTU —) SCOLION
(JAPANESE —) UTA
(LOVE —) ALBA CANSO CANZO FANCY AMORET AUBADE SERENA SERENATA
(MELISMATIC —) DIVISION
(MOCKING —) JIG
(MORNING —) MATIN AUBADE
(MOURNFUL —) DUMP PLAINT ENDECHA
(NEW ZEALAND —) WAIATA
(NIGHT —) COMPLIN
(NUPTIAL —) HYMEN
(PART —) CHACE TROLL CACCIA CANZONET FROTTOLA MADRIGAL
(PASTORAL —) OAT

(PLAIN —) GROUND
(PORTUGUESE —) FADO
(RELIGIOUS —) HYMN CAROL PSALM
SHOUT ANTHEM POLYMNY SIRVENT
(REVOLUTIONARY —) CARMAGNOLE
(SACRED —) MOTET
(SAILOR'S —) CHANTY SHANTY
(SANSKRIT —) GITA
(SINGLE — ON RECORD) CUT
(STUPID —) STROWD
(VINTAGE —) VINATA
(WORK —) HOLLER
SONGBIRD CHAT LARK WREN MAVIS
ROBIN SABIA SIREN VEERY VIREO
BULBUL CANARY LINNET MOCKER
ORIOLE THRUSH CATBIRD WARBLER
ACCENTOR BLUEBIRD BOBOLINK
CARDINAL MEADOWLARK
SONG OF HIAWATHA
(AUTHOR OF —) LONGFELLOW
(CHARACTER IN —) KWASIND
NOKOMIS WENONAH HIAWATHA
CHIBIABOS MINNEHAHA MUDJEKEEWIS
SONG OF ROLAND (AUTHOR OF —)
UNKNOWN
(CHARACTER IN —) ALDA ALORY
MILON OGIER BERTHA FERRAU GERARD
MEDORO MORGAN OBERTO OLIVER
ROLAND SADONE ARGALIA CHARLOT
GANELON GODFREY MALAGIS REINOLD
ASTOLPHO KARAHEUT BRADAMANT
GLORIANDA CHARLEMAGNE
MANDRICARDO
SONOROUS ROUND TONOUS OROTUND
VIBRANT RESONANT RESOUNDING
SONS AND LOVERS (AUTHOR OF —)
LAWRENCE
(CHARACTER IN —) LILY PAUL ANNIE
CLARA DAWES MOREL ARTHUR BAXTER
MIRIAM WALTER LEIVERS WILLIAM
GERTRUDE
SOON ERE ANON EARLY NEWLY SUDDEN
TIMELY BETIMES ERELONG SHORTLY
DIRECTLY SPEEDILY PRESENTLY
SOOT COOM IZLE SMUT BLECK COLLY
GRIME FULIGO SMUTCH
SOOTHE BALM CALM COAX EASE HUSH
LULL ALLAY CHARM HUMOR QUELL
SALVE STILL BECALM PACIFY SETTLE
SMOOTH SOLACE STROKE ASSUAGE
COMFORT COMPOSE CONSOLE FLATTER
MOLLIFY QUALIFY BLANDISH MITIGATE
SOOTHING MILD BALMY BLAND DOWNY
DULCE STILL SWEET ANETIC DREAMY
DULCET GENTLE SMOOTH ANODYNE
BALSAMIC SEDATIVE
SOOTHSAYER SEER AUGUR DIVINE
PYTHON ARUSPEX DIVINER HARUSPEX
SOPHISTICATED WISE BLASE CIVIL
SALTY SVELTE WORLDLY
SOPORIFIC DROWSY OPIATE SLEEPY
HYPNOTIC NARCOTIC SOMNIFIC
SORCERER MAGE BRUJO WITCH
VOODOO WIZARD WARLOCK MAGICIAN
WITCHMAN
SORCERESS BRUJA CIRCE LAMIA SIBYL
WITCH ARMIDA HECATE BABAJAGA

SORCERY OBI MAGIC OBEAH SPELL
PRESTIGE SORTIARY WITCHERY
NECROMANCY
SORDID RAW BASE GAMY MEAN VILE
DIRTY MUCKY SEAMY GRUBBY SQUALID
CHURLISH
SORE BUM BUBA CHAP GALL KIBE OUCH
BLAIN AGNAIL BITTER CANKER FESTER
CHANCRE SCALDING
(— ON HORSE'S FOOT) MELLIT
QUITTER
(ARTIFICIAL —) FOX
(SUMMER —S) CALORIS LEECHES
SORROW RUE WOE BALE CARE DOLE
HARM MOAN RUTH SORE DOLOR GRIEF
MOURN RUING GRIEVE LAMENT MISERY
REGRET STOUND ANGUISH CONDOLE
DEPLORE PENANCE REMORSE TROUBLE
CALAMITY DISTRESS MOURNING
SORROWFUL BAD SAD WAN CHARY
DREAR TRIST WOFUL DISMAL DREARY
RUEFUL BALEFUL DOLEFUL LUCTUAL
UNHAPPY CONTRITE DESOLATE
DOLOROSO MOURNFUL PITIABLE
SORRY BAD SAD HURT VEXED PITIFUL
CONTRITE WRETCHED
SORT KIN LOT COMB KIND RANK SIFT
SUIT BREED GENUS GRADE SPICE
ASSORT GARBLE GENDER KIDNEY
NATURE STRAIN STRIPE FASHION
SPECIES VARIETY CLASSIFY SEPARATE
(— COTTON BY STAPLE) STAPLE
(— MAIL) CASE
(— MERCHANDISE) BRACK
(— OF PERSON) LIKE
SOT LUSH SOAK DRUNK TOPER BLOTTER
DASTARD TOSSPOT DRUNKARD
SOUL AME EGO ALMA ANIMA ATMAN
GHOST HEART SHADE BUDDHI NATURE
PNEUMA PSYCHE SPIRIT SPRITE
INTERNAL
(—S OF THE DEAD) LEMURES
(ANIMAL — IN MAN) NEPHESH
(DISEMBODIED —) KER
(EGYPTIAN IMMORTAL —) BA
(INDIVIDUAL —) JIVA
(LIBERATED —) KEVALIN
(UNIVERSAL —) HANSA
SOUND CRY FIT BLOW FAST FIRM FLOW
GOOD HALE KYLE NOTE SAFE SANE TONE
TRIG WISE BLAST BUGLE CHEEP FLICK
GLUCK GRIND GROPE NOISE PLANG
PROBE RIGHT SLUSH SOLID SPEAK VALID
WHOLE BICKER ENTIRE FATHOM HEARTY
INTACT LABIAL LAGOON ROBUST SIGNAL
SINGLE SONANT SPLASH STABLE STRAIN
STURDY HEALTHY HEARING PERFECT
PHONEME PLUMMET SCRATCH VOCABLE
FLAWLESS FOOTFALL GRINDING
RELIABLE
(— A BAGPIPE) DOODLE
(— BELL) PEAL RING KNELL KNOLL
(— DRUM OR TRUMPET) TUCK
(— FORTH) BOOM
(— IN MIND) FORMAL
(— LIKE THUNDER) BRONTIDE
(— LOUDLY) TANG LARUM

(— MELODIOUSLY) CHARM
(— OF BAGPIPE) DRONE
(— OF BEATING) RATAPLAN
(— OF BELL) DING PEAL RING KNELL
STROKE DINGDONG TINGTANG
(— OF BIRD) JUG CHURR
(— OF CONTEMPT) HUMPH
(— OF CORK) CLOOP CLUNK
(— OF DISAPPROVAL) BOO HOOT
BAZOO
(— OF DOG) BOOK
(— OF DYING PERSON'S VOICE)
TAISCH
(— OF ENGINE) CHUG
(— OF EXPLOSION) BOUNCE
(— OF F) DIGAMMA
(— OF FLUTE) TOOTLE
(— OF HEN) CLUCK
(— OF HOG) GRUNT
(— OF HOOF) CLOP
(— OF HORN) BEEP TOOT
(— OF HORSE) BLOWING
(— OF PLUCKED STRING) TUM
(— OF POURING LIQUID) GLUG
(— OF RAIN) SPAT
(— OF SHEEP) BAA BLEAT
(— OF STEAM ENGINE) CHUFF
(— OF STRAW OR LEAVES) RUSTLE
(— OF THUNDER) CLAP
(— OF TRUMPET) CLARION
(— OF WIND IN TREES) WOOSH
(— OUT) FEEL
(—S HAVING RHYTHM) MUSIC
(ABNORMAL —) BRUIT
(ADVENTITIOUS —) RALE
(BLOWING —) SOUFFLE
(BRAWLING —) CHIDE
(BUBBLING —) BLATHER
(BUZZING —) WHIR WHIRR
(CLICKING —) SNECK
(CONSONANT —) ALVEOLAR
(COOING —) CHIRR TURTUR
(CRACKLING —) RISK
(CRISP —) BLIP
(CRUNCHING —) CRUMP SCRUNCH
(DELICATE —) TINK TINKLE
(DISCORDANT —) JAR BRAY JANGLE
(DULL —) BUFF THUD CLUNK SQUELCH
(EXPLOSIVE —) POP BARK PUFF
REPORT
(FAINT —) PEEP GLIFF WHIST INKLING
(FINAL —) AUSLAUT
(GULPING —) GLUCK
(GUTTURAL —) GROWL
(HARSH —) JAR BRAY BLARE CLASH
CRANK TWANG DISCORD STRIDOR
(HEAVY —) DUMP
(HIGH-PITCHED —) TING
(HISSING —) FIZZ SIZZ SWISH SIZZLE
(HOLLOW —) CHOCK THUNGE
(HUMMING —) HUM BURR DRONE
(INDISTINCT —) BLUR SURD
(INITIAL — OF WORDS) ANLAUT
(JINGLING —) SMIT
(LAPPING —) SLOOSH
(LIGHT REPEATED —) PITAPAT

(LOUD —) PEAL BLARE CLANG CRASH
CLANGOR
(LOW-PITCHED —) BASS
(MEANINGLESS —S) GABBLE
(MEDIAL —) INLAUT
(MENTALLY —) SANE WISE
(MOANING —) SOUGH
(MOURNFUL —) GROAN
(MUSICAL —) CHIME
(NASAL —) ANUSVARA
(PLEASING —) EUPHONY
(RASPING —) BUZZ SKIRR SCROOP
(REPEATED —) ECHO
(RESONANT —) BONG
(REVERBERATING —) PLANG
(RINGING —) CLANG CLANK CLING
TWANG RINGLE DINGDONG
(ROARING —) BEAL
(RUSHING —) SWOOSH HURLING
(RUSTLING —) FISSLE
(SCRAPING —) GRIDE
(SHARP —) POP PING SNAP CHINK
CRAKE KNACK SPANG
(SHORT, HIGH-PITCHED —) BLEEP
(SHRILL —) CHEEP KNACK SKIRL
SCREED SQUEAK STRIDOR
(SHUFFLING —) SCUFFLE
(SIBILANT —) HISS SHISH SHUSH
(SLAPPING —) CLATCH
(SLIGHT —) SWISH
(SOBBING —) YOOP
(SPEECH —) SURD DOMAL TENUE
VOWEL APICAL PHONEME CEREBRAL
(SPLASHING —) LAP CHUNK FLURR
SPLAT SWASH
(SPOKEN —) BREATH
(SQUEAKY —) CREAK
(SQUELCHING —) SQUASH
(STRANGLED —) GLUB GLUG
(SWISHING —) SCHLOOP
(TRAMPING —) STUMP
(TRILLING —) CHIRR CHIZZ HIRRIENT
(TUNEFUL —) HARMONY
(UNPLEASANT —) BLOOP
(VIBRATING —) TIRL
(WARNING —) ALARM SIREN ALARUM
TOCSIN
(WHIRRING —) BIRR FLURR SKIRR
(WHISPERING —) SUSURRUS
(WHISTLING —) STRIDOR
SOUND AND THE FURY
(AUTHOR OF —) FAULKNER
(CHARACTER IN —) HEAD JASON
DILSEY SYDNEY CANDACE COMPSON
QUENTIN BENJAMIN
SOUP BREE KALE SOPA POSOL BORSCH
BILLIBI MARMITE MINESTRA
MINESTRONE
(BARLEY —) SMIGGINS
(CABBAGE —) SHCHI STCHI
(CLEAR —) CONSOMME JULIENNE
(COLD —) SCHAV
(JELLIED —) GAZPACHO
(LARGE QUANTITY OF —) SLASH
(SHINBONE —) SKINK
(THICK —) GUMBO HOOSH PUREE

BISQUE BURGOO CHOWDER GARBURE
POTTAGE HOTCHPOT MORTREWES
(THIN —) BROTH SKILLY
SOUR DRY ACID CRAB DOUR FOXY GRIM
HARD TART TURN ACERB ACRID EAGER
GRUFF ACIDIC BITTER CURDLE RANCID
RUGGED SULLEN ACETOSE ACIDIFY
AUSTERE VINEGARY
(SLIGHTLY —) BLINK BLINKY ACESCENT
SOURCE FONS FONT HEAD MINE RISE
ROOT SEED FOUNT SPAWN SURGE
AUCTOR AUTHOR BOTTOM CENTER
FATHER ORIGIN PARENT RESORT STAPLE
WHENCE FOUNTAIN WELLHEAD
(— OF AID) RECOURSE
(— OF ANCESTRAL LINE) STOCK
(— OF ANNOYANCE) BOGIE HARROW
BUGBEAR
(— OF ASSURANCE) FORTRESS
(— OF CONCERN) BUGABOO
(— OF CONFIDENCE) ANCHOR
(— OF DISPLEASURE) DISGUST
(— OF ENERGY) TAPAS
(— OF HAPPINESS) SUNSHINE
(— OF HARM) CURSE
(— OF HONOR) CREDIT
(— OF INCOME) TITLE REVENUE
(— OF INFORMATION) CHECK
(— OF INSPIRATION) CASTALIA
(— OF INSTRUCTION) BOOK
(— OF LAUGHTER) SPLEEN
(— OF NOURISHMENT) BREAST
(— OF POWER) STRENGTH
(— OF REGRET) SCATHE
(— OF STREAM OR RIVER) FILL
(— OF STRENGTH) HORN
(— OF SUPPLY) SHOP FEEDER ARSENAL
(— OF TROUBLE) HEADACHE
(— OF WATER) BRON SPRING
(— OF WEALTH) GOLCONDA KLONDIKE
(ENCLOSED —) FLOW
(PHYSICAL —) MOTHER
(PRIMARY —) RADIX
SOURNESS ACIDITY ACERBITY
ACRIMONY ASPERITY TARTNESS
VERJUICE

SOUTH AFRICA

BAY: ALGOA FALSE
CAPE: AGULHAS
CAPITAL: CAPETOWN PRETORIA
COIN: CENT RAND POUND FLORIN
LANGUAGE: BANTU HINDI TAMIL TELUGU
BUJARATI
MOUNTAIN: AUX KOP KATHKIN INJASUTI
NATIVE: YOSA BANTU NAMAS PONDO
DAMARA SWAHILI BECHUANA
HOTTENTOT
PROVINCE: NATAL TRANSVAAL
RIVER: MODDER MOLOPO ORANGE
KURUMAM LIMPOPO OLIFANTS
TOWN: AUS MARA STAD BENONI DURBAN
SEVERN UMTATA KOKSTAD SPRINGS
MAFEKING GERMISTON JOHANNESBURG

WATERFALL: HOWICK TUGELA
AUGRABIES

SOUTH CAROLINA

CAPITAL: COLUMBIA
COUNTY: AIKEN HORRY DILLON JASPER
OCONEE SALUDA
ISLAND: EDISTO PARRIS HILTONHEAD
LAKE: MARION MURRAY CATAWBA
WATEREE HARTWELL MOULTRIE
MOUNTAIN: SASSAFRAS
PLATEAU: PIEDMONT
RESERVOIR: SANTEE PINOPOLIS
RIVER: BROAD EDISTO PEEDEE SALUDA
SANTEE ASHEPOO TUGALOS WATEREE
CONGAREE SAVANNAH
STATE BIRD: WREN
STATE FLOWER: JASMINE
STATE TREE: PALMETTO
TOWN: AIKEN GREER UNION BELTON
CAMDEN CHERAW CONWAY DILLON
SALUDA SENECA SUMTER BAMBERG
LAURENS MANNING BEAUFORT
FLORENCE NEWBERRY WALHALLA
GREENVILLE SPARTANBURG

SOUTH DAKOTA

BUTTE: MUD CROW SULLY FINGER SADDLE
THUNDER DEERSEARS
CAPITAL: PIERRE
COUNTY: DAY HYDE BRULE MINER MOODY
SPINK SULLY TRIPP CUSTER JERAULD
YANKTON MELLETTE
LAKE: OAHE BIGSTONE TRAVERSE
MOUNTAIN: BEAR SHEEP TABLE CROOKS
HARNEY MOREAU
RIVER: JAMES MOREAU CHEYENNE
MISSOURI
STATE BIRD: PHEASANT
STATE FLOWER: PASQUE
STATE TREE: SPRUCE
TOWN: LEAD HAYTI HURON LEOLA ONIDA
CUSTER DESMET EUREKA KADOKA
LEMMON MILLER WINNER STURGIS
WEBSTER YANKTON ABERDEEN
DEADWOOD SISSETON

SOUTHERN SUDIC AUSTRAL MERIDIAN

SOUTH KOREA

BAY: KANGHWA
CAPITAL: SEOUL
COIN: WON HWAN
MOUNTAIN: CHIRI
PROVINCE: CHEJU CHOLLA KANGWON
KYONGGI
RIVER: HAN KUM PUKHAN SOMJIN
NAKTONG YONGSAN
TOWN: CHEJU MASAN MOKPO PUSAN
SUWON TAEGU WONJU CHINJU CHONJU

INCHON KUNSAN TAEJON CHONGJU
KWANGJU CHUNCHON

SOUTH VIETNAM

CAPITAL: SAIGON
LANGUAGE: CHAM KHMER RHADE
MEASURE: GANG PHAN THON
MOUNTAIN: BADINH NINHHOA
  KNONTRAN NGOOLINH TCHEPONE
NATIVE: CHAM MALAY
PORT: DANANG SAIGON QUINHON
  NHATRANG
REGION: ANNAM COCHIN
RIVER: BA SONG MEKONG DONGNAI
TOWN: HUE HOIAN ANNHON DANANG
  GIADINH QUINHON SONGCAU TAYNINH
  VINHLOI PHANRANG QUANGTRI
WEIGHT: CAN YET UYEN

SOUTH YEMEN (CAPITAL OF —) ADEN
  (ISLAND OF —) PERIM KAMARAN
  SOCOTRA
  (MONEY OF —) DINAR
  (TOWN OF —) SEIYUN MUKALLA
SOUVENIR RELIC TOKEN FAIRING
  NICKNACK
SOVEREIGN BEY SIR CHAM CHIP FREE
  KHAN QUID SHAH CROWN JAMES NIZAM
  GUINEA KAISER KINGLY MASTER PRINCE
  SHINER SOVRAN SULTAN CROWNED
  MONARCH DOMINANT IMPERIAL
  SUZERAIN
  (DIVINELY —) THEARCHIC
  (FELLOW —) COUSIN
  (HEAVENLY —) TENNO HEAVEN
  (MOSLEM —) SOLDAN
SOVEREIGNTY SWAY CROWN REIGN
  DIADEM EMPIRE THRONE DEMESNE
  DYNASTY KINGDOM MAJESTY SCEPTER
  AUTARCHY DOMINION MONARCHY
  REGNANCY
  (— OF REASON) AUTONOMY
  (JOINT —) SYNARCHY
SOW HOG GILT SEED SHED YELT DRILL
  PLANT STREW GRUMPHY SCATTER
  ENGENDER SEMINATE
SPA BATH CURE HYDRO
SPACE BLUE CORD DENT FACE PALE
  RANK ROOM SIDE VOID ABYSS BLOCK
  CHINK CLEFT FIELD PLACE RANGE
  CANTON HIATUS INDENT MATTER
  ROOMTH ARRANGE COMPASS LEGROOM
  SPATIUM STRETCH INTERVAL
  (— ABOVE EARTH) AIRSPACE
  (— AMONG MUSCLES) SINUS
  (— AROUND HOUSE) AMBIT
  (— AT WHARF) BERTHAGE
  (— BEFORE KILN) LOGIE KILLOGIE
  (— BEHIND ALTAR) FERETORY
  (— BETWEEN BED AND WALL)
  RUELLE
  (— BETWEEN BRIDGE PIERS) LOCK
  (— BETWEEN CASKS) CONTLINE

(— BETWEEN COLUMNS) BAY
(— BETWEEN CONCENTRIC CIRCLES)
ANNULUS
(— BETWEEN DECKS) LAZARET
(— BETWEEN EYE AND BILL) LORE
(— BETWEEN FEATHERS) APTERYLA
(— BETWEEN FLUTINGS) FILET FILLET
GORGERIN
(— BETWEEN FURROWS) RIG
(— BETWEEN PAGES) GUTTER
(— BETWEEN RAILROAD TIES) CRIB
(— BETWEEN SAW TEETH) GULLET
**(— BETWEEN SHIP'S BOWS AND
ANCHOR)** HAWSE
(— BETWEEN STRANDS) CANTLINE
(— BETWEEN TEETH) DIASTEMA
**(— BETWEEN THUMB AND LITTLE
FINGER)** SPAN
(— BETWEEN TIMBERS) SPIRKET
(— BETWEEN TWO WIRES) DENT
(— BETWEEN VEINS OF LEAVES)
AREOLA
(— DEVOID OF MATTER) VACUUM
VACUITY
(— FOR SECRETION) BAG
(— IN CHURCH) KNEELING
(— IN COIL OF CABLE) TIER
(— IN FOREST) GLADE
(— IN MINE) GOB
(— IN THEATER) BOX
(— IN TYPE) CORE
(— OCCUPIED) VOLUME
(— OF TIME) DAY PULL STEAD GHURRY
STITCH INTERVAL
(— ON BILLIARD TABLE) BALK BAULK
(— ON COIN) EXERGUE
(— OVER STAGE) FLIES
(— OVERHEAD) HIGH
(— UNDER STAGE) DOCK
(— USED AS LIVING-ROOM) LANAI
(— WITHIN LIMITS) CONTENT
(AIR —) CENTRUM
(ARCHITECTURAL —) METOPE
PEDIMENT SACELLUM
(BACKGAMMON —) POINT
(BARE — ON BIRD) APTERIUM
(BLANK —) GAP ALLEY LACUNA
(BOUNDLESS —) INFINITE
(BREATHING —) BARLEY
(CLEAR —) FAIRWAY HEADWAY
DAYLIGHT
(COUNTER —) BACKBAR
(CRAMPED —) CUBBY
(EMPTY —) AIR BLANK CAPACITY
(ENCLOSED —) AREA BOWL HATCH
VERGE PARVIS CHAMBER CIRCUIT
CLOSURE COMPASS PARVISE PTEROMA
CLOISTER CONFINES
(EUCLIDEAN —) FLAT
(FLAT —) HOMALOID
(LEVEL —) PLATEA PARTERRE
(NARROW —) SLOT STRAIT
(OPEN —) OUT LAWN ALLEY COURT
LAUND TAHUA MAIDAN AREAWAY
FAIRWAY LOANING APERTURE DAYLIGHT
KNEEHOLE
(OPEN — OF WATER) WAKE

(OVERHANGING —) DOME
(POPLITEAL —) HAM HOCK
(ROOF —) CELL
(SEATING —) CAVEA
(SHELTERED —) KILLOGIE
(STORAGE —) ATTIC
(TRIANGULAR —) SPANDREL
(UNFILLED —) GAP GAPE CAVITY
HOLLOW BREAKAGE
(VAULTED —) ALCOVE
(VERTICAL —) HEADROOM
(WORKING —) COUNTER
(PREF.) SPATIO
SPACIOUS WIDE AMPLE BROAD RANGY
ROOMY BARONIAL
SPADE DIG LILY PEEL PICK SPUD DELVE
DIGGER PADDLE SHOVEL SCAFFLE
SCUPPIT TWISCAR
(LONG NARROW —) LOY
(PEAT —) SLADE SLANE TUSKAR
(PLASTERER'S —) SERVER
(TRIANGULAR —) DIDLE

SPAIN

CAPE: AJO NAO GATA CREUS MORAS
PALOS PENAS PRIOR DARTUCH ORTEGAL
SALINAS TORTOSA ESPICHEL MARROQUI
SACRATIF
CAPITAL: MADRID
ISLAND: IBIZA PALMA GOMERA HIERRO
ALBORAN MAJORCA MINORCA
MALLORCA TAGOMAGO TENERIFE
ISLANDS: CANARY BALEARIC
MOUNTAIN: GATA ANETO ROUCH TEIDE
ESTATS NETHOU TELENO BANUELO
CERREDO PERDIDO ALMANZOR
MONTSENY MULHACEN PENALARA
MOUNTAIN RANGE: CUENCA GREDOS
MORENA TOLEDO ALCARAZ DEMANDA
MONCAYO MALADETA MONEGROS
PYRENEES
PORT: ADRA NOYA VIGO CADIZ GADES
GADIR GIJON PALOS ABDERA CORUNA
MALAGA ALMERIA ALICANTE
BARCELONA
PROVINCE: JAEN LEON LUGO ALAVA
AVILA CADIZ SORIA BURGOS CORUNA
CUENCA GERONA HUELVA HUESCA
LERIDA MADRID MALAGA MURCIA
ORENSE OVIEDO TERUEL TOLEDO
ZAMORA ALMERIA BADAJOZ CACERES
CORDOBA GRANADA LOGRONO
NAVARRA SEGOVIA SEVILLA VIZCAYA
ALBACETE ALICANTE BALEARES
PALENCIA VALENCIA ZARAGOZA
REGION: LEON ARAGON BASQUE MURCIA
CASTILE GALICIA NAVARRE ASTURIAS
CASTILLA VALENCIA
RIVER: SIL TER CEGA EBRO ESLA LIMA
MINO TAJO ADAJA CINCA DOURO
DUERO GENIL JALON JUCAR NAVIA
ODIEL RIAZA SEGRE TAGUS TINTO TURIA
ALAGON ARAGON ERESMA HUERVA
JARAMA ORBIGO SEGURA TOROTE
TOWN: ROA ASPE BAZA ELDA HARO IRUN
JAEN LEON LUGO OLOT REUS ROTA
SAMA VIGO BAENA BEJAR CADIZ CIEZA
CUETA ECIJA EIBAR ELCHE GIJON IBIZA
JEREZ JODAR LORCA OLIVA PALMA
RONDA SIERO UBEDA XERES YECLA
ZAFRA AVILES AZUAGA BILBAO BURGOS
DUENCA GANDIA GERONA GETAFE
GUADIX HELLIN HUELVA HUESCA JATIVA
LERIDA LUCENA MADRID MALAGA
MATARO MERIDA MURCIA ORENSE
OVIEDO TERMEL TOLEDO UTRERA
ZAMORA

SPAN ARCH BEAM PAIR CHORD SWING
BRIDGE EXTEND SPREAD BESTRIDE
(— WITH FINGERS) SPEND
(UNSUPPORTED —) BEARING
SPANIEL TRASY COCKER SUSSEX
CLUMBER BLENHEIM PAPILLON
SPRINGER WATERRUG
SPANK PRAT SCUD SKELP PADDLE
SLIPPER
SPAR BEAM BOOM CLUB GAFF MAST
RAFT SPUR YARD CABER SPRIT BASTITE
DERRICK DOLPHIN JIBBOOM BOWSPRIT
OUTRIGGER MARTINGALE
(BITTER —) DOLOMITE
(HEAVY —) CAUK BARITE
SPARE BONY LEAN NICE SAVE SLIM THIN
FAVOR LANKY LENTEN MEAGER SKIMPY
RESERVE SLENDER PRESERVE
SPARING CHARY SCANT DAINTY FRUGAL
STINGY ECONOMIC PENURIOUS
ABSTEMIOUS
SPARK AIZLE GRAIN SPUNK BLUETTE
FLAUGHT SPARKLE SPARKLET SCINTILLA
(-S OF MOLTEN IRON) NILL
(VITAL —) GHOST LIGHT
SPARKLE SNAP WINK BLINK FLASH
GLINT SHINE GLANCE KINDLE SIMPER
CRACKLE GLIMMER GLISTER GLISTER
GLITTER RADIATE SHIMMER SPANGLE
TWINKLE CORUSCATE
SPARKLING DEWY CRISP QUICK SUNNY
BRIGHT SPUNKY STARRY SHINING
TWINKLY BRILLIANT SCINTILLANT
SPARROW DICKY FINCH HEMPY ISAAC
PADDY SPRIG CHIPPY PHILIP TOWHEE
CHIPPIE FIELDIE HAYSUCK PINNOCK
TITLING ACCENTOR HAIRBIRD WHITECAP
SPARSE BALD THIN MEAGER SCANTY
THRIFTY
SPARTAN LACONIC
SPASM PANG CRICK QUALM FLUTTER
RAPTURE PAROXYSM
(— OF FOOT) PODISMUS
(— OF PAIN) GRIP
(— OF THE IRIS) HIPPUS
(-S OF WHALE) FLURRY
(TONIC —) HOLOTONY
SPASMODIC FITFUL SNATCHY SPASTIC
SPATTER DASH SPURT DABBLE SPLASH
SQUIRT SMATTER SPIRTLE SPLATTER
SPRINKLE
(— WITH FOAM) EMBOSS
(— WITH MUD) JAP BEMUD SPARK

SPEAK ASK CUT SAY CANT CARP MOVE TALK TELL BREAK MOUTH ORATE PARLE SOUND SPIEL UTTER ACCENT PARLEY PATTER SQUEAK TONGUE ADDRESS BESPEAK DECLAIM DELIVER EXCLAIM CONVERSE
(— ABUSIVELY) JAW
(— AFFECTEDLY) MIMP KNACK
(— AGAINST) ACCUSE GAINSAY FORSPEAK
(— ANGRILY) ROUSE CAMPLE
(— AT LENGTH) DISSERT ENLARGE
(— BROKENLY) FALTER
(— CAJOLINGLY) COLLOGUE
(— CONFUSEDLY) HATTER CLUTTER SPLATHER
(— CONTEMPTUOUSLY) SCOFF
(— CRITICALLY) LAUNCH
(— CURTLY) BIRK SNAP
(— EVIL) BLACKEN
(— FAIR) PALP
(— FALSELY) ABUSE
(— FAMILIARLY) HOBNOB
(— FIRST TO) ACCOST
(— FOOLISHLY) PRATE GIBBER
(— HALTINGLY) HACK HAMMER STAMMER
(— HOARSELY) CROAK CROUP
(— ILL OF) KNOCK DEPRAVE DETRACT
(— IMPERFECTLY) LISP
(— IMPUDENTLY) CHEEK
(— IMPULSIVELY) BLURT
(— IN DRAWL) DRANT
(— IN JEST) FOOL
(— IN ONE'S EAR) HARK
(— IN POINTLESS MANNER) DROOL
(— IN STUMBLING WAY) STUTTER
(— IN UNDERTONE) WHISPER
(— IN WHINING VOICE) CANT
(— INDISTINCTLY) FUMBLE JABBER MUFFLE MAUNDER SPLUTTER
(— INEPTLY) BUMBLE
(— INSOLENTLY) SNASH
(— LOUDLY) TANG
(— MINCINGLY) NAB MIMP
(— MONOTONOUSLY) DROLL
(— OF) CALL NEVEN MENTION
(— OUT) LEVEL SHOOT
(— PLAYFULLY) BANTER
(— POMPOUSLY) CRACK
(— PROFUSELY) PALAVER
(— QUERULOUSLY) CREAK
(— RAPIDLY) TROLL GIBBER JABBER SQUIRT CHATTER
(— RESENTFULLY) HUFF
(— RHETORICALLY) DECLAIM
(— SARCASTICALLY) GIRD
(— SHORTLY) JERK
(— SLIGHTINGLY OF) BELITTLE
(— SLOWLY) DRAWL
(— THROUGH THE NOSE) SNAFFLE
(— TRUTH) SOOTHSAY
(— WITH EMPHASIS) DWELL
(— WITH LIPS CLOSED) MUMBLE

SPEAKER VOICE LOCUTOR STYLIST
(ORATORICAL —) SPOUTER
(PUBLIC —) ORATOR STUMPER

SPEAKING STEVEN LOQUENT PARLANCE SPELLING
(— ARTICULATELY) MEROPIC
(— MANY LANGUAGES) POLYGLOT
(EVIL —) PRATING

SPEAR GAD DART PIKE GRAIN LANCE SHAFT STAFF BROACH GIDJEE GLAIVE ASSEGAI BOURDON HARPOON IMPALER JAVELIN TRIDENT GAVELOCK LANCEGAY
(BROKEN —) TRUNCHEON
(EEL —) ELGER PILGER
(FISH —) GIG GAFF TREN POACH FIZGIG GRAINS FISHGIG LEISTER SNIGGER
(SALMON —) WASTER

SPECIAL VERY EXTRA ESPECIAL PECULIAR SPECIFIC

SPECIALIST EXPERT LEGIST ALTAIST FEUDIST GRECIAN OLOGIST SURGEON ARBORIST BOTANIST ETHICIST GEOMETER HEBRAIST LATINIST URBANIST PHYSICIST PEDIATRIST

SPECIES FOLK FORM KIND SORT BROOD CLASS EIDOS GENRE MANNER FEATHER GENOTYPE

SPECIFIC EXPRESS SPECIAL TRIVIAL CONCRETE ESPECIAL

SPECIFY ASSIGN DESIGN DETAIL EXPRESS MENTION INDICATE NOMINATE PRESCRIBE

SPECIMEN TEST ESSAY MODEL CHANCE SAMPLE SWATCH EXAMPLE ISOTYPE NEOTYPE PATTERN SAMPLER ALLOTYPE EXEMPLAR INSTANCE
(ADDITIONAL —) COTYPE
(EXTRAORDINARY —) BENDER
(FEMALE —) GYNETYPE
(FINEST —) PEARL
(LARGE —) ELEPHANT
(POOR —) APOLOGY
(SMALL —) SPRIG

SPECIOUS GAY FALSE FACILE GLOSSY HOLLOW TINSEL PAGEANT SPURIOUS PLAUSIBLE

SPECK DOT PIN PIP MOTE SPOT TICK WHIT FLYSPECK
(— IN LINEN) SPRIT
(— ON FINGERNAIL) GIFT
(BLACK —) DARTROSE

SPECKLED FIGGED MAILED BLOBBED SPECKLY FRECKLED STIPPLED

SPECTACLE POMP SHOW SIGHT CIRCUS DEVICE OBJECT PAGEANT MONUMENT
(ODD —) TRACK
(SORRY —) BYZEN
(WATER —) AQUACADE

SPECTACLES SPECS LUNETS GLASSES GOGGLES WINKERS CHEATERS

SPECTACULAR VIEWY PAGEANT

SPECTATOR FAN VIEWER WITNESS BEHOLDER OBSERVER OVERSEER RAILBIRD

SPECTER BUG MARE BOGIE GHOST POOKA SPOOK TAIPO EMPUSA SHADOW SPIRIT WRAITH BOGGART BUGBEAR PHANTOM RAWHEAD SPECTRE PHANTASM PRESENCE REVENANT

SPECTRAL SPOOKY GHOSTLY SHADOWY

SPECULATE GAMBLE PONDER WONDER CONSIDER RUMINATE THEORIZE
SPECULATOR PIKER GAMBLER PLUNGER SCALPER BOURSIER BUMMAREE OPERATOR
SPEECH LIP SAW SAY COAX RUNE TALE GLOZE LINGO PARLE SPEAK SPIEL VOICE BREATH EPILOG JARGON ORISON REASON SALUTE STEVEN TONGUE ADDRESS BROCARD ORATION VULGATE EPILOGUE LANGUAGE LOCUTION LOQUENCE PARLANCE SONORITY SPEAKING
(— CHARACTERIZED BY SLURRING) SLURVIAN
(— FORM) LEXEME
(— IN GREEK DRAMA) RHESIS
(— IN PLAY) SIDE
(AFFECTED —) CANT
(BITTER —) DIATRIBE
(BOASTFUL —) BLUSTER
(BOMBASTIC —) SQUIRT HARANGUE
(COARSE —) HARLOTRY
(CONFUSED —) SPUTTER
(CONTEMPTUOUS —) FRUMP
(IMPUDENT —) SASS
(IRRITABLE —) SNAP
(JAVANESE —) KRAMA
(LONG —) MONOLOG
(LONG-DRAWN —) TIRADE
(MISLEADING —) PALAVER
(MOCKING —) TRIFLE
(OBSCURE —) ENIGMA
(OFFENSIVE —) INJURY
(PERT —) DICACITY
(PRETENTIOUS —) FUSTIAN
(ROUNDABOUT —) CIRCUIT
(SANCTIMONIOUS —) SNUFFLE
(SLANDEROUS —) EVIL
(VAPID —) WASH
SPEED BAT HIE RIP RUN FLEE FOOT GAIT HIGH PACE PELT POST TILT BLAST HASTE HURRY SMOKE WHIRL CAREER STREAK QUICKEN CELERITY DISPATCH FASTNESS MOMENTUM RAPIDITY VELOCITY ACCELERATE
(— OF NAUTICAL MILE) KNOT
(— OF PITCH) STUFF
(— OF 100 MILES PER HOUR) TON
(— UP) HASTEN CATALYZE EXPEDITE
(AT FULL —) AMAIN
(AUTOMOTIVE —) LOW HIGH DRIVE FIRST THIRD FOURTH SECOND REVERSE
(DRIVING —) SWING
(GOOD —) BONALLY
(HIGH —) CLIP MACH
SPEEDILY SOON APACE PRESTO BETIMES QUICKLY
SPEEDY FAST SOON HASTY QUICK SWIFT SUDDEN EXPEDITE SPEEDFUL POSTHASTE
SPELL GO FIT HEX JAG JINX MOJO RUNE TAKE TIFF TIME TOUR TURN BRIEF CHARM CRAFT MAGIC SPACE ACCESS GLAMOR GRIGRI MAKUTU MANTRA PERIOD STREAK CANTRIP SORCERY EXORCISM MALEFICE

(— OF ACTIVITY) BOUT
(— OF EXERCISE) BREATHER
(— OF LISTLESSNESS) DOLDRUMS
(— OF SHIVERING) AGUE
(— OF WEATHER) SNAP SLANT SEASON
(BREATHING —) BLOW
(BRIEF —) SNATCH
(DRINKING —) FUDDLE
(EVIL —) JINX
(FAINTING —) DROW DWALM
(NIPPING —) SNAPE
(STORMY —) FLAW
(VOODOOISTIC —) WANGA
SPEND COST DROP PASS STOW WEAR DALLY SERVE SHOOT TRADE EXPEND LAVISH OUTRUN CONSUME EXHAUST CONTRIVE DISBURSE
(— FRUITLESSLY) DAWDLE
(— IN IDLENESS) DRONE
(— LAVISHLY) BLUE SPORT DEBAUCH
(— MONEY) MELT
(— RECKLESSLY) BLOW LASH
(— SUMMER) ESTIVATE
(— TIME) DREE FOOL DREIE ENTREAT
(— TIME TEDIOUSLY) DRANT
(— WASTEFULLY) SPILL SQUANDER
SPENDTHRIFT WASTER PANURGE ROUNDER SPENDER WASTREL PRODIGAL PROFLIGATE SCATTERGOOD
SPENT DONE WEARY EFFETE OVERWORN
SPHERE ORB AREA BALL BOWL SHOT GLOBE ORBIT RANGE SCOPE CIRCLE HEAVEN REGION COUNTRY GLOBOID KINGDOM PURVIEW EMPYREAN PROVINCE TERRITORY
(— OF ACTION) AMBIT ARENA WORLD DOMAIN
(— OF ACTIVITY) FIELD FRONT
(— OF AUTHORITY) DIOCESE
(— OF INFLUENCE) DOMAIN SATRAPY
(— OF LIFE) EARTH WORLD STATION
(— OF OPERATION) THEATER THEATRE
(— OF WORK) TITLE
(CELESTIAL —) CYCLE ELEMENT
(ENCOMPASSING —) AMBIENT
(MAGNETIZED —) EARTHKIN TERRELLA
(METAL —) HAMMER
(SMALL —) ORBICLE SPHERULE
(TINKLING —) CROTAL
SPHERICAL GLOBAL ROTUND GLOBATE ORBICAL GLOBULAR
SPICE MACE VEIN AROMA CLOVE TASTE GINGER NUTMEG PEPPER SEASON ALLSPICE CINNAMON SEASONER
SPICY RACY SEXY GAMEY NUTTY SWEET GINGERY PEPPERY FRAGRANT
SPIDER COB ATTID COPPE LOPPE NANCY ANANSI EPEIRA HUNTER KATIPO TRIVET WEAVER ARANEID POKOMOO SKILLET SPINNER ARACHNID ATTERCOP ETTERCAP KARAKURT SOLPUGID VENANTES TARANTULA
SPIGOT TAP SPILE DOSSIL DOZZLE STOPCOCK
SPIKE GAD BARB BROB PICK PIKE PILE SPUR TINE PITON POINT SPEAR SPICA

PRITCH SPADIX PRICKET TRENAIL
TURNPIN STROBILE
(— A CANNON) CLOY
(— OF CEREAL) EAR
(BRACTED —) AMENT
(DRIED —S) CANNABIS
SPILL LET DRIP SHED SLOP SCALE SPILE
SQUAB PURLER SLOBBER
(— FOR LIGHTING PIPES) FIDIBUS
SPIN BIRL DRAW GYRE PURL SCREW
TWIRL TWIST WEAVE WHIRL GYRATE
WAMBLE TWIZZLE
(— AND MAKE HUM) BUM
(— AROUND) SWING
(— ON BASEBALL) STUFF
(— ON BILLIARD BALL) SIDE
(— OUT) SHOOT
(— SILK) THROW
(— SMOOTHLY) SLEEP
(— UNEVENLY) TWITTER
SPINDLE PIN AXLE PIRN SPIT STEM STUD
ARBOR SPIKE SPILL VERGE BOBBIN
BROACH CANNON FUSEAU MANDREL
(AXLE —) ARM
(FOURTH OF —) HASP
(ONE 24TH OF —) HEER
SPINE PIKE PILE SETA SPUR CHINE QUILL
SPEAR SPIKE THORN ACUMEN CHAETA
RACHIS ACANTHA ACICULA FULCRUM
GLOCHIS PRICKLE ROSTRUM SPINULE
STICKLE BACKBONE PELELITH SPICULUM
SPIRAL COIL CURL GYRE SPIN SCREW
GURGES LITUUS SCREWY TWIRLY
VOLUTE HELICAL ROLLING SPIROID
WINDING GYROIDAL HELICOID
(LACEWORK —) PURL
SPIRE CROWN SHAFT SPEAR TAPER
BROACH FLECHE PRICKET SHIKARA
SPIRALE
SPIRIT GO NAG PEP VIM AKUA ALMA
ATUA DASH ELAN FIRE GALL HYLE LIFE
MARE MIND MOOD TONE ZING CHEER
DHOUL DJINN FLING GUACA HAUNT
HEART HUACA JINNI NUMEN PLUCK
POWER SAINT SHRAB SPOOK SPUNK
VERVE BREATH ESPRIT FLECHE INWARD
METTLE MORALE ORISHA PECKER
PNEUMA SPRITE WRAITH ALCOHOL
BRAVERY CONTROL CORDIAL ENTRAIN
MANITOU PIZZAZZ PURUSHA STOMACH
CALVADOS PHANTASM SPIRITUS
(— DWELLING IN JEWEL) AZOTH
(— DWELLING IN MINES) KNOCKER
(— HAUNTING PRINTING HOUSES)
RALPH
(— OF DEAD) CHINDI
(— OF DEATH) CHULPA
(— OF FERTILITY) YAKSHA
(— OF HOSTILITY) ANIMUS
(— OF LOYALTY) PIETAS
(— OF MAN) AKH
(— OF ONE WHO HAS MET VIOLENT
DEATH) PISACHI
(— OF PHYSICAL HEART) AB
(— OF TRAGEDY) COTHURN
(— OF UNBAPTIZED BABE) TARAN

(— WHICH ACTUATES CUSTOMS)
ETHOS
(—S OF LOWER WORLD) INFERI
(—S OF THE DEAD) MANES
(ANCESTRAL —) ANITO KATCHINA
(ARDENT —) ARRACK
(ASTRAL —) AGIEL ASTRAL JOPHIEL
UUCHATON
(AVENGING —) FURY ALECTO ALASTOR
MEGAERA
(CHARACTERISTIC —) VIBE
(COMBATIVE —) SWORD
(DISEMBODIED —) KUEI KWEI SOUL
GHOST LARVA SHADE ASUANG SPECTER
SPECTRE
(DIVINE —) ISVARA ISHVARA
(EARTH —) ERDGEIST
(EFFULGENT —S) ARDORS
(EMANCIPATED —) MUKTATMA
(EVIL —) DEV HAG IMP OKI BAKA BENG
BOKO BOLL DEVA DUSE MARA OKEE
ASURA BUGAN DAEVA DEMON DEVIL
JUMBY OTKON DAITYA DYBBUK LILITH
AHRIMAN BUGGANE CASZIEL INCUBUS
KANAIMA RAKSHAS SHAITAN SKOOKUM
WINDIGO ASMODEUS BAALPEOR
BEELPEOR HOBOMOCO NIGHTMARE
(FAMILIAR —) FLY GENIUS HARPIER
(FEMALE —) DUFFY DUPPY DUSIO
HOLDA UNDINE BANSHEE ATAENSIC
BABAJAGA BELFAGOR BELFAZOR
(FOREST —) MIMING
(FULL OF —) CRANK
(GOOD —) DEVA EUDEMON
(GOVERNING —) ANIMUS
(GUARDIAN —) ANGEL TOTEM FYLGJA
NAGUAL
(HIGH —) GINGER COURAGE
(HIGH —S) CREST GAIETY HEYDAY
ELATION
(HOSTILE —S) LEMURES
(HOUSEHOLD —S) LARES PENATES
(HUMAN —) JIVATMA
(IMPISH —) PO
(IMPURE —) FAINTS
(IN VIGOROUS —S) FIERCE
(LOW —S) DUMP BLUES MEGRIM
DISMALS
(MALEVOLENT —) BHUT GORIC LARVA
(MALICIOUS —) DOBBY
(MALIGNANT —) IMP KER GYRE DEMON
(MANLY —) SPLEEN
(MISCHIEVOUS —) KOBOLD TIKOLOSH
(MOUNTAIN —) RUBEZAHL
(MOVING —) SOUL
(MUSICAL —) BRIO
(NATURE —) NAT
(PARTY —) FACTION
(REFINED —) ELIXIR
(RESOLUTE —) SPRAWL
(ROVING —) RAMPLER
(SEA —) TANGIE
(SENSED —) KARMA
(SOOTHSAYING —) PYTHON
(SUPERNATURAL —) FAMILIAR
(SYLVAN —) LESHY SYLVAN
(TRICKSY —) ARIEL

(TUTELARY —S) DIS LARES
(VITAL —) TUCK
(VOLATILE —) ESSENCE
(WATER —) ARIEL KELPY UNDINE
(WICKED —) IMP THURSE
SPIRITED BRAG FELL GOGO RACY BEANY
CRANK EAGER FIERY FLUSH PEPPY
PROUD SASSY SMART SPICY VIVID
FIERCE GINGER LIVELY PLUCKY SPRUCE
SPUNKY VIVACE ANIMATO DASHING
FORWARD HUMMING NERVOUS PEPPERY
SPIRITY DESIROUS FRAMPOLD SLASHING
SPIRITLESS DEAD MEAN MEEK POOR
TAME AMORT FAINT MILKY SEEDY
SOGGY VAPID ABJECT ANEMIC CRAVEN
JEJUNE LEADEN SODDEN SOFTLY
WOODEN INSIPID LANGUID FECKLESS
FLAGGING LISTLESS
SPIRITUAL ABOVE DEVOUT INWARD
GHOSTLY CHURCHLY INTERNAL
NUMINOUS SUPERIOR
SPIT YEX RACK FROTH SPAWL BROACH
SPITTLE
SPITE ENVY ONDE PIQUE VENOM MALICE
MAUGRE RANCOR SPLEEN
SPITEFUL MEAN CATTY NASTY PETTY
SNAKY MALIGN SULLEN WANTON
WICKED ENVIOUS PEEVISH SNAKISH
VICIOUS WASPISH CANKERED
VENOMOUS
SPLASH LAP DASH GLOB JAUP LUSH
SPAT BLASH FLICK FLOOD PLASH PLOUT
SLOSH DABBLE DOLLOP JABBLE SOZZLE
SQUIRT PLOUTER SPATTER SPIRTLE
SPLURGE SPLATTER SPLUTTER
(— OF COLOR) GOUT
(SLIGHT —) GILP
SPLENDID GAY BRAW FINE NEAT BRAVE
GRAND JOLLY NOBLE PROUD REGAL
ROYAL SHOWY STOUT TOUGH WALLY
COSTLY SPIFFY SUPERB ELEGANT
GALLANT SHINING SUBLIME BARONIAL
CHAMPION COLOSSAL GLORIOUS
GORGEOUS MAJESTIC ORGULOUS
SPANKING STUNNING TERRIFIC
SPLENDOR SUN POMP BLAZE GLARE
GLEAM GLORY SHEEN SHINE FULGOR
LUSTER PARADE CLARITY DISPLAY
JOLLITY PANACHE GRANDEUR RADIANCE
SPLICE JOIN PIECE CROTCH SPLICING
SPLINTER BROOM BURST SHAKE SPALT
SPILE SPILL SPLIT SLIVER SPLINT
SHATTER
SPLIT AX CUT BUCK DUNT MAUL RASH
REND RENT RIFT RIVE SKAG TEAR BLAST
BREAK BURST CHINE SHEAR SMASH
CLEAVE CLOVEN CREASE DIVIDE SCHISM
SUNDER BIVALVE SHATTER CREVASSE
SCISSION SCISSURE
(— FISH) SCROD
(— IN BOWLING) BEDPOSTS
(— OFF) SPALL SPAWL SCREEVED
(— TICKET) SCRATCH
SPOIL MAR ROT BLOT COOK FOIL KILL
PREY ADDLE BLEND BOOTY BOTCH
CROSS DECAY LOUSE QUAIL QUEER
STAIN TOUCH TRASH BOODLE COSSET

CURDLE DEFACE DEFORM INJURE
MANGLE PERISH RAVAGE BEDEVIL
BLEMISH CORRUPT INDULGE PILLAGE
PLUNDER SPOLIUM TARNISH VIOLATE
BANKRUPT CONFOUND DISGRACE
MISGUIDE
SPOILS BAG LOOT SWAG BOOTY SPOLIA
PILLAGE PLUNDER
SPOKE RUNG QUOTH SPAKE LOWDER
SPONDYL
SPONGE FORM MUMP POLE SILK SWAB
CADGE LUFFA SHARK SHIRK SYCON
ASCULA BUMMER LOOFAH MOPPET
ROLLER BLEEDER RADIATE SCOURER
DEADBEAT HEDGEHOG SCROUNGE
PORIFERAN
(YOUNG —) SEEDLING
(SUFF.) AENE
SPOOL COB PIRN REEL SPILL TWILL
BOBBIN COPPIN CARRIER
(— FOR NETS) GURDY
SPOON HORN SHELL COCHLEA MUDDLER
SPINNER STIRRER BARSPOON GOBSTICK
(EUCHARISTIC —) LABIS
(FISHING —) TROLL
(LONG-HANDLED —) LADLE
(SKIMMING —) LINGEL SKIMMER
(SNUFF —) PEN
SPORE CYST SEED AGAMETE AKINETE
ISOLANT SPORULE SWARMER CONIDIUM
GONIDIUM
SPORT FUN GIG KID TOY GAME GAUD
GLEE JEST JOKE LARK PLAY PLOY DALLY
DROLL FREAK MIRTH FROLIC LAUGHS
RACING SKIING BOATING DISPORT
DUCKING FOWLING PASTIME ROLLICK
SAILING FALCONRY PLEASURE
SKYDIVING
(— OF HAWKING) RIVER
(BOISTEROUS —) HIJINKS
(JAPANESE —) KENDO AIKIDO
(ROUGH —) ROMP
(WATER —S) NAUTICS AQUATICS
(WINTER —) SKIJORING
SPORTIVE GAY LARKY MERRY FRISKY
JOCUND LIVELY TOYING WANTON
COLTISH FESTIVE GAMEFUL JESTING
JOCULAR PLAYFUL TRICKSY WAGGISH
FROLICKY PLAYSOME
SPOT BIT DAB BLOT BLUR DIRT DRAB
FLAW MOIL SITE SLUR SMUT SOIL SPAT
TICK BLACK CLOUD FLECK GUTTA JIMMY
PATCH PLACE POINT SMEAR STAIN
SULLY TAINT BLOTCH DAPPLE FOGDOG
MACULE MOTTLE SMUDGE SMUTCH
SPLECK BLEMISH GUTTULA OCELLUS
SMATTER SPATTER SPECKLE SPLOTCH
SPOTTLE STATION STIPPLE TERRAIN
LOCALITY PUNCTULE SPARKLET
(— A SHIELD) GERATE
(— IN CLOTH) YAW
(— IN MINERAL) MACLE
(— IN PAPER) SHINER
(— IN SAW BLADE) BLOB
(— IN STEEL) STAR
(— IN WOOD) WEM
(— IN YARN) MOTE

(— OF INK) MONK
(— OF PAINT) DAUB
(— ON CAT) BUTTON
(— ON EGG) EYE
(— ON FINGERNAIL) GIFT
(— ON FOREHEAD) TILAK
(— ON HAWK) GOUT
(— ON HORSE) RACE SNIP STAR RACHE
(— ON HORSE'S TOOTH) CHARBON
(— ON INSECT WINGS) BULLA
(— ON MOTH'S WINGS) FENESTRA
(— ON PLAYING CARD) PIP
(— ON SUN) FACULA GRANULE
SUNSPOT
(—S IN BOOKS) FOXING
(BARREN —) GALL
(BLIND —) SCOTOMA SCOTOSIS
(BROWN —) SPRAIN SPRAING
(CRUSTY —) SCAB
(ESSENTIAL —) EYE
(FERTILE —) OASIS
(FIRM — IN BOG) HAG
(GREEN — IN VALLEY) HAW
(HALLOWED —) BETHEL
(INFLAMED —) AMPER
(LEAF —) TIKKA BLACKARM
(LIVER —S) CHLOASMA
(LIVID —) TOKEN
(LOW —) DIP SWAMP HOLLOW
(RED —) FLEABITE
(RETIRED —) SHADE
(ROUGH — IN WOVEN GOODS) FAG
(ROUND —) BLOB
(SCABBY —) SCALD
(SECLUDED —) ALCOVE CLOISTER
(SHADY —) SWALE
(SKIN —) MOLE BLISTER FRECKLE
LENTIGO PETECHIA
(SMALL —) DOT PLECK STIGMA
LUNULET SPARKLET
(SOILED —) SLOP
(SORE —) BUBU BOTCH
(SWAMPY —) FLAM
(TIGHT —) JAM JACKPOT
(WEAK —) GALL HOLE CHINK NERVE
(WORN —) FRAY FRET
SPOTLESS FAIR PURE WEMLESS
INNOCENT
SPOTTED PIED MARLY CALICO MACLED
MARLED PARDED SPOTTY TICKED
GUTTATE MOTTLED PIEBALD PINTADO
SPECKLY FRECKLED MACULOSE
SPECKLED STIPPLED
SPOTTY MEALY PATCHY PLATTY SCABBY
SPOUSE EX WIFE BRIDE MATCH PARTY
FELLOW CONSORT HUSBAND
SPOUT JET LIP BEAK GUSH NOSE ORATE
SPILE SPUME SPURT NOZZLE BUBBLER
FOUNTAIN GARGOYLE
SPRAWL LOLL GRABBLE SCAMBLE
SPARTLE SPELDER SCRAMBLE SPRADDLE
STRADDLE
SPRAY FOG HOSE SWISH TWIST SHOWER
SPARGE SPLASH CURTAIN SPAIRGE
SYRINGE INHALANT
(— FROM SMALL WAVES) LIPPER
(— MASH) SPARGE

(— OF GEMS) AIGRETTE
SPREAD BED LAY RUN COAT DRAW TUCK
VEIN WALK APPLY CREEP PASTE SCALE
SLICE SPEND STALK STREW WIDEN
BUTTER EXTEND LAYOUT SETOUT
THRUST UNFOLD UNFURL BROADEN
DISPLAY DISTEND EXPANSE OPENING
SCATTER STRETCH DISPERSE INCREASE
MULTIPLY STRAGGLE
(— ABROAD) TOOT BLAZE DELATE
SPRING DIVULGE EMANATE
(— APART) GAPE
(— AS GOSSIP) BUZZ
(— BY REPORT) BLOW NOISE NORATE
(— DEFAMATION) LIBEL
(— FOR DRYING) TED
(— INTO) INVADE
(— LIKE GRAIN) FLOOR
(— NEWS) HORN
(— ON THICK) COUCH SLATHER
(— OUT) FAN FLOW OPEN ROLL SPAN
SPLAY SPRAY EXPAND FLANGE FRINGE
MANTLE OUTLAY SPRAWL UNLOCK
DIFFUSE DISTENT EXPLAIN FEATHER
DIFFUSED STRAGGLY
(— OUTWARD) FLARE
(— OVER) LAP DASH COVER SUFFUSE
(— PAINT) KNIFE
(— THINLY) BRAY DRIVE TOUCH
SCANTY
(EVENLY —) SUANT
(TAPESTRY-WOVEN —) KILIM
SPREE BAT BUM JAG BLOW BUST LARK
TEAR TIME TOOT BEANO BINGE BURST
SOUSE BENDER BUSTER JUNKET
RANDAN BLOWOFF JAMBOREE
WINGDING
SPRIGHTLY GAY TID AIRY PERT WARM
ALIVE BRISK CANTY CRISP MERRY PERKY
QUICK BLITHE BREEZY JAUNTY LIVELY
SPANKY CHIPPER JOCULAR PLEASANT
SPRING BUG HOP JET URN WAX BATH
BOLT BOUT BUCK BUNT DART FLOW
FONT HAIR HEAD JUMP LEAP RISE SEEP
SKIP SOAK STEM WELL WIND BOUND
DANCE FLIRT FOUNT FRESH ISSUE
LYMPH PRIME QUELL SALLY SPOUT
START SURGE THROW VAULT DERIVE
GAMBOL ORIGIN PIRENE SILOAM SOURCE
VENERO EMANATE ESTUARY FLOUNCE
GAMBADO PROCEED BANDUSIA
CASTALIA FOUNTAIN SPANGHEW
ORIGINATE
(— AWKWARDLY) KEVEL
(— BACK) RECOIL RESULT RETORT
REBOUND
(— DOWN) ALIGHT
(— FORWARD) LAUNCH
(— FROM) DESCEND
(— OF THE YEAR) VER VOAR
(— ON SHEARS) BACKSTAY
(— SEASON) APRIL GRASS BUDTIME
(— SUDDENLY) FLY BOUNCE
(— TO FASTEN NECKLACE) LOCKET
(— UP) ARISE SHOOT SPROUT BURGEON
UPSPRING
(BOILING —) TUBIG

(CARRIAGE —) ROBBIN
(ERUPTIVE —) WALM GEYSER
(GUSHING —) CHARCO
(HOT —) SPRUDEL
(INTERMITTENT —) NAILBOURN
(INTERMITTENT —S) GIPSIES GYPSIES
(LAND —) LAVANT
(MECHANICAL —) RESORT
(MINERAL —) SPA BALNEARY
(SALT —) LICK SALINE
(WARM —S) THERMAE
(WATCH —) SLEEVE
SPRINGTIME VER WARE GERMINAL
SPRINGY WHIPPY ELASTIC FLEXIBLE
SPRINKLE ASH DAMP SHED SHAKE
SPURT WATER DABBLE POUNCE SPARGE
SQUIRT ASPERGE ASPERSE DRIZZLE
SCATTER SKITTER SPARKLE SPATTER
DISPUNGE SPITTING STRINKLE
(— IN BAPTISM) RANTIZE
(— OF RAIN) SPIT
(— SEED) SPRAIN
(— TOBACCO) BLOW
(— WITH FLOUR) DREDGE
(— WITH POWDER) DUST
(— WITH SALT) CORN
(— WITH SAND) SAND
SPRITE ELF HOB PUG PUCK BUCCA FAIRY
PIXIE GOBLIN SPIRIT UMBRIEL
WATERMAN
(WATER —) NIX NIXIE NICKER
SPROUT BUD LAD BROD CION DRAW
TOOT CATCH SHOOT SPEAR SPIRE SPRIT
GERMEN RATOON TELLER BURGEON
COPPICE TENDRON
(— OF BARLEY) TAIL
(FIRST —S) BREER BRAIRD BREIRD
(STUMP —) TILLER
SPRUCE GIM DEFT NEAT POSH SMUG
SPRY TRIG TRIM BRISK COMPT CRISP
FRESH JEMMY NATTY NIFTY SLICK
SMART SPIFF SPRIG DAPPER FINICAL
FOPPISH SMARTEN SMICKER EPINETTE
TITIVATE
SPRY AGILE BRISK QUICK NIMBLE
BOBBISH
SPUR ARM GAD GIG EDGE GAFF GOAD
MOVE STUD TANG ARETE DRIVE PRICK
PRONG ROWEL SPICA BROACH CALCAR
EXCITE FILLIP FOMENT INCITE MOTIVE
OFFSET SICKLE INCITER SCRATCH
GAVELOCK
(— OF COCK) HEEL
(— ON HORSESHOE) CALK
(— TO ACTION) GOOSE
SPURIOUS BAD FAKE SHAM BOGUS
FUNNY PHONY QUEER SNIDE PSEUDO
BASTARD PINCHBECK
SPURN FOOT SCORN REJECT CONTEMN
DECLINE DESPISE DISDAIN
SPURT JET GOUT SPIN BURST CHIRT
PULSE SALLY SPOUT GEYSER SPRING
SPROUT SQUIRT SPATTER
SPUTTER SPIT FIZZLE SOTTER SPATTER
SPLUTTER
SPY PRY ESPY NARK NOSE WORM PERDU
PLANT SCOUT SPOOK WATCH BEAGLE

BEHOLD DESCRY PEEPER SEARCH
SHADOW EXAMINE SPOTTER WATCHER
DISCOVER
(— ON RACEHORSES) TOUT
(— UPON) LAY
(PLANTED —) STOOGE
(POLICE —) SETTER
SQUABBLE MUSS TIFF BRAWL SCRAP
BICKER JANGLE SQUALL BRANGLE
CONTEND QUARREL
SQUAD CREW DECURY TWENTY
PLATOON
SQUALID DINGY DIRTY MANGY SEEDY
FILTHY FROWZY SORDID SCABROUS
SQUALL FRET GUST MEWL ROAR WAUL
FRESH FLURRY SQUAWK BORASCA
TORNADO BLIZZARD
SQUANDER BLOW BURN LASH SPEND
SPILL WASTE LAVISH MUDDLE PALTER
PLUNGE CONSUME DEBAUCH SCAMBLE
EMBEZZLE MISSPEND
SQUARE FIX EDGE EVEN FOUR FULL
QUAD SUIT AGREE CHECK HUNKY PLAIN
PLAZA BLOCKY DINKUM ISAGON PIAZZA
ZENZIC CARREAU CHECKER COMMONS
UPRIGHT QUADRANT QUADRATE
TETRAGON
(— A STONE) PITCH
(— FOR BOWLING SCORE) FRAME
(— OF CANVAS) SKATE
(— OF CLOTH) PANE
(— OF DOUGH) KNISH
(— OF FRAMING) PAN
(— OF GLASS) QUARREL
(— OF LINEN) PALL
(— OF TURF) DIVOT QUADREL
(— OFF) BUTT
(— ON BILLIARD TABLE) CROTCH
(— ON CHESSBOARD) HOUSE POINT
(CARPENTER'S —) NORMA
(CHURCH —) PARVIS
(LINEN —) SUDARIUM
(ONE-MILE —) SECTION
(PATTERN OF —S) DAMIER
(WOVEN —) SINKER
SQUARELY FAIR FULL FLUSH SPANG
FAIRLY DIRECTLY SMACKDAB
SQUASH PEPO GOURD CUCURB CUSHAW
MARROW SIMNEL HUBBARD PUMPKIN
CUCURBIT PEPONIUM ZUCCHINI
SQUAT STUB COWER DUMPY FUBSY
HUNCH PUDGY SQUAB HUNKER STOCKY
STUBBY THICKSET
SQUAWK SCRAWK SQUALL SQUARK
SQUAWL COMPLAIN
SQUEAK PEEP CHEEP CHIRK SCRAWK
SQUEAL
SQUEAL RAT FINK HOWL WHISTLE
SQUEAMISH NICE PAWKY DAINTY
QUAINT QUEASY WAMBLY FINICAL
MAWKISH NAUSEOUS OVERNICE
SQUEEZE EKE HUG JAM NIP CLAM VISE
CREEM CROWD CRUSH PRESS WRING
SQUASH THRONG TWITCH SCRUNCH
SQUINCH COMPRESS CONTRACT
PRESSURE
(— FROM) SPONGE

(— IN) FUDGE
(— INTO) THRIMBLE
(— OUT) PINCH STRAIN
(ECONOMIC —) CRUNCH

SQUINT AWRY GLEE SKEW GOGGLE
SQUINCH SQUINNY

SQUIRE SWAIN DONZEL JUNKER
ARMIGER ESQUIRE YOUNKER HENCHMAN
SERVITOR

SQUIRM CURL TWINE WRING WRITHE
WRESTLE WRIGGLE SQUIGGLE

SQUIRT SCOOT SPIRT SPOUT SPURT
SPRITZ SCOOTER SQUITTER

SRI LANKA

CAPITAL: COLOMBO
COIN: CENT RUPEE
GULF: MANNAR
MEASURE: PARA PARAH AMUNAM
PARRAH
POINT: PEDRO
STRAIT: PALK
TOWN: GALLE KANDY JAFFNA MANNAR
MATARA BADULLA COLOMBO PUTTALAM

STAB DAG JAB DIRK GORE PINK POKE
SHIV KNIFE PRICK PRONG STICK STOKE
BROACH DAGGER PIERCE POUNCE
THRUST BAYONET PRICKADO STILETTO

STABILITY POISE FIXURE BALANCE
FIRMNESS SECURITY CONSTANCY

STABILIZE FIX SET EVEN TRIM POISE
STEADY BALANCE BALLAST STIFFEN

STABLE BYRE FAST FIRM SURE SOLID
SOUND STALL STIFF STOUT LIVERY
SECURE STATIC STEADY STRONG
STURDY DURABLE LASTING OXHOUSE
SETTLED BALANCED IMMOBILE
STANDING PERMANENT
(ROYAL —S) MEWS

STACK MOW SOW PACK POKE GOAVE
SCROO STAKE STALK STOCK COLUMN
FUNNEL STACKAGE
(— BRICKS) CLAMP SCINTLE
(— IN KILN) BOX
(— LUMBER) STICK
(— OF ARMS) PILE
(— OF BRICK) LIFT
(— OF CERAMICS) BUNG
(— OF CORN) SHOCK
(— OF FISH) BULK
(— OF GRAIN) RICK
(— OF HIDES) BED
(— OF PANS) SWEATER
(— OF SHEETS) BOOK
(HAY OR CORN —) HOVEL
(SMALL —) COB CANCH RICKLE
(TILE —) WELL

STAFF ROD TAW CANE CLUB MACE MALL
MAUL PIKE POLE RUNG TREE YARD
CROSS KEVEL PERCH STAVE STICK SUITE
BASTON CLEEKY CROCHE CRUTCH
FAMILY FERULE LITUUS PRITCH WARDER
BOURDON DISTAFF FESTUCA SCEPTER
STADDLE THYRSUS CADUCEUS TIPSTAFF

(— AT END OF NET) BRAIL
(— OF AUTHORITY) VARE VERGE
(— OF COOKS) BOUCHE
(— OF OFFICIALS) OMLAH
(— WITH CROSSPIECE) POTENT
(BISHOP'S —) BAGLE BACULUS
CROSIER PASTORAL
(FIELD MARSHAL'S —) BATON
(FORKED —) LINSTOCK
(GRADUATED —) LIMB
(HOTTENTOT —) KIRVI
(MAGICIAN'S —) RHABDOS
(NEWSPAPER —) DAYSIDE
(NUBIAN —) KUERR
(PILGRIM'S —) BURDEN
(PLASTERER'S —) BEATER
(SHEPHERD'S —) KENT CROOK
(SPARTAN —) SCYTALE
(TEACHING —) FACULTY
(THIEVES' —) FILCH

STAG HART WAPITI BULLOCK KNOBBER
POINTER KNOBBLER
(— OF THE 3D YEAR) SPIRE
(— OF 2ND YEAR) BROCKET
(— OF 8 YEARS OR MORE) ROYAL
(— THAT HAS CAST HIS ANTLERS)
POLLARD
(DEAD —) MORT
(HORNLESS —) HUMMEL
(3-YEAR OLD —) SPADE

STAGE LEG BANK POST APRON ETAGE
GRADE PHASE POINT SCENE STATE
BOARDS DEGREE PERIOD PHASIS
ROSTRUM STADIUM PLATFORM
SCAFFOLD PROSCENIUM
(— FOR DRYING FISH) FLAKE
(— FOR HAY) HEMMEL
(— IN DELIRIUM) TILMUS
(— IN FEVER) FLUSH
(— IN PORCELAIN FURNACE) HOWELL
(— IN TRAVELING) GEST
(— OF CUPOLA) LANTERN
(— OF DEVELOPMENT) ERA BLOSSOM
(— OF FUNGUS) OIDIUM
(— OF GLACIATION) RISS WURM
ACHEN MINDEL
(— OF INSECT) INSTAR
(— OF LIFE) AGE ASHRAMA
(— OF MITOSIS) ANAPHASE PROPHASE
(— OF PERSONALITY) LATENCY
(— OF ROCKET) BOOSTER
(— OF THEATER) SCAENA THEATRON
(— WHERE SLAVES WERE SOLD)
CATASTA
(BOTTOMMOST —) CELLAR
(COMIC —) SOCK
(EARLIEST —) PRIME
(FINAL —) CLOSE FINISH STRETCH
(FIRST —) YOUTH SPRING
(FLOATING —) DUMMY
(FLOOD —) CREST
(GEOLOGICAL —) GUNZ GLACIAL
SENONIAN
(INITIAL —) INFANCY
(LANDING —) STAIR BRIDGE STAITH
STELLING
(MOVING —) PEGMA

(RADIO —) STEP
(THIRD —) AUTUMN
STAGGER REEL ROLL DODGE LURCH PITCH FALTER GOGGLE TOTTER WAMBLE WIGGLE MEGRIMS STAMMER STUMBLE SWAGGER TITUBATE
STAGNANT DEAD DULL INERT STILL STATIC COBWEBBY SLUGGISH STANDING
STAGNATION STASIS TORPOR LANGUOR
STAID SET CIVIL GRAVE SOBER DEMURE STEADY EARNEST SERIOUS DECOROUS
STAIN DYE BLOT BLUR BUFF DIRT DRAB FILE FOIL HURT MOLE RUST SLUR SMUT SOIL SPOT BLACK BRAND CLOUD DIRTY PAINT SMEAR SPECK SULLY TAINT TINGE IMBRUE INFAMY INFECT MACULA SMIRCH SMUDGE SMUTCH SPLASH STIGMA ATTAINT BLEMISH SPATTER SPLOTCH TARNISH BESMIRCH DISCOLOR DISGRACE DISHONOR FLYSPECK MACULATE
(— BLACK) EBONIZE
(— IN LINEN) MELL
(— ON BRICK) SCUMMING
(— WITH BLOOD) ENGORE
STAINED FOXY RUSTY SMUDGY SMUTCHY
(— BY DECAY) DOATY
(— WITH BLOOD) BLOODY IMBRUED
STAINLESS PURE CHASTE INNOCENT
STAIR RUNG STEP DEGREE COCHLEA ESCALIER
(MINING —) LOB
(WINDING —) VICE CARACOL
(PL.) PAIR PITCH FLIGHT DANCERS
STAIRWAY STOOP GREESE PERRON DESCENT ESCALIER
(— ON RIVER BANK) GHAT
(CURVED —) SWEEP
(SHIP'S —) LADDER
(WINDING —) VICE TURNPIKE
STAKE BET HOB LAY SET ANTE BENT GAGE MAIN PALE PAWN POOL PUNT RISK STOB TREE WAGE SPOKE SPRAG STOCK WAGER CHANCE CROTCH GAMBLE HAZARD IMPONE PALING TRUNCH VENTURE
(CART —) RUNG
(COMPULSORY — IN POKER) BLIND
(GAMBLING —) MISE
(POINTED —) SOULE SOWEL PICKET
(SURVEYORS' —) HUB
(TETHERING —) PUTTO
(TINSMITH'S —) TEEST
STALE OLD COLD FLAT PALL SICK WORN BLOWN DUSTY HOARY MOLDY MUSTY TRITE FROWZY MOULDY STUFFY INSIPID STAGNANT
STALK CORN HAFT POLE STEM QUILL SHANK SPIRE STAKE STIPE STUMP COULIS STIPES FUNICLE PEDICEL PETIOLE CAUDICLE PEDUNCLE
(— OF BUCKWHEAT) STRAW
(— OF CRINOID) COLUMN
(— OF GRAIN) RIZZOM
(— OF GRASS) BENT SPEAR

(— OF HAY) RISP
(— OF PLANT) SPINDLE TENACLE
(— OF SPOROGONIUM) SETA
(— OF STAMEN) FILAMENT
(— OF SUGAR CANE) RATOON
(— OF UMBEL) RAY
(—S OF GRAIN) KARBI STRAW
(CABBAGE —) CASTOCK
(CROSSBOW —) TILLER
(DRY —) KEX KECK BENNET
(FLOWER —) SCAPE
(HOLLOW —) BUN KEX KECK
STALL BAY BIN BOX CRIB SPAR BOOTH PITCH STAND CARREL TRAVIS CABINET BUTCHERY STANDING
(— FOR TIME) HAVER STRETCH
(— IN CLOISTER) CAROL
(— IN COAL MINE) BREAST WICKET
(— IN MUD) STOG
(— IN ROMAN CIRCUS) CARCER
(BISHOP'S —) TRIBUNE
(CHURCH —) PEW
(THEATER —) LOGE FAUTEUIL
STALWART STARK STIFF STRONG STURDY VALIANT
STAMINA GUTS SAND BOTTOM
STAMMER HACK STUT GANCH FALTER HACKER HAFFLE HOTTER STUMBLE STUTTER HESITATE SPLUTTER TITUBATE
STAMP COIL DRUB MARK SEAL SNAP TYPE DOLLY FRANK NIXIE PRINT PUNCH STOMP STUNT ACCENT CACHET CLICHE FULLER INDENT PASTER POUNCE SHAPER SIGNET STRIKE CHARACT IMPRESS IMPRINT MINTAGE SPECIAL SQUELCH HALLMARK PUNCHEON
(— AFTER ASSAY) TOUCH
(— BOOK COVER) BLIND
(— FOR CUTTING DOUGH) DOCKER
(— HERRING BARREL) DUNT
(— HIDES) STOCK
(— HOLES) STOACH
(— OUT) SCOTCH
(— WITH DIE) DINK
(BOOKBINDING —) BLOCK FILLET
(CANCELLING —) KILLER
(HALF OF —) BISECT
(HAND —) CANCELER
(OFFICIAL —) CHOP
(POSTAGE —) AIR DUE CAPE FAKE HEAD ERROR LABEL LOCAL BUREAU INVERT AIRMAIL BICOLOR CHARITY CLASSIC REPRINT STICKER ADHESIVE COLONIAL ORIGINAL SPECIMEN PRECANCEL
(REVENUE —) FISCAL TAXPAID
(SMART —) APPEL
STAMPEDE RUSH BLITZ CHUTE DEBACLE STAMPEDO
STAND SET BEAR DESK RACK RANK REST ERECT FRONT KIOSK STALL STICK CASTER ENDURE INSIST PATTEN PILLAR SMOKER STANCE STRIKE TEAPOY TRIPOD CONSIST EPERGNE LECTERN STATION TABORET TROLLEY ATTITUDE BLEACHER COATRACK POSITION SCAFFOLD
(— AT AN ANGLE) CATER

(— AT ATTENTION) BACK
(— BY) SERVE
(— CLOSE) CROWD ENVIRON
(— FASTENED TO MESS TABLE) CROWFOOT
(— FIRM) STAY
(— FOR) DENOTE
(— FOR AUCTIONING) BLOCK
(— FOR BARRELS) JIB THRALL
(— FOR COFFIN) BIER
(— FOR COMPASS) BINNACLE
(— FOR CONFINING HEAT) HASTER HASTENER
(— FOR DRESSES) FRIPPERY
(— FOR DRILL PIPE) FOURBLE
(— FOR FINJAN) ZARF
(— FOR TILES) CRISS
(— FOR WRITING MATERIALS) STANDISH
(— GUARD) COVER
(— IN AWE) FEAR
(— OF FOREST) GROWTH
(— OF PLANTS) STOOL
(— OFF) AROINT
(— ON AND OFF SHORE) BUSK
(— ON END) STARE UPEND
(— ON TWO FEET) BIPOD DUOPOD
(— OUT) CUT TOOT FLAUNT
(— READY) ABIDE
(— STILL) HALT STAY
(— TO SHOOT) ADDRESS
(— TREAT) MUG SHOUT
(— UNSTEADILY) STAGGER
(— UP STIFF) STIVER
(— UP TO) CONFRONT
(— WITH LEGS APART) STRIDE
(CAKE —) CURATE
(CONCESSION —) JOINT
(FIRECLAY —) CRANK
(ONE-NIGHT —) GIG
(PRINTER'S —) BANK FRAME
(PULPIT-LIKE —) AMBO
(RAISED —) PERGOLA
(SCULPTOR'S —) CHASSIS
(SHOOTING —) BUTT
(THREE-LEGGED —) TRIVET
STANDARD FLAG GAGE IDEA MARK
NORM SIGN TEST ALLOY BOGEY CANON
CHECK DRAKE EAGLE GAUGE MODEL
NORMA SCALE STOOL AQUILA BANNER
CORNET FILLER NORMAL SQUARE
STAPLE TRIPOD ANCIENT CLASSIC
DECORUM LABARUM GONFALON
ORIFLAMB ORTHODOX VEXILLUM
(— IN GATE) STRIKE
(— OF ACCURACY) COCKER
(— OF CONDUCT) LINE GNOMON
(— OF PERFECTION) IDEAL
(— OF PITCH) DIAPASON
(— OF QUALITY) GRADE
(—S OF BEHAVIOR) ETHICS
(CONVENTIONAL —) PIETY
(LIGHT —) CARCEL
(NOT —) BASTARD
(TURKISH —) ALEM TOUG
(PL.) LIGHTS HOLSTERS

STANDARD-BEARER CORNET ENSIGN
ALFEREZ ANCIENT SIGNIFER VEXILLARY
STANDING BEING ERECT STATE CREDIT
ESTEEM REGULAR RESPECT PRESTIGE
STANZA CALL ENVOI ENVOY STAFF
STAVE VERSE DIXAIN OCTAVE SEPTET
SESTET SEXTET HUITAIN SEXTAIN
STROPHE TRIOLET CINQUAIN QUATRAIN
QUINTAIN
STAPLE LOOP FLOSS STITCH SHACKLE
STEEPLE VERVELLE
STAR SUN FIRE LAMP ASTER DWARF
EXCEL GIANT SHINE ALNATH ASTRAL
BINARY COUPLE DOUBLE ETOILE LUCIDA
MULLET NITHAM SHINER SPHERE STELLA
BENEFIC DINGBAT ESTOILE GEMINID
STARLET ASTERISK ASTEROID
HEXAGRAM PENTACLE VARIABLE
(COMPANION —) COMES
(DOG —) SEPT SOPT SEPTI SIRIUS
(EVENING —) VENUS HESPER VESPER
EVESTAR HESPERUS
(FEATHER —) COMATULA
(FILM —) VEDETTE
(GUIDING —) LOADSTAR LODESTAR
(MORNING —) VENUS DAYSTAR
PHOSPHOR
(NEW —) NOVA
(OFFICER'S —) PIP
(PULSATING —) CEPHEID
(SHOOTING —) BOLIDE LEONID
METEOR COWSLIP SHOOTER
(SPECIFIC —) YED ADIB ALYA ATIK
CAPH ENIF ENIR IZAR KIED MAIA NAOS
PHAD SADR VEGA WEGA ACRAB ACRUX
AGENA ALCOR ALGOL ALKES ANCHA
ARNEB CHARA DABIH DELTA DENEB
DUBHE GIEDI GUIAM GUYAM HAMAL
HAMUL JUGUM MERAK MIZAR NIBAL
NIHAI PHACD PHAET RIGEL SAIPH SPICA
TEJAT WASAT WEZEN ZOSMA ADHARA
ALHENA ALIOTH ALKAID ALMACH ALTAIR
ALUDRA APOLLO ARIDED CASTOR
CELENO CHELEB DIPHDA ELNATH
ETAMIN GIENAH HYADES KOCHAB
LESUTH MAASYM MARKAB MARKEB
MARSIC MEGREZ MENKAR MENKIB
MEROPE MIRACH MIRFAK MIRZAM
NEKKAR PHECDA POLLUX PROPUS
RANICH SCHEAT SHEDIR SIRIUS THABIT
THUBAN ACUBENS ALBIREO ALCHIBA
ALCYONE ALGENIB ALGIEBA ALGORAH
ALMAACK ALNILAM ALNITAK ALPHARD
ALPHIRK ALSHAIN ANTARES AZIMECH
BUNGULA CANOPUS CAPELLA ELECTRA
GIANSAR GOMELZA GRUMIUM MEBSUTA
MELUCTA MENCHIB MINTAKA MUFRIDE
POLARIS PROCYON REGULUS ROTANIM
RUCHBAR SCHEDAR SEGINUS SHELLAK
STEROPE TARAZED TAYGETA TEGMINE
THEENIM
(THREE —S) KIDS ELLWAND TRIANGLE
(7 —S OF GREAT BEAR) CAR
STARCH AMYL ARUM SAGO STIFF
AMYLUM CONJEE FARINA FECULA
CASSAVA CURCUMA TALIPOT FIXATURE
STARE EYE BORE DARE GAPE GAWK

GAWP GAZE KIKE LOOK PORE GLARE GLOWER GOGGLE EYEBALL
(— IDLY) GOVE
(— VACANTLY) GOWK
(COLD —) FISHEYE

STARK BUCK FAIR HARD CRUDE HARSH NAKED STIFF DESOLATE

START SET BOLT DART DASH HEAD JERK OPEN TURN WHIP ARISE BEGIN BIRTH BREAK BUDGE ENTER FLIRT ONSET RAISE ROUSE THROW BROACH FLINCH OUTSET SETOFF SETOUT STRIKE TWITCH GETAWAY OPENERS OPENING STARTLE SUNRISE COMMENCE CONCEIVE
(— A HORSE) WINCE
(— ASIDE) SHY SKIT DODGE
(— BACK) RESILE
(— BURNING) SPIT KINDLE
(— FERMENTATION) PITCH
(— OF BIRD'S FLIGHT) SOUSE
(— OUT) FRAME INTEND
(— UP) JUMP ASTART
(SUDDEN —) SHY SQUIRT

STARTLE ALARM SCARE SHOCK START BOGGLE FRIGHT FRIGHTEN SURPRISE

STARTLING ALARMING SHOCKING

STARVATION LACK PINE FAMINE

STARVE CLEM FAST FAMINE FAMISH

STATE LAY PUT SAY MODE NAME PORT TERM TIFF POLIS SPEAK TERMS WHACK AGENCY ASSERT ASSURE EMPIRE ESTATE IMPORT NATION PLIGHT POLICY POLITY RENDER RIALTY SOVIET CIVITAS DECLARE DUKEDOM EXPOUND EXPRESS KINSHIP PROPOSE SPECIFY STATION DOMINION HEGEMONY INDICATE KINGSHIP REPUBLIC PREDICAMENT
(— EXPLICITLY) DEFINE
(— FORMALLY) ENOUNCE
(— OF AFFAIRS) CASE ARRAY STATUS
(— OF ALARM) GAST FEEZE SCARE
(— OF AMAZEMENT) STOUND
(— OF ANGER) FUME
(— OF APATHY) STUPOR
(— OF CONCENTRATION) DHARANA SAMADHI
(— OF CONFUSION) FOG FLAP HACK MUSS CHAOS SWIRL HASSLE HUBBUB FLUMMOX
(— OF DISASTER) SMASH
(— OF DISORDER) HELL MUSS FANTAD ANARCHY
(— OF DISTURBANCE) GARBOIL
(— OF DOUBT) MIST
(— OF EAGERNESS) HURRY
(— OF ECSTASY) SWOON
(— OF ENCHANTMENT) SPELL
(— OF ENLIGHTENMENT) BODHI
(— OF EXALTATION) FURY ECSTASY
(— OF EXCITEMENT) FRY FLAP GALE HIGH SNIT STEW FEEZE DITHER HUBBUB FLUSTER SWELTER
(— OF FEAR) FUNK JELLY SCARE
(— OF HAPPINESS) ELYSIUM PARADISE
(— OF HEALTH) EUCRASIA
(— OF HUMILIATION) DUST
(— OF IDEAL PERFECTION) UTOPIA
(— OF INACTION) DEADLOCK
(— OF IRRITABILITY) FUME GALL FANTAD
(— OF JOY) JUBILEE
(— OF MELANCHOLY) GLOOM
(— OF MENTAL INACTIVITY) TORPOR
(— OF MIND) CUE HIP CASE MOOD HUMOR FETTLE
(— OF MISERY) HELL GEHENNA
(— OF NEGLECT) LIMBO
(— OF PERFECTION) SIDDHI
(— OF READINESS) GUARD
(— OF REPOSE) KEF CALM
(— OF RETIREMENT) GRASS
(— OF REVERIE) DUMP
(— OF SLUGGISHNESS) COMA
(— OF SUSPENSE) TRANCE
(— OF SUSPENSION) ABEYANCE
(— OF TRANQUILLITY) KEF PEACE
(— OF UNCERTAINTY) FOG FLUX
(— OF UNREST) FERMENT
(— OF WORRY) TEW SWEAT FANTAD
(— POSITIVELY) AFFIRM
(— UNDER OATH) ALLEGE
(AGITATED —) FUSS SNIT STIR CHURN STORM LATHER SWIVET
(BLISSFUL —) NIRVANA
(DEPRESSED —) GLOOM WALLOW
(DISTURBED —) STIR STORM UNREST
(DOMINANT —) SUZERAIN
(EMOTIONAL —) FEVER FEELING
(HIGHEST —) SUPREME
(HOLY —) IHRAM
(HORIZONTAL —) LEVEL
(LIQUID —) FLUOR FLUIDITY
(LOWEST —) BEDROCK
(MENTAL —) EARNEST DELUSION
(MORBID —) HIP IODISM
(MORMON —) DESERET
(NEUTRAL —) BUFFER
(PROFOUND —) DEPTH
(SWISS —) CANTON
(ULTIMATE —) END

STATELY GRAND LARGO LOFTY NOBLE PROUD REGAL AUGUST PORTLY SOLEMN SUPERB GALLANT BARONIAL IMPOSING MAESTOSO MAJESTIC

STATEMENT SAY BILL WORD AXIOM BRIEF COUNT DIXIT STORY BELIEF DOCKET EXPOSE FACTUM SAYING SPEECH ACCOUNT ADDRESS DISSENT EPITAPH EPITOME FORMULA INVOICE MENTION ABSTRACT ARGUMENT AVERMENT BULLETIN DELIVERY EQUATION JUDGMENT PROPOSAL SENTENCE
(— AS PRECEDENT) AUTHORITY
(— OF OPINION) CHANT
(— OF RELATIONS) THEOREM
(AUTHORITATIVE —) DICTUM
(CASUAL —) REMARK
(CONCISE —) SCHEME APHORISM
(CONDENSED —) RESUME SYNOPSIS
(DEFAMATORY —) LIBEL
(EXAGGERATED —) STRETCH
(FABRICATED —) CANARD

(FINAL — OF ACCOUNT) AUDIT
(FINANCIAL —) BUDGET
(FOOLISH —) INANITY
(FORMAL —) CITATION
(IRRATIONAL —) ALOGISM
(OBSCURE —) ENIGMA
(PLAINTIFF'S —) BODY
(POMPOUS —) BRAG
(PUBLIC —) OUTGIVING
(SELF-CONTRADICTORY —) PARADOX
(SOOTHING —) SALVE
(UNTRUE —) LIE
STATEROOM BIBBY CABIN
STATESMAN GENRO SOLON FATHER
STATIST WARWICK JACOBEAN
WEALSMAN
STATION FIX RUN SET POST RANK ROOM
SEAT STOP BERTH DEPOT PLACE STAGE
STALL STAND DEGREE LOCATE CONTROL
DIGNITY HABITAT OUTPOST GARRISON
POSITION STANDING TERMINAL
TERMINUS
(— IN BASEBALL) BASE
(— IN LIFE) BEING CALLING
(— OF HERON) SEDGE SIEGE
(CONCEALED —) AMBUSH
(CUSTOMS —) CHOKEY
(EXALTED —) PURPLE
(POLICE —) TANNA KOTWALEE
(RADIO —S) CHAIN NETWORK
(RAILWAY —) GARE CABIN
(SIGNALLING —) BANTAY BEACON
(SURVEYING —) STADIA
(TRADING —) FACTORY
(WAY —) TAMBO
STATIONARY SET FAST FIXED STILL
STATIC DORMANT STABILE IMMOBILE
STATUE ICON IDOL IMAGE MOSES
AGALMA BRONZE HERMES MEMNON
XOANON PASQUIN CARYATID
MONUMENT PANTHEUM
(— ENDOWED WITH LIFE) GALATEA
(— OF ATHENA) PALLADIUM
(— OF GIGANTIC SIZE) COLOSSUS
(COLOSSAL —) GOG MAGOG
STATUETTE WAX EMMY OSCAR WINNIE
TANAGRA FIGURINE
STATURE PITCH GROWTH HEIGHT
CAPACITY
STATUS RANK SEAT PLACE STATE
ASPECT FOOTING STATURE POSITION
STANDING SITUATION
(— OF YOUNGER SON) CADENCY
(HIGH —) CACHET
(LEGAL —) CAPUT
(SECONDARY —) BACKSEAT
STATUTE ACT LAW EDICT DECREE
SITTING TANZIMAT
STAUNCH FAST STOUT TRUSTY
FAITHFUL STALWART
STAY DAY LIE BASE HOLD PROP REST
STOP WAIT ABIDE DEFER DELAY DEMUR
DWELL TARRY ARREST ATTEND BIDING
DETAIN REMAIN TIMBER UPHOLD
LAYOVER SOJOURN SUSPEND CONTINUE
MAINSTAY
(— AWAY) SKIP

(— BEHIND) LAG
(— CLEAR) AVOID
(— FOR) AWAIT
(— THE NIGHT) BUNK HOSTLE
(— WITH) STICK
(PRIEST'S —) STATION
(TAILORING —) BRIDLE
STEAD LIEU ROOM VICE PLACE BEHALF
STEADFAST PAT FAST FIRM SURE TRUE
STAID STABLE STEADY CERTAIN
EXPRESS SETTLED STAUNCH VALIANT
CONSTANT FAITHFUL RESOLUTE
STALWART
STEADY GUY BEAU EVEN FIRM SURE
TRIG TRUE LEVEL SOBER TIGHT SMOOTH
STABLE BALLAST EQUABLE STAUNCH
CONSTANT DECOROUS DILIGENT
FAITHFUL RESOLUTE TRANQUIL
UNSHAKEN
(— AT ANCHOR) HOLSOM
STEAL BAG CAB COP FOX GYP LAG NAP
NIM NIP RIG CRIB GLOM HOOK KNAP LIFT
LURK MILL NAIL NICK PICK SLIP ANNEX
BRIBE CREEP FETCH FILCH FRISK GLIDE
HEIST HOIST MOOCH PINCH PLUCK
POACH SHARP SHAVE SLIDE SNAKE
SNARE SNEAK STALK SWIPE COLLAR
CONVEY FINGER HIJACK NOBBLE PILFER
RIPOFF SNITCH THIEVE CABBAGE
PLUNDER PURLOIN SNAFFLE SURREPT
EMBEZZLE SHOPLIFT PLAGIARIZE
(— A GLANCE) GLIME
(— A WATCH) FLIMP
(— ALONG) SLIME SLINK
(— AWAY) LOOP SLINK
(— BY ALTERING BRANDS) DUFF
(— CALVES) NUGGET
(— CATTLE) DUFF RUSTLE
(— COPPER FROM VESSEL'S
BOTTOM) TOSH
(— OFF) RUN
(— SLYLY) SCROUNGE
STEALTHY CATTY PRIVY ARTFUL FELINE
TIPTOE CATLIKE FURTIVE SNEAKING
THIEVISH
STEAM ROKE BLAST SMOKE SWEAT
VAPOR BREATH POTHER CUSHION
STEAMER CLAM LINER TENDER
CUNARDER
STEAMSHIP SCREW STEAM STEAMER
SEATRAIN SHOWBOAT
STEED NAG HORSE MOUNT PEGASUS
SLEIPNER
STEEL RAIL BLOOM BRACE TERNE
WEAPON
(— FOR STRIKING FIRE) ESLABON
(— FOR USE WITH FLINT) FUSIL
FURISON FLEERISH
(— INLAID WITH GOLD) KOFT
KOFTGARI
(DAMASCUS —) DAMASK
(INDIAN —) WOOTZ
(MOLTEN —) HEAT
STEEP SOP BATE BOLD BUCK DEAR DRAW
MASH SOAK STEW BLUFF HEAVY HILLY
SHARP SHEER SOUSE STIFF ABRUPT
BLUFFY CLIFFY DECOCT IMBIBE INFUSE

ARDUOUS CLIVOSE HEADLONG
MACERATE SATURATE STRAIGHT
PRECIPITOUS
STEEPLE SPEAR SPIRE
STEER COX PLY BEEF BULL HELM LEAD
STEM GUIDE SPADO STERN CANNER
RUDDER BULLOCK STOCKER MOSSHORN
NAVIGATE
(— VEHICLE) DRIVE
(HORNLESS —) NOT
(VICIOUS —) LADINO
(WILD —) YAW YEW COWBRUTE
(YOUNG —) STOT
STEERSMAN PILOT WHEEL SHIPMAN
COXSWAIN HELMSMAN STERNMAN
WHEELMAN COCKSWAIN
STEM BUN BASE BEAK CULM CURB NOSE
PIPE RISP ROOT STUD ARISE SCREW
SHANK SHOOT SPIRE STALK STICK
STOCK STRAW THEME TRUNK TUBER
BRANCH DERIVE SCAPUS SPRING
FULCRUM HOPVINE PEDICEL PETIOLE
SARMENT SPINDLE CAULICLE ENGENDER
PEDUNCLE PIPESTEM TIGELLUM
(— OF ARROW) SHAFT
(— OF BANANAS) COUNT
(— OF GLASS) BALUSTER
(— OF GRAPES) RAPE
(— OF HOOKAH) SNAKE
(— OF MATCH) SHAFT
(— OF MUSHROOM) STIPE
(— OF MUSICAL NOTE) TAIL FILUM
VIRGULA
(— OF PIPE) STAPPLE
(— OF PLANT) AXIS RUNT CAULIS
(— OF SHIP) PROW STEMPOST
(— OF TREE) BOLE CAUDEX
(—S OF CULTIVATED PLANTS)
HAULM
(BULBLIKE —) CORM
(DRY WITHERED —) BIRN
(EDIBLE —) EDDO
(GRIEF —) KELLY
(MAIN — OF DEER'S ANTLERS) BEAM
(ORNAMENTAL —) STAVE
(PITHY JOINTED —) CANE
(THORNY —) LAWYER
(TWINING —) BINE
STENCH FOGO FETOR SMELL STINK
WHIFF MEPHITIS
STEP JOG PIP BEMA FOOT LINK PACE
PEEP CORTE FLIER NOTCH POINT STAGE
STAIR TRACE TREAD DEGREE STRIDE
FOOTING GRADINE DEMARCHE
DOORSTEP FOOTPACE FOOTSTEP
PREDELLA
(— ASIDE) DIGRESS
(— BACKWARD) DODGE
(— BY STEP) GRADATIM
(— DOWNWARD) DESCENT
(— FOR GEM MOUNTING) KITE
(— FORWARD) ADVANCE
(— IN A BEARING) BRASS
(— IN BELL RINGING) DODGE
(— IN DOCK) ALTAR
(— IN SELF-ESTEEM) PEG
(— IN SEQUENCE) PLACE

(— IN SOCIAL SCALE) CUT
(— IN TRENCH) BANQUETTE
(— LIVELY) SKELP
(— OF LADDER) RIME RUNG ROUND
RUNDLE
(— OF TUSK) TOOTH
(— PERFORMED BY COMPUTER)
OPERATION
(— SUPPORTING MILLSTONE)
TRAMPOT
(—S OF BOWLER) APPROACH
(ALTAR —S) GRADUAL
(BALLET —) PLIE FOUETTE SISSONNE
(BALLET —S) ALLEGRO
(BOUNDING —) SKIP
(CLUMSY —) STAUP
(DANCE —) DIP PAS SET BUZZ DRAG
DRAW FLAT SHAG SKIP BRAWL CHASS
COULE GLIDE IRISH STOMP BRANLE
CANTER CHASSE DOUBLE INTURN
STRIDE BRANSLE BUFFALO FISHTAIL
GLISSADE PIGEONWING
(FALSE —) HOB SLIP SPHALM SNAPPER
SPHALMA STUMBLE
(FIRST —) STARTER RUDIMENT
(FLIGHT OF —S) GRECE GRICE PERRON
GEMONIES
(HALF —) HALFTONE SEMITONE
(LIGHT —) PITAPAT
(MINING —) LOB STEMPLE
(POMPOUS —) STRUT
(PRIM —) MINCE
(SET OF —S) STILE
(STATELY —) STALK
STEPPENWOLF (AUTHOR OF —)
HESSE
(CHARACTER IN —) HARRY MARIA
HALLER HERMINE
STEREOTYPE CAST CLICHE STEREO
STEREOTYPED CHAIN STAGE TRITE
USUAL STEREO
STERILE DRY DEAD DEAF GELD POOR
BARREN GALLED MEAGER OTIOSE
ASEPTIC BANKRUPT IMPOTENT
STERILITY ATOCIA APHORIA
STERN GRIM HARD POOP ASPER CRUEL
GRUFF HARSH RIGID ROUGH STARK
FLINTY GLOOMY SHREWD STRICT
SULLEN TORVID UNKIND WICKED
AUSTERE STRAIGHT
(— OF SHIP) DOCK APLUSTRE
STERNNESS RIGOR TORVITY SEVERITY
STEVEDORE STOWER TRIMMER
WHARFIE CARGADOR DOCKHAND
STEW FRET ITCH SLUM SWOT BREDI
CURRY SALMI STOVE SWEAT BRAISE
BURGOO MUDDLE PAELLA SEETHE
SIMMER CALDERA GOULASH HARICOT
PUCHERO TERRINE FRIJOADA HOTCHPOT
MORTREUX SLUMGULLION
(— A HARE) JUG
(— IN A SAUCE) DAUBE
(— MADE IN FORECASTLE) HODDLE
(— OF TRAMPS) MULLIGAN
(FISH —) STODGE CHOWDER MATELOTE
(IRISH —) STOVIES
(MUTTON —) NAVARIN

STEWARD HIND VOGT DIWAN GRAVE REEVE FACTOR FARMER GRIEVE SIRCAR SIRDAR BAILIFF CURATOR FLUNKEY GRANGER HUSBAND PROCTOR PROVOST SPENDER APPROVER CONSUMAH HERENACH LARDINER MANCIPLE STEADMAN VILLICUS MAJORDOMO

STICK CAT HEW LUG CHOP CLAM CLUB CRAB GLUE HURL PALE PICK POLE RUNG STAY TREE CLAVE CLEAM CROME DEMUR PASTE PRICK STAFF STAKE STANG STAVE STING STOCK ADHERE BATTLE BROACH CLEAVE CLEEKY CUDGEL INHERE LIBBET MALLET RISSLE STRIKE STRING BATLING GAMBREL HURLBAT KILNRIB BLUDGEON BRINGSEL CATSTICK DIPSTICK SPREADER
(— AS ARCHERY MARK) WAND
(— FAST) JAM JAMB SEIZE FITCHER
(— FASTENED TO DOG'S TAIL) SHANGAN
(— FOR ADMITTING TENANTS) VERGE
(— FOR FIRING CANNON) LINSTOCK
(— FOR KILLING FISH) NOBBLER
(— FOR MAKING FENCE) RADDLE
(— FOR MIXING CHOCOLATE) MOLINET
(— FOR MIXING MORTAR) RAB
(— FOR SNUFF) DIP
(— FOR THATCHING) SPAR GROOM SPELK SPRINGLE
(— IN MUD) STODGE
(— IN OPERATION) FREEZE
(— IT OUT) LAST
(— OF A FAN) BRIN
(— OF CANDY) GIBBY
(— OF CHALK) CRAYON
(— OF ORCHESTRA LEADER) BATON
(— OUT) BUG POKE BULGE SHOOT EXSERT EXTEND EXTRUDE PROTEND
(— REGULATING SLUICEWAY) CATPIECE
(— SEPARATING LUMBER PILES) STICKER
(— TO BEAT CLOTHES) BATLER BATLET
(— TO DISTEND CARCASS) STEND BACKSET
(— TO HOLD BOW) TILLER
(— TO HOLD LOG LOAD) DUTCHMAN
(— TO KEEP ANIMAL QUIET) TWITCH
(— TO MARK CROSSING) BROG
(— TO POKE WITH) POTE
(— TO REMOVE HOOK FROM FISH) GOBSTICK
(— TO STRETCH NET) BRAIL
(— TO STUFF DOLLS) RAMMER
(— TO THROW AT BIRDS) SQUAIL
(— TO TIGHTEN KNOT) WOOLDER
(— TOGETHER) CLOT BLOCK CLING BALTER CEMENT COHERE COAGMENT
(— UP) COCK
(— USED AS POINTER) FESCUE
(BAMBOO —) LATHI LATHEE
(BASKETRY —) LEAGUE
(BENT —) RIFLE

(FIELD HOCKEY —) BULGER CAMMOCK
(FISHING —) GAD
(FORKED —) GROM GROOM
(HOCKEY —) CAMAN HURLY HOCKEY HURLEY SHINNY CAMMOCK CUMMOCK DODDART
(IRON-POINTED —) VALET
(KNOBBED —) BILLET
(LACROSSE —) CROSSE
(LARGE —) MOCK
(MARKING —) LEAD
(ODD —) JAY
(POLISHING —) BUFF
(PRAYER —) PAHO
(PRINTER'S —) SHOOTER
(RANGE-FINDING —) STADIA
(ROUND —) DOWEL SPINDLE
(STIRRING —) MUNDLE POOLER SPURTLE POTSTICK SWIZZLER
(STOUT —) BAT COSH LOWDER
(TALLY —) TAIL
(THROWING —) ATLATL HORNERAH
(TOBACCO —) LATH
(WALKING —) CANE KEBBY WADDY JAMBEE JOCKEY KEBBIE WHANGEE ASHPLANT GIBSTAFF
(PREF.) RHABD(O)

STICKER HINGE LABEL STRIP WAFER PASTER CROSSER

STICKY CAB CLAM ICKY DABBY FATTY GAUMY GLUEY GOOEY GUMMY JAMMY MALMY PUGGY TACKY TOUGH CLAGGY CLAMMY CLARTY CLINGY CLOGGY SMEARY VISCID VISCOUS ADHESIVE TENACIOUS

STIFF BUM HARD TRIG BUDGE RIGID SOLID STARK STOUR TOUGH CLUMSY FORMAL FROZEN STILTY STOCKY STURDY UNEASY WOODEN ANGULAR BUCKRAM COSTIVE STARCHY STILTED RIGOROUS
(SOMEWHAT —) CARKLED

STIFFEN GUM SET SIZE BRACE STRUT TRUSS HARDEN STARCH CONGEAL

STIFFNESS KINK RIGOR STARCH BUCKRAM PRIMNESS RIGIDITY SEVERITY

STIFLE DAMP FUNK SLAY CHOKE CRUSH STUFF MUFFLE QUENCH SMOTHER STRANGLE SUPPRESS THROTTLE

STIFLING CLOSE SMUDGY POTHERY SMOTHERY

STIGMA BLOT FOIL NOTE SLUR SPOT BRAND ODIUM STAIN TAINT BLOTCH BLEMISH

STILETTO BODKIN STYLET PIERCER POINTEL

STILL BUT COY LAY YET CALM HUSH LULL CHECK QUIET WHIST HUSHED PACIFY QUENCH SETTLE SILENT SOOTHE STATIC SUBDUE WITHAL ALEMBIC HOWEVER SILENCE CUCURBIT RESTRAIN STAGNANT SUPPRESS

STILLNESS CALM HUSH REST PEACE LANGUOR SILENCE STATION

STILTED LOFTY STIFF FORMAL POMPOUS

STIMULANT COCA INULA BRACER FILLIP

GINGER CAMPHOR CARDIAC REVIVER
AMMONIAC EXCITANT STIMULUS

STIMULATE FAN HOP KEY PEP FUEL
GOAD HYPO MOVE SEED SPUR STIR
URGE WHET FILIP IMPEL PIQUE PRIME
ROUSE SPARK STING AROUSE BESTIR
EXCITE FILLIP INCITE SPIRIT TICKLE
ANIMATE ENLIVEN INSPIRE PROVOKE
QUICKEN ACTIVATE IRRITATE MOTIVATE
TITILLATE

STIMULATING PERT SEXY BRISK
BRACING PUNGENT EROGENIC EXCITING
GENEROUS INCITANT POIGNANT
STIRRING

STIMULUS CUE AURA BROD EDGE GOAD
HYPO SPUR STING FILLIP MOTIVE
SOURCE IMPETUS

STING NIP BARB BITE BURN GOAD TANG
DEVIL PIQUE PRICK TOUCH NETTLE
ACULEUS IRRITATE STIMULUS

STINGING KEEN SMART PEPPERY
PIQUANT POINTED PRICKLY PUNGENT
ACULEATE NETTLING POIGNANT
SCALDING

STINGY DRY HARD MEAN NEAR CLOSE
TIGHT HUNGRY MEASLY NARROW
SCABBY SCARCE SKIMPY SKINNY STRAIT
CHINTZY MISERLY NIGGARD PENURIOUS
PARSIMONIOUS

STINK FOGO PONG STEW SMELL SMEECH
STENCH MEPHITIS

STINKING FOUL HIGH FETID PUTID
STINKY MALODOROUS

STINT TASK GRIST PINCH SCANT SCRIMP
SCANTLE

STIPEND HIRE ANNAT WAGES SALARY
PENSION PREBEND PROVEND
COMMENDA

STIPULATE ARTICLE PROTEST PROVIDE
COVENANT

STIPULATION IF ANNEX CLAUSE
ARTICLE PREMISE PROVISO COVENANT

STIR DO ADO PUG WAG CARD POKE ROKE
WAKE BUDGE CHURN CREEP FUROR
HURRY POACH RAISE SPARK STING
TEASE TOUCH AROUSE AWAKEN BUBBLE
BUSTLE FLURRY GINGER HUBBUB
JUMBLE PADDLE ROUNCE STODGE
SUMMON TATTER ACTUATE BLATHER
CLUTTER FLUTTER TROUBLE SPLUTTER
(— ABOUT) KNOCK
(— CALICO COLORS) TEER
(— DRINK) MUDDLE SWIZZLE
(— LIQUID) ROG
(— SOIL) CHISEL
(— UP) FAN MIX BUZZ DRUM FUSS
MOVE PROG ROIL TOSS AMOVE AREAR
AWAKE ERECT QUICK ROUSE SNURL
SPOOK STOKE TARRY BESTIR BOTHER
CHOUSE EXCITE INCITE JOSTLE KINDLE
PUDDLE RUMBLE TICKLE UPSTIR
AGITATE ANIMATE COMMOVE DISTURB
PRODDLE PROVOKE STUDDLE TORMENT
UNQUEME DISTRACT
(— UP WITH YEAST) BARM

STIRRING RACY ASTIR DEEDFUL
ROUSING THRILLY EXCITING PATHETIC

STITCH BAR RUN SEW KNIT LOOP PURL
WHIP CABLE CLOSE POINT PREEN PUNTO
FESTON SUTURE TRICOT CROCHET
POPCORN
(— OF CLOTHES) TACK
(NEEDLEPOINT —) BARGELLO

STOCK KIN ROD CANT FILL FUND SEED
SELL STEM BLOOD BROTH CASTE CREAM
FLESH HOARD ISSUE PLANT STORE
STUFF TALON COMMON FUTURE SHARES
STRAIN SUPPLY CAPITAL PILLORY
PROSAPY PROVIDE REPLETE RESERVE
BONEYARD CROSSBAR DIESTOCK
GILLIVER GUNSTOCK ORDINARY
SECURITY PROVISIONS
(— OF ANCHOR) CROSS
(— OF BREEDING MARES) STRUDE
(— OF FOOD) FARE
(— OF GRAIN) COP
(— OF MORPHEMES) LEXICON
(— OF WEAPONS) ARSENAL
(— OF WHIP) CROP
(— OF WINE) CELLAR
(FARM —) BOW
(MEAT —) BLOND BOUILLON
(PLASTIC —) BISCUIT
(RAILROAD —) GRANGER

STOCKADE BOMA PEEL ETAPE ZAREBA
BARRIER TAMBOUR

STOCK EXCHANGE BOURSE COULISSE

STOCKING SOCK SHANK CALIGA
MOGGAN SHINNER
(FOOTLESS —) HOGGER HUSHION
(SOLELESS —) TRAHEEN
(PL.) HOSE NYLONS BUSKINS BOOTHOSE

STOCKY FAT COBBY DUMPY GROSS
SQUAT STOUT CHUNKY STUBBY
BUNTING COMPACT HEAVYSET THICKSET

STODGY STUFFY BOURGEOIS

STOIC IMPASSIVE

STOLEN HOT BENT FURTIVE

STOLID BEEFY BOVINE STUPID WOODEN
DEADPAN PASSIVE

STOMACH MAW CROP GUTS KYTE POKE
TANK WAME BINGY BROOK GORGE
HEART TUMMY CROPPY VENTER GIZZARD
(— OF ANIMAL) CRAW
(— OF CALF) VELL
(— OF RUMINANT) READ RUMEN
BONNET OMASUM PAUNCH ABOMASUM
MANIFOLD RODDIKIN
(PIG'S —) JAUDIE

STONE RAG BOND KLIP KNAR MARK PELT
ROCK STEN TRIG CAPEL CHUCK LAPIS
PITCH SCRAE SCREE SNECK STANE
ASHLAR CEPHAS CLOSER COBBLE
HEADER JUMPER LEDGER PINNER
RUNNER TORSEL DINGBAT DONNOCK
DORNICK KNICKER STANNER SURFACE
CABOCHON DENDRITE LAPILLUS
MACEHEAD MONOLITH SKEWBACK
TOPSTONE
(— ADHERING TO LEAD ORE) KEVEL
(— AS AMULET) HAGSTONE
(— AS IT COMES FROM QUARRY)
RUBBLE
(— AS ROAD MARKER) LEAGUE

(— AT DOOR) RYBAT
(— FOR GLASS-ROLLING) MARVER
(— FOR MOUNTING HORSE) MONTOIR
(— FORMING CAP OF PIER) SUMMER CUSHION
(— HARD TO MOVE) SITFAST
(— IN BLAST FURNACE) DAM
(— IN MEMORY OF DEAD) MONUMENT
(— IN SMALL FRAGMENTS) RATCHEL
(— IN WALL) PARPEN
(— MARKING CENTER OF WORLD) OMPHALOS
(— OF FRUIT) COB PIT NUTLET PYRENE PUTAMEN
(— OF PYRAMID SHAPE) BENBEN
(— PROVIDING CHANGE OF DIRECTION) KNEELER
(— SET IN RING) CHATON
(— SHAPED BY WIND) VENTIFACT
(— SHOT FROM STONE-BOW) JALET
(— TO DEATH) LAPIDATE
(— USED AS MONUMENT) MEGALITH
(— USED IN GAME) DUCK DRAKE
(— WITH INTERNAL CAVITY) GEODE
(—S FROM CRUSHER) TAILINGS
(—S IN WATER) STANNERS
(ARTIFICIAL —) ALBOLITE
(BINDING —) PERPEND THROUGH PIERPONT
(BOND —) GIRDER KEYSTONE
(BOUNDARY —) TERM TERMINUS
(BROKEN —) RIPRAP
(BROKEN — USED FOR ROADS) BALLAST MACADAM
(BUILDING —) SUMMER MITCHEL SPERONE
(CARVED —) CAMEO CUVETTE
(CASTING —) TYMP
(CHINA —) PETUNSE
(CLAY —) LECH
(COPING —) SKEW TABLET TABLING CAPSTONE
(CURLING —) HOG HERD GUARD LOOFIE POTLID
(CYLINDRICAL —) TAMBOUR
(DESERT —) GIBBER
(DRUID —) SARSEN
(DRYING —) STILLAGE
(EDGING —) SETTER
(FLAT —) PLAT DRAKE LEDGER
(FOUNDATION —) BEDDER
(GLITTERING —) DAZE
(GRAVE —) BAUTA STELE
(GREEN —) CALLAIS
(GRINDING —) METATE MULLER
(HOLY —) BEAR BAETYL
(HOPSCOTCH —) PEEVER PALLALL
(IMAGINARY —) ADAMANT
(KIDNEY —) NEPHRITE
(LAST — IN COURSE) CLOSER
(LOOSE —) GLIDDER
(MAGICAL —) BAETYL
(MEMORIAL —) BAUTA EBENEZER
(METEORIC —) ANGRITE AEROLITE AEROLITH NAKHLITE
(MIDDLE —) HONEY

(MIDDLE — OF ARCH) KEY
(MONUMENTAL —) LECH
(PAVING —) PAVER REBATE PITCHER
(PHILOSOPHER'S —) ADROP MAGISTERY
(PRECIOUS —) GEM OPAL RUBY EWAGE JEWEL TOPAZ ADAMAS LIGURE SHAMIR ASTERIA ASTRION CRAPAUD CUVETTE DIAMOND DIONISE EMERALD GELATIA JACINTH OLIVINE SARDINE SARDIUS AMETHYST ASTROITE HYACINTH PANTARBE SAPPHIRE YDRIADES
(PRECIOUS —S) PERRIE
(REFUSE —) ROACH
(ROCKING —) LOGAN
(SACRED —) BAETYL BAETULUS
(SEMIPRECIOUS —) ONYX SARD MURRA GARNET CITRINE TIGEREYE
(SHARPENING —) HONE WHET
(SHOEMAKER'S —) LAPSTONE
(SMALL ROUND —) JACK
(SOFTENED —) SAP
(STEPPING —) GOAT SARN
(STRATIFIED —) FLAG SLAB
(TALISMANIC —) GAMAHE
(TRANSPARENT —) PHENGITE
(UNSQUARED —) BACKING
(UPRIGHT —) BAUTA MENHIR MASSEBAH
STONECUTTER MASON JADDER LAPICIDE SCABBLER SCAPPLER SQUAREMAN
STONEWARE GRES BASALT JASPER BASALTES CANEWARE CHIENYAO
STONY RIGID COBBLY PETROUS LAPIDOSE PETROSAL
STOOL FORM SEAT CROCK HORSE STOLE CURRIE TRIPOD TUFFET COMMODE KNEELER TABORET TRESTLE TUMBREL BARSTOOL
(CLOSE —) TOM
(CUCKING —) THEW
(LOW —) COPPY SUNKIE CREEPIE CRICKET
(3-LEGGED —) BUFFET THRESTLE
STOOL PIGEON NARK SNITCH STOOGE STOOLIE
STOOP BOW BEND LEAN SINK COUCH DEIGN CROUCH DECLINE DESCEND SUCCUMB
(— OF HAWK) SOUSE
STOP COG CUT DIE DIT DOG END KEP MAR NIX BALK BODE COOL DROP EASE HALT HELP HOOK HOLD KILL QUIT REED REST SNUB STAY STEM STOW TENT TRIG WEAR WHOA ABIDE AVAST BELAY BLOCK BRAKE CEASE CHECK CHOKE CHUCK CLAMP CLOSE DELAY EMBAR HITCH PEACE POINT SLAKE SPARE STAND STICK STINT ANCHOR ARREST BIFARA BORROW COLLAR DESIST DETAIN INSTOP PERIOD SCOTCH SQUASH STANCE STIFLE TROMBA BASSOON CAESURA MUSETTE OPPRESS SOJOURN STATION TWELFTH BACKSTOP BOMBARDE PRECLUDE STOPOVER STOPPAGE SUPPRESS SURCEASE

(— AS IF FRIGHTENED) BOGGLE
(— BLAST) DAMP
(— FLOW) BAFFLE STANCH
(— FOR FOOD) BAIT
(— FOR HORSE) BLOW
(— FROM FERMENTING) STUM
(— GROWTH) BLAST
(— GUN BREECH) OBTURATE
(— IN EARLY STAGES) ABORT
(— IN SPEAKING) HAW
(— LEAK) CALK CAULK FOTHER
(— ROWING) EASY
(— SHORT) JIB
(— SWINGING) SET
(— UNDESIREDLY) STALL
(— UP) DAM CALK CLOG CLOY FILL
PLUG CHINK ESTOP STUFF STANCH
OCCLUDE STAUNCH OPPILATE
(— USING) SINK
(— WITH CLAY) PUG
(— WORK) SECURE
(BRIEF —) CALL
(GLOTTAL —) STOD CATCH STOSS
PLOSIVE STOSSTON
(HARPSICHORD —) LUTE
(ROUGH —) ASPIRATA
(SUCTION —) CLICK
(TEMPORARY —) PAUSE SUSPEND
(VOICELESS —) TENUIS
(PREF.) ISCH(O)
STOPPAGE JAM ALLAY CHECK HITCH
STICK STINT ARREST STASIS EMBARGO
REFUSAL SHUTOFF STOPPLE SHUTDOWN
CESSATION
(— OF BLOOD) REMORA
(— OF DEVELOPMENT) ATROPHY
(WORK —) BUND HARTAL LOWSIN
STRIKE
STOPPER WAD BUNG CORK STOP VICE
CHECK STANCH BOUCHON CLOSURE
SHUTOFF STOPGAP STOPPLE TAMPION
STORE CAVE CRIB DECK HOLD KEEP
MASS SAVE SHOP STOW CACHE DEPOT
HOUSE HUTCH STASH STOCK UPLAY
BAZAAR CELLAR GARNER SUPPLY
TIENDA ARSENAL BHANDAR BOOTERY
GROCERY HARVEST HUSBAND REPOSIT
RESTORE SHEBANG BOUTIQUE
EMPORIUM EXCHANGE GARRISON
MAGAZINE WAREROOM WARNISON
(— BEER) AGE LAGER
(— CROP) BARN
(— FODDER) ENSILE
(— IN A MOW) GOVE
(— IN LUMBER CAMP) VAN
(— KEPT BY CHINESE) TOKO
(— OF FOOD) LARDER
(— OF WEALTH) FORTUNE
(— POTATOES) HOG
(— UP) FUND POWDER IMBURSE
SQUIRREL
(ABUNDANT —) MINE
(BREAD —) PANARY
(HIDDEN —) BIKE
(LARGE —) RAFF
(LIQUOR —) GROGGERY
(MILITARY —) DUMP

(READY-TO-EAT FOOD —) DELI
(RESERVE —) SLUICE
(RICH —) ARGOSY
(SMALL —S) SLOPS
STOREHOUSE GOLA CACHE DEPOT
ETAPE ARGOSY ARMORY BODEGA
GODOWN PALACE STAPLE VINTRY
ARSENAL BHANDAR CAMALIG GRANARY
ENTREPOT MAGAZINE TREASURE
(— FOR BREAD) PANARY
(RAISED —) WHATA FUTTAH PATAKA
(UNDERGROUND —) PALACE
MATTAMORE
STOREROOM CAVE GOLA WARD
BODEGA CELLAR DINGLE BOXROOM
BUTTERY GENIZAH LAZARET
(PAWNBROKER'S —) LUMBER
STORK WADER ARGALA JABIRU SIMBIL
HURGILA MAGUARI MARABOU
ADJUTANT MARABOUT OPENBILL
STORM RIG BLOW HAIL HUFF RAGE
RAMP RAVE WIND BLIZZ BRASH DRIFT
FORCE ATTACK EASTER EXPUGN
WESTER BLUSTER BRAVADO DUSTING
PISACHI TORMENT WEATHER
BLOWDOWN CALAMITY UPHEAVAL
WILLIWAW
(— OF BLOWS) STOUR
(DUST —) DEVIL DUSTER HABOOB
KHAMSIN PEESASH SHAITAN
(FURIOUS —) TEMPEST
(HAWAIIAN —) KONA
(SEVERE —) PEELER SNIFTER
(VIOLENT —) FLAW TUFAN CYCLONE
SNORTER
STORMY FOUL RUDE WILD DIRTY DUSTY
GUSTY STARK WINDY WROTH COARSE
RUGGED WINTRY FURIOUS NIMBOSE
RIOTOUS SQUALLY VIOLENT AGITATED
BLUSTERY BOISTEROUS
STORY GAG SAW LORE REDE TALE TEXT
CRACK FABLE PITCH PROSE SPELL SPIEL
STORE FABULA PISTLE SCREED
ADVANCE HAGGADA HISTORY MARCHEN
RECITAL ANECDOTE TREATISE
NARRATIVE
(— FROM THE PAST) LEGEND
(— OF BEEHIVE) SUPER
(— OF BUILDING) DECK FLAT ATTIC
CHESS ETAGE FLOOR PIANO SOLAR
STAGE FLIGHT SOLLAR MANSARD
ENTRESOL MEZZANINE
(— OF HEROES) SAGA
(ABSURD —) CANARD
(ADVENTURE —) YARN
(AMUSING —) BAR DROLLERY
(BIRTH —) JATAKA
(DOLEFUL —) JEREMIAD
(EERIE —) CHILLER
(FAKE —) STRING
(FALSE —) SHAVE CANARD WHOPPER
(LONG, INVOLVED —) MEGILLA
MEGILLAH
(MADE-UP —) FUDGE
(MONSTROUS —) BANGER
(MORBIDLY SENSATIONAL —)
DREADFUL

(MYSTERY —) WHODUNIT
(NEWS —) SIDEBAR
(NEWSPAPER —) LEAD FEATURE
(OLD —) DIDO
(POMPOUS —) BRAG
(PREPOSTEROUS —) CUFFER
(RIBALD —) HARLOTRY
(SATIRICAL —) SKIT
(SHORT —) CONTE NOVELLA
(STALE —) CHESTNUT
(UPPER —) ATTIC GARRET BARBECUE
HYPEROON
STOUT FAT FIRM BONNY BROSY BULKY
BURLY COBBY GREAT HARDY OBESE
PLUMP PODDY STERN BONNIE FLESHY
PORTLY PRETTY PYKNIC ROTUND
SQUARE STRONG STURDY REPLETE
PLUMPISH POWERFUL STALWART
THICKSET
(— PERSON) GURK
STOUTHEARTED GOOD VALIANT
STOVE HOD PLATE CHULHA COCKLE
COOKER HEATER PRIMUS BRASERO
CHAUFFER FRANKLIN POTBELLY
SALAMANDER
(— FOR DRYING GUNPOWDER)
GLOOM
(— ON SHIP) GALLEY
(RUSSIAN —) PEACH
(WARMING —) KANGRI
STOW BIN BOX SET CRAM LADE CROWD
STORE COOPER STEEVE DUNNAGE
STOWAGE BURTON REMBLAI RUMMAGE
STRADDLE SADDLE SPREAD STRIDE
BESTRIDE SPRADDLE
STRAGGLE GAD ROVE TRAIL RAMBLE
SPRAWL TAGGLE WANDER DRAGGLE
MEANDER SCRAMBLE
STRAGGLING RAGGED SCRATCHY
VAGULOUS
STRAIGHT BOLT FAIR FULL GAIN CLEAN
FLUSH RIGHT SHORT SPANG ARIGHT
DIRECT HONEST STRICT REGULAR
UPRIGHT DIRECTLY SEQUENCE
(— AHEAD) ANON PLUMP OUTRIGHT
(— UP AND DOWN) SHEER CLEVER
EVENDOWN
(NOT —) CRAZY
STRAIGHTEN SQUARE UNKINK
COMPOSE RECTIFY STRETCH
(— BY HEATING) SET
(— NEEDLE) RUB
(— RAILS) GAG
STRAIGHTFORWARD EVEN FRANK
LEVEL NAKED PLAIN CANDID DIRECT
HONEST SIMPLE SQUARE JANNOCK
SINCERE EVENDOWN HOMESPUN
OUTRIGHT OPENHEARTED
(NOT —) CROOKED PLAITED
STRAIN LAG TAX TRY TUG ACHE BEND
DASH DRAG HEAT HEFT NOTE PULL RACK
RICK SILE SONG VEIN WORK BRUNT
CHAFE DEMUR DRAIN FORCE HEAVE
PRESS RETCH SHEAR STOCK SURGE
WREST CLENCH DIRECT EXTEND EXTORT
FILTER INTEND KVETCH SPRAIN SPRING
STRESS THRONG DESCANT FATIGUE

STRETCH STROPHE TENSION TORMENT
COLANDER DIAPASON
(— MILK) SIE
(— OF AN ARCH) THRUST
(— OF RAILING LANGUAGE) DIATRIBE
(— ON BUGLE) MOT
(— ON HORN) RECHASE RECHEAT
(— THROUGH COLANDER) COIL
(CONCLUDING —) CADENCE
(MELANCHOLY —) DUMP
(MUSICAL —) FIT SOLO POINT
(MUSICAL —S) TOUCH
(MUTANT —) SALTANT
STRAINED PENT TENSE INTENSE
LABORED INTENDED
STRAINER CAGE ROSE SILE SIEVE TAMIS
TAMMY SEARCH CRIBBLE COLATORY
SEARCHER
(— OF TWIGS) HUCKMUCK
(COFFEE —) GRECQUE
(MILK —) SAY MILSEY
(WICKER —) THEAD
STRAIT CUT GUT BAND BELT FRET NECK
BRAKE CANAL PINCH SOUND FRETUM
NARROW CHANNEL BOSPORUS
JUNCTURE
(IN —S) SET
(LAST —) EXIGENT
(NEWFOUNDLAND —) TICKLER
STRAITEN PINCH SCANT STRAIT
STRAND PLY BANK FLAT WISP BEACH
BRAID CLIFF PRAYA SHORE SINGLE
SLIVER STRAIN SUTURE HAIRLINE
(— OF FIBERS) ROVING
(— OF HAIR) LICK SWITCH
(— OF PROTOPLASM) BRIDGE
STRANGE ODD RUM FELL RARE UNCO
ALIEN EERIE FUNNY KINKY NOVEL QUEER
WOOZY FERLIE QUAINT UNIQUE
CURIOUS ERRATIC HEATHEN ODDBALL
UNHEARD UNKNOWN UNUSUAL
FANCIFUL PECULIAR SINGULAR
UNCOMMON MONSTROUS
(PREF.) XEN(O)
STRANGER COME UNCO ALIEN GUEST
GANGER INMATE INCOMER UNCOUTH
MALIHINI PEREGRIN OUTLANDER
STRANGLE CHOKE SNARL WORRY STIFLE
GARROTE JUGULATE THROTTLE
STRAP TUG BAND CURB GIRD BRACE
GIRTH PATTE RIDER RISER SLING STROP
THONG TRACE VITTA ANKLET BILLET
COLLAR GARTER HALTER HANGER
LATIGO TOGGLE BABICHE BOWYANG
LANYARD LATCHET TICKLER WEBBING
BACKSTAY SQUILGEE WRISTLET
(— AROUND HORSE'S THROAT)
CRIBBER
(— AROUND MAST) DOLPHIN
(— FOR SHIELD) GUIGE ENARME
BRETELLE
(— IN FLAIL) TAPLING
(— OF BRIDLE) REIN
(— OF SENNIT) BACKER
(— ON HAWK'S LEAD) JESS SENDAL
(— WITH SLIT END) TAWS
(ANKLE —) BRACELET

(CARRYING —) METUMP TUMPLINE
(DOOR —) HASP
(MINER'S —) BYARD
(SHOE —) BAR
(STIRRUP —S) CHAPELET
(TIE —) SHANK
(U-SHAPED —) STIRRUP
(PREF.) LIGUL(I)

STRAPPING SWANK BOUNCING CHOPPING SLAPPING SWANKING

STRATAGEM COUP RUSE TURN WILE ANGLE DRAFT FRAUD GUILE KNACK TRICK DECEIT DEVICE POLICY FINESSE SLEIGHT ARTIFICE CONTOISE INTRIGUE LIRIPIPE PRACTICE QUENTISE STRATEGY TRICKERY

STRATEGY GAME FINESSE

STRATUM BED CAP RIB LAIN COUCH ELITE FLOOR LAYER LEDGE SHELF TABLE COUCHE GRAVEL AQUIFER SUBSOIL SUBGRADE
(— OF COAL) BENCH
(— OF FIRECLAY) THILL
(— OF PALE COLOR) FAHLBAND
(— OF SANDSTONE) PINNEL
(— OF SOIL) SOD
(— OF STONE) GIRDLE
(SOCIAL —) CUT
(THIN —) SEAM LENTIL

STRAW BAKU MOTE REED RUSH HAULM STALK YEDDA FESCUE FETTLE PANAMA RIZZOM SIPPER TUSCAN STUBBLE STRAMMEL
(— CUT FINE) CHAFF
(— FOR MAKING HATS) SENNIT BANGKOK LEGHORN SABUTAN
(— FOR THATCHING) YELM
(— TO PROTECT PLANTS) MULCH
(BROKEN —) BHOOSA
(COOKERY —S) PAILLES
(PLAITED —) SENNIT
(WAXED —) STRASS

STRAY ERR ODD ROVE WAIF WALK DRIFT RANGE VAGUE WAVER ESTRAY SWERVE VAGARY WANDER DEVIATE FORLORN DIVAGATE MAVERICK STRAGGLE

STRAYING ASTRAY ERRANT ABERRANT VAGATION

STREAK RAY BAND SEAM VEIN WALE FLECK FREAK GLADE SLASH SMUDGE STRAIN STRAKE STRIPE STIPPLE DISCOLOR
(— CAUSED BY BLOOD) VIBEX
(— IN FABRIC) CRACK SHINER
(— IN GLASS) SKIM
(— IN HAIR) BLAZE
(— IN SKY) ICEBLINK
(— IN WOOD) ROE
(— OF BLUBBER) BLANKET
(— OF LIGHT) STREAM
(— ON BEAST'S FACE) RACE
(— ON SURFACE OF SUN) FACULA
(— WITH FINE STRIPES) LACE
(—S FROM PLANE) CONTRAIL
(BACTERIOLOGICAL —) STROKE
(LOSING —) SLUMP
(THEATRICAL —) HAM

(WHITE —) SHIM

STREAKED ROWY LACED HAWKED SMEARY BRINDLE STRIPED BRINDLED IRONSHOT

STREAM PUP RIO RUN BURN FLOW FLUX FORD GILL KILL PURL SICK SPIN TIDE BAYOU BOGUE BOURN BROOK CREEK DRINK FLARE FLASH FLEAM FLOOD FLUOR FRESH GHYLL PRILL RIVER SWAMP TRAIN ARROYO BOURNE BRANCH BURNIE CANADA FILLER FLUENT GUZZLE OUTLET RUNNEL SLUICE STRAND CHANNEL CURRENT DRIBBLE FLUENCE FRESHET RIVULET AFFLUENT INFLUENT
(— ALONG) SLIDE
(— FULL TO TOP) BANKER
(— OF AIR OR SMOKE) PEW
(— OF ELECTRODES) BEAM
(— OF LAVA) COULEE
(— OF SIRUP) THREAD
(— OF SPEECH) STRAIN
(— OUT) BREAK
(FLOWING —) NYMPH
(HIGH-SPEED —) JET
(SLOW —) OOZE
(SLOW-MOVING —) POW
(SLUGGISH —) LANE
(SMALL —) BECK LAKE SIKE DRAFT RITHE COULEE SICKET SQUIRT STRIPE DRAUGHT GRINDLE
(THIN —) TRICKLE TRICKLET
(TIDAL —) COVE SEAPOOSE
(TRANSIENT —) RILL
(TRICKLING —) DRILL
(TURBID —) DRUVE
(UNDERGROUND —) AAR SWALLET
(VIOLENT —) TORRENT
(WEAK —) DRIP

STREAMER FLAG VANE GUIDON LAPPET PENCEL PENNON SCROLL WIMPLE BANDEROL FILAMENT
(— OF MOSS) WEEPER
(— ON HEADDRESS) LIRIPIPE
(PAPER —S) CONFETTI

STREAMLINED CLEAN SLEEK

STREET ROW RUE WAY GATE PAVE STEM BLOCK CALLE CANON CORSO DRIVE PASEO AVENUE BOWERY CAUSEY TERRACE THROUGH ARTERIAL BROADWAY BYSTREET CHAUSSEE CONTRADA
(— IN BARCELONA) RAMBLA
(— IN FLORENCE) BORGO
(MAIN —) CHAWK TOWNGATE
(NARROW —) CHAR ALLEY CHARE
(PRINCIPAL —) ARTERY
(SIDE —) HUTUNG

STREETCAR TRAMCAR TRAMWAY ELECTRIC

STREET SCENE (AUTHOR OF —) RICE
(CHARACTER IN —) SAM ROSE FRANK STEVE KAPLIN SANKEY WILLIAM MAURRANT

STRENGTH ARM VIR BEEF GRIP GUTS HEAD IRON MAIN THEW BRAWN CRAFT FIBER FORCE HEART JUICE MIGHT NERVE

POWER SINEW VIGOR ENERGY FOISON
MUSCLE STARCH VIRTUE ABILITY
COURAGE STAMINA STHENIA CAPACITY
FIRMNESS VALIDITY
(— OF ACID OR BASE) AVIDITY
(— OF ALE) STRIKE
(— OF CARD HAND) BODY
(— OF CHARACTER) GRISTLE
(— OF CURRENT) AMPERAGE
(— OF SOLUTION) TITER
(— OF SPIRITS) PROOF
(— OF TEA) DRAW
(— OF WILL) BACKBONE
(— OF WINE) SEVE

STRENGTHEN BACK BIND FIRM HELP
PROP STAY BRACE CLEAT FORCE SINEW
STEEL TONIC TRUSS ANNEAL ASSURE
DEEPEN ENDURE ENFIRM HARDEN
MUNIFY SETTLE BUCKRAM CONFIRM
ENFORCE FORTIFY QUICKEN RAMPIRE
SUPPORT THICKEN BUTTRESS ENERGIZE
ENTRENCH HEIGHTEN ROBORATE

STRENUOUS HARD EAGER ARDUOUS
WILLING VIGOROUS

STRESS HIT BIRR BRUNT ICTUS PINCH
SHEAR ACCENT STRAIN THRONG
DOWNBEAT EMPHASIS PRESSURE

STRETCH EKE LAG LIE RUN DRAW LAST
MAIN PASS RACK ROLL SPAN TEND
BOARD BURST SIGHT SPELL SWAGE
VERGE EXTEND LENGTH SMOOTH STRAIN
DISPLAY EXPANSE LENGTHEN STRAIGHT
(— CLOTH) TENTER
(— FORTH) PORRECT
(— INJURIOUSLY) SPRAIN
(— IRREGULARLY) TRAIL
(— LEATHER) DRAFT STAKE DRAUGHT
(— METAL) FORM
(— OF ARMS) FATHOM
(— OF GROUND) BRECK
(— OF LAND) SWALE COMMON GALLOP
PARCEL COMMONS
(— OF ROAD) SIGHT
(— OF SEA) CHOP
(— OF TIME) TIFF
(— OF WALL) CURTAIN
(— OF WATER) GLIDE LEVEL LOGIN
FAIRWAY
(— OUT) GROW SPIN REACH STENT
STRUT TWINE INTEND OUTLIE SPRAWL
SPREAD SPRING DISTEND OUTSPAN
PORTEND ELONGATE
(— THE NECK) CRANE
(GRASSY —) DRINN
(LEVEL —) LAWN

STRETCHER COT GURNEY LITTER
ANGAREP TROLLEY ANGAREEB
BRANCARD

STREW BED SOW CLOT DUST LARD SPEW
CARPET LITTER SPREAD BESTREW
SCATTER
(— WITH BULLETS) SPRAY

STRICT HARD TAUT TRUE CLOSE EXACT
HARSH RIGID STARK STERN TIGHT
GIUSTO SEVERE STRAIT ASCETIC
AUSTERE PRECISE REGULAR RIGOROUS
STRINGENT

(NOT —) LAX SCIOLTO
STRICTLY NARROW STRAIT CLOSELY
PROPERLY
STRICTNESS RIGOR RIGIDITY RIGORISM
SEVERITY
STRIDE SAIL STEP FLOAT STRUT STROKE
BESTRIDE
(— LOFTILY) STALK
(— PURPOSEFULLY) SLING
STRIDENT HARD HARSH BRASSY GLASSY
SHRILL RAUCOUS YELLING GRINDING
STRIFE TUG WAR FEUD PLEA FLITE JIHAD
NOISE BARRAT BICKER BRIGUE DEBATE
MUTINY STRIVE BARGAIN CONTEST
DISCORD DISPUTE QUARREL CONFLICT
CONTRAST STRUGGLE CONTENTION
(CIVIL —) STASIS
STRIKE BAT BOP BOX CUE DUB HIT JOW
LAM PUG WAP BAFF BEAK BEAT BELT
BIFF BLIP BUFF BUMP CLUB COIN COSH
CUFF DINT FANG FLOG FRAP GIRD HURT
KILL KNEE LASH MARK NAIL PUCK ROUT
SLAM SLAP SLOG SOCK SPAR SWAP
SWAT WHOP BATON CATCH CHECK
CHIME CRACK FILIP FLAIL KNOCK PASTE
SKITE SLOSH SMACK SMITE SOUND
SPANK STAMP SWACK SWIPE SWISH
THROW WHALE WHANG AFFECT ATTAIN
BATTER BOUNCE BUFFET FETTLE FILLIP
HAMMER STRICK STRIPE SWITCH
THRASH WALLOP IMPINGE PERCUSS
WHAMPLE WILDCAT STOPPAGE
STRAMASH STRICKLE
(— A WICKET) BREAK
(— ABOUT) FLOP
(— AGAINST) RAM BANG STUMP
ASSAULT COLLIDE
(— AND REBOUND) CAROM
(— CRICKET BALL) EDGE
(— DOWN) LAY FALL SLAY WEND
FLASH FLOOR AFFLICT SIDERATE
(— DUMB) DUMFOUND
(— FEET TOGETHER) HITCH
(— FORCIBLY) GET CLOUT DEVEL
SLASH
(— GENTLY) PAT
(— GOLF BALL) HOOK DRIVE SCLAFF
(— HEAVILY) BASH DUNT DUSH FLOP
SLUG CLUMP SLOUGH CLOBBER
(— IN CURLING) WICK
(— LIGHTLY) BOB DAB SPAT FLICK
(— OF LOCK) KEEPER STRIKER
(— ON HEAD) COP NOBBLE
(— OUT) FAN DELE POKE TAKE CROSS
ELIDE CANCEL DELETE EXPUNGE
OUTLASH EXCUDATE
(— REPEATEDLY) DRUM LICK
(— SHARPLY) CUT SNICK
(— SMARTLY) NAP RAP KNAP
(— TEETH TOGETHER) GNASH
(— TOGETHER) CLASH KNACK
(— UP) LILT YERK RAISE
(— VIOLENTLY) RIP BASH DING PASH
SOUSE BENSEL
(— WITH AMAZEMENT) CONFOUND
(— WITH BAT) DRIVE
(— WITH FEAR) ALARM ASTONISH

(— WITH FIST) PLUG NODDLE
(— WITH FOOT) KICK BUNCH SPURN STAMP
(— WITH HAMMER) CHAP JOWL MELL
(— WITH HORNS) BUNT BUTT HOOK
(— WITH SHAME) ABASH
(— WITH SPEAR) STICK
(— WITH STICK) SQUAIL
(— WITH WHIP) JERK LASH QUIRK
(— WITH WONDER) SURPRISE
(BOWLING —S) DOUBLE
(HUNGER —) ENDURA
(LABOR —) STEEK STICK TURNOUT WALKOUT
(LUCKY —) BONANZA
(MINING —) TREND
(THREE —S) TURKEY
STRIKING FRESH SHOWY VIVID DARING SIGNAL STRONG SALIENT TELLING COLORFUL DRAMATIC KNOCKOUT NOTICEABLE
STRING LAG BAND CORD FILE LACE PAIR SLIP TAPE BRAID POINT SINEW STRAP STRAND TREBLE
(— IN BIRD'S EGG) CHALAZA
(— OF BEADS) ROSARY CHAPLET NECKLACE
(— OF DRUM) SNARE
(— OF FIDDLE) THARM
(— OF FLAGS) HOIST
(— OF LOCK) KEEPER
(— OF LYRE) MESE NETE TRITE HYPATE PARAMESE PARAMETE
(— OF MUSICAL INSTRUMENT) WIRE CHORD DRONE THAIRM CATLING MINIKIN LICHANOSE
(— OF ONIONS) REEVE TRACE
(— OF PHRASES) CENTO
(— OF RAILWAY CARS) SET
(— OF SUGAR CRYSTALS) COB
(— OF VEGETABLES) STRAP
(— OF VERSES) LAISSE
(— OF VIOL) MEAN
(— OF WAGONS) RAKE
(— TOBACCO) SEW
(— UP) KILT
(BONNET —) BRIDE
(OAKUM —) PLEDGET
(ORNAMENTAL —) CORDON
(SURGICAL —) LIGATURE
(VIOLIN —) THAIRM VIBRATOR
(WEAVING —) LEASH
STRINGY ROPY SINEWY WOOLLY THREADY
STRIP BAR TAG BAND BARE BELT GAGE HUSK PEEL ROLL SACK SHIM SKIN CLEAN DRIVE FILET FLAKE GAUGE GLEAN LABEL LINER PANEL PLUME SHEAR SHRED SPOIL STRAP SWATH UNRIG BORDER COLLAR DENUDE DIVEST FILLET FLEECE MATRIX REGLET SCROLL STREAK TARGET UNBARE UNCASE BEREAVE CHANNEL DEPRIVE DESPOIL DISROBE PINRAIL PLUNDER UNCLOAK UNCOVER UNDRESS BOOKMARK DISARRAY FOOTBAND
(— A PLANT) SPRIG

(— BARK) PILL
(— BINDING STALKS TO WALL) TACK
(— BLUBBER FROM WHALE) FLENSE
(— EAR OF CORN) SILK
(— FOR DRAWING CURVED LINES) SPLINE
(— FOR GUIDING PLASTER) BEAD
(— FOR MAKING TUBE) SKELP
(— HANGING AROUND SKIRT) FLOUNCE
(— IN BASKETMAKING) INSIDES
(— IN BEEHIVE) STARTER
(— IN CANING) SPLENT SPLINT
(— IN TYPEWRITER) DRAWBAND
(— OF CANVAS) FOOTBAND
(— OF CLOTH) LIST PATA RIND ROON GUARD BANNER DUTCHMAN
(— OF CORK) SPREADER
(— OF FABRIC) FLIPPER
(— OF FAT) FATBACK LARDOON
(— OF FIELD HOCKEY AREA) ALLEY
(— OF FUR) GROTZEN
(— OF GRASS) VERGE
(— OF HIDE) SPECK DEWLAP
(— OF LAND) BUTT LAND RAIK RAIN RAKE TANG BREAK CREEK SLANG SLIPE SPONG SCREED SELION STRAKE STRIPE FURLONG ISTHMUS CORRIDOR SIDELING
(— OF LEATHER) LAY RAND WELT APRON RANGE THONG BACKSTAY
(— OF LEAVES) TWIST
(— OF LINEN) SETON
(— OF MASONRY) ARCHBAND
(— OF OSIER) SKEIN
(— OF PALM LEAF) CADJAN
(— OF PASTRY) STRAW
(— OF PLANKING) APRON
(— OF PLASTER) SCREED
(— OF PRAIRIE) COVE
(— OF PROVISIONS) FORAGE
(— OF RANK) DEGRADE
(— OF RED CLOTH) COXCOMB
(— OF ROADWAY) LANE
(— OF RUBBER) CUSHION
(— OF TURF) PARKING
(— OF UNPLOWED LAND) GAIR HADE HEADLAND
(— OF WATER) INLET
(— OF WOOD) LAG LAT LATH LIST SHAW SLAT WELT CHINK CLEAT STAVE BATTEN INWALE RADDLE REEPER REGLET FOOTING FURRING STICKER TRACKER FOOTLING
(— OFF) TIRL FLIPE FLYPE SLIPE
(— OFF SKIN) CASE FLAY
(— ON FOLDING DOORS) ASTRAGAL
(— ON PRINTER'S GALLEY) LEDGE
(— ON SQUASH COURT) TELLTALE
(— ON TIRE) CHAFER
(— SEPARATING LINES OF TYPE) LEAD REGLET
(BOUNDARY —) PERIMETER
(CAMOUFLAGING —) GARLAND
(COMIC —) FUNNY
(CONSTRUCTION —S) LAGGING
(CORSET —) BUSK
(DEPENDENT —) LAMBEAU

(DIVIDING —) CLOISON
(HORSESHOE-SHAPED —) BAIL BALE
(IRON IN —S) NAILROD
(MEDIAN —) MALL
(NARROW —) SEAM SLAT SLIP TAPE
REEVE STRAKE
(PAPER —) ORIHON
(PROJECTING —) FEATHER
(RAISED —) RIDGE
(STRENGTHENING —) BEND
(THATCHING —) LEDGER
(UNPLOWED —) BALK
STRIPE BAR RAY BAND BEND PALE SLAT
TRIM WALE WEAL WELT FLECK STRIA
STRIP SWATH VITTA BORDER RIBBON
STREAK STREAM COTTISE TRAVERSE
(— OF CHEVRON) ARC
(— OF COLOR ON CHEEK) FRENUM
(— ON ANIMAL'S FACE) SNIP BLAZE
(— ON FABRIC) CROSSBAR
(— ON MILITARY SLEEVE) SLASH
(— ON SHIELD) ENDORSE
(ENCIRCLING —) ZONE
(PURPLE —) CLAVUS
(SET OF —S) BAR
STRIPED BANDY PALED RAYED WALED
ZONED BARRED CORDED VITTATE
FASCIATE
(— CROSSWISE) BAYADERE
STRIPLING LAD STIRRA YOUNKER
SKIPJACK SHAVELING
STRIPPED BARE NUDE NAKED HUSKED
PICKED PLUMED UNPEELED
STRIVE AIM TRY TUG PAIN TOIL WORK
BANDY DRIVE EXERT FIGHT FORCE
LABOR PRESS BUCKLE BUFFET DEBATE
INTEND STRAIN STRIKE AGONIZE
CONTEST DISPUTE ENFORCE SCUFFLE
CONTRAST ENDEAVOR STRUGGLE
(— AFTER) SEEK FOLLOW CANVASS
(— FOR SUPERIORITY) VIE KEMP
(— IN OPPOSITION) RIVAL CONTEND
(— TO EQUAL) EMULATE
(— TO OVERTAKE) ENSUE
STROKE DAB FIT PAT PET POP RUB BEAT
BLOW CHOP COUP CUFF DASH DENT
DING DINT DUNT FLAP FLOP JERK KERF
LASH LICK PEAL PECK SHOT TILT TIRE
TUCK WELT WHAP WIPE BRUSH DRAFT
FLICK HATCH PULSE SHOCK SLASH
SLING SLIVE SLOSH STRIP SWEEP SWING
SWIPE THROW TOUCH TRICE WHACK
CARESS FONDLE GENTLE GLANCE
PLUNGE SMOOTH STRIPE OUTLASH
SOLIDUS VIRGULE SCORCHER
(— IN PAINTING) HAND
(— IN PENMANSHIP) MINIM
(— IN TENNIS) LET LOB BOAST CHASE
SMASH BRICOLE BACKHAND FOREHAND
OVERHAND
(— OF A LETTER) DUCT STEM SERIF
POTHOOK CROSSBAR
(— OF BAD FORTUNE) CLAP
(— OF BELL) JOW BELL JOWL KNELL
TELLER
(— OF FORTUNE) CAST BREAK BONZER
FELICITY

(— OF LUCK) HIT FLUKE STRIKE
TURNUP CAPTION
(— OF MISFORTUNE) SISERARY
(— OF SCYTHE) SWATH
(— OF SHEARS) SNIP
(— OF WIT) FLIRT
(— OF WORK) BAT CHAR
(— ON THE PALM) LOOFIE
(— WITH CLAW) CLOYE
(BILLIARDS —) SPOT STUN FLUKE
FORCE MASSE HAZARD
(CONNECTING —) LIGATURE
(CRICKET —) CUT GLANCE
(CROQUET —) ROQUET
(CURLING —) INWICK
(CUTTING —) GIRD
(DOUBLE SPINNING —) DRAW
(DRUM —) DRAG
(FINISHING —) NOBBLER
(GOLF —) ODD BAFF BISK HOOK LIKE
BLAST SLICE BISQUE FOOZLE SCLAFF
APPROACH
(HOCKEY —) JOB SCOOP
(JERKY —) STAB
(LIGHTNING —) BOLT
(MEDICAL —) ICTUS APOPLEXY
(MUSICAL —) TACT
(ORNAMENTAL —) FLOURISH
(QUICK —) FLIP
(SKATING —) EDGE MOHAWK
CHOCTAW
(SMART —) FIRK
(SOOTHING —) COY
(SWIMMING —) CRAWL TRUDGEN
SIDESTROKE
(SWINGING —) HEW
(SWORD —) MONTANTO
STROLL IDLE ROAM ROVE JAUNT RANGE
STRAY ROAM GANDER LOUNGE
RAMBLE TODDLE WANDER SAUNTER
TURNOUT STRAVAGE PERAMBULATE
STROLLER SULKY TRAMP SHULER
FLANEUR SHUILER VAGRANT BOHEMIAN
PUSHCHAIR
STRONG FAT FIT HOT FELL FIRM FORT
HALE HARD HIGH IRON KEEN RANK SURE
TRIG TRIM ACRID BONNY FRESH HARDY
HEAVY HUSKY JOLLY LUSTY NERVY
PITHY SHARP SMART SOLID SOUND
STARK STIFF STOUT THEWY VALID VIVID
ARDENT BRAWNY FIERCE MIGHTY
POTENT PRETTY ROBUST RUGGED
SECURE SEVERE SINEWY STABLE
STURDY WIELDY DOUGHTY DURABLE
HUMMING INTENSE LUSTFUL NERVOUS
ATHLETIC MUSCULAR REVERENT
ROBOREAN SPANKING STALWART
STIFFISH VIGOROUS MERACIOUS
STRONGHOLD HOLD KEEP PLACE
TOWER CASTLE WARDER CITADEL
KREMLIN REDOUBT FASTHOLD
FASTNESS FORTRESS
STRUCTURE CAGE FORM MAKE ANNEX
BOOTH CABIN FLOAT HOUSE PEGMA
SETUP SHAPE STOCK BRIDGE FABRIC
GIRDER PREFAB TIMBER COTTAGE
EDIFICE FEATURE GATEWAY MANSION

STADIUM TURNOUT AEDICULA BUILDING
BUTTRESS CRIBWORK ESCORIAL
MOUNTURE SKELETON
(— BUILT IN WATER) PIER
(— CONTAINING KILN) HOVEL
(— EXTENDED INTO SEA) JETTY
(— FOR PIGEONS) COTE
(— FRAMING SHIP) KEELSON
(— IN ROCKS) FLASER
(— OF CARTRIDGE) ANVIL
(— ON ROOF) CUPOLA FEMERELL
(— ON SHIP) BLISTER
(— ON STEAMER) TEXAS
(— PRODUCING SMOOTH OUTLINE)
FAIRING
(— SHELTERING INSECTS) DOMATIUM
(— SUPPORTING AIRSHIP
PROPELLER) PYLON
(— WITHIN SHELL) ENDOCONE
(ANATOMICAL —) BUD APRON CARINA
CRESCENT
(ANTICLINAL —) SWELL
(ARCHED —) FORNIX
(BODILY —) FRAME PHYSIQUE
(BRICK —) KANG HOVEL
(BRONZE AGE —) HENGE
(CABINLIKE —) CABANA
(COMPLEX —) EMBOLUS
(CONELIKE —) PYRAMID
(CONICAL —) BULLET
(CREMATION —) DARGA
(CROWNLIKE —) CORONA
(CRYSTAL —) POLYTYPE
(CYLINDRICAL —) SILO
(DEADENING —) BAFFLE
(DEFENSIVE —) CAT
(FORTIFIED —) CAVALIER
(GENERAL —) GETUP
(HIGH —) TOWER
(HOLLOW —) SHELL
(KNEE-LIKE —) GENU
(LENS-SHAPED —) LENTOID
(LOFTY —) BABEL STEEPLE
(LOGICAL —) EIDOS
(ORGANIZED —) BULK
(ORIENTAL STORIED —) PAGODA
(ORNAMENTAL —) KIOSK
(PLANT —) DISC DISK
(POINTED —) BEAK
(PUEBLO —) KIVA
(RAISED —) CIMBORIO
(RAMSHACKLE —) COOP
(RINGLIKE —) ANNULUS
(RUDE STONE —S) SPECCHIE
(SACRIFICIAL —) ALTAR
(SENTENCE —) SYNTAX
(SHELTERING —) COT
(SICKLE-SHAPED —) FALX
(SLENDER —) HAIR
(STONE —) TAULA
(TEMPORARY —) HUT
(THEATER —) SKENE
(UNDERLYING —) BOTTOM
(UNSTABLE —) COBHOUSE
(WATERTIGHT —) CAMEL
(WHITE —) ALBEDO
STRUGGLE TUG VIE WIN AGON COPE

DEAL FEND GAME PULL TOIL FIGHT
FLING HEAVE LABOR SWORD WORRY
BATTLE BUCKLE BUFFET BUSTLE
COMBAT EFFORT HASSLE JOSTLE
SEESAW STIVER STRIFE STRIVE TUSSLE
AGONIZE CONTEND CONTEST DISPUTE
FLOUNCE WARFARE WRESTLE CONFLICT
ENDEAVOR FLOUNDER SLUGFEST
(— ALONG) HOBBLE
(— CONVULSIVELY) SPRAWL
(— FOR LARGESS) SCAMBLE
(— FORTH) ELUCTATE
(— TO GAIN FOOTING) SCRABBLE
SPROTTLE
(AGONIZED —) THROE
(CONFUSED —) MUSS
(DEATH —) AGONY
(HAND-TO-HAND —) GRAPPLE
(HAPHAZARD —) SCUFFLE
(SPIRITUAL —) PENIEL
(UNCEREMONIOUS —) SCRAMBLE
STRUMPET PUNK TRULL WENCH WHORE
STIVER TOMBOY COCOTTE DOLLYMOP
SUCCUBUS
STRUT JET BRAG COCK POMP SPUR
PRINK SWANK SASHAY SCOTCH STROKE
PEACOCK SWAGGER
STUB BUTT SNAG SPUD STUD CHECK
HINGE STUMP
STUBBLE BUN MANE SHACK ARRISH
EDDISH EEGRASS
STUBBORN BALKY ROWDY STIFF STOUT
TOUGH MULISH STURDY THWART
BULLDOG PEEVISH PIGGISH RESTIVE
WAYWARD WILLFUL OBDURATE
PERVERSE OBSTINATE PIGHEADED
TENACIOUS REFRACTORY
STUD SET BOSS KNOB KNOP KNOT NAIL
SPOT BESET BULLA JOIST ASHLAR
STRING CONTACT QUARTER STANDARD
(— IN BOOT SOLE) SLUG
(— IN WATCH) POTENCE
(— WITH NAILS) CLOUT
(INTERMEDIATE —) PUNCHEON
(ORNAMENTED —) AGLET AIGLET
STUDENT BOY COED PREP SOPH AGGIE
BEJAN GRIND MEDIC PUPIL SIZAR
BURSAR MEDICO PREMED PRIMER
SCOLOG SENIOR CLASSIC DANTEAN
EDUCAND FAILURE INTERNE INTRANT
LEARNER MIDDLER PHARMIC PLUGGER
SCHOLAR STUDIER THEOLOG BOTANIST
COLLEGER DISCIPLE EDUCATOR
HOMERIST PREMEDIC REPEATER
TRANSFER
(— IN TALMUDIC ACADEMY) BAHUR
(— LAST IN CLASS) SPOON
(— OF LOW RANK) TERNAR
(— WHO LIVES IN TOWN) OPPIDAN
(ABNORMALLY ABSORBED —) SAP
(DAY —) EXTERN
(DIVINITY —) STIBBLER
(DRUDGING —) PLUG
(ENGLISH SCHOOL —) BLUE SWOT
ETONIAN OXONIAN SWOTTER BATTELER
(GRADUATE —) FELLOW

(LAW —) PUNEE JURIST LEGIST PUISNE TEMPLAR STAGIARY
(MILITARY —) CADET
(MOSLEM —) SOFTA
(NON-COLLEGIATE —) TOSHER
(PLODDING —) DIG SMUG
(WANDERING —) GOLIARD
(1ST-YEAR —) FUCHS
(3RD-YEAR —) JUNIOR TERTIAN
STUDIOUS BOOKISH CLERKLY DILIGENT SEDULOUS
STUDY CON BOOK CASE SIFT EXAMEN LESSON MUSEUM SURVEY ACCOUNT ANALYZE CANVASS SANCTUM ANALYSIS BOOKWORK CONSIDER EXERCISE MEDITATE SCRUTINY
(— HARD) DIG MUG SAP BONE SMUG STEW SWOT
(ART —) ABBOZZO CROQUIS POCHADE
(BROWN —) REVERIE
(CLAY —) BOZZETTO
(MUSICAL —) ETUDE
(PRELIMINARY —) SKETCH
(UNINTERESTING —) GRIND
STUDY IN SCARLET (AUTHOR OF —) DOYLE
(CHARACTER IN —) HOPE JOHN LUCY HOLMES TOBIAS WATSON FERRIER GREGSON LESTRADE SHERLOCK STAMFORD JEFFERSON STANGERSON
STUFF PAD RAM WAD CRAM CRAP JAZZ TACK TRIG TUCK TUCK WHAT CROWD FORCE KEDGE SQUAB TRADE FABRIC KIBOSH MATTER PAUNCH TACKLE TIMBER BOMBAST ELEMENT MATERIAL
(— AND NONSENSE) HAVERS PICKLE PIFFLE
(— FILLET OF VEAL) BOMBARD
(— FULL) STODGE
(— OF POOR QUALITY SILK) RASH
(— ONESELF) MAST
(— POULTRY) FARCE MARINATE
(— WITH DRESSING) QUILT
(COTTON —) CALICO
(HOUSEHOLD —) GEAR
(INFERIOR —) MOCKADO
(SILKEN —) TARS DIAPHANE
(STICKY —) GOOK
(TASTELESS —) GLOP
(THIN —) CRAPE
(THIN SILK —) LOVE
(WATERY —) BLASH
(WOOLEN —) SAY DUROY TWILLY DRUGGET SAGATHY SHALLOON
(WORTHLESS —) GEAR GLOP HOGWASH
STUFFING PAD TAR FARCE BOMBAST FARCING SAWDUST SALPICON STUFFAGE
STUFFY POKY CLOSE FUBSY WOOLLY AIRLESS
STUMBLE CHIP FALL TRIP LURCH SPURN BUMBLE CHANCE FALTER HAPPEN OFFEND TUMBLE BLUNDER FOUNDER STAMMER STOITER FLOUNDER
STUMP CAG GET SET DOCK GRUB LUMP

SNAG STUB STUD CHUNK SCRAG STICK STOOL SCRUNT SPRONG WICKET RAMPIKE SLEEPER STUMMEL BALDHEAD HUSTINGS
(— AND ROOT) MOCK
(— OF TAIL) STRUNT
(CIGAR —) TOPPER
(CRICKET —) STICKS
(DEAD —) RUNT
(TREE —) MOCK STOW STOCK STOOP ZUCHE DOTARD NUBBIN STOVEN DODDARD
(WALNUT —) BUTT
STUMPY SNUB BUNTY SNUBBED
STUN DIN BOWL DAZE ROCK DAUNT DROWN BEDAZE BENUMB DEADEN DEAFEN NOBBLE STOUND WITHER ASTOUND SANDBAG SILENCE STUPEFY ASTONISH PARALYZE
STUNT GAG KIP FEAT BLAST DWARF STOCK DOLPHIN BACKBEND CATALINA PORPOISE SUPPRESS
(SWIMMING —) SHARK SPIRAL
STUNTED GRUBBY RUNTISH SCRUBBY SCRUFFY
STUPEFIED MAD DAZED DRUNK SILLY SOTTED BEMUSED DOZZLED BESOTTED MINDLESS
STUPEFY FOX DAMP DAZE DRUG DULL GOOF STUN BESOT DAUNT SHEND SMOKE BEMUSE BENUMB FUDDLE MUDDLE STOUND ASTOUND CONFUSE STUPEND ASTONISH BEFUDDLE BEMUDDLE BEWILDER CONFOUND PARALYZE SOMNIATE
STUPENDOUS GREAT IMMENSE ENORMOUS MONSTROUS
STUPID FAT JAY DULL DUMB FOOL HAZY LEWD NUMB SLOW BLUNT BOOBY BRUTE CRASS DENSE DOTED GROSS HEAVY HENT MUZZY SILLY THICK ASSISH BARREN BOVINE CUCKOO DAWKIN DROWSY OBTUSE OPAQUE SIMPLE SODDEN STOLID WOODEN ASININE BRUTISH DOLTISH DUMPISH FATUOUS FOOLISH FOPPISH GAWKISH GULLISH LUMPISH PINHEAD PROSAIC SOTTISH TOMFOOL VACUOUS WITLESS ANSERINE BESOTTED BOEOTIAN CLODDISH DUNCICAL IMBECILE PINHEADED SENSELESS
STUPIDITY BETISE TORPOR BOBBERY DENSITY DUNCERY FATUITY DULLNESS DUMBNESS HEBETUDE STOLIDITY
STUPOR FOG SOG DAMP SOPOR STOUND TORPOR TRANCE LETHARGY NARCOSIS
STURDY BUFF RUDE TALL BURLY CRANK HARDY HUSKY LUSTY SOLID SOUND STARK STIFF STOUT WALLY ROBUST RUGGED SQUARE STABLE STEADY STOCKY STRONG VIRILE UPRIGHT VALIANT STALWART STUBBORN VIGOROUS YEOMANLY
STUTTER BUFF HACK GANCH FAMBLE HABBLE STAMMER
STY PEN QUAT STYE CRUIVE PIGPEN HORDEOLUM

STYLE AIR CUT DUB PEN SAY TON WAY CHIC FACE FORM GARB HAND KIND MODE MOLD NAME RATE VEIN GENRE GETUP GUISE SHAPE STATE SWANK TASTE FORMAT PHRASE STRAIN STYLUS COSTUME DIALECT DICTION FASHION QUALITY EQUIPAGE LANGUAGE

STYLISH CHIC POSH TONY DOGGY NIFTY NOBBY RITZY SASSY SHARP SMART SWELL TIPPY CLASSY DAPPER FLOSSY JAUNTY SWANKY TONISH DASHING DOGGISH GENTEEL KNOWING SWAGGER TOFFISH

STYPTIC ALUM AMADOU MATICO BAROMETZ STANCHER

STYX (FATHER OF —) OCEANUS **(HUSBAND OF —)** PALLAS **(MOTHER OF —)** TETHYS

SUAVE OILY SMUG SOFT BLAND SOAPY SVELT GLOSSY SILKEN SMOOTH URBANE FULSOME POLITIC UNCTUOUS

SUBDUE BOW COW BEAT BEND TAME ACCOY ALLAY CHARM CRUSH DAUNT QUAIL QUASH QUELL SOBER STILL BRIDLE DISMAY EVINCE GENTLE MASTER QUENCH REDUCE SUBMIT ABANDON CAPTURE CHASTEN CONQUER OVERAWE REPRESS SUCCUMB CONVINCE OVERCOME SUPPRESS SURMOUNT VANQUISH

SUBDUED SOFT TAME MUTED SOBER STILL UNDER BROKEN CHASTE GENTLE ASHAMED SOURDINE

SUBJECT DUX ALLY BODY ITEM TEXT PLACE STOOP STUDY THEMA THEME TOPIC GROUND IMPOSE LIABLE PATHIC REDUCE SUBMIT THRALL VASSAL CAITIVE CITIZEN FEODARY FEUDARY SERVILE ELECTIVE INCIDENT OBEDIENT OCCASION SENTENCE

SUBLIME BIG GRAND LOFTY NOBLE AUGUST REFINE SOLEMN WINGED DANTEAN EXALTED EMPYREAN MAGNIFIC MAJESTIC SERAPHIC SPLENDID MAGNIFICENT

SUBMARINE SUB BOAT DIVER GUPPY SUBSEA PIGBOAT

SUBMERGE BOG DIP BURY DIVE DUNK HIDE SINK SOAK DROWN SOUSE SWAMP WHELM DELUGE DRENCH ENGULF IMPLUNGE INUNDATE OVERWHELM

SUBMISSIVE MEEK DEMISS DOCILE DUTIFUL PASSIVE SERVILE SLAVISH SUBJECT OBEDIENT RESIGNED YIELDING **(— TO WIFE)** UXORIOUS

SUBMIT BOW BEND CAVE LEAN OBEY TAKE VAIL DEFER STOOP YIELD ASSENT CRINGE RESIGN KNUCKLE SUCCUMB TRUCKLE **(— FOR CONSIDERATION)** REMIT **(— TAMELY)** EAT **(— TO)** ABIDE STAND SUFFER

SUBPOENA SUMMONS

SUBSCRIBE SIGN ASSENT ASCRIBE CONSIGN SUBSIGN

SUBSCRIPTION APPROVAL SIGNATURE ABONNEMENT

SUBSEQUENT AFTER LATER FUTURE PUISNE ENSUING POSTNATE

SUBSERVIENT OILY VASSAL DUTEOUS SERVILE SLAVISH OFFICIAL

SUBSIDE DIE EBB LIE CALM FALL LULL SINK ABATE ALLAY LAPSE SETTLE ASSUAGE RELAPSE WITHDRAW

SUBSIDY AID BONUS BOUNTY POUNDAGE

SUBSTANCE FAT SUM BODY CORE GIST TACK WHAT AGENT ALLOY BEING METAL OUSIA PROOF SENSE STUFF THING BOTTOM IMPORT MATTER STAPLE WEALTH COLLOID CONTENT ESSENCE MEANING PURPORT REAGENT SUBJECT ADDITIVE ADHESIVE ALLERGEN HARDNESS MATERIAL

SUBSTANDARD BAD BAUCH

SUBSTANTIAL FAT FIRM MEATY PUKKA STOUT ACTUAL BODILY HEARTY SQUARE STABLE STANCH STURDY MASSIVE MATERIAL TANGIBLE

SUBSTANTIATE BACK CONFIRM SUPPORT VALIDATE

SUBSTITUTE SUB MOCK VICE EXTRA PINCH PROXY VICAR BACKUP CHANGE DEPUTY DOUBLE ERSATZ STOOGE COMMUTE REPLACE RESERVE STANDBY STOPGAP DISPLACE MAKESHIFT **(— FOR TEA)** TIA FAHAM **(POOR —)** APOLOGY

SUBSTITUTION SHIFT CHANGE ERSATZ ENALLAGE EXCHANGE NOVATION REPLACEMENT

SUBTERFUGE MASK BLIND CROOK QUIRK SHIFT TRICK CHICANE ARTIFICE PRETENCE

SUBTLE SLY FINE NICE WILY WISE ACUTE ARGUTE ASTUTE CRAFTY SHREWD CUNNING FRAGILE

SUBTLETY FRAUD DECEIT NUANCE FINESSE QUILLET DELICACY FINENESS QUODLIBET REFINEMENT

SUBTRACT BATE PULL TAKE SHAVE DEDUCE DEDUCT DETRACT DIMINISH

SUBURB ANNEX BORGO BARRIO PETTAH BANLIEU ENDSHIP FAUBOURG **(PL.)** SKIRTS ENVIRONS OUTPARTS SUBURBIA

SUBVERT SAP KILL RAZE RUIN EVERT UPSET GAINSAY OVERSET REVERSE OVERTURN

SUCCEED GO HIT FARE RISE WORK CLICK ENSUE PROVE SCORE FOLLOW OBTAIN SECOND THRIVE ACHIEVE INHERIT PREVAIL PROSPER FLOURISH SUPPLANT

SUCCESS GO HIT MAX WIN WOW BANG LUCK SMASH EXPLOIT FORTUNE PROWESS FELICITY GODSPEED **(— IN A MATCH)** GAME **(ACCIDENTAL —)** FLUKE **(BRILLIANT —)** ECLAT **(SUDDEN —)** KILLING **(UNEXPECTED —)** JACKPOT **(WORLDLY —)** ARTHA

SUCCESSFUL HOT MADE SOCK BOFFO LUCKY SPEEDFUL THRIVING

SUCCESSION RUN SUIT ROUND SUITE
TRACK COURSE SEQUEL SERIES STREAM
STRING HEIRDOM ANCESTRY MUTATION
SEQUENCE
(— OF CHANGES) FLUX
(— OF CHORDS) CADENCE
(— OF CRUSTS) CALICHE
(— OF STAGES) CASCADE
(— OF WAVES) CRIMP
(— OF RULERS) DYNASTY
SUCCINCT BRIEF SHORT TERSE CONCISE
LACONIC SUMMARY
SUCCOR AID HELP SERVE SPEED ASSIST
RELIEF RESCUE SUPPLY COMFORT
DELIVER RELIEVE SECOURS SUSTAIN
BEFRIEND
SUCCULENT LUSH JUICY LUSHY PULPY
SAPPY YOUNG FLESHY TENDER
WATERISH
SUCCUMB BREAK QUAIL STOOP YIELD
SUCK SOUK SWIG SWOOP SUCKLE
(— DRY) SOAK
(— UP) DRINK ABSORB TIPPLE
SUCKER CHUB FISH GULL PATSY SOBOL
CUPULE MULLET RATOON REDFIN
SPROUT STOLON TILLER CUTLIPS
LOCULUS OSCULUM PEDICEL BOTHRIUM
LOLLIPOP PUSHOVER REDHORSE
SURCULUS
(SUFF.) BDELLA
SUCKLE FEED MILK SUCK LACTATE
NOURISH

SUDAN

CAPITAL: KHARTOUM
DESERT: NUBIAN
LANGUAGE: GA EWE IBO KRU EFIK MOLE
TSHI YORUBA MANDINGO
MEASURE: UD
MOUNTAIN: KINYETI
NATIVE: DAZA GOLO NUER SERE DINKA
FULAH HAUSA MOSSI NUBIYIN
PROVINCE: DARFUR KASSALA KORDOFAN
REGION: DARFUR KASSALA KORDOFAN
RIVER: NILE
TOWN: WAU JUBA KOSTI MEROE ATBARA
ALUBAYD KASSALA MALAKAL
OMDURMAN
WEIGHT: HABBA

SUDDEN BRASH FERLY HASTY ICTIC
SWIFT ABRUPT FIERCE SNAPPY SPEEDY
HEADLONG SUBITOUS PRECIPITATE
SUDDENLY BOB POP BOLT FLOP SLAP
AMAIN SHORT PRESTO SUBITO
UNAWARES
SUDS BUCK FOAM SAPPLES SOAPSUDS
SUE LAW WOO SUIT IMPLEAD TROUNCE
SUFFER BYE LET BEAR BIDE FIND GAIN
HURT PAIN PINE ALLOW INCUR LABOR
SMART STAND ENDURE PERMIT AGONIZE
SUPPORT SUSTAIN UNDERGO TOLERATE
(— AGONY) THROE
(— AT STAKE) SMOKE
(— DEFEAT) BOW

(— FOR) ABY ABYE ABIDE
(— FROM TIME) AGE
(— GREAT AFFLICTION) GROAN
(— HUNGER) CLEM STARVE AFFAMISH
(— LOSS OF) GIVE
(— PAIN) STOUND ANGUISH
(— PENALTY) SWEAT
(— REMORSE) RUE
(— RUIN) WRECK
(— SYNCOPE) FAINT
(— THROUGH) PASS
(— TO ENTER) ADMIT
SUFFERING BALE COST HURT PAIN RACK
AGONY DOLOR GRIEF SMART PATHIC
PATHOS LANGUOR PASSION PASSIVE
TRAVAIL DISTRESS HARDSHIP
MARTYRDOM
(— FROM HANGOVER) CHIPPY
(— FROM ILL HEALTH) DOWN
(— OF MIND) CARE
(—S OF CHRIST) AGONY
SUFFICE DO LAST COVER REACH SERVE
SATISFY
SUFFICIENCY ENOUGH PLENTY
ADEQUACY ABUNDANCE PLENITUDE
SUFFICIENT DUE FAIR GOOD AMPLE
DECENT ENOUGH PRETTY ADEQUATE
COMPETENT
(BARELY —) SCANT SKIMP NARROW
SCRIMPY
(BE — FOR) COVER
SUFFOCATE CHOKE DROWN STUFF
SWELT STIFLE SMOLDER SMOTHER
STRANGLE THROTTLE
SUFFRAGE VOTE VOICE TONGUE
VERSICLE
SUFFUSE DIP FILL BATHE EMBAY TINGE
INFUSE MANTLE
SUGAR CANDY DIOSE MELIS PIECE
SUCRE THIRD INVERT KETOSE PANELA
GLUCOSE GLYCOSE LACTOSE MALTOSE
MANNOSE PENTOSE SORBOSE SUCROSE
SWEETEN CONCRETE DEXTROSE
FRUCTOSE LEVULOSE
(BROWN —) CARAIBE JAGGARY
DEMERARA JAGGHERY
(COARSE —) RAAB PANOCHA
(CRUDE —) GUR HEAD MELADA
CONCRETE
(INFERIOR —) BASTARD
(SIMPLE —) OSE
(UNREFINED —) CASSONADE
SUGGEST JOG BEAR GIVE HINT IMPLY
OFFER SPEAK ADVISE ALLUDE INDITE
PROMPT SUBMIT DICTATE INSPIRE
INDICATE INTIMATE PROPOUND
(— DRINKING) PROPOSE
(— INSIDIOUSLY) INFUSE
(— STRONGLY) ARGUE
SUGGESTION CUE HINT WIND
ADVICE BREATH MOTION SMATCH
INKLING POINTER PROFFER SOUPCON
WRINKLE INNUENDO INSTANCE
PROPOSAL
SUGGESTIVE ANICONIC PREGNANT
REDOLENT
SUIT DO GO APT FIT GEE HIT SET LIKE

PAIR SEEM SORT ADAPT AGREE APPLY
BEFIT BESIT CLUBS COLOR DRAPE DRESS
FANCY HABIT LEVEL MATCH PLEAD
SAVOR SERVE SHAPE TALLY ANSWER
BECOME COHERE COMPLY HEARTS
PRAYER SPADES SPEECH SQUARE
BEHOOVE COMPORT COSTUME FASHION
PURSUIT REQUEST DIAMONDS SKELETON
STANDARD TAILLEUR TROPICAL
PINSTRIPE
(— AT LAW) ACTO CASE LAWSUIT
(— OF ARMOR) PANOPLY
(— OF MAIL) CATAPHRACT
(DIVER'S —) SCAPHANDER
(SWIMMING —) BATHER BIKINI
MAILLOT

SUITABLE APT FIT PAT ABLE FEAT GAIN
GOOD JUST MEET WELL DIGNE EQUAL
FITTY RIGHT COMELY GAINLY GIUSTO
HABILE HONEST LIABLE LIKELY PROPER
COMMODE CONDIGN CONGRUE FITTING
PLIABLE SEEMING BECOMING DECOROUS
ELIGIBLE HANDSOME ACCORDING
OPPORTUNE
(— FOR MALE AND FEMALE) UNISEX
(EXACTLY —) VERY

SUITCASE BAG CAP GRIP DORLACH
KEESTER

SUITE SET SWEEP TRAIN SERIES PARTITA
RETINUE ENSEMBLE EQUIPAGE

SUITED FIT SEEMLY ADAPTED
CONGENIAL
(POORLY —) CROOK

SUITOR MAN BEAU SUER SWAIN WOOER
GALLANT

SULK PET CHAW CRAB GLUM POUT
FRUMP GROUT GRUMP GROUCH

SULKY CART CHUFF DORTY GOURY
HUFFY CHUFFY GLUMPY GROUTY STUFFY
SULLEN DOGGISH HUFFISH MUMPISH

SULLEN DOUR FOUL GLUM GRIM SOUR
BLACK CHUFF CROSS DUMPY GRUFF
HARSH MOODY STERN SULKY SURLY
CRUSTY DOGGED GLOOMY MOROSE
MULISH SOMBER STUFFY AUSTERE
CRABBED CYNICAL FRETFUL LOURING
LUMPISH PEEVISH CHURLISH FAROUCHE
LOWERING PETULANT SPITEFUL

SULLY BLOT BLUR DASH FOUL SLUR
SMUT SOIL CLOUD DIRTY GRIME SMEAR
SMOKE STAIN TAINT BEFOUL DARKEN
DEFILE SMIRCH SMUTCH ATTAINT
BEGRIME BESMEAR BLEMISH CORRUPT
POLLUTE TARNISH BESMIRCH
BESPATTER

SULTRY CLOSE FLUSH POTHERY
SWELTRY FEVERISH

SUM ALL GOB AGIO CASH DUMP FINE
FUND MASS TALE GROSS KITTY SUMMA
TOTAL WHOLE AMOUNT DEMAND
FIGURE NUMBER DECUPLE SUBSIDY
SUMMARY ENTIRETY QUANTITY
POLYNOMIAL
(— AND SUBSTANCE) TOUR SHORT
UPSHOT
(— AS COMPENSATION FOR
KILLING) MANBOTE

(— FOR REENLISTMENT) GRATUITY
(— FOR SCHOLARSHIP) BURSARY
(— IN BASSET) SEPTLEVA
(— OF) SIGMA
(— OF DETERMINANTS) STIRP
(— OF EXPONENTS) DEGREE
(— OF FACTORS) COMPLEX
(— OF GOOD QUALITIES) ARETE
(— OF MONEY) POT BANK COVER
STOCK BUNDLE ACCOUNT STIPEND
(— OF 25 POUNDS) PONY PONEY
(— OF 3 FARTHINGS) GILL
(— OF 500 POUNDS) MONKEY
(— PAYABLE AT FIXED INTERVALS)
FARM
(— RISKED) STAKE
(— UP) ADD TOT FOOT RECKON
SUBSUME SUMMATE COMPRISE
CONCLUDE PERORATE
(ENTIRE —) SOLIDUM
(EXCESS —) BONUS
(FORFEITED —) DEDIT
(GREAT —) PLUNK SIGHT MICKLE
(LARGE —) GOB SCREAMER
(PETTY —) CENT DIME DRAB
(SMALL — OF MONEY) SPILL DRIBBLE
DRIBLET SHOESTRING
(TRIFLING —) HAY GROAT
(UNEXPENDED —S) SAVINGS
(VECTOR —) GRADIENT

SUMATRA (LANGUAGE IN —) NIAS
(MEASURE OF —) PAAL
(MOUNTAIN IN —) LEUSER KERINTJI
(RIVER IN —) HARI MUSI ROKAN
DJAMBI
(TOWN IN —) ACHIN KUALA MEDAN
NATAL SOLOK DJAMBI LANGSA PADANG
RENGAT BENKULEN BENKULEN

SUMMARY SUM CURT LEAD BRIEF
CHART RECAP SCORE SHORT SUMMA
TOTAL APERCU PRECIS RESUME
CHAPTER CONCISE EPITOME EXTRACT
OUTLINE RUNDOWN VIDIMUS ABSTRACT
ARGUMENT BREVIARY DRUMHEAD
OVERVIEW SUCCINCT SYNOPSIS
(— OF FAITH) SYMBOL
(— OF PRINCIPLES) CREED

SUMMER SHEMU SOMER AESTAS
DORMANT
(OF —) ESTIVAL

SUMMERHOUSE FOLLY KIOSK MAHAL
TUPEK ALCOVE CASINO GAZEBO
PAGODA

SUMMIT SUM TIP TOP VAN ACME APEX
HELM KNAP PEAK ROOF CREST CROWN
SPIRE CULMEN HEIGHT VERTEX ZENITH
PINNACLE MOUNTAINTOP
(— OF TUBE) MOUTH
(— WITHOUT FOREST) BALD
(ROCKY —) KNOT
(ROUND —) DOD
(SNOW-CAPPED —) CALOTTE

SUMMON BAN CRY BUZZ CALL CITE
DRUM HAIL BUGLE CHARM EVOKE KNELL
SOUND ADVOKE COMPEL DEMAND
VOCATE COMMAND CONJURE CONVENE
CONVOKE PROVOKE WHISTLE

(— FOR HIRING) YARD
(— INTO COURT) DEMAND
(— TOGETHER) BAND MUSTER ASSEMBLE
(— UP) FIND GATHER COLLECT
SUMMONS CRY CALL BREVE TICKET BIDDING CALLING STICKER WARNING WARRANT CITATION MONITION
SUMPTUOUS RICH GRAND SHOWY COSTLY DELUXE SUPERB ELEGANT MAGNIFIC SPLENDID MAGNIFICENT
SUN SOL ATEN ATON BASK LAMP STAR SURYA DAYSTAR IOSKEHA PHOEBUS SAVITAR JOUSKEHA
(— MOON AND STARS) HOST
(RISING —) HERAKHTI
SUN ALSO RISES (AUTHOR OF —) HEMINGWAY
(CHARACTER IN —) BILL COHN JAKE MIKE BRETT CLYNE PEDRO ASHLEY BARNES GORTON ROBERT ROMERO FRANCES MICHAEL MONTOYA CAMPBELL GEORGETTE
SUNBONNET TILT UGLY CRESIE KAPPIE SHAKER
SUNBURN GREENING HELIOSIS
SUNDER PART RIVE TWIN BREAK SEVER TWAIN DIVIDE DISALLY DISJOIN DIVORCE DISSEVER SEPARATE
SUNDIAL DIAL GHURRY HOROLOGE SCAPHION SCAPHIUM
(PART OF —) DIAL LINE PLATE GNOMON DIAGRAM
SUNDRY DIVERS DIVERSE SEVERAL
SUNRISE ARIST SUNUP ORIENT
SUNSET SUNFALL
SUNSHADE PARASOL ROUNDEL TIRESOL SOMBRERO
SUNSTROKE HELIOSIS SIRIASIS
SUP EAT DINE FEAST CONSUME SWALLOW
SUPERABUNDANCE FLOOD EXCESS CATARACT PLEONASM PLETHORA PLEURISY
SUPERABUNDANT RANK LAVISH PROFUSE
SUPERB GRAND GOLDEN CLIPPING GORGEOUS SPLENDID
SUPERCILIOUS GRAND PROUD SNIFFY SNIPPY SNOOTY SNOTTY HAUGHTY ARROGANT CAVALIER SUPERIOR
SUPERFICIAL GLIB ECTAL FACIAL FACILE FLIMSY FROTHY GLASSY SLIGHT CURSORY OUTSIDE OUTWARD PASSING SHALLOW SKETCHY SURFACE COSMETIC EXTERNAL DEPTHLESS
SUPERFLUOUS SPARE OTIOSE USELESS NEEDLESS REDUNDANT
SUPERINTEND CON GUIDE OVERSEE PRESIDE
SUPERINTENDENT BOSS SUPE EPHOR SUPER EDITOR VENEUR VIEWER WARDEN CAPTAIN CURATOR EPHORUS MANAGER DIRECTOR OVERSEER SURVEYOR SWINGMAN
SUPERIOR COOL FINE MORE OVER ABBOT ABOVE CHIEF CREAM ELDER ELITE EXTRA FANCY GREAT PRIOR PUKKA SWANK UPPER ABBESS BETTER COCKUP DOMINA FATHER MAHANT SELECT SENIOR STRONG RANKING ABNORMAL DOMINANT GUARDIAN SINGULAR SPLENDID MARVELOUS PARAMOUNT
(— OF CONVENT) HEGUMEN
(— TO) BEFORE
SUPERIORITY DROP HEIGHT MASTERY PROWESS EMINENCE PRIORITY
(MENTAL —) GENIUS
SUPERLATIVE RAVING CURIOUS ROUSING CRASHING OLYMPIAN PEERLESS SWINGING
(ABSOLUTE —) ELATIVE
SUPERNATURAL FEY DIVINE NUMINOUS SUPERIOR MARVELOUS PARANORMAL
SUPERSEDE REPLACE OVERRIDE SUPPLANT
SUPERSTITION FREIT IDOLATRY ABERGLAUBE
SUPERVISE BOSS GUIDE DIRECT GOVERN HANDLE SURVEY FOREMAN OVERSEE PROCTOR ENGINEER OVERLOOK CHAPERONE
SUPERVISION EYE CARE DUTY HAND CHECK CHARGE OVERSIGHT
SUPERVISOR BOSS BULL EPHOR GUIDE SUPER CENSOR WARDEN PROCTOR ALYTARCH CHAIRMAN FLOORMAN MASHGIAH OVERSEER
SUPINE INERT DROWSY LANGUID SERVILE CARELESS INACTIVE INDOLENT LISTLESS SLUGGISH
SUPPER CENA MEAL CUDDY PASCHAL
(HARVEST-HOME —) HOCKEY
(LAST —) MAUNDY
(LORD'S —) NAGMAAL
SUPPLANT FOLLOW REMOVE REPLACE DISPLACE DISPLANT
SUPPLE FLIP OILY SOFT LITHE LIMBER SVELTE SWANKY LISSOME PLIABLE FLEXIBLE
SUPPLEMENT ARM EKE MEND TACK ANNEX SUPPLY BOLSTER CODICIL ADDENDUM APPENDIX
SUPPLEMENTARY ADDED SECOND RIPIENO REMANENT PERIPHERAL
SUPPLICATION CRY VOW LIBEL VENIE APPEAL LITANY PRAYER SYNAPTE ENTREATY PETITION PLEADING ROGATION
SUPPLY FEED FILL GIVE HEEL LEND ARRAY CATER ENDUE EQUIP OFFER SERVE STOCK STORE STUFF YIELD BUDGET DONATE LAYOUT RENDER SUBMIT ADVANCE FURNISH PROVIDE ACCOMMODATE
(— ABUNDANTLY) SWILL
(— ARRANGED BEFOREHAND) RELAY
(— FOR AN OCCASION) GRIST
(— OF MONEY) BANKROLL
(— OF POTENTIAL JURORS) TALES
(— OF REMOUNTS) REMUDA
(— OF TIN) SERVING
(— PROVISIONS) PURVEY

(— WITH CLOTHES) INFIT
(— WITH FUEL) STOKE
(— WITH MONEY) GILD
(— WITH OXYGEN) AERATE
(— WITH WATER) FANG
(CACHED —) CAVE
(CONSTANT —) STREAM
(EXTRA —) RESERVE
(HIDDEN —) HOARD
(INADEQUATE —) DEARTH
(OVERABUNDANT —) SURFEIT
(PLENTIFUL —) CHOICE
(RESERVE —) CUSHION
(RICH —) ARGOSY
(SCANTY —) SCANT
SUPPORT AID ARM BED BOW LEG PEG
RIB TIE TOM ABET AXIS BACK BASE
BEAM BEAR BUOY CRIB FIND FORK HELP
HOLD KEEP LIFT POST PROP RACK REST
STAY STEM STUD STUD ADOPT ANGEL
ATLAS BIPOD BLOCK BRACE BROOK
CARRY CHEER CHOCK CLEAT FAVOR
FLOAT POISE SHORE STAFF STAKE
STEAD STOOP STRUT TOWER VOUCH
WEIGH ANCHOR ASSERT ASSIST
BARROW COLUMN CORSET CRUTCH
DEFEND GARTER PILLAR POTENT SADDLE
SECOND SHIELD SOCKET SPLINT STAYER
STEADY SUFFER TIMBER UPHOLD
UPKEEP ALIMENT ARMREST BACKING
BOLSTER COMFORT CONFIRM ENDORSE
KEEPING NOURISH NURTURE PABULUM
PROTECT RADICAL SPONSOR STIFFEN
STIRRUP SUBSIST SUSTAIN TRESTLE
ADJUMENT ADVOCATE BEFRIEND
BOOKREST BUTTRESS FAIRLEAD
FOOTREST FORESTAY HANDREST
HOLDFAST JACKSTAY KEYSTONE
MAINSTAY MAINTAIN MOUNTING
PEDESTAL PEDIMENT STANDARD
STOCKING STRENGTH SYMPATHY
UNDERLIE UNDERPIN UNDERSET
PATRONAGE MAINTENANCE
(— FOR ANVIL) STOCK
(— FOR BELL CLAPPER) BALDRIC
(— FOR CANOPY) BAIL
(— FOR CATALYST) CARRIER
(— FOR CORSET) BUSK
(— FOR HEAVY MACHINERY)
BUNTING
(— FOR LAUNCHING SHIP) POPPET
(— FOR LEVER) BAIT
(— FOR LIFE-CAR) BAIL
(— FOR MILL) LOWDER
(— FOR MINE PASSAGE) OVERCAST
(— FOR OARLOCK) OUTRIGGER
(— FOR PICTURE HOOKS) CORNICE
(— FOR PIPE) CHAPLET
(— FOR PLATFORM) STEMPLE
(— IN A LATHE) DOCTOR
(— IN PAPERMAKING TUB) DONKEY
(— OF COPING) KNEELER
(— OF MOLD CORE) ARBOR
(— OF RAIL) CHAIR BALUSTER
(— THROUGH BIT AND BRIDLE)
APPUI

(CRUTCHLIKE —) DEADMAN
(ELBOW-SHAPED —) CRANK
(EMBEDDED —) SPURN
(FIREPLACE —) ANDIRON
(INCLINED —) RIDER
(MINING —) CAP FRAME
(PORTABLE —) STOOL
(PRINCIPAL —) BACKBONE
(TEMPORARY —) NEEDLING
(UPRIGHT —) POPPET BANISTER
(WHEELED —) CARRIAGE
(PL.) SHIPWAY
SUPPORTER ALLY ATLAS COHORT
SATRAP APOSTLE BOOSTER DEVOTEE
FAVORER FOUNDER PATROON PROPPER
ADHERENT ESPOUSER FAVORITE
HENCHMAN STALWART UPHOLDER
(CHIEF —) STOOP PILLAR
SUPPOSE SAY SET WIS DEEM READ TAKE
TROW ALLOW COUNT FANCY
GUESS JUDGE OPINE THINK ASSUME
DEVISE DIVINE EXPECT RECKON BELIEVE
DARESAY IMAGINE PRESUME PROPOSE
SURMISE CONCEIVE CONCLUDE
CONSIDER
SUPPOSED ALLEGED ASSUMED
PUTATIVE
SUPPOSITION IDEA FICTION SURMISE
WEENING
SUPPRESS LAY DOWN GULP HIDE HUSH
SINK SLAY SNUB STOP BLACK BURKE
CHOKE CRUSH ELIDE QUASH QUELL
SHUSH STILL CANCEL QUENCH SQUASH
STIFLE CONTAIN CUSHION INHIBIT
OPPRESS REPRESS SILENCE SMOTHER
SQUELCH RESTRAIN STRANGLE
VANQUISH
SUPREMACY PALM PRIMACY DOMINION
OVERRULE
SUPREME HIGH LAST CHIEF VITAL
SUBLIME SUMMARY FOREMOST
GREATEST PEERLESS
SURE COLD SAFE BOUND SECURE STEADY
ASSURED CERTAIN PERFECT COCKSURE
POSITIVE UNERRING
SURETY BAIL BAND BORROW CAUTION
SPONSOR BAILSMAN SECURITY
SURFACE PLAT SIDE BOSOM FLOOR
STONE FINISH ASPHALT BLANKET
COUNTER ENVELOP OUTSIDE STRETCH
CONCRETE EXTERIOR PLATFORM
(— BETWEEN FLUTES OF SHAFT)
ORLO
(— BETWEEN TRIGLYPH CHANNELS)
MEROS
(— IN BEATER) BACKFALL
(— OF BEAM) BACK
(— OF BODY) FLESH HABIT
(— OF COAL) BUTT
(— OF CRICKET FIELD) CARPET
(— OF DIAMOND) SPREAD
(— OF EARTH) DUST GROUND TERRENE
PENEPLAIN
(— OF ESCUTCHEON) FIELD
(— OF GROUND OVER MINE) DAY
(— OF PARACHUTE) CANOPY
(— OF RIFLE BARREL) LAND

(— OF SAWED LUMBER) FUR
(— OF TOOTH) TRITOR
(— OF VAULT) GROIN
(— OF WATER) RYME SCRUFF
(— WITHIN EARTH) GEOID
(CONCAVE —) LAP
(CURVED —) BELLY
(DULL —) MAT MATTING
(EXTERNAL —) PERIPHERY
(FLAT —) BED FLAT AEQUOR PAGINA
(FLOOR —) BOWL
(GEOMETRIC —) TORE CONOID SPHERE
QUARTIC CONICOID CYLINDER HELICOID
PARABOLOID
(GLOSSY —) GLAZE
(GROOVED —) DROVE
(HAIRY —) NAP
(HORIZONTAL —) LEVEL
(INCLINED —) CANT DESCENT
(MINERAL —) DRUSE
(PAVED —) FOOTWALK
(PILE —) FRIEZE
(PLANE —) AREA FACET
(PRINCIPAL —) FACE
(PRINTING —) CUT
(PROTECTIVE —) LAGGING
(ROAD —) MACADAM CORDUROY
(ROUGH —) KEY CRIZZLE STUBBLE
(ROUGHENED —) MAT FOOTGRIP
(SLIPPERY —) GLARE
(SLOPING —) SHELVING
(STRIKING —) BLADE
(UNDER — OF SKI) PALM
(UNGLOSSY PAINT —) FLAT
(UPPER —) NOTAEUM
(UPRIGHT —) JAMB
SURFEIT CLOY FILL GLUT SATE STUFF
ENGLUT SICKEN SATIATE SATIETY
SATURATE REPLETION
SURGE GUST TIDE WASH DRIVE LUNGE
SPURT SWELL BILLOW COURSE SEETHE
WALLOW REDOUND UNDULATE
(— OF ELECTRIC POWER) GLITCH
(SHOREWARD —) SUFF
SURGEON
(ALSO SEE PHYSICIAN AND DOCTOR)
LEECH ARTIST INTERN MEDICO
OPERATOR SAWBONES
SURINAME (CAPITAL OF —)
PARAMARIBO
(RIVER OF —) ITANY MARONI
COPPENAME SARAMACCA COURANTYNE
(TOWN OF —) ALBINA KWATTA
TOTNESS LELYDORP
SURLY BAD ILL GRUM LUNT BLUFF CYNIC
GRUFF ROUGH CRUSTY GRUMPY
MOROSE RUGGED SNARLY SULLEN
CHURLISH
SURMISE DEEM GUESS INFER SUSPECT
MISTRUST
SURMOUNT TOP BEAT CROWN HURDLE
MASTER OVERGO CONQUER SURPASS
OVERCOME
SURPASS CAP TOP BANG BEAT FOIL
HEAD PASS EXCEL OUTDO TRUMP
BETTER EXCEED OUTRUN OUTVIE
OUTWIT OVERDO ECLIPSE OVERTOP

DOMINATE OUTCLASS OUTMATCH
OUTREACH OUTSTRIP SURMOUNT
SURPASSING BEST FINE ABOVE
DOMINANT FRABJOUS TOWERING
SURPLUS OVER PLUS REST EXCESS
SPILTH VELVET OVERAGE OVERRUN
LEFTOVER OVERFLOW
SURPRISE CAP AMAZE SHOCK SNEAK
WAYLAY WONDER ASTOUND PERPLEX
STARTLE ASTONISH BEWILDER
CONFOUND DUMFOUND
SURRENDER LET CEDE CESS FALL QUIT
REMIT YIELD REMISE RENDER RESIGN
SUBMIT ABANDON CONCEDE DELIVER
FORSAKE KAMERAD ABDICATE
ABNEGATE DELIVERY RENOUNCE
SURREPTITIOUS SECRET BOOTLEG
FURTIVE SNEAKING
SURROUND HEM LAP ORB BELT FOLD
GIRD HOOP WRAP BESET BRACE CLASP
EMBAY EMBED FENCE HEDGE CIRCLE
CORRAL ENFOLD ENWRAP GIRDLE
INCASE SWATHE BESIEGE COMPASS
ENCLOSE ENVELOP INVOLVE WREATHE
ENCIRCLE
(— WITH BOOM) CRIB
(— WITH CORD) GIRT
(— WITH MORTAR) GROUT
SURVEILLANCE WATCH SCRUTINY
STAKEOUT OVERSIGHT
SURVEY SEE SCAN VIEW STUDY PERUSE
REGARD REVIEW SEARCH CANVASS
OVERSEE OVERLOOK OVERVIEW
PROSPECT RECONNAISANCE
(— RAPIDLY) GLANCE
(— TIMBER) SKYLOOK
(BRIEF —) APERCU
SURVIVE LAST BILEVE OUTLAST OUTLIVE
SUSCEPTIBLE EASY SOFT LIABLE
FEELING PATIENT TOLERANT
(— TO CHANGE) CASALTY
SUSPECT FEAR DOUBT FANCY GUESS
THINK BELIEVE SUPPOSE DISTRUST
MISDOUBT MISTRUST
SUSPEND CALL HALT HANG SHUT STAY
BREAK CLOSE DEBAR DEFER DEMUR
POISE REMIT SWING DANGLE ADJOURN
EXCLUDE INTERMIT OVERHANG
REPRIEVE SCAFFOLD PRETERMIT
SUSPENDED AFLOAT LATENT HANGING
PENDANT PENSILE HOVERING
SUSPENSION FOG FUME STAY STOP
DELAY DOUBT MAGMA SMOKE CUTOFF
SLURRY AEROSOL FAILURE RESPITE
ABEYANCE EMULSION SHUTDOWN
(— OF JUDGMENT) EPOCHE
(— OF NOISE) HUSH
(— OF RESPIRATION) SYNCOPE
SUSPICION HINT DOUBT SOUPCON
SURMISE DISTRUST JEALOUSY
MISDOUBT MISTRUST
SUSPICIOUS SHY FISHY LEERY QUEER
JEALOUS SUSPECT DOUBTFUL
SUSTAIN ABET BACK BEAR BUOY HELP
HOLD LAST PROP STAY ABIDE CARRY
STAND ASSIST CONVEY ENDURE FOSTER
SECOND SUCCOR SUFFER UPHOLD

BOLSTER NOURISH PROLONG SUPPORT BUTTRESS CONTINUE MAINTAIN PRESERVE

SUSTENANCE GEAR SALT BREAD LIVING RELIEF ALIMENT PABULUM

SVELTE CHIC TRIM LITHE SLEEK SUAVE SMOOTH URBANE SLENDER

SWAB GOB MOP DOSSIL SPONGE SQUILGEE

SWAGGER JET BRAG COCK FACE BOAST BRANK BRAVE STRUT SWANK SWASH BOUNCE PRANCE RENOWN BLUSTER BRAVADO PANACHE ROISTER DOMINEER

SWAGGERER SWAG BUCKO FACER TIGER JETTER BRAVADO HUFFCAP RUFFLER

SWAGGERING HUFFY FACING GASCON HUFFCAP TEARCAT BLUSTERY TIGERISH

SWALLOW SUP BOLT DOWN DROP GLUT GULP SINK TAKE DRINK QUILT SWOOP ENGULF GOBBLE GUZZLE IMBIBE INGEST MARTIN POCKET CONSUME WITCHUCK
(— GREEDILY) BEND SLUP GORGE GULCH SWILL WORRY INHALE
(— HASTILY) SWAP SWOP GLOUP SLUMMOCK
(— IN AGAIN) RESORB
(— UP) GULF SWAMP ABSORB DEVOUR
(— WITH GREEDINESS) ENGORGE
(NOISY —) SLURP
(WOMAN TURNED INTO —) PROCNE

SWAMP BOG FEN FLAT FLOW MIRE MOSS SLUE SOAK SUMP VLEI MARSH SWALE DELUGE DISMAL ENGULF MORASS POCOSIN INUNDATE QUAGMIRE

SWAMPY PUXY BOGGY POOLY QUASHY MOORISH PALUDAL

SWAN COB ELK PEN OLOR CYGNET HOOPER WHOOPER
(FLOCK OF —S) GAME MARK

SWANHILD (FATHER OF —) SIGURD
(MOTHER OF —) GUDRUN

SWAP CHOP TRADE DICKER EXCHANGE

SWARD SOD TURF SWATH SWARTH

SWARM FRY CAST HOST NEST SORT TEEM CLOUD CROWD FLOCK HORDE SNARL RABBLE THRONG OVERRUN
(— IN) FILL
(— OF BEES) BIKE HIVE
(— OF INSECTS) BAND FLIGHT
(— OF PEOPLE) BIKE DRIFT
(THIRD — OF BEES) COLT

SWARTHY DUN DARK BLACK BROWN DUSKY GRIMY MOORY BISTERED

SWASTIKA FYLFOT GAMMADION

SWAY NOD WAG BEAR BEND BIAS HIKE LILT ROCK ROLL RULE SHOG TILT TOSS WAVE CARRY CHARM LURCH POWER REIGN SHAKE SWING WAVER WHEEL AFFECT CAREEN EMPIRE TOTTER WAGGLE COMMAND STAGGER

SWAZILAND (CAPITAL OF —) MBABANE
(COIN OF —) RAND
(LANGUAGE OF —) SISWATI
(MONEY OF —) LILANGENI

(RIVER IN —) USUTU KOMATI MHLATUZE UMBULUZI
(TOWN OF —) STEGI GOLLEL MANZINI PIGGSPEAK PIGGSPEAK

SWEAR VOW DAMN CURSE ADJURE AFFIRM BEDAMN DEPONE OBJURE EXECRATE
(— FALSELY) RAP MOUNT FORSWEAR MANSWEAR

SWEAT DEW WET STEW WASH SUDOR PARBOIL SWELTER PERSPIRATION
(— SKINS) STALE
(DYNAMITE —) LEAK

SWEATER FROCK GANSEY JUMPER WOOLLY CARDIGAN SLIPOVER
(CLOSE-FITTING —) POORBOY
(WOMAN'S SHORT —) SHRINK

SWEDEN

CAPITAL: STOCKHOLM

COIN: ORE KRONA SKILLING

COUNTY: KALMAR OREBRO UPPSALA

DIVISION: AMT LAEN SKANE OREBRO UPPSALA GOTALAND JAMTLAND SWEALAND

GULF: BOTHNIA

ISLAND: OLAND GOTALAND

LAKE: SILJA VANERN MALAREN VATTERN DALALVEN STORAVAN HJALMAREN

MEASURE: AM ALN FOT MIL REF TUM FAMN STOP FODER KANNA KAPPE LINJE NYMIL SPANN STANG TUNNA FATHOM JUMFRU KOLLAST OXHUVUD TUNLAND FJARDING KAPPLAND KOLTUNNA

MOUNTAIN: SARV AMMAR OVIKS HELAGS SARJEK

PROVINCE: KALMAR OREBRO GOTLAND HALLAND UPPSALA ALVSBORG BLEKINGE ELFSBORG JAMTLAND MALMOHUS WERMLAND

RIVER: DAL UME GOTA KLAR LULE KALIX PITEA RANEA LAINIO LJUSNE TORNEA WINDEL ANGERMAN

TOWN: UMEA BODEN BORAS EDANE FALUN GAVLE LULEA MALMO PITEA VISBY YSTAD ARVIKA OREBRO LUDVIKA UPPSALA GOTEBORG NYKOPING VASTERAS

WATERFALL: HANDOL TANNFORSEN

WEIGHT: ASS LOD ORT MARK PUND STEN UNTZ NYLAST LISPUND SKEPPUND

SWEEP DUST SWAY TILT BESOM BROOM DIGHT SCOPE SWIPE SWOOP BREADTH CLEANSE SHADOOF STRICKLE
(— A NET) BEAT
(— MAJESTICALLY) SWAN
(— OF SCYTHE) SWATH SWATHE
(— OFF) SLIPE
(— ON CULTIVATOR) SKIN
(CHIMNEY —) CHUMMY SWEEPY RAMONEUR
(HAY —) BUCK

SWEEPER TOPAZ BHANGI MEHTAR ROADER BROOMER MATRANEE

SWEET DUMP SUCK CREAM DOUCE DULCE FRESH HONEY MERRY SOOTH SPICY BREEZE DULCET FRUITY GENTLE SILKEN SILVER SIRUPY SUGARY DARLING HONEYED MUSICAL SUGARED WINNING WINSOME AROMATIC ENGAGING FLUMMERY LIEBLICH LUSCIOUS NECTARED PLEASANT

SWEETEN CANDY HONEY SUGAR PURIFY CLEANSE DULCIFY FRESHEN MOLLIFY PERFUME MITIGATE

SWEETHEART JO BOY HON JOE LAD SIS BABY BEAU DEAR DOLL DOXY DUCK FAIR GIRL JILL LADY LASS LOVE CHERI COOKY DOLLY FLAME LEMAN LOVER SPARK SWEET COOKIE FELLOW FRIEND MOPSEY PIGEON STEADY AMOROSA BELOVED QUERIDA SWEETIE TOOTSIE LADYLOVE LIEBCHEN MISTRESS TRUELOVE

SWEETMEAT DROP DUMP KISS DULCE FUDGE GOODY PASTE TOFFY BONBON COMFIT DRAGEE DREDGE JUNKET CARAMEL CLAGGUM CONFECT PENUCHE SUCCADE MARZIPAN PASTILLE

SWEETNESS DULCE HONEY SIRUP DOUCEUR SUAVITY FLORIMEL

SWEETSOP ATES ATTA CORAZON SWEETING

SWELL DON NOB BLOW BULB BULK BUMP BUOY DOME FILL GROW PINK RISE TONY WAVE BELLY BLAST BLOAT BULGE FLASH PREEN SMART STRUT DILATE EXPAND GROWTH LOVELY TUMEFY UPRISE AUGMENT BURGEON DISTEND INFLATE SWAGGER
(— OF GUN MUZZLE) TULIP
(— OF WATER) HUSH SURF FLOOD SURGE
(— OUT) BAG POD BUNT DRAW POUT BOSOM BILLOW SPONGE BALLOON BLADDER
(HEAVY —) RUN SEA

SWELLING BIG NOB BOLL BUBO BUMP BURR FROG FULL KNOB KNOT NODE POKE PUFF AMPER BLAIN BOTCH BULGE BUNCH EDEMA MOUSE PROUD SURGE TUMOR BOSOMY BUNCHY CALLUS GROWTH KERNEL PIMPLE RANULA WARBLE AMPULLA CUSHION PUSTULE SURGENT TURGENT UROCELE APOSTEME GLANDULE HEMATOMA NODOSITY
(— IN HORSE'S CHEST) ANTICOR
(— IN HORSE'S MOUTH) LAMPAS
(— IN PLASTER) BLUB
(— OF PLANT TISSUE) GALL
(— OF THE CHEEK) HONE
(— ON ANIMAL'S JOINTS) BUNNY CAPELLET
(— ON HEAD) COWL
(EYE —) STY

SWERVE BOW CUT YAW BIAS FADE SKEW VARY VEER WARP SHEER STRAY DEVIATE DIGRESS DIVERGE

SWIFT FAST FLIT VITE FLEET HASTY LIGHT QUICK RAPID WINDY MARLET NIMBLE RAKING SPEEDY SUDDEN WINGED FLIGHTY SWALLOW SCREAMER SQUEALER

SWIFTLY FAST APACE SNELL LIGHTLY STEEPLY TANTIVY

SWIFTNESS HASTE SPEED CELERITY FASTNESS VELOCITY

SWIM DIP SAIL SPAN TEEM BATHE CRAWL FLOAT GLIDE PLUNGE OVERFLOW
(— IN NEW DIRECTION) MILL
(— IN NUDE) SKINNYDIP
(— TOGETHER) SCHOOL

SWIMMER BATHER NATATOR

SWIMMING POOL POOL THERM PLUNGE PISCINA NATATORY
(— ON LINER) LIDO

SWINDLE CON GYP JOB RIG BILK FAKE HAVE PULL ROOK SCAM BUNCO CHEAT FOIST GOUGE PLANT ROGUE SHARK SHARP SPOOF STING BOODLE BUBBLE FIDDLE HUSTLE NOBBLE FINAGLE THIMBLE FLIMFLAM BAMBOOZLE

SWINDLER DO FOB GYP LEG BILK FYNK HAWK ROOK SKIN CHEAT CROOK ESROC FAKER GREEK HARPY KNAVE MACER ROGUE CHIAUS GOUGER INTAKE RINGER ROOKER SALTER SHAVER VERSER BUBBLER HUSTLER MACEMAN MAGSMAN NOBBLER SHARPER SKELDER SLICKER SPIELER BARNACLE BLACKLEG FINAGLER GILENYER LUMBERER PIGEONER SHELLMAN

SWINE HOG PIG SOW BOAR GILT PORK SUID DUROC ESSEX WHITE GUSSIE POLAND PORKER BUSHPIG PECCARY SUFFOLK CHESHIRE LANDRACE TAMWORTH

SWING HIKE JUMP SWAY TURN SHAKE TREND DANGLE GYRATE HANDLE SWITCH SWIVEL TOTTER JUMPING BRANDISH FLOURISH OSCILLATE
(— A SHIP) SPRING
(— AROUND) JIB SLUE
(— BY BATTER) CUT
(— FROM POSITION) CANT
(— FROM SIDE TO SIDE) JOW
(— FROM THE TIDE) TEND
(— OF PENDULUM) BEAT
(— OF SAIL) JIBE
(— OF SWORD) MOULINET
(— OUT OF LINE) SWAG
(— THE FOREFEET) DISH
(RHYTHMICAL —) LILT
(WILD —) HAYMAKER
(PREF.) OSCILLO

SWIPE COP GLOM SNAKE STEAL VULTURE

SWIRL BOIL EDDY PURL WALM SWALE WREATHE TOURBILLION
(— OF SALMON) BULGE

SWISS FAMILY ROBINSON
(AUTHOR OF —) WYSS
(CHARACTER IN —) JACK EMILY FRITZ ERNEST FRANCIS MONTROSE ROBINSON

SWITCH GAD TAN LASH TWIG WAND BIRCH SHUNT CHANGE CUTOUT DERAIL

DIPPER FERULE LARRUP RATTAN SPRING
HICKORY KIPPEEN SCOURGE POSTICHE
(— FOCUS) FADE
(ELECTRIC —) KEY
(RAILROAD —) GATE POINT

SWITZERLAND

BAY: URI
CANTON: ZUG BERN JURA VAUD BASEL
AARGAU GENEVA GLARUS LUZERN
SCHWYZ TICINO VALAIS ZURICH
GRISONS THURGAU FRIBOURG
OBWALDEN
CAPITAL: BERN BERNE
LAKE: URI ZUG THUN AGERI LEMAN
MORAT BIENNE BRIENZ GENEVA LUGANO
SARNEN WALLEN ZURICH HALLWIL
LUCERNE LUNGERN VIERWALD
MOUNTAIN: JURA RIGI ROSA BLANC
CENIS KARPF LINARD PIZELA BERNINA
BEVERIN GRIMSEL PILATUS ROTONDO
BALMHORN JUNGFRAU
MOUNTAIN PASS: CENIS FURKA ALBERG
MALOJA BRENNER GRIMSEL SIMPLON
SPLUGEN LOTSCHEN
RIVER: AAR INN AARE THUR BROYE
DOUBS LINTH REUSS RHINE RHONE
MAGGIA SARINE TICINO PRATIGAU
TOWN: BALE BERN BIEL BRIG CHUR SION
BASEL VEVEY GENEVA GLARUS LUZERN
SCHWYZ ZURICH FYZABAD HERISAU
LUCERNE LAUSANNE MONTREUX
VALLEY: AAR ZERMATT ENGADINE
WATERFALL: SIMMEN HANDEGG IFFIGEN
DIESBACH GIESSBACH STAUBBACH
TRUMMELBACH
WEIGHT: PFUND CENTNER QUINTAL

SWIVEL SWIPE CASTER TIRRET TOGGLE
TONGUE TRAVERSE
SWOLLEN FULL RANK BLOWN GOUTY
GREAT POBBY PROUD PUFFY TUMID
BRAWNY TURGID BLOATED BULBOUS
GIBBOUS TURGENT TUMOROUS
SWOON KEEL DROWN DWALM FAINT
STOUND TRANCE ECSTASY SYNCOPE
SWOOP DIVE SWAP SOUSE STOOP
POUNCE DESCEND
SWORD FOX BILL FALX IRON SPIT TOOL
TURK BILBO BLADE BRAND DEGEN
GULLY KNIFE PRICK RIPON STEEL BILBOA
DAMASK DUSACK FLORET GLAIVE
HANGER MIMING PINKER PORKER
SMITER TILTER TOLEDO BRANDON
CUTLASS SNICKER SPURTLE TOASTER
BASELARD DAMASCUS FALCHION
FLAMBERG SPADROON SPITFROG
(— OF CHARLEMAGNE) JOYEUSE
(— OF CID) TIZONA
(— OF HERMES) HARPE
(— OF LANCELOT) ARONDIGHT
(— OF ROLAND) DURENDAL
(— OF SIEGFRIED) GRAM BALMUNG

(— OF SIR BEVIS) MORGLAY
(— OF ST. GEORGE) ASCALON
ASKELON
(— USED BY ST. PETER) MALCHUS
(BLUNT —) WAFTER SCHLAGER
(CELTIC —) SAX SAEX
(DOUBLE-EDGED —) KEN PATA
KHANDA SPATHA
(DUELLING —) EPEE SHARP
(DYAK —) PARANG
(FENCING —) EPEE FOIL SABER SABRE
RAPIER
(HALF OF —) FORTE
(JAPANESE —) CATAN KATANA
WACADASH
(LONG —) SPATHA WHIFFLE
(MATADOR'S —) ESTOQUE
(MORO —) BARONG CAMPILAN
(NARROW —) TUCK
(NORMAN —) SPATHA
(PERSIAN —) ACINACES
(POINTLESS —) CURTANA CURTEIN
(RUSTY —) SHABBLE
(SHORT —) DIRK ESTOC KUKRI SKEAN
CREESE CURTAXE WHINGER WHINYARD
(THRUSTING —) ESTOC STOCK
(TWO-HANDED —) ESPADON SPADONE
CLAYMORE
(WOODEN —) WASTER STRICKLE
SWORDSMAN BLADE FENCER SLASHER
THRUSTER
SYCAMORE MAY DAROO COTONIER
LACEWOOD PLANTAIN
SYCOPHANT TOADY FAWNER HANGBY
TAGTAIL PARASITE PICKTHANK
SATELLITE
SYCOPHANTIC FAWNING SERVILE
SLAVISH OBEDIENT
SYLLABLE ARSIS BREVE SHORT DISEME
TRISEME ASSONANT
(— DENOTING ASSENT) OM
(BOBIZATION —) BO CE DI GA GE LO
MA NI
(LAST —) ULTIMA
(LAST — BUT ONE) PENULT
(LONG —) LONG
(MUSICAL —) DI DO FA FI LA LE LI ME
MI RA RE RI SE SI SO TA TE TI TO UT SOL
(REFRAIN —) DILDO
(SHORT —) MORA SHORT
(STRONG —) STRESS
(UNACCENTED —S) THESIS
(UNSTRESSED —) OUTRIDE
SYLLABUS PROGRAM VIDIMUS
HEADNOTE SYNOPSIS PROGRAMME
SYLVAN WOODY FOREST WOODISH
SYMBOL KEY CODE FISH ICON IDOL
MARK SEAL SIGN TYPE BADGE CREST
EAGLE IMAGE TOKEN CIPHER EMBLEM
ENSIGN FIGURE LETTER PNEUME SIGNAL
CONSTANT DIRECTOR IDEOGRAM
LIGATURE SWASTIKA TRISKELE
ORIFLAMME
(— AS ROAD SIGN) GLYPH
(— FOR WAVELENGTH) LAMBDA

(— OF DEATH) CYPRESS
(— OF DISTINCTION) BELT HONOR
(— OF FAITHFUL DEAD) ORANT
(— OF FRANCE) LILY
(— OF LIFE) ANKH
(— OF MONK) COWL
(— OF PHYSICIAN) CADUCEUS
(— OF SPRING) KARPAS
(— OF STRENGTH) HORN
(— OF SUN) DISC
(— OF UNIVERSE) MANDALA
(— REPRESENTING THE ABSOLUTE) TAIKIH
(ALGEBRAIC —) EXPONENT
(CRICKET —) ASHES
(CRUSADERS' —) CROSS
(CURVED —) HOOK
(KOREAN —) TAHGOOK
(MAGIC —) CARACT
(MATHEMATICAL —) KNOWN FACTOR FACIEND OPERAND
(RELIGIOUS —) LABRYS
SYMBOLIC GRAPHIC SHADOWY ANICONIC
SYMBOLIZE TOKEN FIGURE SAMPLE SHADOW TYPIFY BETOKEN EXPRESS PORTEND SIGNIFY
SYMMETRICAL FORMAL DIMERIC REGULAR SHAPELY BALANCED
SYMPATHETIC AKIN SOFT WARM HUMAN KINDLY TENDER PIETOSO SIMPATICO
SYMPATHY PITY RUTH FLESH PHILIA CONSENT EMPATHY RAPPORT AFFINITY KINDNESS
SYMPTOM MARK NOTE SIGN STIGMA INSTANCE

SYNOPSIS BRIEF TABLE EPITOME OUTLINE SUMMARY ABSTRACT ANALYSIS SCENARIO SYLLABUS ABRIDGMENT
SYNTHESIS SUMMA FUSION SYSTASIS
SYNTHETIC ERSATZ PLASTIC SYSTATIC

SYRIA

CAPITAL: DAMASCUS
COIN: POUND TALENT PIASTER
DISTRICT: ALEPPO HAURAN
LAKE: DJEBOID TIBERIAS
MEASURE: MAKUK GARAVA
MOUNTAIN: HERMON LIBANUS
RIVER: ASI BALIKH BARADA JORDAN KNABUR ORONTES EUPHRATES
TOWN: ALEP HAMA HOMS NAWA BUSRA CALNO DERRA HALAB HAMAH IDLIB JERUD RAQQA ALEPPO BALBEL LATAKIA SELEUCIA
WEIGHT: COLA ROTL ARTAL ARTEL RATEL TALENT

SYRINGE GUN HYPO ENEMA DOUCHE SQUIRT
SYRUP DIBS LICK SIRUP ORGEAT FALERNUM QUIDDANY
SYSTEM ISM CREDO FRAME ORDER CIRCLE METHOD SCHEME SYNTAX COMPLEX DUALISM REGIMEN ENSEMBLE OVERRIDE RELIGION UNIVERSE
SYSTEMATIC ORDERLY REGULAR METHODIC
SYSTEMATIZE ORDER CODIFY ORGANIZE METHODIZE

T

T TEE TANGO

TAB JAG TAG BILL COST CHECK FLASH PRICE TALLY WATCH SIGNAL

TABERNACLE PYX HOVEL SACRARY

TABLE PIE RUN BUCK FORM MESS BENCH BOARD CANON CHART PLANK SCALE STALL STONE COMMON SCHEME TABLET TABULA TRIPOD CABARET CONSOLE DRESSER PROJECT SHAMBLE TABLEAU TROLLEY CALENDAR VANITORY NIGHTSTAND
(— FOR BOWING HAT-BODY) HURL
(— FOR GLAZING LEATHER) BANK
(— FOR ORNAMENT) CARTOUCH
(— FOR PHOTOGRAPHIC PLATES) WHIRLER
(— FURNISHED WITH MEAL) SPREAD
(— IN STORE) COUNTER
(— OF ANCESTORS) PEDIGREE
(— OF CONTENTS) INDEX METHOD
(— OF DECLINATIONS) REGIMENT
(— USED IN FELTING A HAT) BASON
(— WITH BRAZIER BENEATH) TENDOUR
(ARITHMETIC —) TARIFF
(ASTROLOGICAL —) SPECULUM
(BOTANIC —) KEY
(CIRCULAR —) ROUNDEL
(COMMUNION —) ALTAR CREDENCE
(DINING —) MAHOGANY
(DRESSING —) TOILET VANITY TOILETTE
(FOLDING —) SERVETTE
(INNER —) HOME
(MASSAGE —) PLINTH
(MUSICAL —) DIAGRAM
(NIGHT —) SOMNO
(PRINCIPAL —) DAIS
(PROFUSELY ORNAMENTED —) PEMBROKE
(SERVING —) WAGON
(SHAKING —) SLIMER
(SMALL —) KURSI STAND TABORET
(STONE —) DOLMEN
(TEA —) TEAPOY
(WRITING —) DESK

TABLEAU LAYOUT PAGEANT PICTURE

TABLELAND PLAT PUNA KARROO PLATEAU BALAGHAT

TABLET ALBUM PIECE SLATE TABLE ABACUS TABULA DIPTYCH PREFORM CARTOUCH CHURINGA MEDALLION
(— BEARING SYMBOL OF CHRIST) PAX
(— FOR PUBLISHING LAWS) PARAPEGM
(— OVER SHOP FRONT) FASCIA
(MEDICATED —) ASPIRIN JELLOID TABELLA

(MEDICINAL —) DISC DISK TROCHE
(MEMORIAL —) BRASS TABUT
(PAINTER'S —) PALETTE
(SQUARE —) ABACK
(UPRIGHT —) STELA
(VOTIVE —) PINAX
(WRITING —) CODICIL TRIPTYCH

TABOO KAPU FORBIDDEN INEFFABLE

TACIT SILENT IMPLICIT

TACITURN DUMB STILL SILENT RESERVED RETICENT

TACK BEAT STAY BASTE FETCH ENTAIL TINGLE SADDLERY
(GLAZIERS' —) BRAD

TACKLE RIG YOKE ATTACK BURTON COLLAR JIGGER RUNNER STEEVE DERRICK HALYARD HARNESS RIGGING PURCHASE
(— FOR RAISING BOAT) FALLS
(— TO HOIST ANCHOR) CAT
(COMBINATION OF —S) JEER JEERS
(FISHING —) TEW OTTER LEDGER

TACT TOUCH ADDRESS CONDUCT DELICACY

TACTFUL POLITIC DISCREET GRACEFUL

TACTLESS BRASH GAUCHE

TAFFY GUNDY TOFFEE CLAGGUM

TAG EAR TAB TAIL LABEL TALLY TOUCH FOLLOW SWATCH TICKET
(— OF A LACE) AGLET
(ANGLING —) TOUCH
(ORNAMENTED —S) FANCY

TAHITI (CAPITAL OF —) PAPEETE
(FORMER NAME OF —) OTAHEITE
(MOUNTAIN IN —) OROHENA

TAIL CAUDA SNAKE FOLLOW RUMPLE SWITCH TAILET TAILLE FANTAIL RATTAIL
(— OF ARTIFICIAL FLY) TOPPING
(— OF BELL CLAPPER) FLIGHT
(— OF BIRD) FAN
(— OF BIRD OR ANIMAL) CUE POLE START
(— OF BOAR) WREATH
(— OF COAT) DOCK
(— OF COMET) BEARD STREAM STREAMER CHEVELURE
(— OF DEER) FLAG SINGLE
(— OF DOG) FLAG STERN
(— OF FISH) UROSOME
(— OF FLY) WHISK
(— OF FOX) BUSH BRUSH FOXTAIL
(— OF HARE OR RABBIT) BUN FUD BUNT SCUT
(— OF HOOD) LIRIPIPE
(— OF HORSE) BOB
(— OF MAN'S TIED HAIR) CLUB
(— OF METEOR) TRAIN
(— OF MUSICAL NOTE) QUEUE
(— OF PUG DOG) TWIST

(— OF SQUIRREL) BUN
(— OF STANZA) CODA
(DRAGON'S —) KETU
(STUMP OF —) STRUNT
(TIP OF —) TAG
TAILOR SNIP BUILD SHRED CUTTER
FULLER SARTOR STITCH BOTCHER
SNIPPER CLOTHIER SEAMSTER
(ITINERANT —) CARDOOER
TAINT MOIL SMUT SPOT VICE CLOUD
STAIN TOUCH DARKEN INFECT SMIRCH
SMUTCH BLEMISH CORRUPT DEBAUCH
ENVENOM POLLUTE TARNISH VITIATE
CONTAMINATE
TAINTED OFF GAMY HIGH BLOWN
RANCID ROTTEN SINFUL SMUTTY
CORRUPT FLYBLOWN

TAIWAN

CAPITAL: TAIPEI
ISLAND GROUP: MATSU PENGHU
QUEMOY
MOUNTAIN: TZUKAO YUSHAN HSINKAO
RIVER: WUCHI TACHIA CHOSHUI HUALIEN
TANSHUI
TOWN: CHIAL TAINAN TAIPEI CHILUNG
KEELUNG PINGTUNG TAICHUNG

TAKE COP HIT NIM NIP NOB BEAR DRAW
GLOM HAVE LEAD TOLL ADOPT BRING
CARRY CATCH FETCH GRASP GRIPE
LATCH SEIZE SNAKE ACCEPT CLUTCH
COTTON DERIVE EXTEND FERRET FINGER
RECIPE SNATCH ATTRACT CAPTURE
RECEIVE
(— ADVANTAGE) DO ABUSE BLUDGE
CLUTCH EXPLOIT
(— AWAY) BATE EASE LIFT TOLL BLEED
HEAVE STEAL ABDUCT CONVEY DEDUCE
DEDUCT DEMISE DEPOSE ELOIGN
EXEMPT REMOVE UNVEST DEPRIVE
DETRACT RETRACT ABSTRACT
DEROGATE DIMINISH SUBTRACT
(— BACK) RECALL RECANT REVOKE
RETRACT
(— CARE) SEE KEEP MIND TEND WARD
NURSE BEWARE GOVERN INTEND
HUSBAND CHAPERON
(— CHANCE) DICE RISK
(— FOR GRANTED) BEG ASSUME
PRESUME
(— FRAUDULENTLY) STEAL STRIKE
(— HOLD) GET BITE GRAB PINCH SEIZE
ARREST
(— IN) IN EAT SUP BITE HOAX KEEP
DRINK ABSORB DEVOUR ENFOLD GATHER
HARBOR INGEST INTAKE MUZZLE
EMBRACE
(— NOTE OF) NB COUNT SMOKE
NOTICE WITNESS
(— OFF) OFF DOFF LIFT VAIL DOUSE
SHUCK STRIP DEDUCT
(— OFFENSE) DORT HUFF
(— ON) HIRE MOUNT START
(— OUT) DELE KILL EXCERPT AIRBRUSH

(— OVER) ABSORB
(— PAINS) BOTHER
(— PART) LEAD FIGHT ENGAGE
(— PLACE) BE DO GO COME GIVE PASS
ARISE BEFALL HAPPEN
(— PLEASURE IN) ENJOY ADMIRE
(— POSSESSION) GRIP ANNEX BESET
SEIZE SPOIL EXTEND CONQUER INHERIT
DISTRAIN
(— REFUGE) HIDE SOIL EVADE HAVEN
WATCH
(— THE PLACE OF) ENSUE SECOND
SUPPLY DISPLACE SUPPLANT
(— UP) ENTER MOUNT ADSORB ASSUME
GATHER HANDLE STRIKE
TALC TALCUM AGALITE STEATITE
TALE SAW JEST REDE TELL CRACK FABLE
SPELL STORY FABULA LEGEND PURANA
FICTION HISTORY ROMANCE ANECDOTE
FOLKTALE TREATISE
(— OF ACHIEVEMENTS) GEST
(— OF FOUR) WARP
(COMIC COARSE —) FABLIAU
(DEVISED —) AITION
(EPIC —) TAIN
(FALSE —) BAM VANITY SLANDER
(FATEFUL —) WEIRD
(FOLK —) NANCY THRENE
(HUMOROUS —S) FACETIAE
(MERRY —) BOURD
(POETIC NARRATIVE —) SAGA
(SENSATIONAL —) BLOOD
(SHORT —) LAI CONTE
TALEBEARER BUZZER GOSSIP TATTLER
TELLTALE
TALENT GIFT HEAD NOUS VEIN DOWER
DOWRY VERVE GENIUS ABILITY FACULTY
CAPACITY CHARISMA
TALENTED ABLE CLEVER GIFTED
TALE OF TWO CITIES
(AUTHOR OF —) DICKENS
(CHARACTER IN —) JOHN JERRY
LORRY LUCIE PROSS BARSAD CARTON
DARNAY JARVIS SYDNEY CHARLES
DEFARGE GASPARD MANETTE STRYVER
CRUNCHER EVREMONDE
TALES OF HOFFMANN
(CHARACTER IN —) ANDRES LUTHER
STELLA ANTONIA CRESPEL LINDORF
MIRACLE OLYMPIA HOFFMANN SCHLEMIL
COPPELIUS GIULIETTA NICALUSSE
DAPERTUTTO SPALANZANI
PITICHINACCHIO
(COMPOSER OF —) OFFENBACH
TALISMAN CHARM IMAGE OBEAH
AMULET SAPHIE SCARAB TELESM
ICHTHYS GREEGREE
TALK GAB JAW RAP SAW SAY YAP BLAT
CANT CARP CHAT CHIN GAFF GIVE GUFF
KNAP TALE WORD CRACK FABLE MOUTH
PARLE PITCH SPEAK SPELL SPIEL
COMMON GAMMON PATTER SERMON
SPEECH STEVEN YABBER ADDRESS
CHINWAG DISCUSS LIPWORK PALABRA
PALAVER PARRALL CAUSERIE COLLOQUY
CONVERSE LANGUAGE PARLANCE
(— ABOUT) HASH

(— BACK) SASS
(— BIG) SWANK BOUNCE
(— BOASTFULLY) GAS BLATTER
(— FOOLISHLY) YAK BLAT FLAP YACK HAVER BABBLE DRIVEL FOOTER FOOTLE GABBLE GIBBER SAWNEY TOOTLE BLATHER BLETHER
(— GLIBLY) PATTER SCREED
(— IDLY) GAB BLAB CHIN GASH FABLE GABBLE JANGLE TATTLE CHATTER GNATTER PRATTLE
(— IMPUDENTLY) SASS
(— INCESSANTLY) YANK BURBLE WAFFLE CHATTER
(— INCOHERENTLY) BABBLE BURBLE HOTTER MITHER MOIDER
(— IRRATIONALLY) RAVE
(— MONOTONOUSLY) DRONE
(— NOISILY) CLAP BLATTER BRABBLE
(— NONSENSE) GAS ROT BLEAT DROOL FUDGE HAVER
(— RAPIDLY) GABBLE JABBER GNATTER
(— TEDIOUSLY) DINGDONG
(— WITH) CONTACT
(ABUSIVE —) HOKER JAWING
(ARROGANT —) GUM BRAG
(BOASTFUL —) BULL GAFF
(EMPTY —) GAS BOSH GASH GLOZE FRAISE BLAFLUM GASSING PRATTLE BALLYHOO GALBANUM MOONSHINE POPPYCOCK
(FOOLISH —) GUP GAFF JIVE BLEAT CLACK FABLE BLETHERS COBBLERS
(IDLE —) GAB BLAB BUFF CHAT GAFF GEST GUFF FABLE GESTE BABBLE CLAVER GOSSIP JANGLE CHATTER CLATTER PALAVER TWATTLE BABBLING BATTOLOGY
(NONSENSICAL —) BLABBER BLATHER FOLDEROL
(RAPID —) GABBLE JABBER CHATTER CLATTER
(SILLY —) BLAH BUFF CLART CACKLE FOOTLE TWADDLE
(SMALL —) CHAT BACKCHAT CHITCHAT
TALKATIVE GASH GLIB CHATTY FLUENT SOCIAL VOLUBLE BIGMOUTH FLIPPANT
TALKER YENTA CAMPER POTGUN CAUSEUR SPIELER
(IDLE —) WHIFFLER
(NOISY —) BLELLUM
(PROFESSIONAL —) JAWSMITH
(SENSELESS —) RATTLE
TALL HIGH LANKY LOFTY STEEP PROCERE
(— AND FEEBLE) TANGLE
(VERY —) TAUNT
TALLOW SUET SEVUM ARMING TAULCH CHERVICE
TALLY TAB NICK SUIT AGREE CHECK COUNT SCORE STICK STOCK STRING SWATCH
TALON FANG SERE UNCE CLUTCH POUNCE UNGUIS WEAPON
TAMBOURINE RIKK TAAR DAIRA TAMBO TABORIN TIMBREL

TAME DEAD MEEK MILD ACCOY BREAK DAUNT MILKY GENTLE INWARD CORRECT INSIPID SUBDUED DOMESTIC
(— FALCON) MAN RECLAIM
TAMING OF THE SHREW
(AUTHOR OF —) SHAKESPEARE
(CHARACTER IN —) SLY BIANCA CURTIS GREMIO GRUMIO TRANIO BAPTISTA LUCENTIO BIONDELLO HORTENSIO KATHARINA PETRUCHIO VINCENTIO CHRISTOPHER
TAMP PUG STEM
TAMPER FIX COOK FAKE FOOL TOUCH DABBLE FIDDLE MEDDLE MONKEY POTTER PUTTER FALSIFY
(— WITH HORSE'S TEETH) BISHOP
TAN ARAB BARK ASCOT TAWNY ORIOLE COCONUT LEATHER SUNBURN
TANCRED (FATHER OF —) OTHO
(LOVER OF —) ERMINIA CLORINDA
(MOTHER OF —) EMMA
TANG NIP FANG VEIN SHANK STING TASTE TWANG RELISH TONGUE⁴
TANGIBLE ACTUAL TACTILE CONCRETE MATERIAL PALPABLE
TANGLE COT TAT FOUL HARL SHAG KNURL SKEIN SNARL THRUM TWINE BURBLE ENTRAP JUNGLE MUCKER SLEAVE BRANGLE THICKET FURBELOW
TANGLED AFOUL TOUSY MESHED SNARLY INTORTED INVOLVED
TANK DAM DIP VAT BOSH SUMP BASIN MIXER STEEP BOILER HOPPER TROUGH BATTERY BREAKER CISTERN FLUSHER SETTLER STEEPER BLEACHER DIGESTOR
(— FOR DYE OR SOAP) BECK
(— FOR FISH) STEW TRUNK PISCINA AQUARIUM STEWPOND
(— IN SHIP) FOREPEAK
(ARMORED —) FLAIL PANZER WHIPPET LANDSHIP
(PAPER MANUFACTURING —) POACHER
(PHOTOGRAPHIC —) CUVETTE
(POTTER'S —) PLUNGER
(RECTANGULAR —) BOWLY
(SALT MANUFACTURING —) GRAINER
(STORAGE —) CHEST
(SUGAR REFINING —) TIGER BLOWUP
(TANNING —) FLOATER
TANKARD JACK STOUP PEWTER POTTLE GODDARD
TANNHAUSER (CHARACTER IN —) VENUS HERMANN WOLFRAM ELISABETH TANNHAUSER
(COMPOSER OF —) WAGNER
TANTALIZE GRIG JADE MOCK TEASE HARASS
TANTALUS (DAUGHTER OF —) NIOBE
(FATHER OF —) AMPHION JUPITER THYESTES
(MOTHER OF —) NIOBE PLUTO
(SON OF —) PELOPS
(WIFE OF —) DIONE CLYTIA EUPRYTO TAYGETE
TANTRUM HISSY TIRRIVEE WINGDING

TANZANIA

CAPITAL: DARESSALAAM
COIN: SENTI SHILINGI
ISLAND: MAFIA PEMBA ZANZIBAR
LAKE: RUKWA
NATIVE: BANTU SUKUMA MAKONDE SWAHILI
REGION: MARA MBEYA PEMBA PWANI TANGA MWANZA RUVUMA TABORA SINGIDA
RIVER: RUVU WAMI RUAHA KAGERA RUFIJI RUVUMA PANGANI MBENKURU
TOWN: WETE KILWA MBEYA MOSHI TANGA ARUSHA DODOMA IRINGA KIGOMA MTWARA MWANZA TABORA MTAWARA MOROGORO ZANZIBAR
VOLCANO: KIBO KILIMANJARO
WATERFALL: KALAMBO
WEIGHT: FARSALAH

TAP BOB DAB PAT TAT TIP COCK DRUB FLIP JOWL TICK FLIRT START TOUCH BROACH DABBLE FAUCET BIBCOCK DRAWOFF HEELTAP PERCUSS
(— A CASK) QUILL STRIKE
(— A DRUM) TUCK
(— FOR A LOAN) TIG
(— ON SHOE) CLUMP UNDERLAY
(— ON THE SHOULDER) FOB
(— REPEATEDLY) DRUM
(— THE GROUND) BEAT
(FENCING —) BEAT
(MASTER —) HOB HUB
(SMART — OF THE FOOT) APPEL
TAPE FERRET GARTER SCOTCH BINDING TELETAPE
(— CARTRIDGE) CASSETTE
(DEMONSTRATION —) DEMO
(FISH —) SNAKE
(LAMP —) WICK
(LINEN —) INKLE
(METALLIC —) GALLOON
(NARROW —) TASTE
(RED —) WIGGERY
TAPER RISE RUSH DRAFT PINCH SCARF SWAGE CIERGE LIGHTER PRICKET SHAMMES DIMINISH ACUMINATE
(— OF A SPRING) DRAW
(— OF PATTERN) STRIP
(— OFF) CEASE TONGUE
TAPERING SHARP SPIRY SPIRAL TERETE FUSIFORM ATTENUATE
TAPESTRY ARRAS TAPIS COSTER DOSSER CEILING GOBELIN HANGING SUSANEE AUBUSSON MORTLAKE
TAPIOCA CASSAVA
TAPROOM SALOON BARROOM BUVETTE TAPHOUSE
TAR PAY BREA BINDER ALKITRAN
(BIRCH —) DAGGETT
(MINERAL —) MALTHA
TARDY LAX LATE SLOW SLACK REMISS LAGGING OVERDUE DILATORY
TARGET AIM BUTT MARK WAND CLOUT

LEVEL ROVER SCOOP WHITE NIVEAU OBJECT SLEEVE SARACEN
(— OF KNEELING FIGURE) SQUAW
(— OF LEVELING STAFF) VANE
(— OF RIDICULE) GAME
(EASY —) SITTER
(RAILROAD SWITCH —) BANNER
(THROWN —) COCKSHY
(TOWED —) DROGUE
(UNIDENTIFIED —) SKUNK
TARNISH DIM BLOT SOIL CLOUD DIRTY STAIN SULLY DARKEN DEFILE INJURE SMIRCH ASPERSE BEGRIME BESMEAR BLEMISH OBSCURE BESMIRCH DISCOLOR
TARO COCO EDDO KALO TALO KAROU COCKER YAUTIA DASHEEN MALANGA
TARRY BIDE STAY STOP ABIDE DALLY DEMUR PAUSE ARREST LINGER REMAIN SOJOURN
TART ACID SOUR BOWLA CUPID EAGER SHARP SNIPPY PIQUANT PUNGENT TURNOVER
TARTNESS ACRITY ACIDITY VERDURE ACERBITY ASPERITY VERJUICE
TARTUFFE (AUTHOR OF —) MOLIERE
(CHARACTER IN —) ARGAS DAMIS ORGON DORINE ELMIRE VALERE CLEANTE MARIANE PERNELLE TARTUFFE
TASK FAG JOB TAX CHAR TOIL CHORE GRIND KNACK LABOR CHARGE PENSUM FATIGUE SWEATER TRAVAIL BUSINESS EXERCISE
(— AS PSYCHOLOGICAL TEST) AUFGABE
(ASSIGNED —) STENT STINT DEVOIR
(DIFFICULT —) BUGGER
(EASY —) PIPE SNAP SETUP
(ONEROUS —) CORVEE
(ROUTINE —) DRUDGE
TASMANIA (CAPITAL OF —) HOBART
(LAKE IN —) ECHO SORELL
(MOUNTAIN IN —) DROME NEVIS BARRON CRADLE LOMOND HUMBOLDT
(RIVER IN —) ESK HUDN TAMAR GORDON JORDAN PIEMAN DERWENT
(TOWN IN —) BURNIE HOBART
TASSEL TAG TUFT LABEL THRUM TARCEL TOORIE CORDELLE
TASTE EAT GAB LAP SIP DASH GOUT HINT SALT TANG TEST TINT WAFT ASSAY DRINK GUSTO HEART PROVE SAPOR SAVOR SHADE SMACK SNACK SPICE TOOTH TOUCH FLAVOR GENIUS LIKING PALATE RELISH SAMPLE SOUPCON THOUGHT APPETITE JUDGMENT SAPIDITY
(— COMBINED WITH APTITUDE) FLAIR
(— IN MATTERS OF ART) FANCY
(BAD —) GOTHISM
(DECIDED —) PENCHANT
(DELICATE —) BREED
(DISCRIMINATING —) SKILL
(GOOD —) DECORUM
(STRONG —) GOO
TASTEFUL NEAT ELEGANT GUSTOSO

TASTELESS DEAF FLAT FLASH MALMY VAPID FATUOUS INSIPID UNSAVORY

TASTY SAPID GUSTABLE TASTEFUL PALATABLE

TATTER RAG TAG SHRED LIBBET TAGRAG FLITTER

TATTERED DUDDY BEATEN TAGGED FORWORN

TATTLE BLAB GASH CLYPE PEACH SNEAK GOSSIP SNITCH CLATTER

TATTLER SNIPE FABLER GOSSIP YELPER TELLTALE

TAUNT BOB DIG CHIP GIBE JAPE JEER JEST MOCK SKIT TWIT CHECK GLAIK SCOFF SCORN DERIDE SARCASM RIDICULE

TAUT SNUG STIFF TIGHT CORDED

TAVERN BAR INN BUSH FONDA TAMBO BISTRO CABACK BUVETTE CABARET CANTEEN OSTERIA TABERNA GASTHAUS ORDINARY TAPHOUSE

TAWDRY CHEAP GAUDY NASTY GILDED TINSEL RAFFISH

TAWNY FUSC DUSKY FULVID TANNED FULVOUS MUSTELINE

TAX LAY LOT CAST CESS DUTY GELT GILD LEVY POLL RATE SCOT SESS TASK TOLL ABUSE AGIST DONUM HANSA MAILL OBROK QUINT STENT VERGI ASSESS AVANIA BURDEN DEMAND EXCISE IMPOST OCTROI PURVEY SENSUS STRAIN SURTAX CONDUCT FINANCE PENSION SCUTAGE STIPEND TRIBUTE AUXILIUM BONAUGHT CARUCAGE CORNBOLE DANEGELD EXACTION EXERCISE OBLATION PESHKASH

TAXICAB CAB HACK CRUISER MOTORCAB

TEA CHA CHA TCHA TSIA ASSAM CHAIS FAHAM HYSON MIANG PEKOE STEEP KEEMUN OOLONG PTISAN SUNGLO LAPSANG REDROOT TWANKAY GOWIDDIE SOUCHONG WORMSEED
(AFRICAN —) CAT KAT QAT KHAT
(BLACK —) BOHEA CONGO OOPAK SYCHEE
(COARSE —) BANCHA
(HIGH-GRADE —) GYOKURO
(MEDICINAL —) TISANE
(MEXICAN —) BASOTE APASOTE
(POOR —) BLASH

TEACH READ SHOW BREED CARRY COACH EDIFY ENDUE LEARN SPELL TRAIN TUTOR INFORM PREACH SCHOOL EDUCATE EXPOUND DOCUMENT INSTRUCT

TEACHER ALIM GURU GUIDE RABBI TUTOR USHER AKHUND DOCENT DOCTOR FATHER MADRIH MENTOR MULLAH PANDIT PUNDIT READER REGENT ACHARYA DOMINIE MUNCHEE PEDAGOG SHASTRI SPONSOR TRAINER DIRECTOR EDUCATOR MAGISTER MISTRESS MAHARISHI PEDAGOGUE PRECEPTOR
(— OF ELOQUENCE) RHETOR
(— OF EMINENCE) MAESTRO
(— OF HIGH LEARNING) SOPHIST
(— OF KORAN) ALFAKI ALFAQUIN
(— OF PAUL) GAMALIEL
(INCA —) AMAUTA
(MOHAMMEDAN —) COJA KHOJA

TEACHING LAW DHARMA DOCENT LESSON TUITION DIDACTIC DOCTRINE TUTELAGE

TEAKETTLE SUKEY CHAFER KETTLE POURIE CRESSET

TEAM SET PLOW SIDE SPAN YOKE DRAFT SWING PLOUGH SEXTET DRAUGHT
(— HARNESSED ONE BEFORE ANOTHER) TANDEM
(— OF CARS) ECURIE
(— OF GLASSWORKERS) SHOP CHAIR
(— OF 3 HORSES ABREAST) TROIKA
(— THAT FINISHES LAST) DOORMAT
(— 2 ABREAST, 1 LEADING) SPIKE UNICORN
(ATHLETIC —) CLUB
(BASEBALL —) NINE
(BASKETBALL —) FIVE
(FOOTBALL —) ELEVEN
(2-HORSE —) PODANGER
(3-HORSE —) RANDEM

TEAR RIP CLAW PULL RACE RASE RASH RAVE RIVE SNAG STUN BREAK PEARL SHARK SPLIT TOUSE CLEAVE HARROW RIPPLE SCHISM WRENCH DISCIND EYEDROP SCRATCH FRACTURE LACERATE LACHRYMA
(— APART) REND TEASE DIVULSE
(— ASUNDER) DIVEL
(— AWAY) AVULSE
(— DOWN) UNPILE DESTROY DEMOLISH
(— IN NEGATIVE) SLUG
(— INTO) LAMBASTE
(— INTO PIECES) DRAW TOLE DEVIL SHRED TEASE LANIATE MAMMOCK
(— INTO SHREDS) HOG DEVIL TATTER
(— OFF) STRIP ABRUPT DISCERP
(— OPEN) PROSCIND
(— UP BY THE ROOTS) ARACHE

TEARFUL SOFT WEEPY LIQUID WATERY MAUDLIN SHOWERY SNIVELLY

TEASE COD FUN MAD RIB TRY VEX BAIT CHIP DRAG FRET HARE HOCK JADE JIVE JOSH LARK RAZZ TOUT WORK CHAFF CHEEK DEVIL RALLY TAUNT WRACK BANTER BOTHER HARASS MOLEST NEEDLE PESTER PLAGUE TORMENT

TEASING CHAFF MERRY BANTER DEVILING QUIZZING

TECHNIQUE FEAT GATE WRINKLE COQUILLE INDUSTRY SPICCATO
(BILLIARD —) FOLLOW
(DANCE —) HEELWORK
(DECORATION —) IKAT
(DRAMATIC —) METHOD
(JUMPING —) SCISSORS
(WRESTLING —) GLIMA
(WRITING —) CUBISM

TEDIOUS DEAD DULL LATE POKY PROSY WEARY BORING PROLIX STODGY IRKSOME OPEROSE PREACHY PROSAIC VERBOSE DRAGGING TIRESOME WEARIFUL

TEDIUM IRK YAWN ENNUI BOREDOM
TEE COCK WITTER BULLHEAD
TEEM FLOW SWIM SWARM ABOUND BUSTLE PULLULATE
TEEMING BIG ALIVE TUMID FERTILE GUSHING ABUNDANT BRAWLING PREGNANT SWARMING
TEETER ROCK WAVER JIGGLE QUIVER SEESAW WOBBLE TREMBLE
TELEGRAM WIRE FLASH FLIMSY
TELEGRAPH WIRE CABLE BUZZER TELEGRAM TELOTYPE
TELEMACHUS (FATHER OF —) ULYSSES
   (MOTHER OF —) PENELOPE
   (SON OF —) LATINUS
TELEPHONE RING PHONE HANDSET
   (PART OF —) PAD BASE CORD DIAL HOLE STOP PLATE CRADLE HANDLE HANDSET PLUNGER SPEAKER EARPIECE RECEIVER MOUTHPIECE TRANSMITTER
TELESCOPE TUBE COUDE GLASS SCOPE FINDER SECTOR ALIGNER BINOCLE TRANSIT PROSPECT SPYGLASS REFRACTOR
TELL SAY DEEM MEAN MOOT READ SHOW BREAK PITCH SPELL TEACH UTTER AUTHOR DEVISE IMPART INFORM RECITE RELATE REPEAT REPORT REVEAL CONFESS DIVULGE NARRATE RECOUNT ACQUAINT
TEMERITY GALL CHEEK NERVE AUDACITY RASHNESS
TEMPER MAD BATE COOL DASH DRAW MOOD TONE ALLOY BLOOD DELAY FRAME GRAIN HUMOR IRISH SAUCE SOBER ADJUST ANIMUS ANNEAL DANDER MASTER MONKEY SEASON STRAIN CHASTEN CLIMATE COURAGE HACKLES STOMACH GRADUATE MITIGATE MODERATE MOORBURN
   (— CLAY) TAMPER
   (— METAL) ALLAY
   (— OF MIND) CUE SPIRIT
   (CAPRICIOUS —) SPLEEN
TEMPERAMENT BLOOD HEART HUMOR NATURE TEMPER STOMACH
TEMPERATE CALM COOL MILD SOFT GREEN SOBER STEADY MODERATE ORDINATE ABSTINENT CONTINENT ABSTEMIOUS
TEMPEST GALE THUD WIND ORAGE STORM TUMULT TORMENT TURMOIL WEATHER
   (AUTHOR OF —) SHAKESPEARE
   (CHARACTER IN —) IRIS JUNO ARIEL CERES ADRIAN ALONSO ANTONIO CALIBAN GONZALO MIRANDA TINCULO PROSPERO STEPHANO FERDINAND FRANCISCO SEBASTIAN
TEMPESTUOUS WILD GUSTY STERN WINDY RUGGED STORMY VIOLENT
TEMPLE WAT FANE NAOS RATH HUACA KIACK MARAE CHANDI HAFFET HERION MANDIR SACRUM SHRINE HERAEUM HERAION VARELLA OLYMPIUM PANTHEON VALHALLA PARTHENON

   (CAVE —) SPEOS
   (FIJI —) BURE
   (HAWAIIAN —) HEIAU
   (SHINTO —) SHA JINJA JINSHA YASHIRO
   (TOWERLIKE —) ZIGGURAT
TEMPORAL CIVIL CARNAL TIMELY EARTHLY PROFANE SECULAR
TEMPORARY FLYING INTERIM STOPGAP EPISODIC EPISODICAL
TEMPT EGG LURE COURT ALLURE ASSAIL ENTICE INVITE SEDUCE SOLICIT SUGGEST
TEMPTATION TRIAL ATTEMPT TESTING SEDUCTION
TENACIOUS FAST ROPEY STIFF TOUGH CLAGGY DOGGED GRIPPY STICKY STRONG VISCID ADHESIVE GRASPING HOLDFAST
TENANT BARON LAIRD COTTER GENEAT HOLDER INMATE LESSEE RENTER SOCMAN VASSAL FEODARY HOMAGER SOCAGER
   (— OF CROWN) THANE
   (LIFE —) LIVIER
   (NEW —) INCOMER
TEND RUN SET BABY BEND DRAW GROW KEEP MAKE MIND MOVE DRESS GROOM NURSE OFFER TREND VERGE WATCH GOVERN INTEND CHERISH CONDUCE DECLINE INCLINE PROPEND
   (— A FIRE) STOKE
   (— IN A CERTAIN DIRECTION) LEAD
   (— TOWARD) AFFECT
TENDENCY SET BENT BIAS HAND TONE VEIN DRAFT DRIFT HABIT KNACK TENOR TREND TWIST ANIMUS COURSE MOTION APTNESS IMPULSE LEANING APTITUDE INSTINCT
   (— IN NATURE) KIND
   (— TO APPROACH) ADIENCE
   (— TO STICK TOGETHER) CLANSHIP
   (— TO WITHDRAW) ABIENCE
TENDER RAW FINE FOND KIND SOFT SORE TAKE TART WARM DEFER FRAIL GREEN MUSHY OFFER DRIVER GENTLE GINGER HUMANE LOVELY SILKEN ADVANCE AMABILE AMOROUS PINNACE PITEOUS PITIFUL PROFFER RUTHFUL COCKBOAT FEMININE LADYLIKE MERCIFUL
TENDERHEARTED HUMAN PITIFUL
TENDERLY FONDLY GENTLY AMOROSO
TENDERNESS CHERTE DELICACY FONDNESS KINDNESS SYMPATHY YEARNING
TENEMENT TACK CHAWL DECKER WARREN HOLDING ROOKERY BUILDING PRAEDIUM
TENET CREDO CREED DOGMA BELIEF GNOMON HOLDING MISHNAH PARADOX DOCTRINE

TENNESSEE

CAPITAL: NASHVILLE
COLLEGE: FISK LANE SIENA BETHEL

BELMONT LAMBUTH LEMOYNE MILLIGAN
TUSCULUM VANDERBILT
COUNTY: DYER KNOX RHEA COCKE GILES
HENRY MEIGS OBION COFFEE GRUNDY
MCMINN SEVIER UNICOI BLEDSOE
FENTRESS
DAM: WILSON WHEELER
LAKE: DOUGLAS CHEROKEE REELFOOT
WATTSBAR
MOUNTAIN: GUYOT LOOKOUT
MOUNTAIN RANGE: SMOKY
RIVER: ELK DUCK CANEY HOLSTON
HIWASSEE CUMBERLAND
STATE BIRD: MOCKINGBIRD
STATE FLOWER: IRIS
STATE TREE: POPLAR
TOWN: ERIN ALAMO ALCOA ERWIN PARIS
CAMDEN CELINA JASPER SELMER
SPARTA BOLIVAR DICKSON JACKSON
MEMPHIS PULASKI GALLATIN KNOXVILLE
CHATTANOOGA

TENON COG PIN STUB TUSK LEWIS
TOOTH DOVETAIL LEWISSON
TENOR FECK TONE VEIN COURSE EFFECT
TENURE CURRENT PURPORT STRENGTH
TENDENCY
TENSE EDGY RAPT TAUT STIFF CORDED
FLINCH FUTURE NARROW STRAIT STRICT
BRITTLE INTENSE PRIMARY FRENETIC
TENSION BENT HEAT DRIVE SPRING
STRAIN STRESS BALANCE
TENT TOP PAWL TELD TILT CABIN LODGE
TUPIK CANVAS DOSSIL BALAGAN
MARQUEE TABERNA PAVILION
(— FOR WOUNDS) PENICIL
(— WHERE GOODS ARE SOLD)
CRAME
(CIRCULAR —) YURT KIBITKA
(INDIAN —) TEPEE WIGWAM
(SAMOYED —) CHUM
(SOUTH AMERICAN —) TOLDO
TENTH DIME DISME TITHE DECIMA
(— OF CENT) MILL
(— OF LINE) GRY
TENUOUS FILMY FOGGY FRAIL SUBTLE
TENDER FRAGILE GASEOUS SLENDER
ETHEREAL GOSSAMER
(TOO —) FINESPUN
TENURE FEU TACK TAKE TERM GAVEL
BARONY SOCAGE BONDAGE CURTESY
FARMAGE SOCCAGE COPYHOLD
FREEHOLD SUITHOLD
TEPID LEW WARM LUKEWARM
TERM HALF NAME WORD RHEMA SPEAK
STYLE HILARY NOTION PARODY EPITHET
SESSION SUBJECT VOCABLE EQUIVOKE
HEADWORD SEMESTER
(— IN JAIL) JOLT
(— IN LOGIC) CONSTANT
(— OF CONTEMPT) SLIPE PILCHER
TITIVIL
(— OF DEFERENCE) AHUNG
(— OF ENDEARMENT) ASTOR CHUCK
COCKY HONEY MOPSY ASTHORE
MACHREE STOREEN

(— OF IMPRISONMENT) LAG LAGGING
STRETCH
(— OF PUNISHMENT) JOB
(— OF REPROACH) GIB BESOM MINGO
RONYON
(— OF SYLLOGISM) EXTREME
ARGUMENT
(ARITHMETICAL —) NOME GNOMON
(UNIVERSAL —) CONCEPT
TERMAGANT JADE RUDAS SHREW
VIXEN VIRAGO
TERMINAL JACK LAST POLE ANODE
DEPOT CATHODE
TERMINATE CUT END CALL HALT KILL
ABORT CEASE CLOSE ISSUE LAPSE
EXPIRE FINISH INCLUDE COMPLETE
CONCLUDE DISSOLVE
(— A SESSION) PROROGUE
TERMINATION END DATE TERM CLOSE
EVENT ISSUE ENDING EXITUS EXPIRY
FINALE PERIOD UPSHOT
TERRACE DAIS STEP XYST BEACH BENCH
OFFSET PERRON LINCHET BARBETTE
CHABUTRA
(LOUNGING —) LANAI
(NATURAL —) MESA
TERRESTRIAL EARTHY EARTHLY
TERRENE SUBLUNAR TELLURIC
TERRIBLE DIRE UGLY AWFUL LURID
DEADLY TRAGIC FEARFUL GHASTLY
HIDEOUS HORRIBLE TERRIFIC TRAGICAL
TERRIER SKYE LHASA SILKY BOSTON
DANDIE RATTER SCOTTIE ABERDEEN
AIREDALE SEALYHAM WIREHAIR
TERRIFIC FINE SWEET FEARFUL
GORGEOUS
TERRIFY AWE COW DARE FLAY APPAL
DREAD SCARE DISMAY FREEZE FRIGHTEN
TERRIFYING GHASTLY HIDEOUS
FLEYSOME TERRIBLE
TERRITORY FEE HAN AREA MARK PALE
BANAT DUCHY FIELD MARCH STATE
BORDER COLONY DOMAIN EMPIRE
GROUND CONFINE COUNTRY DEMESNE
DUKEDOM EARLDOM ENCLAVE REGENCY
SATRAPY CONFINES DISTRICT DOMINION
IMPERIUM SEIGNORY
(MONASTIC —) ABTHANE
TERROR AWE FEAR FRAY ALARM DREAD
PANIC FRIGHT HORROR
TERRORIST GOONDA ALARMIST
SICARIUS
TERSE CURT COMPACT CONCISE
LACONIC POINTED SUMMARY SUCCINCT
TERSENESS BREVITY LACONISM
TEST TRY FEEL TASK ASSAY CANON
CHECK ESSAY GROPE PROBE PROOF
PROVE SENSE SOUND TASTE TOUCH
TRIAL SAMPLE AUSSAGE CONTROL
EXAMINE EXERCISE GAUNTLET
STANDARD
(— CHEESE) PALE
(— EGGS) CANDLE
(— FOR WEIGHT AND FINENESS) PYX
(— GROUND) BOSE
(— OF COURAGE) SCRATCH

(— OF CRINOID) CALYX
(— OF GUILT) CORSNED
(— OF ORE) VAN
(SEVERE —) CRUCIBLE
(SYPHILIS —) KOLMER
TESTIFY SPEAK SWEAR AFFIRM DEPONE
DEPOSE WITNESS
(— FALSELY) MOUNT
TESTIMONY PROBATE WITNESS
EVIDENCE
TESTY PATCHY SPUNKY PEEVISH TETTISH
WASPISH SNAPPISH
TETHER BAND LEASH STAKE PICKET
CABESTRO
(— A HAWK) WEATHER
TEUTON GOTH LOMBARD
TEUTONIC GOTHIC GERMANIC

TEXAS

CAPITAL: AUSTIN
COLLEGE: SMU TCU RICE WILEY BAYLOR
COUNTY: BEE CASS COKE JACK REAL
RUSK VEGA WEBB WISE BEXAR DELTA
ECTOR ERATH GARZA RAINS FANNIN
GOLIAD YOAKUM ZAPATA ZAVALA
HIDALGO REFUGIO ATASCOSA
LAKE: FALCON TEXOMA AMISTAD
MOUNTAIN: GUADALUPE
RIVER: RED PECOS BRAZOS NUECES
TRINITY
STATE BIRD: MOCKINGBIRD
STATE FLOWER: BLUEBONNET
STATE TREE: PECAN
TOWN: GAIL VEGA WACO BRYAN MARFA
OZONA PAMPA TYLER BORGER DALLAS
DENTON ELPASO KILEEN LAREDO
ODESSA QUANAH SONORA ABILENE
HOUSTON LUBBOCK AMARILLO
BEAUMONT FLOYDADA GALVESTON

TEXT BODY MIQRA PURANA SCRIPT
ANTETHEM PERICOPE VARIORUM
(— OF ADVERTISEMENT) COPY
(— OF OPERA) LIBRETTO
(— SET TO MUSIC) ORATORIO
(REVISED —) RECENSION
(SHASTRA —) SRUTI
TEXTILE (ALSO SEE FABRIC) SABA
STUFF GREIGE MOCKADO SAGURAN
SINAMAY TEXTURE TIFFANY
TEXTURE WEB BONE HAND KNIT WALE
WOOF GRAIN FABRIC
(— OF SOAP) FIT

THAILAND

CAPITAL: BANGKOK
COIN: ATT BAHT FUANG TICAL PYNUNG
SALUNG SATANG
ISLAND: PHUKET
ISTHMUS: KRA
MEASURE: WA KEN NIV NMU RAI SAT
SEN SOK WAH YOT KEUP NGAN TANG
YOTE KWIEN LAANG SESTI TANAN

KABIET KAMMEU CHAIMEU ROENENG
CHANGAWN
MOUNTAIN: KHIEO MAELAMUN
MOUNTAIN RANGE: DAWNA
BILAUKTAUNG
NATIVE: LAO THAI
PLAIN: KHORAT
RIVER: CHI NAN PING MENAM MEKONG
MEPING
TOWN: UBON PUKET RANONG AYUDHYA
AYUTHIA BANGKOK LOPBURI RAHAENG
SINGORA SONGKLA KHONKAEN
KIANGMAI THONBURI

THAN AS OR TO BUT NOR TILL
THANKLESS INGRATE SLOWFUL
THANKS TA GRACE MERCI GRAMERCY
THAT AS AT BUT HOW THE WHO LEST
WHAT YOND THOUGH BECAUSE
THATCH NIPA SIRKI THRUM CADJAN
(— OVER BEEHIVE) HOOD
THAW GIVE MELT FRESH DEFROST
THE LA LE THEY THERE
THEATER CINE KINO HOUSE LEGIT
ODEUM SCENE STAGE CINEMA ADELPHI
GUIGNOL ORPHEUM COLISEUM
PANTHEON STRAWHAT PLAYHOUSE
NICKELODEON
(NEIGHBORHOOD —) NABE
(PUPPET —) BUNRAKU
THEATRICAL CAMP HAMMY STAGY
DRAMATIC SCENICAL SINGSONG
THEFT LIFT HEIST PINCH SCORE STEAL
RIPOFF LARCENY PILFERY ROBBERY
BURGLARY STEALING
(LITERARY —) PIRACY
(PETTY —) CRIB PICKERY
THEME BASE IDEA TEXT DITTY LEMMA
MOTIF SCOPE TOPIC MATTER SUBJECT
ANTETHEM
(— OF FUGUE) DUX
(HACKNEYED —) CLICHE
(MAIN —) BURDEN
(STOCK —) TOPOS
THEMIS (DAUGHTER OF —) DICE IRENE
EUNOMIA
(FATHER OF —) URANUS
(HUSBAND OF —) JUPITER
(MOTHER OF —) TERRA
THEOLOGIAN FAQIH ULEMA DIVINE
MUJTAHID
THEOLOGY KALAM IRENICS DIVINITY
POIMENIC POLEMICS
THEORETICAL BOOK PURE CLOSET
ABSTRACT ACADEMIC ARMCHAIR
NOTIONAL
THEORY ISM ETHICS SYSTEM ANIMISM
BIGBANG ESTHETIC HEDONICS IDEALISM
IDEOLOGY PROGRESS SEMANTIC
THERE YARE ALONG VOILA YONDER
THITHER
THEREFORE SO ERGO THEN HENCE
IGITUR THENCE
THEREUPON SO SINCE WITHAL
THEREON THEREUP

THERMOMETER GLASS HYDRA CELSIUS REAUMUR
(PART OF —) BORE BULB LENS SCALE COLUMN GRADUATIONS CONSTRICTION

THESEUS (FATHER OF —) AEGEUS
(MOTHER OF —) AETHRA
(SON OF —) HIPPOLYTUS
(WIFE OF —) PHAEDRA

THESIS ACT THEMA DOWNBEAT LOGICISM THESICLE

THETIS (FATHER OF —) NEREUS
(HUSBAND OF —) PELEUS
(MOTHER OF —) DORIS
(SON OF —) ACHILLES

THICK FAT HAZY BROAD BURLY BUSHY CLOSE CRASS DENSE FOGGY GREAT GROSS MURKY SOLID SQUAB STIFF STOUT COARSE SLABBY STOCKY STODGY TURBID FAMILIAR
(— WITH SMOKE) SMUDGY
(SHORT AND —) SQUAT

THICKEN GEL CLOT KEECH DEEPEN HARDEN ENGROSS STIFFEN

THICKENING FALX LEAR ROUX SWELL CALLUS CLAVATE ATHEROMA CRASSULA
(— OF COAL SEAM) SWELLY
(— OF LETTER STROKE) STRESS

THICKET BOSK SHAW BRAKE CLUMP COPSE COVER HEDGE COVERT JUNGLE SPINNY BOSCAGE COPPICE SPINNEY SALICETUM

THICKNESS PLY BODY LAYER DIAMETER
(— OF CHIP) CUT FEED
(— OF CLOTH) LAY
(— OF METAL) GRIP
(— OF PAPER) BULK CALLIPER UNDERLAY
(ONE — OVER ANOTHER) LAYER
(SECOND —) DOUBLING

THICKSET BEEFY SQUAT STOUT CHUNKY ROBUST STOCKY STUBBY

THIEF NIP PAD LIFT BUDGE CREEP CROOK FAKER GANEF PIKER SNEAK TAKER CLOYER GONOPH LIFTER NIMMER NIPPER PICKER PIRATE ROBBER SNATCH GORILLA GRIFTER HEISTER LADRONE PROWLER SNAPPER SPOTTER STEALER CUTPURSE FINGERER LARCENER PICAROON PICKLOCK PILFERER SNATCHER
(— AT A MINE) CAVER
(CATTLE —) ABACTOR BLOTTER PLANTER RUSTLER
(CLEVER —) KID CANNON
(CRUCIFIED —) DISMAS
(FLASHY —) KIDDY
(MOUNTAIN —) CHOAR
(NIGHT —) SCOURER
(PETTY —) HOOKER SLOCKER
(RIVER —) ACKMAN LUMPER
(SNEAK —) LURCHER
(VAGABOND —) WASTER
(WHARF —) TOSHER
(PREF.) KLEPT(O)

THIEVING MAGPIE, THE
(CHARACTER IN —) NINETTA PODESTA GIANETTO
(COMPOSER OF —) ROSSINI

THIMBLE SKEIN BUSHEL GOBLET SLEEVE CRINGLE

THIN LEW BONY FINE LANK LEAN LIMP RARE SLIM WEAK FRAIL GAUNT GAUZY LATHY PEAKY SHEER SLINK SMALL SPARE WASHY AERIAL BLASHY DILUTE HOLLOW MEAGER PEAKED SEROUS SKINNY SLEAZY SLIGHT SPINNY SUBTLE TENDER TWIGGY WATERY WEAKEN FRAGILE GRACILE HAGGARD SCRAGGY SCRAWNY SHALLOW SLENDER SPIDERY SPINDLY TENUOUS THREADY ARANEOUS EGGSHELL HAIRLINE VAPORISH WATERISH ATTENUATE
(— AND PINCHED) CHITTY
(— OUT) HOE CHOP DISBUD FEATHER
(— SEEDLINGS) SINGLE
(— THE WALLS) IRON

THING JOB RES BABY ITEM SORT WHAT CHOSE AFFAIR ANIMAL DINGUS FELLOW MATTER ARTICLE MINIKIN SHEBANG WHATNOT

THINK LET SEE WIT DEEM FEEL HOLD MEAN MULL MUSE READ TROW WEEN ALLOW FANCY GUESS JUDGE OPINE ESTEEM EXPECT FIGURE IDEATE RECKON BELIEVE IMAGINE REFLECT SUPPOSE COGITATE CONSIDER ENVISAGE
(— BEST) SEEM
(— HARD) YERK
(— OF) MIND PURPENSE
(— OF AS) ACCOUNT
(— OVER) BETHINK
(— UP) INVENT
(— UPON) BROOD
(— WELL OF) APPROVE

THINNESS RARITY EXILITY FINESSE TENUITY EXIGUITY

THIRST DRY CLEM APOSIA DROUGHT DIPSOSIS POLYDIPSIA

THIRSTY DRY ATHIRST DROUGHTY

THITHER TO YON YOND THERE YONDER ULTERIOR

THONG GIRTH LASSO LEASH ROMAL STRAP THUNK LACING LINGEL STRING BABICHE LANIARD LATCHET
(— ON JAVELIN) AMENTUM
(HAWK'S —) BRAIL

THOR THUNAR THUNOR
(FATHER OF —) ODIN
(HAMMER OF —) MJOLLNIR
(MOTHER OF —) JORDH

THORACIC DORSAL

THORN BROD GOAD PIKE STOB BRIAR BRIER PRICK SPIKE SPINE JAGGER ACANTHA PRICKER STICKER

THORNY HARD SPINY PRICKLY SPINOUS

THOROUGH DEEP FIRM FULL SOUND ERRANT HOLLOW STRICT REGULAR COMPLETE INTIMATE

THOROUGHFARE BUND ROAD ALLEY AVENUE STREET BIKEWAY HIGHWAY PARKWAY

THOROUGHGOING ARRANT HEARTY PROPER RADICAL ABSOLUTE PROFOUND TRUEBRED

THOROUGHLY FULL GOOD INLY CLEAN
FULLY DEEPLY GAINLY KINDLY PROPER
RICHLY RIPELY WHOLLY ROUNDLY
SOAKING SOUNDLY HEARTILY INWARDLY
THOUGH AS AND YET ALTHO ALTHOUGH
THOUGHT CARE IDEA MOOD VIEW
FANCY TASTE NOTION PENSEE CONCEPT
COUNSEL OPINION SURMISE
(— OUT) ADVISED
(CAREFUL —) ADVICE ACCOUNT
(FANCIFUL —) CONCEIT
(HIGHEST —) IDEE
(REASONED —) STUDY
(UNCLEAN —) SEWERAGE
(WELL-EXPRESSED —) STROKE
THOUGHTFUL EARNEST PENSIVE
SERIOUS STUDIED STUDIOUS
THOUGHTLESS RASH VAIN DIZZY
VACANT RAMSTAM HEEDLESS RECKLESS
THOUSAND CHI MIL GRAND MILLE
CHILIAD
(FIVE —) EPSILON
(SIX —) DIGAMMA
(TEN —) TOMAN
(10 —) MYRIAD
THRALL SERF GURTH SLAVE CAPTIVE
THRALLDOM BONDAGE SLAVERY
THRASH LAM TAN BANG BEAT BELT
COMB DRUB DUST JERK LICK MILL SOCK
TRIM WHOP YERK BASTE CURRY FLAIL
PASTE SLOSH SWACK SWING THUMP
TWINK WHALE WHANG CUDGEL FETTLE
LARRUP LATHER RADDLE THRESH
THWACK WALLOP LEATHER TROLLOP
TROUNCE BUMBASTE LAMBASTE
THRASHING BELTING LICKING WARMING
WHALING DRUBBING
THREAD BAR CORD DOUP FILE FILM
GOLD LACE PURL ROON SILK CHIVE
FIBER FLOSS HYPHA REEVE SCREW
SHIVE SHOOT SHUTE TWEER TWIRE
TWIST BOTTOM COBWEB COTTON FIBRIL
SINGLE STITCH STRAIN STRAND STRING
TISSUE BABICHE BASTING SPIREME
WARPING ACONTIUM FILAMENT
GOSSAMER LIGATURE RAVELING
(— AROUND BOWSTRING) SERVING
(— IN SEED COATING) SPIRICLE
(— LEGS OF RABBIT) HARL
(— OF SCREW) WORM
(— OF WAX) SWARF
(— USED FOR COCOON) BAVE
(—S THAT CROSS WARP) WEFT
WOOF
(BADLY TWINED —) SLUBBER
(BALL OF —) CLEW CLUE GLOME
(BUTTONHOLE —S) BAR
(COARSE —) GIRD
(COARSEST — IN LACE) GIMP
(COILED —) COP
(FILLING —) PICK
(FLOATING —) PICKOVER
(HARD —) LISLE
(LINEN —) LINE INKLE
(LOOSELY TWISTED —S) BUMP
(METAL —) LAME WIRE
(OAKUM —) PLEDGET

(PULLED —) SNAG
(SHOEMAKER'S —) END LINGEL
(SILK —) TRAM DOUPIONI
(SOFT SHORT —) THRUM
(STRONG —) GOUNAU
(SURGICAL —) SETON
(WARP —) END STAMEN
(WAXED —) TACKER
(WEFT —) PICK SHOT
(40 —S) BEER BIER
THREADBARE BARE SERE TRITE PILLED
SHABBY NAPLESS
THREAT ATTACK MENACE THUNDER
THREATEN BRAG FACE BOAST ATTACK
IMPEND MENACE ENDANGER OVERHANG
(— TO RAIN) SCOUTHER
THREATENING BIG GLUM UGLY ANGRY
SABLE BANEFUL OMINOUS RAMPANT
MINATORY
(— TO RAIN) HEAVY
THREE TREY GIMEL LEASH TRIAS
TERNARY TERNION
(— CENT PIECE) TRIME
(— IN ONE) TRIUNE
(— OF A KIND) GLEEK BRELAN TRIPLET
(GROUP OF —) TRIO TRIAD TRIPLE
TROIKA
(SET OF —) PAIRIAL
THREEFOLD TRINE TERNAL TREBLE
TRIPLE TERNARY TRIPLEX
THREE MUSKETEERS
(AUTHOR OF —) DUMAS
(CHARACTER IN —) ATHOS ARAMIS
WARDES PORTHOS DEWINTER PLANCHET
BONACIEUX CONSTANCE DARTAGNAN
RICHELIEU
THREE SOLDIERS (AUTHOR OF —)
DOSPASSOS
(CHARACTER IN —) DAN RED ANDY
JOHN MABE YVONNE ANDREWS FUSELLI
ANDERSON GENEVIEVE CHRISTFIELD
THRESH COB BEAT LUMP WHIP FLAIL
SPELT STAMP
THRESHOLD HEAD SILL SOLE LIMEN
DOORSILL
THRIFT SAVING VIRTUE ECONOMY
PARSIMONY
THRIFTY CANNY FENDY PUIST FRUGAL
SAVING CAREFUL SPARING
THRILL JAG BANG KICK FLUSH SHOOT
DINDLE STOUND TICKLE TINGLE TREMOR
ENCHANT FRISSON VIBRATE
THRILLING TINGLY VIBRANT PLANGENT
TINGLING
THRIVE GROW RISE PROVE BATTEN
BATTLE PROSPER SUCCEED FLOURISH
THROAT MAW CROP GULA LANE GORGE
HALSE GARGET GULLET GUZZLE RICTUS
CHANNEL JUGULUM WEASAND
THROTTLE
(— OF ANCHOR) CLUTCH
(— OF COROLLA) FAUCES
(— OF FROG) KNEE
(MOUTH AND —) WHISTLE
(SORE —) HOUSTY PRUNELLA
THROB ACHE BEAT DRUM DUNT LEAP
PANT PULSE STOUND STRIKE STROKE

TINGLE WALLOP FLACKER PULSATE
VIBRATE PALPITATE
(— IN PAIN) SHOOT
THROBBING DUNT ATHROB BEATING
PITAPAT VIBRANT PULSATORY
THROE PANG PULL STOUR SHOWER
PAROXYSM
(—S OF DEATH) AGONY
THRONE SEAT ASANA SELLE SIEGE
STALL STATE STOOL SEGGIO SHINZA
TRIBUNE SEGGIOLA SINHASAN
(BISHOP'S —) SEE APSE CATHEDRA
THRONG CREW HEAP HOST ROUT
CROWD FLOCK POSSE PRESS SHOAL
SWARM RESORT THRUST COMPANY
SURROUND
(CONFUSED —) LURRY
THROTTLE GUN CHOKE SCRAG STIFLE
GARROTE STRANGLE
THROUGH BY PER DONE THRU WITH
ROUND AROUND
THROUGHOUT OVER ABOUT ROUND
ABROAD DURING ENTIRE PASSIM
SEMPRE OVERALL
THROW GO DAB HIP PAT PEG PUT SHY
BIFF BUCK CAST CHOP CLOD COOK DART
DASH HAIL HANK HURL HYPE JERK PECK
PICK PURL SEND SKIM TOSS VANG
WARP CHUCK DOUSE FLICK FLING FLIRT
HEAVE PITCH SLING HURTLE INJECT
LAUNCH BUTTOCK COCKSHY VIBRATE
CATAPULT JACULATE
(— ABOUT) BOUNCE
(— ASIDE) DEVEST
(— AWAY) DICE DOFF BANDY WAIVE
PROJECT JETTISON SQUANDER
(— DOWN) DUSH EVEN PILE LODGE
ABJECT FLATTEN
(— FORTH) EJECT
(— FORWARD) LAUNCH
(— IN CRAPS) CRAP PASS CRABS
BOXCARS NATURAL
(— INTO CONFUSION) CLUB FLUTTER
CONFOUND CONVULSE
(— INTO DISORDER) PIE ADDLE BOLLIX
DERANGE DISRUPT EMBROIL
(— OFF) CANT CAST SPILL SLOUGH
CONFUSE UNBURDEN
(— OFF COURSE) EMIT SHED DERAIL
(— OUT) FIRE HOOF BELCH EJECT
ERUPT SPOUT IGNORE EXTRUDE
(— UP) BARF CAVE PICK VOMIT
(— VIOLENTLY) BUZZ DING PASH SOCK
WHOP SMASH HURTLE SPANGHEW
(— WITH GREAT FORCE) BUZZ
SWACK
(FREE —) FOUL
(WRESTLING —) HANK HIPE HYPE
BUTTOCK BACKHEEL
THRUSH POP BREVE FRUSH MAVIS
OUZEL PITTA SABIA SHAMA VEERY
APHTHA JAYPIE KICKUP MISSEL SHRITE
JAYPIET REDWING WAGTAIL BELLBIRD
CHERCOCK FORKTAIL WOODCHAT
THRUST DAB DIG JAB JAG JAM POP
BANG BEAR BORE BUCK BUTT CANT
CHOP CRAM DART DASH FOIN HURL KICK

LICK PICK POKE PROD PUSH SEND SINK
SPAR STAB STOP TILT WHOP BREAK
DRIFT DRIVE EXERT HUNCH LUNGE
POACH POINT PUNCH SHOOT STAVE
STICK STOKE STUFF THROW DARTLE
PLUNGE POUNCE STRAIN STRESS STRIKE
STRIPE BEARING IMPULSE SHOULDER
(— A LANCE) AVENTRE
(— ASIDE) DAFF SHUFFLE
(— AWAY) DOFF SHOVE DETRUDE
ABSTRUDE
(— DOWN) THRING DEPULSE DETRUDE
(— IN) INSERT STRIKE INTRUDE
(— OF ARCH) DRIFT
(— OF EXPLOSION) BLOWOUT
(— ONESELF) CHISEL
(— OUT) POUT REACH STRUT EXSERT
DETRUDE EXTRUDE OBTRUDE PROTRUDE
OBTRUSIVE
(— SUDDENLY) STRIKE
(— THROUGH) ENFILED
(— WITH ELBOW) HUNCH
(— WITH GREAT FORCE) BUZZ
(— WITH NOSE) NUDDLE
(— WITH WEAPON) FOIN SHOVE
(DAGGER —) DAG
(FENCING —) PASS VENY BOTTE PUNTO
VENUE REPOST TIMING PASSADO
RIPOSTE STOCCADO STOCCATA
(MATADOR'S —) ESTOCADA
(SARCASTIC —) GIRD
THUD BAFF DUMP PLOD SWAG POUND
BOUNCE SQUELCH
THUG MUG GOON GORILLA HOODLUM
GANGSTER
THUMB THOOM POLLEX
(BALL OF —) THENAR
THUMP COB DUB BANG BEAT BLOW
BUMP DING DRUB LUMP THUD BLAFF
BLIBE BUNCH CLUNK CRUMP KNOCK
POUND WHELK BOUNCE HAMMER
PUMMEL
THUNDERBOLT BOLT FIRE VAJRA
FULMEN FOULDRE ARTIFACT FIREBOLT
THUS AS SIC THUSLY THISWISE
THWART BALK CROSS SPITE THROW
BAFFLE SCOTCH STYMIE SNOOKER
CONTRAIR TRAVERSE
TIARA MITER REGNUM CIDARIS TIARELLA

TIBET

CAPITAL: LHASA
COIN: TANGA
LAKE: ARU BAM BUM NAM MEMA TOSU
JAGOK TABIA DAGTSE GARHUR KASHUN
SELING TANGRA YAMDOK KYARING
TERINAM TSARING ZILLING JIGGITAI
LANGUAGE: BODSKAD
MOUNTAIN: KAMET SAJUM KAILAS
BANDALA
MOUNTAIN RANGE: KAILAS KUNLUN
HIMALAYA
NATIVE: BHOTIA
RIVER: NAK NAU SAK SONG INDUS
SUTLEJ MATSANG SALWEEN

TOWN: NOH KARAK LHASA GARTOK TOTLING GYANGTSE SHIGATSE

TICK JAR BEAT NICK PEAK PICK PIKE CHALK PIQUE STRAP ACARID PALLET TALAJE ACARIAN ARACHNID GARAPATA

TICKET LOT TAG BLANK CHECK DUCAT FICHE TOKEN BALLOT BILLET COUPON DOCKET POLICY CONTRACT TRANSFER PASTEBOARD
(COMMISSION —) SPIFF
(FREE —) PASS
(LOTTERY —) BLANK HORSE BENEFIT
(SALES —) TRAVELER
(SEASON —) IVORY

TICKLE AMUSE TEASE EXCITE PLEASE THRILL

TICKLISH GOOSEY QUEASY TENDER TOUCHY TRICKY

TIDE FLOW NEAP WAVE AGGER ROUST SPRING SEAFLOOD

TIDINGS NEWS WORD RUMOR SOUND ADVICE MESSAGE
(GLAD —) GOSPEL

TIDY RID COSH NEAT SMUG SNUG TAUT TRIG NATTY NIFTY TIGHT FETTLE POLITE ORDERLY SHIPSHAPE

TIE BOW LAP BAND BEND BIND BOND DRAW KNOT LACE LOCK WISP YOKE ASCOT BRACE NEXUS THROW TRICE TRUSS ATTACH BUNDLE COPULA COUPLE FASTEN LIGATE SECURE FOULARD NECKTIE SHACKLE SLEEPER SPANCEL CROSSTIE STANDOFF STRINGER
(— BENEATH) SUBNECT
(— IN TENNIS) DEUCE
(— IN WRESTLING) DOGFALL
(— KNOT) CAST
(— LEGS) HOBBLE
(— ONIONS) TRACE
(— SCORE) PEELS
(— THE SCORE) EQUALIZE
(— TOGETHER) KNIT LEASH HARNESS
(— UP) SNUB TRAMMEL LIGATURE TWITCHEL
(LEATHER —) WANTY
(MADE-UP —) TECK
(NEEDLEWORK —) BRIDE
(PL.) GILLIES

TIER ROW BANK DECK RANK STORY DEGREE
(— OF CASKS) RIDER
(— OF SEATS) CIRCLE
(— OF SHELVES) STAGE

TIGHT WET FULL HARD SNUG TAUT TIDY TRIG CLOSE DENSE DRUNK TENSE STINGY STRAIT STRICT

TIGHTEN JAM CALK FIRM BRACE CINCH CLOSE SCREW WRENCH STRAITEN

TIGHTFISTED NARROW STINGY

TIGHTLY FAST HARD SHORT STRAIT CLOSELY

TIGHTWAD FIST PIKER STIFF

TILE LUMP SLAT SLATE IMBREX LAPPET TEGULA AZULEJO CARREAU CONDUIT PANTILE STARTER MAINTILE
(— USED IN MOSAIC) ABACULUS
(HEXAGONAL —) FAVUS
(HOLLOW —) BACKING
(HOPSCOTCH —) PEEVER
(LARGE —) DALLE QUARL QUARLE
(MAH JONG —) HONOR SEASON
(ONE-HALF —) HEAD
(PERSIAN —) KASHI
(ROUNDED —) CREASE
(SMALL —) TILETTE
(SQUARE —) QUADREL QUARREL

TILL TO FIT CASH FARM PLOW TOIL DRESS LABOR UNTIL FURROW PLOUGH SHUTTLE

TILLER HELM STERN STOOL HUSBAND KILLIFER

TILT DIP TIP BANK CANT COCK HEEL LIST PEAK TRAP JOUST STOOP TIPUP TOPPLE TOURNEY ATTITUDE QUINTAIN
(— BRICK) HACK
(— IN WATER) DABBLE
(— OF BOWSPRIT) STAVE
(— OF NOSE) KIP

TIMBER CAP LOG RIB BEAM BIBB BUNT CLOG FROG GIRT PUMP SKID SPAR TREE WOOD CAVEL FLOOR GRIPE KEVEL PLATE RIDER SPALE STICK BEARER BRIDGE BUMPER CORBEL FENDER FOREST ROOFER TIMMER BOLSTER CARLING DEADMAN FALLAGE PARTNER RIBBAND TRANSOM CORDWOOD COULISSE
(— BETWEEN TRIMMERS) HEADER
(— CUT TO LENGTH) JUGGLE
(— IN MINE) COG STULL LIFTER DIVIDER JUGGLER
(— KEPT DRY) BRIGHT
(— ON SCAFFOLD) LIGGER PUTLOG
(— ON SLED) BUNK
(— SAWED AND SPLIT) LUMBER
(— SUPPORTING CAP) LEGPIECE
(— SUSTAINING YARDS) MAST
(— TO PROP COAL) BROB
(CONVEX —) CAMBER
(CURVED —) CRUCK
(CUT —) FELL
(FELLED —) HAG
(FLOOR —) JOIST SUMMER
(FLOORING —) BATTEN
(FOUNDATION —) PILE
(FRAMING —) PUNCHEON
(HORIZONTAL —) REASON
(NORWEGIAN —) DRAM
(PHILIPPINE —) LAUAN
(PRINCIPAL — OF VESSEL) KEEL
(ROOF —) LEVER RAFTER
(ROOFING —S) SILE
(SHIPBUILDING —S) STOCKS DEADWOOD HARPINGS
(SHIP'S —) CANT KEEL KNEE RUNG SPUR APRON LEDGE WRONG DAGGER HARPIN LACING SCROLL BRACKET FUTTOCK STEMSON DOGSHORE STANDARD
(SLABBED —) CANT
(SQUARED —) BALK

(SUPPORT —) SILL GIRDER LEDGER
PUNCHEON STRINGER
(SYSTEM OF —S) BOND
(UNCUT —) STUMPAGE
(WEATHERBEATEN —) DRIKI
TIME BELL BOUT HINT TIDE CHARE EPOCH
KALPA SITHE STOUR TEMPO TEMPS
WHILE COURSE KAIROS PERIOD SEASON
TEMPUS CADENCE SESSION MOVEMENT
(— ALLOWED FOR PAYMENT)
USANCE
(— FOR PAYING) KIST
(— FOR PAYMENT) CREDIT
(— GRANTED) FRIST
(— IN SERVICE) AGE
(— INTERVENING) INTERIM MEANTIME
(— OF BEAUTY) BLOOM
(— OF CRISIS) EXIGENT
(— OF DYING) LAST
(— OF EXUBERANCE) CARNIVAL
(— OF HIGHEST STRENGTH) HEYDAY
(— OF LIGHT) DAY
(— OF MATURITY OR DECLINE)
AUTUMN
(— OF OLD AGE) SUNSET
(— OF REST) BREATH SABBATH
(ANOTHER —) AGAIN
(BRIEF —) TINE FLASH THROW
(ENDLESS —) PERPETUITY
(EXTENDED —) TRAIN
(FIXED —) HOUR STEVEN
(FUTURE —) MANANA
(GAY —) FRISK WHOOPEE
(GOOD —) BALL BASH BEANO JOLLY
BARNEY FROLIC HOLIDAY
(HARD —) GYP BUSINESS
(INFINITE —) ABYSS
(LONG —) AGE
(OLD —S) ELD
(POINT OF —) MOMENT
(QUIET —) SLACK
(RIGHT —) TID
(SET —) TRYST
(SHORT —) TIFF SPACE START MINUTE
STOUND
(SPARE —) TOOM LEISURE
(TRIPLE —) TRIPLA
(WORKING —) CORE
TIMELESS AGELESS ETERNAL DATELESS
TIMELY PAT DULY TIDY COGENT TIMEFUL
TOWARDLY SEASONABLE
TIME OF YOUR LIFE (AUTHOR OF —)
SAROYAN
(CHARACTER IN —) JOE TOM NICK
KITTY MCCARTHY
TIMEPIECE DIAL CLOCK TIMER VERGE
WATCH GHURRY PENDULE HOROLOGE
TIMID SHY NESH SELY FAINT PAVID
SCARY AFRAID COWARD ASHAMED
BASHFUL CHICKEN FEARFUL NERVOUS
RABBITY STRANGE TREMBLY COWARDLY
FEARSOME RETIRING TIMOROUS
TIMIDITY SHYNESS TIMERITY FUNKINESS
TIMON OF ATHENS (AUTHOR OF —)
SHAKESPEARE
(CHARACTER IN —) CUPID TIMON
TITUS CAPHIS LUCIUS FLAVIUS PHRYNIA

LUCILIUS LUCULLUS PHILOTUS
TIMANDRA APEMANTUS FLAMINIUS
SERVILIUS VENTIDIUS ALCIBIADES
HORTENSIUS SEMPRONIUS
TIMOR (CAPITAL OF —) DILI
(COIN OF —) AVO PATACA
(ISLAND OF —) MOA LETI LAKOR
(TOWN IN —) KUPANG ATAMBUA
TIMOROUS ASPEN FAINT MILKY TIMID
AFRAID COWISH TREPID FEARFUL
NERVOUS SHEEPISH
TIN JOVE SWELL KHATIN JUPITER PILLION
STANNUM PRILLION
(MESS —) DIXIE
(ROOFING —) TERNE
(SHEET —) LATTEN
TINCTURE DRUG COLOR IMBUE SMACK
STAIN TAINT TINCT ARNICA ELIXIR
INFUSION LAUDANUM PAREGORIC
TINDER SPUNK AMADOU FIREBOX
TINE BAY KNAG SNAG TANG GRAIN POINT
PRONG TOOTH
(ANTLER'S —) RIGHT CROCKET
SURROYAL
TINGE DYE HUE CAST DASH TANG TINT
WOAD COLOR FLUSH IMBUE PAINT
SAVOR SHADE STAIN TAINT TINCT
TOUCH SEASON SMUTCH DISCOLOR
TINCTURE
TINGLE BURN GELL THIRL DINDLE
PRINGLE TRINKLE VIBRATE
TINKER PRIG CAIRD FIDDLE FIDGET
MUGGER KETTLER TRAVELER
TINKLE DINGLE TINGLE TWINKLE
TINT DYE COLOR GRAIN TINCT TINGE
(— IN HORSE'S COAT) BLOSSOM
(— WITH COSMETICS) SURFLE
TINY BITSY BITTY SMALL TEENY WEENY
ATOMIC MINIKIN ATOMICAL
TIP CAP DIP END FEE NEB APEX CAVE
COCK DUMP HEEL KEEL LEAD LIST PALM
PIKE PILE SWAG TILT VAIL POINT SPIRE
STEER CAREEN CENTER TOPPLE WHEEZE
APICULA CUMSHAW DOUCEUR GRIFFIN
POINTER APICULUS BONAMANO
GRATUITY
(— OF ANTENNA) ARISTA
(— OF BILLIARD CUE) LEATHER
(— OF BIRD'S BILL) DERTRUM
(— OF ELBOW) NOOP
(— OF FOX'S BRUSH) CHAPE
(— OF SKI) SHOVEL
(— OF STAMP) SHOE
(— OF TOE) POINTE
(— OF TONGUE) CORONA
(— OF UMBO) BEAK
(— OF WHEAT KERNEL) BRUSH
(— OF WHIP) SNAPPER
(— ON ORGAN PIPE) TOE
(— OVER) TOP PURL OVERSET
(— UP) CANT COUP COWP
(ABRUPT —) MUCRO
(BOW —) HORN
(INWARD —) BANK
(LARGE —S) LARGESS
(RUBBISH —) TOOM

TIPPLE BIB NIP SOT DRAM GILL BIBBER
PUDDLE
TIPPLER SOUSE TOAST WINER BIBBER
BOOZER DRAMMER POTATOR
MALTWORM
TIPSY DRUNK FRESH MUZZY TIGHT
TOTTY TOZIE BUMPSY GROGGY
MUCKIBUS PLEASANT
TIRADE LAISSE SCREED JEREMIAD
PHILIPPIC
TIRE DO FAG LAG SAG BORE CORD FLAT
JADE KILL LABOR SPARE WEARY CASING
SICKEN TUCKER BALLOON EXHAUST
FATIGUE FRAZZLE
(— OUT) HAG FLOG THEAD HARASS
OVERWEARY
(WORN —) CARCASS
TIRED SAD BEAT DEAD BLOWN WEARY
BLEARY BUSHED PLAYED SHAGGED
FATIGATE
TIRESOME DRY FAGGY BORING PROLIX
IRKSOME PROSAIC TEDIOUS BROMIDIC
ENNUYANT
TISSUE FAT CORK PITH TELA GRAFT
TRAMA CALLUS FABRIC FASCIA PHLOEM
SHEATH ADENOID ALBUMEN CAMBIUM
EPITELA HYDROME KLEENEX MESTOME
TEXTURE ADHESION BLASTEMA
ECTODERM ENDODERM
(— OF FUNGUS) CENTRUM
(— SURROUNDING TEETH) GUM
(BLACK —) CLYPEUS
(CONNECTING —) WEB STROMA
TENDON LIGAMENT
(CORK —) SUBER
(FATTY —) LARD GREASE
(HARD —) BONE
(LYMPHOID —) TONSIL
(NERVE —) GANGLION
(SOFT —) FLAB
(VEGETABLE —) ARMOR
(WOOD —) LIGNUM VITRAIN
TITAN BANA LETO MAIA ASURA ATLAS
COEUS CREUS CRIOS DIONE THEIA
CRONOS CRONUS PALLAS PHOEBE
TETHYS THEMIS IAPETUS OCEANUS
HYPERION
TITILLATE AMUSE KITTLE TICKLE
TITLE
(ALSO SEE LEADER, CHIEF,
GOVERNOR, RULER) AGA AYA BAN BEG
BEY DAN FRA MIR PAN ABBA ABBE AGHA
AMIR BABU DAME DEVI EMIR GRAF HERR
KHAN KNEZ NAME ABUNA AMEER
BABOO BEGUM CLAIM CROWN GHAZI
GRACE HAJJI HAKAM HANUM HONOR
MIRZA MPRET NAWAB NEGUS NIZAM
RABBI RIGHT SINGH BASHAW COUSIN
DEGREE DOMINE EPONYM EXARCH
HANDLE LEGEND MASTER MEHTAP
MISTER PESHWA PREFIX SHERIF SQUIRE
ALFEREZ BAHADUR CANDACE CAPTION
DIGNITY EFFENDI EPITHET ESQUIRE
GAEKWAR GRAVITY HEADING HIDALGO
INFANTE KHEDIVE MESSIRE TITULUS
VOIVODE BANNERET EMINENCE
GOSPODIN HIGHNESS HOLINESS

HOSPODAR INTEREST MAGISTER
MAHARAJA MAHARANI MISTRESS
MONSIEUR PADISHAH SUBTITLE
(— OF BOOK) QUARE
(— OF RESPECT) SIR SRI COJA LIEF
MIAN SIDI BURRA KHOJA MADAM SAHIB
SIEUR MADAME MILADY
(BENEDICTINE —) DOM
(MOCK —) IDLESHIP
TITTER GIGGLE SNICKER TWITTER
WHICKER
TITTLE JOT IOTA MINUTE
TITULAR LEGAL NOMINAL HONORARY
TITUS ANDRONICUS (AUTHOR OF —)
SHAKESPEARE
(CHARACTER IN —) AARON CAIUS
TITUS CHIRON LUCIUS MARCUS MUTIUS
TAMORA ALARBUS LAVINIA MARTIUS
PUBLIUS QUINTUS AEMILIUS BASSIANUS
DEMETRIUS VALENTINE SATURNINUS
SEMPRONIUS
TO A AD FOR INTO TILL UNTO UPON
TOAD AGUA BUFO FROG PIPA HYLID
PIPAL ANURAN CRAPON PEEPER
BUFONID CRAPAUD GANGREL HOPTOAD
PADDOCK QUILKIN
TOADY FAWN SUCK COTTON FAWNER
FLUNKY GREASE LACKEY MUCKER
PLACEBO TRUCKLE BOOTLICK LICKSPIT
PARASITE SYCOPHANT
TOAST WET TOSS BREDE SKOAL BIRSLE
BUMPER CHEERS HEALTH PLEDGE
PROSIT CAROUSE CHEERIO LEHAYIM
RESPECT SLAINTE WASSAIL BRINDISI
(— AND ALE) SWIG
(— ONESELF) LEEP
(JACOBITE —) LIMP
TOBACCO CANE CAPA NAVY POKE QUID
ROLL WEED BACCY CUBAN DARKS
FOGUS PETUN SMOKE TABAC TWIST
BRIGHT BURLEY FILLER HAVANA
CRACCUS GORACCO LATAKIA NICOTIA
ORONOKO PERIQUE PIGTAIL SOTWEED
(— AND PAPER) MAKINGS
(— CAKED IN PIPE BOWL) DOTTLE
TOPPER
(— HAVING OFFENSIVE SMELL)
MUNDUNGO
(— IN ROPES) BOGIE
(— MOISTENED WITH MOLASSES)
HONEYDEW
(CAKED —) HEEL
(COARSE —) SHAG SCRAP CAPORAL
(CUT —) CANASTER PICADURA
(DRIED —) TABACUM
(HARD-PRESSED —) NAILROD
(INDIAN —) GAGROOT PUKEWEED
EYEBRIGHT
(INFERIOR —) LUGS
(LADIES' —) CUDWEED
(LOWER LEAVES OF —) FLYING
(MILD —) RETURN
(PERSIAN —) SHIRAZ TUMBEK TUMBEKI
(PERUVIAN —) SANA
(POOR QUALITY —) DOGLEG
(PULVERIZED —) SNUFF
(QUID OF —) CUD

(RAW —) LEAF
(ROLLED —) CARROT
(SMALL PIECE OF —) FIG
(VIRGINIA —) COWPEN VIRGINIA
TOBACCO ROAD (AUTHOR OF —)
CALDWELL
(CHARACTER IN —) ADA LOV DUDE
RICE ELLIE PEARL BENSEY BESSIE
JEETER LESTER
TOBOGGAN COAST CARIOLE
TODDLE DADDLE PADDLE TOTTLE
WADDLE
TO-DO ADO FUSS STIR STINK HOOPLA
FLUSTER FOOFARAW
TOE DIGIT DACTYL HALLUX TRIPPET
POULAINE
(— OF BIRD) HEEL
(LITTLE —) MINIMUS
TOGA GOWN ROBE TRABEA
TOGETHER ONCE SAME ATONE JOINTLY
ENSEMBLE
TOGO (CAPITAL OF —) LOME
(LANGUAGE OF —) EWE TWI MINA
HAUSA KABRAIS LOTOCOLI
(MOUNTAIN IN —) AGOU
(NATIVE OF —) EWE MINA CABRAI
KABRAI OUATCHI
(RIVER IN —) OTI ANIE HAHO MONO
(TOWN IN —) KANDE ANECHO PALIME
SOKODE TSEVIE ATAKPAME
TOIL FAG GRUB HACK MUCK PLOD
TASK WORK LABOR SLAVE DRUDGE
EFFORT HAMMER MOIDER STRIVE
FATIGUE TRAVAIL TURMOIL DRUDGERY
INDUSTRY
TOILET CAN LOO HEAD JOHN BIFFY
CRAPPER BASEMENT BATHROOM
LAVATORY
TOKEN BUCK CENT SIGN TYPE BADGE
CHECK INDEX SCRIP BEAVER CASTOR
COPPER COUPON DOLLAR EMBLEM
MARKER SIGNAL WITTER AUSPICE
COUNTER EARNEST INDICIA MEMENTO
SYMPTOM EVIDENCE INSTANCE
KEEPSAKE MONUMENT
(— OF LUCK) HANDSEL
(— OF RESPECT) SALUTE
(— OF SUPERIORITY) PALM
(— OF VICTORY) LAUREL
(CANADIAN —) HARP
(LOVE —) DRURY AMORET
(PORCELAIN —S) PI
TOLERABLE SOSO PRETTY LIVABLE
BEARABLE PASSABLE PORTABLE
TOLERANT SOFT BROAD BENIGN
PATIENT PLACABLE PERMISSIVE
TOLERATE GO BEAR BIDE HACK HAVE
ABIDE ALLOW BROOK SPARE STAND
STICK ACCEPT ENDURE PARDON PERMIT
SUFFER STOMACH SUSTAIN
TOLL TAX PIKE RENT KNELL EXCISE
OCTROI MULTURE PASSAGE PIERAGE
BERTHAGE WHEELAGE
TOMB BIER CIST MOLE GRAVE HUACA
MAZAR TABUT BURIAL CHULPA DURGAH
GALGAL SAMADH SHRINE THOLOS
TURBEH MASTABA OSSUARY CENOTAPH

CISTVAEN HYPOGEUM MARABOUT
MONUMENT MAUSOLEUM SEPULCHER
(— IN CHURCH) SACELLUM
(— OF MOSLEM SAINT) ZIARAT
(CAVE —) SPEOS
(PREHISTORIC —) KURGAN
TOMBOY RAMP GAMINE HOYDEN
MADCAP TOMRIG
TOM JONES (AUTHOR OF —) FIELDING
(CHARACTER IN —) TOM BETTY JENNY
JONES NANCY BLIFIL GEORGE SOPHIA
SQUARE WATERS BRIDGET WESTERN
THWACKUM ALLWORTHY BELLASTON
PARTRIDGE FITZPATRICK NIGHTINGALE
TOMORROW MANANA MORROW
TOMORN
TOM SAWYER (AUTHOR OF —)
TWAIN CLEMENS
(CHARACTER IN —) AMY JOE SID TOM
FINN HUCK MARY MUFF BECKY POLLY
HARPER POTTER SAWYER DOUGLAS
LAWRENCE ROBINSON THATCHER
TONE DO FA LA MI RE SI TI KEY SOL FLAT
NOTE COLOR FIFTH PRIME SHARP SIXTH
SOUND STYLE DEGREE FOURTH SECOND
MEDIANT PARTIAL ELEVENTH HARMONIC
HEADNOTE SONORITY
(— A DRAWING) STUMP
(— DOWN) DRAB TAME SOFTEN
SUBDUE
(— UP) BRACE
(ACCENTED —) SFORZANDO
(BROKEN —) CRACK
(COMPLEX —) KLANG
(DEEP —) BASS
(DOMINANT —) ANIMUS
(DRAWLING —) DRANT
(HIGH-PITCHED —) PIP
(KEY —) KEYNOTE
(LOUD —) FORTE
(LOW —) SEMISOUN
(MONOTONOUS —) DRONE
(SHARP NASAL —) TWANG
(SIGNIFICANT —) ACCENT
(SINGLE UNVARIED —) MONOTONE
(STRIDENT —) COUAC
(WHINING —) GIRN
(PREF.) PHON(O)
TONGA (CAPITAL OF —) NUKUALOFA
(ISLAND GROUP OF —) TOFUA VAVAU
HAAPAI NIUAFOO TONGATAPU
NIUATOBUTABU
(ISLAND OF —) ONO TOFUA VAVAU
HAAPAI
(TOWN OF —) NEIAFU NEIAFU
TONGS SNAPS SERVER FORCEPS
GRAMPUS SCISSORS
TONGUE GAB CLAP KALI POLE REED
IDIOM VOICE GLOSSA KABYLE KALIKA
LADINO LINGUA SPEECH DIALECT
FEATHER LANGUAGE PLECTRUM
(— IN FLOORING) SPLINE
(— OF BELL) CLAPPER
(— OF JEW'S-HARP) TANG
(— OF LAND) DOAB REACH LANGUE
LANGUET
(— OF MOLLUSC) RADULA

(— OF OXCART) COPE
(— OF SHOE) FLAP KILTIE
(— OF VEHICLE) NEAP SHAFT
(BELLOWS —) GUSSET
(GIVE —) PRATE
(GOSSIPING —) CLACK CLACKER
(PIVOTED —) PAWL

TONIC DO ALOE PICHI BRACER SONANT
SUMBUL BONESET CALAMUS CHIRATA
COLOMBA FUMARIA GENTIAN KEYNOTE
NERVINE ROBORANT TRILLIUM

TONSURE CROWN SHAVE SHEAR
CORONA DIKSHA RASURE

TOO SO ALSO OVER TROP LUCKY OVERLY
LIKEWISE

TOOL
(ALSO SEE IMPLEMENT AND
INSTRUMENT) AX ADZ AWL AXE BIT
BUR DIE DIG GIN GUN HOB KEY LAP LOY
RIP SAW SAX TAP TIP VOL ZAX ADZE
BORE BRAY BURR CLAW COMB DADO
DISC DISK DUPE EDGE FILE FLAY FROE
FROG FROW GAGE HACK HAWK HONE
LEAF LOOM MILL PICK ROLL SATE SEAX
SLED SNAP SPID SPUD STOP TAMP TIER
VISE AUGER BLADE BORAL BORER BRAKE
BRAND BREAK BRUSH BURIN CROZE
DARBY DOLLY DRIFT DRILL DUMMY
EDGER FLAKE FLOAT FLUTE GAUGE
GOUGE GUIDE HARDY HOBBY HOWEL
KNIFE KNURL LEVEL MAKER MISER
MODEL PLANE POINT PRUNT PUNCH
QUIRK SABER SABRE SCREW SHAVE
SHELL SLICE SLICK SNIPE SPADE SPEAR
SPLIT STAKE STAMP STING STOCK STRIG
STYLE SWAGE TEWEL TOYLE UPSET
VALET WAGON BEADER BEATER BIDENT
BIFACE BLADER BODKIN BROACH
BUDGER BUFFER CALKER CHASER
CHISEL CLEAVE COGGLE COLTER CRADLE
CRANNY CUTTER DEVICE DIBBLE DIGGER
DOCTOR DRIVER ENGINE FASCET FERRET
FILLET FLANGE FLORET FLUTER FORMER
FRAISE FULLER GIMLET GLAZER GOFFER
GRAVER GUMMER HACKER HAMMER
HEMMER HOGGER HOLDER HULLER
JIGGER JUMPER LADKIN LASTER LIFTER
NIBBER PALLET PARTER PICKAX PICKER
PLENCH PLIERS PROPER PUPPET REAMER
RIPPER ROCKER RUNNER SAPPER SCRIBE
SCUTCH SEATER SHAPER SHAVER
SHEARS SHOVEL SKIVER SLATER SOCKET
SQUARE STYLET STYLUS SWIVEL
TAGGER TASTER TONGUE TREPAN
TURNER TURREL TWILLY VEINER
WAGGON WIGWAG WIMBLE WORDLE
WORMER YANKEE

TOOTH BIT GAM JAG PEG FANG RASP
SNAG TUSK CRENA IVORY MOLAR PEARL
PRONG RAKER TENON BROACH CANINE
CUTTER JOGGLE TRIGON TRITOR
DENTILE GRINDER INCISOR LATERAL
SURDENT BICUSPID DENTICLE
GAGTOOTH PREMOLAR SAWTOOTH
TRIGONID
(— OF A MOSS) BLEPHARA
(— OF HORSE) DIVIDER

(— OF MOLLUSC) MARGINAL
(— OF PINION) LEAF
(— OF RADULA) UNCINUS
(— ON ROTATING PIECE) WIPER
(ARTIFICIAL —) DUMMY PONTIL
(CANINE —) CUSPID HOLDER LANIARY
CYNODONT DOGTOOTH EYETOOTH
(GEAR —) COG GUB DENT ADDENDUM
SPROCKET
(HARROW —) TINE
(MOLAR —) WANG

TOOTHED SERRATE VIRGATE SERRATED
PECTINATE

TOP CAP COP NUN TIP ACME APEX BEAT
COCK ROOF SKIM BLOOM CHIEF COVER
CREST CROWN FANCY RIDGE SPIRE
TOTUM TRUMP UPPER CAPOTE CULMEN
SUMMIT CACUMEN SPINNER SURMOUNT
TEETOTUM
(— FOR CHIMNEY OR PIPE) COWL
HOOD
(— OF ALTAR) MENSA
(— OF AUTOMOBILE) HEAD HOOD
(— OF CAPSTAN) DRUMHEAD
(— OF FURNACE) ARCH
(— OF GLASS) PRETTY
(— OF HEAD) MOLD PATE MOULD
SCALP VERTEX
(— OF HELMET) SKULL
(— OF HILL) KNAG KNAP KNOLL
(— OF INGOT) CROPHEAD
(— OF MINING SHAFT) PITHEAD
(— OF MOUNTAIN) MAN
(— OF PLANT OR TREE) CROP
(— OF ROOF) DECK
(— OF SPINDLE) COCKHEAD
(— OF THUNDERCLOUD) INCUS
(— OF WAVE) COMB
(— OF WOODEN STAND) CRISS
(—S OF CROP) SHAW
(BOOT —) RUFF
(BOX —) COUPON
(CARRIAGE —) CALASH

TOPER BOUSER CUPMAN POTMAN
SOAKER BOMBARD DRUNKARD
MALTWORM

TOPIC ITEM TEXT HOBBY THEME BURDEN
GROUND MATTER SUBJECT OCCASION

TOPPLE TIP TILT LEVEL TOTTLE

TORCH JACK LAMP LINK PINE WISP
BLAZE BRAND FLARE MATCH LAMPAD
BRANDON CRESSET LUCIGEN FLAMBEAU

TOREADOR TORERO CAPEADOR

TORMENT RAG TRY WOE BAIT BALE
FRET MOIL PAIN PANG PINE RACK TEAR
CURSE DEVIL GRILL HARRY SCALD TEASE
TWIST WRING HARASS HARROW
HECTOR NEEDLE PLAGUE AFFLICT
ANGUISH BEDEVIL CRUCIFY HAGRIDE
PERPLEX TORTURE TRAVAIL LACERATE
MACERATE
(EXTREME —) AGONY

TORN RENT BROKEN BLASTED

TORNADO VORTEX CYCLONE TRAVADO
TWISTER

TORPEDO FISH SHELL SQUIB BATOID
HOAGIE

TORPID FOUL NUMB BROSY INERT SODDEN STUPID LANGUID COMATOSE SLUGGISH

TORPOR COMA SLEEP SWOON ACEDIA ACCIDIE SLUMBER LETHARGY

TORRENT FLOW RUSH FLOOD SPATE STREAM NIAGARA CATARACT
(— OF WORDS) BLATTER

TORRID HOT SULTRY AUSTRAL BOILING

TORTOISE BEKKO COOTER TURTLE EMYDIAN HICATEE MUNGOFA TESTUDO GALAPAGO TERRAPIN

TORTUOUS CRANKY SCREWY SINUATE WRIGGLY SINUATED

TORTURE BOOT CARD FIRE PAIN PANG PINE RACK AGONY SCREW TWIST ENGINE EXTORT IMPALE AFFLICT AGONIZE ANGUISH CRUCIFY PERPLEX TORMENT MARTYRDOM

TORY BANDIT OUTLAW ROBBER PEELITE TANTIVY ABHORRER LOYALIST

TOSS SHY BUNG CANT CAST FLIP PASS SHAG SLAT TOUT CHUCK FLICK FLING HEAVE PITCH THROW BOUNCE DANDLE TOTTER BLANKET
(— A COIN) SKY
(— A JACK) LAG
(— ABOUT) SWAB TAVE POPPLE THRASH THRESH TORFLE WAMPISH
(— ASIDE) BANDY
(— AWAY) BLOW
(— HEAD) CAVE GECK BRANK
(— OF HORSE'S HEAD) CHACK
(— OF THE HEAD) HEEZE
(— OFF) SWAP
(— ON WAVES) SURGE
(— TO AND FRO) WALK
(— TOGETHER CONFUSEDLY) SCRAMBLE
(— WITH THE HORNS) DOSS HIKE

TOTAL SUM TAB TOT MERE COUNT GROSS MOUNT SUMMA UTTER WHOLE ENTIRE GLOBAL OMNIUM TOTTLE EMBRACE GENERAL ABSOLUTE COMPLETE ENTIRETY TEETOTAL

TOTTER ROCK SHAKE WAVER DOTTER FALTER JOGGLE SWERVE WAMBLE WANGLE STAGGER TREMBLE TITUBATE VACILLATE

TOUCH RAP TAG TIP ABUT DASH FEEL KISS MEET PALP PLAY RAKE TACT TAKE GROPE SPICE TAINT TASTE TINGE TRAIT AFFECT ATTAIN CARESS FINGER HANDLE REGARD STRAIN TACTUS ATTINGE CONTACT FEELING PALPATE SOUPCON TINCTURE
(— A KEY) STRIKE
(— BRIEFLY) GLANCE
(— CARESSINGLY) FLATTER
(— CLOSELY) IMPINGE
(— GENTLY) DAB TAT TICK BRUSH
(— LIGHTLY) GRAZE SCUFF SKIFF
(— OF BRUSH) HAND
(— OF COLOR) EYE
(— OF PAINT) GLOB
(— OF PLEASURE) GLISK
(— RIGHTLY) NICK

(— DELICATE) STROKE
(— FINISHING) HOODER COPESTONE
(— PAINTING) ACCENT
(— SLIGHT) SKIFF SMATCH

TOUCHY HUFFY MIFFY TESTY FEISTY KITTLE SPUNKY TENDER TETCHY GROUCHY NERVOUS PEEVISH PEPPERY TEMPERY TICKLISH

TOUGH RUM BHOY HARD TAUT WIRY BUTCH HARDY STIFF STOUT KNOTTY SINEWY STRONG HICKORY BULLYBOY LEATHERY ROUGHNECK TENACIOUS

TOUGHEN TAW ANNEAL ENDURE HARDEN TEMPER
(— METAL) PLANISH

TOUGHNESS TUCK FIBER STRENGTH TENACITY

TOUPEE RUG DOILY SCALP POSTICHE TOPPIECE

TOUR TURN SWING JUNKET SAFARI JOURNEY INVASION PROGRESS
(— OF DUTY) HERD STATION
(CANARY —) GLUCKE

TOURNAMENT TILT JERID TOURNEY BONSPIEL CAROUSEL

TOUSLED TAUTED TOWZIE TUMBLED UNKEMPT

TOUT BRUIT BARKER STEERER

TOW CRIB HAUL PULL TRACK CODILLA CORDELLE

TOWARD AD INTO ANENT AGAINST ADVERSUS GAINWARD

TOWEL CLOUT WIPER DIAPER LAVABO

TOWER PEEL REAR RISE SOAR TOUR BABEL HEAVE MOUNT PYLON SPIRE STUPA TEXAS ASCEND ASPIRE BELFRY CASTLE DONJON RONDEL SPRING TURRET CHULLPA DERRICK LANTERN MIRADOR NURAGHE STEEPLE TALAYOT TOURNEL BARBICAN BASTILLE DOMINEER RONDELLE PEPPERBOX
(— CONTAINING COKE) SCRUBBER
(— FOR SENTINEL) GUERITE
(— OF FORT) SPUR
(— OF MOSQUE) MINARET
(— OF SILENCE) DAKHMA
(— ON SUMMIT) PIKE
(— OVER) DROWN BESTRIDE
(ATTACHED —) DETAIL
(BELL —) CARILLON
(CONNING —) SAIL
(FRACTIONATING —) STILL
(PYRAMIDAL —) VIMANA SHIKARA
(SIEGE —) BRATTICE
(SIGNAL —) BANTAYAN
(WIND —) BADGIR

TOWERING EMINENT SUPERNAL AMBITIOUS

TOWN BYE HAM WON CAMP CITY STAD TOON WICK BAYAN MACHI PLACE SIEGE STAND STEAD VILLE CIUDAD PUEBLO STAPLE BOROUGH OPPIDUM BOOMTOWN HOMETOWN TOWNSHIP
(— DESOLATED) GUBAT
(— FORTIFIED) BURG BURGH ENCEINTE
(— MYTHICAL) QUIVIRA
(— SMALL) SHTETL

(UNFORTIFIED —) BOURGADE
(UNIMPORTANT —) PODUNK
(WALLED —) CHESTER
TOWN HALL HALL CABILDO RATHAUS
TOLBOOTH STADHOUSE
TOWNSHIP DEME DORP BAYAN TREEN
BOROUGH
TOWNSMAN CAD CIT DUDE SNOB
TOWNY BURGHER CITIZEN OPPIDAN
TOWROPE CABLET GUNLINE TOWLINE
CORDELLE
TOY ARK DIE GAY TOP COCK DOLL FOOL
MOVE PLAY BLOCK DALLY FLIRT KNACK
SPORT TRICK BAUBLE DANDLE DOODLE
FIZGIG GEWGAW PRETTY PUPPET
RATTLE SUCKER CRICKET DREIDEL
TANGRAM TRINKET TUMBLER WHIZZER
GIMCRACK KICKSHAW PINWHEEL
SQUAWKER TEETOTUM WINDMILL
ZOETROPE
(— AMOROUSLY) MIRD
(— WITH) PADDLE
(FLYING —) PIGEON
TRACE RUN CAST ECHO HINT LICK MARK
SHOW SIGN TANG TINT BRING GLEAM
GRAIN PRINT SHADE SPICE SPOOR
STAMP TINGE TOUCH TRACK TRAIL
TRAIN DERIVE HARBOR SHADOW SKETCH
SMUTCH STRAIN STREAK GLIMPSE
MENTION REMNANT SOUPCON SYMPTOM
THOUGHT UMBRAGE VESTIGE WHISPER
DESCRIBE FOOTSTEP TINCTURE
(— A BEE) COURSE
(— A CURVE) SWEEP
(— A DESIGN) CALK
(— MATHEMATICALLY) GENERATE
(— OF A HARE) FARE
(— ON CHART) PRICK
(— THE COURSE OF) DEDUCE
(HARNESS —) TUG THEAT TREAT
(MEMORY —) ENGRAM
(SLIGHT —) GHOST STAIN SMATCH
SPARKLE
(SLIGHTEST —) SCINTIL
TRACK DOG PUG RUT WAY CLEW CLUE
FARE FOIL HUNT LANE MARK PATH RACE
RAIL ROAD SHOE VENT CHUTE DRIFT
HOUND LODGE SLIDE SPACE SPOOR
STEAD SWATH TRACE TRAIL TRAIN
TREAD COURSE GROOVE HARBOR
LADDER RUNWAY SLEUTH STREAM
FOOTING PATHWAY TRAFFIC VESTIGE
FOOTSTEP GUIDEWAY WAGONWAY
(— FOR ROPE) CHANNEL
(— GAME) DRAW
(— OF DEER) SLOT STRAIN
(— OF GAME IN GRASS) FOILING
(— OF HARE) FILE
(— OF WOUNDED BEAST) PERSUE
(— ON PRINTING PRESS) BANK
BEARER
(RAILROAD —) LEAD SPUR STUB
SIDING TANGENT APPROACH BACKBONE
(RUNNING —) FLAT CINDERS
(SHORT BRANCH —) RETURN
(SIDE —) LIE HOLE
(TEMPORARY —) SHOOFLY

(WORM —) NEREITE
TRACT AREA BEAT FLAT ZONE CAMPO
CLIME COAST ESSAY FIELD HORST
PATCH SWEEP TRACK BARONY EXTENT
REGION ENCLAVE QUARTER ROYALTY
BROCHURE CAMPAGNA CAMPAIGN
CINGULUM DISTRICT PAMPHLET
PROVINCE TOWNSITE TREATISE
(— KEPT IN NATURAL STATE) PARK
(— OF BARREN LAND) BARREN
DERELICT
(— OF BRAIN FIBERS) PEDUNCLE
(— OF GRASSLAND) PRAIRIE
(— OF LAND) CRU DOAB DUAB DUAR
GORE MARK BLOCK CHASE CLAIM EJIDO
FRITH GRANT LAINE SCOPE SWELL
TALUK EIGHTY ESTATE FOREST GARDEN
ISLAND POLDER STRATH AIRPORT
QUILLET RESERVE TERRAIN BOUNDARY
CLEARING FARMHOLD INTERVAL
SCABLAND SLASHING
(— OF MUDDY GROUND) SLOB
(— OF OPEN UPLAND) DOWN DOWNS
(— OF UNCOVERED ICE) GLADE
(— OF WASTE LAND) HEATH
(BOGGY —) RUNN MORASS
(DRY —) SEARING
(FORESTLESS —) STEPPE
(IRREGULAR —) GORE
(OPEN —) VEGA SLASH
(SANDY —) DEN DENE LANDE
(SHRUBBY —) MONTE
(SWAMPY —) FLOW BAYGALL
(UNOCCUPIED AND UNCULTIVATED
—) DESERT
(WATERLESS —) THIRST
TRACTABLE EASY SOFT TAME BUXOM
DOCILE GENTLE TOWARD DUCTILE
PLIABLE AMENABLE FLEXIBLE OBEDIENT
TOWARDLY YIELDING MALLEABLE
TRACTOR CAT MULE DRAGON BOBTAIL
CRAWLER PEDRAIL AGRIMOTOR
TRADE CHAP DEAL SELL SWAP CRAFT
PRICE TRUCK BARTER CHANGE EMPLOY
HANDLE METIER OCCUPY SCORSE
BARGAIN CALLING CHAFFER SCIENCE
BUSINESS EXCHANGE MERCHANDISE
TRADEMARK CHOP MARK BRAND
COUPON
TRADER BANYA PLIER BALIJA BANYAN
DEALER MONGER CHAPMAN MARWARI
SANGLEY CHANDLER KURVEYOR
MERCHANT OPERATOR
(HORSE —) JOCKEY
(INEXPERIENCED —) LAMB
TRADESMAN CIT BAKAL COOPER
SELLER
TRADITION STORY SUNNA CABALA
SMRITI HALAKAH HEREDITY HERITAGE
TRADUCE SLUR ABUSE DEFAME MALIGN
REVILE VILIFY ASPERSE DETRACT
SLANDER
TRAFFIC DEAL MART TRADE BARTER
PALTER TRAVEL CHAFFER DEALING
PASSAGE BUSINESS COMMERCE
EXCHANGE
(— IN SACRED THINGS) SIMONY

(— IN SLAVES) MAGONIZE
TRAIL PAD PUG DRAG FOIL HUNT PATH
SIGN SLOT BLAZE CRAWL PISTE ROUTE
SPOOR TRACE TRAIN COMING FOLLOW
RUNWAY SHADOW SLEUTH DRAGGLE
(— ALONG) STREEL TRAPES
(— OF A FISH) LOOM
(— OF STAG) ABATURE
(— OUT) STREAM
(— THROUGH MUD) DAGGLE
(DESCENDING —) BAJADA
(MOUNTAIN —) CLIMB
(WAGON —) RUDLOFF
TRAILER SEMI COACH BOXCAR CARAVAN
FLATBED GONDOLA
TRAIN SET TIRE TURN BREED COACH
DRESS DRILL ENTER FOCUS RANGE
TRACE TRADE TRAIL DIRECT GENTLE
INFORM REPAIR SCHOOL SEASON
STRING SUBWAY BRIGADE CARAVAN
EDUCATE PEDDLER RETINUE SHUTTLE
CIVILIZE ELECTRIC EQUIPAGE EXERCISE
HIGHBALL INSTRUCT REHEARSE
(— AN ANIMAL) BREAK
(— FINE) GAUNT
(— FOR CONTEST) POINT
(— FOR FIGHTING) SPAR
(— OF ANIMALS) COFFLE
(— OF ATTENDANTS) CORTEGE
(— OF COMET) TAIL
(— OF EXPLOSIVE) FUSE
(— OF MINING CARS) JAG RUN TRIP
(CAMEL —) KAFILA
(FUNERAL —) CONVOY
(PACK —) CONDUCTA
(RAILROAD —) DRAG HOOK LOCAL
PICKUP EXPRESS FREIGHT LIMITED
RATTLER
TRAINED GOOD MADE ADEPT BROKEN
TRAINING DRILL ASCESIS CULTURE
NURTURE BREEDING
(— IN HUMANITIES) CIVILITY
(— OF HORSE) DRESSAGE
(RELIGIOUS —) SADHANA
TRAIT ITEM MARK VEIN ANGLE CHARM
KNACK ELEMENT HALLMARK
TRAITOR RAT JUDAS APOSTATE
ISCARIOT QUISLING SQUEALER
TRADITOR
TRAITOROUS FALSE FELON APOSTATE
RENEGADE
TRAMP BO BUM PAD HIKE HOBO PUNK
SLOG SWAG VAMP WALK CAIRD PIKER
ROGUE STIFF TRAIK TRASH BAGMAN
GAYCAT JOCKER PICARO STROLL TINKER
TRUDGE DRUMMER FLOATER SWAGMAN
TRAIPSE TROUNCE VAGRANT CLOCHARD
FOOTSLOG STROLLER TRAVELER
VAGABOND
(— ABOUT) WAG
(LONG —) HUMP
TRAMPLE HOX JAM FARE FOIL HOOF
POACH SPURN TRAMP TREAD DEFOUL
SAVAGE OPPRESS OVERRUN OVERRIDE
TRANCE RAPTUS AMENTIA ECSTASY
SAMADHI CATALEPSY
TRANQUIL CALM COOL EASY MILD SOFT

QUIET STILL GENTLE SERENE EQUABLE
PACIFIC RESTFUL PEACEFUL
TRANQUILIZE CALM LULL QUIET STILL
BECALM PACIFY SERENE SETTLE SOFTEN
SOOTHE APPEASE COMPOSE
TRANQUILLITY LEE EASE REST PEACE
QUIET SATTVA HARMONY QUIETUDE
SERENITY
TRANSACT DO PASS AGITATE CONDUCT
PERFORM
TRANSACTION DEAL DEED ACTION
AFFAIR BARGAIN PASSAGE CONTRACT
OPERATION PROCEEDING
TRANSCEND PASS SOAR EXCEED
OVERTOP SURPASS
TRANSCRIPT COPY SCORE DOUBLE
APOGRAPH EXSCRIPT
TRANSFER CEDE GIVE JUMP PASS SALE
SELL TURN CABLE CARRY CROSS REFER
REMIT SHIFT ASSIGN CHANGE DECANT
DONATE REMOVE SWITCH CESSION
CONSIGN DELIVER MIGRATE TRADUCE
DELEGATE DELIVERY DONATION
EXCHANGE TRANSACT NEGOTIATE
(— A RECORDING) OVERDUB
(— DYE) EXHAUST
(— HEAT) CONVECT
(— HOMAGE) ATTORN
(— MOLTEN GLASS) LADE
(— OF ENERGY) FLOW
(— OF PROPERTY) DEED GIFT GRANT
DISPOSAL
(— PIGMENT) FLUSH
TRANSFIX DART PITCH STAKE STICK
SKEWER THRILL
TRANSFORM TURN SHIFT CHANGE
CONVERT FASHION PERMUTE CATALYZE
DISGUISE
TRANSFORMER DIMMER JIGGER
TEASER TOROID BOOSTER
TRANSGRESS ERR SIN BREAK OFFEND
OVERGO DIGRESS DISOBEY VIOLATE
INFRINGE OVERSTEP TRESPASS
TRANSGRESSION SIN SLIP CRIME
FAULT BREACH MISDEED OFFENSE
DELICTUM TRESPASS
TRANSIENT FLEET BUBBLE FLIGHTY
PASSING FLEETING FUGITIVE
MOMENTARY
TRANSITION CUT JUMP LEAP SEGUE
SHIFT PASSAGE
TRANSITORY FLEET FLYING PASSANT
PASSING SLIDING VOLATIC FLEETING
FLITTING VOLATILE MOMENTARY
TRANSLATE PUT DRAW MAKE TURN
RENDER CONVERT EXPOUND CONSTRUE
INTERPRET
TRANSLATION KEY CRIB PONY TROT
GLOSS TARGUM CABBAGE TRADUCT
VERSION VERBATIM
(— OF BIBLE) PESHITO
(— OF THE CLASSICS) JACK
TRANSLUCENT CLEAR LUCID LIMPID
LUCENT HYALINE
TRANSMIT BEAM EMIT SEND CARRY
CONVEY DERIVE EXPORT IMPART

RENDER CONDUCT CONSIGN FORWARD
TRAJECT BEQUEATH DESCRIBE
TRANSPARENT THIN CLEAR FILMY
LUCID BRIGHT LIMPID LUCENT CRYSTAL
FRAGILE HYALINE HYALOID TIFFANY
LUMINOUS LUSTROUS PELLUCID
TRANSPORT JOY BEAR BOAT DRAY
HAUL PASS PORT RIDE SEND SHIP BLISS
CANOE CARRY FERRY CONVEY DEPORT
GALLOP ECSTASY EXPRESS RAPTURE
CARRIAGE DAYDREAM
(— BY PACKHORSE) JAG
(— FOR CRIME) LAG
(— LOGS) BOB
(— ORE) SLUSH
TRANSPORTATION AIR FARE AIRLIFT
BOATAGE FREIGHT TRAJECT TRANSPORT
TRANSPOSITION SHIFT ANSWER
ANAGRAM
TRANSVERSE CROSS FACING THWART
OBLIQUE
TRAP GET GIN PIT FALL HOOK LACE LIME
NAIL TOIL BRAKE CATCH POUND SNARE
SPELL COBWEB EELPOT KEDDAH POCKET
SNATCH FLYTRAP PITFALL RATTRAP
SPRINGE BIRDLIME DEADFALL
(— FOR BIRDS) SCRAPE
(— FOR LARGE GAME) HOPO
(— FOR RABBITS, MICE, ETC) TIPE
TYPE
(— FOR RATS) CLAM
(— FOR SALMON) PUTT
(— FOR SMALL ANIMALS) HATCH
(— FOR THE FEET) CALTROPS
(— IN POKER) SANDBAG
(— IN THEATER) SCRUTO
(— INTO SERVICE) CRIMP
(FISH —) FYKE KILL LEAP WEEL WEIR
CREEL WILLY CORRAL CRUIVE WILLOW
(SAND —) BUNKER
TRAPDOOR DROP SLOT TRAP SCRUTO
VAMPIRE TRAPFALL
TRAPPINGS GEAR ARMORY TOGGERY
EQUIPAGE HOUSINGS CAPARISON
TRASH ROT BOSH GEAR GOOK JUNK
CLART STUFF SWASH THROW WASTE
WRACK BUSHWA KITSCH RAMMEL
REFUSE RUBBLE SCULCH BAGGAGE
GARBAGE RUBBISH CLAPTRAP
FLUMMERY MUCKMENT SKITTLES
TRUMPERY
TRASHY CHEAP FLASH TOSHY TRIPY
PALTRY SHODDY RUBBISH RIFFRAFF
TRAVAIL PAIN TASK TOIL AGONY LABOR
TORMENT
TRAVEL BUS FLY GIG FARE PASS PATH
TOTE TRIP WEND COVER SLOPE THROW
TRACK CRUISE VOYAGE EXPRESS
TRUNDLE WAYFARE PROGRESS
(— ACROSS SNOW) MUSH
(— AIMLESSLY) SAUNTER
(— ALONG GROUND) TAXI
(— AROUND) TURN COAST CIRCLE
GIRDLE COMPASS
(— AT GOOD SPEED) CRACK
(— AT HIGH SPEED) HELL BARREL
SCORCH

(— AT RANDOM) DRIFT
(— BACK AND FORTH) SHUNT
COMMUTE
(— BY OX WAGON) TREK
(— FAST) STREAK
(— IN A VEHICLE) TOOL
(— ON FOOT) HIKE SHANK KNAPSACK
PERAMBULATE PEREGRINATE
(— ON WATER) SAIL
(— OVER) TRANCE TRAVERSE
(— THROUGH) GO
(— THROUGH WOODS) BUSHWACK
(— WITHOUT EQUIPMENT) SIWASH
(DAY'S —) JORNADA JOURNAL
JOURNEY
TRAVELER GOER FARER GUEST HORSE
BAGMAN SAILOR VIATOR CRUISER
DRUMMER PILGRIM SWAGGIE TREKKER
WAYGOER ARGONAUT EXPLORER
OUTRIDER VOYAGEUR WAYFARER
PASSENGER
TRAVERSE GO LIFT MAKE PASS SPAN
WALK COAST COVER CROSS SWEEP
TRACE TRACK COURSE OVERGO TRAVEL
VOYAGE WANDER JOURNEY PERVADE
NAVIGATE OVERPASS
TRAVESTY PARODY SATIRE EXODIUM
BURLESQUE
TRAVIATA, LA (CHARACTER IN —)
FLORA VALERY ALFREDO BERVOIX
DOUPHOL GERMONT GIORGIO VIOLETTA
(COMPOSER OF —) VERDI
TRAY HOD CASE TILL TRUG BATEA
BOARD SUSAN SALVER SERVER WAITER
COASTER CONSOLE
(— FOR CRUMBS) VOIDER
(— FOR DRYING FISH) FLAKE
(— FOR MATCH SPLINTS) CAUL
MONKEY
(— FOR SHELLFISH) FLOAT
(— FOR TYPE) GALLEY
(— TO CATCH OVERFLOW) SAFE
(CIRCULAR —) ROUNDEL
TREACHEROUS FOUL DIRTY FALSE
SNAKY FICKLE HOLLOW ROTTEN YELLOW
SNAKISH PLOTTING
TREACHERY GUILE DECEIT FELONY
PERFIDY TREASON DASTARDY
TREAD PAD BEAT PATH RUNG STEP
TRACK DEFOIL CRAWLER FEATHER
FOOTING FOOTSTEP
(— CLUMSILY) CLUMP BALTER
(— DOWN SHOE HEEL) CAM
(— HEAVILY) SPURN TRAMPLE
(— ON) FOIL
(— TO MUSIC) FOOT
(TIRE —) COVER
TREASURE HOARD PRIZE STORE TROVE
VALUE COFFER GERSUM WEALTH
FINANCE THESAUR GARRISON
(LITTLE —) STOREEN
TREASURE ISLAND (AUTHOR OF —)
STEVENSON
(CHARACTER IN —) BEN JIM PEW
GUNN JOHN BONES HANDS ISRAEL
SILVER HAWKINS LIVESEY SMOLLETT
TRELAWNEY

TREASURER FISC BURSAR FISCAL
BOUCHER HOARDER COFFERER
PROVISOR QUAESTOR
TREASURY FISC KIST CHEST HOARD
PURSE COFFER BURSARY CHAMBER
CHEQUER THESAURY
(PAPAL —) CAMERA
TREAT USE DEAL DOSE LEAD PLAY
COVER GUIDE SERVE SETUP DEMEAN
DOCTOR GOVERN HANDLE REGALO
CONDUCT GARNISH ACTIVATE
TREATISE AGAMA FAUNA FLORA SUMMA
SYLVA TRACT POETRY SYSTEM ALGEBRA
ANATOMY BIOLOGY COMMENT GEOLOGY
GRAMMAR HISTORY PANDECT PHYSICS
ZOOLOGY ALMAGEST BROCHURE
CALCULUS GENETICS GEOMETRY
HORNBOOK PASTORAL PRACTICE
SPECULUM MONOGRAPH
TREATMENT CURE WORK USAGE FACIAL
BEHAVIOR DEMEANOR ENTREATY
(— BY MASSAGE) SEANCE
(— FOR WOOLLENS) SPONGING
(BAD —) MISUSAGE
(COLD —) FREEZE
(COMPASSIONATE —) MERCY
(CRUEL —) SEVERITY
(HARMFUL —) ABUSE
(INHUMAN —) CRUELTY
TREATY ACCORD CARTEL CONCORD
ENTENTE ALLIANCE ASSIENTO
CONCORDAT
TREE TI ACH ADY AMA APA ARN ASH BAY
BEL BEN BUR DAK DAR EBO ELM FIG FIR
GUM HAW KOA KOU LIN OAK SAJ SAL
TAL TUI ULE YEW ACLE AGBA AKEE
AMLA ANAM ANAN ANDA ARAR ASAK
ASOK ATIS ATLE ATTA AULU AUSU BAEL
BAKU BITO BOGO BOOM BREA BURI
BURR CADE COLA CRAB DATE DHAK DILO
DITA DOON EBOE IPIL JACK KINO KOKO
LIME MABI MORA OHIA OMBU PALA PINE
POLE POON SADR SORB SUPA TALA
TAWA TCHE TEAK TEIL TITI TOON TREW
TUNG TUNO UPAS VERA WOOD YATE
YAYA AALII ABETO ABURA ACANA
ACAPU ACOMA AFARA AGATI AGOHO
AKEKI ALAMO ALANI ALDER ALGUM
ALISO ALMON ALMUG AMAGA AMAPA
AMBAK ANABO ANJAN APPLE ARACA
ARBOR ARECA ARJAN ARJUN ARTAR
ASOKA ASPEN ATLEE BABUL BALAO
BALSA BALTA BANAK BEECH BEHEN
BETIS BIRCH BONGO BOREE BOSSE
BUMBO CACAO CARAP CAROB CEBIL
CEDAR CEIBO DADAP DHAVA DHAWA
DILLY DRYAD DURIO ELDER GABUN
GAIAC GENIP GINEP GINKO HAZEL ICICA
IXORA JAMBO JIQUE JIQUI KAPOR
KAPUR KEENA KOKAN KOKIO KOKUM
KONGU KUSAM LANSA LARCH LARIX
LEHUA LEMON LICCA LIMBA LINDE LINER
LINGO MAHOE MAHUA MAMIE MAPLE
MAQUI NARRA NIEPA NURSE OADAL
OSAGE OSIER PACAY PAPAW PECAN
PIPER RAULI ROBLE ROHAN ROWAN
SALAI SAMAN SASSY SCRAG SIMAL

SIRIS SISSU STICK SUMAC TABOG TARFA
TENIO TERAP TIKUR TIMBO TINGI TOONA
TUART ULMUS UMIRI URUCA URUCU
UVITO WAHOO YACAL YACCA YULAN
ZAMAN ACAJOU AHKROT AKEAKE
ALAGAO ALERCE ALERSE ALFAJE
ALMOND ALUPAG AMAMAU AMBASH
AMUGIS AMUYON ANAGAP ANAGUA
ANAQUA ANGICO ANILAO ARALIA
ARANGA ARBUTE AUSUBO AZALEA
BABOEN BACURY BAHERA BAKULA
BALSAM BANABA BANAGO BANANA
BANCAL BANIAN BANYAN BARBAS
BATAAN BIRIBA BOMBAX BONDUC
BONETE BOTONG BRAUNA BUCARE
BUSTIC CALABA CAMARA CANELA
CANELO CAPUMO CARAPA CASSIA
CATIVO CAUCHO CEDRON CHALTA
CHERRY CHICHA CHINAR CHOGAK
CITRON COBOLA COCUYO CUMBER
DATURA DHAMAN DHAURA DHAURI
DRIMYS DURIAN ELCAJA EMBLIC EMBUIA
FEIJOA FILLER FUSTIC GABOON GINGKO
GUAIAC GURJAN GURJUN IDESIA IDIGBO
ILIAHI ILLIPE ILLUPI JAGUEY JUJUBE
KAMALA KEMPAS KINDAL KITTUL
LANSAT LANSEH LAUREL LIGNUM
LINDEN LITCHI LOCUST LONGAN
MAFURA MALLET MAYTEN MEDLAR
MILKER MIMOSA ORANGE PANAMA
PAWPAW PIQUIA POPLAR RAMBEH
ROHUNA RUNNEL SABICU SABINO
SANDAN SANTOL SAPELE SAPOTA
SAPOTE SATINE SAWYER SERAYA
SINTOC SISSOO SOUARI STYRAX
SUMACH SUNDRI TALUTO TAMANU
TARATA TEETEE TIKOOR TIMBER TINGUY
TOATOA TOTARA TUPELO URUCUM
URUSHI UVALHA WABAYO WABOOM
WAHAHE WALNUT WAMARA WAMPEE
WANDOO WATTLE YACHAN YAGHAN
YAMBAN ZAMANG ACHIOTE ACHUETE
AILANTO AKEPIRO AMBATCH AMBOINA
AMUGUIS AMUYONG ANABONG
ANNATTO ANONANG APITONG APRICOT
ARARIBA ARAROBA ARBORET ARBUTUS
AROEIRA ASSAGAI AVOCADO AVODIRE
BANILAD BANKSIA BECUIBA BENZOIN
BILLIAN BOLLING BUBINGA BUCKEYE
BUISSON CADAMBA CAJAPUT CAJUPUT
CANELLA CARAIPE CASTANA CATALPA
CAUTIVO CERILLO CHAMPAC CHECHEM
CHECKER CHENGAL COCULLO CONIFER
CURUPAY CYPRESS DEADMAN DESCENT
DETERMA DHAMNOO EPACRID FRUITER
GONDANG GRIBBLE GUMIHAN HICKORY
HOLLONG HOPBUSH HORMIGO KAMASSI
KAMBALA KICKXIA KITTOOL KOKOONA
KOOMBAR KUMQUAT LOGWOOD
MADRONA MANJACK MARGOSA
NAARTJE PARAIBA PEREIRA PIMENTO
PULASAN PYRAMID RATWOOD
REDWOOD SERINGA SERVICE SHITTAH
SPINDLE STOPPER SUNDARI SURETTE
TANGELO TANGHIN SIRARIH TARATAH
TARWOOD TINDALO TREELET TWISTER
URUNDAY VETERAN WALAHEE WALLABA

WEENONG WONGSHY WONGSKY
YAMANAI YOHIMBE YOHIMBI
(— SYMBOLIZING UNIVERSE)
YGDRASIL
(AUSTRALIAN —) ASH GUM TOON
BELAH BELAR BOREE BUNDY BUNYA
GIDIA HAZEL KARRI NONDA PENDA
SALLY WILGA BAOBAB DRIMYS GIDGEE
GIMLET GYMPIE JARRAH KOWHAI
MARARA PEROBA SALLEE DOGWOOD
GEEBUNG PEEBEEN
(BIG —) SEQUOIA
(EVERGREEN —) FIR YEW PINE SUGI
TAWA ABIES ATHEL CAROB CEDAR
CLOVE HOLLY LARCH LEMON OLIVE
THUJA BALSAM BIBIRU COIGUE COIHUE
KANAGI KAPUKA LOQUAT ORANGE
SPRUCE ARDISIA BEBEERU BILIMBI
CONIFER HEMLOCK JUNIPER MADRONA
MADRONO EUCALYPT
(GUM —) KARI KINO BABUL BALTA
BUMBO ICICA KARRI KIKAR GIMLET
MALLET STORAX TEWART WANDOO
GOMMIER COOLIBAH
(HAWAIIAN —) KOA LEHUA ILIAHI
(JAPANESE —) KAYA KIAKI KEYAKI
KADSURA KATSURA SATSUMA ZELKOVA
(MEXICAN —) ULE AMAPA DRAGO
EBANO SERON CAPULI CATENA CHILTE
CAPULIN COPALCHE
(NEW ZEALAND —) AKE KARO KAWA
MIRO PUKA RATA RIMU TAWA TORU
WHAU HINAU KAORI KAURI MAIRE
MANGI MAPAU MATAI TOWAI AKEAKE
KAMAHI KANUKA KAPUKA KARAKA
KARAMU KAWAKA KONINI MANUKA
PURIRI TARATA TITOKI TOATOA TOTARA
WAHAHE AKEPIRO MANGEAO PUKATEA
TARAIRI TARWOOD
(ORNAMENTAL —) KABIKI LABURNUM
POINCIANA
(PHILIPPINES —) DAO IBA TUA TUI
BOGO DITA IFIL IPIL AGOHO AGOJO
ALMON AMAGA ANABO BAYOG BAYOK
BETIS DANLI GUIJO LAUAN LIGAS TABOG
YACAL ALAGAO ALUPAG AMUYON
ANAGAP ANUBIN ARANGA BANUYO
BATAAN BATETE BATINO BOTONG
DUNGON KATMON LANETE MABOLO
MARANG MOLAVE SAGING TALUTO
AMUGUIS AMUYONG ANABONG
ANOBING ANONANG APITONG BINUKAU
CAMAGON DANGLIN MANCONO MAYAPIS
TINDALO
(POISONOUS —) GUAO UPAS LIGAS
TANGHIN TANQUEN MANCHINEEL
(POLYNESIAN —) MACUDA
(SHADE —) ELM GUAMA CATALPA
HALESIA INKWOOD JOEWOOD
SYCAMORE
(SMALL —) BOX ALDER DWARF NGAIO
AKEAKE CHANAR JOJOBA ARBORET
INKWOOD JOEWOOD STADDLE
(SPINY —) LIME AROMA AROMO HONEY
BOOGUM BUCARE BUMELIA CATECHU
COLORIN LAVANGA COCKSPUR
(TIMBER —) ASH DAR ENG FIR SAL

ACLE ANDA BAKU COCO CUYA EKKI IPIL
PELU PINE TALA TEAK YANG ACAPU
ALMON AMAPA AMATE AMBAY ANJAN
ARACA ARGAN BANAK BIRCH CAROB
CEDAR COCOA CULLA EBONY ERIZO
FOTUI HALDU ICICA IROKO KAURI KHAYA
KIAKI KOKAN MANIU MAPLE MVULE
NARRA ROBLE TIMBO ALERCE ALUPAG
BABOEN BACURY BANABA BANCAL
CARBON CHUPON CORTEZ DAGAME
DEGAME DUKUMA ESPAVE FREIJO
GAMARI GUMHAR IMBUIA JACANA
LEBBEK MUERMO PADAUK SANDAN
SATINE SISSOO
(TROPICAL —) AKE AULU DALI DIKA
EBOE EKKI GUAO INGA MABA MAHO
MAJO PALM SHEA ACKEE BALSA BONGO
COUMA DALLI FOTUI GUAMA GUARA
ICICA ILAMA JIGUA MARIA NEPAL NJAVE
POOLI TARFA ANUBIN BAKULA BALATA
BANANA CASHEW CEDRON CHUPON
GENIPA HACKIA ITAUBA LEBBEK LECYTH
MAMMEE OBECHE PERSEA ANGELIN
ANNATTO CAULOTE COPAIBA DATTOCK
EHRETIA EUGENIA GATEADO GUACIMO
LAPACHO MAJAGUA MOMBINI SANDBOX
SOURSOP SURETTE
TRELLIS TRAIL PERGOLA TARLIES
ESPALIER
TREMBLE QUAKE SHAKE DINGLE DITHER
DODDER FALTER HOTTER QUAVER
QUIVER SHIMMY THRILL WOBBLE
FLICKER SHUDDER STAGGER TWIDDLE
TREMBLING SHAKY DITHER TREMOR
AQUIVER PALSIED QUAKING QUAVERY
QUIVERY
TREMENDOUS BIG AWFUL GIANT
GREAT LARGE ENORMOUS HORRIBLE
TERRIBLE TERRIFIC MONSTROUS
TREMOR RIGOR SHAKE QUIVER THRILL
SHUDDER TREMBLE
TREMULOUS ASPEN QUAKY SHAKY
PALSIED SHIVERY TREMBLY SHIMMERY
TINGLING
TRENCH SAP LINE MOAT RILL BOYAU
DITCH DRAIN FOSSE GRAFT COFFER
FURROW GULLET ACEQUIA CUVETTE
SPREADER
(— BELOW FOREST FIRE) GUTTER
(— FOR BURYING POTATOES) CAMP
(— FOR DRAIN TILES) CHASE
(— FORMED BY BANKING
VEGETABLES) GRAVE
(ARTIFICIAL —) LEAT
(IRRIGATION —) FLOAT SUGSLOOT
TRENCHANT ACID KEEN EDGED SHARP
INCISIVE
TREND BIAS TONE TURN CURVE DRIFT
SENSE SLANT SWING TENOR CURRENT
MOVEMENT TENDENCY
TREPIDATION FEAR ALARM DISMAY
TRESPASS DEBT POACH BREACH INVADE
INTRUDE OFFENSE ENCROACH INFRINGE
TRESS CURL LOCK TAIL BRAID SWITCH
RINGLET
TRESTLE MARE HORSE SAWHORSE
TRIAL TRY BOUT OYER TEST TURN ASSAY

ESSAY GRIEF ISSUE POINT PROOF TASTE
TOUCH ASSIZE EFFORT EQUITY ATTEMPT
HEARING PROVING EXERCISE JUDGMENT
(— BY BATTLE) WAGER
(— BY ORDEAL) ORDALIUM
(— FOR HOUNDS) DERBY
(— OF SPEED) DASH
(— OF STRENGTH) CRUNCH
(EXPERIMENTAL —) TENTAMEN
(RACING —) PREP
(SEVERE —) ORDEAL CRUCIBLE
TRIBE (ALSO SEE NATIVE AND PEOPLE)
AO GI ATI AUS BOH EVE EWE GOG KHA
KIN KRA ROD SUK YAO ADAI AKAN AKHA
AKIM AKKA BAYA BONI CLAN DAGO
GUHA PURU QUNG RACE RAVI REKI
SAHO SEID SHIK SHOR SIOL SOGA SUKU
SUSU TOBA TURI TUSH UBII VEPS VILI
VIRA YANA AEQUI ANGKA APTAL ARAWA
BASSI BATAK BESSI BONGO BROOD
CHANG CINEL DADJO DEDAN DIERI FIRCA
GIBBI HORDE HOUSE ICENI KAJAR
KANDH KEDAR KHOND KIWAI KONGO
KOTAR KREPI LANGO MAGOG MARSI
MBUBA MENDE MENDI MOSSI MUTER
NANDI PHYLE PONDO QUADI SERER
SOTIK STAMM SUEVI TAIPI TAULI TCAWI
TEKKE TELEI TUATH VEPSE VOLOF
WAKHI WARRI WASHO WAYAO YOMUD
ADIGHE AGAWAM AMHARA ANAMIM
ANTEVA APAYAO ARAINS BANYAI
BASOGA BUDUMA BUSAOS CHAMPA
CHAWIA CHORAI DOROBO FAMILY
HERULI KARLUK KEREWA KHAMTI
KONYAK KORANA LOBALE MANGAR
MOLALA NATION NERVII PAHARI PHYLON
POKOMO RAMNES SHAGIA SICULI
SIMEON SUKUMA TAINUI TAMOYO
TCHIAM TELEUT THUSHI TUSHIN TYPEES
VENETI WABENA WABUMA WAGOMA
WAGUHA WAHEHE WARORI WASOGA
WAVIRA ZARAMO ZEGUHA ZENAGA
(— OF ISRAEL) DAN GAD ASHER
REUBEN EPHRAIM ISSACHAR MANASSEH
(CHINESE —S) HU
(PRIVILEGED —) MAKHZAN
(SEA GYPSY —) SELUNG
TRIBULATION AGONY CROSS MISERY
SORROW DISTRESS
TRIBUNAL BAR ROTA BENCH COURT
FORUM JUNTA ACUERDO AREOPAGY
KANGAROO
TRIBUTARY ARM BRANCH FEEDER
AFFLUENT
TRIBUTE AID FEE TAX GELT KUDO LEVY
RENT CANON GAVEL HANSE HOMAGE
IMPOST OVATION PENSION
TRICK BOB COG CON FOB FOX FUB FUN
GIN JIG JOB JILK BITE DIDO DIRT DUPE
FAKE FLAM FLUM FOOL GAFF GAUD
GULL HAVE HOAX JAPE JEST JINK PASS
RUSE SKIT TURN WOOL ANTIC BLINK
CATCH CHEAT CRAFT CROOK CURVE
DODGE ELUDE FEINT FRAUD GRIFT GUILE
KNACK PLANT PRANK SHIFT SLICK
STUNT TWIST WHEEL BAFFLE BANTER
CAUTEL DECEIT DELUDE DOUBLE

EUCHRE HUMBUG JOCKEY JUGGLE
PLISKY SPRING VAGARY WHEEZE
WINNER CHICANE CONCEIT FINESSE
GUILERY KNAVERY SHUFFLE SLEIGHT
ARTIFICE CLAPTRAP CONTOISE
CROTCHET DELUSION FLIMFLAM
INTRIGUE PRACTICE BAMBOOZLE
STRATAGEM
(— OUT) FARD FANGLE FINIFY
(BEGUILING —) WILE
(CARD —) CLUB HEART SPADE STICH
DIAMOND WEAVING
(FRAUDULENT —) RIG TOP
(JUGGLING —) FOIST
(KNAVISH —) DOGTRICK
(LOVE —) AMORETTO
(MEAN —) TOUCH
(MONKEY —) SINGERIE
(OLD —) CONNU
(PETTY —S) CRANS
(SIX —S) BOOK
(SMART —) LIRIPIPE
(STUPID —) SHINE
(VEXING —) CHAW
(WRESTLING —) CHIP CLICK FAULX
FORWARD
TRICKERY GAFF SHAM TRAP WILE
FRAUD HOCUS CAUTEL DECEIT JAPERY
DODGERY FALLACY GULLERY JOUKERY
KNAVERY PAWKERY SLEIGHT ARTIFICE
CHEATING COZENAGE TRUMPERY
TRICKLE DRIP TRILL DRIVEL GUTTER
STRAIN DISTILL DRIBBLE DRIZZLE
TRICKSTER GULL SHAM RASCAL
SLICKER SLEEVEEN TRAMPOSO
TRICKY SLY DODGY GAUDY SNIDE
ARTFUL CATCHY LUBRIC QUIRKY SHIFTY
SMARTY DEVIOUS WINDING FLIMFLAM
JUGGLING SHIFTFUL SKITTISH SLIPPERY
TORTUOUS
TRIFLE ACE DAB PIN SOU BEAN COOT
FICO FOOL HAIR HOOT MESS MOTE PLAY
WHIT DALLY FLIRT FLUKE POINT SPORT
TRICK BREATH DABBLE DAWDLE
DOODAD DOODLE FIDDLE FOOTLE
GEWGAW MONKEY PALTER PICKLE
PIDDLE POTTER PUTTER STIVER WANTON
FEATHER NOTHING THOUGHT TRINKET
FALDERAL FLIMFLAM FOLDEROL
GIMCRACK KICKSHAW MOLEHILL
BAGATELLE
(— WITH) JANK DANDLE DELUDE
NIGGLE
(ATTRACTIVE —) CONCEIT
(LITERARY —) TOY
(MERE —) SONG STRAW
(MEREST —) FIG
(SHOWY —) WALLY
TRIFLER PLAYER WANTON FLANEUR
FOOTLER TWIDDLER WHIFFLER
TRIFLING AIRY IDLE FUNNY INANE LIGHT
PETTY POTTY SILLY SMALL FLIMSY
FUTILE LEVITY LITTLE PALTRY SIMPLE
TOYISH FOOLISH NOMINAL TRIVIAL
COQUETRY FIDDLING FLIMFLAM
FRIPPERY PIDDLING NEGLIGIBLE
TRILBY (AUTHOR OF —) DUMAURIER

(CHARACTER IN —) ALICE GECKO SANDY TAFFY BILLEE TRILBY OFERRALL SVENGALI
TRILL BURR ROLL SHAKE QUAVER THRILL WARBLE ROULADE
TRIM AX CUT LOP NET BEAD CLIP CROP DEFT FEAT HACK LACE NEAT SNUG STOW TACK TOSH TRIG BRAID BRUSH CLEAN DRESS FITTY GENTY KEMPT KNIFE NATTY PREEN PRUNE PURGE SHAVE SHEAR SLEEK SMART TIGHT BARBER DAPPER PICKED REFORM SOIGNE SPRUCE SVELTE CHIPPER FLOUNCE SCISSOR MANICURE ORNAMENT SHIPSHAPE
(— A BOAT) SIT
(— ENDS OF HAIR) SHIRL
(— HEDGE) DUB
(— HIDES) ROUND
(— MEAT) CONDITION
(— SAIL) FILL
(— SEAMS) FETTLE
(— SHOE) FOX
(— TREES) PRIME SWAMP
(— WITH EMBROIDERY) GIMP PANEL
TRIMMING FUR GIMP LACE BRAID COQUE FRILL GUARD INKLE JABOT RUCHE ERMINE LACING PURFLE BEADING CASCADE MARABOU PUFFING ROULEAU FOLDEROL FROUFROU FURBELOW PEARLING PICKADIL SOUTACHE SPAGHETTI
TRINIDAD-TOBAGO (CAPITAL OF —) PORTOFSPAIN
(POINT OF —) GALERA
(RIVER OF —) ORTOIRE
(TOWN OF —) TOCO ARIMA COUVA LABREA MORUGA SIPARIA
TRINITY TRIAD TRINE TRIUNE GODHEAD TRIMURTI
TRINKET TOY DIDO GAUD BIJOU KNACK BAUBLE DEVICE DOODAD GEWGAW BIBELOT TRANKUM GIMCRACK KICKSHAW
TRIP HOP JET JOG TIP FOOT GAIT SKIP TOUR TROT TURN DANCE DRIVE HITCH JAUNT SALLY CRUISE ERRAND FLIGHT HEGIRA OUTING RAMBLE SAFARI VOYAGE JOURNEY STUMBLE
(— ALONG) CHIP LINK
(— BY DOG TEAM) MUSH
(— IN WRESTLING) CHIP CLICK
(— INTO COUNTRY) CAMPAIGN
(— UP) SUPPLANT
(HUNTING —) SHOOT
(PLEASURE —) JUNKET
TRIPOD CAT TRIP SPIDER TEAPOY TRIVET
TRISTAN UND ISOLDE
(CHARACTER IN —) MARK MELOT ISOLDE TRISTAN BRANGANE KURWENAL
(COMPOSER OF —) WAGNER
TRISTRAM SHANDY (AUTHOR OF —) STERNE
(CHARACTER IN —) SLOP TOBY TRIM BOBBY SHANDY WADMAN WALTER YORICK SUSANNAH TRISTRAM
TRITE WORN BANAL CORNY HOARY

MUSTY STALE VAPID BEATEN COMMON HACKNEY TRIVIAL BROMIDIC SHOPWORN
TRITON NEWT TRUMPET
(FATHER OF —) NEPTUNE
(MOTHER OF —) AMPHITRITE
TRIUMPH WIN CROW PALM PREVAIL VICTORY CONQUEST
TRIVET SPIDER TRIPOD TRESTLE BRANDISE
TRIVIAL BALD JERK NICE VAIN BANAL LIGHT PETTY SILLY SMALL FIDFAD PALTRY SLIGHT COMICAL PUERILE SHALLOW DOGGEREL FOOTLING GIMCRACK PIDDLING TRIFLING
(NOT —) SOLID EARNEST
TRIVIALITY FOLLY TRIFLE INANITY IDLENESS NONSENSE NUGACITY
TROILUS (BELOVED OF —) CRESSIDA
(FATHER OF —) PRIAM
(MOTHER OF —) HECUBA
(SLAYER OF —) ACHILLES
TROILUS AND CRESSIDA
(AUTHOR OF —) SHAKESPEARE
(CHARACTER IN —) AJAX HELEN PARIS PRIAM AENEAS HECTOR NESTOR ANTENOR CALCHAS HELENUS TROILUS ULYSSES ACHILLES CRESSIDA DIOMEDES MENELAUS PANDARUS AGAMEMNON ALEXANDER CASSANDRA DEIPHOBUS PATROCLUS THERSITES ANDROMACHE MARGARELON
TROLL HARL SPIN TROW ANGLE TRAWL
TROLLOP DOXY TRULL DOLLOP
TROOP FARE ROUT ROUTE STAND RISALA SCHOOL TROUPE COMPANY
(— OF ARMED MEN) CREW
(— OF FOXES) SKULK
(— OF WORSHIPPERS) THIASUS
(—S ATTACHED TO SOVEREIGN) GUARDS
(—S IN BATTLE ARRAY) SHELTRON
(—S ON WING OF ARMY) ALARES
(ASSAULTING —S) WAVE
(BOMBAY —S) DUCKS
(CAVALRY —) CORNET
(GIRL SCOUT —) SHIP
(LIGHT-ARMED —S) PSILOI
(MOUNTAIN —) ALPINI
(SCOTTISH —) JOCKS
TROPHY BAG EMMY PALM PRIZE SCALP REWARD LAURELS
(WRITING —) HUGO
TROT JOG TRIG FADGE HURRY
TROUBLE ADO AIL ILL IRK MAR VEX WOE BEAT BUSY EARN MASH MOIL PAIN ROUT SORE STIR WORK ANNOY BESET CROSS DUTCH GRIEF LABOR SMITE SPITE TWEAK WORRY BOTHER CUMBER DITHER EFFORT GRIEVE GRUDGE HARASS MOLEST RATTLE SORROW SQUALL UNEASE AFFLICT AGITATE ANXIETY CHAGRIN CONCERN DISEASE DISTURB EMBROIL INFLICT PERTURB SCRUPLE TRAVAIL TURMOIL DARKNESS DISORDER DISQUIET DISTRESS VEXATION
TROUBLED QUEASY CAREFUL FRETFUL HAUNTED AGITATED HARASSED

TROUBLESOME ILL SAD BUSY HARD
PESKY ROWDY TIGHT SHREWD STICKY
THORNY UNEASY HARMFUL PLAGUEY
ANNOYING SPITEFUL UNTOWARD
TROUGH BOX HOD RUN BACK BUNK
COVE DAIL DISH SHOE SINK TRAY VALE
CHUTE DITCH LAVER SHOOT SLIDE
SPOUT GUTTER HARBOR HOPPER
MANGER RUNNER SALTER SLUICE
VALLEY WALLOW CONDUIT TRENDLE
(— FOR ASHES) BAKIE
(— FOR COOLING INGOTS) BOSH
(— FOR PAPER PULP) RIFFLER
(— FOR WASHING ORE) TOM HUTCH
STRIP BUDDLE STRAKE
(— IN MONASTERY) LAVABO
(— OF A WAVE) SULK
(— OF CIDER MILL) CHASE
(— OF ROCK) SYNCLINE
(— OF THE SEA) ALVEUS
(ANNULAR —) CUP
(BAKER'S —) HUTCH
(EAVES —) CANAL CHENEAU
(GLACIAL —) DORR
(ORE —) TYE
(SHEEP-DIPPING —) DUP
(WOODEN —) TRUG BAKIE TROGUE
TROUNCE MOP FLOG TRAMP WHOMP
CUDGEL SHELLAC
TROUSERS BAGS CORDS DUCKS JEANS
KICKS PANTS SLOPS TONGS TREWS
CHINOS DENIMS FLARES SHORTS
SLACKS WHITES BOTTOMS KERSEYS
SHALWAR STRIDES BLOOMERS
BREECHES FLANNELS MOLESKIN
NANKEENS OVERALLS PANTALOONS
TROUT CHAR KELT POGY BROOK BROWN
LAKER SEWEN SHARD FINNOC KIPPER
MYKISS QUASKY TAIMEN TRUCHA
TULADI BOREGAT BROOKIE BROWNIE
COASTER HERLING OQUASSA RAINBOW
HARDHEAD KAMLOOPS SISCOWET
(SMALL —) SCURLING SKIRLING
(YOUNG —) WHITLING
TROVATORE, IL (CHARACTER IN —)
INEZ RUIZ DILUNA AZUCENA LEONORA
MANRICO FERRANDO
(COMPOSER OF —) VERDI
TROWEL HAWK PIPE DARBY
(HEARTSHAPED —) HEART DOGTAIL
(MOLDER'S —) LEAF TAPER
(PLASTERER'S —) FLOAT
TRUANT HOOKY MICHER TRIVANT
VAGRANT
TRUCE PAX BARLEY TREAGUE INDUCIAE
TRUCK DRAG DUCK DUMP RACK BOGIE
BUGGY DOLLY GILLY LORRY TROKE
DIESEL DROGUE DUMPER JITNEY PICKUP
TIPPER TURTLE CARAVAN GONDOLA
SLEEPER TROLLEY TRUNDLE DELIVERY
TRANSFER
(COAL —) DAN
(FIRE —) PUMPER
(LOGGING —) BUNK BUMMER
(MINING —) CORF SKIP BARNEY
(PART OF —) DECK HOOD STEP TANK
TIRE GUARD LIGHT STAKE WHEEL
BUMPER GRILLE MIRROR AIRHORN
CARRIER EXHAUST MUDFLAP BULKHEAD
HEADLIGHT TAILLIGHT COMPRESSOR
WINDSHIELD
(TIMBER —) DRUG WYNN
TRUCULENT MEAN CRUEL HARSH
FIERCE SAVAGE SCATHING
TRUDGE JOG PAD PLOD JAUNT TRACE
TRAMP STODGE TRAIPSE
TRUE SO GOOD JUST LEAL PURE REAL
VERY VRAI PLUMB RIGHT SOOTH SOUND
ACTUAL LAWFUL DEVOTED GENUINE
GERMANE PRECISE SINCERE STAUNCH
FAITHFUL RELIABLE RIGHTFUL UNERRING
(— TO THE FACT) LITERAL
(QUESTIONABLY —) ALLEGED
TRULY YEA EVEN IWIS JUST QUITE
SOOTH TIGHT DINKUM INDEED VERILY
VERAMENT
TRUMP DIX LOW PAM LILY RUFF BASTA
TROMBE MANILLA MATADOR TRIUMPH
SPADILLE
(NOT —S) LAY
(2ND HIGHEST —) MANILLE
TRUMPET LURE TUBA SHELL TRUMP
CORNET KERANA LITUUS TROMBA
BUCCINA CLARINO CLARION KERRANA
SALPINX NARSINGA SOURDINE
(— OF DAFFODIL) CORONA
TRUNCHEON BATON BILLY WARDER
PARTISAN SPONTOON
TRUNK BOX BODY BULK KIST LICH STEM
STUD CABER SHAFT STOCK TORSO
BARREL CAUDEX COFFER LOCKER
CARCASS STOWAGE SARATOGA
(ARTERIAL —) AORTA
(ELEPHANT'S —) SNOUT
(FOSSIL —) CYCAD
(SMALL —) HATBOX
(SPLIT —) PUNCHEON
(SWIM —S) JAMS
(TREE —) BOLE BUTT STICK RICKER
(TREE — OVER 8 INCHES IN
DIAMETER) MAST
(TRIMMED TREE —) LOG
(WORSHIPPED TREE —) IRMINSUL
TRUSS SPAN WARREN DORLACH
(— OF STRAW) WAP
(— UP) KILT
TRUST AFFY HOPE POOL RELY REST TICK
TROW FAITH GROUP TRUTH BELIEF
CARTEL CHARGE CORNER CREDIT
DEPEND TICKET BELIEVE COMBINE
CONFIDE CREANCE SECRECY VENTURE
AFFIANCE CREDENCE MONOPOLY
RELIANCE
TRUSTEE CURATOR FEOFFEE SINDICO
VISITOR ASSIGNEE MUTWALLI
TRUSTWORTHINESS HONOR TRUST
CREDIT HONESTY CREDENCE
TRUSTWORTHY SAFE SURE TRIG
SOOTH SOUND TRIED HONEST SECURE
STABLE TRUSTY COCKSURE CREDIBLE
FIDUCIAL RELIABLE
TRUSTY TRIG FECKFUL STAUNCH
FAITHFUL RELIABLE
TRUTH TAO UNA SOOTH WHITE SATTVA

VERITY LOWDOWN VERITAS VERACITY
VERIDITY
(IDEAL —) CHRIST DHARMA
(IN —) CERTES
(ULTIMATE —) LIGHT SUNYATA
TRUTHFUL TRUE VERY SOOTH HONEST
VERIDIC
TRUTHFULNESS HONESTY VERACITY
SINCERITY
TRY GO SAY HACK PASS SEEK TEST TURN
ASSAY CRACK ESSAY ETTLE GROPE
JUDGE OFFER PROVE SENSE SOUND
TASTE TOUCH WHACK WHIRL ASSAIL
GRIEVE AFFLICT APPROVE ATTEMPT
DISCUSS IMITATE ENDEAVOR STRUGGLE
(— DESPERATELY) AGONIZE
(— FOR GOAL) SHOT
(— HARD) STRIVE
(— OUT) SAMPLE AUDITION
(— TO ATTAIN) AFFECT
(CASUAL —) FLING
(QUICK —) SLAP
TRYING NASTY ARDUOUS CRUCIAL
GRUELING
TUB FAT SOW TUN VAT BOWK COWL
KNOP KNOT TYNE BOWIE ESHIN KIVER
SKEEL STAND BUCKET KEELER TROUGH
TURNEL BREAKER TANKARD KOOLIMAN
(— FOR ALEWIVES) HOD
(— FOR AMALGAMATING ORES)
TINA
(— FOR BREAD) BARGE
(— OF BUTTER) COOL
(— OF HOGWASH) SWILLTUB
(— USED AS DIPPER) HANDY PIGGIN
(— WITH SLOPING SIDES) SHAUL
(BREWER'S —) BACK KEEVE
(LAUNDRY —) WASHTRAY
(MESS —) KID KIT
(MINING —) CORF
(TANNING —) LEACH
(WATER —) DAN JAILER
(WOODEN —) KIT SOE KIMNEL TRINDLE
TUBE BOOT CANE CASE CAST CORE CURL
DRUM DUCT HORN HOSE PIPE REED
CANAL CORER DRAIN GLAND QUILL
SLIDE SPILE SPOUT THECA THIEF TRUMP
VALVE CANNEL CANNON COLUMN
FILTER GULLET HEADER NOZZLE SLEEVE
SYRINX THROAT TRIODE TUBING TUBULE
TUNNEL UPTAKE BLOWGUN CHIMNEY
CONDUIT CUVETTE DROPPER FERRULE
FISTULA HOUSING OOBLAST OVIDUCT
SALPINX SHALLOT SNORTER STOPPLE
ADJUTAGE CORNICLE DIATREME
DRAWTUBE FAIRLEAD GRADUATE
PIPESTEM
(— AT BASE OF PETAL) CALCAR
(— CARRYING BASSOON
MOUTHPIECE) CROOK
(— COVERING TRACE CHAIN) PIPING
(— FOR DEPOSITING CONCRETE)
TREMIE
(— FOR DRINKING MATE) BOMBILLA
(— FOR LINING WELL) WELLRING
(— FOR STIFFENING STRING) TAG

(— FOR TRANSFERRING LIQUID)
SIPHON
(— FOR WINDING THREAD) COP
(— FROM SHIP'S PUMP) DALE
(— IN ENGINE CYLINDER) LINER
(— OF BALLOON) APPENDIX
(— OF GUN) BORE BARREL
(— OF RETORT) BEAK ROSTRUM
(— OF SPIRIT LEVEL) BUBBLE
(— TO LINE A VENT) BOUCHE
(— TWISTED IN COILS) WORM
(— USED IN WHALING) LULL
(AMPLIFIER —) STAGE
(BONE —) SNUFFER
(CAMERA —) ORTHICON
(DISTILLING —) TOWER
(ELECTRO —) BULB
(ELECTRODE —) AUDION PENTODE
(ELECTRON —) DIODE DRIVER TETRODE
KENOTRON KLYSTRON PLIOTRON
TRINISCOPE
(FIREWORKS —) LEADER
(GLANDULAR —) CRYPT
(GLASS —) SIGHT MATRASS
(GLASSBLOWER'S —) BLOWPIPE
(HONEY —) NECTARY SIPHONET
(KNITTED —) STOCKING
(PAPER —) LEADER PASTILLE
(PASTRY —) CORNET
(POLLEN —) SPERMARY
(PRIMING —) AUGET
(RECTIFIER —) IGNITRON
(SILK — OF SPIDER) SPIGOT
(SPEAKING —) GOSPORT
(SUCKING —) STRAW
(SURGICAL —) CANNULA
(THERMOMETER —) STEM
(VACUUM —) DIODE KEYER HEXODE
HEPTODE DYNATRON MAGNETRON
TUBERCULOSIS CON LUPUS CLYERS
DECLINE PHTHISIS SCROFULA
TUBULAR PIPED QUILLED CANNULAR
TUBULE TRACHEA TUBULET TUBULUS
TUCANO BETOYAN
TUCK STUFF TRUSS FLANGE
(— UP) FAKE KILT
TUFT NOB DOWN KNOB KNOP TATE TUFF
WISP BUNCH CREST STUPA WHISK
CATKIN CIRRUS DOLLOP PENCIL TASSEL
TUFFET CIRRHUS PANACHE TOPPING
AIGRETTE FLOCCULE
(— OF BRISTLES) BIRSE
(— OF CLOTH) FAG
(— OF DIRTY WOOL) DAG
(— OF DOWN) FRIEZE
(— OF FEATHERS) EAR HORN HULU
EGRET
(— OF FILAMENTS) BYSSUS
(— OF GRASS) FAG SOP MOCK
HASSOCK TUSSOCK
(— OF HAIR) TOP COMA TUZZ BRUSH
SWITCH COWLICK FEATHER FLOCCUS
SCOPULA TOPKNOT IMPERIAL KROBYLOS
(— OF HAIR ON HORSE'S HOOF)
FETLOCK
(— OF HAY) SOP
(— OF MALE TURKEY) BEARD

(— OF WOOL) FOB TUSK TUZZ FLOCK
(— ON BIRD'S HEAD) COP CUCK EGRET
(— ON BONNET) TOORIE
(— ON PINEAPPLE) CROWN
(— ON SEED PLANT) PAPPUS
(— ON SPIDER'S FEET) SCOPULA
(—S OF ROPE YARN) THRUM
(VASCULAR —) GLOMUS
TUG LUG TOG DRAG HALE HAUL PULL
TOIL TUCK HITCH PLUCK SHRUG
TOWBOAT TUGBOAT
TULIP LILY LILIUM BIZARRE BREEDER
PICOTEE TURNSOLE
TUMBLE COUP SPILL THROW GROVEL
TOPPLE WALTER WAMBLE WELTER
STUMBLE
(— OVER) TIPPLE WALLOP
TUMBLER NUT CLICK GLASS LEVER
WIPER ROLLER ACROBAT TOPPLER
TUMID TURGID BLOATED BULGING
FUSTIAN INFLATED
TUMOR PAP WEN BEAL WART AMPER
BOTCH MYOMA NEVUS PHYMA SWELL
TALPA ANBURY EPULIS GLIOMA GYROMA
INCOME KELOID LIPOMA MYXOMA
NUROMA RISING WARBLE ADENOMA
ANGIOMA CYSTOMA DERMOID DESMOID
FIBROID FIBROMA LUTEOMA MYELOMA
NEUROMA OSTEOMA OSTEOME
SARCOMA TESTUDO THYMOMA
ULONCUS ATHEROMA BLASTOMA
CHLOROMA CHORIOMA EMBRYOMA
GANGLION GLANDULE HEMATOMA
HEPATOMA HOLDFAST LYMPHOMA
MELANOMA MELICERA NEOPLASM
ODONTOMA PHLEGMON PLASMOMA
PSAMMOMA SCIRRHUS SEMINOMA
TERATOID TERATOMA WINDGALL
CHALAZION PAPILLOMA
(— OF EYELID) GRANDO
(— ON HORSES'S LEGS) JARDE
(PUSTULAR —) BLAIN
(SKIN —) OUCH
TUMULT DIN FARE FRAY FUSS MUSS
RIOT ROUT BRAWL BROIL HURLY HURRY
NOISE WHIRL BUSTLE CLAMOR DIRDUM
FRACAS HUBBUB MUTINY RABBLE
RUFFLE SHINDY UPROAR BLUSTER
FERMENT TEMPEST TURMOIL DISORDER
SEDITION STIRRING COMMOTION
PANDEMONIUM
TUMULTUOUS HIGH LOUD RUDE NOISY
ROUGH STORMY FURIOUS HURRIED
RIOTOUS VIOLENT AGITATED CONFUSED
TUNE AIR ARIA NOTE SONG CHARM
CHORD DRANT ATTUNE MAGGOT STRAIN
TEMPER HALLING MEASURE MELISMA
SONANCE HABANERA
(— A HARP) WREST
(— AN INSTRUMENT) STRING
(DANCE —) FURIANT ANGLAISE
GALLIARD
(FOLK —) FADO
(HILLBILLY —) HOEDOWN
(LIGHT —) TOY
(LITTLE —) CATCH
(LIVELY —) LILT SPRING HORNPIPE

(MELANCHOLY —) DUMP
(SACRED —) CHORAL CHORALE
(TRADITIONAL —) TONE
TUNIC COAT JAMA JUPE VEST COTTE
FROCK GIPPO JUPON PALLA CAMISE
CHITON HARDIE KIRTLE TABARD
BLEAUNT SURCOAT COLOBIUM
GANDOURA
(— OF MAIL) HAUBERK
(HOODED FUR —) SOVIK

TUNISIA

CAPE: BON BLANC
CAPITAL: TUNIS
COIN: DINAR
GULF: GABES TUNIS HAMMAMET
ISLAND: DJERBA
LAKE: ACHKEL DJERID BIZERTE
MEASURE: SAA SAH SAAH CAFIZ WHIBA
METTAR
PORT: SFAX GABES TUNIS SOUSSE
BIZERTE
RIVER: MEDJERDA
TOWN: BEJA DOUZ SFAX SUSA GABES
GAFSA THALA MATEUR NABEUL SOUSSE
BIZERTE JENDOUBA KAIROUAN
TEBOURBA ZAGHOUAN
WEIGHT: SAA ROTL ARTAL ARTEL RATEL
UCKIA KANTAR

TUNNEL ADIT BORE CAVE SINK TUBE
DRIFT DRIVE BURROW PIERCE
(— INTO AN IGLOO) TOSSUT
(PROPOSED —) CHUNNEL
TURANDOT (CHARACTER IN —) LIU
CALAF TURANDOT
(COMPOSER OF —) PUCCINI
TURBAN PAT MOAB TUFT LUNGI TOWEL
TUFFE MANDIL KAFFIYEH PUGGAREE
SEERBAND TOLIPANE
TURBID FAT RILY MUDDY ROILY GRUMLY
FECULENT LUTULENT
TURBULENCE FURY UPROAR FERMENT
RIOTING
(— IN WATER) BULLER
TURBULENT HIGH LOUD RUDE WILD
ROILY ROUGH WROTH RUGGED STORMY
UNRULY YEASTY FURIOUS RACKETY
VIOLENT MUTINOUS BOISTEROUS
TURF SOD CESS DELF FLAG FLAT PONE
SUNK SCRAW SWARD FLAUGHT SHIRREL
(— CUT BY GOLF STROKE) DIVOT
(— FOR LINING PARAPET) GAZON
(DRIED — FOR FUEL) VAG
(PARED —) BEAT
(ROUGH —) GOR
(SMALL PIECE OF —) TAB
(THIN LAYER OF —) FLAW
TURGID ERECT TUMID BLOATED
INFLATED PLETHORIC
TURKEY BU9T FLOP STAG BUSTARD
ERECTOR GOBBLER
(BRUSH —) VULTURN TALEGALLA
(MALE —) TOM
(YOUNG —) POULT

TURKEY

CAPE: INCE BAFRA ANAMUR HINZIR KARATAS KEREMPE

CAPITAL: ANKARA

COIN: PARA AKCHA ASPER ATTUN REBIA AKCHEH SEQUIN ZEQUIN ALTILIK BESHLIK PATAQUE PIASTER MEDJIDIE ZECCHINO

DISTRICT: PERA BEYOGLU CILICIA

GULF: COS ANTALYA

LAKE: TUZ VAN EGRIDIR BEYSEHIR

MEASURE: DRA OKA OKE PIK DRAA HATT KHAT KILE ZIRA ALMUD BERRI DONUM KILEH ZIRAI ARSHIN CHINIK DJERIB FORTIN HALEBI PARMAK NOCKTAT

MOUNTAIN: AK ALA KARA HASAN HINIS HONAZ MURAT MURIT ARARAT BINGOL BOLGAR SUPHAN ERCIYAS KARACALI

PROVINCE: MUS VAN AGRI BOLU ICEL KARS ORDU RIZE SERT URFA USAK AYDIN BURSA IZMIR SIIRT ANGORA EYALET

RIVER: DICLE FIRAT GEDIZ HALYS IRMAK KIZIL MESTA SARUS SEIHUN SEYHAN SEYLAN TIGRIS SAKARYA MAEANDER

SEAPORT: ENOS IZMIR MERSIN SAMSUN TRABZON ISTANBUL

TOWN: URFA ADANA BURSA IZMIR KONYA MARAS SIIRT SIVAS AINTAB EDESSA EDIRNE ELAZIG MARASH SAMSUN ERZURUM KAYSERI SCUTARI USKUDAR ISTANBUL STAMBOUL

WEIGHT: OKA OKE DRAM KILE ROTL ARTAL ARTEL CEQUI CHEKE KERAT MAUND OBOLU RATEL BATMAN DIRHEM KANTAR MISKAL DRACHMA QUINTAL YUSDRUM

TURMOIL ADO DIN COIL MOIL TOIL HURLY HURRY TOUSE WHIRL HASSLE POTHER UPROAR WELTER CLUTTER FERMENT RUMMAGE TEMPEST DISQUIET

TURN BOW CUT GEE JAR RUN WIN BOUT BOWL CAST CHOP EDDY GIRO HEAD HINT HURL JAMB KINK PULL PURL ROLL ROVE VEER WAFT WIND ANGLE BLANK CRANK CRASH CROOK ELBOW PIVOT PRICK QUIRK SHIFT SPELL SWING SWIRL TREND TROLL TWINE TWIST WHEEL WREST CIRCLE COURSE DEPEND GRUPPO GYRATE INDENT RESORT ROTATE SPIRAL STRAIN SWIVEL VOLUTE CONVERT CRINKLE DEFLECT DISTURB FLEXION FLEXURE FLOUNCE INCLINE INFLECT PASSADE REVERSE REVOLVE SERPENT SINUATE TWISTER WREATHE TRAVERSE VOLUTION

(— ABOUT) SLEW SLUE SLOUGH WINDLASS

(— AGAINST) CROSS

(— AROUND) GYRE WELT WEND RATCH BEWEND SPHERE

(— ASIDE) ERR WRY DAFF SKEW WARD ABHOR AVERT BLENK DETER EVADE FENCE GLENT SHEER WAIVE BLENCH DEPART DETURN DIVERT SWERVE SWITCH CRINKLE DECLINE DEFLECT DEVIATE DIGRESS DIVERGE PERVERT SCRITHE

(— AT DRINKING) TIRL

(— AWAY) DOFF AVERT CHARE HIELD REPEL DESERT DIVERT REVOLT ABANDON DECLINE REVERSE OVERTURN WITHTURN

(— BACK) KEP ABORT FLYPE RETORT RETURN REVERT REFLECT UNTWIST

(— DOWN) DIP DENY VETO

(— INSIDE OUT) EVERT FLYPE INVERT

(— LEAVES OF BOOK) LEAF TOSS

(— OF AFFAIRS) GO JOB KICK

(— OF DUTY) TOUR SHIFT TRICK

(— OFF) SHUNT DIVERT

(— OUT) GO USH BEAR FALL FARE OUST SORT TAKE CHIVE FUDGE OUTPUT SUCCEED

(— OVER) CANT FLAP FLIP KEEL VETTE VOLVE CLINCH DESIGN AGITATE CAPSIZE OVERSET

(— RAPIDLY) SPIN TIRL GIDDY

(— SOUR) FOX BLINK PRILL BLEEZE CHANGE SOUREN

(— SUDDENLY) FLOP SLUE

(— UPSIDE DOWN) CANT COUP WHELM INVERT QUELME WHELVE WHEMMLE

(SHARP —) DOUBLE WRENCH ZIGZAG HAIRPIN

(SKI —) SWING CHRISTIE TELEMARK

(SUDDEN —) CURL

TURNCOAT APOSTATE RENEGADE

TURNIP BAGA NEEP RAPE NAVEW SWEDE

TURN OF THE SCREW
(AUTHOR OF —) JAMES
(CHARACTER IN —) FLORA MILES PETER QUINT JESSEL

TURNOUT RIG TEAM SETOUT EQUIPAGE

TURNTABLE DECK RACER ROTARY NONSYNC PLAYBACK

TURRET ROUND BELFRY CUPOLA GARRET GAZEBO LOUVER MIRADOR MONITOR BARBETTE BARTIZAN PEPPERBOX

TURTLE EMYD ARRAU JURARA SLIDER THURGI CRAWLER JUNIATA LOGHEAD SNAPPER TORTUGA CHELONID HAWKBILL MATAMATA STINKPOT TERRAPIN TORTOISE

(— HAVING COMMERCIAL SHELL) CHICKEN

(OLD —) MOSSBACK

TUSK GAM CUSK HORN IVORY TOOTH

(— OF WILD BOAR) RAZOR

(ELEPHANT'S —) SCRIVELLO

TUSSLE TUG SCRAP BICKER TUILYIE

TUTELAGE TUTELE YEMSEL NURTURE TEACHING

TUTOR DON ABBE COACH DOCENT FEEDER MASTER PEDANT GRINDER TEACHER PANGLOSS PRECEPTOR

TUVALU (CAPITAL OF —) FUNAFUTI
(ISLAND OF —) NANUMEA NUKUFETAU NUKULAILAI

TWADDLE ROT BOSH FUDGE BABBLE DRIVEL FOOTLE PIFFLE NONSENSE SLIPSLOP TOMMYROT

TWANG TANG PLUCK PLUNK SNUFFLE

TWEEZERS TWIRK TWINGE MULLETS PINCERS VOLSELLA

TWELFTH NIGHT (AUTHOR OF —) SHAKESPEARE
  (CHARACTER IN —) TOBY BELCH CURIO FESTE MARIA VIOLA ANDREW FABIAN OLIVIA ORSINO ANTONIO MALVOLIO AGUECHEEK SEBASTIAN VALENTINE

TWELVE DOZEN DICKER DODECADE

TWENTY KAPH CORGE KAPPA SCORE COOREE

20,000 LEAGUES UNDER THE SEA (AUTHOR OF —) VERNE
  (CHARACTER IN —) NED LAND NEMO PIERRE ARONNAX CONSEIL CONSEIL

TWIG CHAT RISP SLIP WAND YARD BIRCH BRIAR BRIER SHRAG SPRAY SPRIG STICK TWIST VIRGA WITHE FESCUE GREAVE SWITCH WATTLE WICKER TWIGLET
  (— FOR SNUFF) DIP
  (— GROWING FROM STUMP) WAVER
  (— IN BIRD SNARE) SWEEK
  (— WORN AT SACRIFICES) INARCULUM
  (—S FOR BURNING) CHATWOOD
  (—S FOR WATTLING) FRITLES
  (—S MADE INTO BROOM) BESOM
  (BARE —) COW
  (BROKEN —S) BRUSH
  (CUT —) SARMENT
  (DRIED —) CHAD
  (LITTLE —) SURCLE
  (THATCHING —) SCOLLOP
  (WILLOW —) SALLOW ANAPHYTE
  (SUFF.) CLEMA

TWILIGHT EVE DUMPS DIMMET COCKSHUT EVENFALL GLOAMING CREPUSCLE
  (— OF THE GODS) RAGNAROK
  (DARKER PART OF —) DUSK
  (MORNING —) DAWN

TWILL WALE CHINO CADDIS RUSSEL DUNGAREE

TWIN DUAL GEMEL SOSIE DIDYMUS JUMELLE SIAMESE TWINLING

TWINE MAT COIL LACE WIND WRAP TWIRL TWIST INFOLD INTORT ENTWINE SKEENYIE
  (HANK OF —) RAN
  (PITCHED —) WHIPPING

TWINGE PANG PULL SHOOT TOUCH TWANG STOUND
  (— OF CONSCIENCE) SCRUPLE
  (— OF PAIN) GLISK

TWINKLE WINK BLINK BICKER SIMPER WINKLE SPARKLE

TWIRL SPIN TWIST WHIRL TRUNDLE TWIDDLE
  (— OF BAGPIPE) WARBLER

TWIST BOB MAT PLY COIL CURL DRAW KICK PIRL SKEW SLUE TURN WARP WIND WISP CRICK CROOK CURVE GNARL PLAIT REEVE SCREW SNAKE SWIRL THRAW THROW TWEAK TWINE TWIRL WINCE WITHE WREST DETORT HANKLE SLOUGH SPRAIN STRAND WRITHE CHIGNON CRINKLE CRUMPLE DISTORT ENTWINE ENTWIST FLOUNCE SQUINCH TORTURE WREATHE WRIGGLE CLINAMEN CONVOLVE ENTANGLE SQUIGGLE
  (— A ROPE) DALLY
  (— AWAY) WAIVE
  (— BACK) RETORT
  (— FORCIBLY) WRING
  (— IN A ROPE) GRIND SQUIRM
  (— IN GRAIN OF A BOW) BOUGHT
  (— IN ONE'S NATURE) KINK
  (— OF FACE) STITCH
  (— OF HAY) HAYBRAND
  (— OF PAPER) SPILL
  (— OF PEN IN WRITING) QUIRK
  (— OF SPEECH) CRANK
  (— OF THE MOUTH) DRAD
  (— OF TOBACCO) ROLL PIGTAIL
  (— OF YARNS) FORETURN
  (— OUT OF SHAPE) BUCKLE CONTORT
  (— SHARPLY) FEAK
  (— TOGETHER) CABLE RADDLE

TWISTED CAM WRY AWRY KINKY SCREW TORSE WRONG GAUCHE HURLED KNOTTY SCREWY SKEWED SWIRLY THRAWN WARPED CROOKED GNARLED KNOTTED SCREWED TORQUED WREATHY COCKEYED INVOLVED

TWISTING KNECK TWIRLY TWIDDLY SQUIGGLY STREPSIS TORTUOUS

TWITCH TIC FIRK JERK JUMP WINK YANK PLUCK START THRIP TWEAK TWINGE VELLICATE

TWITTER TWIT CHIRM CHIRP GARRE WARBLE CHIRRUP

TWOFOLD DUAL BINAL DUPLE BACKED BIFOLD DOUBLE DUPLEX DIPLOID BIFARIOUS

TWO GENTLEMEN OF VERONA (AUTHOR OF —) SHAKESPEARE
  (CHARACTER IN —) JULIA MILAN SPEED LAUNCE SILVIA THURIO ANTONIO LUCETTA PROTEUS EGLAMOUR PANTHINO VALENTINE

TYCOON SHOGUN TAIKUN

TYMPANUM DRUM EARDRUM EPIPHRAGM

TYNDAREUS (BROTHER OF —) ICARIUS
  (DAUGHTER OF —) PHILOPOE TIMANDRA CLYTEMNESTRA
  (FATHER OF —) OEBALUS PERIERES
  (MOTHER OF —) BATIA GORGOPHONE
  (WIFE OF —) LEDA

TYPE CUT ILK CAST KIND MAKE MOLD NORM SORT BROOD IMAGE MOULD PRINT STAMP EMBLEM KIDNEY LETTER NATURE STRIPE SYMBOL TAKING TIMBER FASHION PARABLE EXEMPLAR
  (— PLACED BOTTOM UP) TURN

(— SET UP) MATTER
(ASSORTMENT OF —) FONT
(DISARRANGED —) PI PIE
(GERMAN —) FRAKTUR
(HEAVY-FACED —) IONIC
(HIGHEST —) PINK
(IDEAL —) CHRIST
(REPRESENTATIVE —) GENIUS
(SET —) STICK
(STYLE OF —) CANON DORIC ELITE
GOUDY GREEK IONIC KABEL ROMAN
BODONI CASLON CICERO GOTHIC
HEBREW ITALIC JENSON MODERN
BOOKMAN BREVIER CENTURY ELZEVIR
EMERALD FULLFACE GARAMOND
TYPEE (AUTHOR OF —) MELVILLE

(CHARACTER IN —) TOM TOBY
MARNOO MEHEVI FAYAWAY KORYKORY
TYPEWRITER MILL TYPER TYPIST
PORTABLE
TYPHOON WIND CYCLONE
TYPICAL FAIR USUAL AVERAGE CLASSIC
PATTERN PERFECT REGULAR
TYPIFY IMAGE EPITOMIZE PERSONIFY
REPRESENT SYMBOLIZE
TYRANNICAL LORDLY SLAVISH
ABSOLUTE DESPOTIC
TYRANNY ROD DESPOTISM
TYRANT ANARCH DESPOT NIMROD
FUEHRER PHARAOH PHALARIS
TYRO HAM BABE COLT PUPIL NOVICE
RABBIT BEGINNER NEOPHYTE

U

U UNCLE UNION

UGANDA

CAPITAL: KAMPALA
LAKE: KYOGA ALBERT EDWARD GEORGE VICTORIA
LANGUAGE: ATESO GANDA LUGANDA SWAHILI
MOUNTAIN: ELGON MARGHERITA
MOUNTAIN RANGE: RUWENZORI
NATIVE: ATESO BANTU LANGO ACHOLI ANKOLE BAGISU BAKIGA BASOGA BATORO BAGANDA BUNYORO LUGBARA NILOTIC SUDANIC
PLATEAU: ANKOLE
PROVINCE: BUGANDA
RIVER: ASWA KAFU PAGER KATONGA
SEAPORT: MOMBASA
TOWN: ARUA JINJA MBALE KITGUM MOROTO TORORO ENTEBBE MOMBASA
WATERFALL: KABALEGA

UGLY FOUL AWFUL CRANKY GORGON HOMELY ORNERY CRABBED GRIZZLY HIDEOUS VICIOUS GRUESOME MONSTROUS
UGLY-TEMPERED SNARLISH
UKULELE UKE TAROPATCH
ULCER FRET KYLE SORE WOLF BOTCH ISSUE RUPIA APHTHA TETTER BEDSORE CHANCRE EGILOPS FISTULA FONTANEL
ULCERATION NOMA CANKER CARIES BEDSORE HELCOSIS
ULTIMATE IT NTH DIRE LAST FINAL SUPREME ABSOLUTE EVENTUAL FARTHEST
ULTIMO PAST
ULTRA EXTREME FANATIC FORWARD
ULYSSES (AUTHOR OF —) JOYCE (CHARACTER IN —) BUCK RUDY BLOOM BREEN MOLLY BLAZES BOYLAN COFFEY GERTIE HAINES MARION DEDALUS LEOPOLD PUREFOY STEPHEN MULLIGAN MACDOWELL (FATHER OF —) LAERTES (MOTHER OF —) ANTICLEA (SLAYER OF —) TELEGONUS (SON OF —) TELEMACHUS (WIFE OF —) PENELOPE
UMBRELLA GAMP MUSH DUMPY BROLLY CHATTA PAYONG PILEUS CHATTAH GINGHAM
UMPIRE JUDGE TRIER ARBITER ODDSMAN
UNABLE UNHABILE POWERLESS
UNACCOMPANIED BARE SOLO ALONE SECCO SINGLE

UNACCUSTOMED UNUSED STRANGE WONTLESS
UNADORNED DRY BALD PLAIN STARK RUSTIC SEVERE SIMPLE AUSTERE LITERAL
UNADULTERATED NET FRANK HONEST VIRGIN GENUINE SINCERE ABSOLUTE
UNAFFECTED EASY REAL PLAIN NATIVE RUSTIC SIMPLE ARTLESS BUCOLIC SINCERE
UNAFRAID BOLD BRAVE DEFIANT
UNALLOYED DEEP SOLID VIRGIN GENUINE
UNANIMOUS SOLID WHOLE UNIVOCAL
UNASSUMING SHY HUMBLE MODEST SIMPLE NATURAL RETIRING
UNATTRACTIVE BLAH UGLY PLAIN HOMELY FRUMPISH
UNAWARE WITLESS HEEDLESS INNOCENT OBLIVIOUS
UNBALANCED DOTTY NUTTY FRUITY UNEVEN FANATIC DERANGED LOPSIDED PIXILATED MOONSTRUCK
UNBECOMING RUDE INEPT PLAIN BENEATH IMPROPER INDECENT UNSEEMLY UNWORTHY
UNBELIEVER PAGAN ATHEIST DOUBTER INFIDEL SCOFFER SKEPTIC
UNBENDING RIGID STARK STERN STIFF OBDURATE RESOLUTE
UNBIASED FAIR JUST DETACHED
UNBIND FREE UNDO UNTIE UNGIRD
UNBLEMISHED FAIR PURE SOUND WHITE ENTIRE SPOTLESS
UNBOLT OPEN UNBAR UNPIN
UNBROKEN FLAT FERAL FLUSH SHEER SOLID SOUND SINGLE REGULAR STRAIGHT
UNBURDEN EMPTY UNLOAD UNSHIP
UNCANNY EERIE SCARY WEIRD CREEPY SPOOKY ELDRITCH
UNCEASING ENDLESS ETERNAL
UNCERTAIN DARK HAZY FLUKY SHADY SHAKY CASUAL CLOUDY FITFUL QUEASY CHANCEY DUBIOUS VARIOUS WILSOME DELICATE FUGITIVE INSECURE SLIPPERY TICKLISH
UNCERTAINTY MIST DOUBT DUBIETY CASUALTY MISTRUST SUSPENSE SKEPTICISM
UNCHANGEABLE FAST STABLE DURABLE ETERNAL
UNCHANGING STATIC ETERNAL UNIFORM CONSTANT
UNCHECKED LIBERAL RAMPANT REINLESS
UNCIVIL RUDE BLUFF ROUGH SURLY COARSE CRUSTY RUGGED IMPOLITE

UNCIVILIZED RUDE WILD SAVAGE BARBARIC IGNORANT

UNCLEAN FOUL VILE BLACK TARRY FILTHY IMPURE DEFILED

UNCLEAR DIM HAZY SHAGGY

UNCLE TOM'S CABIN
(AUTHOR OF —) STOWE
(CHARACTER IN —) EVA TOM BIRD CASSY CHLOE ELIZA HALEY HARRY LOKER MARKS SIMON TOPSY GEORGE HARRIS LEGREE RACHEL SHELBY SIMEON OPHELIA STCLAIR EMMELINE HALLIDAY

UNCLOSE OPE OPEN UNHASP DISCLOSE

UNCOMFORTABLE HOT EVIL POOR HARSH QUEASY STICKY

UNCOMMON MUCH NICE RARE SCARCE SPECIAL STRANGE UNUSUAL SINGULAR

UNCOMPLICATED RURAL HONEST SIMPLE

UNCOMPROMISING ACID FIRM GRIM RIGID STERN STOUT SEVERE STRICT STRONG EXTREME BRASSBOUND

UNCONCEALED BARE OPEN APPARENT

UNCONCERNED COOL EASY BLAND CASUAL CARELESS

UNCONDITIONAL FREE FRANK UTTER SIMPLE ABSOLUTE EXPLICIT

UNCONGENIAL HATEFUL INGRATE KINDLESS

UNCONSCIOUS OUT COLD ASLEEP BLOTTO CUCKOO TORPID UNAWARE WITLESS COMATOSE IGNORANT SENSELESS

UNCONTROLLED FREE MADCAP LIBERAL ABSOLUTE

UNCONVENTIONAL FLAKY GYPSY LOOSE CASUAL DEVIOUS ODDBALL OFFBEAT BOHEMIAN INFORMAL

UNCOUTH RUDE CRUDE ROUGH GOTHIC AWKWARD BOORISH LOUTISH UNGAINLY

UNCOVER BARE DOFF BREAK STRIP DETECT EXHUME SEARCH UNVEIL UNDRAPE UNEARTH DISCLOSE DISCOVER UNMANTLE

UNCTUOUS FAT OILY SLEEK SUAVE GREASY PINGUID

UNCULTIVATED RAW FERAL DESERT FALLOW SAVAGE

UNCULTURED RUDE INCULT ARTLESS

UNDAUNTED BOLD BRAVE MANLY SPARTAN FEARLESS INTREPID

UNDEFILED PURE CHASTE INTACT VIRGIN

UNDER SUB BELOW INFRA NEATH SOTTO

UNDERBRUSH COVERT MAQUIS RAMMEL ABATURE

UNDERCOAT PILE ALPACA SURFACER
(WOOL OF — OF MUSK-OX) QIVIUT

UNDERCUT HOLE LAME POOL NOTCH

UNDERGARMENT SLIP SIMAR SKIRT SMOCK TUNIC WAIST BODICE CORSET GIRDLE CHEMISE DOUBLET DRAWERS BLOOMERS KNICKERS
(WOMAN'S —) PANTIHOSE

UNDERGO PASS SERVE ENDURE SUFFER SUSTAIN

UNDERHAND SLY SHADY SECRET CROOKED OBLIQUE INVOLVED SINISTER SNEAKING

UNDERMINE SAP CAVE ERODE KNIFE WEAKEN SUBVERT ENFEEBLE

UNDERNEATH BELOW BENEATH

UNDERPANTS BRIEFS BLOOMERS KNICKERS

UNDERSHIRT VEST SHIFT SHIRT CAMISA JERSEY SINGLET

UNDERSIDE BOTTOM BREAST
(— OF CLOUD) BASE
(— OF FINGER) BALL
(— OF FLOOR) CEILING
(— OF STAIRCASE) SOFFIT

UNDERSTAND CON DIG GET KEN SEE HAVE MAKE TAKE GRASP REACH SAVVY SEIZE SENSE ACCEPT COTTON FOLLOW UPTAKE DISCERN COMPRISE CONCEIVE CONSTRUE CONTRIVE PERCEIVE

UNDERSTANDING KEN WIT HEAD BRAIN HEART SENSE SKILL ACCORD NOTION REASON TREATY COMPACT CONCEPT ENTENTE INSIGHT MEANING PREHENSION

UNDERTAKE GO TRY DARE OFFER ASSUME ATTEMPT EMBRACE PRETEND CONTRACT
(— RESPONSIBILITY) ACCEPT ANSWER

UNDERTAKING JOB TASK EFFORT SCHEME ATTEMPT CALLING PROJECT VENTURE
(— IN CARDS) CONTRACT
(UNPROFITABLE —) FOLLY

UNDER TWO FLAGS (AUTHOR OF —) OUIDA
(CHARACTER IN —) RAKE CECIL AMAGUE BERTIE CORONA BERKELEY CIGARETTE GUENEVERE ROYALLIEU CHATEAUROY ROCKINGHAM

UNDERWEAR BRIEFS SHORTS SKIVVY UNDIES LONGIES LINGERIE PRETTIES SCANTIES

UNDERWORLD HADES ORCUS SHEOL MICTLAN XIBALBA GANGLAND

UNDETERMINED UNSET DUBIOUS PENDENT DOUBTFUL

UNDEVELOPED CRUDE MORON LATENT SLOVEN IMMATURE JUVENILE

UNDILUTED MERE NEAT PURE NAKED SHEER SHORT STRAIGHT

UNDISCIPLINED WANTON COLTISH

UNDISTINGUISHED GROSS COMMON UNNOBLE FAMELESS NAMELESS

UNDO COOK POOP SLIP DEFEAT UNBIND UNLOCK DESTROY NULLIFY UNRAVEL DECIPHER DISSOLVE UNFASTEN

UNDOMESTICATED WILD FERAL

UNDRESS DOFF PEEL STRIP DIVEST UNCASE UNLACE UNROBE UNARRAY NEGLIGEE

UNDULATE WAVE WAVY FLOAT SWING BILLOW FLICKER

UNDULATING SURGING FLEXUOUS INDENTED

UNDULATION FOLD ROLL WAVE CRIMP TEETER

UNEARTH DIG EXPOSE UNCOVER DISCOVER

UNEARTHLY EERIE WEIRD AWESOME UNCANNY UNGODLY

UNEASINESS ENVY FIDGET NETTLE SORROW AILMENT ANXIETY DISEASE TROUBLE DISQUIET

UNEASY SICKLY FIDGETY NERVOUS RESTIVE UNQUIET WORRIED RESTLESS

UNEDUCATED RUDE SIMPLE IGNORANT

UNEMOTIONAL DRY COLD COOL STOIC STONY

UNEMPLOYED IDLE OTIOSE VACANT LEISURE UNBUSIED

UNENDING ABYSMAL AGELONG CHRONIC ENDLESS UNDYING TERMLESS TIMELESS

UNENLIGHTENED MISTY HEATHEN IGNORANT

UNEQUAL UNEVEN INEQUAL INFERIOR

UNEQUIVOCAL DIRECT SQUARE PERFECT DEFINITE DISTINCT EXPLICIT RESOUNDING

UNEVEN RUDE EROSE JAGGY ROUGH RAGGED RUGGED SPOTTY UNFAIR ERRATIC SCALENE UNEQUAL

UNEVENNESS BUMP WAVE ANOMALY WRINKLE ASPERITY

UNEXCITING DEAD DULL TAME BORING PROSAIC

UNEXPECTED EERIE ABRUPT SUDDEN UNLOOKED

UNFAILING SURE DEADLY UNERRING

UNFAIR FOUL CROOK WRONG BIASED SHABBY UNEVEN UNJUST DEVIOUS PARTIAL UNEQUAL WRONGFUL

UNFAITHFUL INFIDEL TRAITOR DISLOYAL RECREANT

UNFALTERING SURE TRUE STEADY UNERRING

UNFAMILIAR NEW STRANGE UNKNOWN

UNFASTEN FREE OPEN UNDO LOOSE UNPIN UNBIND UNLOCK UNHITCH UNTRUSS

UNFATHOMABLE ABYSMAL ABYSSAL PROFOUND

UNFAVORABLE BAD ILL FOUL HARD POOR UNFAIR UNKIND ADVERSE AWKWARD FROWARD HOSTILE UNHAPPY BACKWARD CONTRARY INIMICAL SINISTER UNKINDLY

UNFEELING COLD DULL HARD CRASS CRUEL HARSH ROCKY STERN STONY BRUTAL LEADEN MARBLE STOLID CALLOUS OBDURATE

UNFEIGNED OPEN TRUE HEARTY CORDIAL NATURAL SINCERE

UNFINISHED RAW CRUDE ROUGH RAGGED IMMATURE INCHOATE

UNFIT BAD SICK COMMON FAULTY DISABLE IMPROPER UNLIKELY

UNFOLD OPEN BREAK BURST DEPLOY EVOLVE EXPAND FLOWER SPREAD UNFURL UNROLL BLOSSOM DEVELOP DISPLAY DIVULGE EXPLAIN UNRAVEL UNWEAVE

UNFORESEEN CASUAL SUDDEN UNAWARE

UNFORTUNATE ILL EVIL POOR TOUGH HAPLESS UNHAPPY UNLUCKY LUCKLESS UNTOWARD

UNFRIENDLY ILL COLD FOUL CHILL BITTER CHILLY FIERCE FROSTY HOSTILE INGRATE INIMICAL

UNFRUITFUL BLUNT ADDLED BARREN EFFETE WASTED STERILE USELESS

UNFURL BREAK SPREAD UNFOLD DEVELOP

UNGAINLY LANKY SPLAY WEEDY CLUMSY AWKWARD BOORISH UNWIELDY

UNGODLY SINFUL WICKED GODLESS IMPIOUS PROFANE

UNGRACEFUL HARD CLUMSY ANGULAR AWKWARD HALTING UNTOWARD

UNGUENT CHRISM POMADE POMATUM UNCTION OINTMENT

UNGULATE HOG PIG DEER HORSE TAKIN TAPIR HOOFED AMBLYPOD ELEPHANT

UNHAPPINESS MISERY SORROW ILLFARE SADNESS UNBLISS

UNHAPPY SAD POOR DISMAL UNLUCKY DEJECTED DOWNBEAT WOBEGONE WRETCHED

UNHEALTHY BAD MORBID QUEASY SICKLY UNHALE

UNHOLY IMPURE WICKED IMPIOUS PROFANE

UNHURRIED EASY SLOW SOFT SOBER

UNIDENTIFIED FACELESS INCOGNITO

UNIFORM EVEN FLAT JUST LIKE SAME SELF SUIT ALIKE CLOTH KHAKI SOLID GLOBAL LIVERY SINGLE STEADY EQUABLE REGULAR SIMILAR SUNTANS CONSTANT MEASURED STANDARD UNIVOCAL

(— IN HUE) FLAT

(LEATHER —) BUFF

(NOT —) SQUALLY

(PRISONER'S —) STRIPES

UNIFORMITY ONENESS EQUALITY EVENNESS MONOTONY SAMENESS

UNIFY MERGE UNITE CEMENT COMPACT UNITIZE COALESCE

UNIMAGINATIVE DULL SODDEN STUPID LIMITED LITERAL PROSAIC PEDANTIC PEDESTRIAN

UNIMPAIRED FRESH SOUND ENTIRE INTACT

UNIMPORTANT PETTY SMALL CASUAL SIMPLE TRIVIAL PIDDLING JERKWATER

UNINFORMED GREEN UNTOLD IGNORANT

UNINHABITED WILD EMPTY DESERT VACANT DESOLATE

UNINSPIRED HACK STODGY DRYASDUST

UNINTELLIGENT DUMB OBTUSE OPAQUE STUPID ASININE FOOLISH VACUOUS WITLESS

UNINTERESTING DRY ARID COLD DRAB DULL FLAT TAME DREAR STALE BORING JEJUNE INSIPID BROMIDIC

UNINTERRUPTED SMOOTH STEADY ENDLESS ETERNAL STRAIGHT

UNION SUM BLOC DUAD ALLOY GROUP
JOINT UNITY FUSION VEREIN COMPACT
CONCERT MEETING ONENESS SOCIETY
ADHESION ALLIANCE COHESION
ESPOUSAL JUNCTION JUNCTURE
SODALITY VINCULUM
(— OF TWO SETS) CUP
(— OF TWO VOWELS) CRASIS
(MARITAL —) BED
(POLITICAL —) ANSCHLUSS
(SEXUAL —) COPULA COUPLING
UNION OF SOVIET SOCIALIST REPU
(SEE RUSSIA)
UNIQUE ODD RARE SOLE ALONE SINGLE
SPECIAL STRANGE ISOLATED SINGULAR
UNIT (ALSO SEE MEASURE) ACE ONE
ATOM BARN KLAN FLOOR HUMIT MONAD
NEPER ADDRESS DIOPTER ELEMENT
ENERGID KLAVERN
UNITE ADD MIX ALLY BAND BIND CLUB
FUSE JOIN KNIT KNOT LINK SEAM CLOSE
GRAFT MERGE UNIFY ATTACH CONCUR
COUPLE EMBODY GATHER LEAGUE
SOLDER SUTURE AMALGAM CLUSTER
COMBINE CONJOIN CONNECT CONSORT
ASSEMBLE COALESCE COMPOUND
CONCRETE FEDERATE
(— BY INTERWEAVING) PLEACH
SPLICE
(— BY THREADS) SEW STITCH
(— CLOSELY) FAY WELD CEMENT
COTTON
(— FOR INTRIGUE) CABAL
(— HOSE) COLLECT
(— IN MARRIAGE) WED SPLICE
SPOUSE
(— METALS) WELD SWEAT
(— TIMBERS) SCARF
UNITED ONE TIED ADDED FUSED JOINT
ALLIED COMBINED CONCRETE
CONJUNCT FEDERATE
UNITED ARAB EMIRATES
(CAPITAL OF —) ABUDHABI
(MONEY OF —) DIRHAM
(MOUNTAINS OF —) HAJAR
(STATE OF —) AJMAN DUBAI SHARJAH
FUJAIRAH
(TOWN OF —) DUBAI JEBEL BURAIMI
SHARJAH
UNITED KINGDOM (SEE ENGLAND)

UNITED STATES
(ALSO SEE SPECIFIC STATES)

LAKE: ERIE MEAD SALT HURON TAHOE
CRATER ONTARIO MICHIGAN SUPERIOR
CHAMPLAIN OKEECHOBEE
MOUNTAIN: BEAR BONA SILL GREEN
OZARK ROCKY UINTA WHITE ANTERO
ELBERT SHASTA SIERRA BELFORD
FORAKER HARVARD MASSIVE RAINIER
SANFORD WASATCH WHITNEY CATSKILL
MCKINLEY WRANGELL BLACKBURN
ADIRONDACK BITTERROOT APPALACHIAN
PRESIDENT: ABE CAL DDE FDR IKE JFK
LBJ FORD POLK TAFT ADAMS GRANT
HARRY HAYES JIMMY NIXON TEDDY
TYLER ARTHUR CARTER HOOVER
MONROE PIERCE REAGAN TAYLOR
TRUMAN WILSON HARDING JACKSON
JOHNSON KENNEDY LINCOLN MADISON
BUCHANAN COOLIDGE FILLMORE
GARFIELD HARRISON MCKINLEY
VANBUREN JEFFERSON ROOSEVELT
EISENHOWER WASHINGTON
VICE PRESIDENT: BURR BUSH FORD KING
ADAMS AGNEW DAWES GERRY NIXON
TYLER ARTHUR COLFAX CURTIS DALLAS
GARNER HAMLIN HOBART MORTON
TRUMAN WILSON BARKLEY CALHOUN
CLINTON JOHNSON MONDALE SHERMAN
WALLACE WHEELER COOLIDGE FILLMORE
HUMPHREY MARSHALL TOMPKINS
VANBUREN FAIRBANKS HENDRICKS
JEFFERSON ROOSEVELT STEVENSON
ROCKEFELLER BRECKINRIDGE
WATERFALL: TWIN AKAKA SEVEN
NARADA RIBBON FEATHER PALOUSE
PASSAIC SLUISKIN YOSEMITE
BRIDALVEIL YELLOWSTONE

UNITY UNION ONENESS IDENTITY
TOTALITY
(— OF SPIRIT AND NATURE)
ABSOLUTE
UNIVERSAL ALL TOTAL WHOLE WORLD
COMMON GLOBAL PUBLIC GENERAL
GENERIC CATHOLIC ECUMENIC
PANDEMIC
UNIVERSE ALL MASS WORLD COSMOS
SYSTEM
(SIDEREAL —) SPACE
UNIVERSITY CAMPUS SCHOOL
ACADEMY COLLEGE STUDIUM VARSITY
UNJUST HARD UNFAIR WICKED UNEQUAL
UNRIGHT WRONGFUL
UNKEMPT ROUGH FROWZY RUGGED
SHAGGY RAFFISH RUFFLED SCRUFFY
TOUSLED DRAGGLED SLIPSHOD
UNCOMBED
UNKIND BAD ILL MEAN VILE CRUEL
HARSH STERN SEVERE
UNKNOWN SEALED SECRET FARAWAY
OBSCURE UNHEARD IGNORANT
UNAWARES UNWITTING
UNLAWFUL ILLEGAL ILLICIT
UNLEARNED GROSS PLAIN BOOKLESS
IGNORANT
UNLESS BUT NISI SAVE WITHOUT
UNLIKE DIFFORM DIVERSE
UNLOAD TIP DROP DUMP HOVEL DECANT
STRIKE UNLADE UNSHIP UNSTOW
DELIVER DEPLETE DETRUCK DISCHARGE
UNLUCKY BAD FAY ILL EVIL FOUL
DISMAL HOODOO WICKED HAPLESS
UNHAPPY UNTOWARD
UNMANAGEABLE RANDY WANTON
RESTIVE CHURLISH REFRACTORY
UNMARRIED ONE LONE SOLE SINGLE
UNMINDFUL SLOWFUL CARELESS
HEEDLESS MINDLESS
UNMISTAKABLE FLAT OPEN BROAD

CLEAR FRANK PLAIN PATENT DECIDED EXPRESS APPARENT DECISIVE MANIFEST UNIVOCAL

UNMITIGATED PURE GROSS ARRANT DAMNED PERFECT REGULAR ABSOLUTE OUTRIGHT

UNMIXED NET DEEP MERE PURE SOLE SHEER UTTER SIMPLE STRAIGHT

UNMOVED CALM COOL FIRM STONY TIGHT SERENE ADAMANT

UNNATURAL EERIE STIFF CLAMMY CREEPY STRANGE UNCANNY VIOLENT ABNORMAL MONSTROUS

UNNECESSARY USELESS NEEDLESS

UNNERVE UNMAN WEAKEN ENERVATE PARALYZE

UNOBSTRUCTED FAIR FREE OPEN PATENT THROUGH APPARENT

UNOBTRUSIVE SHY QUIET MODEST SEDATE DISCREET RETIRING

UNOCCUPIED IDLE VOID BLANK EMPTY WASTE OTIOSE VACANT LEISURE

UNORGANIZED ACOSMIC INCHOATE

UNPALATABLE HARD BITTER BRACKISH

UNPARALLELED ALONE UNIQUE EPOCHAL PEERLESS SINGULAR

UNPERTURBED BLAND STILL

UNPLEASANT BAD ACID EVIL HARD SOUR UGLY VILE AWFUL CRUDE GRIMY HAIRY HARSH MUCKY NASTY ROUGH TOUGH BRUTAL RANCID STICKY BEASTLY GHASTLY DREADFUL HORRIBLE INDECENT SCABROUS UNLOVELY ABOMINABLE

UNPOLISHED RUDE CRUDE ROUGH COARSE RUGGED RUSTIC SAVAGE SHAGGY UNKEMPT

UNPREDICTABLE CHANCY CRANKY ERRATIC

UNPRETENTIOUS HOMEY PLAIN SOBER COMMON HOMELY HUMBLE MODEST SIMPLE DISCREET HOMESPUN

UNPRODUCTIVE DRY SHY ARID DEAD LEAN POOR VAIN BARREN SAPLESS STERILE

UNPROFITABLE BAD DRY DEAD LEAN BARREN BOOTLESS GAINLESS

UNPROGRESSIVE SLOW DORMANT BACKWARD

UNPROPITIOUS ILL EVIL FOUL MALIGN SULLEN ADVERSE OMINOUS

UNQUALIFIED NET BARE FULL MERE PURE VERY PLUMP SHEER UNFIT DIRECT ENTIRE UNABLE IMPLICIT

UNQUESTIONABLE ASSURED CERTAIN DECIDED ABSOLUTE DECISIVE DISTINCT

UNRAVEL UNDO BREAK SOLVE EVOLVE UNFOLD UNKNIT RESOLVE

UNREAL VAIN AERIAL GOTHIC FANCIED SHADOWY CHIMERIC ILLUSORY NOTIONAL VISIONAL

UNREASONABLE ABSURD FANATIC ABSONANT

UNREFINED RAW DARK LOUD BRUTE CRUDE DORIC GROSS COARSE COMMON EARTHY VULGAR BOORISH UNCOUTH UNKEMPT DREADFUL

UNRELATED STRAY UNAKIN UNTOLD EXTREME

UNRELENTING GRIM HARD IRON CRUEL STERN BRASSY SEVERE RIGOROUS

UNRELIABLE FISHY SHADY FICKLE GREASY UNSAFE WILDCAT FECKLESS SLIPPERY

UNRESERVED FREE CLEAN FRANK COMMON EXPLICIT

UNRESPONSIVE DEAD DUMB BARREN SILENT STUBBORN

UNRESTRAINED LAX MAD FREE WILD BROAD FRANK LARGE LOOSE FACILE LAVISH UNTIED WANTON RAMPANT RIOTOUS BARBARIC FAMILIAR FREEHAND ABANDONED LIBERTINE

UNRESTRICTED FREE GLOBAL UNZONED ABSOLUTE

UNRIPE RAW CRUDE GREEN CALLOW UNCURED IMMATURE

UNRUFFLED CALM COOL EASY EVEN QUIET SOBER STILL ASLEEP PLACID SEDATE SERENE SMOOTH DECOROUS

UNRULY HIGH RAMP TOUGH WANTON LAWLESS VICIOUS WAYWARD MUTINOUS REFRACTORY OBSTREPEROUS RAMBUNCTIOUS

UNSAFE HOT FISHY EXPOSED INSECURE PERILOUS

UNSATISFACTORY BAD ILL EVIL POOR CROOK LOUSY WRETCHED

UNSCRUPULOUS CROOK BRAZEN DEVIOUS JACKLEG DEXTROUS RASCALLY

UNSEASONABLE UNRIPE UNTIDY UNCHANCY UNTIMELY

UNSEEMLY HOIDEN UNFAIR IMPROPER INDECENT UNWORTHY

UNSETTLE JAR TURN UNFIX UNSET UPSET DERANGE DISTURB STAGGER UNHINGE DISORDER DISQUIET DISTRACT

UNSETTLED LIGHT SHAKY VAGUE BROKEN FICKLE QUEASY DUBIOUS NOMADIC SHUTTLE RESTLESS UNSTABLE VAGABOND

UNSHAKEN FIRM STEADY UNMOVED CONSTANT RESOLUTE

UNSIGHTLY UGLY AWFUL MESSY HOMELY INDECENT

UNSKILLED PUNY GREEN FECKLESS

UNSKILLFUL ILL EVIL RUDE ARTLESS AWKWARD BUNGLING

UNSOPHISTICATED JAY PURE FRANK GREEN NAIVE SILLY CALLOW SIMPLE BUCOLIC NATURAL HOMEBRED HOMESPUN INNOCENT

UNSOUND BAD ILL EVIL SICK BARMY CRAZY DOTTY SHAKY ABSURD FAULTY FLAWED HOLLOW INFIRM INSANE ROTTEN INVALID RICKETY

UNSTABLE BATTY LOOSE CHOPPY FICKLE FITFUL ROTTEN SHIFTY UNFIRM RICKETY FEVERISH FUGITIVE INSECURE SKITTISH SLIPPERY TICKLISH VARIABLE

UNSTEADY CRANK DOTTY SLACK TIPPY TIPSY FICKLE FLUFFY GROGGY JIGGLY QUAVERY TOTTERY WAYWARD SKITTISH

STAGGERY TICKLISH UNSTABLE VARIABLE

UNSUBSTANTIAL TOY AIRY LIMP THIN WINDY AERIAL BUBBLE FLIMSY SLEAZY SLIGHT UNREAL FRAGILE SHADOWY TENUOUS FINESPUN VAPOROUS

UNSUITABLE INEPT UNAPT UNFIT UNMETE UNGAINLY UNLIKELY

UNSULLIED FAIR PURE CLEAR VIRGIN INNOCENT SPOTLESS VIRGINAL

UNSURE TIMID DOUBTFUL INSECURE

UNSWERVING FIXED LOYAL DIRECT STEADY STURDY STAUNCH

UNSYMPATHETIC DRY HARD STONY FROZEN GLASSY HOSTILE

UNTAMED WILD FERAL SAVAGE

UNTHINKING GLIB BRUTE CASUAL FECKLESS HEEDLESS

UNTIDY DOWDY MESSY LITTERY SCRUFFY DRAGGLED SLOVENLY

UNTIE UNDO UNBIND UNLASH UNLATCH UNTRUSS UNTWINE UNFASTEN

UNTIL AD TO INTO UNTO WHILE PENDING

UNTIRING BUSY SEDULOUS TIRELESS

UNTRIED MAIDEN UNSOUGHT

UNTRUE FALSE WRONG DISLOYAL MENDACIOUS

UNTRUSTWORTHY SHAKY TRICKY UNSURE SLIPPERY

UNTRUTH LIE FABLE FALSITY MENDACITY

UNTWIST FEAZE UNSPIN UNTWIRL

UNUSED IDLE FRESH WASTE MAIDEN VACANT DERELICT INITIATE

UNUSUAL ODD RARE TALL CRAZY EERIE NOVEL UTTER WEIRD SCREWY SINGLE UNIQUE STRANGE ABNORMAL DISTINCT ESPECIAL SINGULAR UNCOMMON UNWONTED PRODIGIOUS

UNVARYING FLAT SAME LEVEL STABLE UNIFORM

UNVEIL REVEAL UNCOVER UNCROWN UNDRAPE UNSCREEN

UNWARY RASH UNAWARE CARELESS HEEDLESS

UNWAVERING FIRM CLEAN LEVEL SOLID GLASSY STABLE EXPRESS STAUNCH

UNWELL BAD ILL EVIL PUNK SICK CROOK SEEDY AILING WICKED

UNWHOLESOME ILL EVIL SICK IMPURE MORBID SICKLY CORRUPT NOISOME NOXIOUS UNCLEAN DISEASED

UNWIELDY BULKY CLUMSY AWKWARD HULKING CUMBROUS UNGAINLY

UNWILLING CHARY LOATH AVERSE BACKWARD GRUDGING

UNWISE FALSE INANE SILLY SIMPLE FOOLISH WITLESS

UNWORLDLY WEIRD ASTRAL SPIRITUAL

UNWORTHY BASE INDIGN BENEATH

UNYIELDING PAT SET DOUR FAST FIRM GRIM HARD RIGID STARK STEEL STIFF STONY TOUGH FLINTY FROZEN GLASSY MARBLE STEELY STURDY ADAMANT AUSTERE OBDURATE OBEDIENT STUBBORN PERTINACIOUS

UP ON ABOUT ASTIR

UPBRAID CHEW RAIL TWIT ABUSE SCOLD TAUNT REPROVE DISGRACE

UPHEAVAL BOIL STORM RUMMAGE

UPHOLD AID ABET BACK FAVOR AFFIRM ASSERT DEFEND BOLSTER SUPPORT SUSTAIN CHAMPION MAINTAIN PRESERVE

UPLIFT TOSS BOOST TOWER UPTHRUST

UPON ON SUR OVER ABOVE AGAINST

UPPER VOLTA (CAPITAL OF —) OUAGADOUGOU

(**LANGUAGE OF —**) BOBO LOBI SAMO MANDE MOSSI

(**MOUNTAIN IN —**) TEMA

(**NATIVE OF —**) BOBO LOBI SAMO BISSA HAUSA MANDE MARKA MOSSI PUEHL TUAREG SENOUFO VOLTAIC YATENGA MANDINGO

(**RIVER IN —**) VOLTA SOUROU

(**TOWN OF —**) PO LEO DORI PAMA YAKO DJIBO GAOUA LAWRA HOUNDE TOUGAN BANFORA

UPRIGHT FAIR GOOD JUST PROP STUD TRUE ERECT GUIDE MORAL RIGHT SETUP DIRECT ENTIRE HONEST SQUARE SINCERE INNOCENT RIGHTFUL STANDARD STANDING STRAIGHT VERTICAL VIRTUOUS

UPRIGHTNESS HONOR TRUTH APLOMB EQUITY HONESTY PROBITY JUSTNESS SINCERITY

UPRISING RIOT MUTINY PUTSCH REVOLT TUMULT REBELLION

UPROAR DIN HELL MOIL RIOT ROUT BABEL FUROR RUMOR CLAMOR FRACAS HUBBUB RANDAN RATTLE RUCKUS RUMPUS TUMULT FERMENT RUCTION TURMOIL BALLYHOO BROUHAHA PANDEMONIUM

UPROOT HACK UNPLANT DISPLANT SUPPLANT

UPSET ILL TIP TOP COUP JUMP ROCK TILT TURN EVERT KNOCK SHAKE SPILL BOTHER DISMAY TOPPLE CAPSIZE DERANGE DISTURB FRAZZLE HAYWIRE PERVERT REVERSE SUBVERT TURMOIL CAPSIZAL OVERTILT OVERTURN TURNOVER OVERTHROW

UPSHOT ISSUE EFFECT SEQUEL OUTCOME

UPSTART SNIP SQUIRT PARVENU ARRIVIST SKIPJACK

UP-TO-DATE MOD MODERN TRENDY ABREAST TODAYISH

UPWARD ALOFT SKYWARD

URBANE CIVIL SUAVE POLITE SVELTE AMIABLE GRACIOUS

URCHIN IMP WAIF ELFIN GAMIN NIPPER

URGE HIE PLY PUT SIC SUE BROD COAX EDGE GOAD MOVE POKE PUSH SPUR WHIP FORCE PRESS PRICK TREAT COMPEL DESIRE EXCITE HUSTLE INDUCE INVITE PROMPT PROPEL THREAT ENFORCE OPPRESS PERSIST SOLICIT SUGGEST ADMONISH PERSUADE

(**— ON**) EGG HAG WHIG ALARM CHIRK

CROWD DRIVE HASTE HURRY IMPEL
ROWEL YOICK ALARUM FILLIP HARDEN
HASTEN INCITE
(— ON A HORSE) HUP CRAM CHUCK
(— STRONGLY) EXHORT SOLICIT
(— WITH VEHEMENCE) DING
URGENCY NEED PRESS STRESS
EXIGENCY INSTANCE PRESSURE
URGENT HOT DIRE LOUD RASH ACUTE
HASTY STRONG BURNING EXIGENT
CRITICAL PRESSING NECESSITOUS
URIAH (WIFE OF —) BATHSHEBA
URINATE WET LEAK EMPTY STALE
PIDDLE EVACUATE MICTURATE
URN JAR EWER KIST VASE CAPANNA
(— FOR MAKING TEA) KITCHEN
SAMOVAR
(— IN KENO) GOOSE
(BURIAL —) OSSUARY
(CINERARY —) DINOS DEINOS
(STONE —) STEEN
URSA MAJOR OKNARI CHARIOT
WAGONER

URUGUAY

CAPITAL: MONTEVIDEO
DEPARTMENT: ROCHA SALTO FLORES
RIVERA ARTIGAS COLONIA DURAZNO
FLORIDA SORIANO
ESTUARY: PLATA
LAKE: MERIN MIRIM DIFUNTOS
MEASURE: VARA LEGUA CUADRA SUERTE
RIVER: MALO MIRIM NEGRO ULIMAR
CUAREIM QUEGUAY YAGUARON
CEBOLLATI
TOWN: MELO AIGUA MINAS PANDO
ROCHA SALTO VERAS RIVERA DURAZNO
FLORIDA MERCEDES PAYSANDU
WEIGHT: QUINTAL

U.S.A. (AUTHOR OF —) DOSPASSOS
(CHARACTER IN —) ANN BEN JOE MAC
MARY WARD DELLA FAINY JANEY
MARGO TRENT FRENCH MAISIE SAVAGE
STAPLE STRANG CHARLEY COMPTON
DOWLING ELEANOR EVELINE RICHARD
SPENCER ANDERSON GERTRUDE
HUTCHINS MCCREARY STODDARD
WILLIAMS ANNABELLE MOOREHOUSE
USAGE USE FORM HABIT CUSTOM
MANNER FASHION PRACTICE
(BAD —) ABUSAGE
(HARD —) GRIEF
(ILL —) ABUSE
(RELIGIOUS —) RITUS
USE CALL DUTY HAVE WISE APPLY AVAIL
GUIDE HABIT SPEND STEAD TREAT
USAGE WASTE BEHOOF EMPLOY FINISH
HANDLE OCCUPY ACCOUNT ENTREAT
IMPROVE PURPOSE SERVICE UTILITY
ACCUSTOM EXERCISE FUNCTION
PRACTICE
(— EXPERIMENTALLY) TRY

(— INDISCRIMINATELY) HACK
(— OF MORE WORDS THAN
NECESSARY) PLEONASM
(— OF SUBTERFUGE) CHICANE
(— UP) EAT TIRE WEAR SHOOT ABSORB
DEVOUR EXPEND GUZZLE PERUSE
CONSUME EXHAUST OVERWEAR
(FRUGAL —) SPARE
(GENERAL —) CURRENCY
(LITURGICAL —) RITE
(UNRESTRICTED —) FREEDOM
(WRONG —) ABUSE
USEFUL GAIN GOOD UTILE HELPFUL
THRIFTY UTENSILE
USEFULNESS USE AVAIL VALUE WORTH
PROFIT MILEAGE UTILITY
USELESS IDLE VAIN VOID EMPTY OTIOSE
TRASHY INUTILE STERILE BOOTLESS
WASTEFUL
USELESSNESS FUTILITY IDLENESS
USHER BOW SHOW CRIER HERALD
SEATER MARSHAL STEWARD
USUAL RIFE COMMON FAMOUS NORMAL
VULGAR WONTED AVERAGE GENERAL
NATURAL REGULAR TYPICAL EVERYDAY
FREQUENT HABITUAL ORDINARY
ORTHODOX ACCUSTOMED
USURP ASSUME INVADE PRESUME
ARROGATE

UTAH

CAPITAL: SALTLAKECITY
COUNTY: IRON JUAB CACHE PIUTE
CARBON SEVIER TOOELE UINTAH
SANPETE
LAKE: SALT SWAN SEVIER
MOUNTAIN: LENA LION WAAS KINGS
PEALE TRAIL FRISCO NAVAJO SWASEY
GRANITE GRIFFIN HAWKINS PENNELL
LINNAEUS
MOUNTAIN RANGE: CEDAR HENRY
HOGUP UINTA WAHWAH TERRACE
CONFUSION
NATIONAL PARK: ZION
RIVER: WEBER JORDAN SEVIER
STATE BIRD: SEAGULL
STATE FLOWER: SEGOLILY
STATE TREE: SPRUCE
TOWN: LOA MOAB OREM DELTA HEBER
KANAB LOGAN MAGNA MANTI NEPHI
OGDEN PRICE PROVO KEARNS TOOELE
VERNAL BRIGHAM BOUNTIFUL
COALVILLE

UTENSIL
(ALSO SEE IMPLEMENT AND TOOL)
HOD BOAT IRON MOLD STEW BAKER
FRYER GRILL KNIFE MOULD RICER SCOOP
SHEET SHELL SIEVE BEATER BEETLE
BREWER COOKER DABBER FUNNEL
GRATER GRILLE KETTLE LINGEL MASKER
POPPER PUSHER SHAKER SIFTER
BRAZIER BROILER DUSTPAN FLIPPER

MUDDLER SKIMMER STEAMER STIRRER
TOASTER GRIDIRON SAUCEPAN
SAUCEPOT SHREDDER STRAINER
UTILITY USE AVAIL USAGE PROFIT
BENEFIT SERVICE
UTILIZE USE EMPLOY ENLIST CONSUME
EXPLOIT HARNESS HUSBAND
UTMOST END NTH BEST LAST MOST
FINAL EXTREME SUPREME
UTTER ASK OUT SAY BARK BLOW BOOM
DEAD EMIT FAIR GASP GIVE HURL MOVE
PASS PURE RANK SEND TELL VENT VERY
COUGH FETCH FRAME FRANK GROSS
ISSUE MOUTH RAISE SHEER SOUND
SPEAK SPELL STARK TOTAL VOICE
ACCENT ARRANT BROACH DIRECT
INTONE PARLEY PROPER TONGUE
BLUSTER BREATHE DELIVER ENOUNCE
EXCLAIM EXPRESS PERFECT ABSOLUTE
COMPLETE CRASHING INTONATE
BLITHERING
UTTERANCE CRY GAB CALL OSSE VOICE

ACCENT ACTION BREATH CHORUS
GIBBER ORACLE PAROLE TONGUE
DELIVERY JUDGMENT LOCUTION
(— FROM A DIVINITY) ORACLE
(— OF PRAISE) MAGNIFICAT
(DEFECTIVE —) STAMMER
(FAINT —) INKLING
(FOOLISH —) DRIVEL
(FOOLISH —S) GUFF
(GUSHING —) EFFUSION
(IMPULSIVE —) BLURT
(INDISTINCT —) BUMBLE
(MALICIOUS —) SLANDER
(OFFENSIVE —) AFFRONT
(PUBLIC —) AIR OUTGIVING
(SHORT —) DITTY
(SOLEMN —) EFFATE EFFATUM
(TRADITIONAL —) AGRAPHON
UTTERLY BONE DEAD PLUMB HOLLOW
MERELY BLANKLY SHEERLY PROPERLY
UZZIAH (FATHER OF —) AMAZIAH
(SON OF —) ATHAIAH JEHONATHAN

V VEE FIVE VICTOR
VACANCY HOLE WANT VACUITY
VACANT IDLE OPEN VOID BLANK EMPTY
INANE HOLLOW DORMANT UNFILLED
VACATE QUIT VOID EMPTY WAIVE
VACANT ABANDON RESCIND ABROGATE
EVACUATE
VACATION REST LEAVE OUTING RECESS
HOLIDAY
VACILLATE WAVE DITHER TEETER
WOBBLE STICKLE HESITATE
VACUOUS DULL BLANK EMPTY SILLY
VACANT
VACUUM GAPE VOID VACANCY VACUITY
VAGABOND BUM VAG HOBO ROGUE
STIFF JOCKEY PICARO TAGRAG TRUANT
ERRATIC GANGREL OUTCAST SWAGMAN
VAGRANT WASTREL BOHEMIAN
FUGITIVE PALLIARD RUNABOUT
VAGARY WHIM FANCY FREAK CAPRICE
CONCEIT
VAGRANT BUM WAIF PIKER ROGUE
STRAG TRAMP ARRANT CASUAL SHAKER
TINKER TRUANT DEVIOUS DRIFTER
ERRATIC FLOATER GANGREL ROGUISH
SWAGMAN TRAMPER PLANETIC
STROLLER VAGABOND
VAGUE LAX DARK HAZY FOGGY FUZZY
GROSS LOOSE MISTY MUDDY WOOZY
CLOUDY DREAMY MYSTIC BLURRED
EVASIVE OBSCURE SHADOWY UNFIXED
CONFUSED NEBULOUS
VAGUELY DIMLY DARKLY DUMBLY
DREAMILY
VAIN MAD IDLE NULL VOID COCKY EMPTY
PROUD SAUCY FLIMSY FUTILE HOLLOW
OTIOSE BIGGITY TRIVIAL BOOTLESS
NUGATORY VAPOROUS WASTEFUL
VAINGLORY POMP GLORY VANITY
ELATION
VALE DALE DELL BACHE ENNIS
VALENTINE (SISTER OF —) GRETCHEN
(SLAYER OF —) FAUST
VALET MAN ANDREW SIRDAR CRISPIN
TIREMAN
VALIANT BOLD BRAG BRAVE LUSTY
PROUD STOUT FIERCE HEROIC DOUGHTY
INTREPID STALWART VIRTUOUS
VALID FAIR GOOD JUST LEGAL SOUND
COGENT LAWFUL BINDING WEIGHTY
FORCIBLE
VALIDATE FIRM SEAL CONFIRM
VALIDITY FORCE VIGOR STRENGTH
VALISE BAG GRIP SATCHEL SUITCASE
VALLEY GUT COVE DALE DELL GILL
HOWE HOYA PARK VALE WADI BACHE
BREAK CHASM HEUGH SLACK SLADE
SWALE BOTTOM CANADA HOLLOW
LAAGTE STRATH GEHENNA

(— BETWEEN CONES OF VOLCANO)
ATRIO
(— IN THESSALY) TEMPE
(— ON MOON'S SURFACE) RILL CLEFT
RILLE
(CIRCULAR —) RINCON
(DEEP —) CANON GRIKE CANYON
(DROWNED —) VIA
(FLAT-FLOORED DESERT —) BOLSON
(GRASSY MOUNTAIN —) HOLE
(MINIATURE —) GULLY
(NARROW —) DENE GLEN GLACK
GOYLE GRIFF KLOOF CLOUGH
(RIVER —) WATER
(SECLUDED —) GLEN DINGLE
(TRENCHLIKE —) COULEE
VALOR MERIT VALUE BOUNTY BRAVERY
COURAGE PROWESS STOMACH
CHIVALRY
VALOROUS BOLD BRAVE VIRTUOUS
VALUABLE DEAR COSTLY PRIZED
WORTHY EMINENT WEALTHY PRECIOUS
SINGULAR
VALUATION VALUE ESTEEM ESTIMATE
TAXATION
VALUE COST FECK RATE TELL AVAIL
CARAT COUNT PRICE STAMP STOCK
VALOR WORTH ASSESS EQUITY ESTEEM
FIGURE MATTER MOMENT PRAISE
REGARD VIRTUE ACCOUNT ADVANCE
CAPITAL CHERISH COMPUTE RESPECT
VALENCY ESTIMATE EVALUATE
GOODWILL SPLENDOR TREASURE
VALIDITY
(— HIGHLY) PRIZE ENDEAR
(— OF ANGLE) EPOCH
(— OF COW) SET
(— OF TIMBER) STUMPAGE
(ABSOLUTE —) MODULUS
(AESTHETIC —) AMENITY
(ESTABLISHED —) PAR
(GOOD —) SNIP
(MATHEMATICAL —) EXTREMUM
(NEGATIVE —) DISVALUE
(TESTED —) ASSAY
VALVE TAP COCK GATE STOP CHOKE
MIXER BOTTLE CUTOUT DAMPER POPPET
SLUICE SUCKER WASHER CLICKET
DRAWOFF PETCOCK REDUCER SHUTOFF
DRAWGATE STOPCOCK THROTTLE
(— OF BARNACLE) SCUTUM
(— OF MUSICAL INSTRUMENT)
PISTON VENTIL
(— OF PUMP BOX) FANG
(THIN —) WAFER
(TRIPLE —) KICKER
VAN FORE LEAD FRONT TRUCK WAGON
CARAVAN
VANDAL HUN SARACEN HOOLIGAN

VANE TEE WEB COCK TAIL WING TARGET
(— OF ARROW) FEATHER
(— OF CONVEYOR BELT) FLIGHT
(— OF FEATHER) WEB FLUE VEXILLUM
(— OF SURVEYING STAFF) TRANSOM
(— OF WINDMILL) FAN FANE TAIL
(COOLING — IN BREWING) FIGHTER
VANISH DIE FLY DROP FADE FLEE MELT
PASS CLEAR SLIDE SCATTER CONQUEST
DISSOLVE EVANESCE
VANITY POMP FOLLY PRIDE EGOISM
CONCEIT FEATHER FOPPERY IDLENESS
PRETENSION
VANITY FAIR (AUTHOR OF —)
THACKERAY
(CHARACTER IN —) JOS PITT BECKY
SHARP AMELIA DOBBIN GEORGE JOSEPH
RAWDON SEDLEY STEYNE CRAWLEY
OSBORNE WILLIAM
VANQUISH WIN BEAT LICK MASTER
SUBDUE THRASH CONQUER SMOTHER
OVERCOME SURMOUNT
VANUATU (CAPITAL OF —) VILA
(ISLAND OF —) EPI EFATE MALEKULA
PENTECOST ESPIRITUSANTO
(MONEY OF —) VATU
(VOLCANO OF —) TANNA LOPEVI
VAPID DRY DULL FADE FLAT STALE TRITE
JEJUNE INSIPID
VAPOR FOG FUME REEK STEW BRUME
HUMOR SMOKE STEAM BREATH
EXHAUST HALITUS
(HOT —) LUNT
(NOXIOUS —) DAMP
VAPORIZE FLASH STEAM AERATE
VARIABLE FREE CHOPPY FICKLE FITFUL
FLUXILE MUTABLE ROLLING STREAKY
UNEQUAL VARIANT FLOATING SHIFTING
SKITTISH UNSTABLE
(EXCEEDINGLY —) PROTEAN
(RANDOM —) STATISTIC
VARIANCE ODDS DISCORD
VARIATION TURN ERROR SHADE
CHANGE JITTER SWITCH DESCANT
SHADING VARIETY DIVISION MUTATION
(— IN AIR PRESSURE) ROBBING
(— IN CURRENT) SURGE
(— IN FREQUENCY) SWINGING
(— IN SPEED) HUNTING
(— OF COLOR) ABRASH
(— OF PUPIL OF EYE) HIPPUS
(— OF SHOE) SPRING
(— OF VOWELS) ABLAUT
(ALLOWABLE —) LEEWAY
(BALLET —) ATTITUDE
(TOPOGRAPHICAL —) BREAK
VARIED DAEDAL SEVERAL VARIOUS
MANIFOLD
VARIEGATED PIED SHOT DAEDAL
MARLED MOSAIC SKEWED BROCKED
CHECKED CLOUDED DAPPLED FREAKED
FRETTED FRECKLED SKEWBALD
VARIETY FORM KIND MODE SORT BRAND
BREED CLASS COLOR SPICE CHANGE
NATURE STRAIN STRIPE SPECIES
VARIOUS MANY DIVERS SUNDRY VARIED
DIVERSE SEVERAL VARIANT MANIFOLD

VARLET BOY LAD COISTREL
VARNISH DOPE JAPAN FIXATIF LACQUER
VEHICLE VERMEIL FIXATIVE
VARY ALTER BREAK DRIFT SHIFT SPORT
CHANGE DIFFER RECEDE DEVIATE
DISSENT DIVERGE DISAGREE
VASE PYX URN OLLA ASKOS CYLIX DINOS
BASKET BOWPOT COTYLA FILLER HYDRIA
KALPIS KRATER LEKANE AMPHORA
AMPULLA CANOPUS PSYKTER SCYPHUS
STAMNOS LECYTHUS
(— FOR PERFUME) CONCH
(— ON PEDESTAL) TAZZA
(—S UNDER THEATER SEATS) SCHEA
VASSAL MAN BOND SERF LIEGE SLAVE
BONDMAN FEODARY HOMAGER SAMURAI
SERVANT SUBJECT
VAST HUGE BROAD GREAT LARGE
COSMIC MIGHTY UNTOLD ABYSMAL
IMMENSE OCEANIC ENORMOUS INFINITE
SPACIOUS
VAT BAC DIP FAT PIT BECK FATE TINE
FETTE ROUND STAND STEEP KIMNEL
MOTHER BLUNGER DRAINER STEEPER
(— USED IN MEASURING SLIPS) ARK
(BREWER'S —) BACK FLOAT KEEVE
UNION CUMMING
(CHEESE —) CHESSET
(COOLING —) KELDER
(DYER'S —) JIG LEAD DYEBECK
(EVAPORATING —) APRON GRAINER
(FERMENTING —) TUN COMB COOM
GYLE KEEL COOMB FLOAT
(TANNER'S —) TAP HANGER SPENDER
(TEXTILE —) KIER
(WINE —) LAKE CUVEE
VAULT COPE JUMP LEAP PEND SKIP
TOMB AZURE CRYPT CELLAR CUPOLA
FORNIX DUNGEON TESTUDO CATACOMB
LEAPFROG
(— IN CEILING) LACUNAR
(— OF HEAVEN) WELKIN
(— OF SKY) CONVEX ZENITH CONCAVE
VAUNT BRAG BOAST BLUSTER GLORIFY
FLOURISH
VEER CUT DIP FLY CHOP SLUE SWAY
TACK SHIFT SWOOP BROACH CHANGE
SWERVE TUMBLE DEVIATE
VEGETABLE PEA YAM BEAN BEET CORN
KALE LEEK OKRA GRASS ONION
SABZI SALAD CARROT CELERY LEGUME
LENTIL POTATO RADISH SQUASH
TOMATO TOPEPO TURNIP BLOATER
CABBAGE CELTUCE LETTUCE PARSNIP
PEASCOD RHUBARB SPINACH BROCCOLI
EGGPLANT RUTABAGA
VEGETATION HERB COVER GREEN
SCRUB GROWTH HERBAGE COVERAGE
PLANTAGE
(DECOMPOSED —) STAPLE
(SCRUB —) BRUSH
VEHEMENCE FURY GLOW HEAT RAGE
WARMTH STRENGTH VIOLENCE
VEHEMENT HOT HIGH KEEN LOUD
ANGRY EAGER FIERY HEFTY ARDENT
BITTER FERVID FIERCE FLASHY HEARTY

HEATED RAGING STRONG FURIOSO
INTENSE VIOLENT
VEHICLE BUS CAB CAR FLY VAN ARBA
AUTO JEEP TAXI WAIN ARABA BRAKE
BUGGY DILLY GUIDE STAGE WAGON
CAMPER DIESEL HEARSE JITNEY MEDIUM
SURREY CARRIER CHARIOT CRUISER
MACHINE MINIBUS OMNIBUS PEDICAB
SHEBANG SHUTTLE SPEEDER STEAMER
TAXICAB TRAVOIS TURNOUT UTILITY
AUTORAIL CARRIAGE CHARETTE
DEADHEAD DELIVERY ELECTRIC
SOCIABLE UNICYCLE MOTORCYCLE
SNOWMOBILE
  (— DRAWN BY BULLOCK) EKKA
  (— FOR COLORS) MEGILP
  (— FOR HAULING) TRACTOR
  (— ON RUNNERS) SLED CARRO SLEDGE
  SLEIGH ICEBOAT AUTOSLED
  (— ON SINGLE RAIL) AEROTRAIN
  (— PULLED BY MAN) BROUETTE
  RICKSHAW
  (— RUNNING ON RAILS) LORRY TRAIN
  (— WITH 3 HORSES ABREAST)
  TROIKA
  (— WITH 3 HORSES BEHIND EACH
  OTHER) RANDEM
  (AMMUNITION —) CAISSON
  (AMPHIBIOUS —) BUFFALO
  (AWKWARD —) ARK
  (CHILD'S —) PRAM WALKER SCOOTER
  STROLLER
  (COVERED —) SEDAN LANDAU
  CARAVAN KIBITKA
  (EARTH-MOVING —) SCOOP
  (LITTLE —) HINAYANA
  (LUMBERING —) TUG TODE
  (MILITARY —) AMTRACK
  (OBSOLETE —) CRATE
  (POOR-QUALITY —) DOG
  (RUSSIAN —) TARANTAS
  (SLEDGE-LIKE —) GAMBO
  (SNOW —) SKIBOB
  (SPACE —) LANDER
  (2-WHEELED —) GIG CART SULKY
  TONGA CISIUM JINGLE LIMBER BICYCLE
  CALECHE CROYDON RICKSHAW
VEIL FALL FILM HIDE MASK WRAP COVER
GLOSS RUMAL SHADE VELUM CHRISM
SHADOW SHROUD WIMPLE CURTAIN
PARANJA CALYPTRA MANTILLA
  (— IN CHURCH) AER ENDOTYS
  ENDOTHYS
  (— ON FUNGI) CORTINA
  (DOUBLE —) YASHMAK
  (HUMERAL —) SUDARY
  (WIDOW'S —) WEEPER
VEILED COVERT LATENT SHROUDED
VEIN BAR CAVA MOOD REEF VENA COMES
MEDIA NERVE VARIX MEDIAL STRAIN
VENULA VENULE AXILLAR JUGULAR
PRECAVA AXILLARY EMULGENT
  (— IN MARBLE) CLOUD
  (— OF LEAF) RIB COSTA MIDRIB
  (— OF MINERAL) STREAK STRINGER
  (— OF ORE) LODE ROKE BUNCH LEDGE

RIDER SCRIN LEADER STRING DROPPER
UNDERSET
  (— OF WING) CUBIT RADIUS CUBITAL
  CUBITUS SUBCOSTA
  (GRANITIC —) ELVAN
  (QUARTZ —) SADDLE
  (VARICOSE —) AMPER
VELOCIPEDE HOBBY STEED TRICAR
BICYCLE RANTOON TRICYCLE
VELOCITY DRIFT CELERITY RAPIDITY
STRENGTH
  (— OF FLOW) CURRENT
  (— OF 1 FOOT PER SECOND) VELO
VELVET PILE PANNE BIRODO VELURE
FRAYING
VENAL CORRUPT HIRELING SALEABLE
VENDIBLE
VEND HAWK SELL MARKET PEDDLE
VENDA (CAPITAL OF —)
THOHOYANDOU
  (TOWN OF —) SIBASA MAKWARELA
VENDOR SELLER ALIENOR HUSTLER
PITCHER VIANDER PITCHMAN VENDITOR
VENEER BURL JAPAN OVERLAY
VENERABLE OLD SAGE HOARY AUGUST
SACRED VETUST ANCIENT VINTAGE
VENERATE FEAR DREAD HALLOW
REVERE RESPECT WORSHIP
VENERATED HOLY SACRED HALLOWED
VENERATION AWE DULIA RESPECT
DEVOTION

VENEZUELA

CAPITAL: CARACAS
COIN: REAL MEDIO FUERTE BOLIVAR
CENTIMO MOROCOTA
GULF: PARIA
MOUNTAIN: PAVA YAVI DUIDA ICUTU
CONCHA CUNEVA PARIMA IMUTACA
MASAITI RORAIMA
NATIVE: CARIB TIMOTE GUARAUNO
RIVER: META APURE CAURA ARAUCA
CARONI CUYUNI GUANARE ORINOCO
ORITUCO PARAGUA SUAPURE VICHADA
GUAVIARE VENTUARI
STATE: LARA APURE SUCRE ZULIA
ARAGUA FALCON MERIDA BOLIVAR
COJEDES GUARICO MONAGAS TACHIRA
YARACUY CARABOBO TRUJILLO
TOWN: AROA CORO ATURES CUMANA
MERIDA BARINAS CABELLO GUAWARE
MARACAY MATURIN CARUPANO
TACUPITA VALENCIA
WATERFALL: ANGEL CUQUENAN

VENGEANCE WRACK ULTION REVENGE
REQUITAL
VENOM GALL ATTER VIRUS POISON
VENOMOUS TOXIC DEADLY BANEFUL
NOXIOUS SNAKISH POISONED VIPERINE
VIRULENT POISONOUS
VENT EMIT HOLE REEK BELCH ISSUE
OUTLET CHIMNEY OPENING ORIFICE
RELEASE APERTURE BREATHER SPIRACLE
VOMITORY

(— IN EARTH'S CRUST) VOLCANO
(VOLCANIC —) BOCCA DIATREME
SOLFATARA
VENTILATE AIR WIND AERATE EXPRESS
VENTURE RUN SET CAST DARE JUMP
LUCK RISK WAGE FLYER SALLY STAKE
WAGER CHANCE DANGER HAZARD
FLUTTER IMPERIL PRESUME ENDANGER
VENTURESOME BOLD RASH RISKY
DARING PARLOUS TEMEROUS
VENUS LOVE VESPER LUCIFER HESPERUS
PHOSPHOR
(FATHER OF —) JUPITER
(HUSBAND OF —) VULCAN
(MOTHER OF —) DIONE
(SON OF —) AMOR CUPID AENEAS
VERACIOUS TRUE VERY SINCERE
FAITHFUL TRUTHFUL
VERACITY TRUTH VERITY FIDELITY
VERANDA LANAI PORCH STOOP PIAZZA
BALCONY GALLERY
VERBATIM DIRECT LITERAL DIRECTLY
VERBOSE WINDY WORDY PROLIX
DIFFUSE WORDISH
VERDANT BOSKY GREEN VIRID
VERDICT WORD ASSIZE FINDING
OPINION DECISION JUDGMENT
VERGE TOP EDGE WAND YARD BRINK
BORDER TRENCH
VERIFY AVER TRUE AUDIT CHECK PROVE
ATTEST RATIFY CONFIRM JUSTIFY
SUPPORT
VERILY YEA AMEN FAITH CERTES INDEED
VERITABLE REAL TRUE VERY ACTUAL
HONEST PROPER GENUINE
VERMILION RED GOYA MINIUM PAPRIKA
PIMENTO VERMEIL CINNABAR
VERMIN FILTH CARRION VARMINT

VERMONT

CAPITAL: MONTPELIER
COLLEGE: BENNINGTON MIDDLEBURY
COUNTY: ESSEX ORANGE ADDISON
ORLEANS WINDSOR LAMOILLE
LAKE: CASPIAN DUNMORE SEYMOUR
CHAMPLAIN
MOUNTAIN: BROMLEY HOGBACK
ASCUTNEY PROSPECT MANSFIELD
MOUNTAIN RANGE: GREEN TACONIC
PRESIDENT: ARTHUR COOLIDGE
RIVER: SAXTONS LAMOILLE NULHEGAN
POULTNEY WINOOSKI
STATE BIRD: THRUSH
STATE FLOWER: CLOVER
STATE TREE: MAPLE
TOWN: BARRE STOWE CHELSEA GRAFTON
NEWFANE RUTLAND BENNINGTON
BURLINGTON
UNIVERSITY: NORWICH

VERNACULAR LINGO COMMON JARGON
PATOIS TONGUE VULGAR DIALECT
VERSATILE HANDY FICKLE MOBILE
FLEXILE
VERSE EPIC LINE RANN SONG BLANK

IONIC METER RHYME STAVE STICH
TANKA ADONIC BURDEN HEROIC JINGLE
PANTUN STANZA ANAPEST DICOLON
ELEGIAC SAPPHIC SAVITRI SOTADIC
TRIPODY TROILUS DACTYLIC DINGDONG
DOGGEREL RESPONSE SINGSONG
TRIMETER VERSICLE MACARONIC
(— FORM) VIRELAY KYRIELLE
(— OF 14 LINES) SONNET
(— OF 2 FEET) DIPODY DIMETER
(— OF 6 FEET) CHOLIAMB SENARIAN
SENARIUS
(— WITH LIMPING MOVEMENT)
SCAZON
(DEVOTIONAL —) ANTIPHON
OFFERTORY
(HINDU —) SLOKA
(JAPANESE —) HAIKAI
(MEDIEVAL —) SIRVENTE
(NONSENSE —S) AMPHIGORY
(UNMELODIOUS —) TERETISM
VERSION EDITION READING TURNING
REDACTION
(SHORT —) BRIEF
(SIMPLIFIED —) KEY
(TRANSLATED —) CONSTRUE
VERTEBRA AXIS RACK ATLAS DORSAL
LUMBAR SACRAL CERVICAL METAMERE
SPONDYLE
VERTEX APEX NODE POLE CROWN
SUMMIT
VERTICAL APEAK ERECT PLUMB SHEER
UPRIGHT COLUMNAR STRAIGHT
VERTIGO TIEGO MEGRIM MIRLIGO
SWIMMING WHIRLING
VERVE DASH ELAN BOUNCE ENERGY
PANACHE VITALITY VIVACITY
VERY SO ALL BIG GAY TOO BRAW DEAD
FULL JUST MAIN MUCH PURE REAL
SAME SELF SUCH TRES WELL AWFUL
BULLY JOLLY MOLTO PESKY RIGHT
SUPER BLAMED DAMNED DEUCED
FREELY GAINLY MAINLY MASTER MIGHTY
POISON PROPER SORELY STRONG
WONDER AWFULLY GREATLY PARLOUS
PRECISE STRANGE DREADFUL
ENORMOUS FAMOUSLY POWERFUL
SPANKING ABSOLUTELY
VESPERS LYCHNIC PLACEBO EVENSONG
VESSEL (ALSO SEE BOAT AND SHIP)
CAN CAT NEF TUB VAT BARK BOAT
BOMB BOWL BRIG BUSH CASK CELL
DISH DUCT HORN HULK LOTA PINT
PROW SAIL SHIP YAWL BARGE BASIN
BIDET BOCAL BOYER CADUS CHURN
CRAFT CRUSE DANDY GUIDE JUBBE
KETCH LAKER LAVER LINER PIECE SCOOP
SMACK STEAM XEBEC BARQUE BARREL
BOILER BOTTLE BUCKET CAIQUE COFFIN
COOLER COPPER CUTTER DECKER
DEINOS DOGGER KERNOS KETTLE
KRATER LANCHA LORCHA MULLER
PACKET PATERA PITHOS POURIE SALTER
SEALER SETTEE SITULA TARTAN TENDER
VESICA BAGGALA BLICKEY CARAVEL
CARRIER CISTERN CLIPPER CORSAIR
CRESSET CUVETTE DRIFTER DROGHER

FELUCCA FLYBOAT FRIGATE GAIASSA
GUNBOAT PATAMAR PINNACE POACHER
REDUCER SCALDER SETTLER SPARGER
STEAMER STEEPER UTENSIL BILANDER
BIRDBATH CORVETTE CRUCIBLE
DECANTER DIGESTER DUTCHMAN
FIREBOAT HELLSHIP HONEYPOT
INKSTAND INRIGGER KEELBOAT
NITRATOR SCHOONER SMUGGLER
SPITTOON
(— FOR COAL) GEORDIE
(— FOR DYE) TOBY
(— FOR HEATING LIQUIDS) ETNA
STOCK STOOP STOUP AMPULLA
BENITIER
(— FOR LIQUID WASTE) DRIP
(— FOR MEASURING ORE) HOPPET
(— FOR MOLTEN METAL) LADLE
(— FOR ORE WASHINGS) LOOL
(— FOR PERFUMES) CENSER
(— FOR PORRIDGE) BICKER
(— FOR SOLDIER'S FOOD) MESSTIN
(— FOR WINE SAMPLING) TASTER
(— HOLDING CONDIMENTS) CRUET
CASTER
(— IN MINE) CORB
(— MADE OF HOLLOW LOG) GUM
(— OF BARK) COOLAMON
(— OF HORN) BUGLE
(— ON TRIPOD) HOLMOS
(— ROWED BY OARS) CATUR GALLEY
(— STATIONED IN ENGLISH
CHANNEL) GROPER
(— USED IN MAKING GLAZE) HILLER
(ABANDONED —) DERELICT
(ARMORED —) CRUISER IRONCLAD
IRONSIDE
(BAPTISMAL —) FONT
(BARGELIKE —) PANGARA
(BLOOD —) AORTA ARTERY BLEEDER
EFFERENT
(BREWER'S —) ROUND
(CANDLEMAKING —) JACK
(CHEMIST'S —) BATH FLASK STILL
BEAKER RETORT
(CHINESE —) JUNK SAMPAN
(CIRCULAR —) KIT
(CLUMSY —) CRAY CRARE HAGBOAT
(COASTING —) DHOW DONI GRAB
PONTIN SHEBAR SHIBAR TRADER
COASTER GRIBANE MISTICO BILLYBOY
HOVELLER
(CODFISHING —) BANKER CODMAN
(DECORATIVE —) AIGUIERE
(DISTILLING —) BODY STILL RETORT
MATRASS CUCURBIT
(DRINKING —) CAP CUP TIN BOOT PECE
FOUNT GLASS GOURD JORUM POKAL
SCALE BICKER CAPPIE CHOPIN COOPER
COOTIE DIPPER DUBBER FIRLOT GOBLET
KITTIE QUAICH RABBIT RUMKIN BIBERON
GALLIOT SCYPHUS SKINKER SKYPHOS
TANKARD CANNIKIN CYLINDER
(DUTCH —) KOFF YANKY HOOKER
SCHUYT

(EARTHEN —) PIG BAYAN PANKIN
TINAGE CRAGGAN
(ELECTROPLATING —) TROUGH
(EUCHARISTIC —) AMA PYX AMULA
PYXIS FLAGON COLUMBA CHRISMAL
CIBORIUM MONSTRANCE
(GLASS —) VERRE UNDINE BALLOON
(HERRING-FISHING —) BUSS
(HOLLOW METALLIC —) BELL
(LADLING —) GAUN
(LARGE-NECKED —) JORDAN
(LATEEN-RIGGED —) DHOW LATEEN
LATEENER
(LEATHER —) BOOT JACK OLPE GIRBA
DUBBER
(LEVANTINE —) JERM SAIC
(LONG-NECKED —) GOGLET GUGLET
(LYMPHATIC —) LACTEAL
(MALAYAN —) PROA COUGNAR
(MELTING —) GRISSET
(OPEN —) LOOM
(PERFORATED —) LEACH
(PINECONE-SHAPED —) THYRSE
(PORTUGUESE —) MULET
(RARE —) SNOW
(SEED —) POD BUTTON BIVALVE
(SERVING —) ARGYLE ARGYLL SERVER
(SHALLOW —) KIVER SKEEL BEDPAN
PANCHION
(SMALL —) CAG HOY VIAL PHIAL VEDET
JIGGER LIEPOT PICARD TINLET YETLIN
FLIVVER VEDETTE YETLING GALLIPOT
(TOP-HEAVY —) CRANK
(TURKISH —) MAHONE
(WHALING —) WHALER SPOUTER
(WICKER —) POT
(WINE —) AMA AMULA TINAGE
(WOODEN —) COG KIT BOSS BAKIE
KIVER BICKER CAPPIE COOTIE DUDDIE
FIRKIN STOUND
VEST GARB GOWN ROBE ATTACH FECKET
JACKET WESKIT
VESTA WAX
(FATHER OF —) SATURN
(MOTHER OF —) RHEA
(SISTER OF —) JUNO CERES
VESTIBULE HALL ENTRY FOYER PORCH
ATRIUM NARTHEX PRONAOS ANTEROOM
VESTIGE TAG MARK SIGN PRINT RELIC
SPARK TRACE TRACK SHADOW
LEFTOVER RUDIMENT TINCTURE
VESTMENT ALB COPE PALL AMICE
COTTA EPHOD FANON RABAT STOLE
ROCHET SAKKOS VAKASS MANIPLE
ORARION PALLIUM CHASUBLE DALMATIC
SCAPULAR SURPLICE
VETERAN VET EMERITUS HARDENED
SEASONED
VETO NIX KILL DISALLOW
VEX FRY FAZE FRET GALL ITCH RILE ROIL
ANGER ANNOY CHAFE GRILL GRIPE
HARRY SCALD SPITE TEASE WORRY
WRACK BOTHER BURDEN CUMBER
GRIEVE GRUDGE HARASS HARROW
NETTLE OFFEND PLAGUE POTHER RUFFLE
AFFLICT BEDEVIL CHAGRIN PERPLEX

PROVOKE TORMENT ACERBATE BULLYRAG IRRITATE
VEXATION MOIL CHAFE ERROR GRIEF PIQUE SPITE STEAM WORRY BOTHER CHAGRIN DISGUST SORENESS
VEXATIOUS MEAN SORE NASTY PESKY ACHING FIERCE THORNY IRKSOME PEEVISH PRICKLY ANNOYING UNTOWARD PESTILENT
VEXED MAD SORE WILD ANGRY ROILY MIFFED GRIEVED
VEXING CHRONIC WAYWARD ANNOYING NETTLING
VIABLE VITAL HEALTHY
VIAL AMPUL CRUET PHIAL CASTER
VIANDS DIET FOOD CHEER VICTUALS
VIBRANT RINGY RESONANT SONOROUS VIGOROUS
VIBRATE JAR WAG BEAT ROCK WHIR PULSE QUAKE SWING THROB TRILL WAVER QUAVER QUIVER SHIMMY SHIVER THRILL TINGLE WARBLE CHATTER FLUTTER STAGGER TREMBLE TWIDDLE RESONATE
VIBRATION BUZZ SWING TRILL QUAVER QUIVER THRILL TREMOR FLUTTER TEMBLOR FREMITUS OSCILLATION
VICAR PROXY DEPUTY ALTARIST STALLARY
VICAR OF WAKEFIELD
(AUTHOR OF —) GOLDSMITH
(CHARACTER IN —) MOSES GEORGE OLIVIA SOPHIA WILMOT DEBORAH ARABELLA BURCHELL PRIMROSE THORNHILL
VICE SIN EVIL CRIME FAULT TAINT ULCER DEFECT OFFENSE INIQUITY
VICEROY EARL NABOB NAWAB EXARCH SATRAP WARDEN PROVOST
VICIOUS BAD ILL EVIL MEAN UGLY VILE ROWDY TOUGH SINFUL STRONG WICKED CORRUPT IMMORAL NAUGHTY DEPRAVED DEVILISH INFAMOUS NEFARIOUS
VICTIM BUTT DUPE GOAT GULL PREY QUARRY CASUALTY
(— FOR SHARPERS) JAY
(INTENDED —) CHUMP
(SACRIFICIAL —) HOST MERIAH
VICTOR COCK CAPTOR MASTER WINNER
VICTORY WIN PALM MASTERY SACKING TRIUMPH WINNING CONQUEST WALKOVER
(EASY —) BREEZE
(OVERWHELMING —) SWEEP
VICTUAL BIT VITTLE
(BROKEN —S) SCRAN
(PL.) KAI BITE CHOW FOOD GRUB PROVENDER PROVISIONS
VIE ENVY JOSTLE STRIVE COMPARE COMPETE CONTEND CONTEST EMULATE
VIEW EYE FACE GLOM BLUSH CATCH SCENE SIGHT VISTA ASPECT GLANCE REGARD SURVEY CONCEIT GLIMPSE LOOKOUT OPINION RESPECT SCENERY THOUGHT EYESIGHT PROSPECT SENTIMENT

(— ATTENTIVELY) GAZE
(— CLOSELY) INSPECT
(— FROM AFAR) DESCRY
(— FROM ANGLE) SLANT
(— WITH SURPRISE) ADMIRE
(BRIEF —) SNAPSHOT
(COMPREHENSIVE —) PANORAMA
(GENERAL —) LANDSKIP
(OPEN —) LIGHT
(PHYSICAL —) INSIGHT
(SATISFYING —) EYEFUL
VIGIL WAKE WATCH AGRYPNIA
VIGILANT AGOG WARY ALERT AWAKE AWARE CHARY SHARP WAKEFUL CAUTIOUS WATCHFUL
VIGOR GO PEP SAP VIM VIR VIS DASH EDGE ELAN PITH SNAP SOUL ARDOR DRIVE FORCE JUICE NERVE OOMPH POWER PUNCH VERVE ENERGY ESPRIT GINGER SPRING STARCH VIGOUR VIRTUS FREEDOM SMEDDUM STAMINA STHENIA FLOURISH STRENGTH TONICITY VITALITY
(MENTAL —) DOCITY SPIRIT
(RENEWED —) REST
VIGOROUS ABLE HALE LIVE SPRY ALIVE EAGER JUICY LUSTY NIPPY PEPPY PITHY SASSY STARK STOUT TOUGH VIVID FLORID HEARTY LIVELY MANFUL POTENT ROBUST RUGGED SINEWY STRONG STURDY CHIPPER CORDIAL FURIOUS HEALTHY VALIANT VIBRANT ZEALOUS ATHLETIC BOUNCING FORCEFUL MUSCULAR SLAMBANG SLASHING VEHEMENT YOUTHFUL TRENCHANT
VIGOROUSLY HARD TIGHT FRESHLY SMARTLY STOUTLY HEARTILY
VILE BAD BASE FOUL RANK CHEAP MUCKY SLIMY ABJECT CRUSTY DRAFTY FILTHY PALTRY SORDID TURPID UNKIND BEASTLY CAITIFF CORRUPT DEBASED HATEFUL IGNOBLE VICIOUS BASEBORN DEPRAVED UNKINDLY
VILIFY ABUSE LIBEL STAIN DEFAME MALIGN REVILE SLIGHT ASPERSE BLACKEN DEBAUCH DETRACT SLANDER TRADUCE REPROACH
VILLA DACHA LODGE CHALET QUINTA TRIANON
VILLAGE BYE HAM BOMA BURG DORP HOME TOWN VILL WICK ALDEA BOURG CASAL PLACE THORP VICUS ALDEIA BARRIO GOTHAM HAMLET BOROUGH CASERIO MISSION
(— IN WHICH BARLEY IS GROWN) BEREWICK
(— OUTSIDE OF FORT) PETTAH
(AFRICAN —) STAD KRAAL
(ARABIAN —) DOUAR
(ARGENTINE —) TOLDERIA
(FRENCH —) BASTIDE
(IMAGINARY —) CRANFORD
(INDIAN —) CASTLE PUEBLO CAMPOODY
(JAPANESE —) MURA BUSTEE
(JAVANESE —) DESSA
(JEWISH —) SHTETL
(MALAY —) KAMPONG

(MAORI —) KAINGA
(MEXICAN —) EJIDO
(NEW ZEALAND FORTIFIED —) PA
(NEWFOUNDLAND —) OUTPORT
(RUSSIAN —) MIR STANITSA
VILLAIN IAGO LOUT SERF DEMON DEVIL
FAGIN FELON HEAVY KNAVE ROGUE
SCAMP SHREW BADDIE SCOUNDREL
VILLAINOUS BAD EVIL KNAVISH
RAFFISH FLAGRANT RASCALLY
MISCREANT
VILLAINY CRIME KNAVERY
VIM ZIP ZING FORCE VIGOR ENERGY
GINGER SPIRIT STARCH VINEGAR
VINDICATE FREE CLEAR RIGHT ACQUIT
AVENGE EXCUSE UPHOLD ABSOLVE
JUSTIFY SUSTAIN MAINTAIN
VINDICTIVE HOSTILE PUNITIVE SPITEFUL
VENGEFUL
VINE AKA FIG HOP IVY BINE SOMA AKEBI
BWAZI GUACO KAIWI KUDZU LIANA
PALAY TIMBO TRAIL TWINE WITHE
BEJUCO CISSUS COBAEA DODDER
ECANDA JICAMA LABLAB PIKAKE
RUNNER TURURI TWINER ULLUCO
WINDER APRICOT BIGROOT BONESET
BRAMBLE CALAMUS CATVINE CERIMAN
CLIMBER COWHAGE COWITCH CUPSEED
EPACRID GHERKIN IPOMOEA LAVANGA
PAREIRA PUMPKIN TRAILER VINELET
YANGTAO
VINEGAR ESILL ACETUM ALEGAR
SOURING BEEREGAR
(— AND HONEY) OXYMEL
VINEYARD CRU COTE VINERY WINEYARD
VINTAGE OLD CUVEE ARCHAIC CLASSIC
OUTMODED
VIOLATE ERR SIN FLAW ABUSE BREAK
CRACK FORCE HARRY WRONG BREACH
DEFILE INVADE OFFEND RAVISH
DEBAUCH FALSIFY OUTRAGE POLLUTE
PROFANE VITIATE DEFLOWER DISHONOR
INFRINGE MISTREAT TRESPASS
VIOLATION SIN DEBT ABUSE CRIME
ERROR FAULT SALLY BREACH INJURY
MISCONDUCT
VIOLENCE FURY RAGE BRUNT FORCE
RIGOR STORM HUBRIS RAPINE STRESS
OUTRAGE FEROCITY SEVERITY
ROUGHHOUSE
VIOLENT HOT HARD HIGH RANK RUDE
WILD ACUTE HEADY HEAVY HEFTY
RABID SHARP SMART STARK STERN
STIFF WROTH FIERCE HEARTY MANIAC
MIGHTY SAVAGE SEVERE STORMY
STRONG STURDY SUDDEN DRASTIC
FURIOUS RAMPANT RUFFIAN TEARING
DIABOLIC FLAGRANT FORCEFUL
MANIACAL RIGOROUS SEETHING
SLAMBANG VEHEMENT
VIOLENTLY HARD AMAIN HOTLY HARDLY
SORELY HOPPING SOUNDLY
VIOLIN KIT ALTO GIGA AMATI CROWD
CRWTH GIGUE REBAB REBEC STRAD
TARAU VIOLA CATGUT CROUTH FIDDLE
CHROTTA CREMONA GUARNERI
VIPER ASP ADDER URUTU DABOIA

JESSUR KATUKA HAGWORM MAMUSHI
CERASTES JARARACA
VIRGIN NEW MAID PURE FRESH CHASTE
MAIDEN VESTAL INITIAL PUCELLE
(— OF PARADISE) HOURI

VIRGINIA

CAPITAL: RICHMOND
COLLEGE: AVERETT HOLLINS MADISON
RADFORD LONGWOOD
COUNTY: LEE BATH PAGE WISE BLAND
CRAIG FLOYD SMYTH SURRY WYTHE
AMELIA LOUISA ACCOMAC HENRICO
PATRICK PULASKI ROANOKE CULPEPER
FLUVANNA TAZEWELL
LAKE: KERR SMITH
MOUNTAIN: CEDAR ELLIOT ROGERS
BALDKNOB
MOUNTAIN RANGE: CLINCH ALLEGHENY
BLUERIDGE
RIVER: DAN JAMES POTOMAC RAPIDAN
STATE BIRD: CARDINAL
STATE FLOWER: DOGWOOD
STATE TREE: DOGWOOD
TOWN: GALAX LURAY SALEM MARION
BEDFORD BRISTOL EMPORIA NORFOLK
PULASKI ROANOKE DANVILLE HOPEWELL
MANASSAS STAUNTON TAZEWELL

VIRGINIA CREEPER CREEPER
WOODBIND WOODBINE
VIRGINIA KNOTWEED JUMPSEED
VIRGINIANS (AUTHOR OF —)
THACKERAY
(CHARACTER IN —) THEO WILL FANNY
HARRY HETTY MARIA MILES ESMOND
GEORGE RACHEL LAMBERT MOUNTAIN
BERNSTEIN CASTLEWOOD WARRINGTON
WASHINGTON
VIRGINITY HONOR CHASTITY PUCELAGE
VIRILE MALE MACHO MANLY
VIRILITY LUST MANHEAD MANHOOD
VIRTUAL IMPLICIT PRACTICAL
VIRTUALLY BUT NEARLY MORALLY
VIRTUE HSIN THEW FAITH GRACE POWER
VALOR WORTH DHARMA CHARITY
JUSTICE PROBITY QUALITY CHARISMA
CHASTITY GOODNESS MORALITY
VIRTUOUS GOOD PURE CIVIL MORAL
PIOUS CHASTE HONEST MODEST
SAINTED SINCERE UPRIGHT STRAIGHT
VIRULENT RANK ACRID RABID DEADLY
MALIGN NOXIOUS WASPISH VENOMOUS
VIRUS VENOM POISON PATHOGEN
SPECIFIC
VISAGE FACE PHIZ IMAGE ASPECT
FASHION
VISCID WAXY GOOEY GLAIRY STICKY
STRINGY VISCOUS
VISCOSITY BODY ROPINESS
VISCOUS LIMY ROPY GOBBY GUMMY
SLIMY STIFF TARRY SIRUPY SLABBY
SMEARY STICKY VISCID SQUISHY
MUCULENT

VISE JACK SHOP CHEEK CLAMP CRAMP WINCH

VISHNU RAMA VASU KALKI KRISHNA BALARAMA BHAGAVAT
(AVATAR OF —) KALKI KURMA BUDDHA MATSYA VAMANA VARAHA KRISHNA NARASINHA PARASHURAMA RAMACHANDRA
(BREAST JEWEL OF —) KAUSTUBHA
(BREASTMARK OF —) SHRIVATSA
(VEHICLE OF —) GARUDA
(WIFE OF —) SHRI LAKSHMI
(WRIST JEWEL OF —) SYAMANTAKA

VISIBLE OUT FAIR SEEN CLEAR EXTANT EVIDENT GLARING OBVIOUS APPARENT EXPLICIT EVIDENT MANIFEST

VISION EYE DREAM FANCY SIGHT FANTAD SEEING SHOWING SPECTER EYESIGHT PROSPECT
(— IN DIM LIGHT) SCOTOPIA
(BLURRED —) SWIMMING
(DEFECTIVE —) ANOPIA
(DOUBLE —) DIPLOPIA
(IMAGINARY —) SHADOW
(IMPERFECT —) CALIGO DARKNESS
(MULTIPLE —) POLYOPIA

VISIONARY AIRY IDEAL ASTRAL SHANDY UNREAL DREAMER UTOPIAN ACADEMIC DELUSIVE FANCIFUL IDEALIST NOTIONAL QUIXOTIC ROMANTIC

VISIT SEE CALL CHAT STAY HAUNT TRYST RESORT RETURN FREQUENT INVASION
(— BETWEEN WHALERS) GAM
(— PERSISTENTLY) INFEST
(— PROFESSIONALLY) ATTEND
(— RELATIVES) COUSIN
(— WRETCHED NEIGHBORHOODS) SLUM
(CEREMONIAL —) SELAMLIK

VISITOR GUEST CALLER VISITANT
(MEALTIME —) SCAMBLER

VISOR BILL BEAVER MESAIL UMBRIL EYESHADE

VISTA VIEW SCENE OUTLOOK PERSPECTIVE

VISUAL OPTIC OCULAR SCOPIC VISORY VISIBLE

VISUALIZE SEE FANCY IDEATE IMAGINE PICTURE CONCEIVE ENVISAGE

VITAL KEY LIVE BASIC CHIEF FRESH LIVELY MOVING VIABLE ANIMATE CAPITAL ESSENTIAL

VITALITY SAP VIM LIFE COLOR GUSTO JUICE OOMPH PULSE PUNCH BREATH ENERGY HEALTH MARROW STARCH STRENGTH

VITAMIN BIOTIN CITRIN NIACIN ADERMIN ANEURIN CHOLINE THIAMIN TORULIN ADVITANT INOSITOL NUTRAMIN ORYZANIN VITAMINE

VITRIOL BLUEJACK COPPERAS
(PL.) SORY

VITRIOLIC SHARP BITING BITTER CAUSTIC MORDANT SCATHING

VITUPERATE RAIL ABUSE CURSE SCOLD BERATE REVILE

VITUPERATIVE ABUSIVE REVILING SHAMEFUL

VIVACIOUS GAY AIRY PERT BRISK MERRY SUNNY ACTIVE BRIGHT LIVELY LIVING SPARKY JOCULAR ANIMATED SPIRITED SPORTIVE

VIVACITY BRIO FIRE LIFE ZEAL ARDOR VERVE VIGOR ESPRIT GAIETY SPIRIT SPARKLE

VIVID DEEP HARD KEEN LIVE RICH BRISK FRESH LURID QUICK RUDDY SHARP GARISH LIVELY LIVING STRONG VISUAL FLAMING GLARING GLOWING GRAPHIC INTENSE PEPPERY VIOLENT COLORFUL DISTINCT DRAMATIC SLASHING STRIKING PICTURESQUE

VIXEN FURY RANDY SCOLD SHREW VIRAGO

VOCABULARY CANT SLANG JARGON DICTION LEXICON WORDBOOK
(FAULTY —) CACOLOGY
(UNDERWORLD —) ARGOT

VOCAL GLIB ORAL FLUENT TONGUED ELOQUENT

VOCATION HOBBY METIER CALLING SCIENCE

VOCIFEROUS LOUD NOISY BAWLING BLATANT BRAWLING STRIDENT

VOGUE CUT FAD TON CHIC MODE RAGE STYLE CUSTOM FASHION

VOICE SAY VOX EMIT GIVE HARP PIPE TONE TURN WISH FROTH LEDEN RAISE RUMOR SOUND UTTER ACTIVE CHOICE STEVEN TAISCH THROAT TONGUE EXPRESS OPINION SONORIZE DIATHESIS
(— PRAISE) SLAVER
(ARTIFICIAL —) FALSETTO
(HOARSE —) FOGHORN
(LOWEST —) BASS BASSO
(MIDDLE —) MOTETUS
(PRINCIPAL —) CANTUS
(PUBLIC —) CRY
(SINGING —) ALTO BASS TENOR SOPRANO BARITONE FALSETTO
(TENOR —) TAILLE
(UPPER —) DESCANT

VOICELESS MUM DUMB HARD MUTE SURD ATONIC SILENT APHONIC

VOID NO BAD FREE MUTE NULL PASS ABYSS BLANK EGEST EJECT EMPTY LAPSE PURGE SPACE WASTE HOLLOW VACANT VACUUM CONCAVE INVALID VACANCY VACUITY EVACUATE
(— OF FEELING) BLATE
(— OF SENSE) INANE
(— OF SUBSTANCE) JEJUNE

VOLATILE LIGHT LIVELY BUOYANT DARTING FLIGHTY GASEOUS FUGITIVE SKITTISH VAPOROSE VAPOROUS FUGACIOUS
(PREF.) PTENO

VOLCANO APO DOME ETNA ASKJA PELEE SHASTA FURNACE FUMAROLE KRAKATOA VESUVIUS
(MUD —) SALSE SALINELLE

VOLITION WILL CHOICE INTENT VELLEITY

VOLLEY CROWD FLIGHT BARRAGE PLATOON BLIZZARD

VOLPONE (AUTHOR OF —) JONSON (CHARACTER IN —) CELIA MOSCA BONARIO CORVINO VOLPONE VOLTORE POLITICK CORBACCIO PEREGRINE

VOLUBLE GLIB WORDY FLUENT

VOLUME BAND BOOK BULK SIZE TOME CODEX SPACE CUBAGE CONTENT CAPACITY CUBATURE SOLIDITY STRENGTH

VOLUMINOUS FULL AMPLE BULKY LARGE BOUFFANT

VOLUNTARY FREE PRELUDE SORTITA WILLFUL WILLING ELECTIVE FREEWILL OPTIONAL POSTLUDE UNFORCED

VOLUNTEER OFFER ENLIST PROFFER

VOLUPTUOUS SULTRY WANTON SENSUAL LUSCIOUS SENSUOUS

VOODOO HEX CHARM OBEAH HOODOO SORCERER

VORACIOUS GREEDY GLUTTON EDACIOUS ESURIENT RAVENING RAVENOUS

VORTEX APEX EDDY GYRE SWIRL WHIRL

VOTE CON ELECT GRACE VOICE BALLOT DIVIDE TONGUE APPROVE SUFFRAGE (— AGAINST) NAY KNIFE NEGATIVE

(— APPROVAL) CONFIRM
(— FOR) AYE PRO SUPPORT
(— OF ASSENT) PLACET

VOUCH ASSURE ATTEST ENDORSE ACCREDIT

VOUCHER CHIT COUPON POLICY TICKET WARRANT

VOUCHSAFE GIVE SEND DEIGN GRANT PLEASE

VOW OATH SWEAR VOUCH BEHEST PLEDGE BEHIGHT PROMISE

VOYAGE SAIL TRIP COURSE CRUISE FLIGHT TRAVEL CARAVAN JOURNEY PASSAGE SAILING

VULGAR LOW LEWD LOUD RUDE BANAL CHEAP FLASH GROSS SLANG TOUGH COARSE COMMON RABBLE BLATANT BOORISH KNAVISH LOWBRED MOBBISH OBSCENE POPULAR PROFANE RAFFISH SECULAR VILLAIN CHURLISH PLEBEIAN

VULGARITY RAUNCH SHODDY FOULNESS

VULNERABILITY GAP EXPOSURE

VULNERABLE NAKED LIABLE EXPOSED PREGNABLE

VULTURE GEIR PAPA GRIPE URUBU CONDOR CORBIE FALCON GRIPHE GRIFFIN AASVOGEL

W

W WAW WHISKEY

WACKY CRAZY INSANE MENTAL ERRATIC

WAD BAT PAD POKE SWAB WISP WAGER PLEDGE

WADDLE WAG TODDLE

WADE FORD SLOSH PLOUTER
   (— IN MUD) LAIR

WAFER HOST ABRET CACHET GAUFRE MATZOH FLATBROD

WAFT PUFF WING WHIFF BECKON WINNOW

WAG LUG NOD WIT CARD CHAP FLAG
WAFF JOKER ROGUE SHAKE TROLL
JESTER WIGWAG FARCEUR HUMORIST
SLYBOOTS

WAGE FEE PAY HIRE LEVY FIGHT EMPLOY ENGAGE
   (— BATTLE) STRIKE

WAGER GO BET LAY PUT SET GAGE
PAWN TOSS PRIZE RAISE STAKE GAMBLE
IMPONE QUINELLA

WAGES FEE PAY UTU HIRE MEED SALARY
PENSION SERVICE STIPEND GRATUITY
LABORAGE PAYCHECK

WAGGISH ARCH DROLL JOCOSE JESTING
JOCULAR ROGUISH HUMOROUS
SPORTIVE

WAGON CAR FLY CART CHAR DRAY
TEAM WAIN BUGGY DILLY TRUCK
CAMION SPIDER CHARIOT COASTER
TUMBREL DEMOCRAT RUNABOUT
   (— WITHOUT SPRINGS) JERKY TELEGA
   (BAGGAGE —) FOURGON
   (COVERED —) VAN CARAVAN TARTANA
LANDSHIP CONESTOGA
   (LUMBER —) GILLY
   (MINING —) TRAM HUTCH ROLLEY
   (ROUNDUP —) HOODLUM
   (RUSSIAN —) TELEGA KIBITKA
   (SCREENED —) ARABA
   (STATION —) MICROBUS SUBURBAN
   (TEA —) SERVER

WAIF STRAY PALTRY IGNOBLE WASTREL

WAIL CRY BAWL HOWL KEEN MOAN
CROON MOURN LAMENT PLAINT
YAMMER ULULATE

WAIN CART WAGON CHARIOT

WAIST BASQUE BLOUSE BODICE HALTER
MIDDLE PIERROT

WAISTCOAT VEST BENJY GILET JERKIN
WESKIT SINGLET CAMISOLE

WAIT BIDE HOLD KEEP PARK STAY TEND
DEFER HOVER TARRY LINGER
   (— FOR) KEEP ABIDE AWAIT ATTEND
EXPECT
   (— ON) HOP SEE SERVE INTEND

WAITER CARHOP FLUNKY GARCON
SALVER TENDER PANNIER SERVITOR

WAIVE DEFER EVADE FORGO ABANDON

DECLINE FORSAKE POSTPONE RENOUNCE
RELINQUISH

WAKE STIR ALERT ROUSE VIGIL WATCH
AROUSE AWAKEN

WAKEFUL ALERT RESTLESS VIGILANT
WATCHFUL

WAKEFULNESS VIGIL WATCH
INSOMNIA

WALES

BAY: SWANSEA CARDIGAN TREMADOC

CAPITAL: CARDIFF

COUNTY: FLINT RADNOR DENBIGH
ANGLESEY CARDIGAN MONMOUTH
PEMBROKE

LAKE: BALA VYRNWY

MEASURE: COVER CANTRED CANTREF
LESTRAD LISTRED CRANNOCK

MOUNTAIN: SNOWDON

MOUNTAIN RANGE: BERWYN CAMBRIAN

PORT: CARDIFF

RIVER: DEE USK WYE TAFF TEME TOWY
TEIFI SEVERN VYRNWY

TOWN: MOLD RHYL ROSS FLINT TOWYN
AMLWCH BANGOR BRECON RUTHIN
CARDIFF NEWPORT RHONDDA SWANSEA
HEREFORD HOLYHEAD PEMBROKE
BRECKNOCK

WATERFALL: CAIN RHAIADR

WALK GO FOOT GAIT HOOF PACE STEP
ALLEY LEAVE MARCH SHANK SLOPE
SPACE TRACK TROOP AVENUE BEHAVE
BOUNCE SASHAY STROKE TODDLE
TRAVEL TRUDGE SHUFFLE TRAIPSE
AMBULATE ARBORWAY TRAVERSE
PROMENADE PEREGRINATE
   (— AFFECTEDLY) PRINK
   (— AIMLESSLY) PAUP
   (— AWKWARDLY) STAUP SHAMBLE
   (— BRISKLY) LEG SKELP
   (— CARELESSLY) JAYWALK
   (— CAUTIOUSLY) STALK
   (— CLUMSILY) JOLL STUMP LOPPET
   (— FOR EXERCISE) HIKE GRIND
   (— HEAVILY) PLOD CLUMP STUMP
TRAMP LAMPER PLODGE
   (— IDLY) DANDER POTTER SAUNTER
   (— LAME) LIMP HIRPLE HOBBLE
   (— LEISURELY) AMBLE DANDER
STROLL
   (— ON) BEAT TREAD
   (— OUT) FLOUNCE
   (— RAPIDLY) LAMP LINK STAVE
   (— SHAKILY) DOTTER
   (— SLOWLY) JET LAG
   (— SMARTLY) LINK

(— UNSTEADILY) REEL DADDLE FALTER STAVER STAGGER STUMBLE
(— WAVERINGLY) SHEVEL WARPLE
(— WITH DIFFICULTY) CRAMBLE LOUTHER
(— WITH STRIDES) STAG
(— WITHOUT LIFTING FEET) SCUFF
(BACKSTAGE —) BRIDGE
(COOL —) FRESCADE
(COVERED —) PAWN PORCH CLOISTER
(FOLIAGE-COVERED —) BERCEAU
(HARD —) STRAM SWINGE
(LIMPING —) GIMP
(POMPOUS —) STRUT
(PUBLIC —) XYST XYSTUS ALAMEDA
(RAISED —) GALLERY
(SHADED —) MALL ARBOR XYSTUS
(TEDIOUS —) TRAIL
WALKER GOER FOOTER TODDLER PEDESTRIAN
WALKING STICK CANE STICK WADDY KEBBIE GIBSTAFF
WALKOUT STRIKE
WALKURE, DIE (CHARACTER IN —) MIME WOTAN FRICKA HUNDING SIEGMUND SIEGLINDE BRUNNHILDE
(COMPOSER OF —) WAGNER
WALL FIN BELT CELL CORE CURB DIKE HEAD MURE PACK SKIN WING FENCE HEDGE MURAL PIRCA SHOJI BAFFLE BATTER CUTOFF DOKHMA PARIES PARPEN SCREEN SHIELD VALLUM CURTAIN ENCLOSE MIZRACH PARAPET PERPEND TAMBOUR SPANDREL
(— ABOVE FACADE) ATTIC
(— AROUND) IMMURE
(— BEHIND ALTAR) REREDOS
(— BETWEEN TWO OPENINGS) PIER
(— CARRYING CUPOLA) DRUM
(— CARRYING ROOF) BAHUT
(— CROSSING RAMPART) SPUR
(— IN HOCKEY RINK) BOARD
(— IN ROMAN ARENA) SPINA
(— IN TRUCK) HEADER
(— OF BLAST FURNACE) DAM INWALL FIREBACK
(— OF CASTLE) BARMKIN
(— OF CLAY) COTTLE
(— OF MINE) FACE
(— OF TENT) KANAT CANAUT
(CIRCULAR —) CASHEL
(CURVED —) SWEEP
(DIVIDING —) SEPTUM
(END — OF BUILDING) GABLE
(FISH —) LEADER
(LOG —) CRIB
(LOW —) BAHUT PODIUM PLUTEUS
(OUTER — OF CASTLE) BAIL BAILEY
(PEAT —) COP
(RETAINING —) CRIB BULKHEAD
(SCARPED —) GHAT
(SECONDARY —) CHEMISE
(SUSTAINING —) RIPRAP
(VENTRAL —) STERNUM
(WING —) AILERON
WALLET JAG POKE BOUGE BULGE SCRIP BUDGET ALFORJA BILLFOLD NOTECASE POCHETTE
WALLOP BEAT SLUG SOCK PASTE POUND IMPACT TROUNCE FLOUNDER LAMBASTE
WALLOW LAIR ROLL SOIL SLOSH GROVEL MUDDLE SWELTER FLOUNDER
WALLPAPER GROUND SCENIC HANGING TENTURE TAPESTRY
WALNUT ACAPU NOGAL TRYMA AKHROT BANNUT
WALRUS MORSE PELAGIAN PINNIPED ROSMARINE
WALTZ MARCH VALSE BOSTON BREEZE FLOUNCE
WAMPUM PEAG HAWOK MONEY SEWAN ROANOKE
WAN DIM PALE SICK FAINT WHITE FEEBLE PALLID SALLOW GHASTLY LANGUID
WAND ROD YARD BATON STAFF STICK VERGE FERULA THYRSE RHABDOS THYRSUS CADUCEUS
(JESTER'S —) BAUBLE
WANDER BUM ERR GAD MAZE MUCK RAVE ROAM ROVE WALK DRIFT GLAIK KNOCK RANGE ROGUE STRAY TAVER WAIVE WAVER CANDER CRUISE FORAGE MITHER MOIDER PALMER PERUSE RAMBLE STROLL SWERVE WILDER TRAFFIC TRAIPSE ABERRATE STRAVAGE
(— ABOUT) DIVAGATE
(— ABSTRACTEDLY) MOON
(— AIMLESSLY) SWAN SLOSH TRACE MEANDER
(— AS A VAGABOND) SHACK
(— AS A VAGRANT) LOITER
(— AT RANDOM) SQUANDER
(— ERRATICALLY) SWASH
(— FROM DIRECT COURSE) STRAGGLE
(— FROM PLACE TO PLACE) WAG
(— IDLY) HAKE LOUT MAUNDER SHACKLE
(— IN DELIRIUM) DWALE
(— IN MIND) DAVER DANDER DELIRE
(— LEISURELY) BUMMEL
(— RESTLESSLY) FEEK
WANDERER WAIF ROVER RANGER PILGRIM RAMBLER FUGITIVE RUNAGATE TRAVELER VAGABOND
WANDERING ERROR STRAY VAGUE ASTRAY ERRANT MOBILE ROVING DEVIOUS NOMADIC ODYSSEY VAGRANT WINDING ABERRANT FLOATING FUGITIVE PLANETIC RAMBLING RESTLESS VAGABOND MIGRATORY PEREGRINE
WANE GO EBB SET ABATE DECAY UNWAX DECLINE DWINDLE DECREASE
WANGLE FAKE SHAKE WIGGLE FINAGLE
WANT HURT LACK LIKE MISS NEED PINE VOID CRAVE FAULT FORGO DEARTH DESIRE PENURY PLIGHT ABSENCE BEGGARY BLEMISH DEFAULT MISEASE POVERTY REQUIRE VACANCY
(— EXCEEDINGLY) DIE
(— OF CONTROL) ACRASY

(— OF ENERGY) ATONY
(— OF GOOD SENSE) FOLLY
(— OF VIGOR) DELICACY
WANTON NAG RIG DAFT IDLE LEWD
DALLY LIGHT SAUCY GIGLET HARLOT
LUBRIC RAKISH TOYING UNRULY
COLTISH FULSOME IMMORAL LUSTFUL
RIOTOUS WAYWARD FLAGRANT
LUSCIOUS PETULANT SKITTISH SLIPPERY
SPORTIVE UNCHASTE
WANTONNESS FOLLY PRIDE SPORT
WAR CAMP FEUD FIGHT SWORD BATTLE
CONTEND CRUSADE CONFLICT
WAR AND PEACE (AUTHOR OF —)
TOLSTOY
(CHARACTER IN —) LISE ELLEN MARYA
ANDREY PIERRE ROSTOV ANATOLE
BEZUHOV KURAGIN KUTUZOV NATASHA
NIKOLAY VASSILY NAPOLEON
BOLKONSKY NIKOLUSHKA
WARBLE SING CAROL CHANT CHIRM
TRILL YODEL DESCANT VIBRATE
WARBLER CHAT WREN PEGGY CANARY
REELER SYLVIA CREEPER FANTAIL
HAYBIRD REDPOLL TROCHIL BLACKCAP
FAUVETTE OVENBIRD PINCPINC
REDSTART REEDBIRD
WARD CARE GUARD WATCH BARRIO
CALPUL DEFEND KEEPING CONTRADA
(— OFF) FEND WEAR AVERT AWARD
FENCE PARRY REPEL STAVE SHIELD
WARDEN DIZDAR PORTER RANGER
REGENT WARNER ALCAIDE CLAVIGER
WARDROBE CLOSET VESTRY ARMOIRE
VESTUARY
WARE CLOTH GOODS FABRICS
SQUANDER
(CERAMIC —) SPODE
(CLOISONNE —) SHIPPO
(ENAMELED —) BILSTON COALPORT
(INFERIOR —S) SLUM
(JAPANESE —) IMARI YAYOI
(JAPANESE CERAMIC —) SETO BIZEN
KARATSU
(MAJOLICA —) DERUTA
(PORCELAIN —) CHINA BERLIN
(UNGLAZED —) BISQUE
WAREHOUSE GOLA HONG ETAPE STORE
BODEGA GODOWN STAITH STOWAGE
ENTREPOT MAGAZINE
WAR-HORSE CHARGER COURSER
TROOPER DESTRIER
WARINESS CAUTION DISTRUST
WARLIKE MARTIAL CAVALIER FIGHTING
MILITARY BELLICOSE
WARLOCK IMP WITCH SPRITE WIZARD
CONJUROR SORCERER
WARM HOT BASK KEEN LEWD MILD
CALID CHAFE EAGER FRESH TOAST
ARDENT DEVOUT FOSTER GENIAL
HEARTY HEATED TENDER CLEMENT
CORDIAL GLOWING THERMAL ZEALOUS
FRIENDLY SANGUINE
(— UP) SCORE
(MODERATELY —) LEW SLACK TEPID
WARMHEARTED KIND TENDER
FRIENDLY GENEROUS

WARMTH GLOW HEAT LIFE ZEAL ARDOR
ENERGY FERVOR ARDENCY PASSION
CALIDITY FERVENCY
WARN ALERT ADVISE EXHORT INFORM
CAUTION COMMAND COUNSEL
ADMONISH THREATEN
WARNING ALARM FLAG CHECK KNELL
BEACON CAVEAT LESSON NOTICE
SIGNAL TIPOFF CAUTION EXAMPLE
MONITOR PRESAGE SUMMONS
MONITION
(— OF DISASTER) DIRE
(ARCHERY —) FAST
(DANGER —) VIGIA
WARP BIAS CAST LIFT ANGLE CHOKE
CROOK KEDGE BUCKLE DEFORM DEFLECT
DISTORT
WARPED WRY BUCKLED GNARLED
WARRANT AMRIT BERAT FIANT PRESS
SANAD VOUCH ASSERT BREVET COUPON
DOCKET ENSURE INSURE PARDON
PERMIT PLEVIN POLICY TICKET JUSTIFY
PRECEPT PROMISE GUARANTY
WARRIOR HERO KEMP RINK BERNE
SEPAD SINGH OSSIAN WARMAN FIGHTER
SOLDIER STARKAD CHAMPION
SHARDANA SWORDMAN
(— OF NOBLE RANK) EARL
(AMERICAN INDIAN —) BRAVE
SANNUP
(BOASTFUL —) RODOMONT
(BRYTHONIC —) LLUDD
(BURGUNDIAN —) HAGEN
(FEMALE —) AMAZON SHIELDMAY
(IRISH —) FENIAN
(KAFFIR —S) IMPI
(MUSLIM —) GHAZI
(NOTED —) THANE THEGN
(SCANDINAVIAN —) BERSERK
(SCOTTISH —) ZERBINO
(TROJAN —) AGENOR
(VALIANT —) TOA
(VIRGIN —) CAMILLA
WARSHIP WAFTER CRUISER MONITOR
SULTANE CORVETTE
WART ANBURY SYCOMA PUSTULE
VERRUCA PAPILLOMA
WARY SHY CAGY WISE AWARE CANNY
LEERY CAREFUL GUARDED PRUDENT
CAUTIOUS VIGILANT WATCHFUL
WASH BOG FEN LAG TUB BEER EDDY
HOSE LAVE SUDS WADI BATHE CLEAN
CLEAR DOLLY ERODE SOUSE SWILL
LOTION PURIFY SLUICE SOZZLE STREAM
CLEANSE LAUNDER SHAMPOO
EYEWATER
(— A GAS) SCRUB
(— AWAY) GULL
(— BY TREADING IN WATER) TRAMP
(— DOWN) SIND SOOGEE
(— FOR GOLD) PAN
(— GIVEN TO SWINE) DRAFF
(— GRAVEL) ROCK
(— IN LYE) BUCK
(— LIGHTLY) RINSE
(— OFF) DETERGE

(— ORE) TYE HUTCH BUDDLE CRADLE STRAKE
(— OUT) SIND ELUTE FLUSH LAVAGE
(— ROUGHLY) SLUSH
(— THOROUGHLY) SCOUR
(— VIGOROUSLY) SLOSH
(— WITH COSMETIC) SURFLE
(DRY —) ARROYO
WASHER BURR DRUM CLOUT BUTTON RONDEL GROMMET COTTEREL SCRUBBER

WASHINGTON

CAPITAL: OLYMPIA
COLLEGE: WHITMAN
COUNTY: ASOTIN KITSAP SKAGIT YAKIMA CLALLAM KITTITAS
DAM: COULEE
LAKE: CHELAN
MOUNTAIN: JACK TUNK ADAMS LEMEI LOGAN MOSES SLOAN QUARTZ SIMCOE STUART OLYMPUS RAINIER SHUKSAN
MOUNTAIN RANGE: KETTLE CASCADE OLYMPIC
RIVER: SNAKE YAKIMA COLUMBIA
SOUND: PUGET
STATE BIRD: GOLDFINCH
STATE TREE: HEMLOCK
TOWN: OMAK PASCO TACOMA YAKIMA EPHRATA EVERETT OTHELLO SEATTLE SPOKANE LONGVIEW

WASP MASON SPHEX BEMBEX DAUBER DIGGER HORNET TREMEX VESPID SCOLIID STINGER
WASPISH TESTY FRETFUL PEEVISH CHOLERIC SNAPPISH
WASTE EAT BURN GNAW JUNK LOSS PASS SACK TEAR DROSS HAVOC SCRAP SLOTH SPILL BANGLE COMMON DEBRIS DESERT DEVOUR DIDDLE DRIVEL ELAPSE EXPEND GARBLE MOLDER MUDDLE PERISH RAVAGE REFUSE SCATHE SPILTH CONSUME EXHAUST FRITTER GARBAGE MULLOCK RUBBISH DEMOLISH SQUANDER
(— AWAY) BATE MELT DECAY DWINE SWAIN SWEAL TRAIK WANZE TABEFY WINDLE DWINDLE FORPINE MISLIKE DISSOLVE EMACIATE FORSPEND MACERATE
(— GRADUALLY) WEAR ABSUME
(— IN DRUNKENNESS) SOT
(— IN RIOT) BEZZLE
(— OF SILK COCOONS) KNUB
(— TIME) FOOL FRIG IDLE DALLY DEFER DRILL DAWDLE DIDDLE FOOTER FOOTLE LOITER DRINGLE FOOSTER GAUSTER
(COAL —) SLUDGE
(COTTON —) FLUKE SLASHER SPOOLER
(FOOD —) SLOP
(LIQUID —) DRIPPING EFFLUENT
(MINING —) GOB GOAF
(WOOL —) FUD MUNGO GARNETT
(YARN —) THRUM EYEBROW

WASTEFUL LAVISH PROFUSE DESOLATE PRODIGAL
WATCH EYE SEE SPY TAB ESPY GLOM HEED LOOK MARK MIND WAKE WARD YARD CLOCK SCOUT SPIAL TIMER VERGE VIGIL WAKEN BEHOLD SENTRY SHADOW TICKER TURNIP OBSERVE OVERSEE STRIKER HOROLOGE SENTINEL SPECTATE
(— FOR) TENT ABIDE AWAIT
(— OVER) HOLD KEEP TEND GUARD ATTEND OVERLOOK
(— QUIETLY) HINT
(— THAT STRIKES) STRIKER REPEATER
(— WITH HINGED COVER) HUNTER
(ALARM —) TATTLER
(CLOSE —) SCRUTINY
(NAUTICAL —) HACK DOGWATCH
(NIGHT —) LYKEWAKE
WATCHFUL ALERT AWARE CANNY CHARY ERECT ANXIOUS GUARDED WAKEFUL VIGILANT OBSERVANT
WATCHMAN FLAG MINA GUARD SCOUT VIGIL ASKARI GHAFIR SERENO WARDER GUARDER WAKEMAN SENTINEL
WATCHTOWER WARD BEACON SENTRY ATALAYA LOOKOUT MIRADOR BARBICAN
WATCHWORD CRY MAXIM PAROLE SIGNAL PASSWORD
WATER EAU AGUA AQUA BATH LAKE POND POOL TIDE WAVE BILGE FLUME LOUGH LYMPH RIVER TEARS PHLEGM SALIVA STREAM AQUATIC JAVELLE IRRIGATE SNOWMELT
(— AFTER BOILING RICE) CONGEE
(— BY CALENDERING) TABBY
(— FOR BREWING) BURN
(— IN SOIL) HOLARD
(— IN WEIR) LASHER
(— REDDISH WITH IRON) RIDDAM
(— SURROUNDED BY ICE) WAKE
(— UNDER PRESSURE) HUSH
(BAPTISMAL —) LAVER
(BARLEY —) PTISAN
(BOTTOM — OF SEA) ABYSS
(BOUNDARY —) SHARD
(BUBBLING —) SPRUDEL
(DEEP —) BALLOW
(DIRTY —) SAUR PUDDLE
(FAST-MOVING —) SOUP
(FEN —) SUDS
(FROZEN —) ICE FROST
(HOLY —) HYSSOP
(HOT —) SOUP
(LIVING —) RASA
(MINERAL —) VICHY SELTZER
(OPEN —) POLYNYA
(QUININE —) TONIC
(RED —) RESP RIDDAM
(ROUGH —) SEA
(SALT —) BRACK BRINE SEAWATER
(SOAPY —) SUDS GRAITH
(SPLASH OF —) FLASH
(STILL —) KELD LOGIN
(SULPHUR —) BAREGE
(SWEETENED —) AMRITA
WATER CLOCK GHURRY CLEPSYDRA
WATERCOURSE

(ALSO SEE STREAM AND RIVER) RUN DIKE LEAT WADI BAYOU BROOK CANAL DITCH DRAIN ARROYO COURSE GUTTER KENNEL CHANNEL

WATERFALL FALL LINN CHUTE FORCE SAULT SPOUT CASCADE CATARACT

WATER HOG BUSHPIG CAPYBARA

WATERLOGGED SOGGY SWAMPY EDEMATOUS

WATERMELON PEPO GOURD MELON CITRUL SANDIA CUCURBIT

WATERSHED BROW DIVIDE SNOWSHED

WATERSPOUT RONE SPOUT VORTEX TWISTER GARGOYLE

WATERWAY GUT DOCK DITCH INLET ARTERY SEAWAY CULVERT HIGHWAY

WATERWHEEL NORIA SAGEER SAKIEH DANAIDE

WATERY WET LASH THIN BOGGY MOIST SAMMY WASHY BLASHY LIQUID SEROUS AQUATIC AQUEOUS HYDROUS PHLEGMY

WAVE FAN FLY SEA BECK FLAG FLAP GUST SULK SWAY WAFT CRIMP FLASH FLOAT PULSE SHAKE SURGE SWELL SWING BILLOW COMBER FLAUNT MARCEL RIPPLE ROLLER WAFFLE BREAKER BRIMMER CRIMPLE FEATHER FLICKER FLUTTER TSUNAMI WHIFFLE BRANDISH FLOURISH UNDULATE WHITECAP
(— ABOUT) WAMPISH
(— OF EXCITATION) IMPULSE
(— OF FLAG) DOT DASH
(— OF SHIP) BONE
(ELECTRIC —) STRAY CARRIER
(HAIR —) PERMANENT
(LARGE —) HEAVY
(TIDAL —) EAGER

WAVER HALT REEL SWAY VARY CHECK DOUBT FLOAT SWING DITHER FALTER QUIVER SWERVE TEETER TOTTER WAFFLE WOBBLE FLICKER FLITTER FLUTTER STAGGER VIBRATE HESITATE VACILLATE

WAVERING WAVY WEAK FICKLE GROGGY WIGGLY DUBIOUS LAMBENT DOUBTFUL FLEXUOUS FLICKERY PENDULOUS

WAVERLEY (AUTHOR OF —) SCOTT
(CHARACTER IN —) EVAN LEAN ROSE VOHR ALICE COSMO DAVIE FLORA DONALD FERGUS STUART CHARLES EVERARD MACIVOR GARDINER PEMBROKE WAVERLEY GELLATLEY MACCOMBICH BRADWARDINE

WAVY UNDE MOIRE SNAKY CRIMPY FLECKY WIGGLY BUCKLED CRINKLY CURVING ROLLING SINUATE UNDULAR FLEXUOUS SQUIGGLY

WAX CERE GROW RAGE BECOME CERESIN CARNAUBA CEROXYLE COCCERIN INCREASE
(— FAINT) APPAL
(— IN HONEYCOMB) CAPPING
(— STRONG) PREVAIL
(CHINESE —) PELA
(COBBLER'S —) CODE

(EAR —) CERUMEN
(SKI —) KLISTER

WAY LAW TAO VIA FARE GAIT KIND LANE LARK PACE PATH ROAD SORT WISE ALLEY FORTH GOING GUISE HABIT MOYEN ROUTE STYLE TRADE ACCESS AVENUE CAREER CHEMIN COURSE MANNER METHOD STREET TRAJET CHANNEL FASHION HIGHWAY PASSAGE APPROACH FOOTPATH VICINITY
(CLEVER —) KNACK
(COVERED —) CORRIDOR
(INDIRECT —) AMBAGES
(LONG —) FAR
(MAJOR —) STEM
(NARROW —) DRANG
(ODD —S) JIMJAMS
(PLANK —) BRIDGE
(RAISED —) BANQUETTE
(ROUNDABOUT —) DETOUR CIRCUIT
(ROUNDABOUT —S) AMBAGES
(SETTLED —) BIAS
(SIDE —) BRANCH
(SLOPING —) RAMP
(UNDEVIATING —) GROOVE

WAYFARER VIATOR PILGRIM TRAVELER PASSENGER

WAYLAY BESET AMBUSH FORSET OBSTRUCT SURPRISE

WAY OF ALL FLESH (AUTHOR OF —) BUTLER
(CHARACTER IN —) JOHN ELIZA ELLEN MARIA PRYER ALLABY ALTHEA ERNEST GEORGE JOSEPH OVERTON SKINNER MAITLAND PONTIFEX THEOBALD CHARLOTTE CHRISTINA

WEAK DIM FOND LAME NICE PALE PUNY SOFT THIN WASH FAINT FLASH JERKY LIGHT REEDY SILLY SLACK WASHY WEARY YOUNG DILUTE DOTISH FEEBLE FLABBY FLAGGY FLIMSY FOIBLE GROGGY INFIRM LITTLE MARCID SICKLY TENDER UNSURE WATERY BRICKLE FLACCID FOOLISH FRAGILE INSIPID INVALID LANGUID PUERILE RICKETY SHALLOW SLENDER SPINDLY TOTTERY UNHARDY DECREPIT FECKLESS FLAGGING HELPLESS IMPOTENT THEWLESS SPINELESS
(— FROM FATIGUE) TANGLE
(— FROM HUNGER) LEER
(— IN RESOLUTION) FRAIL
(MENTALLY —) TOTTY

WEAKEN GO LAG SAP DAMP FAIL HURT MELT PALL SINK THIN ALLAY BLUNT BREAK QUAIL SPEND WATER APPALL DEFEAT DENUDE DILUTE FALTER IMPAIR LESSEN PERISH REDUCE SICKEN SOFTEN CORRODE CORRUPT CRIPPLE DECLINE DEPRESS DISABLE MOLLIFY QUALIFY UNNERVE DIMINISH ENERVATE ENFEEBLE

WEAKLING TOY PULER SOFTIE DILLING RECKLING SOFTLING

WEAKNESS ATONY CRACK FAULT DEFECT FOIBLE ACRATIA FAILING FISSURE FRAILTY LANGUOR ASTHENIA DEBILITY DELICACY FONDNESS

WEALTH WAD GEAR GOLD GOOD MEANS
WORTH GRAITH MAMMON RICHES
FORTUNE RICHDOM WELFARE OPULENCE
PROPERTY TREASURE

WEALTHY FAT BIEN FULL RICH AMPLE
LOADED MONEYED ABUNDANT
AFFLUENT

WEAPON
(ALSO SEE SPECIFIC TYPE OF
WEAPON) ARM BOW GUN BILL BOLO
CLUB DART EPEE FALX FOIL MACE PIKE
ADAGA ARROW BILLY FLAIL KNIFE
LANCE SPEAR STEEL SWORD VOUGE
CANNON CHAKRA DAGGER TOMBOC
BAZOOKA FIREARM HALBERD HARPOON
HURLBAT JAVELIN SHOTGUN ARBALEST
BLUDGEON CROSSBOW FAUCHARD
PARTISAN
(CELTIC —) PALSTAFF
(DEADLY —) DEATH
(LINE OF —S) RIDGE
(PREHISTORIC —) CELT

WEAR KIT BEAR GROW HAVE PASS
CHAFE GUARD VOGUE WEARY BATTER
CONSUME DEFENSE DEGRADE FASHION
FRAZZLE PROCEED WEATHER
(— AN OPENING) BREACH
(— AND TEAR) GAFF SLITE GRUELING
(— AWAY) EAT FADE FRET GALL GNAW
GULL PINE ERODE GULLY SCOUR SPEND
ABRADE CORRODE CONTRIVE
(— DOWN) BRAY GRIND ABRADE
ABRASE GRAVEL
(— FURROWS) GUTTER
(— IN PUBLIC) SPORT
(— OFF) FRAY ABRADE
(— OUT) DO BURN COOK FLOG JADE
TIRE TUCK BREAK SLAVE SPEND HATTER
EXHAUST HACKNEY OVERWEAR
(— SHIP) CAST

WEARISOME DRY DULL HARD SLOW
BORING SODDEN IRKSOME TEDIOUS
TIRESOME TOILSOME

WEARY FAG IRK BORE CLOY PALL POOP
TIRE WEAK WORN BORED SPENT
HARASS PLAGUE SICKLY TUCKER
EXHAUST FATIGUE IRKSOME GRIEVOUS
TIRESOME WRETCHED

WEASEL CANE VAIR HURON SNEAK
STOAT TAYRA ERMINE FERRET FUTTERET
MUSTELIN WHITRACK

WEATHER SKY RAIN TIME COLLA STORM
(FAIR —) SHINE
(HOT AND HUMID —) SIZZARD
(INCLEMENT —) SEASON
(INTERVAL OF FAIR —) SLATCH
(VIOLENT —) ELEMENTS

WEAVE CANE JOIN LACE LOOM REED
SPIN DRAPE PLAIT TWINE UNITE DEVISE
ENTWINE FASHION
(— PATTERNS INTO) BROCADE
(BASKET —) BARLEYCORN
(CARPET —) FLOSSA
(HERRINGBONE —) SUMAK SOUMAK
SHEMAKA
(LATTICE —) TEE
(OPEN —) LENO BAREGE

WEB PLY CAUL MAZE TENT TOIL SKEIN
SNARE TWIST TISSUE ENSNARE
TEXTURE VEXILLUM
(— IN EYE) HAW
(CRANK —) THROW

WED GET BRIDE MARRY ENGAGE PLEDGE
ESPOUSE

WEDDING BRIDAL SPLICE NUPTIAL
WEDLOCK ESPOUSAL MARRIAGE

WEDGE FROE HORN PLUG STOB TRIG
CLEAT QUINE QUOIN COTTER SCOTCH
VOUSSOIR
(— BETWEEN TWO FEATHERS) KEY
(— IN) JAM JAMB
(— OF OATMEAL) FARL
(— TO PREVENT MOTION) CHOCK
(CURVED —) CAM
(WOODEN —) COW GLUT JACK

WEED HOE BURR CHOP CULL DOCK TARE
BLINKS COCKLE DARNEL JIMSON
SPURGE ASHWORT BUGLOSS RAGWEED
RAGWORT SANDBUR VERVAIN
CHADLOCK PURSLANE TOADFLAX

WEEP CRY SOB BAWL LEAK OOZE TEAR
WAIL BEWAIL BOOHOO BUBBLE LAMENT
SHOWER BLUBBER COMPLAIN

WEEPING RAINY BOOHOO LAMENT
OOZING BLUBBER MAUDLIN TEARFUL
DRIPPING LACRIMAL

WEIGH GO SIT HEFT PEIS COUNT HEAVE
HOIST POISE RAISE SCALE ANALYZE
BALANCE LIBRATE CONSIDER EVALUATE
MEDITATE
(— DOWN) LADE SWAY BESET PEISE
CHARGE CUMBER PESTER DEPRESS
FREIGHT OPPRESS OVERLAY ENCUMBER
(— UPON) SIT GRIEVE

WEIGHT
(ALSO SEE MEASURE AND UNIT) KIN
NET RAM SER TOM ATOM BEEF DROP
GRAM HEFT IRON LEAD LOAD MEAL NAIL
ONUS POND PORT ROTL SEAM SEER SINK
WAIT ABBAS GARCE LIVRE PICUL POISE
PRESS SCALE STAMP AUNCEL BURDEN
CHARGE DIRHEM IMPORT MOMENT
PONDER SINKER STRESS BALLAST
GRAVITY PLATINE PLUMMET DEMIMARK
DUMBBELL ENCUMBER PRESSURE
PRESTIGE STRENGTH
(— CARRIED BY HORSE) IMPOST
(— CLOTH) FLOCK
(— FOR HURLING) HAMMER
(— FOR LEAD) FOTHER FOTMAL
(— FOR PRECIOUS STONE) CARAT
(— FOR WOOL) TOD SARPLER
(— FOR WOOL, CHEESE, ETC.) CLOVE
(— OF BROADSIDE) GUNPOWER
(— OF COAL) KEEL
(— OF COFFEE) MAT
(— OF HYDROGEN) CRITH
(— OF METAL) JOURNEY
(— OF ONE 10TH TAEL) MACE
(— OF ONE 100TH TAEL) FEN
(— OF PENDULUM) BOB
(— OF PILE DRIVER) TUP
(— OF RAW SILK) PARI
(— OF SILK OR RAYON) DRAMMAGE

(— OF 100 LBS.) CENTAL CENTENA
CENTNER
(— OF 1000 LIVRES) MILLIER
(— OF 20 OR 21 LBS.) SCORE
(— OF 40 BUSHELS) WEY
(— OF 5 UNCIAE) QUINCUNX
(— ON MINE SWEEPER) KITE
(— ON STEELYARD) PEA
(— ON WATCH CHAIN) FOB
(— TO BEND HOT METAL) DUMPER
(— TO DETECT FALSE COINS) PASSIR
(— TO HINDER MOTION) CLOG
(— WHICH VESSEL CAN CARRY)
TONNAGE
(ABYSSINIAN —) FARASULA
(CARAT —) SILIQUA
(CLOCK —) PEISE
(COUNTERFEIT —) SLANG
(FALSE —) SLANG
(GREATLY VARYING —) MAN MAUND
(HEAVY —) MONKEY
(LIGHT —) SUTTLE
(MONEYER'S —) DROIT
(ORIENTAL —) TAEL CATTY
(SASHCORD —) MOUSE
(SHUFFLEBOARD —) SHIP
(SMALL —) MITE GERAH RIDER
(SPLINE —) DOLPHIN
WEIGHTY GRAVE GREAT HEAVY HEFTY
SOLID VALID COGENT SOLEMN EARNEST
MASSIVE ONEROUS SERIOUS TELLING
GRIEVOUS MATERIAL POWERFUL
PREGNANT PORTENTOUS SIGNIFICANT
WEIRD ODD EERIE CREEPY ELDRICH
UNCANNY UNUSUAL WIZARDLY
WELCOME SEE HAIL ADOPT CHEER
GREET TREAT INVITE SALUTE ACCLAIM
GRATIFY BIENVENU GREETING
ACCEPTABLE
WELD SHUT SWAGE UNITE
WELFARE GOOD HALE SELE WEALTH
BENISON BLESSING
WELL GAY PIT BENE FINE FLOW GOOD
PURE SAFE SINK WINK GREAT MUSHA
QUELL WALLY BUCKET ENOUGH FAIRLY
NICELY OFFSET PUMPER TUNNEL
HEALTHY BOREHOLE FOUNTAIN
WATERPIT
(— AND STRONG) BUNKUM
(— IN GLACIER) MOULIN
(— THROUGH FLOORS OF
WAREHOUSE) FALLWAY
(— UP) WALL WALM DIGHT
(NONPRODUCTIVE —) DUSTER
(OIL —) OILER GASSER GUSHER
SPOUTER WILDCAT STRIPPER
(RECTANGULAR —) BOWLY
(SACRED — AT MECCA) ZEMZEM
(VERY —) BRAWLY CLEVER
WELL-BEING SKIN WEAL HEALTH
WEALTH COMFORT WELFARE
PROSPERITY
WELLBORN GENTLE EUGENIC
WELL-BRED POLITE GENTEEL REFINED
CULTURED
WELL-DRESSED BRAW GASH SMART
BRAWLY

WELL-FOUNDED FIRM GOOD JUST
SOUND WORTHY
WELL-GROOMED SMUG CRISP SOIGNE
WELL-KNOWN FAMOUS KENNED PUBLIC
FAMILIAR PROMINENT
WELL-NIGH ALMOST NEARLY WELLMOST
WELL-PROPORTIONED SUING TRETIS
HANDSOME
WELL-TO-DO ABLE BEIN EASY WARM
WELSHMAN CELT KELT TAFFY BRYTHON
CAMBRIAN
WELT WALE RIDGE STRIP BANDELET
WEN CYST CLYER TALPA TUMOR GOITER
WENCH DILL DOXY DRAB GIRL JADE
MAID MOLL TRUG KITTY MADAM QUEAN
TRULL WHORE BLOUSE DRAZEL POPLET
(CLUMSY —) MODER MODDER MOTHER
MAUTHER
WEND BOW STEER BETAKE DEPART
DIRECT TRAVEL PROCEED
(— ONE'S WAY) MARK
WESTERN SAMOA (CAPITAL OF —)
APIA
(ISLAND OF —) UPOLU MANONO
SAVAII APOLIMA
(MONEY OF —) TALA

WEST INDIES

ISLAND: CAT CUBA LONG ABACO EXUMA
HAITI NEVIS PELEE TURKS ANDROS
BAHAMA CAICOS CAYMAN INAGUA
TOBAGO VIRGIN ACKLINS ANTIGUA
BONAIRE CROOKED CURACAO GRENADA
JAMAICA LEEWARD STKITTS STLUCIA
TORTOLA ANGUILLA BARBADOS
DOMINICA STTHOMAS TRINIDAD
WINDWARD ELEUTHERA MARGARITA
MAYAGUANA STVINCENT GUADELOUPE
HISPANIOLA MARTINIQUE MONTSERRAT
PUERTORICO

WEST VIRGINIA

CAPITAL: CHARLESTON
COLLEGE: SALEM BETHANY CONCORD
MARSHALL BLUEFIELD
COUNTY: CLAY WIRT BOONE HARDY
MINGO ROANE TUCKER UPSHUR
BARBOUR KANAWHA
LAKE: LYNN
RIVER: ELK OHIO KANAWHA POTOMAC
GUYANDOT
STATE BIRD: CARDINAL
STATE FLOWER: RHODODENDRON
STATE TREE: MAPLE
TOWN: ELKINS KEYSER RIPLEY VIENNA
WESTON BECKLEY GRAFTON SPENCER
WEIRTON FAIRMONT WHEELING

WESTWARD HO (AUTHOR OF —)
KINGSLEY
(CHARACTER IN —) YEO JOHN LUCY
ROSE AMYAS FRANK LEIGH DESOTO

GUZMAN EUSTACE OXENHAM RICHARD
GRENVILE SALTERNE AYACANORA

WET DEW DIP SOP DAMP DANK LASH
MOIL SOAK SOFT BATHE DRUNK HUMID
JUICY LEACH MOIST RAINY SLAKE STEEP
TIGHT DAMPEN HUMECT IMBRUE
MADEFY MARSHY QUASHY SHOWER
SPONGY WATERY BLUBBER MOISTEN
IRRIGATE SATURATE SLOBBERY
(— AND STORMY) FOUL
(— LIGHTLY) SPRINKLE
(— THOROUGHLY) SOUSE DRENCH
(SOFTLY —) SQUASHY
(VERY —) SOPPY

WHACK LAM BANG BELT BIFF DEAL
HACK SWACK DEFEAT STROKE THWACK

WHALE CETE ORCA POGGY SPERM
BALEEN BELUGA BLOWER FINNER KILLER
BOWHEAD DOLPHIN FINBACK GRAMPUS
RORQUAL SPOUTER ZIPHIAN CACHALOT
CETACEAN GREYBACK HUMPBACK
PHYSETER THRASHER

WHARF KEY DOCK PIER QUAY SLIP
BERTH JETTY LEVEE STRAND LANDING

WHEAT CORN EMMER FULTZ GRAIN
SPELT SPICA TRIGO CEREAL KANRED
EINKORN KUBANKA POLLARD FRUMENTY
(— BOILED IN MILK) FURMITY
(BEARDED —) RIVETS
(CRACKED —) GROATS
(GRANULATED —) SUJI
(HARD —) DURUM
(PARCHED —) BULGUR

WHEEDLE COG CANT COAX FLUFF GLOZE
JOLLY BANTER CAJOLE SMOOGE
BLARNEY PALAVER BLANDISH
SCROUNGE

WHEEL COG FAN NUT ORB PURL ROLL
ROTA STAR FLUFF IDLER REWET RHOMB
SWING TRUCK CASTER CIRCLE FANNER
HORRAL JAGGER LEADER ROLLER
RUNNER BICYCLE GUDGEON REVOLVE
TRAILER TRINDLE TRUNDLE FOLLOWER
SPROCKET
(— CHARGED WITH DIAMOND
DUST) SLITTER
(— CONTROLLING RUDDER) HELM
(— FOR EXECUTIONS) RAT
(— IN KNITTING MACHINE) BURR
(— IN TIMEPIECE) BALANCE
(— OF LIFE) ZOETROPE
(BUCKET —) LIFTER
(DIAMOND —) SKIVE
(GEAR —) DRIVEN HELICAL
(GRINDING —) SHELL
(GROOVED —) PULLEY SHEAVE SHIVER
(INTERRUPTER —) TICKER
(LOCOMOTIVE —) DRIVER
(METAL —) FILLET
(MILL —) PIRN
(POINTED —) TRACER
(POLISHING —) BOB BUFF SKEIF
BUFFER
(POTTER'S —) LATHE THROW
(SPARE —) STEPNEY
(SPINNING —) TURN CHARKA
(SPUR —) ROWEL

(TANK —) BOGIE
(TOOTHED —) GEAR PINION ROULETTE
(TURBINE —) ROTOR
(TWO PAIRS OF —S) CUTS CUTTS
(VANED —) FLIER FLYER
(WATER —) NORIA SAKIA TYMPANUM

WHEELBARROW GURRY BARROW
CARRIAGE

WHELP CUB PUP SON FAWN PUPPY
KITLING

WHEN AS BUT FRO THAN THEN TILL
SINCE UNTIL ALTHOUGH

WHERE AS FAR PLACE THERE WHITHER
LOCATION

WHEREFORE WHY CAUSE REASON

WHET GOAD HONE TURN GRIND POINT
ROUSE EXCITE INCITE STROKE QUICKEN
SHARPEN

WHETSTONE RUB BUHR SLIP STONE
SHARPER OILSTONE RUBSTONE
STRICKLE

WHIFF FAN BLOW GUFF GUST HINT PUFF
WAFT FLUFF GUSHT SMOKE EXHALE

WHILE AS YET TILL WHEN PIECE SPACE
STEAD UNTIL BEGUILE TROUBLE
OCCASION
(— AWAY) AMUSE FLEET DIVERT
BEGUILE DECEIVE
(LITTLE —) AWEE DRASS

WHIM BEE FAD TOY FLAM KINK CRANK
FANCY FLISK FOLLY FREAK HUMOR
QUIRK MAGGOT VAGARY CAPRICE
CONCEIT WRINKLE CROTCHET

WHIMPER MEWL PULE WAIL BLEAT
WHINE SIMPER YAMMER SNIFFLE
SNUFFLE

WHIMSICAL FAIRY FANCY FLISKY
QUAINT BAROQUE BIZARRE PUCKISH
FANCIFUL HUMOROUS NOTIONAL
VAPOROUS

WHIMSY WHIM FREAK VAGARY CAPRICE
WHIMWHAM

WHINE GIRN MEWL PULE TOOT BLEAT
CROON SNIVEL YAMMER WHIMPER

WHIP CAT EEL GAD BEAT COIL DUST
FLOG GOAD HIDE JEHU JERK LASH LICK
URGE ABUSE BIRCH FLAIL FLICK FLISK
IMPEL ROMAL SLASH STRAP SWING
SWISH TAWSE THONG AROUSE DEFEAT
INCITE LARRUP NETTLE SWITCH THRASH
CHICOTE COWHIDE KURBASH LAMBAST
RAWHIDE SCOURGE SJAMBOK SLASHER
TICKLER CONFOUND FLAGELLA
(— EGGS) CAST
(— IN PIANO ACTION) WIPPEN
(— WITH 3 LASHES) PLET PLETE
(HORSE —) WAND CHABOUK
(JOCKEY'S —) BAT
(RIDING —) CROP DICK QUIRT
(RUSSIAN —) KNOUT

WHIPPING LICK HIDING FANNING
SERVING BIRCHING SKELPING

WHIRL BIRL EDDY FURL GYRE HURL REEL
RUSH SPIN DRILL SKIRL SWIRL TWIRL
TWIST WALTZ WHORL BUSTLE CIRCLE
GYRATE VORTEX REVOLVE TURMOIL
VERTICIL

(— ABOUT) DOZE GURGE
(— IN THE AIR) WARP
WHIRLING GIDDY GYRATION GYRATORY
VORTICAL PIROUETTE
WHIRLPOOL EDDY GULF SUCK GURGE
VORTEX SWALLOW SUCKHOLE
MAELSTROM
WHISK ZIP WHIP FLICK FLISK HURRY
SPEED SWISH SWITCH COWTAIL
WHISKER HAIRLINE VIBRISSA
(PL.) BEARD ZIFFS WEEPER GALWAYS
MOUSTACHE SIDEBURNS
WHISKY RYE BOND CORN IRISH POTEEN
REDEYE SCOTCH BOURBON POPSKULL
USQUABAE MOONSHINE TANGLEFOOT
WHISPER BUZZ HINT RUMOR TRACE
BREATH BREEZE MURMUR TITTLE
SUSURRUS
WHIST MORT VINT QUIET BOSTON
SILENT WHEESHT
WHISTLE BLOW CALL PIPE BUMMER
CUCKOO HOOTER SQUEAL WARBLE
CATCALL BIRDCALL
WHIT BIT JOT RAP ATOM DOIT HOOT
IOTA AUGHT GROAT QUITE SPECK
PARTICLE TWOPENNY
WHITE WAN HOAR LILY PALE ASHEN
BLOND HAOLE HOARY LINEN SNOWY
ALBINO ARGENT BLANCH BRIGHT
BUCKRA ERMINE SILVER WINTRY
CANDENT NIVEOUS INNOCENT
(— AND SMOOTH) IVORINE
(— OF EGG) GLAIR ALBUMEN
(POOR —) YAHOO CRACKER
WHITE COMPANY (AUTHOR OF —)
DOYLE
(CHARACTER IN —) JOHN MAUDE
NIGEL HORDLE LORING SAMKIN ALLEYNE
AYLWARD EDRICSON
WHITEFISH CISCO PILOT BELUGA
CHIVEY POLLAN BLOATER BOWBACK
GWYNIAD LAVARET BLACKFIN
GREYBACK HUMPBACK TULLIBEE
WHITEN CAM CAUM ALBIFY BLANCH
BLEACH BLENCH ETIOLATE
WHITENESS IVORY ALBEDO ARGENT
CANDOR PURITY PALENESS
WHITEWASH LIME BLANCH PARGET
LIMEWASH PALLIATE
WHITTLE CUT PARE CARVE KNIFE
WHIZ BUZZ PIRR SING WHIR SOUGH
WHISH
WHOLE ALL SUM BODY EVEN HALE HULL
BLOCK GREAT GROSS SOLID SOUND
TOTAL TUTTA UNCUT ENTIRE HEALED
INTACT GENERAL INTEGER PERFECT
COMPLETE ENSEMBLE ENTIRETY
INTEGRAL UNBROKEN
(— OF ANY ORGANISM) SOMA
(— OF REALITY) ABSOLUTE
(ORGANIC —) SYSTEM
WHOLEHEARTED HEARTY SINCERE
ZESTFUL COMPLETE IMPLICIT
WHOLESOME GOOD CLEAN SOUND
SWEET BENIGN SAVORY HEALTHY
PRUDENT CURATIVE REMEDIAL
SALUTARY HEALTHFUL

WHOLLY ALL FLAT ONLY CLEAR FULLY
QUITE STARK BODILY FLATLY PURELY
SOLELY ROUNDLY SOLIDLY TOTALLY
DIRECTLY ENTIRELY
WHOOP BOOM HOOT RAISE SHOUT
EXCITE HALLOO
WHOPPING VERY LARGE BANGING
THUMPING WHACKING WALLOPING
WHORE DRAB JILT QUAIL WENCH
HARLOT QUEAN STRUMPET PROSTITUTE
WICK FARM TOWN ANGLE CREEK MATCH
QUICK CORNER LIVING WICKED VILLAGE
FARMSTEAD
(— CLOGGED WITH TALLOW)
ROUGHIE
(LONG WAXED —) TAPER
WICKED BAD SAD DARK EVIL FAST FOUL
LEWD MEAN VILE BLACK CURST FELON
SORRY WRONG CURSED SEVERE SINFUL
UNHOLY UNJUST CAITIFF GODLESS
HEINOUS HELLISH IMMORAL NAUGHTY
NOXIOUS PROFANE UNGODLY UNSOUND
VICIOUS VILLAIN ACCURSED CRIMINAL
DARKSOME DEPRAVED DEVILISH
DIABOLIC FELONOUS FIENDISH
FLAGRANT PERVERSE TERRIBLE
UNKINDLY NEFARIOUS PERNICIOUS
WICKEDNESS ILL SIN EVIL HARM VICE
CRIME GUILT FELONY UNGOOD DEVILRY
DARKNESS DEVILTRY INIQUITY
SATANISM
WICKET GATE HOOP HATCH PITCH
STUMP GUICHET
WIDE FAR LAX DEEP AMPLE BROAD
LARGE ROOMY SLACK ASTRAY SPACIOUS
(— OF) BESIDE
(— OF THE MARK) AWRY WILD
ABROAD
(LONG AND —) SIDE
WIDE-AWAKE FOXY KEEN LIVE ALERT
LEERY KNOWING WAKEFUL WATCHFUL
WIDEN REAM DILATE EXPAND EXTEND
FLANGE FUNNEL BROADEN
WIDENESS WIDTH BREADTH
WIDESPREAD RIFE DIFFUSE GENERAL
POPULAR PROLATE CATHOLIC EXTENDED
PANDEMIC SWEEPING
WIDOW DAME MATRON RELICT
DOWAGER DOWERESS
WIDTH SIDE RANGE SCOPE BREADTH
OPENING FRONTAGE FULLNESS
LATITUDE
(— OF CUT) KERF
(— OF HORSESHOE) COVER
(— OF PALM) HAND
(— OF PAPER) FILL
(— OF PULLEY) FACE
(— OF SHIP) BEAM
(— OF SHIP'S BAND) STRAKE
(— OF TYPE) SET
(— OF WEB) DECKLE
WIELD PLY RUN BEAR APPLY EXERT
SWING EMPLOY GOVERN HANDLE
MANAGE CONTROL
WIFE HEN MRS RIB DORA ENID FRAU
FROW LADY MAMA MATE RANI UXOR
DIRCE DONNA FEMME MATCH MUJER

SQUAW WOMAN EMILIA MATRON
MISSUS MULIER SPOUSE WAHINE
BEDMATE PARTNER DEIANIRA HELPMATE
HELPMEET MISTRESS
(— OF COTTER) COTQUEAN
(— OF KNIGHT OR BARONET) DAME
(— OF MOHAMMEDAN) KHADIJA
(AFFIANCED —) FUTURE
(INDIAN'S —) WEBB
(OLD —) GAMMER

WIG BOB RUG LOCK TETE CAXON MAJOR
SCALP SCOLD PERUKE REBUKE TOUPEE
COMBING SPENCER POSTICHE
(— WITH ROUGHLY CROPPED HAIR)
BRUTUS
(BUSHY —) BUSBY
(GRAY —) GRIZZLE
(WORSTED —) JASEY
(18TH CENTURY —) ADONIS GEORGE

WIGGLE JET HOTCH JIGGLE WABBLE
WANGLE

WIGWAM TIPI LODGE TEPEE WICKIUP

WILD APE MAD FAST RUDE CRAZY FERAL
GIDDY RANDY ROUGH WASTE DESERT
FERINE FIERCE LAVISH MADCAP NATIVE
RANDOM SAVAGE STORMY UNRULY
BERSERK ERRATIC FRANTIC HOWLING
MADDING NATURAL RIOTOUS ABERRANT
BARBARIC DESOLATE FRENETIC
RECKLESS UNTILLED WARRAGAL
BOISTEROUS

WILDCAT CAT BALU EYRA CHATI CHAUS
MANUL TIGER MARGAY SERVAL WAGATI
COLOCOLA

WILD DUCK (AUTHOR OF —) IBSEN
(CHARACTER IN —) GINA EKDAL
SORBY WERLE HANSEN HEDVIG
GREGERS HJALMAR RELLING

WILDERNESS BUSH WILD WASTE
DESERT FOREST SOLITUDE

WILE ART RUSE FRAUD GUILE TRICK
ALLURE DECEIT ENTICE BEGUILE
ARTIFICE TRICKERY

WILL EGO MAY WAY FATE LIST WISH
LEAVE OUGHT SHALL CHOICE CHOOSE
DESIRE DEVICE DEVISE LEGATE LIKING
CODICIL PASSION AMBITION BEQUEATH
VOLITION
(— OF DEITY) DECREE
(— OF GOD) LAW
(— OF LEGISLATURE) ACT
(— TO LIVE) TANGHA
(FREE —) ACCORD
(GOOD —) GREE
(ILL —) ARR ENVY HEST ANIMUS
ENMITY UNTHANK AMBITION

WILLFUL HEADY FEISTY UNRULY
WAYWARD

WILLIAM TELL (AUTHOR OF —)
SCHILLER
(CHARACTER IN —) JOHN TELL FURST
HENRY ARNOLD BERTHA ULRICH WALTER
WERNER GESSLER WILLIAM MATHILDE
BAUMGARTEN
(COMPOSER OF —) ROSSINI

WILLING FAIN FREE GLAD LIEF PRONE

READY MINDED TOWARD CONTENT
UNFORCED

WILLINGLY SOON FREELY GLADLY
LIEFLY FRANKLY READILY

WILLOW ITEA OSIER SALEW SALIX
WITHY DUSTER
(— FOR THATCHING) SPRAYS
(— IN TEXTILES) WOLF
(NATIVE —) COOBA
(SIMPLE —) WHIPPER

WILLOWY SUPPLE SLIPPER DELICATE

WILT EBB SAG DROP FADE FLAG DROOP
SUCCUMB COLLAPSE

WILY SLY FOXY CANNY SLICK ARTFUL
ASTUTE CLEVER CRAFTY QUAINT
SHREWD SUBTLE TRICKY CUNNING
POLITIC VERSUTE

WIN BAG COP HIT DRAW GAIN HAVE
LAND LICK FORCE SCORE ATTACH
CLINCH OBTAIN ACHIEVE ACQUIRE
CONQUER DESERVE HARVEST POSSESS
TRIUMPH OVERCOME
(— AGAINST) BREAK SCOOP
(— AWAY) STEAL DEBAUCH
(— BACK) RECOVER
(— BY GUILE) GET POT BEAR CARRY
RAISE TRAIN GATHER CAPTURE INVEIGLE
PROMERIT
(— EASILY) ROMP
(— NARROWLY) SQUEEZE
(— OVER) DEFEAT DISARM
(— OVERWHELMINGLY) SWEEP

WINCE KICK CHECK CRINGE FLINCH
RECOIL SHRINK

WINCH CRAB JACK REEL GIPSY ROLLER
WINDLE CATHEAD TRAVELER WINDLASS

WIND AIR COP LAP BALL COIL CONE CURL
EAST FIST GALE GUST KINK PUFF ROLL
WEST WRAP BLAST CRANK CREEK
CROOK SPOOL STORM TWINE TWIST
WEAVE WITHE BOTTOM BOUGHT
COLLAR SPIRAL SPIRIT SQUALL WAMPLE
WESTER ZEPHYR BREATHE CRANKLE
CRINKLE CYCLONE ENTWINE EQUINOX
INVOLVE MEANDER SERPENT SINUATE
TEMPEST TWINGLE TWISTER WEATHER
WHIRLER WINDILL DOWNWARD
EASTERLY FAVONIUS
(— ABOUT) WIRE SNAKE
(— AFTER DYEING) BATCH
(— FROM THE ANDES) ZONDA
PAMPERO
(— IN AND OUT) INDENT WINGLE
(— MAGNETS) COMPOUND
(— OF CUBA) BAYAMO
(— OF HAWAII) KONA
(— OF OREGON AND WASHINGTON)
CHINOOK
(— ROPE) WORM WOOLD
(— THREAD OR YARN) QUILL CHEESE
(— TO PREVENT CHAFING) KECKLE
(— WOOL) TREND
(— YARN) BEAM SERVE WINDLE
(—S OF CHILE AND PERU) SURES
(ADRIATIC —) BORA
(BROKEN —) HEAVES
(COLD —) BISE BORA SARSAR BLIZZARD

(COOLING —) IMBAT
(DEAD —) NOSER
(DESERT —) SAMUM GIBLEH SAMIEL
SIMOOM KHAMSIN SIROCCO
(DRYING —) TRADE
(EASTERLY —) LEVANT LEVANTER
(FIERCE —) BUSTER
(GUST OF —) FLAN FLAW
(HEAD —) NOSER MUZZLE
(HIGH —) RIG
(LIGHT GENTLE —) BREEZE
(NORTH —) BISE AQUILO BOREAS
AQUILON MISTRAL
(NORTHEAST —) BURAN GREGALE
(NORTHWEST —) CAURUS MAESTRO
ARGESTES
(PERIODICAL —) ETESIAN MONSOON
(PERSIAN GULF —) SHAMAL SHARKI
(PERUVIAN —) PUNA
(ROARING —) BLORE
(SEVERE —) SNIFTER
(SOUTH —) NOTUS AUSTER
(SOUTHEAST —) EURUS SOLANO
(SOUTHEASTERLY —) SHARKI
SHURGEE
(SOUTHWEST —) CHINOOK LIBECCIO
(STRONG —) BIRR
(VIOLENT —) BUSTER SQUALL
SNORTER
(WARM —) FOEHN CHINOOK SANTANA
(WEST —) ZEPHYR FAVONIUS
ZEPHYRUS
WINDER REEL WINCH DRUMMER
PLUGGER SKEINER SPOOLER
WINDFALL VAIL GRAVY MANNA
BLOWDOWN BUCKSHEE
WINDING MAZY CRANK SPIRE DETOUR
GYRATE SCREWY SPIRAL TWISTY
CRINKLE DEVIOUS MEANDER SINUOUS
SNAKING WRIGGLY
WINDLASS CRAB WINCH TURNEL
TWISTER WILDCAT DRAWBEAM
WINDMILL JUMBO MOTOR COPTER
PINWHEEL
WINDOW BAY EYE ROSE SLIT SLOT
GLAZE GRILL INLET LIGHT OGIVE SIGHT
DORMER PEEPER ROSACE WICKET
BALCONE FENSTER ORIFICE TRANSOM
VENTANA CASEMENT FENESTRA
VENETIAN
(— OF TWO LIGHTS) COUPLET
(BAY —) ORIEL MIRADOR
(BLANK —) ORB
(DORMER —) OXEYE DORMANT
LUCARNE LUTHERN
(HIGH NARROW —) LANCET
(ROUND —) OCULUS ROUNDEL
(SEMICIRCULAR —) FANLIGHT
(TICKET —) GRILLE GUICHET
(TWIN —) AJIMEZ
WINDPIPE WIZEN GUGGLE WEEZLE
TRACHEA WEASAND THROTTLE
WINDY BLOWY GASSY GUSTY HUFFY
STARK SWALE STORMY BREATHY
GUSTFUL VENTOSE VIOLENT
BOISTEROUS
WINE VIN BOIS PALM PORT ROSE GRAPE

KRAMA LUNEL PETER PORTO SHRAB
SOAVE TOKAY VINUM CORTON COUTET
KIJAFA LISBON MASDEU ROCHET
SAUMUR SHIRAZ SOLERA TIVOLI
AMBONNA BARBERA CHACOLI CHATEAU
FALERNO MARSALA MISSION MOSELLE
ORVIETO PALERMO RHENISH ROSOLIO
SERCIAL APERITIF BORDEAUX
DELAWARE MALVASIA MARSALLA
ROCHELLE RULANDER RUMBOOZE
SPARKLER BARDOLINO
(— BOILED WITH HONEY) MULSE
(— FROM VINEGAR) ESILL
(— MIXED WITH WATER) KRASIS
(— OF EXCELLENT QUALITY)
VINTAGE
(— OF SACRAMENT) BLOOD
(AROMATIZED —) DUBONNET
(BANANA —) MARAMBA
(BULK —) CUVEE
(CONSECRATED —) CUP
(FIRST-GROWTH —) LAFITTE
(FRANCONIAN —) STEIN LEISTEN
(GREEK —) RUMNEY RETSINA
(HEATED —) WHITEPOT
(INFERIOR —) PLONK
(JAPANESE —) SAKI
(LIGHT —) BUAL CAPRI BAROLO
CANARY
(MULLED —) GLUHWEIN
(NEW —) MUST
(NEW — BOILED DOWN) CUIT
(PALM —) SAGWIRE
(RED —) MACON TINTA BEAUNE CLARET
CHIANTI HOLLOCK POMMARD ALICANTE
BURGUNDY CABERNET FLORENCE
(REVIVED —) STUM
(RHINE —) HOCK SYLVANER
(SPANISH —) SACK TENT DULCE
OPORTO SHERRY ALICANT BASTARD
TARRAGONA
(STILL —) PONTAC PONTACQ
(SWEET —) TYRE DULCE MULSE
CANARY BASTARD MALMSEY CHARNECO
MUSCATEL
(TENT —) TINTO
(TOKAY —) ESSENCE
(TUSCAN —) VERDEA CHIANTI
FLORENCE
(WHITE —) HOCK SACK CAPRI CASEL
FORST BARSAC MALAGA BROMIAN
CATAWBA CHABLIS CONTHEY LANGOON
ANGELICA BUCELLAS RIESLING
SAUTERNE VERMOUTH
WING ALA ARM FAN FLY OAR RIB VAN
SAIL TAIL ANNEX FLANK PINNA BRANCH
FLETCH FLIGHT PENNON PINION POISER
ELYTRON AEROFOIL BALANCER
DISPATCH
(— OF ARMY) HORN
(— OF BUILDING) ELL JAMB JAMBE
ALETTE FLANKER
(— OF SHELL) AURICLE
(— OF THEATER) COULISSE
TORMENTOR
(— OF TRIPTYCH) VOLET
(—S DISPLAYED) VOL

(BASTARD —) ALULA
(BIRD'S —) FLAG
(FLY'S —S) HALTERES
WINK BAT NAP BLINK FLASH PRINK
SLEEP TWINK FLICKER INSTANT NICTATE
SPARKLE TWINKLE NICTITATE
WINNIE-THE-POOH (AUTHOR OF —)
MILNE
(CHARACTER IN —) ROO KANGA
ROBIN EEYORE PIGLET RABBIT
HEFFALUMP CHRISTOPHER
WINNING SWEET PROFIT GAINING
VICTORY WINSOME CHARMING
(— OF ALL TRICKS) CAPOT SCHWARZ
WINNOW FAN SIFT WIND SIEVE DELETE
REMOVE SELECT SEPARATE
WINSOME GAY BUXOM SWEET
CHARMING CHEERFUL PLEASANT
WINTER BISE SNOW HIEMS DECEMBER
HIBERNATE
WINTERSET (AUTHOR OF —)
ANDERSON
(CHARACTER IN —) MIO CARR GARTH
GAUNT TROCK ESDRAS SHADOW
ROMAGNA MIRIAMNE BARTOLOMEO
WINTER'S TALE (AUTHOR OF —)
SHAKESPEARE
(CHARACTER IN —) DION MOPSA
DORCAS EMILIA CAMILLO LEONTES
PAULINA PERDITA FLORIZEL HERMIONE
ANTIGONUS AUTOLYCUS CLEOMENES
MAMILLIUS POLIXENES ARCHIDAMUS
WINTRY COLD WHITE BOREAL HIEMAL
STORMY BRUMOUS CHILLING HIBERNAL
WIPE BEAT DRUB DUST DIGHT SWIPE
CANCEL SPONGE STRIKE ABOLISH
CLEANSE ABSTERGE SQUEEGEE
(— BEAK OF HAWK) FEAK
(— NOSE) SNITE
(— OFF) SCUFF
(— OUT) ERASE SCRUB SWEEP EFFACE
DESTROY
(— UP) SWAB
WIRE GUY TAP CORE DRAG PURL CABLE
OUTER RISER SNAKE HEATER NEEDLE
STAPLE STOLON STRAND LASHING
SHIFTER FILAMENT STRINGER TELEGRAM
(— BETWEEN TWO VESSELS) SWEEP
(— FOR CUTTING CLAY) SLING
(— FOR SUSTAINING HAIR) PALISADE
(— IN BLASTING CAP) BRIDGE
(— IN CATHETER) STYLET
(— IN WEAVING LOOM) DENT
(— OF GOLD,SILVER OR BRASS)
LAMETTA
(— TO ADJUST WICK) SNUFFER
(— TO CLOSE A BREAK) JUMPER
(— TO REMOVE TUMORS) LIGATURE
(— USED AS POINTER) FESCUE
(— USED IN SPLICING CABLES)
TAPER
(—S BOUND TOGETHER) SELVAGE
(ENAMELED —) LITZ
(FENCE —) DROPPER
(FRAYED —) JAGGER
(GOLD —) KINSEN
(LOOPED —) OESE

(PALLET —) PULLDOWN
(PRIMING —) PICKER EPINGLETTE
(SURGICAL —) STYLET
(VENT —) PRICKER
(4 —S TWISTED TOGETHER) QUAD
WIRY THIN HARDY STIFF KNOTTY SINEWY
STRINGY THREADY

WISCONSIN

CAPITAL: MADISON
COLLEGE: RIPON BELOIT ALVERNO
CARROLL VITERBO CARTHAGE
COUNTY: DOOR VILAS JUNEAU CALUMET
SHAWANO WAUSHARA
LAKE: POYGAN MENDOTA WISSOTA
WINNEBAGO
MOUNTAIN: TIMSHILL SUGARBUSH
RIVER: FOX BLACK STCROIX CHIPPEWA
MENOMINEE
STATE BIRD: ROBIN
STATE FLOWER: VIOLET
STATE TREE: MAPLE
TOWN: ANTIGO BELOIT RACINE WAUSAU
ASHLAND BARABOO KENOSHA MADISON
OSHKOSH PORTAGE SHAWANO
LACROSSE SUPERIOR WAUKESHA

WISDOM WIT LORE SABE SENSE SATTVA
SOPHIA CUNNING MINERVA JUDGMENT
PRUDENCE SAPIENCE
(DIVINE —) WORD THEOMAGY
(ESOTERIC —) GNOSIS
(SUPREME —) PRAJNA
(UNIVERSAL —) PANSOPHY
WISE HEP SLY DEEP KIND SAGE SANE
TURN CANNY SMART SOUND WITTY
CRAFTY QUAINT WITFUL ERUDITE
GNOSTIC KNOWING LEARNED POLITIC
PRUDENT SAPIENT PROFOUND SENSIBLE
WISEACRE SAGE DUNCE GOTHAM
SOLONIST WISEHEAD
WISECRACK JOKE QUIP
WISH CARE GOAL HOPE MIND VOTE
WANT WILL COVET CRAVE DREAM
HEART TASTE VOICE DESIRE FAREWELL
GODSPEED
(DEATH —) DESTRUDO
(SLIGHT —) VELLEITY
WISHFUL EAGER HOPEFUL LONGING
ALLURING
WISHING ANXIOUS DESIROUS
WISHY-WASHY PALE THIN WEAK
BLAND VAPID FEEBLE DILUTED INSIPID
SLIPSLOP
WISP TATE SCRAP SHRED TWIST
(— OF HAY) RISP
(— OF STRAW) WAP WASE DOSSIL
(— OF THATCH) TIPPET
WISTFUL INTENT PENSIVE WISHFUL
MOURNFUL YEARNING
WIT WAG KNOW NOUS SALT BRAIN
HUMOR IRONY SENSE THINK ACUMEN
ESPRIT POLICY SANITY SATIRE WISDOM
CONCEIT CUNNING SARCASM WITWORM
BADINAGE REPARTEE

(BITING —) DICACITY
WITCH HAG HEX MARE BRUJA LAMIA
SIBYL WEIRD WIGHT CARLIN CUMMER
DUESSA HECATE KIMMER PILWIZ
WIZARD CANIDIA HAGGARD HELLCAT
BABAJAGA ERICHTHO SPAEWIFE
VERSIERA
WITCHCRAFT CHARM OBEAH CUNNING
SORCERY BRUJERIA DEVILTRY PISHOGUE
WIZARDRY
WITCH DOCTOR BOCOR GOOFER
WITH BY CUM AVEC CHEZ AMONG ANENT
WITHDRAW GO DROP TAKE AVOID
LOOSE SHIFT CHANGE DESERT DETACH
EFFACE FLINCH RECALL RECANT RECEDE
RETIRE REVOKE SECEDE SHRINK
ABSCOND CONCEAL DETRACT FORSAKE
INVEIGH RETRACT RETREAT SCRATCH
SCUTTLE SECLUDE SEPARATE SUBTRACT
SEGREGATE SEQUESTER
(— FROM) VAIK ABANDON
(— FROM POKER POT) DROP
WITHDRAWAL DRAIN FLIGHT HIDING
SHRINK ABSENCE DUNKIRK PULLOUT
REGRESS RETIRAL RETREAT SCUTTLE
RECESSION REVULSION
(— FROM WORLDLY THINGS)
ABSTRACTION
(— OF BUILDING FACE) SETBACK
(— OF PROMISE) BACKWORD
(— OF SUIT) RETRAXIT
WITHDRAWN SHY ASOCIAL INGROWN
ISOLATED SECLUDED RECESSIVE
ABSTRACTED
WITHER BURN FADE PINE RUST SEAR
STUN WARP BLAST DECAY QUAIL WIZEN
SHRINK WALLOW DECLINE SHRIVEL
LANGUISH PARALYZE
WITHERED DRY ARID SERE CORKY
MARCID BLASTED WIZENED AUTUMNAL
WITHHOLD CURB DENY HIDE KEEP STOP
CHECK ABSENT DETAIN REFUSE RETAIN
ABSTAIN BOYCOTT FORBEAR REPRESS
RESERVE SUSPEND RESTRAIN SUBTRACT
WITHIN IN ONLY INLY INTRA ABOARD
HEREIN INSIDE INDOORS ENCLOSED
INCLUDED
WITHOUT EX BUT OUT FREE SANS SINE
MINUS FAILING OUTSIDE WANTING
OUTDOORS
WITHSTAND BIDE DEFY ABIDE OPPOSE
OPPUGN RESIST CONTEST FORBEAR
CONFRONT
WITLESS MAD SILLY INSANE STUPID
FATUOUS FOOLISH HEEDLESS
SLAPHAPPY
WITNESS SEE PROOF ATTEST BEHOLD
RECORD TESTOR CURATOR TESTIFY
EVIDENCE RECORDER SUFFRAGE
WITTICISM WIT JEER JEST JOKE QUIP
SALLY WHEEZE
WITTY WILY WISE DROLL PAWKY SHARP
SMART CLEVER JOCOSE JOCULAR
HUMOROUS
WIZARD MAGE SEER WITCH DOCTOR
EXPERT CHARMED MAGICAL WARLOCK

WISEMAN CONJUROR MAGICIAN
SORCERER WITCHMAN ARCHIMAGE
WIZENED SERE GIZZEN WEAZEN
WOBBLE COCKLE HOBBLE QUAVER
SHIMMY TEETER WIGGLE TREMBLE
NUTATION
WOBBLY LOOSE SHAKY DRUNKEN
DOUBTFUL
WOE BALE BANE PAIN PINE GRIEF MISERY
SORROW TROUBLE CALAMITY DISTRESS
WOEFUL MEAN DISMAL PALTRY RUEFUL
DIREFUL DOLEFUL RUTHFUL DOLOROUS
PITIABLE WRETCHED
WOLF GLUT LOBO FREKI CHANCO
COYOTE FENRIR KABERU MASHER
SIGRIM
WOMAN DAM EVE HER SHE TEG BABE
BABY FAIR FLAG JANE LADY MAMA
MARY MORT WIFE BLADE BROAD FEMME
FRAIL MAMMA MUJER QUEAN SKIRT
SMOCK TOOTS TWIST CALICO CUMMER
FEMALE GIMMER HEIFER MULIER SISTER
TOMATO VIRAGO WAHINE DISTAFF
PLACKET MISTRESS PETTICOAT
(— DESERTED BY HUSBAND)
AGUNAH
(— OF LOW CASTE) DASI
(— OF RANK) DOMINA
(— OF UNSTEADY CHARACTER) FLAP
CALLET
(— WITH ONE CHILD) UNIPARA
(— WITH 3 CHILDREN) TRIPARA
(ABORIGINAL —) GIN LUBRA
(ABUSIVE —) FISHWIFE
(ALLURING —) DISH
(ATTRACTIVE —) DOLLY SHEBA
LOOKER CHARMER
(AUSTRALIAN —) BINT
(AWKWARD —) ROIL
(BEAUTIFUL —) PERI BELLE HOURI
SIREN SPARK CHERUB EYEFUL
MUSIDORA
(BOISTEROUS —) HOYDEN
(BOLD —) RAMP
(CLEANING —) CHAR
(COARSE —) BEAST RUDAS BLOWZE
RULLION
(COOLIE —) CHANGAR
(COY —) HAGGARD
(CREMATED —) SATI SUTTEE
(DEAR —) PEAT
(DUTCH OR GERMAN —) FRAU FROW
FROKIN FRAULEIN
(ENGAGED —) BONDAGER
(EVIL OLD —) HAG HELLHAG
(EXCITED —) MAENAD
(FASHIONABLE —) MILADY GALLANT
ELEGANTE
(FAT —) BOSS FUSTILUGS
(FINE —) SCREAMER
(FIRST —) EMBLA PANDORA
(FLIRTING —) CHIPPY FIZGIG
(FOOLISH —) TAWPIE
(FORWARD —) STRAP
(GAUDY —) JAY
(GENTLE —) DOVE
(GOSSIPY —) HAIK HAKE BIDDY TABBY

(GOSSIPY, TALKATIVE —) YENTA
(GROSS —) SOW
(GYPSY —) ROMI ROMNI GITANA
(ILL-TEMPERED —) VIXEN CATAMARAN
(IMMORAL —) RIG GITCH FLAPPER
HARLOTRY
(IMPUDENT —) YANKIE
(INDIAN —) SQUAW WENCH KLOOCH
BUCKEEN
(INSPIRED —) PHOEBAD
(ITALIAN —) DONNA
(LASCIVIOUS —) GIGLET
(LEARNED —) PUNDITA CLERGESS
(LEWD —) REP SLUT BITCH HUSSY
HUZZY MALKIN BROTHEL CYPRIAN
(LOOSE —) BAG BIM KIT MOB TIB DRAB
FLAP BIMBO TROLL GILLOT HARLOT
LIMMER BAGGAGE COCOTTE FRANION
TROLLOP
(LOUD-SPOKEN —) RANDY
(LOW OR WORTHLESS —) JADE JURR
BUNTER SLINGDUST
(MARRIED — OF LOWLY STATION)
GOODY
(MASCULINE —) AMAZON RULLION
COTQUEAN
(MEEK —) GRIZEL
(MYTHOLOGICAL —) HEROINE
(NON-JEWISH —) SHIKSA
(OLD —) GIB HEN BABA TROT CRONE
FAGOT FRUMP TROUT BELDAM CARLIN
GAMMER GEEZER GRANNY CARLINE
GRANDAM HARRIDAN
(PEDANTIC —) BLUE
(PERT —) CHIT
(PORTUGUESE —) SENHORA
(PREGNANT —) GRAVIDA
(PRIGGISH —) PRUDE
(RUSTIC —) JOAN
(SCOLDING —) RANDY SHREW
COTQUEAN RIXATRIX
(SHORT OR STUMPY —) CUTTY
(SHOWY —) ANONYMA
(SHREWISH —) JADE HARPY SKELLAT
(SLATTERNLY —) DRAB FLEABAG
SLAMKIN
(SLENDER GRACEFUL —) SYLPH
(SLIPSHOD —) MAUX CLATCH
TROLLIMOG
(SLOVENLY —) BAG DAW SOW SLUT
BESOM TAWPY TROLL TROLLOP
SLATTERN
(SPANISH —) DONA GITANA
(SPANISH-INDIAN —) CHOLA
(SPITEFUL —) CAT FURY BITCH
(SQUAT —) TRUB
(SQUEAMISH —) COCKNEY
(STAID —) MATRON
(STATELY —) JUNO
(STORMY VIOLENT —) FURY
(TRACTABLE —) SHEEP
(UGLY —) HAG GORGON
(UNCHASTE —) JILT
(UNMARRIED —) DAME GIRL SPINSTER
MADEMOISELLE
(VIXENISH —) HARRIDAN
(WANTON —) MINX TRUB PARNEL

(WICKED —) JEZEBEL
(WISE —) VOLVA ALRUNA ALRUNE
(WITHERED —) CRONE
(YOUNG —) BIT BIRD BURD CHIT DAME
DELL DOLL GIRL LASS PUSS BEAST
CHICK FILLY FLUFF TOAST DAMSEL
HEIFER PIGEON SHEILA SUBDEB
BAGGAGE CHICKEN DAMOZEL FLAPPER
WINKLOT DAUGHTER GRISETTE
WOMAN IN WHITE (AUTHOR OF —)
COLLINS
(CHARACTER IN —) ANNE FOSCO
GLYDE LAURA PESCA MARIAN WALTER
FAIRLIE HALCOMBE PERCIVAL
CATHERICK HARTRIGHT
WOMANISH FEMALE FEMININE
LADYLIKE PETTICOAT
WONDER AWE MUSE VERY ADMIRE
MARVEL MIRACLE PORTENT PRODIGY
UNCOUTH SURPRISE
WONDERFUL KEEN NEAT GRAND GREAT
SWELL MIGHTY AMAZING GALLANT
STRANGE GLORIOUS MIRABILE TERRIFIC
WONDROUS
WOO SUE LOVE SEEK SUIT COURT SPARK
SPOON ASSAIL ADDRESS
WOOD (ALSO SEE TREE AND TIMBER)
KIP BOIS BOSK EKKI KIRI MOCK PALO
SHAW SUPA CAHUY CHARK CROWD
FLOUR HURST SHOLA STICK WEALD
ANGILI AUSUBO BRAZIL EKHIMI FOREST
ITAUBA JARANA LUMBER PALING
SPINNY TIMBER APITONG BOSCAGE
COPPICE SATINAY CRANTARA
CALAMANDER
(— FOR CARPENTRY) STUFF
(— FOR REPAIRING HEDGE) TINING
HAYBOTE
(— OF SMALL EXTENT) GROVE
(— OF THE VERA) VENESIA
(— USEFUL FOR TINDER) PUNK SPONK
TOUCHWOOD
(— YIELDING PERFUME) LINALOA
(BLACK —) EBONY
(CONE-SHAPED PIECE OF —) ACORN
(DARK RED —) RATA
(DEAD —) RAMMEL
(DENSIFIED —) STAYPAK
(FLEXIBLE —) EDDER
(FOSSIL —) PINITE PEUCITES
(FRAGRANT —) CEDAR SANDALWOOD
(FUEL —) ESTOVERS
(HARD —) ASH DAO ELM SAL BAKU IPIL
KARI LANA POON ANJAN EBONY GIDYA
KARRI KOKRA MAPLE MAZER ZANTE
BANUYO CAMARA FREIJO GIDGEE
KEMPAS SABICU SAPELE WALNUT
CURUPAY DATTOCK HICKORY GUAIACUM
IRONBARK MAHOGANY
(HEAVY —) DAO EBON EBONY CHENGAL
GUAYABI SUCUPIRA
(LIGHT —) POON BALSA HEMLOCK
(LIMBA —) KORINA
(LOGGED —) CHIP
(LOST —) CHIPPAGE
(LUSTROUS —) LEZA BOARWOOD
(MATCHBOX —) SKILLET

(MOTTLED —) AMBOINA CALAMBOUR
(NUMBER 1 —) DRIVER
(NUMBER 2 —) BRASSIE
(NUMBER 3 —) SPOON
(NUMBER 4 —) CLEEK
(OILY —) BATETE
(OLIVE —) COLLIE
(PETRIFIED —) LITHOXYL ROCKWOOD
(PINKISH —) BOSSE
(REDDISH —) KOA KARI KARRI ARANGA
BANABA CHERRY DUNGON SATINE
KAMBALA
(REDDISH-YELLOW —) GUYO
(ROTTEN —) DADDOCK
(SANDARAC —) ALERCE
(SOFT —) KIRI GABUN GABOON
ELKWOOD AGALLOCH ALBURNUM
GUATAMBU
(WATER-RESISTING —) AMUGIS
(YELLOWISH —) HALDU FUSTIC IDIGBO
KADAMBA KAMASSI GUATAMBU
WOODCHUCK MONAX MARMOT SUSLIK
WEJACK MOONACK GROUNDHOG
WOODCOCK QUIS PEWEE PEWIT SNIPE
BECASSE
WOODEN DRY DULL STIFF CLUMSY
STOLID TIMBER AWKWARD DEADPAN
LIFELESS
WOODPECKER CHAB KATE HECCO
PICUS HECKLE PIANET SPRITE TAPPER
YAFFLE CREEPER FLICKER HICKWAY
LOGCOCK REDHEAD SNAPPER WITWALL
WRYNECK HICKWALL POPINJAY
SAPSUCKER
WOODWIND OBOE FLUTE CORNET
BASSOON PIBGORN PICCOLO CLARINET
WOODWORKER JOINER TURNER
MILLMAN
WOODY BOSKY SYLVAN XYLOID LIGNOSE
LIGNEOUS
WOOER BEAU LOVER SUITOR COURTER
COURTIER PARAMOUR
WOOL HOG VOL WOW BEAT PILE PULU
ROCK FADGE LAINE STUFF ALPACA
ARGALI BOTANY FLEECE JACKET JERSEY
KERSEY LUSTER SLIVER WETHER
COMBING KASHMIR STUBBLE WIGGING
CASHMERE CLOTHING COMEBACK
TOMENTUM
(— AS IT COMES FROM SHEEP)
GREASE
(— FROM DEAD SHEEP) MORTLING
(— FROM LEOMINSTER) ORE
(— FROM RAGS) EXTRACT
(— OF UNDERCOAT OF MUSK-OX)
QIVIUT
(— ON SHEEP'S LEG) GARE BREECH
(— ON SHEEP'S THROAT) HASLOCK
(— WEIGHT) TOD
(COARSE —) ABB SHAG BRAID
COWTAIL
(COTTON —) CADDIS
(DUNGY BIT OF —) FRIB
(FINE GRADE OF —) PICKLOCK
SPINNERS
(GREASY —) TIPPY
(INFERIOR GRADE OF —) HEAD

(KNOT OF —) NOIL
(LAMB'S —) WASSAIL
(LOCK OF —) FLOCK STAPLE
(LONG —) BLUE
(LOW GRADE OF —) LIVERY
(MATTED —) DAG KET SHAG
(PULLED —) SLIPE
(RECLAIMED —) MUNGO SHODDY
(REFUSE —) COT FLOCK PINION
(ROLL OF —) CARDING
(RUSSIAN —) DONSKY
(SMALL PIECE OF —) TATE
(SPUN —) YARN
(WOUND —) TREND
WOOLLY LANATE LANOSE COTTONY
FLOCCOSE PERONATE
WOOZY SICK DRUNK TIGHT VAGUE
BLURRY
WORD MOT NEWS TERM VERB CHEEP
COUCH DILLY GLOSS HOKEY LEMMA
MAXIM ORDER PAROL RUMOR SPELL
ADVERB AVOWAL BREATH COPULA
LATIVE PLEDGE REMARK REPORT SAYING
ACCOUNT ADJUNCT COMMAND
COMMENT DICTION HOMONYM INCIPIT
MESSAGE PALABRA PARONYM PROMISE
PROVERB SYNONYM VOCABLE
CATCHCRY COMPOUND IDEOGRAM
ILLATIVE SYNTAGMA NEOLOGISM
PALINDROME
(— EXPRESSING COMMAND)
JUSSIVE
(— FORMED FROM VOWELS) EUOUAE
(— FROM INITIAL LETTERS)
ACRONYM
(— IN A PUZZLE) LIGHT
(— MISPRONOUNCED) BEARD
(— OF CONCLUSION) AMEN EXPLICIT
(— OF HONOR) PAROLE
(— OF MOUTH) FIDELITY
(— OF OPPOSITE MEANING)
ANTONYM
(— OF SECONDARY RANK) ADNEX
(— OF UNCERTAIN MEANING)
FRINGENT
(— OF UNKNOWN MEANING) KIBBER
ONEYER PRAYFUL PRENZIE
(—S IN LOW TONE) ASIDE
(—S OF OPERA) LIBRETTO
(BIBLICAL — OF DOUBTFUL
MEANING) EZEL FITCH GITTITH
(CHARACTERIZING —) EPITHET
(CODE —) DOG FOX JIG ABLE EASY
ECHO GOLF ITEM KING BRAVO DELTA
HOTEL INDIA SUGAR GEORGE CHARLIE
(EMPTY —S) WAFFLE
(FINE —S) DICK
(GATHERING —) SLOGAN
(HONEYED —S) MANNA
(HYPHENATED —) SOLID
(IDENTIFYING —) LABEL
(LAST — OF SPEECH) CUE
(MAGIC —) ABRACADABRA
(MEANINGLESS —) DERRY
(MEANINGLESS —S) NOISE
(METAPHORICAL —) KENNING
(MNEMONIC —) VIBGYOR

(MYSTIC —) ABRAXAS
(NONSENSE —) RAFF RAFFE FRABJOUS
RUNCIBLE
(ORIGINAL —) STEM
(PARTING —) ENVOI
(QUOTED —) CITATION
(REDUNDANT —) CHEVILLE
(ROOT —) ETYMON PRIMITIVE
(SIGNAL —) NAYWORD SECURITY
(SIGNIFICANT —) ACCENT
(SINGLE —) PHRASE
(SOURCE —) ETYMON
(THIEVES' SLANG —) TWAG WHID
(UNEXPLAINED —) DUCDAME
(UTTERED —S) SPEECH
WORDY PROLIX VERBAL DIFFUSE
VERBOSE WORDISH REDUNDANT
WORK DO GO ACT JOB FRET NOTE OPUS
TASK TEND TOIL ERGON GRIND PRESS
ARBEIT EFFECT HUSTLE OEUVRE RESULT
STRIVE CALLING EXECUTE EXPLOIT
FERMENT MISSION OPERATE PURSUIT
ADVOCACY BUSINESS DRUDGERY
ENDEAVOR FUNCTION INDUSTRY
EXECUTION
(— ACROSS GRAIN) THURM
(— ACTIVELY) LOUSTER
(— AGAINST) KNIFE ATTACK COMBAT
(— AIMLESSLY) FIDDLE
(— CARELESSLY) RABBLE
(— DILIGENTLY) PEG PLUG STRIKE
BELABOR
(— FOR) LABOR SERVE BESWINK
(— FREE) START
(— HARD) TEW MOIL SLOG SWOT
BULLOCK LEATHER
(— HIDES) BEAM
(— INSIDIOUSLY) WORM
(— INTO A MASS) KNEAD
(— LAND) FLOAT
(— OF ACKNOWLEDGED
EXCELLENCE) CLASSIC
(— OF ART) GEM CRAFT ANTIQUE
CAPRICE CREATION EPIPHANY EXERCISE
MANDORLA
(— OF MENIAL KIND) DRUDGE
(— ONE'S WAY) WISE
(— OUT) BLOCK FUDGE SOLVE DESIGN
EVOLVE
(— OVER) DIGEST
(— PERSISTENTLY) HAMMER
(— STEADILY) PLY
(— TO EXHAUSTION) FAG
(— TOGETHER) COACT
(— TRIFLINGLY) PIDDLE
(— UP) SPUNK
(— UPON) TILL LABOR
(— UPWARD) HIKE
(— VIGOROUSLY) BEND
(ANONYMOUS —) ADESPOTA
(BUNGLED —) BOTCH
(CLUMSY —) BOTCH
(COMPLETED —) TRAVAIL
(DAY'S —) DARG DARGUE
(DECORATIVE —) FLOCKING
MARQUETRY
(DULL —) DRUDGERY

(HARD —) TEW MOIL MUCK SWOT
TWIG YERK SWEAT EFFORT MOIDER
LEATHER SLAVERY SLOGGING
(LITERARY —) STUDY CHASER SEQUEL
SERIAL CLASSIC DIPTYCH PRODUCTION
(MANUAL —) FATIGUE
(METAL —) NIELLO
(ORNAMENTAL —) BEADWORK
FILIGREE LEAFWORK
(REFERENCE —) BIBLE SOURCE
(USELESS —) BOONDOGGLE
(WOMAN'S —) DISTAFF
WORKBENCH SIEGE DONKEY TEMPLATE
WORKER
(ALSO SEE WORKMAN AND LABORER)
AGER CARL DOER HAND HIND ICER SCAB
AXMAN BOXER BUTTY DEMAS DRIER
EDGER ENDER FILER FIRER FIXER FLYER
FOXER GLUER GORER HOLER INKER
JERRY LINER LURER MAXIM MINIM
NURSE TAPER TOWER ASHMAN BACKER
BAILER BALLER BANDER BEADER BENDER
BINDER BINMAN BLADER BLOWER
BOILER BONDER BOOKER BOSHER
BRACER BUFFER BUMPER BURNER
BURRER CAPPER CARMAN CASTER
CASUAL CHASER COMBER COOKER
DAYMAN DIPPER DOCKER DOGGER
DOTTER DUMPER ETCHER FACTOR
FAGGER FANMAN FASHER FEEDER
FELLER FILLER FITTER FLAKER FLAMER
FLUTER FLUXER FOILER FOLDER FORCER
FORMER FRAMER FUSER GOFFER
GRADER GUMMER GUTTER HASHER
HEADER HEELER HELPER HEMMER
HOLDER HOOKER HOOPER HOPPER
HUNKIE INKMAN JOGGER JOINER LEAFER
LEASER LEGGER NOILER PUGGER READER
REEDER SCORER SEAMAN SEAMER
SHAKER SKIVER SLAKER SLICER SLIDER
SLOPER STAVER STAYER TOILER TOPPER
BUILDER CREATOR EMPLOYE FIELDER
LABORER OUVRIER
WORKMAN
(ALSO SEE WORKER AND LABORER)
HAND MATE CAGER EXTRA FLINT FLUER
FROCK LAYER MAJOR MIXER POLER
TONER TRIER TUBER BEAMER BLOUSE
BOOMER BOWLER BUCKER BUMMER
COATER DIPPER DRIVER FORKER GAGGER
HANGER LASTER LATHER MASTER
NIPPER OILMAN PUFFER RUNNER
SAMMER SCORER SHAKER SKIVER
SLICER SLIDER SOAKER SPIKER STAGER
STAVER TAPPER TARRER TEEMER TILTER
TIPMAN TIPPER TOPMAN WARMER
WASHER WETTER WRIGHT ARTISAN
DRUMMER HOTSHOT LUDDITE SHOPMAN
(CHIEF —) BOSS
(CLUMSY —) BUNGLER COBBLER
(FELLOW —) BULLY BUTTY
(PROFICIENT —) DEACON
(UNSKILLFUL —) HUNKY BUTCHER
WORKMANLIKE DEFT ADEPT SKILLFUL
WORKMANSHIP HAND FABRIC
FACTURE OVERAGE ARTIFICE ARTISANRY
WORKROOM DEN STUDY ATELIER

WORKSHOP LAB SHED SHOP FORGE SMITHY ATELIER BOTTEGA OFFICINA

WORLD ORB VALE EARTH CAREER PUBLIC KINGDOM MONDIAL CREATION UNIVERSE

WORLDLY LAY CARNAL EARTHY MUNDAL EARTHLY FLESHLY MUNDANE PROFANE SECULAR TERRENE

WORLDWIDE GLOBAL ECUMENIC GLOBULAR PLANETARY

WORM BOB EEL ESS LURG NEMA FLUKE LYTTA SCREW SNAKE NEREID PALMER PALOLO SHAMIR TEREDO VERMIS ANNELID ASCARID SABELLA SERPENT WRIGGLE CEPHALOB CERCARIA CHETOPOD HELMINTH NEMATODE STRONGYL TRICHINA
(— IN HAWKS) FILANDER
(— USED FOR BAIT) TAGTAIL
(AQUATIC —) TUBIFEX
(BLOODSUCKING —) LEECH
(CADDIS —) CADEW PIPER CADBAIT
(FLUKE —) PLAICE
(MEASURING —) LOOPER
(MUD —) IPO LOA
(SHIP —) BROMA COBRA

WORN SERE USED PASSE TRITE MAGGED MIZPAH SHABBY ATTRITE CONTRITE
(— NEXT TO SKIN) INTIMATE
(— OUT) SHOT BANAL JADED SEELY SPENT STALE STANK BEATEN BEDRID BLEARY EFFETE EPUISE SCREWY SHABBY CRIPPLE FORWORN DECREPID FOUGHTEN HARASSED OBSOLETE STRICKEN
(— SMOOTH) BEATEN

WORRY DOG NAG VEX BAIT BITE CARE FAZE FRET FUSS MOIL STEW ANNOY CHOKE HARRY SCALD SHAKE TEASE BOTHER CHIVVY COTTER CUMBER FERRET FIDGET HARASS HECTOR INFEST PESTER PLAGUE POTHER ANXIETY CHAGRIN TROUBLE TURMOIL

WORSHIP GOD CULT PUJA ADORE HONOR NAMAZ WURTH YAJNA CREDIT PRAISE REPUTE REVERE BAALISM ELOHISM ICONISM IDOLIZE VENERATE
(— OF ALL GODS) PANTHEISM
(— OF SHAKESPEARE) BARDOLATRY
(ANCESTOR —) SCIOTHEISM
(FORM OF —) RITUAL
(INFERIOR KIND OF —) DULIA
(SERPENT —) OPHISM
(STAR —) SABAISM

WORSTED GARN JERRY SERGE CUBICA VESSES WHIPCORD

WORTH MEED CARAT MERIT PRICE VALOR VALUE BOUNTY DESERT ESTEEM REGARD RICHES VIRTUE WEALTH DIGNITY SPLENDOR TREASURE VALIDITY
(NET —) CAPITAL

WORTHLESS BAD BUM LOW BALD BARE BASE EVIL IDLE LEWD PUNK SLIM VAIN VILE BLANK DUSTY LOUSY SORRY STRAW WASHY ABJECT CHAFFY CHEESY CRUMMY HOLLOW MEASLY NAUGHT PALTRY RASCAL ROTTEN TRASHY WOODEN BAGGAGE FUSTIAN NOTHING RAFFISH RUBBISH SCABBED USELESS FECKLESS NUGATORY RASCALLY WRETCHED

WORTHY BIG DEAR FAIR GOOD NOBLE PIOUS GENTLE CONDIGN GRADELY ELIGIBLE VALUABLE
(— OF BELIEF) CREDIBLE
(— OF DEVOTION) HOLY
(— OF PRAISE) LAUDABLE

WOUND CUT HEW BITE CLAW GORE HARM HURT MAIM PAIN PINK SCAR SORE TEAR WING GRIEF KNIFE KNOCK SHOOT STICK STING TOUCH BREACH BRUISE CREASE GRIEVE HARROW INJURE LAUNCH LESION OFFEND PIERCE PLAGUE TRAUMA AFFLICT BATTERY GUNSHOT SCRATCH DISTRESS INCISION LACERATE
(— FROM BOAR'S TUSK) GANCH
(— FROM BULL'S HORN) CORNADA
(— FROM RUBBING) GALL
(— IN DEER'S SIDE) FLANKARD
(— MADE BY THRUST) FOIN
(— ON FOOT) FIKE
(— ON HORSE'S ANKLE) CREPANCE
(— WITH POINTED WEAPON) STAB SWORD
(DEEP —) DIACOPE
(MINUTE —) PRICK SCART
(TRIFLING —) FLEABITE

WOUNDED HURT WINGED VULNOSE STRICKEN

WRAITH GHOST SPOOK DOUBLE SHADOW SPECTRE

WRANGLE MOIL SPAR TIFT ARGUE BRAWL CHIDE PLEAD STRUT BICKER DACKER FRATCH HAGGLE HASSLE JANGLE BRANGLE DISPUTE QUARREL SQUABBLE

WRANGLER CAMPER COWBOY GRATER DEBATER OPPONENT

WRAP LAP BIND FURL ROLL AMICE CLOAK SERVE TWINE AFGHAN BURLAP CLOTHE COCOON EMBALE MUFFLE SACQUE ENVELOP INVOLVE SWADDLE
(— CABLE) KECKLE
(— DEAD BODY) CERE
(— ONESELF) HUDDLE
(— UP) HAP MAIL ENROL IMPLY
(— UP HEAD) MOB MOP MOBLE
(— WIRE AROUND FISHING LINE) GANGE
(— WITH BANDAGE) SWATHE

WRAPPER APRON COVER SHAWL SMOCK JACKET ENVELOP OVERALL COVERING
(— FOR BOOK) JACKET
(— FOR CUTLET) PAPILLOTE
(— WORN IN EGYPT) GALABIA

WRATH IRE FURY ANGER CHOLER PASSION VIOLENCE

WRATHFUL ANGRY IRATE WROTH JREFUL RAGING FURIOUS CHOLERIC

WREAK CAUSE AVENGE EXPEND GRATIFY INDULGE INFLICT REVENGE

WREATH LEI ORLE CROWN OLIVE WHORL ANADEM CREASE LAUREL TORTIL

CHAPLET CORONAL CORONET CROWNAL
FESTOON GARLAND

WREATHE BIND WIND TWINE TWIST
WRING INTORT WRITHE CONTORT
ENTWINE INTWIST INVOLVE

WRECK HULK RUIN BLAST CRACK PRANG
SMASH TRASH DESPOIL DESTROY
SHATTER DEMOLISH SABOTAGE
SHAMBLES
(— COMPLETELY) TOTAL
(HUMAN —) DERELICT

WRECKAGE WRACK FLOTSAM
SHAMBLES

WRENCH KEY PIN PULL RACK TEAR
CRICK FORCE THROW TWIST WREST
BEDKEY SPRAIN STRAIN TWEEZE
DISTORT SPANNER TORTURE

WREST REAR REND EXACT FORCE TWIST
EXTORT WRENCH WRITHE
(— AWAY) STRIP DESPOIL

WRESTLE RASSLE SQUIRM TUSSLE
WRITHE GRAPPLE SCUFFLE

WRETCH DOG MISER SLAVE BUGGER
CAITIFF CULLION HILDING BEZONIAN
POLTROON RECREANT SCULLION

WRETCHED EVIL FOUL LORN MEAN
POOR GAUNT SORRY ABJECT DISMAL
MEAGER PALTRY RASCAL SHABBY
SICKLY SORDID WOEFUL ABYSMAL
FORLORN OUTWORN PITIFUL SQUALID
MISERABLE

WRIGGLE EEL RIG LASH WIND SLIDE
SQUIRM WRITHE SNIGGLE TWIDDLE
WRESTLE SQUIGGLE

WRING RACK DRAIN EXACT SCREW
TWIST WREST EXTORT OPPRESS
SQUEEZE TORMENT TORTURE

WRINKLE DRAW FOLD FURL KNIT SEAM
BREAK CRIMP FAULT FRILL BUCKLE
CREASE FURROW PUCKER RUMPLE
SCRIMP WREATH CRINKLE CRUMPLE
FROUNCE CONTRACT RUGOSITY

WRINKLED RUGATE RUGGED RUGOSE
SEAMED CRUMPLED FURROWED
PUCKERED WRIZZLED

WRIT MISE PONE ALIAS BREVE BRIEF
RECTO CAPIAS ELEGIT PLAINT VENIRE
ACCOUNT DETINUE EXIGENT PRECEPT
PROCESS SUMMONS WARRANT
DETAINER DOCUMENT MANDAMUS
MITTIMUS REPLEVIN SUBPOENA
TESTATUM

WRITE INK PEN DRAW READ DRAFT
STYLE AUTHOR INDITE SCRIBE ADDRESS
COMPILE COMPOSE DICTATE SCREEVE
INSCRIBE
(— ADDRESS) BACK
(— BRIEFLY) JOT
(— CARELESSLY) DASH SCRAWL
SCRIBBLE
(— DOWN) SIGN BREVE DENOTE
RECORD AMORTIZE DESCRIBE
(— FURTHER) ADD
(— HASTILY) SCRATCH SCRIBBLE
SQUIGGLE

(— IN A LARGE HAND) ENGROSS
(— IN LARGE CHARACTERS) TEXT
(— ON FRONT OF BILL) ENFACE
(— PASTORAL POEMS) PHILLIS
(— WHAT IS NOT TRUE) FABLE

WRITER (ALSO SEE AUTHOR) PEN BARD
HACK PUFF GHOST AUTHOR HEROIC
MUNSHI NOTARY PENMAN PROSER
SCRIBE YEOMAN ADAPTER ADSMITH
DIARIST GLOSSER GNOMIST HYMNIST
SCRIVER STYLIST TEXTMAN BLURBIST
COMPOSER EPISTLER ESSAYIST
FABULIST MONODIST NOVELIST
PARODIST PSALMIST
(— OF BURLESQUE) GABBER
(FREE-LANCE —) CREEPER
(HACK —) PENSTER
(INCOMPETENT —) BOTCHER
(SATIRICAL —) SILLOGRAPH

WRITHE WIND TWIRL TWIST WRING
SQUIRM WRENCH AGONIZE WRESTLE
WRIGGLE CONVOLVE

WRITING BOOK DITE POEM CADJAN
LEGEND LETTER SCRIPT ARTICLE
DIPLOMA APOCRYPH CONTRACT
DOCUMENT PAMPHLET
(— OF LITTLE VALUE) STUFF SCRIBBLE
(— ON PAPER SCROLL) MAKIMONO
(— ON SILK) KAKEMONO
(— UNDER SEAL) BOND
(BITTER —) DIATRIBE
(CARELESS —) SCRAWL
(CRAMPED —) NIGGLE
(CURSIVE —) JOINHAND
(HINDU —) VEDA
(HUMOROUS —S) FACETIAE
(ILLUMINATED —) FRACTUR
(NORSE —) EDDA
(PRETENTIOUS —) FUSTIAN
(SATIRICAL —) PASQUINADE
(SECRET —) SCYTALE
(SHORT —) SCRIP
(SHORTHAND —) PHONOGRAPHY
(SYLLABIC —) KANA
(VAPID —) WASH
(VERBOSE —) TOOTLE
(WORTHLESS —) TRIPE

WRONG BAD ILL WET AWRY HARM HURT
SORE SOUR AGLEY AMISS CRIME FALSE
GRIEF UNFIT ASTRAY FAULTY INJURE
INJURY OFFEND SINFUL UNTRUE WICKED
ABUSIVE DAMNIFY DEFRAUD IMMORAL
NAUGHTY VIOLATE AGGRIEVE MISTAKEN
PERVERSE
(CIVIL —) TORT
(IMAGINARY —) WINDMILL
(SHOCKINGLY —) MONSTROUS

WRONGDOER SINNER MISDOER
OFFENDER

WRONGFUL UNFAIR UNJUST TORTUOUS
UNLAWFUL

WRY ASKEW TWIST WRING DEFLECT
DISTORT TWISTED SATURNINE

WUTHERING HEIGHTS
(AUTHOR OF —) BRONTE

(CHARACTER IN —) DEAN EDGAR ELLEN JOSEPH LINTON ZILLAH FRANCES HARETON HINDLEY EARNSHAW ISABELLA LOCKWOOD CATHERINE HEATHCLIFF

WYOMING

CAPITAL: CHEYENNE
COUNTY: TETON UINTA GOSHEN BIGHORN LARAMIE NIOBRARA
LAKE: JACKSON
MOUNTAIN: ELK CLOUD GANNET HOBACK FREMONT ATLANTIC SHERIDAN
MOUNTAIN RANGE: TETON ABSARO BIGHORN LARAMIE RATTLESNAKE
RIVER: SNAKE PLATTE POWDER BIGHORN
STATE BIRD: MEADOWLARK
STATE FLOWER: PAINTBRUSH
STATE TREE: COTTONWOOD
TOWN: CODY LUSK CASPER BUFFALO LARAMIE RAWLINS WORLAND GREYBULL KEMMERER SHERIDAN SUNDANCE

X

X EX XRAY
XANTHIC YELLOW
XANTHIPPE NAG SHREW
  (HUSBAND OF —) SOCRATES
XERES JEREZ SHERRY
XERIC DRY
X-RAY UROGRÁM
XUTHUS (ADOPTED SON OF —) ION

(BROTHER OF —) DORUS AEOLUS
(FATHER OF —) HELLEN
(MOTHER OF —) ORSEIS
(SON OF —) ION DURUS ACHAEUS
(WIFE OF —) CREUSA
XYLOPHONE SARON GAMELAN
MARIMBA BALAPHON GIGELIRA
STICCADO

Y

Y WYE YOKE YANKEE

YACHT SAIL SCOW DINGHY SONDER
KEELBOAT

YAHWEH GOD JAHVAH

YAM UBE LIMA TUGUI INAMIA POTATO
BONIATA

YAMMER CRY WAIL SCOLD WHINE
YEARN GRUMBLE WHIMPER

YANK JERK SLAP SNAKE BUFFET

YAP BARK YAWP YELP MOUTH SCOLD
WAFFLE CHATTER KYOODLE

YARD HAW CREW FOLD SKID SPAR TILT
COURT GARTH PATIO STICK CANCHA
HOPPET CURTAIN KNACKERY
(— OF SAWMILL) DUMP
(— WHERE COWS ARE MILKED)
LOANING
(FINAL —) FELL
(GRASSY —) GARSTON
(PAVED —) CAUSEY
(POULTRY —) BARTON
(1-16TH OF A —) NAIL
(1-3RD OF CUBIC —) CARTLOAD
(20 —S) SCORE
(5 AND A HALF —S) ROD

YARDSTICK VERGE METRIC MEASURE
METEWAND STANDARD

YARN END FOX CORD GIMP PIRN SLIP
WEFT WHIP DYNEL FLOSS GRAIN INKLE
PITCH SPIEL ANGORA BERLIN BROACH
CADDIS COTTON CREWEL DACRON
ESTRON FRIEZE MERINO RATINE SAXONY
SINGLE STRAND THREAD VINYON
WOOLEN ACETATE CADDICE GENAPPE
INGRAIN MELANGE RACKING SCHAPPE
VIGOGNE WORSTED BOURETTE CHENILLE
FORTISAN SPINNING ORGANZINE
VIGOUREUX
(— FOR WARP) ABB
(— FROM FLOSS SILK) FLORET
(BITS OF ROPE —) THRUMS
(BUNDLE OF —) PAD
(CONICAL MASS OF —) COP
(ELASTIC —) LASTEX
(EXAGGERATED —) STRETCHER
(FINE SOFT —) ZEPHYR CASHMERE
(LINEN —) SPINEL
(ROLL OF —) PRICK CHEESE
(ROPE —S) SOOGEE
(SILK —) TRAM
(SMALL PIECE OF SPUN —) RABAND
ROBBIN ROPEBAND
(UNEVEN —) BOUCLE

YAW LURCH SHEER BROACH SWERVE

YAWL HOWL DANDY MIZZEN SCREAM
SCHOKKER

YAWN GAP GAPE ABYSM CAVITY TEDIUM
DULLNESS OSCITATE

YAWNING HIANT GAPING OSCITANT

YEA YES TRULY ASSENT REALLY VERILY

YEAR SUN TIME ANNUS WINTER
ZODIAC TOWMOND TZOLKIN
BIRTHDAY
(— OF EMANCIPATION) JUBILEE
(ACADEMIC —) SESSION
(LAST —) FERNYEAR
(MANY —S) AGE
(MAYAN —) TUN HAAB
(ONE BILLION —S) AEON
(SABBATICAL —) JUBILEE
(1000 —S) MILLENARY MILLENNIUM
(4320 MILLION —S) KALPA

YEARBOOK ANNUAL SERIAL
ANNUARY

YEARLING COLT HORNOTINE
(AUTHOR OF —) RAWLINGS
(CHARACTER IN —) LEM ORA JODY
HUTTO PENNY TWINK BAXTER NELLIE
OLIVER WILSON GINRIGHT FORRESTER
WEATHERBY FODDERWING

YEARN YEN ACHE BURN HONE LONG
PANT PINE SIGH CRAVE ASPIRE GRIEVE
HANKER

YEARNING DESIRE HANKER CRAVING
HOMESICK

YEAST BEE BARM KOJI FROTH SPUME
LEAVEN RISING TORULA FERMENT

YEASTY LIGHT FROTHY TRIVIAL
RESTLESS

YEGG ROBBER BURGLAR

YELL CRY CALL HOWL ROAR YOWL
SHOUT TIGER BELLOW HOLLER SCREAM
YAMMER

YELLOW (ALSO SEE COLOR) OR AMBER
BLOND FAVEL JAUNE SHELL ALMOND
BANANA MIMOSA NUGGET OXGALL
BISCUIT JASMINE JONQUIL LEGHORN
LUTEOUS MUSTARD NANKEEN OATMEAL
POPCORN SAFFRON TILLEUL YUCATAN
AUREOLIN ICTEROID MARIGOLD
ORPIMENT PRIMROSE
(— AS BUTTER) BLAKE
(BROWNISH —) FULVID FULVOUS
(GOLDEN —) FLAVID
(GREENISH —) ACACIA
(INDIAN —) PURI PURREE
(LEMON —) GENERALL

YELLOW FEVER VOMITO

YELLOWISH SALLOW ICTERINE
SAFFRONY

YELP CRY YAP YIP BARK KIYI YAWP
BOAST SQUEAL

YEMEN

CAPITAL: SANA SANAA
COIN: RIYAL
PEOPLE: ZAIDI SHAFAI
PORT: MOKA MOCHA
REGION: TIHAMA
TOWN: MOKA DAMAR MOCHA TAIZZ HODEIDA

YEN EYES LONG URGE YEARN DESIRE LONGING
YEOMAN CHURL CLERK WRITER GOODMAN RETAINER BEEFEATER
YES DA IS JA SI AYE YEA YEP YUH YEAH TRULY
YET AND BUT EVEN STILL THOUGH FINALLY HOWEVER
YIELD BOW PAN PLY BEAR BEND CAST CEDE CESS COME CROP FOLD GIVE HEAR QUIT SELL VAIL AGREE ALLOW BRING BUDGE CARRY CAUSE DEFER GRANT LEAVE OFFER STOOP ACCEDE AFFORD BOUNTY BUCKLE COMPLY FOLLOW IMPART OUTPUT RELENT RENDER RETURN SUBMIT SUPPLY SWERVE ABANDON CONCEDE DELIVER FURNISH HARVEST PRODUCE PROVIDE REDOUND SUCCUMB BEGRUDGE FRUITAGE RELINQUISH
  (— FRUIT) ADDLE GRAIN
  (— GRASS) GRAZE
  (— OF FIELD) BURDEN
  (— OF MINE) BONANZA
  (— ON BOND) BASIS
  (— TO) INDULGE
  (— TO TEMPTATION) FALL
  (— UP) LET FORLET
  (— WELL) HIT BLEED
  (MINERAL —) PROSPECT
YIELDING MEEK SOFT WAXY WAXEN BONAIR CAVING FACILE FEEBLE FLABBY LIMBER PLIANT QUAGGY SUPPLE BEARING CESSION FINGENT FLACCID DEDITION LADYLIKE RECREANT
  (— IRREGULARLY) BUNCHY
  (— OF HORSE) FLEXION
  (— STAGE) SEAR
  (— TO IMPULSES) ABANDON
YODEL SONG WARBLE REFRAIN
YOKE BOW DRAG FORK HOOP PAIR POKE SOLE FURCA BANGHY COUPLE INSPAN DRAGBAR HARNESS OPPRESS ADJUGATE
  (— TO HOLD DRILL) CROW
  (— TO RAISE CANNON) BAIL
YOKEFELLOW MATE FELLOW PARTNER
YOKEL BOOR CLUB JAKE JOCK FARMER JOSKIN BUMPKIN HAYSEED WAYBACK ABDERITE CHAWBACON
YOLK CENTER YELLOW ESSENCE LATEBRA VITELLUS PARABLAST
YON YONDER THITHER BACKWARD

YONDER THAT THERE THOSE THITHER
YORE PAST YEARS
YOU CAN'T GO HOME AGAIN
  (AUTHOR OF —) WOLFE
  (CHARACTER IN —) ELSE JACK LLOYD ESTHER GEORGE KOHLER MCHARG WEBBER EDWARDS FOXHALL
YOUNG JUV BIRD DROP BIRTH BROOD FETUS FRUIT GREEN SMALL UNOLD JUNIOR KINDLE JUVENAL IMMATURE YEANLING YOUTHFUL
  (— OF ANY ANIMAL) BABY CALF FOAL JOEY LAMB TOTO
  (— OF BEAST) SLINK
  (— OF BIRD) CHICK
  (— OF CAMEL) COLT
  (— OF DOG) WHELP
  (— OF FISH) FRY
  (— OF SEA TROUT) HERLING
  (VERY —) SUCKING NEPHIONIC SHIRTTAIL
YOUNGER KID LESS JUNIOR PUISNE
YOUNGSTER KID BIRD COLT CHILD YOUTH BUTTON SHAVER URCHIN YOUNKER SPALPEEN
YOUTH BOY BUD IMP LAD CHAP COLT PAGE BAHUR CHABO GROOM HYLAS POULT PRIME SPRIG SWAIN WHELP BOCHUR BURSCH EPHEBE INFANT JUVENT KOUROS MASTER SPRING YONKER CALLANT EPHEBOS GOSSOON JUVENAL PUBERTY SAPLING JUVENILE SPRINGAL
  (— WHO SERVES LIQUORS) GANYMEDE
  (DELINQUENT —) BODGIE
  (IMPUDENT —) SQUIRT
  (INEXPERIENCED —) GUNSEL
  (NON-JEWISH —) SHEGETZ
  (PERT —) PRINCOX
  (RUDE —) HOYDEN
  (SILLY —) CALF SLENDER
  (WELLBORN —) CHILD
YOUTHFUL FRESH GREEN YOUNG BOYISH GOLDEN JUNIOR MAIDEN VIRGIN PUERILE IMMATURE JUVENILE SPRINGAL VIGOROUS
YOUTHFULNESS JEUNESSE
YOWL HOWL WAIL YELL YELP
YUCCA LILY PITA DATIL IZOTE PALMA JOSHUA LILIAL LILIUM PALMITO SOAPWEED

YUGOSLAVIA

CAPITAL: BELGRADE
COIN: PARA DINAR
GULF: KVARNER
LAKE: OHRID PRESPA SCUTARI
MEASURE: RIF AKOV RALO DONUM KHVAT LANAZ STOPA MOTYKA PALAZE RALICO
MOUNTAIN: TRIGLAV DURMITOR
MOUNTAIN RANGE: DINARIC

PEOPLE: SERB CROAT SLOVENE
PORT: KOTOR SPLIT RIJEKA NOVISAD
BELGRADE DUBROVNIK
REGION: BANAT BOSNIA SRBIJA
REPUBLIC: SERBIA CROATIA SLOVENIA
RIVER: UNA DRIM IBAR KRKA SAVA
BOSNA CAZMA DRAVA DRINA RASKA
TAMIS TISZA VRBAS DANUBE MORAVA
VARDAR VELIKA NERETVA
TOWN: NIS AGRAM BUDVA RTANJ SPLIT
TUZLA USKUB BITOLJ MORAVA MOSTAR
OSIJEK PRILEP RAGUSA RIJEKA TETOVO
VARDAR ZAGREB CATTARO NOVISAD
PRIZREN SKOPLJE MONASTIR SARAJEVO
SUBOTICA LJUBLJANA

WEIGHT: OKA OKE DRAMM TOVAR
WAGON SATLIJK

YUKON TERRITORY (CAPITAL OF —)
WHITEHORSE
(LAKE OF —) KLUANE
(MOUNTAIN OF —) LOGAN
(MOUNTAIN RANGE OF —) OGILVIE
STIKINE MACKENZIE
(RIVER OF —) PEEL LEWES LIARD PELLY
WHITE KLONDIKE PORCUPINE
(TOWN OF —) ELSA MAYO BARLOW
DAWSON
YULE NOEL CHRISTMAS

Z

Z ZED ZEE ZETA ZULU ZEBRA IZZARD
(SHAPED LIKE A —) OPENBAND
ZACHARIAH (DAUGHTER OF —)
ABIJAH
(FATHER OF —) JEROBOAM
ZACHARIAS (FATHER OF —)
BARACHIAS
(SON OF —) JOHN
(WIFE OF —) ELISABETH

ZAIRE

CAPITAL: KINSHASA
COIN: SENGI LIKUTA
COINS: MAKUTA
LAKE: KIVU MWERU
LANGUAGE: KIKONGO LINGALA SWAHILI
TSHILUBA
MONEY: ZAIRE
MOUNTAIN RANGE: MITUMBA VIRUNGA
RUWENZORI
PROVINCE: KIVU KASAI SHABA EQUATOR
KATANGA BANDUNDU EQUATEUR
ORIENTAL
RIVER: RUKI CONGO DENGU IBINA KASAI
LINDI ZAIRE LIKATI LOMAMI LUKUGA
UBANGI ARUWIMI LUALABA LULONGA
TOWN: BAYA BOMA LEBO AKETI BUKAVU
KAMINA KIKWIT MATADI BUTEMBO
KANANGA KOLWEZI BAKWANGA
YANGAMBI KISANGANI

ZAMBIA

CAPITAL: LUSAKA
COIN: NGWEE KWACHA
FALLS: VICTORIA
LAKE: MWERU BANGWEULU TANGANYIKA
LANGUAGE: LOZI BEMBA TONGA LUVALE
NYANJA AFRIKAANS
MOUNTAIN RANGE: MUCHINGA
RIVER: KAFUE LUANGWA LUAPULA
ZAMBEZI
TOWN: KITWE NDOLA LUAPULA
LUANSHYA MUFULIRA
WATERFALL: VICTORIA

ZANY FOOL CRAZY TOADY SAWNEY
BUFFOON IDIOTIC CLOWNISH
SCREWBALL
ZANZIBAR (SEE TANZANIA)
ZEAL FIRE MOOD ARDOR FLAME HEART
FERVOR WARMTH DEVOTION GOODWILL
JEALOUSY

ZEALOT BIGOT VOTARY DEVOTEE
FANATIC CANANEAN SERAPHIC
SICARIUS
ZEALOUS HOT HIGH ARDENT FERVID
CORDIAL DEVOTED EARNEST FERVENT
FORWARD JEALOUS PUSHFUL VIGOROUS
PERFERVID RELIGIOUS
ZEALOUSLY FAST INNERLY HEARTILY
ZEBEDEE (SON OF —) JOHN JAMES
(WIFE OF —) SALOME
ZEBRA DAUW EQUID HORSE QUAGGA
SOLIPED
ZEBU BRAGMAN BRAHMIN
(HYBRID OF — AND CATTLE)
CATTABU
(HYBRID OF — AND YAK) ZOBO
ZECHARIAH (DAUGHTER OF —) ABI
ABIJAH
(FATHER OF —) IDDO BEBAI HOSAH
JEHIEL PASHUR ISSHIAH PHAROSH
JEHOIADA JONATHAN BERECHIAH
JEBERECHIAH JEHOSHAPHAT
MESHELEMIAH
(SON OF —) JAHAZIEL
ZENITH ACME PEAK PITCH HEIGHT
SUMMIT VERTEX
ZENOBIA (HUSBAND OF —)
ODENATHUS
ZEPHANIAH (FATHER OF —)
MAASEIAH
(SON OF —) JOSIAH
ZEPHYR FINE SOFT BERLIN BREEZE
ZERBINO (BELOVED OF —) ISABELLA
(COMPANION OF —) ORLANDO
(SISTER OF —) GINEVRA
(SLAYER OF —) MANDRICARDO
ZERO OH NIL BLOB DUCK NULL AUGHT
EMPTY OUGHT ZILCH ABSENT CIPHER
NAUGHT LACKING NOTHING NULLITY
SCRATCH
ZEST EDGE ELAN GUSTO FLAVOR RELISH
STINGO PIQUANCY
ZESTFUL RACY SPICY BREEZY
ZETHUS (BROTHER OF —) AMPHION
(FATHER OF —) JUPITER
(MOTHER OF —) ANTIOPE
ZEUS ZAN SOTER ALASTOR CRONION
KRONION POLIEUS CRONIDES
(BROTHER OF —) HADES POSEIDON
(FATHER OF —) KRONOS
(MOTHER OF —) RHEA
(SISTER OF —) HERA HESTIA DEMETER
(SON OF —) ARES ARCAS ARGUS
AEACUS AGACUS APOLLO HERMES
TITYUS PERSEUS DARDANUS DIONYSUS
HERCULES TANTALUS

(WIFE OF —) HERA JUNO METIS
THEMIS EURYNOME
ZIGZAG BOYAU CRANK BROKEN INDENT
CRANKLE CHEVRONY FLEXUOSE
TRAVERSE

ZIMBABWE

CAPITAL: HARARE SALISBURY
DIVISION: RHODESIA
LANGUAGE: ILA BANTU SHONA NDEBELE
PEOPLE: BANTU MASHOMA MATABELE
BALOKWAKWA
RIVER: SABI GWAII LUNDI LIMPOPO
SANYATI ZAMBEZI
TOWN: GWELO UMTALI BULAWAYO
WATERFALL: VICTORIA

ZINC FAR SPELT ZINCUM SPELTER
TUTENAG EXCLUDER
ZING PEP VIM ZIP DASH SNAP ENERGY
SPIRIT RAZZMATAZZ
ZINNIA CRASSINA
ZION ISRAEL UTOPIA
ZIONIST IRGUNIST
ZIP VIM DASH SNAP FORCE WHISK
BUTTON ENERGY STINGO
ZIPPER FASTENER
(PART OF —) TAB FACE PULL STOP
TAPE CHAIN SLIDE TOOTH
ZIPPORAH (FATHER OF —) REUEL
JETHRO
(HUSBAND OF —) MOSES
(SON OF —) ELIEZER GERSHOM

ZIRCON JARGON AZORITE MALACON
HYACINTH STARLITE
ZITHER KIN CANUN GUSLI CITHARA
GITERNE GITTERN AUTOHARP
GALEMPONG
(JAPANESE —) KOTO
ZODIAC GIRDLE BALDRIC SIGNIFIER
(SECTION OF —) TRIGON
(SIGN OF —) LEO RAM BULL CRAB FISH
GOAT LION ARIES LIBRA SCALE TWINS
VIRGO ARCHER CANCER GEMINI PISCES
TAURUS SCORPIO AQUARIUS CAPRICORN
ZONE BED AREA BAND BEAM BELT HALO
TRACT CIRCLE REGION ZODIAC CLIMATE
HORIZON ZONULET CINCTURE CINGULUM
FRONTIER HABENULA HISTOGEN
(— OF CONFLICT) FRONT
(— OF FLAME) MANTLE
(— OF MINERALS) CORONA
(— OF VENUS) CEST CESTUS
(ABYSSAL —) BASSALIA
(PALEONTOLOGIC —S) ASSISE
(SAFETY —) ISLET ISLAND REFUGE
(STRATOGRAPHIC —) HEMERA
(WELDING —) ROOT
ZOOPHYTE CORAL SPONGE HYDROID
ZOOSPORE MONAD SWARMER ZOOCARP
ZORIL SKUNK CHINCHE POLECAT
MUISHOND
ZOROASTRIAN GABAR PARSI GUEBRE
ZUCCHINI COURGETTE
ZULU CAR TRAIN LUGGER MATABELE
ZUNI CIBOLAN SHALAKO
ZYGOTE OOCYST OOSPERM OOSPORE
SPORONT OOKINETE